THE
PUB
GUIDE
2017

Published by AA Publishing, a trading name of AA Media Limited, whose registered office is Fanum House, Basing View, Basingstoke RG21 4EA. Registered number 06112600.

20th edition September 2016.
© AA Media Limited 2016.

Assessments of AA inspected establishments are based on the experience of the Hotel and Restaurant Inspectors on the occasion of their visit(s) and therefore descriptions given in this guide may contain an element of subjective opinion which may not dictate or influence a reader's own opinion on another occasion. See pages 6–7 for a clear explanation of how, based on our Inspectors' inspection visits, establishments are graded. If the meal or meals were of a sufficient standard, the Inspector or Inspectors during an inspection visit may award the Rosettes; the restaurant concerned may be awarded one of our award levels considered applicable.

AA Media Limited strives to ensure accuracy of the information in this guide at the time of printing. Nevertheless, the Publisher cannot be held responsible for any errors or omissions, or for changes in the details given in this guide, or for the consequences of any reliance on the information provided by the same. This does not affect your statutory rights. Due to the constantly evolving nature of the subject matter the information is subject to change. AA Media Limited is grateful for any advice from readers about necessary updates.

Please contact:
Advertising Sales Department: advertisingsales@theAA.com
Editorial Department: lifestyleguides@theAA.com
AA Hotel and B&B scheme enquiries: 01256 844455

Photographs in the gazetteer are provided by the establishments.

Typeset/Repro: Servis Filmsetting Ltd, Stockport.
Printed and bound in Italy by Printer Trento SRL
Directory compiled by the AA Lifestyle Guides Department and managed in the Lifestyle Information Management System.

Pub descriptions have been contributed by the following team of writers: Jackie Barnes, Phil Bryant, Neil Coates, David Halford and Mark Taylor.

AA Lifestyle Guides would like to thank Liz Haynes and Jo Duggan for their invaluable work in the production of this guide.

Maps prepared by the Mapping Services Department of AA Publishing.

Maps © AA Media Limited 2016.

Contains Ordnance Survey data © Crown copyright and database right 2016.

Information on National Parks in England provided by the Countryside Agency (Natural England).

Information on National Parks in Scotland provided by Scottish Natural Heritage.

Information on National Parks in Wales provided by The Countryside Council for Wales.

A CIP catalogue for this book is available from the British Library.

ISBN: 978-0-7495-7830-5

A05408

Contents

Welcome to the AA Pub Guide 2017

We aim to bring you the country's best pubs, selected for their atmosphere, good beer and great food. Updated every year, this popular and well-established guide includes lots of old favourites, plus many new and interesting destinations for drinking and eating across England, Scotland and Wales.

Who's in the guide?

We make our selection by seeking out pubs that are worth making a detour for – 'destination' pubs – where publicans show real enthusiasm for their trade and offer a good selection of well-kept drinks and great food. We also choose neighbourhood pubs which are supported by locals and prove attractive to passing drivers or walkers. Our selected pubs make no payment for their inclusion in the guide*; they appear entirely at our discretion.

That special place

We find pubs that offer something special: pubs where the time-honoured values of a convivial environment for conversation while supping or eating have not been forgotten. They may be attractive, interesting, unusual or in a good location. Some may be very much a local pub or they may draw customers from further afield, while others appear because they are in an exceptional place. Interesting towns and villages, eccentric or historic buildings and rare settings can all be found within this guide.

Tempting food

We look for menus that show a commitment to home cooking, that make good use of local produce wherever possible, and offer an appetising range of freshly prepared dishes. Pubs presenting well-executed traditional dishes like ploughman's or pies, or those offering innovative bar or restaurant food, are all in the running. In keeping with recent trends in pub food, we are keen to include those where particular emphasis is placed on imaginative modern dishes. Occasionally we include pubs that serve no food, or just snacks, but are distinctive in other ways.

Pick of the Pubs

Some of the pubs included in the guide are particularly special, and we have highlighted these as Pick of the Pubs. For 2017, over 600 pubs have been selected using the personal knowledge of our editorial team, our AA Inspectors, and suggestions from our readers. These pubs have a more detailed description, and this year over 140 have chosen to enhance their entry by purchasing two photographs to create a full-page entry.

Beer and cider festivals

As well as keeping their ales and ciders in tip-top condition throughout the year, many of the pubs in this guide hold beer and cider festivals, either just once a year or on several occasions. If they have told us that they do, we have indicated these events in the pub entries, and where possible have also mentioned the month/s of the year or bank holidays when they are held. You'll find lists of these festivals at the back of the guide.

Tell us what you think

We welcome your feedback about the pubs included, and about the guide itself. We would also be pleased to receive suggestions about good pubs you have visited that do not feature in this guide. A Readers' Report form appears at the back of the guide, so please write in or email us at **lifestyleguides@theAA.com**.

* Once chosen for the guide, pubs may decide to enhance their text entry or include advertising for which there is a charge.

How to use the guide

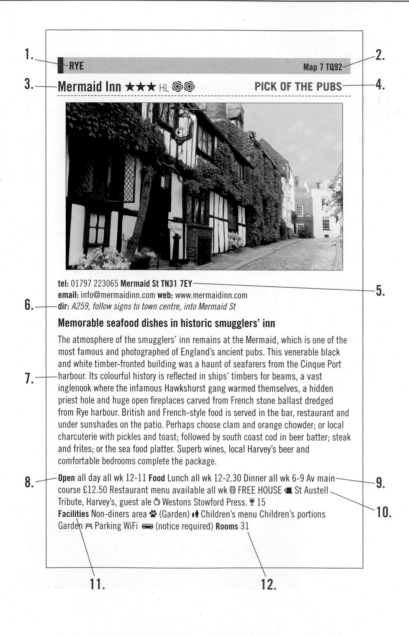

1. RYE

2. Map 7 TQ92

3. Mermaid Inn ★★★ HL ◉◉

4. PICK OF THE PUBS

5. tel: 01797 223065 **Mermaid St TN31 7EY**
email: info@mermaidinn.com web: www.mermaidinn.com

6. dir: *A259, follow signs to town centre, into Mermaid St*

Memorable seafood dishes in historic smugglers' inn

7. The atmosphere of the smugglers' inn remains at the Mermaid, which is one of the most famous and photographed of England's ancient pubs. This venerable black and white timber-fronted building was a haunt of seafarers from the Cinque Port harbour. Its colourful history is reflected in ships' timbers for beams, a vast inglenook where the infamous Hawkshurst gang warmed themselves, a hidden priest hole and huge open fireplaces carved from French stone ballast dredged from Rye harbour. British and French-style food is served in the bar, restaurant and under sunshades on the patio. Perhaps choose clam and orange chowder; or local charcuterie with pickles and toast; followed by south coast cod in beer batter; steak and frites; or the sea food platter. Superb wines, local Harvey's beer and comfortable bedrooms complete the package.

8. **Open** all day all wk 12-11 **Food** Lunch all wk 12-2.30 Dinner all wk 6-9 Av main course £12.50 Restaurant menu available all wk ⊕ FREE HOUSE ◀ St Austell Tribute, Harvey's, guest ale ♻ Westons Stowford Press. ♟ 15

9.

10.

Facilities Non-diners area ✿ (Garden) ♦♦ Children's menu Children's portions Garden ⋒ Parking WiFi ▭ (notice required) **Rooms** 31

11.

12.

1. Location

Guide order Country; county; town or village. Pubs are listed under their town or village name alphabetically within their county, within their country. There is a county map at the back of the guide. Some village pubs prefer to be listed under the nearest town, in which case the village name appears in their address.

2. Map reference

Each town or village is given a map reference – the map page number and a two-figure reference based on the National Grid. For example: **Map 7 TQ92**
7 refers to the page number of the map section at the back of the guide
TQ is the National Grid lettered square (representing 100,000sq metres) in which the location will be found
9 is the figure reading across the top and bottom of the map page
2 is the figure reading down at each side of the map page
London Maps: A Central London map and a Greater London map follow the map section at the back of the guide. The pub location will either appear on Plan 1 or Plan 2.

3. Pub name

Where the name appears in italic type the information that follows has not been confirmed by the pub for 2017.

4. AA ratings/designators/awards

★★☆★ Star rating under AA Hotel or B&B Schemes (see pages 8–9) followed by a designator (i.e. HL) which shows the type of hotel or B&B.

❀ AA Rosette award for food excellence (see page 9).

PICK OF THE PUBS (see page 5)

5. Address and contact details

6. Directions
Brief details are given on how to find the pub.

7. Description

8. Opening times
Times are given for when the pub is open, and closed.

9. Food
Indicates the days and times that food can be ordered, followed by the average price of a main course (as supplied to us by the pub). Please be aware that last orders could vary by up to 30 minutes. We also show if a separate restaurant menu is offered and on what days it is available.

Food Allergies From December 2014 an EU regulation came into force making it easier for those with food allergies to make safer food choices when eating out. There are 14 allergens listed in the regulation, and pubs and restaurants are required to list any of these that are used in the dishes they offer. These may be highlighted on the menus or customers can ask staff for full information. Remember, if you are allergic to a food and are in any doubt, speak to a member of the pub or restaurant's staff.

For further information see www.food.gov.uk/science/allergy-intolerance/label/labelling-changes

10. Brewery and Company
⊕ indicates the name of the brewery to which the pub is tied, or the company that owns it. FREE HOUSE is shown if the pub is independently owned and run.

◀ indicates the principal beers sold by the pub. The pub's top cask or hand-pulled beers are listed. Many pubs have a much greater selection, with several guest beers each week.

ᵟ indicates the real ciders sold by the pub.

♟ indicates the number of wines available by the glass.

11. Facilities
🍴 indicates that the pub serves food outside.

🐾 indicates that the pub has told us they are happy to be described as dog-friendly. If possible we also show whereabouts the dogs are accepted (i.e. bar, restaurant, garden and/or outside area).

👫 indicates that the pub welcomes children and they offer a children's menu and/or children's portions.

Further information in this section shows if the pub has a non-diners' area; holds a beer and/or cider festival; has a children's play area, a garden or outside area; if parking is available; if they accept coach parties and if so, if prior notice is required; if WiFi is available.

Key to Symbols

★★★★	Accommodation rating. See explanation on pages 8 & 9
Ⓤ	Accommodation rating not yet confirmed
❀	Rosettes – The AA's food award. See explanation on page 9
⊕	Name of Brewery; Company; Free House
◀	Principal beers sold
ᵟ	Real ciders sold
♟	At least eight wines available by the glass. The number of wines may be shown beside the symbol
🐾	Dog-friendly pubs: dogs can be accepted in bar, restaurant, garden and/or outside area
👫	Children welcome
🍴	Outside eating area
🚌	Coach parties accepted; pre-booking may be required
🚫💳	Credit and debit cards not accepted
NEW	Pubs appearing in the guide for the first time

12. Rooms
The number of bedrooms is only shown if the pub's accommodation is AA rated.

Notes
🚫💳 Most pubs accept debit or credit cards – we only indicate where this is not the case.

AA classifications and awards

Many of the pubs in this guide offer accommodation. Where a star rating appears next to an entry's name in the guide, the establishment has been inspected by the AA under common Quality Standards agreed between the AA, VisitBritain, VisitScotland and VisitWales. These ratings are for the accommodation, and ensure that the establishment meets the highest standards of cleanliness, with an emphasis on professionalism, proper booking procedures and prompt and efficient service. Some of the pubs in this guide offer accommodation but do not belong to an AA rating scheme; in this case reference to the accommodation is not included in their entry.

AA recognised establishments pay an annual fee that varies according to the classification and the number of bedrooms. The establishments receive an unannounced inspection from a qualified AA Inspector who recommends the appropriate classification. Return visits confirm that standards are maintained; the classification is not transferable if an establishment changes hands.

The annual *AA Hotel Guide* and *AA Bed & Breakfast Guide* give further details of the classification schemes. Details of AA recognised hotels, guest accommodation, restaurants and pubs are also available at theAA.com.

AA hotel classification

Hotels are classified on a 5-point scale, with one star (★) being the simplest, and five stars offering a luxurious service at the top of the range. The AA's top hotels in Britain and Ireland are identified by red stars (★). Hotels with silver stars (★) are highly recommended for their standards of hotel keeping and quality of food within their star rating. In addition to the main **Hotel** (HL) classification which applies to some pubs in this guide, there are other hotel categories which may be applicable to pubs, as follows:

Town House Hotel (TH) – A small, individual city or town centre property.
Country House Hotel – (CHH) Quietly located in a rural area.
Small Hotel (SHL) – Owner-managed with fewer than 20 bedrooms.

AA guest accommodation

Guest accommodation is also classified on a scale of one to five black stars, with one star (★) being the most simple, and five being more luxurious. Gold stars (★) indicate the very best B&Bs, Guest Houses, Farmhouses, Inns, Restaurant with Rooms and Guest Accommodation in the 3, 4 and 5 star ratings. Establishments with silver stars (★) are highly recommended for their levels of hospitality, service and cleanliness within their star rating.
Guest accommodation is designated as follows:

Inn (INN) – Accommodation provided in a fully licensed establishment. The bar will be open to non-residents and food is provided in the evenings.

Bed & Breakfast (B&B) – Accommodation provided in a private house, run by the owner and with no more than six paying guests.

Guest House (GH) – Accommodation provided for more than six paying guests and run on a more commercial basis than a B&B. Usually more services, for example dinner, provided by staff as well as the owner.

Farmhouse (FH) – B&B or guest house rooms on a working farm or smallholding.

Restaurant with Rooms (RR) – Destination restaurant offering overnight accommodation. The restaurant is the main business and is open to non-residents. A high standard of food should be offered, at least five nights a week. A maximum of 12 bedrooms. Most Restaurants with Rooms have been awarded AA Rosettes for their food.

Guest Accommodation (GA) – Any establishment which meets the entry requirements for the Scheme can choose this designator.

U A small number of pubs have this symbol because their star classification was not confirmed at the time of going to press.

Rosette awards

Out of the thousands of restaurants in the British Isles, the AA identifies, with its Rosette awards, around 2,000 as the best. What to expect from restaurants with AA Rosette awards is outlined here; for a more detailed explanation of Rosette criteria please see theAA.com

◉ The best restaurants serving food prepared with care, understanding and skill, using good quality ingredients.

◉◉ Excellent restaurants which aim for and achieve higher standards, better consistency and where greater precision is apparent in the cooking.

◉◉◉ Outstanding restaurants that achieve standards that demand national recognition well beyond their local area.

◉◉◉◉ Amongst the top restaurants in the UK, where the cooking demands national recognition. A passion for excellence, superb technical skills and remarkable consistency are all shown.

◉◉◉◉◉ The pinnacle! Where the cooking compares with the best in the world.

AA Pub of the Year

The prestigious annual awards for the AA Pub of the Year for England, Scotland and Wales have been selected with the help of our AA inspectors and we have chosen three very worthy winners. These pubs stand out for being great all-rounders, combining a convivial atmosphere, well-kept beers and ciders, excellent food, and of course, a warm welcome from the friendly and efficient hosts and their staff.

ENGLAND

THE BOOT ★★★★ ◉
REPTON, DERBYSHIRE   page 131

This place has it all – popular bar, luxury accommodation, award-winning food and it's own microbrewery. The Boot's first occupant in the 17th century was a cobbler who hung a boot outside to attract customers; while mending their footwear he'd offer them a glass of ale and a bowl of pottage, a hospitable idea which obviously took hold. The building has also been used for legal proceedings prior to the completion of the adjacent Court House and for auctions, including one in 1802 when over 700 oak trees were sold (some considered 'fit for the navy'). Fast forward to the 21st century, and after buying this inn, which was in need of some TLC, the current owners took many months to restore and fully refurbish the property. Since re-opening the doors they haven't looked back. At the heart of the inn is the bustling bar where customers can enjoy The Boot's own tip-top condition beers that have travelled all the way from their own brewery in the courtyard. Head brewer Steve Topliss has clocked up 45 years in the brewing industry, including time as head brewer at Tetley's and six years at Guinness. His ales, including Clod Hopper, Repton Cross, Tuffer's Old, Bumble Boots and Wellington, are receiving much praise. The interior's stylish makeover runs through the entire building, including the nine individually designed and elegant en suite bedrooms. The food at The Boot is award-winning too and the chef's confident cooking is demonstrated in his worldwide influenced dishes.

SCOTLAND

THE SHIP INN ★★★★
ELIE, FIFE page 606

The Ship Inn is making a name for itself thanks to the vision and dedication of owners Graham and Rachel Bucknall. Having bought the property in 2014 they immediately set about refurbishing it before reopening in the summer of 2015. The inn is part of a row of old cottages by the harbour. At its heart is the bar where the comfy chairs and sofas beside the open fires and wood-burning stoves make a welcome sight, especially when it's windy and rainy outside. You are more than welcome just to call in for a coffee, but it's worth stopping longer for a pint, a whisky or a meal in the upstairs restaurant with its views of the bay. The same menu is offered throughout the inn – and if you have your dog with you, he or she is very welcome to join you downstairs – water, treats and even dog beds are provided. The food is of the hearty pub variety, but seafood, locally caught, is high on the menu. Graham and Rachel have also created delightful double and twin bedrooms, all with views of Elie Bay and the Firth of Forth. The Ship Inn is unique in the fact that it has the only cricket team in the UK that plays matches on the beach. From May to September, depending on the tide and after the sand has been rolled flat, the Ship's team hosts matches for other Scottish teams and touring teams from all over the world. Who wouldn't want to win the prize of 'your height in beer or soft drinks' – awarded to the batsman who hits a six into the beer garden and to the spectator who catches that ball?

WALES

PENHELIG ARMS ★★★★★ ◉
ABERDYFI, GWYNEDD page 638

Located just over the road from the Dyfi estuary where small boats are anchored, the ever-popular Penhelig Arms commands wonderful views. The estuary forms part of the Ynyslas National Nature Reserve, the feeding ground for thousands of wading birds and a birdwatchers' paradise. Within the Snowdonia National Park, Aberdyfi has long been a popular resort for those seeking both the sea and the mountains. Originally a modest row of fishermens' cottages, the Penhelig Arms became an inn serving travellers and the local community around 1870. Today, it's definitely a great meeting place – the wood-panelled and log fire-warmed Fisherman's Bar is a cosy and friendly bolt-hole for enjoying a pint of Brains ale, a glass of wine or a bite to eat. Alternatively you can head for the brasserie-style dining room to gaze out over the shimmering water while enjoying award-winning dishes; prior booking is highly recommended for a meal here. The menus showcase the very best Welsh produce the chef can find, and the seafood, lamb and beef should all receive a particular mention. When the sun is shining, the sea-wall terrace is a popular place to sit and relax. If you are stopping over, the inn has smart, individually designed en suite bedrooms – the largest being loft-style accommodation on two levels with a private terrace. Throughout the inn, the friendly staff will always go the extra mile to make any visit memorable. All in all, Penhelig Arms is a worthy winner.

Cheers to 20 years

The pub industry has changed a great deal since the AA published its first Pub Guide 20 years ago. Phil Bryant assesses how pubs have adapted to social and cultural changes and how the guide has evolved.

In the early 1970s, Britain's 'Big Six' brewers produced about 80 per cent of the country's beer. They also owned most of the pubs, which enabled them to foist their carbonated keg beer on unappreciative consumers, while conspiring to ditch traditional draught.

For beer drinkers, those were dark days, but it's an ill wind, as they say, for in 1973 the Campaign for Real Ale (CAMRA) began its long crusade in support of just that – real ale. Largely through its efforts most pubs now sell at least one real ale, usually more. So perhaps it's not surprising, that in early 2016 CAMRA announced a possible move beyond its historic focus in favour of "more pressing issues," including the decline of the pub.

Of about 60,500 pubs in 1998, four a week were closing; today there are roughly 48,000, with 27 a week bolting their doors, mostly for ever. About a fifth are owned by brewers, a third by non-brewing pubcos, with the rest independent free houses.

The decline can be attributed to, well, take your pick: the recession, a 40 per cent rise in alcohol duty between 2008 and 2013 (although cuts have been made since), increased competition from trendy bars and restaurants, cheap supermarket alcohol, the smoking ban, and changes in consumer habits. Even so, three in four people believe a well-run pub is as important to community life as a shop or post office.

While pub numbers have plummeted, the AA Pub Guide has grown, both in standing and content. The 365-page first edition reviewed 1,400 pubs, compared with this 20th anniversary edition's 2,161, and 728 pages. With AA inspectors and guide readers recommending more and more pubs for inclusion, the axiom 'survival of the fittest' clearly applies, for these pubs are the best.

The AA editorial team asks landlords for far more information nowadays, as a well-informed reader is more likely to consider visiting a particular pub. In the first guide, The Royal Oak Hotel in Yattendon, Berkshire, merited just 46 words; today it features as a full page 'Pick of the Pubs'. Colour photos now illustrate many entries which also live online at theAA.com.

The first edition of the AA Pub Guide

No longer just a pickled egg

With most pubs now food led, we don't need to trust the ubiquitous, but somewhat unnecessary, 'Good Food' sign, since guidebooks, websites and apps enable us to carry out a sort of due diligence. We can read about the head chef's rise to fame, complete with culinary accolades (including AA Rosettes, of course), and, naturally, their style of cooking.

It was in 1991 that a hitherto ordinary London boozer, The Eagle in Clerkenwell, arguably became the first so-called gastropub (not every landlord's favourite term). By emphasising its food offering it helped kick-start the concept of visiting a pub because it really did promise good tucker.

It's no longer surprising to find a pub, such as Tom and Beth Kerridge's four-AA Rosette Hand & Flowers in Marlow, ranking alongside highly acclaimed restaurants like London's Le Gavroche or The Waterside Inn at Bray. Drinking-led pubs still exist, of course, like The Nutshell in Bury St Edmunds, officially Britain's smallest, with no room for a kitchen – the landlord jokes about its dining area for parties of two or fewer.

The Nutshell in Bury St Edmunds

Now commonplace is the head chef-proprietor who, after years of responding to someone else's instructions in a top kitchen, is at last free to showcase his or her personal style of cooking in their own place and run the show the way they want. Among many examples are Paul Jackson at The Hare Inn, Scawton, North Yorkshire, and Emily Watkins at The Kingham Plough, in Oxfordshire.

With 'food and drink miles' of increasing concern, pubs now talk up the sources of their produce – the more local the better. The Pub Guide frequently finds suppliers' names listed, or a menu offering, say, Hogwhimpering Farm beef, or home-smoked River Twaddle trout. That we don't know such places matters little, because we can assume they'll be nearby. Mind you, the pubs that rear their own pigs, grow their own vegetables, or microbrew their own beer score highest in the source-to-serve stakes.

There's been a huge increase in the number of small breweries and microbreweries. In 1998 there were fewer than 500 breweries nationally but this has since skyrocketed to, at the last count, 1,700 today, producing 11,000 different real ales. This has prompted the Government's community pubs minister Marcus Jones to call Britain "a brewing powerhouse".

For real-ale drinkers this is paradise; for pubs too, particularly free houses, it has been a real boon, as they can spotlight their real ales and how often the line-up changes. And real cider too, a drink once derided as a Zummerzet tipple, has a much higher profile. Naturally, great emphasis is placed on wines, more often than not world sourced, and with rare bins, sometimes costing over £100, no longer the preserve of top restaurants. English wines, however, still seem to struggle for attention, good though they are.

Impressive collections of spirits, primarily malt whiskies, abound. In Devon, The NoBody Inn stocks 280 brands, and

The Cholmondeley Arms, Cheshire

you'll find some 200 at The Inn on Loch Lomond in Argyll & Bute. The Cholmondeley Arms in Cheshire publishes a fascinating 20-page Gin Bible for its trove of more than 200, while 60 gins line up at The Muntjac in Bedfordshire.

Makeovers and reinventions

The words 'refurbishment', 'renovation' and 'makeover' appear often in pub reviews. Usually design-led and eye-wateringly costly, extensive alterations have saved many a lacklustre or even long-closed pub. In 2013, the Upham Brewery, one of a new breed of small pub-owning groups, bought and transformed The Running Horse, a quiet village local near Winchester. "Later years saw the pub run by a succession of landlords," says its website, "many of whom had taken [it] as a route to peaceful semi-retirement." Enough said.

In 1998, The Ship in the hamlet of High Hesleden in County Durham closed. Three years later Sheila and Peter Crosby saw, fell in love with, bought and spent several weeks getting it fit to reopen. "It was hard slog all the way," recalls Sheila. "I wrote 66 cheques in one particular week."

After six years, half a million pounds and many improvements, including a car park, garden, letting rooms and self-catering accommodation, all with sea views, the pub is the beating heart of the village. "We keep it spotlessly clean," says Sheila. "The food is very good, cooked to order, and we're always full Sunday lunchtimes. Our customers come from all over the county and beyond.

The Derby Arms in Cumbria also came back from the dead when Witherslack Community Land Trust bought it. Ainscoughs, a family-owned pub and restaurant group, then took on the lease and renovated the pub, while villagers converted an outbuilding into a community-run shop. Pub general manager Barry Thomas says: "Ainscoughs and the village are very supportive and pub and shop are going from strength to strength."

Yet another success story is the 150-year-old Dragon, formerly The Green Dragon, on the Trent and Mersey Canal in Willington, Derbyshire, now unrecognisable from the run-down pub Derby-based developer Heidi Taylor bought in 2010. "All it needed was a bit of TLC," she explains, "so we extended and renovated it, created a fabulous canal-side beer garden, and renamed it." A 70-seater restaurant and a new bar were added, and in 2014 Heidi bought the next-door cottage to provide B&B accommodation. A huge new kitchen handles the increased business.

Heidi believes she is defying the pub industry slump. As well as The Dragon, she bought and refurbished The Boot in Repton; both pubs are trading successfully, with The Boot's

The Flitch of Bacon, Little Dunmow, Essex

new microbrewery supplying them, and a bar/restaurant/hotel in Melbourne (the Derbyshire one, that is), with ale. "I partly blame breweries for pub closures," Heidi says. "They haven't been investing in pubs for a long time. Many are run down and it puts people off. Also, tied tenants can buy only from their own brewery, so it can be very hard to make money." She adds: "What works for us is investing in our staff, being creative and using common sense."

In rural Essex, despairing of finding somewhere decent locally to eat, acclaimed chef Daniel Clifford of Midsummer House in Cambridge bought the historic, but closed, Flitch of Bacon in Little Dunmow in 2015. "I'd been driving past it for years and always fancied it," he says, "so when the opportunity arose to buy the freehold it was a no-brainer. After gutting it, removing the roof and windows and leaving just four walls, we restored it using the traditional methods and materials of 400 years ago." His sympathetic restoration has given it a new lease of life as a destination pub and restaurant.

Unheard of two decades ago was a local authority's listing of a pub as an Asset of Community Value to protect it from summary demolition or change of use. So far, around 1,250 are thus safeguarded. In some places, local councils have acquired pubs themselves, recognising their important community role. After a pubco sold The Dolphin in Bishampton, Worcestershire, it was closed for nearly a year. In 2013, after the parish council acquired it with a £300,000 government loan, villagers cleaned

it up, and it reopened. New landlord Lee Jones told his local radio station: "The response on opening day was incredible; we had about 300 people in." Understandably, footfall has eased off, but, says Lee: "The village remains very supportive and I'm delighted with the way things are going." It thus makes a welcome return to this guide.

Support from the top

Central government also recognises the community value of pubs. In 2016, Marcus Jones announced a £3.62 million, two-year Community Pub Business Support Programme, jointly funded by the Department for Communities and Local Government, and Power to Change, an independent charitable trust. The objective is to help prevent the threat of closure by supporting 80 community-owned pubs in England.

Looking ahead, closures will inevitably continue, but there's a positive side. We still love our pubs – for offering a rich variety of places to eat, drink and socialise; for often being the centre of community life; for bringing jobs to places that need them; and for sometimes doubling as a much-needed shop or post office. And let's not forget how much overseas tourists love them too.

Marcus Jones again: "There's an increasing confidence in the beer and pubs sector with pubs diversifying, community ownership of public houses starting to take off and a booming brewing industry".

Cheers, Marcus. We'll all drink to that.

Discover Scotland

Kilts, bagpipes, porridge and haggis and so much more. We take a look at what goes into making Scotland such a glorious place.

Spectacular landscapes, buzzing cities, and a lively cultural scene that embraces low comedy as well as high art are key ingredients in the recipe that makes Scotland special. Then there's history and heritage that span not just centuries, but millennia. From the mysterious brochs and stone circles of the far north and the islands to the traces of Roman fortifications, the romantic ruins of scores of medieval castles like Eilean Donan, Urquhart Castle or Dunnottar, and the relatively recent stately homes of monarchs and aristocrats.

Town or country?

If you're a lover of wide open spaces, you'll probably be tempted to head straight for the bens, glens and lochs of regions such as Torridon or Caithness, the high moorland of the Cairngorms, the rolling hills of the Borders, or the dramatic shores of Loch Lomond and Loch Ness. If you're a beachcomber at heart, you'll find long swaths of sandy beach and rocky shoreline on sweeping bays and narrow sea lochs. Island hoppers can explore Orkney and Shetland archipelagos and the remoteness of the Western Isles.

By contrast, Scotland's cities have their own fascinations. There's Edinburgh, with its castle, multiple festivals, and the architectural heritage of Old Town and New Town. Scotland's capital has been given a new vibrancy since devolution and the advent of a new Scottish Parliament. Edinburgh's archrival, Glasgow, makes up for what it lacks in medieval glories with wonderful museums and art galleries like the Kelvingrove Art Gallery and Museum, and the world renowned Burrell Collection, along with unusual spots such as its grandiose hilltop Necropolis. Aberdeen, a key player in the world's energy industry, offers historic attractions like medieval King's College and St Machar's Cathedral. Dundee is in the process of reinventing itself as a 21st-century cultural hub, especially in the rejuvenation of its scenic waterfront. The key attraction of Scotland's fifth city, Stirling, is its castle, made famous by links

Urquhart Castle on Loch Ness

17

Cairngorms National Park

with the stories of William Wallace, Robert the Bruce and the Battle of Bannockburn. Inverness, 'capital of the Highlands', is the gateway to the far north and Loch Ness, home of the legendary monster.

Glorious scenery

Scotland's landscapes range from the hills of the Southern Uplands to the peaks and rolling moorland of the Cairngorms, the forests of Perthshire, the tundra-like peatlands, known as the Flow Country, in Caithness and Sutherland and the fertile farmland of lowland regions such as Tayside, Lothian and Aberdeenshire.

Off Scotland's shores lie hundreds of islands, although less than 100 are inhabited. Some, like Skye, are so close to the mainland that they can be reached in a matter of minutes by road bridge or ferry. Getting to others, such as the Outer Hebrides and Shetland, can involve flying or taking an overnight ferry. Fair Isle, 82 miles from the mainland, is the most remote Scottish island to be inhabited.

Glacial erosion created the deep sea lochs all along the west coast, and also the Great Glen where one of Scotland's longest and deepest bodies of water, Loch Ness, run diagonally from Inverness, at the head of the Moray Firth, to Fort William and Loch Linnhe in the west.

Much of Highland Scotland looks like pristine wilderness, so it may be a surprise to learn that it has been shaped as much by people as by nature. When the first humans arrived, and for many thousands of years afterwards, most of Scotland was covered by thick forest. Gradually, these were felled to create space for farming and to provide firewood and building materials. By the mid-18th century, much of the country was treeless. The huge demand for timber during World War I contributed to further deforestation, but in 1919, the Forestry Commission was set up to create new woodland. Trees were planted all over Scotland and you can see huge swathes of conifers such as Sitka spruce, Scots pine, larch and Douglas fir, but in recent years there has been a drive to create more environmentally sensitive mixed forests of broad-leaved trees such as oak, beech, birch and sycamore as well as conifers.

Abundant wildlife

Scotland's varied landscapes and seascapes shelter a rich diversity of wildlife. On land, herds of red deer roam the moors, while smaller roe deer prefer woodland and forest habitats. Wild boar, hunted to extinction around 500 years ago, have made a comeback in the 21st century. There are at least three breeding populations, all descendants of boar that escaped from farms. Other returnees to the wild include beavers, which were

Scotland's wildlife – Golden Eagle and Red Deer

experimentally reintroduced in south-west Scotland in 2009; reindeer, non-resident for around 800 years, were reintroduced in 1952 and Britain's only free-ranging herd now roams a 10,000-acre expanse of Cairngorms moorland. Wolves, brown bears and lynx all once inhabited Scotland (the last Scottish wolf was shot in 1680) and there have been controversial proposals to reintroduce these predators. Unsurprisingly, some farmers fear for their flocks, but some environmentalists suggest that reintroducing them would help to control wild deer which are now so numerous in some areas that they are considered pests.

Otters have made a successful comeback in recent decades, helped by the cleaning-up of streams and rivers. They're plentiful on rivers such as the Tay, but you're more likely to see them in rock pools at low tide around sea lochs like Loch Morar or Loch Linnhe, or along the Moray Firth.

Two emblematic Scottish mammals aren't doing as well though. The red squirrel's future is threatened by a virus carried by the non-native grey squirrel. Greys aren't as common in Scotland as they are in England, and culling them may be the only way to save the reds. Meanwhile, the Scottish wildcat is endangered by interbreeding with domestic cats – soon there may be not be any pure-bred wildcats outside zoos.

Scotland has more than 400 breeding pairs of golden eagle, but you're more likely to spot kestrels, sparrowhawks and buzzards. Red kites were reintroduced in the 1980s, and if you're very lucky you might see a white-tailed eagle, over the shores of Fife and on the north-west coast.

Puffins, gannets and other seabirds nest in large numbers on islands in the Firth of Forth (such as Bass Rock and Fidra) and vast numbers of migrant waterfowl – including greylag and pink-footed geese – congregate on the tidal estuaries of the Solway Firth and the Firth of Tay in autumn, and huge flocks of barnacle and white-fronted geese from Greenland overwinter on Islay and Jura.

Scotland's waters shelter some amazing sea mammals. Bottlenose dolphins are an everyday sight in the Moray Firth and off the Aberdeenshire coast, and you may even spot migratory humpback and minke whales in Hebridean waters. Grey and common seals bask on the remote shores of western sea lochs, and if you take a stroll along the beach at Tentsmuir, between Dundee and St Andrews, you'll see dozens of them sunbathing on sandbanks at the mouth of the Tay and the River Eden.

A mention should go to everyone's least favourite Scottish creature, and one of the tiniest – the hated midge. These wee bloodsuckers appear in swarms in summer and are a real pest, especially in boggy areas. They seem resistant to insect repellent but they say a layer of baby oil on the skin offers some protection.

Get active: on land and water

For active visitors, the choice of leisure activities is as seemingly endless as are the beaches and mountain vistas of Scotland. Long-distance trails like the West Highland Way and John Muir Way traverse rugged scenery, but there are gentler walks skirting beautiful coastline too, like the Fife Coastal Path. The 282 Munros, mountains over 3,000 feet, prove a big attraction for serious walkers – once 'conquered' they are happy to record their tally which is known as 'Munro Bagging'. Water activities range from canoeing and rafting on lochs and rivers to sea kayaking, sailing and windsurfing. And, of course, there's golf. For keen golfers, playing a round at the Royal and Ancient Golf Club in St Andrews is an experience to savour, but there are other iconic courses like Troon, Turnberry, Gleneagles and Carnoustie, as well as hundreds of other links and greens all over Scotland. Winter snow brings skiers and snowboarders flocking to the Cairngorms National Park and Aviemore becomes the hub of their activities.

True Scottish sustenance

Scottish cuisine is legendary. It's not all porridge, entrails and deep-fried food, of course. Two Scottish specialities immediately come to mind – porridge and haggis. Porridge was traditionally the staple food of rural folk, in its most spartan form this is just oatmeal boiled in water, but the more luxurious version, offered in most Scottish hotels and guest houses, is made with milk. Purists insist porridge should be flavoured with salt, but you can add cream, honey or syrup if you prefer.

The second iconic dish, haggis, is celebrated by Scotland's national bard, Robert Burns, in his *Address to a Haggis* and traditionally consumed in his honour on Burns Night every January, when it is accompanied with bashit neeps (mashed turnip) and tatties (mashed potatoes).

The haggis isn't Scotland's only pudding of course, there's black pudding, made from offal, onions, pig's blood, oatmeal and pork fat; the best, it's claimed, comes from Stornoway on the Isle of Lewis. Fried, sliced black pudding is essential to any full Scottish breakfast, and it's also battered, deep-fried and served with chips in every fish and chip shop in the land. One of the best Scottish desserts is cranachan, a delicious concoction made from whisky-soaked oatmeal, whipped cream and fresh raspberries.

With thousands of miles of coastline, Scotland naturally offers a diverse seafood menu. Loch Fyne, on the west coast, is famous for its oysters. The fishing village of Findon (Finnan), in Aberdeenshire, is the birthplace of the finnan haddie – cold-smoked haddock fillet while Arbroath is the home of the smokie – haddock smoked in its skin and on the bone. Either, or both, of these can go into Cullen skink, a hearty chowder. Scots love pies and savoury pastries like the Forfar bridie, a semi-circular pastry filled with minced beef and onions that can be eaten hot or cold.

Slàinte

Whisky is the national drink, but beer and ale have been brewed in Scotland for more than 2,000 years. There's been a brewing renaissance, with heritage ales flavoured with old-style ingredients such as heather buds, spruce and pine shoots, gooseberry and even seaweed. You'll find distinctive ales from craft breweries such as Williams Brothers, makers of Fraoch Heather Ale, and Harviestoun, brewers of Ola Dubh, a beer that is matured in malt whisky casks.

"Whisky and freedom go together" claimed Robert Burns, and many Scots would agree. Spirit distilled from malted barley is the key ingredient in whisky. Blended Scotch is made by combining this malt spirit with neutral grain alcohol; better blends use higher proportions of malt, but for connoisseurs, blended Scotch doesn't compare with elite single malt whiskies made entirely with malt spirit. The Scotch Whisky Association

insists that both blends and single malts must be aged for at least three years; quality whiskies may be aged for up to 12 years or even more, but it's unlikely that aging for more than 20 years adds any extra depth or flavour.

Each whisky-making region has its own style of single malt, influenced by factors like local water and the fuel used to fire the stills. Whiskies from Islay and Jura have a distinctive peaty, even seaweedy tang, while malts from Speyside are lighter in colour and flavour, with heathery and perhaps flowery notes. A distillery tour followed by a whisky sampling can be one of the high points of a Scottish holiday. There are almost 100 distilleries scattered around Scotland's mainland and islands – too many to visit in one holiday – but more than 40 of them cluster on Speyside. Here you can visit distilleries where world-famous like Glenlivet and Glenfiddich are made, and discover smaller, less well known distilleries like Dallas Dhu. Opening its doors in late 2015, The Isle of Harris Distillers, 'The Social Distillery', offers tours in the summer months, but not as yet any tastings of course – 2019 is the most likely year for that. But they have successfully created their own distinctive gin – a key note to the gin's flavour profile being locally hand-dived sugar kelp. Sláinte, meaning 'health' in gaelic, makes the perfect toast as you raise a glass of the Scottish whisky or gin.

Finally, a word about Scotland's other national drink – Irn-Bru. This caffeine-loaded, fizzy, rusty orange beverage is one of the world's original energy drinks, and is 'made with girders'. It has been produced by Scottish drinks company, AG Barr since 1901 and is now exported around the world. It's renowned as a good hangover remedy, but many also find it goes very well with vodka – this may account for its huge popularity in some places.

In this snapshot of Scotland it's impossible to detail the diversity and fascination of a country which stretches from lowlands to highlands, calm lochs to rugged seascapes, and from snowy winters to long, long summer days. If you haven't visited already, make sure it's added to your 'all-time, best things to do' list.

If you've enjoyed reading this feature, find out more by seeking out *The AA Guide to Scotland*, packed with information on this popular country.

England

BEDFORDSHIRE

BEDFORD
Map 12 TL04

The Embankment

tel: 01234 261332 **6 The Embankment MK40 3PD**
email: embankment@peachpubs.com
dir: *From M1 junct 13, A421 to Bedford. Left onto A6 to town centre. Into left lane on river bridge. Into right lane signed Embankment. Follow around St Paul's Square into High St, into left lane. Left onto The Embankment*

Mock-Tudor riverside pub with a hospitable atmosphere

This imposing pub sits behind an outdoor terrace overlooking the River Great Ouse on the edge of Bedford's beautifully landscaped Embankment gardens. Dating from 1891, the building has been renovated and its Victorian features brought back to life. Among its delights are the open fire, antique mirrors, vintage tables, sofas in racing green and silk lampshades. Food choices range from deli boards to full meals such as free-range pork terrine, piccalilli and sourdough, followed by pan-fried sea bream fillets, saffron and spring onion mash, white wine butter sauce.

Open all day all wk Closed 25 Dec **Food** Lunch all wk 12-6 Dinner all wk 6-10 Set menu available ⊕ CHARLES WELLS/PEACH PUBS ◀ Wells Eagle IPA & Bombardier, Young's ○ Aspall. ▾ 16 **Facilities** Non-diners area ❀ (Bar Outside area) ◀▸ Children's portions Outside area 卅 Parking WiFi ▭ (notice required)

The Knife and Cleaver ★★★★ INN ◉◉

tel: 01234 930789 **The Grove, Houghton Conquest MK45 3LA**
email: info@theknifeandcleaver.com **web:** www.theknifeandcleaver.com
dir: *A6 from Bedford towards Luton. In 5m right to Houghton Conquest. Or B530 from Bedford towards Ampthill left to Houghton Conquest*

Highly regarded rustic pub

The Shuttleworth aeroplane collection and Bletchley Park are easily reached from this pub in a village named after the Conquest family, who lived here between the 13th and 18th centuries. The bar and All Saints Restaurant welcome customers throughout the day, every day, even for just for a pint of Wells Eagle IPA. The choice is good: starters include sharing boards, or single starters of potted shrimps and cucumber on toast; or seared scallops with cauliflower, pork belly and honey glaze: among the mains are smoked haddock risotto; nut roast Wellington; beef bourguignon; and roasted supreme of guinea fowl. Apple and pecan pie or chocolate brownie for afters.

Open all day all wk **Food** all day Set menu available Restaurant menu available all wk ⊕ CHARLES WELLS ◀ Eagle IPA, Courage Directors, guest ale ○ Symonds. ▾ 35 **Facilities** Non-diners area ◀▸ Children's menu Children's portions Family room Garden Outside area 卅 Parking WiFi ▭ (notice required) **Rooms** 9

The Park Pub & Kitchen
PICK OF THE PUBS

tel: 01234 273929 **98 Kimbolton Rd MK40 2PA**
email: info@theparkbedford.co.uk
dir: *M1 junct 14, A509 follow Newport Pagnell signs, then A422, A428 onto A6. Right into Tavistock St (A600). Left into Broadway, 1st left into Kimbolton Rd. Pub 0.5m*

Smart, bright and spacious, a stylish mix of old and new

Built in the 1900s, this fine-looking pub is a stone's throw from Bedford Park, just a little way out of town. The smartly decorated exterior promises a similarly well cared for interior, and you won't be disappointed – fireplaces, flagstone floors and beamed ceilings combine to create a traditional welcoming atmosphere. Beyond the wrap-around bar are a spacious restaurant, relaxing conservatory and airy garden room; this leads to an outdoor area where heaters permit comfortable drinking and dining if there's a chill in the air. Eagle IPA and Bombardier from the town's Wells and Young's brewery are served in the bar, along with over 30 wines sold by the

glass. Most of the pub's suppliers are proudly detailed on the menu, while the kitchen team produces the pub's own bread, pasta, ice creams and chutneys. In addition, snacks and sandwiches with home-cut chips are served on Saturday from 3pm to 6pm.

Open all day all wk 8am-11pm (Sat 9am-11pm Sun 12-10.30) **Food** Lunch Mon-Sat 12-3, Sun 12-8 Dinner Mon-Sat 6-10, Sun 12-8 Set menu available Restaurant menu available all wk ⊕ CHARLES WELLS ◀ Bombardier, Eagle IPA, guest ales ○ Aspall. ▾ 33 **Facilities** Non-diners area ❀ (Bar Garden) ◀▸ Children's portions Garden 卅 Parking WiFi ▭ (notice required)

The Three Tuns

tel: 01234 354847 **57 Main Rd, Biddenham MK40 4BD**
email: info@thethreetunsbiddenham.co.uk
dir: *On A428 from Bedford towards Northampton 1st left signed Biddenham. Into village, pub on left*

Thatched pub with food of a high standard

In a pretty village, this stone-built pub has a large garden with a patio and decking, and a separate children's play area. Owner Chris Smith worked for celebrity chef Jean-Christophe Novelli for a number of years and now produces dishes such as white onion and cumin soup; creamy chicken, bacon and ale pot pie; and pineapple carpaccio with coconut and tarragon sorbet and lime jelly. Each dish on the à la carte is matched with a recommended wine. The two-course set menu is excellent value. In the garden is a long-disused, possibly haunted, morgue, the oldest building hereabouts.

Open all wk 12-3 5.30-late (Fri-Sat all day Sun 12-6) **Food** Lunch Tue-Sat 12-2.30, Sun 12-4 Dinner Tue-Sat 6-9.30 Set menu available Restaurant menu available Tue-Sun ⊕ GREENE KING ◀ IPA, Guinness, guest ale ○ Thatchers Gold. ▾ 16 **Facilities** Non-diners area ◀▸ Children's portions Play area Garden 卅 Parking WiFi ▭ (notice required)

BOLNHURST
Map 12 TL05

The Plough at Bolnhurst ◉
PICK OF THE PUBS

tel: 01234 376274 **Kimbolton Rd MK44 2EX**
email: reservations@bolnhurst.com
dir: *On B660, N of Bedford*

Tudor inn with notable food and wine

This whitewashed 15th-century country inn six miles north of Bedford has fresh, country-style decor coupled with original features such as thick walls, low beams and great open fires. The impressive choice of real ales and inspired wine list are matched by a delicious menu prepared by Raymond Blanc-trained Martin Lee and his team of skilled chefs. The menu is driven by the freshest local and regional produce and specialist foods gathered from all corners. The result is an ever-changing choice of unique dishes, which have gained The Plough an AA Rosette. Start with diver-caught Orkney scallops, grilled leeks, carrot purée and almonds; or pan-fried wood pigeon, pickled beetroot carpaccio, toasted hazelnuts and watercress; follow up with roast John Dory fillet with aubergine purée, courgette, crispy garlic and anchovy potato; or a selection of steaks cooked in the Josper oven. Orange and Grand Marnier nougat glacé with blood orange compôte makes a tempting dessert but do leave room for the cheeseboard, with its fantastic choice of British, Italian and French varieties.

Open Tue-Sat 12-3 6.30-11 (Sun 12-3) Closed 2wks Jan, Mon & Sun eve **Food** Lunch Tue-Sun 12-2 Dinner Tue-Fri 6.30-9, Sat 6.30-9.30 Set menu available ⊕ FREE HOUSE ◀ Adnams Southwold Bitter, Fuller's London Pride, Church End Goats Milk, Black Sheep, Gun Dog Ales Jack's Spaniels ○ Aspall Harry Sparrow. ▾ 15 **Facilities** Non-diners area ❀ (Bar Garden) ◀▸ Children's portions Garden 卅 Parking WiFi ▭ (notice required)

FLITTON
Map 12 TL03

NEW The White Hart

tel: 01525 862022 **Brook Ln MK45 5EJ**
email: phil@whitehartflitton.co.uk
dir: *In village centre, adjacent to church*

One for steak, fish and shellfish lovers

The 13th-century church of St John The Baptist stands on elevated ground right opposite this mostly early 18th-century village pub. Its first beer licence was issued in 1822; today's beers come from the B&T brewery in nearby Shefford. Fresh fish and shellfish are the big thing here, so big in fact that an April shellfish festival has become a calendar fixture. Arctic char, turbot, Dover sole and gilt-head bream dishes all feature on a menu that champions Aberdeen Angus steaks and other meats from the local family butcher. Light snacks include salads of warm Cajun spiced chicken, and goats' cheese with apple and walnut dressing.

Open 12-3 6-12 Closed 2-9 Jan, Sun eve & Mon **Food** Lunch Tue-Sun 12-2 Dinner Tue-Sat 6.30-9 Set menu available Restaurant menu available Tue-Sun ⊕ FREE HOUSE ◾ Banks & Taylor Shefford Bitter & Golden Fox ♂ Aspall. ♟ 18 **Facilities** Non-diners area ❀ (Bar Garden) ♦♦ Children's portions Garden ⋒ Parking WiFi ▭ (notice required)

HARROLD
Map 11 SP95

The Muntjac

tel: 01234 721500 **71 High St MK43 7BJ**
email: muntjacharrold@hotmail.co.uk
dir: *Phone for detailed directions*

Village free house and Indian restaurant

This 17th-century, former coaching inn in a pretty village has a lot on offer. For starters, a bar with six hand-pulls with regularly changing real ales, craft lagers and 60 gins – probably the largest such collection in Bedfordshire. Then there's a pool table and a real fire in winter. A separate restaurant, Harrold's Indian, offers an extensive range of traditional dishes, including tandoori chilli bhuna, duck Darjeeling, and the signature zamir monkfish, to eat in or take away. Chicken and scampi, both with chips, is on the menu for non-Indian-food lovers.

Open Mon-Thu 5.30-11 (Fri 12.30-12 Sat 12-12 Sun 1-10.30) Closed L Mon-Thu **Food** Contact pub for food times Set menu available Restaurant menu available Tue-Sun ⊕ FREE HOUSE ◾ Regularly changing ales. **Facilities** Non-diners area ❀ (Bar Garden) ♦♦ Children's portions Garden Parking ▭ (notice required) **Notes** ⊛

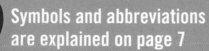

Symbols and abbreviations are explained on page 7

IRELAND
Map 12 TL14

The Black Horse

tel: 01462 811398 **SG17 5QL**
email: info@blackhorseireland.com **web:** www.blackhorseireland.com
dir: *From S: M1 junct 12, A5120 to Flitwick. Onto A507 by Redbourne School. Follow signs for A1, Shefford (cross A6). Left onto A600 towards Bedford. Right at next rdbt, immediately left towards Ireland. Pub on left*

Traditional and modern comfortably combined

Original beams, slate floors, inglenook fireplaces, original artwork and low ceilings combine to create a chic and modern interior in this family-run, 17th-century inn. The flower-rich garden and courtyard offer alfresco dining in the warmer months. Grab a pint of Adnams, or choose from the excellent wine list, and settle down in comfort to appreciate the tempting, seasonally inspired dishes made from locally sourced produce – maybe pan-seared calves' liver with horseradish and spring onion potato scone; Dingley Dell pork loin steak with spiced apple jam; or baked supreme of Atlantic hake with lemon parsley broth and chowder-style vegetables.

Open all wk 12-3 6-12 (Sun 12-6) Closed 25-26 Dec, 1 Jan **Food** Lunch Mon-Sat 12-2.30, Sun 12-5 Dinner Mon-Sat 6.30-10 Set menu available ⊕ FREE HOUSE ◾ Adnams, Sharp's Doom Bar, Fuller's London Pride ♂ Westons Mortimers Orchard. ♟ 16 **Facilities** Non-diners area ♦♦ Children's portions Garden ⋒ Parking WiFi ▭ (notice required)

KEYSOE
Map 12 TL06

The Chequers

tel: 01234 708678 **Pertenhall Rd, Brook End MK44 2HR**
email: chequers.keysoe@tesco.net
dir: *On B660, 7m N of Bedford. 3m S of Kimbolton*

Classic pub grub in a tranquil country pub

This peaceful 15th-century country pub has been in the same safe hands for over a quarter of a century. No games machines, pool tables or jukeboxes disturb the simple pleasures of well-kept ales and great home-made food. The menu offers pub stalwarts like ploughman's; home-made steak and ale pie; chicken curry and rice; chilli con carne and a variety of grilled steaks; and a blackboard displays further choice plus the vegetarian options. For a lighter meal try the home-made chicken liver pâté or soup, garlic mushrooms on toast, or plain or toasted sandwiches.

Open 11.30-2.30 6.30-11 Closed Sun eve, Mon & Tue, Wed L **Food** Lunch Thu-Sun 12-2 Dinner Wed-Sat 6.30-11 Av main course £9 ⊕ FREE HOUSE ◾ Hook Norton, guest ale ♂ Westons Stowford Press. **Facilities** Non-diners area ♦♦ Children's menu Children's portions Play area Family room Garden Parking ▭ (notice required) **Notes** ⊛

LEIGHTON BUZZARD
Map 11 SP92

The Heath Inn ★★★ INN

tel: 01525 237816 **76 Woburn Rd, Heath and Reach LU7 0AR**
email: enquiries@theheathinn.com **web:** www.theheathinn.com
dir: *Phone for detailed directions*

Great cask ales in a traditional setting

Tracy Balen took over this free house on the outskirts of Leighton Buzzard in 2015. The wood-beamed bar is cosy with an open fire, or in summer take your refreshments out to the pretty courtyard garden with its children's play area. Cask ales are well represented from the likes of Tring, Hopping Mad and Vale, ably supported by cider from Westons, draft lagers and quality wines. Food served in the bar or restaurant follows traditional lines with ploughman's, jackets, sandwiches, paninis, grills and pub favourites like bangers and mash; gammon steak, chips and egg; or mushroom risotto.

Open all day all wk **Food** Lunch all wk 12-2.30 Dinner Mon-Sat 6-9 Av main course £10 ⊕ FREE HOUSE ◀ Tring, Hopping Mad, Vale Ö Westons Stowford Press. **Facilities** Non-diners area ❖ (Bar Outside area) ♦i Children's menu Children's portions Play area Outside area ➤ Parking WiFi ☎ (notice required) **Rooms** 16

NORTHILL
Map 12 TL14

The Crown

tel: 01767 627337 **2 Ickwell Rd SG18 9AA**
email: info@crownnorthill.co.uk
dir: *In village centre, adjacent to church*

Greene King pub with a wide-ranging menu

A delightful 16th-century pub with smart, modern interior decor. A number of guest ales are very well kept, and make a delightful companion to almost anything on the menu. Dig into sharing deli boards or sandwiches, baguettes and paninis with fillings such as prawn and avocado, or topside of beef. Or how about mains such as seared sea trout fillet, Lyonnaise potatoes, wilted spinach and sorrel cream; or calves' liver and bacon, bubble-and-squeak and onion gravy? The garden has plenty of tables for alfresco eating, and a children's play area.

Open all day all wk **Food** Lunch Mon-Fri 12-3, Sat 12-10, Sun 12-6 Dinner Mon-Fri 6.30-10, Sat 12-10 ⊕ GREENE KING ◀ IPA & Abbot Ale, Morland Old Speckled Hen, Hardys & Hansons Olde Trip, guest ales Ö Aspall. ♟ 9 **Facilities** Non-diners area ❖ (Bar Garden) ♦i Children's menu Children's portions Play area Garden ➤ Parking WiFi ☎

OAKLEY
Map 11 TL05

Bedford Arms

tel: 01234 822280 **57 High St MK43 7RH**
email: bedfordarmsoakley@btconnect.com
dir: *From A6 N of Bedford follow Oakley signs*

Pretty village inn specialising in fresh fish dishes

Bounded on three sides by the River Ouse in the heart of the pretty village of Oakley, this 16th-century inn is surrounded by beautiful countryside but only a short drive from Bedford. Enjoy a pint of Charles Wells Eagle IPA in the cosy, traditional beamed bar or head to the large garden and decked alfresco dining area for a meal. Fresh fish is a speciality here, and the fish board changes daily to reflect the very best at the market that day. Away from fish there's plenty of choice, from roast rump of lamb or mushroom ravioli to quality sandwiches or pan-seared duck breast. Just let them know if gluten-free dishes are required and they will make sure a wide range is available.

Open all day all wk **Food** Lunch Mon-Sat 12-2.30, Sun 12-4 Dinner Mon-Sat 6-9.30 Restaurant menu available Mon-Sat ⊕ CHARLES WELLS ◀ Eagle IPA, Bombardier Burning Gold, Courage Directors, guest ale Ö Aspall. ♟ 35 **Facilities** Non-diners area ❖ (Bar Garden) ♦i Children's menu Children's portions Garden ➤ Parking WiFi ☎ (notice required)

RAVENSDEN
Map 12 TL05

The Horse & Jockey

tel: 01234 772319 **Church End MK44 2RR**
email: horseandjockey@live.com
dir: *N of Bedford. Phone for detailed directions*

Quiet country pub with a caring approach

Sarah Smith's friendly staff ensure a happy welcome at this quiet country pub, which sits atop a hill next to the village church. Locals and visitors feel equally at home, enjoying an Adnams ale or Aspall cider in the bar, or relaxing in the peaceful garden where birdsong is all that can be heard; the pub supplies fleece blankets for cooler evenings. Sarah's husband Darron runs the kitchen, and is passionate in his distinctly British approach to food. Expect the likes of lobster macaroni to start, chargrilled sirloin or rib-eye steaks to follow, and caramel cheesecake with walnut praline to finish.

Open all wk 12-3 6-11 **Food** Lunch all wk 12-2 Dinner all wk 6-9.30 Set menu available ⊕ FREE HOUSE ◀ Adnams Southwold Bitter & Ghost Ship Ö Aspall. ♟ 26 **Facilities** Non-diners area ❖ (Bar Garden) ♦i Children's portions Garden ➤ Parking WiFi ☎ (notice required)

SALFORD
Map 11 SP93

The Swan
PICK OF THE PUBS

tel: 01908 281008 **2 Warendon Rd MK17 8BD**
email: swan@peachpubs.com
dir: *M1 junct 13, follow signs to Salford*

Smart gastro-pub that appeals to everyone

Located in a pretty village, the tile-hung, Edwardian-era Swan, run by an enthusiastic team, has a lively bar with comfy leather armchairs that make you feel instantly at home, as does the eating area, where the big French doors can be thrown open to the garden. Peer through the feature window into the kitchen to watch the chefs preparing dishes from the best, locally supplied or own-grown ingredients. Sandwiches, snacks and deli boards are available throughout the day. The pub has its own smokehouse so the likes of home-smoked pork loin and home-smoked mackerel appear on the deli boards. Main courses include pumpkin and Swiss chard pancake with gruyère sauce; bangers and mash with sage and onion gravy; or slow-cooked venison bourguignon with parsnip and thyme purée. Puddings are very tempting – who could resist iced apple parfait and warm cinnamon fritter? The restored barn with a large central dining table can be used for a private dinner.

Open all day all wk 11am-mdnt (Sun 11-10.30) Closed 25 Dec **Food** Mon-Sat 12-10, Sun 12-9 ⊕ FREE HOUSE/PEACH PUBS ◀ Sharp's Doom Bar, Black Sheep Ö Aspall. ♟ 12 **Facilities** Non-diners area ❖ (Bar Garden) ♦i Children's portions Garden ➤ Parking WiFi ☎

The Bell
in Studham

Studham is the southern-most village in Bedfordshire & there you'll find the highest lying pub – *The Bell*. The Grade II listed, 500-year-old freehold, is amidst Bedfordshire's finest countryside. With panoramic views and character, this haven is just 10 minutes from Dunstable & Hemel Hempstead and 5 minutes from Dunstable Downs and Whipsnade Zoo.

We pride ourselves on providing 'Food and Gifts we Love' and our team aim to provide a warm welcome… Enjoy home-made pies, Sunday roasts with all the trimmings, freshly beer battered cod & triple cooked chips, to eat in or take-away and '99 soft ice creams! Also authentic pasta dishes, fresh fish & fine meats. Be enticed with the aroma of fresh dough pizzas, cooked in our stone clay oven. Wines are recommended and there's gifts and goodies to buy. Home accessories, clocks, signs, candles, fudge, jams, chutney and more – perfect as a gift or to keep!

Enjoy a 'Brew & Bakery Treat', a snack at lunchtime with our 'Cask 2 Glass Ale'. Free Wi-Fi 'n' revive with fresh 'Bean to Cup' coffees or an evening of champagne. Holding a function or dining with family & friends… *The Bell* is there to welcome you.

The Bell, Dunstable Road, Studham, Bedfordshire LU6 2QG • **Tel:** 01582 872460
Website: www.thebellinstudham.co.uk • **Email:** info@thebellinstudham.co.uk

SOULDROP
Map 11 SP96

The Bedford Arms

tel: 01234 781384 **High St MK44 1EY**
email: bedfordarms.souldrop@gmail.com
dir: *From Rushden take A6 towards Bedford. In 6m right into Stocking Lane to Souldrop. Pub 50mtrs on right*

Good, traditional food at this village free house

There are new owners at this 300-year-old pub, set in a secluded no-through-road village deep in the Bedfordshire countryside. It's a comfortable, cosy and traditional place, with a cottage-style interior and a pleasant beer garden with views across the fields to distant woodland. You'll find a good range of real ales and ciders in the bar, while the restaurant menu covers pub classics like steak and ale pie and ham, egg and chips; a choice of burgers, and various steaks or a mixed grill, while fish mains might include sea bass. Start with pan-seared scallops on garden pea mash; garlic mushrooms; or whitebait.

Open 12-3 4.30-12 (Fri-Sat 12-12 Sun 12-11) Closed Mon (ex BHs) **Food** Lunch Tue-Sat 12-2, Sun 12-4 Dinner Tue-Sat 6-9 Av main course £10 ⊕ FREE HOUSE ◀ Greene King IPA, Black Sheep, Morland Old Speckled Hen, 2 guest ales Ö Evershed's Cider, Thatchers Gold, Saxby's Cider. ₹ 13 **Facilities** Non-diners area ❤ (Bar Garden Outside area) ♦ Children's menu Children's portions Garden Outside area ⋒ Parking WiFi ▦

STANBRIDGE
Map 11 SP92

The Five Bells

tel: 01525 210224 **Station Rd LU7 9JF**
email: fivebells@fullers.co.uk
dir: *A505 from Leighton Buzzard towards Dunstable, turn left to Stanbridge*

Relaxed village pub with large garden

This whitewashed 400-year-old village inn has a bar that features lots of bare wood as well as comfortable armchairs and rustic wood and tiled floors. The modern decor extends to the bright, airy 75-cover dining room with its oak beams and paintings. The inn uses local suppliers whenever possible to offer farm-assured chicken and beef, and sustainable seafood. The menu typically includes dishes such as beer battered cod and chips, and steak and ale suet pudding, which are complemented by light lunches, blackboard daily specials and Sunday roasts. There's also a spacious lawned garden and patio.

Open all day all wk 11-11 (Sun 12-10.30) **Food** Lunch Mon-Fri 12-2.30, Sat 12-10, Sun 12-7 Dinner Mon-Thu 5-9, Fri 5-10, Sat 12-10, Sun 12-7 ⊕ FULLER'S ◀ London Pride, guest ale Ö Westons Stowford Press, Cornish Orchards. ₹ 8 **Facilities** Non-diners area ❤ (Bar Garden) ♦ Children's menu Children's portions Garden ⋒ Parking WiFi ▦ (notice required)

STUDHAM
Map 11 TL01

The Bell in Studham

tel: 01582 872460 **Dunstable Rd LU6 2QG**
email: info@thebellinstudham.co.uk **web:** www.thebellinstudham.co.uk
dir: *M1 junct 9, A5 towards Dunstable. Left onto B4540 to Kensworth, B4541 to Studham*

Real home cooking and more besides

This 500-year-old, Grade II listed pub is surrounded by some of Bedfordshire's prettiest countryside and is close to Dunstable, Dunstable Downs, Whipsnade Zoo and Hemel Hempstead. The welcoming interior is full of beams and stacked logs ready for a winter fire. In summer, grab a table in the large garden and enjoy the panoramic views. From the menu expect sharing boards, home-made pies, roasts with all the trimmings, beer battered cod and triple cooked chips and even '99' ice creams. Authentic pizzas are cooked on the stone clay oven. All around the pub you'll find gifts to buy – T-shirts, clocks and candles to mention but a few.

Open all day all wk **Food** Lunch Mon-Fri 12-2.30, Sat-Sun all day Dinner Mon-Fri 5-9.30, Sat-Sun all day Set menu available ⊕ FREE HOUSE ◀ Greene King IPA, Sharp's Doom Bar, guest ales Ö Thatchers Gold & Heritage. ₹ 10 **Facilities** Non-diners area ❤ (Bar Garden) ♦ Children's portions Garden ⋒ Parking WiFi ▦ (notice required)

See advert on page 27

SUTTON
Map 12 TL24

The John O'Gaunt
PICK OF THE PUBS

tel: 01767 260377 **30 High St SG19 2TP**
email: thejohnogauntsutton@hotmail.co.uk
dir: *From A1 at Biggleswade at rdbt take A6001, straight on at 2 rdbts, right onto B1040. Pub in village centre*

Dog-welcoming village pub

First licensed in 1835, Jago and Jane Hurt's 18th-century free house takes its name from the 1st Duke of Lancaster, son of King Edward III and local lord of the manor. Set back from the road, it's a matter of only yards to an ancient, double-arched packhorse bridge and ford across Potton Brook. Look for Paige, the Hurts' pet Staffie, making a cheeky appearance on the pub sign. Ale pump badges in the bar declare loyalty to Adnams and Woodforde's, with Aspall Harry Sparrow for real-cider drinkers. There's nothing too complicated on Jago's menus: chicken liver parfait with red onion marmalade and toast; pan-fried cod loin with cockles, smoked bacon, capers and new potatoes; pie of the day with hand-cut chips, braised red cabbage and roasted root vegetables; and grills. Open toasted sandwiches are served at lunchtime. Two roasts plus the regular menu on Sundays.

Open 12-3 6.30-11 (Sun 12-6) Closed Mon (ex BH) **Food** Lunch Tue-Sat 12-2, Sun 12-3 Dinner Tue-Sat 6.30-9 ⊕ FREE HOUSE ◀ Woodforde's Wherry, Adnams Broadside & Lighthouse ♻ Aspall Harry Sparrow. ☁ 12 **Facilities** Non-diners area ♣ (Bar Garden) ♦ Children's portions Garden ⋒ Parking WiFi

TILSWORTH
Map 11 SP92

The Anchor Inn

tel: 01525 211404 **1 Dunstable Rd LU7 9PU**
dir: *Exit A5 at Tilsworth. In 1m pub on right at 3rd bend*

Classic Victorian country dining pub with a garden that's great for kids

Dating from 1878, The Anchor is the only pub in the Saxon village of Tilsworth and it boasts an acre of garden including patio seating for alfresco dining and an adventure playground for younger visitors. The pub prides itself on the fresh food and well-kept beers and guest ales. A starter of Barbary duck and port parfait with toasted ciabatta and red onion marmalade might be followed by wild boar and apple sausages with champ and redcurrant gravy; or bacon wrapped chicken breast stuffed with mozzarella, buttered new potatoes and sauce vierge.

Open all day all wk 12-11.30 **Food** Lunch Mon-Fri 12-2.30, Sat 12-9, Sun 12-7 Dinner Mon-Fri 6-9, Sat 12-9, Sun 12-7 Av main course £10-£14 Set menu available ⊕ GREENE KING ◀ Rotating guest ales ♻ Thatchers.
Facilities Non-diners area ♦ Children's menu Children's portions Play area Garden ⋒ Parking WiFi ▦ (notice required)

WOBURN
Map 11 SP93

The Birch at Woburn

tel: 01525 290295 **20 Newport Rd MK17 9HX**
email: info@birchwoburn.com **web:** www.birchwoburn.com
dir: *M1 junct 13, follow A4012 (Woburn) signs at rdbts. From A4012 turn right at T-junct signed Woburn Sands (A5130). Pub on right*

Serious about good, locally sourced food

Close to Woburn Abbey and the Safari Park, this smart family-run bar and restaurant has built its reputation on friendly service and freshly cooked food made from locally sourced ingredients whenever possible; the kitchen team is passionate about sourcing ingredients from local farms and estates. The contemporary restaurant is welcoming and the menu offers dishes such as The Birch chargrilled steak burger in a toasted brioche bun at lunchtime, and pan-fried hake fillet, sage and caramelised onion risotto, toasted almonds and garlic butter in the evening. There's also fresh fish and steaks cooked on the open griddle and traditional roasts on Sundays.

Open 12-3 6-12 Closed 25-26 Dec, 1 Jan, Sun eve **Food** Lunch all wk 12-2.30 Dinner Mon-Sat 6-10 Set menu available ⊕ FREE HOUSE ◀ Sharp's Doom Bar, Adnams ♻ Westons Mortimers Orchard. ☁ 14 **Facilities** Non-diners area ♦ Children's portions Outside area ⋒ Parking ▦ (notice required)

The Black Horse

tel: 01525 290210 **1 Bedford St MK17 9QB**
email: blackhorse@peachpubs.com
dir: *In town centre on A4012*

Georgian coaching inn serving seasonal fare

'Courtyard Garden' it says above the arch through which stagecoaches once entered and left this 18th-century inn, conveniently in the middle of pretty Woburn. Behind the Georgian frontage the cosy bar is lined with old leather-upholstered settles and the chic, relaxing dining area is where locally sourced, modern British menus offer venison from the Duke of Bedford's Woburn Estate; roast free-range chicken breast; Devon mussels and king prawn linguine; caramelised red onion and spinach tart; and daily specials. Bands play live music on the last Friday evening of the month.

Open all day all wk 11-11 (Sat 11am-11.30pm) Closed 25 Dec **Food** Lunch Mon-Fri 12-3, Sat 12-10, Sun 12-9 Dinner Mon-Fri 6-10, Sat 12-10, Sun 12-9 ⊕ GREENE KING/PEACH PUBS ◀ IPA & Abbot Ale, guest ales ♻ Aspall. ☁
Facilities Non-diners area ♣ (Bar Garden) ♦ Children's portions Garden ⋒ Cider festival WiFi ▦ (notice required)

BERKSHIRE

ALDWORTH
Map 5 SU57

The Bell Inn

tel: 01635 578272 **RG8 9SE**
dir: *Just off B4009 (Newbury to Streatley road)*

Well-kept local ales in timewarp setting

Beginning life as a manor hall in 1340, The Bell has reputedly been in the same family for 200 years: ask landlady Mrs Macaulay, she's been here for over 75 years. A 300-year-old, one-handed clock still stands in the taproom 'keeping imperfect time', and the rack for the spit-irons and clockwork roasting jack are still over the fireplace. One might be surprised to discover that an establishment without a restaurant can hold its own in a world of smart gastro-pubs. But The Bell survives thanks to hot, filled rolls and cracking pints of Maggs' Magnificent Mild or a West Berkshire brew or a monthly guest ale plus local farmhouse ciders.

Open Tue-Sat 11-3 6-11 (Sun 12-3 7-10.30) Closed 25 Dec, Mon (open BH Mon L only) **Food** Lunch Tue-Sat 11-2.30, Sun 12-2.30 Dinner Tue-Sat 6-9.30, Sun 7-9 ⊕ FREE HOUSE ◀ Arkell's 3B, West Berkshire Old Tyler & Maggs' Magnificent Mild, Loose Cannon Abingdon Bridge, guest ales ♻ Tutts Clump, Lilley's Pear & Apple, Red Dog. ♟ 10 **Facilities** Non-diners area ♣ (Bar Garden) ♦ Garden ⊨ Parking **Notes** ☺

ASCOT
Map 6 SU96

The Thatched Tavern

tel: 01344 620874 **Cheapside Rd SL5 7QG**
email: enquiries@thethatchedtavern.co.uk
dir: *Follow Ascot Racecourse signs. Through Ascot 1st left (Cheapside). 1.5m, pub on left*

Modern grub in a historic pub

En route to Windsor Castle, Queen Victoria's carriage was allegedly sometimes spotted outside this 400-year-old, flagstone-floored, low-ceilinged pub, while what the history books call 'her faithful servant' John Brown knocked a few back inside. The sheltered garden makes a fine spot to enjoy a Fuller's real ale, a glass of wine and, for lunch, perhaps sausage and red onion marmalade ciabatta or a ploughman's. For something more substantial try warm mackerel fillet, pickled winter vegetables and home-made guacamole, then lemon and thyme marinated corn-fed chicken breast, rustic ratatouille and dauphinoise potatoes.

Open all wk Mon-Thu 12-3 5.30-11 (Fri-Sun all day) **Food** Lunch Mon-Sat 12-2.30, Sun 12-8 Dinner Mon-Sat 6.30-9.30, Sun 12-8 ⊕ FREE HOUSE ◀ Fuller's London Pride, Thatched Best (pub's own from a local brewery), Guinness ♻ Westons Stowford Press. ♟ 11 **Facilities** Non-diners area ♦ Children's portions Garden Parking WiFi

ASHMORE GREEN
Map 5 SU56

The Sun in the Wood

tel: 01635 42377 **Stoney Ln RG18 9HF**
email: info@thesuninthewood.co.uk
dir: *From A34 at Robin Hood Rdbt left to Shaw, at mini rdbt right then 7th left into Stoney Ln. 1.5m, pub on left*

Country pub surrounded by woodland

The Sun is a country pub and restaurant surrounded by beautiful mature woodland; the interior is smart and modern. The menu proffers stone baked pizzas and sharing boards and reliable starters such as duck rillettes, onion chutney and rustic bread; a typical main course might fillet steak, flat mushroom, vine tomato,

rocket, hand-cut chips and Diane sauce. Sticky toffee pudding, salted caramel ice cream and salted caramel sauce might make the perfect finish.

Open all wk 12-11 (Sun 12-10.30) **Food** Lunch Mon-Sat 12-3, Sun 12-5 Dinner Mon-Sat 5.30-9.30 Av main course £8 Restaurant menu available Mon-Sat ⊕ WADWORTH ◀ 6X, Henry's Original IPA, Horizon & Swordfish ♻ Westons Stowford Press, Aspall. ♟ 15 **Facilities** Non-diners area ♣ (Bar Garden) ♦ Children's menu Children's portions Play area Garden ⊨ Parking WiFi

BOXFORD
Map 5 SU47

The Bell at Boxford

tel: 01488 608721 **Lambourn Rd RG20 8DD**
email: paul@bellatboxford.com
dir: *M4 junct 14, A338 towards Wantage. Right onto B4000 to x-roads, signed Boxford. Or from A34 junct 13 towards Hungerford, right at rdbt onto B4000. At x-roads right to Boxford. Pub signed*

Seafood specials in a pretty setting

At the heart of the lovely Lambourn Valley, close to Newbury Racecourse, this mock-Tudor country pub boasts a period main bar in the part of the building dating back to the 17th century, and the very occasional visit from Mr Merritt, the resident ghost. Alfresco dining in flower-laden heated terraces offers hog roasts and barbecues and there's a good range of local ales, and also Stowford Press cider on draught; all 60 wines on the list are available by the glass. Feast on seafood specials (whole lobster available if the season's right); tiger prawn linguine; duck egg, black pudding and hollandaise; and mushroom risotto.

Open all day all wk **Food** Lunch Mon-Fri 12-2.30, Sat-Sun 12-6.30 Dinner Mon-Fri 7-9.30, Sat-Sun 12-6.30, (Pizza all wk 2.30-10.30) Set menu available Restaurant menu available all wk ⊕ FREE HOUSE ◀ West Berkshire Good Old Boy & Mr Chubb's Lunchtime Bitter ♻ Westons Stowford Press, Lilley's Apples & Pears. ♟ 60 **Facilities** Non-diners area ♣ (Bar Garden) ♦ Children's portions Garden Outside area ⊨ Parking WiFi ▦ (notice required)

BRAY
Map 6 SU97

The Crown Inn ◉◉
PICK OF THE PUBS

tel: 01628 621936 **High St SL6 2AH**
email: reservations@thecrownatbray.co.uk
dir: *M4 junct 8, A308(M) signed Maidenhead (Central). At next rdbt, right onto A308 signed Bray & Windsor. 0.5m, left onto B3028 signed Bray. In village, pub on left*

Cosy, Thames-side village inn

Half-timbered outside, this Tudor building is a well-preserved reminder of days long gone, with heavy beams, open fires and all the trimmings. It's been an inn for several centuries; its name possibly derives from regular visits made by King Charles II when visiting Nell Gwynn nearby. Assignations today are firmly rooted in the desire to enjoy the dishes that have gained this Heston Blumenthal-owned pub two AA Rosettes for the distinctly traditional English menu. Diners (restaurant bookings essential, but not for bar meals) may commence with a starter such as Cornish mussels with garlic, apple, cider and parsley; setting the standard for mains like chargrilled Hereford sirloin steak with marrowbone sauce; or roast stone bass fillet with spinach, tomato, shallot and rocket; finishing with apple and plum crumble with vanilla ice cream. The enclosed courtyard is sheltered by a spreading vine, and there's a large garden in which to quaff Caledonian Golden XPA.

Open all day all wk **Food** Lunch Mon-Fri 12-2.30, Sat 12-3, Sun 12-8 Dinner Mon-Thu 6-9.30, Fri-Sat 6-10, Sun 12-8 ⊕ FAT DUCK GROUP ◀ Courage Best Bitter & Directors, Caledonian Flying Scotsman & Golden XPA, guest ales. ♟ 19 **Facilities** Non-diners area ♣ (Bar Garden Outside area) ♦ Children's menu Children's portions Garden Outside area ⊨ Parking WiFi ▦ (notice required)

The Hinds Head ◉◉◉

PICK OF THE PUBS

tel: 01628 626151 **High St SL6 2AB**
email: info@hindsheadbray.com
dir: *M4 junct 8/9 take Maidenhead Central exit. Next rdbt take Bray/Windsor exit. 0.5m, B3028 to Bray*

Old-English fare with a modern twist

This Heston Blumenthal's establishment in Bray has become, not surprisingly, a gastronomic destination, yet the striking 15th-century building remains very much a village local. Its origins as a pub are a little obscure, but the bar's atmosphere created by beams and sturdy oak panelling, log fires, leather chairs, and Windsor & Eton seasonal ales is reassuringly traditional. The main restaurant is on the ground floor, while upstairs are two further dining areas: the Vicar's Room and the larger Royal Room. Having worked alongside the team in the Tudor kitchens at Hampton Court Palace, Heston elaborates on original British cuisine, reintroducing classic recipes from the pub's Tudor roots. Hash of snails; and terrine of pork and Cumbrian ham are indicative starters. Gutsy main courses vary from bone-in sirloin of veal or oxtail and kidney pudding to smoked pollock, cured salmon and prawns fish pie with 'sea and sand'. For seekers of plainer fare there are 28-day aged Hereford prime steaks. Quaking pudding, inspired by a 17th-century sweet jelly recipe, is an ever popular dessert favourite.

Open all wk 11.30-11 (Sun 12-7 Mon 12-11) Closed 25 Dec **Food** Lunch Mon-Sat 12-2.30, Sun 12-4 Dinner Mon-Sat 6.30-9.30 Set menu available Restaurant menu available all wk ⊕ FREE HOUSE ◀ Rebellion IPA & seasonal ales, Windsor & Eton seasonal ale Ö Kentish Pip Vintage Pip. ♀ 15 **Facilities** Non-diners area ❀ (Bar) ♦♦ Children's menu Parking WiFi ▄▄ (notice required)

COLNBROOK Map 6 TQ07

The Ostrich

tel: 01753 682628 **High St SL3 0JZ**
email: enquiries@theostrichcolnbrook.co.uk
dir: *M25 junct 14 towards Poyle. Right at 1st rdbt, over next 2 rdbts. Left at sharp right bend into High St. Left at mini rdbt, pub on left*

900 years of hospitality and still going strong

One of England's oldest pubs can be found, perhaps surprisingly, close to Heathrow and minutes from the M25. Dating from 1106, the vast and rambling Ostrich oozes history. Some of its legends are particularly gruesome, as would befit the heavily timbered façade, cobbled courtyard, wonky oak beams, massive fireplaces and crooked stairs. Yet the interior has acquired a contemporary style, so expect glass doors, a steel bar, chunky furnishings and vibrant colours. The menu of pub food embraces roasted pork belly with blue cheese potato gratin; pesto-crusted cod supreme; grilled salmon fishcake salad; and steak and Spitfire ale pie.

Open all day all wk 12-11 **Food** Lunch Mon-Sat 12-2.30, Sun 12-9 Dinner Mon-Sat 6-9.30, Sun 12-9 ⊕ SHEPHERD NEAME ◀ Master Brew, Spitfire, Whitstable Bay Pale Ale, Shepherd Neame Bishops Finger Ö Symonds. ♀ 10 **Facilities** Non-diners area ♦♦ Children's menu Children's portions Garden ⊟ Parking WiFi ▄▄ (notice required)

COOKHAM Map 6 SU88

The White Oak ◉

tel: 01628 523043 **The Pound SL6 9QE**
email: info@thewhiteoak.co.uk
dir: *From A4 E of Maidenhead take A4094 signed Cookham. Left into High St (B4447) signed Cookham Rise/Cookham Dean. Pass through common. Left at mini rdbt, pub on right*

Modern British menus at friendly pub and restaurant

After a spell in London, Henry and Katherine Cripps returned to their roots to transform and run what is now a successful, contemporary village pub and

restaurant. Diners can tuck into award-winning, daily changing, modern British dishes, so perhaps start with celeriac and blue cheese soup and gorgonzola sippet; or gin and tonic salmon, lime, cucumber, sorrel and caper berries; then roast Cornish cod, samphire, charred cucumber and lemongrass. To finish perhaps, set milk chocolate, honey brittle and hazelnut crumb; or carrot cake, walnuts, sweet pickled sultanas and cream cheese.

Open all day all wk **Food** Lunch Mon-Sat 12-2.30, Sun 12-3.30 Dinner Mon-Sat 6.30-10, Sun 5.30-9 Av main course £9 Set menu available Restaurant menu available all wk ⊕ GREENE KING ◀ IPA & Abbot Ale Ö Aspall. ♀ 24 **Facilities** Non-diners area ♦♦ Children's menu Children's portions Garden ⊟ Parking WiFi

---

COOKHAM DEAN Map 5 SU88

The Chequers Brasserie

PICK OF THE PUBS

tel: 01628 481232 **Dean Ln SL6 9BQ**
email: info@chequersbrasserie.co.uk
dir: *From A4094 in Cookham High St towards Marlow, over rail line. 1m on right*

Historic pub with an established brasserie

Tucked away between Marlow and Maidenhead, The Chequers is in one of the prettiest villages in the Thames Valley. Striking Victorian and Edwardian villas around the green set the tone, while the surrounding wooded hills and dales have earned Cookham Dean a reputation as a centre for wonderful walks. Wooden beams, an open fire and comfortable seating welcome drinkers to the small bar, perhaps to sample Rebellion's fine ales. Dining takes place in the older part of the building, or in the conservatory; a private dining room can be reserved for parties. The menus of expertly prepared dishes are based on fresh, quality ingredients enhanced by careful use of cosmopolitan flavours. A starter of Scotch duck egg, black pudding, red onion jam and a balsamic reduction could be followed by seafood risotto; butternut squash and wild mushroom linguine; or chicken breast wrapped in Parma ham with cream Savoy cabbage and fondant potato.

Open all wk Mon-Fri 10-3 5.30-11 (Sat-Sun all day) ⊕ FREE HOUSE ◀ Rebellion IPA Ö Westons Stowford Press. **Facilities** ♦♦ Children's portions Garden Parking WiFi

---

NEW Uncle Tom's Cabin

tel: 01628 483339 **Hills Ln SL6 9NT**
email: info@uncletomscookham.co.uk
dir: *Contact pub for detailed directions*

Traditional pub with a large garden

The artist Stanley Spencer called Cookham, his birthplace and where he lived most of his life, 'a village in Heaven'. His museum is less than two miles away from this charming, low-beamed 17th-century pub, warmed when nature demands by open fires. A simple menu lists fillet of halibut with saffron and garden pea risotto; rocket pesto-stuffed breast of corn-fed chicken, wrapped in pancetta, with tenderstem broccoli; and mushroom arancini with red pepper coulis and truffle oil. Desserts include sticky toffee pudding with toffee sauce and ice cream; and brie de meaux cheese and biscuits with celery and apple chutney.

Open all wk 11.30-3 5.30-11 **Food** Contact pub for food times Av main course £12-£14 Set menu available Restaurant menu available all wk ⊕ PUNCH TAVERNS ◀ Fuller's London Pride, Rebellion IPA, Courage Best Bitter, Brakspear Ö Westons Stowford Press, Cornish Orchards. **Facilities** Non-diners area ❀ (Bar) ♦♦ Children's portions Garden ⊟ Parking WiFi ▄▄ (notice required)

CRAZIES HILL — Map 5 SU78

NEW The Horns

tel: 0118 940 6041 **RG10 8LY**
email: info@hornsatcrazieshill.co.uk **web:** www.hornsatcrazieshill.co.uk
dir: *Follow signs from A321 NE of Wargrave towards Henley-on-Thames*

Lovely old pub with great food and a welcoming atmosphere

Enthusiastic new licensees Adam and Sandra Purdy have a wealth of experience in the pub trade, and the newly refurbished Horns successfully combines rustic features and contemporary style. You'll find Brakspear and Wychwood Hobgoblin amongst the ales in the bar, while a good selection of dishes is available in the beamed dining room. Start with potted brown shrimps with chive and smoked paprika butter, and move on to a classic steak and mushroom pie with chips and greens. Lemon posset with blackberries and gingerbread rounds things off nicely.

Open 12-3 5-11 (Fri-Sat 12-11 Sun 12-7) Closed Mon **Food** Lunch Tue-Fri 12-2, Sat 12-2.30, Sun 12-5 Dinner Tue-Fri 6-9, Sat 6-9.30 Av main course £14 Set menu available ⊕ BRAKSPEAR ◀ Brakspear, Thwaites, Marston's, Wychwood Hobgoblin ♚ 12 **Facilities** Non-diners area ✿ (Bar Garden) ♦ Children's menu Children's portions Play area Garden ᴙ Parking WiFi ⊟ (notice required)

CURRIDGE — Map 5 SU47

The Bunk Inn ★★★★ INN ◉◉

tel: 01635 200400 **RG18 9DS**
email: info@thebunkinn.co.uk **web:** www.thebunkinn.co.uk
dir: *M4 junct 13, A34 N towards Oxford. Take 1st slip road. At T-junct right signed Hermitage. In approx 1m right at mini rdbt into Long Ln, 1st right signed Curridge*

Village tavern just outside Newbury

One of the oldest village buildings, this inn is owned by the Upham Group so you'll find their brewery's tasty beers at the bar. The log fire-warmed village snug remains a comfy focus for chatter or contemplation, whilst an airy restaurant with eye-catching decor or a heated patio offer alternative locations to sit, sup and study the compact, well-balanced menu. The chefs home-in on local suppliers and create dishes such as glazed pork faggot with black pudding, baked potato purée, Savoy cabbage and honeyed parsnip; and curried Brixham crab and leek omelette. Specials may feature game from the local estates and woods that characterise this green heart of Berkshire.

Open all day all wk **Food** Lunch Mon-Fri 12-2.30, Sat 12-3, Sun 12-3.30 Dinner Mon-Sat 6.30-9.30, Sun 6.30-9 Set menu available Restaurant menu available Mon-Sat ⊕ UPHAM GROUP ◀ Punter, Tipster, 1st Drop & Stakes Ö Orchard Pig. ♚ 9 **Facilities** Non-diners area ✿ (Bar Garden) ♦ Children's menu Children's portions Family room Garden ᴙ Beer festival Parking WiFi ⊟ (notice required) **Rooms** 9

EASTBURY — Map 5 SU37

NEW The Eastbury Plough — PICK OF THE PUBS

tel: 01488 71312 **RG17 7JN**
email: info@eastburyplough.com **web:** www.eastburyplough.com
dir: *M4 junct 14, A338 towards Wantage. In Great Shefford left into Church St. 3m, pub on right*

Passionate about local produce

Eastbury is a pretty downland village, in the 'vale of the racehorse' and the white-painted Plough, is a real local gem. Chef-patron Graham White, owner for four years, is mostly self-taught and his passion for Berkshire produce is very clear. You can eat alfresco when the weather is good, or in the comfortable restaurant. If you'd just like a pint and sandwich that's fine, and you'll be spoilt with excellent choices for both. There's ales from nearby microbreweries, and if you discover that you are particularly fond of one of them and would like to take some home, the inn can provide a takeaway container for your purchase. For a sandwich how about bloomer toast with pink cannon of venison, Barkham Brie, walnuts and chilli jam; or a fish finger bloomer, chunky home-made tartare and crisp cos lettuce? The menu might feature dishes like shin of beef hash with poached duck egg and hollandaise, and mains such as smoked cod loin, dauphinoise potatoes with parsley and bacon velouté; or confit shoulder and rump of lamb, with creamed Savoy cabbage and mustard.

Open 12-4 6-11.30 (Sun 12-10.30) Closed Mon **Food** Lunch Tue-Sat 12-2.15, Sun 12-2.30 Dinner Tue-Sat 6-9.30, Sun 5-8 ⊕ FREE HOUSE ◀ Ramsbury, Sharp's Doom Bar, Loose Cannon, Two Cocks, Eastbury, Siren Craft Ö Cornish Orchards. ♚ 14 **Facilities** Non-diners area ✿ (Bar Garden) ♦ Children's menu Children's portions Play area Garden ᴙ Parking WiFi ⊟ (notice required)

EAST GARSTON — Map 5 SU37

The Queen's Arms Country Inn — PICK OF THE PUBS

tel: 01488 648757 **RG17 7ET**
email: info@queensarmshotel.co.uk
dir: *M4 junct 14, A338 towards Wantage. Turn left in Great Shefford for East Garston*

Stylish pub in the heart of racehorse country

The oldest part of this Lambourn Valley inn was a farmer's cottage in the 18th century; its name derives from being licensed around 1856, the year of Queen Victoria's Silver Jubilee. Freddie Tulloch took over here in August 2015 and has maintained the warm welcome and stylishly traditional setting. In an area with 2,000 racehorses and more than 50 racing yards, this charming pub acts as a quasi-headquarters for British racing with owners, trainers and jockeys among its clientele. With a glass of Doom Bar or Aspall cider in hand, choose from the menu:

ham hock and home-made chutney sandwich; a burger from the bar menu or pub favourites – fish pie or beer battered cod and chips. After a gallop, two courses could be called for: try chicken parfait with toasted brioche, followed by roasted salmon fillet with new potatoes, mango salsa and salad.

Open all day all wk 11am-mdnt **Food** Lunch all wk 12-3 Dinner Mon-Sat 6-9 Restaurant menu available all wk ⊕ FREE HOUSE ◄ Sharp's Doom Bar, Guinness, guest ales Ŏ Aspall. **Facilities** Non-diners area ❖ (Bar Garden) ♦ Children's menu Children's portions Garden ♖ Parking WiFi ◖ (notice required)

FINCHAMPSTEAD   Map 5 SU76

NEW The Greyhound

tel: 0118 973 2269 **Longwater Rd RG40 3TS**
email: info@greyhoundfinchampstead.co.uk
dir: On B3016

Traditional pub with contemporary feel

From the outside, a largely unchanged Victorian, red-brick building with attractive, bargeboarded gables; the interior is an object lesson in how modern design can work successfully in a 19th-century shell. Although owned by Greene King, right of entry is given to guest real ales from breweries such as Siren Craft in the village and Windsor & Eton. Food-wise, honourable mentions may be made of Severn & Wye smoked eel; smoked Gressingham duck breast; pan-fried mackerel fillet; and roast cauliflower and sweet potato tagine. A short lunch selection includes Finchampstead ale rarebit; and Macsween's vegetarian haggis and mushroom ciabatta.

Open all day all wk **Food** Mon-Sat 12-9.30, Sun 12-7 Av main course £15 Set menu available ⊕ GREENE KING ◄ IPA, Windsor & Eton, Truman's, Siren Craft Ŏ Aspall, Hogs Back Hazy Hog. ▾ 30 **Facilities** Non-diners area ❖ (Bar Outside area) ♦ Children's menu Children's portions Family room Outside area ♖ Parking WiFi

---

FRILSHAM   Map 5 SU57

The Pot Kiln ◉   PICK OF THE PUBS

tel: 01635 201366 **RG18 0XX**
email: info@potkiln.org
dir: From Yattendon follow Pot Kiln signs, cross over motorway. 0.25m, pub on right

Locally sourced game dishes drive the menu here

Hidden down narrow lanes, this 18th-century pub can be a bit elusive, but when you find it – and you will – you'll also find it was worth the effort. A former kiln-workers' beer house, the bar has a choice of West Berkshire Brewery ales and Somerset cider. Game and wild food has long fascinated owner Mike Robinson, a passion that lies behind the success of this idyllic red-brick pub. A big draw is the venison from the deer herd that Mike manages nearby. Once out of the pot, it is served in various ways, such as a wild venison Scotch egg; and fallow, bacon and onion pie, mash and January King cabbage. Typical of the tempting dishes on the ever-changing menus are rabbit and foie gras lasagne with wild mushroom cream sauce; and pan-fried red mullet, fennel, cockles and bacon chowder. On summer Sunday evenings, pizzas are cooked in a wood-fired oven in the garden.

Open all wk Mon Fri 12-3 6-11 (Sat-Sun 12-11) Closed 25 Dec **Food** Lunch all wk 12-2.30 Dinner all wk 6.30-8.30 Restaurant menu available all wk ⊕ FREE HOUSE ◄ Brick Kiln, West Berkshire Mr Chubb's Lunchtime Bitter & Maggs' Magnificent Mild Ŏ Thatchers, Cotswold. ▾ 10 **Facilities** Non-diners area ❖ (Bar Garden) ♦ Children's menu Children's portions Play area Garden ♖ Parking WiFi ◖ (notice required)

HAMPSTEAD NORREYS   Map 5 SU57

The White Hart

tel: 01635 202248 **Church St RG18 0TB**
email: the.white.hart@hotmail.co.uk
dir: M4 junct 13, A34 signed Oxford. Left signed Hermitage. Through Hermitage. At T-junct left signed Hampstead Norreys. At mini rdbt in village turn right. Pub on left

Steeped in history and surrounded by beautiful countryside

A charming, traditional building dating back to the 16th-century. Absolutely everything on the menu, from stocks and sauces to the desserts, is made from scratch. Meats come from an award-winning butcher and game-supplier down the road. On the main menu, cod and chips; duck breast; and stuffed mushroom. Look to the specials board for constantly changing dishes such as piri piri pork with sweet potato mash and mango and coriander salsa; roasted monkfish wrapped in Parma ham with chorizo risotto; and minted lamb steak, dauphinoise potatoes with red wine jus. Arrive on the last weekend in June for the annual beer festival.

Open 12-3 6-close (Sat-Sun 12-close) Closed 1 Jan, Mon **Food** Lunch Tue-Sat 12-2.30, Sun 12-3 Dinner Tue-Thu 6-9, Fri-Sat 6-9.30, Sun 6-8.30 ⊕ GREENE KING ◄ Morland Original Ŏ Aspall. **Facilities** Non-diners area ❖ (Bar Garden) ♦ Children's menu Children's portions Play area Garden ♖ Beer festival Parking WiFi ◖ (notice required)

HERMITAGE   Map 5 SU57

The White Horse of Hermitage

tel: 01635 200325 **Newbury Rd RG18 9TB**
email: whitehorsehermitage@gmail.com
dir: 5m from Newbury on B4009. From M4 junct 13 follow signs for Newbury Showground, right into Priors Court Rd, left at mini rdbt, pub approx 50yds on right

Enjoyable home-cooked food and large garden

This family-friendly pub dates back at least 160 years and is run by experienced operator Sarah Sweeney. The White Horse has achieved a solid reputation for its pub food, using the freshest and finest local produce to create a daily menu that typically includes burgers, pies, steaks and other daily specials, all washed down with pints of Abbot Ale or Aspall cider. The interior bar and restaurant is contemporary in decor, and outside you can choose between the Mediterranean-style patio or the large garden, which is equipped with swings and climbing frames for younger visitors.

Open all day all wk **Food** Lunch Mon-Sat 12-3, Sun 12-6 Dinner Mon-Thu 5-9, Fri-Sat 5-9.30, Sun 12-6 Set menu available ⊕ GREENE KING ◄ Abbot Ale & IPA, Guinness, guest ales Ŏ Thatchers, Aspall. ▾ 9 **Facilities** Non-diners area ❖ (Bar Restaurant Garden) ♦ Children's menu Children's portions Play area Garden ♖ Beer festival Cider festival Parking WiFi ◖ (notice required)

HOLYPORT
Map 6 SU87

The Belgian Arms

tel: 01628 634468 **SL6 2JR**
email: reservations@thebelgianarms.com
dir: M4 junct 8, A308(M). At rdbt take A330 signed Ascot. At Holyport village green left signed Bray & Windsor. 1st left into Holyport St. Belgian Arms on right

Earthy decor, friendly staff and classy food

A grassy beer-garden stretches from the secluded patio of this convivial village pub to the duck pond on the green. It's served the pretty village for two centuries; the unique name remembers the service given by local soldiers who fought in Belgium during the Great War. In season a huge twisted wisteria blankets the front of the building; inside, there's an unfussy, restful mix of pastels to the decor. Popular as a destination dining pub, it's also the hub of the community, where drinkers enjoy beers from Brakspear and look forward to the regular live music and entertainment nights.

Open all day all wk Mon 5-9 Tue-Thu 12-3 5-11 Fri-Sat 12-11 Sun 12-9.30
Food Lunch Tue-Sat 12-2.30, Sun 12-4 Dinner Tue-Thu 6.30-9.30, Fri-Sat 6-10, Sun 6-9 Restaurant menu available all wk ⊕ BRAKSPEAR ◗ Brakspear Best & Special, Ringwood Boondoggle Ꝋ Symonds. ♟ 12 **Facilities** Non-diners area ✿ (Bar Garden) ♦ Children's menu Children's portions Garden ⊼ Parking WiFi

HUNGERFORD
Map 5 SU36

The Pheasant Inn

tel: 01488 648284 **Ermin St, Shefford Woodlands RG17 7AA**
email: info@pheasantinnlambourn.co.uk
dir: M4 junct 14, A338 towards Wantage. Left onto B4000 towards Lambourn

Chic pub with good food, now in new hands

Welsh drovers following Roman Ermin Street would stop at what was originally the Board House; later it became The Paraffin House, presumably a profitable sideline to beer at one time. Today, the bar serves Ramsbury Gold and Upham Punter ales, and Symonds Founders Reserve cider. Food style is evidenced by starters of king prawn raviolo with pea shoots, tarragon and celeriac; and mains of pan-fried duck breast with pressed potatoes, creamed leeks, cranberries and roasted figs; rump and sirloin steaks with mushrooms, tomato and hand-cut chips; and pumpkin tortellini with celeriac, fennel, ginger and crispy shallots. For dessert, perhaps caramel pannacotta, pineapple and amaretto biscuits.

Open all day all wk Closed 25 Dec **Food** Lunch all wk 12-2.30 Dinner Mon-Sat 6.30-9.30, Sun 6.30-8.30 Restaurant menu available all wk ⊕ FREE HOUSE ◗ Ramsbury Gold, Upham Punter Ꝋ Symonds Founders Reserve. ♟ 12 **Facilities** Non-diners area ✿ (Bar Restaurant Garden) ♦ Children's menu Children's portions Garden ⊼ Parking WiFi ▭

The Swan Inn ★★★★ INN
PICK OF THE PUBS

tel: 01488 668326 **Craven Rd, Lower Green, Inkpen RG17 9DX**
email: enquiries@theswaninn-organics.co.uk **web:** www.theswaninn-organics.co.uk
dir: S on Hungerford High St, past rail bridge, left to Hungerford Common, right signed Inkpen

Beamed village inn with excellent walks on the doorstep

Idyllically positioned on the North Wessex Downs, this 17th-century pub has its own farm shop, which is the first clue that owners Mary and Bernard Harris are also beef farmers. All the meat on the menu here is organic, with beef from their own farm and chicken from Otter Valley. The beers are organic too, with Jester Bitter from nearby Great Shefford among the regular pumps. Almost everything on the menu is prepared using fresh farm produce, including vegetables and soft fruit. Most pasta is hand made on the premises, maybe making an appearance on the menu as beef ravioli; or ricotta and spinach cannelloni. Other main course choices might include steak and kidney suet pudding; or award-winning home-made sausages and mash. There is an attractive terraced garden and 10 en suite bedrooms.

Open 12-2.30 7-11 (Sat 12-11 Sun 12-4) Closed 23 Dec-1 Feb, Mon, Tue
Food Lunch Wed-Sun 12-2.30 Dinner Wed-Sat 7-9.30 Av main course £12 ⊕ FREE HOUSE ◗ Butts Traditional, Jester & Blackguard Porter, guest ales.
Facilities Non-diners area ♦ Children's menu Children's portions Play area Garden Outside area ⊼ Parking WiFi ▭ (notice required) **Rooms** 10

HURLEY
Map 5 SU88

NEW Dew Drop Inn

tel: 01628 315662 **Honey Ln SL6 6RB**
email: info@dewdrophurley.co.uk
dir: M4 junct 8, A404(M). A4130 signed Hurley. At T-junct left (A4130 signed Hurley). At rdbt 1st left signed Burchetts Green. Right into Honey Ln. Pub at end (single track road) on right

Tucked away down a bridle path

There's hardly another building within sight of this Brakspear pub down a bridle path, just as the asphalt turns to grass. Dog-friendly and presumably horse-friendly too, as it must have been when highwayman Dick Turpin allegedly hid his mount in the cellar. Landlord Luke wonders how, given that he can't even stand up in it. The legend explains why the menu lists a Turpin minced beef and pork burger; other options include deep-fried haloumi with sweet chilli sauce; and a special of venison lasagne with tomato and basil bruschetta. The pub cures its own bacon, makes its own sausages and sells eggs from its own chickens.

Open Closed Mon **Food** Lunch Tue-Fri 12-3, Sat-Sun 12-4 Dinner Tue-Sat 6-9 Av main course £12 ⊕ BRAKSPEAR ◗ Old Ale & Special Ꝋ Symonds. ♟ 9 **Facilities** Non-diners area ✿ (Bar Restaurant Garden) ♦ Children's menu Children's portions Garden ⊼ Parking WiFi

The Olde Bell Inn ★★★★★ INN ◉◉ PICK OF THE PUBS

tel: 01628 825881 **High St SL6 5LX**
email: oldebellreception@coachinginn.co.uk **web:** www.theoldebell.co.uk
dir: *M4 junct 8/9 follow Henley signs. At rdbt take A4130 towards Hurley. Right to Hurley, inn 800yds on right*

Ancient former coaching inn, probably Britain's oldest

In the 12th century what is today's inn was a guest house for pilgrims visiting Hurley's Benedictine priory, its nave surviving to become today's parish church. Sadly, unlike in the 1890s, so it is said, the landlord doesn't stand at the Olde Bell's door every Sunday dishing out free sherry to churchgoers. Although not medieval throughout, it has a good claim to be the country's longest-operating inn, understandably when you see all its nooks, crannies and crooked doors. Meals are served in both the bar and chic dining room, where the banquettes at some tables are softened by Welsh woollen blankets. Bar menu favourites are Cumberland sausages, mash and red onion marmalade; and beef and beer puff pastry pie, while likely to appear on the main menu are pork tenderloin with creamy Stilton and parmesan polenta; pan-fried fillet of sea bass with sweet chilli escabeche; and wild mushroom risotto. Guests are free to roam the charming estate.

Open all day all wk 11am-mdnt (Sun 11-11) **Food** Lunch Mon-Sat 12-2.30, Sun 12.30-3.30 Dinner Mon-Sat 6-9.30, Sun 6.30-9 Av main course £12.50 Set menu available Restaurant menu available all wk ⊕ FREE HOUSE ◀ Rebellion, Theakston ♂ Burrow Hill. ▯ 10 **Facilities** Non-diners area ❀ (Bar Garden) ◆◆ Children's menu Children's portions Play area Garden ⊨ Parking WiFi ☞ **Rooms** 48

The Green Man

tel: 0118 934 2599 **Hinton Rd RG10 0BP**
web: www.greenmanhurst.co.uk
dir: *From Wokingham on A321 towards Twyford. Right after Hurst Cricket Club cricket ground on right into Hinton Rd*

Ever-reliable village retreat

The Green Man is a homely half-timbered cottage pub situated close to the village cricket pitch. Older parts of the building predate its first licence granted in 1602; thick beams were recycled from Tudor warships and offer a memorable interior in this appealing rustic retreat. Brakspear Brewery bitter and seasonal ales continue to keep drinkers happy. Diners can anticipate a seasonally adjusted, solidly British menu with mains like grilled salmon with wild rice risotto; venison Wellington, black cabbage with port and blackcurrant gravy; or potato rösti with broccoli, roasted salsify and crisp duck egg. Sandwiches, jacket potatoes, and lighter meals are also available. There's a tree-shaded beer garden with serene country views.

Open all day all wk **Food** Lunch all wk 12-3 Dinner Mon-Fri 6-9.30, Sat-Sun all day ⊕ BRAKSPEAR ◀ Bitter & Seasonal ales, Wychwood Hobgoblin ♂ Addlestones. ▯ 20 **Facilities** Non-diners area ❀ (Bar Garden) ◆◆ Children's menu Children's portions Play area Garden ⊨ Parking WiFi

---

Bird In Hand Country Inn   PICK OF THE PUBS

tel: 01628 826622 & 822781 **Bath Rd RG10 9UP**
email: info@birdinhand.co.uk
dir: *On A4, 5m W of Maidenhead, 7m E of Reading*

Friendly country pub

Three generations of landlady Caroline Shone's family have run this part 14th-century inn; it's said that George III sometimes stopped here when he resided at Windsor Castle. The choice of real ales in the wood-panelled bar, the oldest part of the pub, runs to two guests in addition to Bingham's locally brewed Twyford Tipple. The 50-bin wine list includes a white and a rosé from nearby Stanlake Park vineyard. In the attractive restaurant, which overlooks a courtyard and fountain, the menu (this also applies in the bar) offers light meals such as scampi and chips; seafood pie; and camembert tart. Classic mains include various steaks; seared calves' liver with crispy bacon and onion rings; or lamb hot pot. There is also an extensive BBQ menu, and a selection of home-made desserts. Beer festivals take place in June and November.

Open all day all wk **Food** all wk 12-10 Av main course £13 ⊕ FREE HOUSE ◀ Binghams Twyford Tipple, Marston's Pedigree, 2 guest ales ♂ Thatchers. ▯ 20 **Facilities** Non-diners area ❀ (Bar Garden) ◆◆ Children's menu Children's portions Garden ⊨ Beer festival Parking WiFi ☞ (notice required)

The Stag

tel: 01488 638436 **Shop Ln RG20 8QG**
dir: *6m from Newbury on B4494*

A great spot after a country walk

The white-painted Stag lies just off the village green in a sleepy downland village, close to the Ridgeway long-distance path and Snelsmore Common, home to nightjar, woodlark and grazing Exmoor ponies. Inside old black-and-white photographs tell of village life many years ago. Traditional home-cooked food is the order of the day, and the special board changes weekly. Sunday lunches are available.

Open 12-3 6-11 Closed Sun eve & Mon **Food** Lunch Tue-Sat 12-2, Sun 12-2.30 Dinner Tue-Sat 6-9 ⊕ FREE HOUSE ◀ Morland Original, West Berkshire Good Old Boy, guest ales ♂ Aspall. **Facilities** Non-diners area ❀ (Bar Garden Outside area) ◆◆ Children's menu Children's portions Garden Outside area ⊨ Parking WiFi ☞ (notice required)

MARSH BENHAM
Map 5 SU46

The Red House

tel: 01635 582017 **RG20 8LY**
email: info@theredhousepub.com
dir: *From Newbury A4 towards Hungerford. Pub signed. in approx 3m. Left onto unclassified road to Marsh Benham*

Thatched country pub with gluten-free menu specialities

Just a stroll (dog walkers welcome) from the Kennet & Avon Canal, this trim thatched pub is tucked away in the verdant Kennet Valley. Indulge in a beer from the respected West Berkshire brewery whilst contemplating views from the sheltered beer garden, or sit beside the log fire, anticipating your choice from the kitchen overseen by experienced French chef-patron Laurent Lebeau. His essentially British menu might include grilled queen scallops with lime and garlic butter, followed by steak and kidney pudding line caught haddock with West Berkshire beer batter and chips. There's a thoughtful gluten-free menu, as well. As for the wines, Laurent chooses well.

Open all day all wk **Food** Mon-Sat 12-9, Sun 12-8 Set menu available ⊕ FREE HOUSE ⬛ West Berkshire Good Old Boy & Mr Chubb's Lunchtime Bitter, Guinness, guest ales ⭕ Aspall Harry Sparrow. **Facilities** Non-diners area ❀ (Bar Garden) ⬤ Children's menu Children's portions Garden ⋔ Parking WiFi ▭ (notice required)

MONEYROW GREEN
Map 6 SU87

The White Hart

tel: 01628 621460 **SL6 2ND**
email: admin@thewhitehartholyport.co.uk
dir: *2m S from Maidenhead. M4 junct 8/9, follow Holyport signs then Moneyrow Green. Pub by petrol station*

Perfect stop for Windsor visitors

The close proximity to the M4 makes this traditional 19th-century coaching inn a popular spot for those heading to nearby Maidenhead and Windsor. The wood-panelled lounge bar is furnished with leather chesterfields, and quality home-made food and award-winning real ales can be enjoyed in a cosy atmosphere with an open fire. Typical mains are grilled chicken and chorizo salad; Argentine rib-eye steak; chilli con carne; and sausage and mash. Sandwiches, jacket potatoes and filled omelettes are offered at lunchtime. There are large gardens to enjoy in summer with a children's playground and petanque pitch.

Open all day all wk **Food** Lunch all wk 12-2.30 Dinner all wk 6-9 ⊕ GREENE KING ⬛ IPA, Morland Old Speckled Hen, guest ales ⭕ Westons Stowford Press. **Facilities** Non-diners area ❀ (Bar Garden) ⬤ Children's menu Children's portions Play area Garden ⋔ Parking WiFi ▭ (notice required)

NEWBURY
Map 5 SU46

The Newbury

tel: 01635 49000 **137 Bartholomew St RG14 5HB**
email: bar@thenewburypub.co.uk web: www.thenewburypub.co.uk
dir: *Phone for detailed directions*

Sophisticated town-centre dining-pub

Formerly the Bricklayers Arms, this popular Newbury pub is now owned by Greene King, whose ales are showcased across the handpumps on the bar. Through the elegant portico from the street there's a spacious bar, lounge and dining areas, and a roof terrace. The charcoal oven is the showpiece of the kitchen and top notch beef and lamb steaks are served with all the proper garnishes and triple cooked chips or fries. Other options might include steamed steak and kidney suet pudding; beer-battered Cornish haddock, crushed peas and skinny fries; or chickpea and coriander burger in a brioche bun.

Open all day all wk **Food** Lunch 12-3 Dinner 5.30-11 Restaurant menu available ⊕ GREENE KING ⬛ Two Cocks Cavalier & Roundhead, West Berkshire Good Old Boy & Mr Swift's Pale Ale ⭕ Westons Stowford Press. 🍷 26 **Facilities** Non-diners area ❀ (Bar Garden) ⬤ Children's portions Garden ⋔ WiFi ▭ (notice required)

See advert on opposite page

OAKLEY GREEN
Map 6 SU97

The Greene Oak ⊛

tel: 01753 864294 **SL4 5UW**
email: info@thegreeneoak.co.uk
dir: M4 junct 8, A308(M) signed Maidenhead Central. At rdbt take A308 signed Bray & Windsor. Right into Oakley Green Rd (B3024) signed Twyford. Pub on left

Thriving dining-pub near Windsor

The refinement that the Metropolitan Pub Company brings, draws those who enjoy a classy yet relaxed style of drinking and dining. On parade in the bar is Guardsman, which was the first new brew in Windsor for 80 years when launched in 2010. Considerable thought lies behind the daily-changing modern menus, as shown by goat's curd and carrot cake, carrots in whey, carrot purée and granola; roast halibut, seaweed dumplings, mussel ragout, monks beard and tapioca; and peanut butter parfait, caramelised bananas and coconut sorbet. Take the children – they have a menu all to themselves.

Open all day all wk Mon-Sat 12-11, Sun 12-7 **Food** Lunch Mon-Sat 12-2.30, Sun 12-5 Dinner Mon-Sat 6.30-9.30 ⊕ METROPOLITAN PUB COMPANY ◖ Greene King IPA, Windsor & Eton Guardsman, Rebellion ♂ Aspall. ♟ 26 **Facilities** Non-diners area ♣ (Bar Garden) ♦♦ Children's menu Children's portions Garden ⌁ Parking WiFi ☞ (notice required)

PALEY STREET
Map 5 SU87

The Royal Oak Paley Street ⊛⊛⊛   PICK OF THE PUBS

tel: 01628 620541 **Littlefield Green SL6 3JN**
email: reservations@theroyaloakpaleystreet.com
dir: M4 junct 8/9a, A308(M) signed Maidenhead (Central). Take A330 to Ascot. In 2m turn right onto B3024 to Twyford. 2nd pub on left

Great food in celebrity-owned, friendly village pub

With a cottagey aspect outside, the interior continues the theme with a distinctly welcoming, nostalgic feel; time-honoured decor and furnishings enhanced by contemporary artwork. Bang up to date is the white pebble and waterfall designer garden, a pleasant, alfresco retreat of shrub and herb planters. The team behind this success story includes former TV chat-show host Sir Michael Parkinson, and his son Nick who brings a wealth of experience to the helm, and having won numerous awards. The head chef sources the best seasonal British produce to create the ever-changing range of dishes such as a starter of smoked herring ravioli, leeks, chilli jam and light curry sauce. Then graduate perhaps to the main event of guinea fowl and ham hock pie and mash with a side order of braised red cabbage and raisins; or Scottish halibut, braised fennel and leeks and sauce bouillabaisse. Definitely leave room for caramel 'snicker', chocolate cremeaux and peanut ice cream. There's ample opportunity to match food and wine, with 25 available by the glass.

Open all wk 12-3 6-11 (Sun 12-4) **Food** Lunch Mon-Sat 12-2.30, Sun 12-3.30 Dinner Mon-Thu 6.30-9.30, Fri-Sat 6.30-10 Set menu available Restaurant menu available all wk ⊕ FULLER'S ◖ London Pride, guest ale. ♟ 25 **Facilities** Non-diners area ♦♦ Children's portions Garden Parking WiFi

PEASEMORE
Map 5 SU47

The Fox at Peasemore   PICK OF THE PUBS

tel: 01635 248480 **Hill Green Ln RG20 7JN**
email: info@foxatpeasemore.co.uk
dir: M4 junct 13, A34 signed Oxford. Immediately left onto slip road signed Chieveley, Hermitage & Beedon. At T-junct left, through Chieveley to Peasemore. Left at phone box, pub signed

Ever-successful village pub

Right opposite the village cricket ground, the imposing Fox draws in spectators with the promise of great microbrewery beers from the likes of West Berkshire Brewery and artisan local ciders from Tutts Clump. It's also a useful stop for ramblers exploring the rolling countryside that cossets this chic, well appointed, village inn. Outside tables skim lanes overlooking rich farmland; or choose a spot in the modern-rustic bar with its polished wooden floor, settles and log-burning stove to consider the confident menu of tried and tested pub classics and contemporary British dishes. Robust favourites include pie of the day or haddock and chips; the carte presents an eclectic choice. Anticipate deep-fried tiger prawns with pickled vegetables and sweet chilli dip to start, trumping this with fillet of beef Wellington with a port and Stilton sauce, savoury potatoes and vegetables; or baked fillet of Shetland cod with herb mash and aromatic tomato sauce.

Open 12-3 6-11 (Sat-Sun 12-late) Closed Mon **Food** Lunch Wed-Fri & Sun 12-2, Sat all day Dinner Wed-Fri & Sun 6-9, Sat all day Set menu available Restaurant menu available Wed-Sun ⊕ FREE HOUSE ◖ Butts Traditional, West Berkshire Good Old Boy ♂ Tutts Clump. ♟ 16 **Facilities** Non-diners area ♣ (Bar Garden Outside area) ♦♦ Children's menu Children's portions Garden Outside area ⌁ Parking WiFi ☞ (notice required)

READING
Map 5 SU77

The Flowing Spring

tel: 0118 969 9878 **Henley Rd, Playhatch RG4 9RB**
email: info@theflowingspringpub.co.uk
dir: 3m N of Reading on A4155 towards Henley

Cosy country pub at the edge of the Chilterns

Unusually this pub is on the first floor, which slopes steeply from one end of the bar to the other; the verandah overlooks Thames Valley countryside. The pub has been recognised for its well-kept ales and cellar, and the menu of no-nonsense pub favourites is backed by a comprehensive range of vegetarian, vegan and gluten-free and dairy-free options. The pub hosts beer festivals, astronomy nights, outdoor live music, stand-up comedy nights and many other exciting events throughout the year. The huge garden is bounded by streams.

Open all day Closed Mon **Food** Lunch Tue-Sun 12-2.30 Dinner Tue-Sat 6-9 Av main course £11.95 ⊕ FULLER'S ◖ London Pride & ESB, George Gale & Co Seafarers, guest ale ♂ Aspall. ♟ 10 **Facilities** Non-diners area ♣ (Bar Restaurant Garden) ♦♦ Children's portions Play area Garden ⌁ Beer festival Cider festival Parking WiFi ☞ (notice required)

The Shoulder of Mutton

tel: 0118 947 3908 **Playhatch RG4 9QU**
email: shoulderofmutton@hotmail.co.uk
dir: *From Reading follow signs to Caversham, take A4155 to Henley-on-Thames. At rdbt left to Binfield Heath, follow brown pub sign, 1st pub on left*

Village pub that is true to its name

A pleasant walled cottage garden, beams and open fire grace this long-established local favourite in tiny Playhatch, close to Caversham Lakes and the River Thames. Beer lovers pop in for ales brewed just up the road by Loddon Brewery, whilst diners travel from afar to indulge in chef-patron Alan Oxlade's astonishing mutton dishes. The 7-hour roasted shoulder of mutton is rightly famous, and the Moroccan-style tagine of mutton leg is worth a mention too; reserve a seat in the airy conservatory and indulge. The wider menu is equally tempting – chicken and wild mushroom pie; slow-cooked Gressingham duck breast, with roast almond, sour cherries and port sauce; and smoked haddock and prawns lasagne.

Open Tue- Sat 12-3 6-11 (Sat 12-3 6.30-11 Sun 12-3) Closed 26 Dec, 2 Jan, Sun eve, Mon **Food** Lunch Tue-Sun 12-2 Dinner Tue-Sat 6.30-9 Restaurant menu available Tue-Sat ⊕ GREENE KING ◖ Ruddles Best, Loddon Ferryman's Gold ♻ Aspall. **Facilities** Non-diners area ♦ Children's portions Garden ⊓ Parking ▭ (notice required)

RUSCOMBE
Map 5 SU77

Buratta's at the Royal Oak

tel: 0118 934 5190 **Ruscombe Ln RG10 9JN**
email: enquiries@burattas.co.uk
dir: *From A4 (Wargrave rdbt) take A321 to Twyford (signed Twyford/Wokingham). Straight on at 1st lights, right at 2nd lights onto A3032. Right onto A3024 (Ruscombe Rd which becomes Ruscombe Ln). Pub on left on brow of hill*

Relaxed pub with its own antiques shop

Originally a one-bar pub, the Royal Oak has been extended over the years and the cottage next door is now the kitchen. With Binghams Brewery and Fuller's London Pride as resident ales, the relaxed restaurant offers a range of meals, from hearty bar snacks and sandwiches to à la carte choices such as black pudding stack with mustard mash, bacon, and peppercorn sauce; or sea bass with Chinese spices, stir-fried noodles with spring onions and carrots. The large garden, complete with resident ducks, is dog friendly, and the pub has its own antiques shop, which is open during restaurant hours. It would seem that nearly everything in the pub is for sale!

Open Tue-Sat 12-3 6-11 (Sun-Mon 12-3) Closed Sun eve & Mon eve **Food** Lunch all wk 12-2.30 Dinner Tue-Sat 7-9.30 ⊕ ENTERPRISE INNS ◖ Fuller's London Pride, Binghams, guest ales. ♟ 12 **Facilities** Non-diners area ♣ (Bar Restaurant Garden) ♦ Children's menu Children's portions Garden ⊓ Parking WiFi ▭ (notice required)

SHURLOCK ROW
Map 5 SU87

The Shurlock Inn

tel: 0118 934 9094 **The Street RG10 OPS**
email: info@shurlockinn.com

Family-friendly village pub serving locally sourced food

This lovely 17th-century pub was bought by a group of villagers a few years ago and hasn't looked back; the stylish interior has retained exposed timbers and an open fireplace. The large family garden and sheltered courtyard are a draw during the warmer months, or you could head to the cosy bar to a enjoy pint of Rebellion, just one of four local ales served. The seasonally-driven menu champions local produce: asparagus, mushroom and baby carrot roulade might be followed by home-made fisherman's pie; or pan-fried calves' liver, colcannon mash and onion gravy. Desserts include lemon cheesecake; and vanilla crème brûlée.

Open all wk 12-3 6-11 (Fri-Sat 12-11 Sun 12-9) **Food** Lunch Mon-Sat 12-2.30, Sun 12-8 Dinner Mon-Sat 6-9.30, Sun 12-8 Av main course £13 Set menu available ⊕ FREE HOUSE ◖ West Berkshire Mr Chubb's, Rebellion ♻ Westons Stowford Press. ♟ 9 **Facilities** Non-diners area ♣ (Bar Garden) ♦ Children's menu Children's portions Play area Garden ⊓ Parking WiFi ▭ (notice required)

SINDLESHAM
Map 5 SU76

The Walter Arms

tel: 0118 977 4903 **Bearwood Rd RG41 5BP**
email: mail@thewalterarms.com
dir: *A329 from Wokingham towards Reading. 1.5m, left onto B3030. 5m, left into Bearwood Rd. Pub 200yds on left*

Welcoming pub with interesting menu of global dishes

A typically solid Victorian building built about 1850 by John Walter III, grandson of the man who founded *The Times* newspaper. The idea was that it should be a working men's club for the workers on the Bearwood Estate, where Walter lived. Now a popular dining pub, the seasonal menus offer traditional English dishes, such as chargrilled rib-eye steak with roasted winter veg; or sausage and mash; as well as pasta, stone-baked pizzas, and seafood and Arabian-style 'smörgåsbord'. If there's still room, spiced sticky toffee pudding or rhubarb and apple crumble should fill you up. The beer garden is a good spot for a pint of Courage Best.

Open all day all wk 12-11 (Sat 12-12) **Food** Lunch Mon-Fri 12-2.30, Sat 12-10, Sun 12-9 Dinner Mon-Fri 6-10, Sat 12-10, Sun 12-9 ⊕ ENTERPRISE INNS ◖ Courage Best Bitter, 2 guest ales ♻ Westons Stowford Press. **Facilities** Non-diners area ♦ Children's menu Children's portions Garden ⊓ Parking WiFi

SONNING
Map 5 SU77

The Bull Inn

tel: 0118 969 3901 **High St RG4 6UP**
email: bullinn@fullers.co.uk
dir: *From Reading take A4 towards Maidenhead. Left onto B4446 to Sonning*

Welcoming olde-worlde inn

Two minutes' walk from the River Thames in the pretty village of Sonning, this black-and-white timbered inn can trace its roots back 600 years or so; it can also boast visits by former owner Queen Elizabeth I and a mention in Jerome K Jerome's classic novel *Three Men in a Boat*. With Fuller's ales on tap, comfy leather chairs and log fires in the grate, The Bull charms locals and visitors alike. It's a great place to eat too, with an interesting menu of British and world cuisine. Dishes could include a slow braised blade of beef; roasted pheasant stew; Greek meze platter; jerk spiced ham; butternut squash gnocchi and chicken fajita wraps.

Open all day all wk 11-11 **Food** all wk 10-9.30 Set menu available Restaurant menu available all wk ⊕ FULLER'S ◖ London Pride, Organic Honey Dew, George Gale & Co HSB, guest ale. ♟ 24 **Facilities** Non-diners area ♣ (Bar Garden) ♦ Children's portions Garden ⊓ Parking WiFi ▭ (notice required)

STANFORD DINGLEY   Map 5 SU57

The Bull Inn

tel: 0118 974 4582 **RG7 6LS**
email: enquiries@thebullinnstanforddingley.co.uk
dir: *M4 junct 12, A4 towards Newbury, A340 towards Pangbourne. 1st left to Bradfield. Through Bradfield, 0.3m left into Back Lane. At end left, pub 0.25m on left*

Historic country inn in the Pang Valley

This pub in the lovely village of Standford Dingley in the Pang Valley, dates from the 15th century, so prepare to 'duck or grouse'. Pump badges promise West Berkshire and Two Cocks ales, and Wyatt's Berkshire Gold cider. For simple rustic surroundings, eat in the Tap Room or the Saloon; the Dining Room is more formal. Choose from dishes featuring rare-breed meats, local game and Brixham-landed fish and shellfish, as well as sandwiches and bar snacks. From May to September, on the second Saturday of the month, classic cars, and their owners, gather in the adjoining meadow.

Open all day all wk **Food** Lunch all wk 12-2.30 Dinner Mon-Sat 6-9.30 Restaurant menu available all wk ⊕ FREE HOUSE ◀ West Berkshire Good Old Boy, Two Cocks Cavalier, Black Sheep Ô Wyatt's Berkshire Gold. ▾ 13 **Facilities** Non-diners area ✿ (Bar Garden) ♦ Children's portions Garden ⌐ Parking WiFi ▭ (notice required)

The Old Boot Inn

tel: 0118 974 4292 **RG7 6LT**
email: johnintheboot@hotmail.co.uk
dir: *M4 junct 12, A4, A340 to Pangbourne. 1st left to Bradfield. Through Bradfield, follow Stanford Dingley signs*

Peaceful situation and well known for good food

Oak beams and half-timbering feature inside this cottagey inn found in the peaceful Pang Valley. The rustic theme continues with log fires and an enormous beer garden rolling back to merge with pastureland backed by wooded hills. The modern conservatory restaurant is light and airy; just the place to settle down with a pint of local Dr Hexters and seek inspiration on the menus. Old school bar meals are the tip of the iceberg, complemented by an à la carte selection and robust specials, perhaps beef Wellington; or lamb shank, mash and vegetables.

Open all wk 11-3 6-11 (Sat-Sun all day) **Food** Lunch all wk 12-2 Dinner all wk 6-9 ⊕ FREE HOUSE ◀ Bass, West Berkshire Dr Hexters, Fuller's London Pride Ô Westons Stowford Press. ▾ 10 **Facilities** Non-diners area ✿ (Bar Garden) ♦ Children's menu Children's portions Play area Garden ⌐ Parking WiFi ▭ (notice required)

SUNNINGHILL   Map 6 SU96

Dog & Partridge

tel: 01344 623204 **92 Upper Village Rd SL5 7AQ**
email: info@dogandpartridgesunninghill.co.uk
dir: *From either A329 or A330 into High St. Into Truss Hill Rd, 1st right into Upper Village Rd, pub on left*

Tucked behind the High Street, but worth finding

If the weather's favourable, make for the courtyard garden, where the fountain gently burbles away as you ease into your Pinot Grigio, or a Windsor & Eton brewery real ale. Start with goats' cheese and spiced apple salad; or maybe smoked salmon with a poached egg. Then, roast stuffed peppers with couscous, feta and courgettes; chargrilled sea bass fillet with creamy mash and golden beetroot carpaccio; or caramelised stuffed pork with chestnut mushrooms and black pudding risotto. For dessert, cheesecake of the day is hard to beat. At lunchtime, you'll find sandwiches, pies, jacket potatoes and pasta on offer.

Open 12-11 (Sun 12-10.30) Closed Mon **Food** Lunch Tue-Sat 12-2.30, Sun 12-7 Dinner Tue-Sat 6-10, Sun 12-7 Restaurant menu available Tue-Sun ◀ Fuller's London Pride, Sharp's Doom Bar, Windsor & Eton Ô Symonds. ▾ 10 **Facilities** Non-diners area ✿ (Bar Garden) ♦ Children's menu Children's portions Garden ⌐ Parking WiFi

---

WALTHAM ST LAWRENCE   Map 5 SU87

The Bell

tel: 0118 934 1788 **The Street RG10 0JJ**
email: info@thebellwalthamstlawrence.co.uk
dir: *On B3024 E of Twyford. From A4 turn at Hare Hatch*

Good ciders and beers at a very old inn

This 14th-century free house is renowned for its ciders and an ever-changing range of real ales selected from small independent breweries. The building was given to the community in 1608 and profits from the rent continue to help village charities. Iain and Scott Ganson have built a reputation for good food and everything possible is made on the premises, including all charcuterie and preparation of game. Start with asparagus risotto with lemon and mint; or sage and butternut squash soup then continue with house-cut pork chop, baby gem, smashed beans, caper and anchovy dressing; or the ever-popular Bell bambi burger. Leave room for treacle tart and crème fraîche ice cream.

Open all wk 12-3 5-11 (Sat 12-11 Sun 12-10.30) **Food** Lunch Mon-Fri 12-2, Sat-Sun 12-3 Dinner all wk 6.30-9.30 ⊕ FREE HOUSE ◀ Loddon Hoppit, 5 guest ales Ô Lilley's Bee Sting Still Perry & Crazy Goat, Westons Old Rosie. ▾ 19 **Facilities** Non-diners area ✿ (Bar Restaurant Garden) ♦ Children's menu Children's portions Garden ⌐ Beer festival Parking

---

WARFIELD   Map 5 SU87

NEW The Cricketers

tel: 01344 882910 **Cricketers Ln RG42 6JT**
email: info@cricketerswarfield.co.uk
dir: *NE of Bracknell*

Informal dining in welcoming surroundings

A white-painted, brick-built country pub dating back to the early 19th century, The Cricketers has been thoughtfully refurbished and extended. There's a patio for outdoor dining in the summer, and a large beer garden (say hello to resident ducks, Cheese and Quackers, if you see them). Family friendly, the pub also welcomes dogs in the bar and garden – canine visitors are welcome to a free dog treat in the porch. The dining room has stripped floor boards and panelling, with comfortable mismatched furniture, and menus feature pub classics like beer battered haddock with chunky chips and mushy peas, while other choices might include braised rabbit, leg, chorizo and Toulouse sausage cassoulet.

Open all day all wk **Food** all wk 12-10 Av main course £9 Restaurant menu available all wk ⊕ METROPOLITAN PUB COMPANY ◀ Windsor & Eton Guardsman, Greene King IPA, Truman's Swift, Hardys & Hansons Grace Ô Aspall. ▾ **Facilities** Non-diners area ✿ (Bar Garden Outside area) ♦ Children's menu Children's portions Garden Outside area ⌐ Parking WiFi ▭ (notice required)

WHITE WALTHAM   Map 5 SU87

The Beehive ◉◉   PICK OF THE PUBS

tel: 01628 822877 **Waltham Rd SL6 3SH**
dir: *M4 junct 8/9, A404, follow White Waltham signs*

A brilliant village pub with exemplary cooking

If choosing a pub involves ticking boxes, then The Beehive will keep you busy. Externally, it's 18th century, stands in a pleasant village, overlooks a cricket pitch and from its beer garden there are distant views of woods and rich pastureland. Inside, while contemporary in style, you just know it has always been the focus of village life. Real ales are from nearby breweries, and the bar also does snacks, such as rollmops and Scotch eggs. More box ticking will be required for award-winning chef Dominic Chapman's menu offering lasagne of wild rabbit with wood blewits and chervil; sea bream with tarka Dhal, cucumber, red onion and coriander salad; and buttermilk pot, raspberries and hazelnut biscuits. His specials could include Cornish brown crab on toast; Cumbrian air-dried ham with fried duck egg and parmesan; and morteau sausage, sauerkraut and celery cress.

Open all wk 11-3 5-11 (Sat 11am-mdnt Sun 12-10.30) Closed 25-26 Dec **Food** Lunch Mon-Fri 12-2.30, Sat 12-9.30, Sun 12-8.30 Dinner Mon-Fri 5-9.30, Sat 12-9.30, Sun 12-8.30 Restaurant menu available all wk ⊕ ENTERPRISE INNS ◄ Fuller's London Pride, Greene King Abbot Ale, Rebellion, Brakspear, Sharp's Doom Bar, Loddon guest ale Ö Sheppy's. ♣ **Facilities** Non-diners area ✿ (Bar Garden) ♠♦ Children's menu Children's portions Garden ⊐ Parking WiFi ▭ (notice required)

WINKFIELD   Map 6 SU97

The Winning Post

tel: 01344 882242 **Winkfield St SL4 4SW**
email: info@winningpostwinkfield.co.uk
dir: *M4 junct 6, A355. 3rd exit at rdbt into Imperial Rd (B3175). Right at lights into Saint Leonards Rd (B3022). At 2nd rdbt 2nd exit into North St signed Winkfield. Through Winkfield, at sharp left bend turn right into Winkfield St. Pub 200yds on right*

Tranquil village pub popular with the racing fraternity

A short canter from Ascot and Windsor racecourses, this charming 18th-century pub has long been a favourite with the equine-inclined. The Winning Post is off the beaten track and surrounded by stunning Berkshire countryside but it's also a convenient pit stop for Heathrow Airport. The open fire and stone floors retain the building's original character and the beer garden offers alfresco opportunities. Enjoy a pint of Tipster & Punter ale as you order from an enticing menu that might offer Windsor Park wood pigeon, blueberries, caper berries and radicchio; and rack of lamb, feta cheese, black olives, cherry tomatoes, spinach and dauphinoise potatoes.

Open all day all wk **Food** Lunch Mon-Thu 12-9.30, Fri-Sat 12-5.30 Dinner Mon-Thu 12-9.30, Sun 7-9 Av main course £18 Restaurant menu available Mon-Sat ⊕ UPHAM GROUP ◄ Tipster & Punter Ö Thatchers. ♣ **Facilities** Non-diners area ✿ (Bar Garden) ♠♦ Children's menu Garden ⊐ Parking WiFi

WINTERBOURNE   Map 5 SU47

The Winterbourne Arms

tel: 01635 248200 **RG20 8BB**
email: mail@winterbournearms.com
dir: *M4 junct 13 into Chieveley Services, follow Donnington signs to Winterbourne. Right into Arlington Ln, right at T-junct, left into Winterbourne*

Idyllic pub with large gardens

Steeped in 300 years of history, warmth and charm, yet only five minutes from the M4, this pretty village pub once housed the village bakery and shop. The real ales may include Ramsbury Gold and West Berkshire Good Old Boy, while 10 wines served by the glass. The traditional and modern British menus and daily-changing specials offer starters like deep-fried butterfly prawns or sautéed lamb's kidneys, followed by pan-fried calves' liver and bacon, which can be enjoyed by candlelight or alfresco in summer. Local game is served in season.

Open all wk 12-3 6-11 (Sun 12-10.30) **Food** Lunch all wk 12-2.30 Dinner Mon-Sat 6-10 Restaurant menu available Mon-Sat ⊕ FREE HOUSE ◄ Ramsbury Gold, West Berkshire Good Old Boy. ♣ 10 **Facilities** Non-diners area ✿ (Bar Garden) ♠♦ Children's portions Garden ⊐ Parking ▭ (notice required)

WOKINGHAM   Map 5 SU86

The Broad Street Tavern

tel: 0118 977 3706 **29 Broad St RG40 1AU**
email: broadstreettavern@wadworth.co.uk
dir: *In town centre, adjacent to Pizza Express*

Family-friendly pub with appealing menu

A handsome detached period building fronted by elegant railings, this town-centre pub offers a friendly atmosphere and spacious indoor and outdoor seating areas. Children and dogs are welcome until 6pm, indeed regular child-centric events are an intrinsic element of the pub's busy social diary, which also includes two ale festivals and one for cider in summer. The menu offers sharing boards and dishes such as chicken or vegetable fajitas; Wadworth-battered fish of the day; broad bean, spinach, pea and mint risotto; and apple tarte Tatin, with custard, cream or ice cream. A set menu is available on Sundays.

Open all day all wk Closed 25 Dec **Food** Lunch Mon-Sat 12-9, Sun 12-5 Dinner Mon-Sat 12-9 Set menu available ⊕ WADWORTH ◄ Swordfish, Horizon, 6X, IPA, The Bishop's Tipple, guest ale Ö Westons Old Rosie. ♣ 15 **Facilities** Non-diners area ✿ (Bar Restaurant Garden) Garden ⊐ Beer festival Cider festival WiFi ▭ (notice required)

The Crooked Billet

tel: 0118 978 0438 **Honey Hill RG40 3BJ**
web: www.crookedbilletwokingham.co.uk
dir: *Phone for detailed directions*

Early 19th-century rural gem

A little tucked away, but once on the right road you really shouldn't miss this cute, white-painted, weatherboarded pub. Brakspear's real ales are accompanied by two monthly guests. Typical dishes include beer-battered pollock with chunky chips and peas; roast chicken breast with braised greens and mushrooms; pan-fried calves' liver with spinach, bacon and onions; and leek, potato and cheddar pie. Winter menus will feature local game. Sandwiches and light meals, such as mussels steamed in cider with shallots and smoked bacon, are available at lunchtime. The cheeseboard is good enough to win a prize.

Open all day all wk **Food** 12-9.30 ⊕ BRAKSPEAR ◄ Brakspear, Wychwood Hobgoblin, guest ales. ♣ 9 **Facilities** Non-diners area ✿ (Bar Garden) ♠♦ Children's menu Children's portions Garden ⊐ Parking WiFi ▭ (notice required)

YATTENDON   Map 5 SU57

The Royal Oak Hotel   PICK OF THE PUBS

See Pick of the Pubs on page 42

See Pick of the Pubs on page 42

PICK OF THE PUBS

The Royal Oak Hotel

YATTENDON   Map 5 SU57

tel: 01635 201325
The Square RG18 0UG
email: info@royaloakyattendon.com
web: www.royaloakyattendon.co.uk
dir: *M4 junct 12, A4 to Newbury, right at 2nd rdbt to Pangbourne then 1st left. From junct 13, A34 N 1st left, right at T-junct. Left then 2nd right to Yattendon*

Village free house with pretty garden

The Domesday Book village of Yattendon was once important enough to have a castle, although it was largely destroyed by Parliamentary forces during the Civil War. There's also a fortune in gold down a deep well, somewhere, hidden by a wealthy family who then fled the village. Locals are still searching. Part of a row of 16th-century cottages, the pub is graced with log fires in the bar, oak beams, and quarry-tiled and wooden floors in the lounge and dining rooms. French windows lead to a walled rear garden with a vine-laden trellis. West Berkshire Brewery is based here and, understandably, Royal Oak owner Rob McGill serves its Good Old Boy and Mr Chubb's Lunchtime Bitter, as well as a guest ale. Abundant local produce from top suppliers is used for seasonal dishes that many a foodie guide has praised. By all means just have a sandwich, or keep browsing and find

starters such as baked scallops thermidor; and Royal Windsor farm pork and game terrine with cranberry, fig and shallot salad. Main course options include wild boar, sage and cider pie with Calvados apple mash; baked Brixham cod, smoky bacon and cheddar sauce, and crispy potatoes; and breaded chicken Kiev with garlic and parsley butter, fries and mixed leaves. For sharing there's côte de boeuf with duck-fat roast potatoes, watercress and béarnaise sauce, while dishes on the feasting menu are worth considering for parties of six or more. There's always something going on, with fortnightly quizzes, rib and crab nights, quarterly seafood weekends and masterclasses in cheese.

Open all day all wk **Food** Lunch Mon-Fri 12-2.30, Sat-Sun 12-3 Dinner Mon-Thu 6.30-9.30, Fri-Sat 6.30-10, Sun 6.30-9 Av main course £17 ⊕ FREE HOUSE ◀ West Berkshire Good Old Boy & Mr Chubb's Lunchtime Bitter, guest ale ♂ Westons Stowford Press. ♟ 10 **Facilities** Non-diners area 🐾 (Bar Restaurant Garden) ∯ Children's menu Children's portions Garden 🚗 Parking WiFi

BRISTOL

BRISTOL
Map 4 ST57

The Albion

tel: 0117 973 3522 **Boyces Av, Clifton BS8 4AA**
email: info@thealbionclifton.co.uk
dir: *From A4 take B3129 towards city centre. Right into Clifton Down Rd. 3rd left into Boyces Ave*

Popular from brunch time through to the evening

This handsome Grade II listed coaching inn dates from the 17th century. Owned by the St Austell Brewery, it's a popular place to enjoy West Country ales and ciders, as well as being a gastro-pub. In the enclosed courtyard you can order jugs of Pimm's in summer or sip mulled cider under heaters in the winter. The modern British cooking uses local produce in dishes such as pan-seared scallops, oyster leaf purée, herb filo pastry and crispy roe; surf and turf with a 4oz fillet steak and grilled king prawns; potato and gorgonzola gnocchi, braised violet artichokes and salted ricotta; and honeycomb cheesecake. A bar and lunch menu offers pub favourites and brioche rolls. There is an annual cider festival in May.

Open all day 10am-mdnt Closed 25-26 Dec, Mon L **Food** Lunch Tue-Fri 12-3, Sat 11-3, Sun 11-3.30 Dinner Tue-Sat 7-10 ⊕ ST AUSTELL BREWERY ◼ Proper Job, Tribute & Cornish Best, Otter Bitter ♙ Thatchers Cheddar Valley & Gold. ♟ 12 **Facilities** Non-diners area ❁ (Bar Outside area) ⚭ Children's portions Outside area ⌁ Cider festival WiFi ⛟ (notice required)

The Alma Tavern & Theatre

tel: 0117 973 5171 **18-20 Alma Vale Rd, Clifton BS8 2HY**
email: info@almatavernandtheatre.co.uk
dir: *Phone for detailed directions*

Traditional pub with its own theatre and good food

Down a leafy side street in the heart of Clifton, this bustling Victorian pub has the unique and added attraction of a small theatre upstairs. The team here continues to draw in the theatre crowd and maintain a pubby atmosphere for the locals, while also enticing others with their good food offering. As well as an appealing lunchtime menu of sandwiches and light bites, the bar menu offers pub classics and a carte that might include pan-seared pigeon breast; with pistachio, raisin and pancetta salad; slow-roasted Welsh lamb; and fire-roasted red pepper, onion marmalade, feta and roast sweet potato parcel.

Open all day all wk **Food** Lunch Mon-Fri 12-3, Sat-Sun 12-5 Dinner Mon-Sat 6-9.30 Av main course £13 Set menu available Restaurant menu available Mon-Fri ⊕ GREENE KING ◼ Bath Ales Gem, Sharp's Doom Bar, St Austell Tribute ♙ Thatchers Gold, Symonds. ♟ 12 **Facilities** Non-diners area ❁ (Bar Garden) ⚭ Children's menu Children's portions Garden ⌁ Beer festival Cider festival WiFi ⛟ (notice required)

NEW The Cross Hands

tel: 0117 965 7759 **1 Staple Hill Rd BS16 5AA**
email: info@thecrosshandsbristol.co.uk **web:** www.thecrosshandsbristol.co.uk
dir: *At junct of Downend Rd & Staple Hill Rd in Fishponds (NE of Bristol city centre)*

Busy neighbourhood inn serving seasonal food

Located four miles from Bristol's busy city centre and convenient for the M32, this refurbished former coaching inn was built in 1853 and remains a draw for local families with its enclosed rear garden and children's play area. Well-kept Bath Ales Gem and Butcombe Bitter fly the flag for local breweries, and there are two real ciders on offer. As well as sandwiches, pizzas and burgers, there is a seasonal à la carte with typical dishes including pork belly, mustard mash, courgette, onions and cider jus; or sea bream, mussel ragout, samphire and Jersey Royals.

Open all day all wk **Food** Lunch Mon-Fri 12-3, Sat 12-5.30, Sun 12-4 Dinner Mon-Sat 5.30-9.30 ⊕ ENTERPRISE INNS ◼ Bath Ales Gem, Butcombe Bitter, 2 rotating guest ales ♙ Thatchers Cheddar Valley, Westons Old Rosie. ♟ 11 **Facilities** Non-diners area ⚭ Children's menu Children's portions Play area Garden ⌁ Beer festival Cider festival WiFi ⛟

See advert on page 44

BRISTOL *continued*

Highbury Vaults

tel: 0117 973 3203 **164 St Michaels Hill, Cotham BS2 8DE**
email: highburyvaults@youngs.co.uk
dir: *A38 to Cotham from inner ring dual carriageway*

Ever-popular unpretentious city escape

A classic little city pub with the character of a Victorian drinking house; lots of dark panelled nooks and crannies, dim lighting, impressive original bar and a cosmopolitan crowd of locals. Condemned Victorian prisoners took their last meals here; today's crowd are more fortunate, revelling in beers such as Bath Ales and chowing down on no-nonsense pub fare like chilli con carne with rice and cheese; lasagne al forno with garlic bread; and fish pie. Gourmet burgers and a selection of pies are also on offer. An added attraction of a rather eccentric nature, is the model train that runs the length of the bar.

Open all day all wk 12-12 (Sun 12-11) Closed 25 Dec eve, 26 Dec L, 1 Jan L
Food Lunch Mon-Fri 12-2, Sat 12-2.30, Sun 12-3 Dinner Mon-Sat 5.30-8.30
Av main course £7.50 ⊕ YOUNG'S ◄ London Gold & Bitter, Bath Ales Gem, St Austell Tribute, guest ales ♂ Addlestones, Thatchers Gold.
Facilities Non-diners area ♦♦ Garden Outside area 宋 WiFi ⇔ (notice required)

The Kensington Arms   PICK OF THE PUBS

tel: 0117 944 6444 **35-37 Stanley Rd BS6 6NP**
email: info@thekensingtonarms.co.uk
dir: *From Redland Rail Station into South Rd, then Kensington Rd. 4th right into Stanley Rd*

Good food in this buzzy backstreet local

In the quiet backstreets of Bristol's leafy Redland district, this Victorian corner pub still attracts discerning local drinkers but the food has a much wider reach. The elegant dining room is packed with mismatched antique furniture, Victorian prints and views into the open kitchen. The modern British food utilises the very best local produce and the menu changes daily, with meat from the region's farms, and fish delivered daily from Cornwall. In the bar, try the burger or venison pie with your pint of Morland Old Golden Hen or Westons Stowford Press cider. Typical restaurant dishes in the evening are starters of mussels, celery and cream; or duck hearts on

toast. These might be followed by Cornish pollack, Tarbais beans and gremolata; or Middle White chop and Agen prunes. Finish with blood orange and rhubarb sorbet; pear and almond tart with bay leaf ice cream; or a selection of artisan cheeses.

Open all day all wk Closed 25 & 26 Dec **Food** Lunch Mon-Fri 12-3, Sat 10-3, Sun 12-4 Dinner all wk 6-10 Av main course £12 Restaurant menu available all wk ⊕ GREENE KING ◄ Morland Old Golden Hen ♂ Westons Stowford Press, Thatchers Gold. ♀ 14 **Facilities** Non-diners area ♣ (Bar Restaurant Outside area) ♦♦ Children's portions Outside area 宋 WiFi ⇔ (notice required)

AMERSHAM	Map 6 SU99

Hit or Miss Inn

tel: 01494 713109 **Penn Street Village HP7 0PX**
email: hit@ourpubs.co.uk
dir: *M25 junct 18, A404 (Amersham to High Wycombe road) to Amersham. Past crematorium on right, 2nd left into Whielden Ln (signed Winchmore Hill). 1.25m, pub on right*

A dining pub that is certainly a hit

Overlooking the cricket ground from which its name is taken, this is an 18th-century cottage-style dining pub. It has a beautiful country garden with lawn, patio and picnic tables for warmer days, while inside you'll find fires, old-world beams, Badger ales and a warm welcome from landlords Michael and Mary Macken, who have been running the pub for over 13 years. Options on the menu range from tempting sandwiches and baked potatoes to dishes like calves' liver with mash, sweet and sour onions and Madeira sauce; or slow-cooked lamb shank with crispy pancetta, broad beans and new potatoes. There are daily specials, Sunday roasts and a children's menu, too. There is a village beer and cider festival in mid July.

Open all day all wk 11-11 (Sun 12-10.30) **Food** Lunch Mon-Fri 12-2.30, Sat 12-3, Sun 12-8 Dinner Mon-Sat 6.45-9.30, Sun 12-8 ⊕ HALL & WOODHOUSE ◄ Tanglefoot, K&B Sussex, Badger Firkin Fox & First Call ♂ Westons Stowford Press. ♀ 14 **Facilities** Non-diners area ♣ (Bar Restaurant Garden) ♦♦ Children's menu Children's portions Garden 宋 Beer festival Cider festival Parking WiFi ⇔ (notice required)

The Hundred of Ashendon

tel: 01296 651296 **Lower End HP18 OHE**
email: info@thehundred.co.uk **web:** www.thehundred.co.uk
dir: *Phone for detailed directions*

An inn where everyone is very welcome

The interiors of The Hundred ooze charisma, thanks to dark polished wood floors, half plastered walls, mismatched furniture and eclectic decorative artefacts. Walkers, cyclists, families with children and dogs – all receive the same warm welcome from chef and landlord Matthew and his partner Pia who are fulfilling their dream here. A splendid array of real ales greets the thirsty, notably Side Pocket for a Toad from Tring Brewery. Daily-changing menus are a good indication of Matthew's kitchen skills: red mullet soup to start, followed by braised duck leg with turnips and green sauce; finish with quince jelly and shortbread if you want to make a proper meal of it.

Open 12-3.30 6-11 Closed Mon **Food** Lunch 12-3 Dinner 6.30-9 Av main course £15 Restaurant menu available Tue-Sun ⊕ FREE HOUSE ◀ Tring Side Pocket for a Toad, XT4, Chiltern Beechwood Bitter, Best Vale IPA ♂ Thatchers. ♟ 10 **Facilities** Non-diners area ♣ (Bar Garden) ♦ Children's portions Garden ⊼ Parking WiFi ▭ (notice required)

The King's Head & Farmer's Bar

tel: 01296 718812 **Market Square HP20 2RW**
email: info@farmersbar.co.uk
dir: *Access on foot only. From Market Square access cobbled passageway. Pub entrance under archway on right*

Brewery tap for the Chiltern microbrewery

This is the award-winning brewery tap for the Chiltern Brewery, one of the oldest microbreweries in the country, which prides itself on serving their beers, plus craft and guest ales, with care and a great deal of knowledge. Special beer celebrations are held throughout the year; wines come from The Rothschild Estate. Enjoy a drink in the ancient cobbled courtyard, or a lunch of home-cooked dishes – venison and wild mushroom Wellington, and pie of the day to name but two. It was in this former coaching inn, dating from 1455, that Henry VIII reputedly wooed Anne Boleyn.

Open all day all wk 11-11 (Sun 12-10.30) Closed 25 Dec **Food** Lunch Mon-Fri 12-2, Sat-Sun 12-3 ⊕ FREE HOUSE/THE CHILTERN BREWERY ◀ Beechwood Bitter, Chiltern Pale Ale, Chiltern Black ♂ Westons Stowford Press. ♟ 12 **Facilities** Non-diners area ♦ Children's menu Children's portions Outside area ⊼ WiFi ▭ (notice required)

The Royal Standard of England   PICK OF THE PUBS

tel: 01494 673382 **Brindle Ln, Forty Green HP9 1XT**
email: theoldestpub@btinternet.com
dir: *A40 to Beaconsfield, right at church rdbt onto B474 towards Penn, left into Forty Green Rd, 1m*

Renowned, historic gabled inn

Really, really tucked away in The Chiltern Hills, this claims to be the oldest free house in England. It all started with the West Saxons, who brewed ale on this site using water from an old Romano-British well that remains in what is now the garden till this day. Ancient blackened timbers, flagstone floors, leaded windows, battle standards, armour and dried hops greet your entry to an interior warmed in winter by log-burners and an inglenook. Chiltern Ale and Windsor & Eton's Conqueror share bar space with farm ciders and a Herefordshire perry. Hearty food includes rib-eye steak, grilled tomato, mushrooms and chips; Welsh lamb shoulder, sauté potatoes and cabbage; and fish pie made with salmon, cod, smoked haddock and prawns. Specials, including local game, appear on a blackboard. Desserts follow a traditionalist path too, with Bramley apple crumble and custard; and Eton Mess. There's a Summer Bank Holiday beer and cider festival.

Open all day all wk 11-11 **Food** Contact pub for food times ⊕ FREE HOUSE ◀ Chiltern Ale, Windsor & Eton Conqueror 1075 ♂ Orchard Pig, Westons Perry, Bridge Farm Artisan Cider. ♟ 11 **Facilities** Non-diners area ♣ (Bar Restaurant Garden) ♦ Children's portions Family room Garden Beer festival Cider festival Parking WiFi ▭

The Lions of Bledlow

tel: 01844 343345 **Church End HP27 9PE**
email: info@thelionsofbledlow.co.uk **web:** www.lionsofbledlow.co.uk
dir: *M40 junct 6, B4009 to Princes Risborough, through Chinnor into Bledlow*

Lovely old pub often in the spotlight

This lovely old free house dates back to the 1500s and is often used as a filming location for dramas such as *Midsomer Murders*, *Miss Marple* and *Restless*. Low beams and careworn flooring give the pub a timeless feeling, underlined by the steam trains chugging past on the heritage railway beyond the village green. Ramblers who drop down from the wooded Chiltern scarp can fill up on generously filled baguettes and rustic home-made meals like beef lasagne with garlic bread; and hot smoked mackerel fillets with salad and boiled potatoes, boosted by daily-changing specials.

Open all wk 11.30-3 6-11 (wknds all day) **Food** Lunch all wk 12-2.30 Dinner Mon-Sat 6.30-9.30, Sun 7-9 ⊕ FREE HOUSE ◀ Wadworth 6X, guest ales ♂ Westons Stowford Press. ♟ 12 **Facilities** Non-diners area ♦ Children's menu Children's portions Family room Garden ⊼ Parking ▭

PICK OF THE PUBS

The Royal Oak

tel: 01628 488611 **Frieth Rd SL7 2JF**
email: info@royaloakmarlow.co.uk
web: www.royaloakmarlow.co.uk
dir: *A4155 from Marlow. 300yds right
signed Bovingdon Green. 0.75m, pub
on left*

Successful pub strong on seasonality

'Dogs, children and muddy boots
welcome' is the friendly motto at this
little old whitewashed pub, just up the
hill from town on the edge of Marlow
Common, and standing in sprawling,
flower-filled gardens. Now refurbished,
the inside is spacious yet cosy, with
dark floorboards, heritage colours, rich
fabrics, and a wood-burning stove. All
this sets the tone for early evening
regulars gathered round a challenging
crossword with a pint of Rebellion from
Marlow, or Mortimers Orchard draught
cider from Westons in Herefordshire. The
imaginative modern British and
international menu, put together with
good food ethics in mind, is designed to
appeal to all, beginning with 'small
plates', such as Wobbly Bottom goats'
cheese, basil quinoa, walnuts and local
damson vinaigrette; and sautéed
mushrooms, parmesan polenta and
hazelnut aïoli. Main courses cover
ground from roast salmon, Bombay
spiced potato cake, Bucksum winter

greens and coconut curry cream; slow-
cooked beef cheek bourguignon with
slow-roast garlic mash; to Jerusalem
artichoke risotto with roast chervil root,
beetroot jelly and toasted almond
dressing. Perhaps treat yourself to warm
pecan pie with burnt orange ice cream
and caramel sauce; or Thai infused rice
pudding with caramelised pineapple,
mango and chilli syrup to finish. An
exclusively European wine list has 24 by
the glass and a wide choice of pudding
wines, including one from the county of
Worcestershire. Outside there's a sunny
summer terrace, pétanque piste and
more than likely, red kites wheeling
around in the sky.

Open all day all wk 11-11 (Sun
12-10.30) Closed 25 Dec **Food** Lunch
Mon-Thu 12-2.30, Fri-Sat 12-3, Sun
12-9.30 Dinner Mon-Thu 6.30-9.30,
Fri-Sat 6-10, Sun 12-9.30 ⊞ SALISBURY
PUBS LTD ◖ Rebellion IPA ○ Westons
Mortimers Orchard. ♟ 24
Facilities Non-diners area ❖ (Bar
Garden) ⋔ Children's portions Garden
Ⴈ Parking WiFi

BOURNE END | Map 6 SU88

NEW The Garibaldi

tel: 01628 522092 **Hedsor Rd SL8 5EE**
dir: *From A4094 (in town centre) into Hedsor Rd. Pub on left*

Community pub serving international food

This 16th-century pub is the hub of the village life and a warm welcome is assured from owner Amanda Baker and her friendly border terrier, Elvis. Four local real ales including Marlow-brewed Rebellion are on offer at the bar, which also dispenses Cornish Orchard cider and up to 15 wines by the glass. The globally-influenced menu might kick off with gin- and coriander-cured salmon with horseradish and lemon before moving on to soy braised pork neck with chilli caramel crackling. Finish with steamed banana and cardamom pudding and chocolate sorbet.

Open all wk 12-3 5-10.30 (Fri-Sat 12-12 Sun 12-10) **Food** Lunch Mon-Sat 12-2.30, Sun 12-4 Dinner Mon-Sat 6-9 Av main course £15 Restaurant menu available all wk ⊕ FREE HOUSE ◀ Rebellion ○ Cornish Orchards. ♀ 15 **Facilities** Non-diners area ✿ (Bar Restaurant Garden) ♦ Children's portions Garden ⋒ Beer festival Cider festival Parking WiFi

BOVINGDON GREEN | Map 5 SU88

The Royal Oak | PICK OF THE PUBS

See Pick of the Pubs on opposite page

BRILL | Map 11 SP61

The Pheasant ★★★★ INN

tel: 01844 239370 **39 Windmill St HP18 9TG**
email: info@thepheasant.co.uk **web:** www.thepheasant.co.uk
dir: *In village centre, by windmill*

Popular pub, B&B and restaurant with stunning views

This friendly 17th-century hilltop country pub and restaurant has wonderful views of Brill Windmill and neighbouring counties. Well worth trying is the pub's own, appropriately named, 'A Very Pleasant Pheasant Ale'. Enticing starter choices might be white bean and onion soup; Cullen skink; or mussels of the week. Then consider braised shoulder steak pie; pan-fried scallops, thermidor sauce and French fries; or honey roast ham, free-range eggs and hand-cut chips. Head for the garden when the weather's good or book for a Thursday curry evening.

Open all day all wk 12-11 (Fri-Sat 12-12 Sun 12-10.30) **Food** Lunch Mon-Fri 12-2.30, Sat 12-6, Sun 12-5 Dinner Mon-Sat 6-9 ⊕ FREE HOUSE ◀ A Very Pleasant Pheasant Ale (pub's own), Chiltern Beechwood Bitter, Vale Brill Gold ○ Symonds, guest ciders. **Facilities** Non-diners area ✿ (Bar Restaurant Garden) ♦ Children's

The Pheasant

menu Children's portions Garden ⋒ Beer festival Cider festival Parking WiFi ⛟ (notice required) **Rooms** 4

See advert on page 48

The Pointer ⊛⊛⊛ | PICK OF THE PUBS

tel: 01844 238339 **27 Church St HP18 9RT**
email: manager@thepointerbrill.co.uk **web:** www.thepointerbrill.co.uk
dir: *M40 junct 9, A41 towards Aylesbury. Right B4011 (signed Thame). Follow Brill signs*

16th-century dining-pub that's a real star turn

In a delightful hilltop village topped by an early surviving post-mill, landlords David and Fiona Howden have made a great success of The Pointer which serves as a pub, a restaurant and a butchers. They support Brill's own Vale brewery and XT Brewing in nearby Thame, whose spent grain feeds the livestock on their own organic farm; Longhorn cattle, rare-breed Middle White pigs and Hampshire Down sheep all live happily on this farm. Typical of the sophisticated cooking by head chef Mini Patel are starters of Jerusalem artichoke soup, fresh black truffle and toasted hazelnuts; and Brixham crab, red beetroot, Bramley apple and New Delhi spices. For the main event perhaps, Longhorn sirloin and Jacob's Ladder (short rib), dripping-cooked chips, bone marrow, hen-of-the-woods mushroom, lovage and port sauce; Shetland cod loin, hand-made pasta, palourde clams, grilled spring onion and sea herbs; or for two to share – Pointer Farm suckling pig, creamed Maris Pipers, farm greens and caramelised apple sauce.

Open all day Closed 1st wk Jan, Mon **Food** Lunch Tue-Sat 12-2.30, Sun 1-5 Dinner Tue-Thu 6.30-9, Fri-Sat 6.30-10 Av main course £12.50 Set menu available Restaurant menu available Tue-Sun ⊕ FREE HOUSE ◀ XT The Pointer, Vale Pale Ale, Rebellion ○ 3Cs Vintage Cider, Willy's. ♀ 13 **Facilities** Non-diners area ✿ (Bar Garden Outside area) ♦ Children's menu Children's portions Garden Outside area ⋒ Parking WiFi ⛟ (notice required)

BUCKINGHAM

Map 11 SP63

The Old Thatched Inn

tel: 01296 712584 **Main St, Adstock MK18 2JN**
email: manager@theoldthatchedinn.co.uk **web:** www.theoldthatchedinn.co.uk
dir: *A413 from Buckingham towards Aylesbury. Approx 4m left to Adstock*

Spacious pub with plenty of original character

Once called the Chandos Arms, this lovely early 18th-century thatched inn still boasts traditional beams and inglenook fireplace. The spacious interior consists of a formal conservatory and a bar with comfy furniture and a welcoming, relaxed atmosphere. Using the freshest, seasonal ingredients from local and regional suppliers, the menu takes in starters like grilled goats' cheese croûte with apple and beetroot chutney; and chicken liver parfait with red onion marmalade; and mains like Cumberland sausages with bubble-and-squeak; roasted rump of lamb with shallot purée; or linguine pasta carbonara.

The Old Thatched Inn

Open all day all wk Closed 26 Dec **Food** Lunch Mon-Fri 12-2.30, Sat 12-3, Sun 12-9 Dinner Mon-Sat 6-9.30, Sun 12-9 Set menu available Restaurant menu available all wk ⊕ FREE HOUSE ◀ Hook Norton Hooky Bitter, Morland Old Speckled Hen, Fuller's London Pride, Timothy Taylor Landlord, Sharp's Doom Bar ⚬ Aspall. ☘ 14 **Facilities** Non-diners area ❖ (Bar) ♦ Children's menu Children's portions Outside area ⊼ Parking WiFi

See advert on opposite page

BUTLER'S CROSS

Map 5 SP80

NEW The Russell Arms

tel: 01296 624411 **2 Chalkside Rd HP17 OTS**
email: therussell@distinctpubs.co.uk
dir: *From A4010 (S of Aylesbury) follow Butlers Cross signs. Pub at x-roads in village*

Village-owned free house

A pub since 1784, it lies below Coombe Hill, second highest point in the Chilterns. It was named after a former owner of the nearby Chequers Estate, which is now better known for being the country retreat of the serving prime minister. Stripped beams, an open fire and a log-burner await the visitor ready for one of 17 wines by the glass, or maybe a pint of Tring brewery's Side Pocket for a Toad, an old Hertfordshire saying alluding to something useless. The menu follows the old 'keep it simple' business dictum, offering dishes along the lines of carrot and coriander soup; braised pork belly; traditional fish pie; pork sausages and mash; and pearl barley risotto.

Open all day 10am-11pm (Sun 12-10-30) Closed Mon **Food** Lunch Tue-Sat 12-2.30, Sun 12-4 Dinner Tue-Sat 6.30-9 ⊕ FREE HOUSE/THE DISTINCT PUB COMPANY ◀ Chiltern Ale, Tring Side Pocket for a Toad ⬮ Aspall. ♟ 17
Facilities Non-diners area ❧ (Bar Garden Outside area) ♦ Children's portions Garden Outside area ⊼ Parking WiFi 🚐 (notice required)

CADMORE END

Map 5 SU79

The Tree at Cadmore

tel: 01494 881183 **HP14 3PF**
email: cadmore@freehotel.co.uk
dir: *M40 junct 5 signed Stokenchurch. In Stokenchurch right onto B482 signed Cadmore End. Pub 2m on left*

International cuisine in a country pub

Close to the M40, but sheltered by woodland, this charming Chilterns pub offers plenty for lovers of Indian and European food. The menu offers starters like murgh masaaledar (battered fried chicken and mango salsa) and pan-fried Cornish scallops with cauliflower purée, baby carrot, crispy pancetta and curry oil. Mains include rolled Norfolk pork belly with mash, braised cabbage, crackling and cider jus; lamb rogan josh; paneer tikka masala; and vegetable cannelloni in tomato and bechamel sauce.

Open all day all wk **Food** Contact pub for food times Restaurant menu available all wk ⊕ MARSTON'S ◀ Brakspear Oxford Gold ⬮ Westons Stowford Press. ♟ 9
Facilities Non-diners area ♦ Children's menu Children's portions Outside area ⊼ Parking WiFi 🚐

CHALFONT ST PETER

Map 6 TQ09

The Greyhound Inn

PICK OF THE PUBS

tel: 01753 883404 **SL9 9RA**
email: reception@thegreyhoundinn.net
dir: *M40 junct 1/M25 junct 16, follow signs for Gerrards Cross, then Chalfont St Peter*

Good food at historic pub

Over the centuries, this old coaching inn has welcomed many a traveller, Oliver Cromwell and Winston Churchill among them. Judge Jeffreys presided over some of his famous assize courts here, often sending miscreants to the gallows overlooking the adjacent River Misbourne. Much of the pub's 14th-century character survives, particularly the massive beams, huge brick chimneys, and imposing panelled and flagstoned bar. Here you can join the villagers supping pints of Sharp's Doom Bar, watch the big game, and order a bar snack at half time. The restaurant specialises in English and continental dishes so perhaps start with the hot and cold Var salmon with asparagus and cream cheese dressing. Next may come a pub favourite such as a home-made burger with back bacon, cheese, fries and relish; or a simple grilled rump steak cooked to your liking. A warm chocolate brownie with orange ice cream makes a satisfying finish.

Open all day all wk Mon-Wed 6.30am-10.30pm (Thu 6.30am-11.30pm Fri 6.30am-1am Sat 7.30am-1am Sun 8.30am-10.30pm) **Food** Lunch Mon-Sat 12-2.30, Sun 12-6 Dinner Mon-Thu 6-9, Fri-Sat 6-9.30, Sun 12-6 Restaurant menu available all wk ⊕ ENTERPRISE INNS ◀ Sharp's Doom Bar, Adnams, Otter Bitter. ♟ 10
Facilities Non-diners area ❧ (Bar Garden) ♦ Children's menu Children's portions Garden ⊼ Parking WiFi

CHESHAM Map 6 SP90

The Swan

tel: 01494 783075 **Ley Hill HP5 1UT**
email: swanleyhill@btconnect.com
dir: *1.5m E of Chesham by golf course*

A warm welcome and a cosy fire

Set in the delightful village of Ley Hill, this beautiful 16th-century pub was once the place where condemned prisoners would drink a 'last and final ale' on the way to the nearby gallows. During World War II, Glen Miller and Clark Gable cycled here for a pint from the Air Force base at Bovingdon. These days, it is a free house offering a warm welcome, real ales and good food, plus a large inglenook fireplace and original beams. Pan-fried fillet of sea bream with Lyonnaise potato, poached baby fennel and roasted cherry tomatoes; steak and kidney pie; or chicken and chorizo tagliatelle are typical choices. Look out for the summer beer festival in August.

Open 12-2.30 5.30-11 (Sun 12-4) **Closed** Mon **Food** Lunch Tue-Sat 12-2.30 Dinner Tue-Sat 6.30-9.30 ⊕ FREE HOUSE ◀ St Austell Tribute, Timothy Taylor Landlord, Tring Side Pocket for a Toad, guest ales. **Facilities** Non-diners area ❧ (Garden) ⭧ Children's menu Garden ⊟ Beer festival Parking WiFi ▥ (notice required)

CUBLINGTON Map 11 SP82

The Unicorn ◉◉

tel: 01296 681261 **High St LU7 0LQ**
email: theunicornpub@btconnect.com **web:** www.theunicornpub.co.uk
dir: *2m N of A418 (between Aylesbury & Leighton Buzzard). In village centre*

Dog- and child-friendly, 17th-century village free house

All the right elements of an English country pub are here: the low-beamed bar, the wooden floors, the real fires, the mismatched furniture and a minimum of four real ales, including XT from Long Crendon and Vale Wychert. You can expect dishes such as deep-fried rabbit with carrot purée; honey-roast ham, duck egg and hand-cut chips; hand-made shortcrust pie of the day; steamed monkfish in Parma ham with pea fritters and lobster bisque; and grilled goats' cheese and field mushroom and honey mustard dressing. Finish with poached clementine with passionfruit posset. There are barbecues on Saturday evenings from May to September.

Open all wk 12-3-5-11 (Fri 10.30am-mdnt Sat 9.30am-mdnt Sun 12-7) **Closed** Sun eve **Food** Lunch Mon-Sat 12-3, Sun 12-4 Dinner Mon-Sat 6.30-9 Av main course £12.40 Set menu available Restaurant menu available all wk (ex Sun eve) ⊕ FREE HOUSE ◀ Timothy Taylor Landlord, Long Crendon XT, Fuller's London Pride, Vale Wychert Ò Westons Stowford Press, Thatchers Gold. **Facilities** Non-diners area ❧ (Bar Garden) ⭧ Children's menu Children's portions Play area Garden ⊟ Parking WiFi ▥ (notice required)

CUDDINGTON Map 5 SP71

The Crown PICK OF THE PUBS

tel: 01844 292222 **Spurt St HP18 0BB**
email: david@djbbars.com
dir: *From A418 between Thame & Aylesbury follow Cuddington signs. Pub in village centre*

Atmospheric pub offering a modern menu with international influences

This thatched and whitewashed listed pub sits in the picturesque village of Cuddington. The Crown's atmospheric interior includes a locals' bar and several low-beamed dining areas lit by candles in the evening. Fuller's London Pride, Adnams and guest ales are on tap, and there's also an extensive wine list, with 12 by the glass. The well thought-out, modern menu might include starters of poached salmon with fennel salad, lemon and black pepper dressing; or roasted red pepper and coriander houmous with toasted date and walnut bread, followed by mains such as beef and ale stew with herb dumplings; aubergine, mozzarella, tomato and basil bake; burger, chips and salad; or braised shoulder of lamb with boulanger potatoes and mulled red wine jus. Look to the blackboard for daily specials or the set menu for good value options. A compact patio area provides outside seating.

Open all wk 12-3 6-11 (Sun all day) **Food** Lunch all wk 12-2.15 Dinner Mon-Sat 6.30-9.15 ⊕ FULLER'S ◀ London Pride, Adnams, guest ales. ⬥ 12 **Facilities** Non-diners area ⭧ Children's portions Outside area ⊟ Parking WiFi ▥ (notice required)

DENHAM Map 6 TQ08

The Falcon Inn ★★★★ INN

tel: 01895 832125 **Village Rd UB9 5BE**
email: mail@falcondenham.com **web:** www.falcondenham.com
dir: *M40 junct 1, follow A40/Gerrards Cross signs. Approx 200yds, right into Old Mill Rd. Pass church on right. Pub opposite village green on left*

The heart and soul of a conservation village

Barely 17 miles away as the crow flies, central London seems light years away from this lovely 16th-century coaching inn opposite the village green. Expect well-kept Brakspear, Timothy Taylor and Fuller's real ales. Brasserie food includes slow-roasted pork belly with wild mushrooms, wilted spinach and truffle mash; or Thai green curry with home-made roti bread. The menu also lists pub classics such as sausages, mash and onion gravy; or beer-battered haddock fillet with mushy peas and chips; check the daily specials too. Other attractions are a south-facing terraced garden and four bedrooms, two of which have original oak beams.

Open all day all wk **Food** Lunch Mon-Sat 11-3, Sun 12-6 Dinner Mon-Sat 5-9.30, Sun 12-6 Av main course £14 Restaurant menu available Mon-Sat ⊕ ENTERPRISE INNS ◀ Timothy Taylor Landlord, Brakspear, Fuller's London Pride Ò Westons Stowford Press, Sharp's Orchard. ⬥ 10 **Facilities** Non-diners area ❧ (Bar Garden) ⭧ Children's portions Family room Garden ⊟ Beer festival Cider festival WiFi ▥ (notice required) **Rooms** 4

DORNEY
Map 6 SU97

The Palmer Arms

tel: 01628 666612 **Village Rd SL4 6QW**
email: chrys@thepalmerarms.com
dir: *From A4 take B3026, over M4 to Dorney*

Community pub with a suntrap garden

Built in the 15th century, with wooden beams and open fires, this family-friendly pub in the pretty conservation village of Dorney is just a short stroll from the Thames Path and Boveney Lock. The interior is contemporary and the menu combines both modern and classic British dishes, which can be accompanied by wines from the comprehensive list. Roasted red onion and goats' cheese tart may precede beef bourguignon with shallots and creamed potatoes; or Cajun chicken burger with avocado, tomato salsa and fries. There is a lighter lunch menu, roasts on Sundays and tasting menu evenings. An early autumn beer festival features local beers and ciders.

Open all day all wk 11am-11.30pm (Sun 12-10.30) **Food** Mon-Fri 12-9, Sat-Sun 12-10 ⊕ GREENE KING ◀ Abbot Ale, IPA & Palmer Arms Ale, Guinness ♖ Aspall. ♟ 18 **Facilities** Non-diners area ✿ (Bar Garden) ♦♦ Children's menu Children's portions Play area Garden ⋈ Beer festival Parking WiFi ➡ (notice required)

EASINGTON
Map 5 SP61

Mole and Chicken
PICK OF THE PUBS

tel: 01844 208387 **HP18 9EY**
email: enquiries@themoleandchicken.co.uk
dir: *M40 juncts 8 or 8a, A418 to Thame. At rdbt left onto B4011 signed Long Crendon & Bicester. In Long Crendon right into Carters Lane signed Dorton & Chilton. At T-junct left into Chilton Rd signed Chilton. Approx 0.75m to pub*

Secluded former cider house with panoramic views

On the Oxfordshire-Buckinghamshire border, Steve and Suzanne Bush's pub was built in 1831 as housing for estate workers, later becoming the village store and beer and cider house. The far-reaching views from its high terraced garden are magnificent, while inside it's a combination of exposed beams, flagged floors and smart, contemporary furniture. Beechwood Bitter and Vale Wychert are on tap, alongside Aspall cider. From a British and eastern Mediterranean-influenced menu, a typical meal would be coriander and white pepper squid, aïoli, chorizo and endive, then braised ox cheek, carrots, horseradish mash, herb crumbs and bone marrow sauce; ending with apple and blackberry crumble and custard. Bar dishes include spaghetti, creamed wild mushrooms, truffle oil and parmesan; and pork belly Thai curry. And if you were wondering about the whimsical name – it recalls two long-gone landlords, 'Moley' and 'Johnny Chick'.

Open all day all wk Mon-Fri 7.30am-11pm (Sat-Sun 8am-mdnt) Closed 25 Dec **Food** Lunch Mon-Sat 12-2.30, Sun 12-4 Dinner Mon-Sat 6.30-9.30, Sun 6-9 Restaurant menu available all wk ⊕ FREE HOUSE ◀ Beechwood Bitter, Vale Wychert ♖ Aspall. **Facilities** Non-diners area ♦♦ Children's menu Children's portions Play area Garden ⋈ Parking WiFi ➡

FARNHAM COMMON
Map 6 SU98

The Foresters

tel: 01753 643340 **The Broadway SL2 3QQ**
email: info@theforesterspub.com
dir: *Phone for detailed directions*

Well-chosen dishes in an eclectic setting

This handsome 1930s building has an interior where old meets new – crystal chandeliers and log fires, real ales and cocktails, glass-topped tables and wooden floors, chesterfields and velvet thrones. Opt for a starter of English asparagus with poached egg and hollandaise sauce, or one of the 'mini dishes' – perhaps prawn popcorn; jam jar sausages; tempura cauliflower; or chorizo pâté. Typical main dishes include lamb cutlets, potato and celeriac terrine, pea parcels, eucalyptus jus; pulled pork and cider risotto; and tasting of duck – pink breast, confit, vanilla creamed potato, lime jus. Carrot and orange pudding; or chilli chocolate profiteroles are sure to appeal for dessert. There are front and rear gardens.

Open all day all wk **Food** Lunch all wk 12-3 Dinner all wk 6.30-10 Set menu available Restaurant menu available all wk ⊕ PUNCH TAVERNS ◀ Fuller's London Pride, Young's, Sharp's Doom Bar, guest ales ♖ Thatchers Gold. ♟ 16 **Facilities** Non-diners area ✿ (Bar Garden) ♦♦ Children's menu Children's portions Garden ⋈ Parking WiFi ➡ (notice required)

FARNHAM ROYAL
Map 6 SU98

The Emperor

tel: 01753 643006 **Blackpond Ln SL2 3EG**
email: emperorpub@gmail.com
dir: *Phone for detailed directions*

A pub for all seasons

Just a short, easy stroll from the fabulous ancient woodland of Burnham Beeches nature reserve, this Victorian village inn seamlessly mixes contemporary comforts with the character of a mature local pub. Polished wood floors and original beams run through the bar, conservatory and weather-boarded barn; there's a log fire in winter and alfresco tables in the summer in a eucalyptus-shaded garden. Rotating real ales satisfy a thirst, whilst the menu of pub classics is elevated by modern dishes like home-made game pâté, or pan-baked cod loin with spinach and champagne sauce. An annual beer festival is held at this family and dog-friendly pub.

Open all day all wk 12-11 (Thu-Sun 12-12) **Food** Lunch Mon-Sat 12-2, Sun 12-3 Dinner Mon-Sat 6-9 ⊕ ENTERPRISE INNS ◀ Fuller's London Pride, Rebellion, 3 guest ales. ♟ 12 **Facilities** Non-diners area ✿ (Bar Garden) ♦♦ Children's menu Children's portions Play area Garden ⋈ Beer festival Parking WiFi ➡ (notice required)

FRIETH
Map 5 SU79

The Prince Albert

tel: 01494 881683 **RG9 6PY**
dir: *4m N of Marlow. Follow Frieth road from Marlow. Straight across at x-roads on Fingest road. Pub 200yds on left*

A peaceful retreat and traditional pub grub

There's no TV, jukebox or electronic games in this cottagey Chiltern Hills pub. What you get instead, surprise, surprise, is just good conversation, probably much as when it was built in the 1700s. In the bar, low beams, a big black inglenook stove, high-backed settles and lots of copper pots and pans; an alternative place to enjoy a pint of Brakspear is a seat in the garden, while admiring the woods and fields. A short menu and regularly changing special board uses locally sourced ingredients for dishes such as smoked mackerel, sautéed potatoes with beetroot and horseradish salad; calves' liver, crispy bacon, onion mash and red wine gravy; and venison stew, creamed leeks and red cabbage.

Open all day all wk 11-11 (Sun 12-10.30) **Food** Lunch Mon-Sat 12.15-2.30, Sun 12.30-3 Dinner Fri-Sat 7.30-9.30 ⊕ BRAKSPEAR ◀ Bitter, seasonal ales ♖ Thatchers Gold. ♟ 9 **Facilities** Non-diners area ✿ (Bar Garden) ♦♦ Children's portions Garden ⋈ Parking WiFi

FULMER
Map 6 SU98

NEW The Black Horse

tel: 01753 663183 **Windmill Rd SL3 6HD**
dir: *M40 junct 1, A40 (Amersham). Then follow Beaconsfield & Gerrards Cross signs. Into Tatling End (over M25), left signed Fulmer (over M40). Pub on left after church*

Old-world charm and hearty eating

Dating back to the 17th century and originally a craftsman's cottage, The Black Horse is a great blend of old-world charm and contemporary decor, lovingly refurbished and extended. The village is close to Pinewood Studios so who knows who you might see if you pop in for a pint of Greene King IPA or something to eat. You'll find pub classics on the menu and a good range of alternative choices, including some ideal for sharing – the baked camembert with ciabatta and apricot chutney, for example. Main courses might include braised blade of beef with colcannon and parsnip chips; or English feta, butternut squash, spinach and pine nut pithivier with pickled red cabbage.

Open all day all wk **Food** Contact pub for food times Restaurant menu available all wk ⊕ GREENE KING ◀ IPA & London Glory, guest ale ♂ Westons Stowford Press. ☘ 20 **Facilities** Non-diners area ❀ (Bar Garden) ♦♦ Children's menu Children's portions Play area Garden ⚲ Parking WiFi ▦

GERRARDS CROSS
Map 6 TQ08

The Three Oaks

tel: 01753 899016 **Austenwood Ln SL9 8NL**
email: info@thethreeoaksgx.co.uk
dir: *From A40 at lights take B416 (Packhorse Rd) signed Village Centre. Over railway. Left signed Gold Hill into Austenwood Ln. Pub on right*

Contemporary gastro-pub with relaxed feel

The Three Oaks, in the heart of affluent Gerrards Cross, is a stylish dining venue with a smart, contemporary feel, yet the vibe is relaxed and informal. Drop by for a pint of local Rebellion Ale or a glass of unoaked Chardonnay and tuck into the cracking value set lunch menu, or perhaps crispy baby squid, Merguez sausage, red pepper and basil mayonnaise, followed by lemon and thyme marinated chicken, black trumpet mushrooms, roast pumpkin, sweetcorn and truffle mayonnaise, and then sticky toffee pudding, Guinness sauce, walnut and Devonshire ice cream. There's a super terrace for alfresco dining.

Open all wk **Food** Lunch Mon-Sat 12-2.30, Sun 12-6 Dinner Mon-Sat 6.30-9.30, Sun 12-6 Set menu available Restaurant menu available all wk ⊕ ENTERPRISE INNS ◀ Fuller's London Pride, Rebellion & IPA ♂ Aspall. ☘ 24 **Facilities** Non-diners area ♦♦ Children's menu Children's portions Garden ⚲ Parking WiFi ▦ (notice required)

GREAT HAMPDEN
Map 5 SP80

The Hampden Arms

tel: 01494 488255 **HP16 9RQ**
email: louise.lucas@outlook.com
dir: *M40 junct 4, A4010, right before Princes Risborough. Great Hampden signed*

Home-cooked food at lovely countryside inn

The large garden of this mock-Tudor free house on the wooded Hampden Estate sits beside the common, where you might watch a game of cricket during the season. Chef-proprietor Constantine Lucas includes Greek signature dishes such as kleftiko with rice or roast potatoes, alongside more traditional choices such as veal escalope, Parma ham with mushroom, sage and white wine sauce; or broccoli and

cauliflower bake with garlic bread; blackboard specials add to the choices. The pub has a secure beer garden, ideal for private functions.

Open all wk 12-3 6-12 **Food** Lunch Mon-Sat 12-2, Sun 12-3 Dinner Mon-Sat 6-9.30, Sun 7-9.30 Set menu available Restaurant menu available all wk ⊕ FREE HOUSE ◀ Chiltern, Rebellion, guest ales ♂ Addlestones. **Facilities** Non-diners area ♦♦ Children's menu Children's portions Family room Garden ⚲ Beer festival Parking WiFi

GREAT KINGSHILL
Map 6 SU89

NEW The Red Lion

tel: 01494 711262 **Missenden Rd HP15 6EB**
email: info@redlion-greatkingshill.co.uk
dir: *On A4128*

All the charms of a country pub

Whoever built this former beer house clearly made good use of flints extracted from Chiltern Hills chalk. An early example, perhaps, of a 'source local' philosophy that continues both for food and real ales. Shellfish options include oysters, which can even be bought singly; prawn, crayfish and smoked salmon cocktail; and king scallops with peas and bacon. 'Classic mains' are country chicken and vegetable pie; Catalan fish stew; and a vegetarian tasting plate. Rump, sirloin and rib-eye steaks are chargrilled with a choice of sauces, and Cajun breaded chicken, bacon and cheeseburger is accompanied by fries and onion rings. Specials change daily.

Open 12-3 6-11 Closed 1-6 Jan, Sun eve & Mon **Food** Lunch Tue-Sun 12-2 Dinner Tue-Sat 6-9 Set menu available Restaurant menu available Tue-Sun ⊕ FREE HOUSE ◀ Rebellion IPA, Chiltern Ale, Binghams ♂ Thatchers. **Facilities** Non-diners area ♦♦ Children's menu Children's portions Garden ⚲ Parking WiFi

GREAT MISSENDEN
Map 6 SP80

The Nags Head ★★★★ INN ❂
PICK OF THE PUBS

See Pick of the Pubs on opposite page

The Polecat Inn
PICK OF THE PUBS

tel: 01494 862253 **170 Wycombe Rd, Prestwood HP16 OHJ**
email: info@thepolecatinn.co.uk
dir: *On A4128 between Great Missenden & High Wycombe*

Wine and beer taken seriously here

This 17th-century Chiltern Hills free house has a timeless quality: flower baskets adorn the exterior, while inside, the small, low-beamed rooms radiating from the bar offer a choice of dining and drinking options. From the village's own Malt The Brewery, which you can visit, comes Prestwood's Best; 30 wines are sold by the glass. Dishes are prepared from local ingredients, including herbs from the huge garden. If you enjoy beef Wellington or magret of duck, you could be in luck; ditto Cumberland sausage; or baked salmon with celeriac dauphinoise, sun-blushed tomatoes and gruyère cheese. Home-made venison and wild rabbit pie, blackboard specials, baguettes and filled jacket potatoes add further choices. Children are well catered for, too. Check with the inn for their summer beer festival dates.

Open all day all wk 11-11 (closed 2.30-6 Jan) **Food** Lunch all wk 12-3 Dinner Mon-Sat 6.30-9 Set menu available ⊕ FREE HOUSE ◀ Brakspear Oxford Gold, Malt The Brewery Prestwood's Best, Rebellion IPA ♂ Thatchers Gold. ☘ 30 **Facilities** Non-diners area ❀ (Bar Restaurant Garden) ♦♦ Children's menu Children's portions Play area Family room Garden ⚲ Beer festival Parking WiFi ▦

PICK OF THE PUBS

The Nags Head ★★★★ INN ❀

GREAT MISSENDEN   Map 6 SP80

tel: 01494 862200
London Rd HP16 0DG
email: goodfood@nagsheadbucks.com
web: www.nagsheadbucks.com
dir: *N of Amersham on A413, left at Chiltern hospital into London Rd signed Great Missenden*

Charming rural pub with excellent Anglo-French cooking

Famous children's author and long-term local resident Roald Dahl was a regular here, which is why you'll find many of his limited-edition prints in the dining room (his award-winning museum is in the village). And over the years many a prime minister, especially Sir Harold Wilson, has called in here en route to Chequers, the premier's official country house retreat not far away. Originally three late 15th-century cottages, whose inhabitants were known as 'bodgers', the Chilterns word for chairmakers in the surrounding beech woods; over time the properties became a popular coaching inn on the London road, which follows the Misbourne Valley. The owning Michaels family have restored it, just as they have their sister pub, the Bricklayers Arms in Flaunden, over the county border in Hertfordshire. Low oak beams and an inglenook fireplace set the scene for the bar and its real ales from local breweries in perhaps Brill, Prestwood or Tring. The Anglo-French

fusion menu abounds with interesting dishes, typical starters being braised chicory and caraway tarte Tatin with warm goats' cheese and honey drizzle; and fresh Cornish white crab and home-smoked salmon with chive cream and blinis. Main courses might be halibut fillet meunière with smoked swordfish shavings, and beetroot and pea beurre blanc; and rump and shredded shoulder of lamb with carrot purée and toasted sunflower seed jus. For dessert look for dandelion and burdock sticky toffee pudding with date mascarpone; or lemon tart with Cassis sorbet. In summer, relax over a drink or a meal in the lovely garden and gaze out towards the hills. Maybe stay overnight in one of the five beautiful bedrooms.

Open all day all wk Closed 25 Dec
Food Lunch Mon-Sat 12-2.30, Sun 12-3.30 Dinner Mon-Sat 6.30-9.30, Sun 6-8.30 Set menu available Restaurant menu available all wk ⊞ FREE HOUSE ◀ Rebellion, Tring, Vale, Malt Missenden Pale Ale, Sharp's Cornish Coaster ⚗ Aspall. ☐ 19 **Facilities** Non-diners area ❖ (Bar Garden) ♦♦ Children's portions Garden ⊼ Parking WiFi ⛌ (notice required) **Rooms** 5

PICK OF THE PUBS

Grouse & Ale

LANE END   Map 5 SU89

tel: 01494 882299 **High St HP14 3JG**
email: info@grouseandale.co.uk
web: www.grouseandale.com
dir: *On B482 in village*

**Smart pub, modern menus,
friendly service**

This was The Clayton Arms for nearly
half a century, named after Sir Robert
Clayton who built it in 1679 on
becoming Lord Mayor of London. Today
the house's spacious spick-and-span
interior mixes cosy corners with
comfortably furnished drinking and
dining areas, to create a smart country
town pub in the true British tradition.
The staff's smiling faces, well cared for
real ales, and impressive modern menus
all combine to make the Grouse & Ale an
inviting venue for family and friends.
With a drink and a menu, relax in the
sun-trap courtyard. Choice is extensive
and high on comfort appeal, but
attention to detail, top quality
ingredients and beautiful presentation
have won awards for the kitchen. Deal
with hungry children first: home-made
fish fingers and skinny chips is a firm
favourite, while pasta with tomato
sauce topped with cheese appeals to
those with more grown-up tastes. Pub
favourites list farmhouse pork
sausages, creamy mash, rich onion
gravy; Guinness-braised shin of beef

pie; and beer-battered haddock with
hand-cut chips, mushy peas and tartare
sauce. With the variety and high gastro
appeal on offer, choosing a three-course
special occasion dinner is not difficult.
Spiced tiger prawn and salmon
fishcakes with pickled cucumber and
pak choi salad makes a mouthwatering
starter. Follow with pan-seared breast of
Gressingham duck served with black
cherry and balsamic sauce with carrot
and potato rösti and sautéed
courgettes. A mixed fruit crumble with a
pot of custard rounds things off nicely
– unless the artisan British cheese
plate is too much of a temptation. As
you would expect from an establishment
that aims to please, the list of coffees
and teas is exemplary.

Open all day all wk **Food** Lunch Mon-Sat
12-2.30, Sun 12-4 Dinner Mon-Sat
6-9.30 ⬡ STAR PUBS & BARS
🍺 Adnams Broadside, Caledonian
Deuchars IPA, Theakston Best Bitter.
🍷 27 **Facilities** Non-diners area 🐾 (Bar
Outside area) 👶 Children's menu
Children's portions Outside area 🪑
Parking WiFi

HEDGERLEY
Map 6 SU98

The White Horse

tel: 01753 643225 **SL2 3UY**
dir: *Phone for detailed directions*

One for the beer festival follower

An ale drinker's paradise if ever there was one, parts of which date back 500 years. With three beer festivals a year (Easter, Spring Bank Holiday and Summer Bank Holiday) and barely a pause between them, this pub can almost claim to run a single year-long celebration, with over 1,000 real ales consumed annually. Real cider and Belgian bottled beers augment the already mammoth range. A large well-kept garden at the rear hosts summer barbecues; otherwise the menu of home-cooked pub favourites ranges from a salad bar with quiches, sandwiches and ploughman's through to curries, chilli, pasta dishes, pies and steaks (lunchtime only).

Open all wk 11-2.30 5-11 (Sat 11-11 Sun 11-10.30) **Food** Lunch Mon-Fri 12-2, Sat-Sun 12-2.30 Av main course £6.50 ⊕ FREE HOUSE ◼ 8 rotating ales ♻ 3 guest ciders. ⚱ 10 **Facilities** Non-diners area ❀ (Bar Garden) ♦ Children's portions Family room Garden ⋈ Beer festival Parking WiFi 🚐

LACEY GREEN
Map 5 SP80

The Whip Inn

tel: 01844 344060 **Pink Rd HP27 0PG**
dir: *1m from A4010 (Princes Risborough to High Wycombe road). Adjacent to windmill*

Traditional pub popular with walkers and cyclists

Standing high above the Vale of Aylesbury in the heart of the Chiltern Hills, the beer garden of this 200-year-old pub overlooks the Lacey Green windmill. Ramblers on the Chiltern Way join locals in appreciating some of 800 different real ales offered each year, as well as real Millwhites cider. A robust menu of home-made classic favourites such as ham, egg and chips and chargrilled steaks seals the deal at this rustic, music- and fruit machine-free country inn. The Whip holds a beer festival twice a year in May and September.

Open all wk all wk **Food** Lunch Mon-Sat 12-2.30, Sun 12-3 Dinner Mon-Sat 6.30-9 ⊕ FREE HOUSE ◼ Over 800 guest ales a year ♻ Thatchers, Millwhites. ⚱ 22 **Facilities** Non-diners area ❀ (Bar Garden) ♦ Children's menu Children's portions Garden ⋈ Beer festival Parking

LANE END
Map 5 SU89

Grouse & Ale
PICK OF THE PUBS

See Pick of the Pubs on opposite page

LITTLE KINGSHILL
Map 6 SU89

The Full Moon

tel: 01494 862397 **Hare Ln HP16 0EE**
email: email@thefullmoon.info
dir: *SW of Great Missenden, accessed from either A413 or A4128*

Perfect for post-walk ales and meals

A popular post-ramble refuelling stop, especially as both dogs and children are warmly welcomed inside, this pub has a wealth of wonderful walks through the Chiltern Hills radiating from its doorstep. It is noted for its tip-top Fuller's London Pride and the weekly-changing guest ales, and the pub throngs during the late June beer festival. Walking appetites will be satisfied with one of the starters to share; one of their home-made burgers; pan-fried marinated wild boar, crushed new potatoes in mushroom sauce; or for the very hungry, The Full Moon grill platter – rib-eye steak, chicken wings, BBQ ribs. The apple toffee fudge cake could round things off nicely.

Open all day all wk **Food** Lunch all wk 12-3 Dinner all wk 6-10 ⊕ PUNCH TAVERNS ◼ Fuller's London Pride, Young's, Adnams, guest ale ♻ Aspall. ⚱ 21 **Facilities** Non-diners area ❀ (Bar Garden) ♦ Children's menu Children's portions Play area Garden ⋈ Beer festival Parking WiFi 🚐 (notice required)

LITTLE MARLOW
Map 5 SU88

The Queens Head

tel: 01628 482927 **Pound Ln SL7 3SR**
email: tqhlittlemarlow@yahoo.co.uk
dir: *From A404 take Marlow exit towards Bourne End. Approx 1m, right by church into Church Rd. Approx 100mtrs right into Pound Ln*

A rose-clad gem of a pub

Dating from the 16th century and called 'Marlow's little secret', this is a pretty collection of buildings from three different periods. Standing opposite the manor house, its beamed, open fire-warmed interior feels immediately welcoming. Since it's just a tankard's throw from the Marlow Rebellion Brewery, expect IPA and from November to January, Roasted Nuts (surely the only real ale named after a bar snack). Starters include pea soup with Whitney crab croquette; or crispy peppered squid with cucumber and fennel salad. Continue to mains like lamb Wellington with spinach purée and dauphinoise potatoes; braised shin of beef with butternut squash purée, celeriac, duck-fat Ratte potatoes and port jus; or roasted haloumi, sweet potato filo roll, spicy tomato jam and watercress salad. Save space for pecan tart and bourbon ice cream for afters.

Open all day all wk Closed 25-26 Dec **Food** Lunch Mon-Fri 12-2.30, Sat-Sun 12-4 Dinner all wk 6.30-9.30 ⊕ PUNCH TAVERNS ◼ Rebellion IPA ♻ Westons Stowford Press. **Facilities** Non-diners area ♦ Children's portions Garden ⋈ Parking WiFi 🚐 (notice required)

LONG CRENDON
Map 5 SP60

The Angel Inn ⓦ
PICK OF THE PUBS

tel: 01844 208268 **47 Bicester Rd HP18 9EE**
email: info@angelrestaurant.co.uk
dir: *M40 junct 7, A418 to Thame, B4011 to Long Crendon. Inn on B4011*

Great food in an exceptional village inn

Situated in the Vale of Aylesbury and close to the rippling Chiltern Hills, the village of Long Crendon was a centre for lace-making in medieval times. Certain buildings retain a real sense of history, including the old courthouse, picturesque rows of cottages and the gabled Angel Inn. This old coaching stop still displays much of its original character with ancient fireplaces and wattle-and-daub walls, alongside modern additions which include an airy conservatory. Refreshments centre on Vale Brewery's Wychert and the village's own XT Brewing Company's ales; the good wine list offers a dozen served by the glass. The AA-Rosette food comprises hand-made dishes cooked to order based on daily deliveries of fresh produce. Typical of these are an oriental vegetable salad with crispy duck and bacon; roast local lamb chump on a summer beans cassoulet; and a rum and raisin cheesecake with almond tuile.

Open all day Closed 1-2 Jan, Sun eve **Food** Lunch all wk 12-2.30 Dinner Mon-Sat 7-9.30 Set menu available Restaurant menu available all wk ⊕ FREE HOUSE ◀ Vale Wychert, XT-4 & XT-6. ⬥ 12 **Facilities** Non-diners area ⬧ Children's portions Garden ⌒ Parking WiFi ⬛ (notice required)

MARLOW
Map 5 SU88

The Coach
PICK OF THE PUBS

3 West St SL7 2LS
dir: *From A404 to Marlow. Pub in town centre*

Oh so stylish enterprise from celebrity chef

In the heart of Marlow, a stone's throw from his award-winning flagship business, The Hand & Flowers, TV chef Tom Kerridge has also created something quite special at The Coach. With its glazed wall tiles, soft leather furnishings and open kitchen, the look is timeless yet contemporary, as is head chef Nick Beardshaw's modern British cooking. So sit yourself down on a bar stool or at a table and decide from the concise menu with headings of 'Meat, No meat and Sweet'. From 'Meat' perhaps choose whole stuffed rotisserie quail, or venison chilli with red wine, chocolate and toasted rice cream. From 'No Meat' be tempted by sea bream fillet with Puy lentils and trompettes; or mushroom 'risotto' Claude Bosi. And then, you must leave room for a 'Sweet' – whisky and rye pudding; or lemon tart and raspberry sorbet are just two options. You can't pre-book to eat here – it's first-come-first-served – so it's all fingers crossed you'll time your visit just right.

Open all day all wk Closed 25 Dec **Food** Lunch all wk 12-2.30 Dinner all wk 6.30-10.30 ⊕ ENTERPRISE INNS ◀ Rebellion IPA, Wells Bombardier Burning Gold, Young's Bitter ⬥ Westons Rosie's Pig. ⬥ 20 **Facilities** ⬧ Children's portions WiFi

The Hand & Flowers ⓦⓦⓦⓦ
PICK OF THE PUBS

tel: 01628 482277 **126 West St SL7 2BP**
email: contact@thehandandflowers.co.uk
dir: *M4 junct 9, A404 to Marlow, A4155 towards Henley-on-Thames. Pub on right*

Unpretentious but highly acclaimed destination pub

Celebrity chef Tom Kerridge and his sculptor wife Beth have without doubt turned their simple concept into reality by making this 18th-century pub the sort of place where they, and everyone else, would like to eat. Four AA Rosettes and a chock-a-

block reservations diary testify to that. Housing all the desired historic features – flagstone floors, old timbers and log fires – the bar offers the unusual opportunity to drink a pint of Roasted Nuts (actually a real ale from Marlow's Rebellion brewery). Sourcing some ingredients from his own allotment, Tom's menus combine modern British and rustic French cooking, such as the duck liver parfait with orange chutney and toasted brioche starter. Mouth-wateringly descriptive mains include loin of Cotswold venison with boudin noir purée, allotment roots, ragout pie and cow puff; and Essex lamb 'bun' with sweetbreads and salsa verde. Booking to eat here is essential and must be arranged months in advance – although it's always worth a call to check for cancellations.

Open 12-2.45 6.30-9.45 (Sun 12-3.15) Closed 24-26 Dec, 1 Jan (dinner), Sun eve **Food** Lunch Mon-Sat 12-2.30, Sun 12-3.15 Dinner Mon-Sat 6.30-9.30 Set menu available ⊕ GREENE KING ◀ Abbot Ale, Morland Old Speckled Hen, Rebellion Roasted Nuts ⬥ Aspall & Perronelle's Blush. ⬥ 17 **Facilities** Non-diners area ⬧ Children's portions Outside area ⌒ Parking WiFi

The Kings Head

tel: 01628 484407 **Church Rd, Little Marlow SL7 3RZ**
email: clive.harvison@sky.com
dir: *M40 junct 4, A4040 S, then A4155 towards Bourne End. Pub 0.5m on right. Or M4 junct 8/9, A404(M) signed High Wycombe. Then A4155 towards Bourne End. Pub 0.5m*

Good range of real ales close to the Thames Path

This charming 16th-century pub with a large garden is only a few minutes' walk from the Thames Path. The open-plan interior features original beams and log fires. A great selection of ales awaits visitors to The Kings Head, including those from the Rebellion Brewery in Marlow. As well as sandwiches, baguettes, paninis and jacket potatoes, the food includes substantial salads, steaks, grilled salmon, chilli con carne, wholetail scampi and aubergine cannelloni. Tell staff you've parked the car, go for a walk and return for a meal.

Open all day all wk Closed 26 Dec **Food** Lunch Mon-Sat 12-2.30, Sun 12-7 Dinner Mon-Sat 6.30-9.30, Sun 12-7 ⊕ ENTERPRISE INNS ◀ Fuller's London Pride, Timothy Taylor Landlord, Adnams Broadside, Rebellion IPA, Otter ⬥ Thatchers Gold, Aspall. ⬥ 13 **Facilities** Non-diners area ⬧ Children's menu Children's portions Garden ⌒ Parking WiFi ⬛ (notice required)

MOULSOE
Map 11 SP94

The Carrington Arms

tel: 01908 218050 **Cranfield Rd MK16 0HB**
email: enquiries@thecarringtonarms.co.uk
dir: *M1 junct 14, A509 to Newport Pagnell 100yds, turn right signed Moulsoe & Cranfield. Pub on right*

Traditional countryside inn which is all about customer choice

Only a short hop from the rush and noise of the M1, the family-run Carrington in the pretty village of Moulsoe combines tradition with modern hospitality. Real ales and a good wine list are a given, but the pub is most famous for its fresh meat counter where customers can talk through their selection with the chef; locally-raised Bedfordshire beef is a highlight. The choice starts with sandwiches and pub favourites, but other options are a modern take on a prawn cocktail, then pink Woburn venison loin with smoked venison boudin, fondant potato with red wine and port jus. The large garden hosts a beer and cider festival in mid June.

Open all day all wk 12-11 **Food** all wk 12-10 Restaurant menu available all wk ⊕ FREE HOUSE ◀ Fuller's London Pride, Marston's Pedigree, guest ales ⬥ Orchard Pig. ⬥ 15 **Facilities** Non-diners area ⬧ Children's portions Garden ⌒ Beer festival Cider festival Parking WiFi ⬛ (notice required)

NEWTON BLOSSOMVILLE   Map 11 SP95

The Old Mill ★★★ INN

tel: 01234 881273 **MK43 8AN**
email: enquiries@oldmill.uk.com **web:** www.oldmill.uk.com
dir: *A509 N of Milton Keynes. Right to village. Or A428 from Bedford. In Turvey, turn left to village*

Much loved village local with reliable cuisine

A handsome stone inn in a village of thatched cottages tucked away in the tranquil Ouse Valley; with its attractive bedrooms, The Old Mill is an ideal base to stay over. The beer range changes with the seasons, whilst the choice on the menu relies heavily on what's available from local suppliers. There's a solid base of pub favourites like sausage and mash with onion gravy and peas; Hunter's chicken with skinny chips and side salad; or smoked haddock and salmon fishcake, wilted spinach with tomato and caper salsa. There's a peaceful, dog-friendly grassy garden, whilst a wood-burner flickers in the cosy bar. Regulars are keep active by playing skittles in the local league.

Open all wk 12-3 5-11 (Fri-Sun 12-11) **Food** Lunch Mon-Sat 12-2.30, Sun 12-4 Dinner Mon-Sat 6-9 Restaurant menu available all wk ⊕ FREE HOUSE ◀ Greene King Ruddles Best, guest ales ♂ Aspall. **Facilities** Non-diners area ✿ (Bar Garden) ♦ Children's menu Children's portions Garden ⊓ WiFi ▦ (notice required) **Rooms** 5

NEWTON LONGVILLE   Map 11 SP83

NEW The Crooked Billet

tel: 01908 373936 **2 Westbrook End MK17 0DF**
email: crookedbilletmk@gmail.com
dir: *M1 junct 13, A421 towards Buckingham. 6m. At Bottledump rdbt 1st left signed Newton Longville. Pub on right in village*

Excellent food a short drive from Milton Keynes

A thatched former farmhouse dating back to 1600, The Crooked Billet is located just south west of Milton Keynes. With log fires in winter and a large garden for warmer months, landlords David Pugh and Alan Ayres have retained the family pub feel for drinkers who can enjoy glasses of Abbot Ale or one of the 17 wines served by the glass. A bar menu offering sandwiches, steaks, burgers and home-made pies runs alongside the à la carte that might include corn-fed chicken, Lyonnaise potatoes, ratatouille and basil pesto. Time a visit for the Early May Bank Holiday beer festival.

Open all day all wk **Food** Lunch Mon-Sat 12-4, Sun 12-5 Dinner Mon-Sat 5-9 Av main course £10 Set menu available Restaurant menu available all wk ⊕ GREENE KING ◀ Abbot Ale, Billet Ale (pub's own) ♂ Symonds Scrumpy Jack. ☗ 17 **Facilities** Non-diners area ♦ Children's menu Children's portions Garden ⊓ Beer festival Parking WiFi ▦

NORTH MARSTON   Map 11 SP72

The Pilgrim

tel: 01296 670969 **25 High St MK18 3PD**
email: info@thepilgrimpub.co.uk **web:** www.thepilgrimpub.co.uk
dir: *From Aylesbury take A413 towards Buckingham. In Whitchurch turn left & follow North Marston sign. Right to North Marston, approx 1m to pub*

Tranquil haven overlooking Aylesbury Vale

A holy well in the village, reputedly the site of many miracles in the Middle Ages, was reason enough for pilgrims to make the journey to North Marston. Brett and Nadia Newman are a husband-and-wife team managing the kitchen and front of house respectively at this 300-year-old pub. They have worked hard to build local loyalty with their burgers, quizzes, curries and open mic – each having a dedicated evening in the month's social calendar. The weekly changing menus feature home-grown produce in dishes such as roast saddle of venison, celeriac purée, potato terrine and braised red cabbage; and free-range chicken breast, green peppercorn sauce and home-made chips.

Open 12-3 5-11 (Fri 12-3 5-12 Sat 12-12 Sun 12-6) Closed Sun eve & Mon **Food** Lunch Tue-Sat 12-2, Sun 12-3 Dinner Tue-Sat 6-9 Restaurant menu available Tue-Sun ⊕ FREE HOUSE ◀ XT 4, Sharp's Doom Bar ♂ Millwhites Hedge Layer, Westons Family Reserve. ☗ 10 **Facilities** Non-diners area ✿ (Bar Garden) ♦ Children's portions Garden ⊓ Parking WiFi ▦ (notice required)

PENN   Map 6 SU99

The Red Lion

tel: 01494 813107 **Elm Rd HP10 8LF**
email: redlionpub@btconnect.com
dir: *Phone for detailed directions*

Traditional village pub popular with Chiltern walkers

Set in the pretty village of Penn, this 16th-century pub is an ideal base for exploring the beautiful Chiltern Hills and nearby Penn Wood. For those in need of more leisurely pursuits, sit on the sunny front terrace overlooking the village green with a pint of Chiltern Beechwood Bitter and watch the world go by. Inside, log fires warm the cosy, antique-strewn bar in winter as good conversation abounds. The food here is home cooked and hearty with dishes including Madras spiced parsnip soup; potted rabbit; coq au vin; suckling pork belly and apple sauce; and cauliflower risotto.

Open all day all wk **Food** all day Restaurant menu available all wk ⊕ ENTERPRISE INNS ◀ Chiltern Beechwood Bitter, guest ales ♂ Westons Mortimers Orchard. ☗ 11 **Facilities** Non-diners area ✿ (Bar Restaurant Garden) ♦ Children's menu Children's portions Garden ⊓ Parking WiFi ▦ (notice required)

SEER GREEN
Map 6 SU99

The Jolly Cricketers

tel: 01494 676308 **24 Chalfont Rd HP9 2YG**
email: amanda@thejollycricketers.co.uk
dir: *M40 junct 2, A355 signed Beaconsfield A40, Amersham. At Pyebush rdbt 1st exit, A40 signed Beaconsfield, Amersham, A355. At rdbt, A355 signed Amersham. Right into Longbottom Ln signed Seer Green. Left into Bottom Ln, right into Orchard Rd, left into Church Rd, right into Chalfont Rd*

Top notch food in a homely setting

Chris Lillitou and Amanda Baker's 19th-century, wisteria-clad free house in the heart of the picture-perfect Seer Green appeals to all-comers: locals chatting over pints of Marlow's Rebellion IPA, quiz addicts on Sunday nights, live music fans, beer festival-goers and dog-walkers. The modern, AA-Rosette menu could include crispy confit Gressingham duck leg with cabbage and carrot slaw; or roasted cauliflower and cumin soup with marinated goats' cheese as typical starters. Follow with pork belly and black pudding with apple purée, coriander potato cake and bok choi; or roasted wood pigeon wrapped in bacon with potato galette. For dessert, maybe sticky toffee pudding with salted popcorn and banana sorbet. Beer festivals are held on Easter weekend and the Summer Bank Holiday in August.

Open all day all wk Mon-Thu 12-11.30 (Fri-Sat 12-12 Sun 12-10.30) **Food** Lunch Mon-Fri 12-2.30, Sat 12-3, Sun 12-7 Dinner Mon-Sat 6.30-9, Sun 12-7 Restaurant menu available all wk ⊕ FREE HOUSE ◀ Rebellion IPA, Fuller's London Pride, Chiltern Beechwood Bitter, Vale VPA ⚲ Millwhites. ₸ 16 **Facilities** Non-diners area ☘ (Bar Garden) ♦ Children's menu Children's portions Garden ⋒ Beer festival Parking WiFi

SKIRMETT
Map 5 SU79

The Frog
PICK OF THE PUBS

tel: 01491 638996 **RG9 6TG**
email: info@thefrogatskirmett.co.uk
dir: *Exit A4155 at Mill End, pub in 3m*

Quality choices in both refreshment and food

An 18th-century coaching inn within the Chilterns Area of Outstanding Natural Beauty, with the Hamble Brook flowing gently behind. In summer the garden is a relaxing place to be, perhaps after a ramble to the famous windmill on nearby Turville Hill. Winter warmth is guaranteed in the charming public bar where oak beams, bare floorboards and leather seating combine with colourful textiles to create a welcoming atmosphere. Where better to settle with a pint of Leaping Frog or Henry's Original IPA? Alternatively 15 wines are sold by the glass, or push the boat out and share a sparkler from the Hambleden vineyard just down the road. Head chef and co-owner Jim Crowe uses superb ingredients in flavoursome dishes to satisfy the most discerning of palates. The menu offers deli boards and perhaps a starter of crisp fried south coast squid; or haggis, neeps and tatties, followed by fillet of pork Wellington; pie of the day; or slow-braised oxtail.

Open 11.30-3 6-11 Closed 25 Dec, Sun eve (Oct-Apr) **Food** Lunch all wk 12-2.30 Dinner all wk 6.30-9.30 ⊕ FREE HOUSE ◀ Leaping Frog, Rebellion IPA, Sharp's Doom Bar, Wadworth Henry's Original IPA ⚲ Thatchers, Sharp's Orchard. ₸ 15 **Facilities** Non-diners area ☘ (Bar Garden) ♦ Children's menu Children's portions Family room Garden ⋒ Parking 🚍

STOKE MANDEVILLE
Map 5 SP81

The Bell

tel: 01296 612434 **29 Lower Rd HP22 5XA**
email: thebell@distinctpubs.co.uk **web:** www.bellstokemandeville.co.uk
dir: *From S & E follow signs from Stoke Mandeville towards Stoke Mandeville Hospital, pub on left in 200yds after primary school. From N & W pass Stoke Mandeville Hospital on left, pub approx 1m on right*

An honest-to-goodness great British dining pub

The Bell has a sign that reads 'Dogs, children and muddy boots welcome', thereby setting the friendly tone of a visit to this traditional country village pub. Physiotherapists caring for those with spinal injuries at nearby Stoke Mandeville hospital have been known to set The Bell as an objective for their newly mobile patients. The reward could be a pint of Wells Bombardier or Symonds cider, with a plate of fresh seasonal food. James Penlington has some star kitchens on his CV, so expect proper bar snacks and hearty full-flavoured meals – typical are crispy fried whitebait, harissa mayonnaise; walnut and goats' cheese cheesecake, balsamic baby onions; pan-fried hake fillet, chickpea and tomato ragout with basil oil; and Orchard View Farm sausages, mash and onion gravy. Be sure to leave a corner for delicious desserts like fruity 'spotted dick' pudding with custard, or frozen mango parfait with coconut and lime biscuit.

Open all day all wk Closed 25-26 Dec **Food** Mon-Sat 12-9.30, Sun 2-8.30 Restaurant menu available all wk ⊕ THE DISTINCT PUB COMPANY ◀ Wells Bombardier, Young's Bitter, guest ale ⚲ Aspall, Symonds. ₸ 16 **Facilities** Non-diners area ☘ (Bar Restaurant Garden) ♦ Children's menu Children's portions Garden ⋒ Parking WiFi 🚍 (notice required)

TURVILLE
Map 5 SU79

The Bull & Butcher
PICK OF THE PUBS

tel: 01491 638283 **RG9 6QU**
email: info@thebullandbutcher.com
dir: *M40 junct 5, follow Ibstone signs. Right at T-junct. Pub 0.25m on left*

Quintessential English pub in the Chilterns

The village of Turville is set in an Area of Outstanding Natural Beauty, and this Grade II listed, 16th-century inn, originally known as the 'Bullen Butcher', (a reference to Henry VIII's treatment of his second wife Anne Boleyn), enjoys beautiful country views. The Well Bar and the Windmill Lounge both feature original beams, open fires and a friendly, laid-back atmosphere. Children and dogs are welcome, and the large sunny garden and patio areas are perfect for alfresco dining. You can expect to find locally sourced produce on the menus, where hearty pub classics rub shoulders with less traditional offerings. Lunch might be a ploughman's or a burger, while dinner might begin with deep-fried whitebait with lemon and garlic aïoli, or ham hock terrine with piccalilli; before moving on to sausage and mash; or braised beef short rib with horseradish mash and curly kale. Round things off with apple tarte Tatin or crème brûlée. There's live music, last Friday of the month.

Open all wk summer 12-11 (Sat noon-1am) winter 12-3 5.30-11 **Food** Lunch Mon-Fri 12-2.30, Sat 12-3, Sun 12-4 Dinner Mon-Sat 6-9, (food served all day in summer) Av main course £12.50 Set menu available ⊕ BRAKSPEAR ◄ Bitter & Oxford Gold, guest ales. ⊈ 36 **Facilities** Non-diners area ✿ (Bar Restaurant Garden) ♦◉ Children's menu Garden ⊓ Parking WiFi ⇌ (notice required)

TURWESTON
Map 11 SP63

The Stratton Arms

tel: 01280 704956 **Main St NN13 5JX**
email: thestrattonarms@aol.com
dir: *From A43 (NE of Brackley) take A422 towards Buckingham. Left to Turweston. Through village, pub on left*

Warmly regarded village local

Just like many of the other buildings in this rather straggly village, the pub is built of mellow local stone. Landlord Philip Caley offers a good range of ales – Bass, London Pride, Otter and more. His menu is full of tried and tested, home-made pub food, such as chilli con carne with rice; wholetail scampi, chips and peas; Barnsley chop and mash; and spinach ricotta cannelloni with jacket potato. Freshly baked pizzas can be taken home to eat. At the far end of its large garden flows the River Great Ouse.

Open all day all wk **Food** Lunch Fri-Sun 12-2 Dinner Fri-Sun 6-9 Av main course £6.50 Set menu available ⊕ ENTERPRISE INNS ◄ Otter, Timothy Taylor Landlord, Fuller's London Pride, Bass, Sharp's Doom Bar ♂ Westons Stowford Press. ⊈ **Facilities** Non-diners area ✿ (Bar Garden Outside area) ♦◉ Children's menu Children's portions Play area Family room Garden Outside area ⊓ Beer festival Parking WiFi ⇌ (notice required)

WEST WYCOMBE
Map 5 SU89

The George and Dragon Hotel

tel: 01494 535340 **High St HP14 3AB**
email: georgeanddragon@live.co.uk
dir: *On A40*

Delightful timber-framed hotel reached through a cobbled archway

After a hard day touring the West Wycombe Caves, and stately houses at Cliveden and Hughenden, relax at this traditional coaching inn located in a National Trust village. The 14th-century inn was once a hideout for highwaymen stalking travellers between London and Oxford; indeed, one unfortunate guest, robbed and murdered here, is rumoured still to haunt its corridors. Reliable real ales include St Austell Tribute and Hook Norton Hooky Gold. The varied menu offers freshly-prepared dishes cooked to order such as grilled fillet of hake with prawns and mussel pesto linguine; red onion, fig and camembert tart with mixed leaves; and beef bourguignon with home-made gnocchi.

Open all day all wk 12-12 (Fri-Sat noon-1am Sun 12-11.30) **Food** Lunch Mon-Sat 12-2.30, Sun 12-6 Dinner Mon-Thu 6-9, Fri-Sat 6-9.30, Sun 12-6 Set menu available Restaurant menu available all wk ⊕ ENTERPRISE INNS ◄ St Austell Tribute, Hook Norton Hooky Gold, Rebellion IPA ♂ Aspall. ⊈ 9 **Facilities** Non-diners area ✿ (Bar Garden) ♦◉ Children's menu Children's portions Play area Family room Garden ⊓ Parking WiFi ⇌ (notice required)

WHEELER END
Map 5 SU89

The Chequers Inn

tel: 01494 883070 **Bullocks Farm Ln HP14 3NH**
email: thechequerswheeler@gmail.com
dir: *4m N of Marlow*

Families welcome at this Fuller's pub

Now in new hands, this picturesque 16th-century inn, with its low-beamed ceilings, roaring winter fires and two attractive beer gardens, is ideally located for walkers on the edge of Wheeler End Common (families and dogs are welcome). An evening menu might offer wild mushroom ragout; or seafood cocktail to start, followed by cod loin, crushed new potatoes, and chorizo, roasted carrot and red pepper purée; or pan-fried Barbury duck breast, poached apple mashed potato, seasonal greens and berry compôte. Chocolate orange bread and butter pudding with custard or vanilla ice cream could round things off.

Open all day 12-12 (Mon-Tue 12-11 Sun 12-8.30) Closed Sun eve **Food** Lunch Wed-Sat 12-3, Sun 12-5 Dinner Tue-Thu 6-9, Fri-Sat 6-9.30 ⊕ FULLER'S ◄ London Pride & ESB, George Gale & Co Seafarers ♂ Cornish Orchards Gold Cider. ⊈ 12 **Facilities** Non-diners area ✿ (Bar Garden) ♦◉ Children's menu Children's portions Garden ⊓ Parking WiFi ⇌ (notice required)

WOOBURN COMMON
Map 6 SU98

Chequers Inn ★★★ HL ◉◉
PICK OF THE PUBS

tel: 01628 529575 **Kiln Ln HP10 0JQ**
email: info@chequers-inn.com web: www.chequers-inn.com
dir: *M40 junct 2, A40 through Beaconsfield towards High Wycombe. Left into Broad Ln, signed Taplow/Burnham/Wooburn Common. 2m to pub*

Pub grub meets fine dining in the Chilterns

The atmosphere of much of this 17th-century coaching inn is still firmly of the past, especially in the open-fired bar, where the hand-tooled oak beams and posts, and timeworn flagstone and wooden floors shrug off the passage of time. Contrast then the 21st-century chic lounge, with leather sofas and chairs, low tables and greenery while outside, sheltering the patio and flowery garden, stands a magnificent old oak tree. Beers are Rebellion IPA and Smuggler and there are 14 wines by the glass. The two AA-Rosette restaurant menu features ever-changing dishes such as calves' liver with olive oil mash, bacon and green beans; coconut crusted cod with wilted spinach and chorizo butter sauce; and Stilton and red onion tart.

Open all day all wk 12-12 **Food** Lunch Mon-Fri 12-2.30, Sat 12-10, Sun 12-9.30 Dinner Mon-Thu 6-9.30, Fri 6-10, Sat 12-10, Sun 12-9.30 Restaurant menu available all wk ⊕ FREE HOUSE ◄ Rebellion IPA & Smuggler, guest ale ♂ Westons Stowford Press. ⊈ 14 **Facilities** Non-diners area ♦◉ Children's menu Children's portions Garden ⊓ Parking WiFi **Rooms** 18

CAMBRIDGESHIRE

ABBOTS RIPTON   Map 12 TL27

The Abbot's Elm ★★★★ INN ◉◉

tel: 01487 773773 **PE28 2PA**
email: info@theabbotselm.co.uk **web:** www.theabbotselm.co.uk
dir: *From A141 or Huntingdon follow Abbots Ripton signs*

Thatched village inn in first-class hands

Situated in the delightful village of Abbots Ripton, the exterior of this pub looks pretty much as it has done over the centuries but step inside and you'll find that the open-plan bar and restaurant are bathed in natural light. In the bar are Oakham Ales JHB and guests, nearly 30 wines by the glass, and lunchtime sandwiches, ploughman's and croque monsieurs. Generous daily-changing menus offer glazed chicken wings with hickory-smoked barbecue sauce; roast cod, baby winter vegetables, saffron and shellfish chowder; and seared calves' liver, grain-mustard mash, creamed cabbage and smoked bacon. Your children and your dog will appreciate the garden space.

Open 11-3 6-10 (Fri 11-3 6-11 Sat all day Sun 11-4) Closed 1st 2wks Jan, Sun eve & Mon (Winter) **Food** Lunch all wk 12-2 Dinner Mon-Sat 6-9 Av main course £13 ⊕ FREE HOUSE ◀ Oakham Ales JHB, Sharp's Doom Bar, guest ales Ö Symonds. ♈ 28 **Facilities** Non-diners area ✿ (Bar Garden) ♦♦ Children's menu Children's portions Garden ♒ Parking WiFi **Rooms** 3

BALSHAM   Map 12 TL55

The Black Bull Inn ★★★★ INN ◉   PICK OF THE PUBS

tel: 01223 893844 **27 High St CB21 4DJ**
email: info@blackbull-balsham.co.uk **web:** www.blackbull-balsham.co.uk
dir: *From S: M11 junct 9, A11 towards Newmarket, follow Balsham signs. From N: M11 junct 10, A505 signed Newmarket (A11), onto A11, follow Balsham signs*

Excellent food and accommodation

Here since the 16th century and still going strong. Stronger than ever, in fact, thanks to the creation of a new dining area in the listed barn, with an oak-panelled, high-vaulted ceiling, a bar with much better lighting than before and a tree-lined sandstone patio out front. The bar serves Adnams and Woodforde's East Anglian real ales and ciders, sandwiches, baguettes and hot meals like burgers, fish and chips, linguine puttanesca and home-made shortcrust pastry pies. Among dishes taken from a winter restaurant menu are braised shin of beef, mussel and black bean Asian dumplings, sesame spinach, soy sauce, and honey and thyme reduction; pan-roasted pork tenderloin rolled in sage crumbs, parsnip purée, parsnip crisps, prunes and whisky sauce; and mushroom and courgette cannelloni with marinated tomatoes and tarragon béchamel. Old favourites, sticky toffee pudding with butterscotch sauce and vanilla ice cream, and lemon meringue tart appear as desserts. A south-facing beer garden awaits at the rear.

Open all day all wk **Food** Lunch Mon-Thu 12-2, Fri-Sat 12-2.30, Sun 12-8 Dinner Mon-Thu 6.30-9, Fri-Sat 6.30-9.30, Sun 12-8 Av main course £13 ⊕ FREE HOUSE ◀ Woodforde's Wherry, Adnams Southwold Bitter, Red & Black, Nethergate Ö Aspall & Harry Sparrow. ♈ 20 **Facilities** Non-diners area ✿ (Bar Garden) ♦ Children's menu Children's portions Garden ♒ Beer festival Parking WiFi ▦ (notice required) **Rooms** 5

BARRINGTON   Map 12 TL34

The Royal Oak

tel: 01223 870791 **31 West Green CB22 7RZ**
email: info@royaloakbarrington.co.uk
dir: *From Barton off M11, S of Cambridge*

Quintessential English pub by village green

One of the oldest thatched and timbered pubs in England, this rambling 16th-century building overlooks a 30-acre village green. With a pretty 'chocolate-box' image on the outside, the smart interior is contemporary in design; the menu lists the classic dishes for which the pub has long been known, such as pie of the day, toad-in-the-hole, beer battered haddock, and aubergine parmigana. In addition there's a regularly changing specials menu, a collection of salads and sandwiches, and a choice of rotating guest ales.

Open all wk 12-3 6-11 (Sun 12-11) **Food** Lunch all wk 12-2 Dinner all wk 6-9 ⊕ FREE HOUSE ◀ 4 rotating guest ales Ö Aspall. ♈ 8 **Facilities** Non-diners area ✿ (Bar Garden) ♦♦ Children's menu Children's portions Garden ♒ Parking WiFi ▦ (notice required)

BOURN   Map 12 TL35

The Willow Tree

tel: 01954 719775 **29 High St CB23 2SQ**
email: contact@thewillowtreebourn.com
dir: *From Royston on A1198, right on B1046 signed Bourn. Pub in village on right (8m from Cambridge)*

Village pub with candlelit restaurant

Just off Ermine Street, the old Roman road from London to York, is Craig and Shaina Galvin-Scott's mansard-roofed village pub. A white picket fence surrounds the street frontage, while in the large rear garden are the majestic eponymous willow tree, a heated terrace, a swing and, when warm, deckchairs. The shabby-chic interior incorporates an open fireplace and a medley of non-matching dining chairs. The menu changes with the seasons and on one spring menu dishes such as grilled sardine on toast; and rabbit escabeche appeared as starters, followed by hake fillet, chorizo, white bean and parsley cassoulet; or Tilbury Meadows rib-eye or fillet steak, hand-cut chips and wild mushroom sauce. A two day music and drink festival is held in June.

Open all day all wk **Food** Lunch Mon-Sat 12-3, Sun 12-8 Dinner Mon-Sat 5.30-9.30, Sun 12-8 Av main course £11 Set menu available ⊕ FREE HOUSE ◀ Abbeydale Moonshine, Lacons, Milton Pegasus, Woodforde's Wherry Ö Addlestones, Aspall. ♈ 20 **Facilities** Non-diners area ✿ (Garden) ♦♦ Children's menu Children's portions Play area Garden ♒ Beer festival Cider festival Parking WiFi ▦ (notice required)

CAMBRIDGE   Map 12 TL45

The Anchor Pub, Dining & River Terrace

tel: 01223 353554 **Silver St CB3 9EL**
email: info@anchorcambridge.com
dir: *Phone for detailed directions*

Popular riverside pub

Bordering Queens' College is a medieval lane, at the end of which stands this attractive pub, right by the bridge over the River Cam. Head for the riverside patio with a local real ale, or an Aspalls cider, and watch rookie punters struggling with their tricky craft – another definition of pole position, perhaps. A good choice of food includes sea bass fillet with pumpkin and sage risotto; honey-glazed Barbary duck leg with parsnip mash; and beer-battered fish and chips. Sandwiches, sausage rolls and Scotch eggs are available too.

Open all day all wk Mon-Thu & Sun 11-11 (Fri-Sat 11am-mdnt) **Food** Lunch Mon-Sat 11.30-4, Sun 11.30-9 Dinner Mon-Sat 5-10, Sun 11.30-9 Restaurant menu available all wk ⊕ METRO COUNTRY PUBS ◧ Rotating guest ales ♻ Aspall Harry Sparrow. ♟ 12 **Facilities** Non-diners area ♦ Children's menu Outside area ⋔ WiFi ⛟ (notice required)

The Old Spring

tel: 01223 357228 **1 Ferry Path CB4 1HB**
email: theoldspring@hotmail.co.uk
dir: Just off Chesterton Rd, (A1303) in city centre, near Midsummer Common

Neighbourhood pub with a lengthy and varied menu

You'll find this bustling pub in the leafy suburb of De Freville, just a short stroll from the River Cam and its many boatyards. The bright and airy interior offers rug-covered wooden floors, comfy sofas and large family tables. Sip a pint of Elgood's Cambridge Bitter, one of the five real ales on tap, or one of 20 wines by the glass while choosing from over a dozen main courses plus specials, perhaps smoked mackerel, beetroot, new potato and spring onion salad; steak ciabatta sandwich with home-made onion marmalade; Cumberland sausage and mash. Sharing plates, sandwiches, wraps and lighter meals add to the choices. Leave some room for pudding though, a chocolate and nut brownie, for example.

Open all day all wk 11.30-11 (Sun 12-10.30) **Food** Lunch Mon-Fri 12-2.30, Sat-Sun 12-9.30 Dinner Mon-Fri 6-9.30, Sat-Sun 12-9.30 Av main course £12 ⊕ GREENE KING ◧ IPA & Abbot Ale, Elgood's Cambridge Bitter, guest ales ♻ Aspall. ♟ 20 **Facilities** Non-diners area ♦ Children's menu Children's portions Outside area ⋔ Parking WiFi ⛟

The Punter

tel: 01223 363322 **3 Pound Hill CB3 0AE**
email: info@thepuntercambridge.co.uk
dir: Phone for detailed directions

Seasonal food and a great atmosphere

Two minutes' walk from the city centre, this former coaching house is popular with post-grads, locals and dog lovers alike who create a happy mood with their chatter and laughter. The interior is an eclectic mix of previously loved hand-me-downs, comfy sofas, sturdy school chairs, and an assortment of pictures and painting jostling for space on the walls. Drinkers can enjoy local ales but it seems it's the food that draws people in. The modern menu might offer mushroom and red wine risotto with crispy leeks; and beef bourguignon, mash and curly kale.

Open all day all wk Closed 25-26 Dec ⊕ PUNCH TAVERNS ◧ Punter (brewed for the pub), Oakham Ales Punter Blonde, guest ales ♻ Addlestones. **Facilities** ❀ (Bar Restaurant Outside area) ♦ Children's portions Outside area WiFi

COTON   Map 12 TL45

The Plough

tel: 01954 210489 **2 High St CB23 7PL**
email: info@theploughcoton.co.uk
dir: M11 juncts 12 or 13. Follow Coton signs

Fine food in Cambridge-edge countryside

Nudging the cricket pitches and grassy recreation ground, this village pub has a new team on board. Savvy diners escaping the hubbub of nearby Cambridge beat a path to the cool, chic interior that creates a relaxing atmosphere in which to enjoy

the modern menus. Lunchtime brings choices such as upmarket pizzas, filled ciabattas, salads, deep-fried whitebait, cured and cooked meats, and baked camembert. Come the evening, expect dishes such as celeriac and white truffle soup; confit duck leg, lentils, bacon and Savoy cabbage; and crème brûlée with boozy prunes. The wine list features around 30 bins and beers are from East Anglian breweries. In summer, children can happily play in the spacious garden.

Open all day all wk **Food** Lunch Mon-Sat 12-3, Sun 12-6 Dinner Mon-Thu 6-9, Fri-Sat 6-9.30, Sun 12-6 ⊕ ENTERPRISE INNS ◧ Sharp's Doom Bar, Adnams Lighthouse, Greene King Ruddles Best, Woodforde's Wherry, rotating guest ales ♻ Aspall. ♟ **Facilities** Non-diners area ❀ (Bar Garden) ♦ Children's menu Children's portions Play area Garden ⋔ Beer festival Parking WiFi ⛟ (notice required)

DRY DRAYTON   Map 12 TL36

The Black Horse

tel: 01954 782600 **35 Park St CB23 8DA**
email: deniseglover@hotmail.co.uk
dir: A14 junct 30, follow signs for Dry Drayton. In village turn right to pub (signed)

Renowned for its ales and good food

Just five miles from Cambridge, The Black Horse has been at the heart of this quiet village for more than 300 years. Gary and Denise Glover and chef Daniel Walker have built a reputation for notable food. Many local ales are showcased in the bar, and local suppliers dominate the menu in the restaurant. A starter of pan-seared pigeon breast, black pudding and game jus might be followed by Aldeburgh stone bass with green lentils, spinach and mussel sauce.

Open 12-3 6-11 (Sat 12-11 Sun 12-4) Closed Mon ⊕ FREE HOUSE ◧ Black Horse, Adnams & Broadside, guest ale ♻ Aspall. **Facilities** ❀ (Bar Garden) ♦ Children's portions Garden Parking WiFi

DUXFORD   Map 12 TL44

The John Barleycorn   PICK OF THE PUBS

tel: 01223 832699 **3 Moorfield Rd CB22 4PP**
email: info@johnbarleycorn.co.uk
dir: Exit A505 into Duxford

Seventeenth-century traditional village pub

Built in 1660, this thatched and whitewashed former coach house became the John Barleycorn in the mid-19th century. The name first appeared in an old folksong as the personification of malting barley and the beer and whisky that results. During World War II the brave young airmen of Group Captain Douglas Bader's Duxford Wing drank here in what today is a softly-lit bar with country furniture, a large brick fireplace, old tiled floor, cushioned pews and hop-adorned beams. Food is a big draw, from the sandwiches and jacket potatoes, to the tzatziki and charcuterie grazing boards; from the smoked Gressingham duck cassoulet with Puy lentils and pancetta, to the chargrilled supreme of tuna marinated in lime and coriander, stir-fried pak choi and ginger and carrot broth; and from the Hereford and Limousin steaks, to the vanilla and strawberry crème brûlée. Eating and drinking on the flower-decorated patio is an extremely pleasant experience.

Open all day all wk **Food** Lunch all wk 12-3 Dinner Mon-Sat 5-9.30, Sun 5-8.30 ⊕ GREENE KING ◧ IPA & Abbot Ale, guest ales ♻ Thatchers. ♟ 12 **Facilities** Non-diners area ❀ (Bar Restaurant Garden) ♦ Children's menu Children's portions Garden ⋔ Parking WiFi ⛟ (notice required)

PICK OF THE PUBS

The Anchor Inn ★★★★ INN 🌹

ELY Map 12 TL58

tel: 01353 778537
Sutton Gault CB6 2BD
email: anchorinn@popmail.bta.com
web: www.anchorsuttongault.co.uk
dir: *From A14, B1050 to Earith, take B1381 to Sutton. Sutton Gault on left*

Enjoyable food at riverside inn beneath big Fenland skies

The Fens were lawless and disease-ridden until, in 1630, the Earl of Bedford commissioned Dutch engineer Cornelius Vermuyden to drain them. By digging the Old and New Bedford Rivers, the Dutchman ended the constant danger of flooding and began the process that created today's rich agricultural landscape. Using thick gault clay, he built raised river banks and beside the New Bedford (or 'The Hundred Foot Drain') constructed the Anchor for his workforce; it has been a pub ever since. Today, low beams, dark wood panelling, scrubbed pine tables, gently undulating tiled floors, antique prints and log fires create the intimate character of this family-run free house. Twelve wines served by the glass and a selection of East Anglian real ales will be found in the bar. The kitchen is proud to source local ingredients for their modern

British cuisine which offers favourites like grilled dates wrapped in bacon with creamy mustard sauce — now served here for 15 years; and pan-fried scallops with butternut squash purée, almonds and curry oil. The daily-changing menus showcase seasonal produce from nearby such as Denham Estate venison, East Anglia tilapia, Sutton strawberries, locally-grown asparagus and locally-made sausages. Sunday roasts — indeed, any meal — may be enjoyed on the terrace overlooking the river. The cathedral cities of Ely and Cambridge are both within easy reach.

Open all wk Mon-Fri 12-2.30 7-10.30 (Sat 12-3 6.30-11 Sun 12-4 6.30-10) Closed 25-26 Dec eve **Food** Lunch Mon-Fri 12-2, Sat-Sun 12-2.30 Dinner Mon-Fri 7-9, Sat 6.30-9.30 Sun 6.30-9 Set menu available ⊕ FREE HOUSE
🍺 Rotating real ales ☕ 12
Facilities Non-diners area
👫 Children's menu Children's portions Garden 🪑 Parking WiFi 🚌 (notice required) **Rooms** 4

ELSWORTH
Map 12 TL36

NEW The George and Dragon

tel: 01954 267236 **41 Boxworth Rd CB23 4JQ**
email: gdelsworth@yahoo.co.uk
dir: *Follow Elsworth signs from either A428 or A14*

Large country pub and restaurant

If you're in Cambridge, Huntingdon or St Ives and fancy a drink or a meal out of town, then head here. Inside it's a good size, with beams and brass and a good real ale selection. Crusty baguettes, sandwiches, ploughman's and omelettes satisfy light lunch expectations, while the main menu offers skewer of barbecued pork belly bites; whole grilled Dover sole; fillet steak Diane; and home-made roasted vegetable lasagne. Fresh seafood is a speciality. 'Home-made' also appears several times to describe desserts, including apple crumble and custard; cheesecake of the day; and strawberry meringue roulade.

Open all wk 12-3 6-11 **Food** Lunch Mon-Sat 12-3, Sun 12-8 Dinner Mon-Sat 6-11, Sun 12-8 Set menu available Restaurant menu available Mon-Sat ⊕ FREE HOUSE ◀ Greene King IPA, Morland Old Speckled Hen, guest ale Ö Aspall. ♥ 14 **Facilities** Non-diners area ❖ (Bar Garden) ♦ Children's menu Children's portions Garden ⊓ Parking WiFi ➡ (notice required)

ELY
Map 12 TL58

The Anchor Inn ★★★★ INN ◉
PICK OF THE PUBS

See Pick of the Pubs on opposite page

FEN DITTON
Map 12 TL46

Ancient Shepherds

tel: 01223 293280 **High St CB5 8ST**
email: marycullen@ancientshepherds.com
dir: *From A14 take B1047 signed Cambridge/Airport*

Popular pub in a peaceful riverside village

Three miles from Cambridge, this heavily beamed pub is a popular dining destination away from the bustle of the city. Built as three cottages in 1540, it was named after the Loyal and Ancient Order of Shepherds that once met here. The pub is free of music, darts and pool, and is a cosy place to sup a pint beside one of the inglenook fires. The bar lunch menu offers an extensive range of filled baguettes as well as jackets and snacks. In the restaurant, perhaps choose marinated crayfish tails; braised lamb shank with minted red wine and rosemary gravy, then apple strudel for dessert. Specials could include fishcakes, lasagne or cannelloni.

Open 12-3 6-11 Closed 1 Jan, Sun eve & Mon **Food** Lunch Tue-Sat 12-2, Sun 12-2.30 Dinner Tue-Sat 7-9 ⊕ PUNCH TAVERNS ◀ Greene King IPA, rotating guest ales Ö Mortimers Orchard. ♥ 8 **Facilities** Non-diners area ❖ (Bar Garden) ♦ Children's portions Garden ⊓ Parking WiFi

FENSTANTON
Map 12 TL36

King William IV

tel: 01480 462467 **High St PE28 9JF**
email: kingwilliamfenstanton@btconnect.com
dir: *On A14 between Hunstanton & Cambridge follow Fenstanton signs*

Rustic village inn with good food

This rambling 17th-century village pub features oak beams, old brickwork and a wonderful central fireplace. Lunchtime offerings include a range of hot and cold sandwiches, wraps and salads as well as a full menu. Starters may include creamy garlic mushrooms or grilled haloumi with melba toast; while mains offer sausages, mash and red wine gravy; or mushroom and spinach lasagne. If you've still got room, go for banoffee tart or chocolate bread and butter pudding with custard. Occasionally, there's live music on a Sunday afternoon.

Open all wk Mon-Thu 12-3 5-11 (Fri-Sun all day) **Food** Lunch all wk 12-2.30 Dinner Mon-Thu 6-9, Fri-Sat 6-9.30 Set menu available Restaurant menu available all wk ⊕ GREENE KING ◀ IPA, guest ales Ö Aspall. ♥ 13 **Facilities** Non-diners area ❖ (Bar Garden) ♦ Children's portions Garden ⊓ Parking WiFi ➡ (notice required)

FORDHAM
Map 12 TL67

White Pheasant ◉◉
PICK OF THE PUBS

tel: 01638 720414 **CB7 5LQ**
email: whitepheasant@live.com
dir: *From Newmarket A142 to Ely, approx 5m to Fordham. Pub on left in village*

Carefully constructed menu of select options

This 18th-century building stands in a fenland village between Ely and Newmarket. While enjoying a pint of Adnams or glass of wine, choose between the dishes of good English fare on the two AA-Rosette menu. Cooking is taken seriously here, with quality, presentation and flavour taking top priority; specials change daily. Starters may include haddock soup, smoked haddock fishcake, egg yolk purée and charred leek; confit duck terrine with fig chutney and pickles; or pork bon bon, braised cheek, celeriac and burnt apple. Followed by beef Wellington, horseradish, wild mushroom, snails and parsley; plaice, truffle gnocchi, roasted squash and brown shrimps. Desserts will prove to be very tempting too – spiced orange pannacotta; or millionniare's shortbread. If you fancy something less sweet then the British cheese selection will fit the bill.

Open Tue-Sat 12-2.30 6.30-9.30 (Sun 12-2.30) Closed Sun eve & Mon **Food** Lunch Tue-Sun 12-2.30 Dinner Tue-Sat 6.30-9.30 Set menu available Restaurant menu available Tue-Sat ⊕ FREE HOUSE ◀ Adnams Ö Aspall Harry Sparrow. ♥ 12 **Facilities** Non-diners area ❖ (Bar Garden) ♦ Children's portions Garden ⊓ Parking WiFi ➡ (notice required)

GLINTON
Map 12 TF10

The Blue Bell

tel: 01733 252285 **10 High St PE6 7LS**
email: info@thebluebellglinton.co.uk **web:** www.thebluebellglinton.co.uk
dir: *Phone for detailed directions*

Contemporary dining and old-world charm

The oak beams and log fires provide a relaxed, old-world feel to this charming 18th-century village pub run by chef Will Frankgate and his wife Kelly. The excellent food at The Blue Bell is more contemporary with innovative new dishes rubbing shoulders with old favourites. Typical choices include marinated Cornish mackerel fillet, pickled turnips, preserved lemon, coriander yogurt; or Gressingham duck breast with carrot purée, braised red cabbage, fondant potato and glazed fig sauce; with steaks, burgers and fish and chips for more traditional palates. Lunchtime sandwiches are also served.

Open all day all wk **Food** Contact pub for food times Set menu available Restaurant menu available all wk ⊕ GREENE KING ◀ IPA, Morland Old Speckled Hen, guest ales. **Facilities** Non-diners area ❖ (Bar Garden) ◀◀ Children's menu Children's portions Garden ☴ Beer festival Parking WiFi ▭ (notice required)

GRANTCHESTER
Map 12 TL45

NEW The Red Lion

tel: 01223 840121 **33 High St CB3 9NF**
email: info@redliongrantchester.co.uk
dir: *M11 junct 11, A1309 signed city centre. In Trumpington at lights into Maris Ln. At T-junct left into Grantchester Rd; pass church in Grantchester on left, next right to pub. Or from M11 junct 12 follow Grantchester signs*

Picture-perfect, and dogs love it here too

Its village location, carefully trimmed thatch, and warm welcome for muddy boots and dogs make the Red Lion popular with Cambridge folk who fancy a Sunday stroll along the Cam's banks. They settle in with a Greene King pint, or mull over the wine list which proffers nearly 30 served by the glass. Food served all day from midday onwards is based on British seasonal produce. Light bites include River Exe mussels in cider with smoked bacon and leek cream sauce. Or try a hearty cassoulet of braised rabbit, Toulouse sausage, chorizo and haricot beans.

Open all day all wk **Food** Lunch all wk 12-6 Dinner all wk 6-9.30 ⊕ GREENE KING ◀ IPA, Nene Valley NVB, Bishop Nick ♂ Aspall. ❦ 27 **Facilities** Non-diners area ❖ (Bar Garden) ◀◀ Children's menu Children's portions Play area Garden ☴ Parking WiFi ▭ (notice required)

The Rupert Brooke

tel: 01223 841875 **2 Broadway CB3 9NQ**
email: info@therupertbrooke.com
dir: *M11 junct 12, follow Grantchester signs*

Idyllic riverside pub with literary links

Named after the English poet who once lived at the Old Vicarage in the pretty village of Grantchester, this is a stylish pub. Located alongside the River Cam, it is just a couple of miles from the centre of Cambridge, which can be accessed via the river path, although some customers are known to arrive by punt. A range of ales including Woodforde's Wherry are dispensed from the bar, which also offers a dozen wines by the glass to accompany enjoyable dishes like wild mushroom and truffle macaroni; and braised collar of ham with duck egg and chips.

Open all day all wk **Food** Lunch all wk 12-2.30 Dinner Mon-Sat 6.30-9.30 ⊕ FREE HOUSE ◀ Woodforde's Wherry, local guest ale ♂ Aspall. ❦ 12
Facilities Non-diners area ❖ (Bar Garden) ◀◀ Children's menu Children's portions Garden ☴ Parking WiFi ▭ (notice required)

GREAT ABINGTON
Map 12 TL54

Three Tuns ★★★★ INN

tel: 01223 891467 **75 High St CB21 6AB**
email: email@thethreetuns-greatabington.co.uk
web: www.thethreetuns-greatabington.co.uk
dir: *A11 onto A1307 (Haverhill). Right signed Abington. Pub on left*

A 16th-century free house with excellent Thai food

A rashly shouted 'Oi!' here might well bring the chef running out from his kitchen, for that's his name. The highly experienced Oi is from Thailand and his huge range of traditional Thai food embraces starters and soups; beef, chicken, duck, pork and prawn stir-fries; classic green, red, yellow, Massaman, Penang and jungle curries; fish dishes, such as sea bass in chilli sauce; pad Thai and other noodle dishes; and vegetables and rice cooked different ways. Among the 200 beers, many from local breweries, available in the bar is Austrian Stiegl lager on tap.

Open all wk 12-2 6-11 (Fri-Sun 12-11) Closed 1 Jan **Food** Lunch Mon-Fri 12-2 Dinner Mon-Sat 6-9.30, Sun 6-9 ⊕ FREE HOUSE ◀ Greene King IPA, Woodforde's Wherry, Adnams ♂ Aspall. **Facilities** ❖ (Bar Garden) ◀◀ Garden ☴ Parking WiFi ▭ (notice required) **Rooms** 9

PICK OF THE PUBS

The Cock Pub and Restaurant

HEMINGFORD GREY   Map 12 TL27

tel: 01480 463609 **47 High St PE28 9BJ**
email: cock@cambscuisine.com
web: www.cambscuisine.com
dir: *Between A14 juncts 25 & 26, follow village signs*

Confident cooking in a pretty village close to the River Ouse

A handsome 17th-century pub on the main street of the charming village of Hemingford Grey, The Cock stands among thatched, timbered and brick cottages. Although it's only a mile from the busy A14, it feels like a world away and it's the ideal place to relax with peaceful views across the willow-bordered Great Ouse. Other than the peaceful location, the detour is well worth taking as the food on offer is excellent – the set lunch menu is a steal. The stylish interior comprises a contemporary bar for drinks only, and a restaurant with bare boards, dark or white-painted beams, wood-burning stoves, and church candles on an eclectic mix of old dining tables. Cooking is modern British, with the occasional foray further afield, and fresh local produce is used in preparing the short, imaginative carte, while daily deliveries of fresh fish dictate the chalkboard menu choice. A typical meal might begin with hazelnut gnocchi with garlic purée, rocket, truffle oil and parmesan; potted rabbit with beetroot chutney and toast; or cod cheek and chorizo risotto with rocket and chilli oil. Follow with a 14oz beef bavette steak with hand-cut chips, fried mushrooms, spinach and blue cheese butter; gurnard with Thai prawn consommé, noodles, pak choi and Thai basil; or aubergine and onion fritters with lentil and spinach dahl, yogurt and coriander; then round off with elderflower and blueberry jelly, honeycomb and white chocolate; or a selection of petits fours. The wine list focuses on the Languedoc-Roussillion region, while longer drinks include a local microbrewery ale such as Great Oakley Wagtail, and Hemingford Grey's own Cromwell cider. A beer festival is held over the mid August weekend.

Open all wk 11.30-3 6-11 **Food** Contact pub for food times Set menu available Restaurant menu available all wk ⊕ FREE HOUSE ◀ Brewster's Hophead, Great Oakley Wagtail, Elgood's Cambridge Bitter Ö Cromwell. ♟ 18 **Facilities** Non-diners area ♦ Children's portions Garden ⋒ Beer festival Parking WiFi 🚐 (notice required)

GREAT WILBRAHAM
Map 12 TL55

The Carpenters Arms

tel: 01223 882093 **10 High St CB21 5JD**
email: contact@carpentersarmsgastropub.co.uk
web: www.carpentersarmsgastropub.co.uk
dir: *From A11 follow "The Wilbraham" signs. Into Great Wilbraham, right at junct, pub 150yds on left*

Traditional free house, microbrewery and French-inspired food

A beer house since 1729, this smart pub restaurant is still brewing – today they're called Crafty Beers, such as Carpenter's Cask and Sauvignon Blonde. Landlords Rick and Heather Hurley previously ran an award-winning restaurant in France, so expect French, Catalan, Italian and even Thai dishes on the menus. Possibilities include beef and ale pie; chestnut, cranberry and mushroom loaf; duck and pork, sausage and bean cassoulet; wild boar and apple burger with apple sauce; and tartiflette, while Sunday roasts remain decidedly English. A Suffolk white features among the world-sourced wine list.

Open 11.30-3 6.30-11 Closed 26 Dec, 1 Jan, 1wk Nov & 1wk Feb, Sun eve, Mon & Tue **Food** Lunch Wed-Sun 12-2.30 Dinner Wed-Sat 7-9 Set menu available ⊕ FREE HOUSE ◀ Crafty Carpenter's Cask & Sauvignon Blonde Ö Aspall.
Facilities Non-diners area ♦♦ Children's menu Children's portions Garden Outside area ⴲ Parking WiFi ☞ (notice required)

HARDWICK
Map 12 TL35

NEW The Blue Lion

tel: 01954 210328 **74 Main St CB23 7QU**
email: info@bluelionhardwick.co.uk
dir: *W of Cambridge. In village centre*

Village inn serving guest ales and locally sourced food

The Blue Lion has been an integral part of Hardwick village life since it began trading as a pub in 1737. A rotating selection of guest ales and 10 wines by the glass keep local drinkers happy and the kitchen prides itself on using local produce including the pub's own rare breed sheep. A starter of crispy lamb on Asian-style salad with chilli, ginger and coriander dressing might be followed by a main course of smoked salmon fillet with chargrilled artichoke, black olive purée and sun-dried tomato tapenade. Look out for the summer beer festival.

Open all day all wk **Food** Lunch Mon-Fri 12-3, Sat 12-9.30, Sun 12-8 Dinner Mon-Thu 6-9, Fri 6-9.30, Sat 12-9.30, Sun 12-8 Av main course £13 ⊕ GREENE KING ◀ Rotating guest ales. ♟ 10 **Facilities** Non-diners area ♣ (Bar Garden) ♦♦ Children's menu Children's portions Play area Garden ⴲ Beer festival Parking WiFi ☞ (notice required)

HEMINGFORD GREY
Map 12 TL27

The Cock Pub and Restaurant
PICK OF THE PUBS

See Pick of the Pubs on page 65

HINXTON
Map 12 TL44

The Red Lion Inn ★★★★ INN ⓦ
PICK OF THE PUBS

tel: 01799 530601 **32 High St CB10 1QY**
email: info@redlionhinxton.co.uk **web:** www.redlionhinxton.co.uk
dir: *N'bound only: M11 junct 9, towards A11, left onto A1301. Left to Hinxton. Or M11 junct 10, A505 towards A11/Newmarket. At rdbt take 3rd exit onto A1301, right to Hinxton*

Country pub, restaurant and B&B with super garden

With many awards for what goes on inside, this 16th-century pink-washed free house and restaurant has much going for it outside too, with a pretty walled garden and dovecote, and a patio overlooking the church. Four local real ales await your order in the low-ceilinged and wood-floored bar; three of them – Woodforde's Wherry, Crafty Sauvignon Blonde and own label Red & Black – are fixtures, the fourth a local guest brew. Over 20 wines are served by the glass. It's good to eat in the bar, but you might prefer the high-raftered, L-shaped restaurant, which is similarly furnished with high-backed settles. The AA Rosette winning menu gives a taste of the modern British approach to food, in starters such as braised pork cheeks with celeriac purée and remoulade; main dishes such as pesto gnocchi with purple sprouting broccoli, tomato concasse and broad beans; and puddings like salted caramel tart.

Open all day all wk **Food** Lunch Mon-Thu 12-2, Fri-Sat 12-2.30, Sun 12-8 Dinner Mon-Thu 6.30-9, Fri-Sat 6.30-9.30, Sun 12-8 Restaurant menu available all wk ⊕ FREE HOUSE ◀ Crafty Sauvignon Blonde, Woodforde's Wherry, Adnams, Red & Black (own ale), guest ales Ö Aspall Harry Sparrow. ♟ 22 **Facilities** Non-diners area ♣ (Bar Garden) ♦♦ Children's menu Children's portions Garden ⴲ Parking WiFi ☞ (notice required) **Rooms** 8

HISTON — Map 12 TL46

Red Lion

tel: 01223 564437 **27 High St CB24 9JD**
dir: M11 junct 14, A14 towards. Exit at junct 32 onto B1049 for Histon

Village pub with good choice of real ales

A pub since 1836, this popular village local on Cambridge's northern fringe has been run by Mark Donachy for more than two decades. A dyed-in-the-wool pub man, Mark's real ales include Oakham Bishops Farewell, as well as Pickled Pig Porker's Snout cider. There are also over 30 different bottled beers from around the world. Expect quality pub food in a traditional environment, along side cheerful service, winter log fires and a good-sized neat garden. Typical of the specials board: steak and kidney suet pudding; and quinoa, sweet potato and black bean chilli. Fresh fish is a draw on Tuesday evenings and Wednesdays. Time a visit for the Easter or early September beer and cider festivals.

Open all day all wk 10.30am-11pm (Fri 10.30am-mdnt Sun 12-11) **Food** Lunch Mon-Sat 12-2.30, Sun 12-5 Dinner Mon-Thu & Sat 6-9.30 Av main course £9.50 ⊕ FREE HOUSE ◀ Oakham Bishops Farewell, Batemans Gold, Adnams Ghost Ship, Tring Side Pocket for a Toad Ŏ Pickled Pig Porker's Snout, Westons Perry. **Facilities** Non-diners area ♦♦ Children's portions Family room Garden ⊼ Beer festival Cider festival Parking WiFi 🚌 (notice required)

HORNINGSEA — Map 12 TL46

The Crown & Punchbowl

tel: 01223 860643 **CB25 9JG**
email: crown@cambscuisine.com **web:** www.thecrownandpunchbowl.co.uk
dir: A14 junct 34, A14 towards Newmarket. Left onto B1047 signed Horningsea. Pub on left in Village

Quaint country pub revamped inside and out

Dating back to 1764, this tiled and whitewashed former coaching inn stands next to a church in a little one-street village on the outskirts of Cambridge. Now part of the Cambscuisine group, the pub underwent a major refurbishment in early 2016 which landscaped a beer garden at the front, enlarged the bar, added a conservatory, and modernised the kitchen. Three real ales include Milton Pegasus and Brewster's Hophead. Seasonal ingredients for modern British dishes may include asparagus, served with a duck egg, capers, lemon and parsley. Typical of the main dishes is a guinea fowl breast stuffed with truffle mousse in red wine sauce.

Open all wk 12-3 6-11 (Fri 12-3 5-11 Sat 12-11 Sun 12-10.30) **Food** Contact pub for food times Set menu available Restaurant menu available all wk ⊕ FREE HOUSE ◀ Milton Pegasus, Brewster's Hophead, guest ale. ₹ 14 **Facilities** Non-diners area ♣ (Bar Outside area) ♦♦ Children's menu Children's portions Outside area ⊼ Parking WiFi

KEYSTON — Map 11 TL07

Pheasant Inn ◉◉ — PICK OF THE PUBS

tel: 01832 710241 **Village Loop Rd PE28 0RE**
email: info@thepheasant-keyston.co.uk
dir: 0.5m from A14, clearly signed, 10m W of Huntingdon, 14m E of Kettering

Thatched 16th-century village inn with excellent food

This pretty thatched pub was bought by the Hoskins family in 1964 and it has been serving good food ever since. Continuing that tradition are today's owners, Simon Cadge and Gerda Koedijk, while John Hoskins, a Master of Wine, compiles the wine list. There's a the large, oak-beamed bar, serving pints of Brewster's Hophead and Digfield Ales Barnwell Bitter, while at the rear, the Garden Room surveys a sunny patio. There's a set menu with two choices at each course; a selection of traditional classics such as home-made black pudding with mash, or steak and chips; or pick something from the à la carte, where roast pigeon with Puy lentils, Jerusalem artichokes and butternut squash; or chargrilled whole John Dory with chickpeas, grilled lemon and samphire might be followed by braised Scotch beef with horseradish mash, wilted greens, confit swede and bourguignon sauce; or pan-fried skate ballotine with saffron potatoes, braised leeks, tiger prawns and citrus dressing. Finish with the excellent cheese selection or damson cheesecake with plum sauce and toasted almonds.

Open 12-3 6-11 (Sun 12-5) Closed 2-16 Jan, Sun eve & Mon **Food** Lunch Tue-Sat 12-2, Sun 12-3.30 Dinner Tue-Sat 6.30-9.30 Set menu available ⊕ FREE HOUSE ◀ Adnams Broadside, Brewster's Hophead, Nene Valley NVB, Digfield Ales Barnwell Bitter Ŏ Aspall. ₹ 16 **Facilities** Non-diners area ♣ (Bar Garden) ♦♦ Children's menu Children's portions Garden ⊼ Parking WiFi 🚌 (notice required)

LITTLE WILBRAHAM — Map 12 TL55

Hole in the Wall ◉◉ — PICK OF THE PUBS

tel: 01223 812282 **2 High St CB21 5JY**
email: info@holeinthewallcambridge.com
dir: Phone for detailed directions

Enjoyable food from an award-winning chef

The name of this 16th-century village pub and restaurant between Cambridge and Newmarket comes from the days when farm workers used to collect their jugs of beer through a hole in the wall so as not to upset the gentry in the bar. Customers nowadays can enjoy ales from the Milton Brewery and the Indian Summer Brewing Company. The heavily-timbered pub is owned by former BBC *MasterChef* finalist Alex Rushmer, and first-class modern British cooking is prepared from fresh local produce. You could explore the five or seven course tasting menus with or without a matched wine flight, or stick to the set menu, with choices like pork rillet, dill pickle and black treacle toast; onion and cider soup, nigella seed dressing; parsley and roasted garlic risotto, mushrooms and watercress; or beer-battered cod, triple cooked chips and peas. Finish with spiced chocolate brownie, burnt white chocolate and cornflake ice cream.

Open 11.30-3 6.30-11 Closed 2wks Jan, 25 Dec, Mon, Tue L, Sun eve **Food** Lunch Wed-Sun 12-2 Dinner Tue-Sat 7-9 Set menu available Restaurant menu available Tue-Sat evenings only ⊕ FREE HOUSE ◀ Milton Brewery, Indian Summer Brewing Co Ŏ Aspall. ₹ 10 **Facilities** Non-diners area ♦♦ Children's portions Garden ⊼ Parking WiFi

The Three Horseshoes PICK OF THE PUBS

tel: 01954 210221 **High St CB23 8AB**
email: 3hs@btconnect.com
dir: *M11 junct 13, 1.5m from A14*

Cutting edge meals in traditional pub

Chimneys of mellow brick pierce the thick thatch of this cute village inn outside Cambridge. Between the reed-roofed main building and the extensive beer garden, a substantial conservatory restaurant bathes in dappled light cast by the mature trees that edge this plot in one of the county's most charming villages. With tasty beers from the likes of City of Cambridge brewery and 22 wines by the glass, the wet side of the business attracts a good following. The meals emerging from the kitchen overseen by chef-patron Richard Stokes take the treat to another level again. A meal could start with Portland crab, peas, grilled corn, pickled samphire and chilli crab aïoli; then mains might offer roast Suffolk cannon and breast of lamb, sweetbread, kidney and wild mushroom ragout, pecorino, peas and pea shoots; or slow-cooked pig cheeks with star anise ginger, chilli, burnt aubergine purée, local bok choy, fried wild rice and pickled namenko and enoki mushrooms. Still room, perhaps, for compressed plums, shortbread crumble, almond cake and cream? Menus change weekly and seasonally; children's portions are available.

Open all wk 11.30-3 6-11 (Sun 11.30-3 6-9.30) **Food** Lunch Mon-Fri 12-2, Sat-Sun 12-2.30 Dinner all wk 6.30-9.30 Restaurant menu available all wk ⊕ FREE HOUSE ◄ Adnams Southwold Bitter, Hook Norton Old Hooky, Smiles Best Bitter, City of Cambridge Hobson's Choice, guest ales Ŏ Westons Stowford Press. ☉ 22
Facilities Non-diners area ◑ Children's portions Garden Outside area ☐ Parking WiFi ☞ (notice required)

The Queen's Head

tel: 01223 870436 **Fowlmere Rd CB22 7PG**
dir: *6m S of Cambridge on B1368, 1.5m off A10 at Harston, 4m from A505*

No nonsense food and good beer in old fashioned pub

The same family has owned and operated this tiny and very traditional village pub for some 50 years. Unchanging and unmarred by gimmickry, the stone-tiled bars, replete with log fires, pine settles and old school benches, draw an eclectic clientele, from Cambridge dons to local farm workers. They all come for tip-top Adnams ale direct from the barrel, the friendly, honest atmosphere and straightforward pub dishes. Food is simple — at lunch, soup, sandwiches and Aga-baked potatoes. In the evening, just soup, toast and beef dripping, and cold platters. Village tradition is kept alive with time-honoured pub games — dominoes, table skittles, shove ha'penny and nine men's Morris.

Open all wk 11.30-2.30 6-11 (Sun 12-2.30 7-10.30) Closed 25-26 Dec **Food** Lunch all wk 12-2.15 Dinner all wk 7-9.30 ⊕ FREE HOUSE ◄ Adnams Southwold Bitter, Broadside, Ghost Ship & Old Ale, guest ales Ŏ Crones, Hogan's. ☉ 10
Facilities Non-diners area ❤ (Bar Outside area) ◑ Children's portions Family room Outside area ☐ Parking ☞ (notice required)

The Horseshoe Inn

tel: 01480 810293 **90 High St PE19 5RH**
email: info@theoffordshoe.co.uk
dir: *Between Huntingdon & St Neots. 1.5m from Buckden on A1*

Inventive cooking at inn close to the river

Behind this substantial, gabled old farmhouse, a long, grassy beer garden stretches to meadows fringing the Great Ouse Valley with its countless ponds and lakes. Tranquil territory in which to sup on a brace of renowned East Anglian real ales, supplemented each mid-summer by a beer festival. At the pub, known locally as The Offord Shoe, the modern, pan-European menu is changed every two months to allow chef-patron Richard Kennedy to utilise seasonal ingredients to the full. Graduate, perhaps, from Maryland-style crab cakes with English mustard mayonnaise to a main course of spiced venison meatballs, tomato and chipotle sauce and cheddar grits; or fried sea bream fillet, spicy lentils, crispy fried okra and coriander yogurt.

Open all wk **Food** Lunch Mon-Fri 12-2.30, Sat-Sun all day Dinner Mon-Fri 6-9.30, Sat-Sun all day Set menu available Restaurant menu available all wk ⊕ FREE HOUSE ◄ Adnams Southwold Bitter, Nethergate Old Growler, Sharp's Doom Bar Ŏ Westons Old Rosie & Rosie's Pig, Cornish Orchards, Pink Lady. ☉ 17
Facilities Non-diners area ❤ (Bar Garden) ◑ Children's portions Play area Garden ☐ Beer festival Parking WiFi ☞ (notice required)

The Brewery Tap

tel: 01733 358500 **80 Westgate PE1 2AA**
email: brewerytap.manager@oakagroup.com
dir: *Opposite bus station*

Award-winning brewpub with local ales and Thai cooking

Home to the multi-award winning Oakham Brewery and one of the largest brewpubs in Europe, this striking pub is located in the old labour exchange on Westgate. Visitors can see the day-to-day running of the brewery through a glass wall spanning half the length of the bar. As if the appeal of the 12 real ales and the vast range of bottled beers was not enough, the kitchen is run by Thai chefs producing delicious and authentic Thai soups, noodle dishes, salads, stir-fries and curries. Look out for live music nights, and DJs on Saturdays.

Open all day all wk Closed 25-26 Dec, 1 Jan **Food** Lunch Mon-Thu 12-2.30, Fri-Sat 12-10.30, Sun 12-3.30 Dinner Mon-Thu 5.30-10.30, Fri-Sat 12-10.30, Sun 5.30-9.30 Av main course £13 Set menu available ⊕ FREE HOUSE ◄ Oakham Inferno, Citra, JHB & Bishops Farewell, guest ales Ŏ Westons Old Rosie, Rosie's Pig, Raspberry Twist & Wyld Wood Vintage. ☉ 10 **Facilities** Non-diners area ❤ (Bar Outside area) ◑ Outside area ☐ WiFi ☞

Charters Bar & East Restaurant

tel: 01733 315700 & 315702 (bookings) **Upper Deck, Town Bridge PE1 1FP**
email: manager@charters-bar.com
dir: *A1/A47 towards Wisbech, 2m to city centre & town bridge (River Nene). Barge moored at Town Bridge (west side)*

Moored barge on the River Nene

The largest floating real ale emporium in Britain can be found moored in the heart of Peterborough. The 176-foot converted barge motored from Holland across the North Sea in 1991, and is now a haven for real-ale and cider-lovers. Twelve handpumps dispense a continually changing repertoire of cask ales, while entertainment, dancing, live music and an Easter beer festival are regular features. The 'East' part of the name applies to the oriental restaurant on the upper deck which offers a comprehensive selection of pan-Asian dishes.

Open all day all wk 12-11 (Fri-Sat noon-2am) Closed 25-26 Dec, 1 Jan **Food** Lunch all wk 12-2.30 Set menu available Restaurant menu available all wk ⊕ FREE HOUSE ◄ Oakham Ales JHB, Bishops Farewell, Citra, Inferno, rotating local guest ales Ŏ Glebe Farm, Westons, Saxby's Cider, Sheppy's. ☉ 11
Facilities Non-diners area ❤ (Bar Garden) ◑ Garden ☐ Beer festival Cider festival Parking WiFi ☞ (notice required)

REACH
Map 12 TL56

Dyke's End

tel: 01638 743816 **CB25 0JD**
dir: *Phone for detailed directions*

At the heart of village life

Located in the centre of the village, overlooking the green, this pub was saved from closure by villagers in the 1990s. They ran it as a co-operative until 2003, when it was bought by Frank Feehan, who further refurbished and extended it. Frank's additions included the Devil's Dyke microbrewery, which continues to be run by owners Catherine and George Gibson. The pub has a strong local following for its food and beers. The menu is seasonal with daily-changing specials, although pub favourites like local sausage, mash and onion gravy; and rib-eye steaks and skinny cut chips are always popular.

Open 12-2.30 6-11 (Sat-Sun 12-11) Closed Mon L **Food** Lunch Tue-Sun 12-2 Dinner Tue-Sun 7-9 Av main course £13 ⊕ FREE HOUSE ◄ Marston's Wainwright, Adnams Southwold Bitter, Sharp's Special Ö Aspall. **Facilities** Non-diners area ❖ (Bar Restaurant Garden) ♦♦ Children's menu Children's portions Garden ⊨ Parking WiFi ▦ (notice required)

SPALDWICK
Map 12 TL17

The George

tel: 01480 890293 **5-7 High St PE28 0TD**
email: info@thegeorgespaldwick.co.uk
dir: *In village centre. Just off A14 junct 18. 5m W of Huntingdon*

Highly-praised village centre inn

Dating from 1679, this former coaching inn is a successful pub and restaurant; it has moved with the times, yet retained its rustic charm and character. The bar, with its low ceilings and wooden floor, serves local real ales and bar snacks, while the restaurant menu majors on all the pub favourites: baked camembert served with home-made marmalade and warm crusty bread; chicken breast wrapped in bacon and stuffed with cream cheese and asparagus; and chocolate brownie served with warm chocolate sauce and vanilla ice cream. Tables on the lawns and a terraced patio are much sought after, especially during the pub's popular annual ale and cider festival.

Open all wk 11.30-3 5.30-11 (Sat 11.30am-mdnt Sun 12-10.30) **Food** Lunch Mon-Sat 12-2.30, Sun 12-7 Dinner Mon-Sat 6-9, Sun 12-7 Restaurant menu available all wk ⊕ PUNCH TAVERNS ◄ Woodforde's Wherry, Timothy Taylor Landlord, Black Sheep. ♥ 9 **Facilities** Non-diners area ❖ (Bar Garden Outside area) ♦♦ Children's menu Children's portions Garden Outside area ⊨ Beer festival Cider festival Parking WiFi ▦ (notice required)

STAPLEFORD
Map 12 TL45

The Rose at Stapleford

tel: 01223 843349 **81 London Rd CB22 5DG**
email: info@rose-stapleford.co.uk
dir: *Phone for detailed directions*

Great home-cooked food and accredited ales

Paul and Karen Beer have woven some magic at The Rose, a traditional village pub close to Cambridge and Duxford Imperial War Museum. Expect a stylish interior, replete with low beams and inglenook fireplaces, and traditional unfussy menus majoring on local produce, fresh Lowestoft fish, and quality Scottish steaks. As well as a good selection of appetisers, typical main dishes include slow-roasted Suffolk pork belly, marinated in cider and sage and served with mashed potatoes, apple purée and seasonal vegetables; and home-made beef lasagne with garlic bread

and mixed salad. For the sweet of tooth, bread and butter pudding with custard is a favourite.

Open all wk 12-3 5.30-11 (Sun 12-10.30) **Food** Lunch Mon-Sat 12-2, Sun 12-8.30 Dinner Mon-Sat 5.30-9.30, Sun 12-8.30 Set menu available Restaurant menu available Mon-Sat ⊕ CHARLES WELLS ◄ Bombardier, Courage Directors, Young's Ö Symonds. ♥ 12 **Facilities** Non-diners area ♦♦ Children's menu Children's portions Garden ⊨ Parking WiFi ▦ (notice required)

STILTON
Map 12 TL18

The Bell Inn Hotel ★★★ HL ◉
PICK OF THE PUBS

tel: 01733 241066 **Great North Rd PE7 3RA**
email: reception@thebellstilton.co.uk web: www.thebellstilton.co.uk
dir: *From A1(M) junct 16 follow signs for Stilton. Hotel on main road in village centre*

Handsome stone inn with historic Stilton pedigree

A Bell Inn has stood here since 1500, although this one, reputedly the oldest coaching inn on the old Great North Road, is mid-17th century, with an impressive stone façade, a splendid inn sign and a fine original interior with an upbeat feel. It once welcomed (or maybe not!) highwayman Dick Turpin, as well as Clark Gable who was stationed nearby in 1943. Famous as the birthplace of Stilton cheese, the pub is again making its own, called Bell Blue – the Stilton cheese sampler is a must. Modern British dishes in the bar/bistro include salt-baked celeriac with air-dried ham, cabbage and yeast flakes; roast and confit lamb with split peas, turnip and English lettuce; Jerusalem artichoke risotto with king oyster mushroom and truffle; ale-battered fish and chips; and chocolate and fig roulade with hazelnut praline and chocolate cake ice cream. All the en suite bedrooms are round the old courtyard – two have four-posters.

Open all wk 12-2.30 6-11 (Sat 12-12 Sun 12-11) Closed 25 Dec **Food** Lunch Mon-Sat 12-2.30, Sun 12-3 Dinner Mon-Sat 6-9.30, Sun 6-9 Av main course £14.95 Restaurant menu available Mon-Sat evening, Sun L ⊕ FREE HOUSE ◄ Greene King IPA, Morland Old Speckled Hen, Oakham Bishops Farewell, Digfield Fool's Nook, guest ales Ö Aspall. ♥ 13 **Facilities** Non-diners area ❖ (Outside area) ♦♦ Children's menu Children's portions Outside area ⊨ Parking WiFi ▦ (notice required)
Rooms 22

STRETHAM
Map 12 TL57

The Lazy Otter ★★★★ INN

tel: 01353 649780 **Cambridge Rd CB6 3LU**
email: thelazyotter@btconnect.com web: www.lazy-otter.com
dir: *Phone for detailed directions*

Welcoming waterside focal point amidst the Fens

A pub here has served fenland watermen for several centuries; today's bustling incarnation is popular with leisure boaters on the River Ouse, which glides past the extensive beer garden, from which are cracking views over the rich farmland. Barley from these acres goes into the good range of East Anglian beers, including the house ale from Milton Brewery; an annual beer and cider festival is also held. The restaurant offers dishes like steak and kidney pudding; ham, egg and chips; seafood linguine; Somerset brie and beetroot tart; and a variety of gourmet burgers including wild boar and apple; and kangaroo.

Open all day all wk 7am-11pm (Sun 8.30am-10.30pm) **Food** Mon-Sat 8am-9pm, Sun 8.30am-9pm Restaurant menu available all wk ⊕ FREE HOUSE ◄ Adnams Broadside, Milton Lazy Otter, Milton Tiki, Oakham JHB, Woodforde's Wherry, guest ales Ö Westons Stowford Press & Old Rosie. ♥ 10 **Facilities** Non-diners area ❖ (All areas) ♦♦ Children's menu Children's portions Play area Garden Outside area ⊨ Beer festival Cider festival Parking WiFi ▦ **Rooms** 3

STRETHAM *continued*

The Red Lion

tel: 01353 648132 **47 High St CB6 3LD**
email: redlion@charnwoodpubco.co.uk
dir: *Exit A10 between Cambridge & Ely into Stretham. Left into High St, pub on right*

Busy local with traditional food

Set in the Cambridgeshire fenlands just a short hop from Ely, this creeper-dressed old coaching inn shares the village centre with the church and medieval cross. The courtyard beer garden is a popular spot on warm days, when beers from the likes of Wychwood hit the spot. The new licensees have further developed the well-liked menu of pub favourites and classic dishes which draws in locals and visitors to the conservatory-style restaurant. Light bites include baked dough balls with garlic and herb butter; whilst mains embrace sharing platters, or perhaps 'piggy three ways' — sausage, chop and belly pork, mash and cabbage.

Open all day all wk **Food** Lunch Mon-Fri 12-2.30, Sat-Sun 12-9 Dinner Mon-Fri 6-9, Sat-Sun 12-9 Av main course £10 ⊕ FREE HOUSE ◀ Greene King IPA, Wychwood Hobgoblin, Adnams, Marston's ♻ Pickled Pig, Thatchers. ▾ 8
Facilities Non-diners area ❀ (Bar Garden) ❢ Children's menu Children's portions Garden ⌑ Parking WiFi ☷ (notice required)

THORNEY   **Map 12 TF20**

Dog In A Doublet   PICK OF THE PUBS

tel: 01733 202256 **Northside PE6 0RW**
email: info@doginad.co.uk
dir: *On B1040 between Thorney & Whittlesey*

A real gem in the Fens

This 16th-century, riverside pub, next to one of the biggest lock gates in Europe, is owned by John McGinn, who, a few years ago, competed in BBC's *MasterChef*. It's a real success story. Local ales and home-made cider draw drinkers to the bar with its open fire, and for food, John is passionate about creating British classics with a twist. The pub has its own chickens and rare-breed pigs that live on land next door, and farm produce is available to buy in the restaurant deli. There's a street food and bar snack menu of 'nibbling snacks' (Swedish juniper and sweet orange roll mops), 'munching snacks' (home-reared sausage hot dog in a blanket) and 'bowls' (Thai beef salad with lemongrass). Turning to the tempting main menu and there could be a starter of black sesame tempura whitebait with korma mayo; and 24-hour lamb shoulder, shepherd's pie sauce, potato purée, cheese and chive hash and pea medley. There's now a five-course tasting lunch and an eight-course tasting menu — a version is offered to vegetarians and vegans too.

Open 12-2.30 5-10 (Sat-Sun 12-10) Closed Mon L & Tue L **Food** Lunch Wed-Thu 12-2, Fri-Sun 12-9 Dinner Mon-Thu 5-9, Fri-Sun 12-9 Set menu available Restaurant menu available all wk ⊕ FREE HOUSE ◀ Marston's Pedigree, KCB 66 ♻ Spinney Abbey Monk & Disorderly, Dog House (own brew). ▾ 20
Facilities Non-diners area ❀ (Bar Garden) ❢ Children's menu Children's portions Play area Garden ⌑ Cider festival Parking WiFi ☷ (notice required)

UFFORD   **Map 12 TF00**

The White Hart ★★★★ INN

tel: 01780 740250 **Main St PE9 3BH**
email: info@whitehartufford.co.uk **web:** www.whitehartufford.co.uk
dir: *From Stamford take B1443 signed Barnack. Through Barnack, follow signs to Ufford*

Pretty pub supplied by the family farm

Salvaged old agricultural tools and other farming memorabilia embellish the bar of this 17th-century country inn. Among its four real ales is Grainstore Brewery's Red Kite, Aspall supplies the cider and 14 wines are by the glass, selected from an extensive cellar. The Orangery, The Pantry and the garden are three of the five dining areas, where options include Portobello mushroom bruschetta with poached hen's egg; slow-braised lamb shank, creamed potatoes and rich mint jus; and roasted vegetable Wellington, parsnip purée and fondant potato. For pudding there might be warm pineapple and coconut upside down cake with passionfruit sorbet.

Open all day all wk Mon-Thu 9am-11pm (Fri-Sat 9am-mdnt Sun 9-9) **Food** Lunch Mon-Sat 12-2.30, Sun 12-4 Dinner Mon-Sat 6-9.30 Av main course £12.95 ⊕ FREE HOUSE ◀ Fuller's London Pride, The Grainstore Red Kite, Oakham Ales JHB ♻ Aspall. ▾ 14 **Facilities** Non-diners area ❀ (Bar Garden) ❢ Children's menu Children's portions Play area Garden ⌑ Parking WiFi ☷ (notice required) **Rooms** 10

WHITTLESFORD   **Map 12 TL44**

The Tickell Arms

tel: 01223 833025 **North Rd CB22 4NZ**
email: tickell@cambscuisine.com **web:** www.cambscuisine.com
dir: *M11 junct 10, A505 towards Saffron Walden. Left signed Whittlesford*

Food prepared and served by a knowledgeable team

Part of the Cambscuisine (that's cuisine from Cambridgeshire) group, this blue-washed village pub stands behind a neat, white picket fence; the car park is entered through wrought-iron gates. Inside the pub are elegant fireplaces, gilt mirrors and whimsical bowler hat-shaped lampshades. Among the four local real ales is Pegasus from Milton Brewery in Cambridge, and from Hemingford Grey comes Cromwell cider. The restaurant serves seasonal modern British and European food from a regularly-changing menu. Examples are Israeli couscous and chive yogurt, roast apple and beetroot; guinea fowl terrine; braised ox cheek, creamed potato, sprout tops and caramelised onions. The tempting fish menu might include hake fillet, bouillabaisse sauce, mussels and fennel.

Open all wk 12-3 6-11 (Sat-Sun all day) **Food** Lunch Mon-Fri 12-2.30, Sat-Sun 12-5 Dinner Mon-Fri 6-11, Sat-Sun 5-11 Set menu available Restaurant menu available all wk ⊕ FREE HOUSE ◀ Milton Pegasus, Brewster's Hophead, Elgood's Cambridge Bitter ♻ Cromwell. ▾ 16 **Facilities** Non-diners area ❀ (Bar Garden) ❢ Children's menu Children's portions Garden ⌑ Beer festival Parking WiFi ☷ (notice required)

CHESHIRE

ALDFORD
Map 15 SJ45

The Grosvenor Arms
PICK OF THE PUBS

tel: 01244 620228 **Chester Rd CH3 6HJ**
email: grosvenor.arms@brunningandprice.co.uk
dir: On B5130, S of Chester

Imposing Victorian pub with village green views

With its red brick and black and white timbering, this higgledy-piggledy Brunning & Price pub was designed by Victorian architect John Douglas, who designed around 500 buildings, many of them in Cheshire. The spacious, open-plan interior includes an airy conservatory and a panelled, book-filled library. The range of real ales from small breweries, such as Phoenix and Weetwood, changes frequently, much to the delight of beer-drinking locals. Venison, pancetta and shallot meatballs in juniper sauce makes an interesting opener to French seafood stew; chicken, ham hock and leek pie; pink-roasted duck breast; and Mexican vegetarian burger. To see Black Forest trifle – not gâteau, note! – on the menu might nevertheless stir the memories of the more mature. A terrace leads into a small, pleasant garden, and on out to the village green.

Open all day all wk **Food** Mon-Thu 12-9.30, Fri-Sat 12-10, Sun 12-9 ⊕ FREE HOUSE/ BRUNNING & PRICE ◀ Original Bitter, Weetwood Eastgate Ale, Phoenix, guest ales ᗡ Westons Stowford Press, Aspall. ☗ 20 **Facilities** Non-diners area ⚘ (Bar Garden) ♦ Children's menu Children's portions Garden ⋈ Parking WiFi

ALLOSTOCK
Map 15 SJ77

The Three Greyhounds Inn

tel: 01565 723455 **Holmes Chapel Rd WA16 9JY**
email: info@thethreegreyhoundsinn.co.uk **web:** www.thethreegreyhoundsinn.co.uk
dir: S from Allostock on A50. Right on B5082 signed Northwich. Over M6, pub on right

A real find at a rural crossroads

This 300-year-old former farmhouse is a stylishly eclectic dining pub. Inside is a warren of atmospheric rooms, replete with exposed beams, rugs on wooden floors, crackling log fires in brick fireplaces, fat candles on old dining tables, and a host of quirky touches to make you smile. Go there for a choice of five local ales and over 50 brandies behind the bar, and some cracking pub food – seafood sharing plate; potted beef with stout piccalilli; cod loin with shrimp butter; duck leg and haricot bean stew; apple and Calvados crumble, and an imaginative choice of sandwiches. Book ahead for the memorable Sunday lunches. Dogs are welcome in the snug and the garden.

The Three Greyhounds Inn

Open all day all wk **Food** all wk 12-9.30 ⊕ FREE HOUSE ◀ Almighty Allostock Ale, Byley Bomber, Merlins Gold, Three Greyhound Bitter, Weetwood Ales Cheshire Cat. ☗ 15 **Facilities** Non-diners area ⚘ (Bar Garden) ♦ Children's portions Garden ⋈ Parking WiFi ▬ (notice required)

ASTON
Map 15 SJ64

The Bhurtpore Inn
PICK OF THE PUBS

See Pick of the Pubs on page 72

BROXTON
Map 15 SJ45

Egerton Arms

tel: 01829 782241 **Whitchurch Rd CH3 9JW**
email: info@egerton-arms.com
dir: On A41 between Whitchurch & Chester

Spacious country pub with a sun-trap garden

Handy for the castle-studded, wooded sandstone ridge that splits Cheshire in two, this gabled roadside restaurant, bar and grill offers diners and drinkers a wholesome choice of Cheshire's finest. Weetwood Brewery ales populate the bar, whilst new owners proffer an eclectic menu of pub grub and modern classics. French trimmed rack of Welsh lamb may hit the spot, whilst cod and crayfish fishcakes are among the extensive fish selection here; there's also a good range of steaks. The airy country-house style interior has a myriad of intriguing local photos, whilst a tree-shaded beer garden is a veritable sun trap.

Open all day all wk 12-11 (Sun 12-10.30) Closed 25 Dec & 31 Dec eve **Food** Mon-Sat 12-9.30, Sun 12-9 Restaurant menu available all wk ⊕ FREE HOUSE ◀ Piffle & Balderdash, Wells Bombardier, Purple Moose Snowdonia, Weetwood Ales. ☗ 22 **Facilities** Non-diners area ♦ Children's menu Children's portions Play area Family room Garden ⋈ Parking WiFi ▬ (notice required)

PICK OF THE PUBS

The Bhurtpore Inn

ASTON Map 15 SJ64

tel: 01270 780917
Wrenbury Rd CW5 8DQ
email: simonbhurtpore@yahoo.co.uk
web: www.bhurtpore.co.uk
dir: *Just off A530 between Nantwich & Whitchurch. Follow Wrenbury signs at x-roads in village*

Friendly traditional inn with real community spirit

A pub since at least 1778, when it was called the Queen's Head. It subsequently became the Red Lion, but it was Lord Combermere's success at the Siege of Bhurtpore in India in 1826 that inspired the name that has stuck. Simon and Nicky George came across it in 1991, boarded-up and stripped out. Simon is a direct descendant of Joyce George, who leased the pub from the Combermere Estate in 1849, so was motivated by his family history to take on the hard work of restoring the interior. Since then, 'award-winning' hardly does justice to the accolades heaped upon this hostelry. In the bar, 11 ever-changing real ales are always available, mostly from local microbreweries, as are real ciders, continental draught lagers and around 150 of the world's bottled beers. An annual beer festival, reputedly Cheshire's largest, is in its 20th year, with around 130 real ales. The pub has

also been shortlisted many times for the 'National Whisky Pub of the Year' award, and there is a long soft drinks menu. Recognition extends to the kitchen too, where unfussy dishes of classic pub fare are prepared. Among the hearty British ingredients you'll find seasonal game, such as venison haunch steak, rosemary roasted potatoes and red wine sauce. Curries and balti dishes are always on the blackboard. Vintage vehicles bring their owners here on the first Thursday of the month, and folk musicians play on the third Tuesday.

Open all day all wk 12-11.30 (Fri-Sat 12-12 Sun 12-11) Closed 25-26 Dec, 1 Jan **Food** Lunch Mon-Thu 12-2, Fri-Sat 12-9.30, Sun 12-8.30 Dinner Mon-Thu 5.30-9.30, Fri-Sat 12-9.30, Sun 12-8.30

Av main course £10 🛢 FREE HOUSE 🍺 Salopian Golden Thread, Abbeydale Absolution, Weetwood Oast-House Gold, Hobsons Twisted Spire, Acorn Yorkshire Pride, Merlins Gold 🍏 Hogan's, Thatchers Cheddar Valley, Wrenbury Cider. 🍷 15 **Facilities** Non-diners area 🐾 (Bar Garden Outside area) 🚸 Children's portions Garden Outside area 🎪 Beer festival Parking WiFi 🚌 (notice required)

BUNBURY
Map 15 SJ55

The Dysart Arms
PICK OF THE PUBS

tel: 01829 260183 **Bowes Gate Rd CW6 9PH**
email: dysart.arms@brunningandprice.co.uk
dir: *Between A49 & A51, by Shropshire Union Canal*

Well presented village pub

Pub group Brunning & Price care hugely about their properties, as is evident here. Named after local landowners, the Earls of Dysart, this classic village pub has open fires, lots of old oak, and properly filled bookcases – not just a random job lot from a jumble sale. Built in the mid-18th century, at one time it was simultaneously farmhouse, abattoir and pub; the abattoir was flattened by a German bomber returning home from a raid on Liverpool docks. Brunning's Original Bitter and Weetwood's Best Cask are likely to be on tap in the bar, with 18 wines by the glass. Around the bar are several dining areas, where starters include Thai crab cakes, and butternut squash tortellini; Greek pork patties are among the light bites; and main courses range from pan-fried trout fillets, to spiced black bean burger, by way of braised lamb shoulder. Views from the pretty garden take in two castles and the parish church.

Open all day all wk 11.30-11 (Sun 12-10.30) **Food** Mon-Sat 12-9.30, Sun 12-9 ⊕ BRUNNING & PRICE ◀ Original Bitter, Weetwood Best Cask, guest ales ♂ Aspall. ♈ 18 **Facilities** Non-diners area ✿ (Bar Garden Outside area) ♦♦ Children's menu Children's portions Garden Outside area ♠ Parking WiFi

BURLEYDAM
Map 15 SJ64

The Combermere Arms

tel: 01948 871223 **SY13 4AT**
email: combermere.arms@brunningandprice.co.uk
dir: *From Whitchurch take A525 towards Nantwich, at Newcastle/Audlem/Woore sign, turn right at junct. Pub 100yds on right*

Classic coaching inn with impressive menu

Local shoots, walkers and town folk frequent this classic 17th-century country inn. Full of character and warmth, it has three roaring fires and a wealth of oak, nooks and crannies, pictures and old furniture. Food options range from light bites such as Shropshire Blue and butternut squash quiche to full meals – maybe smoked pigeon breast with blackberry, hazelnut salad and black pudding croûtons, followed by smoked haddock and salmon fishcakes; or rabbit and prune faggots with celeriac mash, buttered kale and wild mushroom gravy. You could finish with a hot waffle, warm blackberries and salted caramel ice cream. There is a great choice of real ales and ciders, an informative wine list and impressive cheese board.

Open all day all wk 11.30-11 **Food** Sun-Thu 12-9, Fri-Sat 12-10 ⊕ FREE HOUSE/BRUNNING & PRICE ◀ Original Bitter, Weetwood Cheshire Cat, Sharp's Doom Bar, guest ales ♂ Westons Stowford Press, Aspall. ♈ 20 **Facilities** Non-diners area ♦♦ Children's menu Children's portions Garden ♠ Parking WiFi

BURWARDSLEY
Map 15 SJ55

The Pheasant Inn ★★★★★ INN ⊛
PICK OF THE PUBS

See Pick of the Pubs on page 74

CHELFORD
Map 15 SJ87

Egerton Arms

tel: 01625 861366 **Knutsford Rd SK11 9BB**
email: jeremy@chelfordegertonarms.co.uk
dir: *On A537 (Knutsford to Macclesfield road)*

Family-run and family welcoming pub with a deli next door

Sited in Cheshire's best countryside in the affluent area known as the 'golden triangle', the Egerton Arms is efficiently and enthusiastically run by Jeremy Hague.

Low beams, large fireplaces, eccentric antiques and a long bar with brass pumps characterise the interior of this 16th-century building, whose history is closely tied to Lord Egerton and his Tatton Park estate which is nearby. Local real ales are briskly served in the bar, while the 100-seat restaurant caters to hungry families with a comprehensive menu full of pub classics, including deli boards, grills, and pizzas from the stone-baked oven. There's a deli adjoining the pub which sells a wide choice of artisan produce from all over the country.

Open all day all wk **Food** all day Restaurant menu available all wk ⊕ FREE HOUSE ◀ Wells Bombardier, Copper Dragon, local ales ♂ Westons Stowford Press. ♈ 9 **Facilities** Non-diners area ✿ (All areas) ♦♦ Children's menu Children's portions Play area Garden Outside area ♠ Parking WiFi 🚌 (notice required)

CHESTER
Map 15 SJ46

The Brewery Tap

tel: 01244 340999 **52-54 Lower Bridge St CH1 1RU**
email: drink@the-tap.co.uk
dir: *From B5268 in Chester into Lower Bridge St towards river*

Great ale in historic city surroundings

This historic pub is situated in part of Gamul House, named after Sir Francis Gamul, a wealthy merchant and mayor of Chester who built it in 1620. It is reputedly where Charles I stayed when his troops were defeated at Rowton Moor, shortly before the king's final flight to Wales. Relax with a Thirstquencher ale and enjoy the pub's numerous period details, then choose from a menu of hearty favourites such as pork and rabbit rillettes, prune purée, cornichons and toast; pearl barley risotto; and Spanish pig stomach and white bean stew.

Open all day all wk Closed 25-26 Dec **Food** Mon-Sat 12-9.30, Sun 12-9 Av main course £9 ⊕ FREE HOUSE/SPITTING FEATHERS ◀ Thirstquencher, Old Wavertonian Stout ♂ Guest ciders. ♈ 14 **Facilities** Non-diners area ♦♦ WiFi

Old Harkers Arms

tel: 01244 344525 **1 Russell St CH3 5AL**
email: harkers.arms@brunningandprice.co.uk
dir: *Close to railway station, on canal side*

A buzzy city watering hole

Housed in a former Victorian chandler's warehouse beside the Shropshire Union Canal, the tall windows, lofty ceilings, wooden floors and bar constructed from salvaged doors make this one of Chester's more unusual pubs. The bar offers over 100 malt whiskies and ales from a range of breweries. The daily-changing menu from light dishes such as Vietnamese noodle salad through to main courses like slow-cooked beef cheeks, horseradish and tarragon mash, purple sprouting broccoli and rich red wine sauce; honey-roasted ham (served cold) with free-range eggs and chips; roast cod loin, creamed leeks, chargrilled new potatoes and watercress sauce. The pub holds events such as 'Pudding, Pie and Great British Beers Week' in February or March time, where over 20 award-winning ales can be tried, plus a 'Pie and Champion Ale' week in October.

Open all day all wk 10.30am-11pm (Sun 12-10.30) Closed 25 Dec **Food** all wk 12-9.30 Av main course £11.95 ⊕ FREE HOUSE/BRUNNING & PRICE ◀ Brunning & Price Original Bitter, Weetwood Cheshire Cat, Flowers Original, Salopian, Derby, Facer's North Star Porter ♂ Westons Country Perry, Gwynt y Ddraig Black Dragon. ♈ 15 **Facilities** Non-diners area ✿ (Bar Outside area) Outside area ♠ Beer festival Cider festival WiFi

PICK OF THE PUBS

The Pheasant Inn ★★★★★ INN ❀

BURWARDSLEY   Map 15 SJ55

tel: 01829 770434 **CH3 9PF**
email: info@thepheasantinn.co.uk
web: www.thepheasantinn.co.uk
dir: *A41 (Chester to Whitchurch) left signed Tattenhall. Through Tattenhall to Burwardsley. In Burwardsley follow Cheshire Workshops signs*

Popular pub with magnificent rural views

High on the sandstone ridge known as the Peckforton Hills stands Beeston Castle. Enjoying a similarly lofty position on its west-facing slopes overlooking the Cheshire Plain, is this 300-year-old former farmhouse and barn, where only five families have been licensees since it became an alehouse. Such is its elevation that you can see the Welsh hills and two cathedrals, Liverpool's 23 miles away and, much nearer, Chester's. Particularly familiar with the Pheasant are walkers and hikers on the Sandstone Trail long-distance footpath that links Frodsham on the Mersey with Whitchurch in Shropshire. On a fine day the obvious place to be is in the flower-filled courtyard or on the terrace, but when the weather dictates otherwise grab a space by the big open fire in the wooden-floored, heftily-beamed bar. Here you'll find four real ales, three from the Weetwood Brewery near Tarporley. The kitchen makes extensive use of local

produce, while much of the seafood comes from Fleetwood in Lancashire. With the daily-changing restaurant menu offering a wide choice of modern British and European dishes, think about starting with potted Morecombe Bay shrimps; or confit duck leg, rhubarb jam, truffled potato rösti and sauce gribeche. Follow with fillet of lemon sole, rissole potatoes, sauté spinach and shrimp butter sauce; pheasant breast with smoked streaky bacon, butternut squash gratin, chestnut, blackberry jam and sage fritters; or Ridings Reserve beef Wellington, watercress purée, red wine sauce and hand-cut chips. And don't miss the choices on the specials board. Comfortable en suite accommodation is available.

Open all day all wk **Food** Mon-Thu 12-9.30, Fri-Sat 12-10, Sun 12-9 ⊕ FREE HOUSE ◼ Weetwood Old Dog Premium Bitter, Eastgate Ale & Best Bitter, guest ale ♂ Hereford Dry Cider. ♟ 12 **Facilities** Non-diners area ♣ (Bar Restaurant Garden) ♠♦ Children's menu Children's portions Garden ⩊ Parking WiFi 🚌 (notice required) **Rooms** 12

PICK OF THE PUBS

The Cholmondeley Arms

CHOLMONDELEY Map 15 SJ55

tel: 01829 720300 **SY14 8HN**
email: info@cholmondeleyarms.co.uk
web: www.cholmondeleyarms.co.uk
dir: *On A49, between Whitchurch & Tarporley*

Friendly inn with imaginative menus and 200 gins

Set in rolling Cheshire countryside virtually opposite Cholmondeley Castle on the A49, and still part of the Viscount's estate, is this red-brick former schoolhouse. Quirky and eclectic, it's surely one of England's more unusual pubs, the decor and artefacts, including family heirlooms, educational memorabilia, bell tower without and blackboards within add tremendously to the atmosphere of the cavernous interior. It's no longer a draughty institute — owners Tim and Mary Bird have created a warm and inviting interior, with church candles on old school desks, fresh flowers, glowing log fires and a relaxing atmosphere. After exploring the local countryside, visiting the castle, or the fabulous ruins at Beeston, stapled to Cheshire's hilly sandstone spine, it's the perfect place to unwind, sup a pint of Cholmondeley Best or another local guest (only microbrewery beers from a 35-mile radius are stocked), or delve into the mindboggling list of over 200 different gins. Allow time to taste some of the

best produce from Cheshire's burgeoning larder, including seasonal game from the estate. Nibbles to set the scene include venison and chestnut sausage roll before launching into a starter of stuffed pancake of creamed leek, goats' cheese and spinach. Mains are split into 'Old School Favourites' like fish pie with cod cheek, smoked haddock and spinach, whilst seasonal specials may feature rabbit and ham hock broth with baby winter vegetables and smoked bacon and thyme cobbler; or venison loin Wellington with parsnip dauphinoise, glazed carrots and red wine and game sauce. There's a gin festival each year. Please note that children under ten are not allowed after 7pm in the bar, or 9pm in the garden.

Open all day all wk **Food** Lunch Mon-Fri 12-3, Sat 12-9.30, Sun 12-8.45 Dinner Mon-Fri 5.30-8.45, Sat 12-9.30, Sun 12-8.45 ⊕ FREE HOUSE
◀ Cholmondeley Best Bitter, 4 rotating guest ales ♂ Westons Old Rosie, South West Orchards. ♈ 16
Facilities Non-diners area ❧ (Bar Restaurant Garden) ♦♦ Children's portions Garden ⊼ Parking WiFi 🚌 (notice required)

CHESTER *continued*

The Stamford Bridge

tel: 01829 740229 **CH3 7HN**
email: stamfordbridge@hydesbrewery.com
dir: *A51 from Chester towards Tarporley, left at lights, pub on left*

Attractive city-limits inn with good food and beers

This city-outskirts inn has extensive views from its beer garden across the Cheshire Plain. Inside, country-house formality meets cottage homeliness – heavy beams, open fires with precision-cut logs, and well-stocked bookshelves. Lunchtime offers sandwiches, wraps and focaccias, while evening diners can expect a good choice of fish dishes such as whole roasted sea bass, wild rice, pak choi and red Thai sauce; and meat dishes, perhaps toad in the hole; or venison loin; plus steaks, pies and vegetarian options such as tomato and roasted red pepper risotto.

Open all day all wk 12-11 (Sun 12-10.30) Closed 25 Dec & 31 Dec eve **Food** Lunch all wk 12-6 Dinner all wk 6-9.30 ⊕ HYDES BREWERY ◀ Weetwood, Hydes, Woodward & Falconer Balderdash & Piffle. ♟ 14 **Facilities** Non-diners area ♣ Children's menu Children's portions Play area Garden ⌁ Parking WiFi ⛺ (notice required)

CHOLMONDELEY	Map 15 SJ55

The Cholmondeley Arms — PICK OF THE PUBS

See Pick of the Pubs on page 75

CHRISTLETON	Map 15 SJ46

Ring O'Bells

tel: 01244 335422 **Village Rd CH3 7AS**
email: info@ringobellschester.co.uk
dir: *3m from Chester between A51 towards Nantwich & A41 towards Whitchurch*

Chester-fringe pub with local ales and enjoyable food

Much of the appeal of this spruced-up village pub is the scope of events that draw drinkers and diners. Wine tastings, networking events, excellent offers and welcoming staff are just a few of the reasons why people keep on returning, not to mention the choice of outdoor dining areas, particularly the decked suntrap terrace. The bar stocks real ale from Chester's Spitting Feathers brewery, as well as representatives from Cheshire Brew Brothers. Good use of local produce is evident on seasonal menus that might start with pressed chicken and ham hock terrine and continue with home-roasted gammon loin or the famous Bells' fish and chips. There is a beer festival every summer.

Open all day all wk **Food** Lunch Mon-Fri 12-3, Sat-Sun 12-5 Dinner Mon-Thu 5-9, Fri-Sat 5-9.30, Sun 5-8 Av main course £10 ⊕ TRUST INNS ◀ Spitting Feathers, Weetwood, Big Hand, Cheshire Brew Brothers. ♟ **Facilities** Non-diners area ♣ (Bar Restaurant Garden) ♦ Children's menu Children's portions Play area Garden ⌁ Beer festival Parking WiFi ⛺ (notice required)

CHURCH MINSHULL	Map 15 SJ66

NEW The Badger Inn

tel: 01270 522348 **Cross Ln CW5 6DY**
email: info@badgerinn.co.uk
dir: *From A350 between Crewe & Middlewich follow Church Minshull signs*

A friendly welcome and home-cooked food

This brick-built late 18th-century inn was originally known as the Brook Arms after the local lords of the manor. They had a badger, or 'brock' as part of their crest, hence the current name. The pub is popular with walkers and canal boaters from the nearby Shropshire Union Canal, and in the bar you can sample a draught from the local Weetwood Ales. Start your meal with a Scotch egg or Thai-style fishcakes, before moving on to venison Wellington with fondant potato, butternut squash purée and braised red cabbage; or pan-seared calves' liver with black pudding mash, seasonal veggies and red wine jus.

Open all day all wk **Food** all wk 12-9 Av main course £10 Restaurant menu available all wk ⊕ FREE HOUSE ◀ Badger's Best, Titanic Plum Porter, Weetwood Ales Eastgate Ale & Southern Cross. **Facilities** Non-diners area ♣ (Bar Garden) ♦ Children's menu Children's portions Garden ⌁ Parking WiFi ⛺ (notice required)

CONGLETON	Map 16 SJ86

The Plough At Eaton

tel: 01260 280207 **Macclesfield Rd, Eaton CW12 2NH**
email: enquiries@theploughinncheshire.com **web:** www.theploughinncheshire.com
dir: *On A536 (Congleton to Macclesfield road)*

Popular inn with barn restaurant

Set well back from the main road in the hamlet of Eaton, this 400-year-old Cheshire-brick inn is a far cry from its genesis as a farmhouse. With a new licensee arriving in 2015, it continues to be a popular destination dining pub; the restaurant is housed in a remarkable cruck barn moved here from Wales. Choose your refreshment, a pint of Wells Bombardier or a guest ale perhaps, before perusing the monthly changing menu. Here you might find goats' cheese croquette or confit duck leg and spring roll to start, followed by Marrakesh spiced lamb shank; slow-cooked beef short rib; Jalfrezi-style curry and '3 Way Pork' – that's five-hour braised suckling pig.

Open all day all wk 12-12 **Food** all wk all day Av main course £13 Set menu available ⊕ FREE HOUSE ◀ Storm, Wells Bombardier, Tatton, local guest ales ♂ Thatchers. ♟ 10 **Facilities** Non-diners area ♣ (Bar Garden) ♦ Children's menu Children's portions Garden ⌁ Parking WiFi ⛺

PICK OF THE PUBS

The Fishpool Inn

DELAMERE Map 15 SJ56

tel: 01606 883277
Fishpool Rd CW8 2HP
email: info@thefishpoolinn.co.uk
web: www.thefishpoolinn.co.uk
dir: *Phone for detailed directions*

Striking village pub with quirky interior

Idyllically positioned on the edge of the Delamere Forest in the picturesque Cheshire countryside, this 18th-century pub seamlessly blends the traditional with the contemporary. The extensive refurbishment in the pub's recent past created an interior that impresses with its spaciousness. Scrubbed beams and pillars, pale floorboards, and roof windows augmented by downlighters and wall lamps together produce an unexpected light airiness. The decor is rich in furnishings such as chesterfield-style banquettes, solid wood tables and chairs, rugs, and Victorian tilcs. Memorabilia from the Cheshire Polo Club, fishing rods and reels, decorated stags' heads, and even an upside-down skiff are just a few of the artefacts hanging from walls and ceilings in this engagingly quirky interior. The cellar keeps up to eight handpumps busy, with Weetwood's Cheshire Cat in permanent residence alongside a changing selection of local and seasonal real ales. An open-fronted kitchen produces modern British and popular European

food, the latter in the form of thin-crust pizzas from the dedicated Wood Stone oven. Seasonal and regional ingredients are turned into starters of crayfish, Muncaster crab and smoked salmon cocktail; or a tandoori spiced Welsh Valley lamb kofta served with harissa couscous and tzatziki. Main courses follow traditional lines with the likes of scampi with chunky chips; a hand-crafted pie of the day; and a barbecued pulled pork burger served with apple and celeriac slaw. More tradition is displayed on the desserts list, where the words 'crumble', 'trifle', 'sundae' and 'sticky toffee' all tempt the sweet of tooth. Children have their own menu, dogs are welcome, and there's a garden to relax in.

Open all day all wk **Food** Mon-Thu 12-9.30, Fri-Sat 12-10, Sun 12-9 ⊕ FREE HOUSE ◾ Weetwood Ales Best Bitter, Eastgate & Cheshire Cat, guest ales ○ Herefordshire Cider. ☒ 14 **Facilities** Non-diners area ☸ (Bar Garden Outside area) ⵖ Children's menu Children's portions Garden Outside area ⋒ Parking WiFi ☒ (notice required)

COTEBROOK — Map 15 SJ56

Fox & Barrel

tel: 01829 760529 **Foxbank CW6 9DZ**
email: info@foxandbarrel.co.uk
dir: *On A49, 2.8m N of Tarporley*

Countryside pub offering a warm welcome and excellent food

The rather cute explanation for the pub's name is that a fox being chased by the local hunt ran into the cellar, where the landlord gave it sanctuary. And who's to say otherwise? Interior features include a huge open log fire, old beams and half-panelled walls; the snug bar is the perfect spot for a pint of Weetwood. Classic pub food with an adventurous angle includes twice baked Cheshire cheese soufflé; and white onion soup with cheddar and sage as starters; then game suet pudding, garlic mash and juniper sauce; smoked salmon omelette; lamb hotpot with red cabbage; or hand-made goats' cheese gnocchi as main courses. Outside is a secluded landscaped garden surrounded by unspoilt Cheshire countryside.

Open all day all wk Closed 1 Jan, pm 25-26 Dec pm, 31 Dec am **Food** Mon-Sat 12-9.30, Sun 12-9 ⊕ FREE HOUSE ◀ Weetwood Eastgate Ale, Caledonian Deuchars IPA. ▾ 20 **Facilities** Non-diners area ❤ (Bar Garden) ◀ Children's menu Children's portions Garden ⊟ Parking WiFi

DELAMERE — Map 15 SJ56

The Fishpool Inn — PICK OF THE PUBS

See Pick of the Pubs on page 77

FARNDON — Map 15 SJ45

The Farndon ★★★★ INN

tel: 01829 270570 **High St CH3 6PU**
email: enquiries@thefarndon.co.uk web: www.thefarndon.co.uk
dir: *From Wrexham take A534 towards Nantwich. Follow signs for Farndon on left*

Fine food in the tranquil Dee Valley

This most imposing magpie inn commands Farndon's High Street as it winds down to the ancient, haunted stone bridge across the River Dee, which forms the England/Wales border. Coaches stopped here en route between the Midlands and Holyhead; centuries of hospitality are continued in the contemporary, comfy interior, a relaxing mix of colour-washed walls and modern furnishings all warmed by a seasonal roaring fire. Cheshire beers such as Weetwood accompany an impressive menu – the chef's deli platter; smoked haddock fishcakes with tomato salsa; braised ox cheek with bourguignon sauce; and Belgian waffle with rum and raisin ice cream are typical choices from the regularly changing fare. Five boutique guest bedrooms complete the picture.

Open all wk 5-11 (Sat 12-11 Sun 12-10.30) **Food** Lunch Sat 12-9, Sun 12-6 Dinner Mon-Fri 6-9, Sat 12-9.30, Sun 12-6 Restaurant menu available Wed-Sun ⊕ FREE HOUSE ◀ Timothy Taylor Landlord, Weetwood Cheshire Cat & Eastgate Ale, Spitting Feathers Thirstquencher, Sandstone, Big Hand. ▾ 10 **Facilities** Non-diners area ❤ (Bar Garden) ◀ Children's menu Children's portions Garden ⊟ Parking WiFi ⊕ (notice required) **Rooms** 5

GAWSWORTH — Map 16 SJ86

Harrington Arms

tel: 01260 223325 **Church Ln SK11 9RJ**
dir: *From Macclesfield take A536 towards Congleton. Turn left for Gawsworth*

Lovely pub on a working farm

Part farmhouse, part pub, the little-changed interior comprises a main bar serving Robinsons real ales and quirky rooms with open fires and rustic furnishings. Memorable for its impression of timelessness, it dates from 1664 and has been licensed since 1710. On offer is good pub food made extensively from the wealth of local produce, so expect home-made pies; rib-eye, sirloin and gammon steaks; fish and chips; vegetarian dishes; hot sandwiches; plus daily specials and Sunday roasts. Early October sees the annual conker championship here.

Open all wk 12-2.30 5-11.30 (Fri 12-2.30 4.30-12 Sat 12-11.30 Sun 12-11) Closed 25 Dec **Food** Lunch Mon-Fri 12-2.30, Sat 12-9, Sun 12-8 Dinner Mon-Thu 5-8.30, Fri 5-9, Sat 12-9, Sun 12-8 ⊕ ROBINSONS ◀ Unicorn, 1892, Wizard, Guinness, Dizzy Blonde, seasonal ale ♻ Westons Stowford Press. ▾ 8 **Facilities** Non-diners area ❤ (Bar Garden) ◀ Children's portions Garden ⊟ Parking WiFi ⊕ (notice required)

GOOSTREY — Map 15 SJ77

The Crown

tel: 01477 532128 **111 Main Rd CW4 8DE**
email: info@thecrowngoostrey.co.uk
dir: *In village centre. Follow Goostrey signs either from A50, or from A535 in Tremlow Green*

Charming village local with good food and local ales

A traditional pub set in the heart of the Cheshire farming village of Goostrey, The Crown has been an integral part of community life since the 18th century. Beyond its red-bricked façade, the pub's interior retains much charm with old oak beams and real fireplaces. Local breweries including Weetwood and a selection from microbreweries in Cheshire are well represented, perhaps accompanied by home-made crackling. The extensive modern menu takes in Thai green vegetable curry; moules marinière; crisp pork belly; and rib of beef and ale pie. Check with the pub for details of its summer beer festival and its annual gooseberry-growing competition.

Open all wk 11.30-11.30 **Food** Mon-Sat 12-9, Sun 12-8 Av main course £11 ⊕ FREE HOUSE ◀ Weetwood Ales, Timothy Taylor Boltmaker, Jennings Cumberland Ale. ▾ 14 **Facilities** Non-diners area ❤ (Bar Garden Outside area) ◀ Children's menu Children's portions Garden Outside area ⊟ Beer festival Parking WiFi ⊕ (notice required)

GREAT BUDWORTH — Map 15 SJ67

George and Dragon

tel: 01606 892650 **High St CW9 6HF**
email: thegeorge-dragon@btinternet.com
dir: *From M6 junct 19 or M56 junct 10 follow signs for Great Budworth*

Village local steeped in history

Painstakingly restored, this charming inn has many original features, including a stone tablet in the bar dated 1722 and inscribed 'Nil nimium cupito' ('I desire nothing to excess'). Also visible is a verse above a door written by local Arley Hall estate-owner, Rowland Egerton-Warburton, who had the inn remodelled in 1875. Regular real ales are Lees Bitter from Manchester and the pub's own Great Budworth Best Bitter. Start your meal with home-made pâté, or salt and pepper squid with sweet chilli sauce, followed by beer battered fish and chips (cooked in real beef dripping); Thai green curry; or slow cooked lamb shank.

Open all day all wk Food Mon-Sat 11.30-9.30, Sun 12-8.30 Av main course £11.95 Restaurant menu available all wk ⊕ J W LEES ◼ Lees Bitter, Great Budworth Best Bitter, MPA, The Governor. ♟ 12 Facilities Non-diners area ❤ (Bar Outside area) ♦♦ Children's menu Children's portions Outside area ⋒ Parking WiFi ▭ (notice required)

HANDLEY
Map 15 SJ45

The Calveley Arms

tel: 01829 770619 **Whitchurch Rd CH3 9DT**
email: calveleyarms@btconnect.com
dir: *5m S of Chester, signed from A41. Follow signs for Handley & Aldersey Green Golf Course*

Old inn, old beams, great beer

This spruced-up old coaching inn, first licensed in 1636, stands opposite the church with views of the distant Welsh hills. Chock full of old timbers, jugs, pots, pictures, prints and ornaments, the rambling bars provide an atmospheric setting in which to sample some cracking beers and decent pub food. Typically, tuck into lunchtime filled baguettes (tuna mayo, cheese or prawn for example), lamb cutlets, salmon teriyaki, speciality salads, and a good selection of pasta dishes. There are spacious gardens to enjoy in summer.

Open all wk 12-3 6-11 (Sun 12-3 7-11) Food Lunch all wk 12-3 Dinner Mon-Sat 6-9, Sun 7-9 ⊕ ENTERPRISE INNS ◼ Castle Eden Ale, Marston's Pedigree, Theakston Black Bull Bitter, Wells Bombardier, Greene King IPA, Black Sheep ♂ Aspall. Facilities Non-diners area ♦♦ Children's portions Play area Garden Parking ▭

HAUGHTON MOSS
Map 15 SJ55

The Nags Head

tel: 01829 260265 **Long Ln CW6 9RN**
email: manager@nagsheadhaughton.co.uk
dir: *Exit A49 S of Tarporley at Beeston/Haughton sign into Long Ln. 2.75m to pub*

Secluded country inn with finest Cheshire produce

Deep in the Cheshire countryside near to a dramatic wooded sandstone ridge, is this half-timbered country inn. There's no hiding the near-400-year heritage of the place, though; the huge cruck frame and crackling fire create rustic character and charm, which set-off nicely the light, conservatory-inspired dining extension which overlooks the tranquil garden and increasingly rare bowling green. The riches of the northern Welsh Marches are liberally sourced, with great beers from Cheshire's Weetwood brewery matched by the wide-ranging menu – platters, salads, chargrills, sandwiches, and pub classics.

Open all day all wk Food Sun-Thu 12-9, Fri-Sat 12-9.30 Set menu available Restaurant menu available all wk ⊕ FREE HOUSE ◼ Weetwood Ales, Thwaites, Nags 1629, guest ales ♂ Westons Stowford Press. ♟ 10 Facilities ❤ (Bar Garden) ♦♦ Children's menu Children's portions Garden ⋒ Parking WiFi

KERRIDGE
Map 16 SJ97

The Lord Clyde ❀❀❀
PICK OF THE PUBS

tel: 01625 562123 **SK10 5AH**
email: hello@thelordclyde.co.uk
dir: *From Macclesfield A523 towards Poynton. At rdbt follow Bollington sign onto B5090. 1st right into Clark Ln*

Exceptionally good country dining

Tables outside this converted terrace of weavers' cottages look out to the wood-dappled Kerridge Edge, the fringe of the Peak District. There are good local beers in the bar if that's your thing, but it's the restrained and interesting menu that draws

in the diners. Chef-proprietor Ernst van Zyl has worked in some of the world's top restaurants; his seasonally changing menu reflects the very best of Cheshire's produce. Ox cheek and oyster, salsify and kale might kick things off, with monkfish and Brussel sprouts, parsley root and pork skin to follow, showcasing the thoroughly modern approach that's championed here. The wine list is both extensive and impressive. There is now a kitchen table, for up to six people, so you can watch the chefs at work while enjoying your meal.

Open all wk 12-3 5-11 (Fri-Sun all day) Food Lunch all wk 12-3 Dinner all wk 6.30-9 Restaurant menu available Mon-Sat ⊕ PUNCH TAVERNS ◼ Morland Old Speckled Hen, Weetwood Ales Cheshire Cat, Thwaites Original ♂ Westons Stowford Press. ♟ 12 Facilities Non-diners area ❤ (Bar Outside area) ♦♦ Children's portions Outside area ⋒ Parking WiFi ▭ (notice required)

KETTLESHULME
Map 16 SJ97

Swan Inn

tel: 01663 732943 **SK23 7QU**
email: the.swan.kettleshulme@gmail.co.uk
dir: *On B5470 between Whaley Bridge (2m) & Macclesfield (5m)*

Charming village pub renowned for its beer and seafood dishes

Huddled in the shadow of the craggy Windgather Rocks in the Cheshire Peak District, the Swan is a glorious 15th-century village inn. The dining room offers an eclectic and international menu which has interesting dishes such as treacle-cured roasted goose breast, caramelised shallots and apple in red onion jam; and an extensive seafood menu including cod supreme and saffron risotto; and Chinese-style sea bream baked with garlic, ginger, soy and chilli. Local craft ales such as Thornbridge keep ramblers and locals very contented.

Open all wk Mon 5-11 Tue-Sun all day Closed 25-26 Dec, 1 Jan, Mon L Food Lunch Tue 12-8.30, Wed-Sat 12-9, Sun 12-4 Dinner Tue 12-8.30, Wed-Sat 12-9 ⊕ FREE HOUSE ◼ Marston's, Marble, Thornbridge, Phoenix ♂ Thatchers Gold. ♟ Facilities Non-diners area ❤ (Bar Garden Outside area) ♦♦ Children's portions Garden Outside area ⋒ Parking WiFi

KNUTSFORD
Map 15 SJ77

The Dog Inn
PICK OF THE PUBS

tel: 01625 861421 **Well Bank Ln, Over Peover WA16 8UP**
email: info@thedogpeover.co.uk
dir: *S from Knutsford take A50. Turn into Stocks Ln at The Whipping Stocks pub. 2m to inn*

Friendly inn with good food and local ales

This row of cottages housed village industries before being joined together to form a public house in 1860. In summer colourful flowerbeds, tubs and hanging baskets create quite a display, while the interior – rich with dark wood furniture and gleaming brass – generates year-round appeal. A range of cask-conditioned Cheshire ales from Weetwood in Tarporley is supported by a good selection of wines sold by the glass. The menu is strong on comfort food, such as classic prawn cocktail, or corned beef hash with egg and brown sauce. Interspersed are more complex choices such as main courses of sticky sesame chilli beef with cashew nuts and noodle salad; moules frites served with skinny fries and ciabatta; and smoked duck breast and orange salad, with toasted walnuts, sultanas, star anise and orange dressing. Comfort is again the keynote in desserts such as lemon tart with Chantilly cream, or chocolate torte with boozy cherries.

Open all day all wk Food Contact pub for food times ⊕ FREE HOUSE ◼ Weetwood Best Bitter & Cheshire Cat, Hydes. ♟ 10 Facilities Non-diners area ❤ (Bar Garden) ♦♦ Children's menu Children's portions Garden ⋒ Beer festival Parking WiFi ▭

PICK OF THE PUBS

The Bulls Head

MOBBERLEY   Map 15 SJ77

tel: 01565 873395 **Mill Ln WA16 7HX**
email: info@thebullsheadpub.co.uk
web: www.thebullsheadpub.co.uk
dir: *From Knutsford take A537, A5085*
to Mobberley

A 200-year-old pub with lots going on

This little gem thrives as both a village local and also a destination eatery. One attraction is the range of seven real ales from Cheshire microbreweries within 35 miles of the pub — Dunham Massey, Merlin, Redwillow, Storm, Tatton and Wincle — but you'll need more than one visit to make acquaintance with them all. Yet another, Weetwood, brews Mobberley Wobbly (aka Mobb Wobb) exclusively for the pub; it's a pint of this that comes with the 'legendary' hand-crafted steak and ale pie with chips and 'not so mushy' peas. Smart, traditionally styled dining rooms ensure a comfortable and convivial setting for wholesome home-cooked food, including delicious Sunday roasts of prime roast beef sirloin and Yorkshire pudding, served with roast potatoes, red cabbage, seasonal fresh vegetables and gravy. Lunchtime snacks served Monday to Friday until 5pm include a Lancashire Poacher rarebit or home-made haddock fish finger sandwich, both served with dressed salad and a handful of chips. A full meal may start with seafood

crockpot — sustainable white fish, prawns and Scottish salmon in creamy dill and white wine sauce, continue with Rose County calves' liver, smoked bacon, spiced red cabbage, creamy mash and onion gravy. A home-made pudding could be millionnaires' shortbread cheesecake. Wheat-free and gluten-free dishes are also available. The pub hosts two car clubs: the 'Three P' Club, which stands for 'Pub, Porsche and Pint', and for which you have to own, borrow or hire said German vehicle; and the Goodfellows, for which you must own anything but a Porsche. The clubs raise money for local charities including the village church. The pub garden comes into its own for the June Rose Queen Festival.

Open all day all wk **Food** Contact pub for food times Av main course £13 ⊕ FREE HOUSE ◀ Bulls Head Bitter, Mobberley Wobbly Ale, 1812 Overture Ale, White Bull ♨ Westons Stowford Press. ♟ 16 **Facilities** Non-diners area ♣ (Bar Garden) ♦♦ Children's portions Garden ⊓ Beer festival Parking WiFi ⛟ (notice required)

LOWER WITHINGTON
Map 15 SJ87

The Black Swan

tel: 01477 571770 **Trap St SK11 9EQ**
email: enquiries@blackswancheshire.com
dir: From A34 N of Congleton into Giantswood Rd signed Black Swan (brown sign). Pub on right before Lower Withington

Good pub grub in the heart of the Cheshire countryside

Just 15 minutes from Alderley Edge, The Black Swan is a quaint old pub, full of character. The atmosphere is friendly and welcoming, and the eclectic mix of decor and furnishings make for a relaxed setting for something to eat (food is served all day) or just a drink and a chat. Dogs are welcome in the bar and there are plenty of good walks round about. A wood-fired oven in the garden is lit on sunny weekends in the summer, and you can play boules in the pretty beer garden. Menus feature classic pub grub and some modern lighter dishes — lamb shank pie or home-made burgers.

Open all day all wk **Food** Mon-Sat 12-9, Sun 12-6 ⊕ FREE HOUSE ◀ Jennings Cumberland, Red Willow Mucky Duck, guest ales ♻ Westons Stowford Press. ☻ 12 **Facilities** Non-diners area ❅ (Bar Garden) ✚ Children's menu Children's portions Garden ☂ Parking WiFi

MARTON
Map 16 SJ86

The Davenport Arms
PICK OF THE PUBS

tel: 01260 224269 **Congleton Rd SK11 9HF**
email: info@thedavenportarms.co.uk
dir: 2m from Congleton on A34

Charming pub with pleasing home-made dishes

Dating from the 18th century, this former farmhouse with a large garden is steeped in history. It enjoys a picturesque site opposite the oldest half-timbered church still in use in Europe. Inside, many period details make for a comfortable atmosphere. Pull up a leather armchair or flop among cushions on the sofa by the roaring fire in the traditional bar, and choose from the good selection of Cheshire ales. There's something for everyone on the crowd-pleasing menu, all freshly made on the premises. Lunchtime favourites include curry of the day; wraps such as Cajun chicken with lettuce, citrus mayonnaise and sweet chilli; and baguettes. Evening choices could kick off with Portobello mushroom stuffed with goats' cheese accompanied by toasted pine nuts, spinach and red onion marmalade. Follow perhaps with Capesthorne pheasant and game hotpot with braised red cabbage. Alternatively look to the chef's specials list for dishes full of freshly delivered seasonal and local produce.

Open 12-3 6-11 (Fri-Sun 12-11) Closed Mon L (ex BHs) **Food** Lunch Tue-Fri 12-2.30, Sat 12-9, Sun 12-8 Dinner Tue-Fri 6-9, Sat 12-9, Sun 12-8. No food available 25-26 Dec ⊕ FREE HOUSE ◀ Theakston, Black Bull Bitter, Courage Directors, 2 rotating guest ales ♻ Westons Stowford Press. ☻ 9 **Facilities** Non-diners area ❅ (Garden) ✚ Children's menu Play area Garden ☂ Parking WiFi ▭ (notice required)

MOBBERLEY
Map 15 SJ77

The Bulls Head
PICK OF THE PUBS

See Pick of the Pubs on opposite page

The Church Inn
PICK OF THE PUBS

See Pick of the Pubs on page 82

MOULDSWORTH
Map 15 SJ57

The Goshawk

tel: 01928 740900 **Station Rd CH3 8AJ**
email: goshawk@woodwardandfalconer.com
dir: A51 from Chester onto A54. Left onto B5393 towards Frodsham. Into Mouldsworth, pub on left

Old railway inn popular with cyclists and walkers

This sturdy inn has a hint of Edwardian grandeur whilst benefiting from contemporary comforts; print-clad walls and dado rails, comfy sofas and open fires. Its village setting makes the most of the area's delights, including the many miles of footpaths, cycle trails and meres of nearby Delamere Forest; Chester is just one stop away on the train. Local ales draw an appreciative crowd, whilst the wide-ranging menu is matched by an extensive wine list. The menus, that include good fish and vegetarian choices, change every six weeks. The terrace and large grassy beer garden overlooks the well-kept bowling green which is frequently used in the summer months.

Open all day all wk 12-11 (Sun 12-10.30) Closed 25 Dec, 1 Jan ⊕ WOODWARD & FALCONER PUBS LTD ◀ Piffle, Balderdash, Weetwood, Conwy, guest ales. **Facilities** ✚ Children's menu Children's portions Play area Family room Garden Parking WiFi

NANTWICH
Map 15 SJ65

The Thatch Inn

tel: 01270 524223 **Wrexham Rd, Faddiley CW5 8JE**
email: johntribe@gmail.com
dir: From Nantwich follow Wrexham signs, inn on A534 in 4m

Enjoyable food in traditional pub with large beer garden

The Thatch is believed to be one of the oldest pubs in south Cheshire, if not the prettiest. This black-and-white inn has a three-quarter acre garden, while inside there are plentiful oak beams and open fires in winter. Enjoy a pint of Salopian Shropshire Gold with main courses such as barbecue chicken, home-made chips and salad; fish pie; gammon, egg and pineapple; or red Thai chicken curry. Light bites and sandwiches are served until 6pm. Children can choose from their own menu.

Open Mon-Tue 5.30-11, Wed-Thu 12-3 5.30-11, Fri-Sat 12-11, Sun 12-10.30 Closed Mon L & Tue L **Food** Lunch Wed-Fri 12-3, Sat 12-9, Sun 12-8.30 Dinner Mon-Fri 5.30-9, Sat 12-9, Sun 12-8.30 Set menu available Restaurant menu available all wk ⊕ ENTERPRISE INNS ◀ Salopian Shropshire Gold, Timothy Taylor Landlord. **Facilities** Non-diners area ✚ Children's menu Children's portions Play area Garden ☂ Parking WiFi ▭

PARKGATE
Map 15 SJ27

The Boat House

tel: 0151 336 4187 **I The Parade CH64 6RN**
email: boathouse@woodwardandfalconer.com
dir: On B5135, 3m from Heswall

Welcoming pub with unbeatable estuary location

The salt marshes begin right in front of The Boat House, so there's nothing to spoil the views of north Wales across the estuary. Once a thriving Deeside port, Parkgate's silted-up waters are now a nature reserve, although exceptionally high tides do still reach the walls of this striking black-and-white-timbered pub. Real ales include Hydes Original, while for food stay in the bar or head for the Dee-facing dining room. Menus, always with a good fish and seafood selection, might offer seared scallops and pork belly, followed by classic fish pie.

Open all day all wk 12-11 (Sun 12-10.30) **Food** Mon-Sat 12-9.30, Sun 12-9 ⊕ WOODWARD & FALCONER PUBS LTD ◀ Piffle & Balderdash, Brimstage Trapper's Hat, Hydes Original. ☻ 16 **Facilities** Non-diners area ✚ Children's menu Children's portions Outside area ☂ Parking WiFi ▭ (notice required)

PICK OF THE PUBS

The Church Inn

MOBBERLEY Map 15 SJ77

tel: 01565 873178 **WA16 7RD**
email: info@churchinnmobberley.co.uk
web: www.churchinnmobberley.co.uk
dir: *From Knutsford take B5085 towards Wilmslow. In Mobberley left into Church Ln. Pub opposite church*

Local produce drives the menu of this stylish village pub

Tim Bird and Mary McLaughlin have certainly put this old inn back on the map, together with their other pub in the village, The Bulls Head. The Church Inn has a stylish country appeal, pleasing locals and destination diners alike. On the edge of the village and opposite the 12th-century St Wilfrid's church, it is ideally situated between the bustling towns of Wilmslow and Knutsford and only eight miles from Manchester Airport. Surrounded by rolling Cheshire countryside, the attractive summer dining terrace and rear garden lead down to an old bowling green that boasts panoramic views across neighbouring fields. In the bar and boot room, a range of locally sourced ales includes Mallory's Mobberley Best, named after Mobberley-born mountaineer George Mallory; Tatton Brewery's Ale-Alujah may be making a guest appearance. A choice of intimate dining areas provide relaxed and comfortable seating for the perusal of the extensive menu, which includes

country tavern favourites such as steak and marrow burger with mature cheddar, chips, tomato, caramelised onion and cumin chutney. Gluten-free choices are a real strength: start a feast with halloumi, roasted tomatoes, red onion, aubergine, courgettes and sun-blush tomato and red pepper coulis, and follow perhaps with corn-fed chicken breast, tarragon gnocchi, roast baby vegetables with lemon and tarragon sauce. If you can manage a pudding, the home-made vanilla baked brûlée will round things off nicely, or look to a daily-changing board of Cheshire artisan cheeses. Canines are more than welcome in the bar and the boot room; a bowl of dog biscuits, together with dog 'beer' (meat-based stock) to refresh them, are very thoughtful touches.

Open all day all wk **Food** all wk, all day Restaurant menu available all wk ⊕ FREE HOUSE ◀ Dunham Massey Mallory's Mobberley Best, Tatton Brewery Ale-Alujah, guest ales ♻ Ty Gwyn, Apple County Cider, South West Orchards. ♟ 16 **Facilities** Non-diners area 🐾 (Bar Garden) 🚼 Children's portions Garden 🪑 Parking WiFi 🚌 (notice required)

PARKGATE *continued*

The Ship

tel: 0151 336 3931 **The Parade CH64 6SA**
email: info@the-shiphotel.co.uk
dir: *A540 from Chester towards Neston. Left onto B5134 to Neston town centre. At T-junct right onto B5136. Next left onto B5135 to Parkgate. Hotel 50yds on right on The Parade*

Free house with fine views of the Welsh mountains

Parkgate's port is now silted up, but the views from The Parade across what is now the RSPB's Dee Estuary bird reserve to the Welsh coast don't change. With 18th-century origins, The Ship was regularly visited by Lord Nelson and his mistress Lady Hamilton, who had been born in nearby Neston. Real ale names to conjure with in the contemporary bar include Trapper's Hat from Wirral brewery Brimstage and Weetwood Oast-House Gold from Cheshire. Enjoy home-made food by the fire, with options such as pheasant wrapped in pancetta; Cumberland sausage and mash; surf and turf; Thai green curry, and specials.

Open all day all wk Food all wk 12-9 ⊕ FREE HOUSE ◀ Brimstage Trapper's Hat, Weetwood Oast-House Gold, Jennings Cumberland Ale, Tatton Gold. ♟ 15 Facilities Non-diners area ◀ Children's menu Children's portions Outside area ⋈ Parking WiFi ▄ (notice required)

▮ PRESTBURY   Map 16 SJ87

The Legh Arms

tel: 01625 829130 **The Village SK10 4DG**
email: legharms@hotmail.co.uk
dir: *On A538 (New Road)*

Serving good food all day every day

Trendy Prestbury is popular with Premiership footballers and they're lucky to have the gabled and part-timbered Legh Arms on their doorstep. Fine ales from nearby Robinsons Brewery are served in the bar with its oak beams and roaring fires. You'll find simpler fare on offer there, such as salads, sharing platters, sandwiches and pub favourites. For a celeb-spotting special dinner, eat in the restaurant, where dishes use herbs from the pub's own walled garden. You might choose Cheshire game terrine followed by pan-fried calves' liver. The beer garden has a wood-burning stove for cooler nights.

Open all day all wk Food all wk 12-10 ⊕ ROBINSONS ◀ 1892, Hatters & Unicorn. ♟ Facilities Non-diners area ❀ (Garden) ◀ Children's portions Garden ⋈ Parking WiFi

▮ SPURSTOW   Map 15 SJ55

The Yew Tree Inn

tel: 01829 260274 **Long Ln CW6 9RD**
email: info@theyewtreebunbury.com
dir: *400mtrs from A49*

Seriously good ales and food

Built by the Earl of Crewe, this is a sympathetically refurbished 19th-century pub. Inside, the original beams and open fires are a reminder of the pub's history, while the terrace is a more modern addition and perfect for summer dining. Up to eight real ales and two draught ciders testify to the pub's serious attention to quality refreshments, and the Easter weekend beer festival shouldn't be missed. But diners are well rewarded too, with the kitchen producing seasonal menus driven by local produce. Sticky baby back ribs with braised cabbage, fennel and apple make an irresistible starter, and any main course served with beef dripping chips will not disappoint.

Open all day all wk Food Mon-Thu 12-9.30, Fri-Sat 12-10, Sun 12-9 ⊕ FREE HOUSE ◀ Stonehouse Station Bitter, 7 guest ales Ở Westons Stowford Press, guest cider. ♟ 14 Facilities Non-diners area ❀ (Bar Garden Outside area) ◀ Children's menu Children's portions Garden Outside area ⋈ Beer festival Parking WiFi ▄ (notice required)

▮ STYAL   Map 15 SJ88

The Ship Inn

tel: 01625 444888 **Altrincham Rd SK9 4JE**
email: info@theshipstyal.co.uk
dir: *From B5166 N of Wilmslow, left signed Styal into Altrincham Rd*

All that's good in a pub still casting its spell

Styal's history is closely bound to that of the local cotton industry; many of the Ship's customers call in after visiting nearby Quarry Bank Mill. The 350-year-old building was once a shippon, an ancient term for a farm's cattle shed; it became a pub when the farmer owner started brewing for the locals. Happily, craft ales are still high in the pub's attractions, with Weetwood Cheshire Cat and Big Tree Bitter by Dunham Massey usually among the five on offer. There's something for everyone on the menu, with traditional favourites often given a creative spin. Children have their own selection, and are welcome until 8pm. There's a beer festival in the summer.

Open all wk 11-11 (Sun 11-10.30) Food Mon-Sat 12-9, Sun & BHs 12-8 ⊕ FREE HOUSE ◀ Weetwood Best & Cheshire Cat, Dunham Massey Big Tree Bitter, Timothy Taylor Boltmaker, guest ales Ở Hereford Cider. ♟ 11 Facilities Non-diners area ◀ Children's menu Children's portions Garden ⋈ Beer festival Parking WiFi ▄ (notice required)

▮ SWETTENHAM   Map 15 SJ86

The Swettenham Arms   PICK OF THE PUBS

tel: 01477 571284 **Swettenham Ln CW12 2LF**
email: info@swettenhamarms.co.uk
dir: *M6 junct 18 to Holmes Chapel, then A535 towards Jodrell Bank. 3m right (Forty Acre Lane) to Swettenham (NB do not use postcode for Sat Nav; enter Swettenham Lane)*

Haunted 16th-century inn

Concealed from the road by the parish church, this ancient inn stands next door to the renowned Lovell Quinta Arboretum. A comfortable pub full of quiet corners, it draws an appreciative year-round crowd. In the newly refitted bar is a generous selection of real ales, lagers and ciders and 12 wines by the glass. Diners choosing from a winter menu, for example, can expect to find Cheshire gammon with fried duck egg and hand-cut chips; a choice of puff-pastry pies; braised ox cheek with smoked mash and bordelaise sauce; lamb Madras with rice; and Portobello mushroom, pepper, courgette and aubergine stack with white wine sauce. Many dishes benefit from the inn's home-grown vegetables. Sandwiches and ploughman's are available from noon till 6pm, and there's a children's menu. The building itself is tucked into a former Tudor nunnery and has an intriguing record of ghost-sightings. Maybe you'll meet Sarah, the black-clad nun.

Open all wk 11.30am-closc (Closed Mon-Fri 3.30-6 Winter) Food all wk 12-close Av main course £15 ⊕ FREE HOUSE ◀ Timothy Taylor Landlord, Sharp's Doom Bar, Bollington Best, Courage Directors, Moorhouse's Pride of Pendle, Slater's Top Totty, Black Sheep, Beartown, Wells Bombardier, Fuller's London Pride, Tatton, Marston's Wainwright Ở Addlestones, Westons Old Rosie. ♟ 12 Facilities Non-diners area ❀ (Bar Garden) ◀ Children's menu Children's portions Play area Garden ⋈ Parking WiFi ▄ (notice required)

PICK OF THE PUBS

The Bear's Paw ★★★★★ INN 🏵

WARMINGHAM   Map 15 SJ76

tel: 01270 526317
School Ln CW11 3QN
email: info@thebearspaw.co.uk
web: www.thebearspaw.co.uk
dir: *M6 junct 18, A54, A533 towards Sandbach. Follow signs for village*

Refined cooking and stylish accommodation

With its prominent central gable and some nods towards typical Cheshire black-and-white half-timbering, this stylish 19th-century gastro-inn has clearly had a lot of money spent on it. Acres — well it seems like acres — of reclaimed antique oak flooring, leather sofas surrounding a huge open fireplace, bookshelves offering plenty of choice for a good read, and more than 200 pictures and archive photos lining the oak-panelled walls. The bar, in which stands a carved wooden bear with a salmon in its mouth, offers a half dozen cask ales from local microbreweries, including the somewhat appropriate Beartown in Congleton, Weetwood in Tarporley, and Tatton in Knutsford, as well as Hereford Dry Cider. Whether you're sitting out front looking across to the churchyard or in the clubby interior, there's plenty of comfortable dining space in which to sample wholesome, locally sourced food from wide-ranging daily menus that expertly blend the classic with the

modern. Take, for example, starters like goats' cheese crotin, baked balsamic fig and beetroot three ways; or braised venison hash cake with mulled pear purée, pan fried hen's egg and crispy pancetta; and main dishes such as pork, apple and cider pie with hand-cut chips and garden peas; cumin-roasted rump of lamb with harissa-spiced couscous, cucumber and mint yogurt and confit tomato; or pan-seared calves' liver with a crispy haggis fritter, roasted root vegetables, and creamed potato, finished with sultana and sherry jus. Great for sharing are the imaginative deli boards, which come laden with local cheeses, charcuterie or pickled and smoked fish, and don't miss the Sunday roast lunches.

Open all day all wk **Food** Mon-Thu 12-9.30, Fri-Sat 12-10, Sun 12-9 ⊕ FREE HOUSE 🍺 Weetwood Best Bitter, Cheshire Cat & Eastgate Ale, Spitting Feathers, Beartown, Tatton Ö Hereford Dry Cider. 🍷 12
Facilities Non-diners area 🐾 (Bar Restaurant Garden) 👶 Children's menu Children's portions Garden 🪑 Parking WiFi 🚌 (notice required) **Rooms** 17

TARPORLEY Map 15 SJ56

Alvanley Arms Inn ★★★ INN

tel: 01829 760200 **Forest Rd, Cotebrook CW6 9DS**
email: info@alvanleyarms.co.uk **web:** www.alvanleyarms.co.uk
dir: On A49, 1.5m N of Tarporley

A new look at this popular inn

Newly refurbished to a high standard, this lovely 16th-century former coaching inn has a traditional, oak-beamed bar where hand-pulled ales complement freshly prepared dishes, based on ingredients from local family businesses; the chef patron makes his own bread from local Walk Mill flour. Dishes range from starters and light bites like herb-crumbed mushrooms with garlic mayonnaise; and tandoori chicken skewers on naan bread with salad, to sandwiches, salads and pub classics – maybe breaded scampi; lamb tagine; or cottage pie. There are steaks and burgers from the grill and seafood treats like fish pie or paella.

Open all day all wk 12-11 **Food** Lunch Mon-Fri 12-2, Sat-Sun 12-9 Dinner Mon-Fri 6-9, Sat-Sun 12-9 Set menu available Restaurant menu available all wk ⊕ ROBINSONS ◪ Dizzy Blonde, Trooper, Unicorn, guest ales Ò Westons Stowford Press. ♟ 12 **Facilities** Non-diners area ♟ Children's menu Children's portions Garden ⊼ Parking WiFi ⚋ (notice required) **Rooms** 7

The Swan, Tarporley

tel: 01829 733818 **50 High St CW6 0AG**
email: info@theswantarporley.co.uk
dir: From junct of A49 & A51 into Tarporley. Pub on right in village centre

Restored coaching inn where hospitality rules

The 16th-century Swan has been the hub of Cheshire's picturesque Tarporley village for over 500 years; in days gone by it was a convenient resting place for travellers journeying between London and Chester. The Swan opens early – 7am on weekdays, and 8am at weekends. While locals stop by for a pint of Weetwood's Eastgate, the chef prepares local produce for the seasonal menus which change weekly. Bar nibbles include pickled eggs and pork scratchings, while main courses may proffer steak and Guinness pie; sticky sesame beef stir-fry; or warm caramelised onion and broccoli quiche with spinach and walnut salad. Look out for the summer beer festival.

Open all day all wk 7am-11pm (Sat 8am-11pm Sun & BH Mon 8am-10.30pm) **Food** Mon-Sat 12-10, Sun & BH Mon 12-8 ⊕ FREE HOUSE ◪ Weetwood Best Bitter, Cheshire Cat & Eastgate Ale, Timothy Taylor Boltmaker. ♟ 13 **Facilities** Non-diners area ♟ (Bar Garden) ♟ Children's menu Children's portions Family room Garden Outside area ⊼ Beer festival Parking WiFi ⚋ (notice required)

WARMINGHAM Map 15 SJ76

The Bear's Paw ★★★★★ INN ⊛ PICK OF THE PUBS

See Pick of the Pubs on opposite page

WRENBURY Map 15 SJ54

The Dusty Miller

tel: 01270 780537 **CW5 8HG**
email: info@thedusty.co.uk
dir: Phone for detailed directions

Transformed property on Llangollen Canal

This beautifully converted 18th-century corn mill is beside the Llangollen Canal in the rural village of Wrenbury. The pub's large arched windows offer views of passing boats, while a black-and-white lift bridge, designed by Thomas Telford, completes the picture-postcard setting. Alongside a good choice of real ales, the modern British menu, which mainly relies on ingredients from the region, offers frequently changing options to suit everyone.

Open 12-12 Closed Mon **Food** Lunch Tue-Fri 12-3, Sat 12-9.30, Sun 12-8 Dinner Tue-Fri 6-9, Sat 12-9.30, Sun 12-8 ⊕ ROBINSONS ◪ Old Tom & Dizzy Blonde, Ò Westons Stowford Press & Traditional. ♟ 12 **Facilities** Non-diners area ♟ (All areas) ♟ Children's menu Children's portions Garden Outside area ⊼ Parking WiFi ⚋ (notice required)

CORNWALL & ISLES OF SCILLY

ALTARNUN Map 2 SX28

Rising Sun Inn

tel: 01566 86636 **PL15 7SN**
email: risingsuninn@hotmail.co.uk
dir: From A30 follow Altarnun signs onto unclassified road. Through Altarnun & Treween to T-junct. Inn 100yds on left

Moorland free house worth leaving the A30 for

It's still fine to arrive by horse at this inviting, 18th-century moorland inn – there's a hitching post in the car park. On horseback could be the best way home, too, given the real ales from the village's Penpont brewery, Skinner's Betty Stogs, and also Cornish Orchards and Skinner's Press Gang ciders. Lunch and dinner dishes include all kinds, from bangers and mash to lobster (in season). The specials board changes daily, but always focuses on seasonal and locally sourced produce. Home of the original 'Boxeater' steak.

Open all wk 12-2.30 5.30-11 (Sat 12-11 Sun & BHs 12-10.30) **Food** Lunch all wk 12-2 Dinner all wk 6-9 ⊕ FREE HOUSE ◪ Penpont St Nonna's, Skinner's Betty Stogs, guest ales Ò Cornish Orchards, Skinner's Press Gang. ♟ 10 **Facilities** Non-diners area ♟ (Bar Garden) ♟ Children's menu Children's portions Garden ⊼ Beer festival Parking WiFi ⚋ (notice required)

BODINNICK Map 2 SX15

The Old Ferry Inn ★★★ INN

tel: 01726 870237 **PL23 1LX**
email: info@oldferryinn.co.uk **web:** www.oldferryinn.co.uk
dir: From Liskeard on A38 to Dobwalls, left at lights onto A390. After 3m left onto B3359 signed Looe. Right signed Lerryn/Bodinnick/Polruan for 5m

Traditional Cornish pub with splendid estuary views

Daphne du Maurier wrote many of her novels at 'Ferryside', the house next door to this 400-year-old inn by the River Fowey. You can watch people messing about in boats from one of the sun terraces, stay in the bar among the nautical memorabilia, or cosy up in the stone-walled snug. A long list of snacks includes Cornish Pasties, while among the mains are cod in Sharp's ale batter; wholetail scampi and chips; roast chicken breast with local cider, cream and apple sauce; and wild mushroom and thyme penne pasta. The adjacent ferry carries cars over to Fowey town.

Open all day all wk **Food** Lunch all wk 12-3 Dinner all wk 6-9 ⊕ FREE HOUSE ◪ Sharp's Cornish Coaster & Own, guest ale Ò Haye Farm, Sharp's Orchard Cornish Cider. **Facilities** Non-diners area ♟ (Bar Outside area) ♟ Children's menu Family room Outside area ⊼ Parking WiFi **Rooms** 12

BOLINGEY
Map 2 SW75

Bolingey Inn

tel: 01872 571626 **Penwartha Rd TR6 0DH**
email: michaelsanders@bolingeyinn.co.uk
dir: *From B3285 in Perranporth at rdbt into Station Rd. Approx 0.5m right signed Bolingey. Pub 0.5m on right*

Delightful pub associated with Cornwall's former mining industry

In a previous life, the Bolingey Inn was reputedly a count house for the vicinity's mines; doubtless the money men would have appreciated ale on tap without needing to leave the building. 'More landlords than can be researched', the menu tells us, have served here since its change of use, some making structural changes during their tenure. Today the Bolingey charms its clients with its atmosphere, serves four bitters from the likes of Sharp's and Fuller's, and prepares good home-cooked dishes in the kitchen. Most ingredients are sourced locally, with the specials board listing fresh fish options. Beer festivals in April and October.

Open all day all wk **Food** Lunch all wk 12-2 Dinner all wk 6-9.30 ⊕ PUNCH TAVERNS ◀ Sharp's Doom Bar, Greene King Abbot Ale, Butcombe, St Austell Proper Job, Fuller's London Pride ♂ Thatchers. **Facilities** Non-diners area ♥ (Bar Outside area) ♦♦ Children's menu Children's portions Outside area ⋈ Beer festival Parking WiFi ➡ (notice required)

BOSCASTLE
Map 2 SX09

The Wellington Hotel ★★★ HL ◉◉   PICK OF THE PUBS

See Pick of the Pubs on opposite page

CADGWITH
Map 2 SW71

Cadgwith Cove Inn

tel: 01326 290513 **TR12 7JX**
email: garryandhelen@cadgwithcoveinn.co.uk
dir: *A3083 from Helston towards Lizard. Left to Cadgwith*

Local seafood and beer in a former smugglers' haunt

A visit to this 300-year-old pub in the largely unspoilt fishing hamlet on the Lizard coastline will illustrate why it once appealed to smugglers. Relics in the atmospheric bars attest to a rich seafaring history; the cove itself is just across the old pilchard cellar from its sunny front patio. Traditional favourites include fish and chips; crab salad; and vegetarian trio of the day. Quiz nights are on Mondays, folk music on Tuesdays, the Cadgwith Singers perform every Friday and there are seafood buffets on Saturdays throughout the summer; or you could time a visit for the October beer and cider festival.

Open all day all wk **Food** Lunch all wk 12-3 Dinner all wk 6-9 Restaurant menu available all wk ⊕ PUNCH TAVERNS ◀ Sharp's, Skinner's, guest ales ♂ Westons Stowford Press, Thatchers. ⬤ 9 **Facilities** Non-diners area ♥ (Bar Restaurant Outside area) ♦♦ Children's menu Children's portions Outside area ⋈ Beer festival Cider festival WiFi

CHAPEL AMBLE
Map 2 SW97

The Maltsters Arms

tel: 01208 812473 **PL27 6EU**
dir: *A39 from Wadebridge towards Camelford. In 1m left signed Chapel Amble. Pub on right in village*

Traditional home-cooking in charming Cornish village inn

In the pretty Cornish village of Chapel Amble and a short drive from Rock and Port Isaac, The Maltsters Arms oozes old-world charm and character, from slate floors and copper pots to 'mind-your-head' beams and open fires. A pub at the heart of the community with a quiz night and must-book Sunday carvery, the food is home-

cooked and traditional. Pub favourites of burgers and beer-battered fish and chips appear alongside main menu dishes such as roasted cod loin, mussels, prawns and saffron linguine; and local lamb shank with garlic and spring onion mash and redcurrant jus. There's a beer and cider festival on the Spring Bank Holiday weekend in late May.

Open all wk 11-3 6-11 **Food** Lunch all wk 11-3 Dinner all wk 6-9 Set menu available ⊕ FREE HOUSE ◀ Sharp's Doom Bar & Atlantic IPA ♂ Westons Old Rosie. ⬤ 11 **Facilities** Non-diners area ♥ (Bar Outside area) ♦♦ Children's menu Children's portions Outside area ⋈ Beer festival Cider festival Parking WiFi ➡ (notice required)

CONSTANTINE
Map 2 SW72

Trengilly Wartha Inn   PICK OF THE PUBS

tel: 01326 340332 **Nancenoy TR11 5RP**
email: reception@trengilly.co.uk
dir: *Follow signs to Constantine, left towards Gweek until 1st sign for inn, left & left again at next sign, continue to inn*

Friendly, family retreat in a sheltered valley

In this charming 600-year-old inn near the Helford River, Will and Lisa Lea have created a popular bistro and local. The Cornish name means 'a settlement above the trees', although it actually lies at the foot of a densely wooded valley. In the black-beamed bar, ever-changing local real ales might include Penzance Potion No 9, served from the stillage shared with Healey's Cornish Rattler and Ty Gwyn ciders; 15 wines are sold by the glass, and over 40 malts clamour for attention. A typical dish, most likely sourced from a local farm or fishing boat, could be one of the specials, such as spring onion with roasted crab meat; chicken satay with fragrant rice; or wild mushroom and cheddar cheese risotto. Pub classics include 8oz Cornish sirloin steaks with home-made chips and mushrooms; and Thai pork burger with chilli mayonnaise. Meadows surround the pretty beer garden and its vine-shaded pergola.

Open all wk 11-3 6-12 **Food** Lunch all wk 12-2.15 Dinner all wk 6.30-9.30 ⊕ FREE HOUSE ◀ Sharp's, Penzance Potion No 9, guest ales ♂ Healey's Cornish Rattler, Thatchers Gold, Ty Gwyn. ⬤ 15 **Facilities** Non-diners area ♥ (Bar Garden) ♦♦ Children's menu Children's portions Play area Family room Garden ⋈ Beer festival Cider festival Parking WiFi ➡ (notice required)

CRAFTHOLE
Map 3 SX35

The Finnygook Inn

tel: 01503 230338 **PL11 3BQ**
email: eat@finnygook.co.uk
dir: *10m W of Tamar Bridge take A374 S. In 3m right signed Crafthole & follow pub signs. From Torpoint take A374, 5m to Antony. Left in Antony, 1m to T-junct. 3m to Crafthole*

Old coaching inn serving peninsula-brewed beers

This 16th-century pub is located in a hamlet above Portwrinkle's cove-nibbled coast. They say the ghost of smuggler Silas Finny walks the cliffs and byways hereabouts; so, too, do ramblers and visitors seeking to share the local beers from St Austell, Penpont, Harbour and Bays breweries, and tempting fodder available here. The Finnygook serves a host of reliable favourites – Cornish crab, prawn and crayfish cocktail; pork and herb sausages, spring onion mash and caramelised onion gravy; and home-cooked ham, free-range eggs and thick-cut chips – taken by the log fire, in the library room or on the terrace with distant views up the Tamar estuary.

Open all day all wk **Food** Lunch Mon-Sat 12-2.30, Sun 12-5 Dinner Mon-Sat 6-9 ⊕ FREE HOUSE ◀ St Austell Tribute & Proper Job, Penpont Cornish Arvor, Dartmoor, Harbour, Bays, Timothy Taylor Landlord ♂ Thatchers, Healey's Cornish Rattler. ⬤ 10 **Facilities** Non-diners area ♥ (Bar Garden) ♦♦ Children's menu Children's portions Garden ⋈ Parking WiFi ➡ (notice required)

PICK OF THE PUBS

The Wellington Hotel ★★★ HL ◉◉

BOSCASTLE   Map 2 SX09

tel: 01840 250202
The Harbour PL35 0AQ
email: info@wellingtonhotelboscastle.com
web: www.wellingtonhotelboscastle.com
dir: *A30/A395 at Davidstow follow Boscastle signs. B3266 to village. Right into New Rd*

Popular pub and fine dining restaurant on the Cornish coast

This listed 16th-century coaching inn with its castellated tower sits on one of England's most stunning coastlines, at the end of a glorious wooded valley where the rivers Jordan and Valency meet; in 1852 it was renamed in honour of the Duke of Wellington. Known affectionately as 'The Welly' by both locals and loyal guests, it retains much of its original charm as in the traditional Long Bar, complete with minstrels' gallery, where a good selection of Cornish ales, ciders such as Cornish Rattler, and malt whiskies are to be found. Bar snacks here embrace sandwiches and soup of the day, along with small plates. For a proper lunch, look to the blackboard for daily specials or the carte for the likes of beer-battered haddock and chips; slow-cooked pork belly with dauphinoise potatoes, cauliflower and curry oil; and winter vegetable risotto, parmesan and truffle oil. Follow perhaps with prune tart and Armagnac ice cream; or sticky toffee

pudding, toffee sauce and clotted cream. For fine dining, head to the first floor to find the Waterloo Restaurant. The kitchen team prepares fresh local produce – none fresher or more local than the seafood landed by the boats in the harbour a few yards away. Starters may include Cornish mussels with cider and clotted cream, then continue with grilled sea bass, fennel, dill, French beans, potatoes and mustard; and finally summer fruit cheesecake, raspberries and jelly. Children are well catered for with their own menu, and some adult main courses can be served in half-size portions.

Open all day all wk 11-11 **Food** Lunch Mon-Fri 12-3, Sat-Sun 12-9 Dinner Mon-Fri 6-9, Sat-Sun 12-9 Av main

course £13.50 Restaurant menu available Tue-Sat ⊕ FREE HOUSE ◀ St Austell Tribute, Sharp's Doom Bar, Skinner's Betty Stogs ⚬ Cornish Orchards, Healey's Cornish Rattler. **Facilities** Non-diners area ❤ (Bar Garden Outside area) ⁇ Children's menu Children's portions Family room Garden Outside area ⊟ Parking WiFi 🚌 (notice required) **Rooms** 17

CUBERT
Map 2 SW75

The Smugglers' Den Inn

tel: 01637 830209 **Trebellan TR8 5PY**
email: hello@thesmugglersden.co.uk
dir: *From Newquay take A3075 to Cubert x-roads, then right, then left signed Trebellan, 0.5m to inn*

Classic coastal pub with plenty of local seafood

After arriving as the new owners, Jason and Helen Allen quickly stamped their personality on this thatched 16th-century pub, just 15 minutes from Newquay. Popular with locals and visitors alike, the pub comprises a long bar, family room, children's play area, courtyards and huge beer garden. Local ingredients are the cornerstone of the family-friendly menu, which might kick off with Cornish mussels cooked in cider, shallots, garlic and cream. Home-made fish pie; chicken curry; and wild mushroom Stroganoff are typical main courses. Leave a space for the lemon and lime posset.

Open all wk 11.30-3 6-11 (Sun 11-11) **Food** Lunch all wk 12-3 Dinner Mon-Thu & Sun 6-9, Fri-Sat 6-9.30 ⊕ FREE HOUSE ◀ Sharp's Doom Bar, St Austell Tribute, guest ales Ŏ Healey's Cornish Rattler, Thatchers Gold. **Facilities** Non-diners area ❖ (Bar Garden) ◀ Children's menu Play area Family room Garden ⏎ Beer festival Parking WiFi ▄▄▄

DULOE
Map 2 SX25

The Plough

tel: 01503 262556 **PL14 4PN**
email: enquiries@ploughduloe.co.uk
dir: *From A34 to Dobwalls. In Dobwalls follow Duloe signs*

Low-mileage food and cider

Set deep in the Cornish countryside, Richard Shepherd and Louisa Duggie's pub is found in a quiet village midway between the bustling towns of Liskeard to the north and Looe to the south. Duloe is also home to the Cornish Orchards Company, so no surprise to find its ciders on tap alongside St Austell ales in The Plough's bar. Richard and Louisa's use of local produce extends when possible to the menus. A starter of Cornish Yarg and chive croquettes with mulled cider Cumberland sauce, for example, could be followed by a whole gratinated crab with Plough bread and mixed leaves. Finish with ginger parkin and ice cream, or Cornish cheeses with frozen grapes and fig and apple chutney.

Open all wk 12-3 6-11 **Food** Lunch Mon-Sat 12-2, Sun 12-3 Dinner Mon-Sat 6-9, Sun 6-8 Restaurant menu available all wk ⊕ FREE HOUSE ◀ Sharp's Doom Bar, St Austell Tribute, guest ale Ŏ Cornish Orchards Gold Cider.
Facilities Non-diners area ❖ (Bar Restaurant Garden) ◀ Children's menu Children's portions Family room Garden ⏎ Parking WiFi ▄▄▄ (notice required)

FEOCK
Map 2 SW83

The Punchbowl & Ladle

tel: 01872 862237 **Penelewey TR3 6QY**
email: enquiries@puchbowlandladle.com
dir: *From Truro take A39 towards Falmouth, after Shell garage at Playing Place rdbt follow King Harry Ferry signs. 0.5m, pub on right*

Local produce served in this gorgeous thatched inn

Local rumour has it that the fireplace in the bar of this lovely old pub close to the King Harry Ferry was used to burn contraband when customs officers dropped by. Settle down in the cosy low-beamed bar and make your choices from a menu that uses seasonal ingredients sourced from local Cornish suppliers. Typical dishes are slow-braised lamb shank, onion potato cake, crispy kale with carrot and coriander purée; or wild mushroom risotto with leeks and garlic. Salads and sandwiches are also on offer. In summer, head for the suntrap walled garden or patio with a glass of St Austell Proper Job or Cornish Rattler cider.

Open all day all wk **Food** Lunch Mon-Sat 12-2.30, Sun 12-3 Dinner all wk 6-9 ⊕ ST AUSTELL BREWERY ◀ Tribute, Proper Job, Trelawny, HSD & Cornish Best Ŏ Healey's Cornish Rattler. ℙ 16 **Facilities** Non-diners area ❖ (Bar Garden) ◀ Children's menu Children's portions Garden ⏎ Parking WiFi ▄▄▄

FOWEY
Map 2 SX15

The Ship Inn

tel: 01726 832230 **Trafalgar Square PL23 1AZ**
dir: *From A30 take B3269 & A390*

Very old inn situated in Fowey's narrow streets

One of Fowey's oldest buildings, the Ship was built in 1570 by John Rashleigh, who sailed to the Americas with Walter Raleigh. Given Fowey's riverside position, assume a good choice of fish, including River Fowey mussels as a starter or main; and grilled sardines in garlic. Other options include Mr Kittow's pork sausages and mash; spinach, asparagus and wild mushroom risotto. St Austell ales, real fires and a long tradition of genial hospitality add the final touches.

Open all day all wk 11am-mdnt (Fri-Sat 11am-1am) ⊕ ST AUSTELL BREWERY ◀ Tribute & Proper Job, Dartmoor IPA Ŏ Healey's Cornish Rattler & Pear Rattler. **Facilities** ❖ (Bar) ◀ Children's menu Children's portions Family room WiFi

GUNNISLAKE
Map 3 SX47

The Rising Sun Inn

tel: 01822 832201 **Calstock Rd PL18 9BX**
email: therisingsungunnislake@yahoo.co.uk
dir: *From Tavistock take A390 to Gunnislake. Left after lights into Calstock Rd. Inn approx 500mtrs on right*

Traditional picture-postcard pub in a lovely valley

This two-roomed pub has fabulous views from the pretty terraced gardens of the Tamar Valley and the river flowing towards Plymouth. Gunnislake is just in Cornwall, so it's understandable that Dartmoor Brewery's Jail Ale and Legend draught beers are served, while in a nod to neighbouring Devon, so is Otter. Good old British menu favourites include home-made beef chilli and curries; grilled gammon; sustainable cod in Symonds cider batter; and chicken goujons served in a basket. Brie, hazelnut and cranberry Wellington is a vegetarian option. Great walks start and finish from the pub.

Open all day all wk **Food** Contact pub for food times Restaurant menu available all wk ⊕ FREE HOUSE ◀ Exmoor Ales, Driftwood Spars, Otter, Dartmoor Legend & Jail Ale, local guest ales Ŏ Symonds, Thatchers Gold, guest ciders. ℙ 25 **Facilities** Non-diners area ❖ (Bar Garden) ◀ Children's menu Children's portions Play area Garden ⏎ Beer festival Cider festival Parking WiFi ▄▄▄ (notice required)

GUNWALLOE
Map 2 SW62

The Halzephron Inn
PICK OF THE PUBS

tel: 01326 240406 **TR12 7QB**
email: enquiries@halzephron-inn.co.uk
dir: *3m S of Helston on A3083, right to Gunwalloe, through village. Inn on left*

Stunning views and lots of local seafood on the menu

The name of the inn derives from Als Yfferin, old Cornish for 'Cliffs of Hell', an appropriate description for this hazardous stretch of Atlantic coastline. Located high above Gunwalloe Fishing Cove, this 500-year-old, rugged stone inn commands an enviable position, with breathtaking views across Mount's Bay. On sunny days grab a front bench and enjoy a pint of St Austell Tribute while looking out to St Michael's Mount. The two interconnecting bars feature cosy log fires, fishing memorabilia, and watercolours of local scenes. The à la carte and daily changing specials utilise the best Cornish produce available, including fresh seafood. Everything is home made, with the likes of Cornish seafood chowder; and baked camembert with roasted garlic and redcurrant jelly among the starters. Main courses include white crab meat-stuffed chicken breast with creamy dill sauce; steak and ale pie; and rare-cooked pan-fried calves' liver, smoked bacon, creamed potatoes, onion tart and red wine sauce.

Open all day all wk 11-11 (Sun 12-10.30) **Food** Lunch Mon-Sat 12-2.30, Sun 12-3 Dinner all wk 6-9 Av main course £10.95 ⊕ FREE HOUSE ◀ Sharp's Own, Doom Bar & Special, St Austell Tribute, Skinner's Betty Stogs ♂ Thatchers Gold. ♀ 10 **Facilities** Non-diners area ❤ (Bar Garden) ♦♦ Children's menu Children's portions Play area Family room Garden ⊨ Parking WiFi ▄▄ (notice required)

GWEEK
Map 2 SW72

Black Swan ★★★★ INN

tel: 01326 221502 **TR12 6TU**
email: bookings@blackswangweek.co.uk **web:** www. blackswangweek.co.uk
dir: In village centre

Home-cooked food and Cornish beers

This delightful inn is located in the picturesque village of Gweek on the River Helford, a stone's throw from the popular National Seal Sanctuary. The Black Swan has become famous for their sirloin steaks, but also offers signature dishes of steak and Guinness pie with creamy mash, and Cajun chicken breast, chips and peas. There's a choice of regularly changing specials too to widen the options. Not to be missed is a selection of Cornish ales and guest ales. If you'd like to stay over the pub has stylish bedrooms delightfully named Raspberry, Blackberry, Gooseberry and Mulberry.

Open all day all wk **Food** all wk, all day ⊕ PUNCH TAVERNS ◀ Sharp's Doom Bar, Bass, St Austell Tribute, Skinner's Betty Stogs, guest ales ♂ Thatchers, Addlestones. ♀ 9 **Facilities** Non-diners area ❤ (Bar Garden) ♦♦ Children's menu Children's portions Garden ⊨ Parking WiFi ▄▄ (notice required) **Rooms** 4

GWITHIAN
Map 2 SW54

The Red River Inn

tel: 01736 753223 **1 Prosper Hill TR27 5BW**
email: louisa.saville@googlemail.com
dir: Exit A30 at Loggans Moor rdbt, follow Hayle signs. Immediately take 3rd exit at mini rdt onto B3301 signed Gwithian. 2m to pub in village centre

A village pub that offers something for everyone

The name of this 200-year-old pub recalls the colour of the village river when tin was mined locally. Close by runs the South West Coastal Path, and the beach is popular with surfers who, even in their wetsuits, are warmly welcomed here. Among its attractions are up to five, ever-changing Cornish real ales, an Easter weekend beer and cider festival, and food that ranges from steak and Stilton ciabatta or patatas bravas to lamb and rocket salad, steaks and Middle Eastern, Mexican and Indonesian dishes. Vegetarians might choose borlotti bean and chestnut cassoulet. There's live music, curry and quiz nights and a pool table is available in the winter months.

Open 12-11 summer (Tue-Fri 12-2 5.30-11 Sat-Sun 12-11 winter) Closed Mon (winter only) **Food** Lunch all wk 12-2 Dinner all wk 6-9 ⊕ FREE HOUSE ◀ Sharp's Own, Spingo, Cornish Chough, Tintagel Harbour Special ♂ Thatchers Gold, Healey's Cornish Rattler & Cornish Gold. **Facilities** Non-diners area ❤ (Bar Restaurant Garden) ♦♦ Children's menu Children's portions Garden ⊨ Beer festival Cider festival Parking WiFi ▄▄ (notice required)

HALSETOWN
Map 2 SW43

The Halsetown Inn
PICK OF THE PUBS

tel: 01736 795583 **TR26 3NA**
email: info@halsetowninn.co.uk
dir: On B3311, 1m for St Ives

Smart country dining-pub showcasing local produce

Built in 1831, The Halsetown Inn is named after the village's architect and benefactor, James Halse. From the outside, little changes at this stone-built pub, but the interior reveals a more contemporary style although the open fires remain and dogs are welcome. Run by the same team as the award-winning Blas Burgerworks restaurant in St Ives, local produce drives the menus here; typical starters on the concise menu are courgette and charred sweetcorn fritters; pea and Trevaskis Farm smoked ham croquettes with curried mayo. Then for mains, perhaps go for grilled line-caught Wild Harbour Fish Company's fish of the day with saffron mash; or 10-hour braised lamb, tomato and red wine ragù, tagliatelle, spinach and Hasletown ricotta. Puds could be deep-fried vanilla custard, boozy prunes, salted almond praline ice cream and maple syrup; or peanut parfait, banana bread, raspberry jelly, chocolate mousse and honeycomb.

Open 11-3 5.30-close Closed 2-31 Jan, Sun eve **Food** Lunch Mon-Sat 12-2, Sun 12-3 Dinner Mon-Sat 6-9 (5.30-9.30 summer) Set menu available ⊕ PUNCH TAVERNS ◀ Sharp's Doom Bar, Skinner's Betty Stogs ♂ Cornish Orchards. **Facilities** Non-diners area ❤ (Bar Outside area) ♦♦ Children's menu Children's portions Outside area ⊨ Beer festival Parking WiFi ▄▄ (notice required)

HELFORD PASSAGE
Map 2 SW72

The Ferryboat Inn

tel: 01326 250625 **TR11 5LB**
email: manager@ferryboatinnhelford.com
dir: In village centre, 1st turn after Trebah Gardens

Wonderful views and great seafood

There are fabulous views over the Helford estuary from this waterside pub, which dates back 300 years. Whether it's a plate of oysters and a glass of fizz on the sunny, south-facing terrace or a 100% brisket burger, mustard pickles and chips by the warmth of the granite fireplace inside, this is a venue for all weathers. Everything is made on the premises and the Ferryboat burger is especially popular. The pub is owned by Wright Brothers, custodians of the Duchy of Cornwall's oyster farm, so the quality of the shellfish and seafood speaks for itself. If available, perhaps try Cornish brown crab rarebit, white crab and pickled vegetables.

Open all day all wk **Food** Lunch all wk 12-3 Dinner all wk 6-9 (summer 6-10) ⊕ ST AUSTELL ◀ Tribute, Dartmoor, Proper Job ♂ Healey's Cornish Rattler. ♀ 12 **Facilities** Non-diners area ❤ (Bar Restaurant Outside area) ♦♦ Children's menu Children's portions Outside area ⊨ Parking WiFi ▄▄ (notice required)

KINGSAND
Map 3 SX45

NEW The Halfway House Inn

tel: 01752 822279 **Fore St PL10 1NA**
email: info@halfwayinnkingsand.co.uk
dir: *In town centre*

Traditional pub food in traditional surroundings

This property is now firmly in Cornwall; until 1844 the pub was partly in Devon too because the stream running through the garden was the dividing line between the counties. The twin villages of Kingsand and Cawsand were once smuggling hotspots; how easy this is to imagine over a pint of Sharp's Atlantic real ale or Cornish Rattler real cider. Typically, dinner might be pan-fried red mullet with crispy bacon, leeks and cider-apple dressing; steak, stout, chestnut and mushroom pie with herbed suet crust and butternut purée; or harissa, lentil and chickpea burger, pickled cucumber and red pepper; finishing with tarte au citron, or affogato.

Open all day all wk **Food** Lunch Mon-Sat 12-2, Sun 12-3 Dinner all wk 6-9 Restaurant menu available all wk ⊕ FREE HOUSE ◀ Sharp's Atlantic & Doom Bar, St Austell Tribute ♻ Healey's Cornish Rattler, Westons Stowford Press.
Facilities Non-diners area ✿ (Bar Garden) ♦ Children's menu Children's portions Garden ₣ WiFi ▭ (notice required)

LANLIVERY
Map 2 SX05

The Crown Inn
PICK OF THE PUBS

tel: 01208 872707 **PL30 5BT**
email: thecrown@wagtailinns.com
dir: *Signed from A390. Follow brown sign approx 1.5m W of Lostwithiel*

One of Cornwall's oldest pubs

In a moorland village above a tributary of the Fowey River is this former longhouse, with characteristic thick stone walls, low beams, granite and slate floors, open fires and an unusual bread oven. Much of the present building dates from the 12th century, when it housed the stonemasons constructing the nearby church. The pub has been extensively but sympathetically restored over the years; at one point the work uncovered a deep well, now covered by glass, under the porch. With the sea only a few miles away, expect a menu offering plenty of fresh fish and seafood, as well as other local produce. A popular main course is Cornish ale-battered fish with chips, crushed peas and home-made tartare sauce. At lunchtime in warm weather, enjoy a fresh Fowey crab sandwich or a proper Cornish Pasty and a pint of Skinner's Betty Stogs in the lovely garden.

Open all day all wk **Food** Lunch all wk 12-2.30 Dinner all wk 6-9 ⊕ FREE HOUSE ◀ Harbour Amber Ale, Skinner's Betty Stogs, guest ales ♻ Healey's Cornish Rattler.
Facilities Non-diners area ✿ (Bar Garden) ♦ Children's menu Children's portions Garden ₣ Parking WiFi ▭ (notice required)

LOOE
Map 2 SX25

The Ship Inn ★★★ INN

tel: 01503 263124 **Fore St PL13 1AD**
dir: *In town centre*

Busy pub on a narrow street

This lively St Austell Brewery-owned pub stands on a corner in the heart of this charming old fishing town, a minute's walk from the working harbour. Locals and tourists join together in the appreciation of a pint of Tribute, and select their favourites from the menu – a burger or hot baguette for some, while others go for steak and ale pie or hunter's chicken. A quiz is held on Mondays throughout the year, live bands play regularly, and well-equipped bedrooms are available for those wanting to tarry awhile.

Open all day all wk **Food** Contact pub for food times ⊕ ST AUSTELL BREWERY ◀ Tribute, Trelawny, HSD ♻ Healey's Cornish Rattler. ♥ **Facilities** Non-diners area ✿ (Bar) ♦ Children's menu Children's portions Family room **Rooms** 8

MEVAGISSEY
Map 2 SX04

The Ship Inn

tel: 01726 843324 **Fore St PL26 6UQ**
email: shipinnmeva2013@hotmail.co.uk
dir: *7m S of St Austell*

A popular tavern a few steps from the harbour

This 400-year-old inn stands just a few yards from Mevagissey's picturesque fishing harbour, so the choice of fish and seafood dishes comes as no surprise on a menu of home-cooked dishes: moules marinière, beer-battered cod, and oven-baked fillet of haddock topped with prawns and Cornish Tiskey cheese. The popular bar has low-beamed ceilings, flagstone floors and a strong nautical feel.

Open all day all wk 11am-mdnt **Food** Lunch all wk 12-3 Dinner all wk 6-9 ⊕ ST AUSTELL BREWERY ◀ Tribute & Proper Job, guest ale ♻ Healey's Cornish Rattler. ♥ 8 **Facilities** Non-diners area ✿ (Bar) ♦ Children's menu WiFi ▭

MITCHELL
Map 2 SW85

The Plume of Feathers ★★★★ INN
PICK OF THE PUBS

tel: 01872 510387 **TR8 5AX**
email: theplume@hospitalitycornwall.com **web:** www.theplumemitchell.co.uk
dir: *From A30 follow Mitchell signs*

Friendly atmosphere in a historic inn

From the impressive pillared porch at this sturdy old Cornish inn, John Wesley preached the benefits of Methodism to farmers and miners in the 1750s. Elements of the old place still survive, with low beams, wood-burning stove and a natural well in the bar blending with the contemporary artworks on display. As the village inn, it's popular with locals who can rely on regional real ales and farm ciders. The airy conservatory is an appealing place in which to dine, while stylish bedrooms provide the perfect overnight retreat. Local Cornish produce takes centre stage on the modern British menu and there's always a good showing of fish and locally reared meats. To start, consider smoked mackerel and horseradish pâté; advancing then to mains like crispy slow-cooked Cornish pork belly with mustard mash, smoked bacon, peas and baby onion gravy. The raised, tree-shaded beer garden is a tranquil retreat.

Open all day all wk 9am-11pm/mdnt (25 Dec 11-4) **Food** Lunch all wk 12-6 Dinner all wk 6-10 ⊕ FREE HOUSE ◀ Sharp's Doom Bar, Skinner's, St Austell Tribute ♻ Cornish Orchards. ♥ **Facilities** Non-diners area ✿ (Bar Garden) ♦ Children's menu Play area Garden ₣ Beer festival Parking WiFi ▭ (notice required) **Rooms** 13

MYLOR BRIDGE
Map 2 SW83

The Pandora Inn
PICK OF THE PUBS

See Pick of the Pubs on opposite page

PICK OF THE PUBS

The Pandora Inn

MYLOR BRIDGE   Map 2 SW83

tel: 01326 372678
Restronguet Creek TR11 5ST
email: info@pandorainn.com
web: www.pandorainn.com
dir: *From Truro/Falmouth follow A39, left at Carclew, follow signs to pub*

Historic waterside inn

When you visit the Pandora, it's easy to forget you're in the 21st century — its spectacular setting on the edge of Restronguet Creek is timeless. Parts of the inn date back to the 13th century and, with its flagstone floors, low-beamed ceilings and thatched roof it's not difficult to believe that little has changed since that time. While the Pandora's wonderful setting remains unchanged, everything else in this cosy traditional inn is 21st-century comfort and quality. Publicans John Milan and Steve Bellman pay attention to detail in everything — from the food and service, to the decor and furniture, and have established the Pandora as an award-winning pub that aims to give customers an enjoyable and memorable experience whenever they visit. Alongside an excellent wine list and the local ales from St Austell Brewery, chef Tom Milby uses the freshest local and seasonal produce, including fish and shellfish bought from boats landing at

the Pandora's own pontoon. Dine on that very pontoon, at a table by the water's edge, or in one of the series of little rooms inside, perhaps on Cornish shellfish in white wine, garlic, butter, herbs and cream, followed by seared pork cutlet with boulangère potatoes, pan-fried black pudding and a quince and red wine jus. Alternatively, start with seared scallops, winter squash purée, Serrano ham crisps and dill pickled cucumber, then rare-breed 8oz rib-eye steak. Orange marmalade and chocolate chip bread and butter pudding, or steamed honey and pecan nut pudding are two ways to round off a very enjoyable meal.

Open all day all wk 10.30am-11pm
Food all wk 10.30-9.30 🎞 ST AUSTELL BREWERY 🛢 HSD, Tribute, Proper Job & Trelawny ð Healey's Cornish Rattler & Pear Rattler. ♀ 17
Facilities Non-diners area 🐾 (Bar Outside area) 🚻 Children's menu Children's portions Outside area 🪑 Parking WiFi

NEWQUAY
Map 2 SW86

The Lewinnick Lodge Bar & Restaurant ★★★★ RR

tel: 01637 878117 **Pentire Headland TR7 1NX**
email: thelodge@hospitalitycornwall.com **web:** www.lewinnicklodge.co.uk
dir: *From Newquay take Pentire Rd 0.5m, pub on right*

Recommended for its fresh seafood and stunning views

Lewinnick Lodge perches on the cliff top of the Pentire Headland, enjoying a timeless panorama of sea views. This is a destination eatery, but real ales, local cider, crisp wines and premium lagers are all on offer in the bar. Wraps and baps and gourmet burgers can be ordered, but fresh seafood, much of it from Cornish waters, is the menu's key attraction; expect the likes of pan-fried stone bass fillets with patatas bravas, chorizo, spinach, spring onion and salsa verde; or whole roasted plaice with sautéed potatoes, griddled asparagus and cockle butter. Meats from the county include slow-roasted lamb and beef. Leave room for the lemon posset with black forest berries, shortbread and meringue.

Open all day all wk **Food** Lunch all wk 12-5 Dinner all wk 5-10 ⊕ FREE HOUSE ◀ Sharp's Doom Bar, Skinner's Betty Stogs, St Austell Tribute ♂ Cornish Orchards. ᵾ 8 **Facilities** Non-diners area ❖ (Bar Garden) ♦ Children's menu Children's portions Garden ⊼ Parking WiFi ⛟ **Rooms** 11

PAR
Map 2 SX05

The Britannia Inn & Restaurant ★★★★ INN

tel: 01726 812889 **St Austell Rd PL24 2SL**
email: info@britanniainn.com **web:** www.britanniainn.com
dir: *On A390 between Par & St Austell, adjacent to Cornish Market World*

Family-owned and family friendly, with large garden

Sixteenth-century, solidly built free house, where Sharp's Doom Bar, St Austell Tribute and Healey's Cornish Rattler wave the black and white county flag. The three dining areas do likewise by offering prime-cut Cornish steaks and other locally sourced dishes, typically grilled Cornish hake with chorizo, fennel, olives and peppers; breaded scampi with chips and peas; mushroom Stroganoff; and Cajun-spiced salmon steak with garlic mayonnaise. A short pub classics selection is offered at £15 for two, Monday to Saturday, with daily chef's specials adding further choice. The Sunday carvery is popular.

Open all day all wk **Food** all wk 12-9 Av main course £9 ⊕ FREE HOUSE ◀ Sharp's Doom Bar, St Austell Tribute, Bass ♂ Thatchers Gold, Healey's Cornish Rattler. ᵾ **Facilities** Non-diners area ❖ (Bar Garden) ♦ Children's menu Children's portions Play area Family room Garden ⊼ Parking WiFi ⛟ (notice required) **Rooms** 7

The Royal Inn ★★★★ INN

tel: 01726 815601 **66 Eastcliffe Rd PL24 2AJ**
email: info@royal-inn.co.uk **web:** www.royal-inn.co.uk
dir: *A3082 Par, follow brown tourist signs for 'Newquay Branch line' or railway station. Pub opposite rail station*

Welcoming pub on the Rail Ale Trail

This 19th-century inn was named after a visit by King Edward VII to a local copper mine and was originally frequented by travellers and employees of the Great Western Railway. The pub is on the Atlantic Coast Line of the 'Rail Ale Trail', and the building is much extended, with an open-plan bar serving a variety of beers including Tintagel Arthur's Ale. The bar menu offers everything from pizzas and burgers to salads and omelettes, while the restaurant menu includes smoked fish platter; steak, mushroom and ale pie; and battered cod and chips. Fifteen bedrooms are available.

Open all day all wk 11-11 (Sun 12-10.30) **Food** Lunch all wk 12-2 Dinner all wk 6.30-9 ⊕ FREE HOUSE ◀ Sharp's Doom Bar & Special, Cotleigh Barn Owl, Tintagel Arthur's Ale, Bays Devon Dumpling ♂ Healey's Cornish Rattler, Thatchers Gold. ᵾ 13 **Facilities** Non-diners area ❖ (Bar Garden) ♦ Children's menu Children's portions Garden ⊼ Parking WiFi ⛟ (notice required) **Rooms** 15

PENZANCE
Map 2 SW43

The Coldstreamer Inn

tel: 01736 362072 **Gulval TR18 3BB**
email: coldstreamerpenzance@outlook.com
dir: *From Penzance take B3311 towards St Ives. In Gulval right into School Ln. Pub in village centre*

Re-imagined traditional village inn with classy fare

Glimpses of Mount's Bay reward drinkers taking the sun on the terrace at this stone-built village inn on a hillside outside Penzance. With a wood-burner pumping out the heat, the interior is cosy, yet contemporary and welcoming. Tom and Holly Franklin-Pryce took over here in 2015 and augmented the great range of real ales, concentrating on beers from the south-west. The menus are similarly provincial; start with blow-torched squid with rock samphire, or straight in to mains of Newlyn hake with lobster bisque; or gnocchi with porcini and Bath Blue cheese. September sees a beer festival here.

Open all day all wk **Food** Lunch all wk 12-2.30 Dinner all wk 6-9.30 (summer), 6-9 (winter) Av main course £15.95 Restaurant menu available all wk ⊕ PUNCH TAVERNS ◀ Skinner's Ginger Tosser, Bays Topsail, guest ale. **Facilities** Non-diners area ❖ (Bar Outside area) ♦ Children's menu Children's portions Outside area ⊼ Beer festival WiFi ⛟ (notice required)

Dolphin Tavern ★★★ INN

tel: 01736 364106 **Quay St TR18 4BD**
email: dolphin@tiscali.co.uk **web:** www.dolphintavern.com
dir: *From rail station follow road along harbour. Tavern on corner opposite Scilonian Ferry Terminal*

Interesting history and fish always on the menu

Sir Walter Raleigh is said to have smoked the first pipe of tobacco in England at this lovely 16th-century pub, the central part of which was once used as a courtroom by Judge Jeffreys. These days, the Dolphin serves great home-made food accompanied by a full range of St Austell beers, plus accommodation. Fresh, locally caught fish features on the daily specials board, and the menu offers a tempting selection of meat (a house speciality is sizzling Cornish rump steak and chips), vegetarian and children's dishes. Fish lovers should look to the 'From the Boat' section for Newlyn crab and prawn linguine; Ratler battered catch of the day; and grilled hake with Parma ham.

Open all day all wk Closed 25 Dec **Food** Contact pub for food times ⊕ ST AUSTELL BREWERY ◀ HSD, Cornish Best, Tribute ♂ Healey's Cornish Rattler. ᵾ 10 **Facilities** Non-diners area ❖ (Bar Restaurant Garden) ♦ Children's menu Children's portions Family room Garden WiFi ⛟ (notice required) **Rooms** 3

The Turks Head Inn

tel: 01736 363093 **Chapel St TR18 4AF**
email: turks@fsmail.net
dir: *Phone for detailed directions*

Historic tucked-away town pub

This popular terraced side-street local is the oldest pub in Penzance, dating from around 1233, and was the first in the country to be given the Turks Head name. Sadly, a Spanish raiding party destroyed much of the original building in the 16th century, but an old smugglers' tunnel leading directly to the harbour still exists. Wash down hearty pub food — steaks, burgers, fish pie — or perhaps seafood broth, green Thai monkfish curry or braised lamb shank, with a cracking pint of Sharp's Doom Bar, best enjoyed in the sunny flower-filled garden. Don't miss the annual beer festival.

Open all day all wk **Food** Lunch all wk 12-2.30 Dinner all wk 6-10 Av main course £10.95 Set menu available ⊕ PUNCH TAVERNS ◗ Sharp's Doom Bar, Turk's Head Ale ⏺ Westons Old Rosie. ☻ 12 **Facilities** Non-diners area ☙ (Bar Restaurant Garden) ♦♦ Children's menu Children's portions Family room Garden ⌂ Beer festival WiFi ☷ (notice required)

| PERRANUTHNOE | Map 2 SW52 |

The Victoria Inn   PICK OF THE PUBS

tel: 01736 710309 **TR20 9NP**
email: enquiries@victoriainn-penzance.co.uk
dir: *Exit A394 (Penzance to Helston road), signed Perranuthnoe*

Off the beaten track, coastal pub worth finding

Its history spans nine centuries, so this striking pink-washed village inn could be Cornwall's oldest public house. Decorated with seafaring memorabilia, its typically Cornish stone-walled interior attracts families strolling up from Perran Sands and walkers from the South West Coastal Path. Real ales, lager and cider — all from Cornwall — enjoy pride of place in the wood-fire-warmed, softly lit bar; there is even a Cornish wine. After making your choice, take a menu outside to the Mediterranean-style patio garden if the weather is clement. Dishes are modern British in style, again making good use of locally sourced produce. A spring menu revealed courgette and spinach soup with Montgomery Cheddar rarebit; and warm shredded ham hock, cauliflower purée, pineapple salsa and fried duck egg as tasty starters. Continue perhaps with provençal fish and shellfish stew; or garlic and thyme roasted pork cutlet, creamed potato, Savoy cabbage, hogs pudding and apple butter; or spicy prawn and crab tagliatelle. Please note, the inn is closed on Mondays in winter.

Open all day Closed Mon (winter) **Food** Lunch Mon-Sat 12-2, Sun 12-2.30 Dinner all wk 6.30-9 Set menu available ⊕ FREE HOUSE ◗ Sharp's Doom Bar, St Austell Tribute, Skinner's Betty Stogs, Cornish Chough Serpentine ⏺ Healey's Cornish Orchards. ☻ **Facilities** Non-diners area ☙ (Bar Garden) ♦♦ Children's menu Children's portions Garden ⌂ Parking WiFi

| PHILLEIGH | Map 2 SW83 |

Roseland Inn

tel: 01872 580254 **TR2 5NB**
email: contact@roselandinn.co.uk
dir: *From Truro take A39 towards Falmouth. Left onto B3289 towards St Mawes. Left at sharp right bend for Philleigh. Or take King Harry Ferry from Feock (Trelissick) to St Mawes/Roseland peninsula. Onto B3289. At right bend turn left signed Philleigh, 1.5m to pub on left*

Traditional Cornish pub with welcoming, cosy interior

Owner Phil Heslip and chef Brian Green take pride in the quality of the home-prepared modern British cooking at this highly appealing, rural 16th-century inn.

The character of the interior owes much to the low-beamed ceilings, brassware, paintings and prints. Phil brews his ornithologically themed Cornish Shag, Chough to Bits and High-as-a-Kite beers on site. So, in winter cosy up to the fire for a drink or a meal of perhaps slow-roasted shoulder of Cornish lamb, or oven-baked hake with pan-fried new potatoes; in warmer weather head outside to the picnic tables. Just to the west is the famous King Harry Ferry over the River Fal.

Open all wk 11-3 6-11.30 (summer all day) **Food** Lunch all wk 12-2.30 Dinner all wk 6-9 ⊕ PUNCH TAVERNS ◗ Skinner's Betty Stogs, Roseland Cornish Shag, High-as-a-Kite & Chough to Bits, Sharp's Doom Bar ⏺ Westons Stowford Press. **Facilities** Non-diners area ☙ (Bar Garden) ♦♦ Children's menu Children's portions Garden ⌂ Beer festival Parking WiFi ☷ (notice required)

| POLKERRIS | Map 2 SX05 |

The Rashleigh Inn

tel: 01726 813991 **PL24 2TL**
email: jonspode@aol.com
dir: *From A3082 between Fowey & Par follow Polkerris signs*

Right on the beach

Once a coastguard station, this 300-year-old pub at the end of a no-through road to Polkerris Beach faces west, so watching the sun set over St Austell Bay is a delight. In the bar there's a good selection of real ales from the south-west, real cider, local organic soft drinks and a water bowl and Bonio biscuits for visiting dogs. Good, locally sourced food majors on the county's fresh seafood, with river mussels from Fowey, Looe scallops, and local crab. For meat lovers, a prime Cornish sirloin, a home-made burger or the home-made steak and ale pie will hit the spot.

Open all day all wk **Food** Lunch all wk 12-3, snacks 3-5 Dinner all wk 6-9 Av main course £9.95 ⊕ FREE HOUSE ◗ Timothy Taylor Landlord, Skinner's Betty Stogs, St Austell HSD, Otter Bitter, Black Sheep Best Bitter, Bath Ales Gem, guest ales ⏺ Westons Stowford Press, Addlestones. ☻ 9 **Facilities** Non-diners area ☙ (Bar Garden Outside area) ♦♦ Children's menu Children's portions Garden Outside area ⌂ Parking WiFi

| PORT GAVERNE | Map 2 SX08 |

Port Gaverne ★★★★ INN   PICK OF THE PUBS

tel: 01208 880244 **PL29 3SQ**
email: eat@portgavernehotel.co.uk web: www.portgavernehotel.co.uk
dir: *Signed from B3314, S of Delabole via B3267, E of Port Isaac*

The freshest local fish and seafood

This delightful 17th-century inn in pretty Port Gaverne overlooks the secluded cove where women once loaded sea-bound ketches with slate from Delabole's great quarry. With the slate industry long gone, the inn today reaps the reward of being right on the South West Coastal Path, most of whose walkers are ready for a thirst-quenching Cornish-brewed Skinner's Betty Stogs real ale, Rattler cider or a refreshing glass of wine, in the slate-floored, low-beamed bar or small beer garden. Locally supplied produce includes plenty of fresh fish; Porthilly mussels; Port Isaac lobster thermidor. Not everything is from the Atlantic, of course, so look out for braised venison, juniper and ale pie, smoked butter mash and red cabbage; or charcoal-grilled pork T-bone steak with peppercorn sauce. Finish with blueberry and ginger steamed pudding and custard.

Open all day all wk **Food** Lunch all wk 12-2.30 Dinner all wk 6-9 Restaurant menu available all wk ⊕ FREE HOUSE ◗ St Austell Tribute & Proper Job, Timothy Taylor Landlord, Skinner's Betty Stogs ⏺ Healey's Cornish Rattler, Somersby. ☻ 16 **Facilities** Non-diners area ☙ (Bar Garden) ♦♦ Children's menu Children's portions Garden ⌂ Parking WiFi ☷ **Rooms** 15

PORTHLEVEN | Map 2 SW62

The Ship Inn

tel: 01326 564204 **TR13 9JS**
email: manager@theshipinn.org
dir: *From Helston follow signs to Porthleven (B3304), 2.5m. On entering village continue to harbour. Follow road to other side of harbour. 1st left to inn*

Unspoilt pub in an unspoilt fishing port

Dating from the 17th century, this smugglers' inn is actually built into the cliffs, and is approached by a flight of stone steps. It overlooks one of the most picturesque harbours in Cornwall and in summer there's nothing better than sitting with a glass of one of the five ales on offer and watching the fishing boats coming and going; in winter, a log fire warms the interior, while the flames of a second flicker in the separate old smithy private function room. Beer mats and brasses adorn the ceiling and walls. The food is kept simple – fish pies, steak, mussels, crab and catch of the day.

Open all day all wk 11am-11.30pm (Fri-Sun 11am-mdnt) **Food** Lunch all wk 12-2.30 Dinner all wk 6-9 ⊕ FREE HOUSE ◀ Sharp's Doom Bar & Own, Skinner's Porthleven, Rebel Penryn Pale Ale ♂ Cornish Orchards, Sharp's Orchard, Westons Stowford Press. ♀ 8 **Facilities** Non-diners area ♣ (Bar Restaurant Garden) ♦ Children's portions Family room Garden ⊨ WiFi

PORT ISAAC | Map 2 SW98

The Slipway

tel: 01208 880264 **Harbour Front PL29 3RH**
email: slipway@portisaachotel.com
dir: *From A39 take B3314 signed Port Isaac. Through Delabole & Pendoggett, right onto B3267. 2m to Port Isaac, pass Co-op on right, 100mtrs into Back Hill (one way) to harbour (NB no parking by pub; car park at top of village)*

Harbourside pub noted for fish and seafood

This 16th-century, one-time ship's chandlery could hardly be closer to Port Isaac's tiny harbour, so no wonder it has a reputation for seriously good fresh fish and seafood. Cornish Orchards cider, and real ales from Tintagel and Sharp's breweries are on hand pump in the bar, while in the heavy-beamed, galleried restaurant locally sourced dishes include Porthilly mussels; Doom Bar battered fish and chips; roast belly pork; and slow-braised ox cheek. On summer evenings the covered terrace overlooking the harbour is the perfect place to dine and enjoy music from the local bands. Park your car at the top of the village.

Open all day all wk Closed 25 Dec **Food** Lunch all wk 12-2.30 Dinner all wk 6.30-8.30 (9 in summer) Restaurant menu available all wk ⊕ FREE HOUSE ◀ Tintagel Harbour Special, Sharp's Doom Bar ♂ Cornish Orchards. **Facilities** Non-diners area ♣ (Bar Outside area) ♦ Children's menu Children's portions Outside area ⊨ WiFi

PORTREATH | Map 2 SW64

Basset Arms

tel: 01209 842077 **Tregea Ter TR16 4NG**
email: bassettarms@btconnect.com
dir: *From Redruth take B3300 to Portreath. Pub on left near seafront*

Local seafood a speciality

Built as a pub to serve harbour workers, at one time this early 19th-century Cornish stone cottage served as a mortuary for ill-fated seafarers, so there are plenty of

ghost stories. Tin-mining and shipwreck photographs adorn the low-beamed interior of the bar where you can wash down a meal with a pint of Skinner's real ale. The menu makes the most of local seafood, such as deep-fried whitebait; and mussels cooked in creamy white wine and garlic sauce, but also provides a wide selection of alternatives, including steak and kidney pie; and gammon steak, egg, peas, pineapple and chips.

Open all day all wk 11-11 (Fri-Sat 11am-mdnt Sun 11-10.30) **Food** Lunch all wk 12-2, summer 12-3 Dinner all wk 6-9, summer 5-9 ⊕ FREE HOUSE ◀ Sharp's Doom Bar, Skinner's, Dartmoor Legend, St Austell Tribute ♂ Thatchers Gold. **Facilities** Non-diners area ♣ (Bar Outside area) ♦ Children's menu Children's portions Play area Outside area ⊨ Parking WiFi ⊨ (notice required)

ROCK | Map 2 SW97

NEW The Mariners

tel: 01208 863679 **PL27 6LD**
email: info@themarinersrock.com
dir: *On seafront*

Serious about beef

With a great seafront location, views across the Camel Estuary and a menu overseen by award-winning chef Nathan Outlaw, The Mariners is here to offer you 'meat as nature intended' and 'beer brewed without compromise'. The former means all their beef is sourced from the south west, coming from native breeds (what breed you get will depend on when you visit, as all are at their best at different times of the year). Beers come from Sharp's, so you can enjoy a pint of Doom Bar with your dinner. As well as those very particular steaks, cooked on the charcoal grill and served with hand-cut chips, the menu offers treats like potted Cornish crab or beer-cured salmon, before moving on to monkfish curry; grilled plaice, or pork belly with bacon jam and potato terrine.

Open all day all wk **Food** Lunch all wk 12-3 Dinner all wk 6-9 Av main course £15 ⊕ SHARP'S ◀ Atlantic, Doom Bar ♂ Orchard's. ♀ 11 **Facilities** Non-diners area ♣ (Bar Restaurant Outside area) ♦ Children's menu Children's portions Outside area ⊨ WiFi ⊨ (notice required)

RUAN LANIHORNE | Map 2 SW84

The Kings Head

tel: 01872 501263 **TR2 5NX**
email: contact@kings-head-roseland.co.uk
dir: *3m from Tregony Bridge on A3078*

Country pub with delightful summer garden

This traditional country pub set deep in the Roseland countryside has a warm and welcoming atmosphere. Roaring winter fires, beamed ceilings and mulled wine contrast with summer days relaxing on the terrace with a jug of Pimm's, a pint of Betty Stogs or Cornish Orchards cider. Whatever the time of year, the chef responds with seasonal dishes using the best local produce, including roasted chicken breast with five bean and chorizo cassoulet; tiger prawns piri piri and citrus risotto; or apple, leek and cheddar cake. Look out for the signature dish of Ruan duck three ways – confit leg, pan-fried breast and drakes pudding.

Open 12-2.30 6-11 Closed Sun eve, Mon (Oct-Etr) **Food** Lunch 12-2.30 Dinner 6-11 ⊕ FREE HOUSE ◀ Skinner's Betty Stogs, Sharp's Doom Bar, Cotleigh Tawny Owl ♂ Cornish Orchards. ♀ 9 **Facilities** Non-diners area ♦ Children's portions Garden Outside area ⊨ Parking

ST AGNES
Map 3 SW75

Driftwood Spars ★★★★ GA
PICK OF THE PUBS

tel: 01872 552428 **Trevaunance Cove TR5 0RT**
email: info@driftwoodspars.co.uk **web:** www.driftwoodspars.co.uk
dir: *A30 onto B3285, through St Agnes, down steep hill, left at Peterville Inn, follow Trevaunance Cove sign*

Great 16th-century find near coastal path

"I can see the sea" will doubtless be heard from any children in the car as you approach this place, just before St Agnes' relatively secret 'best' beach and redundant harbour. During its time, the whitewashed, three-storey building fulfilled many functions, not least as a smugglers' rendezvous — secret tunnel and all. The roof timbers are spars from a wreck (hence the name), while nautical artefacts recall its time as a chandlery. Assorted furnishings, open fires and dressed stone walls provide additional character in the warren of rooms, including the summer-only, ocean-facing Fitty Pysk seafood bistro. Up to six hand-pulled real ales, including those from the on-site microbrewery, are served in the three fire-warmed bars, as are Rattler Cornish cider and a few English wines. A seasonal bar menu features salt n' pepper squid with sweet chilli sauce; a kilo of Cornish mussels cooked in Driftwood beer with fennel, shallots and cream; twice baked cheese soufflé with smoked cheese sauce. Beer festivals are in mid March and early May.

Open all day all wk 11-11 (Fri-Sat 11am-1am 25 Dec 11am-2pm) **Food** Lunch all wk 12-2.30 Dinner all wk 6-9.30 (winter 6.30-8.30) Restaurant menu available Tue-Sat (peak season) ⊕ FREE HOUSE ◀ Driftwood Spars, Sharp's Doom Bar, guest ales ↺ Healey's Cornish Rattler, Thatchers. ☗ 11 **Facilities** Non-diners area ☙ (Bar Garden Outside area) ⁙ Children's menu Children's portions Garden Outside area ⋒ Beer festival Parking WiFi ▭ (notice required) **Rooms** 15

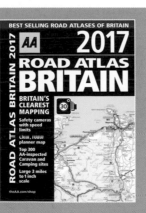

ST EWE
Map 2 SW94

The Crown Inn

tel: 01726 843322 **PL26 6EY**
email: thecrownstewe@hotmail.co.uk
dir: *From St Austell take B3273. At Tregiskey x-roads turn right. St Ewe signed on right*

Local ales and home-cooking in this pretty village inn

Only a mile away from the famous Lost Gardens of Heligan, this attractive 16th-century village inn is the ideal place to refuel, whether it's by the fire in the traditional bar or in the peaceful flower-festooned garden in summer. Quaff a pint of Tribute ale or Healey's Cornish Rattler cider and tuck into the home-cooked food, perhaps traditional prawn cocktail followed by slow-roasted belly pork with apple sauce and cider gravy; BBQ ribs; home-made pie of the day or curry of the day. Lunchtime sandwiches, jacket potatoes and smaller portions of main dishes are also available.

Open all wk 12-3 5.30-close **Food** Lunch all wk 12-2 Dinner Mon-Sat 5.30-9 ⊕ ST AUSTELL BREWERY ◀ Tribute, Cornish Best & Proper Job ↺ Healey's Cornish Rattler. **Facilities** Non-diners area ☙ (Bar Garden) ⁙ Children's menu Children's portions Play area Family room Garden ⋒ Parking WiFi ▭

ST IVES
Map 2 SW54

The Queens ★★ HL ⊛

tel: 01736 796468 **2 High St TR26 1RR**
email: info@queenshotelstives.com **web:** www.queenshotelstives.com
dir: *From rdbt on A30 take A3074 signed St Ives. Through Carbis Bay. In St Ives pass entrance to rail station on right, pass church on corner on right. Road becomes Hugh St. Pub on left (opposite Boots the Chemist)*

Winning combination of fine food and stylish accommodation

There's an easy-going mix of chic and contemporary design with a nod to times past in this thriving hostelry at the heart of the old town. It's worth the stroll from the harbour or the resort's beaches to discover this solid granite-built, late-Georgian building, where local art works vie for attention with local cider, Cornish beers and a great menu inspired by the wealth of the county's larder. A sample lunch menu includes panko-breaded king prawns, fish, Thai salad and sweet chilli sauce; Tribute beer-battered fish 'n' chips; and home-cooked honey-roast ham, free-range eggs and chips. A chalkboard holds much additional promise. Some of the stylish bedrooms have views to Carbis Bay.

Open all day all wk **Food** Lunch Mon-Sat 12-2.30, Sun 12-4 Dinner Mon-Sat 6.30-9.30 Av main course £10 ⊕ ST AUSTELL BREWERY ◀ Tribute, HSD ↺ Healey's Cornish Rattler. ☗ 16 **Facilities** Non-diners area ☙ (Bar Restaurant) ⁙ Children's menu Children's portions WiFi ▭ (notice required) **Rooms** 10

The Sloop Inn ★★★ INN

tel: 01736 796584 **The Wharf TR26 1LP**
email: sloopinn@btinternet.com **web:** www.sloop-inn.co.uk
dir: *On St Ives harbour by middle slipway*

Famous St Ives inn by picturesque harbour

A trip to St Ives wouldn't be complete without visiting this 700-year-old pub perched right on the harbourside. Slate floors, beamed ceilings and nautical artefacts dress some of the several bars and dining areas, whilst the cobbled forecourt is an unbeatable spot for people- and harbour-watching, preferably with a pint of local Doom Bar. The menu majors on local seafood, from line-caught St Ives Bay mackerel and fries to home-made Newlyn cod, smoked haddock and smoked bacon fishcakes. There are also plenty of other options, if fish isn't your dish. Most of the comfortably appointed bedrooms overlook the pretty bay.

Open all day all wk **Food** Lunch all wk 12-3 Dinner all wk 5-10 Restaurant menu available all wk ⊕ ENTERPRISE INNS ◀ Sharp's Doom Bar ↺ Thatchers Gold. ☗ 10 **Facilities** Non-diners area ☙ (Bar Outside area) ⁙ Outside area ⋒ WiFi ▭ (notice required) **Rooms** 22

ST IVES *continued*

The Watermill

tel: 01736 757912 **Lelant Downs, Hayle TR27 6LQ**
email: watermill@btconnect.com web: www.watermillincornwall.co.uk
dir: *Exit A30 at junct for St Ives/A3074, turn left at 2nd mini rdbt*

Converted mill with food to suit everyone

Set in extensive gardens on the old St Ives coach road, with glorious valley views towards Trencrom Hill, The Watermill is a cosy, family-friendly pub and restaurant created in the 18th-century Lelant Mill. The old mill machinery is still in place and the iron waterwheel continues to turn, gravity fed by the mill stream. Downstairs is the old beamed bar and wood-burning stove, while upstairs in the open-beamed mill loft is the atmospheric restaurant where steaks and fish (sea bass, sardines and mackerel perhaps) are specialities. There are beer festivals in June and November with live music all weekend.

Open all day all wk 12-11 (Sun 12-10.30) **Food** Lunch all wk 12-2.30 Dinner all wk 6-9 ⊕ FREE HOUSE ◀ Sharp's Doom Bar, Skinner's Betty Stogs, guest ales Ö Healey's Cornish Rattler. **Facilities** Non-diners area ✿ (Bar Garden) ♦♦ Children's menu Play area Garden ⋈ Beer festival Parking WiFi ▭

▌ ST KEW — Map 2 SX07

St Kew Inn

tel: 01208 841259 **Churchtown PL30 3HB**
email: stkewinn@btconnect.com
dir: *From Wadebridge N on A39. Left to St Kew*

A chocolate-box village pub with plenty of local seafood

Visit this 15th-century, stone-built pub in summer and you will be rewarded with flower tubs and creepers enhancing its pretty façade, whilst traditional features inside include a huge open fire. Cornish St Austell beers and Rattler cider are the prime refreshments, while menus proffer carefully sourced British dishes, often featuring local fish and seafood. Choose between four eating areas – five if you include the garden – when ordering your lunchtime snack. Alternatively, in the evening try seared squid, fennel, chorizo and orange, and follow with seafood gratin; or chicken, bacon and mushroom pie, sautéed potatoes and peas.

Open all wk 11-3 5.30-11 (summer all day) **Food** Lunch all wk 12-2, summer all day Dinner all wk 6-9, summer all day Av main course £13.50 Set menu available ⊕ ST AUSTELL BREWERY ◀ Tribute, HSD, Proper Job Ö Healey's Cornish Rattler. **Facilities** Non-diners area ✿ (Bar Garden) ♦♦ Children's menu Children's portions Family room Garden ⋈ Parking

▌ ST MAWES — Map 2 SW83

The Victory Inn — PICK OF THE PUBS

tel: 01326 270324 **Victory Hill TR2 5DQ**
email: contact@victory-inn.co.uk
dir: *A3078 to St Mawes. Pub adjacent to harbour*

Seafood takes top billing on the menus

Named after Nelson's flagship, this friendly fishermen's local near the harbour adopts a modern approach to its daily lunch and dinner menus. You may eat downstairs in the traditional bar, or in the modern and stylish first-floor Seaview Restaurant (white walls, white linen and wicker chairs), with a terrace that looks across the town's rooftops to the harbour and the River Fal. High on the list of ingredients is fresh seafood – all from Cornish waters – the choice changing daily to include crab risotto, fisherman's pie, and beer-battered cod and hand-cut chips, with chicken breast cordon bleu, lamb shank Provençale, and curry or casserole of the day among the other favourites. Wines are all carefully chosen and excellent in quality, as are the real ales from Cornwall's own Roseland, Sharp's and Skinner's breweries. There is outside seating with views over the harbour. Booking for meals is definitely advisable in the summer.

Open all day all wk 11-3 6-11 (summer all day) **Food** Lunch all wk 12-2.30 Dinner all wk 6-9 ⊕ PUNCH TAVERNS ◀ Skinner's Betty Stogs, Sharp's Doom Bar, Roseland Cornish Shag Ö Westons Stowford Press. **Facilities** Non-diners area ✿ (Bar Garden) ♦♦ Children's menu Children's portions Garden ⋈ WiFi ▭

▌ ST MAWGAN — Map 2 SW86

The Falcon Inn ★★★★ INN — PICK OF THE PUBS

See Pick of the Pubs on opposite page

▌ ST MERRYN — Map 2 SW87

The Cornish Arms — PICK OF THE PUBS

tel: 01841 532700 **Churchtown PL28 8ND**
email: reservations@rickstein.com
dir: *From Padstow follow signs for St Merryn, up hill, pub on right*

Simple British pub food the Rick Stein way

St Merryn, just outside Padstow, is home to this ancient village pub, part of the Stein portfolio. Situated across the road from the parish church and overlooking a peaceful valley, the pub has remained very much the village boozer certainly to the happiness of the locals. The Cornish Arms oozes character, with slate floors, beams and roaring log fires, and they've kept the food offering equally traditional. A sample menu starts with grilled piri piri sardines; or butternut squash and thyme soup, continues with steak and ale pie; or lamb curry; and ends in sunken chocolate cake with clotted cream. Wash it down with a glass of Chalky's Bite, named after the scene-stealing Jack Russell that appeared in his owner's earlier TV programmes. Check with the pub for details of themed nights and the beer and mussels festival in March.

Open all day all wk 11.30-11 **Food** Lunch all wk 12-2.30 Dinner all wk 6-8.30 Av main course £12.45 Set menu available ⊕ ST AUSTELL BREWERY ◀ Tribute, Proper Job, Trelawny, Chalky's Bite Ö Healey's Cornish Rattler. ♟ 12 **Facilities** Non-diners area ✿ (Bar Restaurant Garden) ♦♦ Children's menu Children's portions Garden ⋈ Beer festival Parking WiFi ▭

PICK OF THE PUBS

The Falcon Inn ★★★★ INN

ST MAWGAN Map 2 SW86

tel: 01637 860225 **TR8 4EP**
email: thefalconinnstmawgan@gmail.com
web: www.thefalconinnstmawgan.co.uk
dir: *From A30 (8m W of Bodmin) follow signs to Newquay Airport. Turn right 200mtrs before airport terminal into St Mawgan, pub at bottom of hill*

Traditional Cornish village inn

This wisteria-clad, stone-built inn situated in the Vale of Lanherne is just four miles from Newquay. Although it can trace its ancestry back to 1758, it's probably older, given that by 1813 it had been renamed more than once. Since about 1880, however, it has clung to its current name, an allusion to the nearby estate's coat of arms. The flagstone-floored, winter log-fire-warmed interior is cosy and relaxing, while outside is a large, attractive garden with a magnificent magnolia tree and a cobbled courtyard. In the bar you'll find a rotating roster of predominantly West Country real ales and ciders, and a dozen wines served by the glass. Lunchtime could bring a starter of feta and beetroot muhammara (a Levantine dip) with pistachio dukkah with rustic toast and dressed salad leaves; something more conventional like smoked duck mousse pâté with piccalilli and toast; or just an appetising sandwich. There's also a good choice of home-made hot dishes, such as steak and kidney suet-crust pie with new potatoes and vegetables. In the more formal restaurant, the evening menu could prompt you to start with spiced home-cured salmon, onion bhaji and chilli herb salad; or maybe Cornish goats' cheese arancini with golden beetroot carpaccio, beetroot jelly and apple salad. Your main course options might then include trio of Primrose Herd rare breed pork sausages, spring onion and smoked cheese mash with real ale gravy; and beer-battered Newlyn hake with chips and mushy peas. A late July beer and cider festival is one of several fun events.

Open all wk 11-3 6-11 (Jul-Aug all day) Closed 25 Dec (open 12-2) **Food** Lunch all wk 12-2 Dinner all wk 6-9 Av main course £11 ⊕ FREE HOUSE ◖ Rotating real ales ♻ Rotating real ciders. ♟ 12 **Facilities** Non-diners area ❖ (Bar Garden) ⅙ Children's menu Children's portions Garden ⋈ Beer festival Cider festival Parking WiFi ⛟ **Rooms** 3

ST TUDY
Map 2 SX07

St Tudy Inn

tel: 01208 850656 **PL30 3NN**
email: hello@harbourkitchen.com
dir: *Follow St Tudy signs from A39 between Camelford & Wadebridge. Pub in village centre*

Welcoming pub with concise menus

Emily Scott, one of Cornwall's most admired female chefs, owns this much-loved village pub. The building's exterior stonework and interior warm terracotta decor create a welcoming ambience. Emily's short and sweet menus with no-nonsense pricing indicate treats in store: snacks such as Welsh rarebit; starters like celeriac, fennel and orange soup; a main course of sea bream with herb dressing, new potatoes and watercress; and puddings such as flourless chocolate cake with crème anglaise are typical. Doom Bar and Sharp's Orchard cider are the bar's staples.

Open 12-3 6-12 Closed Sun eve & Mon ⊕ FREE HOUSE ◀ Sharp's Doom Bar ☼ Sharp's Orchard. **Facilities** ❄ (Bar Outside area) ◗ Children's portions Outside area Parking WiFi

SALTASH
Map 3 SX45

The Crooked Inn ★★★★ INN

tel: 01752 848177 **Stoketon Cottage, Trematon PL12 4RZ**
email: info@crooked-inn.co.uk **web:** www.crooked-inn.co.uk
dir: *Phone for detailed directions*

Family-run inn with good food and great children's facilities

Overlooking the lush Lyher Valley and run by the same family for many years, this delightful inn once housed staff from Stoketon Manor, whose ruins lie on the other side of the courtyard. It is set in 10 acres of lawns and woodland, yet is only 15 minutes from Plymouth. There is an menu offering something for everyone – Mediterranean meze; confit of belly pork; and home-made soup of the day fits the light bites and starters' bill; then for a main course how about their 'famous' suet pudding smothered in gravy; rack of roasted ribs; Thai chicken curry; a prime steak; or warm Manuka smoked duck salad? There's a children's playground and a treehouse. The spacious bedrooms are individually designed.

Open all day all wk 11-11 (Sun 12-10.30) Closed 25 Dec **Food** Lunch all wk 11-2.30 Dinner all wk 6-9.30 Av main course £9.95 ⊕ FREE HOUSE ◀ St Austell HSD, Dartmoor Jail Ale, guest ales ☼ Thatchers Gold, Cornish Orchards. ▾ 9 **Facilities** Non-diners area ❄ (All areas) ◗ Children's menu Children's portions Play area Garden Outside area 🏠 Parking WiFi 🚌 **Rooms** 15

ISLES OF SCILLY

See Tresco

TORPOINT
Map 3 SX45

Edgcumbe Arms
PICK OF THE PUBS

tel: 01752 822294 **Cremyll PL10 1HX**
dir: *Phone for detailed directions*

A 15th-century pub with glorious views over the Tamar estuary

Close to the foot ferry from Plymouth, this inn next to Mount Edgcumbe Country Park offers fabulous views from its bow window seats and waterside terrace, which take

in Drakes Island, the Royal William Yard and the marina. Real ales from St Austell like Tribute, plus Healey's Cornish Rattler cider, and quality home-cooked food are served in a series of rooms, which are full of character with American oak panelling and flagstone floors. The same extensive menu is offered throughout and dishes are a mixture of international and traditional British pub favourites: pork and chicken liver pâté; or salt and pepper squid to start, followed by beef and Merlot pie, chicken Rossini; or smoked haddock rarebit. Vegetarian options might include gnocchi in tomato and herb sauce. Sandwiches, loaded potato skins and platters are also available. The inn has a courtyard garden.

Open all day 11-11 Closed Jan-Feb Mon & Tue eve **Food** all wk 12-8.30 ⊕ ST AUSTELL BREWERY ◀ Tribute, Proper Job, Trelawny ☼ Healey's Cornish Rattler. ▾ 10 **Facilities** Non-diners area ❄ (Bar Garden) ◗ Children's menu Children's portions Garden 🏠 Parking WiFi 🚌 (notice required)

TREBARWITH
Map 2 SX08

The Mill House Inn
PICK OF THE PUBS

tel: 01840 770200 **PL34 0HD**
email: management@themillhouseinn.co.uk **web:** www.themillhouseinn.co.uk
dir: *From Tintagel take B3263 S, right after Trewarmett to Trebarwith Strand. Pub 0.5m on right*

Family-friendly inn with good food and live entertainment

Set in seven acres of woodland on the north Cornish coast, close to Tintagel Castle, the Mill House is half a mile from the surfing beach at Trebarwith Strand, one of the finest in Cornwall. The log fires in this atmospheric stone building – a charming former corn mill dating from 1760 – warm the residents' lounge and slate-floored bar, where wooden tables and chapel chairs help create a relaxed, family-friendly feel. Locally brewed real ales are supplied by Sharp's and Tintagel breweries, and the ciders are Cornish Orchards and Healey's Cornish Rattler. Lunches, evening drinks and barbecues are particularly enjoyable out on the attractive terraces, while a more intimate dinner in the Millstream Restaurant might involve firecracker prawns with mango, pickled radish, coriander and pomegranate dressing; followed by sea trout with crushed potatoes, kale, roasted banana shallots and mussel and tarragon cream; or slow-roasted pork belly with cauliflower purée and sauerkraut. Regular live entertainment events feature local musicians and comedians.

Open all day all wk 11-11 (Fri-Sat 11am-mdnt Sun 12-10.30) **Food** Lunch Mon-Sat 12-2.30, Sun 12-3 Dinner all wk 6.30-8.30 Restaurant menu available all wk evening ⊕ FREE HOUSE ◀ Sharp's Doom Bar, Tintagel Cornwall's Pride, Castle Gold & Arthur's Ale ☼ Cornish Orchards, Healey's Cornish Rattler. **Facilities** Non-diners area ❄ (Bar Garden) ◗ Children's menu Children's portions Play area Family room Garden 🏠 Parking WiFi 🚌 (notice required)

The Port William

tel: 01840 770230 **Trebarwith Strand PL34 0HB**
email: portwilliam@staustellbrewery.co.uk
dir: *From A39 onto B3314 signed Tintagel. Right onto B3263, follow Trebarwith Strand signs, then brown Port William signs*

Stunning location by the sea

Occupying one of the best locations in Cornwall, this former harbourmaster's house lies directly on the coastal path, 50 yards from the sea, which means the views of the Trebarwith Strand are amazing. There is an entrance to a smugglers' tunnel at the rear of the ladies' toilet! Obviously there's quite an emphasis on fresh fish, but there's no shortage of other options. A typical menu starts with pulled pork with smoky barbecue sauce and toasted croûton, or sautéed Cornish mushrooms with peppercorn sauce and crumbled blue cheese; then moves on to mains such as gourmet burger with chunky chips; ocean pie; local mussels; or vegetable red Thai curry. If you've room, check the specials board for the desserts of the day.

Open all day all wk 10am–11pm (Sun 10am–10.30pm) **Food** all wk 12–9 ⊕ ST AUSTELL BREWERY ◀ Tribute, Proper Job & Trelawny, guest ales ○ Healey's Cornish Rattler & Berry Rattler. ♀ 8 **Facilities** Non-diners area ☙ (Bar Restaurant Garden) ♦ Children's menu Children's portions Family room Garden ♬ Parking WiFi

---

TREBURLEY Map 3 SX37

The Springer Spaniel PICK OF THE PUBS

tel: 01579 370424 **PL15 9NS**
email: enquiries@thespringerspaniel.org.uk
dir: *On A388 halfway between Launceston & Callington*

Popular dining-pub in Cornish village setting

Set above the valley of the River Inny in the pretty hamlet of Treburley, a few miles south of Launceston. This 18th-century pub is owned and run by Anton Piotrowski, a former winner of BBC's *MasterChef The Professionals*. Anton heads a close-knit team dedicated to serving guests with top-notch ales, ciders and food. A tree-shaded garden to the rear is a pleasant place to relax with a pint of Healey's Cornish Rattler cider or Jail Ale from the increasingly popular Dartmoor Brewery. Choosing from the menu of pub classics and specials may be a struggle, although a pleasant one. A robust start could be game terrine with pickles and toast; or a pheasant and bacon Scotch egg with home-made brown sauce. Follow perhaps with roast guinea fowl, pearl barley and green beans. Dessert selections may include chocolate and orange bread and butter pudding; and lemon curd cheesecake.

Open all day all wk Closed 25–26 Dec **Food** Lunch Mon–Thu 12–3, Fri–Sun all day Dinner Mon–Thu 6–9, Fri–Sun all day ⊕ FREE HOUSE ◀ St Austell Tribute, Dartmoor Jail Ale ○ Thatchers, Healey's Cornish Rattler. **Facilities** Non-diners area ☙ (Bar Garden) ♦ Children's portions Garden ♬ Parking WiFi (notice required)

TREGADILLETT Map 3 SX28

Eliot Arms

tel: 01566 772051 **PL15 7EU**
email: humechris@hotmail.co.uk
dir: *From Launceston take A30 towards Bodmin. Then follow brown signs to Tregadillett*

Creeper-covered inn with lots of nostalgia

The extraordinary decor in this charming creeper-clad coaching inn, dating back to 1625, includes Masonic regalia, horse brasses and grandfather clocks. It was believed to have been a Masonic lodge for Napoleonic prisoners, and even has its own friendly ghost. Customers can enjoy real fires in winter and lovely hanging

baskets in summer. Food, based on locally sourced meat and fresh fish and shellfish caught off the Cornish coast, is served in the bar or bright and airy restaurant. Expect home-made soups, pie and curry of the day; steak and chips; chargrills; and home-made vegetarian dishes.

Open all day all wk 11.30–11 (Fri–Sat 11.30am–mdnt Sun 12–10.30) **Food** Lunch Mon–Fri 12–2, Sat–Sun 12–9 Dinner Mon–Fri 6–9, Sat–Sun 12–9 ⊕ FREE HOUSE ◀ St Austell Tribute, Wadworth 6X, guest ale ○ Symonds. ♀ 9 **Facilities** Non-diners area ☙ (Bar Outside area) ♦ Children's menu Children's portions Family room Outside area Parking WiFi (notice required)

TRESCO (ISLES OF SCILLY) Map 2 SV81

The New Inn ★★★★ INN ◉ PICK OF THE PUBS

tel: 01720 422849 **New Grimsby TR24 0QQ**
email: newinn@tresco.co.uk web: www.tresco.co.uk
dir: *By New Grimsby Quay*

Sub-tropical splendour and local bounty at the very edge of Britain

Just a few steps away from this old inn is the quay at New Grimsby and the first of a string of white-sand beaches that garland this sub-tropical island in the Atlantic. Very much at the heart of Tresco's community, the pub hosts three ale and cider festivals during the summer months, and live music throughout the year. Visitors from the mainland receive a hearty welcome as they settle at the bar, which is partly created from shipwreck salvage. It lends a rustic maritime ambience entirely suited to the imbibing of ales brewed on St Mary's. Delicious Scillonian provender from both land and sea are the mainstays of the pub's menu, which has been awarded an AA Rosette. The 'surf and turf' combination of Bryher lobster and chargrilled Tresco beefsteak is a no-brainer, while the savoury delicacy of a Cornish pork and Tresco partridge sausage roll may suffice for the smaller appetite.

Open all day all wk (Apr–Oct) phone for winter opening **Food** Lunch all wk 12–2 Dinner all wk 6.30–9 ⊕ FREE HOUSE ◀ Skinner's Betty Stogs, Ales of Scilly, St Austell Tribute ○ Healey's Cornish Rattler, Cornish Gold, Skreach. ♀ 14 **Facilities** Non-diners area ☙ (Bar Restaurant Garden) ♦ Children's menu Children's portions Garden ♬ Beer festival Cider festival WiFi **Rooms** 16

TRURO Map 2 SW84

Old Ale House

tel: 01872 271122 **7 Quay St TR1 2HD**
email: robin@skinnersbrewery.com
dir: *In town centre*

Architecturally distinctive city-centre pub

Close to the old riverside quays, this bare-boarded, heavily-beamed pub is a Skinner's Brewery tap, so a reliable pint is a cert; guest ales and Truro-made Apple Slayer and Lyonesse real ciders are first-rate too. A collaboration between Skinner's and Devon's River Cottage-trained chefs lies behind the upstairs restaurant, that showcases Cornwall's best produce. Menus offer spicy chorizo and fennel sausage roll; Cornish rarebit on toast; butternut squash Wellington; and 100% Cornish mackerel burger, winter leaves, chunky tartare sauce and wedges. Enjoy lemon posset or apple and cobnut crumble for afters.

Open all day all wk 11–11 (Fri–Sat 11am–1am Sun 12–10.30) Closed 25–26 Dec, 1 Jan **Food** Lunch all wk 12–2.30 Dinner 5.30–9 Av main course £10 Restaurant menu available all wk ⊕ ENTERPRISE INNS ◀ Skinner's Betty Stogs, Porthleven, Lushingtons Cornish Pale Ale & Heligan Honey, guest ales ○ Cornwall Cider Co Apple Slayer & Lyonesse. ♀ 9 **Facilities** Non-diners area ☙ (Bar) ♦ Children's menu WiFi (notice required)

VERYAN
Map 2 SW93

The New Inn

tel: 01872 501362 **TR2 5QA**
email: newinnveryan@gmail.com
dir: *From St Austell take A390 towards Truro, in 2m left to Tregony. Through Tregony, follow signs to Veryan*

Traditional home cooking and good ales

This unspoiled pub started life as a pair of cottages in the 16th century. In the centre of a pretty village on the Roseland Peninsula, The New Inn has open fires, a beamed ceiling, a single bar serving St Austell ales and a warm, welcoming atmosphere. Sunday lunch is a speciality but other choices during the week might include steak and St Austell ale pie; mushroom Stroganoff; Cornish ham with free range eggs and fries; or creamy tarragon chicken with fresh veg and new potatoes. Traditional puddings take in warm chocolate fudge cake; zingy lemon cheesecake; and sticky toffee pudding – some served with Cornish clotted cream.

Open all day all wk 12-3 5.30-11 (Sun 12-3 7-11) Closed 25 Dec **Food** Lunch all wk 12-2 Dinner Mon-Sat 6.30-9, Sun 7-9 Set menu available ⊕ ST AUSTELL BREWERY ◀ Tribute, Proper Job, Cornish Best ↻ Healey's Cornish Rattler, Cloudy Apple. ₹ **Facilities** Non-diners area ❀ (Bar Garden) ♦ Children's menu Children's portions Garden ⋒ WiFi ☶ (notice required)

WADEBRIDGE
Map 2 SW97

The Quarryman Inn

tel: 01208 816444 **Edmonton PL27 7JA**
email: thequarryman@live.co.uk
dir: *From A39 (W of Wadebridge) follow Edmonton sign (opposite Royal Cornwall Showground)*

Tucked away in the Cornish countryside

Close to the famous Camel Trail, this family-owned free house was originally a group of 18th-century slate workers' cottages, built around a courtyard. A bow window featuring a stained-glass quarryman adds character to this unusual inn. The pub's menus change frequently, but look out for regular house speciality hake, monkfish, prawns and River Camel mussels Portuguese-style, cooked and served in a copper cataplana. The pub is also popular for their chargrilled prime sizzling steaks served on a platter with mushrooms, tomatoes, onions and chips. Enjoy one of the good range of beers and ciders in the slate courtyard.

Open all day all wk 12-11 **Food** Lunch all wk 12-2.30 Dinner all wk 6-9 ⊕ FREE HOUSE ◀ Timothy Taylor Landlord, Sharp's, Skinner's, Otter, guest ales ↻ Cornish Orchards Gold Cider. **Facilities** Non-diners area ♦ Children's menu Children's portions Garden ⋒ Parking WiFi ☶ (notice required)

The Ship Inn

tel: 01208 813845 **Gonvena Hill PL27 6DF**
email: info@shipinnwadebridge.com
dir: *From A39 (E of River Camel) at rdbt follow Rock sign. Straight on at mini rdbt, pass Wadebridge School, inn on right at bottom of the hill*

A local with a busy social diary

Naval paraphernalia is only to be expected within a pub called The Ship, and this one in Wadebridge is no exception. But it's not overdone, instead lending an air of quiet sophistication to this popular local. Dating back to the 16th century, the interior's three levels are warmed by two open fires in winter; a decking area outside is much sought-after in summer. Local ales populate the bar, as do local suppliers

on the menus. Smoked mackerel, beetroot, new potatoes, horseradish and watercress makes a good start to a meal, followed by Porthilly mussels, fennel, onion, Thatcher's cider and thin chips; or chicken breast, macaroni cheese, asparagus and truffle oil.

Open all wk 12-2.30 5-11 **Food** Lunch 12-2 Dinner Sun-Thu 5-9, Fri-Sat 5-9.30 (no food Sun eve in winter) Set menu available ⊕ PUNCH TAVERNS ◀ Sharp's Atlantic IPA & Doom Bar, Padstow Windjammer, Harbour IPA. ₹ 12 **Facilities** Non-diners area ❀ (Bar) ♦ Children's menu Children's portions Outside area ⋒ Parking WiFi ☶ (notice required)

WIDEMOUTH BAY
Map 2 SS20

Bay View Inn

tel: 01288 361273 **Marine Dr EX23 0AW**
email: thebayviewinn@aol.com
dir: *Adjacent to beach*

Ocean views and good food

Dating back around 100 years, this welcoming, family-run pub was a guest house for many years before becoming an inn in the 1960s. True to its name, the pub has fabulous views of the rolling Atlantic. It also has three dining areas: Driftwood Restaurant, which has patio doors that lead out onto a decking area; Surf Restaurant, with its atmospheric lighting and quirky paintings; and Beach Hut Restaurant, running along the front of the original building. Menus make excellent use of local produce, as in the signature dish of fish pie; Cornish gammon steak; or Big Bad Boy Bay View Burger – Cornish mince steak topped with red onion marmalade. Other choices include home-made pies and casseroles.

Open all day all wk **Food** Mon-Sat 12-9, Sun 12-8 ⊕ FREE HOUSE ◀ Skinner's Spriggan Ale, Sharp's Doom Bar, St Austell Tribute ↻ Somersby, Cornish Orchards. ₹ 14 **Facilities** Non-diners area ❀ (Bar Garden) ♦ Children's menu Children's portions Play area Garden ⋒ Parking WiFi ☶ (notice required)

ZENNOR
Map 2 SW43

The Tinners Arms
PICK OF THE PUBS

tel: 01736 796927 **TR26 3BY**
email: tinners@tinnersarms.co.uk
dir: *Take B3306 from St Ives towards St Just. Zennor approx 5m*

Timeless village inn with local ales and good food

Its closeness to the South West Coastal Path almost guarantees that muddy-booted walkers will be found among the Tinners Arms' clientele, enjoying the timelessness of its stone floors, low ceilings, cushioned settles, winter open fires and the revivifying Cornish real ales or Burrow Hill cider from Somerset. Built of granite in 1271 for masons working on ancient St Senara's church next door (famous for its richly carved Mermaid Chair), many may welcome the fact that the only pub in the village has no TV, jukebox or fruit machine, nor can a mobile phone signal reach it. Based on ingredients from local suppliers, a winter supper menu offers moules marinière; grilled goats' cheese and couscous salad; venison and chorizo stew, creamy mash and curly kale; and winter berry crumble with ice cream or custard. Sandwiches, ploughman's and light meals are available at lunchtime. Outside is a peaceful garden and large terrace with sea views.

Open all day all wk **Food** Lunch all wk 12-3 Dinner all wk 6.30-9 (ex Sun & Mon eve winter) Av main course £14 ⊕ FREE HOUSE ◀ Zennor Mermaid, St Austell Tinners Ale & Tribute ↻ Burrow Hill. ₹ 10 **Facilities** Non-diners area ❀ (Bar Restaurant Garden) ♦ Children's menu Children's portions Garden ⋒ Parking WiFi

CUMBRIA

AMBLESIDE
Map 18 NY30

Drunken Duck Inn
PICK OF THE PUBS

tel: 015394 36347 **Barngates LA22 0NG**
email: info@drunkenduckinn.co.uk
dir: *From Kendal on A591 to Ambleside, then follow Hawkshead sign. In 2.5m inn sign on right, 1m up hill*

Traditional 17th-century inn with classic Lakeland views

A good story lies behind the name of the inn. When a 19th-century landlady found her ducks blotto in the road after a beer leak 'contaminated' their feed, she thought they were dead and began plucking them. When they came round, she was so full of remorse she knitted them all warm Hawkshead yarn waistcoats. The inn stands at a crossroads above Ambleside with splendid views towards Windermere. Ales from the on-site Barngates brewery are served on a Brathay slate counter in the oak-floored, hop-hung bar, where wooden settles with Herdwick wool coverings, sketches, prints and enamel signs further contribute to the character. Add candlelight and a log fire, and what more could you want? Ideally the menu, of course, which offers a possible dinner of hake, pickled radish and brown shrimps; beef shin and stout suet pudding, carrot, swede and red cabbage; and egg custard tart with blood orange sorbet. Behind lies a tranquil garden with its own tarn.

Open all day all wk Closed 25 Dec **Food** Lunch all wk 12-4 Restaurant menu available ⊕ FREE HOUSE ◖ Barngates Cracker Ale, Chesters Strong & Ugly, Tag Lag, Cat Nap, Brathay Gold. ♟ 17 **Facilities** Non-diners area ⬩♦ Children's portions Garden ⇌ Parking WiFi

Wateredge Inn

tel: 015394 32332 **Waterhead Bay LA22 0EP**
email: stay@wateredgeinn.co.uk
dir: *M6 junct 36, A591 to Ambleside, 5m from Windermere station*

Family-run inn on the shores of Lake Windermere

The Wateredge Inn was converted from two 17th-century fishermen's cottages, and now offers a stylish bar and restaurant. With large gardens and plenty of seating running down to the lakeshore, the inn has been run by the same family for nearly 30 years. The lunch menu offers sandwiches, salads, pub classics and slates – platters of smoked fish, charcuterie or cheese and antipasti. Meanwhile the dinner menu has choices ranging from baby pork back ribs to Cumbrian lamb hotpot, and chicken curry. Specials and a children's menu are also available.

Open all day all wk 10.30am-11pm Closed 23-26 Dec **Food** Lunch Mon-Fri 12-2.30, Sat-Sun 12-4 Dinner all wk 6-9 ⊕ FREE HOUSE ◖ Theakston, Barngates Tag Lag & Cat Nap, Watermill Collie Wobbles ♻ Symonds. ♟ 15 **Facilities** Non-diners area ⬩ (Bar Garden) ⬩♦ Children's menu Children's portions Garden ⇌ Parking WiFi

APPLEBY-IN-WESTMORLAND
Map 18 NY62

Tufton Arms Hotel
PICK OF THE PUBS

tel: 017683 51593 **Market Square CA16 6XA**
email: info@tuftonarmshotel.co.uk
dir: *In town centre*

Elegant coaching inn with renowned fish dishes

This imposing, gabled building sits at the foot of Appleby's main street, close to the River Eden below the curvaceous fells of the wild North Pennines. There's an elegant, country house feel to the public rooms, where co-owner Teresa Milsom's design skills shine through, with astonishing attention to detail producing classic atmosphere and contemporary comforts. At the heart of the hotel, overlooking a cobbled mews courtyard, is the Conservatory Fish Restaurant, where David Milsom and his kitchen team's cuisine is complemented by a serious wine list. The menu covers all bases, with lamb shank, belly pork or home-made steak and ale pie as comforting standards, and local game presented as available. It's for the fresh fish dishes, however, that the Tufton has a particular reputation. Daily deliveries from Fleetwood are crafted into starters like smoked haddock and mushroom hotpot baked in cheese sauce; progressing to mains of seafood tagliatelle, or pan-fried hand-picked crab and salmon cake. Beer connoisseurs may enjoy the hotel's own house ale.

Open all day all wk 7.30am-11pm Closed 25-26 Dec **Food** Lunch all wk 12-2 Dinner all wk 6.30-9 ⊕ FREE HOUSE ◖ Tufton Arms Ale, Cumberland Corby Ale. ♟ 15 **Facilities** Non-diners area ⬩ (Bar) ⬩♦ Children's portions Outside area ⇌ Parking WiFi ▭

BASSENTHWAITE
Map 18 NY23

The Pheasant ★★★ HL ⊛
PICK OF THE PUBS

See Pick of the Pubs on page 102

BEETHAM
Map 18 SD47

The Wheatsheaf at Beetham
PICK OF THE PUBS

tel: 015395 62123 **LA7 7AL**
email: info@wheatsheafbeetham.com
dir: *On A6, 5m N of M6 junct 35*

Family-owned traditional village free house

In the 17th century, this was a farmhouse and the farmer's wife would feed the labourers; it later became a coaching inn. Today its long history of providing refreshment continues with an intriguing offer from owners Jean and Richard Skelton: order a main course and pay just 1p for your starter or dessert. So, having raided the piggy bank, what do your pennies buy? Among the starters are chicken and pork pâté with home-made chutney; and goats' cheese and tomato tart. Main courses include pan-fried minute steak with mushroom, onion, potato and red wine ragout; and home-made fish pie with haddock and prawns, mash and melted cheese. A dessert could be rich warm chocolate fudge cake and cream; or apple crumble and custard. The Old Tap Bar offers Marston's Wainwright, Tirril Queen Jean and Cross Bay Nightfall real ales, as well as Kingstone Press cider.

Open all day all wk 10am-11pm Closed 25 Dec **Food** Mon-Sat 12-9, Sun 12-8.30 Set menu available Restaurant menu available all wk ⊕ FREE HOUSE ◖ Marston's Wainwright, Tirril Queen Jean, Cross Bay Nightfall ♻ Kingstone Press.
Facilities Non-diners area ⬩♦ Children's menu Children's portions Outside area ⇌ Parking WiFi ▭ (notice required)

PICK OF THE PUBS

The Pheasant ★★★ HL ✸

BASSENTHWAITE Map 18 NY23

tel: 017687 76234 **CA13 9YE**
email: info@the-pheasant.co.uk
web: www.the-pheasant.co.uk
dir: A66 to Cockermouth, 8m N of
Keswick on left

Accomplished food in peaceful Lake District setting

At the foot of the Sale Fell and close to Bassenthwaite Lake, this 17th-century former coaching inn occupies a peaceful spot in the Lake District and is surrounded by lovely gardens. Once a farmhouse, the pub today combines the role of traditional Cumbrian hostelry with that of an internationally renowned modern hotel. Even so, you still sense the history the moment you walk through the door – the legendary foxhunter John Peel, whose "view halloo would awaken the dead", according to the song, was a regular here. In the warmly inviting bar, with polished parquet flooring, panelled walls and oak settles, hang two of Cumbrian artist and former customer Edward H Thompson's paintings. Here, you can order a pint of Coniston Bluebird or Hawkshead Bitter, or cast your eyes over the extensive selection of malt whiskies. The high standard of food, recognised by an AA Rosette, is well known for miles around; meals are served in the attractive beamed restaurant, bistro, bar and lounges overlooking the

gardens. Light lunches served in the lounge and bar include open sandwiches, baguettes and potted shrimps on toast, as well as main courses such as Cumberland sausages, buttered Savoy cabbage and mashed potato; smoked haddock with light cheese sauce, spinach and poached egg; and pan-fried supreme of guinea fowl. A three course dinner in the restaurant could feature beetroot-cured gravad lax, beetroot jelly and horseradish cream; crispy confit of Gressingham duck, cabbage and bacon, potato terrine and plum compôte; and pistachio and cherry Arctic roll. Treat the family to afternoon tea with home-made scones and rum butter. The Pheasant can get pretty busy, so booking ahead for meals may be required.

Open all day all wk Closed 25 Dec
Food Lunch all wk 12-4.30 Dinner all wk 6-9 Restaurant menu available Tue-Sun
🛢 FREE HOUSE ◀ Coniston Bluebird Bitter, Cumberland Corby Ale, Hawkshead Bitter ☼ Thatchers Gold.
🍷 12 **Facilities** Non-diners area 🐾 (Bar Garden) 🧒 Children's menu Children's portions Garden 🪑 Parking WiFi
Rooms 15

BOOT
Map 18 NY10

Brook House Inn ★★★★ INN
PICK OF THE PUBS

tel: 019467 23288 **CA19 1TG**
email: stay@brookhouseinn.co.uk **web:** www.brookhouseinn.co.uk
dir: M6 junct 36, A590 follow Barrow signs. A5092, then A595. Pass Broughton-in-Furness, right at lights to Ulpha. Cross river, next left signed Eskdale to Boot. (NB not all routes to Boot are suitable in bad weather conditions)

Tranquil location for tempting, home-made food

Few locations can rival this: Lakeland fells rise behind the inn to England's highest peak, while golden sunsets illuminate tranquil Eskdale. Footpaths wind to nearby Stanley Ghyll's wooded gorge with its falls and red squirrels, and the charming La'al Ratty narrow-gauge railway steams to and from the coast. It's a magnet for ramblers and cyclists, so a small drying room is greatly appreciated by them. Up to seven real ales are kept, including Yates Best Bitter and Langdale from Cumbrian Legendary Ales, and an amazing selection of 175 malt whiskies. Home-made food prepared from Cumbria's finest showcases the menus, so temper the drizzle with a warming bowl of home-made soup, or grilled scallops with cheese, garlic and lemon, followed by wild mushroom and fettuccine; beef and beer pie; or smoked haddock on mashed potato with leeks. Raspberry meringues or chocolate fudge cake with hot berry sauce, make a fine finish. This great community pub also takes a full role in the famous Boot Beer Festival each June.

Open all day all wk Closed 25 Dec **Food** Contact pub for food times Set menu available ⊕ FREE HOUSE ◀ Hawkshead Windermere Pale, Cumbrian Legendary Langdale, Yates Best Bitter, guest ales ♂ Westons. ♚ 10 **Facilities** Non-diners area ♦ Children's menu Children's portions Family room Garden ⋒ Beer festival Parking WiFi ▭ **Rooms** 8

BORROWDALE
Map 18 NY21

The Langstrath Country Inn

tel: 017687 77239 **CA12 5XG**
email: info@thelangstrath.com
dir: From Keswick take B5289, through Grange & Rosthwaite, left to Stonethwaite. Inn on left after 0.5m

Picturesque village inn, a favourite with ramblers

Sitting in the stunning Langstrath Valley in the heart of the Lakes and on the coast-to-coast and Cumbrian Way walks, this lovely family-run, 16th-century inn was originally a miner's cottage. It is an ideal base for those attempting England's highest peak, Scafell Pike, and the restaurant is ideally positioned to maximise the spectacular views. Here hungry ramblers enjoy high-quality Lakeland dishes based on local ingredients. A typical choice could include pheasant, duck, chicken and pistachio terrine; home-made steak and ale pie; chicken, wild boar, salami and leek steamed suet pudding; and oven-baked salmon fillet with Mediterranean vegetables. Local cask-conditioned ales include some from the Keswick Brewery.

Open all day 12-10.30 Closed Dec & Jan, Mon **Food** Lunch Tue-Sun 12-2.30 Dinner Tue-Sun 6-9 ⊕ FREE HOUSE ◀ Jennings Bitter & Cocker Hoop, Keswick Thirst Rescue, Theakston Old Peculier ♂ Thatchers Gold. ♚ 9 **Facilities** Non-diners area ♣ (Bar Garden) ♦ Children's menu Children's portions Garden ⋒ Parking WiFi ▭ (notice required)

BOWLAND BRIDGE
Map 18 SD48

Hare & Hounds Country Inn
PICK OF THE PUBS

tel: 015395 68333 **LA11 6NN**
email: info@hareandhoundsbowlandbridge.co.uk
dir: M6 junct 36, A590 signed Barrow. Right onto A5074 signed Bowness & Windermere. Approx 4m at sharp bend left & follow Bowland Bridge sign

Fabulous views and local produce

Very much at the heart of the community, this 17th-century coaching inn even hosts the Post Office on Tuesday and Thursday afternoons. In the pretty little hamlet of Bowland Bridge, not far from Bowness, the pub has gorgeous views of Cartmel Fell. Its traditional country-pub atmosphere is fostered by the flagstone floors, stacked logs, wooden tables and mis-matched chairs. Strong links with local suppliers bring exclusively reared pork and lamb to the menu, and an excellent range of Cumbrian ales to the bar. At lunchtime hot or cold sandwiches are available, in addition to hearty plates such as Fell House Farm trio of lamb cutlets with mint and rosemary gravy; or a special of home-made cottage pie stuffed with minced Tulithwaite Hall beef and topped with creamy mash. Also home made are desserts such as individual rhubarb and ginger crumble, served with your choice of cream, ice cream or custard.

Open all day all wk 12-11 Closed 25 Dec **Food** Lunch Mon-Fri 12-2, Sat 12-9, Sun 12-8.30 Dinner Mon-Fri 6-9, Sat 12-9, Sun 12-8.30 Restaurant menu available all wk ⊕ FREE HOUSE ◀ Tirril, Coniston, Ulverston, Hawkshead, Kirkby Lonsdale ♂ Cowmire Hall. ♚ 10 **Facilities** Non-diners area ♣ (Bar Garden) ♦ Children's menu Children's portions Garden ⋒ Parking WiFi ▭ (notice required)

BRAITHWAITE
Map 18 NY22

Coledale Inn

tel: 017687 78272 **CA12 5TN**
email: info@coledale-inn.co.uk
dir: M6 junct 40, A66 signed Keswick. Approx 18m. Exit A66, follow Whinlatter Pass & Braithwaite sign, left on B5292. In Braithwaite left at pub sign, over stream bridge to inn

An atmospheric place to finish a walk

Originally a woollen mill, the refurbished Coledale Inn dates from around 1824 and had stints as a pencil mill and a private house before becoming the inn it is today. The interior is attractively designed, whilst footpaths leading off from the large gardens make it ideal for exploring the nearby fells. Two homely bars serve a selection of local ales while traditional lunch and dinner menus are served in the dining room. Typical choices include duo of black pudding and haggis; chilli con carne; rosemary and garlic chicken; and hot chocolate and fudge cake; there's further options on the specials board.

Open all day all wk **Food** Lunch Mon-Fri 12-2, Sat-Sun 12-6 Dinner all wk 6-9 Av main course £11 Set menu available ⊕ FREE HOUSE ◀ Cumberland Corby Ale, Hesket Newmarket, Yates, Keswick, Tirril, Geltsdale, Marston's. ♚ 8 **Facilities** Non-diners area ♣ (Bar Garden) ♦ Children's menu Children's portions Play area Garden ⋒ Parking WiFi ▭ (notice required)

BRAITHWAITE *continued*

The Royal Oak ★★★★ INN

tel: 017687 78533 **CA12 5SY**
email: tpfranks@hotmail.com **web:** www.royaloak-braithwaite.co.uk
dir: *M6 junct 40, A66 towards Keswick, approx 18m (bypass Keswick), exit A66 left onto B5292 to Braithwaite. Pub in village centre*

Delightful country pub surrounded by beautiful landscapes

Surrounded by high fells and beautiful scenery, The Royal Oak is set in the centre of the village and is the perfect base for walkers. The interior is all oak beams and log fires, and the menu offers hearty pub food, such as slow-roasted pork belly and apple flavoured mash; Thai red chicken curry; smoky bacon and chorizo sausage pasta; and giant Yorkshire pudding filled with Cumberland sausage casserole, all served alongside local ales, such as Sneck Lifter or Cumberland Ale. Visitors can extend the experience by staying over in the comfortable en suite bedrooms.

Open all day all wk **Food** Lunch all wk 12-2 Dinner all wk 6-9 ⊕ MARSTON'S ◀ Jennings Lakeland Stunner, Cumberland Ale, Cocker Hoop & Sneck Lifter. ♈ 8 **Facilities** Non-diners area ♦♦ Children's menu Children's portions Garden ⌐ Parking WiFi ⛺ **Rooms** 10

BRAMPTON   Map 21 NY56

Blacksmiths Arms ★★★★ INN

tel: 016977 3452 **Talkin CA8 1LE**
email: blacksmithsarmstalkin@yahoo.co.uk **web:** www.blacksmithstalkin.co.uk
dir: *M6 junct 43, A69 E. 7m, straight on at rdbt, follow signs to Talkin Tarn then Talkin Village*

Attractive free house serving good home-cooked food

With cartwheels lined up outside, this former smithy faces a small green by the crossroads in the centre of the village. On its doorstep is northern Cumbria's wildly beautiful countryside. The menu of good, traditional home cooking makes extensive use of fresh local produce for smoked haddock and spring onion fishcakes; creamy chicken and leek pie; liver and bacon casserole; Barnsley double lamb chop; and fisherman's pie. At lunchtime a choice of sandwiches, paninis and baked potatoes is offered. Four real ales are always available; there's a beer garden, and out front a couple of tables with seating.

Open all day all wk 12-12 **Food** Lunch all wk 12-2 Dinner all wk 6-9 Av main course £9.95 ⊕ FREE HOUSE ◀ Yates, Black Sheep, guest ales. ♈ 16 **Facilities** Non-diners area ♦♦ Children's menu Children's portions Garden ⌐ Parking WiFi **Rooms** 8

CARTMEL   Map 18 SD37

The Masons Arms

tel: 015395 68486 **Strawberry Bank LA11 6NW**
email: info@masonsarmsstrawberrybank.co.uk
dir: *M6 junct 36, A590 towards Barrow. Right onto A5074 signed Bowness/Windermere. 5m, left at Bowland Bridge. Through village, pub on right*

Attractive inn in a beautiful spot

An atmospheric, charmingly decorated pub with a stunning location overlooking the Winster Valley and beyond, The Masons Arms has an atmospheric interior with low, beamed ceilings, old fireplaces and quirky furniture. Waiting staff manoeuvre through the busy bar, dining rooms and heated, covered terraces carrying popular dishes such as warm pitta bread and home-made houmous to nibble; Masons Arms ribs with sticky sauce and fries; or Cullen skink to start; followed by smoked

haddock, scampi and lemon fishcakes; or braised belly pork with sage jus. If there's room, try some apple and blackberry crumble, jam roly poly or honeycomb cheesecake. Wash it down with a pint of Marston's Wainwright.

Open all day all wk 9.30am-11pm **Food** Lunch Mon-Fri 12-2.30, Sat-Sun 12-9 Dinner Mon-Fri 6-9, Sat-Sun 12-9 ⊕ FREE HOUSE/INDIVIDUAL INNS LTD ◀ Marston's Wainwright, Hawkshead Bitter, guest ales ♂ Kingstone Press. ♈ 12 **Facilities** Non-diners area ♦♦ Children's menu Children's portions Outside area ⌐ Parking WiFi

---

CLIFTON   Map 18 NY52

George and Dragon   PICK OF THE PUBS

tel: 01768 865381 **CA10 2ER**
email: enquiries@georgeanddragonclifton.co.uk
dir: *M6 junct 40, A66 towards Appleby-in-Westmorland, A6 S to Clifton*

Historic pub majoring on local produce

This lovely pub is more peaceful today than it was in 1745, when the retreating army of 'Bonnie' Prince Charlie was defeated in the nearby village of Clifton. The pub is set on the historic Lowther Estate near Ullswater, where a ruined castle-mansion is set at the heart of pasture, woodland and fells alongside the rushing River Lowther and pretty village of Askham. Meticulously renovated by owner Charles Lowther, this is a traditional inn with contemporary comforts, and the appealing menu majors on the bountiful produce of the estate. Beef is from pedigree Shorthorns; pork from home-reared rare breed stock; while game and most fish is local. Settle in with a pint of Hawkshead Bitter and secure a starter of terrine of smoked venison with salt-baked celeriac, followed by braised Galloway beef pavé, smoked potato purée, and roasted root vegetables; or pan-fried fillet of grey mullet, Parmentier potatoes, salsify, and caramelised queen scallops. Sharing plates, salads, sandwiches and burgers all vie for space on the menu. There is a secluded courtyard and garden.

Open all day all wk Closed 26 Dec **Food** Lunch all wk 12-2.30 Dinner all wk 6-9 Set menu available ⊕ FREE HOUSE ◀ Hawkshead Bitter, Eden Gold, Cumberland Corby Blonde ♂ Westons Stowford Press. ♈ 17 **Facilities** Non-diners area ❄ (Bar Garden) ♦♦ Children's menu Children's portions Garden ⌐ Parking WiFi

---

COCKERMOUTH   Map 18 NY13

The Trout Hotel ★★★★ HL

tel: 01900 823591 **Crown St CA13 0EJ**
email: enquiries@trouthotel.co.uk **web:** www.trouthotel.co.uk
dir: *In town centre*

Town-centre hotel overlooking the River Derwent

Until he was eight, the poet William Wordsworth lived next door, although then this 17th-century building was a private house. Much remains to remind us of its heritage: stone walls, exposed beams, marble fireplaces, restored plasterwork, period stained-glass, and a carefully-preserved oak staircase. At the bar ales from town brewery Jennings are joined by Carlisle-brewed guest, Corby Blonde. Fresh, locally sourced ingredients drive the menu, from smoked haddock fishcake, made with Thornby Moor Stumpies goats' cheese, to Cumbrian beef sirloin fajitas. A drink or a meal in the gardens overlooking the River Derwent is an enjoyable way of passing time.

Open all day all wk **Food** all wk 12-9.30 Restaurant menu available all wk ⊕ FREE HOUSE ◀ Jennings Cumberland Ale, Cooper Hoop, Cumberland Corby Blonde ♂ Thatchers. ♈ 24 **Facilities** Non-diners area ♦♦ Children's menu Children's portions Garden ⌐ Parking WiFi ⛺ (notice required) **Rooms** 49

PICK OF THE PUBS

The Punch Bowl Inn ★★★★★ INN ❁❁

CROSTHWAITE Map 18 SD49

tel: 015395 68237 **LA8 8HR**
email: info@the-punchbowl.co.uk
web: www.the-punchbowl.co.uk
dir: *M6 junct 36, A590 towards Barrow, A5074, follow Crosthwaite signs. Pub by church*

Luxury Lake District inn and restaurant

Very much a destination dining inn, the Punch Bowl stands alongside the village church in the delightfully unspoilt Lyth Valley. The slates on the bar floor, which were found beneath the old dining room, complement the Brathay slate bar top and antique furnishings. Ales from Cumbrian microbreweries include Tag Lag from Barngates Brewery, and Bluebird from Coniston. The restaurant has comfortable leather chairs, polished oak floorboards and an eye-catching stone fireplace. Two rooms off the bar add extra space for eating or relaxing with a pint and the daily paper in front of an open fire. Head chef Scott Fairweather focuses on the best local and seasonal produce, winning two AA Rosettes for his expertise. Sourcing ingredients extensively from the area's estates, farms and coastal villages, the lunch and dinner menus in both the bar and the restaurant might begin with traditional steak tartare with Bloody Mary dressing; or twice-baked mature cheddar soufflé with wilted spinach. For

the main event, choose from the likes of roast cod loin cooked in Thatchers cider with mussels, leeks, bacon and mash; or roast venison haunch with parsnip, blue cheese, blackberry and apple. If potatoes are a must, choose between twice-cooked chips or sautéed with crème fraîche and spring onions. Desserts are accomplished, and tempt with uncommon flavours: vanilla cheesecake with mulled wine, blackcurrant and liquorice, for example; or dark chocolate delice with parsnip, yogurt and cranberry. In addition to a good list of dessert wines, champagne is available by the glass. Individually furnished guest rooms featuring freestanding roll-top baths can be booked.

Open all day all wk **Food** Lunch Mon-Fri 12-5.30, Sat-Sun 12-4 Dinner all wk 5.30-9 Av main course £17
⊕ FREE HOUSE ◀ Barngates Tag Lag, Coniston Bluebird Bitter ⚘ Thatchers Gold. ♟ 12 **Facilities** Non-diners area ❧ (Bar Garden) ♛ Children's menu Children's portions Garden ⌲ Parking WiFi **Rooms** 9

CONISTON
Map 18 SD39

The Black Bull Inn & Hotel
PICK OF THE PUBS

tel: 015394 41335 & 41668 **1 Yewdale Rd LA21 8DU**
email: ian@conistonbrewery.com
dir: *M6 junct 36, A590. 23m from Kendal via Windermere & Ambleside*

Four-hundred-year-old Lake District heartland pub

Beside a stream, or beck as they say round here, stands this traditional Lakeland pub. Its bare stone walls, oak beams, log-burning stove and part-slate floor all contribute to its appeal, while of further interest, at least to beer drinkers, is its own microbrewery's Bluebird Bitter, commemorating Donald Campbell's attempts on the world water speed record; it also brews Old Man Ale, named for the local 2,634-ft mountain. Those out walking all morning or all day can look forward to sandwiches or filled jacket potatoes. Chances are they'll want something heartier, such as roast rib of beef with Yorkshire pudding and gravy; poached sole fillets with dill and cucumber cream; or roast loin and belly of pork with sage and onion stuffing, crackling and gravy.

Open all day all wk Closed 25 Dec **Food** all wk 12-9 Av main course £10 ⊕ FREE HOUSE ◀ Coniston Bluebird Bitter, Bluebird Premium XB, Old Man Ale, Winter Warmer Blacksmiths Ale, Special Oatmeal Stout ♂ Broadoak Premium Perry & Moonshine, Gwynt y Ddraig Haymaker, guest ciders. ♀ 10 **Facilities** Non-diners area ♣ (Bar Garden) ♦♦ Children's menu Children's portions Family room Garden 🎋 Beer festival Parking WiFi ⇔ (notice required)

CROSTHWAITE
Map 18 SD49

The Punch Bowl Inn ★★★★★ INN ◉◉ PICK OF THE PUBS

See Pick of the Pubs on page 105

ELTERWATER
Map 18 NY30

The Britannia Inn
PICK OF THE PUBS

tel: 015394 37210 **LA22 9HP**
email: info@britinn.co.uk
dir: *In village centre*

Village inn well placed for Lake District walkers

Walks and mountain-bike trails head off in all directions from the front door of this free house in the Langdale Valley, just a short drive from Ambleside, Grasmere, Windermere, Hawkshead and Coniston. Built as a farmhouse and cobbler's more than 500 years ago, the whitewashed building only became an inn some 200 years back and the bar area is essentially a series of small, cosy rooms with low-beamed oak ceilings and winter coal fires. Bar staff pull pints of guest beers nineteen to the dozen, as well as the house special brewed by Coniston. An even wider selection of real ales is available during the two-week beer festival in mid-November. The inn offers a wide choice of fresh, home-cooked food, with an evening meal typically featuring grilled sea bass fillet; or home-made chicken, ham and leek pie. Dine alfresco in the garden and take in the views of the village and tarns.

Open all day all wk 10.30am-11pm **Food** all wk 12-9.30 ⊕ FREE HOUSE ◀ Jennings Bitter, Coniston Bluebird Bitter & Britannia Inn Special Edition, Dent Aviator, Hawkshead Bitter, guest ales. **Facilities** Non-diners area ♣ (Bar Garden) ♦♦ Children's menu Children's portions Garden 🎋 Beer festival WiFi

ENNERDALE BRIDGE
Map 18 NY01

Shepherds Arms

tel: 01946 861249 **Kirkland Rd CA23 3AR**
email: shepherdsarmshotel@btconnect.com **web:** www.shepherdsarms.com
dir: *From A66 at Cockermouth take A5086 to Egremont. 7.3m, left towards Ennerdale. Through Kirkland Down to Ennerdale Bridge*

Cumbrian hospitality in a remote valley

Popular with coast-to-coast walkers and cyclists of various nationalities, the bar is usually populated by a cosmopolitan crowd mixing merrily with locals. In fact, this was once a village-centre farmhouse which also dispensed beer to the local farmers and travellers. Today, an excellent array of Cumbrian ales is served, alongside plates of good home-made food based on local produce. All appetites are catered for, starting with lunchtime snacks and finishing with robust dinner dishes such as pork belly and black pudding; or duck breast with a port and marmalade reduction.

Open all day all wk (winter times may vary) Closed 25-26 Dec **Food** Lunch all wk 12-5 Dinner all wk 5-9 ⊕ FREE HOUSE ◀ Cumbrian Legendary Ales Loweswater Gold, Yates Best Bitter, Ennerdale Blonde, Hesket Newmarket High Pike, Stringers Wolf Warrior. **Facilities** Non-diners area ♦♦ Children's portions Outside area 🎋 Parking WiFi ⇔ (notice required)

FAUGH
Map 18 NY55

The String of Horses Inn

tel: 01228 670297 **CA8 9EG**
email: info@stringofhorses.com
dir: *M6 junct 43, A69 towards Hexham. In approx 5m right at 1st lights at Corby Hill/ Warwick Bridge. 1m, through Heads Nook, in 1m sharp right. Left into Faugh. Pub on left down hill*

Traditional coaching inn in historic area

Close to Hadrian's Wall in the peaceful village of Faugh, this traditional 17th-century Lakeland inn may be tucked away but it's just 10 minutes from Carlisle. There are oak beams, wood panelling, old settles and log fires in the restaurant, where imaginative pub food is on offer, and in the bar, where you'll find real ales from the Allendale and Hesket breweries. Creamy tomato and basil soup; spicy prawn casserole; Moroccan lamb tagine; chilli lasagne; and half shoulder of lamb with mint gravy admirably represent what's on a typical menu.

Open Tue-Sun 6-11 Closed Mon **Food** Dinner Tue-Sun 6-8.30 Av main course £12.95 ⊕ FREE HOUSE ◀ Allendale Pennine Pale, Hesket Red Pike ♂ Westons Family Reserve. ♀ 8 **Facilities** Non-diners area ♦♦ Children's menu Outside area Parking WiFi ⇔ (notice required)

GRASMERE
Map 18 NY30

The Travellers Rest Inn

tel: 015394 35604 **Keswick Rd LA22 9RR**
email: stay@lakedistrictinns.co.uk **web:** www.lakedistrictinns.co.uk
dir: A591 to Grasmere, pub 0.5m N of Grasmere

Old-world charm and a mountain backdrop

Located on the edge of picturesque Grasmere and handy for touring and exploring the ever-beautiful Lake District, the Travellers Rest has been a pub for more than 500 years. Inside, a roaring log fire complements the welcoming atmosphere of the beamed and inglenook bar area. Along with ales like Sneck Lifter, an extensive menu of traditional home-cooked fare is offered, ranging from steak and kidney pudding with potatoes and vegetables, to roasted aubergine with haricot bean ratatouille. Leave room for sticky toffee pudding or red berry sundae.

Open all day all wk 12-11 **Food** all wk 12-9.30 Set menu available ⊕ FREE HOUSE ◀ Jennings Bitter, Cocker Hoop, Cumberland Ale & Sneck Lifter, guest ales. ♀ 10 **Facilities** Non-diners area ♣ (Bar Garden) ♦ Children's menu Children's portions Family room Garden ⊟ Parking WiFi ▭

GREAT SALKELD
Map 18 NY53

The Highland Drove Inn
PICK OF THE PUBS

tel: 01768 898349 **CA11 9NA**
email: highlanddrove@kyloes.co.uk
dir: M6 junct 40, A66 E'bound, A686 to Alston. 4m, left onto B6412 for Great Salkeld & Lazonby

Convivial village pub deep in the pretty Eden Valley

On an old drove road, this 300-year-old country inn recalls the long-vanished days when hardy Highland cattle were driven across open water from Scotland's Western Isles to markets in England. A reputation for high-quality food might suggest it's a destination pub, as indeed it is, but it's more than that, because locals love it too,

one attraction being a cask-conditioned ale called Kyloes Kushie. The attractive brick and timber bar, where snacks are available, is furnished with old tables and settles; the more formal dining takes place upstairs in the hunting lodge-style restaurant, where a verandah offers fine country views. The kitchen depends on locally-sourced game, fish and meat, examples including venison rendang, an Indonesian curry with coconut milk and spices; Cumbrian lamb shank slow-braised in Guinness; and duck breast marinated in pineapple, chilli and soy sauce.

Open Tue-Fri 12-2 (all wk 6pm-mdnt Sat noon-2am) Closed 25 Dec, Mon L **Food** Lunch Tue-Sun 12-2 Dinner all wk 6-9 ⊕ FREE HOUSE ◀ Theakston Black Bull Bitter, Best & Traditional Mild, Eden Brewery Kyloes Kushie, guest ale Ö Symonds. ♀ 10 **Facilities** Non-diners area ♣ (Bar Garden) ♦ Children's menu Children's portions Garden ⊟ Parking WiFi ▭ (notice required)

HAWKSHEAD
Map 18 SD39

Kings Arms ★★★ INN

tel: 015394 36372 **The Square LA22 0NZ**
email: info@kingsarmshawkshead.co.uk **web:** www.kingsarmshawkshead.co.uk
dir: M6 junct 36, A590 to Newby Bridge, right at 1st junct past rdbt, over bridge, 8m to Hawkshead

Homely inn in Beatrix Potter village

In the charming square at the heart of this Lakeland village, made famous by Beatrix Potter who lived nearby, this 16th-century inn throngs in summer. In colder weather, bag a table by the fire in the traditional carpeted bar, quaff a pint of Hawkshead Bitter and tuck into lunchtime food such as hot Cumberland sausage with a jacket potato and gravy, or evening meals along the lines of Morecambe Bay potted shrimps; or Lakeland tapas followed by baked chicken supreme; or lamb, black pudding and chunky vegetable casserole. Look out for the carved figure of a king in the bar. Cosy, thoughtfully equipped bedrooms are available.

Open all day all wk 11am-mdnt **Food** Lunch all wk 12-2.30 Dinner all wk 6-9.30 ⊕ FREE HOUSE ◀ Hawkshead Gold & Bitter, Coniston Bluebird Bitter, Cumbrian Legendary, guest ales. ♀ 10 **Facilities** Non-diners area ♣ (Bar Outside area) ♦ Children's menu Children's portions Outside area ⊟ Beer festival WiFi ▭ (notice required) **Rooms** 8

The Queen's Head Inn & Restaurant ★★★★ INN ⊛
PICK OF THE PUBS

tel: 015394 36271 **Main St LA22 0NS**
email: info@queensheadhawkshead.co.uk **web:** www.queensheadhawkshead.co.uk
dir: M6 junct 36, A590 to Newby Bridge, 1st right, 8m to Hawkshead

Excellent food and hospitality in the southern Lakes

Hawkshead has impressive literary links – William Wordsworth attended the local grammar school, and Beatrix Potter lived just up the road. The 17th-century Queen's Head on the village's main street is a stone's throw from Esthwaite Water and surrounded by fells and forests. Behind the pub's flower-bedecked exterior, low oak-beamed ceilings, wood-panelled walls, slate floors and welcoming fires create a relaxed, traditional setting. Ales include Hartleys Cumbria Way and Robinsons Double Hop, and nearly a dozen wines are served by the glass. Local suppliers are proudly listed on the menu, which brims with their fresh, quality ingredients. At lunchtime, sandwiches such as steak and blue cheese with red onion marmalade refuel the ramblers. In the evening you might start with beetroot-cured salmon and horseradish mayonnaise; or king scallops, black pudding and apple purée; and continue with slow-cooked milk-fed Lakeland lamb shoulder, rosemary infused creamed potatoes, burnt onion, chantenay carrots, mint and redcurrant jus. Coconut and tonka bean pannacotta could be one of the desserts.

Open all day all wk 11am-11.45pm (Sun 12-11.45) **Food** Lunch Mon-Sat 12-3, Sun 12-4 Dinner all wk 6-9 ⊕ ROBINSONS ◀ Double Hop, Hartleys Cumbria Way, guest ale. ♀ 11 **Facilities** Non-diners area ♣ (Bar Garden) ♦ Children's menu Garden ⊟ WiFi ▭ (notice required) **Rooms** 13

HAWKSHEAD *continued*

The Sun Inn ★★★★ INN

tel: 015394 36236 **Main St LA22 ONT**
email: rooms@suninn.co.uk **web:** www.suninn.co.uk
dir: *N'bound on M6 junct 36, A591 to Ambleside, B5286 to Hawkshead. S'bound on M6 junct 40, A66 to Keswick, A591 to Ambleside, B5286 to Hawkshead*

A popular hostelry in a busy village

This listed 17th-century coaching inn is at the heart of the charming Hawkshead village and makes a great base for exploring the Lakes. The wood-panelled bar has low, oak-beamed ceilings, and hill walkers and others will enjoy the log fires, real ales and locally sourced food. Choices range from fresh Scottish mussels in white wine, garlic and cream sauce, to venison terrine with wild mushrooms, chestnuts and pancetta for starters; and for mains from pan-seared hake fillet with colcannon potatoes, cabbage and seafood chowder, to butternut squash and goats' cheese risotto with roasted pine nuts and rocket.

Open all day all wk 10am-mdnt **Food** Lunch all wk 12-2.30 Dinner all wk 6-9 ⊕ FREE HOUSE ◀ Jennings, Bowness Bay Swan Blond, Watermill Collie Wobbles, guest ale. **Facilities** Non-diners area ✿ (Bar Garden) ◀▶ Children's menu Children's portions Garden ⊟ Beer festival WiFi ⊨ **Rooms** 8

IRTHINGTON   Map 21 NY46

NEW The Golden Fleece ★★★★ INN ⊛

tel: 01228 573686 **Ruleholme CA6 4NF**
email: info@thegoldenfleececumbria.co.uk **web:** www.thegoldenfleececumbria.co.uk
dir: *On A689 between Carlisle & Brampton. Just E of Carlisle Airport*

Home-from-home where the Romans trod

A stone's throw from Hadrian's Wall and the Stanegate Roman road, this inn is sited in a truly beautiful part of the country. Step inside and the log fire glow is matched by the warmth of welcome and service. A Golden Fleece ale brewed by Dent or the Corby range by Cumberland suit ale lovers, while wine lovers can choose from over a dozen wines served by the glass. British classics prepared to AA Rosette standard are heart-warming too – expect the likes of Cumbrian wild game terrine with fried quail's egg and ale chutney, followed by a chargrilled steak or slow-braised lamb shoulder with roasted roots and parsley mash.

Open all wk noon-close (Nov-Mar Mon-Fri 4pm-close Sat-Sun noon-close) Closed 25 Dec, 1st wk Jan **Food** Lunch Sat 12-9, Sun 12-3 (Apr-Oct Mon-Sat 12-9, Sun 12-3) Dinner Mon-Fri 4-9, Sat 12-9, Sun 5.30-9 (Apr-Oct Mon-Sat 12-9, Sun 5.30-9) ⊕ FREE HOUSE ◀ Cumberland Corby Blonde, Dent Golden Fleece. ♈ 16
Facilities Non-diners area ✿ (Bar Garden) ◀▶ Children's menu Children's portions Play area Garden ⊟ Parking WiFi ⊨ (notice required) **Rooms** 8

KENDAL   Map 18 SD59

The Punch Bowl ★★★★ INN

tel: 015395 60267 **Barrows Green LA8 0AA**
email: punch-bowl@hotmail.co.uk **web:** www.thepunchbowla65.com
dir: *M6 junct 36, A65. Pub in 5m on left*

A 'proper' Lakeland pub

If, when heading for The Lakes, your route involves leaving the M6 at junction 36, this is the first pub you'll encounter. In the inviting bar the real ales change frequently, and you can play pool, darts and dominoes. Committed to local sourcing, the kitchen has a mantra: "Proud to serve proper pub food in decent portions". Expect cheesy leek-stuffed chicken; steak and Theakston's ale pie; gently baked salmon fillet; roasted and stuffed bell pepper; chargrills and gourmet burgers.

Expect good wines: the three top men at the pub's wine merchant have knocked up 100 years' experience between them.

Open all day all wk 12-11 **Food** Lunch Mon-Fri 12-3, Sat 12-9, Sun 12-8 Dinner Mon-Fri 6-9, Sat 12-9, Sun 12-8 ⊕ HEINEKEN ◀ Theakston, guest ales. ♈ 10
Facilities Non-diners area ✿ (Bar Garden) ◀▶ Children's menu Children's portions Garden ⊟ Parking WiFi ⊨ (notice required) **Rooms** 2

KESWICK   Map 18 NY22

The George ★★★★ INN

tel: 017687 72076 **3 Saint John's St CA12 5AZ**
email: rooms@thegeorgekeswick.co.uk **web:** www.thegeorgekeswick.co.uk
dir: *M6 junct 40, A66, filter left signed Keswick, pass pub on left. At x-roads left into Station St, inn 150yds on left*

Imposing coaching inn with plenty of character

Keswick's oldest coaching inn is a handsome 17th-century building in the heart of this popular Lakeland town. Restored to its former glory, retaining its traditional black panelling, Elizabethan beams, ancient settles and log fires, it makes a comfortable base from which to explore the fells and lakes. Expect to find local Jennings ales on tap and classic pub food prepared from local ingredients. Typical dishes include brie and almond wedges or haggis fritters with creamy whisky sauce to start; then there could be main dishes such as pumpkin and red onion tagine; local pheasant breast stuffed with Cumberland sausage and wrapped in bacon; or caramelised duck breast on potato rösti, or Mediterranean vegetable and goats' cheese lasagne. There are 12 comfortable bedrooms available.

Open all day all wk **Food** Lunch Mon-Thu 12-2.30, Fri-Sun 12-4.30 Dinner all wk 5.30-9 Restaurant menu available all wk ⊕ JENNINGS ◀ Bitter, Cumberland Ale, Sneck Lifter & Cocker Hoop, guest ales. ♈ 10 **Facilities** Non-diners area ✿ (Bar) ◀▶ Children's menu Children's portions Parking WiFi ⊨ (notice required) **Rooms** 12

The Horse & Farrier Inn   PICK OF THE PUBS

tel: 017687 79688 **Threlkeld Village CA12 4SQ**
email: info@horseandfarrier.com
dir: *M6 junct 40, A66 signed Keswick, 12m, right signed Threlkeld. Pub in village centre*

Classic Lakeland inn with hard-to-beat views

From this lovely, late 17th-century Lakeland inn at the foot of Blencathra there are wonderful views across to the Helvellyn range. Within its thick, whitewashed stone walls you'll find slate-flagged floors, beamed ceilings and open log fires, with hunting prints decorating the traditional bars and panelled snug. Cockermouth's Jennings and a guest brewery supply the real ales. The pub has a reputation for good food, dependent on a long-standing commitment to local, seasonal produce and continuing with its preparation in the 'gleaming kitchen'. Restaurant starters include buffalo mozzarella, vine tomato and air-dried prosciutto; and breaded garlic mushrooms. Likely contenders among the mains could be smoked haddock, chive mash; lasagne; mushroom Stroganoff; bean and celery chilli; or lamb shoulder braised in Jennings Cumberland Ale. Six walks start or end here, including ones to Blencathra and Skiddaw.

Open all day all wk 7.30am-mdnt **Food** all wk 12-9 ⊕ JENNINGS ◀ Bitter, Sneck Lifter & Cumberland Ale, guest ale ♂ Westons Stowford Press. ♈ 10
Facilities Non-diners area ✿ (Bar Garden) ◀▶ Children's menu Children's portions Family room Garden ⊟ Parking WiFi ⊨ (notice required)

The Kings Head   PICK OF THE PUBS

See Pick of the Pubs on opposite page

PICK OF THE PUBS

The Kings Head

KESWICK   Map 18 NY22

tel: 017687 72393 **Thirlspot CA12 4TN**
email: stay@lakedistrictinns.co.uk
web: www.lakedistrictinns.co.uk
dir: *M6 junct 40, A66 to Keswick then A591, pub 4m S of Keswick*

Lovely valley views south of Keswick

In the heart of the Lake District, Helvellyn, the third highest peak in England, towers above this 17th-century coaching inn; the long, whitewashed building and its delightful beer garden enjoy great views of the surrounding fells, while indoors the traditional bar features old beams and an inglenook fireplace. In addition to several regulars from the Cumberland brewery, there are guest real ales and a fine selection of wines and malt whiskies. In the bar, paninis, sandwiches and jacket potatoes head the lunchtime options, which also feature a deli board, a ploughman's and an old-fashioned pork, Stilton and red onion marmalade pie with piccalilli and salad garnish. It's in the restaurant, which looks out to the glacial valley of St Johns in the Vale that dinner might begin with ham and foie gras terrine, toasted bloomer and pickles; wild mushroom, Stilton and walnut tart, salad and basil pesto; or a hunter's skillet of pan-fried chicken

livers, wild mushrooms, bacon and garlic croûte. A meal might continue with lemon- and herb-crusted sea bass, dauphinoise potatoes, baby vegetables and garlic butter; haddock in Jennings beer batter, hand-cut chunky chips, tartare sauce and mushy peas; or root vegetable and butterbean stew. Finish with mixed winter berry crumble and crème anglaise; or 'original' Cumbrian sticky toffee pudding with vanilla ice cream. There's a separate set price steak menu on offer Mondays to Saturdays, with Sunday lunches featuring roast Cumbrian beef, pork and chicken, a poached salmon fillet and a vegetarian option.

Open all day all wk 11-11 **Food** all wk 12-9.30 Set menu available Restaurant menu available all wk 🛢 FREE HOUSE 🍺 Jennings Bitter, Cumberland Ale, Sneck Lifter & Cocker Hoop, guest ales. 🍷 9 **Facilities** Non-diners area 🐾 (Bar Garden) 👪 Children's menu Children's portions Family room Garden 🏕 Parking WiFi 🚌 (notice required)

PICK OF THE PUBS

The Royal Oak at Keswick ★★★★ INN

KESWICK   Map 18 NY22

tel: 017687 74584 **Main St CA12 5HZ**
email: relax@royaloakkeswick.co.uk
web: www.royaloakkeswick.com
dir: *M6 junct 40, A66 to Keswick town centre to war memorial x-roads. Left into Station St. Inn 100yds*

Popular inn at the heart of walking country

One of Thwaites' Inns of Character, on the corner of a pedestrian-only street leading to Keswick's busy market square, this friendly 18th-century coaching inn combines modern amenities with charming reminders of its past. In the 19th century, when it was known as Keswick Lodge, Coleridge, Wordsworth, Tennyson, Ruskin, Shelley and other literary titans either met or passed through here, as the plaque on an outside wall testifies. By its very nature the Lake District attracts outdoor types, so today's inn is understandably popular with walkers, climbers, sailors and cyclists. That dogs are permitted in the bar, and in some of the bedrooms, will please their owners (and probably Buster too). In the bar the real ales to remind you of your location are Wainwright and Lancaster Bomber; also on tap are representatives from the Thwaites brewery's seasonal range, Kingstone Press cider and 12 wines by the glass. The kitchen's careful sourcing

of ingredients ensures sustainability as well as quality, all the way from sandwiches on fresh crusty bread to dishes such as steak and ale pie. Among the starters are salt and pepper calamari with lemon and garlic mayonnaise; and home-cured gravad lax with pink grapefruit and rocket salad. Sharing platters come in butcher's, fishmonger's and vegetable antipasti varieties; from the grill come sirloin, rib-eye and rump steaks, pork chops, gammon steaks and burgers. For those with a sweet tooth, baked vanilla cheesecake, seasonal berries and basil sugar; and lemon posset are tempting options. Beer and food pairing options are marked on the menu.

Open all day all wk 9am-mdnt
Food Mon-Sat 11-10, Sun 12-9
⊕ THWAITES INNS OF CHARACTER
🍺 Wainwright, Original, Lancaster Bomber 🍏 Kingstone Press. ☆ 12
Facilities Non-diners area
🐾 (Bar Restaurant) 🚼 Children's menu Children's portions WiFi 🚌 (notice required) **Rooms** 19

KESWICK *continued*

Pheasant Inn

tel: 017687 72219 **Crosthwaite Rd CA12 5PP**
dir: *On A66 Keswick rdbt towards town centre, 60yds on right*

Local food and ales, an ideal stop after a Lakeland walk

An open-fired, traditional Lakeland inn, owned by Jennings Brewery, so expect their regular range on tap, and a monthly guest. For the seasonal menus, the kitchen produces home-cooked, locally sourced food, including starters of whitebait with home-made tartare sauce; and 'gooey' baked camembert with ciabatta dipping sticks and chilli, red onion and tomato relish. Follow with a favourite like the chef's beef Madras, or a special (of which there are many), such as prime Cumbrian rump steak; wild boar ragout; and Lakeland lamb shank, garlic and spring onion mash with red wine, rosemary and cranberry jus.

Open all day all wk Closed 25 Dec **Food** Lunch all wk 12-2 Dinner all wk 6-9 Av main course £12 ⊕ JENNINGS ◀ Bitter, Cumberland Ale, Cocker Hoop & Sneck Lifter, Pheasant Ale, guest ale ⚬ Thatchers Gold. ♟ 8 **Facilities** Non-diners area ❀ (Bar Garden) ♦ Children's menu Garden ⊨ Parking WiFi

The Royal Oak at Keswick ★★★★ INN PICK OF THE PUBS

See Pick of the Pubs on opposite page and advert below

KIRKBY LONSDALE	Map 18 SD67

The Pheasant Inn ★★★★ INN ◉ PICK OF THE PUBS

tel: 01524 271230 **Casterton LA6 2RX**
email: info@pheasantinn.co.uk web: www.pheasantinn.co.uk
dir: *M6 junct 36, A65 for 7m, left onto A683 at Devils Bridge, 1m to Casterton centre*

Peaceful inn with lovely views of the fells

Below the fell on the edge of the beautiful Lune Valley is this sleepy hamlet with its whitewashed 18th-century coaching inn. It's perfectly situated for exploring the Dales, the Trough of Bowland and the Cumbrian Lakes. The Wilson family and staff ensure a warm welcome in the bar and stylish oak-panelled dining room. Guest ales and beers from Theakston can be sampled while perusing the interesting menu

which mixes home-grown seasonal produce from valley farms with favourite recipes from foreign fields: starters, for example, include panko-coated king prawns with carrot and mouli noodles; or black pepper smoked mackerel with creamed cheese and smoked salmon roulade. Follow that with tenderloin of pork with black truffle risotto; or pheasant breast wrapped in smoked bacon with onion stuffing. The excellent dessert choice ranges from old fashioned sticky toffee pudding, to brandy and apricot parfait. Food can be served on the lawn in fine weather.

Open all day all wk **Food** Lunch all wk 12-2 Dinner all wk 6-9 ⊕ FREE HOUSE ◀ Theakston, Tirril, guest ales. ♟ 8 **Facilities** Non-diners area ❀ (Bar Garden Outside area) ♦ Children's menu Children's portions Garden Outside area ⊨ Parking WiFi **Rooms** 10

The Sun Inn ★★★★ RR ◉◉ PICK OF THE PUBS

tel: 01524 271965 **Market St LA6 2AU**
email: email@sun-inn.info web: www.sun-inn.info
dir: *M6 junct 36, A65 for Kirkby Lonsdale. 5m to mini rdbt, 1st exit, left at next junct. At bottom of hill right, inn on left*

Terrific period inn with top-notch menu

JMW Turner captured the town's beauty on canvas; John Ruskin did the same in prose. Kirkby Lonsdale retains immense character and charm, beautifully evidenced in the classic period building that is The Sun Inn. It burrows back from a pretty pillared frontage into a comfy mix of low-slung beams, oak and flagstone flooring and cosy alcoves focussed on a feature fireplace at the heart of the pub. The enthusiastic owners are keen supporters of locally produced goods; expect beer from the town's microbrewery to accompany the uplifting bill of fare sourced from the surrounding countryside. Sam Carter's accomplished, modish bar and dinner menus feature starters such as suckling pig, orange gel, red chicory and crispy black pudding which complements a main dish of hay-smoked roe deer with caramelised chicory, creamed potato and red cabbage gel. Eleven bedrooms make The Sun an ideal base from which to explore the Lake District and Yorkshire Dales.

Open Mon 3-11, Tue-Sun 10am-11pm Closed 25 Dec, Mon L **Food** Lunch Tue-Sun 12-3 Dinner all wk 6.30-9 Set menu available ⊕ FREE HOUSE ◀ Kirkby Lonsdale, Marston's Wainwright, Hawkshead Bitter ⚬ Kingstone Press. ♟ 9 **Facilities** Non-diners area ❀ (Bar) ♦ Children's portions WiFi **Rooms** 11

PICK OF THE PUBS

Kirkstile Inn ★★★★ INN

LOWESWATER   Map 18 NY12

tel: 01900 85219 **CA13 0RU**
email: info@kirkstile.com
web: www.kirkstile.com
dir: *From A66 Keswick take Whinlatter Pass at Braithwaite. Take B5292, at T-junct left onto B5289. 3m to Loweswater. From Cockermouth B5289 to Lorton then Loweswater. At red phone box left, 200yds to inn*

Traditional pub set among woods, fells and lakes

Stretching as far as the eye can see, the woods, fells and lakes are as much a draw today as they must have been in the inn's infancy some 400 years ago. The beck below meanders under a stone bridge, with oak trees clinging to its banks and the mighty Melbreak towering impressively above. Tucked away next to an old church, this classic Cumbrian inn stands just half a mile from the Loweswater and Crummock lakes. It makes an ideal base for walking, climbing, boating and fishing. The whole place has an authentic, traditional and well-looked-after feel, with whitewashed walls, low beams, solid polished tables, cushioned settles, a well stoked fire and the odd horse harness to remind you of times gone by. You can call in for afternoon tea, but better still would be to taste one of the Cumbrian Legendary Ales – Loweswater Gold, Grasmoor Dark Ale, Esthwaite

Bitter – brewed by landlord Roger Humphreys in Esthwaite Water near Hawkshead. Robust and wholesome dishes to satisfy the most hearty appetites are freshly prepared using produce from local suppliers listed on the menu. For a light lunchtime meal, tuck into an Arnold Bennett omelette with dressed leaves; or a tatie pot – Lakeland lamb stew with vegetables, potatoes, and pickled red cabbage. In the evening, start with a Cumbrian duck egg wrapped in Cumberland sausagemeat, black pudding and herb breadcrumbs, served with a fennel and orange salad. To follow look to the specials board for the Cumbrian steak or fish of the day. Finish nicely with a mixed berry and elderflower jelly, or choose the Cumbrian cheeseboard.

Open all day all wk Closed 25 Dec
Food Lunch all wk 12-2, light menu 2-4.30 Dinner all wk 6-9 ⊕ FREE HOUSE
🛢 Cumbrian Legendary Ales Loweswater Gold, Esthwaite Bitter, Grasmoor Dark Ale & Langdale
Ŏ Westons Stowford Press. ⏛ 9
Facilities Non-diners area 👪 Children's menu Children's portions Family room Garden 🌳 Beer festival Parking
Rooms 10

LITTLE LANGDALE
Map 18 NY30

Three Shires Inn ★★★★ INN
PICK OF THE PUBS

tel: 015394 37215 **LA22 9NZ**
email: enquiry@threeshiresinn.co.uk **web:** www.threeshiresinn.co.uk
dir: Exit A593, 2.3m from Ambleside at 2nd junct signed 'The Langdales'. 1st left 0.5m. Inn in 1m

Popular stop-over in a wonderful setting

A slate-built Lake District hostelry sitting comfortably amidst the dry-stone walls and thick hedges along the winding lane to the Wrynose and Hardknott Passes. The pub is Lakeland through and through, from its Cumbrian-sourced food to real ales such as Cumbrian Legendary Melbreak Bitter and Coniston Old Man. Ian Stephenson and his family have run it for over 30 years, and everyone, including dogs, is made welcome in the beamed bar. A light lunch may comprise soup of the day and a ploughman's, or a plate of Cumberland sausage with fresh vegetables and chips. When it's cold there's a fire; when it's warm the place to settle is in the landscaped garden, where fell views are a bonus. For an evening meal, start with pan-fried scallops with Stornaway black pudding mousse; follow with a Cartmel Valley venison and cranberry burger; and finish with a selection of Lakeland ice creams. Comfortable accommodation includes self-catering options.

Open 11-3 6-10.30 Dec-Jan, 11-10.30 Feb-Nov (Fri-Sat 11-11) Closed 25 Dec, part of Jan, May be closed some days in Dec & Jan **Food** Lunch all wk 12-2 (ex 24-25 Dec) Dinner all wk 6-8.45 (ex mid-wk Dec-Jan) ⊕ FREE HOUSE ◀ Cumbrian Legendary Melbreak Bitter, Jennings Bitter & Cumberland Ale, Coniston Old Man Ale, Hawkshead Bitter, Ennerdale Blonde. **Facilities** Non-diners area ❤ (Bar Garden) ♦ Children's menu Children's portions Garden ⋒ Parking WiFi **Rooms** 10

LOWESWATER
Map 18 NY12

Kirkstile Inn ★★★★ INN
PICK OF THE PUBS

See Pick of the Pubs on opposite page

LOW LORTON
Map 18 NY12

The Wheatsheaf Inn

tel: 01900 85199 & 85268 **CA13 9UW**
email: j.williams53@sky.com
dir: From Cockermouth take B5292 to Lorton. Right onto B5289 to Low Lorton

Good beers, good food and good views

Occasionally, landlord Mark Cockbain crosses the lane from his white-painted, 17th-century pub to fish for salmon and trout in the River Cocker. For visitors it's the panoramic views of the lush Vale of Lorton from the child-friendly beer garden that matter. The quaint, open-fired bar looks like a gamekeeper's lodge: "We like our locals to feel at home," says Mark's wife, Jackie. Real ales from Jennings in Cockermouth also help in that respect. On the menu are sticky sesame ribs; lemon pepper chicken goujons; local trout with lime, almond and parsley butter; and chilli con carne in a tortilla basket. The end of March is beer festival time.

Open Tue-Sun Closed Mon & Tue eve in Jan & Feb **Food** Lunch Fri 12-2, Sat 12-3, Sun 12-8.30 Dinner Tue-Sat 6-8.30, Sun 12-8.30 ⊕ MARSTON'S ◀ Pedigree, Jennings Bitter & Cumberland Ale, Brakspear Oxford Gold ♂ Scrumpy Jack. **Facilities** Non-diners area ❤ (Bar Garden) ♦ Children's menu Children's portions Family room Garden ⋒ Beer festival Parking ▰

LUPTON
Map 18 SD58

The Plough Inn ★★★★★ INN ⦿
PICK OF THE PUBS

tel: 015395 67700 **Cow Brow LA6 1PJ**
email: info@theploughatlupton.co.uk **web:** www.theploughatlupton.co.uk
dir: M6 junct 36, A65 towards Kirkby Lonsdale. Pub on right in Lupton

Affectionately held in the locals' hearts

Below Farleton Knott, a hill from which locals once warned of Scottish unrest, stands this apparently simple roadside pub. Any notion of simplicity, however, is quickly dispelled on entering this stylish 1760s inn. Oak beams, leather sofas, colourful rugs and antique furniture impart a farmhouse feel. Brathay slate tops the bar, where Lakeland brewers such as Tirril and Bowness Bay augment Kirkby Lonsdale's own Monumental ale; more than a dozen wines are served by the glass. Polished oak floors lead into the restaurant, where open fires and wood-burning stoves do a sterling job when needed. Food is served from noon through to 9pm, with quality and local provenance the keynotes. Home-made pork pie and piccalilli; or sharing platters (fisherman's; the ploughman's; and baked camembert) kick things off maybe, then continue with free-range pork belly, parsnip purée, red cabbage, crackling, creamy mash and red wine gravy; or wild boar and damson sausages, caramelised onion mash, green beans and red wine sauce. Puddings will tempt too, vanilla crème brûlée, juniper berry biscotti and gin and tonic sorbet; and chilled chocolate fondant, honeycomb and peanut butter ice cream.

Open all day all wk **Food** all wk 12-9 ⊕ FREE HOUSE ◀ Kirkby Lonsdale Monumental, Marston's Wainwright, Tirril, Bowness Bay ♂ Kingstone Press. ♥ 14 **Facilities** Non-diners area ❤ (Bar Garden) ♦ Children's menu Children's portions Garden ⋒ Parking WiFi **Rooms** 6

NEAR SAWREY
Map 18 SD39

Tower Bank Arms
PICK OF THE PUBS

See Pick of the Pubs on page 114

OUTGATE
Map 18 SD39

Outgate Inn

tel: 015394 36413 **LA22 0NQ**
email: theoutgateinn@btconnect.com
dir: M6 junct 36, by-passing Kendal, A591 towards Ambleside. At Clappersgate take B5285 to Hawkshead, Outgate 3m

Traditional welcoming Cumbrian inn with a secluded beer garden

For 80 years until 1921, aerated waters were produced in this 18th-century building, sourced from deep underground. It's owned by Robinsons Brewery, so Hartleys Cumbrian XB and Dizzy Blonde are the real ale mainstays. The regularly changing menus and specials feature a wide selection of freshly-made dishes made from locally sourced ingredients. Consider choosing beer-battered haggis fritters with tomato and onion chutney; chicken, chorizo and red lentil casserole; or burger of the day. Vegetarian and gluten-free options are available. Several Lakeland walks start here; since they also finish here, the real fire is often a welcome sight.

Open all day all wk Closed 2wks Jan **Food** Lunch all wk 12-5 Dinner all wk 5-8 Av main course £10.95 ⊕ ROBINSONS ◀ Dizzy Blonde, Hartleys Cumbrian XB ♂ Westons Stowford Press. **Facilities** Non-diners area ❤ (Bar Restaurant Garden) ♦ Children's menu Children's portions Garden ⋒ Parking WiFi ▰ (notice required)

PICK OF THE PUBS

Tower Bank Arms

NEAR SAWREY Map 18 SD39

tel: 015394 36334 **LA22 0LF**
email: towerbankarms@aol.com
web: www.towerbankarms.co.uk
dir: *On B5285 SW of Windermere. 1.5m
from Hawkshead. 2m from Windermere
via ferry*

Popular rustic pub

This 17th-century village pub on the
west side of Lake Windermere is owned
by the National Trust (although run
independently), as is Beatrix Potter's old
home, Hill Top, which can be found just
behind the inn. It has been known as
the Tower Bank Arms for over a century
and Potter illustrated it perfectly in her
Tale of Jemima Puddleduck, although
history fails to record whether she ever
slipped in for a drink during a break
from sketching. This cosy, bustling inn
is popular not only with visitors to Hill
Top, but also walkers, cyclists,
holidaymakers and locals. In the low-
beamed slate-floored main bar are an
open log fire, fresh flowers and ticking
grandfather clock. Local brews on
hand pump embrace Langdale from
Cumbrian Legendary and Brodie's Prime
from Hawkshead; alternatively a good
selection of ciders and wines are served
by the glass. If you are looking to eat,
menus for both lunch and dinner are
served throughout the premises. The
style is very much hearty country fare
based on local produce. At midday,

warm ciabattas of steak and sautéed
onions, or smoked chicken with
Cumbrian brie and red onion
marmalade, are sufficient for some;
others may plump for a traditional
lunchtime plate of deep-fried beer-
battered haddock with home-made
chips and mushy peas. For dinner,
asparagus tempura with blue cheese
dip makes a tasty vegetarian starter.
Follow perhaps with braised shoulder of
Lakeland lamb, bubble-and-squeak and
vegetables. Finish in style with a warm
chocolate brownie, berries, banana ice
cream and salted caramel sauce. Food
and drink can be served in the garden,
where the panorama of farms, fells and
fields makes a relaxing vista.

Open all wk (all day Etr-Oct) Closed one

day mid wk Jan & Dec, Mon Nov-early Feb
(ex Xmas & New Year) **Food** Lunch all wk
12-2 Dinner Mon-Sat 6-9, Sun & BH 6-8
(Mon-Thu Oct-Apr) Av main course £12.75
🛢 FREE HOUSE 🛢 Hawkshead Bitter &
Brodie's Prime, Cumbrian Legendary Ales
🍏 Westons Wyld Wood Organic Vintage,
Country Perry, Rosie's Pig & Old Rosie. 🍷 9
Facilities Non-diners area 🐾 (Bar Garden)
🚼 Children's menu Children's portions
Garden 🎋 Parking 🚐 (notice required)

PICK OF THE PUBS

The Black Swan ★★★★ INN

RAVENSTONEDALE   Map 18 NY70

tel: 015396 23204 **CA17 4NG**
email: enquiries@blackswanhotel.com
web: www.blackswanhotel.com
dir: *M6 junct 38, A685 E towards Brough; or A66 onto A685 at Kirkby Stephen towards M6*

One of Lakeland's best family-run inns

In a pretty conservation village, this handsome, multi-gabled Victorian inn is proudly run by enterprising owners Alan and Louise Dinnes. There are friendly bars, a lounge warmed by an open fire and tranquil riverside gardens below Wild Boar Fell and the headwaters of the River Eden where you might spot a red squirrel or two. An acclaimed real ale line-up features regulars from the Black Sheep brewery and from Timothy Taylor and rotating local guests. Meals may be eaten in both bar areas, the lounge or in either of the two beautifully decorated restaurants. As with the beers, reliance on local produce is key, which is evident in the names of some of the dishes. There's a wealth of experience in the kitchen, so maybe try trio of Cumbrian lamb with fondant potatoes, minted cabbage, peas, artichoke purée, baby turnip and rosemary jus; pan-fried salmon and clams, potato and butternut squash rösti, purple sprouting broccoli

and creamy saffron sauce; and wild mushroom, leek, chestnut and spinach crêpes, Stilton and truffle cream sauce, toasted almonds and curly kale. A children's option is Whitby scampi, fries, peas and home-made tartare sauce. On a memorable day in 2008 HRH Prince Charles opened the Black Swan's on-site village store where essential groceries, stationery and locally-made gifts, crafts and organic soaps and toiletries — as used in the guest rooms — are on sale. A beer festival is held in the garden in the summer. In such a lovely area of the country it is certainly worth stopping over in one of the inn's individually designed bedrooms.

Open all day all wk 8am-1am **Food** all day from 8am Dinner all wk 6-9 Av main course £12 Set menu available ⊕ FREE HOUSE ◫ Black Sheep Best Bitter, John Smith's Extra Smooth, Timothy Taylor, Guinness, rotating local guest ales ♻ Westons Stowford Press. ♟ **Facilities** Non-diners area ☙ (Bar Garden) ᛙ Children's menu & portions Play area Garden ⧖ Beer festival Parking WiFi ⛟ (notice required) **Rooms** 16

PENRITH
Map 18 NY53

Cross Keys Inn

tel: 01768 865588 **Carleton Village CA11 8TP**
email: crosskeys@kyloes.co.uk
dir: *From A66 in Penrith take A686 to Carleton Village, inn on right*

Lovely views and traditional food

This old drovers' and coaching inn at the edge of Penrith offers sweeping views to the nearby North Pennines from the upstairs restaurant where timeless, traditional pub meals are the order of the day; Scottish wholetail battered scampi or Cumberland lamb hotpot for example. Kyloes Grill here is particularly well thought of, with only Cumbrian meats used. Beers crafted in nearby Broughton Hall by Tirril Brewery draw an appreciative local clientele, warming their toes by the ferocious log-burner or laying a few tiles on the domino tables.

Open all wk Mon-Fri 12-2.30 5-12 (Sat-Sun all day) ⊕ FREE HOUSE ◼ Tirril 1823, guest ale. **Facilities** ✿ (Bar Garden) ⁌ Children's menu Children's portions Garden Parking WiFi

RAVENGLASS
Map 18 SD09

NEW The Inn at Ravenglass

tel: 01229 717230 **Ravenglass CA18 1SQ**
email: info@penningtonhotels.com
dir: *From A595 between Whitehaven & Broughton-in-Furness follow Ravenglass signs. Under 2 rail bridges to pub on left*

Lake District inn with fabulous estuary views

On the western side of the Lake District, in the National Park's only coastal village, this 17th-century inn is located on the edge of the estuary where the Rivers Irt, Mite and Esk meet before entering the Irish sea. Locally landed and sustainably sourced fish and seafood appear on the daily-changing menus, which might kick off with smoked salmon, cod and king prawn fishcakes and move on to halibut, pistachio risotto and smoked ham hock fritters. Watch the sun set over the estuary with a pint of Coniston Bluebird, one of three real ales available in the bar.

Open all wk 5-11 (Fri-Sun 12-11.30) **Food** Lunch Fri-Sun 12-5 Dinner all wk 5-9 Av main course £12.95 Restaurant menu available Tue-Sun ⊕ FREE HOUSE ◼ Coniston Bluebird Bitter, Independent Lakeland Breweries Gold Wing. ♟ 12 **Facilities** Non-diners area ✿ (Bar Outside area) ⁌ Children's menu Outside area Parking WiFi ☛ (notice required)

RAVENSTONEDALE
Map 18 NY70

The Black Swan ★★★★ INN   PICK OF THE PUBS

See Pick of the Pubs on page 115

The Fat Lamb Country Inn ★★★★ INN PICK OF THE PUBS

tel: 015396 23242 **Crossbank CA17 4LL**
email: enquiries@fatlamb.co.uk **web:** www.fatlamb.co.uk
dir: *On A683 between Sedbergh & Kirkby Stephen*

Old-fashioned hospitality and idyllic countryside

Tables outside this 350-year-old former coaching inn come with some of the most outstanding views in England. Vast fells create an undulating patchwork that completely surrounds the stone inn. A source of the River Lune here has been

tapped to create the heart of the inn's own nature reserve, where sightings have included otters, roe deer and countless upland birds. Rambling parties can pop in for breakfast before tackling the local trails; less-active travellers can explore the very traditional interior of the inn, where quirks like a huge aircraft propeller and a stuffed ram's head provoke comment. Lounge at the bar near the old Yorkshire range, quaff Yorkshire beer and peruse a menu of pub stalwarts and daily-changing specials that cater for most diets. Look for slow-roast pulled beef cooked in a barbecue sauce served with horseradish rösti potato and parsnip crisps; or pan-seared salmon fillet with Morecambe Bay shrimps. Twelve en suite rooms complete the picture here.

Open all day all wk **Food** Lunch Mon-Fri 12-2, Sat-Sun 12-6 Dinner all wk 6-9 ⊕ FREE HOUSE ◼ Black Sheep Best Bitter ♙ Symonds. **Facilities** Non-diners area ✿ (Bar Garden) ⁌ Children's menu Children's portions Play area Garden Parking WiFi ☛ (notice required) **Rooms** 12

The King's Head

tel: 015396 23050 **CA17 4NH**
email: enquiries@kings-head.com
dir: *M6 junct 38, A685 towards Kirkby Stephen. Approx 7m, right to Ravenstonedale. Pub 200yds on right*

Set in beautiful rolling Cumbrian countryside

It's hard to believe that this old whitewashed pub was, at one time, closed for three years. There are real fires in the restaurant, where a three-course lunch or evening meal might be wood pigeon breast with celeriac remoulade; braised belly of pork with black pudding potato cake; and sticky toffee pudding. Vegetarians will find dishes such as Cumberland farmhouse cheese and onion soufflé; and wild mushroom and courgette bouché. Three regularly-changing real ales and eight wines by the glass are served in the open-plan bar. Cyclists will appreciate the lock-up facility for their bikes.

Open all day all wk Closed 25 Dec **Food** Lunch all wk 12-6 Dinner all wk 6-9 ⊕ FREE HOUSE ◼ 3 regularly changing guest ales. ♟ 8 **Facilities** Non-diners area ✿ (Bar Garden) ⁌ Children's menu Children's portions Garden Parking WiFi ☛ (notice required)

SANTON BRIDGE
Map 18 NY10

Bridge Inn

tel: 019467 26221 **CA19 1UX**
email: info@santonbridgeinn.co.uk
dir: *From A595 at Gosforth follow Eskdale & Wasdale sign. Through Santon to inn on left. Or inn signed from A595 S of Holmkirk*

Old country inn – that's no lie

The Lake District was formed, not by ice or volcanic action, but by large moles and eels. Actually, that's a lie, one of the many told in this comfortable old inn at the annual World's Biggest Liar competition, held every November. No doubt pints of Jennings Sneck Lifter, Cocker Hoop and Thatchers Gold help to inspire such outrageous fibbing. The chef's specials are chalked up on the board. The inn, in the beautiful valley of Wasdale, is licensed for civil marriages, when, hopefully, "I do" is not a lie!

Open all day all wk **Food** all wk 12-9 ⊕ FREE HOUSE/JENNINGS ◼ Cumberland Ale, Sneck Lifter, Cocker Hoop, guest ales ♙ Thatchers Gold. ♟ 10 **Facilities** Non-diners area ✿ (Bar Outside area) ⁌ Children's menu Children's portions Family room Outside area Parking WiFi ☛ (notice required)

SATTERTHWAITE
Map 18 SD39

The Eagles Head

tel: 01229 860237 **LA12 8LN**
email: theeagleshead@gmail.com
dir: *Phone for detailed directions*

Traditional food and local beers in family-run Lake District pub

More than 400 years old, The Eagles Head occupies a lovely spot in the tiny village of Satterthwaite in the Grizedale Forest. A traditional, family-run Cumbrian inn with a crackling log fire in winter and pretty beer garden for sunnier days, the pub has a good reputation for serving tip-top quality beers from local microbreweries such as Hawkshead and Barngates. Local meat and vegetables, as well as fish from the east coast appear in straightforward, enjoyable dishes. Whole Lakeland trout with new potatoes and salad; and Cumberland sausage, mash and onion gravy are typical main courses.

Open all day all wk **Food** Lunch Mon-Fri 12-3, Sat-Sun all day Dinner Mon-Fri 5-9, Sat-Sun all day ⊕ FREE HOUSE ◆ Hawkshead Pale, Cumbrian Legendary Ales Loweswater Gold, Barngates Cracker Ale, Ulverston ♂ Westons Stowford Press. **Facilities** Non-diners area ❖ (Bar Garden) ♦ Children's menu Children's portions Garden ⋒ Beer festival Parking WiFi ▥ (notice required)

SEATHWAITE
Map 18 SD29

Newfield Inn

tel: 01229 716208 **LA20 6ED**
dir: *From Broughton-in-Furness take A595 signed Whitehaven & Workington. Right signed Ulpha. Through Ulpha to Seathwaite, 6m (NB it is advisable not to use Sat Nav)*

Classic walkers' pub with view-filled garden

Tucked away in the peaceful Duddon Valley, Wordsworth's favourite, is this 16th-century cottage-style pub, now in new hands. Hugely popular with walkers and climbers, the slate-floored bar regularly throngs with parched outdoor types quaffing pints of local ales. Served all day, food is hearty and traditional and uses local farm meats; the choice ranges from hot and cold sandwiches, salads and lunchtime snacks like beer-battered fish and chips, to pie and mash; chicken supreme; Cumberland sausages; and sticky toffee pudding. Retreat to the garden in summer and savour cracking southern fells views, or come for the beer festival in October.

Open all day all wk **Food** all wk 12-9 ⊕ FREE HOUSE ◆ Cumberland Corby Ale, Jennings Cumberland Ale & Sneck Lifter, Barngates Cat Nap. ☗ 8 **Facilities** Non-diners area ❖ (Bar Garden) ♦ Children's menu Children's portions Play area Garden ⋒ Beer festival Parking ▥ (notice required)

SEDBERGH
Map 18 SD69

The Dalesman Country Inn

tel: 015396 21183 **Main St LA10 5BN**
email: info@thedalesman.co.uk
dir: *M6 junct 37, A684 to Sedbergh. Inn in town centre*

Good food and local ales in the Lakes

A 30-minute drive from Windermere, this family-run 16th-century coaching inn in the pretty market town of Sedbergh is an ideal base for Lake District walkers. A range of ales such as Timothy Taylor Landlord and Tetley's are served in the character bar with its warming log-burner. Once the village smithy, the restaurant serves seasonal food showcasing local producers. Try the award-winning

Cumberland sausages or the lamb and root vegetable casserole with mash and pickled red cabbage. Alternatively, the home-made gourmet pizzas are a popular choice, as are the 'native breed' steaks.

Open all day all wk **Food** all wk 12-9 ⊕ FREE HOUSE ◆ Timothy Taylor Landlord, Tetley's ♂ Thatchers Gold. ☗ 14 **Facilities** Non-diners area ♦ Children's menu Children's portions Outside area ⋒ WiFi ▥

STAVELEY
Map 18 SD49

NEW The Beer Hall at Hawkshead Brewery

tel: 01539 825260 **Mill Yard LA8 9LR**
email: chris@hawksheadbrewery.co.uk
dir: *From A591 NE of Kendal, follow Staveley signs*

Extraordinary brewery tap at the edge of the Lake District

Through the vast picture windows of this striking modern building in Staveley's old mill yard are grand views of the fells tumbling to the village. Immediately to hand, the brewing process can be glimpsed through glass dividing walls; the award-winning beers emanating from here can be enjoyed with tapas-style food selected to complement each beer style. More substantial meals celebrate down-to-earth pub-grub like cheese, onion and potato pie. The Beer Hall's modern, airy interior hosts an open mic and music session every Sunday, whilst brewery tours are available four days a week. Beer festivals occur in March and July.

Open all wk 12-6 (Fri-Sat 12-11 Sun 12-8) Closed 25-26 Dec, 1 Jan **Food** Lunch Mon-Thu 12-3, Fri-Sat 12-8.30, Sun 12-6 Dinner Fri-Sat 12-8.30 ⊕ FREE HOUSE ◆ Hawkshead Bitter, Lakeland Gold, Red, Windermere Pale & Cumbrian 5 Hop ♂ Thistly Cross Traditional, Pure North Original. **Facilities** Non-diners area ❖ (Bar Restaurant Outside area) ♦ Children's portions Outside area ⋒ Beer festival Parking WiFi ▥

TEMPLE SOWERBY
Map 18 NY62

The Kings Arms ★★★ INN

tel: 017683 62944 **CA10 1SB**
email: enquiries@kingsarmstemplesowerby.co.uk
web: www.kingsarmstemplesowerby.co.uk
dir: *M6 junct 40, E on A66 to Temple Sowerby. Inn in town centre*

Hostelry in charming village

In 1799, when Temple Sowerby was known as 'The Queen of Westmorland Villages', romantic poets William Wordsworth and Samuel Coleridge began their tour of the Lake District at this 17th-century coaching inn on the Penrith to Appleby turnpike. The kitchen serves a mix of old favourites and more modern options, including deep-fried breaded Whitby scampi; Moroccan lamb tagine; Thai red chicken curry; butter-grilled salmon steak; Cumberland sausage with mustard mash; and lasagne. There's also a good vegetarian choice, home-made desserts and a children's menu.

Open all wk 10-3 6-11 **Food** Lunch all wk 12-2 Dinner all wk 6-9 Av main course £11.50 ⊕ FREE HOUSE ◆ Black Sheep, guest ales ♂ Westons Stowford Press. **Facilities** Non-diners area ❖ (Bar Garden) ♦ Children's menu Children's portions Garden ⋒ Parking WiFi ▥ (notice required) **Rooms** 8

The Farmers

tel: 01229 584469 **Market Place LA12 7BA**
email: roger@thefarmers-ulverston.co.uk
dir: *In town centre*

A warm welcome and crowd-pleasing pub grub

Perhaps the oldest inn in the Lake District, there's a hospitable welcome here at The Farmers, whether in the traditionally decorated restaurant with its oak beams and impressive views of the Crake Valley or in the 14th-century stable bar complete with a log fire and original slate floors. The wide-ranging menus include meat or seafood deli boards for sharing; slow-cooked belly pork with black pudding, local sausage, buttered and gravy; piri piri chicken with feta, coriander and sweet potato mash; and Cumbrian mature cheese, broccoli and leek pie. Local ales include Hawkshead Bitter and there's both beer and cider festivals annually.

Open all day all wk **Food** Lunch all wk 9-3 Dinner all wk 6-9 ⊕ FREE HOUSE ◀ Hawkshead Bitter, John Smith's, Courage Directors, Yates, Cumbrian Legendary Ales Loweswater Gold ♻ Symonds. ᵧ 12 **Facilities** Non-diners area ♦ Children's menu & portions Garden ⋒ Beer festival Cider festival WiFi ▭ (notice required)

Old Farmhouse

tel: 01229 480324 **Priory Rd LA12 9HR**
email: oldfarmhouse@hotmail.co.uk
dir: *From A590 in Ulverston take A5087 signed Bardsea. Pub on right*

Community-focused pub in a converted barn

Located just south of the town and a short distance from Morecambe Bay, the Old Farmhouse is a busy pub housed within a beautifully converted barn. Its very popular restaurant in the main barn area offers an extensive traditional menu — choose a classic such as their celebrated Cumberland pie, or an Aberdeen Angus, chicken or fish burger; Cumberland meatballs and linguine; or grilled mackerel fillets, and leave room for the apple and cinnamon crumble. Local Cumbrian ales, a sun-trap courtyard garden, a big screen for live sports and a function room for private hire complete the picture.

Open all day all wk **Food** all wk 12-9 Set menu available Restaurant menu available all wk ⊕ FREE HOUSE ◀ Ulverston Harvest Moon, Lancaster Blonde, Cumberland, Sharp's Doom Bar, Copper Dragon. ᵧ 9 **Facilities** Non-diners area ♣ (Bar Garden Outside area) ♦ Children's menu Children's portions Garden Outside area ⋒ Parking WiFi ▭

The Stan Laurel Inn

tel: 01229 582814 **31 The Ellers LA12 0AB**
email: thestanlaurel@aol.com
dir: *M6 junct 36, A590 to Ulverston. Straight on at Booths rdbt, left at 2nd rdbt in The Ellers, pub on left after Ford garage*

Local ales and hearty food

When the old market town of Ulverston's most famous son — the comic actor Stan Laurel — was born in 1890, this town-centre pub was still a farmhouse with two cottages surrounded by fields and orchards. Owners Trudi and Paul Dewar serve a selection of locally brewed real ales and a full menu of traditional pub food plus a specials board. Take your pick from dishes such as BBQ baby back ribs; chicken forestière; liver, bacon and onions; chill con carne; steak and ale pie; and the ever popular 'Stan's renowned lasagne'.

Open Mon 7pm-11pm Tue-Thu 12-2.30 6-11 Fri-Sat 12-2.30 6-12 Sun 12-11.30 Closed Mon L **Food** Lunch Tue-Sat 12-2, Sun 12-8 Dinner Tue-Sat 6-9, Sun 12-8 ⊕ FREE HOUSE ◀ Thwaites Original, Ulverston, Barngates, Salamander. **Facilities** Non-diners area ♣ (Bar Outside area) ♦ Children's menu Children's portions Outside area ⋒ Parking WiFi

Wasdale Head Inn ★★★★ INN

tel: 019467 26229 **CA20 1EX**
email: reception@wasdale.com **web:** www.wasdale.com
dir: *From A595 follow Wasdale signs. Inn at head of valley*

Welcoming inn surrounded by record breakers

Dramatically situated at the foot of England's highest mountain, adjacent to England's smallest church and not far from the deepest lake, this Victorian inn is reputedly the birthplace of British climbing — photographs decorating the oak-panelled walls reflect the passion for this activity. Ritson's Bar is named after Will Ritson who was awarded the very first title of 'The World's Biggest Liar'. Expect local ales and hearty food such as Cumbrian rarebit or pea and ham soup; followed by fish and chips; lamb stew and dumplings; or salmon burger in teriyaki sauce. The Wasdale Head Show and Shepherd's Meet, which is held on the second Saturday in October, is a great reason to hang up the climbing boots for a day and maybe stay over in one of the comfortable bedrooms.

Open all day all wk **Food** all wk 12-8.30 Restaurant menu available Wed-Sun ⊕ FREE HOUSE ◀ Cumbrian Legendary Ales Loweswater Gold & Esthwaite Bitter, Jennings, Hesket Newmarket High Pike ♻ Westons. **Facilities** Non-diners area ♣ (Bar Garden) ♦ Children's menu Children's portions Garden ⋒ Beer festival Parking **Rooms** 20

Eagle & Child Inn

tel: 01539 821320 **Kendal Rd, Staveley LA8 9LP**
email: info@eaglechildinn.co.uk
dir: *M6 junct 36, A590 towards Kendal then A591 towards Windermere. Staveley 2m*

Free house with a riverside beer garden

Surrounded by miles of excellent walking, cycling and fishing country in a quiet village, this friendly inn shares the same name with several pubs in Britain, which refers to a legend of a baby found in an eagle's nest during the time of King Alfred. The rivers Kent and Gowan meet at the pub's gardens with its picnic tables for outdoor eating and local-ale drinking. Dishes include ingredients from village suppliers, such as slow-roasted lamb shank, Cumberland sausage and hunter's chicken. Non-meat choices might be Malaysian vegetable curry or roast vegetable pasta.

Open all day all wk **Food** Lunch Mon-Fri 12-2.30, Sat-Sun 12-9 Dinner Mon-Fri 6-9, Sat-Sun 12-9 ⊕ FREE HOUSE ◀ Hawkshead Bitter, Yates Best Bitter, Tirril, Coniston, Dent, Jennings Cumberland ♻ Westons, Thatchers Gold, guest cider. ᵧ 10 **Facilities** Non-diners area ♣ (Bar Restaurant Garden) ♦ Children's menu Children's portions Garden ⋒ Parking WiFi ▭

The Brown Horse Inn

tel: 015394 43443 **LA23 3NR**
email: steve@thebrownhorseinn.co.uk
dir: *On A5074 between Bowness-on-Windermere & A590 (Kendal to Barrow-in-Furness road)*

An inn of many talents

The decor at this 1850s inn, in the beautiful and tranquil Winster Valley, has a subtly modern edge. It is virtually self-sufficient: vegetables and free-range meat come from the owners' surrounding land, and ales are brewed on site. The innovative cooking is a contemporary take on traditional fare and dinner could see a starter of grilled Bury black pudding, fried duck egg, powdered bacon and home-made brown sauce. Mains range from Lakes Blonde beer-battered cod, chips and pea purée to their gammon plate – grilled steak and pulled ham hock, slow-cooked egg, home-made chips and piccalilli and pineapple relish.

Open all day all wk **Food** Lunch Mon-Fri 12-2, Sat-Sun, BHs & School Hols 12-4 Dinner all wk 6-9 Av main course £14 ⊕ FREE HOUSE ⬛ Winster Valley Best Bitter, Old School, Hurdler, Chaser, Dark Horse & Lakes Blonde ♖ Thatchers. ♟ 12 **Facilities** Non-diners area ♣ (Bar Outside area) ♦ Children's menu Children's portions Play area Outside area ♬ Beer festival Parking WiFi ▭ (notice required)

▮ WITHERSLACK   Map 18 SD48

NEW The Derby Arms

tel: 015395 52207 **LA11 6RH**
email: info@thederbyarms.co.uk
dir: *From Sizergh take A590 towards Barrow-in-Furness. From dual carriageway turn right at Witherslack sign. Pub on left in village*

Treasured village asset

Some years ago, not wanting The Derby Arms to close, the village bought it, later selling the lease to the Ainscough pub and restaurant group. Now extensively restored, part is now a community-run shop. The bar maintains a good roster of local real ales and a wide choice of wines by the glass. Potted shrimps from Morecambe Bay only a few miles south might prove the perfect starter, then steak and ale shortcrust pastry pie, the meat coming from the pub's own organic herd; battered fillet of haddock; or wild mushroom risotto, ending with home-made apple crumble. Live music sessions are held at least once a month.

Open all day all wk **Food** Lunch Mon-Fri 12-2, Sat 12-9, Sun 12-8 Dinner Mon-Fri 6-9, Sat 12-9, Sun 12-8 Av main course £11 Set menu available Restaurant menu available all wk ⊕ FREE HOUSE ⬛ Bowness Bay Swan Blond, Marston's Wainwright, Cumbrian Legendary Ales Esthwaite Bitter, Dent Rambrau, Eden Best ♖ Kingstone Press. ♟ 9 **Facilities** Non-diners area ♣ (Bar Outside area) ♦ Children's menu Children's portions Outside area ♬ Parking WiFi ▭ (notice required)

▮ WORKINGTON   Map 18 NY02

The Old Ginn House

tel: 01900 64616 **Great Clifton CA14 1TS**
email: enquiries@oldginnhouse.co.uk
dir: *Just off A66, 3m from Workington & 4m from Cockermouth*

Converted farm building offering good food

When this was a farm, ginning was the process by which horses were used to turn a grindstone that crushed grain. It took place in the rounded area known today as the Ginn Room and which is now the main bar, serving local ales. The dining areas, all butter yellow, bright check curtains and terracotta tiles, rather bring the Mediterranean to mind, although the extensive menu and specials are both cosmopolitan and traditional. The pub has a good reputation for steaks but others options are cod loin, streaky bacon and smoked cheese sauce; whole shoulder of lamb marinated in mint, honey and garlic; pan-fried sea bass fillet with cracked black pepper and lemon butter. A good vegetarian choice is available.

Open all day all wk Closed 24-26 Dec, 1 Jan **Food** Lunch all wk 12-2 Dinner all wk 6-9.30 ⊕ FREE HOUSE ⬛ John Smith's, Coniston Bluebird Bitter, local guest ales. **Facilities** Non-diners area ♦ Children's menu Children's portions Garden ♬ Parking WiFi ▭ (notice required)

▮ YANWATH   Map 18 NY52

The Yanwath Gate Inn

tel: 01768 862386 **CA10 2LF**
email: info@yanwathgate.co.uk
dir: *Phone for detailed directions*

Known for its Cumbrian craft beers and good food

Taken over by Simon Prior at the end of 2015, this 17th-century coaching inn is well placed for excursions to the shores of Ullswater or the great fells of the high Pennines. Its favoured location in an area of country estates and the rich pasturelands of the Eden Valley, holds the promise of great food and drink. Some of the best Cumbrian microbrewery beers from the likes of Yates and Barngates draw guests into the beamed, country-style interior. Menus change monthly and may include bouillabaisse; or rack of lamb, mustard mash, root veg and port gravy.

Open all day all wk **Food** Lunch all wk 12-2.30 Dinner all wk 6-9 ⊕ FREE HOUSE ⬛ Barngates, Yates, guest ales ♖ Westons Old Rosie. ♟ 12 **Facilities** Non-diners area ♣ (Bar Garden) ♦ Children's menu Garden ♬ Parking WiFi

▮▮ DERBYSHIRE

▮ ASHOVER   Map 16 SK36

The Crispin Inn

tel: 01246 590911 **Church St S45 0AB**
dir: *From Matlock take A632 towards Chesterfield. Right onto B6036 to Ashover*

Popular village pub with a past

Ashover was the scene of a confrontation between Cavaliers and Roundheads during the English Civil War; a sign on the front wall of this 14th-century pub tells of its bit-part role in the skirmish. Jennings delivers its real ales from Cumbria, Brakspear from Oxfordshire, and Marston's from Burton upon Trent. There's plenty of good pub food to be had, including hot torpedo cobs and ciabattas; jacket potatoes; seafood platter; home-made lasagne and chips; pan-fried liver and bacon; and beef and ale with dumplings. Other options are specials such as kangaroo, ostrich, wild boar and speciality sausages, and dishes suitable for vegetarians and vegans.

Open all wk 12-3 6-11.30 (Sun 12-11.30) Closed 25 Dec **Food** Lunch all wk 12-2 Dinner Tue-Sat 6-9 ⊕ MARSTON'S ⬛ Jennings Cumberland Ale & Cocker Hoop, Brakspear Oxford Gold, Marston's Pedigree. ♟ **Facilities** Non-diners area ♣ (Bar Garden) ♦ Children's portions Garden ♬ Parking WiFi ▭ (notice required)

The Old Poets Corner

tel: 01246 590888 **Butts Rd S45 0EW**
email: enquiries@oldpoets.co.uk
dir: *From Matlock take A632 signed Chesterfield. Right onto B6036 to Ashover*

Ever-popular pub with great walks all around

It's no wonder that ale and cider aficionados flock to this traditional village local; it dispenses eight ciders, and ten cask ales including choices from the Ashover Brewery behind the pub. The March and October beer festivals see these numbers multiply. There's live music here twice a week, quizzes, special events and Sunday night curries. Hearty home-cooked pub dishes range from chicken, bacon and BBQ melt to trio of local sausages with creamed potatoes, red onion gravy and seasonal veg. Walk it all off in the scenic Derbyshire countryside.

Open all day all wk **Food** Lunch Mon-Fri 12-2, Sat all day, Sun 12-3 Dinner Mon-Thu 6.30-9, Fri 6-9.30, Sat all day, Sun 6-9 ⊕ FREE HOUSE ⬛ Ashover, Oakham, guest ales ♖ Broadoak Perry & Moonshine, Westons Old Rosie, Ashover & Poets' Pippin. **Facilities** Non-diners area ♣ (Bar Outside area) ♦ Family room Outside area ♬ Beer festival Cider festival Parking WiFi ▭

BAKEWELL
Map 16 SK26

The Monsal Head Hotel

tel: 01629 640250 **Monsal Head DE45 1NL**
email: enquiries@monsalhead.com
dir: *A6 from Bakewell towards Buxton. 1.5m to Ashford. Follow Monsal Head signs, B6465 for 1m*

An all-rounder in the Peak District

Only a few minutes from Chatsworth House and the famous railway viaduct at Monsal Head, the hotel's Stables bar reflects its earlier role as the home of railway horses collecting passengers from Monsal Dale station. It has a rustic ambience with an original flagstone floor, seating in horse stalls and a log fire – the perfect place to enjoy a range of cask ales from microbreweries such as Tollgate. The Longstone restaurant is spacious and airy with large windows to appreciate the views, again with an open fire in the colder weather. The menu demonstrates an extensive use of local produce. Breakfasts and morning coffee are available everyday, and the same menu is offered in the bar, restaurant and the large outdoor seating area.

Open all day all wk 8am-mdnt ⊕ FREE HOUSE ◖ Wincle, Pennine Brewery Co, Tollgate Brewery, Welbeck Abbey Brewery Ŏ Symonds. **Facilities** ❀ (Bar Garden Outside area) ◖ Children's menu Children's portions Garden Outside area Parking

BAMFORD
Map 16 SK28

The Yorkshire Bridge Inn
PICK OF THE PUBS

See Pick of the Pubs on opposite page and advert below

BARROW UPON TRENT
Map 11 SK32

Ragley Boat Stop

tel: 01332 703919 **Deepdale Ln, off Sinfin Ln DE73 7FY**
email: pippa@king-henrys-taverns.co.uk
dir: *Phone for detailed directions*

Canalside pub ideal for watching the world go by

This timbered and whitewashed free house features a lovely garden sloping down to the Trent and Mersey Canal. A huge balcony overlooking the canal and the grassy garden complete with picnic benches are both great spots for a quiet drink. The smart, spacious interior is cool and contemporary with muted colours, stripped wood and plenty of comfy sofas. The menu of freshly prepared dishes has choices to suit every appetite. Beef in all its forms is a major attraction; alternatively international flavours abound in dishes such as vegetable fajitas, chicken korma, swordfish steak, and a Cajun chicken and ribs combo.

Open all day all wk 11.30-11 **Food** all wk 12-10 ⊕ FREE HOUSE/KING HENRY'S TAVERNS ◖ Greene King IPA, Marston's Pedigree, Guinness. ☗ 16
Facilities Non-diners area ◖ Children's menu Children's portions Garden Parking ⊟

BEELEY
Map 16 SK26

The Devonshire Arms at Beeley ★★★★ INN ⊛
PICK OF THE PUBS

tel: 01629 733259 **Devonshire Square DE4 2NR**
email: res@devonshirehotels.co.uk web: www.devonshirebeeley.co.uk
dir: *B6012 towards Matlock, pass Chatsworth House. After 1.5m turn left, 2nd entrance to Beeley*

Chatsworth Estate scene of Royal trysts

Surrounded by classic Peak District scenery, this handsome, 18th-century former coaching inn often welcomed Charles Dickens and, so rumour has it, King Edward VII often entertained his mistress, Alice Keppel, here. The original part of the inn is much the same as they would remember it, with low-beamed ceilings, wooden settles, flagstone floors and open fires in winter. Far more 21st century are the floor-to-ceiling windows in the bright, stripey-chaired Brasserie, which overlooks a brook and the village square, while up a few steps in the Malt Vault is the 'big table', ideal for family get-togethers. Among chef-patron Alan Hill's modern British dishes are harissa-glazed Scottish salmon; Chatsworth Estate venison haunch bourguignon; and parsnip and winter squash tarte Tatin. Alan makes good use of local produce, including game, while his Barter Board offers estate-brewed and other local beers in exchange for villagers' home-grown produce.

Open all day all wk **Food** Lunch Mon-Thu 12-2.30, Fri-Sun 12-3 Dinner Mon-Sat 6-9.30, Sun 6-9 ⊕ FREE HOUSE/DEVONSHIRE HOTELS & RESTAURANTS ◖ Peak Chatsworth Gold, Thornbridge Jaipur, Theakston Old Peculier Ŏ Aspall. ☗ 10
Facilities Non-diners area ◖ Children's menu Children's portions Garden ⩲ Parking WiFi **Rooms** 14

PICK OF THE PUBS

The Yorkshire Bridge Inn

BAMFORD   Map 16 SK28

tel: 01433 651361
Ashopton Rd S33 0AZ
email: info@yorkshire-bridge.co.uk
web: www.yorkshire-bridge.co.uk
dir: *From Sheffield A57 towards Glossop,
left onto A6013, pub 1m on right*

In the heart of wonderful Peak District walking country

Named after the old packhorse bridge over the River Derwent, this early 19th-century free house is only a short distance away from the Ladybower Reservoir. Between 1935 and 1943, when it was created, two local villages were drowned and during periods of drought it's possible to see the remains of one of them. It was in 1943 that the RAF's 617 Squadron, known as 'The Dambusters', used Ladybower and two other nearby reservoirs for testing Barnes Wallis's famous bouncing bombs, later to destroy two important German dams. Back inside, views from the beamed and chintz-curtained bars take in the peak of Whin Hill, making it a jolly good spot for enjoying a pint of the unique Bombs Gone specially brewed for the inn at the Bradfield Brewery, and good-quality pub food made with fresh local produce. Sandwiches are all freshly prepared, with fillings from home-baked ham to hot tuna melt. Main meal starters include home-made cream of chicken

soup; chicken liver pâté; or an ocean pot of smoked haddock, salmon and cod in white wine sauce. Next could come a home-made shortcrust steak and kidney pie; chilli con carne; grilled sea bass fillets with prawn and lemon butter, new potatoes and vegetables; or fresh dressed Filey crab salad. If you've walked to one of the reservoirs and back, look to the grill for a calorie replacing T-bone, sirloin or gammon steak, cooked to your liking without demur from a chef who doesn't insist on doing it his way. Bakewell pudding, or New York vanilla cheesecake finish a meal off well. A beer and cider festival is held in mid-May.

Open all day all wk **Food** Lunch Mon-Sat 12-2.30, Sun 12-8.30 Dinner Mon-Thu

5.30-8.30, Fri-Sat 5-9, Sun 12-8.30 Av main course £10.25 ⊞ FREE HOUSE ◀ Peak Ales Bakewell Best Bitter, Bradfield Farmers Blonde, Farmers Bitter & Bombs Gone, Abbeydale Moonshine, Kelham Island Easy Rider ♻ Thatchers. ♟ 11 **Facilities** Non-diners area ♦ Children's menu Children's portions Garden ⩕ Beer festival Cider festival Parking WiFi ⛟ (notice required)

BIRCHOVER
Map 16 SK26

The Druid Inn
PICK OF THE PUBS

tel: 01629 653836 **Main St DE4 2BL**
email: r.innes228@btinternet.com
dir: *From A6 between Matlock & Bakewell take B5056 signed Ashbourne. In approx 2m, left to Birchover*

Well-appointed village inn with dynamic menu choices

Set on a wooded ridge at the fringe of a pretty Peak District village, this classic stone-built inn has been here for over four centuries. The all-day menus make the place an ideal retreat for ramblers exploring the evocative stone circles and rock formations of the local vales and moors. It's also increasingly popular as a dining destination. Home-in first on the great selection of top-notch real ales – Blue Monkey and Abbeydale amongst many – and grab a seat on the terrace before studying a revelatory menu that offers both stalwart pub grub choices and cutting-edge dishes. Prosecco and lemon thyme risotto, taleggio bonbons is a great starter; chased up by mains like Dixie's three little piggies – cheek, fillet and belly – with apple and black pudding; or perhaps confit salmon and cucumber, candied garlic, tikka spices, apple and snow peas. The blackboard menus change weekly and are complemented with occasional specialist taster menus.

Open all day noon–late Closed 25-26 Dec, 1 Jan, Mon **Food** Tue-Sat 12-9, Sun 12-8 ⊕ FREE HOUSE ◀ Abbeydale, Cumbrian Legendary Ales, Hawkshead, Oakham Ales, Blue Monkey, Sarah Hughes, guest ales ○ Hogan's. **Facilities** Non-diners area ❀ (Bar Restaurant Garden) ◀ Children's menu Children's portions Family room Garden ㅠ Beer festival Parking WiFi ☵ (notice required)

Red Lion Inn

tel: 01629 650363 **Main St DE4 2BN**
email: red.lion@live.co.uk
dir: *5.5m from Matlock, off A6 onto B5056*

Good beer plus Sardinian dishes on the menu

Built in 1680, the Red Lion's old well, now glass-covered, still remains in the taproom. Follow a walk to nearby Rowter Rocks and cosy up in the oak-beamed bar with its exposed stone walls, scrubbed oak tables and worn quarry-tiled floor. Quaff a pint of locally brewed Nine Ladies or one of the other weekly-changing real ales on tap, and refuel with a plate of home-cooked food. Start with a Sardinian speciality from owner Matteo Frau's homeland, perhaps a selection of cured meats, cheese and olives, then follow with pork loin medallions with lemon, caper and sage butter, or field mushroom tarte Tatin with Birchover Blue cheese. Their Sardinian evenings prove popular.

Open 12-2.30 6-11.30 (Sat & BH Mon 12-12 Sun 12-11) Closed Mon in winter ex BHs **Food** Lunch Mon-Fri 12-2.30, Sat 12-9, Sun-12-8 Dinner Mon-Fri 6-9, Sat 12-9, Sun-12-8 Set menu available ⊕ FREE HOUSE ◀ Birchover Bircher Best, Cork Stone, Robin Hood's Stride & Nine Ladies ○ Traditional Local ciders.
Facilities Non-diners area ◀ Children's portions Garden Beer festival Cider festival Parking WiFi ☵

BONSALL
Map 16 SK25

The Barley Mow

tel: 01629 825685 **The Dale DE4 2AY**
email: david.j.wragg@gmail.com
dir: *S from Matlock on A6 to Cromford. Right onto A5012 (Cromwell Hill). Right into Water Ln (A5012). Right in Clatterway towards Bonsall. Left at memorial into The Dale. Pub 400mtrs on right*

Good food, real ales and fast fowl

There are several reasons to visit this intimate, former lead miner's cottage: Bonsall is apparently Europe's UFO capital; the pub hosts the World Championship Hen Races; and landlords Colette and David display an unshakeable commitment to

Peak District and other regional real ales, as their beer festivals help to confirm. The simple menu is all about home-cooked pub grub, such as ham, egg and chips; scampi and chips; extra-mature rump steak; chicken curry; sausages and mash; beef chilli; and gammon steak.

Open 6-11 (Sat-Sun 12-12) Closed Mon (ex BHs) ⊕ FREE HOUSE ◀ Thornbridge, Whim, Abbeydale, Blue Monkey ○ Hecks, Westons Perry. **Facilities** ❀ (Bar Restaurant Outside area) ◀ Children's menu Children's portions Beer festival Outside area Parking WiFi

BRADWELL
Map 16 SK18

The Samuel Fox Country Inn ★★★★★ INN ◉◉

tel: 01433 621562 **Stretfield Rd S33 9JT**
email: enquiries@samuelfox.co.uk web: www.samuelfox.co.uk
dir: *M1 junct 29, A617 towards Chesterfield onto A623 (Chapel-en-le-Frith). B6049 to Bradwell. Pub on left*

Fine food and real ales in the Hope Valley

In the heart of the Peak District National Park and handy for the Pennine Way, this village inn is named after the local man credited with inventing the steel-ribbed umbrella – hence the pub sign showing a fox sheltering beneath one. Owner and experienced chef, James Duckett ensures that there's a warm welcome and pleasant atmosphere for villagers and visitors alike. Contemporary notes creep into the food, which is firmly based on fresh local produce. Expect the likes of goats' cheese and potato terrine with pickled beets; spiced cod fillet, chickpea curry, spinach and sweet potato; and slow-roasted belly pork, cauliflower, celeriac and red wine sauce.

Open 12-3 6-11 Closed 2-27 Jan, Mon & Tue **Food** Lunch Fri-Sat 12-2.30, Sun 1-8 (Sun 1-4 in winter) Dinner Wed-Sat 6-9, Sun 6-8 Set menu available Restaurant menu available Wed-Sun ⊕ FREE HOUSE ◀ Bradfield, Kelham Island, Intrepid, Pennine ○ Thatchers Heritage, Westons. ☗ 12 **Facilities** Non-diners area ◀ Children's menu Children's portions Outside area ㅠ Parking WiFi **Rooms** 4

CASTLETON
Map 16 SK18

The Peak Hotel

tel: 01433 620247 **How Ln S33 8WJ**
email: info@thepeakhotel.co.uk
dir: *On A6187 in centre of village*

Plenty on offer at this Peak District magnet

The Peak Hotel is where to aim for after climbing Lose Hill, or walking along the Hope Valley. Standing below Peveril Castle, this 17th-century stone building is a real magnet, seducing visitors with its leather armchairs, open log fires and locally brewed cask beers, real ciders, wines by the glass and a large selection of craft gins; alternative places to recover are the restaurant/coffee shop and raised sun terrace. Regional ingredients are used to good effect in dishes such as drunken duck pâté with real ale chutney; steak and ale casserole with dumplings; and a hearty sandwich filled with Derbyshire beef and horseradish.

Open all day all wk **Food** Lunch all wk 12-5 Dinner all wk 5-9 ⊕ PUNCH TAVERNS ◀ Kelham Island Easy Rider, Bradfield Farmers Blonde, Moonshine, guest ales ○ Westons Old Rosie & Stowford Press. ☗ 9 **Facilities** Non-diners area ❀ (All areas) ◀ Children's menu Children's portions Garden Outside area ㅠ Beer festival Cider festival Parking WiFi ☵ (notice required)

PICK OF THE PUBS

Old Hall Inn

CHINLEY Map 16 SK08

tel: 01663 750529
Whitehough SK23 6EJ
email: info@old-hall-inn.co.uk
web: www.old-hall-inn.co.uk
dir: *B5470 W from Chapel-en-le-Frith. Right into Whitehough Head Ln. 0.8m*

An ideal stop for serious walkers

Prime Peak District walking country surrounds this family-run, 16th-century pub attached to Whitehough Hall. Within easy reach are the iconic landscape features of Kinder Scout, Mam Tor and Stanage Edge, popular with climbers and fell-walkers who head here for refreshment following their exertions. And no wonder. The drinks list is as long as your arm, with local breweries to the fore; beers from Abbeydale, Kelham Island, Phoenix, Storm and many more all have their enthusiasts, which makes for a lively atmosphere in the bar. Sheppy's from Somerset is among the real ciders and perries (note: a beer and cider festival is held on the third weekend in September). All manner of bottled beers, particularly Belgian wheat, fruit and Trappist varieties, a remarkable choice of malts and gins and around 80 wines round off the excellent drinks range. Food service is busy too: the pub opens into the Minstrels' Gallery restaurant in the old manor house, where a short seasonal menu and daily specials offer freshly

made 'small plates' of white onion and tarragon risotto; celeriac and apple soup with celery salt croûtons; and traditional prawn cocktail. Move on to Thai-style breaded haddock goujons with home-made chilli jam, dressed salad and noodles; or confit duck leg, Parmentier potatoes and curly kale with port and shallot sauce. Then there are pub classics, such as steak and ale pudding with home-made chips, garden peas and a pot of gravy; Lancashire hotpot with braised red cabbage and crusty bread; and cheese, leek and apple pie with mash and peas. Half a dozen desserts, among them apple and cinnamon walnut crumble, round off the wide-ranging menu.

Open all day all wk **Food** Lunch Mon-Sat 12-2, Sun 12-7.30 Dinner Mon-Thu 5-9, Fri-Sat 5-9.30, Sun 12-7.30 Av main course £10 Set menu available ⊞ FREE HOUSE ◀ Marston's, Thornbridge, Phoenix, Abbeydale, Storm, Kelham Island, Red Willow Ŏ Thatchers, Sheppy's, Westons. ♉ 12 **Facilities** Non-diners area ❀ (Bar Garden) ⋕ Children's menu & portions Garden ♬ Beer & Cider festival Parking WiFi ⛟

CASTLETON *continued*

Ye Olde Nags Head

tel: 01433 620248 **Cross St S33 8WH**
email: info@yeoldenagshead.co.uk
dir: *A625 from Sheffield, W through Hope Valley, through Hathersage & Hope. Pub on main road*

A warm welcome and crowd-pleasing food

Close to Chatsworth House and Haddon Hall, this traditional 17th-century coaching inn is situated in the heart of the Peak District National Park. The owner continues to welcome thirsty travellers, and the miles of wonderful walks and country lanes favoured by walkers and cyclists means that there are plenty of them willing to occupy the cosy bars warmed by open fires. The interior is a successful mix of contemporary and traditional, a theme also reflected on the menu: expect a variety of stone-baked pizzas, sandwiches, salads, grills and sharing platters. Main dishes include beef, ale and potato pie, and classic nut roast topped with roast tomato sauce and goats' cheese. There's also a beer festival in the summer.

Open all day all wk **Food** all wk 12-9 Av main course £12 ⊕ FREE HOUSE ◀ Timothy Taylor Landlord, Buxton Kinder Sunset, Kelham Island Riders on the Storm, Black Sheep, Sharp's Doom Bar, Bradfield Farmers Blonde, Guinness ♂ Westons Old Rosie, Rosie's Pig, Family Reserve. **Facilities** Non-diners area ✿ (Bar) ●♦ Children's menu Children's portions Beer festival Parking WiFi ⇔

CHESTERFIELD	Map 16 SK37

Red Lion Pub & Bistro ★★★★ HL ◉◉ PICK OF THE PUBS

tel: 01246 566142 **Darley Rd, Stone Edge S45 0LW**
email: dine@peakedgehotel.co.uk **web:** www.peakedgehotel.co.uk
dir: *Phone for detailed directions*

Innovative food close to good walking country

Dating back to 1788, the Red Lion is located on the edge of the beautiful Peak District National Park. It has seen many changes over the years but retains much character – the original wooden beams and stone walls are complemented by discreet lighting and comfy leather armchairs which add a contemporary edge. Striking black-and-white photographs decorate the walls, whilst local bands liven up the bar on Thursday evenings. Meals are served in the bar and bistro, or beneath umbrellas in the large garden. Seasonal produce drives the menu and the chefs make everything, from sauces to the chips. Typical choices might start with scallops, butternut squash purée, peanut brittle and pink grapefruit; or carrot soup, clotted cream pannacotta, carrot crisps and baby coriander, followed by beef skirt, oxtail croquettes, bone marrow, mirepoix and roast onion purée; or halibut, seaweed butter, kimchi and crab dumplings.

Open all day all wk **Food** Sun-Thu 12-9, Fri-Sat 12-9.30 ⊕ FREE HOUSE ◀ Guest ales. ♟ 12 **Facilities** Non-diners area ●♦ Children's menu Children's portions Garden ⋒ Parking WiFi ⇔ (notice required) **Rooms** 27

CHINLEY	Map 16 SK08

Old Hall Inn

PICK OF THE PUBS

See Pick of the Pubs on page 123

The Paper Mill Inn

tel: 01663 750529 **Whitehough SK23 6EJ**
email: info@papermillinn.co.uk
dir: *In village centre*

A cosy haven for beer drinkers

Run by the same team as the adjacent Old Hall Inn, the pub is a veritable haven for beer and sport lovers. Flagstone floors, open fires and sporting events on TV combine to create a highly satisfactory ambience for customers enjoying real ales such as Thornbridge, or a world beer from the list of many; the choice peaks at the festival in September, which also features draught ciders. The main restaurant is over at the Old Hall Inn.

Open all wk 5-11 (Sat-Sun 12-11) **Food** Contact pub for food times ⊕ FREE HOUSE ◀ Thornbridge, Marston's. **Facilities** Non-diners area ✿ (Bar Restaurant Outside area) ●♦ Outside area ⋒ Beer festival Cider festival Parking WiFi ⇔

DALBURY	Map 10 SK23

The Black Cow ★★★★ INN ◉

tel: 01332 824297 **The Green DE6 5BE**
email: info@blackcow.co.uk **web:** www.theblackcow.co.uk
dir: *From A52 (W of Derby) take B5020 signed Mickleover. On left bend turn right signed Long Ln & Longford. Left signed Lees Dalbury. Pub on left in village. (NB if using Sat Nav follow directions not postcode)*

Recommended for its hospitality, accommodation and cuisine

Facing the village green and its iconic red telephone box, this free house champions real ales from county-based Dancing Duck, Mansfield and Mr Grundy's breweries. In the one AA-Rosette restaurant, award-winning head Danny Edwards' seasonal menus might feature pulled pork faggots, buttered greens, creamed potato with Guinness and shallot gravy. Since this is Derbyshire, expect Bakewell tart with crème anglaise to make an appearance. Tastefully decorated guest rooms offer free WiFi. A small store/farm shop even sells ramblers' and cyclists' requirements.

Open all wk 12-3 5-close (Sat & Sun 12-close) **Food** Lunch Mon-Fri 12-2, Sat 12-9.30, Sun 12-4 Dinner Mon-Thu 6-9, Fri 6-9.30, Sat 12-9.30 ⊕ FREE HOUSE ◀ Guest ales. ♟ 10 **Facilities** Non-diners area ●♦ Children's menu Children's portions Play area Family room Garden Outside area ⋒ Beer festival Parking WiFi ⇔ (notice required) **Rooms** 7

DOE LEA (HARDWICK PARK)	Map 16 SK46

Hardwick Inn

tel: 01246 850245 **Hardwick Park, DOE LEA S44 5QJ**
email: hardwickinn@hotmail.co.uk
dir: *M1 junct 29, A6175. 0.5m left signed Stainsby/Hardwick Hall. After Stainsby, 2m, left at staggered junct. Follow brown tourist signs*

Step back in time at this village inn

Dating from the 15th century and built of locally quarried sandstone, this striking building was once the lodge for Hardwick Hall (NT) and stands at the south gate of Hardwick Park, not far from Chesterfield. Owned by the Batty family for three generations, the pub has a rambling interior and features period details such as mullioned windows, oak beams and stone fireplaces. Traditional food takes in a popular carvery roast, a salad bar, hearty home-made pies and casseroles, as well as fish and vegetarian dishes. A handy pitstop for anyone battling along the M1.

Open all day all wk **Food** Mon-Sat 11.30-9.30, Sun 12-9 Set menu available ⊕ FREE HOUSE ◀ Theakston Old Peculier, Bess of Hardwick, Black Sheep, Peak Ales Chatsworth Gold, guest ales ♂ Symonds Scrumpy Jack, Westons Old Rosie. ♟ 10 **Facilities** Non-diners area ✿ (Bar Garden) ●♦ Children's menu Children's portions Play area Family room Garden ⋒ Parking ⇔

ELMTON
Map 16 SK57

The Elm Tree

tel: 01909 721261 **S80 4LS**
email: enquiries@elmtreeelmton.co.uk
dir: *M1 junct 30, A616 signed Newart through 5 rdbts. Through Clowne, right at staggered x-roads into Hazelmere Rd to Elmton*

Contemporary dining pub with a passion for local produce

Food is very much the focus at this 17th-century pub tucked away in pretty Elmton. Chef-patron Chris Norfolk is passionate about sourcing seasonal and fully traceable produce from local suppliers, including fruit and vegetables from neighbour's gardens, and everything, from bread, pasta and pastry, is made on the premises. Changing menus (served all day) may deliver Elmton game terrine with pickled vegetables; partridge with creamed cabbage and bacon, hand-cut chips and blackberry gravy; or warm rice pudding, mulled berry sorbet and home-made marshmallows. There's a contemporary feel in the stone-floored bar and The Library, The Study and The Gallery private dining rooms that prove ideal for larger parties.

Open all day Closed Tue **Food** Mon, Wed-Sat 12-9, Sun 12-6 Set menu available ⊕ PUNCH TAVERNS ◀ Black Sheep, Kelham Island Easy Rider, Elm Tree Bitter ♂ Westons Old Rosie & Perry. ♟ **Facilities** Non-diners area ♥ (Bar Garden) ♦♦ Children's portions Play area Garden ☶ Parking ⛟ (notice required)

EYAM
Map 16 SK27

Miners Arms

tel: 01433 630853 **Water Ln S32 5RG**
email: info@theminersarmseyam.co.uk
dir: *Off B6521, 5m N of Bakewell*

Children, dogs and walkers all welcome

This welcoming 17th-century inn and restaurant was built just before the plague hit Eyam; the village tailor brought damp cloth from London and hung it to dry in front of the fire so releasing the infected fleas. The pub gets its name from the local lead mines of Roman times. Owned by Greene King, there's always the option to pop in for a pint of their IPA or Ruddles Best bitter, or enjoy a meal. A beer festival is held three times a year.

Open all wk Mon 12-3 5.30-11 Tue-Sun 12-11 **Food** Lunch Mon-Sat 12-2, Sun 12-3 Dinner Mon 6-8, Tue-Fri 6-9, Sat 7-9 ⊕ GREENE KING ◀ IPA, Ruddles Best, guest ales ♂ Westons Old Rosie. **Facilities** Non-diners area ♥ (Bar Garden) ♦♦ Children's menu Children's portions Garden ☶ Beer festival Parking WiFi ⛟ (notice required)

FENNY BENTLEY
Map 16 SK14

The Coach and Horses Inn

tel: 01335 350246 **DE6 1LB**
email: coachandhorses2@btconnect.com **web:** www.coachandhorsesfennybentley.co.uk
dir: *On A515 (Ashbourne to Buxton road), 2.5m from Ashbourne*

17th-century coaching inn offering good, honest cooking

A cosy refuge in any weather, this family-run, 17th-century coaching inn stands on the edge of the Peak District National Park. Besides the beautiful location, its charms include stripped wood furniture and low beams, real log-burning fires plus a welcoming and friendly atmosphere. Expect a great selection of real ales and hearty good home cooking that uses the best of local produce. A typical menu includes pork trio – pork belly, loin chop and traditional Cumberland sausage, apple cider sauce, mushroom, leeks and new potatoes; spicy five bean and vegetable casserole, grilled haloumi and herbed rice; or seared pavé of fresh salmon with pesto dressing, potato stack and fine green beans. Hot and cold sandwiches and baguettes provide lighter options.

Open all day all wk 11-11 (Sun 12-10.30) **Food** all wk 12-9 ⊕ FREE HOUSE ◀ Marston's Pedigree, Oakham JHB, Peak Swift Nick, Whim Hartington Bitter, Derby. **Facilities** Non-diners area ♦♦ Children's menu Family room Garden ☶ Parking ⛟ (notice required)

FOOLOW
Map 16 SK17

The Bulls Head Inn ★★★★ INN

tel: 01433 630873 **S32 5QR**
email: wilbnd@aol.com **web:** www.thebullatfoolow.co.uk
dir: *Just off A623, N of Stoney Middleton*

Traditional English country inn serving good food

In an upland village surrounded by a lattice-work of dry-stone walls, this 19th-century former coaching inn is the epitome of the English country pub. With open fires, oak beams, flagstone floors, great views, good food and beer, and accommodation, the much used adjective 'traditional' was never more appropriate. The bar stocks Black Sheep and Peak Ales. At lunchtime snacks and sandwiches come to the fore, but a weekly-changing blackboard is the backbone of the dining options. A sizzling crab ramekin makes a great starter, to be followed perhaps by sautéed calves' liver with mushrooms and caramelised onions.

Open 12-3 6.30-11 (Sun all day) Closed Mon (ex BHs) **Food** Lunch Tue-Sun 12-2 Dinner Tue-Sun 6.30-9 ⊕ FREE HOUSE ◀ Black Sheep, Peak, Adnams, Tetley. **Facilities** Non-diners area ♥ (Bar) ♦♦ Children's menu Children's portions ☶ Parking ⛟ **Rooms** 3

FROGGATT
Map 16 SK27

The Chequers Inn ★★★★ INN ◉◉ PICK OF THE PUBS

tel: 01433 630231 **Froggatt Edge S32 3ZJ**
email: info@chequers-froggatt.com **web:** www.chequers-froggatt.com
dir: On A625, 0.5m N of Calver

A traditional Peak District free house

You'll enjoy visiting this 16th-century pub on a wooded hillside below the gritstone escarpment of Froggatt Edge. Timber floors, antiques and blazing log fires help to make a pint of Chatsworth Gold, brewed on the Duke of Devonshire's nearby estate, irresistible. The kitchen's loyalty to all things locally produced or supplied is reflected in dishes such as pan-roasted pigeon breast with brown bread purée, pickled wild mushrooms, brioche wafer, lamb's lettuce and jus; salt-and-pepper duck breast with Savoy cabbage, caraway seed, salt-baked celeriac and red wine and orange reduction; and pan-fried sea bass with saffron fondant, crispy chicken wing, sautéed pancetta, samphire and chicken and tarragon velouté. In addition to a range of classics and lunchtime sandwiches, frequently changing blackboard specials include vegetarian options. A steep woodland footpath from the pub's elevated 'secret' garden leads up to Froggatt Edge itself.

Open all day all wk Closed 25 Dec **Food** Lunch Mon-Fri 12-2.30, Sat-Sun 12-9 Dinner Mon-Fri 6-9, Sat-Sun 12-9 ⊕ FREE HOUSE ◀ Kelham Island Easy Rider, Peak Ales Bakewell Best Bitter & Chatsworth Gold, Bradfield Farmers Blonde, guest ales. ♀ 10 **Facilities** ♦️ Children's portions Garden ⊼ Parking WiFi **Rooms** 7

GREAT HUCKLOW
Map 16 SK17

The Queen Anne Inn ★★★ INN

tel: 01298 871246 **SK17 8RF**
email: angelaryan100@aol.com **web:** www.queenanneinn.co.uk
dir: A623 onto B6049, exit at Anchor pub towards Bradwell, 2nd right to Great Hucklow

Great hospitality in a country setting

The inn dates from 1621, and the premises have held a licence for over 300 years; the names of all the landlords are known. The sheltered south-facing garden enjoys wonderful open views, and it's an ideal space for children during the warmer months. Inside you'll find an open fire in the stone fireplace, an ever-changing range of cask ales, and a short menu of popular pub dishes. These embrace starters of Thai fishcake with salad and dip; or duck pancakes with hoisin sauce; and main courses of beef rendang with rice; steak and ale pie; brie and beetroot tart; or home-baked ham salad and new potatoes.

Open 12-2.30 5-11 (Fri-Sun 12-11) Closed Mon **Food** Lunch Tue-Sun 12-2 Dinner Tue-Thu 6-8.30, Fri-Sat 6-9, Sun 6-8 Av main course £9.95 Set menu available Restaurant menu available Tue-Sun ⊕ FREE HOUSE ◀ Tetley's Cask, Bass, local guest ales ♂ Westons Stowford Press. ♀ 9 **Facilities** Non-diners area ♥ (Bar Garden) ♦️ Children's menu Children's portions Family room Garden ⊼ Parking WiFi ➡ (notice required) **Rooms** 2

GREAT LONGSTONE
Map 16 SK27

The White Lion

tel: 01629 640252 **Main St DE45 1TA**
email: info@whiteliongreatlongstone.co.uk
dir: Take A6020 from Ashford-in-the-Water towards Chesterfield. Left to Great Longstone

Stylish pub in an unspoilt Peak District village

Whether arriving on foot, on two wheels, or on four legs, visitors to Great Longstone's White Lion are sure to recuperate from their exertions. Sitting under the mass of Longstone Edge not far from Bakewell, Greg and Libby Robinson's pub has a peaceful outside patio and dog-welcoming snug bar. Very much food focussed,

the monthly-changing menus use locally-sourced produce whenever possible. A fixed-price two- or three-course lunch represents excellent value: a starter of prosciutto wrapped poached egg; or sweet potato rösti could be followed by pan-seared gilt-head bream with saffron potatoes, shredded kale and lemon and ginger syrup; or a choice of flatbread pizzas.

Open all wk 12-3 6-9 (Sat 12-9 Sun 12-8) **Food** Contact pub for food times Set menu available ⊕ ROBINSONS ◀ Dizzy Blonde, Robinsons Unicorn ♂ Westons Stowford Press. **Facilities** Non-diners area ♥ (Bar Outside area) ♦️ Children's menu Children's portions Outside area ⊼ Parking WiFi ➡ (notice required)

GRINDLEFORD
Map 16 SK27

The Maynard ★★★ HL ◉◉ PICK OF THE PUBS

See Pick of the Pubs on opposite page

HARDSTOFT
Map 16 SK46

COCO Bar Bistro at the Shoulder ★★★★ INN

tel: 01246 850276 **Deep Ln S45 8AF**
email: book@cocoattheshoulder.co.uk **web:** www.cocoattheshoulder.co.uk
dir: From B6039 follow signs for Hardwick Hall. 1st right into car park

Inviting menu in Derbyshire countryside inn

In new hands since June 2015, this 300-year-old pub, just ten minutes from the M1, is an ideal stop when exploring the Peak District and Sherwood Forest. Peak Ales' Bakewell Best Bitter is one of the local beers available in the bar, with its open log fires. The kitchen sources ingredients locally where possible, including the 30-day aged steaks cooked on the grill. The modern tapas menu offers plenty of choices whether you are sharing them or ordering them as a starter. Kick off with patatas bravas before charred chicken breast, tagliatelle, herb and tomato sauce.

Open all day all wk 12-11 **Food** Lunch Mon-Sat 12-5, Sun 12-6 Dinner Mon-Thu 5-9, Fri-Sat 5-9.30 Av main course £9.95 ⊕ FREE HOUSE ◀ Peak Bakewell Best Bitter, guest ales ♂ Symonds, Old Mout. ♀ 12 **Facilities** Non-diners area ♥ (Bar Restaurant Outside area) ♦️ Children's menu Children's portions Outside area ⊼ Parking WiFi ➡ (notice required) **Rooms** 4

HARTINGTON
Map 16 SK16

The Jug & Glass Inn ★★★ INN

tel: 01298 84848 **Ashbourne Rd SK17 0BA**
email: enquiries@jugandglass.biz **web:** www.jugandglass.biz
dir: From Buxton take A515 towards Ashbourne. Approx 10m to pub

Family-run hostelry in High Peak walking country

An ideal base for hiking the trails of Derbyshire's Peak District, strolling through the streets of Ashbourne and Bakewell, or visiting famous sights such as Chatsworth. Ales include Church End, and Whim from nearby Hartington, while the menu lists all the comfort food you could wish for: starters of lemon sole goujons or prawn cocktail; cottage pie, chilli con carne, steak and kidney pudding, and pan-fried lamb's liver are among the traditional and home-made main courses; dessert lovers are spoilt for choice with favourites such as profiteroles, apple crumble and treacle sponge. Nine newly-appointed bedrooms and superb views complete the picture.

Open 12-3 6-10 (Fri-Sat 12-10.30 Sun 12-9.30) Closed Mon-Tue **Food** Lunch Wed-Thu 12-3, Fri-Sat 12-8.30, Sun 12-7.30 Dinner Wed-Thu 6-8.30, Fri-Sat 12-8.30, Sun 12-7.30 ⊕ FREE HOUSE ◀ Church End, Whim Hartington. **Facilities** Non-diners area ♥ (Bar Garden Outside area) ♦️ Children's menu Children's portions Garden Outside area ⊼ Parking WiFi ➡ (notice required) **Rooms** 9

PICK OF THE PUBS

The Maynard ★★★ HL ❀❀

GRINDLEFORD   Map 16 SK27

tel: 01433 630321 **Main Rd S32 2HE**
email: info@themaynard.co.uk
web: www.themaynard.co.uk
dir: *M1 junct 30, A619 into Chesterfield,
then onto Baslow. A623 to Calver, right
into Grindleford*

Fine-dining Peak District hotel with a fine dining restaurant

Chatsworth House, the family seat of the Dukes of Devonshire, and the Blue John Cavern near Castleton, are just two of the renowned attractions near this impressive inn. Built in 1908 below the steep, wooded crags of Froggatt Edge, it's decorated in a contemporary style, although oak panelling, golden chandeliers and stained-glass windows help to declare Edwardian origins. Local artists display their work around the walls alongside photos of Peak District scenes. Leather sofas and log fires await in the Longshaw Bar, where real ales include Abbeydale Moonshine and Peak Ales Bakewell Best, the latter brewed on the Chatsworth Estate. The bar offers terrine of the day and prawn cocktail as starters, followed perhaps by bangers and mash, or beer-battered fish and chips. Another way to find out why The Maynard has earned two AA Rosettes is to dine in the restaurant overlooking the garden and beyond; here

seasonal menus might offer fillet of beef carpaccio; smoked aubergine risotto; pan-roast breast of quail and confit leg; oven-roast, home-smoked salmon fillet; and spiced carrot and chickpea blinis; desserts include Braeburn apple pannacotta; and iced quince parfait. On a Sunday a roast or fish lunch might begin with teriyaki salmon fishcake; or goats' cheese bavarois. The large garden offers striking panoramas across moorland and the Derwent Valley, a super backdrop for those getting married here. Beautifully appointed en suite bedrooms offer a king-size bed, flat-screen TV, and tea and coffee facilities. Dogs are most welcome.

Open all day all wk Closed 25 Dec, 1 Jan **Food** all day Restaurant menu available all wk ⊕ FREE HOUSE ◨ Abbeydale Moonshine, Peak Ales Bakewell Best Bitter. **Facilities** Non-diners area ❀ (Bar) ♦♦ Children's menu Garden ⊼ Parking WiFi 🚌 (notice required) **Rooms** 10

HASSOP
Map 16 SK27

The Old Eyre Arms

tel: 01629 640390 **DE45 1NS**
email: nick@eyrearms.com
dir: On B6001 N of Bakewell

A perfect Peak District escape

In a village-edge location between the formality of Chatsworth's vast estate, bold gritstone edges and the memorable wooded limestone dales of Derbyshire's River Wye, this comfortably unchanging, creeper-clad old inn ticks all the right boxes for beers and food. Real ales from Peak Ales and Bradfield breweries couldn't be more local, whilst all meals are prepared in-house: kick off with prawn cocktail or onion bhaji, and follow with lamb cooked in coconut, black pepper and Indian spices; rainbow trout baked with butter and almonds; or aubergine and mushroom lasagne to take the chill off a long ramble. Oak beams and furnishing and log fires complete the picture.

Open all wk 11-3 6-11 Closed 25-26 Dec, 2wks in Jan **Food** Lunch Mon-Fri 12-2, Sat 12-2.30, Sun 12-8 Dinner Mon-Sat 6-9, Sun 12-8 Set menu available ⊕ FREE HOUSE ◀ Peak Ales Swift Nick & Chatsworth Gold, Black Sheep Ale, Bradfield Farmers Blonde ♻ Westons Stowford Press. ♟ 9 **Facilities** Non-diners area ♦♦ Children's menu Children's portions Garden ⋒ Parking

HATHERSAGE
Map 16 SK28

The Plough Inn ★★★★ INN ◉ PICK OF THE PUBS

See Pick of the Pubs on opposite page

The Scotsmans Pack Country Inn

tel: 01433 650253 **School Ln S32 1BZ**
email: scotsmans.pack@btinternet.com
dir: From A6187 in Hathersage turn at church into School Lane

A warm welcome for locals and visitors alike

Set in the beautiful Hope Valley on one of the old packhorse trails used by Scottish 'packmen', this traditional inn is a short walk from Hathersage church and Little John's Grave. Weather permitting, head outside onto the sunny patio, next to the trout stream. The pub offers a good choice of hearty daily specials — six starters, ten mains and eight desserts — perhaps best washed down with a pint of Burton Bitter. This is a perfect base for walking and touring the Peak District.

Open all day all wk **Food** all wk 12-9.30 ⊕ MARSTON'S ◀ Burton Bitter, Pedigree, Marston's Wainwright, Ringwood Boondoggle ♻ Thatchers Gold. ♟ 10 **Facilities** Non-diners area ♦♦ Children's menu Children's portions Family room Garden ⋒ Parking WiFi 🚌

HAYFIELD
Map 16 SK08

The Royal Hotel

tel: 01663 742721 **Market St SK22 2EP**
email: enquiries@theroyalathayfield.com
dir: From A624 follow Hayfield signs

Village-centre pub on the Peak District border

Up in the High Peak, below the windswept plateau of Kinder Scout, the hotel dates from 1755. Its period charm still very evident, one place to relax with a pint of Thwaites Original or Happy Valley Kinder Falldown is the oak-panelled, log-fired bar. Others are the Cricket Room, popular with the local cricket team, whose ground is next door, and the Ramblers Bar which has hiking boots strung along the beams. The bar menu keeps things simple: a choice of four different pies; chicken curry; Derbyshire ham, free-range eggs, peas and chips; Derbyshire Dales lamp hotpot, pickled red cabbage and crusty bread. There's also a separate sandwich menu. Meals can be served on the patio overlooking the moorland.

Open all day all wk Mon-Thu 11-11 (Fri-Sat 11am-11.30pm Sun 11-10.30) **Food** Lunch Mon-Fri 12-2.30, Sat 12-9, Sun 12-7 Dinner Mon-Fri 6-8, Sat 12-9, Sun 12-7 Av main course £9.50 Set menu available ⊕ FREE HOUSE ◀ Thwaites Original, Happy Valley Kinder Falldown ♻ Westons Stowford Press, Thatchers Green Goblin, Hogan's. ♟ **Facilities** Non-diners area ♣ (Bar Outside area) ♦♦ Children's menu Children's portions Family room Outside area ⋒ Beer festival Parking WiFi 🚌 (notice required)

HOGNASTON
Map 16 SK25

The Red Lion Inn

tel: 01335 370396 **Main St DE6 1PR**
email: enquiries@redlionhognaston.uk **web:** www.redlionhognaston.uk
dir: From Ashbourne take B5035 towards Wirksworth. Approx 5m follow Carsington Water signs. Turn right to Hognaston

Traditional country pub awash with character

Here in 1997 to attend a wedding, John F Kennedy's son and his wife stayed at this whitewashed, 17th-century village pub overlooking Carsington Water. With beams, bare brick, old photos, bric-a-brac and antique furniture spread liberally around an open-fire warmed interior, traditional character isn't hard to find. Settle with a pint, perhaps from the Wincle Brewery in Cheshire, and start considering the menu, on which might appear fresh Conwy mussels cooked in dark ale; oven-roasted sea bass with beurre blanc sauce; chicken breast and leg with garlic sauce; and wild mushroom arancini. In the garden is a boules court.

Open all wk 12-2.30 6-11 **Food** Lunch all wk 12-2.30 Dinner all wk 6.30-9 summer, 6-8.30 winter Av main course £10 ⊕ FREE HOUSE ◀ Marston's Pedigree, Wincle, Whim Hartington IPA, Leatherbritches. ♟ 10 **Facilities** Non-diners area ♣ (Bar Restaurant Garden) ♦♦ Children's portions Garden ⋒ Parking WiFi

PICK OF THE PUBS

The Plough Inn ★★★★ INN ❀

HATHERSAGE Map 16 SK28

tel: 01433 650319 & 650180
Leadmill Bridge S32 1BA
email: sales@theploughinn-hathersage.co.uk
web: www.theploughinn-hathersage.co.uk
dir: M1 junct 29, take A617W, A619, A623, then B6001 N to Hathersage

Stylish, riverside award-winner with extensive menu

The 16th-century Plough stands in nine acres by the River Derwent, where the modern-by-comparison (in other words, 18th-century) three-arched Leadmill Bridge carries the Derwent Valley Heritage Way over a mildly turbulent stretch of river. Inside, smart red tartan carpets harmonise well with the open fires and wooden beams of the bar, where you'll find hand-pulled local ales and 15 wines by the glass. From the extensive bar menu come field mushroom bruschetta with aubergine purée, feta cheese and rocket; steak and kidney pudding with hand-cut chips (or mash) and mushy peas; and grills, pastas and pizzas. The restaurant menu pushes the boat out with the more elaborate feuilleté of scallops with radicchio and liquorice sauce; poached fillet of beef with fondant potato, buttered squash purée, buttered kale and horseradish and ginger cream; and orzo with white beans, confit fennel, courgettes, goats' cheese, and orange and tarragon dressing. Roast meats are only part of the Sunday line-up, with fillet of plaice in real ale batter, twice-cooked fries, garden peas and tartare sauce; and baked poussin with Spanish-style rice is also on offer. The Plough's well-stocked cellar combines Old and New World wines, from France to Chile westbound, and New Zealand eastbound. Overnight guests may stroll through the landscaped grounds before retiring to one of the bedrooms in the inn itself, or in the converted barn across the cobbled courtyard.

Open all day all wk 11-11 (Sun 12-10.30) Closed 25 Dec **Food** all wk 12-9.30 Av main course £16 Set menu available ⊕ FREE HOUSE ◼ Black Sheep, local ales. ♈ 15
Facilities Non-diners area 🐾 (Bar Restaurant Garden) 🧒 Children's menu Children's portions Garden 🪑 Parking WiFi **Rooms** 6

HOPE
Map 16 SK18

The Old Hall Hotel

tel: 01433 620160 **Market Place S33 6RH**
email: info@oldhallhotelhope.com
dir: *On A6187 in town centre*

Fine old inn with a tea room and café

For generations Hope Hall, as this early 16th-century building was once called, was the Balguy family seat. In 1730 it became an inn, The Cross Daggers, then in 1876 it was renamed The Hall Hotel. In the 18th century a cattle market was held here; today, on bank holidays, the Hope Valley Beer and Cider Festival draws the crowds. Main menus promise dishes such as chicken supreme with chestnut purée, creamed cabbage and roast garlic pomme purée; king prawn and crab claw tagliatelle; and steak and ale pie with garden peas and beef dripping chips. For lunch there's also soup and sandwiches, hot ciabattas and light bites.

Open all day all wk Food Lunch all wk 12-5 Dinner all wk 5-9 ⊕ HEINEKEN/
THEAKSTON ◀ Theakston Best, Old Peculier & 2 craft ales, Castle Rock Harvest Pale, Adnams, Caledonian Deuchars IPA, 2 guest ales ♂ Guest ciders. ♥ 10
Facilities Non-diners area ♣ (Bar Garden Outside area) ♦♦ Children's menu Children's portions Garden Outside area ⋈ Beer festival Cider festival Parking WiFi ▭ (notice required)

HURDLOW
Map 16 SK16

The Royal Oak

tel: 01298 83288 & 07866 778847 **SK17 9QJ**
email: hello@peakpub.co.uk
dir: *From A515 between Buxton & Ashbourne follow Hurdlow signs*

Popular pitstop for walkers and cyclists on the Tissington Trail

Situated in the southern Peak District, this warm-hearted hostelry welcomes one and all, at any time of day. Tired ramblers and cyclists head straight for the pumps, where five real ales include locals such as Whim Hartington, Thornbridge and Peak Ales. Families with children and dogs add to the fun, arriving in the knowledge that generous plates of home-cooked pub food are served throughout the day. Most ingredients are seasonal and sourced within 20 miles of the pub from suppliers with trusted reputations. Look out for the likes of millionaire's fish pie; wild mushroom and Stilton risotto; pork fillet, Grand Marnier cream sauce and black pudding mash; or blackened Cajun salmon with lemon oil dressing. Sharing platters for two or three are also available.

Open all day all wk Food Mon-Fri 10-9, Sat-Sun 8.30am-9pm Av main course £9-£20 ⊕ FREE HOUSE ◀ Whim Hartington Bitter, Thornbridge, Buxton, Wincle, Peak Ales ♂ Aspall. Facilities Non-diners area ♣ (Bar Restaurant Garden) ♦♦ Children's menu Children's portions Garden ⋈ Parking WiFi ▭ (notice required)

INGLEBY
Map 11 SK32

The John Thompson Inn & Brewery

tel: 01332 862469 **DE73 7HW**
email: nick@johnthompsoninn.com
dir: *From A38 between Derby & Burton upon Trent take A5132 towards Barrow upon Trent. At mini rdbt right onto B5008 (signed Repton). At rdbt 1st exit into Brook End. Right into Milton Rd. Left, left again to Ingleby*

Friendly brewpub serving hearty lunches

A pub since 1968, this 15th-century former farmhouse took its name from licensee and owner John Thompson. Now run by son Nick, it is a traditional brewpub set in idyllic countryside beside the banks of the River Trent with views of the neighbouring National Forest. Inside, a wealth of original features make it an atmospheric place to enjoy a pint of home-brewed JTS XXX and tuck into lunches

ranging from sandwiches to a roast beef carvery or a trio of cheese and pasta broccoli bake. Finish with home-made bread and butter pudding.

Open Tue-Fri 11-2.30 6-11 (Sat-Sun 11-11) Closed Mon Food Lunch Tue-Sun 12-2 ⊕ FREE HOUSE ◀ John Thompson JTS XXX, St Nick's, Gold, Rich Porter. ♥ 9
Facilities Non-diners area ♦♦ Children's portions Family room Garden Parking WiFi ▭

KIRK IRETON
Map 16 SK25

Barley Mow Inn

tel: 01335 370306 **DE6 3JP**
email: barley.mow@w3z.co.uk
dir: *Phone for detailed directions*

Step back in time at this traditional pub

Built on the edge of the Peak District National Park by the Storer family of yeomen farmers in the 16th century, the building became an inn during the early 1700s. The imposing free house has remained largely unchanged over the years. Six nine-gallon barrels of beer stand behind the bar, with cheese and pickle or salami rolls and bar snacks on offer at lunchtime. Tea and coffee are always available. If you bring your dog it must be kept on a lead at all times. Close to Carsington Water, there are good walking opportunities on nearby marked paths.

Open all wk 12-2 7-11 (Sun 12-2 7-10.30) Closed 25 Dec, 1 Jan Food Lunch 12-2 ⊕ FREE HOUSE ◀ Whim Hartington Bitter, rotating ales ♂ Thatchers Gold.
Facilities Non-diners area ♦♦ Garden Parking Notes ◉

LITTLE HAYFIELD
Map 16 SK08

Lantern Pike

tel: 01663 747590 **45 Glossop Rd SK22 2NG**
email: tomandstella@lanternpikeinn.co.uk
dir: *On A624 between Glossop & Chapel-en-le-Frith*

Welcoming pub in hilly terrain

Set in a tiny mill village at the edge of the Kinder Scout moors and below the shapely Lantern Pike hill, site of an Armada beacon, the sublime views from the beer garden of the wooded Peak District hills are reason enough to seek out this fine pub. Add a well-considered selection of real ales and an ever-changing menu — perhaps seafood pâté; home-cured peppered mackerel; braised lamb shank, mash, veg with rosemary and red wine jus; chicken linguine; and if you time your visit right, there'll be new season, de-shelled Whitby crab — and it's little wonder that this ultra-traditional 170-year-old inn is a highly popular destination for diners and outdoor pursuits enthusiasts alike. Unique *Coronation Street* ephemera add fascination for the faithful.

Open Mon 5-12, Tue-Fri 12-3 5-12 (Sat-Sun all day) Closed 25 Dec, Mon L
Food Lunch Tue-Fri 12-2.30, Sat-Sun 12-8.30 Dinner Mon 5-8, Tue-Fri 5-8.30, Sat-Sun 12-8.30 Av main course £10 Restaurant menu available all wk ⊕ ENTERPRISE INNS ◀ Timothy Taylor Landlord, Abbeydale Moonshine. Facilities Non-diners area ♦♦ Children's menu Children's portions Garden ⋈ Parking WiFi ▭ (notice required)

LITTON
Map 16 SK17

Red Lion Inn

tel: 01298 871458 **SK17 8QU**
email: theredlionlitton@aol.com
dir: *Just off A623 (Chesterfield to Stockport road), 1m E of Tideswell*

Pub paradise beside the village green

This is a tiny pub in a terrace of stone-built cottages which has served locals and visitors to this pretty White Peak village for two centuries. The warren of hobbit-sized rooms ooze character, shadows cast by log-fires flit across the low beams, murmuring village chit-chat and happy ramblers returning from nearby limestone gorges add to the timeless atmosphere. Beers from local microbreweries such as Peak Ale and Abbeydale major on the bar, whilst diners can happily chomp away on homity pie, or braised blade of beef with cheddar cheese and bacon mash. Space constraints mean that children under six cannot be accommodated inside the pub.

Open all day all wk **Food** Sun-Mon 12-8, Tue-Sat 12-9 ⊕ ENTERPRISE INNS ◀ Abbeydale Absolution, Peak Ales Bakewell Best Bitter, 2 guest ales Ö Orchard Pig. ♈ 10 **Facilities** Non-diners area ❀ (Bar Restaurant Outside area) Outside area ㅿ Beer festival WiFi

MATLOCK — Map 16 SK35

The Red Lion ★★★ INN

tel: 01629 584888 **65 Matlock Green DE4 3BT**
email: info@theredlionmatlock.co.uk
dir: From Chesterfield, A632 into Matlock, on right just before junct with A615

An all-rounder in the heart of Derbyshire's county town

This friendly, family-run free house makes a good base for exploring local attractions like Chatsworth House, Carsington Water and Dovedale. Spectacular walks in the local countryside help to work up an appetite for bar lunches, or great tasting home-cooked dishes in the homely restaurant. On Sunday there's a popular carvery with freshly cooked gammon, beef and turkey. In the winter months, open fires burn in the lounge and games room, and there's a boules area in the attractive beer garden for warmer days. Some of the ales from the bar were brewed on the Chatsworth Estate. There are six comfortable bedrooms.

Open all day all wk **Food** Lunch Tue-Fri 12-2 Dinner Tue-Sat 6-9 Restaurant menu available Tue-Sat ⊕ FREE HOUSE ◀ Morland Old Speckled Hen, Peak, guest ales. **Facilities** Non-diners area Children's menu Children's portions Garden ㅿ Beer festival Cider festival Parking WiFi ▥ **Rooms** 6

PILSLEY — Map 16 SK27

The Devonshire Arms at Pilsley ★★★ INN

tel: 01246 583258 **High St DE45 1UL**
email: enquiries@devonshirepilsley.co.uk **web:** www.devonshirepilsley.co.uk
dir: From A619, in Baslow, at rdbt take 1st exit onto B6012. Follow signs to Chatsworth, 2nd right to Pilsley

Traditional inn on the Chatsworth Estate

Set in an estate village amidst the rolling parkland that surrounds Chatsworth House, the 'Palace of The Peaks', this fabulous old stone pub is an ideal base for visiting Matlock Bath and Castleton. There are open fires, Peak Ales from the estate's brewery and meats, game and greens from the adjacent estate farm shop, all sourced from these productive acres at the heart of the Peak District. After a day's exploration, tuck into chicken liver pâté, Chatsworth Farm Shop chutney and melba toast; braised lamb Henry, mint mash, pea and caper sauce; and sticky toffee pudding, toffee sauce and salted caramel ice cream then stay over in the luxurious accommodation designed by the Duchess of Devonshire.

Open all day all wk **Food** Lunch all wk 12-2.30 Dinner all wk 5-9 ⊕ FREE HOUSE ◀ Thornbridge Jaipur, Peak Ales Bakewell Best Bitter, Chatsworth Gold & Swift Nick, guest ales Ö Thatchers Gold. **Facilities** Non-diners area ♦● Children's portions Outside area ㅿ Parking WiFi **Rooms** 13

REPTON — Map 10 SK32

AA PUB OF THE YEAR FOR ENGLAND 2016–2017

NEW The Boot ★★★★ INN ◉ **PICK OF THE PUBS**

tel: 01283 346047 **12 Boot Hill DE65 6FT**
email: info@thebootatrepton.co.uk **web:** www.thebootatrepton.co.uk
dir: From junct A50 & A38 follow Repton & Willington (B5008) signs. In Willington follow Repton sign. Under railway bridge. At cross in Repton left into Brook End, pub on right

Renovated inn with excellent food and own beers

The Boot's first occupant in the 17th century was a cobbler who hung a boot outside to attract customers; while mending their footwear he'd offer them a glass of ale. Today there's no point bringing your shoes in for new soles, but ale is most certainly still offered – Clod Hopper, Tuffer's Old porter and Bumble Boots (a summer ale) are brewed on site. Now renovated and refurbished, the inn makes a good choice for a drink, a meal and for overnight luxury accommodation if you're in this lovely part of the country. They provide first-class meals, beginning with a champagne breakfast. On their classics menu you'll find the Boot burger, pastrami, smoked bacon and Swiss cheese; gammon, eggs and pineapple; and T-bone, rib-eye, fillet or bavette steaks. Turning to the à la carte, duck and foie gras parfait, smoked duck hams, oats and orange, followed by 'fish du jour' with cockles, caramelised onion, artichoke and hazelnuts might take your fancy. Chocolate, Boot beer and banana torte with peanut brittle makes an unusual dessert. There's a beer festival in August.

Open all day all wk **Food** Contact pub for food times Av main course £12 Set menu available Restaurant menu available Mon-Sat ⊕ FREE HOUSE ◀ Boot Beer Clod Hopper, Repton Cross, Tuffer's Old, Bumble Boots & Wellington Ö Aspall, Westons Country Perry, Saxon Ruby Tuesday, Sandford Orchards Strawberry Lane. ♈ 12 **Facilities** Non-diners area ❀ (Bar Garden) ♦● Children's menu Children's portions Garden ㅿ Beer festival Parking WiFi **Rooms** 9

ROWSLEY — Map 16 SK26

The Grouse & Claret ★★★★ INN

tel: 01629 733233 **Station Rd DE4 2EB**
web: www.grouseclaretpub.co.uk
dir: On A6 between Matlock & Bakewell

Angling connections and a menu for everyone at this popular pub

A venue popular with local anglers, this 18th-century pub takes its name from a fishing fly. Situated at the gateway to the Peak District National Park, it is handy for visits to the stately homes of Haddon Hall and Chatsworth House. After quenching the thirst with a pint of Wychwood Hobgoblin, the comprehensive menu promises a selection of well-priced and tasty pub meals: beef lasagne; golden breaded scampi; piri piri chicken; a selection of burgers; ham and eggs; or chicken, gammon and mustard pie. From the dessert choices there's jam roly poly pudding or lemon and mandarin sponge. Dogs are very welcome in the outside areas.

Open all day all wk **Food** Mon-Sat 11.30-10, Sun 11.30-9 Av main course £8 Set menu available ⊕ MARSTON'S ◀ Pedigree, Wychwood Hobgoblin, guest ale. ♈ 16 **Facilities** Non-diners area ❀ (Outside) ♦● Children's menu Children's portions Play area Garden ㅿ Beer festival Parking WiFi ▥ **Rooms** 8

SHARDLOW
Map 11 SK43

The Old Crown Inn

tel: 01332 792392 **Cavendish Bridge DE72 2HL**
email: jamesvize@hotmail.co.uk
dir: *M1 junct 24, A50 signed Stoke & Shardlow. Take slip road signed B6540. At rdbt right, follow Shardlow sign. Left at Cavendish Bridge sign to inn*

Traditional inn with regular evening events

Up to nine real ales are served at this family-friendly pub on the south side of the River Trent, where there's a beer festival twice a year. Built as a coaching inn during the 17th century, it retains its warm and atmospheric interior. Several hundred water jugs hang from the ceilings, while the walls display an abundance of brewery and railway memorabilia. Food is lovingly prepared by the landlady; main meals focus on pub classics such as home-made steak and kidney pie; ham, eggs and chips; lasagne; curry; steaks; vegetarian dishes, and daily specials. There's also a good choice of baguettes, sandwiches and jackets. Monday night is quiz night; folk music on the first and third Tuesday of every month; curry night on Wednesdays.

Open all wk 11am-11.30pm (Mon 3-11 Fri-Sat 11am-12.30am Sun 11-11) **Food** Lunch Tue-Fri 12-2, Sat 12-8, Sun 12-3 Dinner Tue-Fri 5-8, Sat 12-8 Set menu available ⊕ MARSTON'S ◀ Pedigree & Old Empire, Jennings Cocker Hoop, guest ales Ŏ Thatchers Gold. **Facilities** Non-diners area ✿ (Bar Restaurant) ♦ Children's menu Children's portions Play area Garden ⌐ Beer festival Cider festival Parking ☞ (notice required)

SHIRLEY
Map 10 SK24

The Saracen's Head

tel: 01335 360330 **Church Ln DE6 3AS**
email: info@saracens-head-shirley.co.uk
dir: *A52 from Ashbourne towards Derby. Right in 4m to Shirley*

A pub where traditional meets contemporary

Overlooking the front garden and village street, the 1791-built Saracen's Head takes its name from the family crest of Sewallis de Scyrle (pronounced Shirley), a Holy Land crusader. All dishes are made on the premises from local, ethical sources. Starting with creamy garlic button mushrooms, it's an easy move to, say, slowly braised beef bourguignon with creamy mash and vegetables; or warm cheddar and caramelised onion quiche. For a quintessential country pub experience, visit on a Sunday at lunchtime.

Open all wk 11-3 6-11 (Sun 11-10.30) **Food** Lunch Mon-Sat 12-2, Sun 12-2.30 Dinner all wk 6-9 ⊕ GREENE KING ◀ IPA, St Edmunds, Morland Old Speckled Hen, guest ales. **Facilities** Non-diners area ✿ (Bar Garden) ♦ Children's portions Garden ⌐ Parking WiFi ☞ (notice required)

STANTON IN PEAK
Map 16 SK26

The Flying Childers Inn

tel: 01629 636333 **Main Rd DE4 2LW**
dir: *From A6 (between Matlock & Bakewell) follow Youlgrave signs. Onto B5056 to Ashbourne. Follow Stanton in Peak signs*

Enchanting old-style village pub

Above this instantly likeable, charmingly old-fashioned village pub looms Stanton Moor, riddled with Neolithic stone monuments. At the heart of a pretty old Peak District estate village, The Flying Childers was named after a champion racehorse

owned by the 4th Duke of Devonshire. Little log fires warm the cosy, beamed interior, where settles and magpie-furniture fit an absolute treat. The lunchtime-only menu is small but perfectly formed: home-made soups, casseroles, filled cobs, toasties, and hearty ploughman's, all with locally sourced ingredients. Local real ales, a beer garden and a great welcome for canine companions, too.

Open all wk Mon-Tue 7pm-11pm, Wed-Thu & Fri 12-2 7-11, Sat-Sun 12-3 7-11 **Food** Lunch Wed-Sun 12-2 ⊕ FREE HOUSE ◀ Wells Bombardier, guest ales. **Facilities** ✿ (Bar Garden) ♦ Garden Parking **Notes** ⊜

TIDESWELL
Map 16 SK17

The George

tel: 01298 871382 **Commercial Rd SK17 8NU**
email: andrewrowe@rowe-erices.cl
dir: *A619 to Baslow, A623 towards Chapel-en-le-Frith, 0.25m*

Charming coaching inn with traditional food

Well placed for exploring the Peak District National Park and visiting Chatsworth, this delightful stone-built coaching inn is in the shadow of the village church, the 'Cathedral of the Peak'. The simple menu focuses on traditional pub food – lunchtime sandwiches; starters such as prawn cocktail; and vegetarian bean chilli with guacamole. Mains include grilled salmon steak with dill butter, new potatoes and mixed salad; sweet honey- and mustard-glazed ham with chips and peas; beer-battered cod fillet; and vegetarian burger with cheddar cheese, chips and salad. Home-made apple and fruit crumble comes with custard, cream or ice cream.

Open all day all wk **Food** Lunch all wk 12-3 Dinner all wk 5-9 Av main course £8 ⊕ GREENE KING ◀ Hardys & Hansons Ŏ Aspall. **Facilities** Non-diners area ✿ (Bar Restaurant Outside area) ♦ Children's menu Children's portions Outside area ⌐ Parking WiFi ☞ (notice required)

WILLINGTON
Map 10 SK22

NEW The Dragon ★★★★ INN

tel: 01283 704795 **11 The Green DE65 6BP**
email: info@thedragonatwillington.co.uk web: www.thedragonatwillington.co.uk
dir: *From junct of A50 & A38 follow Willington & Repton signs onto B5008. At x-roads in Willington left into The Green. Pub on left*

Character, charm and a great restaurant

Following sympathetic refurbishment, the 150-year-old Dragon has changed considerably from the one its owners bought in 2010. New features are a beer garden, which borders the Trent & Mersey Canal, and a 70-seater restaurant in the adjacent cottage. A much larger kitchen is now capable of providing a wide range of dishes, such as turbot with thyme rösti potato, mussel and pancetta velouté; slow-cooked short rib of beef with smoked garlic mash, kale and bourguignon garnish; and risotto, bubble-and-squeak, crispy egg and rocket salad. An August beer festival features real ales from the Boot brewery a mile away in Repton.

Open all day all wk **Food** Contact pub for food times Av main course £11 Set menu available Restaurant menu available Mon-Sat ⊕ FREE HOUSE ◀ Boot Beer Clod Hopper, Sharp's Doom Bar, Marston's Pedigree, Bass Ŏ Thatchers, Westons Stowford Press & Country Perry. ♀ 10 **Facilities** Non-diners area ✿ (Bar Garden) ♦ Children's menu Children's portions Play area Garden ⌐ Beer festival Parking WiFi **Rooms** 7

WOOLLEY MOOR
Map 16 SK36

The White Horse Inn

tel: 01246 590319 **Badger Ln DE55 6FG**
dir: *From A61 at Stretton take B6014, then B6036 Woolley Moor*

Spick and span bar and restaurant near Matlock

This 200-year-old pub sits in two acres of gardens amidst beautiful countryside; the nearby Ogston Reservoir is where Dame Ellen MacArthur learned her sailing skills. The building's interior has been meticulously updated, with exposed solid stone walls and precisely laid flagstone floors providing the backdrop for an abundance of polished tables and chairs in both the bar area and bright garden conservatory. Peak Ales are well kept and wines sold by the glass are numerous, but this is primarily a food destination. Cauliflower and Stilton soup makes a flavoursome starter, to be followed perhaps by crispy pork belly with spring onion mash and smoked bacon sauce; or butternut squash, pea and rosemary risotto.

Open all wk 12-3 5.30-11 (Sun 12-5) **Food** Lunch Mon-Sat 12-1.45, Sun 12-4 Dinner Mon-Sat 6-8.45 Set menu available Restaurant menu available all wk ⊕ FREE HOUSE ◀ Peak Ales Bakewell Best Bitter & Chatsworth Gold. ☻ 13 **Facilities** Non-diners area � Children's portions Garden ⊓ Parking WiFi ⛟ (notice required)

YOULGREAVE
Map 16 SK26

The Farmyard Inn

tel: 01629 636221 **DE45 1UW**
email: suzidayfarmyard@hotmail.co.uk
dir: *Phone for detailed directions*

A little gem in the Peak District National Park

This old farmhouse, which became an inn in 1829, looks south across Bradford Dale and its picturesque stretches of tree-hung, crystal-clear water. Warm and friendly, the bar offers two guest real ales and a good selection of wines by the glass. Home-made, locally-sourced dishes include Derbyshire mushrooms with grilled blue cheese; warm black pudding and bacon salad; fish pie with North Atlantic prawns; Derbyshire homity pie filled with leek and apple; and red bean, tomato and brazil nut flan. The area abounds with walks and places to visit, such as Chatsworth and Haddon Hall.

Open all wk 5pm till late (Sat-Sun 12 till late) **Food** Lunch Sat-Sun 12-3 Dinner Mon-Sat 5-9, Sun 6-9 ⊕ GREENE KING ◀ Abbot, IPA Gold, Morland, guest ales ☻ Aspall, Thatchers Gold. ☻ 9 **Facilities** ⛞ (Bar Restaurant Garden) ⮑ Children's menu Children's portions Garden ⊓ Parking WiFi ⛟ (notice required)

DEVON

ASHBURTON
Map 3 SX77

The Rising Sun ★★★ INN

tel: 01364 652544 **Woodland TQ13 7JT**
email: admin@therisingsunwoodland.co.uk web: www.therisingsunwoodland.co.uk
dir: *From A38 E of Ashburton follow Woodland & Denbury signs. Pub on left, approx 1.5m*

Family-friendly pub with large garden near Dartmoor

This former drovers' pub is in the hands of the capable Reynolds family who welcome everyone including families and visitors with dogs. Surrounded by gorgeous countryside, and with a large garden in which to sup a pint of Dartmoor Jail Ale, it's on the edge of Dartmoor National Park. Renowned for their pies, chips and specials board, they also offer light snacks at lunchtime, and a great children's menu. Sample specials include pork belly with vanilla mashed potatoes, spinach and caramelised apple jus; and braised lamb shoulder with colcannon and black trumpet mushrooms.

Open 12-3 6-11 (Sun 12-3 6.30-11) Closed Mon (ex BH) **Food** Lunch Tue-Sat 12-2.15, Sun 12-2.30 Dinner Mon-Thu 6-9, Fri-Sat 6-9.30, Sun 6.30-9 ⊕ FREE HOUSE ◀ Dartmoor Jail Ale, guest ales ☻ Annings Fruit Cider, Thatchers Gold. **Facilities** Non-diners area ⛞ (Bar Restaurant Garden) ⮑ Children's menu Children's portions Play area Garden ⊓ Parking WiFi ⛟ (notice required) **Rooms** 4

AVONWICK
Map 3 SX75

The Turtley Corn Mill
PICK OF THE PUBS

tel: 01364 646100 **TQ10 9ES**
email: eat@turtleycornmill.com
dir: *From A38 at South Brent/Avonwick junction, take B3372, then follow signs for Avonwick, 0.5m*

Seasonal menus in an idyllic riverside setting

Set among six acres of gardens and fields on the edge of Dartmoor, including a lake complete with ducks and its own small island, this sprawling old free house was originally a corn mill and spent many years as a chicken hatchery before being converted to a pub. The interior is light and fresh with old furniture and oak and slate floors. You'll find plenty of newspapers and books to browse through while enjoying a whisky or supping a pint of Doom Bar. The daily-changing modern British menus for breakfast/brunch, lunch and dinner are extensively based on local produce from around the pub's idyllic location. Choices from a sample menu start with terrine of pork, apple and black pudding; or salad of heritage beetroot and goats' curd; continue with smoked haddock and chive fishcakes; or red wine braised oxtail with mustard, mash and vegetables; and wind up with poached apricot open tart, or cappuccino pannacotta.

Open all day all wk Closed 25 Dec **Food** all wk 12-10 Set menu available ⊕ FREE HOUSE ◀ St Austell Tribute, Sharp's Doom Bar, Summerskills Start Point, guest ales ☻ Thatchers. ☻ 10 **Facilities** Non-diners area ⛞ (Bar Restaurant Garden) ⮑ Children's portions Garden ⊓ Parking WiFi

BAMPTON
Map 3 SS92

The Swan ★★★★ INN ◉◉
PICK OF THE PUBS

tel: 01398 332248 **Station Rd EX16 9NG**
email: info@theswan.co **web:** www.theswan.co
dir: *M5 junct 17, A361 towards Barnstaple. At rdbt NW of Tiverton take A396 to Bampton*

A warm welcome and seriously good food

Originally used as accommodation by masons and other craftsmen enlarging the church in 1450, this inn has a contemporary style despite its considerable age; the bread oven and original fireplace remain. The inn is popular with walkers and cyclists as it is just six miles from Exmoor National Park, so it's a pretty good idea to make for The Swan after being out and about in the fresh air. At the solid oak counter you'll find Devon Storm, Otter and Proper Job real ales and Ashridge Devon Gold cider. If you're staying for a something to eat, then Brock Hall Farm goats' cheese fritter, beetroot and orange gets a meal off to a good start, followed by smoked Creedy Carver duck breast, salt baked celeriac purée, quail Scotch egg and vermouth sauce; or Brixham cod fillet, Bombay potato, pea purée and curry essence. Desserts shouldn't be overlooked – sticky ginger pudding, toffee sauce and vanilla ice cream; or spiced plum and port crumble. The inn is open on Mondays but food isn't served.

Open all day all wk Mon-Thu 12-11 (Fri-Sat 12-12 Sun 12-10.30) Closed 25 Dec **Food** Lunch Tue-Sat 12-2, Sun 12-2.30 Dinner Tue-Sat 6-9.30 Av main course £13.50 ⊕ FREE HOUSE ◀ Red Rock Devon Storm, Otter, St Austell Proper Job Ö Ashridge Devon Gold. ▾ **Facilities** Non-diners area ❖ (Bar Restaurant Outside area) ᶿᶠ Children's menu Children's portions Family room Outside area ⋒ Parking WiFi ⇦ (notice required) **Rooms** 3

BEER
Map 4 SY28

Anchor Inn

tel: 01297 20386 **Fore St EX12 3ET**
email: 6403@greeneking.co.uk
dir: *A3052 towards Lyme Regis. At Hangmans Stone take B3174 into Beer. Pub on seafront*

Enjoy sea views and sample fresh fish

A traditional inn overlooking the bay in the picture-perfect Devon village of Beer, this pretty colour-washed pub is perfectly situated for walking the Jurassic coastline. Fish caught by local boats features strongly on the menu, or the tempting starters might include ham hock and black pudding terrine or nachos, followed by roasted pork belly with black treacle and bourbon glaze; salmon and spring onion fishcakes; or roasted butternut squash and feta couscous. Leave space for Bramley apple pie or gingerbread, pear and caramel crumble pudding.

Open all day all wk 8am-11pm **Food** all wk 12-10 Set menu available ⊕ GREENE KING ◀ IPA & Abbot Ale, Otter Ale Ö Aspall, Symonds Scrumpy Jack. ▾ 14 **Facilities** Non-diners area ❖ (Bar Garden) ᶿᶠ Children's menu Garden ⋒ WiFi ⇦ (notice required)

BEESANDS
Map 3 SX84

The Cricket Inn ★★★★ INN ◉
PICK OF THE PUBS

tel: 01548 580215 **TQ7 2EN**
email: enquiries@thecricketinn.com **web:** www.thecricketinn.com
dir: *From Kingsbridge take A379 towards Dartmouth. At Stokenham mini rdbt turn right to Beesands*

This seaside inn is a must for seafood lovers

The Cricket Inn first opened its doors in 1867 and has since survived storms, a World War II bomb and a mudslide. Located in a small South Hams fishing village, the inn encompasses a dog-friendly bar serving West Country ales, an AA-Rosette restaurant with sea views, and bright and airy accommodation. Cooking just metres from the beach and clear waters of Start Bay, the head chef works closely with local fishermen who bring their catch straight to the kitchen door. From the menu, start with crispy cuttlefish, wild garlic aïoli and watercress; goats' cheese mousse, spiced carrot purée, pickled carrots and ginger breadcrumb; or scallops, pork belly, apple purée, crispy pig's head and crackling. Continue with a seafood pancake stuffed with scallops, prawns and cod; fish pie; or truffled mac and cheese, all made with produce from the Devonshire countryside and its waters.

Open all wk 11-3 6-11 (May-Sep all day) Closed 25 Dec **Food** Lunch all wk 12-2.30 Dinner all wk 6-8.30 Restaurant menu available all wk ⊕ HEAVITREE ◀ Otter Ale & Bitter, St Austell Tribute Ö Aspall, Heron Valley, Thatchers. ▾ 12 **Facilities** Non-diners area ❖ (Bar Restaurant) ᶿᶠ Children's menu Children's portions Outside area ⋒ Parking WiFi **Rooms** 7

BICKLEIGH
Map 3 SS90

Fisherman's Cot

tel: 01884 855237 **EX16 8RW**
email: info@fishermanscot-bickleigh.com
dir: *Phone for detailed directions*

Riverside hostelry popular with locals and visitors alike

Just a short drive from Tiverton and Exmoor, this well-appointed thatched inn stands by Bickleigh Bridge over the River Exe. With food all day and beautiful gardens, The Waterside Bar is the place for doorstep sandwiches, pies, snacks and afternoon tea, while the restaurant incorporates a carvery (on Sunday) and carte menus. Expect dishes such as Thai green chicken curry; chilli and lime sea bass fillets with pilau rice and roasted vegetables; slow-cooked lamb shank in rosemary, redcurrant and red wine jus; chuck steak chilli con carne; and for dessert, lemon meringue.

Open all day all wk 11-11 (Sun 12-10.30) **Food** all wk 12-9 ⊕ MARSTON'S ◀ Pedigree, Ringwood Ö Thatchers. ▾ 8 **Facilities** Non-diners area ❖ (Bar Garden) ᶿᶠ Children's portions Garden ⋒ Parking WiFi ⇦ (notice required)

BISHOPSTEIGNTON

NEW Cockhaven Arms ★★★ INN

tel: 01626 775252 **TQ14 9RF**
web: www.cockhavenarms.co.uk
dir: *From A380 onto A381 towards Teignmouth. Follow brown signs for pub*

Pub classics and a warm welcome

This friendly pub, dating back to the 16th century with later additions, is set in the quiet village of Bishopsteignton, at the foot of Haldon Moor and overlooking the lovely Teign Estuary. Full of history, it has plenty of original features, including the gallery landing, beams, and fireplaces. Menus are strong on local produce and pub classics, and you should definitely book for Sunday lunch. At lunchtime there are ciabatta sandwiches and toasties, jacket potatoes and omelettes available, while in the evening you might start with breaded whitebait or a sharing platter, followed by scampi and chips, gammon steak; or slow-cooked lamb shoulder in maple syrup glaze with creamy mash and local veggies.

Open all day all wk **Food** Lunch all wk 12-2 Dinner all wk 6.30-9.30 ⊕ FREE HOUSE ◼ Otter Bitter, Butcombe. ♚ 14 **Facilities** Non-diners area ❤ (Bar Garden) ♦♦ Children's menu Children's portions Garden ⊼ Parking WiFi ▦ (notice required) **Rooms** 10

BLACKAWTON   Map 3 SX85

The George Inn ★★★ INN

tel: 01803 712342 **Main St TQ9 7BG**
email: tgiblackawton@yahoo.co.uk **web:** www.blackawton.com
dir: *From Totnes on A381 through Halwell. Left onto A3122 towards Dartmouth, turn right to Blackawton at Forces Cross*

Family-friendly village pub close to Dartmouth

In the South Hams village of Blackawton, The George is an ideal base for visitors to nearby Totnes, Kingsbridge and Dartmouth, as well as Woodlands Leisure Park. The pub gained its name during George III's reign but it was rebuilt after a fire in 1939, after which it became the rallying point for the forced evacuation of the parish in World War 2 Now a family-friendly and dog-friendly pub with comfortable accommodation, it's a place to relax with a real ale and choose from a traditional menu, based on local produce, that includes pizzas, curries and pub classics.

Open all wk 12-3 5-11 (Sun 12-3 7-10.30, Sun 12-3 Jan) **Food** Lunch all wk 12-2 Dinner Mon-Sat 6-9, Sun 7-9 Av main course £10-£15 ⊕ FREE HOUSE ◼ Teignworthy Spring Tide, St Austell Tribute, guest ales ♂ Thatchers Gold, Healey's Cornish Rattler. ♚ 12 **Facilities** Non-diners area ❤ (Bar Restaurant Outside area) ♦♦ Children's menu Children's portions Play area Garden Outside area ⊼ Beer festival Parking WiFi **Rooms** 4

BRAMPFORD SPEKE   Map 3 SX99

The Lazy Toad   PICK OF THE PUBS

tel: 01392 841591 **EX5 5DP**
email: thelazytoad@outlook.com
dir: *From Exeter take A377 towards Crediton 1.5m, right signed Brampford Speke*

Thatched village country inn

Dating from the late 18th century, when the village farrier and wheelwright worked in the cobbled courtyard, this oak-beamed Grade II listed pub is run by Harriet and Mike Daly who welcome all comers, including dogs on leads in the bar and the walled beer garden. Polished slate tiles surround a bar serving ales from the likes of Otter and the Exeter Brewery, Sandford Orchards ciders from Crediton, and wines from Sharpham near Totnes, and Camel Valley near Bodmin. A smallholding behind the pub supplies vegetables, fruits and herbs for dishes on the short, daily changing menus. These offer starters of crispy squid with lime, pickled carrot salad and chilli jam; and mains of roasted faggots, creamed mash potato, runner beans and red wine gravy; or white bean stew with root vegetables.

Open 12-3 6-11 (Sun 12-4) Closed 1wk Jan, Sun eve, Mon **Food** Lunch Tue-Sat 12-2, Sun 12-2.30 Dinner Tue-Sat 6.30-9 ⊕ FREE HOUSE ◼ Otter Bitter, St Austell Tribute, O'Hanlon's Yellow Hammer, Exeter Avocet ♂ Sandford Orchards Devon Red & Devon Mist. ♚ 12 **Facilities** Non-diners area ❤ (Bar Garden Outside area) ♦♦ Children's menu Children's portions Garden Outside area ⊼ Beer festival Cider festival Parking WiFi

BRANSCOMBE   Map 4 SY18

The Fountain Head

tel: 01297 680359 **EX12 3BG**
email: thefountainhead@btconnect.com
dir: *From Seaton on A3052 towards Sidmouth left at Branscombe Cross to pub*

Often packed with walkers and locals

This 500-year-old forge and cider house is a true rural survivor, in a peaceful village just a short walk from the coastal path. The traditional worn flagstones, crackling log fires, rustic furnishings, village-brewed beers from Branscombe Vale, and the chatty atmosphere (no intrusive music or electronic games here) charm both locals and visitors. Hearty pub food includes home-made duck liver and orange pâté with ginger and pear chutney; Cajun spiced chicken breast, parsnip mash, caramelised red onion, wild mushrooms and red wine dressing. There's a spit-roast and barbecue every Sunday evening between July and September. Don't miss the midsummer beer festival.

Open all wk 11-3 6-11 (Sun 12-10.30) **Food** Lunch all wk 12-2 Dinner all wk 6.30-9 ⊕ FREE HOUSE ◼ Branscombe Vale Branoc, Jolly Geff & Summa That ♂ Westons, Pip. **Facilities** Non-diners area ❤ (Bar Restaurant Garden) ♦♦ Children's menu Children's portions Family room Garden ⊼ Beer festival Parking ▦ (notice required)

BRANSCOMBE *continued*

The Masons Arms

PICK OF THE PUBS

tel: 01297 680300 **EX12 3DJ**
email: masonsarms@staustellbrewery.co.uk
dir: *Exit A3052 towards Branscombe, down hill, Masons Arms at bottom of hill*

Ancient pub close to the sea

Just a 10-minute stroll from the beach and located in a picturesque village, the peaceful gardens of this inn have sea views across a picturesque valley. Creeper-clad, it dates from 1360 when it was a cider house. Back then it was a smugglers' haunt and its interior has barely changed since those days: slate floors, stone walls, ships' beams, an old jail railing and a huge open fireplace used for spit roasts on Sundays all add to the time-warp charm. Food is a serious business here; where possible all ingredients are grown, reared or caught locally. Kick off with a starter of steamed River Exe mussels, white wine, garlic, cream, parsley and rustic bread and follow it with the baked pie of the day or a chargrilled Devonshire steak.

Open all day all wk 11-11 (Sun 12-10.30) **Food** Lunch all wk 12-2.15 Dinner all wk 6.30-9 ⊕ ST AUSTELL BREWERY ◀ Tribute & Proper Job, Otter ♻ Thatchers Gold, Healey's Pear Rattler. ♥ 14 **Facilities** Non-diners area ✿ (Bar Outside area) ♦♦ Children's menu Children's portions Outside area ⊨ Parking WiFi

---

■ **BRENDON**   Map 3 SS74

Rockford Inn

tel: 01598 741214 **EX35 6PT**
email: enquiries@therockfordinn.com
dir: *A39 through Minehead follow signs to Lynmouth. Left to Brendon*

Popular Exmoor hideaway

Standing alongside the East Lyn River in the tucked-away Brendon Valley, this traditional 17th-century free house stands at the heart of Exmoor and is handy for several walking routes. Thatchers ciders complement local cask ales such as Barn Owl and Devon Darter, and there's a choice of good home-made pub meals. Venison casserole cooked with shallots, chantenay carrots and port; wild mushroom and leek crumble; and steak and Devon Blue shortcrust pie are typical menu choices; the specials board changes daily. Eat in the garden in warm weather, or head inside to the open fire when the weather changes.

Open all day all wk **Food** Lunch all wk 12-2.30 Dinner all wk 6-8.30 ⊕ FREE HOUSE ◀ Cotleigh Barn Owl & 25, St Austell Tribute, Clearwater Proper Ansome, Devon Darter & Real Smiler, Exmoor ♻ Thatchers, Addlestones. **Facilities** Non-diners area ✿ (Bar Restaurant Garden) ♦♦ Children's menu Children's portions Garden ⊨ Parking WiFi

---

■ **BROADHEMBURY**   Map 3 ST10

The Drewe Arms

tel: 01404 841267 **EX14 3NF**
email: info@drewearmsinn.co.uk
dir: *M5 junct 28, A373 towards Honiton. Left to Broadhembury*

Renowned time-warp in pretty village

Tucked away in the Blackdown Hills, but only five miles from Honiton, this ancient building has a delightfully quirky interior with original beams, sisal flooring and wood-burning stove. Otter Amber and Branscombe Vale Branoc are among the five Devon ales dispensed from the convivial bar, alongside local Tricky cider and an extensive wine list. On a no-frills menu featuring daily-changing specials, a starter of home-made chicken liver and date pâté with caramelised red onion and toast might be followed by oven-roasted duck breast with celeriac mash, braised red cabbage and port sauce. Easter Bank Holiday is beer festival time.

Open all day all wk **Food** Lunch all wk 12-3 Dinner all wk 6-9 Av main course £10 ⊕ FREE HOUSE ◀ Otter Amber & Ale, Exeter Avocet, Bays Devon Dumpling, Branscombe Vale Branoc ♻ Tricky. **Facilities** Non-diners area ✿ (Bar Garden) ♦♦ Children's menu Children's portions Garden ⊨ Beer festival WiFi

---

■ **BUCKLAND MONACHORUM**   Map 3 SX46

Drake Manor Inn

tel: 01822 853892 **The Village PL20 7NA**
email: drakemanor@drakemanorinn.co.uk
dir: *From A386 (Plymouth) turn left before Yelverton, follow signs to Buckland Monachorum. Left into village, on left next to church*

Ancient inn known for its warm welcome and good food

Dating back to the 12th century, when it was home to masons working on nearby St Andrew's church, this very old house is run by Mandy Robinson, who prides herself on running a 'proper pub', with a menu of locally-sourced delights. Start with duck and chilli jam spring rolls; follow on with grilled gammon ham, double free-range eggs, chips and peas; or seafood pancake – a medley of fish and shellfish in white wine, garlic and cream sauce. There's a lovely cottage garden to the side of the pub, and a wood-burner blazing in the winter.

Open all wk Mon-Thu 11.30-2.30 6.30-11 (Fri-Sat 11.30-11.30 Sun 12-11) **Food** Lunch Mon-Fri 12-2, Sat-Sun 12-2.30 Dinner Sun-Thu 7-9.30, Fri-Sat 7-10 Av main course £10 ⊕ PUNCH TAVERNS ◀ Dartmoor Jail Ale, Sharp's Doom Bar, Otter Amber ♻ Thatchers Gold & Heritage. ♥ 9 **Facilities** Non-diners area ✿ (Bar Garden) ♦♦ Children's menu Children's portions Family room Garden ⊨ Parking WiFi

---

■ **BUTTERLEIGH**   Map 3 SS90

The Butterleigh Inn

tel: 01884 855433 **EX15 1PN**
email: thebutterleighinn1@btconnect.com
dir: *M5 junct 28, B3181 signed Cullompton. In Cullompton High St right signed Butterleigh. 3m to pub*

Regularly changing real ales and home-made food

Set in a delightful village opposite the 13th-century St Matthew's church and in the heart of the rolling Devon countryside, the 400-year-old Butterleigh is a traditional free house. There is a mass of local memorabilia throughout this friendly local, where customers can choose from a selection of changing real ales including Dartmoor Jail Ale, ciders including Devon Scrumpy from Sandford Orchards, and around 15 malt whiskies. Expect home-made dishes such as chicken supreme with Devon cider, mushroom and cream sauce; chicken and king prawn linguine; steak and ale pie; and curry of the week. On fine days, the garden is very popular.

Open 12-2.30 6-11 (Fri-Sat 12-2.30 6-12 Sun 12-3) Closed Sun eve, Mon L **Food** Lunch Tue-Sat 12-2 Dinner Tue-Sat 7-9 Av main course £10.50 ⊕ FREE HOUSE ◀ Cotleigh Tawny Owl, Otter Ale & Amber, Dartmoor IPA & Jail Ale, guest ale ♻ Sandford Orchards Devon Scrumpy, Sheppy's, Winkleigh Sam's. ♥ 9 **Facilities** Non-diners area ✿ (Bar Garden) ♦♦ Children's portions Garden ⊨ Parking WiFi

---

■ **CHAGFORD**   Map 3 SX78

NEW The Chagford Inn

tel: 01647 433109 **7 Mill St TQ13 8AW**
email: thechagfordinn@gmail.com
dir: *From A30 at Whiddon Down follow Chagford signs onto A382. Right onto B3206 signed Chagford*

Excellent locally sourced food on Dartmoor

Set within the glorious Dartmoor National Park, this blue-washed pub has an artistic bent with regular exhibitions of new artists and also life drawing classes.

Close links with neighbouring farms means a steady supply of quality local meat and the kitchen adopts a nose-to-tail philosophy. A typical meal might start with roast ox heart, white anchovies, capers and aïoli before moving on to venison ragù with linguine, wild mushrooms and watercress. If fish is your thing, try the Brixham hake fillet with Jerusalem artichokes, fondant potato and saffron. Wash it down with a pint of Dartmoor Legend.

Open all day all wk **Food** Lunch Mon-Sat 12-2.30, Sun 12-3 Dinner Mon-Sat 6-9, Sun 6-8.30 Set menu available Restaurant menu available all wk ⊕ ENTERPRISE INNS ⬛ Dartmoor Legend, Otter Bitter ♂ Thatchers Heritage. ⬤ 10 **Facilities** Non-diners area ⬤ (Bar Restaurant Garden) ⬤ Children's portions Garden ⌂ WiFi

CHALLACOMBE
Map 3 SS64

NEW Black Venus Inn

tel: 01598 763251 **EX31 4TT**
email: blackvenus@hotmail.co.uk
dir: On B3358

Local ales and good food in the heart of Exmoor

Named after an extinct breed of sheep, this 16th-century stone-built pub occupies a wonderful location in the Exmoor National Park. Surrounded by many excellent walks, the low-beamed pub welcomes dogs and children, particularly in the school summer holidays when the pub opens all day. This is a pub passionate about beer so there's always two local cask ales on tap — among them Cotleigh Golden Seahawk and Exmoor Fox — to accompany robust dishes such as home-made chilli con carne; beef and ale pie; or braised lamb shank with redcurrant and rosemary gravy, potatoes and vegetables.

Open all wk 12-2.30 5.30-11 Closed 25 Dec **Food** Lunch all wk 12-2.30 Dinner all wk 5.30-9 ⊕ FREE HOUSE ⬛ Cornish Best, Cotleigh Golden Seahawk, Exmoor Ales Fox ♂ Thatchers Gold. ⬤ 10 **Facilities** Non-diners area ⬤ (Bar Garden) ⬤ Children's menu Children's portions Play area Garden ⌂ Parking WiFi

CLOVELLY
Map 3 SS32

Red Lion Hotel ★★ HL
PICK OF THE PUBS

tel: 01237 431237 **The Quay EX39 5TF**
email: redlion@clovelly.co.uk **web:** www.clovelly.co.uk
dir: From Bideford rdbt, A39 to Bude, 10m. At Clovelly Cross rdbt right. Park at Visitor Centre. Walk to hotel at bottom of hill

Excellent home-cooked food in unspoilt fishing village

This charming whitewashed hostelry sits right on the quay in Clovelly, the famously unspoilt 'village like a waterfall', which descends down broad steps to a 14th-century harbour. Guests staying in the whimsically decorated bedrooms can fall asleep to the sound of waves lapping the shingle. Originally a beer house for fishermen and other locals, the Red Lion has plenty of character and offers Cornish ales such as Sharp's Doom Bar in its snug bar, where you can rub shoulders with the locals. Alternatively, you could settle in the Harbour Bar, and sample the home-cooked food, the modern seasonal menu specialising in fresh seafood, which is landed daily right outside the door. Choose pan-fried fillet of sea bass with cream bean cassoulet, or opt for medallions of wild venison, or beetroot risotto served with parsnip chips.

Open all day all wk **Food** Lunch all wk 12-2.30 Dinner all wk 6-8.30 Av main course £8-£10 Set menu available Restaurant menu available all wk ⊕ FREE HOUSE ⬛ Sharp's Doom Bar, Clovelly Cobbler, Guinness ♂ Thatchers, Somersby. **Facilities** Non-diners area ⬤ (Bar Outside area) ⬤ Children's menu Children's portions Family room Outside area ⌂ Parking WiFi ⬛ (notice required) **Rooms** 17

CLYST HYDON
Map 3 ST00

The Five Bells Inn

tel: 01884 277288 **EX15 2NT**
email: info@fivebells.uk.com
dir: B3181 towards Cullompton, right at Hele Cross towards Clyst Hydon. 2m turn right, then sharp right at left bend at village sign

Pretty 16th-century pub with tempting food

The pub and the church were neighbours until early last century, when the rector's objections forced the inn to move into this old thatched farmhouse, its new name intended as a raspberry to the rector. Otter and Butcombe real ales hold sway in the bar — note the original counter. Exposed brick and cream-papered walls are adorned with signed Exeter Chiefs rugby shirts, and there's a German-style 'stammtisch', or regulars' table. Simple pub food includes home-made Scotch duck egg; home-cured wild Escot venison; lightly curried Skrei cod fillet; and River Exe mussels in Berry Farm cider. The inn is very child friendly. The beer festival is held during the second week of August.

Open all wk 12-3 6-12 (Sun 12-10) **Food** Lunch Mon-Sat 12-2, Sun 12-5 Dinner Sun-Thu 6-9, Fri-Sat 6-9.30 Av main course £18.50 Set menu available ⊕ FREE HOUSE ⬛ Otter Ale & Amber, Butcombe Bitter ♂ Berry Farm. ⬤ 9 **Facilities** Non-diners area ⬤ (Bar Garden Outside area) ⬤ Children's menu Children's portions Garden Outside area ⌂ Beer festival Cider festival Parking WiFi ⬛ (notice required)

COCKWOOD
Map 3 SX98

The Anchor Inn

tel: 01626 890203 **EX6 8RA**
email: scott.anchor@hotmail.co.uk **web:** www.anchorinncockwood.com
dir: From A379 between Dawlish & Starcross follow Cockwood sign

Waterside pub specialising in seafood

This 450-year-old inn overlooks a small landlocked harbour on the River Exe and was once the haunt of smugglers. There is even a friendly ghost with his dog. In summer, customers spill out onto the verandah and harbour wall, while real fires, nautical bric-à-brac and low beams make the interior cosy in winter. For fish dish lovers, the comprehensive menu will make decisions difficult — there are over 20 different ways to eat mussels, and plenty of scallop dishes and fish platters. Meat-eaters and vegetarians are not forgotten. Sample main courses include homity pie; Asian spiced marinated tuna, fried tempura style; pan-fried Gressingham duck breast with tomato, leek and bell pepper sauce; and scampi and chips. Beer festivals twice a year around Easter and Halloween.

Open all day all wk 11-11 (Sun 12-10.30 25 Dec 12-2) **Food** Mon-Sat 12-10, Sun 12-9.30 Restaurant menu available all wk ⊕ HEAVITREE ⬛ Otter Ale, St Austell Tribute & Proper Job, Dartmoor Jail Ale, 3 guest ales. **Facilities** Non-diners area ⬤ (Bar Outside area) ⬤ Children's menu Children's portions Outside area ⌂ Beer festival Parking ⬛ (notice required)

PICK OF THE PUBS

Royal Castle Hotel ★★★ HL 🌹

DARTMOUTH Map 3 SX85

tel: 01803 833033
11 The Quay TQ6 9PS
email: enquiry@royalcastle.co.uk
web: www.royalcastle.co.uk
dir: *In town centre, overlooking inner harbour*

Historic pub and hotel with great estuary views

An iconic 17th-century building in the centre of this bustling town, the Royal Castle Hotel commands a prime site overlooking the Dart estuary. Originally four Tudor houses built on either side of a narrow lane, which now forms the lofty hallway, this handsome old coaching inn offers plenty of original features in the shape of period fireplaces, spiral staircases, oil paintings and priest holes. The choice of real ales from local breweries includes Dartmoor Jail Ale and Otter Amber, and there is an impressive number of carefully selected wines served by the glass; a wider range of high quality wines appears on the Castle Collection list. A supporter of Taste of the West's 'buy local' campaign, the kitchen showcases plenty of Devon produce on both the all-day bar menu and the Grill Room restaurant. Typical choices in the pubby Harbour Bar and Galleon Lounge might take in local crab sandwiches; baked Little Wallop goats' cheese salad; and Donald Russel chargrilled sirloin steaks. With its lovely

river views, the AA Rosette-awarded Grill Room upstairs is a great setting to enjoy starters such as ham hock ballotine with shimeji mushroom à la grecque and pancetta crisp; or Brixham crab ravioli, asparagus, broad beans and ginger velouté. These might be followed by walnut-crusted pork loin, butternut squash purée, spring greens, glazed pork belly, onions and wholegrain mustard; their famous chateaubriand for two served with hand-cut chips, baked tomato, field mushrooms, garlic butter and a choice of sauce; or whole Torbay sole with clams, mussels and chive vinaigrette. Finish, perhaps, with lemon tart and raspberry compôte, raspberry coulis and clotted cream; or glazed dark chocolate cheesecake with hazelnut ice cream.

Open all day all wk 8am-11pm
Food all wk 11.30-10 Restaurant menu available all wk 🛢 FREE HOUSE
🍺 Dartmoor Jail Ale, Otter Amber, Sharp's Doom Bar 🍏 Thatchers Gold, Orchard's. 🍷 25
Facilities Non-diners area 🐾 (Bar)
🚼 Children's menu Children's portions Family room WiFi **Rooms** 24

COLEFORD

Map 3 SS70

The New Inn ★★★★ INN   PICK OF THE PUBS

tel: 01363 84242 **EX17 5BZ**
email: enquiries@thenewinncoleford.co.uk **web:** www.thenewinncoleford.co.uk
dir: *From Exeter take A377, 1.5m after Crediton left for Coleford, 1.5m to inn*

Local ales and food in secluded Devon valley

The attractive 13th-century building with thatched roof makes a perfect home for this friendly inn. The ancient slate-floored bar with its old chests and polished brass blends effortlessly with fresh white walls, original oak beams and simple wooden furniture in the dining room. Set beside the River Cole, the garden is perfect for alfresco summer dining, when you can ponder on the pub's history: it was used by travelling Cistercian monks long before Charles I reviewed his troops from a nearby house during the English Civil War. Menus change regularly, and special events such as 'posh pies week' or 'sea shanty evening' are interspersed throughout the year. Home-made bar food includes a range of soups, omelettes and platters, while a larger meal might include roast guinea fowl breast, redcurrant sauce with raspberry and Madeira; seasonal game pie; or aubergine moussaka with tomato and fresh basil. The pub's talking Amazon Blue parrot, called Captain, has been a famous fixture here for some 30 years, greeting bar regulars and guests booking into the six well-appointed bedrooms.

Open all wk 12-3 6-11 (Sun 12-3 6-10.30) **Food** Lunch all wk 12-2 Dinner all wk 6-9 Av main course £10 Restaurant menu available all wk ⊕ FREE HOUSE ◀ Sharp's Doom Bar, Otter Ale Ō Winkleigh Sam's, Thatchers Gold. ♀ 15
Facilities Non-diners area ✿ (Bar Garden Outside area) ♦♦ Children's menu Children's portions Garden Outside area ⌐ Parking WiFi ➡ (notice required)
Rooms 6

DARTMOUTH

Map 3 SX85

Royal Castle Hotel ★★★ HL ◉   PICK OF THE PUBS

See Pick of the Pubs on opposite page

DODDISCOMBSLEIGH

Map 3 SX88

The NoBody Inn ★★★★ INN ◉   PICK OF THE PUBS

See Pick of the Pubs on page 140

DOLTON

Map 3 SS51

Rams Head Inn

tel: 01805 804255 **South St EX19 8QS**
email: info@theramsheadinn.co.uk **web:** www.theramsheadinn.co.uk
dir: *8m from Torrington on A3124*

Traditional pub in Devon's lovely countryside

This beautiful 17th-century free house, with a new owner, has been refurbished yet retains much of its original character with huge old fireplaces, bread ovens and log burners. The inn's central location places it on many inland tourist routes, whilst the Tarka Trail and Rosemoor Gardens are both nearby. Expect a selection of cask ales on tap, accompanied by freshly cooked, locally sourced dishes that are served at lunchtime and in the evening. A typical meal might start with River Exe mussels in cider, followed by home-made steamed suet pudding; or 8oz Exmoor rump steak and triple cooked chips.

Open 11.30-3 6-11 (Fri-Sat 12-12 Sun 12-8 Winter Mon-Thu 5-10 Fri-Sat 11.30-2.30 5-11 Sun 12-6) Closed 4-31 Jan **Food** Lunch all wk 12-2.30 (Etr-Sep) Dinner Mon-Sat 6.30-9 Av main course £15 Restaurant menu available Tue-Sat ⊕ FREE HOUSE ◀ Sharp's Own, guest ales Ō Winkleigh, Cloudy Apple. ♀ 14
Facilities Non-diners area ✿ (All areas) ♦♦ Children's portions Garden Outside area ⌐ Parking WiFi ➡ (notice required)

EAST ALLINGTON

Map 3 SX74

The Fortescue Arms

tel: 01548 521215 **TQ9 7RA**
email: reception@thefortescuearms.com
dir: *Phone for detailed directions*

Pretty free house in a South Hams village

Named after a local landowner, this 19th-century pub retains the charms of yesteryear with wooden tables, flagstone floors and beamed ceilings. Open fires burn in winter, warming the informal and candlelit interior where a range of proper ales is served. Expect popular home-made fare: Welsh rarebit; creamy garlic mushrooms; slow-cooked lamb shank, creamy mash, seasonal vegetables; trio of Yarde Farm pork sausages; and chicken and vegetable curry. The quiet and comfortable cottage garden is a great place to eat if you're visiting this Area of Outstanding Natural Beauty on a fine day.

Open 12-3 6-11 (Sat-Sun all day Tue 6-11) Closed Mon & Tue L (ex BH) **Food** Lunch Wed-Sun 12-2 Dinner Tue-Sun 6-9 Av main course £9.95 ⊕ FREE HOUSE ◀ Dartmoor Legend & Jail Ale, St Austell Trelawny Ō Westons Stowford Press. ♀ **Facilities** Non-diners area ✿ (Bar Restaurant Garden) ♦♦ Children's menu Children's portions Garden ⌐ Beer festival Cider festival Parking WiFi ➡ (notice required)

PICK OF THE PUBS

The NoBody Inn ★★★★ INN ❀

DODDISCOMBSLEIGH   Map 3 SX88

tel: 01647 252394 **EX6 7PS**
email: info@nobodyinn.co.uk
web: www.nobodyinn.co.uk
dir: *3m SW of Exeter Racecourse (A38)*

All the old-world charm you could want

For over 400 years, this old building has stood in the rolling countryside between the Haldon Hills and the Teign Valley. Remodelling over the centuries has reflected its several roles, including a long spell as a centre for parish affairs and meeting place until in 1838 Pophill House, as it was then known, formally became The New Inn. Among the five landlords since was the poor chap in 1952 whose body undertakers mistakenly left in the mortuary, so that his funeral went ahead with an empty coffin – which is how the inn acquired its name. Inside, providing all the expected old-world charm, are low ceilings, blackened beams, an inglenook fireplace and antique furniture. The bar serves 30-odd wines by the glass, selected from a range of more than 250 bins, some quite rare, and the shelves groan under the weight of a mind-boggling 280 whiskies, mostly malts. Branscombe Vale brewery supplies NoBody's Bitter, with other Devon and Cornwall guest ales adding to the choice. Crisp white napkins define the

restaurant, where the seasonally changing menus, awarded an AA Rosette, rely extensively on fine Devon produce. A typical lunch or dinner would be beetroot carpaccio, Vulscombe goats' cheese mousse, candied walnuts and celery and apple salad; followed by herb-crusted confit sea bream fillet and mussel chowder; or the ever-popular steak and NoBody ale pie; and, to finish, pistachio olive oil cake with raspberry sorbet. Daily specials might be panko crumb squid and sweet chilli mayo; and rack of Devon lamb, oregano crust, pesto mash, roast butternut squash and Madeira jus. If you want a bar snack, there's homity pie; and ploughman's, featuring Sharpham Brie, Devon Blue or Devon Oke cheese.

Open all day all wk 11-11 (Sun 12-10.30) **Food** Lunch Mon-Sat 12-2.30, Sun 12-3 Dinner Mon-Thu 6-9, Fri-Sat 6-9.30, Sun 7-9 ⊞ FREE HOUSE ◀ Branscombe Vale NoBody's Bitter, guest ales ♂ Winkleigh Sam's Poundhouse Crisp, Sandford Orchards Devon Red. ♟ 28
Facilities Non-diners area ☙ (Bar Garden) ♦♦ Children's portions Garden ⋒ Cider festival Parking **Rooms** 5

EAST DOWN
Map 3 SS64

NEW Pyne Arms

tel: 01271 850055 **EX31 4LX**
email: info@pynearms.co.uk
dir: *Follow East Down & pub signs from A39 between Blackmoor Gate & Barnstaple*

Family-run pub on the edge of Exmoor

Just seven miles from Barnstaple, the Pyne Arms is a popular stop for walkers visiting nearby Arlington Court (NT) and Exmoor National Park. The pub was taken over by the Pannell family, who renovated the place whilst retaining its character and long tradition of feeding visitors well. Enjoy locally brewed Exmoor Stag ale or Thatchers Gold cider as you consider choices on a menu that might include steak and ale pie; home-made faggots with roasted root vegetable gravy and creamed mash potato; or Exmoor Ale battered cod, hand-cut chips, mushy peas and tartare sauce.

Open 12-3 5-close (Mon 5-close, Sat-Sun 12-close) Closed 6-23 Jan, Mon L **Food** Contact pub for food times ⊕ FREE HOUSE ◼ Exmoor Ales Gold & Stag, St Austell Tribute ♂ Thatchers Gold & Somerset Haze. **Facilities** Non-diners area ❀ (Bar Outside area) ♦ Children's menu Children's portions Outside area ⋒ Parking WiFi ⛟ (notice required)

EAST PRAWLE
Map 3 SX73

The Pigs Nose Inn

tel: 01548 511209 **TQ7 2BY**
email: info@pigsnoseinn.co.uk
dir: *From Kingsbridge take A379 towards Dartmouth. After Frogmore turn right signed East Prawle. Approx 5m to pub in village centre*

A 500-year-old inn overlooking the village green

Smugglers used to store their shipwreck booty here but, rather than hiding contraband, the owners today prefer to demonstrate their adherence to old-fashioned values by banning juke boxes and games machines, and by their provision of a 'knitting corner', games and toys. Devon-sourced real ales are served straight from the barrel in the wonderfully cluttered bar. Food here is never a 'minuscule blob on an oversized square plate', but is good helpings of traditional pub grub, such as chicken curry; scampi and chips; cod and chips; and vegetarian Mediterranean pasta. There's also a dogs' menu!

Open 12-3 6-11.30 Closed Sun (Nov-Mar) **Food** Lunch all wk 12-2 Dinner all wk 6.30-9 Av main course £7 ⊕ FREE HOUSE ◼ The South Hams Eddystone & Devon Pride, Otter ♂ Thatchers Heritage. **Facilities** Non-diners area ❀ (Bar Restaurant Outside area) ♦ Children's menu Children's portions Play area Family room Outside area ⋒ WiFi ⛟ (notice required) **Notes** ☺

EXETER
Map 3 SX99

The Hour Glass

tel: 01392 258722 **21 Melbourne St EX2 4AU**
email: ajpthehourglass@yahoo.co.uk
dir: *M5 junct 30, A370 signed Exeter. At Countess Weir rdbt 3rd exit onto Topsham Rd (B3182) signed City Centre. In approx 2m left into Melbourne St*

Quirky end-of-terrace pub with friendly staff

This distinctively shaped backstreet pub has built a reputation for its friendly service and inventive food, not to mention its rotating local ales and great choice of ciders. Expect beams, wood floors, an open fire and resident cats in the bar, where hand-pulled pints of Bath Ales or Exeter Avocet are in top condition. The short

chalkboard menu changes every six weeks or so, and everything — including the bread — is prepared from scratch in the kitchen. Choose from the likes of celeriac and Bramley soup with Devon Blue; ham hock croquettes; or venison borscht with mash.

Open 12-2.30 5-close (Sat-Sun all day Mon 5-close) Closed 25-26 Dec, 2 Jan, Mon L **Food** Lunch Tue-Fri 12-2.15, Sat-Sun 12-3 Dinner Mon-Sat 5.30-9.30, Sun 5.30-9 ⊕ ENTERPRISE INNS ◼ Otter Bitter, Exeter Avocet, Bath Ales Special Pale Ale, rotating local ales ♂ Burrow Hill, Sandford Orchards, Ashridge. ⬤ 24 **Facilities** Non-diners area WiFi

The Rusty Bike

tel: 01392 214440 **67 Howell Rd EX4 4LZ**
email: tiny@rustybike-exeter.co.uk
dir: *Phone for detailed directions*

Truly unique pub keeping the food local

The kitchen team here showcase the wealth of excellent local produce and they aim to keep the food miles to a minimum. Having established strong ties with local farmers and gamekeepers they can rely on top quality ingredients for dishes such as their venison burger; and black pudding beignet, juniper cured venison fillet and blackberry vinegar. All fish used is line caught — so perhaps try the smoked haddock, parsley and cheddar risotto; or cèviche of hand-dived scallops, cucumber, lemon, watercress and horseradish snow. Beer and cider aficionados will also enjoy the Fat Pig Brewery's own creations, Fat Pig Ham 69, Phat Nancy's, Pigmalion Ale, John Street Ale and Rusty Pig cider.

Open all wk 5-11 (Fri-Sat 5-12 Sun 12-11) **Food** Lunch Sun 12-7 Dinner Mon-Sat 6-10, Sun 12-7 ⊕ FREE HOUSE ◼ Fat Pig Ham 69, John Street Ale, Phat Nancy's IPA, Pigmalion, & Steam Hammer ♂ Rusty Pig. ⬤ 18 **Facilities** Non-diners area ❀ (Bar Restaurant Outside area) ♦ Children's portions Outside area WiFi ⛟ (notice required)

EXTON
Map 3 SX98

The Puffing Billy
PICK OF THE PUBS

tel: 01392 877888 **Station Rd EX3 0PR**
email: enquiries@thepuffingbilly.co.uk
dir: *A376 signed Exmouth, through Ebford. Follow signs for pub, right into Exton*

Smart modern setting for seasonal British food

The whitewashed building might be 16th century and the 19th-century name refers to the nearby railway line, but the food here is absolutely 21st century, served in a chic, modern dining pub-restaurant. Taken over in 2015 by the St Austell Brewery, the traditional exterior disguises the crisp, clean lines and finish within, where reliable West Country beers such as Branscombe Vale Branoc, combined with an appealing menu, combine to make The Puffing Billy a favourite destination dining bar. The home-cooked dishes are seasonal and locally sourced so along with pub classics you can expect the likes of fennel and orange-cured salmon, poached king prawns and chicory salad; and beef short rib and Portobello mushroom pie with horseradish mash, buttered kale and chantenay carrots. The neighbouring Exe estuary and the distant upwellings of Dartmoor's hills and woods may be glimpsed from the tables at the front.

Open all day all wk **Food** Lunch 12-2.15 Dinner 6-9.15 Av main course £14 Set menu available Restaurant menu available Mon-Sat ⊕ ST AUSTELL ◼ Branscombe Vale Branoc, Hanlons Yellow Hammer, St Austell Tribute ♂ Sandford Orchards Devon Red, Thatchers Gold. ⬤ 15 **Facilities** Non-diners area ❀ (Bar Garden) ♦ Children's menu Children's portions Garden ⋒ Parking WiFi ⛟ (notice required)

GEORGEHAM Map 3 SS43

The Rock Inn

tel: 01271 890322 **Rock Hill EX33 1JW**
email: therockgeorgeham@gmail.com
dir: *From A361 at Braunton follow Croyde Bay signs. Through Croyde, 1m to Georgeham. Pass shop & church. Turn right (Rock Hill), inn on left*

A mixture of dining options at this popular inn

Handy for the famous surfing beaches at Woolacombe, this old inn is also a lovely watering hole for walkers and cyclists. Its friendly atmosphere, comprising a mix of happy banter from the locals and gentle jazz played at lunchtime, adds to the enjoyment of a pint selected from the five ales on offer, including Exmoor Gold. Choose between the bar, the slightly more contemporary lower bar, or a bright conservatory. The tasty menu is hard to resist, extending from a lunch of shredded duck wraps, to dinner dishes such as linguine with tiger prawns, mussels, chilli, garlic and white wine.

Open all day all wk 11am-mdnt **Food** Lunch Mon-Sat 12-2.30, Sun 12-9 Dinner Mon-Sat 6-9.30, Sun 12-9 ◼ Timothy Taylor Landlord, Exmoor Ale & Gold, St Austell Tribute, Sharp's Doom Bar, Otter, Braunton Bitter ♂ Thatchers Gold & Haze. ♟ 12 **Facilities** Non-diners area ❀ (Bar Garden) ♦ Children's menu Children's portions Garden ⌂ Parking WiFi 🚌

HAYTOR VALE Map 3 SX77

The Rock Inn ★★★★ INN ◉◉   PICK OF THE PUBS

tel: 01364 661305 **TQ13 9XP**
email: info@rock-inn.co.uk **web:** www.rock-inn.co.uk
dir: *A38 from Exeter, at Drum Bridges rdbt take A382 for Bovey Tracey, 1st exit at 2nd rdbt (B3387), 3m left to Haytor Vale*

An oasis of calm and comfort on wild Dartmoor

Just inside Dartmoor National Park, below the Haytor Rocks, this beamed and flagstoned 18th-century coaching inn occupies a stunning location within wonderful walking country. The traditional interior is full of character, with antique tables, settles, prints and paintings, a grandfather clock, and pieces of china above the two crackling fireplaces. After a day's exercise, healthy appetites can be satisfied with some robust and contemporary British cooking, which uses top-notch local produce in attractively presented dishes. From the fixed-price dinner menu, carrot and tarragon soup could be followed by pan-fried salmon fillet with samphire, and rounded off with sticky toffee pudding, caramel sauce and the county's famous clotted cream. West Country cheeses are a particular feature, as are Devon Mist or Ashridge Devon Gold ciders from the bar. In fair weather, your chosen refreshment can be enjoyed alfresco in the courtyard or in the peaceful garden across the lane.

Open all day all wk 11-11 (Sun 12-10.30) Closed 25-26 Dec **Food** Lunch all wk 12-2 Dinner all wk 7-9 Set menu available Restaurant menu available all wk ⊕ FREE HOUSE ◼ Dartmoor Jail Ale & IPA ♂ Sandford Orchards & Devon Mist, Ashridge Devon Gold. ♟ 12 **Facilities** Non-diners area ❀ (Garden) ♦ Children's menu Children's portions Family room Garden ⌂ Parking WiFi **Rooms** 9

HONITON Map 4 ST10

The Holt ◉◉   PICK OF THE PUBS

tel: 01404 47707 **178 High St EX14 1LA**
email: enquiries@theholt-honiton.com
dir: *Phone for detailed directions*

A chic pub, restaurant and smokehouse

Successfully run by brothers Joe and Angus McCaig, this popular split-level establishment is just where the High Street crosses a stream called The Gissage.

The downstairs bar is stocked with the full range of Otter beers from nearby Luppitt, ciders from Honiton's own Norcotts, and Joe's wine selection; it's also where the open-plan kitchen is; for the candlelit, two AA-Rosette restaurant, head upstairs. The cooking style is modern British, with regularly changing menus showcasing local suppliers in a big way and making good use of meats and fish from Angus's smokehouse. Tapas is served at lunchtime and in the evening, and daily specials supplement main dishes such as hot and sour broth with sea bass, squid, prawns, bamboo shoots and coriander; and oak-smoked duck leg confit, roasted winter vegetables, mash and mustard sauce. Cookery classes are held here too.

Open 11-3 5.30-12 Closed 25-26 Dec, Sun & Mon **Food** Lunch Tue-Sat 12-2 Dinner Tue-Sat 6.30-9 ⊕ FREE HOUSE ◼ Otter Bitter, Ale, Bright, Amber, Head ♂ Aspall, Thatchers Gold, Norcotts Cider. ♟ 9 **Facilities** Non-diners area ❀ (Bar) ♦ Children's portions Beer festival WiFi 🚌

The Railway

tel: 01404 47976 **Queen St EX14 1HE**
email: sue@gochef.co.uk/therailwayhoniton@icloud.com
dir: *From High St into New St (Lloyds bank on corner). 1st left into Queen St (follow road to right). Pub on left. Or from A35 (at Copper Castle) into Pine Park Rd. 1st right (Pine Park Rd), over railway bridge, pub on right*

Local ale and good food in this friendly town pub

The Railway dates back to 1869, when it was built as a cider house for thirsty GWR workers. Melanie and Jean Sancey offer their visitors a warm, family-friendly atmosphere. Whether it's in the bar with its cosy log-burner and range of real ales, or in the restaurant, the appealing menu offers plenty of choice including meze and gourmet pizzas; there is an emphasis on quality local ingredients. A typical starter of chicken liver parfait with blood orange, ginger bread and watercress might be followed by hake and mussels with leek, pancetta, parsley and new potatoes.

Open 12-3 6-close (Sun 12-4) Closed Mon **Food** Lunch Tue-Sat 12-2, Sun 12-3 Dinner Tue-Sat 6-9 Av main course £12-£16 Restaurant menu available all wk ⊕ FREE HOUSE ◼ St Austell Proper Job, Bath Ales Gem, Branscombe Vale Branoc, Hanlons Yellow Hammer ♂ Bath Ciders Bounders, Thatchers, Cornish Orchards, Orchard Pig. ♟ 12 **Facilities** Non-diners area ❀ (Bar Outside area) ♦ Children's menu Children's portions Outside area ⌂ Parking

IDDESLEIGH Map 3 SS50

The Duke of York   PICK OF THE PUBS

tel: 01837 810253 **EX19 8BG**
email: john@dukeofyorkdevon.co.uk
dir: *Phone for detailed directions*

High on a hill with views of the tors

In a tiny village of pretty cottages, this thatched, cob and stone inn is where local author Michael Morpurgo embarked on his novel *War Horse*, following conversations in front of the fire with a First World War veteran. Another literary link is Henry Williamson's *Tarka the Otter*, the Tarka Trail now passes the pub door. An enticing range of real ales includes Bays Topsail from Paignton, and Winkleigh cider from that Devon village. Around 640 years old, the interior bursts at the seams with signs of antiquity: ancient beams and pillars, huge inglenooks and timeworn furniture. The short menu typically offers a three-course meal of smoked duck breast with avocado and mixed leaf salad; whole brill stuffed with prawns, and rich white wine and parsley sauce; and Dunstaple Farm ice cream. Daily specials appear on a blackboard. There's a beer festival in August.

Open all day all wk 11-11 **Food** all wk 11-10 Av main course £10 Restaurant menu available all wk ⊕ FREE HOUSE ◼ Adnams Broadside, Bays Topsail, guest ales ♂ Winkleigh. ♟ 10 **Facilities** Non-diners area ❀ (Bar Garden) ♦ Children's menu Children's portions Garden ⌂ Beer festival WiFi 🚌 (notice required)

KILMINGTON
Map 4 SY29

The Old Inn

tel: 01297 32096 **EX13 7RB**
email: oldinnk@gmail.com
dir: *From Axminster on A35 towards Honiton. Pub on left in 1m*

Delightful Devon longhouse offering classic pub meals

This thatched Devon longhouse dates from 1650, when it was a staging house for changing post horses, and stands beside the A35 just west of Axminster. Weary travellers will find a cosy, beamed interior with a relaxed atmosphere, crackling log fires, and a fine range of local ales on tap. Order a pint of Otter or Thatchers Gold to accompany a traditional pub meal, perhaps a baked aubergine with Mediterranean vegetables and sweet potato, topped with a three-cheese crust; or a jacket potato with a choice of toppings. The south-facing garden is the venue for the Spring Bank Holiday beer festival in late May. A change of hands in late 2015.

Open all day all wk 8am–11pm **Food** all wk 8am–9pm ⊕ FREE HOUSE ◀ Otter Bitter, Branscombe Vale Branoc ♂ Thatchers Gold. ⚱ 10 **Facilities** Non-diners area ❖ (Bar Garden) •♦ Children's menu Children's portions Garden ⩋ Beer festival Parking WiFi ➡ (notice required)

KINGSBRIDGE
Map 3 SX74

The Crabshell Inn

tel: 01548 852345 **Embankment Rd TQ7 1JZ**
email: info@thecrabshellinn.com
dir: *A38 towards Plymouth, follow signs for Kingsbridge*

Gourmet pizzas and great views

Set waterside on an old quay beside the gorgeous Kingsbridge Estuary; a dizzy mix of vessels, wildlife and glorious views captivate those lucky enough to moor up here, either actually or metaphorically. Both mariners and landlubbers can enjoy a variety of events here, where paddleboarding is a popular pastime. More restful is the practice of supping Devonshire beers from the likes of Dartmoor Brewery or an ultra-local farm cider, whilst contemplating the 15-strong menu of gourmet pizzas created here. The daily menu is equally impressive; scallop mornay with leek mash and watercress salad, a case in point.

Open all day all wk **Food** all wk 12–9 ⊕ FREE HOUSE ◀ Sharp's Doom Bar, St Austell Proper Job & Tribute, Dartmoor Jail Ale, Crabshell Bitter ♂ Thatchers Gold & Haze, Heron Valley. ⚱ 14 **Facilities** Non-diners area ❖ (Bar Restaurant Garden) •♦ Children's menu Children's portions Family room Garden ⩋ Parking WiFi ➡ (notice required)

KINGSKERSWELL
Map 3 SX86

Bickley Mill Inn
PICK OF THE PUBS

tel: 01803 873201 **TQ12 5LN**
email: info@bickleymill.co.uk
dir: *From Newton Abbot take A380 towards Torquay. Left, follow Stoneycombe signs. Then follow Bickley Mill signs*

A charming mix of old and new in a rural mill

With the resorts and beaches of the English Riviera just to the east and the wilderness of Dartmoor an easy drive to the west, this country pub in the Stoneycombe Valley started life as a flour mill some 700 years ago. Lovingly converted into a homely inn, the owners have effortlessly blended the old with on-trend contemporary design and furnishings. Thirsty ramblers can rest easy beside a roaring log fire in the bar, supping beers from local microbreweries like Teignworthy and Otter. The stimulating menu melds modern British and international dishes, with the ingredients favouring Devon suppliers. A typical

starter may be crispy squid with lemon and garlic mayonnaise; cured-meats boards, Spanish tapas vegetables and crusty bread, followed by pan-fried calves' liver, mash, red onion marmalade and rich onion gravy; or smoked and poached haddock fishcakes, tartare sauce, chunky chips and mixed salad leaves. Alfresco dining takes advantage of a tree-shaded garden above the inn.

Open all day all wk **Food** Lunch Mon-Sat 12-2.30, Sun 12-3 Dinner Mon-Sat 6-9, Sun 6-8 ⊕ FREE HOUSE ◀ Otter Ale, Teignworthy, Bays. ⚱ 12 **Facilities** Non-diners area ❖ (Bar Garden) •♦ Children's menu Children's portions Garden ⩋ Parking WiFi ➡

KINGS NYMPTON
Map 3 SS61

The Grove Inn
PICK OF THE PUBS

tel: 01769 580406 **EX37 9ST**
email: eatdrink@thegroveinn.co.uk
dir: *2.5m from A377 (Exeter to Barnstaple road). 1.5m from B3226 (South Molton road). Follow brown pub signs*

Classic English village free house

Commanding the crossroads in a peaceful village, The Grove has all the requisites of a typical Devon pub – thatched roof, whitewashed exterior, beamed ceilings, bare stone walls, rustic furnishings, flagstone floors, winter log fires and even on occasions, Morris dancers. Just like many other properties in the village, it's listed. The kitchen takes full advantage of fresh produce from nearby farms and the coast to feature in dishes such as individual north Devon fillet of beef Wellington with dauphinoise potatoes and seasonal vegetables; West Country mackerel in real ale batter with chips and mushy peas; and vegetable curry with mango chutney, rice and poppadom. All wines, even fizz, are served by the glass, beers come from regional breweries and there's a collection of 65 single malts from around the world. Dogs are allowed in the bar. A beer and cider festival takes place in July.

Open 12-3 6-11 (Sun 12-4 7-10 BH 12-4) Closed Mon L (ex BHs) **Food** Lunch Tue-Sat 12-2, Sun 12-3 Dinner Tue-Sat 6.30-9 ⊕ FREE HOUSE ◀ Exmoor Ale, Skinner's Betty Stogs, Otter Ale, Chuffin' Ale, Hunter's Devon Dreamer, Exe Valley DOBS Best Bitter ♂ Winkleigh Sam's Dry, Autumn Scrumpy, Skorpian Black. ⚱ 26 **Facilities** Non-diners area ❖ (Bar Outside area) •♦ Children's menu Children's portions Outside area ⩋ Beer festival Cider festival WiFi ➡ (notice required)

KINGSTON
Map 3 SX64

The Dolphin Inn

tel: 01548 810314 **TQ7 4QE**
email: info@dolphininn.eclipse.co.uk
dir: *From A379 (Plymouth to Kingsbridge road) take B3233 signed Bigbury-on-Sea, at x-roads straight on to Kingston. Follow brown inn signs*

Off the beaten track for precious tranquillity

Church stonemasons lived here in the 15th century, and later it was taken over by fishermen and their families. The inn is close to the beautiful Erme estuary and the popular surfing beaches of the South Hams. Teignworthy Spring Tide is one of several real ales, alongside Thatchers cider. Home-made food includes chicken liver parfait with red onion jam; devilled crab tartlet with bay leaf salad; trio of sausages, mash and onion gravy; twice-baked cheese soufflé with creamed spinach; and pineapple tarte Tatin with rum raisin ice cream. A circular walk from the pub takes in woodland, the estuary and the South West Coastal Path.

Open 12-3 6-11 (Sun 12-3 7-10.30) Closed Sun eve & Mon winter **Food** Lunch Mon-Sat 12-3, Sun 12-2.30 Dinner all wk 6-9 Av main course £10 Set menu available Restaurant menu available Tue-Sun evenings (ex Sun eve in winter) ⊕ PUNCH TAVERNS ◀ Exmoor Ale, Teignworthy Spring Tide, Sharp's Doom Bar, Otter, Dartmoor Jail Ale ♂ Thatchers. **Facilities** Non-diners area ❖ (Bar Restaurant Garden) •♦ Children's menu Children's portions Play area Family room Garden ⩋ Parking WiFi

KNOWSTONE
Map 3 SS82

The Masons Arms @@
PICK OF THE PUBS

tel: 01398 341231 **EX36 4RY**
email: enqs@masonsarmsdevon.co.uk
dir: *Follow Knowstone signs from A361*

Village local crossed with high-end restaurant

A thatched 13th-century inn on the edge of Exmoor, where excellent food and drink are preceded by a genuinely warm welcome. Villagers and visiting walkers mix happily in the low-beamed bar, where pints of Cotleigh Tawny Owl and Sam's Poundhouse cider are supped around the warmth of the huge fireplace. The bright rear dining room offers long views, an extraordinary ceiling mural, and food worthy of two AA Rosettes. Chef and owner Mark Dodson can boast cooking under the guidance of Michel Roux, and runs his own monthly masterclass which culminates in a two-course lunch. As befits the menu's sophisticated adult tastes, the dining room is out of bounds for under 5s in the evening. Typical of choices are seared peppered tuna with oriental salad; loin of venison with red wine pear and blue cheese gratin; and spiced pumpkin crème brûlée with cinnamon ice cream.

Open 12-2 6-11 Closed 1st wk Jan, Feb half term & last wk Aug, Sun eve & Mon **Food** Lunch Tue-Sun 12-2 Dinner Tue-Sat 6-11 Set menu available Restaurant menu available Tue-Sun ⊕ FREE HOUSE ◀ Cotleigh Tawny Owl ♂ Winkleigh Sam's Poundhouse. ☖ 10 **Facilities** Non-diners area ✿ (Bar Garden Outside area) Children's portions Garden Outside area ⋒ Parking WiFi

LIFTON
Map 3 SX38

The Arundell Arms ★★★ HL @@
PICK OF THE PUBS

tel: 01566 784666 **PL16 0AA**
email: reservations@arundellarms.com web: www.arundellarms.com
dir: *1m from A30 dual carriageway, 3m E of Launceston*

Internationally acclaimed fishing and country sports hotel

A spit from Cornwall, this former coaching inn has a 250-year-old cock-fighting pit in the garden, and from the car park you can see the window bars of the cells of the neighbouring old police station. The Courthouse Bar dispenses the aptly named Dartmoor Jail Ale, and Ashridge cider; sensibly priced wines come from around the world. Holding two AA Rosettes for many years, Devon-born Master Chef of Great Britain Steve Pidgeon's restaurant makes good use of produce from local shoots and estates, the hotel's kitchen garden and villagers; he'll cook fish caught by guests, too. Menus feature pan-fried grey mullet; roast best-end of English lamb; fillet of Aylesbury duck; and vegetable croustade provençale. There's also a five-course 'Taste of the West' menu. With Dartmoor close by, the big decisions are: lunch? dinner? breakfast? or all three? Professional advice is available for guests using the inn's fishing beats on the Tamar and six tributaries.

Open all wk 12-3 6-11 **Food** Lunch all wk 12-2 Dinner all wk 6-10 Restaurant menu available all wk ⊕ FREE HOUSE ◀ St Austell Tribute, Dartmoor Jail Ale, guest ales ♂ Ashridge. ☖ 9 **Facilities** Non-diners area ✿ (Bar Garden) ♦ Children's menu Children's portions Garden ⋒ Parking WiFi **Rooms** 24

LUSTLEIGH
Map 3 SX78

The Cleave Public House

tel: 01647 277223 **TQ13 9TJ**
email: ben@thecleavelustleigh.uk.com
dir: *From Newton Abbot take A382, follow Bovey Tracey signs, then Moretonhampstead signs. Left to Lustleigh*

Delightful thatched pub beside the village cricket pitch

Set on the edge of Dartmoor National Park, and dating from the 16th century, this thatched, family-run pub is the only one in the village and is adjacent to the cricket pitch. It has a traditional snug bar, with beams, granite flooring and log fire; to the rear, formerly the old railway station waiting room, is now a light and airy dining

area leading to a lovely cottage garden. The pub/bistro has gained a reputation for an interesting and varied, daily-changing menu. Dishes include Ligurian fish stew; River Teign mussels; sausages in ale gravy with bubble-and-squeak; or hand-made pumpkin ravioli with sage butter and balsamic onions. If you're thinking of taking your dog inside the pub, please just call ahead on the day to check it's alright with the landlord.

Open all day all wk 11-11 (Sun 12-9) **Food** Mon-Sat 12-9, Sun 12-6 ⊕ HEAVITREE ◀ Otter Ale, Bitter, guest ales ♂ Aspall. **Facilities** Non-diners area ✿ (Bar Garden) ♦ Children's menu Children's portions Garden ⋒ Parking WiFi

LUTON (NEAR CHUDLEIGH)
Map 3 SX97

The Elizabethan

tel: 01626 775425 **Fore St TQ13 0BL**
email: contact@elizabethaninn.co.uk web: www.elizabethaninn.co.uk
dir: *Between Chudleigh & Teignmouth*

Good honest Devon food and drink

Known locally as the Lizzie, this smart, welcoming 16th-century free house attracts diners and drinkers alike. There's a great selection of West Country ales like Teignworthy Reel Ale to choose from, as well as local Reddaway's Farm cider. Sit beside a log fire in winter or in the pretty beer garden on warmer days. The pub prides itself on using the best local ingredients. The regularly-changing menus includes salad bowls, risottos and traditional dishes, while the daily specials boards might offer River Teign mussels; fish and chips; and roasted red peppers filled with Mediterranean risotto. A monthly-changing set menu on weekdays and a take-away menu are both offered.

Open all wk 12-3 6-11.30 (Sun all day) Closed 25-26 Dec, 1 Jan **Food** Lunch Mon-Sat 12-2, Sun 12-8.30 Dinner Mon-Sat 6-9.30, Sun 12-8.30 Set menu available ⊕ FREE HOUSE ◀ Teignworthy Reel Ale, Sharp's Doom Bar, Otter Amber ♂ Reddaway's Farm, Winkleigh Sam's Poundhouse. ☖ **Facilities** Non-diners area ✿ (Bar Garden) ♦ Children's menu Children's portions Garden ⋒ Parking WiFi

See advert on opposite page

The Elizabethan

Whether you're popping in for a drink and a chat with friends, dining or collecting a takeaway, you will always receive a warm welcome at "The Lizzie".

Since 2002 Nick and Anne have been the Proprietors of this Free House and together with their Manager Matt Goldsworthy and loyal staff work hard at maintaining its reputation for good food and service. Originally a farmhouse the pub can trace its title back to Elizabethan times and since 1840 has been a Licensed Premises; first known as The Albert Inn then renamed The Elizabethan in 1953 to celebrate the Queen's Coronation. Situated in the farming community of Luton it is only a 5 minute drive away from either the A380 or B3192.

When choosing from the Special Boards, Bar Menu or the Weekday Set Menu you will become aware of just how many of the tempting dishes are made with very local ingredients. Meat and vegetables, herbs and, when in season, game comes from suppliers based in the surrounding countryside, and fresh fish is delivered daily direct from Brixham Fish Market. All these are then used in the dishes prepared by Nick and team of chefs using classic, traditional and their own recipes and they rightly pride themselves for producing "good, honest Devon Food". Having been awarded the Cask Marque for well-kept beers and cellar a good pint of beer is guaranteed. There is always a choice of two real ales available, as well as an array of other drinks to tempt you including award-winning Reddaway's Cider which is made in the village by a neighbouring farmer.

The Elizabethan is open every day for food which is served 12 noon to 2 pm and from 6 pm to 9.30pm and ALL DAY on Sundays when the Special Roast Menu is added to the extensive choice.

Extra Information:
- Large car park
- Pub garden
- Children's menu available and highchairs
- Takeaway menu
- Dogs allowed in bar area only and garden
- Free WiFi

Fore Street, Luton, Nr Newton Abbot, Devon TQ13 0BL • **Tel:** 01626 775425
Email: contact@elizabethaninn.co.uk • **Website:** www.elizabethaninn.co.uk

LYNMOUTH
Map 3 SS74

Rising Sun Hotel ★★ HL ◉
PICK OF THE PUBS

tel: 01598 753223 **Harbourside EX35 6EG**
email: reception@risingsunlynmouth.co.uk **web:** www.risingsunlynmouth.co.uk
dir: M5 junct 25 follow Minehead signs. A39 to Lynmouth

Historic inn with literary connections

Overlooking Lynmouth's tiny harbour and bay is this 14th-century thatched smugglers' inn. In turn, overlooking them all, are Countisbury Cliffs, the highest in England. The building's long history is evident from the uneven oak floors, crooked ceilings and thick walls. Literary associations are plentiful: R D Blackmore wrote some of his wild Exmoor romance, *Lorna Doone*, here; the poet Shelley is believed to have honeymooned in the garden cottage, and Coleridge stayed here too. Immediately behind rises Exmoor Forest and National Park, home to red deer, wild ponies and birds of prey. With moor and sea so close, game and seafood are in plentiful supply; appearing in dishes such as braised pheasant with pancetta, quince and Braunton greens; and roast shellfish – crab, mussels, clams and scallops in garlic, ginger and coriander. At night the oak-panelled, candlelit dining room is an example of romantic British inn-keeping at its best.

Open all day all wk 11am-mdnt Closed 25 Dec **Food** Lunch all wk 12-2.30 Dinner all wk 6-9 ⊕ FREE HOUSE ◀ Exmoor Gold & Stag, Sharp's Doom Bar, guest ales ♂ Thatchers Gold & Cheddar Valley, Addlestones,. ♈ **Facilities** Non-diners area ☙ (Bar Outside area) Outside area ⋒ WiFi ➾ **Rooms** 14

MARLDON
Map 3 SX86

The Church House Inn

tel: 01803 558279 **Village Rd TQ3 1SL**
dir: From Torquay ring road follow signs to Marldon & Totnes, follow brown signs to pub

Grade II listed 18th-century inn with contemporary touches

Built as a hostel for the stonemasons of the adjoining village church, this ancient country inn dates from 1362. It was rebuilt in 1740 and many features from that period still remain, including beautiful Georgian windows; happily some of the original glass is intact despite overlooking the cricket pitch. These days it has an uncluttered, contemporary feel with additional seating in the garden. The menu might include smoked fish platter with salad and crusty bread; pan-fried tiger prawns cooked in coriander and walnut oil; or slow-cooked lamb shoulder with redcurrant sauce. Sandwiches and baguettes too – perhaps prawn with rocket mayonnaise; or English cheddar with home-made pear and ginger chutney.

Open all wk 11.30-2.30 5.30-11 (Fri-Sat 11.30-2.30 5.30-11.30 Sun 12-3 5.30-10.30) **Food** Lunch all wk 12-2 Dinner all wk 6.30-9.30 ⊕ FREE HOUSE ◀ St Austell Tribute, Teignworthy Gundog, Dartmoor Legend ♂ Thatchers Somerset Haze. ♈ 12 **Facilities** Non-diners area ☙ (Bar Garden) ⋔ Children's portions Garden ⋒ Parking WiFi

MEAVY
Map 3 SX56

The Royal Oak Inn

tel: 01822 852944 **PL20 6PJ**
email: info@royaloakinn.org.uk
dir: B3212 from Yelverton to Princetown. Right at Dousland to Meavy, past school. Pub opposite village green

At the heart of the community in Dartmoor village

This traditional 15th-century inn is situated by a village green within Dartmoor National Park. Flagstone floors, oak beams and a welcoming open fire set the scene at this free house popular with cyclists and walkers. Local cask ales, ciders and fine wines accompany the carefully sourced ingredients in a menu ranging from lunchtime light bites to hand-battered cod and chips; a local steak – rib-eye, sirloin or rump; with chocolate and ginger tart or an ice cream sundae to finish. The beer and cider festival takes place on the Summer Bank Holiday in late August.

Open all day all wk **Food** Lunch Mon-Fri 12-2.30, Sat-Sun 12-3 Dinner all wk 6-9 ⊕ FREE HOUSE ◀ Dartmoor Jail Ale & IPA, Meavy Oak Ale, guest ale ♂ Westons Old Rosie, Sandford Orchards Scrumpy & Old Kirton, Black Rat Perry. ♈ 12 **Facilities** Non-diners area ☙ (Bar Garden) ⋔ Children's menu Children's portions Garden ⋒ Beer festival Cider festival WiFi ➾ (notice required)

MODBURY
Map 3 SX65

California Country Inn
PICK OF THE PUBS

See Pick of the Pubs on opposite page

MORETONHAMPSTEAD
Map 3 SX78

The Horse

tel: 01647 440242 **George St TQ13 8PG**
email: hello@thehorsedartmoor.co.uk
dir: In village centre

One for those who enjoy Italian food

Once virtually derelict, The Horse is an object lesson in pub revival, as its beautiful dining room, Mediterranean-style courtyard and stunning barn conversion testify. The chesterfield-furnished bar offers Devon-brewed real ales and ciders, and the same menu as the restaurant, which could mean antipasto to share; tapas choices; hand-rolled gourmet pizzas; or hand-made meatballs in rich tomato sauce, while the courtyard smokery is responsible for smoked pastrami, salmon and salt beef. Other choices might be moules frites; chicken Caesar salad; or chargrilled 21-day hung Dartmoor rib-eye. Local folk musicians have a sing-song on the last Monday of every month.

Open all wk 12-3.30 5-12 (Mon 5-12) Closed 25 Dec **Food** Lunch Tue-Sun 12.30-2.30 Dinner all wk 6.30-9 (pizza only Sun-Mon) ⊕ FREE HOUSE ◀ Dartmoor Legend & IPA, Otter Ale, Pedigree New World Pale Ale ♂ Addlestones, Symonds. ♈ 12 **Facilities** Non-diners area ☙ (Bar Outside area) ⋔ Children's menu Children's portions Outside area ⋒ WiFi ➾ (notice required)

NEWTON ABBOT
Map 3 SX87

The Wild Goose Inn

tel: 01626 872241 **Combeinteignhead TQ12 4RA**
email: wildgooseinndevon@gmail.com
dir: From A380 at Newton Abbot rdbt take B3195 (Shaldon road) signed Milber, 2.5m to village, right at pub sign

Family-run free house with a sunny walled garden

An integral part of the village street scene, this former farmstead was first licensed as the Country House Inn in 1840; then, in the 1960s, when geese began intimidating customers, it acquired a new name. Dartmoor Brewery's Jail Ale and Sandford Orchards Devon Mist cider represent the county in the bar. New owners offer home-made pub food that includes game stew with herb dumplings at lunchtime, and in the evening ale-battered pollack, triple-cooked chips and mushy peas; pan-fried chicken breast with bacon jam, fondant potatoes and braised lettuce; and hay-baked heritage vegetables with violet potatoes. Tapas, pie and quiz nights are worth catching.

Open all wk 12-3 5.30-11 (Sun 12-3 7-11) **Food** Lunch all wk 12-2.30 Dinner Mon-Sat 6-9 ⊕ FREE HOUSE ◀ Sharp's Atlantic & Doom Bar, Dartmoor Jail Ale ♂ Sandford Orchards Devon Mist. **Facilities** Non-diners area ☙ (Bar Garden) ⋔ Children's menu Children's portions Family room Garden ⋒ Parking WiFi

PICK OF THE PUBS

California Country Inn

MODBURY   Map 3 SX65

tel: 01548 821449
California Cross PL21 0SG
email: enquiries@californiacountryinn.co.uk
web: www.californiacountryinn.co.uk
dir: *On B3196 (NE of Modbury)*

A real find in the South Hams area

This centuries-old inn stands in some of the most tranquil countryside in southern England, just a few miles from Dartmoor to the north and the cliffs and estuaries of the coast to the south. In fact, this Area of Outstanding Natural Beauty encompasses the hills and vales which can be seen from the pub's landscaped gardens. Dating from the 14th century, its unusual name is thought to derive from local adventurers in the mid-19th century who heeded the call to 'go west' and waited at the nearby crossroads for the stage to take them on the first part of their journey to America's west coast. They must have suffered wistful thoughts of home when recalling their local pub, with its wizened old beams, exposed dressed stone walls and a fabulous, huge stone fireplace. Old rural prints and photographs, copper kettles, jugs, brasses and many other artefacts add to the rustic charm of the whitewashed pub's atmospheric interior. A family-run free house, the beers on tap are likely to include Sharp's and St Austell, the wine list has award-winning Devon wines

from nearby Sharpham Vineyard, and the good-value house wines come from Chile. Having won accolades as a dining pub, head chef Tim Whiston's food is thoughtfully created and impressively flavoursome. Most ingredients are sourced from the bounty of the local countryside and waters, with meats from a supplier in nearby Loddiswell. Meals can be taken from the bar menu, but why not indulge in the à la carte menu from the inn's dining room? Appetising starters include twice baked goats' cheese soufflé, and the main course selection may include roasted monkfish, smoked bacon, potato and sweetcorn chowder. The special board adds to the choices.

Open all day all wk **Food** Lunch Mon-Sat 12-2.15, Sun 12-2.30 Dinner Mon-Sat 6-9, Sun 6-8.30 Restaurant menu available Wed-Sun eve ⊕ FREE HOUSE ◀ Dartmoor Jail Ale, Sharp's Doom Bar, St Austell Tribute ⚲ Thatchers Somerset Haze & Gold, Hunt's. ♟ 12
Facilities Non-diners area ♣ (Bar Garden) ♦♦ Children's menu Children's portions Family room Garden ⚞ Parking WiFi ▭

NEWTON ST CYRES — Map 3 SX89

The Beer Engine

tel: 01392 851282 **EX5 5AX**
email: info@thebeerengine.co.uk
dir: *From Exeter take A377 towards Crediton. Signed from A377 towards Sweetham. Pub opposite rail station, over bridge*

Ever popular brewpub

This pretty whitewashed free house has new owners. It sits on the banks of the River Creedy, opposite the Tarka Line, and is popular with walkers. Home to one of Devon's oldest microbreweries, it offers a selection of four cask ales and a range of seasonal specials. Menus focus on hearty home-cooked British food – of which 85-90% is gluten free. Dishes might include home-made Scotch eggs; steak and ale pie; and confit duck leg. Save some room for the sticky toffee pudding, made with ale from the pub.

Open all day all wk Mon-Sat 11-11 (Sun 12-10.30) **Food** Lunch Mon-Sun 12-3 Dinner Mon-Sun 6-9.30 Av main course £12 ⊕ FREE HOUSE ◀ The Beer Engine Piston Bitter, Rail Ale, Sleeper Heavy, Silver Bullet Ö Green Valley Cyder, Dragon Tears, Sandford Orchards Devon Red & Devon Mist. ▾ 10 **Facilities** Non-diners area ❅ (Bar Garden) ◀ Children's portions Garden ➤ Parking WiFi ➤ (notice required)

NOSS MAYO — Map 3 SX54

The Ship Inn — PICK OF THE PUBS

tel: 01752 872387 **PL8 1EW**
email: ship@nossmayo.com
dir: *5m S of Yealmpton. From Yealmpton take B3186, then follow Noss Mayo signs*

Waterside free house popular with sailing enthusiasts

Surrounded by wooded hills, Noss Mayo lies on the south bank of the tidal Yealm; opposite is Newton Ferrers. The waterside location means you can, if you wish, sail to this deceptively spacious pub, which has been superbly renovated using reclaimed local stone and English oak. Log fires, wooden floors, old bookcases and dozens of local pictures characterise the interior spaces. The cellar keeps a good range of beers, mostly from brewers that know the Ship well. Whether eating in the bar, panelled library or by the river, daily-changing home-made dishes include starters like grilled flat mushroom topped with Welsh rarebit, or chicken liver pâté with red onion marmalade and toast; and mains such as seared scallops with bacon and sautéed potatoes; or oven-baked cod with smoked haddock and saffron chowder. For chicken curry and rice; steak and kidney pie; or ploughman's and baguettes, see the bar menu. Dogs are allowed downstairs.

Open all day all wk **Food** Mon-Sat 12-9.30, Sun 12-9 ⊕ FREE HOUSE ◀ Dartmoor Jail Ale & IPA, St Austell Tribute & Proper Job, Palmers. ▾ 13 **Facilities** Non-diners area ❅ (Bar Garden) ◀ Children's portions Garden ➤ Parking

OTTERY ST MARY — Map 3 SY19

The Talaton Inn

tel: 01404 822214 **Talaton EX5 2RQ**
dir: *A30 to Fairmile, then follow signs to Talaton*

Black-and-white timbered, traditional inn

This well-maintained timber-framed 16th-century inn is run by a brother and sister partnership. There is a good selection of real ales (Otter Ale, Otter Amber) and malts, and a fine collection of bar games. The regularly-changing evening blackboard menu might include beer battered calamari or seasoned whitebait; home-cooked ham with eggs and chunky chips; Cornish brie, tomato and mushroom frittata; or a choice of steaks. Lunchtime special deals are available and at Sunday lunchtimes (booking advisable), as well as the popular roast, there is also a pie and vegetarian choice. There is a patio for summer dining, plus bingo, quizzes, and themed food nights. In winter, tables must be booked for Wednesday evenings.

Open 12-3 7-11 Closed Mon **Food** Lunch Tue-Sun 12-2 Dinner Wed-Sat 7-9 Av main course £4.95-£7.25 Set menu available ⊕ FREE HOUSE ◀ Otter Ale & Amber, Sharp's Doom Bar, guest ale Ö Westons Stowford Press. **Facilities** Non-diners area ❅ (Bar Outside area) ◀ Children's menu Children's portions Outside area ➤ Parking ➤ (notice required)

PLYMTREE — Map 3 ST00

The Blacksmiths Arms

tel: 01884 277474 **EX15 2JU**
email: blacksmithsplymtree@yahoo.co.uk
dir: *From A373 (Cullompton to Honiton road) follow Plymtree signs. Pub in village centre*

Well-kept ales and locally-sourced food

Alan and Susie Carter have been at the helm for a numbers of years and the pub has become the hub of this idyllic Devon village. A traditional free house with exposed beams and log fire, it has a reputation for serving quality food using local ingredients, and is known for generous portions of classics like game pie and local steaks, as well as curries, sharing platters and fish dishes. Up to 14 well-kept local ales include Otter Amber, and there is a fine selection of wines. A beer and music festival is held in July. A large beer garden and alfresco dining area complete the picture.

Open Tue-Fri 6-11 (Sat 12-11 Sun 12-4) Closed Mon, Tue-Fri L, Sun eve **Food** Lunch Sat-Sun 12-2 Dinner Tue-Sat 6-9 ⊕ FREE HOUSE ◀ Otter Amber, St Austell Proper Job & Tribute, Sharp's Doom Bar & Atlantic Ö Thatchers Gold, Healey's Cornish Rattler. ▾ 8 **Facilities** Non-diners area ❅ (Bar Restaurant Garden) ◀ Children's menu Children's portions Play area Family room Garden ➤ Beer festival Parking WiFi ➤ (notice required)

RATTERY — Map 3 SX76

Church House Inn

tel: 01364 642220 **TQ10 9LD**
email: info@thechurchhouseinn.co.uk
dir: *1m from A38 (Exeter to Plymouth road) & 0.75m from A385 (Totnes to South Brent road)*

Centuries of conversation and hospitality

Some customers at the Church House Inn encounter the wandering spirit of a monk; fortunately for new owners, the Edwards family, he seems to be friendly. Tracing its history as far back as 1028, this venerable inn burgeons with brasses, bare beams, large fireplaces and other historic features. In the character dining room, dinner might start with spiced lamb koftas, tabbouleh salad, cucumber and mint yogurt. It might continue with roast fillet of gurnard, smoked pancetta, grilled baby gem, ratatouille and basil oil. There is a large garden and patio where you can enjoy a pint of Dartmoor Jail Ale.

Open all wk 11.30-11 (Sun 11.30-10) **Food** Lunch all wk 12-2.30 Dinner all wk 6.30-9 Restaurant menu available all wk ⊕ FREE HOUSE ◀ Dartmoor Jail Ale, Otter, guest ale Ö Thatchers Gold. ▾ 10 **Facilities** Non-diners area ❅ (Bar Garden) ◀ Children's menu Children's portions Garden ➤ Parking WiFi ➤ (notice required)

RINGMORE — Map 3 SX64

NEW The Journey's End Inn

tel: 01548 810205 **TQ7 4HL**
email: thejourneysend@btinternet.com
dir: *From Exeter take A38 towards Plymouth. Left onto A3121 signed Modbury. Left onto A379 signed Modbury. From Modbury High St follow Ringmore & St Anne's Chapel signs. In St Anne's Chapel at Old Chapel Inn (on right) turn right signed Ringmore. Inn's car park opposite church on left. Walk 200yds downhill to pub*

International food in the South Hams

A short walk from the coastal path at Ayrmer Cove, this 13th-century village inn was built by monks and the original fires are still lit during the winter months.

There are five different areas for drinkers and diners, plus a large beer garden, so there is plenty of space to enjoy local ales such as Otter Amber. Irish owner-chef Conor Heneghan worked in Australia and Thailand and his travels are reflected in dishes like crisp duck leg, hoisin sauce, cucumber, spring onion and steamed pancakes, which might be followed by charred swordfish steak, sweet potato, chilli and prawn salad.

Open 12-3 6-11 (Sat-Sun all day) Closed Mon (ex BH) **Food** Lunch Tue-Sun 12-2.30 Dinner Tue-Sun 6-8.30 Av main course £10 Restaurant menu available Tue-Sat ⊕ FREE HOUSE ◖ Otter Ale & Amber, Sharp's Doom Bar. **Facilities** Non-diners area ✿ (Bar Garden) ♦♦ Children's menu Children's portions Garden ⋒ Beer festival Cider festival Parking WiFi 🚐 (notice required)

| ROBOROUGH | Map 3 SS51 |

NEW The New Inn

tel: 01805 603247 **EX19 8SY**
email: info@thenewinnroborough.co.uk
dir: From Great Torrington take B3227 signed South Molton. Right signed Kingscott, through Kingscott to Roborough. Or from A377 (W of Portsmouth Arms) follow High Bickington & Burrington signs. At x-roads left signed Roborough. Pub on right

Excellent locally sourced food and ales

Magda and James Berry run this handsome thatched inn that has been part of daily life in this idyllic village since the 16th century. Whether you choose a spot near the log fire or out on the sunny patio in summer, this rural inn offers a friendly welcome. Local breweries and cider makers are well represented, with Teignworthy Gundog and Lilley's Merry Monkey among the favourite tipples. Local produce drives the menu, with typical dishes such as rock mussels in garlic and white wine sauce; and Elston Farm Cumberland sausages, mash and onion gravy. A beer and cider festival is held on the last weekend in September.

Open all wk 12-3 5-11 (Mon-Tue 5-11 Fri-Sat 12-11 Sun 12-10.30) **Food** Lunch Wed-Thu 12-3, Fri-Sat 12-10, Sun 12-9 Dinner Mon-Thu 6-9.30, Fri-Sat 12-10, Sun 12-9 Av main course £12.95 Set menu available ⊕ FREE HOUSE ◖ Exmoor Ale, Teignworthy Gundog, Hunter's Half Bore Ô Winkleigh Sam's, Lilley's Merry Monkey Scrumpy, Brooksy's. **Facilities** Non-diners area ✿ (Bar Outside area) ♦♦ Children's menu Children's portions Outside area ⋒ Beer festival Cider festival Parking WiFi 🚐 (notice required)

| ROCKBEARE | Map 3 SY09 |

Jack in the Green Inn ⦿⦿   PICK OF THE PUBS

tel: 01404 822240 **London Rd EX5 2EE**
email: info@jackinthegreen.uk.com
dir: M5 junct 29, A30 (dual carriageway) towards Honiton. Left onto B3184 (old A30) to Rockbeare

Top notch pub food for everyone

Empty plates, diners' contented smiles and two AA Rosettes testify to the Jack's well-deserved reputation for upmarket modern British food, but this family-friendly roadside pub also offers good West Country brews on tap. The smart interior with its low beamed rooms, soft brown leather chairs and a wood-burning stove create a contemporary pub atmosphere. In the restaurant, the simple philosophy is to serve the best seasonal Devon produce in stylish surroundings. Local artisan producers underpin chef Matthew Mason's innovative menus with punchy flavours, be it game from local shoots, or salad leaves and seasonal vegetables from growers just six miles away. A three-course 'Totally Devon' selection could start with game terrine with spiced fruit chutney and toasted brioche. Next may come slow-braised pork belly with honey and roasted butternut squash, and last but not least spiced pumpkin brûlée and stem ginger ice cream; or Sharpham Brie with pickled apples and hazelnut toasts.

Open all wk 11-3 5.30-11 (Sun 12-11) Closed 25 Dec-5 Jan **Food** Lunch Mon-Sat 12-2, Sun 12-9 Dinner Mon-Sat 6-9, Sun 12-9 Av main course £13.50 Set menu available Restaurant menu available all wk ⊕ FREE HOUSE ◖ Otter Ale & Amber, Sharp's Doom Bar, Butcombe Bitter, Hanlons Firefly & Yellow Hammer Ô Dragon Tears, Luscombe, St Georges. ♟ 12 **Facilities** Non-diners area ♦♦ Children's menu Children's portions Family room Outside area ⋒ Parking WiFi 🚐 (notice required)

| SALCOMBE | Map 3 SX73 |

The Victoria Inn

tel: 01548 842604 **Fore St TQ8 8BU**
email: info@victoriainn-salcombe.co.uk **web:** www.victoriainn-salcombe.co.uk
dir: In town centre, overlooking estuary

Friendly town pub with excellent local seafood

Tim and Liz Hore's dog-friendly pub has something unique among Salcombe's licensed premises – a large garden with sun terraces, children's play area and even chickens. Where better to sit and enjoy a warm summer evening with a drink in hand? Inside, there is a mix of traditional seating and comfy sofas, and a roaring open fire in winter. The menu is built around the owners' appreciation of the high-quality produce growing on their doorstep, both from the sea and the lush surrounding countryside. They have built close relationships with local suppliers and the pub is proud of its reputation for seasonal home-cooked food.

Open all day all wk 11.30-11 Closed 25 Dec **Food** all wk 12-9 ⊕ ST AUSTELL BREWERY ◖ Tribute, Proper Job, guest ales Ô Healey's Cornish Rattler. ♟ 20 **Facilities** Non-diners area ✿ (Bar Garden) ♦♦ Children's menu Children's portions Play area Garden ⋒ WiFi

See advert on page 150

Fore Street , Salcombe, TQ8 8BU   01548 842604   www.victoriainn-salcombe.co.uk

A genuine family-friendly pub run by Tim & Liz Hore . Tradition, quality and value are in every aspect of our business and we believe in going the extra inch, every time for every guest, welcoming every customer who walks through the door as a new friendship waiting to happen.

Our award winning menu is developed and built around our love of the fantastic produce we have right here on our doorstep - both from the sea and the lush surrounding countryside. We have built great relationships with local suppliers who know what produce is excellent as the seasons change and we change our menus accordingly. We even have a few chickens at the bottom of our garden who contribute their eggs – food doesn't get fresher than that!

The bar stocks great St Austell ales, a good selection of wines, champagnes and premium spirits with a great gin and Prosecco menu! Families are welcomed with boxes of toys and books, a play area in the garden and dogs aren't left out either with an 'A la Bark' menu just for them.

SANDFORD

Map 3 SS80

The Lamb Inn ★★★★ INN

tel: 01363 773676 **The Square EX17 4LW**
email: thelambinn@gmail.com web: www.lambinnsandford.co.uk
dir: *A377 from Exeter to Crediton. 1st right signed Sandford & Tiverton. Left, left again, up hill. 1.5m left into village square*

A thriving community local that offers a lot

Set in a sleepy Devon village, the pub's upstairs room is used as an art gallery, skittle alley, cinema, theatre, venue for open-mic nights, conferences and a meeting room for village groups. Downstairs, expect to find three log fires, candles on scrubbed tables and an imaginative chalkboard menu. Mark Hildyard has worked hard at making this 16th-century former coaching inn a cracking all-round pub. Using the best Devon produce, top-notch dishes may include oxtail tortellini, seared scallop, celeriac remoulade, red wine jus; Chinn's sausages and mash, seasonal vegetables and onion gravy; roast breast and confit leg of poussin, wild garlic gnocchi, watercress and charred leeks. Everyone is welcome, including dogs and walkers in muddy boots.

Open all day all wk 11am–11.30pm **Food** Lunch all wk 12.30-2.30 Dinner all wk 6.30-9.30 ⊕ FREE HOUSE ◀ Otter Bitter, Hanlons Yellow Hammer, Dartmoor Jail Ale & Legend, Skinner's, St Austell Proper Job ♂ Sandford Orchards. ♟ 9
Facilities Non-diners area ❀ (Bar Restaurant Garden) ♦ Children's portions Garden ⊫ Beer festival WiFi ▄ (notice required) **Rooms** 7

SHEBBEAR

Map 3 SS40

The Devil's Stone Inn

tel: 01409 281210 **EX21 5RU**
email: churst1234@btinternet.com
dir: *From Okehampton turn right opposite White Hart, follow A386 towards Hatherleigh. At rdbt outside Hatherleigh take Holsworthy road to Highampton. Just after Highampton right, follow signs to Shebbear*

A village pub with an interesting history

Reputedly one of England's most haunted pubs, The Devil's Stone Inn was a farmhouse before it became a coaching inn some 400 years ago. The pub's name comes from the village tradition of the turning the Devil's Stone (situated opposite the pub), which happens every year on 5th November. Country sports lovers use this pub as a base for their activities; it is especially a haven for fly-fishermen, with beats, some of which the pub owns, on the middle and upper Torridge. The beamed and flagstone-floored interior has several open fires. Locally sourced and home-cooked food, a selection of real ales and ciders, a games room, separate dining room and large garden complete the picture.

Open all wk 12-3 6-11 (Fri-Sun all day fr 12) **Food** Lunch all wk 12-2.30 Dinner all wk 6-9.30 Restaurant menu available all wk ⊕ FREE HOUSE ◀ St Austell Tribute, Wadworth 6X, Black Tor ♂ Healey's Cornish Rattler, Thatchers Gold.
Facilities Non-diners area ❀ (Bar Garden) ♦ Children's menu Children's portions Play area Garden ⊫ Parking WiFi ▄ (notice required)

SIDBURY

Map 3 SY19

The Hare & Hounds

tel: 01404 41760 **Putts Corner EX10 0QQ**
email: contact@hareandhounds-devon.co.uk web: www.hareandhounds-devon.co.uk
dir: *From Honiton take A375 signed Sidmouth. In approx 0.75m pub at Seaton Rd x-roads*

Whitewashed free house serving classic pub dishes

Behind the whitewashed walls of this traditional Devon free house you'll find a comfortable interior with wooden beams and winter log fires. There's also a large garden and an extension which both enjoy fantastic views down the valley to the sea at Sidmouth. Besides the daily carvery, the extensive menu features classic pub dishes and snacks. Main course options include beef lasagne and steak and kidney pudding, as well as fish dishes and vegetarian options. The permanent cask ales are brewed less than 10 miles away by the Otter Brewery. Please note, children aren't allowed in the bar area.

Open all day all wk 10am-11pm (Sun 11-10.30) Closed 25 Dec eve **Food** all wk 12-9 ⊕ FREE HOUSE ◀ Otter Bitter & Ale, St Austell Tribute, guest ales ♂ Wiscombe Suicider. **Facilities** Non-diners area ❀ (Bar Garden Outside area)
♦ Children's menu Children's portions Play area Garden Outside area ⊫ Parking WiFi

SIDMOUTH

Map 3 SY18

Blue Ball Inn

PICK OF THE PUBS

tel: 01395 514062 **Stevens Cross, Sidford EX10 9QL**
email: enquiries@blueballinnsidford.co.uk
dir: *M5 junct 30, A3052, through Sidford towards Lyme Regis, inn on left*

Family-friendly pub with a warm welcome

Postcard-pretty under its thatched roof, the 14th-century cob-and-flint Blue Ball in Sidford is popular with locals and visitors alike. Lovingly maintained, colourful and attractive gardens surround the inn. A wide selection of freshly prepared food from traditional beer battered fish and chips, and steak and kidney pudding to a wide range of fresh fish including crab, lobster, sole and mussels; in addition there are many other dishes from the regularly changing specials board. The wine list ranges from new world and more traditional choices that will suit all pockets. The real ales include local Otter Bitter, St Austell Tribute, Sharp's Doom Bar and Bass. The inn is within easy reach of the M5, A303 and Exeter, and just minutes from stunning walks inland and along the coast. Families are very welcome here.

Open all day all wk Closed 25 Dec eve **Food** Lunch all wk 12-2.30 Dinner all wk 6-9 Set menu available ⊕ PUNCH TAVERNS ◀ Otter Bitter, St Austell Tribute, Sharp's Doom Bar, Bass, guest ale ♂ Thatchers Gold. ♟ 13 **Facilities** Non-diners area ❀ (Bar Garden) ♦ Children's portions Garden Outside area ⊫ Parking WiFi ▄

SLAPTON
Map 3 SX84

The Tower Inn
PICK OF THE PUBS

See Pick of the Pubs on opposite page

SOUTH POOL
Map 3 SX74

The Millbrook Inn
PICK OF THE PUBS

tel: 01548 531581 **TQ7 2RW**
email: info@millbrookinnsouthpool.co.uk **web:** www.millbrookinnsouthpool.co.uk
dir: *A379 from Kingsbridge to Frogmore. In Frogmore right signed South Pool. 2m to village*

French country cooking meets good pub grub

This quaint white-painted 16th-century village pub is little more than a good mooring rope's throw from South Pool creek on the Salcombe estuary. No surprise then that it attracts boat-owners from all along the coast. Its compact courtyard with bench tables is to one side, while at the rear a small terrace overlooks a pretty stream and fields. Open fires warm the two traditionally decorated beamed bars, where South Hams ales such as Wild Blonde await. Menus tempt with top-notch auberge-type food prepared by a French chef using the best South Hams meats and fish. A starter of escargots sees a plate of pan-fried snails and wild mushrooms flambéed with cognac served on toasted brioche with a garlic butter sauce. Delights among the main courses may include bouillabaisse; and game – rabbit, perhaps, in the form of confit leg, liver and kidney kebab, and loin wrapped in pancetta.

Open all day all wk 12-11 (Sun 12-10.30) **Food** Lunch all wk 12-5 Dinner all wk 7-9 Av main course £18 Set menu available Restaurant menu available all wk ⊕ FREE HOUSE ◀ South Hams Pandemonium & Wild Blonde, guest ales ♂ Thatchers Heritage & Gold. **Facilities** Non-diners area ♣ (Bar Restaurant Garden) •♦ Children's portions Garden Outside area ⊼ WiFi ☰ (notice required)

SPARKWELL
Map 3 SX55

The Treby Arms ◉◉
PICK OF THE PUBS

See Pick of the Pubs on page 154

SPREYTON
Map 3 SX69

The Tom Cobley Tavern
PICK OF THE PUBS

tel: 01647 231314 **EX17 5AL**
dir: *From A30 at Whiddon Down take A3124 towards North Tawton. 1st right after services, 1st right over bridge*

Fabulous views and a huge range of ales

Close to the village green in this village of cob and thatch cottages, guests in the tree-shaded beer garden here can enjoy views across to the distant moors of northern Dartmoor. It was from this pub one day in 1802 that Thomas Cobley and his companions set forth for Widecombe Fair, an event immortalised in song; his cottage still stands in the village. The inn's unspoilt main bar has a roaring log fire, cushioned settles, and benefits from a stillage where an impressive selection of casks of Devon microbrewery beers are always on tap. Being a firmly traditional Devon pub, there are draught ciders here too, all served from the unusual thatched bar. Time-honoured hearty English fare is the mainstay of the menus, and there's a

particularly strong suite of vegetarian and vegan dishes. Mushroom, brie and cranberry Wellington; duck and cherry pie; or steak and kidney suet pudding give a flavour of the home-cooked dishes here.

Open 12-3 6-11 (Sun 12-4 7-11 Mon 6.30-10.30 Fri-Sat 12-3 6-12) Closed Mon L **Food** Lunch Tue-Sun 12-2 Dinner all wk 7-9 ⊕ FREE HOUSE ◀ Teignworthy Gundog, St Austell Tribute & Proper Job, Dartmoor Jail Ale & Legend, Plain Ales ♂ Sam's Cider, Winkleigh, Westons Stowford Press, Healey's Berry Rattler & Pear Rattler, Sandford Orchards, Gwynt y Ddraig, Lilley's. **Facilities** Non-diners area ♣ (Bar Garden Outside area) •♦ Children's menu Children's portions Garden Outside area ⊼ Parking WiFi ☰ (notice required)

STAVERTON
Map 3 SX76

Sea Trout Inn

tel: 01803 762274 **TQ9 6PA**
email: info@theseatroutinn.co.uk
dir: *From A38 take A384 towards Totnes. Follow Staverton & Sea Trout Inn sign*

Long, white-painted pub offering a modern British menu

This stunning family-run 15th-century coaching inn close to the River Dart ticks all the boxes for an authentic country pub, from the delightful Stag's Bar and stylish restaurant to the log fires and beautiful beer garden. Apart from the occasional puff of a steam train drifting across from the South Devon Railway, this village inn is the epitome of tranquillity. Your only stress might be choosing what to order from the extensive menu combining pub classics, sharing platters and daily specials with lots of local produce from the area. Wash it all down with well-kept Palmers ales or a Thatchers Gold cider.

Open all day all wk **Food** Lunch Mon-Fri 12-2, Sat 12-2.30, Sun 12-3 Dinner Mon-Thu 6-9, Fri-Sat 6-9.30, Sun 6.30-9 ⊕ PALMERS ◀ 200, Copper Ale, Best Bitter & Dorset Gold ♂ Thatchers Gold. ♀ 11 **Facilities** Non-diners area ♣ (Bar Garden) •♦ Children's menu Children's portions Garden ⊼ Parking WiFi ☰ (notice required)

STOKE FLEMING
Map 3 SX84

The Green Dragon Inn

tel: 01803 770238 **Church Rd TQ6 0PX**
email: pcrowther@btconnect.com
dir: *From A379 (Dartmouth to Kingsbridge coast road) follow brown pub sign, into Church Rd. Pub opposite church*

A haven of boating memorabilia

Opposite the village church, this South Hams pub has many seafaring connections, being only two miles from Dartmouth. Although there has been a building on this site since the 12th century, the first recorded landlord took charge in 1607. The interior is decorated in a seafaring theme with charts and sailing pictures. Local beers such as Otter and Exmoor slake the thirst of walkers, whilst the great-value menu can satisfy the largest of appetites with hearty baguettes, wild boar terrine; venison burgers; trawlerman's fish pie; Thai green curry or a West Country sirloin steak.

Open all wk 11.30-3 5.30-11 (Sun 12-3.30 6.30-10.30) Closed 25-26 Dec **Food** Lunch all wk 12-2 Dinner all wk 6.30-8.30 ⊕ HEAVITREE ◀ Otter Ale, Exmoor Ale, St Austell Tribute, guest ales ♂ Aspall, Addlestones. ♀ 10 **Facilities** Non-diners area ♣ (Bar Garden) •♦ Children's menu Children's portions Play area Garden ⊼ Parking WiFi

PICK OF THE PUBS

The Tower Inn

SLAPTON Map 3 SX84

tel: 01548 580216
Church Rd TQ7 2PN
email: towerinn@slapton.org
web: www.thetowerinn.com
dir: *Exit A379 S of Dartmouth, left at Slapton Sands*

West Country ales and seasonal menus

Tucked up a narrow driveway behind cottages and the church in this unspoilt Devon village, the ancient ivy-clad tower (which gives this charming 14th-century inn its name) looms hauntingly above the pub. It is all that remains of the old College of Chantry Priests — the pub was built to accommodate the artisans who constructed the monastic college. Six hundred years on and this truly atmospheric village pub continues to welcome guests and the appeal, other than its peaceful location, is the excellent range of real ales on tap and the eclectic choice of modern pub grub prepared from locally sourced ingredients, which include smoked fish from Dartmouth, quality Devon-reared beef, and fresh fish and crab landed at Brixham. Expect hearty lunchtime sandwiches alongside the ploughman's platter and mussels in cider cream broth. A typical evening meal may take in Devon crab gnocchi, tenderstem broccoli, spinach and crab bisque; or

pan-roasted pigeon, celeriac, apple with walnut dressing; followed by 12-hour braised ox cheek, butternut squash, onion, wild mushroom and kale; or bouillabaisse with mussels, clams, tiger prawns, saffron potato, fish of the day and aïoli. Round off with pear and Amaretti tart and wash down with a pint of Otter Bitter or St Austell Proper Job. Stone walls, open fires, low beams, scrubbed oak tables and flagstone floors characterise the welcoming interior, the atmosphere enhanced at night with candlelit tables. There's a splendid landscaped rear garden, perfect for summer alfresco meals. Visitors exploring Slapton Ley Nature Reserve and Slapton Sands should venture inland to seek out this ancient inn.

Open 12-3 6-11 (Sun 6-10.30) Closed 1st 2wks Jan, Sun eve in winter
Food Lunch all wk 12-2.30 Dinner all wk 6.30-9.30 ⊞ FREE HOUSE ◀ Butcombe Bitter, Otter Bitter, St Austell Proper Job, The South Hams Devon Pride ♂ Addlestones, Sharp's Orchard.
Facilities Non-diners area ✿ (Bar Restaurant Garden) ♦ Children's menu Children's portions Garden ⩙ Beer festival Parking WiFi 🚌

PICK OF THE PUBS

The Treby Arms ✿✿

SPARKWELL Map 3 SX55

tel: 01752 837363
1 Newton Row PL7 5DD
email: trebyarms@hotmail.co.uk
web: www.thetrebyarms.co.uk

Village pub that punches above its weight

This once humble, 17th-century, end-of-terrace local has successfully become a destination dining pub due to the initiative and hard work of chef-patron Anton Piotrowski and his wife Clare. Anton's achievement as a BBC *MasterChef* in 2012 has undoubtedly helped to ramp up interest, so booking is essential if you want to experience his inspired cooking. But first the bar, where Dartmoor Jail Ale shares counter space with beers from St Austell and Hunter's, and Symonds and Thatchers ciders. The restaurant's achievement of two AA Rosettes acknowledges the passion Anton and his staff have for their food, all, it goes without saying, prepared, cooked and presented to a very high standard. They use fresh seasonal produce, including locally-caught fish, estate game and village allotment vegetables, for the daily carte and set menus. A typical three-course option might be smoked haddock, parsnip purée, confit egg yolk and curried cornflakes; Dover sole with tartare

beurre blanc, pickled cockles and potato purée; and sticky toffee pudding, butter beer, caramelised banana and honeycomb ice cream. Turn to the carte for Cornish red mullet with chorizo jam, parsley emulsion, crispy capers, and honey-glazed duck breast with triple-cooked chips, game cabbage ball and duck gravy. As it says on the menu 'a meal isn't complete without a dessert', so you could try the apple parfait with cider syrup, Granny Smith apple, apple sorbet and salted toffee apple purée. Alternatively, there's a cheeseboard, on which Sharpham Rustic from Totnes is one choice. Anton also puts together five- and 11-course taster menus with wines.

Open Mon-Thu 12-3 6-11 (Fri-Sun 12-11) Closed 25-26 Dec & 1-2 Jan **Food** Lunch Mon-Thu 12-2, Fri-Sun 12-9 Dinner Mon-Thu 6-9, Fri-Sun 12-9 Set menu available Restaurant menu available all wk ⊕ FREE HOUSE ◀ St Austell Tribute, Hunter's, Dartmoor Jail Ale & IPA ♂ Thatchers, Symonds, Rekorderlig. **Facilities** Non-diners area ✿ (Bar Outside area) ♦♦ Children's portions Outside area 🚗 Parking WiFi

STOKENHAM
Map 3 SX84

NEW The Tradesman's Arms

tel: 01548 580996 **TQ7 2SZ**
email: thebar@thetradesmansarms.com
dir: *Signed from A379 between Kingsbridge & Dartmouth*

Good food in one of Devon's most picturesque villages

Formerly a brewhouse and cottages, this part-thatched 14th-century pub stands in the pretty village of Stokenham, just one mile from stunning Slapton Sands. Tables in the beer garden overlooking the village green and church are highly prized in summer, with a log-burning fire warming the beamed bar in colder months. Local ales such as Otter keep the drinkers happy, whilst bar meals and sandwiches are supplemented by a full menu that might start with pan-fried wood pigeon breast, carrot slaw, redcurrant gel and red wine jus followed by Cajun-spiced lamb rack with pea and chickpea falafel.

Open all wk 11-3 6-11 **Food** Lunch all wk 12-2 Dinner all wk 6-9 Av main course £11 Restaurant menu available all wk ⊕ FREE HOUSE ◀ Otter Ale, St Austell Tribute. ♥ 8 **Facilities** Non-diners area ✿ (Bar Garden) ♦ Children's menu Children's portions Garden ⌱ Parking WiFi ▥ (notice required)

TAVISTOCK
Map 3 SX47

The Cornish Arms

tel: 01822 612145 **15-16 West St PL19 8AN**
email: info@thecornisharmstavistock.co.uk
dir: *Phone for detailed directions*

Cosy and welcoming pub on the edge of Dartmoor

Historically the last coaching inn before reaching Cornwall, The Cornish Arms is run by husband and wife team John and Emma Hooker. Whether inside the modern but cosy interior or out in the garden, guests will find a wide-ranging and unpretentious menu of pub favourites, from roast loin of venison, pork belly, parsnip and spiced prune; to blue cheese and walnut tart, soft poached egg and new potatoes. Round things off with buttermilk pannacotta or rhubarb trifle. The bar is well stocked with ales including St Austell's Trelawny and ciders such as Cornish Rattler, and the real ale and cider festival in August is a must-attend occasion for visitors.

Open all day all wk **Food** Lunch Mon-Sat 12-6, Sun 12-3 Dinner Mon-Sat 6-9.30, Sun 6-9 Av main course £14 ⊕ ST AUSTELL ◀ Tribute, Proper Job & Trelawny ♂ Healey's Cornish Rattler, Sandford Orchards Devon Mist. **Facilities** Non-diners area ✿ (Bar Garden Outside area) ♦ Children's menu Children's portions Garden Outside area ⌱ Beer festival Cider festival Parking WiFi ▥ (notice required)

Peter Tavy Inn

tel: 01822 810348 **Peter Tavy PL19 9NN**
email: chris@wording.freeserve.co.uk
dir: *From Tavistock take A386 towards Okehampton. In 2m right to Peter Tavy*

Dartmoor inn recommended for its pies

It is thought this inn was originally built in the 15th century as a Devon longhouse for the stonemasons rebuilding the village church. On the western flanks of Dartmoor, it is likely that it became a pub by the early 17th century and a further floor was added. It is now as much a draw for its range of local real ales and ciders as it is for its food, much of it sourced locally. The pies are popular main dishes, but other choices could be venison casserole with Stilton dumpling; chicken curry; lamb rump with mint and gooseberry gravy; and grey mullet fillet with prawn and saffron risotto.

Open all wk 12-3 6-11 (Sun 12-3 6-10.30); all day Etr-Autumn Closed 25 Dec **Food** Lunch all wk 12-2 Dinner all wk 6.30-9 Av main course £10.95 ⊕ FREE HOUSE ◀ Dartmoor Jail Ale, Branscombe Vale Summa This, Tavy Ideal Pale Ale ♂ Winkleigh Sam's Poundhouse Dry & Crisp. ♥ 9 **Facilities** Non-diners area ✿ (Bar Restaurant Garden) ♦ Children's menu Children's portions Garden ⌱ Parking WiFi

THURLESTONE
Map 3 SX64

The Village Inn

tel: 01548 563525 **TQ7 3NN**
email: enquiries@thurlestone.co.uk
dir: *Take A379 from Plymouth towards Kingsbridge, at Bantham rdbt take B3197, right signed Thurlestone, 2.5m*

Minutes from the beach and South West Coastal Path

Recycling came naturally to the 16th-century builders of The Village Inn, for they used timbers salvaged from wrecked Spanish Armada warships. Run by the Grose family, who also own the nearby Thurlestone Hotel, this inn's interior is smart with traditional touches. The menu offers freshly prepared sandwiches and salads; signature dishes such as West Country kedgeree; pub classics including scampi, chips and peas; and daily blackboard specials. Palmers Best, Doom Bar and guest ales are on tap. Children and dogs are welcome. Live entertainment is arranged throughout the year.

Open all wk 11.30-3 6-11.30 (Sat-Sun, summer & school holidays all day) **Food** Lunch Mon-Fri 12-2.30, Sat-Sun 12-9 Dinner Mon-Fri 6-9, Sat-Sun 12-9 ⊕ FREE HOUSE ◀ Palmers Best Bitter, Sharp's Doom Bar, guest ale ♂ Heron Valley, Thatchers, Rekorderlig. **Facilities** Non-diners area ✿ (Bar Restaurant Outside area) ♦ Children's menu Children's portions Outside area ⌱ Parking WiFi ▥ (notice required)

TIPTON ST JOHN
Map 3 SY09

The Golden Lion
PICK OF THE PUBS

See Pick of the Pubs on page 156

TOPSHAM
Map 3 SX98

Bridge Inn
PICK OF THE PUBS

tel: 01392 873862 **Bridge Hill EX3 0QQ**
email: tom@cheffers.co.uk
dir: *M5 junct 30 follow Sidmouth signs, in approx 400yds right at rdbt onto A376 towards Exmouth. In 1.8m cross mini rdbt. Right at next mini rdbt to Topsham. 1.2m, cross River Clyst. Inn on right*

True brewing heritage with royal approval

This 'museum with beer' is substantially 16th century, although its constituent parts vary considerably in age. Most of the fabric is local stone, while the old brewhouse at the rear is traditional Devon cob. Four generations of the same family have run it since great grandfather William Gibbings arrived in 1897, and it remains eccentrically and gloriously old fashioned. Usually around 10 real ales from local and further-flung breweries are served straight from their casks, the actual line-up varying by the week. There are no lagers and only a few wines, two from a local organic vineyard. Traditional, freshly prepared lunchtime bar food includes granary ploughman's, pork pies, veggie or meat pasties, and sandwiches, all made with local ingredients. Queen Elizabeth II visited in 1998; it is believed this is the only time she has officially stepped inside an English pub.

Open all wk 12-2 6-10.30 (Fri-Sat 12-2 6-11 Sun 12-2 7-10.30) **Food** Lunch all wk 12-2 ⊕ FREE HOUSE ◀ Branscombe Vale Branoc, Adnams Broadside, Exe Valley, Hanlons, Teignworthy, Jollyboat Plunder. **Facilities** Non-diners area ✿ (Bar Garden) ♦ Garden ⌱ Parking **Notes** ⊛

PICK OF THE PUBS

The Golden Lion

TIPTON ST JOHN   Map 3 SY09

tel: 01404 812881 **EX10 0AA**
email: info@goldenliontipton.co.uk
web: www.goldenliontipton.co.uk
dir: *Phone for detailed directions*

Mediterranean slant to excellent menus

Michelle and Francois Teissier have been at the helm of this welcoming Devon village pub for over a decade. So many things contribute to its traditional feel – the low wooden beams and stone walls, the winter log fire, the art-deco prints and Tiffany lamps, not to mention the paintings by Devonian and Cornish artists. And there's the bar, of course, where locally brewed Otter ales are the order of the day. Chef-patron Franky (as everyone calls him) trained in classical French cooking at a prestigious establishment in the Loire Valley, a grounding that accounts today for his rustic French, Mediterranean and British menus. Their delights may include home-smoked duck salad with onion marmalade; chunky fish soup with rouille and croutons; crevettes with garlic butter; moules frites; steak frites; escargots de Bourgogne; magret de canard; and crayfish salad with lime and garlic dressing. Given that the genteel seaside town of Sidmouth is just down the road, the seafood specials depend totally on that day's catch – cod, hake and sea bass are all

candidates. Tempting white and granary bread sandwiches are filled with fresh Lyme Bay crab, mature cheddar or home-cooked ham. The Sunday lunch menu offers roast West Country beef with Yorkshire pudding; roast lamb with mint sauce; and winter vegetable crêpe. As Franky sums up: 'When Michelle and I took over in 2003, our aim was to create a friendly, inviting village pub offering great value, high-quality food made from the freshest ingredients; with our combination of rustic French dishes and traditional British food with a Mediterranean twist, there's something for everyone!' Outside there is a grassy beer garden and walled terrace area with tumbling grapevines.

Open 12-2.30 6-11 (Sun 12-2.30)
Closed Sun eve **Food** Lunch all wk 12-2
Dinner Mon-Sat 6.30-8.30 ⊕ HEAVITREE
🛢 Bass, Otter Ale & Bitter. 🍷 12
Facilities Non-diners area 👫 Children's menu Children's portions Garden 🎋
Parking 🚌 (notice required)

TOPSHAM *continued*

The Globe

tel: 01392 873471 **34 Fore St EX3 0HR**
email: theglobe@staustellbrewery.co.uk
dir: *M5 junct 30, A379 to Topsham. At rdbt take B3182. In Topsham at mini rdbt straight ahead into Fore St. Pub approx 500yds on left*

16th-century coaching inn in appealing estuary town

Rich textures and colours meet the eye on entering this sympathetically updated old inn, close to the River Exe. You can enjoy a pint of Tribute in the comfortable fire-warmed bar, while the wood-panelled Elizabethan restaurant makes excellent use of locally grown, reared or caught ingredients. There are chargrilled West Country rump and fillet steaks on offer; as well as dishes like pan-seared sea bass fillet, basil butter, warm salad Niçoise, and tomato jelly; or oven-roasted pork belly with apple fondant, black pudding, buttered mash and green beans. Daily-changing specials make the most of West Country produce too.

Open all day all wk **Food** all day ⊕ ST AUSTELL ◀ Tribute, Proper Job & Trelawny ♂ Thatchers Gold. ▼ 10 **Facilities** Non-diners area ♣ (Bar Outside area) ♦ Children's menu Children's portions Outside area ⊼ Parking WiFi ▭ (notice required)

TORCROSS | Map 3 SX84

Start Bay Inn

tel: 01548 580553 **TQ7 2TQ**
email: clair@startbayinn.co.uk
dir: *Between Dartmouth & Kingsbridge on A379*

Ancient pub serving the very freshest seafood

Located on the beach and with a freshwater reserve on its other side, the patio of this 14th-century inn overlooks the sea. The fishermen working from Start Bay deliver their catch direct to the kitchen; so does a local crabber, who leaves his catch at the back door to be cooked by the pub. The former landlord (father of landladies Clair and Gail) continues to dive for scallops. Be in no doubt therefore about the freshness of the seafood on the specials board. Look also for locally sourced steaks, burgers from the local butcher, and Salcombe Dairy ice creams. Ploughman's, sandwiches and jackets are also available.

Open all day all wk 11.30-11 **Food** Lunch all wk 11.30-2.15 Dinner all wk 6-9.30 winter, 6-10 summer, all day in holidays Av main course £10 ⊕ HEAVITREE ◀ Otter Ale & Bitter, St Austell Tribute & Trelawny, guest ale ♂ Heron Valley, Addlestones. ▼ 8 **Facilities** Non-diners area ♦ Children's menu Children's portions Family room Garden ⊼ Parking WiFi

TORQUAY | Map 3 SX96

Cary Arms ★★★★★ INN | PICK OF THE PUBS

tel: 01803 327110 **Babbacombe Beach TQ1 3LX**
email: enquiries@caryarms.co.uk **web:** www.caryarms.co.uk
dir: *On entering Teignmouth, at bottom of hill at lights, right signed Torquay/A379. Cross river. At mini rdbt follow Babbacombe signs. Pass Babbacombe Model Village, through lights, left into Babbacombe Downs Rd, left into Beach Rd*

Beachside inn that has it all

Right on the beach, the whitewashed Cary Arms is a real find in Babbacombe Bay. This 'boutique inn' is so much more than just a pub; unwind in the beamed bar with its original stone walls, perhaps with a pint of Otter Ale in hand, contemplating the stunning views across the bay; stay in one of the luxury sea-facing bedrooms; and sample the delicious food from the daily-changing menu. The watchwords in the kitchen are freshness and seasonality, underpinned by a respect for local ingredients. Pan-fried Brixham scallops, pea purée and crispy Parma ham might be followed by Dunterton Farm steak, Otter Ale and mushroom pie, dauphinoise potatoes and red wine jus; and trio of Gribbles sausages with mash and red onion jus. If it's a glorious summer's day, eat in the terraced gardens leading to the water's edge.

Open all wk 12-4 6-11 **Food** Lunch all wk 12-3 Dinner all wk 6.30-9 Restaurant menu available all wk ⊕ FREE HOUSE ◀ Otter Ale, Bays Topsail, Hunter's Devon Dreamer ♂ Sandford Orchards Devon Mist & Devon Red. ▼ 11
Facilities Non-diners area ♣ (Bar Restaurant Garden) ♦ Children's menu Children's portions Family room Garden ⊼ WiFi **Rooms** 12

TOTNES | Map 3 SX86

The Durant Arms | PICK OF THE PUBS

tel: 01803 732240 **Ashprington TQ9 7UP**
email: info@durantarms.co.uk
dir: *From Totnes take A381 towards Kingsbridge, 1m, left for Ashprington*

Village free house high above the River Dart

A 1725-built village pub that goes from strength to strength after its relaunch a couple of years ago. The stylish bar 'in all its solid-oak glory' has a wood-burning stove and the original stone-flag floor — here you'll find West Country ales and ciders, and award-winning Luscombe organic soft drinks and wines from Sharpham Vineyard just down the hill (tours are available). Ingredients sourced from in and around Totnes appear on a seasonal menu listing home-cooked dishes such as seared wood pigeon breast, pickled samphire and red wine reduction; mackerel fillets with warm tomato, shallot and potato salad; and grass-fed 8oz sirloin and triple cooked chips. Waving the flag for the desserts section might be sticky toffee and port pudding, toffee sauce and vanilla ice cream; or chocolate and rum marquise with rhubarb sauce. Simple snacks, sandwiches and salads are available at lunchtime. Doors from the dining room lead to a sheltered courtyard.

Open 11-3 6-11 Closed Mon (out of season) **Food** Lunch Tue-Sat 12.30-2.30, Sun 12-3 Dinner Tue-Sat 6-9 Set menu available ⊕ FREE HOUSE ◀ Noss Beer Works, Otter, guest ales ♂ Sandford Orchards Devon Red. ▼ 12 **Facilities** Non-diners area ♣ (Bar Restaurant Outside area) ♦ Children's menu Children's portions Outside area ⊼ Beer festival WiFi ▭ (notice required)

TOTNES *continued*

Royal Seven Stars Hotel

tel: 01803 862125 **The Plains TQ9 5DD**
email: enquiry@royalsevenstars.co.uk **web:** www.royalsevenstars.co.uk
dir: *From A382 signed Totnes, left at 'Dartington' rdbt. Through lights towards town centre, through next rdbt, pass Morrisons car park on left. 200yds on right*

Town centre favourite

This Grade II listed property in the heart of Totnes has three character bars and a grand ballroom. The champagne bar, an addition to the TQ9 brasserie, is where bubbly is served by the glass or bottle from 5pm onwards, along with cocktails and wines. Excellent local brews and ciders are always on tap. Quality food at affordable prices is another strength – expect the likes of herb-crusted lamb rump, butternut squash purée and roasted root veg; truffle-infused tagliatelle with wild mushroom and parmesan sauce; pan-roasted sea bass with orange braised fennel, roasted chicory and fondant potatoes; and a choice of steaks from the grill.

Open all day all wk **Food** all wk 11-9.30 Set menu available Restaurant menu available Mon-Sat ⊕ FREE HOUSE ◀ Sharp's Doom Bar, Bays Gold, Jail Ale, guest ales Ď Thatchers, Orchard's, Ashridge. ♟ 26 **Facilities** Non-diners area ❖ (Bar Outside area) ♦️ Children's menu Children's portions Family room Outside area ♬ Beer festival Cider festival Parking WiFi

Steam Packet Inn

tel: 01803 863880 **St Peter's Quay TQ9 5EW**
email: steampacket@buccaneer.co.uk
dir: *Exit A38 towards Plymouth, 18m. A384 to Totnes, 6m. Left at mini rdbt, pass Morrisons on left, over mini rdbt, 400yds on left*

Popular inn on the River Dart

Named after the passenger, cargo and mail steamers that once plied the Dart, this riverside pub (alongside which you can moor your boat) offers great views, particularly from the conservatory restaurant and heated waterside patio, where there is plenty of seating. A real log fire warms the bar in the colder months. The choices at lunch and dinner might include chicken liver and pistachio terrine with apple and fig chutney; sloe gin-cured salmon, beetroot and walnut salad and horseradish cream; beef bourguignon, creamed mash and fine beans; and Thai fish curry, plus daily fish specials on the blackboard. Look out for the three-day beer festival in mid-May, occasional live music and summer barbecues. A change of hands.

Open all day all wk **Food** Lunch Mon-Fri 12-2.30, Sat 12-3, Sun 12-8 Dinner Mon-Sat 6-9.30, Sun 12-8 ⊕ FREE HOUSE/BUCCANEER ◀ Sharp's Doom Bar, Dartmoor Jail Ale, guest ale Ď Westons Stowford Press & GL, Ashridge. ♟ 11
Facilities Non-diners area ❖ (Bar Garden) ♦️ Children's menu Garden ♬ Beer festival Parking WiFi ▭ (notice required)

The White Hart Bar & Restaurant PICK OF THE PUBS

tel: 01803 847111 **Dartington Hall TQ9 6EL**
email: bookings@dartingtonhall.com
dir: *A38 onto A384 towards Totnes. Turn at Dartington church into Dartington Hall Estate*

Focal point on an 880-acre estate

Surrounded by landscaped gardens and leafy woodland paths, the White Hart is part of the splendid 14th-century Dartington Hall, home of a famous arts trust. Ancient tapestries, open fires, flagstones, Gothic chandeliers and limed oak settles characterise the interior. Devonshire and Cornish real ales and Dartington's own cider are available in the bar; outside there's a patio. Starters on Anuj Thakur's menu include line-caught mackerel escabeche; Exmouth mussels; and Vulscombe goats' cheese. Further local sourcing is evident from mains such as Devon lamb rump with polenta, charred courgette and gazpacho fondue; Salcombe and Dartmouth-reared pork with salsify, ham hock bon bon and toasted-nut muesli; and roasted butternut with wild mushrooms and Sharpham cheese. Desserts are few, but delicious nonetheless – chocolate mousse with Cointreau sorbet; glazed lemon tart with clotted cream; roast pineapple with Breton sablé biscuit; and sticky toffee pudding with honeycomb ice cream. Curries are served every Thursday night.

Open all day all wk 12-11 **Food** Lunch all wk 12-3 Dinner all wk 5.30-9 Av main course £15 Set menu available ⊕ FREE HOUSE ◀ St Austell Tribute & Proper Job, Hunter's Elmhirst, guest ale Ď Ashridge Dartington Gold, Sandford Orchards Devon Red. ♟ 18 **Facilities** Non-diners area ♦️ Children's menu Children's portions Garden Outside area ♬ Parking WiFi ▭ (notice required)

TRUSHAM Map 3 SX88

Cridford Inn PICK OF THE PUBS

tel: 01626 853694 **TQ13 ONR**
email: reservations@vanillapod-cridfordinn.com
dir: *From A38 exit at junct for Teign Valley, right, follow Trusham signs for 4m*

Historic pub near Dartmoor with great food

Over a thousand years of history are packed into the rough stone walls and thatched roof of this heritage gem of a pub, right down to the medieval masons' marks still visible above the bar. Find a seat on the terrace beneath mature trees for views over the Teign Valley. You can eat in either the bar, where Teignworthy is one of the local brewery's showcased, or the popular Vanilla Pod restaurant, where food with an excellent local pedigree and seasonal flavours delights locals and visitors alike. Start with Tregida smoked salmon and pickled beetroot, or River Teign mussels poached in dry white wine, garlic, onion, tarragon and cream; follow with rabbit pie; honey-baked ham with free-range eggs and chunky chips; or classic chilli con carne with basmati and coriander rice. Home-made desserts include raspberry marshmallow cheesecake or steamed lemon and golden syrup sponge pudding with crème anglaise.

Open all wk 11-3 6.15-11 (Sat 11-11 Sun 12-10.30) **Food** Lunch Mon-Fri 12-2.30, Sat & Sun (Mar-Sep) all day, Sun (Oct-Feb) 12-3 Dinner all wk 7-9.30 ⊕ FREE HOUSE ◀ Sharp's Doom Bar, Teignworthy, guest ales Ď South West Orchards. ♟ 10 **Facilities** Non-diners area ❖ (Bar Garden Outside area) ♦️ Children's menu Children's portions Family room Garden Outside area ♬ Parking WiFi ▭ (notice required)

PICK OF THE PUBS

The Digger's Rest

WOODBURY SALTERTON Map 3 SY08

tel: 01395 232375 **EX5 1PQ**
email: bar@diggersrest.co.uk
web: www.diggersrest.co.uk
dir: *2.5m from A3052. Signed from Westpoint Showground*

Picturesque thatched pub offering the best of seasonal produce

The Digger's Rest has been welcoming drinkers for more than 500 years. This pretty free house is just a few minutes' drive from the Exeter junction of the M5, and stands in the delightful east Devon village of Woodbury Salterton. Originally a cider house, its vintage can be identified from the thatched roof, thick stone and cob walls, heavy beams and log fire. These days, choice on the bar is much wider but real cider is still well represented by Westons and Symonds. Real ales feature Otter Ale from Devon with guest appearances of other West Country brews such as Exeter Avocet. Wine fans will appreciate the list created by the independent wine merchant, Tanners of Shrewsbury. The menus make the best of seasonal produce, with local sourcing playing a big role in freshness and quality control, and English and West Country organic produce used wherever possible. The kitchen is also committed to supporting farmers who practise good husbandry. Menus feature fish landed at Brixham and Looe, West Country beef hung for 21 days and pork from a farm just up the road. As well as the main menu there is a blackboard which features dishes created from prime cuts or rarer seasonal ingredients. Start perhaps with crispy whole camembert, seasonal chutney, crusty ciabatta, walnut and rocket salad; or smoked mackerel and dill fish cakes, lemon mayonnaise and crispy kale; before moving on to crispy Creedy Carver duck leg, Savoy cabbage and bacon, creamy mash and red wine jus; beer-battered cod fillet, chunky chips and garden peas; or potato and garlic gnocchi, tomato sauce, spinach, pesto and goats' cheese. It's worth timing a visit for the May beer and cider festival.

Open all wk 11-3 5.30-11 (Sat 11-11

Sun noon-10.30pm) **Food** Lunch all wk 12-2.15 Dinner all wk 6-9 Av main course £12 Set menu available ⌑ FREE HOUSE ◖ Otter Ale, Hanlons Yellow Hammer, Exeter Avocet, Hunter's Crack Shot ⌒ Westons & Stowford Press, Symonds. ♟ 10 **Facilities** Non-diners area ❧ (Bar Restaurant Garden) ❧ Children's menu & portions Garden ㅈ Beer & cider festival Parking WiFi ⛟ (notice required)

TUCKENHAY
Map 3 SX85

The Maltsters Arms

tel: 01803 732350 **TQ9 7EQ**
email: maltsters@tuckenhay.com
dir: *A381 from Totnes towards Kingsbridge. 1m, at hill top turn left, follow signs to Tuckenhay, 3m*

Arrive by road or river at this waterside pub and restaurant

A white-painted, 18th-century inn standing just where tidal Bow Creek tapers to an end. Predictably, it was once a malthouse, malt being one of many commodities handled on the wide quay, now a lovely place to sit with a pint of Otter or Bays Topsail and admire the steep wooded river banks. Dine in the restaurant overlooking the creek, in the bar, or the fire-warmed Dart Cabin on seasonal, locally sourced home-smoked fish and shellfish; Exmoor venison; or Creedy Carver duck breast. To finish a meal, try the West Country cheeses. Events include an annual beer festival, live music and winter quizzes.

Open all day all wk Mon-Thu & Sun 9am-11pm (Fri-Sat 9am-mdnt) **Food** Lunch Mon-Fri 12-2.30, Sat-Sun all day (summer all wk all day) Dinner Mon-Fri 6-9, Sat-Sun all day (summer all wk all day) ⊕ FREE HOUSE ◀ Otter Ale, Bays Topsail, guest ale ☍ Thatchers Gold & Somerset Haze. �images10 **Facilities** Non-diners area ♥ (Bar Restaurant Garden) ♦ Children's menu Children's portions Garden ♒ Beer festival Parking WiFi

TYTHERLEIGH
Map 4 ST30

The Tytherleigh Arms

tel: 01460 220214 **EX13 7BE**
email: tytherleigharms@gmail.com
dir: *Between Chard & Axminster on A358*

Local produce at a smart 16th-century inn

This 16th-century coaching inn on the borders of Devon, Dorset and Somerset still retains plenty of original features, including beamed ceilings and huge fires, which make for a lovely setting if you are popping in for a pint of Branoc ale, or making a beeline for the daily-changing menu. Local produce drives the menu, whether it's tenderloin of pork with caramelised apple, white onion purée, charred baby leeks, fondant potato and black pudding; or fillet of gurnard with smoked salmon and pea hash, horseradish cream and poached egg. If there's room, have a go at lemon posset or steamed ginger pudding.

Open 11-4 6-12 Closed 25 Dec, Sun eve winter **Food** Lunch Mon-Fri 12-2.30, Sat 12-3, Sun 12-4 Dinner Mon-Fri 6-9.30, Sat 6-10, Sun 6-9 ⊕ FREE HOUSE ◀ Otter Ale & Amber, Branscombe Vale Branoc ☍ Thatchers Gold, Orchard Pig Truffler, Perry's Barn Owl. ♦ 10 **Facilities** Non-diners area ♥ (Bar Garden) ♦ Children's portions Garden ♒ Parking WiFi

Looking for a beer or cider festival?
Check our listings at the end of this guide

WIDECOMBE IN THE MOOR
Map 3 SX77

The Rugglestone Inn
PICK OF THE PUBS

tel: 01364 621327 **TQ13 7TF**
email: enquiries@rugglestoneinn.co.uk
dir: *From village centre take road by church towards Venton. Inn down hill on left*

Pretty, wisteria-clad Dartmoor pub

Originally a cottage, this unaltered Grade II listed building was converted to an inn around 1832. Set in the picturesque village of Widecombe in the Moor, the pub is surrounded by tranquil moorland and streams; the Rugglestone stream rises behind the pub, and Widecombe's famous church acts as a beacon for ramblers and riders seeking out the inn's rural location. Cosy little rooms and comforting wood-burners encourage appreciative visitors and locals alike to tarry awhile and sup ales such as Dartmoor Legend; farmhouse ciders such as Ashridge are stillaged behind the snug bar and tapped straight from the barrel. The filling fare is a decent mix of classic pub staples and savoury dishes, keeping the cold away in winter or fulfilling a summer evening's promise in the streamside garden. The Rugglestone platter of ham, cheddar and Stilton served with salad, pickles, home-made coleslaw and crusty bread is a great Dartmoor experience.

Open all wk Mon-Thu 11.30-3 6-11.30 Fri 11.30-3 5-12 Sat 11.30am-mdnt Sun & BH 12-11 **Food** Lunch all wk 12-2 Dinner all wk 6.30-9 ⊕ FREE HOUSE ◀ Teignworthy Rugglestone Moor, Dartmoor Legend, guest ales ☍ Ashton Press, Ashridge, Hunt's. ♦ 10 **Facilities** Non-diners area ♥ (Bar Restaurant Garden) ♦ Children's menu Children's portions Garden ♒ Parking ▭ (notice required)

WOODBURY SALTERTON
Map 3 SY08

The Digger's Rest
PICK OF THE PUBS

See Pick of the Pubs on page 159

YEALMPTON
Map 3 SX55

Rose & Crown
PICK OF THE PUBS

tel: 01752 880223 **Market St PL8 2EB**
email: info@theroseandcrown.co.uk
dir: *Phone for detailed directions*

Classy dining among enticing countryside

Close to the pretty Yealm Estuary and the seductive wilderness of southern Dartmoor, foodies make a bee-line here to experience Simon Warner's modern British cooking. There's a cool, airy, bistro-like atmosphere in this classy dining pub at the heart of the South Hams. Village locals and beer-lovers can sample beers from the St Austell Brewery stable, perhaps in the walled courtyard garden with its fishpond and fountain, but it is as a destination dining pub that the Rose & Crown shines out. The menu proffers traditional classics with an extra touch of class, allowing the kitchen's focus on quality and local supply to be maintained. A choice of pub favourites such as curry of the day or home-made burger runs alongside starters such as Yealmpton artichoke soup; or pan-fried South Devon scallops. Mains include five-spiced crispy duck leg with egg noodles; and blue cheese and walnut tart.

Open all day all wk **Food** Lunch all wk 12-2.30 Dinner all wk 6.30-9.30 Set menu available Restaurant menu available all wk ⊕ ST AUSTELL BREWERY ◀ Tribute & Proper Job, Bath Ales Gem, Dartmoor Jail Ale ☍ Thatchers Gold, Healey's Cornish Rattler. **Facilities** Non-diners area ♥ (Bar Garden) ♦ Children's menu Children's portions Garden ♒ Parking WiFi ▭ (notice required)

DORSET

ASKERSWELL
Map 4 SY59

The Spyway Inn ★★★★ INN

tel: 01308 485250 **DT2 9EP**
email: spywaytime@hotmail.com web: www.spyway-inn.co.uk
dir: *From A35 follow Askerswell sign, then follow Spyway Inn sign*

Oak beams, cask ales and stunning views

Handy for Dorchester and Bridport, this old beamed country inn offers magnificent views of the glorious Dorset countryside. Close to West Bay, who's memorable cliffs have been made even more memorable by two series of *Broadchurch*, the pub boasts a landscaped beer garden with a pond, stream and children's play area. It all makes for a lovely setting to enjoy a glass of Otter Ale and sample locally sourced, home-made fare like slow-roast belly pork with cider sauce; pan-fried fillets of sea bass with Savoy cabbage and bacon; or steak and ale pie. Accommodation is also available.

Open all wk 12-3 6-close Food Lunch all wk 12-3 Dinner all wk 6-9 ⊕ FREE HOUSE ◑ Otter Ale, Bitter ♂ West Milton, Kingcombe Cider. ▾ 10 Facilities Non-diners area ◕ Children's menu Children's portions Play area Garden ⋒ Parking WiFi ➡ (notice required) Rooms 3

BOURTON
Map 4 ST73

The White Lion Inn

tel: 01747 840866 **High St SP8 5AT**
email: office@whitelionbourton.co.uk
dir: *Off A303, opposite B3092 to Gillingham*

Beautiful inn with popular ales and dishes

Dating from 1723, the White Lion is a beautiful stone-built, creeper-clad Dorset inn. The bar is cosy with beams, flagstones and an open fire. Here you will find a range of real beers and ciders, and menus drawing on the wealth of quality local produce. Starters range from devilled kidneys on toast, to Jackson's of Newton Abbot smoked haddock with spinach and creamy gruyère sauce. Select a main course from the classics list, such as Barclay's Butchers stack: Cumberland sausage, faggot and bacon with mash and gravy; or the half-pound cheese burger with chips and salad.

Open all day all wk Food Lunch Mon-Sat 12-2, Sun 12-4 Dinner all wk 6-9 ⊕ FREE HOUSE ◑ Otter Amber, St Austell Tribute ♂ Thatchers, Rich's Farmhouse. Facilities Non-diners area ◕ (Bar Restaurant Garden) ◕ Children's menu Children's portions Garden ⋒ Parking WiFi ➡ (notice required)

BRIDPORT
Map 4 SY49

The Shave Cross Inn ★★★★★ INN   PICK OF THE PUBS

tel: 01308 868358 **Shave Cross, Marshwood Vale DT6 6HW**
email: roy.warburton@virgin.net web: www.theshavecrossinn.co.uk
dir: *From Bridport take B3162. In 2m left signed Broadoak & Shave Cross, then follow Marshwood signs*

Caribbean food in the heart of Hardy country

Off the beaten track down narrow lanes in the beautiful Marshwood Vale, deep in Thomas Hardy country, this thatched 14th-century cob-and-flint inn was once a resting place for pilgrims and other monastic visitors on their way to Whitchurch Canonicorum to visit the shrine to St Candida and St Cross. While they were at the inn they had their tonsures trimmed, hence the pub's name. Step inside the cosy bar to find low beams, stone floors, a huge inglenook fireplace, rustic furnishings, and local Dorset ale on tap, as well as real farm ciders. The food here is both unusual and inspirational, with a strong Caribbean influence together with dishes originating as far afield as Fiji. A starter of jerk chicken salad with plantain, crispy bacon and aïoli might be followed by a main course of hot and spicy Cuban seafood bouillabaisse or Jamaican jerk pork tenderloin with pineapple compôte.

Open 11-3 6-11.30 Closed Mon (ex BHs) ⊕ FREE HOUSE ◑ Branscombe Vale Branoc, Dorset, local guest ales ♂ Westons Old Rosie, Thatchers, Pitfield Thunderbolt. Facilities ◕ (Bar Garden) ◕ Children's menu Children's portions Play area Garden Parking WiFi Rooms 7

BUCKHORN WESTON
Map 4 ST72

Stapleton Arms   PICK OF THE PUBS

See Pick of the Pubs on page 162

CATTISTOCK
Map 4 SY59

Fox & Hounds Inn

tel: 01300 320444 **Duck St DT2 0JH**
email: lizflight@yahoo.co.uk
dir: *On A37, between Dorchester & Yeovil, follow signs to Cattistock*

Popular inn in pretty Dorset village

Expect a bar full of locals, families, dogs and even chickens under foot at this attractive pub. Situated in a picturesque village, the 17th-century inn has a welcoming and traditional atmosphere engendered by ancient beams, open fires in winter and huge inglenooks, one with an original bread oven. Palmers ales are on tap, along with various ciders, while home-made meals embrace Dorset charcuterie boards; fresh fish, 'proper' double crusted pies and excellent steaks. Regular events include folk music and poetry.

Open 12-2.30 6-11 (Sun 12-10) Closed Mon L Food Lunch Tue-Sun 12-2 Dinner Mon-Sat 7-9, Sun 6-8 Av main course £10.95 ⊕ PALMERS ◑ Best Bitter, Copper Ale, 200, Dorset Gold ♂ Thatchers Gold, Sheppy's, Dorset Orchard Apple Bee. Facilities Non-diners area ◕ (Bar Restaurant Garden) ◕ Children's portions Play area Garden ⋒ Parking WiFi ➡ (notice required)

CERNE ABBAS
Map 4 ST60

The New Inn

tel: 01300 341274 **14 Long St DT2 7JF**
email: info@thenewinncerneabbas.co.uk
dir: *Take A352 from Dorchester to Cerne Abbas. Pub in village centre*

Old coaching inn serving accomplished cooking

The village of Cerne Abbas has a reasonable claim to be one of the prettiest in England, with its delightful stone buildings and thatched cottages. In the past, it was famous for brewing – at one time there were 16 pubs here. One that remains is the New Inn, a beautifully restored 16th-century coaching inn, now with new landlords. There's a mix of contemporary British and pub classic dishes on offer – pressed ham, globe artichoke and truffle terrine with piccalilli; slow-roast pork belly and crackling, braised red cabbage, apple sauce and champ; or mushroom 'Scotch egg' with curly kale, Jerusalem artichoke and mustard dressing. Wednesday nights are steak nights.

Open all wk 12-3 5-11 (summer 12-11) Closed 25-26 Dec Food Lunch all wk 12-2 (summer all wk 12-3) Dinner all wk 7-9 (summer all wk 6.30-9.30) Restaurant menu available all wk ⊕ PALMERS ◑ IPA, Copper, Dorset Gold ♂ Dorset Orchards Apple Bee & First Press, Thatchers Gold. ▾ 12 Facilities Non-diners area ◕ (Bar Garden) ◕ Children's menu Children's portions Garden ⋒ Parking WiFi

PICK OF THE PUBS

Stapleton Arms

BUCKHORN WESTON   Map 4 ST72

tel: 01963 370396 **Church Hill SP8 5HS**
email: relax@thestapletonarms.com
web: www.thestapletonarms.com
dir: *3.5m from Wincanton in village centre*

Serious about cider, ale and local produce

Clean, modern lines within belie the Georgian exterior of this progressive village inn. It sits on the edge of Blackmore Vale in Thomas Hardy's rolling Dorset countryside, classic walking country enjoyed by many of the inn's patrons. With a multitude of artisanal producers on the doorstep, it's no surprise that the bar majors on farmhouse ciders – Orchard Pig, Ashton and guests are among a handful on offer, along with a tantalising range of earthy apple juices. The pub hosts an annual beer festival, always a good indication of a serious attitude to ales. Handles pulling pints from Butcombe brewery in Bristol and regional guests are complemented by a comprehensive range of world bottled beers. The pub's stylish and unstuffy attitude creates a welcoming and relaxing ambience in which to enjoy these drinks. For more of Dorset's larder, look no further than the menu, overflowing with fresh and local produce, ethically raised and delivered with minimum food miles. Light bites in the bar range from pickled beetroot,

walnuts and goats' curd salad, to Dorset salmon terrine with roast tomatoes and toasted brioche; and lamb koftas with tzatziki, flatbread and watercress salad. Sandwiches are prepared with home-made bread and quality fillings such as salt beef, sauerkraut, sliced cheese and Russian dressing. Lunchtime classics include griddled beef and Cajun chicken with triple-cooked chips; and wild mushroom strudel with spinach purée, roast cherry tomatoes and Madeira jus. For a dinner treat, try sesame tuna steak, chilli pak choi, baby corn and udon noodles; or ballotine of chicken stuffed with olive tapenade, chorizo and tomato orzo pasta. Round off with salted caramel chocolate torte with cherries.

Open all wk 11-3 6-11 (Sun 12-10.30) **Food** Lunch all wk 12-3 Dinner all wk 6-10 ⊞ FREE HOUSE ◀ Butcombe, Plain Ales ♻ Thatchers Cheddar Valley & Gold, Orchard Pig, Ashton Press, guest ciders. ♇ 30 **Facilities** Non-diners area ❤ (Bar Garden) ♦ Children's menu Children's portions Play area Garden ⊼ Beer festival Parking WiFi 🚌 (notice required)

PICK OF THE PUBS

The Anchor Inn ★★★★ INN

CHIDEOCK　　　Map 4 SY49

tel: 01297 489215 **Seatown DT6 6JU**
email:
contact@theanchorinnseatown.co.uk
web: www.theanchorinnseatown.co.uk
dir: *From A35 in Chideock turn opposite
church & follow single track road for
0.75m to beach*

Almost on the beach

Locals know it as the 'sea town of
Chideock', although to call a pub and a
few cottages a town is perhaps a bit
ambitious. This former smugglers'
haunt lies on a long shelving pebble
beach, part of the Jurassic Coast,
surrounded by National Trust land. The
only thing that separates – that too is
hardly the right word – the pub from the
waves is the South West Coast Path as
it drops down to sea level from Golden
Cap, the highest point on England's
south coast. A large sun terrace and
cliffside beer garden overlooking Lyme
Bay help to make the Anchor a popular
destination, but there's a good-size car
park, just as the road morphs into
shingle. Sample dishes include salmon
tataki, sesame, chilli, ginger and soy; or
carrot 'spaghetti', smoky tomato sauce,
black garlic purée and coriander. On a
blustery winter's day, a lamb shoulder
shepherd's pie with crushed potato and
swede, and root vegetables should help
to restore order; at any time, though, see

if the kitchen has prepared Jurassic
Coast bouillabaisse with rouille and
sourdough bread. Alternatives include
various platters: there's the Farmhand,
consisting of local cheeses; the
Fisherman, whose composition,
depending on the day you visit, might be
treacle-cured salmon, roll-mop herring,
potted shrimp and crispy cockles; or you
could go for the Scotch egg and pork
pie-based Huntsman. Finish with cinder
toffee popcorn parfait with rum-torched
banana and hot melted chocolate; or
maybe warmed Kingston black-treacle
tart with vanilla ice cream. The wine list
is short, but there should be enough
choice for most tastes; real ales are all
from Palmers of Bridport.

Open all day all wk 10am-11pm
Food Lunch all wk 12-9 (12-3 Dec-Feb)
Dinner all wk 12-9 (6-9 Dec-Feb)
⊕ PALMERS ◼ 200, Best Bitter, Copper
Ale & Dorset Gold ⚙ Thatchers Gold,
Appleby. **Facilities** Non-diners area
❖ (Bar Restaurant Garden)
♦ Children's menu Children's portions
Family room Garden ⌖ Parking WiFi
Rooms 3

CHEDINGTON
Map 4 ST40

Winyard's Gap Inn

tel: 01935 891244 **Chedington Ln DT8 3HY**
email: enquiries@winyardsgap.com
dir: *5m S of Crewkerne on A356*

Extravagant views, craft ciders and seasonal produce

Situated beside National Trust woodlands in a corner of the Dorset Area of Outstanding Natural Beauty, the old inn's garden commands an extraordinary view across Somerset from the eponymous gap in the sinuous chalk hills. The two counties provide the wherewithal for the August cider festival here, whilst beers from Exmoor and Otter breweries anoint the bar, with its solid rustic seating and tables and a log-burner for the winter nip. The impressive 'Ultimate Ploughman's' takes in the cheeses of the area, or enjoy twice-baked Red Leicester soufflé with tarragon crème fraîche, then pan-fried sea bass fillets with new potatoes, samphire and clam chowder. Leave space for cider mulled plum frangipane tart, or lime and ginger crunch.

Open all wk 11.30-3 6-11 (Sat-Sun 11.30-11) Closed 25-26 Dec **Food** Lunch Mon-Sat 12-2 Dinner all wk 6-9 Set menu available Restaurant menu available all wk ⊕ FREE HOUSE ◀ Sharp's Doom Bar, Dorset Piddle, Exmoor Ale, Otter Ale Ö Thatchers Gold, Westons Old Rosie & 1st Quality, Dorset Nectar. ♀ 12 **Facilities** Non-diners area ♣ (Bar Garden) ♦♦ Children's menu Children's portions Garden ⊼ Cider festival Parking WiFi ☍ (notice required)

CHETNOLE
Map 4 ST60

The Chetnole Inn

tel: 01935 872337 **DT9 6NU**
email: enquiries@thechetnoleinn.co.uk
dir: *A37 from Dorchester towards Yeovil. Left at Chetnole sign*

Tranquil village pub with garden overlooking fields

This is a bright and airy village inn situated opposite a pretty church deep in Thomas Hardy country. Plenty of walks thread their way through the rich countryside; it's handy, too, for the historic town of Sherborne. The flagstone-floored snug, bar and restaurant make an ideal setting for the West Country meats and Bridport-landed seafood that fill the British menu. Choose perhaps pan-roasted chicken breast with cherry vine tomatoes and asparagus, or the home-made beefburger, and enjoy at a table in the tree-shaded garden, home to the pub's hens. Local beers include Yeovil Ales Star Gazer and Wriggle Valley Copper Hoppa.

Open 12-3 6-close Closed Sun eve **Food** Lunch all wk 12-2 Dinner Mon-Sat 6.30-9 ⊕ FREE HOUSE ◀ Sharp's Doom Bar, Yeovil Ales Star Gazer, Wriggle Valley Copper Hoppa Ö Burrow Hill, Thatchers Gold. ♀ 9 **Facilities** Non-diners area ♣ (Bar Garden) ♦♦ Children's menu Children's portions Garden ⊼ Parking WiFi ☍ (notice required)

CHIDEOCK
Map 4 SY49

The Anchor Inn ★★★★ INN
PICK OF THE PUBS

See Pick of the Pubs on page 163 and advert below

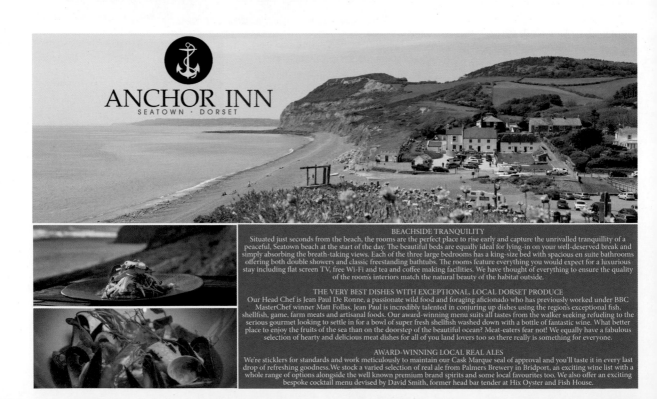

CHURCH KNOWLE
Map 4 SY98

The New Inn

tel: 01929 480357 **BH20 5NQ**
email: maurice@newinn-churchknowle.co.uk
dir: *From Wareham take A351 towards Swanage. At Corfe Castle right for Church Knowle. Pub in village centre*

16th-century, part-thatched village inn

The Estop family have been here for over three decades, landlord Maurice being only the fourth licensee in 150 years. The inn's old-world charm includes inglenook fireplaces and a brick alcove once the farmhouse oven. Real ales include Dorset Jurassic and guests, with draught ciders too. Son and head chef Matthew Estop makes much of locally caught fish and seafood (especially evident on the summer menu) – hake, Dover sole, black bream, gurnard, mussels and crab – as well as local meats, in the restaurant and the carvery. Blue Vinny cheese soup is a popular, long-standing fixture. Don't expect a wine list, because customers can browse for the right bottle in the 'Wine Shack'.

Open 10-3 6-11 (10-3 5-11 summer) Closed Mon (Jan-Feb) **Food** Lunch all wk 12-2.15 Dinner all wk 6-9.15 (5-9.15 summer) Set menu available ⊕ PUNCH TAVERNS ◼ Dorset Jurassic, Sharp's Doom Bar, St Austell Tribute, guest ales ♂ Westons Old Rosie, Stowford Press & Traditional. ☗ 10 **Facilities** Non-diners area ♣ (Garden Outside area) ⛟ Children's menu Children's portions Play area Family room Garden Outside area ⚲ Parking WiFi ▭ (notice required)

CRANBORNE
Map 5 SU01

The Inn at Cranborne ★★★★ INN

tel: 01725 551249 **5 Wimborne St BH21 5PP**
email: info@theinnatcranborne.co.uk **web:** www.theinnatcranborne.co.uk
dir: *On B3078 between Fordingbridge & Wimborne Minster*

Hearty food and Dorset ales in a delightful village

Jane Gould searched long and hard for somewhere she could realise her vision of a traditional English country pub. Since finding this 17th-century, former coaching inn she has skilfully transformed it into a must-visit destination in Cranborne Chase, nearly 400-square miles of rolling chalk downland. Badger First Gold shares bar space with Dorset and Somerset ciders. Choose a table near one of the wood-burning stoves for something hearty from the daily-changing menu, such as roast

local venison with celeriac three ways and juniper jus; home-cured peppered duck with poached baby pear and blackberries; or spelt and barley risotto with roasted squash, toasted pumpkin seeds and Old Winchester cheese crisp.

The Inn at Cranborne

Open all day all wk **Food** Lunch Mon-Fri 12-2, Sat-Sun 12-2.30 Dinner Mon-Thu 6-9, Fri-Sat 6-9.30 Av main course £12 ⊕ HALL & WOODHOUSE ◼ Badger First Gold, guest ales ♂ Westons Stowford Press, Badger Pearwood & Applewood. ☗ 10 **Facilities** Non-diners area ♣ (All areas) ⛟ Children's menu Children's portions Garden Outside area ⚲ Beer festival Parking WiFi ▭ (notice required) **Rooms** 9

See advert below

EAST MORDEN   Map 4 SY99

The Cock & Bottle   PICK OF THE PUBS

tel: 01929 459238 **BH2O 7DL**
email: cockandbottle@btconnect.com
dir: *From A35 (W of Poole) turn right onto B3075, pub 0.5m on left*

Crowd-pleasing range of ales and food options

The low-beamed ceilings and wealth of nooks and crannies are a reminder that
parts of this Dorset longhouse were built around 400 years ago. The simply
furnished locals' bar is comfortably rustic, with a large wooden settle on which to
while away a winter's evening beside the cosy log fire. The fine range of real ales
from the nearby Hall & Woodhouse brewery is also available in the lounge bar, while
a modern restaurant at the back completes the picture. The ever-changing menu
ranges from light lunches and bar meals to pub favourites. The carte menu choices
might include a starter of crispy duck and green onion spring roll, cucumber and
sweet and sour sauce. Moving on, rabbit pie; steak and kidney pudding; and lamb
shank are typical main course options, and home-made desserts like dark and
white chocolate terrine make a fitting finale. There are lovely pastoral views over the
surrounding farmland.

Open 11.30-2.30 6-11 (Sun 12-3) Closed Sun eve **Food** Lunch all wk 12-1.45 Dinner
Mon-Sat 6-8.45 Restaurant menu available all wk ⊕ HALL & WOODHOUSE
◀ Badger Dorset Best & Tanglefoot, guest ale. **Facilities** Non-diners area ☺ (Bar
Restaurant Garden) ◄ Children's menu Children's portions Play area Garden ☐
Parking ▥

EVERSHOT   Map 4 ST50

The Acorn Inn ★★★★ INN ◉   PICK OF THE PUBS

See Pick of the Pubs on opposite page and advert below

FARNHAM   Map 4 ST91

The Museum Inn ★★★★ INN ◉◉   PICK OF THE PUBS

tel: 01725 516261 **DT11 8DE**
email: enquiries@museuminn.co.uk **web:** www. museuminn.co.uk
dir: *From Salisbury take A354 to Blandford Forum, 12m. Farnham signed on right. Pub in
village centre*

Country pub with a lively locals bar

In the 19th century this part-thatched country pub on Cranborne Chase served
visitors to General Augustus Pitt-Rivers' small archaeological and anthropological
museum, now relocated to Oxford. The interior features the original inglenook
fireplace, flagstone floors, a fashionable mismatch of furniture and a book-filled
sitting room. If you're passionate about your real ales or ciders, the bar will oblige
with Sixpenny 6D Best, Ringwood Best and Orchard Pig. Local estates and farms
supply many of the ingredients for dishes awarded two AA Rosettes, among which
might be sliced prosciutto and salami with olives and cabbage salad; seared tuna
Niçoise with aged balsamic; and wild nettle risotto with wild mushrooms and
mascarpone. An interesting dessert is peanut butter and Amarula (a South African
cream liqueur) baked Alaska with banana bread. Pitt-Rivers also created Larmer
Tree Gardens, a public pleasure garden, on his Rushmore Estate near Tollard Royal.

Open all day all wk **Food** Lunch Mon-Sat 12-2.30, Sun 12-3 Dinner Sun-Thu 6.30-9,
Fri-Sat 6.30-9.30 Av main course £16.95 ⊕ CIRRUS INNS ◀ Sixpenny 6D Best,
Fuller's London Pride, Ringwood Best Bitter, guest ale ♂ Orchard Pig. ♟ 12
Facilities Non-diners area ☺ (Bar Outside area) ◄ Children's menu Children's
portions Outside area ☐ Parking WiFi ▥ (notice required) **Rooms** 8

The Acorn Inn

28 Fore Street, Evershot, Dorset DT2 0JW
Tel: 01935 83228 • Website: www.acorn-inn.co.uk • Email: stay@acorn-inn.co.uk

An unspoilt 16th-century coaching inn, set deep in the heart of Hardy's Wessex, and featured in his novel *Tess
of the d'Urbervilles* – perfect for exploring the delights of the legendary Jurassic Coast. Ten individually designed
and recently refurbished rooms, three with four poster beds. The feel is comfortable and traditional with strikingly
modern bathrooms. With two bars, skittle alley and a restaurant, it's equally popular with drinkers and diners alike –
not just a local, or a gastro-pub, but both! The highly rated menu features dishes that make inspired use of the finest
seasonal produce, from local and sustainable sources.

PICK OF THE PUBS

The Acorn Inn ★★★★ INN ❀

EVERSHOT   Map 4 ST50

tel: 01935 83228 **DT2 0JW**
email: stay@acorn-inn.co.uk
web: www.acorn-inn.co.uk
dir: *From A37 between Yeovil &
Dorchester, follow Evershot & Holywell
signs, 0.5m to inn*

Surrounded by upspoilt rolling countryside

In *Tess of the d'Urbervilles*, Wessex novelist and poet Thomas Hardy called this pretty, 16th-century inn the 'Sow and Acorn'; he also featured it in two other novels. He'd still recognise it, especially its unusual porch, old beams, low ceilings, oak panelling, flagstone floors and carved Hamstone fireplaces. And he'd appreciate the bedroom names that are taken from locations in his books. Run impressively by Jack and Alex Mackenzie, the inn is a big draw locally, with two lively bars stocking real ales from Devon and Dorset breweries and brewpubs, Thatchers Somerset Haze cider, 39 wines by the glass and an impressive stock of malt whiskies. And that's not all, because there are quiz nights and occasional yard-of-ale-drinking challenges too. In the softly lit AA Rosette restaurant you'll find smartly laid tables, terracotta tiles and an elegant stone fireplace carved with oak leaves and, no great surprise, acorns. Sustainability, localness and seasonality govern a modern British

menu of Cornish crab with lime, coriander and chilli bruschetta, and balsamic dressing; chargrilled 10oz rump steak with smoked bacon, artichoke gratin, buttered tenderstem broccoli, triple-cooked chips and béarnaise sauce; and parsnip and carrot rösti with roasted sweet potato, spinach, leek and mushroom ragout, and spiced tomato sauce. A fish specials board changes daily, while lunch and bar menus offer sandwiches, a charcuterie sharing platter, roasted pork and leek sausages, burgers and ploughman's. The pub also features a lovely old skittle alley and a beer garden. Good walks radiate from the village, so make sure you put those wellies in the car.

Open all day all wk 11am-11.30pm
Food Lunch all wk 12-2 Dinner all wk 7-9 Av main course £10 Restaurant menu available all wk ⊕ FREE HOUSE ◀ Otter, rotating guest ales ☼ Thatchers Somerset Haze. ☗ 39
Facilities Non-diners area ❖ (Bar Garden) ⅋ Children's menu Children's portions Family room Garden ⩎ Parking WiFi ☲ (notice required) **Rooms** 10

FERNDOWN
Map 5 SU00

The Kings Arms

tel: 01202 577490 **77 Ringwood Rd, Longham BH22 9AA**
email: thekingsarmslongham@yahoo.co.uk
dir: *On A348*

Free house serving tempting food

The Kings Arms has gained a good local reputation for its British classics, especially beef, and other locally-sourced dishes prepared by chefs Mark Miller and Tim Butler. From their main menu come a variety of steaks, including a 100-day aged, grain-fed rib-eye, and a Chateaubriand for sharing. Also, seafood bouillabaisse; prosciutto-wrapped venison cannon; pan-fried calves' liver; chicken and chorizo risotto; and Blue Vinny and butternut squash tarte Tatin are tempting. Duo of pork with apple and apricot stuffing; and duck breast with stir-fry vegetables and saffron rice might appear on the specials menu. The bar usually keeps three real ales, among them Ringwood Best, from a few miles east, and various traditional ciders. Some 15 wines are by the glass, the reds chosen very much with the beef dishes in mind.

Open all day all wk **Food** Sun-Thu 12-9, Fri-Sat 12-9.30 Set menu available ⊕ FREE HOUSE ◀ Ringwood Best, Otter Ale, Fuller's London Pride, Timothy Taylor ♂ Westons. ♚ 15 **Facilities** Non-diners area ♣ (Bar Outside area) ♦ Children's portions Outside area ⋒ Parking WiFi ➡ (notice required)

FONTMELL MAGNA
Map 4 ST81

The Fontmell ★★★★ INN

tel: 01747 811441 **SP7 0PA**
email: info@thefontmell.com **web:** www.thefontmell.com
dir: *Halfway between Shaftesbury & Blandford Forum, on A350*

Smart inn with seasonally inspired menus

On the A350, between Shaftesbury and Blandford Forum is The Fontmell, a stylish and comfortable country pub, complete with a stream flowing between the bar and the dining room. Linger over a pint of one of the weekly changing guest ales at the bar, or curl up on the sofa and peruse the newspapers. Most visitors and guests cannot resist chef/patron Tom Shaw's frequently changing menus which feature flavour packed dishes such as goats' cheese soufflé with wild mushroom ragout; pan-fried pork belly with langoustines, caramelised cauliflower and cumin purée; or pan-fried sea trout with spinach, samphire, crab fritter and prawn bisque. From Monday to Thursday a set menu is available at lunchtime.

Open all day all wk **Food** Lunch Mon-Thu 12-2, Fri-Sun 12-2.30 Dinner Mon-Thu 6-9, Fri-Sat 6-9.30, Sun 6-8.30 ⊕ FREE HOUSE ◀ Keystone Mallyshag, seasonal ale, rotating guest ales ♂ Rotating guest ciders. ♚ 13 **Facilities** Non-diners area ♣ (Bar Garden) ♦ Children's menu Children's portions Garden ⋒ Parking WiFi **Rooms** 6

GILLINGHAM
Map 4 ST82

The Kings Arms Inn

tel: 01747 838325 **East Stour Common SP8 5NB**
email: nrosscampbell@aol.com
dir: *4m W of Shaftesbury on A30*

Family-run pub with a Scottish flavour

Scottish touches – paintings by artist Mavis Makie, quotes by Robert Burns, the presence of haggis, skirlie and cranachan on the menus, and a wide choice of

single malts – reflect the origin of this inn's landlord and landlady. A 200-year-old, family-run village free house where Victorian fireplaces sit comfortably alongside modern wooden furniture and subtly coloured fabrics, it offers an extensive choice of dishes ranging from Puy lentil and mixed vegetable burger in a brioche bun with tomato chutney, to steak and kidney baked suet pudding with red wine gravy, vegetables and chips. Look out for the £7 pub lunch specials.

Open all wk 12-3 5.30-11.30 (Sat-Sun 12-12) **Food** Lunch Mon-Sat 12-2.30, Sun 12-9.15 Dinner Mon-Sat 5.30-9.15, Sun 12-9.15 Av main course £12 Restaurant menu available all wk ⊕ FREE HOUSE ◀ Sharp's Doom Bar, St Austell Tribute, Butcombe. ♚ **Facilities** Non-diners area ♣ (Bar Garden) ♦ Children's menu Children's portions Family room Garden ⋒ Parking WiFi ➡ (notice required)

HINTON ST MARY
Map 4 ST71

NEW The White Horse Inn

tel: 01258 472723 **DT10 1NA**
email: mjpimm@aol.com
dir: *From A357 in Sturminster Newton take B3092 (over bridge) signed Gillingham. At x-roads in Hinton St Mary turn right, pub on left*

Variety, value, and its own craft brew

For a taste of old England, you should seek out this small village and its 400-year-old pub. If you need an excuse, come to ghost-hunt or for the summer beer festival when the White Horse Craft Brewery comes into its own. You will probably meet Pepper, the pub dog, who likes to meet other dogs. Food is sourced from local farms and suppliers – the mixed platter of salami, for example, is made in Dorset and served with home-made bread. Among other options, all of which are priced to please, are home-made pork faggots with mash, fresh vegetables and real gravy.

Open 12-3 6-11 Closed Sun eve, Mon **Food** Lunch Tue-Sun 12-2.30 Dinner Tue-Sat 6-9 Av main course £9.95 ⊕ FREE HOUSE ◀ Own Craft Brewery ♂ Thatchers, Orchard Pig. ♚ 9 **Facilities** Non-diners area ♣ (Bar Restaurant Garden) ♦ Children's portions Garden Beer festival Parking WiFi ➡ (notice required)

LYME REGIS
Map 4 SY39

The Mariners ★★★★ INN

tel: 01297 442753 **Silver St DT7 3HS**
email: enquiries@hotellymeregis.co.uk **web:** www.hotellymeregis.co.uk
dir: *A35 onto B3165 (Lyme Rd). The Mariners is pink building opposite road to The Cobb (Pound Rd)*

Try the local seafood specials

Once a coaching inn in the 17th century, this restored property in the heart of the town is steeped in Lyme's fossil history, having once been home to the Philpot sisters, famed as collectors in the early 19th century. Beatrix Potter is said to have stayed here too, reputedly writing *The Tale of Little Pig Robinson* – The Mariners is illustrated in the book. The building combines traditional character with modern style. Simple menus feature the best of local seafood and other quality ingredients in dishes such as fillet of Weymouth sea bass, tomato and olive risotto and lobster oil; pork fillet, courgette provençale, crushed new potatoes and oregano jus; and lemon and lime parfait with chilled berry soup. Only bottled beers are available.

Open all day all wk **Food** Lunch all wk 12-2 Dinner all wk 6.30-9 Set menu available Restaurant menu available all wk ⊕ FREE HOUSE ◀ Otter Bright, Mighty Hop Mighty Red IPA & Mariners Ale ♂ Thatchers Gold. ♚ 9 **Facilities** Non-diners area ♣ (Bar Garden) ♦ Children's menu Children's portions Garden ⋒ Parking WiFi ➡ (notice required) **Rooms** 14

MILTON ABBAS
Map 4 ST80

The Hambro Arms ★★★★ INN

tel: 01258 880233 **DT11 OBP**
email: info@hambroarms.com **web:** www.hambroarms.com
dir: *From A354 (Dorchester to Blandford road), exit at Milborne St Andrew to Milton Abbas*

A thriving pub in an unusual village

Many Dorset picture-postcards feature the 36 near-identical, late 18th-century thatched cottages of Milton Abbas, replacements for a nearby hamlet demolished by the privacy-seeking, landowning Earl of Dorchester. Built at the same time, the whitewashed pub thrives, its bar and outside tables perfect for a lunchtime snack, and the elegant Library Restaurant offering a full carte. Start with home-made duck liver and whisky pâté, or share a Mediterranean meze, including salami, chorizo, sun-dried tomatoes and Manchego cheese. Then pan-fried breast and confit leg of Bryanston pheasant; pistachio- and almond-crusted salmon; or wild mushroom and blue cheese risotto. Catch the July beer festival.

Open 11.30-3 6-11 (Sat-Sun 11.30-11.30) Closed Mon Oct-Mar **Food** Lunch Mon-Fri 12-2.30, Sat 12-3, Sun 12-7.30 Dinner Mon-Thu 6-9, Fri-Sat 6-9.30, Sun 12-7.30 ⊕ ADMIRAL TAVERNS ◀ Sharp's Doom Bar, Otter Bitter, guest ales ♂ Thatchers Gold. ♟ 8 **Facilities** Non-diners area ♦ Children's menu Children's portions Garden ⋈ Beer festival Parking WiFi ➡ **Rooms** 4

MOTCOMBE
Map 4 ST82

The Coppleridge Inn ★★★ INN

tel: 01747 851980 **SP7 9HW**
email: thecoppleridgeinn@btinternet.com **web:** www.coppleridge.com
dir: *Take A350 towards Warminster for 1.5m, left at brown tourist sign. Follow signs to inn*

Former farmhouse in beautiful surroundings

Chris and Di Goodinge took over this 18th-century farmhouse and farm about 25 years ago and converted it into the pub you see today. As well as retaining the flagstone floors and log fires, they have kept the farm's 15 acres of meadow and woodland, where they raise their own cattle. The bar offers a wide range of real ales, as well as a decent choice of food. Start with smoked trout salad with prawns and avocado; continue with venison and cranberry cobbler with blue cheese scones and roasted roots; and finish off with brioche bread and butter pudding with vanilla mascarpone. Ten spacious bedrooms are situated around a converted courtyard and there is a secure children's playground.

Open all day all wk **Food** Lunch all wk 12-2.30 Dinner all wk 6-9 Av main course £12 ⊕ FREE HOUSE ◀ Butcombe Bitter, Wadworth 6X, Fuller's London Pride, Sharp's Doom Bar, Ringwood Best Bitter ♂ Ashton Press, Thatchers. ♟ 10 **Facilities** Non-diners area ♦ (Bar Garden) ♦ Children's menu Children's portions Play area Family room Garden ⋈ Parking WiFi ➡ (notice required) **Rooms** 10

NETTLECOMBE
Map 4 SY59

Marquis of Lorne

tel: 01308 485236 **DT6 3SY**
email: info@themarquisoflorne.co.uk
dir: *From A3066 (Bridport-Beaminster road) approx 1.5m N of Bridport follow Loders & Mangerton Mill signs. At junct left past Mangerton Mill, through West Milton. 1m to T-junct, straight over. Pub up hill, approx 300yds on left*

Recommended for its interesting menus and lovely views

In a picturesque hamlet and close to the market town of Bridport, the Marquis of Lorne has beautiful views. Built as a farmhouse in the 16th century and converted into a pub in 1871, it is now run by Steve and Tracey Brady. They have renewed the focus on local produce throughout the menus, and locally brewed Palmers ales are on tap. Lightly sautéed soft herring roes with capers and parsley makes an interesting starter, while international influences are at play in main courses of 'sticky' beef with Indonesian-style salad; and grilled vegetable lasagne with lovage pesto. Look out for special dinner evenings. The attractive gardens are family friendly, too.

Open all wk 12-2.30 6-11 **Food** Lunch all wk 12-2 Dinner all wk 6-9 Av main course £20-£25 ⊕ PALMERS ◀ Copper Ale, Best Bitter, Dorset Gold. ♟ 9 **Facilities** Non-diners area ♦ (Bar Garden) ♦ Children's menu Children's portions Play area Garden ⋈ Parking WiFi ➡ (notice required)

PIDDLEHINTON
Map 4 SY79

The Thimble Inn

tel: 01300 348270 **DT2 7TD**
email: info@thimbleinn.co.uk
dir: *Take A35 W'bound, right onto B3143, Piddlehinton in 4m*

Thatched village local in huge grounds

This 18th-century pub and restaurant is run by French-trained chef Mark Ramsden and his wife Lisa. The stunning interior features antique furniture, sandstone and oak floors and a glass-covered well. Its patio overlooks the River Piddle, or Puddle, as prim Victorians preferred to call it. Mark uses the best local produce for dishes such as curried parsnip soup; pan-fried chicken livers with thyme, brioche and port reduction; steak, ale and mushroom pot pie; salmon fillet with potato and spinach hash; Black Forest sundae; and warm Dorset apple cake and vanilla custard.

Open all wk 11.30-3 6-11 (Sat-Sun 11.30-11) Closed Mon (Nov-Feb) **Food** Lunch Mon-Fri 12-3, Sat-Sun 12-9 Dinner Mon-Fri 6-9, Sat-Sun 12-9 Restaurant menu available all wk ⊕ PALMERS ◀ Copper Ale, Best Bitter, Tally Ho! & Dorset Gold ♂ Thatchers Gold, Dorset Orchard First Press & Apple Bee. ♟ 10 **Facilities** Non-diners area ♦ (Bar Garden) ♦ Children's menu Children's portions Garden ⋈ Parking WiFi ➡ (notice required)

PIDDLETRENTHIDE
Map 4 SY79

The Poachers Inn

tel: 01300 348358 **DT2 7QX**
email: info@thepoachersinn.co.uk
dir: *6m N from Dorchester on B3143. At church end of village*

Good range of food and garden with swimming pool

Located in the pretty little village of Piddletrenthide in the heart of Thomas Hardy country, this 17th-century riverside pub is perfectly situated for exploring west Dorset and the Jurassic Coast. The kitchen makes good use of Dorset suppliers to create both classic pub meals — honey-roast ham with egg and chips; or pie of the day; or contemporary alternatives such as braised pork belly, cider and Bramley apple reduction and parsnip chips for the extensive menu. Relax with a glass of ale in the beer garden, which even has a heated swimming pool to enjoy throughout the summer. Details of three circular walks are available at the bar.

Open all day all wk 8am-mdnt **Food** Lunch all wk 12-2.30 Dinner all wk 6-9.30 Set menu available ⊕ FREE HOUSE ◀ Sharp's Doom Bar, Morland Old Speckled Hen, Greene King Ruddles County ♂ Thatchers Gold. ♟ 9 **Facilities** Non-diners area ♦ (Bar Garden) ♦ Children's menu Children's portions Garden ⋈ Parking WiFi ➡ (notice required)

PLUSH

Map 4 ST70

The Brace of Pheasants ★★★★ INN

tel: 01300 348357 **DT2 7RQ**
email: info@braceofpheasants.co.uk web: www.braceofpheasants.co.uk
dir: *A35 onto B3143, 5m to Piddletrenthide, then right to Mappowder & Plush*

Village inn popular with walkers

Tucked away in a fold of the hills in the heart of Hardy's beloved county, this pretty 16th-century thatched village inn is an ideal place to start or end a walk. With its welcoming open fire, oak beams and fresh flowers, it is the perfect setting to enjoy a selection of real ales and ciders and 18 wines by the glass. Food options might include pan-fried lamb's kidneys with mustard cream sauce or local venison steak with red wine reduction. The inn offers eight en suite bedrooms, four above the pub and four in the old skittle alley.

Open all wk 12-3 7-11 **Food** Lunch all wk 12-2.30 Dinner all wk 7-9 ⊕ FREE HOUSE ◀ Flack Manor Flack's Double Drop, Palmers, Ringwood Best Bitter, Sunny Republic, guest ales ♂ Westons Traditional, Purbeck Dorset Draft, Cider by Rosie. ♀ 18 **Facilities** Non-diners area ♣ (Bar Restaurant Garden) ◀ Children's portions Garden ♫ Parking WiFi ➛ (notice required) **Rooms** 8

POOLE

Map 4 SZ09

The Plantation

tel: 01202 701531 **53 Cliff Dr, Canford Cliffs BH13 7JF**
email: info@the-plantation.co.uk
dir: *From A35 between Poole & Bournemouth into Archway Rd (leads to Canford Cliffs Rd). At mini rdbt left into Haven Rd, right into Cliff Drive*

Fresh and refreshing pub and restaurant

Light and airy interiors in classic colonial style characterise this beautifully appointed pub and restaurant. Within the Poole conservation area and close to some of Bournemouth's best beaches, The Plantation is ideally sited for visitors sampling the delights of this picturesque coast. At the bar Upham ales are ably supported by Orchard Pig's range of bottled ciders, while short menus showcase high quality, fresh, local and seasonal ingredients. A typical three-course choice could begin with treacle-cured salmon, horseradish, rye and apple cracker; continue with glazed beef cheek with tongue ragù, confit potato, shiitakes and port sauce; and finish with gingerbread, blackberry and eggnog trifle.

Open all day all wk **Food** Lunch 12-3 Dinner 6-9.30 Restaurant menu available all wk ⊕ FREE HOUSE/UPHAM GROUP ◀ Upham Punter, Tipster & Stakes ♂ Orchard Pig Reveller, Charmer & Truffler. ♀ 15 **Facilities** Non-diners area ♣ (Bar Garden Outside area) ◀ Children's menu Children's portions Garden Outside area ♫ Parking WiFi ➛ (notice required)

POWERSTOCK

Map 4 SY59

Three Horseshoes Inn

PICK OF THE PUBS

tel: 01308 485328 **DT6 3TF**
email: threehorseshoespowerstock@live.co.uk
dir: *3m from Bridport off A3066 (Beaminster road)*

Good reputation for locally-sourced food

This pretty late-Victorian inn is owned by Palmers, a part-thatched brewery in nearby Bridport. The food owes much to the kitchen's devotion to seasonal, locally sourced ingredients, some from the garden and some foraged from surrounding hedgerows. Daily-changing menus lean towards game dishes in winter and fresh fish in summer, but inventiveness is present all year round. Your visit may coincide with starters of Dorset snails with pancetta, garlic and red wine; or gruyère and thyme soufflé. For mains, try wild boar sausages, braised red cabbage and Apple

Bee Cider gravy; or roast hake fillet with brown shrimp and lemon butter. Those with a sweet tooth should look to the blackboards for the dessert choices – tarte Tatin with cinnamon ice cream for example. The pub patio and terraced garden look out over the village, above which rises the National Trust's Eggardon Hill Fort.

Open 12-3 6.30-11.30 (Sun 12-3 6.30-10.30) Closed Mon L **Food** Lunch Tue-Sat 12-2.30, Sun 12-3 Dinner all wk 6.30-9.30 ⊕ PALMERS ◀ Best Bitter, Copper Ale, Tally Ho! & 200 ♂ Dorset Orchards Apple Bee. **Facilities** Non-diners area ♣ (Bar Restaurant Garden) ◀ Children's portions Garden ♫ Parking WiFi

PUNCKNOWLE

Map 4 SY58

The Crown Inn

tel: 01308 897711 **Church St DT2 9BN**
email: email@thecrowninndorset.co.uk
dir: *From A35 through Litton Cheney to Puncknowle. Or from Swyre on B3157 follow Puncknowle signs*

Chocolate-box thatched inn

This picturesque 16th-century pub was once the haunt of smugglers on their way from nearby Chesil Beach to visit prosperous customers in Bath. There's a traditional, welcoming atmosphere within the rambling, child- and dog-friendly bars with their log fires, comfy sofas and low beams. Home-cooked food ranges from pizzas, tapas slates and multi-grain sandwiches to seasonally changing dishes like fish pie; chickpea and roasted vegetable tagine; and local pork belly with cranberry and apple compôte. Enjoy a glass of real ale or one of the wines by the glass with a meal, or while playing one of the many traditional board games that are dotted around the pub. The lovely garden overlooks the Bride Valley.

Open all wk all day (Nov-Etr 11-3 5.30-10.30) **Food** Lunch Mon-Sat 12-2.30, Sun 12-9 (summer), Sun 12-8 (winter) Dinner Mon-Sat 6-9 Av main course £12 ⊕ PALMERS ◀ Best Bitter, 200, Copper Ale, seasonal ales ♂ Thatchers Gold, Dorset Orchard First Press. **Facilities** Non-diners area ♣ (Bar Restaurant Garden) ◀ Children's menu Children's portions Garden ♫ Parking WiFi ➛ (notice required)

SHAPWICK

Map 4 ST90

The Anchor Inn

tel: 01258 857269 **West St DT11 9LB**
email: anchor@shapwick.com
dir: *From Wimborne or Blandford Forum take B3082. Pub signed*

Village-owned pub with great local food

Rescued by a village collective, the Anchor is now home to the Magrath family. 'Our landlords are our neighbours,' they point out 'it doesn't get much more independent than that!' And this independence pays off, with all their produce sourced from within a 20-mile radius of the village. For lunch you could go for the venison burger, or the house ham, egg and chips; they also do filled baguettes and chips. At dinner, start with smoked duck breast, pomegranate seed and hazelnut salad before moving on to braised and roasted beef brisket with confit cabbage mash, truffle butter and caramelised onions; or salt and vinegar batter cod fillet.

Open all day Closed Sun eve **Food** Lunch all wk 12-3 Dinner Mon-Sat 6-9.30 Set menu available Restaurant menu available ⊕ FREE HOUSE ◀ Sharp's Doom Bar, local guest ales ♂ Westons Stowford Press, Aspall. ♀ 20 **Facilities** Non-diners area ♣ (Bar Restaurant Garden) ◀ Children's menu Children's portions Garden ♫ Parking WiFi ➛ (notice required)

SHERBORNE

Map 4 ST61

The Kings Arms ★★★★★ INN ⊛

PICK OF THE PUBS

See Pick of the Pubs on opposite page

PICK OF THE PUBS

The Kings Arms ★★★★★ INN ®

SHERBORNE Map 4 ST61

tel: 01963 220281
North Rd, Charlton Horethorne DT9 4NL
email: admin@thekingsarms.co.uk
web: www.thekingsarms.co.uk
dir: On A3145, N of Sherborne. Pub in village centre

Enjoyable food in elegantly converted pub

Midway between Sherborne and Wincanton, The Kings Arms was first licensed in 1813. While it retains its original grand frontage, the owners, Sarah and Tony Lethbridge, have completely transformed the interior from cellar to loft into a chic country pub and modern restaurant with boutique-style bedrooms. First port of call for most, of course, is usually the bar, where Butcombe and Wadworth real ales, and Lawrence's cider from nearby Corton Denham, all have their devotees. Of the 50 wines, 13 are sold by the glass. Stay in the bar if you're looking for a light snack in relaxed surroundings, otherwise go through a light, airy atrium to the more formal self-contained, Georgian-mirrored dining room, where black and brown leather, high-backed chairs are set round chunky wooden tables. From here, doors open on to an extensive dining terrace overlooking the countryside. The cooking style, traditional and modern British with world influences, results in an AA

Rosette awarded menu, for which everything is made in-house, including breads, pastas and ice creams. Starters range from cream of sweetcorn butternut and chestnut soup, to chicken Caesar salad with parmesan shavings. The charcoal grill is kept busy with pork, rib-eye and venison steaks, although there are plenty of alternatives such as free-range Creedy Carver duck leg; pan-fried hake; and beetroot risotto on the menu. Pudding favourites include baked apple and blackcurrant crumble; Bakewell tart with raspberry ripple ice cream; and West Country cheeses. Children's dishes include salmon fishcake with hand-cut chips, and tagliatelle with roasted tomato sauce. A game of croquet in the garden is unlikely to prove too strenuous.

Open all day all wk **Food** Lunch all wk 12-2.30 Dinner Mon-Thu 7-9.30, Fri-Sat 7-10, Sun 7-9 Av main course £12
⊕ FREE HOUSE ◀ Butcombe, Wadworth 6X ♻ Lawrence's. ♟ 13
Facilities Non-diners area ♣ (Bar Garden) ♦♦ Children's menu Children's portions Garden ⋒ Parking WiFi ▭ (notice required) **Rooms** 10

PICK OF THE PUBS

The Cricketers

SHROTON OR IWERNE COURTNEY Map 4 ST81

tel: 01258 860421 **DT11 8QD**
email: info@thecricketersshroton.co.uk
web: www.heartstoneinns.co.uk
dir: *7m S of Shaftesbury on A350, turn right after Iwerne Minster. 5m N of Blandford Forum on A360, past Stourpaine, in 2m left into Shroton. Pub in village centre*

Award-winning free house in secluded gardens

Under Hambledon Hill, where General Wolfe trained his troops before his assault on Quebec in 1759, lies what maps show as both Iwerne Courtney and Shroton; ask locals for the latter when looking for this early 20th-century pub and you'll be pointed in the right direction. Built to replace a much earlier establishment, over the years it has become not only a real community local, but also a popular pit-stop for walkers on the Wessex Way, who, since the path passes conveniently right by, are rarely so unwise as to wander through without stopping for Joe and Sally Grieves' genuine hospitality. In the light, open-plan interior, where in winter there's a cosy log-burner, the real beers are Butcombe and Otter Bitter, while wine drinkers will find up to nine by the glass; there's no separate restaurant. The menu changes seasonally and makes use of home-cooked, locally

sourced ingredients to offer starters or light options such as grilled onglet steak; and spiced tomato crumble. Main dishes include braised ox cheek, horseradish and orange dumpling, roasted shallots and carrots with red wine sauce; and pan-fried buffalo's liver and bacon. For vegetarians there's twice-baked cheddar soufflé; and macaroni, porcini and parmesan. Sandwiches are available at lunchtime, and on Sunday a choice of roast meats is always on offer; specials are forever changing. Events include occasional summer barbecues and a beer festival weekend with live music. The pub is proud of its long association with the Shroton Cricket Club, from which it takes its name.

Open all wk 12-3 6-11 (Sun 12-10.30)
Food Lunch all wk 12-2.30 Dinner Mon-Thu 6.30-9, Fri-Sat 6.30-9.30
🛢 FREE HOUSE 🍺 Butcombe, Otter Bitter 🍎 Westons Stowford Press. 🍷 9
Facilities Non-diners area 🚼 Children's menu Children's portions Garden 🪑 Beer festival Parking WiFi 🚐 (notice required)

SHROTON OR IWERNE COURTNEY
Map 4 ST81

The Cricketers
PICK OF THE PUBS

See Pick of the Pubs on opposite page

STRATTON
Map 4 SY69

Saxon Arms

tel: 01305 260020 **DT2 9WG**
email: rodsaxonlamont1@yahoo.co.uk
dir: *3m NW of Dorchester on A37. Pub between church & village hall*

Thatched flint-stone pub serving good food

Popular with villagers as much as visiting fishermen, cycling clubs and ramblers, this handsome, thatched flint-stone free house is ideally situated for riverside walks. Flagstone floors, a wood-burning stove and solid oak beams create a comfortable setting for a traditional English inn that offers a friendly welcome, a range of well-kept real ales and simple, carefully cooked food. Menu choices include grilled Portobello mushroom filled with Dorset Blue Vinny and salad; duo of diver-caught Portland scallops and cod fillet with butternut squash purée and chive butter sauce; pan-fried duck breast with sweet chilli stir-fry; and lemon and lime tart with summer berry compôte. There's also a deli counter and a selection of baguettes and jackets.

Open all wk 11-3 5.30-late (Fri-Sun 11am-late) **Food** Lunch Mon-Thu 11-2.15, Fri-Sat 11.30-9.30, Sun 12-9 Dinner Mon-Thu 6-9.15, Fri-Sat 11.30-9.30, Sun 12-9 Av main course £10.95 Set menu available ⊕ FREE HOUSE ◨ Fuller's London Pride, Palmers Best Bitter, Greene King Abbot Ale & Ruddles, Otter, Ringwood, Timothy Taylor, Butcombe, guest ales ○ Westons Stowford Press, guest ciders. ♈ 15 **Facilities** Non-diners area ♣ (Bar Garden) ♦♦ Children's menu Children's portions Garden ⋒ Parking WiFi ⊜ (notice required)

STUDLAND
Map 5 SZ08

The Bankes Arms Hotel

tel: 01929 450225 **Watery Ln BH19 3AU**
dir: *B3369 from Poole, take Sandbanks chain ferry, or A35 from Poole, A351 then B3351*

Creeper-clad 16th-century pub close to Studland Bay

Standing above the wide sweep of Studland Bay, this 16th-century creeper-clad inn was once a smugglers' dive. Nowadays the pub hosts an annual four-day festival in mid-August, featuring live music and some 200 beers and ciders that include award-winning ales from its own Isle of Purbeck brewery. Fresh fish and seafood salads are a speciality, but slow-braised lamb shank with rosemary mash; chilli con carne; and a daily curry are other examples from the menu.

Open all day all wk 11-11 (Sun 11-10.30) Closed 25 Dec **Food** Lunch all wk 12-3 (summer & BHs 12-9.30) Dinner Mon-Sat 6-9.30, Sun 6-9 (summer & BHs 12-9.30) ⊕ FREE HOUSE ◨ Isle of Purbeck IPA & Fossil Fuel, Studland Bay Wrecked, Solar Power ○ Broadoak. **Facilities** Non-diners area ♣ (Bar Restaurant Garden) ♦♦ Children's menu Garden ⋒ Beer festival Cider festival WiFi ⊜

SYDLING ST NICHOLAS
Map 4 SY69

The Greyhound Inn
PICK OF THE PUBS

tel: 01300 341303 **26 High St DT2 9PD**
email: info@dorsetgreyhound.co.uk
dir: *From A37 (Yeovil to Dorchester road), exit at staggered x-roads signed Sydling St Nicholas & Cerne Abbas*

Good food in the heart of Hardy country

Deep in Thomas Hardy country, this 18th-century pub is tucked away among pastel-hued flint and stone houses in a valley formed by Sydling Water. With many lovely walks starting from the pub, the staff are accustomed to welcoming muddy-booted families and wet dogs. Relax in the open-plan bar with a pint of Trelawny, a glass of Sandford Orchards Devon Red craft cider, or one of over 20 wines sold by the glass. Next, choose where to eat: the bar, with its open fire; the conservatory with oak, fruitwood and scrubbed wood tables and a deep chesterfield; the restaurant with an exposed well; or the suntrap front terrace. The food is modern British in approach, and menus change daily. Look to the specials list for fresh fish, the pub's strength; it's ordered the night before from the quaysides in Weymouth and Bridport. There's a good vegetarian selection too.

Open all wk 11-3 5.30-late (Sun 12-late, summer & BH hours may vary) **Food** Lunch Mon-Sat 12-2.30, Sun 12-5 Dinner Mon-Sat 6-9.30 Set menu available ⊕ FREE HOUSE ◨ Fuller's London Pride, St Austell Proper Job & Trelawny, Otter Ale ○ Sandford Orchards Devon Red, Westons Old Rosie. ♈ 22 **Facilities** Non-diners area ♣ (Bar Garden Outside area) ♦♦ Children's portions Garden Outside area ⋒ Parking WiFi

TARRANT MONKTON
Map 4 ST90

The Langton Arms ★★★★ INN
PICK OF THE PUBS

tel: 01258 830225 **DT11 8RX**
email: info@thelangtonarms.co.uk **web:** www.thelangtonarms.co.uk
dir: *A31 from Ringwood, or A357 from Shaftesbury, or A35 from Bournemouth*

Family-friendly thatched inn surrounded by beautiful countryside

Located in countryside immortalised by Thomas Hardy and a short walk from the village church, The Langton Arms is a lovely 17th-century thatched inn. Inside are two bars, each of which is a relaxing place to savour a pint from the ever-changing range of outstanding local ales and ciders. Traditional pub dishes are served in the bars, as well as in the Stables restaurant and conservatory. Expect choice West Country fare made from local produce – sourced in Dorset whenever possible, including beef from the owners' own herd at Rawston Farm. In addition to beef, main course options could include fillet of sea bass with wilted spinach; or roast belly pork with crackling and cider gravy. Children, if you can persuade them to leave the fully-equipped play area, are spoilt for choice with their own menu or smaller portions from the adult carte. Comfortable bedrooms are situated around an attractive courtyard.

Open all day all wk **Food** Lunch Mon-Fri 12-2.30, Sat-Sun all day Dinner Mon-Thu 6-9.30, Fri 6-10, Sat-Sun all day ⊕ FREE HOUSE ◨ Local guest ales ○ Purbeck Dorset Draft, Westons Stowford Press. ♈ 10 **Facilities** Non-diners area ♣ (Bar Garden) ♦♦ Children's menu Children's portions Play area Family room Garden ⋒ Parking WiFi ⊜ (notice required) **Rooms** 6

PICK OF THE PUBS

The Rose and Crown Inn, Trent ★★★★★ INN

TRENT   Map 4 ST51

tel: 01935 850776 **DT9 4SL**
email: info@theroseandcrowntrent.co.uk
web: www.theroseandcrowntrent.co.uk
dir: *Just off A30 between Sherborne & Yeovil*

Much loved by generations of locals and visitors

When 14th-century workmen were building the slender church spire, one of only three of such vintage in Dorset, this is where they lived. Now ivy-clad, it owes more to its days as a farmhouse in the 18th century than to its medieval origins, but the beams and flagstone floors of this Dorset gem don't date. Located on the Ernest Cook Trust estate that surrounds Trent, the inn has a lounge with a large, log-surrounded open fire and comfortable leather sofa; the main bar looks out over fields, and from the restaurant you can survey the valley of the Trent Brook. At the bar, Wadworth's ales usually include 6X, Henry's Orinigal IPA, Horizon and The Bishop's Tipple, with a guest alongside. If your visit coincides with lunchtime hunger pangs, a good range of lighter bites and pub classics has something for every appetite: an open steak sandwich is served with tarragon and tomato relish, green salad and chips; battered south coast cod comes with tartare, triple-cooked chips and mushy peas; and Andrew Barclay sausages are

served in the time-honoured fashion with mash and onion gravy. Essential to the country cooking appeal of the regularly changing main menus are starters of cream of Jerusalem artichoke soup with chives and gruyère gougères; roasted pigeon breast with red watercress, pomegranate and Serrano ham; and warm salt and pepper squid salad with puffed rice, cucumber, spring onion and Asian chilli dressing. Main courses may feature grilled calves' liver, potato rösti, buttered spinach, sage fritters and smoked bacon and onions; or oriental-style belly of pork in a miso and ginger broth, bok choi and prawn dumplings. Leave room for warm maple syrup pancakes with salted caramel and pecan ice cream. Award-winning Read's roaster coffee is served too.

Open all day all wk **Food** Lunch Mon-Sat 12-2.30, Sun 12-3 Dinner all wk 6-9 ⊕ WADWORTH ◀ 6X, Henry's Original IPA, Horizon & The Bishop's Tipple, guest ale ♂ Addlestones, Thatchers Gold. ♇ 25 **Facilities** Non-diners area ♣ (Bar Restaurant Garden) ♦ Children's menu Children's portions Family room Garden ⊼ Parking WiFi 🚌 (notice required) **Rooms** 3

TRENT
Map 4 ST51

The Rose and Crown Inn, Trent ★★★★★ INN

PICK OF THE PUBS

See Pick of the Pubs on opposite page

WEST BEXINGTON
Map 4 SY58

The Manor Hotel

tel: 01308 897660 **DT2 9DF**
email: relax@manorhoteldorset.com
dir: *On B3157, 5m E of Bridport. In Swyre turn opposite The Bull Inn into 'No Through Road'*

Cosy old pub overlooking Chesil Beach

Overlooking the Jurassic Coast's most famous feature, Chesil Beach, parts of this 16th-century manor house are thought to date from the 11th century. It offers an inviting mix of flagstones, Jacobean oak panelling, roaring fires and a cosy cellar bar serving Otter ales and locally sourced dishes. Eat in the Manor Restaurant or in the Cellar Bar. With a drink in hand study the chalkboards displaying modern British dishes; perhaps mackerel pâté followed by pan-fried venison steak and triple cooked celeriac chips. The large free car park is a bonus.

Open all wk 11.30-3 6-10 Closed 1st 2wks Jan **Food** Lunch all wk 12-2 Dinner Mon-Sat 6.30-9, Sun 6-8 ⊕ FREE HOUSE ◼ Otter Ale & Bitter Ö Thatchers Gold, Lilley's. ♟ 10 **Facilities** Non-diners area ❧ (Bar Garden) ⊪ Children's menu Garden 🎋 Parking WiFi ▦ (notice required)

WEST LULWORTH
Map 4 SY88

Lulworth Cove Inn

tel: 01929 400333 **Main Rd BH20 5RQ**
email: lulworthcoveinn@hall-woodhouse.co.uk
dir: *From A352 (Dorchester to Wareham road) follow Lulworth Cove signs. Inn at end of B3070, opposite car park*

A short stroll from Lulworth Cove and the Jurassic Coast

Lulworth Cove's famous horseshoe bay is just steps away from the front door of this inn. It was once a distribution point for the mail service arriving by stagecoach, plus many smugglers' stories can be heard. Ramblers can sate their appetites from the extensive menu, which features light bites, filled baguettes and jacket potatoes, as well as main course dishes like the ever popular steak and Tanglefoot ale pie; haddock smokie pie; and crisp parmesan chicken.

Open all day all wk **Food** all wk 12-9 ⊕ HALL & WOODHOUSE ◼ Badger Ö Westons Stowford Press. ♟ 10 **Facilities** Non-diners area ❧ (Bar Restaurant Garden) ⊪ Children's menu Children's portions Garden 🎋 WiFi ▦

WEST STOUR
Map 4 ST72

The Ship Inn

tel: 01747 838640 **SP8 5RP**
email: mail@shipinn-dorset.com
dir: *On A30, 4m W of Shaftesbury (4m from Henstridge)*

Combining old and new in a rural setting

Walkers can explore the footpaths, which pass through the picturesque Dorset countryside surrounding this coaching inn built in 1750. The main bar has a traditional flagstone floor, low ceiling and log fire, while the lounge bar has stripped oak floorboards and chunky farmhouse furniture. Both offer a selection of beers and ciders, with weekly-changing guest ales. There's a good variety of sandwiches available at lunchtime – smoked salmon and crayfish being just one. An evening menu includes goats' cheese potato and chive croquettes; mixed seafood platter; aubergine, brie, chicory and red pepper tarte Tatin; and steak, mushroom and Blue Vinny shortcrust-lid pie. Outside there's a suntrap patio and large child-friendly garden. Perhaps time your visit for the beer and cider festival in August.

Open all wk 12-3 6-11.30 (Sat-Sun 12-11.30) **Food** Lunch all wk 12-2.30 Dinner Mon-Sat 6-9 Av main course £12.95 Set menu available ⊕ FREE HOUSE ◼ Palmers IPA, Sharp's Doom Bar, Ringwood Fortyniner, Butcombe, guest ale Ö Thatchers Cheddar Valley & Heritage, Westons Stowford Press, Orchard Pig, Landshire Cider. ♟ 13 **Facilities** Non-diners area ❧ (Bar Garden) ⊪ Children's menu Children's portions Garden 🎋 Beer festival Cider festival Parking WiFi

WEYMOUTH
Map 4 SY67

The Old Ship Inn

tel: 01305 812522 **7 The Ridgeway DT3 5QQ**
email: info@theoldshipupwey.co.uk
dir: *3m from Weymouth town centre, at bottom of The Ridgeway*

Weymouth views and real ales

Thomas Hardy refers to this 400-year-old pub in his novel *Under the Greenwood Tree*, and copper pans, old clocks and a beamed open fire create a true period atmosphere. Expect a good selection of real ales of tap, perhaps Dorset Jurassic, St Austell Proper Job and Sharp's Doom Bar, with Addlestones cloudy cider as an alternative. A frequently changing menu of good home-cooked pub food offers crispy whitebait; grilled goats' cheese bruschetta; the ever popular pork belly braised in Addlestones cider with black pudding and dauphinoise potatoes; home-made pie of the day; and parmesan crusted cod. On sunny days bag a bench in the garden and enjoy the views across Weymouth.

Open all wk Mon 5-11 Tue-Fri 12-3 5-11 Sat 12-11 Sun 12-10 **Food** Lunch Tue-Sat 12-2.30, Sun 12-6 Dinner Mon-Sat 6-9, Sun 12-6 ⊕ PUNCH TAVERNS ◼ Sharp's Doom Bar, Ringwood Best Bitter, Dorset Jurassic, St Austell Proper Job, Wadworth 6X, guest ales Ö Addlestones, Westons Stowford Press, Thatchers Somerset Haze. ♟ 13 **Facilities** Non-diners area ❧ (Bar Garden) ⊪ Children's menu Children's portions Garden 🎋 Parking WiFi ▦

WEYMOUTH *continued*

The Red Lion

tel: 01305 786940 **Hope Square DT4 8TR**
email: info@theredlionweymouth.co.uk web: www.theredlionweymouth.co.uk
dir: *Opposite Brewers Quay*

Rums, real ale and extensive food choices

Directly opposite the old Devenish Brewery in the heart of Weymouth, this former brewery tap has long been a famous ale house, popular with locals and visitors, and with strong links with the local RNLI – it is after all the lifeboat crew's nearest pub. Expect a comfortably rustic feel to the rambling rooms, with wood floors, candles on scrubbed tables, eclectic furnishings, period fireplaces, walls adorned with lifeboat pictures and artefacts, newspapers to peruse, and a cracking bar serving 80 rums, five ales and traditional ciders. To eat, there are platters to share; a pint or half pint of prawns; proper surf 'n' turf; and the 'legendary' home-made steak and Life Boat Ale pie, chips and 'not so mushy' peas.

Open all day all wk 11-11 (Fri-Sat 11am-mdnt Sun 12-10.30) **Food** Lunch all wk 12-3, Apr-Sep all day Dinner all wk 6-9, Apr-Sep all day ⊕ FREE HOUSE ◀ Otter Brewery Life Boat Ale, Dorset Jurassic, Sharp's Doom Bar, St Austell Tribute ♂ Westons Traditional Scrumpy & Country Perry. ▾ 12 **Facilities** Non-diners area ♣ (Outside area) ♦♦ Children's menu Children's portions Outside area ⊫ WiFi ➡ (notice required)

WORTH MATRAVERS   Map 4 SY97

The Square and Compass

tel: 01929 439229 **BH19 3LF**
dir: *Between Corfe Castle & Swanage. From B3069 follow signs for Worth Matravers*

Lovely pub with beer but no bar and limited food

Award-winning West Country beers and ciders come straight from the barrel here and food is limited to just pasties and pies. Little has changed at this stone-built pub for the past century, during which time it has been run by the same family. It is tucked-away and boasts a simple interior with no bar, just a serving hatch and an abundance of flagstone floors, oak panels and a museum of local artefacts and fossils from the nearby Jurassic Coast. On the first Saturday in October there's a beer and pumpkin festival, and in early November there's a cider festival.

Open all wk 12-3 6-11 (summer & Fri-Sun 12-11) **Food** Contact pub for food times ⊕ FREE HOUSE ◀ Palmers Copper Ale, Wessex Longleat Pride, Hatty Browns Mustang Sally ♂ Hecks Farmhouse, home-made cider. **Facilities** Non-diners area ♣ (All areas) ♦♦ Garden Outside area Beer festival Cider festival ➡ **Notes** ☺

COUNTY DURHAM

AYCLIFFE   Map 19 NZ22

The County

tel: 01325 312273 **13 The Green, Aycliffe Village DL5 6LX**
email: info@thecountyaycliffevillage.com
dir: *A1(M) junct 59, off A167 into Aycliffe Village*

Picturesque village green setting

Prettily perched on the village green, this inn's smart restaurant and terrace are lovely places to eat, as is the homely bar where you can sup a pint of Black Sheep or Cocker Hoop. With superb local produce on the doorstep, the seasonally changing menus offer the likes of baked goats' cheese and spinach tart; or chicken liver and almond pâté with spiced Indian tomato chutney, then loin of venison, roasted salsify, spinach and chocolate and sweet chilli jus; or home-made steak and ale shortcrust pastry pie.

Open all day all wk Closed 25-26 Dec, 1 Jan, 1st 2wks Aug **Food** Lunch Mon-Sat 12-2, Sun 12-7 Dinner Mon-Sat 5.30-9, Sun 12-7 Restaurant menu available all wk ⊕ FREE HOUSE ◀ Cocker Hoop, Black Sheep, Yorkshire Dales, Hawkshead ♂ Kingstone Press. ▾ 10 **Facilities** Non-diners area ♦♦ Children's portions Outside area ⊫ Parking WiFi

---

BARNARD CASTLE   Map 19 NZ01

The Morritt Hotel ★★★★ HL ☺☺   PICK OF THE PUBS

tel: 01833 627232 **Greta Bridge DL12 9SE**
email: relax@themorritt.co.uk web: www.themorritt.co.uk
dir: *From A1(M) at Scotch Corner take A66 towards Penrith, in 9m exit at Greta Bridge. Hotel over bridge on left*

Country house atmosphere

Georgian grandeur to the creeper-clad exterior; country house character and contemporary comforts inside; this classic, large coaching inn has commanded a bridge over the River Greta for three centuries. In Victorian times Charles Dickens passed through; he likely based a scene in *Nicholas Nickelby* here. In the bar, an eye-catching mural of Dickensian characters was painted by 'Guinness' artist Jack Gilroy; the practice of promoting local artists continues, with regularly changing works of art on display. A change of hands in early 2016 ensured continuity both of the stylish accommodation and the award-winning food, which is rich with local pickings. Bar meals such as fish pie or braised shoulder of pork are served in the Dickens Bar and Bistro; the more gracious Gilroy's Dining Room has a changing menu which might offer wood pigeon starter followed by hoggit loin, salt-baked leg, wild garlic purée and gnocchi, and mint jus; or sea bass with crispy chicken wing and French peas. Local real ales and a good selection of bins seal the deal.

Open all day all wk 7am-11pm (Sun 7am-10.30pm) **Food** Lunch all wk 12-6 Dinner all wk 6-9 Av main course £12 Restaurant menu available Tue-Sun ⊕ FREE HOUSE ◀ Timothy Taylor Landlord, rotating local guest ales. ▾ 12 **Facilities** Non-diners area ♣ (Bar Garden) ♦♦ Children's menu Children's portions Play area Family room Garden ⊫ Beer festival Parking WiFi ➡ **Rooms** 26

Three Horseshoes ★★★★ INN

tel: 01833 631777 **5-7 Galgate DL12 8EQ**
email: info@three-horse-shoes.co.uk web: www.three-horse-shoes.co.uk
dir: *In town centre on A67*

Local produce in family-run pub

In the centre of the historic market town of Barnard Castle, the Three Horseshoes is an ideal base for walkers exploring the nearby Teesdale Valley and the North Pennines. The Green family successfully run this popular 17th-century coaching inn. Enjoy a pint of real ale as you scan the menus. Start with deep-fried breaded brie; or lamb kofta, then follow on with chicken carbonara; Malayan chicken curry; lasagne, or something from the chargrill. Sandwiches and salads are available during the day.

Open all day all wk **Food** Lunch Mon-Sat 11.30-3, Sun 12-4 (early bird menu Mon-Fri 3-6.30) Dinner Mon-Sat 5-9 Set menu available ⊕ FREE HOUSE ◄ Wychwood Hobgoblin, Ringwood Boondoggle. ☕ 12 **Facilities** Non-diners area ◄ Children's menu Children's portions Garden Outside area ⊟ Parking WiFi ▬ **Rooms** 11

| CASTLE EDEN | Map 19 NZ43 |

Castle Eden Inn

tel: 01429 835137 **Stockton Rd TS27 4SD**
email: info@castleedeninn.com
dir: *Phone for detailed directions*

Great reputation for locally sourced good food

The village of Castle Eden was mentioned in the Domesday Book (although it seems there is no evidence that there was a castle there at the time) and the inn dates from the 18th century. You'll find Castle Eden Ale and Timothy Taylor Landlord in the bar, and the kitchen has certainly built a good reputation for dishes such as ox tongue, pickles and croûtons; North Sea smoked salmon and prawn fishcakes with sweetcorn chowder; bacon and black pudding salad with free-range poached egg; and marmalade roast bacon loin, mustard mash and leeks. The pub's events calendar is pretty full and includes a beer festival in early summer.

Open all day all wk 11am-mdnt (Sun 12-10.30) **Food** Lunch Mon-Sat 12-2.30, Sun 12-5.30 Dinner Mon-Thu 5-9, Fri-Sat 5-9.30 Set menu available Restaurant menu available all wk ⊕ ENTERPRISE INNS ◄ Castle Eden Ale, Timothy Taylor Landlord ♂ Rekorderlig. ☕ 10 **Facilities** Non-diners area ♣ (Bar Garden) ◄ Children's menu Children's portions Family room Garden ⊟ Beer festival Cider festival Parking WiFi ▬ (notice required)

| CHESTER-LE-STREET | Map 19 NZ25 |

NEW The Lambton Worm ★★★★ INN

tel: 0191 387 1162 **52 North Rd DH3 4AJ**
email: info@thelambton.com web: www.thelambton.com
dir: *A1(M) junct 63, A693 towards Stanley. At next rdbt take A167 signed Birtley. Pub on left*

Brewery tap for Sonnet 43 craft ales

All six of Sonnet 43's core beers are on tap at The Lambton Worm. *Sonnet 43* is Elizabeth Barrett Browning's best-known poem and the inspiration behind the Lambton operation; the pub seeks to answer the poem's opening question 'How do I love thee?' in its approach to food, drink and accommodation. The ales are paired with dishes of 'good honest food that makes the heart sing'. Braised beef brisket, for example, followed by home-made rice pudding, both match well with a pint of their Bourbon Milk Stout. If wine is preferred, more than a dozen are served by the glass.

Open all day all wk **Food** Mon-Sat 12-9, Sun 12-7 Av main course £9 Set menu available Restaurant menu available Mon-Sat ⊕ SONNET 43 BREWHOUSE ◄ Sonnet 43, guest ales. ☕ 16 **Facilities** Non-diners area ◄ Children's menu Children's portions Garden Outside area ⊟ Parking WiFi ▬ (notice required) **Rooms** 14

The Moorings Hotel

tel: 0191 370 1597 **Hett Hill DH2 3JU**
email: info@themooringsdurham.co.uk
dir: *A1(M) junct 63 to Chester-le-Street. Take B6313. Hotel on left*

Tranquil Tees Valley setting

Handy both for the fascinating open air museum at Beamish and the historic heart of Chester-le-Street, this thriving hotel bar attracts much custom from ramblers and riders enjoying the glorious countryside. Thirsts are quenched by beers from the respected microbrewery at the Beamish complex, whilst keen appetites will be satisfied by dishes created from the freshest local and seasonal produce. The menu of modern classics and daily specials ranges across the spectrum, from breaded cod, haddock and crayfish tail fishcakes with ratatouille to sirloin steak and garlic butter tiger prawns, finishing with sticky toffee and date pudding with caramel cream sauce.

Open all day all wk **Food** Mon-Thu 11.45-9, Fri-Sat 11.45-9.30, Sun 11.45-8.30 Av main course £8 Set menu available Restaurant menu available Fri-Sun ⊕ FREE HOUSE ◄ The Stables Beamish Hall Bitter, Rudgate Battle Axe, guest ales. **Facilities** ◄ Children's menu Children's portions Family room Garden Outside area ⊟ Parking WiFi

| COTHERSTONE | Map 19 NZ01 |

The Fox and Hounds

tel: 01833 650241 **DL12 9PF**
email: mail@cotherstonefox.co.uk
dir: *4m W of Barnard Castle. From A66 onto B6277, pub signed*

Picturesque village setting

At the heart of beautiful Teesdale and just a stone's throw from the river's wooded gorge, The Fox and Hounds is huddled above one of the village greens in pretty Cotherstone. Beams, open fires and thickly cushioned wall seats tempt you to linger at this 360-year-old coaching inn, admiring the local photographs and country pictures while you sip a pint of Black Sheep Best Bitter or Symonds cider. From the menu, tuck into dishes made from the best of fresh, local ingredients: cheese-filled chicken baked in creamy leek sauce; gammon steak, sausage, black pudding with fried egg and chips; or pan-fried lamb's liver and gravy, for example.

Open all wk 12-2.30 6-11 (Sun 12-2.30 6-10.30) Closed 25-26 Dec, Mon L, Tue L, Wed L winter **Food** Lunch all wk 12-2 Dinner all wk 6-8.30 Av main course £10 ⊕ FREE HOUSE ◄ Black Sheep Best Bitter & Ale, York Yorkshire Terrier, Daleside, Hawkshead Lakeland Gold, Rudgate ♂ Aspall, Symonds, Westons Rosie's Pig. ☕ 8 **Facilities** Non-diners area ♣ (Restaurant Outside area) ◄ Children's menu Children's portions Outside area ⊟ Parking WiFi ▬ (notice required)

COXHOE
Map 19 NZ33

The Italian Farmhouse

tel: 0191 377 3773 **DH6 4HX**
email: coxhoe@theitalianfarmhouse.co.uk
dir: Phone for detailed directions

Traditional Victorian pub with a separate Italian restaurant

New landlord Mark Hird now runs what used to be the Clarence Villa. It remains the home of Sonnet 43 Brewhouse, named for "How do I love thee?", the famous poem by Elizabeth Barrett Browning, who was born locally in 1806. The brewery's full range of craft beers is served in the bar, as is familiar pub grub such as meat, fish and vegetable 'planks'; burgers and pizzas; beer-battered cod and chips; chicken, leek and mushroom pie; and honey- and bourbon-glazed pork belly. The menu recommends Sonnet 43's Bourbon Milk Stout as an accompaniment to profiteroles, tiramisù and other puddings.

Open all day all wk **Food** Mon-Sat 12-9, Sun 12-8 Set menu available Restaurant menu available all wk ⊕ FREE HOUSE/TAVISTOCK HOSPITALITY ◀ Sonnet 43 American Pale Ale, Steam Beer, Bourbon Milk Stout, India Pale Ale & Blonde Beer. ♚ 12 **Facilities** Non-diners area ♦♦ Children's menu Children's portions Garden Outside area ⋒ Parking WiFi ➡ (notice required)

DARLINGTON
Map 19 NZ21

Number Twenty 2

tel: 01325 354590 **22 Coniscliffe Rd DL3 7RG**
email: no22@btconnect.com
dir: In town centre, off A67

An ale drinkers' heaven with microbrewery

Looking just like other shop fronts in the street, the door of Number Twenty 2 opens to reveal a classic Victorian pub. Multiple awards recognise that real ales are the name of the game here – up to 13 being pulled at busy times; expect to find Bull Premium and White Boar among them. Even more interesting perhaps is the ouput from the onsite microbrewery and nano-distillery. Add to all this, nine continental beers, wines chosen for easy quaffing, and a select list of fine spirits and you have a drinker's paradise. Whether by popular demand or applied common sense, a seating area known as 'the canteen' is where light bites, soups, gourmet burgers and toasted sandwiches are served from midday until 7pm.

Open all day Closed 25-26 Dec, 1 Jan & BH Mon, Sun **Food** Mon-Sat 12-7 ⊕ FREE HOUSE ◀ The Village Brewer White Boar Bitter, Bull Premium Bitter & Old Raby ♖ Kingstone Press, guest ciders. ♚ 22 **Facilities** Non-diners area ♦♦ WiFi

DURHAM
Map 19 NZ24

Victoria Inn

tel: 0191 386 5269 **86 Hallgarth St DH1 3AS**
dir: In city centre

Traditional red brick street pub at the heart of the city

This unique, listed inn has scarcely changed since it was built in 1899 – not a jukebox, pool table or TV to be found. Just five minutes' walk from the cathedral, it has been carefully nurtured by the Webster family for over 40 years. Small rooms warmed by coal fires and a congenial atmosphere include the tiny snug, where a portrait of Queen Victoria still hangs above the upright piano. You'll find a few simple snacks to tickle the taste buds, but it's the cracking well-kept local ales, single malts, and over 40 Irish whiskies that are the main attraction.

Open all wk 11-11 **Food** Contact pub for food times ⊕ FREE HOUSE ◀ Wylam Gold Tankard, Durham Magus, Big Lamp Bitter, Fyne Ales Jarl, Hill Island, Saltaire Blonde. **Facilities** Non-diners area ♚ (Bar Restaurant) ♦♦ Family room Parking WiFi ➡

FIR TREE
Map 19 NZ13

Duke of York Inn

tel: 01388 767429 **DL15 8DG**
email: info@dukeofyorkfirtree.co.uk
dir: On A68, 12m W of Durham. From Durham take A690 W. Left onto A68 to Fir Tree

A warm welcome, modern interior and good food

On the tourist route (A68) to Scotland, the Duke of York is a former drovers' and coaching inn dating from 1749. It is appointed inside and out to a high standard, keeping the traditional country feel with contemporary touches. Look for Camerons Black Sheep to accompany the food served all day. There's light bites, sandwiches and omelettes plus main menu choices such as the signature dish of chicken in creamy leek and pancetta sauce with crushed potatoes; or full rack of smokey BBQ baby ribs and hand-cut chips.

Open all day all wk **Food** all wk 12-9 Set menu available ⊕ CAMERONS BREWERY ◀ Black Sheep Best Bitter, guest ales. **Facilities** Non-diners area ♚ (Bar Garden) ♦♦ Children's menu Children's portions Garden ⋒ Parking WiFi ➡

FROSTERLEY
Map 19 NZ03

The Black Bull Inn

tel: 01388 527784 **DL13 2SL**
email: blackbullfrosterley@gmail.com
dir: From A68 onto A689 towards Stanhope. Left into Frosterley. Inn adjacent to railway station

Great ales with bells on

Uniquely, this family-run, independent country pub has its own church bells – not to mention a great range of real ales to enjoy after a spot of bell-ringing. Located next to Weardale steam railway station, it has cosy, music-free rooms, a stone-flagged bar and open fires in Victorian ranges. The ad hoc beer festivals demonstrate unwavering backing for local microbreweries, while the kitchen is equally supportive of the regional suppliers behind the food. A meal might take in potted North Shields crab; pan-roasted pheasant breast, apricot and walnut stuffing, potato and squash dauphinoise and red cabbage; and sticky toffee pudding with ginger ice cream.

Open all day Closed Sun eve, Mon (Tue & Wed in winter) **Food** Lunch Thu-Sat 12-3, Sun 12-2.30 Dinner Thu-Sat 7-9, (summer Tue & Wed extended opening hours) ⊕ FREE HOUSE ◀ Allendale, Wylam, Consett, York, Jarrow ♖ Wilkins Farmhouse, Westons. **Facilities** ♚ (Bar Restaurant Garden) ♦♦ Children's portions Garden ⋒ Beer festival Cider festival Parking WiFi ➡ (notice required)

HESLEDEN
Map 19 NZ43

NEW The Ship Inn ★★★★ INN

tel: 01429 836453 **High Hesleden TS27 4QD**
email: sheila@theshipinn.net **web:** www.theshipinn.net
dir: From A19 at Castle Eden take B1281 towards Blackhall Colliery. Turn right signed Hesleden. Pub on left

The hamlet's beating heart

It took six years of hard work, not to mention money, for Peter and Sheila Crosby to breathe new life into this once-derelict, but now fine-looking, 1910 pub. The bar's seven changing real ales are of considerable appeal; so too are its freshly prepared, locally sourced dishes, among which favourites are the black pudding and haggis medley starter, and main courses of surf and turf; chargrilled rump of Yorkshire lamb; and, for vegetarians, baked sweet bell peppers. On Wednesdays to Fridays, Early Bird two-course specials include a bottle of wine.

Open 6-11 (Sat 12-3 6-11 Sun 12-8) Closed Mon, Tue-Fri L **Food** Lunch Sat-Sun 12-3 Dinner Tue-Sat 5.30-9 Set menu available Restaurant menu available Tue-Sat

FREE HOUSE Rotating guest ales Symonds Scrumpy Jack.
Facilities Non-diners area Children's menu Children's portions Play area Family room Garden Parking WiFi (notice required) **Rooms** 9

HURWORTH-ON-TEES **Map 19 NZ30**

The Bay Horse

tel: 01325 720663 **45 The Green DL2 2AA**
email: mail@thebayhorsehurworth.com
dir: *From A66 at Darlington Football Club rdbt follow Hurworth sign*

Fine dining in pretty Tees Valley village

Savvy diners may get 'Bitter and Twisted' as it's one of the real ales on hand to satisfy devotees seeking out the culinary magic conjured up by talented chef-proprietors Jonathan Hall and Marcus Bennett. The ancient pub retains considerable character enhanced by carefully chosen period furnishings. Thoroughly modern cuisine sets this ambience off to a tee. At dinner expect starters like white crab meat with mango ketchup, avocado, brown crab mousse, prawn beignets and prawn crisps, and mains such as rack of venison with roast apple purée, shallot and venison croquettes, roasted shallots, shallot tart fine and Madeira jus; or roasted stone bass with fish burger, pickled cucumber, mussel and saffron chowder, cauliflower purée and a brown shrimp butter. There's a good vegetarian choice too.

Open all day all wk Closed 25-26 Dec **Food** Lunch Mon-Sat 12-2.30, Sun 12-4 Dinner all wk 6-close Av main course £19 Set menu available Restaurant menu available Mon-Sat & Sun eve FREE HOUSE Harviestoun Bitter & Twisted, Timothy Taylor, The Village Brewer White Boar Bitter. 12 **Facilities** Non-diners area Children's menu Garden Parking WiFi

The Otter & Fish

tel: 01325 720019 **1 Strait Ln DL2 2AH**
email: r.weeks@btconnect.com **web:** www.otterandfish.co.uk
dir: *Phone for detailed directions*

Contemporary style and traditional food

Overlooking the River Tees in the picturesque village of Hurworth, close to the North Yorkshire border, this pub has been family owned and run for 10 years or so. The place has a relaxed and welcoming contemporary style, with an emphasis on good food and great service. Traditional bar meals are available, as well as a full carte, offering plenty of choice, from venison haunch with caramelised cauliflower, French beans, fondant potato and thyme pancetta jus; or pork fillet and black pudding roulade wrapped in Parma ham with confit belly, sprouts and broad beans; to broccoli, pea and leek linguine; or mushroom and chilli carbonara.

Open all wk **Food** Lunch Mon-Sat 12-2, Sun 12-5 Dinner Mon-Sat 6-9 Set menu available Restaurant menu available Mon-Sat FREE HOUSE Black Sheep Westons Stowford Press. **Facilities** Non-diners area Children's menu Children's portions Outside area Parking WiFi (notice required)

HUTTON MAGNA **Map 19 NZ11**

The Oak Tree Inn PICK OF THE PUBS

tel: 01833 627371 **DL11 7HH**
dir: *From A1 at Scotch Corner take A66 W. 6.5m, right for Hutton Magna*

Excellent cooking with a pedigree

Books by Raymond Blanc, Gordon Ramsay, Stéphane Reynaud and other top chefs casually repose around this whitewashed, part 18th-century free house. They suggest that food is taken seriously here – seriously enough to warrant two AA Rosettes, that's for sure. Responsible are Alastair and Claire Ross, he with a CV listing The Savoy, Leith's and a London private members' club. In the simply furnished dining room, Alastair's refined dishes change daily, combining classic techniques and modern flavours to offer such starters as celeriac and parmesan soup; or warm pork belly and black pudding salad. Then, maybe fillet of sea bass with roast scallops, tenderstem broccoli and leek risotto; or best end of lamb with olive oil and chorizo mashed potato. As well as fine real ales from Timothy Taylor and Jennings, there are world-sourced bottled beers, a serious wine list, and over 20 malt whiskies.

Open 6-11 (Sun 5.30-10.30) Closed Xmas & New Year, Mon **Food** Contact pub for food times Restaurant menu available Tue-Sun FREE HOUSE Jennings Cumberland Ale, Timothy Taylor Landlord, Copper Dragon. 10
Facilities Non-diners area (Bar) Parking

LONGNEWTON **Map 19 NZ31**

Vane Arms

tel: 01642 580401 **Darlington Rd TS21 1DB**
email: thevaneatlongnewton@gmail.com **web:** www.thevaneatlongnewton.com
dir: *W end of Longnewton, just off A66 (midway between Stockton-on-Tees & Darlington)*

Village pub with new landlord

This 18th-century pub has neither jukebox, pool or gaming machine, and the TV is on only for special events; background music plays quietly in the lounge. Sensibly priced home-made restaurant food includes haloumi stuffed pepper; crispy salmon and haddock fishcakes; butternut squash risotto; short-crust steak, mushroom and Black Sheep ale pie; and steamed spotted dick with bay leaf custard and seasonal berries. Grill night is Tuesday, French cuisine and tapas are available on alternate Wednesday evenings, roasts on Sunday, and there is a mini beer festival in July. A large garden looks towards the Cleveland Hills and the North Yorkshire Moors.

Open 12-2 5-11 (Mon 5-11 Fri-Sat 12-2 5-12 Sun 12-11) Closed Mon L **Food** Lunch Tue-Sat 12-2, Sun 12-3 Dinner Tue-Sat 5-9 Set menu available Restaurant menu available all wk FREE HOUSE Black Sheep Best Bitter, guest ales Somersby.
Facilities Non-diners area (Garden) Children's portions Garden Beer festival Parking WiFi (notice required)

MICKLETON
Map 18 NY92

The Crown

tel: 01833 640381 **DL12 0JZ**
email: info@thecrownatmickleton.co.uk
dir: B6277 from Barnard Castle. Approx 6m to Eggleston. Follow Mickleton signs

In the upper Tees Valley

This old stone inn stands on Mickleton's main street, surrounded by the heather-covered moors of the North Pennines Area of Outstanding Natural Beauty. Candlelight and a log-burning stove illuminate the interior, lovingly maintained by the Rowbotham family whom, it's good to report, are enthusiastic supporters of local craft breweries, such as Cumberland, Jarrow and Sonnet 43. The menu might catch your eye with steamed Shetland mussels and bacon and cider cream sauce; broad bean, garden pea and goats' cheese salad with lemon and mint dressing; twice-cooked Simpson's Aberdeen Angus beef steak and chunky chips; and strawberry cheesecake and fresh strawberry ice cream. The dog-friendly garden is a real treat.

Open all day 11am-mdnt **Closed** 1st 2wks Jan, Mon-Tue (Jan-Apr) **Food** all wk 12-9 Av main course £10 ⊕ FREE HOUSE ◀ Cumberland Corby Ale, Jarrow Rivet Catcher, Sonnet 43 Steam Beer. ☻ 9 **Facilities** Non-diners area ✿ (All areas) ♦ Children's portions Garden Outside area ⌁ Parking WiFi ➣ (notice required)

NEWTON AYCLIFFE
Map 19 NZ22

Blacksmiths Arms

tel: 01325 314873 **Preston le Skerne, (off Ricknall Lane) DL5 6JH**
dir: Exit A167 (dual carriageway) at Gretna Green pub signed Great Stanton, Stillington & Bishopton, into Ricknall Ln. Blacksmiths Arms 0.5m

Fondly regarded village pub

Rachel and Peter Walton arrived at 'The Hammers', as its regulars call it, in February 2016. For a light starter there's Caesar salad, or the slightly more substantial pan-fried chorizo, red wine and honey. Home-made pie of the day comes with hand-cut chips and peas, as does battered cod but with tartare sauce too. The Blacksmiths burger is always a good bet. Speciality dishes include chicken breast stuffed with brie wrapped in Parma ham, dauphinoise potatoes and creamy herb sauce; pan-fried sea bass on a warm salad of chorizo, cherry tomatoes, green beans and new potatoes; and leek and mushroom risotto with crème fraîche, parmesan and dressed rocket.

Open 11.30-2.30 6-11 (Sun 12-10.30) **Closed** 1 Jan, Mon **Food** Lunch Tue-Sat 11.30-2, Sun 12-10.30 Dinner Tue-Sat 6-9, Sun 12-10.30 ⊕ FREE HOUSE ◀ Guest ales. ☻ 10 **Facilities** Non-diners area ♦ Children's menu Play area Garden ⌁ Parking ➣ (notice required)

ROMALDKIRK
Map 19 NY92

The Rose & Crown ★★★ HL ◉◉
PICK OF THE PUBS

See Pick of the Pubs on opposite page

SEAHAM
Map 19 NZ44

The Seaton Lane Inn ★★★★ INN

tel: 0191 581 2036 **Seaton Ln SR7 0LP**
email: info@seatonlaneinn.com **web:** www.seatonlaneinn.com
dir: S of Sunderland on A19 take B1404 towards Houghton-le-Spring. In Seaton turn left for pub

Traditional pub with stylish, contemporary interior and good food

With a traditional bar area as well as a stylish restaurant and lounge, this boutique-type inn offers four real ales to keep the regulars happy, served from the central bar. The menu proffers dishes such as smooth chicken liver parfait; and classic Caesar salad with hot kiln smoked salmon flakes as starters, followed by beef cheeks braised in stout, mash and honey-roasted carrots; fillet of monkfish cassoulet; Thai vegetable risotto; or Wallington Estate prime rib-eye steak. Bedrooms are modern, spacious and smartly furnished.

Open all day all wk 7am-mdnt **Food** all wk 7am-9.30pm Set menu available Restaurant menu available all wk ⊕ FREE HOUSE ◀ Black Sheep, Firebrick. ☻ 10 **Facilities** Non-diners area ✿ (Bar Garden Outside area) ♦ Children's menu Children's portions Garden Outside area ⌁ Parking WiFi ➣ **Rooms** 18

SHINCLIFFE
Map 19 NZ24

Seven Stars Inn

tel: 0191 384 8454 **DH1 2NU**
email: info@sevenstarsinn.co.uk
dir: A1(M) junct 61, A177 towards Durham. Approx 2m to Shincliffe. Pub in village centre

Country inn with walks to Durham city

In a peaceful village a short hop from Durham's historic city centre, the family-run Seven Stars has been refreshing travellers since it was built as a coaching inn in 1724. The cosy traditional bar with open fire offers ales from the Durham Brewery, while the separate restaurant serves modern British dishes with occasional international influences. Expect the likes of crayfish tail salad; black pudding fritters; beef and Durham Magus ale pie; and lemon pannacotta with blackberries. Lighter lunchtime bites include pork and leek sausages with chunky apple sauce, and sandwiches, and from 5.30pm, home-made, stone-baked hand-rolled pizzas.

Open all day **Closed** Mon L **Food** Lunch Tue-Sun 12-2 Dinner Mon-Sat 5.30-9, Sun 6-8 Set menu available ⊕ ENTERPRISE INNS ◀ Timothy Taylor Landlord, Black Sheep Best Bitter, Durham Magus. ☻ 10 **Facilities** Non-diners area ✿ (Bar Outside area) ♦ Children's menu Children's portions Outside area ⌁ WiFi ➣ (notice required)

PICK OF THE PUBS

The Rose & Crown ★★★ HL ❀❀

ROMALDKIRK   Map 19 NY92

tel: 01833 650213 **DL12 9EB**
email: hotel@rose-and-crown.co.uk
web: www.rose-and-crown.co.uk
dir: *6m NW from Barnard Castle on B6277*

A real rural dining pub with a long pedigree

Overlooking the village's old stocks and water pump, this creeper-clad stone built coaching inn stands on the village green, while next door is the Saxon church known as 'The Cathedral of the Dale'. Step inside the 18th-century pub to be greeted by fresh flowers, varnished oak panelling, old beams, and gleaming copper and brass artefacts, then enter the quirky little bar and you'll encounter oak settles, a vast dog grate, old prints, carriage lamps and rural curios. In the secluded lounge you can retire to a wing-backed chair and be lulled by the ticking of a grandfather clock, with maybe a glass of Marston's Wainwright or Black Sheep. The chefs use the best local produce sourced from Teesdale farms and sporting estates, as well as fish from the north-east coast, to create their imaginative, seasonal menus. Drop in at lunchtime for a just light bite or from the à la carte choose perhaps a home-made steak and ale pie or a seasonally inspired fish dish such as

pan-roasted fillet of hake with brown shrimp fritter, Jerusalem artichoke, kale and rosemary cream. In the evening food can be enjoyed either in the bar area or in the oak-panelled restaurant. The cuisine style combines modern British cooking with a nod to the traditional Dales setting of The Rose & Crown. Typical dinner menu dishes are charred mackerel with compressed cucumber, pickled artichoke and artichoke broth; and pan-fried venison, mini venison cottage pie, baby carrots, kale, root vegetable purée and thyme jus. The service is professional yet friendly and the overall ambience is relaxed and comfortable.

Open all day all wk Closed 24-26 Dec & 1wk Jan **Food** Lunch all wk 12-2.30 Dinner all wk 6.30-9 Restaurant menu available all wk ⊕ FREE HOUSE
🍺 Black Sheep Best Bitter, Marston's Wainwright Ö Kingston. ♀ 9
Facilities Non-diners area 🐾 (Bar Outside area) 👶 Children's portions Outside area 🅿 Parking WiFi **Rooms** 14

STANLEY
Map 19 NZ15

The Stables Pub and Restaurant

tel: 01207 288750 & 233733 **Beamish Hall Hotel, Beamish DH9 OYB**
email: info@beamish-hall.co.uk
dir: *A693 to Stanley. Follow signs for Beamish Hall Country House Hotel & Beamish Museum. Left at museum entrance. Hotel on left 0.2m after golf club. Pub within hotel grounds*

Own-brewed beer and ever-popular food

The stone-floored, beamed bar is the perfect spot to sample the pub's own real ales, brewed on site at their microbrewery. The beer festival in the third week of September will get you even more closely acquainted, while a cider festival is held during the second weekend of December. The pub, in the former mansion house stables, was a courtyard for alfresco eating and drinking, but if the weather's on the chilly side there's always the option to cheer up your day by enjoying a drink by a roaring fire. Regional producers supply the best local ingredients from which are crafted exemplary meals. Try perhaps Thai crab cakes with lime and chilli jam; followed by the trio of Knitsley Farm sausages, buttered mash, Beamish Ale gravy and crispy onion rings; or a classic fish pie and winter greens.

Open all day all wk Mon-Thu 11-11 (Fri-Sat 11am-mdnt Sun 11-10.30) **Food** Mon-Thu 12-9, Fri-Sat 12-9.30, Sun 12-8 Set menu available Restaurant menu available all wk ⊕ FREE HOUSE ◀ The Stables Beamish Hall Bitter, Beamish Burn Brown Ale, Old Miner Tommy, Silver Buckles Ŏ Gwynt y Ddraig Haymaker & Farmhouse Pyder. ♈
Facilities Non-diners area ❀ (Garden) ♦♦ Children's menu Children's portions Play area Garden ⋒ Beer festival Cider festival Parking WiFi ⛟

THORPE THEWLES
Map 19 NZ32

The Vane Arms

tel: 01740 630458 **TS21 3JU**
email: tom@thevanearms.com
dir: *Take A177 from Stockton-on-Tees towards Sedgefield. Left to Thorpe Thewles*

Long-established pub

In a picturesque village named after the Vane-Tempest family of Nynyard, high up the valley, this handsome pub has served the peaceful Tees Valley for over 200 years. Tables out-front overlook the green, and Village Brewer's White Boar is served in the bar as well as guest ales. Expect roaring fires in winter and a large garden for whiling away a summer evening. The menu changes seasonally with a focus on locally sourced ingredients – hot haggis Scotch egg; and pork, pistachio and prune terrine to start, then braised venison shank, roast winter veg and wild mushroom jus; beer-battered North Sea cod with chips, tartare sauce and Yorkshire caviar; or perhaps a 32oz côte de boeuf for two to share. There's a beer festival in June.

Open 12-2 5-11 (Sat 12-11 Sun 12-5) Closed Sun eve & Mon **Food** Lunch Tue-Sat 12-2, Sun 12-4 Dinner Tue-Sat 5.30-9 Av main course £13.50 ⊕ FREE HOUSE ◀ The Village Brewer White Boar Bitter, rotating guest ales Ŏ Aspall. ♈ 12
Facilities Non-diners area ♦♦ Children's portions Garden Outside area ⋒ Beer festival Parking

WINSTON
Map 19 NZ11

The Bridgewater Arms

tel: 01325 730302 **DL2 3RN**
email: paul.p.grundy@gmail.com
dir: *Exit A67 between Barnard Castle & Darlington, onto B6274 into Winston*

Former schoolhouse serving fresh seafood

Set in a former schoolhouse, this Grade II listed pub is decorated with original photographs of the building and its pupils. It prides itself on offering high quality, simple meals made with local produce, particularly seafood. Cheddar and spinach soufflé, followed by confit leg of duck with garlic mash and red wine sauce is a

typical meal, while fishy offerings could include tiger prawn and monkfish curry with pilau rice; and grilled cod chunk, spring onion mash, mussels and curry cream. Afterwards, the historic Winston Bridge and beautiful views to the church are a short stroll away.

Open 12-2.30 6-11 Closed 25-26 Dec, 1 Jan, Sun & Mon **Food** Lunch Tue-Sat 12-2 Dinner Tue-Sat 6-9 Av main course £14 ⊕ FREE HOUSE ◀ Timothy Taylor Landlord, Marston's, Cumberland, Mithril Ales, Rudgate Ŏ Thatchers. ♈ 15
Facilities Non-diners area ♦♦ Children's portions Outside area ⋒ Parking WiFi

ESSEX

ARKESDEN
Map 12 TL43

Axe & Compasses
PICK OF THE PUBS

See Pick of the Pubs on opposite page

AYTHORPE RODING
Map 6 TL51

Axe & Compasses

tel: 01279 876648 **Dunmow Rd CM6 1PP**
email: axeandcompasses@msn.com
dir: *From A120 follow signs for Dunmow*

Nostalgic pub with great home cooking

The owners of this weather-boarded, 17th-century pub like to create a 'nostalgic pub experience'. In the bar, ales from brewers such as Adnams, are backed by Westons ciders. David Hunt, a skilled self-taught chef, uses the best of seasonal produce and loves to offer dishes such as prawn and crayfish cocktail; butternut squash, chestnut and mushroom risotto; calves' liver and bacon; steak in ale puff pastry pie; and confit pork belly with apple mash. The pub also serves breakfast daily and offers a great range of bar snacks such as pork crackling with warm apple sauce or a home-made Scotch egg.

Open all day all wk 9am-11.30pm (Sun 9am-11pm) **Food** Bkfst all wk 9am-11.30am Lunch Mon-Sat 12-2.30, Sun 12-8 Dinner Mon-Sat 6-9.30, Sun 12-8 ⊕ FREE HOUSE ◀ Sharp's Doom Bar, Adnams Broadside & Lighthouse, guest ale Ŏ Westons Old Rosie, Rosie's Pig & Cider Twist Raspberry. ♈ 15
Facilities Non-diners area ❀ (Bar Garden) ♦♦ Children's menu Children's portions Garden ⋒ Parking WiFi ⛟ (notice required)

BELCHAMP ST PAUL
Map 13 TL74

The Half Moon

tel: 01787 277402 **Cole Green CO10 7DP**
email: enquiries@halfmoonbelchamp.co.uk
dir: *From Braintree take A131 towards Halstead. Left onto A1017 to Great Yeldham. In Great Yeldham follow 'The Belchamps' signs. Approx 4m to pub*

Delightful thatched free house overlooking village green

Many pubs claim to be quintessentially English; this one deserves the claim. Dating from the 1520s, many of its original features, including low beams, leaded windows and an open fire have survived – no wonder scenes in TV's *Lovejoy* were filmed here. Locally sourced, freshly made food maintains an ever-changing seasonal menu offering such dishes as steak and kidney pudding; wild boar and apple sausages; and warm sundried tomato, shallot and parmesan tartlet. Essex-brewed beers are in the bar and again in August for the bank holiday beer and cider festival.

Open all wk 12-3 6-11 (Sat-Sun 12-11) **Food** Lunch Tue-Fri 12-2.30, Sat 12-3, Sun 12-5 Dinner Tue-Sat 6-9 ⊕ FREE HOUSE ◀ Greene King IPA, Sharp's Doom Bar, Mighty Oak, Colchester, Nethergate, Woodforde's, guest ales Ŏ Westons, Gwynt y Ddraig, Orchard Pig. ♈ 8 **Facilities** Non-diners area ♦♦ Children's portions Family room Garden ⋒ Beer festival Cider festival Parking WiFi ⛟ (notice required)

PICK OF THE PUBS

Axe & Compasses

ARKESDEN Map 12 TL43

tel: 01799 550272 **High St CB11 4EX**
email: axeandcompasses@mail.com
web: www.axeandcompasses.co.uk
dir: *From Buntingford take B1038 towards Newport, left for Arkesden*

Lovely inn with hints of Greek on the menus

The Axe & Compasses is the centrepiece of this sleepy, picture-postcard village, whose narrow main street runs alongside gentle Wicken Water, spanned by a succession of footbridges giving access to white, cream and pink cottages. The thatched central part of the pub dates from 1650; the right-hand extension was added during the early 19th century and is now the public bar. It's run by Themis and Diane Christou from Cyprus, who between them have knocked up a good few awards for the marvellous food they cook here. Easy chairs and settees, antique furniture, clocks and horse brasses fill their comfortable lounge and, in winter, there's an open fire. The pumps of Greene King and a guest ale hold sway in the bar, or it might be with a pint of Thatchers Gold cider that you have a sandwich or light meal, such as crunchy squid with lime and chilli mayonnaise. In the softly lit restaurant area, which seats 50 on various levels, and where agricultural implements adorn the old beams, the slightly

Greek-influenced menus offer a good selection of starters, including feta cheese parcels with sweet cherry tomato dressing; and king prawns and green-lipped mussels grilled with garlic butter. There's a good choice of main courses too, examples being lamb kebabs with Greek salad, chips or rice and pitta bread; fresh salmon and smoked haddock fishcakes with dill and lemon butter sauce; lamb's liver and bacon; and a large pancake filled with mushrooms cooked in cream and parmesan cheese. Round off with a dessert from the trolley. The wine list is easy to navigate, with house reds and whites coming in at modest prices. On fine days drinkers and diners head for the patio.

Open all wk 12-2.30 6-11 (Sun 12-3 6-10.30) **Food** Lunch all wk 12-2 Dinner all wk 6.30-9.15 Av main course £12.95 Restaurant menu available all wk
🍺 GREENE KING 🍺 IPA, Hardys & Hansons Olde Trip, guest ale
Ŏ Thatchers Gold. 🍷 14
Facilities Non-diners area 🚻 Children's portions Outside area 🚗 Parking WiFi
🚌 (notice required)

BLACKMORE END
Map 12 TL73

NEW The Bull at Blackmore End

tel: 01371 851740 **CM7 4DD**
email: info@thebullatblackmoreend.co.uk
dir: *N of Braintree*

Fifteenth-century pub rescued and restored

In 2010, the Grade II listed Bull was closed and under threat from developers. Bought by villagers Colin and Belinda Coleman, a beautiful restoration and lots of hard work have seen it back to its rightful place at the heart of the community. The restaurant is the focus of the operation and offers pub classics like ham, egg and chips as well as an à la carte menu featuring starters like pan-seared scallops with lemon-infused samphire, and mains such as home beer-battered fish of the day with chips and peas. Lime and mango posset with shortbread fingers rounds things off nicely.

Open all day Closed Mon **Food** Lunch Tue-Sun 12-3 Dinner Tue-Sun 6-9 Set menu available Restaurant menu available Tue-Sun ⊕ FREE HOUSE ◀ Sharp's Doom Bar, Adnams Southwold Bitter, Shalford, guest ales ♂ Aspall. ☻ 12
Facilities Non-diners area ⚬⬦ Children's menu Children's portions Play area Garden ⋒ Parking WiFi ☷ (notice required)

BROXTED
Map 12 TL52

NEW The Prince of Wales

tel: 01279 850256 **Brick End CM6 2BJ**
email: bar@princeofwalesbroxted.co.uk
dir: *M11 junct 8, A120 towards Braintree, follow Stansted Airport signs. At 2nd rdbt follow Broxted sign. Right, through Molehill Green. Right at T-junct to pub on left*

A warm welcome and home-cooked pub grub

A friendly, traditional village inn with cosy log fires, offering up to six real ales from local breweries (Bishop Nick Ridley's Rite, maybe, or Heresy), and serving home-cooked pub grub all day. The Sunday roasts are popular. There's a great garden for summer days, when the hanging baskets are overflowing with flowers, and the meal deal (Tuesday-Friday, 12-5) is a real bargain. Otherwise the menu features all the pub food classics, from home-cooked ham, egg and chips; gammon steak with egg or pineapple; pie of the day; cod, chips and peas; lasagne; and a cracking all-day breakfast.

Open all day Closed Mon **Food** Contact pub for food times ⊕ FREE HOUSE ◀ Greene King IPA, Bishop Nick Heresy & Ridley's Rite, guest ales ♂ Aspall, guest cider. ☻
Facilities Non-diners area ⚬ (Bar Garden) ⬦ Children's menu Garden ⋒ Parking WiFi ☷ (notice required)

BURNHAM-ON-CROUCH
Map 7 TQ99

Ye Olde White Harte Hotel

tel: 01621 782106 **The Quay CMO 8AS**
email: whitehartehotel@gmail.com
dir: *Along high street, right before clocktower, right into car park*

Quayside hotel with an old world atmosphere

Situated on the waterfront overlooking the River Crouch, the hotel dates from the 17th century and retains many original features, including beams and fireplaces. It also has its own private jetty. Enjoy fresh local produce and fish in The Waterside Restaurant, or eat in the bar or on the terrace. The dining room offers a wide range of starters, as well as main course options that include vegetarian dishes and a daily roast. A typical menu starts with chicken liver and port pâté; or stuffed mushrooms, then continues with rosemary-crusted rack of lamb; pan-fried skate wing; or brie-stuffed chicken breast wrapped in bacon; then ends up in profiteroles with hot chocolate sauce; or baked white chocolate and strawberry cheesecake.

Open all day all wk **Food** Lunch all wk 12-2.15 Dinner all wk 6.30-9 Av main course £9.20 Restaurant menu available all wk ⊕ FREE HOUSE ◀ Adnams Southwold Bitter, Crouch Vale Brewers Gold. **Facilities** ⚬ (Bar Outside area) ⬦ Children's portions Outside area ⋒ Parking WiFi ☷ (notice required)

CASTLE HEDINGHAM
Map 13 TL73

The Bell Inn
PICK OF THE PUBS

See Pick of the Pubs on opposite page

CHRISHALL
Map 12 TL43

The Red Cow

tel: 01763 838792 **11 High St SG8 8RN**
email: thepub@theredcow.com
dir: *M11 junct 10, A505 towards Royston. 2m, pass pet crematorium, 1st left signed Chrishall. 3.5m, pub in village centre*

Recommended for local game dishes

Conveniently positioned between Saffron Walden and Royston, this 500-year-old thatched pub is very much the hub of the local community. Ales such as Nelson's Revenge, and ciders from Aspall, are locally brewed or from East Anglia. The seasonally changing restaurant carte typically offers prawn mornay with crusty bread, followed by Barbary duck breast with dauphinoise potatoes and butternut squash purée. The pub's social calendar is full to bursting, with music (or 'moosic' to use one of the pub's favoured beef-based puns) particularly high on the agenda. If a quieter life is preferred, a proper English afternoon tea is served at weekends.

Open 12-3 6-12 (Sat 12-12 Sun 12-11) Closed Mon **Food** Lunch Tue-Sun 12-3 Dinner Tue-Thu 6-9, Fri-Sat 6-9.30 ⊕ FREE HOUSE ◀ Adnams Southwold Bitter, Woodforde's Wherry & Nelson's Revenge, Morland Old Speckled Hen, Purity Mad Goose, Sharp's Doom Bar, Timothy Taylor Landlord ♂ Aspall Harry Sparrow.
Facilities Non-diners area ⚬ (Bar Garden) ⬦ Children's menu Children's portions Play area Garden ⋒ Beer festival Parking WiFi ☷ (notice required)

CLAVERING
Map 12 TL43

The Cricketers
PICK OF THE PUBS

tel: 01799 550442 **CB11 4QT**
email: info@thecricketers.co.uk
dir: *M11 junct 10, A505 E, A1301, B1383. At Newport take B1038*

Famous dining pub in rural Essex

Inevitably some foodies will seek out The Cricketers in the lovely village of Clavering hoping that Jamie Oliver may be calling in on his parents that day. Landlords Trevor and Sally Oliver have been pulling pints and cooking classy food here for over 30 years; Jamie now supplies The Cricketers' kitchen with vegetables and herbs from his certified organic garden nearby. The menu almost rings with the now-famous Oliver focus on flavour. Properly hung meat and the freshest of fish are givens, along with tasty leaves. A starter of five spice Telmara Farm duck salad could be followed by a plate of Prior's Hall Farm pork belly, slow-roasted and served on a baked apple purée with rösti potato, crispy crackling and spring greens. Food aside, The Cricketers has been a community local for nearly 500 years. A refreshing pint of Nethergate Old Growler supped beneath the beams is justification enough for a visit.

Open all day all wk Closed 25-26 Dec **Food** Lunch Mon-Sat 12-2, Sun 12-8 Dinner Mon-Sat 6.30-9.30, Sun 12-8 ⊕ FREE HOUSE ◀ Adnams Broadside, Southwold Bitter & Ghost Ship, Nethergate Old Growler ♂ Aspall, Somersby. ☻ 17
Facilities Non-diners area ⬦ Children's menu Children's portions Garden ⋒ Parking WiFi ☷ (notice required)

PICK OF THE PUBS

The Bell Inn

CASTLE HEDINGHAM　　Map 13 TL73

tel: 01787 460350
Saint James St CO9 3EJ
email: enquiries@hedinghambell.co.uk
web: www.hedinghambell.co.uk
dir: *On A1124 N of Halstead, right to Castle Hedingham*

British and Turkish cooking in a traditional village local

A 15th-century former coaching inn situated in the charming medieval village of Castle Hedingham, The Bell has been run by the Ferguson family for over 45 years. From the late 1700s the pub was a popular stop for coaches en route between Bury St Edmunds and London and it remains a traditional pub serving good quality real ales and honest food using local ingredients including herbs and vegetables from the pub's own allotment at the back. Exposed stone walls, heavy beams and real log fires create a welcoming atmosphere in which to enjoy a Mighty Oak Maldon Gold, Adnams Southwold Bitter or one of the guest ales. The Turkish chef puts his stamp on the menu, with Mediterranean fish nights on Mondays, and Turkish stone-baked pizzas on Wednesdays, Thursdays and Fridays. In the summer, the wood-fired oven and barbecue are fired up for guests to enjoy Middle Eastern dishes and fish specials alfresco in the walled patio and hop garden, once home to

cock-fighting, croquet and quoits. At lunchtime, Italian paninis are one option, alongside favourites such as ploughman's. Otherwise, enjoy unpretentious dishes like grilled lamb shish and sweet red pepper in a tortilla wrap with bulgur wheat; salmon and broccoli fishcakes with salad and potato salad; lemon roast chicken with root vegetables; or lentil pottage pie (a vegan alternative to cottage pie); with chocolate brownie for afters. Half-size portions of many dishes are available for younger visitors. The annual July beer festival that showcases up to 40 ales proves popular, as is live music every Friday night and jazz on the last Sunday of the month.

Open all wk 12-3 5.30-11 (Fri-Sat

12-12 Sun 12-11) Closed 25 Dec eve
Food Lunch Mon-Fri 12-2, Sat 12-2.30, Sun 12-3 Dinner Sun-Mon 7-9, Tue-Sat 7-9.30 🛢 GRAY & SONS ◀ Mighty Oak Maldon Gold, Adnams Southwold Bitter, guest ales ♂ Aspall, Delvin End.
Facilities Non-diners area 🐾 (Bar Restaurant Garden) 👫 Children's menu Children's portions Play area Family room Garden 🎍 Beer festival Parking WiFi 🚌 (notice required)

COLCHESTER
Map 13 TL92

The Rose & Crown Hotel ★★★ HL

tel: 01206 866677 **East St CO1 2TZ**
email: info@rose-and-crown.com **web:** www.rose-and-crown.com
dir: M25 junct 28, A12 N. Follow Colchester signs

Ancient, black-and-white oak-framed hotel

Just a few minutes' stroll from Colchester Castle, this beautiful timber-framed building dates from the 14th century and is believed to be the oldest hotel in the oldest town in England. The Tudor bar with its central roaring fire is a great place to relax with a drink. Food is served in the Oak Room or the Tudor Room brasserie, an informal alternative serving classic bar food. Typically, start with pulled lamb samosa with coriander and honey yogurt, then follow with pan-fried sea bass with pistachio nut crust, seared cucumbers and sesame and saffron potato. Leave room for the sherry and strawberry trifle.

Open all wk 10-2.30 5-11 **Food** Lunch all wk 12-2.30 Dinner all wk 6.30-9.30 Av main course £13.50 ⊕ FREE HOUSE ◀ Rose & Crown Bitter, Tetley's Bitter, Adnams Broadside. **Facilities** Non-diners area ♦♦ Children's portions Family room Outside area Parking WiFi ▭ **Rooms** 39

COPFORD GREEN
Map 7 TL92

The Alma

tel: 01206 210607 **CO6 1BZ**
email: mail@thealma.org.uk
dir: From rdbt junct of A12 & A120 follow Colchester signs. At next rdbt follow Copford sign (B1408). In Copford right into School Rd. Pub 0.75m on left

Traditional country village pub for all-comers

On the edge of Copford Green, the staff at The Alma warmly welcome their guests, with or without their children and dogs. A Greene King house, there are always four ales and various lagers to choose from; its beer credentials are confirmed by the festival held here every Spring Bank Holiday weekend. The menus are crowd-pleasers too, featuring main dishes such as steak and ale pie, mash and seasonal vegetables; poached smoked haddock, creamed potatoes and spinach; and mushroom and cheese strudel with tomato and vegetable stew. Children are well catered for with smaller portions from the main menu, or their own choices such as creamy pasta carbonara.

Open all wk 12-3 5-close **Food** Lunch all wk 12-3 Dinner all wk 6-9 Set menu available Restaurant menu available Wed-Sun ⊕ GREENE KING ◀ IPA & Abbot, Red Fox Hunter's Gold, guest ales Ŏ Aspall. **Facilities** Non-diners area ❖ (Bar Garden Outside area) ♦♦ Children's menu Children's portions Play area Garden Outside area ⋈ Beer festival Parking WiFi ▭

DANBURY
Map 7 TL70

NEW The Griffin

tel: 01245 699024 **64 Main Rd CM3 4DH**
email: info@griffindanbury.co.uk
dir: A12 onto A414 towards Maldon. Pub at top of hill on left in Danbury

Dining-pub with character on the hill

A 400-year-old hostelry on the hill in the middle of the village. The attractive black and white timber-framed exterior is an introduction to the wealth of scrubbed beams inside, some of which are reputed to have been sourced when the nearby church was under construction. This pub ticks all the gastro-chic boxes, with Adnams ales on tap and a menu embracing most crowd pleasers. Sharing boards, starters of moules marinière, and stone-baked pizzas are all here. Specials may proffer a poached fillet of turbot stuffed with prawn mousse, and rich chocolate truffle tart for dessert.

Open all day all wk **Food** Lunch Mon-Sat 12-3, Sun 12-6 Dinner Mon-Fri 6-9, Sat 6-10, Sun 12-6 Av main course £12 Set menu available Restaurant menu available all wk ⊕ FREE HOUSE ◀ Adnams Southwold Bitter, Broadside & IPA. **Facilities** Non-diners area ♦♦ Children's menu Children's portions Garden Outside area ⋈ Parking WiFi ▭ (notice required)

DEDHAM
Map 13 TM03

Marlborough Head Inn

tel: 01206 323250 **Mill Ln CO7 6DH**
email: jen.pearmain@tiscali.co.uk
dir: E of A12, N of Colchester

Comfortable and cosy inn serving hearty food

Tucked away in glorious Constable Country, this 16th-century building was once a clearing-house for local wool merchants. In 1660, after a slump in trade, it became an inn. Today it is as perfect for a pint, a sofa and a newspaper as it is for a good home-cooked family meal. Traditional favourites such as deep-fried whitebait; steak and kidney pie; and breaded whole tail scampi appear on the menu, plus fish is given centre stage on Fridays. There is a terrace and walled garden to enjoy in the warmer weather and an open log fire to sit beside in winter.

Open all day all wk 11.30-11 **Food** Contact pub for food times ⊕ PUNCH TAVERNS ◀ Greene King IPA, Adnams Southwold Ŏ Aspall. ₹ 12 **Facilities** Non-diners area ❖ (Bar Garden) ♦♦ Children's menu Children's portions Family room Garden ⋈ Parking WiFi ▭ (notice required)

The Sun Inn ★★★★★ INN ⊛⊛
PICK OF THE PUBS

tel: 01206 323351 **High St CO7 6DF**
email: office@thesuninndedham.com **web:** www.thesuninndedham.com
dir: From A12 follow signs to Dedham for 1.5m, pub on High Street

A centuries-old inn with Mediterranean-influenced cuisine

With its smart yellow-painted exterior and exposed timbers, this lovely old inn is independently owned and there are two informal bars, an open dining room, a snug oak-panelled lounge and three open fires. So take your pick of where to enjoy your chosen refreshment, be it a pint of Adnams Broadside or Aspall Harry Sparrow cider; for wine drinkers, the choice extends beyond two dozen served by the glass. Locally sourced seasonal ingredients drive the daily-changing menu of traditional Mediterranean-style dishes, many with a strong Italian influence. Two AA Rosettes have been awarded for tastebud-tingling dishes such as venison casserole, Chianti, swede, wet polenta and thyme; and line-caught Mersea cod fillet roasted with marjoram and capers, chickpeas, Swiss chard, tomatoes and mint. In summer, head to the suntrap terrace and walled garden overlooked by the church tower.

Open all day all wk 11-11 Closed 25-27 Dec **Food** Lunch Mon-Thu 12-2.30, Fri-Sun 12-3 Dinner Sun-Thu 6.30-9.30, Fri-Sat 6.30-10 ⊕ FREE HOUSE ◀ Crouch Vale Brewers Gold, Adnams Broadside, 2 guest ales Ŏ Aspall Harry Sparrow. ₹ 25 **Facilities** Non-diners area ❖ (Bar Garden) ♦♦ Children's menu Children's portions Garden ⋈ Parking WiFi **Rooms** 7

EDNEY COMMON
Map 6 TL60

NEW The Green Man

tel: 01245 248076 **Highwood Rd CM1 3QE**
dir: Take A414 (S of Chelmsford) towards Harlow. At rdbt left signed Highwood. Pub on right in Edney

Flower-filled tubs and a friendly atmosphere

A classic red brick Grade II listed building dating back to 1730, The Green Man offers a comfortable beamed dining room, and regularly changing menus, featuring freshly prepared, often local produce in a wide range of dishes, including their signature 20 hour-cooked lamb shank with swede mash and rosemary jus. There's a beer garden with a natural pond and a lovely sunny courtyard for alfresco dining, and dinner could start with chicken liver parfait and toasted ciabatta; or roast pigeon breast with bacon, swede and pearl barley risotto. Main courses might include roast belly of pork with snow crab cakes and apple chutney; or Loch Duart salmon ballotine with lobster mousse and pea purée.

Open 12-3 6-11.30 (Sun 12-7) Closed Sun eve, Mon **Food** Lunch Tue-Sun 12-3 Dinner Tue-Sat 6-9.30 Av main course £14.95 Set menu available Restaurant menu available Tue-Sun ⊕ FREE HOUSE ◀ Greene King London Glory, Sharp's Doom Bar ♂ Aspall. ♟ 8 **Facilities** Non-diners area ♦♦ Children's menu Children's portions Garden ⋈ Parking WiFi ▦ (notice required)

FEERING   Map 7 TL82

The Sun Inn

tel: 01376 570442 **Feering Hill CO5 9NH**
email: hello@sunninnfeering@.co.uk
dir: On A12 between Colchester & Witham. Village 1m

Black and white timbered pub at heart of village

A pretty pub dating from 1525 with heavily carved beams to prove it, this Grade II listed building has two inglenook fireplaces and a large garden and courtyard. The traditional bar, which sells Shepherd Neame's real ales, has no TV or games machines. Home-cooked pub classics are backed by mains like beef, mushroom and Stilton pie, and haddock in ale batter with chips, peas and tartare sauce. Three roasts, together with other options, are offered on Sundays.

Open all wk Sat-Sun all day ⊕ SHEPHERD NEAME ◀ Master Brew, Spitfire & Bishops Finger, Whitstable Bay Pale Ale, guest ales ♂ Thatchers Heritage. **Facilities** ❀ (Bar Garden) ♦♦ Children's menu Children's portions Garden Parking WiFi

FINGRINGHOE   Map 7 TM02

The Whalebone

tel: 01206 729307 **Chapel Rd CO5 7BG**
email: info@thewhaleboneinn.co.uk
dir: Phone for detailed directions

British cuisine and breathtaking views

This Grade II listed 18th-century free house enjoys beautiful views from its position at the top of the Roman River Valley. Its name comes from the bones of a locally beached whale, which were once fastened above the door of the pub. Wooden floors, exposed beams, bespoke furniture, a roaring fire and unique artwork all combine to create a feeling of warmth and character. Hearty British fare is prepared from local ingredients, along with Adnams and Woodforde's ales. A lunchtime snack can be enjoyed in one of the garden pavilions. The menu options smoked haddock, red gurnard and leek chowder; twice-cooked crispy Suffolk pork belly; and four-hour-cooked rich cottage pie.

Open all wk 12-3 5.30-11 (Sat 12-11 Sun 12-10.30 Winter Sun 12-6) **Food** Lunch Mon-Sat 12-2.30, Sun 12-5 Dinner Mon-Thu 6.30-9, Fri-Sat 6.30-9.30 Av main course £15.95 Restaurant menu available all wk ⊕ FREE HOUSE ◀ Adnams Southwold Ritter, Woodforde's Wherry, 2 guest ales ♂ Aspall. ♟ 13 **Facilities** Non-diners area ❀ (Bar Restaurant Garden) ♦♦ Children's menu Children's portions Play area Family room Garden ⋈ Parking ▦ (notice required)

FULLER STREET   Map 6 TL71

The Square and Compasses

tel: 01245 361477 **CM3 2BB**
email: info@thesquareandcompasses.co.uk **web:** www.thesquareandcompasses.co.uk
dir: From A131 (Chelmsford to Braintree) take Great Leighs exit, enter village, right into Boreham Rd. Left signed Fuller St & Terling. Pub on left

A prominent feature of village life

This beautifully restored 17th-century village pub is set in lovely countryside just 10 minutes from Chelmsford. Originally two farm cottages, the free house still retains its original beams and inglenook fireplaces, with antique furnishings. The locally sourced food is straightforward, served alongside a good selection of beers and ciders such as Crouch Vale Essex Boys ale and Dudda's Tun Kentish cider. As well as pub classics, the daily-changing specials might include crab cake with lime, chilli and coriander, followed by roast chump of lamb marinated in thyme and garlic with rosemary roasted crushed new potatoes, red wine and thyme sauce.

Open all day all wk 11.30-11.30 **Food** Lunch Mon-Fri 12-2, Sat 12-2.30, Sun 12-6 Dinner Mon-Sat 6.30-9.30, Sun 12-6 ⊕ FREE HOUSE ◀ Crouch Vale Brewers Gold & Essex Boys, Mighty Oak Maldon Gold & Captain Bob ♂ Berties, Celtic Marshes Thundering Molly, Abrahalls, Herefordshire, Dudda's Tun Kentish Cider. ♟ 14 **Facilities** Non-diners area ❀ (Bar Garden) ♦♦ Children's portions Garden ⋈ Parking

FYFIELD
Map 6 TL50

The Queen's Head

tel: 01277 899231 **Queen St CM5 0RY**
email: sglamprecht@gmail.com
dir: *M11 junct 7, A414 towards Chelmsford. In Chipping Ongar at rdbt left to Fyfield on B184*

Family-run free house with river garden

With a history dating back to the 15th century, The Queen's Head is a traditional free house with log fires, a private dining room and riverside garden. Ales from Adnams are backed up by backed by Aspall cider and a wide-ranging choice of wines.The kitchen's modern British approach produces starters such as blow-torched confit salmon; and crispy aromatic quail with sweet and sour tamarind. Scan the daily specials board for the likes of potted crab followed by pan-fried skate wing with caper beurre noisette.

Open 11-3.30 6-11 (Sat 11am-11.30pm Sun 12-10.30) Closed 26 Dec, Mon **Food** Lunch Tue-Fri 12-2.30, Sat 12-4, Sun 12-6 Dinner Tue-Sat 6.30-9.30, Sun 12-6 Set menu available Restaurant menu available Tue-Sun ⊕ FREE HOUSE ◄ Adnams Southwold Bitter & Broadside, guest ale Ŏ Aspall. ♀ 17 **Facilities** Non-diners area ◆ Children's portions Garden ⋈ Beer festival Parking WiFi ▰ (notice required)

GESTINGTHORPE
Map 13 TL83

The Pheasant ★★★★★ INN ⊛
PICK OF THE PUBS

See Pick of the Pubs on opposite page

GOLDHANGER
Map 7 TL90

The Chequers Inn

tel: 01621 788203 **Church St CM9 8AS**
email: chequersgoldhang@aol.com
dir: *From B1026, 500mtrs to village centre*

'Low' pub in a riverside village

Built in 1410, The Chequers can be found next to the church in picturesque Goldhanger, on the River Blackwater. The pub name comes from a chequerboard used by the tax collector in the pub many, many years ago. At around 30 feet above sea level, it reputedly has the 'lowest' bar in Britain, where you can enjoy perhaps a pint of Adnams Ghost Ship. Several rooms decorated with farming and fishing implements surround the bar area. Pride is taken in the preparation and presentation of food, which includes whole sea bass baked with with fennel and thyme; lamb and mint suet pudding; and aubergine, butternut and walnut bake. There are beer festivals in March and September.

Open all day all wk **Food** Lunch all wk 12-3 Dinner Mon-Sat 6.30-9 ⊕ PUNCH TAVERNS ◄ Young's Bitter, Crouch Vale Brewers Gold, Adnams Ghost Ship, Sharp's Atlantic, St Austell Proper Job, guest ale Ŏ Westons Traditional & Perry. ♀ 13 **Facilities** Non-diners area ❀ (Bar Garden) ◆ Children's menu Children's portions Garden ⋈ Beer festival Parking WiFi ▰ (notice required)

GREAT TOTHAM
Map 7 TL81

The Bull at Great Totham ★★★★ RR ⊛⊛
PICK OF THE PUBS

tel: 01621 893385 **2 Maldon Rd CM9 8NH**
email: reservations@thebullatgreattotham.co.uk **web:** www.thebullatgreattotham.co.uk
dir: *Exit A12 at Witham junct to Great Totham*

A highly regarded destination gastro-pub and restaurant

The Bull, overlooking the cricket green, is a 16th-century coaching inn and proud holder of two AA Rosettes. It offers not far short of 20 fine wines by the glass, real ales from Adnams and Greene King, and a bar menu of baguettes, sausage and mash, and beer-battered cod tail. Named after the ancient tree in the lavender-filled garden is the fine-dining Willow Room, where you might start with crispy duck egg, Russian salad and truffle dressing then follow with marinated loin of venison, pear, braised red cabbage, fondant potatoes and chocolate jus; or the Bull's mixed grill – beef medallion, sausages, gammon and fried egg. If you're a vegetarian, the pan-fried aubergine and goats' cheese roulade and tomato sauce might take your fancy. Finish in style warm chocolate fondant and vanilla ice cream. Musical and themed dining evenings and other events are held frequently.

Open all day all wk **Food** Lunch Mon-Fri 12-3 (light bites till 5.30), Sat 12-10, Sun 12-6.45 Dinner Mon-Thu 5.30-9, Fri 5.30-10, Sat 12-10, Sun 12-6.45 Set menu available Restaurant menu available Mon-Fri ⊕ FREE HOUSE ◄ Adnams, Greene King. ♀ 17 **Facilities** Non-diners area ❀ (Bar Garden Outside area) ◆ Children's menu Children's portions Play area Garden Outside area ⋈ Parking ▰ (notice required) **Rooms** 4

HASTINGWOOD
Map 6 TL40

Rainbow & Dove

tel: 01279 415419 **Hastingwood Rd CM17 9JX**
email: rainbowanddove@hotmail.co.uk
dir: *Just off M11 junct 7*

Little pub with a varied history

Dating back to at least the 16th century, the Rainbow & Dove was a farmhouse, staging post, village shop and post office before it became a pub. English Heritage has given it Grade II historical building status. There are cask-conditioned real ales, a selection of whiskies and a good wine list. Menus revolve around fresh seasonal produce and the owners have their own smallholding where rare and traditional pigs, goats, geese, chickens and quail are reared. On the snack menu you'll find ciabattas, baguettes, sandwiches and jacket potatoes, but if it's something more substantial that you require then the carte lists dishes such as sharing platters; carpaccio of wild venison; stuffed rabbit loin; fresh, whole, grilled lemon sole; Tuscan-style roast pork belly; and asparagus, broad bean and roasted garlic risotto.

Open 11.30-3 6-11 (Sun 12-7 Mon 11.30-3.30) Closed Sun eve, Mon eve **Food** Lunch Mon-Sat 12-2.30, Sun 12-5 Dinner Tue-Sat 6-9 Restaurant menu available all wk ⊕ FREE HOUSE ◄ Rotating guest ales Ŏ Aspall. ♀ 10 **Facilities** Non-diners area ❀ (Bar Garden) ◆ Children's menu Children's portions Garden ⋈ Beer festival Parking ▰ (notice required)

PICK OF THE PUBS

The Pheasant ★★★★★ INN ✿

GESTINGTHORPE Map 13 TL83

tel: 01787 465010
Audley End, Church St CO9 3AU
email: thepheasantpb@aol.com
web: www.thepheasant.net
dir: *A131 from Sudbury towards Castle Hedingham. Right, follow Castle Hedingham sign, through Gestingthorpe to Audley End*

Gastro-pub with top-notch plot-to-plate cooking

A previous winner of the AA Pub of the Year for England, The Pheasant has become a total success story thanks to the dedicaton of hands-on owners James and Diana Donoghue. On the Essex and Suffolk border and surrounded by lovely countryside, this stylish gastro-pub is blessed in that James was an award-winning garden designer and he has created a kitchen garden which now provides a steady and abundant supply of seasonal organic fruit and vegetables for the restaurant. The one-acre garden is located across the road from the pub and produces soft fruits, onions, leeks, artichokes, beetroots, courgettes and various herbs and lettuces. Potatoes destined for the chips, mash and Sunday lunch roasties are grown ten miles away in Wormingford and the kitchen staff peel ten sacks of them a week. Enterprising James even keeps bees and he also smokes his own fish,

much of it sourced from south coast day boats and delivered up to four times a week. Starters typically include grilled goats' cheese with a green salad and sweet chilli dressing; and tempura tiger prawns with garlic mayonnaise dip, followed by mains of garlic chicken, new potatoes and kale; Gressingham duck breast with orange and fennel salad; or home-made pie of the day with hand-cut chips. Home-made apple and cider crumble; and sticky toffee pudding with caramel sauce and honeycomb crunch ice cream are two typical desserts. Accompany your meal with a pint of Adnams ale or the pub's own Pheasant Bitter, brewed by Woodforde's in Norfolk. Alternatively, enjoy a glass of Suffolk-made Aspall cider.

Open all day all wk Closed 1st 2wks Jan **Food** Lunch all wk 12-2.30 Dinner all wk 6.30-9.30 ⊕ FREE HOUSE ◀ Adnams Southwold Bitter, Woodforde's Pheasant Bitter, guest ales ♂ Aspall.
Facilities Non-diners area
❀ (Bar Garden Outside area)
✦ Children's portions Garden Outside area 🖵 Parking WiFi 🚌 (notice required) **Rooms** 5

HATFIELD BROAD OAK
Map 6 TL51

The Duke's Head

tel: 01279 718598 **High St CM22 7HH**
email: info@thedukeshead.co.uk **web:** www.thedukeshead.co.uk
dir: M11 junct 8, A120 towards Great Dunmow. Right into B183 to Hatfield Broad Oak. Pub on left at 1st bend in village

Friendly village dining-pub

Standing behind a white-painted picket fence, this 185-year-old pub's proprietors are Justin and Liz Flodman. Spacious, with two wood-burners, the pub's customers can enjoy good wines by the glass, real ales from Essex and surrounding counties, and Justin's seasonal modern British food. Maybe choose spiced lamb kofta kebab; or crispy paprika whitebait to start; then move on to local Churchgate Farm sausages, creamy mash and thyme and shallot gravy; free-range chicken saltimbocca; or a Turkish dish of baked 'imam bayildi' (which translates as 'the imam swooned', allegedly at his wife's cooking). For dessert you might like to try banana and chocolate bread and butter pudding; or lemon syllabub.

Open all day all wk Closed 25-26 Dec **Food** Lunch Mon-Fri 12-2.30, Sat 10.30-10, Sun 10.30-9 Dinner Mon-Thu 6.30-9.30, Fri 6.30-10, Sat 10.30-10, Sun 10.30-9 Av main course £13.75 Set menu available ⊕ ENTERPRISE INNS ◀ Greene King IPA, Sharp's Doom Bar, Timothy Taylor Landlord, Purity Mad Goose Ö Aspall. ♀ 25 **Facilities** Non-diners area ♣ (Bar Garden) ♦♦ Children's menu Children's portions Garden ⌷ Parking WiFi ▦ (notice required)

HATFIELD HEATH
Map 6 TL51

The Thatcher's

tel: 01279 730270 **Stortford Rd CM22 7DU**
email: thethatcherspub@yahoo.co.uk
dir: In village on A1060 (Bishop's Stortford road)

Quaint old pub serving home-made food

A pretty, thatched 16th-century pub overlooking the village green with oak beams and a welcoming inglenook wood-burning stove. Enjoy a glass of wine (11 are offered by the glass) or a pint from the Mighty Oak brewery among others at the bar. The dishes are all prepared on the premises and might start with tempura duck spring rolls, Asian salad and hoi sin sauce; or dressed crab on toast, followed by roast Brixham skate, mash, wilted spinach, caper and lemon butter; hand-made minced Essex beefburger, brioche bun and French fries; or wild mushroom ravioli, woodland mushroom cream sauce, black truffle oil. Lighter lunches and 'sandwich and soup' add to the choices.

Open all day all wk 11.30-11 **Food** Lunch all wk 12-3 Dinner all wk 5-9 ⊕ FREE HOUSE ◀ St Austell Tribute, Nethergate, Mighty Oak, Adnams. ♀ 11 **Facilities** Non-diners area ♦♦ Children's menu Children's portions Family room Garden ⌷ Parking WiFi ▦ (notice required)

HORNDON ON THE HILL
Map 6 TQ68

Bell Inn
PICK OF THE PUBS

tel: 01375 642463 **High Rd SS17 8LD**
email: info@bell-inn.co.uk
dir: M25 junct 30 or 31 follow Thurrock signs

Historic family-run inn with plenty of talking points

In the same family since 1938, this 15th-century coaching inn is steeped in history – you might notice hot cross buns hanging from the original king post supporting the ancient roof timbers. Every year the oldest willing villager hangs another one, an unusual tradition that dates back 100 years to when the pub changed hands on a Good Friday. In the wood-panelled bar, regular brews like Crouch Vale Brewers Gold are backed by a selection of changing guest ales. The lunchtime bar menu offers sandwiches and light meals but booking is essential in the popular restaurant, where the daily-changing menu is driven by seasonal produce. Confit venison and Essex wood pigeon terrine; and prawn bisque for starters perhaps, followed by sautéed calves' liver and bacon, Puy lentil, sautéed chorizo with spinach and caramelised onions; or salmon fillet, saffron aïoli, carrot, leek and mooli spaghetti, crayfish ravioli and mussel velouté.

Open all day all wk 11-11 (Sun 12-10.30) Closed 25-26 Dec **Food** Lunch all wk 12-1.45 Dinner Mon-Fri 6.30-9.45, Sat 6-9.45, Sun 7-9.45 Av main course £10.95 Restaurant menu available all wk ⊕ FREE HOUSE ◀ Greene King IPA, Crouch Vale Brewers Gold, Sharp's Doom Bar, Bass, guest ales. ♀ 16 **Facilities** Non-diners area ♣ (Bar Garden) ♦♦ Children's portions Garden ⌷ Parking WiFi

INGATESTONE
Map 6 TQ69

The Red Lion

tel: 01277 352184 **Main Rd, Margaretting CM4 0EQ**
dir: From Chelmsford take A12 towards Brentwood. Margaretting in 4m

A proper English pub

Emphatically a traditional inn and not a restaurant (although it does sell quality food), the 17th-century Red Lion is best described as a 'quintessential English pub'. The bar is decorated in burgundy and aubergine, the restaurant in coffee and cream. From an extensive menu choose prawn tostada; home-made balti curry; or classic moules marinière. Wash it down with a pint of Greene King IPA or one of the guest ales. Every Thursday you can get two steaks and a bottle of wine for £28.

Open all wk 12-11 (Sun 12-6) **Food** Lunch all wk 12-3 Dinner Mon-Sat 6-9 Restaurant menu available all wk ⊕ GREENE KING ◀ IPA, 4 weekly changing guest ales Ö Westons Stowford Press. ♀ 14 **Facilities** Non-diners area ♦♦ Children's menu Children's portions Play area Garden ⌷ Parking WiFi ▦ (notice required)

LANGHAM
Map 13 TM03

The Shepherd

tel: 01206 272711 **Moor Rd CO4 5NR**
email: info@shepherdlangham.co.uk
dir: A12 from Colchester towards Ipswich, take 1st left signed Langham

Stylish village food pub in Constable Country

In the pretty village of Langham, deep in Constable Country on the Suffolk/Essex border, is this Edwardian pub. Richard and Esther Brunning run this family-friendly and stylish free house that's open all day. Adnams and Woodforde's are among the ales served at the bar, alongside an extensive list of wines. A typical meal could take in beetroot-cured gravad lax with lemon crème fraîche; followed by lamb curry platter; or beef, bacon and red wine pie, then crème brûlée or sticky toffee pudding.

Open all day all wk **Food** Lunch all wk 12-3 Dinner Tue-Sat 6-9 Restaurant menu available Mon-Sun (excl Mon eve) ⊕ FREE HOUSE ◀ Adnams Southwold & Ghost Ship, Woodforde's Wherry Ö Aspall. **Facilities** Non-diners area ♣ (Bar Garden) ♦♦ Children's menu Children's portions Garden ⌷ Parking WiFi ▦ (notice required)

LITTLE BURSTEAD
Map 6 TQ69

The Dukes Head

tel: 01277 651333 **Laindon Common Rd CM12 9TA**
email: enquiry@dukesheadlittleburstead.co.uk
dir: *From Basildon take A176 (Noah Hill Rd) N toward Billericay. Left into Laindon Common Rd to Little Burstead. Pub on left*

Welcoming pub known for its themed food events

Smart interiors and a friendly team characterise the atmosphere in this large hostelry between Brentwood and Basildon. Chunky wood tables, leather-upholstered stools and relaxing armchairs surround the open fire in the bar area, where the ales vie for selection with an excellent range of wines served by the glass. Modern British food ranges from pizzas and pastas to the chef's daily specials.

Open all day all wk **Food** Mon-Sat 12-10, Sun 12-9 Set menu available ⊕ MITCHELLS & BUTLERS ◄■ Sharp's Doom Bar, Adnams Southwold Bitter, guest ales Ö Aspall. ♚ 21 **Facilities** Non-diners area ✿ (Bar Garden) ♦️ Children's menu Children's portions Garden ⊼ Parking WiFi ☛ (notice required)

LITTLEBURY
Map 12 TL53

The Queens Head Inn Littlebury

tel: 01799 520365 **High St CB11 4TD**
email: queensheadlittlebury@aol.com
dir: *M11 junct 9A, B184 towards Saffron Walden. Right onto B1383, S towards Wendens Ambo*

Popular community pub with good home-made food

This beautiful, family-run former coaching inn with open fires, exposed beams and one of only two remaining full-length settles in England is very much at the centre of the local community. The chefs prepare good home-made dishes and fish is a major focus – Goan fish curry and Italian-style cod loin with new potatoes being just two choices. So expect a menu of popular favourites from fresh baguettes, beef and Merlot pie; and a choice of home-made gourmet burgers; and for dessert, cheesecake of the day; or chocolate brownie. A large beer garden with a children's play area confirms its family-friendly credentials.

Open all day all wk Mon-Thu 12-11.30 Fri-Sat 12-12 Sun 12-10.30 **Food** Lunch Mon-Sat 12-2.30, Sun 12-4 Dinner Mon-Sat 6-9.30 Restaurant menu available all wk ⊕ GREENE KING ◄■ IPA, Morland Old Speckled Hen, guest ales Ö Westons Stowford Press, Aspall. ♚ 9 **Facilities** Non-diners area ✿ (Bar Garden) ♦️ Children's menu Children's portions Play area Garden ⊼ Beer festival Parking WiFi ☛

LITTLE CANFIELD
Map 6 TL52

The Lion & Lamb

tel: 01279 870257 **CM6 1SR**
email: info@lionandlamb.co.uk
dir: *M11 junct 8, B1256 towards Takeley & Little Canfield*

Perfect for a pre-flight meal

Ideal for business or leisure, this former coaching inn was built on what used to be the main East Coast road. Now a traditional country pub and restaurant, it's a popular stop for travellers on the way to Stansted Airport. Inside are oak beams, winter log fires and plenty of real ales, although the large and well-furnished garden is the place to relax in summer. A typical meal from might be smoked chicken with beetroot, watercress and avocado; grilled skate wing, salad and chips or new potatoes; or roasted vegetable risotto, parmesan and basil oil.

Open all day all wk 11-close (Sun 12-close) Closed 1 Jan **Food** Mon-Sat 11-10, Sun 12-10 Restaurant menu available all wk ⊕ GREENE KING ◄■ IPA, Morland Old Golden Hen, guest ales Ö Aspall Harry Sparrow. ♚ 11 **Facilities** Non-diners area ♦️ Children's menu Children's portions Play area Garden ⊼ Parking WiFi ☛

LITTLE DUNMOW
Map 6 TL62

NEW The Flitch of Bacon
PICK OF THE PUBS

tel: 01371 821660 **The Street CM6 3HT**
email: manager@flitchofbacon.co.uk
dir: *From A120 E'bound take B1008 signed Thaxted. At next rdbt take B1256 signed Rayne. Right signed Little Dunmow. Or from A120 W'bound follow signs for B1256 (Stebbing). Over A120, left at T-junct. Left signed Little Dunmow*

Sympathetically restored destination dining pub

After driving past this property for some time, award-winning chef Daniel Clifford could see its potential, so when the 'for sale' sign went up he bought it. Many of the staff who formerly worked at his five AA-Rosette Midsummer House in Cambridge, can now be found here. Little Dunmow is where Flitch Trials originated, a flitch being a side of bacon awarded to couples who could swear to not regretting their marriage for a year and a day. The trials are now held in Great Dunmow every four years, but you can visit this rejuvenated village pub as often as you like, whether just to sample Bishop Nick real ales or Jake's Orchard nettle cider, or to eat. On chef-patron Danny Gill's menus – a starter of beetroots baked on open coals with golden beetroot marmalade, hazelnut shortbread and goats' cheese; or there's the more familiar chicken and duck liver parfait with quince and toasted brioche. Mains include slow-roasted loin of venison, celeriac and elderberries; and beer-battered pollack, chips and mushy peas. Then, to follow, pistachio soufflé with coconut rice pudding, passionfruit and mango perhaps. There's a kitchen table, for two, positioned just beside the pass.

Open all day Closed Mon **Food** Lunch Tue-Sat 12-2.30, Sun 12-6.30 Dinner Tue-Sat 6.30-9, Sun 12-6.30 Av main course £15 Set menu available Restaurant menu available Tue-Sun ⊕ FREE HOUSE ◄■ Bishop Nick 1555 & Heresy, Greene King IPA Ö Hush Heath Jake's Orchard. ♚ 10 **Facilities** Non-diners area ✿ (Bar Garden) ♦️ Children's menu Children's portions Garden ⊼ Parking WiFi ☛ (notice required)

LITTLEY GREEN
Map 6 TL71

The Compasses

tel: 01245 362308 **CM3 1BU**
email: compasseslittleygreen@googlemail.com
dir: *Phone for detailed directions*

Unspoilt country local deep in rural Essex

A few years ago Joss Ridley left London and a top job so he could snap up this pub to revive the family link with the former Ridley Brewery, and he hasn't looked back. The traditional inn stands in a sleepy hamlet and thrives selling tip-top ales straight from the barrel, including Bishop Nick, brewed by Joss's brother Nelion, and fresh, hearty pub food. Using local ingredients, the menu and chalkboard specials include filled 'huffer' baps, ploughman's, and beer battered cod and chips. The interior is timeless and unspoilt, the garden large and peaceful.

Open all wk 12-3 5.30-11.30 (Thu-Sun all day) **Food** Lunch Mon-Fri 12-2.30, Sat-Sun 12-9.30 Dinner Mon-Fri 7-9.30, Sat-Sun 12-9.30 ⊕ FREE HOUSE ◄■ Bishop Nick, Crouch Vale, guest ales Ö Hogan's, guest ciders. **Facilities** Non-diners area ✿ (Bar Restaurant Garden) ♦️ Children's portions Garden ⊼ Beer festival Parking WiFi ☛ (notice required)

MANNINGTREE
Map 13 TM13

The Mistley Thorn ◉◉
PICK OF THE PUBS

tel: 01206 392821 **High St, Mistley CO11 1HE**
email: info@mistleythorn.co.uk
dir: *From Ipswich A12 junct 31 onto B1070, follow signs to East Bergholt, Manningtree & Mistley. From Colchester A120 towards Harwich. Left at Horsley Cross. Mistley in 3m*

Coastal village inn where seafood's a speciality

This 18th-century coaching inn overlooks the Stour Estuary at almost its widest point. During 2016 the back of the building underwent a major refurbishment which introduced a new exhibition kitchen and enlarged the dining area. There's no doubt that diners comprise the majority of customers, but Adnams ales and a choice of 17 wines served by the glass can be enjoyed at the bar in the relaxed and casual ambience. Fresh and locally-sourced ingredients are the highlights of the daily-changing two-AA Rosette menu. The emphasis is on seafood, which sees the likes of Mersea rock oysters served with shallot and ginger mignonette; a smoked fish trio with mustard dill sauce; and chargrilled dayboat squid 'a la plancha' with chilli, garlic, lemon oil and herbs. Non-fishy alternatives include chargrilled Suffolk Red Poll beef with hand-cut, skin-on fries; and home-made potato gnocchi with spinach, hazelnut pesto and pine nuts.

Open all wk 12-2.30 6.30-9.30 (Fri 6-9.30 Sat-Sun all day) **Food** Lunch Mon-Fri 12-2.30, Sat-Sun & BHs 12-5 Dinner Mon-Thu 6.30-9.30, Fri-Sun 6-9.30 Set menu available Restaurant menu available all wk ⊕ FREE HOUSE ◀ Adnams Southwold Bitter & Ghost Ship. ♟ 17 **Facilities** Non-diners area ❄ (Bar Restaurant) ◀◀ Children's menu Children's portions Parking WiFi

MARGARETTING TYE
Map 6 TL60

The White Hart Inn

tel: 01277 840478 **Swan Ln CM4 9JX**
email: liz@thewhitehart.uk.com **web:** www.thewhitehart.uk.com
dir: *From A12 junct 15, B1002 to Margaretting. At x-roads in Margaretting left into Maldon Rd. Under rail bridge, left. Right into Swan Ln, follow Margaretting Tye signs. Follow to pub on right*

Two popular beer festivals held here

Parts of this pub, sitting proudly on a green known locally as Tigers Island, are 250 years old. Landlady Liz and her team revel in offering a great choice of the best regional and local beers and ciders. The pub's interior, all match boarding, old pictures, brewery memorabilia, dark posts, pillars, beams and fireplaces, oozes character, while the solidly traditional menu and specials board shout quality. Start with an Italian meat platter, and move on to lamb's liver and bacon casserole;

grilled extra mature rib-eye steak; or grilled haddock served on creamy spring onion mash with a wild mushroom fricasée.

Open 11.30-3 6-12 (Sat-Sun 12-12) Closed 25 Dec, Mon (Jan-Apr) **Food** Lunch Tue-Fri 12-2.30, Sat 12-3, Sun 12-7.30 Dinner Tue-Thu 6-9, Fri-Sat 6-9.30, Sun 12-7.30 ⊕ FREE HOUSE ◀ Adnams Southwold Bitter & Broadside, Mighty Oak IPA & Oscar Wilde Mild, guest ales ○ Aspall, Rekorderlig. ♟ 10 **Facilities** Non-diners area ❄ (Bar Restaurant Garden) ◀◀ Children's menu Family room Garden ⩩ Beer festival Parking WiFi 🚌 (notice required)

MATCHING TYE
Map 6 TL51

NEW The Fox Inn

tel: 01279 731335 **The Green CM17 OQS**
email: foxinn.matching@gmail.com
dir: *From A414 in Harlow take B183 towards Sheering. At 2nd rdbt 2nd exit (Churchgate Street). At T-junct left (The Matchings). Over motorway. Pub on right in village centre*

Village pub that's gone from strength to strength

Known to have been licensed by 1809, the Gibson family took over this 18th-century pub in 2002. In the lofty, timbered restaurant a huge open fireplace spanned by a wide bressumer beam supports a hefty brick chimney that disappears into the rafters. The menus strike all the right notes for those who like their food both simply prepared and described, thus lamb's liver, bacon, mash and onion gravy; gammon, eggs and chips; baked salmon fillet, new potatoes and mixed vegetables; and home-made vegetable lasagne. Adnams Southwold and Shepherd Neame Spitfire are among the real ales to be found in the bar, as are 12 wines by the glass.

Open all wk 11.30-3.30 6-11.30 (Sun noon-11) Closed 26 Dec **Food** Lunch Mon-Fri 12-2.30, Sat 12-3, Sun 12-4 Dinner Mon-Sat 6.30-9.30, Sun 4-8 Av main course £12 ⊕ FREE HOUSE ◀ Shepherd Neame Spitfire, Greene King IPA, Timothy Taylor Landlord, Sharp's Doom Bar, Adnams Southwold Bitter. ♟ 12 **Facilities** Non-diners area ❄ (Bar Garden) ◀◀ Children's menu Children's portions Garden ⩩ Beer festival Parking WiFi 🚌 (notice required)

MESSING
Map T TL81

The Old Crown

tel: 01621 815575 **Lodge Rd CO5 9TU**
email: theoldcrownmessing@hotmail.co.uk
dir: *From Chelmsford: A12 junct 23, B1024 (Kelvedon). In Kelvedon right onto B1023 (Maldon). Left to Messing. From Colchester: A12 junct 24, B1024 (Kelvedon) left onto B1023*

Bistro pub in a lovely village

After many years as regulars, Malcolm and Penny Campbell took over this lovely old pub a few years back. The Old Crown calls itself a 'bistro pub' and is right in the heart of the lovely village of Messing, proving very popular with walkers and cyclists. Dogs are welcome in the bar and the atmosphere throughout is warm and cosy, with open fires in the winter and outside tables in summer. The food is all home cooked and sourced locally whenever possible, and there's a delicatessen on site. There's plenty of choice on the handwritten menu — from warm pigeon breast and sautéed wild mushroom bruschetta, to lamb curry; steamed game pudding; or cassoulet of belly pork, pancetta and Toulouse sausages.

Open all day all wk **Food** Lunch 12-2.30 Dinner 6-9.30 Set menu available Restaurant menu available Mon-Sat ⊕ FREE HOUSE ◀ Adnams Southwold Bitter & Broadside, Crouch Vale ○ Aspall Harry Sparrow. **Facilities** Non-diners area ❄ (Bar Outside area) ◀◀ Children's portions Outside area ⩩ Parking WiFi 🚌 (notice required)

MOUNT BURES
Map 13 TL93

The Thatchers Arms

tel: 01787 227460 **Hall Rd CO8 5AT**
email: hello@thatchersarms.co.uk
dir: *From A12 onto A1124 towards Halstead. Right immediately after Chappel Viaduct. 2m, pub on right*

Bustling rural pub with well thought-out menus

There's something for all comers at this cheery country pub in the lovely Stour Valley, a perfect rural setting for weddings, birthdays and celebrations of all types in a function room and private patio area. Challenge the quoits beds in the beer garden, or ramble on paths that Constable may once have walked; the pub even hosts cinema nights, quiz nights and theatre productions. Popular with locals and visitors drawn to the real ales and interesting wines, delicious home-cooked dishes include pasta carbonara; slow-cooked lamb shank with minted mash and braised red cabbage; and Thai green prawn and squid curry.

Open all day all wk **Food** Lunch Mon-Fri 12-2.30, Sat 12-9, Sun 12-8 Dinner Mon-Fri 6-9, Sat 12-9, Sun 12-8 Set menu available Restaurant menu available all wk ⊕ FREE HOUSE ◀ Adnams Southwold Bitter, Crouch Vale Brewers Gold, guest ales ♂ Aspall Harry Sparrow. ♚ 11 **Facilities** Non-diners area ❀ (Bar Restaurant Garden) ♦ Children's menu Children's portions Garden ⌂ Beer festival Parking WiFi ▭ (notice required)

MOUNTNESSING
Map 6 TQ69

The George & Dragon

tel: 01277 352461 **294 Roman Rd CM15 0TZ**
email: enquiry@thegeorgeanddragonbrentwood.co.uk
dir: *In village centre*

Flavoursome food in a laid-back dining-pub

Spruced-up in true contemporary pub style, the interior of this 18th-century former coaching inn successfully blends bold artwork, colourful leather chairs and chunky modern tables with preserved original wooden floors, exposed beams and brick fireplaces. In this relaxed and convivial setting tuck into Mediterranean-inspired British dishes from an extensive menu that should please all tastes and palates. There are sharing platters, salads, pasta dishes, stone-baked pizzas and main courses like chicken, ham and crème fraîche pie; and four-bone rack of English lamb, asparagus, chorizo, peas, baby onions, dauphinoise potatoes and jus.

Open all day all wk **Food** all wk 12-10 Av main course £15 Set menu available ⊕ MITCHELLS & BUTLERS ◀ Sharp's Doom Bar, St Austell Tribute ♂ Aspall. ♚ 21 **Facilities** Non-diners area ❀ (Bar Garden Outside area) ♦ Children's menu Children's portions Garden Outside area ⌂ Parking WiFi ▭ (notice required)

NEWNEY GREEN
Map 6 TL60

The Duck Pub & Dining

tel: 01245 421894 **CM1 3SF**
email: theduckinn1@btconnect.com
dir: *From Chelmsford take A1060 (Sawbridgeworth). Straight on at mini rdbt, 4th left into Vicarage Rd (signed Roxwell & Willingate), left into Hoe St, becomes Gravelly Ln, left to pub*

Peace and quiet at a quintessential country inn

Formed from two agricultural cottages, this 17th-century inn is situated in the tiny hamlet of Newney Green. The friendly Duck offers up to six real ales, including weekly guests, and menus that reflect the region's produce. Choose from the extensive menu in the beamed dining room; start with giant duck pancake and

hoisin sauce; or deep-fried brie with quince jelly and dressed leaves; then move on to mains like steak and ale pie; beef casserole and fluffy dumplings; or scampi and chips. Soak up the sun in the garden with its children's play area.

Open all day Closed Mon **Food** Tue-Sun 12-9.30 ⊕ FREE HOUSE ◀ Woodforde's Wherry, Adnams Broadside, Sharp's Doom Bar, guest ales. ♚ 14 **Facilities** Non-diners area ♦ Children's menu Children's portions Play area Family room Garden ⌂ Parking WiFi ▭

NORTH FAMBRIDGE
Map 7 TQ89

The Ferry Boat Inn

tel: 01621 740208 **Ferry Ln CM3 6LR**
email: ferryboatinn1@btconnect.com
dir: *From Chelmsford take A130 S, then A132 to South Woodham Ferrers, then B1012. Turn right to village*

Traditional riverside village inn

Believed to have been an inn for at least 200 years, the 500-year-old weatherboarded building was originally three fishermen's cottages. Known locally as the FBI, the pub sits beside a yacht haven on the River Crouch. Low beams and winter fires characterise the bars where pints of Greene King, Mighty Oak Maldon Gold and Sharp's Doom Bar are pulled. Food follows pub grub lines but is home-cooked and good value; look out for specials served all day, deals for OAPs, steaks on Tuesdays and curries on Thursdays. Next door is the 600-acre Essex Wildlife Trust nature reserve, a winter feeding ground for flocks of Brent geese.

Open all day all wk 12-11.30 (Winter Mon-Thu 12-3 6-11 Fri-Sun 12-11) **Food** Lunch Mon-Thu 12-2.30, Fri-Sun all day Dinner Mon-Thu 6-8.30, Fri-Sun all day ⊕ FREE HOUSE ◀ Greene King IPA & Abbot Ale, Mighty Oak Maldon Gold, Sharp's Doom Bar. **Facilities** Non-diners area ❀ (Bar Garden) ♦ Children's menu Children's portions Family room Garden Outside area ⌂ Parking WiFi ▭ (notice required)

PATTISWICK
Map 13 TL82

The Compasses at Pattiswick
PICK OF THE PUBS

tel: 01376 561322 **Compasses Rd CM77 8BG**
email: info@thecompassesatpattiswick.co.uk
dir: *A120 from Braintree towards Colchester. After Bradwell 1st left to Pattiswick*

Destination pub, an ideal rural retreat

Set in the heart the beautiful north Essex countryside, and only a mile from the A120, is this dining-pub that developed from two farm workers' cottages more than a century ago. Flagstone floors, eclectic furniture and a relaxing colour palette all create a stylish interior; the welcome is genuine and the service, professional. The kitchen sources quality produce from local suppliers, including the surrounding estate, for the variety of well cooked food – from classic pub favourites such as fish and chips, through to more complex dishes, perhaps trio of Dingley Dell pork – belly, cheek and fillet with prunes in Armagnac, fondant potato, parsnips and kale. A roaring log fire makes a welcoming sight in winter after a long walk, while in summer the large garden is inviting. Families are very well catered for here, with a play area and toy box to keep little diners entertained. A private dining room with its own patio is available for a maximum of 22 people.

Open all wk 12-3 5.30-11 (Sat 12-3 5.30-12 Sun 12-4) **Food** Lunch Mon-Sat 12-2.30, Sun 12-3 Dinner Mon-Thu 6-9.30, Fri-Sat 6-9.45 Av main course £13.50 Set menu available Restaurant menu available all wk ⊕ FREE HOUSE ◀ Woodforde's Wherry, Adnams Southwold Bitter ♂ Aspall. ♚ 10 **Facilities** Non-diners area ❀ (Bar Garden) ♦ Children's menu Children's portions Play area Garden Parking WiFi ▭ (notice required)

PELDON

Map 7 TL91

The Peldon Rose

tel: 01206 735248 **Colchester Rd CO5 7QJ**
email: enquiries@thepeldonrose.co.uk
dir: On B1025 Mersea Rd, just before causeway

Historic inn, modern food

Contraband was once big business at this early 15th-century inn, understandably given its proximity to The Strood, which bridges the network of channels and creeks separating mainland Essex from Mersea Island. You can easily imagine the smugglers in the original-beamed bar with its leaded windows, but less so in the contemporary conservatory leading to the garden. A well-deserved reputation for good food begins with regularly changing menus offering dishes such as chicken and chorizo terrine; and beetroot-cured salmon as starters, and main courses of Thai-style vegetable linguine; Moroccan-style lamb tagine; and beer-battered fish and chips.

Open all day all wk Closed 25 Dec ∰ FREE HOUSE ◀ Adnams Southwold Bitter, Woodforde's Wherry, IPA, guest ales ♂ Aspall. **Facilities** ♦ Children's menu Children's portions Garden Parking

PURLEIGH

Map 7 TL80

The Bell

tel: 01621 828348 **The Street CM3 6QJ**
email: kirsten@purleighbell.co.uk
dir: Between Chelmsford & Burnham-on-Crouch on B1010. (5m S of Maldon). In Purleigh, pub on top of hill adjacent to church

Some of the best views in Essex

A direct ancestor of George Washington is believed to have lived here in 1634 when he was the local rector. The building was old even then, going back to the 14th century. Purleigh Hill on which it stands is only 45 metres above sea level, but still high enough for sweeping views south. Drink Essex- and Suffolk-brewed real ales or try neighbouring New Hall Vineyard's Sauvignon Blanc in the inglenook fireplace-warmed bar. Daily menus and weekly specials boards inspire with deep-fried camembert with cranberry sauce; guinea fowl with chasseur sauce; and monkfish with whisky provençale sauce.

Open 11.30-3 6-11 (Sat 12-3.30 6-11 Sun 12-5) Closed Sun eve, Mon (ex BHs) **Food** Lunch Tue-Fri 12-2, Sat 12-2.30, Sun 12-4 Dinner Tue-Fri 7-9, Sat 6.30-9 Restaurant menu available ∰ FREE HOUSE ◀ Crouch Vale Brewers Gold, Adnams IPA, Mighty Oak Captain Bob ♂ Aspall. ☑ 13 **Facilities** Non-diners area ❖ (Bar Restaurant Garden) ♦ Children's menu Children's portions Garden ⋤ Parking WiFi ⬛ (notice required)

RICKLING GREEN

Map 12 TL52

The Cricketers Arms

tel: 01799 543210 **CB11 3YG**
email: info@thecricketersarmsricklinggreen.co.uk
dir: M11 junct 10, A505 E. 1.5m, right onto B1301, 2.2m, right onto B1383 at rdbt. Through Newport to Rickling Green. Right into Rickling Green Rd, 0.2m to pub, on left

Classic village green pub – perfect for cricket fans

Well-placed for Saffron Walden and Stansted Airport, this inn enjoys a peaceful position overlooking the village green and cricket pitch in sleepy Rickling Green. The rambling bar and dining rooms have a comfortable, contemporary feel, with squashy sofas by the log fire providing the perfect winter evening refuge for tucking into vegetarian tapas; locally caught rabbit with mustard sauce; Thai fishcake with clam broth; or oven baked whole sea bass with ginger and lemongrass cream. Arrive early on summer weekends to bag a table on the terrace – a popular spot in which to relax with a pint of Doom Bar and watch an innings or two.

Open all day all wk **Food** Lunch Mon-Thu 12-3, Fri-Sat 12-10, Sun 12-8 Dinner Mon-Thu 6-10, Fri-Sat 12-10, Sun 12-8 Set menu available ∰ PUNCH TAVERNS ◀ Sharp's Doom Bar, Woodforde's Wherry, guest ale ♂ Westons Stowford Press. ☑ 10 **Facilities** Non-diners area ❖ (Bar Outside area) ♦ Children's menu Children's portions Outside area ⋤ Parking WiFi ⬛ (notice required)

RIDGEWELL

Map 12 TL74

NEW Kings Head

tel: 01440 788331 **CO9 4RU**
dir: From Braintree take A131 towards Sudbury. In High Garrett left onto A1017 signed Haverhill. Through Gosfield, Castle Hedingham & Great Yeldham to Ridgewell

Fifteenth-century free house on the Essex/Suffolk border

With a pink-washed exterior, this building is full of original charm and character, notably its impressive beams, open inglenook fireplaces and tiled and oak floors. No regular real ales in the two bars, but four different ones every week, and five ciders and perries, including Waltzing Wasp made from a 1907 press in nearby Sible Hedingham. Typically on the menu are toasted white crab and gruyère cheese baguette; Gloucester Old Spots sausage toad-in-the-hole and mash; oven-baked cod, roasted peppers, leeks and carrots; and chicken breast burger. Dogs are welcome in the bar and private walled garden.

Open 6-10.30 (Fri 12-3 5-11 Sat 12-11 Sun 12-9) Closed Mon-Tue, Wed L, Thu L **Food** Lunch Fri-Sun 12-3 Dinner Wed-Sun 6-9 ∰ FREE HOUSE ◀ Rotating guest ales ♂ Delvin End Waltzing Wasp. **Facilities** Non-diners area ❖ (Bar Garden) ♦ Children's menu Children's portions Garden ⋤ Parking WiFi

SAFFRON WALDEN

Map 12 TL53

The Crown Inn ★★★ INN

tel: 01799 522475 **Little Walden CB10 1XA**
email: pippathecrown@aol.com web: www.thecrownlittlewalden.co.uk
dir: 2m from Saffron Walden on B1052

A family-friendly beamed country pub

The Crown's rural situation just outside the pretty market town of Saffron Walden makes it a good choice for local businessmen in need of a change of scene, and for families wanting to tire out children and dogs on one of the many walks in the surrounding countryside. Mums and dads can return for a well-earned glass of Adnams Broadside or a glass of wine, and hungry children can choose from the half dozen options on their dedicated menu. The short but reasonably priced menus embrace all the classic pub grub dishes. There's live jazz on Wednesday evenings.

Open all wk 11.30-2.30 6-11 (Sun 12-10.30) **Food** Lunch Mon-Sat 11.30-2, Sun 12-3 Dinner Tue-Sat 6.30-9 ∰ FREE HOUSE ◀ Woodforde's Wherry, Adnams Broadside, Greene King Abbot Ale, guest ales. **Facilities** Non-diners area ❖ (Bar Restaurant Outside area) ♦ Children's menu Children's portions Outside area ⋤ Parking WiFi ⬛ (notice required) **Rooms** 3

Old English Gentleman

tel: 01799 523595 **11 Gold St CB10 1EJ**
email: goodtimes@oldenglishgentleman.com **web:** www.oldenglishgentleman.co.uk
dir: *M11 junct 9a, B184 signed Saffron Walden. Left at High St lights into George St, 1st right into Gold St (one-way system)*

A warm, friendly town-centre local

Regulars call Jeff and Cindy Leach's 19th-century, town centre pub the OEG, an informality which the top-hatted dandy on the sign over the front door might frown upon. Ancient beer taps line a wall of the central bar area, which extends into a dining space with a log-burner and air conditioning, while outside is a heated patio garden. Resident ales Adnams Southwold and Woodforde's Wherry are backed up by changing guests and Aspall cider; a portfolio that earns customers' respect. Hearty main meals include beer-battered catch of the day; OEG pie of the week; and sausages and mash. For a lighter bite try a panini or hand-cut sandwiches.

Open all day all wk **Food** Lunch all wk 12-2.30 ◖ Woodforde's Wherry, Adnams Southwold Bitter, 2 guest ales ♂ Aspall. ♟ 10 **Facilities** Non-diners area ♣ (Bar Outside area) ⋔ Outside area ⊼ WiFi

STANSTED AIRPORT

See Little Canfield

STANSTED MOUNTFITCHET   Map 12 TL52

The Cock Public House

tel: 01279 812964 **30 Silver St CM24 8HD**
email: info@thecockatstansted.co.uk
dir: *Phone for detailed directions*

Family-run and proudly traditional

The Cock sits on a busy road running through Stansted Mountfitchet, but today's locals are given just the same warm welcome as their ancestors received when it opened for business back in the 1800s. The pub hosts quizzes, live music and charity events, as well as private parties; Greene King ales and home-cooked pub food are its keys to success. Snacks include sandwiches, paninis and jackets, while a typical three-course choice could embrace deep-fried brie; pumpkin and red onion tagine; or pesto-filled chicken breast and tomato, pepper and onion sauce; and apple crumble or bread and butter pudding to finish.

Open all day all wk **Food** Lunch Mon-Sat 12-2.30, Sun 12-6 Dinner Mon-Sat 6-9 Sun 12-6 Av main course £9-£10 Set menu available Restaurant menu available all wk ⊕ GREENE KING ◖ IPA & Abbot, Morland Old Speckled Hen. ♟ 10 **Facilities** Non-diners area ⋔ Children's menu Children's portions Play area Garden Outside area ⊼ Parking WiFi ⛟ (notice required)

STISTED   Map 13 TL72

NEW The Dolphin

tel: 01376 321143 **CM77 8EU**
email: info@thedolphinpub.co.uk
dir: *On A120 between Braintree & Coggeshall*

Attractive and traditional country hostelry

The Dolphin was originally four cottages dating from the 16th-century, one of which was an alehouse, that over time have become a single attractive building. Midway between Braintree and Colchester, The Dolphin makes a great refreshment stop, serving food and drink all day every day. Greene King ales, Aspall's cider, popular home-cooked pub fare, warming log fires and friendly staff are all attributes here. Children have their own menu, washed down with unlimited squash. Dedham Vale beef is grilled to your liking, or look to the specials list for the likes of twice-roasted pork belly, Bramley apple and ham mash with wholegrain mustard sauce.

Open all day all wk **Food** all wk 12-9.30 ⊕ GREENE KING ◖ IPA, Morland Original, Ruddles Best ♂ Aspall Harry Sparrow. **Facilities** Non-diners area ♣ (Bar Garden Outside area) ⋔ Children's menu Children's portions Garden Outside area ⊼ Parking WiFi ⛟ (notice required)

STOCK
Map 6 TQ69

The Hoop ◉

tel: 01277 841137 **21 High St CM4 9BD**
email: thehoopstock@yahoo.co.uk **web:** www.thehoop.co.uk
dir: On B1007 between Chelmsford & Billericay

Traditional pub with a focus on food

This 15th-century free house on Stock's village green is every inch the traditional country pub, offering a warm welcome, authentic pub interiors and a pleasing absence of music and fruit machines. There's an emphasis on food here, with dishes ranging from traditional pie, mash and liquor to pan-fried calves' liver with crispy bacon, creamy mash and home-cooked onion rings. You could finish with treacle tart and ice cream, or citrus bread pudding. The annual beer festival (late May) has been going from strength to strength for over 30 years; you'll have over 100 real ales to choose from, not to mention fruit beers, perries and more.

Open all day all wk **Food** Lunch Mon-Fri 12-2.30, Sat 12-9.30, Sun 12-5 Dinner Mon-Thu 6-9, Fri 6-9.30, Sat 12-9.30 Restaurant menu available Tue-Sat ⊕ FREE HOUSE ◖ Adnams Southwold Bitter, Crouch Vale Brewers Gold, Young's, Wibblers, guest ales Ö Thatchers Gold. ♟ 14 **Facilities** Non-diners area ☙ (Bar Garden) ♦♦ Children's portions Garden ⊓ Beer festival WiFi

WENDENS AMBO
Map 12 TL53

The Bell

tel: 01799 540382 **Royston Rd CB11 4JY**
dir: Phone for detailed directions

Traditional old English pub with beams galore

First mentioned in 1576 as a farm, evidence of its great age is everywhere, particularly the fine Elizabethan chimney stack. Other attributes include acres of gardens, a willow-edged pond, a woodland walk, play equipment, open fires and a resident ghost. Then there's the traditional country pub food, such as the hugely popular Bell beef and real ale pie; lamb Marrakesh; battered 'catch of the day'; and roasted vegetable and goats' cheese strudel. Cask ales and real ciders are always on tap. Ambo, incidentally, means 'both' in Latin and reflects a 17th-century merging of parishes.

Open all day Closed Mon L (winter) **Food** Lunch Tue-Thu 12-2, Fri-Sat 12-3, Sun 12-4 Dinner Tue-Sat 6-9 Set menu available ⊕ FREE HOUSE ◖ Woodforde's Wherry, Oakham Ales JHB, Adnams, guest ales Ö Thatchers Cheddar Valley. **Facilities** Non-diners area ☙ (Bar Garden) ♦♦ Children's menu Children's portions Play area Garden ⊓ Parking WiFi ⟺ (notice required)

WIDDINGTON
Map 12 TL53

NEW Fleur de Lys

tel: 01799 543280 **CB11 3SG**
dir: M1 junct 9A, follow Newport (B1383) signs. After Newport turn left signed Widdington. 2m to pub on left

Family- and dog-friendly village free house

Terracotta-painted, low-beamed, and with a fine inglenook fireplace, the Fleur is over 500 years old. A games room is essential in a pub, say the landlords, which is why you'll find one here, accommodating a dartboard, full-size pool table and jukebox. Regional brews such as Woodforde's Wherry and Adnams are usually accompanied by guest ales and Rosie's Pig cloudy cider. Huge doorstep sandwiches are served with hand-cut chips, while the fish and chips has been dubbed 'whale and chips', so make sure you're hungry. Other dishes include Dedham Vale beefburger; sausage and mash; creamy mushroom, chestnut and spinach fricassée; and specials.

Open 12-3 6-11 (Mon 6.30-11 Fri-Sat 12-11.30 Sun 12-10) Closed 1 Jan, Mon L **Food** Lunch Tue-Sat 12-2.30, Sun 12-3 Dinner Wed-Sat 6.30-9 Av main course £12 Restaurant menu available Tue-Sun ⊕ FREE HOUSE ◖ Adnams Southwold Bitter, Woodforde's Wherry, 2 rotating guest ales Ö Westons Rosie's Pig. ♟ 8 **Facilities** Non-diners area ☙ (Bar Garden) ♦♦ Children's portions Garden ⊓ Parking

WOODHAM MORTIMER
Map 7 TL80

Hurdlemakers Arms

tel: 01245 225169 **Post Office Rd CM9 6ST**
email: info@hurdlemakersarms.co.uk
dir: From Chelmsford A414 to Maldon (Danbury). 4.5m, through Danbury into Woodham Mortimer. Over 1st rdbt, 1st left, pub on left. Behind golf driving range

Family-run pub with a great beer festival

This pretty old village institution slumbers contentedly beside a lane in tranquil countryside just inland from Maldon's creeks and sea-marshes. Muscular posts and rippling beams inside hint at the age of the building, which is much older than its first licence in 1837. There's a simply enormous garden here, dappled with ancient fruit trees; an ideal location for their June beer festival. Year-round treats on the bar include beers from Dark Star and Wibblers, who also provide the local cider. The consummate menu covers all bases: pigeon pie; walnut and almond roast; and smoked haddock Florentine are typical choices on the locally sourced bill of fare.

Open all day all wk 12-11 (Sun 12-9) **Food** Lunch Mon-Fri 12-3, Sat 12-9.30, Sun 12-8 Dinner Mon-Fri 6-9.30, Sat 12-9.30, Sun 12-8 ⊕ GRAY & SONS ◖ Mighty Oak, Farmers, Wibblers, Dark Star, guest ales Ö Rotating guest ciders. ♟ 8 **Facilities** Non-diners area ♦♦ Children's menu Children's portions Play area Garden ⊓ Beer festival Parking WiFi ⟺

GLOUCESTERSHIRE

ALDERTON
Map 10 SP03

The Gardeners Arms

tel: 01242 620257 **Beckford Rd GL20 8NL**
email: gardeners1@btconnect.com
dir: M5 junct 6, A46 towards Evesham. At rdbt take B4077 signed Stow. Left to Alderton

Tapas, fresh fish and seasonal specials

Operating as a pub since the 16th century, this pretty, family-run, thatched free house is popular with walkers, cyclists and car clubs. You can play boules in the large beer garden, and traditional games in the stone-walled bar, where Cotswold Way numbers among the real ales. Menus change with the seasons, as you might expect from a pub with the word 'gardener' in its name. The Gardeners Arms offers a fixed menu that changes fortnightly – the food is hearty and traditional, including the likes of pork belly, lamb chump and bacon, fish and chips, and beef topside with roasted turnips. There's a beer and cider festival in August.

Open all wk 9.30-2.30 5.30-10 (Fri 9.30-2.30 5.30-12 Sat 9.30-10.30 Sun 10-8) Closed 3 days in Jan **Food** Lunch all wk 12-2 Dinner all wk 5.30-9 Av main course £12.95 Set menu available ⊕ FREE HOUSE ◀ Sharp's Doom Bar, Prescott Track Record, Wickwar Cotswold Way, Gloucester, local guest ales ♂ Westons Stowford Press. ☕ **Facilities** Non-diners area ♣ (Bar Garden Outside area) ♦ Children's menu Children's portions Garden Outside area ⌂ Beer festival Cider festival Parking WiFi ▦ (notice required)

ALMONDSBURY — Map 4 ST68

The Swan Hotel

tel: 01454 625671 **14 Gloucester Rd BS32 4AA**
email: garth@swanhotelbristol.com
dir: M5 junct 16, A38 to Almondsbury

Comfortable village pub with full events calendar

On the outskirts of Bristol, parts of this former coaching inn date back to the 16th century and its hilltop position offers views of the Bristol Channel. Head chef Ross Hunter champions local produce and keeps things interesting with Monday Pie Nights, Tuesday Pizza Nights and on Thursdays it's Fish and Fizz. The daily menu might offer ham hock, mustard and prune terrine; chicken and chorizo burgers; cider and tarragon braised chicken; pan-fried lamb's liver with bubble-and-squeak cake; and rabbit pot pie. For dessert there could be Bakewell tart; double chocolate brownie or even, a beetroot parfait. The pub holds a beer and cider festival in July.

Open all day all wk **Food** Lunch all wk 12-4 Dinner Mon-Sat 4-9.30, Sun 4-9.30 Av main course £15 ⊕ MARSTON'S ◀ Pedigree, Wychwood Hobgoblin, Ringwood Old Thumper ♂ Thatchers Gold & Cheddar Valley, Westons Stowford Press. ☕ 12 **Facilities** Non-diners area ♦ Children's menu Children's portions Play area Garden ⌂ Beer festival Cider festival Parking WiFi ▦ (notice required)

ASHLEWORTH — Map 10 SO82

The Queens Arms   PICK OF THE PUBS

tel: 01452 700395 **The Village GL19 4HT**
dir: From Gloucester N on A417 for 5m. At Hartpury, right at Broad St to Ashleworth. Pub 100yds past village green

Rural free house offering an interesting menu

Set between rolling hills and the River Severn in a delightful rural village, this 16th century inn is owned by Tony and Gill Burreddu. Although alterations have been made over the years, the original beams and iron fireplaces have been kept, simply complemented with comfortable armchairs, antiques and a gallery of local artists' work. As a free house, the Queens offers ales from a range of breweries including Brecon Brewing and Shepherd Neame. Tony and Gill have built a loyal customer base and an excellent reputation for imaginative dishes made from the best local produce. Specials board entries may include a starter of filo prawns with sweet and sour sauce; a main course of Greek lamb studded with garlic and herbs, braised in rich red wine gravy and served with mint yogurt; and Cape brandy pudding – a South African speciality made with light sponge and brandy-soaked dates.

Open 12-3 7-11 Closed 25-26 Dec, 1 Jan, Sun eve & Mon (ex BHs wknds) **Food** Lunch Tue-Sun 12-2 Dinner Tue-Sat 7-9 ⊕ FREE HOUSE ◀ Timothy Taylor Landlord, Donnington BB, Brains The Rev. James, Shepherd Neame Spitfire, Sharp's

Doom Bar, Brecon Brewing Gold Beacons ♂ Westons Stowford Press. ☕ 14 **Facilities** Non-diners area ♦ Garden ⌂ Parking

---

BARNSLEY — Map 5 SP00

The Village Pub ★★★★★ INN   PICK OF THE PUBS

See Pick of the Pubs on page 198

BERKELEY — Map 4 ST69

The Malt House ★★★ INN

tel: 01453 511177 **Marybrook St GL13 9BA**
email: the-malthouse@btconnect.com **web:** www.themalthouse.uk.com
dir: M5 junct 13/14, A38 towards Bristol. Pub on main road towards Sharpness

Village charm in the pretty Vale of Berkeley

At the heart of historic Berkeley, close to the remarkable castle and the Edward Jenner (the pioneer immunologist) Museum, this village free house is a popular place with walkers on the spectacular Severn Way along the nearby estuary shoreline; comfy accommodation and good food tempt overnight stops here. Ease into the copiously beamed old bar and consider a menu rich with modern British dishes — steak and ale pie; lamb shank; or halibut steak with sweet chilli dip will satisfy; there's a good vegetarian selection including nut roast, a specials board and a great sausage choice.

Open all wk Mon-Thu 6-11 (Fri 6-12 Sat 12-12 Sun 12-3) **Food** Lunch Sat-Sun 12-2 Dinner Mon-Sat 6.30-8.30 ⊕ FREE HOUSE ◀ Theakston Best Bitter, Wickwar Cotswold Way ♂ Westons Stowford Press, Thatchers Gold. **Facilities** Non-diners area ♦ Children's menu Children's portions Garden ⌂ Parking WiFi ▦ (notice required) **Rooms** 9

PICK OF THE PUBS

The Village Pub ★★★★★ INN

BARNSLEY   Map 5 SP00

tel: 01285 740421 **GL7 5EF**
email: reservations@thevillagepub.co.uk
web: www.thevillagepub.co.uk
dir: *On B4425 4m NE of Cirencester*

Non-touristy traditional local in an Area of Outstanding Natural Beauty

Not to be mistaken for its younger Yorkshire namesake, Barnsley is one the prettiest chocolate box villages in the Cotswolds and its only pub is as smart and well-mannered as the locals. The interior is warmly furnished and decorated, as befits the flagstones, oak floorboards, exposed timbers and open fireplaces. Also contributing to its appeal is a contemporary approach to English pub food, holder of an AA Dinner Award, with regularly-changing, largely locally-sourced menus. Vegetables, for example, come from 17th-century Barnsley House across the road. Starters include wild rabbit and ham hock terrine, pickled mushrooms and windfall chutney; or smoked mackerel pâté, toast, soft-boiled egg and watercress. Main course choices might include local pheasant, celeriac gratin, wild mushrooms and curly kale; Cornish sea bream with chorizo, red pepper and chickpeas; and rosemary and garlic marinated Black Angus sirloin steak with hand cut chips and béarnaise sauce. Desserts deliver plenty of comfort

value in the shape of banoffee bread and butter pudding with vanilla ice cream or custard; or chocolate nemesis with fruit and nut ice cream, perhaps accompanied by one of several sweet and fortified wines. A carefully curated board of British cheeses might include Cotswold-made Simon Weaver Brie or award-winning Perl Las blue cheese from Wales. Bar snacks of quail and black pudding Scotch eggs or onion bhaji and pickle go well with a pint of North Cotswold Shagweaver or Happy Daze cider, or perhaps one of the 16 wines served by the glass from a concise but interesting list.

Open all day all wk all wk 7am-11pm
Food Sun 12-9. Lunch Mon-Fri 12-2.30,

Sat 12-3 Dinner Mon-Sat 6-9.30,
Av main course £15 ⊞ FREE HOUSE
◀ North Cotswold Brewery Cotswold Best & Shagweaver, Yubberton Yawnie
Ŏ Symonds Founders Reserve & Scrumpy Jack, Gwynt y Ddraig Happy Daze. ♇ 16 **Facilities** Non-diners area
♣ (Bar Restaurant Outside area)
♦♦ Children's portions Outside area ⋈ Parking WiFi 🚐 (notice required)
Rooms 6

BIBURY
Map 5 SP10

Catherine Wheel ★★★★ INN

tel: 01285 740250 **Arlington GL7 5ND**
email: info@catherinewheel-bibury.co.uk web: www.catherinewheel-bibury.co.uk
dir: *On B4425, W of Bibury*

Welcoming Cotswold inn offering a crowd-pleasing menu

The beautiful Cotswold-stone building, stable courtyard and orchard date back to the 15th century but plenty of historical features remain. This former blacksmith's has changed hands many times since J Hathaway opened it as an inn in 1856 but a warm welcome, a good selection of accredited ales such as Hook Norton and quality food remain its hallmarks. The appetising menu might include ham hock and chicken terrine; and Asian-marinated beef short ribs. Classics such as steak and red wine pie; and Gloucester Old Spots sausages and mash satisfy more traditional tastes.

Open all day all wk 9am-11pm **Food** Lunch Mon-Fri 3-6, Sat 12-9.30, Sun 12-9 Dinner Mon-Fri 6-9.30, Sat 12-9.30, Sun 12-9 ⊕ FREE HOUSE/WHITE JAYS LTD ◼ Sharp's Doom Bar, Hook Norton ⊙ Westons Stowford Press, Aspall. ♟ 9 **Facilities** Non-diners area ❖ (Bar Garden) ♦♦ Children's menu Children's portions Garden ⋒ Parking WiFi ☛ (notice required) **Rooms** 4

BIRDLIP
Map 10 SO91

The Golden Heart

tel: 01242 870261 **Nettleton Bottom GL4 8LA**
email: info@thegoldenheart.co.uk
dir: *On A417 (Gloucester to Cirencester road). 8m from Cheltenham. Pub at base of dip in Nettleton Bottom*

Traditional pub with some exotic dishes

A traditional 17th-century Cotswold-stone inn that was once a drovers' resting place, this lovely pub boasts stunning views of the valley from the terraced gardens. The main bar is divided into four cosy areas with log fires and traditional built-in settles. Excellent local ales and ciders are backed by a good selection of wines, while the extensive menus demonstrate commitment to local produce, particularly prize-winning meat from the region. Perhaps try Gloucester Old Spots sausages with mash and onion gravy; wild boar and apple burger; or Thai king prawn curry. The more adventurous should aim for kangaroo steak marinated in chilli and honey glaze. A good range of vegetarian, vegan and gluten-free options are available.

Open all day all wk **Food** all wk 11-11 ⊕ FREE HOUSE ◼ Otter Bitter, Cotswold Lion, Brakspear, Jennings, Flying Monk, Wychwood ⊙ Westons, Ilenney's, Thatchers. ♟ 10 **Facilities** Non-diners area ❖ (Bar Restaurant Garden) ♦♦ Children's portions Family room Garden ⋒ Parking WiFi ☛

BISLEY
Map 4 SO90

The Bear Inn

tel: 01452 770265 **George St GL6 7BD**
email: info@bisleybear.co.uk
dir: *Phone for detailed directions*

Striking 17th-century inn serving traditional food

Now run by David and Amanda Terry, there has been a pub here for almost 400 years. Stories and legends abound here and there is even a priest hole halfway up the inglenook fireplace. The pub's original character and charm is still evident, from the friendly bar serving pints of Wells Bombardier beer to the dining room where food is traditional and comforting. If one of the weekly pie specials or Tuesday night curries doesn't take your fancy, the likes of home-made beef lasagne; mushroom and chestnut Stroganoff; or beer-battered haddock and chips surely will.

Open all day all wk **Food** Lunch all wk 12-3 Dinner all wk 6-9 ⊕ PUNCH TAVERNS ◼ Wells Bombardier & Golden, Butcombe, St Austell Tribute ⊙ Westons Stowford Press. **Facilities** Non-diners area ❖ (Bar Garden) ♦♦ Children's menu Children's portions Family room Garden ⋒ Parking WiFi ☛ (notice required)

BLAISDON
Map 10 SO71

The Red Hart Inn

tel: 01452 830477 **GL17 OAH**
dir: *Take A40 (NW of Gloucester) towards Ross-on-Wye. At lights left onto A4136 signed Monmouth. Left into Blaisdon Lane to Blaisdon*

Village inn with tranquil country views

On the fringe of the Forest of Dean, this old whitewashed pub exudes the charm of a village local, all flag-stoned floors, log fire, low beams and dog-friendly too. Four guest ales whet the whistle of passing ramblers, whilst those dining out will appreciate the quality pork raised by the pub's owners. Look out for Mediterranean vegetable pasta bake; herb stuffed loin of pork with mustard mash and cider gravy; or duck breast with Cassis sauce. Specials introduce dishes featuring venison or pheasant to the well-balanced menu, taken in the bar or restaurant. The sunny garden is a good place to sit with a glass of local cider.

Open all wk 12-3 6-11.30 (Sun 12.30-4 7-11) **Food** Lunch all wk 12-2.15 Dinner all wk 6.30-9 ⊕ FREE HOUSE ◼ Bespoke, Otter, 3 guest ales ⊙ Westons Stowford Press, Traditional & 1st Quality. **Facilities** Non-diners area ❖ (Bar Garden) ♦♦ Children's menu Children's portions Play area Garden ⋒ Parking WiFi ☛ (notice required)

BLEDINGTON
Map 10 SP22

The Kings Head Inn ★★★★ INN ⊛ PICK OF THE PUBS

tel: 01608 658365 **The Green OX7 6XQ**
email: info@kingsheadinn.net web: www.kingsheadinn.net
dir: *On B4450, 4m from Stow-on-the-Wold*

Sublime Cotswold free house

It's axiomatic that people make pubs – on both sides of the bar. They certainly do here. On one side, long-term owners Archie and Nicola Orr-Ewing; on the other, their customers, drawn by a reputation for well-kept real ales and top-quality, locally sourced food. Facing the village green, this stone-built pub dates back to the 15th century; it's been called the quintessential Cotswolds inn. Original structure survives in the low-beamed ceilings, flagstone floors, exposed stone walls and an inglenook fireplace. On the beer pumps, the labels of Hooky Bitter, Purity Gold and Wye Valley appear alongside local lagers; 10 wines are served by the glass. Among choices in the AA Rosette restaurant are deep-fried Windrush goats' cheese salad; vodka-and-tonic soft-shell crab; wood pigeon tart; seafood and saffron risotto; and Tamworth pork and black pudding burger. For dessert, how about affogato?

Open all day all wk Closed 25-26 Dec **Food** Lunch Mon-Fri 12-2, Sat-Sun 12-3 Dinner Sun-Thu 6.30-9, Fri-Sat 6.30-9.30 ⊕ FREE HOUSE ◼ Hook Norton Hooky Bitter, Purity Gold, Wye Valley, Butcombe, Butts, Bath Ales, guest ales ⊙ Westons Stowford Press. ♟ 10 **Facilities** Non-diners area ♦♦ Children's menu Children's portions Garden ⋒ Parking WiFi **Rooms** 12

BOURTON-ON-THE-HILL
Map 10 SP13

Horse and Groom
PICK OF THE PUBS

tel: 01386 700413 **GL56 9AQ**
email: greenstocks@horseandgroom.info
dir: *2m W of Moreton-in-Marsh on A44*

Elegant inn offering excellent locally-sourced food

The Greenstock brothers run this handsome Grade II listed Cotswold stone pub and it is both a serious dining destination and a friendly place for a drink. The building combines a contemporary feel with plenty of original period features and the mature garden is a must-visit in summer with its panoramic hilltop views. The beer selection mixes local brews such as Goffs Jouster and over 20 carefully selected wines are served by the glass. The blackboard menu changes daily, providing plenty of appeal for even the most ardent regulars. With committed local suppliers backed up by the pub's own abundant vegetable patch, the kitchen has plenty of good produce to work with. A typical menu might feature Cornish fish soup, rouille, gruyère and crispy toasts; then shin of Dexter beef ragù, home-made pappardelle pasta; or grilled Middlewhite pork chop, creamed celeriac purée and chorizo crumbs; followed by peanut butter, Nutella and chocolate mousse tart; or Granny G's toffee meringue.

Open 11-3 6-11 Closed 25 Dec, Sun eve **Food** Lunch all wk 12-2 Dinner Mon-Sat 7-9 ⊕ FREE HOUSE ◀ Wye Valley Bitter, Purity Pure UBU, Goffs Jouster, Cotswold Wheat Beer, Stroud Organic Ö Hogan's, Pearsons. ♟ 21 **Facilities** Non-diners area ♦♦ Children's portions Garden ⌐ Parking WiFi

BROCKHAMPTON
Map 10 SP02

Craven Arms Inn

tel: 01242 820410 **GL54 5XQ**
email: cravenarms@live.co.uk
dir: *From Cheltenham take A40 towards Gloucester. In Andoversford, at lights, left onto A436 signed Bourton & Stow. Left, follow signs for Brockhampton*

Secluded village setting in fine walking country

Inside and out, this set-back, gabled old village inn glows with mellow honeyed stone; log fires, beams and mullioned windows add to the charm of its setting beneath the gently undulating horizon of the Cotswolds. Drinkers appreciate the selection of real ales; ciders and perry from regional orchards; and the mid-September beer festival. Diners can self-cook their fish, steaks or haloumi on hot-rocks at the table, or choose from the list of starters and bar meals. Here you may find baked Cotswold Blue Brie with fig chutney; steak and ale pie, vegetables with new potatoes or chips; or salmon and dill fishcake with sweet chilli mayonnaise. There's a gluten-free menu too.

Open 12-3 6-11 Closed Sun eve & Mon **Food** Lunch Tue-Fri 12-2, Sat 12-2.30, Sun 12-3 Dinner Tue-Thu 6.30-9, Fri-Sat 6.30-9.30 ⊕ FREE HOUSE ◀ Otter, Butcombe Legless Bob Ö Westons Stowford Press, Dunkertons. ♟ 9 **Facilities** Non-diners area ✿ (Bar Garden) ♦♦ Children's menu Children's portions Garden ⌐ Beer festival Parking WiFi ☛ (notice required)

CHELTENHAM
Map 10 SO92

The Gloucester Old Spot

tel: 01242 680321 **Tewkesbury Rd, Piff's Elm GL51 9SY**
email: eat@thegloucesteroldspot.co.uk
dir: *On A4019 on outskirts of Cheltenham towards Tewkesbury*

Traditional pub run by enthusiastic owners

Simon and Kate Daws' free house ticks all the boxes with its quarry tile floors, roaring log fires, farmhouse furnishings and real ales such as Wye Valley; they also own another Cheltenham pub, The Royal Oak Inn. Local ciders and perries are on offer at the bar. The baronial dining room takes its inspiration from the local manor, and game and rare-breed pork make an appearance on a menu that includes crispy pressed pork shoulder with seared scallops, parsnip purée and salsa verde; and black pudding stuffed pork fillet with pork liver faggot and devilled pig's kidney sauce. The lovely gardens are just the place for enjoying a drink or lunch, or a perhaps a barbecue that is available for private groups.

Open all day all wk Closed 25-26 Dec **Food** Lunch Mon-Sat 12-2, Sun 12-8 Dinner Mon-Sat 6-9, Sun 12-8 Set menu available ⊕ FREE HOUSE ◀ Timothy Taylor Landlord, Purity Mad Goose, Wye Valley HPA & Butty Bach, Butcombe Bitter Ö Thatchers, Westons Stowford Press, Black Rat. **Facilities** Non-diners area ✿ (Bar Garden) ♦♦ Children's menu Children's portions Garden ⌐ Beer festival Cider festival Parking WiFi ☛ (notice required)

The Royal Oak Inn

tel: 01242 522344 **The Burgage, Prestbury GL52 3DL**
email: eat@royal-oak-prestbury.co.uk
dir: *From town centre follow signs for Winchcombe/Prestbury & Racecourse. In Prestbury follow brown signs for inn from Tatchley Ln*

Welcoming pub recommended for its beer and cider festivals

Close to Cheltenham's famous racecourse, this 16th-century pub was once owned by England cricket legend Tom Graveney. Current owners Simon and Kate Daws, who have been here for 15 years, also own The Gloucester Old Spot. Enjoy well-kept local cask ales, real ciders and delicious food in the snug, the comfortable dining room or the heated patio overlooking a pretty beer garden. Menus and blackboard specials might list pan-fried wood pigeon breast, and black pudding salad; baked ratatouille lasagne; and spiced roast lamb rump, fondant potato, sauté kale and ras el hanout seasoned tomato sauce. There is a beer and sausage festival on the Spring Bank Holiday and a cider festival on the Summer Bank Holiday.

Open all day all wk Closed 25 Dec **Food** Lunch Mon-Sat 12-2, Sun 12-8 Dinner Mon-Sat 6-9, Sun 12-8 ⊕ FREE HOUSE ◀ Timothy Taylor Landlord, Purity Mad Goose, Butcombe Bitter Ö Thatchers, Westons Stowford Press, Sandford Orchards Devon Red. **Facilities** Non-diners area ♦♦ Children's menu Children's portions Garden ⌐ Beer festival Cider festival Parking WiFi

NEW Sandford Park Alehouse

tel: 01242 574517 **GL50 1DZ**
email: spalehouse@gmail.com
dir: *SE end of High St*

Town centre pub with over a hundred beers on offer

The large garden of this handsome Grade II listed pub backs on to Sandford Park with its landscaped gardens and lido, which makes it ideal for visitors to Cheltenham town centre. A pub that takes its beers very seriously, there are 10 handpumps and 16 taps set aside for ale, not to mention around 100 bottled beers. The beer theme continues with the food, which might include Flemish stew of beef shin, slowly cooked in Belgian brown ale; or haddock fried in Belgian beer batter. Other choices include curry of the day; Polish sausage and mash; and chicken schnitzel.

Open all day all wk Closed 25-26 Dec, 1 Jan **Food** Lunch all wk 12-2.30 Dinner all wk 5.30-9 Av main course £7.95 ⊕ FREE HOUSE ◀ Oakham Ales Citra, Wye Valley Butty Bach, Purity Mad Goose Ö Guest Cider. ♟ 10 **Facilities** Non-diners area ✿ (Bar Garden) Garden ⌐ Cider festival WiFi ☛ (notice required)

CHIPPING CAMPDEN
Map 10 SP13

The Bakers Arms

tel: 01386 840515 **Broad Campden GL55 6UR**
email: info@bakersarmscampden.co.uk
dir: *1m from Chipping Campden*

Sublime Cotswold pub with friendly welcome

Ease into the compact little bar here, squeeze into a space near the eye-catching inglenook and live the Cotswold dream, with local Stanney Bitter mirroring the colour of the mellow thatched stone cottages in this picture-postcard hamlet. The patio, terrace and garden are all ideal on summer evenings in this most tranquil spot, lost amidst lanes and tracks below tree-fringed hilltops. The traditional, well-considered menu may offer a creamy beetroot risotto starter with chicken, ham and leek pie or lamb shank to follow; the intimate dressed-stone walled restaurant area is a peaceful retreat from the popular bar.

Open 11.30-2.30 5.30-close (Fri-Sat 11.30-11 Sun 12-10.30) Closed 25 Dec, Mon L (ex BH) **Food** Lunch Tue-Sat 12-2, Sun 12-4 Dinner Mon-Sat 6-8 Av main course £9.50 ⊕ FREE HOUSE ◀ Stanway Stanney Bitter, Wickwar, Wye Valley, North Cotswold Windrush ♂ Thatchers Heritage. **Facilities** Non-diners area ❤ (Bar Garden) ♦♦ Children's menu Children's portions Play area Garden ⊨ Parking WiFi ▭ (notice required)

The Kings ★★★★ RR ❀❀
PICK OF THE PUBS

tel: 01386 840256 **The Square GL55 6AW**
email: info@kingscampden.co.uk web: www.kingscampden.co.uk
dir: *Phone for detailed directions*

Wide choice of dining options in charming town centre pub

Facing the square of one of England's prettiest towns, this sympathetically restored old townhouse is packed with character, the oldest parts including the 16th-century stone mullioned windows on the first floor. The bar not only offers real ales but also daily papers and traditional pub games, but no noisy gaming machines. Bar snacks include a good range of sandwiches and baguettes, while main meals are served in the informal bar brasserie or more formal AA-Rosette restaurant overlooking the square. A sample dinner menu offers some imaginative delights: citrus-cured salmon, buttermilk, horseradish, cucumber and tempura prawn; or butter-roast parsnip, beer-braised shallot, honey and crispy leeks to start. Mains include pollock with salt cod croquette and parsley purée; or the venison dish of loin and pie with blackberry, smoked beetroot and kale. The large grassed garden and dining terrace is surprising to find in a town centre pub. Individually decorated bedrooms offer period features with plenty of modern comforts too.

Open all day all wk 7am-11pm (Sat-Sun 8am-11pm) **Food** Lunch all wk 12-2.30 Dinner all wk 6.30-9.30 Av main course £13 Set menu available Restaurant menu available all wk ⊕ FREE HOUSE ◀ Hook Norton Hooky Bitter ♂ Thatchers Gold. � 10 **Facilities** Non-diners area ♦♦ Children's menu Children's portions Garden Outside area ⊨ Parking WiFi ▭ (notice required) **Rooms** 19

Noel Arms Hotel
PICK OF THE PUBS

tel: 01386 840317 **High St GL55 6AT**
email: reception@noelarmshotel.com
dir: *On High St, opposite Town Hall*

Delightful inn with its own curry club

The Noel Arms is one of the oldest hotels in the Cotswolds, a place where traditional appeal has been successfully preserved and interwoven seamlessly with contemporary comforts. Charles II reputedly stayed in this golden Cotswold-stone

16th-century coaching inn. It was through the carriage arch that packhorse trains used to carry bales of wool, the source of Chipping Campden's prosperity, to Bristol and Southampton. Absorb these details of the hotel's history while sipping a pint of North Cotswold brewery's Windrush Ale in front of the log fire in Dover's Bar; read the papers over a coffee and pastry in the coffee shop; and enjoy brasserie-style food in the restaurant. An alternative to the modern English dishes is brought by Indunil Upatissa who creates his trademark curries daily, and enthusiasts arrive for his Curry Club on the last Thursday evening of every month.

Open all day all wk **Food** Lunch all wk 12-2 Dinner all wk 6.30-9.30 ⊕ FREE HOUSE ◀ North Cotswold Brewery Cotswold Best & Windrush Ale, Hook Norton Old Hooky ♂ Westons Stowford Press. ☷ **Facilities** Non-diners area ❤ (Bar) ♦♦ Children's menu Children's portions Outside area ⊨ Parking WiFi ▭

Seagrave Arms ★★★★ RR ❀❀
PICK OF THE PUBS

tel: 01386 840192 **Friday St, Weston Subedge GL55 6QH**
email: enquiries@theseagravearms.com web: www.seagravearms.co.uk
dir: *From Moreton-in-Marsh take A44 towards Evesham. 7m, right onto B4081 to Chipping Campden. Left at junct with High St. 0.5m, straight on at x-roads to Weston Subedge. Left at T-junct*

Prime Cotswold country inn where quality counts

Built as a farmhouse around 1740 and Grade II listed, this handsome Georgian building in Cotswold stone is approached between a display of neatly trimmed, globe-shaped bushes in stone planters. In the bar you'll find real ales from Hook Norton and guest breweries, and 3Cs cider from Northampton. The same menu is served in the bar and the restaurant, and a garden and sheltered courtyard offer alfresco dining options. Local sourcing and sustainability are the basic tenets behind compact seasonal menus. Expect asparagus from Evesham, pork from Gloucester Old Spots pigs, local venison, Dexter beef and Cotswold lamb; pheasant, wild duck and partridge are delivered after winter shoots. A typical choice could begin with salt hake Scotch egg, bacon and tomato, perhaps followed by ox cheek, chips, charred onion, carrot and smoked garlic. Finish with warm chocolate and rosemary mousse and orange ice cream.

Open all day all wk **Food** Lunch Mon-Fri 12-2.30, Sat 12-9.30, Sun 12-8 Dinner Mon-Sat 6-9.30, Sat 12-9.30, Sun 12-8 Set menu available ⊕ CIRRUS INNS ◀ Hook Norton, guest ale ♂ Orchard Pig, 3Cs Vintage Cider. ☷ 11 **Facilities** Non-diners area ❤ (Bar Garden) ♦♦ Children's menu Children's portions Garden ⊨ Parking WiFi **Rooms** 8

The Volunteer Inn

tel: 01386 840688 **Lower High St GL55 6DY**
email: info@thevolunteerinn.net
dir: *From Shipston on Stour take B4035 to Chipping Campden*

Cotswold character and cuisine with a twist

The beautiful, honey-coloured Cotswold stone glowing beside Chipping Campden's main street continues within; the convivial, log-fire warmed stone floored bar a welcoming retreat for guests hunting through the town's antique shops or pausing on a stroll along the Cotswold Way footpath. Once a recruiting centre for volunteer militia, today's clients sign on for some very interesting dishes from the Maharaja Restaurant located here. As well as traditional dishes like dhansak, bhuna, jalfrezi and so on, there are less well known options like nowabi lamb, jalil hash, begun bhari and moglai chicken. The grassy beer garden is a quiet town centre retreat.

Open all wk Mon-Thu 3-12 (Fri-Sun 11am-late) **Food** Contact pub for food times ⊕ FREE HOUSE ◀ Sharp's Doom Bar ♂ Westons Stowford Press. **Facilities** Non-diners area ♦♦ Children's portions Play area Family room Garden WiFi ▭ (notice required)

CIRENCESTER
Map 5 SP00

The Crown of Crucis
PICK OF THE PUBS

tel: 01285 851806 **Ampney Crucis GL7 5RS**
email: reception@thecrownofcrucis.co.uk
dir: On A417 to Lechlade, 2m E of Cirencester

Quintessential Cotswold coaching inn

Five minutes' drive out of Cirencester will bring you to this 16th-century former coaching inn; it overlooks a cricket green, and Ampney Brook meanders past its lawns. Its name is derived from the 'crucis' or ancient cross in the churchyard. Although modernised, the interior still feels old, and the traditional beams and log fires create a warm, friendly atmosphere. Atlantic and Wickwar are among the real ales, along with some 17 wines served by the glass. Sandwiches, salads, pastas and grills are served from midday, while in the evening the restaurant's dinner menu proffers popular pub dishes such as starters of breaded whitebait with salad and tartare sauce; or smoked mackerel pâté with toasted home-made brioche. Move on to a special of herb-crusted cod loin with spring onion and pea risotto and tomato salsa; or a dish from the chargrill stove: pan-fried calves' liver with crispy bacon, bubble-and-squeak cake and Madeira sauce.

Open all day all wk Closed 25 Dec **Food** Lunch all wk 12-5 Dinner all wk 5-10 ⊕ FREE HOUSE ◀ Crown Bitter, Sharp's Doom Bar & seasonal ales, Wickwar, Atlantic ⚙ Westons Stowford Press. ♟ 17 **Facilities** Non-diners area ♣ (Bar Garden) ♦ Children's menu Children's portions Garden ⤢ Parking WiFi ⛟ (notice required)

The Fleece at Cirencester ★★★★★ INN

tel: 01285 658507 **41 Dyer St, Market Place GL7 2NZ**
email: relax@thefleececirencester.co.uk **web:** www.thefleececirencester.co.uk
dir: In centre of Cirencester

Cotswold dining pub with royal links

This is a 17th-century coaching inn, once visited by Charles II. The bar, restaurant and lounge retain their original charms with wooden beams, a log fire and an outdoor courtyard for long summer days. A range of excellent Thwaites ales is offered. The extensive menu features deli boards; chargrilled steaks; and mains of roasted butternut squash risotto; or blade of beef cooked in ale with parsnip and potato mash. There are 28 bedrooms if you want to extend your visit and explore the Cotswolds.

The Fleece at Cirencester

Open all day all wk **Food** Lunch all wk 12-6 Dinner Mon-Sat 6-9.30, Sun 6-8.30 ⊕ THWAITES INNS OF CHARACTER ◀ Marston's Wainwright, guest ales ⚙ Westons Stowford Press, local guest cider. ♟ 10 **Facilities** Non-diners area ♣ (Bar Outside area) ♦ Children's menu Children's portions Outside area ⤢ Parking WiFi **Rooms** 28

See advert below

PICK OF THE PUBS

The Yew Tree

CLIFFORD'S MESNE   Map 10 SO72

tel: 01531 820719
GL18 1JS
email: info@yewtreeinn.com
web: www.yewtreeinn.com
dir: *From Newent High Street follow signs to Clifford's Mesne. Pub at far end of village on road to May Hill*

Child-friendly pub serving fresh, home-made food

Although not immediately apparent as you arrive – and you might need the sat nav to help you do so – this now-family-owned, former cider house dates back to the 1600s. Indeed, the interior suggests as much. Because it stands on the slopes of May Hill (National Trust), Gloucestershire's highest point, the views from the terrace are excellent, especially on a clear day, when you can see the River Severn, the Malvern Hills and the Welsh mountains. Of course, you might prefer to stay in the quarry-tiled interior, where log fires do their stuff in winter, while all year round the beer pump badge-festooned bar serves a good choice of real ales, such as Wye Valley, and a real cider or two. The Clarke family who run the pub offer a seasonal menu of fresh, home-made food inspired by their time spent abroad, as well as plenty of British classics. For lunch there might be chicken satay, sausage and mash or homity pie, which if you're not familiar with it is an open pie of garlic-mashed potato, red onion, cheddar cheese, a hint of cayenne pepper, cannellini beans in sage passata sauce, and a side salad. For dinner, perhaps Oolong-marinated sea bass; a classic chicken and mushroom pie; chilli con carne; crispy duck with sweet chilli noodles; or nut roast, with a generous helping of New York cheesecake or orange pannacotta to finish. Children will enjoy the play area whatever the month, while in October adults will relish the beer and cider festival.

Open all day Closed Mon, Tue L, Sun eve **Food** Lunch Wed-Sat 12-2, Sun 12-3 Dinner Tue-Sat 6-9 Av main course £11 ⊕ FREE HOUSE ◧ Wye Valley HPA & Butty Bach, Sharp's Doom Bar, local ales ♻ Westons Stowford Press, Jolter Press. ⬥ 14 **Facilities** Non-diners area ❀ (Bar Restaurant Garden) ♦♦ Children's menu & portions Play area Garden ⊼ Beer & cider festival Parking WiFi 🚌 (notice required)

CLEEVE HILL
Map 10 SO92

The Rising Sun

tel: 01242 676281 **GL52 3PX**
email: 9210@greeneking.co.uk
dir: *On B4632, 4m N of Cheltenham*

Hilltop inn offering stunning vistas

On a clear day you can see south Wales from this Victorian property on Cleeve Hill, which also boasts views across Cheltenham and the Malverns. Whether you are staying overnight or just popping in to relax, settle in the bar or, in summer, out in the garden, which is well furnished with trestle tables and benches. The wide ranging menu includes British beef and ale pie; fish and chips; sandwiches; wraps; ciabattas; steaks and grills; burgers; jacket potatoes; and roasts on Sundays.

Open all day all wk **Food** Contact pub for food times ⊕ GREENE KING ◀ IPA, Abbot Ale ♂ Aspall. ☘ 15 **Facilities** Non-diners area ◀ Children's menu Children's portions Family room Garden ⊼ Parking WiFi ☰ (notice required)

CLIFFORD'S MESNE
Map 10 SO72

The Yew Tree
PICK OF THE PUBS

See Pick of the Pubs on page 203 and advert on opposite page

COATES
Map 4 SO90

The Tunnel House Inn
PICK OF THE PUBS

tel: 01285 770280 **Tarlton Rd GL7 6PW**
email: info@tunnelhouse.com
dir: *A433 from Cirencester towards Tetbury, 2m, right towards Coates, follow brown inn signs*

Delightfully timeless Cotswold village inn

Built for the navvies who spent five years constructing the two-mile long Sapperton Tunnel, this rural inn overlooks the entrance to the tunnel which hasn't been navigated by a barge since 1911. Three winter log fires warm the curio-filled bar, where oddities include an upside-down table suspended from the ceiling. Food, all home cooked, is served every day from noon onwards and you may eat in the bar or restaurant, starting perhaps with prawns and smoked salmon platter, followed by wild mushroom risotto. The garden is tailor-made for relaxing with a pint of one of the mostly local guest real ales or ciders, while enjoying the views over the fields. A children's play area and delightful walks add to the pub's popularity.

Open all day all wk 12-11pm **Food** Lunch Mon-Fri 12-2.30, Sat-Sun 12-9 Dinner Mon-Fri 6-9, Sat-Sun 12-9 Set menu available ⊕ FREE HOUSE ◀ Uley, guest ales ♂ Thatchers Cheddar Valley & Heritage, Westons Stowford Press. ☘ 9 **Facilities** Non-diners area ◀ (All areas) ◀ Children's menu Children's portions Play area Family room Garden Outside area ⊼ Beer festival Cider festival Parking WiFi ☰

COLD ASTON
Map 10 SP11

The Plough Inn

tel: 01451 822602 **GL54 3BN**
email: hello@coldastonplough.com
dir: *In village centre*

Country pub enjoying a new lease of life

Locals Nick and Laura Avery successfully run the 17th-century Plough that is full of period charm – Cotswold flagstones, oak beams and a big open fire make it look very smart indeed. Rotating real ales, such as local Stroud Budding, are served from casks, and there are real ciders, too. Try devilled lamb's kidneys on toast; followed by Gloucester Old Spots sausages, mash and onion gravy; or beer-battered

haddock, chips and crushed peas; then custard tart, nutmeg and fresh summer berries. A charcoal oven cooks perfect steaks and fish.

Open 12-3 6-11 (Sat-Sun all day) Closed 1-16 Jan, Mon **Food** Lunch Tue-Sun 12-3 Dinner Tue-Sun 6.30-9 ⊕ FREE HOUSE ◀ Cotswold Spring Stunner, Stroud Budding, Wye Valley Butty Bach ♂ Aspall Spadger, Orchard Pig Reveller. **Facilities** Non-diners area ◀ (Bar Restaurant Outside area) ◀ Children's portions Outside area ⊼ Parking WiFi ☰ (notice required)

COLEFORD
Map 4 SO51

The Dog & Muffler Inn

tel: 01594 832444 **Joyford, Berry Hill GL16 7AS**
web: www.dogandmuffler.co.uk
dir: *Phone for detailed directions*

Traditional food in the heart of the forest

Set in the ancient and beautiful Forest of Dean, where wild boar and deer roam free, The Dog & Muffler was once a cider house with its own orchard and cider press; the press can still be found in the large garden. Once a favourite watering hole of playwright Dennis Potter, visitors can now mingle with locals supping pints of Wye Valley ale or one of several ciders on offer. The seasonally changing menu offers the dishes such as duck with Morello cherry sauce; crackled belly of pork with fresh apple sauce; briam (an oven-roasted Mediterranean vegetable dish); beef lasagne and prize-winning pies.

Open 12-3.30 6-11.30 Closed Mon **Food** Lunch Tue-Sun 12-3 Dinner Tue-Sun 6-9.30 Av main course £11 Set menu available ⊕ FREE HOUSE ◀ Wye Valley Butty Bach, Sharp's Doom Bar ♂ Westons Stowford Press, Lilley's Apples & Pears. ☘ 14 **Facilities** Non-diners area ◀ (Bar Restaurant Garden) ◀ Children's menu Children's portions Garden ⊼ Parking WiFi ☰ (notice required)

See advert on page 206

THE YEW TREE INN
FREE HOUSE

PUBLIC HOUSE ~ RESTAURANT ~ COFFEE SHOP

At the Yew Tree we are highly invested in keeping our ingredients locally sourced. All of our meats are bought from Andy Creese's Butcher shop in Newent just down the road, and our vegetables are sourced fresh from various farms within a few miles radius.

The menu changes with the seasons to ensure our food is the freshest quality available. We'll often have a selection of specials available in addition to the menus.

Beginning at 10am, Tuesday through Saturday we offer tea, coffee and an assortment of cakes, scones and cookies from our Coffee Shop.

Some of our favorites will include victoria sponge, chocolate cake, carrot cake and many more. Come on by to check out our daily selection!

We hold regular exciting events from quiz nights to live music; check out our calendar online for more details.

The Yew Tree Inn
Clifford's Mesne
Newent
Gloucestershire
GL18 1JS

E / info@yewtreeinn.com
T / 01531 820 719
W / yewtreeinn.com/

 /yewtreeinn

THE Dog & Muffler INN

A warm and welcoming inn in the magical Forest of Dean.

Originally a Cider House, with its own cider apple orchard and a cider press which can still be seen in the garden. It has been extended over the years and the interior has been designed to make you feel completely at ease.

Relax and enjoy the large open garden with shady parasols in summer, or settle down by a roaring log fire in winter.

COLESBOURNE
Map 10 SP01

The Colesbourne Inn

tel: 01242 870376 **GL53 9NP**
email: colesbourneinn@wadworth.co.uk
dir: *Midway between Cirencester & Cheltenham on A435*

Georgian country inn full of character

This handsome, stone-built inn is just a short meadow walk from the source of the Thames; you can sit in the two-acre grounds with a pint of Wadworth 6X or Swordfish and savour the glorious country views. Dating back to 1827, the inn oozes historic charm and character with its original beams and roaring log fires aplenty. The seasonal menus combine traditional pub classics, including fish and chunky chips, with modern ideas, perhaps pan-seared sea bass, stir-fried chilli, ginger and spring onion, warm potato salad, tomato and seasonal vegetables; lamb and mint burger, toasted brioche bun with goats' cheese and red onion relish; or red pepper and sun-blushed tomato tart, sautéed potatoes with rocket and parmesan salad.

Open all day all wk **Food** Mon-Sat 12-9.30, Sun 12-8 Set menu available Restaurant menu available all wk ⊕ WADWORTH ◀ 6X, Horizon & Swordfish ♂ Westons Stowford Press. ⬤ 20 **Facilities** Non-diners area ☙ (Bar Garden) ●◀ Children's portions Garden ⊼ Parking WiFi ⬛ (notice required)

COWLEY
Map 10 SO91

The Green Dragon Inn ★★★★ INN   PICK OF THE PUBS

See Pick of the Pubs on page 208

CRANHAM
Map 10 SO81

The Black Horse Inn

tel: 01452 812217 **GL4 8HP**
dir: *A46 towards Stroud, follow signs for Cranham*

A great rest-stop for walkers

Near the Cotswold Way and the Benedictine Prinknash Abbey, in a small village surrounded by woodland and commons, this inn is popular with walkers, the cricket team and visiting Morris dancers. The new owners serve traditional pub food such as steak and ale pie with chips and peas; grilled salmon with hollandaise sauce and jacket potato; and chicken casserole with roast potatoes and vegetables. Among the real ales are Stroud Tom Long, Wye Valley Bitter and Wickwar BOB, and there are real ciders too in the cosy, open-fire-warmed bar. The lunchtime bar menu offers sandwiches, jacket potatoes, ploughman's and pasties

Open 12-2 6.30-11 (Sun 12-2 8.30-11) Closed Mon (ex BHs L) **Food** Lunch Tue-Sun 12-2 Dinner Tue-Sat 6.30-9 ⊕ FREE HOUSE ◀ Wye Valley Bitter, Stroud Tom Long, Wickwar BOB ♂ Gwatkin. ⬤ 8 **Facilities** Non-diners area ☙ (Bar Outside area) ●◀ Children's portions Outside area ⊼ Parking ⬛ (notice required)

DURSLEY
Map 4 ST79

The Old Spot Inn   PICK OF THE PUBS

tel: 01453 542870 **Hill Rd GL11 4JQ**
email: enquiries@oldspotinn.co.uk
dir: *From Tetbury on A4135 (or Uley on B4066) into Dursley, round Town Hall. Straight on at lights towards bus station, pub behind bus station. Or from Cam to lights in Dursley immediately prior to pedestrianised street. Right towards bus station*

Excellent beer at popular village local

This classic 18th-century free house is a real ale champion, so it's worth a visit to savour the tip-top brews on hand pump. The pub sits smack on the Cotswold Way, and is formed from three terraced farm cottages known as 'pig row'. Ale festivals are held in May and October; the one in May also showcases ciders, and fans of fermented apple juice enjoy the weekly alternating choice at the bar. Devoid of

modern-day intrusions, the rustic and traditional low-beamed bars are havens of peace, with just the comforting sound of crackling log fires and the hubbub of chatting locals filling the rambling little rooms. Wholesome and home-made fodder ranges from doorstep sandwiches – the soft brie and smoked back bacon is served with cranberry sauce – to grazing planks and home-made puds.

Open all day all wk 11-11 (Sun 12-11) **Food** Lunch Mon-Sat 12-3, Sun 12-4 Av main course £10.95 ⊕ FREE HOUSE ◀ Old Ric, Butcombe, Otter, guest ales ♂ Rotating guest ciders. ⬤ 8 **Facilities** Non-diners area ☙ (Bar Garden) ●◀ Children's portions Family room Garden ⊼ Beer festival Cider festival Parking WiFi ⬛ (notice required)

EBRINGTON
Map 10 SP14

The Ebrington Arms ★★★★ INN ◉◉ PICK OF THE PUBS

tel: 01386 593223 **GL55 6NH**
email: reservations@theebringtonarms.co.uk **web:** www.theebringtonarms.co.uk
dir: *From Chipping Campden on B4035 towards Shipston on Stour. Left to Ebrington signed after 0.5m*

Home-brewed ales at this quintessential village pub

The large inglenook fireplaces of this charming old pub recall the building's days as the village bakery. Built in 1640, this award-winning Cotswold gem has an abundance of character thanks to the heavy beams and original flagstones in both the bar and Old Bakehouse dining room. Very much the hub of community life, lucky locals (and even luckier visitors too, of course) are spoilt for choice as the pub brews three of its own beers: Yubberton Yubby, Yawnie and Goldie, which sit alongside others such as Stroud's and Hogans cider, as well as more than a dozen whiskies. Recognised with two AA Rosettes, the pub's menu offers the likes of Oxford Blue, Conference pear, celery, walnuts and chicory salad, which could be followed by belly of pork, spring cabbage, chorizo and creamed potato. Leave a space for dessert of pistachio iced parfait, almond and blackberry.

Open all day all wk noon-close **Food** Lunch Mon-Sat 12-2.30, Sun 12-3.30 Dinner Mon-Thu 6-9, Fri-Sat 6-9.30, Sun 6-8.30 ⊕ FREE HOUSE ◀ Stroud Budding Pale Ale, North Cotswold Windrush Ale, Prescott Hill Climb, Yubberton Yubby Bitter, Yawnie & Goldie ♂ Hogan's. ⬤ 9 **Facilities** Non-diners area ☙ (Bar Garden) ●◀ Children's menu Children's portions Garden ⊼ Beer festival Parking WiFi ⬛ (notice required) **Rooms** 5

EWEN
Map 4 SU09

The Wild Duck

tel: 01285 770310 **GL7 6BY**
email: reservations@thewildduckewen.com
dir: *From Cirencester take A429 towards Malmesbury. At Kemble left to Ewen. Inn in village centre*

Cotswold pub with an excellent food and local ales

Built from honeyed Cotswold stone in 1563, this pub close to the Cotswold Water Park reopened after a stylish refurbishment under new owners, The Lucky Onion, in October 2015. The extensive choice of real ales and ciders includes Otter Amber, Hook Norton Hooky and Dunkertons Premium Organic cider, with a large number of wines by the glass. The kitchen keeps a close eye on the seasons and makes a point of using local suppliers. A starter of creamed mustard veal kidneys on sourdough toast might be followed by Cotswold White chicken and leek pie with creamed potatoes and buttered chard; or faggots and gravy.

Open all day all wk **Food** Lunch Mon-Sat 12-3, Sun 12-4 Dinner Mon-Fri 6-9.30, Sat 6-10, Sun 6-9 Set menu available ⊕ FREE HOUSE ◀ Butcombe Bitter, Cotswold Lion Best in Show, Hook Norton Hooky Bitter, Otter Amber, Manchester Brewing Co Factory Pale Ale ♂ Dunkertons Premium Organic. ⬤ 32 **Facilities** Non-diners area ☙ (Bar Restaurant Garden) ●◀ Children's menu Children's portions Garden ⊼ Beer festival Parking WiFi ⬛ (notice required)

PICK OF THE PUBS

The Green Dragon Inn ★★★★ INN

COWLEY Map 10 SO91

tel: 01242 870271
Cockleford GL53 9NW
email: green-dragon@buccaneer.co.uk
web: www.green-dragon-inn.co.uk
dir: *Phone for detailed directions*

Cotswolds inn featuring Mouseman furniture

With a pretty rose and creeper-covered Cotswold-stone façade, this building was recorded as an inn in 1675. However it was 1710 before Robert Jones, a churchwarden, became the first landlord, splitting his time between pew and pulling pints for the next 31 years. Today the secluded patio overlooking a lake is an obvious spot to head for in summer. Step inside the stone-flagged Mouse Bar and you will notice that each piece of English oak furniture features a carved mouse, the trademark of Robert Thompson, the Mouseman of Kilburn. He died in 1955, but North Yorkshire craftsmen continue the tradition. There's even one of the little beggars running along the bar edge in front of the Butcombe, Hook Norton and Sharp's beer handles. A range of lunchtime sandwiches includes coronation chicken, while light meals have popular appeal: braised faggots with mashed potato and onion gravy, for example; or home-cooked ham with two free-range fried eggs and fries. Weather permitting, food and drink can be served on the patio. A typical evening meal choice could start with warm chicken liver, pigeon breast and quail egg salad with smoked bacon and croûtons. Continue with an oven-roasted hake fillet with a herb cheese crust. Children are catered for with a range of favourites. The comfortable and individually furnished en suite bedrooms, and the St George's Suite (which has its own sitting room overlooking Cowley lakes), make the Green Dragon an ideal base for exploring the Cotswolds; the local Miserden Gardens and Chedworth Roman Villa should not be missed.

Open all day all wk Closed 25 Dec eve, 26 Dec eve & 1 Jan eve **Food** Lunch Mon-Fri 12-2.30, Sat 12-3, Sun 12-3.30 Dinner all wk 6-9.30 Av main course £15 ⊕ FREE HOUSE/BUCCANEER ◀ Hook Norton, Butcombe, Sharp's Doom Bar, guest ale ⌕ Westons Stowford Press. ☕ 12 **Facilities** Non-diners area ✦ Children's menu Outside area ㅠ Parking WiFi ☎ **Rooms** 9

FRAMPTON MANSELL

Map 4 SO90

The Crown Inn ★★★★ INN

PICK OF THE PUBS

tel: 01285 760601 **GL6 8JG**

email: enquiries@thecrowninn-cotswolds.co.uk web: www.thecrowninn-cotswolds.co.uk

dir: *A419 halfway between Cirencester & Stroud*

A handsome Cotswold inn perfect for whiling away an hour or two

Right in the heart of the village, the Crown is surrounded by the peace and quiet of the Golden Valley. Once a simple cider house, it's a classic 17th-century Cotswold-stone inn that's full of old-world charm, with honey-coloured stone walls, beams and open fireplaces where logs blaze in winter. Plenty of seating in the large garden allows for contemplative supping during the warmer months. Gloucestershire beers, such as Stroud Organic and Laurie Lee's Bitter, are usually showcased alongside others from the region, and a good choice of wines by the glass is served in the restaurant and three inviting bars. Fresh local food with lots of seasonal specials is the carte's promise. Brioche and cheddar toastie with steamed egg yoke, parmesan cream, roasted cherry tomato and herb salad is a tasty starter, to be followed perhaps by roasted chicken with bacon, silverskin onions and mushrooms. For non-meat eaters, spinach and ricotta pasta bake with roasted field mushrooms is ideal.

Open all day all wk 12-11 Closed 25 Dec **Food** Lunch Mon-Sat 12-2.30, Sun 12-8.30 Dinner Mon-Sat 6-9.30, Sun 12-8.30 Av main course £12 ⊕ FREE HOUSE ◀ Butcombe Bitter, Uley Laurie Lee's Bitter, Stroud Organic, guest ales Ò Westons Stowford Press, Addlestones, guest ciders. ♥ 16 **Facilities** Non-diners area ♣ (Bar Restaurant Garden) ♦ Children's portions Garden ☐ Parking WiFi ☐ **Rooms** 12

GLOUCESTER

Map 10 SO81

Queens Head

tel: 01452 301882 **Tewkesbury Rd, Longford GL2 9EJ**

email: info@queensheadlongford.co.uk

dir: *On A38 (Tewkesbury to Gloucester road) in Longford*

A cracking line-up at the locals' bar

This pretty 250-year-old half-timbered pub and restaurant is just out of town, but cannot be missed in summer when it is festooned with hanging baskets. Inside, a lovely old flagstone-floored locals' bar proffers a great range of real ales and ciders. The owners believe in giving their diners high-quality, freshly prepared food that is great value for money. Menus tempt with modern British food: Isle of Man Scallops and black pudding; half a boned roasted Peking duck, cashew nuts, spring onions, pak choi, noodles and black bean sauce; lime-seared scallops, prawns and mussels in creamy white wine sauce. Smart casual dress and no children under 12 years is the order of the day here.

Open all wk 11-3 5.30-11 **Food** Lunch all wk 12-2 Dinner all wk 6.30-9.30 ⊕ FREE HOUSE ◀ Wye Valley Butty Bach, Sharp's Doom Bar, Skinner's Betty Stogs, Otter, Butcombe Gold Ò Ashton Press, Westons Stowford Press. ♥ **Facilities** Non-diners area Parking WiFi ☐ (notice required)

GREAT BARRINGTON

Map 10 SP21

The Fox Inn

PICK OF THE PUBS

tel: 01451 844385 **OX18 4TB**

email: info@foxinnbarrington.com

dir: *From Burford take A40 towards Northleach. In 3m right signed The Barringtons, pub approx 0.5m on right*

Seasonal food in riverside Cotswold pub

With a garden overlooking the River Windrush, this busy centuries-old former coaching house is a perfect base for lovely walks and cycle rides in summer. Set in the picturesque Windrush Valley, the pub is popular with race-goers visiting

Cheltenham. A quintessential Cotswold inn built of mellow local stone, the bar proffers a range of well-kept Donnington beers and a concise wine list. The conservatory dining bar and alfresco eating area contribute to the friendly and relaxed atmosphere. Landlord Paul Porter's enthusiasm for tasty food shines through with the menu's descriptions: examples are 'our famous' twice-cooked belly of pork with stuffing, apple compôte, sauté potatoes and vegetables; and a 'classic' pan-fried Barbary duck breast with orange and marmalade gravy. Vegetarians are well catered for, with typical dishes including spinach, leek and chestnut pie. Barbecues are held in summer.

Open all day all wk 11am-close **Food** Lunch Mon-Fri 12-2.30, Sat-Sun all day Dinner Mon-Fri 6.30-9.30, Sat-Sun all day ⊕ DONNINGTON ◀ BB, SBA, Gold Ò Westons Stowford Press & Perry, Addlestones. **Facilities** Non-diners area ♣ (Bar Garden) ♦ Children's portions Garden ☐ Parking WiFi ☐

HAM

Map 4 ST69

The Salutation Inn

tel: 01453 810284 **GL13 9QH**

dir: *S of Berkeley towards Stone*

Genuine rural free house close to the Severn Estuary

Landlord Peter Tiley says "What makes the Sally so special isn't the range of quality ales and ciders, the heritage pub games, the humble bar snacks, the cosy bars with log fires, or the genuine community spirit. It's something intangible". Maybe he's right, although those tangible features sound pretty good. His own beers – Tiley's Pale Ale and Tiley's Porter – now sit alongside others. Food is available only at lunchtime when, in addition to the permanent ploughman's, and Gloucestershire ham, home-laid eggs and chips, he offers a not-so-humble 'third dish', perhaps 'ham from Ham', hay-baked, cider-soaked belly of pork from his own Gloucester Old Spots pigs; or Cornish beer-battered hake, hand-cut chips, Yorkshire caviar (aka mushy peas) and tartare sauce.

Open 12-2.30 5-11 (Sat 12-11 Sun 12-10.30) Closed Mon L **Food** Lunch Tue-Sun 12-2.30 Av main course £8.95 ⊕ FREE HOUSE ◀ Butcombe Bitter, Bristol Beer Factory, Cotswold Spring, Severn Vale, Wye Valley, Tiley's Pale Ale & Porter Ò Tom Olivers, Barnes & Adams, Wilkins Farmhouse. **Facilities** Non-diners area Garden ☐ Parking WiFi ☐ (notice required)

HINTON

Map 4 ST77

The Bull at Hinton

tel: 0117 937 2332 **SN14 8HG**

email: info@thebullathinton.co.uk

dir: *From M4 junct 18, A46 to Bath, 1m turn right 1m, down hill. Pub on right*

Village inn on the southern edge of the Cotswolds

Just 20 minutes from both Bath and Bristol, this 17th-century, stone-built former farmhouse and dairy is packed with original character, with beams in the bar and dining room, flagstone floors, inglenook fireplaces, old pews and big oak tables. Meals are freshly prepared using ingredients mostly from local producers and suppliers (and from home-grown produce), meaning that a typical menu might feature spicy salmon fish cakes; followed by sticky BBQ ribs or spring green risotto; and finally passionfruit pannacotta. The south-facing terrace and garden is where to be when the sun's out.

Open 12-3 6-11.30 (Fri 12-3 6-12 Sat-Sun 12-12) Closed Mon (ex BHs) **Food** Lunch Tue-Fri 12-2.30, Sat 12-9, Sun 12-6 (BHs 12-2.30) Dinner Tue-Fri 6-9, Sat 12-9, Sun 12-6 ⊕ WADWORTH ◀ 6X, Henry's Original IPA, The Bishop's Tipple, guest ale Ò Thatchers Gold, Westons Stowford Press. ♥ 11 **Facilities** Non-diners area ♣ (Bar Garden) ♦ Children's menu Play area Garden ☐ Parking WiFi ☐ (notice required)

LECHLADE ON THAMES   Map 5 SU29

The Trout Inn

tel: 01367 252313 **St Johns Bridge GL7 3HA**
email: chefpjw@aol.com
dir: *A40 onto A361 then A417. From M4 junct 15, A419, then A361 & A417 to Lechlade*

Extensive menu served in an ancient inn

When workmen constructed a new bridge over the Thames in 1220, they also built an almshouse to live in. It became an inn in 1472, and its flagstone floors and beams give the interior great character. The extensive menu features meat, fish and vegetarian options, as well as pizzas, filled jacket potatoes and burgers. This family-friendly pub offers smaller portions for children, who also have their own separate menu. The large garden often hosts live jazz, an annual steam week and a beer festival, both in June, plus a riverfolk festival in July.

Open all day all wk 11-11 Closed 25 Dec **Food** Lunch Mon-Sat 12-2, Sun 12-2.30 Dinner Mon-Thu 7-9.30, Fri 7-10, Sun 7-8.30 ⊕ ENTERPRISE INNS ◀ Courage Best Bitter, Sharp's Doom Bar, guest ales Ò Addlestones, Westons Stowford Press, Thatchers Gold. ♈ 15 **Facilities** Non-diners area ❀ (Bar Garden) ♦♦ Children's menu Children's portions Play area Family room Garden ⊨ Beer festival Parking WiFi ⇔ (notice required)

LEIGHTERTON   Map 4 ST89

The Royal Oak

tel: 01666 890250 **1 The Street GL8 8UN**
email: info@royaloakleighterton.co.uk
dir: *M4 junct 18, A46 towards Stroud. After Dunkirk continue on A46. Right signed Leighterton*

Pub majoring on local, seasonal produce

Set in a picture-postcard Cotswold village, close to Westonbirt Arboretum, this pub thrives as a popular dining venue. The bright, contemporary bar and dining room successfully blends exposed beams, open fires and antiques with modern furnishings. Enjoy a pint of Bath Ales with a lunchtime sandwich or platter or dive into the main menu. Food is classic British and everything is made on the premises from local ingredients. In addition to pub classics (fish and chips, burgers and pies) typically, tuck into lobster ravioli and vermouth butter sauce; game casserole with juniper berry dumplings; and ginger and cinnamon sponge, warm poached apples and whipped cream.

Open 12-3 5.30-11 (Sat 12-11 Sun 12-10.30) Closed Mon ⊕ FREE HOUSE ◀ Bath Ales Gem, Butcombe Adam Henson's Rare Breed, guest ales Ò Westons Stowford Press, Sherston, Wilce's Herefordshire. **Facilities** ❀ (Bar Garden) ♦♦ Children's menu Children's portions Garden Parking WiFi

LONGHOPE   Map 10 SO61

The Glasshouse Inn

tel: 01452 830529 **May Hill GL17 0NN**
email: glasshouseinn@gmail.com
dir: *From A40 approx 8m SE of Ross-on-Wye, follow signs for May Hill. Through May Hill to pub on left*

Gimmick-free traditional pub

The Glasshouse gets its name from Dutch glassmakers who settled locally in the 16th century but its origins can be traced back further, to 1450. A gimmick-free traditional pub, it is located in a fabulous rural setting with a country garden and an elegant interior. The inn serves a range of real ales including Butcombe and Sharp's Doom Bar, plus home-cooked dishes such as fish pie; cod and chips; beef

curry; steak and kidney served in Yorkshire puddings; and chilli. At lunch you can also choose from a range of sandwiches, ploughman's lunches or basket meals of chips with the likes of scampi or sausage. There's a choice of roasts at Sunday lunch – booking is advisable.

Open 11.30-3 7-11 (Sun 12-3) Closed Sun eve **Food** Lunch all wk 12-2 (booking required for parties of 6 or more) Dinner Mon-Sat 7-9 (booking required for parties of 6 or more) ⊕ FREE HOUSE ◀ Sharp's Doom Bar, Butcombe Ò Westons Stowford Press. ♈ 12 **Facilities** Garden ⊨ Parking WiFi

LOWER SLAUGHTER   Map 10 SP12

The Slaughters Country Inn ★★★★★ INN ⊚⊚

PICK OF THE PUBS

tel: 01451 822143 **GL54 2HS**
email: info@theslaughtersinn.co.uk **web:** www.theslaughtersinn.co.uk
dir: *Between Stow-on-the-Wold & Bourton-on-the-Water on A429 follow 'The Slaughters' signs*

Much-loved Cotswold-stone village inn

Formerly Washbourne Court, and once a crammer school for Eton, this handsome inn stands close to the River Lye, soon to join the Windrush and eventually the Thames. Well positioned for exploring the Cotswolds, Bourton-on-the-Water is within walking distance and Cheltenham is only a 30-minute drive away. The spacious beamed bar and stone mullioned windows are a good example of how to successfully balance the appealing qualities of a 17th-century building with the demands of the 21st century. Two AA Rosettes signify that good food is paramount, from sandwiches and light bites to the chargrilled Hereford flat iron steak with watercress and fries. In between might come pan-fried sea bream, spiced lentils, shrimps, cauliflower and coriander dressing; roast duck, spiced carrot purée, turnip and confit leg pastilla. A final flourish might be baked pear clafoutis with caramel ice cream.

Open all day all wk **Food** Lunch all wk 12-3 Dinner all wk 6.30-9 ⊕ FREE HOUSE ◀ Brakspear, Wychwood Hobgoblin. ♈ 11 **Facilities** Non-diners area ❀ (Bar Garden) ♦♦ Children's menu Children's portions Garden ⊨ Parking WiFi ⇔ (notice required) **Rooms** 31

MARSHFIELD   Map 4 ST77

The Catherine Wheel

tel: 01225 892220 **39 High St SN14 8LR**
email: roo@thecatherinewheel.co.uk
dir: *M4 junct 18, A46 signed Bath. Left onto A420 signed Chippenham. Right signed Marshfield*

Traditional Cotswold inn with sunny patio

On the edge of the Cotswolds, this mainly 17th-century inn has the expected exposed brickwork and large open fireplaces offset by a simple, stylish decor. Menus are also simple and well presented, with favourites at lunchtime including steak and kidney pie; and jacket potatoes. In the evening look forward to potted smoked mackerel, lemon and herb pâté or tomato and goats' cheese tartlets, followed perhaps by venison stew and thyme dumplings or fish pie. A small but sunny patio is a lovely spot for a summertime pint of Butcombe Bitter or Thatchers cider.

Open all day all wk **Food** Lunch Mon-Fri 12-2, Sat-Sun 12-3 Dinner Mon-Thu 6.30-9, Fri-Sat 6.30-9.30, Sun 6-8.30 ⊕ FREE HOUSE ◀ Butcombe Bitter, Fuller's London Pride, Cotswold Spring Stunner Ò Ashton Press, Thatchers. ♈ 10 **Facilities** Non-diners area ❀ (Bar Garden) ♦♦ Children's portions Garden ⊨ Parking WiFi ⇔ (notice required)

PICK OF THE PUBS

The Weighbridge Inn

MINCHINHAMPTON   Map 4 SO80

tel: 01453 832520 **GL6 9AL**
email: weighbridge123@yahoo.co.uk
web: www.weighbridgeinn.co.uk
dir: *On B4014 between Nailsworth & Avening*

Recommended for its freshly made pies

Parts of this whitewashed free house date back to the 17th century, when it stood adjacent to the original packhorse trail between Bristol and London. While the trail is now a footpath and bridleway, the road in front (now the B4014) became a turnpike in the 1820s. The innkeeper at the time ran both the pub and the weighbridge for the local woollen mills — serving jugs of ale in between making sure tolls were paid. Associated memorabilia and other rural artefacts from the time are displayed around the inn, which has been carefully renovated to retain original features, like exposed brick walls and open fires. Up in the restaurant, which used to be the hayloft, the old roof timbers reach almost to the floor. The inn prides itself on its decent ales and ciders, and the quality of its food, with everything cooked from scratch. Starters to get the taste buds going could be Welsh rarebit or ham hock terrine. The hearty main courses include a 16oz

T-bone steak and chips; pan-seared lamb rump; and the Weighbridge burger. Lighter meals are available, such as salads, ploughman's lunch and doorstep sandwiches. The Weighbridge is also the home of 'the famous 2 in 1 pies', one half containing a filling of your choice from a selection of seven (such as steak and mushroom, or chicken, ham and leek) and topped with pastry, the other half home-made cauliflower cheese — all cooked to order and available to take away or even bake at home. Typical desserts are gooey chocolate brownie; fruit crumble; and crème brûlée. From the patios and sheltered, landscaped garden the Cotswolds are in full view.

Open all day all wk 12-11 (Sun 12-10.30) Closed 25 Dec **Food** all wk 12-9.30 ⊞ FREE HOUSE ◀ Wadworth 6X, Uley Old Spot, Flying Monk Elmers, Prescott, Bath Ales ☼ Westons Rosie's Pig, Severn. ♟ 15
Facilities Non-diners area ❧ (Bar Restaurant Garden) ♦♦ Children's menu Children's portions Family room Garden ⊼ Parking WiFi 🚐 (notice required)

MEYSEY HAMPTON
Map 5 SP10

The Masons Arms

tel: 01285 850164 **28 High St GL7 5JT**
email: masonsatmeysey@gmail.com
dir: *6m E of Cirencester off A417, beside village green*

Family- and dog-friendly village pub

Sitting proudly on the village green in the heart of the Cotswolds village of Mersey Hampton, this 17th-century, stone-built inn used to be owner Paul Fallows' local pub. Now running it, he has transformed it into a bustling community pub with a warming log fire in the large inglenook, and well-kept Arkell's ales, and Thatchers ciders in the convivial beamed bar. Good value home-made food includes garlic and herb mushrooms on toast with dressed rocket; and honey-roasted Wiltshire ham, two free-range eggs and chips.

Open all day all wk 8.30-3 5-11 (Sat-Sun all day) **Food** Lunch Mon-Fri 12-2, Sat 12-9, Sun 12-8 Dinner Mon-Fri 6-9, Sat 12-9, Sun 12-8 ⊕ ARKELL'S ◀ Wiltshire Gold, Three B's ○ Thatchers, Old Mout. ▼ 12 **Facilities** Non-diners area ✿ (Bar Garden) ♦ Children's menu Children's portions Garden ⊼ Beer festival WiFi ☞ (notice required)

MINCHINHAMPTON
Map 4 SO80

The Weighbridge Inn
PICK OF THE PUBS

See Pick of the Pubs on page 211

NETHER WESTCOTE
Map 10 SP22

The Feathered Nest Country Inn ★★★★★ INN ◉◉◉
PICK OF THE PUBS

See Pick of the Pubs on opposite page

NEWENT
Map 10 SO72

Kilcot Inn ★★★★ INN

tel: 01989 720707 **Ross Rd, Kilcot GL18 1NA**
email: info@kilcotinn.com **web:** www.kilcotinn.com
dir: *M50 junct 3, B4221 signed Newent. Approx 2m to pub on left*

Welcoming country inn offering great hospitality

A restored country inn on the borders of Gloucestershire and Herefordshire, the Kilcot offers the best traditions of hospitality, food and drink. From the selection of local real ales and ciders on tap to the high quality produce used in the dishes in the bar and restaurant, there is something for everyone. The menu might include mussels in white wine, cream, garlic and parsley, followed perhaps by shoulder of Welsh lamb with dauphinoise potatoes, slow-roast beets and confit carrot. Outdoor seating is available, including a pleasant garden area to the rear.

Open all day all wk Closed 26 Dec & 1 Jan **Food** Lunch all wk 12-2.30 Dinner Mon-Wed 6-9, Thu-Sat 6-9.30 ⊕ FREE HOUSE ◀ Wye Valley Butty Bach, Marston's EPA ○ Westons Stowford Press, Old Rosie, Mortimers Orchard. **Facilities** Non-diners area ✿ (Bar Garden Outside area) ♦ Children's menu Children's portions Play area Family room Garden Outside area ⊼ Parking WiFi ☞ (notice required) **Rooms** 4

NORTHLEACH
Map 10 SP11

The Wheatsheaf Inn

tel: 01451 860244 **West End GL54 3EZ**
email: reservations@cotswoldswheatsheaf.com
dir: *Just off A40 between Oxford & Cheltenham*

Stylish pub worth seeking out

A beautiful Cotswold-stone 17th-century inn on the square of the pretty former wool town of Northleach, The Wheatsheaf is everything anyone could wish for, with flagstone floors, beams, log fires and a vibrant, smartened-up feel throughout. It's the perfect place for enjoying bracing walks then chilling out in the bar with the papers or sampling some seriously good food. Monthly menus evolve with the season and may take in twice baked soufflé; wood pigeon saltimbocca; ox tail, rib and oyster pie, mash and roasted beets; and roast cod loin, Puy lentils, root vegetables and pancetta.

Open all day all wk **Food** Lunch all wk 12-3 Dinner Sun-Thu 6-9.30, Fri-Sat 6-9.45 Set menu available ⊕ FREE HOUSE ◀ Hook Norton Old Hooky, Butcombe Bitter, Sharp's Cornish Coaster ○ Dunkertons Premium Organic. ▼ 15
Facilities Non-diners area ✿ (Bar Restaurant Garden) ♦ Children's menu Children's portions Play area Garden ⊼ Parking WiFi ☞ (notice required)

OAKRIDGE LYNCH
Map 4 SO90

NEW The Butchers Arms

tel: 01285 760371 **GL6 7NZ**
email: alison@butchersarmsoakridge.com
dir: *From A419 between Cirencester & Chalford, to Frampton Mansell then Oakridge Lynch*

Stunning village inn popular with Cotswold walkers

Tucked away in glorious *Cider with Rosie* country, and convenient for the Cotswold market towns of Stroud and Cirencester, this beautiful 18th-century inn was once the village butchers and abattoir. Thick stone walls and solid oak beamed ceilings add to the timeless country home feel, as do farmhouse kitchen tables and three real ales including Wadworth 6X. Surrounded by excellent walks, lunchtime meals of ploughman's salad and steak sandwiches keep welly-wearing visitors happy, with cottage pie; moules frites; and pan-fried duck breast with caramelised onion and thyme mash, red cabbage and plum sauce also on offer.

Open 12-3 6-11 Closed Mon (ex BHs) **Food** Lunch Tue-Sun 12-2 Dinner Tue-Sat 6-9 ⊕ WADWORTH ◀ Henry's Original IPA, 6X, guest ale. ▼ 9 **Facilities** Non-diners area ✿ (Bar Garden) ♦ Children's menu Children's portions Garden ⊼ Parking WiFi ☞ (notice required)

PICK OF THE PUBS

The Feathered Nest Country Inn ★★★★★ INN ❀❀❀

NETHER WESTCOTE   Map 10 SP22

tel: 01993 833030 **OX7 6SD**
email: info@thefeatherednestinn.co.uk
web: www.thefeatherednestinn.co.uk
dir: *A424 between Burford &
Stow-on-the-Wold, follow signs*

Award-winning food in a beautiful rural location

The views over the Evenlode Valley from
this old malthouse in picturesque
Nether Westcote on the Gloucestershire-
Oxfordshire border are marvellous.
Thoughtfully designed, the inn retains
its original character, especially in the
log-fired bar, where rotating local real
ales — maybe Severn Vale's Nibley, or
Prescott's Hill Climb — can be found.
Local produce forms the backbone of the
menus, with herbs and vegetables
grown in the kitchen garden. Kuba
Winkowski's modern British cuisine
brings a daily set lunch menu for
relaxed eating in the bar, or on the
sycamore tree-shaded garden terrace.
Blackboard specials have included kid
with chickpeas, puntarella, aubergine,
apricot and ras el hanout; and wood
pigeon with beetroot, tortellini,
buckwheat, winter truffle and
consommé. The seasonal carte's modern
take on classic combinations leads to
starters of suckling pig with Granny
Smith apple, celeriac slaw, mustard and

vintage cider; and albacore tuna with
turnip, mooli, wasabi, miso, ponzu
sauce and sesame seeds. Or from the
charcoal grill, maybe 8oz Iberico pork
pluma with chunky chips, chorizo, garlic
mushroom, romesco sauce and mixed
leaf salad. Do leave room for desserts,
such as rhubarb, blood orange, ginger
nut and yogurt shard. Afternoon tea and
Sunday lunch are also served.
Individually decorated bedrooms with
comfortable beds and antiques are
available; the pub makes an excellent
base from which to explore the quaint
and charming villages nearby. Look out
for enjoyable events that run throughout
the year, including jazz evenings, flower
workshops and a vintage car rally.

Open all day Closed 25 Dec, Mon
Food Lunch Tue-Sat 12-2.30, Sun
12-3.30 Dinner Tue-Sat 6.30-9.30 Set
menu available ⊞ FREE HOUSE
◖ Rotating local ales Ď Aspall Harry
Sparrow. ♟ 19 **Facilities** Non-diners area
❖ (Bar Garden) ⋔ Children's menu
Children's portions Family room Garden
⛱ Parking WiFi **Rooms** 4

OLDBURY-ON-SEVERN
Map 4 ST69

The Anchor Inn

tel: 01454 413331 **Church Rd BS35 1QA**
email: info@anchorinnoldbury.co.uk
dir: *From N: A38 towards Bristol, 1.5m then right, village signed. From S: A38 through Thornbury*

Family-friendly pub on the Severn Way

Just before a tree-lined stream called Oldbury Pill enters the Severn Estuary is the stone-built Anchor, its more recent near-500-year-old history recalled in old photos and fishing and farming bric à brac. The bar line-up includes guest real ales, Ashton ciders, perries and 16 wines by the glass. Doors from the light, bright dining room lead out to a beautiful garden. On the good-value bar and main menu are baked lasagne; Gloucestershire pork 'snorkers', mash and peas; roasted guinea fowl breast, shallot and red wine sauce; smoked haddock and salmon pie; and goats' cheese, spinach, pine nut and red onion filo tart.

Open all wk Mon-Thu 11.30-2.30 6-11 (Fri-Sat 11.30am-mdnt Sun 12-10.30) **Food** Lunch Mon-Fri 12-2, Sat 12-2.30, Sun 12-3 Dinner Mon-Sat 6-9, Sun 6-8.30 Set menu available ⊕ FREE HOUSE ◀ Bass, Butcombe Bitter, St Austell Trelawny, guest ales ♂ Ashton Press & Still, Thatchers. ☙ 16 **Facilities** Non-diners area ♦♦ Children's menu Family room Garden ⋒ Parking ⇌ (notice required)

PAINSWICK
Map 4 SO80

The Falcon Inn ★★★★ INN

tel: 01452 814222 **New St GL6 6UN**
email: info@falconpainswick.co.uk **web:** www.falconpainswick.co.uk
dir: *On A46 in centre of Painswick, opposite St Mary's church*

Historic inn with wide-ranging menus

Dating from 1554, this pub spent over 200 years as a courthouse and occupies a lovely spot in the heart of the town and opposite the church with its iconic 99 yew trees (legend has it that if a 100th tree is planted, it never grows). Expect a good choice of local real ales, including Hook Norton, Wye Valley HPA and various guest ales. Lunch and dinner menus are varied, offering something for everyone. A typical dinner might start with a Greek-inspired sharing platter or chicken liver parfait with apple and plum chutney and move on to blade of beef and bean cassoulet with dauphinoise potatoes.

Open all day all wk 10am-11pm **Food** Lunch Mon-Sat 12-2.30, Sun 12-3 Dinner Mon-Sat 6.30-9.30, Sun 6.30-9 ⊕ PARSNIP INNS LTD ◀ Hook Norton, Wye Valley HPA, guest ales ♂ Westons Stowford Press. ☙ 10 **Facilities** Non-diners area ♣ (All areas) ♦♦ Children's menu Children's portions Garden Outside area ⋒ Parking WiFi ⇌ (notice required) **Rooms** 11

POULTON
Map 5 SP00

The Falcon Inn
PICK OF THE PUBS

See Pick of the Pubs on opposite page and advert below

SAPPERTON
Map 4 SO90

The Bell at Sapperton
PICK OF THE PUBS

tel: 01285 760298 **GL7 6LE**
email: info@bellsapperton.co.uk
dir: *From A419 between Cirencester & Stroud follow Sapperton signs*

Village free house, very much part of the community

The Cotswold stone exterior of this village inn has been quietly mellowing for over 300 years. Still gently maturing are the beamed ceilings, unrendered walls, polished flags, bare boards and open fireplaces inside. Liquid refreshments start with ranges of teas and coffees, and continue with real ales from Butcombe, Hook Norton, Otter and Stroud; Stowford Press cider, a dozen wines by the glass and 20 spirits conclude a broad selection. The menu also displays variety, with nibbles and sharing boards giving way to starters such as devilled lamb's kidneys on toast with mustard cream sauce; and main courses such as braised ox cheek with roasted carrots and horseradish mash. Round off with a boozy Black Forest knickerbocker glory. Meals are served in four cosy dining areas, each with its own individual character. A secluded rear courtyard and a landscaped front garden make fine-weather alfresco dining a pleasure.

Open all day all wk 11-11 (Sun 12-9) Closed 25 Dec **Food** Lunch Mon-Sat 12-2.30, Sun 12-4 Dinner Mon-Sat 6-9.30 ⊕ FREE HOUSE ◀ Flying Monk, Otter Bitter, Hook Norton Hooky Bitter, Butcombe, Stroud Budding ♂ Westons Stowford Press. ☙ 12 **Facilities** Non-diners area ♣ (Bar Restaurant Garden) ♦♦ Children's menu Children's portions Garden ⋒ Beer festival Parking WiFi

PICK OF THE PUBS

The Falcon Inn

POULTON   Map 5 SP00

tel: 01285 851597 & 850878
London Rd GL7 5HN
email: bookings@falconinnpoulton.co.uk
web: www.falconinnpoulton.co.uk
dir: *From Cirencester 4m E on A417 towards Fairford*

Informal atmosphere and locally brewed cask ales

Slap-bang in the middle of this pretty Cotswold village, with its lovely stone cottages, the Falcon is a charming old pub, run with loads of passion and enthusiasm by Gianni Gray and Natalie Birch. When they took over they had a vision of what makes a great village pub that truly fits in at the heart of the community – 'a friendly place where you can relax, enjoy a good pint or a nice glass of wine and eat amazing food at a reasonable price,' and this is what they've set out (very successfully) to achieve. You can expect genuine dedication to local produce, ensuring a reliable pint of real ale from some of the area's independent breweries, enjoyed in a pub that marries contemporary comforts with age-old tradition. The fresh, vibrant menu changes every month to make the most of what's available locally. The set price lunch menu is great value, while the à la carte offers more options. Kick things off with apple and treacle-cured salmon with

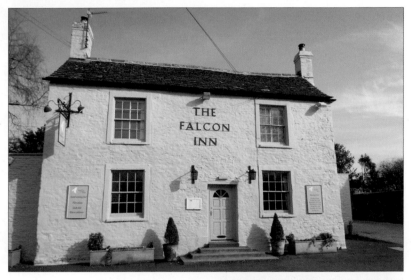

cucumber and horseradish; chargrilled quail with lentils, creamed kale and pine nuts; or twice-baked crab soufflé, before moving on to fillet of hake with cassoulet of cannellini beans, chorizo, grilled artichokes and cherry tomatoes; slow-cooked Kelmscott pork belly with creamy mash, sauerkraut and glazed baby carrots; or butternut squash and ricotta tortellini with roast squash, crispy sage and beurre noisette. There's a good range of steaks as well, and for dessert you could go for steamed orange marmalade pudding with a lightly spiced custard, or chocolate fondant with toasted coconut, mango and chilli gel and coconut sorbet. You can have the cheese board with three cheeses, or five if you've got room for more.

Open Tue-Sat 12-3 5-11 (Sun 12-4) Closed 25 Dec, Mon **Food** Lunch Tue-Sat 12-2.15, Sun 12-2.30 Dinner Tue-Sat 6-9 Set menu available 🛢 FREE HOUSE 🍺 Hook Norton Hooky Bitter, guest ale 🍏 Westons Stowford Press. 🍷 11 **Facilities** Non-diners area 👫 Children's menu Children's portions Garden 🪑 Parking WiFi

PICK OF THE PUBS

The Butchers Arms

SHEEPSCOMBE Map 4 SO81

tel: 01452 812113 **GL6 7RH**
email: mark@butchers-arms.co.uk
web: www.butchers-arms.co.uk
dir: *1.5m S of A46 (Cheltenham to Stroud road), N of Painswick*

Rural Cotswold gem with stunning views

Tucked into the western scarp of the Cotswolds and reached via narrow winding lanes, pretty Sheepscombe radiates all of the mellow, sedate, bucolic charm you'd expect from such a haven. The village pub, dating from 1670 and a favourite haunt of *Cider with Rosie* author Laurie Lee, lives up to such expectations and then some. Views from the gardens are idyllic whilst within is all you'd hope for: log fires, clean-cut rustic furnishings, village chatter backed up by beers from Prescotts of Cheltenham, Wye Valley and Otter. Walkers, riders and locals all beat a path to the door beneath the pub's famous carved sign showing a butcher supping a pint of ale with a pig tied to his leg. The pub takes its name from its association with Henry VIII's Royal Deer Park, which was located nearby, when deer carcasses were hung in what is now the bar. The fulfilling fodder here includes locally sourced meats, including beef from Beech Farm; the beef, ale, mushroom and Stilton shortcrust pastry pie is a perennial

favourite, as is the home-made burger – try one with a Double Gloucester and bacon topping. Alternative main courses take in cottage pie or salmon, cod, lemon and dill fishcakes and specials like home-made faggots, wholegrain mustard mash, mushy peas, bacon and onion gravy; or mushroom, spinach, Stilton and chestnut tartlet. Nibblers can graze on a delicious fish finger sandwich; others can share an oven-baked camembert or a farmhouse platter, while those thinking of tucking into the memorable Sunday roasts should book well ahead. To drink, there's a cracking range of ales, and Westons Stowford Press and Rosie's Pig ciders. Following a sympathetic extension, there is now more room to enjoy the delights of this lovely pub.

Open all wk 11.30-2.30 6.30-11 (Sat 11.30-11.30 Sun 12-10.30) **Food** Lunch Mon-Fri 12-2.30, Sat-Sun all day Dinner Mon-Sat 6.30-9.30, Sun 6.30-8 (ex Sun Jan & Feb) ⊕ FREE HOUSE ◖ Prescott Hill Climb, Otter Bright, St Austell Proper Job, Wye Valley HPA ⚘ Westons Stowford Press & Rosie's Pig. **Facilities** Non-diners area ❖ (Bar Garden) ♦♦ Children's menu Children's portions Garden ⋒ Cider festival Parking WiFi

SHEEPSCOMBE
Map 4 SO81

The Butchers Arms
PICK OF THE PUBS

See Pick of the Pubs on opposite page

SOMERFORD KEYNES
Map 4 SU09

The Bakers Arms

tel: 01285 861298 **GL7 6DN**
email: enquiries@thebakersarmssomerford.co.uk
dir: *Exit A419 signed Cotswold Water Park. Cross B4696, 1m, follow signs for Keynes Park & Somerford Keynes*

Chocolate-box Cotswold pub

The beautiful Bakers Arms dates from the 17th century and was formerly the village bakery; it still has its low-beamed ceilings and inglenook fireplace. Only a stone's throw from the Thames Path and Cotswold Way, the pub is a convenient watering hole for walkers. The home-cooked food on offer runs along the lines of baguettes, light lunches and pub favourites – a pot of whitebait with aïoli; honey-baked ham, two fried eggs and chips; home-made vegetable curry; and 8oz Forest of Dean boar burger with rosemary salted chips. The mature gardens are ideal for alfresco dining, with discreet children's play areas.

Open all day all wk 12-11 **Food** Lunch Mon-Sat 12-9, Sun 12-4 Dinner Mon-Sat 12-9, Sun 6-8 ⊕ ENTERPRISE INNS ◀ Butcombe Bitter, Flying Monk Elmers, Sharp's Doom Bar ♻ Addlestones, Somersby, Westons Stowford Press. **Facilities** Non-diners area ❄ (Bar Restaurant Garden) ♦ Children's menu Children's portions Play area Garden ♫ Parking WiFi ➡ (notice required)

SOUTHROP
Map 5 SP10

The Swan
PICK OF THE PUBS

tel: 01367 850205 **GL7 3NU**
email: admin@theswanatsouthrop.co.uk
dir: *Follow Southrop signs from A361 between Lechlade & Burford*

Beautifully appointed, early 17th-century Cotswolds inn

Overlooking the green, The Swan is clearly the village focal point. Ivy covers the external walls, while those in the stone-floored bar and restaurant are painted white, soft grey-blue or left unrendered. A good real ale line-up includes North Cotswold Brewery's Shagweaver and Sharp's Atlantic, with 15 wines by the glass. Owner Jerry Hibbert's close links with local food producers underlines his ethos of 'home grown, home made and produce driven'. Try a glass of blood orange and rose geranium fizz while deciding which of the tempting dishes appeals most. Perhaps it'll will be oxtail ravioli and rosemary butter; or Matt's Scotch egg to start; then slow-cooked Southrop Manor Estate lamb shoulder shepherd's pie' with buttered kale; Cornish hake fillet, pelourde clams, monk's beard and Noilly Prat; or charred rosemary polenta, salt-baked vegetables, garlic and capers. Don't overlook the desserts though, rhubarb and almond puff pastry tart with clotted cream; or lemon meringue pie with candied peel perhaps.

Open 12-2.30 6-11 (Sat 12-3 6-11 Sun 12-4) Closed Sun eve **Food** Lunch Mon-Fri 12-2.30, Sat 12-3, Sun 12-3.30 Dinner Mon-Thu 6-9, Fri-Sat 6-9.30 Restaurant menu available all wk ⊕ FREE HOUSE ◀ Sharp's Doom Bar & Atlantic, Otter, North Cotswold Shagweaver ♻ Westons Stowford Press. ☂ 15 **Facilities** Non-diners area ❄ (Bar Restaurant Garden) ♦ Children's menu Children's portions Garden ♫ WiFi ➡ (notice required)

STANTON
Map 10 SP03

The Mount Inn

tel: 01386 584316 **Old Snowshill Rd WR12 7NE**
email: info@themountinn.co.uk
dir: *Follow Stanton signs from B4632 between Broadway & Winchcombe*

Amazing sunsets and local ales

In a tranquil, picture-perfect hillside setting at the top of a no-through-road Cotswold village, memorable views from the patio here stretch west to the crinkly top of Bredon Hill in the Vale of Evesham, with shimmering glimpses of the distant Black Mountains. In the ultra-traditional interior, ramblers and discerning diners may enjoy locally-brewed Donnington beers whilst perusing a punchy menu which mixes pub stalwarts with an ever-changing specials board. Locally-grown asparagus; or smoked haddock chowder might be an entrée; progressing then to beef suet pudding, oyster fritter and rich thyme jus. Leave room for warm Tuscan orange polenta cake.

Open 12-3 6-11 Closed 1wk Jan, Mon (Oct-Apr) **Food** Lunch 12-2 Dinner 6-9 Av main course £14 ⊕ DONNINGTON ◀ BB, SBA & Gold ♻ Westons Mortimers Orchard & Stowford Press. **Facilities** Non-diners area ❄ (All areas) ♦ Children's portions Garden Outside area ♫ Parking WiFi

STOW-ON-THE-WOLD
Map 10 SP12

The Bell at Stow

tel: 01451 870916 **Park St GL54 1AJ**
dir: *In town centre on A436*

Handsome Cotswold pub with modern British dishes

This ivy-clad stone pub in lovely Stow offers a warm welcome to all, including dogs. Open-plan with flagstone floors, beamed ceilings and log fires, it's a relaxed setting to enjoy a pint of Young's Special or one of the 10 wines sold by the glass. Seafood dominates the daily-changing specials boards – typical dishes including seafood linguine; battered Atlantic cod and chips; and seafood chowder. Non-fish options might be pan-seared Gressingham duck breast with caramelised chicory; or slow-braised lamb shoulder, minted haricot beans and rosemary and thyme fondant potato.

Open all day all wk 11-11 **Food** Mon-Sat 12-9.30, Sun 12-9 Restaurant menu available all wk ⊕ YOUNG'S ◀ Bitter & Special, guest ales. ☂ 10 **Facilities** Non-diners area ❄ (Bar Garden) ♦ Children's portions Garden ♫ Parking WiFi

The Porch House ★★★★★ INN ⓐⓐ **PICK OF THE PUBS**

tel: 01451 870048 **Digbeth St GL54 1BN**
email: james@porch-house.co.uk **web:** www.porch-house.co.uk
dir: *A429 into Stow, off main square at end of Digbeth St*

Award-winning, historic Cotswold inn

In the centre of pretty Stow-on-the-Wold, this stone-built inn claims to be the oldest pub in England. Parts of the historic building date back to 947AD, when it is believed to have been a hospice built by the order of Aethelmar, Duke of Cornwall, on land belonging to Evesham Abbey. More recent additions include vast 16th-century fireplaces and low 'mind your head' beams. The Porch has a relaxed feel about the place, especially the bar which dispenses a range of real ales, including several from the pub's brewery owners Brakspear. Served in the bar, conservatory and dining room, the food is a worthy recipient of two AA Rosettes. A typical dinner meal might begin with grilled Devon sardines, heritage tomatoes and sourdough toast; or twice-baked cheese soufflé, with leeks and wholegrain mustard and lead onto Butts Farm calves' liver, creamed potato, bacon, spring cabbage and red wine; with white chocolate millefeuille, white rum and strawberries to finish.

Open all day all wk **Food** Lunch all wk 12-3 Dinner all wk 6-9.30 ⊕ BRAKSPEAR ◀ Bitter, Oxford Gold, Special, Ringwood Boondoggle. ☂ **Facilities** Non-diners area ❄ (Bar Garden Outside area) ♦ Children's menu Children's portions Garden Outside area ♫ Parking WiFi ➡ (notice required) **Rooms** 13

STROUD
Map 4 SO80

Bear of Rodborough Hotel ★★★ HL ⊛ PICK OF THE PUBS

tel: 01453 878522 **Rodborough Common GL5 5DE**
email: info@bearofrodborough.info **web:** www.cotswold-inns-hotels.co.uk/bear
dir: From M5 junct 13 follow signs for Stonehouse then Rodborough

Surrounded by 300 acres of National Trust land

Located amidst the rolling, windswept grassland of Rodborough Common with its far-reaching views of the Stroud Valley and Severn Vale, and cattle roaming free in the summer months, this 17th-century former alehouse takes its name from the bear-baiting that used to take place nearby. Head to the bar for a pint of Wickwar before seeking a seat on the York stone terrace or in the gardens with their walled croquet lawn. The bar menu has many delights, such as afternoon tea, sharing platters and ploughman's, and fond favourites: fisherman's pie, cornfed chicken supreme and chargrilled steaks. Look to the Library Restaurant for a more formal affair, where you can try smoked Scottish scallops with butternut squash and chorizo; followed by rump of lamb and braised shoulder, dauphinoise potatoes, wilted spinach and rosemary jus; and lastly raspberry crème brûlée with a cassis smoothie and vanilla, all the while enjoying panoramas of the Cotswold countryside. Guest rooms are distinctively furnished and decorated with rich fabrics.

Open all day all wk 10am-11pm **Food** Lunch all wk 12-3 Dinner all wk 6.30-9.30 Restaurant menu available all wk ⊕ FREE HOUSE ◀ Butcombe, Stroud, Wickwar Ö Ashton Press. ₹ 10 **Facilities** Non-diners area ❖ (Bar Garden) ♦ Children's menu Children's portions Play area Garden ⊨ Parking WiFi ⚌ (notice required) **Rooms** 46

Bisley House

tel: 01453 751328 **Middle St GL5 1DZ**
email: info@bisleyhousecafe.co.uk
dir: From A419 rdbt follow hospital signs. 1st right into Field Road. 3rd left into Whitehall (leads to Middle St). Pub on right

Town centre pub designed for family dining

Built in Victorian times, this bar and restaurant was given a fresh look two years ago. It takes its regular real ales from Stroud Brewery, including their ever-popular Budding, while draught lager and cider come from Bourton-on-the-Water's Cotswold Brewery. Smoked Scottish salmon with lemon mayonnaise might begin lunch or dinner, followed by pan-fried hake with white wine and saffron sauce; an 8oz rib-eye steak with mushrooms and cherry tomatoes; or Moroccan spiced vegetable tagine with roasted baby courgettes and heritage carrots. On the extensive wine list are bins from France, Italy and Spain, chosen to complement the cooking's Mediterranean flavours.

Open Tue-Fri 4-11 (Sat 11-11, Sun 11-6) Closed 1st 2wks Jan, Mon **Food** Lunch Sat-Sun 12-3 Dinner Wed-Sat 6-9 ⊕ FREE HOUSE ◀ Stroud Budding, Beerd Monterey Ö Cotswold. ₹ **Facilities** Non-diners area ❖ (Bar Restaurant Garden) ♦ Children's menu Children's portions Garden ⊨ WiFi

The Ram Inn

tel: 01453 873329 **South Woodchester GL5 5EL**
dir: A46 from Stroud to Nailsworth, right after 2m into South Woodchester, follow brown tourist signs

17th-century inn with splendid Cotswold views

In winter the warmth from its huge fireplace might prove more appealing than standing on the terrace of this 17th-century Cotswold-stone inn, admiring the splendid views. Originally a farm, it became an alehouse in 1811 and is still full of historic little gems. Typical dishes are starters of black pudding tapas, Scotch egg, chorizo chips or chicken goujons, followed by main courses such as fillet steak, beer-battered cod or haddock, or the Woodchester Whopper burger. Paninis are also served at lunchtime.

Open all day all wk **Food** Lunch Mon-Thu 12-2, Fri-Sun 12-3 Dinner Mon-Sat 6-9 Av main course £10 ⊕ FREE HOUSE ◀ Otter Amber, St Austell Proper Job & Tribute, Flying Monk Elmers, guest ales Ö Westons Stowford Press, Lilley's Apples & Pears & Bee Sting Pear, Pheasant Plucker. **Facilities** Non-diners area ❖ (Bar Restaurant Garden) ♦ Children's menu Children's portions Garden ⊨ Parking WiFi ⚌ (notice required)

TETBURY
Map 4 ST89

Gumstool Inn
PICK OF THE PUBS

See Pick of the Pubs on opposite page

The Priory Inn ★★★ SHL
PICK OF THE PUBS

tel: 01666 502251 **London Rd GL8 8JJ**
email: info@theprioryinn.co.uk **web:** www.theprioryinn.co.uk
dir: M4 junct 17, A429 towards Cirencester. Left into B4014 to Tetbury. Over mini rdbt into Long St, pub 100yds after corner on right

Family-friendly Cotswold pub and hotel

An enormous 'walk-around' open log fire greets visitors to this thriving place. Its high exposed beams date from the 16th century, when it was the stable-block and grooms' cottages for the neighbouring priory. Local microbreweries, typically Uley and Cotswold Lion, supply the real ales; a white wine and a sparkling rosé come from a vineyard in Malmesbury; and damson brandy, sloe gin and quince liqueur are made on the banks of the River Severn. Meals in the bare-boarded, beamed bar and more contemporary restaurant use fresh ingredients sourced from within a 30-mile radius – for risotto with cavolo nero, almonds and cheese pesto; roasted half pheasant with redcurrant sauce; or Wagyu beefburger with Double Gloucester cheese, bacon jam and thousand island dressing. Diners can also design their own wood-fired pizzas.

Open all day all wk 7am-11pm (Fri 7am-mdnt Sat 8am-mdnt Sun 8am-11pm) **Food** Bkfst all wk 7-10.30 Lunch Mon-Thu 12-3, Fri-Sun & BH all day Dinner Mon-Thu 5-10, Fri-Sun & BH all day ⊕ FREE HOUSE ◀ Uley Bitter, Cotswold Lion, guest ale Ö Thatchers Gold, Cotswold, guest cider. ₹ 13 **Facilities** Non-diners area ❖ (Bar Garden) ♦ Children's menu Children's portions Play area Family room Garden ⊨ Parking WiFi ⚌ (notice required) **Rooms** 14

The Royal Oak Tetbury

tel: 01666 500021 **1 Cirencester Rd GL8 8EY**
email: stay@theroyaloaktetbury.co.uk
dir: From town centre at mini rdbt by Market House (yellow building) into Chipping St. Pass car park on right. Royal Oak on right at bottom of hill

An impressive Arts and Crafts-style free house and dining room

For owners Chris York and Kate Lewis, restoration of this Cotswolds inn was a labour of love, a feeling shared by the team of craftsmen and other experts. Stroud Brewery's Tom Long, Bath Ales Gem, the rotating Moor Beer's Nor'Hop and So'Hop, and Severn cider occupy the bar pumps. Organic bar food includes Workers' Pot, a hearty stew and, if you dine 'up in the rafters', shellfish linguine with tomato chowder sauce; pan-fried duck breast with Thai potato rösti; real ale battered fish of the day; and porcini mushroom and herb burger. The monthly changing menus feature vegan choices too.

Open all day all wk Closed 1st wk Jan Mon-Thu **Food** Lunch Mon-Sat 12-2.30, Sun 12-5 Dinner Mon-Sat 5-9.30 ⊕ FREE HOUSE ◀ Bath Ales Gem, Stroud Brewery Tom Long, Moor Beer So'Hop & Nor'Hop Ö Severn. ₹ 10 **Facilities** Non-diners area ❖ (Bar Garden) ♦ Children's menu Children's portions Garden ⊨ Beer festival Cider festival Parking WiFi ⚌ (notice required)

PICK OF THE PUBS

Gumstool Inn

TETBURY   Map 4 ST89

tel: 01666 890391
Calcot GL8 8YJ
email: reception@calcot.co
web: www.calcot.co
dir: *3m W of Tetbury at junct of A4135 & A46*

Stylish dining-pub with good wine choices

Now a stylish and popular free house that's part of Calcot & Calcot Spa this stone farmhouse was originally built by Cistercian monks in the 14th century. The buzzy and comfortable Gumstool Inn has a proper country-pub atmosphere and stocks a good selection of West Country ales such as Butcombe Bitter and Wadworth 6X, as well as Symonds cider. An excellent choice of more than 20 wines is offered by the glass or bottle. The food here is top-notch and there is a pronounced use of local suppliers and seasonal produce. A typical meal might kick off with starters of twice-baked Arbroath smokies and Montgomery Cheddar cheese soufflé; chicken liver parfait with red onion and fig chutney and grilled brioche; or Calcot smoked salmon with beetroot and caper remoulade with horseradish cream. Among the main courses may be found Gressingham duck breast with sautéed potatoes, pak choi, chestnuts and

prunes; Gloucestershire sausages with mash, red onion jam and crispy shallots; or roasted salmon fillet with brandade mashed potato and anchovy, caper and herb butter. Another option might be to order something from the fireside grill — perhaps organic Black Angus beefburger with bacon jam, gherkins, mature Cheddar and onion mayonnaise or calves' liver with pancetta, sage, creamy mashed potato and capers. Leave a space for the apple and rhubarb crumble with ice cream or the old-fashioned but comforting treacle tart. In the summer, grab a table on the pretty, flower-filled sun terrace, while indoor winter evenings are warmed with log fires.

Open all day all wk **Food** Lunch Mon-Fri 12-2, Sat 12-2.30, Sun 12-4 Dinner Mon-Sat 6-9.30, Sun 6-9
🛢 FREE HOUSE 🍺 Butcombe Bitter, Wadworth 6X 🍏 Symonds. 🍷 24
Facilities Non-diners area 👫 Children's menu Children's portions Play area Family room Garden 🎪 Parking WiFi 🚌 (notice required)

TETBURY *continued*

Snooty Fox Hotel ★★★ SHL

tel: 01666 502436 **Market Place GL8 8DD**
email: res@snooty-fox.co.uk **web:** www.snooty-fox.co.uk
dir: *In town centre opposite covered market hall*

Draw up a chair by the log fire

Occupying a prime spot in the heart of Tetbury, this 16th-century coaching inn and hotel retains many of its original features. Sit in a leather armchair in front of the log fire with a pint of Flying Monk Elmers and take a look at the menu. Start with chicken liver pâté with red onion chutney and toast; black pudding hash with apple, streaky bacon, poached egg and spiced date ketchup; or roasted stuffed figs with goats' cheese. Continue with seared fillet of sea trout with lemongrass, chilli sauce and creamy coconut sauce; haddock, chips and mushy peas; or mushroom, haloumi and red pepper burger.

Open all day all wk **Food** Lunch all wk 12-3, snacks 3-6 Dinner all wk 6-9.30 Av main course £14 ⊕ FREE HOUSE ◀ Wadworth 6X, Butcombe Bitter, Flying Monk Elmers, Wickwar, St Austell Tribute, Stroud ♂ Ashton Press, Thatchers Heritage, Pheasant Plucker. ♀ **Facilities** Non-diners area ♣ (Bar Restaurant Outside area) ♦♦ Children's menu Children's portions Outside area ⋈ WiFi ▬ (notice required) **Rooms** 12

| UPPER ODDINGTON | Map 10 SP22 |

The Horse & Groom Inn   PICK OF THE PUBS

tel: 01451 830584 **GL56 0XH**
email: info@horseandgroom.uk.com
dir: *1.5m S of Stow-on-the-Wold, just off A436*

Cotswold-stone inn specialising in local beer and food

In a conservation village in the Evenlode Valley, this pretty 16th-century inn has been owner-operated for more than a decade. The bar boasts pale polished flagstones, stripped stone walls, oak beams in the ochre ceiling, and a double-sided inglenook fireplace. Well-kept ales, cider and lager from the Cotswold Brewing Company, plenty of wines by the glass and 20 malt whiskies add up to a faultless choice of drinks. After ordering liquid refreshment, take a menu out to the terrace or walled garden for a seat beneath a green parasol. Three courses of classic but imaginative pub food could start with smoked salmon and crayfish, red chard and lemon mayo. Follow perhaps with a popular choice like Gloucester Old Spots sausages with mustard mash; or confit Gressingham duck leg with egg noodles, stir-fry and sweet and sour sauce. Puddings may include a chocolate marquise with meringue, toasted almonds and brandy crème anglaise.

Open all wk 12-3 5.30-11 (Sun 12-3 6.30-10.30) **Food** Lunch all wk 12-2 Dinner Mon-Sat 6.30-9, Sun 7-9 ⊕ FREE HOUSE ◀ Wye Valley Bitter & HPA, Goffs Tournament, Prescott Hill Climb, Otter Bitter, North Cotswold Shagweaver ♂ Cotswold. ♀ 25 **Facilities** Non-diners area ♣ (Bar Restaurant Garden) ♦♦ Children's menu Children's portions Garden ⋈ Parking WiFi ▬ (notice required)

| WINCHCOMBE | Map 10 SP02 |

The Lion Inn ★★★★ INN ◉

tel: 01242 603300 **37 North St GL54 5PS**
email: reception@thelionwinchcombe.co.uk **web:** www.thelionwinchcombe.co.uk
dir: *In town centre (parking in Chandos St)*

Shabby-chic, friendly and caring town centre hostelry

A buzzy, welcoming watering hole in the pretty town of Winchcombe, The Lion Inn has 15th-century origins, and care has been taken to maintain the building's quirky

charms. Lovers of wine and real ale are spoilt for choice in the spacious and relaxed bar – a pint of Brakspear Oxford Gold or Prescott Hill Climb might be just the thing. On the award-winning menu you might find lobster and squid ink tagliatelle with lemongrass and coriander sauce; or confit pork belly to begin, followed by calves' liver, herb pancakes and greens with lemon and white wine sauce.

Open all day all wk **Food** Lunch all wk 12-3 Dinner all wk 6-9.30 ⊕ FREE HOUSE ◀ Brakspear Oxford Gold, Wye Valley Butty Bach, Prescott Hill Climb ♂ Thatchers Gold. ♀ 12 **Facilities** Non-diners area ♣ (Bar Garden) ♦♦ Children's portions Garden ⋈ WiFi **Rooms** 7

GREATER MANCHESTER

| CHORLTON-CUM-HARDY | Map 15 SJ89 |

The Horse & Jockey

tel: 0161 860 7794 **Chorlton Green M21 9HS**
email: info@horseandjockeychorlton.com
dir: *M60 junct 7, A56 towards Stretford. Right onto A5145 towards Chorlton. After lights, 2nd right into St Clements Rd. Pub on left on green*

Facing Chorlton's wooded town green

Assuming this Tudor pub's interior designers had a free hand when it was last refurbished, they certainly made the most of it. Wherever you look – the bar, the restaurant, the rooms, the beer garden – the results are impressive. The pub doubles as the home of the Bootleg Brewery, run by an all-too-rare female head brewer. The brewery is open to the public on occasions such as their Oktoberfest. Home-made gourmet pies; Lancashire lamb hotpot; seafood platter; hanging kebabs; and burger boards all feature on a comprehensive menu.

Open all day all wk **Food** Mon-Sat 12-10, Sun 12-8 ⊕ JOSEPH HOLT ◀ Bootleg Chorlton Pale Ale, Twisted Groove & Urban Fox ♂ Westons Stowford Press. ♀ **Facilities** Non-diners area ♣ (Bar Outside area) ♦♦ Children's menu Children's portions Outside area ⋈ Beer festival WiFi ▬

| DELPH | Map 16 SD90 |

The Old Bell Inn ★★★★ INN ◉

tel: 01457 870130 **5 Huddersfield Rd OL3 5EG**
email: info@theoldbellinn.co.uk **web:** www.theoldbellinn.co.uk
dir: *M62 junct 22, A672 to Denshaw junct (signed Saddleworth). Left onto A6052 signed Delph. Through Delph to T-junct. Left onto A62, pub 150yds on left*

Historic coaching inn with excellent food

Did highwayman Dick Turpin rest here en route to the gallows in York? Possibly. More certain is that in 1835 a young Queen Victoria stayed here when visiting that city. If you're dining, starters might include Fleetwood smoked haddock and leek chowder; steamed Welsh mussels with tomato and chorizo; and duck liver and gin parfait. Moving on to mains you may find pressed shoulder of Yorkshire lamb with rosemary fondants; poached and roasted Goosnargh chicken breast with chorizo dauphinoise; and seasonal fish and seafood pie. For something rather different, try snout-to-tail suckling pig. Finish with a slate of Lancashire, Yorkshire and European cheeses.

Open all day all wk **Food** Lunch all wk 12-5 Dinner Mon-Sat 5-9.30, Sun 5-9 Av main course £10.95 Set menu available Restaurant menu available all wk ⊕ FREE HOUSE ◀ Timothy Taylor Landlord & Golden Best, Black Sheep Best Bitter, guest ales ♂ Thatchers. ♀ 10 **Facilities** Non-diners area ♦♦ Children's menu Children's portions Garden Outside area ⋈ Parking WiFi ▬ (notice required) **Rooms** 18

DIDSBURY
Map 16 SJ89

The Metropolitan

tel: 0161 438 2332 **2 Lapwing Ln M20 2WS**
email: info@the-metropolitan.co.uk
dir: M60 junct 5, A5103, right into Barlow Moor Rd, left into Burton Rd. Pub at x-roads. Right into Lapwing Ln for car park

Airy Victorian railway hotel and gastro-pub

'The Met' is well situated in the leafy suburb of West Didsbury on the old Midland Railway line into Manchester. Its Victorian heritage – decorative floor tiling, ornate windows and huge airy interior filled with antique tables, chairs and deep sofas – attracts a mainly young and cosmopolitan crowd. The drinks choice matches customer demand with nearly 30 wines sold by the glass, popular beers and bottled craft ciders. The bar and terrace menu offers pizzas and salads, while the restaurant carte is high on brasserie appeal: confit duck and kale hash with fried duck egg and brown sauce, for example; and the famous Met burger made from 28-day aged beef.

Open all day all wk 11.30-11 (Wed-Thu 11.30-11.30 Fri-Sat 11.30am-mdnt Sun 12-11) Closed 25 Dec **Food** Bkfst Mon-Fri 10am-11.45am, Sun 10am-11.30am Lunch Mon-Thu 12-9.30, Fri-Sat 12-10, Sun 12-9 Dinner Mon-Thu 12-9.30, Fri-Sat 12-10, Sun 12-9 ⊕ ENTERPRISE INNS ◀ Timothy Taylor Landlord, Caledonian Deuchars IPA, Guinness ♂ Orchard Pig, Cornish Heritage. ♥ 28
Facilities Non-diners area ♦ Children's menu Children's portions Outside area ⅋ Parking WiFi ▥ (notice required)

LITTLEBOROUGH
Map 16 SD91

The White House

tel: 01706 378456 **Blackstone Edge, Halifax Rd OL15 0LG**
dir: On A58, 8m from Rochdale, 9m from Halifax

A favourite with walkers and cyclists

Known as The White House for over 100 years, this 17th-century coaching house is on the Pennine Way, 1,300 feet above sea level – it has panoramic views of the moors and Hollingworth Lake far below. Not surprising then, that it attracts walkers and cyclists who rest up and sup on Black Sheep and Theakston Best Bitter. A simple menu of pub grub ranges from sandwiches and salads, to grills, international and vegetarian dishes, and traditional mains such as home-made steak and kidney pie, and haddock and prawn Mornay.

Open all wk Mon-Sat 12-3 6-10 (Sun 12-10.30) Closed 25 Dec **Food** Lunch Mon-Sat 12-2, Sun 12-9 Dinner Mon-Sat 6.30-9.30, Sun 12-9 ⊕ FREE HOUSE ◀ Theakston Best Bitter, Black Sheep, guest ales. **Facilities** Non-diners area ♦ Children's menu Children's portions Outside area Parking WiFi ▥

MANCHESTER
Map 16 SJ89

Marble Arch

tel: 0161 832 5914 **73 Rochdale Rd M4 4HY**
dir: In city centre (Northern Quarter)

Victorian pub popular with ale aficionados

A listed building famous for its sloping floor, glazed brick walls and barrel-vaulted ceiling, the Marble Arch is a fine example of Manchester's Victorian heritage. Part of the award-winning organic Marble Brewery, the pub was built in 1888 by celebrated architect Alfred Darbyshire for Manchester brewery B&J McKenna. An established favourite with beer aficionados and offering six regular ales and eight seasonal house beers, the pub offers a well-considered menu of pub favourites and ever-changing specials including Sunday lunches. The Marble Arch hosts its own beer festivals.

Open all day all wk Closed 25 Dec **Food** Mon-Sat 12-8.45, Sun 12-7.45 ⊕ FREE HOUSE ◀ Marble Manchester Bitter, Lagonda IPA, Ginger Marble, Pint & Earl Grey IPA ♂ Moonshine. **Facilities** Non-diners area ✿ (Bar Garden) ♦ Garden ⅋ Beer festival WiFi

MARPLE BRIDGE
Map 16 SJ98

Hare & Hounds

tel: 0161 427 4042 **19 Mill Brow SK6 5LW**
email: haremillbrow@gmail.com
dir: From A626 in Marple Bridge (at lights at river bridge) follow Mellor signs into Town St. 1st left into Hollins Ln. Right at T-junct into Ley Ln. Pub 0.25m on left

Idyllic rural retreat in lovely countryside

Tucked away in a secluded hamlet in the hills fringing the Peak District, this comfortable community local first opened its doors in 1805. It retains much of the character of days gone by and is a popular stop with ramblers exploring the countless paths threading the ridges, moors and wooded cloughs hereabouts. Roaring winter fires take away the chill, or you could settle down outside with a glass of Stockport-brewed Robinsons beer and anticipate freshly cooked mains such as wild mushroom, smoked garlic and spinach risotto; or venison pie with roasted root vegetables, braised red cabbage and gravy, with bread and butter pudding with double cream to finish.

Open Mon-Tue 5-10 (Wed-Thu 5-12 Fri 12-3 5-12 Sat 12-12 Sun 12-10) Closed Mon-Thu L **Food** Lunch Fri-Sat 12-2, Sun 1-7 Dinner Wed-Sat 6-9.30, Sun 1-7 Av main course £15 ⊕ ROBINSONS ◀ Unicorn, Hatters, Dizzy Blonde, seasonal ales ♂ Westons Stowford Press. **Facilities** Non-diners area ✿ (Bar Restaurant Outside area) ♦ Children's portions Outside area ⅋ Parking WiFi

MELLOR
Map 16 SJ98

Oddfellows Arms

tel: 0161 449 7826 **73 Moor End Rd SK6 5PT**
email: info@oddfellowsmellor.com **web:** www.oddfellowsmellor.com
dir: In village centre

Stylish pub with good food and local ales

A pub since 1803, the 'Oddies' was taken over by a group of regulars who set about restoring it to its 17th-century splendour. Situated in the High Peak National Park, the pub boasts three log burners, oak floors and a stylish upstairs dining room. In the bar, cask ales such as Abbeydale Deception keep drinkers happy but the excellent food attracts diners from far and wide. Local produce drives the menu, with typical dishes that include chicken liver parfait with plum and cinnamon chutney; steak and kidney pudding; and Baileys crème brûlée.

Open 4-late (Fri-Sun 12-late) Closed Mon **Food** Lunch Fri 12-3, Sat 12-9.30, Sun 12-8 Dinner Tue 5-8, Wed 5-9, Thu-Fri 5-9.30, Sat 12-9.30, Sun 12-8 ⊕ FREE HOUSE ◀ Marston's Pedigree, Abbeydale Deception, Thornbridge Jaipur ♂ Thatchers Gold. ♥ 13 **Facilities** Non-diners area ✿ (Bar Outside area)
♦ Children's menu Children's portions Family room Outside area ⅋ Parking ▥ (notice required)

The Roebuck Inn

tel: 0161 624 7819 **Strinesdale OL4 3RB**
email: sehowarth1@hotmail.com
dir: *From Oldham Mumps Bridge take Huddersfield Rd (A62), right at 2nd lights into Ripponden Rd (A672), 1m right at lights into Turfpit Ln, 1m*

Country pub not far from Oldham

A thousand feet up in Strinedale on the edge of Saddleworth Moor, this traditionally styled inn provides a menu with plenty of choice. Among the options are lamb's liver and onion; steak, kidney and ale suet pudding; roast beef and Yorkshire pudding; mushroom, cranberry, nut and brie Wellington with cranberry sauce; deep-fried haddock in batter served with peas; or a large seafood salad. Beers come from a variety of local breweries.

Open all wk 12-3 5-11 (Fri-Sun 12-11) **Food** Lunch all wk 12-2.15 Dinner all wk 5-9.15 Set menu available Restaurant menu available all wk ⊕ FREE HOUSE ◀ Greenfield Silver Owl, Copper Dragon Best Bitter. ♀ 9 **Facilities** Non-diners area ❖ (Bar Garden) ⬤ Children's menu Children's portions Play area Garden Parking WiFi ⬛

The White Hart Inn ★★★★ INN ❀❀ PICK OF THE PUBS

tel: 01457 872566 **51 Stockport Rd, Lydgate OL4 4JJ**
email: bookings@thewhitehart.co.uk **web:** www.thewhitehart.co.uk
dir: *From Manchester A62 to Oldham. Right onto bypass, A669 through Lees. In 500yds past Grotton, at brow of hill right onto A6050*

Charming dining pub on the edge of The Pennines

There's been a pub here since 1788, when its huge cellars were used for brewing. From its hilltop location, Manchester and the Cheshire plain are spread out below, and on a good day even the Welsh Mountains and Snowdonia are visible. Owner Charlie Brierley has blended the period charm of its beams, exposed stonework and open fireplaces with contemporary decor, especially in The Brasserie, where among the cosmopolitan dishes are Whitby crab cocktail with mango, black beans and chilli; pot au feu; grilled lemon sole with brown shrimps and almond butter; and slow-cooked ox cheek with potato butter and kale. The two- and three-course set lunch and early evening menus are good value, as is chef's seven-course Dining Room tasting menu. Sunday's set lunch includes either a roast meat, a fish or a vegetarian dish.

Open all day all wk Closed 26 Dec, 1 Jan **Food** Lunch Mon-Sat 12-2.30, Sun 12-8 Dinner Mon-Sat 6-9.30, Sun 12-8 Av main course £15 Set menu available Restaurant menu available Wed-Sat eve ⊕ FREE HOUSE ◀ Timothy Taylor Landlord & Golden Best, JW Lees Bitter, Marston's Wainwright ♂ Westons Mortimers Orchard. ♀ 9 **Facilities** Non-diners area ⬤ Children's menu Garden ⌂ Beer festival Parking WiFi **Rooms** 12

The King's Arms

tel: 0161 839 3605 **11 Bloom St M3 6AN**
email: kingsarmssalford@gmail.com
dir: *Phone for detailed directions*

Impressive Victorian pub with Bohemian atmosphere

Redevelopment has swept away much of old Salford. Fortunately this striking street-corner edifice survives intact amidst the concrete, steel and glass, across the River Irwell from Manchester's gleaming centre. It's a grass-roots venue

renowned for arts, festivals and creative exhibitions. The change of management is currently building on the King's unique appeal – musical and theatrical performers continue almost non-stop in the busy function room, refreshed by the bar's six guest ales and two draught ciders – celebrated with a festival in September.
A major introduction is Aunty Hilda's Kitchen, which serves a short list of home-made favourites from tea-time to supper between Wednesday and Saturday.

Open all day all wk **Food** Lunch Wed-Sat 12-4, Sun 1-6 Dinner Wed-Sat 4-8, Sun 1-6 Set menu available ⊕ FREE HOUSE ◀ 6 changing guest ales ♂ 2 changing guest ciders. ♀ **Facilities** Non-diners area ❖ (Bar Restaurant Garden) ⬤ Children's menu Children's portions Garden ⌂ Beer festival Cider festival WiFi ⬛ (notice required)

The Arden Arms

tel: 0161 480 2185 **23 Millgate SK1 2LX**
email: steve@ardenarms.com
dir: *M60 junct 27 to town centre. Across mini rdbt, at lights turn left. Pub on right of next rdbt behind Asda*

Good food in town-centre pub of outstanding heritage interest

This late-Georgian coaching inn just has to be seen. Essentially unchanged since a 1908 brewery makeover, it retains its classic multi-roomed layout, fine curved wooden bar, tiled floors and tiny snug. Out back is a cobbled courtyard, used for music gigs on summer Saturdays; in the cellar are mortuary slabs from the time when inquests were held here. If you're eating, look for beef, herb and garlic sausages and mash; grilled gammon steak and egg; Caribbean fish stew; mushroom Stroganoff; Moroccan spiced lamb lasagne; Robinsons beer-battered cod, chips and mushy peas; and daily-changing specials. Hot and cold sandwiches at lunchtime, and on Sundays there's always a traditional roast.

Open all wk 12-12 Closed 25-26 Dec, 1 Jan **Food** Lunch Mon-Fri 12-2.30, Sat 12-4, Sun 12-6 Dinner Thu-Sat 6-9, Sun 12-6 Av main course £9.95 ⊕ ROBINSONS ◀ Unicorn, Trooper, 1892, Dizzy Blonde, Double Hop, seasonal ales ♂ Westons Stowford Press. ♀ 9 **Facilities** Non-diners area ❖ (All areas) ⬤ Garden Outside area ⌂ WiFi

The Lord Raglan

tel: 0161 764 6680 **Nangreaves BL9 6SP**
dir: *M66 junct 1, A56 to Walmersley. Left into Palatine Drive, left into Ribble Drive, left into Walmersley Old Rd to Nangreaves*

Recommended for its own microbrewery beers

The rambling, stone-built Lord Raglan is set beside a cobbled lane high on the moors above Bury, at the head of a former weaving hamlet, where lanes and tracks dissipate into deep, secluded gorges rich in industrial heritage. Beers brewed at the on-site Leyden microbrewery may be taken in the garden, where the throaty cough of steam engines on the East Lancashire Railway echoes off the River Irwell's steep valley sides below the towering Peel Monument. Reliable, traditional pub grub and changing specials take the edge off walkers' appetites. Try the chicken and mushroom pie, hot steak sandwich, or grilled halibut steak served with a lime and tomato salsa. There are beer festivals in the summer and autumn.

Open all wk 12-2.30 6-11 (Fri-Sun all day) **Food** Lunch Mon-Thu 12-2, Fri-Sat 12-9, Sun 12-8 Dinner Mon-Thu 6-9, Fri-Sat 12-9, Sun 12-8 ⊕ FREE HOUSE ◀ Leyden Nanny Flyer, Crowning Glory, Light Brigade, Black Pudding ♂ Wilce's Herefordshire. ♀ 10 **Facilities** ❖ (Bar Garden) ⬤ Children's menu Children's portions Garden Beer festival Parking WiFi ⬛

HAMPSHIRE

ALTON
Map 5 SU73

The Anchor Inn ★★★★ INN @@   PICK OF THE PUBS

tel: 01420 23261 **Lower Froyle GU34 4NA**
email: info@anchorinnatlowerfroyle.co.uk **web:** www.anchorinnatlowerfroyle.co.uk
dir: *From A31 follow Bentley signs*

Celebrating the traditional English country inn

A 16th-century, tile-hung farmhouse forms the nucleus of the Anchor. The stylish interior is all low ceilings, exposed beams, wooden floors and open fires, suggesting that little has changed for decades. In the intimate snug and saloon bar you'll find Marston's beers taking pride of place. The restaurant's two AA Rosette award recognises the quality of the regularly changing, locally sourced food that at dinner could be octopus carpaccio, crispy pig's ears, pickled grapes and spiced tomato; followed by hay-baked hake, sweet potato, asparagus, roasted palm hearts and red wine jus; or roasted cauliflower and truffle tortellini, coco bean cassoulet and confit shallot. For dessert, how about rhubarb pannacotta, salsa, pistachio tuile and rhubarb soup; or chocolate cake, raspberry sorbet and popcorn? Spacious and beautifully designed bedrooms, friendly and efficient service and on-the-doorstep country walks complete the picture.

Open all day all wk **Food** Lunch Mon-Sat 12-2.30, Sun 12-4 Dinner Mon-Sat 6.30-9.30, Sun 6-8 ⊕ FREE HOUSE/CIRRUS GROUP ◀ Triple fff, Marston's, guest ale ♂ Hogs Back Hazy Hog. ♟ 9 **Facilities** Non-diners area ♣ (Bar Garden) ♦♦ Children's menu Children's portions Garden ⋒ Parking WiFi ➡ **Rooms** 5

AMPFIELD
Map 5 SU42

White Horse at Ampfield

tel: 01794 368356 **Winchester Rd SO51 9BQ**
email: whitehorseinn@hotmail.co.uk
dir: *From Winchester take A3040, then A3090 towards Romsey. Ampfield in 7m. Or M3 junct 13, A335 (signed Chandler's Ford). At lights right onto B3043, follow Chandler's Ford Industrial Estate then Hursley signs. Left onto A3090 to Ampfield*

Traditional village inn once frequented by pilgrims

With roots as a pilgrims' inn in the 16th century, the timber-framed White Horse is the only pub in the village in which The Rev W. Awdry, *Thomas the Tank Engine's* creator, lived as a boy. The building is home to three large inglenooks, the one in the public bar having an iron fireback decorated with the crest of Charles I and hooks on which to hang bacon sides for smoking. Typical dishes are mushroom mille feuille with mixed bean and chickpea cassoulet and pea purée; roast chicken breast with sweet chilli and honey sauce; and smoked trout with new potatoes and salad.

Open all day all wk 11-11 (Sun 12-9) **Food** Lunch Mon-Sat 12-2.30, Sun 12-4 Dinner Mon-Sat 6-9 ⊕ GREENE KING ◀ IPA, Morland Old Speckled Hen & Original ♂ Aspall. ♟ 14 **Facilities** Non-diners area ♣ (Bar Garden Outside area) ♦♦ Children's menu Children's portions Play area Garden Outside area ⋒ Parking WiFi ➡ (notice required)

AMPORT
Map 5 SU34

The Hawk Inn

tel: 01264 710371 **SP11 8AE**
email: info@hawkinnamport.co.uk
dir: *From Andover towards Thruxton on A303 exit signed Hawk Conservancy & Amport. 1m to Amport. Or A303 onto A343 (S of Andover) follow Abbots Ann & Amport signs*

Both modern and traditional British food

On warmer days, the terrace area of The Hawk Inn is a draw with its views towards Pill Hill Brook. In the light and spacious interior of adjoining rooms, the bar offers Upham Punter real ale, while a meal could feature chilli and garlic king prawns, fennel, grapefruit and cucumber to start, followed by pork and black pudding hash with fried duck egg and honey and mustard dressing; or wild garlic and potato frittata with cherry tomato, rocket and red onion salad. Apple, sultana and cinnamon crumble with stem ginger ice cream is one way to finish.

Open all day all wk **Food** Lunch Mon-Sat 12-2.30, Sun 12-3 Dinner Sun-Thu 6-9, Fri-Sat 6-9.30 ⊕ FREE HOUSE/UPHAM GOUP ◀ Punter, Tipster, Stakes, guest ale ♂ Orchard Pig Reveller. ♟ 14 **Facilities** Non-diners area ♣ (Bar Outside area) ♦♦ Children's menu Children's portions Outside area ⋒ Parking WiFi

ANDOVER
Map 5 SU34

Wyke Down Country Pub & Restaurant

tel: 01264 352048 **Wyke Down, Picket Piece SP11 6LX**
email: info@wykedown.co.uk
dir: *3m from Andover town centre on A303 follow signs for Wyke Down Caravan Park*

Converted barn and conservatory dining

A diversified farm on the outskirts of Andover, this pub and restaurant has new landlords who took over in January 2016. The pub started in a barn over 25 years ago and the restaurant was built some years later. Typical dishes are a smoked fish board; crab linguine; beef, onion, bacon and London Pride steamed pudding; and mixed bean chilli. Smaller portions, jacket potatoes and baguettes are available too. You might want to time your visit for a summer Sunday car boot sale, held in an adjacent field.

Open all wk 12-3 6-11 **Food** Lunch all wk 12-2 Dinner Sun-Tue 6-8, Wed-Sat 6-9 ⊕ FREE HOUSE ◀ Fuller's London Pride ♂ Cornish Orchards. **Facilities** Non-diners area ♦♦ Children's menu Children's portions Play area Garden ⋒ Parking WiFi ➡ (notice required)

BALL HILL
Map 5 SU46

The Furze Bush Inn

tel: 01635 253228 **Hatt Common, East Woodhay RG20 ONQ**
email: info@furzebushinn.co.uk
dir: *From Newbury take A343 (Andover Road), pub signed*

Hearty food in a handy location

A popular rural free house, this is a perfect place for refreshment following a day at the Newbury Races, walking the Berkshire Downs, or visiting Highclere Castle. The bar menu offers a good range of favourites, such as medallions of pork fillet with cider sauce, black pudding and mustard mashed potato; chicken Madras curry; gourmet minted lamb burger with brie; steak and kidney suet pudding; and warm chocolate fudge cake for afters. There's a large front garden, a children's play area and a rear patio with parasols – perfect for summer drinking.

Open all day all wk **Food** Lunch Mon-Fri 12-3, Sat 12-9, Sun 12-8.30 Dinner Mon-Fri 5-9, Sat 12-9, Sun 12-8.30 Av main course £10 Restaurant menu available all wk ⊕ FREE HOUSE ◀ Greene King Abbot Ale, Hook Norton Hooky Bitter, Cheddar Ales Gorge Best. ♟ 9 **Facilities** Non-diners area ♦♦ Children's menu Play area Garden ⋒ Beer festival Parking WiFi ➡

BAUGHURST
Map 5 SU56

The Wellington Arms ◉◉
PICK OF THE PUBS

See Pick of the Pubs on opposite page

BEAULIEU
Map 5 SU30

The Drift Inn

tel: 023 8029 2342 **Beaulieu Rd SO42 7YQ**
email: bookatable@driftinn.co.uk
dir: *From Lyndhurst take B3056 (Beaulieu Rd) signed Beaulieu. Cross railway line, inn on right*

Family-friendly New Forest inn

This inn is surrounded by the glorious New Forest National Park. The word 'drift' refers to the centuries-old, twice a year, round-up of the 3,000-plus free-wandering ponies. Beers from Ringwood on the western side of the forest and a guest ale are served in the bar, while in the restaurant the menu lists tandoori rubbed salmon with Bombay-style potatoes; seasonable vegetable Wellington with creamed garlic and parmesan mash; shepherd's pie; and a selection of sandwiches, baguettes and jacket potatoes. Outside are two children's play areas and large gardens, although no one minds if you come inside wearing walking boots or wellies and with your dog in tow.

Open all day all wk 10am-11pm (Sat 9am-11pm Sun 9am-10.30pm) **Food** Lunch all wk 12-3 (Etr-Oct 12-9) Dinner all wk 6-9 (Etr-Oct 12-9) Set menu available ⊕ FREE HOUSE ◀ Ringwood Best Bitter, Old Thumper & Fortyniner, guest ales Ö Thatchers. **Facilities** Non-diners area ❤ (Bar Restaurant Garden) ♦♦ Children's menu Children's portions Play area Garden ⊼ Beer festival Cider festival Parking WiFi ➡ (notice required)

BENTLEY
Map 5 SU74

The Bull Inn

tel: 01420 22156 **GU10 5JH**
email: enquiries@thebullinnbentley.co.uk
dir: *2m from Farnham on A31 towards Winchester*

Period details and an extensive menu

Exposed beams, real fires and plenty of alfresco seating make this 15th-century coaching inn well worth a visit. There's also a great selection of food. Lunch choices brings The Bull platter, sandwiches, salads and a two-course lunch special; the à la carte menu includes an 8oz Boyne Valley British sirloin steak, chips and garlic butter; and honey- and mustard-glazed Orchard Gold ham, two fried eggs and chips. There's a good selection of wines, and real ales such as Fuller's London Pride, Ringwood Best Bitter and St Austell Tribute.

Open all day all wk 11-11 (Sun 12-10.30) Closed 1 Jan **Food** Lunch Mon-Sat 12-2.30, Sun 12-7 Dinner Tue-Sat 6-9.30, Sun 12-7 ⊕ ENTERPRISE INNS ◀ Fuller's London Pride, St Austell Tribute, Ringwood Best Bitter Ö Aspall. ₹ 9 **Facilities** Non-diners area ❤ (Bar Outside area) ♦♦ Children's menu Children's portions Outside area ⊼ Parking WiFi ➡ (notice required)

BISHOP'S WALTHAM
Map 5 SU51

The Hampshire Bowman

tel: 01489 892940 **Dundridge Ln SO32 1GD**
email: info@hampshirebowman.com
dir: *From Bishop's Waltham on B3035 towards Corhampton. Right signed Dundridge. 1.2m to Pub*

Rustic rural gem lost down lanes

A true rural local, set in 10 acres beside a country lane in rolling downland, this unassuming Victorian pub remains delightfully old fashioned. In the beamed,

simply furnished and brick-floored bar you'll find time-honoured pub games and barrels of beer on racks behind the bar. Ale-lovers come for foaming pints of Bowman Ales Swift One or Oakleaf Quercus Folium, or a glass of heady Black Dragon cider, best enjoyed in the rambling orchard garden. Soak it up with a traditional bar meal, perhaps ham, egg and chips; liver and bacon with mash and shallot jus; or fish and chips. Don't miss the beer and cider festival in late July.

Open all day all wk **Food** Lunch Mon-Thu 12-2, Fri-Sun 12-9 Dinner Mon-Thu 6-9, Fri-Sun 12-9 ⊕ FREE HOUSE ◀ Bowman Ales Swift One, Oakleaf Quercus Folium, guest ales Ö Gwynt y Ddraig Black Dragon, Lilley's Crazy Goat, guest ciders. ₹ 10 **Facilities** Non-diners area ❤ (Bar Restaurant Garden) ♦♦ Children's menu Children's portions Play area Garden ⊼ Beer festival Cider festival Parking WiFi ➡ (notice required)

BOLDRE
Map 5 SZ39

The Hobler Inn

tel: 01590 623944 **Southampton Rd, Battramsley SO41 8PT**
email: hobler@alcatraz.co.uk
dir: *From Brockenhurst take A337 towards Lymington. Pub on main road*

New Forest pub popular with families

On the main road between Brockenhurst and Lymington, The Hobler has a large grassed area and trestle tables ideal for families visiting the New Forest. The Hobler Inn is more London wine bar with its stylish leather furniture than a village local, but still serves a well-kept pint of Ringwood ale. The food is locally sourced and freshly cooked. A meal might kick off with pan-fried tiger prawns in tomato, garlic and chilli, before moving on to slow-cooked shank of lamb with creamy mash, red onion gravy and vegetables. Eton Mess is one typical dessert.

Open all day all wk 10am-11pm **Food** Mon-Sat 12-9.30, Sun 12-9 Set menu available ⊕ ENTERPRISE INNS ◀ Ringwood Razorback, guest ale Ö Aspall. ₹ 10 **Facilities** Non-diners area ♦♦ Children's menu Garden Parking WiFi ➡ (notice required)

The Red Lion
PICK OF THE PUBS

tel: 01590 673177 **Rope Hill SO41 8NE**
email: redlionboldre@gmail.com
dir: *M27 junct 1, A337 through Lyndhurst & Brockenhurst towards Lymington, follow Boldre signs*

15th-century pub for all seasons

Mentioned in the Domesday Book, The Red Lion sits at the crossroads in the ancient village of Boldre. The rambling interior contains cosy, beamed rooms, log fires and rural memorabilia; the rooms glow with candlelight on antique copper and brass. Expect a genuinely warm welcome and traditional values, with Ringwood ales on offer at the bar. The kitchen places an emphasis on traditional meals made using the very best of the forest's produce. Typical starters include tea-smoked Hampshire trout with home-made potato salad; and twice baked goats' cheese soufflé, then lamb shank slow-braised with redcurrant, rosemary and honey, mash and root vegetables; and free-range chicken supreme, crispy bacon, smoked cheese sauce and chunky chips. In the summer, you can eat outside on the herb patio.

Open all wk 11-3 5.30-11 (Sun 12-8) (summer Sat 11-11) Closed 25 Dec **Food** Lunch Mon-Sat 12-2.30, Sun 12-8 (summer Sat 12-9.30) Dinner Mon-Sat 6-9.30, Sun 12-8 (summer Sat 12-9.30, winter Mon-Thu 6-9) ⊕ FREE HOUSE ◀ Ringwood Best Bitter & Fortyniner, Guinness, guest ales Ö Thatchers Gold. ₹ 15 **Facilities** Non-diners area ❤ (Bar Restaurant Garden) ♦♦ Children's portions Garden ⊼ Parking WiFi ➡ (notice required)

PICK OF THE PUBS

The Wellington Arms ❀❀

BAUGHURST   Map 5 SU56

tel: 0118 982 0110
Baughurst Rd RG26 5LP
email: hello@thewellingtonarms.com
web: www.thewellingtonarms.com
dir: *From A4, E of Newbury, through Aldermaston. At 2nd rdbt 2nd exit signed Baughurst, left at T-junct, pub 1m*

Drawing discerning diners from miles around

Hidden down a maze of lanes in peaceful countryside between Basingstoke and Newbury is the stylish 'Welly', once used as a hunting lodge by the Duke of Wellington. Inside are wooden tables, tiled floors and attractively patterned curtains and blinds. Since arriving here over a decade ago, Jason King and Simon Page have never looked back. Their ethos is simple: local, well-priced and delicious food. Jason's award-winning, daily chalkboard menus offer plenty of interest and imagination and much of the produce is organic and local or home grown, since they are dedicated to keeping down the food miles. Salad leaves, herbs and vegetables are grown in the pub's polytunnel and raised vegetable beds, free-range eggs come from their rare-breed and rescue hens, and there are also pedigree Jacob sheep, Tamworth pigs and five beehives. Begin with roasted home-grown

pumpkin soup with toasted pumpkin seeds and sour cream; or home-cured ham hock, fennel and parsley terrine, English mustard mayonnaise and sourdough toast. Follow with roast fillet of Brixham cod with preserved lemon crust, sautéed marsh samphire and Puy lentils; or chargrilled Orchard Farm pork chop, sticky red cabbage, mash and parsnip crisps. Any home-made dessert will make the perfect finish — perhaps Eccles cake stuffed with dried fruit and 'Welly' honey, with Lancashire cheese or custard. The dining room is rather small so booking is certainly advisable. The well-tended garden acts as an extension for diners when the sun shines; if the weather is on the chilly side, ask to borrow a warm mohair rug.

Open 12-3 6-11 (Sun 12-3) Closed Sun eve **Food** Lunch all wk 12-3 Dinner Mon-Sat 6-9 Set menu available Restaurant menu available all wk 🛢 FREE HOUSE ◾ Longdog, West Berkshire, Wild Weather Ales Ŏ Tutts Clump. 🍷 9 **Facilities** 🐾 (Bar Restaurant Garden) 👶 Children's portions Garden ⚘ Parking WiFi 🚐 (notice required)

BRAISHFIELD
Map 5 SU32

The Wheatsheaf

tel: 01794 368652 **SO51 0QE**
email: thewheatsheafbraishfield@aol.co.uk
dir: *On A3090 from Romsey towards Winchester, left for Braishfield*

Dog-friendly pub with great beer

Close to the Test Valley Way, The Wheatsheaf welcomes walkers, cyclists and especially dogs. Your four-legged friends will appreciate the barrel of treats on the bar while you sample a pint of Sharp's Doom Bar or Flack's Double Drop. The pub has lovely gardens and great views, and there's always something going on – live music and 'jam' nights, quiz nights, theme nights, and 'pie nite' where there's a choice of nine or more home-made pies. In the summer there are barbecues and an annual bottled cider festival. Sandwiches, jackets, baguettes and ploughman's are available, or try one of the other traditional pub dishes such as gammon steak, double egg, chips and peas.

Open all day all wk **Food** Lunch Mon-Sat 12-2, Sun all day **Dinner** Mon-Sat 6-9, Sun all day ⊕ ENTERPRISE INNS ◀ Sharp's Doom Bar, Flack Manor Flack's Double Drop, St Austell Tribute ♂ Thatchers. ♟ 10 **Facilities** Non-diners area ♣ (Bar Garden) ♦ Children's menu Children's portions Play area Garden ♍ Beer festival Cider festival Parking WiFi ▭ (notice required)

BRAMBRIDGE
Map 5 SU42

NEW The Dog & Crook

tel: 01962 712129 **Church Ln SO50 6HZ**
email: karenp.brooks@hotmail.co.uk
dir: *M3 junct 12, A335 towards Eastleigh. At next rdbt into Allbrook Hill signed Brambridge. Right, follow brown pub sign*

Good pub grub and more

Worth a visit when in the Winchester/Southampton area, the 18th-century Dog & Crook provides a wide choice of food. Begin with Welsh rarebit and buttered leeks, or Brussels pâté, then choose between, say, beef Stroganoff with rice, spinach and onions, and grilled pork chop with fondant potato, green bean and pea fricassée, and apple jus. Beer-battered haddock is a pub favourite, and spinach and ricotta tortellini is popular with vegetarians. There's also a special fish menu. For dessert try white chocolate and redcurrant cheesecake with vanilla ice cream, or sponge pudding of the day.

Open all wk 12-3 5-11 (Fri-Sun 12-11) **Food** Lunch all wk 12-3 **Dinner** all wk 5-9 Av main course £12 Restaurant menu available all wk ⊕ ENTERPRISE INNS ◀ Wadworth 6X, Bowman Ales Swift One, Shepherd Neame Spitfire ♂ Aspall, Kingstone Press. ♟ 14 **Facilities** Non-diners area ♣ (Bar Restaurant Garden) ♦ Children's menu Children's portions Garden ♍ Parking WiFi ▭ (notice required)

BRANSGORE
Map 5 SZ19

The Three Tuns Country Inn ◉
PICK OF THE PUBS

tel: 01425 672232 **Ringwood Rd BH23 8JH**
email: threetunsinn@btconnect.com
dir: *1.5m from A35 Walkford junct. 3m from Christchurch & 1m from Hinton Admiral railway station*

A 'must-visit' on a day out in the New Forest

'Chocolate' and 'box' come to mind on first seeing this flower-adorned, thatched, 17th-century inn. In a south-facing garden, surrounded by fields, trees and grazing

ponies, it's just beyond the edge of the New Forest National Park. AA Rosette-standard food is served in all five public areas, including the comfortable, fire-warmed lounge bar that offers Ringwood beers and cider from Burley, both nearby. There's a large outdoor terrace, a 60-seat restaurant and the oak-beamed snug offers biscuits and water for your dog. Menu favourites of spiced chicken Maryland, and steamed steak and kidney suet pudding, join specials of fish and lobster from the coast at Mudeford; braised rabbit with spätzle pasta; and linguine with buffalo mozzarella from ex-Formula One racing driver Jody Scheckter's organic farm. A cider festival takes place during the summer holidays, followed by a beer festival at the end of September.

Open all day all wk 11-11 (Sun 12-10.30) **Food** Lunch Mon-Fri 12-2.15, Sat-Sun 12-9.15 **Dinner** Mon-Fri 6.30-9.15, Sat-Sun 12-9.15 Set menu available Restaurant menu available all wk ⊕ ENTERPRISE INNS ◀ St Austell Tribute, Ringwood Best Bitter & Fortyniner, Exmoor Gold, Otter Bitter, Timothy Taylor, Skinner's Betty Stogs & Cornish Knocker ♂ Rekorderlig, Thatchers Gold & Katy, New Forest Traditional, Westons Stowford Press. ♟ 9 **Facilities** Non-diners area ♣ (Bar Garden Outside area) ♦ Children's menu Children's portions Garden Outside area ♍ Beer festival Cider festival Parking WiFi ▭ (notice required)

BROOK
Map 5 SU21

The Bell Inn ★★★★ INN ◉

tel: 023 8081 2214 **SO43 7HE**
email: bell@bramshaw.co.uk web: www.bellinnbramshaw.co.uk
dir: *M27 junct 1, B3079 signed Brook. Inn 1m on right*

Sumptuous hostelry serving New Forest delights

Owned by the same family for generations, this lavishly furnished inn is more akin to a country house than a pub. Stately in its dimensions, it has a garden with forest views, comfortable dining areas, a huge bar and accommodation for those just can't tear themselves away. In the bar you'll find local ales from Ringwood and Romsey's Flack Manor Brewery, and the AA Rosette menu has its focus firmly on modern British dishes of fresh, local and seasonal provender. Start perhaps with Lymington Bay crab cakes; continue with a trio of lamb rump, rack and faggot; and finish with warm carrot cake, or apple crumble parfait.

Open all day all wk **Food** Lunch 12-3 **Dinner** 6-9.30 Set menu available Restaurant menu available all wk ⊕ FREE HOUSE ◀ Ringwood Best Bitter, Flack Manor Flack Catcher, guest ales ♂ Thatchers, Aspall. **Facilities** Non-diners area ♣ (Bar Restaurant Garden) ♦ Children's menu Children's portions Family room Garden ♍ Parking WiFi ▭ (notice required) **Rooms** 27

BROUGHTON
Map 5 SU33

NEW The Tally Ho

tel: 01794 301280 **High St SO20 8AA**
email: carolyntallyho@yahoo.co.uk
dir: *From x-roads on A30 between Stockbridge & Salisbury take B3084 signed Broughton. Follow pub signs in village*

Idyllic village pub

For walkers and cyclists on the Clarendon Way between the cathedral cities of Winchester and Salisbury, the 300-year-old Tally Ho couldn't be better located. Originally a doctor's surgery before becoming a pub in 1832, it now belongs to top record producer Chris Thomas. Four real ales, among them Ringwood and Cheddar, are on tap as perfect accompaniments to doorstep sandwiches, such as the Broughton Big Boy. Top quality, locally raised meats include buffalo, pork, lamb and venison, with pan-roasted halibut and Selsey crab to appeal to fish lovers. There's create-your-own pizza nights on Thursdays, and roasts on Sundays.

Open all day all wk **Food** Lunch all wk 12-2 Dinner all wk 6-9 Av main course £12.95 Restaurant menu available Fri-Sat ⊕ FREE HOUSE ◼ Ringwood Best Bitter, Butcombe, Cheddar Ales Ö Thatchers Heritage. ♟ 13 **Facilities** Non-diners area ❈ (Bar Garden) ◖◗ Children's menu Children's portions Play area Garden ⊞ Beer festival Cider festival WiFi 🚌 (notice required)

BURLEY
Map 5 SU20

The Burley Inn

tel: 01425 403448 **BH24 4AB**
dir: *4m SE of of Ringwood*

Favoured forest village setting

A great base from which to explore the tracks, paths and rides of the surrounding New Forest National Park, this imposing Edwardian edifice, in neat grounds behind picket fencing, is one of a small local chain of dining pubs combining the best of local real ales – Flack's Double Drop being one – with homely, traditional pub grub from an extensive menu. Toast wintery toes before log fires or relax on the decking patio, looking forward to olde English fish pie or venison casserole, with key lime pie to finish, whilst idly watching free-roaming livestock amble by on the village lanes.

Open all day all wk Closed 25 Dec **Food** all wk 12-9 ⊕ FREE HOUSE ◼ Flack Manor Flack's Double Drop, guest ales Ö Aspall. ♟ 10 **Facilities** Non-diners area ❈ (Bar Outside area) ◖◗ Children's menu Children's portions Outside area ⊞ Parking WiFi 🚌

CADNAM
Map 5 SU31

Sir John Barleycorn

tel: 023 8081 2236 **Old Romsey Rd SO40 2NP**
email: sjb@alcatraz.co.uk
dir: *From Southampton M27 junct 1 into Cadnam*

The oldest inn in the New Forest

The name of this friendly thatched establishment comes from a folksong celebrating the transformation of barley to beer. It is formed from three 12th-century cottages, one of which was reputedly home to the charcoal burner who discovered the body of King William Rufus who was killed by an arrow while hunting

in 1100AD. Beers on offer are Fuller's London Pride and HSB, while ciders are represented by Westons Stowford Press. The menu has something for everyone with quick snacks and sandwiches, a children's menu and dishes like pan-fried sea bass fillet with prawn and spinach risotto; and honey-roast ham, fried eggs and chunky chips.

Open all day all wk 11-11 **Food** Mon-Sat 12-9, Sun 12-8 Set menu available ⊕ FULLER'S ◼ London Pride, George Gale & Co HSB, guest ales Ö Westons Stowford Press, guest cider. ♟ 10 **Facilities** Non-diners area ◖◗ Children's menu Children's portions Family room Garden ⊞ Parking WiFi 🚌 (notice required)

CHALTON
Map 5 SU71

The Red Lion

tel: 023 9259 2246 **PO8 0BG**
email: redlion.chalton@fullers.co.uk
dir: *Just off A3 between Horndean & Petersfield. Follow signs for Chalton*

Traditional English pub with South Downs views

Said to be the oldest pub in Hampshire, dating back to 1147, when it was built to house craftsmen constructing St Michael's church opposite. It retains an olde worlde English charm, with a thatched roof, whitewashed exterior, brass knick-knacks, beams and roaring fires. A large purpose-built dining room is kept busy serving plates of pub grub. The expansive garden gives lovely views of the South Downs, and there's a beer festival on the last weekend in July.

Open all day all wk 11.30-11 (Sun 12-10.30) **Food** Mon-Sat 12-9, Sun 12-8 ⊕ FULLER'S ◼ London Pride, George Gale & Co Seafarers & HSB, guest ales Ö Cornish Orchards, Rekorderlig. ♟ 20 **Facilities** Non-diners area ❈ (Bar Garden) ◖◗ Children's menu Children's portions Garden ⊞ Beer festival Parking WiFi 🚌 (notice required)

CHARTER ALLEY
Map 5 SU55

The White Hart Inn

tel: 01256 850048 **White Hart Ln RG26 5QA**
email: enquiries@whitehartcharteralley.com
dir: *M3 junct 6, A339 towards Newbury. Right signed Ramsdell. Right at church, then 1st left into White Hart Ln*

A must for lovers of good beer

When this free house opened in 1818, on the northern edge of the village overlooking open farmland and woods – just as today – it must have delighted the woodsmen and coach drivers visiting the farrier next door. Real ale pumps lined up on the herringbone-patterned, brick-fronted bar can include Triple fff Moondance, Red Cat Prowler and Bowman Swift One. The regularly changing menu features many pub favourites – steak and Stilton pie; slow-roasted pork belly; and as fresh fish is delivered twice a week all the way from Cornwall, there'll be beer-battered cod and chips.

Open Mon 7-11 Tue-Wed 12-2.30 7-11 Thu-Fri 12-2.30 5.30-11 Sat 12-3 6.30-11 Sun 12-4 Closed 25-26 Dec, 1 Jan, Mon L, Sun eve **Food** Lunch Tue-Sun 12-2 Dinner Tue-Sat 7-9 Av main course £12 ⊕ FREE HOUSE ◼ Triple fff Moondance, Bowman Swift One, Red Cat. ♟ 9 **Facilities** Non-diners area ❈ (Bar Garden Outside area) ◖◗ Children's menu Children's portions Family room Garden Outside area ⊞ Beer festival Parking WiFi 🚌 (notice required)

CHAWTON

Map 5 SU73

The Greyfriar

tel: 01420 83841 **Winchester Rd GU34 1SB**
email: hello@thegreyfriar.co.uk web: www.thegreyfriar.co.uk
dir: *Just off A31 near Alton. Access to Chawton via A31/A32 junct. Follow Jane Austen's House signs. Pub opposite*

Old-fashioned values and family-friendly

Opposite Jane Austen's House Museum stands this 16th-century pub. As well as its friendly atmosphere and delightful village setting, the south-facing suntrap garden is another draw. The pub is Fuller's-owned and offers London Pride and Gale's Seafarers along with great food. An extensive sample menu includes ham hock terrine; and breaded Japenese prawns for starters, followed by a sharing board (Mediterranean or smoked salmon); chilli con carne; red Thai curry; and grilled Asian pork chop. Finish with sticky toffee pudding or lemon posset. Sandwiches and jackets are also available for lunch.

Open all day all wk 12-11 (Sun 12-10.30) **Food** Lunch Mon-Sat 12-2.30, Sun 12-7 Dinner Mon-Sat 6-9.30, Sun 12-7 Restaurant menu available all wk ⊕ FULLER'S ◼ London Pride, George Gale & Co seafarers, seasonal ales ♂ Aspall. ♥ **Facilities** Non-diners area ❀ (Bar Restaurant Garden) ♦♦ Children's portions Garden ⊓ Parking WiFi ▭ (notice required)

CHERITON

Map 5 SU52

The Flower Pots Inn

tel: 01962 771318 **SO24 OQQ**
dir: *A272 towards Petersfield, left onto B3046, pub 0.75m on right*

Popular village pub with its own microbrewery

Known almost universally as The Pots, this pub was once a farmhouse and home to the head gardener of nearby Avington Park. These days, local beer drinkers know the pub well for its award-winning Flowerpots Bitter and Goodens Gold, brewed across the car park in the microbrewery. Simple home-made food includes hearty filled baps, toasted sandwiches, jacket potatoes, cheese and meat ploughman's and different hotpots – chilli con carne, lamb and apricot, steak and ale, spicy mixed bean. A large, safe garden, with a covered patio, allows children to let off steam (under 14s are not allowed in the bar).

Open all wk 12-2.30 6-11 (Sun 12-3 7-10.30) **Food** Lunch all wk 12-1.45 Dinner Mon-Sat 7-8.45 ⊕ FREE HOUSE ◼ Flowerpots Bitter, Goodens Gold and Perridge Ale ♂ Westons Old Rosie. **Facilities** Non-diners area ❀ (Bar Garden) Garden Parking **Notes** ⊗

The Hinton Arms

tel: 01962 771252 **Petersfield Rd SO24 ONH**
email: info@hintonarms.co.uk
dir: *A272 between Petersfield & Winchester*

Great food and colourful floral displays

Weary walkers, cyclists, well-behaved children and dogs are all very welcome at this privately owned bar and restaurant. So too are those interested in the English Civil War keen to follow the trail to the nearby site of the Battle of Cheriton, fought in 1644. Food is a high point, especially the game and fresh fish; portions are reputedly generous. Seasonal menus cover all bases, with dishes such as Malaysian chicken korma; Atlantic wholetail scampi; gammon steak and eggs; sausages and mash; and mushroom Stroganoff. Their real ale policy favours those brewed in Hampshire.

Open all wk 10-3 6-11 (Sat-Sun 10am-11pm) **Food** Lunch Mon-Sat 12-2.30, Sun 12-9.30 Dinner Mon-Sat 6-9.30, Sun 12-9.30 ⊕ FREE HOUSE ◼ Itchen Valley Hampshire Rose, Bowman Ales Swift One & Wallops Wood ♂ Westons Stowford Press. ♥ 12 **Facilities** ❀ (Bar Garden) ♦♦ Children's menu Children's portions Play area Garden ⊓ Parking WiFi ▭ (notice required)

CLANFIELD

Map 5 SU71

The Rising Sun Inn ★★★ INN

tel: 023 9259 6975 **North Ln PO8 ORN**
email: enquiries@therisingsunclanfield.co.uk web: www.therisingsunclanfield.co.uk
dir: *A3(M) then A3 towards Petersfield. Left signed Clanfield. Follow brown inn signs*

Traditional village inn just inside the South Downs National Park

Although it looks two centuries old, the flint-faced Rising Sun was actually built in the 21st century. Apparently, in 1960, its predecessor was constructed in one day, even serving its first pint at 6pm. Today the bar sells a variety of real ales and ciders, as well as a good selection of single malt whiskies. The menu focuses on pub favourites such as beer-battered cod; pan-fried lamb's liver, bacon and onion gravy; ham, egg and chips; and Thai green curry. Vegetarian options, baguettes, sandwiches, jacket potatoes and ploughman's are there too. Tuesday night is steak night, curries are on Thursday and it's Friday for music. The B&B accommodation is popular with walkers and cyclists on the South Downs Way.

Open all day all wk **Food** all wk 12-9 ⊕ ENTERPRISE INNS ◀ George Gale & Co HSB, Ringwood Best Bitter, Sharp's Doom Bar, Timothy Taylor Landlord, guest ales ♂ Westons Old Rosie, Thatchers Gold. ♀ 15 **Facilities** Non-diners area ✿ (All areas) ♦♦ Children's menu Children's portions Garden Outside area ⋔ Beer festival Parking WiFi ▭ (notice required) **Rooms** 3

CROOKHAM VILLAGE　　　　　　　　　Map 5 SU75

The Exchequer

tel: 01252 615336 **Crondall Rd GU51 5SU**
email: bookings@exchequercrookham.co.uk
dir: M3 junct 5, A287 towards Farnham for 5m. Left to Crookham Village

Welcoming dining pub with top-notch ales

Amongst the quiet villages of north Hampshire in the beautiful setting of Crookham Village, this whitewashed free house is just a stone's throw from the A287. The Exchequer serves carefully chosen wines and local ales straight from the cask, and offers a great seasonal menu with dishes featuring the best local produce. Start with a sharing board of meze or perhaps a sweet pepper and goats' cheese tart. Main course dishes include crushed new potato, salmon and smoked haddock fishcake; and roast chicken breast wrapped in Parma ham and stuffed with pâté. Leave room for blackberry and apple crumble with custard. Sandwiches and pub classics are available at lunchtime.

Open all wk 12-3 6-11 (Fri-Sun 11-11) Closed 25 Dec **Food** Lunch Mon-Thu 12-2.30, Fri-Sun 12-9.30 Dinner Mon-Thu 6-9.30, Fri-Sun 12-9.30 ⊕ FREE HOUSE ◀ Andwell, Hogs Back TEA, guest ales ♂ Hogs Back Hazy Hog. ♀ 10 **Facilities** Non-diners area ✿ (Bar Garden Outside area) ♦♦ Children's menu Children's portions Garden Outside area ⋔ Parking WiFi

---

DROXFORD　　　　　　　　　　　　　Map 5 SU61

The Bakers Arms ◉　　　　　　PICK OF THE PUBS

tel: 01489 877533 **High St SO32 3PA**
email: enquiries@thebakersarmsdroxford.com
dir: 10m E of Winchester on A32 between Fareham & Alton. 7m SW of Petersfield

Small village pub with first-rate food

This is an unpretentious, white-painted pub with abundant country charm – the staff are friendly and the locals clearly love the place. The Bowman Brewery a mile away supplies the bar with Swift One and Wallops Wood, so why look any further afield, asks owner Adam Cordery. Also in the bar you'll find home-made Cornish pasties, pickled eggs and onions, and hot filled baguettes, while over the big log fire a blackboard lists the day's AA-Rosette standard main dishes. Among these will be the day's pie, burgers, sausages or steaks; and maybe roasted pheasant breast with pheasant bon bon; creamy goats' cheese, chestnut and spinach linguine; and baked Devon crab with skinny fries and lemon mayo. Adam shoots game or grows much of the produce himself.

Open 11.45-3 6-11 (Sun 12-3) Closed Sun eve **Food** Lunch all wk 12-2 Dinner Mon-Sat 7-9 ⊕ FREE HOUSE ◀ Bowman Ales Swift One & Wallops Wood, guest ales ♂ Thatchers. ♀ 11 **Facilities** Non-diners area ✿ (Bar Restaurant Garden) ♦♦ Children's portions Garden ⋔ Parking WiFi

---

DUMMER　　　　　　　　　　　　　Map 5 SU54

The Queen Inn

tel: 01256 397367 **Down St RG25 2AD**
email: clivechalcraft@btinternet.com
dir: From M3 junct 7 follow Dummer signs

Traditional country inn just minutes from the M3

Dine by candlelight at this 16th-century, low-beamed inn with a huge open log fire. Fresh hands since the end of 2015 have maintained the real ale portfolio of Doom

Bar, Otter and guests, and the menu continues to offer a wide choice: chargrilled rump and fillet steaks; burgers, including one so-called 'bad boy' jalapeño and cheese; teriyaki salmon with stir-fried noodles; chef's curry of the day; and five-bean chilli with rice. Children are welcome to have a small portion of what mum and dad have chosen, but can fall back on their own menu if all appeals fail. Two roasts on Sundays and a specials board.

Open all wk 11-3 6-11 (Sun 12-3 7-10.30) **Food** Lunch all wk 12-2.30 Dinner Mon-Sat 6.30-9.30, Sun 7-9 ⊕ ENTERPRISE INNS ◀ Otter Bitter, Sharp's Doom Bar, guest ale ♂ Thatchers Gold, Westons Stowford Press. ♀ 9 **Facilities** Non-diners area ♦♦ Children's menu Children's portions Garden Parking WiFi

---

The Sun Inn

tel: 01256 397234 **Winchester Road A30 RG25 2DJ**
email: info@suninndummer.com
dir: M3 junct 7, A30 (Winchester Rd) towards Basingstoke. Left onto A30 towards Winchester. Inn on right

Certainly worth a detour from a motorway journey

The Sun has stood for many years alongside the main coaching route from London to Exeter, today's A30. Passing traffic is not a problem since most West Country travellers now use the M3, accessible from nearby junction 7. Moondance from Triple fff takes pole position in the bar, while in the restaurant the young chef's well-conceived menu might list hand dived scallops with cauliflower, couscous, bacon and mixed peppers; pan-fried duck breast with sweet potato fondant, parsnips, roasted pecans and red wine jus; Brickworth Down bone-in sirloin steak with triple-cooked chips, alongside pub classics such as Bracken Farm pork sausages and mash. A lovely garden lies at the back.

Open all wk 12-11 **Food** Lunch Mon-Fri 12-2.30, Sat-Sun 12-3 Dinner Mon-Sat 6-9 Av main course £15.95 ⊕ FREE HOUSE ◀ Triple fff Moondance, Sharp's Doom Bar ♂ Symonds. ♀ 8 **Facilities** Non-diners area ✿ (Bar Garden) ♦♦ Children's portions Play area Garden ⋔ Parking WiFi ▭

DUNBRIDGE　　　　　　　　　　　　Map 5 SU32

The Mill Arms ★★★★ INN

tel: 01794 340401 **Barley Hill SO51 0LF**
email: mill.arms@btconnect.com **web:** www.millarms.co.uk
dir: From Romsey take A3057 signed Stockbridge & Winchester. Left onto B3084 through Awbridge to Dunbridge. Pub on left before rail crossing

Smart country pub offering good food not far from the River Test

This attractive Victorian country inn has flagstone floors, oak beams and open fires – it's traditional and welcoming, and in a great location in the heart of the Test Valley close to the River Test, one of the finest chalk streams in the world. Not surprisingly, the pub is popular with fly fishermen from far and wide. On the menu you'll find everything from patatas bravas and chorizo, to a good choice of sandwiches, as well as more substantial dishes like game cobbler or beer battered fish and chips. There's also a function room, a skittle alley and large landscaped gardens.

Open all day Closed 25 Dec, Sun eve **Food** Lunch Mon-Sat 12-3, Sun 12-4 Dinner Mon-Sat 6-9 ⊕ ENTERPRISE INNS ◀ Flack Manor Flack's Double Drop, guest ales ♂ Symonds, Westons Rosie's Pig. ♀ 10 **Facilities** Non-diners area ✿ (Bar Restaurant Garden) ♦♦ Children's menu Children's portions Garden ⋔ Parking WiFi ▭ (notice required) **Rooms** 6

DURLEY Map 5 SU51

The Robin Hood

tel: 01489 860229 **Durley St SO32 2AA**
email: robinhooddurley@gmail.com

A village pub with lots of personality

The Robin Hood is a friendly, welcoming place. There's a cosy seating area with comfy sofas, not one but two open fires and loos which are hidden behind a false bookcase door. The garden is huge, with a play area for children that includes a pirate ship. If you're (sadly) too old to make use of that, there's a decked area with lovely country views for relaxing with drinks and for alfresco dining. In the bar you'll find Black Sheep and Timothy Taylor Landlord, and on the menu and specials board are dishes such as smoked haddock and gruyère fishcakes with chive sauce; puff pastry steak and ale pie, new crushed potatoes and veg; and black cherry Bakewell and clotted cream.

Open all wk 11-3 5.30-11 (Sun 11-10.30) Closed 25 Dec **Food** Lunch Mon-Sat 12-2, Sun 12-8.30 Dinner Mon-Thu 6-9, Fri-Sat 6-9.30, Sun 12-8.30 ⊕ GREENE KING ◀ Timothy Taylor Landlord, Black Sheep, Robin Hood House Bitter (own brew), guest ales ♂ Aspall. ♟ 14 **Facilities** Non-diners area ❅ (Bar Garden Outside area) ♦♦ Children's menu Children's portions Play area Garden Outside area ⋒ Parking WiFi ▦ (notice required)

EAST BOLDRE Map 5 SU30

Turfcutters Arms

tel: 01590 612331 **Main Rd SO42 7WL**
email: enquiries.turfcutters@gmail.com
dir: *From Beaulieu take B3055 towards Brockenhurst. Left at Hatchet Pond onto B3054 towards Lymington, turn left, follow signs for East Boldre. Pub approx 0.5m*

Off the beaten track and offering good value food

Five miles south of Beaulieu, this New Forest pub, easily recognised by its white picket fence, attracts cyclists, ramblers, dog-walkers and locals all year round. In winter the open fires warm the cockles, while the lovely garden comes into its own in summer. Good beer including Ringwood and draught ciders such as Thatchers complement a menu of unpretentious pub grub including baguettes, jacket potatoes and main meals such as curry of the day; Billingsgate fish pie; home-cooked Hampshire ham, a brace of free-range eggs and chips; and veggie quiche of the day. Children have their own menu, and canine treats are handed out at the bar. Maybe time a visit for their annual beer festival.

Open all day all wk **Food** Lunch Mon-Fri 12-2.30, Sat 12-3, Sun 12-8 Dinner Mon-Tue 6-8, Wed-Sat 6-9, Sun 12-8 Av main course £11.95 Set menu available ⊕ ENTERPRISE INNS ◀ Ringwood Best Bitter, Fortyniner, guest ales ♂ Thatchers Gold. **Facilities** Non-diners area ❅ (Bar Restaurant Garden) ♦♦ Children's menu Children's portions Play area Garden ⋒ Beer festival Parking WiFi ▦ (notice required)

EAST END Map 5 SZ39

The East End Arms

PICK OF THE PUBS

tel: 01590 626223 **Main Rd SO41 5SY**
email: manager@eastendarms.co.uk
dir: *From Lymington towards Beaulieu (past Isle of Wight ferry), 3m to East End*

Striking all the right notes

On the southern edge of the New Forest National Park, just a short stroll from the Solent and close to the delightful village of Buckler's Hard, The East End Arms is a happy mix of community village inn and restaurant, with menus drawing on local produce and changing daily. The inviting Foresters Bar is pleasingly old-fashioned, with flagstoned floors and roaring fire adding to the pleasure of a gravity-drawn pint of ale, or a bottle of Thatchers cider. Lunchtime sandwiches are served on granary or white bloomer with French fries or crisps. The bright and airy restaurant is decorated with photographs of musicians, reflecting the past of the pub's owner, Dire Straits' bass player John Illsley. Starters such as ham hock and pigeon terrine could be followed by garlic and thyme roast poussin with wild mushrooms, Savoy cabbage and Parmentier potatoes.

Open all wk 11.30-3 5-11 (Fri-Sat 11.30-11 Sun 12-10.30) **Food** Lunch all wk 12-2.30 Dinner Mon-Sat 7-9 ⊕ FREE HOUSE ◀ Ringwood Best Bitter & Fortyniner, weekly changing guest ales ♂ Thatchers Gold. **Facilities** Non-diners area ❅ (Bar Garden Outside area) ♦♦ Children's portions Garden Outside area ⋒ Parking WiFi

EAST MEON Map 5 SU62

Ye Olde George Inn

tel: 01730 823481 **Church St GU32 1NH**
email: yeoldegeorge@live.co.uk
dir: *S of A272 (Winchester to Petersfield road). 1.5m from Petersfield turn left opposite church*

Medieval inn set in a lovely village

In the beautiful countryside of the Meon Valley, the setting for this delightful 15th-century coaching inn is hard to beat. The village boasts a magnificent Norman church where tapestry designs similar to Bayeux can be found. If you want heavy beams, inglenook fireplaces and wooden floors, look no further – they're all here, creating an ideal atmosphere for enjoy a pint of Badger First Call or Westons cider. The kitchen team make everything in house for their monthly-changing menus (except the ice cream which is made on a local farm) – so expect dishes such as salt and pepper squid; potato skin and leek soup, poached egg and parmesan crisp; Casterbridge 28-day aged rib-eye steak with triple-cooked chips; and roasted cod loin with pea, chorizo and mint risotto. There are tables outside on the pretty patio.

Open all wk 11-3 6-11 (Sun 11-10) Closed 25 Dec, 26 Dec eve & 1 Jan eve **Food** Lunch Mon-Sat 12-2.30, Sun 12-3 Dinner Mon-Sat 6.30-9.30, Sun 6.30-9 ⊕ HALL & WOODHOUSE ◀ K&B Sussex, Tanglefoot, Badger First Call ♂ Westons Stowford Press. ♟ 9 **Facilities** Non-diners area ❅ (Bar Outside area) ♦♦ Children's menu Children's portions Outside area ⋒ Parking WiFi ▦ (notice required)

EASTON Map 5 SU53

The Chestnut Horse

tel: 01962 779257 **SO21 1EG**
email: info@thechestnuthorse.com
dir: *M3 junct 9, A33 towards Basingstoke, then B3047. 2nd right, 1st left*

Hidden away in the idyllic Itchen Valley

This gem of a 16th-century pub has an abundance of traditional English character and atmosphere. Old tankards hang from the low-beamed ceilings in the two bar areas, and a large open fire is the central focus through the winter months. Hall & Woodhouse beers, such as Pickled Partridge and Chestnut Horse Special, along with Westons ciders, can be enjoyed in the bar or the garden. A typical menu starts with goats' cheese open ravioli with fig purée, rocket salad and balsamic dressing; or herrings à la Baltique; then continues with seafood broth with crusty bread; or herb-crusted rack of lamb with olive tapenade and sweetbreads. Walnut sticky toffee pudding, or apple and rhubarb crumble round things off nicely.

Open all wk 12-3.30 5.30-11 (Fri-Sat 12-11.30 Sun 12-10.30) **Food** Lunch Mon-Sat 12-2.30, Sun 12-8 Dinner Mon-Sat 6-9.30, Sun 12-8 Set menu available ⊕ HALL & WOODHOUSE ◀ Badger First Gold & Pickled Partridge, Chestnut Horse Special ♂ Westons Stowford Press & Old Rosie. ♟ 12 **Facilities** Non-diners area ❅ (Bar Garden) ♦♦ Children's menu Children's portions Garden ⋒ Beer festival Parking WiFi ▦

EAST STRATTON
Map 5 SU54

Northbrook Arms

tel: 01962 774150 **SO21 3DU**
email: thenorthbrook@aol.co.uk
dir: *Follow brown pub sign from A33, 4m S of junct with A303*

Social centre of a small but perfectly formed village

Memo to Hollywood: if you need an English pub location, look no further. Bang opposite the village green and architecturally perfect, it endears itself to local bar-proppers with six or seven real ales and three ciders, a May beer festival and a September cider celebration. The compact menu gets the thumbs up too, with dishes such as spicy duck parcels with chilli and apple purée; wild mushroom and thyme mille feuille; baked lemon and pepper salmon; and buttermilk pudding with cardamom strawberries. There are light bites and deli options such as Indian potato cake, and smoked cod Scotch egg.

Open all day all wk **Food** Lunch all wk 12-3 Dinner all wk 6-9 ⊕ FREE HOUSE ◀ Otter, Bowman Swift One, Flack Manor Flack's Double Drop, Amber Sharp's Cornish Coaster, Alfred's Saxon Bronze Ò Aspall, Mr Whiteheads, Westons Stowford Press. ₹ 12 **Facilities** Non-diners area ❤ (All areas) ◀ Children's menu Children's portions Play area Garden Outside area ⧟ Beer festival Cider festival Parking WiFi ⛟ (notice required)

EMSWORTH
Map 5 SU70

The Sussex Brewery

tel: 01243 371533 **36 Main Rd PO10 8AU**
email: info@sussexbrewery.com
dir: *On A259, E of Emsworth towards Chichester*

Friendly roadside pub with a winning ale-and-sausage combination

No prizes for guessing this pub was once a brewery, and this ethos continues with its pride in offering good honestly-priced food and drink served by friendly staff in a happy atmosphere. Young's ales sit beside guests, with Addlestones and Thatchers ciders served too. Locally made sausages form the backbone of the menu, and have done for many a year; differing flavours, including a special made with Young's bitter, are served with creamy mash, caramelised onions and gravy. Equally in demand are light bites such a bucket of whitebait with home-made tartare sauce, and main courses like ale-battered hake with chips.

Open all day all wk **Food** Lunch Mon-Sat 12-2.30, Sun 12-3 Dinner Mon-Sat 6-9, Sun 6.30-9 Restaurant menu available all wk ⊕ YOUNG'S ◀ London Gold & Special, St Austell Tribute, Courage Directors Ò Addlestones, Thatchers. ₹ 12 **Facilities** Non-diners area ❤ (Bar Outside area) ◀ Children's portions Outside area ⧟ Parking WiFi ⛟ (notice required)

EVERSLEY
Map 5 SU76

The Golden Pot
PICK OF THE PUBS

tel: 0118 973 2104 **Reading Rd RG27 0NB**
email: info@golden-pot.co.uk
dir: *Between Reading & Camberley on B3272 approx 0.25m from Eversley cricket ground*

Innovative home-cooked food and local craft beers

Set beside meadows in the Long River valley, this creeper-clad pub, a jigsaw of interlinked cottages, has the charm of ages past. Three centuries of tradition ooze from the run of public spaces and the atmospheric, beamed 'The Pottery' restaurant suite. A double-sided warming fire connects the bar and restaurant, while outside the Snug and Vineyard, surrounded by colourful tubs and hanging baskets, are just

the ticket for summer relaxation. Licensee Gary Pope is a strong supporter of microbrewery beers and sources an impressive range of bitters from brewers such as Ascot and Hammerpot. The inspiring menu here is equally eclectic, with starters such as duck rillettes with shallot purée and roasted garlic setting the standard. Mains can include pan-fried partridge breasts, creamed cabbage and bacon with parsnip purée. 21-day aged Angus steaks are a house speciality, whilst a phenomenal range of fish is sourced daily from Brixham's fishmarket. The wine list has 36 bins to choose from.

Open all day all wk 11.30-11 **Food** Lunch Mon-Fri 12-2.30, Sat-Sun all day Dinner Mon-Fri 5.30-10, Sat-Sun all day Restaurant menu available all wk ⊕ FREE HOUSE ◀ Andwell, Bowman, Ascot, Rebellion, Windsor & Eton, Upham Ale, Church End, Longdog Ales, Hammerpot Ales, guest ale Ò Rekorderlig, Aspall, Henney's, Westons Stowford Press. ₹ 9 **Facilities** Non-diners area ❤ (Bar Garden) ◀ Children's menu Children's portions Garden ⧟ Beer festival Cider festival Parking WiFi ⛟ (notice required)

EVERSLEY CROSS
Map 5 SU76

The Chequers

tel: 0118 402 7065 **RG27 0NS**
email: thechequers@peachpubs.com
dir: *On B3272 (W of Yateley) in village centre*

Welcoming and warm-hearted dining-pub

Belonging to the Peach Pubs group, which pursues the tenet of 'small is beautiful', The Chequers welcomes all-comers from breakfast onwards. Quality is the focus for all aspects of the operation, from ales such as Hogs Back to a carte packed with seasonal goodies. The deli boards are generous: choose either the butcher's board, the veggie board, the cheese board or the fish board. Brasserie-type dishes range from Devon crab and artichoke gratin with crusty bread as a starter to Cornish lamb cutlets and broad bean houmous, parmentier potatoes and tomato and mint salsa; or Hampshire honey-glazed ham hock and sauerkraut with beer gravy for a main course.

Open all day all wk Closed 25 Dec **Food** Mon-Sat 12-10, Sun 12-9 ⊕ FREE HOUSE/ PEACH PUBS ◀ Hogs Back TEA, Sharp's Doom Bar Ò Aspall. ₹ **Facilities** Non-diners area ❤ (Bar Garden) ◀ Children's portions Garden ⧟ Beer festival Parking WiFi ⛟ (notice required)

EXTON
Map 5 SU62

The Shoe Inn

tel: 01489 877526 **Shoe Ln SO32 3NT**
email: theshoeexton@googlemail.com
dir: *On A32 between Fareham & Alton*

Good food with many ingredients from the pub's own garden

On warmer days, you can enjoy views of Old Winchester Hill from the garden of this popular pub in the heart of the Meon Valley. Food is key – local ingredients include those from its ever-expanding herb and vegetable garden. A typical selection of dishes could include local home-made pea and ham soup; Southdown lamb's liver, bacon, onion gravy and mashed potato; beer battered haddock, hand-cut chips and mushy peas. The bar offers well-kept Wadworth ales, weekly changing guest ales, and 11 wines served by the glass.

Open all wk 11-3 6-11 (Sat-Sun all day) Closed 25 Dec **Food** Lunch all wk 12-2.15 Dinner all wk 6-9 ⊕ WADWORTH ◀ 6X, Henry's Original IPA, The Bishop's Tipple, guest ales Ò Westons Stowford Press. ₹ 11 **Facilities** ❤ (Bar Garden) ◀ Children's menu Children's portions Garden ⧟ Parking

FORDINGBRIDGE
Map 5 SU11

The Augustus John

tel: 01425 652098 **116 Station Rd SP6 1DG**
email: enquiries@augustusjohnfordingbridge.co.uk
dir: *12m S of Salisbury on A338 towards Ringwood*

Village pub with artistic associations

The Welsh painter Augustus John lived in Fordingbridge until his death in 1961; he was a regular when the pub served the now long-vanished, adjacent railway station. Today, under landlord Bryan Greenwood, Ringwood and guest real ales continue to attract locals and visitors. So too do such characteristic dishes as ham hock and parsley terrine, pickled vegetables and sourdough toast; free-range pork schnitzel, black pudding, fried duck egg, parsley butter and warm potato salad; and sea bass, purple sprouting broccoli with chorizo and mussel sauce.

Open all wk 12-2.30 6-10.30 (Fri-Sat 12-2.30 5-11.30 Sun 12-3 7-10) **Food** Lunch all wk 12-2.30 Dinner Mon-Sat 6.30-9 (booking advised Fri-Sun) Set menu available ⊕ MARSTON'S ◀ Ringwood Best Bitter & Fortyniner, guest ale ♻ Westons Stowford Press, Addlestones. **Facilities** Non-diners area ✿ (Bar Garden) ♦ Children's menu Children's portions Garden ﹄ Parking WiFi ▄ (notice required)

FREEFOLK
Map 5 SU44

The Watership Down Inn

tel: 01256 892254 **RG28 7NJ**
email: enquiries@watershipdowninn.com
dir: *From Whitchurch take B3400 towards Basingstoke. Pub in 1.5m*

19th-century Test Valley country pub with large garden

The downland that Richard Adams made famous in his classic 1972 novel lies four miles north of here. The inn's country-style interior features oak and quarry-tile flooring, a wood-burner and hardwood bar, from where some 100 different locally brewed real ales are offered – over time, of course. The wine list is similarly comprehensive. At lunchtime snails in garlic butter may be available; more conventional possibilities are beer-battered haddock, and home-made pie of the day. Evening choices could well include brie-filled chicken supreme in Parma ham; an 8oz rib-eye steak; and wild mushroom, thyme and pumpkin risotto.

Open all wk 12-3 6-11 (Fri-Sun all day) ⊕ FREE HOUSE ◀ Rotating guest ales. **Facilities** ✿ (Bar Garden) ♦ Children's menu Children's portions Play area Garden Parking WiFi

HANNINGTON
Map 5 SU55

The Vine at Hannington

tel: 01635 298525 **RG26 5TX**
email: info@thevineathannington.co.uk
dir: *Follow Hannington signs from A339 between Basingstoke & Kingsclere*

A favourite with walkers and cyclists

Given the nature of North Hampshire's rolling chalk downland, you can expect rambling and cycling devotees to patronise this gabled Victorian inn. A wood-burning stove heats the spacious, traditionally furnished bar areas and conservatory. Seasonal menus and daily specials feature three platters – vegetarian, antipasti meat and fish; chicken or Vegetable tikka masala;

home-baked ham, egg and chips; broccoli and cauliflower cheesy bake; and The Vine beefburger with cheddar or blue cheese. Sharp's Doom Bar and guest ales, 11 wines by the glass as well as teas, coffee and hot chocolate are always available. There is a large, secure garden with a children's play area.

Open 12-3 6-11 (Sat all day Sun 12-5) Closed Mon **Food** Lunch Tue-Sat 12-2, Sun 12-4 Dinner Tue-Sat 6-9 ⊕ PUNCH TAVERNS ◀ Sharp's Doom Bar, guest ales ♻ Thatchers Gold. ♇ 11 **Facilities** Non-diners area ✿ (Bar Restaurant Garden) ♦ Children's menu Children's portions Play area Family room Garden ﹄ Beer festival Parking WiFi ▄ (notice required)

HAVANT
Map 5 SU70

The Wheelwright's Arms

tel: 023 9247 6502 **27 Emsworth Rd PO9 2SN**
email: info@wheelwrightshavant.co.uk
dir: *A27 into Emsworth Rd towards Havant. Pub on right*

Character pub in capable hands

The Upham Group are owners of this handsome, twin-gabled pub and they supply the real ales – Tipster, Punter and Stakes which are made using only English hops; the cider is Orchard Pig Reveller. At lunch there's honey- and mustard-glazed ham; ale-battered hake; or fried Havant rabbit perhaps. For dinner, pressed smoked mackerel, River Test trout and saffron potato terrine with Alresford watercress; then steak and kidney suet pudding; and finally Wheelwright's waffle, strawberries and cream. Picking up on the pub's name, over-65s can choose from the Pounds & Penny Farthings menu, children from one called Trikes.

Open all day all wk **Food** Lunch 12-3 Dinner 6-9.30 ⊕ UPHAM GROUP ◀ Punter, Tipster & Stakes ♻ Orchard Pig Reveller. ♇ 10 **Facilities** Non-diners area ✿ (Bar Restaurant Outside area) ♦ Children's menu Children's portions Outside area ﹄ Parking WiFi ▄ (notice required)

HAWKLEY
Map 5 SU72

The Hawkley Inn ★★★★ INN

tel: 01730 827205 **Pococks Ln GU33 6NE**
email: info@hawkleyinn.co.uk **web:** www.hawkleyinn.co.uk
dir: *From A3 (Liss rdbt) towards Liss on B3006. Right at Spread Eagle, in 2.5m left into Pococks Ln*

Friendly pub with seriously good food

An inn sign saying 'Free Hoose' owes something to the moose head hanging above one of the fires. It sums up this pub's quirky decor and relaxed atmosphere. With seven beer engines, the pub is well known to local real ale enthusiasts and cider lovers; a festival takes place over June's first weekend. If not eating, you can just enjoy your drink in the garden or on a wooden bench (with cushions) right beside the narrow country lane. Menus change daily, and along with pub classics, proffer the likes of pan-fried sea bass, asparagus, crisp Parma ham and pesto; or pork belly with pea purée, butternut squash and sauté potatoes. These, and the vegetarian specials, are all locally sourced and freshly prepared on the premises, and any dietary need can be catered for.

Open all wk Mon-Fri 12-3 5.30-11 (Sat-Sun all day) **Food** Lunch Mon-Sat 12-2, Sun 12-4 Dinner Mon-Sat 6-9 Set menu available ⊕ FREE HOUSE ◀ 7 constantly changing ales ♻ Aspall, Thatchers. ♇ 17 **Facilities** Non-diners area ✿ (Bar Restaurant Garden) ♦ Children's portions Garden ﹄ Beer festival WiFi ▄ (notice required) **Rooms** 5

HERRIARD — Map 5 SU64

The Fur & Feathers

tel: 01256 384170 **Herriard Rd RG25 2PN**
email: bookings@thefurandfeathers.co.uk
dir: *From Basingstoke take A339 towards Alton. After Herriard follow pub signs. Turn left to pub*

Bag a table in the garden when the weather allows

Its high-ceilinged Victorian proportions translate into light and airy spaces for drinkers and diners, and comfort too, with log-burning fireplaces at each end of the bar. Purpose-built 120 years ago for local farm workers, The Fur & Feathers has to this day obligations in the upkeep of the church roof. In the bar, a trio of ales are rotated, and menus of modern British cooking of local sourced ingredients are perused. Typical dishes are the fish platter — smoked mackerel pâté, smoked salmon, bubbly-battered prawns, large shell-on prawn and sweet chilli dipping sauce; Herriard-shot pheasant casserole, mini pheasant leg pie, creamy mash and vegetables; and twice baked Lyburn's Old Winchester cheese and chive soufflé. A large garden hosts entertainment, and is home to chickens laying eggs for the pub's kitchen.

Open Tue-Thu 12-3 5-11 (Fri-Sat 12-11 Sun 12-6) Closed 1wk end of Dec, Sun eve & Mon **Food** Lunch Tue-Sat 12-2, Sun 12-3 Dinner Tue-Sat 6.30-9 Restaurant menu available Tue-Sun ⊕ FREE HOUSE ◀ Local ales, rotating Flack Manor Flack's Double Drop, Hogs Back, Sharp's, Wild Weather Ales, Long Dog, Red Cat ♂ Hogs Back Hazy Hog, Sharp's Orchard. ☻ 28 **Facilities** Non-diners area ♣ Children's menu Children's portions Garden ⌁ Parking WiFi ▥ (notice required)

HIGHCLERE — Map 5 SU45

The Yew Tree ★★★★ RR ◉◉

tel: 01635 253360 **Hollington Cross, Andover Rd RG20 9SE**
email: info@theyewtree.co.uk **web:** www.theyewtree.co.uk
dir: *M4 junct 13, A34 S, 4th junct on left signed Highclere/Wash Common, turn right towards Andover A343, inn on right*

Delightful 17th-century pub

After visiting nearby Highclere Castle, where *Downton Abbey* was filmed, have lunch here. Or vice versa. Either way, enjoy its high standards of food and service, starting in the bar with tartan high back seats and comfy leather chairs, which offers 13 wines by the glass, real ales from the Two Cocks Brewery and Orchard Pig Reveller cider. Admired for his locally sourced fresh fish and game, chef Simon Davis presents frequently-changing menus featuring bar snacks, sharing plates and, typically, salt and pepper Brixham squid with mango, chilli and lime dressing; Laverstoke Park mozzarella crostini with chargrilled aubergine; and wild line-caught black bream with squid and potato chowder.

Open all day all wk **Food** Lunch all wk 12-2.30 Dinner Mon-Sat 6.30-9.30, Sun 7-8.30 ⊕ CIRRUS INNS ◀ Two Cocks Cavalier, Ringwood Best Bitter, Ramsbury Gold ♂ Orchard Pig Reveller. ☻ 13 **Facilities** Non-diners area ♣ (Bar Restaurant Garden) ♦ Children's menu Children's portions Garden ⌁ Parking WiFi ▥ (notice required) **Rooms** 8

HOOK — Map 5 SU75

The Hogget

tel: 01256 763009 **London Rd, Hook Common RG27 9JJ**
email: home@hogget.co.uk
dir: *M3 junct 5, A30, 0.5m, between Hook & Basingstoke*

Value for money just off the M3

Just off the London Road, The Hogget goes from strength to strength, and its reputation for good food and service continues to grow. Ringwood Razorback or Fortyniner can be found at the bar. In addition to sandwiches, nibbles and sharing options there are carefully prepared English favourites such as chicken Milanese;

slow-cooked oxtail ragù tagliatelle; roasted pumpkin and thyme risotto; and pub favourites, typically beef chilli con carne; and pie of the day.

Open all wk 12-3 5.30-11 (Sat 12-11 Sun 12-10.30) Closed 25-26 Dec **Food** Lunch all wk 12-2.30 Dinner all wk 6.30-9 Av main course £11-£14 ⊕ MARSTON'S ◀ Ringwood Razorback & Fortyniner, guest ales ♂ Stowford Press. ☻ 12 **Facilities** Non-diners area ♣ (Bar Outside area) ♦ Children's menu Children's portions Outside area ⌁ Parking WiFi

HOUGHTON — Map 5 SU33

The Boot Inn

tel: 01794 388310 **SO20 6LH**
email: bootinnhoughton@btconnect.com
dir: *Phone for detailed directions*

Quality pub dining with fishing by arrangement

The River Test is renowned as one of the world's best fly fishing waters, and The Boot enjoys a tranquil location on its banks. The 18th-century timber-framed bar serves a choice of beers and ciders, while its restaurant strives to serve good food without earning the gastro-pub sobriquet. In the bar you can choose from a selection of baguettes, salads, or the likes of faggots with crushed new potatoes, bacon, peas and onion gravy; while the restaurant offers three cheese and cherry tomato tart; roasted vegetable linguine with pesto and garlic bread; or haddock mornay with mash, broad beans and prawns.

Open all wk 10-3 6-11 **Food** Lunch all wk 12-2 Dinner Tue-Sat 6.30-9 Restaurant menu available Lunch all wk, Dinner Tue-Sat ⊕ FREE HOUSE ◀ Ringwood Best Bitter, Flack Manor Flack's Double Drop, Red Cat Scratch ♂ Westons Stowford Press. ☻ 10 **Facilities** Non-diners area ♣ (Bar Garden Outside area) ♦ Children's menu Children's portions Garden Outside area ⌁ Parking WiFi ▥ (notice required)

HURSLEY — Map 5 SU42

The Dolphin Inn

tel: 01962 775209 **SO21 2JY**
email: thedolphinhursley@mail.com
dir: *Phone for detailed directions*

16th-century coaching inn close to South Downs National Park

Like most of the village, this old coaching inn with magnificent chimneys once belonged to the Hursley Estate, which is now owned by IBM. It was built between 1540 and 1560, reputedly using timbers from a Tudor warship called HMS *Dolphin* (today's less glamorous 'ship' is a shore establishment in Gosport). In the beamed bars you'll find Ringwood Razorback, Sharp's Doom Bar and Timothy Taylor Landlord plus Aspall and Stowford Press ciders. In addition to sandwiches, baguettes and jacket potatoes, favourites include sausage and mash; lamb's liver and bacon; and beer battered cod and chips.

Open all day all wk Mon-Sat 11-11 (Sun 12-10.30) **Food** Lunch Mon-Sat 12-2.30, Sun 12-8.30 Dinner Mon-Thu 6-9, Fri-Sat 6.30-9.30, Sun 12-8.30 Av main course £10 ⊕ ENTERPRISE INNS ◀ Ringwood Razorback, Sharp's Doom Bar, Timothy Taylor Landlord ♂ Thatchers, Aspall, Westons Stowford Press. ☻ 12 **Facilities** Non-diners area ♣ (Bar Garden) ♦ Children's menu Children's portions Play area Family room Garden ⌁ Beer festival Parking ▥ (notice required)

The Kings Head ★★★★ INN ◉

tel: 01962 775208 **Main Rd SO21 2JW**
email: enquiries@kingsheadhursley.co.uk **web:** www.kingsheadhursley.co.uk
dir: *On A3090 between Winchester & Romsey*

Country tavern with touches of luxury

A picturesque drive out of Winchester brings you to this creeper clad Georgian coaching inn, now managed by Mark and Penny Thornhill. Their enthusiasm for all things local shines through in their warm hospitality, and the pub is a member of

continued

HURSLEY *continued*

the Sustainable Restaurant Association. Ales include Flack Manor, while those in need of a sharpener should look to the list of 25 gins. Lunchtime small plates may include asparagus ravioli with Old Winchester cheese shavings. For dinner, a partridge and rabbit vol-au-vent with roasted Hursley pear purée could be followed by slow-roasted haunch of Hampshire venison. Round off with crème caramel with rum-soaked golden raisins and candied orange peel.

Open all day all wk 7.30am-11pm **Food** all wk 12-9 Av main course £15 Set menu available ⊕ CIRRUS INNS ◼ Sharp's Doom Bar, Ringwood, Flack Manor, guest ale ♻ Orchard Pig. ⏦ 10 **Facilities** Non-diners area ✿ (Bar Garden) ♦◗ Children's menu Children's portions Garden ⋒ Beer festival Parking WiFi ▭ (notice required) **Rooms** 8

HURSTBOURNE TARRANT	Map 5 SU35

NEW The George and Dragon ★★★★ INN ◉

tel: 01264 736277 **The Square SP11 0AA**
email: info@georgeanddragon.com **web:** www.georgeanddragon.com
dir: *On A343 in village centre*

Stylishly reborn old coaching inn

On the old coach road between Newbury and Andover, the 16th-century George and Dragon reopened its doors in 2014 following a year-long restoration. The big bay window is where travellers would eat and drink while keeping an eye out for their coach, well known for its all-too-brief stops. House beer is Betteridge's brewed about a hundred metres away, the cider is Purbeck's Dorset Draft, and carefully chosen wines are available by the glass and carafe. On the easy-to-digest, seasonal menu might be venison carpaccio with smoked parsnip purée; roasted monkfish with pulled pork raviolo and bean, pea and pancetta broth; and Isle of Wight Blue cheese gnocchi.

Open all day all wk **Food** Lunch Mon-Sat 12-2.30, Sun 12-3 Dinner Mon-Sat 6-9.30, Sun 6-9 Av main course £12 Set menu available ⊕ FREE HOUSE ◼ Betteridge's, Upham Punter, Andwell King John ♻ Purbeck Dorset Draft. ⏦ 12 **Facilities** Non-diners area ✿ (All areas) ♦◗ Children's menu Children's portions Garden Outside area ⋒ Parking WiFi ▭ (notice required) **Rooms** 8

LEE-ON-THE-SOLENT	Map 5 SU50

The Bun Penny

tel: 023 9255 0214 **36 Manor Way PO13 9JH**
email: bar@bunpenny.co.uk **web:** www.bunpenny.co.uk
dir: *From Fareham take B3385 to Lee-on-the-Solent. Pub 300yds before High St*

Classic country free house close to the water

A short walk from the waterfront, this former farmhouse occupies a prominent position on the road into Lee-on-the-Solent. Every inch a classic country free house,

it has a large patio area at the front and an extensive back garden that's ideal for summer relaxation, while real fires and cosy corners are welcome in winter. Otter beer is sold alongside ales from the local breweries. A typical meal might be a home-made deep filled shortcrust pie; a pub favourite like slow-cooked pork belly with apple and thyme; or one of the fresh fish dishes. Tapas, sandwiches, wraps, salads and omelettes are offered too.

Open all day all wk 11-11 (Fri-Sat 11am-mdnt Sun 12-10) **Food** Lunch Mon-Sat 12-2.30, Sun 12-7 Dinner Mon-Sat 6-9, Sun 12-7 ⊕ FREE HOUSE ◼ Otter Bitter, Oakleaf Hole Hearted, St Austell Tribute, guest ales ♻ Westons. ⏦ 13 **Facilities** Non-diners area ✿ (Bar Garden) ♦◗ Children's menu Children's portions Garden ⋒ Cider festival Parking WiFi ▭ (notice required)

LISS	Map 5 SU72

The Jolly Drover ★★★★ INN

tel: 01730 893137 **London Rd, Hillbrow GU33 7QL**
email: thejollydrover@googlemail.com **web:** www.thejollydrover.co.uk
dir: *From station in Liss at mini rdbt right into Hill Brow Rd (B3006) signed Rogate, Rake, Hill Brow. At junct with B2071, pub opposite*

Just out of town at the top of the hill

This pub was built in 1844 by a drover, Mr Knowles, to offer cheer and sustenance to other drovers on the old London road. For over 20 years it has been run by Anne and Barry Coe, who welcome all-comers to enjoy the large log fire, secluded garden, a choice of real ales and home-cooked food. The same menu is served in the bar and restaurant. Dishes include roast beef and Yorkshire pudding; 'Hodgepodge Pie' (pork, veal and lamb); chicken breast with bacon and Stilton sauce; and grilled whole plaice with white wine and parsley sauce. Gluten-free and vegetarian choices are also available.

Open all wk 10.30-3 5.30-11 (Sun 12-4) Closed 25-26 Dec, 1 Jan, Sun eve **Food** Lunch Mon-Sat 12-2.15, Sun 12-2.30 Dinner Mon-Sat 7-9.30 Restaurant menu available all wk ⊕ ENTERPRISE INNS ◼ Sharp's Doom Bar, Timothy Taylor Landlord, guest ale. ⏦ 10 **Facilities** Non-diners area ♦◗ Children's portions Garden ⋒ Parking WiFi ▭ (notice required) **Rooms** 6

LITTLETON	Map 5 SU43

The Running Horse ★★★★ INN ◉◉   PICK OF THE PUBS

See Pick of the Pubs on opposite page

PICK OF THE PUBS

The Running Horse ★★★★ INN ❀❀

LITTLETON Map 5 SU43

tel: 01962 880218
88 Main Rd SO22 6QS
email: info@runninghorseinn.co.uk
web: www.runninghorseinn.co.uk
dir: *3m from Winchester, 1m from Three Maids Hill, signed from Stockbridge Rd*

Upmarket village pub and restaurant

Belonging to the Upham Group, this judiciously restored and rejuvenated, mid-1850s country pub lies in a favoured village to the north-west of Winchester. Before its acquisition it had been run by a succession of landlords, many of whom, says Upham had opted "for a leisurely lifestyle in lovely Littleton after hectic years in busy Southampton pubs". A bit of a generalisation, perhaps, but fear not, things are different today as the pub's new lease of life came with a thoroughly professional team — and it shows. The light, spacious interior proves just what a good designer can achieve: contrasting wall colours, wooden flooring, bookcases crammed with old tomes, and a large hatch revealing the kitchen. Needless to say, the real ales are from the Upham brewery, although guest ales get a look-in too. Cider fans will find Orchard Pig, and wine drinkers a good selection by the glass. Two AA Rosettes prove the continuing high quality and careful preparation of the

food — all from trusted local suppliers. Look out for starters of smoked salmon ballotine with salmon eggs and chive Chantilly; and black pudding Scotch egg with HP mayonnaise. To follow might be salt beef hash, January king cabbage and poached egg; cassoulet with Toulouse sausage, lamb neck, confit duck leg and duck-fat crumbs; and butternut risotto with pickled onion, gorgonzola and gremolata. For dessert, dark chocolate and salt caramel fondant and hazelnut ice cream; or plum fool, yuzu curd and ginger crumb. An open area at the front features a cosy thatched cabana, and at the rear are tables and benches, beyond which overnight accommodation is arranged around the garden.

Open all day all wk Closed 25 Dec eve **Food** Lunch Mon-Sat 12-2.30, Sun 12-3.30 Dinner Mon-Sat 6.30-9.30, Sun 6.30-9 Restaurant menu available all wk 🛢 FREE HOUSE/UPHAM GROUP ▦ Tipster, Punter & Stakes, guest ale Ŏ Orchard Pig. ♟ 12
Facilities Non-diners area 🐾 (Bar Garden) 🍴 Children's menu Children's portions Garden 🎋 Beer festival Parking WiFi 🚐 (notice required) **Rooms** 9

| LOVEDEAN | Map 5 SU61 |

The Bird in Hand

tel: 023 9259 1055 **269 Lovedean Ln PO8 9RX**
email: enquiries@lovedeanbirdinhand.co.uk **web:** www.lovedeanbirdinhand.co.uk
dir: A3(M) junct 2, A3 signed Portsmouth. At next rdbt left (A3/Portsmouth). Right into Lovedean Ln (signed Lovedean). Pub on left

Country pub with inspiring menus

This Tudor-look, 200-year-old pub marks the village edge, from where cornfields and copses ripple across the gently rolling Hampshire countryside. At the start of World War II, locals are rumoured to have drunk beer out of the FA Cup, which was despatched here for safe-keeping by the then-holders, Portsmouth. Today's drinkers lack such silverware, but still have great local beers to sample. The inspiring, multiple menus include generous dairy-free and gluten-free selections for bar or restaurant consumption. Main menu options include starters like seared baby squid with pea and ham arancini; or warm smoked duck with black pudding and green beans. Follow with pie of the day; slow-roasted lamb shank; or vegetarian lasagne, with coconut rice pudding with spiced apple relish to finish.

Open all day all wk **Food** Lunch Mon-Sat 12-3, Sun 12-7.30 Dinner Mon-Sat 6-9.30, Sun 12-7.30 ⊕ ENTERPRISE INNS ◀ Ringwood Best Bitter, Bowman Ales Wallops Wood, Havant Finished, guest ales ⚘ Westons Stowford Press. ♚ 11
Facilities Non-diners area ✿ (Bar Garden) ♦♦ Children's menu Children's portions Garden ⊼ Parking WiFi ▭ (notice required)

See advert on opposite page

| LOWER SWANWICK | Map 5 SU40 |

The Navigator

tel: 01489 572123 **286 Bridge Rd SO31 7EB**
email: info@thenavigatorswanwick.co.uk
dir: M27 junct 8, A3024 signed Bursledon. 1st exit at next rdbt onto A27 (Bridge Rd). Cross river, pub 300yds on left

Food-driven hostelry on the River Hamble

With its prime location on the magnificent marina front at Lower Swanwick, The Navigator's ambience reflects the strong sea-faring traditions of this area. It's one owned by the Upham Group, so no surprise to find ales from its own brewery behind the bar. The food ticks all the boxes too, so a sample dinner menu, for example, details pan-fried scallops wrapped in pancetta, crispy chorizo and celeriac purée; herb crusted cod fillet, crushed new potatoes, purple sprouting broccoli and smoked cod roe cream; and braised blade of beef, carrot purée, buttered kale, fondant potato and red wine jus.

Open all day all wk **Food** Lunch Mon-Sat 12-2.30, Sun 12-3.30 Dinner Mon-Sat 6.30-9.30, Sun 6.30-9 ⊕ UPHAM GROUP ◀ Tipster, Punter & Stakes. ♚ 10
Facilities Non-diners area ✿ (Bar Outside area) ♦♦ Children's menu Children's portions Outside area ⊼ Parking WiFi ▭ (notice required)

| LOWER WIELD | Map 5 SU64 |

The Yew Tree   PICK OF THE PUBS

tel: 01256 389224 **SO24 9RX**
dir: A339 from Basingstoke towards Alton. Turn right for Lower Wield

Good selection of fine wines and local ales

Set in wonderful countryside, opposite a picturesque cricket pitch, the popular and enthusiastic landlord's simple mission statement promises 'Good honest food; great local beers; fine wines (lots of choice); and, most importantly, good fun for one and all'. There are 20 guest ale brewers on rotation, including Bowman Ales, Flowerpots and Hogs Back. Most of the food is sourced from Hampshire or neighbouring counties, and the menu reflects the seasons while keeping the regular favourites 'to avoid uproar'. Sample dishes include gorgonzola and crispy bacon salad; or smoked trout and horseradish pâté, toast and lime pepper mayo, followed by Graves butchers' Lincolnshire sausages, parsley mash and onion gravy; or teriyaki cod, noodles, pak choi with sweet plum and hoisin sauce. Finish off with gooseberry, apple and berry crumble for afters. There is an annual cricket match and sports day in summer, and quizzes in the winter months.

Open Tue-Sat 12-3 6-11 (Sun all day) Closed 1st 2wks Jan, Mon **Food** Lunch Tue-Sun 12-2 Dinner Tue-Sat 6.30-9, Sun 6.30-8.30 ⊕ FREE HOUSE ◀ Flowerpots Cheriton Pots, Bowman Swift One, Triple fff Moondance, Hogs Back TEA, Hop Back GFB, Andwell Gold Muddler. ♚ 14 **Facilities** Non-diners area ✿ (Bar Garden) ♦♦ Children's menu Children's portions Garden Parking WiFi

LYMINGTON Map 5 SZ39

The Walhampton Arms

tel: 01590 673113 **Walhampton Hill SO41 5RE**
email: enquiries@walhamptonarms.co.uk **web:** www.walhamptonarmslymington.co.uk
dir: *From Lymington take B3054 towards Beaulieu. Pub in 2m*

Popular carvery and a menu to please everyone

Originally a farm building in the early 19th-century that included a model dairy supplying Walhampton Estate, this busy, friendly and relaxed New Forest pub serves real ales from Ringwood, with guest ales from local microbreweries throughout the year. This pub is also known for its excellent value carvery and pub menu favourites such as steak and ale pie; beer-battered cod, chips and peas; and home-made beef chilli nachos.

Open all day all wk 11-11 (Sun 12-10.30) **Food** Tue-Sat 12-9, Sun-Mon 12-8 ⊕ FREE HOUSE ◄ Ringwood Best Bitter, local guest ales. ♀ 10 **Facilities** Non-diners area ❖ (Bar Outside area) ♦ Children's menu Children's portions Outside area ⊼ Parking WiFi ▭ (notice required)

LYNDHURST Map 5 SU30

New Forest Inn

tel: 023 8028 4690 **Emery Down SO43 7DY**
email: info@thenewforestinn.co.uk
dir: *M27 junct 1 follow signs for A35/Lyndhurst. In Lyndhurst follow signs for Christchurch, turn right at Swan Inn towards Emery Down*

Friendly 18th-century inn with large garden

New Forest ponies occasionally wander into this traditional local, a distraction that only serves to enhance its friendly atmosphere. There's incumbents Fortyniner, Flack's Double Drop and Aspall cider on tap. The menu showcases a multitude of items – doorstep sandwiches, snacks, chargrills, toasted paninis, vegetarian and chef's choices. In there somewhere are smoked haddock kedgeree with poached egg; pork cutlet with ratatouille and mash; herb crusted salmon fillet on chorizo and pea risotto; and leek and gruyère tart. The beer festival is in July.

Open all day all wk **Food** Mon-Sat 11.30-9.30, Sun 12-9 ⊕ ENTERPRISE INNS ◄ Ringwood Fortyniner, Flack Manor Flack's Double Drop, guest ales ♂ Aspall. ♀ 12 **Facilities** Non-diners area ❖ (Bar Restaurant Garden) ♦ Children's menu Children's portions Garden ⊼ Beer festival Cider festival Parking WiFi ▭ (notice required)

The Oak Inn

tel: 023 8028 2350 **Pinkney Ln, Bank SO43 7FD**
email: oakinn@fullers.co.uk
dir: *From Lyndhurst signed A35 to Christchurch, follow A35 for 1m, left at Bank sign*

Reliable oasis on New Forest trails

At the heart of the National Park, patrons enjoying Gales ales in the garden of this bare-boarded, bric-à-brac full country pub may idly watch local residents' pigs snuffling for acorns, New Forest ponies grazing or even fallow deer fleetingly flitting amidst the trees. It's a popular stop with cyclists and walkers exploring the forest's tracks, breaking for a while to partake of the enticing menu which is strong on meals prepared using produce of the parish; perhaps a doorstop sandwich with New Forest ham and Loosehanger cheese, or cider-braised pork belly, celeriac and sage purée, gratin potatoes and spiced apple compôte as a main. Booking for meals is advised. Children are welcome, but only 10 years and over are permitted after 6pm.

Open all wk Mon-Fri 11.30-3 5.30-11 (Sat 11.30-11 Sun 12-10.30) **Food** Lunch Mon-Fri 12-2.30, Sat 12-9.30, Sun 12-9 Dinner Mon-Fri 6-9.30, Sat 12-9.30, Sun 12-9 ⊕ FULLER'S ◄ London Pride, George Gale & Co HSB & Seafarers ♂ Cornish Orchards. ♀ 12 **Facilities** Non-diners area ❖ (Bar Restaurant Garden) ♦ Children's menu Children's portions Garden ⊼ Parking WiFi

PICK OF THE PUBS

The Gamekeepers

MAPLEDURWELL   Map 5 SU65

tel: 01256 322038 & 07786 998994
Tunworth Rd RG25 2LU
email: info@thegamekeepers.co.uk
web: www.thegamekeepers.co.uk
dir: *M3 junct 6, A30 towards Hook. Right across dual carriageway after The Hatch pub. Pub signed*

Charming 19th-century village pub with a large garden

In 1841, what was then a cottage housed shoemaker Joseph Phillips, his wife Elizabeth, four children, his brother and a farm labourer. Around 1854, this being the date on two fireplace bricks in the dining room, one also with JP, the other with EP, it seems probable that Joseph decided shoes were career limiting and converted his cottage into a beer house, The Queen's Head. This name survived until 1973, when it became The Gamekeepers; present owners Phil and Sandra Costello arrived 30 years later. Standing alone down a leafy lane in a village comfortably beyond Basingstoke's eastern limits, the weatherboarded pub has a low-beamed, flagstone-floored interior and a covered well. The bar is certain to offer a choice of Hampshire-brewed real ales, Norcotts real cider from Devon, as well as 10 wines by the glass. On settling into a leather sofa to study the menu, you'll find starters typified by bouillabaisse; and wild boar and herb terrine with

quince and pear chutney. Among the mains look for chargrilled venison fillet with blue cheese and pink peppercorn butter, dauphinoise potatoes, shimeji mushrooms and red wine jus; pan-roasted Gressingham duck breast with potato gratin, heritage carrots, greens and port and redcurrant jus; and pan-fried fillet of hake with sauté potatoes, celeriac purée, greens and beurre rouge sauce. A vegetarian option of 'Sicilian' tagliatelle comes with pesto, sundried tomatoes, spinach, wild mushrooms, olives, parmesan and warm rustic bread. To round off, perhaps choose sticky toffee pudding with custard, or the Hampshire cheeseboard.

Open all wk Mon-Fri 11-2.30 5.30-11 (Sat 11-11 Sun 11-10.30) Closed 31

Dec, 1 Jan **Food** Lunch Mon-Fri 11-2.30, Sat-Sun 11-9.30 Dinner Mon-Fri 5.30-9.30, Sat-Sun 11-9.30 Restaurant menu available all wk ⊞ FREE HOUSE ◀ Andwell, Flack Manor, Longdog, Upham, West Berkshire ♂ Sharp's Orchard, Norcotts Cider, Westons Stowford Press. ♟ 10 **Facilities** Non-diners area ♣ (Bar Garden) ♦♦ Children's portions Garden ⋒ Parking WiFi 🚐 (notice required)

| **MAPLEDURWELL** | Map 5 SU65 |

The Gamekeepers · PICK OF THE PUBS

See Pick of the Pubs on opposite page

| **MARCHWOOD** | Map 5 SU31 |

The Pilgrim Inn

tel: 023 8086 7752 **Hythe Rd SO40 4WU**
email: pilgrim.inn@fullers.co.uk
dir: *M27 junct 2, A326 towards Fawley. Follow brown sign for inn, turn left into Twiggs Lane. At T-junct right into Hythe Rd. Pub on right*

Very dog-friendly pub on edge of New Forest National Park

What is now the Pilgrim was originally three 18th-century cottages, but although considerably expanded, altered and refurbished since, its thatched roof, exposed beams, stone walls and log fire still create an inviting look and homely feel. Fuller's previous manager has moved on, but another first-class boss has taken over, so you can still expect the same professional approach. The family-friendly menu of classic pub favourites and modern dishes typically offers steak and London Pride ale pie; roasted rump of Hampshire lamb; lemon and thyme roast chicken; and roasted butternut squash. Among the desserts are pear frangipane tart; and spiced apple and macadamia nut crumble. They are very dog-friendly here too.

Open all day all wk **Food** Lunch Mon-Fri 12-3, Sat-Sun 12-6 Dinner Mon-Fri 6-9, Sat 6-9.30, Sun 6-8 ⊕ FULLER'S ◀ London Pride, Gales HSB. ₹ 17 **Facilities** Non-diners area ❖ (Bar Garden) ♦ Children's menu Children's portions Garden ☛ Parking WiFi ▄ (notice required)

| **MICHELDEVER** | Map 5 SU53 |

Half Moon & Spread Eagle

tel: 01962 774339 **Winchester Rd SO21 3DG**
email: hmoonseagle@gmail.com
dir: *From Winchester take A33 towards Basingstoke. In 5m left after Class tractors. Pub 1m on right*

Traditional pub with large garden in thatched village

Highly experienced landlords successfully maintain 'the real village pub feel' here, while also attracting customers from well beyond the parish boundary. The only pub in the country with this name, incidentally, it comprises a beamed central bar, a pool room and a restaurant, although the convivial bar has tables too. Interesting guest beers change frequently. In addition to sandwiches, jackets, salads and ploughman's expect home-cooked dishes like sausages, mash and peas; steak and ale pie; rack of ribs, fries and home-made coleslaw; and nachos and chilli.

Open 12-3 6-10.30 (Fri 12-3 6-12 Sat 12-12 Sun 12-8) Closed Mon (winter) **Food** Lunch Tue-Sat 12-3, Sun 12-4 Dinner Tue-Sat 6-9 Av main course £10 ⊕ GREENE KING ◀ London Glory, Moon Best, 3 guest ales ♂ Westons Stowford Press. ₹ 12 **Facilities** Non-diners area ❖ (Bar Garden) ♦ Children's menu Children's portions Play area Garden ☛ Parking WiFi ▄ (notice required)

| **NEW ALRESFORD** | Map 5 SU53 |

The Bell Inn

tel: 01962 732429 **12 West St SO24 9AT**
email: info@bellalresford.com
dir: *In village centre*

Small, family-run free house in charming town centre

A well-restored former coaching inn in Alresford's Georgian main street, where Hampshire real ales hold their own against contenders from Cornwall and Devon, and 18 wines are available by the glass. The bar dining area and candlelit restaurant offer game terrine, apple, pear and fig chutney; and smoked haddock and mussel chowder to start; then steak and Guinness pie, mash, greens and gravy; and confit of French duck leg, dauphinoise potatoes, spinach and cassis sauce. There's a good value two-course menu available at various times during the week. Station Road. opposite the inn. leads to the famous Watercress Line railway.

Open all day Closed Sun eve **Food** Lunch Mon-Sat 12-3, Sun 12-4 Dinner Mon-Sat 6-9 Set menu available Restaurant menu available Lunch all wk ⊕ FREE HOUSE ◀ Sharp's Doom Bar, Itchen Valley, Otter Bitter, Bowman Ales Swift One, Irving Frigate Golden Bitter ♂ Aspall, Thatchers. ₹ 18 **Facilities** Non-diners area ❖ (Bar Outside area) ♦ Children's menu Children's portions Outside area ☛ WiFi ▄ (notice required)

| **NORTHINGTON** | Map 5 SU53 |

The Woolpack Inn ★★★★ INN ⊛ · PICK OF THE PUBS

tel: 01962 734184 **Totford SO24 9TJ**
email: info@thewoolpackinn.co.uk web: www.thewoolpackinn.co.uk
dir: *From Basingstoke take A339 towards Alton. Under motorway, turn right (across dual carriageway) onto B3046 signed Candovers & Alresford. Pub between Brown Candover & Northington*

Welcoming country inn with cracking food and local ales

Set in stunning Hampshire countryside, this brick and flint drovers' inn has a sense of calm modernity while still retaining the classic feel of a country pub. Standing in a tiny hamlet in the peaceful Candover Valley, The Woolpack welcomes walkers and their dogs, families, cyclists and foodies. Ales change weekly, while an up-market wine list will please the cognoscenti. Eat in the traditional bar, where rugs on tiled or wood floors and a roaring log fire create a relaxing atmosphere; alternatives are the smart dining room or a terrace. The bar menu proffers classics such as pie of the day or bangers and mash with onion gravy. Typical dining room main courses are confit pork belly, smoked bacon and potato gratin; or spiced winter vegetable hotpot, carrot and onion fritters and garlic flatbread.

Open all day all wk **Food** Lunch Mon-Thu 12-2.30, Fri-Sun 12-3 Dinner Mon-Sat 6.30-9, Sun 5.30-8.30 Set menu available ⊕ FREE HOUSE ◀ Palmers Copper Ale, The Ramshead (pub's own), weekly changing guest ale ♂ Thatchers Gold. ₹ 11 **Facilities** Non-diners area ❖ (Bar Restaurant Garden) ♦ Children's menu Children's portions Play area Garden ☛ Parking WiFi ▄ (notice required) **Rooms** 7

| **NORTH WALTHAM** | Map 5 SU54 |

The Fox · PICK OF THE PUBS

See Pick of the Pubs on page 240

| **OLD BASING** | Map 5 SU65 |

The Crown

tel: 01256 321424 **The Street RG24 7BW**
email: sales@thecrownoldbasing.com
dir: *M3 junct 6 towards Basingstoke. At rdbt right onto A30. 1st left into Redbridge Ln, to T-junct. Right into The Street, pub on right*

Village local with well-kept ales

Just outside Basingstoke is the picturesque village of Old Basing, in the heart of which is The Crown. Reliable and popular national ales are backed by a good wine list. Here, they take great pride in the fact that every dish is prepared from scratch in the pub's kitchen. Food takes the form of bar snacks like filled rolls, salads and deli boards, and on the main menu, a typical choice could be a starter of crispy breaded Tunworth cheese with Doom Bar chutney, followed by crisp belly of lamb with cauliflower purée and spiced lentils. Lemon posset or warm coffee and walnut sponge both make for a delicious finale.

Open all wk 12-3 5-11 (Fri-Sat 12-12 Sun 12-7) Closed 1 Jan **Food** Lunch Mon-Thu 12-2, Fri-Sun 12-2.30 Dinner Mon-Thu 6-9, Fri-Sat 6-9.30 Restaurant menu available ⊕ ENTERPRISE INNS ◀ Sharp's Doom Bar, St Austell Tribute, Ringwood Razorback ♂ Thatchers Gold. ₹ 9 **Facilities** Non-diners area ❖ (Bar Garden) ♦ Children's menu Children's portions Garden ☛ Parking WiFi ▄ (notice required)

PICK OF THE PUBS

The Fox

NORTH WALTHAM   Map 5 SU54

tel: 01256 397288 **RG25 2BE**
email: info@thefox.org
web: www.thefox.org
dir: *M3 junct 7, A30 towards Winchester. North Waltham signed on right. Take 2nd signed road, then 1st left at Y junct*

Family-friendly pub with a large garden

Built as four farm cottages in 1624, a feature of the bar in this peaceful village pub is its collection of miniatures — over 1,100 so far, and counting. It's an easy place to get to whether travelling on the A303 or the M3. The Fox welcomes families, as you might guess from the children's adventure play area in the extensive beer garden which blazes with colour in summer when the pretty flower borders and hanging baskets are in bloom. In the bar, landlord Rob MacKenzie serves well-looked after real ales from Sharp's, Brakspear, West Berkshire and a guest brewery, and an impressive malt whisky selection among which you'll find the relatively scarce Auchentoshan, Dalmore and Singleton. Bar choices include a ciabatta bacon butty; and steak and beef sausage pie and mash. Rob's wife Izzy is responsible for the monthly menus and daily specials board in the tartan-carpeted restaurant, which list the house specialities of cheese soufflé,

and Hampshire venison served with glazed shallots, field mushrooms, spinach, creamed swede, sauté potatoes and port glaze. Among typical main courses there might be sea bass with coriander butter; lobster and crab risotto; or, in season, pan-fried pheasant breast and confit leg in apricot and wine sauce with dauphinoise potatoes and steamed green beans. Home-made desserts are tempting too — there's pineapple Alaska; passionfruit crème brûlée; and bread and butter pudding with caramelised apples, toffee sauce and ice cream. The Fox's events calendar features monthly wine tasting dinners.

Open all day all wk 11-11 Closed 25 Dec **Food** Lunch all wk 12-2.30 Dinner all wk 6-9.30 Restaurant menu available all wk ⊕ FREE HOUSE ◧ West Berkshire Good Old Boy, Brakspear, Sharp's Doom Bar & guest ale ⏾ Aspall. ♟ 14 **Facilities** Non-diners area ❧ (Bar Garden) ♦♦ Children's menu Children's portions Play area Garden ⊼ Parking WiFi 🚌 (notice required)

OVINGTON
Map 5 SU53

The Bush
PICK OF THE PUBS

tel: 01962 732764 **SO24 ORE**
email: bushinn@wadworth.co.uk
dir: *A31 from Winchester towards Alton & Farnham, approx 6m, left to Ovington. 0.5m to pub*

On the banks of the River Itchen

On the banks of the River Itchen, in the pretty village of Ovington, this rose-covered pub is tucked down a short track that's part of the historic Pilgrim's Way running from nearby Winchester to Canterbury. Small rooms off the bar are characterised by subdued lighting, dark-painted walls, sturdy tables and chairs, high-backed settles, and trout-fishing and other rustic artefacts. Add the comforting log fire and one of Wadworth's real ales and the result is, well, pub heaven. Under new management since December 2015, the menu takes in boards, salads, sandwiches, small plates and main courses. Asian-style sesame duck and roasted squash salad, honey, soy and ginger dressing might be followed by home-made steak, porcini mushroom and peppercorn pie, buttered mash and seasonal greens. Finish with classic egg custard tart, clotted cream and fruit compôte or a board of British cheeses.

Open all wk 11-3 6-11 (Sat 11-11 Sun 12-10.30) **Food** Lunch Mon-Sat 12-2.30, Sun 12-8 (summer holidays all wk) 12-9.30 Dinner Mon-Sat 6-9, Sun 12-8 (summer holidays all wk) 12-9.30 ⊕ WADWORTH ◀ 6X, IPA, Horizon, seasonal ales Ö Westons Rosie's Pig. ♟ 21 **Facilities** Non-diners area ♥ (Bar Restaurant Garden) ♦♦ Children's menu Children's portions Garden ⋒ Parking WiFi

PETERSFIELD
Map 5 SU72

The Old Drum ★ ★ ★ ★ INN

tel: 01730 300208 **16 Chapel St GU32 3DP**
email: hello@theolddrum.com web: www.theolddrum.com
dir: *From A3 follow town centre signs (Winchester Rd). At mini rdbt, 2nd exit. Over rail crossing, 3rd right into Chapel St. Pub on right*

A contemporary pub in the centre of town

When Petersfield's oldest pub was refurbished they discovered original 16th-century features including a superb beamed ceiling and, of perhaps less pulse-racing potential, a tongue-and-groove 1960s ceiling. The bar where author H G Wells once sat with a pint of mild now serves Dark Star and Bowman Ales along with Orchard Pig and Purbeck Dorset Draft ciders. The food too has moved considerably on from H G's pickled-egg-if-he-was-lucky days to include smoked Scottish salmon tartare, dill mustard sauce and warm blinis; saffron risotto with Williams pears and chargrilled wild mushrooms; grilled fish of the day, Maris Piper chips, crushed petit pois and tartare sauce; and tarte Tatin with vanilla ice cream. The new owners are continuing with a long term refurbishment.

Open all day all wk 10am-11pm (Fri-Sat 10am-mdnt Sun 10-8) **Food** Lunch Mon-Sat 12-3.30, Sun 12-4 Dinner Tue-Sat 6-9 Av main course £14 ⊕ FREE HOUSE ◀ Dark Star Hophead, Bowman Ales Wallops Wood, guest ales Ö Purbeck Dorset Draft, Orchard Pig Philosopher. ♟ 12 **Facilities** Non-diners area ♥ (Bar Garden) ♦♦ Children's menu Children's portions Garden ⋒ Beer festival WiFi **Rooms** 5

The Trooper Inn
PICK OF THE PUBS

tel: 01730 827293 **Alton Rd, Froxfield GU32 1BD**
email: info@trooperinn.com
dir: *From A3 follow A272 Winchester signs towards Petersfield (NB do not take A272). 1st exit at mini rdbt for Steep. 3m, pub on right*

Within the South Downs National Park

It calls itself the Pub on the Hill and, at an elevation of 220 metres, it's entitled to, although it sits in a dip. Allegedly a recruiting centre during the run-up to WWI, it

backs on to Ashford Hangers National Nature Reserve. Inside are winter log fires, a spacious bar and a charming restaurant with a vaulted ceiling and wooden settles. Hampshire real ales Ballards and Ringwood Best are served in the bar, and the menu offers a wide range of tempting dishes – free-range chicken and pork terrine; smoked salmon and dill pâté ; Saida's Mococcan chicken couscous; squash, butternut and leek stew; and The Trooper's speciality, slow-cooked half shoulder of lamb. Among the desserts are pistachio meringue with Turkish Delight ice cream; and gin and sorbet martini. There's a mid-week set menu too.

Open 12-3 6-11 Closed Xmas & New Year (contact pub for details), Sun eve & Mon L (ex BH Mon L) **Food** Lunch Tue-Sat 12-2, Sun 12-2.30 Dinner Mon-Fri 6.30-9, Sat 7-9.30 Set menu available ⊕ FREE HOUSE ◀ Ringwood Best Bitter, Ballards, local guest ales. **Facilities** Non-diners area ♥ (Bar Restaurant Garden) ♦♦ Children's menu Children's portions Garden ⋒ Parking WiFi ᕫ (notice required)

RINGWOOD
Map 5 SU10

NEW The Railway

tel: 01425 473701 **35 Hightown Rd BH24 1NQ**
email: ringwoodrailway@gmail.com
dir: *From A31 (N of Ringwood) follow Ringwood signs onto B3347. At next rdbt 2nd exit signed Winkton. At next rdbt 2nd exit into Christchurch Rd. 2nd right into Hightown Rd*

Family-friendly pub in the New Forest

In the market town of Ringwood, this family-run pub has a traditional and unspoilt feel with locals huddled around the bar drinking Hampshire-brewed Ringwood Best. With a beautiful garden complete with play area and vegetable patch, The Railway is family-friendly and younger visitors get to choose from their own menu. The American-influenced menu takes in home-made burgers, 'posh' hot dogs and pub classics like cottage pie with greens and gravy; or maple-glazed ham, chips and eggs from the pub's own hens. Time a visit for the Early May Bank Holiday beer festival and a cider festival in August.

Open all day all wk **Food** all day Av main course £7 ⊕ FREE HOUSE ◀ Ringwood Best Bitter, Otter, St Austell Tribute, Stonehenge Ales, Downton Ö Symonds, Mr Whitehead's. ♟ 12 **Facilities** Non-diners area ♥ (Bar Restaurant Garden) ♦♦ Children's menu Children's portions Play area Family room Garden ⋒ Beer festival Cider festival WiFi

ROCKBOURNE
Map 5 SU11

The Rose & Thistle

tel: 01725 518236 **SP6 3NL**
email: enquiries@roseandthistle.co.uk
dir: *Follow Rockbourne signs from either A354 (Salisbury to Blandford Forum road) or A338 at Fordingbridge*

Pretty, quintessentially English pub

A spectral presence is occasionally abroad here; hardly surprising that the spirit of a former landlord is loathe to leave such an idyllic thatched pub at the fringe of the New Forest. For mortal visitors it's the lure of the local beers, the discovery of top-notch home cooking and the bright, shrubby cottage garden that will detain them. In chillier weather they can settle inside to be warmed by huge log fires. A tasty lunchtime snack might be a crayfish tail sandwich with avocado and salad; or a Welsh rarebit; but for something more substantial choose homity pie and onion gravy; confit rare breed pork belly, spring onion mash, black pudding and cider jus; or oven roasted Dorset lamb rump, confit smoked garlic and redcurrant jus.

Open all wk 11-3 6-11 (Sat 11-11 Sun 12-8) **Food** Lunch all wk 12-2.15 Dinner Mon-Sat 7-9.15 ⊕ FREE HOUSE ◀ Ringwood Best, Sharp's Doom Bar, Butcombe Bitter Ö Westons, Black Rat. ♟ 10 **Facilities** Non-diners area ♥ (Bar Garden) ♦♦ Children's portions Garden ⋒ Parking WiFi ᕫ (notice required)

ROMSEY
Map 5 SU32

The Three Tuns ⊛
PICK OF THE PUBS

tel: 01794 512639 **58 Middlebridge St SO51 8HL**
email: manager@the3tunsromsey.co.uk
dir: *From Romsey bypass (A27) follow town centre sign. Left into Middlebridge St*

Award-winning market-town pub, near Broadlands

This 300-year-old pub is owned by the same team as Winchester's much-praised Chesil Rectory restaurant. A traditional feel is created by smart wood panelling, vintage chandeliers and botanical prints, along with low oak beams and open fireplaces, and you can enjoy a pint of Romsey's own Flack Manor's Double Drop, Ringwood or a guest ale. A simple British menu depends on local ingredients for seasonal classics, sharing platters and Sunday roasts. For a starter, maybe Hampshire black pudding with poached egg and mustard cream; followed by Swiss chard and lentil dumplings shallots and parsley pesto, perhaps, or the Three Tuns pie of the day with mashed potatoes and gravy. Puddings might feature honey carrot cake with beetroot ice cream, or rhubarb cheesecake and white chocolate shavings.

Open all wk 12-3 5-11 (Fri-Sun 12-11) summer all day (Sun 11-10.30) **Food** Lunch Mon-Thu 12-2.30, Fri-Sun 12-3 Dinner Mon-Thu 6-9, Fri-Sat 6-9.30 Av main course £12.50 ⊕ ENTERPRISE INNS ◀ Ringwood Best Bitter, Flack Manor Flack's Double Drop, 2 guest ales Ö Westons Stowford Press. ☗ 11 **Facilities** Non-diners area ❄ (Bar Garden) ♦ Children's portions Garden ⊟ Cider festival Parking WiFi

ROTHERWICK
Map 5 SU75

The Coach and Horses

tel: 01256 768976 **The Street RG27 9BG**
email: ian027@btinternet.com
dir: *Follow brown signs from A32 (Hook to Reading road)*

A cosy, welcoming and unpretentious atmosphere

Close to the church in Rotherwick – a picturesque village that has appeared in TV's *Midsomer Murders* – parts of this smart, cream-washed inn can be traced back to the 17th century. With log fires in winter, board games, exposed brickwork and red-and-black tiled or wooden floors, the interior is pleasingly traditional. The south-facing garden with views of fields is a draw in the summer as a place for a relaxed pint of Badger First Call or a sensibly priced meal; in summer wood-fired pizzas are available. Look out for visiting Morris dancers throughout the summer, and visits by vintage tractors and classic cars.

Open 12-3 5-11 (Sat 12-11 Sun 12-6) Closed Sun eve & Mon **Food** Lunch Tue-Sat 12-3, Sun 12-3.30 (booking advisable Sun) Dinner Tue-Sat 6-9 ⊕ HALL & WOODHOUSE ◀ Badger First Call, Tanglefoot Ö Westons Stowford Press & Old Rosie. ☗ 9 **Facilities** Non-diners area ❄ (Bar Restaurant Garden) ♦ Children's menu Children's portions Garden ⊟ Parking WiFi 🚌 (notice required)

SELBORNE
Map 5 SU73

The Selborne Arms

tel: 01420 511247 **High St GU34 3JR**
email: info@selbornearms.co.uk
dir: *From A3 take B3006, pub in village centre*

Microbrewery delights in a friendly village pub

A huge chimney, known as a baffle entry, blocks your way on entering this 17th-century pub. You have to turn left or right, but it doesn't matter which, for either way you'll find homely bars with hop-strewn beams, a huge fireplace, Bowman Ales Swift One, Ringwood Fortyniner, local guest ales and Mr Whitehead's cider. The menu will please those who enjoy, for example, Welsh rarebit with Suthwyk Ale; local hand-made pork sausages and mash; smoked Scottish salmon salad; or Hampshire beefburger. A beer festival takes place on the first weekend in October. Eighteenth-century naturalist and author Gilbert White lived at The Wakes just up the road.

Open all wk 11-3 6-11 (Sat 11-11 Sun 12-11) **Food** Lunch Mon-Sat 12-2, Sun 12-3 Dinner Mon-Sat 7-9, Sun 7-8.30 ⊕ FREE HOUSE ◀ Ringwood Fortyniner, Bowman Ales Swift One, local guest ales Ö Mr Whitehead's. ☗ 10 **Facilities** Non-diners area ♦ Children's menu Children's portions Play area Garden ⊟ Beer festival Parking WiFi 🚌 (notice required)

SILCHESTER
Map 5 SU66

Calleva Arms

tel: 0118 970 0305 **Little London Rd, The Common RG7 2PH**
email: thecalleva@gmail.com
dir: *A340 from Basingstoke, signed Silchester*

A country pub in the finest tradition

The ancient walls of Calleva Atrebatum, known today as Silchester Roman Town, are some of the best preserved in Britain. The ruins are not far away from this 19th-century Fuller's pub overlooking the common and cricket pitch. Two bar areas, with a log-burner in the middle, lead to a pleasant conservatory and pretty garden. A full lunch and evening menu includes baguettes, ciabattas, baked jacket potatoes and fresh salads; home-made pie of the day; hand-carved Wiltshire ham, eggs and chips; beer-battered hake fillet; and wild mushroom risotto. Daily specials broaden the choice.

Open all day all wk **Food** Lunch Mon-Fri 12-2.30, Sat 12-9, Sun 12-6 Dinner Mon-Fri 5.30-9, Sat 12-9, Sun 12-6 ⊕ FULLER'S ◀ London Pride, George Gale & Co HSB & Seafarers, Fuller's Oliver's Island, Guinness Ö Westons Stowford Press. ☗ 11 **Facilities** Non-diners area ❄ (Bar Garden) ♦ Children's portions Garden ⊟ Parking WiFi 🚌 (notice required)

SPARSHOLT
Map 5 SU43

The Plough Inn
PICK OF THE PUBS

See Pick of the Pubs on opposite page

STEEP
Map 5 SU72

Harrow Inn
PICK OF THE PUBS

tel: 01730 262685 **GU32 2DA**
dir: *From A272 in Petersfield into Inmans Ln (diagonally opposite garage) to Sheet. In Sheet turn left opposite church into School Ln, over A3 by-pass bridge. Inn signed on right*

Real ales, hearty food and serious charity fundraiser

This 16th-century tile-hung gem is situated in a lovely rural location and has changed little over the years. The McCutcheon family has run it since 1929; sisters Claire and Nisa, both born and brought up here, are now the third generation with their names over the door. Tucked away off the road, it comprises two tiny bars – the 'public' is Tudor, with beams, tiled floor, inglenook fireplace, scrubbed tables, wooden benches, tree-trunk stools and a 'library'; the saloon (or Smoking Room, as it is still called) is Victorian. Beers are dispensed from barrels, there is no till and the toilets are across the road. Food is no-nonsense in keeping too: ham and pea soup; hot Scotch eggs (some days); cheddar ploughman's; and various quiches. The large garden has plenty of tables surrounded by country-cottage flowers and fruit trees. Quiz nights raise huge sums for charity, for which Claire's partner Tony grows and sells flowers outside. Ask about the Harrow Cook Book, a collection of customers' recipes on sale for charity. Children are welcome in the garden but not inside the pub.

Open 12-2.30 6-11 (Sat 11-3 6-11 Sun 12-3 7-10.30) Closed Sun eve in winter **Food** Lunch all wk 12-2 Dinner all wk 7-9 Av main course £11-£20 ⊕ FREE HOUSE ◀ Ringwood Best Bitter, Hop Back GFB, Bowman, Dark Star Hophead, Flack Manor Flack's Double Drop, Langham Hip Hop Ö Thatchers Heritage. **Facilities** Non-diners area ❄ (Bar Garden Outside area) Garden Outside area ⊟ Parking **Notes** ⊛

PICK OF THE PUBS

The Plough Inn

SPARSHOLT   Map 5 SU43

tel: 01962 776353
Woodman Ln SO21 2NW
dir: *B3049 from Winchester towards Salisbury, left to Sparsholt, 1m*

Ever-popular inn down a country lane

Built as a coach house to serve Sparsholt Manor opposite, this village pub just a few miles from Winchester has been a popular local alehouse for more than 150 years. Inside, the main bar and dining areas blend harmoniously together, with farmhouse-style pine tables, wooden and upholstered seats, stone jars, miscellaneous agricultural implements, wooden wine box end-panels and dried hops. Wadworth of Devizes supplies all the real ales, and there's a good wine selection. Lunchtime regulars know that 'doorstep' is a most apt description for the great crab and mayonnaise, beef and horseradish and other sandwiches, plus good soups and chicken liver parfait. The dining tables to the left of the entrance look over open fields to wooded downland, and it's at this end of the pub you'll find a daily changing blackboard offering dishes such as salmon and crab fishcakes with saffron sauce; lamb's liver and bacon with mash and onion gravy; beef, ale and

mushroom pie; and whole baked camembert with garlic and rosemary. The menu board at the right-hand end of the bar offers the more substantial venison steak with celeriac mash and roasted beetroot; roast pork belly with bubble-and-squeak, five spice and sultana gravy; chicken breast filled with goats' cheese mousse; and fillet of sea bass with olive mash. Puddings include sticky toffee pudding and crème brûlée. The Plough is very popular, so it's best to book for any meal. The delightful flower- and shrub-filled garden has plenty of room for children to run around and play in. There's a jazz night on the first Sunday in August and carol singing with Father Christmas on 23rd December.

Open all wk 11-3 6-11 (Sun 12-10.30) Closed 25 Dec **Food** Lunch Mon-Sat 12-2.30, Sun 12-8.30 Dinner Mon 6-8.30, Tue-Thu 6-9, Fri-Sat 6-9.30, Sun 12-8.30 ⊕ WADWORTH ◀ Henry's Original IPA, 6X, The Bishop's Tipple, Horizon. ♀ 15 **Facilities** Non-diners area ☙ (Bar Garden) ♦♦ Children's menu Children's portions Play area Family room Garden ⋈ Parking WiFi

STOCKBRIDGE Map 5 SU33

The Greyhound on the Test ★★★★ RR ◎◎

tel: 01264 810833 **31 High St SO20 6EY**
email: info@thegreyhoundonthetest.co.uk web: www.thegreyhoundonthetest.co.uk
dir: *In village centre*

High quality food and accommodation

Hampshire's famous fly-fishing river runs right behind this early 19th-century free house on Stockbridge's wide, picturesque high street. The wood-floored interior is laid out with interestingly styled tables and chairs under a beamed ceiling, while en route to the restaurant local artist Soraya French's artwork is on show. Very much a dining pub, The Greyhound has two AA Rosettes, so expect high quality in dishes such as Broughton buffalo carpaccio; best end of lamb, haggis and faggots; monkfish and scallop céviche; and roasted celeriac soup with honey and chestnut. Saturday's regular special is Barbary duck breast.

Open all day all wk Closed 25-26 Dec **Food** Lunch 12-3 Dinner 6.30-9 Set menu available ⊕ FREE HOUSE ◀ Rotating guest ales. **Facilities** Non-diners area ✿ (Bar Garden) ◀ Children's portions Garden ⊼ Parking WiFi ▰ (notice required) **Rooms** 10

Mayfly

tel: 01264 860283 **Testcombe SO20 6AZ**
dir: *Between A303 & A30, on A3057. Between Stockbridge & Andover*

Famous pub on the River Test

Standing right on the banks of the swiftly flowing River Test, the Mayfly is an iconic drinking spot and a very popular place. Inside the beamed old farmhouse with its traditional bar and bright conservatory you'll find a choice of draught ciders and up to six real ales. All-day bar food might include grilled black pudding and poached egg; chicken and five bean chilli; baked sea bream stuffed with fennel and red peppers; or steak and Stilton pie. Be sure to arrive early to guarantee a space in the small car park, and on warm spring and summer days to grab a bench on the large riverside terrace.

Open all day all wk 10am-11pm **Food** all wk 11.30-9 ⊕ FREE HOUSE ◀ George Gale & Co Seafarers & HSB ♂ Aspall, Thatchers Green Goblin & Gold. ♥ 20 **Facilities** Non-diners area ✿ (Bar Restaurant Garden) ◀ Children's portions Garden ⊼ Parking WiFi ▰

The Peat Spade Inn ★★★★ INN ◎ PICK OF THE PUBS

tel: 01264 810612 **Longstock SO20 6DR**
email: info@peatspadeinn.co.uk web: www.peatspadeinn.co.uk
dir: *Phone for detailed directions*

Test Valley pub famous for its fishing connections

Owned by the successful Upham Pub Company, The Peat Spade stands very close to the River Test. Nearby is Stockbridge, sometimes referred to as the country's fly-fishing capital. A gabled, red-brick Victorian building, its unusual windows overlook a peaceful village lane and thatched cottages. In the cosy fishing- and shooting-themed bar and dining room the short, daily changing menu lists dishes reliant on local and regional suppliers. Among them at lunchtime may be dry-aged beefburger, wild mushrooms, truffle mayonnaise, fries and mixed leaves; Punter ale-battered hake and chips; or handpicked Portland crab on toast. The dinner menu might offer pan-fried fillet of salmon, pink fir potatoes, peas, samphire, cucumber and wasabi butter sauce; and slow-cooked rump of lamb, belly croquette, dauphinoise potatoes, baby carrots and rosemary jus. Outside is a sheltered and enclosed terrace.

Open all day all wk 11-11 (Sun 11-10.30) **Food** Lunch all wk 12-2.30 Dinner all wk 6.30-9.30 Set menu available ⊕ FREE HOUSE/UPHAM GROUP ◀ Punter & Sprinter, guest ale. ♥ 11 **Facilities** Non-diners area ✿ (Bar Restaurant Garden) ◀ Children's menu Children's portions Garden ⊼ Parking WiFi ▰ (notice required) **Rooms** 8

The Three Cups Inn ★★★★ INN ◎ PICK OF THE PUBS

tel: 01264 810527 **High St SO20 6HB**
email: manager@the3cups.co.uk web: www.the3cups.co.uk
dir: *M3 junct 8, A303 towards Andover. Left onto A3057 to Stockbridge*

Charming pub with low beams and a river in the garden

It's said that the name of this 15th-century, timber-framed pub comes from an Old English phrase for a meeting of three rivers, but there's only one here – The Test, known as 'the birthplace of modern fly fishing'. You might even spot a brown trout or two while sitting on the patio in the charming rear garden. There's a log fire to warm the low-beamed bar, where you'll find local ales Itchen Valley and Flowerpots. Menus feature modern European and traditional dishes, so you could start things off with beetroot-cured trout with horseradish pannacotta, smoked trout Scotch egg, beetroot purée and lemon oil; or white crab mayonnaise and brown crab pâté with avocado purée and toast. Mains might include wild mushroom risotto; pheasant and root vegetable stew with sage dumplings; or confit pork belly and braised shoulder. Finish with pannetone bread and butter pudding with salted caramel ice cream, orange curd and toasted almond brittle; or choose from the great selection of local cheeses. Suites provide excellent overnight accommodation.

Open all day all wk 10am-11pm (Fri-Sun 8am-11pm) **Food** Lunch all wk 12-2.30 Dinner all wk 6-9.30 Restaurant menu available all wk ⊕ FREE HOUSE ◀ Itchen Valley Fagins, Young's Bitter, Flowerpots, guest ales ♂ Westons Stowford Press. ♥ 12 **Facilities** Non-diners area ✿ (Bar Garden) ◀ Children's menu Children's portions Garden ⊼ Parking WiFi ▰ (notice required) **Rooms** 8

SWANMORE Map 5 SU51

The Rising Sun

tel: 01489 896663 **Hill Pound SO32 2PS**
email: therisingsunswanmore@gmail.com
dir: *M27 junct 10, A32 through Wickham towards Alton. Left into Bishop's Wood Rd, right at x-roads into Mislingford Rd to Swanmore*

Homely pub with extensive menu

Tucked in the heart of the beautiful Meon Valley, this 17th-century coaching inn has winter fires, low beams, uneven floors and lots of nooks and crannies. In summer, enjoy a pint of Ringwood Best or Flowerpots Goodens Gold in the secluded rear garden. Home-cooked food makes good use of locally sourced ingredients in simple snacks such as a sandwiches and salads through to full meals along the lines of devilled whitebait; or creamy garlic mushrooms followed by pie of the day or spicy curry of the day. The new owners say there'll be a beer festival in mid September.

Open all wk 11.30-3 5.30-11 (Sun 12-7.30) **Food** Lunch Mon-Sat 12-2, Sun 12-6 Dinner Mon-Sat 6-9, Sun 12-6 Set menu available ⊕ FREE HOUSE ◀ Ringwood Best Bitter, Flowerpots Goodens Gold, local guest ales ♂ Pheasant Plucker, Lilley's Bee Sting Pear. ♥ 13 **Facilities** Non-diners area ✿ (Bar Garden) ◀ Children's menu Children's portions Garden ⊼ Beer festival Parking ▰ (notice required)

TANGLEY Map 5 SU35

The Fox Inn

tel: 01264 730276 **SP11 0RU**
email: info@foxinntangley.co.uk
dir: *From rdbt (junct of A343 & A3057) in Andover follow station signs (Charlton Rd). Through Charlton & Hatherden to Tangley*

Local ales and spicy treats in rural seclusion

Curiously, among the team at The Fox Inn, is a former chef to the Thai Royal Family who now dedicates his skills to providing a startling menu to pub-goers who adventure along the country lanes that cross outside this secluded inn in the North Wessex Downs Area of Outstanding Natural Beauty. Their reward is a superb setting beside coppice woodland with relaxing views across sloping arable fields that stretch to the horizons. This 300-year-old brick and flint cottage has been a pub since 1830; inside it is largely furnished in a casual-contemporary style featuring an unusual log-end bar design, where guests may enjoy a wide choice of genuine Thai dishes and some fine local beers.

Open all day all wk 12-11 (Sun 12-10.30) Closed 25 Dec **Food** Lunch all wk 12-2.30 Dinner Mon-Sat 6-9.30, Sun 6-9 Av main course £10 Set menu available Restaurant menu available all wk ⊕ FREE HOUSE ◀ Ramsbury Gold, Flack Manor Flack's Double Drop, Upham Punter, Red Rock Devon Coast, Two Cocks Leveller ♂ Symonds. ♟ 12 **Facilities** Non-diners area ✿ (All areas) ♦♦ Children's menu Children's portions Garden Outside area ⚲ Parking WiFi ▭ (notice required)

THRUXTON   Map 5 SU24

The White Horse Inn & Restaurant ★★★ INN

tel: 01264 772401 **Mullens Pond SP11 8EE**
email: enquiries@whitehorsethruxton.co.uk **web:** www.whitehorsethruxton.co.uk
dir: *S of Thruxton. Phone for detailed directions*

Thatched, 15th-century pub with lovingly-tended garden

There's plenty of old-time, Grade II listed atmosphere in this Test Valley pub, thought to date from around 1450. The spacious bar does its bit for local breweries by offering Romsey's Flack Manor Flack's Double Drop, and King John from Andwell, near Basingstoke. Australian chef-patron Norelle Oberin shows her hand with twice-baked mature cheese soufflé; chorizo and lamb croquettes with saffron mayo; herb-crusted lamb rump, new potatoes, seasonal greens and mint jus; and roast cherry tomato, feta and thyme risotto. For dessert try one of the ice creams or sorbets, or coffee crème brûlée perhaps. Baguettes and sandwiches are available at lunchtime.

Open all day all wk **Food** Lunch all wk 12-3 Dinner Mon-Sat 6-9 Set menu available Restaurant menu available all wk ⊕ FREE HOUSE ◀ Sharp's Doom Bar, Andwell King John, Flack Manor Flack's Double Drop ♂ Thatchers. ♟ 24 **Facilities** Non-diners area ✿ (Bar Garden) ♦♦ Children's menu Children's portions Garden ⚲ Parking WiFi **Rooms** 4

TICHBORNE   Map 5 SU53

The Tichborne Arms   PICK OF THE PUBS

tel: 01962 733760 **SO24 0NA**
email: tichbornearms@xln.co.uk
dir: *Follow pub signs from B3046, S of A31 between Winchester & Alresford*

In a village with a tale to tell

Not as old as its thatched roof might suggest, for this village pub was built in the mid-20th century to replace its burnt-down predecessor. If the pub's name rings a bell, it's probably because of the famous 1870s trial of The Tichborne Claimant, a crooked East End butcher pretending to be heir to a local baronetcy, and the subject of a 1998 film, starring John Gielgud. Antiques, prints and other artefacts attractively clutter the rustically furnished, dried-hop-strung bar, so there's plenty to look at as you relax with a pint of Hop Back or Red Cat real ale, or JJ's SuEcider (sic). Owner-chef Patrick Roper's short daily menus may well feature fillet of sea bream with creamy prawn sauce; medallions of pork tenderloin with apple and cider sauce; and mushroom tagliatelle, as well as at least one vegetarian option. A beer festival takes place in the tree-shaded garden over the Summer Bank Holiday weekend in August.

Open all wk Mon-Fri 11.45-3 (Mon 6-9, Tue-Thu 6-10.30, Fri 6-11, Sat 11.45-11, Sun 12-7.30) **Food** Lunch Mon-Fri 12-2, Sat 12-2.30, Sun 12-4 Dinner Tue-Sat 6-9 Set menu available Restaurant menu available all wk ⊕ FREE HOUSE ◀ Hop Back, Palmers, Bowman, Red Cat, Flack Manor, Stonehenge Ales ♂ JJ's SuEcider. ♟ 10 **Facilities** Non-diners area ✿ (Bar Restaurant Garden) ♦♦ Children's portions Garden ⚲ Beer festival Parking WiFi ▭ (notice required)

TWYFORD   Map 5 SU42

NEW The Bugle Inn

tel: 01962 714888 **Park Ln SO21 1QT**
email: rooms@bugleinntwyford.co.uk
dir: *M3 junct 11, B3335, 1.5m to Twyford*

Interesting food in a delightful village

This charming 18th-century coaching inn was sold for development in 2002 but rescued after the villagers stepped in. It re-opened six years later and has never looked back. A good selection of snacks and sandwiches is available at lunchtime, or you can choose from the main menu. A meal might begin with a salad — maybe Hampshire goats' cheese and roasted beetroot, before moving on to dressed Mudeford crab with Jersey Royal, pea and avocado salad; or roasted John Dory, served with gently spice aubergine and spinach 'caviar'. Boozy bread and butter pudding finishes things off nicely.

Open all day all wk **Food** Contact pub for food times Av main course £19 ⊕ FREE HOUSE ◀ Bowman Ales Swift One, Timothy Taylor Landlord ♂ Aspall. ♟ **Facilities** Non-diners area ♦♦ Children's portions Outside area ⚲ Beer festival Parking WiFi

Find out more about the AA's accommodation rating schemes on page 8

UPPER CLATFORD
Map 5 SU34

Crook & Shears

tel: 01264 361543 **SP11 7QL**
dir: *Phone for detailed directions*

Quiet village inn with picture postcard credentials

Old photographs show the thatched and whitewashed exterior looking much as it did 100 years ago, when the Crook & Shears first became a pub; parts of the building date to the 17th century, when it was probably built as a farmhouse. The interiors ooze character, ideal surroundings in which to enjoy a quiet pint of Ringwood or glass of wine. Menus are wholesome and traditional, ranging from freshly baked baguettes and jacket potatoes at lunchtime, to pub favourites in the evening such as breaded garlic mushrooms; home-made steak and ale pie; and jam roly poly. Food and drink can be served in the large rear garden.

Open 12-3 6-11 (Fri-Sat 12-3 6-12 Sun 12-3 7-10.30) Closed Mon L **Food** Lunch Tue-Sun 12-2.30 Dinner Tue-Sat 6.30-9 Av main course £10.95 ⊕ ENTERPRISE INNS ◀ Ringwood Best Bitter, Otter Ale Ō Thatchers Gold. ♟ 10 **Facilities** Non-diners area ♣ (Bar Garden) ♦ Children's portions Play area Garden ⊼ WiFi ➡ (notice required)

UPPER FROYLE
Map 5 SU74

The Hen & Chicken Inn

tel: 01420 22115 **GU34 4JH**
email: info@henandchicken.co.uk
dir: *2m from Alton towards Farnham on A31. Adjacent to petrol station. Signed from A31*

Character coaching inn off the A31

Highwaymen, hop-pickers and high clergy have all supped and succoured here in this noble, three-storey Georgian road house. They'd still recognise some of the comfortably traditional interior – timeless panelling, beams, old tables and inglenook; maybe, too, the little wooden barn in a corner of the grassy garden, standing on its painted staddle stones. The reliable country menu is strong on local produce and vegetables from the garden; start with calamari; or home-made Scotch egg; then move onto hunter's chicken; sausage and mash; sweet pepper and goats' cheese tart; or a gourmet burger. It may be hard to resist the apple and cherry pie.

Open all day all wk 9am-11pm **Food** all wk 12-9 Av main course £10 ⊕ HALL & WOODHOUSE ◀ Badger Tanglefoot & First Call, K&B Sussex Ō Westons Stowford Press & Rosie's Pig. **Facilities** Non-diners area ♣ (Bar Garden) ♦ Children's menu Children's portions Play area Garden ⊼ Parking WiFi ➡ (notice required)

WARNFORD
Map 5 SU62

The George & Falcon ★★★★ INN

tel: 01730 829624 **Warnford Rd SO32 3LB**
email: reservations@georgeandfalcon.com web: www.georgeandfalcon.com
dir: *M27 junct 10, A32 signed Alton. Approx 10.5m to Warnford*

Country inn with modern cuisine

The lively little River Meon slides past the garden of this imposing inn, first recorded over 400 years ago. The cosy, fire-warmed snug is the place to settle with a pint of Ringwood Fortyniner and reflect on a grand winter walk on nearby Old Winchester Hill; or discover the terrace and consider the enticing modern choices including those on the good value, set menus – perhaps a charcuterie board; baked camembert; lamb Wellington; pie and mash; chocolate brownie; and vanilla cheesecake. Six en suite bedrooms complete the scene.

Open all day all wk 11-11 (Oct-Mar 11-3 6-11) **Food** Lunch all wk 11-3 Dinner all wk 6-9 Set menu available Restaurant menu available all wk ⊕ MARSTON'S ◀ Ringwood Best Bitter & Fortyniner Ō Thatchers Gold. ♟ 9

Facilities Non-diners area ♣ (Bar Restaurant Garden) ♦ Children's menu Children's portions Family room Garden ⊼ Parking WiFi ➡ (notice required) **Rooms** 6

WELL
Map 5 SU74

The Chequers Inn

tel: 01256 862605 **RG29 1TL**
email: thechequers5@hotmail.co.uk
dir: *From Odiham High St into King St, becomes Long Ln. 3m, left at T-junct, pub 0.25m on top of hill*

Locally renowned little cracker

A lovely country pub with a multitude of low beams testifying to its 15th-century origins. Paul and Nicola Sanders have a proven track record of running successful pubs and their forte is preparing classic English dishes and daily specials based on fresh fish, steaks and duck, and serving well-kept pints of Hall & Woodhouse ales. A brasserie menu proffers the likes of Cornish battered cod fillet, while the carte overflows with favourites such as crispy breaded brie, and skate wing with black butter. Eat and drink by a log fire, out front under sheltered grapevines, or on the decked area in the rear garden, overlooking the countryside.

Open all wk 12-3 6-11 (Fri-Sun & Jun-Sep all day) **Food** Lunch Mon-Fri 12-3, Sat 12-9.30, Sun 12-8 Dinner Mon-Fri 6-11, Sat 12-9.30, Sun 12-8 Av main course £15 Restaurant menu available all wk ⊕ HALL & WOODHOUSE ◀ Badger First Gold & Tanglefoot, seasonal ales Ō Westons Stowford Press, Badger Applewood & Pearwood. ♟ 12 **Facilities** Non-diners area ♣ (Bar Garden Outside area) ♦ Children's portions Garden Outside area ⊼ Parking WiFi ➡ (notice required)

WEST MEON
Map 5 SU62

The Thomas Lord ⊛
PICK OF THE PUBS

tel: 01730 829244 **High St GU32 1LN**
email: info@thethomaslord.co.uk
dir: *M3 junct 9, A272 towards Petersfield, right at x-roads onto A32, 1st left*

Country inn with impressive cricket connections

Thomas Lord was the eponymous founder of Lord's Cricket Ground. He retired to the pretty village of West Meon in 1830 and is buried in the churchyard. This beautifully restored pub has a bar decorated with cricketing memorabilia and well furnished with drinkers' tables and chairs; it's an agreeable setting for well-kept seasonal and guest ales, or a chilled glass of white chosen from the sophisticated range of wines. Herbs, salads and vegetables are grown in the pub's own garden; otherwise the kitchen is supplied by local farms and small-scale producers; the result is a menu of seasonal delights. A typical meal might start with smoked mackerel rillette, scorched mackerel, cucumber and wasabi, followed by confit pork belly, perhaps, or haunch of venison wrapped in pancetta, blue cheese, cabbage, chestnut and pear.

Open all day all wk **Food** Lunch Mon-Fri 12-2.30, Sat 12-3, Sun 12-4 Dinner Mon-Thu 6-9.30, Fri-Sat 6-10, Sun 6-9 Av main course £14 Set menu available ⊕ FREE HOUSE/UPHAM GROUP ◀ Upham Ales, seasonal & guest ales Ō Orchard Pig. ♟ 14 **Facilities** Non-diners area ♣ (Bar Garden) ♦ Children's portions Garden ⊼ Parking WiFi ➡ (notice required)

WEST TYTHERLEY
Map 5 SU22

The Black Horse

tel: 01794 340308 **The Village SP5 1NF**
email: theblackhorsepublichouse@gmail.com
dir: *In village centre*

A village pub for all

Nathaniel and Vanessa Clift have taken over the reins of The Black Horse, a traditional 17th-century former coaching inn. It's a proper village community pub, with a skittle alley, regular quiz nights and an oak-beamed bar where locals sup pints of Butcombe, Fuller's and Red Cat ales by the fire, or wherever they like. On the menu: baguettes and jacket potatoes; hand-made game pie; scampi, chips and peas; sea bass fillets with lemon and caper butter; chicken tikka with onion bhajis, omelette and basmati rice; and Hunter's chicken and vegetable lattice. Sunday roasts are good value. Well-behaved children and dogs welcome, and muddy boots ignored.

Open 12-3 6-11 (Sun 12-7) Closed Mon L & Tue L **Food** Lunch Wed-Sun Dinner Tue-Sun ⊕ FREE HOUSE ◖ Hop Back, Butcombe, Fuller's London Pride, Red Cat ♻ Westons Stowford Press, Cornish Orchards. **Facilities** Non-diners area ❧ (Bar Restaurant Garden) ♦♦ Children's menu Children's portions Play area Garden ⊼ Parking WiFi ⟳ (notice required)

WEST WELLOW
Map 5 SU21

The Rockingham Arms
PICK OF THE PUBS

tel: 01794 324798 **Canada Rd SO51 6DE**
email: info@rockinghamarms.co.uk
dir: *M27 junct 2, A36 towards Salisbury. In Wellow left into Canada Rd*

Dog-friendly pub that's full of character

This pub on the edge of Canada Common in the New Forest (under new ownership) is going from strength to strength. Its 1840 origin is still evident from the outside, although the pleasingly modernised interior today retains few clues. No worries if you've been out and about in the forest with your dog, as he or she is more than welcome to accompany you inside and even be treated with one of the dog biscuits kept in a jar on the bar. The pub sources food from local suppliers and serves comforting home-cooked food along with New Forest real ales. You could just choose a warming cup of home-made soup, a simple sandwich and skinny fries, or opt for three courses — cold smoked trout, crostini and wasabi mayonnaise; chef's pie of the day, creamy mash and seasonal greens; and caramelised lemon tart, raspberry sorbet and clotted cream. There also a gluten-free menu. Please note, booking is essential for coach parties.

Open all day all wk **Food** Lunch all wk 12-3 Dinner Mon-Sat 6-9, Sun 6-8 ⊕ FREE HOUSE ◖ Ringwood Best Bitter, Upham Ale, local guest ale ♻ Orchard Pig. **Facilities** Non-diners area ❧ (Bar Restaurant) ♦♦ Children's menu Children's portions Garden ⊼ Parking WiFi ⟳ (notice required)

WHITCHURCH
Map 5 SU44

The White Hart ★★★ INN

tel: 01256 892900 **Newbury St RG28 7DN**
email: thewhitehart.whitchurch@arkells.com **web:** www.whiteharthotelwhitchurch.co.uk
dir: *On B3400 in town centre*

Tasty pub grub near the source of the River Test

Strategically located where the old London to Exeter and Oxford to Southampton roads cross, this was Swindon brewery Arkell's first Hampshire pub. Dating from 1461, its rich history includes patronage by the late Lord Denning, Master of the Rolls, who was born opposite. What he dined on is unknown, but today's menu lists jacket potatoes; steak and ale pie; Somerset pork casserole; beer-battered fish and chips; and sizzling home-made fajitas. For vegetarians, there's three-cheese macaroni, and vegetable Madras. Just over the road is Whitchurch Silk Mill, the oldest of its type in the UK in its original building, and still using 19th-century machinery.

Open all day all wk **Food** Lunch all wk 12-2 Dinner Mon-Sat 6-9 ⊕ ARKELL'S ◖ 3B & Wiltshire Gold ♻ Westons Stowford Press. **Facilities** Non-diners area ❧ (Bar Restaurant Outside area) ♦♦ Children's menu Family room Outside area ⊼ Parking WiFi **Rooms** 10 **Notes** ⊜

WICKHAM
Map 5 SU51

Greens Restaurant & Bar

tel: 01329 833197 **The Square PO17 5JQ**
dir: *M27 junct 10, A32 to Wickham*

Hardy perennial of the pub world

It's hard to miss Greens' black-and-white timbered building, standing prominently on a corner of Wickham's medieval market square, the second largest in England. Its proprietors for 30 years, Frank and Carol Duckworth still use their original slogan — 'Nothing is too much trouble', a promise evident in the modern British seasonal menus and, more importantly, on the plate. Starters include pork croquette with chipotle ketchup and crackling; and salmon and hake fishcake; while main dish options are seared hake fillet with mussel and clam saffron chowder; or aubergine parmigiana with rocket and marinated artichokes. Bowmans, in nearby Droxford, supplies two of its prize-winning ales.

Open 10-3 6-11 (Sat 11-11 Sun & BH 12-5 May-Sep all day) Closed 19-20 May, Sun eve & Mon **Food** Lunch Tue-Sat 12-2.30, Sun 12-5 Dinner Tue-Sat 6-9.30 ⊕ FREE HOUSE ◖ Bowman Ales Wallops Wood & Swift One. ♀ 12 **Facilities** Non-diners area ♦♦ Children's portions Garden ⊼

WINCHESTER
Map 5 SU42

The Black Boy

tel: 01962 861754 **1 Wharf Hill SO23 9NQ**
email: enquiries@theblackboypub.com
dir: *Off Chesil St (B3300)*

Traditional pub with the emphasis firmly on local ales

This old fashioned whitewashed pub in the ancient capital of Wessex is a decidedly beer-led hostelry. As well as three regular regional ales from the Cheriton, Alfred's and Hop Back breweries, The Black Boy offers two Hampshire guests, perhaps from Bowman or Itchen Valley; a small selection of good wine is also available. The interior features old wooden tables and a quirky decor with all manner of objects hanging from the ceiling, while the short daily menu on the blackboard could include sandwiches, home-made burgers and fish and chips. There is a sheltered garden with patio heaters.

Open all day all wk **Food** Lunch Wed-Fri 12-2, Sat-Sun 12-2.30 Dinner Tue-Sat 7-9 Av main course £9.50 ⊕ FREE HOUSE ◖ Flowerpots Cheriton Pots, Bowman Ales Swift One, Hop Back Summer Lightning, Alfred's Saxon Bronze, guest ales ♻ Westons Stowford Press, Lilley's Apples & Pears & Star Gazer. **Facilities** Non-diners area ❧ (All areas) ♦♦ Garden Outside area ⊼ WiFi

The Golden Lion

99 Alresford Road, Winchester, Hants SO23 0JZ • **Tel:** 01962 865512
Website: www.thegoldenlionwinchester.co.uk • **Email:** bridphelan@me.com

We warmly invite you to *The Golden Lion Pub*, Winchester, for our cosy vintage style interiors, excellent home cooked food and great Irish welcome! We are located just on the eastern edge of the city, within very easy reach of the M3, the A272 and the A34, and just a 10 minute walk into the beautiful heart of the city with all of its historic attractions and wealth of independent shops. We have a large car park as well as patio areas and beer gardens to the front and back, including a special enclosed area for doggies to have a run. We also have disabled access and facilities inside. We are a TV and gaming machine free zone so that you can relax in our friendly atmosphere and enjoy our great background music. We also welcome children who are eating with their parents/guardians.

We are very proud to have received many awards for the services that we offer, including 'The Casque Mark' and 'Master Cellerman' for our real ales, the certificate of 'Excellent' for our food hygiene, and we have won many awards for our floral displays and hanging baskets. We were very honoured to have been awarded as the Wadworth Brewery 'Retailer of the Year'. We were also delighted to receive the Quality Assured Award in Hampshire Hospitality Awards 2014 and the 'Certificate of Excellence' from TripAdvisor.

We have regular live music sessions such as Bluegrass music on the last Tuesday evening of the month, and Irish music on the second Thursday evening of the month.

Our 'Regal Room' is also available, and would be perfect for any occasion; a birthday, a small wedding, a christening and many more! We offer a large range of buffet menus and set-menus, afternoon cream tea and corporate breakfasts, details for all of these can be found on our website. We cater for pre-booked coach parties too, with parking available, for group meals.

Follow us on Facebook at facebook.com/goldenlionwinchester
Or on Twitter @GoldenLionWinch

We very much look forward to welcoming you very soon!

WINCHESTER *continued*

The Golden Lion

tel: 01962 865512 **99 Alresford Rd SO23 0JZ**
email: bridphelan@me.com web: www.thegoldenlionwinchester.co.uk
dir: *From Union St in town centre follow 'All other routes' sign. At rdbt 1st exit into High St. At rdbt 1st exit into Bridge St (B3404) signed Alton/Alresford, (becomes Alresford Rd)*

Charming, dog-friendly pub

This 1932-built pub on the outskirts of Winchester is well known for its wonderful floral displays in the summer months. Brid and Derek Phelan are strong on Irish charm and pride themselves on offering good, home-cooked food. Typically you can tuck into steak and ale pie; home-cooked ham, egg and chips; poached salmon. Vegetarian options, a short vegan menu and a gluten-free menu are also available. The pub has a large beer garden, smoking shelter, large car park and the new Regal Room for functions for up to 40 people.

Open all wk Mon-Sat 11.30-3 5.30-11 (Sun 12-10.30) **Food** Lunch all wk 12-2.30 Dinner all wk 6-9 ⊕ WADWORTH ◀ 6X, Henry's Original IPA, seasonal ales ♂ Westons Stowford Press. ▼ 8 **Facilities** Non-diners area ♣ (Bar Restaurant Garden) ♦ Children's menu Children's portions Garden ⋒ Parking WiFi ▭ (notice required)

See advert on opposite page

The Green Man

tel: 01962 866809 **53 Southgate St SO23 9EH**
email: greenmanwinchester@gmail.com
dir: *Phone for detailed directions*

Cool, quirky and central

With its retro-furnished bar, Jayne Gillin's Green Man is one of her five city bars and restaurants, all showing her enviable talent for trendy makeovers. Upstairs is an Edwardian-style dining room with rich fabrics, candelabras and chandeliers, while The Outhouse, formerly the skittle alley, is now a cool, 1930s industrial-style function room, where platter suppers, pitchers of wine and buckets of beer are served at a huge refectory table. The evening menu offers dishes such as the Green Man burger with seasoned fries; cod fillet, mussel and saffron velouté; porchetta and sautéed greens; or fish and chips, mushy peas, tartare sauce and pickles.

Open all day all wk 12-12 (Sun-Mon 12-10.30) Closed 25-26 Dec **Food** Lunch all wk 12-3 Dinner all wk 6-10 Av main course £13 ⊕ GREENE KING ◀ St Edmunds, Morland ♂ Aspall. ▼ 16 **Facilities** Non-diners area ♦ Children's portions WiFi

The Old Vine ★ ★ ★ ★ INN

tel: 01962 854616 **8 Great Minster St SO23 9HA**
email: reservations@oldvinewinchester.com web: www.oldvinewinchester.com
dir: *M3 junct 11, follow Saint Cross & City Centre signs. 1m, right at Green Man pub right into Saint Swithun St, bear left into Symonds St (one-way). Right into Great Minster St (NB for Sat Nav use SO23 9HB)*

Cathedral views and top hospitality

An elderly vine rambles all over the street frontage of this elegant pub, built on Saxon foundations in the 18th century. Directly opposite is Winchester's fine cathedral and the City Museum. There are four guest beers, including local ales, in the oak-beamed bar, where you can eat sandwiches, salads and light meals. Freshly prepared, in the restaurant are, typically, starters like pork and chive Scotch egg with piccalilli; home-cured Scottish salmon with mustard and dill dressing; or twice-baked blue cheese and walnut soufflé; followed by creamy crab and prawn bake; West Country mussels steamed in Somerset cider, shallots, bacon and crème fraîche; or pea and asparagus ravioli with pea pureé and mushrooms. Puddings include fruity summer berry pudding; vanilla cheesecake with raspberry coulis; and butterscotch and treacle sponge pudding. At the back of the pub you'll find a flower-filled patio.

Open all day all wk Closed 25 Dec **Food** Lunch Mon-Thu 12-2.30, Fri-Sun 12-6 Dinner Mon-Sat 6.30-9.30, Sun 6.30-9 ⊕ ENTERPRISE INNS ◀ Guest ales. ▼ 11 **Facilities** Non-diners area ♣ (Bar Outside area) ♦ Family room Outside area ⋒ WiFi **Rooms** 6

The Wykeham Arms ★ ★ ★ ★ INN ◉◉ PICK OF THE PUBS

See Pick of the Pubs on page 250

PICK OF THE PUBS

The Wykeham Arms ★★★★ INN ◉◉

tel: 01962 853834
75 Kingsgate St SO23 9PE
email: wykehamarms@fullers.co.uk
web: www.wykehamarmswinchester.co.uk
dir: *Near Winchester College &*
Winchester Cathedral

Sophisticated pub in Winchester's historic heart

It's quite hard to convey just how much character The Wyk has. For it's more than a pub and a restaurant with accommodation; it's a Winchester institution. Beyond the cathedral from the High Street, with Winchester College as a neighbour, this 270-year-old building is entered from the pavement through curved, etched-glass doors straight into two bars, one dead ahead, the other to your left. Both have open fires and are furnished with old pine tables and redundant college desks. Everywhere, and that's no understatement – are portraits and prints, pewter tankards and miscellaneous ephemera. It all creates a warm feeling – gemütlichkeit as they say in Germany. Perhaps this is why it attracts such a varied clientele - business people, barristers, clergy, college dons, ladies who lunch, tourists and, yes, locals, for this is a desirable residential quarter. You may eat in the bars, but serious dining is done in tucked-away rooms, where modern

British menus ring the seasonal changes to include crispy Kings Somborne egg, pickled mushrooms, shallots and cep purée; and pan-seared scallops, hazelnut crumb, sesame purée and compressed apple as typical starters. Equally representative are main dishes of roast halibut, parmentiers, black cabbage, capers and beef cromesquis; and braised blade of beef, snails, carrots and burnt aubergine purée. 'Home Comforts' include confit pork belly, chorizo hash and roast swede. Finish with warm treacle tart, bay leaf ice cream and citrus curd. It's one of the Fuller's flagship pubs, although there's guest real ales too, perhaps one from the nearby Flowerpots microbrewery. The wine list is impressive.

Open all day all wk **Food** Lunch all wk 12-3 Dinner all wk 6-9.30 Set menu available Restaurant menu available all wk ⊕ FULLER'S ◼ London Pride, George Gale & Co HSB & Seafarers, Flowerpots Goodens Gold, guest ales. ♟ 20 **Facilities** Non-diners area ☻ (Bar Outside area) Outside area ☍ Parking WiFi **Rooms** 14

HEREFORDSHIRE

AYMESTREY
Map 9 SO46

The Riverside Inn
PICK OF THE PUBS

tel: 01568 708440 **HR6 9ST**
email: theriverside@btconnect.com
dir: *On A4110, 18m N of Hereford*

Friendly hostelry in countryside setting

Built in 1580, this character inn started catering to the passing sheep drovers in 1700; it's midway along the Mortimer Trail, just by the ford across the River Lugg. All the country pursuits are here: choose between 10 circular walks and look out for otters, kingfishers, herons and deer on the way. The wood-panelled interior with low beams and log fires makes a cosy setting for the enjoyment of ales such as Wye Valley Butty Bach and Hobsons Best; ciders include Westons and Robinsons. The pub's vegetable, herb and fruit garden is the source of many ingredients for the seasonal menus – Shropshire ham hock terrine, pickled apple relish and caramelised walnuts might precede seared freshwater trout fillet, parsley and almond gremolata and cauliflower purée; Heritage carrot, Monkland cheese and leek risotto; or slow-cooked Herefordshire beef, oxtail sauce, smoked mash and salt-baked shallots.

Open Tue-Sat 11-3 6-11 (Sun 12-3) Closed 26 Dec, 1 Jan, Sun eve, Mon L, Mon eve in winter **Food** Lunch Tue-Sun 12-2.15 Dinner Tue-Sat 7-9 Restaurant menu available Tue-Sun evening ⊕ FREE HOUSE ◀ Wye Valley Bitter & Butty Bach, Hobsons Best Bitter Ŏ Westons Stowford Press, Robinsons Flagon. **Facilities** Non-diners area ❀ (Bar Restaurant Garden) ❖ Children's portions Garden ⅋ Parking WiFi ⛟ (notice required)

BREDWARDINE
Map 9 SO34

The Red Lion ★★★ INN

tel: 01981 500303 **HR3 6BU**
email: info@redlion-hotel.com web: www.redlion-hotel.com
dir: *Take A438 from Hereford towards Eardisley. Follow signs for Bredwardine*

Tranquil rural pub serving enjoyable local food

Handy for both Hereford and Hay-on-Wye, the 17th-century Red Lion is tucked away in the sleepy hamlet of Bredwardine, set against a backdrop of fields and cider orchards. Once a coaching inn, the lounge was used as the courtroom for the circuit judge, although these days the only judgement being passed is on the well-kept Butty Bach beer and Gwatkin cider, and the highly-regarded food. A starter of lime and garlic marinated pigeon breast with spinach, tomato and coriander salsa might precede lamb, beetroot and black pudding casserole.

Open all wk 12-2.30 6.30-11 **Food** Lunch 12-2 Dinner 7-9 ⊕ FREE HOUSE ◀ Wye Valley Bitter & Butty Bach Ŏ Westons Stowford Press, Gwatkin. **Facilities** ❀ (Bar Garden) ❖ Children's portions Garden ⅋ Parking WiFi **Rooms** 10

BROMYARD DOWNS
Map 10 SO65

The Royal Oak

tel: 01885 482585 **HR7 4QP**
email: info@royaloakbromyard.com
dir: *From A44 at Bromyard take B4203 towards Stourport-on-Severn. Approx 1.5m, pub signed*

Definitely one for the walking fraternity

A 300-year-old, black-and-white free house, 200 metres above sea level and the only pub left on the lovely Bromyard Downs. Breweries not too far away supply Shropshire Lad, Black Pear and Pure Gold real ales. A look at the menu reveals a comforting list of home-made dishes, including steak and kidney pie; beef chilli; and Stilton, leek and apple crumble. Curries make a good showing too, with Thai green, chicken tikka masala and vegetable balti. Batting for the fish team are breaded wholetail scampi; plaice goujons; and battered haddock. Burgers, jacket potatoes, sandwiches, baguettes and salads are other possibilities.

Open 12-3 6-10/11 Closed 25 Dec, Sun eve & Mon **Food** Lunch Tue-Sun 12-3 Dinner Tue-Sat 6-9 ⊕ FREE HOUSE ◀ Wood's Shropshire Lad, Malvern Hills Black Pear, Purity Pure Gold. ❦ 9 **Facilities** Non-diners area ❀ (Bar Garden) ❖ Children's menu Children's portions Play area Garden ⅋ Parking ⛟ (notice required)

CAREY
Map 10 SO53

Cottage of Content

tel: 01432 840242 **HR2 6NG**
dir: *From x-roads on A49 between Hereford & Ross-on-Wye, follow Hoarwithy signs. In Hoarwithy branch right, follow Carey signs*

Cracking inn secluded in the Wye Valley

Lost along narrow lanes in bucolic countryside close to the meandering River Wye, this pretty streamside inn (with lovely views from the garden) has been licensed for 530 years. Now, as then, local ciders and beers flow from the bar which boasts log fire and flagged floors, with heavy timbering and traditional furnishings. Making the most of the county's produce, the concise menu might offer chicken liver, pork and brandy pâté, or goats' cheese and red onion marmalade tartlet; followed by Cajun-spiced chicken breast, bacon-wrapped green beans and sweet potatoes; or griddled Hereford fillet steak with all the trimmings. Save room for the rich chocolate pot with Baileys cream and chocolate biscotti. The pub opens at 5.30 on Fridays, with a tapas menu available from 5.30-7pm.

Open 12-2 6.30-11 (times vary summer & winter) Closed 1wk Feb, 1wk Oct, Sun eve, Mon (Tue winter only) **Food** Lunch Tue-Sat 12-2 Dinner Tue-Sat 6.30-9.30 Restaurant menu available Tue-Sun Lunch, Tue-Sat Dinner ⊕ FREE HOUSE ◀ Wye Valley Butty Bach, Hobsons Best Bitter Ŏ Ross-on-Wye, Carey Organic, Westons Stowford Press & Mortimers Orchard. **Facilities** Non-diners area ❖ Children's menu Children's portions Garden ⅋ Parking ⛟ (notice required)

CLIFFORD
Map 9 SO24

The Castlefields

tel: 01497 831554 **HR3 5HB**
email: info@thecastlefields.co.uk
dir: *On B4352 between Hay-on-Wye & Bredwardine*

Traditional country pub and restaurant in Golden Valley

After hours spent browsing in nearby Hay-on-Wye, the 'Town of Books', a 10-minute drive will get you to this family-run, 16th-century former coach house. The interior is furnished with elegantly modern tables and chairs, although a reminder of the pub's long life is the glass-covered, 39ft-deep well. Home-cooked, locally-sourced food served all day includes roast half-duck with orange sauce; pan-fried liver and crispy bacon; tagliatelle carbonara; wholetail scampi; and lots of grills. Wednesday is curry night and traditional roasts are served on Sundays. Doom Bar and Butty Bach will be found in the bar.

Open all day 11.45am-close Closed Mon (Nov-Feb) **Food** Tue-Sat 12-9, Sun 12-8 Restaurant menu available Tue-Sun ⊕ FREE HOUSE ◀ Sharp's Doom Bar, Wye Valley Butty Bach Ŏ Westons Stowford Press. ❦ **Facilities** Non-diners area ❀ (Bar Garden) ❖ Children's menu Children's portions Play area Garden ⅋ Parking WiFi ⛟ (notice required)

COLWALL
Map 10 SO74

NEW The Wellington Inn

tel: 01684 540269 **Chances Pitch WR13 6HW**
email: thewellingtoninn@btinternet.com
dir: *Between Ledbury & Malvern on A449*

A pub and restaurant with the right balance

Located on the western face of the Malvern Hills, the Wellington sits in an Area of Outstanding Natural Beauty – its garden enjoys panoramic views of unspoilt countryside and magnificent sunsets. Originally a coaching inn where horses were added to passing coaches to ensure successful negotiation of the hill. The ethos here is to keep the bar for drinkers, and seat diners in one of the three dedicated eating areas. So while locals quaff pints of Goffs, seated diners enjoy their choices from the specials board: roast red onion and Bleu d'Auvergne tartlet to start, perhaps, followed by pavé of local venison with creamed Savoy cabbage, watercress, pommes Anna and juniper jus.

Open 12-3 6.30-11 Closed Closed BHs eve, Sun eve **Food** Lunch Mon-Sat 12-2, Sun 12-2.30 Dinner Mon-Sat 6.30-9 ⊕ FREE HOUSE ◀ Goffs Tournament, Gloucester Gold, Butcombe Adam Henson's Rare Breed Ö Westons Stowford Press. ♥ 12 **Facilities** Non-diners area ❀ (Bar Garden) ♦❙ Children's portions Garden ⋒ Parking WiFi ▭ (notice required)

EARDISLEY
Map 9 SO34

The Tram Inn

tel: 01544 327251 **Church Rd HR3 6PG**
email: info@thetraminn.co.uk
dir: *On A4111 at junct with Woodeaves Rd*

Family- and dog-friendly free house with a beautiful garden

With its name recalling a 19th-century, narrow-gauge, horse-drawn railway, this 16th-century inn is one of Eardisley's many traditional, black-and-white-timbered buildings. Wood-burning stoves warm the bar for the Wye Valley Butty Bach drinkers who, in summer, might be found playing boules in the garden. Landlords Mary and Kerry Vernon like to champion their 28-day-aged steaks. And quite right too, as a visit will confirm, although they'd understand if instead you chose cheddar and mixed herb sausages, rich tomato sauce and sweet potato chips; roasted loin of pork with stuffing, crackling and apple sauce; or one of their steak, ale and button mushroom pies.

Open 12-3 6-12 (Fri-Sat 12-3 6-12.30 Sun 12-3 7-11) Closed Mon (ex BHs) **Food** Lunch Tue-Sun 12-3 Dinner Tue-Sat 6-9 ⊕ FREE HOUSE ◀ Wye Valley Butty Bach, Hobsons Best Bitter Ö Westons Stowford Press, Dunkertons Organic. **Facilities** Non-diners area ❀ (Bar Garden) ♦❙ Children's portions Garden ⋒ Parking WiFi ▭ (notice required)

EWYAS HAROLD
Map 9 SO32

The Temple Bar Inn ★★★★ INN ◉◉

tel: 01981 240423 **HR2 0EU**
email: phillytemplebar@btinternet.com **web:** www.thetemplebarinn.co.uk
dir: *From Pontrilas on A465 take B4347 to Ewyas Harold. 1m turn left into village centre. Inn on right*

Smart village pub popular with walkers and cyclists

Just a few miles from the Welsh border, The Temple Bar Inn is a popular pit-stop for walkers and cyclists exploring the Black Mountains and Herefordshire Trail. Painstakingly restored by the Jinman family, this handsome building was first licensed in the 1850s but before that it had been a court house, corn exchange,

school room and stable. It is now very much the hub of the community, with locals popping in for pints of Wye Valley ales or foodies enjoying well-executed classics such as pan-fried chicken breast stuffed with chorizo; aubergine parmigiana with fig and toasted pine nut salad; or pan-fried sea trout with crushed new potatoes and lemon beurre blanc.

Open all wk 11-3 5-close (Sat-Sun & BH 11am-close) Closed 25 Dec **Food** Lunch Mon-Sat 12-2.30 Dinner Wed-Sat 5-7 Av main course £8.50-£11.95 Restaurant menu available Wed-Sat 7-9, Sun Lunch ⊕ FREE HOUSE ◀ Wye Valley Butty Bach, Ludlow Gold, Butcombe Bitter, Otter, Kingstone Classic Bitter Ö Westons Stowford Press & Gold Label. **Facilities** Non-diners area ❀ (Bar Outside area) ♦❙ Children's portions Outside area ⋒ Parking WiFi ▭ (notice required) **Rooms** 3

GARWAY
Map 9 SO42

Garway Moon Inn ★★★★ INN

tel: 01600 750270 **HR2 8RQ**
email: info@garwaymooninn.co.uk **web:** www.garwaymooninn.co.uk
dir: *From Hereford S on A49. Right onto A466, right onto B4521. At Broad Oak turn right to Garway*

Eat, drink and relax in this privately owned country inn

A family-run free house dating back to 1750, overlooking the peaceful and picturesque common. Ask at the bar for three circular walks which will take you to a Knights Templar church of 1180, Skenfrith Castle, and panoramic views of Garway Hill. A good selection of real ales includes Butcombe and Otter Brewery, with Westons cider also on tap. Traditional pub food is based on high quality local ingredients – many of the producers are regulars in the bar. Share a platter of charcuterie or go for a starter of salmon and dill fishcakes or lamb meatballs served in a potjie (a small cooking pot; pronounced 'poykey'), followed by locally sourced steak; a hearty home-made pastry pie or one of their famous espetadas.

Open all wk Mon-Tue 6-11 (Wed-Fri 12-2.30 5-11 Sat-Sun 11-11) Closed Mon L & Tue L **Food** Lunch Wed-Sun 12-2.30 Dinner Tue-Sun 6-9.30 Restaurant menu available Tue-Sun ⊕ FREE HOUSE ◀ Wye Valley Butty Bach & HPA, Butcombe, Kingstone Brewery, Otter Ö Westons Stowford Press. **Facilities** Non-diners area ❀ (Bar Garden) ♦❙ Children's menu Children's portions Play area Family room Garden ⋒ Parking WiFi ▭ (notice required) **Rooms** 3

HAREWOOD END
Map 10 SO52

NEW Harewood End Inn

tel: 01989 730637 **HR2 8JT**
email: inn@theharewoodend.com
dir: *On A49 between Hereford & Ross-on-Wye*

Family-run traditional country inn

Much restored since coaching inn days, the pub is, give or take a house or two, pretty much all there is to Harewood End. The wood-walled and wood-floored interior is decorated with old enamel signs, including a period gem showing a rubicund, besmocked yokel enjoying his pint. Talking of which, look for ales from local brewers like Kel Paul, Purity and Wobbly. Menus offer plenty of choice at both lunchtime and dinner, with beer-battered hake; jerk sweet potato and black bean curry; mustard-glazed ham and free-range eggs; and Portobello mushroom provençale stew. Separate gluten-free menus offer a generous choice too. The shady garden's a delight.

Open 12-3 6-10.30 (Fri-Sat 12-3 6-11 Sun 12-3.30 6-10) Closed Mon **Food** Lunch Tue-Sat 12-2, Sun 12-2.30 Dinner Tue-Sat 6.30-9, Sun 7-9 Av main course £12 Set menu available ⊕ FREE HOUSE ◀ St Austell Tribute, local guest ale Ö Westons Stowford Press, Somersby. **Facilities** Non-diners area ♦❙ Children's menu Children's portions Garden Outside area ⋒ Parking WiFi ▭ (notice required)

HOARWITHY
Map 10 SO52

The New Harp Inn

tel: 01432 840900 **HR2 6QH**
email: booking@thenewharpinn.co.uk **web:** www.thenewharpinn.co.uk
dir: *From Ross-on-Wye take A49 towards Hereford. Turn right for Hoarwithy*

A real country pub

The New Harp's slogan reads: 'Kids, dogs and muddy boots all welcome' — and it's certainly popular with locals, fishermen, campers and visitors to the countryside. Situated on the River Wye in an Area of Outstanding Natural Beauty, the pub has extensive gardens and a real babbling brook. Begin your visit with a local real ale or the home-produced cider. The menu includes starters such as leek and feta cake, tomato and olive tapenade; treacle and port-smoked salmon; then for mains, the 'drunken bunny' — rabbit, vegetable and Shiraz shortcrust pie; beer-battered Cornish cod and hand-cut chips; or an 8oz hanger steak. There's also a board for specials. Look out for bank holiday beer festivals and a cider festival on the Summer Bank Holiday.

The New Harp Inn

Open all wk 12-3 6-11 (Fri-Sun all day) **Food** Lunch Mon-Fri 12-3, Sat-Sun all day Dinner Mon-Fri 6-9, Sat-Sun all day Av main course £12 Set menu available Restaurant menu available all wk ⊕ FREE HOUSE ◀ Wye Valley Bitter, Butty Bach & Dorothy Goodbody's Country Ale, Otter, Sharp's Doom Bar, Wood's Shropshire Lad, Ledbury ales ⚘ Westons Stowford Press & Gold Label, Mortimers Orchard, New Harp Reserve. ♞ 10 **Facilities** Non-diners area ☻ (All areas) ♥ Children's menu Children's portions Garden Outside area ⌇ Beer festival Cider festival Parking WiFi ▭

See advert below

The New Harp Inn
Address: Hoarwithy, Hereford HR2 6QH
Tel: 01432 840900 • **Website:** www.thenewharpinn.co.uk

The New Harp Inn Hoarwithy is a true country pub the way it should be, hidden in the remote village of Hoarwithy in the Wye Valley Area of Outstanding Natural Beauty. The Harp offers fantastic rustic-styled home-cooked food, using only local and organic produce where possible, with real ales, local ciders and a good selection of wines and varied soft drinks. If you are looking for beer battered Cornish fish & homemade chips, a Hereford steak or even a sandwich on homemade bread then the New Harp Inn Hoarwithy is the place for you. We also specialise in fish and have an excellent selection of fish available on our market fish blackboard. Enjoy the countryside in Hoarwithy. We have extensive views, a babbling brook, very large gardens, covered alfresco dining area and a large car park. Well behaved children are welcome, as are our four-legged friends (dog friendly). All food is produced by our "Award Winning" chefs, from the humble chip through to our salted caramel ice cream, we can cater for any dietary requirements and offer an excellent selection for Coeliacs and vegetarians. We also have a shop on site. Good Beer Guide.

Find us on facebook: www.facebook.com/newharpinn • www.facebook.com/groups/newharpinn
Twitter: twitter.com/NewHarpInn@NewHarpInn

| **KENTCHURCH** | Map 9 SO42 |

The Bridge Inn

tel: 01981 240408 **HR2 0BY**
email: bridgeinnkentchurch@hotmail.co.uk
dir: *From A465 between Hereford & Abergavenny onto B4347 at Pontrilas signed Kentchurch. Pub on right*

Delightful 400-year-old pub on the River Monnow

Before going in, take a look at the inn sign. It shows Jack O' Kent, a legendary hero of the Welsh Marches who regularly took on the devil and usually got the better of him. From the beer garden stretching 100 metres along the banks of the river, which here forms the England-Wales border, enjoy fine views of the Black Mountains. The simple menu offers traditional and not-so-traditional pub food, typified by panko-battered squid rings; duck spring rolls; Mediterranean vegetable risotto; steak and Otter pie; and chicken supreme with mushroom and vermouth sauce. In addition, there are specials and regular Oriental, Italian and tapas themed nights.

Open 12-2 6-11 Closed 2nd wk Feb & 1st 2wks Oct, Mon & Tue **Food** Lunch Wed-Sun 12-2 Dinner Wed-Sat 6-9 Restaurant menu available Wed-Sat ⊕ FREE HOUSE ◀ Greene King Ruddles Best. **Facilities** Non-diners area ♦◀ Children's menu Children's portions Garden ⋈ Parking WiFi ⛟ (notice required)

| **KILPECK** | Map 9 SO43 |

The Kilpeck Inn

tel: 01981 570464 **HR2 9DN**
email: booking@kilpeckinn.com **web:** www.kilpeckinn.com
dir: *From Hereford take A465 S. In 6m at Belmont rdbt left towards Kilpeck. Follow church & inn signs*

A warm welcome awaits at this green inn

A few minutes' walk from Kilpeck's famous Romanesque church, this 250-year-old whitewashed pub is run by chef patron Ross Williams. Commendably green, the pub uses a wood-pellet burner for underfloor heating and solar panels for hot water. The bar stocks local real ales from Wye Valley brewery, and draught cider from Robinsons in Tenbury, as well as Herefordshire-made Gun Dog Gin. Typical dishes might include wood pigeon breast, apple and blackberry and toasted cob nuts; and pig cheeks braised with cider apples, celeriac mash and cavolo nero. Leave a space for lemon posset, orange mascarpone cream and gingernut crumb.

Open 12-2.30 5.30-11 (Sun 12-4) Closed 25 Dec, Sun eve, Mon L **Food** Lunch Tue-Sat 12-2, Sun 12-3 Dinner Mon-Sat 6-9 Av main course £12 ⊕ FREE HOUSE ◀ Wye Valley Butty Bach & Bitter, guest ale ♂ Westons Stowford Press, Robinsons. ☗ 8 **Facilities** Non-diners area ❤ (Bar Garden) ♦◀ Children's menu Children's portions Garden ⋈ Parking WiFi ⛟ (notice required)

| **KINGTON** | Map 9 SO25 |

The Stagg Inn and Restaurant ◉◉ PICK OF THE PUBS

tel: 01544 230221 **Titley HR5 3RL**
email: reservations@thestagg.co.uk
dir: *Between Kington & Presteigne on B4355*

Part-medieval old drovers' pub

With many accolades, including two AA Rosettes, to its credit, this well-established and celebrated rural gastro-pub stands where the wooded ridges of west Herefordshire nudge the Welsh border. Locals congregate in the small bar to chat, snack and drink beers from Ludlow and Wye Valley, and Herefordshire real ciders. The rambling layout incorporates several dining areas, where a starter of pan-fried Presteigne trout with celeriac, apple and radish might be followed by roasted, locally shot partridge with pickled cauliflower and pearl barley; or shallot and goats' cheese tart with onion purée, kale and noisette potatoes. A specials board extends the options, while Sunday's set lunch could introduce you to Herefordshire beef, with roast topside served with roast potatoes and Yorkshire pudding. And if you've never had a Herefordshire wine, try a white or rosé from nearby Broadfield Court Vineyard.

Open 12-3 6.30-11 Closed 25-27 Dec, 2wks Nov, 2wks Jan & Feb, Mon & Tue **Food** Lunch Wed-Sun 12-3 Dinner Wed-Sun 6.30-9 Av main course £13.50 Restaurant menu available Wed-Sat, Sun Dinner ⊕ FREE HOUSE ◀ Ludlow Gold, Wye Valley Butty Bach ♂ Dunkertons, Westons & Mortimers Orchard, Robinsons. ☗ 12 **Facilities** Non-diners area ❤ (Bar Garden Outside area) ♦◀ Children's menu Children's portions Garden Outside area ⋈ Parking WiFi

---

| **LEDBURY** | Map 10 SO73 |

The Talbot

tel: 01531 632963 **14 New St HR8 2DX**
email: talbot.ledbury@wadworth.co.uk
dir: *From A449 in Ledbury into Bye St, 2nd left into Woodley Rd, over bridge to junct, left into New St. Pub on right*

Beautiful inn in historic town

This higgledy-piggledy marvel is one of the stars of Ledbury's extensive suite of amazing half-timbered buildings. Parts of it date back to 1550; the interior of the coaching inn oozes the character of great age, with fine beams and panelling in the refined dining room. Holes caused by musket shot fired during a Civil War skirmish are just another quirky talking point of the gabled building, where Wadworth's beers slake the thirst of ramblers fresh from the challenging local countryside. Indulge in starters like baked mushroom with goats' cheese and caramelised red onion chutney; or chicken liver parfait with crostini and plum and apple chutney; follow with Somerset brie and beetroot tart; honey-glazed ham with eggs, tomatoes and chips; or confit pork belly with bubble-and-squeak and black pudding. If the weather permits, sit in the sun-trap courtyard garden.

Open all day all wk **Food** Lunch all wk 12-3 Dinner Mon-Sat 5.30-9, Sun 5-8 ⊕ WADWORTH ◀ 6X, Henry's Original IPA & Wadworth guest ales, Wye Valley Butty Bach ♂ Westons Stowford Press, Wyld Wood Organic & Perry, Thatchers Gold. ☗ 15 **Facilities** Non-diners area Children's portions Garden ⋈ WiFi

The Trumpet Inn

tel: 01531 670277 **Trumpet HR8 2RA**
email: thetrumpetinn@mail.com
dir: *4m from Ledbury, at junct of A438 & A417*

Beamed inn dating from the Middle Ages

This very striking half-timbered inn has stood at a rural crossroads for upwards of 600 years. The name recalls Georgian times when stagecoach guards blew a horn to warn of their approach. A warm welcome remains at the heart of today's pub; whether it's the cheery open fires in the well-beamed and posted interior or a filling meal from the accomplished menu of both traditional and modern dishes. Perhaps a smoked salmon and chive pâté with beetroot and horseradish chutney starter followed by mains such as spaghetti and meatballs; local butcher, Mr Waller's sausages and mash or a vegetarian choice from the specials board.

Open all day all wk 11-11 (Sun 11-10.30) **Food** Lunch Mon-Sat 12-3, Sun 12-8 Dinner Mon-Sat 6-9, Sun 12-8 Av main course £8.95 Set menu available ⊕ WADWORTH ◀ 6X, Henry's Original IPA, guest ales Ö Westons Stowford Press. **Facilities** Non-diners area ❖ (Bar Garden) ♦♦ Children's portions Garden ⊓ Parking WiFi ▤ (notice required)

The Grape Vaults

tel: 01568 611404 **Broad St HR6 8BS**
email: saxonp@pobroadband.co.uk
dir: *Phone for detailed directions*

In the heart of the town centre

This unspoilt, 15th-century pub is so authentic that even its fixed seating is Grade II listed. Its many charms include a small, homely bar complete with a coal fire. A good selection of real ale is a popular feature, and includes microbrewery offerings. The unfussy food encompasses favourites like cottage pie, lasagne, chicken curry and various fresh fish and vegetarian choices. There are also plenty of jackets, baguettes, omelettes and other lighter meals available. No jukebox, gaming machines or alcopops but there is live music every Sunday from 3pm to 6pm.

Open all day all wk 11-11 **Food** Lunch Sun-Thu 12-2, Fri-Sat 12-9 Dinner Mon-Thu 5.30-9, Fri-Sat 12-9 ⊕ FREE HOUSE ◀ Ludlow Best, Mayfields, Wood's, Malvern Hills, guest ales Ö Westons Stowford Press. ☗ 10 **Facilities** Non-diners area ❖ (Bar Restaurant) ♦♦ Children's portions WiFi **Notes** ⊜

The Comet Inn

tel: 01981 250600 **Stoney St HR2 9NJ**
email: thecometinn-madley@hotmail.co.uk
dir: *6m from Hereford on B4352*

Hearty food served in converted cottages with plenty of character

Set at a crossroads deep in rural Herefordshire, the space-age parabolic dishes of the Madley Earth Station and the distant smudge of the Black Mountains provide contrasting skylines visible from the large grounds of this convivial local. Now refurbished, it still retains much of the character of the old cottages from which it was converted 150 years ago. Vicky Willison, the enthusiastic and welcoming owner (almost ten years at the pub), prepares hearty home-cooked food which can be enjoyed in the conservatory off the main bar. In winter, sit beside a roaring fire and in summer enjoy the large, well-kept garden.

Open all wk 12-3 6-11 (Fri-Sun & BHs all day) **Food** Lunch all wk 12-3 Dinner Mon-Sat 6-9 (Sun bookings only) Av main course £8.95 Restaurant menu available all wk (Sun eve bookings only) ⊕ FREE HOUSE ◀ St George's, Hereford, Otter, Bespoke, Brecon Brewery Ö Westons Stowford Press. **Facilities** Non-diners area ♦♦ Children's menu Children's portions Play area Garden ⊓ Parking WiFi ▤ (notice required)

The Bridge Inn

tel: 01981 510646 **HR2 OJW**
email: thebridgeinn@hotmail.com
dir: *From Peterchurch take B4348 towards Hereford, turn right in Vowchurch to Michaelchurch Escley. At T-junct in village turn left*

A truly welcoming inn by a river

With its 16th-century origins, traditional wood-burning stoves and friendly atmosphere, this delightful riverside inn exudes a warm welcome. It makes an ideal base for exploring the Golden Valley, the Brecon Beacons National Park and Offa's Dyke. Cask-conditioned ales and a selection of local ciders are bar highlights; over the Bank Holiday weekend in August, a festival celebrates both forms of refreshment. Heartwarming dishes on their interesting menus are Persian lamb served with za'atar potatoes and steamed vegetables; steak frites; and Escleyside pie – beef, bacon and Butty Bach beer pie with hand-cut chips. If you have room you could be tempted by plum crumble or sticky toffee pudding.

Open all wk 12-3 5.30-10 (Sat-Sun all day) **Food** Lunch Tue-Fri 12-2.30, Sat-Sun 12-3 Dinner Mon-Thu 5.30-8.30, Fri-Sat 5.30-9.30, Sun 5.30-8 Restaurant menu available all wk ⊕ FREE HOUSE ◀ Wye Valley Butty Bach Ö Gwatkin Pyder & Yarlington Mill, Westons Wyld Wood. ☗ 20 **Facilities** Non-diners area ❖ (Bar Garden) ♦♦ Children's menu Children's portions Garden ⊓ Beer festival Cider festival Parking WiFi ▤ (notice required)

The Boot Inn

tel: 01568 780228 **SY8 4HN**
email: hello@thebootinnorleton.co.uk **web:** www.thebootinnorleton.co.uk
dir: *Follow A49 S from Ludlow (approx 7m) to B4362 (Woofferton), 1.5m off B4362 turn left. Inn in village centre*

Atmospheric hostelry with many tall tales

A black and white, half-timbered, 16th-century village inn characterised by a large inglenook fireplace, oak beams, mullioned windows, and exposed wattle-and-daub. Herefordshire real ales and Robinsons cider accompany dishes such as slow-cooked belly pork; line-caught sea bass; and wild mushroom and spinach linguine. In the back room is a painting from which the figure of one-time regular Joe Vale was obliterated after arguing with the landlord. Occasionally, old Joe's ghost returns.

Open all wk 12-3 5.30-11 (Sat-Sun all day) **Food** Lunch Mon-Sat 12-2, Sun 12-3 Dinner all wk 6.30-9 ⊕ FREE HOUSE ◀ Hobsons Best Bitter, Wye Valley, local guest ales Ö Robinsons, Thatchers Gold. **Facilities** Non-diners area ❖ (Bar Garden) ♦♦ Children's menu Play area Garden ⊓ Beer festival Cider festival Parking ▤

PICK OF THE PUBS

The Saracens Head Inn ★★★★ INN

SYMONDS YAT (EAST) Map 10 SO51

tel: 01600 890435 **HR9 6JL**
email: contact@saracensheadinn.co.uk
web: www.saracensheadinn.co.uk
dir: A40 onto B4229, follow Symonds at East signs, 2m

Former cider mill in an unrivalled location

Occupying a stunning position on the east bank of the River Wye where it flows into a steep wooded gorge on the edge of the Royal Forest of Dean, The Saracens Head can be reached by the inn's own ferry, which still operates by hand, just as it has for the past 200 years. Symonds Yat East ('yat' being the local name for a gate or pass) was named after Robert Symonds, a Sheriff of Herefordshire in the 17th century, and has been designated an Area of Outstanding Natural Beauty. There's a relaxed atmosphere throughout the 16th-century inn, from the bar (serving Wye Valley ales), the cosy lounge and stylish dining room, and two sunny terraces overlooking the Wye. If you come at lunchtime, try roasted topside, horseradish and watercress sandwich, or bacon, brie and cranberry baguette. Seasonal menus and daily specials boards offer both the traditional and modern: ham hock, prune and fennel terrine, ginger breaded quail's egg, and cognac poached cherry jelly could be followed by hand-made Monmouthshire faggots, mash, mushy peas and red wine gravy. Main courses at dinner might include Toulouse sausage and duck cassoulet; or trio of Welsh lamb – garlic and rosemary lamb cutlet, sweet potato shepherd's pie and lamb frickadella. Complete your meal with one of the home-made desserts on the blackboard or you might opt for a slate of three local cheeses – Hereford Hop, Per Las and Tintern – served with grapes, crackers, and quince and rose petal jelly. A stay in one of the ten en suite bedrooms is a must if you're exploring this area.

Open all day all wk Closed 25 Dec
Food Lunch all wk 12-2.30 Dinner all wk 6.30-9 🛢 FREE HOUSE 🍺 Wye Valley HPA & Butty Bach, Bespoke Saved by the Bell, Sharp's Doom Bar, Kingstone Llandogo Trow, Wickwar BOB ♨ Westons Stowford Press & Country Perry. 🍷 10
Facilities Non-diners area 🐾 (Bar Garden) 👫 Children's menu Children's portions Garden ⌇ Parking WiFi
Rooms 10

PEMBRIDGE

Map 9 SO35

New Inn

tel: 01544 388427 **Market Square HR6 9DZ**
dir: *From M5 junct 7 take A44 W through Leominster towards Llandrindod Wells*

Traditional inn for good beer and home-cooked food

Formerly a courthouse and jail, and close to the site of the last battle of the War of the Roses, this 14th-century black and white timbered free house has been under the same ownership for over 30 years. Worn flagstone floors and winter fires characterise the cosy bar, and in summer customers spill out into the pub's outdoor seating area on the Old Market Square. Don't expect to find any background music or a TV screen. Home-cooked English fare, using local produce, might include beef steak and ale casserole with horseradish dumplings; hot game pie with Cumberland sauce; or garlic and cheese stuffed chicken wrapped in bacon.

Open all wk 11-2.30 6-11 (summer 11-3 6-11) Closed last wk Feb **Food** Lunch all wk 12-2 Dinner all wk 6.30-9 Av main course £10 ⊕ FREE HOUSE ◀ Hobsons Town Crier, Sharp's Doom Bar, Hook Norton, Three Tuns, Ludlow ♂ Westons Stowford Press & Wyld Wood Organic, Dunkertons. ♀ 10 **Facilities** Non-diners area ♦♦ Children's portions Family room Outside area ⊟ Parking

STAPLOW

Map 10 SO64

The Oak Inn   PICK OF THE PUBS

tel: 01531 640954 **HR8 1NP**
email: oakinn@wyenet.co.uk
dir: *M50 junct 2, A417 to Ledbury. At rdbt take 2nd exit onto A449, then A438 (High St). Take B4214 to Staplow*

17th-century pub in the heart of rural Herefordshire

Set in bucolic Herefordshire countryside richly endowed with orchards and hopyards. The Oak enjoys an enviable location close to the lovely old market town of Ledbury, with the striking ridge of the Malvern Hills a sublime horizon. Ramblers can enjoy a walk along the nearby course of the former Herefordshire and Gloucestershire Canal before retiring to the lovingly extended cottage-style pub, complete with log-burning stoves, flagstone floors and old wooden beams adorned with hops. Both the drinks and food menus draw lavishly on the county's larder; beers from Ledbury and Wye Valley breweries adorn the bar, whilst local cider adds interest. Dishes from the starter menu include Madgett's Farm (Wye Valley) chicken liver and brandy parfait, whilst a sharing platter includes Severn and Wye smoked Var salmon. Juniper-braised blade of Herefordshire beef, roasted beetroot, carrots and wild berry sauce examples the comfortable mains menu here. Dogs are very welcome both inside and in the orchard-side garden.

Open all day all wk **Food** Lunch Mon-Sat 12-2.30, Sun 12-3 Dinner Mon-Sat 6.30-9.30, Sun 7-8.30 ⊕ FREE HOUSE ◀ Bathams Best Bitter, Ledbury Gold, Wye Valley Bitter, guest ales ♂ Westons Stowford Press, Robinsons. **Facilities** Non-diners area ❖ (Bar Restaurant Garden) ♦♦ Children's portions Garden ⊟ Parking WiFi

SYMONDS YAT (EAST)

Map 10 SO51

The Saracens Head Inn ★★★★ INN   PICK OF THE PUBS

See Pick of the Pubs on opposite page and advert below

The Saracens Head Inn

Symonds Yat East, Ross-on-Wye, Herefordshire HR9 6JL   Tel: 01600 890435
Website: www.saracensheadinn.co.uk · Email: contact@saracensheadinn.co.uk

For centuries the *Saracens Head Inn* has occupied its spectacular position on the east bank of the River Wye, where the river flows into a steep wooded gorge. The Inn's own ferry across the river still operates by hand, just as it has for the past 200 years.

There's a relaxed atmosphere throughout the Inn, from the flagstoned bar to the cosy lounge and dining room. The riverside terraces are a great place to watch the world go by.

The Inn has a reputation for high quality food, using fresh local ingredients where possible, with a regularly changing menu and daily specials – not to mention a tempting choice of 6 real ales (featuring local breweries), and freshly-ground coffee.

Symonds Yat East is situated in an Area of Outstanding Natural Beauty on the edge of the Forest of Dean, so a stay in one of the ten guest bedrooms is a must for exploring the unspoilt local countryside.

The Wye Valley Walk passes the Inn, as does the Peregrine cycle trail. Walking, cycling, mountain biking, river cruises, canoeing, kayaking, climbing and fishing are all available nearby.

PICK OF THE PUBS

The Mill Race

WALFORD   Map 10 SO52

tel: 01989 562891
HR9 5QS
email: enquiries@millrace.info
web: www.millrace.info
dir: *B4234 from Ross-on-Wye to Walford. Pub 3m on right*

Pub near the River Wye where local produce truly is local

The village is sometimes known as Walford-on-Wye to distinguish it from another of the same name in the north of the county. The pub is close to the River Wye, just upstream from the picturesque gorge at Symonds Yat, and the Forest of Dean. On the other bank is Goodrich Castle, home to 'Roaring Meg', the only surviving Civil War mortar, which the Parliamentarians used to breach its walls. A refurbishment has left the beamed and flagstoned pub even more comfortable inside, especially now that banquette seating has replaced church chairs in the rustically furnished dining areas. Warm up by one of the wood-burners, or maybe relax on the terrace and watch the buzzards drifting overhead. Just under two miles away on its own 1,000-acre farm estate, the pub rears free-range beef and game. It also grows its own animal feed, some fruit and vegetables, while the woodland conjures up wild boar, rabbits, deer, wild garlic and mushrooms.

Dedicated local producers look after the rest. Dinner might typically begin with Hereford Hop rarebit with spiced fruit chutney; or devilled mackerel fillet, cucumber, mint and cumin seeds; followed by cider-braised pork belly, apple, black pudding and wholegrain mashed potato; whole Cornish plaice, parsley crust, lemon and herb butter; or root vegetable and chestnut pie, creamed celeriac and kale. Steaks are aged for a minimum of 30 days and there is a separate pizza menu that offers a slice (or several slices) of Italy. Wines from Herefordshire appear on the globe-spanning list.

Open all wk 11.30-3 6-10.30 (Sat 12-11.30 Sun 12-11) **Food** Lunch Mon-Sat 12-2, Sun 12-4 Dinner Mon-Fri 6.30-9, Sat-Sun 6.30-9.30 Av main course £13 ⊕ FREE HOUSE ◀ Wye Valley Bitter & Butty Bach, Gloucester Priory Pale, Hillside Legless Cow & Pinnacle ♂ Westons Stowford Press. ♟ 25 **Facilities** Non-diners area ☺ (Bar Garden) ♦♦ Children's portions Garden ⊼ Parking WiFi 🚌 (notice required)

TILLINGTON
Map 9 SO44

The Bell

tel: 01432 760395 **HR4 8LE**
email: glenn@thebellinntillington.co.uk
dir: *From A4103 (N Hereford) follow Tillington sign*

Village pub with something for everybody

Amidst blossoming fruit trees (in the spring, that is) this traditional, village pub has been run since 1988 by the Williams family. With two bars, one with an open fire and a screen for sporting events, dining room, extensive gardens, patio and grassed play area, it offers something for everybody. Home-made ciders are served alongside Herefordshire ales such as brews from Wye Valley. Prepared from locally-sourced ingredients are the sandwiches, light lunches, and dishes such as venison casserole; crab and prawn spaghetti; pork belly with apple and black pudding fritter; and fish pie. If you have a sweet tooth, go for the Mars Bar cheesecake or pecan pie.

Open all day all wk **Food** Lunch Mon-Fri 12-2.30, Sat all day, Sun 12-3 Dinner Mon-Fri 6-9.30, Sat all day ⊕ FREE HOUSE ◀ Hobsons Town Crier, Wye Valley Bitter, local ales ⚖ Tillington Belle & Tinker Belle (pub's own). **Facilities** Non-diners area ❤ (Bar Garden) ♦ Children's menu Play area Garden ⇌ Parking WiFi ⚌ (notice required)

WALFORD
Map 10 SO52

The Mill Race
PICK OF THE PUBS

See Pick of the Pubs on opposite page

WALTERSTONE
Map 9 SO32

Carpenters Arms

tel: 01873 890353 **HR2 0DX**
email: carpentersarms1@btinternet.com
dir: *Exit A465 between Hereford & Abergavenny at Pandy*

Step back in time inside the cosy Carpenters

Located on the edge of the Black Mountains and overlooked by Offa's Dyke, there's plenty of character in this 300-year-old pub that's been owned by the Watkins family for three generations. You'll find beams, antique settles and a leaded range with an open fire that burns all winter; a perfect cosy setting for enjoying a pint of Ramblers Ruin. Popular food options include a steak with pepper or Stilton sauce; crispy battered cod; gammon steak with pineapple or an egg; and vegetarian lasagne. Ask about the large choice of home-made desserts. There are a few tables outside which can be a suntrap in summer.

Open all wk 12-3, 7-11 Closed 25 Dec **Food** Contact pub for food times ⊕ FREE HOUSE ◀ Wadworth 6X, Breconshire Golden Valley & Ramblers Ruin ⚖ Westons. **Facilities** Non-diners area ♦ Children's portions Play area Family room Garden Parking ⚌ Notes ⊛

WELLINGTON
Map 10 SO44

The Wellington

tel: 01432 830367 **HR4 8AT**
email: thewellingtoninn@btinternet.com
dir: *Exit A49 into village centre. Pub 0.25m on left*

Country pub ideal for families

The garden of this pub is sunny and secure, an ideal venue for enjoying a pint of the local brew or a glass of wine. If the weather is inclement, the pub's restaurant and conservatory are also at the disposal of family groups. Here, a typical lunch could comprise potted crab, cottage pie topped with cheddar mash, and sticky toffee pudding. Dinner choices include seared scallops, pancetta and apple and mustard sauce; steak au poivre and chunky chips; and chocolate pudding cake with clotted cream. Ales include local ones such as from the Wye Valley Brewery in Herefordshire.

Open 12-2.30 5.30-11 Closed Mon **Food** Lunch Tue-Sun 12-3 Dinner Tue-Sat 6-9.30 ⊕ FREE HOUSE ◀ Wye Valley Butty Bach & HPA, Butcombe, guest ales ⚖ Westons. ⚑ 9 **Facilities** Non-diners area ❤ (Bar Garden) ♦ Children's portions Garden ⇌ Beer festival Parking WiFi ⚌ (notice required)

WELLINGTON HEATH
Map 10 SO74

NEW The Farmers Arms

tel: 01531 634776 **Horse Rd HR8 1LS**
email: farmersarms@gmail.com
dir: *Take B4214 from Ledbury towards Bromyard. Right signed Wellington Heath*

Good food in a beautiful country setting

You'll find this friendly place just outside Ledbury, in the village of Wellington Heath, surrounded by beautiful countryside – it's good walking country if you want to work up an appetite. Inside you'll find pale walls and mis-matched furniture, well-kept ales from the Wye Valley brewery, and home-cooked, fresh food. Menus feature pub classics like sausage and mash or steak and ale pies, a choice of grills, or something a bit different, maybe jerk sweet potato and black bean curry with home-made flatbread. Finish with chocolate tart with cherry sauce.

Open 12-3 5.30-11 (Tue 5.30-11 Sat-Sun 12-10.30) Closed Mon, Tue L **Food** Lunch Wed-Sun 12-2 Dinner Tue-Sun 6-9.30 Set menu available Restaurant menu available Tue-Sun ⊕ FREE HOUSE ◀ Hillside, Otter, Wye Valley ⚖ Oliver's, Westons, Wilce's. **Facilities** Non-diners area ❤ (Bar Restaurant Outside area) ♦ Children's portions Outside area ⇌ Beer festival Cider festival Parking WiFi ⚌ (notice required)

WOOLHOPE
Map 10 SO63

The Crown Inn

tel: 01432 860468 **HR1 4QP**
email: kitchen@thecrowninn.pub
dir: *B4224 to Mordiford, left after Moon Inn. Pub in village centre by church*

Locally sourced food and great choice of ciders and perries

A traditional village free house with large gardens, The Crown Inn is popular with walkers and well supported by locals and visitors alike. Excellent food and drink are a priority here, with good ales as well as 24 local ciders and perries. Typical starter dishes on the concise menu could be crispy chilli beef with coriander salad; or twice baked Hereford Hop soufflé with creamy garlic mushrooms. Follow on with pheasant, leek and bacon pie, creamed mash and flower sprouts; beer battered Cornish whiting, chunky chips, mushy peas and tartare sauce; or hand-cut Ledbury côte de beouf. There is an outside summertime bar in the garden on Saturday nights and an Early May Bank Holiday beer and cider festival.

Open all wk 12-2.30 6-11 (Sat-Sun all day) **Food** Lunch all wk 12-2 Dinner all wk 6-9 Av main course £11 Set menu available ⊕ FREE HOUSE ◀ Wye Valley HPA, Ledbury Bitter, guest ales ⚖ Westons Stowford Press, Home Milled cider. ⚑ 8 **Facilities** Non-diners area ♦ Children's menu Children's portions Play area Garden ⇌ Beer festival Cider festival Parking WiFi ⚌ (notice required)

HERTFORDSHIRE

The Greyhound Inn

tel: 01442 851228 **19 Stocks Rd HP23 5RT**
email: greyhound@aldbury.wanadoo.co.uk
dir: *Phone for detailed directions*

A traditional village inn offering good food in a relaxed atmosphere

The village's ancient stocks and duck pond are popular with film-makers who frequently use Aldbury as a location, allowing the pub's customers the chance to witness every clap of the clapperboard. In the oak-beamed restaurant, the comprehensive menu includes salads and platters, as well as pan-fried sea bass on braised fennel, kale, yellow peppers and rösti; venison and root vegetables casseroled in red wine; king prawn spaghetti; or rump of lamb on Savoy cabbage and bacon with dauphinoise potatoes. Among the desserts are bread and butter pudding with custard; and dark chocolate and orange mousse with Chantilly cream. The bar snacks are a local legend, especially when accompanied by Badger Dorset Best or Tanglefoot ale.

Open all day all wk 11.30-11 (Sun 12-10.30) Closed 25 Dec **Food** Lunch Mon-Fri 12-2.30, Sat 12-9.15, Sun 12-7.30 Dinner Mon-Fri 6.30-9.30, Sat 12-9.15, Sun 12-7.30 Av main course £16 Set menu available ⊕ HALL & WOODHOUSE ◀ Badger Dorset Best, Tanglefoot, K&B Sussex. ☐ 13 **Facilities** Non-diners area ❀ (Bar Garden) ♦♦ Children's menu Children's portions Family room Garden Outside area ⌂ Parking WiFi ▭ (notice required)

Valiant Trooper

tel: 01442 851203 **Trooper Rd HP23 5RW**
email: valianttrooper@gmail.com
dir: *A41 at Tring junct, follow rail station signs 0.5m, at village green turn right, 200yds on left*

Pretty pub with good food

Named in honour of the Duke of Wellington who allegedly discussed strategy with his troops here, this old pub has been enjoyed by lucky locals for centuries. Located in the quintessential Chilterns' village of Aldbury, beneath the beech woods of Ashridge Park, the Trooper's bar proffers six real ales. Bar food encompasses jackets, sandwiches, ploughman's and pub favourites, while the restaurant menu features dishes like steak and Tring Ale pie; and beer-battered fish, mushy peas and hand-cut chips.

Open all day all wk 12-11 (Sun 12-10.30) **Food** Lunch Mon-Fri 12-3, Sat 12-9, Sun 12-4 Dinner Tue-Fri 6-9, Sat 12-9 ⊕ FREE HOUSE ◀ Tring Side Pocket for a Toad, Chiltern Beechwood, local guest ales ♂ Lilley's Apples & Pears, Millwhites Hedge Layer, Westons, Mr Whitehead's Rum Cask. ☐ **Facilities** Non-diners area ❀ (Bar Garden) ♦♦ Children's portions Play area Garden Parking WiFi ▭ (notice required)

Jolly Waggoner

tel: 01438 861350 **SG2 7AH**
email: info@churchfarmardeley.co.uk
dir: *From Stevenage take B1037, through Walkern, in 2m right to Ardeley*

Ancient village pub with a 'one-mile menu'

All meat on the Jolly Waggoner's menu, including heritage varieties and rare breeds, is traditionally reared at Church Farm across the road, together with over 100 different vegetables, fruits and herbs. As Church Farm runs this 500-year-old pub, the food on offer is truly local, being sourced from within a one-mile radius. Start with sweet potato curry or macaroni cheese, and continue with slow-cooked shoulder of lamb or pan-fried salmon fillet from the market menu. Regular beers

are Buntingford and Fuller's London Pride. The annual beer festival takes place in August.

Open all day all wk 12-11.30 **Food** Lunch Mon-Fri 12-2, Sat 12-9, Sun 12-7 Dinner Mon-Fri 6.30-9, Sat 12-9, Sun 12-7 ⊕ FREE HOUSE ◀ Buntingford Highwayman, Fuller's London Pride, Adnams Broadside, Dark Star, Mauldons Mole Trap, Tring ♂ Aspall. ☐ 13 **Facilities** Non-diners area ❀ (Bar Garden) ♦♦ Children's menu Children's portions Garden ⌂ Beer festival Parking WiFi ▭ (notice required)

NEW Bushel & Strike

tel: 01462 742394 **15 Mill St SG7 5LY**
email: info@busheland strike.co.uk
dir: *Opposite church in village centre*

Food-centred but still very much a local

Billed as a country pub and eating house, the Bushel & Strike was built in 1854 as a brewery for this picturesque village. The provenance of the pub's name is difficult to identify, but it enjoys a growing reputation for well-kept Charles Wells beers, a genuine warm welcome, and chef/landlord Martin Nisbet's excellent food; Martin's partner Lucy, a local girl, also brought a wealth of experience from the hospitality industry when they took over the pub in 2014. Set lunch menus from Tuesday to Friday present the likes of cream of Jerusalem artichoke soup; grilled bavette steak with seasonal vegetables and chips; and home-made ice creams and sorbets.

Open all day Closed Mon (ex BHs) **Food** Lunch Tue-Sat 12-2.30, Sun 12-6 Dinner Tue-Sat 6-9, Sun 12-6 Set menu available Restaurant menu available Tue-Sun ⊕ CHARLES WELLS ◀ Eagle IPA, Young's Bitter, Courage Directors ♂ Symonds. ☐ 12 **Facilities** Non-diners area ❀ (Bar Restaurant Garden) ♦♦ Children's menu Children's portions Play area Garden ⌂ Parking WiFi ▭ (notice required)

The Three Tuns ★★★★ INN ◉

tel: 01462 743343 **6 High St SG7 5NL**
email: info@thethreetunsashwell.co.uk **web:** www.thethreetunsashwell.co.uk
dir: *A1(M) junct 10, A507 (Baldock) then follow Ashwell signs*

Popular destination pub

Behind this early 19th-century inn are Ashwell Springs, source of The Cam, the river that from here heads for nearby Cambridge. A handsome brick building, the pub has a pergola-shaded patio and lovely gardens to the rear. For lunch try a Crumps steak sandwich, or omelette Arnold Bennett. Poached Dingley Dell pork tenderloin; sea bass fillet, smoked parsnip purée, pear, purple potatoes, vanilla poached crayfish and passionfruit; and warm vegetable salad are dinner possibilities. Highlighted on the menu as favourites are pan-fried calves' liver; tempura-battered fish and chips; and steak frites. Potential dessert candidates include sticky toffee pudding, and iced lemon parfait. Wines are from Argentina to New Zealand, by way of Austria.

The Three Tuns

Open all day all wk **Food** Lunch Mon-Sat 12-3, Sun 12-5 Dinner Mon-Thu 6-9, Fri-Sat 6-10 Av main course £13.95 Set menu available ⊕ GREENE KING ◀ St Austell Tribute, Hogs Back TEA, Hook Norton Old Hooky Ò Thatchers. ♟ **Facilities** Non-diners area ✿ (Bar Garden Outside area) ♦♦ Children's menu Children's portions Garden Outside area ⋈ Parking WiFi ▬ (notice required) **Rooms** 3

■ AYOT GREEN   Map 6 TL21

The Waggoners ◉

tel: 01707 324241 **Brickwall Close AL6 9AA**
email: laurent@thewaggoners.co.uk
dir: *Ayot Green on unclassified road off B197, S of Welwyn*

Modern French cuisine in the Hertfordshire countryside

Close to the large, traditional village green and with good English real ales flowing in the beamed bar, it comes as a surprise that the menu has a strong French bent to it. Cue the Gallic owners, whose culinary skills have gained an AA Rosette for their inspired cuisine at this former waggoners' and coaching stop in the low Hertfordshire hills. Menus may include mussels marinière; macaroni and cheese with parmesan crisp and salad; crispy monkfish cheeks; hot green beans and button mushroom salad with sautéed minute steak; or potted duck confit with hot caramelised onions. The wine list stretches to 100 bins.

Open all day all wk **Food** Lunch all wk 12-2.45 Dinner all wk 6.30-9.30 Set menu available Restaurant menu available all wk ⊕ PUNCH TAVERNS ◀ Fuller's London Pride, St Austell Tribute, Adnams Broadside, Greene King Abbot Ale & IPA, Sharp's Doom Bar Ò Westons Stowford Press. ♟ 50 **Facilities** Non-diners area ✿ (Bar Garden Outside area) ♦♦ Children's portions Garden Outside area ⋈ Parking WiFi ▬ (notice required)

■ BERKHAMSTED   Map 6 SP90

The Old Mill

tel: 01442 879590 **London Rd HP4 2NB**
email: theoldmill@peachpubs.com
dir: *At east end of London Rd in town centre*

Historic waterside pub buzzing throughout the week

Owned by Peach Pubs, this imposing, multi-gabled old mill building is right beside the Grand Union Canal. Ghosts of its former life add character to the pub; the mill race off the River Bulbourne still flows by the secluded courtyard, whilst absorbing photos and ephemera are spread throughout the part-beamed rooms. Beers from the Tring Red Squirrel Brewery feature at the bar in the thoughtfully updated interior, where modern British dishes lead on the well balanced menu. Expect dishes like mulled Cornish lamb casserole; or roasted cod supreme with River Exe mussel and bacon chowder. Vegetarian choices are equally inspired.

Open all day all wk Closed 25 Dec **Food** Lunch Mon-Sat 12-6, Sun 12-9 Dinner Mon-Sat 6-10, Sun 12-9 Set menu available ⊕ PUNCH/PEACH PUBS ◀ Tring Side Pocket

for a Toad, Greene King IPA, guest ales Ò Aspall. ♟ 16 **Facilities** Non-diners area ✿ (Bar Garden) ♦♦ Children's portions Garden ⋈ Parking WiFi ▬ (notice required)

■ BISHOP'S STORTFORD   Map 6 TL42

Water Lane Bar and Restaurant

tel: 01279 211888 **31 Water Ln CM23 2JZ**
email: reservations@waterlane.co
dir: *From A1250 in town centre at mini rdbt into North St. 2nd left into Barrett Ln (one way). At T-junct left into Water Lane*

Slickly converted brewery proud of their food sourcing

Just off the main street in the market town of Bishop's Stortford, the old Hawkes Brewery, founded in 1780, underwent a total restoration, with contemporary fixtures and fittings now enhancing the retained original features. It's a dog-free zone that welcomes families, who are entertained on occasion by a resident magician as they dine in the vaulted cellar bar or high-ceilinged restaurant. Pick from a rotating choice of craft ales and speciality cocktails as you tuck into the likes of wild mushroom, truffle and spinach ravioli with poached duck egg, perhaps followed by lemongrass and chilli steamed salmon.

Open all day all wk **Food** Lunch Mon-Sat 12-10, Sun 10-4 Dinner Mon-Sat 12-10 Av main course £14 Set menu available Restaurant menu available all wk ⊕ FREE HOUSE ◀ Craft ales Ò Symonds. ♟ **Facilities** Non-diners area ♦♦ Children's menu Children's portions Outside area ⋈ WiFi ▬ (notice required)

■ BRAUGHING   Map 12 TL32

The Golden Fleece

tel: 01920 823555 **20 Green End SG11 2PG**
email: pub@goldenfleecebraughing.co.uk web: www.goldenfleecebraughing.co.uk
dir: *A10 N from Ware. At rdbt right onto B1368 signed Braughing. Approx 1m to village*

Lovingly village inn on the way to Cambridge

This Grade II listed Georgian coaching is successfully run by Peter and Jessica Tatlow who bought it at auction and then renovated it. Their hard work clearly paid off as the pub has gained a good reputation for its local real ales and ciders, but also its food, which specialises in gluten- and dairy-free dishes. The menu changes every month, but popular dishes are brought back time and time again. Pork, chorizo, pink peppercorn and olive terrine; pulled beef Wellington; and harissa-coated salmon fillet with preserved lemons are typical choices, and the monthly tapas night is a popular fixture on the last Wednesday of each month.

Open all wk 11.30-3 5.30-11 (Fri 11.30-3 5.30-12 Sat 11.30am-midnt Sun 12-10) Closed 25 Dec **Food** Lunch Mon-Sat 12-2.30, Sun 12-6 Dinner Mon-Thu 6-9, Fri-Sat 7-10, Sun 12-6 Set menu available ⊕ FREE HOUSE ◀ Adnams, Nethergate, Buntingford, Mauldons, Church End, Cottage Ò Aspall Harry Sparrow. ♟ 15 **Facilities** Non-diners area ♦♦ Children's menu Children's portions Play area Garden ⋈ Parking WiFi ▬ (notice required)

BROOKMANS PARK
Map 6 TL20

Brookmans

tel: 01707 664144 **Bradmore Green AL9 7QW**
email: brookmans@peachpubs.com
dir: *A1000 from Hatfield towards Potters Bar. Right signed Brookmans Park. Through Bradmore Green. Pub on right*

Enjoyable local food in a buzzy village hub

Built as a hotel in the 1930s, Brookmans may no longer offer a bed for the night but it remains the social hub of the village. Racing Green leather upholstery and silk lampshades add a touch of class to the bar, where a rotating choice of guest ales is complemented by 15 wines by the glass. Local produce and named suppliers drive the modern British menu and daily specials, which might include chilli and lime crab cake with wasabi mayo; Cornish lamb casserole and creamy mash, finishing off with Valrhona white chocolate cheesecake and Baileys cream.

Open all day all wk Closed 25 Dec **Food** Lunch all wk 12-6 Dinner Mon-Sat 6-10, Sun 6-9 Set menu available ⊕ FREE HOUSE/PEACH PUBS ◀ Sharp's Doom Bar, guest ales Ŏ Aspall. ☗ 15 **Facilities** Non-diners area ❄ (Bar Garden) ᛁᛱ Children's portions Play area Garden ᚛ Parking WiFi ➡ (notice required)

BUNTINGFORD
Map 12 TL32

The Sword Inn Hand ★★★★ INN

tel: 01763 271356 **Westmill SG9 9LQ**
email: theswordinnhandrestaurant@gmail.com **web:** www.theswordinnhand.co.uk
dir: *Off A10, 1.5m S of Buntingford*

Welcoming travellers since the 14th century

This old inn provides an excellent stopping off point halfway between London and Cambridge. Inside are the original oak beams, flagstone floors and open fireplace; outside is a large garden and pretty patio. As a free house, there is a varied selection of real ales from the likes of Woodforde's and Timothy Taylor. Fresh produce is delivered daily for a good selection of bar snacks including salads, omelettes, sandwiches and light dishes. Taken from a typical evening menu are Moroccan spiced lamb koftas with mint yogurt dip; and spiced chargrilled sticky chilli pork fillet. Smart accommodation is available.

Open all wk 12-3 5-11 (Fri-Sat all day Sun 12-7) **Food** Lunch Mon-Sat 12-2.30, Sun 12-4 Dinner Mon-Sat 6.30-9 Set menu available ⊕ FREE HOUSE ◀ Timothy Taylor Landlord, Woodforde's Wherry, Adnams Southwold Bitter Ŏ Westons Stowford Press. ☗ 9 **Facilities** Non-diners area ᛁᛱ Children's menu Children's portions Play area Garden ᚛ Parking WiFi ➡ **Rooms** 4

BUSHEY
Map 6 TQ19

The Horse & Chains

tel: 020 8421 9907 **79 High St WD23 1BL**
email: info@thehorseandchains.co.uk
dir: *Phone for detailed directions*

Family-run and a clear hit with locals

First referred to in 1698, its location halfway up a hill was ideal for wagoners and their horses needing refreshment. Although sympathetically redesigned, its great age remains evident, particularly the big open fireplace that dwarfs its modern wood-burner. If more than a sandwich, bar snack or sharing platter is called for, then maybe confit duck leg cassoulet with creamy mashed potatoes; oven-baked

cod with Devon crab risotto; or a salad will do the trick. Theme nights include fish (Mondays), mussels (Tuesdays), tapas, and Greek. Between 5 and 6.30pm on Saturdays buy a starter, main or dessert and get another free.

Open all day all wk **Food** Lunch all wk 12-6 Dinner all wk 6-10 Av main course £14 Set menu available Restaurant menu available all wk ⊕ ENTERPRISE INNS ◀ Sharp's Doom Bar, Wells Bombardier Burning Gold. ☗ 19 **Facilities** Non-diners area ❄ (Bar Garden) ᛁᛱ Children's menu Children's portions Garden ᚛ Parking WiFi ➡ (notice required)

COTTERED
Map 12 TL32

The Bull at Cottered

tel: 01763 281243 **SG9 9QP**
email: darren.perkins@tiscali.co.uk
dir: *On A507 in Cottered between Buntingford & Baldock*

Charming, traditional village local

The four key things that sum up this member of the Greene King portfolio — low beams, antique furniture, cosy fires and teamwork. Then, of course, there's the food. You can eat in one of two traditional bars with open fires, in the pretty beamed dining room, or in the large, well-kept gardens. Everything that can be is home made and the brasserie-style cooking is typified by starters of grilled haloumi Caesar salad; and smoked salmon and prawn parcel; then fillet of sea bass with chilli, ginger, soya and garlic; loin of lamb with roasted chorizo and tomato sauce; or wild mushroom risotto. Look out for regular music evenings (mainly tribute acts).

Open all wk 11.30-3 6.30-11 (Sun 12-10.30) **Food** Lunch Mon-Sat 12-2, Sun 12-4 Dinner Mon-Sat 6.30-9.30, Sun 6-9 Av main course £16 Restaurant menu available all wk ⊕ GREENE KING ◀ IPA & Abbot Ale. ☗ **Facilities** Non-diners area ᛁᛱ Children's portions Garden Outside area ᚛ Parking WiFi ➡ (notice required)

DATCHWORTH
Map 6 TL21

The Tilbury ◉◉
PICK OF THE PUBS

tel: 01438 815550 **Watton Rd SG3 6TB**
email: info@thetilbury.co.uk
dir: *A1(M) junct 7, A602 signed Ware & Hertford. At Bragbury End right into Bragbury Ln to Datchworth*

Lovely country pub serving exciting food

This pub in a little village south of Stevenage goes from strength to strength thanks to brothers James and Tom Bainbridge and a very experienced and welcoming team. The large terrace and garden are ideal for enjoying a drink or meal on sunny days, and inside there are several dining areas, including private dining options. The self-taught and award-winning head chef is passionate about sourcing the best ingredients for his exciting modern British dishes. You could opt for a pub classic such as game cottage pie, or look to the à la carte choices such as pheasant breast, wild mushrooms and pickled mustard seeds; braised rabbit, carrot cake and jus (a witty combination); chicken breast and wings, waffle, chicken jus and thyme cream; and goats' cheese fondant, kale, braised baby onions, peas and lettuce. A set menu is available at both lunch and dinner, and there is an extensive wine list.

Open 12-2.30 5.30-11 (Sat noon-2am Sun 12-5) Closed Sun eve & Mon **Food** Lunch Tue-Sun 12-2 Dinner Tue-Sat 6-9.30 Set menu available Restaurant menu available Tue-Sun ⊕ BRAKSPEAR ◀ Bitter Ŏ Westons Wyld Wood Organic, Symonds. ☗ 12 **Facilities** Non-diners area ᛁᛱ Children's menu Children's portions Garden ᚛ Parking WiFi ➡ (notice required)

PICK OF THE PUBS

The Bricklayers Arms ❁

FLAUNDEN　　　　　　　　Map 6 TL00

tel: 01442 833322
Hogpits Bottom HP3 0PH
email: goodfood@bricklayersarms.com
web: www.bricklayersarms.com
dir: *M25 junct 18, A404 (Amersham road). Right at Chenies for Flaunden*

Country inn with Anglo-French cuisine

The creeper-clad Bricklayers Arms evolved from early 18th-century cottages that, in 1832, the former Benskin's brewery had part-converted into an alehouse. Additional conversions took place in the 1970s, with remaining outbuildings and barn becoming the restaurant more recently. Like The Nags Head 10 miles away in Flaunden, it's owned by the Michaels family. Featuring in many films and TV programmes, the pub is a favourite with locals, walkers, horse-riders and, well, just about everyone, an obvious reason being the array of locally brewed real ales. Past the ivy-covered façade is an immaculate interior, with low beams, exposed brickwork, open fires and candlelight, although on a warm, sunny day a drink or a meal in the terraced, flower-filled garden would be hard to beat. Traditional English and French cooking in the award-winning restaurant is masterminded by head chef Claude Pallait, whose starters include pan-fried tiger prawns with

crayfish salad and cockles in Pernod flambé with warm potatoes, Puy lentils and mixed chicory leaves; or maybe share a charcuterie board. Follow with pan-fried grey partridge breasts with lovage, wilted courgettes and chestnut jus; steak, mushroom and ale pie with chive mash and vegetables; or lemon sole and Scottish salmon medallion, fennel and chardonnay cream and yellow courgette fritters. A good variety of puddings includes rhubarb and apple tart with ice cream; crème brûlée; and several sorbets. With nearly 120 wines and champagnes to browse, the ideal accompaniment for your meal will jump off the page.

Open all day all wk 12-11.30 (Sun 9.15am-10.30pm 25 Dec 12-3)

Food Lunch Mon-Sat 12-2.30, Sun 12-3.30 Dinner Mon-Sat 6.30-9.30, Sun 6.30-8.30 Av main course £16 Set menu available Restaurant menu available all wk ⊕ FREE HOUSE ◀ Tring Side Pocket for a Toad, Rebellion, Chiltern Beechwood Bitter, Paradigm Brewery Touch Point ♂ Aspall, Thatchers Gold. ♟ 20 **Facilities** Non-diners area ♣ (Bar Garden) ♦♦ Children's portions Garden ⌔ Parking WiFi

EPPING GREEN
Map 6 TL20

The Beehive

tel: 01707 875959 **SG13 8NB**
email: squirrell15@googlemail.com
dir: *B158 from Hertford towards Hatfield. Left signed Little Berkhamsted. Left at war memorial signed Epping Green*

Popular family-run country free house

Weatherboarded under a tiled roof, this family-run pub has held a liquor licence for over 200 years. Hanging baskets and window boxes adorn the frontage, while the interior feels traditional to the core, with black beams, a log-burner and ornamental brasses; outside is decked and grassed. Fresh fish is a speciality — maybe poached fish pie; sea bass fillets; or conventional fish and chips. Among the meats are chicken, ham hock and leek pie; lamb shoulder in minted gravy; bacon and brie beefburger; steaks and specials. Vegetarians and coeliacs have a good choice too. On the beer pumps are Greene King and a changing guest ale.

Open all wk Mon-Sat 12-3 5.30-11 (Sun 12-10.30) **Food** Lunch Mon-Sat 12-2.30, Sun 12-4 Dinner Mon-Sat 6-9.30, Sun 6-8.30 Restaurant menu available all wk ⊕ FREE HOUSE ◑ Greene King IPA & Abbot Ale, guest ale. ♟ 12 **Facilities** Non-diners area ♦ Children's portions Garden ⊸ Parking WiFi ⊜ (notice required)

FLAUNDEN
Map 6 TL00

The Bricklayers Arms ◉
PICK OF THE PUBS

See Pick of the Pubs on page 263

HEMEL HEMPSTEAD
Map 6 TL00

Alford Arms
PICK OF THE PUBS

See Pick of the Pubs on opposite page

HERONSGATE
Map 6 TQ09

The Land of Liberty, Peace and Plenty

tel: 01923 282226 **Long Ln WD3 5BS**
email: beer@landoflibertypub.com
dir: *M25 junct 17, follow Heronsgate signs. 0.5m, pub on right*

Top-quality beers and ciders in single-bar pub

Named after a Chartist settlement established in Heronsgate in 1847, this inn is believed to have the second longest pub name in the British Isles. A traditional pub with a large garden and covered decked area, the cosy single bar has a buzz of conversation from locals. The focus here are the real ales and real ciders, all of which can be enjoyed with bar snacks of pork pies, pasties and pots of nuts. Please note that no children or the use of mobile phones are allowed in the bar. Regular events and beer festivals are held during the year.

Open all wk 12-11 (Fri-Sat 12-12) **Food** Contact pub for food times ⊕ FREE HOUSE ◑ 10 guest ales ♂ 4 guest ciders or perries. **Facilities** Non-diners area ♣ (Bar Garden) Garden ⊸ Beer festival Parking WiFi ⊜ (notice required)

HERTFORD HEATH
Map 6 TL31

The College Arms

tel: 01992 558856 **40 London Rd SG13 7PW**
email: info@thecollegearmshertfordheath.com
dir: *From A10 onto A1170 towards Hoddesdon. At rdbt left towards Ware. At next rdbt left signed Hertford Heath*

Dog-friendly village pub with good food

With links to the old East India Company College, now Haileybury College, the pub backs on to woodland, making it an ideal halfway house for walkers. Thoughtful

renovation is particularly evident inside, where exposed brickwork, large rugs and gentlemen's-club-style wingback chairs are harmoniously juxtaposed. An easy-to-digest menu suggests pork dumplings with rocket salad as a starter; pork belly with Savoy cabbage, braised beetroot and mash; and sausages and mash as mains; then chocolate brownie, Italian meringue and chocolate ice cream for dessert. All the cheeses are from The Cheese Plate in Buntingford and Sunday roasts are all served with large Yorkshire puddings.

Open all day all wk **Food** Lunch Mon-Sat 12-3, Sun 12-7 Dinner Mon-Fri 6-9, Sat 6-9.30, Sun 12-7 ⊕ PUNCH TAVERNS ◑ Adnams Ghost Ship, guest ale ♂ Thatchers Gold. ♟ 17 **Facilities** Non-diners area ♣ (Bar Garden) ♦ Children's menu Children's portions Play area Garden ⊸ Parking WiFi ⊜ (notice required)

HEXTON
Map 12 TL13

The Raven

tel: 01582 881209 **SG5 3JB**
email: theraven@emeryinns.com
dir: *5m W of Hitchin. 5m N of Luton, just outside Barton-le-Clay*

Family-friendly pub

This neat 1920s pub is named after Ravensburgh Castle in the neighbouring hills. Comfortable bars witness the serving of four weekly-changing guest ales, perhaps Fuller's London Pride or Greene King IPA, while outside a large garden with heated terrace and a play area ensure family friendliness. Extensive menus and blackboard specials embrace pub classics, salads, jackets, baguettes and wraps, vegetarian options, fish dishes and 'combination' meat plates like ribs and/or steak with Cajun chicken, and surf 'n' turf. So a three-course meal could see garlic and herb king prawns; or chicken liver pâté; steak, mushroom and ale pudding; or whole rack of barbecue spare ribs; and sticky figgy pudding to finish.

Open all day all wk **Food** all wk 12-9 ⊕ FREE HOUSE ◑ Greene King IPA, Morland Old Speckled Hen, Fuller's London Pride, Timothy Taylor Landlord, Sharp's Doom Bar. ♟ 24 **Facilities** Non-diners area ♦ Children's menu Children's portions Play area Garden ⊸ Parking WiFi ⊜ (notice required)

HITCHIN
Map 12 TL12

Hermitage Rd.

tel: 01462 433603 **20-21 Hermitage Rd SG5 1BT**
email: reservations@hermitagerd.co.uk
dir: *From lights on B656 in town centre into Hermitage Rd*

A bar, restaurant and coffee house

Once a ballroom and nightclub, this is not your typical town-centre pub. Although original features survive, like the high vaulted ceiling and arched windows, the stage once graced by Sixties pop stars is now a dining area. Also part of the transformation is the open-plan kitchen, from which come harissa-glazed salmon with sweet potato, broccoli, bok choy and cashew nuts; Norfolk mussels with white wine and parsley cream; and wild mushroom, tarragon and truffle risotto. There's a strong selection of local steaks from the grill, and a roast on Sunday. Local brews from Brancaster are complemented by a globe-trotting wine list.

Open all day all wk **Food** Mon-Sat 12-9.30, Sun 12-8 Av main course £12.50 Restaurant menu available all wk ⊕ FREE HOUSE ◑ Adnams Southwold Bitter, Sharp's Doom Bar, Brancaster, guest ales ♂ Symonds Founders Reserve. ♟ 12 **Facilities** Non-diners area ♦ Children's menu Children's portions WiFi ⊜ (notice required)

PICK OF THE PUBS

Alford Arms

HEMEL HEMPSTEAD ·   Map 6 TL00

tel: 01442 864480 **Frithsden HP1 3DD**
email: info@alfordarmsfrithsden.co.uk
web: www.alfordarmsfrithsden.co.uk
dir: *From Hemel Hempstead on A4146,*
2nd left at Water End. 1m, left at T-junct,
right in 0.75m. Pub 100yds on right

Professional but relaxed pub with understated style

The Alford Arms has now re-opened after a devastating fire in early 2016. With a flower-filled garden overlooking the green in the untouched hamlet of Frithsden, this pretty Victorian pub is surrounded by National Trust woodland and has historic Ashridge Park on its doorstep. Cross the threshold and you'll immediately pick up on the warm and lively atmosphere, derived from the buzz of conversation, some soft jazz in the background, and from the rich colours and eclectic mix of old furniture and antique pictures in the dining room and bar from Tring's well known salerooms. Also from Tring is real ale called Side Pocket for a Toad, which shares bar space with Sharp's Doom Bar and Chiltern Brewery's Beechwood Bitter. The seasonal menus and daily specials are a balance of modern British with more traditional and international dishes, all prepared from fresh local produce whenever possible. There's a great choice of light dishes or 'small plates',

from Scotch broth to rabbit and pistachio terrine, pear and elderflower chutney and sourdough crunch. The equally imaginative 'big plates' include ale-glazed pork fillet, braised barley, roast shallots and carrot crush; baked sea trout, superfood grain risotto, caramelised orange, chicory and saffron vinaigrette; and spiced Potash Farm coq au vin with parsnip purée. Banana and praline spring roll with cinnamon ice cream and toffee sauce; and steamed treacle sponge with vanilla bean custard are just two ways to finish, or there's also home-made sorbets and ice creams, and the plate of British cheeses with toasted seed lavosh, water biscuits and local hedgerow chutney.

Open Mon-Sat 11-11 Sun 12-10.30
Closed 25-26 Dec **Food** Lunch Mon-Thu 12-2.30, Fri-Sat 12-3, Sun 12-9.30 Dinner Mon-Thu 6.30-9.30, Fri-Sat 6-10, Sun 12-9.30 🛢 SALISBURY PUBS LTD
🍺 Sharp's Doom Bar, Tring Side Pocket for a Toad, Chiltern Beechwood Bitter
Ö Westons Mortimers Orchard.
Facilities 🐾 (Bar Garden) 🚻 Children's portions & menu Garden Parking WiFi

HITCHIN *continued*

The Highlander

tel: 01462 454612 **45 Upper Tilehouse St SG5 2EF**
email: info@highlanderhitchin.co.uk
dir: *From Hitchen centre take A505 towards Luton. Pub on right*

English pub and French bistro in entente cordiale

Close to Hitchin's historic town centre, with rustic charm intact, open fire, and secluded garden with terrace, The Highlander continues to thrive in the capable hands of the Prutton family, who have run this Grade II listed pub for nearly 40 years. Today's partnership between Charlotte Prutton and Eric Ransinangue has introduced a French flavour to proceedings. Excellent real ales such as Tring's Side Pocket for a Toad are on tap (a beer festival is hosted in late May), the wine list is eco-friendly, and there is an extensive choice of malt whiskies. Concise menus worthy of a French bistro complete the picture, proposing the likes of duck leg confit with Sardalaise potatoes and red wine jus; or saffron, rocket and pea risotto with parmesan crisp.

Open all wk 12-3 6-11 (Fri-Sat all day Sun 12-4.30 7-10.30) **Food** Lunch Mon-Thu 12-2, Fri-Sun 12-2.30 Dinner Mon-Sat 6.30-9 ⊕ FREE HOUSE ◾ Greene King IPA, Tring Side Pocket for a Toad, XT 1,2,3,4, The 3 Brewers Special. ♀ **Facilities** ✿ (Bar Restaurant Garden) ♦ Children's portions Garden ⋒ Beer festival Parking WiFi ▭ (notice required)

The Fox and Hounds

PICK OF THE PUBS

tel: 01279 843999 **2 High St SG12 8NH**
email: info@foxandhounds-hunsdon.co.uk **web:** www.foxandhounds-hunsdon.co.uk
dir: *From A414 between Ware & Harlow take B180 in Stanstead Abbotts N to Hunsdon*

Mediterranean-inspired menu in a renowned gastro-pub

Eye-catching features at this family-run free house include the unusual white-tiled bar-back, and a striking poster reading 'Nous sommes les soiffards', which, tactfully translated, suggests a fondness for drink. Chef James and wife Bianca run things and together they've created an easy-going place, where Adnams and local ales hold court at the bar, and lunch and dinner can be taken in the elegant, chandeliered dining room. James uses a Josper charcoal oven to cook Isle of Man queenie scallops and seaweed butter; and Scotch Black Angus côte de boeuf, but you could also try the shepherd's pie and mashed swede or roast fillet of cod, fennel, saffron potatoes and mussel bourride. Finish with apple tart fine, caramel sauce and vanilla ice cream or griottine cherry and almond tart. Outside is a tree-shaded garden with a covered terrace.

Open 12-4 6-11 Closed 25-26 Dec, Sun eve, Mon & BHs eve (Tue after BHs) **Food** Lunch Tue-Sat 12-2.30, Sun 12-3.30 Dinner Tue-Sat 6-9 Set menu available ⊕ FREE HOUSE ◾ Adnams Southwold Bitter & Broadside, local ales ♂ Aspall. ♀ 9 **Facilities** Non-diners area ✿ (Bar Garden) ♦ Children's menu Children's portions Play area Garden ⋒ Parking WiFi

The Nags Head

tel: 01279 771555 **The Ford SG11 2AX**
email: paul.arkell@virgin.net
dir: *M11 junct 8, A120 towards Puckeridge & A10. Left at lights in Little Hadham. Pub 1m on right*

Along the country byways just south of Little Hadham

This warm and relaxed country pub was built in 1595 and still retains its traditional atmosphere, with an old bakery oven and a good range of real ales at the bar. Fish dishes such as poached skate wing with black butter and capers feature strongly on the full à la carte menu, which also includes a choice of steaks and vegetarian meals. At lunchtime, sandwiches and jacket potatoes offer a lighter alternative to hot main courses. Sit out the front on a good day and enjoy the countryside.

Open all wk 11.30-2.30 6-11 (Sun 12-10.30) Closed 26 Dec **Food** Lunch Mon-Sat 12-2, Sun all day Dinner Mon-Sat 6-9, Sun all day Set menu available Restaurant menu available all wk ⊕ GREENE KING ◾ Abbot Ale, Ruddles IPA, Morland Old Speckled Hen. ♀ 12 **Facilities** Non-diners area ♦ Children's menu Children's portions Garden ⋒ WiFi ▭

NEW Hermit of Redcoats

tel: 01438 747333 **Titmore Green SG4 7JR**
email: info@hermitofredcoats.co.uk
dir: *A1(M) junct 8 into Stevenage Rd signed Little Wymondley. 1st left signed Todd's Green. At rdbt left under road bridge. At next rdbt 2nd exit. Pub on right*

Smart, traditional pub on the village green

The hermit was James Lucas, who died in 1874. After meeting Lucas, Charles Dickens wrote *Tom Tiddler's Ground*, a short story based on him. At the front a picket fence encloses a pergola, tables and chairs; inside, the scene is set by painted quotations on the walls, old bottles on the mantelpiece, that sort of thing. Try house bitter Tirrells Hermit, one of 17 wines by the glass or maybe a gin – 52 varieties and counting – while your dog enjoys a complimentary biscuit. On the menu could be Dorset crab; sirloin steak, halibut or potato gnocchi; and the comforting puding of spotted dick.

Open all day all wk **Food** Lunch Mon-Sat 12-2.30, Sun 12-3.30 Dinner Mon-Sat 6-9 ⊕ GREENE KING ◾ Tirrells Hermit, rotating guest ales ♂ Aspall. ♀ 17 **Facilities** Non-diners area ✿ (Bar Garden) ♦ Children's portions Garden ⋒ Parking WiFi

The Sun at Northaw

tel: 01707 655507 **1 Judges Hill EN6 4NL**
email: reservations@thesunatnorthaw.co.uk
dir: *M25 junct 24, A111 to Potters Bar. Right onto A1000, becomes High Street (B156). Follow to Northaw, pub on left*

Pretty inn with a skilled chef patron

A Grade II listed inn on a picturesque village green, The Sun has gained a reputation for its real ale, with up to seven available at any time. There is also an excellent wine list to complement cooking from chef and owner Oliver Smith, whose menus are driven by local, seasonal produce. An appetiser of smoked sprats and horseradish might precede a starter of potted beef, pickled prunes and Yorkshire pudding, followed by a main course of venison saddle, swede, haggis mash, wild cabbage and sloe gin. Finish with salted caramel rice pudding, rum and raisins.

Open 12-4 5-11 Closed Sun eve & Mon (ex BHs then closed Tue) **Food** Lunch Tue-Sun 12-4 Dinner Tue-Sat 6-10 Set menu available ⊕ FREE HOUSE ◾ Adnams,

Buntingford, Saffron, Nethergate, Red Squirrel RSX ☼ Millwhites, Aspall. ⚱ 13
Facilities Non-diners area ❄ (Bar Garden) ⚭ Children's menu Children's portions
Garden ⛺ Parking WiFi

The Hoops Inn

tel: 01279 843568 **SG10 6EF**
email: reservations@hoops-inn.co.uk
dir: *From Ware on B1004 towards Bishop's Stortford right onto unclassified road to Perry Green*

Stylish inn with links to famous sculptor

The slightly surreal aspect of the villagescape here is courtesy of renowned sculptor Henry Moore, past resident of the parish, whose vast works dot the area. A subtle blend of cottagey and chic ensure the pub, part of the Moore Foundation Charity, caters for most tastes. A new licensee here has maintained the commitment to real ale, with a great beer garden in which to sit and sup, and tweaked the menus to offer a blend of traditional and modern dishes. Slow roasted pork ribs; tapas plates; or daily-changing specials add to the flavoursome mix; Sunday roasts are a speciality.

Open all day 11.30-11 Closed Mon, Tue **Food** Lunch Wed-Sat 12-3, Sun 12-6 Dinner Wed-Sat 5-9.30, Sun 12-6 Restaurant menu available Wed-Sun ⊕ FREE HOUSE ◀ Adnams Southwold Bitter, Guinness ☼ Aspall. **Facilities** Non-diners area ⚭ Children's menu Children's portions Garden ⛺ Parking WiFi ▭ (notice required)

Martins Pond

tel: 01442 864318 **The Green HP4 2QQ**
dir: *A41 onto A416 signed Chesham, follow signs to Berkhamsted town centre. At lights straight over into Lower Kings Rd. Pass station, into Station Rd. Left at pub on opposite side of village green*

Innovative food and good walks directly from the pub

The unusual name refers to the village green where this welcoming pub is located. A section of Grim's Dyke, an ancient bank-and-ditch earthwork, is clearly visible nearby. By comparison the pub – dating from 1924 – is relatively new, but there's been a public house here since the 17th century. These days it's a good destination for home-cooked food such as smoked salmon pâté with lemon purée and pickled cucumber followed by pan-roasted chicken breast, chorizo gnocchi, tomato and bacon sauce and rocket pesto.

Open all day all wk Closed 26 Dec **Food** Lunch Mon-Sat 12-2.30, Sun 12-4 Dinner Mon-Sat 6-9 ⊕ FREE HOUSE ◀ Fuller's London Pride, Red Squirrel. ⚱ 13 **Facilities** Non-diners area ❄ (Bar Garden) ⚭ Children's portions Garden ⛺ Parking WiFi

The Holly Bush

tel: 01727 851792 **AL2 3NN**
email: info@thehollybushpub.co.uk
dir: *Village accessed from A4147 & A405*

Country pub with old-world charm

Close to St Albans with its Roman ruins and good local walks, there is a delightfully welcoming atmosphere at this picturesque 17th-century pub, which is tucked away in a peaceful hamlet. Wooden benches and tables, antique dressers, log fires and exposed beams set the interior style and there's a large enclosed garden. Both traditional and modern pub fare is offered. At lunch there's ploughman's, baked potatoes, garden salads, deli platters, burgers and toasted sandwiches; while on the evening menu there might be lamb kofta, feta cheese salad, pittas and tzatziki, followed by Belgian waffle, clotted cream ice cream and maple syrup.

Open all wk 12-2.30 6-11 (Sun 12-3) **Food** Lunch Mon-Sat 12-2, Sun 12-2.30 Dinner Wed-Sat 6-9 Av main course £11 ⊕ FULLER'S ◀ London Pride, ESB, George Gale & Co Seafarers, seasonal ales. **Facilities** Non-diners area ⚭ Garden ⛺ Parking WiFi ▭ (notice required)

The Cock Inn

tel: 01923 282908 **Church Ln WD3 6HH**
email: enquiries@cockinn.net
dir: *M25 junct 18, A404 signed Chorleywood, Amersham. Right follow signs to Sarratt. Pass church on left, pub on right*

Welcoming rustic pub oozing character and charm

A warm and friendly welcome is guaranteed at this traditional village inn standing opposite Sarratt's Norman church. Originally called the Cock Horse, this 17th-century pub is in the heart of the Chess Valley, an area favoured by walkers. It has head-cracking low beams, an inglenook fireplace and Hall & Woodhouse ales at the bar, while the ancient timbered barn houses the restaurant. Expect classic pub dishes such as cottage pie; pork and leek sausages; or liver and bacon casserole. Light bites and sandwiches are served in the bar or garden.

Open all day all wk **Food** Lunch Mon-Fri 12-2.30, Sat 12-9, Sun 12-5 Dinner Mon-Fri 6-9, Sat 12-9, Sun 12-5 Restaurant menu available Tue-Sun ⊕ HALL & WOODHOUSE ◀ Badger First Call, Tanglefoot, K&B Sussex, guest ale ☼ Westons Stowford Press. **Facilities** Non-diners area ❄ (Bar Restaurant Garden) ⚭ Children's menu Children's portions Play area Garden ⛺ Parking WiFi ▭ (notice required)

| THERFIELD | Map 12 TL33 |

The Fox and Duck

tel: 01763 287246 **The Green SG8 9PN**
email: info@thefoxandduck.co.uk
dir: *From Royston take A505 towards Baldock. At rdbt left signed Therfield. 1st right signed Therfield*

Lovely old pub in great walking country

A quintessential country pub with plenty of original features – flagstone floors and exposed beams – The Fox and Duck is right on the village green in picturesque Therfield and ideally situated for walking the Icknield Way, which passes directly outside. Ramblers and walking groups use the pub as a start and finish point, stopping in for a pint of IPA or one of the rotating guest ales. Food wise, there's a bar menu and a carte and you can mix and match from either, maybe starting with chicken liver parfait and moving on to a trio of pork – loin, braised cheek and white pudding.

Open 12-3 5.30-11.30 (Sat-Sun all day) Closed Mon (ex BH) ⊕ GREENE KING ◀ IPA, rotating guest ales Ö Aspall, Rekorderlig. **Facilities** ❖ (Bar Garden) ♦ Children's menu Children's portions Play area Garden Parking WiFi

---

| WATTON-AT-STONE | Map 6 TL31 |

The Bull

tel: 01920 831032 **High St SG14 3SB**
email: info@thebullwatton.co.uk
dir: *A602 from Stevenage towards Ware. At rdbt follow Watton-at-Stone sign. Right at mini rdbt (Datchworth & Walkern) into High St. Pub on right*

Village pub infused with love and vitality by local family

The Bramley family were living in this pretty village when The Bull became available. Using their experience in managing gastro-pubs, they've made sure that this inn once again extended warm hospitality to all-comers. Families gather for Christmas carols around the huge inglenook fireplace, Morris dancers entertain in summer, and beer and cider festivals are hosted in May and October. Seasonality is also key to the kitchen's work, together with the provenance of high-grade ingredients; rare breed meats, for example, are reared just outside the village. So expect menus of hearty British fare such as pork belly with black pudding and apple bon bons; duck leg cassoulet with Toulouse sausage, root vegetables, haricot beans and fondant potato; or butternut squash and pea pappardelle.

Open all day all wk **Food** Lunch Mon-Sat 12-3, Sun 12-6 Dinner Mon-Sat 6-10, Sun 12-6 Set menu available Restaurant menu available Mon-Sat ⊕ PUNCH TAVERNS ◀ Sharp's Doom Bar, Adnams Ghost Ship, guest ale Ö Thatchers Gold. ❣ 10 **Facilities** Non-diners area ❖ (Bar Garden Outside area) ♦ Children's menu Children's portions Play area Garden Outside area ☿ Beer festival Cider festival Parking WiFi (notice required)

| WELWYN | Map 6 TL21 |

The Wellington ★★★★★ INN ⊛

tel: 01438 714036 **High St AL6 9LZ**
email: info@wellingtonatwelwyn.co.uk **web:** www.wellingtonatwelwyn.co.uk
dir: *A1(M) junct 6 to Welwyn*

Stylish village pub with notable food

Opposite the Saxon church in the attractive village of Welwyn, this 13th-century coaching inn offers six comfortable bedrooms alongside its one AA-Rosette food. Inside, it's cosy and stylish but when the weather allows, grab a table on the terrace

or enjoy a drink by the river at the bottom of the garden. There is plenty of choice when it comes to food, from lunchtime sandwiches and wraps to sharing plates and ambitious modern British dishes listed on the 'clipboard' menus and blackboard specials. A notable 37 wines are sold by the glass.

Open all day all wk **Food** Lunch Mon-Fri 12-3, Sat-Sun 12-10 Dinner Mon-Fri 5.30-10, Sat-Sun 12-10 Set menu available Restaurant menu available all wk ⊕ GREENE KING ◀ Morland Old Speckled Hen, Wellington Ale Ö Aspall. ❣ 37 **Facilities** Non-diners area ♦ Children's menu Children's portions Garden ☿ Parking WiFi (notice required) **Rooms** 6

| WEST HYDE | Map 6 TQ09 |

The Oaks

tel: 01895 822118 **Old Uxbridge Rd WD3 9XP**
email: info@theoakspub.co.uk
dir: *From rdbt on A412 between Rickmansworth & Denham into Chalfont Ln. At T-junct right, pub on left*

Brewers' Tudor-style country pub

Surrounded by a white picket-fence, The Oaks stands on a corner, with lakes and woodland behind; handy for an outing from Harefield, Chalfont St Peter, Rickmansworth or Denham. Expect to find St Austell and Rebellion IPA on hand pump along with guest ales. A typical meal could be brochette of fried wild mushrooms, house-smoked cheddar and shallots followed by haddock in Symonds cider batter, chips, peas and home-made tartare sauce; a 28-day-aged rump, sirloin or rib-eye steak; or honey-roast ham hock with beetroot and potato gratin, mustard and cider sauce. Snacks include spiced barbecue chicken and pulled pork sandwiches. Among the desserts, quince crème caramel is quite unusual.

Open all day all wk **Food** Contact pub for food times Set menu available ⊕ ENTERPRISE INNS ◀ St Austell Tribute, Rebellion IPA, guest ales. ❣ 16 **Facilities** Non-diners area ❖ (Bar Garden) ♦ Children's menu Children's portions Garden ☿ Parking WiFi (notice required)

| WESTON | Map 12 TL23 |

The Cricketers

tel: 01462 790273 **Damask Green Rd SG4 7DA**
email: info@thecricketersweston.co.uk
dir: *Phone for detailed directions*

Good food at this family-friendly pub

The warmest of welcomes is assured at The Cricketers, whether for adults with or without children, muddy boots and dogs. The open fire, range of ales and Symonds cider, and menu of home-cooked pub food meld into the pub's relaxed ambience. As well as wood-fired pizzas baked to order in the cricket ball-themed oven, try the sweet chilli glazed pork belly ribs; or lemongrass, lime and coconut lamb curry. Excellent green credentials and menus meeting gluten-free and other dietary requirements complete the picture, with the large garden and kids' play area especially popular in the summer.

Open all wk 12-2.30 5.30-11 (Fri-Sat 12-11 Sun 12-10) **Food** Lunch Mon-Fri 12-2.30, Sat-Sun all day (takeaway service 12-9.30) Dinner Mon-Fri 6-9.30, Sat-Sun all day Av main course £12 ⊕ FREE HOUSE ◀ Woodforde's Wherry, Sharp's Doom Bar, Adnams Bitter Ö Symonds. **Facilities** Non-diners area ❖ (Bar Restaurant Garden) ♦ Children's menu Children's portions Play area Garden ☿ Beer festival Parking WiFi (notice required)

WILLIAN
Map 12 TL23

The Fox ◉◉
PICK OF THE PUBS

tel: 01462 480233 **SG6 2AE**
email: info@foxatwillian.co.uk
dir: A1(M) junct 9 towards Letchworth, 1st left to Willian, pub 0.5m on left

Fine dining pub with a smart, contemporary interior

Sitting opposite the village pond and right next to the church, this imposing 18th-century pub is an award-winning destination, attracting locals, walkers and cyclists alike. A clean, crisp look defines the interior, while the laid-back bar, restaurant atrium, enclosed courtyard and two beer gardens are all pleasant places to settle down with the modern British menus. In the bar and restaurant, expect East Anglian ales such as Adnams Southwold Bitter accompanying fresh fish brought in from Norfolk and plenty of other produce sourced locally. There's lots of choice on the menus – from bar snacks such as venison croquettes with pickled red cabbage and brown sauce, to main courses of Toulouse sausages with root vegetable and lentil ragù; or braised shoulder of lamb with roast potatoes and seasonal veg. Look out for 'bin end' wine deals and the popular themed food nights that take place throughout the year.

Open all day all wk **Food** Lunch Mon-Thu 12-2.30, Fri-Sat 12-9, Sun 12-3 Dinner Mon-Thu 6.30-9, Fri-Sat 12-9 Av main course £12.95 Restaurant menu available Mon-Sat & Sun Lunch ⊕ FREE HOUSE ◖ Adnams Southwold Bitter, Woodforde's Wherry, Sharp's Doom Bar, Brancaster Best Ŏ Symonds. ♟ 12 **Facilities** Non-diners area ☻ (Bar Garden Outside area) ♦♦ Children's portions Garden Outside area ⋒ Beer festival Parking WiFi ▭ (notice required)

ISLE OF WIGHT

ARRETON
Map 5 SZ58

The White Lion

tel: 01983 528479 **Main Rd PO30 3AA**
email: whitelioniow@gmail.com
dir: On A3056 (Blackwater to Shanklin/Sandown road)

Traditional pub food and reliable real ales

A 200-year-old coaching inn in the heart of Arreton village. Reliable ales like Doom Bar and Timothy Taylor Landlord are the top refreshments, while prices on the short wine list are commendably affordable. Food ranges from paninis and sandwiches to light bites and children's choices, and then on to classic starters, favourites main courses, and traditional desserts. A typical choice could kick off with blue cheese and Ventnor Bay crab beignets with port and Stilton sauce. Next may come the short-crust pie of the day from the blackboard, with a home-made berry Pavlova with crème Chantilly to finish.

Open all day all wk 11.30-11 (Sun 12-10.30) **Food** all wk 12-9 Set menu available ⊕ ENTERPRISE INNS ◖ Sharp's Doom Bar, Timothy Taylor Landlord. **Facilities** Non-diners area ☻ (Bar Garden) ♦♦ Children's menu Children's portions Family room Garden ⋒ Parking

BEMBRIDGE
Map 5 SZ68

The Crab & Lobster Inn ★★★★ INN

tel: 01983 872244 **32 Forelands Field Rd PO35 5TR**
email: info@crabandlobsterinn.co.uk **web:** www.crabandlobsterinn.co.uk
dir: From High St in Bembridge, 1st left after Boots into Forelands Rd. At right bend, left into Lane End Rd, 2nd right into Egerton Rd. At T-junct left into Howgate Rd. Road bears right & becomes Forelands Field Rd, follow brown inn signs

Great sea views and seafood at beamed inn

This inn is bedecked with flower baskets in summer and the stunning coastal location beside Bembridge Ledge means the raised deck and patio is a perfect place to sup locally brewed Goddards Fuggle-Dee-Dum bitter whilst watching yachts and fishing boats out in the eastern approach to the Solent. Locally caught seafood is one of the pub's great attractions, with dishes such as dressed crab; cold seafood platter; moules marinière; and Thai cod and prawn fishcakes. There are of course pub favourites, seasonal and vegetarian dishes too, and sandwiches at lunchtime. Some of the light and airy bedrooms have outstanding sea views.

Open all day all wk 11-11 (Sun 11-10.30) **Food** Lunch all wk 12-2.30 (wknds & BHs all day) Dinner Sun-Thu 6-9, Fri-Sat 6-9.30 (wknds & BHs all day) ⊕ ENTERPRISE INNS ◖ Sharp's Doom Bar, Goddards Fuggle-Dee-Dum, guest ales Ŏ Westons Stowford Press. ♟ 12 **Facilities** Non-diners area ☻ (Bar Garden) ♦♦ Children's menu Children's portions Garden ⋒ Parking WiFi **Rooms** 5

The Pilot Boat Inn

tel: 01983 872077 **Station Rd PO35 5NN**
email: george@thepilotboatinn.com
dir: Follow B3395 (Embankment Rd) around harbour. Pub on junct with Station Rd

Welcoming harbourside local beside coastal footpath

With a startling, quirky look of a beached ark, this lively pub makes the most of its setting beside Bembridge Harbour, with an ever-varying choice of daily seafood specials progressing straight from creel to galley. Slow-cooked lamb shank with all the trimmings is another staple at this accommodating local in what is said to be England's largest village, where beers from the Isle of Wight's own Goddards Brewery keep seafarers old and new in chatty mode. A winter fire warms the brightly appointed interior, dressed with nautical and other flags, whilst Morris dancers may brighten up a summer's afternoon.

Open all day all wk **Food** Lunch all wk 12-2.30 Dinner all wk 6-8.30 Restaurant menu available all wk ⊕ FREE HOUSE ◖ Goddards Ale of Wight Ŏ Westons Old Rosie & Stowford Press. **Facilities** Non-diners area ☻ (Bar Restaurant Garden) ♦♦ Children's menu Children's portions Garden ⋒ Parking WiFi ▭ (notice required)

NEW The Spinnaker ★★★★ INN

tel: 01983 872840 **1 Steyne Rd PO35 5UH**
email: info@thespinnakeriow.co.uk **web:** www.thespinnakeriow.co.uk
dir: From A3055 onto B3395 towards Bembridge. After rdbt road becomes Steyne Rd, pub on right

Edwardian inn serving island produce

After a complete refurbishment, The Spinnaker is a warmly glowing beacon of hospitality on the island's east coast. Goddard's, the island brewer, furnishes the bar with Fuggle-Dee-Dum, just as the island's farmers and fishermen deliver most of the fresh produce used by the kitchen. Pub favourites such as local pork sausages and grilled steaks from island herds are a cut above the norm. And where better to sit down to a plate of Bembridge crab, smoked salmon, shell-on prawns and smoked mackerel? Look to the specials board for lobster or the day's fresh fish dish. Fourteen refurbished and fully equipped en suite bedrooms complete the picture here.

Open all day all wk **Food** Contact pub for food times Av main course £12 Restaurant menu available ⊕ FREE HOUSE ◖ Goddards Fuggle-Dee-Dum Ŏ Symonds. ♟ 12 **Facilities** Non-diners area ♦♦ Children's menu Children's portions Garden ⋒ Parking WiFi ▭ (notice required) **Rooms** 14

BONCHURCH | Map 5 SZ57

The Bonchurch Inn

tel: 01983 852611 **Bonchurch Shute PO38 1NU**
email: gillian@bonchurch-inn.co.uk
dir: *Signed from A3055 in Bonchurch*

Family-run free house with an Italian emphasis

Tucked away in a secluded Dickensian-style courtyard, this small inn is in a quiet, off-the-road location. In fact, little has changed here since this former coaching inn and stables was granted a licence in the 1840s. Food is available lunchtime and evenings in the bar; choices range from sandwiches and salads to plenty of daily-fresh fish (sea bass, pollock and crab among the choices) and traditional meat dishes. Italian specialities are a prominent feature on account of the owners' heritage; try one of the pizzas, perhaps the Adrian special (mushroom, olive, salami, spinach, bolognese, chilli and Stilton); spinach cannelloni, or tagliatelle carbonara. Desserts also have an Italian bias – perhaps zabaglione, tiramisù or cassata. If you want something not-so-Italian, there's still plenty of choice.

Open all wk 12-3 6.30-11 Closed 25 Dec **Food** Lunch all wk 12-2 Dinner all wk 6.30-9 ⊕ FREE HOUSE ◄ Courage Best Bitter, Wells Bombardier. **Facilities** Non-diners area ✿ (Bar Outside area) ◄ Children's menu Children's portions Family room Outside area ♠ Parking WiFi

COWES | Map 5 SZ49

Duke of York Inn ★★★ INN

tel: 01983 295171 **Mill Hill Rd PO31 7BT**
email: bookings@dukeofyorkcowes.co.uk **web:** www.dukeofyorkcowes.co.uk
dir: *In town centre*

Pub with a nautical theme

A former coaching inn close to Cowes town centre, ferry terminals and the marina, the Duke of York has been run by the Cass family for over 40 years. Even sopping wet yachtsmen are made welcome here. Fuggle-Dee-Dum from the island's Goddards Brewery is one of several real ales, with the rest coming from the mainland. Quality home-cooked food with an emphasis on fresh seafood available in the bar and restaurant includes oven-baked sea bass, poached salmon in parsley sauce, and traditional battered cod. Possible alternatives are a variety of pie, bangers and mash, spaghetti bolognaise, and BBQ pork ribs, all home made, as well as daily blackboard specials, vegetarian choices and Sunday roasts.

Open all day all wk **Food** all wk 12-10 Restaurant menu available Mon-Sat & Sun evening ⊕ ENTERPRISE INNS ◄ Goddards Fuggle-Dee-Dum, Sharp's Doom Bar, Ringwood Best Bitter Ö Westons 1st Quality & Old Rosie. **Facilities** Non-diners area ✿ (Bar Restaurant Outside area) ◄ Children's menu Children's portions Outside area ♠ Parking WiFi ▄▄▄ **Rooms** 13

How have pubs changed over the last 20 years? See page 12

FISHBOURNE | Map 5 SZ59

The Fishbourne ★★★ INN

tel: 01983 882823 **Fishbourne Ln PO33 4EU**
email: info@thefishbourne.co.uk **web:** www.thefishbourne.co.uk
dir: *From East Cowes ferry terminal to rdbt. 3rd exit signed Ryde & Newport. At T-junct left onto A3021 signed Ryde & Newport. At next rdbt 1st exit signed Newport. At next rdbt 1st exit onto A3054 signed Ryde. Left at lights into Fishbourne Ln signed Portsmouth. Pass ferry terminal to pub*

Top-quality eating in a pub environment

Time your ferry crossing to Portsmouth carefully and, since it's down the same cul-de-sac as the Wightlink terminal, you'll be able to visit this mock-Tudor dining pub. A design-savvy approach to furnishing is apparent in the spacious bar, where there are smart leather sofas, and in the elegant dining area; lunchtime sees sandwiches, baguettes, seafood specialities, deli boards and sharing platters, as well as old favourites like fish and chips, and sausages and mash. Daily-changing blackboard specials may include pork and leek sausages with mash and gravy; pie of the day; and warm chicken and bacon salad with boiled egg and ranch dressing. The en suite bedrooms are stylishly decorated with light and airy decor and modern amenities.

Open all day all wk **Food** Lunch all wk 12-2.30 Dinner all wk 6-9.30 (varies with season) ⊕ ENTERPRISE INNS ◄ Goddards Fuggle-Dee-Dum, Sharp's Doom Bar, Ringwood Best Bitter Ö Symonds. ♟ 12 **Facilities** Non-diners area ◄ Children's menu Children's portions Garden ♠ Parking WiFi **Rooms** 5

FRESHWATER | Map 5 SZ38

The Red Lion

tel: 01983 754925 **Church Place PO40 9BP**
email: info@redlion-freshwater.co.uk
dir: *In Old Freshwater follow signs for All Saints Church*

Friendly village pub a short walk from Yarmouth Harbour

Its two big gables and red-brick walls give no indication of its great age but, like the neighbouring church, the pub's origins go back to the 11th century. Landlord Mark McDonald serves Fuggle-Dee-Dum and Sharp's Doom Bar in the shiny-flagstoned bar, where settles and sofas partner well-scrubbed pine tables. Meals feature herbs and vegetables from the pub's large garden, and many other ingredients are from elsewhere on the island or its coastal waters. Menu fixtures include crab mornay with toasted ciabatta; beer-battered fresh fish; daily changing pies; and home-made tagliatelle. Further choice is afforded by specials.

Open all wk 11-11 (Sun 11-10.30) **Food** Lunch 12-2.30 Dinner 6-9 ⊕ ENTERPRISE INNS ◄ Fuggle-Dee-Dum, Sharp's Doom Bar, West Berkshire Good Old Boy, St Austell Proper Job Ö Symonds, Westons Stowford Press, Lilley's Apples & Pears. ♟ 12 **Facilities** Non-diners area ✿ (Bar Garden) ◄ Garden ♠ Parking WiFi

GODSHILL | Map 5 SZ58

The Taverners | PICK OF THE PUBS

tel: 01983 840707 **High St PO38 3HZ**
dir: *Phone for detailed directions*

Village pub incorporating its own food shop

Godshill is surely the island's prettiest village, and The Taverners fits the heritage jigsaw perfectly. With heavy ribbed beams and posts, slab flooring, log fires and scrubbed rustic furnishings it's the archetypical village inn. There's a toddlers' play area in the garden, adjoining the vegetable plots, and the pub has its own shop selling top-notch wines and artisanal goods. Real ales and village-made cider are stalwarts in the bar, while meats and dairy products all come from Isle of Wight farmers, fish are from local waters, island fruit and vegetables are used when in season, and much else is locally caught, shot or foraged. Time-honoured pub grub is a given, including burgers, fish and chips and home-made beef and ale pie; the daily-changing specials might include grilled ox tongue with sauerkraut and smoked potato puree, or smoked haddock fishcakes, followed by partridge with bacon, celeriac purée, black cabbage and straw potatoes; or slow-roast pork belly, home-made faggot, red cabbage and bubble-and-squeak. For pudding try the baked honey semolina with rhubarb and vanilla ice cream.

Open all day all wk Closed 1st 3wks Jan **Food** Lunch all wk 12-3 Dinner Mon-Thu 6-9, Fri-Sat 6-9.30 Av main course £12 ⊕ PUNCH TAVERNS ◖ Taverners Own, Sharp's Doom Bar, Brains The Rev. James, Black Sheep, Butcombe Ŏ Godshill, Symonds. ☂ 10 **Facilities** Non-diners area ❧ (Bar Garden) ⅰ Children's menu Children's portions Play area Garden ⌤ Parking WiFi ⇥ (notice required)

HULVERSTONE — Map 5 SZ38

The Sun Inn at Hulverstone

tel: 01983 741124 **Main Rd PO30 4EH**
dir: *Between Mottistone & Brook on B3399*

Village-edge inn in stunning location

All flagstones, floorboards, beams, settles and wood-burners, this lovely ancient thatched pub, now in new hands, occupies an enviable position in the gently rolling countryside towards the western tip of the island. With fabulous English Channel views from the pleasant garden here, customers can enjoy a wide variety of ales and choose from a menu that has something for everyone. Expect to find moules marinière, home-made Ventnor crab cake; seafood mixed grill; vegetable lasagne; and 10oz rump steak with all the trimmings, whilst the specials board highlights the pie of the day. Gluten free-dishes are marked on the menu. There's live music on Wednesdays, Fridays, Saturdays and Sundays.

Open all day all wk **Food** all wk 12-9 ⊕ ENTERPRISE INNS ◖ Brakspear, Sharp's Doom Bar, Greene King Abbot Ale, Young's, rotating ales. **Facilities** Non-diners area ❧ (Bar Garden) ⅰ Children's portions Garden ⌤ Parking WiFi ⇥ (notice required)

NEWPORT — Map 5 SZ48

The Stag

tel: 01983 522709 **Stag Ln PO30 5TW**
email: info@stagpub.com
dir: *On A3020 between Cowes & Newport*

Family dining pub

There's been a change of hands at this pub, located in the middle of the island. Pale-coloured wood predominates in the attractive long bar, where Sharp's Doom Bar takes the lead along with guest ales and sandwiches and baguettes come with dressed salad or chips. Other dishes include a trio of Isle of Wight sausages, mash and gravy; chicken and chorizo tagliatelle; classic, BBQ or sweet chilli half rotisserie chicken; and a mixed grill.

Open all day all wk **Food** Lunch Mon-Fri 12-2.30, Sat-Sun 12-9 Dinner Mon-Fri 6-9, Sat-Sun 12-9 Av main course £10 ⊕ PUNCH TAVERNS ◖ Sharp's Doom Bar, guest ales. ☂ 12 **Facilities** Non-diners area ❧ (Bar Garden) ⅰ Children's menu Children's portions Play area Garden ⌤ Parking WiFi ⇥ (notice required)

NINGWOOD — Map 5 SZ38

Horse & Groom

tel: 01983 760672 **Main Rd PO30 4NW**
email: info@horse-and-groom.com
dir: *On A3054 (Yarmouth to Newport road)*

Great for families with young children

Just a couple of miles west of Yarmouth on the Newport road, this large landmark pub is certainly family-friendly. There's a pleasant garden with a large children's play area, and an extensive and well-priced kids' menu. Food is served daily from noon until 9pm, and the offering ranges from jacket potatoes and light bites to pub favourites like home-made lasagne; steak and ale pie; and sticky toffee pudding plus a specials board offering seasonal specialities. Four-footed family members are also welcome on the stone and wood-floor indoor areas.

Open all day all wk **Food** all wk 12-9 ⊕ ENTERPRISE INNS ◖ Ringwood, Sharp's Doom Bar Ŏ Westons Stowford Press, Somersby. ☂ 11 **Facilities** Non-diners area ❧ (Bar Restaurant Garden) ⅰ Children's menu Children's portions Play area Garden ⌤ Parking WiFi ⇥ (notice required)

NITON — Map 5 SZ57

Buddle Inn

tel: 01983 730243 **St Catherines Rd PO38 2NE**
email: sayhi@buddleinn.co.uk
dir: *From Ventnor take Whitwell Rd (signed Niton). In Whitwell left after church into Kemming Rd (signed Niton). In Niton, left opposite Norris (shop), right into St Catherines Rd*

Popular with hikers and ramblers

With the English Channel on one side and the coastal path on the other, this 16th-century, former cliff-top farmhouse and smugglers' inn is one of the island's oldest hostelries. The interior has the full traditional complement — stone flags, oak beams and a large open fire, great real ales on tap, and muddy boots are welcome. Expect hearty home-made food, deep-filled Buddle pies, a large specials board full of seasonal dishes, and a great variety of freshly caught local fish.

Open all day all wk 12-10.30 (Wed 12-11 Fri-Sat 12-11.30) ⊕ ENTERPRISE INNS ◖ Sharp's Doom Bar, Yates' Dark Side of the Wight & Buddle Inn, Timothy Taylor Landlord Ŏ Westons Old Rosie. **Facilities** ❧ (All areas) ⅰ Children's menu Children's portions Garden Outside area Parking

NORTHWOOD — Map 5 SZ49

Travellers Joy

tel: 01983 298024 **85 Pallance Rd PO31 8LS**
email: karnagestocker38@icloud.com
dir: *Phone for detailed directions*

Family-friendly inn popular with everyone

A little way inland from Cowes, this 300-year-old alehouse is now in new hands. The appeal is to all-comers — from walkers and cyclists to locals and tourists, especially families. In addition to Island Wight Gold ale on hand pump there's a great selection of real ciders and a beer festival in October too. Classic home-made pub dishes are the mainstays of the menu, with local sourcing and seasonal availability playing their part. Expect the likes of salt and pepper squid; half a pint of shell-on prawns; pie or pudding of the day with creamy mash; home-made Italian meatballs; and sweet potato, Puy lentil and spinach goulash.

Open all day all wk 12-12 **Food** Lunch Mon-Sat 12-3, Sun 12-9 Dinner Mon-Sat 6-9, Sun 12-9 ⊕ FREE HOUSE ◖ Island Wight Gold, Brains The Rev. James, guest ales Ŏ Biddenden Bushels, Westons Stowford Press, Old Mout. ☂ 9
Facilities Non-diners area ❧ (Bar Garden) ⅰ Children's menu Children's portions Play area Garden ⌤ Beer festival Parking WiFi ⇥ (notice required)

PICK OF THE PUBS

The New Inn

SHALFLEET   Map 5 SZ48

tel: 01983 531314 **Main Rd PO30 4NS**
email: info@thenew-inn.co.uk
web: www.thenew-inn.co.uk
dir: *6m from Newport towards Yarmouth on A3054*

Recommended for their seafood

Set on the National Trust-owned Newtown River estuary, this charming whitewashed pub is an absolute mecca for sailing folk. One of the island's best-known dining pubs, The New Inn's name refers to how it rose phoenix-like from the charred remains of an older hostelry, which burnt down in 1743. Original inglenook fireplaces, flagstone floors and low-beamed ceilings give the place bags of character. The waterside location sets the tone for the menu; the inn has a reputation for excellent seafood dishes, with lobster and cracked local crab usually available. Daily specials are chalked on blackboards around the place. Further seafood options may include a pint of shell-on prawns with citrus-dressed baby leaf salad and locally baked bread; local ale battered fish of the day with chips, peas and home-made chunky tartare sauce; or fisherman's pie made with fresh and smoked fish and lemon and tarragon sauce topped with mashed potato and melted IOW Gallybagger cheese. Meat lovers could try the home-made pie of the day or

hand-carved honey and clove-glazed local ham, two fried Brownrigg eggs and chips. Vegetarians can enjoy the likes of grilled courgette stuffed with couscous, feta cheese and pine nuts, and butternut squash purée. There's also a list of dishes for 'smaller appetites', including chicken goujons; or locally reared 5oz sirloin steak with chips and peas — but if it's a light lunch you're seeking, be sure to consider the best-selling hand-picked crabmeat sandwiches and baguettes or the ploughman's featuring local cheeses and home-made chutneys. At the bar you'll find Goddards Fuggle-Dee-Dum and Cornish Sharp's Doom Bar among others, Westons Rosie's Pig cider and over 60 worldwide wines.

Open all day all wk **Food** Lunch Mon-Sat 12-2.30, Sun 12-3 Dinner all wk 6-9.30 (varies with season) 🛢 ENTERPRISE INNS 🍺 Goddards Fuggle-Dee-Dum, Sharp's Doom Bar 🍏 Westons Rosie's Pig. 🍷 13 **Facilities** 🐾 (Bar Garden) 👫 Children's menu Children's portions Garden 🎍 Parking WiFi

PICK OF THE PUBS

The Crown Inn

SHORWELL Map 5 SZ48

tel: 01983 740293
Walkers Ln PO30 3JZ
email: enquiries@crowninnshorwell.co.uk
web: www.crowninnshorwell.co.uk
dir: *Left at top of Carisbrooke High Street. Shorwell approx 6m*

Family-friendly village pub beside a delightful stream

A traditional country pub in the pretty village of Shorwell, a short hop south-west from Newport. After World War II, the Crown was one of the first pubs to boast an island-wide trade thanks to the entertainment value of its then landlord, Vivian 'Nutty' Edwards, who entertained customers nightly with his music hall approach to tales from his army days; Nutty retired in the 1960s to become the island's last Chelsea Pensioner. Today's owners, Nigel and Pamela Wynne, are continuing this heritage of welcoming hospitality, with a family-friendly approach throughout the all-day operation. The rear garden boasts a children's play area, bounded by a spring-fed stream where trout, ducks and moorhens can be spotted. Parts of the Crown date from the 17th century, although its varying floor levels suggest many subsequent alterations. The most recent building work has increased the floor area significantly, but the pub's character has been preserved with log fires burning and

antique furniture in abundance. Real ales include Goddards that's brewed on the island, while cider comes from Healey's Farm in Cornwall. If you overindulge, you might glimpse the female ghost who is friendly but shows her disapproval of customers playing cards by throwing them on the floor (the cards, that is, not the customers). The kitchen makes good use of locally sourced lamb, beef, game and fish in daily specials. Otherwise pub staples include lasagne, curries, scampi or beer-battered fish with chips, a range of pizzas, and sausages with mash. Steaks, gammon and burgers from the chargrill are understandably popular, but vegetarian choice is good too with dishes such as wild mushroom and spinach gratin.

Open all day all wk **Food** all wk 12-9.30 Av main course £11 ⊕ ENTERPRISE INNS ◀ Sharp's Doom Bar, Adnams Broadside, Goddards, St Austell Tribute ♂ Westons Stowford Press, Healey's. ♟ 12 **Facilities** Non-diners area ♣ (Bar Restaurant Garden) ♦ Children's menu Children's portions Play area Garden ⊼ Parking WiFi 🚐 (notice required)

SEAVIEW Map 5 SZ69

The Boathouse ★★★★ INN

tel: 01983 810616 **Springvale Rd PO34 5AW**
email: info@theboathouseiow.co.uk **web:** www.theboathouseiow.co.uk
dir: *From Ryde take A3055. Left onto A3330, left into Puckpool Hill. Pub 0.25m on right*

Watch the ocean liners from this seaside location

At the rather chic and certainly aptly-named Seaview, the powder-blue-painted Boathouse overlooks the eastern Solent. The setting really is spectacular. Well-kept ales and an extensive global wine listing complement specials boards that make the most of freshly landed local fish. Other choices include lunchtime baguettes and sandwiches; Isle of Wight reared rump and rib-eye steaks; whole cracked crab salad; cold seafood platter for two; and the Boathouse fisherman's pie. Children might like dishes such as sausages with chips and peas; or breaded wholetail scampi, chips, peas and home-made tartare sauce. Sea views are available in some of the stylish en suite bedrooms.

Open all day all wk 9am-11pm (varies with season) **Food** Lunch all week 12-2.30 Dinner all week 6-9.30 (varies with season) Set menu available ⊕ PUNCH TAVERNS ◖ Sharp's Doom Bar, Goddards ♂ Symonds. ♥ 13 **Facilities** Non-diners area ◖♦ Children's menu Children's portions Garden ⊨ Parking WiFi **Rooms** 4

Seaview Hotel ★★★ HL ⊛ PICK OF THE PUBS

tel: 01983 612711 **High St PO34 5EX**
email: reception@seaviewhotel.co.uk **web:** www.seaviewhotel.co.uk
dir: *B3330 from Ryde, left signed Puckpool, along seafront, hotel on left*

Great combination of coastal views and island produce

One of life's great pleasures has to be sitting on the terrace outside here, sipping beer from Wight brewers like Yates and drinking in the views over racing dinghies to one of the Solent's remarkable sea forts. Warm and welcoming, The Pump Bar is a hidden gem and perfect for ladies who lunch, old friends spinning yarns or families chilling out; its decor reflects the seaside location with a quirky selection of lobster pots, oars, masts and other nautical memorabilia. Fittingly, seafood features strongly on the menu, with a smoked haddock Scotch egg with curry mayonnaise starter or Ale of Wight fish and chips ticking all the right boxes. The owners raise deer, highland cattle and pigs on their farm, ensuring traceability and top quality for the carte and specials. Salt-beef hash, spinach, fried egg and HP sauce; poached pigs' cheeks, Savoy cabbage and mash; and cheddar and stout rarebit, fried hen's egg and pickled red onion are typical of the choices.

Open all wk 10-3 6-11 ⊕ FREE HOUSE ◖ Goddards, Island Ales, Yates ♂ Westons Stowford Press. **Facilities** ❀ (Bar Restaurant Outside area) ◖♦ Children's menu Children's portions Outside area Parking WiFi **Rooms** 20

SHALFLEET Map 5 SZ48

The New Inn PICK OF THE PUBS

See Pick of the Pubs on page 272

SHORWELL Map 5 SZ48

The Crown Inn PICK OF THE PUBS

See Pick of the Pubs on page 273

WHIPPINGHAM Map 5 SZ59

The Folly

tel: 01983 297171 **Folly Ln PO32 6NB**
email: 7771@greenking.co.uk
dir: *Phone for detailed directions*

Extensive menus and a large beer garden

The Folly stands beside the River Medina and you can, if you wish, travel here from Cowes on the pub's own waterbus. In the bar are timbers from the hull of an old barge, and even the restaurant tables are named after boats. The menus offer a wide choice of lighter bites – sandwiches and jacket potatoes – as well as burgers, steaks and classic pub grub such as sausage and mash; and breaded Whitby scampi tails. In addition, there are sharing platters, and international mains such as sizzling fajitas; salad Niçoise; and spicy aubergine and roasted beetroot curry. Wednesday evening is 'Get Spicy' curry night and from Mondays to Fridays, the 'Great Value' meal option is popular.

Open all day all wk **Food** Lunch all wk 12-5 Dinner all wk 5-10 ⊕ GREENE KING ◖ Abbot Ale, IPA, Morland Old Speckled Hen, ♂ Aspall, Westons Stowford Press. ♥ 19 **Facilities** Non-diners area ❀ (All areas) ◖♦ Children's menu Children's portions Garden Outside area ⊨ Parking WiFi ⬛ (notice required)

KENT

APPLEDORE Map 7 TQ92

NEW The Black Lion

tel: 01233 758206 **15 The Street TN26 2BU**
email: blappledore@aol.com

Family-run free house serving locally caught fish

In the historic village of Appledore, this free house has a rotating selection of ales and ciders, as well as 35 wines by the glass. Ray and Sandra Cottingham have run The Black Lion for the past 21 years and they have built up a great reputation for their food, especially local fish. A typical meal might include tiger prawns sautéed with garlic, ginger and spring onion; grilled lemon sole with peas and potatoes; and Romney Marsh lamb pie. Time a visit for a bank holiday, when the chefs cook a giant paella and pig roast on the pub's forecourt.

Open all day all wk **Food** Lunch Mon-Thu 11.30-3, Fri-Sat 11.30-9.30, Sun 12-9 Dinner Mon-Thu 6-9.30, Fri-Sat 11.30-9.30, Sun 12-9 Restaurant menu available all wk ⊕ FREE HOUSE ◖ Tonbridge Rustic, Sharp's Doom Bar, Goacher's ♂ Biddenden, Thatchers. ♥ 35 **Facilities** Non-diners area ◖♦ Children's menu Children's portions Outside area ⊨ Parking WiFi ⬛ (notice required)

BADLESMERE Map 7 TR05

The Red Lion

tel: 01233 740320 **Ashford Rd, Badlesmere Lees ME13 0NX**
email: theredlionbadlesmere@gmail.com
dir: *M2 junct 6, A251 towards Ashford. Approx 5m to Badlesmere Lees*

Family- and dog-friendly free house with large garden

Built as a farmhouse in 1546, and an inn since 1728, today's pub is known for affordable home-cooked food and locally brewed beers, and as a live-music venue. Diners after something regional should try a Kentish huffkin, a traditional stone-ground flour bread roll with Kentish Blue cheese and spiced plum chutney. Or there's lamb hotpot and moglai lamb curry – the animals reared on the Kentish salt-marshes. Alternatives are locally shot pheasant in rich red wine and port sauce; fresh cod, smoked haddock and salmon fish pie; and breadcrumb-topped cauliflower, broccoli and leeks with mature cheddar sauce.

Open all day 12-11 (Sun-Mon 12-7) Closed Sun eve & Mon eve ⊕ FREE HOUSE ◀ Gadds' The Ramsgate No 7, Shepherd Neame Master Brew ♂ Kentish Pip. **Facilities** ❀ (Bar Restaurant Garden) ♦♦ Children's menu Children's portions Garden Parking WiFi

---

BEARSTED — Map 7 TQ85

The Oak on the Green

tel: 01622 737976 **Bearsted Green ME14 4EJ**
email: headoffice@villagegreenrestaurants.com
dir: *In village centre*

Beefy treats beside the village green

Kentish hops drape the beams in this lively old pub, which dates from 1665 and is known for its good quality menu and the sometimes unusual real ales. The oak-shaded terrace overlooks a corner of the immense village green and cricket pitch, great for those long summer evenings. The kitchens were once the village gaol; escaping from them today are freshly-prepared dishes with a distinct nod towards Scottish beef – the steaks are impressive, from the 28- to 35-day dry-aged rib-eye to the 28-day dry-aged fillet. For dessert, try the apple tarte Tatin or banoffee pie.

Open all day all wk Closed 25 Dec **Food** Mon-Sat 12-10.30, Sun 12-10 ⊕ FREE HOUSE ◀ Harvey's Sussex Best Bitter, Old Dairy Red Top, guest ale ♂ Biddenden. ♀ **Facilities** Non-diners area ❀ (Bar Restaurant Outside area) ♦♦ Children's menu Children's portions Outside area ⊨ Parking WiFi ➡

BENENDEN — Map 7 TQ83

The Bull at Benenden — PICK OF THE PUBS

tel: 01580 240054 **The Street TN17 4DE**
email: enquiries@thebullatbenenden.co.uk
dir: *From A229 onto B2086 to Benenden. Or from Tenterden take A28 S towards Hastings. Right onto B2086*

One for all the family plus dogs and horses

Overlooking the green in a lovely Wealden village, home of a famous girls' school, the early 17th-century Bull was built around a huge chimney. Other noteworthy architectural features include chinoiserie windows, an enormous brick inglenook fireplace and a rounded wooden bar – no wonder the antique furniture looks so at home. Guest ales join Larkins from Kent and Dark Star and Harvey's from Sussex, with Biddenden-brewed Bushels cider on tap. Sandwiches, ploughman's and sharing platters head the traditional pub-grub menu, on which you'll also find home-cooked ham with two free-range eggs; beer-battered haddock and chips; 'Mr Bull's' burgers; and daily specials such as wild mushroom and goats' cheese millefeuille. Don't overlook the selection of filo and shortcrust pastry pies, and suet puddings. For children there's wholetail scampi, chipolatas with mash and vegetables, and pasta, as well as colouring pens and paper, and high chairs. Outside is a 'secret' garden.

Open all day all wk 12-12 **Food** Lunch Mon-Sat 12-2.30, Sun 12-4 Dinner Mon-Sat 6-9.20 Set menu available ⊕ FREE HOUSE ◀ Dark Star Hophead, Larkins, Harvey's, guest ales ♂ Biddenden Bushels. ♀ 9 **Facilities** Non-diners area ❀ (Bar Garden) ♦♦ Children's menu Children's portions Garden ⊨ Parking WiFi ➡ (notice required)

BIDBOROUGH — Map 6 TQ54

The Kentish Hare ⊛⊛ — PICK OF THE PUBS

tel: 01892 525709 **95 Ridborough Ridge TN3 0XB**
email: enquiries@thekentishhare.com
dir: *Phone for detailed directions*

Family-friendly pub with top notch food

Brothers James and Chris Tanner have numerous prestigious assignments to their names and The Kentish Hare is one of them. The smart building, saved from demolition a few years ago, is distinctive – grey walls, a hare motif and white weatherboarding on the outside lead to a stylish modern interior. In the bar, you'll find house-brewed real ale The Kentish Hare alongside Harvey's Sussex, and Jake's Orchard cider from the Hush Heath Estate; there is an excellent choice of wines by the glass too. The kitchen team care passionately about where their food comes from (in this case Kent, of course) and you can expect some difficult choices ahead. From bar menu, sticky mini chorizo; devilled whitebait; and mushroom arancini could precede Speldhurst sausages, mash and gravy; or a Caesar salad. A la carte choices start with 'little dishes' such as tuna carpaccio with ginger dressing; and jigged squid and roast garlic aïoli, followed by the 'main event' dishes of poached hake fillet, tarka dal, carrot purée, cockle popcorn and coconut; pork belly, cauliflower, pickled mushrooms and braised pig's cheek; and mushroom and black truffle risotto.

Open 11-3 5-11 (Sat 11-11 Sun 11-4) Closed 2-9 Jan, Sun eve & Mon **Food** Lunch Tue-Sun 12-2.30 Dinner Tue-Sat 6-9.30 Set menu available Restaurant menu available Tue-Sun ⊕ FREE HOUSE ◀ Harvey's, The Kentish Hare ♂ Hush Heath Jake's Orchard. ♀ 30 **Facilities** Non-diners area ♦♦ Children's menu Children's portions Garden ⊨ Parking WiFi

---

BIDDENDEN — Map 7 TQ83

The Three Chimneys — PICK OF THE PUBS

tel: 01580 291472 **Hareplain Rd TN27 8LW**
email: info@thethreechimneys.co.uk
dir: *From A262 midway between Biddenden & Sissinghurst, follow Frittenden signs. (Pub visible from main road). Pub immediately on left*

Pretty village pub with excellent cooking

Its original small-roomed layout and old-fashioned furnishings make this 15th-century timbered pub a classic. Further atmosphere is provided by low beams, wood-panelled walls, worn brick floors, log fires, evening candlelight and nothing electronic except the till. From the Garden Room and conservatory customers can access the secluded heated patio and huge shrub-filled garden. Bar snacks are served all day, but the kitchen is at the top of its game so a meal here should not disappoint. You could start with warm mushroom, bacon, brie and caramelised onion tart; or salmon and smoked haddock fishcakes. Continue with Wilkes pork and sage sausages, mash, spring greens with port and red onion gravy. Harvey's and Adnams ales and the heady (8.4 per cent ABV) Biddenden cider are tapped direct from the cask. The village sign depicts The Biddenden Maids, who were conjoined twins born here in 1100.

Open all day all wk 11.30-11 **Food** Lunch all wk 12-3 (bar menu 3-6.30) Dinner all wk 6.30-9.30 Restaurant menu available all wk ⊕ FREE HOUSE ◀ Harvey's Sussex Old Ale, Adnams ♂ Biddenden. ♀ 10 **Facilities** Non-diners area ❀ (Bar Garden) ♦♦ Children's portions Garden ⊨ Parking WiFi

BRABOURNE
Map 7 TR14

The Five Bells Inn

tel: 01303 813334 **The Street TN25 5LP**
email: visitus@fivebellsinnbrabourne.com
dir: *5m E of Ashford*

Blowing the trumpet for fine Kent produce

Environmental responsibility is important to the owners of this old village inn which trims the North Downs. Locally sourced wood supplies 25% of the energy here, whilst most of the food and drink is traceable locally. Thus the beers travel the few miles from Goacher's Maidstone brewery, ciders are from Biddenden, meats arrive from Kent's Romney Marsh or the Alkham Valley, and fish from the Dungeness Fish Hut. Tempting in ramblers from the popular walking country hereabouts may be fish finger club sandwiches; wood-oven-roasted pork ribs (for two); chargrilled beef steaks; and sticky date pudding with butterscotch sauce. The on-site deli and shop is a trove of all things comestible and Kentish.

Open all day all wk **Food** Mon-Thu 8am-9.30pm, Fri-Sat 8am-10pm, Sun 8am-9pm ⊕ FREE HOUSE ◀ Goacher's, Hopdaemon, Brabourne Stout, Romney Marsh Brewery, Harvey's Sussex Best Bitter, guest ales Ō Biddenden. **Facilities** Non-diners area ❖ (All areas) ◈ Children's portions Garden Outside area ♣ Parking WiFi ➡ (notice required)

BROOKLAND
Map 7 TQ92

NEW The Woolpack Inn

tel: 01797 344321 **Beacon Ln TN29 9TJ**
email: thewoolpackinn@outlook.com
dir: *From A259 between Rye & Brenzett follow Midley sign into lane to pub on left*

Family-run, with crowd-pleasing menu

Mother and son team Tracey and Daniel Ray took over the Woolpack in 2015. It's named after the wool smugglers of yesteryear, and its old-fashioned appeal has been left largely intact. A perfect stop for ramblers then, with or without children and dogs. There's nothing passé about the quality of the Shepherd Neame ales at the bar, and the copious menu reflects today's popular tastes: home-made lasagne; burgers; various fish with chips and salad; locally-sourced steaks are carefully cooked to order. Sit out in one of the two large beer gardens in summer, where food can be served at your chosen picnic bench.

Open all wk 11-3 6-10.30 (Sat 11-11 Sun 12-10) **Food** Lunch Mon-Fri 12-2.30, Sat-Sun 12-9 Dinner Mon-Fri 6-9, Sat-Sun 12-9 Av main course £8.95 ⊕ SHEPHERD NEAME ◀ Master Brew, Spitfire Gold Ō Symonds. **Facilities** Non-diners area ❖ (Bar Garden) ◈ Children's menu Family room Garden ♣ Parking ➡ (notice required)

CANTERBURY
Map 7 TR15

The Chapter Arms

tel: 01227 738340 **New Town St, Chartham Hatch CT4 7LT**
email: info@chapterarms.com
dir: *A28 from Canterbury towards Ashford. Right signed Chartham Hatch. 1m to pub*

An acre of gardens and a talented kitchen team

This charming and picturesque free house was once three cottages owned by Canterbury Cathedral's Dean and Chapter – hence the name. It sits on the North Downs Way overlooking apple orchards and oast houses. The à la carte includes chicken liver, brandy and herb pâté; and salmon fishcakes to start, followed by slow-roasted pork shoulder with caramelised apple sauce; wild mushroom, leek and

spinach Stroganoff; or smoked haddock, poached egg and spinach. A barbecue is available for special events. Look out for the Spoofers' Bar, where you can enjoy a game of spoof; The Chapter Arms hosted the World Spoofing Championships a few years ago and was featured in Rory McGrath and Will Mellor's TV programme *Champions of the World*.

Open 11-3 6-11 (Sun 12-5) Closed Mon **Food** Lunch Tue-Sun 12-2.30 Dinner Tue-Sat 6.30-9 Av main course £12 Set menu available Restaurant menu available Tue-Sun ⊕ FREE HOUSE ◀ Greene King IPA & London Glory, seasonal ales Ō Thatchers. ☎ 10 **Facilities** Non-diners area ❖ (Bar Garden) ◈ Children's menu Children's portions Play area Garden ♣ Parking WiFi ➡

The Dove Inn ◉
PICK OF THE PUBS

tel: 01227 751360 **Plum Pudding Ln, Dargate ME13 9HB**
email: bookings@thedovedargate.co.uk
dir: *6m from Canterbury; 4m from Whitstable. Phone for detailed directions*

Friendly village pub that welcomes walkers, families and dogs

About half-way between Faversham and Whitstable, this single-gabled 18th-century village inn stands amid wooded hills and fruit orchards – this is the Garden of England, after all. Its matchboarded, wooden-floored interior is warmed by a log-burner, creating agreeably comfortable surroundings in which to enjoy a Shepherd Neame ale and AA-Rosette food. A fixed price menu gives ample choice at each stage. Start perhaps with whitebait and tartare sauce; continue with roast turkey breast with roast potatoes and parsnips, buttered carrots and greens; and finish with chocolate chip and orange bread and butter pudding. The carte may proffer home-made salmon fishcake, followed by golonka – the Polish term for ham hock, cooked in Kentish ale and served with home-made sauerkraut. Outside is a gorgeous cottage garden complete, appropriately, with dovecote and doves; and a pitch for summer games of 'bat and trap', an old pub game that survives in Kent.

Open Mon-Sat all day (Sun 12-6) Closed Mon **Food** Lunch Wed-Sat 12-2.30 Dinner Wed-Sat 6.30-9 Restaurant menu available all wk ⊕ SHEPHERD NEAME ◀ Master Brew, Spitfire, Whitstable Pale Ale, seasonal ales. ☎ 10 **Facilities** Non-diners area ❖ (Bar Garden) ◈ Children's portions Garden ♣ Parking WiFi ➡ (notice required)

Duke of Cumberland ★★★ INN

tel: 01227 831396 **The Street, Barham CT4 6NY**
email: info@dukeofcumberland.co.uk **web:** www.dukeofcumberland.co.uk
dir: *A2 from Canterbury towards Dover. Follow Barham signs. In village centre into The Street. Pub 200yds on left*

Pub grub in a village near Canterbury

A traditional country inn, the Duke of Cumberland was built in 1749 and has been licensed to sell ale since 1766. It's named after the commander of the English army victorious at Culloden, although no one knows exactly why. You'll find a good choice of ales in the bar, including Greene King IPA and Harvey's Sussex Best. If you're peckish there's a selection of sandwiches available, or go all out with crispy whitebait followed by a 10oz rib-eye steak and chips, or the Duke burger. There's a great children's play area, and bedrooms if you want to stay over. There's a beer festival in July or August.

Open all day all wk 12-11 (Fri-Sat 12-12 Jan-Feb Mon-Fri 12-3 5.30-11) **Food** Lunch Mon-Fri 12-3, Sat-Sun 12-9 Dinner Mon-Fri 6-9, Sat-Sun 12-9 Set menu available ⊕ PUNCH TAVERNS ◀ Greene King IPA, Harvey's Sussex Best Bitter, guest ales Ō Thatchers Gold. **Facilities** Non-diners area ❖ (Bar Garden) ◈ Children's menu Children's portions Play area Garden Beer festival Parking WiFi ➡ (notice required) **Rooms** 3

PICK OF THE PUBS

The Red Lion

CANTERBURY   Map 7 TR15

tel: 01227 721339
Stodmarsh Rd, Stodmarsh CT3 4BA
email: info@theredlionstodmarsh.com
web: www.theredlionstodmarsh.com
dir: *From Canterbury take A257 towards Sandwich, left into Stodmarsh Rd to Stodmarsh*

Perfect country pub in a pretty village

Owned since late 2015 by four friends, The Red Lion is one for the bird-watchers, although as we've probably all watched birds in our time, that means everyone. It happens to be close to Stodmarsh National Nature Reserve, the largest in the south east, whose reed-beds are home to bitterns, marsh harriers, ducks and waders. So, if nearby Canterbury's medieval streets, lovely as they are, get too busy, this could be where to head. From the front it looks like two gable-ended buildings, one weatherboarded, the other tile hung, joined in the middle by the entrance. This configuration may be explained by the fact that, while originally 15th century, it was rebuilt in 1801 following a fire. The low-ccilinged, boarded and stone-floored interior, with library book wallpaper, could remind one of home, albeit a home with a fair sprinkling of old scales, copper pots, jugs, baskets, horseshoes and tea-lights. To all this add log fires in winter, a secluded,

flowery garden for other times and a bar that dispenses changing real ales, such as Gadds' from Ramsgate or Old Dairy from Tenterden. Pave the way for a meal with a taster of tempura vegetables or share a charcuterie board, then choose a typical starter of sizzling king prawns in garlic and chilli oil; or woodland mushroom bruschetta, followed by a Kentish lamb with carrot and caraway purée, dauphinoise potatoes, seasonal greens and lamb jus; gilt-head sea bream with crushed new potatoes, courgette linguine and sauce vièrge; or, for two, whisky-cured pork ribs with home-made barbecue sauce, onion rings, corn on the cob and salad. For something sweet to finish, there's treacle tart with lemon sorbet; or apple and pear crumble with crème anglaise.

Open all day all wk 11-11 (Sat 11am-11.30pm Sun 12-10.30)
Food Lunch Mon-Sat 12-3, Sun 12-9 Dinner Mon-Thu 6-9, Fri-Sat 6-9.30, Sun 12-9 ⊞ FREE HOUSE ◀ Greene King IPA, Guinness, guest ales ☼ Somersby. ♟ 15
Facilities Non-diners area ✿ (Bar Restaurant Garden) ♦♦ Children's menu Children's portions Garden ⊼ Parking WiFi ▥ (notice required)

CANTERBURY *continued*

The Granville

tel: 01227 700402 **Street End, Lower Hardres CT4 7AL**
email: us@thegranvillecanterbury.co.uk
dir: *On B2068, 2m from Canterbury towards Hythe*

Ever-changing art at pub with contemporary character

As well as a striking feature central fireplace/flue, this light and airy pub not far from Canterbury displays an interesting series of roll-over art exhibitions and installations (lino cuts, photographs, sculptures). Ample parking, a patio and large beer garden where summer barbecues take place make this Shepherd Neame pub good for families and dogs, whilst locals head for the public bar. The kitchen team has a confident approach to utilising the best that Kent and the enfolding seas can provide. You could start with warm salad of teal, beetroot and orange, followed perhaps by roast venison haunch with celeriac and wild mushrooms; or roast cod fillet with tartare sauce. Finish with roast plums on French toast with cinnamon ice cream.

Open all day all wk **Food** all wk 12-9.30 Set menu available Restaurant menu available all wk ⊕ SHEPHERD NEAME ◀ Master Brew, seasonal ale ♻ Thatchers. **Facilities** Non-diners area ♣ (Bar Garden) ⦿ Children's portions Garden ⌙ Parking WiFi

The Red Lion  PICK OF THE PUBS

See Pick of the Pubs on page 277 and advert on opposite page

CHILHAM   Map 7 TR05

The White Horse

tel: 01227 730355 **The Square CT4 8BY**
email: thewhitehorsechilham@outlook.com
dir: *Take A28 from Canterbury then A252, in 1m turn left*

One of the most photographed pubs in Britain

The White Horse is situated opposite Chilham Castle in the 15th-century village square that is a delightfully haphazard mix of gabled, half-timbered houses, shops, and inns dating from the late Middle Ages — it's often used as a film location. This 'chocolate box' inn offers a traditional atmosphere and a wide selection of real ales from breweries like Sharp's and Shepherd Neame. The modern cooking is based on fresh local produce. The bar menu offers sandwiches, ploughman's and dishes like pie of the week and vegetable curry. An evening menu might tempt with duo of Ardennes and Brussels pâté; chicken cake and home-made lemon mayo; and dark and white chocolate mousse.

Open all day all wk 12-12 (Tue-Thu 12-11) Closed 25 Dec eve **Food** Lunch Mon-Fri 12-3, Sat 12-10, Sun 12-8 Dinner Mon-Thu 5-9, Fri 5-10, Sat 12-10, Sun 12-8 ⊕ ENTERPRISE INNS ◀ Shepherd Neame Master Brew, Sharp's Doom Bar, guest ale. ☡ 10 **Facilities** Non-diners area ♣ (All areas) ⦿ Children's menu Children's portions Garden Outside area ⌙ Beer festival Parking WiFi ▦ (notice required)

CHIPSTEAD   Map 6 TQ55

George & Dragon

tel: 01732 779019 **39 High St TN13 2RW**
email: info@georgeanddragonchipstead.com
dir: *Phone for detailed directions*

Sincerity in everything is the watchword here

The delights of this 16th-century village gastro-pub are easily summarised: the welcoming open fires, the heavy oak beams and solid furnishings; the splendidly beamed upstairs restaurant; and the tree-house-inspired private dining room. Then there's Westerham Brewery's specially-produced George's Marvellous Medicine ale; and finally, the food, using top free-range or organic meats from farms in Kent and neighbouring counties, and sustainable fish from south-east coastal waters. Daily-changing menus might list grilled skate wing with lemon and caper butter; seared haunch of Chart Farm venison with Jerusalem artichoke and truffle; and beetroot and goats' cheese risotto.

Open all day all wk 11-11 **Food** Lunch Mon-Fri 12-3, Sat-Sun 12-4 Dinner Mon-Sat 6-9.30, Sun 6-8.30 ⊕ FREE HOUSE ◀ Westerham George's Marvellous Medicine & Grasshopper ♻ Westons Stowford Press. ☡ 18 **Facilities** Non-diners area ♣ (Bar Garden) ⦿ Children's menu Children's portions Play area Garden ⌙ Parking WiFi ▦ (notice required)

CRANBROOK   Map 7 TQ73

The George Hotel

tel: 01580 713348 **Stone St TN17 3HE**
email: georgehotel@shepherd-neame.co.uk
dir: *From A21 follow signs to Goudhurst. At large rdbt take 3rd exit to Cranbrook (A229). Hotel on left*

Former courthouse offers brasserie and restaurant dining

One of Cranbrook's landmark buildings, the 14th-century George Hotel traditionally served visiting buyers of locally-made Cranbrook cloth. Magistrates held court here for over 300 years, and today the sophisticated interior mixes period features with contemporary decor. The brasserie menu offers a take on classic English cuisine — wild boar sausages with mash, perhaps; while in the restaurant diners can sample modern English dishes like trio of pork — slow-roast belly, braised cheek, Savoy cabbage and pancetta parcel, with heritage carrots.

Open all day all wk **Food** Lunch all wk 12-3 Dinner Mon-Sat 6-9.30, Sun 6-9 Set menu available Restaurant menu available all wk ⊕ SHEPHERD NEAME ◀ Master Brew, Spitfire, Whitstable Bay, seasonal ales ♻ Symonds. ☡ 10 **Facilities** Non-diners area ♣ (Bar Outside area) ⦿ Children's menu Children's portions Outside area ⌙ Parking WiFi ▦ (notice required)

Stodmarsh Road, Stodmarsh, Nr Canterbury,
Kent, CT3 4BA
W: www.theredlionstodmarsh.com
T: 01227 721339

@RLatStodmarsh

The Red Lion at Stodmarsh is the perfect country pub to enjoy delightful food together with fine wines, local beers, ales and ciders.

Set in the countryside just outside of Canterbury, next to Stodmarsh National Nature Reserve, The Red Lion is the perfect location to spend all and every occasion, whether a family Sunday lunch, a romantic dinner for two or a dog-walkers' drink by the fire.

With a cellar of over 60 wines, we aim to be able to provide a tipple for all tastes and budgets.
Our menu is constantly changing, depending on what the Chefs bring back from the market each morning, whether that be locally reared lamb to freshly caught oysters.

With comfortable bedrooms and hearty breakfasts, this is the perfect place to stay for a perfect experience of the Kent countryside. The eclectic restaurant is full of snug tables and benches, books on window sills, tankards hanging from beams, with various old stone bottles and lamps dotted about, full and empty wine bottles and a big log fire.

DARTFORD
Map 6 TQ57

The Rising Sun Inn ★★★ INN

tel: 01474 872291 **Fawkham Green, Fawkham, Longfield DA3 8NL**
email: enquiries@risingsun-fawkham.com web: www.risingsun-fawkham.com
dir: *0.5m from Brands Hatch Racing Circuit & 5m from Dartford*

Traditional 16th-century pub opposite the village green

Standing on the green in a picturesque village not far from Brands Hatch, The Rising Sun is a 16th-century building, which has been a pub since 1702. Inside you will find a bar full of character, complete with inglenook log fire, and Inglenooks restaurant where home-made traditional house specials and a large fresh fish menu, using the best local produce, are served. Among the mains you may find a selection of steaks; pork fillet with Stilton, bacon and chives wrapped in Parma ham; veal with paprika sauce; and lamb shank with a redcurrant jus. There is also a front patio and garden for alfresco dining in warmer weather, plus comfortable en suite bedrooms if you would like to stay over.

Open all day all wk **Food** Contact pub for food times Set menu available Restaurant menu available all wk ⊕ FREE HOUSE ◀ Courage Best Bitter & Directors, Fuller's London Pride, Sharp's Doom Bar. ♀ 9 **Facilities** Non-diners area ◀◗ Children's portions Garden ⊼ Parking WiFi ➡ (notice required) **Rooms** 5

FAVERSHAM
Map 7 TR06

Albion Taverna

tel: 01795 591411 **29 Front Brents ME13 7DH**
email: albiontaverna@uesltd.co
dir: *Phone for detailed directions*

Mexican and English cook house on the waterfront

Located next to the Shepherd Neame Brewery near the Faversham swing bridge, the Albion Taverna looks directly onto the attractive waterfront area. The colourful menu is a combination of Mexican and English dishes. On the Mexican side are fajitas and quesadillas with a choice of fillings, enchiladas, nachos, Mexican ribs, huevos rancheros, chicken Veracruz and beef chilli tacos. English options include smoked salmon and avocado salad; and white pepper skate wing and chunky chips. You can even stay in the Mexican mood with a dessert of churros (hot doughnuts with a rich chocolate fudge sauce). There is an annual hop festival in early September.

Open all wk 12-3 6-11.30 (Sat-Sun 12-11.30) **Food** Lunch all wk 12-2.30 Dinner all wk 6-10 Av main course £10 ⊕ SHEPHERD NEAME ◀ Master Brew, Whitstable Bay, Early Bird, IPA, Spitfire Gold, Late Red Ⓣ Thatchers Gold. ♀ **Facilities** Non-diners area ◀ (Garden) ◀◗ Children's menu Children's portions Play area Garden ⊼ Beer festival Parking WiFi ➡ (notice required)

Shipwright's Arms
PICK OF THE PUBS

tel: 01795 590088 **Hollowshore ME13 7TU**
dir: *A2 through Ospringe then right at rdbt. Right at T-junct then left opposite Davington School, follow signs*

Walk in the footsteps of pirates, smugglers and sailors

The creekside Shipwright's Arms was first licensed in 1738, when the brick and weather boarded pub's remote location on the Swale Marshes made it a popular haunt for briny ne'er-do-wells; it's been a favoured watering hole for sailors and fishermen ever since. Best reached on foot or by boat, the effort in getting here is well rewarded, as this charming and unspoilt tavern oozes historic character. Step back in time in the relaxed and comfortable bars, which boast nooks and crannies, original timbers, built-in settles, well-worn sofas, wood-burning stoves, and a wealth of maritime artefacts. Locally-brewed Goacher's ales are tapped straight from the cask, and make for a perfect match with simple, traditional bar food such as baguettes and jacket potatoes. Alternatively look to the specials board for fresh fish, or the carte for the likes of beef casserole with large Yorkshire pudding; tomato and spinach risotto; and moules frites. In summer come and support the pub's Bat and Trap team.

Open all wk 11-3 6-10 (Sat 11-11; Sun 12-6 in winter 12-10.30 in summer) **Food** Lunch Mon-Sat 11-2.30, Sun 12-2.30 Dinner Tue-Sat 7-9 (no food Tue-Thu eve in winter) ⊕ FREE HOUSE ◀ Goacher's, Harveys, local ales. ♀ 12 **Facilities** Non-diners area ◀ (Bar Garden) ◀◗ Children's menu Children's portions Family room Garden ⊼ Parking ➡

GOODNESTONE
Map 7 TR25

NEW The Fitzwalter Arms

tel: 01304 840303 **The Street CT3 1PJ**
email: fitz840303@gmail.com
dir: *In village centre*

Many great walks finish here

This appealing pub was built in 1589 as the bailiff's lodge for the Goodnestone estate and gardens, to which it still belongs. Known as 'the Fitz' to locals, it welcomes many muddy boots and dogs as people discover this and other beautiful buildings in the village or finish a long walk. Log fires, wooden floors, exposed brick walls and beams adorned with Kentish hops characterise the interior; Shepherd Neame ales are ideally conditioned by chalk cellars. Home-cooked pub fare includes Jeanette's family recipe for a spicy Welsh rarebit. Alternatively go for the comfort of a cottage pie with seasonal vegetables, or scampi and chips.

Open all day all wk **Food** Lunch all wk 12-4 Dinner all wk 6-9 Av main course £9 Set menu available ⊕ SHEPHERD NEAME ◀ Master Brew, Whitstable Bay Pale Ale. ♀ 10 **Facilities** Non-diners area ◀ (Bar Restaurant Garden) ◀◗ Children's menu Children's portions Play area Garden ⊼ WiFi ➡ (notice required)

Follow us on twitter
@TheAA_Lifestyle

PICK OF THE PUBS

The Star & Eagle ★★★★ INN

GOUDHURST   Map 6 TQ73

tel: 01580 211512 **High St TN17 1AL**
email: starandeagle@btconnect.com
web: www.starandeagle.co.uk
dir: *Just off A21 towards Hastings. Take
A262 into Goudhurst. Pub at top of hill
adjacent to church*

Traditional and European cooking in an old timbered inn

From The Star & Eagle's lofty position in
this Wealden hill village, some of the
orchards and hop fields that originally
earned Kent the sobriquet 'Garden of
England' stretch out below. The parish
church next door is higher than the Star,
but only just. The rambling inn dates
from the 14th century, when surviving
vaulted stonework suggests it may have
been a monastery. Four centuries later
the infamous Hawkhurst Gang of
smugglers and thieves drank and
plotted here, until angry villagers finally
sent them packing. Always on offer in
the bar are Harvey's Sussex from its
brewery in Lewes, guest ales, Biddenden
cider and 14 wines by the glass.
Suitably armed, as it were, with a full
glass, choose between fine traditional
and European dishes prepared by head
chef Scott Smith and team in the big-
beamed, split-level restaurant. An
Iberian influence evident in tapas, such
as gambas al ajillo (king prawns
sautéed in garlic, chillies and white
wine); hot Spanish chorizo, avocado and

lime on toast; and house speciality of
Rioja-braised shoulder of lamb, owes
much to owners Enrique and Karin
Martinez. But if you prefer to stay on
home soil, mains include Cumberland
sausage, sage, chive mash and onion
gravy; ginger chicken with white wine
cream sauce, rice and wilted spinach;
sautéed calves' liver with bacon, crispy
onions, chive mash, butter, cream and
cracked black pepper; and Scottish
salmon en croûte with creamy
mushroom sauce and herb-roast
potatoes. A blackboard displays daily
specials. Some of the desserts reveal a
continental influence: tiramisù sundae;
warm Belgian chocolate pudding; and
crème brûlée. Or choose a selection of
Kentish cheeses served with biscuits,
grapes and chutney.

Open all day all wk 11-11 (Sun 12-3
6.30-10.30) **Food** Lunch all wk 12-2.30
Dinner all wk 7-9.30 🛢 FREE HOUSE
🛢 Harvey's, Brakspear, Marston's
Pedigree, guest ale 🍎 Biddenden. 🍷 14
Facilities Non-diners area 👥 Children's
menu Children's portions Family room
Outside area 🪑 Parking WiFi 🚌
Rooms 10

GOUDHURST
Map 6 TQ73

Green Cross Inn

tel: 01580 211200 **TN17 1HA**
dir: *A21 from Tonbridge towards Hastings left onto A262 towards Ashford. 2m, Goudhurst on right*

Dining pub specialising in seafood

In an unspoiled corner of Kent, close to Finchcocks Manor, and originally built to serve the Paddock Wood to Goudhurst railway line, this thriving dining pub specialises in fresh seafood. Arrive early to bag a table in the dining room, prettily decorated with fresh flowers, and tuck into grilled skate wing, halibut with cream and spinach sauce; seafood paella; or go for the slow-roasted pork belly with crackling, gravy and apple sauce, followed by pineapple sorbet or lemon chiffon; all freshly prepared by the chef-owner who is Italian and classically trained.

Open all wk 12-3 6-11 Closed Sun eve **Food** Lunch all wk 12-2.30 Dinner Mon-Sat 7-9.45 Restaurant menu available all wk ⊕ FREE HOUSE ◀ Harvey's Sussex Best Bitter, Guinness Ö Biddenden. **Facilities** ♦♦ Children's portions Garden ⊼ Parking WiFi ➡ (notice required)

The Star & Eagle ★★★ INN
PICK OF THE PUBS

See Pick of the Pubs on page 281

GRAVESEND
Map 6 TQ67

The Cock Inn

tel: 01474 814208 **Henley St, Luddesdowne DA13 0XB**
email: andrew.r.turner@btinternet.com
dir: *Phone for detailed directions*

Adults-only pub with cask-conditioned English ales

Dating from 1713, this whitewashed free house in the beautiful Luddesdowne Valley has two traditional beamed bars with wood-burning stoves and open fires. Always available are eight well-kept real ales, Köstritzer and other German beers, and not a fruit machine, jukebox or TV in sight. All food, only served at lunchtime, is ordered at the bar: expect filled submarine rolls and basket meals. As an adults-only pub, no-one under 18 is allowed inside or in the garden.

Open all day all wk 12-11 (Sun 12-10.30) **Food** Lunch all wk 12-3 ⊕ FREE HOUSE ◀ Adnams Southwold Bitter, Broadside & Lighthouse, Goacher's Real Mild Ale, St Austell Trelawny, Truman's Swift. **Facilities** Non-diners area ❧ (Bar Restaurant Garden) Garden ⊼ Parking

HALSTEAD
Map 6 TQ46

Rose & Crown

tel: 01959 533120 **Otford Ln TN14 7EA**
email: info@roseandcrownhalstead.co.uk
dir: *M25 junct 4, A21, follow London (SE), Bromley & Orpington signs. At Hewitts Rdbt 1st exit onto A224 signed Dunton Green. At rdbt 3rd exit into Shoreham Ln. In Halstead left into Station Rd, left into Otford Ln*

Bustling community local

This handsome Grade II listed pub, situated in the lee of the North Downs, is all a good village pub should be; traditional pub games including bat and trap, family friendly, supporting local microbreweries (with no less than three beer festivals held each year) and a welcoming base for walks into the peaceful countryside on the doorstep. With a lively bar, peaceful lounge, Stables Restaurant and tranquil garden to suit all tastes, home-made pub grub is the icing on the cake, from home-made venison and ale pie to breaded plaice, chips and peas.

Open all day all wk **Food** all wk 12-11 Set menu available ⊕ FREE HOUSE ◀ Larkins Traditional, Elgood's Rose & Crown Best, guest ales Ö Symonds. ☗

Facilities Non-diners area ❧ (Bar Garden Outside area) ♦♦ Children's menu Children's portions Play area Garden Outside area ⊼ Beer festival Parking WiFi ➡

HAWKHURST
Map 7 TQ73

The Great House
PICK OF THE PUBS

tel: 01580 753119 **Gills Green TN18 5EJ**
email: enquiries@thegreathouse.net
dir: *Just off A229 between Cranbrook & Hawkhurst*

Family-friendly free house in the heart of the Kentish Weald

Tucked away along a lane in a tranquil hamlet is this eye-catching Kentish weatherboard inn. Over 400 years old, it displays equally appealing character in the range of rooms that cater well both for drinkers – beers from the ever-reliable Harvey's Brewery are stocked – and diners. With beams and trusses; open fires and stone floors; country furniture and very eclectic decor, there's a relaxed atmosphere here. This spreads informally through the three dining areas; whilst an orangery and secluded terrace suggest undertones of the Mediterranean linking to the peaceful beer garden. The menus combine classic English dishes with a dash of French brasserie-style cooking. Offering starters like seared pigeon and fig salad; mains run to Kentish wild boar burger with fried duck egg, streaky bacon, smoked cheddar and pickled red cabbage; or beer-battered fish and chips. Accompanying a meal can be Kentish cider and wines, and the pub hosts a beer festival every year.

Open all day all wk 11.30-11 **Food** Lunch Mon-Fri 12-3, Sat-Sun 12-9.45 Dinner Mon-Fri 6-9.45, Sat-Sun 12-9.45 Av main course £15.50 ⊕ FREE HOUSE ◀ Harvey's, Sharp's Doom Bar, Guinness Ö Biddenden, Aspall. ☗ 20
Facilities Non-diners area ❧ (All areas) ♦♦ Children's menu Children's portions Garden Outside area ⊼ Beer festival Parking WiFi

Smugglers' Alehouse

tel: 01580 752306 **Moor Hill TN18 4PF**
email: info@thesmugglersalehouse.co.uk
dir: *On A229, S of Hawkhurst*

Newly-opened real ale den

Opened in 2016, the Smugglers' Alehouse (formerly The Black Pig) focuses on the wet side of the business. An eclectic array of tavern tables and chairs, oxblood pews and pewter jugs revive memories of the notorious era when contraband smuggling was all the rage in this area. Expect to find half a dozen regional brewers on tap, backed by a lager, a stout, a cider or three and a good choice of wines and soft drinks. To mop up your chosen refreshment, nibbles, nachos, the 'seven guinea bounty' (a ploughman's), a chilli, and a hot dish of the day are always available. Take note of the unusual opening hours when planning a visit.

Open all wk 3pm-close (Sat-Sun noon-close) **Food** Contact pub for food times ⊕ FREE HOUSE ◀ Dark Star Hophead, Larkins Traditional, Old Dairy Copper Top, Harvey's Ö Biddenden. **Facilities** Non-diners area ❧ (Bar Garden) ♦♦ Children's menu Children's portions Garden ⊼ WiFi ➡ (notice required)

HODSOLL STREET
Map 6 TQ66

The Green Man

tel: 01732 823575 **TN15 7LE**
email: the.greenman@btinternet.com
dir: *Between Brands Hatch & Gravesend off A227*

Recommended for its fish dishes

The picturesque village of Hodsoll Street on the North Downs, surrounded by beautiful Kent countryside, is home to this 300-year-old, family-run pub, much loved for its decent food and real ales. There's a large garden for warmer weather, and Sharp's Doom Bar and Timothy Taylor Landlord are a couple of the four real ales on tap. Food is prepared to order using fresh local produce, and the evening menu includes a wide variety of fish, such as whole plaice, skate wing and smoked haddock, as well as dishes like roast lamb shank, steak and kidney filo parcel, and various steaks.

Open all wk 11-2.30 6-11 (Fri-Sun all day) **Food** Lunch Mon-Thu 12-2, Fri-Sun all day Dinner Mon-Thu 6.30-9.30, Fri-Sun all day Set menu available ⊕ FREE HOUSE ◄ Timothy Taylor Landlord, Harvey's, Sharp's Doom Bar, guest ale ♂ Thatchers Gold. ♞ 8 **Facilities** Non-diners area ♥ (Bar Restaurant Garden) ♦♦ Children's menu Children's portions Play area Garden ♜ Parking WiFi ▦

HOLLINGBOURNE
Map 7 TQ85

The Dirty Habit
PICK OF THE PUBS

tel: 01622 880880 **Upper St ME17 1UW**
email: enquiries@thedirtyhabit.net
dir: M20 junct 8, follow A20 signs, then Hollingbourne signs on B2163. Through Hollingbourne, pub on hill top on right

Historic watering hole on the Pilgrims Way

There's been a pub on this site since the 11th century, and it was later frequented by pilgrims plodding from Winchester to the shrine of Thomas à Becket at Canterbury. The building retains much period charm – look, for instance, at the long Georgian oak bar and panelling, and the Victorian furniture, all beautifully restored by skilled local craftsmen. Harvey's of Lewes is one of the real ales on tap, and there's cider from Aspall too. The Monks Corner, with oak beams to the apex and a bread oven in the corner, is ideal for private dining, while outside is a quiet terrace. The kitchen prepares dishes such as fish, tapas and meat sharing boards; salt and pepper squid with lemon mayo; Aga-cooked Bedgebury game stew (rabbit, partridge and venison), new potatoes and seasonal vegetables; king prawn and chorizo linguine; and fig pudding with honeycomb ice cream.

Open all day all wk **Food** Lunch Mon-Thu 12-3, Fri-Sat 12-9.30, Sun 12-8.30 Dinner Mon-Thu 5.30-9, Fri-Sat 12-9.30, Sun 12-8.30 ⊕ ENTERPRISE INNS ◄ Harvey's, Timothy Taylor Landlord, Sharp's Doom Bar, guest ale ♂ Aspall. ♞ 28 **Facilities** ♥ (Bar Outside area) ♦♦ Children's menu Children's portions Outside area ♜ Parking WiFi

---

The Windmill

tel: 01622 889000 **32 Eyhorne St ME17 1TR**
email: reservations@thewindmillbyrichardphillips.co.uk
dir: M20 junct 8, A20 towards Lenham. Straight on at 1st rdbt, left at 2nd rdbt into Eyhorne St

Community pub with great food.

The Windmill, found in the beautiful village of Hollingbourne, is one of chef Richard Phillips' collection of pubs and restaurants. Full of distinctive character and very much part of the local community, it's the ideal place for a relaxing lunch, a quiet drink (Doom Bar, Hoppin' Robin or Flintlock Pale Ale are the real ales on offer) or a more formal dinner. On the menu might be salt and pepper squid with soy ponzu sauce to nibble on while you choose perhaps roasted Jerusalem artichoke velouté, salt baked artichoke and white truffle, followed by free-range duck, slow-cooked breast and confit leg, Merlot-braised red cabbage, roasted red onions and girolle mushrooms, butternut squash and grain mustard sauce.

Open all day all wk **Food** all wk 11am-mdnt Av main course £15 Set menu available Restaurant menu available all wk ⊕ ENTERPRISE INNS ◄ Sharp's Doom Bar, Rockin' Robin Hoppin Robin, Coach House Flintlock Pale Ale ♂ Aspall, Westons Stowford Press. ♞ **Facilities** Non-diners area ♥ (Bar Garden) ♦♦ Children's menu Children's portions Play area Garden ♜ Beer festival Parking WiFi ▦ (notice required)

ICKHAM
Map 7 TR25

The Duke William ★★★★ INN

tel: 01227 721308 & 721244 **The Street CT3 1QP**
email: goodfood@dukewilliam.biz **web:** www.thedukewilliammickham.com
dir: A257 Canterbury to Sandwich. In Littlebourne left opposite The Anchor, into Nargate St. 0.5m right into Drill Ln, right into The Street

Quintessential Kentish pub in village setting

New owners here have preserved all aspects of the pub's authenticity while introducing new menus for both drink and food. Famed as it is for hops, the Garden of England hosts some fine microbreweries and you can sample three of them – Tonbridge, Wantsum and Romney Marsh – at the Duke's bar; also on tap is cider from the Kent Cider Company. The focus on 'local' applies equally to the ingredients for the kitchen's new menus. A typical three-course choice could be potted Dungeness shrimps with toasted sourdough; Romney Marsh lamb neck curry; and a selection of Kent Simply ice creams.

Open all day all wk **Food** Lunch Mon-Fri 12-3, Sat 11-3, Sun 11-5 Dinner Mon-Fri 6.30-9.30, Sat 6.30-10 Restaurant menu available all wk ⊕ FREE HOUSE ◄ Shepherd Neame Whitstable Bay, Tonbridge Rustic, Wantsum, Romney Marsh Brewery, guest ale ♂ Aspall, Kent. ♞ 9 **Facilities** Non-diners area ♥ (Bar Garden) ♦♦ Children's menu Children's portions Play area Garden ♜ WiFi ▦ (notice required) **Rooms** 4

IGHTHAM
Map 6 TQ55

The Harrow Inn
PICK OF THE PUBS

tel: 01732 885912 **Common Rd TN15 9EB**
dir: 1.5m from Borough Green on A25 to Sevenoaks, signed Ightham Common, left into Common Rd. Inn 0.25m on left

Worth seeking out for imaginative food

Tucked away down country lanes, yet easily accessible from both the M20 and M26, this creeper-hung, stone-built free house dates back to at least the 17th century. The two-room bar area has a great brick fireplace, open to both sides and piled high with logs, while the restaurant's vine-clad conservatory opens on to a terrace that's ideal for a pint of Loddon Hoppit or Gravesend Shrimpers and warm weather dining. Menus vary with the seasons, and seafood is a particular speciality: fish lovers can enjoy dishes such as crab and ginger spring roll; swordfish with Cajun spice and salsa; or pan-fried fillets of sea bass with lobster cream and spinach. Other main courses may include baked sausage with gammon, fennel, red onions and garlic; and tagliatelle with wild mushroom, fresh herb, lemongrass and chilli ragout. The car park is fairly small, although there's adequate street parking.

Open 12-3 6-11 Closed 1wk between Xmas & New Year, Sun eve & Mon-Wed **Food** Lunch Thu-Sun 12-2 Dinner Thu-Sat 6-9 Restaurant menu available Thu-Sun ⊕ FREE HOUSE ◄ Loddon Hoppit, Gravesend Shrimpers. ♞ 9 **Facilities** Non-diners area ♦♦ Children's portions Family room Outside area ♜ Parking

IVY HATCH Map 6 TQ55

The Plough at Ivy Hatch PICK OF THE PUBS

See Pick of the Pubs on opposite page

LAMBERHURST Map 6 TQ63

The Vineyard PICK OF THE PUBS

tel: 01892 890222 **Lamberhurst Down TN3 8EU**
email: enquiries@thevineyard.com
dir: *From A21 follow brown Vineyard signs onto B2169 towards Lamberhurst. Left, continue to follow Vineyard signs. Straight on at x-roads, pub on right*

Robust Anglo-French cooking with good ale and wines to match

Built more than 300 years ago, original elements of this country roadside pub are reflected in the quirky stuffed boar's head mounted above the huge brick-built fireplace. Leather sofas, wingback and parlour chairs mix easily with the rustic look and chunky wooden furniture, whilst the eye is taken by a mural illustrating the well-established wine-making craft in the area. The pub is next door to one of England's oldest vineyards and there's a carefully chosen wine list and 20 served by the glass. Fans of the hop are rewarded with firkins from microbreweries such as Old Dairy. From the kitchen comes a pleasing mix of top-notch traditional English and regional French brasserie dishes: seared scallop with sweet potatoes and cumin purée to start, then wild mushroom and tarragon open lasagne; or stone bass fillet with roasted squash, wilted spinach, and crayfish hollandaise, finishing with iced plum pudding parfait with poached pear and chocolate shavings.

Open all day all wk 11.30-11 **Food** Lunch Mon-Fri 12-6, Sat-Sun 12-9.30 Dinner Mon-Fri 6-9.45, Sat-Sun 12-9.30 Av main course £15.50 ⊕ FREE HOUSE ◀ Sharp's Doom Bar, Harvey's, Old Dairy Ŏ Aspall. ♥ 20 **Facilities** Non-diners area ♣ (Bar Garden Outside area) ♦ Children's portions Garden Outside area ⊼ Parking WiFi

LEYSDOWN-ON-SEA Map 7 TR07

The Ferry House Inn ★★★★ INN ⊛

tel: 01795 510214 **Harty Ferry Rd ME12 4BQ**
email: info@theferryhouseinn.co.uk **web:** www.theferryhouseinn.co.uk
dir: *From A429 towards Sheppey. At rdbt take B2231 to Eastchurch. From Eastchurch High St into Church Rd. At rdbt into Rowetts Way signed Leysdown. Right into Harty Ferry Rd to village*

A family-owned, delightfully remote island pub

Named for the ferry that crossed the Swale to the mainland until the onset of World War II, this 16th-century pub stands in three acres of terraced lawns. The views over the water to Faversham, Whitstable and the North Downs alone are worth the journey, while its open log fires, wooden beams and solid oak floors add to the tally. And then there's the one-AA Rosette food, with the inn's membership of 'Produced in Kent' meaning locally caught fish of the day; game from the Harty Estate, beef and lamb from their family farm in Eastchurch and fresh produce from the inn's kitchen garden.

Open all day all wk Mon-Fri 11-11 (Sat all day, Sun 11-5) Closed 24-31 Dec **Food** Lunch Mon-Fri 12-2.30, Sat & Sun 12.30-4 Dinner Mon-Sat 6.30-9 Set menu available ⊕ FREE HOUSE ◀ Whitstable, Old Dairy, guest ales Ŏ Sheppy's. ♥ **Facilities** Non-diners area ♦ Children's menu Children's portions Play area Family room Garden ⊼ Parking WiFi ▭ (notice required) **Rooms** 5

LINTON Map 7 TQ75

The Bull Inn

tel: 01622 743612 **Linton Hill ME17 4AW**
email: food@thebullatlinton.co.uk
dir: *S of Maidstone on A229 (Hastings road)*

Rural pub ideal for alfresco eating and drinking

Built in 1674, this part-timbered former coaching inn stands high on the Greensand Ridge, with wonderful views and sunsets over the Weald. The award-winning garden includes two oak gazebos and a large decked area for alfresco bistro dining and afternoon tea. Inside there is an imposing inglenook fireplace, lots of beams and a bar serving Shepherd Neame ales. The wide-ranging menu offers hearty sandwiches and pub classics – lasagne; lamb's liver and bacon; and home-made pie of the week – perfect sustenance for walkers tackling the Greensand Way. The inn offers seasonal menus, daily delivered seafood, and home-made desserts.

Open all day all wk 11am-11.30pm (Sun 12-10.30) **Food** all wk 12-9 Set menu available ⊕ SHEPHERD NEAME ◀ Master Brew, Kent's Best, Late Red Ŏ Thatchers Gold. **Facilities** Non-diners area ♣ (Bar Garden) ♦ Children's menu Children's portions Garden ⊼ Parking WiFi ▭

LOWER HALSTOW Map 7 TQ86

The Three Tuns

tel: 01795 842840 **The Street ME9 7DY**
email: info@thethreetunsrestaurant.co.uk
dir: *From A2 between Rainham & Newington turn left, follow Lower Halstow sign. At T-junct right signed Funton & Iwade. Pub on right*

Quality dining, pub grub and Kentish real ales

Built in 1468 and licensed to sell ale since 1764, Chris and Carol Haines's traditional fire-warmed bar is paradise for lovers of local real ales and cider. They stock Millis Kentish Best, Goacher's Real Mild and Dudda's Tun Kentish Cider, while Summer Bank Holiday sees the Kentish Ale and Cider Festival, with a hog-roast, seafood and live music. Farms supply much of the food on the ever-changing restaurant menu, such as pan-fried marinated fillet of plaice, Parmentier potatoes, roasted Mediterranean vegetables, prawn and sun-dried tomato butter; or corn-fed chicken supreme with goats' cheese and cranberry stuffing, wild mushroom, potato cake and tarragon sauce. There's a large beer garden.

Open all day all wk **Food** all wk 12-9 ⊕ FREE HOUSE ◀ Millis Brewing Co Kentish Best, Goacher's Real Mild Ale, guest ales Ŏ Dudda's Tun Kentish Cider, Core Fruit Products Hard Core. ♥ 10 **Facilities** Non-diners area ♣ (Bar Garden) ♦ Children's menu Children's portions Garden ⊼ Beer festival Cider festival Parking WiFi ▭ (notice required)

PICK OF THE PUBS

The Plough at Ivy Hatch

IVY HATCH   Map 6 TQ55

tel: 01732 810100
High Cross Rd TN15 0NL
email: miles@theploughivyhatch.co.uk
web: www.theploughivyhatch.co.uk
dir: *Exit A25 between Borough Green &
Sevenoaks, follow Ightham Mote signs*

Village pub near the National Trust's Ightham Mote

This 17th-century, tile-hung pub in the picturesque village of Ivy Hatch is but a short walk from the National Trust's Ightham Mote, Britain's best-preserved medieval manor house. From spring to autumn, The Plough keeps its own pigs and chickens in a cobnut coppice in the back garden. During the week it's open for breakfast and a wide range of teas and coffees. In the bar, the real ales come from a select roster of Kentish breweries, and food includes sandwiches with chips or soup; and a choice of fish, ploughman's and deli farm charcuterie boards. On the daily-changing restaurant menus are British- and European-style dishes featuring rare-breed steaks (Longhorn T-bones, Dexter sirloin and Shorthorn burgers) seafood, game and, courtesy of those pigs, country pork terrines; home-made bacon, pork and apple burgers; and mouth-watering, slow-cooked legs and shoulders. Looking to other options, a starter of gin cured salmon, pickled cherries and dill cream cheese might be

followed by a main course of Chart Farm venison bourguignon with thyme and rosemary dumplings; polenta-coated deep-fried squid with chilli, parsley, aïoli and mixed leaves; or smoked chicken Caesar salad. Desserts include Seville orange curd and cinnamon mille feuille with passionfruit and orange sorbet; and chocolate fondant with vanilla ice cream and chocolate sauce. There are many excellent walks through the countryside surrounding The Plough, and the road- and mountain-biking opportunities are excellent too. Muddy boots and cycling gear, if not necessarily de rigueur, are definitely not frowned upon and wearers caught in the rain will be able to dry off either in front of the winter open fire, or, if the sun's out, on the terrace.

Open all day all wk 9am-11pm (Sat 10am-11pm Sun 10-6) Closed 26 Dec **Food** Lunch Mon-Sat 12-2.45, Sun 12-5.30 Dinner Mon-Sat 6-9.30 ⊕ FREE HOUSE ◀ Tonbridge Coppernob & Rustic, Old Dairy Red Top, Ringwood Best Bitter ⚙ Thatchers Gold. ♟ 10 **Facilities** Non-diners area ❖ (Bar Restaurant Garden) ✦ Children's menu Children's portions Garden ⌁ Parking WiFi 🚌 (notice required)

MAIDSTONE
Map 7 TQ75

The Black Horse Inn ★★★★ INN

tel: 01622 737185 **Pilgrim's Way, Thurnham ME14 3LD**
email: info@wellieboot.net web: www.wellieboot.net
dir: *M20 junct 7, A249, right into Detling. Turn opposite Cock Horse Pub into Pilgrim's Way*

Charming free house on the Pilgrim's Way

Tucked beneath the North Downs on the Pilgrim's Way, this 18th-century former forge welcomes guests with an open log fire in the colder months. Dine in the conservatory restaurant that has garden views or in the cosy candlelit restaurant. Real ales change weekly and the kitchen uses local ingredients in fish or meat sharing plates, or in mains like roast beef, stuffing and Yorkshire pudding; or slow-roasted belly of pork and stuffed loin of pork, served with carrot purée, black pudding mashed potatoes, stuffed cabbage leaf and cider and apple sauce; a daily-changing specials board adds to the choices.

Open all day all wk **Food** Lunch all wk 12-6 Dinner all wk 6-10 Av main course £14.95 Restaurant menu available all wk ⊕ FREE HOUSE ◀ Greene King IPA, Wychwood Hobgoblin, Westerham Grasshopper, Harvey's Sussex Best Bitter, Black Sheep ♂ Biddenden. ♀ 21 **Facilities** Non-diners area ♣ (Bar Garden) ♦♦ Children's menu Children's portions Garden ⊼ Parking ☷ (notice required) **Rooms** 27

MARKBEECH
Map 6 TQ44

The Kentish Horse

tel: 01342 850493 **Cow Ln TN8 5NT**
email: theoldhouse007@aol.com
dir: *3m from Edenbridge & 7m from Tunbridge Wells*

Popular free house in the Garden of England

Britain's only Kentish Horse honours Invicta, the county's prancing white stallion. Popular with ramblers and cyclists, the locals rate it too, partly because Chiddingstone-brewed Larkins and Lewes-brewed Harvey's are available, with guest ales on high days and holidays. Owners Trevor and Tina Jobson serve home-cooked, traditional food, such as pan-fried lamb's liver and onions; beer-battered fresh fillet of haddock; and tagliatelle with Stilton and mushroom cream sauce. The four-acre grounds include an extensive garden and a children's play area, and you also get a terrific view over Winnie the Pooh's home, Ashdown Forest.

Open all day all wk **Food** Lunch Mon-Sat 12-2.30, Sun 12-3 Dinner Tue-Sat 6.30-9.30 ⊕ FREE HOUSE ◀ Harvey's, Larkins, guest ales ♂ Westons Stowford Press, Symonds. **Facilities** Non-diners area ♣ (Bar Garden) ♦♦ Children's menu Children's portions Play area Garden Parking ☷ (notice required)

MATFIELD
Map 6 TQ64

The Poet at Matfield

tel: 01892 722416 **Maidstone Rd TN12 7JH**
email: info@thepoetatmatfield.co.uk
dir: *From Tonbridge on A21 towards Hastings left onto B2160 signed Paddock Wood. Approx 1.5m to pub on left in Matfield*

Smart village inn with impressive literary links

Named after poet Siegfried Sassoon, who was born in this quintessentially English village just outside Tunbridge Wells, this Grade II listed pub is more than 350 years old. The pub, now with new landlords, retains its original character with the beams and antiques, but comfortable leather chesterfield sofas and armchairs add an elegant edge. Harvey's Sussex Best Bitter and guest ales can be found at the bar.

Open all day Closed Mon **Food** Lunch Tue-Sat 12-2.30, Sun 12-4 Dinner Tue-Sat 6-9 Set menu available ⊕ ENTERPRISE INNS ◀ Harvey's Sussex Best Bitter, guest ale. ♀ 12 **Facilities** Non-diners area ♣ (Bar Garden) ♦♦ Children's portions Garden ⊼ Parking WiFi ☷ (notice required)

NEW The Wheelwrights Arms

tel: 01892 722129 **The Green TN12 7JX**
dir: *From A21 between Pembury & Lamberhurst take B2160 to Matfield. Pub on left*

Weatherboarded, traditional free house

Overlooking Kent's largest village green, the four-century-old Wheelrights really deserves to be called a quintessential English pub. A cliché perhaps, but apart from being exceptionally pretty, its qualifications also include seven weekly changing real ales, a cider from the village and an impressive range of gins. For an idea of what food to expect, take pressing of duck leg with prunes, pistachios and pickled fennel; roast rump of lamb with confit breast, makhani sauce with cashews, Bombay aloo, lamb samosa and raita; and spiced Yorkshire rhubarb with meringue, rhubarb sponge and home-made stem ginger and rhubarb ice cream. A worthy fish alternative would be pan-roast loin of cod and clams.

Open all day Closed Mon **Food** Lunch Tue-Sun 12-2.15 Dinner Tue-Sun 6.30-8.45 Av main course £16 ⊕ FREE HOUSE ◀ Rotating local guest ales ♂ Symonds, Charrington's. ♀ 12 **Facilities** Non-diners area ♣ (Bar Restaurant Outside area) ♦♦ Children's menu Outside area ⊼ Beer festival Parking WiFi ☷ (notice required)

OARE
Map 7 TR06

The Three Mariners

tel: 01795 533633 **2 Church Rd ME13 0QA**
email: info@thethreemarinersoare.co.uk
dir: *M2 junct 7, A2 towards Sittingbourne. Through Ospringe. At rdbt right onto B2045 (Western Link). At T-junct left signed Oare. 2nd pub on right*

Coastal pub popular with walkers and bird-watchers

Dating back to the late 18th century, the Grade II listed Three Mariners occupies an enviable position in the village of Oare just outside Faversham. With the Saxon Shore Way, the Swale Heritage Trail and the marshes close by, this coastal pub is popular with walkers and wildlife enthusiasts. Log fires warm the bar in winter, whilst the sunny terrace is a real draw in summer. Enjoy a pint of local Shepherd Neame or Whitstable Bay Pale Ale and order from a menu that might include fish soup, aïoli and croûtons; red mullet fillets, piquillo peppers, salsa verda and sablée potatoes; or calves' liver, mash, vegetables and beetroot and cassis jus. Cinnamon-coated Nutella gnocchi doughnuts and vanilla ice cream to finish perhaps.

Open all day all wk 12-11 (Sun 12-10) Closed 24 Dec eve & 25 Dec eve **Food** Contact pub for food times Set menu available Restaurant menu available all wk ⊕ SHEPHERD NEAME ◀ Master Brew, Late Red, Early Bird & Whitstable Bay Pale Ale ♂ Thatchers Gold. ♀ 13 **Facilities** ♣ (Bar Garden Outside area) ♦♦ Children's portions Garden Outside area ⊼ Parking

PICK OF THE PUBS

The Bottle House Inn

PENSHURST   Map 6 TQ54

tel: 01892 870306
Coldharbour Rd TN11 8ET
email: info@thebottlehouseinnpenshurst.co.uk
web: www.thebottlehouseinnpenshurst.co.uk
dir: *A264 W from Tunbridge Wells onto B2188 N. After Fordcombe left towards Edenbridge & Hever. Pub 500yds after staggered x-roads*

Historic pub off the beaten track

During 1492, the year Columbus landed in America, the uniquely named Bottle House was being built as an estate farmhouse, which helps to put its great age in context. Down a country lane, it wasn't until 1806 that it was granted a licence to sell ale and cider, later also becoming a shop, a farrier's and a cobbler's. In 1938 a refurbishment exposed hundreds of old bottles –thus the name. Later improvements have included sandblasting ancient oak beams back to their natural colour, exposing brickwork and painting walls in neutral shades. At the copper-topped bar counter there's a contingent of beers from Kentish breweries Larkins, Tonbridge, Westerham and Whitstable, with Sussex-brewed Weltons joining the line-up, as well as 19 wines by the glass. The menus in the stylish dining room capitalise on the abundant supply of local produce, so the chef's

recommendations change accordingly. For instance, there might be a starter of panko-breaded tiger prawns, or light dishes such as eggs Benedict; and creamy chorizo, pine nut and spinach linguine. Main courses include venison and bacon cottage pie, mustard mash and winter vegetables; butter-roasted chicken supreme with chorizo; Cajun hake fillet with creamy mash, buttered spinach, crispy bacon, peas and parmesan cream; and roasted cauliflower, spinach and hazelnut carbonara. Among the home-made desserts you're likely to find salted caramel brûlée; and chocolate brownie with toffee sauce and vanilla ice cream. When the weather's favourable, there's a good-sized patio area with umbrellas.

Open all day all wk 11-11 (Sun 11-10.30) Closed 25 Dec **Food** Mon-Sat 12-10, Sun & BH 12-9 ⊕ FREE HOUSE 🍺 Larkins Traditional, guest ales from Westerham, Tonbridge, Whitstable & Weltons Brewies. ♟ 19 **Facilities** 🐾 (Bar Outside area) 👶 Children's menu Children's portions Outside area 🪑 Parking WiFi 🚌 (notice required)

PENSHURST
Map 6 TQ54

The Bottle House Inn
PICK OF THE PUBS

See Pick of the Pubs on page 287

PLUCKLEY
Map 7 TQ94

The Dering Arms
PICK OF THE PUBS

tel: 01233 840371 **Station Rd TN27 ORR**
email: jim@deringarms.com
dir: *M20 junct 8, A20 to Ashford. Right onto B2077 at Charing to Pluckley*

Great selection of seafood dishes

Creeper-clad stone gables and arched windows mark out this imposing building as something special. There's a touch of Victorian Gothic about this eye-catching pub, built originally as a hunting lodge. The grandeur remains inside too, with open fires, bare boards, scrubbed old tables and a hop-bine dressed bar groaning with venerable hand pumps. The separate clubroom has comfy settees, log-burner and a baby grand just itching to be played. It's a popular destination for seafood lovers, with ever-changing dishes filling the specials board. A starter of duck rillettes; or half a pint of shell-on prawns could be followed by grilled skate wing with caper butter; or whole crab salad. If you really want to push the boat out, and the time of year is right, ask for the fruits de mer – just give the chef 24 hours' notice. Drinkers are rewarded with a fine cellar, plus a selection of Kentish ales and ciders.

Open Mon-Fri 11.30-3.30 6-11 (Sat 9am-11pm Sun 12-4) Closed 26-27 Dec, Sun eve **Food** Lunch Mon-Fri 12-2.30, Sat 12-3, Sun 12-4 Dinner Mon-Sat 6.30-9 Restaurant menu available all wk ⊕ FREE HOUSE ◀ Goacher's Best Dark Ale, Gold Star Ale, Old Ale, Dering Ale ♂ Biddenden, Hush Heath Jake's Orchard, Wise Owl. ♀ 11 **Facilities** Non-diners area ❖ (Bar Garden) ♦♦ Children's portions Family room Garden ⋒ Parking WiFi

ROLVENDEN
Map 7 TQ83

The Bull

tel: 01580 241212 **1 Regent St TN17 4PB**
email: info@thebullinnrolvenden.co.uk
dir: *Just off A28, approx 3m from Tenterden*

The beer garden overlooks the village cricket pitch

This handsome, tile-hung village inn dates, in part, back to the 13th century and is located close to the walled garden that inspired Frances Hodgson Burnett's classic tale *The Secret Garden*. Handy, too, for steam trains of the Kent and East Sussex Railway, there's a welcome focus on local beers and produce, with a heart-warming, pubby menu. Look out for warm chicken and chorizo salad with sun-blushed tomatoes to start, followed by calves' liver and bacon or wild boar sausages with wholegrain mustard mash and tomato confit. There's a lovely beer garden overlooking the village cricket ground.

Open all day all wk **Food** Lunch all wk 12-3 Dinner all wk 6-10 Restaurant menu available Mon-Sat ⊕ FREE HOUSE ◀ Red Top, Harvey's, Old Dairy Gold Top ♂ Westons Stowford Press. ♀ 12 **Facilities** Non-diners area ❖ (Bar Garden) ♦♦ Children's menu Children's portions Garden ⋒ Beer festival Parking WiFi ▭ (notice required)

SANDWICH
Map 7 TR35

George & Dragon Inn

tel: 01304 613106 **Fisher St CT13 9EJ**
email: enquiries@georgeanddragon-sandwich.co.uk
dir: *Between Dover & Canterbury (park at Quay Car Park, walk through Fisher Gate to Fisher St)*

Charming family-run pub serving modern British food

Built in 1446, ale was first sold here in 1549, but was only licensed under the name of George & Dragon in 1615. This town centre pub oozes charm and character, with its wood floors and open fires, and makes a welcome pit stop when exploring historic Sandwich on foot. Run by two brothers, you can refuel with a pint of well-kept Wantsum, Otter or a guest ale. On the monthly-changing evening menu, you might find mushrooms and spinach on a toasted onion and walnut scone with blue cheese; followed by rump of lamb with goats' cheese and olive mash; or braised venison and boar faggot with blackberries, mash and steamed cabbage. Head outside to the picturesque suntrap courtyard in summer.

Open all day 11-11 (Sun 12-4) Closed Sun eve **Food** Lunch all wk 12-2 Dinner Mon-Sat 6-9 Set menu available ⊕ ENTERPRISE INNS ◀ Wantsum, Otter Amber, Butcombe, guest ales ♂ Aspall. ♀ 9 **Facilities** Non-diners area ❖ (Bar Garden) Garden ⋒ WiFi

SELLING
Map 7 TR05

The Rose and Crown

tel: 01227 752214 **Perry Wood ME13 9RY**
email: info@roseandcrownperrywood.co.uk
dir: *From A28 right at Badgers Hill, left at end. 1st left signed Perry Wood*

Pretty country pub with a long history

The ghost of Hammond Smith, murdered after a boozy day in 1889, may join you for a pint but don't let his friendly presence detract from the pleasure of this rambling, low-beamed 16th-century inn. Packed with character via the inglenooks, horse brasses and corn dollies, Goldings hops are draped around a bar offering Harvey's and Adnams real ales plus Biddenden cider. Descend to the restaurant for home-cooked Kent fish pie; confit duck; game pie; or brie, bacon and walnut jacket potato. The flower-festooned garden is made for summer eating and drinking enjoyment.

Open 12-3 6.30-11 (Sat-Sun all day) Closed 25-26 Dec eve, 1 Jan eve, Mon **Food** Lunch Tue-Sun 12-2 Dinner Tue-Sat 6.30-9 Av main course £9 ⊕ FREE HOUSE ◀ Adnams Southwold Bitter, Harvey's Sussex Best Bitter, guest ale ♂ Westons Stowford Press, Biddenden. **Facilities** Non-diners area ❖ (Bar Restaurant Garden) ♦♦ Children's menu Children's portions Play area Garden ⋒ Parking ▭ (notice required)

SHIPBOURNE
Map 6 TQ55

The Chaser Inn

tel: 01732 810360 **Stumble Hill TN11 9PE**
email: enquiries@thechaser.co.uk
dir: *N of Tonbridge take A227 towards Shipbourne. Pub on left*

Popular pub with famous connections

Once a haunt for stars such as Richard Burton and Elizabeth Taylor, The Chaser Inn is an informal, relaxed village inn, next to the church and overlooking the common. Well-kept real ales are complemented by an extensive menu of sandwiches, light bites and main courses such as honey mustard ham with free-range eggs and chunky chips; seafood stew; or chicken and leek pie with creamy mash. There is a lovely beer garden and the covered courtyard comes into its own in the winter months. The pub takes its name from its long association with the nearby Fairlawne racing stables.

Open all day all wk 10am-mdnt **Food** Mon-Sat 12-9.30, Sun 12-9 ⊕ WHITING & HAMMOND ◼ Greene King IPA, Larkins Traditional, guest ales ○ Aspalls, Isobel. **Facilities** Non-diners area ❖ (Bar Garden) ᵼ Children's portions Garden ⊼ Parking WiFi ➡ (notice required)

SISSINGHURST — Map 7 TQ73

The Milk House

tel: 01580 720200 **The Street TN17 2JG**
email: fresh@themilkhouse.co.uk
dir: *In village centre*

Excellent locally-sourced food in convivial village inn

In picturesque Sissinghurst, this 16th-century, former hall house is very much the hub of the village. With its timber beams and Tudor fireplace, the pub has considerable charm and locals supping pints of Kentish-brewed Old Dairy Brewery ale mingle with destination diners tempted by the acclaimed food. Most of the produce comes from a 20-mile radius of the pub and dishes such as navarin of Romney Marsh lamb with root vegetables and minted pearl barley; or sumac-crusted sea bass, avocado purée and quinoa, cucumber, pomegranate and parsley salad sit happily alongside innovative home-made pizzas and a top-notch children's menu.

Open all day all wk **Food** 12-9 Av main course £9 Restaurant menu available all wk ⊕ ENTERPRISE INNS ◼ Old Dairy, Harvey's, Westerham, Tonbridge, Dark Star ○ Symonds, Orchard Pig, Rubens Curious Apple, Hush Heath Jake's Kentish Cider, Turner's, Gibbet Oak. ⚑ 18 **Facilities** Non-diners area ❖ (Bar Garden) ᵼ Children's menu Children's portions Play area Garden ⊼ Beer festival Cider festival Parking WiFi

SMARDEN — Map 7 TQ84

The Chequers Inn — PICK OF THE PUBS

tel: 01233 770217 **The Street TN27 8QA**
email: spaldings@thechequerssmarden.com
dir: *From Maidstone take A229. Left through Sutton Valence & Headcorn. Left signed Smarden. Pub in village centre*

Ancient pub with courtyard and lovely gardens

The former weavers' village of Smarden has around 200 buildings of architectural and historical interest, one of which is the clapboarded 14th-century Chequers Inn. Its beautiful landscaped garden features a large carp pond and an attractive south-facing courtyard. Ales brewed by Harvey's, Sharp's, Fuller's, Wadworth and the Old Dairy Brewery are served in the low-beamed bars. Seasonal ingredients are sourced locally for the menus of traditional and modern food. Typical of the restaurant choices are starters of potted ham with piccalilli; home-made Scotch egg; whole lemon sole, lemon and caper butter, green vegetables and new potatoes; and rabbit pie, braised cabbage and bacon. The bar menu, carte and children's menu are all served on Sundays too, when traditional beef, lamb and pork roasts are joined by gammon and turkey.

Open all day all wk **Food** Lunch all wk 12-3 Dinner all wk 6-9 Restaurant menu available all wk ⊕ FREE HOUSE ◼ Sharp's Doom Bar, Fuller's London Pride, Wadworth 6X, Old Dairy, Harvey's ○ Westons Stowford Press. **Facilities** Non-diners area ᵼ Children's menu Children's portions Garden ⊼ Parking WiFi ➡

SPELDHURST — Map 6 TQ54

George & Dragon — PICK OF THE PUBS

tel: 01892 863125 **Speldhurst Hill TN3 0NN**
email: julian@speldhurst.com
dir: *Phone for detailed directions*

Kentish ales and fine food in ancient timber-framed inn

This venerable building has surveyed the heart of the village for at least 800 years. Its gables, pitched roof, cruck frame and immense chimney recall another age; the interior is just as captivating, with huge, head-cracking beams and wizened posts sewing the treasure together. Roaring fires dismiss a winter chill, whilst outdoor areas are pleasing places to sit on lazy summer days after an exploration of the High Weald Area of Outstanding Natural Beauty in which the pub is located. Local beers from Larkins share top billing at the bar. Much of the food prepared here is equally parochial in provenance – Ashdown Forest, the Downs and cheeses from Sussex amongst areas championed. Enjoy a braised pork knuckle with celeriac remoulade starter, then follow with a classic pub dish like salt marsh shepherd's pie; loin of Buckhurst Park roe deer; or pan-fried sea bream with piquillo pepper and roasted tomato cassoulet. Seasonally available produce means the menus vary pleasingly throughout the year.

Open all day all wk **Food** Lunch all wk 12-2.30 Dinner Mon-Sat 7-9.30 Av main course £13.50-£16.50 Set menu available ⊕ FREE HOUSE ◼ Harvey's Sussex Best Bitter, Brakspear, Larkins ○ Aspalls. ⚑ 11 **Facilities** Non-diners area ❖ (Bar Garden) ᵼ Children's portions Family room Garden ⊼ Parking WiFi ➡

STALISFIELD GREEN — Map 7 TQ95

The Plough Inn

tel: 01795 890256 **ME13 0HY**
email: info@theploughinnstalisfield.co.uk
dir: *From A20 (dual carriageway) W of Charing follow Stalisfield Green signs. Approx 2m to village*

Downland pub with a passion for Kentish produce

The Plough Inn is a splendid, 15th-century Wealden hall house situated by the green in an unspoilt hamlet high up on the North Downs. A real country pub, it enjoys far-reaching views across the Swale estuary and is worth seeking out for the array of Kentish drinks – microbrewery beers, ciders and juices – and a choice of dishes on the constantly changing menus and blackboard specials. Kick off an enjoyable evening meal with a kir royale followed by wild rabbit risotto, crispy loin and Swiss chard emulsion, then pan-roasted duck breast, celeriac sauerkraut, sweet potato purée, cavolo nero and brandied cherry sauce. End with chestnut sponge, roast rhubarb and rhubarb ice cream perhaps.

Open 12-3 5-11 (Sat 12-11 Sun 12-6) Closed Mon **Food** Lunch Tue-Fri 12-2, Sat 12-3, Sun 12-3.30 Dinner Tue-Sat 6-9 Set menu available Restaurant menu available Tue-Sun ⊕ FREE HOUSE ◼ Dragon's Tail, Musket, local guest ales ○ Biddenden Bushels, Kent, Hush Heath Jake's Orchard, Staplehurst. ⚑ 13 **Facilities** Non-diners area ❖ (Bar Restaurant Garden) ᵼ Children's menu Children's portions Play area Family room Garden ⊼ Beer festival Parking ➡ (notice required)

STOWTING
Map 7 TR14

The Tiger Inn

tel: 01303 862130 **TN25 6BA**
email: info@tigerinn.pub
dir: *Phone for detailed directions*

Classic village pub with rustic charm and hearty food

Lost down winding lanes in a scattered North Downs hamlet, the 250-year-old Tiger Inn oozes traditional character and rural charm. The front bar is delightfully rustic and unpretentious, with stripped oak floors, two warming wood-burning stoves, old cushioned pews and scrubbed old pine tables. Mingle with the locals at the bar with a pint of Master Brew or the pub's own Tiger Bitter, then order a hearty meal from the inviting chalkboard menu — perhaps Romney Marsh rack of lamb with redcurrant jus; whole Dover sole; and chicken, ham and leek pie with shortcrust pastry. In summer dine alfresco on the suntrap front terrace. There are super walks all around.

Open all day Closed Mon & Tue (ex BH Mon) **Food** Lunch Wed-Sat 12-9, Sun 12-5 Dinner Wed-Sat 12-9 ⊕ FREE HOUSE ◀ Shepherd Neame Master Brew, Tiger Bitter, guest ales. ♟ 10 **Facilities** Non-diners area ✿ (Bar Garden) ♦♦ Children's menu Children's portions Garden ⊼ Parking WiFi ▭

TUDELEY
Map 6 TQ64

The Poacher & Partridge

tel: 01732 358934 **Hartlake Rd TN11 0PH**
email: enquiries@thepoacherandpartridge.com
dir: *A21 S onto A26 E, at rdbt turn right. After 2m turn sharp left into Hartlake Rd, 0.5m on right*

Stylish rural pub with good food

Set amongst Kentish orchards, this pretty country pub has a rustic, down-to-earth feel with sturdy old wood furniture and unique features such as a beautiful old wine cellar and deli kitchen. Outside, you'll discover a large garden, with a children's play area, ideal for a refreshing summer pint of Harvey's from the wide selection of local ales and ciders. Traditional English, continental and wood-fire dishes appear on the menu, perhaps lamb kofta; baked camembert; wood-fired pizzas; slow-roast lamb shank, crushed potato, curly kale and red wine jus; butternut squash tortellini; and a superfood salad.

Open all day all wk 11.30-11 **Food** all wk 12-9 Av main course £15 ⊕ FREE HOUSE ◀ Sharp's Doom Bar, Timothy Taylor, Musket, Harvey's, Old Dairy ♢ Thatchers Gold, Aspall, Biddenden. ♟ 30 **Facilities** Non-diners area ✿ (Bar Garden) ♦♦ Children's menu Children's portions Play area Garden ⊼ Parking WiFi ▭ (notice required)

TUNBRIDGE WELLS (ROYAL)
Map 6 TQ53

The Crown Inn

tel: 01892 864742 **The Green, Groombridge TN3 9QH**
email: crown.inn.groombridge@gmail.com
dir: *Take A264 W of Tunbridge Wells, then B2110 S*

Good food and bags of character

In the 18th century this charming free house was the infamous headquarters for a gang of smugglers who hid their casks of tea in the passages between the cellar and Groombridge Place, later home to Sir Arthur Conan Doyle. Doyle made this 16th-century pub his local and today, its low beams and an inglenook fireplace are the setting for some great food and drink. Favourites include trio of local pork sausages, mash, kale and red onion gravy; beer battered fish and chips, peas and home-made tartare sauce, and daily specials based on fresh local produce. Eat alfresco during the summer months.

Open all day all wk **Food** Lunch Mon-Fri 12-2.30, Sat 12-9, Sun 12-5 Dinner Mon-Fri 6-9, Sat 12-9 ⊕ FREE HOUSE ◀ Harvey's Sussex Best Bitter, Black Cat, Larkins ♢ Westons Stowford Press. **Facilities** Non-diners area ✿ (Bar Garden) ♦♦ Children's menu Children's portions Play area Garden ⊼ Parking WiFi ▭ (notice required)

Sankey's

tel: 01892 511422 **39 Mount Ephraim TN4 8AA**
email: sankeys@sankeys.co.uk
dir: *Phone for detailed directions*

Cask ales and beers from around the world

A respected family business in the Tonbridge area for over 50 years, Sankey's houses a unique collection of enamel signs, family memorabilia and antique church pews. But the focal points are the large open fire encircled with comfy armchairs, and the bar. Here you will need time to peruse the 23 draught options, which include ales from the town's brewery such as Coppernob, and from overseas such as Denmark's Mikkeller; also among the taps are two cider specials. A mouth-watering selection of pub favourites will soak up your refreshment, or head down to the old cellars for a feast of fish in the Seafood Brasserie.

Open all day all wk **Food** Lunch Mon-Fri 12-3, Sat-Sun 12-5, Dinner all wk 6-10 Set menu available Restaurant menu available Tue-Sat ⊕ FREE HOUSE ◀ Tonbridge Coppernob, Brewdog, Mikkeller, Larkins, rotating guest ales ♢ Westons Stowford Press, guest ciders. ♟ 12 **Facilities** Non-diners area ✿ (Bar Garden Outside area) ♦♦ Children's menu Children's portions Garden Outside area ⊼ Beer festival WiFi ▭

WESTERHAM
Map 6 TQ45

Grasshopper on the Green

tel: 01959 562926 **The Green TN16 1AS**
email: info@grasshopperonthegreen.com
dir: *M25 junct 5, A21 towards Sevenoaks, then A25 to Westerham. Or M25 junct 6, A22 towards East Grinstead, A25 to Westerham*

Local brews and modern home-cooked cuisine

Overlooking Westerham's pretty green, the more-than-800-year-old Grasshopper takes its name from the arms of local merchant Thomas Gresham, founder of London's Royal Exchange in 1565. The bar's low-beamed ceilings, hung with antique jugs, and its winter log fire are particularly appealing, as are Westerham brewery's Grasshopper and British Bulldog real ales. House specials include home-made steak and ale pie and the 'Winston Whopper' home-made burger, while regular cast members include grilled fresh tuna, lemon butter and capers; and slow-roasted lamb shank with red wine and rosemary jus. Ask long-term hosts Neale and Anne Sadler for directions to Chartwell (NT), Sir Winston Churchill's former home.

Open all day all wk **Food** all wk 12-9.30 ⊕ FREE HOUSE ◀ Adnams Broadside, Harvey's Sussex Best Bitter, Courage Best Bitter, Westerham British Bulldog BB & Grasshopper ♢ Symonds. ♟ 12 **Facilities** Non-diners area ✿ (Bar Garden) ♦♦ Children's menu Children's portions Play area Garden ⊼ Parking WiFi ▭ (notice required)

WEST MALLING
Map 6 TQ65

The Farm House
PICK OF THE PUBS

tel: 01732 843257 **97 The High St ME19 6NA**
email: enquiries@thefarmhouse.biz
dir: *M20 junct 4, S on A228. Right to West Malling. Pub in village centre*

Modern dining-pub with style

Well positioned in the heart of the Kentish market town of West Malling, with a pretty walled garden overlooking 15th-century stone barns. The handsome Elizabethan building offers a friendly welcome, whether stopping for refreshment in the stylish bar or eating in one its two dining areas. Local seasonal ingredients are expertly used in menus with a strong French influence. So a glass of wine may be called for — choose from 20 sold by the glass. In addition to the tapas or fish sharing boards typical starters are smoked haddock and caper fishcakes. Main courses vary from pub favourites such as a mixed grill, to slow-cooked Moroccan chickpea stew; and Kentish wild rabbit and Aspall cider pie. Puddings could be chocolate and chilli tart; and apple tarte Tatin. Sandwiches and paninis are served until 6pm.

Open all day all wk 10am-11pm **Food** Lunch Mon-Thu 10-3, Fri-Sat 10-9.45, Sun 10-9.30 Dinner Mon-Thu 6-9.45, Fri-Sat 10-9.45, Sun 10-9.30 ⊕ ENTERPRISE INNS ◼ Harvey's, Sharp's Doom Bar, Guinness ♻ Biddenden, Aspall. ♟ 20 **Facilities** Non-diners area ♦ Children's menu Garden ⛏ Parking WiFi

---

WEST PECKHAM | Map 6 TQ65

The Swan on the Green

tel: 01622 812271 **The Green ME18 5JW**
email: bookings@swan-on-the-green.co.uk
dir: From A228 from West Malling towards Tonbridge, at rdbt take B2016 (Wrotham). At x roads left to West Peckham. Pub opposite church

Well-crafted home brews and modern food

First licensed over 330 years ago, The Swan on the Green's microbrewery has revived the 18th-century principles of 'pure ale', using only natural and, when possible, local ingredients for its eight craft ales; these are colourfully celebrated during the pub's October beer festival when Morris dancing may hinder through-traffic. A full menu includes starters such as blue crab and lobster risotto; pan-seared scallops with bacon and spinach; and boar ham and vegetable winter broth. From the mains choose caramelised red onion sausages and mash; or fillet of hake with tiger prawns. Home-made puddings may proffer American-style pancakes with either maple syrup or berry compôte with ice cream.

Open all wk 12-3 6-late **Food** Lunch 12-2 Dinner 6.30-9 ⊕ FREE HOUSE ◼ Swan Fuggles & Trumpeter ♻ Biddenden Bushels. **Facilities** ❄ (Bar Restaurant) ♦ Children's portions Outside area ⛏ Beer festival Parking (notice required)

WHITSTABLE | Map 7 TR16

Pearson's Arms

tel: 01227 773133 **Sea Wall CT5 1BT**
email: info@pearsonsarmsbyrichardphillips.co.uk
dir: In town centre. On one-way system, left at end of High St

Relaxed seafront hostelry serving the county's best

Once owned by the infamous Kray twins, this beach-facing pub was built to accommodate workers building the railway line between the town and Canterbury – now a popular rambling route called the Crab and Winkle Way. Today, this friendly pub proffers all good Kentish things, including ales such as Timothy Taylor Landlord, and Symonds cider; drinks can be served in plastic cups for taking to the beach. Chef Richard Phillips' flavoursome food is fresh and also sourced as locally as possible: fresh Whitstable rock oysters with sherry vinegar shallots and tabasco could precede a plate of roast saddle of Kentish rabbit; or organic salmon and crab fishcake.

Open all day all wk **Food** Mon-Sat 12-9.30 Set menu available Restaurant menu available all wk ⊕ ENTERPRISE INNS ◼ Timothy Taylor Landlord, Whitstable IPA, Harvey's Sussex Best Bitter ♻ Aspall, Symonds. ♟ 16 **Facilities** Non-diners area ❄ (Bar) ♦ Children's menu Children's portions WiFi (notice required)

WROTHAM | Map 6 TQ65

The Bull ★★★★ INN ◉◉ | PICK OF THE PUBS

tel: 01732 789800 **Bull Ln TN15 7RF**
email: info@thebullhotel.com **web:** www.thebullhotel.com
dir: M20 junct 2, A20 (signed Paddock Wood, Gravesend & Tonbridge). At rdbt 3rd exit onto A20 (signed Wrotham, Tonbridge, Borough Green, M20 & M25). At rdbt take 4th exit into Bull Ln (signed Wrotham)

Ancient pub featuring micro-beers

World War II pilots once relaxed at this 14th-century inn – stamps on the restaurant ceiling mark downed German planes. These days, guest ales from microbreweries such as Pressure Drop and Burning Sky are supported by a vast wine list offering 23 by the glass. A Big Green Egg BBQ is the workhorse of the two AA-Rosette kitchen and it's used for smoking, slow roasting and grilling. Be tempted by a starter of pan-fried pigeon breast, bacon crumb, game croquette, liquorice-pickled baby veg; or roasted butternut squash soup, balsamic reduction and toasted pumpkin seeds, and follow on with venison fillet, game stew with mash, greens, macadamia nut purée, roasted parsnip and pears; 10-hour smoked beef rib; or a pub classic of ham, egg and hand-cut chips. The bar menu offers the likes of salted beef sandwich, sauerkraut and melted gruyère.

Open all day all wk **Food** Lunch Mon-Fri 12-2.30, Sat 12-9, Sun 12-8 Dinner Mon-Fri 6-9, Sat 12-9, Sun 12-8 Av main course £11 Restaurant menu available all wk ⊕ FREE HOUSE ◼ Dark Star Hophead, Old Dairy Red Top, guest ales ♻ Burrow Hill Perry & Cider. ♟ 23 **Facilities** Non-diners area ❄ (Bar Garden) ♦ Children's menu Children's portions Garden ⛏ Parking WiFi (notice required) **Rooms** 11

LANCASHIRE

ALTHAM | Map 18 SD73

The Walton Arms

tel: 01282 774444 **Burnley Rd BB5 5UL**
email: oldgit277@msn.com
dir: M65 junct 8, A678, pub between Accrington & Padiham

Popular pub serving good pub food

A long-established way-station on an ancient highway linking Yorkshire and Lancashire, this sturdy, stone-built dining pub oozes history. Pilgrims to Whalley Abbey called at an inn here when Henry VII was king. Beams and brasses, rustic furniture and slabbed stone floors welcome today's pilgrims intent on sampling the comprehensive menu, either as a bar meal or in the atmospheric dining room. Typical choices include sea bass fillets, crayfish, chorizo and lemon risotto; spinach, cherry tomato and mozzarella suet pudding; or the inn's signature dish – shoulder of local lamb with roasted vegetables.

Open 12-2.30 5.30-11 (Sun 12-10.30) Closed Mon **Food** Lunch Tue-Fri 12-2, Sun 12.30-7.30 Dinner Tue-Thu 6-8.30, Fri-Sat 6-9, Sun 12.30-7.30 Set menu available Restaurant menu available Tue-Sun ⊕ J W LEES ◼ Bitter, Game On. ♟ 16 **Facilities** Non-diners area ❄ (Bar Outside area) ♦ Children's menu Children's portions Outside area ⛏ Parking (notice required)

BARLEY
Map 18 SD84

Barley Mow ★★★★ INN

tel: 01282 690868 **BB12 9JX**
email: info@barleymowpendle.co.uk web: www. seafoodpubcompany.com
dir: *M65 junct 13, at rdbt exit onto A682. Left into Pasture Ln, right into Ridge Ln, continue on Barley New Rd. Turn right*

Upmarket diners' pub with good walks all around

Owned by the Seafood Pub Company, the Barley Mow is located at the start and end of a lovely walk on Pendle Hill, after which you should be in need of a glass of Wainwright ale and a hearty meal. The menu has an excellent choices from the Robata grill, which might be employed to produce dishes such as prawn and chorizo skewer with paprika potatoes, guacamole, charred corn and tomato salsa; or 12oz gammon rib-eye, fried egg, onion rings and fries. Steamed syrup sponge with proper custard is one traditional end to a meal.

Open all day all wk Mon-Thu 7.30am-11pm Fri-Sat 8.30am-mdnt Sun 8.30am-10pm **Food** Mon-Thu 12-8.30, Fri-Sat 11.30-9.30, Sun 11.30-8.30 Av main course £9 ⊕ FREE HOUSE/SEAFOOD PUB CO ◀ Marston's Wainwright, Timothy Taylor Landlord, Moorhouses Pride of Pendle ♂ Kingstone Press. ▼ 8
Facilities Non-diners area ✿ (All areas) ◆ Children's menu Children's portions Garden Outside area ⚲ Parking WiFi ⛟ (notice required) **Rooms** 6

NEW The Pendle Inn

tel: 01282 614805 **Barley Ln BB12 9JX**
email: pendleinn@hotmail.co.uk
dir: *M65 junct 13, A6068 signed Fence. In Fence follow brown pub signs. Through Newchurch-in-Pendle to Barley. Pub on left in village*

Log-fire-warmed home of the Pendle Witches

The brooding, whaleback shape of Pendle Hill looms up behind this imposing, stone-built inn. They specialise in home-made Lancashire pub favourites here, such as steak and ale pies; pesto-grilled cod fillet with creamy mash; and wild mushroom linguine in white wine cream. Don't miss lamb from the owner's Barley House Farm 100 yards away. Equally, thoughts might turn to honey-glazed duck breast; spicy peri peri chicken; or Cumberland sausages and mash. Burnley's Moorhouse brewery and local micros supply some of the bar's six cask ales, while all the wines are available by the glass.

Open all wk 12-3 5-9 Jan-Mar (all day Summer) **Food** Lunch all wk 12-3 Dinner all wk 5-8.30 Av main course £9 Set menu available ⊕ FREE HOUSE ◀ Moorhouses Pride of Pendle & White Witch, Marston's Wainwright ♂ Kingstone Press. ▼ 9
Facilities Non-diners area ✿ (Bar Garden) ◆ Children's menu Children's portions Play area Garden ⚲ Parking WiFi ⛟ (notice required)

BASHALL EAVES
Map 18 SD64

NEW The Red Pump Inn

tel: 01254 826227 **Clitheroe Rd BB7 3DA**
email: enquiries@theredpumpinn.co.uk
dir: *From Clitheroe take B6243 to Bashall Eaves*

Destination pub for steak lovers

The Ribble Valley and the Forest of Bowland are hardly short of high-quality pubs and restaurants. The Red Pump's USP is its lack of pretentiousness – it aims to keep things simple and serve 'seriously good' food. Beef is the speciality here – dry-aged for about 40 days, the meat originates from Longhorn, Shorthorn and Galloway cattle carefully reared on grass. Lamb, pork and chicken are also simply cooked, while fish-lovers will find pan-fried sea bass; fish and chips; or a salad of home-cured salmon and Atlantic prawn an ideal choice. Three cask ales in the Snug include Bowland and Moorhouses brews.

Open all day Closed Jan, Mon **Food** Lunch Tue-Sun 12-2 Dinner Tue-Sun 6-9 Av main course £12.50 Restaurant menu available Tue-Sun ⊕ FREE HOUSE ◀ Bowland Hen Harrier, Moorhouses White Witch. ▼ 10 **Facilities** Non-diners area ✿ (All areas) ◆ Children's portions Family room Garden Outside area ⚲ Beer festival Parking WiFi

BILSBORROW
Map 18 SD53

Owd Nell's Tavern

tel: 01995 640010 **Guy's Thatched Hamlet, Canal Side PR3 0RS**
email: info@guysthatchedhamlet.com
dir: *M6 junct 32 N on A6. In approx 5m follow brown tourist signs to Guy's Thatched Hamlet*

Canalside eating and drinking

Owned and run by the Wilkinson family for over 35 years, this authentic tavern sits by the Lancaster Canal within Guy's Thatched Hamlet. Flagged floors, low beamed ceilings and whitewashed walls add to the ambience, as do well-kept cask ales including the pub's own Owd Nell's Canalside Bitter and Moorhouse Pendle Witch. The home-made food is typified by steak and kidney pudding; hot roasted local beef sandwiches; and fish, chips and mushy peas. The pub hosts numerous events throughout the year, including a beer and cider festival in the last weekend of July and an early September oyster festival.

Open all day all wk 7am-2am Closed 25 Dec **Food** all wk 12-9 Av main course £9.50 Restaurant menu available all wk ⊕ FREE HOUSE ◀ Moorhouse's Pendle Witches Brew, Owd Nell's Canalside Bitter, Bowland, Copper Dragon, Black Sheep, Marston's Wainwright, Cross Bay ♂ Thatchers Heritage & Cheddar Valley. ▼ 20
Facilities Non-diners area ✿ (Bar Garden Outside area) ◆ Children's menu Children's portions Family room Garden Outside area ⚲ Beer festival Cider festival Parking WiFi ⛟ (notice required)

BLACKBURN
Map 18 SD62

The Clog and Billycock ◉
PICK OF THE PUBS

tel: 01254 201163 **Billinge End Rd, Pleasington BB2 6QB**
email: enquiries@theclogandbillycock.com
dir: *M6 junct 29 to M65 junct 3, follow Pleasington signs*

Landmark village pub that ticks all the boxes

Out on Blackburn's western fringes, this pub is well placed for walks through pleasantly wooded countryside. Owned by the Ribble Valley Inns group, the unusual name celebrates the favourite attire of an early 20th-century landlord, a billycock being a felt hat. Wall lights fashioned from old weaving shuttles, lamps from cobblers' shoe stretchers, and artwork by north-west artist, Nicholas Saunders add to the character of the pub, where real ales include Thwaites Original and Wainwright. Holder of an AA Rosette, the kitchen concentrates on robust British cooking and regional produce. Warm Morecambe Bay shrimps with blade mace butter and toasted English muffin might precede slow-cooked Cumbrian lamb shank, purple sprouting broccoli, hot pot potatoes, mint jelly and rosemary gravy. Finish with jam roly poly and custard or home-made rice pudding. If the weather's good, eat and drink outdoors on the dining terrace.

Open all wk 12-11 (Sun 12-10) **Food** Lunch Mon-Fri 12-2, Sat & BHs 12-9, Sun 12-8.30, (afternoon bites Mon-Fri 2-5.30) Dinner Mon-Thu 5.30-8.30, Fri 5.30-9, Sat & BHs 12-9, Sun 12-8.30 Set menu available ⊕ RIBBLE VALLEY INNS ◀ Thwaites Original & The 1865, Marston's Wainwright ♂ Kingstone Press. ▼ 11
Facilities Non-diners area ✿ (Bar Outside area) ◆ Children's menu Outside area ⚲ Parking WiFi

PICK OF THE PUBS

The Millstone at Mellor ★★★★★ INN ⚜⚜

BLACKBURN   Map 18 SD62

tel: 01254 813333
Church Ln, Mellor BB2 7JR
email: relax@millstonehotel.co.uk
web: www.millstonehotel.co.uk
dir: *M6 junct 31, A59 towards Clitheroe, past British Aerospace. Right at rdbt signed Blackburn/Mellor. Next rdbt 2nd left. At top of hill on right*

Country-edge inn with excellent cuisine

This handsome coaching inn stands in an old village at the edge of Mellor Moor above Blackburn. With the beautiful Ribble Valley and Forest of Bowland Area of Natural Beauty to the north, Pendle Hill nearby and the half-timbered wonder that is Samlesbury Hall just along the lanes, it's little wonder that this inn is a popular place. It's very much a village inn at the heart of the community and the skills of the kitchen have repeatedly gained two AA Rosettes in recognition of the innovative take on classic dishes. Warm up by the log fire in the well-appointed bar or relax in the oak-panelled Miller's restaurant, perhaps picking at the nibbles board – Thwaites ale Lancashire rarebit, perhaps, or Szechuan pepper chicken goujons – and pondering the attractive menu options. The selection of starters ranges from Earl Grey tea-smoked duck breast, rocket, pea shoots and berry coulis to pig's head terrine

with orchard fruit chutney; or settle for one of the sharing boards. Mains reflect the strong tradition of good pub food, with a home-made steak burger, toasted brioche bun and thick cut chips, and Bowland steak, kidney and Wainwright ale pudding proving very popular options. Seared rump of Pendle lamb, crushed new potatoes, broad beans, sugar peas with shallot and butter showcases the wonderful local produce. Leave room for poached pear, seasonal berry soup and soured cream; or one of the locally produced ice creams. Walkers passing from the local footpath network can expect beers from the local Thwaites brewery, founded over 200 years ago by Daniel Thwaites, who is buried in the churchyard nearby this, one of his first pubs.

Open all day all wk **Food** Mon-Sat 12-9.30, Sun 12-9 Av main course £9.95
🛢 THWAITES INNS OF CHARACTER
🍺 Original, Wainwright, 13 Guns
🍏 Kingstone Press. 🍷 10
Facilities Non-diners area
👪 Children's menu Children's portions Outside area 🪑 Parking WiFi
Rooms 23

BLACKBURN *continued*

The Millstone at Mellor ★★★★★ INN ◎◎

PICK OF THE PUBS

See Pick of the Pubs on page 293 and advert below

| BLACKO | Map 18 SD84 |

Moorcock Inn

tel: 01282 614186 **Gisburn Rd BB9 6NG**
email: moorcockinn@gmail.com
dir: *M65 junct 13, A682, inn halfway between Blacko & Gisburn*

Country pub with many walks around

Beyond the folly of Blacko Tower, high on the road towards Gisburn on the Upper Admergill area, lies this family-run, 18th-century inn with traditional log fires, splendid views towards the Pendle Way and locally brewed cask ales in the bar. There's a wide choice on the menu and specials board including salads and sandwiches, and vegetarian and children's meals. Hearty main dishes include corn beef hash with sautéed potatoes, Savoy cabbage and pickled beetroot; seafood lasagne; pan-fried Bowland rump steak in creamy peppercorn or mushroom and red wine sauce; and spinach and ricotta tortellini.

Open 12-2 6-9 (Sat 12-9 Sun 12-6) Closed Mon **Food** Lunch Tue-Fri 12-2, Sat 12-9, Sun 12-6 Dinner Tue-Fri 6-9, Sat 12-9, Sun 12-6 ⊕ FREE HOUSE ◂ Reedley Hallows Ŏ Kingstone Press. **Facilities** Non-diners area ❖ (Bar Restaurant Outside area) ♦♦ Children's menu Children's portions Outside area ⋒ Parking ➡ (notice required)

| BURROW | Map 18 SD67 |

The Highwayman ◎◎

PICK OF THE PUBS

tel: 01524 273338 **LA6 2RJ**
email: enquiries@highwaymaninn.co.uk
dir: *M6 junct 36, A65 to Kirkby Lonsdale. A683 S. Burrow approx 2m*

Flying the flag for regional produce

Part of the Ribble Valley Inns group, The Highwayman is a stylishly appointed 18th-century coaching inn with craggy stone floors, warm wooden furniture and log fires. Marston's Wainwright is the real ale, Kingstone Press supplies draught cider, and

wine expert Craig Bancroft chooses the extensive wine list of which 10 are served by the glass. Sitting in Lancashire but only a few miles from the Cumbrian and Yorkshire borders, the inn has won a Green Tourism award and also two AA Rosettes for its use of local and regional ingredients. Experienced chef Jason 'Bruno' Birkbeck, who trained with owner Nigel Haworth, prepares a classic fish pie served with cheesy mash; another pie, made with Cumbrian lamb shanks and topped with butter puff pastry, is accompanied by rosemary and sea-salt potato wedges. Butterflies and birds love the terraced gardens, where there is comfortable seating and outdoor heating.

Open all day all wk 12-11 (Sun 12-10.30) **Food** Lunch Mon-Fri 12-2, Sat-Sun 12-9 Dinner Mon-Thu 5.30-8.30, Fri-Sat 5.30-9, Sat-Sun 12-9 Set menu available ⊕ FREE HOUSE ◂ Thwaites Wainwright Ŏ Kingstone Press. ☂ 10 **Facilities** Non-diners area ❖ (Bar Garden Outside area) ♦♦ Children's menu Garden Outside area ⋒ Parking WiFi

---

| CARNFORTH | Map 18 SD47 |

The Longlands Inn and Restaurant

tel: 01524 781256 **Tewitfield LA6 1JH**
email: info@longlandshotel.co.uk
dir: *Phone for detailed directions*

Confident cooking of local produce

Although very much Lancastrian, this traditional country inn is only minutes away from the Cumbria border. With its nooks and crannies, old beams and uneven floors, this family-run dog-friendly inn stands next to Tewitfield Locks on the Lancaster Canal. The bar, with Tirril ales on tap, rocks to live bands on Mondays while hungry music lovers consume plates of stone-baked pizzas and pasta. Otherwise look to the restaurant for good country cooking and local produce, twice-baked Garstang Blue cheese soufflé; smoked salmon and crayfish terrine; pan-seared sea bass, spiced Morecambe Bay shrimp butter, falafel and roasted cauliflower; Cumberland pork sausages, bubble-and-squeak, with OSB ale, sage and onion gravy. Children are well catered for too.

Open all day all wk **Food** Lunch Mon-Fri 12-2.30, Sat 12-4, Sun 12-9 Dinner Mon-Sat 6-9.30, Sun 12-9 ⊕ FREE HOUSE ◂ Tirril Old Faithful, Black Sheep, Bowland Hen Harrier, Old School Brewery. ☂ 9 **Facilities** Non-diners area ❖ (Bar Garden) ♦♦ Children's menu Garden ⋒ Parking WiFi ➡ (notice required)

With a heritage dating back to 1871 the Yew Tree is steeped in history and countryside charm. Original flagstone floors, touches of British Tweed and natural oak furniture create an unpretentious and relaxing ambience in which to enjoy the finest in freshly cooked local produce.

Yew Tree Inn, Dill Hall Brow, Heath Charnock, Lancashire, PR6 9HA
Tel: 01257 480344   Email: greg@yewtreeinnanglezarke.co.uk

CHIPPING
Map 18 SD64

Dog & Partridge

tel: 01995 61201 **Hesketh Ln PR3 2TH**
dir: *M6 junct 31A, follow Longridge signs. At Longridge left at 1st rbdt, straight on at next 3 rdbts. At Alston Arms turn right. 3m, pub on right*

Tudor pub with a restored barn restaurant

Dating back to 1515, this pleasantly modernised rural pub in the Ribble Valley enjoys delightful views of the surrounding fells. The barn has been transformed into a welcoming dining area, where home-made food on the comprehensive bar snack menu is backed by a specials board featuring fresh fish and game dishes. A typical menu shows a starter of deep-fried garlic mushrooms; and chilled melon with cream curry sauce; then mains of braised pork chops with home-made apple sauce and stuffing; poached salmon with prawn sauce; roast duckling; or home-made steak and kidney pie.

Open 11.45-3 6.45-11 (Sat 11.45-3 6-11 Sun 11.45-10.30) Closed Mon **Food** Lunch Tue-Sat 12-1.45, Sun 12-3 Dinner Wed-Fri 7-8.30, Sat 6.30-8.30, Sun 3.30-8 Set menu available Restaurant menu available Tue-Sun ⊕ FREE HOUSE ◑ Marston's EPA, Moorhouse's Pride of Pendle, Tetley's Dark Mild, guest ales. ☻ 8 **Facilities** Non-diners area ◑ Children's menu Children's portions Parking WiFi ⇌ (notice required)

CHORLEY
Map 15 SD51

The Yew Tree Inn

tel: 01257 480344 **Dill Hall Brow, Heath Charnock PR6 9HA**
web: www.yewtreeinnanglezarke.co.uk
dir: *Take A6 from Chorley towards Manchester. In Anderton, at lights, left into Babylon Rd. Over M61, 1st left signed Anglezarke. Pub on right*

Secluded pub-restaurant in stunning setting

This stone-built country inn stands at the fringe of Bolton's remarkable lakeland; a string of reservoirs wrapped around the foot of the West Pennine Moors. No surprises, then, that the peaceful beer garden is a target for ramblers slaking their thirst with beers from the local Blackedge Brewery. At heart The Yew Tree is a popular destination dining pub, with hearty British dishes to the fore — typically pan-roasted lamb cannon, parsley root purée, Jerusalem artichoke and spring cabbage; or Chateaubriand for two and hand-cut chips. Log fires warm the light interior of this rural retreat; whilst Good Friday sees a beer and cider festival here.

The Yew Tree Inn

Open 12-3 6-9.30 (Fri 12-3 6-10.30 Sat 12-10.30 Sun 12-8) Closed Mon **Food** Lunch Tue-Fri 12-3, Sat 12-9.30, Sun 12-6.30 Dinner Tue-Thu 6-9, Fri 6-9.30, Sat 12-9.30, Sun 12-6.30 Set menu available ⊕ FREE HOUSE ◑ Blackedge Anglezarke, Rivington Brewing Company Bodacious & Most Excellent ♻ Herefordshire Cider, South West Orchards Raspberry Craft Cider. ☻ 15 **Facilities** ♣ (Bar Garden Outside area) ◑ Children's menu Children's portions Garden Outside area ⋈ Beer festival Cider festival Parking WiFi

See advert on page 295

CLAUGHTON
Map 18 SD54

Fenwick Arms Steak and Seafood Pub ★★★★ INN

tel: 01524 221157 **Hornby Rd LA2 9LA**
email: info@fenwickarms.co.uk **web:** www.fenwickarms.co.uk
dir: *M6 junct 34, A683. Follow Kirkby Lonsdale signs. Approx 5m to pub on left*

Great seafood and local steaks

Joycelyn Neve founded her Seafood Pub Company on the back of her family's long-standing maritime associations. One of her several pubs, this 250-year-old inn, with open fires, low-beamed ceilings and oak-planked floors, combines its traditional role with that of specialist fish, seafood and steak restaurant. Top quality produce arrives daily from the family business in Fleetwood, to emerge from the kitchen perhaps as pickled cockles with spiced vinegar as a snack; salt and pepper squid; and Goan king prawn and chicken curry. From the Robata grill you could choose 28-day dry-aged, grass-fed Lancashire beef steak with proper chips; or a peppered tuna steak.

Open all day all wk **Food** Lunch all wk 12-5 Dinner all wk 5-10 Av main course £12 ⊕ FREE HOUSE/SEAFOOD PUB CO ◑ Marston's Wainwright, Timothy Taylor, Moorhouse's. ☻ 24 **Facilities** Non-diners area ♣ (Bar Garden Outside area) ◑ Children's menu Children's portions Garden Outside area ⋈ Parking WiFi ⇌ (notice required) **Rooms** 9

CLITHEROE
Map 18 SD74

The Assheton Arms ★★★★★ RR PICK OF THE PUBS

tel: 01200 441227 **Downham BB7 4BJ**
email: info@asshetonarms.com **web:** www.asshetonarms.com
dir: A59 to Chatburn, then follow Downham signs

Historic village inn with seafood specialities

A pub since 1872, when it was called the George and Dragon, The Assheton Arms was originally a farmhouse brewing beer for its workers. Renamed in 1950, the current name honours Ralph Assheton, Lord Clitheroe, for his contribution during World War II. Now it's owned by the Seafood Pub Company, which refreshed the stylish restaurant while preserving its traditional village inn credentials. You'll find a great choice of real ales in the bar, including Moorhouse's Pride of Pendle, and local sourcing is key, with fresh fish and seafood supplied daily. The 'little plates and pub snacks' are great – pickled cockles with spiced vinegar, say, or pitta bread with houmous. Starters might take in devilled crab, salmon and brown shrimps with radish and cress salad, or spicy quinoa cakes with sweet potato, chargrilled spring onions, dried tomatoes and tzatziki. There's a daily specials board and a Robata grill – steaks are 28-day dry-aged Lancashire beef – or main courses might include haddock and chips; cod tagine with crab koftas, toasted couscous, pickled lemon, pomegranate and rose petal harissa.

Open all day all wk 7.30am-11pm (Sat 8am-mdnt, Sun 8am-10.30pm) **Food** Lunch Mon-Sat 12-5, Sun 12-8.30 Dinner Mon-Thu 5-9, Fri-Sat 5-10, Sun 12-8.30 Av main course £11 ⊕ FREE HOUSE/SEAFOOD PUB CO ◀ Marston's Wainwright, Black Sheep, Timothy Taylor, Moorhouse's Pride of Pendle Ö Thatchers Gold. ♀ 10 **Facilities** Non-diners area ❄ (Bar Garden Outside area) ♦ Children's menu Children's portions Garden Outside area ♣ Parking WiFi ☎ (notice required) **Rooms** 12

ELSWICK
Map 18 SD43

The Ship at Elswick

tel: 01995 672777 **High St PR4 3ZB**
email: mail@theshipatelswick.co.uk
dir: M55 junct 3, A585 signed Fleetwood. Right onto Thistleton Rd (B5269). 1m to pub

Former farmhouse in a quiet village, offering hearty food

In a quiet village on the Fylde and handy both for Blackpool and the quieter resorts of Cleveleys and Fleetwood, this former farmhouse is now a reliable village local and dining inn. From Fleetwood comes some of the fish featured on the very traditional menu here; start with smoked salmon and crayfish fishcakes; or black pudding, chorizo and poached egg, then follow with Lancashire lamb hot pot; or corned beef hash; and finally apple pie and custard. There are also pasta choices, salads and a Sunday roast. The owners are proud to use Lancashire produce in most of their dishes, although one of the beers on hand pump is Yorkshire's Black Sheep.

Open all day all wk **Food** Mon-Sat 12-9, Sun 12-8 Av main course £10 ⊕ PUNCH TAVERNS ◀ Jennings Cumberland Ale, Black Sheep, guest ales. ♀ 8 **Facilities** Non-diners area ♦ Children's menu Children's portions Play area Garden ♣ Parking WiFi ☎

ENTWISTLE
Map 15 SD71

NEW The Strawbury Duck

tel: 01204 852013 **Overshores Rd BL7 0LU**
email: info@thestrawburyduck.co.uk
dir: At x-roads in Edgworth follow Entwistle rail station signs. Left signed The Strawbury Duck & Entwistle Station. Over reservoir, over railway bridge to pub

Rustic inn with modern menu

Way up in the hills between the Entwistle and Wayoh reservoirs, The Strawbury Duck has long been a landmark pub. Although magnificently modernised, it hasn't said farewell to its old beams and open fire, nor forgotten that pictures and comfortable chairs help make a pub particularly welcoming. No surprise to find an ale called Strawbury Duck in the bar, nor indeed Pride of Pendle and Blond Witch. Pub classics like home-made pie, and Southern fried chicken in a basket vie for attention with beer-battered fresh fish of the day; pub-raised rare-breed Saddleback sausage and mash; and chargrilled steaks. Sweeping views are available from the beer garden.

Open all day all wk **Food** Mon-Fri 12-8.45, Sat-Sun 12-8 Av main course £12.95 Restaurant menu available all wk ⊕ FREE HOUSE ◀ Marston's Wainwright, Moorhouse's Pride of Pendle & Blond Witch, Lancaster Strawbury Duck Ale Ö Thatchers. **Facilities** Non-diners area ❄ (All areas) ♦ Children's menu Children's portions Family room Garden Outside area ♣ Parking WiFi ☎ (notice required)

FENISCOWLES
Map 18 SD62

Oyster & Otter
PICK OF THE PUBS

tel: 01254 203200 **631 Livesey Branch Rd BB2 5DQ**
email: info@oysterandotter.co.uk
dir: M65 junct 3, right at lights, right at mini rdbt into Livesey Branch Rd

Seafood-led gastro-pub with global influences

This clapboard and stone-fronted pub is run by former Fleetwood fish wholesaler Chris Neve, who comes from a long line of North Sea and Irish Sea trawlermen. His daughter Joycelyn studied the coastal food industry in South America before becoming head of operations here, and the third lynch-pin is executive chef Antony Shirley, formerly head chef at Raffles in the West Indies. This Blackburn-fringe pub may look more New England than Lancashire mill-town but the menu gets its inspiration from all over the world. You might try fish starters such as crab sausage roll; or salt and pepper squid, while main courses include Malaysian seafood curry. Alternatively, there's baby back ribs with orange, rosemary and chilli; crispy duck legs with dauphinoise potatoes and bourguignon sauce. The Monday to Saturday lunch club dishes include a barbecued pulled pork bun; and spicy chicken salad.

Open all day all wk **Food** Lunch all wk 12-5 Dinner Sun-Thu 5-9, Fri-Sat 5-10 ⊕ THWAITES/SEAFOOD PUB CO ◀ Marton's Wainwright, Lancaster Bomber, Original Ö Kingstone Press. ♀ 9 **Facilities** Non-diners area ♦ Children's menu Children's portions Garden Outside area ♣ Parking WiFi ☎ (notice required)

FORTON
Map 18 SD45

The Bay Horse Inn
PICK OF THE PUBS

tel. 01524 791204 **LA2 0HR**
email: craig@bayhorseinn.com
dir: *M6 junct 33 take A6 towards Garstang, turn left for pub. Pub approx 1m from M6*

Stylish family-run inn with imaginative menu

In one direction lanes percolate through to the sea-marshes of Morecambe Bay; in the other the destination is the Forest of Bowland, a magical landscape of moors, crags and gorge-like valleys. Rural Lancashire at its most sublime. There's good Lancashire beer here too, from Moorhouse's in Burnley, perhaps supped in the extended gardens which lead to open fields where pheasants and deer can often be spotted. Mismatched furniture and a handsome stone fireplace with roaring winter log fire characterise the inn, offering a tantalising flavour of the small coaching inn it once was. The kitchen, managed by chef-patron Craig Wilkinson, makes full use of the wealth of produce the county has to offer. So from the concise menu be tempted by a starter of treacle-cured salmon with apple purée, samphire and radish; progress then to roast chicken breast with dry-cured bacon, mash, asparagus and truffle butter, and round off with warm orange and almond sponge with vanilla ice cream.

Open 12-3 6-12 Closed Mon-Tue (ex BHs L) **Food** Lunch Wed-Sat 12-2, Sun 12-3 Dinner Wed-Sat 6.30-9, Sun 6-8 Av main course £15 Set menu available ⊕ FREE HOUSE ◀ Moorhouse's Pendle Witches Brew, Timothy Taylor Golden Best, guest ale. � 8 **Facilities** Non-diners area ✿ (Bar Garden) ✦ Children's portions Garden ☂ Parking WiFi

GREAT ECCLESTON
Map 18 SD44

Farmers Arms

tel: 01995 672018 **Halsalls Square PR3 0YE**
email: info@greatecclestonpub.co.uk
dir: *M55 junct 3, A585, A586 to Great Eccleston. From High St into Chapel St, pub on left*

Family-friendly dining-pub specialising in seafood

Just off the main Garstang to Blackpool road, this two-storey pub-restaurant belongs to the Seafood Pub Company. It was set up by Joycelyn Neve who decided to capitalise on her family's long-standing involvement with deep-sea fishing. Naturally, there's plenty of fish and seafood on the menu, from spicy crab bisque with rarebit on toast as a starter to haddock and prawn fish pie. Other options might be Korean fried chicken with lime, ginger and chilli; and pot pie of Goosnargh chicken, ham hock and leeks with green beans and 'proper' chips. Under the 'Sweet Tooth' heading, try the warm peanut butter doughnut with maple syrup and raspberries.

Open all day all wk **Food** Lunch all wk 12-5 Dinner Sun-Thu 5-9, Fri-Sat 5-10 Av main course £12 ⊕ FREE HOUSE/SEAFOOD PUB CO ◀ Timothy Taylor Landlord, Marston's Wainwright, Moorhouses White Witch ♂ Aspall. � 24 **Facilities** Non-diners area ✿ (Bar Garden Outside area) ✦ Children's menu Children's portions Garden Outside area ☂ Parking WiFi ▄▄ (notice required)

HEST BANK
Map 18 SD46

Hest Bank Inn

tel: 01524 824339 **2 Hest Bank Ln LA2 6DN**
email: chef.glenn@btinternet.com
dir: *From Lancaster take A6 N, after 2m left to Hest Bank*

Historic inn with lots to offer

First licensed in 1554, this former coaching inn is awash with history: it was occupied by Cromwell's officers in the Civil War and was also the haunt of highwaymen. Comedian Eric Morecambe used to drink at the canalside Hest Bank, which offers cask ales and a wide selection of meals all day, with local suppliers playing an important role in maintaining food quality. The good value menu ranges from traditional pub favourites such as venison and beef cobbler; and flash-fried lamb's liver, as well as seasonal specials. Enjoy a pint of Marston's Wainwright in the terraced garden. Wednesday evening is quiz night, while steak night is every Thursday.

Open all day all wk 11.30-11.30 (Sun 11.30-10.30) **Food** Lunch Mon-Fri 12-3, Sat 12-9, Sun 12-8 Dinner Mon-Fri 5-9, Sat 12-9, Sun 12-8 ⊕ PUNCH TAVERNS ◀ Marston's Wainwright, Black Sheep Best Bitter, guest ales. **Facilities** Non-diners area ✿ (Bar Garden) ✦ Children's menu Children's portions Play area Garden ☂ Parking WiFi ▄▄ (notice required)

LANCASTER
Map 18 SD46

The Borough

tel: 01524 64170 **3 Dalton Square LA1 1PP**
email: jodie@theboroughlancaster.co.uk
dir: *Phone for detailed directions*

Superb Lancashire produce in town house pub

This Grade II Georgian pub, in the city centre, with a Victorian frontage has wooden floors, chunky tables, chesterfield sofas, warm green hues and masses of light from a huge bay window. All this creates a friendly, relaxed vibe for enjoying their own microbrewery's Borough Pale, Dark and Bitter and a quality food offering. Using top-notch ingredients from local suppliers, including meat and eggs from surrounding farms, the seasonal menu may take in BBQ pulled pork croquettes; Morecambe Bay mariners' pie; and the chance of 'building' your own burger from the grill section. Platters are available, and home-made desserts include sticky toffee pudding.

Open all wk 8am-11pm (Fri noon-12.30am Sat 8am-12.20am) ⊕ FREE HOUSE ◀ Borough Brewery Bitter, Pale & Dark, Lancaster Amber, Young's Bitter, Wells Eagle IPA, Bowland Hen Harrier. **Facilities** ✿ (Bar Garden) ✦ Children's menu Garden WiFi

The Sun Hotel and Bar
PICK OF THE PUBS

tel: 01524 66006 **LA1 1ET**
email: info@thesunhotelandbar.co.uk
dir: *6m from M6 junct 33*

Famous for its hospitality over the centuries

The oldest building in Lancaster, The Sun was first licensed as 'Stoop Hall' in 1680 as the town's premier coaching inn. Generals from the occupying Jacobean Army lodged here in 1745, and the artist JMW Turner stayed whilst making sketches of Heysham in 1812. Original features include a bottomless well and beautiful old door. The bar is frequented throughout the day; from hotel guests and business breakfasters, to shoppers enjoying mid-morning coffee or brunch, and customers tucking into the locally sourced food at lunch and dinner, as well as wine and ale connoisseurs. The experienced kitchen brigade prepares sea bass niçoise; baby carrot and fennel risotto; and sausages and mash. The extensive cheese board menu is especially popular, and also includes cold meats, pâtés and fish. There is a patio for alfresco dining in warmer weather, regular quiz nights and an annual beer festival in the summer.

Open all day all wk from 7.30am-late **Food** Lunch Mon-Sat 12-3, Sun 12-8 Dinner Mon-Thu 4-9, Fri-Sat 4-8, Sun 12-8 ⊕ FREE HOUSE ◀ Lancaster Amber, Black, Red & Blonde, guest ales ♂ Kingstone Press. � 23 **Facilities** Non-diners area ✦ Children's menu Children's portions Garden ☂ Beer festival WiFi ▄▄ (notice required)

PICK OF THE PUBS

Toll House Inn ★★★★ INN

LANCASTER Map 18 SD46

tel: 01524 599900 **Penny St LA1 1XT**
email: relax@tollhouseinnlancaster.co.uk
web: www.tollhouseinnlancaster.co.uk
dir: *In city centre*

Quirkily elegant, canal-side townhouse offering top Lancashire produce

Right in the centre of the city, the listed Toll House Inn was once a Corporation Toll House. Demolished in 1901, it was then rebuilt as two separate pubs, which Thwaites Brewery joined together again in 2007 to create a grand 28-room inn with a bar. Its wonderfully high ceilings make it feel light and modern, although retained period features can be seen everywhere, from the listed staircase to the servant bell hooks, and from the stained-glass windows to the unusual listed wardrobe in one of the bedrooms. The atmosphere is quirkily elegant, with wooden floors throughout, modern yet cosy furniture in the bar area and a stylish, contemporary feel in the bedrooms. The kitchen team prepare all the food on the premises; served all day, their seasonal menus make the most of the excellent Lancashire produce that's available right on their doorstep. The popular menu includes crab and haddock fishcakes; and chicken liver pâté to start, and classics such as steak and

real ale pudding; and Lancashire cheese and onion pie. They also serve their now famous 'hanging kebabs', as well as a selection of sharing boards (Butcher's, Cheese and Vegetable Antipasti and Fishmonger's) and salads. From The Grill section on the menu you might opt for a 28-day aged fillet or rib-eye steak or a gammon chop. Interestingly on the menu, the Thwaites beer sommelier has identified some dishes that can be paired perfectly with beer. For pudding perhaps try the lime and ginger cheesecake; sticky toffee pudding; or strawberry and white chocolate mousse. Toll House Inn is situated next to the Lancaster Canal so it's the ideal place from which to explore the county and its rich history.

Open all day all wk 9am-mdnt
Food all wk 11.30-9 ⊕ THWAITES INNS OF CHARACTER ◖ Wainwright, 13 Guns & Original, Hawkshead Lakeland Gold, Tirril Old Faithful ♂ Kingstone Press, Aspall. ⚲ 13 **Facilities** Non-diners area ⵌ Children's menu Children's portions Garden ⼍ Beer festival Cider festival WiFi ⛟ (notice required) **Rooms** 28

LANCASTER *continued*

Toll House Inn ★★★★ INN   PICK OF THE PUBS

See Pick of the Pubs on page 299 and advert below

The White Cross

tel: 01524 33999 **Quarry Rd LA1 4XT**
email: twcpub@yahoo.co.uk
dir: *S on one-way system, left after Town Hall. Over canal bridge, on right*

Enjoy good food as canal boats go by

Set in a 130-year-old former cotton mill warehouse on the edge of the Lancaster Canal, The White Cross is a short stroll from the city centre. A regularly changing selection of up to 14 cask ales includes beers from Copper Dragon, Timothy Taylor and Theakston breweries, but food is an equal draw at this popular waterfront venue. Look out for starters like poached egg duck egg Royale; or pan-fried king scallops and black pudding, then follow with Cajun marinated chicken fillet burger; haddock and chips; or honey roast duck breast with spiced Puy lentils, baby fondant potatoes and crispy fennel. If there's still room after all that, try warm sticky toffee and date pudding; or 'crumble of the week.' Sandwiches, grills, salads and deli boards are also available. A beer and pie festival takes place in late April.

Open all day all wk **Food** all wk 12-9 Av main course £7-£12 ⊕ ENTERPRISE INNS ◪ Copper Dragon Golden Pippin, Timothy Taylor Landlord, Theakston Old Peculier ☼ Westons Stowford Press & Old Rosie, Ribble Valley Gold. ♗ 13 **Facilities** Non-diners area ◖◗ Children's menu Children's portions Garden ⋈ Beer festival Parking WiFi ▭ (notice required)

LANESHAW BRIDGE   Map 18 SD94

The Alma Inn ★★★★ INN

tel: 01282 857830 **Emmott Ln BB8 7EG**
email: reception@thealmainn.com **web:** www.thealmainn.com
dir: *M65, A6068 towards Keighley. At Laneshaw Bridge left into Emmott Ln. 0.5m, inn on left*

Country inn serving local produce

With magnificent views to Pendle Hill from tables on the paved patio, this old, hill-top stone inn deep in the Lancashire countryside is a real find. The rambling interior has some fine panelling, real fires and stone floors, whilst chic accommodation and extensive dining facilities mean it's popular for weddings. Reliable beers from Moorhouse's slake the thirst after a decent stroll. The wide-ranging contemporary menu covers most bases, from starters like king scallops Benedict; or turkey spring rolls via mains of pies, puddings, pasta and risotto dishes to the butcher's selection choices of horseradish sirloin of beef with Yorkshire pudding; or smoked garlic and red wine sausages and mash. Jam roly poly with custard is a filling final fling.

Open all day all wk **Food** all wk 12-9 Av main course £13.95 ⊕ FREE HOUSE ◪ Moorhouse's Pride of Pendle, guest ales ☼ South West Orchards. ♗ 10 **Facilities** Non-diners area ✿ (Bar Restaurant Garden) ◖◗ Children's menu Children's portions Garden ⋈ Parking WiFi ▭ **Rooms** 9

LITTLE ECCLESTON   Map 18 SD44

The Cartford Inn   PICK OF THE PUBS

See Pick of the Pubs on opposite page

LONGRIDGE   Map 18 SD63

Derby Arms ★★★★ INN

tel: 01772 782370 **Chipping Rd PR3 2NB**
email: info@derbyarmslongridge.co.uk **web:** www.seafoodpubcompany.com

One for fish and seafood aficionados

A delightful village inn owned by Joycelyn Neve's Seafood Pub Company, with a central bar leading into three dining rooms, two with feature fireplaces. A tap room is set aside for bar games. Its very ownership dictates fish by the boatload – for instance, spicy crab and brandy bisque with rarebit on toast; salt and pepper squid with rice wine and ginger dipping sauce; and smoked haddock, bubble-and-squeak, poached egg and wholegrain mustard sauce. In addition, expect Goosnargh chicken, ham hock and leek pot pie; and pig on a stick – slow-cooked pork belly with chorizo and pork sausage, rosemary potatoes and apple sauce.

Open all day all wk **Food** Sun-Thu 12-9, Fri-Sat 12-10 Av main course £11 ⊕ FREE HOUSE/SEAFOOD PUB CO ◪ Marston's Wainwright, Timothy Taylor Landlord, Copper Dragon ☼ Kingstone Press. ♗ 10 **Facilities** Non-diners area ◖◗ Children's menu Children's portions Garden Outside area ⋈ Parking WiFi ▭ (notice required) **Rooms** 6

PICK OF THE PUBS

The Cartford Inn

LITTLE ECCLESTON Map 18 SD44

tel: 01995 670166 **PR3 0YP**
email: info@thecartfordinn.co.uk
web: www.thecartfordinn.co.uk
dir: *N of A586 (W of Great Eccleston)*

A 17th-century inn with eclectic interiors and excellent food

Set in an idyllic location adjoining a toll bridge across the tidal Rive Wyre, this award-winning 17th-century coaching inn enjoys extensive views over the countryside towards the Trough of Bowland and the Lake District. Owners Julie and Patrick Beaume have created a relaxed family-run inn. Its stylish and contemporary interior is an appealing blend of striking colours, natural wood and polished floors, whilst the smart open fireplace and an eclectic selection of furniture adds a comfortable and relaxed feel to the bar lounge. If your arrival coincides with coffee or tea time, you won't be disappointed. Coffees are blended with beans from Guatemala, El Salvador, Ethiopia and Sumatra; teas range from the house blend Irish breakfast, to a decaf Ceylon, green chai, or hedgerow tisane. There's a choice of eating areas – the Riverside Lounge, Fire Lounge and alcove, and outside on the terrace – where you can enjoy an imaginative range of dishes based on quality ingredients from local suppliers. Lunchtime sees plates of Goosnargh

duck salad served with roasted heritage carrots, fried ginger, plum, beetroot, dressed with chipotle and honey; or a French baguette of bavette steak with pickled shallots, horseradish relish, fries and salad. A typical three-course choice could start with potted confit rabbit, and continue with a Lancashire hotpot or the day's delivery of fish from Fleetwood Docklands. Round off with a Lancashire parkin tart with liquorice purée, white chocolate and spiced syrup. The Cartford Inn makes an ideal base from which to explore the surrounding area; Lancaster, the Royal Lytham Golf Club, and Blackpool with its Winter Gardens and Grand Theatre are all within easy reach.

Open all day Closed 25 Dec, Mon L
Food Lunch Tue-Sat 12-2, Sun 12-8.30 Dinner Mon-Thu 5.30-9, Fri-Sat 5.30-10 ⊕ FREE HOUSE ◧ Moorhouse's Pride of Pendle, Hawkshead Lakeland Gold, Giddy Kipper ♂ Westons Stowford Press.
Facilities Non-diners area ᵻ Children's menu Children's portions Garden ⩇ Parking WiFi

NEWTON-IN-BOWLAND
Map 18 SD65

Parkers Arms
PICK OF THE PUBS

tel: 01200 446236 **BB7 3DY**
email: enquiries@parkersarms.co.uk
dir: *From Clitheroe take B6478 through Waddington to Newton-in-Bowland*

Imaginative cooking and delightful countryside views

In a beautiful hamlet amidst the rolling hills of the Trough of Bowland, this Georgian dining inn is just yards from the River Hodder and enjoys panoramic views over Waddington Fell. It celebrates its rural location by serving the best Lancashire produce. This includes ales from the local breweries, meats raised on nearby moorland, vegetables from Ribble Valley farms and fresh fish from nearby Fleetwood. French chef-patron Stosie Madi even forages for ingredients herself. The simple, but elegant, modern dishes on the daily-changing, seasonal menu include Goosnargh corn-fed chicken and leek pie; slow-braised shin of Bowland beef in ale with creamed mash; and fillet of sea bass with pea gnocchi and lemon reduction. Pudding could be 'Wet Nelly', a classic north-west dessert originally created for Lord Nelson in Liverpool and reworked by co-owner Kathy Smith.

Open 12-3 6-close (Sat-Sun & BH 12-close) Closed Mon (Tue in winter) **Food** Lunch Tue-Sun 12-3 Dinner Tue-Sun 6-8.30 Set menu available Restaurant menu available Tue-Sun ⊕ FREE HOUSE/ENTERPRISE ◀ Lancaster, Bowland Ŏ Westons Stowford Press. **Facilities** Non-diners area ❖ (Bar Restaurant Garden) ⋕ Children's menu Children's portions Garden ⋒ Parking WiFi ▭ (notice required)

PARBOLD
Map 15 SD41

The Eagle & Child
PICK OF THE PUBS

tel: 01257 462297 **Maltkiln Ln, Bispham Green L40 3SG**
dir: *M6 junct 27, A5209 to Parbold. Right onto B5246. 2.5m, Bispham Green on right*

A country dining pub in a pretty and peaceful location

This thriving village inn is set in the tranquil valley of the River Douglas and close to some lovely rambles on Parbold Hill. A pub that caters admirably for all-comers, the emphasis is on high-quality modern cooking using locally sourced seasonal produce. On the restaurant menu crispy duck egg, home-cured spiced bacon, celeriac and dashi is a typical opening gambit. Progress to roast breast of Goosnargh chicken, winter truffle and olive mash, Scottish morels; or pan-fried halibut steak, Puy lentils and warm salad of olives, tomatoes and capers. The bar menu is equally appealing; perhaps steak, ale and mushroom pie, mushy peas and triple-cooked chips. The traditionally styled pub is a popular village local, with an ever-changing array of beers from local microbreweries and farmhouse ciders, while the annual Early May Bank Holiday beer festival attracts up to 2,000 people to a huge marquee.

Open all day all wk 12-11 (Sun 12-10.30) **Food** Lunch all wk 12-2 Dinner Sun-Thu 5.30-8.30, Fri-Sat 5.30-9 Av main course £10.50 Set menu available Restaurant menu available ⊕ FREE HOUSE ◀ Moorhouse's White Witch, Thwaites Original, Southport Golden Sands, George Wright Cheeky Pheasant, Bowland Hen Harrier, guest ales Ŏ Kingstone Press, Farmhouse Cider Scrumpy. ₹ 10
Facilities Non-diners area ❖ (Bar Restaurant Garden) ⋕ Children's menu Children's portions Family room Garden ⋒ Beer festival Parking WiFi ▭ (notice required)

PENDLETON
Map 18 SD73

The Swan with Two Necks

tel: 01200 423112 **BB7 1PT**
email: swanwith2necks@yahoo.co.uk
dir: *Exit A59 between Whalley & Chatburn follow Pendleton signs, 0.5m to pub*

Charming inn set in a beautiful stone-built Lancashire village

Hidden away in the pretty village of Pendleton, the award-winning Swan with Two Necks is a traditional village inn dating back to 1722. Pendleton sits under Pendle Hill, which is famous for its tales of witches, and that's not the only curious piece of history attached to this place; the inn's name refers to the tradition of marking the necks of swans belonging to the Worshipful Company of Vintners with two 'nicks' to distinguish them from swans belonging to the king or queen. Of course you won't find swan on the menu here, but this pub is renowned for its ales and ciders, so be sure to try the likes of Phoenix Wobbly Bob or Ribble Valley Gold along with a home-made pie or a dish of beef in red wine.

Open 12-3 6-11 (Sat 12-11, Sun 12-10.30) Closed 25 Dec, Mon L **Food** Lunch Tue-Sat 12-1.45, Sun 12-6 Dinner Mon 6-8, Tue-Sat 6-8.30, Sun 12-6 ⊕ FREE HOUSE ◀ Phoenix Wobbly Bob, Copper Dragon Golden Pippin, Prospect Nutty Slack, Marble, Salamander Ŏ Westons Traditional & Country Perry, Ribble Valley Gold. ₹ 14
Facilities Non-diners area ⋕ Children's menu Children's portions Garden ⋒ Parking WiFi ▭ (notice required)

RAMSBOTTOM
Map 15 SD71

Eagle + Child

tel: 01706 557181 **3 Whalley Rd BLO ODL**
email: glen@eagle-and-child.com
dir: *M66 junct 1, A56 towards Edenfield. Pub on left in outskirts of Ramsbottom*

A unique social enterprise

Youngsters are introduced to the hospitality and horticultural industries at this pub with a social purpose. The result of landlord Glen Duckett's vision, with wholehearted support from the Thwaites Brewery, the pub has won many local and national food awards. An acre of 'incredible edible' beer garden is a work in progress, but is already inspiring children and the pub's clientele to grow, cook and eat delicious high quality produce with minimum food miles. Look out for Lancashire sausage with Bury black pudding; Double Bomber cheese and onion pie; Lancashire hotpot and braised red cabbage; and Goosnargh turkey pie with clapshot.

Open all day all wk **Food** Lunch Mon-Fri 12-2.30, Sat 12-9.30, Sun 12-7 Dinner Mon-Fri 5-9, Sat 12-9.30, Sun 12-7 Set menu available ⊕ THWAITES ◀ Lancaster Bomber & Wainwright Ŏ Westons Rosie's Pig. **Facilities** Non-diners area ❖ (Garden) ⋕ Children's menu Children's portions Play area Garden ⋒ Beer festival Parking WiFi ▭ (notice required)

SLAIDBURN
Map 18 SD75

Hark to Bounty Inn

tel: 01200 446246 **Townend BB7 3EP**
email: manager@harktobounty.co.uk
Good beer in a lovely location

If you're wondering about the unusual name of this pub, the story goes that in the 19th century the local squire, out hunting one day with his hounds, stopped at the pub for a drink. Disturbed by prolonged baying from the pack, he could hear above the noise his favourite dog, prompting him to call out 'Hark to Bounty!' It is located in the pretty village of Slaidburn in the Forest of Bowland, an Area of Outstanding Natural Beauty and perfect for walking, fishing, bird-watching and cycling. Have a pint of Theakston's Old Peculier and check out the pub classics on the menu – a prawn cocktail; home-made beef lasagne; gammon, eggs, pineapple ring and chips; and beer-battered Irish Sea haddock, mushy peas and chips.

Open all day Closed Tue **Food** Lunch Wed-Sat & Mon 12-2, Sun 12-8 Dinner Wed-Thu & Mon 6-8, Fri-Sat 6-9 (winter), Wed-Sat & Mon 6-9 (summer), Sun 12-8 ⊕ FREE HOUSE ◀ Theakston Best Bitter & Old Peculier, Lancaster Blonde. **Facilities** Non-diners area ❖ (Bar Restaurant Garden) ⋕ Children's menu Children's portions Garden ⋒ Parking WiFi ▭ (notice required)

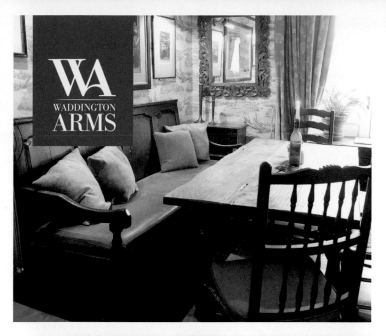

Eat, Drink, Sleep.

Located beside an ancient stone bridge over a babbling brook at the heart of the picture postcard village of Waddington, the Waddington Arms is the hub of this vibrant little community and an ideal base for a multitude of walks - from a gentle countryside amble, to pretty riverside walks or challenging hikes up into the fells to the north of the village.

Fabulous food from well thought out menus is served for lunch and dinner seven days a week and six beautiful bedrooms provide a comfortable base for exploring the Ribble Valley by car or on foot.

Waddington, Clitheroe, Lancashire, BB7 3HP
01200 423262 | www.waddingtonarms.co.uk

TOCHOLES

Map 15 SD62

The Royal Arms

tel: 01254 705373 **Tockholes Rd BB3 OPA**
dir: *M65 junct 4, follow Blackburn signs. Right at lights, 1st left. Up hill left at Three B's Brewery into Tockholes Rd. Pub in 1m on left*

Rich with pickings from Lancashire microbreweries

High in the West Pennine Moors is this appealing old stone pub situated in a tiny fold of mill-workers' cottages. There's an engaging hotchpotch of furnishings in the fire-warmed, flagstoned and beamed rooms together with fascinating old photos of the local villages in their mill-town heyday. Take a glass of ale out to tables on the lawn and study the regularly changing menu of home-cooked goodies, such as lamb kleftico, and braised steak in red wine. There are walks from the door – drop into Roddlesworth Woods or you can climb to the imposing Jubilee Tower on nearby Darwen Hill.

Open all wk 12-11 (Mon 4-8 Sun 12-10.30) **Food** Lunch Tue-Fri 12-2, Sat 12-3, Sun 12-5.30 Dinner Wed-Sat 6-8.45 Restaurant menu available Wed-Sun ⊕ FREE HOUSE ◼ Banks's Bitter, Copper Dragon Golden Pippin, Moorhouse's Pendle Witches Brew, Three B's, York Dark Knight, guest ales. **Facilities** Non-diners area ❄ (Bar Garden) ◖ Children's menu Children's portions Garden ⊓ Parking WiFi ▭ (notice required)

WADDINGTON

Map 18 SD74

The Lower Buck

tel: 01200 423342 **Edisford Rd BB7 3HU**
email: manager@lowerbuck.co.uk
dir: *From A671 at rdbt onto B6478 (Well Terrace) signed Waddington. In Waddington at x-roads left into Waddow View. At T-junct right signed Bashall Eaves. At next T-junct right, pub on left*

Easily missed gem in a 'Best Kept Village'

In the chocolate box village of Waddington, winner of 'Best Kept Village' on several occasions, look for St Helen's church and you'll find The Lower Buck just behind it. The 250-year-old pub is affectionately run by Andrew Warburton, without music or fruit machines disturbing the peace. The emphasis is on warmth of welcome, five excellent ales – with award-winning Bowland AONB among them – and a classic pub menu of quality dishes. Choose to eat superior sandwiches such as hot topside of beef with fried onions; board and platters; Bowand Bakery pies; or a hearty dish of Lancashire hotpot; or Cowman's of Clitheroe Cumberland sausage and mash.

Open all day all wk **Food** Lunch Mon-Fri 12-2.30, Sat-Sun 12-9 Dinner Mon-Fri 5-9, Sat-Sun 12-9 Av main course £10 ⊕ FREE HOUSE ◼ Bowland Hen Harrier, AONB, Pheasant Plucker, Timothy Taylor Landlord, guest ales ♂ Ribble Valley Gold. ▾ 10 **Facilities** Non-diners area ❄ (Bar Outside area) ◖ Children's menu Children's portions Outside area ⊓ WiFi ▭

Waddington Arms

tel: 01200 423262 **West View, Waddington Rd BB7 3HP**
email: info@waddingtonarms.co.uk **web:** www.waddingtonarms.co.uk
dir: *In village centre*

Local produce drives the menu here

Close to the A59, this former coaching inn occupies an enviable position in the heart of the Ribble Valley. In the bar and on the pavement outside cushioned wickerwork chairs are ideal for watching village life and perfect for relaxing with a pint of Bowland Hen Harrier. Dining is available throughout, including two cosy side rooms off the main bar. Strong on local specialities, the menu offers Goosnargh duck Wellington with potato gratin, chestnut mushrooms and Madeira sauce; and curry-spiced cod loin with saag aloo and basmati rice.

Open all day all wk **Food** Lunch Mon-Fri 12-2.30, Sat 12-9.30, Sun 12-9 Dinner Mon-Fri 6-9.30, Sat 12-9.30, Sun 12-9 ⊕ FREE HOUSE ◼ Bowland Hen Harrier & AONB, Lancaster Blonde ♂ Aspall. ▾ 14 **Facilities** Non-diners area ❄ (Bar Garden) ◖ Children's menu Children's portions Play area Family room Garden ⊓ Parking WiFi ▭ (notice required)

See advert on page 303

PICK OF THE PUBS

The Inn at Whitewell ★★★★★ INN ❀

WHITEWELL   Map 18 SD64

tel: 01200 448222
Forest of Bowland BB7 3AT
email: reception@innatwhitewell.com
web: www.innatwhitewell.com
dir: *From B6243 follow Whitewell signs*

Historic inn with spectacular valley views

This must be one of the most idyllically located inns in England. The River Hodder swirls by verdant meadows abutting wooded clefts in the glorious Forest of Bowland. Here the partly 13th-century inn slumbers by a tiny Georgian chapel, with slippery paths down to stepping stones across the torrent. All around the high moors, pastures and estates burst with provisions destined for the inn's renowned kitchen. The engaging multi-roomed interior is liberally decorated with antiques, ephemera and pictures; there's also an independent wine shop. All in all, there is plenty to entertain the residential guests who book into one of the individually designed, luxury period bedrooms. Jamie Cadman's enduring passion for quality local produce shines through in consistently good dishes, which have been awarded an AA Rosette. A light lunch could comprise potted Cornish crab with toasted sourdough, cucumber pickle and avocado purée; or garlic and thyme roasted flat mushrooms, tapenade

toast, and tomato and shallot ketchup. At dinner, the à la carte features starters such as seared king scallops, pancetta with pea purée, which can lead to main dishes of whole roast Goosnargh corn-fed lemon thyme poussin with thyme, sage and onion croquette, bread sauce and gravy; or pan-fried gnocchi, roast pepper and spinach, plum tomato sauce, toasted pine nuts, parmesan shavings and basil oil. For fish lovers, the kitchen's signature fish pie and beer-battered haddock, chips and mushy peas will do the trick. Puddings are traditional and home made. Ramblers dropping in from the heights will delight in beers from Timothy Taylor and Hawkshead, enjoyed on a terrace with the fabulous fell views.

Open all day all wk 10am-1am
Food Lunch all wk 12-2 Dinner all wk 7.30-9.30 Restaurant menu available all wk evenings only ⊕ FREE HOUSE
◀ Timothy Taylor Landlord, Bowland, Copper Dragon, Moorhouse's, Hawkshead Ŏ Dunkertons Premium Organic. ☙ 16 **Facilities** Non-diners area ❧ (Bar Garden) ❧ Children's portions Garden ⊼ Parking WiFi ⊟ (notice required) **Rooms** 23

WEST BRADFORD — Map 18 SD74

NEW Three Millstones

tel: 01200 443339 **Waddington Rd BB7 4SX**
email: millstonesinn@live.com
dir: *From A59 between Wiswell & Gisburn follow Waddington signs. At rdbt 2nd exit signed West Bradford (over railway crossing, then River Ribble), at T-junct in Waddington left. Pub on left*

Enjoyable locally sourced food in welcoming village inn

Dating back to the 19th century, this Grade II listed building is one of the oldest in the picturesque village of West Bradford and only a few minutes from Clitheroe and the A59. With two real fires and a bar dispensing local ales such as Worsthorne Chestnut Mare, the pub has a genuinely warm and relaxed atmosphere. Owner-chef Matthew Frost uses predominantly local suppliers for dishes like warm pulled pork salad, black pudding fritter, apple and wholegrain mustard dressing, which might be followed by roast organic Goosnargh chicken breast, wild mushroom risotto, chive and white wine sauce.

Open 12-3 6-10 (Sun 12-6) Closed Mon, Tue **Food** Lunch Wed-Sat 12-2, Sun 12-5 Dinner Wed-Sat 6-9 Av main course £16 Set menu available Restaurant menu available Wed-Sun ⊕ FREE HOUSE ◀ Reedley Hallows, Worsthorne Chestnut Mare. **Facilities** Non-diners area ◀◀ Children's menu Children's portions Parking WiFi ⊞ (notice required)

WHALLEY — Map 18 SD73

The Three Fishes ◉ — PICK OF THE PUBS

tel: 01254 826888 **Mitton Rd, Mitton BB7 9PQ**
email: enquiries@thethreefishes.com
dir: *M6 junct 31, A59 to Clitheroe. Follow Whalley signs, B6246, 2m*

Contemporary hostelry championing local food and drink

People have stopped for refreshment at this inn for more than two centuries and although the focus is now on the AA Rosette-standard food, well-kept pints of Bowland and Thwaites ales can still be supped in the bar. As you settle with your refreshment of choice, you'll notice black-and-white photographs of local food producers on the walls. Some new cooking techniques have been introduced in the quest to keep pace with trends, but owner Nigel Haworth has retained many classics, and even reinstated old favourites such as Lancashire hotpot. Well-trained staff are adept at friendly and professional service, ushering starters of sticky pulled Bowland venison and twice-baked Lancashire cheese soufflés from kitchen to table. Next may come wild rabbit pie or breast of Goosnargh chicken with mash and red wine sauce. Dessert choices may include Bramley apple tart or rhubarb and lemon verbena trifle.

Open all day all wk 12-11 (Sun 12-10.30) **Food** Sun-Thu 12-9, Fri-Sat 12-9.30 Set menu available ⊕ FREE HOUSE ◀ Bowland Hen Harrier, Thwaites Original, Reedley Hallows Pendleside ♂ Westons Stowford Press. ▼ 11 **Facilities** Non-diners area ❖ (Bar Garden) ◀◀ Children's menu Garden ⊼ Parking WiFi

WHEELTON — Map 15 SD62

The Dressers Arms

tel: 01254 830041 **Briers Brow PR6 8HD**
email: info@dressersarms.co.uk
dir: *M61 junct 8, A674 to Blackburn. Follow sign for pub on right*

Dog-friendly, welcoming fires and good pub grub

Until the 1960s, this was the smallest pub in Lancashire. The long, low, creeper-festooned old gritstone building is crammed with local photos, collectables and artefacts spread through a clutch of separate drinking areas; partly flagged floors

are warmed by roaring fires in winter. Its appeal is enhanced by the choice of ales and a reliable raft of home-made pub grub: perhaps a beef and onion sandwich, a salad or a jacket potato will hit the spot; otherwise look to the main for beef lasagne, chilli con carne, braised lamb shank, sea bass risotto, a T-bone steak or grilled aubergine, courgette and pepper stack.

Open all day all wk **Food** all wk 12-9 ⊕ FREE HOUSE ◀ Dressers Bitter, Black Sheep ♂ Westons. ▼ 20 **Facilities** Non-diners area ❖ (Bar Restaurant Garden) ◀◀ Children's menu Children's portions Family room Garden ⊼ Parking WiFi ⊞

WHITEWELL — Map 18 SD64

The Inn at Whitewell ★★★★★ INN ◉ PICK OF THE PUBS

See Pick of the Pubs on page 305

LEICESTERSHIRE

BLABY — Map 11 SP59

NEW The Bakers Arms

tel: 0116 278 7253 **The Green LE8 4FQ**
email: ccsmart@hotmail.co.uk
dir: *From A426 (S of Leicester) at rdbt (with Northfield Park on left) into Sycamore St. 2nd left into Wigston Rd. Pub on left*

Oldest pub in the county

When neighbouring All Saints Church was under construction in 1485 its builders needed a hostel, so they built what about half a millennium later became Ye Olde Bakers Arms. Its bakehouse, last used in the 1920s, still features the original ovens. Bar snacks are written on chalk boards; restaurant dishes include halibut bouillabaisse; stuffed parcel of Norfolk turkey breast; blade of Leicestershire beef; and butternut squash and Stilton Wellington. Sharing slates include 'Seaside' and antipasti. It's an Everard's house, so expect the Leicester brewery's Tiger and Beacon real ales, while also from the county comes Bottle Kicking cider.

Open all day all wk **Food** Lunch Mon-Sat 12-3, Sun 12-4 Dinner Mon-Sat 5-9 Set menu available Restaurant menu available Mon-Sat ⊕ EVERARDS ◀ Tiger, Original & Beacon ♂ Westons, Bottle Kicking Cider Company. ▼ 14 **Facilities** Non-diners area ◀◀ Children's portions Garden ⊼ Beer festival Cider festival

BREEDON ON THE HILL — Map 11 SK42

The Three Horseshoes

tel: 01332 695129 **Main St DE73 8AN**
email: ian@thehorseshoes.com
dir: *5m from M1 junct 23a. Pub in village centre*

Welcoming old pub with a chocolate workshop next door

Originally a farrier's, the buildings here are around 250 years old; the pub has been here for at least a century, while the main kitchen, a farm shop and a chocolate workshop now occupy the smithy and stables in the courtyard. Inside, numerous original features and old beams are supplemented by antique furniture, and sea-grass matting completes the warm and welcoming atmosphere. A typical menu presents mains such as beef and red wine casserole; cod with caper butter; and duck breast with cabbage and bacon. Try bread and butter pudding or treacle oat tart for dessert.

Open 11.30-2.30 5.30-11 (Sun 12-3) Closed 25-26 & 31 Dec-1 Jan, Sun eve & Mon **Food** Lunch Tue-Sat 12-2, Sun 12-3 Dinner Tue-Sat 6-9 Restaurant menu available Tue-Sun ⊕ FREE HOUSE ◀ Marston's Pedigree, guest ales. **Facilities** Non-diners area ❖ (Bar Garden) ◀◀ Children's portions Garden ⊼ Parking

BRUNTINGTHORPE

Map 11 SP68

The Joiners

tel: 0116 247 8258 **Church Walk LE17 5QH**
email: stephen@thejoinersarms.co.uk
dir: *4m from Lutterworth*

Food-led village pub

Yesteryear's modest village pub is today's popular eating place, thanks to Stephen and Tracy Fitzpatrick and their dedicated team. You'll find stripped oak beams, flagstone floors, an open fire and candles. Menus change constantly, with ingredients sourced from wherever Stephen thinks best — beef from Scotland, seafood from Cornwall, black pudding from Clonakilty. A typical example lists medallions of beef fillet with dauphinoise potatoes and Diane sauce; calves' liver with smoked bacon and garlic mash; monkfish in Parma ham with butternut squash and sage risotto; and goats' cheese and beetroot orzo. Every Tuesday there's a three-course fixed-price 'Auberge Supper' (booking is essential).

Open 12-2 6.30-11 Closed Mon **Food** Lunch Tue-Sun 12-2 Dinner Tue-Sat 6.30-9.30 Set menu available ⊕ FREE HOUSE ◀ Sharp's Doom Bar. 🍷 16 **Facilities** Non-diners area Outside area ⊼ Parking WiFi 🚌 (notice required)

BUCKMINSTER

Map 11 SK82

Tollemache Arms

tel: 01476 860477 **48 Main St NG33 5SA**
email: info@tollemache-arms.co.uk **web:** www.tollemache-arms.co.uk
dir: *4m from A1, between Colsterworth & Melton Mowbray on B676*

Family-friendly village dining pub

An imposing 19th-century stone-built country inn in the centre of a lovely village. It's run by brother and sister Peter and Sarah Turner, who have built a reputation for warm hospitality and good home cooking. Flower-decorated tables on wood-boarded floors, old pews and an open fire characterise the rustic yet contemporary ambience. Local Oakham and Grainstore Breweries furnish two of the ales, and a good wine selection includes bubbly served by the glass. Sit with a menu in the bar, the restaurant or the intimate library, and choose from starters such as battered tiger prawns, and mains like roasted lamb fillet.

Tollemache Arms

Open Tue-Thu 11-3 6-11 (Fri 11-3 5-11 Sat 11-11 Sun 12-5) Closed Sun eve, Mon **Food** Lunch Tue-Fri 12-3, Sat 12-9, Sun 12-4 Dinner Tue-Thu 6-9, Fri 5-9, Sat 12-9 Restaurant menu available Tue-Sun ⊕ FREE HOUSE ◀ Oakham Ales JHB, The Grainstore Red Kite, guest ale. 🍷 11 **Facilities** Non-diners area ❀ (Bar Garden Outside area) 🍴 Children's menu Children's portions Garden Outside area ⊼ Parking WiFi 🚌 (notice required)

COLEORTON

Map 11 SK41

George Inn

tel: 01530 834639 **Loughborough Rd LE67 8HF**
email: janice@jwilkinson781.orangehome.co.uk
dir: *A42 junct 13 onto A512*

Relaxing country pub in National Forest

A comfortable old local bristling with homely touches, with crackling log-burners in the main rooms and a tree-shaded beer garden looking over the rich pasturelands of this corner of Leicestershire. It's at the heart of the extensive National Forest, whilst Calke Abbey is a leisurely drive away. Bright and airy inside, with colourwash and panelled walls and nooks and crannies to explore, Marston's Pedigree complements the sturdy menu. Kick in with goats' cheese and poached pear, following up with wild boar sausages or steak and ale pie with Stilton; some gluten-free options are available too.

Open 12-3 5.30-11 (Fri-Sat 12-11 Sun 12-4) Closed Sun eve, Mon ⊕ FREE HOUSE ◀ Marston's Pedigree, guest ales ⚬ Thatchers Gold. **Facilities** 🍴 Children's menu Children's portions Play area Garden Parking WiFi

EVINGTON

Map 11 SK60

The Cedars

tel: 0116 273 0482 **Main St LE5 6DN**
email: pippa@king-henrys-taverns.co.uk
dir: *From Leicester take A6 towards Market Harborough. Left at lights, onto B667 to Evington. Pub in village centre*

'Something for everyone' menus

At The Cedars you can choose to eat in the restaurant with its panoramic windows overlooking the fountain and pond, dine alfresco in the gardens, or just enjoy a drink in the lounge bar with its leather sofas and relaxed atmosphere. The menu of freshly prepared dishes offers something for everyone — small and large appetites alike. Choose from steaks, grills and burgers, as well as traditional favourites such as fish pie, vegetarian options and international dishes like lamb rogan josh. Smaller plates include paninis, salads and jackets. For dessert, the chocolate fudge cake or pecan pie is a treat for those with a sweet tooth.

Open all day all wk 11.30-11 **Food** all wk 12-10 ⊕ FREE HOUSE/KING HENRY'S TAVERNS ◀ Greene King IPA, Marston's Pedigree, Guinness. **Facilities** Non-diners area 🍴 Children's menu Children's portions Garden ⊼ Parking WiFi 🚌

| GILMORTON | Map 11 SP58 |

NEW Grey Goose

tel: 01455 552555 **Lutterworth Rd LE17 5PN**
email: manager@greygoosegilmorton.co.uk
dir: *From A426 in Lutterworth into Gilmorton Rd signed Gilmorton. Over M1. Pub on left in village*

Good food served in this modern pub

Close to the A426, the Grey Goose is a light and airy, contemporary pub popular with families. Real ales and ciders are joined by 30 wines by the glass in the bar with its log-burning fire, although the emphasis here is as much about the food. Start with warm and spicy sweet chilli beef salad, perhaps, before moving on to the organic salmon fillet with fluffy mash and creamed leeks. A comforting dessert of winter berry mess with crushed meringue and whipped cream is one way to finish. Monday is pizza, pasta and risotto night.

Open all wk 12-3 6-11 (Sun 12-7) **Food** Lunch Mon-Sat 12-2, Sun 12-6.30 Dinner Mon-Sat 6-9, Sun 12-6.30 Av main course £11.95 Set menu available Restaurant menu available Mon-Sat ⊕ FREE HOUSE ◀ Sharp's Doom Bar, Wells Bombardier ⚲ Aspall. ♟ 30 **Facilities** Non-diners area ♦ Children's menu Children's portions Outside area ⊨ Parking WiFi 🚗 (notice required)

| GRIMSTON | Map 11 SK62 |

The Black Horse

tel: 01664 812358 **3 Main St LE14 3BZ**
email: amanda.wayne@sky.com
dir: *Phone for detailed directions*

Family pub in the countryside

At the foot of the hill dropping from the medieval church, The Black Horse commands the sloping green in this peaceful village outside Melton Mowbray. The trim, flowery garden, alfresco dining area and rich, warm interior reflect this village setting, where Leicestershire produce leads on the highly traditional menu. Steak and ale pie; lamb shank; or chicken breast with Stilton and bacon are classic dishes, whilst daily specials, a snack menu, fresh fish dishes and a vegetarian board enliven the choice. On the beer front, two weekly-changing guest ales complement regional favourites.

Open all wk 12-3 6-11 (Sun 12-6) **Food** Lunch Mon-Sat 12-2, Sun 12-3 Dinner Mon-Sat 6-9 ⊕ FREE HOUSE ◀ Marston's Pedigree, Adnams, guest ales ⚲ Thatchers Gold. **Facilities** Non-diners area ♣ (Bar Garden Outside area) ♦ Children's menu Children's portions Garden Outside area ⊨ WiFi 🚗

| HUNGARTON | Map 11 SK60 |

NEW The Black Boy

tel: 0116 259 5410 **Main St LE7 9JR**
email: theblack.boy@btconnect.com
dir: *From Leicester take A47 towards Peterborough. In Thurnby left at lights into Station Rd signed Scraptoft. At T-junct right signed Beeby. In Beeby at x-roads right signed Hungarton. Pub on right in village*

Choice local ales and home-cooked fare

About 200 years old, The Black Boy took its name from the image on the landowner's coat of arms when it was built. It's set in beautiful countryside and a magnet for walkers; dogs, though, must be kept outside. The bar hosts a varied selection of beers, some with very low ale miles such as Langton's Inclined Plane (named after the Foxton boat lift), and Grainstore's Ten Fifty from Rutland. Look to the chalkboard for the week's home-cooked dishes. Typical of these are goats' cheese and red onion tart; lamb's liver with bacon, mash and onion gravy; and sticky toffee pudding.

Open all wk 12-3 6-11 (Mon 6-11 Sun 12-5) **Food** Lunch Tue-Sat 12-2, Sun 12-4 Dinner Mon-Sat 6-9 Av main course £10 ⊕ FREE HOUSE ◀ The Grainstore Ten Fifty,

Fuller's London Pride, Sharp's Doom Bar, Adnams Ghost Ship, Marston's Pedigree, Timothy Taylor Landlord, Langton Inclined Plane ⚲ Westons Stowford Press. ♟ 9 **Facilities** Non-diners area ♦ Children's menu Children's portions Garden ⊨ Parking WiFi 🚗 (notice required)

| KNOSSINGTON | Map 11 SK80 |

The Fox & Hounds

tel: 01664 452129 **6 Somerby Rd LE15 8LY**
dir: *4m from Oakham in Knossington*

Cosy, inviting interior and good food

High-quality food and helpful, friendly service are the hallmarks of this 500-year-old pub. Set in the leafy village of Knossington close to Rutland Water, the building retains lots of traditional features, and the large rear garden and sitting area are ideal for alfresco summer dining. All food is freshly cooked to order and comes with fresh vegetables and potatoes of the day. Children are welcome for Sunday lunches.

Open Tue-Fri 6-11 (Sat 6.30-11 Sun 12-4) Closed Sun eve & Mon **Food** Dinner Tue-Sat 6.30-9 ⊕ ENTERPRISE INNS ◀ Fuller's London Pride. **Facilities** Non-diners area ♣ (Bar Garden Outside area) Garden Outside area ⊨ Parking WiFi 🚗 (notice required)

| LEICESTER | Map 11 SK50 |

The Rutland & Derby

tel: 0116 262 3299 **Millstone Ln LE1 5JN**
email: rutlandandderby@ssoosh.co.uk
dir: *Phone for detailed directions*

City centre pub that pleases on many levels

Everything here seems carefully considered, and nothing is without some special quality. Handy for city-centre attractions, and not far from the city's rugby ground, the pub is worth seeking out for a craft ale such as Everards, a glass of wine from the 20 on offer, or a carefully prepared cocktail. Attention to detail is evident too in the food. Ethically sourced ingredients feature in flavoursome dishes such as goats' cheese and beetroot salad with couscous; honey and mustard chargrilled lamb; and Rutland fried chicken with 'proper' mash and creamed corn. Hand-stretched and stone-cooked flatbreads are a speciality: meatball, mozzarella, field mushroom, white sauce and rocket makes a winning combination. Pub tapas is also a treat.

Open all day Closed Sun **Food** Contact pub for food times ⊕ FREE HOUSE ◀ Everards Tiger & Sunchaser, guest ale ⚲ Westons, Orchard Pig. ♟ 20 **Facilities** Non-diners area ♦ Children's portions Garden ⊨ Beer festival Cider festival WiFi 🚗 (notice required)

| LONG WHATTON | Map 11 SK42 |

The Falcon Inn

tel: 01509 842416 **64 Main St LE12 5DG**
email: enquiries@thefalconinnlongwhatton.com
dir: *M1 junct 24, A6 (Derby Rd) to Kegworth. Left into Whatton Rd to Long Whatton*

A change of owners, a change of style

The refurbished Falcon is located in the heart of a pretty village and is convenient for access to, or from, the M1. It can be described as a family-friendly, traditional English country pub with lots of character, from the teacup lights to the chairs 'made of suits and ties'. A good selection of local ales is on offer, alongside an extensive menu showcasing locally-sourced produce – the dishes are pub classics with a twist, they say.

Open all day all wk **Food** Lunch Mon-Sat 12-2.30, Sun 12-8.30 Dinner Mon-Sat 5.30-9.30, Sun 12-8.30 Restaurant menu available all wk ⊕ EVERARDS ◀ Tiger & Original, guest ale. **Facilities** Non-diners area ♦ Children's portions Garden Outside area ⊨ Parking WiFi 🚗 (notice required)

The Royal Oak ★★★★ INN ⊛   PICK OF THE PUBS

tel: 01509 843694 **26 The Green LE12 5DB**
email: enquiries@theroyaloaklongwhatton.co.uk **web:** www.theroyaloaklongwhatton.co.uk
dir: *M1 junct 24, A6 to Kegworth. Right into Whatton Road (becomes Kegworth Ln) to Long Whatton. From Loughborough, A6 towards Kegworth. Left onto B5324, right into Hathern Rd leading to The Green*

Stylish village inn, good food and local beers

Ideally situated in a picturesque village close to Loughborough and East Midlands Airport, The Royal Oak is an award-winning pub, offering high quality, locally sourced food. Charnwood ales, brewed just four miles down the road, are on offer in the smart bar, and the carefully selected wine list has 15 by the glass. In the stylish AA-Rosette restaurant diners can expect some tough decisions – Ribblesdale superior goats' cheese soufflé; sharing platter of mixed tapas; pork belly and black pudding roulade with crispy crackling or a pub classic such as home-made burger of the day. Leave room for desserts like the Nutella cheesecake; or spiced pineapple tarte Tatin with rum and raisin ice cream. An annual summer beer festival offers 30 real ales and 10 ciders. The impeccably furnished guest bedrooms are in a separate building.

Open all day all wk **Food** Lunch Mon-Sat 12-2.30, Sun 12-4 Dinner Mon-Sat 5.30-9.30, Sun 6-8.30 ⊕ FREE HOUSE ◀ St Austell Tribute, Bass, Charnwood Vixen, guest ales Ö Westons Old Rosie, Thatchers. ♚ 15 **Facilities** Non-diners area ♦♦ Children's menu Children's portions Garden ⊨ Beer festival Cider festival Parking WiFi **Rooms** 7

▮ LUTTERWORTH   Map 11 SP58

The Man at Arms

tel: 01455 552540 **The Green, Bitteswell LE17 4SB**
email: pippa@king-henrys-taverns.co.uk
dir: *From Lutterworth take Lutterworth Rd towards Ullesthorpe. Turn left at small white cottage. Pub on left after college on village green*

Contemporary decor and hearty pub grub

Close to the market town of Lutterworth, this large village pub is named after a bequest by the Dowse Charity to the nearby village of Bitteswell in return for providing a 'man at arms' for times of war. It was the first pub bought by the King Henry's Taverns group; now, 30 years later, it has a smart, contemporary interior, all clean lines, wooden floorboards and high-backed leather seats, and shares a common menu with its sister pubs. Along with traditional favourites, there are international, fish and vegetarian dishes. Sizeable options include the Titanic Challenge – a rump steak weighing some three pounds.

Open all day all wk 11.30-11 **Food** all wk 12-10 ⊕ FREE HOUSE/KING HENRY'S TAVERNS ◀ Greene King IPA, Wells Bombardier, Bass, Guinness. ♚ 16 **Facilities** Non-diners area ♦♦ Children's menu Children's portions Garden Parking ⊟

▮ MOUNTSORREL   Map 11 SK51

The Swan Inn

tel: 0116 230 2340 **10 Loughborough Rd LE12 7AT**
email: danny.harwood@hotmail.com
dir: *On A6 between Leicester & Loughborough*

17th-century cottage beside the river

Originally built as two terraced cottages in 1688, this Grade II listed free house stands on the banks of the River Soar and has a secluded riverside garden, ideal for summer sipping and dining. Exposed beams, flagstone floors and roaring winter log fires characterise the cosy bar and dining areas. Fine wines and cask-conditioned beers from Black Sheep accompany a varied, weekly-changing menu of British and European classics, as well as light lunches and snacks – Moroccan spiced potted lamb, chutney and toast; home-made beef and Stilton pie, herbed

mash and gravy; or chicken, bacon and mushroom penne carbonara. Children are welcome only until 8pm unless they're eating along with adults.

Open all wk 12-2.30 5.30-11 (Fri 12-2.30 4.30-12 Sat 12-12 Sun 12-11) **Food** Lunch Mon-Sat 12-2, Sun 12-4 Dinner Mon-Sat 6.30-9.30 Av main course £7.50 Set menu available Restaurant menu available all wk ⊕ FREE HOUSE ◀ Black Sheep Best Bitter, Greene King Abbot Ale, Morland Old Speckled Hen, Castle Rock Harvest Pale, guest ales Ö Symonds, guest ciders. **Facilities** Non-diners area ♣ (Bar Garden) ♦♦ Children's portions Garden ⊨ Beer festival Parking WiFi

---

▮ MOWSLEY   Map 11 SP68

The Staff of Life   PICK OF THE PUBS

tel: 0116 240 2359 **Main St LE17 6NT**
dir: *M1 junct 20, A4304 to Market Harborough. Left in Husbands Bosworth onto A5199. In 3m turn right to pub*

Fresh look for a charming village inn

Tucked away in the countryside, this pub has been in the same hands for over a decade during which time it has been very well looked after. Were they to return, the former residents of this well-proportioned Edwardian house would surely be amazed by the transformation of their home into such an appealing community local. The bar has high-backed settles, a flagstone floor and large wood-burning stove. Look up to see not only a fine wood-panelled ceiling but also, not quite where you'd expect it, the wine cellar. The dining area overlooking the garden offers dishes using the best of British seasonal produce, with a strong emphasis on local game: duck liver pâté and plum chutney or seared wood pigeon breast wrapped in bacon with black pudding are typical starters. Follow with roast leg of lamb with apricot and rosemary stuffing, or smoked salmon and dill fish cakes with aïoli mayonnaise.

Open Mon-Fri 6-close (Sat 12-3 6-close Sun 12-10.30) Closed Mon-Fri L **Food** Lunch Sat 12-2.15, Sun 12-3 Dinner Tue-Sat 6-9.15 Set menu available ⊕ FREE HOUSE ◀ Marston's Wainwright, Okells, Sharp's Doom Bar. ♚ 19 **Facilities** Non-diners area ♦♦ Children's portions Garden Outside area ⊨ Parking WiFi ⊟ (notice required)

▮ REDMILE   Map 11 SK73

The Windmill

tel: 01949 842281 **4 Main St NG13 0GA**
email: kirsten.rutt@btopenworld.com
dir: *From A52 between Bingham & Grantham follow signs for Redmile. Pub in village centre*

Lovely village pub with TV connections

Located in the centre of Redmile, three miles from the A52 and within walking distance of Belvoir Castle, The Windmill featured in the TV series *Auf Wiedersehen Pet* and still draws fans of the show. A comfortable lounge bar with a fireplace is a cosy place to enjoy a pint of Oldershaw Heavenly Blonde, or head to the magnificent sunny terrace at the front. Lunchtime sandwiches and snacks are augmented by a full lunch and dinner menu, which might start with smoked haddock, salmon and prawn fishcakes and move on to braised Derbyshire beef with creamed potato and roast root vegetables.

Open all day Closed Mon **Food** Lunch Tue-Fri 12-2, Sat 12-9, Sun 12-6 Dinner Tue-Fri 5-9, Sat 12-9, Sun 12-6 Set menu available Restaurant menu available all wk ⊕ FREE HOUSE ◀ Oldershaw Heavenly Blonde, Adnams Ghost Ship Ö Aspall Harry Sparrow. ♚ **Facilities** Non-diners area ♦♦ Children's menu Children's portions Outside area ⊨ Parking WiFi ⊟ (notice required)

SADDINGTON
Map 11 SP69

The Queens Head

tel: 0116 240 2536 **Main St LE8 0QH**
email: info@queensheadsaddington.co.uk **web:** www.queensheadsaddington.co.uk
dir: *M1 junct 20, A4304 signed Market Harborough. At Husbands Bosworth left onto A5199 signed Leicester. In 4m right signed Saddington. Pub in village centre*

Country pub and kitchen with views

Set in the rolling hills of south Leicestershire with views over Saddington Reservoir, this spacious family-friendly pub promises a welcoming and relaxing experience. Everards and a brace of guest ales, plus 11 wines by the glass and guest ciders, are the prime refreshments, while the work of Chris Lewis-Sharman in the kitchen pleases all-comers. A lighter menu offers the likes of goats' cheese and walnut roulade, spicy tomato and garlic coulis; pan-fried sea bass, Thai potato cake, sweet chilli salsa, deep-fried tiger prawns; and lemon and lime pannacotta with berry compôte. Children have their own menu, and there's plenty of room to play outside.

Open all wk 12-11 (Sun 12-10 Mon 12-2.30 5.30-10 Tue 12-2.30 5.30-11) **Food** Lunch Mon-Fri 12-2.30, Sat 12-9.30, Sun 12-6 Dinner Mon-Fri 5.30-9, Sat 12-9.30 Restaurant menu available Mon-Sat ⊕ EVERARDS ◼ Tiger, guest ales ᵭ Guest ciders. ₹ 11 **Facilities** Non-diners area ❤ (Bar Garden) ◗◗ Children's menu Children's portions Play area Garden ⊓ Parking WiFi ▦ (notice required)

SHAWELL
Map 11 SP58

The White Swan
PICK OF THE PUBS

tel: 01788 860357 **Main St LE17 6AG**
email: info@whiteswanshawell.co.uk
dir: *M6 junct 1, A426, at rdbt into Gibbet Ln (by garage) to Shawell. Or M1 junct 19, A5 towards Nuneaton. Under M6, at rdbt into Gibbet Ln (by garage)*

High-quality food close to the M1

Rory McLean and Samantha Laye successfully run this character pub with its log-burning fires and cosy snug. Between Rugby and Lutterworth, in the pretty village of Shawell, the pub is just a few minutes from the M1, making it a perfect place to stop for a pint of local Dow Bridge Gladiator ale or Aspall cider. Chef Rory used to cook in some of London's most notable restaurants and his modern British food is worth a detour. A starter of game Scotch egg, celeriac remoulade and soused vegetables might precede curried monkfish, spiced red lentils, coconut and coriander. Finish with rhubarb Bakewell tart and cardamom pannacotta or a plate of four cheeses. The fixed-price lunch menu might feature fishcake with asparagus, poached egg and hollandaise or beer-battered haddock, chips and peas.

Open all day Closed Mon **Food** Lunch Tue-Sun 12-2.30 Dinner Tue-Sun 6-9.30 Set menu available Restaurant menu available Tue-Sun ⊕ FREE HOUSE ◼ Dow Bridge Acris & Gladiator, Church End Goats Milk ᵭ Aspall. ₹ 37 **Facilities** Non-diners area ❤ (Bar Outside area) ◗◗ Children's menu Children's portions Outside area ⊓ Beer festival Parking WiFi ▦ (notice required)

SILEBY
Map 11 SK61

The White Swan

tel: 01509 814832 **Swan St LE12 7NW**
email: tamiller56@googlemail.com
dir: *From Leicester A6 towards Loughborough, right for Sileby; or take A46 towards Newark-on-Trent, left for Sileby*

A reputation for home-cooked food

Behind the unassuming exterior of this 1930s building, you'll find a refurbished free house of character. Menus change weekly, and there are blackboard specials, too. Favourites include duck and vegetable pancakes with hoi sin sauce; breaded mushrooms with garlic dip; Colston Bassett chicken breast with creamy leek and Stilton sauce; and beef, ale and mushroom puff pastry pie. There's a good range of gourmet 8oz beefburgers with various toppings, and if you've still got room, you could try and fit in a chocolate brownie or chocolate tiffin for afters. Sunday lunch is also a popular event and dogs are welcome in the snug bar.

Open Fri & Sun 12-1.30 Tue-Sat 6-11 Closed 1-5 Jan, Sun eve & Mon (Tue-Thu L) **Food** Lunch Fri & Sun 12-1.30 Dinner Tue-Sat 7-8.30 Av main course £12 ⊕ FREE HOUSE ◼ Sharp's Doom Bar, guest ales. ₹ 8 **Facilities** Non-diners area ❤ (Bar Outside area) ◗◗ Children's menu Children's portions Outside area ⊓ Parking WiFi

SOMERBY
Map 11 SK71

Stilton Cheese Inn

tel: 01664 454394 **High St LE14 2QB**
web: www.stiltoncheeseinn.co.uk
dir: *From A606 between Melton Mowbray & Oakham follow signs to Pickwell & Somerby. Enter village, 1st right to centre, pub on left*

Village pub surrounded by beautiful countryside

An attractive, mellow sandstone building dating from the 17th century, whose interior frequently prompts customers to liken it to stepping back in time. Its reputation for good food stems from dishes such as deep-fried fillet of cod; home-made cottage pie; grilled beef and gammon steaks; chilli con carne; macaroni cheese, and regularly changing specials. Stilton comes as a cheese option for a ploughman's, and for a steak sauce topping. In addition to the food, also attracting custom is the wide selection of wines by the glass or mini-bottle, and locally brewed real ales from Belvoir, The Grainstore, Newby Wyke and others. Furthermore, there's a choice of 25-plus malt whiskies.

Open all wk 12-3 6-11 (Sun 12-3 7-11) **Food** Lunch all wk 12-2 Dinner Mon-Sat 6-9, Sun 7-9 Av main course £9.95 ⊕ FREE HOUSE ◼ The Grainstore Ten Fifty, Brewster's Hophead, Belvoir Star, Oakham Ales JHB, Newby Wyke Kingston Topaz ᵭ Westons Old Rosie & Bounds. ₹ 15 **Facilities** Non-diners area ◗◗ Children's menu Children's portions Family room Garden ⊓ Parking ▦ (notice required)

STATHERN
Map 11 SK73

Red Lion Inn

tel: 01949 860868 **Red Lion St LE14 4HS**
email: info@theredlioninn.co.uk
dir: *From A1 (Grantham), A607 towards Melton, turn right in Waltham, right at next x-roads then left to Stathern*

An inn for all seasons

A change of hands in 2016 turned the Red Lion into a fully fledged country-style dining pub operating seven days a week. The traditional flagstoned bar warmly welcomes with an open fire, beams, oak doors and comfy seating. Ales from Fuller's and Brewster's are joined by an astounding wine collection of which some 25 can be served by the glass. A small snug connects to a long, narrow restaurant and on out to a sun-trap lawn and patio. Menus range from tasty bar food such as a home-made smoked haddock Scotch egg, to inventive à la carte dishes such as halibut fillets served with bouillabaisse risotto.

Open all day all wk 12-11 **Food** Lunch Mon-Sat 12-2.30, Sun 12-6 Dinner Mon-Sat 6-9 Av main course £16 Set menu available ⊕ FREE HOUSE ◀ Brewster's Marquis, Fuller's London Pride, Castle Rock Harvest Pale ♂ Aspall, Sheppy's, Westons. ☐ 25 **Facilities** Non-diners area ☀ (Bar Garden Outside area) ◀ Children's menu Children's portions Garden Outside area ☐ Parking WiFi ⊕ (notice required)

SUTTON CHENEY
Map 11 SK40

Hercules Revived

tel: 01455 699336 **Main St CV13 0AG**
email: info@herculesrevived.co.uk **web:** www.herculesrevived.co.uk
dir: *Phone for detailed directions*

Great British produce at revitalised village inn

Hercules was an 18th-century racehorse and — the story goes — his 'revival' has led to him becoming an innkeeper — described as a 'strong silent type and rarely seen'. Whether or not it's run by a horse, this 17th-century inn has undergone its own revival; there's a relaxed bar and simple dining on the ground floor, with a cosy and elegant restaurant upstairs. Local producers supply pretty much everything. A winter evening menu might include a seafood platter for grazing, as well as classics like slow-braised beef with cheddar mash, hot pickled red cabbage and bacon; or maybe teriyaki salmon, carrot, ginger and potato rösti, with toasted sesame and broccoli.

Hercules Revived

Open all day all wk **Food** Lunch all wk 12-2.30 Dinner all wk 6-9 ⊕ FREE HOUSE ◀ Church End What The Fox's Hat, Tunnel Brewery Henry Tudor ♂ Thatchers Gold. ☐ 12 **Facilities** Non-diners area ☀ (Bar Outside area) ◀ Children's portions Outside area ☐ Beer festival Parking ⊕ (notice required)

See advert below

SWITHLAND — Map 11 SK51

The Griffin Inn

tel: 01509 890535 **174 Main St LE12 8TJ**
email: lee@oddjohn.co.uk
dir: *From A46 into Anstey. Right at rdbt to Cropston. Right at x-roads, 1st left, 0.5m to Swithland. Follow brown signs for inn*

Unpretentious food in a traditional walkers' inn

Parts of this welcoming, traditional, family-run country inn date back to the 15th century. There are three cosy bar areas serving a range of real ales, two dining rooms, a skittle alley, large patio and 'secret' garden with a stream. Menus and a wide range of specials offer unfussy, good-value internationally inspired food including moules marinière; chicken and chorizo linguine; traditional Spanish paella; and rhubarb and ginger sponge, lemon curd and vanilla ice cream. Dogs are only allowed in one room near the bar. The area is popular with walkers heading for Swithland Woods, Beacon Hill and the Old John folly, and there's also a steam railway nearby.

Open all day all wk **Food** Lunch Mon-Thu 12-2, Fri-Sun 12-9 Dinner Mon-Thu 6-9, Fri-Sun 12-9 ⊕ EVERARDS ◀ Tiger & Original, Adnams Southwold Bitter, 2 guest ales Ŏ Symonds, 2 guest scrumpies. ♥ 15 **Facilities** Non-diners area ❖ (Bar Garden) ⊪ Children's menu Children's portions Garden ☲ Parking WiFi ➾

THORPE LANGTON — Map 11 SP79

The Bakers Arms

tel: 01858 545201 **Main St LE16 7TS**
dir: *Take A6 S from Leicester then left signed 'The Langtons', at rail bridge continue to x-roads. Straight on to Thorpe Langton. Pub on left*

Intimate thatched pub with great fish nights

A pretty thatched pub set in an equally pretty village, The Bakers Arms has the requisite low beams, rug-strewn quarry-tiled floors, large pine tables and open fires. Its weekly-changing menu of modern pub food has gained it a keen local following. Expect dishes like crevettes with asparagus, soft boiled eggs and garlic mayonnaise; confit of duck with red pepper and ginger marmalade; and apple and cinnamon crêpes with vanilla ice cream. Fish lovers should be sure to visit on a Thursday, when fish specials might include pan-fried sea bass fillets with spinach and chive butter sauce. The area is popular with walkers, riders and mountain bikers.

Open 6.30-11 (Sat 12-2.30 6.30-11 Sun 12-2.30) Closed 1-7 Jan, Sun eve, Mon **Food** Contact pub for food times Restaurant menu available all wk ⊕ FREE HOUSE ◀ Langton Bakers Dozen Bitter. ♥ 9 **Facilities** Non-diners area Garden ☲ Parking WiFi

WELHAM — Map 11 SP79

The Old Red Lion

tel: 01858 565253 **Main St LE16 7UJ**
email: pippa@king-henrys-taverns.co.uk
dir: *NE of Market Harborough take B664 to Weston by Welland. Left to Welham*

Tranquil setting in rolling countryside

The airy, split-level, contemporary interior of today's pub blends well with vestiges of its origins as a coaching inn. Polished floorboards, leather seating and open fire are a welcome retreat for ramblers drifting in from the area's popular walking routes. Views from the windows stretch across this rural corner of Leicestershire where the River Welland meanders through rich pastureland. One of a small chain of local dining pubs; the menu covers all bases, from British classics such as calves' liver and bacon; a seafood platter; a variety of steaks 'for the larger appetite', a choice of international dishes such as spicy Cajun chicken, and

vegetarian options, perhaps vegetable enchiladas; and a nut loaf. Beers include Marston's Pedigree.

Open all day all wk 11.30-11 **Food** all wk 12-10 ⊕ FREE HOUSE/KING HENRY'S TAVERNS ◀ Greene King IPA, Marston's Pedigree, Fuller's London Pride, Guinness. ♥ 15 **Facilities** Non-diners area ⊪ Children's menu Children's portions Outside area ☲ Parking WiFi ➾

WOODHOUSE EAVES — Map 11 SK51

The Curzon Arms

tel: 01509 890377 **44 Maplewell Rd LE12 8QZ**
email: info@thecurzonarms.com
dir: *M1 junct 23, A512 towards Loughborough. Right signed Nanpantan. Through Nanpantan to Woodhouse Eaves*

Contemporary but still pleasingly old-fashioned village pub

Traditional and lounge bars, a restaurant, wood-burning stoves, wooden floors, a large terrace and a beer garden just about sum up this Charnwood Forest pub. Other essentials are the four rotating real ales, hand-picked wines and seasonal British food, with monthly changing, well-compiled menus offering light bar meals, three-course dinners and 'funky' bar snacks. Possible choices include rabbit, carrot and leek stew; crispy risotto balls with chilli and tomato dressing; whole baked sea bream; confit leg of Gressingham duck; Woodhouse honey and mustard roast ham; and pan-fried polenta cake with winter vegetable ragout. For dessert, maybe Baileys crème brûlée with mulled berry compôte.

Open all wk 12-3 5.30-12 (Fri-Sat 12-12 Sun 12-11.30) **Food** Lunch Mon-Fri 12-2.30, Sat 12-9, Sun 12-6 Dinner Mon-Fri 5.30-9.30, Sat 12-9, Sun 12-6 Av main course £12 Set menu available ⊕ ENTERPRISE INNS ◀ Sharp's Doom Bar, Timothy Taylor Landlord. ♥ 16 **Facilities** Non-diners area ❖ (Bar Garden) ⊪ Children's menu Children's portions Garden ☲ Parking WiFi ➾ (notice required)

The Wheatsheaf Inn

tel: 01509 890320 **Brand Hill LE12 8SS**
email: richard@wheatsheafinn.net **web:** www.wheatsheafinn.net
dir: *M1 junct 22, follow Quorn signs*

Old village inn at heart of Charnwood Forest

A rambling, creeper dressed stone inn (it was a quarrymen's watering hole 200 years ago) that has a comfortably traditional bar and 'The Mess' dining area based on RAF connections. Charnwood Forest's stirring countryside is all around and the Great Central Railway (steam) is close-by. Explorers may choose to sit in the flowery courtyard garden, indulging in Timothy Taylor Landlord bitter and select from an ever-changing menu, perhaps haddock in beer batter with mushy peas, fries and home-made tartare sauce; the always popular Woodhouse smokies; and the Wheatsheaf burger. There's a decent list of wines to accompany.

Open all wk 12-3 6-11 (Sat 12-11 Sun 12-4) Closed Sun eve **Food** Lunch Mon-Fri 12-2.30, Sat 12-3, Sun 12-4 Dinner Mon-Fri 6-9.15, Sat 6-9.30 ⊕ FREE HOUSE ◀ Greene King Abbot Ale, Timothy Taylor Landlord, Adnams Broadside, Tetley's Smoothflow, Marston's Pedigree, guest ale ○ Thatchers. ♈ 16
Facilities Non-diners area ☻ (Bar Garden) ♦♦ Children's menu Children's portions Garden ⋒ Parking WiFi ▰ (notice required)

WYMESWOLD   Map 11 SK62

The Windmill Inn

tel: 01509 881313 **83 Brook St LE12 6TT**
email: info@thewindmillwymeswold.com
dir: *From A46 N of Six Hills left onto A606 signed Wymeswold. In village left into Church Ln, left into Brook St. Or from M1 junct 24, A6 signed Loughborough & Kegworth, A6006 to Wymeswold*

Family-friendly local with large beer garden

It may be a traditional village inn but the Windmill has a contemporary feel in both the bar and restaurant, with a mix of wood and stone tiled floors, wood-burners, warm heritage colours and comfortable seating creating the informal scene. Monthly menus combine pub classics with modern British dishes, perhaps root vegetable, tomato and orzo stew, followed by chicken katsu curry with spiced cabbage and egg noodles; or the pie of the week; and apple and granola crumble with vanilla custard to finish. Dogs and children are welcome, and there's a lovely garden for alfresco dining.

Open all wk 12-3 5.15-11.30 (Mon 12-3 5.15-11 Fri-Sat 12-12 Sun 12-9) **Food** Lunch Mon-Thu 12-2.30, Fri-Sat 12-9.30, Sun 12-5 Dinner Mon 5.30-9, Tue-Thu 5.30-9.30, Fri-Sat 12-9.30 Set menu available ⊕ FREE HOUSE ◀ Sharp's Doom Bar, Castle Rock Harvest Pale, guest ale ○ Symonds. ♈ **Facilities** Non-diners area ☻ (Bar Garden Outside area) ♦♦ Children's menu Children's portions Family room Garden Outside area ⋒ Parking WiFi

WYMONDHAM   Map 11 SK81

The Berkeley Arms

tel: 01572 787587 **59 Main St LE14 2AG**
email: info@theberkeleyarms.co.uk
dir: *In town centre*

Locally sourced, freshly prepared meals and fine wines

Having fulfilled their long-held ambition to own a pub, Neil and Louise Hitchen have seen their appealing, stone-built Berkeley Arms go from strength to strength. They are dedicated to sourcing fresh, local produce for the daily-changing menus. So a winter menu starts with roast parsnip soup with parsnip chips; pork and black pudding pâté with apple compôte and toast; and continues with whole roasted partridge with fondant potato and honey-roasted parsnips; or braised shoulder of venison with mash, caramelised walnuts and poached pear. Leave a little room for apple and blackberry crumble with blackberry sorbet. Well thought out two- and three- course lunches are served on Sundays.

Open 12-3 6-11 (Sun 12-5) Closed 1st 2wks Jan & 2wks summer, Sun eve & Mon **Food** Lunch Tue-Sat 12-2, Sun 12-3 Dinner Tue-Sat 6.30-9.30 Set menu available ⊕ FREE HOUSE ◀ Castle Rock Harvest Pale, Batemans XB, Marston's Pedigree ○ Westons Stowford Press. ♈ 10 **Facilities** Non-diners area ☻ (Bar Garden) ♦♦ Children's portions Garden ⋒ Parking

LINCOLNSHIRE

BARNOLDBY LE BECK   Map 17 TA20

The Ship Inn

tel: 01472 822308 **Main Rd DN37 0BG**
email: the_ship_inn@btinternet.com
dir: *M180 junct 5, A18 past Humberside Airport. At Laceby Junction rdbt (A18 & A46) straight over follow Skegness/Boston signs. Approx 2m turn left signed Waltham & Barnoldby le Beck*

Traditional village pub with coal fires and great seafood

Set in a picturesque village on the edge of the Lincolnshire Wolds, this 300-year-old inn has always attracted an interesting mix of customers, from Grimsby's seafarers to aviators from the county's World War II airstrips. The bar is filled with maritime bric-à-brac and serves a grand choice of ales such as Black Sheep or Tom Wood's, and there's also a beautiful garden. Seafood is a speciality, so tuck into seared scallops, chorizo, aïoli and sun blush tomatoes; and whole salt-crusted sea bass, chilli salsa, coriander rice and pak choi. Meat lovers are sure to enjoy dishes such as slow-roast lamb shank, creamed potato, sautéed cabbage and redcurrant reduction.

Open 12-3 6-11 (Fri-Sat 12-3 6-12 Sun 12-5) Closed 25 Dec, Sun eve **Food** Lunch Mon-Sat 12-2, Sun 12-5 Dinner Mon-Sat 6-9 Av main course £13 ◀ Black Sheep Best Bitter, Tom Wood's, Guinness ○ Thatchers Gold. ♈ 9 **Facilities** Non-diners area ☻ (Garden) ♦♦ Children's portions Garden ⋒ Parking WiFi ▰ (notice required)

BASTON   Map 12 TF11

NEW White Horse Baston

tel: 01778 560923 **4 Church St PE6 9PE**
email: info@thewhitehorsebaston.co.uk
dir: *From Peterborough take A15 towards Sleaford. After Market Deeping turn right signed Baston, 2nd right into Church St, pub on right*

Thriving 18th-century village survivor

In 2013, local farmer Mark Richardson bought what for 40 years had been The Spinning Wheel. He and his team transformed it, importing beams from an old barn, floorboards to form a ceiling, and a decorative piece of sycamore trunk for the Snug. It got its old name back, too. His farm supplies meats so expect, for example, seared pork medallion; brisket and ale fritter; braised shin of beef; and chargrilled sirloin steak. Other prospects are roasted hake fillet, salsify, sautéed beets and caramelised chicory; game of the week; and sweet potato and coconut curry. Put the first weekend in July's beer festival on your calendar.

Open 4-11 (Wed-Thu 12-11 Fri-Sat 12-12 Sun 12-10.30) Closed Mon L & Tue L **Food** Lunch Wed-Fri 12-2.30, Sat 12-9, Sun 12-6 Dinner Tue-Fri 5.30-9, Sat 12-9, Sun 12-6 ⊕ FREE HOUSE ◀ Castle Rock Harvest Pale, Adnams Southwold Bitter. ♈ 11 **Facilities** Non-diners area ☻ (Bar Garden) ♦♦ Children's menu Children's portions Garden ⋒ Beer festival Parking WiFi ▰

BELCHFORD
Map 17 TF27

The Blue Bell Inn

tel: 01507 533602 **1 Main Rd LN9 6LQ**
email: bluebellbelchford@gmail.com
dir: *From Horncastle take A153 towards Louth. Right signed Belchford*

In the heart of the Lincolnshire Wolds

Pantiles on the roof, white walls reflecting the sun, this family-run free house stands on the Viking Way long-distance path from the Humber to Rutland Water. Diners from all over the county are attracted by its many culinary temptations, among them smoked salmon confit fishcake; pork, chicken and pistachio terrine; apple and cranberry Lincolnshire sausages, mash and onion gravy; steak and ale casserole; and pan-fried gilt-head bream, chive buttered mash and lobster bisque. Anyone just after a glass of wine or pint of Wainfleet-brewed Batemans XXXB, Greene King IPA or a guest beer, will find plenty of armchairs to sink into.

Open all wk 11.30-2.30 6.30-11 (Sun 12-10.30) Closed 2nd & 3rd wk Jan **Food** Lunch all wk 12-2 Dinner all wk 6.30-9 ⊕ FREE HOUSE ◀ Batemans XXXB, Greene King IPA, guest ale. **Facilities** Non-diners area ❖ (Bar Garden) ♦ Children's menu Children's portions Garden ♫ Parking WiFi

BURTON COGGLES
Map 11 SK92

The Cholmeley Arms
PICK OF THE PUBS

tel: 01476 550225 **Village St NG33 4JS**
email: berrylesley@aol.com
dir: *From A1 at Colsterworth onto A151 towards Corby Glen. Left onto B1176 signed Burton Coggles*

Tread in royal footsteps in this village free house

It 1086, William the Conqueror's Domesday Book noted that a path of coggles, or cobbles, ran through the area. Half a millennium later, politician Sir Henry Cholmeley, whose descendants still live in the village, bought the Easton Estate, which owns the inn, and whose 'lost' walled gardens are worth visiting. There'll be no need to puzzle over mysterious culinary terms on the comprehensive, clear-cut menu, so start with traditional smoked haddock and prawn chowder; or melon with fresh fruits and mango sorbet. Then move easily into lambs' liver with creamy mash potato and caramelised onion gravy; fresh Grimsby haddock with either garden or mushy peas, chips and salad; or Mediterranean roasted vegetable bake topped with mozzarella. When the Prince of Wales and The Duchess of Cornwall visited the inn and associated farm shop in connection with His Royal Highness's Pub is the Hub initiative, they presented the landlords, John and Lesley Berry, with a commemorative barrel top.

Open 12-3 5-11 (Sun 12-11) Closed Mon L & Tue L **Food** Lunch Wed-Sat 12-2.30, Sun 12-3.30 Dinner Mon-Sat 6-8.30 ⊕ FREE HOUSE ◀ John Smith's Extra Smooth, Guinness, guest ales Ò Thatchers Gold. **Facilities** Non-diners area ❖ (Bar Garden) ♦ Children's menu Children's portions Garden ♫ Parking WiFi

CAYTHORPE
Map 11 SK94

NEW Red Lion

tel: 01400 272632 **High St NG32 3DN**
email: john@redlioncaythorpe.org.uk
dir: *SE of Newark-on-Trent*

Quality cooking in stylish pub

Old world charm combines with contemporary comforts in this refurbished 17th-century inn. Grab one of the comfortable armchairs by the open fire and enjoy a glass of Adnams ale or one of nine wines served by the glass as you agonise over menu choices. Pub classics of shepherd's pie, and steak and ale pudding may be one way to go, but then you could kick off with smoked salmon and crayfish risotto followed by slow-roasted barbecue pork ribs with apple and celeriac coleslaw and hand-cut chips. Make sure you leave a space for baked banana cheesecake.

Open 12-3 6-11 (Sun 12-4) Closed Sun eve **Food** Lunch Mon-Sat 12-2, Sun 12-3 Dinner Mon-Thu 6-9, Fri-Sat 6-9.30 Av main course £12 Set menu available ⊕ PUNCH TAVERNS ◀ Adnams Southwold Bitter, Everards Tiger. ⚑ 9 **Facilities** Non-diners area ♦ Children's portions Outside area ♫ Parking WiFi ⊟ (notice required)

CLEETHORPES
Map 17 TA30

The Nottingham House ★★★★ INN

tel: 01472 505150 **5-7 Seaview St DN35 8EU**
email: nottinghamhousehotel@gmail.com web: www.nottinghamhousehotel.com
dir: *Phone for detailed directions*

Real ale haven in seaside town centre

To locals this is The Notts, an intimate, family-run pub in narrow Seaview Street, from which you can indeed see the briny. Landlords Anne and Roger Gott speak of the "amazing views across the Humber Estuary" that can be enjoyed from upstairs. A strong commitment to real ales and ciders is evident in the bar, where, in addition, 25 wines are sold by the glass. Menus offer pub grub – for example, fish and chips – and dishes such as pan-fried Gressingham duck with red wine and redcurrant gravy; paupiettes of plaice stuffed with smoked salmon and spinach; and three-cheese vegetable bake.

Open all day all wk **Food** Lunch Wed-Sun 12-3 Dinner Wed-Sat 5-7 Set menu available Restaurant menu available Wed-Sun 12-3 & 6-9 ⊕ PUNCH TAVERNS ◀ Tetley's Bitter & Dark Mild, Wychwood Hobgoblin, Timothy Taylor Landlord, Guinness Ò Westons Old Rosie, Rosie's Pig, Perry & Raspberry Twist. ⚑ 25 **Facilities** Non-diners area ❖ (Bar) ♦ Children's menu Children's portions Family room Beer festival Cider festival WiFi ⊟ (notice required) **Rooms** 3

COLEBY
Map 17 SK96

NEW The Bell at Coleby

tel: 01522 813778 **3 Far Ln LN5 0AH**
email: enquiries@thebellatcoleby.com
dir: *7m S of Lincoln on A607 towards Grantham*

Thriving village dining pub

Down a quiet cul-de-sac just off the long distance walking path, The Viking Way, is Paul Vidic's friendly dining pub. Rapidly gaining in popularity since its relaunch a few years, the pub has three elegant yet informal dining areas. Paul is passionate about the food he creates, and his accomplished menu offers starters such as baked seafood thermidor, and chicken liver and smoked bacon pâté; and typical mains of panache of sea bass, turbot and salmon; roast rack of lamb; and spinach, ricotta and walnut ravioli. Among some reassuringly familiar desserts are baked American-style cheesecake with blackcurrant ice cream and berry compôte; and caramelised lemon tart with strawberry and raspberry sorbet.

Open 5.30-11 (Sun 12-3) Closed Mon-Tue **Food** Lunch Sun 12-3 Dinner Wed-Sat 5.30-9.30 Set menu available Restaurant menu available Wed-Sat ⊕ FREE HOUSE ◀ Timothy Taylor Landlord & Boltmaker ○ Thatchers, Aspall. ▼ 12 **Facilities** Non-diners area Outside area ⊟ Parking

CONINGSBY — Map 17 TF25

The Lea Gate Inn

tel: 01526 342370 **Leagate Rd LN4 4RS**
email: theleagateinn@hotmail.com
dir: *From Coningsby take A153 towards Horncastle. Right onto B1192 signed Boston. Pub on left*

The oldest licensed premises in the county

Dating from 1542, this was the last of the Fen Guide Houses that provided shelter before the treacherous marshes were drained. Among the oak-beamed pub's features are a priest's hole, low ceilings, a very old inglenook fireplace, extensive gardens and a yew tree dating from the 1600s. The same family has been running the pub for over 30 years and they source their produce locally (including game in season). All food is home made, and dishes on the seasonal menu could include wild game pie, slow-roasted blade of beef, fisherman's pie and double-dipped full rack of BBQ ribs. Wednesday night is steak night.

Open all wk 11.30-3 6-11 (Sun 12-10.30) **Food** Lunch Mon-Sat 11.45-2, Sun 12-9 Dinner Mon-Sat 6-9, Sun 12-9 ⊕ FREE HOUSE ◀ Timothy Taylor Landlord, guest ales ○ Thatchers. ▼ 10 **Facilities** Non-diners area ♣ (Bar Garden) ♦ Children's menu Children's portions Play area Garden ⊟ Parking WiFi ▭

CORBY GLEN — Map 11 SK92

NEW Woodhouse Arms

tel: 01476 552452 **2 Bourne Rd NG33 4NS**
email: info@thewoodhousearms.co.uk
dir: *From A1 between Stamford & Grantham onto A151 signed Bourne & Corby Glen*

Friendly pub in a pretty village

The village of Corby Glen is a lovely setting for this cosy, welcoming pub, which has alfresco dining for the summer and roaring fires in the winter. In the bright and airy restaurant, you could share a baked camembert, or try the calves' liver and pork terrine, with Parma ham, sourdough toast and apple and apricot chutney; then take in toad-in-the-hole with mash and onion gravy; fillet of sea bream with saffron crushed potatoes, tomato and mussel broth; or rack of lamb with a pistachio and orange crust and dauphinoise potatoes. Finish with the Woodhouse cheese plate, or the hot chocolate fondant with poached black cherries and vanilla ice cream.

Open all day all wk Closed 25-27 Dec **Food** Lunch all wk 12-2 Dinner all wk 6-9 Av main course £10.95 ⊕ FREE HOUSE ◀ Greene King Abbot Ale, Black Sheep, Timothy Taylor Landlord. **Facilities** Non-diners area ♦ Children's menu Garden ⊟ Parking WiFi ▭ (notice required)

DRY DODDINGTON — Map 11 SK84

Wheatsheaf Inn

tel: 01400 281458 **NG23 5HU**
email: info@wheatsheafdrydoddington.co.uk
dir: *From A1 between Newark-on-Trent & Grantham. Turn into Doddington Ln for Dry Doddington*

Village inn with a good selection of ales

This pantile-roofed inn looks across the green to the village church with its leaning tower. Picnic settles around the pub entrance encourage resting for a while to contemplate this timeless view with a pint in hand – Abbot Ale, Timothy Taylor Landlord and guest ales are all on hand pump inside. The inn's age is uncertain, but the pre-Jurassic era stones used to build it are around 200-million-years old. Its ancient beams are warmed in winter by a roaring log-burner. Seasonal plates of classic pub food may embrace home-made game pie with hand-cut chips and mushy peas; or pan-roasted hake fillet with lemon and thyme linguine. A change of hands.

Open all day 12-3 5-11 (Sat-Sun 12-11) Closed Mon **Food** Lunch Tue-Sat 12-3, Sun 12-6 Dinner Tue-Sat 6-9, Sun 12-6 Set menu available ⊕ FREE HOUSE ◀ Timothy Taylor Landlord, Greene King Abbot Ale & IPA, guest ales ○ Aspall. ▼ 14 **Facilities** Non-diners area ♣ (Bar Garden) ♦ Children's menu Children's portions Garden ⊟ Beer festival Parking WiFi ▭ (notice required)

FULBECK — Map 17 SK95

The Hare & Hounds

tel: 01400 273322 **The Green NG32 3JJ**
email: reservations@hareandhoundsfulbeck.com
dir: *On A607, N of Grantham*

Village pub with imaginative food

Overlooking an attractive village green, this is a 17th-century, Grade II listed pub where a log fire keeps the chills away in winter; on warmer days, an outside eating area awaits. The beer pumps in the bar announce Adnams Broadside and Woodforde's Wherry among others. The chef and his team work with only the best locally sourced ingredients, producing a typical three-course dinner of curried smoked haddock risotto with poached egg and crispy pancetta; breast of chicken with pan haggerty, green beans and wild mushroom sauce; and Baileys crème brûlée. Pub classics include Lincolnshire sausages with mash and onion gravy; and barbecued sticky ribs. A change of hands.

Open 12-2 5.30-11 (Sun 12-4) Closed Sun eve **Food** Lunch Mon-Sat 12-2, Sun 12-3 Dinner Mon-Sat 6-9 ⊕ FREE HOUSE ◀ Adnams Broadside, Harvey's Pale, Wadworth 6X, Woodforde's Wherry. ▼ 11 **Facilities** Non-diners area ♦ Children's menu Children's portions Family room Outside area ⊟ Parking WiFi

---

The Chequers

tel: 01406 366700 **PE12 OAJ**
email: info@the-chequers.co.uk **web:** www.the-chequers.co.uk
dir: *From A17 between Holbeach & Sutton Bridge left at rdbt onto B1359 (signed Gedney Dyke)*

Destination eatery with beguiling warmth

You can just sit at the spotless bar and enjoy a pint of Woodforde's Wherry, but chances are most people arriving here will have booked a table. The contemporary decor, crisp white napery and smartly dressed front of house staff all indicate a quality food destination. That said, dogs are welcome in the bar, children have their own menu, and the welcome from the staff matches the warmth of the atmosphere. So choose your refreshment and settle down to enjoy the labours of a highly-qualified kitchen brigade – roast saddle of venison; roast sea bass in a Thai-style broth; and butternut squash and feta cheese bake are indicative dishes. If you aren't too full, try the vanilla poached apple with blackberries and hazelnut crumble.

Open 11.30-3 5-11 Closed Mon & Tue **Food** Lunch Wed-Sat 12-2.30, Sun 12-3 Dinner Wed-Sat 6-9 Set menu available Restaurant menu available Wed-Sun ⊕ FREE HOUSE ◀ Woodforde's Wherry, guest ales ♨ Aspall. ♈ 12
Facilities Non-diners area ♣ (Bar Garden) ♦ Children's menu Children's portions Garden ⌁ Parking WiFi ▭

The Black Horse

tel: 01775 840995 **66 Siltside, Gosberton Risegate PE11 4ET**
dir: *From Spalding take A16 towards Boston. Left onto A152. At Gosberton take B1397 to Gosberton Risegate. Pub set back from road*

No poker faces at this friendly Fenland local

This lovely creeper-clad hostelry is tucked away in a village outside Spalding. Poker and nap nights feature in the pub's social calendar along with quiz nights, and indoor barbecues if the weather is unaccommodating. Huddle up to the wood-burning stove with a pint of Black Sheep or Fuller's London Pride while perusing the extensive choices of pub grub on the menu. All the favourites are here, from starters of whitebait or prawn cocktail, to main plates of scampi with chips and peas, or pie of the day. Chef's home-made cheesecake with fruit coulis and honeycomb ice cream rounds things off nicely.

Open Wed-Thu 5.30-10.30 (Fri-Sat 12-2 5.30-10.30 Sun 12-10.30) Closed Mon-Tue ⊕ FREE HOUSE ◀ Black Sheep, Fuller's London Pride. **Facilities** ♦ Children's portions Garden Parking WiFi

---

NEW The New Inn ★★★★ INN ◉◉　　PICK OF THE PUBS

tel: 01469 569998 **2 High St DN37 8JL**
email: enquiries@thenewinngreatlimber.co.uk **web:** www.thenewinngreatlimber.co.uk
dir: *From rdbt on A180 follow Brigg & Humber Airport signs. Pass airport, pub on right in Great Limber*

Smart rooms and sharp cooking

This Grade II listed inn, set in the heart of the Brocklesby Estate, has been welcoming locals and travellers alike for nearly 240 years. Today, there are 10 boutique-style bedrooms, and the smart, modern restaurant, which has been awarded two AA Rosettes, offers modern British menus using fine produce, some of it from the estate's organic kitchen garden. A meal might kick off with roast Gressingham duck breast, crispy leg croquettes, cherries and almonds; followed by chicken, ham and leek pie with mustard cream and new potatoes from the estate. Lemon tart with marmalade ice cream to finish, or local cheeses with plum bread. The bar is a delightful place to enjoy a pint of Tom Wood's Best Bitter or one of the 12 glasses served by the glass. The decor has country-style chic – stacked logs, painted wood panelling, long wooden tables, bentwood chairs and cosy library corners. Here you can also choose lunchtime sandwiches or maybe just a home-made beefburger with Stilton rarebit and fries.

Open all day all wk **Food** Lunch Tue-Sun 12-2 Dinner all wk 6.30-9 Av main course £15 Set menu available Restaurant menu available all wk ⊕ FREE HOUSE ◀ Batemans XXXB, Sharp's Doom Bar, Tom Wood's Best Bitter. ♈ 12
Facilities Non-diners area ♣ (Bar Garden) ♦ Children's portions Garden ⌁ Parking WiFi ▭ **Rooms** 10

The Brownlow Arms ★★★★★ INN ◉

tel: 01400 250234 **High Rd NG32 2AZ**
email: armsinn@yahoo.co.uk **web:** www.thebrownlowarms.com
dir: *From A607 (Grantham to Sleaford road), Hough-on-the-Hill signed from Barkston*

Country-house-style village inn

This 17th-century stone inn ticks all the boxes. Named after former owner Lord Brownlow, it still looks, inside and out, every inch the country house it once was. Enjoy a pint of Timothy Taylor Landlord or Black Sheep in the convivial bar, while browsing the menu for AA-Rosette standard dishes such as black treacle pork tenderloin, cider and maple braised belly, butter mash, parsnip purée, crackling and red wine jus; and pan-seared steak, hand-cut chips with sauce au poivre or garlic butter. The landscaped terrace invites outdoor drinking and dining, although please note that children must be eight or over to be allowed in the pub, and only at lunchtime from Wednesday to Saturday.

Open Wed-Sat 12-2.30 Tue-Sat 6pm-11pm Sun 12-3 Closed 25-26 Dec, Mon, Sun eve **Food** Lunch Wed-Sat 12-2, Sun-12-2.30 Dinner Tue-Sat 6-9 Set menu available Restaurant menu available Tue-Sat eve ⊕ FREE HOUSE ◀ Timothy Taylor Landlord, Black Sheep. ⬤ 10 **Facilities** Non-diners area Children's portions Garden ⋒ Parking WiFi **Rooms** 5

The Inn on the Green

tel: 01522 730354 **34 The Green LN1 2XT**
email: enquiries@innonthegreeningham.co.uk **web:** www.innonthegreeningham.co.uk
dir: *From Lincoln take A15 signed Scunthorpe. Left into Ingham Ln signed Ingham, Cammeringham. Right onto B1398 (Middle St), left to Ingham*

Village favourite offering some excellent pub food

This lovely old limestone building stands on the corner of a pretty village green at the foot of Lincoln Edge. Drinkers relaxing at garden tables and enjoying a real ale from Laneham or Grantham may be startled by the Red Arrows, practicing from nearby RAF Scampton. The pub's two bars and restaurant area exude the character that has gained it Grade II listing; an appealing destination in which to enjoy highly individual seasonal dishes crafted by a talented kitchen team. Perhaps there will be pan-seared cod with laksa and coconut rice; blade of beef, horseradish croquette and charred chicory; lemon curd and lavender meringue; or white chocolate croissant bread and butter pudding. A summer beer festival is held.

Open 11.30-3 6-11 (Sat 11.30-11 Sun 12-10.30) (Sat 11.30-3 6-11 in winter) Closed Mon **Food** Lunch Tue-Sat 12-2, Sun 12-3.30 Dinner Tue-Sat 6-8.45 Set menu available Restaurant menu available Tue-Sat ⊕ FREE HOUSE ◀ Horncastle, Sharp's Doom Bar, Springhead Outlawed, Oldershaw Heavenly Blonde ⟡ Thatchers Gold, Rekorderlig. ⬤ 10 **Facilities** Non-diners area ⚭ Children's portions Garden ⋒ Beer festival Parking WiFi ⛟ (notice required)

NEW The Griffin Inn

tel: 01476 550201 **Bulby Rd NG33 4JG**
email: chris@thegriffininrham.co.uk
dir: *From A151 between Colsterworth & Bourne follow Irnham signs*

An 18th-century country estate inn

Newly refurbished to an excellent standard, the handsome 18th-century stone-built Griffin Inn makes an ideal refreshment stop if you are touring Lincolnshire's deepest countryside. Speciality teas such as Kandula Pink Ceylon and Ebony Chai are served with shortbread, as is coffee in your preferred format. If visiting at lunchtime, Oakham Ales and two other local brews will be found on tap, which can be soaked up with bar snacks, 'doorstep' sandwiches, or a plate of gammon, egg and chips

perhaps. In the evening, a bolognese burger and bucket of chips could be rounded off with rhubarb crumble and custard.

Open 12-3 6-11 Closed Mon-Tue **Food** Lunch Wed-Sun 12-3 Dinner Wed-Sun 6.30-9 Av main course £8 Restaurant menu available Wed-Sat eve ⊕ FREE HOUSE ◀ Oakham Ales JHB, 2 local guest ales ⟡ Aspall. **Facilities** Non-diners area ⚭ Garden ⋒ Parking WiFi ⛟ (notice required)

Queens Head

tel: 01529 305743 & 307194 **Church Ln NG34 9NU**
email: info@thequeensheadinn.com **web:** www.thequeensheadinn.com
dir: *Follow brown tourist board signs for pub from A17 (dual carriageway)*

Offering ales brewed in a windmill

Heavy beams, open log fires, antique furnishings and original watercolours – this destination dining pub fulfils the brief when it comes to original features and traditional character. The French-trained chef-proprietor prepares everything on site, from breads to desserts, and local ingredients get star billing on the extensive seasonal menus. You could perhaps choose a platter of Lincolnshire stuffed chine and haslet, mixed pickles and home-made chutney; locally shot pigeon and red wine pie; or Thai garlic and coriander salmon fillet with buttered noodles. The good choice of desserts might include sticky toffee and date pudding, butterscotch sauce, toffee ice cream and custard. Wash it down with a glass of wine from a well-considered list or a Lincolnshire ale from the 8 Sail Brewery, brewed in Heckington Windmill.

Open all wk 12-3 6-11 (Sun 12-11) **Food** Lunch Mon-Sat 12-2.30, Sun 12-8.30 Dinner Mon-Fri 6-9.30, Sat 6-10, Sun 12-8.30 Av main course £9.95 Set menu available Restaurant menu available all wk ⊕ FREE HOUSE ◀ Batemans XB, 8 Sail Brewery, Black Sheep, guest ales. ⬤ 9 **Facilities** Non-diners area ⚘ (Bar Outside area) ⚭ Children's menu Children's portions Outside area ⋒ Parking WiFi ⛟ (notice required)

See advert on page 318

KIRTON IN LINDSEY
Map 17 SK99

The George

tel: 01652 640600 **20 High St DN21 4LX**
email: enquiry@thegeorgekirton.co.uk
dir: *From A15 take B1205, turn right onto B1400*

Country inn near Ermine Street

Lincoln and the Wolds are within easy reach of this extensively restored yet traditional pub. The 18th-century former coaching inn serves locally brewed ales and seasonally changing menus. Customers can dine in the comfortable bar area or in the informal restaurant. Favourite starters such as prawn cocktail, and bar meals such as lasagne with salad and hand-cut chips, are topped by regularly changing specials such as chicken schnitzel with a brandy and mushroom sauce; and game and blackcurrant pie. The inn is closed on Sundays (although available for hire).

Open 5-11 Closed Sun **Food** Dinner Mon-Sat 5-9 ⊕ FREE HOUSE ◼ Rotating guest ales. **Facilities** Non-diners area ◗◾ Children's menu Children's portions Play area Garden Outside area WiFi ▭

LINCOLN
Map 17 SK97

The Pyewipe

tel: 01522 528708 **Fossebank, Saxilby Rd LN1 2BG**
email: enquiries@pyewipe.co.uk
dir: *From Lincoln on A57 towards Worksop, pub signed in 0.5m on left*

Waterside inn with home-made food

There's a great view of nearby Lincoln Cathedral from the grounds of this waterside inn, which takes its name from the local dialect for lapwing. Set in four wooded acres beside the Roman-built Fossedyke Navigation, it serves real ales and home-made, locally sourced food. Expect dishes such as partridge and black pudding stack with red wine sauce; pork belly with cider and grain mustard sauce and mash; or loin of cod poached in Thai broth with noodles and stir-fried vegetables. There is a beer garden and riverside patio where you can enjoy your meal, a refreshing ale or a glass of wine.

Open all day all wk 11-11 **Food** all wk 12-9 ⊕ FREE HOUSE ◼ Guest ales. **Facilities** Non-diners area ◗◾ Children's portions Garden ⋈ Parking WiFi ▭

The Victoria

tel: 01522 541000 **6 Union Rd LN1 3BJ**
email: jonathanjpc@aol.com
dir: *From city outskirts follow signs for Cathedral Quarter. Pub 2 mins' walk from all major up-hill car parks. Adjacent to West Gate of Lincoln Castle*

Good real ales in the city

Situated right next to the West Gate entrance of the castle and a short stroll from Lincoln Cathedral, a long-standing drinkers' pub with a range of real ales, including three changing guest beers, ciders and perries. As well as the fantastic views of the castle, the pub also offers home-prepared food including hot baguettes and filled rolls. House specials include sausage and mash, various pies, chilli con carne and home-made lasagne. Facilities include a large beer garden with children's play area.

Open all day all wk 11am-mdnt (Fri-Sat 11am-1am Sun 12-12) **Food** Lunch all wk 12-2.30 Av main course £5.95 ⊕ BATEMANS ◼ Gold & XB, Timothy Taylor Landlord, Castle Rock Harvest Pale, guest ales Ŏ Westons Old Rosie & Country Perry. **Facilities** Non-diners area ❀ (Bar Garden) ◗◾ Children's portions Play area Garden ⋈ WiFi ▭ (notice required)

Wig & Mitre
PICK OF THE PUBS

tel: 01522 535190 **32 Steep Hill LN2 1LU**
dir: *At top of Steep Hill, adjacent to cathedral & Lincoln Castle car parks*

Old-fashioned values and contemporary cuisine

Just yards from the magnificent edifice of Lincoln Cathedral, this two-storey pub has a pedigree nearly as long; parts of it date back over 700 years. It's the ideal place for a quick pick-me-up snack, drink or leisurely meal from breakfast to evening. Notably music-free; instead you'll find a reading room, eclectic decor and furnishings – note the caricatures and prints of clergy and lawyers – and own-brewed beers and those from local breweries slake the thirst. The daily-changing set menu adds modern twists to traditional dishes. Thus roast rump of lamb comes with pine nut and herb couscous and minted yogurt; or slow-cooked pork collar with Lincolnshire sausage bread pudding, creamed white beans and sage may be listed. Daily blackboard specials considerably extend the choice and include vegetarian and gluten-free options. Gourmet evenings (pre-booking essential) are regularly held, while wine-lovers have a choice of 24 by the glass.

Open all day all wk 8.30am-mdnt Closed 25 Dec **Food** all wk 8.30am-10pm Set menu available Restaurant menu available all wk ⊕ FREE HOUSE ◀ Oakham Ales JHB, Black Sheep, pub's own beers Ò Aspall. ▾ 24 **Facilities** Non-diners area ❤ (Bar) ♦♦ Children's menu Children's portions WiFi

LITTLE BYTHAM
Map 11 TF01

The Willoughby Arms

tel: 01780 410276 **Station Rd NG33 4RA**
email: info@willoughbyarms.co.uk
dir: *B6121 (Stamford to Bourne road), at junct follow signs to Careby & Little Bytham, inn 5m on right*

Former railway property now a traditional inn

This beamed, traditional stone country inn started life as the booking office and waiting room for Lord Willoughby's private railway line. These days it has a fresher look whilst retaining its traditional charms. Expect a good selection of real ales – including several from local microbreweries – with great, home-cooked food available every lunchtime and evening. Dishes may include steak and kidney pie, Lincolnshire sausage and mash, or meat or vegetable lasagne. Omelettes, jacket potatoes, and hot and cold baguettes are also on offer. As well as a cosy bar with open fire, and a light and airy sun lounge, there is also a large beer garden with stunning views to enjoy on warmer days. A summer holiday beer festival is held.

Open all day all wk 12-11 **Food** Lunch Mon-Sat 12-2, Sun 12-3 Dinner all wk 6-9 ⊕ FREE HOUSE ◀ Hopshackle Simmarillo, Abbeydale Absolution Ò Aspall, Westons Stowford Press, guest cider. ▾ 10 **Facilities** Non-diners area ❤ (Bar Garden) ♦♦ Children's menu Children's portions Garden ⋒ Beer festival Parking WiFi 🚌 (notice required)

MARKET RASEN
Map 17 TF18

The Advocate Arms ★★★★★ RR ◉◉

tel: 01673 842364 **2 Queen St LN8 3EH**
email: info@advocatearms.co.uk **web:** www.advocatearms.co.uk
dir: *In town centre*

Convenient town-centre location

This 18th-century, three-storey corner property in the town centre has a contemporary veneer. Until 11am there's a wide choice of breakfasts, including kippers and eggs Benedict, then for lunch there are sandwiches (smoked salmon and beetroot mayo), three free-range egg omelettes, salads (chicken, asparagus and croûtons) and light bites (soufflé of the day), or more substantial main meals. These may include smoked lamb carpaccio; baked cod provençal; and blood orange and plum tart.

Open all day all wk **Food** Lunch all wk 12-6 Dinner all wk 6-9.30 Av main course £7.50 Set menu available Restaurant menu available Mon-Sat ⊕ FREE HOUSE ◀ Wells Bombardier, Greene King IPA, Sharp's Doom Bar Ò Aspall, Westons Rosie's Pig. ▾ 12 **Facilities** Non-diners area ♦♦ Children's menu Children's portions Outside area ⋒ Parking WiFi 🚌 (notice required) **Rooms** 10

MINTING
Map 17 TF17

The Sebastopol Inn
PICK OF THE PUBS

tel: 01507 578577 **Church Ln LN9 5RS**
email: thesebastopol@hotmail.co.uk
dir: *From A158 from Lincoln towards Horncastle. After Wragby follow signs for Minting on right*

Cosy old inn with excellent food

First licensed in 1836, the Sebastopol is located in the picturesque village of Minting. Head chef and co-owner Nick Reed has built an excellent reputation for great food that can be enjoyed in a relaxed and comfortable atmosphere. For his modern menus of beautifully presented dishes, Nick sources the highest quality ingredients from the best local producers, and wild foods from the surrounding countryside appear too. Perhaps choose a starter of pig's head fritter, apple, mustard and chive blossom; or cured line-caught mackerel, beetroot, horseradish, dulse and miso gel. Then turn your attention to Minting Park Farm brisket, smoked barley risotto, fermented mushroom, pickled spring onion and chive oil; wood pigeon (may contain shot!) poached in pine butter, Jerusalem artichoke three ways, rowan and apple jelly, pine oil; or grilled halibut, lemon skin purée, hash brown, crisp air-dried pork belly, smoked halibut emulsion, fermented mushroom and broccoli. Desserts are no less tempting so save room for set yogurt, fennel, liquorice poached pear and ginger crumb; or the simply described 'lemon, meringue, thyme'.

Open Wed-Sat 12-2.30 6-11 (Sun 12-4) Closed 2-3wks from 1 Jan, Mon-Tue **Food** Lunch Wed-Sun 12-1.45 Dinner Wed-Sat 6-10 Av main course £15 ⊕ FREE HOUSE ◀ Batemans, Tom Wood's, Springhead, Horncastle, Oldershaw, Milestone Ò Skidbrooke. **Facilities** Non-diners area ❤ (Bar Garden) ♦♦ Children's menu Garden ⋒ Parking

PARTNEY
Map 17 TF46

Red Lion Inn

tel: 01790 752271 **PE23 4PG**
email: enquiries@redlioninnpartney.co.uk
dir: *On A16 from Boston, or A158 from Horncastle*

Sound reputation for good, home-cooked food

Here is a welcoming village inn especially to walkers and cyclists due to its location, just below the Lincolnshire Wolds; many inevitably more than ready for pint of Black Sheep, or a glass of chilled wine. The pub's solid reputation for home-cooked food can be attributed to dishes such as their 16oz Grimsby haddock, chips, garden or mushy peas; shortcrust pie of the day; and BBQ rack of pork ribs. A formidable selection of desserts includes puddings, sponges, sundaes and tarts.

Open 12-2 6-11 (Sun 12-2 6-10.30) Closed Mon **Food** Lunch Tue-Sun 12-2 Dinner Tue-Sun 6-9 Av main course £10 ⊕ FREE HOUSE ◀ Black Sheep, Tetley's, Guinness, guest ales. **Facilities** Non-diners area ♦♦ Children's menu Children's portions Outside area ⋒ Parking WiFi 🚌 (notice required)

RAITHBY

Map 17 TF36

Red Lion Inn

tel: 01790 753727 **PE23 4DS**
dir: *A158 from Horncastle, through Hagworthingham, right at top of hill signed Raithby*

Quiet village setting, cosy in winter, garden in summer

This traditional beamed village pub, parts of which date back 300 years, is situated on the edge of the Lincolnshire Wolds, a great place for walking and cycling. Inside is a wealth of character with log fires providing a warm welcome in winter. Dine in one of the four bars or in the comfort of the restaurant. A varied menu of home-made dishes is prepared using fresh local produce — sea bass with stir-fried vegetables; roast guinea fowl with tomato, garlic and bacon; and medallions of beef with peppercorn sauce. Meals can be enjoyed in the garden in the warmer months.

Open 12-2 6-11 (Mon 7-11) Closed Mon L **Food** Lunch Tue-Sun 12-2 Dinner Tue-Sat 7-8.30 ⊕ FREE HOUSE ◀ Thwaites, Batemans ○ Thatchers Gold.
Facilities Non-diners area ◆◆ Children's menu Children's portions Outside area ╦ Parking ▩ (notice required)

SCAMPTON

Map 17 SK97

NEW Dambusters Inn

tel: 01522 531333 **23 High St LN1 2SD**
email: info@dambustersinn.co.uk
dir: *4m N of Lincoln on B1398*

TV-free hostelry with historic links

Packed with artefacts, the pub hails the achievements of RAF Bomber Command's 617 Squadron, *The Dambusters*, in 1943. In 1999, when this 200-year-old farmhouse became a pub, three survivors of that mission pulled the first pints. It's home to landlord Greg's microbrewery, whose real ales are among the six on offer. Grimsby haddock appears on the menu, as do steak and ale casserole; grilled fresh tuna; and leek and cheese crumble. Greg advises visitors not to miss the artwork in the lavatories. RAF Scampton, home of the Red Arrows, is next door, and their training flights may occasionally rattle the glasses.

Open all day 12-11 (Tue 12-10.30 Fri-Sat 12-12 Sun 12-7.30) Closed Mon **Food** Lunch Tue Sat 12-2.30, Sun 12-3.30 Dinner Tue-Thu 6-8.30, Fri-Sat 5.30-8.30 Restaurant menu available Tue-Sun ⊕ FREE HOUSE ◀ Brewster's Hophead, Marston's Lancaster Bomber, Thornbridge Jaipur, Greg's ○ Black Rat Perry, Abrahalls Slack Alice & Lily the Pink. ♥ 9 **Facilities** Non-diners area ☻ (Bar Restaurant Outside area) ◆◆ Children's portions Outside area ╦ Beer festival Parking WiFi ▩ (notice required)

SOUTH FERRIBY

Map 17 SE92

NEW Hope and Anchor

tel: 01652 635334 **Sluice Rd DN18 6JQ**
email: info@thehopeandanchorpub.co.uk **web:** www.thehopeandanchorpub.co.uk
dir: *From A15 onto A1077 signed South Ferriby. In South Ferriby follow Winterton sign. Pub on right before River Ancholme*

Estuaryside location with extravagant views

Tucked amidst creeks and moorings where the River Ancholme meets the Humber Estuary; panoramic views from the patio and restaurant encompass the waterways and nearby Humber Bridge. An appealingly, updated 19th-century inn, with much exposed brickwork and a log-burning stove, this is a popular stop for birdwatchers and dog-walkers. Lincolnshire-brewed beers hit the spot and a happy mix of seasonal cuisine and traditional pub grub celebrates local produce, including from the pub's own acreage; Lincolnshire pheasant with creamed sprouts and polenta may feature. Charcoal-grilled steaks are the speciality of the house; the belted Galloway meat is matured in an ageing-cabinet on-site.

Open all day Closed 28-30 Dec, 1-8 Jan, Mon **Food** Lunch Tue-Thu 12-3, Fri-Sat 12-10, Sun 12-6 Dinner Tue-Thu 5-9, Fri-Sat 12-10, Sun 12-6 Av main course £12 ⊕ FREE HOUSE ◀ Theakston, Tom Wood's ○ Symonds. ♥ 10
Facilities Non-diners area ☻ (Bar Outside area) ◆◆ Children's menu Children's portions Outside area ╦ Parking ▩

See advert on opposiite page

The Hope and Anchor Pub,
Sluice Road, South Ferriby,
North Lincolnshire, DN18 6JQ
T: 01652 635334
E: info@thehopeandanchorpub.co.uk
W: www.thehopeandanchorpub.co.uk

Informal hospitality at its best. The beautiful 19th century pub, run by Slawek Mlkolajczyk, is nestled at the heart of the South Ferriby community. The Hope & Anchor offers a traditional yet unique approach to food and drinks. It offers a combination of traditional seasonal cuisine and historic dishes. Priding itself on using locally sourced ingredients, including vegetables grown from its own field; it does not compromise on quality.

Offering panoramic, picturesque views of the Humber in the restaurant, guests at the Hope & Anchor can enjoy exceptional pub food whilst watching the local wildlife or staring into the stunning sunset. The bar area has cosy armchairs and a beautiful fire to keep you warm through the winter months. Summer sees the extensive beer garden filled with people enjoying a perfectly pulled pint in the refreshing breeze coming from the Humber.

The Hope & Anchor only uses exceptional quality produce and really pride themselves on the high quality of their steaks. Sourced from the Lake District, the Hope & Anchor have decided that the Belted Galloway is their cattle of choice due to their superior quality. The steaks are stored in the state of the art MaturMeat cabinet and cooked on a charcoal Josper giving the meat a superbly smoky flavour. They welcome a broad range of guests who appreciate the simple, yet satisfying things in life, whether it be a "cheeky" pint after a dog walk, sailing in via the Humber, or just to enjoy great wine and great food.

The Bustard Inn & Restaurant ® PICK OF THE PUBS

tel: 01529 488250 **44 Main St NG34 8QG**

email: info@thebustardinn.co.uk

dir: *A15 from Lincoln. Right onto B1429 for Cranwell, 1st left after village, straight across A17 to South Rauceby*

Grade II listed pub with award-winning cooking

Situated above Lincoln Edge, at the heart of a pretty stone-built estate village, this imposing building dates from 1860. The pub's name is based on the legend that the last indigenous great bustard was shot nearby in 1845 by the local lord of the manor. In the beer garden and courtyard, sample a pint of Batemans XB or Timothy Taylor Landlord. The light and airy interior is divided between the bar and an elegant restaurant, with dressed stone walls, beamed ceiling and tapestry chairs; an ornate oriel window looks out on to the lovely garden. Head chef Phil Lowe's AA-Rosette cooking draws on local produce where possible. There's a snacking and sharing menu, or look to the full carte for the likes of smoked salmon with pickled cucumber followed by pan-fried chicken with Stilton dumpling. The words 'sticky toffee'and 'bread and butter pudding' are easily spotted in the list of favourite desserts.

Open 12-3 5.30-11 (Sat 12-11 Sun 12-3.30) Closed 1 Jan, Sun eve, Mon **Food** Lunch Tue-Sat 12-2.30, Sun 12-3 Dinner Tue-Sat 6-9.30 Set menu available ⊕ FREE HOUSE ◀ Batemans XB, Timothy Taylor Landlord, Guinness, guest ale ♂ Aspall. ♟ 15 **Facilities** Non-diners area ♦♦ Children's menu Children's portions Garden ⅋ Parking WiFi ➡ (notice required)

Blue Cow Inn & Brewery

tel: 01572 768432 **High St NG33 5QB**

email: enquiries@bluecowinn.co.uk

dir: *Between Stamford & Grantham on A1*

Own-brewed real ale and pub classics

Licensee Simon Crathorn has been brewing the award-winning Blue Cow Best Bitter at the small brewery here for more than 10 years – ask for a free viewing, subject to availability. The pub was renamed 'blue' by erstwhile owner the Duke of Buckminster nearly 400 years ago, on account of his political allegiance to his king. Low beams, flagstone floors and dressed-stone walls characterise the ancient interior, with crackling log fires to take the edge off the fenland breezes; any remaining chill may be generated by the pub's ghosts – a lady and a dog. Snacks, salads and sandwiches are offered, as well as mains like gammon steak, sausages and scampi.

Open all day all wk 11-11 **Food** Lunch all wk 12-2.30 Dinner all wk 6-9.30 ⊕ FREE HOUSE ◀ Blue Cow Best Bitter, Sharp's Doom Bar, Castle Rock Vulcan Bomber. ♟ 10 **Facilities** Non-diners area ♣ (All areas) ♦♦ Children's menu Children's portions Family room Garden Outside area ⅋ Parking WiFi ➡ (notice required)

The Bull & Swan at Burghley ★★★★ INN ®

tel: 01780 766412 **High St, St Martin's PE9 2LJ**

email: enquiries@thebullandswan.co.uk **web:** www.thebullandswan.co.uk

dir: *A1 onto B1081 (Carpenters Lodge junct). Signed Stamford & Burghley. 1m, pub on right*

Memorable meals in a magnificent market town setting

Commanding a prime position on one of historic Stamford's most stunning streets, this gabled coaching inn is recognised by the AA for both its top-notch

accommodation and its very good food. Tucked behind the mellow stone façade is a comfy, traditional destination which appeals to all-comers, where dining is to the fore but beer lovers aren't short-changed. Local brewers The Grainstore is one reliable supplier to the bar, whilst produce from this corner of Lincolnshire plump out the enticing menu. Opt for a starter such as crispy whitebait in Bloody Mary sauce; or seared scallops with black pudding and pink apple, then move on to wild mushroom, chestnut and broad bean lasagne with truffle greens and wild rocket; or Norfolk Black turkey with all the trimmings.

Open all day all wk **Food** Lunch Mon-Fri 12-2.30, Sat 12-10, Sun 12-9 Dinner Mon-Thu 6-9.30, Fri 6-10, Sat 12-10, Sun 12-9 Av main course £12.95 ⊕ FREE HOUSE ◀ Nene Valley Blond Session BSA, Adnams Southwold Bitter, The Grainstore Triple B, Sharp's Doom Bar ♂ Westons Stowford Press. **Facilities** Non-diners area ♣ (Bar Outside area) ♦♦ Children's menu Children's portions Outside area ⅋ Parking WiFi **Rooms** 9

The George of Stamford ★★★★ HL ® PICK OF THE PUBS

tel: 01780 750750 **71 St Martins PE9 2LB**

email: reservations@georgehotelofstamford.com **web:** www.georgehotelofstamford.com

dir: *From Peterborough take A1 N. Onto B1081 for Stamford, down hill to lights. Hotel on left*

Magnificent period inn located in heritage town

One of England's most renowned old coaching inns, it shares a stunning streetscape of imposing silver-limestone houses and villas tumbling down to the River Welland. Many period films and TV programmes have been filmed here. The George, with its extraordinary gallows sign (erected as a welcome to some and a warning to others), was built in 1597 to extend an earlier inn, elements of which survive in the crypt and walled garden. In the York Bar northbound coach passengers waited while horses were changed; the London Room fulfilled the same purpose for those heading south. The York Bar menu offers sandwiches, ploughman's, toasties and light dishes such as minestrone soup; and smoked Scottish salmon with capers. In the slightly more formal Garden Room expect the likes of 'a taste of Asian chicken' (Thai green curry, deep-fried tempura, peanut satay and aromatic basmati rice); steak and kidney pudding; beetroot risotto; or push the boat out and opt for the Grand Brittany platter comprising half lobster, crab, oyster, king prawn, mussels, clams, shell-on prawns and whelks. Local beers from The Grainstore and a considerable choice of 24 wines by the glass may accompany.

Open all day all wk 11-11 (Sun 12-11) **Food** Lunch all wk 12-2.30 Set menu available Restaurant menu available all wk ⊕ FREE HOUSE ◀ Adnams Broadside, The Grainstore, Bass, guest ales ♂ Aspall. ♟ 24 **Facilities** Non-diners area ♦♦ Children's portions Garden Outside area ⅋ Parking WiFi **Rooms** 45

The Tobie Norris   PICK OF THE PUBS

tel: 01780 753800 **12 Saint Pauls St PE9 2BE**
email: tobie@kneadpubs.co.uk
dir: *From A1 to Stamford on A6121, becomes West St, then East St. After right bend right into Saint Pauls St*

Lively pub with new owners

Named after Tobias Norris, who bought it in 1617 for use as a bell foundry, this splendidly restored and renovated medieval hall house dates back to 1280. Adnams Southwold Bitter and Castle Rock Harvest Pale are permanent fixtures in the wood-floored bar, while guest ales are rotated regularly. Having started maybe with a plate of pigs in blankets with mustard mayonnaise, your main course, from the rather imaginative menu, could be venison Wellington; lime and chilli beef salad; roasted cauliflower, red lentil and coconut curry with rice and honey flatbread; or roasted chicken and leek pie. Stone-baked pizzas are cooked in ovens imported from Italy, their toppings ranging from spicy beef brisket to duck. Puddings include passionfruit cheesecake and spiced apple crumble. A large enclosed patio is ideal on warmer days. Note that, lunchtimes apart, there's a strict over 18s-only policy.

Open all day all wk **Food** Lunch all wk 12-2.30 Dinner all wk 6-9 ⊕ FREE HOUSE ◖ Adnams Southwold Bitter, Castle Rock Harvest Pale, guest ales ☉ Guest cider. ♟ 18 **Facilities** Non-diners area ☘ (Bar Garden) ♦♦ Garden ⋈ WiFi

SUSWORTH   Map 17 SE80

The Jenny Wren Inn

tel: 01724 784000 **East Ferry Rd DN17 3AS**
email: info@jennywreninn.co.uk
dir: *Phone for detailed directions*

Good food by the River Trent

With an upstairs function room overlooking the River Trent, this beamed and wood-panelled former farmhouse has buckets of character. No better place then for the sampling of special cocktails and nibbles served every evening; ale lovers can stick to the likes of Morland Old Speckled Hen. The pub gains much praise for its food, especially for dishes involving line-caught fresh fish. Otherwise the kitchen team create both traditional pub favourites, to be enjoyed in the ground-floor lounge with open fire. Salads; steak and ale pie; fish pie; and ratatouille and cheese pie all make an appearance on the menu.

Open all wk 12-2 5.45-10.30 (Sat-Sun 12-10.30) ⊕ FREE HOUSE ◖ Morland Old Speckled Hen, Sharp's Doom Bar. **Facilities** ☘ (Bar Garden) ♦♦ Children's menu Children's portions Family room Garden Parking WiFi

TEALBY   Map 17 TF19

The Kings Head

tel: 01673 838347 **11 Kingsway LN8 3YA**
email: sol.newunion@googlemail.com
dir: *At lights in Market Rasen take B1203 (Jameson Bridge St) to Tealby*

The oldest thatched pub in Lincolnshire

Dating from around 1367, The Kings Head stands in an ample garden in a pretty village where former resident and songwriter Bernie Taupin was apparently inspired by the colour of the Lincolnshire stone to pen *Goodbye Yellow Brick Road* for his mate, Elton John. Dogs are welcome in the bar, where the line-up includes real ales from Marston's, Ringwood, Jennings and Wychwood plus ciders. Sausage and mash; and brie, cherry tomato, cranberry and broccoli bake appear on the bar menu, while

in the converted barn restaurant the mains listing includes slow-cooked lamb shank; pancetta wrapped chicken breast; and vegetable bake.

Open all day all wk **Food** Tue-Sat 12-9, Sun-Mon 12-7 Set menu available Restaurant menu available all wk ⊕ MARSTON'S ◖ Pedigree, Ringwood Boondoggle, Jennings Cumberland, Wychwood Hobgoblin ☉ Thatchers Gold, Rekorderlig. ♟ 9 **Facilities** Non-diners area ☘ (Bar Garden) ♦♦ Children's portions Garden ⋈ Parking WiFi ⛺

THEDDLETHORPE ALL SAINTS   Map 17 TF48

Kings Head Inn

tel: 01507 339798 **Mill Rd LN12 1PB**
email: lordandladyhutton@hotmail.co.uk
dir: *From A1031 between Mablethorpe & Theddlethorpe, turn left into Mill Rd. Pub on right*

Ultra-low ceilings and old world charm

Two miles from the beach and close to a nature reserve, this thatched 16th-century inn is a sight for sore eyes. Inside are charming bars with traditional furnishings and very low ceilings. All food is locally sourced and vegetables are home grown. Fish is a speciality in the summer; game in the winter. Dishes range from spicy crab cakes; or Lincolnshire venison salad for starters, to hunters' pie; steaks; lamb Henry; and three little piggies (belly pork, sausage and cider-marinated chop) for mains.

Open 12-3 6-11 (Sat 12-11 Sun 12-10.20 summer; Sun 12-5 winter) Closed Mon & Tue (winter) **Food** Lunch Sun-Fri 12-2.30, Sat all day Dinner Sun-Fri 6-9, Sat all day Av main course £9.95 Restaurant menu available Wed-Sat ⊕ FREE HOUSE ◖ Batemans XB ☉ Thatchers Gold, Skidbrooke. **Facilities** Non-diners area ☘ (Bar Garden) ♦♦ Children's menu Children's portions Family room Garden ⋈ Beer festival Parking WiFi ⛺ (notice required)

WEST DEEPING   Map 12 TF10

NEW The Red Lion

tel: 01778 347190 **48 King St PE6 9HP**
email: theredlionwestdeeping@live.co.uk
dir: *Between Stamford & Market Deeping on A1175 follow West Deeping & pub signs*

Good food and spooky sightings in this vibrant village inn

Only 10 minutes from Peterborough, this 16th-century stone-built former cow barn is set in the heart of West Deeping, a picturesque Lincolnshire village. An open fire, exposed brickwork and beams add to the character of the pub, as does the friendly ghost of an old man reputed to have once lived there. As well as pub classics of fish and chips or burgers, the menu offers sharing boards and main courses such as dandelion and burdock braised ham, chips, peas and eggs; or salsa verde pasta with fresh tomatoes, peppers, red onions and mushrooms.

Open 12-3 6-12 (Sun 12-4) Closed Sun eve, Mon **Food** Lunch Tue-Sat 12-2, Sun 12-4 Dinner Tue-Sat 6-9 Av main course £10 Set menu available ⊕ FREE HOUSE ◖ Fuller's London Pride, 2 rotating local guest ales. **Facilities** Non-diners area ♦♦ Children's menu Children's portions Play area Garden ⋈ Parking WiFi ⛺ (notice required)

WOODHALL SPA — Map 17 TF16

Village Limits Country Pub, Restaurant & Motel

tel: 01526 353312 **Stixwould Rd LN10 6UJ**
email: info@villagelimits.co.uk
dir: *At rdbt on main street in Woodhall Spa follow Petwood Hotel signs. Pub 500yds past Petwood Hotel*

Tranquil location beside country park

Handily placed for the southern hills of the Lincolnshire Wolds, and 80 years of aircraft heritage at nearby RAF Coningsby, this friendly pub is on the outskirts of the Edwardian spa town. It's a little country inn that excels at offering beers from Tom Wood's and Dixon's and meals which champion the best of locally sourced ingredients. Creamy garlic and Stilton sautéed mushrooms set the scene for beer-battered Grimsby haddock; chicken supreme, roast tomatoes, thyme, goats' cheese and toasted pine nuts; and a selection of steaks with cherry vine tomatoes and battered onion rings. Keep an eye on the specials board for the latest dishes.

Open 11.30-3 6.30-11 Closed 26 Dec-2 Jan, Mon L **Food** Lunch Tue-Sun 11.30-2 Dinner all wk 6.30-9 Av main course £10 ⊕ FREE HOUSE ◀ Batemans XB, Tom Wood's Best Bitter, Dixon's Major Bitter ♂ Thatchers. ♀ 8 **Facilities** Non-diners area ♦ Children's menu Children's portions Garden ⏢ Parking WiFi

WOOLSTHORPE — Map 11 SK83

The Chequers Inn ★★★★ INN ⚜ PICK OF THE PUBS

tel: 01476 870701 **Main St NG32 1LU**
email: justinnabar@yahoo.co.uk **web:** www.chequersinn.net
dir: *Approx 7m from Grantham. 3m from A607, follow heritage signs for Belvoir Castle*

Country dining pub in charming surroundings

Leicestershire, Lincolnshire and Nottinghamshire all meet not far from this 17th-century coaching inn overlooking the village cricket pitch. From here you can see Belvoir Castle, a mile or so away. Five real fires warm the interior, and a well-stocked bar does a good line in real ales. Dine in the Snug & Bar, the contemporary Dining Room or the Bakehouse Restaurant, which still features the oven from village bakery days. On the menu may be grilled mackerel fillet, aubergine purée, cucumber, olive and celery salsa; and pan-fried duck breast, beetroot and spring onion mash, confit orange and braised chicory. Representing the pub classics category are home-made pies; beer-battered fish; and sausages, mash and onion gravy. Typical puddings are apple and berry crumble with custard, and lemon meringue pie with raspberry sorbet.

Open all day all wk **Food** Lunch Mon-Sat 12-2.30, Sun 12-4 Dinner Mon-Sat 6-9.30, Sun 6-8.30 Av main course £10.95 ⊕ FREE HOUSE ◀ Rotating guest ales ♂ Guest cider. ♀ 30 **Facilities** Non-diners area ♦ (Bar Garden) ♦ Children's menu Children's portions Garden ⏢ Parking WiFi ⛟ (notice required) **Rooms** 4

Find out more about the AA's awards for food excellence on page 9

LONDON

E1

NEW The Culpeper PLAN 1 G4 PICK OF THE PUBS

tel: 020 7247 5371 **40 Commercial St E1 6LP**
email: bookings@theculpeper.com
dir: *Nearest tube stations: Aldgate East & Liverpool Street*

Classic pub with a rooftop garden in cosmopolitan East End

Many of London's Victorian street-corner pubs have a unique architectural style – this is one of them. It's named after 17th-century Spitalfields herbalist, physician and astrologer Nicholas Culpeper. The pub's huge windows help to illuminate original features in the large open interior, and from the bar a curving staircase leads up to a more formal first-floor eating area and kitchen, which makes good use of herbs and vegetables grown in a rooftop greenhouse. The short, daily-changing menu typically offers burrata, orange, braised Treviso lettuce and pine nuts as a starter; then lamb sirloin, dauphinoise potatoes, parsnip, anchovy and mint salad; and poached rhubarb, frangipane and pistachio ice cream. Real East End beer Truman's Runner might well be among those on hand pump, and 10 wines are by the glass. A bar and dining room on the roof are bookable during the summer for private functions.

Open all day all wk Closed 24-30 Dec **Food** Lunch Mon-Fri 12-3, Sat 11-3, Sun 12-6 Dinner Mon-Sat 6-10.30, Sun 12-6 Av main course £12 Restaurant menu available Tue-Sat ⊕ ENTERPRISE INNS ◀ Purity Mad Goose, Truman's Runner. ♀ 10 **Facilities** Non-diners area ♣ (Bar Garden) ♦ Garden ⏢ WiFi

Town of Ramsgate PLAN 2 G3

tel: 020 7481 8000 **62 Wapping High St E1W 2PN**
email: peter@townoframsgate.co.uk
dir: *Nearest tube: Wapping*

River Thames gem full of history

Wood panelling, snob screens, leaded windows and a secluded terrace with views across the river; the oldest Thames-side pub makes the most of its heritage and setting. Tucked away amidst converted warehouses, the name recalls the days when fishermen from Ramsgate landed their fresh catches on nearby steps before heading off to market. Its robust past includes use by press-gangs and a visit by the ill-fated Captain Bligh on his way to view HMS *Bounty*. Today's guests are ensured a far more positive outcome, with traditional pub meals including a hand-made cheese and bacon burger; a sharing sausage platter with chips, Yorkshire pudding and gravy; chicken and leek pie; and lasagne.

Open all day all wk 12-12 (Sun 12-11) **Food** Lunch all wk 12-4 Dinner Sun-Thu 5-9, Fri-Sat 5-10 ⊕ FREE HOUSE ◀ Fuller's London Pride, Sharp's Doom Bar, Young's ♂ Cornish Orchards Gold Cider. ♀ 13 **Facilities** Non-diners area ♣ (Bar Garden) ♦ Garden ⏢ WiFi ⛟ (notice required)

E9

The Empress ⚜⚜ PLAN 2 G4 PICK OF THE PUBS

tel: 020 8533 5123 **130 Lauriston Rd, Victoria Park E9 7LH**
email: info@empresse9.co.uk
dir: *From Mile End Station turn right into Grove Rd, leads into Lauriston Rd*

Café, bar and restaurant pleasing a Bohemian clientele

A classic mid-Victorian East End corner pub, with Gothic revival windows at first-floor level and lofty ceilings. A long bar serves ale and cider from that venerable East End brewer, Truman's. Neighbourhood suppliers are important to The Empress, with meats and fish from Victoria Park suppliers Ginger Pig and Jonathan Norris respectively, and coffee from Climpson & Sons. Head chef Elliott Lidstone's great value bar snacks include whitebait and spicy aïoli; puffed pork skin and fennel salt; and cecina. Among the thoughtful mains are dishes such as smoked eel, blood orange, radicchio and hazelnuts; hake with black lentils, cauliflower purée and smoked almonds; or braised goat, harissa, sumac and yogurt. The short list of sweet things may include vanilla pannacotta, rhubarb and almonds. There are roasts on Sundays, a popular weekend brunch menu and a meal deal on Monday evenings.

Open all day all wk Closed 25-26 Dec **Food** Lunch all wk 12-3.30 Dinner all wk 6-10.15 ⊕ FREE HOUSE ◀ East London Foundation Bitter, Truman's Runner ♂ Aspall, Truman's Côte Breton Brut. ♀ 16 **Facilities** Non-diners area ♣ (Bar Outside area) ♦ Children's menu Children's portions Outside area ⌂ WiFi ▭

E14

The Grapes   PLAN 2 G3

tel: 020 7987 4396 **76 Narrow St, Limehouse E14 8BP**
email: info@thegrapes.co.uk
dir: *Phone for detailed directions*

Dickensian pub on the Thames

In *Our Mutual Friend*, Charles Dickens immortalised this old Thames-side pub as the Six Jolly Fellowship Porters. While he might recognise the wood-panelled, Victorian long bar and The Dickens Snug, where as a child he reputedly danced on a table, much of surrounding Limehouse has changed beyond recognition. Sir Ian McKellan is a joint leaseholder of The Grapes which is in an area with many literary and artistic connections. Served in the tiny upstairs dining room are dishes such as devilled whitebait; smoked salmon and haddock fishcakes; fresh pan-fried swordfish, marinated in lemon and olive oil; grilled chicken burger; and the Sir Ian meaty shepherd's pie. Salads, and sandwiches are always available, and there are Sunday roasts. Sorry, no one under 18 years is permitted.

Open all day all wk Closed 25-26 Dec, 1 Jan **Food** Lunch Mon-Fri 12-2.30, Sat 12-9.30, Sun 12-3.30 Dinner Mon-Fri 6.30-9.30, Sat 12-9.30 Restaurant menu available Mon-Sat ⊕ GREENE KING ◀ Timothy Taylor Landlord, Adnams Southwold Bitter, Black Sheep, guest ales ♂ Aspall. **Facilities** Non-diners area ♣ (Bar Outside area) Outside area ⌂

The Gun ◉   PLAN 2 G3   PICK OF THE PUBS

tel: 020 7515 5222 **27 Coldharbour, Docklands E14 9NS**
email: info@thegundocklands.com
dir: *From West Ferry Rd into Marsh Wall to mini rdbl. Turn left, over bridge, 1st right into Coldharbour. Nearest tube stations: Canary Wharf, South Quay & Blackwall*

A surviving riverside gem

Contrasting skylines are revealed from this historic Thames-side pub; adjoining is a terrace of dockers' cottages that overlook the nearby lock, backed by frozen-in-time crane jibs. Dwarfing these are the skyscrapers of Canary Wharf, whilst across the river is the distinctive domed shape of the O2 Arena. Lord Nelson and Lady Hamilton secretly met at The Gun, and the pub still retains a restrained naval and shipping heritage that adds character to the range of panelled dining rooms and snugs. Diners drawn to the AA-Rosette menu can anticipate tempting dishes prepared by a highly capable kitchen team. From a choice of menus come first courses like venison, rabbit and pistachio terrine; and confit wild boar collar. Mains choices may include slow-braised Dexter beef cheek; Herdwick lamb rump with smoked bacon, kidney and lentil stew, or 45-day aged rare breed steaks. The chefs look to nearby Billingsgate Market for the best fish and seafood. Guest beers, several beer festivals and a great wine list complement the award-winning menus.

Open all wk 11am-mdnt (Sun 11-11) Closed 25-26 Dec **Food** Lunch Mon-Sat 12-3, Sun 12-9.30 Dinner Mon-Sat 6-10.30, Sun 12-9.30 ⊕ ETM GROUP ◀ Jugged Hare Pale Ale, guest ales ♂ Symonds. ♀ 22 **Facilities** Non-diners area ♦ Children's portions Outside area ⌂ Beer festival WiFi ▭ (notice required)

EC1

The Bleeding Heart Tavern ◉◉   PLAN 1 E4
PICK OF THE PUBS

tel: 020 7242 8238 **19 Greville St EC1N 8SQ**
email: bookings@bleedingheart.co.uk
dir: *Close to Farringdon tube station, at corner of Greville St & Bleeding Heart Yard*

City pub with award-winning bistro food

Dating from 1746 when drunkenness and debauchery were rife in the area, this historic tavern once offered a straw-lined back room where inebriated customers could sleep things off until the morning after the night before. Nowadays, early morning visitors can enjoy full English breakfasts, with croissants and baguettes from its own bakery. Drinks-wise, holding court are traditional ales from Adnams, Aspall cider and an impressive wine list with 450 choices from around the globe. Downstairs in the wood-panelled restaurant you'll find dishes such as rabbit and ham hock terrine, apple and raisin chutney and honey mustard dressing; crispy-fried Cornish squid, red chilli, coriander and lime; fillet of hake with tenderstem broccoli, fennel and brown shrimps; and slow-cooked Suffolk lamb shank, spinach, tomato and rosemary jus. Desserts include treacle tart with whisky Jersey cream; or passionfruit cheesecake.

Open all day 7am-11pm Closed BHs, 10 days at Xmas, Sat-Sun **Food** Mon-Fri 11.30-10.30 Set menu available Restaurant menu available Mon-Fri ⊕ FREE HOUSE ◀ Adnams Southwold Bitter, Broadside, Fisherman, May Day ♂ Aspall. ♀ 17 **Facilities** Non-diners area WiFi

The Eagle   PLAN 1 E5

tel: 020 7837 1353 **159 Farringdon Rd EC1R 3AL**
dir: *Nearest tube: Angel or Farringdon. Pub at north end of Farringdon Rd*

One of trendy Clerkenwell's best

A trailblazer in the early 1990s and paving the way for what we now except as stylish gastro-pubs, The Eagle is still going strong. The lofty interior includes a wooden-floored bar and dining area, a mishmash of vintage furniture, and an open-to-view kitchen that produces a creatively modern, twice-daily changing blackboard menu and tapas selection which revel in bold, rustic flavours. Typical of the range are courgette and potato soup; grilled Merguez sausages, pomegranate couscous and tzatziki; smoked haddock chowder and pancetta; grilled tuna, oven potatoes and aïoli.

Open all day 12-11 (Sun 12-5) Closed BHs L (1wk Xmas), Sun eve **Food** Lunch Mon-Fri 12-3, Sat 12-3.30, Sun 12.30-4 Dinner Mon-Sat 6.30-10.30 Av main course £12 ⊕ FREE HOUSE ◀ Wells Eagle IPA & Bombardier, Hackney Ales ♂ Westons, Addlestones. ♀ 15 **Facilities** Non-diners area ♣ (Bar) ♦ Children's portions

The Jerusalem Tavern   PLAN 1 E4

tel: 020 7490 4281 **55 Britton St, Clerkenwell EC1M 5UQ**
email: thejerusalemtavern@hotmail.com
dir: *100mtrs NE of Farringdon tube station; 300mtrs N of Smithfield*

Historic inn with St Peter's Brewery cask and bottled beers

Owned by Suffolk's St Peter's Brewery, this tavern has close links to Samuel Johnson, Oliver Goldsmith, David Garrick and the young Handel, who used to drink here on his visits to London. The current premises date from 1720 although the shop frontage dates from about 1810, when it was a workshop for Clerkenwell's various watch and clock craftsmen. Its dimly lit Dickensian bar, with bare boards, rustic wooden tables, old tiles, candles, open fires and cosy corners, is the perfect film set – which is what it has been on many occasions. A classic pub in every sense, it offers the full range of cask and bottled beers from St Peter's Brewery, as well as a range of simple pub fare.

Open all day 11-11 Closed 25 Dec-1 Jan, Sat-Sun ⊕ ST PETER'S BREWERY ◀ St Peter's (full range) ♂ New Forest Traditional, Oliver's, Once Upon a Tree Tumpy Ground. **Facilities** ♣ (Bar) Outside area WiFi

EC1 *continued*

The Peasant   PLAN 1 E5   PICK OF THE PUBS

tel: 020 7336 7726 **240 Saint John St EC1V 4PH**
email: eat@thepeasant.co.uk
dir: *Nearest tube: Farringdon. Pub on corner of Saint John St & Percival St*

Victorian pub with reputation for good food

One of the first gastro-pubs, this dining institution stands opposite tree-shaded gardens in the heart of Clerkenwell. With imposing brickwork and a balustrade outside, the eye-catching interior emphasises the Victorian grandeur of the pub with its decorative tiling, plasterwork ceiling, mosaic floor and great horseshoe mahogany bar. The first-floor restaurant continues the theme, with bold chandeliers and a quirky collection of arty circus memorabilia. Beer hounds will not be disappointed by the selection of real ales, including beers from Crouch Vale brewery, whilst Bounders cider quenches a sharper thirst. The good value bar menu indulges most tastes, kicking in with starters typified by squid tempura and chilli aïoli; pheasant burger; and Denham Estate sausages, mash and caramelised onion gravy. The restaurant has a set menu (2 or 3 courses) of modern European-inspired dishes — coq au vin, pancetta, mash and mixed greens catches the eye.

Open all day all wk Closed 24 Dec-2 Jan, BHs **Food** all wk 12-11 Restaurant menu available ⊕ FREE HOUSE ◧ Crouch Vale Brewers Gold, Bath Ales Gem, guest ales ☼ Bath Ciders Bounders, Westons Wyld Wood Organic, Original Sin. ♟ 15 **Facilities** Non-diners area ◀♦ Children's portions Garden ➡ (notice required)

Ye Olde Mitre   PLAN 1 E4

tel: 020 7405 4751 **1 Ely Court, Ely Place EC1N 6SJ**
email: yeoldemitre@fullers.co.uk
dir: *From Chancery Lane tube station exit 3 to Holborn Circus, left into Hatton Garden. Pub in alley between 8 & 9 Hatton Garden*

Historic, hidden away pub

Built in 1546, extended in 1781, in the shadow of the palace of the Bishops of Ely, this quirky historic corner pub is in Ely Court, off Hatton Garden. It is often used as a film location. Choose from at least six ales in the magnificent wood-panelled rooms, with a range of bar snacks or 'English tapas' that includes toasted sandwiches, pork pies, Scotch eggs, sausage rolls and picked eggs. Please note that this pub, without music and bar TVs, is closed at weekends and Bank Holidays. Beer festivals are held in May, August and December.

Open all day Closed 25 Dec, 1 Jan, BHs, Sat-Sun (ex 1st wknd Aug) **Food** Mon-Fri 11.30-9.30 ⊕ FULLER'S ◧ London Pride, George Gale & Co Seafarers, Caledonian Deuchars IPA, Adnams Broadside, guest ales ☼ Biddenden Bushels, Orchard Pig Philosopher, Gwynt y Ddraig Black Dragon. ♟ 8 **Facilities** Non-diners area Garden ⏡ Beer festival WiFi

EC2

The Princess of Shoreditch   PLAN 1 F4

tel: 020 7729 9270 **76-78 Paul St EC2A 4NE**
email: info@theprincessofshoreditch.com
dir: *Nearest tube: Old Street*

Well-known City gastro-pub

Dating back to 1742, this popular place is a lively pub with three rotating ales on hand pump, around 40 bottled beers and canned craft beers and a range of wines. On the pub menu there's steamed Scottish mussels in chilli, garlic and parsley; and shepherd's pie and roasted root vegetables. There is a 42-seater candlelit dining

room accessed via a spiral staircase where the regularly changing menu might feature 35-day aged Hereford rib of beef to share with maple glazed carrots and buttered kale, followed by spiced sultana ice cream, honeycomb and orange jelly.

Open all day all wk Closed 24-26 Dec **Food** Lunch Mon-Fri 12-3, Sat 12-4, Sun 12-9 Dinner Mon-Sat 6.30-10, Sun 12-9 Av main course £14.50 Restaurant menu available Mon-Sat ⊕ ENTERPRISE INNS ◧ Hackney, Redemption, East London, Truman's ☼ Aspall Premier Cru & Waddlegoose Lane. ♟ 17 **Facilities** Non-diners area ◀♦ Children's portions Outside area WiFi

EC4

The White Swan ◉   PLAN 1 E4   PICK OF THE PUBS

tel: 020 7242 9696 **108 Fetter Ln, Holborn EC4A 1ES**
email: info@thewhiteswanlondon.com
dir: *Nearest tube: Chancery Lane. From station towards St Paul's Cathedral. At HSBC bank left into Fetter Ln. Pub on right*

Handsome pub on legal London's eastern fringe

This exquisitely fitted-out City pub comprises a traditional ground-floor bar, a galleried mezzanine, and a first-floor dining room. For its cosmopolitan selection of bottled beers and lagers, Adnams on tap, Addlestones cider and a dozen wines by the glass, it has to be the bar, of course, whose cream-coloured walls provide the backdrop for leather-covered stools and assorted tables, chairs and banquettes. Modern British dishes here include spiced goat Scotch egg with mint yogurt; and pie of the day, mash greens and gravy. Upstairs is the beautifully restored dining room with mirrored ceiling and linen-clad tables, where the day's choices might include pan-fried monkfish cheeks, octopus, cauliflower and chia seed couscous (fish comes in daily from Billingsgate); crisp veal sweetbreads, bubble-and-squeak, girolles and Madeira jus; or 45-day aged Cumbrian Shorthorn steaks with triple cooked chips. Finish with banana and rosemary soufflé with chocolate ice cream. Please note, the pub is closed at weekends.

Open all day Closed 25-26 Dec, wknds & BHs, Sat-Sun **Food** Lunch Mon-Fri 12-3 Dinner Mon-Fri 6-10 Av main course £20 Set menu available Restaurant menu available Mon-Fri ⊕ PUNCH TAVERNS ◧ Adnams ☼ Addlestones. ♟ 12 **Facilities** Non-diners area ◀♦ Children's menu Children's portions WiFi ➡ (notice required)

N1

The Albion   PLAN 2 F4

tel: 020 7607 7450 **10 Thornhill Rd, Islington N1 1HW**
email: bookings@the-albion.co.uk
dir: *From Angel tube station, cross road into Liverpool Rd past Sainsbury's, continue to Richmond Ave. Left. At junct with Thornhill Rd turn right. Pub on right*

Spacious walled garden for alfresco drinking

This is a Georgian gem of a pub in the Barnsbury conservation area of Islington that continues to serve good food using top-notch British produce. In winter, log fires warm the pub's tastefully furnished interior, with the large walled garden and wisteria-covered pergola drawing the crowds in summer. The daily-changing menu includes roast pork tenderloin, wild garlic mash, rhubarb compôte and crab apple jus; whole roast sea bass, Atlantic prawns and chorizo; and pearl barley and celeriac risotto, squash, gorgonzola and roast garlic.

Open all day all wk **Food** Lunch Mon-Fri 12-3, Sat 12-4, Sun 12-9 Dinner Mon-Sat 6-10, Sun 12-9 ⊕ PUNCH TAVERNS ◧ Sharp's Doom Bar, guest ales ☼ Symonds. ♟ 12 **Facilities** Non-diners area ❤ (Bar Restaurant Garden) ◀♦ Children's menu Children's portions Garden ⏡ WiFi ➡ (notice required)

The Charles Lamb PLAN 2 F4

tel: 020 7837 5040 **16 Elia St, Islington N1 8DE**
email: charleslamb@suttonvale.co.uk
dir: *From Angel station turn left, at junct of City Rd turn left. Pass Duncan Terrace Gdns, left into Colebrooke Row. 1st right*

A really friendly London local

Named after a local writer who lived in Islington in the 1830s, this is a cracking neighbourhood pub. Locals beat a path to the door for microbrewery ales and the hearty, home-cooked comfort food listed on the daily chalkboard menu. Traditional British and French dishes are the order of the day, perhaps – steak anglaise; or truffle mushroom Wellington, buttered Jersey Royals and kale. Sunday roasts are very popular.

Open all wk Mon & Tue 4-11 Wed-Fri 12-11 Sat 11-11 Sun 12-11 Closed 23 Dec-1 Jan **Food** Lunch Wed-Fri 12-3, Sat 12-4, Sun 12-6 Dinner Mon-Sat 6-9.30, Sun 7-9 ⊕ FREE HOUSE ◀ Dark Star Hophead, Ripple Steam Farmhouse Pale Ale ♂ Newton Court Gasping Goose. ♥ 9 **Facilities** Non-diners area ♣ (Bar Restaurant Outside area) ♦♦ Outside area ⋈ WiFi

The Drapers Arms ◉ PLAN 2 F4 PICK OF THE PUBS

tel: 020 7619 0348 **44 Barnsbury St N1 1ER**
email: nick@thedrapersarms.com
dir: *Turn right from Highbury & Islington station, into Upper St. Barnsbury St on right opposite Shell service station*

Neighbourhood pub in trendy Islington

Standing beside a quiet tree-lined street of attractive Georgian terraced housing, backed by a tranquil paved patio garden and distinguished by tasteful, cool colourwash above the wood-floored bar, this popular neighbourhood local appeals to all-comers. Founded in the 1830s by one of London's trade guilds, the pub's current owners marry up the best of fine dining with an appealing range of real ales and cider. Plump for a beer from Dark Star or Windsor & Eton breweries – or maybe one of 16 wines by the glass – and prepare to tackle the ever-changing menu. Both lunchtime and evening choices are equally rewarding. Exceptional starters may include duck hearts, snails and black cabbage on toast, trumped by a main of cod, grilled leeks and crab broth. A choice for two could include whole mallard with red cabbage and duck fat potatoes. The modern, edgy menu also retains classics like steaks or slow-cooked lamb shoulder, with comfort-food gingerbread pudding with whipped cream and oats to finish.

Open all day all wk Closed 25-26 Dec **Food** Lunch Mon-Fri 12-3, Sat 12-4, Sun 12-8.30 Dinner Mon-Fri 6-11, Sat 7-11, Sun 12-8.30 ⊕ FREE HOUSE ◀ Harvey's Sussex, Sambrook's Wandle, Truman's Runner, Dark Star Hophead, Windsor & Eton Windsor Knot, Cornish Crown Bitter, Portobello Star ♂ Westons Stowford Press & Wyld Wood Organic, Orchard Pig. ♥ 16 **Facilities** Non-diners area ♣ (Bar Garden) ♦♦ Children's portions Garden ⋈ WiFi

The Pig and Butcher PLAN 2 F4

tel: 020 7226 8304 **80 Liverpool Rd, Islington N1 0QD**
email: crackling@thepigandbutcher.co.uk
dir: *Nearest tube: Angel*

Lovely ales and food 'like Granny used to make'

Before The Pig and Butcher was built in the mid-1800s, the fields here were grazed by livestock on its way to Smithfield. Owner Jack Ross, together with Head Chef Michael Chan, embrace this history by receiving carcasses direct from the farm and then butchering on site. Rare breeds such as White Park cattle, Iron Age pigs and Hebridean lamb are specialities, along with game and vegetables from Kent and

south coast fish. In winter, meats are brined, cured, smoked and braised, while summer sees the specially built charcoal grill glowing. As well as meat dishes look out for Cornish stone bass with corn, smoked pancetta and black cabbage; and Temple Farm Special Reserve chicken pie, mash and hispi.

Open all wk 5-11 (Thu 5-12 Fri-Sat noon-1am Sun 12-11) Closed 24-26 Dec **Food** Lunch Fri 12-3.30, Sat 12-4, Sun 12-9 Dinner Mon-Sat 6.30-10, Sun 12-9 Av main course £16-£17 ⊕ ENTERPRISE INNS ◀ Bath Ales Gem, Sharp's Doom Bar, Sambrook's Wandle. ♥ 22 **Facilities** Non-diners area ♣ (Bar Outside area) ♦♦ Children's portions Outside area ⋈ WiFi

Smokehouse ◉◉ PLAN 2 F4

tel: 020 7354 1144 **63-69 Canonbury Rd N1 2DG**
email: info@smokehouseislington.co.uk
dir: *Phone for detailed directions*

Meat-eaters can't go wrong here

Situated in Islington's prestigious Canonbury district but moments away from the hustle and bustle of Upper Street, this successful gastro-pub serves food steered by award-winning chef Neil Rankin who smokes, barbecues and roasts on Big Green Eggs, offset smokers and a Robata grill. Using the finest ingredients sourced from small, family-owned farms, the Smokehouse offers a refined take on BBQ dishes. You'll find dishes like chopped brisket roll and gochujang; and smoked pork belly, brown shrimp, udon and pear miso. Expect to find a range of 20 craft beers on tap and a further 60 by the bottle; the wine list showcases only wines from small, family-owned vineyards.

Open Mon-Wed 5-11 (Thu-Fri 5-mdnt Sat 11am-mdnt Sun & BHs 12-10.30) Closed 24-26 Dec, Mon-Fri L (ex BHs) **Food** Lunch Sat 12-4, Sun 12-9 Dinner Mon-Sat 6-10, Sun 12-9 ⊕ NOBLE INNS ◀ Rotating craft ales ♂ Aspall Waddlegoose Lane, Lilley's Apples & Pears. ♥ 15 **Facilities** Non-diners area ♣ (Bar Garden) ♦♦ Children's portions Garden ⋈ WiFi ⛭ (notice required)

N6

The Flask PLAN 2 E5 PICK OF THE PUBS

tel: 020 8348 7346 **77 Highgate West Hill N6 6BU**
email: theflaskhighgate@london-gastros.co.uk
dir: *Nearest tube: Archway or Highgate*

Landmark gastro-pub with links to Dick Turpin

High on Highgate Hill, The Flask may now be a gastro-pub with a big reputation but its name was made long ago when Dick Turpin frequented it. This Grade II listed pub, dating back to 1663 and made famous by Byron, Keats, Hogarth and Betjeman, has become a London landmark. It retains much of its character and cosy atmosphere and a maze of small rooms is served by two bars, one of which still has the original sash windows. Fuller's and guest real ales from newer London breweries are on offer alongside two dozen bottled ales and ciders, and some sensibly priced wines. Starters include salt and pepper squid with chilli mayonnaise; and crispy pig's cheeks, chorizo salad and pickled vegetables, while typical mains are pheasant, cannellini bean and mushroom ragù and wilted spinach; and pan-fried sea bass, mussel and pea velouté, runner beans and spinach. For dessert, try the lime tart. The large front garden is especially popular in the summer.

Open all day all wk 12-11 (Sun 12-10.30) **Food** Lunch Mon-Sat 12-4, Sun 12-7 Dinner Mon-Sat 6-10, Sun 12-7 ⊕ FULLER'S ◀ London Pride, ESB, guest ales ♂ Cornish Orchards Gold. ♥ 13 **Facilities** Non-diners area ♣ (Bar Restaurant Garden) ♦♦ Garden ⋈ WiFi ⛭ (notice required)

NW1

The Chapel   PLAN 1 B4

tel: 020 7402 9220 **48 Chapel St NW1 5DP**
email: thechapel@btconnect.com
dir: *By A40 Marylebone Rd & Old Marylebone Rd junct. Off Edgware Rd by tube station*

A popular child-friendly gastro-pub

The Chapel has a bright, open-plan interior of stripped floors and pine furniture, and boasts one of central London's largest enclosed pub gardens – great for the children to let off steam. Owners Alison McGrath and Lakis Hondrogiannis take delivery of the freshest produce for daily-changing menus featuring internationally influenced dishes, as well as Mediterranean antipasti and canapés. A sample menu lists creamy cauliflower soup with bacon and walnuts; rabbit pie; slow-cooked pork belly with braised lentils, buttered spinach and thyme sauce; and risotto with wild mushrooms, aubergines and peppers. There's a good choice of wines by the glass.

Open all day all wk Closed 25-26 Dec, 1 Jan, Etr **Food** Lunch Mon-Sat 12-2.30, Sun 12-3 Dinner all wk 7-10 Av main course £13 Set menu available ⊕ FREE HOUSE ◀ Black Sheep, Shepherd Neame Whitstable Bay Pale Ale ⚙ Somersby. ♟ 15 **Facilities** Non-diners area ♣ (Bar Restaurant Garden) ♦ Children's menu Children's portions Garden ⌂ WiFi ▭ (notice required)

The Prince Albert   PLAN 2 F4

tel: 020 7485 0270 **163 Royal College St NW1 0SG**
email: info@princealbertcamden.com
dir: *From Camden tube station follow Camden Rd. Right into Royal College St, 200mtrs on right*

Organic food at character pub

Picnic tables furnish the small paved courtyard, while The Prince Albert's wooden floors and bentwood furniture make a welcoming interior for customers and their four-legged friends. Real ales there are, but you may fancy a refreshing glass of wine and there's plenty of choice. Bar dishes range from home-made sticky pork ribs; salmon Scotch eggs; and octopus, chorizo and onion stew; these can be followed by home-made steak and kidney pie, burgers and relish, or fish and chips. Two or three times a year the pub holds a three-day real ale festival.

Open all day all wk **Food** Lunch Mon-Fri 12-3, Sat 12-5, Sun 12-8 Dinner Mon-Sat 6-10, Sun 12-8 Set menu available ⊕ FREE HOUSE ◀ Dark Star, Sambrook's, Adnams, Redemption, guest ales ⚙ Westons Stowford Press. ♟ 14 **Facilities** Non-diners area ♣ (Bar Garden) ♦ Children's portions Garden ⌂ Beer festival Cider festival WiFi ▭ (notice required)

NW5

The Bull and Last   PLAN 2 E5

tel: 020 7267 3641 **168 Highgate Rd NW5 1QS**
email: info@thebullandlast.co.uk
dir: *From Kentish Town tube station N into Highgate Rd. (4 mins' walk from Gospel Oak Station)*

Tempting menus and many wines by the glass

A popular free house, owned and run by an enthusiastic young team, in a Grade II listed building, a stone's throw from Hampstead Heath. Children and dogs are welcome too, so this really is a relaxing place to sample one of the guest ales or one of the many wines sold by the glass. Wondering whether to eat? A glance at the home-made dishes on the menu will make up your mind – who can resist mouth watering starters like confit rabbit, smoked eel and ham hock terrine with sour apple purée? Move on to roast cod, hazelnut pesto, Roscoff onions, monk's beard and white kale; or Denham Vale aged côte de boeuf for two if you're determined to push the boat out. Summer picnic hampers and take-away ice creams are also available.

Open all day all wk 12-11 (Fri-Sat 12-12 Sun 9am-11pm, 12-10.30) Closed 23-25 Dec **Food** Lunch Mon-Fri 12-3, Sat-Sun 9am-11am (bkfst), 12.30-4 Dinner Mon-Sat 6.30-10, Sun 6.30-9 ⊕ FREE HOUSE/ETIVE PUBS LTD ◀ 4 rotating guest ales ⚙ Addlestones, guest cider. ♟ 17 **Facilities** Non-diners area ♣ (Bar Outside area) ♦ Children's menu Children's portions Outside area ⌂ WiFi

NW6

The Salusbury Pub and Dining Room   PLAN 2 D4

tel: 020 7328 3286 **50-52 Salusbury Rd NW6 6NN**
email: info@thesalusbury.co.uk
dir: *100mtrs left from Queen's Park tube & train station (5 mins' walk from Brondesbury Station)*

A community local serving good value fare

A stone's throw from Queen's Park tube, this pub serves the local community well, admitting dogs and children and serving kiddy-sized portions from the uncomplicated menu. Small plates come cold (Dorset crab, quail's egg and watercress) or hot (devilled lamb's kidneys on toast), while main dishes are robust and classically British: grilled Barnsley chop with grain mustard mash and broccoli; or Guinness-braised ox cheek with pearl barley. Desserts may feature Bramley apple and quince crumble with clotted cream. Along with the food, Greene King ales, Aspall cider and a good range of wines can all be served on the outside patio.

Open all day all wk 12-11 (Thu-Sat 12-12 Sun 12-10.30) Closed 25-26 Dec ⊕ FREE HOUSE ◀ Greene King Abbot Ale & IPA, Moncada Notting Hill ⚙ Aspall, Rekorderlig. **Facilities** ♣ (Bar Outside area) ♦ Children's portions Family room Outside area WiFi

NW8

The New Inn   PLAN 2 E4

tel: 020 7722 0726 **2 Allitsen Rd, St John's Wood NW8 6LA**
email: thenewinn@gmail.com
dir: *Exit A41 by St John's Wood tube station into Acacia Rd, last right, to end on corner*

British favourites meet international tapas

Colourful flower baskets and troughs break the lines of this street-corner pub, where pavement tables are a popular retreat for locals supping Abbot Ale, Aspall cider or a choice from the extensive wine list. This convivial Regency inn is well-placed for nearby Regent's Park and Lord's Cricket Ground. In the elegant restaurant, diners indulge in the sharing boards, the global tapas selection, fresh salads or a traditional main like bangers and mash or rack of ribs. Desserts include tiramisù and home-made ice creams. There is also a 'Little People's' menu.

Open all day all wk 7.30am-11pm (Fri 7.30am-mdnt Sat 8am-mdnt Sun 8.30am-10.30pm) **Food** all day Restaurant menu available all wk ⊕ GREENE KING ◀ Abbot Ale, IPA, guest ales ⚙ Aspall, Kopparberg, Rekorderlig. ♟ 14 **Facilities** Non-diners area ♣ (Bar Restaurant) ♦ Children's menu Children's portions WiFi ▭

SE1

The Garrison   PLAN 1 G2   PICK OF THE PUBS

tel: 020 7089 9355 **99-101 Bermondsey St SE1 3XB**
email: info@thegarrison.co.uk
dir: *From London Bridge tube station, E towards Tower Bridge 200mtrs, right into Bermondsey St. Pub in 100mtrs*

Friendly neighbourhood dining-pub

No doubt this green-tiled, street-corner pub was once a popular local for generations of workers at the Surrey Docks. The docks are no more, Bermondsey has gone up-market, and The Garrison, too, has moved with the times and has new owners. The pub's 21st-century restyling comprises an idiosyncratic mix of decorative themes and antique knick-knacks. The place pulsates from breakfast through to the evening. Start the day with avocado on sourdough toast, porridge, or pancakes. At lunch there are 'small plates' – pumpkin, goats' curd and radicchio salad, say, or larger dishes like lentil, apple and walnut Wellington. Desserts may include baked ricotta cheesecake or Bramley apple and blackberry crumble. In the evening check out the smoked haddock and leek brandade with croûton soldiers; followed by seared hake with curried celeriac, Swiss chard, crab bisque and lemon pickle. Menus change every couple of months; ales rotate more frequently.

Open all day all wk 8am-11pm (Fri 8am-mdnt Sat 9am-mdnt Sun 9am-10.30pm) Closed 25-26 Dec **Food** Lunch Mon-Fri 12-3, Sat 12.30-4, Sun 12-9 Dinner Mon-Sat 6-10.30, Sun 12-9 Av main course £16 Restaurant menu available all wk ⊕ FREE HOUSE ◀ Rotating guest ales Ö Aspall Cyderkyn. ♥ 17 **Facilities** Non-diners area 🐾 (Bar) ♦ Children's portions WiFi

---

The George Inn   PLAN 1 F3

tel: 020 7407 2056 **77 Borough High St SE1 1NH**
email: 7781@greeneking.co.uk
dir: From London Bridge tube station, take Borough High St exit, left. Pub 200yds on left

Unique former haunt of Charles Dickens

The coming of the nearby railway meant demolition of part of what is now London's sole surviving example of a 17th-century, galleried coaching inn, but what's left is impressive. National Trust-owned, it still features some very old woodwork, like the simple wall seats. Serving thirsty Londoners for centuries, the pub is mentioned in Dickens's *Little Dorrit*. As well as Greene King ales and rotating guests, George Inn Ale is the house beer. Classic pub grub is the order of the day.

Open all day all wk 11-11 (Sun 12-10.30) Closed 25-26 Dec ⊕ GREENE KING ◀ IPA, George Inn Ale, guest ales Ö Aspall. **Facilities** ♦ Children's portions Garden WiFi

---

The Market Porter   PLAN 1 F3

tel: 020 7407 2495 **9 Stoney St, Borough Market, London Bridge SE1 9AA**
dir: Close to London Bridge Station, in Borough market

A real ale pub with a Harry Potter connection

With as apt a name as you could wish for, this Borough Market pub is blessed with a really good atmosphere, especially on Thursdays, Fridays and Saturdays, when the retail market operates. Harry Potter fans will surely know that the inn became the 'Third Hand Book Emporium' in one of the films. The exceptional choice of real ales includes the resident Harvey's, and 14 other ales which rotate on a weekly or even daily basis. Unusually there are also guest ciders. Apart from sandwiches and bar snacks there are dishes such as steak, ale and mushroom pie; cod and pancetta fishcakes; and for vegetarians, wild mushroom and baby leaf spinach risotto. On weekdays the pub opens its doors at 6am. Children are welcome before 6pm.

Open all day all wk 6am-9am, 11-11 (Sat 12-11 Sun 12-10.30) Closed 25-26 Dec, 1 Jan **Food** Lunch Mon-Thu 12-3, Fri-Sun 12-5 Set menu available Restaurant menu available all wk ⊕ FREE HOUSE ◀ Harvey's Sussex Best Bitter, international ales, guest ales Ö Traditional Scrumpy, Westons Old Rosie, guest ciders. ♥ 10 **Facilities** Non-diners area ♦ Children's portions Outside area 🚌 (notice required)

■ **SE5**

NEW The Camberwell Arms   PLAN 2 F3

tel: 020 7358 4364 **65 Camberwell Church St SE5 8TR**
email: enquiries@thecamberwellarms.co.uk
dir: Nearest tube stations: Brixton & Oval

Imaginative food in a lively South London bar

More elegant than its neighbours in a lively shopping street, this late Victorian pub is frequented by an enthusiastic crowd of drinkers and diners. Attractions include

the wood-floored bar, its craft beers, organic and biodynamic wines, Breton cider and a generous lunch menu featuring Dexter beef ragout with gnocchi, black cabbage and parmesan; and salt marsh lamb kleftiko and Greek salad. In the evening, equally distinctive options include brown shrimps and kohlrabi on a buttered crumpet; cuttlefish in ink with roasted peppers and orzo pasta; and Delica pumpkin, coconut and chick pea curry with raita and barbecued naan.

Open all day Closed 23-28 Dec, 1-3 Jan, Mon L **Food** Lunch Tue-Sat 12-2.30, Sun 12-4 Dinner Mon-Sat 6-10 Av main course £13-£16 ⊕ ENTERPRISE INNS ◀ Brockley Pale Ale, St Austell Tribute Ö Symonds, Cidre Breton. **Facilities** Non-diners area 🐾 (Bar Outside area) ♦ Children's portions Outside area WiFi

---

The Crooked Well   PLAN 2 F3

tel: 020 7252 7798 **16 Grove Ln, Camberwell SE5 8SY**
dir: Nearest tube: Denmark Hill

Neighbourhood restaurant and bar is a Camberwell beauty

Set up and run by three friends, each with stacks of restaurant experience in the kitchen or front of house, this Victorian, street corner pub has rapidly earned some worthy plaudits for its food. A penchant for home-cooked British classics, such as rabbit and bacon pie (for two), still allows continental influences to not so much creep in as enter with brio – for example, roast lamb with spiced aubergine and tzatziki; rose harissa toasted couscous; and coley with tagliatelle and salsa verde. Regularly involved with community events, it offers mums' (and dads') mornings, jazz nights, BYO wine on Mondays and 50% discount on steaks Wednesday evenings.

Open all day all wk Closed 25-27 Dec, Mon L **Food** Lunch Tue-Sat 12.30-3, Sun 12.30-4 Dinner Mon-Thu 6.30-10, Fri-Sat 6.30-10.30, Sun 7-9 Set menu available Restaurant menu available all wk ⊕ FREE HOUSE ◀ Butcombe Bitter, Dark Star American Pale Ale Ö Addlestons. ♥ 10 **Facilities** Non-diners area 🐾 (Bar Restaurant Outside area) ♦ Children's menu Children's portions Outside area 🚫 WiFi 🚌 (notice required)

■ **SE10**

Greenwich Union Pub   PLAN 2 G3

tel: 020 8692 6258 **56 Royal Hill SE10 8RT**
email: theunion@meantimebrewing.com
dir: From Greenwich DLR & main station exit by main ticket hall, turn left, 2nd right into Royal Hill. Pub 100yds on right

Surely a beer-drinker's idea of heaven

In the heart of Greenwich's bustling Royal Hill, this pub's comfortable leather sofas and flagstone floors help to keep its original character intact. Interesting craft beers from the award-winning Meantime Brewing Company, along with lagers from around the world and a beer garden, make this a popular spot. All the food is freshly prepared and sourced locally where possible: fish from Billingsgate Market, and bread from the Greenwich itself. The lunch menu includes sandwiches, and favourites like ham hock, egg and chips, while at dinner you could opt for pigs in blankets; mussels in Gueze beer sauce; marinated pork steak with sweet potato, sage and onion mash; or soft shell crab, baby gem, artichoke heart, red pepper, with tabasco buerre blanc sauce.

Open all day all wk 12-11 (Fri-Sat 12-11 Sun 12-10.30) **Food** all wk 12-10 ⊕ FREE HOUSE ◀ Meantime Pale Ale & Chocolate Porter, Pilsner, Yakima Red Ö Sheppy's. **Facilities** Non-diners area 🐾 (Bar Restaurant Garden) ♦ Children's portions Garden 🚫 WiFi

SE10 *continued*

North Pole Bar & Restaurant PLAN 2 G3 **PICK OF THE PUBS**

tel: 020 8853 3020 **131 Greenwich High Rd, Greenwich SE10 8JA**
email: info@northpolegreenwich.com
dir: *Right from Greenwich rail station, pass Novotel. Pub on right*

The complete package in Greenwich

Dating from 1849, the name originated with the Victorian obsession for polar exploration, and North Pole Road adjoins the pub. It's a stylish, contemporary venue, offering a complete night out under one roof, with a bar, restaurant and basement club. Outside in the beer garden (which is also home to a shisha lounge) is seating for well over 100 people. Refreshments range from international beers such as Staropramen to cocktails, while the all-day bar menu features tapas, platters, sandwiches, grills and salads. The Piano restaurant attracts both visitors and loyal locals with its seasonally changing, modern European à la carte and brasserie menus: Thai-style haddock and crayfish cake, lime curry mayo; roast duck breast, braised red cabbage, roast parsnip and port reduction; pumpkin, mascarpone, mushroom risotto; and seared tuna, sweet chilli pea lentils, horseradish purée and herb oil. Please note, a dress code applies.

Open all day all wk noon-2am **Food** all wk 12-10 Set menu available Restaurant menu available all wk ⊕ FREE HOUSE ◀ Wells Bombardier, Morland Old Speckled Hen ♉ Aspall. ♟ 9 **Facilities** Non-diners area ♣ (All areas) ♦ Children's menu Children's portions Garden Outside area ⊼ WiFi ⛟ (notice required)

SE16

The Mayflower PLAN 2 G3

tel: 020 7237 4088 **117 Rotherhithe St SE16 4NF**
email: mayflowerrotherhithe@gmail.com
dir: *Phone for detailed directions*

Historic pub with fine Thames views

Named after the famous ship that set sail from Rotherhithe in 1620 with the Pilgrim Fathers on board, this historic Thameside pub is packed with reminders of life in the 16th century. Original fireplaces and timber floors add to the timeless character of this pub, which boasts wonderful river views from the upstairs restaurant and the jetty outside. Over a pint of Scurvy Ale, one of several beers on tap, order from the extensive menu. Typical dishes include Gloucester Old Spots sausages and mash with black pudding and onion gravy; and asparagus and pea risotto. Look to the specials board for the pie of the day.

Open all day all wk **Food** Lunch 12-9.30 Dinner 6-9.30 ⊕ FREE HOUSE ◀ Mayflower Scurvy Ale, Dark Star Hophead, Thwaites 13 Guns, Purity Pure UBU, Okells, St Austell Tribute ♉ Aspall. ♟ 12 **Facilities** ♣ (Bar Outside area) ♦ Children's portions Outside area ⊼ WiFi ⛟ (notice required)

SE18   Map 6 TQ47

NEW Dial Arch

tel: 020 3130 0700 **Dial Arch Buildings, The Warren, Royal Arsenal SE18 6GH**
email: dialarch@youngs.co.uk
dir: *Nearest station: Woolwich Arsenal*

Enjoyable food in an elegant waterside building

In the heart of the swanky Royal Arsenal Riverside development alongside the Thames, this Young's brewery-owned pub occupies a historic and elegant building dating from Georgian times. Up to 30 wines served by the glass and a range of Young's ales are dispensed from the long bar, and food is served throughout, including the attractive terrace. A typical meal might start with lemon mackerel

fillet, toasted sourdough, caramelised apple and beetroot and move on to slow-braised feather blade of beef with creamy mashed potato, cavolo nero and red wine shallots. Flatbreads and sharing boards are also available.

Open all day all wk **Food** Contact pub for food times ⊕ YOUNG'S ◀ Bitter & Special ♉ Aspall. ♟ 30 **Facilities** Non-diners area ♣ (Bar Outside area) ♦ Children's menu Children's portions Outside area ⊼ WiFi ⛟ (notice required)

SE21

The Rosendale PLAN 2 F2

tel: 020 8761 9008 **65 Rosendale Rd, West Dulwich SE21 8EZ**
email: info@therosendale.co.uk
dir: *Nearest station: West Dulwich*

Transformed mid-Victorian coach house

Part of a group of very successful south London pubs, The Rosendale likes keeping things simple but interesting, so the formidably-stocked bar might include Moor Nor' Hop, a Bristol brew, but also Harvey's Sussex classic bitter, several real ciders, and a mind-boggling range of rums, tequilas and vodkas. Traditional British food, using top-quality ingredients such as meats from the owners' farm in Hampshire, includes bar snacks like chicken and chorizo with saffron mayo, and more substantial beetroot risotto, goats' cheese beignet, blood orange drizzle; confit duck leg, squash terrine, spinach and apricot jus; and artisan pizzas with toppings that include merguez, capers, olives, tomato, mozzarella and duck eggs.

Open all day all wk Closed 26 Dec **Food** Lunch Mon-Fri 12-3.30, Sat 12-4, Sun 12-9 Dinner Mon-Thu 6-10, Fri-Sat 6-10.30, Sun 12-9 ⊕ FREE HOUSE ◀ Moor Nor' Hop, Adnams Ghost Ship, Harvey's Sussex Best Bitter, Timothy Taylor Landlord, Brixton Atlantic APA, London Beer Factory ♉ Wilkins Farmhouse, Hecks, Sandford Orchards, Thatchers. ♟ 27 **Facilities** Non-diners area ♣ (Bar Garden) ♦ Children's menu Children's portions Play area Garden ⊼ WiFi ⛟

SE22

The Palmerston ⊛ PLAN 2 F2

tel: 020 8693 1629 **91 Lordship Ln, East Dulwich SE22 8EP**
email: info@thepalmerston.co.uk
dir: *2m from Clapham, 0.5m from Dulwich Village (10 mins' walk from East Dulwich station)*

Smart London corner pub serving excellent modern food

A striking corner-plot destination dining pub in leafy Dulwich, heavy on the wood panelling, with stripped floorboards and some great floor tiling. The kitchen creates modern British menus with a Mediterranean twist. Start with game terrine with piccalilli or Colchester native oysters before moving on to fricassée of rabbit with sherry, sweetcorn, monk's beard and oregano; or walnut gnocchi with gorgonzola cream and rocket. Affable locals pop in for some flavoursome beers, too, from the likes of Timothy Taylor, and perhaps one of the 30-plus wines offered by the glass. Occasional photographic exhibitions add to the interior's flair.

Open all day all wk Closed 25-26 Dec, 1 Jan **Food** Lunch Mon-Fri 12-2.30, Sat-Sun 12-3.30 Dinner Mon-Sat 7-10, Sun 7-9.30 Set menu available Restaurant menu available all wk ⊕ ENTERPRISE INNS ◀ Sharp's Doom Bar, Harvey's, Timothy Taylor Landlord, Sambrook's Wandle ♉ Cornish Orchards Gold. ♟ 32 **Facilities** Non-diners area ♣ (Bar Outside area) ♦ Children's portions Outside area ⊼ Beer festival Cider festival WiFi ⛟ (notice required)

SE23

The Dartmouth Arms   PLAN 2 G2

tel: 020 8488 3117 **7 Dartmouth Rd, Forest Hill SE23 3HN**
email: dartmouth@innpublic.com
dir: *100mtrs from Forest Hill Station*

Smart Georgian pub with modern British cuisine

The original patrons of today's stylish pub would have been boatmen from the Croydon Canal, which ran behind the pub until 1836. Georgian features remain in this popular meeting place, where good beers like Golden from Brockley Brewery quench the thirst. A cosmopolitan choice of menu dishes caters for most tastes; a starter may be duck and pistachio terrine with cranberry confit and grilled sourdough. Mains range from venison sausages, sweet potato mash, sticky onions and gravy to cod fillet with Puy lentils, bacon and spinach. Orange posset with poached rhubarb and shortbread biscuit should take care of a sweet tooth.

Open all wk Closed 25-26 Dec, 1 Jan **Food** Lunch Mon-Fri 12-3.30, Sat 12-9.30, Sun 12-4 Dinner Mon-Fri 6-9.30, Sat 12-9.30, Sun 5-9 ⊕ ENTERPRISE INNS ◀ Adnams, Brockley Golden, guest ale Ò Westons Stowford Press. ₹ 9 **Facilities** Non-diners area ❄ (Bar Garden) ⭑ Garden ⨅ Parking WiFi ▭

SW1

NEW The Alfred Tennyson   PLAN 1 B2

tel: 020 7730 6074 **10 Motcomb St SW1X 8LA**
dir: *Nearest tube: Knightsbridge*

Design-led, elegant corner pub

Previously The Pantechnicon Rooms, inspired by the early 19th-century, Greek revival-style building a hundred yards away, this poetically renamed pub is very, very Belgravia. For a drink, a quick breakfast, lunch or supper, stay in the casual ground-floor bar; for something more formal ascend to the dining room, with open fires and big sash windows overlooking the cobbled street. The menu offers rock oysters with shallot dressing; spicy crumbed Goosnargh chicken burger, avocado and blue cheese; Norfolk Horn shepherd's pie and cheddar mash; pan-fried fillet of salmon, Jersey Royals, caramelised onions, samphire and romesco sauce; and stuffed globe artichoke with smoked aubergine and minted yogurt.

Open all day all wk 8am-11pm (Sat 9am-11pm Sun 9am-10pm) **Food** Contact pub for food times ⊕ FREE HOUSE ◀ Canopy Beer Co, The Cubitt 1788 Ò Westons Mortimers Orchard. ₹ 23 **Facilities** Non-diners area ❄ (Bar Outside area) ⭑ Children's menu Children's portions Outside area ⨅ WiFi

The Buckingham Arms   PLAN 1 D2

tel: 020 7222 3386 **62 Petty France SW1H 9EU**
email: buckinghamarms@youngs.co.uk
dir: *Nearest tube: St James's Park*

Forever popular for good beer and top pub food

This elegant Young's pub retains much of its old charm including etched mirrors and period light fittings in the bar. Close to Buckingham Palace, it is popular with pretty much everyone: tourists, business people, politicians, media types and real ale fans. Expect a good range of simple pub food, including grazers (perhaps breaded brie with raspberry and rosemary dip), sandwiches and hearty favourites such as sausages and mash, steak and ale pie and West Country beefburgers.

Open all day 11-11 (Sat & Sun (summer) 11-6) Closed 25-26 Dec, Sun (winter) **Food** Lunch Mon-Fri 12-9, Sat-Sun 12-5 Dinner Mon-Fri 12-9 ⊕ YOUNG'S ◀ Bitter & Special, Wells Bombardier, London Gold, guest ales Ò Aspall. ₹ 15 **Facilities** Non-diners area ❄ (Bar) ⭑ WiFi

The Nags Head   PLAN 1 B2   PICK OF THE PUBS

tel: 020 7235 1135 **53 Kinnerton St SW1X 8ED**
dir: *Phone for detailed directions*

Step back in time at this mews pub

This pub was built in the early 19th century to cater for below-stairs staff and stable hands working in this quiet Belgravia mews near Harrods. With its Dickensian frontage and an interior like a well-stocked bric-à-brac shop, The Nags Head stubbornly resists any contemporary touches. It's a mobile-free zone, and you are politely requested to hang coats and bags on the hooks provided. Compact and bijou, its front and back bars are connected by a narrow stairway and boast wooden floors, low ceilings and panelled walls covered with photos, drawings, and mirrors; other adornments include helmets, model aeroplanes, and even penny-slot machines. The atmosphere is best described as 'entertaining' if you're in the right mood. The waist-high bar is another oddity, but the full Adnams range is served, along with a good value menu of traditional pub grub – real ale sausages, roast of the day; and chilli con carne.

Open all day all wk 11-11 **Food** all wk 11-9.30 ⊕ FREE HOUSE ◀ Adnams Southwold Bitter, Broadside, Fisherman, Regatta & Old Ale Ò Aspall. **Facilities** Non-diners area ❄ (Bar) ⭑ Outside area ⨅

The Orange Public House & Hotel   PLAN 1 C1

tel: 020 7881 9844 **37 Pimlico Rd SW1W 8NE**
email: reservations@theorange.co.uk
dir: *Nearest tube: Victoria or Sloane Street*

An ornate corner building offering rustic and uncomplicated food

The Orange comprises a number of light and airy adjoining rooms, which have a rustic Tuscan feel with their muted colours and potted orange trees on stripped wooden boards. Well-heeled locals quaff local ales and Italian wines while selecting from menus of modern European dishes. Wood-fired pizzas and oven roasts lead the way, but the carte is full of good things: chilli salt squid and spiced lime dressing; Jerusalem artichoke gnocchi, gorgonzola, purple sprouting broccoli and walnut granola; Cornish mussels with Guinness and smoked bacon broth. Welsh rarebit; baked spinach and feta pie, pomegranate, beluga lentils, candied beetroot and lemon thyme to list but a few. The pub is recognised for its approach to sustainability.

Open all day all wk 8am-11.30pm (Sun 8am-10.30pm) **Food** Lunch all wk 12-6 Dinner all wk 6-10 ⊕ FREE HOUSE ◀ Canopy Journeyman & Cubitt 1788 Ò Westons Mortimers Orchard. ₹ 23 **Facilities** Non-diners area ⭑ Children's menu Children's portions Outside area ⨅ WiFi

The Thomas Cubitt   PLAN 1 C2

tel: 020 7730 6060 **44 Elizabeth St SW1W 9PA**
email: reservations@thethomascubitt.co.uk
dir: *Nearest tube: Victoria or Sloane Square*

Distinguished pub in fashionable district

Norfolk-born builder Thomas Cubitt developed Belgravia as a stuccoed rival to swanky Mayfair. This exclusive, white-painted corner pub draws a discerning crowd to its country-house-style interior featuring open fireplaces, detailed panelling and a superb hand-made, oak counter. Floor-to-ceiling glass doors open out on to tables and chairs on the street. In the bar, where excellent real ales are resident. From the menu here enjoy rock oysters; and dry-aged rib-eye, celeriac remoulade, truffle and parmesan fries perhaps. Upstairs the dining room offers dishes such as suckling Middle White pig, haggis, stuffed trotter, turnips and pommes Anna to share; and roasted and smoked cauliflower kale, crispy quail's egg and cocoa husk. Booking is essential for the memorable Sunday roast.

Open all day all wk 12-11 (Sun 12-10.30) **Food** all wk all day Restaurant menu available Mon-Sat ⊕ FREE HOUSE ◀ Canopy Journeyman & Cubitt 1788 Ò Westons Mortimers Orchard. ₹ **Facilities** Non-diners area ⭑ Children's menu Children's portions Outside area ⨅ ▭ (notice required)

SW1 *continued*

The Wilton Arms   PLAN 1 B2

tel: 020 7235 4854 **71 Kinnerton St SW1X 8ED**
email: wilton@shepherd-neame.co.uk
dir: *Between Hyde Park Corner & Knightsbridge tube stations*

Cosy pub serving Shepherd Neame ales

Known locally as The Village Pub, this early 19th-century hostelry's other name is a reference to the 1st Earl of Wilton. In summer it is distinguished by fabulous flower-filled baskets and window boxes. High settles and bookcases create cosy, individual seating areas in the air-conditioned interior, and a conservatory covers the old garden. Shepherd Neame ales, including Spitfire, accompany traditional pub fare – ploughman's, sandwiches, burgers, sausages with bubble-and-squeak and onion gravy; and home-made specials such as pies, curries, lasagne and chilli con carne add to the choices.

Open all day all wk Closed 25-26 Dec, BHs **Food** Lunch Mon-Sat 12-3 Dinner Mon-Fri 5.30-9 Av main course £8.50 ⊕ SHEPHERD NEAME ◀ Spitfire & Bishops Finger, Oranjeboom ☽ Symonds. �; 8 **Facilities** Non-diners area ☆ (Bar Outside area) ♦️ Children's portions Outside area ♬ WiFi ▦

SW3

Coopers Arms   PLAN 1 B1

tel: 020 7376 3120 **87 Flood St, Chelsea SW3 5TB**
email: coopersarms@youngs.co.uk
dir: *From Sloane Square tube station, into King's Rd. Approx 1m W, opposite Waitrose, turn left. Pub half way down Flood St*

Classy Chelsea pub offering a genial welcome

Just off the King's Road and close to the river, this pub sees celebrities rubbing shoulders with the aristocracy and blue collar workers. The stuffed Canadian moose brings a character of its own to the bar, where at least five real ales grace the pumps. Food is served both in the main bar area and in the first-floor Albert Room, which also plays host to private dinners and parties. The menu offers a range of modern British classics, including beef and bone marrow burger and a pie of the day. There is a weekly Tuesday quiz night.

Open all day all wk 12-11 (Sun 12-10.30) **Food** Lunch Mon-Fri 12-3, Sat 12-10, Sun 12-7 Dinner Mon-Fri 5-10, Sat 12-10, Sun 12-7 Av main course £12 Set menu available ⊕ YOUNG'S ◀ Special & Bitter, Sambrook's Wandle, Sharp's Doom Bar, guest ales ☽ Aspall. �; 15 **Facilities** Non-diners area ☆ (Bar Garden) ♦️ Children's menu Children's portions Garden WiFi

SW4

The Stonhouse   PLAN 2 E2

tel: 020 7819 9312 **165 Stonhouse St SW4 6BJ**
email: info@thestonhouse.co.uk
dir: *Nearest tube: Clapham Common*

Modern local on a residential side street

Mark Reynolds bought The Stonhouse in 2015 and has taken it back to a free house after years of pub company ownership. Tucked discreetly away between Clapham's Old Town and its busy High Street, this impressively transformed corner local has an elegant bar where Sambrook's Pumphouse Pale Ale vies for real ale drinkers' attention alongside Timothy Taylor Landlord. In the log-fire-warmed dining area, the brasserie-style menu is skewed towards modern British food, in particular steaks. The regularly changing menu could feature seared scallops, spiced lentils and crispy pancetta; or chargrilled rack of lamb, ratatouille, minted gravy.

Open all day all wk Closed 26 Dec **Food** Lunch Mon-Fri 12-3.30, Sat 11-4, Sun 12-9 Dinner Mon-Sat 6-10.30, Sun 12-9 ⊕ FREE HOUSE ◀ Timothy Taylor Landlord, Sambrook's Pumphouse Pale Ale ☽ Westons Stowford Press. �; 20 **Facilities** Non-diners area ☆ (Bar Garden) ♦️ Children's menu Children's portions Garden ♬ WiFi ▦ (notice required)

SW6

The Atlas   PLAN 2 E3   **PICK OF THE PUBS**

tel: 020 7385 9129 **16 Seagrave Rd, Fulham SW6 1RX**
email: reservations@theatlaspub.com
dir: *2 mins' walk from West Brompton tube station*

Traditional London pub with a walled garden

Located in a trendy part of town where a great many pubs have been reinvented to become diners or restaurants, The Atlas is one of only a handful of London pubs to have a walled garden. Just around the corner from West Brompton tube, this traditional, relaxed local remains true to its cause with a spacious bar area split into eating and drinking sections. Typical menus might feature starters such as salsify and roast garlic soup with crispy chorizo; or roast pheasant and ham hock terrine with spiced pineapple chutney and toast. Tempting mains demonstrate some Italian influences in dishes such as 'osso buco' braised shin of veal with risotto alla Milanese; or prosciutto and wild mushroom lasagne. There are good choices on the wine list, with around 15 by the glass for those who want to match different dishes.

Open all day all wk 12-12 Closed 24-31 Dec **Food** Lunch Mon-Fri 12-2.30, Sat 12-4, Sun 12-10 Dinner Mon-Sat 6-10, Sun 12-10 ⊕ FREE HOUSE ◀ Fuller's London Pride, guest ales ☽ Symonds. �; 15 **Facilities** Non-diners area ☆ (Bar Restaurant Garden) ♦️ Children's portions Garden ♬ WiFi ▦ (notice required)

The Harwood Arms ◉◉   PLAN 2 E3   **PICK OF THE PUBS**

tel: 020 7386 1847 **Walham Grove SW6 1QP**
email: admin@harwoodarms.com
dir: *Phone for detailed directions*

Tip-top dining pub in leafy Fulham

The combined talents of chef Brett Graham and TV chef Mike Robinson, who also owns The Pot Kiln in Berkshire, have transformed this neighbourhood pub in leafy Fulham into a top dining venue. The inspired British cooking makes it worthy of two AA Rosettes, but the Harwood remains a proper pub. Microbrewery ales are on tap, the atmosphere is vibrant and friendly, and bar snacks like venison rissoles with Oxford sauce, or crispy garlic potatoes, can be ordered. The kitchen's passion about the provenance and seasonality of ingredients is key to its success; the pub is renowned for its game and wild food, predominantly from Berkshire, where Mike shoots on various estates. The short, daily-changing menu may list whipped rabbit liver with crispy chicken skin, balsamic onions and thyme hobnobs; or Berkshire wood pigeon faggots with carrots cooked in bone marrow to start. Then for mains, Cornish sea bream, leeks, Jerusalem artichoke and pickled mussels; or loin of Tamworth pork with bacon marmalade, cider pickled cabbage and apple. Finishing up with warm malted chocolate cake with pearl barley and lovage ice cream.

Open all day 12-11 (Mon 5.30-11) Closed 24-27 Dec, 1 Jan, Mon until 5.30pm **Food** Lunch Tue-Sat 12-3, Sun 12-3 Dinner all wk 6.30-9.30 ⊕ ENTERPRISE INNS ◀ Sambrook's Wandle, Bath Ales Gem, guest ales. �; 20 **Facilities** Non-diners area ☆ (Bar Restaurant) ♦️ Children's portions WiFi ▦ (notice required)

The Jam Tree   PLAN 2 E3

tel: 020 3397 3739 **541 King's Rd SW6 2EB**
email: chelsea@thejamtree.com
dir: *Nearest tube: Imperial Wharf or Fulham Broadway*

Quirky pub with a vibrant night life

Number two in The Jam Tree pub family, this Chelsea sibling echoes the quirkiness of its Clapham sister. Antique mirrors, personalised artworks, old chesterfields and mismatched furniture give the interior a decidedly individual look. The modern British menu offers goan pork vindaloo; marinated hanger steak; poached chicken and broccoli; game pie; and crisp sea bass fillet with squash, spinach and brown shrimp beurre noisette. A long cocktail list, barbecues, Sunday roasts, plasma screen and resident DJs could be additional reasons for visiting.

Open all day all wk **Food** Lunch Mon-Fri 12-3, Sat-Sun 11-5 Dinner Mon-Fri 6-10, Sat 5-10, Sun 5-9 Av main course £15 ⊕ FREE HOUSE ◀ Guest craft beers Ö Symonds. ♈ 9 **Facilities** Non-diners area ♣ (Bar Restaurant Garden) ♦♦ Children's menu Children's portions Garden ⋒ WiFi

The Malt House   PLAN 2 E3

tel: 020 7084 6888 **17 Vanston Place, Fulham SW6 1AY**
email: reservations@malthousefulham.co.uk **web:** www.malthousefulham.co.uk
dir: *Nearest tube: Fulham Broadway*

A quietly situated, upmarket Fulham pub

Situated just five minutes from the Fulham Broadway tube station, this 18th-century building, still has its old name – The Jolly Maltster - on a gable-end. The kitchen's policy is to source the ingredients from independent local suppliers for the modern dishes they serve. To convey an idea of the style, starters include London gin-cured salmon gravad lax, honey and mustard dressing, beetroot gel and quails' eggs; and whipped goats' cheese, figs, Marcona almonds, truffle honey and pitta bread; and for mains, roasted hake in Serrano ham, saffron risotto, charred broccoli, lemon, chilli and garlic; and slow-cooked charred spring lamb shoulder, imam bayildi and coriander yogurt.

Open all day all wk Closed 25 Dec **Food** Lunch Mon-Sat 12-3, Sun 12-9 Dinner Mon-Sat 6-10, Sun 12-9 ⊕ BRAKSPEAR ◀ Bitter, Marston's Pedigree Ö Symonds. **Facilities** Non-diners area ♣ (Bar Restaurant Garden) ♦♦ Children's menu Children's portions Garden ⋒ WiFi ▭ (notice required)

The Sands End Pub   PLAN 2 E3

tel: 020 7731 7823 **135-137 Stephendale Rd, Fulham SW6 2PR**
email: enquiries@thesandsend.co.uk
dir: *From Wandsworth Bridge Rd (A217) into Stephendale Rd. Pub 300yds at junct with Broughton Rd*

Local, seasonal produce drives the menu here

A stylish country pub in the city is how fashionable Fulham foodies regard this much-loved neighbourhood gem. Expect to find scrubbed farmhouse tables, wooden floors, locals quaffing pints of real ale, chalkboard menus listing terrific bar snacks (the Scotch eggs are legendary). British seasonal cooking makes use of foraged produce and even vegetables from the pub's allotment, resulting in dishes like, slow-cooked duck egg with wild mushroom tart, confit leeks and pancetta crisps to start; confit lamb belly, charred broccoli, provençal red peppers, black olives and rosemary to follow; and pecan pie, clotted cream ice cream and salted caramel for afters.

Open all day all wk Closed 25 Dec **Food** Lunch Mon-Fri 12-3, Sat 10.30-4, Sun 10.30-9, snacks all day Dinner Mon-Sat 6-10, Sun 10.30-9 Set menu available ⊕ FREE HOUSE ◀ Otter Bitter, Bath Ales SPA, Sharp's Cornish Coaster Ö Aspall. ♈ 24 **Facilities** Non-diners area ♣ (Bar Restaurant Outside area) ♦♦ Children's portions Outside area ⋒ WiFi

The White Horse   PLAN 2 E3   PICK OF THE PUBS

tel: 020 7736 2115 **1-3 Parson's Green, Fulham SW6 4UL**
email: bookings@whitehorsesw6.com
dir: *140mtrs from Parson's Green tube station*

Beer Academy at the 'Sloaney Pony'

With a triangular walled front terrace overlooking Parson's Green, the late 18th-century, former coaching inn and Victorian gin palace is a substantial sandstone pub. It's a destination for lovers of British pub food and interesting real ales and wines, with a restaurant in the former coach house, an upstairs bar, and a luxurious private dining area. The interior is a pleasing blend of polished mahogany and wooden and flagstone floors, open fires and contemporary lighting. Bar snacks are very tempting – tempura cauliflower, chilli mayo; and pan-fried chorizo being just two to get you started. Every dish on the menu comes with a recommended beer to drink, such partnering forming part of the pub's Beer Academy Courses. For instance, a starter of salt and pepper squid with spiced mayonnaise is paired with Goose Island 312; and a main of steak focaccia with caramelised onion, should be washed down with Adnams Broadside. It's good for Sunday brunch, summer barbecues and its four annual beer festivals – American, European, British and Old Ale. At any one time the pub has at least 135 bottled beers from around the world.

Open all day all wk **Food** all wk 12-10.30 ⊕ MITCHELLS & BUTLERS ◀ Adnams Broadside, Harvey's Sussex Best Bitter Ö Aspall. ♈ 20 **Facilities** Non-diners area ♣ (Bar Garden) ♦♦ Children's menu Children's portions Garden ⋒ Beer festival WiFi

SW8

NEW Canton Arms   PLAN 2 F3

tel: 020 7582 8710 **177 South Lambeth Rd SW18 1PX**
dir: *Nearest tube: Stockwell & Vauxhall. Pub on corner of South Lambeth Rd & Aldebert Terrace*

Local boozer turned upmarket eatery

The Canton Arms can be found midway between Stockwell and Vauxhall tube stations. Pavement trestle tables are much sought after on summers' evenings by office workers refreshing themselves at the end of the day. The pub's interior is typical of its kind, with dark walls, mismatched furniture and well-trodden floorboards. Pints of Timothy Taylor Landlord and Skinner's Betty Stogs are dispensed at the darkwood bar. Chalkboards abound, displaying everything from snacks to specials. Head for the restaurant at the back for a meal of devilled crab with chilli, ginger and garlic, followed by roast Hampshire porchetta with roasties and apple sauce.

Open all day Closed 24 Dec-2 Jan, Mon L **Food** Lunch Tue-Sat 12-2.30, Sun 12-4 Dinner Mon-Sat 6-10 ⊕ ENTERPRISE INNS ◀ Timothy Taylor, Skinner's Betty Stogs ⚬ Addlestones. **Facilities** Non-diners area ❅ (Bar Outside area) ⁂ Outside area ☶ WiFi

SW10

The Hollywood Arms   PLAN 1 A1   PICK OF THE PUBS

tel: 020 7349 7840 **45 Hollywood Rd SW10 9HX**
email: hollywoodarms@youngs.co.uk
dir: *From Chelsea & Westminster Hospital in Fulham Rd into Hollywood Rd opposite, 200mtrs on right*

Stylish mid-terrace gem of a pub

Deep in Chelsea, this mid 17th-century building was once the home of the Middletons, owners of land in England, Barbados and America's Deep South. To one side, a gated archway leads to a small mews where horses were once stabled. The elegant interior was a runner-up in the prestigious Restaurant & Bar Design Awards, in part for the splendid first-floor Blanchard Room, named after a balloonist who in 1784 ascended from the grounds of the house and landed in Romsey. The ground-floor bar serves Meantime's London-brewed real ales and rather special wines released by Young's brewery (to obtain, discreetly ask a member of staff). Spiced parsnip and apple soup with sourdough toast is a possible starter, with 'posh' chicken Kiev, champ, autumn greens and smoked bacon; or market fish of the day to follow. Finish with sticky toffee pudding and Meantime London Stout-flavoured ice cream. Please note, no children after 7pm.

Open all day all wk 11am-11.30pm (Thu-Sat 11am-mdnt Sun 11-10.30) **Food** Lunch Mon-Fri 12-4, Sat-Sun 12-10 Dinner Mon-Fri 5.30-10.30, Sat-Sun 12-10 ⊕ YOUNG'S ◀ Wells Bombardier, Young's, Meantime ⚬ Aspall. ⚑ 12
Facilities Non-diners area ❅ (Bar Restaurant) ⁂ Children's portions Outside area ☶ Beer festival Cider festival WiFi ▭ (notice required)

SW11

The Bolingbroke Pub & Dining Room   PLAN 2 E2

tel: 020 7228 4040 **172-174 Northcote Rd SW11 6RE**
email: info@thebolingbroke.com
dir: *Nearest tube: Clapham South or Clapham Junction*

Family-friendly dining pub

This refined dining pub stands in a road known colloquially as 'Nappy Valley', due to its popularity with well-heeled young families. Named after the first Viscount

Bolingbroke, who managed to be both brilliant politician and reckless rake, the pub caters admirably for children and adults alike. Expect modern British fare along the lines of beetroot and goats' cheese tarte Tatin with balsamic glaze followed by braised beef cheeks with haggerty potatoes and red cabbage. Weekend brunch includes boiled egg and soldiers for the very young.

Open all day all wk Closed 25-26 Dec ⊕ FREE HOUSE ◀ Timothy Taylor Landlord, Sambrook's Junction ⚬ Aspall. **Facilities** ❅ (Bar Restaurant Outside area) ⁂ Children's menu Children's portions Outside area WiFi

The Fox & Hounds   PLAN 2 E2   PICK OF THE PUBS

tel: 020 7924 5483 **66 Latchmere Rd, Battersea SW11 2JU**
email: foxandhoundsbattersea@btopenworld.com
dir: *From Clapham Junction exit into High St, turn left, through lights into Lavender Hill. After post office, left at lights. Pub 200yds on left*

Known for its international wine list and Mediterranean food

From the moment you step through the door of this archetypal Victorian corner pub, you'll feel like one of the locals. This is one of those timeless pubs that London still has in abundance, its style simple with bare wooden floors, an assortment of furniture, walled garden, extensive patio planting and a covered and heated seating area. Regulars head here for the good selection of real ales and an international wine list. Fresh ingredients arrive daily from the London markets, enabling the Mediterranean-style menu and specials to change accordingly; all prepared in the open-to-view kitchen. So, you might start with cauliflower and sweet onion soup with saffron; or roast pheasant and ham hock terrine with spiced pineapple chutney. Follow with steamed sea bream fillet, grilled purple sprouting broccoli and romesco sauce; or grilled Italian sausages, mash and red onion marmalade. A traditional British lunch is served on Sundays.

Open 12-3 5-11 (Mon 5-11 Fri-Sat 12-11 Sun 12-10.30) Closed 24-28 Dec, Mon L **Food** Lunch Fri 12.30-3, Sat 12.30-4, Sun 12-10.30 Dinner Mon-Sat 6.30-10, Sun 12-10.30 ⊕ FREE HOUSE ◀ St Austell Tribute, Sambrook's, Hogs Back, Twickenham Fine Ales ⚬ Cornish Orchards. ⚑ 14 **Facilities** Non-diners area ❅ (Bar Restaurant Garden) ⁂ Children's portions Garden ☶ WiFi ▭ (notice required)

SW12

The Avalon   PLAN 2 E2

tel: 020 8675 8613 **16 Balham Hill SW12 9EB**
email: info@theavalonlondon.com
dir: *Nearest tube: Clapham South*

Elegant, comfortable and relaxing

Named after the mythical isle of Arthurian legend, the attractions of this Balham member of the Renaissance Group of south London pubs are far from fairytale. For example, there's a three-tiered rear garden that comes alive on summer days, the bar stocks Timothy Taylor Landlord and Mortimers cider, and the wine list offers many by the glass. On top of that, house policy is to serve beef aged in-house, sustainable fish from English waters, and free-range pork and chicken from the group's own farm. Bar meals include meze platter; Welsh rarebit; fish and chips; and croque monsieur.

Open all day all wk **Food** Lunch Mon-Fri 12-3.30, Sat 12-4, Sun 12-9 Dinner Mon-Sat 6-10.30, Sun 12-9 ⊕ ENTERPRISE INNS ◀ Timothy Taylor Landlord, guest ales ⚬ Mortimers. ⚑ 15 **Facilities** Non-diners area ❅ (Bar Restaurant Garden) ⁂ Children's menu Children's portions Family room Garden ☶ WiFi

PICK OF THE PUBS

The Victoria ★★★★ RR ❀❀

SW14   **PLAN 2 C2**

tel: 020 8876 4238 **10 West Temple Sheen, East Sheen SW14 7RT**
email: bookings@thevictoria.net
web: www.thevictoria.net
dir: *Nearest station: Mortlake*

Family-friendly and a real charmer

In a great location just a couple of minutes from the wide open spaces of Richmond Park, The Victoria is a friendly, welcoming place, with everything you might look for in a restaurant with rooms. There are comfortable bedrooms and a bright and airy conservatory dining room, plus a sunny courtyard and a leafy garden with a safe children's play area. And of course, as it's run by TV chef Paul Merrett and restaurateur Greg Bellamy, you can expect award-winning culinary delights. The modern menu strikes just the right note, with a thoughtful selection of dishes, from comforting classics to something a bit more inventive. Have a pint of Timothy Taylor Landlord or Orchard Pig Reveller cider in the bar – or maybe one of the interesting non-boozy drinks – rhubarb lemonade, for example – to kick off a meal that might start with the artisan charcuterie board with pickles and focaccia, maybe, or buratta with fennel, blood orange pistachio and basil oil; or crispy pork head and hock terrine,

smoked apple purée, quince and bitter leaves. You might move on to a steak – the 28-day aged 7oz South Devon rib-eye, maybe, with triple-cooked chips; or Jerusalem artichoke ravioli with artichoke crisps, wild mushrooms and Granny Smith. Desserts might range from vanilla buttermilk pannacotta with poached Yorkshire rhubarb and almond tozzetti biscuit; to warm banana bread with caramelised banana, toffee sauce and puffed wild rice. If you can't quite squeeze in a full-sized dessert they offer a mini version – perhaps sticky toffee pudding with caramel sauce and vanilla ice cream; or the cheese board, complete with fruit and nut bread and quince paste, is worth a look.

Open all day all wk Closed 1 Jan

Food Bkfst Sat 8.30am-10.30am Brunch Sat 11-3, Lunch Mon-Fri 12-2.30, Sun 12-4 Dinner Mon-Fri 6-10, Sat 5-10, Sun 5-8 Set menu available Restaurant menu available Mon-Sat 🛢 ENTERPRISE INNS ◀ Fuller's London Pride, Timothy Taylor Landlord, guest ale Ⓒ Orchard Pig Reveller. ♟ 28 **Facilities** Non-diners area 🐾 (Bar Garden) 🕯 Children's menu & portions Play area Garden 🎋 Parking WiFi 🚌 (notice required) **Rooms** 7

SW13

The Brown Dog PLAN 2 D2

tel: 020 8392 2200 **28 Cross St, Barnes SW13 OAP**
email: info@thebrowndog.co.uk
dir: Phone for detailed directions

Pleasant family oasis a short detour from the Thames

Given the pub's name, it would be odd if The Brown Dog did not welcome canines, albeit that the resident dog is black. The pub also welcomes children, which is perhaps surprising given its location in the exclusive back streets of Barnes and the gastro nature of its operation. St Austell Tribute and rotating guest ales and Orchard Pig cider testify to its drinking credentials, along with a wine list designed to match an enticing menu. Here you'll find oysters among the starters, main courses boasting Tamworth pork or aged Scottish beef, and traditional sweets such as apple and rhubarb crumble with vanilla ice cream. A granite-slabbed terrace furnished with bench tables and parasols completes this altogether rather pleasant establishment.

Open all day all wk **Food** Lunch Mon-Fri 12-3, Sat-Sun 12-4 Dinner Mon-Fri 6.30-10, Sat 6-10, Sun 6-9 ⊕ FREE HOUSE ◀ St Austell Tribute, rotating guest ales ◌ Orchard Pig, Cidre Breton. ♟ 18 **Facilities** Non-diners area ♣ (Bar Restaurant Garden) ♦ Children's menu Children's portions Family room Garden ⊼ WiFi

SW14

The Victoria ★★★★ RR ◉◉ PLAN 2 C2 **PICK OF THE PUBS**

See Pick of the Pubs on page 335

SW15

Prince of Wales PLAN 2 D2

tel: 020 8788 1552 **138 Upper Richmond Rd, Putney SW15 2SP**
email: princeofwales@foodandfuel.co.uk
dir: From East Putney station turn left, pub on right. From Putney Station, left into High St, left into Upper Richmond Rd; pub on left

Victorian pub serving good beer and interesting food

Just two minutes from East Putney tube station, this Victorian corner pub attracts a mix of drinkers and foodies. In the cosy front bar, you can enjoy pints of Sambrook's Wandle and Purity Mad Goose with the locals or head to the rear dining room with its skylight and eclectic country-style decor of stuffed animals and wall-mounted antlers. The food here is not lacking ambition – a starter of crispy pig's cheeks with spicy sweet and sour sauce might be followed by pan-seared brill, squid ink risotto, crab-stuffed cucumber and red wine reduction.

Open all day all wk **Food** Lunch all wk 12-3 Dinner all wk 6-10 Set menu available ⊕ PUNCH TAVERNS/FOOD & FUEL ◀ Purity Mad Goose, Sambrook's Wandle ◌ Aspall, Addlestones. ♟ 30 **Facilities** Non-diners area ♣ (Bar Outside area) ♦ Children's portions Outside area ⊼ WiFi ⛟ (notice required)

The Spencer PLAN 2 D2 **PICK OF THE PUBS**

tel: 020 8788 0640 **237 Lower Richmond Rd, Putney SW15 1HJ**
email: info@thespencerpub.com
dir: Corner of Putney Common & Lower Richmond Rd, opposite Old Putney Hospital

Well-kept ales and family-friendly food

This landmark pub occupies a lofty position on green and leafy Putney Common. Its close proximity to the Thames makes it a popular base for boat race enthusiasts. The beer garden here is part of the common and the pub's picnic benches are hotly contested by those in search of an alfresco lunch. A light, bright and airy interior

belies the rather traditional look of the place; revamped a few years ago, locals are welcomed at the bar where Timothy Taylor and Fuller's are the pick of the beers. Meals, in the bar or restaurant area, are traditional favourites embracing salads, pasta, burgers, shepherd's pie, and BBQ ribs with fries and home-made slaw. The extensive breakfast menu served from 9am is popular with early morning dog walkers and cyclists; the New Yorker – a golden waffle with two fried eggs and crispy bacon rashers – will set you up for the day.

Open all day all wk Mon-Sat 9am-mdnt (Sun 11-11) **Food** Mon-Sat 12-10, Sun 12-9 ⊕ FREE HOUSE ◀ Fuller's London Pride, Sharp's Doom Bar, Timothy Taylor Landlord, Guinness ◌ Aspall Draught. ♟ 20 **Facilities** Non-diners area ♣ (Bar Restaurant Garden) ♦ Children's menu Children's portions Play area Garden ⊼ WiFi ⛟

SW18

The Earl Spencer PLAN 2 E2 **PICK OF THE PUBS**

tel: 020 8870 9244 **260-262 Merton Rd, Southfields SW18 5JL**
dir: Exit Southfields tube station, into Replingham Rd, left at junct with Merton Rd, to junct with Kimber Rd

Sophisticated Edwardian gastro-pub

This grand Edwardian pub is a popular drinking and dining venue, especially during 'Wimbledon Fortnight', but that still leaves 50 other weeks for its attractions to work their magic. The log fires and polished wood furnishings make their contribution, but for many it's the great choice of refreshments – real ales and lagers including Belleville Amber and Meantime London Lager, ciders and global wines, of course, but not forgetting the Merton Mule, a cocktail of vodka, ginger beer, ginger ale and crushed lime. Another big draw is the daily-changing menu on which everything is home made, including the bread. Start with pork rillette, celeriac remoulade, cornichons and toast. For a main course, poached sea trout, smoked garlic and pea purée and Jersey Royals makes an enjoyable spring treat. Finish with buttermilk pudding, poached Yorkshire rhubarb, or dark chocolate and hazelnut terrine with crème fraîche.

Open all wk 4-11 (Fri-Sat 11am-mdnt Sun 12-10.30) Closed 25-26 Dec **Food** Lunch Fri-Sat 12.30-3, Sun 12.30-4 Dinner Mon-Sat 7-10.30, Sun 7-9.30 ⊕ ENTERPRISE INNS ◀ Sambrook's Wandle, Wimbledon Tower SPA, East London Foundation Bitter, By The Horns The Mayor of Garratt, Meantime Yakima Red, Freedom Organic Helles, guest ales ◌ Aspall, Westons Old Rosie & Wyld Wood Organic. ♟ 17 **Facilities** Non-diners area ♣ (Bar Restaurant Garden) ♦ Garden Outside area ⊼ WiFi

The Roundhouse PLAN 2 E2

tel: 020 7326 8580 **2 Northside, Wandsworth Common SW18 2SS**
email: info@theroundhousewandworth.com
dir: Phone for detailed directions

Recommended for its London microbrewery ales

Between Clapham Junction and Wandsworth, The Roundhouse has the ambience of a friendly local, with a round black walnut bar, open kitchen, and eclectic art on the walls. Ales come from two local microbreweries, including Sambrook's Wandle – an ale named after a nearby river. The short, daily-changing menu may take in pan-fried sea bass; rump of venison; goose leg confit and a chargrilled steak sandwich. Finish with apple and wild berry crumble.

Open all day all wk Mon-Thu 12-11 (Fri-Sat 12-12 Sun 12-10.30) Closed 25-26 Dec **Food** Lunch Mon-Fri 12-3, Sat 12-4, Sun 12-4.30 Dinner Mon-Sat 6-9.30, Sun 6-9 Av main course £13 Set menu available ⊕ FREE HOUSE ◀ Sambrook's Wandle, Bells Roundhouse India Red Ale, guest ales ◌ Symonds, Westons Mortimers Orchard. ♟ 16 **Facilities** Non-diners area ♣ (Bar Garden) ♦ Children's menu Children's portions Garden ⊼ WiFi ⛟ (notice required)

SW19

Fox & Grapes ● PLAN 2 D1

tel: 020 8619 1300 **9 Camp Rd, Wimbledon Common SW19 4UN**
email: reservations@foxandgrapeswimbledon.co.uk
web: www.foxandgrapeswimbledon.co.uk
dir: *Just off Wimbledon Common*

Ever-successful pub on a secluded edge of Wimbledon Common

The Fox & Grapes' success from day one was more or less assured by the pedigree of its chefs. Step inside to a large open-plan interior of parquet flooring, wood panelling, scrubbed wooden tables. Certainly you can enjoy a pint of Doom Bar or Wye Valley, as many dog-walkers do, or consult the wine carte for the small selection of sustainable, organic and biodynamic wines. But award-winning cooking remains the prime attraction, so booking is advisable. A typical dinner menu offers oak-smoked mackerel rillettes, red onion jam and granary toast; and ham hock terrine, beetroot and horseradish tapenade. Followed by roasted duck breast, smoked onion purée, and figs roasted in prosciutto; or seared salmon fillet, white wine and mussel velouté, peas and samphire.

Open all day all wk Closed 25 Dec **Food** Lunch Mon-Sat 12-3, Sun 12-9 Dinner Mon -Sat 6-9.30, Sun 12-9 ⊕ ENTERPRISE INNS ◀ Sharp's Doom Bar, Wye Valley Ò Symonds. **Facilities** Non-diners area ❖ (Bar Restaurant) ◀◀ Children's menu Children's portions WiFi ▦ (notice required)

W1

French House PLAN 1 D4

tel: 020 7437 2477 **49 Dean St, Soho W1D 5BG**
dir: *Nearest tube: Piccadilly Circus; Tottenham Court Road; Covent Garden. Pub at Shaftesbury Avenue end of Dean St*

The rich and famous beat a path to this Soho spot

This legendary Soho watering hole was known as the Maison Francais a hundred years ago; it was patronised by General de Gaulle during the Second World War, and later by Dylan Thomas, Francis Bacon, Dan Farson and many other louche Soho habitués. Run by Lesley Lewis for over 27 years, the small, intimate and very atmospheric bar only serves half pints of Theakston, Meteor, Kronenbourg and Guinness. The upstairs is a second bar, offering more informal drinking space; this area is also used as an art gallery. Bar food is served only from Monday to Friday.

Open all day all wk 12-11 (Sun 12-10.30) **Food** Lunch Mon-Fri 12-4 Av main course £10 ⊕ FREE HOUSE ◀ Budweiser Budvar, Kronenbourg, Leffe, Meteor, Theakston, Guinness Ò Truman's Côte Breton Brut. ☻ 22 **Facilities** Non-diners area WiFi

The Grazing Goat PLAN 1 B4

tel: 020 7724 7243 **6 New Quebec St W1H 7RQ**
email: reservations@thegrazinggoat.co.uk
dir: *Behind Marble Arch tube station, off Seymour St*

Stylish London dining pub with plenty of character

Just minutes away from Oxford Street and Marble Arch, this classy, six-storey pub is full of period features including open fireplaces, oak floors and solid oak bars. The name is not mere whimsy; goats did once graze around here because the first Lady Portman was allergic to cow's milk. Expect modern British, seasonal cooking – maybe chilli salt squid, smoked chilli and lime dressing; or the pub's own house-cured meats with marinated olives, bocconcini, spiced apple chutney and tomato relish (to share), followed by hot-smoked salmon, potato and caper salad, lemon confit and horseradish dressing; cottage pie, chantenay carrots and gravy; or roast pheasant, sweet potato dauphinoise, kale, bread sauce and pomegranate jus. For dessert – Yorkshire rhubarb with white chocolate, cashew macaron; or chocolate tart, poached pear and hazelnut. Floor-to-ceiling glass doors are opened in warmer weather for alfresco dining.

Open all day all wk 7.30am-11.30pm (Sun 7.30am-10.30pm) **Food** Contact pub for food times ⊕ FREE HOUSE ◀ Crate Brewery Pale Ale, Canopy The Cubitt 1788 & Journeyman Ò Westons Mortimers Orchard. ☻ 20 **Facilities** Non-diners area ◀◀ Children's portions ⋈ WiFi ▦ (notice required)

The Portman PLAN 1 B4

tel: 020 7723 8996 **51 Upper Berkeley St W1H 7QW**
email: manager@theportmanmarylebone.com
dir: *From Marble Arch into Great Cumberland Place, 3rd left into Upper Berkeley St*

Stylish central London pub with a seasonal British menu

Tucked between today's hustle of Oxford Street and the elegant shops of Marylebone, prisoners once stopped here for a final drink on their way to the gallows at Tyburn Cross. These days, this friendly central London pub is the perfect place for weary shoppers and tourists to refuel on a glass of wine or pint of beer and seasonal British classics served all day, 365 days a year. Beer battered fish and chips, Thai chicken curry, and the pie of the day are popular choices in the ground-floor pub but for a fine dining experience there's a restaurant upstairs where meals are served by way of an unpretentious silver service.

Open all day all wk **Food** all day Set menu available Restaurant menu available all wk ⊕ FREE HOUSE ◀ St Austell Proper Job, Timothy Taylor, guest ale Ò Aspall. ☻ 15 **Facilities** Non-diners area ❖ (Bar Outside area) ◀◀ Children's menu Children's portions Outside area ⋈ WiFi ▦ (notice required)

W4 | Map 6 TQ27

The City Barge PLAN 2 C3

tel: 020 8994 2148 **27 Strand on the Green W4 3PH**
email: info@citybargechiswick.com

Fantastic location by the Thames

Slap bang next to the Thames in Chiswick, The City Barge dates in part to the 14th century. With three open fires, old prints on the walls and photographs of the river and the famous Thames barges, it's certainly full of character. There's a private dining room overlooking the water, and loads of outside seating so you can enjoy a pint of Greene King IPA or the house bitter, Argey Bargey, in the sunshine. On the menu perhaps, Mediterranean charcuterie; miso-glazed duck leg; moules marinière; trio of lobster (tail thermidor, claw fritter and lobster and basil risotto), or braised rabbit and smoked ham hock pappardelle.

Open all day all wk **Food** Contact pub for food times Set menu available Restaurant menu available all wk ⊕ FREE HOUSE/METROPOLITAN PUBS ◀ Greene King IPA, Argey Bargey (house bitter) Ò Truman's Cote Breton. ☻ 20 **Facilities** Non-diners area ❖ (Bar Garden Outside area) ◀◀ Children's menu Children's portions Garden Outside area ⋈ Beer festival Cider festival Parking WiFi ▦ (notice required)

W4 *continued*

The Swan   PLAN 2 D3   PICK OF THE PUBS

tel: 020 8994 8262 **1 Evershed Walk, 119 Acton Ln, Chiswick W4 5HH**
email: reservations@theswanpub.com
dir: *At end of Evershed Walk*

Many real ales and cooking with a Mediterranean accent

A friendly dining-pub, The Swan is a perfect choice for all seasons. Its welcoming wood-panelled interior embraces all-comers in winter, and a large lawned garden and patio are popular in summer. A garden room can be booked for special occasions. Good food is at the heart of the operation; you can sit and eat wherever you like. The menu of modern, mostly Mediterranean cooking has a particularly Italian influence. Start perhaps with pan-fried grey mullet with courgette, gnocchi and basil butter; next could be penne with spicy Italian sausage and tomato ragout, with oregano and cream. A short choice of desserts may include chocolate terrine with marshmallow, honeycombe and orange mascarpone. It's a cuisine that lends itself to tasty vegetarian options: an excellent example is a starter of butternut squash, parsnip crisps, golden raisins and smoked cheddar with leaves.

Open all wk 5-11.30 (Sat 12-11.30 Sun 12-11) Closed 24-28 Dec **Food** Lunch Sat 12.30-10.30, Sun 12.30-10 Dinner Mon-Thu 6-10, Fri 6-10.30, Sat 12.30-10.30, Sun 12.30-10 Av main course £15 ⊕ FREE HOUSE ◀ Fuller's London Pride, St Austell Tribute, Dark Star Hophead, Sambrook's, Twickenham Fine Ales, Otter Bitter ♂ Cornish Orchards, Orchard Pig Reveller. ☗ 12 **Facilities** Non-diners area ❤ (Bar Garden) ♦♦ Children's portions Garden ⌂ WiFi

---

▌ W5

The Grove ◉   PLAN 2 C3

tel: 020 85672439 **The Green, Ealing W5 5QX**
email: info@thegrovew5.co.uk
dir: *Nearest tube: Ealing Broadway*

Cosmopolitan food, cosmopolitan West London

Now in new hands, the well-positioned Grove lies between Ealing Broadway's shops and the famous film studios. In addition to the bar and restaurant there's an outdoor dining area and a large terrace. The menu's cosmopolitan tone comes from such items as a starter of scallop raviolo with brown shrimps, samphire and chilli butter, while the British side is represented by slow-cooked Hampshire pork belly with white beans, pancetta, celeriac and cider stew; and beer-battered North Sea haddock, hand-cut chips and mushy peas. At least three roasts and a full menu is served throughout Sunday. Beer festivals are held in February and October.

Open all day all wk **Food** Lunch 12-4 Dinner 6-10 Restaurant menu available all wk ⊕ METROPOLITAN PUBS ◀ Dark Star Hophead, Twickenham Naked Ladies, Portobello Chestnut Ale, Truman's Runner, Greene King IPA. ☗ 17 **Facilities** Non-diners area ❤ (Bar Garden) ♦♦ Children's menu Children's portions Garden ⌂ Beer festival WiFi ▭

▌ W6

Anglesea Arms ◉   PLAN 2 D3   PICK OF THE PUBS

tel: 020 8749 1291 **35 Wingate Rd W6 0UR**
email: theangleseaarmsw6@gmail.com
dir: *Phone for detailed directions*

Reliable experience in west London

Built in 1866, this traditional Victorian corner pub is thriving in the hands of Richard and George Manners, whose experience with seven other London pubs has

stood them in good stead. The Anglesea Arms' reputation has grown steadily, thanks to a rotating choice of real ales in the bar, a global wine list to suit every taste and pocket, and a concise menu of carefully prepared food. The ambience too plays its part. Located between Shepherd's Bush and Hammersmith, the bar's sofas make for cosy fireside drinking, there's an intimate dining area at the rear, and the outdoor terrace is popular in summer. Chef Phil Harrison mixes British and continental ingredients to great effect. A typical three-course choice could begin with smoked mackerel rillettes, pickled cucumber and rye bread; followed by slow-cooked duck leg with mash, kale and onions; and finish with malted caramel pears, whipped mascarpone, tarragon and meringues.

Open all wk 5-11 (Fri-Sat 12-11 Sun 12-10.30) Closed 24-26 Dec **Food** Lunch Fri-Sat 12-3, Sun 12-9 Dinner Mon-Sat 6-10, Sun 12-9 ⊕ ENTERPRISE INNS ◀ Rotating guest ales. ☗ 20 **Facilities** Non-diners area ❤ (Bar Garden) ♦♦ Children's menu Children's portions Garden ⌂

The Dartmouth Castle   PLAN 2 D3   PICK OF THE PUBS

tel: 020 8748 3614 **26 Glenthorne Rd, Hammersmith W6 0LS**
email: dartmouth.castle@btconnect.com
dir: *Nearest tube: Hammersmith. 100yds from Hammersmith Broadway*

Corner pub with a reputation for imaginative cooking

The Dartmouth Castle is very much a place to relax in, serving a good range of refreshments and plates of very appealing food. It's a child-free zone after 7pm too, adding to its appeal for those seeking a quiet evening pint. Sambrook's make their mark with ales such as Wandle; alternatives are Cornish Orchards cider amidst a generous choice of cosmopolitan bottled ciders, beers and lagers; more than a dozen wines are sold by the glass. From the menu, expect imaginative flavours in starters such as roast pheasant and ham hock terrine; or seared scallops with Jerusalem artichoke purée. Move on to a main course of pan-fried venison fillet or slow-cooked guinea fowl, and finish with apple and rhubarb crumble.

Open all day 12-11 (Sat 5-11 Sun 12-10.30) Closed Etr, 23 Dec-2 Jan, Sat L **Food** Lunch Mon-Fri 12-2.30, Sun 12-9.30 Dinner Mon-Sat 6-10, Sun 12-9.30 ⊕ FREE HOUSE ◀ Sharp's Doom Bar, Sambrook's Wandle, Otter Bitter, St Austell Tribute, guest ales ♂ Cornish Orchards, Symonds Founders Reserve. ☗ 15 **Facilities** Non-diners area ❤ (Bar Restaurant Garden) ♦♦ Garden ⌂ WiFi

---

The Hampshire Hog   PLAN 2 D3

tel: 020 8748 3391 **225-227 King St W6 9JT**
email: info@the-hog.com
dir: *Nearest tube: Hammersmith & Ravenscourt Park*

Stylish dining-pub with its own pantry of home-made delights

Located between Chiswick and Hammersmith, this corner gastro-pub may be Victorian on the outside but it's stylishly contemporary within, with wood floors, white walls and an airy conservatory. With three additional private dining rooms and outdoor tables, there are plenty of options when it comes to eating here and the seasonal menu might include lemon, ricotta, basil and cherry tomato tart; onglet steak (served rare), parsnip crisps and chimichurri sauce; and sparkling champagne pannacotta with rose meringue. Health conscious customers can look to the salads, and gluten free options are available too. Brunch is served from 10am until midday and home-made products can be bought from the pub's pantry.

Open all day all wk 10am-11pm (Sun 10am-9pm) Closed 26 Dec **Food** Lunch Mon-Sat 12-4, Sun & BHs 12.30-4.30 Dinner Mon-Sat 6-10.30, Sun 6-8.30 Set menu available Restaurant menu available all wk ⊕ STAR PUBS & BARS ◀ Caledonian 80/- & Deuchars IPA ♂ Symonds. **Facilities** Non-diners area ❤ (Bar Garden) ♦♦ Children's menu Children's portions Garden ⌂ WiFi ▭ (notice required)

The Stonemasons Arms PLAN 2 D3

tel: 020 8748 1397 **54 Cambridge Grove W6 0LA**
email: stonemasonsarms@fullers.co.uk
dir: *From Hammersmith tube station into King St, 2nd right into Cambridge Grove, pub at end*

Creative cooking and artwork to admire

This family friendly pub wraps round the end of a terrace of elegant houses in leafy Hammersmith. Handy for leading cultural venues and good transport links, the curious rustic-Georgian ambience of the pub is enhanced by a rolling display of artworks by local artists in the upstairs gallery restaurant. On the beer front are reliable quaffs from the Fuller's stable, complemented by an extensive list of 20 wines by the glass. Bar menus impress, covering the whole gamut from butternut squash and root veg crumble to pancetta, chorizo and white bean cassoulet; a set evening menu will add to the tricky decisions that need to be made.

Open all day all wk 11-11 (Sun 12-10.30) **Food** Lunch Mon-Fri 12-3, Sat 12-10, Sun 12-9 Dinner Mon-Fri 6-10, Sat 12-10, Sun 12-9 Av main course £12 Set menu available Restaurant menu available Mon-Sat ⊕ FULLER'S ◄ London Pride & Organic Honey Dew, Wild River, Frontier, Peroni, Guinness Ò Cornish Orchards. ⌻ 20 **Facilities** Non-diners area ❖ (Bar Outside area) ♦ Children's menu Children's portions Outside area ⋒ WiFi ⛟ (notice required)

W8

The Scarsdale PLAN 2 E3

tel: 020 7937 1811 **23A Edwardes Square, Kensington W8 6HE**
email: scarsdale@fullers.co.uk
dir: *From Kensington High Street tube station turn left. 0.5m (10 mins' walk) left into Edwardes Square after Odeon Cinema*

19th-century character pub in quiet area

The Scarsdale is a 19th-century free-standing building with colourful hanging baskets and window boxes spilling into the small terraced patio, in a leafy road just off Kensington High Street. The Frenchman who developed the site was supposedly one of Bonaparte's secret agents, but more recently – the 1970s and 80s – The Scarsdale played a role as the local watering hole for Bodie and Doyle, in ITV's *The Professionals*. A typical restaurant menu offers slow-roasted shoulder of lamb with flageolet beans, red wine, rosemary sauce, mash and veg; chargrilled chicken ciabatta sandwich with spinach, bacon, avocado and chips; or fish pie with leek and cheesy mash. There is also an equally tempting bar menu, and an impressive wine list.

Open all day all wk 12-11 (Sun 12-10.30) **Food** Mon-Sat 12-10, Sun 12-9.30 ⊕ FULLER'S ◄ London Pride, George Gale & Co Seafarers, guest ales Ò Cornish Orchards. ⌻ 20 **Facilities** Non-diners area ❖ (Bar Garden) Garden ⋒ WiFi

The Windsor Castle PLAN 2 E3

tel: 020 7243 8797 **114 Campden Hill Rd W8 7AR**
email: enquiry@thewindsorcastlekensington.co.uk
web: www.thewindsorcastlekensington.co.uk
dir: *From Notting Hill tube station into Bayswater Rd towards Holland Park. Left into Campden Hill Rd*

Eccentric and therefore not to be missed

One legend has it that Windsor Castle could be seen from the upstairs windows when this eponymous pub was built in the 1830s. Such stories add to the fascination of this pub, where wood panelling separates three areas inexplicably called Campden, Private and Sherry. Enjoy a pint of Timothy Taylor Landlord or Aspall cider as you choose from a menu that might include steak, pancetta and Porter ale pie; pan-fried sea bass, heritage potatoes, sautéed kale and lobster thermidor sauce; or cod and chips. Canine (and the occasional feline) visitors have their own 'dogstation' corner with toys and treats.

Open all wk 12-11 (Sat 10am-11pm Sun 12-10.30) **Food** Lunch Mon-Sat 12-10, Sun 12-9 (Brunch Sat 10am-noon) Dinner Mon-Sat 12-10, Sun 12-9 ⊕ MITCHELLS & BUTLERS ◄ Timothy Taylor Landlord, rotating guest ales Ò Aspall. ⌻ 21 **Facilities** Non-diners area ❖ (Bar Restaurant Garden) ♦ Children's menu Children's portions Garden ⋒ Beer festival Cider festival WiFi ⛟ (notice required)

W9

The Waterway   PLAN 2 E4

tel: 020 7266 3557 **54 Formosa St W9 2JU**
email: info@thewaterway.co.uk
dir: *From Warwick Avenue tube station into Warwick Av, turn left into Formosa St*

Canalside pub with a great range of drinks

Enjoying a lovely setting in Maida Vale, The Waterway offers great alfresco
opportunities with is outdoor terrace, where popular barbecues are held in summer.
In colder weather, the bar is a great place to relax with its sumptuous sofas and
open fires. There is a good choice of drinks, including many wines and a couple of
champagnes by the glass, as well as draught beers and non-alcoholic cocktails.
The menus offer British and European food – wild mushroom and kale risotto; roast
duck breast with butternut squash purée, confit garlic and kale; or Guinness
braised Irish lamb stew with colcannon mash and winter greens. Apple and pear
crumble or baked vanilla and lemon cheesecake make a great way to finish.

Open all day all wk 11am-mdnt (Sat 10-mdnt Sun 10am-11pm) **Food** all day
Av main course £12.50 Set menu available Restaurant menu available all wk
⊕ ENTERPRISE INNS ◀ Sharp's Doom Bar, Fuller's London Pride, Skinner's Cornish
Knocker, Red Squirrel Redwood American IPA ♻ Aspall. ♱ 16
Facilities Non-diners area ♦♦ Children's menu Children's portions Garden ⋒ WiFi ▭

W11

Portobello Gold   PLAN 2 E3

tel: 020 7460 4900 **95-97 Portobello Rd, Notting Hill W11 2QB**
email: reservations@portobellogold.com
dir: *From Notting Hill Gate tube station follow signs to Portobello Market*

A touch of gold in Notting Hill

Many famous visitors have called in or become regulars at this quirky Notting Hill
pub/wine bar/brasserie in the heart of famous Portobello Road Market. The menus
here always list game and seafood, including bar snacks of rock oysters and
charcuterie. All dishes are prepared from scratch on the premises and typical
choices might include Thai-style steamed mussels followed by wild mushroom
linguine, parmesan and rocket. With the landlord's wife an established wine writer,
around 20 wines by the glass should be no surprise. The pub also offers an
interesting range of British ales and European beers and cocktails.

Open all day all wk **Food** all day Set menu available ⊕ ENTERPRISE INNS ◀ Harvey's
Sussex, guest ales ♻ Thatchers Gold, Katy & Spartan. ♱ 18
Facilities Non-diners area ♥ (Bar) ♦♦ Children's portions ⋒ WiFi ▭ (notice
required)

The Red Lemon   PLAN 2 D4

tel: 020 7229 5963 **45 All Saints Rd, Notting Hill W11 1HE**
email: info@theredlemon.co.uk
dir: *Nearest tube stations: Westbourne Park & Ladbroke Grove*

Music, food and beer in Notting Hill

The Red Lemon, as its now called, has been a pub for 130 years and has seen
plenty of changes in Notting Hill. Embracing its setting, music is important here,
and the clientele is a mix of locals, young professionals, and musicians and artists,
some of whom are responsible for the art on the walls. The pub and restaurant
areas are separate, so the bar feels properly pub-like. Modern takes on pub classics
might bring choices like spiced crab on toast followed by ham, fried duck egg and
chips. They do Sunday roasts as well.

Open all day Closed Mon **Food** Tue-Wed 12-10, Thu-Sat 12-10.30, Sun 12-8.30
⊕ FREE HOUSE ◀ Portobello ♻ Addlestones, Orchard Pig. ♱ 14 **Facilities** ♥ (Bar
Restaurant Outside area) ♦♦ Children's menu Children's portions Outside area ⋒
WiFi ▭

W12

Princess Victoria   PLAN 2 D3

tel: 020 8749 5886 **217 Uxbridge Rd W12 9DH**
email: info@princessvictoria.co.uk **web:** www.princessvictoria.co.uk
dir: *Nearest tube: Shepherd's Bush Market*

Former 'gin palace' keeping its heritage alive

The building dates from 1829 when it was the terminus of a tram route from Acton.
Not until it was rebuilt in 1872 did it take on its new vocation and grand 'gin
palace' appearance thanks to architect William Bruton; he was known as 'the
supreme music hall artist of pub architects'. In keeping with this heritage, today's
Princess Victoria maintains a close relationship with a local gin distillery –
Sipsmiths in Chiswick; the Gin Palace Extravaganza, a distillery tour, followed by a
meal at the pub is an ever popular feature of their busy social diary. The brasserie-
style menu ranges from fine charcuterie to steaks from the charcoal oven served
with triple-cooked chips.

Open all day all wk Closed 24-28 Dec **Food** Lunch Mon-Sat 12-3, Sun 12-4.30
Dinner Mon-Sat 6.30-10.30, Sun 6.30-9.30 Set menu available Restaurant menu
available all wk ⊕ FREE HOUSE ◀ Timothy Taylor Landlord, Portobello Pale
♻ Addlestones, Orchard Pig Reveller, Westons Wyld Wood Organic. ♱ 20
Facilities Non-diners area ♥ (Bar Garden) ♦♦ Children's menu Children's portions
Garden ⋒ Parking WiFi ▭ (notice required)

W14

The Albion   PLAN 2 D3

tel: 020 7603 2826 **121 Hammersmith Rd, West Kensington W14 0QL**
email: info@thealbionpub.com
dir: *Near Kensington Olympia & Barons Court tube stations*

Old pub with a great atmosphere

If you've been wandering around Olympia all day head across the road to The Albion
for a pint of London Pride, St Austell Tribute or one of the many wines by the glass.
A fine old pub that takes its name from HMS *Albion*, it has the look and feel of an
old ship, with bare floor boards and long, scrubbed wooden tables. The menu
features a selection of burgers and salads, with jackets, sandwiches and omelettes
available at lunchtime. Other choices are sausages, mash, rich onion gravy; Cajun
chicken; home-made steak and ale pie; and battered fish and chips. There is an
August beer festival.

Open all day all wk **Food** Lunch Mon-Fri 12-3 Dinner all wk 5-10 ⊕ HEINEKEN
◀ Fuller's London Pride, St Austell Tribute, guest ales ♻ Symonds. ♱ 13
Facilities Non-diners area ♥ (Bar Restaurant Outside area) Outside area ⋒ Beer
festival WiFi ▭ (notice required)

The Cumberland Arms   PLAN 2 D3   **PICK OF THE PUBS**

tel: 020 7371 6806 **29 North End Rd, Hammersmith W14 8SZ**
email: thecumberlandarmspub@btconnect.com
dir: *From Kensington Olympia tube station turn left. At T-junct right into Hammersmith Rd. 3rd left into North End Rd, 100yds pub on left*

Gastro-pub with a locals' atmosphere

At the heart of cosmopolitan Hammersmith and handy for Olympia, this eye-catching diners' pub, generously dressed with colourful summer hanging baskets and boxes, is a popular place for people-watching. Bag a bench beside the adjacent flowery enclave on sunny days, or head inside where mellow furniture and stripped floorboards characterise the interior. Friendly staff, a comprehensive wine list and well-kept ales (St Austell Tribute, Skinner's Betty Stogs, Exmoor Gold) are the draw for those seeking after-work refreshment. But it's also a great place for sampling enticing cuisine with an Italian accent from a regularly updated menu and specials selection. Starters embrace Jerusalem artichoke and pancetta salad; and bruschetta al pomodoro. Among the mains are penne with Italian sausage ragù; salmon and dill fishcakes; and pan-roast fillet of sea bass with shaved fennel, olive and orange salad. Desserts are few but sweet: sticky date pudding with caramel, perhaps, or chocolate brownie with ice cream.

Open all day all wk 12-11 (Sun 12-10.30 Thu-Fri 12-12) Closed 24 Dec-1 Jan **Food** Lunch Mon-Sat 12-3, Sun 12-9.30 Dinner Mon-Sat 6-10, Sun 12-9.30 ⊕ FREE HOUSE ◼ Exmoor Gold, Sharp's Doom Bar, Skinner's Betty Stogs, St Austell Tribute. ♟ 16 **Facilities** Non-diners area ❖ (Bar Restaurant Garden) ♦ Children's portions Garden ᴨ WiFi ▭ (notice required)

WC1

The Bountiful Cow   PLAN 1 E4   **PICK OF THE PUBS**

tel: 020 7404 0200 **51 Eagle St, Holborn WC1R 4AP**
email: manager@roxybeaujolais.com
dir: *230mtrs NE from Holborn tube station, via Procter St. Walk through 2 arches into Eagle St. Pub between High Holborn & Red Lion Square*

Homage to the cow

Pub cookbook author Roxy Beaujolais runs this 'public house devoted to beef', her second pub venture following the delightful Seven Stars in WC2. Two floors are crowded with framed pictures of cows, bullfights, cowgirls, diagrams of meat cuts and posters of cow-themed films; jazzy but discreet music adds to an atmosphere halfway between funky bistro and stylish saloon. The well kept ales are from Adnams or guest breweries, and the short but estimable wine list includes equally gutsy reds. The value-priced menu features Bountyburgers and perfectly grilled and tender aged steaks; the meat is sourced from a trusted Smithfield Market supplier. Starters of garlic fried prawns or octopus salad, and desserts like Belgian apple tart with vanilla ice cream might open and close the proceedings, with an oak steak board platter for two in between. Booking for all meals is advisable.

Open all day 11-11 (Sat 12-11) Closed 25-26 Dec, 1 Jan, BHs, Sun **Food** Mon-Sat 12-10.30 ⊕ FREE HOUSE ◼ Adnams Southwold Bitter, guest ales ♂ Aspall. ♟ **Facilities** Non-diners area ❖ (Bar Outside area) ♦ Outside area ᴨ WiFi ▭ (notice required)

The Easton   PLAN 1 E5

tel: 020 7278 7608 **22 Easton St WC1X 0DS**
email: info@theeastonpub.co.uk
dir: *Nearest tube stations: Farringdon; Angel; Kings Cross*

Modern dining in deepest Clerkenwell

Near the famous Sadlers Wells Theatre a short distance from Farringdon tube, this pub with pavement benches is also just a stroll away from EC1's Exmouth Market. Timothy Taylor, Truman's and Hackney Pale Ale are the top real ales. A dozen tasty bar snacks tempt with the likes of porcini arancini; mini smoked haddock fishcakes with tartare sauce; and smoked ham croquettes with aïoli. These indicate the modern approach to cosmopolitan ingredients found on the seasonally-changing main menu, in dishes such as rabbit ravioli with parmesan; pan-fried pollock fillet; and asparagus, tarragon and goats' cheese pie.

Open all day all wk ⊕ FREE HOUSE ◼ Timothy Taylor Landlord, Truman's Runner, Hackney Pale Ale ♂ Westons Stowford Press, Cidre Breton. **Facilities** ❖ (Bar Restaurant Outside area) ♦ Children's menu Outside area WiFi

The Lady Ottoline   PLAN 1 E4

tel: 020 7831 0008 **11A Northington St WC1N 2JF**
email: info@theladyottoline.com **web:** www.theladyottoline.com
dir: *Nearest tube: Chancery Lane*

Classic London corner pub and dining rooms

A blue plaque marks the house in nearby Gower Street where Bloomsbury aristocrat and society hostess Lady Ottoline Morrell lived. Her memory also lives on in this attractive corner pub with a log fire, where rotating real ales, bottled craft beers, several real ciders, and nine wines by the glass are always at the ready. Mount the stairs to the cosy dining rooms for good seasonal British food. Start with canapés, or tomato salad with black olives and Lincolnshire poacher cheese; continue with Cornish plaice, peas, smoked bacon and caper butter; or chicken, leek and mushroom pie with spring greens; and finish up with sticky toffee pudding and vanilla ice cream; or dark chocolate and honey mousse with a hazelnut cookie.

Open all wk 12-11 (Sun 12-5) Closed 25 Dec-2 Jan, BHs **Food** Lunch Mon-Fri 12-3, Sat 12-4, Sun 12-5 Dinner Mon-Sat 6.30-10 Set menu available ⊕ PUNCH TAVERNS ◼ Portobello Star, Sambrook's Wandle, Adnams ♂ Addlestones, Aspall, Hoxton. ♟ 9 **Facilities** Non-diners area ❖ (Bar Outside area) ♦ Children's portions Outside area ᴨ WiFi

Norfolk Arms   PLAN 1 D5

tel: 020 7388 3937 **28 Leigh St WC1H 9EP**
email: info@norfolkarms.co.uk
dir: *Nearest tube: Russell Square, King's Cross St Pancras & Euston*

Classic London corner pub offering international tapas

Set amidst the elegant terraces of Bloomsbury, this eye-catching partly tile-fronted Victorian pub brings a taste of Spain and the Med to this cosmopolitan corner of London. Its gastro-pub credentials — braised beef cheeks with celeriac mash or whole sea bream with sautéed spinach examples of such — are greatly enhanced by the extensive tapas menu that draws an appreciative clientele from a wide area. Chorizo in cider; fried paprika pork belly; roast biodynamic pumpkin or saganaky (baked feta) give a flavour of the ever-changing tastes of the moment. Mainstream beers and 10 wines by the glass accompany the food, whilst private dining facilities are available.

Open all day all wk Closed 25-26, 31 Dec & 1 Jan **Food** Lunch Mon-Fri 12-3, Sat 12-4, Sun 12-10.15 Dinner Mon-Sat 6-12.15, Sun 12-10.15 Set menu available ⊕ STAR PUBS & BARS ◼ Theakston XB, Greene King IPA. ♟ 10 **Facilities** Non-diners area ❖ (Bar) ♦ Children's portions ᴨ WiFi

WC2

The Seven Stars   PLAN 1 E4   PICK OF THE PUBS

tel: 020 7242 8521 **53 Carey St WC2A 2JB**
email: roxy@roxybeaujolais.com
dir: *From Temple tube station turn right. 1st left into Arundel St. Right into Strand (walking). Left into Bell Yard. 1st left into Carey St*

A real one-off – stylish saloon style and market driven dishes

The Seven Stars may never have seen better days in its 415 years of existence. Since Roxy Beaujolais took over this Grade II listed pub behind the Royal Courts of Justice 17 years ago, delicate and undisruptive primping has produced nothing but accolades. Look out for the mullioned glass dumbwaiter, designed by Roxy's architect husband, that looks tactfully historic, and the cat, named Ray Brown, who wears a ruff just as his predecessor did. Strengthened by its personalities and ambience, The Seven Stars is considered the ideal pub – the food is simple but well executed, the ales are kept perfectly, the wines are few but very good, and the staff are welcoming and efficient. Roxy cooks most of the time here. The day's dishes, listed on the blackboard, change according to what's best in the market and what tickles Roxy's fancy. Examples are cured herring and potato salad; chicken liver pâté; goose rillettes; linguine with chorizo and crayfish; oxtail and mash; chicken and potato pie; and braised beef ribs.

Open all day all wk 11–11 (Sat 12–11 Sun 12–10.30) Closed 25–26 Dec, 1 Jan **Food** Mon–Fri 12–9.30, Sat–Sun 1–9.30 Av main course £11.50 ⊕ FREE HOUSE ◧ Adnams Southwold Bitter & Broadside, Sambrook's Wandle, Sharp's Cornish Coaster Ŏ Aspall. **Facilities** Non-diners area WiFi

The Sherlock Holmes   PLAN 1 D3

tel: 020 7930 2644 **10 Northumberland St WC2N 5DB**
email: hello@sherlockholmes-stjames.co.uk
dir: *From Charing Cross tube station into Villiers St. Through 'The Arches' (runs underneath Charing Cross station) straight across Craven St into Craven Passage to Northumberland St*

Themed pub serving comforting pub grub

Painted black with etched glass windows and colourful hanging baskets, this traditional corner pub is chock-full of Holmes memorabilia, including photographs of Conan Doyle, mounted pages from manuscripts, and artefacts and pieces recording the adventures of the Master Detective. There's even a replica of Holmes' and Watson's sitting room and study. This split-level establishment has a bar on the ground floor and on the first floor an intimate covered roof garden and the restaurant. There's Sherlock Holmes Ale to drink, hot and cold bar food plus a menu offering Holmesian food choices like Rupert Everett's smoked salmon, Mrs Hudson's home-made steak and ale pie, Mary Sunderland's Cumberland sausages, and (non-Holmesian) vanilla and mascarpone cheesecake for afters.

Open all day all wk Closed 25 Dec **Food** all wk 11–10 ⊕ GREENE KING ◧ IPA, Sherlock Holmes Ale, Watson's Golden Ale, Abbot Ale, guest ales Ŏ Mortimers Orchard. ⬤ 14 **Facilities** Non-diners area ◖◗ Outside area 🚗 WiFi 🚌 (notice required)

GREATER LONDON

CARSHALTON   Map 6 TQ26

The Sun

tel: 020 8773 4549 **4 North St SM5 2HU**
email: thesuncarshalton@googlemail.com
dir: *From A232 (Croydon Rd) between Croydon & Sutton, turn into North St signed Hackbridge (B277). Pub on right at x-roads*

Stylish pub with excellent real ales and good food

This imposing corner-plot pub stands close to the heart of Carshalton village. The enclosed walled garden area houses a wood-fired pizza oven, whilst a private dining room is ideal for group gatherings. Both wet and food sides of the business are increasingly popular; six real ales, such as Sharp's Doom Bar, Brighton Bier and Slater's attract beer lovers – there's a summer beer festival, too. The tempting menu encourages diners to tarry a while in the modish interior. Commence with green tea-cured mackerel, wasabi tomato, pickled fennel and coal mayo; leaving room for mains such as confit duck leg, pecan and sultana couscous, maple parsnip and pomegranate dressing; or squid, mussel and clam linguine.

Open all day all wk **Food** Lunch Mon–Fri 12–3, Sat 12–10, Sun 12–8 Dinner Mon Fri 6–9.30, Sat 12–10, Sun 12–8 Set menu available Restaurant menu available ⊕ FREE HOUSE ◧ Sharp's Doom Bar, Brighton Bier, Slater's Ŏ Aspall. ⬤ 14 **Facilities** Non-diners area ❀ (Bar Restaurant Garden) ◖◗ Children's menu Children's portions Family room Garden 🚗 Beer festival WiFi 🚌 (notice required)

CHELSFIELD   Map 6 TQ46

The Bo-Peep

tel: 01959 534457 **Hewitts Rd BR6 7QL**
dir: *M25 junct 4 (Bromley exit). At rdbt follow Well Hill sign. Pub approx 500yds on right*

Traditional home cooking close to the M25

Turn off the ever hectic M25 and within just five minutes you could be enjoying the tranquillity of this 14th-century inn. The low timber beams and inglenook in the bar offer plenty of original character, and Adnams, Sharp's Doom Bar, and Westerham (when possible) are on tap to quench your thirst. Just about everything is home cooked and typical dishes include belly of pork with cider jus; and fillet of sea bass with ratatouille. On sunny days, take a table in the large garden and admire the views.

Open all day all wk **Food** Contact pub for food times Av main course £12 Set menu available ⊕ ENTERPRISE INNS ◧ Adnams, Sharp's Doom Bar, Westerham's Beers on rotation Ŏ Thatchers. ⬤ 12 **Facilities** ❀ (Bar Garden) ◖◗ Children's portions Garden 🚗 Parking WiFi

The Five Bells   PICK OF THE PUBS

tel: 01689 821044 **BR6 7RE**
dir: *M25 junct 4, A224 towards Orpington. In approx 1m turn right into Church Rd. Pub on left*

Country pub with good food and live music

The Five Bells is a whitewashed Grade II listed building that dates from the late 17th century and takes its name from the magnificent bells at the church just up the road. Set in a protected conservation village, it's handy for the M25 as well as many lovely walks. There are two bars: one is a dog-friendly front bar boasting an original inglenook fireplace; the other is the dining room, leading out to the patio and extensive garden, which comes complete with a children's play area. The seasonal menu complements the real ales and wines on offer: maybe start with pork belly and crackling with black pudding, or a traditional prawn cocktail, followed by beer-battered cod and chips; freshly-made pie of the day; or lamb hotpot. Sandwiches, baguettes, ciabattas and pizzas are available too, and beer festivals take place at Easter and in October along with regular live music and quizzes.

Open all day all wk **Food** Lunch all wk 12-2.45 Dinner Thu-Sat 6.30-8.45 Av main course £11.50 Restaurant menu available Thu-Sat eve ⊕ ENTERPRISE INNS ◀ Courage Best Bitter, Sharp's Doom Bar, Otter, Jennings Cumberland. ♟ 13 **Facilities** Non-diners area ✿ (Bar Garden) ♦ Children's menu Children's portions Play area Garden ⋒ Beer festival Parking WiFi ⛟ (notice required)

HAREFIELD
Map 6 TQ09

The Old Orchard

tel: 01895 822631 **Park Ln UB9 6HJ**
email: old.orchard@brunningandprice.co.uk
dir: M25 junct 17, follow Harefield signs. Before Harefield follow pub signs

No other buildings in sight, just lakes and countryside

An early 20th-century country house that became a B&B in the Sixties, a Seventies' dance venue and then a restaurant, until Brunning & Price bought and transformed it. The outside looks good, and the inside can hold its head high too, with open fires, honest-to-goodness furniture and a decent bar, where the six real ales include Tring Brewery's Side Pocket for a Toad, and whiskies top 140. Daily menus offers dishes such as sweetcorn pannacotta, Moroccan croquette, avocado and coriander salsa, sweet chilli popcorn; bouillabaisse; pork tenderloin green curry with lemongrass cauliflower cake; and smoked salmon and haddock fishcakes. An outside bar and barbecue function in the summer.

Open all day all wk **Food** Mon-Sat 12-10, Sun 12-9.30 ⊕ FREE HOUSE ◀ Tring Side Pocket for a Toad, Brunning & Price Original Bitter, Mighty Oak Oscar Wilde ♻ Thistly Cross, Aspall, Westons Old Rosie & Stowford Press. ♟ 18 **Facilities** Non-diners area ✿ (Bar Restaurant Garden) ♦ Children's menu Children's portions Play area Garden ⋒ Beer festival Parking WiFi ⛟ (notice required)

RICHMOND UPON THAMES

The White Swan   PLAN 2 C2

tel: 020 8940 0959 **26 Old Palace Ln TW9 1PG**
email: info@whiteswanrichmond.co.uk
dir: Nearest tube: Richmond

Excellent food in the heart of Richmond

Tucked away from Richmond's bustling high street, The White Swan dates back to 1777. Whether it's for a pint of Timothy Taylor Landlord in the cosy bar with its open fire or a meal in the upstairs dining room or suntrap garden, this is a pub to suit every occasion. The kitchen has gained a good reputation for its daily-changing menus. A typical meal might feature Thai-spiced salmon and smoked haddock fish cakes, followed by puff pastry chicken and ham pie with mixed vegetables. Look out for pub dog Jake, a friendly Springer Spaniel. Please note, only those 18 years and over are permitted after 6.30pm.

Open all day all wk **Food** Lunch Mon-Wed 12-2.30, Thu-Fri 12-2.45, Sat 12-3.30, Sun 12.30-3.30 Dinner Mon 6.30-8.45, Tue 6.30-9.15, Wed-Sat 6.30-9.30, Sun 6.30-8.30 ⊕ FREE HOUSE ◀ Sharp's Doom Bar, Timothy Taylor Landlord, Otter Bitter, St Austell Tribute ♻ Aspall, Orchard Pig. ♟ 18 **Facilities** Non-diners area ✿ (Bar Restaurant Outside area) ♦ Children's portions Outside area ⋒ WiFi

MERSEYSIDE

BARNSTON
Map 15 SJ28

Fox and Hounds

tel: 0151 648 7685 **107 Barnston Rd CH61 1BW**
email: info@the-fox-hounds.co.uk
dir: M53 junct 4, A5137 to Heswall, onto A551 signed Barnston

Home-cooked food in friendly village pub

In the quaint village of Barnston can be found the Fox and Hounds. Built in 1911, the pub's Edwardian character is preserved in its leaded windows, pitch-pine woodwork and open fire. In the Snug, the original bar, are impressive collections of bric-à-brac including 200 horse brasses, 30 brewery clocks and 66 flying ducks. A good variety of real ales includes Theakston and Timothy Taylor; a huge range of malts appeals to whisky aficionados; and Rosie's Llandegla cider is made over the border in North Wales. The frequently-changing menu always includes favourites such as steak pie, curries, sausages and mash, and cottage pie, along with sharing plates, lighter bites, toasted paninis and open sandwiches. Traditional Sunday roasts showcase Welsh lamb and beef.

Open all day all wk 11am-11.30pm (Sun 11-10.30) **Food** Lunch Mon-Thu 12-2, Fri-Sat 12-8, Sun 12-7 Dinner Tue-Thu 5-8, Fri-Sat 12-8, Sun 12-7 Av main course £8.95 ⊕ FREE HOUSE ◀ Theakston Best Bitter & Old Peculier, Brimstage Trapper's Hat, Timothy Taylor ♻ Aspall, Rosie's Llandegla. ♟ 15 **Facilities** Non-diners area ✿ (Bar Garden) ♦ Children's portions Garden ⋒ Parking WiFi ⛟ (notice required)

GREASBY
Map 15 SJ28

Irby Mill

tel: 0151 604 0194 **Mill Ln CH49 3NT**
email: info@irbymill.co.uk
dir: M53 junct 3, A552 signed Upton & Heswall. At lights onto A551 signed Upton & Greasby. At lights left into Arrowe Brook Rd. At rdbt 3rd exit into Mill Ln

Former miller's cottage serving local produce

An eye-catching, solid, sandstone-block built old miller's cottage (the windmill was demolished in 1898, the pub opened in 1980) just a short jog from the airy heights of Thurstaston Common at the heart of The Wirral Peninsula. One of the area's best choices of real ales meets an exceptional, very pubby menu strong on Wirral produce – 'Muffs' sausage and mash comes with black pudding, peas, mushrooms, gravy and onion rings and could be followed by Nicholls of Parkgate ice cream or Belgian waffles. Popular with ramblers and Sunday diners, there's a suntrap grassy garden for summer; a log fire for the winter.

Open all day all wk **Food** Mon-Sat 12-9, Sun 12-8 ⊕ STAR PUBS & BARS ◀ Wells Bombardier, Greene King Abbot Ale, Brains The Rev. James, 5 guest ales. ♟ 12 **Facilities** ✿ (Bar Garden) ♦ Children's menu Children's portions Garden ⋒ Parking WiFi ⛟

HESWALL
Map 15 SJ28

The Jug and Bottle

tel: 0151 342 5535 **Mount Av CH60 4RH**
email: info@the-jugandbottle.co.uk
dir: *From A540 in Heswall. At lights into The Mount, 1st left into Mount Ave*

Good locally-sourced food on the Wirral Peninsula

In the heart of Heswall, on the spectacular Wirral Peninsula with its views towards Liverpool and North Wales, 'The Jug' (as the locals call it) is tucked away off the main road but convenient for the M56. With two open fires and surrounded by gardens, this traditional country pub offers a warm welcome all year round, serving good food in the dining room and a range of real ales including local Brimstage Trapper's Hat. Locally-sourced food is served lunchtimes and evenings, typical choices being fisherman's pie with spring greens; and braised oxtail suet pudding with horseradish mash and ale gravy.

Open all day all wk **Food** Lunch Mon-Fri 12-2.30, Sat 12-9.30, Sun 12-8 Dinner Mon-Thu 5.30-9, Fri-5.30-9.30, Sat 12-9.30, Sun 12-8 ⊕ FREE HOUSE ◼ Brimstage Trapper's Hat, guest ales. **Facilities** Non-diners area ✿ (Bar Garden) ♦ Children's menu Children's portions Garden ⌒ Parking WiFi ☷

HIGHTOWN
Map 15 SD30

The Pheasant Inn

tel: 0151 929 2106 **20 Moss Ln L38 3RA**
email: enquiry@thepheasanthightown.co.uk
dir: *From A565 take B5193, follow signs to Hightown*

A different event every day of the week

This attractive pub with a whitewashed wooden exterior is a former alehouse with a sunny garden. It's just minutes from Crosby Beach, where sculptor Antony Gormley's famous 100 cast-iron figures gaze out to sea. Surrounded by fields and golf courses, the pub retains an original brick in the restaurant wall dated 1719. In the bar these days you'll find Marston's Wainwright alongside Aspall ciders. The menu is changed twice a year so expect dishes like pulled lobster brioche roll with twice-cooked chunky chips and thermidor dip; or slow-cooked pork belly, seared scallops with sticky ginger beer glaze and black pudding. There are also the legendary Sunday platter, fish suppers on 'Fin and Fizz' Fridays, and retro dining evenings.

Open all day all wk 12-11 (Sun 12-10.30) **Food** Lunch all wk 12-6 Dinner all wk 6-9.30 Set menu available Restaurant menu available all wk ⊕ MITCHELLS & BUTLERS ◼ Marston's Wainwright ☼ Aspall Draught & Organic. ▾ 30 **Facilities** Non-diners area ✿ (Bar Garden) ♦ Children's menu Garden ⌒ Parking WiFi

LIVERPOOL
Map 15 SJ39

The Monro

tel: 0151 707 9933 **92 Duke St L1 5AG**
email: mail.monro@themonrogroup.com
dir: *Phone for detailed directions*

Elegant pub offering fresh, locally sourced food

In 1746, merchant John Bolton built himself a finely-proportioned house, which today is this popular city pub. Bolton later entered history as a combatant in Liverpool's last recorded duel (he was the victor). The elegance of the interior would make him feel very nostalgic, although he might struggle with the concept of naming beers Boondoggle (Ringwood), Cocker Hoop (Jennings) and GingerBeard (Wychwood). Examples from a monthly-changing menu include six-hour confit of pork belly, celeriac mash, apple purée and purple sprouting broccoli; and guinea fowl ballotine, fondant potato, winter vegetables and red wine jus.

Open all day all wk Closed 25-26 Dec, 1 Jan ⊕ FREE HOUSE ◼ Ringwood Boondoggle, Jennings Cocker Hoop, Wychwood GingerBeard ☼ Thatchers Katy. **Facilities** ♦ Children's menu Children's portions Garden WiFi

NORFOLK

BAWBURGH
Map 13 TG10

Kings Head ★★★★ INN ◉◉
PICK OF THE PUBS

tel: 01603 744977 **Harts Ln NR9 3LS**
email: anton@kingsheadbawburgh.co.uk **web:** www.kingsheadbawburgh.co.uk
dir: *From A47 take B1108 W towards Watton. Right signed Bawburgh*

Worth finding after exploring nearby Norwich

Old English roses and lavender fragrance the lanes in front of this low, rambling 17th-century pub, set in a cosy village of flint and brick cottages beside the River Yare. Behind the roadside brick house rambles an eye-catching half-timbered cottage, complete with bulging walls, wooden floors and log fires. Leather sofas and a vaguely rustic mix of furnishings add to the charm which attracts customers keen to engage with Pamela and Anton Wimmer's enticing menu of pub favourites and something that little bit special. The busy kitchen team relies on East Anglian suppliers for virtually all the ingredients; grilled pigeon breast, salted popcorn, sweetcorn purée and toasted seeds is a typically uplifting starter. There's plenty of seafood on the monthly-changing menu – witness the steamed salmon with warm salad of green beans, courgettes and peas. Gluten free options and daily specials add to the choices.

Open all day Closed Sun eve Oct-Apr **Food** Lunch Mon-Sat 12-2, Sun 12-4, summer Sun 12-3 Dinner Mon-Sat 5.30-9, summer Sun 6-9 ⊕ FREE HOUSE ◼ Adnams Southwold Bitter & Broadside, Woodforde's Wherry, guest ale ☼ Aspall. ▾ 11 **Facilities** Non-diners area ✿ (Bar Garden) ♦ Children's menu Children's portions Garden ⌒ Parking WiFi ☷ (notice required) **Rooms** 6

BLAKENEY
Map 13 TG04

The Kings Arms

tel: 01263 740341 **Westgate St NR25 7NQ**
email: kingsarmsnorfolk@btconnect.com
dir: *From Holt or Fakenham take A148, then B1156 for 6m to Blakeney*

Very old pub in lovely seaside village

Tucked away in a popular fishing village close to north Norfolk's coastal path (Peddars Way), this thriving free house is the perfect refreshment stop following an invigorating walk, time spent birdwatching, or a boat trip to the nearby seal colony. Open all day and run by the same family for 40 years, it serves an excellent selection of real ales, including Norfolk-brewed Woodforde's Wherry that is backed by menus featuring locally caught fish and seasonal seafood. Perhaps locally gathered mussels in rich garlic cream sauce; cod, prawn and bacon chowder; steak and Adnams ale suet pudding; and braised Norfolk pheasant, herb stuffing, chipolatas, thyme and bacon jus.

Open all day all wk Closed 25 Dec eve **Food** 8.30am-9.30pm ⊕ FREE HOUSE ◼ Morland Old Speckled Hen, Woodforde's Wherry, Marston's Pedigree, Adnams Southwold Bitter, Greene King. ▾ 10 **Facilities** Non-diners area ✿ (Bar Restaurant Garden) ♦ Children's menu Children's portions Play area Family room Garden ⌒ Parking WiFi ☷

The White Horse Blakeney
PICK OF THE PUBS

tel: 01263 740574 **4 High St NR25 7AL**
email: blakeney@adnams.co.uk
dir: *From A148 (Cromer to King's Lynn road) onto A149 signed to Blakeney*

Popular pub in fishing village

Since the 17th century, this former coaching inn has been tucked away among Blakeney's flint-built fishermen's cottages, a short, steepish amble up from the small tidal harbour. The tastefully appointed, Adnams-stocked bar is stylish yet informal, the conservatory is naturally bright – both are eating areas, where the same menu and daily specials apply. Locally sourced food is a given, especially the lobster, crab and mussels from village fishermen, meats and game from Norfolk estates, soft fruit, salads, asparagus and free-range eggs from local smallholders, while rod- and line-caught mackerel and sea bass find their way through the kitchen door in summer. For a light lunch choose perhaps a ciabatta sandwich, a seasonal salad; Letzer's smoked cod and Cajun fishcake with mango dressing; or crispy squid rings with tom-yum mayo. For something a bit more substantial, how about a White Horse classic – Norfolk spring lamb hotpot; or roast hake, creamed mash, braised fennel, sauté wild mushrooms and crab bisque?

Open all day all wk 10.30am-11pm (Sun 10.30-10.30) **Food** Lunch all wk 12-2.30 Dinner Mon-Sat 6-9, Sun 6-8 ⊕ ADNAMS ◄ Southwold Bitter, Broadside & Ghost Ship ☼ Aspall. ♟ 14 **Facilities** Non-diners area ✿ (Bar Restaurant) ♦ Children's menu Children's portions Family room Outside area ⊨ Parking WiFi

■ BLICKLING   Map 13 TG12

NEW Buckinghamshire Arms

tel: 01263 732133 **NR11 6NF**
email: contact@bucksarms.co.uk
dir: From A140 at rdbt (S of Aylsham) into Norwich Rd signed Aylsham. Through Aylsham centre, follow to Blickling. Pub on right (adjacent to Blickling Hall)

Friendly welcome at this former coaching inn

Visitors to Blickling Hall often discover 'the Bucks' right next door. It's owned by the National Trust, leased by Colchester Inns, and run by a friendly team headed by Andy Snowling. The relaxed and unassuming ambience is in definite contrast to the stately pile a few minutes' walk away. Customers can pop in for coffee or tea with cake, or a traditional roast on Sundays. Ale lovers will find Norfolk brewer Woodforde's at the bar, along with a menu of pub dishes built around the county's produce. Typical of these are Swannington ham and sausages; or mixed Norfolk shellfish and seafood platter served with steamed samphire and garlic mayo.

Open all day all wk Closed 25 Dec **Food** Lunch all wk 12-2.30 Dinner Sun-Thu 6-8.30, Fri-Sat 6-9 Av main course £12 ⊕ FREE HOUSE ◄ Timothy Taylor Landlord, Woodforde's ☼ Aspall. ♟ 10 **Facilities** Non-diners area ✿ (Bar Garden Outside area) ♦ Children's menu Garden Outside area ⊨ Parking ⬛ (notice required)

■ BRANCASTER   Map 13 TF74

The Ship Hotel

tel: 01485 210333 **Main Rd PE31 8AP**
email: manager@shiphotelnorfolk.co.uk
dir: On A149 in village centre

Nautical pub serving cracking food

Set in a prime coastal location close to Brancaster Beach, TV chef and hotelier Chris Coubrough's stylish establishment continues to attract walkers, beach bums and families with its appealing menus of modern pub food prepared from fresh produce sourced from local farmers and fisherman. Be tempted by crab and preserved lemon risotto, or pan-roasted chicken breast, tagliatelle, chorizo and olive arrabiatta. Wash it down with a pint of Jo Coubrough's own brewery's Bitter Old Bustard or Aspall Harry Sparrow cider and relax in the gorgeous bar and dining rooms, where you can expect rug-strewn wood floors, wood-burning stoves, shelves full of books, quirky antiques, scrubbed wooden tables and a distinct nautical feel.

Open all day all wk **Food** Lunch 12-2.30 (school holidays, menu available 3-6) Dinner 6-9 ⊕ FREE HOUSE/FLYING KIWI INNS ◄ Jo C's Norfolk Kiwi & Bitter Old Bustard, Adnams Southwold Bitter, Woodforde's ☼ Aspall Harry Sparrow. ♟ 19 **Facilities** Non-diners area ✿ (Bar Outside area) ♦ Children's menu Children's portions Garden Outside area ⊨ Parking WiFi ⬛ (notice required)

■ BRANCASTER STAITHE   Map 13 TF74

The Jolly Sailors

tel: 01485 210314 **PE31 8BJ**
email: info@jollysailorsbrancaster.co.uk
dir: On A149 (coast road) midway between Hunstanton & Wells-next-the-Sea

Children, muddy boots and dogs welcome

Focal point of the village, the 18th-century 'Jolly' is the brewery tap for the Brancaster microbrewery, both being run by father and son team, Cliff and James Nye. In the Harbour Snug you can look out over the water, read local books, and play darts and board games. The Nyes' Brancaster ales aren't obligatory – you'll also find Adnams and Woodforde's, 12 wines by the glass, a selection of cocktails and 30 rums. Pub food is typified by open-fired pizzas (make-your-own, eat in or take away), plus from the blackboard and the smokehouse choices: smokehouse brisket chilli con carne; steak and ale pie; half a pint of Jolly smoked prawns; and fish, chips, peas and home-made tartare sauce. The beach-themed ice cream hut in the garden is an attraction in the summer. A beer and music festival is held in June.

Open all wk Mon-Thu 12-3 6-11 Fri 12-3 5-11 Sat 12-11 Sun 12-10.30 (all day Easter-late summer) Closed 25 Dec **Food** Lunch (winter) Mon-Fri 12-2, Sat-Sun 12-9 Dinner (winter) Mon-Thu 6-9, Fri 5-9, Sat-Sun 12-9 (contact pub for details of spring & summer food times) Av main course £10.95 ⊕ FREE HOUSE ◄ Brancaster Brewery, Woodforde's Wherry, Adnams ☼ Symonds. ♟ 12 **Facilities** Non-diners area ✿ (Bar Restaurant Garden) ♦ Children's menu Children's portions Play area Garden ⊨ Beer festival Parking WiFi ⬛ (notice required)

The White Horse ★★★ HL ◉◉   PICK OF THE PUBS

tel: 01485 210262 **PE31 8BY**
email: reception@whitehorsebrancaster.co.uk **web:** www.whitehorsebrancaster.co.uk
dir: A149 (coast road), midway between Hunstanton & Wells-next-the-Sea

Stylish inn with stunning coastal views

The White Horse offers stunning vistas over glorious tidal marshes across to Scolt Head Island, a four-mile long sandbar that's home to a nature reserve rich in birdlife. Reflecting the view, interior colours are muted and natural, with beach-found objects complemented by contemporary artworks. Scrubbed pine tables and high-backed settles in the bar create a welcoming atmosphere, while alfresco dining in the sunken front garden is a popular warm-weather option, perhaps accompanied by a pint of Adnams Ghost Ship. While the bar menu lists such things as tapas boards, superfood salad, and root vegetable crumble, the extensive, daily-changing menu in the airy conservatory restaurant (with two AA Rosettes) champions the freshest local seafood, delivered directly to the kitchen by the fishermen and the 'mussel men' next door. Typically on a winter menu, sourced herrings, cucumber and sauerkraut; or salt-baked celeriac cannelloni, Puy lentils and cauliflower velouté could precede duo of hogget, fondant potato, Brancaster Beer carrot and braised red cabbage; or gurnard fillets, pink fir potatoes, capers, shallots, gherkins, spinach and dashi. Leave room for lemon tart, goats' curd mousse and raspberry.

Open all day all wk 11-11 (Sun 12-10.30) **Food** all wk (from 9am for breakfast) 11am-9pm Av main course £11.95 Restaurant menu available all wk ⊕ FREE HOUSE ◄ Brancaster Brewery ales, Woodforde's Wherry, Adnams Ghost Ship ☼ Aspall. ♟ 12 **Facilities** Non-diners area ✿ (Bar Garden Outside area) ♦ Children's menu Children's portions Garden Outside area ⊨ Beer festival Parking WiFi ⬛ (notice required) **Rooms** 15

BURNHAM THORPE
Map 13 TF84

The Lord Nelson
PICK OF THE PUBS

tel: 01328 738241 **Walsingham Rd PE31 8HN**
email: enquiries@nelsonslocal.co.uk web: www.nelsonslocal.co.uk
dir: *B1355 (Burnham Market to Fakenham road), pub 9m from Fakenham & 1.75m from Burnham Market*

Soak up over 370 years of atmosphere

This pub started life in 1637 as The Plough and was renamed The Lord Nelson in 1798, to honour Horatio Nelson who was born in the village. Located opposite the delightful village cricket ground and bowling green, it has an atmospheric interior that has changed little over the past 370 plus years; you can even sit on Nelson's own high-backed settle. Drinks are served from the taproom, with real ales drawn straight from the cask. In the cosy bar you can also partake in unique rum-based tipples such as Nelson's Blood. The kitchen aims to cook dishes with balance between flavours, so that the quality of the ingredients shines. A typical meal is farmhouse pâté with toast and red onion marmalade followed by pan-fried salmon in a green herb crust with beurre blanc and duchess potatoes, with apple pie and vanilla ice cream for dessert. Children will enjoy the huge garden.

Open all wk 12-3 6-10 (Jul-Aug & BHs 12-10.30) **Food** Lunch all wk 12-2.30 Dinner all wk 6-9 ⊕ GREENE KING 🍺 Abbot Ale, Woodforde's Wherry Ò Aspall. 💯 12 **Facilities** Non-diners area 🐾 (Bar Garden) 👭 Children's menu Play area Garden ⊼ Parking WiFi 🚍

BURSTON
Map 13 TM18

The Crown

tel: 01379 741257 **Mill Rd IP22 5TW**
email: enquiries@burstoncrown.com
dir: *NE of Diss*

Very much a locals' pub serving inventive food

Steve and Bev Kembery have transformed their 16th-century pub by the green into a cracking community pub, drawing locals in for top-notch ale and food, organising the village fête, hosting three beer festivals a year, and offering a weekly busker's night and regular theme nights. As well as a decent pint of Adnams, you can just opt for nachos with spicy tomato salsa and melted cheese; or 'a very Norfolk platter' charcuterie board. If you want something more substantial, try one of their sandwiches — jerk chicken with lime and chilli mayo; home-made beef lasagne; pie of the week; Thai vegetable curry; or Filipino pork tagolog.

Open all day all wk **Food** Lunch Tue-Sat 12-2, Sun 12-4 Dinner Tue-Sat 6.30-9 Av main course £11 Restaurant menu available Tue-Sun ⊕ FREE HOUSE 🍺 Adnams Southwold Bitter & Old Ale, Elmtree Burston's Cuckoo, Morland Old Speckled Hen, Green Jack Orange Wheat Beer Ò Aspall. **Facilities** Non-diners area 🐾 (Bar Garden) 👭 Children's menu Children's portions Play area Garden ⊼ Beer festival Parking WiFi 🚍 (notice required)

CASTLE ACRE
Map 13 TF81

NEW The Ostrich Inn ★★★★ INN

tel: 01760 755398 **Stocks Green PE32 2AE**
email: info@ostrichcastleacre.com web: www.ostrichcastleacre.com
dir: *From A1065 N of Swaffham follow Castle Acre signs. Pub in village centre, near church*

An impressive 16th-century coaching inn

The Ostrich has stood on Castle Acre's green for over four centuries and looks all the better for its longevity; even the walls and ceilings that defied the ancient spirit level and plumb line are a delight. The decor is rich and warm, the bar bright. From a winter menu come duck and sweet potato hash cake with soft poached egg; braised ham hock, grain mustard mash, pineapple purée, charred corn, crispy hen's egg and cider sauce; and Ostrich Ale-battered haddock, chunky chips, mushy peas with tartare sauce. A June beer festival is held in the beautiful garden, which even finds room for a sandpit and a beach hut.

Open all day all wk **Food** Lunch all wk 12-3 Dinner all wk 6-9 Av main course £13 ⊕ GREENE KING 🍺 IPA & Ostrich Ale Ò Aspall. 💯 11 **Facilities** Non-diners area 🐾 (Bar Garden) 👭 Children's menu Children's portions Play area Garden ⊼ Beer festival Cider festival Parking WiFi 🚍 **Rooms** 6

CLEY NEXT THE SEA
Map 13 TG04

The George ★★★★ INN
PICK OF THE PUBS

tel: 01263 740652 **High St NR25 7RN**
email: info@thegeorgehotelatcley.co.uk web: www.thegeorgehotelatcley.co.uk
dir: *On A149 through Cley next the Sea, approx 4m from Holt*

Village hostelry popular with birdwatchers

An ornithological focal point for many years, The George's beer garden backs on to the salt marshes of the north Norfolk coast, a renowned paradise for birdwatchers. Close to the famous Cley Windmill and Blakeney Harbour, The George is a welcoming place, proffering several real ales at the bar, including Yetman's. You can snack in the lounge bar or dine in the light, painting-filled restaurant. The daily-changing dishes offer the best of local ingredients, and fish and seafood is a real strength. Starters include potted pheasant, orange jelly, toasted ciabatta and mixed leaves, with pan-seared sea bass fillets, pea and smoked tomato pearl barley risotto, brown shrimp and dill velouté one of the typical main courses. Birdwatchers can bring in their dogs, which are welcome in the bar and front restaurant, as are children, who get to choose from their own menu.

Open all day all wk 10.30am-11.30pm **Food** Mon-Thu 11.30-9, Fri- Sat 11.30-9.30, Sun 11.30-8.30 ⊕ FREE HOUSE 🍺 Greene King Abbot Ale, Woodforde's Wherry, Winter's, Yetman's, guest ales Ò Aspall. 💯 11 **Facilities** Non-diners area 🐾 (Bar Restaurant Garden) 👭 Children's menu Garden ⊼ Parking WiFi 🚍 (notice required) **Rooms** 10

CROMER
Map 13 TG24

The Red Lion Food and Rooms ★★★★ INN

tel: 01263 514964 **Brook St NR27 9HD**
email: info@redlion-cromer.co.uk web: www.redlion-cromer.co.uk
dir: *From A149 into Cromer, on one-way system, pass church on left. 1st left after church into Brook St. Pub on right*

Interesting beers on Norfolk's conservation coastline

A firm fixture of the charming Victorian resort of Cromer; guests can gaze through the inn's front windows directly over the fine beach to the sturdy pier. Fishing boats drawn up on the shingle bank may provide the wherewithal for the pub's renowned seafood dishes — try the fish chowder, Norfolk ale battered cod or Cromer crab — whilst sharing platters overflow with produce from Norfolk's generous inland larder. The playful menu has suggestions for wines to accompany dishes, whilst beer-lovers will delight at a choice that includes cutting edge local breweries like Wolf and Cromer's own Poppyland. Some of the bedrooms have sea views.

Open all day all wk **Food** Lunch Mon-Fri 12-2.30, Sat-Sun 12-9.30 Dinner Mon-Fri 6-9.30, Sat-Sun 12-9.30 ⊕ FREE HOUSE ◀ Green Jack Lurcher Stout, Woodforde's Nelson's Revenge, Humpty Dumpty Railway Sleeper, Adnams Broadside, Wolf, Poppyland ♂ Westons, Aspall. ♟ 10 **Facilities** Non-diners area ♣ (Bar) ♦ Children's menu Children's portions Parking WiFi ▦ (notice required) **Rooms** 15

EATON
Map 13 TG20

The Red Lion

tel: 01603 454787 **50 Eaton St NR4 7LD**
email: admin@redlion-eaton.co.uk
dir: Off A11, 2m S of Norwich city centre

The menus offer a seemingly endless choice

This heavily beamed 17th-century coaching inn has bags of character, thanks to its Dutch gable ends, panelled walls, suit of armour and inglenook fireplaces. The covered terrace enables customers to enjoy one of the real ales or a glass of wine outside during the summer months. Everyone will find something that appeals on the extensive menus, which include plenty of fish options: pan-fried fillet of brill with roasted shellfish bisque sauce; chargilled swordfish loin with avocado and sun-dried tomato salad; and non-piscatorian dishes like teriyaki glazed pork loin ribs with coleslaw and corn on the cob; or slow-baked Swannington lamb shoulder kleftico style. There's a light meals and snack menu too.

Open all day all wk **Food** Lunch all wk 12-2.15 Dinner all wk 6.30-9 ◀ Adnams Southwold Bitter, Woodforde's Wherry, Fuller's London Pride ♂ Aspall. ♟ 10 **Facilities** ♦ Children's portions Outside area ⋒ Parking WiFi

---

FAKENHAM
Map 13 TF92

The Wensum Lodge Hotel

tel: 01328 862100 **Bridge St NR21 9AY**
email: enquiries@wensumlodge.fsnet.co.uk
dir: In town centre

Idyllic riverside hostelry with fishing

Dating from around 1700, this building was originally the grain store for the adjoining mill idyllically located by the River Wensum. Just three minutes' walk from Fakenham, this lovely place has a stream flowing through its garden and offers guests free fishing on the river. An ideal base for cycling, birdwatching, fishing and horse racing, the pub serves a range of real ales that are complemented by home-cooked food, with baguettes, jacket potatoes and an all-day breakfast on the light bite menu. From the carte menu, a typical meal might start with whitebait or home-made soup and follow with home-cooked slow-roast lamb shank.

Open all day all wk **Food** Lunch all wk 12-3 Dinner all wk 6.30-9 Set menu available Restaurant menu available all wk ⊕ FREE HOUSE ◀ Greene King Abbot Ale & IPA, Old Mill Traditional Bitter, Adnams, Elmtree Beers ♂ Thatchers Gold. **Facilities** Non-diners area ♣ (Bar Garden Outside area) ♦ Children's menu Children's portions Garden Outside area ⋒ Parking WiFi ▦

GREAT HOCKHAM
Map 13 TL99

The Eagle

tel: 01953 498893 **Harling Rd IP24 1NR**
email: mail@hockhameagle.com
dir: From Thetford take A1075 to Great Hockham. Right into Harling Road. Pub on left

Good choice of beer and classic pub grub

A traditional country pub in the picturesque village of Great Hockham, close to Thetford Forest and just 10 minutes from the motor racing circuit at Snetterton. Children and dogs are welcome, and as well as seating out the front there's an

enclosed rear courtyard. The bars serve five real ales, including Woodforde's Wherry and Morland Old Speckled Hen as well as rotating guest ales. Classic pub food is what's on the menu – Sheringham steak and ale pie; ham, egg and chips, or lasagne. There's a weekly-changing specials board, and you can 'build your own burger' from a selection including pork and apple.

Open all wk 12-2.30 6-11 (Fri-Sat 12-12 Sun 12-10.30) **Food** Lunch Mon-Thu 12-2, Fri 12-9, Sat-Sun 12-6 Dinner Fri 12-9, Sat-Sun 12-6 ⊕ FREE HOUSE ◀ Adnams Southwold Bitter, Woodforde's Wherry, Morland Old Speckled Hen, Greene King Abbot Ale, guest ale. **Facilities** Non-diners area ♣ (Bar Outside area) ♦ Children's menu Children's portions Outside area ⋒ Parking WiFi

---

GREAT MASSINGHAM
Map 13 TF72

The Dabbling Duck

tel: 01485 520827 **11 Abbey Rd PE32 2HN**
email: info@thedabblingduck.co.uk
dir: From King's Lynn take either A148 or B1145 then follow Great Massingham signs. Or from Fakenham take A148 signed King's Lynn. Or from Swaffham take A1065 towards Cromer, then B1145 signed King's Lynn

Stylish village-owned inn

The Dabbling Duck on Great Massingham's glorious green thrives as a community local and a stylish inn. Head for the high-backed settles by the raised log fire to peruse the papers with pork scratchings and apple ketchup and a pint of Aspall cider, Woodforde's Wherry or Adnams Ghost Ship. Then move to a scrubbed table in one of the comfortably rustic dining areas, or the garden, and choose beetroot gravad lax, pickled beetroot, crème fraîche and rye cracker; or salt hake Scotch egg, sardine ketchup and n'duja mayonnaise to start, followed by cod, 'Norwich' carrot, sea buckthorn, nasturtium and cobnuts; or Dingley Dell pork belly, piccalilli purée, carrots, cauliflower, apple and cucumber. There are shelves groaning with books and board games, rugs on tiled floors and the atmosphere is informal and relaxed. Everything adds up to create a cracking village pub.

Open all day all wk 8am-11pm **Food** Lunch all wk 12-2.30 Dinner Mon-Thu & Sun 6.30-9, Fri-Sat 6-9.30 ⊕ FREE HOUSE ◀ Woodforde's Wherry, Beeston Worth the Wait, Adnams Broadside & Ghost Ship ♂ Aspall, Thatchers. **Facilities** Non-diners area ♣ (Bar Garden Outside area) ♦ Children's menu Children's portions Play area Garden Outside area ⋒ Parking WiFi ▦ (notice required)

GREAT RYBURGH
Map 13 TF92

The Blue Boar Inn ★★★ INN

tel: 01328 829212 **NR21 ODX**
email: eat@blueboar-norfolk.co.uk **web:** www.blueboar-norfolk.co.uk
dir: From Fakenham take A1067 towards Norwich. Approx 4m right to Great Ryburgh

Good food in pretty Wensum Valley inn

Lots to see at this character, listed village inn; beyond the beer garden is a notable round-towered medieval church (once linked to the pub by a secret tunnel), whilst inside are quarry-tile floors, beams and a vast inglenook, spread through a jumble of levels marking alterations to this popular local pub over the centuries. It was used as a recruiting station during the Napoleonic Wars; all that's required of today's visitors is to enjoy the local Yetman's beers and indulge the richly varied, Norfolk-based menu, which may include cassoulet of chicken leg and sausage, or pot roast half guinea fowl.

Open 6-11 (Sun 12-6) Closed Tue **Food** Lunch Sun 12-4.30 Dinner Wed-Sat & Mon 6.30-9 ⊕ FREE HOUSE ◀ Adnams Southwold Bitter, Winter's Golden & Revenge, Staropramen, Yetman's, Guinness ♂ Addlestones, Westons Stowford Press, Aspall. ♟ 8 **Facilities** Non-diners area ♦ Children's menu Children's portions Play area Family room Garden ⋒ Parking WiFi ▦ **Rooms** 6

HEVINGHAM — Map 13 TG12

Marsham Arms Coaching Inn

tel: 01603 754268 **Holt Rd NR10 5NP**
email: info@marshamarms.co.uk
dir: *On B1149 (N of Norwich Airport), 2m, through Horsford towards Holt*

Charming inn serving ales from the taproom

Victorian philanthropist and landowner Robert Marsham built the Marsham Arms as a roadside hostel for poor farm labourers, and some original features, including the wooden beams and large open fireplace are still evident. Real ales are served straight from the barrel. The seasonal menu uses fresh local produce and may include Thai green vegetable curry; haddock fillet with cheddar and leek gratin; and slow-roasted pork belly with crunchy crackling, creamy mash, apple purée, cider and sage sauce. The spacious garden has a paved patio, and the inn holds a Green Tourism award.

Open all day all wk **Food** all day Av main course £10.95 Set menu available ⊕ FREE HOUSE ◼ Adnams Southwold Bitter & Broadside, Woodforde's Wherry, Mauldons, Grain Best Bitter, Humpty Dumpty Ò Aspall. ♟ 10 **Facilities** Non-diners area ♥ (Bar Restaurant Garden) ♦♦ Children's menu Children's portions Garden ⊫ Parking WiFi ▥ (notice required)

HEYDON — Map 13 TG12

Earle Arms

tel: 01263 587376 **The Street NR11 6AD**
email: theearlearms@gmail.com
dir: *Signed between Cawston & Corpusty on B1149 (Holt to Norwich road)*

One for fans of the turf

H, the landlord and chef, is responsible for the horseracing memorabilia throughout this 16th-century, Dutch-gabled free house on the village green. As part-owner of a racehorse, he will gladly give you a tip, but says it's probably best not to go nap on it. The privately owned conservation village of Heydon is often used for filming, and many a star of the big and small screen has enjoyed the Earle's off-the-pier-fresh seafood, game from local estates and locally reared meats. A beer festival is held in May.

Open 11-3 6-11 (Sun all day) Closed Mon **Food** Lunch Tue-Sun 12-2 Dinner Tue-Sun 6-8.30 Av main course £11 Restaurant menu available Tue-Sun ⊕ FREE HOUSE ◼ Woodforde's Wherry, Adnams, guest ales Ò Addlestones. ♟ 16 **Facilities** Non-diners area ♦♦ Children's menu Children's portions Garden ⊫ Beer festival Parking WiFi ▥ (notice required)

HOLT — Map 13 TG03

The Pigs — PICK OF THE PUBS

See Pick of the Pubs on opposite page

HUNSTANTON — Map 12 TF64

The Ancient Mariner Inn ★★★★ HL

tel: 01485 536390 **Golf Course Rd, Old Hunstanton PE36 6JJ**
email: gm@lestrangearms.co.uk web: www.traditionalinns.co.uk
dir: *Exit A149, 1m N of Hunstanton. Turn left at sharp right bend by pitch & putt course*

Coastal setting with great views and local walks

Summer evenings can be spectacular here; when the sun sets across the sands of The Wash, the light matches the golds of the real ales enjoyed by drinkers in the peaceful gardens, up to seven beers may be on tap. Equally enticing is the menu of modern pub classics such as trio of local sausages; beef lasagne; or slow-roast lamb shank; daily fish specials boost the choice. The appealing flint and brick inn is creatively incorporated into the stable block of a Victorian hotel, the stylish rooms of which are popular with visitors to the beautiful Norfolk Coast Area of Outstanding Natural Beauty.

Open all day all wk **Food** all wk 12-9 ⊕ FREE HOUSE ◼ Adnams, Theakston, Wychwood, Shepherd Neame, Sharp's, Woodforde's Ò Symonds. ♟ 10 **Facilities** Non-diners area ♥ (Bar Garden) ♦♦ Children's menu Children's portions Play area Family room Garden ⊫ Beer festival Parking WiFi ▥ (notice required) **Rooms** 43

The King William IV Country Inn & Restaurant ★★★★ INN

tel: 01485 571765 **Heacham Rd, Sedgeford PE36 5LU**
email: info@thekingwilliamsedgeford.co.uk web: www.thekingwilliamsedgeford.co.uk
dir: *A149 to Hunstanton, right at Norfolk Lavender in Heacham onto B1454, signed Docking. 2m to Sedgeford*

Food and drink to please all tastes

Tucked away in the village of Sedgeford, this free house has been an inn for over 175 years. It's conveniently close to the north Norfolk coastline and the Peddars Way. Made cosy by winter log fires, it has four dining areas, plus a covered alfresco terrace where you may enjoy a local crab salad in the summer months. You'll find five real ales on tap, and extensive menus (including one for vegetarians) to please everyone: salmon fishcakes or smoked duck mousse for starters, and steak and Adnams Ale pie; or grilled sea bream and brown shimps to follow. Events include quiz Mondays and curry Tuesdays.

Open all day 11-11 (Sun 12-10.30) Closed Mon L (ex BHs) **Food** Lunch Tue-Sat 12-2, Sun 12-2.30 Dinner all wk 6.30-9 Set menu available Restaurant menu available all wk ⊕ FREE HOUSE ◼ Woodforde's Wherry, Adnams Southwold Bitter, Greene King Abbot Ale, Morland Old Speckled Hen, guest ale Ò Aspall Harry Sparrow. ♟ 9 **Facilities** Non-diners area ♥ (Bar Garden) ♦♦ Children's menu Children's portions Family room Garden ⊫ Parking WiFi ▥ (notice required) **Rooms** 9

HUNWORTH — Map 13 TG03

The Hunny Bell — PICK OF THE PUBS

tel: 01263 712300 **The Green NR24 2AA**
email: hunnybell@hotmail.com
dir: *From Holt take B1110. 1st right to Hunworth*

Dog-friendly pub offering a warm welcome

Run by a husband and wife team, this 18th-century, whitewashed and pantile-roofed pub belongs to the local Stody Estate, famed for its rhododendron and azalea gardens. The front patio overlooks the large village green and there's a spacious garden at the rear; or stay in the wooden-floored bar, where well-behaved dogs can become buddies with Sheamus, the pub's half Irish Wolfhound, half German Shepherd cross. The two menus – Seasonal and Favourites – make good use of Norfolk's seafood, such as the warm fillet of Cley-smoked mackerel starter with apple and fennel remoulade. Among the mains are chargrilled lemon and thyme chicken, sautéed potatoes and wild garlic dressing; chargrilled Aberdeen Angus sirloin steak, jenga chips, garlic aïoli, slow-roast tomato, field mushroom and salad; and red onion and mozzarella tart, mixed leaf salad and aged balsamic.

Open all wk 12-3 6-11 (Fri-Sat 12-3 6-12) **Food** Lunch all wk 12-2 Dinner Sun-Thu 6-8.30, Fri-Sat 6-9 ⊕ FREE HOUSE/COPPERBEECH INNS LTD ◼ Woodforde's Wherry, Greene King & Abbot Ale, Hunny Bell Cask Ale, guest ales Ò Aspall. ♟ 10 **Facilities** Non-diners area ♥ (Bar Garden Outside area) ♦♦ Children's menu Children's portions Garden Outside area ⊫ Beer festival Parking ▥ (notice required)

PICK OF THE PUBS

The Pigs

HOLT Map 13 TG03

tel: 01263 587634 **Norwich Rd, Edgefield NR24 2RL**
email: info@thepigs.org.uk
web: www.thepigs.org.uk
dir: *From Norwich A140 (Airport). Pass airport on right, left onto B1149 at rdbt. Approx 16m to Edgefield*

Bustling village local with pig-inspired menus

Bought by three ambitious co-owners nearly ten years ago, this 17th-century country inn on the edge of a lovely village has been transformed into a thriving local and celebration of all things Norfolk, both on the plate and in the glass. The lovely tranquil setting at the fringe of the village allows for a peaceful garden, whilst locals barter their fresh fruit and vegetables over the bar for a pint or two, practise darts or bar billiards and quaff the Old Spot bitter brewed by local Wolf Brewery — what else. An impressively versatile menu emerges from the kitchen, utilising forgotten cuts of locally sourced meat and produce from the pub's adjoining allotment. If it's genuine 'nose to tail' dining you're looking for, the honey, Colman's mustard and marmalade glazed pork ribs, followed by the slow-cooked belly of pork with smoky bacon beans, apple chutney, black pudding and crackling should fit the

bill. Tapas-style starters called 'Iffits' include deep-fried 'popcorn' cockles, and a Kilner jar of potted pork which are ideal for sharing. If pork-based treats aren't your thing, then venison faggots with roast chestnut and leek mash; or East coast mussels with Old Spot ale, leeks, parsley sauce and bread to dunk may tempt, along with fish options such as deep-fried line-caught haddock, mushy peas, beef dripping chips and tartare sauce. Leek, wild mushroom and pine nut pot barley stew is one of the meat-free choices. Leave room for one of the tempting desserts, perhaps cinnamon rice crumble with vanilla shortbread. The children's indoor playroom and outdoor Piggleplay play area both prove very popular.

Open all day all wk 8am-11pm
⊕ FREE HOUSE ◀ Woodforde's Wherry, Greene King Abbot Ale, Wolf Old Spot, Adnams Broadside & Southwold Bitter ⌀ Aspall. **Facilities** ❧ (Bar Outside area) ⁑ Children's menu Children's portions Play area Family room Outside area Parking WiFi

INGHAM
Map 13 TG32

The Ingham Swan ★★★★ RR ◎◎ PICK OF THE PUBS

tel: 01692 581099 **Swan Corner, Sea Palling Rd NR12 9AB**
email: info@theinghamswan.co.uk web: www.theinghamswan.co.uk
dir: *From A149 through Stalham to Ingham*

Picture-postcard dining inn

From the tiny village of Ingham you can follow meandering lanes to the nearby Norfolk Coast Area of Outstanding Natural Beauty and a string of broadland nature reserves, renowned for rare birds. Before you head off though, you should check out The Swan. This ancient, flint-built pub and the majestic church that adjoins it are all that survive of the once-flourishing Ingham Priory. Slumbering beneath trim thatch, the inn was carefully transformed into a destination dining pub and restaurant a while ago, but drinkers are always welcome at the bar for real ales from the local Grain Brewery. Chef-patron Daniel Smith trained at Le Gavroche in London and Blakeney's Morston Hall, and he sticks to his Norfolk roots with an award-winningly creative, modern menu, packed with seasonal local produce. A lazy lunch could start with Cromer crab salad or Yorkshire Blue and chicken dumpling with leeks and asparagus, followed by pan-roast sea bass with samphire, prawns and beans; or honey-baked guinea fowl breast with cabbage, potato and mushrooms. The menu includes useful matching wine suggestions.

Open all wk 11-3 6-11 Closed 25-26 Dec **Food** Lunch Mon-Sat 12-2, Sun 12-3 Dinner all wk 6-9 Set menu available Restaurant menu available all wk ⊕ FREE HOUSE ◀ Woodforde's Wherry, Nelson's Revenge, Grain Oak & Redwood ♂ Aspall. ♀ 10 **Facilities** Non-diners area ♦ Children's portions Garden ﬔ Parking ₪ (notice required) **Rooms** 4

ITTERINGHAM
Map 13 TG13

The Walpole Arms

tel: 01263 587258 **NR11 7AR**
email: info@thewalpolearms.co.uk web: www.thewalpolearms.co.uk
dir: *From Aylsham towards Blickling. After Blickling Hall take 1st right to Itteringham*

Dining pub with inventive food

Owned by a local farming family, this renowned rural dining venue is tucked away down narrow lanes on the edge of sleepy Itteringham, close to the National Trust's Blickling Hall. Its oak-beamed bar offers local Woodforde's and Adnams ales on tap, while menus champion top-notch meats and produce from the family farm and local artisan producers. Typical dishes include poached duck egg with spinach, black pudding crumb and butter sauce; the Walpole Pigs board – ham hock terrine, pork rillette fritter, pork belly, and black pudding with pickled pear, apple jelly and focaccia; and beef ribs with sauté potatoes and carrots. Leave room for vanilla crème brûlée; baked Alaska; or sticky toffee pudding.

Open all wk 12-3 6-11 (Sat 12-11 Sun 12-5) **Food** Lunch Mon-Sat 12-2.30, Sun 12-3 Dinner Mon-Sat 6-9.15 Set menu available ⊕ FREE HOUSE ◀ Adnams Broadside & Southwold Bitter, Woodforde's Wherry, guest ales ♂ Aspall. ♀ 20 **Facilities** Non-diners area ♥ (Bar Garden) ♦ Children's menu Children's portions Garden ﬔ Parking WiFi ₪ (notice required)

KING'S LYNN
Map 12 TF62

The Stuart House Hotel, Bar & Restaurant

tel: 01553 772169 **35 Goodwins Rd PE30 5QX**
email: reception@stuarthousehotel.co.uk
dir: *Follow signs to town centre, pass under Southgate Arch, immediate right, in 100yds turn right*

Small, independent free house

In a central, but nevertheless quiet location, this place, in attractive grounds, is one of the town's favoured eating and drinking places. Top-notch East Anglian ales and traditional snacks are served in the bar, and there's a separate restaurant menu typically featuring Norfolk sausages with creamy mash and red onion gravy; pan-fried fillet of sea bass with herbed sauté potatoes; sweet chilli beef with noodles; and vegetable Kiev with garlic butter sauce. Daily specials, like everything else, are home cooked from fresh local produce. Events include regular live music, murder mystery dinners and a July beer festival.

Open all wk 5-11 **Food** Dinner all wk 6-9.30 ⊕ FREE HOUSE ◀ Oakham Ales JHB, Timothy Taylor Landlord, Adnams, Woodforde's ♂ Aspall. **Facilities** Non-diners area ♥ (Bar Garden) Children's portions Play area Garden Beer festival Parking WiFi ₪ (notice required)

LARLING
Map 13 TL98

Angel Inn
PICK OF THE PUBS

tel: 01953 717963 **NR16 2QU**
email: info@angel-larling.co.uk
dir: *5m from Attleborough; 8m from Thetford*

Family-run inn with a range of ales and enjoyable food

On the edge of Breckland and Thetford Forest Park, this 17th-century former coaching inn has been run for more than 80 years by three generations of the Stammers family and has a good local feel and warm welcome. In the beamed public bar, a jukebox, dartboard and fruit machine add to the traditional feel, while the oak-panelled lounge bar has dining tables with cushioned wheel-back chairs, a wood-burner and a collection of water jugs. Five ales, including Crouch Vale Brewers Gold, are served, as well as more than a hundred whiskies. Menus make good use of local ingredients, with lighter snacks including sandwiches, jacket potatoes, ploughman's, burgers and salads. Typically among the mains are tiger prawn balti; chicken and bacon fusilli; lamb chops with mint sauce; or Stilton and mushroom bake. Look out for the August festival, with over 100 real ales.

Open all day all wk 10am-mdnt **Food** Sun-Thu 12-9.30, Fri-Sat 12-10 Av main course £11.95 Set menu available ⊕ FREE HOUSE ◀ Adnams Southwold Bitter, Crouch Vale Brewers Gold, Timothy Taylor Landlord, Mauldons, Lacons ♂ Aspall, Crone's, Banham, Norfolk Kingfisher. ♀ 10 **Facilities** Non-diners area ♦ Children's menu Children's portions Play area Garden ﬔ Beer festival Parking WiFi ₪

LETHERINGSETT Map 13 TG03

The Kings Head PICK OF THE PUBS

tel: 01263 712691 **Holt Rd NR25 7AR**
email: info@kingsheadnorfolk.co.uk
dir: *On A148, 1m from Holt. Pub on corner*

Vintage-chic dining-pub recommended for its outdoor areas

From the outside this looks to be a grand, manor-like building, but step through the door to find elegant, rustic-chic decor throughout the rambling dining areas that radiate from the central bar, with warm heritage hues, rugs on terracotta tiles, feature bookcases, an eclectic mix of old dining tables, and squashy sofas and leather chairs fronting blazing winter log fires. The atmosphere is informal, the beer on tap is Woodforde's Wherry, and the modern British food is prepared from top-notch ingredients supplied by local farmers, fisherman and artisan producers. This translates to pub favourites such as pan-fried sea bass fillet with crushed new potatoes, greens and brown shrimp butter; wild mushroom risotto; and beer-battered haddock with garden peas and hand-cut chips. This pub has superb alfresco areas including an excellent children's garden and a gravelled front terrace with benches and brollies.

Open all day all wk 11-11 **Food** Lunch all wk 12-2.30, BHs all day Dinner Mon-Sat 6.30-9.30, Sun 6.30-8, BHs all day FREE HOUSE Adnams, Norfolk Moon Gazer, Woodforde's Wherry, guest ales Aspall. 14 **Facilities** Non-diners area (Bar Restaurant Garden) Children's menu Children's portions Play area Garden Parking WiFi

MORSTON Map 13 TG04

NEW The Anchor PICK OF THE PUBS

tel: 01263 741392 **The Street NR25 7AA**
dir: *On A149 (Blakeney Rd) in village centre*

Seaside village pub in good hands

A dream come true for former school buddies Harry Farrow and Rowan Glennie, who reunited to buy and refurbish this popular pub. Not yet 30, the lads still have plenty of joint experience behind them, which they put to impressive effect in both the bar, where Norfolk breweries Winter's and Woodforde's, and Suffolk's Adnams provide the real ales, and the restaurant. With East Anglian produce, particularly fish and game, being the kitchen's priority, try chunky smoked haddock and brown shrimp chowder with sourdough bread, followed by roasted loin of venison with Anna potatoes, beetroot purée, spinach, piccolo parsnips and jus. Or there's the vegetarian home-made cheddar gnocchi, butternut squash, wild mushrooms and rocket and pine nut pesto. Round off with local apple and rhubarb crumble and home-made custard. Sixteen wines are sold by the glass, although bottles won't break the bank. Inside you can buy tickets for a boat trip to see the seals just along the coast at Blakeney Point.

Open all wk 9am-late **Food** Bkfst 9am-11am Lunch Mon-Sat 12-3, Sun 6-8.30 Dinner Mon-Sat 6-9, Sun 6-8.30 Av main course £14 FREE HOUSE Woodforde's Wherry, Adnams, Winter's Aspall. 16 **Facilities** Children's menu Garden Parking WiFi

MUNDFORD Map 13 TL89

Crown Hotel

tel: 01842 878233 **Crown Rd IP26 5HQ**
email: info@the-crown-hotel.co.uk **web:** www.the-crown-hotel.co.uk
dir: *A11 to Barton Mills onto A1065 through Brandon to Mundford*

By the small but perfectly formed village green

Roofed with traditional Norfolk pantiles, this historic inn on the edge of Thetford Forest dates from 1652. Originally a hunting lodge, it has also served as a magistrate's court. Today it's a popular pub with two restaurants, the Old Court and the Club Room, whose menus might propose Jimmy Butler's slow-roasted pork belly with dauphinoise potatoes; leek, mushroom and spinach crumble with crispy cheddar topping; herb-crusted salmon fillet with roasted tomato and red pepper sauce; and baked apple and rhubarb ice cream. In addition to Woodforde's Wherry, guest ales and wines by the glass, the bars stock over 50 malt whiskies. The pub being on a slight rise, the garden is at first-floor level.

Open all day all wk 10.30am-mdnt **Food** Lunch all wk 12-3 Dinner all wk 6.30-10 FREE HOUSE Courage Directors, Greene King Ruddles County, Hardys & Hansons Olde Trip, Woodforde's Wherry, guest ales. 9 **Facilities** Non-diners area (Bar Garden) Children's portions Garden Parking WiFi

NORWICH Map 13 TG20

Adam & Eve

tel: 01603 667423 **Bishopsgate NR3 1RZ**
email: theadamandeve@hotmail.com
dir: *Behind Anglican Cathedral, adjacent to Law Courts*

Historic city-centre bolt hole

This enchanting, brick-and-flint built inn sits beneath trees at the fringe of the grounds of Norwich's Anglican Cathedral, the builders of which lodged at the pub, licensed since 1249. It's a refreshing step back in time, free of electronic diversions whilst rich with beers from Woodforde's and Wolf breweries; spirits here include ghosts of lingering, long-gone former locals. Who can blame them when the food is as rewarding as the ales; visitors resting on a tour of Norwich's finest can expect no-nonsense quality pub classics like filled large Yorkshire pudding, trawlerman's pie, home-made curry or chilli. The hanging basket displays are stunning.

Open all day all wk 11-11 (Sun 12-10.30) Closed 25-26 Dec, 1 Jan **Food** Lunch Mon-Sat 12-7, Sun 12-5 Dinner Mon-Sat 12-7 ENTERPRISE INNS Adnams Southwold Bitter, Theakston Old Peculier, Wolf Golden Jackal, Woodforde's Sundew Aspall. 11 **Facilities** Outside area Parking WiFi (notice required)

NORWICH *continued*

The Reindeer Pub & Kitchen   PICK OF THE PUBS

tel: 01603 612995 **1O Dereham Rd NR2 4AY**
email: enquiries@thereindeerpub.co.uk
dir: *Phone for detailed directions*

Dining-pub where real ales share star billing with the food

Dan and Katie Searle say they focus on the food as much as the beer, although there are still more than 20 ales on offer. The head chef is passionate about British produce and you can expect to find anything from Norfolk pigeon, Puy lentil ragù and game crisps; black treacle Blythburgh pork loin, Earl Grey prunes, spiced red cabbage, to Channel hake supreme, garlic Scottish mussel and clam broth. Also available all day is a tapas menu including home-made Swannington pork crackling; plates of British cured meats and cheeses; and black pudding Scotch egg. Leave room for desserts such as dark chocolate tart, poached prunes and chocolate ice cream; or spiced apple and pepper cake, spiced cider jelly and star anise anglaise. Wash it all down with one of several real ales from breweries such as Dark Star and Elgood's. Look out for the summer beer festival.

Open all day Closed Mon **Food** Lunch Tue-Sat 12-3, Sun 12-8 Dinner Tue-Sat 6-10, Sun 12-8 Av main course £10 ⊕ ELGOOD'S & SONS ◀ Elgood's, Dark Star, Thornbridge, Green Jack, Humpty Dumpty, Magic Rock, BrewDog, Oakham ♂ Westons & Bounds, Orchard Pig. ♀ 12 **Facilities** Non-diners area ❖ (Bar Garden) ♦ Children's menu Children's portions Garden ☰ Beer festival Parking WiFi ☷ (notice required)

Ribs of Beef

tel: 01603 619517 **24 Wensum St NR3 1HY**
email: enquiries@ribsofbeef.co.uk
dir: *From Tombland (in front of cathedral) turn left at Maids Head Hotel. Pub 200yds on right on bridge*

City centre local with cask ales and river views

On record as an alehouse back in the 18th century, this building has been used variously as an antiques shop, electrical store and fashion boutique, before Roger and Anthea Cawdron took over some three years ago. The pub is popular for its range of cask ales, excellent wines, traditional English food using locally sourced produce and comfy leather seats. The varied menus offer 'old favourites' like home-made Scotch egg, pickle and salad; breaded wholetail scampi; salmon and dill fishcakes; and beef and ale stew alongside sandwiches, wedges and jacket potatoes. Sit outside on the jetty during the warmer months and enjoy the fabulous river views. There's live music on Saturdays.

Open all day all wk 11-11 (Fri-Sat 11am-1am) **Food** Lunch Mon-Fri 12-2.30, Sat-Sun 12-5 ⊕ FREE HOUSE ◀ Woodforde's Wherry, Adnams Ghost Ship, Oakham JHB, Fuller's London Pride, Wolf Golden Jackal ♂ Kingfisher Norfolk Cider, Westons Old Rosie. ♀ 9 **Facilities** Non-diners area ❖ (Bar Garden Outside area) ♦ Children's menu Children's portions Family room Garden Outside area ☰ WiFi ☷ (notice required)

SALTHOUSE   Map 13 TG04

The Salthouse Dun Cow

tel: 01263 740467 **Coast Rd NR25 7XA**
email: info@salthouseduncow.com
dir: *On A149 (coast road). 3m E of Blakeney, 6m W of Sheringham*

An ideal retreat overlooking salt marsh scenery

In a quiet coastal village within an Area of Outstanding Natural Beauty, this traditional brick and flint pub probably originated as a cattle barn built around

1650. Today it overlooks some of Britain's finest salt marshes, so expect to share it, particularly the front garden, with birdwatchers and walkers. The interior decor seems to reflect the surrounding farmland and seascapes with brick walls, bare floorboards and a wood-burning stove. Local suppliers provide high quality produce for select menus prepared from scratch, especially fresh shellfish and game from local shoots. Samphire, asparagus and soft fruit are all sourced within five miles.

Open all day all wk Closed 25 Dec **Food** all wk 12-9 ⊕ PUNCH TAVERNS ◀ Woodforde's Wherry, Adnams, guest ales ♂ Aspall. ♀ 19 **Facilities** Non-diners area ❖ (Bar Restaurant Garden) ♦ Children's menu Children's portions Garden ☰ Parking WiFi ☷ (notice required)

SHERINGHAM   Map 13 TG14

The Two Lifeboats

tel: 01263 823144 **2 High St NR26 8JR**
email: bridget@thetwolifeboats.co.uk
dir: *In town centre*

Traditional pub a few yards from the beach

Once the local Fisherman's Mission building and a coffee shop, this seafront pub was named in honour of the two lifeboats that rescued a crew of eight from a Norwegian brig in the late 19th century. This is a traditional pub where you can either quaff pints of Adnams Broadside alongside the locals or grab a table to enjoy home-cooked dishes such as creamy smoked salmon and dill linguine; lamb's liver and bacon with mustard mash; or roasted butternut squash and red pepper risotto.

Open all day all wk **Food** Lunch all wk 12-3, summer all day Dinner all wk 6-9, summer all day ⊕ PUNCH TAVERNS ◀ Adnams Broadside & Ghost Ship, Woodforde's Wherry, Sharp's Doom Bar ♂ Aspall. ♀ **Facilities** Non-diners area ❖ (Bar Outside area) ♦ Children's menu Children's portions Outside area ☰ WiFi ☷ (notice required)

SNETTISHAM   Map 12 TF63

The Rose & Crown ★★★★ INN ⊛   PICK OF THE PUBS

tel: 01485 541382 **Old Church Rd PE31 7LX**
email: info@roseandcrownsnettisham.co.uk **web:** www.roseandcrownsnettisham.co.uk
dir: *10m N from King's Lynn on A149 signed Hunstanton. At Snettisham rdbt take B1440 to Snettisham. Left into Old Church Rd, inn on left*

Everything you'd expect from a north Norfolk free house

Roses round the door, fresh seafood and an AA Rosette – just some of what Anthony and Jeannette Goodrich's splendid inn offers. Built in the 14th century for craftsmen working on the beautiful village church, its rose-hung façade conceals twisting passages and hidden corners, heavy oak beams, uneven red-tiled floors and inglenooks. Three charming bars offer Adnams, Ringwood and Woodforde's real ales on tap and 26 wines by the glass. Locally supplied produce includes shellfish and samphire from Brancaster, beef from salt marsh-raised cattle, game shot by men in wellies who drink in the back bar, asparagus and strawberries from farmers, and herbs from village allotments. Lunch and dinner menus typically offer venison and black pudding Scotch egg, parsnip and apple remoulade; hot smoked mackerel, spiced butternut and pomegranate; pan-fried hake fillet, local cockle and clam chowder, carrot spaghetti and watercress; and cherry cheesecake, toasted almonds and popcorn sauce.

Open all day all wk **Food** Lunch all wk 12-6.30 Dinner Mon-Thu 6.30-9, Fri-Sat 6.30-9.30, Sun 6.30-8.30 Av main course £13 ⊕ FREE HOUSE ◀ Adnams Broadside, Woodforde's Wherry, Ringwood Boondoggle, guest ales ♂ Aspall. ♀ 26 **Facilities** Non-diners area ❖ (Bar Restaurant Garden) ♦ Children's menu Children's portions Play area Family room Garden ☰ Parking WiFi **Rooms** 16

PICK OF THE PUBS

Chequers Inn

THOMPSON Map 13 TL99

tel: 01953 483360
Griston Rd IP24 1PX
email: richard@thompsonchequers.co.uk
web: www.thompsonchequers.co.uk
dir: *Exit A1075 between Watton & Thetford*

Breckland pub well off the beaten track

If you can't place Breckland, it's that region of gorse-covered sandy heath straddling south Norfolk and north Suffolk. Within its boundaries you'll find this splendid, long and low, thatched 17th-century inn, and worth finding it is for its peaceful location and unspoilt charm. In the 18th century manorial courts were held here, dealing with rents, letting of land, and petty crime. It's more fun here today. Beneath its steeply-raked thatch lies a series of low-ceilinged, interconnecting rooms served by a long bar at which the principal real ales are Adnams Southwold Bitter, Greene King IPA and Wolf Ale. The overall impression of the interior is of skew-whiff wall timbers, squat doorways, open log fires, rustic old furniture and farming implements. Although not long, the main menu more than adequately covers most bases, with starters of pan-fried mushrooms in Stilton and cream sauce; local asparagus with crispy pancetta and hollandaise sauce; and Cranworth

smoked salmon with dill and lemon mayonnaise. Its seven or eight main dishes may well include seafood tagliatelle with tomato and herb sauce; Chinese-spiced roast belly of pork with stir-fried vegetables and noodles; and roast vegetable and Portobello mushroom puff pastry pie. To add to one's choice, there are specials — typically breast of chicken stuffed with smoked salmon, and steak and kidney pudding. Finally, dessert — perhaps home-made apple crumble; treacle and almond tart; or chocolate profiteroles. You'll find picnic tables in the large rear garden, where dogs are welcome. The inn is an ideal base for walking the Peddars Way and the Great Eastern Pingo Trail - a string of lakelets (the pingos) left behind after the Ice Age.

Open all wk 11-3 6-11 (Sun all day)
Food Lunch Mon-Sat 12-2, Sun all day Dinner Mon-Sat 6.30-9, Sun all day ⊕ FREE HOUSE ◀ Adnams Southwold Bitter, Wolf Ale, Greene King IPA, Woodforde's Wherry Ö Thatchers, Aspall. ♟ 8 **Facilities** Non-diners area ✿ (Bar Garden) ✚ Children's menu Children's portions Garden ⋈ Beer festival Parking WiFi ▭ (notice required)

STANHOE
Map 13 TF83

NEW The Duck Inn

tel: 01485 518330 Burnham Rd PE31 8QD
email: info@duckinn.co.uk

Good local produce and local beers

Close to the North Norfolk coast, The Duck Inn is run by Ben and Sarah Handley, who have established it as a pub that showcases the region's produce, down to the Elgood's Cambridge Bitter and Aspall cider. Local references are stamped all over the menu, whether it's Thornham oysters, Brancaster mussels or Lakenham Creamery ice creams. Start with sautéed duck hearts, chicken liver parfait, brioche and pickled cherries before moving on to pan-seared ox liver, smoked mash, pancetta, onions and beef jus. Leave room for the treacle and walnut tart with coconut ice cream.

Open all day all wk Closed 25 Dec Food Lunch Mon-Sat 12-2.30, Sun 12-8 Dinner Mon-Sat 6.30-9, Sun 12-8 ⊕ ELGOOD'S ◀ Cambridge Bitter Ö Aspall. ♥ 12 Facilities Non-diners area ✿ (Bar Garden) ♦ Children's menu Children's portions Garden ⊨ Parking WiFi

STOKE HOLY CROSS
Map 13 TG20

The Wildebeest
PICK OF THE PUBS

tel: 01508 492497 82-86 Norwich Rd NR14 8QJ
email: wildebeest@animalinns.co.uk
dir: From A47 take A140, left to Dunston. At T-junct turn left, pub on right

Seasonality and traceability in peaceable surroundings

Set in a village just far enough out of Norwich to enjoy tranquillity, The Wildebeest is a haven of refined eating and drinking. The interior is a feast in itself, rich with beams, aged floorboards, solid wood tables and dark ochre leather-clad dining chairs. The pub's reputation for fine food has been built over many years, and continues today in the hands of chef-patron Daniel Smith. Settle on a bar stool for a pint of Adnams Southwold or Greene King Abbot Ale; or select a wine from the dozen sold by the glass while perusing the menu. Land on a nearby farm is given over to the cultivation of much of the kitchen's seasonal produce. The Norfolk coast sees deliveries of Brancaster mussels and diver-caught scallops. A typical main course is Dijon-roasted loin of lamb with crispy lamb breast, charred fillet, fondant potato, smoked garlic purée and braised red cabbage. Finish with a lemon slice and Italian meringue.

Open all wk 11.30-3 6-11 (Sat-Sun all day) Food Lunch Mon-Sat 12-2, Sun 12-3 Dinner Mon-Sat 6-9, Sun 6-8 Set menu available ⊕ FREE HOUSE ◀ Adnams Southwold Bitter, Morland Old Speckled Hen, Greene King Abbot Ale Ö Aspall. ♥ 12 Facilities Non-diners area ♦ Children's portions Garden ⊨ Parking WiFi

STOW BARDOLPH
Map 12 TF60

The Hare Arms
PICK OF THE PUBS

tel: 01366 382229 PE34 3HT
email: trishmc@harearms222.wanadoo.co.uk
dir: From King's Lynn take A10 to Downham Market. After 9m village signed on left

Handsome country pub with a good vegetarian selection

Peacocks and hens roam the garden of this ivy-clad pub. It was named after the Hare family, who purchased Stow Bardolph estate in 1553 and still play an important part locally. The fascinating memorabilia that Trish and David McManus have collected during four decades here are on display throughout the music-free, L-shaped bar, where two guest ales partner those of Greene King. There's plenty to contemplate on the menu, so take your time in choosing between, perhaps pigeon breast with black pudding or shell-on Greenland prawns with garlic mayo for starters, or, as a main, between local Old English sausages and mash and, say, beef lasagne. Another good read is the daily specials menu, featuring grilled sardines; camembert to share; pork and prune casserole; and venison Wellington. Vegetarian eyes will spot spicy bean and carrot patties; mushroom and three cheese lasagne; and the haloumi and roast vegetable burger.

Open all wk 11-2.30 6-11 (Sat & BH Mon 11-11 Sun 12-10.30) Closed 25-26 Dec Food Lunch Mon-Fri 12-2, Sat-Sun & BH Mon 12-10 Dinner Mon-Fri 6.30-10, Sat-Sun & BH Mon 12-10 Av main course £12 ⊕ GREENE KING ◀ Abbot Ale & IPA, Morland Old Speckled Hen, guest ales Ö Aspall. ♥ 9 Facilities Non-diners area ♦ Children's menu Children's portions Family room Garden ⊨ Parking WiFi ▭ (notice required)

THOMPSON
Map 13 TL99

Chequers Inn
PICK OF THE PUBS

See Pick of the Pubs on page 353

THORNHAM
Map 12 TF74

The Orange Tree
PICK OF THE PUBS

tel: 01485 512213 High St PE36 6LY
email: email@theorangetreethornham.co.uk
dir: *Phone for detailed directions*

Contemporary dining pub in a coastal village

Formerly a smugglers' haunt, this 400-year-old whitewashed inn has evolved over the years into the stylish family-run country pub it is today. Standing in the centre of the village opposite the church, The Orange Tree is a useful stop for walkers on the Peddars Way. Develop an appetite with a stroll to the local staithe, where working fishing boats still come and go through the creeks of Brancaster Bay, before returning for a pint of East Anglian-brewed ale. Chef Philip Milner makes the most of freshly landed local seafood but it's not just the fish that justifies his claim that the restaurant is the jewel in The Orange Tree's crown; the pub has a long-established relationship with local suppliers, and most of the meat is sourced from the Sandringham Estate. Children will love the climbing frame in the pub's garden.

Open all day all wk Food all wk 12-9.30 ⊕ PUNCH TAVERNS ◀ Woodforde's Wherry, Adnams Southwold Bitter, guest ales Ö Aspall. ♥ 29 Facilities Non-diners area ✿ (Bar Garden) ♦ Children's menu Children's portions Play area Garden ⊨ Parking WiFi ▭

TITCHWELL
Map 13 TF74

Titchwell Manor Hotel ★★★ HL ⊚⊚⊚ PICK OF THE PUBS

tel: 01485 210221 PE31 8BB
email: margaret@titchwellmanor.com web: www.titchwellmanor.com
dir: *A149 between Brancaster & Thornham*

Sublime sea views and extraordinary cuisine

Elegant, bold, contemporary; descriptions both of the interior of the substantial Victorian farmhouse here and the brasserie-style cuisine that has gained three AA Rosettes for Eric Snaith and his team. This smart destination dining inn glories in an enviable situation at the heart of North Norfolk's heritage coast. Premier bird-watching and rambling opportunities are strung along the bays and salt marshes fringing the fields opposite; ideal appetite-builders. Select a spot in the Eating Rooms, bar, sea-view terrace or tranquil conservatory and indulge in a Pandora's box of food choices. Your first choice from an autumn menu could be Norfolk quail terrine, honey soused veg and prune as a starter. Typical main dishes are sea trout fillet, parsley, lardo and smoked mousse; loin and belly of Houghton venison, roast pumpkin, chocolate and salsify. Desserts complete the treats here – perhaps lemon and cucumber tart; or poached rhubarb and honeycomb bavarois. Children can have fun choosing from their own menu – how about prawn cocktail; crisp salmon squares; and chocolate brownie?

Open all day all wk Food Lunch all wk 12-5.30 Dinner all wk 6-9.30 Set menu available Restaurant menu available all wk ⊕ FREE HOUSE ◀ Woodforde's Wherry Ö Aspall. ♥ 17 Facilities Non-diners area ✿ (Bar Garden) ♦ Children's menu Children's portions Garden ⊨ Parking WiFi ▭ (notice required) Rooms 27

PICK OF THE PUBS

Wiveton Bell ★★★★ INN ❀

WIVETON　　　Map 13 TG04

tel: 01263 740101
Blakeney Rd NR25 7TL
email: wivetonbell@me.com
web: www.wivetonbell.com
dir: *A149 from Blakeney towards Cley next the Sea. Right into Wiveton Rd signed Cley Spy. Approx 1m to pub*

Tranquil country pub championing local fish and game

Immaculately spruced-up though it is, and while rightly renowned for its cuisine, the Bell remains faithful to its roots as a traditional village pub. This means that, even in full walking gear (dog in tow) you are welcome to drift in for just a pint of Woodforde's Wherry, or Norfolk Moon Gazer, and nobody will suggest you should be better dressed, or have left Rex in his basket. In a village pub so close to the unspoilt salt marshes of the North Norfolk coast – an Area of Outstanding Natural Beauty – and just 10 minutes' walk from Blakeney nature reserve, that's a wise approach. Built in the 18th century, it features earthy, heritage-coloured walls, stripped beams, chunky tables and oak-planked floors, with further character imbued by local artworks lining the walls of the bar and conservatory dining room. On a winter's evening head for the tables close to the inglenook fireplace, where, by the light of the masses of

candles, your meal might begin with smoked haddock and sweetcorn chowder; or caramelised beetroot and local goats' cheese curd with honey and mustard dressed leaves, pickled walnuts and beetroot crisp. For a main course try the 'Cley Smoke House' smoked trout linguine, dill cream sauce and parmesan; or six-hour braised salt marsh beef blade, smoked mash potato, purple sprouting broccoli, mushroom duxelle and red wine jus. Local shiitake mushroom risotto, truffle oil and Smoked Dapple crisp is a vegetarian option. To finish, try the treacle-dipped ginger parkin with vanilla ice cream. On a Sunday there's an excellent choice of roasts, but booking is essential.

Open all day all wk Closed 25 Dec
Food Lunch all wk 12-2.15 Dinner all wk 6-9 ⊞ FREE HOUSE ◀ Woodforde's Wherry, Norfolk Moon Gazer, Yetman's Ŏ Aspall. ♀ 14
Facilities Non-diners area
♟ Children's menu Children's portions Garden Outside area ⌫ Parking WiFi
Rooms 6

WARHAM ALL SAINTS
Map 13 TF94

Three Horseshoes

tel: 01328 710547 **NR23 1NL**
email: mail@warhamhorseshoes.co.uk
dir: *From Wells A149 to Cromer, then right onto B1105 to Warham*

Memorable heritage pub with great pies and ales

In a row of brick-and-flint sits this timeless village pub. Its rambling layout, quarry-tile floor, and period-piece rooms recall long-gone taverns; the bar is still lit by gas mantles. Beers from the likes of Wolf and Woodforde's breweries are gravity-served from barrels stillaged behind the servery. Vintage posters, clay pipes, photographs and memorabilia adorn the walls, whilst a curious green and red dial in the ceiling turns out to be a rare example of Norfolk Twister, an ancient drinking game. As befits such a rural pub, generous home-made pies star on the chalkboard menu, along with fish from the nearby coast.

Open all wk 12-2.30 6-11 **Food** Lunch all wk 12-2 Dinner all wk 6-8 ⊕ FREE HOUSE ◀ Woodforde's Wherry, Nelson's Revenge, Wolf Ale, Moon Gazer Ö Whin Hill. **Facilities** Non-diners area ✿ (Bar Garden) ◀∥ Children's portions Family room Garden ☰ Parking ▭ (notice required)

WELLS-NEXT-THE-SEA
Map 13 TF94

The Crown Hotel
PICK OF THE PUBS

tel: 01328 710209 **The Buttlands NR23 1EX**
email: crownhotel@flyingkiwiinns.co.uk
dir: *10m from Fakenham on B1105*

Modern dishes and locally brewed beers

Owned by TV chef Chris Coubrough, this 17th-century former coaching inn overlooks a tree-lined green. Contemporary decor blends effortlessly with the bar's ancient beams and other old-world charms, leaving the modern marketing punnery of Fakenham brewer Jo Coubrough ('the bird who brews') to bring you back to the future with real ales called Bitter Old Bustard and Knot Just Another IPA. Whether you eat in the bar, the restaurant, the Orangery, or outside with its great views, the menus offer modern British and internationally influenced dishes. Gluten, meat and dairy free dishes are handily collected into dedicated menus. A selection of options include starters like quail eggs and curried mayonnaise; or butternut, cranberry and brie filo parcel with Cumberland sauce; and mains like Holkham venison with butternut and ginger risotto and buttered kale; or seared sea bass with crab, fennel and lemon linguine. There could be cinnamon apple puff with ice cream; or kiwi and passionfruit Pavlova with fruit coulis for afters.

Open all day all wk **Food** Lunch all wk 12-2.30 Dinner all wk 6.30-9.30 ⊕ FREE HOUSE/FLYING KIWI INNS ◀ Adnams Southwold Bitter, Jo C's Norfolk Kiwi, guest ale Ö Aspall. ▼ 14 **Facilities** Non-diners area ✿ (Bar Outside area) ◀∥ Children's menu Children's portions Outside area ☰ WiFi

Find out more about this county with *The AA Guide to Norfolk & Suffolk* – see shop.theAA.com

WINTERTON-ON-SEA
Map 13 TG41

Fishermans Return

tel: 01493 393305 **The Lane NR29 4BN**
email: enquiries@fishermansreturn.com web: www.fishermansreturn.com
dir: *8m N of Great Yarmouth on B1159*

Just round the corner from sandy beaches

This dog-friendly, 350-year-old brick and flint built free house stands close to long beaches and National Trust land, making it the ideal spot to finish a walk. Guest ales support Woodforde's Norfolk Nog and Wherry behind the bar, whilst the menus range from popular favourites like beef lasagne; cottage pie; fisherman's platter, sirloin steak; and burgers. Look out for fish and seafood specials on the daily-changing blackboard, where freshly caught mackerel or sea bass may be on offer. The pub hosts a beer festival on Summer Bank Holiday in August.

Open all wk 11-2.30 5.30-11 (Sat-Sun 11-11) **Food** Lunch all wk 12-2.30 Dinner all wk 6-9 ⊕ FREE HOUSE ◀ Woodforde's Wherry & Norfolk Nog, Greene King Skippers Tipple & IPA, guest ales Ö Westons Stowford Press & Old Rosie Scrumpy, local ciders. ▼ 9 **Facilities** Non-diners area ✿ (Bar Restaurant Garden) ◀∥ Children's menu Children's portions Play area Family room Garden ☰ Beer festival Cider festival Parking WiFi ▭

WIVETON
Map 13 TG04

Wiveton Bell ★★★★ INN ◉
PICK OF THE PUBS

See Pick of the Pubs on page 355

WOODBASTWICK
Map 13 TG31

The Fur & Feather Inn

tel: 01603 720003 **Slad Ln NR13 6HQ**
dir: *From A1151 (Norwich to Wroxham road), follow brown signs for Woodforde's Brewery. Pub adjacent to brewery*

An idyllic thatched country pub ideal for beer lovers

A weeping willow and duckpond in the garden; a creeper-clad façade beneath rolling reed-thatched roof; oh, and a brewery right next door. This pub-lovers' nirvana gets better, with an interior wrested from a brace of artisan's cottages still blissfully free of electronic entertainment. Here, Woodforde's beers from across the yard are gravity dispensed from barrels on the bar stillage. Work up an appetite exploring the Bure Valley's broads just across the fields before selecting from the classic pub-grub menu. Pies, puddings, fish and a good vegetarian choice all feature; the top-notch locally made burgers are renowned.

Open all day all wk **Food** Mon-Fri 11-9, Sat-Sun 10-9 ⊕ WOODFORDE'S LTD ◀ Wherry, Bure Gold, Norfolk Nog, Nelson's Revenge, Mardler's Mild, guest ales. ▼ 12 **Facilities** Non-diners area ◀∥ Children's menu Garden ☰ Parking WiFi ▭ (notice required)

NORTHAMPTONSHIRE

ASHBY ST LEDGERS
Map 11 SP56

The Olde Coach House Inn ★★★★ INN

tel: 01788 890349 **CV23 8UN**
email: info@oldecoachhouse.co.uk web: www.oldecoachhouse.co.uk
dir: *M1 junct 18 follow A361/Daventry signs. Village on left*

Good food in a memorable village setting

This mellow stone inn (The OCH) sits amidst thatched cottages in the lovely estate village here; until a century ago it was a farmhouse. Today it's an engaging mix of contemporary and rustic, with a strong emphasis on comfort; deep leather furnishings tempt you to linger by log fires, wondering at the function of the archaic rural artefacts on display. The courtyard dining area is a popular place to sample the extensive fare which ranges from home-made, stone-fired pizzas and 'design your own' grazing boards to dishes such as baked wild sea bass, chorizo, butter beans and crushed new potatoes. Fifteen boutique-style bedrooms are available.

Open all day all wk **Food** Lunch Mon-Sat 12-2.30, Sun 12-8 Dinner Mon-Sat 6-9.30, Sun 12-8 Av main course £12 Set menu available Restaurant menu available all wk ⊕ CHARLES WELLS ◀ Bombardier, Young's. ♀ 12 **Facilities** Non-diners area ☻ (Bar Garden Outside area) ♦♦ Children's menu Children's portions Play area Garden Outside area ⊼ Parking WiFi ➠ (notice required) **Rooms** 15

AYNHO
Map 11 SP53

The Great Western Arms

tel: 01869 338288 **Station Rd OX17 3BP**
email: info@great-westernarms.co.uk
dir: *From Aynho take B4031 (Station Road) W towards Deddington. Turn right to pub*

Run by a young and friendly bunch

The Great Western Railway company disappeared in 1948, but its name lives on in this foliage-covered inn between the line it built to Birmingham, and the Oxford Canal. It's a Hook Norton pub, so the brewery's range of ales is well represented; 10 wines are sold by the glass, and there's a packed whisky and spirit shelf. Good things on chef-patron René Klein's menus include his creamy chicken curry; venison, pheasant, cranberry and port pie; Cajun-dusted salmon fillet; and leek and cheese sausages. There is a pretty courtyard and garden.

Open all day all wk 11-11 Closed 25 Dec **Food** Lunch Mon-Sat 12-2.30, Sun 12-9 Dinner Mon-Sat 6-9, Sun 12-9 ⊕ HOOK NORTON ◀ Old Hooky, Hooky Bitter, Lion, guest ales ♂ Westons Perry, Old Rosie & Stowford Press. ♀ 10 **Facilities** Non-diners area ☻ (Bar Garden) ♦♦ Children's menu Children's portions Garden ⊼ Parking WiFi ➠ (notice required)

BRAUNSTON
Map 11 SP56

The Admiral Nelson

tel: 01788 891900 **Dark Ln NN11 7HJ**
dir: *Phone for detailed directions*

Canal-side free house saved by one family's determination

Despite its enviable position beside the Grand Union Canal, The Admiral Nelson has suffered a chequered history. Originally a 1730s farm building, the pub's custom waned as canal traffic declined; but fast forward to today, and the Davis family have certainly turned its fortunes around. Four hand pumps offer three guest ales and Admiral Ale, specially made by the local MerriMen microbrewery. The chef, Liam (son of the owners), applies the same care to the provenance of the kitchen ingredients; the village butcher supplies much of the meat and home-made pork pies, and he makes full use of produce from the nearby water buffalo farm. A big event on the pub's calendar is the music festival in August.

Open all day all wk 12-11 **Food** Lunch 12-3 Dinner 6-9 Restaurant menu available Tue-Sat ⊕ FREE HOUSE ◀ MerriMen Admiral Ale, rotating guest ales ♂ Addlestones, Westons Stowford Press. **Facilities** Non-diners area ☻ (Bar Garden) ♦♦ Children's menu Children's portions Garden ⊼ Parking WiFi ➠ (notice required)

CRICK
Map 11 SP57

The Red Lion Inn

tel: 01788 822342 **52 Main Rd NN6 7TX**
dir: *M1 junct 18, A428, 0.75m, follows signs for Crick from rdbt*

Village inn in trusted hands for many years

An old gabled, thatched, coaching inn of mellow ironstone standing beside the pretty main street just a stone's throw from Crick's ancient church. Exposed beams, low ceilings and open fires characterise this village free-house, family-run for over 35 years. Local beers plus those from Adnams and Wells are available here, with classic pub meals the order of the day. Faggots in onion gravy; breaded haddock, chips and peas; lasagne, hash browns and salad; mushroom and pepper Stroganoff give an idea of the dishes on offer.

Open all wk 11-2.30 6-11 (Sun 12-3 7-11) **Food** Lunch all wk 12-2 Dinner Mon-Sat 6.30-9 ⊕ FREE HOUSE ◀ Adnams Southwold Bitter, Wells Bombardier, guest ales. **Facilities** Non-diners area ☻ (Bar Restaurant Garden) ♦♦ Children's menu Children's portions Garden ⊼ Parking WiFi

DUDDINGTON
Map 11 SK90

NEW Royal Oak

tel: 01780 444267 **High St PE9 3QE**
email: theroyaloakduddington@gmail.com
dir: *From Peterborough take A47 towards Leicester. Approx 14m to Duddington*

In the quiet Welland Valley

Built of locally quarried limestone, the interior of this family-run hotel has been given a heritage-respecting makeover. The bar's leather chairs and sofas offer as ideal a place as any for a pint of Grainstore's GB Best, perhaps, or Ossett Silver King. Main menu attractions at lunchtime could be chicken, ham hock and leek pie; or beef and red wine stew with spring onion mash. In the evening a more expansive menu offers seafood tagliatelle in tomato and chilli sauce; 21-day-aged Scottish rib-eye steak with hand-cut chips and side salad; and sweet potato and black bean curry with basmati rice.

Open all wk 11-3 6-11 (Fri-Sat 11-11 Sun 11-10) **Food** Lunch Mon-Thu 12-2.30, Fri-Sun 12-6 Dinner Mon-Thu 6.30-9.30, Fri-Sat 6-9.30, Sun 6-9 Av main course £12 Set menu available Restaurant menu available Mon-Sat ⊕ FREE HOUSE ◀ St Austell Proper Job, The Grainstore GB Best, Fuller's London Pride, Ossett Silver King. ♀ 12 **Facilities** Non-diners area ♦♦ Children's menu Children's portions Garden Outside area ⊼ Parking WiFi ➠ (notice required)

EAST HADDON

Map 11 SP66

The Red Lion

PICK OF THE PUBS

tel: 01604 770223 **Main St NN6 8BU**
email: nick@redlioneasthaddon.co.uk
dir: *Just off A428*

Refined destination village dining-pub

There's something about the yellow Northamptonshire stone and thatched roof of Nick Bonner and Ren Aveiro's Red Lion that declares 'classic English village pub'. Classic ideas in the food too, from a starter of ham hock and black pudding fritter with piccalilli mayonnaise; or whipped goats' cheese, beetroot and walnut salad with sloe gin dressing, to mains of roasted hake with gnocchi and spicy tomato and chorizo casserole; or slow-cooked lamb shoulder, Greek-style salad and mint yogurt. Home-made doughnuts with warm jam sauce will prove more than tempting for dessert. As an accompaniment, a reasonably priced glass of Pinot Grigio or Malbec, or maybe a pint of Bombardier. In the grounds, overlooking rolling countryside, Nick and fellow director Wendy Carter run Shires Cookery School.

Open all day all wk 11-11 **Food** Lunch Mon-Fri 12-2.30, Sat-Sun all day Dinner Mon-Fri 6-9, Sat-Sun all day ⊕ CHARLES WELLS ◀ Bomardier, Young's. ♞ 14
Facilities Non-diners area ♦♦ Children's menu Children's portions Garden ⊫ Parking WiFi ☞ (notice required)

FARTHINGHOE

Map 11 SP53

The Fox

tel: 01295 713965 **Baker St NN13 5PH**
email: info@foxfarthinghoe.co.uk
dir: *M40 junct 11, A422, towards Brackley. Approx 5.5m to Farthinghoe*

Relaxed and friendly village pub close to Silverstone

This Charles Wells pub, now under new management, has a well furnished beer garden to the front, and an interior gleaming with scrubbed and polished wood, mismatched chairs and well-worn floorboards. Customer service is as before, friendly and welcoming, and the relaxed atmosphere also remains unchanged. Ales from the Charlie Wells stable are as dependable as ever, and new menus follow traditional lines. Lunchtime sandwiches served with chips, soup or salad augment a short list of favourites: a starter of baked garlic mushrooms could be followed by liver, bacon and mash, then rounded off with a fruit crumble.

Open all day all wk **Food** Lunch all wk 12-2.30 Dinner all wk 6-9.30 ⊕ CHARLES WELLS ◀ Courage Directors, Young's, Guinness, guest ale ♂ Aspall. ♞ 12
Facilities Non-diners area ❀ (Bar Garden) ♦♦ Children's portions Garden ⊫ Parking WiFi ☞ (notice required)

FARTHINGSTONE

Map 11 SP65

The Kings Arms

PICK OF THE PUBS

tel: 01327 361604 **Main St NN12 8EZ**
email: paul@kingsarms.fsbusiness.co.uk
dir: *M1 junct 16, A45 towards Daventry. At Weedon take A5 towards Towcester. Turn right signed Farthingstone*

Attractive village pub with wildlife-loving garden

Tucked away in perfect walking country, this stone-built 300-year-old free house is close to Canons Ashby, an Elizabethan manor house run by the National Trust. The pub's quirky garden is full of interesting recycled items, decorative trees and shrubs, and secluded corners. Paul and Denise Egerton grow their own salads and herbs here, and it's also a haven for wildlife – 50 different species of bird, 200 species of moth and 20 of butterfly have all been spotted. Walkers and their dogs relax on the terrace when it's warm; in winter, real fires warm the stone-flagged interior. Up to five real ales and Westons Old Rosie cider are on tap. Food is honestly priced and wholesome: soups, baguettes, home-made salmon fishcakes, and

sausage and bean casserole are some of the choices, along with vegetarian options. Weekend bar lunches include quality platters of meat, fish or British cheeses.

Open 7-11.30 (Fri 6.30-12 Sat 12-12 Sun 12-5 9-11) Closed Mon **Food** Lunch Sat-Sun 12-2.30 Dinner last Fri in month or special events Av main course £9 ⊕ FREE HOUSE ◀ Vale VPA, St Austell Trelawny, Marston's Wainwright, Adnams Ghost Ship ♂ Westons Old Rosie. **Facilities** Non-diners area ❀ (Bar Restaurant Garden) ♦♦ Children's portions Family room Garden ⊫ Parking WiFi

FOTHERINGHAY

Map 12 TL09

The Falcon Inn

tel: 01832 226254 **PE8 5HZ**
email: info@thefalcon-inn.co.uk **web:** www.thefalcon-inn.co.uk
dir: *From A605 between Peterborough & Oundle follow Fotheringhay signs*

Popular locals' inn with designer garden

This attractive 18th-century, stone-built pub stands in gardens overlooking the stunning church. It's a real local, the Tap Bar regularly used by the village darts team, their throwing arms lubricated by pints of Fool's Nook ale. The menus in both the bar and charming conservatory restaurant rely extensively on locally sourced ingredients. In the spring, restaurant offerings are smoked ham hock and rabbit terrine and piccalilli to start, followed by lamb three ways – roast loin, confit shoulder and sweetbreads with pommes Anna, niçoise vegetables and red pepper jus. Hopefully there'll still be room for lemon curd tartlet with honey ice cream.

Open all day 12-11 (Sun 12-4 Jan-May) Closed Sun eve Jan-May **Food** Lunch Mon-Sat 12-2, Sun 12-3 (Sun 12-4 Jan-May) Dinner Mon-Sat 6-9 (Sun 6-8 Apr-Dec) Set menu available Restaurant menu available all wk ⊕ FREE HOUSE ◀ Greene King IPA, Digfield Fool's Nook, Fuller's London Pride ♂ Aspall. ♞ 14
Facilities Non-diners area ❀ (Bar Garden) ♦♦ Children's menu Children's portions Garden ⊫ Beer festival Parking WiFi ☞ (notice required)

GREAT EVERDON

Map 11 SP55

NEW The Plough Inn

tel: 01327 361606 **High St NN11 3BL**
email: theploughinn.everdon@icloud.com
dir: *In village centre*

Potter with your pint among plants

Pub? Or antiques showroom? You decide. But after enjoying one of the many lovely walks around the village, the Plough's customers enjoy the relaxed ambience created by vintage furniture, collectables and plants on sale from barns in the garden. Gun Dog Ales, Sharp's Doom Bar and 10 wines served by the glass are the most requested refreshments, while the simple menu of pub grub is attractively priced. On Sundays, the traditional roast offers Kim's own organic lamb or Everdon rib of beef with all the trimmings, followed by treacle or Bakewell tart. The garden and terrace are well furnished, and enjoy lovely views over rolling Northamptonshire countryside.

Open all day all wk **Food** Lunch all wk 12-3 Dinner Fri 7-10 ⊕ FREE HOUSE ◀ Gun Dog Ales Jack's Spaniels, Sharp's Doom Bar, Greene King IPA, guest ales. ₹ 10 **Facilities** Non-diners area ♣ (Bar Garden) ♦ Children's portions Play area Garden ⋒ WiFi ⊜ (notice required)

HINTON-IN-THE-HEDGES   Map 11 SP53

NEW Crewe Arms

tel: 01280 705801 **Sparrow Corner NN13 5NF**
email: enquiries@crewearms.co.uk
dir: From A422 between Banbury & Brackley follow Hinton-in-the-Hedges signs

Traditional local in a Domesday-listed village

The two small gardens of this traditional village pub are often populated by the village cricket team on summer weekends, refreshing themselves with pints of beautifully conditioned ales. The pub dates from the 15th century so there's a cosy interior divided into four areas, warmed by log fires in winter. Food from local suppliers is turned into a menu of reasonably-priced home-made favourites. A typical three-course selection could comprise field mushrooms on toast with garlic butter; pan-fried sea bass with ratatouille and basil; and a Hinton crumble or chocolate brownie.

Open all day all wk **Food** Lunch all wk 12-3 Dinner all wk 6-9 Av main course £11 ⊕ FREE HOUSE ◀ Hook Norton Hooky Bitter, Caledonian Deuchars IPA, Tring Side Pocket for a Toad ♂ Symonds. ₹ 10 **Facilities** Non-diners area ♣ (Bar Garden) ♦ Children's portions Garden ⋒ Parking WiFi ⊜ (notice required)

KILSBY   Map 11 SP57

The George

tel: 01788 822229 **Watling St CV23 8YE**
dir: M1 junct 18, follow A361 & Daventry signs. Pub at rdbt junct of A361 & A5

A great local with home-cooked food

A warm welcome and great local atmosphere characterise this village pub, which has a traditional public bar and a high-ceilinged wood-panelled lounge opening into a smarter but relaxed area with solidly comfortable furnishings. The lunch bar menu includes sandwiches, filled baguettes and a selection of home-made dishes. The evening menu majors on home-made, hearty dishes such as boeuf bourguignon; pork loin and mushroom Stroganoff; lamb shank braised in red wine; and sea bass, Italian tomato, olives and caper sauce. A children's menu is always available. There is a new function room, large car park and an attractive garden for sunny days.

Open all wk 11.30-3 5.30-11.30 (Sun 12-5 6-11) **Food** Lunch Mon-Sat 12-2, Sun 12-3 Dinner Mon-Sat 6-9, Sun 6-8.30 Set menu available Restaurant menu available all wk ⊕ PUNCH TAVERNS ◀ Fuller's London Pride, Adnams Southwold Bitter, Timothy Taylor Landlord. ₹ 10 **Facilities** Non-diners area ♦ Children's menu Children's portions Garden ⋒ Parking WiFi ⊜ (notice required)

LITTLE BRINGTON   Map 11 SP66

The Saracens Head

tel: 01604 770640 **Main St NN7 4HS**
email: info@thesaracensatbrington.co.uk
dir: M1 junct 16, A45 to Flore. In Flore 1st right signed the Bringtons. Straight on at x-roads to Little Brington, pub on left

Old village inn with modern dishes

Barrel tables and beams; quarry tile and bareboard floors; leaded windows and a fierce wood-burner; the Saracens has character in droves. This 17th-century

building of mellow ironstone slumbers in a tiny village where lucky locals enjoy a changing range of beers that includes some from local microbreweries. It's a popular stop too, for horse riders using the network of local bridleways, who can hitch-up in the garden for more sedate views of the countryside. It's a menu of modern British dishes and there's a tapas menu from Mondays to Thursdays.

Open all day all wk ⊕ FREE HOUSE ◀ Greene King IPA, Timothy Taylor Landlord, guest ale. **Facilities** ♣ (Bar Garden) ♦ Children's portions Garden Parking WiFi

---

LITTLE HOUGHTON   Map 11 SP85

Four Pears

tel: 01604 890900 **28 Bedford Rd NN7 1AB**
email: info@thefourpears.com
dir: From Northampton take A428 towards Bedford. Left signed Little Houghton

Smartly renovated village inn with appealing menu

In a peaceful, ironstone-built village just outside Northampton, this 400-year-old hostelry was rescued from closure by local residents a few years ago. The fresh, contemporary design owes little to the past. Rather; tip-top real ales are supped in the smart, light bar area, where dog-walkers straying from the nearby Nene Valley lakes will find a warm welcome. The refined, soft-furnishing rich lounge captures the essence of the dining pub; a comfy retreat where bistro meets pub-grub. Start with pan-fried pigeon breast, mixed grains, baked pears, pancetta and caramel dressing, or go straight for braised cod cheeks, broad beans, smoked bacon, pea shoots and pommes frites in the bright restaurant area popular with families.

Open all day all wk **Food** Lunch all wk 12-2.30 Dinner Mon-Sat 6-9.15 Restaurant menu available Mon-Sat ⊕ FREE HOUSE ◀ St Austell Tribute, Fuller's London Pride, Phipps IPA ♂ Westons Stowford Press. ₹ **Facilities** Non-diners area ♣ (Bar Outside area) ♦ Children's portions Outside area ⋒ WiFi ⊜ (notice required)

NASSINGTON   Map 12 TL09

The Queens Head Inn ★★★★ INN ◉   PICK OF THE PUBS

tel: 01780 784006 **54 Station Rd PE8 6QB**
email: info@queensheadnassington.co.uk **web:** www.queensheadnassington.co.uk
dir: Exit A1 at Wansford, follow Yarwell & Nassington signs. Through Yarwell. Pub on left in Nassington

Traditional inn with great food

The sun-trap garden of this striking Collyweston-stone inn slopes to a meander of the River Nene. Savvy boaters moor up here to join customers who drive miles to engage with a menu that has gained AA-Rosette recognition. Fires warm the interior in winter and you can dine alfresco on the patio. Settle into the comfy, beamed interior with a glass of Oakham JHB beer and contemplate a choice of invigorating classics exampled by Middlewhite belly pork with cider sauce, or sea bass fillets with ginger and chilli. The trump card is a notable range of luxury steaks, including Wagyu rib-eye and prime American USDA 150-day, corn-fed Black Angus sirloin. The Queen Head's diary is always full and includes events such as seafood week and the Great British game week. Sumptuous accommodation is also available here.

Open all day all wk 11-11 (Sat 11am-mdnt Sun 12-11) **Food** Lunch Mon-Sat 12-2.30, Sun 12-8 Dinner Mon-Sat 6-9, Sun 12-8 Av main course £13.50 Restaurant menu available all wk ⊕ FREE HOUSE ◀ Greene King IPA, Oakham JHB. ₹ 8 **Facilities** Non-diners area ♣ (Bar Garden) ♦ Children's menu Children's portions Garden ⋒ Parking WiFi ⊜ (notice required) **Rooms** 10

Althorp Coaching Inn

tel: 01604 770651 **Main St, Great Brington NN7 4JA**
email: althorpcoachinginn@btconnect.com
dir: *From A428 pass main gates of Althorp House, left before rail bridge.
Great Brington 1m*

Thatched pub with old-world charm and locally sourced food

Occupying a lovely position in the pretty village of Great Brington on the Althorp
Estate, this 16th-century stone coaching inn has original decor throughout. A brick
and cobbled courtyard is surrounded by stable rooms, and the enclosed flower
garden is a peaceful spot in which to sample one of the real ales and ciders from a
wide selection that includes Phipps IPA and Somersby cider. The restaurant
specialises in traditional English cooking based on local produce. Start with game
terrine, port jelly and toast, followed perhaps by slow-cooked pork belly, braised red
cabbage, parsnip purée and red wine jus.

Open all day all wk 11-11 (Sat-Sun 11am-mdnt) **Food** Lunch Mon-Thu 12-3, Fri-Sat
12-9.30, Sun 12-8 Dinner Mon-Thu 6-9.30, Fri-Sat 12-9.30, Sun 12-8 ⊕ FREE
HOUSE ◼ Greene King IPA, Phipps IPA, Sharp's Doom Bar, St Austell Tribute
Ŏ Somersby, guest ciders. ♛ 10 **Facilities** Non-diners area ❧ (Bar Garden)
♦♦ Children's menu Children's portions Garden ⌗ Beer festival Parking WiFi
🚌 (notice required)

The Hopping Hare ★★★★ INN ◉

tel: 01604 580090 **18 Hopping Hill Gardens, Duston NN5 6PF**
email: info@hoppinghare.com **web:** www.hoppinghare.com
dir: *Take A428 from Northampton towards West Haddon. Left into Hopping Hill Gardens,
pub signed*

Top family-owned pub

The mildly eccentric pub signage reflects the 'hopping' element; as it's hard to
explain, a visit will clarify. Having seen, enter the bar, where several national real
ales accompany Saxby's cider, made on a local farm, and around 11 wines by the
glass. For her modern British dishes, head chef Jennie Bowmaker hand-picks her

suppliers, so knows how her meats were reared, her fish caught, and her vegetables
grown. The result: honey and sesame roasted heritage carrots, blue cheese,
chargrilled pear, chicory, rocket, smoked walnuts, pickled grapes and pomegranate
mollasses, and that's just a starter! Main dishes could include slow-braised beef
shortrib, sautéed leeks with wholegrain mustard, roasted garlic mashed potato,
crispy shallots and green peppercorn jus; or a more prosaic but no less tasty, maple
ham, egg and chips. Sandwiches, omelettes and salads are also available.

The Hopping Hare

Open all day all wk **Food** Mon-Sat 12-10, Sun 12-8.30 Set menu available
Restaurant menu available all wk ⊕ FREE HOUSE ◼ Black Sheep, Adnams
Broadside, Towcester Mill Ŏ Aspall, Somersby, Saxby's Cider. ♛ 11
Facilities Non-diners area ♦♦ Children's portions Outside area ⌗ Parking WiFi
🚌 (notice required) **Rooms** 20

The White Horse

tel: 01604 781297 **Walgrave Rd NN6 9QX**
email: info@whitehorseold.co.uk
dir: *From A43 (between Kettering & Northampton) follow Walgrave signs. Through
Walgrave to Old*

Beautifully restored village-centre pub with lovely beer garden

Whimsical sayings ("The road to success is under construction"), leather sofas,
stacked logs and a book exchange characterise the interior of this stylishly
designed steam-driven mill. Micro-brewed real ales rarely need to travel far, as for
instance Gun Dog from Woodford Halse, and Whistling Kite from Kettering. Seasonal
dishes are prepared fresh daily plus there's favourites such as a classic fish and
chips, burgers and steaks. A doggy bag is willingly offered if you can't finish. Over
the Summer Bank Holiday weekend in August there's a beer and cider festival.

Open 12-3 5-11 (Sat 12-11 Sun 12-7) Closed Mon (ex BH) **Food** Contact pub for food
times Restaurant menu available Tue-Sun ⊕ FREE HOUSE ◼ Phipps, Langton, Nene
Valley, Whistling Kite, Gun Dog Ales Ŏ Westons, Saxby's Cider. ♛ 11
Facilities Non-diners area ❧ (Bar Garden Outside area) ♦♦ Children's portions Garden
Outside area ⌗ Beer festival Cider festival Parking WiFi 🚌 (notice required)

OUNDLE
Map 11 TL08

The Chequered Skipper

tel: 01832 273494 **Ashton PE8 5LD**
email: enquiries@chequeredskipper.co.uk
dir: *A605 towards Oundle, at rdbt follow signs to Ashton. 1m, turn left into Ashton*

Well known for their pizzas

The Chequered Skipper has a traditional thatched exterior complemented by a contemporary interior. Located opposite the green in the model village of Ashton, built for the estate workers in the 1880s, the pub plays its part well, with timeless oak floor and beams, and a collection of butterfly display cases diverting attention from a bar stocking locally brewed beers (two beer festivals a year). The menu mixes speciality pizzas and traditional English and European dishes — pork and liver pâté might be followed by braised shoulder of lamb with dauphinoise potatoes.

Open all wk 11.30-3 6-11 (Sat 11.30-11 Sun 11.45-11) **Food** Lunch Mon-Fri 12-2, Sat 12-2.30, Sun 12-3 Dinner Mon-Sat 6.30-9.30, Sun 6.30-9 ⊕ FREE HOUSE ◀ Rockingham Ale, Brewster's Hophead, Oakham. ⬥ 8 **Facilities** Non-diners area ❀ (Bar Garden) ♦ Children's portions Garden Beer festival Parking WiFi ▭ (notice required)

PAULERSPURY
Map 11 SP74

NEW Barley Mow

tel: 01327 811086 **53 High St NN12 7NA**
email: info@barleymow.pub
dir: *From A5 between Milton Keynes & Towcester follow Paulerspury signs (at BP Garage). 0.75m to pub on left*

Attractive old village centre pub with games room

The description 'idyllic rural spot' may be a tad overworked, but it certainly applies to the Barley Mow in Paulerspury. Surrounded by thatched cottages and beautiful farmland, it's been the village centre watering hole since at least the 17th century. Among the traditional features is a Northamptonshire skittles table, and a large fireplace with wood-burner; a more recent addition is a games room with darts and table tennis. Adnams, two guests and a beer garden satisfy ale enthusiasts. The menu tempts with a starter of port and Long Clawson Stilton mushrooms on toast, followed perhaps by Matt's fried chicken with twice-cooked chips and coleslaw.

Open 12-2 5-11 (Mon 5-11 Fri 12-2 5-12 Sat 12-12 Sun 12-9) Closed Mon L **Food** Lunch Tue-Sat 12-2, Sun 12-4 Dinner Tue-Sat 5-9 Av main course £11.50 ⊕ ENTERPRISE INNS ◀ Adnams Broadside, guest ales. **Facilities** Non-diners area ❀ (Bar Garden) ♦ Children's menu Children's portions Garden ⊓ Parking WiFi ▭ (notice required)

SIBBERTOFT
Map 11 SP68

The Red Lion
PICK OF THE PUBS

tel: 01858 880011 **43 Welland Rise LE16 9UD**
email: andrew@redlionwinepub.co.uk
dir: *From Market Harborough take A4304, through Lubenham, left through Marston Trussell to Sibbertoft*

A real passion for good wine

The interior of this friendly 300-year-old free house is an appealing blend of contemporary and classic decor, with oak beams, leather upholstery and a smartly turned-out dining room. Andrew and Sarah Banks have built a loyal following here thanks to their special passion for wine: over 200 bins appear on the list, 20 labels are served by the glass, and an annual wine festival is a high point in the pub's busy calendar. After tasting, all wines can be bought at take-home prices, avoiding the guesswork of supermarket purchases. The monthly-changing and reasonably priced menu is served in both bar and restaurant, and could feature devilled whitebait, or pork belly and black pudding bites; fish pie with cheesy mash or an 8oz sirloin with hand-cut chips; and caramelised orange cheesecake or treacle sponge and custard.

Open 5-11 (Sat 12-3 6-11 Sun 12-6) Closed Mon-Fri L & Sun eve **Food** Lunch Sun 12-3 Dinner Mon-Sat 6.30-9.30 Av main course £10 Set menu available ⊕ FREE HOUSE ◀ St Austell Tribute, Greene King Abbot Ale ♂ Aspall, Westons, Healey's Cornish Rattler. ⬥ 20 **Facilities** Non-diners area ❀ (Garden) ♦ Children's menu Children's portions Play area Garden ⊓ Parking WiFi ▭ (notice required)

STAVERTON
Map 11 SP56

The Countryman

tel: 01327 311815 **Daventry Rd NN11 6JH**
email: thecountrymanstaverton@gmail.com **web:** www.thecountrymanstaverton.co.uk
dir: *On A425 between Daventry & Southam*

Quality modern cooking in traditional village coaching inn

Built in traditional Northamptonshire ironstone, this lovely 17th-century coaching inn retains plenty of original character courtesy of log fires and beamed ceilings. A wide choice of beers keep beer fans happy, while the seasonal menu showcases regional produce. Start with smoked haddock fishcakes with creamed leeks; or braised rabbit leg with Puy lentils and bacon, then move on to wild mushroom and spinach 'cottage pie' and seasonal vegetables; or smoked salmon, tiger prawn and tenderstem broccoli linguine.

Open all wk Mon 12 3 6 10 Tue-Sat 12-3 6-11 (Sun 12-10) Closed 3-12 Jan **Food** Lunch Mon-Sat 12-2.30, Sun 12-9 Dinner Mon-Sat 6-9.30, Sun 12-9 Set menu available ⊕ FREE HOUSE ◀ Gun Dog Ales, Church End, Great Oakley. ⬥ 9 **Facilities** Non-diners area ❀ (Bar Outside area) ♦ Children's menu Children's portions Outside area ⊓ Parking WiFi ▭ (notice required)

STOKE BRUERNE   Map 11 SP74

The Boat Inn

tel: 01604 862428 **NN12 7SB**
email: enquiries@boatinn.co.uk **web:** www.boatinn.co.uk
dir: *In village centre, just off A508 & A5*

Family-run free house on the Grand Union Canal

Trim thatch topping a long, low building of golden limestone makes this canal-side pub stand out at the heart of the canal system. The busy locks here, together with the National Canal Museum directly opposite, are reflected in the decor; lots of old photos, paintings and ephemera – one bar is shaped like a narrowboat. A wide range of beers will satisfy a thirst, whilst food can be enjoyed in bars, bistro or elegant restaurant. Traditional pub grub is the foundation of robust bar meals; the carte menu in Woodwards Restaurant includes pan-fried trio of fish (salmon, red mullet and sea bass) with balsamic stir-fried vegetables; slow-cooked devilled rump of lamb; and mushroom and tarragon strudel with Madeira sauce.

Open all day all wk 9.30am-11pm (Sun 9.30am-10.30pm) **Food** all wk 9.30-9.30 Set menu available Restaurant menu available all wk ⊕ FREE HOUSE ◀ Banks's Bitter, Marston's New World, Wychwood Hobgoblin, Jennings Cumberland Ale, Ringwood Boondoggle Ö Thatchers Traditional. ♀ 10 **Facilities** Non-diners area ✿ (Bar Outside area) ♦♦ Children's menu Children's portions Outside area ♯ Parking WiFi ➠ (notice required)

THORNBY   Map 11 SP67

The Red Lion

tel: 01604 740238 **Welford Rd NN6 8SJ**
email: enquiries@redlionthornby.co.uk
dir: *A14 junct 1, A5199 towards Northampton. Pub on left in village*

An oasis just off the main road

Weary A14 travellers should earmark this 400-year-old village pub that's just a mile from junction 1. In winter months a log fire warms the traditional interior and its wall of pictures of the pub from bygone days. It's hospitably run by Simon and Louise Cottle, who consult the locals on their choice of four ales; Vale of Welton cider is here too. The menu of freshly prepared dishes includes lunchtime rustic ciabattas; in the evening settle down to a pavé of hot smoked salmon with cucumber and dill risoni, followed by pan-roasted chicken breast with braised baby gem. The glorious summer garden hosts a beer festival on the last weekend in July.

Open all wk 12-3 5-11 (Mon 5-10 Sat-Sun 12-11) **Food** Lunch Tue-Fri 12-2, Sat 12-3, Sun 12-5 Dinner Tue-Sat 6-9 ⊕ FREE HOUSE ◀ Adnams, Black Sheep, The Grainstore, Purity, Nobby's, Fuller's London Pride, Timothy Taylor Ö Westons Stowford Press, Vale Of Welton. **Facilities** Non-diners area ✿ (Bar Garden) ♦♦ Children's portions Garden ♯ Beer festival Parking WiFi ➠ (notice required)

TITCHMARSH   Map 11 TL07

The Wheatsheaf at Titchmarsh

tel: 01832 732203 **1 North St NN14 3DH**
email: enquiries@thewheatsheafattitchmarsh.co.uk
dir: *A14 junct 13, A605 towards Oundle, right to Titchmarsh. Or from A14 junct 14 follow signs for Titchmarsh*

Pretty village pub with smart, modern interior

There's a perfect balance of traditional and contemporary styles at this stone-built village pub. A wide selection of real ales is on offer in the bar and can be enjoyed beside one of the two open fires. Freshly prepared dishes might include smoked paprika Scotch egg, celeriac remoulade, tomato and red pepper coulis; venison bourguignon shortcrust pastry pie, mash, chantenay carrots and gravy; or Thai green vegetable curry. Among the desserts there could be apple and cinnamon crème brûlée; or chilled lemon soufflé. Dessert wine pairings appear on the à la carte. Real ales include Sharp's Doom Bar, Butcombe, and Fuller's London Pride.

Open all wk 12-3 6-11 (Sat 12-11 Sun 12-8) **Food** Lunch Mon-Thu 12-2, Fri-Sat 12-2.30, Sun 12-5 Dinner Mon-Sat 6-9.30 Set menu available Restaurant menu available all wk ⊕ FREE HOUSE ◀ Greene King IPA, Sharp's Doom Bar, Fuller's London Pride, Butcombe, guest ales Ö Aspall. ♀ 11 **Facilities** Non-diners area ✿ (Bar Garden) ♦♦ Children's menu Children's portions Garden ♯ Parking WiFi ➠ (notice required)

TOWCESTER   Map 11 SP64

The Folly Inn

tel: 01327 354031 **London Rd NN12 6LB**
email: info@follyinntowcester.co.uk **web:** www.follyinntowcester.co.uk
dir: *On A5 opposite Towcester Racecourse*

Quintessential thatched country inn for foodies

Sitting beside the A5 opposite Towcester Racecourse, the Folly beckons with its picture-postcard looks, flower-filled hanging baskets and coaching lamps. The interior reveals all the hallmarks of a proper diners' pub, with neatly laid tables in a clean and fresh setting. Lunchtime classics range from roasted pork belly and crackling, to mushroom, brie, spinach and cranberry Wellington. Dinner could feature Perkins Lodge Farm steaks or pan-fried chicken breast stuffed with crab meat and wrapped in Parma ham. Desserts are tried and tested favourites such as blueberry and buttermilk pannacotta or sticky toffee pudding. If a glass of ale in the extensive rear garden is all that's required, three of the county's most cherished breweries are on tap.

The Folly Inn

Open 12-2.30 6-9.30 (Sun 12-7.30) Closed Mon **Food** Contact pub for food times Restaurant menu available Tue-Sun ⊕ FREE HOUSE ◀ Gun Dog Ales, Towcester Mill, Whittlebury. **Facilities** ❀ (Bar Garden) ♦ Children's menu Children's portions Garden ⋒ Parking WiFi

The Saracens Head

tel: 01327 350414 **219 Watling St NN12 6BX**
email: saracenshead.towcester@greeneking.co.uk
dir: *M1 junct 15A, A43 towards Oxford. Take A5 signed Towcester*

400 years old and immortalised by Charles Dickens

This imposing building dates back over 400 years, and is featured in Charles Dickens' first novel, *The Pickwick Papers*. The same home comforts that Dickens enjoyed when visiting Towcester have been updated to modern standards, and discerning customers will find excellent service in the restored pub. Starters might be panko-breadcrumbed calamari rings; or chicken liver pâté with cherry compôte, followed by a main course of beef and ale pie, mash and vegetables; or leek, potato and spring onion homity pie. Sandwiches, jackets, wraps and ciabattas are all available too.

Open all day all wk 11-11 (Fri-Sat 11am-mdnt) ⊕ GREENE KING/OLD ENGLISH INNS ◀ Abbot Ale & IPA, Morland Old Speckled Hen, guest ale. **Facilities** ♦ Children's menu Children's portions Garden Parking WiFi

UPPER BODDINGTON   Map 11 SP45

Plough Inn

tel: 01327 260364 **32 Warwick Av NN11 6DH**
email: enquiries@ploughinnboddington.co.uk
dir: *Phone for detailed directions*

Traditional thatched village inn close to Silverstone

Just one mile from the tranquillity of Boddington reservoir with its fishing and sailing club, this charming 18th-century thatched coaching inn is also convenient for Silverstone race circuit. Set within lovely Northamptonshire countryside, the Plough is at the heart of village life in Upper Boddington. A traditional pub with flagstones and log-burner, this free house serves several real ales, which can be enjoyed in the snug or 'Doll's Parlour'. In the dining room, enjoy dishes such as fish pie; sticky rack of ribs; or butternut squash and pumpkin risotto. Look out for the Summer Bank Holiday beer festival in August.

Open all wk 5.30-11 (Fri 5-12 Sat 12-12 Sun 12-10.30) **Food** Lunch Sat 12-2.30, Sun 12-4 Dinner Tue-Sat 6-9 ⊕ FREE HOUSE ◀ Shepherd Neame Spitfire, Greene King IPA, local guest ales. **Facilities** Non-diners area ❀ (Bar Outside area) ♦ Children's menu Children's portions Outside area ⋒ Beer festival Parking WiFi ▭ (notice required)

WADENHOE   Map 11 TL08

The King's Head   PICK OF THE PUBS

tel: 01832 720024 **Church St PE8 5ST**
email: info@wadenhoekingshead.co.uk
dir: *From A605, 3m from Wadenhoe rdbt. 2m from Oundle*

Pretty riverside village pub

For over 400 years, travellers and locals have been able to drink and eat at this part-thatched, stone-built inn by the River Nene in unspoilt Wadenhoe. The facilities may be modern, but the old-world charm is still there. For instance, sit in the shade of the ancient pollarded willow trees and enjoy the lazy pastime of gongoozling, that is, watch the narrowboats negotiating the nearby lock, not always correctly. The quarry-tiled and bare-boarded bar features heavy oak-beamed ceilings, pine furniture, open log fires and local beers. On the lunchtime menu find sandwiches, pies and home-made burgers and mains such as roast supreme of salmon. In the evening you can feast like a king on pan-fried duck breast; chicken and mushroom pot pie; or goats' cheese and caramelised onion tart. Pub classics include Gloucestershire Old Spots sausages and mash; and scampi, chips and garden peas.

Open Tue-Sat 12-3 6-11, Sun 12-6 (Summer Mon-Sat 12-11, Sun 12-9) Closed Sun eve & Mon (Winter) **Food** Lunch Mon-Sat 12-2, Sun 12-6 Dinner all wk 6-9 Set menu available ⊕ FREE HOUSE ◀ King's Head Bitter, Digfield Barnwell Bitter, Nobby's Swift Nick ♂ Gaymers. ♟ 11 **Facilities** Non-diners area ❀ (Bar Garden Outside area) ♦ Children's portions Garden Outside area ⋒ Parking WiFi ▭ (notice required)

WESTON   Map 11 SP54

The Crown   PICK OF THE PUBS

tel: 01295 760310 **Helmdon Rd NN12 8PX**
email: mike.foalks@live.co.uk
dir: *Accessed from A43 or B4525*

Community-focused village pub

This delightful 16th-century inn fulfils a role as a true community pub, with a reputation for its family- and dog-friendly attitude, its excellent beers and a range of high-quality, locally-sourced, 'nothing-out-of-a-packet' dishes. The interior is modern and styled in calming colours. A seasonal menu might well feature the following – twice baked cheddar cheese soufflé, blushed tomato, red onion and walnut salad; Thai-style fishcakes with sweet chilli, coriander and lime crème fraîche; beer battered codling fillet, mushy peas and home-cut chips; slow-braised blade of beef, beetroot dauphinoise, charred broccoli and green peppercorn jus; and cheddar, leek and feta sausages, spring onion mash, spring greens and red onion gravy.

Open all wk 12-3 5-11 (Fri-Sat 12-11 Sun 12-5) Closed Mon L **Food** Lunch Tue-Sun 12-3 Dinner Mon-Sat 6-9.30 ⊕ FREE HOUSE ◀ Hooky, St Austell Tribute, Sharp's Doom Bar ♂ Thatchers Gold. **Facilities** Non-diners area ❀ (Bar Garden) ♦ Children's menu Children's portions Garden ⋒ Parking WiFi ▭ (notice required)

WOODNEWTON

Map 11 TL09

The White Swan

tel: 01780 470944 **22 Main St PE8 5EB**
dir: *Phone for detailed directions*

Popular village pub with contemporary interior

When Ian Simmons bought this 19th-century, stone-built pub it was in a bad way, with heavy shutters on the windows and doors, having closed down no less than three times in five years. But with his dedication and strong local support, The White Swan really is making a name for itself. Beer drinkers will find Sharp's Doom Bar and Fuller's London Pride. On the menu, start with goats' cheese and caramelised onion bruschetta; or pan-fried scallops with black pudding bon bons; then continue with boeuf bourguignon; venison cottage pie; smoked haddock, chive mash and poached egg; or mushroom, brie and cranberry Wellington with fennel and leek croquette. Young ones can choose from their own dedicated menu.

Open 12-3 6-11 (Sat 12-11 Sun 12-10.30) Closed Mon L, Sun eve Jan-Etr **Food** Lunch Tue-Sun 12-2.30 Dinner all wk 6-9.30 (Mon-Sat 6-9.30 Jan-Etr) Av main course £9 Set menu available Restaurant menu available throughout ⊕ FREE HOUSE ◀ Fuller's London Pride, Sharp's Doom Bar. ♚ 9 **Facilities** Non-diners area ✿ (Bar Garden Outside area) ♦♦ Children's menu Children's portions Garden Outside area ⊨ Parking WiFi ▨▨ (notice required)

NORTHUMBERLAND

ALNWICK

Map 21 NU11

The Hogs Head Inn ★★★ INN

tel: 01665 606576 **Hawfinch Dr NE66 2BF**
email: info@hogsheadinnalnwick.co.uk web: www.hogsheadinnalnwick.co.uk
dir: *From S: A1 onto A1068 signed Alnwick. 3rd exit at rdbt. Under A1, right at BP garage. From N: A1 onto A1068 signed Alnwick. 1st left, right at BP garage (NB older Sat Nav systems may not recognise pub's postcode)*

Notable local food at family-friendly pub

Named after the pub featured in the Harry Potter books, this inn is just minutes from Alnwick Castle, which became *Hogwarts* in the first two films. Close to Alnwick Garden, the Hogs Head is an ideal base for exploring Northumberland, and food at this family-friendly pub is served all day. North East produce appears throughout the menu – belly pork and black pudding served with peppercorn sauce and crispy crackling; chicken and pancetta tagliatelle in creamy garlic sauce; or chickpea and coriander burger are typical dishes. Save space for treacle sponge and custard, and wash it down with a pint of Hadrian Border Tyneside Blonde.

Open all day all wk **Food** all wk 7.30am-9pm ⊕ FREE HOUSE ◀ Black Sheep Best Bitter, Hadrian Border Tyneside Blonde, Tetley's Gold ♉ Somersby. ♚ **Facilities** Non-diners area ♦♦ Children's menu Children's portions Play area Garden Outside area ⊨ Parking WiFi ▨▨ (notice required) **Rooms** 53

AMBLE

Map 21 NU20

The Wellwood

tel: 01665 714646 **High St NE65 0LD**
email: enquiries@wellwoodamble.co.uk
dir: *At junct of A1068 & High St in Amble*

Traditional meals served alongside Indian classics

On the stunning Northumberland coast in an Area of Outstanding Natural Beauty, The Wellwood started life as a farmhouse and it's the oldest building in Amble. Walkers and locals mingle in the bar over pints of cask ales, whilst diners have very different options, with a restaurant, dining room and carvery. As well as a bar menu and traditional pub favourites like bangers and mash and steak pie, there are dishes such as mussels in spiced tomato and basil sauce; tempura battered goats' cheese fritters; a brace of Craster kippers with brown bread, new potatoes and garden peas; supreme of chicken; and locally sourced sirloin, fillet or rump steaks.

Open all day all wk **Food** Lunch all wk 12-3 Dinner all wk 5-9 Av main course £5-£9 Set menu available Restaurant menu available all wk ⊕ PUNCH TAVERNS ◀ Wells Bombardier, Black Sheep. ♚ 10 **Facilities** Non-diners area ✿ (Bar Garden) ♦♦ Children's menu Children's portions Family room Garden ⊨ Parking WiFi ▨▨ (notice required)

BARRASFORD

Map 21 NY97

The Barrasford Arms ◉

tel: 01434 681237 **NE48 4AA**
email: contact@barrasfordarms.co.uk
dir: *From A69 at Hexham take A6079 signed Acomb & Chollerford. In Chollerford by church turn left signed Barrasford*

A destination food pub

Chef Tony Binks's village inn can be found close to Hadrian's Wall deep in the glorious Northumbrian countryside, with spectacular views of the Tyne Valley. Most beat a path to Tony's door for his short and imaginative menus. But the Barrasford retains a traditional pub atmosphere, and local Wylam and Hadrian Border ales are on tap in the time-honoured bar to refresh locals, passing walkers and cyclists. A typical lunchtime choice may comprise twice-baked cheddar cheese soufflé followed by 'very local' pheasant, bacon and shallot pie with creamy mash. Finish with a vanilla crème brûlée served with home-made shortbread.

Open 12-3 6-11 (Sat-Sun all day) Closed 1st wk Jan, Mon **Food** Lunch Tue-Sun 12-2.30 Dinner Tue-Sat 6.30-9 Set menu available ⊕ FREE HOUSE ◀ Wylam Gold Tankard, Hadrian Border Gladiator. **Facilities** Non-diners area ♦♦ Children's portions Garden ⊨ Parking WiFi ▨▨ (notice required)

BEADNELL

Map 21 NU22

The Craster Arms ★★★★ INN

tel: 01665 720272 **The Wynding NE67 5AX**
email: michael@crasterarms.co.uk web: www.crasterarms.co.uk
dir: *Exit A1 at Brownieside signed Preston. Left at T-junct signed Seahouses. Right signed Beadnell village. Pub on left*

Within walking distance of beautiful beaches

In the 15th century, the English in this neck of the woods built small fortified watch towers to warn of Scottish invasions – this was one of them. Since becoming a pub in 1818 its role has widened to offer not just food, drink and accommodation, but a programme of live entertainment, including the Crastonbury music festival (an RNLI fundraiser), and a beer and cider festival (last weekend in July). Sandwiches, baguettes, paninis, salads and hot meals are available at lunchtime; in the evening there's braised lamb shank; Thai green chicken curry; crab fishcake and other local seafood. Seasonal blackboard specials are worth considering too, of course.

Open all day all wk 11-11 **Food** all wk 11-9 ⊕ PUNCH TAVERNS ◀ Camerons Strongarm, Black Sheep, Mordue Workie Ticket ♉ Westons Traditional Scrumpy & Old Rosie. **Facilities** Non-diners area ✿ (Bar Garden) ♦♦ Children's menu Children's portions Garden ⊨ Beer festival Cider festival Parking WiFi ▨▨ **Rooms** 3

BLANCHLAND

Map 18 NY95

The Lord Crewe Arms ★★★ CHH ◉   PICK OF THE PUBS

See Pick of the Pubs on opposite page

PICK OF THE PUBS

The Lord Crewe Arms ★★★ CHH ⊛

BLANCHLAND Map 18 NY95

tel: 01434 675469 **DH8 9SP**
email: enquiries@lordcreweblanchland.co.uk
web: www.lordcrewearmsblanchland.co.uk
dir: *From Hexham take B6306 to Blanchland. Approx 10m*

Memorable village hotel with reliable menu

High in the Durham Dales, Blanchland is an exquisite little estate village of honey-coloured limestone houses. What is now The Lord Crewe was built as the Abbot's lodge, guest house, dining room and kitchens for the monks of the Norman Blanchland Abbey. Although the abbey was dissolved in 1539 it took until the 1720s before the buildings became an inn, after which it swiftly became popular with miners exploiting the rich deposits of lead up on the moors. It belongs to the group that owns Calcot Manor, Barnsley House and The Village Pub in Gloucestershire, so you can expect the team here to know exactly how to create an enjoyable experience in an historic setting. The bar is in the vaulted crypt, a hugely atmospheric space formed by thick stone walls, lit by 'candle-style' chandeliers, and offering Northumbrian ales, including the inn's own appropriately named Lord Crewe Brew. At lunch the bar and two restaurants might offer smoked haddock rarebit on toast with a fried egg as a starter, and braised lamb on the bone with root vegetables as a main. In the evening you might contemplate a selection including black pudding with crushed apple potatoes and mustard gravy as your starter, followed by Yorkshire mallard with Weardale game dumpling and whipped celeriac; or grilled whole Dover sole with caper butter and charlotte potatoes. Finish with Bakewell pudding with vanilla ice cream, or sea buckthorn posset. You can eat in the beautiful gardens, surrounded by the ancient walls and imagine the monks strolling around all those centuries ago.

Open all day all wk 11-11 **Food** Lunch Mon-Fri 12-2.30, Sat 12-3, Sun 12-3.30 Dinner all wk 6-9 ⊕ FREE HOUSE ◀ Wylam Gold Tankard, Lord Crewe Brewe (pub's own), Cumberland Corby Ale. ♟ 9 **Facilities** Non-diners area ♦♦ Children's menu Children's portions Garden ⋈ Parking WiFi 🚌 (notice required) **Rooms** 21

CARTERWAY HEADS
Map 19 NZ05

The Manor House Inn
PICK OF THE PUBS

tel: 01207 255268 **DH8 9LX**
email: themanorhouseinn@gmail.com
dir: *A69 W from Newcastle, left onto A68 then S for 8m. Inn on right*

Head out of town for this popular all-rounder

When a day out in Newcastle or Durham is over and you fancy a drink or meal out of town, a 30-minute drive will get you to this former coaching inn. As the stone walls, low-beamed ceiling and massive timber support in the bar might suggest, it was built in the mid 18th century. From its lofty position, there are great views of both the Derwent Valley and reservoir. Jostling for real ale drinkers' attention are Old Speckled Hen and local brews. The restaurant is divided into two and the larger area welcoming families with children. Most produce is local and includes game and wild fish from hereabouts. Suggested dishes include toasted walnut, red wine poached pear and Stilton salad; and premium Cumberland sausage and mash, garden peas and rich onion gravy; and crispy real ale battered cod with home-made chips. There's an annual beer festival at the end of August.

Open all day all wk 12-11 (Sun 12-10.30) Closed 26 Dec, 1st Mon in Jan **Food** Mon-Sat 12-9, Sun 12-8 summer 12-7 winter ⊕ ENTERPRISE INNS ◄ Morland Old Speckled Hen, Wylam, Allendale, Consett, Cullercoats Ale Works ♂ Westons Old Rosie. ₱ 12 **Facilities** Non-diners area ♣ (Bar Garden) ♦ Children's menu Children's portions Garden ☷ Beer festival Cider festival Parking WiFi ➡ (notice required)

CHATTON
Map 21 NU02

Percy Arms ★ ★ ★ ★ INN

tel: 01668 215244 **Main Rd NE66 5PS**
email: enquiries@percyarmschatton.co.uk **web:** www.percyarmschatton.co.uk
dir: *From A1 between Warenford & Belford, onto B6348 signed Chatton*

Classy pub in tranquil village

On a low grassy bank with tables and benches, this beautifully appointed pub, with an underlying theme of game birds and animals, reflects the owner's refined approach to styling. The dog-friendly, L-shaped bar is filled with chesterfields, tartan-covered chairs, hunting-scene drapes, horns, horseshoes, riding crops and wellies, all within range of an open fire. Popular real ales such as Allendale Golden Plover are served in the bar. Expect dishes like black pudding Scotch egg; pan-rendered duck breast, sticky red cabbage, tea-soaked raisins and pickled raspberry jus; wild mushroom, white wine and tarragon risotto; and lamb rump with fondant potato, mulled red cabbage and redcurrant jus.

Open all day all wk **Food** Lunch Mon-Sat 12-3, Sun 12-8 Dinner Mon-Sat 6-9, Sun 12-8 ⊕ FREE HOUSE ◄ Allendale Golden Plover. **Facilities** Non-diners area ♣ (Bar) ♦ Children's menu Children's portions Garden ☷ Parking WiFi ➡ (notice required) **Rooms** 5

CORBRIDGE
Map 21 NY96

The Angel of Corbridge

tel: 01434 632119 **Main St NE45 5LA**
email: info@theangelofcorbridge.com
dir: *0.5m off A69, signed Corbridge*

Historic coaching inn in Roman garrison town

A handsome, white-painted inn overlooking the widest part of Main Street. Formerly the King's Head, it was extended in the 18th century and from 1752 was the town's posting inn until the railway station opened in 1835. The lounge has a log fire, but the real hub is the bar where Hadrian Border and Wylam ales, and all-day food are available. For a more formal meal it has to be the Barn Restaurant and its herb-crusted loin and confit shoulder croquette of 'own farm' lamb, smoked almond and blackberry purée; Northumberland beef sirloin steak; beer-battered North Shields cod, hand-cut chips and mushy peas; or potato and chive gnocchi.

Open all day all wk 11-11 (Fri-Sat 11am-mdnt Sun 11-10.30) **Food** Lunch Mon-Sat 12-9, Sun 12-8 Dinner Mon-Sat 12-9, Sun 12-8 Av main course £14 Set menu available Restaurant menu available Mon-Fri ⊕ FREE HOUSE ◄ Hadrian Border Tyneside Blonde, Wylam Angel, local ales. ₱ 12 **Facilities** Non-diners area ♦ Children's menu Children's portions Outside area ☷ Parking WiFi ➡ (notice required)

CRASTER
Map 21 NU21

The Jolly Fisherman

tel: 01665 576461 **Haven Hill NE66 3TR**
email: info@thejollyfishermancraster.co.uk
dir: *Exit A1 at Denwick. Follow Seahouses signs, then 1st sign for Craster*

Fine harbourside location

The charm of this historic stone-flagged, low-beamed pub remains undimmed. When it's cold, relax by an open fire; at any time admire impressive Dunstanburgh Castle from the delightful beer garden. When the pub opened in 1847, Craster was a thriving fishing village; now only a few East Coast cobles leave harbour, mostly for the herring that, once smoked, become the famous kippers. Menu choices could be warm crab toasts with sweetcorn chowder; the fishboard – crab pot, salmon fillet, kipper pâté, smoked salmon, prawns, rollmop herring; venison, pigeon and pheasant game pie; and lemon posset with fresh fruit. At the bar are Black Sheep and Mordue Workie Ticket bitter.

Open all day all wk 11-11 **Food** Lunch Mon-Sat 11-3, Sun 12-3 Dinner Mon-Sat 5-8.30 winter, 5-9 summer, Sun 5-9 ⊕ PUNCH TAVERNS ◄ Mordue Workie Ticket, Black Sheep, Timothy Taylor Landlord, guest ale. ₱ 12 **Facilities** Non-diners area ♣ (Bar Garden) ♦ Children's menu Children's portions Garden ☷ Parking WiFi ➡ (notice required)

EGLINGHAM
Map 21 NU11

NEW The Tankerville Arms

tel: 01665 578444 **15 The Village NE66 2TX**
email: info@tankervillearms.com
dir: *Follow Eglingham signs from A697 (between Powburn & Wooperton) or from Alnwick take B6346 to Eglingham, approx 6m*

Local ales and good food in the heart of Northumberland

The picturesque Northumbrian village of Eglingham is just eight miles from Alnwick, handily located for walkers exploring the Cheviot Hills, people fishing the Tweed and its tributaries, and tourists visiting the many attractions in the area – Alnwick Castle, Hadrian's Wall and Lindisfarne Castle, for example. The Tankerville Arms is a charmingly traditional country inn offering local ales from the Hadrian Border Brewery and well-conceived modern British food. A meal might kick off with local pigeon salad with black pudding and bacon; or smoked haddock and spring onion fishcake with spinach and garlic sauce, followed by twice-cooked Ingram Valley lamb with nettle mash, redcurrant jus and fresh mint sauce; or butternut squash risotto with fresh goats' curd and crispy sage.

Open all wk noon-close (Mon-Tue 5pm-close) **Food** Lunch Wed-Sun 12-9 Dinner Mon-Tue 6-9, Wed-Sun 12-9 Av main course £10 ⊕ FREE HOUSE ◄ Hadrian Border Tyneside Blonde & Secret Kingdom ♂ Old Mout. **Facilities** Non-diners area ♣ (Bar Garden) ♦ Children's menu Children's portions Family room Garden ☷ Parking WiFi ➡ (notice required)

PICK OF THE PUBS

The Pheasant Inn ★★★★ INN

FALSTONE Map 21 NY78

tel: 01434 240382
Stannersburn NE48 1DD
email: stay@thepheasantinn.com
web: www.thepheasantinn.com
dir: *A69, B6079, B6320, follow signs for Kielder Water*

Perfect base for Northumbrian adventures

In the early 17th century, long, long before nearby Kielder Water and Kielder Forest were created, agricultural workers drank at a beer-house in Stannersburn. This ivy-clad country inn is that beer-house, now finding itself where the Northumberland National Park meets the Border Forest Park, and surrounded by verdant valleys, high moors and tranquil woodlands. It's well positioned too for cycle tracks, a sculpture trail, an observatory, endless walks and wildlife watching, including red squirrels. What you see today is what Walter, Irene and Robin Kershaw have achieved since they acquired it, then rather run down, over 30 years ago. Most spaces in the two bars have been filled with historic Northumberland memorabilia, and on the exposed stone walls that support the blackened beams are photos of yesteryear's locals working at forgotten trades like blacksmithing and coalmining. In winter, log fires cast flickering shadows across the furniture.

The restaurant, with pale mushroom-coloured walls and furnished in medium oak, looks out over the countryside; this is where to sit down and choose from the daily-changing traditional British menu, which makes the most of what Northumbria has to offer. Sweet marinated herrings make a tasty starter, to be followed perhaps by fresh fish of the day from North Shields Fish Quay; or a hearty home-made game and mushroom pie. Excellent beers from Wylam Brewery and Timothy Taylor may cloud the mind, but not the dark night skies, which make the area a mecca for astronomers. There is a tranquil stream-side garden.

Open 11-3 6-11 Closed 25-27 Dec, Mon-Tue (Nov-Feb) **Food** Lunch Mon-Sat 12-2.30 Dinner all wk 6.30-8.30 (Etr-Oct 6-8.30) ⊕ FREE HOUSE ◄ Timothy Taylor Landlord, Wylam Gold Tankard, Rocket, Red Kite, Red Shot & Angel. **Facilities** Non-diners area ⭢ Children's menu Children's portions Play area Family room Garden Outside area ⌐ Parking WiFi **Rooms** 8

ELLINGHAM
Map 21 NU12

NEW The Pack Horse Inn

tel: 01665 589292 **NE67 5HA**
email: enquiries@packhorseinn-ellingham.co.uk
dir: *From A1 follow Ellingham signs*

Little gem set in wonderful countryside

The landlady here must have been one of the youngest in the UK when she starting running the inn at the age of 22. But the Pack Horse today is fully-fledged after a complete but character-preserving refurbishment. Nearly 200 jugs hang from exposed beams in the bar, log fires burn in the grates, and the restaurant has comfortable seating with solid wood tables. Black Sheep and Timothy Taylor beers are well-kept, while the carefully considered menu features Ellingham rare breed meats. The garden has been landscaped too, producing seasonal vegetables for the kitchen and a sunny spot for the summer trade.

Open 12-2 6-11 (Mon 6-11) Closed Feb, Mon L **Food** Lunch Tue-Sun 12-2 Dinner Mon-Sat 6-9 Av main course £12.95 ⊕ FREE HOUSE ◀ Timothy Taylor Landlord, Black Sheep Best Bitter. **Facilities** Non-diners area ✿ (Bar Garden) ♦◆ Children's menu Children's portions Garden ☎ WiFi ☞ (notice required)

FALSTONE
Map 21 NY78

The Pheasant Inn ★★★★ INN
PICK OF THE PUBS

See Pick of the Pubs on page 367 and advert on opposite page

FELTON
Map 21 NU10

The Northumberland Arms

tel: 01670 787370 **The Peth, West Thirston NE65 9EE**
email: thenorthumberlandarmsfelton@gmail.com
dir: *Take A1 from Morpeth towards Alnwick. Turn right, follow Felton signs*

Upmarket local and refined eatery

A solid stone-built coaching inn in a picturesque village beside the River Coquet, and just 25 minutes from Newcastle. It was built in the 1820s by Hugh Percy, 3rd Duke of Northumberland, as a place for horses to rest and guests to freshen up before being received at Alnwick Castle. In the bar locals and tourists alike sup pints of Northumbrian brewed beers. The kitchen sources local ingredients for dishes such as smoked bacon lardons, black pudding and poached egg salad; or ham hock terrine with tomato and chilli jam; confit duck leg, sticky red cabbage, fondant potato, green beans and red wine jus; and pea and mint risotto, crumbed goats' cheese and baby leaf salad.

Open all day all wk **Food** Lunch Mon-Sat 12-3, Sun 12-8 Dinner Mon-Sat 6-9, Sun 12-8 Av main course £11 ⊕ FREE HOUSE ◀ Northumbrian Ales ♂ Symonds. **Facilities** Non-diners area ✿ (Bar) ♦◆ Children's menu Children's portions Outside area ☎ Parking WiFi ☞ (notice required)

HAYDON BRIDGE
Map 21 NY86

The General Havelock Inn

tel: 01434 684376 **Ratcliffe Rd NE47 6ER**
email: generalhavelock@aol.com
dir: *On A69, 7m W of Hexham*

Free house overlooking the River Tyne

Built in the 1760s, this riverside inn is named after a 19th-century British Army officer and is popular with locals and local celebrities. In a converted stone barn, the restaurant overlooks the river where otters can often be spotted. The real ales are all sourced locally: Cumberland Corby Blonde and Wylam Collingwood are but two. Owner and chef Gary Thompson makes everything by hand and local ingredients are the foundation of his dishes, which include cod with boulangère potatoes, and lamb shank braised in red wine on mash. In summer, the patio area is covered by a marquee.

Open 12-2.30 7-12 (Sun 12-10.30) Closed Mon **Food** Lunch Tue-Sun 12-2.30 Dinner Tue-Sat 7-9 Av main course £10 Set menu available Restaurant menu available Tue-Sat ⊕ FREE HOUSE ◀ High House Farm Nel's Best, Wylam Collingwood, Mordue Workie Ticket, Cumberland Corby Blonde, Cullercoats Lovely Nelly, Jarrow Rivet Catcher. ☕ 15 **Facilities** Non-diners area ✿ (Bar Garden) ♦◆ Children's portions Family room Garden ☎ WiFi ☞ (notice required)

HEDLEY ON THE HILL
Map 19 NZ05

The Feathers Inn
PICK OF THE PUBS

See Pick of the Pubs on page 370

HEXHAM
Map 21 NY96

Battlesteads Hotel & Restaurant ★★★ HL
PICK OF THE PUBS

tel: 01434 230209 **Wark NE48 3LS**
email: info@battlesteads.com web: www.battlesteads.com
dir: *10m N of Hexham on B6320 (Kielder road)*

Utterly charming pub, hotel and restaurant

Hadrian's Wall lies to the south of this converted 18th-century farmhouse; surrounding it are some of the country's finest livestock herds, game-shooting and fishing; and Britain's darkest night skies are overhead. There are three dining options: the bar serving, among others, Nel's Best real ale from High House Farm brewery, and Sandford Orchards cider; the conservatory, overlooking the walled herb, salad leaf, fruit and vegetable garden; and the softly-lit main restaurant, decorated with old railway travel posters. Among head chef Eddie Shilton's primarily modern British dishes are venison bourguignon; baby leek and smoked brie pie; hake and chips; and autumn vegetable tagine with bulgar wheat and harissa. Desserts include their ever popular whisky and marmalade bread and butter pudding. Given half a chance, owner Richard Slade will show visitors his carbon-neutral heating system and other 'green' features. Check with them for the summer beer festival date.

Open all day all wk **Food** Lunch all wk 12-3 Dinner all wk 6.30-9.30 Set menu available Restaurant menu available all wk ⊕ FREE HOUSE ◀ Durham Magus, High House Farm Nel's Best, guest ales ♂ Sandford Orchards. ☕ 15 **Facilities** Non-diners area ✿ (Bar Garden) ♦◆ Children's portions Garden ☎ Beer festival Parking WiFi ☞ (notice required) **Rooms** 22

The Pheasant Inn
Kielder Water

Stannersburn, Nr Kielder Water, Falstone, Hexham,
Northumberland, NE48 1DD
T. + 44 (0)1434 240 382
E. stay@thepheasantinn.com
W. thepheasantinn.com/

The Pheasant Inn

From the moment you step inside The Pheasant Inn you'll be treated to the warmest of welcomes. Found in the heart of the Northumberland countryside near Kielder Water, we are a family run Country Inn with Bed and Breakfast, offering comfortable accommodation, hearty home cooked food, good beers and wines.

Accommodation

All of our guest rooms are en-suite and located around a quiet courtyard garden. Each room is peaceful, light and airy, designed with homely comfort in mind.

Bar & Restaurant

The Pheasant Inn combines the character and charm of a traditional Coaching Inn, with oak beams and open fires. Our kitchen is open 7 days a week serving delicious traditional British food. With beautiful views over the Northumberland countryside, The Pheasant Inn is ideally placed for visiting all that Northumberland and the Borders have to offer.

PICK OF THE PUBS

The Feathers Inn

HEDLEY ON THE HILL   Map 19 NZ05

tel: 01661 843607 **NE43 7SW**
email: info@thefeathers.net
web: www.thefeathers.net
dir: *A695 towards Gateshead. In Stocksfield right into New Ridley Rd. Left at Hedley on the Hill sign to village*

Microbrewery ales and cracking food

This small 200-year-old stone-built free house is set high above the Tyne Valley, and gives splendid views across the Cheviot Hills. Once frequented by lead miners and cattle drovers, all visitors are charmed by the friendly and relaxed atmosphere created by the owners. It's also worth the detour for its rotating choice of microbrewery ales; relax and sup Wylam Red Kite or Northumberland Pit Pony beside a welcoming wood-burning stove. Old oak beams, rustic settles, and stone walls decorated with local photographs set the informal scene. There's a good selection of traditional pub games like shove ha'penny and bar skittles; you'll find a good collection of cookery books as well. The impressive daily menu makes sound use of the freshest local ingredients — including game from local shoots, rare breed local cattle and Longhorn beef — to create great British classics as well as regional dishes from the north east. For a snack, order a sandwich of cold roast rib of Haydon Bridge beef with

horseradish. Starters may include Sand Hutton asparagus with crisp fried Wylam duck egg and sorrel mayonnaise; or Northumbrian cheese rarebit with apple and rhubarb chutney. Typical of the lunchtime main courses are a Gunnerton Dexter beefburger with Doddington's cheese, brioche bun, gherkins, burger sauce, chunky chips and celeriac coleslaw. The evening menu may feature the likes of Medomsley Hebridean lamb chops served with buttered leeks, heritage carrots and braised pearl barley; or local game pie with wild mushrooms, creamy mash and buttered greens. Desserts line up an equally appealing selection such as creamy rice pudding with poached quince and boozy prunes; or apple and almond tart with clotted cream.

Open all wk 12-11 (Mon-Wed 6-11 Sun 12-10.30) No food 1st 2wks Jan **Food** Lunch Thu-Sat 12-2, Sun 12-4.30 Dinner Wed-Sat 6-8.30 Av main course £12 Set menu available ⊕ FREE HOUSE ◀ Mordue Workie Ticket, Wylam Red Kite Northumberland Pit Pony, Orkney Red MacGregor ♂ Westons 1st Quality & Old Rosie. ♀ **Facilities** Non-diners area ♦♦ Children's portions Outside area ⊼ Beer festival Cider festival Parking WiFi

HEXHAM *continued*

Dipton Mill Inn   PICK OF THE PUBS

tel: 01434 606577 **Dipton Mill Rd NE46 1YA**
email: ghb@hexhamshire.co.uk
dir: *2m S of Hexham on HGV route to Blanchland, B6306, Dipton Mill Rd*

Converted mill that now brews its own beer

Surrounded by farmland and woods, with footpaths for pleasant country walks, and not far from Hadrian's Wall and other Roman sites, this former farmhouse was rebuilt some 400 years ago and has a pretty millstream running right through the gardens. The Dipton Mill is home to Hexhamshire Brewery ales, which include Devil's Water and Whapweasel, plus Blackhall English Stout. All dishes are freshly prepared from local produce where possible, and a wide range of sandwiches includes a gourmet selection. Lunch or dinner could start with smoked salmon and prawns, or soup, and mains might include haddock baked with tomatoes and basil, or lamb steak braised in wine and mustard. A good selection of vegetarian options includes ratatouille with couscous. Dessert brings comforting favourites such as fruit crumble, Pavlova or chocolate rum truffle torte, plus a good selection of Northumberland and Durham cheeses. Salads and ploughman's are always available.

Open 12-2.30 6-11 (Sun 12-3) Closed 25 Dec, Sun eve **Food** Lunch all wk 12-2 Dinner Mon-Sat 6.30-8 Av main course £7.50 ⊕ FREE HOUSE ◀ Hexhamshire Shire Bitter, Devil's Water, Devil's Elbow, Whapweasel, Blackhall English Stout, Seasonal ales ♂ Westons Old Rosie. ☂ 15 **Facilities** Non-diners area ♣ (Garden) ♦ Children's portions Garden ⊟ WiFi ➡ (notice required)

Miners Arms Inn

tel: 01434 603909 **Main St, Acomb NE46 4PW**
email: minersarms2012@gmail.com
dir: *2m W of Hexham on A69*

Traditional food in peaceful family-run village pub

The Greenwell family took over this 18th-century village pub near Hadrian's Wall a few years ago, and it's very much a family business with David and Elwyn helped by their son and two daughters. Visitors can enjoy the open-hearth fire, the sunny beer garden, or simply sit out front soaking up life in this peaceful village. Among the choice of ales, local Wylam Gold Tankard is always available, with guest beers available every week. Mainly locally sourced dishes, including haggis and black pudding with peppercorn sauce; and home-made steak and ale pie typify the traditional food. Quiz nights take place on the last Wednesday of the month and there's a popular key draw and supper every Sunday night.

Open all wk 4-12 (Sat-Sun 12-12) **Food** Lunch Sat 12-8, Sun 12-2.30 Dinner Tue-Fri 4-8, Sat 12-8 Av main course £8.95 ⊕ FREE HOUSE ◀ Wylam Gold Tankard, Yates Best Bitter, Acton Ales, guest ale ♂ Westons Stowford Press.
Facilities Non-diners area ♣ (Bar Garden) ♦ Children's menu Children's portions Garden ⊟ Beer festival ➡ (notice required)

Rat Inn   PICK OF THE PUBS

tel: 01434 602814 **Anick NE46 4LN**
email: info@theratinn.com
dir: *2m from Hexham. At Bridge End (A69) rdbt, take exit signed Oakwood. Inn 500yds on right*

A humdinger of a pub

Facing a small, triangular green in a tiny hamlet of stone cottages, the terraced, tree-shaded garden of this convivial old drovers' inn looks out over the River Tyne as it curves round to the Roman town of Corbridge. The nearness of Hadrian's Wall has long made people wonder whether some of its stones were liberated to build the pub. Wonder yourself in the flagstone-floored, beamed bar over a glass of High House Farm Nel's Best or Wylam Gold Tankard. The bar itself is fashioned from a great oak sideboard, chamberpots hang from the ceiling and a cast-iron range may blaze away. Appearing on the daily-changing menu might be rillette of Craster kipper with potato and horseradish salad; pan-fried North Sea coley with squid, creamed leeks and salsify; peppered Northumbria steak with chips and roasted tomato; and parsnip and wild mushroom pan haggerty. A small conservatory offers the best views from indoors.

Open all day all wk **Food** Lunch Tue-Sat 12-2, Sun 12-3 Dinner Tue-Sat 6-9 ⊕ FREE HOUSE ◀ Cumberland Corby Ale, High House Farm Nel's Best, Hexhamshire Shire Bitter, Timothy Taylor Landlord, Wylam Gold Tankard ♂ Westons Old Rosie. ☂ **Facilities** Non-diners area ♦ Children's portions Garden ⊟ Parking WiFi

---

▮ LONGFRAMLINGTON   Map 21 NU10

The Anglers Arms   PICK OF THE PUBS

tel: 01665 570271 & 570655 **Weldon Bridge NE65 8AX**
email: info@anglersarms.com
dir: *Take A697 N of Morpeth signed Wooler & Coldstream. 7m, left to Weldon Bridge*

Still welcoming visitors after 250 years

Since the 1760s, this part-battlemented, three-storey, former coaching inn on the road to and from Scotland has commanded the picturesque Weldon Bridge over the River Coquet. It belongs to John and Julie Young, whose knick-knacks and curios, pictures and fishing memorabilia are liberally distributed within. On the bar top pump badges declare the availability of Timothy Taylor Landlord, Theakston Best Bitter and Greene King brews. A comprehensive menu suggests, for example, kipper salad – warm Craster kippers, new potatoes, endive and soft poached egg with Caesar dressing, followed by Tournedos Flodden – prime fillet steak and Stilton wrapped in bacon with garlic sauce; or glazed ham hock with vine tomatoes, chunky chips and cheese sauce. The carefully tended half-acre of garden is perfect for outdoor eating and includes a children's play park. It is possible to fish for brown trout, salmon and sea trout on the pub's own one-mile stretch of the Coquet.

Open all day all wk 11-11 (Sun 12-10.30) **Food** all wk 12-9.30 ⊕ FREE HOUSE ◀ Timothy Taylor Landlord, Morland Old Speckled Hen, Greene King Abbot Ale, Theakston Best Bitter. **Facilities** Non-diners area ♣ (Bar Garden Outside area) ♦ Children's portions Play area Family room Garden Outside area ⊟ Parking ➡ (notice required)

The Granby Inn ★★★ INN

tel: 01665 570228 **NE65 8DP**
email: info@thegranbyinn.co.uk **web:** www.thegranbyinn.co.uk
dir: *In village centre*

Popular with visitors to the Northumbrian coast

Once a coaching inn, this family-run pub just north of Morpeth is perfectly situated for exploring the stunning Northumbrian coast and the ancient town of Alnwick. Dating back around 250 years, The Granby Inn prides itself on being a traditional pub for a pint in the cosy bar but the food attracts diners from all over. Local sourcing extends to meat from a nearby butcher and fish from North Shields, all of which turns up in dishes such as home-made black pudding with tomato and chilli jam; poussin confit legs, Kiev, skin crackling, wild garlic purée and chicken jus; and steak and ale pie with braised cabbage.

Open all wk 11.30-3 6-11 (Sat-Sun 12-11) Closed 25-26 Dec & 1 Jan **Food** Lunch 12-3 Dinner 6-9 Set menu available ⊕ FREE HOUSE ◀ Worthington's, Caffrey's Irish Ale. **Facilities** ♦ Children's menu Children's portions Outside area ⊟ Parking WiFi ➡ (notice required) **Rooms** 5

LONGHORSLEY
Map 21 NZ19

Linden Tree ★★★★ HL ◎◎

tel: 01670 500033 **Linden Hall NE65 8XF**
email: lindenhall@macdonald-hotels.co.uk web: www.macdonald-hotels.co.uk/lindenhall
dir: *From A1 onto A697, 1m N of Longhorsley*

The 19th-hole after a round of golf

The friendly and informal Linden Tree stands within the 450-acres that surround Linden Hall, an impressive Georgian mansion that is a popular golf and country club. A sunny patio makes a relaxed setting for lunch in summer and the brasserie-style menu makes good use of Scottish produce. Dishes might include kipper pâté; spatchcock poussin, buttered baby potatoes, garden salad and garlic and lemon butter; or slow-cooked lamb shank, creamed potatoes and minted spring vegetable broth. Platters for sharing, sandwiches and grills are available too. Round off a long day with a nightcap in the golfers' lounge.

Open all day all wk Mon-Sat 11-11 (Sun 11-10.30) **Food** all wk 12-9 ⊕ FREE HOUSE ◀ Mordue, guest ale. ☕ 10 **Facilities** Non-diners area ❅ (Bar Garden) ☝ Children's menu Children's portions Play area Garden ⊨ Parking WiFi ▭ (notice required) **Rooms** 50

LOW NEWTON BY THE SEA
Map 21 NU22

The Ship Inn

tel: 01665 576262 **The Square NE66 3EL**
email: forsythchristine@hotmail.com
dir: *NE from A1 at Alnwick towards Seahouses*

Good, simple food and home-brewed beers

There's a very salty tang about this pretty, late-1700s inn – of course there is, since it overlooks Newton Haven's sandy beach. Then there are the names of their real ales: Sea Coal, Sea Wheat, Ship Hop Ale and Sandcastles at Dawn, all in fact, with Dolly Day Dream brewed next door. The barrels then have to be rolled all of 15 feet to the cellar; from here they are pumped to the small bar, where you can expect plenty of locally caught fresh and smoked fish; toasted sandwiches; ploughman's; bacon, mushroom and tomato stottie (a local flat loaf); and hand-picked crab.

Open all wk (seasonal variations - please phone pub for details) Closed 24-26 Dec **Food** Lunch all wk 12-2.30 Dinner Wed-Sat 7-8 ⊕ FREE HOUSE ◀ The Ship Inn Sea Coal, Dolly Day Dream, Sea Wheat, Ship Hop Ale, Sandcastles at Dawn. **Facilities** ❅ (Bar Restaurant Garden) ☝ Garden

LUCKER
Map 21 NU13

NEW The Apple Inn

tel: 01668 213824 **NE70 7JL**
email: j.johnson@stablewoodgroup.com
dir: *At Warenford on A1 follow Lucker signs*

Family-owned village pub

Larger villages than tiny Lucker have lost their pub, but the Apple, which reopened in 2015, is in good hands. Beer drinkers in the wooden-floored bar enjoy Alnwick Brewery's Amber and Gold real ales, while diners in the tartan-carpeted restaurant relish Craster kippers; Whitby scampi; and local black pudding and melted Northumbrian Nettle cheese stack. Or, they might consider chicken casserole with roasted mini vegetables and sage dumplings; lamb shank with creamy mash, seasonal vegetables and minted gravy; or hand-made burgers. Some children might prefer toad-in-the-hole or battered fish and chips. There's plenty of room for eating and drinking outside too.

Open 5-11 (Sat 12-11 Sun 12-6 open all day BHs & in holiday season) Closed Wed-Thu in winter **Food** Lunch Sat 12-8.30, Sun 12-5 Dinner Mon-Tue & Fri 5-8.30, Sat 12-8.30 Av main course £10.95 ⊕ FREE HOUSE ◀ Alnwick Amber Ale & Gold.

Facilities Non-diners area ❅ (Bar Garden Outside area) ☝ Children's menu Children's portions Garden Outside area ⊨ Parking WiFi ▭ (notice required)

MILFIELD
Map 21 NT93

The Red Lion Inn

tel: 01668 216224 **Main Rd NE71 6JD**
email: iain@redlionmilfield.co.uk web: www.redlionmilfield.co.uk
dir: *On A697, 9m S of Coldstream (6m N of Wooler)*

Historic inn serving comfort food and guest ales

Dating back to the 1700s, sheep drovers from the northern counties stayed at this stone building before it was used as a stopover for the mail stagecoach en route from Edinburgh and London. Well placed for salmon and trout fishing on the River Tweed and for shooting on the Northumberland estates, the Red Lion offers a relaxing atmosphere, good guest beers and wholesome food. Start with sautéed duck and chorizo with a green bean salad; or garlic wild mushrooms on toasted brioche before enjoying a classic steak and ale pie; or poached salmon fillet with smoked salmon and pea risotto. Finish with one of the home-made desserts. There's also a beer festival the last weekend in June.

Open all wk 11-2 5-11 (Sat 11-11 Sun 11-10.30) (summer all day) **Food** Lunch all day all wk summer, winter Mon-Fri 11-2, Sat-Sun 11-9 Dinner all day all wk summer, winter Mon-Fri 5-9, Sat-Sun 11-9 ⊕ FREE HOUSE ◀ Black Sheep, Guinness, guest ales ⭗ Westons, guest cider. **Facilities** Non-diners area ☝ Children's menu Children's portions Outside area Beer festival Parking WiFi ▭

MORPETH
Map 21 NZ28

St Mary's Inn ★★★★★ INN

tel: 01670 293293 **Saint Mary's Ln, St Mary's Park NE61 6BL**
email: hello@stmarysinn.co.uk web: www.stmarysinn.co.uk
dir: *From A1 into Stannington into Church Rd. At T-junct right into Green Ln, into St Mary's Park*

Spacious yet embracing cure for all ills

Occupying the site of a former hospital, this eponymously named pub continues the caring tradition – with hospitality. In-patients have been known to make a speedy recovery while relaxing by the real fires, and enjoying the pub's cosy corners and colourful spaces. Four real ales, including a pale ale brewed especially by Wylam Breweries, 17 wines by the glass, and a huge range of whiskies are dispensed at the huge oak bar. All-day sustenance ranges from good old-fashioned bar snacks such as corned beef and potato pie with brown sauce, to steaming plates of mince and dumplings with seasonal vegetables. Afternoon tea is a speciality.

Open all day all wk **Food** all day Restaurant menu available Mon-Sat ⊕ FREE HOUSE ◀ Wylam St Mary's Ale, Anarchy Citra Star ⭗ Gwynt y Ddraig Black Dragon. ☕ 17 **Facilities** Non-diners area ❅ (Bar Garden Outside area) ☝ Children's menu Children's portions Garden Outside area ⊨ Parking WiFi **Rooms** 11

NETHERTON
Map 21 NT90

The Star Inn

tel: 01669 630238 **NE65 7HD**
dir: *7m from Rothbury*

Old fashioned inn, tip-top cask ales but no food

Little has changed at this timeless gem since the Wilson-Morton family took over in 1917. Lost in superb remote countryside north of Rothbury, The Star Inn retains many period features and the bar is like stepping into someone's living room, comfortable and quiet, with no intrusive fruit machines or piped music. Don't expect any food though, just cask ales in the peak of condition, served from a hatch in the entrance hall. This inn is a real find — just check the days of the week when it's open though.

Open Tue-Wed & Sun 7.30pm-10.30pm (Fri-Sat 7.30pm-11pm) Closed Mon, Thu ⊕ FREE HOUSE ◀ Guest ales in summer, bottle beers in winter.
Facilities Non-diners area Outside area Parking ➡ (notice required) **Notes** ⊛

NEWBROUGH
Map 21 NY86

NEW Red Lion Inn

tel: 01434 674226 **Stanegate Rd NE47 5AR**
email: redlionnewbrough@hotmail.co.uk
dir: *From Haydon Bridge take B6319 signed Chollerford (adjacent to rail line). At T-junct left onto Stonegate Rd signed Haydon Bridge. Pub on right. Or from Hexham take A69 towards Haydon Bridge. Follow Fourstones & Newbrough signs. Through Fourstones to pub on right*

A handsome retreat

Part 12th century, this solid-looking, stone-built former coaching inn sympathetically accommodates 21st century needs. The bar area is spacious, with original wood and stonework, open log fires and comfortable chairs. Ales come from local breweries such as Allendale, Alnwick and Firebrick, while wines come from further afield — all over the world, in fact. Light and main meals are available at lunchtime; in the evening look for crab and lobster ravioli; twice-cooked belly pork; and tomato and red onion tarte Tatin. The Stanegate Room celebrates local arts and crafts. An outside seating area looks over the surrounding countryside.

Open all day all wk Closed 25 Dec **Food** Lunch Tue-Sun 12-2 Dinner Tue-Sat 6-9 (6-8 in winter) Restaurant menu available Tue-Sat ⊕ FREE HOUSE ◀ Allendale Golden Plover & Pennine Pale, Firebrick, Alnwick, Mordue Northumbrian Blonde ♂ Symonds. **Facilities** Non-diners area ◀◀ Children's menu Children's portions Outside area ➡ Parking WiFi ➡ (notice required)

NEWTON
Map 21 NZ06

Duke of Wellington Inn ★★★★★ INN

tel: 01661 844446 **NE43 7UL**
email: info@thedukeofwellingtoninn.co.uk **web:** www.thedukeofwellingtoninn.co.uk
dir: *From Corbridge A69 towards Newcastle. 3m to village*

Hillside, traditional country pub

Just off the A69 near Corbridge, this early 19th-century coaching inn overlooks the Tyne Valley and has stunning views, and is a handy base for exploring the National Park and Hadrian's Wall. The building's original oak and stone construction is complemented by modern furniture and fabrics that create a comfortable pub. On offer are local ales, a comprehensive wine list and enjoyable dishes such as beetroot smoked salmon; or pineapple and prawn cocktail, followed by lamb stew with red cabbage, carrots and new potatoes; or open wild mushroom lasagne. The stone floored bar has a roaring log fire during the colder months but when the sun shines there is ample space on the terrace to enjoy refreshments. Dogs are welcome in the bar and garden.

Open all day all wk 8am-11pm **Food** all wk 12-9 Set menu available ⊕ FREE HOUSE ◀ Hadrian Border Tyneside Blonde, Timothy Taylor Landlord. ⚑ 11
Facilities Non-diners area ☙ (Bar Garden) ◀◀ Children's menu Children's portions Garden ➡ Parking WiFi ➡ (notice required) **Rooms** 7

NEWTON-ON-THE-MOOR
Map 21 NU10

The Cook and Barker Inn ★★★★ INN PICK OF THE PUBS

tel: 01665 575234 **NE65 9JY**
email: info@cookandbarkerinn.co.uk **web:** www.cookandbarkerinn.co.uk
dir: *0.5m from A1 S of Alnwick*

Traditional Northumbrian country inn with far-reaching views

For spectacular views of the North Sea coast and the Cheviot Hills, head for the Farmer family's creeper-covered, flower-adorned, stone-built pub and restaurant. Phil Farmer also runs Hope House Farm eight miles away, source of the organic beef, lamb and pork that feature on the various menus — 'forest and field', grills and roasts, and Oriental; there's also a seafood selection. A suggested dinner starter of seared West Coast scallops, black pudding, fresh green pea purée, and red wine reduction might be followed by either rack of Hope House Farm lamb with parsnips, petit pois, and redcurrant and pork wine sauce; or roasted sea bass fillet, prawn and crab risotto, and tempura herbs. Real ale drinkers can expect — indeed, should be pleased — to find Bass on the bar, as well as Timothy Taylor Landlord and Black Sheep. The en suite bedrooms are smartly furnished, some retaining original exposed beams.

Open all day all wk 12-11 **Food** Lunch all wk 12-2 Dinner all wk 6-9 Set menu available Restaurant menu available all wk ⊕ FREE HOUSE ◀ Timothy Taylor Landlord, Black Sheep, Bass ♂ Kopparberg. **Facilities** Non-diners area ◀◀ Children's portions Garden ➡ Parking WiFi ➡ (notice required) **Rooms** 18

NORTH SHIELDS
Map 21 NZ36

NEW The Staith House

tel: 0191 270 8441 **57 Low Lights NE30 1JA**
email: thestaithhouse@gmail.com
dir: *Phone pub for detailed directions*

Great local produce on the regenerated Fish Quay

John Calton used to dream of owning his own place on the North Shields fish quay. After working with some of Europe's top chefs his dream finally came true in 2013, when he took on this historic pub, inspired by local produce and the area's recent regeneration. Regular tasting menus are offered, or you can explore the best the region has to offer from the carte. Roast marinated beetroot salad, maybe, or a haggis Scotch egg, to start, mains might include Orchard Farm pig belly, 'bashed root veg', black pudding, Savoy cabbage and crackling. Please note, children are welcome until 7pm.

Open all day all wk Closed 25-26 Dec, 1-2 Jan **Food** Lunch Mon-Fri 12-3, Sat 12-3.30, Sun 12-5 Dinner Mon-Fri 6-9, Sat 6-9.30 Av main course £14 ⊕ HEINEKEN ◀ Theakston Lightfoot, Robinsons Dizzy Blonde, Caledonian Deuchars IPA. ⚑ 10
Facilities Non-diners area ☙ (Bar Outside area) ◀◀ Children's portions Outside area ➡ Parking WiFi

SEAHOUSES

Map 21 NU23

The Bamburgh Castle Inn ★★★ INN

tel: 01665 720283 **NE68 7SQ**
email: enquiries@bamburghcastleinn.co.uk **web:** www.bamburghcastleinn.co.uk
dir: *A1 onto B1341 to Bamburgh, B1340 to Seahouses, follow signs to harbour*

Harbourside inn with superb Farne Islands views

With its prime location on the quayside giving wraparound sea views as far as the Farne Islands, this is surely one of the best situated pubs anywhere along Northumberland's stunning coast. Dating back to the 18th century, the inn has been transformed in more recent times to offer superb bar and dining areas plus seating outside. Children and dogs are welcomed, and pub dishes of locally sourced food represent excellent value. Typical of these are Cointreau chicken liver pâté; slow-cooked shoulder of lamb, mash and minted jus; and Northumberland pheasant Stroganoff.

Open all day all wk **Food** all wk 8am-9pm ⊕ FREE HOUSE ◀ Black Sheep, Hadrian Border Farne Island Ŏ Somersby. ▮ 11 **Facilities** Non-diners area ✿ (Bar Restaurant Garden) ✦ Children's menu Children's portions Family room Garden ⊟ Parking WiFi ▄ (notice required) **Rooms** 33

The Olde Ship Inn ★★★★ INN   PICK OF THE PUBS

tel: 01665 720200 **9 Main St NE68 7RD**
email: theoldeship@seahouses.co.uk **web:** www.seahouses.co.uk
dir: *Lower end of main street above harbour*

Family-owned inn with a nautical theme

Built on farmland around 1745, this stone-built inn with rooms has been in the present owners' family for the past century. Set above the bustling old harbour of Seahouses, the Olde Ship's interior is lit through stained-glass windows and the main saloon bar is full of character, its wooden floor made from ships' decking. A range of whiskies is supplemented by a selection of real ales, such as Hadrian Border Farne Island and Black Sheep. The inn's corridors and boat gallery are an Aladdin's cave of antique nautical artefacts, ranging from a figurehead to all manner of ship's brasses and dials. Bar food includes locally caught seafood and home-made soups. In the evenings, starters like salt and pepper squid; or pork terrine with apricot and gherkins might be followed by gammon and chips; chicken and mushroom casserole; or fresh crab salad. Some of the bedrooms have views of the Farne Islands.

Open all day all wk 11-11 (Sun 12-11) **Food** Lunch all wk 12-2.30 Dinner all wk 7-8.30 (no Dinner late Nov-late Jan) ⊕ FREE HOUSE ◀ Greene King Ruddles, Courage Directors, Hadrian Border Farne Island, Morland Old Speckled Hen, High House Farm Nel's Best, Black Sheep, Theakston Ŏ Westons Old Rosie & Family Reserve. ▮ 10 **Facilities** Non-diners area ✦ Children's menu Children's portions Family room Garden ⊟ Parking WiFi **Rooms** 18

SLAGGYFORD

Map 18 NY65

The Kirkstyle Inn

tel: 01434 381559 **CA8 7PB**
email: mail@andrewmarkland.plus.com
dir: *Just off A689, 6m N of Alston*

Wonderful views of the South Tyne Valley

Slaggyford has no shop or school, but when the South Tynedale Railway, currently being restored, reaches the village it will again have a station and its first trains since 1976. Thankfully, it already has the 18th-century Kirkstyle Inn, named after the stile into the adjacent churchyard and blessed with wonderful views of the river. In winter a log fire heats the bar, where among the real ales are Yates Best Bitter and a summer brew named after the inn. On the menu are the very popular local sausages with Alston honey mustard as well as classic British pub dishes, like lasagne; steak and ale pie; and cod and chips. Friday is steak night.

Open 12-3 6-11 Closed Mon & Tue in winter **Food** Lunch Tue-Sun 12-2 Dinner Tue-Sat 6-8.30 ⊕ FREE HOUSE ◀ Kirkstyle Ale, Yates Best Bitter, Guinness. **Facilities** Non-diners area ✿ (Bar Outside area) ✦ Children's portions Outside area ⊟ Parking WiFi ▄ (notice required)

WARDEN

Map 21 NY96

The Boatside Inn

tel: 01434 602233 **NE46 4SQ**
email: sales@theboatsideinn.com **web:** www.theboatsideinn.com
dir: *From A69 W of Hexham, follow signs to Warden Newborough & Fourstones*

A traditional haven for walkers and cyclists

Standing beneath Warden Hill at the confluence of the North and South Tyne rivers, The Boatside is surrounded by woodland footpaths and bridleways, and has fishing rights on the river. The name of this stone-built country free house harks back to the days when a rowing boat ferried people across the river before the bridge was built. The inn has now been refurbished following the terrible flooding in the winter of 2015. Black Sheep, Wylam and Mordue ales are on offer in the bar with its log fire and dart board. Meals are served in the conservatory, restaurant or snug, and include sharing platters (Tex mex; from the sea; and party); fish pie; curry of the day; lamb hotpot; and poacher's pie (slow cooked minced venison and wild boar). The Boatside welcomes children and dogs too.

Open all day all wk 11-11 (Sun 11-10.30) **Food** Mon-Sat 11-9, Sun 12-8 ⊕ FREE HOUSE ◀ Black Sheep, Caffrey's Irish Ale, John Smith's, Mordue, Wylam. **Facilities** Non-diners area ✿ (Bar Garden) ✦ Children's menu Children's portions Garden ⊟ Parking WiFi ▄ (notice required)

WARENFORD
Map 21 NU12

The White Swan
PICK OF THE PUBS

tel: 01668 213453 **NE70 7HY**
email: dianecuthbert@yahoo.com
dir: *100yds E of A1, 10m N of Alnwick*

Worth a detour from the main road

This 200-year-old coaching inn stands near the original toll bridge over the Waren Burn. Formerly on the Great North Road, the building is now just a stone's throw from the A1. Inside, you'll find thick stone walls and an open fire for colder days; in summer, there's a small sheltered seating area outside, with further seats in the adjacent field. The Dukes of Northumberland once owned the pub, and its windows and plasterwork still bear the family crests. Visitors and locals alike enjoy the welcoming atmosphere, fine wines and Northumbrian ales. The modern British dishes are created in-house from the county's produce; the bread, preserves and desserts are home made too. Try perhaps pheasant and black pudding terrine with black grape, apricot and cumin chutney; and seared duck breast, apple and hazelnut fricassée with anise velouté. Vegetarians are well catered for, with interesting dishes like baked tower of aubergine, courgette, onion, sweet pepper and mushroom with beetroot sorbet and blue cheese.

Open all wk Mon-Sat 12-2.30 5.30-10 (Sun 12-10) **Food** Lunch all wk 12-2.30 Dinner all wk 6-9 ⊕ FREE HOUSE ◀ Caledonian, Hadrian Border Tyneside Blonde, Greene King IPA. ♟ 10 **Facilities** Non-diners area ✿ (Bar Garden) ♦ Children's menu Children's portions Garden ⊨ Parking WiFi 🚐

NOTTINGHAMSHIRE

BEESTON
Map 11 SK53

The Victoria

tel: 0115 925 4049 **Dovecote Ln NG9 1JG**
email: vichotel@btconnect.com
dir: *M1 junct 25, A52 E. Turn right at Nurseryman PH, right opposite Rockaway Hotel into Barton St, 1st left, adjacent to railway station*

Excellent range of beers, ciders, whiskies and trains

This free house combines a welcoming atmosphere with great food and a wide choice of traditional ales and ciders, continental beers and lagers, many wines by the glass and single malt whiskies. The Victoria dates from 1899 when it was built next to Beeston Railway Station, and the large, heated patio garden is still handy for a touch of train-spotting. Main courses could include steak bordelaise; sauté of fresh monkfish and king prawns with mild Thai sauce; or smoked haddock with spinach and prawn lasagne. There are just as many options for vegetarians. Check out the dates of the annual beer festivals — Easter, last two weeks in July, and again in October.

Open all day all wk 10.30am-11pm (Fri-Sat 10.30am-mdnt Sun 12-11) Closed 26 Dec **Food** Lunch Sun-Tue 12-9, Wed-Sat 12-9.30 ⊕ FREE HOUSE ◀ Timothy Taylor Boltmaker, Castle Rock Harvest Pale, Everards Tiger, Holden's Black Country Bitter, Dancing Duck, guest ales Ö Thatchers Traditional, Broadoak, Gwynt y Ddraig. ♟ 25 **Facilities** Non-diners area ✿ (Bar Garden) ♦ Children's portions Garden ⊨ Beer festival Parking WiFi

BLIDWORTH
Map 16 SK55

Fox & Hounds

tel: 01623 792383 **Blidworth Bottoms NG21 0NW**
email: hello@foxblidworth.co.uk **web:** www.foxblidworth.co.uk
dir: *From Ravenshead towards Blidworth on B6020, right to Blidworth*

Country pub with theatrical leanings

A fusion of blues, creams, reds and smart furniture and fabrics give this pub a modern feeling without taking away the traditional country-style character that stems from its early 19th-century origins. For nearly 100 years the locals have performed a 'Plough Play' in the pub every January, recalling the days when Blidworth Bottoms was a larger community with shops and a post office. The Greene King ales are reliable as ever, and the menu delivers well-priced dishes of popular home-made favourites, such as beef casserole and herb dumplings or cottage pie.

Open all day all wk 11.30-11.30 (Fri-Sat 11.30am-mdnt) **Food** all wk 11.30-9 ⊕ GREENE KING ◀ Morland Old Golden Hen, Hardys & Hansons Best Bitter & Olde Trip, Black Sheep, seasonal guest ales Ö Thatchers Gold. ♟ 9 **Facilities** Non-diners area ✿ (Bar Garden) ♦ Children's menu Children's portions Play area Garden ⊨ Parking 🚐

CAR COLSTON — Map 11 SK74

The Royal Oak

tel: 01949 20247 **The Green NG13 8JE**
email: rich-vicky@btconnect.com
dir: *From Newark-on-Trent on A46 follow Mansfield, then Car Colston signs. From rdbt N of Bingham on A46 follow Car Colston sign. Left at next rdbt signed Car Colston*

Good pub food and an intriguing past

Some experts attribute origins as a hosiery factory to this 200-year-old inn, citing as evidence its unusual vaulted brick ceiling, undoubtedly capable of supporting any weighty textile machinery above. Much older is the centurion, perhaps from the nearby Roman-British town of Margidunum, whose ghost you may run into. Normally on duty in the bar is owner Richard Spencer, dispensing his carefully tended Burton, Brakspear and Ringwood real ales, while Vicky, his wife (a dab hand chef) is in the kitchen preparing dishes such as fresh beer-battered or oven-baked haddock; shepherd's pie; and her very popular steak pies.

Open all day all wk **Food** Lunch Mon-Sat 12-2.15, Sun 12-4 Dinner Mon-Sat 6-8.45 Av main course £9.95 ⊕ MARSTON'S ◄ Burton Bitter, Brakspear Bitter, Ringwood Boondoggle, guest ales. ☕ 13 **Facilities** Non-diners area ❀ (Bar Garden) ⬥ Children's portions Garden ⊓ Parking WiFi ☛ (notice required)

CAUNTON — Map 17 SK76

Caunton Beck — PICK OF THE PUBS

tel: 01636 636793 **NG23 6AB**
email: email@cauntonbeck.com
dir: *6m NW of Newark on A616 to Sheffield*

A village pub-restaurant open early until late

Tucked away deep in the rich farmlands of the Trent Valley, this beck-side village inn is one of a small chain of quality dining pubs owned by the Hope family. An imposing rose arbour, created by a former vicar of the village church across the water, is part of the much extended 16th-century cottages at the core of the pub. Fans of the hop can expect a glass of Black Sheep alongside further guest ales; wine-lovers have a choice of 24 by the glass. Beams, oak floorboards and rustic farmhouse-style furnishings characterise the traditional-style interior; outside is a sheltered terrace and lawned garden. The modern, mostly pan-European main menu changes regularly, offering a stimulating choice to satisfy most palates. Starters might be teriyaki salmon fillet with shredded bok choy; leading to pan-seared red mullet, crayfish and chorizo-spiced paella; or panko pork schnitzel. A daily-changing set menu is now available and gourmet evenings add further spice to the mix.

Open all day all wk 9am-10.30pm Closed 25 Dec **Food** all wk 9am-10pm Set menu available Restaurant menu available all wk ⊕ FREE HOUSE ◄ Black Sheep, Oakham Ales JHB, Guinness, guest ales ♻ Westons Stowford Press. ☕ 24 **Facilities** Non-diners area ❀ (Bar Garden Outside area) ⬥ Children's menu Children's portions Garden Outside area ⊓ Parking WiFi

COLSTON BASSETT — Map 11 SK73

The Martin's Arms — PICK OF THE PUBS

See Pick of the Pubs on opposite page

EDWINSTOWE — Map 16 SK66

Forest Lodge ★★★★ INN

tel: 01623 824443 **4 Church St NG21 9QA**
email: reception@forestlodgehotel.co.uk **web:** www.forestlodgehotel.co.uk
dir: *A614 towards Edwinstowe, onto B6034. Inn opposite church*

Coaching inn at the edge of Robin Hood territory

This 18th-century coaching inn stands on the edge of Sherwood Forest opposite the church where Robin Hood is supposed to have married Maid Marian. Sympathetically restored by the Thompson family over the past decade or so, it includes stylish accommodation and a comfortable restaurant and bar. Award-winning cask ales are always on tap in two beamed bars warmed by open fires. An impressive baronial-style dining hall is an ideal setting for wholesome fare that changes to reflect the seasons; be sure to consider the venison pavé, leek textures, black pudding, fondant potatoes and stout reduction on a winter menu. All-time favourites are on offer too of course, and include beef and ale pie; home-made beef chilli; and battered fish fillet and hand-cut chips.

Open all wk 11.30-3 5.30-11 (Fri 11.30-3 5-11 Sun 12-3 6-10.30) Closed 1 Jan **Food** Lunch all wk 12-2 Dinner all wk 6-9 ⊕ FREE HOUSE ◄ Wells Bombardier, Kelham Island Pale Rider, Forest Lodge English Pale Ale, Ossett Silver King. **Facilities** Non-diners area ⬥ Children's menu Children's portions Garden Outside area ⊓ Parking WiFi ☛ (notice required) **Rooms** 13

FARNDON — Map 17 SK75

The Farndon Boathouse ⊕ — PICK OF THE PUBS

tel: 01636 676578 **Off Wyke Ln NG24 3SX**
email: info@farndonboathouse.co.uk
dir: *From A46 rdbt (SW of Newark-on-Trent) take Fosse Way signed Farndon. Right into Main St signed Farndon. At T-junct right into Wyke Ln, follow Boathouse signs*

Delightful riverside pub

Should you arrive here on a mystery tour, you might not guess that the tranquil, wooded view from the terrace of this modern bar and restaurant is the River Trent. The setting is perfect for this old-boathouse-styled pub, with wood cladding, chunky exposed roof trusses, stone floors and warehouse-style lighting. The food reflects a philosophy that champions home cooking and local sourcing, with herbs and salad leaves from the pub garden, and meats, fish and cheeses often smoked in-house. Wide-ranging menus offer over four different sharing boards; a starter or main called The Mussel Pot; pizzas, burgers, and steaks; and other choices like pan-fried sea bass fillet, beetroot and watercress risotto and salsa verde. There are pie nights, monthly ladies' nights, and live music every Sunday evening. In the events calendar is a Beaujolais Breakfast (10am-4pm) — a five course breakfast that includes a half bottle of Beaujolais nouveau.

Open all day all wk 10am-11pm **Food** Lunch Mon-Sat 12-3, Sun 12-8 Dinner Mon-Sat 6-9.30, Sun 12-8 Set menu available ⊕ FREE HOUSE ◄ Greene King IPA, guest ales ♻ Aspall. ☕ 20 **Facilities** Non-diners area ⬥ Children's menu Children's portions Garden ⊓ Parking WiFi ☛ (notice required)

PICK OF THE PUBS

The Martin's Arms

COLSTON BASSETT   Map 11 SK73

tel: 01949 81361 **School Ln NG12 3FD**
email: martins_arms@hotmail.com
web: www.themartinsarms.co.uk
dir: *Exit A46 between Leicester &*
Newark

Traditional 18th-century pub with seasonally inspired menus

At the heart of village life since the 18th century, the pub takes its name from Henry Martin, MP for Kinsale in County Cork, who was the local squire in the early 19th century. In the pretty village of Colston Bassett in the Vale of Belvoir, this striking Grade II listed building occupies a quintessentially English spot on the corner of a leafy cul-de-sac close to an old cross. Overlooked by the church spire, the one-acre garden incorporates a croquet lawn. Close to National Trust land, the pub is surrounded by ancient trees in the estate parkland to which it belonged until 1990, when the current owners, Jack Inguanta and Lynne Strafford Bryan, bought it, undertaking to maintain its character and unique atmosphere. This they have clearly managed to do, since much of the interior will transport you straight back in time, especially the Jacobean fireplaces and the period furnishings. The bar has an impressive range of real ales, with Castle Rock Harvest Pale waving the flag for the county, while

another local 'brew' is elderflower pressé from Belvoir Fruit Farms. With new head chef Andrew Brookes at the helm, bread, preserves, sauces, terrines, soups, pasta and much, much more are all made on site. Classic pub dishes include a pie of the day; fish and chips and a beefburger teamed with Colston Bassett's world-famous Stilton, while starters from the à la carte might include smoked salmon, yuzu, pickled fennel, barbecue cucumber and seaweed cracker. For mains, locally shot pheasant with apple and black pudding sausage roll, grains, celeriac and truffle, mushroom ketchup. Finish with duck egg custard tart, rhubarb, white chocolate and pistachio Arctic roll.

Open all wk 12-3 6-11 (Sun 12-4 7-11)

Closed 25 Dec eve & 26 Dec eve
Food Lunch Mon-Sat 12-2, Sun 12-2.30
Dinner Mon-Sat 6-9.30 Restaurant
menu available Mon-Sat ⊕ FREE HOUSE
◀ Marston's Pedigree, Bass, Greene
King IPA, Timothy Taylor Landlord, Castle
Rock Harvest Pale Ò Aspall, Cornish
Orchards. � **Facilities** Non-diners area
♦ Children's portions Family room
Garden ᗡ Parking WiFi 🚌 (notice
required)

HARBY
Map 17 SK87

Bottle & Glass

tel: 01522 703438 **High St NG23 7EB**
dir: *S of A57 (Lincoln to Markham Moor road)*

Compact and convivial old free house

One of the Exceedingly Small group's three pubs, the Bottle & Glass is in the village where Edward I's wife, Eleanor, died in 1290. With flagged floors and heavy beams, it offers beers brewed on the premises and London Gold and Black Sheep real ales, and a generous 24 wines by the glass. Starters on the short, seasonal lunch and dinner menu include twice baked soufflé with Stilton and leeks; and beer-battered squid with garlic and herb mayonnaise. Mains typically include grilled wild sea bass, leek mash, buttered spinach and beurre blanc; and slow-cooked lamb shoulder, fondant potato, green beans, redcurrant and mint sauce. On sunny days stake an early claim for a terrace table.

Open all day all wk 10am-11pm Closed 25 Dec **Food** Mon-Fri & Sun 10-9.30, Sat 10-10 Set menu available Restaurant menu available all wk ⊕ FREE HOUSE ◀ London Gold, Black Sheep ⌂ Aspalls. ♚ 24 **Facilities** Non-diners area ♨ (Bar Garden) ♦♦ Children's menu Children's portions Play area Garden ⊼ Parking WiFi

KIMBERLEY
Map 11 SK44

The Nelson & Railway Inn

tel: 0115 938 2177 **12 Station Rd NG16 2NR**
dir: *M1 junct 26, A610 to Kimberley*

Family-run former railway inn

This popular village pub has been in the capable hands of the same family for very many years. Originally dating from the 17th-century with Victorian additions, it sits next door to the Hardys & Hansons Brewery that supplies many of the beers. Sadly the two nearby railway stations that once made it a railway inn are now derelict. Interesting brewery prints and railway signs decorate the beamed bar and lounge. A hearty menu of pub favourites includes ploughman's and hot rolls, as well as grills and pub classics like lasagne, scampi and chips, chilli con carne and home-made steak and ale pie.

Open all day all wk 11am-mdnt **Food** Lunch Mon-Fri 12-2.30, Sat 12-9, Sun 12-6 Dinner Mon-Fri 5.30-9, Sat 12-9, Sun 12-6 Restaurant menu available all wk ⊕ GREENE KING ◀ Hardys & Hansons Best Bitter, Cool & Dark Mild, Nottingham EPA, 2 local guest ales. **Facilities** Non-diners area ♨ (Bar Garden) ♦♦ Children's menu Children's portions Family room Garden ⊼ Beer festival Parking WiFi

LAXTON
Map 17 SK76

The Dovecote Inn

tel: 01777 871586 **Cross Hill NG22 0SX**
email: hello@thedovecoteinn.com
dir: *Exit A1 at Tuxford through Egmanton to Laxton*

Superb local produce features on the menus

Like most of the village of Laxton, the 18th-century Dovecote Inn is Crown Estate property, belonging to the Royal Family. There's a delightful beer garden with views of the church, while the interior has a bar as well as three cosy wining and dining rooms. The seasonally changing menus and daily changing specials board could include baked goats' cheese, roasted fig, wild rocket, walnuts and honey dressing; Thoresbury Estate wild venison burger with caramelised onions; home-made steak and ale shortcrust pastry pie; and pear, dark chocolate and marzipan strudel. The gourmet themed nights are extremely popular and booking is essential.

Open all wk 11.30-3 5.30-11 (Sat 11.30-3 6-11 Sun 12-10.30) **Food** Lunch Mon-Sat 11.30-3, Sun all day Dinner Mon-Fri 5.30-11, Sat 6-11, Sun all day Av main course £12.95 Set menu available ⊕ FREE HOUSE ◀ Castle Rock Harvest Pale, Black Sheep Best Bitter, Timothy Taylor Landlord, guest ales. ♚ 24 **Facilities** Non-diners area ♦♦ Children's menu Children's portions Garden ⊼ Parking WiFi ▭ (notice required)

MORTON
Map 17 SK75

The Full Moon Inn
PICK OF THE PUBS

tel: 01636 830251 **Main St NG25 0UT**
email: bookings@thefullmoonmorton.co.uk
dir: *A617 from Newark towards Mansfield. Past Kelham, left to Rolleston & follow signs to Morton*

Pretty red-brick pub with year-round appeal

All pantiles, pale bricks and creeper, this long-established inn stands at the village centre just a short hop from the magnificent Minster at nearby Southwell amidst the rich cornfields of the Trent Valley. Within, it's a contemporary and comfortable pub, with exposed old beams and brickwork retained from the original 18th-century cottages, scattered with reclaimed panelling and furniture. It's a relaxing locale in which to chill out with a glass of wine or a pint of Doom Bar. What's more it's both child and dog-friendly, with a grassy, tree-shaded garden an additional bonus for summer days. Good pub tucker features on the menus: leek and potato soup; goats' cheese fondue, figs, pomegranate seeds, garlic croûtons; braised blade of beef, parmesan mash, peas, crumbled bacon and red wine jus; celeriac and spinach risotto, soft hen's egg and watercress; and beer-battered haddock, chunky chips, pea purée and tartare sauce.

Open all wk fr 10am **Food** Lunch Mon-Fri 12-2, Sat 12-3, Sun 12-5 Dinner Mon-Fri 5.30-9, Sat 6-9.30 Set menu available ⊕ FREE HOUSE ◀ Sharp's Doom Bar, Timothy Taylor, guest ales. ♚ 9 **Facilities** Non-diners area ♨ (Bar Garden) ♦♦ Children's menu Children's portions Play area Family room Garden ⊼ Parking WiFi ▭ (notice required)

NEWARK-ON-TRENT
Map 17 SK75

The Prince Rupert

tel: 01636 918121 **46 Stodman St NG24 1AW**
email: rupert@kneadpubs.co.uk
dir: *5 mins' walk from castle, on entry road to Market Sq*

Brimming with character and charm

Full of charm and character, the 15th-century Prince Rupert is one of Newark's most historic pubs. Expect old beams, wood floors, crackling log fires and cosy corners in the series of small downstairs rooms; make sure you explore upstairs, as the ancient architectural features are stunning. To drink, Oakham Ales JHB and Brains The Rev. James take pride of place alongside constantly changing choices while menus take in pub classics such as game and ale casserole, and excellent stone-baked pizzas. There are regular live music events and beer and cider festivals in the summer months.

Open all day all wk Mon-Tue 11-11 Wed-Thu 11am-mdnt Fri-Sat 11am-1am Sun 12-11 Closed 25 Dec **Food** Lunch Mon-Fri 12-2.30, Sat 12-5, Sun 12-8 Dinner Mon-Sat 6-9, Sun 12-8 ⊕ FREE HOUSE ◀ Brains The Rev. James, Oakham Ales JHB, rotating guest ales. ♚ 16 **Facilities** Non-diners area ♨ (Bar Restaurant Outside area) ♦♦ Outside area ⊼ Beer festival Cider festival WiFi ▭

NOTTINGHAM
Map 11 SK53

The Hand and Heart

tel: 0115 958 2456 **65-67 Derby Rd NG1 5BA**
email: handandheart@ntlworld.com
dir: On A610 (2 mins' walk from Canning Circus)

Great beer in a fascinating building

This Georgian building was a brewery before becoming a pub in Victorian times. Beer was brewed in the converted stables and stored in the sandstone cave below, which is now an atmospheric restaurant. Famous for its excellent selection of real ales, The Hand and Heart holds two beer festivals a year, spring and autumn, and in the bar you can sample Round Heart from the Dancing Duck Brewery as well as the Maypole Brewery's Little Weed, and six changing guest ales. The tempting menu choices could include slow-braised oxtail on the bone, root veg stew, Stilton mash and parsnip crisps; herb puff pastry topped steak, smoked bacon and local ale pie; and lemon battered fish and chips with minted peas.

Open all day all wk 12-11 (Thu 12-12 Fri-Sat 12-late Sun 12-10.30) Closed 25-26 Dec & 1 Jan **Food** Mon-Sat 12-9.30, Sun 12-9 Set menu available ⊕ FREE HOUSE ◀ Dancing Duck Round Heart, Maypole Little Weed, guest ales ♂ Guest ciders. ⚑ 18 **Facilities** Non-diners area ♣ (Bar Outside area) Outside area ⚲ Beer festival Cider festival WiFi ➡

Ye Olde Trip to Jerusalem
PICK OF THE PUBS

tel: 0115 947 3171 **1 Brewhouse Yard, Castle Rd NG1 6AD**
email: 4925@greeneking.co.uk
dir: In town centre

Medieval gem with history aplenty

Castle Rock, upon which stands Nottingham Castle, is riddled by caves and passageways cut into the sandstone. The builders of this unusual pub made the most of this, incorporating some of the caves into the design of the inn, one of Britain's oldest – founded in AD1189. The name recalls that soldiers, clergy and penitents gathered here before embarking on the Crusade to the Holy Land – doubtless they drank to their quest at the castle's beerhouse before their trip to Jerusalem. Centuries of service impart instant appeal, from the magpie collection of furnishings in the warren of rooms to the unique Rock Lounge, and quirks such as the cursed galleon and the fertility chair. Beers from the Nottingham Brewery feature strongly, accompanying a reliable menu of old favourites like slow-cooked pork belly and Scottish scampi, to tapas style dishes, sharing plates, lighter mains and fish such as oven-baked cod, crayfish and spinach fishcakes. Several annual beer festivals are held.

Open all day all wk 11-11 (Fri-Sat 11am-mdnt) Closed 25 Dec **Food** all wk 11-10 ⊕ GREENE KING ◀ IPA, Hardys & Hansons Olde Trip, Nottingham guest ales ♂ Aspall. ⚑ 13 **Facilities** Non-diners area ♦ Garden Beer festival WiFi ➡ (notice required)

RUDDINGTON
Map 11 SK53

NEW The Ruddington Arms

tel: 0115 984 1628 **56 Wilford Rd NG11 6EQ**
email: info@theruddingtonarms.com
dir: From A52 (S of Nottingham) onto A60 signed Ruddington

Village pub showcasing local produce

Five miles south of Nottingham in the village of Ruddington, this refurbished pub has built up a reputation for its locally-sourced products, whether it's the pints of quirkily-named Ruddy Good Ale or the regionally-inspired food. Toasted sandwiches, melts and light bites are served throughout the afternoon, with the à la carte served lunchtimes and evenings. Typical dishes include Lincolnshire Poacher and spinach soufflé; roast monkfish tail coconut curry, fragrant rice, herb salad and toasted almonds; or slow-cooked pork shoulder, black pudding croquettes, rhubarb and ginger compôte. Leave room for blood orange posset with lemon curd, poppy seeds and granola.

Open all day all wk **Food** Lunch Mon-Thu 12-5, Fri-Sun 10-5 Dinner all wk 5.30-9 ⊕ STAR PUBS ◀ Ruddy Good Ale, Castle Rock Harvest Pale, guest ales ♂ Symonds. ⚑ **Facilities** Non-diners area ♣ (Bar Outside area) ♦ Children's menu Children's portions Outside area ⚲ Parking WiFi

---

SOUTHWELL
Map 17 SK75

The Hearty Goodfellow

tel: 01636 919176 **NG25 0HQ**
email: info@heartygoodfellowpub.co.uk
dir: From Newark-on-Trent take A617 towards Mansfield. At lights left to Southwell. Pub on right on A612

Traditional cask ale house and award-winning garden

Close to the picturesque centre of Southwell, a stone's throw from the Minster and racecourse. Inside, a warm and caring welcome embraces one and all, including children and dogs. Settle back with a pint of Hearty Blonde, the house beer, or try a Fiery Fox cider for a change. Light bites include a posh fish-finger sandwich; for a 'Hearty' alternative, look to the home-made beef and ale pie in shortcrust pastry; or the burger with garlic sauce. Children eat proper food too, choosing either from a Little Darlings menu or smaller portions from the main menu. Ales in July and cider in February are celebrated in two annual festivals.

Open all wk Mon-Thu 11-3 5-11 (Fri-Sun 11am-mdnt) **Food** Lunch Mon-Thu 12-2.30, Fri-Sat 12-9, Sun 12-4 Dinner Mon 5-8, Tue-Thu 5-9, Fri-Sat 12-9 Set menu available ⊕ EVERARDS ◀ Welbeck The Hearty Blonde, Tiger, Castle Rock, rotating guest ales ♂ Gwynt y Ddraig Fiery Fox. ⚑ 11 **Facilities** Non-diners area ♣ (Bar Restaurant Garden) ♦ Children's menu Children's portions Play area Garden ⚲ Beer festival Cider festival Parking WiFi ➡ (notice required)

TUXFORD
Map 17 SK77

The Fountain

tel: 01777 872854 **155 Lincoln Rd NG22 0JQ**
email: thefountaintuxford@aol.co.uk
dir: Phone for detailed directions

Family-oriented pub with a good local reputation

Now under new management, The Fountain makes a convenient pit-stop off the A1(M) for frazzled parents and their hungry children. Unpretentious pub grub at reasonable prices is the deal here, but a 'fresh is best' attitude and support for local growers drive the inn's ethos nonetheless. Some look no further than stone-baked pizzas and meal deals on the kiddies' menu. But chicken liver pâté and steak and ale pie are home made; steaks chargrilled to order can be served with the special house salad; and the specials list may proffer a goat curry. On tap are beers from Welbeck Abbey Brewery.

Open all day all wk **Food** Lunch Mon-Thu 12-3, Fri-Sat 12-9, Sun 12-6 Dinner Fri-Sat 12-9 Av main course £8 ⊕ FREE HOUSE ◀ Welbeck Abbey Brewery. ⚑ 12 **Facilities** Non-diners area ♦ Children's menu Children's portions Play area Garden ⚲ Parking WiFi ➡ (notice required)

TUXFORD *continued*

The Mussel & Crab

tel: 01777 870491 **Sibthorpe Hill NG22 OPJ**
email: musselandcrab1@hotmail.com **web:** www.musselandcrab.com
dir: *From Ollerton/Tuxford junct of A1 & A57. N on B1164 to Sibthorpe Hill. Pub 800yds on right*

A huge choice of seafood dishes

Bruce and Allison Elliott-Bateman turned this quirky pub in landlocked Nottinghamshire into a renowned seafood restaurant. Beautifully fresh fish and seafood dominate the menu, with food served in a multitude of rooms; the piazza room is styled as an Italian courtyard and the beamed restaurant is big on rustic charm. Over a dozen blackboards offer ever-changing fish dishes, as well as 'things that don't swim'. You could select po pei mussels, followed by lobster thermidor, twice baked soufflé or locally shot pheasant – braised leg and breast wrapped in pancetta.

Open all wk 11-3 6-11 **Food** Lunch Mon-Sat 11-2.30, Sun 11-3 Dinner Mon-Sat 6-10, Sun 6-9 Set menu available ⊕ FREE HOUSE ◀ John Smith's, Black Sheep, Guinness ♂ Somersby. ♟ 16 **Facilities** Non-diners area ♣ (Bar Garden) ♦ Children's menu Family room Garden ⋈ Parking

UPTON   Map 17 SK75

Cross Keys

tel: 01636 813269 **Main St NG23 5SY**
email: info@crosskeysatupton.co.uk
dir: *From A617 W of Newark-on-Trent onto A612 towards Southwell. Pub in village centre*

A 16th-century pub for everyone

Open fires, cosy alcoves, beamed ceilings and candles in the evenings – in a nutshell, that's the Cross Keys. Co-owner Steve Hussey, with partner Alison Ryan, is also head brewer/owner at nearby Maythorne's Mallard microbrewery, which supplies the real ales, with Somerset's Broadoak providing cider and perry. On the ever-changing weekly menu, classically trained French chef Franck Morisseau specialises in fish, such as curried cod loin topped with king prawns and his famous fish ragout. Local sourced produce also goes into other options such as venison steak with port and red wine jus, dauphinoise potatoes and braised red cabbage; and veggie stack in blue cheese sauce.

Open Tue 5-11, Wed-Thu 12-3 5-11 (Fri-Sat 12-12, Sun 12-11) Closed Mon **Food** Lunch Wed-Sat 12-3, Sun 12-4 Dinner Tue-Sat 5-8.30 ⊕ FREE HOUSE ◀ Mallard Drake & Duck 'n' Dive ♂ Broadoak Moonshine & Perry. ♟ 10 **Facilities** Non-diners area ♣ (Bar Garden) ♦ Children's portions Garden ⋈ Parking WiFi 🚌 (notice required)

ABINGDON-ON-THAMES   Map 5 SU49

The Brewery Tap

tel: 01235 521655 **40-42 Ock St OX14 5BZ**
email: thebrewerytap@gmail.com
dir: *Phone for detailed directions*

Town-centre favourite with a beer garden

This predominantly late 17th-century pub, has been in the aptly-named Heritage family for nearly 25 years. Flagstone floors and open fireplaces characterise the interior, where the bar staff dispense a changing line-up of six guest ales along with a good choice of ciders. Bar snacks range from grilled jalapeño peppers to pork crackling, while classic dishes include home-made pies and the 'Made in America' dishes prove ever popular. Sunday roasts are a big thing, followed between 5pm and 7pm by live music. Beer and cider festivals are held in March and October.

Open all day all wk **Food** Lunch all wk 12-3 Dinner Mon-Sat 6-9 ⊕ REDSTAR PUB CO ◀ Rotating guest ales ♂ Thatchers Heritage, Westons Old Rosie, Hogs Back Hazy Hog. ♟ 12 **Facilities** Non-diners area ♣ (Bar Restaurant Garden) ♦ Children's menu Children's portions Garden ⋈ Beer festival Cider festival Parking WiFi

ASHBURY   Map 5 SU28

NEW The Rose & Crown ★★★ INN

tel: 01793 710222 **3 High St SN6 8NA**
email: bookings@roseandcrowninn.co.uk **web:** www.roseandcrowninn.co.uk
dir: *Take B4000 from Shrivenham signed Sevenhampton. At x-roads in Ashbury turn right, pub on left. Or from Lambourn take B4000 to Ashbury. Left at x-roads to pub*

Dog-friendly village inn popular with walkers

In the heart of the historic village of Ashbury, The Rose & Crown dates back to the 16th century when it was a coaching inn. Refurbished in 2013, it still retains plenty of original features including open fires and the patio terrace is a real draw in the summer. Local produce drives the menu, with typical dishes including Wiltshire ham, hand-cut chips and fried eggs; linguine with prawns, squid, chilli, garlic, tomato and basil; or curry of the day. Walkers exploring the nearby Ridgeway National Trail can refuel with a glass of Arkell's Wiltshire Gold, and dogs are welcome to join their owners in the bar.

Open all wk 12-3 5.30-11 (Apr-Oct all day) **Food** Lunch Mon-Thu 12-2, Fri-Sun 12-3 Dinner all wk 6.30-9.30 Av main course £12.95 Restaurant menu available all wk ⊕ ARKELL'S ◀ 3B, Wiltshire Gold ♂ Westons Stowford Press. ♟ 10 **Facilities** Non-diners area ♣ (Bar Garden) ♦ Children's menu Children's portions Play area Family room Garden ⋈ Beer festival Cider festival Parking WiFi 🚌 (notice required) **Rooms** 8

Find out more about this area with *The AA Guide to The Cotswolds* – see shop.theAA.com

PICK OF THE PUBS

The Vines

BLACK BOURTON   Map 5 SP20

tel: 01993 843559
Burford Rd OX18 2PF
email: info@vineshotel.com
web: www.vinesblackbourton.co.uk
dir: *A40 at Witney onto A4095 to
Faringdon, 1st right after Bampton to
Black Bourton*

Stylish village retreat with modern British food

Built of Cotswold stone, The Vines is discreetly set back from the road behind a screen of bushes. During the 1940s, it would have heaved as dozens of American airmen based at nearby Brize Norton packed themselves in and learnt to love English beers. Today, spacious and smartly decorated and furnished, it belongs to Ahdy and Karen Gerges, who maintain its excellent reputation. Leather sofas in the spacious lounge area by the log fire are the perfect place for a pint of Old Hooky from the Hook Norton brewery about 24 miles away, or maybe you'd prefer to drift patio-wards with a glass of wine for a game of Aunt Sally, a time-honoured pub game involving throwing sticks at an old woman's head (wooden of course). The menu lists imaginative, internationally influenced, modern British dishes, all freshly prepared from locally sourced produce. Typical starters include

deep-fried breaded brie wedges with cranberry dip; spaghetti with clams in rich garlic and parsley sauce; and a special, bresaola and parmesan salad. Loin of pork stuffed with sage and onion is served with rosemary and garlic potatoes and red wine sauce; and grilled rib-eye steak comes with chips, grilled mushrooms, tomatoes and peppercorn sauce. Other possibilities are venison steak with mash, garlic, red wine and rosemary sauce, and fish of the day. Typical home-made puddings are lemon posset; and warm chocolate brownie with ice cream. A good selection of Old and New World wines is always available. Food and drink can be served in the garden.

Open Mon Sat 5-11 Closed L all wk, Sun eve **Food** Dinner Mon-Sat 6-9 Av main course £13 🍺 FREE HOUSE 🍺 Hook Norton Old Hooky, Tetley's Smoothflow Ö Westons Stowford Press.
Facilities Non-diners area 🐾 (Garden) 🚻 Children's menu Children's portions Garden 🎪 Parking WiFi 🚌 (notice required)

BANBURY
Map 11 SP44

The Wykham Arms

tel: 01295 788808 **Temple Mill Rd, Sibford Gower OX15 5RX**
email: info@wykhamarms.co.uk
dir: *Between Banbury & Shipston-on-Stour off B4035*

Attractive village inn with modern menu

A beautiful thatched, mellow stone pub in a hilly village of venerable, reed-roofed cottages at the edge of The Cotswolds. With roses round the door and a cosy courtyard for long summer evenings, it's the idyllic rural inn. With a brace and more of real ales, including one from local brewers Whale, proprietors and classically trained chefs Damian and Debbie Bradley skilfully produce a regularly changing menu of contemporary dishes. Start perhaps with seared pigeon breast, black pudding and apple compôte; or go straight to a main dish like grilled aged sirloin steak, thin chips, sauté mushrooms and sweet balsamic baby onions; or south coast sea bass fillet with pad Thai-style noodles.

Open 12-3 6-11 Closed 25 Dec, Mon (ex BHs) **Food** Lunch Tue-Sun 12-2.30 Dinner Tue-Sat 6-9.30 Av main course £12 Restaurant menu available Tue-Sat ⊕ FREE HOUSE ◼ Wye Valley HPA, St Austell Trelawny, Whale Ale Brewery, Guinness ♂ Aspall. ♀ 20 **Facilities** Non-diners area ♣ (Bar Garden Outside area) ♦♦ Children's portions Family room Garden Outside area ⋒ Parking WiFi

Ye Olde Reindeer Inn

tel: 01295 270972 **47 Parsons St OX16 5NA**
email: thereindeerbanbury@gmail.com
dir: *1m from M40 junct 11, in town centre just off market square. Car park access via Bolton Rd*

Town pub with interesting history

Cotswold-brewed beers from the renowned Hook Norton Brewery draw in a lively local clientele to this historic pub right at the core of old Banbury, just a stone's throw from the Cross of nursery-rhyme fame. Its origins go back to Tudor times, and during the Civil War, Oliver Cromwell himself is believed to have directed his commanders in the richly panelled Globe Room. Weekly events include live music, steak nights and quizzes. Enjoy good, solid pub grub in the traditional, time-worn, classic interior or indulge in a game of Aunt Sally in the flower-decked courtyard. A sampling of dishes includes venison pie, fish and chips, bangers and mash, and sticky toffee pudding and custard.

Open all day all wk Mon-Thu 11-11 (Fri-Sat 11am-mdnt Sun 12-10.30) Closed 25 Dec **Food** Lunch all wk 12-3 Dinner Mon-Sat 6-9 Av main course £10 ⊕ HOOK NORTON ◼ Hooky Bitter, Old Hooky, Hooky Lion, Hooky Mild ♂ Westons Stowford Press. ♀ 16 **Facilities** Non-diners area ♣ (All areas) ♦♦ Children's menu Children's portions Family room Garden Outside area ⋒ Beer festival Cider festival Parking 🚌 (notice required)

BEGBROKE
Map 11 SP41

The Royal Sun

tel: 01865 374718 **2 Woodstock Road West OX5 1RZ**
email: theroyalsun@hotmail.co.uk
dir: *From Oxford take A44 towards Woodstock. Approx 5m to Begbroke*

Pub classics in an Oxfordshire village

A stone-built inn, dating from the 17th century, and handy for Woodstock and Blenheim Palace. Sir Winston Churchill (who was born at the Palace) and the Duke of Marlborough used to ride to the pub for a drink — and if it was good enough for them, then surely it's good enough for anyone. There's a cosy bar and a smart restaurant where you'll find dishes like boxed camembert, roasted in garlic and rosemary, with onion jam and sliced baguette; confit duck, crispy bacon, beetroot, honey and walnut salad; hand-raised beef and Guinness pie, braised cabbage,

creamy mash and red wine gravy; and caramelised lemon tart with raspberry sorbet.

Open all day all wk 12-3 5.30-11 (Sun 12-6) **Food** Lunch Mon-Sat 12-3, Sun 12-4 Dinner Mon-Sat 6-9 ⊕ PUNCH TAVERNS ◼ Hook Norton Hooky Bitter, Marston's Lancaster Bomber ♂ Westons Stowford Press. ♀ 9 **Facilities** Non-diners area ♦♦ Children's menu Children's portions Garden ⋒ Parking WiFi 🚌 (notice required)

BESSELS LEIGH
Map 5 SP40

NEW The Greyhound

tel: 01865 862110 **OX13 5PX**
email: greyhound@brunningandprice.co.uk
dir: *On A420 between Oxford & Fyfield*

Handsome country pub with a delightful garden

The best efforts to date the Cotswold-stone Greyhound suggest it's around 400 years old, when it was a coaching inn and forge. A plaque records how 19th-century landlord Alfred White began here what survives as Britain's oldest church-bell-hanging company. The Greyhound is set well back from a main road and in terms of appearance Central Casting couldn't have done better. Locally brewed beers are in the bar, and there's a good wine list. A comprehensive all-day menu leads you from steamed mussels to bread and butter pudding, by way of Greek lamb patties; cider-braised pig's cheeks; deep-fried haddock in beer batter; and sweet potato and cauliflower curry.

Open all day all wk **Food** Contact pub for food times ⊕ FREE HOUSE ◼ Brunning & Price Original Bitter, Loose Cannon Abingdon Bridge, White Horse Wayland Smithy ♂ Aspall, Thatchers. ♀ **Facilities** Non-diners area ♣ (Bar Garden) ♦♦ Children's portions Garden ⋒ Parking WiFi

BLACK BOURTON
Map 5 SP20

The Vines
PICK OF THE PUBS

See Pick of the Pubs on page 381

BLOXHAM
Map 11 SP43

The Elephant & Castle

tel: 01295 720383 **OX15 4LZ**
email: bloxhamelephant1@btconnect.com
dir: *Take A361 from Banbury towards Chipping Norton, 1st left after shops in Bloxham*

Traditional Cotswold stone coaching inn

Locals play Aunt Sally or shove-ha'penny in this 15th-century coaching inn's big wood-floored bar, whilst the lounge boasts a bar-billiards table and a large inglenook fireplace. External features include an arch that used to straddle the former Banbury to Chipping Norton turnpike; at night the gates of the pub were closed, and no traffic could get over the toll bridge. Today the menu offers toasties and baguettes, and favourites like scampi, crispy cod and vegetarian shepherd's pie. The bar serves seasonal and guest ales as well as Westons ciders. The beer festival in May is part of the Bloxfest Music Festival.

Open all wk 10-3 6-12 (Fri 10-3 5-2am Sat 10am-2am Sun 10am-mdnt) **Food** Lunch Mon-Sat 12-2 Av main course £6 ⊕ HOOK NORTON ◼ Hooky Bitter & Seasonal ales, guest ales ♂ Westons 1st Quality, Old Rosie, Wyld Wood, Perry & Rosie's Pig, Thatchers, Hogan's Picker's Passion & Panking Pole. **Facilities** Non-diners area ♣ (Bar Restaurant Garden) ♦♦ Children's menu Children's portions Family room Garden ⋒ Beer festival Cider festival Parking WiFi 🚌

BRIGHTWELL BALDWIN
Map 5 SU69

The Nelson
PICK OF THE PUBS

See Pick of the Pubs on opposite page

PICK OF THE PUBS

The Nelson

BRIGHTWELL BALDWIN   Map 5 SU69

tel: 01491 612497 **OX49 5NP**
email: info@thenelsonbrightwell.co.uk
web: www.thenelsonbrightwell.co.uk
dir: *Off B4009 between Watlington &*
Benson

Country inn and restaurant with pretty terraced garden

In Nelson's day the pub was known as the Admiral Nelson but when, in 1797, the great man was elevated to the peerage, the pub's name was elevated accordingly. In 1905 the inn closed following complaints about over-indulgent estate workers, but several years later the building was bought by a couple who gave it a complete makeover. The Lord Nelson finally reopened on Trafalgar Day 1971, but today it's known simply as The Nelson. As you approach down the lane, look for the union flags flying patriotically outside. Its quiet position makes it a great getaway for a country walk before opening time. The interior is full of fresh flowers, and tables lit by candles in the evening are warmed by a splendid inglenook fireplace. In summer the pretty terraced garden with its weeping willow is popular for alfresco eating and drinking; seafood lovers should check out the dates of the annual crab and lobster festival. All food is freshly cooked, using local produce where possible. Starters might include local

pigeon breast with smoked bacon and black pudding; or paprika-dusted whitebait with lemon and caper mayo. Main courses reflect the pub's proudly British traditions: expect the likes of rack of English lamb, dauphinoise potatoes, and spinach with rosemary and red wine jus; or chunky cod fillet with mixed bean cassoulet and skinny fries. Vegetarian options have much appeal: goats' cheese en croute, roasted peppers and tomato with balsamic glaze and dressed salad. If refreshment is all that's required, ales include Loose Cannon from Abingdon, or North Yorkshire's much respected Black Sheep. Weston's ciders and around 20 wines served by the glass complete the drinks line-up.

Open 12-3 6-11 (Sun 12-4) Closed 25 Dec, Sun eve **Food** Lunch Mon-Sat 12-2, Sun 12-3.30 Dinner Mon-Sat 6-10 Set menu available ⊞ FREE HOUSE
◀ Rebellion IPA, Loose Cannon, Black Sheep ♂ Westons Stowford Press. ♇ 20
Facilities Non-diners area ♣ (Bar Garden Outside area) ♦♦ Children's portions Garden Outside area ☐ Parking WiFi ▭ (notice required)

BRIGHTWELL-CUM-SOTWELL
Map 5 SU59

The Red Lion

tel: 01491 837373 **The Street OX10 0RT**
email: mark@redlion.biz
dir: *From A4130 (Didcot to Wallingford road) follow Brightwell-cum-Sotwell signs. Pub in village centre*

Friendly village pub

This picture-postcard thatched and timbered 16th-century village pub is not only pretty but also a cracking community local. Behind the bar, beers come from the likes of West Berkshire, and Loddon breweries, while a choice of wine comes from the very local Brightwell Vineyard. The pub holds a beer festival (with live music) for two days every summer. Hearty, traditional pub food is freshly prepared from local produce. Look to the chalkboard for the famous short-crust pastry pies of the day, or the main menu for things like lasagne, pork tenderloin with black pudding and caramelised apple, or vegetable chilli. Don't miss the Sunday roast lunches.

Open all wk 12-3 6-11 **Food** Lunch all wk 12-2 Dinner Tue-Sat 6.30-9 ⊕ FREE HOUSE ◀ West Berkshire Good Old Boy, Loddon Hoppit ♻ Symonds Founders Reserve, Tutts Clump. **Facilities** Non-diners area ♥ (Bar Garden) ♦ Children's menu Children's portions Garden ⋈ Beer festival Parking WiFi

BROUGHTON
Map 11 SP43

Saye and Sele Arms

tel: 01295 263348 **Main Rd OX15 5ED**
email: mail@sayeandselearms.co.uk
dir: *From Banbury Cross take B4035 to Broughton. Approx 3m*

Peaceful retreat in historic village

Sheltered by a spinney fringing the grounds buffering the extraordinary moated medieval Broughton Castle, this inn, parts of which date back 700 years, is named after the titled family who still call the manor home. Age-polished flagstones, wizened beams and gleaming brasses greet customers who can indulge in a range of real ales, in good weather in the sheltered garden where an Aunt Sally pitch – a muscular Oxfordshire pub game – confronts the curious. Many travel to sample chef-patron Danny McGeehan's shortcrust pies – lamb and apricot, a good example; an accomplished menu of British standards considerably extends the choices.

Open 11.30-2.30 7-11 (Sat 11.30-3 7-11 Sun 12-5) Closed 25 Dec, Sun eve **Food** Lunch Mon-Sat 12-2 Dinner Mon-Sat 7-9.30 Set menu available ⊕ FREE HOUSE ◀ Brains The Rev. James, Sharp's Doom Bar, Skinner's Betty Stogs, St Austell Tribute, 2 guest ales ♻ Westons Stowford Press, Thatchers Dry. ₹ 9 **Facilities** Non-diners area ♦ Children's portions Garden ⋈ Parking WiFi ➡ (notice required)

Symbols and abbreviations are explained on page 7

BURCOT
Map 5 SU59

The Chequers

tel: 01865 407771 **OX14 3DP**
email: enquiries@thechequers-burcot.co.uk
dir: *On A415 (Dorchester to Abingdon road) between Clifton Hampden & Dorchester*

Classic British food by the river

Once a staging post for boats on the Thames, this 400-year-old thatched and timber-framed pub is run by chef-patron Steven Sanderson. Locals supply game during the winter, and neighbours' gardens and allotments also yield their bounty. In the kitchen, Steven devises straightforward British classics for his seasonal menus, using carefully chosen meats, fish from Devon and Cornwall markets, mussels from the Norfolk coast, and oysters from Scotland and Jersey. Try diver-caught Orkney scallops with black pudding, parsnip purée, crackling and red wine jus followed by the trio of beef with horseradish mash.

Open all day 12-11 (Sun 12-8) Closed Mon **Food** Lunch Tue-Sat 12-2.30, Sun 12-6 Dinner Tue-Sat 6.15-9 Set menu available Restaurant menu available all wk ⊕ FREE HOUSE ◀ Loose Cannon Abingdon Bridge, Two Cocks, West Berkshire ♻ Westons Stowford Press. ₹ 10 **Facilities** Non-diners area ♦ Children's menu Children's portions Garden ⋈ Parking WiFi ➡ (notice required)

BURFORD
Map 5 SP21

The Angel at Burford ★★★★ INN ⊛

tel: 01993 822714 **14 Witney St OX18 4SN**
email: enquiries@theangelatburford.co.uk web: www.theangelatburford.co.uk

Well presented 16th-century coaching inn

This welcoming Hook Norton house continues to lure real ale drinkers with pints of perfectly kept Hooky, but it also draws the food crowd. The menu offers an all-day bar menu, including a charcuterie board, sandwiches and burgers, alongside the main à la carte. Try the twice baked Manchego soufflé; or beef fillet carpaccio to start; then free-range chicken supreme; smoked haddock kedgeree; or 8oz aged rib-eye steak. If you still have room, treacle tart and Chantilly cream is one choice for those with a sweet tooth. Look out for the summer beer festival.

Open all day all wk **Food** Lunch all wk 12-6 Dinner all wk 6-9.30 Av main course £12.50 Restaurant menu available all wk ⊕ HOOK NORTON BREWERY ◀ Hooky Bitter ♻ Westons Stowford Press. **Facilities** Non-diners area ♥ (Bar Restaurant Garden) ♦ Children's menu Children's portions Garden ⋈ Beer festival WiFi ➡ (notice required) **Rooms** 3

The Highway Inn

tel: 01993 823661 **117 High St OX18 4RG**
email: info@thehighwayinn.co.uk
dir: *From A40 onto A361*

Charming pub in a picturesque Cotswold town

An attractive inn of medieval origin at the heart of pretty Burford; the secluded courtyard garden to the rear is a blissful retreat from the hurly-burly of this ancient town. Beers from the likes of Hook Norton, together with local cider are the order of the day. The relaxing interior, with lots of dressed stone, open fire, bric-à-brac and cosy corners is popular with diners drawn to the unfussy, high-quality menu of seasonal dishes. Cotswold largesse is exampled by mains like oven-roasted breast of pheasant with game jus; home-made pies and the renowned rack of ribs. A beer festival takes place at the beginning of June.

Open all day all wk Mon-Sat 10am-11pm (Sun 12-11) Closed 1st 2wks Jan **Food** Lunch all wk 12-2.30 Dinner all wk 6-9 Set menu available Restaurant menu available all wk ⊕ FREE HOUSE ◀ Hook Norton Hooky Bitter, guest ale ♻ Westons Stowford Press, Cotswold. ₹ 15 **Facilities** Non-diners area ♥ (Bar Outside area) ♦ Children's menu Children's portions Outside area ⋈ Beer festival WiFi

The Inn for All Seasons ★★★ INN   PICK OF THE PUBS

tel: 01451 844324 **The Barringtons OX18 4TN**
email: sharp@innforallseasons.com **web:** www.innforallseasons.com
dir: *3m W of Burford on A40*

Excellent fresh fish specials and extensive wine list

This 17th-century inn has a long history and once witnessed the dispatch of
Cotswold stone for buildings like St Paul's Cathedral. The pub's unusual name was
chosen by former owner Jeremy Taylor, who had worked on the film *A Man for All
Seasons* as a horse choreographer. The Sharp family took over in the mid-1980s
and the interior is a veritable treasure trove of ancient oak beams, leather chairs
and interesting memorabilia. The bar offers St Austell ales, as well as an extensive
wine list. Matthew Sharp selects seasonal local produce for his European cuisine;
he also offers one of the area's best specials boards for fresh fish, with daily
deliveries from Brixham. Main course meat options include roast rack of Cotswold
lamb, tomato and lentil ragout, confit new potatoes, fine beans and basil jus. Finish
with orange cheesecake, poached rhubarb and ginger.

Open all wk 11-3 6-11 (Fri-Sat 11-11) **Food** Lunch all wk 12-3 Dinner all wk
6.30-9.30 Av main course £16 Restaurant menu available all wk ⊕ FREE HOUSE
◀ St Austell Tribute, Shepherd Neame Master Brew ♂ Kingstone Press. ♈ 16
Facilities Non-diners area ❖ (Bar Garden) ♦ Children's menu Children's portions
Play area Family room Garden ⊨ Parking WiFi ▬ **Rooms** 10

The Lamb Inn ★★★ SHL ◉◉◉   PICK OF THE PUBS

tel: 01993 823155 **Sheep St OX18 4LR**
email: info@lambinn-burford.co.uk **web:** www.cotswold-inns-hotels.co.uk/lamb
dir: *M40 junct 8, follow A40 & Burford signs, 1st turn, down hill into Sheep St*

Cotswold charm and lots of style

In a tranquil side street in this attractive Cotswolds town, the 15th-century Lamb is
a dyed-in-the-wool, all round award winner. A welcoming atmosphere is generated
by the bar's flagstone floor, log fire, cosy armchairs, gleaming copper, brass and
silver and, last but not least, Hook Norton and Wickwar real ales. In fact, old-world
charm and stylish interiors are a feature throughout. Take, for example, the elegant
columns and mullioned windows of the courtyard-facing restaurant, where new
chef Peter Galeski presents enticing menus, based extensively on local produce.
Starters such as seared scallops, maple-cured pancetta, roast pumpkin purée and
puffed wild rice could be followed by loin of venison, baby parsnips, red cabbage
purée, ceps, plum, venison pot and juniper berry jus. If you have room for dessert,
choose perhaps white peach soup and compressed peach, chocolate granola and
passionfruit sorbet. The Garden and Fireside menu offers simpler fare — deli
boards; salads; 31-day aged steaks; and dishes such as moules marinière and
braised lamb shank, mash and seasonal vegetables. An extensive cellar holds over
100 wines.

Open all day all wk **Food** all wk 12-9.30 Av main course £15 Set menu available
Restaurant menu available all wk ⊕ FREE HOUSE ◀ Hook Norton Hooky Bitter,
Wickwar Cotswold Way ♂ Cotswold. ♈ 16 **Facilities** Non-diners area ❖ (Bar Garden
Outside area) ♦ Children's menu Children's portions Garden Outside area ⊨
Parking WiFi **Rooms** 17

The Maytime Inn ★★★★ INN

tel: 01993 822068 **Asthall OX18 4HW**
email: info@themaytime.com **web:** www.themaytime.com
dir: *Phone for detailed directions*

Pleasing combination of traditional ambience and eclectic food

Dominic Wood heads up the young and passionate team in this 17th-century
countryside pub that once had its own smithy. You'll find it in the pretty Cotswold
village of Asthall, where the Mitford sisters were raised. The church is worth a visit,
and the manor often hosts public events. There's a large selection of gin (65 and
counting), well-conditioned cask ales, craft beers and ciders plus around 20 wines
by the glass. The ambitious kitchen uses only the finest, fresh local ingredients to
dishes such as seared pigeon breast, blackberry and Puy lentils; pea and broad
bean risotto; and sage and wild boar burger.

Open all day all wk **Food** Lunch all wk 12-3 Dinner all wk 6-9.30 Restaurant menu
available all wk ⊕ FREE HOUSE ◀ Otter Amber, Loose Cannon Abingdon Bridge,
North Cotswold Windrush, Hook Norton Hooky Bitter ♂ Gwynt y Ddraig Black Dragon
& Haymaker, Westons Old Rosie, Pheasant Plucker. ♈ 20 **Facilities** Non-diners area
❖ (All areas) ♦ Children's portions Garden Outside area ⊨ Parking WiFi ▬ (notice
required) **Rooms** 6

BURFORD *continued*

The Mermaid

tel: 01993 822193 **78 High St OX18 4QF**
email: themermaidburford@btconnect.com
dir: *In Burford from A40 rdbt onto A361 signed Chipping Norton. Pub in centre of High St by pedestrian crossing*

Historic town-centre and family-friendly pub

With a long history dating back to the 14th century, an interior with character is only to be expected. The Mermaid certainly does not disappoint. Part of the building once housed a bakery, and today the baker's fireplace still radiates a warmth to match the welcome extended to guests, their children and dogs. Add in the crooked beams, flagstone floors, a candle-lit first-floor restaurant, a choice of four real ales and home-cooked food, and it's no wonder the pub is popular with townspeople and visitors alike. Fresh fish dishes and home-made pies are a speciality, and vegetarian and gluten-free menus are available.

Open all day all wk **Food** Lunch Mon-Fri 11-2.30, Sat 10-9.30, Sun 10-9 Dinner Mon-Fri 6-9 (9.30 in summer), Sat 10-9.30, Sun 10-9 ⊕ GREENE KING ◀ IPA, Morland Old Speckled Hen, Hardys & Hansons Olde Trip. ♥ 10
Facilities Non-diners area ♣ (Bar Outside area) ◀ Children's menu Children's portions Family room Outside area ⌁ WiFi ☎ (notice required)

■ **CHALGROVE**   Map 5 SU69

The Red Lion Inn   PICK OF THE PUBS

tel: 01865 890625 **The High St OX44 7SS**
dir: *B480 from Oxford ring road, through Stadhampton, left then right at mini rdbt. At Chalgrove Airfield right into village*

Historic pub overlooking the village green

Other than the occasional quack of inquisitive ducks, the medieval village of Chalgrove may be tranquil these days but that wasn't the case in 1643 when Prince Rupert clashed with John Hampden's Parliamentarian forces during the first Civil War. The stream-side beer garden of this old inn overlooks the compact green at the heart of the village, where thatched cottages slumber not far from the church which is, unusually, the owner of the pub. In the bar, select from the great range of draught beers complementing the appealing menu created from the best local ingredients by chef-patron Raymond Sexton. The choice may include roulade of smoked salmon with cream cheese and chives, an appetiser for lemon sole fillets 'simply grilled in a little butter', or slow-cooked pork belly with braised vegetables and roast gravy. Finish with sticky toffee pudding or warm treacle tart courtesy of Suzanne Sexton, an accomplished pastry chef.

Open all wk 11-3 6-12 (Fri-Sat 11-3 6-1am Sun all day) **Food** Lunch Mon-Sat 12-2, Sun 12-3 Dinner Mon-Sat 6-9.30 ⊕ FREE HOUSE ◀ Fuller's London Pride, Butcombe, guest ales ♂ Westons Stowford Press, local cider. ♥ 11
Facilities Non-diners area ♣ (Bar Garden) ◀ Children's menu Children's portions Play area Garden ⌁ ☎ (notice required)

■ **CHARLBURY**   Map 11 SP31

The Bull Inn   PICK OF THE PUBS

tel: 01608 810689 **Sheep St OX7 3RR**
email: eat-drink-sleep@bull-inn.com
dir: *M40 junct 8, A40, A44 follow Woodstock/Blenheim Palace signs. Through Woodstock take B4437 to Charlbury, pub at x-roads in town*

Imaginative cooking and Cotswold ales

Presiding over Charlbury's main street, this handsome stone-fronted 16th-century free house, now with new owners, is a conveniently short hop from Woodstock,

Blenheim Palace and other attractions of the Cotswolds. Outside, their vine-covered terrace is a lovely backdrop for a drink or meal in summer. The bar offers Bull Bitter (brewed for the pub) and weekly guest ales. The concise menus might feature beetroot- and gin-cured salmon, cucumber and horseradish cream; steak tartare, cornichons, capers and crème fraîche; local venison, green wheat, spinach and rose harissa; or gilt-head bream, purple sprouting broccoli, samphire and caper butter. For dessert perhaps, forced rhubarb and pear crumble and vanilla ice cream; or sticky toffee pudding, toffee sauce and clotted cream.

Open all wk 10am-11pm (Fri-Sat 10am-12.30am) **Food** all wk all day ⊕ FREE HOUSE ◀ Bull Bitter (brewed for pub), guest ales ♂ Thatchers Gold. ♥ 10
Facilities Non-diners area ◀ Children's portions Garden ⌁ Parking

---

■ **CHASTLETON**   Map 10 SP22

The Greedy Goose

tel: 01608 646551 **Salford Hill GL56 0SP**
email: info@thegreedygoosemoreton.co.uk
dir: *From Chipping Norton towards Moreton-in-Marsh on A44, pub at x-roads junct with A436*

Attractive country pub guarding a crossroads

With no immediate neighbours, The Greedy Goose looks lonely, but it knows how to attract customers. The interior, all intriguingly patterned walls, swathes of polished wood flooring, elegant striped-fabric chairs and much else point to the talents of an interior design pro. A large, part-covered patio also reflects professional design input. In the bar North Cotswold Brewery Windrush Ale, Cotswold Best and Shagweaver monopolise the real ale pumps. The menu favours 'modern, fresh and hearty' dishes such as local sausages with horseradish mash; Moroccan lamb tagine; 'succulent' fish pie; and butternut squash and goats' cheese risotto. Stone-baked pizzas can be ordered to go.

Open all wk **Food** Lunch all wk 12-3 Dinner Mon-Sat 6-9, Sun 6-8 ⊕ FREE HOUSE ◀ North Cotswold Brewery Cotswold Best, Windrush Ale & Shagweaver ♂ Thatchers Gold. **Facilities** Non-diners area ♣ (Bar Garden) ◀ Children's menu Children's portions Family room Garden ⌁ Parking WiFi ☎ (notice required)

■ **CHECKENDON**   Map 5 SU68

The Highwayman ◉   PICK OF THE PUBS

tel: 01491 682020 **Exlade St RG8 0UA**
email: thehighwaymaninn@btconnect.com
dir: *On A4074 (Reading to Wallingford road)*

Desirable food below Chiltern beech woods

The wooded hills of the Chilterns, criss-crossed by bridleways and footpaths, form a constant horizon drifting above the rural location of this attractive old building. Just a stone's throw away is the remarkable Maharaja's Well at nearby Stoke Row, a bracing circular ramble from the inn. Bare brick and beams predominate in the airy interior, interspersed by alcoves and warmed by log-burning stoves in this much updated 16th-century inn, where contented regulars sup beers supplied from the nearby Loddon brewery. The menu is eclectic and strong on locally sourced raw materials. The speciality here is pies; chicken and mushroom bacon pie or game pie may tempt as a follow-up to a cod and crab fishcake starter. Alternatively a bracing walk is well-rewarded with grilled sea bass, greens, croquette potato and brown shrimps, whilst the steaks are from the Royal Windsor Estate. A peaceful rear garden and suntrap terrace aid laid-back summer drinking.

Open 12-3 6-11 (Sun 12-6) Closed 25 Dec, Mon **Food** Lunch Tue-Sat 12-2, Sun 12-3 Dinner Tue-Sat 6-9 Set menu available ⊕ FREE HOUSE ◀ Fuller's London Pride, Loddon Hoppit, Rebellion, guest ale ♂ Tutts Clump. ♥ 11 **Facilities** Non-diners area ♣ (Bar Garden) ◀ Children's portions Garden Outside area ⌁ Parking WiFi ☎ (notice required)

PICK OF THE PUBS

Bear & Ragged Staff ❀

CUMNOR   Map 5 SP40

tel: 01865 862329
28 Appleton Rd OX2 9QH
email: enquiries@bearandraggedstaff.com
web: www.bearandraggedstaff.com
dir: *A420 from Oxford, right onto B4017
signed Cumnor*

Old World charm and modern menus

In typically tranquil Oxfordshire countryside, this 16th-century, stone-built dining pub has a rich history, not least having served as a billet for troops during the English Civil War. While the soldiers were here, Richard Cromwell, son of Oliver and Lord Protector of England, allegedly chiselled away the Royal Crest that once adorned the lintel above one of the doors in the bar, and Sir Walter Scott mentions this very Bear & Ragged Staff in his novel, *Kenilworth*. The chefs here take full advantage of the fresh, seasonal game available from local estates and shoots, since the surrounding woods and farmland teem with pheasant, partridge, deer, muntjac, rabbit, duck and pigeon. From the kitchen come hearty, country-style casseroles, stews, steaks, bangers and mash and other pub classics. Install yourself in one of the traditional bar rooms, all dressed stone and warmed by log fires, relax on the stone-flagged patio, or settle in the comfortable restaurant and ask for the eminently

manageable menu. Create your own sharing platter from a choice of items to begin; then move on to guinea fowl with pumpkin purée, turnip tops, hazelnuts and sage; whole Cornish mackerel with lemon and herb crumb, salsify, leeks and crispy capers; or venison haunch with smoked potato purée, baby beetroot and winter berries. Afterwards there are artisan cheeses with crackers, celery, chutney and grapes, or, for the sweet-toothed, lemon posset with macerated raspberries and ginger biscuit; apple, cinnamon and sultana bread and butter pudding with Calvedos crème anglaise; or Valrhona chocolate and Guinness cake with chocolate sauce and salted caramel ice cream. The Bear has a climbing frame for children and dogs are welcome in the bar area.

Open all day all wk **Food** Contact pub for food times Restaurant menu available all wk ⊕ GREENE KING ◖ Morland Old Speckled Hen, Guinness, guest ales ♂ Aspall, Hogan's. ♟ 20
Facilities Non-diners area ♣ (Bar Outside area) ♦ Children's menu Children's portions Play area Garden Outside area ⋒ Parking WiFi 🚌 (notice required)

CHINNOR
Map 5 SP70

The Sir Charles Napier ◉◉◉
PICK OF THE PUBS

tel: 01494 483011 Spriggs Alley OX39 4BX
dir: M40 junct 6, B4009 to Chinnor. Right at rdbt to Spriggs Alley

An amazing dining experience among the Chiltern beechwoods

Despite being well and truly hidden down rural Oxfordshire lanes, this one is definitely worth seeking out. Named after the British Army general who became commander-in-chief in India in the 19th century, this sublime flint-and-brick destination dining inn is just 10 minutes from the M40. Locally-felled timber fuels the fires in the bars, while further neighbourhood exploitation is evidenced by the hedgerow and field-sourced herbs, fungi, berries and game. You can eat inside, on the vine-covered terrace or under the cherry trees beside Michael Cooper's big, black marble sculptures and watch red kites soaring overhead. Once you negotiated their extensive and highly praised wine list take a look at the blackboards and seasonally inspired menus. Here you could find dishes such as Cornish crab, kohlrabi, white soy and coriander; venison tartare with coal oil and charred focaccia; yuzu-glazed Goosnargh duck, confit leg, croustillant, carrot and cumin; roast stone bass with linguine, mussels and samphire; and braised ox cheek, horseradish mash, oyster beignet and red wine jus.

Open 12-4 6-12 (Sun 12-6) Closed 25-26 Dec, Mon, Sun eve Food Lunch Tue-Fri 12-2.30 Dinner Tue-Fri 6.30-9 Av main course £14.50 Set menu available Restaurant menu available Tue-Sun ⊕ FREE HOUSE ◀ Rebellion. ▼12 Facilities Non-diners area ◉ Children's menu Children's portions Garden ☂ Parking WiFi

CHURCH ENSTONE
Map 11 SP32

The Crown Inn
PICK OF THE PUBS

tel: 01608 677262 Mill Ln OX7 4NN
email: crown_inn@btconnect.com
dir: From A44 at Enstone (15m N of Oxford) onto B4030 signed Church Enstone

Box-ticking Cotswold-stone village pub

If log fires in an inglenook, old village photos on the walls of a traditional rustic bar, and a beamed dining room sound like your type of pub, then look no further. Similarly, if you'd enjoy a pint of Hook Norton Hooky Bitter, or a glass of Pinot Grigio on a cottage garden terrace overlooking thatched, honey-coloured stone cottages, Tony and Caroline Warburton's 17th-century inn will tick even more boxes. The couple have a well-earned reputation for food, based partly on Tony's speciality, fish, although steak pie is also given top billing. In the slate-floored conservatory, the compact menu might offer fettuccine with mushrooms, rocket, pesto and cream; and roast belly of Cotswold pork, with apple sauce, crackling and cider gravy. Among the day's specials might be breaded John Dory fillets with chips and mushy peas; or winter vegetable, sweet potato, bean and spinach curry with rice.

Open all wk 12-3 6-11 (Sun 12-4) Closed 26 Dec, 1 Jan Food Lunch all wk 12-2 Dinner Mon-Sat 7-9 Av main course £11 Set menu available ⊕ FREE HOUSE ◀ Hook Norton Hooky Bitter, Timothy Taylor Landlord, Wychwood Hobgoblin ♂ Westons Stowford Press. ▼8 Facilities Non-diners area ◉ Children's portions Garden ☂ Parking

CUMNOR
Map 5 SP40

Bear & Ragged Staff ◉
PICK OF THE PUBS

See Pick of the Pubs on page 387

The Vine Inn

tel: 01865 862567 11 Abingdon Rd OX2 9QN
email: info@vineinncumnor.com
dir: A420 from Oxford, right onto B4017

Well kept ales and a large garden

A vine does indeed clamber over the whitewashed frontage of this 18th-century village pub. In 1560, nearby Cumnor Place was the scene of the suspicious death of the wife of Lord Robert Dudley, favourite of Elizabeth I; the house was pulled down in 1810. There's a selection of rotating real ales in the carpeted bar, and a typical starters include traditional prawn cocktail; whitebait; or calamari and salad; followed by a meat, fish or oven-baked camembert sharing plate; or perhaps chilli con carne or one of the burger choices. Children love the huge garden.

Open all wk 12-3 6-11.30 (Fri-Sun all day) ⊕ PUNCH TAVERNS ◀ Sharp's Doom Bar, Brakspear, Hobgoblin, guest ales ♂ Somersby. Facilities ❀ (Bar Garden) ◉ Children's menu Children's portions Play area Garden Parking WiFi

DEDDINGTON
Map 11 SP43

Deddington Arms ★★★ HL
PICK OF THE PUBS

tel: 01869 338364 Horsefair OX15 0SH
email: deddarms@oxfordshire-hotels.co.uk web: www.deddington-arms-hotel.co.uk
dir: M40 junct 11 to Banbury. Follow signs for hospital, then towards Adderbury & Deddington, on A4260

Good country pub fare in a 16th-century inn

Overlooking Deddington's pretty market square, this striking 16th-century former coaching inn boasts a wealth of timbering, flagstone floors, numerous nooks and crannies, crackling winter log fires and sought-after window seats in the beamed bar. Here you can savour a glass of Hook Norton or Somersby cider while perusing the menu. Eat in the bar or head for the elegant dining room, where you can kick off a meal with feta and tabouleh salad; or smoked halibut with shaved fennel and orange. Continue with another fish course – baked fillet of cod with Puy lentils, wilted greens and parsley juice. Desserts are old favourites ranging from black cherry and dark chocolate baked Alaska to sticky toffee pudding with toffee sauce and vanilla ice cream. The cheese selection tempts with notable products from around the UK, such as Colston Bassett Stilton, Welsh Bomber Cheddar, Miss Muffet from Cornwall, Waterloo from Berkshire and North Yorkshire's Ribblesdale.

Open all day all wk 11am-mdnt (Sun 11-11) Food Lunch all wk 12-2.30 Dinner all wk 6-9.30 Av main course £13-£16 Set menu available Restaurant menu available all wk ⊕ FREE HOUSE ◀ Adnams, Hook Norton, 2 guest ales ♂ Somersby. ▼8 Facilities Non-diners area ◉ Children's menu Children's portions Parking WiFi ▭ (notice required) Rooms 27

NEW The Unicorn Inn ★★★ INN ◉

tel: 01869 338838 Market Place OX15 0SE
email: info@unicorndeddington.co.uk web: www.unicorndeddington.co.uk
dir: On A4260 between Oxford & Banbury

Newly refurbished and making a name for itself

Historians date the inn to the 17th century, although the façade you see is a 19th-century addition. A well-kept cellar supplies the charming bar and snug, both with open and warming fireplaces. The lunch menu embraces sandwiches, burgers, starters and mains, among which look for Loch Duart salmon and smoked haddock fishcake, and Kelmscott pork sausages with mustard mash. A similar dinner menu line-up in the contemporary restaurant might additionally include roast breast of Norfolk chicken with wild mushroom, smoked bacon and pearl barley risotto; and fillet of sea bream with new potatoes, wilted greens and brown shrimp butter sauce. The garden is a good size.

Open all day all wk 12-close **Food** Lunch Mon-Sat 12-2.30, Sun 12-4 Dinner Mon-Thu 6.30-9, Fri-Sat 6.30-9.30 Av main course £14 Set menu available ⊕ CHARLES WELLS ◖ Eagle IPA & Bombardier ♂ Symonds. ₹ 12 **Facilities** Non-diners area ✿ (Bar Garden) ◖◗ Children's menu Children's portions Garden ⋈ Beer festival WiFi ▦ (notice required) **Rooms** 6

DORCHESTER (ON THAMES)   Map 5 SU59

The George   PICK OF THE PUBS

See Pick of the Pubs on page 390

DUNS TEW   Map 11 SP42

NEW The White Horse

tel: 01869 340272 **OX25 6JS**
email: info@dunstewwhitehorse.co.uk
dir: *Take A4260 from Banbury towards Adderbury. Right signed Duns Tew. Pub on left in village. Or from M40 junct 10, A43, B430 to Ardley. Right signed Somerton. Through Somerton & North Aston to x-roads. Straight across signed Duns Tew*

Home-made food in a fabulous Cotswold pub

A beautiful Cotswold stone pub, dating from the 17th century and full of wonderful period features – panelling, beams, and open fires. Newly refurbished with love and care, The White Horse is welcoming and friendly. You'll find three real ales in the blue-tiled bar, and top-quality British produce on the menus. Everything's home made, seasonal, and thoughtfully prepared. Smoked haddock fishcakes come with lemon and watercress, and soy and ginger pork belly with pickled carrot, radish and coriander.

Open all day all wk **Food** Lunch all wk 12-2.30 (ex Mon in winter) Dinner all wk 6-9 Av main course £12.50 Set menu available Restaurant menu available all wk ⊕ GREENE KING ◖ Ruddles ♂ Aspall. ₹ **Facilities** Non-diners area ✿ (Bar Garden Outside area) ◖◗ Children's portions Garden Outside area ⋈ Parking WiFi ▦ (notice required)

EAST HENDRED   Map 5 SU48

Eyston Arms

tel: 01235 833320 **High St OX12 8JY**
email: info@eystonarms.co.uk
dir: *Just off A417 (Wantage to Reading road)*

A family-owned local favourite

Owned, appropriately, by the Eyston family, who have lived in the village since 1443, this old inn stands just north of the prehistoric track known as The Ridgeway. With some of its original look revealed by renovations, the pub greets its customers with a huge log fire, flagstone floor, simple polished tables, leather chairs and cartoons of its regulars. The bar stocks real ales from Wadworth and Hook Norton. Chef Maria Jaremchuk's ever-changing menus may feature seafood pasta; chargrilled steaks; and wild boar burgers while carefully cultivated contacts with south coast fishermen mean excellent fish specials.

Open all day all wk 11-3 6-11 (Fri-Sat 11-11 Sun 11-9) **Food** Lunch Mon-Sat 12-2, Sun 12-4 Dinner Mon-Sat 6-9 Av main course £16 Set menu available Restaurant menu available Mon-Sat ⊕ FREE HOUSE ◖ Hook Norton, Wadworth 6X ♂ Aspall, Westons Stowford Press. **Facilities** ✿ (Bar Restaurant Outside area) ◖◗ Children's portions Garden Outside area ⋈ Parking WiFi

FARINGDON   Map 5 SU29

The Lamb at Buckland   PICK OF THE PUBS

tel: 01367 870484 **Lamb Ln, Buckland SN7 8QN**
email: thelambatbuckland@googlemail.com
dir: *Just off A420, 3m E of Faringdon*

Hearty, well-made food and friendly service

So often the word 'Cotswold' prefixes 'stone', but today it can also appear on the labels of the gin, vodka and lager available at the 17th-century Lamb, because they're all made in nearby Bourton-on-the-Water. The pub lies down a cul-de-sac in a group of similar-vintage cottages. Owners Richard and Shelley Terry are experienced chefs, although Shelley is usually front-of-house. Localness is paramount, as testified, for example, by the real ales, the game shot by a pub regular, and the many vegetables grown in the kitchen garden. Typical dishes include twice baked cheese soufflé with apple salad; locally-sourced venison sausages, creamed potato, caramelised onions and red wine jus; smoked haddock fillet, buttered spinach and sweetcorn cream; and pan-roasted duck breast, spiced sticky pear, cavolo nero and fondant potato. Among the desserts are ice peanut butter parfait with chocolate sauce; and orange and almond tart. Steak Night is every Wednesday.

Open all wk 11.30-3 6-11 Closed Sun eve, Mon **Food** Lunch Tue-Sat 12-2, Sun 12-3 Dinner Tue-Sat 7-9 Av main course £12 ⊕ FREE HOUSE ◖ Flying Monk, Ramsbury Gold, West Berkshire Good Old Boy, Loose Cannon Abingdon Bridge. ₹ 12 **Facilities** Non-diners area ✿ (Bar Restaurant Garden) ◖◗ Children's portions Garden ⋈ Parking WiFi

The Trout Inn ★★★★ INN ◉   PICK OF THE PUBS

tel: 01367 870382 **Buckland Marsh SN7 8RF**
email: info@troutinn.co.uk **web:** www.troutinn.co.uk
dir: *A415 from Abingdon signed Marcham, through Frilford to Kingston Bagpuize. Left onto A420. 5m, right signed Tadpole Bridge. Or M4 (E'bound) junct 15, A419 towards Cirencester. 4m, onto A420 towards Oxford. 10m, left signed Tadpole Bridge*

Famous Thames-side free house in new hands

It's not just trout that grace the walls in this lovely stone pub by an ancient bridge over the River Thames; for instance, there's a rather fine rhino-headed lamp bracket and sundry stags' heads too. The Trout is inevitably popular with boaters, and walkers from the Thames Path that runs along the bank opposite the pub's garden, a pleasant space clearly intended for those nursing a pint of locally brewed Abingdon Bridge, Ramsbury Bitter or Wayland Smithy, or a chilled Pinot Grigio. Maintaining the menu requires fish and seafood to arrive daily from Cornwall, game from area shoots, and fruit, herbs and vegetables from local growers. Try charred pollack Thai curry with pak choi and pistachios; guinea fowl with sweet potato and buttered leeks; or chargrilled rainbow trout with crayfish butter and fries. Kelmscott Manor, the remarkable home of 19th-century artist and designer, William Morris, is up the road.

Open all day all wk **Food** Lunch all wk 12-2.30 Dinner Mon-Sat 6.30-9, Sun 6.30-8.30 Av main course £17 ⊕ FREE HOUSE ◖ Ramsbury Bitter, Young's Bitter, White Horse Wayland Smithy, Loose Cannon Abingdon Bridge, Prescott Chequered Flag ♂ Orchard Pig Reveller. ₹ 15 **Facilities** Non-diners area ✿ (Bar Restaurant Garden) ◖◗ Children's menu Children's portions Garden ⋈ Parking WiFi **Rooms** 6

PICK OF THE PUBS

The George

DORCHESTER (ON THAMES) Map 5 SU59

tel: 01865 340404 **25 High St OX10 7HH**
email: georgedorchester@relaxinnz.co.uk
web: www.georgedorchester.relaxinnz.co.uk
dir: *From M40 junct 7, A329 S to A4074
at Shillingford. Follow Dorchester signs.
From M4 junct 13, A34 to Abingdon then
A415 E to Dorchester*

Take a step back in time at this friendly inn

The multi-gabled, 15th-century George stands in the old town's picturesque high street, opposite the 12th-century Dorchester Abbey. Believed to be one of the country's oldest coaching inns, it has been a welcome haven for many an aristocrat, including Sarah Churchill, the first Duchess of Marlborough, while much later the non-aristocratic author D H Lawrence favoured it with his presence. Oak beams and inglenook fireplaces characterise the interior, while the elevated restaurant offers a secret garden with a waterfall. The Potboys Bar, apparently named after the Abbey bell-ringers, is a traditional taproom and therefore unquestionably the right place to enjoy a pint from one of the six breweries that make up The George's roll of honour while tucking into pasta carbonara with garlic bread; bangers and mash with gravy; or an 8oz rump steak with fat chips from the bar menu. Food is all locally sourced: the

Abbey gardens, for example, supply all the herbs, customers contribute the occasional home-grown vegetables, and local shoots provide pheasants. In Carriages Restaurant the menu offers confit of crisp belly pork with Puy lentils, local Toulouse sausages and crushed new potatoes; coq au vin with roasted garlic croûtons and celeriac mash; fresh and smoked fish pie with potato and cheddar cheese glaze; and butternut squash risotto with red onion, fresh herbs, white truffle oil and parmesan shavings. Expect white chocolate and marmalade bread and butter pudding with Disaronno custard, and Eton Mess for dessert. There are extensive gardens to enjoy.

Open all day all wk 7am-mdnt
Food Lunch all wk 12-3 Dinner all wk 6-9 ⊕ CHAPMANS GROUP ▪ Wadworth 6X, Skinner's Betty Stogs, Fuller's London Pride, Sharp's Doom Bar, Butcombe, Hook Norton ☼ Westons Stowford Press. **Facilities** Non-diners area ♦ Children's menu Children's portions Garden Outside area ⊼ Beer festival Parking WiFi 🚌

FILKINS
Map 5 SP20

The Five Alls
PICK OF THE PUBS

tel: 01367 860875 **GL7 3JQ**
email: info@thefiveallsfilkins.co.uk
dir: *Between Lechlade & Burford, just off A361*

A class act in the Cotswolds

The Five Alls, in picture-postcard Filkins, is very successfully run by Sebastian and Lana Snow. The pub's interior oozes warmth and style, with rugs on stone floors, flickering candles on old dining tables, and a leather chesterfield fronting the log fire – the perfect spot to relax with a pint and the papers. The bar bustles with locals, walkers and cyclists supping pints of Brakspear Oxford Gold or Wychwood Hobgoblin and tucking into proper bar snacks (devilled kidneys or a plate of Serrano ham perhaps), while the concise modern British menu bristles with quality, locally sourced ingredients, draws diners from far and wide across the Cotswolds. Typically, you'll find roast rare beef salad; potted shrimps; and eggs Benedict, florentine or royale as a starter, then for the main event, confit duck leg, braised red cabbage, watercress and rösti potato; blackened cod with bok choy, glass noodles, ginger, chilli and scallions; or tagliata of beef with roasties, wild mushrooms and parmesan shavings.

Open all day Closed 25 Dec, Sun eve **Food** Lunch all wk 12-2.30 Dinner Mon-Sat 6-9.30 Set menu available Restaurant menu available all wk ⊕ BRAKSPEAR ⬛ Oxford Gold, Ringwood, Wychwood Hobgoblin Ò Thatchers.
Facilities Non-diners area ❄ (Bar Restaurant Garden) ❙❙ Children's menu Children's portions Play area Garden ⋔ Parking WiFi 🚌

FRINGFORD
Map 11 SP62

The Butchers Arms

tel: 01869 277363 **OX27 8EB**
email: tg53@sky.com
dir: *4m from Bicester on A4421 towards Buckingham*

Charming pub next to the village green

Flora Jane Thompson, author of *Lark Rise to Candleford,* was born at Juniper Hill, a couple of miles from this pretty, creeper-covered pub, and her first job was in the Post Office in Fringford. In her writings, Juniper Hill became Lark Rise, Fringford became Candleford Green, and Buckingham and Banbury metamorphosed into Candleford. Handpumps dispense Doom Bar, Hooky and Black Sheep, while the menu, on chalk boards, offers a good traditional selection including home-made pies; liver, bacon and onions; king prawns; and mussels. There's a senior citizens lunch offer six days a week. You can watch the cricket from the patio and in June there's a beer festival.

Open all day all wk **Food** Lunch Mon-Sat 12-2.30 Dinner Tue-Sat 6.30-9 Av main course £10.95 ⊕ PUNCH TAVERNS ⬛ Sharp's Doom Bar, Black Sheep, Hook Norton Hooky Bitter Ò Thatchers Katy, Westons Stowford Press. **Facilities** Non-diners area ❄ (Bar Outside area) ❙❙ Children's menu Children's portions Outside area ⋔ Beer festival Parking WiFi 🚌 (notice required)

FYFIELD
Map 5 SU49

The White Hart ◉◉
PICK OF THE PUBS

See Pick of the Pubs on page 392

GALLOWSTREE COMMON
Map 5 SU68

The Reformation

tel: 0118 972 3126 **Horsepond Rd RG4 9BP**
email: info@therefpub.com
dir: *From A4074 between Reading & Wallingford follow signs for Gallowstree Common*

Diners, drinkers, children, muddy boots and dogs all very welcome

Set in an Area of Outstanding Natural Beauty, this friendly pub is a busy place, with plenty going on. There are regular charity 'tractor runs' and barbecues in the summer, live music monthly, and themed dining evenings, as well as beer festivals in May and October. You'll find very well-kept Brakspear ales here, and guests too, and the classic pub menu, with ingredients sourced locally where possible, might feature pan-fried scallops with chilli jam; or potted Devon crab with ginger and spring onion; and mains such as wild mushroom pie; or pork belly with chorizo, black pudding, leek hash and a fried duck egg; with sticky toffee pudding to finish. Their philosophy? 'We're a pub that serves food, not a restaurant that serves beer.'

Open 12-3 5.30-11 (Sat 12-4 6-11 Sun 12-5) Closed Sun eve & Mon **Food** Lunch Tue-Fri 12-2.30, Sat-Sun 12-4 Dinner Tue-Sat 6-9 ⊕ BRAKSPEAR ⬛ Bitter, Wychwood Hobgoblin, seasonal ales Ò Symonds, Orchard Pig. ⬤ 11
Facilities Non-diners area ❄ (Bar Restaurant Garden) ❙❙ Children's menu Children's portions Play area Family room Garden ⋔ Beer festival Parking WiFi 🚌 (notice required)

GORING
Map 5 SU68

The Miller of Mansfield ★★★★ RR ◉◉ PICK OF THE PUBS

tel: 01491 872829 **High St RG8 9AW**
email: mary.galer@millerofmansfield.com **web:** www.millerofmansfield.com
dir: *From Pangbourne take A329 to Streatley. Right on B4009, 0.5m to Goring*

A beautiful focal point for the village

Run by Nick and Mary Galer, this creeper-clad 18th-century coaching inn is set in an upmarket village just a hop, step and a jump from the River Thames, with the rolling Berkshire and Oxfordshire countryside beyond. Shiny wooden floors, fat candles on scrubbed tables, log fires and local ales Good Old Boy and Old Hooky characterise the bar, while a restaurant overview must mention its Philippe Starck-influenced design. Menus full of flavour have earned two AA Rosettes but remain keenly priced. Who would quibble with a nibble of proper sausage rolls and brown sauce? A typical fixed-price lunch could comprise whipped Baron Bigod cheese with quince jam and tomato relish, candied hazelnuts and treacle toast; whole roasted local partridge with bacon and shallot potato cake, Brussels tops, Jerusalem artichokes and partridge sauce; followed by Cox apple tart with Calvados crème fraîche. In the evening, look to the carte for a crispy free-range egg with cured salmon, smoked onions and black pudding, with maybe slow-cooked ling with buttered potatoes, parsley purée, mussels and clams for a main course.

Open all day all wk **Food** Lunch Mon-Sat 12-2.30, Sun 12-3.30 Dinner Mon-Sat 6-9, Sun 6-8 Set menu available ⊕ ENTERPRISE INNS ⬛ Hook Norton Old Hooky, West Berkshire Good Old Boy Ò Aspall, Thatchers. ⬤ 11 **Facilities** Non-diners area ❄ (Bar Outside area) ❙❙ Children's menu Children's portions Outside area ⋔ Parking WiFi 🚌 (notice required) **Rooms** 13

PICK OF THE PUBS

The White Hart ❀❀

FYFIELD   Map 5 SU49

tel: 01865 390585
Main Rd OX13 5LW
email: info@whitehart-fyfield.com
web: www.whitehart-fyfield.com
dir: *7m S of Oxford, just off A420
(Oxford to Swindon road)*

Confident cooking in picturesque village inn

Mark and Kay Chandler's 500-year-old former chantry house is steeped in history and has been a pub since 1580 when St John's College in Oxford leased it to tenants but reserved the right to 'occupy it if driven from Oxford by pestilence' — so far this has not been invoked! The building is breathtaking and boasts a grand hall with a 15th-century arch-braced roof, original oak beams, flagstone floors, and huge stone-flanked windows. For a table with a view there's still a splendid 30ft high minstrels' gallery overlooking the restaurant. Study the wonderful history and architecture over a pint of local Loose Cannon Abingdon Bridge, Loddon Hullabaloo or Sharp's Doom Bar, or one of the 14 wines served by the glass in the character bar — in winter arrive early to bag the table beside the roaring fire. Awarded two AA Rosettes for his food, chef/owner Mark is steadfast in his pursuit of fresh, seasonal food from trusted local suppliers and their own kitchen garden provides a regular

supply of fruit and vegetables. Mark's cooking reveals a high level of technical skill and his menus change daily, perhaps featuring rabbit, langoustine and artichoke crumble, wild garlic crust; or sweet potato and orange soup among the starters. To follow, try slow-roasted belly of Kelmscott pork, apple, carrots, celeriac purée, crackling and cider jus; or roast skate wing, sea vegetables, new potatoes and cockle butter. Then sticky rum and date sponge, hazelnut tuille, caramelised bananas. Fish, antipasti or meze sharing boards are great for nibbles. The lunchtime set menu is great value.

Open 12-3 5.30-11 (Sat 12-11 Sun 12-10.30) Closed Mon (ex BHs)
Food Lunch Tue-Sat 12-2.30, Sun

12-3.30 Dinner Tue-Sat 6.45-9.30, Set menu available ⊕ FREE HOUSE
🍺 Sharp's Doom Bar, Loddon Hullabaloo, Loose Cannon Abingdon Bridge, guest ales Ö Thatchers Cheddar Valley & Gold. ♍ 14
Facilities Non-diners area
👫 Children's menu Children's portions Play area Garden ☐ Parking WiFi
🚌 (notice required)

GREAT TEW
Map 11 SP42

The Falkland Arms
PICK OF THE PUBS

tel: 01608 683653 **OX7 4DB**
email: falklandarms@wadworth.co.uk
dir: *Off A361, 1.25m, signed Great Tew*

Ancient inn replete with English character

Named after Lucius Carey, 2nd Viscount Falkland, who inherited the manor of Great Tew in 1629, this venerable creeper-clad inn (now in new hands), at the end of a charming row of Cotswold-stone cottages, is a classic. Its wooden floors, exposed beams, high-backed settles, low stools and an inglenook fireplace characterise the intimate bar; a huge collection of beer and cider mugs and jugs hangs from the ceiling. Wadworth ales vary from the well-known such as 6X, to various seasonals from the brewery's Victorian Brew House and Beer Kitchen. The menu mixes modern with traditional, but attention to the provenance of ingredients is an overriding factor here. Small plates include faggots, mashed potatoes with onion gravy. The butcher's board presents pork pie, chicken liver pâté, honey-roast ham, Scotch egg, chutney and rustic bread. Expect to find poached salmon or pan-seared chicken breast among the main courses. Finish with bread and butter pudding or a seasonal fruit crumble.

Open all day all wk 8am-11pm **Food** Lunch all wk 12-2.30 Dinner all wk 6.30-9.30 ⊕ WADWORTH ◀ 6X, Henry's Original IPA & Horizon, guest ales ♂ Thatchers Heritage. ♎ 14 **Facilities** Non-diners area ❤ (Bar Restaurant Garden) ♦♦ Children's portions Garden ☎ Beer festival WiFi ☎ (notice required)

HAILEY
Map 11 SP31

The Lamb Inn ◉◉
PICK OF THE PUBS

tel: 01993 708792 **Steep Hill, Crawley OX29 9TW**
email: lambcrawley@yahoo.co.uk
dir: *From Witney (B4047), follow signs for Crawley*

Pretty village inn popular with walkers

Popular with walkers because of its routes from Minster Lovell and the Windrush River, this 18th-century village pub is located just outside Witney. Oak beams and Cotswold-stone walls are reminders of the pub's vintage, although a BBQ and brick pizza oven in the garden indicate a more contemporary approach to hospitality. Ales brewed nearby can be found on the hand pumps, with Somerset cider also on tap, perhaps with a bar snack of home-made pork scratchings or chilli rice crackers. Local produce drives the menu, from a starter of Carney goats' cheese, poached pear, gingerbread, beetroot and truffle honey to a main course of Butt's Farm rare breed pork belly, creamed cabbage and bacon, mustard, champ potatoes, rhubarb and cider gravy. Leave space for one of the comforting puddings – perhaps dark chocolate with roasted banana, bayleaf ice cream and lime.

Open 12-3 6-11 (Sat-Sun all day) Closed Mon & Tue **Food** Lunch Wed-Thu 12-2, Fri-Sat 12-2.30, Sun 12.30-2.30 Dinner Wed-Thu 6.30-9, Fri-Sat 6.30-9.30, Sun 7-9 Restaurant menu available Wed-Sun (ex Sun L) ⊕ BRAKSPEAR ◀ Bitter & Oxford Gold ♂ Thatchers Gold. ♎ 13 **Facilities** Non-diners area ❤ (Bar Garden) ♦♦ Children's menu Children's portions Garden ☎ Parking WiFi ☎ (notice required)

HAMPTON POYLE
Map 11 SP51

The Bell
PICK OF THE PUBS

tel: 01865 376242 **OX5 2QD**
email: contactus@thebelloxford.co.uk
dir: *From N: exit A34 signed Kidlington, over bridge. At mini rdbt turn right, left to Hampton Poyle (before slip road to rejoin A34). From Kidlington: at rdbt (junct of A4260 & A4165) take Bicester Rd (Sainsbury's on left) towards A34. Left to Hampton Poyle*

Good food and welcoming, professional staff

A centuries-old inn that is independent and privately owned, and conveniently sited for Oxford, Bicester Village shopping outlet and Blenheim Palace. The charms of its oak beams and time-worn flagstone floors are complemented by the dining area with an open kitchen featuring an eye-catching wood-burning oven, from which are produced rustic pizzas and other dishes. These, along with burgers and salads, are served in the bar at any time. There are plenty of other dishes to choose from including game terrine with cornichons, caramelised shallots and toast; and cold rare beef sirloin with celeriac remoulade, string chips, mustard and horseradish. Finish with ginger and lemon syrup sponge with rhubarb compôte and custard. Should you have a well-behaved dog, he or she will be welcome to join you in the bar or out on the delightful south-facing terrace.

Open all day all wk 7am-11pm **Food** Lunch Mon-Sat 12-2.30, Sun 12-3 Dinner Sun-Thu 6-9, Fri-Sat 6.30-9.30 Set menu available ⊕ FREE HOUSE ◀ Hook Norton Hooky Bitter, Wye Valley Butty Bach, Sharp's Doom Bar ♂ Thatchers Gold. ♎ 10 **Facilities** Non-diners area ❤ (Bar Garden Outside area) ♦♦ Children's portions Family room Garden Outside area ☎ Parking WiFi ☎ (notice required)

HARWELL
Map 5 SU48

The Hart of Harwell

tel: 01235 834511 **High St OX11 0EH**
email: info@hartofharwell.com
dir: *In village centre, accessed from A417 & A4130*

Village pub with unusual wells and great food

Several old wells were found during renovations of this 15th to 16th-century pub, and one now serves as a dining table. You can peer down it while eating – an unusual diversion. The modern bar's stable of Greene King real ales is supplemented by regularly-changing guests. Sandwiches are served at lunchtime only, while the main menu covers both lunch and dinner, so either meal could feature a pulled pork, pickles and toast starter, followed by, say, treacle baked ham with egg, chips and peas; or perhaps beef and Guinness pie with cabbage and mash; and, to end, ginger pear and black cherry crumble with vanilla custard.

Open all wk 12-3 5.30-11 (Fri-Sat 12-12 Sun 12-11) ⊕ GREENE KING ◀ Morland Old Speckled Hen & Original, Hardys & Hansons Olde Trip, Guinness ♂ Thatchers Gold. **Facilities** ❤ (Bar Garden) ♦♦ Children's menu Children's portions Garden Parking WiFi

PICK OF THE PUBS

The Cherry Tree Inn ★★★★ INN ❀

tel: 01491 680430
Stoke Row RG9 5QA
email: enquiries@thecherrytreeinn.co.uk
web: www.thecherrytreeinn.co.uk
dir: *B481 towards Reading & Sonning Common 2m, follow Stoke Row sign*

British and European food at smart inn

Originally three flint cottages, the 400-year-old Cherry Tree's interior has strong colours and modern, comfortable furnishings that look good alongside the original flagstone floors, beamed ceilings and fireplaces. Brakspear's Bitter and Special and seasonal ales are on handpump in the bar, where there is also a good range of malt whiskies, chilled vodkas and wines by the glass. An eat-anywhere policy means freedom to enjoy any of the British and European dishes in the bar, restaurant or large garden. Local produce is used throughout the menu, with items such as lobster, oysters and game available in season. Try and decide between a starter of rabbit and black pudding terrine with cherry chutney; or salmon and green bean Thai fishcakes with a green onion salad perhaps, before moving onto red pepper marinated sea bass fillet, crushed potatoes and coriander oil; Barbary duck breast, braised red cabbage and dauphinoise potatoes; or spiced bean goulash, deep fried courgette and tomato bulgar wheat. Desserts are no less tempting – mocha profiteroles dipped in white chocolate; and kiwi and lime cheesecake to name just two. Chalkboards offer daily specials, and Sunday roasts feature Scottish prime beef, Yorkshire pudding, roast potatoes, fresh vegetables and home-made horseradish. Children may eat in the dining rooms until 8pm, choosing from a menu that includes grilled fresh chicken and chips; pork and leek sausages and mash; and fish and chips. The large south-facing garden makes fine-weather dining a pleasure. All around is the Chilterns Area of Outstanding Natural Beauty.

Open all day all wk **Food** Lunch Mon-Fri 12-3, Sat-Sun all day Dinner Mon-Fri 6.30-10, Sat-Sun all day 🍺 BRAKSPEAR 🍺 Brakspear & Special, guest ale 🍎 Symonds. 🍷 **Facilities** Non-diners area 🐾 (Bar Restaurant Garden) 👨‍👧 Children's menu Children's portions Garden 🍺 Beer festival Parking WiFi 🚐 (notice required) **Rooms** 4

Map 5 SU78

The Cherry Tree Inn ★★★★ INN 🏵   PICK OF THE PUBS

See Pick of the Pubs on opposite page

The Little Angel

tel: 01491 411008 **Remenham Ln RG9 2LS**
email: enquiries@thelittleangel.co.uk **web:** www.thelittleangel.co.uk
dir: *M4 juncts 8 & 9, A404, A4130 to Henley, then towards Maidenhead. Pub on left*

Spacious and busy pub with an inviting interior

This large whitewashed pub, just over the famous bridge from the town, gets pretty packed, especially at weekends. The chic interior features wooden floorboards, duck-egg blue tones with warming accents, an open fire, and spacious bar and dining areas. Other attractions are the well-compiled wine list, the Brakspear ales, and the exceptional modern menu, which is changed quarterly. Try game terrine with celeriac remoulade and toasted Lawler's bread; pan-fried black bream fillet with braised fennel, samphire and sauce vièrge; and poached pear in mulled red wine, with fig and sherry frozen yogurt. Sundays are 'unbelievably busy' so booking is essential, but don't worry, lunch is served all day.

Open all day all wk 11-11 (Fri-Sat 11am-mdnt Sun 12-10) **Food** Lunch Mon-Fri 12-3, Sat-Sun all day Dinner Mon-Fri 7-10 Set menu available Restaurant menu available all wk ⊕ BRAKSPEAR ◀ Brakspear, Oxford Gold, Guinness, seasonal ales ♂ Symonds. ♟ 11 **Facilities** Non-diners area ♣ (Bar Restaurant Garden) ♦♦ Children's menu Children's portions Garden ⊓ Parking WiFi ▄▄ (notice required)

See advert on page 396

The Three Tuns

tel: 01491 410138 & 01865 891118 **5 The Market Place RG9 2AA**
email: info@threetunshenley.co.uk
dir: *In town centre. Parking nearby*

Known for its warm and friendly service

One of the oldest pubs in town, the cosy, matchboarded front bar has scrubbed tables, an open fire and Brakspear Brewery prints from a bygone era. Successfully run by Mark and Sandra Duggan, this is a bustling drinking and dining spot. From the cosy and intimate dining room, a passageway leads to the suntrap terrace garden. Freshly sourced local produce (the butcher is only next door) underpins menus both traditional and modern – salt and chilli squid with saffron aïoli; pan-fried calves' liver, bacon and onions; and a chargrilled 8oz rib-eye steak with home-cut chips. There is live music every Sunday evening in the front bar.

Open all day 11.30-11 (Sat 11am-mdnt Sun 11-10) Closed 25 Dec, Mon (ex BHs) **Food** Lunch Tue-Sat 12-3, Sun 12-4 Dinner Tue-Sat 6-9.45 Set menu available ⊕ BRAKSPEAR ◀ Special, Oxford Gold & Bitter ♂ Symonds. ♟ 20 **Facilities** Non-diners area ♣ (Bar Garden Outside area) ♦♦ Children's portions Garden Outside area ⊓ ▄▄ (notice required)

The White Hart   PICK OF THE PUBS

tel: 01491 641245 **High St, Nettlebed RG9 5DD**
email: whitehart@tmdining.co.uk
dir: *On A4130 between Henley-on-Thames & Wallingford*

History and tradition blend with stylish modernity

Royalist and parliamentary soldiers frequently lodged in taverns during the English Civil War; this 15th-century inn reputedly billeted troops loyal to the King. During the 17th and 18th centuries the area was plagued by highwaymen, including the notorious Isaac Darkin who was eventually caught, tried and hung at Oxford Gaol. Today the beautifully restored property is favoured by a stylish crowd who appreciate the chic bar and restaurant. Heading the beer list is locally-brewed Brakspear, backed by popular internationals and a small selection of cosmopolitan bottles. Food comprises typically English dishes interspersed with South African offerings such as grilled boerewors, polenta and sheeba sauce; bobotie; and Cape Malay curry. A wide choice of steaks take centre stage on the menu – tournedos Rossini, and surf 'n' turf are included. For dessert you'll see stalwarts such as Eton Mess; banoffee pie; and hot chocolate sponge.

Open all day all wk 7am-11pm (Sun 8am-10pm) **Food** Lunch Mon-Sat 12-3, Sun 12-8 Dinner Mon-Sat 6-10, Sun 12-8 Av main course £14 ⊕ BRAKSPEAR ◀ Brakspear, Oxford Gold, Guinness. ♟ 20 **Facilities** Non-diners area ♣ (Bar Outside area) ♦♦ Children's menu Children's portions Outside area ⊓ Parking ▄▄ (notice required)

Map 11 SP52

The Muddy Duck   PICK OF THE PUBS

See Pick of the Pubs on page 397

THE LITTLE ANGEL
Henley on Thames

Henley on Thames, South Oxfordshire is just an hour from London & home to the famous Little Angel Pub. Just 80 yards from Henley Bridge & the famous Royal Regatta course on the River Thames, it is renowned the world over. One of the largest & most individual pubs in the area, the focus here is a cracking bar, fantastic food & good times. Open every day, all day & serving only the best local & seasonal food, this award winning pub is one of the busiest in the region & is as happy hosting thousands during regatta week in July, as it is a romantic table for two! A uniquely designed pub, it has several individual areas that can cater for parties of all sizes & with a large car park for its patrons, is highly prized in the town. Daily specials boards deliver delicious foodie treats, as does the daily bar food offer, including enormous home made Scotch eggs that are superb. Cosy in the winter but equally loved for its large patio garden for al fresco dining or drinks. Overlooking the quintessential Henley Cricket Club grounds, you could do worse than while away an afternoon with a good lunch, chilled bottle of rosé & good company. Whether you are enjoying a day trip, passing through or partaking in one of the large annual events in the town, you would not want to pass The Little Angel & not pop in. Their friendly & efficient staff will take great care of you.

THE LITTLE ANGEL REMENHAM LANE   HENLEY ON THAMES   OXON   RG9 2LS
01491 411 008   ENQUIRIES@THELITTLEANGEL.CO.UK   WWW.THELITTLEANGEL.CO.UK

PICK OF THE PUBS

The Muddy Duck

HETHE Map 11 SP52

tel: 01869 278099 **Main St OX27 8ES**
email: dishitup@themuddyduckpub.
co.uk
web: www.themuddyduckpub.co.uk
dir: *From Bicester towards Buckingham
on A4421 left signed Fringford. Through
Fringford, right signed Hethe, left
signed Hethe*

Family-run rural pub and restaurant

The Muddy Duck is family-owned and run
by a close-knit team who are big on
friendly, efficient service and high food
standards – without the pompous style.
This stone-built village pub is a
sympathetic combination of old and new.
Real ales are likely to include old
favourites Hooky, Landlord and Tribute,
from a cellar looked after by the
knowledgeable Iain, himself a former
innkeeper. The refurbished pub is a lively,
welcoming place to enjoy a pint by the
open fire, along with nibbles such as
crispy pickled onion rings; honey mustard
sausages with chorizo; sweet and salty
pork crackling sticks; and hazelnut
houmous with toasted tortilla strips.
For more of a dining experience, take a
reassuring peek through the kitchen
viewing window before checking out the
menu. It's divided into starters and
salads, pub classics and 'main event'
courses, with home-made desserts to
finish. The Harris family is high on

animal welfare, big on free-range and
zero tolerance on short-cuts – in their
words 'all fresh, no ping-and-ding here';
the only thing that comes frozen is the
ice cream, and that's made by them, too.
The rich offering of starters could include
sautéed chicken livers with spiced
brioche, braised onions and bacon
crumbs; or grilled haloumi, watermelon,
crunchy seeds, gordal olives and honey.
Of the classics, you can pimp your
cheeseburger with a sticky beef rib or
blue cheese; the Cornish white fish with
fat-cut chips is served with tartare sauce
and watercress. Big hearted mains might
be venison loin with thyme and garlic
potatoes and sautéed spring greens; and
slow-cooked lamb shoulder with tomato
olives and capers. There's a terrace area
for year-round outdoor dining.

Open all wk 11-11 **Food** Lunch Mon-Sat
12-2.30, Sun 12-4 Dinner Mon-Sat 6-9
Restaurant menu available all wk
⊕ FREE HOUSE ◀ Timothy Taylor
Landlord & Boltmaker, St Austell Tribute,
Hook Norton Hooky Bitter Ō Westons
Stowford Press. **Facilities** Non-diners
area 🐾 (Bar Garden) 🚼 Children's
portions Garden ⊞ Parking WiFi

HIGHMOOR
Map 5 SU78

Rising Sun

tel: 01491 640856 **Witheridge Hill RG9 5PF**
email: info@risingsunwitheridgehill.co.uk
dir: *From Henley-on-Thames take A4130 towards Wallingford. Take B481, turn right to Highmoor*

Intimate, cottagey pub in the Chilterns

Next to the green in a Chilterns' hamlet, you approach this 17th-century pub through the garden. Inside, you'll find richly coloured walls, low-beamed ceilings and open fires. Chalkboards tell you which guest ales are accompanying Brakspear Bitter, or Westons Wyld Wood Organic, the incumbent cider. The three-section restaurant is a cosy place to dine on steak and Guinness puff pastry pie; slow-cooked belly of pork with black pudding mash, crackling and cider jus; Thai style beef, chilli, vegetable and coriander stir-fry; or traditional fish and chips. Check dates of outdoor music events.

Open all wk Mon-Fri 12-3 5-11 (Sat 12-11 Sun 12-7) **Food** Lunch Mon-Fri 12-2, Sat-Sun 12-3 Dinner Mon-Sat 6.30-9 Restaurant menu available all wk ⊕ BRAKSPEAR ◀ Brakspear Bitter, guest ales ᵇ Westons Wyld Wood Organic, Orchard Pig Reveller, Thatchers Gold. ♟ 10 **Facilities** Non-diners area ✿ (Bar Garden) ♦ Children's menu Children's portions Family room Garden ⍭ Parking WiFi ⛒ (notice required)

KINGHAM
Map 10 SP22

The Kingham Plough ★ ★ ★ ★ INN ⊛⊛⊛ PICK OF THE PUBS

tel: 01608 658327 **The Green OX7 6YD**
email: book@thekinghamplough.co.uk **web:** www.thekinghamplough.co.uk
dir: *B4450 from Chipping Norton to Churchill. 2nd right to Kingham, left at T-junct. Pub on right*

Relaxed and upmarket village inn with an imaginative menu

Multi award-winning chef-proprietor Emily Watkins, together with head chef Ben Dulley, continue to raise the culinary stakes at this eye-catching old stone village coaching inn. The pub effortlessly satisfies a role as both welcoming local and destination dining inn. The discerning bar-hound can revel in great beers from small breweries such as Purity; relaxing in a beamed bar that features real fires, a pub dog and Sunday quizzes, perhaps snacking on snails and mushrooms with garlic butter on toast. The ever-evolving menu of British dishes is based on carefully-sourced local produce. The kitchen's three AA Rosette distinction results from consummate starters such as twice-baked pumpkin soufflé with Windrush goats' cheese. The mains' menu may field treats like Tamworth pork belly with pheasant sausage, caramelised onions, red haricot beans, pork and pheasant consommé. Finish with frozen pear parfait, warm gingerbread and sloe gin jelly.

Open all day all wk Closed 25 Dec **Food** Mon-Sat 12-9, Sun 12-8 Restaurant menu available all wk ⊕ FREE HOUSE ◀ Wye Valley HPA, Purity Mad Goose, Cotswold Wheat Beer, Hook Norton ᵇ Ashton Press. **Facilities** Non-diners area ✿ (Bar Garden) ♦ Children's menu Children's portions Garden ⍭ Parking WiFi **Rooms** 6

The Wild Rabbit ★ ★ ★ ★ ★ RR ⊛⊛⊛ PICK OF THE PUBS

tel: 01608 658389 **Church St OX7 6YA**
email: theteam@thewildrabbit.co.uk **web:** www.thewildrabbit.co.uk
dir: *In centre of village*

Organic produce and celebrity clientele

From the family behind nearby Daylesford Organic, The Wild Rabbit has already been dubbed 'the poshest pub in Britain' due to its A-list celebrity customers. The 18th-century Cotswold inn has stripped back walls, open fires and simple handcrafted furniture. Local Hook Norton is one of seven beers on tap, and the impeccably sourced wine list displays more than a dozen served by the glass. Three AA Rosettes have been awarded for the seasonal menu which features Daylesford's organic produce, served in the bar and on the terrace all day. Try duck egg, truffle purée, slow-cooked bacon and crispy sourdough; or glazed short rib with sautéed bacon, button mushrooms, baby onions, straw potatoes and red wine sauce. Desserts showing the same attention to detail may include Braeburn apple cheesecake with sorrel and caramelised honey. A beer festival over the Spring Bank Holiday is as good a pretext as any to do a little star gazing.

Open all day all wk Closed 1st wk Jan **Food** Lunch all wk 12-2.30 Dinner all wk 7-9.30 Restaurant menu available all wk ⊕ FREE HOUSE ◀ Hook Norton, Timothy Taylor Landlord, Sharp's Doom Bar, Otter ᵇ Westons Stowford Press. ♟ 14 **Facilities** Non-diners area ✿ (Bar Outside area) ♦ Children's menu Children's portions Outside area ⍭ Beer festival Parking WiFi **Rooms** 12

KIRTLINGTON
Map 11 SP42

The Oxford Arms

tel: 01869 350208 **Troy Ln OX5 3HA**
email: enquiries@oxford-arms.co.uk
dir: *Take either A34 or A44 N from Oxford, follow Kirtlington signs*

Homely village pub serving unpretentious good food

Dating from 1862, this attractive stone-built village inn prides itself on providing a warm welcome mirrored by its real log fire. In summer, head to the patio for alfresco dining near the kitchen garden that produces a supply of herbs, salad leaves and soft fruits. Inside, freshly-cut flowers and wax-encrusted church candles on the tables adds a rustic touch to proceedings. Everything in the kitchen is made from scratch from local produce. Start perhaps with organic salmon gravad lax or pork pie with green tomato chutney before enjoying slow-roasted belly of pork with black pudding and lentils.

Open all wk Closed 26 Dec **Food** Lunch Mon-Sat 12-3, Sun 12-4 Dinner Mon 6-11, Tue-Sun 6.30-10.30 Av main course £15 ⊕ PUNCH TAVERNS ◀ Hook Norton Hooky Bitter, McMenamins Black Ship Dunkel ᵇ Symonds. ♟ 12 **Facilities** Non-diners area ✿ (Bar Restaurant Garden) ♦ Children's portions Garden ⍭ Parking

LOWER SHIPLAKE
Map 5 SU77

The Baskerville ★★★★ INN ◉　　PICK OF THE PUBS

tel: 0118 940 3332 **Station Rd RG9 3NY**
email: enquiries@thebaskerville.com web: www.thebaskerville.com
dir: *Just off A4155, 1.5m from Henley-on-Thames towards Reading, follow signs at War Memorial junct*

Relaxed pub in Thames-side village

Maybe, like many, you'll have reached this modern-rustic pub along the Thames Path, which briefly leaves the river to run through Lower Shiplake and passes two minutes from its door. The dog-friendly bar is adorned with sporting memorabilia and is home to real ales from the nearby Loddon and Marlow breweries, and some 17 wines by the glass. Food-wise, there's plenty of modern British choice on the bar menu and the carte, including devilled lamb's kidneys with crispy shallots; and Cornish rope-grown mussels with smoked bacon as starters; and mains such as bouillabaisse; braised Chiltern lamb shank with champ mash; and feta and spinach puff pastry roll with salsa verde. For lunch, maybe an open sandwich or chargrilled chicken and Caesar salad. The wine list extends to 60 bins, while owner Allan Hannah betrays his Scottish origins with over 40 malt whiskies. Summer Sunday barbecues are held in the pub's attractive garden.

Open all day all wk 11-11 (Sun 12-10.30) Closed 1 Jan **Food** Lunch Mon-Sat 12-6, Sun 12-3.30 Dinner Mon-Thu 6-9.30, Fri-Sat 6-10 Set menu available Restaurant menu available all wk ◖ Loddon Hoppit & Ferryman's Gold, Sharp's Doom Bar, Rebelllion IPA ♂ Thatchers. ♟ 17 **Facilities** Non-diners area ♣ (Bar Garden) ♦ Children's menu Children's portions Play area Garden ⋔ Parking WiFi **Rooms** 4

MARSH BALDON
Map 5 SU59

Seven Stars

tel: 01865 343337 **The Green OX44 9LP**
email: info@sevenstarsonthegreen.co.uk
dir: *From Oxford ring road onto A4074 signed Wallingford. Through Nuneham Courtenay. Left, follow Marsh Baldon signs*

Thriving community-owned pub

After several closures the exasperated Marsh Baldon residents dug deep into their pockets and bought the historic 350-year-old pub on the pretty village green. Today the Seven Stars has a smart interior, local ales on tap and a modern pub menu offering a good range of dishes prepared from fresh local ingredients. Typical dishes include risottos, sausages and mash, classic Sunday roasts, and specials like fish pie and sticky toffee pudding. For summer, there's a gorgeous garden and a beer festival. The area has several interesting walks and Oxford Arboretum is a five-minute walk away.

Open all day all wk **Food** Mon-Sat 12-9, Sun 12-7 ⊕ FREE HOUSE ◖ Fuller's London Pride, Loose Cannon Abingdon Bridge, Loddon Hoppit, Shotover Prospect, Village Idiot, White Horse ♂ Aspall. ♟ 9 **Facilities** Non-diners area ♣ (Bar Garden) ♦ Children's menu Children's portions Garden ⋔ Beer festival Parking WiFi ⛟ (notice required)

MIDDLETON STONEY
Map 11 SP52

Best Western The Jersey Arms ★★ HL

tel: 01869 343234 **OX25 4AD**
email: jerseyarms@bestwestern.co.uk web: www.jerseyarms.com
dir: *M4 junct 9 or 10, A34 onto B340*

British food in a historic property

Until 1951, when a family called Ansell bought it, this 13th-century country inn belonged to the Jersey Estate. In 1985 the Ansells sold it to Donald and Helen Livingston, making them only its third set of owners since 1243. It is just three minutes from Bicester Village shopping outlet if you want to call in for refreshments after grabbing a few bargains. Food can be taken in the Bar & Grill where the British menu is supplemented by daily specials. Start with creamy garlic mushrooms with herbs, then move onto slow-roasted shoulder of pork with sage and onion sauce; steak and kidney pudding; or classic spaghetti bolognese. Afters of bread and butter pudding or warm apple pancake with ice cream will finish things off nicely.

Open all day all wk **Food** Lunch all wk 12-2 Dinner all wk 6.30-9 Av main course £9.75 Restaurant menu available all wk ⊕ FREE HOUSE ◖ Flowers. ♟ 9 **Facilities** Non-diners area ♦ Children's menu Garden ⋔ Parking WiFi **Rooms** 20

MILCOMBE
Map 11 SP43

The Horse & Groom Inn ★★★★ INN

tel: 01295 722142 **OX15 4RS**
email: horseandgroominn@gmail.com web: www.thehorseandgroominn.co.uk
dir: *From A361 between Chipping Norton & Bloxham follow Milcombe signs. Pub at end of village*

A traditional Cotswold pub with daily-changing menus

The 17th-century Horse & Groom still has many traditional elements such as stone floors, a wood-burning stove, and delightful snug area, but is very much in the 21st century otherwise. The contemporary dining room seats 50, and the daily-changing menus are bursting with dishes created from local produce. Start off with roasted cauliflower and Oxford Blue cheese soup; followed by beef, mushroom and Guinness pie; Thai green chicken curry; or pulled pork and roasted vegetable lasange. Vegetarians have interesting choices too – grilled goats' cheese croûton with basil pesto dressing; or lentil, cashew and vegetable bake, perhaps.

Open 12-3 6-11 (Sun 12-5) Closed 25 Dec eve & 26 Dec, Sun eve **Food** Lunch Mon-Sat 12-2.30, Sun 12-3 Dinner Mon-Sat 6-9 Av main course £9 ⊕ PUNCH TAVERNS ◖ Sharp's Doom Bar, Hook Norton Hooky Bitter, Young's Bitter, Black Sheep. ♟ 11 **Facilities** Non-diners area ♣ (Bar Outside area) ♦ Children's menu Children's portions Outside area ⋔ Parking WiFi ⛟ (notice required) **Rooms** 4

MILTON
Map 5 SU49

The Plum Pudding

tel: 01235 834443 **44 High St OX14 4EJ**
email: jez@theplumpuddingmilton.co.uk
dir: *From A34 (Milton Interchange) follow Milton signs. 1st left (signed Milton) into High St*

Proper village free house serving old-breed pork

The name 'Plum Pudding' derives from the nickname of the Oxford Sandy and Black Pig, one of the oldest of British breeds and bred in this area. The dog-friendly bar of this pub stocks local and regional ales such as Loose Cannon, and the Plum Pudding's pork specialities may include glazed ham, free-range eggs and chips, and different flavours of specially made sausages. Alternatives such as filled baguettes and sandwiches, home-made beefburger, aged steaks and scampi and chips appear on a menu of confirmed pub favourites. Beer festivals are held in April and October.

Open all wk 11.30-2.30 5-11 (Fri-Sun all day) **Food** Lunch Mon-Sat 12-2, Sun 12-3 Dinner Mon-Sat 6-9 ⊕ FREE HOUSE ◄ Loose Cannon, Brakspear, Ringwood, guest ales. **Facilities** Non-diners area ☻ (Bar Restaurant Garden) ♦♦ Children's portions Garden ⊨ Beer festival Parking WiFi ☞

MURCOTT
Map 11 SP51

The Nut Tree Inn ◉◉
PICK OF THE PUBS

tel: 01865 331253 **Main St OX5 2RE**
dir: *M40 junct 9, A34 towards Oxford. Left onto B4027 signed Islip. At Red Lion turn left. Right signed Murcott, Fencott & Charlton-on-Otmoor. Pub on right in village*

Village local and destination dining venue

Local lad Mike North grew up dreaming of owning this thatched 15th-century free house overlooking the pond. Some 10 years ago his dream came true when he and Imogen, then his fiancée, bought it. Oak beams, wood-burners and unusual carvings are the setting for a range of ales, one of which from Tring delights in the name of Side Pocket for a Toad. But, as the Norths point out, real ales and an award-winning list of world wines don't pay the bills. So Mike and his team have built an excellent local trade and an enviable destination dining reputation for cooking that has won two AA Rosettes. Commitment begins outside, where two thirds of an acre of the pub's grounds are devoted to a kitchen garden. A typical menu promises diver-caught Scottish scallops with cauliflower couscous, followed by roasted breast of Tidenham duck 'Marco Polo'; ginger pannacotta with poached Yorkshire rhubarb ends an excellent meal.

Open all day Closed 2wks from 27 Dec, Sun eve, Mon & Tue **Food** Lunch Wed-Sat 12-2.30, Sun 12-3 Dinner Wed-Sat 7-9 Restaurant menu available Wed-Sun L, Wed-Sat evening ⊕ FREE HOUSE ◄ Vale Best Bitter, Fuller's London Pride, Brains The Rev. James, Shepherd Neame Spitfire, Oxfordshire Ales Pride of Oxford, Tring Side Pocket for a Toad. ☻ 15 **Facilities** Non-diners area ♦♦ Children's portions Garden ⊨ Parking ☞ (notice required)

NORTH HINKSEY VILLAGE
Map 5 SP40

The Fishes

tel: 01865 249796 **OX2 0NA**
email: fishes@peachpubs.com
dir: *From A34 S'bound (dual carriageway) left at junct after Botley Interchange, signed North Hinksey & Oxford Rugby Club. From A34 N'bound exit at Botley Interchange & return to A34 S'bound, then follow as above*

Victorian pub with a huge garden

A short walk from Oxford city centre, this attractive tile-hung pub stands in three acres of tranquil wooded grounds running down to Seacourt Stream, with a decking area, an outdoor tipi and a large garden. Providing plenty of shade, these grounds are ideal for barbecues and picnics, which can be ordered at the bar. Seasonal menus of modern British dishes include Enderby smoked haddock risotto with a poached free-range egg; superfood salads; roast and pan-fried sustainable fish; and steaks from butcher Aubrey 'by Royal Appointment' Allen. Soups, sandwiches, deli boards and a handful of mains are served all day. Also seasonal, are the interesting English and French cheese selections.

Open all day all wk Closed 25 Dec **Food** Lunch 12-2.30 Dinner 6.30-9.30 ⊕ GREENE KING/PEACH PUBS ◄ Morland Old Speckled Hen, Greene King IPA ♂ Aspall. ☻ **Facilities** Non-diners area ☻ (Bar Garden) ♦♦ Children's portions Play area Garden ⊨ Beer festival Cider festival Parking WiFi ☞

NORTHMOOR
Map 5 SP40

The Red Lion
PICK OF THE PUBS

tel: 01865 300301 **OX29 5SX**
email: info@theredlionnorthmoor.com
dir: *A420 from Oxford. At 2nd rdbt take 3rd exit onto A415. Right after lights into Moreton Ln. At end turn right, Pub on right*

Popular pub with own kitchen garden

A pretty 17th-century pub with a large garden set on the skew in the middle of the village; experts have deduced from the positioning of its wooden beams and open fireplaces that it was originally two cottages. Experienced publicans Ian Neale and Lisa Lyne have established a good reputation and the pub goes from strength to strength. They have transformed the pub's land into a productive kitchen garden producing seasonal fruit and vegetables for their menus, and their chickens do their part too, laying a surplus of eggs. The tempting modern menus might offer a starter of venison carpaccio, hazelnuts, home-grown Jerusalem artichokes and Brussel sprout leaves; or beetroot- and vodka-cured salmon, pickled beetroot, horseradish and rye bread crisps. Following on could be Densham's Cumberland sausages, potato rösti, veg and onion gravy; gilt-head bream fillet, parsnip panisse, parsnip purée, girolle mushrooms and watercress; or a pub classic – devilled lamb's liver, mash, seasonal veg and mustard sauce.

Open all wk 11-3 6-11 (Sat all day Sun 12-4) **Food** Lunch Mon-Sat 12-2.30, Sun 12-3.30 Av main course £6- £13 Restaurant menu available Mon-Sat ⊕ FREE HOUSE ◄ Wychwood Hobgoblin, Brakspear, Hook Norton Lion, guest ale ♂ Thatchers Gold. ☻ 11 **Facilities** Non-diners area ☻ (All areas) ♦♦ Children's menu Children's portions Garden Outside area ⊨ Beer festival Parking WiFi ☞ (notice required)

OXFORD　　　　　　　　　　　　　　　　Map 5 SP50

The Magdalen Arms

tel: 01865 243159 **243 Iffley Rd OX4 1SJ**
email: info@magdalenarms.co.uk
dir: *On corner of Iffley Rd & Magdalen Rd*

Busy food pub with a boho vibe

Just a short stroll from Oxford city centre, this bustling food pub is run by the same team as Waterloo's hugely influential Anchor & Hope gastro-pub. There is a similar boho feel to the place with its dark red walls and vintage furniture and the nose-to-tail menu will be familiar to anybody who knows the pub's London sibling. Expect the likes of wild rabbit and pork rillettes; twice-baked cep and parmesan soufflé; braised ox cheek, suet dumplings and horseradish cream; rib of beef, béarnaise, chips and salad; and sticky toffee pudding with double cream. Real ales are complemented by a vibrant modern wine list. There's books and wooden bricks for children in the sofa area.

Open 11-11 (Mon 5-11 Sun 12-10.30) Closed BHs, 24-26 Dec, Mon L **Food** Lunch Tue-Sat 12-2.30, Sun 12-3 Dinner Mon-Fri 5.30-10, Sat 6-10, Sun 6-9.30 Av main course £14 ⊕ STAR PUBS & BARS ◀ Caledonian XPA & Deuchars IPA, Lion, Wychwood ♂ Symonds. ₹ 16 **Facilities** Non-diners area ❤ (Bar Garden) ✦ Children's portions Garden ♬ WiFi 🚌 (notice required)

NEW The Old Bookbinders Ale House

tel: 01865 553549 **17-18 Victor St, Jericho OX2 6BT**
email: info@oldbookbinders.co.uk
dir: *From St Giles into Beaumont St. At lights right into Walton St. 6th left into Cranham St. At end left into Canal St, pub on left*

A fascinating family-run pub serving good French food

Built in 1869 for workers from Oxford University Press in the city's Jericho area, 'The Bookies' featured in the first episode of real ale-loving TV detective *Morse* and more recently in The Hairy Bikers' *Pubs That Built Britain* series. Its quirky decoration includes a train set on the ceiling, a barrel of 'help-yourself' monkey nuts and things French, courtesy of Gallic patron Michel. The menu offers Burgundy snails in garlic butter; shredded duck pâté; fillet of sole roulade with spinach in cream and champagne sauce; fillet of pork in port, lime and garlic sauce; and a range of sweet and savoury crêpes. There are six real ales on offer. Well-behaved students, children and dogs are more than welcome to this delightful corner pub.

Open 12-12 (Tue-Wed 4pm-mdnt Sun 12-11) Closed Mon, Tue L, Wed L **Food** Lunch Thu-Sat 12-2.15, Sun 12-7.30 Dinner Tue-Sat 5.30-9.15, Sun 12-7.30 Set menu available Restaurant menu available Tue-Sun ⊕ GREENE KING ◀ Morland Old Speckled Hen, Bookies Best. **Facilities** Non-diners area ❤ (Bar Restaurant Outside area) ✦ Outside area ♬ Beer festival WiFi 🚌 (notice required)

The Punter

tel: 01865 248832 **7 South St, Osney Island OX2 0BE**
email: info@thepunteroxford.co.uk
dir: *Phone for detailed directions*

Quirky Thames-side treasure

If feeling famished on your tour of Oxford, then seek out this rustically-cool pub on Osney Island in the heart of the city – it enjoys a magnificent and very tranquil spot beside the river. The decor is eclectic and interesting, with much to catch the eye, from rugs on flagstone floors and mismatched tables and chairs to bold artwork on whitewashed walls. Come for a relaxing pint of Punter Ale by the river or refuel on something tempting from the daily menu – pork goulash with pitta bread; potato gnocchi with swimmer crab and samphire sauce; rabbit cacciatore with polenta and fine beans; or chestnut and gorgonzola risotto with fried sage leaves.

Open all day all wk **Food** Lunch Mon-Fri 12-3, wknds all day Dinner Mon-Fri 6-10, wknds all day ⊕ GREENE KING ◀ The Punter Ale ♂ Addlestones. ₹ 12
Facilities Non-diners area ❤ (Bar Restaurant Garden) ✦ Children's portions Garden ♬ WiFi

The Rickety Press

tel: 01865 424581 **67 Cranham St OX2 6DE**
email: info@thericketypress.com
dir: *Phone for detailed directions*

In the heart of historic Jericho

The Rickety Press is run by the same three old school friends as The Rusty Bicycle in east Oxford. Deceptively spacious, there's a large conservatory restaurant, a snug and a bar serving Arkell's real ales, handpicked wines, coffees and teas, while the spicy aroma of mulled wine fills the winter air. The menu runs along the lines of Snackin' and Sides; Burgers & Buns; Wood-Fired Pizza, and Bowls. Under those heading you might find – cheese and truffle chips or pulled pork tots; the dodo, the angry Texan and moo and blue burgers; Mr Melanzane or Pepper Pig pizzas; and rabbit food and chop chop in the bowls section. Food can be taken away too.

Open all day all wk ⊕ ARKELL'S ◀ 3B, Moonlight, Kingsdown. **Facilities** ❤ (Bar) ✦ Children's menu Children's portions WiFi

The Rusty Bicycle

tel: 01865 435298 **28 Magdalen Rd OX4 1RB**
email: info@therustybicycle.com
dir: *From Oxford ring road into Iffley Rd towards city centre. Right into Magdalen Rd*

Great community local with fine pies

You can't miss the hanging sign for this quirky suburban pub – look for a 1950s grocer's bike swinging high above Magdalen Road's pavement. Inside the design is decidedly eccentric and Edwardian. This is a community pub in a very cosmopolitan part of the city, with the ambition of catering for all-comers. The plan appears to work well, with grand beers from owners Arkell's Brewery and carefully chosen guests coupled with a menu that is both traditional and eclectic. Look for burgers (including cod, pulled pork and black bean and mushroom varieties); sourdough pizzas (meat-eaters, vegetarian and vegans catered for); snacks and salads. Bareboard floors, amusing signage, real fires and eclectic furnishing, this is one to discover and savour at length.

Open all day all wk Closed 25-26 Dec **Food** Lunch Mon-Fri 12-2.30, Sat-Sun 10-3 Dinner all wk 6-9.30 ⊕ ARKELL'S ◀ 3B, Moonlight & Wiltshire Gold, Hoperation IPA ♂ Westons Old Rosie & Stowford Press. ₹ 8 **Facilities** Non-diners area ❤ (Bar Restaurant Garden) ✦ Children's menu Children's portions Garden ♬ WiFi 🚌

Turf Tavern

tel: 01865 243235 **4 Bath Place, off Holywell St OX1 3SU**
email: 8004@greeneking.co.uk
dir: *Phone for detailed directions*

The hidden haunt of dons and students over many centuries

A jewel of a pub, and consequently one of Oxford's most popular, although it's not easy to find, as it is approached through hidden alleyways, which, if anything, adds to its allure. Previously called the Spotted Cow, it became the Turf in 1842, probably in deference to its gambling clientele; it has also had brushes with literature, film and politics. The Turf Tavern is certainly one of the city's oldest pubs, with some 13th-century foundations and a 17th-century low-beamed front bar. Three beer gardens help ease overcrowding, but the 11 real ales and reasonably priced pub grub keep the students, locals and visitors flowing in.

Open all day all wk 11-11 (Sun 12-10.30) Closed 25 Dec **Food** Mon-Sat 11-9, Sun 12-9 ⊕ GREENE KING ◀ Guest ales ♂ Westons Old Rosie, Lilley's Apples & Pears, guest ciders. **Facilities** ❤ (Bar Garden) ✦ Garden ♬ WiFi 🚌

PISHILL
Map 5 SU78

The Crown Inn
PICK OF THE PUBS

tel: 01491 638364 **RG9 6HH**
email: enquiries@thecrowninnpishill.co.uk
dir: A4130 from Henley-on-Thames, right onto B480 to Pishill

Coaching inn with thatched barn

A pretty 15th-century brick and flint former coaching inn, The Crown began life in medieval times, serving ale to the thriving monastic community, then providing refuge to Catholic priests escaping Henry VIII's tyrannical rule. Fast-forward to the Swinging 60s, and the neighbouring thatched barn housed a nightclub hosting George Harrison, Dusty Springfield and other big names from the world of pop. In the pub itself, the bar is supplied by mostly local breweries, typically Brakspear. Lunch and dinner are served from Wednesdays through to Sunday lunchtime and may be enjoyed inside, where there are three log fires, or in the picturesque garden overlooking the valley. Depending on the season, you might find pan-roasted lamb rump, wild garlic purée, potato and heritage carrot dauphinoise, sautéed samphire and lamb jus; or pan-fried chicken supreme wrapped in Parma ham. In late September, there's a beer festival.

Open 12-3 6-11 (Sun 12-3.30) Closed 25-26 Dec, Sun eve **Food** Lunch Wed-Sat 12-2.30, Sun 12-3 Dinner Wed-Sat 6.30-9 ⊕ FREE HOUSE ◀ Brakspear, guest ale Ô Westons Stowford Press. **Facilities** Non-diners area ❤ (Bar Garden) ⱡ Children's portions Garden ⊨ Beer festival Parking WiFi ⬛ (notice required)

RAMSDEN
Map 11 SP31

The Royal Oak
PICK OF THE PUBS

See Pick of the Pubs on opposite page

SHILTON
Map 5 SP20

Rose & Crown

tel: 01993 842280 **OX18 4AB**
dir: From A40 at Burford take A361 towards Lechlade on Thames. Right, follow Shilton signs on left. Or from A40 E of Burford take B4020 towards Carterton

Well-supported village local and destination food pub

A traditional Cotswold-stone inn dating back to the 17th century, whose two rooms retain their original beams and are warmed by a wood-burner and an open log fire. In the bar, Hook Norton Old Hooky might well partner Young's Bitter and Ashton Press cider. As their pedigrees might lead you to expect, chef-landlord Martin Coldicott, who trained at London's Connaught Hotel, and head chef Mike Evans, prepare above average, but simply presented food, typically cod fillet with mussel and prawn risotto; steak, ale and mushroom pie; or aubergine parmigiana baked with mozzarella. Bread and butter pudding or sticky toffee pudding for afters. You may eat and drink in the garden if the weather's nice.

Open all wk 11.30-3 6-11 (Sat-Sun & BH 11.30-11) **Food** Lunch Mon-Fri 12-2, Sat-Sun & BH 12-2.45 Dinner all wk 7-9 ⊕ FREE HOUSE ◀ Butcombe, Hook Norton Old Hooky, Loose Cannon, Wye Valley, Young's Bitter Ô Ashton Press, Westons Wyld Wood Organic. ⱡ 10 **Facilities** Non-diners area ❤ (Bar Garden) ⱡ Garden ⊨ Parking WiFi

SHIPLAKE
Map 5 SU77

The Plowden Arms

tel: 0118 940 2794 **Reading Rd RG9 4BX**
email: info@doffandbow.co.uk
dir: On A4155, 4m from Reading (2m from Henley-on-Thames)

Family-welcoming hostelry offering refreshments from a bygone era

Between Henley-on-Thames and Reading, The Plowden Arms takes its name from the family who occupied Shiplake Court (now Shiplake College) in the 17th century. Period features, original beams and a working fireplace are the setting for Brakspear beers, draught ciders, and a menu that takes its inspiration from forgotten dishes of bygone times. The recipe for Alexis Soyer's Lamb 'Reform', for example, dates from 1839; and the pudding of Barley cream (on the menu with blackcurrant compôte) was first created in 1859 by Robert Kemp Philp. Other dishes that might tempt are devilled kidneys on toast; and whole roast poussin, onion cake, baby vegetables and Madeira gravy.

Open 11-2.30 5-11 (Sun 12-4 7-10.30) Closed Mon **Food** Lunch Tue-Sat 12-2, Sun 12-3.30 Dinner Tue-Sat 6-10, Sun 7-9 ⊕ BRAKSPEAR ◀ Bitter, Ringwood Boondoggle Ô Addlestones, Thatchers Heritage. ⱡ 13 **Facilities** Non-diners area ❤ (Bar Garden) ⱡ Children's menu Children's portions Garden ⊨ Parking

SHIPTON-UNDER-WYCHWOOD
Map 10 SP21

The Shaven Crown Hotel

tel: 01993 830500 **High St OX7 6BA**
email: relax@theshavencrown.co.uk
dir: On A361, halfway between Burford & Chipping Norton

Historic inn overlooking the picturesque village green and church

This 14th-century coaching inn was built by the monks of Bruern Abbey as a hospice for the poor. Following the Dissolution of the Monasteries, Elizabeth I used it as a hunting lodge before giving it to the village in 1580, when it became the Crown Inn. Thus it stayed until 1930, when a brewery with a sense of humour changed the name as homage to the familiar monastic tonsure. Its interior is full of original architectural features, like the Great Hall. Light meals and real ales are served in the bar, while the restaurant offers modern English dishes.

Open all wk 11-11 (Sun 11-4) **Food** Lunch all wk 12-2.30 Dinner Mon-Sat 6-9.30 Restaurant menu available all wk ⊕ FREE HOUSE ◀ Hook Norton Ô Westons Stowford Press. ⱡ 10 **Facilities** Non-diners area ❤ (Bar Garden) ⱡ Children's menu Children's portions Garden ⊨ Parking WiFi ⬛ (notice required)

STANFORD IN THE VALE
Map 5 SU39

The Horse & Jockey

tel: 01367 710302 **25 Faringdon Rd SN7 8NN**
email: info@horseandjockey.org
dir: On A417 between Faringdon & Wantage

Stylish village inn with home comforts

A wealth of exposed stone, leather-clad armchairs, and dark wood dining furniture characterise the interior of this stylish 16th-century inn. Children and dogs are made as welcome as their parents, and with a range of pizzas on the menu they are unlikely to leave hungry (the children, that is). Other hearty pub fare options are steaks, beer battered fish and chips, fisherman's pie, wild mushroom Stroganoff, cheese and leek puff pastry parcel, and chicken, Parma ham and black olive tagliatelle. A take-away service operates for those in a rush, but if it's just a quiet pint you are looking for, head to the beer garden to sup a Hook Norton Hooky or Belhaven Black.

Open all wk 11-3 5-12 (Fri-Sat 11am-12.30am Sun 12-11) **Food** Lunch 12-2.30 Dinner 6-9 Av main course £10.95 ⊕ GREENE KING ◀ Greene King ales, Hook Norton Hooky Bitter, Belhaven Black. ⱡ 8 **Facilities** Non-diners area ❤ (Bar Garden) ⱡ Children's portions Play area Garden ⊨ Parking WiFi

PICK OF THE PUBS

The Royal Oak

RAMSDEN   Map 11 SP31

tel: 01993 868213 **High St OX7 3AU**
email: info@royaloakramsden.com
web: www.royaloakramsden.com
dir: *B4022 from Witney towards Charlbury, right before Hailey, through Poffley End*

Award-winning pub near many lovely walks

Built of Cotswold stone and facing Ramsden's fine parish church, this former 17th-century coaching inn is a popular refuelling stop for walkers exploring nearby Wychwood Forest and visitors touring the pretty villages and visiting Blenheim Palace. Whether you are walking or not, the cosy inn oozes traditional charm and character, with its old beams, warm fires and stone walls, and long-serving landlords John and Jo Oldham provide a very warm welcome. A free house, it dispenses beers sourced from local breweries, such as Hook Norton Hooky Bitter and Old Hooky, alongside Flying Monk and Wye Valley. Somerset's Original Cider Company supplies the bar with Pheasant Plucker cider, alongside Mortimers Orchard from Herefordshire. With a strong kitchen team, the main menu, built on the very best of fresh local and seasonal ingredients, regularly features a pie of the week topped with puff pastry, or the popular steak and kidney suet pudding; there

are popular choices such as starters of oven-baked baby brie; devilled lamb's kidneys with Dijon mustard sauce; or chargrilled aubergine, sun-dried feta cheese and piquant tomato sauce. Typical mains are confit of duck, Puy lentils, garlic potatoes, red berry and quince sauce; seafood pot au feu; Gymkhana Club curry, a traditional Sri Lankan dish, served with rice and pickles; and a choice of Aberdeen Angus steaks and burgers. Carefully selected by the owner, the wine list has over 200 wines, specialising in those from Bordeaux and Languedoc, with 30 of them served by the glass. Every Thursday evening there is a special offer of steak, with a glass of wine and dessert included.

Open all wk Mon-Fri 11.30-3 6.30-11 (Sat 11.30-11 Sun 12-10.30) Closed 25 Dec **Food** Lunch all wk 12-2 Dinner Mon-Fri 7-9.45, Sat-Sun 12-9.30 ⊕ FREE HOUSE ◖ Hook Norton Old Hooky & Hooky Bitter, Wye Valley, Loose Cannon Abingdon Bridge, Flying Monk ♂ Pheasant Plucker, Mortimers Orchard. ♟ 30 **Facilities** Non-diners area ♣ (Bar Outside area) ♟ Children's portions Outside area ⊼ Parking

---

STEEPLE ASTON   Map 11 SP42

The Red Lion

tel: 01869 340225 **South Side OX25 4RY**
email: redlionsa@aol.com
dir: *0.5m off A4260 (Oxford Rd). Follow brown tourist signs for pub*

Unspoilt 18th-century pub popular with walkers

In an elevated position in the village, this Hook Norton brewery pub offers a number of options: in front of the fire in the bar; in the comfortably furnished, oak-beamed Garden Room; or head for the pretty suntrap terrace, not least for its view of the delightful Cherwell Valley. In addition to generous Sunday roasts, other locally sourced dishes include salads; thin-crust, stone-baked pizzas; Aberdeen Angus burgers; risottos; roast rump of lamb with redcurrant and rosemary; and fresh haddock with or without batter, triple-cooked chips and mushy peas. Children and dogs are welcome.

Open all wk 12-3 5.30-11 (Sat 12-11 Sun 12-5) Closed Sun eve from 5pm **Food** Lunch all wk 12-2.30 Dinner Mon-Sat 6-9 ⊕ HOOK NORTON ◼ Hooky Bitter, Lion & seasonal ales ♂ Westons Stowford Press. ♟ 11 **Facilities** Non-diners area ♣ (Bar Outside area) ♦ Children's portions Outside area � Parking WiFi ⚏ (notice required)

STOKE ROW   Map 5 SU68

Crooked Billet   **PICK OF THE PUBS**

tel: 01491 681048 **RG9 5PU**
dir: *From Henley towards Oxford on A4130. Left at Nettlebed for Stoke Row*

Excellent menu in a 17th-century pub with ample character

Down a narrow, winding lane, lined with beech and oak trees, this mid 17th-century pub was one of notorious highwayman Dick Turpin's hideouts. Since he was involved with the landlord's daughters that makes sense. Many of its finest features are unchanged, including the low beams, tiled floors, open fires and the absence of a bar – beer is drawn directly from casks in the cellar. Local produce and organic fare are the kitchen's mainstays, with set lunches typified by seared Cornish sardines, tomato and anchovy salsa, samphire and green herb oil; slow-roast local Saddleback pork belly, creamed mash potato, pickled red cabbage, broccoli and jus; and lemon tart, raspberry coulis and cream. From the carte come stone bass, seared diver scallops, roast sweet potato, kale, lemon and parsley butter and crispy capers; and chicken breast baked in pancetta, lemon and chestnut stuffing with rösti potato, young carrots and winter greens.

Open all wk 12-3 7-12 (Sat-Sun 12-12) **Food** Lunch Mon-Fri 12-2.30, Sat 12-10.30, Sun 12-10 Dinner Mon-Fri 7-10, Sat 12-10.30, Sun 12-10 Set menu available ⊕ BRAKSPEAR ◼ Organic Best Bitter. ♟ 10 **Facilities** Non-diners area ♦ Children's portions Garden ⌒ Parking

---

STONESFIELD   Map 11 SP31

The White Horse

tel: 01993 891063 **The Ridings OX29 8EA**
email: jalloyd@btinternet.com
dir: *From Oxford take A44 towards Chipping Norton. After Woodstock left signed Charlbury. Through Stonesfield to T-junct, pub opposite*

Contemporary country inn serving great pub classics

Originally built as two mine-workers' cottages, this Cotswold-stone free house dates back to the 19th century and is situated in the village of Stonesfield, handy for exploring Woodstock, Blenheim Palace, and Oxford. The atmosphere is welcoming at this family and dog-friendly contemporary country pub, with its wood-burning stove and cosy seating. The menus are strong on pub classics like roast topside of beef, Yorkshire pudding and goose-fat roast potatoes; or pan-fried sea bass with ratatouille. A double chocolate brownie with ice cream for pudding seals the deal.

Open 5-11 (Sat 12-3 6-11 Sun 12-3) Closed Lunch Tue-Fri, Sun eve & Mon **Food** Lunch Sat-Sun 12-2 Dinner Fri-Sat 6-9 Set menu available Restaurant menu available Fri-Sun ⊕ FREE HOUSE ◼ Ringwood Best Bitter ♂ Westons Stowford Press. **Facilities** Non-diners area ♣ (Bar Garden Outside area) ♦ Children's portions Garden Outside area ⌒ Parking WiFi

---

SWERFORD   Map 11 SP33

The Mason's Arms

tel: 01608 683212 **Banbury Rd OX7 4AP**
email: admin@masons-arms.com
dir: *Between Banbury & Chipping Norton on A361*

Large beer garden ideal for families

Here at The Mason's Arms, Jamie Bailey and Louise Robertson continue their successful track record of running pubs. This one is a 300-year-old, stone-built former Masonic lodge, situated in the Cotswolds; it retains its traditional, informal feel and the large garden has stunning views of the surrounding area. Jamie's modern European cooking concentrates on local produce whenever possible and there is an emphasis on fish on the specials board, which might offer pan-fried tiger prawns with chilli and chorizo followed by pan-fried red mullet with crab meat and samphire linguine. Non-fish options include coq au vin and venison Wellington.

Open all wk 10-3 6-11 (Sun 12-dusk) **Food** Lunch Mon-Sat 12-2.30, Sun 12-dusk Dinner Mon-Fri 7-9, Sat 7-9.30 Set menu available ⊕ FREE HOUSE ◼ Jennings Cumberland Ale , Brakspear ♂ Thatchers Gold. ♟ 15 **Facilities** Non-diners area ♣ (Bar Garden) ♦ Children's menu Children's portions Garden ⌒ Parking WiFi ⚏ (notice required)

SWINBROOK   Map 5 SP21

The Swan Inn ★★★★ INN ◉◉   **PICK OF THE PUBS**

tel: 01993 823339 **OX18 4DY**
email: info@theswanswinbrook.co.uk **web:** www.theswanswinbrook.co.uk
dir: *A40 towards Cheltenham, left to Swinbrook*

Tranquillity and class at Cotswold boutique inn

Hidden in the Windrush Valley you will find the idyllic village of Swinbrook where time stands still. Owners Archie and Nicola Orr-Ewing took on the lease of this dreamy, wisteria-clad stone pub from the late Dowager Duchess of Devonshire. The Swan is the perfect English country pub – it stands by the River Windrush near the village cricket pitch, overlooking unspoilt Cotswold countryside. It gets even better inside: the two cottage-style front rooms, replete with worn flagstones, crackling log fires, low beams and country furnishings, lead through to a cracking bar and classy conservatory extension. First-class pub food ranges from simple bar snacks (beef dripping, gherkins and toasted bread) to more substantial main courses of pork belly, black pudding, streaky bacon, creamy mash and sage jus; and confit duck leg, roast sweet potato, green beans, spinach and hazelnut pesto. You won't want to leave, so book one of the stunning en suite rooms in the restored barn.

Open all wk 11.30-11 Closed 25 Dec **Food** Lunch Mon-Fri 12-2, Sat 12-2.30, Sun 12-3 Dinner Mon-Sat 7-9, Sun 7-8.30 ⊕ FREE HOUSE ◼ Hook Norton, guest ales ♂ Aspall, Westons Wyld Wood Organic, Cotswold. ♟ 9 **Facilities** Non-diners area ♣ (Bar Restaurant Garden) ♦ Children's menu Children's portions Garden ⌒ Parking WiFi **Rooms** 6

TETSWORTH
Map 5 SP60

The Old Red Lion

tel: 01844 281274 **40 High St OX9 7AS**
email: info@theoldredliontetsworth.co.uk
dir: *From Oxford ring road at Headington take A40. Follow A418 signs (over M40). Right onto A40 signed Milton Common & Tetsworth*

Village pub ideal for early birds

An airy, contemporary pub with traditional flourishes, ideal for trippers heading for the nearby Chilterns. Birdwatchers seeking red kites can stop by before or after hitting the hills, whilst cricketers inspecting the wicket on the adjacent village green pitch can call from mid-morning onwards. Not content with two restaurant areas and a bustling bar to run, the owners also host a village shop here. Beers from local microbreweries hit the spot, whilst timeless pub grub meals like sausage and mash fill the gap. Summer barbecues are popular, and there's a mini beer festival every Easter.

Open all day all wk **Food** Lunch Mon-Thu & Sat 10-10, Fri 11am-mdnt, Sun 12-3.30 (open for breakfast 7am-11.30am) Dinner Mon-Thu & Sat 10-10, Fri 11am-mdnt ⊕ FREE HOUSE ◄ Loose Cannon Brewery, White Horse, XT 4 ♂ Somersby. ♀ 8 **Facilities** Non-diners area ✿ (Bar Outside area) ♦♦ Children's menu Children's portions Family room Garden Outside area ⋒ Beer festival Parking WiFi ▄▄

THAME
Map 5 SP70

The James Figg

tel: 01844 260166 **21 Cornmarket OX9 2BL**
email: thejamesfigg@peachpubs.com
dir: *In town centre*

Buzzing town centre free house with a beer garden

This pub's traditional interior of dark wood floors and a double-sided open fire also houses a curving bar stocking ales such as Purity Mad Goose. Snacks include home-made pork scratchings, Scotch eggs, sandwiches and granary baps. Further 'simple and tasty' possibilities are burger and chips; a range of pizzas; roast of the day; beer-battered fish and chips; and honey- and mustard-glazed ham, egg and chips. Beyond The Stables function room you'll find a private garden. The pub's name? James Figg, born in Thame in 1684, was the bare-knuckle boxer who Jack Dempsey called the 'father of modern boxing'.

Open all day all wk 11am-mdnt Closed 25 Dec **Food** Lunch Mon-Sat 12-8.30, Sun 12-6 Dinner Mon-Sat 12-8.30, Sun 12-6 ⊕ FREE HOUSE/PEACH PUBS ◄ Purity Mad Goose, Sharp's Doom Bar ♂ Aspall Draught & Harry Sparrow. ♀ 10 **Facilities** Non-diners area ✿ (Bar Garden) ♦♦ Children's portions Garden ⋒ Parking WiFi

The Thatch

tel: 01844 214340 **29-30 Lower High St OX9 2AA**
email: thatch@peachpubs.com
dir: *From rdbt on A418 into Oxford Rd signed town centre. Follow into Thame High St. Pub on right*

Half-timbered pub with a sunny courtyard garden

Originally a row of cottages in the heart of Thame's high street, this thatched pub remains a cosy warren of rooms with inglenook fireplaces and antique furniture. If you make it past the bar without being tempted by coffee, cakes or a pint of Doom Bar, you'll find yourself in the restaurant overlooking the garden. The kitchen focuses on the best seasonal ingredients – a starter of game terrine with spiced apple chutney might be followed by venison pavé with dauphinoise potatoes, maple

and thyme roasted parsnips, and juniper jus. There is a beer festival during National Cask Ale Week (September-October time).

Open all day all wk Closed 25 Dec **Food** all wk 12-10 ⊕ PEACH PUBS ◄ Vale Wychert & Best Bitter, Sharp's Doom Bar ♂ Aspall. ♀ 16 **Facilities** Non-diners area ✿ (Bar Garden) ♦♦ Children's portions Garden ⋒ Beer festival Parking WiFi ▄▄ (notice required)

TOOT BALDON
Map 5 SP50

The Mole Inn ●
PICK OF THE PUBS

tel: 01865 340001 **OX44 9NG**
email: info@themoleinn.com
dir: *5m SE from Oxford city centre off B480*

A destination pub in beautiful countryside

Toot is derived from an Old English word for a look-out place; Baldon from Bealda's Hill, so the curious village name makes sense when you know. The lovely 300-year-old Mole is a Grade II listed pub that Gary and Jenny Witchalls have put firmly on the foodie map. Leather sofas, stripped beams, solid white walls and terracotta floors provide the perfect background for a leisurely meal. The Mole's Pleasure is just one of the real ales a beer drinker should enjoy before or with a starter (or main) of spicy lamb meatballs with tomato dressing, Greek yogurt and chargrilled ciabatta; followed by grilled fish of the day with new potatoes, baby leaf and cherry tomato salad, and house dressing; and ending with sticky date pudding with toffee sauce and vanilla ice cream. Food and drink is also served in the garden.

Open all day all wk 12-12 (Sun 12-11) Closed 25 Dec **Food** Lunch all wk 12-2.30 Dinner all wk 7-9.30 Set menu available Restaurant menu available all wk ⊕ FREE HOUSE ◄ The Mole's Pleasure, Fuller's London Pride, Shepherd Neame Spitfire, Hook Norton, Guinness ♂ Westons Stowford Press. ♀ 11 **Facilities** Non-diners area ♦♦ Children's menu Children's portions Garden ⋒ Parking WiFi

UFFINGTON
Map 5 SU38

The Fox & Hounds ★★★★ INN

tel: 01367 820680 **High St SN7 7RP**
email: enquiries@uffingtonpub.co.uk web: www.uffingtonpub.co.uk
dir: *From A420 (S of Faringdon) follow Fernham or Uffington signs*

Traditional food and good beer in timeless village inn

Amidst the thatched cottages and 13th-century church in the charming village of Uffington, The Fox & Hounds boasts unrivalled views of The Ridgeway and the Uffington White Horse. Writer John Betjeman once lived across the road from the pub and JRR Tolkein was a frequent visitor – legend has it that St George slew the dragon at nearby Dragon Hill. This is a traditional free house with a range of well-kept real ales; the home-cooked food includes a tapas menu, pub favourites and daily specials; the Sunday roasts are ever popular. Contact the pub for details of its summer beer festival and live music events.

Open all day all wk 11-11 (Sun 12-10.30) **Food** Lunch Mon-Fri 12-2, Sat-Sun & BHs 12-3 (ex 25 Dec) Dinner Mon-Sat 6-9 Av main course £11 ⊕ FREE HOUSE ◄ Local ales ♂ Thatchers. **Facilities** Non-diners area ✿ (Bar Restaurant Garden) ♦♦ Children's menu Children's portions Garden ⋒ Beer festival Parking WiFi ▄▄ (notice required) **Rooms** 2

WATLINGTON — Map 5 SU69

NEW The Fat Fox Inn ★★★ INN ⊕

tel: 01491 613040 **13 Shirburn St OX49 5BU**
email: info@thefatfoxinn.co.uk **web:** www.thefatfoxinn.co.uk
dir: *In town centre*

Seasonal food attracting the customers

At the foot of the Chiltern Hills, parts of this building date back to Tudor times, although much of it is Georgian. An inglenook fireplace with wood-burning stove warms the bar, where locals can enjoy a pint of Brakspear Oxford Gold or 16 wines by the glass. South Oxfordshire producers supply the kitchen with seasonal ingredients for the short, daily-changing menu which has an AA Rosette to its name. Confit pork belly, seared scallops and celeriac might precede duck breast, potato fondant, feta, poached egg, artichoke and balsamic jus. Finish with baked lemon tart and wild berry ice cream.

Open all day all wk **Food** Lunch Mon-Fri 12-2.30, Sat-Sun 12-3 Dinner Mon-Sat 6.30-9, Sun 7-9 Av main course £15 ⊕ BRAKSPEAR ◾ Bitter, Oxford Gold, guest ale ♂ Symonds. ♟ 16 **Facilities** ❧ (Bar Garden) ♦ Children's portions Garden ☂ Parking WiFi ▭ (notice required) **Rooms** 9

WEST HANNEY — Map 5 SU49

Plough Inn

tel: 01235 868909 **Church St OX12 0LN**
email: p.curtis@wanadoo.fr
dir: *From Wantage take A338 towards Oxford. Inn in 1m*

Friendly village free house

Thatched with four 'eyebrows', the Plough dates from around 1525, when it was a row of cottages. The landlord enjoys responsibility for such things as choosing the six rolling real ales and organising the Easter, Spring and Summer bank holiday beer festivals. From the kitchen come home-cooked, seasonal dishes such as pan-seared devilled lamb's kidneys, coriander, smoked bacon and spring onions; and slow-cooked pork belly with creamy mash, red onions and glazed apples. For a treat in summer, dine in the pretty walled garden.

Open all wk 12-3 5-12 (Sat-Sun all day) **Food** Lunch Tue-Sun 12-2 Dinner Tue-Sun 6-9 Set menu available ⊕ FREE HOUSE ◾ St Austell Tribute, Greene King IPA, Loose Cannon, local guest ales. ♟ 10 **Facilities** Non-diners area ❧ (Bar Garden) ♦ Children's portions Garden ☂ Beer festival Parking WiFi ▭ (notice required)

WITNEY — Map 5 SP31

The Fleece

tel: 01993 892270 **11 Church Green OX28 4AZ**
email: fleece@peachpubs.com
dir: *In town centre*

Good surroundings and good craic

Overlooking, as the address suggests, the green in front of St Mary's church, this fine Georgian pub was where, in the late 1940s, Dylan Thomas enjoyed a drink or two when he was living nearby. Then, it was also Clinch's brewery; today it's a Peach Pub, serving Greene King and guest ales. The packed menu takes a while to study, so here are some advance suggestions: share a cold cuts or fish deli board, or single-handedly tackle classic fish stew; sea trout fillet with horseradish potato cake, caper and almond butter sauce; or roasted Tidenham duck breast, with carrot and potato rösti, wilted spinach and honey and thyme jus. Another thought is a steak from Aubrey Allen, the Queen's appointed butcher.

Open all day all wk Closed 25 Dec **Food** Lunch all wk 12-2.30 Dinner Mon-Sat 6-10, Sun 6-9 Set menu available ⊕ GREENE KING/PEACH PUBS ◾ IPA, Morland Old Speckled Hen, guest ale ♂ Aspall Draught, guest cider. ♟ **Facilities** Non-diners area

❧ (Bar Outside area) ♦ Children's portions Outside area ☂ Parking WiFi ▭ (notice required)

Old Swan & Minster Mill ★★★★★ INN ⊕

tel: 01993 774441 **Minster Lovell OX29 0RN**
email: enquiries@oldswanandminstermill.com **web:** www.oldswanandminstermill.com
dir: *N'bound: M40 junct 8, A40 (S'bound M40 junct 9, A34) towards Oxford. From Oxford ringroad follow Cheltenham signs. 14m, follow Carterton & Minster Lovell signs. Through Minster Lovell, right at T-junct, 2nd left signed Old Swan & Minster Mill*

Romantic bolthole in the heart of the Cotswolds

Idyllically situated alongside the River Windrush in the thatched village of Old Minster, this 600-year-old inn was a favourite of Sir Winston Churchill, whose ancestral home is nearby Blenheim Palace. Over the past 30 years, the de Savary family has transformed the place into a luxurious destination, whether it's just for a quiet pint, a meal or overnight stay. In the high-ceilinged, beamed restaurant, pub classics are served alongside more innovative daily specials. A starter of River Windrush crayfish and Devon crab cocktail might be followed by pan-roasted Burford chicken and Madeira jus.

Open all wk 12.30-3 6.30-9 (Fri-Sat 12.30-3 6.30-9.30) **Food** Lunch all wk 12.30-3 Dinner all wk 6.30-9 ⊕ FREE HOUSE ◾ Brakspear Bitter & Oxford Gold, Wychwood Hobgoblin ♂ Westons Stowford Press. **Facilities** Non-diners area ❧ (Bar Garden Outside area) ♦ Children's menu Children's portions Play area Garden Outside area ☂ Parking WiFi **Rooms** 60

WOLVERCOTE — Map 5 SP40

NEW Jacobs Inn

tel: 01865 514333 **130 Godstow Rd OX2 8PG**
email: info@jacobs-inn.com
dir: *From A40 rdbt into Godstow Rd signed Wolvercote. Over railway line, pub on left in village*

Robust British cooking in a friendly Cotswold inn

This comfortable, relaxed pub near Oxford is as welcoming and friendly as you please. Bring the kids and the dog and settle down on a chesterfield with a pint (the choice of ales changes daily) while you peruse the menu. Great local produce features (they keep their own pigs) and there's a large garden with a pizza kitchen in the summer. Start with smoked salmon and anchovy terrine with crème fraîche and toasted sourdough, or duck rillettes; then tuck into spiced squash pie with creamed leeks and peas, or rump of lamb with minted gravy.

Open all day all wk Closed 25 Dec **Food** Contact pub for food times Set menu available Restaurant menu available all wk ⊕ MARSTON'S ◾ Brakspear Bitter, Wychwood Hobgoblin ♂ Thatchers Heritage. ♟ 10 **Facilities** Non-diners area ♦ Children's menu Children's portions Garden ☂ Parking WiFi ▭ (notice required)

The Trout Inn

tel: 01865 510930 **195 Godstow Rd OX2 8PN**
dir: *From A40 at Wolvercote rdbt (N of Oxford) follow signs for Wolvercote, through village to pub*

Ever-popular waterside inn

The Trout was already ancient when Lewis Carroll, and later CS Lewis took inspiration here; centuries before it had been a hospice for Godstow Nunnery, on the opposite bank of the Thames. It featured in several episodes of *Inspector Morse*, and has long been a favourite with Oxford undergraduates. Its leaded windows, great oak beams, flagged floors and glowing fireplaces make it arguably the area's most atmospheric inn. On a summer day bag a table on the terrace by the fast flowing water to enjoy a pint and something from the menu that pleases everyone — 18-hour slow cooked British corned salt beef hash; stone-baked pizzas; and beer-battered line-caught cod and twice cooked chunky chips are possibilities.

Open all day all wk 11–11 **Food** Mon-Sat 12-10, Sun 12-9 Set menu available ⊕ FREE HOUSE ◀ Brakspear Bitter, Sharp's Doom Bar, guest ales ○ Aspall. ♟ 21 **Facilities** Non-diners area ❀ (Bar Garden) ♦♦ Children's menu Children's portions Garden ⟁ Parking WiFi ▭

WOOLSTONE   Map 5 SU28

The White Horse

tel: 01367 820726 **SN7 7QL**
email: info@whitehorsewoolstone.co.uk
dir: *Exit A420 at Watchfield onto B4508 towards Longcot signed Woolstone*

Thatched pub with literary connections

Built in Elizabethan times, this ancient, black-and-white timbered village pub appears as if on cue after an invigorating walk along the Ridgeway and White Horse Hill (NT) Uffington. It is said that Thomas Hughes (of *Tom Brown's Schooldays* fame) penned some of his works here; indeed, one is called *The Scouring of the White Horse*. Upholstered stools line the traditional bar, and the fireplace conceals two priest holes which you can see if you don't mind getting your knees grubby. A weekday lunch could be Cajun spiced chicken burger with smoked Applewood cheese, or smoked haddock kedgeree with poached egg. For dinner, how about pan-fried turbot with fresh Lamorna crab, chilli and tomato linguine? The pub has a garden, although dogs are welcome throughout.

Open all day all wk 11–11 **Food** Lunch all wk 12-2.30 Dinner Mon-Sat 6-9 Restaurant menu available all wk ⊕ ARKELL'S ◀ Moonlight & Wiltshire Gold, 3B, Guinness ○ Westons Stowford Press, Thatchers. ♟ 12 **Facilities** Non-diners area ❀ (Bar Restaurant Garden) Garden ⟁ Parking WiFi ▭ (notice required)

WYTHAM   Map 5 SP40

White Hart

tel: 01865 244372 **OX2 8QA**
email: whitehartwytham@wadworth.co.uk
dir: *From A34 (NE of Oxford) follow Wytham signs*

Smart, sleepy-village pub

Although 17th century, the White Hart's contemporary interior sits well with the big old fireplace and all those 400-year-old stone flags. The management's marketing stance is that it's as happy to serve a pint of real ale as it is a sit-down meal. But if you are hungry perhaps start with pan-fried wood pigeon breast, roast beetroot, black pudding and lamb's lettuce; or home-smoked cod fritters with saffron aïoli, and follow on with chargrilled 8oz British sirloin steak, hand-cut chips, creamed spinach, rosemary roast tomato and red wine, shallot and thyme butter; wild mushroom and samphire risotto; or tapenade crusted cod fillet with sweet potato and red onion rösti. In summer, dine on the Mediterranean-style terrace.

Open all wk 12-3 6-11 (Sat-Sun 12-11, all day Apr-Oct) **Food** Lunch Mon-Sat 12-3, Sun 12-4.30 Dinner Mon-Sat 6-9 Restaurant menu available all wk ⊕ WADWORTH ◀ Henry's Original IPA & 6X, guest ales ○ Westons Stowford Press. ♟ 15 **Facilities** Non-diners area ❀ (Bar Garden) ♦♦ Children's menu Children's portions Garden ⟁ Beer festival Cider festival Parking WiFi ▭ (notice required)

RUTLAND

BARROWDEN   Map 11 SK90

Exeter Arms

tel: 01572 747365 **LE15 8EQ**
dir: *From A47 turn at landmark windmill, village 0.75m S. 6m E of Uppingham & 17m W of Peterborough*

Heart of the village and heart of Rutland, too

There are new owners at this 17th-century, stone-built free house, which overlooks the village green, duck pond and open countryside. Tom and Joanne Wade are new to the industry, but their daughter, Jessica, who runs front of house, has plenty of experience, having worked at various pubs and hotels in the area. They're keen to keep things friendly and welcoming, with real ale in the spacious traditional bar as well as 11 wines by the glass. Out front is a shaded patio, while the large rear garden has sufficient room for a petanque piste. On the menu, you can expect locally-sourced, seasonal produce.

Open all day Closed Sun eve, Mon **Food** Contact pub for food times Set menu available ⊕ FREE HOUSE ◀ Oakham Ales Grainstore Cooking, Sharp's Doom Bar & Atlantic IPA. ♟ 11 **Facilities** Non-diners area ❀ (Bar Garden) ♦♦ Children's menu Children's portions Garden ⟁ Parking WiFi ▭ (notice required)

BRAUNSTON   Map 11 SK80

The Blue Ball

tel: 01572 722135 **6 Cedar St LE15 8QS**
email: blueballbraunston@gmail.com
dir: *From Oakham N on B640. Left into Cold Overton Rd, 2nd left into West Rd, into Braunston Rd (becomes Oakham Rd). In village 2nd left into Cedar St. Pub on left opposite church*

A warm welcome at a pretty thatched inn

The 17th-century thatched Blue Ball, only a few miles from Rutland Water, makes an excellent stopping-off point for cyclists and walkers. Landlord Dominic Way looks after his ales, as locals in the beamed and cosy bar will testify. Seasonal and local ingredients go into classics, and modern dishes such as seared pigeon, beetroot purée, chorizo and dressed salad; marinated swordfish loin, lemon and parsley potato cake and home-made salsa; and Bates Butchers' sausages-of-the-week, mash, braised red cabbage and gravy. There is a Sunday roast menu and young diners are welcome to order small portions of most dishes, confirming the pub's family-friendly credentials. Vegetarian and special diets are catered for.

Open 12-2.30 6-11 (Fri 12-2.30-5.30-11 Sat 12-11 Sun 12-8) Closed 25 Dec, Mon (ex BHs) **Food** Lunch Tue-Fri 12-1.45, Sat 12-2, Sun 12-3 Dinner Tue-Sat 6.30-9 Set menu available ⊕ MARSTON'S ◀ EPA & Burton Bitter, Jennings Cumberland Ale, guest ales ○ Thatchers Gold, Westons Stowford Press. ♟ 10 **Facilities** Non-diners area ♦♦ Children's portions Outside area ⟁ WiFi ▭ (notice required)

CLIPSHAM
Map 11 SK91

The Olive Branch ★★★★ INN ⊛   PICK OF THE PUBS

tel: 01780 410355 **Main St LE15 7SH**
email: info@theolivebranchpub.com **web:** www.theolivebranchpub.com
dir: 2m from A1 at B664 junct, N of Stamford

Award-winning hostelry on the fringe of the Wolds

Investigate the bar here for its range of bottled beers, ales from the Grainstore brewery in nearby Oakham, and Sheppy's cider. Note the unusual nurdling chair – used for an archaic pub game when coins are thrown into a hole in the seat – just one of a range of artefacts enriching the interior of this one-time terrace of farm workers' cottages. The pub's name originated when a local squire made a peace offering by opening the inn in 1890 after closing another in the village. Chef and co-owner Sean Hope has earned an AA Rosette for his well-balanced, fiercely local menus. There might be starters like duck and beetroot terrine with pickled walnut and pomegranate salad, or pub-cured bresaola with pickled vegetables and goats' curd; followed by whole roast partridge with game chips, or black olive crusted fillet of salmon with saffron risotto. Finish with refreshing green tea pannacotta with lemongrass meringue and lemon and chilli granita.

Open all wk 12-3.30 6-11 (Sat 12-11 Sun 12-10.30) Closed 25 Dec eve **Food** Lunch Mon-Sat 12-2, Sun 12-3 Dinner Mon-Sat 6.30-9.30, Sun 7-9 Set menu available Restaurant menu available all wk ⊕ FREE HOUSE/RUTLAND INN COMPANY LTD ◀ The Grainstore Olive Oil, Timothy Taylor Landlord ◌ Westons Mortimers Orchard. ♟ 16 **Facilities** Non-diners area ♥ (Bar Garden) ♦♦ Children's menu Children's portions Garden ⏁ Parking WiFi **Rooms** 6

GREETHAM
Map 11 SK91

The Wheatsheaf

tel: 01572 812325 **1 Stretton Rd LE15 7NP**
email: enquiries@wheatsheaf-greetham.co.uk
dir: From A1 follow signs for Oakham onto B668 to Greetham, pub on left

Homely refuge with an emphasis on locally sourced food

Set sideways to the road, this 18th-century, stone-built village pub is lovingly run by Carol and Scott Craddock. Carol notched up more than 20 years working in several renowned kitchens before coming here to put her wide experience to excellent use. She changes her modern British menu weekly, and cooks using locally sourced meats and high quality sustainable fresh fish; she makes bread daily, too. A typical dinner might feature pork and sage terrine with onion confit and toast; or baked snails in garlic and parsley butter for starters, then smoked haddock fillet with champ potato, poached egg and chive butter sauce; or crispy pork belly, chorizo, sautéed potatoes, roast root veg and apple sauce for the main course. Rutland-brewed real ales are served in the bar.

Open 12-3 6-close (Fri-Sun all day) Closed 1st 2wks Jan, Mon (ex BHs) **Food** Lunch Tue-Fri 12-2, Sat 12-2.30, Sun 12-3 Dinner Tue-Sat 6.30-9 Set menu available ⊕ PUNCH TAVERNS ◀ Greene King IPA, Oldershaw Newton's Drop, Brewsters Decadence, Oakham Ales Inferno, Grainstore Triple B. ♟ 11
Facilities Non-diners area ♥ (Bar Garden) ♦♦ Children's menu Children's portions Garden ⏁ Parking WiFi

LYDDINGTON
Map 11 SP89

The Marquess of Exeter ★★★★ INN ⊛

tel: 01572 822477 **52 Main St LE15 9LT**
email: info@marquessexeter.co.uk **web:** www.marquessexeter.co.uk
dir: A1(N) exit towards Leicester/A4. At rdbt onto A47 towards Leicester. At Uppingham rdbt onto A6003/Ayston Rd. Through Uppingham to Stoke Rd. Left into Lyddington, left into Main St. Pub on left

Smart village inn with great food

Run by renowned local chef Brian Baker, this old village inn fits seamlessly into Lyddington's long, yellow-brown ironstone streetscape. Stylish, contemporary design works well together with traditional pub essentials, to wit, beams, flagstone floors and winter fires. Modern British menus offer starters like Asian prawn broth; or the charcuterie plate with rocket and marinated shallots, and main courses such as pan-fried calves' liver, steamed new potatoes, crispy Parma ham and onion dressing; and Brian's signature sharing dish of grilled rib of Derbyshire beef with frites and béarnaise sauce. Add a shady garden and the mix is complete for an enjoyable visit.

Open all day all wk 11-11 (Sat 11am-mdnt Sun 12-10.30) Closed 25 Dec **Food** Lunch Mon-Sat 12-2.30, Sun 12-3 Dinner Mon-Sat 6.30-9.30, Sun 6-9 Set menu available Restaurant menu available Mon-Sat ⊕ MARSTON'S ◀ The Marquess Bitter, guest ale ◌ Thatchers. ♟ 14 **Facilities** Non-diners area ♥ (Bar Garden) ♦♦ Children's menu Children's portions Garden ⏁ Parking WiFi ⊞ (notice required) **Rooms** 17

Old White Hart

tel: 01572 821703 **51 Main St LE15 9LR**
email: mail@oldwhitehart.co.uk
dir: From A6003 between Uppingham & Corby take B672. Pub on main street

17th-century inn in a rural conservation village

This free house opposite the village green is constructed from honey-coloured sandstone like the surrounding cottages, and has original beamed ceilings and stone walls. Owners Stuart and Holly East have been running the pub for over 16 years and have built a reputation for food. Dishes served in the restaurant include crayfish and smoked salmon thermidor; roast rabbit with spinach tagliatelle and wild mushrooms, and a selection of vegetarian choices. On warm days customers take their pints of Nene Valley bitter or Aspall cider out into the gardens or onto the covered patio. The inn also has a floodlit petanque pitch.

Open all wk 12-11 (Sun 12-4 7-10.30) Closed 25 Dec, 26 Dec eve **Food** Lunch Mon-Sat 12-2, Sun 12-2.30 Dinner Mon-Sat 6.30-9 (Sun 6-8 summer) ⊕ FREE HOUSE ◀ Greene King IPA, The Grainstore, Nene Valley, KCB ◌ Aspall. ♟ 10
Facilities Non-diners area ♦♦ Children's portions Play area Garden ⏁ Parking WiFi ⊞ (notice required)

MANTON — Map 11 SK80

The Horse and Jockey

tel: 01572 737335 **2 St Marys Rd LE15 8SU**
email: enquiries@horseandjockeyrutland.co.uk
dir: *Exit A6003 between Oakham & Uppingham signed Rutland Water South Shore. 1st left in Manton into St Marys Rd*

Handy refuelling stop by Rutland Water

Privately owned, this pleasing, stone-built village free house is a popular pitstop for cyclists and ramblers investigating the recreational tracks around Rutland Water. The innate charm of the traditional, stone-floored, beamed interior complements the well-kept Rutland-brewed beers and robust pub food. The wholesome home-cooked menu is strong on produce with local provenance and baguettes and salads are also on offer for those looking for a lighter option at lunch. Typical dishes from the main menu include black pudding fritters with red onion chutney; steak and ale pie; and roasted aubergine topped with vegetables and chickpeas.

Open all day all wk **Food** Lunch all wk 12-9 (Apr-Sep) all wk 12-2.30 (Oct-Mar) Dinner all wk 12-9 (Apr-Sep) all wk 6-9 (Oct-Mar) ⊕ FREE HOUSE ◀ The Grainstore Cooking & Ten Fifty, Fall at the First (pub's own), guest ales ♂ Jollydale, Aspall, Kopparberg. ▼ 12 **Facilities** Non-diners area ❦ (Bar Garden) ◀ Children's menu Children's portions Garden ⊟ Parking WiFi ▦ (notice required)

MARKET OVERTON — Map 11 SK81

The Black Bull

tel: 01572 767677 **2 Teigh Rd LE15 7PW**
email: enquiry@blackbullrutland.co.uk
dir: *From Oakham take B668 to Cottesmore. Left signed Market Overton*

Convivial village local with good food

Just six miles from Rutland Water nature reserve and a short drive from Stamford and Nottingham, The Black Bull occupies a lovely spot in the picturesque village of Market Overton. Once a coach house, the thatched pub offers a traditional atmosphere with real fires and sumptuous sofas, although walking boots, children and dogs are as welcome as diners. Local produce fills the frequently changing menu here, including steaks from a nearby farm and lamb from Launde Abbey. Sample dishes include fresh crab cakes, dill, white wine and cream sauce; and trio of pork sausages, mash and rich onion pan gravy.

Open 12-3 6-12 (Sun 12-6) Closed Sun eve & Mon **Food** Lunch Tue-Sat 12-2.30, Sun 12-3 Dinner Tue-Sat 6-9.30 ⊕ FREE HOUSE ◀ Black Sheep, Grainstore Rutland Bitter ♂ Thatchers Gold, Westons Old Rosie, Scrambler. **Facilities** Non-diners area ❦ (Bar Outside area) ◀ Children's menu Children's portions Outside area Cider festival Parking WiFi ▦ (notice required)

NORTH LUFFENHAM — Map 11 SK90

NEW The Fox Country Pub

tel: 01780 720991 **1 Pinfold Ln LE15 8LE**
email: info@thefoxrutland.co.uk
dir: *From A6003 follow Manton signs. Right signed Lyndon. Through Lyndon to North Luffenham. Pub on left. Or from A6121 follow North Luffenham signs*

Picturesque setting for a summer beer festival

An attractive 18th-century double-fronted stone building in one of Rutland's oh-so-picturesque villages. Now in Jason Allen's caring hands and with an extensive refurbishment behind it, the Fox welcomes all-comers at its locally

crafted oak bar, where stone-flagged floors are warmed by log-burners. Ample choice of refreshments includes four rotating real ales, and 16 wines sold by the glass. Find a spot in the lounge for a relaxed snack, or peruse the menu in the tastefully decorated restaurant. Fresh, locally sourced ingredients are the basis of home-cooked dishes such as steak and mushroom pie; pork loin with Stilton and pears; and Bakewell tart.

Open 12-2.30 5.30-11 (Mon-Tue 5.30-11 Sat-Sun 12-11) Closed Mon & Tue L **Food** Contact pub for food times ⊕ FREE HOUSE ◀ The Grainstore, Oakham Ales, Tydd Steam, 4 rotating guest ales ♂ Aspall. ▼ 16 **Facilities** Non-diners area ❦ (Bar Garden Outside area) ◀ Children's menu Children's portions Garden Outside area ⊟ Beer festival Parking WiFi ▦ (notice required)

OAKHAM — Map 11 SK80

The Grainstore Brewery

tel: 01572 770065 **Station Approach LE15 6RE**
email: enquiries@grainstorebrewery.com
dir: *Adjacent to Oakham rail station*

The largest brewery in the smallest county

One of the best brew pubs in Britain, The Grainstore Brewery is housed in a three-storey Victorian grain store next to Oakham railway station. William Davis and Peter Atkinson's brewing company uses the finest quality hops and ingredients to make the beers and ciders that can be sampled in the pub's taproom. Food is wholesome and straightforward, with the ales playing an important part in recipes for Rutland Panther chilli con carne and pork and Ten Fifty sausages. A full diary of events includes live music, the annual Summer Bank Holiday Rutland beer festival and the Spring Bank Holiday cider and sausage festival in late May. Tours of the brewery can be arranged.

Open all day all wk Mon-Fri 11am-mdnt (Sat-Sun 8.30am-mdnt) **Food** Lunch Mon-Fri 11-3, Sat 9-9, Sun 9-5 Dinner Mon-Fri 6-9, Sat 9-9 ⊕ FREE HOUSE ◀ The Grainstore Rutland Panther, Triple B, Ten Fifty, Rutland Beast, Nip, Cooking, seasonal beers ♂ Lady in Pink, Hornet. **Facilities** Non-diners area ❦ (Bar Restaurant Outside area) ◀ Children's menu Children's portions Outside area ⊟ Beer festival Cider festival Parking WiFi ▦ (notice required)

SOUTH LUFFENHAM — Map 11 SK90

The Coach House Inn

tel: 01780 720166 **3 Stamford Rd LE15 8NT**
email: thecoachhouse123@aol.com
dir: *On A6121, off A47 between Morcroft & Stamford*

Former stables serving well-kept real ales

Horses were once stabled here while weary travellers enjoyed a drink in what is now a private house next door. This elegantly appointed, attractive stone inn offers a comfortable 40-cover dining room and a cosy bar serving Adnams, Morland and Greene King beers. A short, appealing menu may include starters like deep-fried ham bites with cheese fondue; home made duck liver pâté, or goats' cheese and red onion tartlet, and follow on with pork chop with champ potato and asparagus; duck breast with savoury flapjack; or Thai chicken curry.

Open 12-2 5-11 (Sat 12-11, Sun 12-5) Closed 25 Dec, 1 Jan, Sun eve, Mon L **Food** Lunch Tue-Sun 12-2 Dinner Mon-Sat 6.30-9 ⊕ FREE HOUSE ◀ Morland Old Speckled Hen, Adnams, Greene King IPA, St Austell Tribute, The Grainstore Triple B, Guinness ♂ Aspall. **Facilities** Non-diners area ❦ (Bar Garden Outside area) ◀ Children's portions Garden Outside area ⊟ Parking WiFi ▦ (notice required)

PICK OF THE PUBS

King's Arms Inn ★★★★ INN ❀❀

tel: 01572 737634 **Top St LE15 8SE**
email: info@thekingsarms-wing.co.uk
web: www.thekingsarms-wing.co.uk
dir: *1m off B6003 between Uppingham & Oakham*

A 17th-century inn with its own smokehouse

The Family Goss — as they like to style themselves — have run this attractive stone-built free house since 2004, and their expertise is evident. Dating from 1649, its flagstone floors, low-beamed ceilings and two open fires are original. The bar is well stocked with snacks, including home-made salamis, biltong and pork scratchings, any of which would happily accompany a sloe gin, elderflower vodka or Zermatter mulled wine, all made here with locally foraged or donated berries and fruit. Real ales come from Grainstore, Marston's and Shepherd Neame; the very local Fynburys real cider is also stocked. Chef James Goss has earned two AA Rosettes for his seasonal menus — his 'buy local' policy relies heavily on a network of farmers, millers, brewers, hunters and fishermen; sea fish are all wild or line-caught from British waters. Lunchtime snacks include onion soup topped with grilled vintage Lincolnshire Poacher croûte; and crispy black pudding fritters with the house relish. A smokehouse platter results from the pub's smokery

which James was able to set up after experience of air-drying and fish-curing in Switzerland and Denmark. Typical of robust winter dishes are hare loin tournedos with beetroot and chocolate purée, pomme rissole, roots and kale; and stuffed corn-fed pheasant suprême, with Jerusalem artichoke purée, root vegetable and potato terrine, and mushrooms à la crème. Leave some space for fruit crumble, custard and cinnamon yogurt ice cream. A Bin Ends blackboard lists fine, affordable wines, while a Farmers Market board in the Snug promotes locally grown fruit and vegetables. The eight spacious letting rooms are located opposite the pub.

Open 12-3 6.30-11 (Mon 6.30-10 Fri 12-3 5-11 Sat all day Sun 12-3) **Food** Lunch

Tue-Sun 12-2 Dinner Mon 6.30-8, Tue-Thu 6.30-8.30, Fri-Sat 6.30-9 Av main course £12.50 Restaurant menu available Tue-Sat ⊕ FREE HOUSE ◼ Shepherd Neame Spitfire, The Grainstore Cooking, Marston's Pedigree ♂ Fynsburys Rutland Cider. ♟ 33 **Facilities** Non-diners area ❀ (Bar Outside area) ◗◖ Children's menu Children's portions Outside area ☲ Parking WiFi ⛟ (notice required) **Rooms** 8

STRETTON
Map 11 SK91

The Jackson Stops Country Inn
PICK OF THE PUBS

tel: 01780 410237 **Rookery Rd LE15 7RA**
email: robertknowles1@sky.com
dir: *From A1 follow Stretton signs, 1st right into village*

Timeless pub with seasonal dishes

There can be few pubs in the country that have acquired their name by virtue of a 'For Sale' sign. One was planted outside the pub for so long during a change of ownership that the locals dispensed with the old name in favour of the name of the estate agent on the board. Since taking over Robert and Mandy Knowles have certainly made their mark at this long, low, stone-built partly thatched building dating from 1721. Inside, the pub has plenty of offer: stone fireplaces with log fires, quarry-tiled floors, scrubbed wood tables and five intimate dining rooms. In the timeless and beamed snug bar, real ales such as Grainstore Ten Fifty lift the heart, boding well for excellent value dishes like flaky pastry Burgundy beef pie; Gressingham duck breast with bubble-and-squeak mash; or pan-fried fillet of sea bass with squash risotto, tiger prawns and roast chorizo.

Open 12-3 6-10.30 (Sun 12-3.30) Closed Sun eve, Mon **Food** Lunch Tue-Sat 12-3, Sun 12-3.30 Dinner Tue-Sat 6.30-9.30 Set menu available Restaurant menu available Tue-Sun ⊕ FREE HOUSE ◀ The Grainstore Cooking & Ten Fifty ♂ The Grainstore ciders. ☙ 10 **Facilities** Non-diners area ❧ (Bar Garden) ♦❧ Children's menu Children's portions Garden ☷ Parking WiFi ☷ (notice required)

WHITWELL
Map 11 SK90

The Noel @ Whitwell

tel: 01780 460347 **Main Rd LE15 8BW**
email: info@thenoel.co.uk
dir: *Between Oakham & Stamford on A606, N shore of Rutland Water*

North shore village pub for everyone

The part-thatched village inn stands just a 15-minute stroll from the north shore of Rutland Water, so worth noting if you are walking or pedalling the lakeside trail and in need of refreshment. The friendly, smart bar and dining room both have a stylish modern feel and feature flagstone floors, heritage colours and a warming winter log fires. Expect to find local Grainstore ales on tap and a wide-ranging menu listing pasta and salad dishes alongside The Noel's chicken, leek and bacon pie; Thai green prawn curry and Moroccan vegetable couscous.

Open 12-3 6-close Closed Mon **Food** Lunch Tue-Sat 12-2, Sun 12-3 Dinner Tue-Sat 6.30-9 Restaurant menu available Tue-Sat ⊕ ENTERPRISE INNS ◀ The Grainstore Rutland Bitter ♂ Westons Stowford Press. ☙ 10 **Facilities** Non-diners area ❧ (Bar Garden) ♦❧ Children's menu Children's portions Garden ☷ Parking WiFi ☷ (notice required)

WING
Map 11 SK80

King's Arms Inn ★★★★ INN ◉◉
PICK OF THE PUBS

See Pick of the Pubs on opposite page

SHROPSHIRE

ADMASTON
Map 10 SJ61

The Pheasant Inn at Admaston

tel: 01952 251989 **TF5 0AD**
email: info@thepheasantadmaston.co.uk
dir: *M54 junct 6, A5223 N. At 4th rdbt left onto B5063 to Admaston. Pub on left*

Stylish country inn with good children's menu

Dating from the 19th century, this lovely old country pub offers stylish interior decor and a real fire, which add character to the dining areas. The large enclosed garden is ideal for families and there is a good menu for children under ten. Grown-ups certainly aren't overlooked, either — the kitchen uses the best local produce in dishes such as Shropshire Blue and caramelised onion horn, which might be followed by Wickstead aged sirloin steak with balsamic tomatoes, watercress salad and chips. Steamed chocolate pudding, and banana and pecan tart are just two options for dessert. Dogs are allowed in the bar only between 2.30pm and 5.30pm.

Open all day all wk 11-11 (Thu 11am-11.30pm Fri-Sat 11am-mdnt) **Food** Lunch Mon-Fri 12-2, Sat 12-9.15, Sun 12-7 Dinner Mon-Fri 6-9, Sun 12-7 Set menu available ⊕ ENTERPRISE INNS ◀ Salopian Shropshire Gold, Greene King IPA, Guinness. ☙ 10 **Facilities** Non-diners area ❧ (Garden Outside area) ♦❧ Children's menu Children's portions Play area Garden Outside area ☷ Parking WiFi ☷

BASCHURCH
Map 15 SJ42

The New Inn

tel: 01939 260335 **Church Rd SY4 2EF**
email: eat@thenewinnbaschurch.co.uk
dir: *8m from Shrewsbury, 8m from Oswestry*

Shropshire beers plus the best local produce on the menus

Near the medieval church, this stylishly modernised whitewashed village pub is a focal point for all things Welsh Marches, with beers from nearby Oswestry's Stonehouse brewery amongst the ales stocked, meats from the village's Moor Farm or Shrewsbury's renowned market, and cheeses from a Cheshire supplier. In addition to the interesting sandwich menu, the tempting fare might include a sharing platter (seafood or deli); a starter of chicken and duck liver pâté, spiced plum chutney and toasted sourdough; followed by pan-fried sea bass fillet, with warm salad of butter beans, chorizo and tomatoes; or slow-roasted shoulder of lamb with leek and roasted garlic mash.

Open Tue-Fri 11-3 6-11 (Sat 11-11 Sun 12-6) Closed 26 Dec, 1 Jan, Mon **Food** Lunch Tue-Sat 12-2, Sun 12-3 Dinner Tue-Sat 6-9 ⊕ FREE HOUSE ◀ Banks's Bitter, Stonehouse Station Bitter, Hobsons Best Bitter, Marston's New World ♂ Thatchers Gold. ☙ 13 **Facilities** Non-diners area ❧ (Bar Outside area) ♦❧ Children's menu Children's portions Outside area ☷ Parking WiFi

BISHOP'S CASTLE

Map 15 SO38

NEW The Castle ★★★★ INN

tel: 01588 638403 **Market Square SY9 5BN**
email: stay@thecastlehotelbishopscastle.co.uk
web: www.thecastlehotelbishopscastle.co.uk
dir: *Between Lydham & Clun exit A488 to Bishop's Castle*

Multiple choices for customer relaxation

In an elevated position off a quiet square, The Castle's beer garden offers panoramic views over Shropshire countryside. This is one option for customers at this imposing stone-built inn dating from 1719. The Castle is a veritable haven of hospitality, warmed by three log fires in the cooler months. Three bars serve an excellent choice of real ales such as Clun Pale, and a dozen wines by the glass. The oak-panelled restaurant serves plates of sustainably produced south Shropshire food. Choose from the likes of Jacob's Ladder (short rib) of beef with horseradish gnocchi, or slow-roasted pork belly. A beer and cider festival is hosted in early July.

Open all day all wk **Food** Lunch all wk 12-2.30 Dinner all wk 6.30-8.45 Av main course £11-£15 Restaurant menu available all wk ⊕ FREE HOUSE ◖ Three Tuns, Clun Pale Ale, Hobsons Best Bitter, Six Bells Big Nev's ♂ Robinsons Flagon. ♀ 12 **Facilities** Non-diners area ♣ (Bar Restaurant Garden) ♦ Children's menu Children's portions Play area Family room Garden ⋈ Beer festival Cider festival Parking WiFi **Rooms** 12

The Three Tuns Inn

PICK OF THE PUBS

tel: 01588 638797 **Salop St SY9 5BW**
email: timce@talk21.com
dir: *From Ludlow take A49 through Craven Arms, left onto A489 to Lydham, A488 to Bishop's Castle, inn at top of town*

Historic inn famed for its home-brewery ales

The memorable time-warp town of Bishop's Castle tumbles down steep hills at the fringe of Shropshire's Clun Forest. A sheep market centre for centuries; traders from the time of King Charles I onwards have enjoyed the hospitality of The Three Tuns, where England's oldest brewery, licensed in 1642, continues to produce beers in its eye-catching tower brewery; Rantipole and Cleric's Cure just two of a suite of accomplished offerings. The engaging warren of rooms is generally music and games machine free, although regular live jazz, rock, classical music and morris dancing events prove very popular. The pub hosts a beer festival as part of the town's renowned summer festival each July. Timber frames, beams and redoubtable fireplaces add tremendous character, whilst a glass-sided dining room overlooks the sun trap, flower-bedecked brewery yard. Menus are as diverse as the beers; witness roast loin of hake with saffron and shellfish bisque; or slow-cooked 'three pork and bean' casserole; with banana parfait and peanut brittle to finish.

Open all day all wk **Food** Lunch all wk 12-2.30 Dinner Mon-Sat 6.30-9 ⊕ STAR PUBS & BARS ◖ Three Tuns XXX, Cleric's Cure, 1642, Rantipole & Stout. ♀ 12 **Facilities** Non-diners area ♣ (Bar Restaurant Outside area) ♦ Children's menu Children's portions Outside area Beer festival WiFi

BRIDGNORTH

Map 10 SO79

Halfway House Inn ★★★ INN

tel: 01746 762670 **Cleobury Rd, Eardington WV16 5LS**
email: info@halfwayhouseinn.co.uk web: www.halfwayhouseinn.co.uk
dir: *M54 junct 4, A442 to Bridgnorth. Or M5 junct 4, A491 towards Stourbridge. A458 to Bridgnorth. Follow tourist signs on B4363*

An old-world coaching inn

This 16th-century coaching inn was renamed in 1823 after the very young Princess Victoria stopped here en route between Shrewsbury and Worcester; when she asked where she was, came the diplomatic reply, 'halfway there ma'am'. An original Elizabethan mural has been preserved behind glass for all to enjoy, and the pub is renowned for a good selection of regional real ales, 40 malts, and around 100 wines. A dinner menu might offer home-made duck liver pâté; deep-fried brie with hot redcurrant sauce; or breaded wholetail scampi and home-made tartare sauce to start, followed by Shropshire beef with onions and mushrooms braised in Guinness and ale; 16oz Astbury Falls rainbow trout with lemon and rosemary butter; or home-made chicken curry, rice, poppadum, naan bread and pickles.

Open all wk 5-11.30 (Fri-Sat 11am-11.30pm Sun 11-7) Closed Sun eve Nov-Mar **Food** Lunch Fri-Sun 12-2 Dinner Mon-Sat 6-9 Av main course £9.95 Set menu available Restaurant menu available all wk ⊕ FREE HOUSE ◖ Holden's Golden Glow, Wood's Shropshire Lad, Guinness ♂ Westons Stowford Press. ♀ 10 **Facilities** Non-diners area ♣ (Bar Garden) ♦ Children's menu Children's portions Play area Garden ⋈ Parking WiFi ⌷ (notice required) **Rooms** 10

NEW The Kings Head and Stable Bar

tel: 01746 762141 **Whitburn St WV16 4QN**
email: info@thekingsheadbridgnorth.co.uk
dir: *Town centre*

Fantastic old building in a busy little town

A splendid example of a heavily-timbered 17th-century coaching inn, built (or possibly rebuilt) after Bridgnorth's Great Fire in 1646. In the summer you can make the most of the weather in the small courtyard, while in the winter the three fires keep things cosy. Have a pint of Hobsons Town Crier or Twisted Spire while you peruse the menu, and chose from a good selection of modern British dishes, maybe starting with a black pudding Scotch egg with crisp smoked bacon and home-made brown sauce, followed by half a roast Aylesbury duck, served on or off the bone; or smoked hake with a cheddar and mustard crust, crisp fried poached egg and mashed potato.

Open all day all wk **Food** Lunch Mon-Fri 12-2.30, Sat 12-4, Sun 12-8.30 Dinner Mon-Sat 6-9.30, Sun 12-8.30 ⊕ FREE HOUSE ◖ Hobsons Town Crier & Twisted Spire, Wye Valley HPA. **Facilities** Non-diners area ♣ (Bar Outside area) ♦ Children's portions Outside area ⋈ WiFi ⌷ (notice required)

BUCKNELL
Map 9 SO37

Baron at Bucknell

tel: 01547 530549 **SY7 OAH**
email: info@baronatbucknell.co.uk **web:** www.baronatbucknell.co.uk
dir: *From Bromfield on A49 onto A4113 towards Knighton. Through Leintwardine. Right to Bucknell. Cross rail line, left & follow brown signs for inn*

Home-made food in great walking country

A stone's throw from Ludlow in the lovely Shropshire Hills Area of Outstanding Natural Beauty, the Baron sits at the foot of Bucknell Mynd. It's beautifully peaceful and there are plenty of great walks if you need to work up an appetite. Good home-made food is what they promise here, and you can eat either in the charming restaurant or the airy conservatory. Start with warm black pudding, bacon and croûton salad, maybe, before moving on to honey-glazed gammon steak, or steak, mushroom and Guinness pie. There's a pizza menu, too, and a choice of sandwiches and toasted paninis is available at lunchtime.

Open 6pm-10.30pm (Fri 12-3 6-11 Sat 12-11 Sun 12-6) Closed 2wks Jan, Lunch Mon-Thu & Sun eve **Food** Lunch Fri-Sun 12-2.30 Dinner Mon-Sat 6-8.30 ⊕ FREE HOUSE ◼ Wye Valley Bitter & Butty Bach, Wood's Shropshire Lad ♨ Robinsons Flagon, Westons Stowford Press. **Facilities** Non-diners area ✿ (Bar Garden) ◑♦ Children's menu Children's portions Garden ⊓ Parking WiFi 🚐 (notice required)

CARDINGTON
Map 10 SO59

The Royal Oak

tel: 01694 771266 **SY6 7JZ**
email: inntoxicated@gmail.com
dir: *From Church Stretton on A49, take B4371 towards Much Wenlock. Through Hope Bowdler, right signed Cardington. Or from Much Wenlock, take B4371 towards Chruch Stretton. Turn right at Cardington sign*

Historic pub in a conservation village

Reputedly the oldest continuously licensed pub in Shropshire and set in a conservation village, this free house can trace its roots to the 15th century. The rambling low-beamed bar with vast inglenook (complete with cauldron, black kettle and pewter jugs) and comfortable beamed dining room are refreshingly undisturbed by music, TV or games machines. Choose from the excellent cask ales and ponder your choice of sustenance: good-value home-made fare includes devilled kidneys with home-made onion rings; Shropshire fidget pie (gammon cooked with spiced cider and apples with a puff pastry top); fish pie; and mushroom and spinach lasagne.

Open 12-2.30 6-11 (Sat-Sun 12-11) (Nov-Mar 12-2.30 6-11 Sat 12-11 Sun 12-4) Closed Mon (ex BH L) & Sun eve Nov-Mar **Food** Lunch Tue-Sun 12-2.30 Dinner Tue-Sun 6-9 (Tue-Sat 6-9 Nov-Mar) ⊕ FREE HOUSE ◼ Ludlow Best, Three Tuns XXX, Wye Valley Butty Bach, Sharp's Doom Bar, Hobsons Town Crier. **Facilities** Non-diners area ✿ (Bar Outside area) ◑♦ Children's menu Outside area ⊓ Parking WiFi 🚐 (notice required)

CHURCH STRETTON
Map 15 SO49

The Bucks Head ★★★★ INN

tel: 01694 722898 **42 High St SY6 6BX**
email: lnutting@btinternet.com **web:** www.the-bucks-head.co.uk
dir: *12m from Shrewsbury & Ludlow*

Traditional pub in the Shropshire Hills

The small market town of Church Stretton is sandwiched between the Long Mynd and Wenlock Edge, and the charming old Bucks Head is without doubt where to stay to explore these impressive landscape features. The pub is known for several essential things: its comfortable, AA four-star accommodation, its well-kept Marston's, Banks's and guest ales, and its restaurant. Where possible, the kitchen uses local fresh meat, poultry and vegetables to create their dishes.

Open all day all wk **Food** Lunch all wk 12-2.30 Dinner Mon-Sat 6-9, Sun 6-8.30 ⊕ MARSTON'S ◼ Pedigree, Banks's Bitter, 3 guest ales. ♟ 9
Facilities Non-diners area ◑♦ Children's menu Children's portions Garden ⊓ WiFi 🚐 (notice required) **Rooms** 4

The Crown Inn   PICK OF THE PUBS

tel: 01299 270372 **Hopton Wafers DY14 ONB**
dir: *On A4117, 8m E of Ludlow, 2m W of Cleobury Mortimer*

Delightful old coaching inn with three restaurants

The exterior of this 16th-century coaching inn pushes the description 'creeper-clad' to its limit, and delightful it looks as a result. Birmingham to Ludlow mail coaches used to take on extra horses here for the steep climb up the hill. Much of its period past is evident inside – in the bar, for example, and in Poachers Dining Area, where you'll find exposed beams, stonework and a large inglenook fireplace. The two other eating areas are the Shropshire Restaurant, overlooking the countryside, and the Rent Room, with pine kitchen-style seating, sofas and more rural views. A typical three-course meal might start with pea and mint risotto; smoked haddock, salmon and spring onion fishcake; or Cajun chicken salad; then chef's pie of the day; wholetail breaded scampi, chunky chips and garden peas; or pork medallions stuffed with apricots and sage; and finally, chocolate brownie and chocolate sauce. The wine list, selected by a local merchant, includes a range of fine ports, Armagnacs and Cognacs.

Open all day all wk **Food** Lunch Mon-Fri 12-2, Sat 12-2.30, Sun 12-8 Dinner Mon-Fri 6-9, Sat 6-9.30, Sun 12-8 Set menu available Restaurant menu available all wk ⊕ FREE HOUSE ◀ Hobsons Best Bitter, guest ales. ♀ 25 **Facilities** Non-diners area ❖ (Bar Garden) ♦ Children's menu Children's portions Play area Garden Parking ▭

The White Horse Inn

tel: 01588 640305 **The Square SY7 8JA**
email: pub@whi-clun.co.uk **web:** www.whi-clun.co.uk
dir: *On A488 in village centre*

Home to the Clun Brewery

In the beautiful Shropshire Hills, this gloriously unspoilt and unpretentious village inn oozes character with beams, wizened wood and slab floors. Three beers brewed in their own microbrewery, the Clun, together with others selected from Shropshire's many craft breweries provide the line-up at the bar. This 'green' pub offers visitors

drawn to AE Housman's 'Quietest place under the sun' heart-warming pub grub, derived from very local suppliers. The traditional suet puddings are a speciality or you could try venison and red wine casserole; or parmesan and dill crusted salmon perhaps; while leaving some room for a home-made dessert of apple, calvados and sultana crumble. Regular events take place here, including the Clun Valley Beer Festival on the first weekend in October.

The White Horse Inn

Open all day all wk **Food** Lunch Mon-Sat 12-2, Sun 12.30-2.30 Dinner all wk 6.30-8.30 Av main course £11 ⊕ FREE HOUSE ◀ Clun Pale Ale, Citadel & Loophole, Wye Valley Butty Bach, Hobsons Best Bitter, guest ales ♂ Robinsons Flagon, Thistly Cross Whisky Cask. **Facilities** Non-diners area ❖ (Bar Garden) ♦ Children's menu Children's portions Garden ⋈ Beer festival WiFi ▭ (notice required)

The Sun Inn

tel: 01584 861239 **Corfton SY7 9DF**
email: normanspride@btconnect.com
dir: *On B4368, 7m N of Ludlow*

Family-run pub with an innovative microbrewery

First licensed in 1613, this historic pub is close to the towns of Ludlow and Bridgnorth, and handy for the ramblers' paradise of Clee Hill and Long Mynd. It's been run by the Pearce family since 1984, and from 1997 landlord Norman Pearce has been brewing the Corvedale ales in what was the pub's old chicken and lumber shed, using local borehole water; Herefordshire's Gwatkin cider is another thirst-quenching option. Teresa Pearce uses local produce in a delicious array of traditional dishes – lamb curry, steak, fish pie, beef in ale in a giant Yorkshire pudding. There are also vegetarian and some vegan options.

Open all wk 12-2 6-11 (Sun 12-3 7-11) **Food** Lunch Mon-Sat 12-2, Sun 12-2.45 Dinner Mon-Sat 6-8, Sun 7-8 Av main course £10 ⊕ FREE HOUSE ◀ Corvedale Norman's Pride, Golden Dale & Farmer Rays, Dark & Delicious, Coniston Special Oatmeal Stout ♂ Gwatkin. ♀ 8 **Facilities** Non-diners area ❖ (Bar Garden Outside area) ♦ Children's menu Children's portions Play area Garden Outside area ⋈ Parking WiFi ▭ (notice required)

CRESSAGE
Map 10 SJ50

The Riverside Inn

tel: 01952 510900 **Cound SY5 6AF**
email: info@theriversideinn.net
dir: *On A458. 7m from Shrewsbury, 1m from Cressage*

Great river views from the conservatory and garden

This inn sits in three acres of gardens alongside the River Severn, offering its customers delightful river views both outdoors and from a modern conservatory. Originally a vicarage for St Peter's church in the village, the building also housed a girls' school and a railway halt before becoming a pub in 1878. The inn is popular with anglers. The monthly-changing menu might open with curried beef pancake; or chicken liver pâté, followed by perhaps beef bourguignon; turkey and ham pie; or vegetarian chilli. Comforting desserts include golden syrup sponge. Their own brew, Riverside Inn Bitter, is available in the cosy bar.

Open all day all wk **Food** all wk 12-9 ⊕ FREE HOUSE ◧ Riverside Inn Bitter, guest ales. ♞ **Facilities** Non-diners area ❖ (Bar Garden Outside area) ♦ Children's menu Garden Outside area ⊓ Parking WiFi

GRINSHILL
Map 15 SJ52

NEW The Inn at Grinshill ★ ★ ★ ★ INN ⊛⊛

tel: 01939 220410 **High St SY4 3BL**
email: info@theinnatgrinshill.co.uk **web:** www.theinnatgrinshill.co.uk
dir: *From Shrewsbury take A49 towards Whitchurch. Left signed Grinshill. Pub in village centre*

Much-restored coaching inn

A handsome Georgian inn with two later additions, whose successively lower rooflines help to create an attractive architectural grouping. Rising opposite is Grinshill Hill itself, source of the sandstone used for the surrounds of 10 Downing Street's famous door. Old Prickly (brewed to support the British Hedgehog Preservation Society) and Old Speckled Hen real ales introduce a wildlife element in the traditional, part-panelled and fire-warmed bar. Meals are served in several dining areas both inside and in the garden, the short menu including vermouth-cured salmon; cheeseburger; pie of the day; sausages and mash; pan-seared mackerel; and butter-poached celeriac with wild mushrooms. Conclude with chocolate brownie and home-made ice cream.

Open all day 8am-11pm Closed Sun eve, Mon-Tue **Food** Lunch Wed-Sat 12-2.30, Sun 12-3 Dinner Wed-Sat 6-9.30 Av main course £15 Restaurant menu available Fri eve & Sat eve ⊕ FREE HOUSE ◧ Hobsons Old Prickly, Ludlow Gold, Morland Old Speckled Hen, Greene King IPA Ò Thatchers, Kopparberg. ♞ 13 **Facilities** Non-diners area ❖ (Bar Garden) ♦ Children's portions Family room Garden ⊓ Parking WiFi ➡ (notice required) **Rooms** 6

HODNET
Map 15 SJ62

The Bear at Hodnet

tel: 01630 685214 **TF9 3NH**
email: reception@bearathodnet.co.uk
dir: *At junct of A53 & A442 turn right at rdbt. Inn in village centre*

Former coaching inn with a ghostly tale

With old beams, open fireplaces and secret passages leading to the church, this black-and-white-timbered, former coaching inn was once known for its bear-baiting pit. In the 1680s, a landlord threw Jasper, a regular down on his luck, out into a bitterly cold night. Within hours both were dead, Jasper from hypothermia, the landlord from fright, as if he'd seen a ghost, which legend suggests was Jasper. Food includes prawn cocktail with rosemary and sea salt focaccia; breaded whitebait; 'proper' chicken and mushroom pie with wholegrain mash, seasonal greens and red wine gravy; triple chocolate brownie, white chocolate sauce and coconut ice cream.

Open all day all wk 12-11 (Sun 12-9) Closed 1 Jan **Food** Lunch Mon-Sat 12-3, Sun 12-4 Dinner Mon-Sat 6-9 Av main course £12.95 Set menu available ⊕ FREE HOUSE ◧ Salopian Shropshire Gold, Black Sheep, rotating guest ales Ò Aspall. ♞ 10 **Facilities** Non-diners area ❖ (Bar Garden) ♦ Children's menu Children's portions Play area Garden ⊓ Parking WiFi ➡ (notice required)

LEEBOTWOOD
Map 15 SO49

NEW The Pound

tel: 01694 751477 **SY6 6ND**
email: info@thepound.org.uk
dir: *On A49 between Church Stretton & Longnor*

Great food and drink in the oldest house in the village

Have a pint of Ludlow Gold or Stonehouse Station Bitter and you'll be following in the footsteps of all those who've enjoyed a drink here since the thatched building (which dates to around 1457) became an inn in 1823. It's a comfortable, relaxed place, and the bright, airy dining room has a contemporary feel while making the most of original features. There's also a garden with a patio for alfresco dining. The menu includes a 'classics' section featuring beer battered cod and triple-cooked chips, fish pie and rib-eye steak, as well as starters like fresh crab salad with pink grapefruit, avocado and apple; or wild garlic and bacon soup. Mains might include rare breed pork, ham hock croque monsieur; heritage carrots, thyme and honey; or blue cheese, chestnut and beetroot ravioli, shallot and pine nut dressing.

Open 11-3 6-11 Closed Sun eve, Mon **Food** Lunch Tue-Fri 12-2, Sat-Sun 12-2.30 Dinner Tue-Sat 6-9 Av main course £14 ⊕ ENTERPRISE INNS ◧ Ludlow Gold, Stonehouse Station Bitter, Three Tuns 1642. **Facilities** Non-diners area ♦ Children's portions Garden ⊓ Parking WiFi ➡ (notice required)

LITTLE STRETTON
Map 15 SO49

The Green Dragon

tel: 01694 722925 **Ludlow Rd SY6 6RE**
email: enquiries@greendragonlittlestretton.co.uk
web: www.greendragonlittlestretton.co.uk
dir: *A49 from Shrewsbury towards Ludlow. 1m after Church Stretton right to Little Stretton. Pub in village centre*

Traditional village pub in prime walking country

Close to the Long Mynd in the Shropshire Hills and backing on to Small Batch Valley, the 16th-century Green Dragon is in a prime location for walkers and campers but also convenient for the busy market town of Ludlow 14 miles away. Grab a seat near the log-burner in the bar and enjoy a glass of Wye Valley Butty Bach ale or one of the traditional ciders. Local produce appears on the traditional menu in the form of Paddy Ryan's faggots and peas with mash and onion gravy, or Bert Butler's beef in Butty Bach with herb dumplings.

Open all day all wk **Food** Mon-Sat 11.30-9, Sun 11.30-8 ⊕ FREE HOUSE ◄ Wye Valley Butty Bach, Bass, Ludlow Gold, Hobsons Best Bitter, guest ales ♂ Westons Stowford Press, Robinsons, Green Dragon Special Cellar, guest ciders. ▾ 10 **Facilities** Non-diners area ❤ (Bar Garden) ♦ Children's menu Children's portions Play area Garden 🚌 Parking WiFi ☎ (notice required)

The Ragleth Inn

tel: 01694 722711 **Ludlow Rd SY6 6RB**
email: wendyjd65@hotmail.com
dir: *From Shrewsbury take A49 towards Leominster. At lights in Church Stretton turn right. 3rd left into High St. Continue to Little Stretton. Inn on right*

Country inn serving home-cooked favourites

This 17th-century country inn sits midway between Shrewsbury and Ludlow in beautiful countryside at the foot of the Long Mynd hills. Its pretty exterior overlooks a large beer garden with plenty of wooden benches and a children's play area. Inside are two traditional bars and a restaurant with oak beams, antiques and inglenook fireplaces. A good range of ales includes Wye Valley Butty Bach and Wrekin Gold, with Mortimers Orchard pleasing cider lovers. Food follows classic pub grub lines, though the specials menu may list fresh calamari with sweet chilli; or medallions of pork, black pudding and Dijon sauce.

Open all wk Closed 25 Dec **Food** Lunch Mon-Sat 12-2.15, Sun all day Dinner Mon-Sat 6.30-9, Sun all day ⊕ FREE HOUSE ◄ Ludlow Gold, Wrekin Gold, Wye Valley Butty Bach, Hobsons, Three Tuns, Sharp's Doom Bar ♂ Mortimers Orchard. **Facilities** Non-diners area ❤ (Bar Garden Outside area) ♦ Children's menu Children's portions Play area Garden Outside area 🚌 Parking WiFi ☎ (notice required)

LUDLOW
Map 10 SO57

The Charlton Arms ★★★★★ INN ◉   PICK OF THE PUBS

tel: 01584 872813 **Ludford Bridge SY8 1PJ**
email: reservations@thecharltonarms.co.uk web: www.thecharltonarms.co.uk
dir: *On B4361 from Ludlow towards Leominster (S of River Teme)*

Enjoyable Anglo-French food and local ale

Since taking over the pub a few years ago, Frenchman Cedric Bosi and his wife Amy have quickly established it as one of Ludlow's must-visit food pubs. Whether it's dogs, children or muddy-booted walkers, everybody is made to feel welcome at this pub on the banks of the River Teme. Well-kept local ales such as Hobsons Best Bitter keep beer drinkers happy and there are 14 wines by the glass. The food is excellent – a typical meal might start with Cornish crab raviolo, pink grapefruit, samphire and beurre blanc; or saag aloo soup, spiced potato bon bon and raita, and continue with Skrei cod, razor clams, chorizo and chickpeas; ox cheek, watercress pomme mousseline, baby onions, mushrooms and sour cream; or truffled mushroom risotto and aged parmesan. To end a great meal perhaps choose treacle tart, stem ginger ice cream or chocolate marquise, cherry and pistachio. Nine en suite bedrooms are available, some have wonderful views over the river.

Open all day all wk **Food** Lunch all wk 12-3 Dinner Mon-Sat 6-9.15, Sun 6-8.30 ⊕ FREE HOUSE ◄ Hobsons Best Bitter, Ludlow Gold, Wye Valley Butty Bach ♂ Thatchers Gold, Westons Mortimers Orchard. ▾ 14 **Facilities** Non-diners area ❤ (Bar) ♦ Children's portions Outside area 🚌 Parking WiFi ☎ (notice required) **Rooms** 9

The Clive Bar & Restaurant with Rooms ★★★★★ RR ◉

PICK OF THE PUBS

tel: 01584 856565 **Bromfield SY8 2JR**
email: info@theclive.co.uk **web:** www.theclive.co.uk
dir: *2m N of Ludlow on A49, between Hereford & Shrewsbury*

Handsome Georgian building with classy bar and restaurant

A former farmhouse, this place has been a pub since the early 1900s, when it catered for thirsty workers on the Earl of Plymouth's estate. Clive of India lived on the estate in the 18th century, hence the name. Today it is a mix of contemporary style with original features still evident. The bar comprises two areas: an 18th-century lounge with log fire and Clive's original coat of arms; and a more contemporary upper part that leads out to a courtyard with tables and parasols. You'll find Hobsons ales at the bar, plus ciders such as Robinsons Flagon, and 16 wines served by the glass. Lunchtime bar snacks served with home-cut chips proffer the likes of croque monsieur or a smoked salmon and cream cheese sandwich; while a three-course choice in the evening could comprise pan-fried scallops with prawns, saffron risotto, petit pois and chorizo; followed by bubble-and-squeak with wild mushrooms, cabbage, chestnuts, poached egg and wholegrain mustard sauce. If there's still room try strawberry and buttermilk pannacotta; or apple crumble with granola crust and custard. Tastefully converted period outbuildings provide accommodation.

Open all day all wk Closed 25-26 Dec **Food** Lunch Mon-Fri 12-3, Sat-Sun 12-6.30 Dinner Mon-Sat 6.30-10, Sun 6.30-9.30 Restaurant menu available all wk ⊕ FREE HOUSE ◀ Hobsons Best Bitter, Ludlow Gold Ō Dunkertons, Thatchers Old Rascal, Robinsons Flagon. ♟ 16 **Facilities** Non-diners area ❀ (Bar Garden) ♦♦ Children's portions Garden ⋒ Parking WiFi ▄▄ (notice required) **Rooms** 14

The Navigation Inn

tel: 01691 672958 **SY10 8JB**
email: info@thenavigation.co.uk **web:** www.thenavigation.co.uk
dir: *From Shrewsbury take A5 to Mile End Services. A483 (Welshpool), 2nd left signed Knockin. Approx 1.5m to Maesbury Marsh*

Country position beside the Montgomery Canal

Otherwise known as 'the Navvy', this canal-side pub maximises the appeal of its red-brick and stone-built industrial heritage; the restaurant was a canal warehouse in the 18th century. Comfortable sofas, a wealth of beams, log fire and piano all add to the bar's appeal, not to mention the range of Oswestry's Stonehouse ales on tap. Outside in summer, benches on the patio by the canal are much sought after. The kitchen applies strong ethical standards to the sourcing of its meats and fish, and deals directly with local producers whenever possible. A typical menu choice could be baked camembert with roasted garlic, followed by Welsh beef Wellington with wild mushrooms.

Open 12-2 6-11 (Sun 12-6) Closed 1st 2wks Jan, Sun eve-Tue L **Food** Lunch 12-2 Dinner 6-8.30 Av main course £12 Set menu available Restaurant menu available Tue-Sun eve ⊕ FREE HOUSE ◀ Stonehouse Cambrian Gold & Station Bitter, Wood's Shropshire Lad, Joule's Slumbering Monk Ō Westons Stowford Press. ♟ 11 **Facilities** Non-diners area ❀ (Bar Outside area) ♦♦ Children's menu Children's portions Outside area ⋒ Parking WiFi ▄▄ (notice required)

The Lowfield Inn

tel: 01743 891313 **SY21 8JX**
email: lowfieldinn@tiscali.co.uk
dir: *From Shrewsbury take B4386 towards Montgomery. Through Westbury & Brockton. Pub on right in 13m just before Marton*

Successful modern interpretation of old village inn

In a stunning location below the west Shropshire Hills, this pub combines the atmosphere of a friendly village local with a fierce support for microbreweries dotted along the England/Wales border – Monty's and Three Tuns beers are regularly stocked, as are a range of decent ciders. Modern British pub grub is the order of the day – wild mushroom Stroganoff; pork and leek sausages with mash; or beer battered cod and chips. They also do a 'pie of the day', as well as a selection of sandwiches. The eye-catching brick bar, comfy seating, slab floor, log-burner and duck pond add to the character of this village favourite.

Open all day all wk **Food** all wk 12-9.30 Set menu available ⊕ FREE HOUSE ◀ Three Tuns XXX & 1642, Monty's Moonrise & Mojo, Wood's Shropshire Lad, Salopian Shropshire Gold Ō Inch's Stonehouse, Westons Old Rosie, Gwynt y Ddraig Dog Dancer. ♟ 18 **Facilities** Non-diners area ❀ (Bar Restaurant Garden) ♦♦ Children's menu Children's portions Garden ⋒ Parking WiFi ▄▄

The Sun Inn

tel: 01938 561211 **SY21 8JP**
email: suninnmarton@googlemail.com
dir: *On B4386 (Shrewsbury to Montgomery road), in centre of Marton*

Convivial free house respected for its food

Probably about 300 years old, the attractive, stone-built Sun Inn stands on a corner in a quiet hamlet. Offa's Dyke Path runs nearby on its 177-mile route from Sedbury Cliffs on the Severn estuary to Prestatyn. The Gartell family runs this pub very much as a convivial local, with darts, dominoes, regular quiz nights and Hobsons real ales from Cleobury Mortimer. It's well respected as a dining venue, with the Gartells offering modern British dishes such as braised local venison with liquorice and blackcurrant, red cabbage, beetroot and parsnip chips; roast whole sea bass with peppers and salsa verde; or butternut squash, sweet potato, peppers and pak choi in mild coconut curry.

Open 12-3 7-12 Closed Sun eve, Mon, Tue L **Food** Lunch Wed-Sat 12-2.30 Dinner Tue-Fri from 7pm Av main course £12.95 Set menu available Restaurant menu available Tue-Sat ⊕ FREE HOUSE ◀ Hobsons Best Bitter, guest ales Ō Oldfields Orchard. ♟ 8 **Facilities** Non-diners area ❀ (Bar) ♦♦ Children's portions Outside area ⋒ Parking ▄▄ (notice required)

MUCH WENLOCK
Map 10 SO69

NEW Gaskell Arms ★★★ SHL

tel: 01952 727212 **High St TF13 6AQ**
email: maxine@gaskellarms.co.uk **web:** www.gaskellarms.co.uk
dir: *M6 junct 10A onto M54, exit at junct 4, follow signs for Ironbridge, Much Wenlock & A4169. Hotel at junct of A458 & High St*

Medieval town's venerable coaching inn

This inn was originally part of the Much Wenlock estate and its current name and heraldic shield refer to the Yorkshire Milnes-Gaskell family who acquired it in the mid-1800s. Bought by the Sheldon family 30 years ago, it continues to change with the times. The stabling has been turned into accommodation, and modifications have revealed the best of its architectural features. Ponder then, as you relax with a pint of Worcestershire Way, how many four-horse carriages were welcomed outside the bay windows before the railways came. For the hungry, the menu of classic pub dishes continues the tradition of seeing all-comers happily refreshed.

Open all day all wk **Food** Lunch all wk 12-2.30 Dinner all wk 6.30-9 Av main course £10 Set menu available Restaurant menu available all wk ⊕ FREE HOUSE ◀ Wye Valley Butty Bach, Hobsons Town Crier, Bewdley Worcestershire Way, Salopian Shropshire Gold Ő Symonds. **Facilities** Non-diners area ♦♦ Children's menu Children's portions Garden Outside area ⋒ Parking WiFi ⛐ (notice required) **Rooms** 14

MUNSLOW
Map 10 SO58

The Crown Country Inn ★★★★ INN ⊛⊛

PICK OF THE PUBS

See Pick of the Pubs on opposite page

NEENTON
Map 10 SO68

NEW The Pheasant at Neenton

tel: 01746 787955 **WV16 6RJ**
email: info@pheasantatnneenton.co.uk
dir: *On B4364 (Bridgnorth to Ludlow road)*

Thriving village inn run by the local community

Closed and derelict for a decade, this 18th-century village pub was bought by the local community, restored to its former glory and reopened. So very much the hub of this picturesque village, just six miles from Bridgnorth, chef Mark Harris creates daily-changing menus around the seasonal local ingredients available. A starter of eight-hour bourbon-glazed barbecue pork ribs with slaw might be followed by pan-fried line-caught coley fillet, leek, pea and spinach risotto. Wash it all down with one of several local ales, perhaps Hobsons Twisted Spire or Ludlow Gold.

Open all wk 12-3 6-11 (Sat 12-11 Sun 12-10) **Food** Lunch Mon-Sat 12-3, Sun 12-5 Dinner Mon-Sat 6-9 ⊕ FREE HOUSE ◀ Hobsons Twisted Spire, Wye Valley HPA, Ludlow Gold, Exmoor Ales Gold, Salopian Darwin's Origin. ♟ 16 **Facilities** Non-diners area ♣ (Bar Garden Outside area) ♦♦ Children's menu Children's portions Garden Outside area ⋒ Parking WiFi

NESSCLIFFE
Map 15 SJ31

The Old Three Pigeons

tel: 01743 741279 **SY4 1DB**
email: info@3pigeons.co.uk
dir: *Phone for detailed directions*

Rural roadside pub with resident ghost

The spirits of Sir Humphrey Kynaston and his horse Beelzebub are said to return occasionally to this ancient watering hole in deepest Shropshire; a local 'Robin Hood', he was outlawed by Henry VII and in 1493 ultimately pardoned by Henry VIII. Red leather-clad armchairs, a forest of black beams and local real ales set the charming ambience, while the menu's broad range of pub dishes pleases all tastes and appetites. Starters range from black pudding Scotch egg with mixed salad to button mushroom and blue cheese crumble with crusty bread. Typical main courses are herby lamb cobbler with mixed greens; crispy chicken burger topped with pulled pork and mozzarella; and grilled salmon with beetroot risotto, asparagus and crisp leeks. Vegetarians are also well catered for.

Open all day all wk 12-11 **Food** Lunch 12-2 Dinner 6-9 ⊕ FREE HOUSE ◀ Stonehouse Station Bitter, Ness Ales. ♟ 10 **Facilities** Non-diners area ♣ (Bar Garden) ♦♦ Children's menu Children's portions Garden ⋒ Parking WiFi ⛐ (notice required)

NORTON
Map 10 SJ70

The Hundred House ★★★★ INN ⊛⊛ PICK OF THE PUBS

tel: 01952 580240 **Bridgnorth Rd TF11 9EE**
email: reservations@hundredhouse.co.uk **web:** www.hundredhouse.co.uk
dir: *On A442, 6m N of Bridgnorth, 5m S of Telford centre*

Award-winning pub with quirky features

Lapped by astonishing gardens, this creeper-clad old Shropshire brick inn dates in part to the 14th century. From its village location, lanes and paths filter down through verdant countryside into the depths of the Severn Gorge. It's from the same countryside that the land-based ingredients for the two AA-Rosette menu are garnered. Order a glass of local microbrewery beer and relax in the warren of lavishly decorated bars and dining rooms, replete with quarry-tiled floors, exposed brickwork, beamed ceilings and Jacobean oak panelling. Both à la carte and specials menus are rich in fish and game choices to accompany a starter like black pudding, apple and chorizo stack with smoked cheese sauce and crispy onion rings. Move on to main dishes like rack of lamb with moussaka, harissa sauce and rich lamb jus; or smoked pheasant breast stuffed with walnut and fresh sage, and served with orange and red wine sauce. Memorable, antique-rich accommodation is the icing on the cake here.

Open all day all wk 10am-11pm Closed 25 Dec eve **Food** Lunch all wk 12-2.30 Dinner all wk 6-9.30 Restaurant menu available all wk ⊕ FREE HOUSE ◀ Ironbridge, Three Tuns, Ludlow, Big Shed Engineers Best Ő Westons Old Rosie. ♟ 10 **Facilities** Non-diners area ♣ (Bar Garden) ♦♦ Children's menu Children's portions Family room Garden ⋒ Parking WiFi ⛐ (notice required) **Rooms** 9

PICK OF THE PUBS

The Crown Country Inn ★★★★ INN ❀❀

MUNSLOW   Map 10 SO58

tel: 01584 841205 **SY7 9ET**
email: info@crowncountryinn.co.uk
web: www.crowncountryinn.co.uk
dir: *On B4368 between Craven Arms &*
Much Wenlock

Dedication to hospitality and serving excellent food

The Grade II listed Crown has stood in its lovely setting below the limestone escarpment of Wenlock Edge since Tudor times. An impressive three-storey building, it served for a while as a Hundred House, a type of court, where the infamous 'Hanging' Judge Jeffreys sometimes presided over proceedings. Could it be that the black-swathed Charlotte, whose ghost is sometimes seen in the pub, once appeared before him? The main bar retains its sturdy oak beams, flagstone floors and prominent inglenook fireplace, and on offer are beers from the Three Tuns Brewery, as well as Thatchers and Stowford Press ciders. Owners Richard and Jane Arnold are well known for their strong commitment to good food, Richard being not only head chef but Shropshire's only Master Chef of Great Britain, a title he has cherished for many years. Meals based on top-quality local produce from trusted sources are served in the main bar, the Bay dining area, and the Corvedale restaurant, the former court room. These may include

dishes such as smoked salmon and chive fishcake with celeriac remoulade, red pepper jam and fennel herb dressing; home-made black pudding croquettes with Boston beans and crispy bacon; confit of lamb shoulder and home-made faggot, fondant potato, creamed cabbage and smoked onion; and spice-crusted roast cod loin with vegetable dhal and coriander pesto. Sundays here are deservedly popular, as are the Tuesday and Wednesday steak nights and regular pie and pudding nights when a typical dinner might start with toasted garlic and herb bread; followed by steak, mushroom and ale steamed suet pudding; and to finish, apple and raisin crumble. Three large bedrooms are in a converted Georgian stable block.

Open Tue-Sat 12-3.30 6.45-11 (Sun 12-3.30) Closed Xmas, Sun eve, Mon **Food** Lunch Tue-Sun 12-2 Dinner Tue-Sat 6.45-8.45 Restaurant menu available Tue-Sat ⊕ FREE HOUSE ◀ Three Tuns 1642, Corvedale Golden Dale, Ludlow Best, local guest ales ♉ Thatchers Gold, Westons Stowford Press. ♓ 8 **Facilities** Non diners area 🐾 (Bar) 🕴 Children's portions Play area Garden ⛺ Parking WiFi 🚌 (notice required) **Rooms** 3

OSWESTRY
Map 15 SJ22

The Bradford Arms

tel: 01691 830582 **Llanymynech SY22 6EJ**
email: robinbarsteward@tesco.net
dir: *5.5m S of Oswestry on A483 in Llanymynech*

Tip-top ales at a Welsh Borders pub

Once part of the Earl of Bradford's estate, between Oswestry and Welshpool, this 17th-century coaching inn is ideally situated for golfing, fishing and walking. It is well known as a community pub serving first-class real ales. Eating in the spotless, quietly elegant bar, dining rooms and conservatory is a rewarding experience, with every taste catered for. For lunch try beef Stroganoff; or chilli con carne; while a typical dinner menu features hunter's chicken; lamb casserole; or pork medallions.

Open all wk 11.30-3 5-12 **Food** Lunch all wk 11.30-2 Dinner all wk 5.30-9 Av main course £8.95 Set menu available Restaurant menu available all wk ⊕ FREE HOUSE ◀ Black Sheep Best Bitter, 2 guest ales ♂ Westons Stowford Press. **Facilities** Non-diners area ❖ (Bar Outside area) ⦁ Children's menu Children's portions Outside area ⊼ Parking WiFi ▱ (notice required)

PAVE LANE
Map 10 SJ71

The Fox

tel: 01952 815940 **TF10 9LQ**
email: fox@brunningandprice.co.uk
dir: *1m S of Newport, just off A41*

Grand Edwardian pub offering Shropshire ales

Behind The Fox's smart exterior are spacious rooms and little nooks wrapped around a busy central bar, where there is an original wooden fireplace, and plenty of Shropshire real ales demanding attention. The menu offers sandwiches and light meals such as steamed mussels or wild mushroom ravioli, as well as pan-fried chicken breast, chorizo and sun-blushed tomato risotto with butternut squash velouté; game suet pudding with steamed greens; pork and red onion marmalade sausages with mash and gravy; and warm crispy beef salad. Enjoy the gently rolling countryside and wooded hills from the lovely south-facing terrace with its patio tables and large grassy area.

Open all day all wk 11-11 (Sun 11-10.30) **Food** all day ⊕ FREE HOUSE/BRUNNING & PRICE ◀ Wood's Shropshire Lad, Holden's Golden Glow, Three Tuns XXX, Purple Moose Snowdonia, Salopian Oracle ♂ Aspall. ♔ 12 **Facilities** Non-diners area ❖ (Bar Garden) ⦁ Children's menu Children's portions Play area Garden ⊼ Beer festival Cider festival Parking WiFi

PORTH-Y-WAEN
Map 15 SJ22

The Lime Kiln

tel: 01691 839599 **SY10 8LX**
email: fjpriamoltd@gmx.co.uk
dir: *From Oswestry take A483 towards Welshpool. Right at Llynclys x-roads. Pub on right*

Last pub in England, first in Wales

Below a wooded hillside stands this unassuming white-painted pub, with padded stools lining the counter in the homely bar, and cushioned wooden settles and leather sofas offering more relaxing seating. The Stonehouse Brewery in Oswestry supplies the beer. Menu suggestions in the simply furnished dining area include pan-fried scallops, black pudding chorizo and shallot brunoise; and braised steak in Cognac and peppercorn sauce. Hidden in the undergrowth nearby are the old lime kilns.

Open 12-3 5-close (Sun 12-close Mon 5-close) Closed Mon L **Food** Lunch Tue-Sat 12-3, Sun 12-8 Dinner Mon-Sat 5-9, Sun 12-8 ⊕ FREE HOUSE ◀ Stonehouse Station Bitter ♂ Stonehouse Sweeney Mountain. **Facilities** Non-diners area ❖ (Bar Restaurant Garden) ⦁ Children's portions Garden ⊼ Parking WiFi ▱ (notice required)

PULVERBATCH
Map 15 SJ40

NEW The White Horse Inn

tel: 01743 718247 **SY5 8DS**
email: admin@thewhitehorsepulverbatch.co.uk
dir: *From Shrewsbury at rdbt on B4380 into Longden Rd signed Longden. Approx 7m to Pulverbatch*

Dog-friendly pub in the lovely Shropshire Hills

Restored to its former glory, the 15th-century White Post was a farmhouse until the 19th century. By the front door some old doggerel reads: "Cathercott upon the hill, Wilderly down in the dale, Churton for pretty girls, Pulverbatch for good ale". Whoever wrote it would appreciate today's Shropshire-brewed Hobsons Twisted Spire and Joules Pale Ale. Home-reared pork and lamb are menu mainstays, alongside fillet of sea bass with chorizo and white bean broth; ballotine of chicken stuffed with smoked bacon; and butternut squash, celeriac and cashew nut tagine. Events include a Sunday beer festival at Summer Bank Holiday Weekend in August.

Open 12-2 5.30-11 (Sat-Sun 12-11) Closed 2nd 2wks in Jan, Mon **Food** Lunch Tue-Sun 12-2 Dinner Tue-Sun 6-9 Av main course £10.95 ⊕ FREE HOUSE ◀ Hobsons Twisted Spire, Joules Pale Ale ♂ Aspall, Westons Stowford Press. ♔ 10 **Facilities** Non-diners area ❖ (Bar Restaurant Outside area) ⦁ Children's menu Children's portions Outside area ⊼ Beer festival Parking WiFi ▱ (notice required)

SHREWSBURY
Map 15 SJ41

The Boat House

tel: 01743 231658 **New St SY3 8JQ**
email: info@boathouseshrewsbury.co.uk **web:** www.boathouseshrewsbury.co.uk
dir: *From A458 & A488 rdbt (N of River Severn) follow A488 (Porthill & Bishops Castle). 1st left into New St. Pub on left by suspension footbridge*

Riverside ambience and serious Shropshire fare

Paths from the medieval heart of the town drift through Quarry Park and across a footbridge to this half-timbered retreat beside a great loop of the River Severn at Shrewsbury. Lounge on the huge riverside terrace or make a base in the beamed, rambling, airy interior where real ales from Shropshire's best microbreweries, including Three Tuns and Ludlow Gold should delight the most discerning beer-lover. Dishes from the grill are specialities of the house, using meats with a largely Welsh Marches provenance. Otherwise perhaps start with ham hock and pea terrine with piccalilli purée; or wild mushroom and thyme soup, then tuck into steak and ale pie, sauté curly kale, peas and carrots; and finish with lemon posset and raspberry sorbet.

Open all day all wk **Food** Lunch Mon-Thu 12-2.30, Fri-Sat 12-10, Sun 12-9 Dinner Mon-Thu 6-10, Fri-Sat 12-10, Sun 12-9 ⊕ ENTERPRISE INNS ◀ Salopian Shropshire Gold, Three Tuns, Wood's Shropshire Lad, Purity Mad Goose, Ludlow Gold. ♔ **Facilities** ⦁ Children's portions Garden Outside area ⊼ Parking WiFi

Lion & Pheasant Hotel ★★★ TH ◉◉ PICK OF THE PUBS

tel: 01743 770345 **50 Wyle Cop SY1 1XJ**
email: info@lionandpheasant.co.uk **web:** www.lionandpheasant.co.uk
dir: *From S & E: pass abbey, cross river on English Bridge to Wyle Cop, hotel on left. From N & W: follow Town Centre signs onto one-way system to Wyle Cop. Hotel at bottom of hill on right*

Boutique hotel luxury in historic market town

The handsome façade of this family-owned hotel and free house graces medieval Wyle Cop, shortly before the street becomes English Bridge over the River Severn. A coolly elegant look is evident throughout, from the ground floor public areas to the spacious, well-equipped bedrooms upstairs. Just off the reception is the wood-floored café-style bar, which leads to the flagstoned Inglenook Bar, serving locally brewed Salopian Shropshire Gold, an extensive choice of cocktails and gins and a full range of main meals and snacks. On the first floor is the split-level restaurant, where dishes like cured salmon, sauce gribiche, watercress and lemon; Welsh lamb loin and crisp shoulder, wild garlic, roast carrots, potato mousse, goats' cheese and lamb sauce; and lychee duck egg custard tart, sugar glass and rice pudding ice cream help to maintain their two AA-Rosette status.

Open all day all wk Closed 25-26 Dec **Food** Lunch 12-2.30 Dinner 6-9.30 ⊕ FREE HOUSE ◼ Salopian Shropshire Gold, guest ales ○ Robinsons, Westons Stowford Press. ♀ 13 **Facilities** Non-diners area ♦ Children's menu Children's portions Garden ⊼ Parking WiFi ▭ (notice required) **Rooms** 22

The Mytton & Mermaid Hotel PICK OF THE PUBS

tel: 01743 761220 **Atcham SY5 6QG**
email: reception@myttonandmermaid.co.uk
dir: *M54 junct 7, follow Shrewsbury signs, at 2nd rdbt take 1st left signed Ironbridge & Atcham. In 1.5m hotel on right after bridge*

Attractive riverside coaching inn

The River Severn slides past the grounds of this substantial Georgian coaching inn. On one hand is the ancient stone church; on the other a stunning old bridge arching gracefully over the waters. From waterside benches and the grassy garden are restful views of this favoured corner of rural Shropshire. Dating from 1735, the inn is tastefully appointed throughout; the lovingly updated interior reflects the essence of long-past mail-coach days. There's a relaxed feel about the place, especially the bar which features a wood floor, scrubbed tables, comfy sofas and an open log fire plus Salopian Shropshire Gold and Sharp's Doom Bar beers. Dining opportunities make the most of the generous larder of the Marches so on the bar menu you could find pressed chicken and red pepper terrine; home-made Glamorgan sausages, sage and thyme mash; and Cajun-spiced sirloin steak salad. Smaller meals might include home-smoked breast of pigeon, and deli boards add further spice. For dessert perhaps try the raspberry and Limoncello cheesecake; or warm treacle tart.

Open all day all wk 7am-11pm **Food** Lunch Mon-Sat Brunch 9am-noon, Sun Brunch 9am-11.30am, Lunch 12-6 Dinner Mon-Sat 6-10, Sun 6-9 ⊕ FREE HOUSE ◼ Salopian Shropshire Gold, Sharp's Doom Bar, Three Tuns, guest ale. ♀ 12 **Facilities** Non-diners area ♦ Children's menu Garden ⊼ Parking WiFi ▭ (notice required)

The Prince of Wales

tel: 01743 343301 **30 Brynner St SY3 7NZ**
email: queenprince117@yahoo.co.uk
dir: *Phone for detailed directions*

Traditional food and award-winning local ales

Tucked down the back streets of Belle Vue in the heart of Shrewsbury, The Prince of Wales is run by Victoria Price who restored this friendly pub to its former glory. A rotating choice of guest ales has already won the pub several awards and the commitment to real ale continues with February and May beer festivals. Enjoy your pint in the bar or the large sun-trap beer garden overlooking the local bowling green. The traditional food menu includes baguettes, ploughman's, pie of the day, home-made lasagne and local sausages, egg and chips. On the days that Shrewsbury Town FC are playing at home, the pub opens for extra hours.

Open 5pm-mdnt (Fri-Sun 12-12) Closed Lunch Mon-Thu **Food** Lunch Fri 12-2 Av main course £5 Set menu available ⊕ FREE HOUSE/RED OAK TAVERNS ◼ Salopian Golden Thread, St Austell Tribute, Marston's Wainwright, Greene King IPA, Hobsons Twisted Spire, Three Tuns Mild ○ Westons Rosie's Pig. ♀ 10 **Facilities** Non-diners area ♣ (Bar Garden) ♦ Children's menu Children's portions Garden ⊼ Beer festival Parking WiFi ▭ (notice required)

■ STIPERSTONES	Map 15 SJ30

The Stiperstones Inn

tel: 01743 791327 **SY5 0LZ**
email: inn@stiperstones.net
dir: *Phone for detailed directions*

Beautiful location for pub grub

Built in the mid-16th century, the Stiperstones has been a pub since the 1840s and is full of charm and character. Set in the heart of the south Shropshire hills, in an Area of Outstanding Natural Beauty, it's ideally placed for walking the Stiperstones Ridge or the Long Mynd. Afternoon tea is available as well as more traditional pub offerings. Local ales can be found in the two bars, and a comprehensive menu includes favourites such as salads and jacket potatoes, as well as steaks, curries and ribs; or try the steak and kidney pudding. For dessert don't miss the famous whinberry crumble.

Open all day all wk **Food** all wk 12-9 ⊕ FREE HOUSE ◼ Wood's, Stonehouse, Hobson's, Three Tuns, Six Bells ○ Westons Stowford Press. **Facilities** Non-diners area ♣ (Bar Garden) ♦ Children's portions Garden ⊼ Parking WiFi ▭ (notice required)

UPTON MAGNA
Map 10 SJ51

NEW The Haughmond ★★★★ INN ⚜⚜

tel: 01743 709918 **Pelham Rd SY4 4TZ**
email: contact@thehaughmond.co.uk **web:** www.thehaughmond.co.uk
dir: *From A49 rdbt (NE of Shrewsbury) take B5062 signed Newport. Right signed Upton Magna*

Stylish community pub with inventive cooking

Named after the popular local landmark Haughmond Hill, this refurbished coaching inn has reclaimed its position at the heart of the local community since Martin and Melanie Board took over. Occupying a mezzanine in a newly converted barn, the upmarket Basil's restaurant offers such dishes as goats' cheese pannacotta, ginger and beetroot; and pan-fried duck breast, duck hash and blood orange jus. Alternatively, order fish and chips; steak and oxtail pie; or squash and cashew nut tart in the bar. Local Salopian Shropshire Gold is one of the regular ales on tap, and there are 10 wines by the glass.

Open all day all wk **Food** Lunch all wk 12-3 Dinner all wk 6-9 Av main course £16 Set menu available Restaurant menu available Wed-Sat ◀ Salopian Shropshire Gold, Exmoor Ales Antler ♂ Aspall. ♉ 10 **Facilities** Non-diners area ♦ Children's portions Garden ♔ Beer festival Parking WiFi **Rooms** 5

WELLINGTON
Map 10 SJ61

The Old Orleton Inn

tel: 01952 255011 **Holyhead Rd TF1 2HA**
email: aapub@theoldorleton.com
dir: *From M54 junct 7 take B5061 (Holyhead Rd), 400yds on left on corner of Haygate Rd & Holyhead Rd*

Rustic cooking in an 18th-century coaching inn

Although Paul Turpin-Ottley, landlord of this 17th-century former coaching inn, enjoys pasta, curry and Thai food, he doesn't offer them here because, as he says, they're available everywhere. Instead, he prefers an 'informal rustic style' of cookery, which means a wide-ranging menu of simply cooked, seasonal British dishes, sometimes with a European influence. Typically, these include Staffordshire supreme sirloin; Shropshire 'fidget' faggots; classic oxtail hotpot with basil dumplings; beer-battered cod; and split pea and whole-nut cottage pie. Real ales come from Hobsons brewery in Cleobury Mortimer. Walkers exploring this neck of the Shropshire countryside often head for the nearby Wrekin hill.

Open 12-3 5-11 (Sun 12-4) Closed 1st 2wks Jan, Sun eve **Food** Lunch Mon-Sat 12-2.30, Sun 12-4 Dinner Mon-Sat 6-9.30 Av main course £15 ⊕ FREE HOUSE ◀ Hobsons Best Bitter, Town Crier ♂ Westons Stowford Press. ♉ 10 **Facilities** Non-diners area Garden ♔ Parking WiFi ▭ (notice required)

WENTNOR
Map 15 SO39

The Crown Inn

tel: 01588 650613 **SY9 5EE**
email: thecrowninnwentnor@gmail.com
dir: *From Shrewsbury A49 to Church Stretton, follow signs over Long Mynd to Asterton, right to Wentnor*

A lovely village pub set in a beautiful landscape

Deep amid the Shropshire Hills, this inviting 16th-century timbered inn is popular with walkers who warm themselves at wood-burning stoves in winter and on the outside decking in the summer; here you can sup Three Tuns bitter and gaze at the Long Mynd's lofty ridge. The pub's homely atmosphere, enhanced by beams and horse brasses, makes eating and drinking here a pleasure. Meals are served in the bar or separate restaurant; expect pub classics like garlic mushrooms and chicken balti with rice, chips and naan bread.

Open all day all wk **Food** all wk 12-9.30 ⊕ FREE HOUSE ◀ Brains The Rev. James, Hobsons Old Henry, Three Tuns, Wye Valley Butty Bach ♂ Westons Scrumpy. ♉ 8 **Facilities** Non-diners area ❀ (Bar Garden) ♦ Children's menu Children's portions Play area Garden ♔ Beer festival Parking WiFi ▭ (notice required)

WISTANSTOW
Map 9 SO48

NEW The Plough Inn

tel: 01588 673251 **SY7 8DG**
email: plough.inn@aol.co.uk
dir: *From A49 between Ludlow & Church Stretton onto A489 signed Newtown. Under railway bridge. 1st right, pub signed*

Village pub popular with families, walkers and cyclists

Built, like much of the village, of local sandstone, this is pub is next door to it's own brewery – Wood's. Predictably, Shropshire Lad is one of its real ales. Playing pool, darts and dominoes and answering quiz questions – all are possible here, maybe with an ale from next door, a Snails Bank Herefordshire cider or one of the 10 wines by the glass. There's also a children's games room. Seasonal menus, backed by specials, tempt with dishes such as pheasant breast stuffed with black pudding, wrapped in bacon with creamy mash and apple sauce; smoked haddock fillet with poached egg; and two-tiered vegetable lasagne with chips and salad.

Open 11.30-3 5.30-11 (all day Fri-Sun) Closed Tue **Food** Lunch Wed-Mon 11.30-2.30 Dinner Wed-Mon 6-8.30 Av main course £10.50 ⊕ WOOD'S BREWERY ◀ Wood's ♂ Herefordshire cider, Snails Bank Tumbledown, Westons Gold Label. ♉ 10 **Facilities** Non-diners area ❀ (Bar Outside area) ♦ Children's menu Children's portions Family room Outside area ♔ Parking WiFi ▭ (notice required)

SOMERSET

ASHCOTT
Map 4 ST43

Ring O'Bells

tel: 01458 210232 **High St TA7 9PZ**
email: info@ringobells.com
dir: *M5 junct 23 follow A39 & Glastonbury signs. In Ashcott turn left, at post office follow church & village hall signs*

Traditional family-run village free house

Successfully run by the same family for more than 25 years, this independent free house dates in parts from 1750, and the interior reflects this with beams, split-level bars, an old fireplace and a collection of bells and horse brasses. The pub is close to the Somerset Levels, the RSPB reserve at Ham Wall and the National Nature Reserve at Shapwick Heath. Local ales and ciders are a speciality, while all food is made on the premises. Expect good-value dishes and daily specials such as Somerset brie fritters with cranberry sauce; fillets of sole stuffed with lemon and prawns with cheese sauce; or spinach and feta cheese parcels with onion relish.

Open all wk 12-2.30 7-11 (Sun 12-2.30 7-10.30) **Food** Lunch all wk 12-2 Dinner all wk 7-10 Av main course £11 Set menu available ⊕ FREE HOUSE ◀ Rotating local guest ales ♻ Wilkins Farmhouse, Orchard Pig. ⟟ 8 **Facilities** Non-diners area ✤ (Bar Garden) ♦♦ Children's menu Children's portions Play area Garden ⏟ Parking WiFi ⛟ (notice required)

ASHILL
Map 4 ST31

Square & Compass ★★★★ INN

tel: 01823 480467 **Windmill Hill TA19 9NX**
email: squareandcompass@tiscali.co.uk **web:** www.squareandcompasspub.com
dir: *Exit A358 at Stewley Cross service station onto Wood Rd. 1m to pub in Windmill Hill*

Friendly rural pub with high-quality accommodation

Beautifully located overlooking the Blackdown Hills, this traditional family-owned country pub has been a labour of love for owners Chris and Janet Slow for over 18 years. A warm and friendly atmosphere pervades the bar with its hand-made settles and tables. Exmoor and St Austell ales head the refreshments list, while reasonably priced and freshly made meals are prepared in the state-of-the-art kitchen. In addition to classic pub dishes, steaks and grills, the chef's specials may tempt with smoked haddock, prawn and leek bake, honey and mustard glazed lamb noisettes; or country chicken casserole. The inn offers AA-rated accommodation, and the barn next door hosts weddings and regular live music.

Open 12-3 6.30-late (Sun 7-late) Closed 25-26 Dec, Tue-Thu L **Food** Lunch Fri-Mon 12-2 Dinner all wk 7-9.30 ⊕ FREE HOUSE ◀ St Austell Tribute & Trelawny, Exmoor ♻ Burrow Hill. **Facilities** Non-diners area ✤ (Bar Restaurant Garden) ♦♦ Children's menu Children's portions Garden ⏟ Parking WiFi **Rooms** 8

AXBRIDGE
Map 4 ST45

Lamb Inn

tel: 01934 732253 **The Square BS26 2AP**
dir: *10m from Wells & Weston-Super-Mare on A370*

Plenty of pub favourites at this old inn

Parts of this rambling 15th-century building were once the guildhall, but it became an inn in 1830. The bars are heated by log fires and offer Butcombe ales; there's also a skittle alley and large terraced garden. All the food is home made, ranging from pan-roast stuffed chicken breast to beef bourguignon, with burgers, jacket potatoes and a ploughman's offering a lighter option. Opposite is the medieval King John's Hunting Lodge, so christened in 1905 by an owner who chose to ignore the fact that John had died over two centuries before it was built.

Open all day all wk **Food** Lunch Mon-Thu 12-2.30, Fri-Sat 12-3, Sun 12-6 Dinner

---

Mon-Thu 6-9, Fri-Sat 6-9.30, Sun 12-6 ⊕ BUTCOMBE ◀ Butcombe Bitter, guest ales ♻ Thatchers Cheddar Valley, Ashton Press, Wilkins Farmhouse. ⟟ 10 **Facilities** Non-diners area ✤ (Bar Garden) ♦♦ Children's portions Garden ⏟ WiFi ⛟ (notice required)

BABCARY
Map 4 ST52

Red Lion ★★★★ INN

tel: 01458 223230 **TA11 7ED**
email: redlionbabcary@btinternet.com **web:** www.redlionbabcary.co.uk
dir: *NE of Yeovil. Follow Babcary signs from A303 or A37*

Pretty pub with a great range of food

Rich colour-washed walls, heavy beams and simple wooden furniture characterise this beautifully appointed, thatched free house that has six, AA-rated en suite bedrooms. The bar offers a great selection of real ales, and you can dine there, in the restaurant or in the garden. The daily menus run from pub favourites such as sausage and mash and honey roasted ham, egg and hand-cut chips through to roasted pork belly, cavolo nero, pomme purée and honey and cider jus; or duck breast, potato and pancetta terrine, heritage carrots and broccoli. All bread is baked on the premises and local suppliers are used as much as possible – they have a 24-hour 'port to plate' policy for the fish that's supplied from Brixham.

Open all wk 12-3 6-12 **Food** Lunch all wk 12-2.30 Dinner Mon-Sat 7-9.30 ⊕ FREE HOUSE ◀ Teignworthy, Otter, Bays, Yeovil Ales ♻ Mallets, Orchard Pig. ⟟ 12 **Facilities** Non-diners area ✤ (Bar Garden) ♦♦ Children's portions Play area Garden ⏟ Parking WiFi ⛟ **Rooms** 6

BATH
Map 4 ST76

The Blathwayt Arms

tel: 01225 421995 **Lansdown BA1 9BT**
email: info@blathwaytarms.co.uk **web:** www.blathwaytarms.co.uk
dir: *2m N of Bath, next to Bath Racecourse*

Classic country pub, traditional fare, interesting ales

Named after William Blathwayt, the 17th-century politician who established the War Office as an official government department. Blathwayt effectively became the country's first Minister for War; his National Trust country house a few miles from the pub is known for its deer park. With its welcoming approach to dogs, children and muddy boots, this is a proper pub serving anything from a pint of Otter to a plate of Blathwayt steak and ale pie. Mulled wine is supped around log fires in winter, while barbecues in summer are prepared in the large garden, which has a children's play area and overlooks Bath Racecourse.

Open all day all wk **Food** Lunch Mon-Thu 12-9, Fri-Sat 12-9.30, Sun 12-6 Dinner Mon-Thu 12-9, Fri-Sat 12-9.30, Sun 12-6 ⊕ FREE HOUSE/HEARTSTONE INNS LTD ◀ Otter Bitter, Abbey Ales Bellringer ♻ Westons Wyld Wood. ⟟ 9 **Facilities** Non-diners area ✤ (Bar Garden) ♦♦ Children's menu Children's portions Play area Garden ⏟ Parking WiFi ⛟ (notice required)

BATH *continued*

The Chequers ⦿⦿

tel: 01225 360017 **50 Rivers St BA1 2QA**
email: info@thechequersbath.com **web:** www.thechequersbath.com
dir: *In city centre, near Royal Crescent & The Circus*

Smart city dining-pub

A beautifully appointed gastro-pub that's been serving customers since sedan-chair carriers first quenched their thirst here in 1776. A short walk from The Circus and the Royal Crescent, The Chequers' reputation for excellent ales and great food has made it a firm favourite with city locals and visitors alike; booking is advisable. The upstairs restaurant has the look and feel of the ground floor rooms; a large window into the kitchen introduces an air of modern theatricality to the enjoyment of such dishes as ham hock terrine with pickled vegetables or pheasant pie with chips.

Open all day all wk 12-11 Closed 25 Dec **Food** Lunch Sat 12-2.30, Sun 12-6 Dinner Mon-Sat 6-9.30, Sun 12-6 Restaurant menu available all wk ⊕ ENTERPRISE INNS ◧ Butcombe Bitter, Bath Ales Gem ♂ Westons Wyld Wood Organic, Symonds Founders Reserve. ♚ 26 **Facilities** ♦♦ Children's portions Outside area ⊓ WiFi ▭ (notice required)

The Garricks Head

tel: 01225 318368 **7-8 St John's Place BA1 1ET**
email: info@garricksheadpub.com
dir: *Adjacent to Theatre Royal. Follow Theatre Royal brown tourist signs*

City centre pub with a dining room and outside terrace

Once the home of Beau Nash, the celebrated dandy who put the spa city on the map, The Garricks Head is named after 18th-century theatrical powerhouse David Garrick, and is adjacent to the Theatre Royal, for whose customers it provides pre-show dining facilities. The bar has a lot to commend it: a selection of natural wines from Europe, four real ales, Somerset ciders, and the largest selection of single malt whiskies in Bath. The food, locally sourced as far as possible, includes pub classics such as steak and chips or pie of the day, while the carte features wood pigeon with compressed fennel, carrot and pomegranate; poached hake with cavolo nero; artichoke risotto with parmesan crisp and truffle oil; and rhubarb and ginger fool or lemon posset to finish.

Open all day all wk Closed 25-26 Dec **Food** Lunch Mon-Sat 12-3, Sun 12-4 Dinner Mon-Sat 5.30-10, Sun 5.30-9 Av main course £16.50 Set menu available Restaurant menu available all wk ⊕ FREE HOUSE ◧ Otter Bitter, Palmers, Milk Street Funky Monkey ♂ Honey's Midford Cider, Broadoak Kingston Black. ♚ 20 **Facilities** Non-diners area ♣ (All areas) ♦♦ Children's menu Children's portions Garden Outside area ⊓ WiFi ▭ (notice required)

The Hare & Hounds ⦿

tel: 01225 482682 **Lansdown Rd BA1 5TJ**
email: info@hareandhoundsbath.com **web:** www.hareandhoundsbath.com
dir: *Phone for detailed directions*

Visit for the view, stay to eat and drink

Only a mile from Bath city centre, The Hare & Hounds sits high on Lansdown Hill with stunning views over the valley to Solsbury Hill. Happily the feast for the eyes extends to the pub's food and drink – so tarry awhile with an eponymous pint of ale or one of over 30 wines served by the glass. The welcome is warm, the staff and service friendly, and the food unpretentiously good. In summer the terrace is much sought after for alfresco dining as you'd expect; typical dishes honey-baked figs with goats' cheese, rocket and walnuts; venison shepherd's pie with spiced red cabbage; and sticky toffee pudding with butterscotch sauce.

Open all day all wk **Food** Lunch all wk 12-3 Dinner all wk 6-9 Restaurant menu available all wk ⊕ STAR PUBS ◧ Butcombe, Caledonian Hare & Hounds (pub's own) ♂ Symonds. ♚ 31 **Facilities** Non-diners area ♣ (Bar Restaurant Garden) ♦♦ Children's menu Children's portions Play area Garden ⊓ Parking WiFi ▭ (notice required)

PICK OF THE PUBS

The Marlborough Tavern ❀❀

BATH   Map 4 ST76

tel: 01225 423731
35 Marlborough Buildings BA1 2LY
email: info@marlborough-tavern.com
web: www.marlborough-tavern.com
dir: *200mtrs from W end of Royal Crescent*

Agreeable hostelry well placed for Bath's best attractions

Just round the corner from the famous Royal Crescent, this 18th-century pub once refreshed foot-weary sedan-chair carriers. Today's clientele is more likely to need a break from the rigours of traipsing around Bath's shops, for which the Marlborough is handily placed. The interior is contemporary yet retro, with an abundance of mismatched chairs, sturdy solid wood tables and scrubbed floorboards. At the rear is a walled and trellised courtyard terrace, a secluded little spot that's ideal for whiling away a warm summer's evening. Butcombe and Box Steam Brewery's Piston Broke are the prime ales dispensed in the spotless bar, with Orchard Pig cider also very popular; the wine selection comprising 26 sold by the glass offers something for everyone. The lunch menu pleases too by not straying far from popular and traditional pub classics, such as beer battered haddock with triple-cooked chips, mushy peas and tartare sauce. Other light bites range from sandwiches served with fries

and salad; a 6oz Ruby Red beef burger with fries, relish and coleslaw, to roasted tomatoes and rosemary soup with basil and crème fraîche. A typical three-course dinner may start with salt and pepper squid, garlic aïoli and dressed leaves; or pork rillette, apricot chutney, salad and ginger brioche. Next may come pan-fried stone bass, smoked haddock chowder, sautéed courgettes, samphire and crispy Parma ham; or duo of pork, crispy black pudding stuffing, broccoli purée, green beans, wholegrain mustard mash and red wine jus. Finish with lemon posset, almond crumble, candied orange and shortbread The must-book Sunday lunches might include roasted Berkshire Boar belly of pork with crackling, apple sauce and all the trimmings.

Open all day all wk 8am-11pm (Sat-Sun 9am-11pm) Closed 25 Dec **Food** Lunch all wk 12-2.30 Dinner all wk 6-9.30 Set menu available Restaurant menu available all wk 🛢 FREE HOUSE 🍺 Butcombe Bitter, Box Steam Piston Broke 🍎 Orchard Pig. 🍷 26 **Facilities** Non-diners area 🚼 Children's menu Children's portions Garden 🪑 WiFi 🚌 (notice required)

BATH *continued*

The Hop Pole PICK OF THE PUBS

tel: 01225 446327 **7 Albion Buildings, Upper Bristol Rd BA1 3AR**
email: hoppole@bathales.co.uk
dir: *On A4 from city centre towards Bristol. Pub opposite Royal Victoria Park*

An oasis of calm plus top notch beer and food

A delightful pub in a great setting, just off the River Avon towpath and opposite Royal Victoria Park. Described as both 'a country pub in the heart of a city', and as a 'secret oasis', it has a stripped-down, stylish interior and a spacious beer garden with a grapevine canopy. Bath Ales supplies many beers from its stable – here you'll find Barnsley, Gem and Special Pale Ale. Home cooked food is the order of the day, from bar snacks to main meals such as slow-roast gammon with fried eggs, 'proper chips' and pineapple chutney; free-range chicken, mushroom and bacon pie; market fish of the day fresh from the West Country; and wild mushroom and roast winter squash Wellington, braised hispi cabbage and new potatoes.

Open all day all wk 12-11 (Fri-Sat 12-12) **Food** Lunch Mon-Thu 12-3, Fri & Sat 12-9.30, Sun 12-8 Dinner Mon-Thu 6-9.30, Fri & Sat 12-9.30, Sun 12-8 Set menu available ⊕ BATH ALES ◀ Gem, Special Pale Ale & Barnsley, guest ales ⓞ Bath Ciders Bounders & Traditional. ⬤ 16 **Facilities** Non-diners area ✿ (Bar Garden Outside area) ♦ Children's menu Children's portions Garden Outside area ⌂ WiFi ▭ (notice required)

King William PICK OF THE PUBS

tel: 01225 428096 **36 Thomas St BA1 5NN**
email: info@kingwilliampub.com
dir: *At junct of Thomas St & A4 (London Rd), on left from Bath towards London. 15 mins' walk from Bath Spa rail station*

Modern British cooking and well-kept local ales

A short stroll from the city centre on a busy main road, this unassuming Bath stone building offers a happy mix of destination dining inn and locals' pub. In the cosy snug and traditional bar, real ale buffs will generally find a regular Palmers ale, supplemented by guest beers from local microbreweries such as Stonehenge, Milk Street and Yeovil. The kitchen creates traditional dishes, with a contemporary twist, from locally produced seasonal ingredients. A winter dinner menu offers the likes of a starter of curried parsnip soup and Bertinet; or chicken and black pudding terrine, Waldorf salad and rosemary focaccia then a main course of duck breast, lentils, black cabbage, smoked prune sauce; or slow-cooked pork belly, white beans, sage pesto, chicory and cider syrup. Rhubarb sponge and stem ginger ice cream is one highly comforting end to an evening, matched by a carefully chosen wine list.

Open all wk 12-3 5-close (Sat-Sun 12-close) Closed 25-26 Dec **Food** Lunch all wk 12-2 Dinner Mon-Sat 6-10, Sun 6-9 Av main course £16.50 Set menu available Restaurant menu available all wk ⊕ FREE HOUSE ◀ Stonehenge Danish Dynamite, Palmers Dorset Gold, Milk Street Funky Monkey, Yeovil Ales Star Gazer ⓞ Pheasant Plucker, Westons Wyld Wood Organic, Orchard Pig, Honey's Midford Cider. ⬤ 14 **Facilities** Non-diners area ✿ (Bar) ♦ Children's portions WiFi ▭ (notice required)

The Marlborough Tavern ◉◉ PICK OF THE PUBS

See Pick of the Pubs on page 425

See Pick of the Pubs on page 425

NEW The Rising Sun Inn ★★★ INN

tel: 01225 425918 **3-4 Grove St BA2 6PJ**
email: therisingsunbath@gmail.com web: www.therisingsunbath.co.uk
dir: *M4 junct 18, A46. Follow A4 & Bath signs at rdbt. At lights left into Bathwick St. Over river bridge, 1st right into St Johns Rd. Becomes Grove St, pub on left*

Hidden gem in Bath's city centre

Close to Pulteney Bridge and a short walk from the Bath's rugby ground, this Georgian pub is tucked away but well worth seeking out. Traditional but with fresh, modern decor and a peaceful courtyard garden, the atmosphere is friendly whether you just pop in for a pint of Sharp's Doom Bar or Thatchers Gold cider or stop longer for the home-made food. Light bites of chilli con carne and macaroni cheese bake sit alongside sandwiches and jacket potatoes, but those with larger appetites may well be tempted by steak and ale pie; Gloucester Old Spots sausages and mash; or spinach and falafel burgers.

Open 11-3 5-11 (Fri-Sat all day) Closed Mon **Food** Lunch Tue-Sat 12-2.30, Sun 12-4.30 Dinner Tue-Sat 5.30-9 Av main course £8.50 ⊕ PUNCH TAVERNS ◀ Bass, Sharp's Doom Bar ⓞ Thatchers Gold, Westons Stowford Press. ⬤ 10 **Facilities** Non-diners area ✿ (Bar Restaurant Garden) ♦ Children's portions Garden ⌂ WiFi **Rooms** 5

The Star Inn

tel: 01225 425072 **23 Vineyards BA1 5NA**
email: landlord@star-inn-bath.co.uk
dir: *On A4, 300mtrs from centre of Bath*

The city's oldest pub offering ales from its only brewery

Set amid glorious Georgian architecture and first licensed in 1760, the impressive Star Inn is one of Bath's oldest pubs and is of outstanding historical interest, with a rare and totally unspoiled interior. Original features in the four drinking areas include 19th-century Gaskell and Chambers bar fittings, a barrel lift from the cellar, and even complimentary pinches of snuff found in tins in the smaller bar. Long famous for its pints of Bass served from the jug, these days Abbey Ales from Bath's only brewery are also popular. Fresh filled rolls are available and free snacks on Sundays. A beer festival focusing on Cornish beers is held twice a year.

Open all wk 12-2.30 5.30-12 (Fri-Sat noon-1am Sun 12-12) **Food** Contact pub for food times ⊕ PUNCH TAVERNS ◀ Abbey Bellringer, Bath Star, Twelfth Night & White Friar, Bass ⓞ Thatchers Cheddar Valley. **Facilities** Non-diners area ✿ (Bar Restaurant) ♦ Beer festival WiFi ▭

BAWDRIP Map 4 ST33

The Knowle Inn

tel: 01278 683330 **TA7 8PN**
email: bookings@theknowleinn.co.uk
dir: *M5 junct 23 or A39 from Bridgwater towards Glastonbury*

A true community pub with amazing views

This 16th-century pub on the A39 sits beneath the Polden Hills and has far-reaching views across Sedgemoor to the Quantocks and Blackdown Hills. The live music, skittles and darts are popular with locals, while the seafood specials and Mediterranean-style garden attract visitors from further afield for summer alfresco meals. A full range of sandwiches and light meals is backed by pub favourites such as creamy garlic mushrooms; deep-fried cod fillet; celery and cashew nut roast; smoked haddock with cheese and tomato topping; grilled steak with all the trimmings; and Malteser cheesecake.

Open all day all wk 11-11 **Food** Lunch all wk 11-2.30 Dinner all wk 6-9 ⊕ ENTERPRISE INNS ◀ Otter, guest ales ⓞ Thatchers. **Facilities** Non-diners area ✿ (Bar Garden) ♦ Children's menu Children's portions Garden ⌂ Parking WiFi ▭ (notice required)

BECKINGTON
Map 4 ST85

Woolpack Inn

tel: 01373 831244 **BA11 6SP**
email: 6534@greeneking.co.uk
dir: *Just off A36 near junct with A361*

Former coaching inn with smart interior

This charming, stone-built coaching inn, now in new hands, dates back to the 1500s. Standing in the middle of the village and a short drive from Bath, inside there's an attractive, flagstone floor in the bar and outside at the back, a delightful terraced garden. The menu offers sandwiches, jacket potatoes, burgers, steaks and dishes such as beef and ale pie; breaded scampi tails; traditional sausage and mash; and slow-cooked lamb shank. The evening menu is extensive.

Open all day all wk 11-11 (Sun 11-10) **Food** Lunch Mon-Fri 12-3, Sat-Sun 12-10 Dinner Mon-Fri 6-10, Sat-Sun 12-10 Set menu available ⊕ OLD ENGLISH INNS & HOTELS ◀ Greene King IPA, Butcombe, guest ale Ŏ Thatchers, Rekorderlig. ⦿ 14 **Facilities** Non-diners area ❖ (Bar Garden) ♦ Children's menu Children's portions Garden ⋒ Parking WiFi 🚌

BISHOP SUTTON
Map 4 ST55

The Red Lion

tel: 01275 333042 **Sutton Hill BS39 5UT**
email: redlionbishopsutton@aol.com
dir: *Between Pensford & Clutton on A37 take A368 to Bishop Sutton*

Innovative seasonal dishes in village pub

This has fast become a real little gem of a pub; many visitors comment on its friendliness, the efficiency of its staff and how much they enjoy eating and drinking here. In the bar, Bath Ales Gem single-handedly raises the flag for Somerset. The menus offer choices such as Camelot Vale blue cheese and onion tart, truffle honey dressing and walnut salad; or wild boar salami with fennel and apple salad to start, followed by pappardelle pasta and venison ragù; pot roast belly of lamb; and salmon, crayfish and cod bake. There's also the 'classic stuff' as they call dishes such as thick slices of Walsh's ham, double fried egg, chips and chunky piccalilli; and a 12oz dry-aged (for a minimum of 31 days) T-bone steak.

Open all wk 12-2.30 4.30-11 (Fri-Sun 12-12 Mon 5-11) **Food** Contact pub for food times ⊕ PUNCH TAVERNS ◀ Courage Best Bitter, Fuller's London Pride, Sharp's Doom Bar, Bath Ales Gem Ŏ Thatchers Dry & Gold. ⦿ **Facilities** Non-diners area ❖ (All areas) ♦ Children's portions Play area Garden Outside area ⋒ Parking WiFi 🚌 (notice required)

BISHOPSWOOD
Map 4 ST21

Candlelight Inn

tel: 01460 234476 **TA20 3RS**
email: info@candlelight-inn.co.uk
dir: *From A303 SW of Newtown, right a x-roads signed Bishopswood & Churchinford. Pub on right in village*

Remote pub with excellent food

Debbie Lush and Tom Warren run this rustic rural inn tucked away deep in the Blackdown Hills. A 17th-century flint-built pub with wooden floors, crackling log fires and a warm and friendly atmosphere, locals gather here for tip-top pints of Exmoor or Branscombe ale drawn straight from the cask. Food will not disappoint, with everything made on the premises, including vegetables grown in the pub's garden. Follow creamy cauliflower soup or devilled lamb's kidney on toast with venison haunch with mash and vegetables; plaice fillets with brown crab mousse; or smoked cheddar and leek cannelloni, leaving room for sticky toffee pudding with toffee sauce and double cream.

Open 12-3 6-11 (Sun all day) Closed 25-27 Dec, Mon **Food** Lunch Tue-Fri 12-2, Sat-Sun 12-2.30 Dinner Tue-Thu & Sun 7-9, Fri-Sat 7-9.30 Set menu available ⊕ FREE HOUSE ◀ Otter Bitter, Bass, Exmoor, Branscombe Ŏ Thatchers, Sheppy's, Tricky. ⦿ 9 **Facilities** Non-diners area ❖ (Bar Garden) ♦ Children's portions Garden ⋒ Beer festival Parking WiFi 🚌 (notice required)

BLAGDON HILL
Map 4 ST21

The Blagdon Inn

tel: 01823 421296 **Honiton Rd TA3 7SG**
email: nigel@blagdoninn.co.uk **web:** www.blagdoninn.co.uk
dir: *From Taunton, through Trull, over M5, to pub on right*

On the edge of the Blackdown Hills

Just three miles from Taunton, on the edge of the Blackdown Hills, this friendly family pub and restaurant uses locally sourced produce including the pub's very own livestock. Chef Scott Simpson's menus specialise in local game and sustainable line-caught fish from Lyme Bay. Kick off with cider-cured salmon, apple gel, apple crisps and apple blossom before moving on to chicken, leek and ham pie with chargrilled baby vegetables, mashed potato and chicken jus; or gnocchi, truffled butternut squash purée and beetroot granola. Leave room for apple crumble and Calvados.

Open 12-3 5-11 (Sun 12-4) Closed Sun eve & Mon **Food** Lunch Tue-Sun 12-2.30 Dinner Tue-Sat 6-9 Restaurant menu available Tue-Sun ⊕ FREE HOUSE ◀ Butcome, Otter Bitter & Amber Ŏ Thatchers Gold, Katy, Rose, Red, Vintage, Old Rascal & Somerset Haze, Sheppy's. ⦿ **Facilities** Non-diners area ❖ (Bar Restaurant Garden) ♦ Children's menu Children's portions Garden ⋒ Parking WiFi 🚌 (notice required)

CATCOTT
Map 4 ST33

The Crown Inn

tel: 01278 722288 **1 The Nydon TA7 9HQ**
email: catcottcrowninn@aol.com
dir: *M5 junct 23, A39 towards Glastonbury. Turn left to Catcott*

Venerable ale house with good home-cooked food

Originally a beer house serving local peat-cutters, this low-beamed, flagstoned pub in the Somerset levels is perhaps 400 years old. The winter log fire takes the chill off Bristol Channel winds; in summer the half-acre beer garden is great for families and sun worshippers. Food is plentiful, imaginative and home made; typical options include spicy battered chilli beef; lasagne; and cheesecake. Look out for specials such as fish pie au gratin; game casserole; or teriyaki belly pork. A good range of cask ales and ciders from regional suppliers completes the picture.

Open 12-2.30 6-late Closed Mon L **Food** Lunch Tue-Sun 12-2 (booking advisable Sun) Dinner all wk 6-9 Set menu available Restaurant menu available all wk ⊕ FREE HOUSE ◀ Sharp's Doom Bar, St Austell Proper Job, Molegrip Core Ŏ Pheasant Plucker, Thatchers. ⦿ 10 **Facilities** Non-diners area ❖ (Bar Garden) ♦ Children's menu Children's portions Garden ⋒ Parking WiFi 🚌 (notice required)

CHEW MAGNA | Map 4 ST56

The Bear and Swan ★★★★★ INN | PICK OF THE PUBS

tel: 01275 331100 **South Pde BS40 8SL**
email: thebearandswan@ohhcompany.co.uk **web:** www.ohhpubs.co.uk
dir: A37 from Bristol. Turn right signed Chew Magna onto B3130. Or from A38 turn left on B3130

Much loved by locals and visitors alike

On the main street in the bustling village of Chew Magna, a short hop from Bristol Airport, this early 18th-century pub boasts a warm and friendly atmosphere. Inside, the oak-beamed rooms with scrubbed wooden floors and diverse collection of reclaimed tables, chairs and assorted artefacts all contribute to its charm. Fuller's London Pride and Butcombe Bitter take pride of place at the bar alongside a real Somerset cider and a list of well selected wines. The restaurant has a good choice of fish, game, seafood, meats and vegetarian dishes. You might choose to start with pan-fried scallops, butternut squash, chorizo and pea shoots before moving on to roast duck breast with garlic roasted celeriac, beetroot, carrots, spinach and plum chutney, or wild mushroom risotto. Home-made desserts like passionfruit cheesecake with raspberry sorbet will appeal to a sweet tooth. Look out for the spring into summer beer and cider festivals.

Open all day all wk 9am-mdnt Closed 24-25 Dec **Food** 9am-10pm Set menu available Restaurant menu available all wk ⊕ FULLER'S ◀ London Pride, Butcombe Bitter, guest ale Ò Thatchers Gold, Cornish Orchards. ♟ 12 **Facilities** Non-diners area ♣ (Bar Garden) ♦♦ Children's menu Children's portions Garden ⊨ Beer festival Cider festival Parking WiFi ▭ (notice required) **Rooms** 4

The Pony and Trap ⊛⊛ | PICK OF THE PUBS

tel: 01275 332627 **Knowle Hill, Newton BS40 8TQ**
email: info@theponyandtrap.co.uk
dir: Take A37 S from Bristol. After Pensford turn right at rdbt onto A368 towards Weston-super-Mare. In 1.5m right signed Chew Magna & Winford. Pub 1m on right

Country cottage pub-restaurant with award-winning cuisine

From the grassy beer garden of this appealing old country pub on a low ridge above the Chew Valley are gorgeous views across pastures and pocket woodlands. It's from these tranquil acres of north Somerset that most of the produce used to create the two AA-Rosette cuisine is provenanced; beer from the respected Butcombe Brewery is equally local. Brother and sister team of Josh and Holly Eggleton have now celebrated a decade here, during which tenure they've built a tremendous reputation for the invigorating menus based on a mantra of field-to-fork simplicity. The daily-changing à la carte may offer a starter of rabbit terrine, celeriac remoulade, apple and Butcombe chutney; a mains like venison faggot, hash brown, squash and kale; or fillet of brill with brown shrimp, celery, Savoy cabbage and seaweed butter. To finish, perhaps sticky ale pudding with salted caramel sauce and stout ice cream. The six-course tasting menu with wine pairings is a real treat.

Open all wk 12-2.30 7-11 (Fri-Sat 12-2.30 6-11 Sun 12-11) **Food** Lunch Mon-Sat 12-2.30, Sun 12-9 Dinner Sun-Thu 7-9.30, Fri-Sat 6-9.30 ⊕ FREE HOUSE ◀ Butcombe Bitter, guest ale Ò Ashton Press. ♟ 26 **Facilities** Non-diners area ♣ (Bar Garden) ♦♦ Children's portions Garden ⊨ Parking WiFi

CHURCHILL | Map 4 ST45

The Crown Inn

tel: 01934 852995 **The Batch BS25 5PP**
dir: From Bristol take A38 S. Right at Churchill lights, left in 200mtrs, up hill to pub

Rural village pub with lovely gardens

This gem of a pub was once a stop on what was then the Bristol to Exeter coach road. A good selection of real ales is served straight from the cask in the two flagstone-floored bars, where open fires blaze on cold days. The freshly prepared bar lunches include sandwiches, soups, salads and ploughman's, all made from the best local ingredients. In fact the beef comes straight from the fields that can be seen from the pub's windows. You can enjoy a meal in the beautiful gardens in warmer weather, perhaps beef casserole; chilli; or cauliflower cheese.

Open all day all wk 11-11 (Fri 11am-mdnt) **Food** Lunch all wk 12-2.30 ⊕ FREE HOUSE ◀ Palmers IPA, Bass, RCH Hewish IPA, Bath Ales Gem, St Austell Tribute, Butcombe, Otter, guest ale Ò Thatchers, Ashton Press, Healey's Cornish Rattler, Bath Ciders Bounders. **Facilities** Non-diners area ♣ (Bar Garden Outside area) ♦♦ Children's portions Garden Outside area ⊨ Parking WiFi ▭ Notes ⊚

CLAPTON-IN-GORDANO | Map 4 ST47

The Black Horse | PICK OF THE PUBS

tel: 01275 842105 **Clevedon Ln BS20 7RH**
email: theblackhorse@talktalkbusiness.net
dir: M5 junct 19, A369 to Portishead. At rdbt left onto B3124. At 3rd rdbt left to Clapton-in-Gordano

Real ales, short lunchtime menu, families welcome

The bars on one of the windows of this attractive, whitewashed inn near Bristol are a reminder that the Black Horse's Snug Bar was once the village lock-up. Built in the 14th century, the pub features low beams, flagstone floors, wooden settles, and old guns above the big open fireplace. Real ales served straight from the barrel include local Butcombe Bitter and Bath Ales Gem, whilst cider fans will rejoice at the sight of Thatchers Heritage. The small kitchen in this listed building limits its output to traditional pub food served at lunchtimes only (Monday to Saturday). The repertoire includes hot and cold filled baguettes and rolls; home-made soup of the day; daily specials, and classics like lamb hot pot and corned beef hash. The large rear garden includes a children's play area, and there's a separate family room.

Open all day all wk **Food** Lunch Mon-Sat 12-2.30 ⊕ ENTERPRISE INNS ◀ Courage Best Bitter, Bath Ales Gem, Butcombe Bitter, Exmoor Gold, Otter Bitter Ò Thatchers Heritage & Dry. ♟ 8 **Facilities** Non-diners area ♣ (Bar) ♦♦ Play area Family room Garden ⊨ Parking WiFi

CLUTTON | Map 4 ST65

The Hunters Rest ★★★★ INN | PICK OF THE PUBS

See Pick of the Pubs on opposite page

PICK OF THE PUBS

The Hunters Rest ★★★★ INN

CLUTTON   Map 4 ST65

tel: 01761 452303
King Ln, Clutton Hill BS39 5QL
email: info@huntersrest.co.uk
web: www.huntersrest.co.uk
dir: *On A37 follow signs for Wells through Pensford, at large rdbt left towards Bath, 100mtrs right into country lane, pub 1m up hill*

Traditional country inn with excellent views

Dating from 1750, The Earl of Warwick's former hunting lodge offers far-reaching views across the Cam Valley to the Mendip Hills and the Chew Valley towards Bristol. When the estate was sold in 1872, the building became a tavern serving the growing number of coal miners working in the area, but all the mines closed long ago and the place has been transformed into a popular and attractive inn. Paul Thomas has been running the place for more than 25 years, during which time he has established a great reputation for good home-made food, real ales – typically Butcombe, Bath Ales Gem and Otter – and a well-stocked wine cellar. The menu includes chicken liver and chorizo pâté; smoked trout and prawn cocktail; giant pastries called oggies, which might come with a variety of fillings, such as beef steak and Stilton, mixed smoked fish, cauliflower cheese, and not

for the faint hearted they say – the Welsh Dragon, casseroled beef with fiery chillies, peppers and tomatoes. Other dishes may include Somerset faggots with caramelised onion gravy; baked lamb rump, root vegetable mash, buttered greens with red wine and rosemary gravy; and curry of the day. From the specials blackboard there's a selection of daily delivered, Brixham-landed fish – sea bass fillet, pea and ham risotto; or beer-battered cod being just two options perhaps. Finish with a popular dessert such as hot chocolate pudding; Bakewell tart; or chocolate and honeycomb cheesecake. In summer you can sit out in the landscaped grounds, and if a longer visit is on the cards the inn has very stylish en suite bedrooms.

Open all day all wk **Food** all wk 12-9.45 Av main course £11 ⊕ FREE HOUSE
◄ Bath Ales Gem, Otter Ale, Butcombe Ŏ Broadoak, Thatchers. ♀ 10
Facilities Non-diners area ♣ (Bar Restaurant Garden) ♦ Children's menu Children's portions Play area Family room Garden Parking WiFi ☞ (notice required) **Rooms** 5

| COMBE HAY | Map 4 ST75 |

The Wheatsheaf Combe Hay — PICK OF THE PUBS

tel: 01225 833504 **BA2 7EG**
email: info@wheatsheafcombehay.co.uk
dir: *From Bath take A369 (Exeter road) to Odd Down, left at Park & Ride & immediately right towards Combe Hay. 2m to thatched cottage, turn left*

Great food in silver screen country

Settled on a hillside brushing the verdant valley where the cinema classic *The Titfield Thunderbolt* was filmed, this long, whitewashed pub has served the village for over 250 years. Its rustic charm is enhanced by country-chic furnishings and decor; massive wooden tables, sporting prints and open log fires offer a timeless scene whilst the valley view terraced garden makes an ideal spot for outdoor drinking and dining. The wet side of the business offers ciders matured just down the lane and beers from Butcombe brewery. The chef and his team put West Country produce at the heart of the menus, so expect starters such as rabbit pasty, rabbit liver parfait and carrot ketchup, and confident mains like slow-roast belly of Somerset pork, ham hock hash, pig's cheek, black pudding and spring onions. Equally zesty bar snacks are available, whilst a set market menu is very popular.

Open 10.30-3 6-11 (Sun 11-5.30) Closed 25-26 Dec & 1st wk Jan, Sun eve, Mon (ex BHs) **Food** Lunch Tue-Sat 12-2 Dinner Tue-Sat 6.30-9 Set menu available Restaurant menu available Tue-Sat ⊕ FREE HOUSE ◀ Butcombe Bitter, Otter, guest ale ♂ Thatchers, Honey's Midford Cider Honey & Daughter, Ashton Press. ♟ 13 **Facilities** Non-diners area ❄ (Bar Restaurant Garden) ♦♦ Children's menu Children's portions Garden ⩑ Parking WiFi

| COMPTON DANDO | Map 4 ST66 |

The Compton Inn

tel: 01761 490321 **Court Hill BS39 4JZ**
email: paul@huntersrest.co.uk
dir: *From A368 between Chelwood & Marksbury follow Hunstrete & Compton Dando signs*

Confident cooking in a picturesque location

A former farmhouse, the Grade II listed Compton Inn has only been a pub since World War II, but it has been sympathetically restored. Located in picturesque Compton Dando, with its imposing church and hump-backed bridge crossing the River Chew, it is only a few miles from the bustling city of Bristol. It's an ideal bolt-hole to enjoy local ale and cider, and well-cooked dishes like pork loin, roasted apple and black pudding, sauté potatoes, vegetables and cider and mustard sauce; or 12oz gammon steak and free-range eggs. For pudding try Bailey's crème brûlée.

Open all day all wk 12-11 (Sun-Mon 12-9.30) **Food** Lunch Mon-Sat 12-2.15, Sun 12-5 Dinner Mon-Sat 6.15-9.15 Av main course £12.50 Restaurant menu available all wk ⊕ PUNCH TAVERNS ◀ Sharp's Doom Bar, Butcombe Bitter, guest ale ♂ Thatchers Traditional & Dry. ♟ 10 **Facilities** Non-diners area ❄ (Bar Restaurant Garden) ♦♦ Children's menu Children's portions Garden ⩑ Parking WiFi (notice required)

| CORTON DENHAM | Map 4 ST62 |

The Queens Arms ★★★★★ INN ◉◉ PICK OF THE PUBS

See Pick of the Pubs on opposite page

| CRANMORE | Map 4 ST64 |

The Strode Arms

tel: 01749 880450 **BA4 4QJ**
email: info@thestrodearms.co.uk
dir: *S of A361, 3.5m E of Shepton Mallet, 7.5m W of Frome*

Country pub in pretty setting

The Strode Arms, now in new hands, is a stone-built 18th-century inn, packed with character — there's an open fire in winter and a sun-trap front terrace in the warmer months. The pub sits in the centre of the village, opposite the duck pond handy for the market towns of Frome and Shepton Mallet. Expect classics like prawn cocktail and rib-eye steaks alongside home-smoked sliced duck with warm noodle salad, and pot-roasted monkfish and Parma ham with Lyonnaise potatoes and wilted spinach; or pan-fried medallion of beef with grain mustard mash, caramelised shallots and red wine sauce.

Open all wk 12-3 5-11 **Food** Lunch all wk 12-2.30 Dinner Mon-Sat 6-9 Set menu available Restaurant menu available all wk ⊕ WADWORTH ◀ Horizon, Henry's Original IPA, 6X, The Bishop's Tipple, Strong in the Arm & Swordfish ♂ Thatchers Gold, Kingstone Press. **Facilities** Non-diners area ❄ (Bar Garden) ♦♦ Children's menu Children's portions Play area Family room Garden ⩑ Parking WiFi (notice required)

| CREWKERNE | Map 4 ST40 |

The George Inn ★★★ INN

tel: 01460 73650 **Market Square TA18 7LP**
email: georgecrewkerne@btconnect.com **web:** www.thegeorgehotelcrewkerne.co.uk
dir: *Phone for detailed directions*

400 years of hospitality in busy market town

Situated in the heart of Crewkerne, The George has been welcoming travellers since 1541, though the present hamstone building dates from 1832, and the current landlord has held sway since 1994. Thatchers Gold cider sits alongside the real ales in the bar, while the kitchen produces an array of popular dishes for bar snacks and more substantial meals from the daily specials board. Vegetarian and vegan meals are always available. Comfortable en suite bedrooms are traditionally styled and include four-poster rooms.

Open all day all wk **Food** Lunch all wk 12-2 Dinner all wk 7-9 Restaurant menu available all wk ⊕ FREE HOUSE ◀ Exmoor Ales, Sharp's Doom Bar ♂ Thatchers Gold. ♟ 8 **Facilities** Non-diners area ♦♦ Children's menu Children's portions Outside area ⩑ WiFi **Rooms** 13

The Manor Arms

tel: 01460 72901 **North Perrott TA18 7SG**
email: bookings@manorarms.net
dir: *From A30 (Yeovil to Honiton) take A3066 towards Bridport. North Perrott 1.5m*

A bastion of tradition in the country

On the Dorset/Somerset border, this 16th-century Grade II listed pub and its neighbouring hamstone cottages overlook the green in the conservation village of North Perrott. The inn has been lovingly restored and an inglenook fireplace, flagstone floors and oak beams are among the charming features inside. Dogs and children are welcome, there's a good beer garden for warmer days, and plenty of rambling opportunities on the doorstep. To accompany ales like Butcombe, and Ashton Press cider, expect wholesome traditional food such as steak and ale pie, pan-fried lamb's liver, and beer-battered cod. There is also a specials board, and every month sees a different theme night.

Open 12-2 6-11 Closed Sun eve **Food** Lunch all wk 12-2 Dinner Mon-Sat 6.30-9 ⊕ FREE HOUSE ◀ Butcombe, St Austell Trelawny, Fuller's London Pride ♂ Ashton Press. **Facilities** Non-diners area ❄ (Bar Garden) ♦♦ Children's menu Children's portions Garden ⩑ Parking WiFi

PICK OF THE PUBS

The Queens Arms ★★★★★ INN ❀❀

CORTON DENHAM   Map 4 ST62

tel: 01963 220317 **DT9 4LR**
email: relax@thequeensarms.com
web: www.thequeensarms.com
dir: *A303 follow signs for Sutton Montis,*
South Cadbury & Corton Denham.
Through South Cadbury, 0.25m, left, up
hill signed Corton Denham. Left at hill
top to village, approx 1m. Pub on right

Award-winning country pub serving excellent food

Below the Blackdown Hills, just over the Dorset border in Somerset, stands this late 18th-century, stone-built, one-time cider house. Beneath the beams in the bar and separate dining room are grand open fireplaces, leather chairs and sofas, and old scrubbed tables set with tasteful china. The bar offers the pub's own ale, Legless Liz, alongside Otter and Exmoor beers, local farm ciders, apple juices and a remarkable range of bottled beers, gins, malts, world spirits and liqueurs; even the 60-bin wine list includes six champagnes. Owners Gordon and Jeanette Reid champion high-quality local produce, measuring the distance their food travels more in metres than miles; the back of the menu illustrates just how close some suppliers are, like their own farm in Sutton Montis. Settle in with a Margarita on the rocks, then start with Redlake Somerton beetroot-cured trout with crab, cucumber and soda bread;

followed by North Dorset 28-day-aged rib-eye steak with foie gras butter, roasted garlic and hand-cut chips; butter-poached breast, braised leg and confit thigh of guinea fowl with celeriac, quince and charred broccoli; or Cornish mussels steamed in cider and chorizo with home-made bread. Typically imaginative puddings include, for example, yogurt and saffron pannacotta with spiced winter fruits and gingerbread; and chocolate marquise with popcorn, marshmallow and caramel. The sheltered terrace and sunny garden are perfect for outdoor eating and drinking. Muddy boots and dogs are no problem here. In July there's a beer festival. Breakast is available to non residents from 7.30am-9.30am.

Open all day all wk **Food** Lunch all wk 12-3 Dinner Mon-Sat 6-9.30, Sun 6-9 Restaurant menu available all wk ⌾ FREE HOUSE ▬ Exmoor Ales, Gyle 59 Legless Liz, Otter Ale, Bath Ales Gem, guest ales ⌀ Thatchers Gold, Hecks, Wilkins Farmhouse, Burrow Hill, Orchard Pig. ⬥ 14 **Facilities** Non-diners area ❖ (Bar Garden) ⫯ Children's menu Children's portions Garden ⊞ Beer festival Parking WiFi **Rooms** 8

CROSCOMBE
Map 4 ST54

The George Inn

tel: 01749 342306 & 345189 **Long St BA5 3QH**
email: pg@thegeorgeinn.co.uk
dir: *On A371 midway between Shepton Mallet & Wells*

Traditional food and two beer festivals

This 17th-century village pub has a traditional look with real hops, a large inglenook fireplace and family grandfather clock. In addition to a good range of local ales there's real ciders too, including Orchard Pig and Thatchers Gold. Tempting food appears on the menu — perhaps devilled lamb's kidneys on ciabatta croûton; or deep-fried brie with crème de cassis cranberry chutney to start, followed by chargrilled tuna, king prawn and sweet pepper skewers; ballotine of rabbit stuffed with black pudding; or goats' cheese and caramelised onion tart. The garden terrace incorporates an all-weather patio and children's area next to a function room, skittle alley and wood-fired pizza oven. There are beer festivals on the weekend nearest to St George's Day (23rd April) and in mid-October; steak nights on Wednesdays and a five-curry buffet the last Thursday of each month.

Open all wk 11-3 6-11 (Fri 11-3 5-12 Sat 11am-mdnt Sun 11.30-11) **Food** Lunch Mon-Fri 12-2.30, Sat 12-9, Sun 12-8 Dinner Mon-Fri 6-9, Sat 12-9, Sun 12-8 ⊕ FREE HOUSE ◀ Butcombe Bitter, Timothy Taylor Landlord, Blindmans, Hop Back Summer Lightning, Cheddar Ales Potholer, St Austell HSD Ŏ Thatchers Cheddar Valley & Gold, Orchard Pig, Stone's Bittersweet. ₱ 9 **Facilities** Non-diners area ❅ (Bar Garden) ⚬ Children's menu Children's portions Play area Family room Garden ⟘ Beer festival Parking WiFi ▭ (notice required)

DINNINGTON
Map 4 ST41

Dinnington Docks

tel: 01460 52397 **TA17 8SX**
email: hilary@dinningtondocks.co.uk
dir: *S of A303 between South Petherton & Ilminster*

Traditional locals' pub in a small hamlet

This traditional village pub on the old Fosse Way has been licensed for over 250 years and has no loud music, pool tables or fruit machines to drown out the conversation. Inside you will find pictures, signs and memorabilia of its rail and maritime past. Good-quality cask ales and farmhouse cider are served, and freshly prepared food including the likes of crab cakes, faggots, snapper, steak, and lamb shank for two feature on the menu. There's a carvery every Sunday, and the pub is located in an ideal place for cycling and walking.

Open all wk 11.30-3 6-12 (Fri-Sun all day) **Food** Lunch all wk 12-2 Dinner all wk 7-9 ⊕ FREE HOUSE ◀ Butcombe Bitter, guest ales Ŏ Burrow Hill, Westons, Thatchers Gold. **Facilities** Non-diners area ❅ (Bar Garden) ⚬ Children's menu Children's portions Play area Family room Garden ⟘ Parking ▭

DULVERTON
Map 3 SS92

The Bridge Inn

tel: 01398 324130 **20 Bridge St TA22 9HJ**
email: info@thebridgeinndulverton.com
dir: *M5 junct 27, A361 towards Barnstaple. In Tiverton take A396 signed Dulverton. Left onto B3222 to Dulverton. Pub by river in village*

Walkers' choice on the southern edge of Exmoor

Well-behaved dogs are welcome at this early-Victorian pub, and the resident canine, Milly, keeps a stash of gravy bones behind the bar for visiting dogs. Not only are dogs welcome, but well-behaved fans of award-winning cask ales, worldwide craft beers, sensibly priced wines and traditional pub food are also in luck. Favourites include venison sausage cassoulet; fish pie; and beetroot gnocchi with sage and spinach butter, pine nuts and pea shoots. Grazing plates of meats, and River Exe mussels are designed as both main courses or for sharing. A beer festival is held over the Spring Bank Holiday in late May.

Open all wk 12-11 summer (Mon 12-3 Tue-Thu 12-3 6-11 Fri-Sun 12-11 winter) Closed 25 Dec **Food** Lunch all wk 12-2.30 Dinner all wk 6-9 ⊕ FREE HOUSE ◀ Exmoor Ale, St Austell Proper Job, Otter Ale Ŏ Addlestones. ₱ 12 **Facilities** ❅ (Bar Restaurant Garden) ⚬ Children's menu Children's portions Garden ⟘ Beer festival Parking WiFi ▭ (notice required)

DUNSTER
Map 3 SS94

The Luttrell Arms Hotel
PICK OF THE PUBS

See Pick of the Pubs on opposite page

The Stags Head Inn

tel: 01643 821229 **10 West St TA24 6SN**
email: info@stagsheadinnexmoor.co.uk
dir: *From A39 take A396 to Dunster. Pub on right*

Cosy, welcoming pub on edge of Exmoor

Dunster Castle dominates this historic village, the Gateway to Exmoor National Park. The inn itself is 16th century, as a fresco in a bedroom depicting Henry VIII as the devil confirms. The bar stocks Somerset real ciders and ales, including Exmoor Ale brewed in Wiveliscombe. Sandwiches and a ploughman's are served at lunchtime, while the main menu presents sweet potato, spinach and almond curry; coriander and garlic chicken; and pork, fennel and sage pie. This small inn has limited seating, so reservations for dinner and Sunday lunch are recommended.

Open all day all wk 12-11 **Food** all wk 12.30-9 ⊕ FREE HOUSE ◀ Exmoor Ale, Otter Ale, local guest ales Ŏ Addlestones, Thatchers Gold. **Facilities** Non-diners area ❅ (Bar Restaurant Garden) ⚬ Children's menu Children's portions Garden ⟘ Cider festival WiFi ▭ (notice required)

EAST BOWER
Map 4 ST33

The Bower Inn

tel: 01278 422926 **Bower Ln TA6 4TY**
email: enquiries@thebowerinn.co.uk
dir: *M5 junct 23, A39 signed Glastonbury & Wells. Right at lights signed Bridgwater. Over motorway, left into Bower Ln to pub on left*

Attractive 18th-century building in a picturesque cottage garden

The Bower Inn was converted from a private family home to a restaurant in the 1980s, then following two years of closure, it attracted the attention of Peter and Candida Leaver, who purchased and renovated it. Business is good, both in the bar (mind the tiger!), where Somerset's Butcombe and Devon's Otter real ales are served, and in the contemporary restaurant, renowned for home-made food such as goats' cheese risotto with parmesan and truffle oil; smoked haddock and cheddar fish cakes; lasagne with garlic ciabatta; and beefburger with blue cheese and jalapeño pepper jam.

Open 12-3 6-11 Closed Mon L **Food** Lunch Tue-Sun 12.30-2.30 Dinner Mon-Sat 6.30-9, Sun 6.30-8 ⊕ FREE HOUSE ◀ Otter, Butcombe. **Facilities** Non-diners area ❅ (Bar Garden) ⚬ Children's menu Children's portions Garden ⟘ Parking WiFi ▭ (notice required)

PICK OF THE PUBS

The Luttrell Arms Hotel

DUNSTER Map 3 SS94

tel: 01643 821555 **High St TA24 6SG**
email: enquiry@luttrellarms.co.uk
web: www.luttrellarms.co.uk
dir: *From A39 (Bridgwater to Minehead),
left onto A396 to Dunster (2m from
Minehead)*

Ancient free house in memorable location

Dramatically sited on a wooded hill, Dunster Castle, the Luttrell family home for 600 years until 1976, looks down over the film-set village, where stands the imposing sandstone-built Luttrell Arms, and in the near distance, the Bristol Channel. In the street outside is the early 17th-century, timber-framed, octagonal Yarn Market. One of Britain's oldest post-houses, it retains its galleried courtyard, fine plasterwork ceiling, stone-mullioned windows, wood-panelled walls and open fireplaces; it was from here that Oliver Cromwell directed the siege of Dunster Castle during the English Civil War. Until the 1950s one would book a table by telephoning Dunster 2; the Luttrells had the pleasure of answering "Dunster 1". You can see the castle from the inn's hidden garden; here's as good a place as any to savour a pint of Exmoor Ale from nearby Wiveliscombe, or Thatchers Cheddar Valley cider, while perusing the menu. The Old Kitchen Bar offers hot ciabattas and sandwiches; chef's pie of

the day; and two types of ploughman's. In Psalter's restaurant, the choice is narrower but more sophisticated, with a typical winter menu starting with beetroot and vodka cured salmon, home-made fennel bread and lemon mayonnaise; and mains such as grilled fillet of bream with pineapple salsa, herbed new potatoes and seasonal salad; duck and noodle stir-fry with bok choy and plum sauce; and green vegetable risotto topped with a poached egg and parmesan. A trio of local sausages with champ mash and green beans; or ham, egg and chips keeps pub food traditionalists happy. Children get to choose from their own menu — perhaps scampi, chips and peas; or pasta with tomato sauce.

Open all day all wk 8am-11pm
Food all wk 11.30-9.30 Av main course £11 Restaurant menu available all wk
⊕ FREE HOUSE ◀ Exmoor Ale, Sharp's Doom Bar, guest ale ♂ Thatchers Cheddar Valley. ♟ 12
Facilities Non-diners area ❤ (Bar Garden) ♦♦ Children's menu Children's portions Family room Garden ꭴ Beer festival Cider festival WiFi 🚌

EAST HARPTREE · Map 4 ST55

Castle of Comfort

tel: 01761 221321 **BS40 6DD**
email: castleofcomfort@yahoo.com
dir: On B3134

Traditional home cooking on the Mendips

During Judge Jeffreys' time in the 17th century, prisoners from nearby Wells jail were taken to the Castle of Comfort for their last meal and a pint before being hanged at Gibbets Brow. Thankfully, modern-day visitors to this charming country pub on top of The Mendips can enjoy their time without the worry of being taken away. Local Butcombe beer and Thatchers cider are amongst the regularly changing options at the bar, with local produce appearing in straightforward, enjoyable dishes like lamb chops with mushrooms and onions; ham, egg and chips; and chicken Kiev.

Open all wk 12-3 6-11 **Food** Lunch 12-2 Dinner 6.30-9 ⊕ FREE HOUSE ◖ Butcombe Bitter, Sharp's Doom Bar, guest ale ♂ Thatchers, guest ciders. ♟ 9 **Facilities** Non-diners area ❤ (Bar Garden Outside area) ◖ Children's menu Children's portions Play area Garden Outside area ⊟ Parking 🚐 (notice required)

EXFORD · Map 3 SS83

The Crown Hotel ★★★ HL ⊚   PICK OF THE PUBS

tel: 01643 831554 **TA24 7PP**
email: info@crownhotelexmoor.co.uk **web:** www.crownhotelexmoor.co.uk
dir: From M5 junct 25 follow Taunton signs. Take A358 then B3224 via Wheddon Cross to Exford

Dedicated to produce from the South West

A family-run, 17th-century coaching inn in the heart of Exmoor National Park, the Crown is a comfortable mix of elegance and tradition. With three acres of its own grounds and a tributary of the infant River Exe flowing through the woodland, it's popular with visiting outdoor pursuit enthusiasts. But the cosy bar is also very much the social hub of the village, where many of the patrons enjoy the range of Exmoor Ales from Wiveliscombe just down the road. The AA-Rosette cuisine promises much, especially with Exmoor's profuse organic produce on the doorstep and the kitchen's close attention to sustainable sources. A typical selection from the bar menu could include ham hock and leek terrine with cider chutney and toasted brioche; pan-fried sea bass, spaghetti in tomato fondue with sauce vierge; and creamy rice pudding with salted caramel with roasted pecan nuts.

Open all day all wk 12-11 **Food** Lunch all wk 12-2.30 Dinner all wk 5.30-9.30 Av main course £12.95 Restaurant menu available all wk ⊕ FREE HOUSE ◖ Exmoor Ale & Gold, guest ales ♂ Thatchers Gold, St Austell Copper Press. ♟ 10 **Facilities** Non-diners area ❤ (Bar Garden Outside area) ◖ Children's portions Garden Outside area ⊟ Parking WiFi 🚐 (notice required) **Rooms** 16

Follow us on Facebook
www.facebook.com/TheAAUK
Find us on
Facebook

FAULKLAND · Map 4 ST75

Tuckers Grave

tel: 01373 834230 **BA3 5XF**
dir: From Bath take A36 towards Warminster. Right onto A366, through Norton St Philip towards Faulkland. In Radstock, left at x-roads, pub on left

The smallest pub in Somerset in a lovely countryside setting

Tapped Butcombe ale and Cheddar Valley cider draw local aficionados to this unspoilt rural gem. Somerset's smallest pub has a tiny atmospheric bar with old settles but no counter, or music, TV or jukebox either. Lunchtime sandwiches are available, and a large lawn with flower borders makes an attractive outdoor seating area, with the countryside adjacent. The 'grave' in the pub's name is the unmarked one of Edward Tucker, who hung himself here in 1747.

Open 11.30-3 6-11 (Sun 12-3 7-10.30) Closed 25 Dec, Mon L **Food** Contact pub for food times ⊕ FREE HOUSE ◖ Fuller's London Pride, Butcombe Bitter ♂ Thatchers Cheddar Valley. **Facilities** ◖ Family room Garden ⊟ Parking Notes ⊛

HASELBURY PLUCKNETT · Map 4 ST41

The White Horse at Haselbury   PICK OF THE PUBS

tel: 01460 78873 **North St TA18 7RJ**
email: whitehorsehaselbury@hotmail.co.uk **web:** www.thewhitehorsehaselbury.co.uk
dir: Just off A30 between Crewkerne & Yeovil on B3066

Rural pub offering French and British classics

Owners Rebecca and Richard Robinson, once part of the London restaurant scene, were drawn back to this lovely part of the country and now run this pub that was once a rope works and flax store, then a cider house. Richard sources the majority of the produce for his French and British dishes from within a few miles. You'll get an idea of the cooking style from dishes such as a starter of flame-grilled mackerel, tea-smoked beignets and gooseberries; and braised beef cheek and tongue with provençale tomato and salsa verde followed by cod with Dorset snails, Alsace bacon, garlic and parsley; or Creedy Carver duck breast, parsnip, apple purée, English feta, watercress and raspberry. Given Richard and Rebecca's pledge that the 'great British pub experience is important to them', they equally welcome those who just want something simple, like a Dexter beefburger and hand-cut chips, for example. Real ales are from Otter, Palmers, Teignworthy and other breweries, with ciders from Burrow Hill and Thatchers.

Open 12-2.30 6.30-11 Closed Sun eve, Mon **Food** Lunch Tue-Sun 12-3 Dinner Tue-Sat 6.30-9.30 Set menu available Restaurant menu available Tue-Sun ⊕ FREE HOUSE ◖ Palmers Best Bitter, Otter Ale, Teignworthy, Wadworth 6X, Sharp's Doom Bar, Butcombe ♂ Thatchers, Burrow Hill. ♟ 10 **Facilities** Non-diners area ❤ (Garden) ◖ Children's menu Children's portions Garden ⊟ Beer festival Cider festival Parking WiFi 🚐 (notice required)

HINTON ST GEORGE
Map 4 ST41

The Lord Poulett Arms
PICK OF THE PUBS

tel: 01460 73149 **High St TA17 8SE**
email: reservations@lordpoulettarms.com
dir: *2m N of Crewkerne, 1.5m S of A303*

Welcoming inn with lots of charm

A pub since 1680, this handsome stone village inn has that certain something, from its thatched roof and secluded garden to the wisteria-draped pergola tucked in next to an old Fives court. Then inside, a magpie-mix of polished antique furniture distributed judiciously across timeworn boarded floors, shiny flagstones and a vast fireplace pumping out the heat into tastefully decorated rooms. The inner bar is popular with locals, not least because it dispenses pints of Butcombe, Otter and Trelawny, and West Country ciders straight from the cask. Food is a step or three above pub grub too, with starters such as Cornish mussels in curry and coconut sauce served with coriander flatbread. Follow this with roast rump of Somerset lamb with lamb shoulder shepherd's pie, Savoy cabbage and rosemary jus. The desserts can have unexpected flavours such as chai-infused pannacotta, pink grapefruit salad with sea salt and black pepper shortbread.

Open all day all wk 12-11 Closed 25-26 Dec, 1 Jan **Food** Lunch all wk 12-2.30 Dinner all wk 6.30-9.15 Set menu available ⊕ FREE HOUSE ◀ St Austell Trelawny, Otter, Butcombe Ỗ Thatchers Gold, Perry's. ♀ 11 **Facilities** Non-diners area ♣ (Bar Garden) ♦ Children's menu Garden ⇌ Beer festival Cider festival Parking WiFi

HOLCOMBE
Map 4 ST64

The Holcombe Inn ★★★★★ INN ⊛
PICK OF THE PUBS

tel: 01761 232478 **Stratton Rd BA3 5EB**
email: bookings@holcombeinn.co.uk **web:** www. holcombeinn.co.uk
dir: *On A367 to Stratton-on-the-Fosse, take concealed left turn opposite Downside Abbey signed Holcombe, take next right, pub 1.5m on left*

Known for great food and glorious sunsets

A 17th-century, Grade II listed inn with views of nearby Downside Abbey, this is where to find some of the county's top locally-produced food, represented on the AA-Rosette menus. Start with a pint of Bath Ales Gem in the log-fired, flagstone-floored bar, where local Orchard Pig cider is on tap and wines by the glass are plentiful. At lunch settle for a thick-cut farmhouse, white, granary of wholemeal sandwiches (Wye Valley smoked salmon with herb cream cheese, or a classic BLT perhaps); a pick 'n' mix ploughman's; a charcuterie board; or a salad. Then, a typical evening meal might start with crispy duck samosa with hoisin, soy and honey reduction; or pan-seared scallops with chorizo and cauliflower purée , followed by slow-cooked lamb shank, creamy mash, seasonal veg and wholegrain mustard gravy; or pan-seared brill fillet, prawn and herb risotto and sautéed samphire. Linger in the evening as the sunsets can be rather special here.

Open all wk 12-3 6-11 (Fri-Sun all day) **Food** Lunch Mon-Thu 12-2.30, Fri-Sun all day Dinner Mon-Thu 6.30-9.30, Fri-Sun all day ⊕ FREE HOUSE ◀ Otter Ale, Bath Ales Gem, Butcombe Ỗ Thatchers, Orchard Pig, Hecks. ♀ 17
Facilities Non-diners area ♣ (Bar Garden) ♦ Children's menu Children's portions Garden ⇌ Parking WiFi ⛺ **Rooms** 10

HOLTON
Map 4 ST62

The Old Inn

tel: 01963 32002 **BA9 8AR**
email: enquiries@theoldinnrestaurant.co.uk
dir: *Exit A303 signed Wincanton. At rdbt left onto A371. At 2nd rdbt left, then right to Holton*

Convivial village inn with enjoyable food

In the safe hands of locally renowned chef Sue Bloxham, this sympathetically restored coaching inn is at the heart of this small village near Wincanton. With Wessex produce to the fore, you'll be assured of tip-top beers from local microbrewers; an ideal accompaniment to a considered selection of tapas choices or a dish from the dependable modern European menu. Smoked chicken salad with honey and mustard dressing, or venison burger with melted brie, baby tomatoes give a flavour of the range. Fish is delivered daily so time a visit for the popular Fish Friday night.

Open all wk 12-3 6-11 (Sat 12-11 Sun 12-10.30) **Food** Lunch Tue-Sat 12-2.30, Sun 12-3 Dinner Tue-Sat 6.30-9 Set menu available Restaurant menu available ⊕ FREE HOUSE ◀ Butcombe, Otter, Palmers Ỗ Gold Rush & Farmhouse Light, Ashton Press. ♀ 10 **Facilities** Non-diners area ♣ (Bar Outside area) ♦ Children's menu Children's portions Outside area ⇌ Parking WiFi ⛺ (notice required)

HUISH EPISCOPI
Map 4 ST42

Rose & Crown (Eli's)

tel: 01458 250494 **TA10 9QT**
dir: *M5 junct 25, A358 towards Ilminster. Left onto A378. Huish Episcopi in 14m (1m from Langport). Pub near church in village*

The pub with no bar but plenty of real ales

Locked in a glorious time-warp, this 17th-century thatched inn, affectionately known as Eli's, (named after the current licensees' grandfather) has been in the same family for over 150 years. Don't expect to find a bar counter, there's a flagstoned taproom where customers congregate. In the four parlour rooms you'll find an upright piano, dart board, time-honoured pub games, books and old family photographs. Home-made food includes popular steak and ale pie; pork, apple and cider cobbler, cauliflower cheese, soups and ploughman's lunches. There's a pool table and jukebox in a large function room. Other attractions include a children's outdoor play area, skittle alley, regular quizzes and live music nights and on Fridays, an organic food co-op.

Open all wk 11.30-3 5.15-11.30 (Fri-Sat 11.30-11.30 Sun 12-10.30) Closed 25 Dec eve **Food** Lunch all wk 12-2 Dinner Mon-Sat 5.30-7.30 ⊕ FREE HOUSE ◀ Teignworthy Reel Ale, rotating guest ales Ỗ Burrow Hill, Thatchers Gold, Westons Stowford Press, Harry's Cider. **Facilities** Non-diners area ♣ (Bar Garden) ♦ Play area Family room Garden ⇌ Parking WiFi ⛺ **Notes** ⊛

The Bull Inn

tel: 01935 840400 **The Square BA22 8LH**
dir: *From A303 between Sparkford & Ilminster take A37 signed Ilchester. At rdbt left onto B3151. Pub in village on left*

Unpretentious town centre watering hole for sports fans

Sitting in the heart of Ilchester's town square, the Bull is a traditional free house serving Yeovil Ales along with Thatchers cider. The menu is an unpretentious choice of favourite pub grub plates, but meats are supplied by local butchers and fresh fish is delivered daily from Brixham. It's properly child-friendly too, but note that the Bull opens at 2pm, serves food from 3pm, and stays open until way after bedtime. There are large TV screens for sporting events plus a pool table and a skittle alley.

Open all wk 2pm-mdnt Closed 25 Dec, 1 Jan **Food** Dinner Mon-Sat 3-9 ⊕ FREE HOUSE ◀ Yeovil Ales, guest ales Ö Thatchers Gold. ♀ 10 **Facilities** Non-diners area ☆ (Bar Restaurant Garden) ♦ Children's menu Children's portions Garden ⊼ Beer festival Cider festival WiFi 🚐

Ilchester Arms

tel: 01935 840220 **The Square BA22 8LN**
email: mail@ilchesterarms.com
dir: *From A303 take A37 signed Ilchester & Yeovil, left at 2nd Ilchester sign. Pub 100yds on right*

Smart hostelry close to A303

An elegant Georgian-fronted house with lots of character, this establishment was first licensed in 1686. Between 1962 and 1985 it was owned by the man who developed Ilchester cheese, and its association with good food continues: chef-proprietor Brendan McGee takes pride in producing modern British dishes such as pigeon with cauliflower purée; chicken liver pâté with red onion marmalade; Dexter beef steak cooked in ale with creamy mash; and medallions of venison, pumpkin purée, peppered sprouts, dauphinoise potatoes and red wine jus. There is a lovely walled garden.

Open all day all wk 7am-11pm Closed 26 Dec **Food** Lunch all wk 12-2.30 Dinner Mon-Sat 7-9 Restaurant menu available Mon-Sat ⊕ FREE HOUSE ◀ Yeovil Ales, local ales Ö Sharp's Orchard. ♀ 14 **Facilities** Non-diners area ☆ (Bar Garden) ♦ Children's menu Children's portions Play area Family room Garden ⊼ Beer festival Cider festival Parking WiFi 🚐

New Inn ★★★★ INN

tel: 01460 52413 **Dowlish Wake TA19 ONZ**
email: newinn-ilminster@btconnect.com **web:** www.newinn-ilminster.co.uk
dir: *From Ilminster follow Kingstone & Perry's Cider Museum signs, in Dowlish Wake follow pub signs*

Recommended for its home-cooked food and local cider

Deep in rural Somerset, this 350-year-old stone-built pub is tucked away in the village of Dowlish Wake, close to Perry's thatched Cider Mill and Museum. Inside are two bars (serving Perry's Cider, of course) with wood-burning stoves and a restaurant, where menus of home-cooked food capitalise on the quality and freshness of local produce. You could opt for a signature dish of prawn and butter-glazed salmon fillet; or perhaps stick to pub favourites like a giant Yorkshire pudding filled with pork sausages, served with new potatoes, vegetables and gravy. There are four guest rooms situated in an annexe overlooking the large secluded garden.

Open all wk 11.30-3 6-11 **Food** Lunch all wk 12-2.30 Dinner all wk 6-8.45 ⊕ FREE HOUSE ◀ Butcombe Bitter, Otter Ale Ö Perry's, Thatchers Gold. ♀ 10 **Facilities** Non-diners area ☆ (All areas) ♦ Children's menu Children's portions Garden Outside area ⊼ Parking WiFi 🚐 (notice required) **Rooms** 4

The Hood Arms

tel: 01278 741210 **TA5 1EA**
email: info@thehoodarms.com
dir: *From M5 junct 23/24 follow A39 to Kilve. Village between Bridgwater & Minehead*

Enjoyable food and beer betwixt the sea and the hills

Just an ammonite's throw from Kilve's fossil-rich beach, the Quantock Hills rise up behind this family-run 17th-century coaching inn. Real ales to enjoy in the beamed bar or in the garden include Exmoor Gold and Otter Head, plus local ciders, any of which will happily accompany a ciabatta roll or something from the main menu, such as roast chump of lamb with dauphinoise potatoes, wilted greens and port jus; seafood linguine in tomato and white wine sauce; butternut squash, spinach, pine nut and parmesan risotto; or pork cutlet with fondant potato, Savoy cabbage and apple cider sauce. Specials are chalked up daily.

Open all day all wk 11-11 **Food** Lunch Mon-Sat 12-2, Sun 12-3 Dinner Mon-Sat 6-9, Sun 6-8 ⊕ FREE HOUSE ◀ Otter Head, Exmoor Gold, Fuller's London Pride, Guinness, guest ales Ö Thatchers Gold, Rich's. ♀ 12 **Facilities** Non-diners area ☆ (Bar Garden) ♦ Children's menu Children's portions Play area Family room Garden ⊼ Parking WiFi

---

Kingsdon Inn

tel: 01935 840543 **TA11 7LG**
email: enquiries@kingsdoninn.co.uk
dir: *A303 onto A372, right onto B3151, right into village, right at post office*

Former cider house with very good food

Once a cider house, this pretty thatched pub is furnished with stripped pine tables and cushioned farmhouse chairs, and there are enough open fires to keep everywhere well warmed. The three charmingly decorated, saggy-beamed rooms have a relaxed and friendly feel. Hosts Adam Cain and Cinzia Iezzi have a wealth of experience in some of the UK's most respected hotels and restaurants, and they have made food a key part of the Kingsdon's appeal. Menus make excellent use of seasonal, local and often organic produce – maybe home-smoked duck breast, crispy duck beignet, duck liver parfait and toasted gingerbread; and twice-cooked pork belly, creamed potato, apple purée, winter vegetables, sautéed spinach and cooking juices.

Open all wk 12-3 6-11 (Fri-Sat 12-3 6-11.30 Sun 12-4 7-10.30) **Food** Lunch Mon-Sat 12-2, Sun 12-4 Dinner Mon-Sat 6.30-9, Sun 7-9 ⊕ FREE HOUSE/GAME BIRD INNS ◀ Butcombe Adam Henson's Rare Breed & Bitter Ö Thatchers, Ashton Press, Orchard Pig Reveller. ♀ 10 **Facilities** Non-diners area ☆ (Bar Garden) ♦ Children's menu Children's portions Garden ⊼ Parking WiFi 🚐 (notice required)

The Bird in Hand

tel: 01275 395222 **17 Weston Rd BS41 9LA**
email: info@bird-in-hand.co.uk
dir: *Phone for detailed directions*

Stylish pub with a warm atmosphere and good food

Just to the west of Bristol, this pub's clean lines haven't smothered its former village-pub feel. To the left is the bar area, home of Bath Ales Gem, St Austell Tribute and guest ales; to the right the dining area. Here, with fish and shellfish delivered daily, meat sourced locally where possible, and much neighbourhood foraging, is a monthly-changing, modern British menu listing pork belly, parsnips, pearl barley and kale; cod, wild mushrooms and salsify; and Jerusalem artichoke risotto, goats' cheese and gremolata. Home-made snacks include Scotch eggs and sausage rolls.

Open all day all wk **Food** Lunch all wk 12-3 Dinner all wk 6-9 Restaurant menu available Mon-Sat ⊕ FREE HOUSE ◀ St Austell Tribute, Bath Ales Gem, 2 guest ales. ☘ 13 **Facilities** ❤ (Bar Outside area) ◀ Children's portions Outside area ⋈ WiFi ▭ (notice required)

LONG SUTTON
Map 4 ST42

The Devonshire Arms ★★★★ INN ⊛ PICK OF THE PUBS

tel: 01458 241271 **TA10 9LP**
email: info@thedevonshirearms.com web: www.thedevonshirearms.com
dir: *Exit A303 at Podimore rdbt onto A372. 4m, left onto B3165*

Excellent food and beers in a former hunting lodge

Wisteria, acers and lavender surround the walled courtyard at the rear of this lovely pub; croquet, boules and Jenga can be played by all the family on the garden's terraced lawns. Ales include regulars such as Cheddar Potholer, Otter Bitter and Adam Henson's Rare Breed from Butcombe. Burrow Hill and village-pressed Harry's are the draught ciders, and the wine list offers 10 by the glass. Locally sourced ingredients in modern British dishes have helped the Devonshire achieve an AA Rosette. Both lunch and dinner menus share a starter of fried, walnut-encrusted Somerset goats' cheese with beetroot and balsamic onions; and a main course of pan-fried hake, caper mash, greens, cockles with white wine and cream sauce. For the truly hungry, look to finish with the West Country cheeseboard accompanied by bread, oatcakes, water biscuits and quince jelly; otherwise take comfort in a sticky toffee pudding with Somerset cider brandy ice cream.

Open all wk 12-3 6-11 Closed 25-26 Dec, 1 Jan **Food** Lunch all wk 12-2.30 Dinner all wk 7-9.30 ⊕ FREE HOUSE ◀ Cheddar Potholer, Butcombe Adam Henson's Rare Breed, Otter Bitter ⚭ Burrow Hill, Harry's Cider. ☘ 10 **Facilities** Non-diners area ❤ (Bar Outside area) ◀ Children's menu Play area Garden Outside area ⋈ Parking WiFi **Rooms** 9

LOWER GODNEY
Map 4 ST44

The Sheppey

tel: 01458 831594 **BA5 1RZ**
email: hi@thesheppey.co.uk
dir: *From Wells towards Wedmore on B3139. Through Bleadney. Left into Tilleys Drove to Godney. Or from Glastonbury & Street take B3151 to Meare, follow Godney signs*

Enticing combination of ales, ciders, art and music

On the Somerset Levels and only a hippy's dance away from Glastonbury, The Sheppey sits beside its eponymous river like a cider barn crossed with a private members' club. The ales and craft beers are reassuringly real – around a dozen to tease the taste buds. Cider is taken seriously too – 10 barrels sit atop the bar, so there's no danger of running out as happened in 1976 resulting in a loss of trust by the locals towards the then landlords. The modern menu offers twists on various international dishes. Start perhaps with duo of octopus (crispy and slow-cooked), chorizo, samphire, clams and spiced tomato glaze; then follow with half-roast chicken, bulgar wheat pilaf, gherkin salad with roasted mango ketchup. Round a good meal off with orange and almond polenta cake, poached kumquats with saffron and cardamom cream.

Open all wk 12-2.30 5.30-12 (Sat all day Sun 12-6.30) **Food** Lunch all wk 12-2.30 Dinner Mon-Sat 6.30-9.30 Restaurant menu available all wk ⊕ FREE HOUSE ◀ Glastonbury Ales, Cheddar Ales, Arbor ⚭ Wilkins, Sheppeys own, Hecks, Harry's Cider, Tricky. **Facilities** Non-diners area ❤ (All areas) ◀ Children's menu Children's portions Family room Garden Outside area ⋈ Beer festival Cider festival Parking WiFi ▭ (notice required)

LOWER LANGFORD
Map 4 ST46

The Langford Inn ★★★★ INN

tel: 01934 863059 **BS40 5BL**
email: langfordinn@aol.com web: www.langfordinn.com
dir: *M5 junct 21, A370 towards Bristol. At Congresbury turn right onto B3133 to Lower Langford. Village on A38*

Traditional and international food

This acclaimed Mendip's pub and restaurant is owned by the Cardiff brewery, Brains, so expect a decent pint of SA in the bar. Brains beers are joined by local Butcombe ales in the bar, which is adorned with local memorabilia. The daily-changing menu proffers traditional dishes such as beef and ale pie; cod and chips; and a selection of grilled steaks; but rogan josh chicken curry; sizzling beef with oyster sauce; and vegetarian cottage pie offer something a little different. There's a good choice of 24 wines by the glass to accompany your meal. The inn also offers accommodation in converted 17th-century barns.

Open all day all wk **Food** Sun-Thu 12-9, Fri-Sat 12-9.30 Set menu available ⊕ BRAINS ◀ SA, Butcombe, Guinness ⚭ Thatchers Gold & Katy. ☘ 24 **Facilities** Non-diners area ❤ (Bar Garden) ◀ Children's menu Children's portions Garden Parking WiFi ▭ (notice required) **Rooms** 7

LOWER VOBSTER
Map 4 ST74

Vobster Inn ★★★★ INN ⊛⊛ PICK OF THE PUBS

tel: 01373 812920 **BA3 5RJ**
web: www.vobsterinn.co.uk
dir: *4m W of Frome*

Historic village pub with Spanish twist

Set in four acres of glorious countryside in the pretty hamlet of Lower Vobster, it is believed the inn originated in the 16th century and was used by King James II and his army of Royalists prior to the battle of Sedgemoor in 1685. For lunch, choose baked petit camembert, cranberry and toast; toasted bloomer bacon sarnie; or eggs fried in chorizo oil, hash browns and black pudding. On the main menu you may find scallop and squid ink risotto; wild boar sausage with apple mash; and roast rump of venison, beluga and bacon lentils. All desserts are home made like lemon posset with lemon curd; and orange and Oreo cheesecake with red wine syrup. Look out for their special events. Individually furnished bedrooms are available.

Open 12-3 6.30-11 Closed Sun eve & Mon **Food** Lunch Tue-Sun 12-2 Dinner Tue-Thu & Sat 7-9, Fri 6.30-9 ⊕ FREE HOUSE ◀ Butcombe Bitter, Morland Old Golden Hen ⚭ Orchard Pig, Thatchers Gold. ☘ 10 **Facilities** Non-diners area ❤ (Bar Garden) ◀ Children's menu Children's portions Family room Garden ⋈ Parking WiFi ▭ (notice required) **Rooms** 4

MARTOCK
Map 4 ST41

The Nag's Head Inn

tel: 01935 823432 **East St TA12 6NF**
dir: *Phone for detailed directions*

Hamstone former cider house offering good grub, skittles and beer

This 16th-century former cider house is set in a lovely hamstone street in a picturesque south Somerset village. The large rear garden is partly walled and has pretty borders and trees. Ales, wines and home-cooked food are served in both the public and lounge/diner bars, where crib, dominoes, darts and pool are available. A sample menu includes Cajun chicken, burgers, quiche and sizzling garlic butter rump steak. The pub also has a separate skittle alley. There's a poker evening on Tuesday, and Sunday evening is quiz night.

Open all wk 12-3 6-11 (Fri-Sun 12-12) **Food** Lunch all wk 12-2 Dinner Mon-Tue 6-8, Wed-Sat 6-9 ⊕ FREE HOUSE ◾ Yeovil Ruby, local guest ales ⬤ Thatchers Gold, Westons Stowford Press. **Facilities** Non-diners area ❤ (Bar Restaurant Garden) ♦ Children's menu Children's portions Family room Garden ⊼ Parking WiFi ⬛ (notice required)

MELLS
Map 4 ST74

The Talbot Inn

tel: 01373 812254 **Selwood St BA11 3PN**
email: info@talbotinn.com
dir: *A362 from Frome towards Radstock. Left signed Mells, Hapsford & Great Elm. Right at T-junct in Mells. Inn on right*

Traditional yet stylish coaching inn

In coaching days, this 15th-century inn was the stop before Wells. Perhaps some passengers mistakenly alighted here in Mells, a bonus for the innkeepers of the day. It has a main bar, snug and map rooms, all open for classic pub food and Talbot Ale. Across a cobbled courtyard is the Coach House Grill Room, where chef Pravin Nayar's fish and meats are grilled over a charcoal fire and, on Sundays, whole roast chickens and suckling pigs are carved at the table. His bar snacks – including deep-fried rabbit legs, and duck hearts on toast – are clearly not ordinary. Other options include stout-braised veal cheek with buttermilk mash and caramelised king cabbage; and lightly-cured trout with leeks, lemon and fregola.

Open all day all wk 9am-11pm **Food** Lunch all wk 12-3 Dinner all wk 6-9.30 ⊕ FREE HOUSE ◾ Butcombe, Talbot Ale, guest ales ⬤ Ashton Press, Orchard Pig. ▾ 10 **Facilities** Non-diners area ❤ (Bar Restaurant Garden) ♦ Children's menu Children's portions Garden ⊼ Parking WiFi

MILVERTON
Map 3 ST12

The Globe ★★★ INN ⬤
PICK OF THE PUBS

tel: 01823 400534 **Fore St TA4 1JX**
email: info@theglobemilverton.co.uk **web:** www.theglobemilverton.co.uk
dir: *On B3187*

Friendly, family-run inn close to Exmoor

Run by Mark and Adele Tarry for the past decade, this old coaching inn is a firm part of the community in Milverton. From the outside, the pub has all the character expected of a Grade II listed building, but the uncluttered interior is contemporary with paintings by local artists, a wood-burning stove and a tranquil sun terrace providing for all seasons. Local real ales are one of Mark's passions so expect tip-top local ales like Exmoor and Otter and heady cider from Sheppy's. The extensive menu makes good use of West Country produce and ranges from lunchtime

sandwiches and ham, egg and chips, to evening specials such as spiced lamb and feta filo parcels with harissa and yogurt; Creedy Carver duck breast with ratatouille and crushed new potatoes. If you're in the area to explore the Quantock Hills and Exmoor stay over in one of the comfortable bedrooms at The Globe.

Open 12-3 6-11 (Fri-Sat 12-3 6-11.30) Closed Sun eve, Mon L **Food** Lunch Tue-Sun 12-2 Dinner Mon-Sat 6.30-9 ⊕ FREE HOUSE ◾ Exmoor Ale, Butcombe Bitter, Otter Bitter, Exeter Brewery ales, guest ales ⬤ Sheppy's, Thatchers Gold. ▾ 9 **Facilities** Non-diners area ❤ (Bar Outside area) ♦ Children's menu Outside area ⊼ Parking WiFi **Rooms** 3

MONKTON COMBE
Map 4 ST76

Wheelwrights Arms

tel: 01225 722287 **Church Ln BA2 7HB**
email: bookings@wheelwrightsarms.co.uk
dir: *SE of Bath*

Lovely valley and village setting for old pub

Sit in the lavender-scented garden with an Otter beer, or cosy up to the snug's log fire with a glass of Honey's cider in this attractive village inn set on the slopes of the Avon Valley just outside Bath. Handy for ramblers straying from the Kennet & Avon Canal towpath walk, the accomplished menu of home-prepared, locally sourced dishes means it's also a popular dining inn. Start with ham fritters and gruyère fondue; or consider a sharing plate of whole oven-baked camembert. Mains may be shellfish linguine; smoked chicken stew; or a minute steak, mustard mayo and red onion compôte sandwich, whilst desserts such as chocolate cake and orange mascarpone make a memorable finale. The extensive wine list is equally satisfying.

Open all day all wk **Food** Lunch Mon-Fri 12-2, Sat-Sun 12-3 Dinner all wk 6-10 Set menu available Restaurant menu available all wk ⊕ FREE HOUSE ◾ Butcombe, Otter ⬤ Honey's Midford Cider Honey & Daughter. ▾ 10 **Facilities** ♦ Children's portions Garden ⊼ Parking WiFi ⬛ (notice required)

MONTACUTE
Map 4 ST41

The Kings Arms Inn

tel: 01935 822255 **49 Bishopston TA15 6UU**
email: info@thekingsarmsinn.co.uk
dir: *From A303 onto A3088 at rdbt signed Montacute. Inn in village centre*

17th-century village pub with cosy bar and good food

The hamstone-built Kings Arms has stood in this picturesque village, at the foot of Mons Acutus (thus, supposedly, Montacute) since 1632. Along with cask ales and fine wines, you can eat in several places as there are two restaurant areas, a bar/lounge, and a large beer garden which has games for both adults and children. Seasonal dishes based on locally sourced produce are offered on both the traditional bar menu and the à la carte. Perhaps try ham hock and pea pie with champ mash and gravy; slow-braised shoulder of lamb with minted jus; or grilled salmon fillet with ginger and crayfish tail sauce. There are plenty of events to watch out for.

Open all day all wk 7.30am-11pm **Food** Lunch all wk 12-3 Dinner all wk 6-9 Restaurant menu available all wk ⊕ GREENE KING ◾ Ruddles Best & IPA, Morland Old Speckled Hen, Timothy Taylor Landlord ⬤ Thatchers. ▾ 11 **Facilities** Non-diners area ❤ (Bar Garden Outside area) ♦ Children's menu Children's portions Play area Garden Outside area ⊼ Parking WiFi ⬛

The Phelips Arms

tel: 01935 822557 **The Borough TA15 6XB**
email: thephelipsarms@hotmail.com
dir: *From Cartgate rdbt on A303 follow signs for Montacute*

Pub classics in a classic setting

About 1598 Sir Edward Phelips, Master of the Rolls and the prosecutor during the Gunpowder Plot trial, built Montacute House, now owned by the National Trust. Next door, overlooking the village square, stands this 17th-century hamstone building, offering well-kept Palmers beers and Thatchers cider. The main menu features their ever popular shortcrust steak and ale pie, triple-cooked chips and peas; traditional beef lasagne; and hand-carved sliced gammon, free-range eggs and those tempting triple-cooked chips. Sandwiches and jacket potatoes are available too. The pub, with its beautiful walled garden, featured in the 1995 film *Sense and Sensibility* and the more recent BBC drama series, *Wolf Hall*.

Open all wk 12-2.30 6-11 (Sun 12-5) **Food** Lunch Mon-Sat 12-2, Sun 12-4 Dinner Mon-Sat 6.30-9 ⊕ PALMERS 🍺 Best Bitter, 200, Copper Ale, Tally Ho! & Dorset Gold ♉ Thatchers Gold, Dorset Orchard First Press. ♟ 10 **Facilities** Non-diners area ♥ (Bar Restaurant Garden) 🚼 Children's menu Children's portions Garden Parking WiFi 🚌

NORTH CURRY   Map 4 ST32

The Bird in Hand

tel: 01823 490248 **1 Queen Square TA3 6LT**
dir: *M5 junct 25, A358 towards Ilminster, left onto A378 towards Langport. Left to North Curry*

Low beams, warming fires, friendly service

Cheerful staff provide a warm welcome to this friendly 300-year-old village inn, which boasts large inglenook fireplaces, flagstone floors, and exposed beams. The place is very atmospheric at night by candlelight, and the blackboard menus feature local produce, including game casserole, curries and bubble-and-squeak with sausage, bacon, eggs and mushrooms. The à la carte menu always has two or three fresh fish dishes, steaks and home-made desserts. In season you can expect local game, as well as local lamb, chicken and pork. On Sunday, roast lunch is available.

Open all wk 12-3 6-11 (Fri 12-3 5.30-12 Sat 12-3 6-12) Closed 25 Dec eve & 26 Dec eve **Food** Lunch Mon-Sat 12-2, Sun 12-3 Dinner Sun-Thu 6.45-9, Fri-Sat 7-9.30 Restaurant menu available all wk ⊕ FREE HOUSE 🍺 Otter Bitter & Ale, Exmoor Gold, Morland Old Speckled Hen, Greene King IPA Gold, North Curry Gold & The Withyman ♉ Parsons Choice, Ashton Press, Thatchers Gold. ♟ 9 **Facilities** Non-diners area ♥ (Bar Outside area) 🚼 Children's portions Outside area ⌨ Parking WiFi

---

NUNNEY   Map 4 ST74

The George at Nunney

tel: 01373 836458 **Church St BA11 4LW**
email: info@thegeorgeatnunney.co.uk
dir: *From A361 (between Shepton Mallet & Frome) follow Nunney signs. 0.5m to pub in village centre*

The hub of the village's lively community

With views of 14th-century moated castle ruins, and a babbling brook and waterfall directly opposite, this rambling inn, run by the Hedges family, has the added attractions of landscaped gardens and a winter log fire. The stylish interior merges contemporary with traditional; the beamed bar has a choice of Wadworth ales, Thatchers cider and fine wines. Sandwiches are available at lunchtime and there are roasts on Sundays.

Open all day all wk **Food** all wk 12-9.30 ⊕ WADWORTH 🍺 6X, Henrys IPA, guest ale ♉ Thatchers Gold. ♟ 8 **Facilities** Non-diners area ♥ (Bar Restaurant Garden) 🚼 Children's menu Children's portions Family room Garden ⌨ Parking WiFi 🚌 (notice required)

OAKHILL   Map 4 ST64

The Oakhill Inn ★★★★ INN ◉   PICK OF THE PUBS

tel: 01749 840442 **Fosse Rd BA3 5HU**
email: info@theoakhillinn.com **web:** www.theoakhillinn.com
dir: *On A367 between Stratton-on-the-Fosse & Shepton Mallet*

Mendips inn with a coveted AA Rosette

This smart stone-built inn stands on a corner in the middle of the village and from the landscaped garden you can see the village church and the Mendip Hills. Spacious yet cosy, old but contemporary, inside, the duck-egg blue interior features a display of over 20 clocks. Real ales from Butcombe and Palmers keep bar-top company with Thatchers Gold and Pheasant Plucker ciders. The award-winning food conforms to free-range, organic and local-sourcing principles so, even though the menus are brief, the dishes are certainly not short on quality. Consider a three-course meal of Wiltshire ham hock, soft boiled egg and watercress salad; slow-roast lamb rump, risotto and roast roots; and white chocolate cheesecake with raspberry coulis. The bar menu offers a good choice of sandwiches, steaks, pizzas, fish and chips and a ploughman's.

Open all wk 12-3 5-11 (Sat-Sun 12-12) **Food** Lunch Mon-Sat 12-3, Sun 12-9 Dinner Mon-Sat 6-9, Sun 12-9 Av main course £16.50 Set menu available Restaurant menu available all wk ⊕ FREE HOUSE 🍺 Butcombe Bitter, Palmers, guest ale ♉ Pheasant Plucker, Lilley's Sunset, Thatchers Gold. ♟ **Facilities** Non-diners area ♥ (All areas) 🚼 Children's menu Children's portions Garden Outside area ⌨ Parking WiFi 🚌 (notice required) **Rooms** 5

OVER STRATTON   Map 4 ST41

The Royal Oak

tel: 01460 240906 **TA13 5LQ**
email: info@the-royal-oak.net
dir: *Exit A303 at Hayes End rdbt (South Petherton). 1st left after Esso garage signed Over Stratton*

Real ales and home-cooked food

With X-shaped tie-bar ends securing its aged hamstone walls, a thatched roof, blackened oak beams, flagstones, log fires, old church pews and settles, this 17th-century former farmhouse certainly looks like a textbook example of an English country pub. First licensed in the 1850s, the bar dispenses real ales from Hall & Woodhouse in Blandford, Dorset. With different prices for small or normal appetites, home-cooked dishes on the menu range from chicken tikka lahoori, via salmon en croûte, to beef and bacon pie. Added attractions are the good value two-course set lunch menu and large patio for enjoying in warmer weather.

Open Tue-Sun Closed Mon **Food** Lunch Tue-Sun 12-2 Dinner Tue-Sun 6-9 Set menu available ⊕ HALL & WOODHOUSE 🍺 Badger Dorset Best, Tanglefoot, K&B Sussex. **Facilities** Non-diners area ♥ (Bar Garden) 🚼 Children's menu Children's portions Garden Parking

PITNEY
Map 4 ST42

The Halfway House

tel: 01458 252513 **TA10 9AB**
dir: *On B3153, 2m from Langport & Somerton*

One for lovers of real ales and ciders

A delightfully old fashioned rural pub, The Halfway House has three homely rooms boasting open fires, books and traditional games, but no music or electronic games. This free house is largely dedicated to the promotion of quality brews, with an annual beer festival in March and cider festival in August. Eight to twelve top ales and ciders are served, including Teignworthy Reel Ale and Kingston Black cider. The home-cooked rustic fare is made using local ingredients. Sandwiches, pies, fish and chips, game casserole and soups are served at lunchtimes, while a great range of English pub food and specials are available for dinner. Sundays lunches stretch from 1 until 5.

Open all wk 11.30-3 4.30-11 (Fri 11.30-3 4.30-12 Sat-Sun all day) **Food** Lunch Mon-Sat 12-2.30, Sun 1-5 Dinner Mon-Sat 7-9.30 ⊕ FREE HOUSE ◀ Otter Bright, Hop Back Summer Lightning, Teignworthy Reel Ale, Dark Star American Pale Ale ♂ Kingston Black, Wilkins Farmhouse, Gold Rush, Harry's Cider. 🍷 8
Facilities Non-diners area ❤ (Bar Garden) ♦ Children's portions Play area Garden Beer festival Cider festival Parking WiFi

PORLOCK
Map 3 SS84

The Bottom Ship

tel: 01643 863288 **Porlock Weir TA24 8PB**
email: enquiries@shipinnporlockweir.co.uk
dir: *Phone for detailed directions*

Thatched inn in lovely Porlock Weir location

Enjoy superb views across the Bristol Channel to south Wales from the suntrap terrace of this thatched waterside pub, best enjoyed after an exhilarating coastal path stroll. Ales in the beamed bar all originate in the South West, and Rich's cider is also on tap. Home-made food using fresh local produce includes most pub favourites, with a range of sandwiches and baguettes at lunchtime backed up by such hot plates as home-made lasagne; lemon chicken; and local sausage and mash. Children have their own menu, and dogs are welcome inside and out. Don't miss the ale and cider festival in early July.

Open all day all wk 9am-10.45pm **Food** Lunch all wk 12-2.30 Dinner all wk 6-8.30 Av main course £9 ⊕ FREE HOUSE ◀ Exmoor Ale & Stag, Otter Amber, guest ales ♂ Thatchers, Rich's. 🍷 9 **Facilities** Non-diners area ❤ (Bar Garden) ♦ Children's menu Children's portions Garden Beer festival Cider festival Parking WiFi

The Ship Inn

tel: 01643 862507 **High St TA24 8QD**
email: enquiries@shipinnporlock.co.uk
dir: *A358 to Williton, then A39 to Porlock. 6m from Minehead*

Picture-postcard inn with sea-faring tales to tell

Reputedly one of the oldest inns on Exmoor, this 13th-century free house stands at the foot of Porlock's notorious hill, where Exmoor tumbles into the sea. In the past it's attracted the sinister attentions of Nelson's press gang, but now its thatched roof and traditional interior provide a more welcoming atmosphere. Regularly changing menus include an appealing selection of hot and cold baguettes, sandwiches, ciabattas, and hot dishes from creamy haddock, leek and pea risotto, to Exmoor venison casserole. There's also a beer garden and children's play area.

Open all day all wk 9am-mdnt **Food** Lunch all wk 12-2.30 Dinner Sun-Thu 6.30-8.30, Fri-Sat 6-9 Av main course £10 ⊕ FREE HOUSE ◀ St Austell Tribute & Proper Job, Exmoor Ale & Beast, Cotleigh Tawny Owl, Otter, guest ales ♂ Thatchers

& Cheddar Valley, Rich's. 🍷 9 **Facilities** Non-diners area ❤ (Bar Garden) ♦ Children's menu Children's portions Play area Garden Parking WiFi

RIMPTON
Map 4 ST62

NEW The White Post

tel: 01935 857525 **BA22 8AR**
email: be@thewhitepost.com
dir: *From rdbt on A303 (SW of Sparkford) take A359 signed Sherborne. Through West Camel & Marston Magna. Left onto B3148 signed Sherborne. Pub on right*

Highly praised family-run pub

Believed to be the country's only remaining pub to straddle two counties, it's only fair that one real ale and one cider – Butcombe and Orchard Pig, respectively – should come from Somerset, and ditto – DBC and Dabinett – from Dorset. Appearing on the thoroughly modern menus could be sea bass with samphire, crab tortellini, crab bisque, caviar and saffron mayo; lamb rump with confit Maris Piper potatoes, textures of onion, seared liver and roasted lamb sauce; and, requiring a deeper dig into the wallet, 50-day-hung, salt-chamber rib-eye with dripping-cooked chips and black-garlic ketchup. To finish, carpaccio of pineapple, iced passionfruit, coconut jelly, pink praline and coriander.

Open 12-3 6-close Closed Sun eve & Mon **Food** Lunch Tue-Sun 12-3 Dinner Tue-Sat 6-9 Restaurant menu available Tue-Sun ⊕ FREE HOUSE ◀ Butcombe, Dorset ♂ Orchard Pig, Purbeck Dorset Dabinett. 🍷 10 **Facilities** Non-diners area ❤ (Bar Garden) ♦ Children's menu Children's portions Garden Parking WiFi ▭ (notice required)

SHEPTON BEAUCHAMP
Map 4 ST41

Duke of York

tel: 01460 240314 **North St TA19 0LW**
email: sheptonduke@tiscali.co.uk
dir: *N of A303 between Ilchester & Ilminster*

Traditional village pub with plenty of reasons to visit

Husband and wife team Paul and Hayley Rowlands have established a good reputation over the years at this 17th-century free house. The bar stocks good West Country ales and local ciders, and the restaurant's traditional menu pleases locals and tourists alike with confit chicken terrine with spiced gooseberry and fresh coriander, griddled cider and mustard sausages with red onion gravy and buttered mash, and pan-fried lamb's liver and bacon. Lunchtime sandwiches are also available. Gardens, a skittle alley, two steak nights a week, a Sunday carvery and the occasional beer festival round off the attractions of this homely pub.

Open all day Mon 5pm-11pm Tue-Wed 3.30pm-11pm Thu-Sun 12-12 Closed Mon L **Food** Lunch Thu-Sun 12-2 Dinner Tue-Sat 6.45-9 Av main course £9.95 ⊕ FREE HOUSE ◀ Teignworthy Reel Ale, Otter Ale & Bright, Sharp's Doom Bar ♂ Thatchers Gold. 🍷 9 **Facilities** Non-diners area ❤ (Bar Garden) ♦ Children's menu Children's portions Family room Garden Beer festival Parking WiFi ▭ (notice required)

SHEPTON MALLET
Map 4 ST64

The Natterjack Inn ★★★★ INN

tel: 01749 860253 **BA4 6NA**
email: natterjack@btconnect.com web: www.thenatterjackinn.co.uk
dir: *Between Castle Cary & Shepton Mallet on A371*

Family-owned hostelry with railway connection

Originally the Railway Hotel, which hosted passengers and goods yard workers on the Somerset and Dorset line for 100 years before closure in the 1960s. Its current name is based in a legend that a live toad was added to the cider barrel before the bung was inserted. In the capable hands of Adrian and Kate Brixey, the pub offers

Butcombe and guest ales, along with Ashton Press cider and a dozen wines by the glass. The menu proffers staples like liver and bacon with black pudding and mash; round off with one of Kate's home-made desserts such as warm chocolate fudge cake with clotted cream ice cream.

Open all wk 11.30-3.30 6-11.30 Food Lunch 12-2.30 Dinner 6.30-9.30 Av main course £10-£15 ⊕ FREE HOUSE ◀ Bath Ales Gem, Butcombe, guest ale Ở Ashton Press, Orchard Pig Reveller. ♟ 12 Facilities Non-diners area ✿ (Bar Restaurant Garden) ♦ Children's menu Children's portions Garden ⌁ Parking WiFi ▬ (notice required) Rooms 5

The Three Horseshoes Inn — PICK OF THE PUBS

tel: 01749 850359 Batcombe BA4 6HE
email: info@thethreehorseshoesinn.com
dir: Take A359 from Frome to Bruton. Batcombe signed on right. Pub by church

Local produce drives the enjoyable menu here

Squirrelled away in the rural Batcombe Vale, this honey-coloured stone inn enjoys a peaceful position with a lovely rear garden overlooking the old parish church. The long and low-ceilinged main bar has exposed stripped beams, a huge stone inglenook with log fire, and is tastefully decorated, with pale blue walls hung with old paintings. From gleaming handpumps on the bar come pints of local brews including Plain Ales Innocence. Menus draw on the wealth of fresh seasonal produce available, including surplus vegetables from local allotments. Lunches take in sandwiches, simply grilled south coast sardines; and 'bunny' (that's locally shot) biryani'. Choice at dinner extends to cottage pie with Westcombe Cheddar mash; slow-roasted Somerset pork belly; and home-smoked braised brisket. Desserts include local rhubarb crumble cake; or a board of local cheeses.

Open all wk Mon-Fri 11-3 6-11 (Sat 11-11 Sun 12-10.30) Food Lunch all wk 12-2.30 Dinner Mon-Sat 6-9.30, Sun 6-9 Av main course £12 ⊕ FREE HOUSE ◀ Butcombe Bitter, Plain Ales Innocence, Wild Beer Ở Rich's Farmhouse, Ashton Press, Worley's, guest ciders. ♟ 8 Facilities Non-diners area ✿ (Bar Garden) ♦ Children's menu Children's portions Garden ⌁ Beer festival Cider festival Parking WiFi ▬ (notice required)

The Waggon and Horses — PICK OF THE PUBS

tel: 01749 880302 Old Frome Rd, Doulting Beacon BA4 4LA
email: waggon.horses09@googlemail.com
dir: 1.5m NE of Shepton Mallet. From Shepton Mallet take A37 N towards Bristol. At x-roads right into Old Frome Rd (follow brown pub sign)

Family-run pub with a large enclosed garden

By a lonely crossroads with views towards Glastonbury Tor from its perch high in the Mendip Hills, this long, whitewashed building was a coaching inn in the 18th century. Its arched doorway once led into the blacksmith's forge. Beers include Butcombe and Box Steam Brewery's Chuffin' Ale, with real ciders from Wilkins Farmhouse and Ashton Press. A bar menu lists lunchtime baguettes, jacket potatoes, ploughman's and cheesy chips, while among traditional, home-cooked mains are steak and ale pie; lasagne with chips and garlic bread; freshly made smoked salmon tagliatelle; and a range of beef and gammon steaks. Vegetarian lasagne is served with chips and garlic bread. Friday night is (motor) Bike Night, the second Wednesday of the month is Acoustic Night, and an Italian food evening is held on the last Thursday with a guest chef.

Open all wk Mon-Sat 12-2.30 6-11 (Sun 12-3 6-10) Food Lunch Mon-Sat 12-2.30, Sun 12-3 Dinner Mon-Sat 6-9, Sun 6-8 ⊕ FREE HOUSE ◀ Butcombe, Box Steam Brewery Chuffin' Ale Ở Wilkins Farmhouse, Ashton Press. Facilities Non-diners area ✿ (Bar Garden) ♦ Children's menu Children's portions Garden ⌁ Parking WiFi ▬

SOMERTON — Map 4 ST42

The White Hart

tel: 01458 272273 Market Place TA11 7LX
email: info@whitehartsomerton.com
dir: In village centre

500-year-old inn beside pretty market place

Chic modern lines blend easily with old beams, wooden flooring, matchboarding and other timeless features to produce a quality dining pub where beer drinkers aren't left on the back foot and children and dogs are welcome. Bath Ales and Cheddar beers, together with farmhouse ciders ensure the place is a thriving local; a great place to sup is the sheltered beer garden here. Typical dishes on the menu are crispy pig's cheek Scotch egg, pickled vegetables and Dijon dressing; Cornish crab and wild garlic cakes with feta and orange salad; whole wood-roasted Lyme Bay lemon sole, pink fir potatoes, spinach and gherkin, caper and dill butter; and chocolate brownie sundae.

Open all day all wk 9am-11pm (Sun 9am-10.30pm) Food all wk 12-10 ⊕ FREE HOUSE/DRACO PUB COMPANY ◀ Cheddar Ales Potholer, Bath Ales Gem, guest ales Ở Thatchers Gold, Orchard Pig, Harry's Cider. ♟ Facilities Non-diners area ✿ (Bar Garden) ♦ Children's menu Children's portions Garden ⌁ WiFi ▬ (notice required)

STANTON WICK — Map 4 ST66

The Carpenters Arms — PICK OF THE PUBS

See Pick of the Pubs on page 442

STOGUMBER — Map 3 ST03

The White Horse

tel: 01984 656277 High St TA4 3TA
email: info@whitehorsestogumber.co.uk
dir: From Taunton take A358 to Minehead. In 8m left to Stogumber, 2m into village centre. Right at T-junct & right again. Pub opposite church

Village local off the beaten track

This traditional free house on the edge of the Quantock Hills is ideally situated for walkers and visitors travelling on the West Somerset Steam Railway and who alight at Stogumber station. Formerly the village's Market Hall and Reading Room, the dining room is now the place to study a menu of home-cooked dishes such as Caribbean pork with apple, mango and ginger; steak and kidney pudding; or local gammon steak, egg and chips. Enjoy local ales such as Otter Bitter in the pretty courtyard garden.

Open all day all wk 12-2.30 4.30-12 (Sat-Sun 12-12) Food Lunch all wk 12-2 Dinner all wk 7-9 Av main course £9.50 ⊕ FREE HOUSE ◀ St Austell Proper Job, Otter Bitter, local & guest ales Ở Thatchers, Healey's Cornish Rattler, Lilley's Apples & Pears. ♟ 10 Facilities Non-diners area ✿ (Bar Restaurant Garden) ♦ Children's menu Children's portions Garden ⌁ Parking WiFi ▬ (notice required)

PICK OF THE PUBS

The Carpenters Arms

STANTON WICK   Map 4 ST66

tel: 01761 490202 **BS39 4BX**
email: carpenters@buccaneer.co.uk
web: www.the-carpenters-arms.co.uk
dir: *From A37 at Chelwood rdbt take A368 signed Bishop Sutton. Right to Stanton Wick*

Good food and local ale in peaceful hamlet

Well placed for visiting Bath, Bristol and Wells or, by the same token, if you're already in one of these cathedral cities, then this quiet hamlet is close enough to consider making for. A low-slung, stone-built, pantile-roofed free house overlooking the Chew Valley, it was converted from a row of miners' cottages, dating from when the Somerset coalfield was in production. Beyond the flower-hung porch, the rustic bar displays low beams, old pews, squashy sofas, and precision-cut logs stacked neatly in the large fireplace. An appealing music-free place, it's where a pint of local Butcombe Bitter, Cornish Doom Bar or a guest ale will always go down well, whether inside or on the attractively landscaped patio. The menus change regularly to make the best of West Country-sourced produce, appearing perhaps as a starter of tomato, basil and mozzarella salad; chicken liver and wild mushroom pâté; or smoked salmon with lemon, capers

and black pepper. For a main course, try mussel, prawn and crayfish linguine with white wine and chive cream sauce; Thai chicken curry with steamed coriander-flavoured rice; or whole roasted pepper with Mediterranean vegetable ragout topped with gratinated goats' cheese, new potatoes and dressed mixed salad. Sunday, of course, means a choice of roasts, but fish and vegetarian dishes are there for the asking too. Among the home-made desserts are treacle tart and clotted cream; and white chocolate and raspberry cheesecake. Not an overlong wine list, but a good range. If you have your walking boots, nearby Chew Valley Lake is an established wildlife haven.

Open all day all wk 11-11 (Sun 12-10.30) Closed 25-26 Dec
Food Lunch Mon-Sat 12-2.30, Sun 12-9 Dinner Mon-Thu 6-9.30, Fri-Sat 6-10, Sun 12-9 Av main course £15.95 Restaurant menu available all wk
⊕ FREE HOUSE ◖ Butcombe Bitter, Sharp's Doom Bar. ♟ 10
Facilities Non-diners area ♟♦ Children's menu Children's portions Outside area ♫ Parking WiFi 🚐 (notice required)

Map 4 ST43

STREET

The Two Brewers ★★★★ INN

tel: 01458 442421 **38 Leigh Rd BA16 OHB**
email: thetwobrewers@yahoo.com **web:** www.thetwobrewers.co.uk
dir: *In town centre. From High St into Leigh Rd. 400mtrs to pub*

A country pub in a town

Located in a quiet area of Street, this country-style, creeper-clad stone inn is an ideal touring base, with the fascinating Somerset Levels and the medieval glories of Glastonbury within easy reach. Over the years more than 500 guest beers have shared billing with the local favourite St Austell Tribute. Robust and traditional pub meals — some available as child portions — are the order of the day here; lasgane, chilli con carne, and Mediterranean pasta are home cooked, as are the changing daily specials. A final flourish could be a Somerset apple cake. The pub is proudly music and fruit-machine free; there's a grassy garden where dogs are welcome. En suite accommodation is available.

Open all wk 11-3 6-11 (Sun 11.30-3 6-10.30) Closed 25-26 Dec **Food** Lunch all wk 12-2 Dinner all wk 6-9 Av main course £7 ⊕ FREE HOUSE ◢ St Austell Tribute, 3 guest ales ⚬ Westons Stowford Press. **Facilities** Non-diners area ◑ Children's menu Children's portions Garden ⼓ Parking WiFi **Rooms** 3

TAUNTON   Map 4 ST22

NEW The Hankridge Arms

tel: 01823 444405 **Hankridge Way TA1 2LR**
email: bookings@thehankridgearms.com
dir: *M5 junct 25, A358 (Minehead). At next rdbt take 2nd left into Heron Gate. At next rdbt 2nd left into Hankridge Way. With Sainsburys on left, pub on right at mini-rdbt*

Bustling bar and restaurant in a retail and leisure park

Although not a huge town, Taunton has expanded considerably since this former farmhouse was built in the 16th century. Eventually becoming derelict, it was rescued by Blandford brewery Hall & Woodhouse, whose expert attentions ensured that many of its original features remain visible. Starters on the wide-ranging menu include continental meat platter; and deep-fried salt and pepper squid; mains could be poached fillet of West Country salmon; rib-eye and sirloin steaks; pan-fried escalope of veal; and wild rocket, mushroom, spring onion and sun-blushed tomato risotto. Mature gardens and a courtyard could, for some, be welcome relief following a shopping expedition next door.

Open 11-3 5-11 (Sun 11-4) Closed 25-26 Dec, Sun eve **Food** Lunch all wk 12-2 Dinner Mon-Sat 5-9 Set menu available ⊕ FREE HOUSE ◢ Badger First Call ⚬ Westons Stowford Press. ⚑ 14 **Facilities** Non-diners area ✿ (Bar Garden Outside area) ◑ Children's portions Garden Outside area ⼓ Parking WiFi ▭ (notice required)

The Hatch Inn

tel: 01823 480245 **Village Rd, Hatch Beauchamp TA3 6SG**
email: info@thehatchinn.co.uk
dir: *M5 junct 25, S on A358 for 3m. Left to Hatch Beauchamp, pub in 1m*

A good reputation for quality pub food and ales

Surrounded by splendid Somerset countryside, the pub dates back to the mid-1700s and has its share of ghostly occupants. The inn prides itself on its friendly, community atmosphere and the quality of its wines and West Country beers. Wholesome home-made food is served, prepared from seasonally changing, local produce, with a good choice of snacks and pub classics for the early afternoon and evening; meals shown on the dinner menu could be Scotch egg Benedict; or lightly

curried rabbit terrine to start, followed by pork fillet stuffed with feta and lemon; and beetroot and red wine risotto.

Open all day 9-3 5-11 (Sat 12-12 Sun 12-4) Closed Sun eve, Mon **Food** Lunch Tue-Sun 12-3 Dinner Tue-Sat 6-9 ⊕ FREE HOUSE ◢ St Austell Tribute, local guest ales ⚬ Thatchers Gold & Somerset Haze, guest cider. ⚑ 9 **Facilities** Non-diners area ✿ (Bar Outside area) ◑ Children's menu Children's portions Outside area ⼓ Parking WiFi ▭ (notice required)

TINTINHULL   Map 4 ST41

The Crown and Victoria Inn ★★★★ INN ⚙

PICK OF THE PUBS

tel: 01935 823341 **14 Farm St BA22 8PZ**
email: info@thecrownandvictoria.co.uk **web:** www.thecrownandvictoria.co.uk
dir: *1m S of A303. Adjacent to Tintinhull Garden (NT)*

Excellent food served in this family-friendly inn

Three hundred years old, and run by Isabel Thomas and Mark Hilyard, this lovely pub occupies an enviable position amidst the sweeping willow trees in its tranquil beer garden. The beer pumps belong exclusively to West Country real ales, such as Butcombe, Cheddar and Yeovil, while from the wine list, 10 are sold by the glass. Locally-sourced food, much of it organic and free-range, feature on the AA-Rosette menus. Typical starters might include wild mushrooms on toast; or ham hock terrine, capers, parsley and real ale chutney. Mains could include roast topside of beef with Yorkshire pudding; roast leg of lamb with roast potatoes; pan-fried chicken supreme with leek and pancetta cream sauce; or mushroom Wellington. Finish with blueberry and apple crumble or a board of West Country cheeses. Five spacious, well-equipped bedrooms complete the picture.

Open all wk 10-4 5.30-late **Food** Lunch all wk 12-2.30 Dinner Mon-Sat 6.30-9.30 ⊕ FREE HOUSE ◢ Sharp's Doom Bar, Butcombe, Cheddar, Cotleigh, Yeovil ⚬ Ashton Press. ⚑ 10 **Facilities** Non-diners area ✿ (Bar Garden) ◑ Children's menu Children's portions Garden ⼓ Parking WiFi ▭ **Rooms** 5

TRISCOMBE   Map 4 ST13

The Blue Ball Inn   PICK OF THE PUBS

tel: 01984 618242 **TA4 3HE**
email: enq@blueballinn.info
dir: *From Taunton take A358 past Bishops Lydeard towards Minehead*

Inventive dishes with top quality, traceable ingredients

Although the 18th-century Blue Ball is still down the same narrow lane in the Quantock Hills, some years ago it moved into a pretty thatched barn across the road. The inn looks south to the Brendon Hills and serves regional ales such as Exmoor Stag, along with Thatchers and Mad Apple ciders. The food focus is on reliably sourced, fully traceable produce, and cooking to order is the order of the day. Share a board of nibbles at lunchtime, or choose your filling for a fresh sandwich made with home-baked bread. Look to the restaurant carte for a proper three-course treat: Fowey River mussels with white wine, garlic and thyme; slow-cooked shank of lamb with Moroccan spices, couscous, apricots and pistachios; and a sticky toffee pudding with butterscotch and Somerset clotted cream.

Open 12-10.30 Closed 25 Dec, Sun eve **Food** Lunch all wk 12-3 Dinner Mon-Sat 6.30-9 ⊕ FREE HOUSE ◢ Exmoor Stag, St Austell Tribute, Sharp's Doom Bar ⚬ Thatchers Gold, Mad Apple. ⚑ 10 **Facilities** Non-diners area ✿ (Bar Garden) ◑ Children's menu Children's portions Garden ⼓ Parking WiFi ▭ (notice required)

WAMBROOK

Map 4 ST20

The Cotley Inn

tel: 01460 62348 **TA20 3EN**
email: contact@cotleyinnwambrook.co.uk
dir: *Take A30 from Chard towards Yarcombe. At thatched roundhouse turn left to Wambrook. Pub on right*

Local fare served in Grade II listed building

Situated in classic Somerset countryside, The Cotley makes an ideal watering hole for lovers of peace and quiet. Walkers with, or without, their dogs enjoy open fires in winter, and the raised terrace in summer with views over surrounding hills. Formerly the New Inn, it was bought and re-named the Cotley by Colonel Eames, after the Cotley Harriers. With a pint of Exmoor in hand, choose from pub fare such as home-made beef lasagne, or look to the regularly changing specials for dishes like plaice fillet stuffed with prawns and crabmeat. With spirit calmed and body replete, depart for a visit to the lovely gardens of Cricket St Thomas a short drive away.

Open 12-3 6-11 Closed Sun eve & Mon L **Food** Lunch Tue-Sat 12-2, Sun 12-2.30 Dinner Mon-Sat 6.30-9 ⊕ FREE HOUSE ◀ Otter Bitter & Amber, Exmoor Ales Fox ♻ Guest cider. **Facilities** ❄ (Bar Garden) ♦️ Children's menu Children's portions Garden ⊓ Parking

WEDMORE

Map 4 ST44

The George Inn ★★★★ INN

tel: 01934 712124 **Church St BS28 4AB**
email: info@thegeorgewedmore.co.uk **web:** www.thegeorgewedmore.co.uk
dir: *M5 junct 22, follow Bristol & Cheddar signs (A38). From dual carriageway right, follow signs for Mark, then Wedmore. Pub in village centre*

Home-from-home philosophy at pretty village inn

At this former coaching inn all the original features, artwork, old and new furniture blend seamlessly, and there are four different dining areas, each with a warming open fire lit in the winter months. Food is sourced as locally and seasonally as possible – perhaps start with half a roasted quail with celeriac purée, braised red cabbage and game jus; or tian of white crab, smoked trout and crayfish. Mains include pork, honey and cider sausages; sea bass, cod, lime and ginger fishcakes; or venison and winter root veg stew with wilted spinach and home-made chips. As it's a free house, expect cask ales from Butcombe and Sharp's, and Wilkins Farmhouse real cider, together with an ever-changing choice of craft beers. Stylish accommodation is available.

Open all day all wk **Food** Lunch Mon-Fri 12-2, Sat-12-3, Sun 12-8 Dinner Mon-Sat 6-9, Sun 12-8 Set menu available Restaurant menu available all wk ⊕ FREE HOUSE ◀ Butcombe, Sharp's Doom Bar ♻ Thatchers, Symonds, Wilkins Farmhouse. **Facilities** Non-diners area ❄ (Bar Garden Outside area) ♦️ Children's menu Children's portions Play area Garden Outside area ⊓ Beer festival Cider festival Parking WiFi 🚌 (notice required) **Rooms** 4

The Swan

tel: 01934 710337 **Cheddar Rd BS28 4EQ**
email: info@theswanwedmore.com
dir: *In village centre*

Busy village pub with all-day food

Open fires, stripped wood floors and big mirrors now greet visitors to what in the early 1700s was a beer house, then by the mid 19th century had developed into a hotel. This free house stocks the bar with Cheddar Ales Potholer, Bath Ales Gem and Thatchers Gold cider. In the kitchen, head chef Tom Blake, ex-River Cottage Canteen, is in charge of a team producing cider-steamed Dorset clams with watercress, soy and peanut dressing; merguez-spiced chickpea and butternut stew; and chargrilled Somerset rib-eye steak, roasted garlic parsley butter and hand-cut chips.

Open all day all wk **Food** Contact pub for food times ⊕ FREE HOUSE/DRACO PUB COMPANY ◀ Cheddar Ales Potholer, Bath Ales Gem ♻ Thatchers Gold. ♚ 12 **Facilities** Non-diners area ❄ (Bar Garden) ♦️ Children's menu Children's portions Garden ⊓ Parking WiFi

WELLS

Map 4 ST54

The Crown at Wells ★★★★ INN

tel: 01749 673457 **Market Place BA5 2RP**
email: eat@crownatwells.co.uk **web:** www.crownatwells.co.uk
dir: *On entering Wells follow signs for Hotels & Deliveries. Left at lights into Sadler St, left into Market Place. For car park pass Bishop's Palace entrance, post office & town hall*

Centuries-old coaching inn in a central spot

This 15th-century inn overlooks the Market Place and is a stone's throw from the magnificent cathedral and easily spotted by pretty hanging baskets; Penn Barr with tall leaded windows, is named after William Penn, a Quaker who preached from The Crown and who later gave his name to Pennsylvania. Very good pub dishes are offered food-wise in this bar – duck confit with chorizo and pancetta cassoulet being just one. Similar food appears on the Anton's Bistrot menu, but alternative choices include a starter of crayfish salad, aïoli and croûtons, and mains like slow-cooked pork belly marinated in cider and fennel seeds; mushroom and onion Stroganoff; or pan-fried sea bass. There are also 15 en suite bedrooms.

Open all day all wk Closed 25 Dec **Food** Lunch all wk fr noon Dinner Mon-Sat 6-9.30, Sun 6-9 Av main course £10 Restaurant menu available all wk ⊕ FREE HOUSE ◀ Sharp's Doom Bar, Glastonbury Holy Thorn, Butcombe, St Austell Tribute, Palmers Dorset Gold ♻ Ashton Press, Thatchers Old Rascal. ♚ 11 **Facilities** Non-diners area ❄ (Bar Outside area) ♦️ Children's menu Children's portions Outside area ⊓ Parking WiFi 🚌 (notice required) **Rooms** 15

The Fountain Inn

PICK OF THE PUBS

tel: 01749 672317 **1 Saint Thomas St BA5 2UU**
email: eat@fountaininn.co.uk
dir: *In city centre, at A371 & B3139 junct. Follow signs for The Horringtons. Inn on junct of Tor St & Saint Thomas St*

A dining-pub with a quirky interior

The tower of Wells Cathedral protrudes above the rooftops a short distance away from this attractive, three-storey, blue-shuttered pub with pretty window boxes. The interior is appealing, too, with a large open fire in the big, comfortable bar, interesting bric-à-brac, discreet music and board games. Owner Tessa Hennessey, who once had her own restaurant in South Africa, is one of the two chefs, the other being the Fountain's long-serving Julie Pearce. Together they maintain a winning repertoire of high quality, home-cooked food, among which are crispy squid with garlic mayo; chicken and butternut Madras curry with coconut rice; grilled salmon with seasonal stir-fry vegetables; and filo parcel with feta, sun-blushed tomatoes, olives and pine nuts. Some of these you'll also find at lunchtime, alongside savoury crêpes, and home-made lasagne. A meal could finish with pear tarte Tatin, or home-made cranberry and almond Bakewell tart. Off-street parking is available opposite the inn.

Open 12-3 6-10.30 (Fri 12-3 6-11 Sat 12.30-3.30 6-11 Sun 12-3.30 7-10) Closed 26 Dec, Mon L **Food** Lunch Tue-Fri 12-2, Sat-Sun 12-2.30 Dinner Mon-Sat 6-9, Sun 7-9 Restaurant menu available all wk ⊕ PUNCH TAVERNS ◀ Butcombe Bitter, Sharp's Atlantic, Bath Ales Gem, guest ales ♻ Thatchers, Westons Stowford Press. **Facilities** Non-diners area ♦️ Children's menu Children's portions Parking WiFi 🚌 (notice required)

PICK OF THE PUBS

Crossways Inn ★★★★ INN

WEST HUNTSPILL   Map 4 ST34

tel: 01278 783756 **Withy Rd TA9 3RA**
email: info@crosswaysinn.com
web: www.crosswaysinn.com
dir: *M5 juncts 22 or 23 on A38*

Good beer and cider choices plus classic pub food

A family-run 17th century, tile-hung coaching inn ideally positioned for visitors to the Somerset Levels or walkers looking for a cosy respite from the rigours of the Mendip Hills. Warmed by two open log fireplaces, the inviting, wavy-beamed interior has an array of fine old photos of the area. Draw close to the bar to inspect the ever-rotating selection of excellent beers, often from microbreweries in Somerset, such as Exmoor and Cotleigh. The beer choice increases significantly during the pub's popular Summer Bank Holiday beer festival in August. Cider drinkers are spoiled for choice, too, with Thatchers on tap and Rich's Cider created at a local farm just a couple of miles away. The classic food here also tends to be very locally sourced, like Somerset rump and sirloin steaks, which come with home-made peppercorn, Stilton or white wine and mushroom sauce. Faggots and mash, curry of the day, Somerset ham, eggs and chips are all popular options, but you will need to check the specials board for the daily pie. If fish is your thing, the cod and prawns in garlic

butter with spinach is hard to resist. The pasta section of the menu offers beef lasagne, spaghetti bolognese and, for vegetarians, there's Stilton and broccoli crêpe. Lighter meals include sandwiches, baguettes, ploughman's and jacket potatoes. Desserts include Alabama chocolate fudge cake and toffee and Dime Bar crunch pie. Under-10s can have a menu of their own, including sandwiches, chicken nuggets, fish fingers and cottage pie. In summer, the large enclosed beer garden and children's play area comes into its own, as does the heated gazebo.

Open all day all wk Closed 25 Dec
Food Lunch all wk 12-2.30 Dinner all wk 6-9 🛢 FREE HOUSE ◧ Exmoor Stag, Cotleigh Snowy, Sharp's Doom Bar, Otter

Ale, RCH Double Header, Moor, Butcombe, Cheddar Gorge Best Ô Thatchers Gold, Dry & Heritage, Rich's. 🍷 16 **Facilities** Non-diners area 🐾 (Bar Restaurant Garden) 👫 Children's menu Children's portions Play area Family room Garden 🪑 Beer festival Parking WiFi 🚌 (notice required) **Rooms** 7

WEST BAGBOROUGH — Map 4 ST13

The Rising Sun Inn

tel: 01823 432575 **TA4 3EF**
dir: *Phone for detailed directions*

Quantocks' pub serving West Country ales

There's been a change of hands at this traditional, 16th-century village pub that lies in an Area of Outstanding Natural Beauty. Found down a narrow lane, this old building was rebuilt around the original cob walls; inside the decor is smart and inviting. A good choice of ales and food, both sourced from local suppliers, is on offer. Dishes include salt and pepper squid; Gloucester Old Spots pork sausages with scrumpy sauce; and aged prime fillet steaks. Daily specials flag up fresh fish options and seasonal choices such as locally reared spring lamb. A gallery restaurant above the bar is ideal for private functions.

Open all wk 10.30-3 6-11 **Food** Lunch all wk 12-2 Dinner all wk 6.30-9.30 Restaurant menu available all wk ⊕ FREE HOUSE ◀ Exmoor Ale, St Austell Tribute, guest ales. ♈ 8 **Facilities** Non-diners area ♣ (Bar) ♦ Children's portions Outside area ☂ WiFi

WEST CAMEL — Map 4 ST52

The Walnut Tree — PICK OF THE PUBS

tel: 01935 851292 **Fore St BA22 7QW**
email: info@thewalnuttreehotel.com
dir: *Exit A303 between Sparkford & Yeovilton Air Base at x-roads signed West Camel*

Family-run village pub with good reputation for food

The Boatwright family took over this country inn in August 2015 and its location just half a mile from the A303 makes it an ideal pit stop for weary travellers driving to and from the West Country. The eponymous tree provides the terrace with welcoming dappled shade on warm sunny days, while inside the black-beamed, part-oak, part-flagstone-floored bar sets the scene. As well as a carefully chosen wine list, West Country-brewed Sharp's real ales (and Thatchers Gold cider from Somerset) can accompany seasonal, locally sourced dishes in the comfortable, wood-panelled restaurant. Typical starters of potted shrimps, brown toast and baby gem salad; or sweet potato and coconut soup might precede main courses of pan-roasted salmon, warm roasted beetroot and spinach salad or slow-cooked pork belly, black pudding, apple sauce, fine beans and fondant potato. A menu of light bites is also served.

Open 11-3 6-11 Closed 25-26 Dec, 1 Jan, Sun eve, Mon L **Food** Lunch Tue-Sun 12-2 Dinner Mon-Sat 6-9 Restaurant menu available Tue-Sat ⊕ FREE HOUSE ◀ Sharp's ♂ Thatchers Gold. **Facilities** Non-diners area ♦ Children's portions Garden ☂ Parking WiFi

WEST HUNTSPILL — Map 4 ST34

Crossways Inn ★★★★ INN — PICK OF THE PUBS

See Pick of the Pubs on page 445

WEST MONKTON — Map 4 ST22

The Monkton Inn — PICK OF THE PUBS

tel: 01823 412414 **Blundells Ln TA2 8NP**
dir: *M5 junct 25 to Taunton, right at Creech Castle for 1m, left into West Monkton, right at Procters Farm, 0.5m on left*

Pretty little pub offering hearty meals

A little bit tucked away on the edge of the village, this convivial pub is run by Peter and Val Mustoe who, for many years, lived in South Africa. Once inside you'll undoubtedly be struck by the polished floorboards, stone walls, log fire, leather sofas, smart dining furniture, in fact, by the whole set-up. At the bar you'll be able to order Exmoor and Sharp's real ales, as well as your food, but meals are served only in the restaurant or on the patio. Lunch could be ostrich burger with hand-cut chips; or cottage pie and side salad, while the dinner menu offers tapas to share; grilled kingclip fillet with lemon butter; pork tenderloin with apple and cider sauce; or vegetarian choices of risotto and vegetable curry. Gluten free dishes are available too. Peter and Val say they are child, dog and horse friendly.

Open all wk 12-3 6-11 **Food** Lunch all wk 12-2 Dinner Tue-Sat 6-9, Sun-Mon 6-8 Restaurant menu available all wk ⊕ ENTERPRISE INNS ◀ Sharp's Doom Bar, Exmoor Ale, Otter Ale ♂ Thatchers Gold, Orchard Pig. ♈ 10 **Facilities** Non-diners area ♣ (Bar Garden Outside area) ♦ Children's menu Children's portions Play area Garden Outside area ☂ Parking WiFi ⛟ (notice required)

WINSCOMBE — Map 4 ST45

NEW The Woodborough Inn

tel: 01934 844167 **Sandford Rd BS25 1HD**
email: contact@woodborough-inn.co.uk **web:** www.woodborough-inn.co.uk
dir: *M5 junct 21, A370 (Weston-Super-Mare). At 2nd rdbt take A371 (Wells). Under motorway, in Banwell follow Winscombe signs. In Winscombe, under railway bridge, pub at x-roads on left*

Appealing menus and local ales in the Mendips

Slap bang in the centre of the bustling village of Winscombe, surrounded by the Mendip Hills, The Woodborough is close to Weston-super-Mare and conveniently located for Bristol Airport. The pub is also popular with cyclists using the Strawberry Line cycle way which passes the door. With a large comfortable bar and separate restaurant, a log-burner makes this a cosy space and the village hub. Locally brewed Butcombe Bitter and Thatchers Traditional cider keep drinkers satisfied, whilst a typical meal might start with beetroot-cured gravad lax with horseradish and dill cream, followed by beef Stroganoff with rice.

Open all day all wk 10.30am-11pm (Sun 12-10.30) **Food** Lunch Mon-Sat 12-2.15, Sun 12-3 Dinner Mon-Sat 6-9.30, Sun 6-8 ⊕ FREE HOUSE ◀ Butcombe, St Austell Tribute, Otter Bitter ♂ Thatchers Traditional. ♈ 14 **Facilities** Non-diners area ♦ Children's menu Children's portions Outside area ☂ Beer festival Parking WiFi ⛟ (notice required)

WINSFORD

Map 3 SS93

The Royal Oak Exmoor ★★★★ INN

tel: 01643 851455 **TA24 7JE**
email: enquiries@royaloakexmoor.co.uk **web:** www.royaloakexmoor.co.uk
dir: Follow Winsford signs from A396 (Minehead to Tiverton road)

Local ales and seasonal produce in a delightful setting

Previously a farmhouse and dairy, the Royal Oak is a stunningly attractive thatched inn in one of Exmoor's prettiest villages, huddled beneath the rising moors beside the River Exe. Inside its all big fires, comfy chairs, restrained paraphernalia and restful decor. So, all the better to enjoy the twin treats of good honest Exmoor beers and rich local produce on the seasonal bar and restaurant menus, including slow-braised lamb shank with pan-fried gnocchi and red wine jus; butternut squash risotto cake; and deep-fried scampi in stout batter and chips.

The Royal Oak Exmoor

Open all wk 11-3 6-11 **Food** Lunch all wk 12-2 Dinner all wk 6-9 ⊕ FREE HOUSE
🍺 Exmoor Ale & Gold, guest ale ♂ Thatchers, Addlestones, Orchard Pig.
Facilities Non-diners area 🐾 (Bar Garden) 🚸 Children's menu Children's portions Garden Outside area 🚗 Parking WiFi **Rooms** 14

See advert below

The Royal Oak Inn

tel: 01643 831506 **TA24 7QP**
email: enquiries@royaloakwithypool.co.uk
dir: *Phone for detailed directions*

Local food and ales in village pub with literary links

Only four miles from the historic Tarr Steps, the Royal Oak Inn has been the hub of the pretty Exmoor village of Withypool for over 300 years. During that time, the pub has welcomed some notable guests including RD Blackmore, who stayed here whilst writing *Lorna Doone*. In the two bars with their real fires and wheelback chairs, join the locals over a pint of Exmoor Gold, or head to the restaurant for seasonal dishes such as roasted stuffed crown of pheasant with juniper jus; or steak and Exmoor Ale pie.

Open 12-3 6-11 (Summer all wk 12-11) Closed Mon in winter **Food** Lunch all wk 12-3 Dinner all wk 6.30-9 ⊕ FREE HOUSE ◀ Exmoor Ale & Gold, guest ale Ö Sheppy's, Thatchers, Shepton Mallet Cider. ⚑ 10 **Facilities** Non-diners area ❤ (Bar Outside area) ♦❧ Children's menu Children's portions Outside area ⋒ Parking WiFi ▭ (notice required)

The Burcott Inn

tel: 01749 673874 **Wells Rd BA5 1NJ**
email: ian@burcottinn.co.uk
dir: *2m from Wells on B3139*

Homely stone-built inn offering a friendly welcome

On the edge of a charming village just two miles from the cathedral city of Wells, the age of this 300-year-old pub is confirmed by the low-beamed ceilings, flagstone floors and log fires. Another notable feature is its copper-topped bar with five real ales and Thatchers Gold on handpull. Here, you can have a snack or a daily special, while in the restaurant typical dishes include starters such as garlic mushrooms; pan-fried tiger prawns or warm mushroom and walnut salad; and main dishes like apricot chicken breast or poached salmon fillet. There are also specials board choices. The large enclosed garden enjoys views of the Mendip Hills.

Open 12-2.30 6-11 (Sun 12-3) Closed 25-26 Dec, 1 Jan, Sun eve & Mon **Food** Lunch Tue-Sun 12-2 Dinner Tue-Sat 6.30-9 Restaurant menu available Tue-Sun ⊕ FREE HOUSE ◀ Teignworthy Old Moggie, RCH Pitchfork, Hop Back Summer Lightning, Cheddar Potholer, Butts Barbus barbus Ö Thatchers Gold. **Facilities** Non-diners area ♦❧ Children's menu Children's portions Family room Garden ⋒ Parking ▭ (notice required)

Wookey Hole Inn

tel: 01749 676677 **High St BA5 1BP**
email: mail@wookeyholeinn.com
dir: *Opposite Wookey Hole caves*

A top selection of beers and noteworthy cuisine

Located opposite the famous caves, this family-run inn is outwardly traditional, although the interior looks and feels very laid-back. Somerset and continental draught and bottled beers include Glastonbury Ales Love Monkey and fruity Belgian Früli; local Wilkins Farmhouse tempts cider-heads. The menu offers something for everyone, from starters like tempura tiger prawns with sweet chilli jam; duck liver parfait with orange peel jelly; or butternut squash and sage soup; to mains like red peppers stuffed with couscous; or roast cod fillet with cauliflower mash. Try to leave space for hot date and walnut pudding with toffee sauce; or caramelised poached pear with cinnamon ice cream.

Open all day Closed 25-26 Dec, Sun eve **Food** Lunch all wk 12-2.30 Dinner Mon-Sat 7-9.30 ⊕ FREE HOUSE ◀ Glastonbury Ales Love Monkey, Cheddar Ales, Yeovil, Cottage Ö Wilkins Farmhouse. **Facilities** Non-diners area ❤ (Bar Garden) ♦❧ Children's menu Children's portions Garden ⋒ Parking WiFi ▭ (notice required)

The Battleaxes ★★★★ INN

tel: 01275 857473 **Bristol Rd BS48 1LQ**
email: thebattleaxes@flatcappers.co.uk web: www.flatcappers.co.uk
dir: *Take A370 from Bristol towards Weston-Super-Mare. Exit for B3130 signed Wraxall. Pub on left in village*

Fab building with great local ales

Built in 1882, The Battleaxes was originally staff quarters for the many servants working for the Gibbs family, who owned the now National Trust-run Tyntesfield Estate. A great example of Gothic Revival architecture, the pub is owned by Flatcappers, a small local pub company. Have a pint of Butcombe Bitter or Flatcapper Ale while you peruse the menu. Breakfast is served between 8 and 12, but if it's lunch or dinner you're after, no problem. Black pudding Scotch egg might be a good place to start, followed by steak and chips; or roast Loch Duart salmon; desserts might include vanilla rice pudding with poached rhubarb, or a choice of West Country cheeses.

Open all day all wk **Food** Contact pub for food times Set menu available ⊕ FREE HOUSE ◀ Three Castles Flatcapper Ale, Butcombe Bitter, Bath Ales Dark Side, Bristol Beer Factory Ö Bath Ciders Bounders, Westons Stowford Press. **Facilities** Non-diners area ❤ (Bar Garden) ♦❧ Children's menu Children's portions Garden ⋒ Parking WiFi ▭ (notice required) **Rooms** 6

The Half Moon Inn ★★★ INN

tel: 01935 850289 **Main St, Mudford BA21 5TF**
email: enquiries@thehalfmooninn.co.uk web: www.thehalfmooninn.co.uk
dir: *A303 at Sparkford onto A359 to Yeovil, 3.5m on left*

Long menu with something for everyone

The exposed beams and flagstone floors retain the character of this painstakingly restored 17th-century village pub just north of Yeovil. Cornish beers are on tap and there are 10 wines by the glass to accompany the extensive menu of home-cooked food, which includes pub classics and main meals such as garlic cream cheese stuffed chicken breast with white wine sauce; oven-roasted barbecue pork ribs; or smoked haddock, cheese and chive mash, mornay sauce and poached egg. Sandwiches, hot paninis and jackets are also available. The large cobbled courtyard is ideal for alfresco dining and spacious, well-equipped bedrooms are also available.

Open all day all wk Closed 25-26 Dec **Food** Sun-Mon 11-9, Tue-Sat 11-9.30 ⊕ FREE HOUSE ◀ St Austell Proper Job & HSD Ö Thatchers Gold, Black Rat. ⚑ 10 **Facilities** Non-diners area ♦❧ Children's menu Children's portions Outside area ⋒ Parking WiFi ▭ (notice required) **Rooms** 14

The Masons Arms ★★★★ INN   PICK OF THE PUBS

tel: 01935 862591 **41 Lower Odcombe BA22 8TX**
email: paula@masonsarmsodcombe.co.uk web: www.masonsarmsodcombe.co.uk
dir: *A3088 to Yeovil, right to Montacute, through village, 3rd right after petrol station to Lower Odcombe*

Strong green credentials and a microbrewery

Once a cider house and bolt-hole for local quarry workers, Paula and Drew's thatched, 16th-century pub serves an exclusive clutch of real ales – Odcombe No 1, Spring and Roly Poly – all specially brewed by Drew. The couple are big on green initiatives and grow many of their own vegetables and fruit, and also offer organic, vegetarian, biodynamic and Fairtrade wines. Another string to Drew's bow is the modern British cooking that lies behind the dishes on his seasonal and daily-changing menus. Start with monktail with seared scallops, pea purée, pancetta crisp and truffle oil; then move on to starters like butternut squash, goats' cheese and spinach lasagne; venison casserole with rosemary dumplings and charred baby leeks; or battered fish of the day with triple-cooked, rustic chips and tartare sauce. Finish with apple and stem ginger bread and butter pudding with crème anglaise. The comfortable en suite letting rooms are set back from the road, overlooking the pretty garden.

Open all wk 12-3 6-12 **Food** Lunch all wk 12-2 Dinner all wk 6.30-9.30 ⊕ FREE HOUSE ◀ Odcombe No 1, Spring, Roly Poly, Winters Tail, Half Jack Ō Thatchers Gold & Heritage. ℙ 8 **Facilities** Non-diners area ✿ (Bar Restaurant Garden) ☀ Children's menu Children's portions Garden ⊫ Parking WiFi **Rooms** 6

STAFFORDSHIRE

ALSTONEFIELD   Map 16 SK15

The George   PICK OF THE PUBS

tel: 01335 310205 **DE6 2FX**
email: emily@thegeorgeatalstonefield.com
dir: *7m N of Ashbourne, signed Alstonefield to left off A515*

An unspoilt, family-run pub in a Peak District village

Emily Brighton's family has run The George for three generations and it's a must-visit for the many walkers passing the door. Located up above Dovedale, this pretty, stone-built pub offers a bar with a fire, historic artefacts, portraits of locals and a wide choice of real ales, including Banks's Sunbeam and Jennings Cumberland. There's an original simplicity about the dining room and snug, with their lime-plastered walls, farmhouse furniture, candlelight and fresh flowers. The kitchen's passion for locally sourced food is evident from the organic garden, source of abundant vegetables, salad leaves and herbs. A winter lunch menu might offer pheasant rillettes, celeriac remoulade, cornichons and toast; or smoked Scottish salmon, winter coleslaw and horseradish cream, followed by pappardelle, crème fraîche, woodland mushroom and roast squash; or a venison burger. Leave a space for apple and blackberry crumble with custard.

Open all wk Mon-Thu 11.30-3 6-11 (Fri-Sat 11.30-11 Sun 12-9.30) Closed 25 Dec **Food** Lunch all wk 12-2.30 Dinner Mon-Sat 6.30-9, Sun 6.30-8 Av main course £16 ⊕ MARSTON'S ◀ Burton Bitter & Pedigree, Jennings Cumberland Ale, Brakspear Oxford Gold, Banks's Sunbeam, guest ale Ō Thatchers. ℙ 10 **Facilities** Non-diners area ✿ (Bar Garden) ☀ Children's portions Garden ⊫ Parking

BARTON-UNDER-NEEDWOOD   Map 10 SK11

The Waterfront

tel: 01283 711500 **Barton Marina DE13 8DZ**
email: info@waterfrontbarton.co.uk web: www.waterfrontbarton.co.uk
dir: *Exit A38 onto B5016 towards Barton-under-Needwood. 1st left signed Barton Turn. 1st right into Barton Marina*

Large modern pub overlooking a marina

This pub is part of a purpose-built marina complex, and is constructed with reclaimed materials to resemble a Victorian canalside warehouse. Overlooking busy moorings, it offers beers specially brewed for the pub and a fair few cocktails. Dine in the contemporary conservatory from an extensive menu of snacks, oven-fired pizzas, and old favourites like chicken balti; braised beef ribs; and moules marinière. Vegetarians might like the Ch'ish (battered halloumi) and chips. Children over five are welcome. A walk along the Trent & Mersey towpath leads to the nearby National Memorial Arboretum, the UK's Centre of Remembrance.

Open all day all wk Sun-Thu 10am-11pm (Fri-Sat 10am-1am) Closed 25 Dec **Food** 12-9.30 Restaurant menu available Sun-Sat ⊕ FREE HOUSE ◀ St Austell Tribute, Marston's Pedigree, Sharp's Doom Bar, Castle Rock Harvest Pale Ō Thatchers, Orchard Pig Reveller. ℙ 20 **Facilities** Non-diners area ☀ Garden ⊫ Parking WiFi ⇔ (notice required)

See advert on page 450

CAULDON
Map 16 SK04

Yew Tree Inn

tel: 01538 309876 **ST10 3EJ**
email: info@yewtreeinncauldon.co.uk
dir: From either A52 or A523 follow brown tourist signs for 'Yew Tree Historical Inn'

Affectionately known as the 'junk shop with a bar'

This is an Aladdin's Cave of a pub with a collection of antiques and curios which includes Queen Victoria's stockings, a 3,000-year-old Grecian urn, penny-farthings and Victorian polyphons. Sit on church pews or on a grand settee and settle for a pint of Burton Bridge or a guest ale, then turn to the modest yet hearty menu to decide on a traditional Staffordshire pie, stew or a Staffordshire oatcake. Family owned since 1961, the Yew Tree is a popular meeting place for owners of vintage cars and motorcycles — rallies are held throughout the summer on the events field. Time a visit for the July beer festival.

Open all wk 12-3 6-11 (Sat 12-12 Sun 12-11) **Food** Lunch Mon-Fri 12-3, Sat-Sun 12-9 Dinner Mon-Fri 6-9, Sat-Sun 12-9 Av main course £7 ⊕ FREE HOUSE ◀ Burton Bridge, Rudgate Ruby Mild, guest ales Ŏ Abrahalls, guest ciders. ♥ 9
Facilities Non-diners area ✿ (Bar Garden Outside area) ♦♦ Children's portions Play area Family room Garden Outside area ☎ Beer festival Cider festival Parking WiFi ➡ (notice required)

CHEADLE
Map 10 SK04

The Queens at Freehay

tel: 01538 722383 **Counslow Rd, Freehay ST10 1RF**
email: mail@queensatfreehay.co.uk
dir: From Cheadle take A552 towards Uttoxeter. In Mobberley left, through Freehay to pub at next rdbt. Freehay also signed from B5032 (Cheadle to Denstone road)

Family-run pub tucked away in a quiet village

Surrounded by mature trees and well-tended gardens, this 18th-century, family-run pub and restaurant has a refreshing, modern interior and it's just four miles from Alton Towers. Ringwood Fortyniner and the more local Alton Abbey are among the beers on hand pump in the bar. With a good reputation for food, its main menu is supplemented by daily chef's specials on the fresh fish and meat boards. Expect chicken liver, bacon and rosemary pâté; or herb-breaded brie to start, followed by Moroccan harissa chicken; or perhaps a fillet or rib-eye steak served with tomato, mushrooms and crispy deep-fried onions. At lunchtimes there are light bite options such as scampi and chips; and pork sausage, egg and chips.

Open all wk 12-3 6-11 (Sun 12-4 6.30-11) Closed 25-26, 31 Dec-1 Jan **Food** Lunch Mon-Sat 12-2, Sun 12-2.30 Dinner Mon-Sat 6-9.30, Sun 6.30-9.30 Av main course £12.95 Restaurant menu available all wk ⊕ FREE HOUSE ◀ Peakstones Rock Alton Abbey, Marston's Pedigree & Oyster Stout, Ringwood Fortyniner Ŏ Thatchers. ♥ 10
Facilities Non-diners area ♦♦ Children's portions Garden ☎ Parking WiFi

---

The Waterfront

Barton Marina, Barton-under-Needwood, Staffordshire DE13 8DZ
Tel: 01283 711500 · **Website:** www.waterfrontbarton.co.uk

The Waterfront pub opened in 2007. With the inspired use of reclaimed timber and brick, stone flags and period lighting, this privately-owned free house replicates the style of a Victorian canal-side warehouse. The vaulted bar serves an extensive range of real ales, premium lagers, fine wines, cocktails and malt whiskies.

Sensibly priced pub food, freshly cooked to order, is served in the restaurant, bar and lounge, and on the terrace overlooking the idyllic 300-berth Marina. The 50-seat contemporary conservatory, known as the Quarterdeck, is popular with diners and for private parties.

On the first floor, the Crow's Nest function room is available to hire for weddings, celebrations or for business use. This spacious and elevated room boasts a dance floor and a well-stocked bar, and the open balcony offers splendid views across the marina.

The Mill at Worston

Worston Lane, Great Bridgeford, Staffordshire ST18 9QA • **Tel:** 01785 282710
Website: www.themillatworston.co.uk • **Email:** info@themillatworston.co.uk

It is quite rare to stumble across a hidden gem as unique as *The Mill at Worston*. Nestled in some of our best Staffordshire countryside it sits beside the River Sow and has spectacular grounds, yet it is easily accessible, being just five minutes from junction 14 of the M6. The building itself is a 200-year-old watermill and it has been tastefully converted retaining many features from its milling days. Thus, the lounge is dominated by the impressive original 10-foot pit wheel and full of character with enormous original beams spanning the ceiling and log burning stoves providing warmth on autumn and winter evenings. *The Mill at Worston* is cask marque accredited and has four cask ales on rotation, featuring beers from many local micro-breweries including Titanic, Lymestone and Peakstones.

The Mill at Worston is an avid supporter of local sourcing, and nearby farms and suppliers feature strongly on their menu. Starters include grilled black pudding topped with poached egg laced with a mustard dressing and oven-baked field mushroom filled with welsh rarebit and served with rustic bread. For your main course our weekly specials currently feature such temptations as salmon au poivre with sauté potatoes, chargrilled vegetables and chervil hollandaise and mint glazed lamb cutlets with leek and potato cake, roast beetroot and spinach. If you've still got room desserts start from £4.25 and include the highly recommended sticky toffee pudding made to The Mill's own recipe, or for those wanting something more adventurous why not try the raspberry and basil cheesecake? Alternatively, the cheeseboard features traditional favourites, along with more local produce. Service is friendly and attentive without being too formal, making *The Mill at Worston* the perfect place to relax with family and friends.

The Mill at Worston serves food all day, seven days a week from 12pm. The venue's restaurant is open Wednesday to Saturday evenings from 6pm, and 12pm–4pm on Sundays when customers can enjoy a traditional Sunday carvery. Reservations are advisable, especially at peak times.

Directions to *The Mill at Worston* and further information can be downloaded from www.themillatworston.co.uk.

COLTON
Map 10 SK02

The Yorkshireman
PICK OF THE PUBS

tel: 01889 583977 **Colton Rd WS15 3HB**
email: theyorkshireman@wine-dine.co.uk
dir: *From A51 rdbt in Rugeley follow rail station signs, under rail bridge, to pub*

Try real ales from the local microbrewery

The pub's name derives from an erstwhile White Rose landlord, although the heritage of this edge-of-town pub opposite Rugeley's Trent Valley railway station is lost in the mists of time. Some believe it was a tavern built to serve the new railway in the 19th century, and it's certainly been a meeting place for farmers and soldiers. Walk through the doors today to find a panelled and wood-floored dining pub with eclectic furnishings including faux Stubbs paintings. Real ales from Blythe Brewery include Palmer's Poison, which commemorates the town's very own 19th-century mass murderer. Seasonal menus using top Staffordshire produce are changed regularly, but an indicative choice could start with Yorkshire crab, prawn and salmon cocktail; continue with a fillet of lemon sole stuffed with green beans and wrapped in Parma ham; and finish with traditional bread and butter pudding with vanilla custard.

Open all wk 12-2.30 5.30-10 (Sat 12-11 Sun 12-6) **Food** Lunch Mon-Sat 12-2.30, Sun 12-6 Dinner Mon-Sat 6-9, Sun 12-6 Set menu available ⊕ FREE HOUSE
◀ Blythe Bagots Bitter & Palmer's Poison ◌ Symonds. ♈ 14
Facilities Non-diners area ✿ (Bar Garden) ♦ Children's portions Garden ⌂ Parking WiFi ▭ (notice required)

ELLASTONE
Map 10 SK14

The Duncombe Arms

tel: 01335 324275 **Main Rd DE6 2GZ**
email: hello@duncombearms.co.uk **web:** www.duncombearms.co.uk
dir: *From Ashbourne take A515 towards Lichfield. 1m, take A52 towards Leek. Approx 1m left onto B5032 signed Ellastone. In village turn left, pub on left*

Smart village pub in the Dove Valley

George Eliot set her first novel *Adam Bede* in Ellastone. In this bucolic corner of Staffordshire, between the wooded Dove Valley and the shapely Weaver Hills, is where you'll find The Duncombe Arms, a notable dining pub. Classic and contemporary architecture now blend seamlessly in the sturdy old inn. Over a glass of Duncombe Ale or Addlestones cider consider a comforting menu of pub stalwarts enhanced with modern dishes; start with braised pig's head terrine before enjoying perhaps pan-fried Icelandic cod fillet, rope-grown mussels, crispy potatoes and warm tartare sauce. Finish with toffee bread and butter pudding and Granny Smith sorbet. The wine list is extensive.

The Duncombe Arms

Open all day all wk **Food** Lunch Mon-Sat 12-2.30, Sun 12-8 Dinner Mon-Thu 6-9, Fri-Sat 5.30-10, Sun 12-8 Set menu available Restaurant menu available all wk
⊕ FREE HOUSE ◀ Marston's Pedigree, Duncombe Ale, Timothy Taylor Landlord ◌ Addlestones, Aspall Premier Cru. ♈ 21 **Facilities** Non-diners area ✿ (Bar Garden) ♦ Children's menu Children's portions Garden ⌂ Parking WiFi ▭ (notice required)

GREAT BRIDGEFORD
Map 10 SJ82

The Mill at Worston

tel: 01785 282710 **Worston Ln ST18 9QA**
email: info@themillatworston.co.uk **web:** www.themillatworston.co.uk
dir: *M6 junct 14, A5013 signed Eccleshall. 2m to Great Bridgeford. Turn right signed Worston Mill. Or from Eccleshall on A5013 towards Stafford. 3m to Great Bridgeford, turn left to Mill*

A restored corn mill serving good food

Documents can trace a mill on this site from 1279. The building that now occupies this rural spot beside the River Sow dates from 1814, when it was in daily use as a corn mill. Visitors can still see the original wheel and gearing that powered the mill stone. Drop in for meals that range from ciabatta or baguette sandwiches, jacket potatoes and grills to home-made steak and ale pie, wild mushroom carbonara and roasted field mushrooms with Welsh rarebit, all washed down with a pint of Greene King IPA perhaps? The pretty gardens, with duck pond, make a great place for alfresco eating in the warmer months.

The Mill at Worston

Open all day all wk Closed 26 Dec **Food** Lunch all wk 12-6 Dinner Sun-Thu 6-9, Fri-Sat 6-10 Set menu available Restaurant menu available ⊕ FREE HOUSE ◪ Morland Old Speckled Hen, Greene King IPA, rotating guest ales. ☗ 12
Facilities Non-diners area ⬥ Children's menu Children's portions Play area Garden ⋒ Parking WiFi ▭ (notice required)

See advert on page 451

HAUGHTON | Map 10 SJ82

NEW The Bell

tel: 01785 780301 **ST18 9EX**
email: allyheath@btconnect.com
dir: *On A518 between Stafford & Newport*

Popular roadside pub

'A village pub' says the sign on the front of the building, which, with the parish church only a couple of hundred yards away, indeed it is. Real ales include Marston's Pedigree and Timothy Taylor Landlord, are accompanied by a more local guest. Pub classics of wholetail breaded scampi; chilli con carne; and honey-baked ham and eggs are popular; so too are specials such as Thai fish curry with green peppers, coconut milk and basmati rice; Barnsley chops with rosemary mash and redcurrant and mint gravy; and duo of duck with Kirsch and rich berry sauce. Monthly steak nights are a big draw.

Open all wk 12-3 5-12 (Fri-Sun 12-12) **Food** Lunch Mon-Sat 12-2, Sun 12-4 Dinner Tue-Sat 6-9 Av main course £9.50 Set menu available ⊕ ENTERPRISE INNS ◪ Timothy Taylor Landlord, Marston's Pedigree, guest ales ♻ Thatchers Gold. ☗ 17
Facilities Non-diners area ⬥ Children's menu Children's portions Garden ⋒ Beer festival Cider festival Parking WiFi ▭ (notice required)

KING'S BROMLEY | Map 10 SK11

NEW The Royal Oak

tel: 01543 410022 **Manor Rd DE13 7HZ**
email: royaloak13@outlook.com
dir: *On A515*

Village pub with no airs and graces

Overseeing the crossroads in the centre of the village, this is a true community pub. Owned by Marston's, you can expect big brand ales like Pedigree, Wainwright and Ringwood, as well as guests; bar snacks include sandwiches and jacket potatoes. Among lunch or dinner starters are whitebait, fresh salad and garlic mayonnaise; and breaded brie, cranberry purée and dressed salad. From the grill come Hunter's

chicken with bacon, cheese, chips, peas and barbecue sauce; and mixed grill – 4oz rump steak, 6oz gammon steak, two sausages and chicken breast. Other options are beer-battered haddock, chips and mushy peas; liver, onions and mash; and penne arrabbiata.

Open all day all wk **Food** Contact pub for food times ⊕ MARSTON'S ◪ Pedigree, Wainwright, Ringwood Boondoggle, guest ale ♻ Thatchers Gold.
Facilities Non-diners area ⬥ (Bar Garden) ⬥ Children's menu Children's portions Garden ⋒ Parking WiFi ▭ (notice required)

LEEK | Map 16 SJ95

Three Horseshoes Country Inn ★★★★ INN ◉◉

tel: 01538 300296 **Buxton Rd, Blackshaw Moor ST13 8TW**
email: enquiries@3shoesinn.co.uk **web:** www.3shoesinn.co.uk
dir: *On A53, 3m N of Leek*

Award-winning food at a well known inn

A family-run inn in the Peak District National Park, the Three Horseshoes offers breathtaking views of the moorlands, Tittesworth reservoir and rock formations from the attractive gardens. Inside this creeper-covered inn are ancient beams, gleaming brass, rustic furniture and wood fires in the winter, with a good selection of real ales. Using the best Staffordshire produce, visitors can choose from wide ranging lunch and dinner menus of British dishes in the Bar and Grill, Bar Carvery, The Stables restaurant, or refurbished Kirks Restaurant. Delicious afternoon teas are also available.

Open all day all wk **Food** Contact pub for food times Restaurant menu available ⊕ FREE HOUSE ◪ Morland Old Speckled Hen, Sharp's Doom Bar, Marston's Pedigree, Blue Moon, guest ales. ☗ 12 **Facilities** Non-diners area ⬥ Children's menu Children's portions Play area Garden ⋒ Parking WiFi ▭ (notice required) **Rooms** 26

STAFFORD | Map 10 SJ92

The Holly Bush Inn | PICK OF THE PUBS

See Pick of the Pubs on page 455 and advert on page 454

STOURTON | Map 10 SO88

The Fox Inn

tel: 01384 872614 & 872123 **Bridgnorth Rd DY7 5BH**
email: foxinnstourton@gmail.com
dir: *5m from Stourbridge town centre. On A458 (Stourbridge to Bridgnorth road)*

Forty-plus years behind the bar

Stefan Caron has been running this late 18th-century inn for more than 40 years. In unspoilt countryside on an estate once owned by Lady Jane Grey, it retains the style of an old country pub, with church pews in the bar, where Black Country brewers Bathams and Wye Valley put on a double act. Menus variously offer chicken balti; fresh tagliatelle; Tex Mex, a rib-eye steak with chilli and mozzarella; pie of the day with peas and chunky chips; and beer-battered cod with mushy peas. The large garden with weeping willow, gazebo and attractive patio area are the external attractions.

Open all wk 10.30-3 5-11 (Sat-Sun 10.30am-11pm) **Food** Lunch Mon-Sat 12-2.30, Sun 12.30-7 Dinner Tue-Sat 7-9.30, Sun 12.30-7 ⊕ FREE HOUSE ◪ Bathams, Wye Valley HPA, Guinness ♻ Robinsons, Thatchers. **Facilities** Non-diners area ⬥ (Garden) ⬥ Children's menu Children's portions Garden ⋒ Parking WiFi ▭ (notice required)

THE HOLLY BUSH INN
SCRUMPTIOUS FOOD & QUAFFABLE ALES

The Holly Bush buys its fresh fish and meats as whole cuts direct from market and does all its own butchery and fishmongery, also practicing many other traditional cooking skills within its kitchen such as home-smoking fish and dry-aging cuts of meats to develop taste and tenderness. The Holly Bush has also recently started growing some of its own fruit and vegetables within its garden.The family operated inn also rewards its customers with a preferred customer loyalty card scheme which offers 5p back in every pound spent and other benefits such as a free bottle of house wine, when taken with a meal for two, on the card holder's birthday.
The Holly Bush Inn also offers promotional nights such as pizza & pasta night which showcases fresh hand-crafted pizza, cooked in its traditional wood-fired outdoor pizza oven and homemade pasta dishes.

PICK OF THE PUBS

The Holly Bush Inn

STAFFORD   Map 10 SJ92

tel: 01889 508234 **Salt ST18 0BX**
email: geoff@hollybushinn.co.uk
web: www.hollybushinn.co.uk
dir: *From Stafford on A518 towards*
Weston. Left signed Salt. Pub on left

Ancient pub with second oldest licence in England

This thatched inn is situated in the village of Salt, which has been a settlement since the Saxon period. It is thought to be only the second pub in the country to receive, back in Charles II's reign, a licence to sell alcohol, although the building itself may date from 1190. When landlord Geoff Holland's son Joseph became a joint licensee six days past his 18th birthday, he was the youngest person ever to be granted a licence. The pub's comfortably traditional interior contains all the essential ingredients: heavy carved beams, open fires, attractive prints and cosy alcoves. The kitchen has a strong commitment to limiting food miles by supporting local producers, and to ensuring that animals supplying meat have lived stress-free lives. The main menu features dishes such as breaded whole-tail scampi; grilled pork chops with cheese, beer and mustard topping; free-range supreme of chicken with Guinness; mixed grill; and Greek lamb, namely roast shoulder with red wine, herbs and spices and Greek salad. Look to the blackboards for the day's vegetarian options. Lunchtime and evening specials change every session, with examples including Cajun spiced beef tortilla wrap with sautéed peppers, onions and sautéed potatoes; grilled panini filled with bacon, mozzarella, Stilton and tomato; pan-fried fresh monkfish tails in creamy smoked bacon and button mushroom sauce; and trio of home-made sausages — venison and chilli, beef and horseradish, pork, apple and cider — with colcannon mash and caramelised baby carrots. Seasonal puddings include traditional bread and butter pudding, and apple crumble. During the warmer months hand-made pizzas are cooked in a wood-fired brick oven. June and September are the months for beer and cider festivals.

Open all day all wk 12-11 (Sun 12-10.30) Closed 25-26 Dec
Food Lunch Mon-Sat 12-9.30, Sun 12-9 Av main course £11 ⊞ ADMIRAL TAVERNS ▣ Marston's Pedigree, Adnams, guest ales. ♉ 12
Facilities Non-diners area
⋔ Children's menu Children's portions Garden ⋈ Beer festival Cider festival Parking WiFi

SUMMERHILL

Map 10 SK00

Oddfellows in the Boat

tel: 01543 361692 **The Boat, Walsall Rd WS14 0BU**
email: info@oddfellowsintheboat.com
dir: *A461 (Lichfield towards Walsall). At rdbt junct with A5 (Muckley Corner) continue on A461. 500mtrs, U-turn on dual carriageway back to pub*

An ale-lover's dream

Just four miles from Lichfield, this light and airy pub with country pine furnishings once served bargees on the now-disused 'Curly Wyrley' Canal to the rear. Real ale lovers can enjoy what amounts to a rolling beer festival all year thanks to an ever-changing choice from local microbreweries. Locally sourced dishes are prepared in an open kitchen and chalked up daily. Typical choices include black and white pudding fritters with Puy lentils; slow-cooked blade of beef and bourguignon sauce; smoked haddock kedgeree; and cappuccino Pavlova with whipped Irish cream. There is a large, attractive beer garden to enjoy on sunny days.

Open all wk 11-3 6-11 (Sun 12-11) Closed 25 Dec **Food** Lunch Mon-Sat 12-2.15, Sun 12-8.15 Dinner Mon-Sat 6-9.30, Sun 12-8.15 Restaurant menu available all wk ⊕ FREE HOUSE ◀ Backyard The Hoard, Blythe Staffie, 3 guest ales. ♥ 13 **Facilities** Non-diners area ♦♦ Garden ⋈ Beer festival Parking WiFi

SWYNNERTON

Map 10 SJ83

NEW The Fitzherbert Arms

tel: 01782 796782 **ST15 0RA**
email: info@fitzherbertarms.co.uk **web:** www.fitzherbertarms.co.uk
dir: *M6 junct 15, follow Eccleshall (A519) signs. At rdbt left onto A51 (Stone), 1st right signed Swynnerton. Pub in village centre*

Book in for a port tasting class

This brick-built village pub narrowly escaped closure. Instead it underwent a complete revamp when pub entrepreneurs Mary Mclaughlin and Tim Bird entered into a joint venture with Lord Stafford's estate. Reopened in 2016, the richly furnished interior is warmed by three log fires. Artefacts from the village smithy include tables made from old anvils, a blacksmith's furnace and water troughs. Ales sourced within a 35-mile radius include Titanic Brewery's stout. A speciality of the house is port, with over 30 sold by the bottle and a dozen of which can be tasted by the glass. Uncomplicated dishes of modern British food embrace pub favourites, seasonal specials, and home-made puddings. The pub is member of the Sustainable Restaurant Association.

The Fitzherbert Arms

Open all day all wk **Food** all wk until 9.30pm Av main course £13 ⊕ FREE HOUSE ◀ Weetwood Ales Fitzherbert Best, Titanic Stout ♂ Apple County Cider, Ty Gwyn. ♥ **Facilities** Non-diners area ♣ (Bar Garden Outside area) ♦♦ Children's portions Garden Outside area ⋈ Parking WiFi

TAMWORTH

Map 10 SK20

The Globe Inn ★★★ INN

tel: 01827 60455 **Lower Gungate B79 7AT**
email: info@theglobetamworth.com **web:** www.theglobetamworth.com
dir: *Phone for detailed directions*

Early 20th-century free house under new ownership

The Globe's elegant restored frontage dates from a 1901 brewery rebuild. The interior, also revamped, still retains its period look, particularly the grand wooden bar and the fireplaces. Three guest ales accompany Bass and Holden's Black Country Mild. Snacks include wraps, ciabattas, sandwiches, burgers and jackets, while among the starters are loaded potato skins with cheese and bacon; and popcorn shrimps with sweet chilli dip. Divided into grills and classics, the menu lists sirloin steak, mushroom and chips; cottage pie; chicken curry; scampi and chips; and vegetable lasagne. Belgian chocolate meringue roulade appears among the puddings.

Open all day all wk 11-11 (Thu-Sat 11am-mdnt Sun 12-11) Closed 25 Dec, 1 Jan **Food** Lunch Mon-Sat 11-2, Sun 12-4 Dinner Mon-Sat 6-9 Set menu available Restaurant menu available Mon-Sat ⊕ FREE HOUSE ◀ Bass, Holden's Black Country Mild, guest ales. **Facilities** Non-diners area ♦♦ Children's menu Children's portions Parking WiFi ⛟ (notice required) **Rooms** 18

PICK OF THE PUBS

The Crown Inn

WRINEHILL Map 15 SJ74

tel: 01270 820472 **Den Ln CW3 9BT**
email: info@thecrownatwrinehill.co.uk
web: www.thecrownatwrinehill.co.uk
dir: *On A531, 1m S of Betley. 6m S of Crewe; 6m N of Newcastle-under-Lyme*

Great ales and food at this family-run village pub

In the picturesque village of Wrinehill, The Crown is just six miles south of Crewe and the same distance from Newcastle-under-Lyme so it's well located for visitors crossing the borders of Staffordshire and Cheshire. The Davenhill family bought this 19th-century former coaching inn back in 1977 and it is now run by Anna and Mark Condliffe, the daughter and son-in-law of long-serving licensee Charles Davenhill. With an open-plan layout the pub retains its oak beams and famously large inglenook fireplace, always a welcome feature. The bar does a good line in well-kept real ales, with always a choice of seven, two each from Jennings and Marston's, one from Salopian Ales and every week two microbrewery guests including their own 'Legend' ale; 15 wines are offered by the glass. Food is a major reason for the success of The Crown, not just for its consistent quality but for the generosity of the portions. Regularly changing menus are jam-packed with choice: from modestly priced light meals, such as home-made

veggie chilli and rice; or marinated chicken tikka kebabs with onions, mushrooms and red and green peppers, to head chef Steve's trademark minced beef or vegetable lasagne al forno or his 'legendary' beef and ale pie with a hint of Stilton. Anna, a vegetarian herself, recognises that choice should extend beyond mushroom Stroganoff, so alternatives such as Cheddar cheese and onion pasty with balsamic roasted cherry tomatoes, caramelised onion chutney and potatoes will always make a showing on the menus. For pudding, try home-made raspberry Bakewell with cream; or a slice of Bramley apple pie with hot custard. On their own menu, children will find locally produced pork and leek sausage with mash, peas and gravy; or scampi, chips and peas.

Open 12-3 6-11 (Sun 12-4 6-10.30) Closed 25-26 Dec, Mon L **Food** Lunch Tue-Fri 12-2, Sat-Sun 12-3 Dinner Sun-Thu 6-9, Fri 6-9.30, Sat 6-10 ⊛ FREE HOUSE ◖▮ Marston's Pedigree & Burton Bitter, Jennings Sneck Lifter, Legend, Salopian, guest ales ♂ Hogan's, Lyme Bay. ♟ 15 **Facilities** Non-diners area ♦♦ Children's menu Children's portions Outside area ⊼ Parking ⛟ (notice required)

The Trooper

tel: 01543 480413 **Watling St WS14 0AN**
email: info@thetrooperwall.co.uk
dir: *Phone for detailed directions*

Free house on a hillside overlooking Roman site

The Trooper is a Victorian pub in the Roman village of Wall, built on the original line of Watling Street, now superseded by the A5. Open fires welcome you to the bar, where you'll find local ales including Black Country brewer Holden's Golden Glow. There's a great terrace for fine days and the modern rustic restaurant serves mature Longhorn and Wagyu steaks and those from local Hereford suppliers, plus fresh pizza from the wood-fired oven. The large rear garden has a children's play area and views of Lichfield Cathedral's lofty spire.

Open all day all wk **Food** Lunch all wk 12-5 Dinner all wk 5-9.30 Set menu available Restaurant menu available all wk ⊕ FREE HOUSE ◀ Marston's Pedigree, Holden's Golden Glow, Black Sheep, Morland Old Speckled Hen, Bass, Backyard, Church End ○ Aspall, Westons Stowford Press. ♀ 11 **Facilities** Non-diners area ❖ (Bar Garden) ♦ Children's menu Children's portions Play area Garden ⊟ Beer festival Parking WiFi ➡

The Royal Oak

tel: 01335 310287 **DE6 2AF**
email: info@royaloakwetton.co.uk
dir: *A515 from Ashbourne towards Buxton, left in 4m signed Alstonfield. In Alstonfield follow Wetton sign*

Old pub in astonishing Peak District countryside

This long-established watering-hole in a pretty White Peak village continues to offer the most hospitable, time-honoured welcome to all; the landlord also says that muddy boots (a rack is provided) and friendly dogs are ok by him. To set the scene – flagged floors, beams and open fire within, and tables outside that promise views to tree-studded limestone pastures. Tracks and byways wend down into the amazing gorge of the River Manifold, riddled by caves amidst memorable ash woods. No surprise then that the pub is popular with ramblers happy to sample beers from local producers like Whim. Filling pub stalwarts populate the menu here; Staffordshire chicken, and rustic beef and Guinness casserole are cases in point.

Open all day 12-close Closed Mon-Tue in winter **Food** Lunch Mon-Thu 12-3, Fri-Sun 12-close Dinner Mon-Thu 6-close, Fri-Sun 12-close ⊕ FREE HOUSE ◀ Whim Ales Hartington IPA, local guest ales ○ Thatchers Gold. **Facilities** Non-diners area ❖ (Bar Restaurant Garden) ♦ Children's menu Family room Garden ⊟ Parking WiFi ➡ (notice required)

NEW The Dog Inn

tel: 01543 432601 **2 Main St WS14 9JU**
email: jamiehalfpint@gmail.com
dir: *From A51 between Lichfield & Tamworth follow Whittington signs*

Friendly village local serving unpretentious food

In the heart of the pretty village of Whittington, Jamie Lowe took over The Dog Inn in November 2015. With its open fire and separate restaurant, this whitewashed 18th-century pub appeals to local drinkers and diners. The no-frills cooking sticks to old favourites such as toad-in-the-hole with grain mustard mash and red onion gravy,

which might be followed by the home-made pie of the day or a gammon steak with roasted tomato, flat mushroom, fried egg, pineapple and chilli salsa. A traditional roast is served every Sunday lunchtime.

Open all day all wk 12-11 (Fri-Sat 12-12 Sun 12-10.30) **Food** Lunch Tue-Sat 12-3, Sun 12-5 Dinner Tue-Sat 5-9 Set menu available ⊕ PUNCH TAVERNS ◀ Sharp's Doom Bar, Greene King Abbot Ale, Bass ○ Westons Stowford Press. ♀ 10 **Facilities** Non-diners area ❖ (Bar Outside area) ♦ Children's menu Children's portions Outside area ⊟ Parking WiFi ➡ (notice required)

The Crown Inn   PICK OF THE PUBS

See Pick of the Pubs on page 457

The Hand & Trumpet

tel: 01270 820048 **Main Rd CW3 9BJ**
email: hand.and.trumpet@brunningandprice.co.uk
dir: *M6 junct 16, A351, follow Keele signs, 7m, pub on right in village*

Smart pub with alfresco area overlooking the water

A deck to the rear of this relaxed country pub overlooks sizeable grounds, which include a large pond. The pub has a comfortable interior with original floors, old furniture, open fires and rugs. Six cask ales and over 70 malt whiskies are offered, along with a locally sourced menu. Typical dishes on the comprehensive menu are crispy duck leg with egg noodle salad; crab and samphire quiche with lemon and crème fraîche potato salad; Buttercross Farm pork and black pudding sausages, mash, buttered greens and onion gravy; smoked haddock, red mullet and mussel chowder with bacon and sweetcorn dumplings; and apple and treacle pudding, apricot compôte and clotted cream. A children's menu is available. There is a cider festival and a hog roast in August.

Open all day all wk 11.30-11 (Sun 11.30-10.30) **Food** all wk 12-10 ⊕ FREE HOUSE/BRUNNING & PRICE ◀ Original, Timothy Taylor Boltmaker, Salopian Oracle ○ Aspall. ♀ 12 **Facilities** Non-diners area ❖ (Bar Garden) ♦ Children's menu Children's portions Garden ⊟ Cider festival Parking

The Parrot and Punchbowl Inn & Restaurant

tel: 01728 830221 **Aldringham Ln IP16 4PY**
dir: *On B1122, 1m from Leiston, 3m from Aldeburgh, on x-roads to Thorpeness*

Former smugglers' haunt, now a welcoming pub and restaurant

If you thought bizarre pub names were a late 20th-century fad, think again. Originally called The Case is Altered, this 16th-century pink-washed smugglers' inn became The Parrot and Punchbowl in 1604 when Aldringham was a centre for smuggled contraband. East Anglian-brewed ales from Adnams and Woodforde's, and Suffolk's Aspall cider all feature in the bar line-up. The good-value menu offers chicken liver pâté with chutney and toast; steak and kidney pudding; lasagne; bangers and mash; and steaks. Daily specials and vegetarian meals also have very reasonable price tags. There are roasts on Sundays and quiz nights.

Open all wk 12-2.30 6-11 (Sun 12-4) **Food** Lunch all wk 12-2 Dinner Mon-Sat 6.30-9 Restaurant menu available Tue-Sun ⊕ ENTERPRISE INNS ◀ Woodforde's Wherry, Adnams, guest ale ○ Aspall. ♀ 12 **Facilities** Non-diners area ❖ (Bar Garden) ♦ Children's menu Children's portions Play area Family room Garden ⊟ Parking WiFi ➡

PICK OF THE PUBS

The Old Cannon Brewery ★★★ INN

BURY ST EDMUNDS　　Map 13 TL86

tel: 01284 768769
86 Cannon St IP33 1JR
email: info@oldcannonbrewery.co.uk
web: www.oldcannonbrewery.co.uk
dir: From A14 junct 43 follow signs to Bury St Edmunds town centre, 1st left at 1st rdbt into Northgate St, 1st right into Cadney Ln, left at end into Cannon St, pub 100yds on left

Free house with long brewing history

Brewing started at this Victorian pub over 160 years ago. Today it's brewing still, an independent brewpub in Suffolk where you can see beer being brewed on a regular basis. Indeed, dominating the bar are two giant stainless steel brewing vessels, fount of Old Cannon Best Bitter, Gunner's Daughter and seasonal and special occasion beers, augmented by ever-rotating regular and other guest ales. In keeping with having a brewery inside the bar-cum-dining room, the decor and furnishings are easy on the eye, with rich, earth-coloured walls, wooden floors and scrubbed tables. Exploiting the obvious pun, the menu is headed 'Cannon Fodder', among which, all freshly prepared from local produce, are starters and light dishes of confit chicken and leek parfait with spiced pear chutney, and main meals of chicken tagine; Gunner's Daughter sausage and colcannon mash, onion gravy and beer

batter pudding; and gluten-free hen egg hash with tomato velouté. The daily-changing specials board offers at least three more options. The possibility of a home-made pudding or a British cheeseboard is worth planning ahead for; otherwise, try a lighter locally produced ice cream. For the really keen, the pub offers a Brew Day experience giving two people the opportunity to work alongside the brewer, loading the malt, creating the wort and adding the hops, all during normal production hours. An August beer festival and tours of the brewery are added attractions. Overnight guests stay in the converted old brewery, just across the courtyard. Since the pub is tucked away in the back streets, follow the website directions carefully.

Open all day all wk 12-11 (Sun 12-10.30) Closed 26 Dec & 1 Jan **Food** Lunch Mon-Sat 12-9, Sun 12-3 Dinner Mon-Sat 12-9 ⊕ FREE HOUSE ◀ The Old Cannon Best Bitter & Gunner's Daughter & seasonal ales, Adnams Southwold Bitter, guest ales Ŏ Aspall. ♟ 12
Facilities Non-diners area Garden ⋒ Beer festival Parking WiFi **Rooms** 7

BRANDESTON
Map 13 TM26

NEW The Queen

tel: 01728 685307 **The Street IP13 7AD**
email: info@thequeenatbrandeston.co.uk
dir: *From A12 take B1078 (Clopton). Right signed Easton. Through Easton & Kettleburgh. Pub on right in Brandeston*

Appealing, modernised village pub

When Alexander Aitchison and Lillie Fulford arrived at the old Queen's Head Inn in 2015, they gave it a more modern look, a shorter name and a new lease of life. Alexander's venison, beetroot, carrot and sorrel makes an interesting starter; follow with lamb with salsify, onions, mushrooms and leeks; and lastly lemon, honey and almond meringue. A reasonably priced wine list partners real ales from mostly East Anglian breweries, such as Adnams and Grain. The pair plan to grow their own fruit and vegetables in the field behind the pub.

Open all day Closed Mon **Food** Lunch Tue-Sun 12-2.30 Dinner Tue-Sun 6-9 ⊕ FREE HOUSE ◀ Adnams Southwold Bitter, Grain Redwood, Timothy Taylor Landlord ♂ Aspall. ♀ 24 **Facilities** Non-diners area ♣ (Bar Restaurant Garden) ♦♦ Children's portions Garden Parking WiFi

BROMESWELL
Map 13 TM35

NEW The Unruly Pig
PICK OF THE PUBS

tel: 01394 460310 **Orford Rd IP12 2PU**
email: brendan@theunrulypig.co.uk
dir: *From A12 rdbt (N of Woodbridge) take A1152 through Melton. Over railway crossing. At rdbt take B1084 towards Orford. Pub on left*

Stylish Suffolk pub with an enthusiastic kitchen team

Close to the National Trust's Sutton Hoo, Rendlesham Forest and the lovely medieval town of Woodbridge, The Unruly Pig is a 16th-century Suffolk inn. The style is a pleasing mixture of traditional and contemporary, with original oak beams, sloping ceilings, log-burners and an eclectic mix of pop and local art on the walls. In the cosy bar you'll find Adnams and Greene King ales, while in the wood-panelled dining rooms the monthly-changing menus offer a good choice – and there are separate gluten-free and vegetarian menus. Starters might feature salmon rillette with fennel, horseradish and capers; or smoked duck hash with poached duck egg and broccoli; and main courses range from sage and thyme stuffed rabbit loin with baked polenta and cauliflower, to whole grilled sea bream with black olive hollandaise, crispy capers and baked potatoes.

Open all wk 12-3 6-10.30 (Sat all day Sun 12-8) **Food** Lunch Mon-Fri 12-3, Sat 12-6, Sun 12-8 Dinner Mon-Sat 6-9.30, Sun 12-8 Av main course £13 Set menu available ⊕ PUNCH ◀ Adnams Southwold Bitter, Greene King IPA ♂ Aspall. ♀ 40 **Facilities** Non-diners area ♣ (Bar Garden Outside area) ♦♦ Children's menu Children's portions Play area Garden Outside area ⊼ Parking WiFi

BUNGAY
Map 13 TM38

NEW The Castle Inn

tel: 01986 892283 **35 Earsham St NR35 1AF**
email: markandtanya@thecastleinn.net
dir: *From A143 into Broad St (A144) signed Bungay. At junct right (around island), last exit into Earsham St. Pub on left*

Welcoming hostelry in venerable building

Records going back over 400 years testify to the Castle's roots as an alehouse – even if its name has changed several times. Since buying the pub some 10 years ago, Mark and Tanya Hougham have made a great success of things due to their hard work and enthusiasm. Today the Castle is known for simply cooked food based on fresh locally-sourced ingredients, and Suffolk ales from Earl Soham and Cliff Quay. Mussels in one form or another are likely to appear among the starters, while the concise list of main courses will include well-aged beef, and perhaps a classic fish pie with cod, smoked haddock, capers, shallots, parsley and peas.

Open 12-10 (Wed-Sat 12-10 Sun & Tue 12-4 in winter) Closed 1st 2wks Jan, Sun eve (Sun & Tue eve, Mon in winter) **Food** Lunch all wk 12-2.30 (Tue-Sun 12-2.30 in winter) Dinner Mon-Fri 6-9 (Wed-Sat 6-9 in winter) Av main course £14.50 Set menu available Restaurant menu available Tue-Sun ⊕ FREE HOUSE ◀ Earl Soham Victoria, Cliff Quay Sea Dog ♂ Aspall. **Facilities** Non-diners area ♣ (Bar Garden) ♦♦ Children's menu Children's portions Garden ⊼ Parking WiFi ⊨ (notice required)

BURY ST EDMUNDS
Map 13 TL86

The Nutshell

tel: 01284 764867 **17 The Traverse IP33 1BJ**
dir: *Phone for detailed directions*

Officially the smallest pub in Britain

Measuring just 15ft by 7ft, this unique pub has been confirmed as Britain's smallest by *Guinness World Records*; and somehow more than 100 people and a dog managed to fit inside in the 1980s. It has certainly become a tourist attraction and there's lots to talk about while you enjoy a drink – a mummified cat and the bar ceiling which is covered with paper money. There have been regular sightings of ghosts around the building, including a nun and a monk who apparently weren't praying! No food is available, though the pub jokes about its dining area for parties of two or fewer.

Open all day all wk **Food** Contact pub for food times ⊕ GREENE KING ◀ IPA & Abbot Ale, guest ales. **Facilities** Non-diners area WiFi ⊨ (notice required) **Notes** ⊜

The Old Cannon Brewery ★★★ INN
PICK OF THE PUBS

See Pick of the Pubs on page 459

CHILLESFORD
Map 13 TM35

The Froize Inn

tel: 01394 450282 **The Street IP12 3PU**
email: dine@froize.co.uk
dir: *On B1084 between Woodbridge (8m) & Orford (3m)*

Adnams free house near heritage coast

Nobody really knows what a froize is, or was. A savoury French pancake? Or Suffolk dialect for a friar? Anyhow, it's what this pantiled dining pub is called. No printed menus here, simply changing blackboards listing dishes and sharing boards based on the best seasonal and local ingredients. At the hot buffet counter you choose your main dish. Perhaps, Suffolk lamb, Moroccan style; roast breast of guinea fowl, smoke bacon, roots and redcurrants; or wild sea trout with crayfish risotto. A champion of 'Great British' puddings, chef-patron David Grimwood's sunken chocolate pudding; or marmalade bread and butter pudding could prove irresistible.

Open Tue-Sun Closed Mon **Food** Contact pub for food times Restaurant menu available Tue-Sun ⊕ FREE HOUSE ◀ Adnams ♂ Aspall. ♀ 12 **Facilities** ♦♦ Children's portions Garden ⊼ Parking WiFi ⊨ (notice required)

PICK OF THE PUBS

The Ship at Dunwich ★★ SHL ⬡

DUNWICH   Map 13 TM47

tel: 01728 648219
Saint James St IP17 3DT
email: info@shipatdunwich.co.uk
web: www.shipatdunwich.co.uk
dir: *N on A12 from Ipswich through Yoxford, right signed Dunwich*

Coastal pub renowned for its fish and chips

Dunwich was at one time a medieval port of some size and importance, but the original village was virtually destroyed by a terrible storm in 1326. Further storms and erosion followed and now the place is little more than a hamlet beside a shingle beach. Two minutes' stroll from the briny, the Ship at Dunwich is a well-loved old smugglers' inn overlooking the salt marshes and sea; today it's popular with walkers and birdwatchers visiting the nearby RSPB Minsmere reserve. The Ship keeps Dunwich on the map with its ancient fig tree in the garden, hearty meals, and ales from Brandon's, Earl Soham and Green Jack — to name just three of the local brews on offer; look out for ale festivals held on bank holiday Sundays. The delightfully unspoilt public bar appeals with nautical bric-à-brac, a wood-burning stove in a huge fireplace, flagged floors and simple wooden furnishings. The Ship is locally renowned for its fish and chips, which include a choice of cod,

whiting, plaice or hake. Beetroot and vodka home-cured salmon with beetroot relish, horseradish cream, house bread and Charlie's leaves is tempting. Or skip the starter for a reed cutter's platter: a delicious plate of Blythburgh free-range baked ham, Suffolk Shipcord or Binham Blue cheese with pickles, coleslaw, dressed salad and crusty roll. Hot dishes include slow-cooked Blythburgh pork belly with leek gratin, Lyonnaise potatoes, apple and date purée and red wine gravy. Desserts continue in similar robust vein — Colin's sticky toffee pudding with custard, cream or ice cream is one example.

Open all day all wk **Food** Lunch all wk 12-3 Dinner all wk 6-9 🛢 FREE HOUSE ◀ Adnams Southwold Bitter, Humpty

Dumpty, Brandon Rusty Bucket, Earl Soham, Green Jack, Grain Norfolk Brewery, Woodforde's, St Peter's Ö Aspall. 🍷 9 **Facilities** Non-diners area 🐾 (Bar Restaurant Garden) 👪 Children's menu Children's portions Family room Garden 🍺 Beer festival Parking WiFi 🚌 (notice required) **Rooms** 16

CRATFIELD
Map 13 TM37

The Cratfield Poacher

tel: 01986 798206 **Bell Green IP19 OBL**
email: cratfieldpoacher@yahoo.co.uk
dir: *B1117 from Halesworth towards Eye. At Laxfield right, follow Cratfield signs. Or, A143 from Diss towards Bungay. Right at Harleston onto B1123 towards Halesworth. Through Metfield, 1m, right, follow Cratfield signs*

Family-run free house in rural location

A pub for the past 350 years, this handsome longhouse in deepest rural Suffolk is off the beaten track but well worth the detour. Boasting some impressive exterior plasterwork pargeting, it is just as charming inside, with low beams and tiled floors. There's always six draught beers available, often from the Adnams and Oakham breweries, plus local Aspall cider. Home-cooked food, such as smoked mackerel salad and shepherd's pie, with daily-changing specials complete the pleasing picture at this proper village local, which is the hub of the community.

Open 12-2.30 6-12 (Sat-Sun all day) Closed Mon, Tue L **Food** Lunch Fri 12-2.30 (Sat-Sun all day) Dinner Tue-Fri 6-9 (Sat-Sun all day) Set menu available ⊕ FREE HOUSE ◀ Crouch Vale Brewers Gold, Oakham JHB, Earl Soham Victoria Bitter & Gannet Mild, Adnams Ö Aspall. **Facilities** Non-diners area ✿ (Bar Garden) ♦ Children's menu Children's portions Garden ⋒ Parking ⇌ (notice required)

DENNINGTON
Map 13 TM26

Dennington Queen

tel: 01728 638241 **The Square IP13 8AB**
email: denningtonqueen@yahoo.co.uk
dir: *From Ipswich A14 to exit for Lowestoft (A12). Then B1116 to Framlingham, follow signs to Dennington*

Village centre pub worth seeking out

A 16th-century inn with bags of old-world charm including open fires, a coffin hatch, a bricked-up tunnel to the neighbouring church and a ghost. Locally brewed Aspall cider accompanies real ales from Adnams, plus Black Sheep, Timothy Taylor and Sharp's ales. Suggestions from the modern British menu include moules marinière; confit leek, blue cheese and sage bruschetta; seared calves' liver, bacon, parsley mash and onion gravy; and pan-seared sea bass fillet, coriander rösti and herb oil. A typical dessert might be chocolate fudge cake, pecan nut sauce and vanilla mascarpone.

Open all wk 12-3 6.30-10.30 **Food** Lunch all wk 12-2 Dinner all wk 6.30-9 Set menu available ⊕ FREE HOUSE ◀ Adnams, Timothy Taylor, Black Sheep, Sharp's Doom Bar, Wadworth Ö Aspall. **Facilities** Non-diners area ✿ (Bar Garden) ♦ Children's menu Children's portions Garden ⋒ Parking WiFi ⇌ (notice required)

DUNWICH
Map 13 TM47

The Ship at Dunwich ★★ SHL ◉
PICK OF THE PUBS

See Pick of the Pubs on page 461

EARL SOHAM
Map 13 TM26

Victoria

tel: 01728 685758 **The Street IP13 7RL**
email: vic@earlsohamvictoria.com
dir: *From A14 at Stowmarket take A1120 towards Yoxford, cross A140 at Stonham, through Pettaugh on A1120 to Earl Soham. Pub on right*

Microbrewery beers at their best

Sandwiched amidst a range of cottages in a peaceful village above the Vale of Deben, this uncompromisingly unchanging country pub ticks all the right boxes for lovers of traditional locals. The new licensee remains fiercely supportive of the microbrewery that started life in the pub's old chicken shed and now brews from larger premises opposite. Bitters, specials and a stout all keep appreciative villagers and visitors very happy in an unfussy, wood-burner-warmed interior where quiet conversation and village banter are bedfellows. Filling pub meals may include slow-roast lamb; corned beef hash or a good choice of vegetarian specials like creamy leek flan.

Open all wk 11.30-3 5.30-11 **Food** Lunch all wk 12-2 Dinner all wk 6.30-9 ⊕ EARL SOHAM BREWERY ◀ Earl Soham Victoria Bitter, Albert Ale, Brandeston Gold, Sir Roger's Porter Ö Aspall. **Facilities** Non-diners area ✿ (Bar Garden) ♦ Children's portions Garden ⋒ Parking WiFi ⇌ (notice required)

ELVEDEN
Map 13 TL88

Elveden Inn ★★★★★ INN
PICK OF THE PUBS

tel: 01842 890876 **Brandon Rd IP24 3TP**
email: enquiries@elvedeninn.com **web:** www.elvedeninn.com
dir: *From Mildenhall take A11 towards Thetford. Left onto B1106, pub on left*

Stylish inn showcasing produce from the estate

Located on the Elveden Estate, home to a direct descendent of the Guinness family, this village inn has a relaxed and contemporary bar, several dining areas, and six luxury bedrooms. Expect a family-friendly atmosphere, blazing log fires in winter, a range of guest ales on tap, and a modern pub menu that brims with produce sourced from the estate farm and surrounding area. Whether eating inside, or outside on the large patio area, a meal could kick off with warm pigeon breast, silverskin onion, lardon and endive salad with red wine syrup; or caramelised onion and mature cheddar croquettes with red pepper relish. Then confit rabbit leg, sage and onion dauphinoise potato, roasted carrot and Dijon mustard sauce; wild mushroom, vegetarian parmesan and chive risotto; slow-roasted Suffolk pork belly, colcannon, sautéed greens and Aspall cider cream sauce. Finish with espresso crème brûlée; or sticky Guinness pudding with clotted cream and cinder toffee. Children can choose from their own selection of 'fawn-size' portions.

Open all day all wk **Food** Mon-Sat 7.30am-9pm, Sun 7.30am-8pm Set menu available Restaurant menu available Sun ⊕ FREE HOUSE ◀ Adnams Southwold, Elveden IPA, local guest ales Ö Aspall. ☂ 30 **Facilities** Non-diners area ✿ (Bar Restaurant Garden) ♦ Children's menu Children's portions Play area Garden ⋒ Beer festival Cider festival Parking WiFi ⇌ (notice required) **Rooms** 6

EYE
Map 13 TM17

The White Horse Inn ★★★★ INN

tel: 01379 678222 **Stoke Ash IP23 7ET**
email: mail@whitehorse-suffolk.co.uk **web:** www.whitehorse-suffolk.co.uk
dir: *On A140 between Ipswich & Norwich*

Family-run inn with good food

Midway between Norwich and Ipswich, this 17th-century coaching inn is set amid lovely Suffolk countryside. The heavily timbered interior accommodates an inglenook fireplace, two bars and a restaurant. An extensive menu is supplemented by lunchtime snacks, grills and daily specials from the blackboard. Try salmon pâté or smoked duck salad to start. Main courses include red pepper and goats' cheese lasagne; honey and mustard chicken; venison casserole; chicken Madras; and baked salmon with sage and parmesan crust. There are 11 spacious motel bedrooms in the grounds, as well as a patio and secluded grassy area.

Open all day all wk 7am-11pm (Sat 8am-11pm Sun 8am-10.30pm) **Food** Contact pub for food times ⊕ FREE HOUSE ◀ Greene King Abbot Ale, Adnams, Woodforde's Wherry Ö Aspall. **Facilities** Non-diners area ♦ Children's menu Children's portions Play area Garden Parking WiFi ⇌ **Rooms** 11

FRAMLINGHAM
Map 13 TM26

The Railway

tel: 01728 724760 **9 Station Rd IP13 9EA**
email: info@therailwayframlingham.co.uk
dir: *In village centre on B1116*

Good food and beer in smart village pub

The picturesque market town of Framlingham is the delightful location for this dog-friendly pub, now in new hands. The Railway is stylish inside with a real fire in colder months, and a lovely enclosed garden at the rear is the perfect spot for alfresco summer eating and drinking. In the bar you'll find Adnams Southwold Bitter and Ghost Ship. A meal might begin with deep-fried whitebait; or baked camembert that's ideal for sharing, followed by steak and ale pie; spicy beef chilli; full rack of BBQ ribs; oven-roasted vegetable lasagne.

Open all day all wk **Food** Lunch all wk 12-2.30 Dinner Mon-Sat 6-8.30 Set menu available ⊕ FREE HOUSE ◀ Adnams Southwold Bitter & Ghost Ship Ô Aspall. **Facilities** Non-diners area ❤ (Bar Restaurant Garden) ◀ Children's menu Children's portions Garden ⊓ WiFi ▦ (notice required)

The Station Hotel

tel: 01728 723455 **Station Rd IP13 9EE**
email: framstation@btinternet.com
dir: *Bypass Ipswich towards Lowestoft on A12. Approx 6m, left onto B1116 to Framlingham*

Known for its bold and flavoursome dishes

Built as part of the local railway in the 19th century, The Station Hotel has been a pub since the 1950s, outliving the railway which closed in 1962. Inside, you will find scrubbed tables and an eclectic mix of furniture. During the last decade it has established a fine reputation for its gutsy and earthy food listed on the ever-changing blackboard menu. Lunch may start with smoked haddock kedgeree, or lobscouse (a Welsh beef dish), then continue with seared venison fillet and wild mushroom risotto; steamed steak and mushroom suet pudding; or something cooked in the wood-fired pizza oven. Several of the beers are supplied by Suffolk brewery, Earl Soham and there is a beer festival in mid July.

Open all wk 12-2.30 5-11 (Sun 12-3 7-10.30) **Food** Lunch all wk 12-2 Dinner Mon-Thu 6.30-9, Fri-Sat 6.30-9.30, Sun 7-9 ⊕ FREE HOUSE ◀ Earl Soham Victoria Bitter, Albert Ale & Gannet Mild, Veltins, Crouch Vale, Guinness Ô Aspall. **Facilities** ❤ (All areas) ◀ Children's portions Garden Outside area ⊓ Beer festival Parking WiFi ▦

GREAT BRICETT
Map 13 TM05

The Veggie Red Lion
PICK OF THE PUBS

tel: 01473 657799 **Green Street Green IP7 7DD**
email: janwise@fsmail.net
dir: *4.5m from Needham Market on B1078*

Smart country inn with innovative approach to meals

Snuggled beside a thicket secluded in the rich wheat-fields outside Ipswich; Jan Wise's stylish country pub continues to attract discerning diners keen to experience the many-faceted menu of vegetarian and vegan dishes. The rustic heritage and real ales here reward lovers of traditional pubs, but it's the considered selection of dishes based on local produce that draws the accolades. The animal, fish and fowl-free fare benefits from Jan's long years of dedication to promoting alternatives to the catering mainstream. Starters might see Red Lion spring rolls; crispy garlic mushrooms; or butterbean, lemon and sage soup setting a standard. Mains tempt with dishes such as roasted mushroom Wellington; spicy bean burrito; butterbean,

okra and apricot tagine; or creamy squash and king oyster mushroom pie. Rich, moreish puddings such as spiced summer pudding or lemon posset complete the repast. There's a garden here and a terrace for alfresco dining. Booking ahead is recommended.

Open 12-3 6-11 Closed Sun eve & Mon **Food** Lunch Tue-Sun 12-2 Dinner Tue-Sat 6-9 ⊕ HAWTHORN LEISURE ◀ Greene King IPA, Morland Old Speckled Hen, rotating guest ales Ô Aspall. **Facilities** Non-diners area ❤ (Bar Garden) ◀ Children's menu Children's portions Play area Garden ⊓ Parking WiFi

HADLEIGH
Map 13 TM04

NEW The Hadleigh Ram

tel: 01473 822880 **5 Market Place IP7 5DL**
email: info@thehadleighram.co.uk
dir: *From High St into Market Place, pub on left*

Stylish pub a short drive from Ipswich

In the market town of Hadleigh, this elegant dining-pub pushes all the right buttons when it comes to contemporary rustic chic. Distressed wooden beams, duck egg blue paintwork and antique furniture add to the stylish look of the place where a range of menus is served, including an excellent choice for vegetarians. A typical meal here might kick off with pan-fried Scottish halibut, prawn bisque, steamed greens and chive oil, followed by masala rump of lamb, smoked yogurt, aubergine, couscous, mint and radicchio. Tonka bean pannacotta, coconut arancini, pineapple sorbet and tropical salsa is one way to finish.

Open all day all wk **Food** Lunch all wk 12-2.30 Dinner Mon-Thu 6-9, Fri-Sat 6-10 Av main course £16.50 Set menu available ⊕ GREENE KING ◀ IPA & Abbot Ale Ô Aspall. ▮ 24 **Facilities** Non-diners area ◀ Children's menu Children's portions Outside area ⊓ WiFi ▦ (notice required)

HAWKEDON
Map 13 TL75

The Queen's Head
PICK OF THE PUBS

tel: 01284 789218 **Rede Rd IP29 4NN**
dir: *From A143 at Wickham St, between Bury St Edmunds & Haverhill, follow Stansfield sign. At junct left signed Hawkedon. 1m to village*

Thriving village local with a butcher's shop

Off-the-beaten track by the green in a picture-book village deep in rural Suffolk, The Queen's Head is worth seeking out for its classic 15th-century character and charm – inglenook fireplace, stone floors, head-cracking timbers, scrubbed wooden tables – and top-notch hearty pub food prepared from the best local ingredients. Pork, beef, venison, poultry and wild boar are sourced from local farms – they are hung and butchered at the butcher's shop in the pub grounds. This may translate to venison carpaccio; pork chops with Stilton, pear and sage; and pot-roasted beef with red wine and red onion marmalade; with butterscotch and almond pudding among the desserts. Sunday roast lunches, traditional bar snacks, and pizzas baked in the stone oven complete the culinary picture. A thriving community local, it also offers live music, game and wine tasting dinners and other social evenings.

Open 5-11 (Fri-Sun 12-11) Closed Mon-Thu L **Food** Lunch Fri-Sun 12-2.30 Dinner Wed-Thu 6-9, Fri-Sun 6.30-9 ⊕ FREE HOUSE ◀ Woodforde's Wherry, Adnams, guest ales Ô Guest ciders. **Facilities** Non-diners area ❤ (Bar Garden) ◀ Children's portions Garden ⊓ Parking WiFi

HOLBROOK
Map 13 TM13

The Compasses

tel: 01473 328332 **Ipswich Rd IP9 2QR**
email: info@thecompassesholbrook.co.uk
dir: From A137 S of Ipswich, take B1080 to Holbrook, pub on left. From Ipswich take B1456 to Shotley. At Freston Water Tower right onto B1080 to Holbrook. Pub 2m right

New owners making this the heart of the community

On the spectacular Shotley peninsula bordered by the rivers Orwell and Stour, this traditional 17th-century country pub, now with new owners and a refurbished restaurant, offers a reasonably priced, traditional menu with plenty of choice. Typical starters include smoked mackerel pâté; or prawn and crayfish cocktail. Follow this with home-made lasagne; pan-seared lamb's liver and bacon; spinach, sweet potato and feta cheese pancake; or traditional ham, eggs and chips. There's a separate children's menu.

Open all wk 11.30-3 6-11 (Sun 12-10.30) **Food** Lunch Mon-Sat 11.30-3, Sun 12-9 Dinner Mon-Sat 6-9, Sun 12-9 ⊕ PUNCH TAVERNS ◼ Adnams Southwold Bitter, guest ales ⚬ Aspall. ♜ 12 **Facilities** Non-diners area ◖◗ Children's menu Children's portions Play area Garden ⊞ Parking WiFi ▭ (notice required)

HONEY TYE
Map 13 TL93

The Lion

tel: 01206 263434 **CO6 4NX**
email: info@thelioncolchester.com
dir: On A134 midway between Colchester & Sudbury

Good food in dining pub with alfresco options

This traditional country dining pub occupies an enviable spot in an Area of Outstanding Natural Beauty. The spacious restaurant is decorated in a modern, comfortable style and the bar has low-beamed ceilings and a wood-burner. The reasonably priced food here is sourced locally and the menu changes with the seasons. Start with twice-baked goats' cheese soufflé, perhaps, before a main course of oven-roasted rump of new season lamb with pearl barley risotto and salsa verde. The Lion has a walled beer garden for alfresco eating and drinking in the summer.

Open all day 11-11 Closed Mon **Food** Tue-Sun 12-9 Set menu available ⊕ FREE HOUSE ◼ Adnams ⚬ Westons. ♜ 9 **Facilities** Non-diners area ◖◗ Children's menu Children's portions Garden ⊞ Parking WiFi ▭ (notice required)

INGHAM
Map 13 TL87

The Cadogan ★★★★ INN ◉

tel: 01284 728443 **The Street IP31 1NG**
email: info@thecadogan.co.uk **web:** www.thecadogan.co.uk
dir: A14 junct 42, 1st exit onto B1106. At rdbt take 1st exit (A134). 3m to Ingham. Pub on right

A welcoming place to stay or dine

A friendly and inviting pub with seven en suite bedrooms for those who want to stay longer, The Cadogan sits just four miles from the centre of Bury St Edmunds. The kitchen places an emphasis on seasonality and local produce; for something lighter there's grazing boards at both lunch and dinner (cheese; seafood; deli and puds). Dinner menu options could be duck liver parfait, Cumberland gel and brioche; or Suffolk Gold rarebit and cranberry toast to start, followed by mushroom cottage pie with blue cheese mash and caramelised onion ketchup; Cajun sea bass with potato rösti and braised fennel; or venison and wild hare stew. Open all day, the pub has a large garden, with a children's play area, perfect for alfresco dining.

Open all day all wk Closed 25-26 Dec & 31 Jan eve **Food** Lunch Mon-Sat 12-2.30, Sun 12-8.30 Dinner Mon-Sat 6-9.30, Sun 12-8.30 ⊕ GREENE KING ◼ Abbot Ale, Brewshed Pale Ale ⚬ Aspall. ♜ 18 **Facilities** Non-diners area ◖◗ Children's menu Children's portions Play area Garden ⊞ Parking WiFi ▭ (notice required) **Rooms** 7

IPSWICH
Map 13 TM14

The Fat Cat

tel: 01473 726524 **288 Spring Rd IP4 5NL**
email: fatcatipswich@btconnect.com
dir: From A12 take A1214 towards town centre, becomes A1071 (Woodbridge Road East). At mini rdbt 2nd left into Spring Rd

One for the beer lover

Good beer and conversation are the two main ingredients in this a traditional free house. The Fat Cat is a mecca for beer aficionados, with a friendly atmosphere in the homely bar and a raft of real ales served in tip-top condition from the taproom behind the bar. The head-scratching choice — up to 18 every day — come from Adnams, Woodforde's and Crouch Vale and a host of local and national breweries. Six real ciders, bottled Belgian beers, whiskies, gins and wine add to the considerable array. There's just simple bar snacks to accompany like home-made Scotch eggs, sausage rolls, pork pies and filled rolls. Please note, children are not allowed inside or in the garden.

Open all day all wk **Food** Contact pub for food times ⊕ FREE HOUSE ◼ Adnams Old Ale, Skinner's Betty Stogs, Green Jack Gone Fishing, Crouch Vale Yakima Gold, Oakham Inferno, Hop Back Summer lightning, guest ales ⚬ Aspall, Westons, Lilley's Cider Barn, Gwynt y Ddraig. ♜ 8 **Facilities** Non-diners area ♥ (Bar Garden) Garden WiFi ▭ (notice required)

LAXFIELD
Map 13 TM27

The Kings Head (The Low House)
PICK OF THE PUBS

tel: 01986 798395 **Gorams Mill Ln IP13 8DW**
email: marketing@bruisyardhall.co.uk
dir: On B1117

Discover an authentic old pub with no bar

This unspoilt thatched 16th-century alehouse is a rare Suffolk gem that oozes charm and character. Locals know it as the Low House because it lies in a dip below the churchyard. Tip-top ales are served straight from the cask in the original taproom — this is one of the few pubs in Britain without a bar. Now run by Paul Rous and David Newstead, the home-made approach to food continues. Typical dishes are roast black pudding with a soft poached egg; and panko-crumbed white crab and black tiger prawn fishcakes to start, followed by pan-fried skate wing, burnt caper and parsley butter with hand-cut chips; or grilled Cumberland sausages, bubble-and-squeak and caramelised onion gravy. Beer festivals in May and September are unforgettable occasions thanks to the beautiful situation of the pub overlooking the river; its grounds, with rose gardens and an arbour, were formerly the village bowling green.

Open all wk 12-3 6-11 (Sat 8am-11pm Sun 8am-7pm) **Food** Lunch Mon-Fri 12-2, Sat 8am-9pm, Sun 8-4.30 Dinner Mon-Fri 6-9, Sat 8am-9pm ⊕ ADNAMS ◼ Southwold Bitter, Broadside & Ghost Ship ales, guest ales ⚬ Aspall. ♜ 11 **Facilities** Non-diners area ♥ (Bar Garden) ◖◗ Children's menu Children's portions Play area Family room Garden ⊞ Beer festival Parking WiFi ▭ (notice required)

MILDENHALL
Map 12 TL77

The Bull Inn ★★★★★ INN ◉
PICK OF THE PUBS

See Pick of the Pubs on opposite page

PICK OF THE PUBS

The Bull Inn ★★★★★ INN ❀

MILDENHALL Map 12 TL77

tel: 01638 711001
The Street, Barton Mills IP28 6AA
email: reception@bullinn-bartonmills.com
web: www.bullinn-bartonmills.com
dir: *Exit A11 between Newmarket & Mildenhall, signed Barton Mills*

An independent, quirky inn with something to suit everyone

With its fine roofline, dormer windows and old coaching courtyard, this rambling 16th-century building certainly looks like a traditional roadside inn. Stepping inside this historic building you'll be wowed by an amazing interior that blends original oak beams, wooden floors and big fireplaces with funky fabrics, designer wallpapers and bold colours. This, along with their dedication, is how family owners Cheryl, Wayne and Sonia have created a success story, making the bar, with scrubbed pine tables and cosy seats by a winter fire, the hub of the building (and indeed the village). Here you can study the menus, perhaps with one of the 11 wines by the glass, or an East Anglian real ale from Adnams, Wolf or Humpty Dumpty. Menus evolve with the seasons, with every effort made to reduce 'food miles' by sourcing locally. In the AA Rosette dining rooms you can do no better than choose Lowestoft

haddock in Adnams beer batter with double cooked chips and pea purée; roast breast of Gressingham duck, potato and thyme rösti, piccolo parsnips and sautéed spinach with port and onion jus; or The Bull's 'famous' MOO pie filled with slow-cooked fillet steak in locally-brewed Rusty Bucket ale, with creamy mashed potato and roasted root vegetables. They say people travel miles for the pub's legendary sticky toffee pudding, rock salt caramel and toffee ice cream, so that's a must to finish an excellent meal. Bar meals include classics like Newmarket sausages with mash and caramelised red onion gravy; and chicken curry with basmati rice.

Open all day all wk 8am-11pm Closed 25-26 Dec **Food** Sun-Thu 12-9, Fri-Sat 12-9.30 (bkfst all wk 8-12) ⊕ FREE HOUSE ◀▮ Adnams Broadside, Greene King IPA, Brandon Rusty Bucket, Humpty Dumpty, Wolf ♻ Aspall. ♟ 11
Facilities Non-diners area ♦♦ Children's menu Children's portions Garden ⩊ Parking WiFi ▦ (notice required)
Rooms 15

PICK OF THE PUBS

The Packhorse Inn ★★★★★ INN

NEWMARKET   Map 12 TL66

tel: 01638 751818
Bridge St, Moulton CB8 8SP
email: info@thepackhorseinn.com
web: www.thepackhorseinn.com
dir: *A14 junct 39, B1506 signed Newmarket. Left onto B1085 to Moulton*

Stylish country pub near Newmarket

Those who seek out dining establishments with top notch food should head here, one of Suffolk's most highly acclaimed. Former banker and founder of Chestnut Inns, Philip Turner owns it, having reopened it following a six-month renovation and changing its name from the Kings Head in homage to the adjacent medieval, pedestrian-only bridge across the River Kennet. Just two miles from Newmarket Racecourse, this smart, family-friendly country pub and restaurant attracts all — locals, out-of-town race-goers and everyone in between — to its large dining and bar area and individually designed, en suite bedrooms. The emphasis is on quality, locally sourced food and drink, including game from shoots, lamb from Moulton, beers from Woodforde's and guest breweries, and Harry Sparrow cider from the Suffolk village of Aspall. Fish has to travel a little further of course, but mainly fish from British waters are

sought. The concise but appealing, regularly changing menus might start with cauliflower velouté, grilled mackerel and apple; truffled goats' cheese, pear, hazelnut and beetroot salad; or maybe breast of pigeon, confit leg, beetroot and radish. Among the mains might be fillet of stone bass, braised chicory, razor clams and carrot; loin of Suffolk venison, boulangère potato, parsnip, broccoli and blackberries (for two to share); butternut squash cannelloni and chestnut; and breast of Suffolk chicken, white beans, mushrooms and pancetta. Finish with vanilla rice pudding, roasted hazelnut and pear; or blackberry cheesecake, apple sorbet and honey granola.

Open all day all wk **Food** Lunch all wk 12-2.30 Dinner all wk 7-9.30
⊕ FREE HOUSE ◼ Woodforde's Wherry, guest ales ♻ Aspall Harry Sparrow. ♟ 19
Facilities Non-diners area ☸ (Bar Restaurant Garden) ⑪ Children's portions Garden ☶ Parking WiFi ☷ (notice required) **Rooms** 8

MONKS ELEIGH
Map 13 TL94

NEW The Swan Inn

tel: 01449 763163 **The Street IP7 7AU**
email: info@theswaninnmonkseleigh.co.uk
dir: *On A1141 between Lavenham or Hadleigh. Pub in village centre*

Smart thatched village inn

This cream-washed old inn, the only survivor from the four here a century ago, stands on a corner opposite the village green. Lowish beams in the bar might catch any particularly tall arrival distracted by thoughts of a pint of one of the East Anglian ales, such as Brewers Gold, or a cider from the Suffolk village of Aspall. Fricassée of wild mushrooms, poached egg, horseradish mayo and micro herbs might be the ideal way to start a meal, followed perhaps by a gourmet duck burger; pan-fried salted cod with quinoa risotto; pork three ways; or ratatouille tartlet with goats' cheese. Banoffee pie or warm sticky toffee pudding to finish.

Open all day Closed Mon **Food** Lunch Tue-Fri 12-3, Sat 12-9.30, Sun 12-6 Dinner Tue-Fri 6-9.30, Sat 12-9.30 Av main course £12.50 Set menu available Restaurant menu available Tue-Sun ⊕ FREE HOUSE ◀ Adnams Southwold Bitter, Crouch Vale Brewers Gold, Greene King IPA, Woodforde's Ö Aspall. ♟ 12
Facilities Non-diners area ♣ (Bar Garden Outside area) ♦ Children's menu Children's portions Garden Outside area ⌐ Parking WiFi ▭ (notice required)

NAYLAND
Map 13 TL93

Anchor Inn
PICK OF THE PUBS

tel: 01206 262313 **26 Court St CO6 4JL**
email: info@anchornayland.co.uk
dir: *Take A134 from Colchester towards Sudbury for 3.5m, through Great Horkesley, at bottom of hill right into Horkesley Rd. Pub on right after bridge*

Eclectic modern dining in Constable Country

The inn, which enjoys a peaceful setting beside the alder-fringed meadows of the River Stour, is said to be the last remaining place from which press-gangs recruited their 'volunteers' in this area. Today's customers can rest easy, perhaps recovering from strolls around the idyllic village, which is close to the heart of 'Constable Country'. The Anchor is a light, airy destination where local and regional ales change monthly; the riverside decking and garden are ideal spots to tarry a while. The head chef presides over a progressive menu of pub favourites and modern European dishes, so anticipate smoked fish platter (the inn has its own smokehouse); trio of Kerridge sausages and mash; battered 'catch of the day' with hand-cut chips; a range of pizzas; and for dessert, lemon posset with lime and lavender jelly.

Open all wk 11-11 (Sun 11-10.30) **Food** Lunch Mon-Fri 12-2.30, Sat-Sun 12-4 Dinner Mon-Sat 6-9.30, Sun 6-8 ⊕ FREE HOUSE/EXCLUSIVE INNS ◀ Greene King IPA, Adnams, local & guest ales Ö Aspall. ♟ 10 **Facilities** Non-diners area ♣ (Bar Garden) ♦ Children's menu Children's portions Garden ⌐ Beer festival Parking WiFi ▭ (notice required)

NEWMARKET
Map 12 TL66

The Packhorse Inn ★★★★★ INN
PICK OF THE PUBS

See Pick of the Pubs on opposite page

PRESTON ST MARY
Map 13 TL95

NEW The Six Bells

tel: 01787 247440 **The Street CO10 9NG**
email: info@thesixbellspreston.com
dir: *From Lavenham take A1141 towards Bury St Edmunds. Right into Preston Rd signed Brettenham & Preston. At x-roads right. In Preston St Mary right into The Street to pub on right*

Restored Suffolk pub with great local produce

Newly restored, this charming Grade II listed pub is just outside Lavenham in a pretty village and is open from Wednesdays to Sundays. The huge garden is a bonus in the summer, and a good choice of ale is offered in the bar. In the dining room you'll find a daily-changing lunch and dinner menu, using strictly local and seasonal ingredients. Expect starters like beetroot, autumn vegetable and goats' curd salad, or pheasant terrine, with mains taking in Blythburgh pork belly and faggot with chicory and apple; or Adnams ale-battered haddock with hand-cut chips and mushy peas.

Open all day Closed Mon, Tue **Food** Lunch Wed-Sat 12-3, Sun 12-5 Dinner Wed-Thu 6-9.30, Fri-Sat 6-10.30 Set menu available Restaurant menu available Wed-Sun ⊕ FREE HOUSE ◀ Adnams Southwold Bitter, The Old Cannon, Six Bells Ö Aspall. ♟ 12 **Facilities** Non-diners area ♣ (Bar Restaurant Garden) ♦ Children's menu Children's portions Play area Family room Garden ⌐ Parking WiFi ▭ (notice required)

REDE
Map 13 TL85

The Plough

tel: 01284 789208 **IP29 4BE**
dir: *On A143 between Bury St Edmunds & Haverhill*

Interesting menus in Suffolk's highest spot

Easily identified by an old plough and a weeping willow at the front, this part-thatched, 16th-century pub is tucked away on the pretty village green in Rede. On long-standing landlord Brian Desborough's ever-changing blackboard menu look for lamb braised in Rioja red wine with vegetables and chorizo; crab au gratin; and diced chicken breast with creamy Stilton and celery sauce. The bar serves Fuller's, Adnams, Ringwood and Sharp's ales and 10 wines by the glass. At 128 metres above sea level, Rede is Suffolk's highest point – verified by Guinness World Records.

Open all wk 11-3 6-12 (Sun 12-3) **Food** Lunch all wk 12-2 Dinner Mon-Sat 6-9 ⊕ ADMIRAL TAVERNS ◀ Fuller's London Pride, Ringwood Best Bitter, Sharp's Cornish Coaster, Adnams Ö Aspall. ♟ 10 **Facilities** Non-diners area ♦ Children's portions Garden ⌐ Parking WiFi ▭ (notice required)

SIBTON
Map 13 TM36

Sibton White Horse Inn ★★★★ INN ⊕ PICK OF THE PUBS

See Pick of the Pubs on page 468

PICK OF THE PUBS

Sibton White Horse Inn ★★★★ INN 🏵

tel: 01728 660337
Halesworth Rd IP17 2JJ
email: info@sibtonwhitehorseinn.co.uk
web: www.sibtonwhitehorseinn.co.uk
dir: *A12 at Yoxford onto A1120, 3m to Peasenhall. Right opposite butchers, inn 600mtrs*

Delightful, award-winning inn

Off the beaten track in the heart of the Suffolk countryside, yet, it's just five minutes from the A12 at Yoxford and 10 miles from the coast. This rustic 16th-century inn retains much of its Tudor charm and incorporates stone floors, exposed brickwork and ships' timbers believed to have come from Woodbridge shipyard. A free house, the bar with its raised gallery is the place to enjoy a pint of Adnams Southwold, Green Jack Trawlerboys or Woodforde's Once Bittern. There is a choice of dining areas to sample the award-winning food, while the secluded courtyard has a Mediterranean feel when the sun comes out. Owners Neil and Gill Mason are committed to producing high-quality food from fresh local ingredients — and to prove it they grow many of their own vegetables behind the pub. At lunch, you can order from the menu or from the selection of light bites and sandwiches. At dinner, starters may include leek and potato soup, and tempura tiger prawns

with red pepper, butternut squash and cashew nut salad, and chilli aïoli. Treats to follow might well be roast saddle of lamb, dauphinoise potato, buttered kale, roast beetroot, wild garlic pesto and port jus; pan-roasted sea bass with Bombay potato, cauliflower, spinach, mango raita and curry cream; or sweet potato and smoked paprika soufflé with purple sprouting broccoli, chargrilled potato, toasted almond and saffron aïoli. Finish, perhaps, with banana and beer sponge with toasted marshmallow, caramelised banana, toffee sauce, hazelnut praline and banana ice cream. The children's menu is for lunchtime only; six-year-olds and over are permitted in the evening.

Open 12-2.30 6.30-11 (Sun 12-3.30 6.45-10.30) Closed 26-27 Dec, Mon L **Food** Lunch Tue-Sat 12-2, Sun 12-2.30 Dinner Mon-Sat 6.30-9, Sun 7-8.30 🌐 FREE HOUSE 🍺 Adnams Southwold Bitter, Woodforde's Once Bittern, Green Jack Trawlerboys Best Bitter ♂ Aspall. 🍷 9 **Facilities** Non-diners area 🐾 (Bar Garden) 👬 Children's menu Children's portions Garden 🪑 Beer festival Parking WiFi **Rooms** 6

SNAPE
Map 13 TM35

The Crown Inn
PICK OF THE PUBS

tel: 01728 688324 **Bridge Rd IP17 1SL**
email: snapecrown@tiscali.co.uk
dir: *A12 from Ipswich towards Lowestoft, right onto A1094 towards Aldeburgh. In Snape right at x-roads by church, pub at bottom of hill*

Ancient village inn dedicated to using local produce

Getting on for 600 years old and once the haunt of smugglers using the nearby River Alde, this village stalwart shelters beneath a most extraordinary saltbox pantile roof. Inside, the public area threads beneath vast old beams and across mellow brick floors to cosy corners and an inglenook enclosed by the arms of a huge double settle. Folk musicians regularly take over this area for informal gigs; far more renowned is the nearby Snape Maltings complex which attracts international performers. Pre- or post-concert meals are available for such concert goers. The Crown's owners Teresa and Garry Cook run their own livestock smallholding behind the pub, ensuring a very local supply chain. This is enhanced by locally sourced Limousin beef, seafood from Orford boats, game from nearby shoots, village vegetables and foraged specialities. Menus change frequently, but a sample features ham hock and leek macaroni cheese; pheasant Wellington with truffle sauce; and sirloin beef steak with field mushroom, vine tomatoes, onion rings and chips.

Open all wk 12-3 6-11 **Food** Lunch all wk 12-2.30 Dinner all wk 6-9.30 ⊕ ADNAMS ◧ Southwold Bitter, Broadside, seasonal ales ♂ Aspall. ♈ 12
Facilities Non-diners area ❖ (Bar Garden) ♦♦ Children's portions Garden ☎ Parking WiFi ☞ (notice required)

Plough & Sail

tel: 01728 688413 **Snape Maltings IP17 1SR**
dir: *On B1069, S of Snape. Signed from A12*

Drawing in the crowds in Snape

Local twins, Alex (front of house) and Oliver (chef) Burnside own this pink, pantiled old inn at the heart of the renowned Snape Maltings complex; it's handy for cultural and shopping opportunities and close to splendid coastal walks. The interior is a comfy mix of dining and avant-garde destination pub; local ales and a good bin of wines accompany a solid menu, featuring a Mediterranean fish soup with rouille, gruyère and crostini, and home-made potted shrimps on toast to start; followed by seasonal fish pie; Gressingham duck (breast and confit leg), spiced pear, celeriac purée, sprouting broccoli and potato rösti; or Adnams beer-battered fish and chips with crushed minted peas. A blackboard of specials adds to the choice.

Open all day all wk **Food** Lunch all wk 12-2.30 Dinner all wk 6-9 ⊕ FREE HOUSE ◧ Adnams Broadside, Southwold Bitter, Ghost Ship, guest ale ♂ Aspall. ♈ 10
Facilities Non-diners area ❖ (Bar Garden) ♦♦ Children's menu Children's portions Garden ☎ Parking WiFi ☞ (notice required)

SOMERLEYTON
Map 13 TM49

The Duke's Head

tel: 01502 733931 & 730281 **Slug's Ln NR32 5QR**
email: dukeshead@somerleyton.co.uk
dir: *From A143 onto B1074 signed Lowestoft & Somerleyton. Pub signed from B1074*

Rural estate-owned pub worth finding

Tucked away down Slug's Lane on the edge of the village, this smart pub overlooks the Somerleyton Estate. Tara Smyth took over the reins in July 2015 and it is renowned locally for its imaginative seasonal menus, which champion game and estate-reared meats. A thriving dining-pub, the relaxed bar and eating areas fill early with those in the know. A typical meal might begin with ham hock and split pea broth and continue with roast rump and cheek of beef, Jerusalem artichoke risotto and hispi cabbage. Savour the views over a pint of Woodforde's Wherry in the garden in the summer months.

Open all day all wk **Food** Lunch Mon-Sat 12-2.30, Sun 12-5 winter, 12-8 summer Dinner Mon-Sat 6.30-9, Sun 12-8 summer Av main course £11.50 ⊕ FREE HOUSE ◧ Adnams, Woodforde's Wherry, guest ales ♂ Aspall. ♈ 12
Facilities Non-diners area ❖ (Bar Restaurant Garden) ♦♦ Children's menu Children's portions Play area Garden ☎ Beer festival Cider festival Parking WiFi ☞ (notice required)

SOUTHWOLD
Map 13 TM57

The Harbour Inn

tel: 01502 722381 **Blackshore Quay IP18 6TA**
email: info@harbourinnsouthwold.co.uk
dir: *From A12 (N of Blythburgh) take A1095 (Southwold). In Southwold right into York Rd to Southwold Harbour*

Traditional old fishermen's pub with river and marsh views

In contrast to pubs that don't tolerate wellies indoors, in winter this one actually recommends them because it stands right by the water, sometimes in it, as the sobering flood-level markers testify. Inside are two snug, photograph-plastered bars, the upper, nautically themed one with a wood-burner, while in the lower one staff must stoop to serve pints of Adnams through a hatch. Fish dishes take high priority here. The menu begins with little taster dishes to 'pick, mix and share' – potted shrimps; cockle popcorn; roll herrings being just three; then you could choose an 'other fishiness' dish – grilled spiced mackerel fillet; or clam, king prawn, smoked haddock and potato chowder perhaps. Meat eaters are not left out with dishes such as pulled beef brisket in a toasted brioche bun with BBQ sauce.

Open all day all wk **Food** 12-9 Av main course £13 ⊕ ADNAMS ◧ Southwold Bitter, Broadside, Ghost Ship & Spindrift ♂ Aspall. ♈ 12 **Facilities** Non-diners area ❖ (Bar Garden) ♦♦ Children's menu Children's portions Family room Garden ☎ Parking ☞ (notice required)

The Randolph
PICK OF THE PUBS

tel: 01502 723603 **41 Wangford Rd, Reydon IP18 6PZ**
email: reception@therandolph.co.uk
dir: *A12 onto A1095 towards Southwold. Left into Wangford Rd*

Family run with locally brewed beers

Easily walkable from Southwold, this majestic pub was built in 1899 by the town's well-known Adnams Brewery, whose directors were pally with Lord Randolph Churchill, Sir Winston's father. Showing no real sign today of its late-Victorian origins, the light and airy bar is furnished with contemporary high-backed chairs and comfortable sofas; the well-protected garden is lovely in the sun. In the bar and restaurant a concise modern British menu offers starters of smoked duck breast with celeriac remoulade, caper and raisin tapenade; or timbale of Bloody Mary soused herrings with dill cream cheese. Mains include poached smoked haddock, cheese, spring onion and grain mustard sauce; steamed steak and kidney suet pudding; and Moroccan pot-roasted chicken with apricot couscous and pomegranate yogurt. Children can opt to select from their own menu.

Open all day all wk **Food** Lunch all wk 12-2 Dinner all wk 6.30-9 Restaurant menu available all wk ⊕ ADNAMS ◧ Southwold Bitter, Explorer, Old Ale & Ghost Ship ♂ Aspall. **Facilities** Non-diners area ♦♦ Children's menu Children's portions Garden ☎ Parking WiFi ☞ (notice required)

STOKE-BY-NAYLAND
Map 13 TL93

The Angel Inn ★★★★★ INN ◉
PICK OF THE PUBS

tel: 01206 263245 **CO6 4SA**
email: info@angelinnsuffolk.co.uk **web:** www.angelinnsuffolk.co.uk
dir: *From Colchester take A134 towards Sudbury, 5m to Nayland. Or from A12 between juncts 30 & 31 take B1068, then B1087 to Nayland*

Charming coaching inn in Constable Country

This substantial old inn has served the sublime village of gabled colour-washed houses and tall, slim chimneys since well before local lad John Constable put brush to canvas to capture the beauty of deepest rural Suffolk. Careful modernisation, like the air-conditioned conservatory, patio and sun terrace, harmonise happily with the ancient charm of The Angel's beamed bars, log fires and snug areas. The Well Room restaurant area, with its lofty, timbered ceiling and 52-ft deep well, is an astonishing centrepiece. Modern dishes and robust classics share billing on the seasonally-inspired menu which has gained head chef Mark Allen an AA Rosette. From the à la carte, consider chargrilled swordfish; pan-fried calves' liver and bacon; or warm caramelised onion and goats' cheese tart. There is a choice of grills cooked over oak and chicory on their Big Green Egg. Luxurious accommodation here offers scope for extended exploration of the scenic Stour Valley.

Open all day all wk 11-11 (Sun 11-10.30) **Food** Lunch Mon-Fri 12-3.30, Sat 12-9.30, Sun 12-9 Dinner Mon-Fri 6-9.30, Sat 12-9.30, Sun 12-9 Set menu available Restaurant menu available all wk ⊕ FREE HOUSE/EXCLUSIVE INNS ◀ Adnams Southwold Bitter, Greene King, Nethergate, 2 guest ales ♻ Aspall, Thatchers. ♟ 12 **Facilities** Non-diners area ✿ (Bar Garden) ♦♦ Children's menu Children's portions Family room Garden Outside area ⊟ Parking WiFi ▭ (notice required) **Rooms** 6

The Crown ★★★ SHL ◉◉
PICK OF THE PUBS

tel: 01206 262001 **CO6 4SE**
email: info@crowninn.net **web:** www.crowninn.net
dir: *Exit A12 signed Stratford St Mary & Dedham. Through Stratford St Mary 0.5m, left, follow signs to Higham. At village green left, left again, 2m, pub on right*

Delightful combination of village pub and boutique hotel

Slap bang in the heart of Constable Country and handy for the timeless villages of Lavenham, Kersey and Long Melford, this 16th-century free house sits above the Stour and Box Valleys on the Suffolk and Essex border. The stylish dining areas are informal, and there's a great choice of local ales in the contemporary bar. These are matched by an award-winning cellar of some 250 bins; over 30 of them can be bought by the glass. Tasty seasonal and local produce underpins a modern British menu. Typical starters are steamed Shetland mussels with saffron, white wine, chilli, herbs and toasted almonds; and potted Long Melford rabbit with carrot salad and walnut bread. Children are welcome but dining is for adults only after 8pm. Dinner might feature Jerusalem artichoke and feta tart, toasted hazelnuts and apple and watercress salad; or steak and Guinness pie with blue cheese and walnut mash. Finish with blood orange meringue pie or tiramisù cake. Eleven luxury en suite bedrooms complete the jewels in this crown.

Open all day all wk 7.30am-11pm (Sun 8am-10.30pm) Closed 25-26 Dec **Food** Lunch Mon-Sat 12-2.30, Sun 12-9 Dinner Mon-Thu 6-9.30, Fri-Sat 6-10, Sun 12-9 Set menu available Restaurant menu available all wk ⊕ FREE HOUSE ◀ Adnams Southwold Bitter, Crouch Vale Brewers Gold, Woodforde's Wherry, guest ales ♻ Aspall. ♟ 32 **Facilities** Non-diners area ♦♦ Children's menu Children's portions Outside area ⊟ Parking WiFi **Rooms** 11

STOWMARKET
Map 13 TM05

The Buxhall Crown

tel: 01449 736521 **Mill Rd, Buxhall IP14 3DW**
email: mail@thebuxhallcrown.co.uk
dir: *B1115 from Stowmarket, through Great Finborough to Buxhall*

Charming rural pub with exceptional menu

The curious jigsaw that is an old country cottage and a Georgian farmhouse fit together seamlessly here, resulting in an appealing country pub set amidst the cornfields of deepest Suffolk. With a wealth of beams, log-burners and two contrasting areas in which to relax, indulge in a glass of Suffolk-brewed beer and find your bearings on an invigorating menu that caters for both grazers and gastronomes. With a commitment to local produce, distinguished dishes from the carte menu may include roast partridge breast; seared king scallops or pan-roasted venison, with bread and butter pudding a final flourish.

Open 12-3 7-11 (Sat 12-3 6.30-11) Closed Sun eve & Mon **Food** Lunch Tue-Sun 12-2 Dinner Tue-Fri 7-9, Sat 6.30-9 ⊕ FREE HOUSE ◀ Adnams Southwold Bitter & Broadside ♻ Aspall. ♟ 12 **Facilities** Non-diners area ✿ (Bar Restaurant Garden) ♦♦ Children's portions Garden Parking WiFi ▭ (notice required)

STRADBROKE
Map 13 TM27

The Ivy House

tel: 01379 384634 **Wilby Rd IP21 5JN**
email: stensethhome@aol.com
dir: *Phone for detailed directions*

Interesting ales and wines in a pretty pub

Around the corner from Stradbroke's main street, is this Grade II listed thatched pub that dates from the Middle Ages. Real ales on hand pump and wine from the Adnams wine cellar are the draw here. The weekly-changing menu makes good use of local and seasonal produce to offer both British and Asian-style dishes, and in warmer weather you can sit outside at the front or in the garden. Typical options include teriyaki-marinated chicken skewers with salsa to start; and pan-fried calves' liver with Suffolk dry-cured bacon, mash and onion gravy as a main course. Leave room for dark chocolate cake with praline ice cream. Curries and other dishes are available to take away.

Open all wk 12-3 6-11 **Food** Contact pub for food times ⊕ FREE HOUSE ◀ Adnams, Greene King, Fuller's London Pride ♻ Aspall. **Facilities** Non-diners area ✿ (Bar Garden) Garden ⊟ Parking WiFi

PICK OF THE PUBS

The Westleton Crown ★★★ HL ✿✿

WESTLETON Map 13 TM46

tel: 01728 648777 **The Street IP17 3AD**
email: info@westletoncrown.co.uk
web: www.westletoncrown.co.uk
dir: A12 N, turn right for Westleton just
after Yoxford. Hotel opposite on entering
Westleton

Classic dishes with a twist and fine local ales

Opposite the churchyard, this red-brick, former coaching inn is essentially 18th century, although some sources say its origins are considerably older. The RSPB's Minsmere coastal nature reserve is about two miles away, and Suffolk's glorious Heritage Coast is also within easy reach. The pub retains plenty of character and rustic charm, complemented by all the comforts of contemporary living. In addition to winter real log fires, you'll find locally brewed ales, including Brandon Rusty Bucket and Adnams Southwold Bitter, as well as a good wine list, with 20 available by the glass. The 'hearty' and 'sophisticated' food, to quote the Crown, includes daily specials and classic dishes, freshly prepared from top local produce, all on the menu in the cosy, dog-friendly bar, the elegant dining room, and the garden room. Sandwiches are made with home-baked bread.

A more substantial meal might comprise pressed ham hock terrine, spiced plum chutney and toasted brioche; Moroccan braised lamb shank, coriander couscous and vegetable tagine; or grilled fillet of sea bass, herb-crushed new potatoes, ratatouille and basil pesto; followed perhaps by warm ginger pudding, kumquat confit, vanilla ice cream and toffee sauce. For vegetarians, perhaps four-cheese macaroni with sautéed wild mushrooms; or sweet potato, baby spinach, parmesan and wild rocket risotto. Retire to one of the 34 comfortably and individually styled bedrooms. Outside, the large terraced gardens are floodlit in the evening.

Open all day all wk 7am-11pm (Sun 7.30am-10.30pm) **Food** Lunch all wk 12-2.30 Dinner all wk 6.30-9.30 ⊕ FREE HOUSE ◀ Adnams Southwold Bitter, Brandon Rusty Bucket Ŏ Aspall Harry Sparrow. ♀ 20 **Facilities** Non-diners area ❀ (Bar Garden) ♦♦ Children's menu Children's portions Garden ☲ Parking WiFi ▭▭ (notice required) **Rooms** 34

SWILLAND
Map 13 TM15

Moon & Mushroom Inn

tel: 01473 785320 **High Rd IP6 9LR**
email: moonandmushroom@gmail.com
dir: Take B1077 (Westerfield road) from Ipswich. Approx 6m, right to Swilland

Tranquil escape in deepest Suffolk

The delightful sight of several firkins of East Anglian beer stillaged enticingly behind the bar welcomes drinkers to this 400-year-old free house in the Suffolk countryside. Diners, too, relish the prospect of indulging in home-cooked specials such as Suffolk fish pie with salmon, cod, haddock and prawns; or slow-roasted breast of lamb with lamb croquettes and redcurrant gravy. In times gone by the pub was reputedly a staging post for the dispatch of convicts to Australia, and the records at Ipswich Assizes do indeed show that a previous landlord was deported for stealing two ducks and a pig. Today's guests are able to linger longer in the colourful, cottagey interior or the fragrant rose garden here.

Open Tue-Sat & Sun L Closed Sun eve & Mon **Food** Lunch Tue-Sat 12-2, Sun 12-2.30 Dinner Tue-Sat 6.30-9 Set menu available Restaurant menu available Tue-Sat ⊕ FREE HOUSE ◀ Nethergate Suffolk County, Woodforde's Wherry & Admiral's Reserve, Wolf Ale & Golden Jackal, Earl Soham Brandeston Gold & Victoria Bitter Ŏ Aspall. **Facilities** Non-diners area ❀ (Bar Garden) ♦ Children's portions Garden ⟑ Beer festival Parking WiFi ⛟ (notice required)

THORPENESS
Map 13 TM45

The Dolphin Inn

tel: 01728 454994 **Peace Place IP16 4NA**
email: dolphininn@hotmail.co.uk
dir: A12 onto A1094 & follow Thorpeness signs

At the community's heart and close to never-ending beaches

A stone's throw from the shingle of Suffolk's Heritage Coast and in a conservation area, this community-focused free house replaced a 1910 predecessor, destroyed by fire in 1995. At the bar are real ales from Adnams and Brandon, nearly 20 wines by the glass, and bourbons and single malts in abundance. Look forward to dressed crab salad; potted brown shrimps; seared Gressingham duck breast with sweet potato mash; grilled sea bass fillet; and lemon and elderflower cheesecake. After a bracing walk on the beach sit beside the fire and enjoy a pint of the local brew; in summer, barbecues are held in the huge garden.

Open 11-3 6-11 (Sat-Sun 11-11) Closed Sun eve & Mon in winter **Food** Lunch all wk 12-2.30 Dinner all wk 6.30-9.30 Set menu available ⊕ FREE HOUSE ◀ Adnams Southwold Bitter & Broadside, Brandon Rusty Bucket, Mauldons Midsummer Gold, Woodforde's Wherry Ŏ Aspall. ⏣ 18 **Facilities** Non-diners area ❀ (Bar Garden) ♦ Children's menu Children's portions Garden ⟑ Parking WiFi ⛟

TUDDENHAM
Map 13 TM14

The Fountain

tel: 01473 785377 **The Street IP6 9BT**
email: fountainpub@btconnect.com
dir: From Ipswich take B1077 (Westerfield Rd) signed Debenham. At Westerfield turn right for Tuddenham

Informal bistro-style eating in a 16th-century country pub

Only three miles north of Ipswich, in a lovely village, is this 16th-century country pub that combines old fashioned pub hospitality with an informal bistro-style restaurant. The menu changes frequently and there is an emphasis on local produce in dishes such as pan-seared scallops, crispy pancetta and celeriac purée;

chargrilled Dingley Dell pork cutlet with macaroni cheese and buttered curly kale; and free-range chicken saltimbocca, dauphinoise potatoes and a seasonal vegetable medley. Wash it all down with pints of Adnams ale and Aspall cider, or one of the nine wines served by the glass.

Open all wk 12-3 6-11 (Sun 12-8) **Food** Lunch Mon-Sat 12-2, Sun 12-7 Dinner Mon-Fri 6-9, Sat 6-9.30, Sun 12-7 Set menu available Restaurant menu available all wk ⊕ FREE HOUSE ◀ Adnams Ŏ Aspall. ⏣ 9 **Facilities** Non-diners area ♦ Children's menu Children's portions Garden ⟑ Parking WiFi

UFFORD
Map 13 TM25

The Ufford Crown

tel: 01394 461030 **High St IP13 6EL**
email: max@theuffordcrown.com
dir: Just off A12 between Woodbridge & Wickham

Friendly, family-run village pub and restaurant

Step though the doors of Max and Polly Durrant's handsome property and you'll find a spacious restaurant, cosy bar, stylish lounge area and, at the rear, a terrace and garden, where there's plenty to keep children amused. Adnams and Earl Soham badges adorn the real ale pumps, with Aspall cider alongside. A glass of sloe gin fizz would make a great intro for lunch or dinner here. Gifted chef Will Hardiman has a reputation for using all cuts of meat, including sweetbreads and ox cheeks, and Lowestoft-landed fish. Heavily reliant on seasonal produce from local suppliers, his daily-changing menus might feature pork rillettes, red onion marmalade, fried quail's egg and salad; half a local lobster, garlic butter and fries; and bavette of Ketley beef.

Open 12-3 5-11 (Sat-Sun all day) Closed Tue **Food** Lunch Mon & Wed-Sat 12.30-2, Sun 12-3 Dinner Mon & Wed-Sat 6.30-9, Sun 6-8 ⊕ FREE HOUSE ◀ Adnams Southwold Bitter, Earl Soham Brandeston Gold & Victoria Bitter Ŏ Aspall. ⏣ 15 **Facilities** Non-diners area ❀ (Bar Garden) ♦ Children's menu Children's portions Play area Garden Outside area ⟑ Parking WiFi ⛟ (notice required)

WALBERSWICK
Map 13 TM47

The Bell Inn

tel: 01502 723109 **Ferry Rd IP18 6TN**
email: info@bellinnwalberswick.co.uk
dir: From A12 take B1387 to Walberswick, after village green turn right into track

Old inn where the menu captures top Suffolk produce

There's plenty of character here, with 600 years of history, oak-beamed ceilings, hidden alcoves, worn flagstone floors and open fires. Close to the Southwold ferry, the Suffolk Coastal Path and the marshes, the pub has a family-friendly garden overlooking a creek and the beach; here too is the Barn Café, offering everything for a picnic. Firm favourites on the menu are deep-fried breaded whitebait; Suffolk smokies; steak, ale and mushroom shortcrust pastry pie; and apple and cinnamon pannacotta crumble. Well-behaved dogs are welcome.

Open all day all wk **Food** Lunch all wk 12-2.30 Dinner all wk 6-9 Av main course £14 ⊕ ADNAMS ◀ Southwold Bitter, Broadside, Spindrift, Ghost Ship Ŏ Aspall. ⏣ 15 **Facilities** Non-diners area ❀ (Bar Garden) ♦ Children's menu Children's portions Family room Garden ⟑ Parking WiFi ⛟ (notice required)

WESTLETON
Map 13 TM46

The Westleton Crown ★★★ HL ◉◉ PICK OF THE PUBS

See Pick of the Pubs on page 471

WHEPSTEAD
Map 13 TL85

The White Horse ◉
PICK OF THE PUBS

tel: 01284 735760 **Rede Rd IP29 4SS**
dir: *From Bury St Edmunds take A143 towards Haverhill. Left onto B1066 to Whepstead. In Whepstead right into Church Hill, leads into Rede Rd*

Delightful East Anglian pub with a loyal following

In the valley of the little River Lark and at the hub of easy country rambles, this centuries-old pub oozes character. A series of cosy rooms splay from the huge hand-thrown brick chimney breast, radiating below generous beams that were cut 400 years ago. The bright, spacious interior makes a great space for the display and sale of artworks by local painters. With a large, copper-topped bar, part-tiled floors and restful decor, you feel instantly at home, while nostalgic touches like the Tuck Shop – which sells ice cream, sweets and chocolate – appeal to adults and children alike. Highly regarded chef-patron Gary Kingshott synthesises wholesome contemporary dishes from local produce, receiving the accolade of one AA Rosette for dishes such as steamed hake with samphire and butter sauce; or pork and harissa sausage with saffron mash. Finish with butterscotch and raisin tart, then ponder the rest of the day in the huge grassy beer garden.

Open 11.30-3 7-11 Closed 25-26 Dec, Sun eve **Food** Lunch all wk 12-2 Dinner Mon-Sat 7-9.30 ⊕ FREE HOUSE ◢ Adnams Southwold Bitter & Broadside, guest ale Ⓒ Aspall. ♟ 10 **Facilities** Non-diners area ❁ (Bar Garden) ◆♦ Children's portions Garden Parking ▦

WOODBRIDGE
Map 13 TM24

Cherry Tree Inn ★★★★ INN

tel: 01394 384627 **73 Cumberland St IP12 4AG**
email: andy@thecherrytreepub.co.uk **web:** www.thecherrytreepub.co.uk
dir: *Phone for detailed directions*

Classically appealing hostelry with a caring approach

The Cherry Tree Inn features a large central counter, and several distinct seating areas amidst the twisting oak beams. The focus on customer care manifests subtly in many ways: the availability of board games; play equipment for children in the large enclosed garden; wheelchair access; dog friendliness; free WiFi. Winner of an AA Dinner Award, there are many gluten-free options among the locally-sourced and home-cooked menu dishes. The year sees around eight guest ales rotate, with Adnams and Aspall cider in permanent residence; a beer festival in early July confirms the pub's ale credentials.

Open all day all wk 10.30am-11pm **Food** Mon-Sat 12-9, Sun 12-8 ⊕ ADNAMS ◢ Adnams ales, guest ales Ⓒ Aspall. ♟ 11 **Facilities** Non-diners area ❁ (Bar Outside area) ◆♦ Children's menu Children's portions Play area Garden Outside area ▱ Beer festival Parking WiFi ▦ (notice required) **Rooms** 3

WOODDITTON
Map 12 TL65

The Three Blackbirds

tel: 01638 731100 **36 Ditton Green CB8 9SQ**
email: info@threeblackbirds.co.uk
dir: *From Newmarket High Street (Cambridge end) take B1061 opposite Shell garage. In 300yds turn left, 2.5m to Woodditton. At x-roads turn right, pub 300yds on right*

Exciting food and local ales in beautiful thatched village inn

Mentioned in the Domesday Book, the beautiful village of Woodditton is just three miles from Newmarket, and the thatched Three Blackbirds dates from 1642. The two cosy oak-beamed bars offer a range of real ales and diners can choose between the restaurant and private dining room to sample a daily-changing menu packed

with local produce. Perhaps Dullingham sausages and mash, buttered greens and onion gravy; pearl barley, roasted pumpkin and sage risotto; or local steaks from the grill that are followed by treats like home-made profiteroles filled with Baileys Irish cream.

Open all wk 12-3 5-11 (Fri 12-3 5-12 Sat 12-3 5.30-12 Sun 12-7) **Food** Lunch Mon-Sat 12-2.30, Sun 12-4 Dinner Mon-Sat 6.30-9.30 Restaurant menu available Mon-Sat ⊕ FREE HOUSE ◢ Adnams Best Bitter, Woodforde's Wherry, Sharp's Doom Bar, regional ales Ⓒ Aspall. ♟ 17 **Facilities** Non-diners area ❁ (Bar Garden Outside area) ◆♦ Children's menu Children's portions Garden Outside area ▱ Parking WiFi ▦ (notice required)

SURREY

ABINGER
Map 6 TQ14

The Abinger Hatch

tel: 01306 730737 **Abinger Ln RH5 6HZ**
email: manager@theabingerhatch.com
dir: *A25 from Dorking towards Guildford. Left to Abinger Common*

Quintessentially English pub with something for everyone

Plenty of variety is the key here, from the children's choices to dishes based on fresh locally sourced produce. Traditionally English from its beams to its flagstone floors, the pub enjoys a light and airy atmosphere. There's lots of space outside too, with capacious car parking and a huge garden where a summer barbecue, wood-burning oven and outdoor bar make for a truly relaxing experience. Typically on the menu are dishes such as mushroom and goats' cheese tartlet; and smoked mackerel pâté to start, followed by pan-fried veal liver, mash, bacon, onion gravy and seasonal vegetables; or the chef's pie of the day.

Open all day all wk **Food** Lunch all wk 12-6 Dinner Mon-Thu 6-9, Fri-Sat 6-10, Sun 6-8 ⊕ FREE HOUSE ◢ Ringwood Razorback & Fortyniner, Cottage, guest ales Ⓒ Thatchers. ♟ 14 **Facilities** Non-diners area ❁ (Bar Restaurant Garden) ◆♦ Children's menu Children's portions Garden ▱ Parking WiFi ▦ (notice required)

ALBURY
Map 6 TQ04

William IV

tel: 01483 202685 **Little London GU5 9DG**
dir: *Off A25 between Guildford & Dorking (for detailed directions contact pub)*

16th-century free house on a quiet country lane

Deep in the wooded Surrey Hills yet only a few miles from Guildford, this 16th-century free house provides 'proper pub food' made from mostly local produce. Look out for dishes of free-range pork (raised by landlord Giles) written on the blackboards, but also worth considering are the liver and bacon, beer-battered cod and chips, and pan-fried Cajun chicken, all served in the bar and dining room. Young's and two Surrey breweries supply the real ales. It is great walking and riding country, and the attractive garden is ideal for post-ramble relaxation.

Open all wk 11-3 5.30-11 (Sat 11-11 Sun 12-11) **Food** Lunch all wk 12-2 Dinner Mon-Sat 7-9 ⊕ FREE HOUSE ◢ Young's, Hogs Back, Surrey Hills Ⓒ Westons Stowford Press, Addlestones. **Facilities** Non-diners area ❁ (Bar Garden) ◆♦ Children's portions Garden ▱ Parking WiFi ▦ (notice required)

Jolly Farmer Inn

tel: 01483 893355 **High St GU5 0HB**
email: enquiries@jollyfarmer.co.uk
dir: *From Guildford take A281 (Horsham road). Bramley 3.5m S of Guildford*

Welcoming and friendly pub

A 16th-century coaching inn steeped in character and history, this friendly family-run free house clearly has a passion for beer. Besides the impressive range of Belgian bottled beers, you'll always find up to eight constantly-changing cask real ales on the counter. The pub offers a high standard of food all freshly cooked, with daily specials board, featuring dishes such as half a pint of tiger prawns (or a pint for a main course); 12-hour braised lamb shank, almond, apricot and mint couscous and sprouting broccoli; and chocolate and honey tart, pistachio praline and crème fraîche.

Open all day all wk 11-11 **Food** Lunch all wk 12-2.30 Dinner all wk 6-9.30 Av main course £11 ⊕ FREE HOUSE ◀ 8 guest ales ♂ Westons Stowford Press, Aspall. ♚ 16 **Facilities** Non-diners area ❀ (Bar Outside area) ♦♦ Children's portions Outside area ⋒ Parking WiFi ⛟ (notice required)

The Dog & Pheasant

tel: 01428 682763 **Haslemere Rd GU8 5UJ**
email: info@dogandpheasant.com
dir: *From Godalming take A286 towards Haslemere. Pub approx 4.5m*

A truly English country pub

Four open fires warm this picturesque 15th-century pub, where over the inglenook fire on Wednesday nights the chef grills steaks and fish. Sixteen wines are served by the glass and real ales are sourced from Surrey to Cornwall. In addition to grills, sandwiches and ploughman's, the menu offers Applewood smoked goats' cheese and thyme mousse; crispy devilled whitebait; slow-cooked beef and Guinness puff pastry pie; crab and crayfish linguine; and home-cooked honey-mustard ham, Chapel Farm eggs and skin-on chips. A 'cover drive' away from the lovely garden is the cricket pitch, the Surrey Hills beyond.

Open all day all wk **Food** Lunch Mon-Fri 12-2.30, Sat-Sun 12-4 Dinner Mon-Fri 6-9.30, Sat 5-9.30 ⊕ FREE HOUSE ◀ Sharp's Atlantic, Hogs Back, Sharp's Doom Bar ♂ Hogs Back Hazy Hog. ♚ 16 **Facilities** Non-diners area ❀ (Bar Garden) ♦♦ Children's menu Children's portions Play area Garden ⋒ Parking WiFi ⛟ (notice required)

The Crown Inn ★★★★★ INN

tel: 01428 682255 **The Green GU8 4TX**
email: enquiries@thecrownchiddingfold.com **web:** www.thecrownchiddingfold.com
dir: *On A283 between Milford & Petworth*

Pretty as a picture timbered inn, more than 700 years old

Set by the village green and church, this beautifully appointed inn is one of the county's oldest buildings. It oozes charm and character, featuring ancient panelling, open fires, distinctive carvings, huge beams, and eight comfortable bedrooms. In addition to the house beer, Crown Bitter, ales come from Surrey, Hampshire and London breweries. Food ranges from enticing snacks like houmous and toasted pitta bread; and haggis bon bons with chive mayonnaise, to dishes

such as devilled kidneys on toast; rabbit cacciatore, polenta and green beans; and Crown favourites – pie of the week; and gammon steak, double egg and fries.

Open all day all wk **Food** Lunch Mon-Thu 12-2.30, Fri-Sat 12-10, Sun 12-9 Dinner Mon-Thu 6.30-10.30, Fri-Sat 12-10, Sun 12-9 Set menu available ⊕ FREE HOUSE/ FGH INNS ◀ Crown Bitter, Fuller's London Pride, Triple fff Moondance, Hogs Back. ♚ 12 **Facilities** Non-diners area ♦♦ Children's menu Children's portions Outside area ⋒ Parking WiFi **Rooms** 8

The Swan Inn   PICK OF THE PUBS

tel: 01428 684688 **Petworth Rd GU8 4TY**
email: info@theswaninnchiddingfold.com
dir: *From A3 follow Milford/Petworth/A283 signs. At rdbt 1st exit onto A283. Slight right onto Guildford & Godalming bypass. Right into Portsmouth Rd, left (continue on A283), to Chiddingfold*

Cosmopolitan food and drink in stylish village inn

Rebuilt in the 1880s and under new management since September 2015, the Swan today offers weary travellers a friendly and relaxed welcome. Located among the Surrey Hills, The Swan is typical of the coaching inns that once served customers travelling to or from the south coast. In the bar, temptations include local ales such as Upham Brewery's Punter, and from an international list, there are 18 wines served by the glass. The daily-changing menu has broad appeal; a typical meal might kick off with chicken and foie gras terrine, apricot chutney and pickled mustard seeds. That might be followed by a main course of crayfish linguini, chilli, garlic and spring onions. For dessert perhaps choose banana bread and butter pudding with poppy seed ice cream, or the carefully sourced cheeseboard.

Open all day all wk 10am-11pm (Sun 11-10.30) **Food** Lunch all wk 12-3 Dinner Mon-Sat 6.30-9.30, Sun 6.30-9 ⊕ FREE HOUSE/UPHAM GROUP ◀ Punter, Stakes, Tipster & Sprinter, guest ale ♂ Hogs Back Hazy Hog. ♚ 18 **Facilities** Non-diners area ❀ (Bar Garden) ♦♦ Children's menu Children's portions Garden ⋒ Beer festival Parking WiFi

The Plough Inn   PICK OF THE PUBS

tel: 01306 711793 **Coldharbour Ln RH5 6HD**
email: landlord@ploughinn.com
dir: *M25 junct 9, A24 to Dorking. A25 towards Guildford. Coldharbour signed from one-way system*

Well-established pub moving with the times

Set in the heart of the Surrey Hills Area of Outstanding Natural Beauty, this charming 17th-century coaching inn has been brought bang up to date. Since John and Becky Hopper took it over in September 2015, refurbishment has created a new bar, kitchen and shop; even the car park has been greatly improved. Nearby Leith Hill, the highest point in south-east England at 965 feet, makes the pub a popular watering hole for walkers and cyclists needing sustenance after their exertions. The hill lends its name to the pub's own on-site craft brewery. The menu proffers good country fare sourced locally if possible, so start with potted crab with chive butter and granary toast, and continue with lamb rump, served pink, with Moroccan couscous and herb-whipped Greek yogurt; and finish with lemon and lime cheesecake. Lighter lunches include a ploughman's and assorted sandwiches.

Open all day all wk 11.30am-close **Food** Lunch Mon-Fri 12-2.45, Sat 12-9, Sun 12-4.45 Dinner Mon-Fri 6-9, Sat 12-9 ⊕ FREE HOUSE ◀ Leith Hill Crooked Furrow, Hogs Back, John Thompson Gold ♂ Biddenden, Hogs Back Hazy Hog. ♚ 10 **Facilities** Non-diners area ♦♦ Children's menu Children's portions Garden Outside area ⋒ Parking WiFi ⛟ (notice required)

COMPTON
Map 6 SU94

The Withies Inn

tel: 01483 421158 **Withies Ln GU3 1JA**
dir: *Phone for detailed directions*

Eclectically furnished old village inn

This low-beamed inn has slumbered beside the wooded common for five centuries, maturing into a popular, cosy village local enhanced by an intimate restaurant area, where seasonal specials tumble from the menu. Start off with seafood crêpe mornay; mushrooms in garlic butter; or paw paw with fresh crab; then move on to mains like escalope of veal Marsala; mushroom Stroganoff; grilled calves' liver with bacon and onions; or poached halibut with prawns and brandy sauce. After you've finished you could take a stroll in the lovely surrounding countryside, or relax in the garden with a pint of TEA (Traditional English Ale) from the local Hogs Back Brewery.

Open 11-3 6-11 (Fri-Sat 11-11) Closed Sun eve **Food** Lunch all wk 12-2.30 (Fri-Sat 12-3) Dinner Mon-Sat 6-10 Restaurant menu available all wk ⊕ FREE HOUSE ◀ Hogs Back TEA, Greene King IPA, Adnams, Sharp's Doom Bar ⌀ Hogs Back Hazy Hog. ▾ 12 **Facilities** Non-diners area ♦ Children's portions Garden ⌂ Parking WiFi ▭ (notice required)

CRANLEIGH
Map 6 TQ03

The Richard Onslow

tel: 01483 274922 **113-117 High St GU6 8AU**
email: hello@therichardonslow.co.uk
dir: *From A281 between Guildford & Horsham take B2130 to Cranleigh, pub in village centre*

A classy village dining-pub

This grand old tile-hung pub stands at the heart of what claims to be England's largest village. While necessarily updating the interior, owners Peach Pubs worked hard to retain its period appeal, particularly the original brick inglenook in the bar, where you can enjoy Surrey-brewed Shere Drop (named after a nearby village) and Firebird Heritage XX real ales. With the emphasis firmly on top-notch seasonal produce, and meat supplied a very reliable butcher, expect Cornish lamb rump; dry-aged steaks from British grass-fed cattle; fillet of Loch Duart salmon; breast of chicken with crispy bread pudding; and pappardelle of sprouting broccoli, pine nuts, sun-dried tomato and Wensleydale Blue cheese.

Open all day all wk Closed 25 Dec **Food** Mon-Sat 12-10, Sun 12-9 ⊕ FREE HOUSE/ PEACH PUBS ◀ Surrey Hills Shere Drop, Firebird Heritage XX ⌀ Hogs Back Hazy Hog, Aspall. ▾ **Facilities** Non-diners area ♦ (Bar Outside area) ♦ Children's portions Outside area ⌂ Beer festival Parking WiFi ▭ (notice required)

DUNSFOLD
Map 6 TQ03

The Sun Inn

tel: 01483 200242 **The Common GU8 4LE**
email: suninn@dunsfold.net
dir: *A281 through Shalford & Bramley, take B2130 to Godalming. Dunsfold in 2m*

Traditional village pub charm

After 14 years at the helm, Chris and Yvonne Lindesay finally bought the freehold of this 17th-century inn in September 2015. With tables and benches on the green opposite, the pub is well within earshot of "Howzat!" from the adjacent cricket pitch. Beams and blazing fires add to the character of the pub, which offers a line-up of eight real ales including Adnams and Harvey's. The inn's own vegetable garden contributes generously to daily menus, typically featuring courgette and brie soup; chilli con carne; and chicken and chorizo pie. Dogs will certainly appreciate the free biscuits kept in the bar.

Open all day all wk **Food** Lunch all wk 12-2.30 Dinner Mon-Sat 7-9.15, Sun 7-8.30 ⊕ FREE HOUSE ◀ Sharp's Doom Bar, Harvey's Sussex, Adnams, Marston's Wainwright, local guest ales ⌀ Westons Scrumpy, Old Rosie & Stowford Press. ▾ 10 **Facilities** Non-diners area ♦ (Bar Garden) ♦ Children's menu Children's portions Garden ⌂ Parking WiFi ▭ (notice required)

EASHING
Map 6 SU94

The Stag on the River

tel: 01483 421568 **Lower Eashing GU7 2QG**
email: bookings@stagontherivereashing.co.uk
dir: *From A3 S'bound exit signed Eashing, 200yds over river bridge. Pub on right*

A good meeting place by the river

Located on the banks of the River Wey, this comfortable, well-appointed village inn takes full advantage, with a large garden and separate patio. Fixtures on hand pump in the bar are Hogs Back TEA (Traditional English Ale) and their own Red Mist Ale, other local beers rotate. A seasonal menu might begin with home-made black pudding and pork Scotch egg; or a charcuterie sharing plate. Main courses include chicken and chorizo pie with sweet potato mash; or braised beef shin in red wine sauce. For dessert try apple and toffee strudel with locally-made ice cream.

Open all day all wk Closed 25 Dec **Food** Lunch Mon-Sat 12-3, Sun 12-8.30 Dinner Mon-Sat 6-9, Sun 12-8.30 ⊕ FREE HOUSE ◀ Hogs Back TEA, Red Mist, guest ales ⌀ Hogs Back Hazy Hog. ▾ 12 **Facilities** Non-diners area ♦ (Bar Garden) ♦ Children's menu Children's portions Garden ⌂ Parking WiFi

EAST CLANDON
Map 6 TQ05

The Queens Head

tel: 01483 222332 **The Street GU4 7RY**
email: bookings@queensheadeastclandon.co.uk
dir: *4m E of Guildford on A246. Signed*

Village pub with a tree-shaded garden

With the North Downs Way (linking Farnham and the White Cliffs of Dover) nearby, you can expect fleece-clad backpackers alongside the locals here. Surrey, Kent and Hampshire real ales are part of the appeal, together with top quality locally sourced food in dishes such as ham hock terrine with home-made piccalilli. Surrounding farms and suppliers contribute to the main course dishes too – black pudding sausages and mash; and British steak ale and mushroom pie.

Open all wk 12-3 6-11 (Sat 12-11 Sun 12-9) **Food** Lunch Mon-Fri 12-2.30, Sat 12-9.30, Sun 12-8 Dinner Mon-Thu 6-9, Fri 6-9.30, Sat 12-9.30, Sun 12-8 Set menu available ⊕ FREE HOUSE ◀ Hogs Back TEA, Red Mist, guest ales ⌀ Hogs Back Hazy Hog. ▾ 13 **Facilities** Non-diners area ♦ (All areas) ♦ Children's menu Children's portions Garden Outside area ⌂ Parking WiFi ▭

EFFINGHAM
Map 6 TQ15

The Plough

tel: 01372 458121 **Orestan Ln KT24 5SW**
email: info@theplougheffingham.co.uk
dir: *Between Guildford & Leatherhead on A246*

Ever-reliable walkers' favourite

Hidden gems once discovered can lose their sparkle, but not this super little Surrey Hills pub. New improvements, courtesy of the landlord's wife, have made the dining room and bar more comfortable; outside is a pretty garden and terrace, where walkers and cyclists are often to be found nursing Naked Ladies, Redheads (both real ales, you understand) and Shere Drop. Monthly-changing menus offer contemporary and traditional favourites, such as pan-roasted duck breast with leek and bread pudding; cod fillet with clams and cockles; and Cumberland sausages with spring onion mash. The National Trust's Polesden Lacey and the Royal Horticultural Society's Wisley Gardens are nearby.

Open all wk 11-3 5.30-11 (Sun 12-5.30) Closed 25-26 Dec & 31 Dec eve **Food** Lunch Mon-Sat 12-2.30, Sun 12-4.30 Dinner Mon-Thu 6.30-9.30, Fri-Sat 6.30-10 ⊕ YOUNG'S ◀ Special, Twickenham Fine Ales, Redhead, Naked Ladies & Grandstand, Surrey Hills Shere Drop ♻ Aspall. ☗ 16 **Facilities** Non-diners area ◀◀ Children's menu Children's portions Garden Outside area ⊟ Parking WiFi

ELSTEAD
Map 6 SU94

The Woolpack

tel: 01252 703106 **The Green, Milford Rd GU8 6HD**
email: info@woolpackelstead.co.uk
dir: *A3 S, take Milford exit, follow signs for Elstead on B3001*

Village local with an Italian flavour

Originally a wool exchange dating back to the 17th century, the attractive tile-hung Woolpack continues to display weaving shuttles and other artefacts relating to the wool industry. You'll also find open log fires, low beams, high-backed settles, comfortable window seats and cask-conditioned ales including local Hogs Back TEA and Ringwood Fortyniner. The menu features Italian dishes from the owners' home country, plus there's a sandwich menu and a wide selection of stone-baked pizzas. The surrounding common land attracts ramblers galore, especially at lunchtime.

Open all wk 12-3 5.30-late (Sun 12-late) ⊕ PUNCH TAVERNS ◀ Ringwood Fortyniner, Hogs Back TEA, Sharp's Doom Bar ♻ Westons Stowford Press. **Facilities** ◀ (Bar Garden) ◀◀ Children's menu Children's portions Play area Garden Parking WiFi

ENGLEFIELD GREEN
Map 6 SU97

The Fox and Hounds

tel: 01784 433098 **Bishopsgate Rd TW20 0XU**
email: marketing@thefoxandhoundsrestaurant.com
dir: *M25 junct 13, A30 signed Basingstoke & Camberley. Right at lights onto A328 signed Englefield Green. With village green on left, left into Bishopsgate Rd*

Friendly pub by Windsor Great Park

Dating back to 1780, this pub is ideally situated next to the Bishopsgate entrance to Windsor Great Park in the village of Englefield Green. Enjoy a pint of Brakspear bitter in the stylish bar or a slap-up meal in the light and elegant conservatory restaurant. The locally sourced ingredients create a wide ranging choice of dishes, from wild mushrooms, toasted brioche and crispy hen's egg to the Hampshire pork tenderloin, cabbage and bacon with Calvados jus. Leave room for one of the home-made desserts or the tasting plate of puddings that's for sharing. Summer barbecues are popular events.

Open all day all wk 8am-11pm **Food** all wk 12-9.30 Set menu available Restaurant menu available all wk ⊕ FREE HOUSE/BRAKSPEAR ◀ Brakspear Bitter & Oxford Gold ♻ Symonds. ☗ 14 **Facilities** Non-diners area ◀ (Bar Garden) ◀◀ Children's menu Children's portions Garden ⊟ Parking WiFi ➡ (notice required)

FARNHAM
Map 5 SU84

The Bat & Ball Freehouse
PICK OF THE PUBS

tel: 01252 792108 **15 Bat & Ball Ln, Boundstone GU10 4SA**
email: info@thebatandball.co.uk
dir: *From A31 (Farnham bypass) onto A325 signed Birdworld. Left at Bengal Lounge. At T-junct right, immediately left into Sandrock Hill Rd. 0.25m left into Upper Bourne Ln. Follow signs*

A mid-Victorian free house well worth seeking out

A little tricky to find – it's down a long cul-de-sac – but you'll be pleased you persevered. It's a real community pub, with terracotta floors, oak beams, a warming fire and cricketing memorabilia, while in the garden you'll find a patio with picnic tables, a vine-topped pergola and a children's fort. Six frequently-changing real ales come from regional microbreweries, and the ciders are Thatchers and the local Hazy Hog. Lizzy, daughter of owners Kevin and Sally Macready, masterminds a menu comprising both modern and traditional dishes. After a starter of smoked duck carpaccio, maybe, main courses might include chicken and ham pie; roasted belly pork with smoky maple baked beans and winter pecan slaw; or a rib-eye steak. A huge choice of ales and ciders is laid on during the beer, cider and music festival during the second weekend in June.

Open all day all wk 11-11 (Sun 12-10.30) **Food** Lunch Mon-Fri 12-2.15, Sat 12-9.30, Sun 12-8.30 Dinner Mon-Fri 7-9.30, Sat 12-9.30, Sun 12-8.30 ⊕ FREE HOUSE ◀ Hogs Back TEA, Triple fff, Bowman, Ballards, Andwell, Arundel, Weltons, Itchen Valley ♻ Thatchers, Hogs Back Hazy Hog. ☗ 8 **Facilities** Non-diners area ◀ (All areas) ◀◀ Children's menu Children's portions Play area Family room Garden Outside area ⊟ Beer festival Cider festival Parking WiFi

The Spotted Cow at Lower Bourne

tel: 01252 726541 **Bourne Grove, Lower Bourne GU10 3QT**
email: thespottedcow@btinternet.com
dir: *From Farnham town centre, cross rail line, onto B3001. Right into Tilford Rd, up hill, at lights straight on, Bourne Grove 3rd right*

Idyllic woodland and garden setting

Set in four acres of secluded, woodland-shaded grounds and two gardens, one of which is enclosed and especially suitable for young children, The Spotted Cow is a perfect place to unwind. Try a pint of TEA from nearby Hogs Back Brewery and consider the ever-changing menu of tried-and-tested favourites, all made fresh on the premises. Sandwiches and jackets are on the bar lunch menu, while regularly-changing specials could include oven-baked salmon with braised fennel; tomato, brie and spinach risotto; and the 'ultimate' veggie burger – roasted aubergine, beef tomato, onion marmalade and breaded goats' cheese in a brioche bun.

Open all wk 12-3 5.30-11 (Sat 12-11 Sun 12-10.30) ⊕ FREE HOUSE ◀ Timothy Taylor Landlord, Hogs Back TEA, Sharp's Doom Bar ♻ Addlestones. **Facilities** ◀ (Bar Garden) ◀◀ Children's portions Play area Garden Parking WiFi

NEW The Wheatsheaf

tel: 01252 717135 **19 West St GU9 7DR**
email: bookings@thewheatsheaffarnham.co.uk
dir: *In town centre*

Contemporary style in a traditional town centre pub

This relaxed red brick pub has had a very stylish makeover, all pale grey paintwork and eclectic furnishings. Have a pint of local or craft beer, or check out the G&T Club (every Wednesday). Local, sustainable food is the kitchen's motto, and they offer light lunches and a gluten-free menu as well as the seasonal à la carte. Share a deli board, or start with English venison and green pepper salami with fig compôte, dressed rocket and beetroot syrup; move on to lentil, spinach and mushroom cottage pie with parmesan mash; or grilled fillet of sea bass with saffron and spring onion risotto and spiced crayfish butter.

Open all day all wk 11-11 (Fri-Sat 11am-mdnt Sun 11-10.30) Closed 25 Dec **Food** Contact pub for food times ⊕ FREE HOUSE ◀ Hogs Back TEA, Andwell Red Mist, Triple fff Alton's Pride Ö Hogs Back Hazy Hog. ♉ 14 **Facilities** Non-diners area ♣ (Bar Restaurant Outside area) ♦♦ Children's menu Children's portions Outside area ⊨ WiFi ▭ (notice required)

| FOREST GREEN | Map 6 TQ14 |

The Parrot Inn   PICK OF THE PUBS

tel: 01306 621339 **RH5 5RZ**
email: drinks@theparrot.co.uk
dir: *B2126 from A29 at Ockley, signed Forest Green*

Inviting 17th-century country pub with its own farm

Overlooking the village green and cricket pitch, this tile-hung Surrey pub is friendly and welcoming. The low-beamed bar, complete with flagstone floor and huge brass fireplace, is delightfully traditional, and French doors lead to a sheltered, paved terrace. Owner Linda Gotto raises rare-breed pigs, Shorthorn cattle and Dorset sheep at her farm in nearby Dorking, and you can buy some of her produce in Butchers Hall, an on-site farm shop. You'll also find it on the plate in the restaurant, along with other quality ingredients. Kick things off with Middle White pork and pistachio terrine with toast and chutney; or pigeon pastrami and buttered kale on toasted rye bread, before a main of chargrilled hogget chops, Lyonnaise potatoes and kale; pot-roasted guinea fowl, chestnut mushrooms, fine beans, baby potatoes and smoked bacon sauce; or herb-baked hake with roasted fennel, white bean and chervil sauce.

Open all day all wk Closed 25 Dec **Food** Lunch Mon-Sat 12-3, Sun 12-5 Dinner Mon-Thu 6-9.30, Fri-Sat 6-10 Av main course £14 ⊕ FREE HOUSE ◀ Ringwood Best Bitter & Old Thumper, Timothy Taylor Landlord, Dorking DB Number One, Fuller's London Pride Ö Aspall, Hogs Back Hazy Hog. ♉ 14 **Facilities** Non-diners area ♣ (Bar Garden) Children's portions Garden ⊨ Parking WiFi

---

| GUILDFORD | Map 6 SU94 |

The Weyside

tel: 01483 568024 **Millbrook GU1 3XJ**
email: weyside@youngs.co.uk
dir: *From Guildford take A281 towards Shalford. Pub on right*

When in Guildford, definitely one to head for

Overlooking the River Wey, this is one humdinger of a pub. The decor, the furnishings, the accessorising – all have been conceived and applied by people who understand good interior design. There are plenty of places to eat and drink, not

least on the waterside decking (first grab some bread from the bowl on bar to feed the ducks). There's even a 'dog corner', with beds, treats and towels. Typical menu items are pan-seared bavette steak with horseradish crème fraîche; 8oz piri-piri pork steak, chorizo and tomato crushed potatoes, basil dressing; and Young's beer-battered cod, rustic chips and garden peas.

Open all day all wk **Food** Sun-Fri 12-9, Sat 12-10 ⊕ YOUNG'S ◀ Bitter & Special Ö Aspall. ♉ 15 **Facilities** Non-diners area ♣ (Bar Garden) ♦♦ Children's menu Children's portions Garden ⊨ WiFi

---

| HASLEMERE | Map 6 SU93 |

The Wheatsheaf Inn ★★★ INN

tel: 01428 644440 **Grayswood Rd, Grayswood GU27 2DE**
email: thewheatsheaf@aol.com **web:** www.thewheatsheafgrayswood.co.uk
dir: *From Haslemere take A286 to Grayswood, approx 7.5m*

Woodland-edge setting in the Surrey Hills

The Wheatsheaf Inn is a very distinctive, part hang-tiled Edwardian pub with enough vegetation to give Kew Gardens a run for its money. The hanging-basket festooned verandah, creeper-covered pergola and patio and colourful garden just invite a lingering visit with a pint of Sharp's Atlantic to hand, relaxing after a walk in the enfolding Surrey Hills beloved by Tennyson. There's opportunity to stay overnight here in one of the comfy rooms so creating an added excuse to engage with a wide-ranging menu of pub classics and thoughtful specials. Kick in with warmed brie, Cumberland sauce and rustic bread, moving along to hake fillet in real ale batter with chips; or honey-glazed ham with egg and chips. There's also a selection of steaks, sandwiches and salads, but be sure to leave room for some sticky toffee pudding, or apple and rhubarb crumble.

Open all wk 11-3 6-11 (Sun 12-3 7-10.30) **Food** Lunch all wk 12-2 Dinner all wk 7-9.45 Av main course £10.95 ⊕ FREE HOUSE ◀ Fuller's London Pride, Sharp's Doom Bar & Atlantic, Greene King Abbot Ale Ö Aspall. **Facilities** Non-diners area ♣ (Bar Garden) ♦♦ Children's menu Children's portions Garden ⊨ Parking WiFi **Rooms** 7

| HORSELL | Map 6 SU95 |

NEW The Red Lion

tel: 01483 768497 **123 High St GU21 4SS**
email: info@redlionhorsell.co.uk
dir: *In village centre*

Village pub with stunning garden

Less than a mile from Woking, this smart village pub is very much at the heart of the community, but it attracts diners from all over Surrey. The beautiful garden is a major draw in the summer, but real fires and sumptuous sofas and armchairs make it a cosy place in winter. Enjoy one of the 14 wines served by the glass or a pint of well-kept real ale before heading to the restaurant. Crispy fried sesame king prawns, wasabi and lime mayonnaise might be followed by pork belly, creamy mash, spiced plums, buttered kale and red wine jus.

Open all day all wk **Food** Lunch all wk 12-5 Dinner all wk 5-10 Av main course £12 ⊕ STAR PUBS ◀ Butcombe, Fuller's London Pride, St Austell Tribute, guest ale Ö Symonds. ♉ 14 **Facilities** Non-diners area ♣ (Garden) ♦♦ Children's menu Children's portions Garden ⊨ Parking WiFi ▭ (notice required)

LEIGH
Map 6 TQ24

The Plough

tel: 01306 611348 **Church Rd RH2 8NJ**
email: sarah@theploughleigh.wanadoo.co.uk
dir: *Phone for detailed directions*

Ramblers' retreat in the Surrey countryside

Some parts of this appealing, architecturally mixed-up building are known to date from the 15th century, whilst the popular locals' bar with its fire and traditional pub games is somewhat younger. Situated by a large green bordered by old houses and the medieval church, The Plough today is a cracking village pub. Beers from the Hall & Woodhouse list slake the thirst of walkers enjoying exploration of the Surrey Weald, whilst the popular pub grub menu of bangers and mash or fish and chips is supplemented by chicken fillet, Black Forest ham or lamb steak dishes. The home-made pies also prove very popular.

Open all wk 11-11 (Sun 12-11) **Food** all wk 12-9 ⊕ HALL & WOODHOUSE ◀ Badger Dorset Best, Tanglefoot, K&B Sussex Ò Westons Rosie's Pig. ⚑ 11
Facilities Non-diners area ❤ (Bar Garden) ♦️ Children's menu Children's portions Garden ㅈ Parking WiFi ☞

The Seven Stars

tel: 01306 611254 **Bunce Common Rd, Dawes Green RH2 8NP**
email: info@7starsleigh.co.uk
dir: *S of A25 (Dorking to Reigate road)*

Timeless tavern with high-quality food

This early 17th-century tile-hung tavern is tucked away in the rural southern reaches of the Mole Valley, its charm enhanced by the absence of games machines, TV screens and piped music. The older bar is centred on an inglenook fireplace at one end and a log-burning stove at the other. The food served is of high quality and is prepared by a team of chefs using local produce whenever possible. Typical dishes include pork and herb terrine, which might be followed by steak and ale pie or supreme of chicken. At the front is a garden for those with a drink, at the side a patio and garden for diners, and there's ample parking space.

Open all wk 12-11 (Sun 12-10) ⊕ PUNCH TAVERNS ◀ Fuller's London Pride, Young's, Harvey's Sussex, guest ales Ò Westons Mortimers Orchard. **Facilities** ❤ (Bar Garden) ♦️ Children's menu Children's portions Garden Parking

LONG DITTON
Map 6 TQ16

The Ditton
PICK OF THE PUBS

tel: 020 8339 0785 **64 Ditton Hill Rd KT6 5JD**
email: goodfood@theditton.co.uk
dir: *Phone for detailed directions*

Suburban local not far from Hampton Court

With its large, south-facing beer garden, The Ditton is clearly a popular community local. Playing their part of course are beers from Sambrook's, Surrey Hills and Truman's and a good choice of wines by the glass. A typical menu offers ciabattas, wraps and jacket potatoes; potato skins topped with Stilton and bacon; toad-in-the-hole with bubble-and-squeak, fried onions and gravy; and vegetable lasagne with garlic bread and dressed salad. Fish dishes are there too, such as breaded

wholetail scampi; as well as beef and Cajun chicken burgers; and home-made, hand-stretched pizzas. Children's main courses arrive with an ice lolly. Those irresistible old favourites, sticky date and toffee pudding, and chocolate and caramel tart, both with Yorvale vanilla ice cream, are characteristic desserts. Skittle alley league nights are every Monday, and quiz nights are Tuesday. Summer barbecues are held in the garden and live music backs a popular June beer and cider festival.

Open all day all wk 12-11 **Food** Lunch Mon-Sat 12-9, Sun 12-5 Dinner Mon-Sat 12-9 ⊕ ENTERPRISE INNS ◀ Sharp's Doom Bar, Sambrook's Wandle, Surrey Hills Shere Drop, Truman's Swift, Otter Bitter. ⚑ 10 **Facilities** Non-diners area ❤ (Bar Garden) ♦️ Children's menu Children's portions Play area Garden ㅈ Beer festival Cider festival Parking WiFi ☞ (notice required)

MICKLEHAM
Map 6 TQ15

The Running Horses

tel: 01372 372279 **Old London Rd RH5 6DU**
email: info@therunninghorses.co.uk
dir: *M25 junct 9, A24 towards Dorking. Left signed Mickleham & B2209*

Lovely country inn below Box Hill

Built in the 16th century, the inn had an important role as a coaching house, but it also sheltered highwaymen – a tiny ladder leading to the roof space was discovered during alterations. The inn acquired its name in 1825 after two horses, Colonel and Cadland, running in the Derby at Epsom, passed the post together. They appear on the inn sign, and the bars are named after them. Food includes home-smoked salmon; devilled kidneys; twice baked cheddar soufflé; Brixham bouillabaisse; grilled spatchcock chicken; and crisp roast pork belly with champ mash. Chunky sandwiches are available at lunchtime.

Open all day all wk 12-11 (Sun 12-10.30) **Food** Lunch Mon-Fri 12-2.30, Sat-12-3, Sun 12-6 Dinner Mon-Thu 6-9, Fri-Sat 6-10, Sun 12-6 Restaurant menu available all wk ⊕ BRAKSPEAR ◀ Bitter & Special, Fuller's London Pride, Ringwood, Dead Heat Derby Ò Symonds. ⚑ 9 **Facilities** Non-diners area ❤ (Bar Garden) ♦️ Children's menu Children's portions Garden ㅈ WiFi

NEWDIGATE
Map 6 TQ14

The Surrey Oaks

tel: 01306 631200 **Parkgate Rd RH5 5DZ**
email: visit-us@surreyoaks.co.uk
dir: *From A24 follow signs to Newdigate, at T-junct turn left, pub 1m on left*

Excellent beers in lovely country pub

This former wheelwright's shop is over 440 years old and still has wood fires burning in the inglenook fireplaces and original flagstones in the bar. At the bar counter you'll find Surrey Hills Shere Drop which is brewed just six miles from the pub. Much of the food on the seasonal menu is cooked in the wood-fired oven, including the steak burger and fish pie. A separate list of 'Daily Doings' features specials from the butchers, fishmongers and gamekeepers.

Open all wk 11.30-2.30 5.30-11 (Sat 11.30-11 Sun 12-9) ⊕ FREE HOUSE ◀ Surrey Hills Ranmore Ale & Shere Drop, guest ales Ò Snails Bank Tumbledown, Sandford Orchards Shaky Bridge, guest perry. **Facilities** ❤ (Bar Garden) ♦️ Children's portions Play area Garden Parking WiFi

RIPLEY
Map 6 TQ05

The Anchor ⑳⑳

tel: 01483 211866 **High St GU23 6AE**
email: info@ripleyanchor.co.uk **web:** www.ripleyanchor.co.uk
dir: *M25 junct 10, A3 towards Guildford, then B2215 to Ripley*

Great food in a historic building

In the late 19th century, as cycling became increasingly popular, Ripley became a well-known stop on the London-Portsmouth road, and The Anchor was a favourite port of call. One of the town's most historic pubs, it was built as an almshouse in the early 16th century. Local and regional produce features on the menus, appearing in dishes such as warm soft poached egg, roast artichoke, charred broccoli and maple syrup; pan-fried gurnard fillet, salt-baked celeriac, parsley root, chard with white grape and parsley sauce; roast leek tart and king oyster mushroom; and Black Forest chocolate mousse, poached cherries and cherry sorbet.

Open all day Closed 25 Dec, Mon **Food** Contact pub for food times Set menu available ⊕ FREE HOUSE ◖ Timothy Taylor Landlord ⚘ Henney's Vintage. ☗ 14 **Facilities** Non-diners area ◖◗ Children's menu Children's portions Outside area ⧖ Parking

SHAMLEY GREEN
Map 6 TQ04

The Red Lion

tel: 01483 892202 **The Green GU5 0UB**
email: debbieersser@gmail.com
dir: *On B2128 between Guildford & Cranleigh*

Classic pub in the Surrey Hills

Film location scouts looking for a pub on a village green will find a prime candidate here. Although 17th century, it has been a pub only since the 1800s; before that it may have been tea rooms. Rich red ceilings and high-backed, red-upholstered settles help create that quintessential warm pubby feeling. A typical carte proposes warm bacon and scallop salad; griddled haloumi with Mediterranean vegetables and pesto; duck stir-fry with Chinese vegetables, chilli and noodles; veal schnitzel cooked in lemon garlic butter, fried egg, fries and salad. Sandwiches, salads, jackets, and ploughman's add to the choices.

Open all day all wk **Food** Lunch Mon-Fri 12-2.30, Sat-Sun 12-3 Dinner Mon-Sat 6.30-9.30, Sun (Apr-Oct) 6.30-8.30 ⊕ PUNCH TAVERNS ◖ Young's IPA, Sharp's Doom Bar & Atlantic, Arundel Sussex Gold ⚘ Aspall, Westons Stowford Press. ☗ 11 **Facilities** Non-diners area ◖ (Bar Garden) ◖◗ Children's menu Children's portions Garden ⧖ Parking WiFi

SOUTH GODSTONE
Map 6 TQ34

Fox & Hounds

tel: 01342 893474 **Tilburstow Hill Rd RH9 8LY**
email: info@foxandhounds.org.uk
dir: *M25 junct 6, A22 to South Godstone. Right into Harts Ln. At T-junct right into Tilburstow Hill Rd*

Haunted country pub with rural views

Dating in part to 1368, the Fox & Hounds has been a pub since 1601. Allegedly, yet eminently believably, 17th-century pirate-turned-smuggler John Trenchman haunts the building, having been ambushed and fatally wounded nearby. The restaurant's large inglenook and the bar's real fire add to the old-world charm. Food-wise there's plenty to choose from, including a potted duck liver and Cointreau pâté starter; mains of haggis, neeps and tatties; fisherman's pie; and hunter's chicken with bacon and barbecue sauce, as well as specials. Landlady Ellie Conway travels weekly to the south coast for her fish. A large garden features a pirate ship play area that will keep children happy.

Open all day all wk **Food** all wk 12-9 ⊕ FREE HOUSE ◖ Greene King Abbot Ale & IPA, guest ales. ☗ 12 **Facilities** Non-diners area ◖ (Bar Garden) ◖◗ Children's menu Children's portions Play area Garden ⧖ Parking WiFi ◻ (notice required)

STOKE D'ABERNON
Map 6 TQ15

The Old Plough

tel: 01932 862244 **2 Station Rd KT11 3BN**
email: info@oldploughcobham.co.uk
dir: *From A245 into Station Rd. Pub on corner*

Friendly, smart community pub

Contemporary decor and traditional lines blend easily at this mature dining inn in the Mole Valley. In earlier times it was the village courthouse; it also features in the Sherlock Holmes story *The Adventure of The Speckled Band*. Local drinkers take summer shade in the peaceful garden and quaff beers from Surrey Hills brewery. Fulfilling meals are at the heart of the business, with a core menu available all day, supplemented by lighter bites available to 5.30pm in both bar and restaurant. A starter of crispy fried sesame king prawns then twice-cooked pork belly, creamy mash, spiced plums, buttered kale and red wine jus are tempting examples of the modern cuisine. Children are welcome in the restaurant area until 7.30pm.

Open all day all wk Closed 26 Dec **Food** 12-9.30 ⊕ FULLER'S ◾ London Pride, Surrey Hills Shere Drop, George Gale & Co Seafarers ♂ Aspall. ♟ 18 **Facilities** Non-diners area ❤ (Bar Garden) ♦ Children's menu Children's portions Garden ⌁ Parking WiFi ▱

THURSLEY
Map 6 SU93

NEW The Three Horseshoes

tel: 01252 703268 **Dye House Rd GU8 6QD**
dir: *From A3 between Hindhead & Milford follow Thursley signs. Pub on left*

Sixteenth-century pub in great walking country

Popular with walkers exploring the Devil's Punchbowl and Thursley Common, this lovely pub can be found in the little village of Thursley. It's been sustaining travellers and locals since the 16th century, and was rescued from five years' closure in 2004 by a group of villagers who didn't want to lose the heart of their community. It has a fantastic garden and patio for alfresco dining, and menus might feature heirloom tomato bruschetta; or chicken liver parfait followed by pan-fried calves' liver with smoked bacon; sausage and mash; or butternut squash risotto with gorgonzola. A good choice of sandwiches is also available.

Open all wk 12-3 5.30-11 (Sat 12-11 Sun 12-10) **Food** Lunch Mon-Sat 12-2.15, Sun 12-3 Dinner Mon-Sat 7-9.15 Av main course £13 ⊕ FREE HOUSE ◾ Hogs Back TEA, Soul of the Shoes. ♟ 12 **Facilities** Non-diners area ❤ (Bar Garden) ♦ Children's portions Play area Garden ⌁ Parking WiFi ▱ (notice required)

TILFORD
Map 5 SU84

The Duke of Cambridge

tel: 01252 792236 **Tilford Rd GU10 2DD**
email: amy.corstin@redmistleisure.co.uk
dir: *From Guildford on A31 towards Farnham follow Tongham, Seale, Runfield signs. Right at end, follow Eashing signs. Left at end, 1st right (signed Tilford St). Over bridge, 1st left, 0.5m*

Family-friendly pub offering wholesome local fodder

Set among pine trees with a lovely garden and terrace, this attractive pub in the Surrey countryside welcomes all, children and dogs included. Expect Surrey ales and locally sourced food on their seasonal menus. Typical you'll find hearty deli boards; slow-cooked Tilford beef and Red Mist Ale pie; and Hampshire steaks. In

May, fundraising for a local charity is just one excuse for holding a beer and music festival. The Garden Bar & Grill is a particular highlight in summer (weather permitting).

Open all wk 11-3 5-11 (Sat 11-11 Sun 12-10.30) Closed 25 Dec & 31 Dec eve **Food** Lunch Mon-Fri 12-2.30, Sat 12-3.30, Sun 12-8.30 Dinner Mon-Fri 6-9, Sat 6-9.30 ⊕ FREE HOUSE/RED MIST LEISURE LTD ◾ Hogs Back, Red Mist guest ales ♂ Hogs Back Hazy Hog. ♟ 15 **Facilities** ❤ (Bar Restaurant Garden) ♦ Children's menu Children's portions Play area Garden ⌁ Beer festival Parking WiFi

WEST CLANDON
Map 6 TQ05

The Onslow Arms

tel: 01483 222447 **The Street GU4 7TE**
email: info@onslowarmsclandon.co.uk
dir: *On A247, S of railway line*

Eye-catching village pub with cosmopolitan appeal

Cyclists and ramblers, drinkers and diners all mix seamlessly at this vibrant and smart community local. The visually striking building retains much character, with a wealth of beams, huge open fire, squashy sofas and chairs set in a light, cool interior. Relax within or on the sheltered terrace with a glass of Tillingbourne Brewery bitter and choose from an all-day menu which offers a great mix of comfort meals and contemporary dishes. Bang bang peanut chicken satay makes a great starter, followed by pan-fried calves' liver, smoked streaky bacon, creamy mash, wilted spinach and sage jus.

Open all day all wk 11-11 (Wed & Fri-Sat 11am-11.30pm Sun 11-10.30) Closed 26 Dec **Food** Sun-Thu 12-9.30, Fri-Sat 12-10 ⊕ FREE HOUSE/PEARMAN PUBS LTD ◾ Surrey Hills Shere Drop, Sharp's Cornish Coaster, Tillingbourne Brewery Ales, Onslow Arms Ale ♂ Mortimers Orchard. ♟ 18 **Facilities** Non-diners area ❤ (Bar Garden) ♦ Children's menu Children's portions Garden ⌁ Parking WiFi ▱

WEST END
Map 6 SU96

The Inn West End ★★★★ INN
PICK OF THE PUBS

See Pick of the Pubs on opposite page

WINDLESHAM
Map 6 SU96

The Half Moon

tel: 01276 473329 **Church Rd GU20 6BN**
email: c@sturt.tv
dir: *M3 junct 3, A322 follow Windlesham signs into New Rd; right at T-junct into Church Rd, pub on right*

Old-fashioned values and friendly service

Family-owned since 1909, Helga and Conrad Sturt's slate-floored, low-beamed, 17th-century free house offers the traditional country pub experience, including locally brewed Hogs Back real ale and Lilley's Bee Sting Pear cider from Somerset. There's plenty of choice at lunchtime, while dinner options include baked camembert with chilli jam; red Thai curry; calves' liver and smoked bacon with bubble-and-squeak; braised venison and ale ragout; and smoked trout salad. Go past the patio terrace into the well-kept beer garden with its children's play area.

Open all day all wk 11-11 ⊕ FREE HOUSE ◾ Sharp's, Theakston, Fuller's, Timothy Taylor, Hogs Back, Palmers, Dark Star ♂ Lilley's Bee Sting Pear, Westons Old Rosie. **Facilities** ❤ (Bar Garden Outside area) ♦ Children's menu Children's portions Play area Garden Outside area Parking WiFi

PICK OF THE PUBS

The Inn West End ★★★★ INN

WEST END   Map 6 SU96

tel: 01276 858652
42 Guildford Rd GU24 9PW
email: greatfood@the-inn.co.uk
web: www.the-inn.co.uk
dir: *On A322 towards Guildford. 3m from M3 junct 3, just beyond Gordon's School rdbt*

Destination restaurant and friendly local pub with bedrooms

It has been said that Gerry and Ann Price's renowned village pub out-manoeuvres many a competitor. One particular attraction is its special wine events, linked to its own on-site wine shop (open on request) whose wide range includes Pinot Noir and Claret collections, magnums of reds, bin ends and own-label Labradouro Tinto, created by Gerry, who loves the Douro region of Portugal, and his Labrador dog. But don't let this passion deter you from just slipping in for a pint of West Berkshire Good Old Boy, local Thurstons Horsell Gold, or Aspall cider, with a newspaper in the bar or out on the clematis-hung terrace overlooking the garden and boules pitch. The modern interior is open plan with wooden floors, crisp linen-clothed tables and an open fire. In the newly revamped kitchen, the brigade make great use of fish from the coast and game from Windsor Great Park, or

shot by Gerry himself. Seasonal menus reveal all with such dishes as Royal pigeon breasts with white pudding, baby beets and port reduction; wild mushroom, chestnut and spinach risotto, rocket and truffle oil; pan-fried selection of fresh British fish with crushed new potatoes, seasonal greens and lemon beurre blanc; and seared calves' liver with haggis mash, spinach, crispy bacon and port jus. At lunchtime, consider pairing Cornish mussels and hand-cut chips with a glass of white Rioja. There's a comprehensive bar menu, too. Weekly fish nights, monthly quizzes and 12 boutique bedrooms further enhance the overall package. Children over five years old are welcome for meals.

Open all wk 7.30am-11pm (Sat 8.30am-11pm Sun 8.30am-10.30pm) **Food** Lunch Mon-Sat 12-2.30, Sun 12-3 Dinner Mon-Sat 6-9.30, Sun 6-9 🍺 FREE HOUSE 🍺 Fuller's London Pride, Dark Star Hophead, Thurstons Horsell Gold, West Berkshire Good Old Boy Ō Aspall. 🍷 15 **Facilities** Non-diners area 🐾 (Bar) Children's portions Garden 🍺 Beer festival Parking WiFi **Rooms** 12

EAST SUSSEX

ALCISTON
Map 6 TQ50

Rose Cottage Inn
PICK OF THE PUBS

tel: 01323 870377 **BN26 6UW**
email: ian@alciston.freeserve.co.uk
dir: Off A27 between Eastbourne & Lewes

Home-cooked food in a pretty cottage

Expect a warm welcome at this traditional village pub, housed in a 17th-century flint cottage complete with roses round the door and a lovely front garden. At the foot of the South Downs, ramblers will find it a good base for long walks in unspoilt countryside, especially along the old traffic-free coach road to the south. With its oak beams and sloping walls and ceilings, the inn has been in the same family for over 40 years, and is well known for its good, home-cooked food, including organic vegetables and local meats, poultry and game. A typical menu starts with smoked salmon cornet filled with prawns; or grilled flat mushrooms marinated in garlic and fresh herbs. Follow with honey-roasted ham with poached egg and chips; confit of duck with cherry and brandy sauce and mash; or traditional beef lasagne.

Open 11.30-3 6.30-11 Closed 25-26 Dec, Sun eve **Food** Lunch all wk 12-2 Dinner Mon-Sat 7-9.30 Restaurant menu available Mon-Sat evening ⊕ FREE HOUSE ◀ Harvey's Sussex Best Bitter, Burning Sky Plateau ♂ Biddenden. ♥ 8 **Facilities** Non-diners area ✿ (Bar Garden Outside area) Children's portions Garden Outside area ⨼ Parking WiFi

ALFRISTON
Map 6 TQ50

George Inn

tel: 01323 870319 **High St BN26 5SY**
email: info@thegeorge-alfriston.com
dir: Phone for detailed directions

Period inn in a lovely location

First licensed to sell beer as far back as 1397, this splendid Grade II listed flint and half-timbered inn is set in a picturesque village with the South Downs Way passing its front door. The heavy oak beams and ancient inglenook fireplace add plenty of character to the bar, whilst the kitchen serves delights such as rustic boards to share; smoked mackerel pâté on toast; crab cakes with saffron mayonnaise; tomato and spinach-stuffed chicken supreme with polenta cakes; Thai green vegetable curry; and banoffee pie or apple compôte, Calvados cream and shortbread to finish. A network of smugglers' tunnels leads from the pub's cellars.

Open all day all wk Closed 25-26 Dec **Food** all wk 12-9 ⊕ GREENE KING ◀ Abbot Ale, Hardys & Hansons Olde Trip, Dark Star Hophead ♂ Aspall. ♥ 14 **Facilities** Non-diners area ✿ (Bar Restaurant Garden) ◗♦ Children's menu Children's portions Garden ⨼ WiFi (notice required)

NEW The Star Inn ★★★★ INN

tel: 01323 840495 **High St BN26 5TA**
email: nicky.osborne@thestaralfriston.co.uk **web:** www.thestaralfriston.co.uk
dir: From A27, at Drusillas rdbt, follow Alfriston signs. Pub on right in High St

Confident cooking in historic village inn

Originally a hostelry for pilgrims making their way from Battle to Chichester, this timber-framed 13th-century pub has a wealth of features including a lion figurehead from a 17th-century shipwreck. Refurbished in 2015, the heavy beams and real fires are still present and correct, with the 37 elegant bedrooms and restaurant offering a more contemporary comforts. Order a pint of locally brewed Harvey's ale as you choose from a locally-sourced menu that includes steamed clams with spaghetti, pancetta, chilli and white wine, perhaps followed by pan-fried organic lamb's liver, mash, greens, bacon and roast onion gravy.

Open all day all wk **Food** Lunch all wk 12-2 Dinner all wk 6-9 ⊕ FREE HOUSE ◀ Harvey's, Long Man ♂ Westons Stowford Press, Old Mout. ♥ 10 **Facilities** Non-diners area ✿ (Bar Garden) ◗♦ Children's menu Children's portions Garden ⨼ Parking WiFi (notice required) **Rooms** 37

ASHBURNHAM PLACE
Map 6 TQ61

Ash Tree Inn

tel: 01424 892104 **Brownbread St TN33 9NX**
email: ashtreeinn@gmail.com
dir: From Eastbourne take A271 at Boreham Bridge towards Battle. Next left, follow pub signs

Country pub that welcomes walkers

Deep in the Sussex countryside on the delightfully named Brownbread Street, the 400-year-old Ash Tree is a hub of local activity, hosting everything from quiz nights to cricket club meetings. It boasts a warm and bright interior, replete with stripped wooden floors, four fireplaces (two of them inglenooks), exposed beams and a friendly local atmosphere. Expect to find Harvey's ale on tap and traditional home-cooked meals such as battered tiger prawns with sweet chilli dip; or soup of the day followed by steak and kidney pudding or ham, free-range eggs and chips. Dishes are created from locally caught fish and seafood and locally produced meat and game. Walkers and dogs are welcome.

Open 12-4 7-11 (Sat 11.30am-mdnt) Closed Mon pm (Sun pm winter) **Food** Lunch Mon-Sat 12-2.30, Sun 12-4 (summer Sun 12-5) Dinner Tue-Thu 7-9, Fri-Sat 6-9 (summer Fri-Sat 6-9.30) Av main course £12 ⊕ FREE HOUSE ◀ Harvey's Sussex Best Bitter, guest ales ♂ Westons Stowford Press. **Facilities** Non-diners area ✿ (Bar Restaurant Garden) ◗♦ Children's portions Garden ⨼ Parking WiFi (notice required)

BERWICK
Map 6 TQ50

The Cricketers Arms
PICK OF THE PUBS

tel: 01323 870469 **BN26 6SP**
email: info@cricketersberwick.co.uk
dir: At x-roads on A27 (between Polegate & Lewes) follow Berwick sign, pub on right

Popular with South Downs walkers

Previously two farmworkers' cottages dating from the 16th century, this flintstone building was an alehouse for 200 years, until around 50 years ago Harvey's of Lewes, Sussex's oldest brewery, bought it and turned it into a 'proper' pub. The Grade II listed building, in beautiful cottage gardens, is close to many popular walks – the South Downs Way runs along the crest of the chalk scarp between here and the sea. Three beamed, music-free rooms with stone floors and open fires are simply furnished with old pine furniture. A short menu of home-made food includes pork and pistachio terrine; and home-cured gravad lax as starters. Their home-made burger is an ever-popular main course, as are winter favourites such as a shortcrust pie with a variety of fillings (look to the blackboard for daily choices); and pork and herb sausages (served with a free-range egg and chunky chips) from the local butcher in Seaford. Nearby is Charleston Farmhouse, the country rendezvous of the Bloomsbury Group of writers, painters and intellectuals, and venue for an annual literary festival.

Open all wk Mon-Fri 11-3 6-11 Sat 11-11 Sun 12-9 (Etr-Sep Mon-Sat 11-11 Sun 12-10.30) Closed 25 Dec **Food** Lunch Oct-Apr Mon-Fri 12-2.15, Sat-Sun 12-9, Etr-Sep all wk 12-9 Dinner Oct-Apr Mon-Fri 6.15-9, Sat-Sun 12-9, Etr-Sep all wk 12-9 Av main course £12 ⊕ HARVEY'S OF LEWES ◀ Sussex Best Bitter, Armada Ale & IPA ♂ Thatchers, Westons Stowford Press. ♥ 12 **Facilities** ✿ (Bar Garden) ◗♦ Children's portions Family room Garden ⨼ Parking WiFi (notice required)

BLACKBOYS
Map 6 TQ52

The Blackboys Inn

tel: 01825 890283 **Lewes Rd TN22 5LG**
email: info@theblackboys.co.uk
dir: *From A22 at Uckfield take B2102 towards Cross in Hand. Or from A267 at Esso service station in Cross in Hand take B2102 towards Uckfield. Village 1.5m*

Hamlet pub known for its Sunday roasts

This inn was named after the local charcoal-burners, or the soot-caked 'blackboys', with whom the 14th-century pub was once a favourite. Today's well-scrubbed visitors enjoy beers from Harvey's of Lewes in one of two bars, and in the restaurant, vegetables from the garden, game from local shoots, and fish from Rye and Hastings. Typical dishes include pork Stroganoff with linguine; chicken, mushroom and leek pie; and bouillabaisse. Outside are rambling grounds with resident ducks and an orchard. There are quiz nights and open mic nights.

Open all day all wk 12-11 (Sun 12-10) ⊕ HARVEY'S OF LEWES ◀ Sussex Best Bitter, Sussex Hadlow Bitter, Sussex Old Ale, seasonal ales. **Facilities** ❤ (Bar Restaurant Garden) ◀❙ Children's menu Children's portions Garden Parking WiFi

BRIGHTON & HOVE
Map 6 TQ30

The Basketmakers Arms

tel: 01273 689006 **12 Gloucester Rd BN1 4AD**
email: bluedowd@hotmail.co.uk
dir: *From Brighton station main entrance 1st left (Gloucester Rd). Pub on right at bottom of hill*

Leave The Lanes to the tourists and find this cracker

Peter Dowd has run his Victorian back-street local with passion and pride for nearly 30 years. Tucked away in the bohemian North Laine area, quirky customer messages left in vintage tins on the walls have made the pub a local legend. Expect to find a splendid selection of Fuller's and guest ales, around 100 malt whiskies and rarely seen vodkas, gins and bourbons. The menu lists popular plates, whose affordability is noteworthy. Sandwiches, baguettes, cheesy chips and garlic bread are some of the snack options. For a larger appetite, choose from good quality steaks, a range of burgers, and locally caught fish. The specials board changes daily.

Open all day all wk 11-11 (Fri-Sat 11am-mdnt Sun 12-11) **Food** all wk 12-9 ⊕ FULLER'S ◀ London Pride, ESB, Bengal Lancer, HSB & Seafarers, Castle Rock Harvest Pale, Butcombe, guest ales. **Facilities** ❤ (Bar Restaurant) ◀❙ Outside area ⊓ WiFi

NEW The Chimney House

tel: 01273 556708 **28 Upper Hamilton Rd BN1 5DF**
email: info@chimneyhousebrighton.co.uk
dir: *From B2122 at Seven Dials rdbt into Dyke Rd, right into Old Shoreham Rd, 2nd left into Buxton Rd, pub on right at end*

Innovative cooking of local and foraged ingredients

Just north of Seven Dials in the residential area of Port Hall, this convivial Brighton pub keeps the neighbours happy with locally brewed Harvey's and Arundel Sussex Gold ales. Close links with Sussex producers, growers and foragers means a menu that changes with the seasons. A starter of breadcrumbed pig's head, rosehip and hazelnuts might be followed by a main course of hogget breast with carrots, onion, chervil and watermint. Leave a space for innovative desserts such as cherry plum blossom, milk, hay, sorrel and birch syrup.

Open all day 12-11 Closed 25-26 Dec, Mon **Food** Lunch Tue-Fri 12-3, Sat 12-4, Sun 12-5 Dinner Tue-Wed 6-9, Thu-Sat 6-9.45 Av main course £13 ⊕ PUNCH TAVERNS ◀ Harvey's Sussex Best Bitter, Arundel Sussex Gold Ö Westons Stowford Press. ⬙ **Facilities** Non-diners area ❤ (Bar Outside area) ◀❙ Children's menu Children's portions Outside area ⊓ WiFi ▭ (notice required)

The Ginger Pig

tel: 01273 736123 **3 Hove St, Hove BN3 2TR**
email: gingerpig@gingermanrestaurants.com
dir: *From A259 (seafront) into Hove St*

Excellent food and local ale

Very much a food pub, The Ginger Pig puts a lot of emphasis on seasonality and has a strong reputation for game and local sea food. The monthly-changing menu might offer starters including crispy lamb belly with braised chickpeas; or grilled octopus with hot Nduja sausage and Grelot onion; while for a main course you could have hogget hot pot, Brussels sprout tops and anchovy butter; whole lemon sole with salt-baked kohl rabi, grapefruit dressing and tarragon; or pork roast fillet with lardo di Colonnata, black pudding, celeriac purée, rhubarb chutney and mustard greens. Follow that with roast pineapple with black sesame ice cream perhaps. There's a grand old bar at the front serving great cocktails and well-kept local ales, like Bedlam, Brighton Bier or Dark Star.

Open all day all wk Closed 25 Dec **Food** Lunch 12-2.30 Dinner 6.30-10 Av main course £6-£9 Set menu available Restaurant menu available all wk ⊕ FREE HOUSE ◀ Bedlam, Dark Star, Brighton Bier, Gun Brewery Pale Ale, Burning Sky Plateau. ⬙ 20 **Facilities** Non-diners area ❤ (Bar Garden) ◀❙ Children's menu Children's portions Garden ⊓ WiFi ▭ (notice required)

The Urchin

tel: 01273 241881 **15-17 Belfast St BN3 3YS**
email: hello@urchinpub.co.uk
dir: *From A259 (coast road) into Hove St (A2023). Right into Blatchington Rd at lights. 4th right into Haddington St, right into Malvern St, left into Belfast St to pub (one-way system)*

Specialist craft beer and shellfish combo

Now well established as part of Brighton's star-studded eating and drinking scene, this has become a popular destination for enjoying a drink and the best seafood. Expect over 100 craft and speciality beers in addition to local real ales and wines to accompany your choice of shellfish. On the concise list of eating options, mussels, scallops, prawns, crab and lobster are the core ingredients, prepared classically with flavourings of garlic, chilli, coconut, tomato, lemongrass and coriander as appropriate. Worth seeking out.

Open all day all wk ⊕ ENTERPRISE INNS ◀ Harvey's Sussex Best Bitter, Dark Star Hophead, guest ale Ö Symonds. **Facilities** ❤ (Bar Garden) ◀❙ Garden WiFi

CHELWOOD GATE
Map 6 TQ43

The Red Lion

tel: 01825 740836 & 740265 **Lewes Rd RH17 7DE**
email: redlion@outlook.com
dir: *On A275*

Popular Ashdown Forest destination

An attractive pub built in the early 1800s that includes among its famous visitors Prime Minister Harold Macmillan and President John F Kennedy. Although it is owned by Kent brewer Shepherd Neame, Harvey's of Lewes also gets a look in on the bar. A full menu is served in the conservatory dining room and on the patio, while a more limited selection applies at tables in the extensive gardens. Typical dishes are beer-battered cod and chips with mushy peas; steak burger with Emmental cheese, chunky chips and chef's burger relish; and risotto of butternut squash with fresh sage and goats' cheese.

Open all day all wk 11-11 (Fri-Sat 11am-mdnt Sun 11-10.30) **Food** Mon-Thu 12-9, Fri-Sat 12-9.30, Sun 12-8 Av main course £10.95 ⊕ SHEPHERD NEAME ◀ Spitfire, Harvey's Sussex Best Bitter Ö Thatchers Gold. **Facilities** Non-diners area ❤ (Bar Garden) ◀❙ Children's menu Children's portions Play area Garden ⊓ Parking WiFi ▭

PICK OF THE PUBS

The Coach and Horses

DANEHILL   Map 6 TQ42

tel: 01825 740369 **RH17 7JF**
email: coachandhorses@danehill.biz
web: www.coachandhorses.danehill.biz
dir: *From East Grinstead, S through Forest Row on A22 to junct with A275 right on A275, 2m to Danehill, left into School Ln, 0.5m, pub on left*

Family-run country pub offering more than just beer

On the edge of Ashdown Forest, The Coach and Horses opened in 1847 when it was a simple alehouse with stabling. Today it ticks all the boxes for an attractive countryside inn. If you fancy a ramble to work up a thirst or an appetite, ask about the three routes that start at the pub door. Upon your return, you'll find a sunny child-free terrace at the rear dominated by an enormous maple tree; children can play in the peaceful front garden, where the undulating South Downs dominate the horizon. Understated and unspoilt, the pub's interior has retained the typical twin bar layout, with vaulted ceilings, wood-panelled walls and stone and oak flooring lending their quiet charm. The pub's dog lazing on a bar rug sets a friendly tone, along with locals supping weekly-changing guest ales from the likes of Long Man and Dark Star; local Danehill Black Pig cider is also popular, and English sparkling wines come from the Bluebell vineyard just up the road.

Relax with your drink or settle with a menu in the dedicated eating area. Dishes are traditionally English, but the cooking scores highly with the freshness of ingredients sourced as locally as possible. A good list of lighter lunches includes sweetcorn fritters with cherry tomato salsa, lime and red chilli dip; and pork rillettes with capers, cornichon, salad and toast. For those of good appetite, a starter of Horsted Keynes wild duck pastrami with caraway pickled white cabbage could be followed by pan-roasted bream with sautéed ginger, shallot, tenderstem broccoli, sesame soy dressing and straw potatoes. Typical of the desserts are apple and rhubarb crumble with vanilla ice cream; and pistachio rice pudding with lemon curd and milk chocolate.

Open all wk 12-3 5.30-11 (Sat-Sun 12-11) Closed 26 Dec **Food** Lunch Mon-Fri 12-2, Sat 12-2.30, Sun 12-3 Dinner Mon-Thu 6.30-9, Fri-Sat 6.30-9.30 Set menu available ⊕ FREE HOUSE ◀ Harvey's, Hammerpot, Dark Star, Isfield Brewery, Hurst Brewery, Long Man Best Bitter, guest ales ♂ Black Pig, Thatchers Gold. ♀ 8 **Facilities** Non-diners area ❀ (Bar Garden) ♦♦ Children's menu & portions Play area Garden ⊓ Parking WiFi

CHIDDINGLY
Map 6 TQ51

The Six Bells

tel: 01825 872227 **BN8 6HE**
dir: *E of A22 between Hailsham & Uckfield. Turn opposite Golden Cross pub*

Popular pub with vintage car, music and jazz events

Inglenook fireplaces and plenty of bric-à-brac are to be found at this large free house, which is where various veteran car and motorbike enthusiasts meet on club nights. This is a popular pub with walkers who are out on the many great routes round here including the Vanguard Way. Enjoy live music on Tuesday, Friday and Saturday evenings plus jazz at lunchtime on Sundays. The jury in the famous 1852 Onion Pie Murder trial sat and deliberated in the bar before finding the defendant, Sarah Ann French, guilty of poisoning her husband.

Open all wk 10-3 6-11 (Fri-Sun all day) **Food** Lunch Mon-Thu 12-2.30, Fri-Sun all day Dinner Mon-Thu 6-9.30, Fri-Sun all day ⊕ FREE HOUSE ◀ Courage Directors, Harvey's Sussex Best Bitter, guest ales. **Facilities** Non-diners area ♣ (Bar Garden) ♦♦ Children's portions Family room Garden Parking 🚌

DANEHILL
Map 6 TQ42

The Coach and Horses
PICK OF THE PUBS

See Pick of the Pubs on opposite page

DITCHLING
Map 6 TQ31

The Bull ★★★★★ INN ⊕
PICK OF THE PUBS

See Pick of the Pubs on page 486

EAST CHILTINGTON
Map 6 TQ31

The Jolly Sportsman ⊕

tel: 01273 890400 **Chapel Ln BN7 3BA**
email: info@thejollysportsman.com
dir: *From Lewes take A275, left at Offham onto B2166 towards Plumpton, into Novington Ln, after approx 1m left into Chapel Ln*

Award-winning rustic food and local ales to match

Isolated but well worth finding, Bruce Wass's dining pub enjoys a lovely garden setting on a peaceful dead-end lane looking out to the South Downs. The bar retains some of the character of a Victorian alehouse, with Long Man Best Bitter & Long Blonde on tap, while the dining room strikes a cool, modern-rustic pose. Well-sourced food shines on daily-changing menus, served throughout the pub, from calves' liver in bacon and shallot sauce with colcannon, broccoli and potatoes, to Thai chickpea cakes with crispy aubergine and tofu kofta, garlic spinach, mint yogurt and pepper coulis. Good value fixed-price and children's menus are also available.

Open Tue-Sat 12-3 5.45-11 (Sat all day in summer Sun 12 5) Closed 25 Dec, Sun eve & Mon **Food** Lunch Tue-Sat 12-2.30, Sun 12-3.30 Dinner Tue-Sat 6-9.30 Set menu available ⊕ FREE HOUSE ◀ Long Man Best Bitter & Long Blonde ♂ Orchard Pig. ♟ 14 **Facilities** Non-diners area ♣ (Bar Garden) ♦♦ Children's menu Children's portions Play area Garden Parking WiFi

EAST DEAN
Map 6 TV59

The Tiger Inn
PICK OF THE PUBS

tel: 01323 423209 **The Green BN20 0DA**
email: tiger@beachyhead.org.uk
dir: *From A259 between Eastbourne & Seaford. Pub 0.5m*

Village inn with splendid downland views

Set beside the large sloping green in one of the prettiest old villages on the South Downs, it's just a short stroll along downland paths from the inn to the magnificent coastal walk at the renowned Seven Sisters cliffs. The pub was once the base for smugglers landing contraband at the cove at nearby Birling Gap. The interior recalls such heady days, with log fires, beams, stone floors and ancient settles. With beers from the pub's own Beachy Head microbrewery, the best local brews are guaranteed – 'Legless Rambler' celebrates walkers on the adjacent South Downs Way footpath. The menu too is laden with the promise of local ingredients cooked to hearty recipes. Fresh fish features in several choices; or look for pan-fried duck breast with new potatoes, vegetables and rhubarb and ginger sauce. Steamed puddings lead the sweet choice, while the daily specials board extends the appealing culinary fest.

Open all day all wk **Food** Lunch all wk 12-3 Dinner all wk 6-9 ⊕ FREE HOUSE/ BEACHY HEAD BREWERY ◀ Legless Rambler & Original Ale, Harvey's, Long Man Long Blonde & Crafty Blonde ♂ Kingstone Press. ♟ 10 **Facilities** Non-diners area ♣ (Bar Garden) ♦♦ Children's menu Children's portions Garden Parking WiFi

ERIDGE GREEN
Map 6 TQ53

The Nevill Crest and Gun

tel: 01892 864209 **Eridge Rd TN3 9JR**
email: nevill.crest.and.gun@brunningandprice.co.uk
dir: *On A26 between Tunbridge Wells & Crowborough*

Intriguingly named pub with a long history

This uniquely named, tile-hung pub was built on land owned by the Nevill family, the Earls of Abergavenny. So the 'Crest' is easily explained; a cannon that once stood outside accounts for the 'Gun'. The hamlet's balancing act on the Kent-Sussex border is reflected in the real ales dispensed in the low-beamed, wooden-floored bar: all ales are sourced from the two counties, giving a local feel to the whole affair. A springtime Sunday lunch menu offers carrot and coriander soup to start; mains like venison and rabbit meatballs with red wine and tomato ragù; or trout with pan-fried gnocchi, rainbow chard, clams and seaweed butter; and clementine and chocolate tart with green apple sorbet for dessert.

Open all day all wk 11.30-11 (Sun 12-10.30) **Food** all wk 12-9 Av main course £12.95 ⊕ FREE HOUSE ◀ Hurst, Old Dairy, Larkins, Black Cat ♂ Aspall, Biddenden. ♟ 16 **Facilities** Non-diners area ♣ (Bar Garden Outside area) ♦♦ Children's menu Children's portions Play area Garden Outside area Parking WiFi 🚌 (notice required)

PICK OF THE PUBS

The Bull ★★★★★ INN ❀

tel: 01273 843147 **2 High St BN6 8TA**
email: info@thebullditchling.com
web: www.thebullditchling.com
dir: *From Brighton on A27 take A23,
follow Pyecombe/Hassocks signs, then
Ditchling signs, 3m*

Old inn with contemporary feel

Perfect for visitors to the South Downs
National Park, within which The Bull
stands, this cosy 450-year-old inn has
been sympathetically restored with open
fires, bare floorboards and candlelit
scrubbed tables. With three bars and
dining areas, locals and visitors alike
settle comfortably in their chosen spot.
Choices continue with The Bull's drinks
list: 13 craft beers and local ales
include Bedlam from the pub's own
brewery, and there's a London stout on
draught too; ciders are well represented
with the county's own Silly Moo as well
as those from the West Country; wines
served by the glass exceed 20 in
number; and there are even half a dozen
house cocktails. If it's good food you're
after, the friendly, knowledgeable staff
will help you order from head chef Dion
Scott's AA-Rosette menu, which
showcases local produce from Sussex
farms and estates, as well as
vegetables, fruit and herbs from the
pub's own abundant kitchen garden.
Starters could include fig, goats' cheese

and rocket salad with pine nuts and
port reduction; or cured salmon with dill
potato pancake, fennel and beetroot
salad. Roast partridge, served with
Savoy cabbage, chestnuts, bacon and
juniper is a warming winter main
course. On Sundays the popular roasts
come with all the trimmings; or try the
smoked haddock chowder with poached
duck egg for a change. Desserts are firm
favourites along the lines of chocolate
brownie with vanilla ice cream; and rice
pudding with poached quince. You can
walk it all off with a trek over the South
Downs — routes recommended at the bar
will take you beyond the village and up
onto the hills of Ditchling Beacon.

Open all day all wk 11-11 (Sun
11-10.30) **Food** Mon-Fri 12-2.30, 6-9.30
Sat 12-9.30, Sun 12-9 Av main course
£14 ⬤ FREE HOUSE ◧ Bedlam
Benchmark, Timothy Taylor Landlord,
Dark Star ⬥ Cornish Orchards, Orchard
Pig, Silly Moo Cowfold Cider. ☞ 23
Facilities Non-diners area ☙ (Bar
Garden) ♟ Children's menu Children's
portions Play area Garden ⌂ Parking
WiFi **Rooms** 4

PICK OF THE PUBS

The Hatch Inn

HARTFIELD Map 6 TQ43

tel: 01342 822363
Coleman's Hatch TN7 4EJ
email: nickad@mac.com
web: www.hatchinn.co.uk
dir: *A22 at Forest Row rdbt, 3m to Coleman's Hatch, right by church*

Award-winning pub in the heart of Ashdown Forest

If AA Milne could populate Ashdown Forest with a bear called Winnie the Pooh, a tiger called Tigger and a kangaroo called Kanga, why shouldn't llamas and reindeer live here? Well, they do, on a farm in nearby Wych Cross. The Hatch is an eye-catching old inn sitting at one of the medieval gates into what was then dense woodland, with its valuable iron and timber reserves. Built around 1430, the part-weatherboarded building may have been cottages for iron workers, although it has been a pub for nearly 300 years. It was no doubt much appreciated by dry-throated charcoal burners who also used to work in these parts, and probably by smugglers too. Today the classic beams and open fires draw an appreciative crowd to sample beers from Fuller's, Larkins and Harvey's. Food is a fusion of classic and modern, for which proprietor Nicholas Drillsma and partner Sandy Barton have built an enviable reputation. Their daily-changing menus are complemented by an extensive wine list, including 10 served by the glass. With plenty of local suppliers to draw on, fresh seasonal produce is used in just about every dish. An exception but brimming with appeal is the lunchtime meze platter of houmous, kalamata olives, tzatziki, sun-blushed tomatoes, pan-fried halloumi and pitta breads. A three-course evening dinner selection could commence with carpaccio of tuna with pineapple salsa and sweet basil dressing. Local ingredients come into their own with main course choices: south coast cod, deep-fried in Harvey's beer batter, hand-cut fries, pea purée and tartare sauce; or new season lamb with dauphinoise potatoes, roast vegetables and a port and redcurrant reduction.

Open all wk 11.30-3 5.30-11 (Sat-Sun all day) **Food** Lunch all wk 12-2.15 Dinner Mon-Thu 7-9.15, Fri-Sat 7-9.30 (25 Dec drinks only) Av main course £15 ⊞ FREE HOUSE ◀ Harvey's & Sussex Old Ale, Fuller's London Pride, Larkins, Black Cat ⌣ Westons Stowford Press. ♟ 10 **Facilities** Non-diners area 🐾 (Bar Restaurant Garden) ⚬ Children's portions Play area Garden ⋈ WiFi

EWHURST GREEN
Map 7 TQ72

The White Dog

tel: 01580 830264 **Village St TN32 5TD**
email: info@thewhitedogewhurst.co.uk
dir: *On A21 from Tonbridge towards Hastings, left after Hurst Green signed Bodiam. Straight on at x-roads, through Bodiam. Over rail crossing, left for Ewhurst Green*

Family-run country inn overlooking Bodiam Castle

This tile-hung village pub is either the first in, or the last out of the village, depending on which way you are travelling. Its age is more apparent from the interior, particularly the huge fireplace, old oak beams and stone floors. Four hand-pumps dispense regularly-changing, mostly Sussex real ales and some 20 wines are available by the glass. The seasonal menus show how dependent the kitchen is on the local area: for example, roasted scallops with a ginger, chilli, garlic and soy butter; chargrilled chump of lamb, mustard mash with rosemary and garlic oil; linguine vongole with whole fresh clams; and Kentucky-fried rabbit with carrot purée and pesto potatoes.

Open all day all wk **Food** Lunch all wk 12-2.30 Dinner all wk 6.30-9.30 Av main course £10 Restaurant menu available all wk ⊕ FREE HOUSE ◀ Harvey's, Growler Brewery Top Dog, Rother Valley Level Best, Pig and Porter Ashburnham Pale Ale, Ewhurst Ales ♻ Double Vision. ₹ 20 **Facilities** Non-diners area ✿ (Bar Garden Outside area) ♦♦ Children's menu Children's portions Play area Garden Outside area ⋒ Beer festival Cider festival Parking WiFi ➡ (notice required)

FLETCHING
Map 6 TQ42

The Griffin Inn
PICK OF THE PUBS

tel: 01825 722890 **TN22 3SS**
email: info@thegriffininn.co.uk
dir: *M23 junct 10, A264 to East Grinstead, then A22, in Maresfield take A275. Village signed on left*

Popular for its huge gardens and lovely country views

The unspoilt village of Fletching overlooks the Ouse Valley. This imposing Grade II listed inn has landscaped gardens with views over Ashdown Forest, the Sussex Downs and 'Capability' Brown-designed Sheffield Park Gardens. You might just hear a steam whistle, for the heritage Bluebell Railway is little more than a mile away. The 16th-century interior simply oozes charm from its beams, panelling, settles and log fires. The bar's handles dispense the best of local ales, while the already generous wine list has grown since the introduction of the pub's highly popular wine club, which organises tastings, special dinners and excursions. Walkers and cyclists arriving to join destination diners will revel in the menu, created from the freshest of local produce. Look out for gambas crostini, garlic, chilli, white wine and parsley, or Devon crab cakes to start; follow with king prawn, chorizo and squid ink spaghetti; pan-roasted skate wing; or harissa lamb shank and buckwheat pie. On fine summer days the barbecue is fired up and food can be served on the terrace.

Open all day all wk 12-11 (Sat 12-12) Closed 25 Dec **Food** Lunch Mon-Fri 12-2.30, Sat-Sun 12-3 Dinner all wk 7-9.30 Av main course £15 Set menu available Restaurant menu available all wk (ex Sun eve) ⊕ FREE HOUSE ◀ Harvey's Sussex Best Bitter, Hepworth & Co, Black Cat, Gun Brewery Pale Ale ♻ Symonds. ₹ 16 **Facilities** Non-diners area ✿ (Bar Garden) ♦♦ Children's menu Children's portions Play area Garden ⋒ Parking WiFi

GUN HILL
Map 6 TQ51

The Gun
PICK OF THE PUBS

tel: 01825 872361 **TN21 0JU**
email: enquiries@thegunhouse.co.uk
dir: *From Heathfield on A267 after Horam turn right into Chiddingly Rd (signed Chiddingly). Follow to pub on left*

First-class food in a charming setting

Felons and miscreants were brought to face justice in this local courthouse centuries ago; today discerning drinkers and diners seek out this rambling, steeply-roofed old inn. Located high in the Sussex Downs, extensive views reward those who sit in the tranquil tree-shaded garden with a Musket ale or Biddenden cider in hand. Inside, lots of beams, wooden floors and open log fireplaces picked out in old brick characterise an interior dressed with rustic furnishings. A beautifully panelled dining room is a particular draw, whilst numerous hideaway niches and corners offer dining privacy. When surveying the menu, some get no further than the tapas sharing board with its wild boar Scotch egg, chipolatas and prunes, chilli tiger prawns, devilled whitebait, and flatbread along with a salad of apple, celery and walnuts. Wood-fired sourdough pizzas are also much in demand. Beer-battered fish with chips followed by Bramley apple and quince crumble reassures the traditionalists.

Open all wk 11.30-3 5.30-11 (Sun 11.30-10.30) **Food** Lunch Mon-Fri 12-2.45, Sat 12-9.30, Sun 12-8.30 Dinner Mon-Thu 5.30-9, Fri 5.30-9.30, Sat 12-9.30, Sun 12-8.30 Av main course £15 ⊕ FREE HOUSE ◀ Sharp's Doom Bar, Harvey's, Musket, Timothy Taylor, Guinness ♻ Biddenden, Aspall. ₹ 14 **Facilities** Non-diners area ✿ (All areas) ♦♦ Children's menu Children's portions Play area Garden Outside area ⋒ Parking WiFi

HARTFIELD
Map 6 TQ43

Anchor Inn

tel: 01892 770424 **Church St TN7 4AG**
email: info@anchorhartfield.com
dir: *On B2110*

Friendly free house in the Ashdown Forest

This family-orientated pub is in the heart of 'Winnie the Pooh' country. It was built in 1465 and was at one time a workhouse before it became a pub in the late 19th century. Locals meet in the front bar with its stone floors and heavy wooden beams, plus the inglenook fireplace and library area give the back bar a more intimate feel. As well as hot and cold snacks, main courses such as Cumberland sausages and mash or battered haddock, chips and peas satisfy heartier appetites. Friday evening is steak night. The front verandah and large garden are a bonus on warm sunny days. Look out for the early May beer festival.

Open all day all wk **Food** Lunch Mon-Sat 12-3, Sun 12-6 Dinner Mon-Thu & Sat 6-9, Fri 6-9.30 ⊕ FREE HOUSE ◀ Harvey's Sussex Best Bitter, Larkins, Westerham, Timothy Taylor ♻ Westons Stowford Press. **Facilities** Non-diners area ✿ (All areas) ♦♦ Children's menu Children's portions Play area Garden Outside area ⋒ Beer festival Parking WiFi ➡ (notice required)

The Hatch Inn
PICK OF THE PUBS

See Pick of the Pubs on page 487

PICK OF THE PUBS

The Middle House

MAYFIELD Map 6 TQ52

tel: 01435 872146 **High St TN20 6AB**
email: info@themiddlehousemayfield.co.uk
web: www.themiddlehousemayfield.co.uk
dir: *E of A267, S of Tunbridge Wells*

Historic timber-framed hostelry

Once described as 'one of the finest examples of a timber-framed building in Sussex', this Grade I listed 16th-century village inn dominates Mayfield's High Street. It has been here since 1575, when it was built for Sir Thomas Gresham, Elizabeth I's Keeper of the Privy Purse and founder of the London Stock Exchange. The entrance hall features a large ornately carved wooden fireplace by master carver Grinling Gibbons. Wattle-and-daub infill, a splendid oak-panelled restaurant and secret priest holes complete the period appeal. A private residence until the 1920s, it is now a family-run business. Real ale drinkers do well here; the handsome choice embraces half a dozen of the nation's favourite brewers, from Harvey's in Lewes to Theakston in North Yorkshire via Adnams in Suffolk. As in all good kitchens, the meats, poultry, game and vegetables come from local farms and producers. The lunchtime menu includes sandwiches, wraps and ploughman's. Alongside are salads constructed by nationality (British, Russian, Italian for example); fish

choices such as baked sea trout fillet or roast wild halibut; and Middle House classics such as lamb's liver, crispy bacon, creamed potato and onion gravy. Pub favourites among the starters, mains and desserts include chicken liver pâté with herb brioche; slow-roasted belly of Mayfield pork with pear and orange purée, crackling, vegetables and a sauce of local cider and sage; and a seasonal crumble with cream or crème anglaise. It is not just the building that has been described in superlative terms — the private chapel in the restaurant is regarded as 'one of the most magnificent in England'. Step out onto the lovely terraced gardens to enjoy views of the rolling countryside.

Open all day all wk **Food** Lunch Mon-Thu 12-2.15, Fri-Sun all day Dinner Mon-Thu 6.30-9.30, Fri-Sun all day ⊕ FREE HOUSE ◄ Harvey's Sussex Best Bitter, Greene King Abbot Ale, Black Sheep Best Bitter, Theakston Best Bitter, Adnams Southwold Bitter, Sharp's Doom Bar, Fuller's London Pride ♨ Aspall. ♟ 9 **Facilities** Non-diners area ♦♦ Children's menu Children's portions Play area Garden ⋔ Parking WiFi

HASTINGS & ST LEONARDS
Map 7 TQ80

NEW The Crown

tel: 01424 465100 **64-66 All Saints St TN34 3BN**
email: hello@thecrownhastings.co.uk
dir: *From A259 in Hastings into Rock-A-Nore Rd. Parking available at end. Walk along All Saints St to pub on right*

Popular home-from-home in the old town

A relaxed ambience is the keynote here, with daily papers, open fires and board games for all the family; dogs are welcome too. Yet there's entertainment if you want it – The Crown hosts quiz nights, craft evenings, storytelling, exhibitions and gigs. The drinks choice embraces teas and coffees as well as East Sussex ales, ciders and gins. Honestly-priced dishes are home-cooked from traceable sources – organic meat from Winchelsea, fish from Sonny's boat at the bottom of the road, and vegetables from Rye. A fillet of plaice with caper hash brown and pickles, followed by Brighton gingerbread pudding with toffee sauce will set you up for a nice cliff-top walk.

Open all day all wk **Food** Lunch all wk 12-6 Dinner Mon-Sat 6-10, Sun 6-9.30 Av main course £12 ⊕ FREE HOUSE ◀ Old Dairy, Hastings, Franklins, The Three Legs, Downlands Ò Orchard Pig, Turner's, Hunt's, Wobblegate. ♀ 14 **Facilities** Non-diners area ❤ (Bar Restaurant Outside area) ♦ Children's portions Outside area ⋈ Cider festival WiFi ⛺

HEATHFIELD
Map 6 TQ52

Star Inn

tel: 01435 863570 **Church St, Old Heathfield TN21 9AH**
email: susiechappelle@aol.co.uk
dir: *From A265 between Cross in Hand & Broad Oak right onto B2096 signed Old Heathfield. Right signed Old Heathfield. At T-junct into School Hill. In Old Heathfield left into Church St*

Creeper-clad inn with great views and a welcoming interior

Built as an inn for the stonemasons who constructed the 14th-century church, this creeper-clad stone building has a stunning summer garden that affords impressive views across the High Weald. Equally appealing is the atmospheric, low-beamed main bar with its rustic furnishings and huge inglenook fireplace – all very cosy and welcoming in winter. The regularly-changing chalkboard menu lists fresh fish and seafood from the day boats in Hastings. Other choices could be carpaccio of venison; spiced roasted vegetable soup; local bavette steak, skinny fries and escargot garlic butter; and toffee waffle cheesecake.

Open all day all wk **Food** Lunch Mon-Sat 12-2.30, Sun 12-3 Dinner Mon-Sat 7-9.30, Sun 6-8.30 ⊕ FREE HOUSE ◀ Harveys, Young's, Whitstable Bay Pale Ale, John Smith's, guest ale Ò Thatchers. ♀ 10 **Facilities** Non-diners area ❤ (All areas) ♦ Children's menu Children's portions Garden Outside area ⋈ Parking WiFi ⛺ (notice required)

ICKLESHAM
Map 7 TQ81

The Queen's Head

tel: 01424 814552 **Parsonage Ln TN36 4BL**
dir: *Between Hastings & Rye on A259. In Icklesham into Parsonage Ln. Pub on right*

A must for real ale lovers

This 17th-century tile-hung and oak-beamed pub enjoys magnificent views from its gardens of the Brede Valley and as far as the coast at Rye, and has been in the same hands for more than 30 years. The traditional atmosphere has been preserved, with vaulted ceilings, large inglenook fireplaces, split-level floors, church pews, antique farm implements, and a bar from the old Midland Bank in Eastbourne. Customers are kept happy with up to 10 real ales, an annual beer festival in October, and menus ranging from salads, sandwiches and ploughman's to a comprehensive main menu selection which includes chicken, chorizo, tomato and basil pasta; pan-fried soft herring roe with toast and garnish; and spinach and roasted vegetable lasagne.

Open all day all wk 11-11 (Sun 11-10.30) Closed 25 & 26 Dec (eve) **Food** Lunch Mon-Fri 12-2.30, Sat-Sun 12-9.30 Dinner Mon-Fri 6-9.30, Sat-Sun 12-9.30 Av main course £9.95 ⊕ FREE HOUSE ◀ Rother Valley Level Best, Greene King Abbot Ale, Harvey's Sussex Best Bitter, Ringwood Fortyniner, Dark Star Ò Biddenden, Westons Rosie's Pig. ♀ 12 **Facilities** Non-diners area ❤ (Bar Restaurant Garden) ♦ Children's menu Children's portions Play area Garden ⋈ Beer festival Parking WiFi ⛺ (notice required)

MAYFIELD
Map 6 TQ52

The Middle House
PICK OF THE PUBS

See Pick of the Pubs on page 489

PILTDOWN
Map 6 TQ42

The Peacock Inn
PICK OF THE PUBS

tel: 01825 762463 **Shortbridge Rd TN22 3XA**
email: enquiries@peacock-inn.co.uk
dir: *Just off A272 (Haywards Heath to Uckfield road) & A26 (Uckfield to Lewes road)*

Pretty black and white pub with seasonally inspired menus

Mentioned in Samuel Pepys' diary, The Peacock Inn dates from 1567 and is well known for its food and warm welcome – and it's full of old-world charm, both inside and out. Long Man Best and a guest ale keep beer-lovers happy. For the hungry there are starters such as baked camembert; shredded confit of duck salad; or Sussex smokie – smoked haddock with cream and mustard sauce; followed by steak, Guinness and mushroom pie; or wild mushroom risotto. Leave room for desserts such as tiramisù cheesecake with coffee ice cream, or winter berry brûlée and biscotti. The large rear patio garden is a delightful spot in summer.

Open all wk 11-3 6-11 (Sun all day) Closed 25-26 Dec **Food** Lunch Mon-Sat 12-3, Sun 12-8 Dinner Mon-Sat 6-9.30, Sun 12-8 ⊕ FREE HOUSE ◀ Harvey's Sussex Best Bitter, Long Man Best Bitter, guest ale Ò Westons Stowford Press. ♀ 8 **Facilities** Non-diners area ❤ (Bar Garden) ♦ Children's menu Children's portions Garden ⋈ Parking

The Cock

This is a 16th century family run dining pub where the landlords still find time to personally greet both new and returning customers. Walk into the pub and you are met by a huge blackboard that seems to list every pub dish that has ever existed! Should that not be enough choice then this is supplemented by a daily Specials Board and at lunchtimes (ex Sundays) sandwiches, rolls & Ploughman's – we try to offer something for all tastes, appetites and budgets and are also able to cater for coeliacs and vegans. The pub is well renowned for its wide choice of homemade dishes featuring locally produced ingredients, such as Steak & Ale Pie, Venison Sausages and Chicken Florentina. Vegetarians are well catered for with 6 regular Vegetarian dishes, 3 of which are prepared to Vegan standards. A variety of fish and steaks are always featured and a favourite is Val's Purse (named after the Landlady!) – Sirloin Steak stuffed with Stilton and with a Creamy Mushroom Sauce. There is always a choice of Sunday Roast with all the 'Trimmings' and if you still have room there are lovely homemade traditional puddings like Rhubarb Crumble, Sticky Toffee & Date Sponge with our own Butterscotch Sauce, Eton Mess or award winning Ice Creams from Downsview Farm (Toffee-Apple as featured on *The Apprentice*) available every day. And, if there is a dish that you particularly want, with a bit of notice, we will try to provide it.

The Specials Board is always well stocked with locally produced fare, representing the seasons – asparagus in Spring, Game in Autumn/Winter (Venison, Pheasant, Partridge, Guinea Fowl, etc), Winter warmers (Sausage casserole, Lamb's Hearts, Oxtail etc) and fresh salads and quiches in the Summer.

There is a well-stocked bar that always features Harvey's Best Bitter, together with two locally produced seasonal guests from The Hogsback Brewery, Hammerpot, WJ King, together with a number of locally emerging micro-breweries – details of which can be found on the pub's continually updated website at www.cockpub.co.uk. In addition, there is a choice of 12 wines by the glass, including Pinot Grigio, Sauvignon Blanc, Shiraz and Merlot, all at £4.20 per 175 ml glass plus Hot Mulled Wine in the winter and a wide selection of liqueurs, together with a selection of 12 Malt Whiskies.

There are three dining areas, which can accommodate up to 65 covers, plus the Bar area that can seat a further twelve people. The bar is a wonderful unspoilt area with original oak beams, a flagstone floor and an Inglenook fireplace, where a log fire can be found from October to April. Well-behaved children are welcomed in the restaurant and garden, keeping the bar for those who would like a quiet drink or bite to eat.

The garden has plenty of space to enjoy fine weather with patio areas and grass and views to the South Downs and if you are lucky spectacular sunsets on clear evenings. The pub welcomes dogs in the garden and bar area with dog chews and water bowls. The pub's own spaniels Tally & Bailey can often be seen returning through the bar after a walk on the nearby Wellingham Walk.

The Cock Inn takes its name from the bygone era when a spare horse (The Cock Horse) was kept ready at the foot of a steep hill to assist another horse with a heavy load up the hill. Old maps show that there was stabling in the car park area up until the later 1800s. The Cock Horse, of course, was immortalised in the favourite children's nursery rhyme that depicted Queen Elizabeth I riding into Banbury Cross aboard a large white stallion, after the Queen's carriage had broken a wheel on the steep climb up the hill.

Built in the mid-16th century, The Cock has always been a thriving Coaching Inn. Although none of the original stables remain, it was once a mustering point during The Civil War, prior to the siege of Arundel.

The main bar and interior has changed little since Cromwell's time, with low oak beams and Inglenook fireplace. In its earliest days, four rooms within the building were licensed separately, each room identified by a small porcelain plate bearing a number. Two of these plates can still be seen in the main bar.

Uckfield Road, Ringmer, Lewes, East Sussex BN8 5RX • Tel: 01273 812040 • Email: matt@cockpub.co.uk
Website: www.cockpub.co.uk • Twitter: @CockInnRingmer • Facebook: TheCockInnRingmer

The Cock

tel: 01273 812040 **Uckfield Rd BN8 5RX**
email: matt@cockpub.co.uk **web:** www.cockpub.co.uk
dir: *Just off A26 approx 2m N of Lewes just outside Ringmer*

Step back in time at this historic pub

This 16th-century inn takes its name from the time when a 'cock horse' was a spare horse used by coachmen to pull heavy loads – immortalised in the nursery rhyme *Ride a Cock Horse to Banbury Cross*. A mustering point during the Civil War, the interior of the main bar is pretty much unaltered since Cromwell's time, with oak beams, flagstone floors and a blazing fire in the inglenook. Harvey's, and two local guest ales accompany a truly extensive menu. Main courses include venison sausages with mash and onion gravy; and salmon fillet with cream and watercress sauce. A good vegetarian choice is always available.

Open all wk 11-3 6-11.30 (Sun 11-11) Closed 26 Dec **Food** Lunch Mon-Fri 12-2, Sat 12-2.30, Sun 12-8.30 Dinner Mon-Sat 6-9.30, Sun 12-8.30 ⊕ FREE HOUSE
◀ Harvey's Sussex Best Bitter, local guest ales. ☘ 12 **Facilities** Non-diners area
☙ (Bar Garden) ♦♦ Children's menu Children's portions Play area Garden ☷ Parking WiFi ☷ (notice required)

See advert on page 491

The George Tap

tel: 01797 222114 **98 High St TN31 7JT**
email: stay@thegeorgeinrye.com
dir: *M20 junct 10, A2070 to Brenzett, A259 to Rye*

16th-century inn in pretty Sussex town

This town centre inn can trace its origins back to 1575. Inside it offers a fascinating mix of old and new, with an exquisite original Georgian ballroom and plenty of antique and contemporary furnishings and locally produced art. In the bar, the draw is beers from Dark Star and Harvey's breweries and a tasty, light bar menu. Diners can enjoy daily fresh fish from local boats; perhaps sweetcorn chowder or salt and pepper squid, followed by classic fish and chips with mushy peas. Alternatively, try delicious grilled lamb from the wood charcoal oven or classic steak frites.

Open all day all wk **Food** Lunch all wk 12-3 Dinner all wk 6-9 ⊕ FREE HOUSE
◀ Dark Star American Pale Ale, Harvey's Sussex Best Bitter. ☘ 18
Facilities Non-diners area ♦♦ Children's menu Children's portions Garden ☷ WiFi ☷

Mermaid Inn ★★★ HL ◉◉   PICK OF THE PUBS

tel: 01797 223065 **Mermaid St TN31 7EY**
email: info@mermaidinn.com **web:** www.mermaidinn.com
dir: *A259, follow signs to town centre, into Mermaid St*

Memorable seafood dishes in historic smugglers' inn

The atmosphere of the smugglers' inn remains at the Mermaid, which is one of the most famous and photographed of England's ancient pubs. This venerable black and white timber-fronted building was a haunt of seafarers from the Cinque Port harbour. Its colourful history is reflected in ships' timbers for beams, a vast inglenook where the infamous Hawkshurst gang warmed themselves, a hidden priest hole and huge open fireplaces carved from French stone ballast dredged from Rye harbour. British and French-style food is served in the bar, restaurant and under sunshades on the patio. Perhaps choose clam and orange chowder; or local charcuterie with pickles and toast; followed by south coast cod in beer batter; steak and frites; or the sea food platter. Superb wines, local Harvey's beer and comfortable bedrooms complete the package.

Open all day all wk 12-11 **Food** Lunch all wk 12-2.30 Dinner all wk 6-9 Av main course £12.50 Restaurant menu available all wk ⊕ FREE HOUSE ◀ St Austell Tribute, Harvey's, guest ale ♨ Westons Stowford Press. ☘ 15
Facilities Non-diners area ☙ (Garden) ♦♦ Children's menu Children's portions Garden ☷ Parking WiFi ☷ (notice required) **Rooms** 31

The Ypres Castle Inn — PICK OF THE PUBS

tel: 01797 223248 **Gun Garden TN31 7HH**
email: info@yprescastleinn.co.uk
dir: Behind church & adjacent to Ypres Tower

A well-kept secret in the ancient town of Rye

Known locally as 'The Wipers', the pretty Ypres Castle Inn sits beneath the castle's ramparts and has been providing hospitality since 1640. As you'd expect with such a long pedigree, the atmosphere is relaxed and friendly, and the reading room is stocked with an eclectic literary mix and children's games. The bar, featuring the original timber frame of the building, serves Larkins and Harvey's, plus Biddenden cider, all to be savoured beside the log fire. There are magnificent views of Romney Marsh and the River Rother from the garden; the Rye Bay fishing fleet moors close by. Light bites include baguettes, ciabattas and bruschettas; popular choices are smoked haddock, salmon and pea fishcakes; local sausages and mash; or locally caught fish and chips. Booking is advisable for the traditional Sunday roasts. The pub hosts live music on Friday nights, Sundays and in the garden in summer.

Open all day Closed Mon in winter **Food** Lunch all wk 12-3 Dinner Mon-Thu & Sat 6-9, Fri 6-8 ⊕ FREE HOUSE ◀ Harvey's Sussex Best Bitter, Larkins Best Bitter, Adnams, Westerham Brewery, Long Man, guest ales ♂ Biddenden Bushels, Westons Stowford Press, Rekorderlig. **Facilities** Non-diners area ♣ (Bar Restaurant Garden) ♦ Children's menu Children's portions Garden ➤ Beer festival WiFi ⊜ (notice required)

SALEHURST — Map 7 TQ72

Salehurst Halt — PICK OF THE PUBS

tel: 01580 880620 **Church Ln TN32 5PH**
dir: 0.5m from A21 (Tunbridge Wells to Hastings road). Exit at Robertsbridge rdbt to Salehurst

Free house with hop growing connections

Built in the 1860s, when it was known as the Old Eight Bells. Legend puts the name change down to a church organist who commuted to the village from Bodiam, necessitating a new halt on the Robertsbridge to Tenterden line. Despite use by many a hop-picker thereafter, the steam railway eventually closed. Today the hop crop is sold to Harvey's in Lewes, and returned as one of the ales sold by the pub – its traditional cellar is much prized for maintaining ale in top condition. The hop-growing farm also supplies the pub's meats, including Buster's burgers. The landscaped garden has a wonderful terrace with beautiful views over the Rother Valley; here a wood-fired pizza oven runs almost continually during the summer, with orders taken at the garden counter. Before leaving, have a stroll around this picturesque hamlet and the 12th-century church.

Open all day Closed Mon **Food** Contact pub for food times ⊕ FREE HOUSE ◀ Harvey's Sussex Best Bitter, Dark Star, Old Dairy, guest ales ♂ Biddenden Bushels, East Stour. **Facilities** Non-diners area ♣ (Bar Restaurant Garden) ♦ Children's portions Garden ➤ WiFi

THREE LEG CROSS — Map 6 TQ63

The Bull

tel: 01580 200586 **Dunster Mill Ln TN5 7HH**
email: enquiries@thebullinn.co.uk
dir: From M25 exit at Sevenoaks toward Hastings, right at x-roads onto B2087, right onto B2099 through Ticehurst, right for Three Leg Cross

Home-cooked food and large family-friendly garden

The Bull started life as a Wealden hall house in 14th century, reputedly one of the oldest dwellings in the country, and is set in a hamlet close to Bewl Water. The interior is crammed with oak beams, inglenook fireplaces, quarry-tiled floors, and a mass of small intimate areas in the bar. The extensive gardens include a duck pond, petanque pitch, aviary and children's play area, making them popular with families. Menus offer pub favourites ranging from freshly baked baguettes and bar snacks to hearty dishes full of comfort, such steak and kidney suet pudding and honey roast ham, egg and chips.

Open all day all wk 12-12 **Food** Lunch all wk 12-2.30 Dinner Tue-Sat 6.30-9.30 Av main course £12 Restaurant menu available all wk ⊕ FREE HOUSE ◀ Harvey's Sussex Best Bitter & Armada Ale, Timothy Taylor Landlord, guest ales ♂ Westons Stowford Press, Symonds. ♟ 9 **Facilities** Non-diners area ♣ (Bar Garden) ♦ Children's menu Children's portions Play area Garden ➤ Beer festival Parking WiFi ⊜ (notice required)

TICEHURST — Map 6 TQ63

The Bell — PICK OF THE PUBS

tel: 01580 200234 **High St TN5 7AS**
email: info@thebellinticehurst.com
dir: From A21 follow signs for Ticehurst. Pub in village centre

A village inn to make you smile

This eye-catching gabled and tile-hung village centre inn is equally appealing inside, with heavy beams, huge brick-and-timber inglenook, rug-strewn bare board flooring and antiquey furnishings dappling the main rooms. Funky design touches abound, from the top hat lampshades and pillar of books in the bar, to the tubas for urinals in the Gents and the stuffed squirrel that appears to hold up a ceiling. A cosy snug is furnished with leather chesterfields and shelves of books, and the Stable with a Table is an inspired function room with long sunken table and benches, perfect for the pub's regular debate evenings and demonstration dinners. Regular entertainment events add another strand to this very popular old coaching inn. Beers from Harvey's and guest breweries populate the handpulls. Menu choices are a cut above the ordinary; starters may include pan-seared scallops with honey and carrot purée and chorizo; versatile mains typically cover wild mushroom risotto with Kentish Blue Cheese; or home-made fish stew with fennel, aïoli and gruyère.

Open all day all wk **Food** Lunch all wk 12-3 Dinner all wk 6-9.30 Restaurant menu available all wk ⊕ FREE HOUSE ◀ Harvey's, Old Dairy, seasonal guest ales ♂ Symonds. ♟ 12 **Facilities** Non-diners area ♣ (Bar Garden) ♦ Children's menu Garden ➤ Parking WiFi ⊜ (notice required)

UCKFIELD
Map 6 TQ42

NEW The Highlands Inn

tel: 01825 762989 **Eastbourne Rd TN22 5SP**
email: highlandsinnuckfield@gmail.com **web:** www.ridleyinns.co.uk
dir: *From rdbt (junct of A22 & A26) into Lewes Rd signed Ridgewood. Pub on right*

A relaxed pub for all the family

Family-run, family-friendly and fully refurbished, the Highlands has a light and modern feel to its largely open plan interior. Seating varies from chesterfield-style sofas to leather-clad armchairs, tartan-clothed banquettes and high stools. At the bar, optics have been dispensed with, so all spirits are hand-measured. Harvey's and two local guest ales are on hand pump. The menu comprises home-made pub fare, with steaks, burgers, platters, and pub classics such as hunter's chicken – chargrilled breast topped with bacon, smoked cheddar and barbecue sauce. A trio of vegetarian options and a home-cooked children's menu complete the picture.

Open all day all wk 11-11 (Fri-Sat 11am-mdnt Sun 11-10.30) **Food** Lunch Mon-Sat 12-2.30, Sun 12-6 Dinner Mon-Sat 6-9.30 ⊕ FREE HOUSE ◼ Harvey's Sussex Best Bitter, local guest ales ♂ Westons Stowford Press, guest ciders. ☐ 11
Facilities Non-diners area ✤ (Bar Garden Outside area) ◉ Children's menu Children's portions Play area Garden Outside area ⋒ Parking WiFi ▥ (notice required)

See advert on opposite page

WARBLETON
Map 6 TQ61

NEW The Black Duck

tel: 01435 830636 **Church Hill TN21 9BD**
email: theblackduck@hotmail.co.uk
dir: *From Heathfield take A265 towards Hawkhurst. Right onto B2096 signed Old Heathfield, right signed Warbleton*

Popular local with picnic benches and ghostly legends

The Black Duck was so named by owners Gary and Nicola Kinnell a few years ago, to commemorate all those poor birds used as chimney sweeps in medieval times. The pub's somewhat modern-looking exterior belies its venerable age, confirmed inside by scrubbed beams, timber framing and an inglenook fireplace and bread oven at the heart of the building. A huge cellar keeps Harvey's beers in tip-top condition. The menu proposing popular pub fare is backed by a dozen specials every day, including several vegetarian options. The rear beer garden with picnic benches enjoys lovely views over rolling downland.

Open 12-3 5.30-11 (Fri-Sat 12-11 Sun 12-6) Closed Sun eve, Mon **Food** Lunch Tue-Sat 12-2.15, Sun 12-2.45 Dinner Tue-Sat 6.30-9.15 Av main course £10-£11 ⊕ FREE HOUSE ◼ Harvey's Sussex Best Bitter ♂ Aspall. ☐ 9
Facilities Non-diners area ✤ (Bar Restaurant Garden) ◉ Children's menu Children's portions Garden ⋒ Parking

WILMINGTON
Map 6 TQ50

The Giants Rest

tel: 01323 870207 **The Street BN26 5SQ**
email: giantsrest@hotmail.com
dir: *2m from Polegate on A27 towards Brighton*

An ideal spot for South Downs walkers

This traditional country pub is set back off the A27 in a pretty village close to the famous chalk figure of the Long Man of Wilmington. A family-owned Victorian free house, the pub is ideally situated for walkers exploring the South Downs Way. Furnished with pine tables and pews, the bar is decorated with Beryl Cook prints. Local ales from The Long Man brewery in nearby Litlington accompany a blackboard menu of traditional classics and daily specials. Typical choices include flaked smoked haddock, salmon and hake fishcakes; African-style sweet potato, spinach, courgette and peanut stew; and Selmeston game pie with new potatoes and seasonal veg.

Open all wk 12-3 6-11 (Sun all day) **Food** Lunch Mon-Sat 12-2, Sun all day Dinner Mon-Sat 6.30-9, Sun all day ⊕ FREE HOUSE ◼ Long Man Best Bitter, Long Blonde, Old Man, American Pale Ale, Sussex Pride & Copper Hop ♂ Aspall, South Downs. ☐ 10 **Facilities** Non-diners area ✤ (Bar Restaurant Garden) ◉ Children's portions Garden ⋒ Parking WiFi ▥

THE HIGHLANDS INN

Great food to satisfy everyone, at Uckfield's favourite family pub

Eastbourne Road, Uckfield, East Sussex TN22 5SP
01825 762989

You can be assured of a warm welcome at The Highlands Inn, with a broad selection of delicious, high-quality food to suit all **tastes and dietary requirements, all home-made and** locally-sourced. You'll also find a great selection of drinks including some personally selected real ales.

The Highlands Inn, Uckfield is the sister pub to The Cock Inn, Ringmer, under the umbrella of Ridley Inns, a small local chain of **family-run pubs in East Sussex**

WITHYHAM
Map 6 TQ43

The Dorset Arms
PICK OF THE PUBS

tel: 01892 770278 **Buckhurst Park TN7 4BD**
email: enquiries@dorset-arms.co.uk
dir: *4m W of Tunbridge Wells on B2110 between Groombridge & Hartfield*

Good food in this buzzy village local

Licensed over 250 years ago, the pub was named after the heads of the local landowning family, the Dukes and Earls of Dorset. The centuries-old building is a jigsaw of styles, with slender chimney stacks, sharp gables, white weatherboarding and careworn tiles. The interior doesn't disappoint with its comfy period mix of flagstoned and oak-boarded floors, vast open fireplace and undulating beams. The Dorset Arms remains at heart a true village local, with darts, and good Sussex and Kent ales from Harvey's and Larkins; wines served by the glass include three sparklers. The kitchen's output is also a major draw, with eggs, sausages and organic beef sourced from the Buckhurst Estate. Starters include Scotch egg with mustard mayonnaise, then choose a main from the likes of chicken breast with tarragon cream sauce; or venison burger with blue cheese and pommes frites. Classic English puddings include spotted dick and custard.

Open all day all wk 12-11 (Sun 12-10.30) **Food** Lunch Mon-Fri 12-2.30, Sat 12-9, Sun 12-8 Dinner Mon-Fri 6-9, Sat 12-9, Sun 12-8 Av main course £13 ⊕ FREE HOUSE ◾ Harvey's Sussex Best Bitter, Larkins, Black Cat, guest ales ♂ Aspall. ☻ 18 **Facilities** Non-diners area ☻ (Bar Garden Outside area) ⁙ Children's portions Garden Outside area ⏚ Parking WiFi

WEST SUSSEX

ALBOURNE
Map 6 TQ21

The Ginger Fox ◉◉

tel: 01273 857888 **Muddleswood Rd BN6 9EA**
email: gingerfox@gingermanrestaurants.com
dir: *On A281 at junct with B2117*

Pretty, thatched pub with no neighbours

The South Downs look glorious from the beer garden, where children can play safely, and mums and dads can admire the raised vegetable seed-bed while relaxing with a drink. Inside, walls and beams are painted in beige and oatmeal, a gentle contrast perhaps to the golden colour of a pint of Bedlam, the real ale brewed up nearby Shaves Wood Lane. Local beef from Redlands Farm may be on the menu, specifically a fillet with bacon and mushroom croquette, roasted parsnip purée, braised red cabbage and duck fat chips. Another possibility is spiced fillet of cod, cuttlefish, Puy lentils and curry sauce.

Open all day all wk Closed 25 Dec **Food** Lunch Mon-Fri 12-2, Sat 12-3, Sun 12-4 Dinner Mon-Fri 6-10, Sat 6.30-10, Sun 6-9 Set menu available Restaurant menu available all wk ⊕ FREE HOUSE ◾ Bedlam, Dark Star Partridge Best Bitter, Long Man ♂ Orchard Pig Reveller, Tiny Rebel Rocksteady. ☻ 27 **Facilities** Non-diners area ☻ (Bar Garden) ⁙ Children's menu Play area Garden ⏚ Parking WiFi ⛟ (notice required)

AMBERLEY
Map 6 TQ01

The Bridge Inn

tel: 01798 831619 **Houghton Bridge BN18 9LR**
email: bridgeamberley@btinternet.com **web:** www.bridgeinnamberley.com
dir: *5m N of Arundel on B2139. Adjacent to Amberley rail station*

Traditional downland free house in South Downs National Park

Over the road from this charming period pub is the fascinating Amberley Museum; adjacent is Houghton Bridge over the River Arun. The pub has a long association with the museum's industrial heritage theme as quarrymen and limekiln workers once bought their beer here. What attracts people to the pub today are its candlelit bar's log fires, real ales from Harvey's, Langham and Skinner's breweries, the sheltered garden with views of the South Downs countryside, and the extensive menu. This offers pub classics and daily specials, including fish, steaks, Mediterranean and vegetarian dishes.

Open all day all wk 11-11 (Sun 12-9) **Food** Lunch Mon-Fri 12-2.30, Sat-Sun 12-4 Dinner Mon-Sat 6-9, Sun 5.30-8 ⊕ FREE HOUSE ◾ Skinner's Betty Stogs, Harvey's Sussex Best Bitter, Langham Hip Hop, guest ales ♂ Westons Stowford Press. **Facilities** Non-diners area ☻ (Bar Garden Outside area) ⁙ Children's menu Children's portions Garden Outside area ⏚ Parking WiFi ⛟ (notice required)

ANGMERING
Map 6 TQ00

NEW The Lamb at Angmering

tel: 01903 774300 **The Square BN16 4EQ**
email: info@thelamb-angmering.com
dir: *From A27 onto A280 to Rustington, right into Water Ln. Pub in village centre*

Seasonal food and local ales close to Goodwood races

Situated between Chichester and Brighton, 25 minutes' drive from the Goodwood Estate, The Lamb is well positioned and also popular for visitors to nearby Arundel.

Head chef Richard Cook prides himself on creating appealing seasonal menus and fresh local fish arrives daily, destined for the specials board. Over a pint of Sussex Gold, enjoy a starter of pressed ham hock, quail's egg, pineapple and watercress, perhaps followed by black bream, chorizo, artichokes, sauté potatoes, mussels and saffron sauce. If it's pub classics you're after, try the beer-battered local fish and hand-cut chips or home-made beefburger.

Open all day all wk **Food** Lunch all wk 12-3 Dinner Mon-Sat 6.30-9 Set menu available ◀ Arundel Sussex Gold. ♟ 19 **Facilities** Non-diners area ❀ (Bar Outside area) ✦ Children's menu Children's portions Outside area ⊼ Parking WiFi

---

ASHURST	Map 6 TQ11

The Fountain Inn   PICK OF THE PUBS

tel: 01403 710219 **BN44 3AP**
email: mail@fountainashurst.co.uk
dir: On B2135, N of Steyning

Traditional village pub with some famous customers

The South Downs and the village duck pond can be seen from the terrace of this lovely 16th-century listed building, which comes complete with wonky floorboards, inglenook fireplaces, beams and skittle alley. Acting legend Laurence Olivier was once a regular and Paul McCartney loved the place so much he filmed part of the video for *Wonderful Christmas Time* here. Local beers from Harvey's accompany the freshly cooked pub food that attracts walkers, cyclists, locals and those from further afield. At lunchtime there are light bites, or at lunch or dinner you could opt for the full three courses; maybe game terrine with malted toast, farmhouse chutney and dressed leaf salad, followed by sausages, onion jam, buttered mash and red wine gravy. If you still have space, finish with brioche and butter pudding with crème anglaise. Look out for live music events.

Open all day all wk 11-11 (Sun 11-10.30) **Food** Lunch Mon-Fri 12-2.30, Sat-Sun 12-9.30 Dinner Mon-Fri 6-9.30, Sat-Sun 12-9.30 ⊕ ENTERPRISE INNS ◀ Harvey's Sussex, Sharp's Doom Bar, Fuller's, seasonal & guest ales Ö Symonds. ♟ **Facilities** Non-diners area ❀ (Bar Garden) ✦ Children's menu Children's portions Play area Garden ⊼ Parking WiFi ⊟ (notice required)

BOSHAM	Map 5 SU80

The Anchor Bleu

tel: 01243 573956 **High St PO18 8LS**
email: theanchorbleu@gmail.com
dir: From A27 (SW of Chichester) take A259. Follow Fishbourne signs, then Bosham signs

Harbourside pub with plenty of real ales

If you park your car opposite The Anchor Bleu, check the tide times at this 17th-century inn, as that area floods during most high tides. Flagstone floors, low beams, an open log fire, an upstairs dining room with views and two terraces, one overlooking Chichester Harbour, add to the charm of this popular pub. A good choice of real ales is on offer, including Ringwood Fortyniner. Dishes are based on locally sourced, seasonal ingredients, such as Blackdown venison steak, salt and pepper squid, and brie and artichoke tartlet. Meals can be taken on the terraces during warmer weather. Reservations are recommended.

Open all wk all day (Mon-Thu 11.30-3 6-11 Nov-Mar) **Food** Lunch Mon-Sat 12-3, Sun all day Dinner all wk 6-9.30 ⊕ ENTERPRISE INNS ◀ Ringwood Fortyniner, Otter Ale, Hop Back Summer Lightning, Flowerpots Cheriton Pots, Woodforde's Wherry Ö Symonds. ♟ 10 **Facilities** Non-diners area ❀ (Bar Garden) ✦ Children's menu Children's portions Garden ⊼ WiFi ⊟ (notice required)

BURGESS HILL
Map 6 TQ31

The Oak Barn

tel: 01444 258222 **Cuckfield Rd RH15 8RE**
email: enquiries@oakbarnrestaurant.co.uk **web:** www.oakbarnrestaurant.co.uk
dir: *Phone for detailed directions*

British produce in a restored barn

As its name suggests, this popular pub-restaurant occupies a 250-year-old barn that has been lovingly restored using salvaged timbers from wooden ships. Brimming with charm, the interior is rich in oak flooring, authentic wagon wheel chandeliers, and fine stained glass. Lofty raftered ceilings, a galleried restaurant, and leather chairs fronting a huge fireplace add to the atmosphere. Here, and in the bar and enclosed courtyard, you'll find sandwiches, pub classics and an à la carte menu at lunch and dinner. Sup a pint of Harvey's or Guinness and tuck into dishes created from seasonal British ingredients.

Open all day all wk 10am-11pm (Sun 11-11) **Food** Lunch all wk 12-2.30 Dinner all wk 6-9.30 Set menu available Restaurant menu available all wk ⊕ FREE HOUSE ◀ Dark Star, Harvey's, Fuller's London Pride, Guinness. ♥ 8
Facilities Non-diners area ♦♦ Children's portions Garden Outside area ⊨ Parking WiFi

See advert on page 497

BURPHAM
Map 6 TQ00

The George at Burpham
PICK OF THE PUBS

tel: 01903 883131 **Main St BN18 9RR**
email: info@georgeatburpham.co.uk
dir: *Exit A27 1m E of Arundel signed Burpham, 2.5m, pub on left*

Thriving village pub

Built in 1736, this popular pub stands opposite the 11th-century parish church, one of whose features is a lepers' window from which the afflicted could watch mass. Head for the bar with its wood-burning stove, safe in the knowledge that Sussex-sourced real ales, soft drinks and even champagne are waiting. The menus are changed daily so there's always something different to try. There's bar snacks such as a hot smoked salmon and crème fraîche sandwich; starters of salt and pepper squid with chilli mayonnaise; and mains that include potato gnocchi with spinach and wild mushroom sauce; mussels in cream, garlic and white wine sauce; house beefburger in a brioche bun with chips; a naked burger with poached egg and salad, or a haloumi burger with guacamole, sweet peppers and sweet potato fries. Puddings and Sussex cheeses tempt too.

Open all wk 10.30-3 6-11 (Sat 10.30am-11pm Sun 10.30-5.30) **Food** Lunch Mon-Fri 12-2.30, Sat 12-3, Sun 12-5.30 Dinner Mon-Fri 6-9, Sat 6-9.30 Av main course £15 Set menu available ⊕ FREE HOUSE ◀ Arundel, guest ales ♂ Aspall. ♥ 25
Facilities Non-diners area ♥ (Bar) ♦♦ Children's menu Children's portions Outside area ⊨ Parking WiFi ⊟ (notice required)

CHARLTON
Map 6 SU81

The Fox Goes Free ★★★★ INN
PICK OF THE PUBS

See Pick of the Pubs on opposite page

CHICHESTER
Map 5 SU80

The Bull's Head ★★★★ INN

tel: 01243 839895 **99 Fishbourne Road West PO19 3JP**
email: enquiries@bullsheadfishbourne.net **web:** www.bullsheadfishbourne.net
dir: *A27 onto A259, inn 0.5m on left*

Good range of well-kept real ales

Only three minutes' walk from Chichester harbour, this traditional roadside pub with large open fire has been a hostelry since some time in the 17th century, and before that it was a farmhouse. Its position just outside Chichester is perfect for anyone visiting Fishbourne Roman Palace and Bosham Harbour. Traditional home-cooked food is based on locally sourced ingredients and baguettes and jacket potatoes are on offer as a lighter option; there's a chef's daily-changing special menu too. The pub serves five real ales all in tip-top condition. Live music, special events and private functions are hosted throughout the year. The comfortable en suite accommodation (each room has a private entrance) is light and airy with modern decor and furnishings.

Open all wk 11-3 5.30-11 (Sat 11-11 Sun 12-11) **Food** Lunch Mon-Sat 12-2, Sun 12-3 Dinner Mon-Thu 6-9, Fri-Sat 6-9.30, Sun 6-8 Restaurant menu available ⊕ FULLER'S ◀ London Pride, ESB, HSB, George Gale & Co Seafarers, guest ales ♂ Aspall. ♥ 10 **Facilities** Non-diners area ♥ (Bar Outside area) ♦♦ Children's menu Children's portions Outside area ⊨ Parking WiFi ⊟ (notice required) **Rooms** 4

PICK OF THE PUBS

The Fox Goes Free ★★★★ INN

CHARLTON　　　　　　Map 6 SU81

tel: 01243 811461 **PO18 0HU**
email: enquiries@thefoxgoesfree.com
web: www.thefoxgoesfree.com
dir: *A286, 6m from Chichester towards Midhurst*

Friendly pub with William III, racing world and WI connections

Standing in unspoilt countryside at the foot of the South Downs, this lovely old brick and flint free house was a favoured hunting lodge of William III. With its three huge fireplaces, old pews and brick floors, the 17th-century building simply exudes charm and character. The pub, which hosted the first English Women's Institute meeting in 1915, lies close to the Weald and Downland Open Air Museum, where 50 historic buildings from around southern England have been reconstructed. Goodwood Estate is also close by, and the Fox attracts many customers during the racing season, the annual Festival of Speed and Revival. Away from the high life, you can watch the world go by from the solid timber benches and tables to the front, or relax under the apple trees in the lawned rear garden. Lest all this sounds rather extravagant, you'll find the Fox a friendly and welcoming drinkers' pub with a good selection of real ales that includes the eponymous Fox Goes Free bitter. Whether

you're looking for a quick bar snack or something more substantial, the daily-changing menus offer something for every taste. Bar meals include the ever reliable crispy battered fresh fish and chips with minted garden peas and home-made chunky tartare sauce. Another lunchtime speciality is a baked ciabatta or Greek flatbread with a choice of toppings. Salads include the Fox Caesar salad – gem lettuce, parmesan, home-made dressing and served with either chicken or king prawns. At dinner time, start with honey and mustard sticky pork belly with apple and beetroot slaw, and follow with garlic and rosemary pan-roasted lamb with red onion jus and bubble-and-squeak.

Open all day all wk 11-11 (Sun 12-11) Closed 25 Dec eve **Food** Lunch Mon-Fri 12-2.30, Sat-Sun 12-10 Dinner Mon-Fri 6.30-10, Sat-Sun 12-10 Av main course £10.50 Restaurant menu available all wk ⊕ FREE HOUSE ◀ The Fox Goes Free, Langham Hip Hop. ⍭ Addlestones, Aspall. ⍙ 15 **Facilities** Non-diners area ❤ (Bar Garden) ♦♦ Children's menu Children's portions Garden ⍥ Parking WiFi ⛟ (notice required) **Rooms** 5

CHICHESTER *continued*

The Earl of March ◉   PICK OF THE PUBS

tel: 01243 533993 **Lavant Rd, Lavant PO18 OBQ**
email: info@theearlofmarch.com
dir: *On A286, 1m N of Chichester*

Country-plush ambience on the edge of a National Park

The current Earl is the founder of the Festival of Speed and the Goodwood Revival, held on the nearby family estate of the Dukes of Richmond. In the pub in 1803 William Blake wrote the words to *Jerusalem*; today's visitors can enjoy much the same memorable South Downs' views that influenced his verse. The excellent dishes, courtesy of Giles Thompson, former executive chef at London's Ritz Hotel, depend on local estates and the nearby English Channel. Taking the Earl's Menu, dinner might comprise roast pumpkin and chestnut gnocchi with burnt apple and goats' curd, followed by pan-fried pork fillet, white bean and wild mushroom cassoulet, cavolo nero, rösti and port wine jus; or whole lemon sole meunière, pommes Anna, sautéed sprouting broccoli and sauce béarnaise; and end with pudding of the day. Plenty of bar and lighter meals are offered too.

Open all day all wk **Food** Lunch all wk 12-2.30 winter, 12-9 summer Dinner all wk 12-9 summer Av main course £10 Set menu available Restaurant menu available all wk ⊕ ENTERPRISE INNS ◀ Harvey's, Otter, Timothy Taylor Landlord, guest ale ♂ Westons Stowford Press, Aspall. ♟ 24 **Facilities** Non-diners area ❀ (Bar Garden) ♦♦ Children's menu Children's portions Garden ☌ Parking WiFi

The George & Dragon Inn ★★★ INN

tel: 01243 785660 **51 North St PO19 1NQ**
email: info@georgeanddragoninn.co.uk **web:** www.georgeanddragoninn.co.uk
dir: *Near Chichester Festival Theatre. Phone for detailed directions*

Stylish pub in the heart of Chichester

The George & Dragon stands next to the site of the original north walls' gatehouse in historic Chichester, and is well positioned near the Old Town Cross and cathedral. It dates from the early 18th century and today you'll find open fires, comfortable sofas and a courtyard to enhance the family-friendly feel. In the light and airy conservatory dining room, the menus reveal traditional pub favourites such as breaded whitebait, rump of lamb or pork belly.

Open all day all wk Closed 25-26 Dec, 1 Jan **Food** Lunch Mon-Fri 12-3, Sat-Sun 12-5 Dinner Mon-Sat 5-9 Restaurant menu available all wk ⊕ PUNCH TAVERNS ◀ Sharp's Doom Bar, Timothy Taylor Landlord ♂ Westons Old Rosie. ♟ 10 **Facilities** Non-diners area ❀ (Bar Outside area) ♦♦ Children's menu Children's portions Outside area ☌ WiFi ☎ (notice required) **Rooms** 10

Royal Oak Inn ★★★★★ INN ◉◉   PICK OF THE PUBS

See Pick of the Pubs on opposite page

Coach & Horses

tel: 023 9263 1228 **The Square PO18 9HA**
dir: *On B2146, S of Petersfield. In village centre*

Appealing South Downs honeypot

David and Christiane Butler have run their 17th-century coaching inn in this pretty South Downs village since 1985. Popular with walkers, cyclists and, let's face it, anyone looking for good food and drink, its unspoiled Victorian bar, with two open fires, is widely known for championing local microbreweries like Ballards. The oldest part of the pub, with many exposed beams, is the restaurant, where you'll find dishes such as chicken, mushroom and tarragon pie; avocado and spinach bake; lamb rump with dauphinoise potatoes; steak and kidney pie; crackling pork belly, and local game choices in season.

Open Tue-Sun 11.30-3 6-11 Closed Mon **Food** Lunch Tue-Sun 12-2 Dinner Tue-Sun 7-9 ⊕ FREE HOUSE ◀ Ballards Best Bitter, Bowmans, guest ales ♂ Thatchers. **Facilities** Non-diners area ❀ (Bar Outside area) ♦♦ Children's portions Outside area ☌ WiFi ☎ (notice required)

The Talbot

tel: 01444 455898 **High St RH17 5JX**
email: info@thetalbotcuckfield.co.uk
dir: *B2036 into village centre*

Smart village pub showcasing the local larder

Once a staging post for travellers on the road between London and Brighton, The Talbot is still the hub in the historic village of Cuckfield. It's now a contemporary pub and restaurant that prides itself on making the most of the local larder, whether it's Dark Star ales or seasonal dishes such as pigs' cheeks, Puy lentils and home-made apple jelly; blackened salmon, chorizo, sugar snap and fennel velouté, saffron fondant with tomato and herb dressing; and blackcurrant crème brûlée with pistachio biscotti.

Open all day all wk ⊕ FREE HOUSE ◀ Harvey's Sussex Best Bitter, Dark Star, guest ales ♂ Symonds. **Facilities** ❀ (Bar Garden) ♦♦ Children's menu Children's portions Garden WiFi

The Crown Inn

tel: 01403 710902 **Worthing Rd RH13 8NH**
email: crowninndialpost@aol.com
dir: *8m S of Horsham. Village signed from A24*

Local ales and just about everything is home made

The Crown Inn is a free house owned and run by Penny and James Middleton-Burn. Nicely positioned opposite the village green, the pub has an excellent reputation for home-made and seasonal food, together with well-kept ales: a house brew by Long Man is supported by others from the likes of Hammerpot and Bedlam. Chef James and his team make nearly everything from scratch, from soups, pâtés and home-ground steak burgers to puddings, ice creams and sorbets. Hard to resist is the hand-crafted steak, kidney and local ale pie; or look to the daily specials board for a Sussex smokie – smoked haddock, spinach, mash and fish velouté.

Open 12-3 6-11 (Sun 12-4) Closed Sun eve (contact pub for Xmas opening times) **Food** Lunch Mon-Sat 12-2, Sun 12-3 Dinner Mon-Thu 6-9, Fri-Sat 6-9.30 Set menu available ⊕ FREE HOUSE ◀ Long Man American Pale Ale, Bedlam Brewery, Hammerpot ♂ Thatchers Gold. **Facilities** Non-diners area ❀ (Bar Restaurant Garden) ♦♦ Children's portions Garden ☌ Parking ☎ (notice required)

PICK OF THE PUBS

Royal Oak Inn ★★★★★ INN ❀❀

CHICHESTER　　　　Map 5 SU80

tel: 01243 527434
Pook Ln, East Lavant PO18 OAX
email: info@royaloakeastlavant.co.uk
web: www.royaloakeastlavant.co.uk
dir: *2m N of Chichester. Exit A286 to East Lavant centre*

A smart dining pub with luxury accommodation

Starting life two centuries ago as a farmhouse, the Royal Oak is set within the South Downs National Park and is just up the hill from Goodwood racecourse; it is also perfectly situated for the nearby cathedral city of Chichester. The creeper-clad Georgian inn is at the heart of the beautiful, historic village of East Lavant and is known for offering great food to visitors and locals alike. The brick-lined restaurant and beamed bar achieve a crisp, rustic brand of chic: details include chunky wooden tables, leather chairs, open fires, fresh flowers, candles, and wine attractively displayed in alcoves set into the walls. Local Sussex Gold and Horsham Best ales, whiskies and Gospel Green Champagne cider are among the thirst-quenchers on offer. The seasonal menu is an easy mix of modern European dishes and English classics with a twist, and much of the produce is grown by villagers in return for pints. The lovely patio is the perfect place to enjoy pork and apricot

ballotine, with spiced apricot compôte; or beetroot, orange and sorrel risotto perhaps accompanied by one of the 20 wines by the glass. Progress then to a main dish of guinea fowl breast, rösti potatoes, wilted greens with pancetta and wild mushroom jus; seared hake, white bean, chorizo and fennel cassoulet; or a 28-day aged rib-eye steak, thick hand cut chips, baked cherry tomatoes, roast field mushroom with a choice of sauces. Typical desserts are mascarpone and blueberry cheesecake with hedgerow compôte; and Madagascan vanilla seed crème brûlée. There are luxury guest rooms with large, comfortable beds and en suite bathrooms.

Open all day all wk 7am-11.30pm
Food Lunch all wk 11.30-3.30 Dinner all wk 5.30-9.30 Set menu available Restaurant menu available all wk
⊕ FREE HOUSE ◀ Skinner's Betty Stogs, Sharp's Doom Bar, Arundel Sussex Gold, WJ King Horsham Best ◐ Gospel Green Champagne & Cidermakers, Thatchers Gold. ♀ 20 **Facilities** Non-diners area
♛ Children's portions Garden ᛗ Parking WiFi **Rooms** 8

DUNCTON
Map 6 SU91

The Cricketers

tel: 01798 342473 **GU28 0LB**
email: ruthboichot@hotmail.co.uk
dir: *On A285, 3m from Petworth, 8m from Chichester*

Ideal rest stop when exploring the South Downs

Named to commemorate its one-time owner John Wisden, the first-class cricketer and creator of the famous sporting almanac, this attractive whitewashed pub sits in beautiful gardens behind Goodwood. Dating to the 16th century, with an inglenook fireplace, the inn has hardly changed over the years. Well-kept real ales include Arundel Sussex Gold, while the blackboard menu offers lunchtime sandwiches and traditional favourites, home-cooked from locally sourced ingredients. Look for the likes of a trio of Old English sausages, mash and onion gravy; sizzling pork, pear and parsnip skillet; and confit duck leg, bubble-and-squeak with spiced orange dressing. Children are welcome and there's a menu to suit younger tastes.

Open all day all wk **Food** Lunch Mon-Fri 12-2.30, Sat-Sun 12-9 Dinner Mon-Fri 6-9, Sat-Sun 12-9 Av main course £11.95 ⊕ FREE HOUSE ◀ Triple fff Moondance, Dark Star Partridge Best Bitter, Arundel Sussex Gold, guest ale Ö Thatchers & Heritage. **Facilities** Non-diners area ❀ (Bar Restaurant Garden) ✦ Children's menu Children's portions Garden ⊭ Parking

EARTHAM
Map 6 SU90

The George

tel: 01243 814340 **PO18 0LT**
email: bookings@thegeorgeeartham.com **web:** www.thegeorgeeartham.com
dir: *From A283 (Petworth to Chichester Rd) follow Eartham signs. Inn on right. Or from A27 follow Great Ballard & Eartham signs*

Privately owned free house with 'good, honest British food'

First appearing on an 1840 tithe map, this appealing pub is a tad off the beaten track in a quiet South Downs National Park village. Open fires act as magnets on cold days, on warm ones it's the pretty garden that attracts. Devoted to British produce, mostly local, one of its real ales is Langham Hip Hop, from nine crow-flying miles away. The menu's an easy read, with confit duck leg, fondant potato, braised red cabbage and spiced orange jus; seared sea bass fillet, pancetta, crushed lemon-scented new potatoes with sweet and sour Grand Marnier sauce as typical dishes.

The George

Open all day Closed Mon **Food** Lunch 12-3 Dinner 6-9 ⊕ FREE HOUSE ◀ Langham Hip Hop, Otter The George, rotating guest ales Ö Westons Old Rosie & Mortimers Orchard. ♟ 12 **Facilities** Non-diners area ❀ (Bar Garden) ✦ Children's portions Garden ⊭ Beer festival Parking WiFi ▭

See advert on opposite page

EAST GRINSTEAD
Map 6 TQ33

The Old Dunnings Mill

tel: 01342 821080 **Dunnings Rd RH19 4AT**
email: enquiries@olddunningsmill.co.uk
dir: *From High St into Ship St. At mini rdbt right into Dunnings Rd. Pub on right*

Good food and local ale in converted water mill

A pub of two halves, parts of the ODM date from the original 16th-century flour mill that inspired its name, while the rest was added in the 1970s. As it's a Harvey's pub, you'll find their real ales in the bar, while on the menu look for the dishes such as salt and pepper baby squid, pink peppercorn mayo and burnt lime; Harvey's stout and white crabmeat Welsh rarebit with poached egg; and hop and barley sausages, smokey mash potato and crispy onions. The front garden is fenced, and a stream, which powers a working water-wheel, runs under the covered decking. The ODM holds beer festivals in June and September.

Open all day all wk **Food** Lunch Mon 12-3, Tue-Sun 12-9 Dinner Mon 6-9, Tue-Sun 12-9 Av main course £14 ⊕ HARVEY'S OF LEWES ◀ Sussex Best Bitter Ö Thatchers Gold Apple. **Facilities** Non-diners area ❀ (Bar Restaurant Garden) ✦ Children's menu Children's portions Garden ⊭ Beer festival Parking WiFi ▭

ELSTED
Map 5 SU81

The Three Horseshoes

tel: 01730 825746 **GU29 0JY**
dir: *A272 from Midhurst towards Petersfield, left in 2m signed Harting & Elsted, 3m to pub on left*

Game is a speciality here

With views across fields and woods, this 16th-century former drovers' alehouse is one of those quintessential English country pubs that Sussex specialises in. Tucked below the steep scarp slope of the South Downs National Park, expect unspoilt cottage-style bars, brick and quarry tiled floors, low beams, latch doors, a vast inglenook, and a mix of antique furnishings. On fine days the extensive rear garden, with roaming bantams, is hugely popular. Tip-top real ales, including local Ballards, are drawn from the cask, and a daily-changing blackboard menu offers classic country cooking with game abundant in season and treacle tart being a typical dessert.

Open all wk 11-2.30 6-11 (Sun 12-3 7-10.30) **Food** Lunch all wk 12-2 Dinner Mon-Sat 6.30-9, Sun 7-8.30 summer only ⊕ FREE HOUSE ◀ Ballards Best Bitter, Bowman Wallops Wood, Flowerpots, Young's, Langham Hip Hop Ö Westons Stowford Press. **Facilities** Non-diners area ❀ (Bar Garden) ✦ Children's portions Garden ⊭ Parking

The George Eartham

t: 01243 814 340
e: info@thegeorgeeartham.com
w: www.thegeorgeeartham.com

The George is a quintessentially English Pub that serves good honest food. With its breathtaking setting on the South Downs National Park, it is a sanctuary for peace and tranquillity: somewhere to indulge yourself in an unspoilt environment. At The George, everything we do echoes our passion and our desire to share them: our aspiration is to create an "experience" which is both truly satisfying and distinctively English.

The George takes food provenance very seriously and prides itself on its high quality locally sourced seasonal menu. Also on offer is a selection of traditional roasts for Sunday lunch. In our well-kept cellar we include a wide range of quality wines, local real ales and English artisan lagers.

The first and possibly only pub in West Sussex or England to sell ONLY British Real Ales, Lagers, Stout, Porter, Ciders & Mead & Wines and Spirits from Britain, The Commonwealth & USA.

FERNHURST
Map 6 SU82

The Red Lion

tel: 01428 643112 **The Green GU27 3HY**
email: jcredlionfernhurst@gmail.com
dir: *Just off A286 midway between Haslemere & Midhurst*

Tempting menu in South Downs village

In the dimpled shade of a huge maple, this attractive stone-and-whitewashed inn overlooks a corner of the green in this peaceful village set in the wooded hills of the South Downs National Park. Cricketers from the nearby ground amble here to enjoy Fuller's beers and guest ales, settling in the oak-beamed, fire-warmed heart of the 16th-century building to select from a menu finely balanced between good pub grub (fish and chips, grills) and enticing diversions such as jerk pulled pork; and BBQ piri piri half chicken, winter slaw and chunky chips. Finish with home-made bread and butter pudding perhaps.

Open all day all wk 11.30–11 (Sun 11.30–10.30) **Food** Lunch all wk 12–3 Dinner all wk 6–9.30 ⊕ FULLER'S ◀ ESB & London Pride, George Gale & Co Seafarers, guest ale Ŏ Westons Stowford Press. ▮ 8 **Facilities** Non-diners area ✿ (Bar Garden) ⌖ Children's menu Children's portions Garden ⌂ Parking WiFi ⊟ (notice required)

HENLEY
Map 6 SU82

Duke of Cumberland Arms
PICK OF THE PUBS

tel: 01428 652280 **GU27 3HQ**
email: info@thedukeofcumberland.com
dir: *From A286 between Fernhurst & Midhurst take single-track road signed Nicholsons & Aspinals. Pub on right*

'Pretty as a picture' inn with good beers and good food

In an absolutely delightful setting, this beautiful, 16th-century pub, perched on a wooded hillside in the South Downs National Park is a real gem. Inside are flagstones, brick floors, scrubbed tables, and ales served straight from the barrels Harvey's and Langham breweries deliver them in. There's a terrace, and the gardens are lovely, with fabulous views of the Weald, pools of trout, and plenty of places to sit, whether you're having a pint or stopping for something more substantial. The first-rate menus impress at lunchtime with braised oxtail, horseradish mash, curly kale and red wine jus; or grilled south coast mackerel fillet open sandwich, while in the evening you might be choosing from salt and pepper squid, garlic mayonnaise, wasabi nut dust and toasted sesame seeds; or pig's head ballotine, smoked potato croquette, quail's egg and brown sauce to start followed by Selsey crab thermidor; or an 8oz grain-fed sirloin steak, with roasted tomato, mixed leaf, peppercorn sauce and chunky chips.

Open all day all wk **Food** Lunch all wk 12–2 Dinner Tue-Sat 7–9 Av main course £18.95 ⊕ FREE HOUSE ◀ Harvey's Sussex, Langham Best Bitter & Hip Hop Ŏ Westons Stowford Press. ▮ **Facilities** Non-diners area ✿ (Bar Garden) ⌖ Children's portions Garden ⌂ Parking WiFi

HEYSHOTT
Map 6 SU81

Unicorn Inn
PICK OF THE PUBS

tel: 01730 813486 **GU29 ODL**
email: unicorninnheyshott@hotmail.co.uk
dir: *Phone for detailed directions*

A favourite with walkers and cyclists plus great views

Enjoying stunning views of the South Downs from its beautiful, south-facing rear garden, Jenni Halpin's 18th-century free house is the perfect spot to relax on sunny day with a pint of Adnams. This sleepy Sussex village is in the National Park, so it's a fair bet that you'll share the pub with walkers and cyclists (and, of course, some locals) seeking out the home-cooked food listed on seasonal menus that make sound use of locally sourced produce. The bar, with beams and a large log fire, is particularly atmospheric, while the subtly lit, cream-painted restaurant is where you can sample fresh fish from Selsey, or dishes like grilled pork belly with Stilton sauce; rib-eye steak; fish pie; or pheasant breast with apricot and date stuffing. Good sandwiches (perhaps roast beef and horseradish) and popular Sunday lunches complete the pleasing picture.

Open all day Tue-Sat (Sun 12–4) Closed Sun eve & Mon (except BHs & summer) **Food** Lunch Tue-Sat 11.30–2, Sun 12–2.30 Dinner Tue-Sat 6–9.30 Set menu available Restaurant menu available Tue-Sun ⊕ FREE HOUSE ◀ Adnams, Sharp's Doom Bar, Arundel Sussex Gold Ŏ Westons Stowford Press. **Facilities** Non-diners area ✿ (Bar Garden) ⌖ Children's menu Children's portions Garden ⌂ Parking WiFi ⊟ (notice required)

HORSHAM
Map 6 TQ13

The Black Jug

tel: 01403 253526 **31 North St RH12 1RJ**
email: black.jug@brunningandprice.co.uk
dir: *Phone for detailed directions*

Recommended for its eclectic menu

This handsome, tile-hung and gabled pub has served the discerning clientele of Horsham town centre for around 200 years. With a trim garden and copious flower displays outside; the interior is a delightful mix of panelling, classic time-worn pub furniture and a warm atmosphere free of music and gaming machines. Up to six beers and some cracking traditional ciders slake the thirst, whilst an indulgent, quality menu may feature pan-fried pigeon breast with black pudding and celeriac purée to start; and a main of warm crispy beef salad with satay sauce, pickled ginger and lotus root crisps; or cauliflower, aubergine and paneer dahl. Light bites, sandwiches, a children's menu, and a tempting range of puddings are available too. Please note that although dogs are welcome they are not allowed in the conservatory area.

Open all day all wk **Food** Contact pub for food times ⊕ BRUNNING & PRICE ◀ Harvey's, Caledonian Deuchars IPA, rotating guest ales Ŏ Aspall, Westons Stowford Press, rotating guest ciders. ▮ 19 **Facilities** Non-diners area ✿ (Bar Garden Outside area) ⌖ Children's menu Children's portions Garden Outside area ⌂ Cider festival WiFi

HORSTED KEYNES
Map 6 TQ32

The Crown Inn
PICK OF THE PUBS

tel: 01825 791609 **The Green RH17 7AW**
email: info@thecrown-horstedkeynes.co.uk
dir: *From A272 at North Chailey (E of Haywards Heath) take A275 towards East Grinstead. In Daneshill left signed Horsted Keynes*

Great food in a lovely old building

The Crown dates back to the 16th century, and has been serving locals and travellers for more than 250 years. Back in 2003 a lightning strike caused serious damage, and large parts of the building were destroyed. Fortunately the oldest parts were untouched and, after being closed for five years, it finally reopened. In 2013 Mark Raffan, former co-owner of Gravetye Manor, took over and has brought elegant yet relaxed fine dining to this cosy, traditional inn. There are comforting real fires in winter and a glorious patio garden overlooking the village cricket green for warmer days. Have a pint of Harvey's Sussex Best Bitter while you check out the inviting menu. Kick off with warm roasted figs, pancetta and Stilton, port wine reduction and toasted pine nuts, and then enjoy creamy chicken, mushroom and leek pie, autumn greens, chips or mash. Finish with passionfruit and white chocolate cheesecake, mango chilli salsa and mango sorbet.

Open 12-3 5-11 (Sat 12-11 Sun 12-9) Closed 25 Dec, Mon **Food** Lunch Tue-Fri 12-2, Sat 12-2.30, Sun 12-4 Dinner Tue-Thu 6-9, Fri-Sat 6-9.30 Restaurant menu available all wk ⊕ FREE HOUSE ◼ Harvey's Sussex Best Bitter, Sharp's Doom Bar. ♟ 10 **Facilities** Non-diners area ♣ (Bar Garden Outside area) ♦ Children's menu Children's portions Garden Outside area ⊼ Parking WiFi ➡ (notice required)

HURSTPIERPOINT
Map 6 TQ21

The New Inn

tel: 01273 834608 **76 High St BN6 9RQ**
email: info@thenewinnhurst.com
dir: *In village centre*

Bustling village local with large beer garden

Despite its name, The New Inn actually dates back as far as 1450 and it has been a hub of the village ever since. Just off the A23 to the north of the South Downs National Park, this bustling village is also a short hop from Brighton. Whether it's one of the four areas in the pub or in the pretty beer garden, this friendly and lively pub is a great place to enjoy a glass of local Harvey's or Orchard Pig cider and tuck into a home-made burger and French fries; monkfish Thai green curry; or Cumberland sausage, mash and onion gravy.

Open all day all wk **Food** Lunch all wk 12-3 Dinner all wk 6-9 Restaurant menu available all wk ⊕ PUNCH TAVERNS ◼ Harvey's ♂ Aspall, Orchard Pig. ♟ 10 **Facilities** Non-diners area ♣ (Bar Garden) ♦ Children's menu Children's portions Play area Garden ⊼ WiFi ➡

KINGSFOLD
Map 6 TQ13

The Dog and Duck

tel: 01306 627295 **Dorking Rd RH12 3SA**
email: info@thedoganduck.fsnet.co.uk
dir: *On A24, 3m N of Horsham*

Children and dogs very welcome

The Dog and Duck is a 16th-century family-run and family-friendly country pub serving enjoyable food like cottage pie, home-made curry and chicken and bacon pie, washed down with Dorset Best. There's plenty of children's play equipment in the huge garden and three very large fields that encourage canines and energetic owners to stretch their legs. The rest of the year sees the diary chock-full of celebratory events, including the charity fundraising beer festival, summer camp, hallowe'en party and firework display.

Open all day Closed Mon eve **Food** Lunch Mon 12-3, Tue-Sat 12-8.30, Sun 12-6 Dinner Tue-Sat 12-8.30, Sun 12-6 ⊕ HALL & WOODHOUSE ◼ Badger K&B Sussex, Dorset Best, seasonal ales ♂ Westons Stowford Press. **Facilities** Non-diners area ♣ (Bar Garden) ♦ Children's menu Children's portions Play area Garden ⊼ Beer festival Cider festival Parking ➡ (notice required)

The Owl at Kingsfold

tel: 01306 628499 **Dorking Rd RH12 3SA**
email: info@theowl-kingsfold.co.uk **web:** www.theowl-kingsfold.co.uk
dir: *On A24, 4m N of Horsham*

In a hamlet just 20 minutes from the sea

A traditional country free house with wooden beams, flagstone floors and log burners. It occupies a prominent roadside site in the village, with plenty of parking and a garden with views to the Surrey Hills; composer Ralph Vaughan Williams reputedly arranged the hymn *Kingsfold* here. There are three real ales to choose from, while the frequently changing lunch menu might include Ardennes pâté with cranberry compôte; or filo wrapped king prawns to start, followed by home-made chilli con carne; pork fillet with mustard, honey and whisky cream sauce; or smoked cod loin with chorizo, potato and peas; a specials board adds to the choices.

Open all day all wk 11-11 **Food** Lunch Mon-Sat 12-2.30, Sun 12-6 Dinner Mon-Sat 5.30-9, Sun 12-6 ⊕ FREE HOUSE ◼ St Austell Tribute, rotating guest ales ♂ Westons. ♟ 12 **Facilities** Non-diners area ♦ Children's menu Children's portions Garden ⊼ Parking WiFi

KIRDFORD
Map 6 TQ02

NEW The Half Moon Inn

tel: 01403 820223 **Glasshouse Ln RH14 0LT**
email: info@halfmoonkirdford.co.uk
dir: *A281 from Horsham to Broadbridge Heath. A264 towards Guildford. At rdbt left into Stane St signed Billinghurst. At 2nd rdbt 2nd exit onto A272 to Wisborough Green. Right to Kirdford*

Hub of the village with cooking to order

The kitchen's promise here is 'always local, always seasonal and always prepared from scratch'. The chef will even cook your favourite dish if it's phoned through a day in advance. Expect the likes of chargrilled steaks, and classics such as a prawn cocktail followed by oven-roasted honey mustard gammon with two free-range eggs and chips. Food aside, the Half Moon is still an idyllic village local with garden and picnic benches; a summer weekend beer festival is planned. So if it's just refreshment you are seeking, the Langham and Firebird ales along with more than a dozen wine choices should meet your needs.

Open all day all wk **Food** Lunch Mon-Sat 12-2.30, Sun 12-3.30 Dinner Mon-Sat 6-9 Set menu available ⊕ ENTERPRISE INNS ◀ Firebird Heritage XX, Langham Hip Hop & Best Bitter, Shepherd Neame Spitfire & Whitstable Bay Pale Ale. ☿ 16 **Facilities** Non-diners area ❄ (Bar Restaurant Garden) ✦ Children's menu Children's portions Garden ⊼ Beer festival Parking WiFi ▭ (notice required)

LAMBS GREEN
Map 6 TQ23

The Lamb Inn

tel: 01293 871336 & 871933 **RH12 4RG**
email: lambinnrusper@yahoo.co.uk
dir: *6m from Horsham between Rusper & Faygate. 5m from Crawley*

Unspoilt village local with a long list of ciders and beers

Landlords Ben and Chris run a successful modern business within the ancient framework of their unspoilt, rustic country pub. They serve some great local beers and ciders in the beamed bar — too many to list, sadly, but there's Dark Star Hophead for one, while from Somerset comes Westons Old Rosie. As much as possible, menus feature locally sourced produce, typical dishes being Sussex steak and ale pie; wild rabbit casserole; chargrilled sirloin steak; and pan-seared swordfish steak with chorizo, cherry tomatoes and sherry.

Open all wk Mon-Thu 11.30-3 5.30-11 (Fri-Sat 11.30-11 Sun 12-10.30) Closed 25-26 Dec **Food** Lunch Mon-Thu 12-2, Fri-Sat 12-9.30, Sun 12-9 Dinner Mon-Thu 6.30-9.30, Fri-Sat 12-9.30, Sun 12-9 Av main course £13.50 Set menu available ⊕ FREE HOUSE ◀ WJ King Kings Old Ale, Weltons Old Cocky, Langham LSD, Dark Star Hophead & Partridge Best Bitter Ò Westons Stowford Press & Old Rosie, Biddenden, Rekorderlig. ☿ 12 **Facilities** Non-diners area ❄ (Bar Outside area) ✦ Children's menu Children's portions Outside area ⊼ Parking WiFi ▭ (notice required)

LODSWORTH
Map 6 SU92

The Halfway Bridge Inn ★★★★★ INN ◉
PICK OF THE PUBS

tel: 01798 861281 **Halfway Bridge GU28 9BP**
email: enquiries@halfwaybridge.co.uk **web:** www.halfwaybridge.co.uk
dir: *Between Petworth & Midhurst, adjacent to Cowdray Estate & Golf Club on A272*

Excellent food on South Downs National Park's doorstep

This renovated, 17th-century traditional pub and contemporary dining inn stands roughly equidistant from Midhurst, home of the Cowdray Estate and British polo, and Petworth, with its National Trust mansion. Travellers stopping at this inn will find tastefully furnished rooms with beamed ceilings, log fires and peaceful patio

and garden. Those seeking a truly local pint will find real ales from Langham, brewed a mile away, and Sussex Gold from the Arundel Brewery. Lighter meals include linguine carbonara with bacon, mushroom and parmesan; and open sandwiches, ciabattas and salads. From the mains selection there might be rolled belly of pork, bubble-and-squeak, kale and mustard cream sauce; or pan-fried fillet of sea trout, leek and chive crushed potato, buttered spinach and white wine cream sauce. Leave room for one of the tempting desserts, perhaps white chocolate rice pudding, rhubarb compôte and rhubarb syrup.

Open all day all wk 11-11 **Food** Lunch Mon-Fri 12-2.30, Sat-Sun 12-6 Dinner Mon-Thu 6-9.30, Fri-Sat 6-10, Sun 6-9 Av main course £9.50-£12.50 Restaurant menu available all wk ⊕ FREE HOUSE ◀ Langham, Arundel Sussex Gold, Sharp's Doom Bar Ò Thatchers. ☿ 24 **Facilities** Non-diners area ❄ (Bar Garden) ✦ Children's menu Children's portions Garden ⊼ Parking WiFi **Rooms** 7

LOWER BEEDING
Map 6 TQ22

The Crabtree

tel: 01403 892666 **Brighton Rd RH13 6PT**
email: info@crabtreesussex.com
dir: *On A281 between Cowfold & Horsham, opposite South Lodge Hotel*

Good, seasonal food in the lovely Sussex countryside

Visit the family-run Crabtree and you'll be following in the footsteps of author and poet Hilaire Belloc who was often to be found here. The inn, originally built in 1539, is located in beautiful countryside which is where the pub sources the vast majority of their produce. Trusty local companies supply meat from high welfare farms and the daily caught fish and shellfish come via the harbour at nearby Shoreham. Start perhaps with cured salmon with yuzu, fennel, soy and ginger, followed by braised pork shoulder with mash, buttered greens and apple purée; or poached stuffed plaice fillets with wild mushrooms, curried mussel velouté, crispy mussels, braised fennel and fine beans. The enticing dessert menu might include crab apple and walnut crumble; peach, apricot and thyme tarte Tatin; or apple and sultana strudel.

Open all day all wk **Food** all wk 12-9 Set menu available Restaurant menu available all wk ⊕ HALL & WOODHOUSE ◀ Badger Tanglefoot, K&B Sussex Ò Westons Stowford Press, Wobblegate, Silly Moo Cowfold Cider. ☿ 20 **Facilities** Non-diners area ❄ (Bar Garden) ✦ Children's portions Garden ⊼ Parking WiFi

LURGASHALL
Map 6 SU92

The Noah's Ark

tel: 01428 707346 **The Green GU28 9ET**
email: amy@noahsarkinn.co.uk
dir: *B2131 from Haslemere follow signs to Petworth/Lurgashall. A3 from London towards Portsmouth. At Milford take A283 signed Petworth. Follow signs to Lurgashall*

16th-century inn at the height of country chic

In a picturesque village beneath Blackdown Hill, this attractive 16th-century inn overlooks the cricket green. The pretty, shabby-chic interior is full of warmth thanks to the charm of old beams, a large inglenook fireplace, muted colours, pale wooden furniture, fresh flowers and the enthusiasm of its owners. In addition to the Greene King ales is a regularly changing guest, and the traditional British food with a contemporary twist uses seasonal ingredients carefully sourced from the best local suppliers. The menu is concise but enticing: shrimp bisque fritter and garlic mayo may precede a main course of 10oz Sussex rib-eye steak, chips, salad and onion rings; or black tiger prawn and Parma ham linguine.

Open all day all wk 11-11 (Sun 12-10 summer Sun 12-8 winter) **Food** Lunch Mon-Sat 12-2.30, Sun 12-3 Dinner Mon-Sat 7-9.30 Av main course £14 ⊕ GREENE KING ◀ IPA & Abbot Ale, guest ale Ò Westons Stowford Press. **Facilities** Non-diners area ❄ (Bar Garden) ✦ Children's menu Children's portions Garden ⊼ Parking WiFi ▭ (notice required)

MAPLEHURST
Map 6 TQ12

The White Horse

tel: 01403 891208 **Park Ln RH13 6LL**
dir: *5m SE of Horsham, between A281 & A272*

Village-brewed cider and local ales prove a draw

This rural free house has been under the same family ownership for over 30 years and lies deep in the Sussex countryside. It offers a welcome haven free from music and fruit machines. Hearty home-cooked pub food, such as their popular chilli; and ham, free-range egg and chips plus an enticing selection of five real ales are served over what is reputed to be the widest bar counter in Sussex. Sip a pint of Harvey's or Weltons whilst admiring the rolling countryside from the large, quiet, south-facing garden. Village-brewed cider is a speciality.

Open 12-2.30 6-11 (Sun 12-3 7-11) Closed Mon L (ex BH) **Food** Lunch Tue-Sun 12-2 Dinner Mon-Sat 6-9, Sun 7-9 ⊕ FREE HOUSE ◀ Harvey's Sussex Best Bitter, Weltons Pridenjoy, guest ales Ö JB, Westons Perry, Silly Moo Cowfold cider, Garden Cider, local cider. ♀ 11 **Facilities** Non-diners area ♣ (Bar Garden) ♦ Children's menu Children's portions Play area Family room Garden ⇱ Parking WiFi ☞ (notice required) **Notes** ⊕

OVING
Map 6 SU90

The Gribble Inn

tel: 01243 786893 **PO20 2BP**
dir: *From A27 take A259. After 1m left at rdbt, 1st right to Oving, 1st left in village*

Thatched pub with its own microbrewery

This charming 16th-century thatched inn has its own microbrewery, and it is a peaceful spot to sup any of the own-brewed real ales on tap; any of the six ales can be taken away – quantities from just two pints to 20 litres. There are two open log fires, low beams and a pretty cottage garden. From the menu, enjoy traditional pub food such as slow-roasted pork belly; pork and herb sausages with creamy mash; and fruit crumble and custard. The inn hosts summer and winter beer festivals, and there is also a skittle alley. The inn is named after school teacher, Rose Gribble, who up until her death, lived in the building.

Open all day all wk Mon-Sat 11-11 (Sun 12-9) **Food** Mon-Sat all day, Sun 12-4 Av main course £12 ⊕ HALL & WOODHOUSE ◀ Gribble Ale, Reg's Tipple, Pig's Ear, Fuzzy Duck, Plucking Pheasant & Sussex Quad Hopper & Gribble Wobbler Ö Westons Stowford Press & Rosie's Pig. ♀ 20 **Facilities** Non-diners area ♣ (Bar Garden) ♦ Children's menu Children's portions Family room Garden ⇱ Beer festival Parking

PETWORTH
Map 6 SU92

The Angel Inn ★★★★ INN

tel: 01798 344445 & 342153 **Angel St GU28 0BG**
email: enquiries@angelinnpetworth.co.uk **web:** www.angelinnpetworth.co.uk
dir: *From Petworth centre take A283 E towards Fittleworth, pub on left*

A real gem in a delightful town

Bowed walls, exposed beams, head-cracking doorways and sloping floors all testify to the Angel's medieval origins, especially in the bedrooms. So too do the ships' beams and three open fireplaces, one of which is used to spit-roast joints of meat. Petworth's Langham Brewery supplies real ales. The modern British menu changes every six weeks. Expect dishes such as crispy confit of duck with cherry liqueur sauce; Sussex wild venison casserole; The Angel fish pie; and warm Thai beef salad. The walled patio garden can be a real sun-trap.

Open all day all wk 10.30am-11pm (Sun 11.30-10.30) **Food** Lunch all wk 12-2.30 Dinner Mon-Sat 6.30-9.30, Sun 6-9 ⊕ FREE HOUSE ◀ Langham, guest ales Ö Aspall, Addlestones. ♀ 25 **Facilities** Non-diners area ♣ (Bar Garden) ♦ Children's menu Children's portions Garden ⇱ Parking WiFi **Rooms** 6

POYNINGS
Map 6 TQ21

Royal Oak
PICK OF THE PUBS

tel: 01273 857389 **The Street BN45 7AQ**
email: mail@royaloakpoynings.pub
dir: *From A23 onto A281 signed Henfield & Poynings*

Dining pub in downland village

In a pretty South Downs National Park village and close to the remarkable Devil's Dyke, this pub occupies a lovely spot that's handy for glorious downland walks. In summer, the wonderful garden boasts excellent barbecue facilities and serene rural views. Beyond the handsome exterior, the contemporary decor inside is an effortless blend of solid oak floors, old beams hung with hop bines and sumptuous sofas. In the bar, Harvey's Sussex Best Bitter sits alongside Westons cider, and the accessible wine list includes New and Old World wines with up to 14 by the glass. The menu changes seasonally and is driven by local produce. Booking ahead for meals is advised. Gregarious grazers will appreciate the shared charcuterie platter of Serrano ham, Milano salami, pastrami, piccalilli, caper berries and olives with warm ciabatta; then mains could be beef, mushroom and ale pie; Royal Oak fish pie; twice baked pork belly; or hand-made Sussex beefburger. Puddings are no less tempting – perhaps the trio of bananas could round off an excellent meal.

Open all day all wk 11-11 (Sun 12-10.30) **Food** all wk 12-9.30 ⊕ FREE HOUSE ◀ Harvey's Sussex Best Bitter, guest ale Ö Westons Family Reserve & Stowford Press. ♀ 14 **Facilities** Non-diners area ♣ (Bar Restaurant Garden) ♦ Children's menu Children's portions Play area Garden ⇱ Parking WiFi ☞ (notice required)

ROWHOOK
Map 6 TQ13

The Chequers Inn ⊛
PICK OF THE PUBS

tel: 01403 790480 **RH12 3PY**
email: thechequersrowhook@googlemail.com
dir: *From Horsham A281 towards Guildford. At rdbt take A29 signed London. In 200mtrs left, follow Rowhook signs*

Award-winning food in delightful country pub

A striking, 400-year-old higgledy-piggledy pub with a classic interior of flagstoned floor, low beams and blazing fire in the inglenook. The Chequers Inn is run by Master Chef of Great Britain Tim Neal, also the holder of an AA Rosette. The bar offers Firebird Heritage XX and Long Man Best Bitter on tap and an impressive wine list to partner dishes of quality from the menu. These can be eaten either in the bar or in the restaurant. You could snack on baked ciabatta, smoked bacon and Somerset brie; and a ploughman's proffers Sussex Charmer cheese with ham, pickles and bread. Harvey's beer-battered fish and chips with mushy peas; or home-made sausages with mashed potatoes and onion gravy are among the tasty crowd-pleasing hot dishes. Tim delights in using only the best local produce, often sourcing seasonal wild mushrooms and even truffles from the generous woodlands around the hamlet of Rowhook.

Open 11.30-3.30 6-11.30 (Sun 12-3.30) Closed 25 Dec, Sun eve & BHs eve **Food** Lunch all wk 12-2 Dinner Mon-Sat 7-9 Av main course £10.50 Restaurant menu available all wk ⊕ FREE HOUSE ◀ Harvey's Sussex, Long Man Best Bitter, Firebird Heritage XX Ö Thatchers Gold. ♀ 10 **Facilities** Non-diners area ♣ (Bar Garden) Children's portions Garden ⇱ Parking WiFi

SHIPLEY
Map 6 TQ12

The Countryman Inn
PICK OF THE PUBS

See Pick of the Pubs on opposite page

SLINDON
Map 6 SU90

The Spur

tel: 01243 814216 **BN18 ONE**
email: thespurslindon@btinternet.com
dir: *From A27 take A29 signed Slindon*

Pretty pub with lovely garden for alfresco drinking and eating

On top of the rolling South Downs, just outside the village of Slindon, this 17th-century pub is a an ideal stopping-off point on a day out in the country. It has been praised for its friendly atmosphere and for generous portions of food. Outside are large gardens and a courtyard, inside is an open-plan bar and restaurant, warmed by log fires. Daily-changing bar meals are marked up on the blackboard, and may include home-made chicken and ham pie; lasagne; or beer-battered fish and chips. A skittle alley and function room are also available.

Open all wk 11.30-3 6-11 (Sun 12-10) **Food** Lunch Mon-Sat 12-2, Sun 12-8 Dinner Mon-Tue 7-9, Wed-Sat 7-9.30, Sun 12-8 Av main course £11.95 Set menu available ⊕ FREE HOUSE ◀ Sharp's Doom Bar, Courage Directors Ô Thatchers Gold. ♀ 12 **Facilities** Non-diners area ❖ (Bar Garden) ♦♦ Children's menu Children's portions Garden ⋈ Beer festival Parking ▭

SOUTH HARTING
Map 5 SU71

The White Hart

tel: 01730 825124 **The Street GU31 5QB**
email: info@the-whitehart.co.uk
dir: *From Petersfield take B2146 to South Harting*

A stylish interior at this cosy inn

An engaging mix of beams and timber framing, log-burners, rustic furnishings, deep leather chairs and an eye-catching stone fireplace set the scene at this 16th-century inn at the heart of a pretty village in the South Downs. Ramblers diverting from the nearby long-distance footpath sup beers from Upham Brewery's tasty range, kept well by the licensees who also tempt with a good menu. Home cooking and local producers ensure that both standard dishes and ever-changing specials have something for all tastes. Crispy duck salad, pomegranate, red onion and roast garlic mayo; or a meat and fish sharing board could kick things off, before moving on to pan-fried hake, wild mushrooms, watercress, new potatoes, clams and bacon marinière perhaps. Views from the garden encompass the rolling downland edges.

Open all day all wk **Food** Lunch all wk 12-3 Dinner Mon-Thu 6-9, Fri-Sat 6-9.30, Sun 6-8.30 ⊕ FREE HOUSE/UPHAM GROUP ◀ Upham Punter & Sprinter, guest ale Ô Somersby. ♀ 9 **Facilities** Non-diners area ❖ (Bar Garden Outside area) ♦♦ Children's menu Children's portions Garden Outside area ⋈ Parking WiFi

STEDHAM
Map 5 SU82

Hamilton Arms/Nava Thai Restaurant

tel: 01730 812555 **Hamilton Arms, School Ln GU29 0NZ**
email: hamiltonarms@hotmail.com **web:** www.thehamiltonarms.co.uk
dir: *Follow Stedham sign from A272 between Midhurst & Petersfield. Pub on left in village*

Well known for the excellent Thai food

Opposite the village common, this whitewashed free house serves authentic Thai food and beers — but if you prefer you can opt for English bar snacks and ales, including the Hamilton's own draught Armless. Thai food devotees will be spoilt for choice — the extensive menu features soups, salads and curries such as beef in coconut milk and bamboo shoots. For vegetarians the choice includes mushroom soup flavoured with lemongrass, lime leaves and chillies, perhaps followed by fried broccoli with garlic and oyster sauce. The pub is home to the Mudita Trust, which helps abused and underprivileged children in Thailand.

Open all day Closed Mon (ex BHs) **Food** Lunch Tue-Sun 12-2.30 Dinner Tue-Sun 6-10 Av main course £9 Set menu available Restaurant menu available Tue-Sun ⊕ FREE HOUSE ◀ Fuller's London Pride, Triple fff Alton's Pride, Hamilton Armless, Dark Star Hophead, Skinner's Betty Stogs. ♀ 8 **Facilities** Non-diners area ❖ (Bar Garden) ♦♦ Children's menu Children's portions Play area Garden ⋈ Parking WiFi ▭

TILLINGTON
Map 6 SU92

The Horse Guards Inn ★★★★ INN ⊛ PICK OF THE PUBS

tel: 01798 342332 **GU28 9AF**
email: info@thehorseguardsinn.co.uk **web:** www.thehorseguardsinn.co.uk
dir: *From Petworth towards Midhurst on A272. 1m, right signed Tillington. Inn 300mtrs*

South Downs National Park village dining pub

This 350-year-old inn's name recalls the day when Household Cavalry horses were rested in the parkland opposite. The tasteful interior features sagging beams, stripped floorboards, open fires (on one of which you can roast chestnuts), antique furnishings, fresh flowers and candles. The fine range of real ales includes nearby Langham brews, and the wine carte will satisfy a serious oenophile. The compact, seasonal menu often incorporates goodies from Sussex hedgerows and seashores. Begin with breaded cod tongues, aïoli, caper berries and lemon. Excellent steaks feature alongside main dishes such as Persian-style pork shoulder and potato curry, onion raita, kachumber salad and parsnip bhaji. Deckchairs, sheepskin-covered benches and even straw bales provide seating in the tree-shaded garden.

Open all day all wk Closed 25-26 Dec **Food** Lunch Mon-Fri 12-2.30, Sat 12-3, Sun 12-3.30 Dinner all wk 6.30-9 ⊕ ENTERPRISE INNS ◀ Harvey's Sussex Best Bitter, Langham Hip Hop, Guinness Ô Westons Stowford Press & Old Rosie. ♀ 16 **Facilities** Non-diners area ❖ (Bar Restaurant Garden) ♦♦ Children's menu Children's portions Garden ⋈ WiFi ▭ (notice required) **Rooms** 3

PICK OF THE PUBS

The Countryman Inn

SHIPLEY   Map 6 TQ12

tel: 01403 741383
Countryman Ln RH13 8PZ
email: countrymaninn@btinternet.com
web: www.countrymanshipley.co.uk
dir: *A272 at Coolham into Smithers Hill Ln. 1m, left at T-junct*

A real old fashioned, traditional pub that ticks all the boxes

Alan Vaughan and his family, having run this traditional rural free house for around 30 years, certainly know a thing or two about pleasing their customers. Surrounding the inn is the Knepp Castle Estate, 3,500 acres devoted to nature conservation through regeneration and restoration projects. In the pub's log fire-warmed bar, you'll find cask-conditioned beers from Sussex-brewed Harvey's, as well as ales from smaller microbreweries such as Hurst and Greyhound. Making their way to the kitchen are fish landed at Shoreham and Newhaven, the two closest ports; free-range meats from local farms; game from the Knepp Estate; vegetables and salads grown in the pub's own half-acre garden; and, through a 'swop shop' arrangement with villagers, unusual ingredients such as quince, kohlrabi or romanesco. Surplus garden produce can be purchased in the bar. Choose from six fillings for the Countryman sandwiches made with the day's artisan bread. Starters and light bites include

potted crab and prawns with melba toast; and grilled Golden Cross goats' cheese with caramelised fig salad. Classic favourites range from a beef and mushroom pie in shortcrust pastry, served with chips and garden peas; to a bacon, sage and onion roly-poly accompanied by home-grown vegetables and dauphinoise potatoes. Desserts don't disappoint traditionalists either, with the likes of banoffee pie or crème caramel. Children are welcome in the restaurant, although the inn doesn't have a separate play area or family dining room. In the garden, weather permitting, an open-air kitchen serves grills, ploughman's and other snacks. In the pub's own farm shop you can buy free-range eggs and home-made preserves, pickles and relishes.

Open all wk 10-4 6-11 **Food** Lunch all wk 11.30-3.30 Dinner all wk 6-9.30 Restaurant menu available all wk
⬤ FREE HOUSE 🍺 Harvey's, Langham, Shepherd Neame, Long Man, Greyhound, Hurst, guest ales 🍏 Thatchers Gold.
🍷 18 **Facilities** Non-diners area
👪 Children's portions Garden 🪑 Parking WiFi

WALDERTON
Map 5 SU71

The Barley Mow

tel: 023 9263 1321 **PO18 9ED**
email: info@thebarleymowpub.co.uk
dir: *From Chichester take B2178 (East Ashling). Through East Ashling (road becomes B2146). In Funtington right into Hares Ln signed Walderton. At T-junct right. 0.5m to Walderton. Turn right at Walderton village sign, pub 100yds on left*

Popular Sunday carvery and pretty garden

Famous locally for its skittle alley, this 18th-century pub, now with new owners and a new chef, is a favourite with walkers, cyclists and horse-riders. Its secluded, stream-bordered garden is a real sun-trap and inside is a log-fire-warmed bar. Booking is strongly advised for the popular Sunday carvery. Nearby Kingley Vale Nature Reserve contains a grove of some of Britain's oldest trees.

Open all day all wk 11-11 ⊕ FREE HOUSE ◀ Tichbourne, 4 rotating guest ales Ö Westons Stowford Press, Aspall. **Facilities** ❤ (Bar Garden) ⊀ Children's menu Children's portions Garden Parking WiFi

WARNINGLID
Map 6 TQ22

The Half Moon

tel: 01444 461227 **The Street RH17 5TR**
email: info@thehalfmoonwarninglid.co.uk
dir: *1m from Warninglid & Cuckfield junct on A23 & 6m from Haywards Heath*

Family-owned country inn that's welcoming whatever the season

This picture-perfect Grade II listed building dates from the 18th century and has been sympathetically extended to preserve its traditional feel. Look out for the glass-topped well as you come in. Enjoy a pint of Harvey's or a real cider while perusing the menu, which offers specials and pub classics. Try chicken and rabbit liver parfait with red onion marmalade; pan-fried sea bass fillet, beetroot purée, orange braised chicory and sauté potatoes; wild mushroom, sun-blushed tomato and mozzarella potato gnocchi; or calves' liver, smoked bacon, bubble-and-squeak, kale and onion gravy. The pub garden is home to a 250-year-old cider press.

Open all wk 11.30-3 5.30-11 (Sun 12-8) Closed 25 Dec eve **Food** Lunch Mon-Sat 12-2, Sun 12-3 Dinner Mon-Sat 6-9.30 ⊕ FREE HOUSE ◀ Harvey's Sussex & Old Ale, Adnams Broadside Ö Aspall. ♟ 12 **Facilities** Non-diners area ❤ (Bar Garden) ⊀ Children's menu Children's portions Family room Garden ⋔ Parking WiFi 🚌 (notice required)

WEST ASHLING
Map 5 SU80

The Richmond Arms ◉

tel: 01243 572046 **Mill Rd PO18 8EA**
email: richmondarms@gmail.com
dir: *Phone for detailed directions*

Raising the beer and pizza game

Thatched flint cottages and a quiet millpond characterise this old village. The Richmond Arms is young by comparison, but this welcoming pub is drawing custom from far afield with its attractive combination of cheerful interiors, Harvey's beers, sumptuous wine carte, and interesting menus. You might start with crispy rare salmon tempura roll with orange blossom and soy; followed by slow-cooked hare lasagne; beef brisket with winter slaw; or BBQ pheasant with fragrant Kashmiri

spices. Outside there's the WoodFired family-friendly bar with a vintage Citroën van that houses a wood-fired pizza oven, stoked up on Friday and Saturday evenings.

Open 11-3 6-11 Closed 23 Dec-12 Jan, 23-30 Jul, Sun eve, Mon & Tue **Food** Lunch 12-2.30 Dinner 6-9.30 ⊕ FREE HOUSE ◀ Harvey's Sussex Hadlow Bitter, Star of Eastbourne, Armada Ale & Tom Paine Ale Ö Aspall. ♟ 14 **Facilities** Non-diners area ❤ (Bar Outside area) ⊀ Children's menu Children's portions Outside area ⋔ Parking WiFi 🚌

WEST DEAN
Map 5 SU81

The Dean Ale & Cider House ★★★★ INN

tel: 01243 811465 **Main Rd PO18 0QX**
email: thebar@thedeaninn.co.uk **web:** www.thedeaninn.co.uk
dir: *Between Chichester & Midhurst on A286*

Contemporary community pub on the downs

In a village between the South Downs and Chichester Harbour, this 200-year-old country dining inn is a great place to relax and unwind but also handy for race-goers to nearby Goodwood. It maintains a community pub ethos, with drinkers revelling in the choice of real ales including Dark Star Hophead. With a home-based smokery preserving meat, fish and cheese, the kitchen team produces an arresting range of pub stalwarts and modern dishes, using materials derived from the local area. Start with ham hock terrine and grape chutney before sea bass fillet, potato cake and tarragon sauce.

Open all day Closed Mon (Sep-May) **Food** Lunch Mon-Fri 12-3, Sat & Sun 12-5 Dinner Mon-Sat 5-9.30 Restaurant menu available all wk ⊕ FREE HOUSE ◀ Dark Star Hophead, The Dean Ale Ö Westons Old Rosie. ♟ 9 **Facilities** Non-diners area ❤ (Bar Garden) ⊀ Children's menu Children's portions Garden ⋔ Beer festival Parking WiFi 🚌 (notice required) **Rooms** 6

WEST HOATHLY
Map 6 TQ33

The Cat Inn
PICK OF THE PUBS

tel: 01342 810369 **North Ln RH19 4PP**
email: thecatinn@googlemail.com
dir: *From East Grinstead centre take A22 towards Forest Row. Into left lane, into B2110 (Beeching Way) signed Turners Hill. Left into Vowels Ln signed Kingscote & West Hoathly. Left into Selsfield Rd, forward into Chapel Row, right into North Ln*

Village hospitality at its best

A 16th-century tile-hung pub in a great walking area, set high on the Sussex Weald close to the Ashdown Forest. In the old bar you'll find two inglenook fireplaces, oak beams, oak panelling and wooden floors, and the sort of buzzy atmosphere village pubs are so good at generating. Local breweries in Groombridge (Black Cat), Litlington (Long Man), Lewes (Harvey's) and Chiddingstone (Larkins) deliver the excellent beers. The well-lit dining rooms are furnished with wooden dining chairs and tables on pale wood-strip flooring, while hops, china platters and brass and copper ornaments decorate the walls in homely style. Glass doors from the contemporary garden room open onto a terrace. The menu tempts with an excellent choice of English or cosmopolitan flavours. Starters, for example, include a pan-fried pigeon breast with heritage beetroot, goat's curd, blackberries and hazelnut dressing; or a Spanish tapas board for two to share. Youngsters over seven are welcome.

Open all day 12-11.30 Closed Sun eve **Food** Lunch Mon-Thu 12-2, Fri-Sun 12-2.30 Dinner Mon-Thu 6-9, Fri-Sat 6-9.30 ⊕ FREE HOUSE ◀ Harvey's Sussex Best Bitter, Black Cat, Larkins, Long Man Ö Westons Stowford Press. ♟ 10 **Facilities** Non-diners area ❤ (Bar Garden) ⊀ Children's portions Garden ⋔ Parking WiFi

WEST WITTERING
Map 5 SZ79

NEW The Lamb Inn

tel: 01243 511105 **Chichester Rd PO20 8QA**
email: info@thelambwittering.co.uk
dir: *From Chichester take A286 signed Witterings. At mini rdbt right signed Wittering B2179. Pub on right*

Pub classics close to the beach

Just a mile from the beach at West Wittering and set in lovely rural surroundings, this pretty redbrick, tile-hung pub dates to the 19th century. They're serious about their food here and the menu offers a good selection of interesting dishes. You could start with pulled pork rillette, crackling and apple sauce, and move on to a sharing platter — whole baked rosemary and honey camembert, maybe, or if you don't want to share there are pub classics like slow-cooked sticky beef rib with French fries; or pan-fried sea bream with crushed new potatoes.

Open 11.30-2.30 5.30-11 (Sat 11.30-11 Sun 11.30-5 Mar-Oct all day) Closed Sun eve Nov-Feb **Food** Lunch Mon-Fri 12-2, Sat 12-3, Sun 12-3.30 Dinner Mon-Sat 6-9 (Sun Mar-Oct 6-8) Av main course £13.50 ⊕ HALL AND WOODHOUSE ◪ Harvey's Sussex, Badger First Call, guest ale. ☝ 8 **Facilities** Non-diners area ❄ (Bar Garden) ♦ Children's menu Children's portions Play area Garden ⛱ Parking ☎ (notice required)

TYNE & WEAR

NEWCASTLE UPON TYNE
Map 21 NZ26

The Bridge Tavern

tel: 0191 261 9966 **7 Akenside Hill NE1 3UF**
email: contact@thebridgetavern.com **web:** www.thebridgetavern.com
dir: *On A167 at Tyne Bridge*

Amazing location for bespoke beers beneath the Tyne Bridge

Built between the stanchions of the iconic Tyne Bridge, there has been an alehouse on this site for two hundred years — the original building being demolished to make way for the bridge and then rebuilt afterwards. There's a working microbrewery on site, where they brew bespoke, never repeated ales available exclusively in the pub. On the menu you'll find great bar snacks — pickled eggs with celery salt, and pork fried peanuts, for example, plus hearty dishes like ox cheek with bone marrow, toast and pickled walnuts; calves' liver and bacon; or beer battered haddock with triple cooked chips.

The Bridge Tavern

Open all day all wk 12-12 (Fri-Sat noon-1am Sun 12-11) Closed 25 Dec **Food** Mon-Thu 12-9, Fri-Sun 12-7 ⊕ FREE HOUSE ◪ Wylam Tavernale. ☝ 10 **Facilities** Non-diners area ❄ (Bar Restaurant Outside area) ♦ Children's menu Children's portions Outside area ⛱ Beer festival WiFi ☎ (notice required)

NEW The Broad Chare

tel: 0191 211 2144 **25 Broad Chare, Quayside NE1 3DQ**
email: enquiries@thebroadchare.co.uk
dir: *Phone for detailed directions*

A properly welcoming pub hits the spot

The pub's own-label brew, The Writer's Block, is just one of several real ale choices at the polished oak bar in this proper pub. Dog Dancer and Happy Daze ciders are here too, along with a dozen wine choices, world bottled beers and a quirky collection of whiskies. Expect service with a smile from the proprietor and his team, for the atmosphere here is genuinely friendly. Settle on a high bar stool or leather banquette, or head to the upstairs dining room to eat. Dishes of proper food include creamed smoked haddock, celery and fennel; and grilled calves' liver with onions and bacon.

Open all day all wk Closed 25-26 Dec, 1 Jan **Food** all wk 11-11 Av main course £12 Restaurant menu available all wk ⊕ FREE HOUSE ◪ Wylam The Writer's Block, Bass, Timothy Taylor Landlord Ò Gwynt y Ddraig Dog Dancer & Happy Daze. ☝ **Facilities** Non-diners area ❄ (Bar) ♦ Children's menu Children's portions WiFi

Crown Posada

tel: 0191 232 1269 **31 Side NE1 3JE**
dir: *Phone for detailed directions*

Great local beer in a fantastic setting

This glorious Grade II listed building is one of the most famous pubs in Newcastle. The façade is Victorian, there's an elaborately panelled entrance and original stained glass windows, and the music comes courtesy of a 1940s gramophone. You can get a freshly made sandwich and a packet of crisps, but beer's the thing here. Check out the well-kept real ales; Allendale Pennine Pale, Hadrian Border Tyneside Blonde or Blackgate Bitter, and three guest ales.

Open all day all wk **Food** Contact pub for food times ⊕ SIR JOHN FITZGERALD ◪ Allendale Pennine Pale, Hadrian Border Tyneside Blonde & Blackgate Bitter, guest ales. **Facilities** Non-diners area Beer festival WiFi

WARWICKSHIRE

ALDERMINSTER
Map 10 SP24

The Bell ★★★★ INN ⊕
PICK OF THE PUBS

See Pick of the Pubs on opposite page

ALVESTON
Map 10 SP25

The Baraset Barn
PICK OF THE PUBS

tel: 01789 295510 **1 Pimlico Ln CV37 7RJ**
email: barasetbarn@lovelypubs.co.uk
dir: *Phone for detailed directions*

200-year-old history with contemporary refinements

Barn is what it's called, because barn is what it was. The original flagstones reflect its 200 years of history, but now it's a light and modern gastro-pub, the dramatic interior styled in granite, pewter and oak. Stone steps lead from the bar to the main dining area with brick walls and high oak beams, while the open mezzanine level offers a good view of the glass-fronted kitchen. The menu successfully blends classic British with Mediterranean ideas, such as sharing plates of meze. A sample of starters includes smoked haddock fishcake, poached egg, wilted spinach and hollandaise; and bourbon and maple syrup glazed baby back ribs. Follow with chicken Kiev with watercress and garlic butter; ricotta and vegetable Wellington; or crispy Korean chicken salad. The patio garden is perfect for outdoor dining.

Open all day 11-11 (Fri-Sat 11am-mdnt Sun 12-6) Closed 1 Jan, Sun eve **Food** Lunch Mon-Sat 12-2.30, Sun 12-3.30 Dinner Mon-Sat 6.30-9.30 Set menu available Restaurant menu available all wk ⊕ FREE HOUSE ◀ Purity Gold. **Facilities** Non-diners area ❄ (Bar Garden) ♦ Children's portions Garden ⊓ Parking WiFi ▭

ARDENS GRAFTON
Map 10 SP15

The Golden Cross
PICK OF THE PUBS

tel: 01789 772420 **Wixford Rd B50 4LG**
email: info@thegoldencross.net
dir: *Phone for detailed directions*

Pretty pub with prized faggots

This traditional 18th-century country inn is the place to go to if you like faggots. The original recipe went missing but was then rediscovered; the tasty savouries are served with creamy mashed potato, mushed peas and onion gravy. Eat them in the pastel-toned dining room with attractive plasterwork on the ceiling, or in the rug-strewn, flagstone-floored and heavily beamed bar. The seasonally changing main menu of pub favourites is augmented by a daily changing specials board; ingredients for the freshly prepared dishes are sourced from best quality local suppliers. The single menu served throughout proffers a starter such as haddock and spring onion fishcake with dressed leaves and tartare sauce. Comforting mains include beef or chicken burgers served on a toasted bap with tomato and red pepper relish, double-dipped hand-cut chips and rocket salad. Sharing tapas platters brim with either fish or meats. Oven-baked camembert with red onion jam, olives and toasted farmhouse bread is a popular vegetarian option.

Open all wk Mon-Thu 12-3 5-11 (Fri-Sat 12-12 Sun 12-10.30) **Food** Lunch Mon-Fri 12-2.30, Sat 12-9, Sun 12-8 Dinner Mon-Fri 5-9, Sat 12-9, Sun 12-8 Set menu available ⊕ CHARLES WELLS ◀ Bombardier, Purity, guest ales Ö Thatchers Heritage. ⚑ 10 **Facilities** Non-diners area ❄ (Bar Garden) ♦ Children's menu Children's portions Garden ⊓ Parking WiFi ▭ (notice required)

The King's Head

The King's Head is a 15th Century Grade II listed pub in the beautiful village of Aston Cantlow. An historic building, said to have held Shakespeare's parents wedding breakfast, the property is steeped in history. Ideally placed in between Henley-in-Arden and Stratford-upon-Avon, it is easily accessible from the motorway network and only 20mins from the NEC arenas. Owned and Managed by Chef Proprietor Brett Sandland, the King's Head offers food and drink to suit all. From traditional fish and chips, to the signature dish of duck mixed grill, the pub caters for those wanting a quick bite in the bar, to those wanting a more formal dinner for a special occasion. The pub also caters for celebrations and weddings of all sizes, and offers live music in the garden over bank holidays. With real fires in the bar, the atmosphere is welcoming and they allow dogs in the bar and garden. Children have their own menu too. The pub is open all day, everyday, for food until 9.30pm (8pm Sundays)

21 Bearley Road, Aston Cantlow, Henley-in-Arden, Warwickshire B95 6HY • Tel: 01789 488242 • Website: thekh.co.uk

PICK OF THE PUBS

The Bell ★★★★ INN ❀

ALDERMINSTER Map 10 SP24

tel: 01789 450414 **CV37 8NY**
email: info@thebellald.co.uk
web: www.thebellald.co.uk
dir: *On A3400, 3.5m S of
Stratford-upon-Avon*

Country pub chic with great food

Part of the Alscot Estate, this striking Georgian coaching inn is set in the heart of a picturesque village between Stratford-upon-Avon and Shipston on Stour. The interior is a refreshing mix of contemporary comforts and rustic charm, with the historic core of beamed ceilings, blazing log fires and flagged floors combining well with bold colours and stylish fabrics and the modern dining courtyard. The inn is located beside a grassy garden, and the riverside meadow that ripples down to the River Stour is perfect for enjoying summer picnics. The restaurant oozes charm and is cunningly designed into quirky zones, each with its own distinct atmosphere. Time to enjoy a pint of North Cotswold Windrush or the inn's locally-brewed Alscot Ale and nibble on a self-selected grazing platter, perhaps laden with falafel, grilled halloumi, feta, olives, tzatziki and tabbouleh salad, before considering the indulgent daily-changing menu. Typically, begin with pan-seared wood pigeon, black rice salad, carrot and turnip with pumpkin muffin, then follow with pan-seared

scallops and bream with truffle oil mash, wild mushrooms, cavolo nero and bacon crumble. Round off with apple and passion fruit mousse with champagne sorbet, or a plate of local cheeses with home-made chutney. In the bar, sandwiches are served with hand-cut chips and salad, or you can try a Bell classic, perhaps the 10oz chargrilled rump steak with peppercorn sauce, or jerk-spiced Warwickshire pulled pork with red slaw in a brioche bun. Much of the produce is local, with vegetables and herbs harvested from Alscot's historic kitchen garden, and game and venison is reared on the estate.

Open all day all wk 9.30-3 6-11 (Fri-Sat 9.30am-11pm) **Food** Lunch Mon-Thu

12-2.30, Fri-Sun 12-3 Dinner Mon-Thu 6.30-9, Fri-Sat 6.30-9.30, Sun 6.30-8.30 Av main course £10 Set menu available Restaurant menu available all wk ⊕ FREE HOUSE ◀ Alscot Ale, North Cotswold Windrush ♂ Robinsons. ♟ 12 **Facilities** Non-diners area ✿ (Bar Garden Outside area) ♦♦ Children's menu Children's portions Garden Outside area ⊼ Parking WiFi 🚌 (notice required) **Rooms** 9

ARMSCOTE
Map 10 SP24

The Fuzzy Duck ★★★★ INN ◉
PICK OF THE PUBS

tel: 01608 682635 **Ilmington Rd CV37 8DD**
email: info@fuzzyduckarmscote.com web: www.fuzzyduckarmscote.com
dir: *From A429 (Fosse Way) N of Moreton-in-Marsh follow Armscote signs*

Innovative modern cooking in stylish village pub

In the picturesque hamlet of Armscote, a few miles south of Stratford-upon-Avon, this building once housed the local blacksmith before becoming a coaching inn in the 18th century. The pub is owned by the family behind the Baylis & Harding toiletries company; its range of luxury products take pride of place in the stylish bedrooms. In the buzzy bar, contemporary furnishings combine with exposed beams, flagstone floors and original fireplaces to create a relaxed setting to enjoy local ales such as Purity Mad Goose. The seasonal menu majors on local produce and robust, innovative dishes. Try the pork pie with date chutney; duck liver parfait; or leek and wild mushroom tart to start, followed by lamb shank with buttered mash, green beans and lamb gravy; or local venison pie. An attractive courtyard garden is a peaceful spot for alfresco dining but if the weather turns, you might be able to make use of the pub's quirky Hunter welly loan service.

Open 12-11 (Sun 12-5) Closed Sun eve, Mon **Food** Lunch Tue-Sat 12-2.30, Sun 12-3 Dinner Tue-Thu 6.30-9, Fri-Sat 6-9 Restaurant menu available Tue-Sat ⊕ FREE HOUSE ◀ Purity Mad Goose, guest ales ♂ Aspall, Westons Mortimers Orchard. ₹ 11 **Facilities** Non-diners area ♣ (Bar Restaurant Garden) ♦♦ Children's menu Children's portions Family room Garden ╕ Parking WiFi **Rooms** 4

ASTON CANTLOW
Map 10 SP16

The King's Head

tel: 01789 488242 **21 Bearley Rd B95 6HY**
email: info@thekh.co.uk web: www.thekh.co.uk
dir: *Exit A3400 between Stratford-upon-Avon & Henley-in-Arden. Follow Aston Cantlow signs*

Rustic Tudor pub steeped in history

Flanked by a huge spreading chestnut tree and oozing historic charm, this impressive black-and-white timbered Tudor building has been appointed in a modern style. Tastefully rustic inside, with lime-washed low beams, huge polished

flagstones, painted brick walls, old scrubbed pine tables and crackling log fires, it draws diners for innovative pub food. Tuck into pub classics such as fish and chips; and sausage and mash, or choose from the à la carte dishes such as pan-fried fillet of stone bass with sesame seed crust; pork and prawn wontons with ginger cream, followed by chocolate pot with orange shortbread biscuit. If you don't want alcohol, try one of the specialist teas on offer. There's also an area for alfresco dining.

The King's Head

Open all day all wk **Food** Mon-Sat 12-9.30, Sun 12-8 ⊕ ENTERPRISE INNS ◀ Purity Gold, Greene King Abbot Ale, M&B Brew XI ♂ Aspall. ₹ 12 **Facilities** Non-diners area ♣ (Bar Garden) ♦♦ Children's menu Children's portions Garden ╕ Parking WiFi ⬛ (notice required)

See advert on page 512

BROOM
Map 10 SP05

The Broom Tavern

tel: 01789 778199 **32 High St B50 4HL**
email: enquiries@thebroomtavern.co.uk
dir: *From A46 onto B439 towards Bidford-on-Avon. Left into Victoria Rd to Broom. In Broom left into High St. Pub on right*

Historic food pub with links to Shakespeare

Reputed to be one of Shakespeare's drinking haunts, The Broom is a timber-framed, 16th-century pub in a pretty village. This venerable inn has great charm and character, with log fires in winter and three sunny beer gardens for alfresco drinking in the summer. Chef patron Fritz Ronnenburg showcases the best local produce and offers locally-brewed ales including Purity Mad Goose. Everything is made on the premises and a typical meal might include organic Scottish salmon 'three ways' with samphire, Jerusalem artichoke, potato, lemon and belly pork lardons, followed by breast of Gressingham duck, gastronome potatoes, confit duck straws, local Mudwalls Farm vegetables and winter berry sauce.

Open all wk 12-3 5-11 (Sat-Sun all day) **Food** Lunch Mon-Sat 12-2.30, Sun 12-6 Dinner Mon-Sat 6-9.30, Sun 12-6 ⊕ FREE HOUSE ◀ Sharp's Doom Bar, Wye Valley Butty Bach, Purity Mad Goose & Pure Gold ♂ Hogan's, Westons. ₹ 10 **Facilities** Non-diners area ♣ (Bar Garden) ♦♦ Children's menu Children's portions Garden ╕ Beer festival Cider festival Parking WiFi ⬛ (notice required)

EARLSWOOD

Map 10 SP17

Bull's Head

tel: 01564 700368 **7 Limekiln Ln B94 6BU**
email: relax@bullsheadearlswood.co.uk **web:** www.bullsheadearlswood.co.uk
dir: *M42 junct 4, A34 signed Birmingham & Solihull. Left signed Chiswick Green. Through Chiswick Green, straight on at x-roads into Vicarage Rd. Left at T-junct signed Earlswood. On right bend turn left into Salter St. Pub on left*

Village food pub with large sun terrace

In the charming rural setting of Earlswood, near Solihull, the Bull's Head was built in the 18th century to house navvies building the Stratford-upon-Avon canal. Rumoured to be haunted by the ghost of a lime kiln worker, it comprises a cluster of whitewashed cottages and became a pub in 1832. Popular with walkers, the pub is owned by the Daniel Thwaites Brewery and retains much of its original charm courtesy of log fires and a large sun terrace. Enjoy a glass of Lancaster Bomber as you choose from an extensive menu offering pizzas, deli boards, salads and chargrilled steaks.

Bull's Head

Open all day all wk **Food** Bkfst 9am-11.30am Lunch all wk 12-10 Dinner all wk 12-10 ⊕ THWAITES INNS OF CHARACTER ◀ Lancaster Bomber, Wainwright, guest ales. ☗ 11 **Facilities** Non-diners area ❖ (Bar Garden) ♦ Children's menu Children's portions Garden ⋈ Parking WiFi ▭ (notice required)

See advert below

EDGEHILL
Map 11 SP34

Castle at Edgehill ★★★★ RR 🏵️🏵️

tel: 01295 670255 **OX15 6DJ**
email: enquiries@castleatedgehill.co.uk **web:** www.castleatedgehill.co.uk
dir: *M40 junct 11, A422 towards Stratford-upon-Avon. 6m to Upton House, next right, 1.5m to Edgehill*

A most unusual country pub

In 1742, a man called Sanderson Miller built this curious castellated property on top of Edgehill to mark the centenary of the English Civil War's first major skirmish. In 1822 it became an alehouse; fast-forward a hundred years and it was acquired by the Hook Norton Brewery, whose real ales you'll find to this day in the two bars. There are four dining areas including a glass-protected balcony with panoramic views. The modern menus are inviting and include dishes such as potted Cornish crab, mushroom loaf and samphire cream; and blade of beef, horseradish purée, shallots, broad beans, onion rings and garlic potato.

Open all day all wk **Food** Lunch Mon-Sat 12-2.30, Sun 12-4 Dinner Mon-Sat 6-9 ⊕ HOOK NORTON 🍺 Hooky Bitter, Old Hooky Ŏ Westons Old Rosie.
Facilities Non-diners area 🐾 (Bar Garden) ♦♦ Children's menu Children's portions Garden 🍺 Beer festival Cider festival Parking WiFi 🚌 (notice required) **Rooms** 4

ETTINGTON
Map 10 SP24

The Chequers Inn
PICK OF THE PUBS

tel: 01789 740387 **91 Banbury Rd CV37 7SR**
email: hello@the-chequers-ettington.co.uk
dir: *Take A422 from Stratford-upon-Avon towards Banbury. Ettington in 5m, after junction with A429*

Tastefully decorated country inn serving classic fare

Thought to have once been a courthouse and probably named after the old chequer tree that used to stand in front of the building, this locals' pub is an elegant place to eat and drink. Go for a pint of Prescott Chequered Flag or Banks's Bitter in the bar, before moving on to the dining room, decorated in French style with ornate mirrors and chairs, rich tapestries and comfortable armchairs. A choice of interesting sandwiches might include grilled brie and apple chutney; or BBQ pulled pork flatbread with rocket, and there are classics like beef chilli con carne; and cheeseburger with gherkins. For something more substantial, kick off proceedings with chicken and wild mushroom galatine with tarragon mayonnaise; followed by crispy confit duck leg, fondant potato, buttered cabbage and plum jus; or artichoke, fennel and saffron ravioli, Pernod spinach cream. Puddings may include cinnamon sponge, warm apple rose and ginger syrup.

Open 12-3 5-11 (Sat 12-11 Sun 12-6) Closed Sun eve, Mon **Food** Lunch Tue-Fri 12-2.30, Sat 12-9.30, Sun 12.30-3.30 Dinner Tue-Fri 6.30-9.30, Sat 12-9.30 ⊕ FREE HOUSE 🍺 Chequers Pale Ale, Banks's Bitter, Prescott Chequered Flag Ŏ Aspall, Thatchers Gold. 🍷 8 **Facilities** Non-diners area 🐾 (Bar Garden) ♦♦ Children's menu Children's portions Garden 🍺 Parking WiFi 🚌 (notice required)

FARNBOROUGH
Map 11 SP44

The Kitchen at Farnborough

tel: 01295 690615 **OX17 1DZ**
email: dining@thekitchenfarnborough.co.uk
dir: *M40 junct 11 towards Banbury. Right at 3rd rdbt onto A423 signed Southam. 4m onto A423. Left onto single track road signed Farnborough. Approx 1m, right into village, pub on right*

Stylish pub with tempting food

This Grade II listed, 16th-century property on the National Trust-owned Farnborough Park Estate has had change of name, a full refurbishment and a fresh ethos under the new team. The bar serves Purity Brewery ales, Cotswold Cider Company No Brainer and Sideburn, and plenty of wines by the glass. The frequently changing menus reflect the seasons, with close links with local suppliers and good use of ingredients grown in the pub's own kitchen garden. Dorset scallops, peas, black pudding, wild garlic and lemon might be followed by smoked honey roast pork belly, watercress, apples, butter mash and English mustard sauce.

Open 10-3 6-11 (Sat-Sun all day) Closed Tue-Wed, Thu L **Food** Lunch Mon & Fri-Sat 12-3, Sun 12-4 Dinner Mon & Thu-Sat 6-10, Sun fr 4 Set menu available Restaurant menu available all wk ⊕ FREE HOUSE 🍺 Purity Gold & Pure UBU Ŏ Cotswold Sideburn & No Brainer. 🍷 12 **Facilities** Non-diners area 🐾 (Bar Garden) ♦♦ Children's menu Children's portions Play area Garden 🍺 Parking WiFi 🚌 (notice required)

GAYDON
Map 11 SP35

The Malt Shovel

tel: 01926 641221 **Church Rd CV35 0ET**
email: malt.shovel@btconnect.com
dir: *M40 junct 12, B4451 to Gaydon*

Village pub that gets it right

Richard and Debi Morisot's 16th-century village pub has a reputation for being friendly and reliable, qualities that have helped to make their venture a success. Another plus is the range of real ales, usually from Sharp's, Everards, Fuller's, Hook Norton, Timothy Taylor or Wadworth. Menu options include smoked haddock Welsh rarebit; wild boar and apple sausages braised in Calvados and cider; three cheese vegetable lasagne; and bread and butter pudding with cream, custard or ice cream. If all you want is a lunchtime snack, there are chunky granary sandwiches, baguettes and hot paninis. Well-behaved children and dogs are welcome and can play with Molly, the Morisot's Jack Russell.

Open all wk 11-3 5-11 (Fri-Sat 11-11 Sun 12-10.30) **Food** Lunch all wk 12-2 Dinner all wk 6.30-9 Av main course £11 ⊕ ENTERPRISE INNS 🍺 Fuller's London Pride, Timothy Taylor Landlord, Everards Tiger, Wadworth 6X, Hook Norton, Sharp's Doom Bar Ŏ Thatchers Gold, Westons Stowford Press. 🍷 11 **Facilities** Non-diners area 🐾 (Bar Outside area) ♦♦ Children's portions Outside area 🍺 Parking WiFi 🚌 (notice required)

HENLEY-IN-ARDEN
Map 10 SP16

The Bluebell 🏵️🏵️

tel: 01564 793049 **93 High St B95 5AT**
email: info@bluebellhenley.co.uk
dir: *Opposite police station on A3400 in town centre*

Innovative food in pub with plenty of character

This rambling, half-timbered old coaching inn has fronted Henley's picturesque High Street for over 500 years. Behind the property is a secluded, lavender-scented beer-garden, where beers from Hooky or Purity can be enjoyed in the warmer months. The punchy, seasonal menus have gained the award of two AA Rosettes. Typically, expect a starter of braised pig cheek, lobster bisque, apple and bacon followed by halibut, butter bean and chorizo cassoulet; or shoulder of lamb, broccoli, tomato, yellow carrots and creamed potatoes. Chocolate mousse cake and raspberry sorbet to finish.

Open all day Closed Mon **Food** Tue-Thu 12-11, Fri-Sat 12-12, Sun 12-7 ⊕ FREE HOUSE 🍺 Purity Pure UBU & Mad Goose, Hook Norton Hooky Bitter, Guinness, 2 rotating guest ales Ŏ Hogan's. 🍷 12 **Facilities** Non-diners area 🐾 (Bar Restaurant Garden) ♦♦ Children's portions Garden 🍺 Parking WiFi

HUNNINGHAM
Map 11 SP36

The Red Lion

tel: 01926 632715 **Main St CV33 9DY**
dir: *From Leamington Spa take B4453, through Cubbington to Weston under Wetherby. Follow Hunningham signs (turn sharp right as road bends left towards Princethorpe)*

Popular village inn next to the river

In the heart of rural Warwickshire, beside a 14th-century bridge, this 17th-century country pub's beer garden leads down to the River Leam and offers views of sheep and cows grazing. Inside, it's 'modern country-style' with different areas to eat in. Enjoy a pint of Red Lion House Special ale as you choose from the appealing menu, which might start off with Thai crab cakes, sweetcorn and chilli relish or chicken liver parfait, apricot chutney and brioche. Typical main courses include fish pie and creamed leeks; and game and pancetta casserole with smoked cheddar dumplings and roasted garlic mash. Leave room for Bakewell tart with raspberry ripple ice cream. A change of hands.

Open all day all wk Mon Sat 11-11 (Sun 11-10.30) **Food** all wk 12-9 Av main course £12.95 Set menu available ⊕ GREENE KING/METROPOLITAN PUB CO ◄ IPA, Abbot Ale, Red Lion House Special, guest ales ♂ Thatchers Gold. **Facilities** Non-diners area ♥ (Bar Garden) ♦ Children's menu Children's portions Garden ⌂ Parking WiFi ▦ (notice required)

ILMINGTON
Map 10 SP24

The Howard Arms ★★★★★ INN ⊛　PICK OF THE PUBS

tel: 01608 682226 **Lower Green CV36 4LT**
email: info@howardarms.com **www.** www.howardarms.com
dir: *Exit A429 or A3400, 9m from Stratford-upon-Avon*

A popular base for walkers

Overlooking the lower green and pastures at the fringe of this charming North Cotswolds village, the 400-year-old Howard Arms is a great base for local walks, detailed in a guide here in support of church funds, and handy for the renowned National Trust gardens at Hidcote, just along the lane. Well-appointed residential rooms allow guests to indulge these passions at leisure. The flagstoned bar, diverse mix of timeworn furnishings and open-plan dining room create a civilised yet informal atmosphere; a crackling log fire ensures additional warmth for much of the year. Top notch beers from the likes of Purity wet the whistle; whilst fine food sleuths will be rewarded with a stylish menu drawing on local, seasonal produce as available. Kick in with duck liver parfait, rabbit and apricot ballotine, plum jam and toast; leaving room for mains ranging from pub classic fish and chips to modern dishes like pan-fried fillet of stone bass with polenta, kale and beetroot; or Stilton arancini, polenta chips, ratatouille and roast garlic.

Open all day all wk **Food** Lunch Mon-Sat 12-3, Sun 12-8 Dinner Mon-Sat 6-9.30, Sun 12-8 ⊕ FREE HOUSE ◄ Wye Valley Bitter, Hook Norton Old Hooky, Purity, Timothy Taylor ♂ Orchard Pig. ♟ 30 **Facilities** Non-diners area ♥ (Bar Garden) ♦ Children's portions Garden ⌂ Parking WiFi ▦ (notice required) **Rooms** 8

KENILWORTH
Map 10 SP27

The Almanack

tel: 01926 353637 **Abbey End North CV8 1QJ**
email: almanack@peachpubs.com
dir: *Exit A46 at Kenilworth & brown Castle sign, towards town centre. Left into Abbey Hill (B4104) signed Balsall Common. At rdbt into Abbey End. Opposite Holiday Inn*

New look all-day eatery

The refurbished Almanack has a modern and bright bar area with pale grey walls, comfortable armchairs, bar tables, herringbone parquet floors and mesh bar

lighting. Metal screens divide the bar from the eatery with its leather booths and tones of blue teal and red; there's a new chef's table here too. Serving food from brunch through to the evening, the dishes on the menu might be BBQ brisket and sweet potato hash with free-range egg and almond milk porridge; chargrilled lamb chops and lamb shoulder cassoulet with cavolo nero and salsa verde; and for dessert, pie of the day, or iced gin and tonic parfait.

Open all day all wk 8am-11pm (Thu-Sat 8am-mdnt Sun 8am-11pm) Closed 25 Dec **Food** Lunch all wk 12-6 Dinner all wk 6-10 Set menu available ⊕ FREE HOUSE/ PEACH PUBS ◄ Purity Pure UBU & Gold, Sharp's Doom Bar ♂ Aspall. ♟ 16 **Facilities** Non-diners area ♥ (Bar Outside area) ♦ Children's portions Outside area ⌂ WiFi ▦ (notice required)

LADBROKE
Map 11 SP45

NEW The Bell Inn

tel: 01926 811224 **Banbury Rd CV47 2BY**
email: enquiries@thebellinnladbroke.co.uk
dir: *Follow Ladbroke signs from A423 (S of Southam)*

Village pub with a bright future

Once a four-pub village, only the attractive, white-painted Bell has stood the test of time. Run with flair by husband and wife Huw and Ruth Griffiths, it lies way back from the road, with a tree-shaded garden and tables to one side. Real design flair is evident inside. Beers change frequently, sometimes to include the locally brewed What the Fox's Hat. Representing a broad menu, options are crispy duck spring roll; various burgers, including bean with grilled haloumi; pie of the day; supreme of pheasant wrapped in bacon with juniper mousse; and seared pavé of salmon with Puy lentil and spinach cassoulet.

Open 12-3 5.30-11 Closed Sun eve & Mon **Food** Lunch Tue-Sun 12-2 Dinner Tue-Sat 6.30-9.30 Av main course £15.95 Set menu available ⊕ FREE HOUSE ◄ Ringwood Boondoggle, Church End What The Fox's Hat. ♟ 15 **Facilities** Non-diners area ♥ (Bar Garden Outside area) ♦ Children's menu Children's portions Garden Outside area ⌂ Parking WiFi ▦ (notice required)

LAPWORTH
Map 10 SP17

The Boot Inn
PICK OF THE PUBS

tel: 01564 782464 **Old Warwick Rd B94 6JU**
email: thebootinn@lovelypubs.co.uk
dir: *Phone for detailed directions*

Stylish country pub by canal

Precision-cut logs and soft modern furnishings meet the eye in this convivial, 16th-century former coaching inn beside the Grand Union Canal. Beyond its smart interior is an attractive garden, on cooler days under a canopied patio with heaters. Free-house status means a good choice of real ales in the shape of Purity Pure UBU, Sharp's Doom Bar and Wye Valley HPA. But for many the draw is the brasserie-style food, and there's lots to choose from. For example, the first course could be Thai chicken patties with papaya salad, miso aïoli and black pepper crackers; mains include chargrilled 28-day-matured Hereford rib-eye steak with roast tomato, crispy onions, skin-on chips and béarnaise sauce; and South Indian spiced spit chicken with sweet potato and coconut curry with saffron and cashew pilaf. Children and well-behaved dogs are welcome.

Open all day all wk 11-11 (Thu-Sat 11am-mdnt Sun 12-10.30) **Food** Lunch Mon-Sat 12-2.30, Sun 12-4.30 Dinner Mon-Sat 6.30-9.30, Sun 6.30-9 Set menu available ⊕ FREE HOUSE ◄ Purity Pure UBU, Wye Valley HPA, Sharp's Doom Bar ♂ Sharp's Orchard. ♟ 9 **Facilities** Non-diners area ♥ (Bar Garden) ♦ Children's menu Children's portions Garden ⌂ Parking WiFi ▦ (notice required)

LAPWORTH *continued*

Navigation Inn

tel: 01564 783337 **Old Warwick Rd B94 6NA**
email: info@navigationlapworth.co.uk
dir: *On B4439 (Old Warwick Rd) between Lapworth & Rowington*

Family-run traditional pub with canalside beer garden

Right by Bridge 65 on the Grand Union Canal, the Navigation has a long history of refreshing narrowboat crews, walkers and cyclists. Keeping draught ales, lagers and ciders in optimum condition is second nature to landlord and former brewery engineer, Mark Ainley. Note to beer-hunters: unique to the pub is Coventry-brewed Lapworth Gold; also unique is Guinness on hand-pull, something Mark's expertise enabled him to devise. Fresh, home-made food served in the comfortable interior includes sandwiches and wraps with chips and dressed salad; sausages and mash, garden peas and onion gravy; wild mushroom tagliatelle; and home-made Angus beefburger with all the trimmings.

Open all day all wk **Food** Lunch Mon-Fri 12-3, Sat 12-9.30, Sun 12-8 Dinner Mon-Fri 6-9.30, Sat 12-9.30, Sun 12-8 Set menu available Restaurant menu available all wk ⊕ ENTERPRISE INNS ◼ Lapworth Gold, Timothy Taylor Landlord, Purity Mad Goose, Wadworth 6X, Guinness ♻ Thatchers Gold, Aspall. ♀ 9
Facilities Non-diners area ✿ (Bar Garden) ♦♦ Children's menu Children's portions Garden ⊼ Parking WiFi ▄

LEAMINGTON SPA (ROYAL)   Map 10 SP36

NEW The Drawing Board

tel: 01926 330636 **18 Newbold St CV32 4HN**
email: hello@thedrawingboard.pub
dir: *Contact pub for detailed directions*

Fusion food in eclectic surroundings

Calling itself 'an urban bar/restaurant', The Drawing Board offers a fascinatingly eclectic experience, a relaxed, friendly atmosphere and quirky contemporary surroundings, as well as a good range of real ale and craft beers, and interesting global fusion-inspired dishes. On the menu you'll find all sorts, from tapas and small plates to 'bits in buns' plus the usual starters and mains. Try the spam fritters with mustard mayo; or maybe something more substantial – Asian spiced goats' cheese with pickled fig, rocket, port and balsamic syrup to begin, followed by seared king scallops 'aloo gobi' with saffron potatoes, cauliflower fritter, golden sultanas and beurre noisette; or smoked fillet of Welsh Black beef with wild mushrooms, truffled turnips, potato croquant and Madeira jus.

Open all day all wk **Food** Lunch all wk 12-3 Dinner all wk 5.30-9.30 Av main course £15 ⊕ FREE HOUSE ◼ Black Sheep Golden Sheep, Purity Pure UBU, Sharp's Doom Bar, North Cotswold Winter Solstice ♻ Gwynt y Ddraig Black Dragon. ♀ 18
Facilities Non-diners area ✿ (All areas) ♦♦ Children's menu Children's portions Garden Outside area ⊼ Parking WiFi

The Moorings at Myton

tel: 01926 425043 **Myton Rd CV31 3NY**
email: info@themoorings.co.uk
dir: *M40 junct 14 or 13, A452 towards Leamington Spa. At 4th rdbt after crossing canal, pub on left*

Anglo-French cuisine in waterside location

This food-led pub beside the Grand Union Canal is a popular stop for boaters on England's arterial waterway. Diners may look forward to dishes created by Raymond Blanc protégés Charles Harris and Nigel Brown, whose ever-evolving Anglo-French menu relies on local suppliers for the ingredients. A sharing charcuterie board is a substantial starter; mains include 28-day dry-aged Aberdeenshire steaks, or perhaps pan-fried duck breast, confit duck leg croquette, herb rösti, wilted spinach

and orange jus. Fruit ciders, a decent wine list and beer from Warwickshire craft brewery slip down easily on the waterside terrace.

Open all day all wk **Food** Lunch all wk 12-2.30 Dinner all wk 6-9.30 ⊕ CHARLES WELLS ◼ Bombardier, Young's London Gold, Courage Directors, Warwickshire Darling Buds. ♀ 13 **Facilities** Non-diners area ✿ (Bar Garden) ♦♦ Children's menu Children's portions Family room Garden ⊼ Parking WiFi ▄ (notice required)

LONG COMPTON   Map 10 SP23

The Red Lion ★ ★ ★ ★ INN ◉   PICK OF THE PUBS

tel: 01608 684221 **Main St CV36 5JS**
email: info@redlion-longcompton.co.uk **web:** www.redlion-longcompton.co.uk
dir: *On A3400 between Shipston on Stour & Chipping Norton*

Cotswold character and award-winning cuisine

Wooded ridges ripple along the horizons enfolding this attractive north Cotswolds village. Ramblers challenge a web of recreational trails hereabouts, while folklorists home-in on the mysterious Rollright Stones monument just to the south. Explorers in-the-know then make a bee-line for the village's Red Lion pub. Its Georgian coaching inn origins bequeath an appealing mix of beams, stone-flags and honey-coloured stone, matchboarding, inglenook and log fires. The seasonal menu, complemented by daily specials, has the award of one AA Rosette for the considered mix of classic and contemporary dishes, and may offer starters such as smoked duck salad with poached pears, prosciutto and rocket. Progress then with vegetable and lentil cottage pie; or whole roasted sea bass with baby leaf spinach, grain mustard and tarragon butter. In summer, the shrubby beer garden is just the place to enjoy beers from Hook Norton and Wickwar breweries. Dogs are well-liked here, in fact pigs' ears are available as snacks for your four-legged friend; whilst well-appointed accommodation is on hand for those on short breaks.

Open all wk Mon-Thu 10-2.30 6-11 (Fri-Sun all day) **Food** Lunch Mon-Thu 12-2.30, Fri-Sat 12-9.30, Sun 12-9 Dinner Mon-Thu 6-9, Fri-Sat 12-9.30, Sun 12-9 Av main course £15 Set menu available ⊕ FREE HOUSE ◼ Hook Norton Hooky Bitter, Wickwar Cotswold Way, guest ale ♻ Symonds. ♀ 11 **Facilities** Non-diners area ✿ (All areas) ♦♦ Children's menu Play area Garden Outside area ⊼ Parking WiFi **Rooms** 5

OFFCHURCH   Map 11 SP36

The Stag at Offchurch

tel: 01926 425801 **Welsh Rd CV33 9AQ**
email: info@thestagatoffchurch.com
dir: *From Leamington Spa take A425 towards Southam. At Radford Semele left into Offchurch Ln to Offchurch*

Picturesque pub with progressive menu

The Stag is a charming thatched pub in a classic English village. Considerably modernised, it balances the feel of times long-gone with contemporary flourishes; diners, ramblers and locals all flock to the restaurant and bar. The imaginative menu offers plenty of choice – Berkswell cheese soufflé; Jimmy Butler's free-range pork belly, hog's pudding mousse, apple and sage potato cake, petit pois à la Francais. The head chef specialises in locally raised, 28-day, dry-aged Aberdeenshire beef steaks.

Open all day all wk **Food** Lunch all wk 12-2.30 Dinner all wk 6-9.30 ⊕ FREE HOUSE ◀ Hook Norton, Warwickshire ♂ Somersby. ⬥ 13 **Facilities** Non-diners area ♨ (Bar Garden) ◀ Children's menu Children's portions Garden ⌂ Parking WiFi

---

OXHILL
Map 10 SP34

The Peacock

tel: 01295 688060 **Main St CV35 0QU**
email: info@thepeacockoxhill.co.uk
dir: *From Stratford-upon-Avon take A422 towards Banbury. Turn right to Oxhill*

Destination pub in picturesque village

This 16th-century, stone-built pub, now in new hands, effortlessly combines its historic past with a relaxed modern atmosphere. Hand-pulled ales come from St Austell, Marston's and Wye Valley, and the food reflects the kitchen's focus on meats and vegetables from local farms, and fresh fish from Devon and Cornwall. Meal ideas include a pie of the day; roast chump of lamb, olive crushed potatoes, basil and mint pesto; and pan-fried fillet of hake, sun-blushed tomato mash, mange tout and black olive tapenade. There is also an extensive menu of lunchtime sandwiches and baguettes.

Open all day all wk 12-11 **Food** Lunch Mon-Sat 12-2, Sun 12-8 Dinner Mon-Sat 6-9, Sun 12-8 Set menu available ⊕ FREE HOUSE ◀ Marston's Pedigree, St Austell Tribute, Sharp's Doom Bar, Wye Valley HPA, Salopian Darwin's Origin, Brakspear Bitter ♂ Thatchers Gold, Healey's Cornish Rattler. ⬥ 12 **Facilities** Non-diners area ♨ (Bar Garden) ◀ Children's menu Children's portions Garden ⌂ Parking WiFi ▬ (notice required)

PRESTON BAGOT
Map 10 SP16

The Crabmill

tel: 01926 843342 **B95 5EE**
email: thecrabmill@lovelypubs.co.uk
dir: *M40 junct 16, A3400 towards Stratford-upon-Avon. Take A4189 at lights in Henley-in-Arden. Left, 1.5m pub on left*

Richly varied menu in converted cider mill

Handy for a stroll in superb countryside alongside the Stratford-upon-Avon Canal, this carefully renovated former rural mill, where crab apples were perhaps mashed into cider, is a fine destination dining-pub presented in a modern rustic style. Colourwash, comfy seating and light beams offer an airy, informal interior. The menu changes with the seasons, but a sample meal may start with smoked haddock and leek fishcake; or corned beef and sweet potato hash; then continue with wild mushroom, spinach, mascarpone, sage and lemon gnocchi with granola and pumpkin seeds; or beef, chestnut mushroom and Stinking Bishop cheese pie.

Open all day 11-11 Closed Sun eve **Food** Lunch Mon-Thu 12-3, Fri-Sat 12-5, Sun 12-4 Dinner Mon-Sat 6-9.30 Set menu available ⊕ FREE HOUSE ◀ Purity Gold & Pure UBU, Sharp's Doom Bar, guest ale ♂ Sharp's Orchard. ⬥ 14 **Facilities** Non-diners area ♨ (Bar Garden) ◀ Children's menu Children's portions Garden ⌂ Parking WiFi

---

STRATFORD-UPON-AVON
Map 10 SP25

The One Elm
PICK OF THE PUBS

tel: 01789 404919 **1 Guild St CV37 6QZ**
email: theoneelm@peachpubs.com
dir: *From rdbt on A46 take A3400 (Birmingham Rd) towards town centre. Pass Tesco, through lights, pub after mini rdbt on left*

Quirky decor and a Mediterranean-style courtyard

Handy for the Avon, the popular canal and the Shakespearean attractions of Stratford, the pub is named after a long-gone town boundary landmark. Opening at 11am every day there's an informal, almost continental feel about the place, amplified by the chic, contemporary look of the interior, a hallmark of the innovative Peach Pub Company which owns The One Elm. Explore beyond the stylish, light and bright interior and you'll find a secluded courtyard, the ideal retreat in which to sup beers from Purity, Church Farm and other carefully selected microbreweries in the area. The central, open-to-view kitchen serves dining areas to two floors and offers a versatile menu of modern European dishes, seasonally adjusted. A measure of this could be Enderby smoked haddock and spring onion carnaroli rice risotto; or free-range chicken breast with Iberico chorizo and roasted red pepper sizzler. Various deli boards offer a good taster of meats, fish, cheese or vegetarian options, and there's a generous, well-balanced wine list.

Open all day all wk 11-11 (Fri-Sat 11am-mdnt Sun 11-11) Closed 25 Dec **Food** Lunch all wk 12-6 Dinner all wk 6-10 Av main course £12 Set menu available ⊕ FREE HOUSE/PEACH PUBS ◀ Purity Pure UBU & Gold, Sharp's Doom Bar, Church Farm Harry's Heifer, guest ales ♂ Aspall. ⬥ 14 **Facilities** Non-diners area ♨ (Bar Garden) ◀ Children's menu Children's portions Garden ⌂ Parking WiFi ▬ (notice required)

TANWORTH IN ARDEN
Map 10 SP17

The Bell Inn

tel: 01564 742212 **The Green B94 5AL**
email: thebell@realcoolbars.com
dir: *M42 junct 8, A435 signed Evesham. Left signed Portway & Tanworth (Penn Ln). To T-junct, left signed Tanworth. 1st right signed Tanworth. Inn in village centre*

A popular village pub of both real and TV vintage

Older visitors might remember (or perhaps try to forget) a TV soap called *Crossroads*, many of whose outdoor scenes were shot in Tanworth, doubling as 'Kings Oak'. The pub overlooks the small village green and war memorial, and has stood here since the 17th century, so the cool grey tones of the thoroughly modern bar area might come as a surprise. Starters include liver, brandy and mushroom pâté and goats' cheese with parsley mousse on ciabatta; mains might be grilled sea bass on marinated peppers; tagliatelle with broccoli and pine nuts; or pub classics like Cumberland sausage and mash.

Open all day all wk **Food** Lunch Mon-Sat 12-2.30, Sun 12-8 Dinner Mon-Sat 6.30-9, Sun 12-8 ⊕ ENTERPRISE INNS ◀ Timothy Taylor Landlord ♂ Sandford Orchards Devon Mist. ⬥ **Facilities** Non-diners area ♨ (Bar Outside area) ◀ Children's menu Children's portions Outside area ⌂ Parking WiFi ▬ (notice required)

TEMPLE GRAFTON
Map 10 SP15

The Blue Boar Inn ★★★ INN

tel: 01789 750010 **B49 6NR**
email: info@theblueboar.co.uk **web:** www.theblueboar.co.uk
dir: From A46 (Stratford to Alcester) turn left to Temple Grafton. Pub at 1st x-roads

Historic inn with Cotswolds views

The oldest part of this former ale house and now thriving village inn dates back to the early 1600s and includes a 35-foot deep well, now glassed over and illuminated, set into a flagstone floor and home to goldfish. Warmth in the bar and restaurant comes from four open fires, while in the summer there is a patio garden with views of the Cotswold Hills. Extensive menus include seafood linguine; spinach and asparagus risotto; and honey-roasted duck breast, dauphinoise potatoes, sautéed baby spinach and plum sauce. Wash it down with a pint of Boondoggle from the Ringwood Brewery. There are 14 attractive bedrooms.

Open all day all wk 12-11.30 **Food** Lunch Mon-Fri 12-3, Sat 12-10, Sun 12-9 Dinner Mon-Fri 6-10, Sat 12-10, Sun 12-9 Av main course £9.95 Set menu available Restaurant menu available all wk ⊕ MARSTON'S ◀ Wychwood Hobgoblin, Banks's Bitter, Jennings, Ringwood Boondoggle Ŏ Thatchers Gold. ♀ 10
Facilities Non-diners area ♣ (Bar Garden) ♦╢ Children's menu Children's portions Garden ⇌ Parking WiFi ▭ (notice required) **Rooms** 14

WARWICK
Map 10 SP26

The Rose & Crown
PICK OF THE PUBS

tel: 01926 411117 **30 Market Place CV34 4SH**
email: roseandcrown@peachpubs.com
dir: M40 junct 15 follow signs to Warwick. Pass castle car park entrance, up hill to West Gate, left into Bowling Green St, 1st right, follow one-way system to T-junct, right into Market Place, pub visible ahead

Vibrant and stylish town-centre gastro-pub

Overlooking Warwick's market place, The Rose & Crown's outside tables are in pole position for people-watching while sinking that pint of Purity UBU or Harry Sparrow Cider. The seasonally changing menus and daily specials rely on top quality ingredients – 28-day aged beef from the Warwickshire's butcher who holds The Queen's Royal Warrant, lamb from Cornwall, free-range chickens and sustainably managed fish. In keeping with the pub's own fresh image are dishes such as salt and pepper squid, crunchy salad, lemongrass and chilli dressing; Devon crab and artichoke gratin with crusty bread; Cornish lamb chop and confit belly, mini moussaka, sautéed potatoes and salsa verde; and roasted monkfish, spring vegetables and mussels, with saffron and lemon sauce. Banoffee profiteroles with hot chocolate sauce; and warm treacle tart with clotted cream and golden syrup both make for great ways to end a meal.

Open all day all wk 7am-11pm (Sat 8am-mdnt Sun 8am-11pm) Closed 25 Dec **Food** Lunch all wk 12-6 Dinner Mon-Sat 6-10, Sun 6-9 ⊕ FREE HOUSE/PEACH PUBS ◀ Purity Pure UBU & Gold, Sharp's Doom Bar Ŏ Aspall Draught & Harry Sparrow. ♀
Facilities Non-diners area ♣ (Bar) ♦╢ Children's portions Outside area ⇌ WiFi ▭ (notice required)

The Pheasant
~ Eating House ~

Tel: 01455 220 480   **Fax:** 01455 221 296
Website: www.thepheasanteatinghouse.com
Email: thepheasant01@hotmail.com

A warm welcome greets you at this 17th-century inn, idyllically situated beside a brook in the picturesque village of Withybrook.

The Pheasant is a popular freehouse, full of character. An inglenook fireplace and farming implements add to the warm cosy atmosphere.

A chalkboard displays daily and seasonal specials, complementing a wealth of food choices from an extensive menu. Examples of daily specials includes fresh fish such as traditional cod and haddock ranging to dover sole, lemon sole or lobster (preordered); local game; pasta and homemade pies. Vegetarian dishes are also available. Outside the umbrella'd patio area adjacent to the brook accommodates up to 100 people – perfect for a leisurely lunch or a thirst quenching pint of real ale after a walk in the beautiful surrounding countryside.

WELFORD-ON-AVON · Map 10 SP15

The Bell Inn · PICK OF THE PUBS

tel: 01789 750353 **Binton Rd CV37 8EB**
email: info@thebellwelford.co.uk
dir: *Phone for detailed directions*

An enjoyably civilised pub

Legend has it that William Shakespeare, having been drinking here with dramatist Ben Jonson, contracted fatal pneumonia after returning to Stratford-upon-Avon in the pouring rain. It's a matter owners Colin and Teresa Ombler leave others to debate, while they focus on providing quality drink and food at this early 16th-century pub. For example, there are always four real ales and 16 wines served by the glass. Starters and light meals include avocado and smoked crispy bacon salad; and crispy fried whitebait dusted with cayenne pepper. Main courses include Thai vegetable curry with basmati rice; or oven-roasted cod, creamy asparagus penne pasta with crispy Serrano ham. Don't miss the banoffee sundae dessert. Each distinct space in the Bell displays its own character, with flagstones in one, and oak flooring in another; there's antique wood panelling in the bar, and three open fires, one an inglenook.

Open all wk 11.30-3 6-11 (Sat 11.30-11 Sun 12-10.30) **Food** Lunch Mon-Fri 11.30-2.30, Sat-Sun all day Dinner Mon-Thu 6-9.30, Fri 6-10, Sat-Sun all day ⊕ ENTERPRISE INNS ◀ Hobsons Best Bitter, Purity Gold & Pure UBU, Morland Old Speckled Hen. ☕ 16 **Facilities** Non-diners area ◀❧ Children's menu Children's portions Garden ☂ Parking WiFi 🚐 (notice required)

WITHYBROOK · Map 11 SP48

The Pheasant Eating House

tel: 01455 220480 **Main St CV7 9LT**
email: thepheasant01@hotmail.com **web:** www.thepheasanteatinghouse.com
dir: *7m NE of Coventry, on B4112*

Crowd-pleasing pub grub in an idyllic location

A warm welcome awaits you at this 17th-century inn, idyllically situated beside the brook where withies were once cut for fencing, hence the village's name, Withybrook. The Pheasant is a popular free house, cosy and full of character with an inglenook fireplace, farm implements and horse-racing photographs on display. The chalkboard flags up specials, complementing a wealth of food choices from the extensive main menu. Take your pick from a range of steak and chicken grills (including fillet, rump and T-bone steaks; chicken Kiev, and Cajun chicken); a half

roast duck with orange or plum sauce; and home-cooked lamb shank with root vegetables. Outside, the patio area is perfect for a leisurely lunch or a thirst-quenching pint of real ale after a walk in the beautiful countryside.

The Pheasant Eating House

Open all wk 11-3 6-11.30 (Sun & BH 11-11) Closed 25-26 Dec **Food** Lunch Mon-Sat 12-2, Sun 12-9 Dinner Mon-Sat 6.30-9.30, Sun 12-9 ⊕ FREE HOUSE ◀ Courage Directors, Theakston Smooth Dark, John Smith's Extra Smooth, Wells Bombardier. ☕ 16 **Facilities** Non-diners area ◀❧ (Garden Outside area) ◀❧ Children's menu Children's portions Garden Outside area ☂ Parking WiFi 🚐 (notice required)

See advert on opposite page

WEST MIDLANDS

BARSTON · Map 10 SP27

The Malt Shovel at Barston · PICK OF THE PUBS

See Pick of the Pubs on page 522

BIRMINGHAM · Map 10 SP08

The High Field

tel: 0121 227 7068 **22 Highfield Rd, Edgbaston B15 3DP**
email: highfield@peachpubs.com

Classy pub making its mark

The Peach Pubs Company renovated and extended this white-painted, early 20th-century Edgbaston villa to become a smart gastro-pub. With two patios to catch plenty of sun, a leafy garden and a light, contemporary orangery, it's rapidly grown to be very popular. Modern brasserie-style dishes, some available all day, include cheese, butcher's, fish and veggie boards; 28-day aged steaks; 'slow and low' dishes such as mustard-glazed pork chop, devilled beans and slaw; and rhubarb and custard tart with mascarpone. Warwickshire brewery Purity supplies UBU and Pure Gold, alongside two changing guest ales and Aspall cider. Sundays offer far more than just roasts.

Open all day all wk 8am-11pm (Fri-Sat 9am-mdnt Sun 9am-11pm) Closed 25 Dec **Food** Lunch 12-6 Dinner 6-10 Restaurant menu available evenings ⊕ FREE HOUSE/ PEACH PUBS ◀ Timothy Taylor Landlord, Purity Pure Gold & UBU Ö Aspall. ☕ 16 **Facilities** Non-diners area ◀❧ (Bar Garden) ◀❧ Children's portions Garden ☂ Parking WiFi 🚐 (notice required)

PICK OF THE PUBS

The Malt Shovel at Barston

BARSTON   Map 10 SP27

tel: 01675 443223 **Barston Ln B92 0JP**
email: themaltshovelatbarston@gmail.com
web: www.themaltshovelatbarston.com
dir: *M42 junct 5, A4141 towards Knowle.*
Left into Jacobean Ln, right at T-junct
(Hampton Ln). Left into Barston Ln,
0.5m

Smart, busy inn down the country lanes

The Malt Shovel is an airy, well designed free house with modern soft furnishings and interesting artefacts. An early 20th-century, stylishly converted mill building, it sits comfortably in the countryside outside Solihull. Natural wood and pastel colours characterise the interiors and flowers decorate the unclothed tables in the tiled dining area. The bar is cosy and relaxed with winter log fires, and there's an attractive garden for outdoor dining; at weekends, the restaurant in the adjacent converted barn is opened. The extensive choice of modern British dishes makes the best of fresh seasonal ingredients, and, predictably, the daily fish specials board is popular with lovers of seafood — perhaps tempura soft shell crab, shiitake mushrooms, bok choy and satay sauce; or line-caught mackerel, free-range slow roast pork belly and buttered Savoy cabbage. A look through the imaginative menu finds starters such as chicken and chorizo patties with

guacamole, tortilla chips and sour cream; or wild pigeon breast, pear and vanilla purée, balsamic shallot and pine nuts. Main course dishes are just as appetising: there could be Jamaican spiced slow roast lamb, sweet potato, mango and ginger beer shot; salmon fishcakes, spinach, free-range poached eggs and tarragon hollandaise; and open camembert Wellington, fire-roasted peppers, artichoke hearts and courgettes. As for desserts, you could easily be tempted by salted caramel chocolate torte with caramel sauce; or gooseberry bread and butter pudding. A board of English and European cheeses with grapes, celery, red onion chutney and artisan crackers will fill any remaining corners.

Open all day all wk **Food** Lunch Mon-Sat 12-2.30, Sun 12-4 Dinner Mon-Sat 6-9.30 Av main course £16.95
⊕ FREE HOUSE ◀ St Austell Tribute, M&B Brew XI, Sharp's Doom Bar, Black Sheep. ♀ 15 **Facilities** Non-diners area
❀ (Bar Garden) ♦♦ Children's menu Children's portions Garden ⊼ Parking WiFi

BIRMINGHAM *continued*

The Old Joint Stock

tel: 0121 200 1892 **4 Temple Row West B2 5NY**
email: oldjointstock@fullers.co.uk
dir: *Opposite main entrance to St Philip's Cathedral, just off Colmore Row*

Great for pies and pre-theatre drinks

A pub with its own theatre and art gallery, its high-Victorian Gothic interior incorporates an immense domed ceiling, stately-home fittings and towering mahogany island bar. Originally a library and later a bank, this impressively colonnaded building was designed by the same architect as part of St Philip's Cathedral opposite. Pies take up a chunk of the menu, which also features seared duck breast and pomegranate salad; pan-fried sea bass fillet with pearl barley and butterbean casserole, chorizo, salsa verde; and apple and blackberry crumble with custard. Please note, no children are allowed after 6pm.

Open all day all wk **Food** all wk 12-10 ⊕ FULLER'S ◼ London Pride, ESB, Oliver's Island Golden Ale. ♀ 16 **Facilities** Non-diners area ♦♦ Family room Outside area ⊨ WiFi ➡ (notice required)

CHADWICK END   Map 10 SP27

The Orange Tree   PICK OF THE PUBS

tel: 01564 785364 **Warwick Rd B93 0BN**
email: theorangetree@lovelypubs.co.uk
dir: *3m from Knowle towards Warwick*

Informal modern revival with landscaped gardens

Part of the small, Warwickshire-centred Lovely Pubs chain, The Orange Tree adopts the house style of a light, modern interior, open kitchen, wooden floors, log fires and, here at least, old beams and antique mirrors. Wide-ranging menus group dishes according to type: 'grazing and sharing', 'hoof and fin', 'feather and fur' and 'pasta and flour'. Such generics embrace Mumbai meze of spiced aubergine dip, masala houmous, Bombay potato and spinach pakora; beef steak, stout, mushroom and black pudding pie; spit-roast chicken with winter slaw and fries; and king prawn and crab tagliatelle with chilli, spring onion and white wine cream. Puddings include sticky toffee pudding with butterscotch sauce and clotted cream; and Belgian waffle with banana, maple and walnut ice cream. Go for a 2-for-1 pizza deal (lunchtime and very early evening) on Monday to Fridays.

Open all day all wk 11-11 **Food** Lunch Mon-Sat 12-2.30, Sun 12-7 Dinner Mon-Sat 6-9.30, Sun 12-7 Set menu available ⊕ FREE HOUSE ◼ Sharp's Doom Bar, Greene King IPA, Purity Pure UBU. ♀ 10 **Facilities** Non-diners area ♣ (Bar Garden) ♦♦ Children's menu Children's portions Play area Garden ⊨ Parking WiFi ➡ (notice required)

HAMPTON IN ARDEN   Map 10 SP28

The White Lion Inn   PICK OF THE PUBS

tel: 01675 442833 **10 High St B92 0AA**
email: info@thewhitelioninn.com
dir: *M42 junct 6, A45 towards Coventry. At rdbt take A452 towards Leamington Spa. At rdbt take B4102 towards Solihull. Approx 2m to Hampton in Arden*

Classic English and French dishes side by side

Once a farmhouse, this 17th-century, timber-framed pub first acquired a drinks licence in the early 1800s. Its bright, modern interior is today furnished with wicker chairs and decorated with fresh flowers. Landlord Chris Roach and his partner Fanfan draw on their considerable experience of working in or visiting restaurants, bistros and gastro-pubs throughout England and France to present an ever-appealing combination of classic English pub grub and simple French bistro-style food. St Malo Black pudding or honey and mustard ham hock terrine would both

make a good starter; a main of moules of the day and frites, or boeuf bourgouignon could continue the Gallic approach; or go Italian with mushroom and pesto linguine. At lunch there are also sandwiches and Les Croques (Monsieur and Madame among the choices). Real ales include St Austell Proper Job and Castle Rock Harvest Pale.

Open all day all wk noon-12.30am (Sun 12-10.30) **Food** Lunch Mon-Sat 12-2.30, Sun 12-4 Dinner Mon-Sat 6.30-9.30 Set menu available Restaurant menu available all wk ⊕ PUNCH TAVERNS ◼ M&B Brew XI, Sharp's Doom Bar, Hobsons Best, Castle Rock Harvest Pale, St Austell Proper Job, Banks's Mild ♂ Westons Stowford Press, Aspall. ♀ 11 **Facilities** Non-diners area ♣ (Bar Restaurant Garden) ♦♦ Children's menu Children's portions Garden ⊨ Parking WiFi ➡ (notice required)

SEDGLEY   Map 10 SO99

Beacon Hotel & Sarah Hughes Brewery
PICK OF THE PUBS

tel: 01902 883380 **129 Bilston St DY3 1JE**
dir: *Phone for detailed directions*

Enjoy a pint of ale brewed on the premises

Home of the Sarah Hughes Brewery, the Beacon Hotel is a restored Victorian tap house that has barely changed in 150 years. Proprietor John Hughes reopened the adjoining Sarah Hughes Brewery in 1987, 66 years after his grandmother became the licensee. The rare snob-screened island bar serves a simple taproom, with its old wall benches and a fine blackened range; a super cosy snug replete with a green-tiled marble fireplace, dark woodwork, velvet curtains and huge old tables; and a large smoke-room with an adjoining, plant-festooned conservatory. On a tour of the brewery you can see the original grist case and rare open-topped copper that add to the Victorian charm and give unique character to the brews. Flagship beers are Sarah Hughes Dark Ruby, Sedgley Surprise & Amber, with seasonal bitter and two guest beers from small microbreweries also available. Food in the pub is limited to filled cob rolls but there is a designated children's room and play area, as well as a large garden.

Open all wk 12-2.30 5.30-11 (Sat-12-3 6-11 Sun 12-3 7-10.30) **Food** Contact pub for food times ⊕ FREE HOUSE ◼ Sarah Hughes Dark Ruby, Sedgley Surprise & Amber, guest ales. **Facilities** Non-diners area ♦♦ Play area Family room Garden Outside area ⊨ Parking ➡ (notice required) **Notes** ⊕

WEST BROMWICH   Map 10 SP09

The Vine

tel: 0121 553 2866 **Roebuck St B70 6RD**
email: theteam@thevine.co.uk
dir: *M5 junct 1, follow West Bromwich/A41 signs. 1st left into Roebuck St. Pub at end on corner*

Spicy meals near West Brom's football ground

Certainly not the most attractive approach road to this pub, but keep going. Beers from reliable well-loved stalwarts such as Bathams and Holden's help this thriving, edge-of-town free house shine out. Equally adept at attracting customers to fill the surprisingly large open-plan interior and conservatory-style dining area is the remarkable menu created by Suki Patel, based around a pick 'n' mix of firm Indian favourites. Channa massala, saag aloo, curried goat, kotmari lamb and mutter paneer all appear. The indoor barbecue is extremely popular, and there's also a range of traditional pub grub dishes like beef in ale pie, and fish and chips.

Open all wk 11.30-2.30 5-11 (Fri-Sat 12-11 Sun 12-10) **Food** Lunch Mon-Fri 11.30-2.30, Sat-Sun 12-10 Dinner Mon-Fri 5-10, Sat-Sun 12-10 Av main course £6 ⊕ FREE HOUSE ◼ Bathams, Holden's, Wye Valley, Burton Bridge.
Facilities Non-diners area ♦♦ Garden ⊨ Beer festival Cider festival WiFi ➡ (notice required)

WILTSHIRE

The Blue Boar

tel: 01672 540237 **20 The Green SN8 2EN**
email: theblueboar@mail.com
dir: *From Salisbury take B4192 to Aldbourne. Or M4 junct 14 take A338 to Hungerford, B4192 to Aldbourne & follow brown signs*

The sort of pub to dream about when abroad

This Wadworth-owned, 16th-century pub stands on the village green, itself distanced from traffic, with views of pretty houses, the church and a Celtic cross. It couldn't wish for a better location, so outdoor drinking and eating are a particular pleasure, although there will be times when the two open fires inside beckon. Home-prepared food includes sandwiches and baguettes; chicken liver pâté; roast chicken breast with sage and onion stuffing; and leek, cheddar and mustard tart. Landlords Michael and Joanne Hehir hold a beer festival over the first weekend in June, while local enthusiasts periodically relive wartime days when an American parachute regiment was billeted locally.

Open all wk 11.30-3 5.30-11 (Fri-Sun 11.30-11) **Food** Lunch Mon-Fri 12-2, Sat 12-2.30, Sun 12-4 Dinner Mon-Sat 6.30-9 ⊕ WADWORTH ◆ 6X & Henry's Original IPA, guest ales ♂ Westons Stowford Press. **Facilities** Non-diners area ♥ (Bar Garden) ♦♦ Children's menu Children's portions Garden ♠ Beer festival Cider festival WiFi ⬚ (notice required)

The Crown Inn

tel: 01672 540214 **The Square SN8 2DU**
email: bookings@thecrownaldbourne.co.uk
dir: *M4 junct 15, N on A419, signed Aldbourne*

Classic village-square pub in popular ramblers' area

This imposing coaching inn has served the village for over 400 years, and retains much period feel in the well-beamed old bar. In World War 2 American NCOs made it their mess-room; today's regulars and visitors may enjoy the home-prepared food that majors on ingredients sourced from local suppliers. The intriguing sounding 'Share a piggy' (for a minimum of two) is a board of pork belly, black pudding and crispy pork shoulder served with crispy potatoes, seasonal veg and cider gravy; or you could chose the daily changing 'Ultimate Pie', a burger or home-made stone-baked pizza. There are beer festivals each May and September and a cider festival is held in July.

Open all day all wk 12-12 **Food** all wk, all day Restaurant menu available all wk ⊕ ENTERPRISE INNS ◆ Timothy Taylor Landlord, Shepherd Neame Spitfire, Ramsbury Gold, Sharp's Doom Bar, guest ales ♂ Westons Stowford Press, Aspall. ☞ 16 **Facilities** Non-diners area ♥ (Bar Garden) ♦♦ Children's menu Children's portions Play area Garden ♠ Beer festival Cider festival Parking WiFi ⬚ (notice required)

The Boot Inn

tel: 01722 790243 **High St SP3 4TN**
email: cathy@theboot.pub
dir: *From either A303 (Deptford to Winterbourne Stoke) or A36 (Deptford to Salisbury) take B3083 to Berwick St James. Pub in village centre*

Worth a detour if you're on the A303

Here in their picturesque 16th-century property, formally trained chefs and landlords Giles and Cathy Dickinson aim to provide 'traditional British food', all home-made or locally sourced as far as possible. It's a Wadworth house which, as all the Devizes brewery's disciples know, means 6X and Henry's Original IPA. The Dickinson's say you won't find curry, chilli, lasagne or 'expensive gastro-pub concoctions'; instead, there's dishes like chicken liver and brandy pâté; Westcombe Cheddar and spring onion tartlet; roast rump of treacle-cured Stokes Marsh Farm beer with horseradish Yorkshire pudding; garlic and rosemary slow-roasted leg of Wiltshire lamb; and apple and blackberry crumble; or marmalade bread and butter pudding to finish.

Open 12-3 6-11 (Fri-Sat 12-3 6-12 Sun 12-4) Closed 1-13 Feb, Sun eve & Mon **Food** Lunch 12-2.15 Dinner 6.30-9.15 Av main course £14 ⊕ WADWORTH ◆ Henry's Original IPA & 6X. ☞ 9 **Facilities** Non-diners area ♥ (Bar Restaurant Garden) ♦♦ Children's menu Children's portions Garden ♠ Parking

The Talbot Inn

tel: 01747 828222 **The Cross SP7 0HA**
dir: *From Shaftesbury take A30 towards Salisbury. Right to Berwick St John. Pub 1.5m*

Traditional pub with lots of character

The Talbot Inn used to be three cottages, one of them the village shop, before becoming an alehouse in 1835. This typical old English country free house in the beautiful Chalke Valley dates from the 17th century and has the beams, low ceilings and huge inglenook fireplace so typical of its kind. Good home-cooked food might include grilled Cajun-style chicken breast with Creole salad and sautéed potatoes; slow-roast pork belly, black pudding, sage and onion stuffing and crackling; and Moroccan tagine with lemon herb couscous.

Open 12-2.30 6.30-11 (Sun 12-4) Closed Sun eve & Mon **Food** Lunch Tue-Sun 12-2 Dinner Tue-Sat 6.30-9 ⊕ FREE HOUSE ◆ Ringwood Best Bitter, Wadworth 6X, Sixpenny Handley IPA ♂ Westons Stowford Press. **Facilities** ♥ (Bar Garden) ♦♦ Children's menu Garden ♠ Parking

The Royal Oak

tel: 01793 790481 **Cues Ln SN6 8PP**
email: royaloak@helenbrowningorganics.co.uk
dir: *M4 junct 15, A419 towards Swindon. At rdbt right into Pack Hill signed Wanborough. In Bishopstone left into Cues Ln. Pub on right*

Rustic, relaxed and friendly pub with its own organic farm

The delightful Royal Oak stands tucked away in a glorious village below the Wiltshire Downs, and you can expect a cracking community atmosphere, Arkell's ales, Westons ciders, roaring log fires and daily-changing menus. Almost 60 per cent of produce comes from Helen Browning's own organic farm, with the rest sourced from three other local organic farms and allotments. A three-course dinner could be pork rillettes, cornichons and dressed leaves; 40-day aged beef fillet with sauce béarnaise, hand-cut chips and salad; and caramelised apple and raspberry upside down cake with star anise custard. The child-friendly garden has a Wendy house and rope swing.

Open all wk 12-3 6-11 (Sat 12-12 Sun 12-10) **Food** Lunch Mon-Sat 12-3, Sun 12-7 Dinner Mon-Sat 6-9.30, Sun 12-7 ⊕ ARKELL'S ◆ 3B, Wiltshire Gold, guest ales ♂ Westons Stowford Press, Wyld Wood Organic & Organic Pear. ☞ 12 **Facilities** Non-diners area ♥ (All areas) ♦♦ Children's menu Children's portions Play area Garden Outside area ♠ Parking WiFi ⬚ (notice required)

PICK OF THE PUBS

The Tollgate Inn ★★★★ INN

BRADFORD-ON-AVON Map 4 ST86

tel: 01225 782326 **Holt BA14 6PX**
email: laura@tollgateinn.co.uk
web: www.tollgateinn.co.uk
dir: *M4 junct 18, A46 towards Bath,
then A363 to Bradford-on-Avon, then
B3107 towards Melksham, pub on right*

Sixteenth-century country inn with large grounds

Bradford-on-Avon was once at the heart of a thriving woollen textile industry, which is why one part of this stone-built village inn used to be a weaving shed, another the weavers' own chapel. Oak-floored and sofa-furnished, the main bar serves Ashton Press and Toodle Pip ciders, real ales from local breweries like Box Steam and Butcombe, and nigh on 20 wines by the glass. The two dining rooms, one upstairs in the old chapel, offer a seasonal menu based on the principle: 'If it isn't local, there will be a damn good reason why!' Expect therefore hand-reared, free-range meats from the farm opposite, day-boat fish from Lyme Bay and Brixham, and vegetables from nearby Bromham. A smoked haddock and anchovy fishcake comes with tartare dressing; and spinach, feta and herb roll with cucumber yogurt and red onion salad. Main courses include Cumberland sausages with bubble-and-squeak, braised red cabbage and red onion gravy; slow-roast pork belly with apple

crisps, caramelised onion purée, mustard mash and honeyed carrots; and vegetarian risotto of the day. Listed among the daily specials are various dishes of the day, such as ham, pea and vegetable pie; pan-roasted pork loin steak; and fillet of roasted salmon. For dessert you could be fairly certain of chocolate and hazelnut brownie with ice cream and chocolate sauce; or date and walnut sticky toffee pudding. Sandwiches available at lunchtime include smoked salmon and crayfish, and tenderised striploin steak with caramelised onions; quiche of the day is another possibility. Wines are selected from all over the world. Pub quizzes are every other Tuesday and there's live music every Friday in July.

Open 9am-11.30pm (Sun 9-4.30) Closed 25 Dec, Sun eve **Food** Lunch Mon-Fri 12-2, Sat 12-9, Sun 12-2.30 Dinner Tue-Sat 6.30-9 Av main course £11-£15 ⊞ FREE HOUSE ◀ Butcombe Adam Henson's Rare Breed, Box Steam Piston Broke, Fuller's London Pride ♂ Ashton Press, Toodle Pip. ♀ 19 **Facilities** Non-diners area ♦ Children's menu & portions Garden ⊼ Parking WiFi ⊞ (notice required) **Rooms** 5

BOX
Map 4 ST86

The Northey Arms ★★★★★ INN ⊕

tel: 01225 742333 **Bath Rd SN13 8AE**
email: thenorthey@ohhcompany.co.uk **web:** www.ohhcompany.co.uk
dir: A4 from Bath towards Chippenham, 4m. Between M4 juncts 17 & 18

Contemporary inn close to Bath

The former station hotel, built by Brunel for the workers who were building Box Tunnel, was transformed from a shabby roadside drinking pub to a stylish inn by Mark Warburton. The contemporary interior makes good use of wood and flagstone flooring, high-backed oak chairs, leather loungers and handcrafted tables around the bar, where inviting sandwiches (roast ham, tomato and mustard; or cheese with salad and chutney) and pub classics like haddock and chips hold sway. The main menu ranges from veal chop with red cabbage, lyonnaise potatoes, roasted mushrooms and parmesan; or baked pepper with caponata salad, goats' cheese and asparagus; to the pub's speciality fish dishes and great steaks. Swish bedrooms complete the picture.

Open all day all wk Closed 25 Dec **Food** all wk 12-9.30 Av main course £13.50-£28 ⊕ FREE HOUSE ◀ Butcombe, Wadworth 6X, guest ale Ò Ashton Press, Kingstone Press. ☕ 16 **Facilities** Non-diners area ❤ (Bar Restaurant Garden) ♦♦ Children's menu Children's portions Garden ⊫ Parking WiFi **Rooms** 5

The Quarrymans Arms

tel: 01225 743569 **Box Hill SN13 8HN**
email: pub@quarrymans-arms.co.uk
dir: On A4 between Box & Corsham, follow brown signs for pub

Former miners' pub with excellent views

Superb views of the Box Valley can be enjoyed from this 300-year-old pub, from where you can also see Solsbury Hill. A display of Bath stone-mining memorabilia bears witness to the years Brunel's navvies spent driving the Great Western Railway through Box Tunnel (spot the bar's replica fireplace) deep beneath the pub. The resultant honeycomb of Bath stone workings attract potholers and cavers, who slake their thirsts on local ales and ciders, and replace lost calories with venison noisettes with port and rosemary sauce; poached cod loin with garlic mash; or something from the comprehensive vegetarian selection. 'Mini ale weeks' are held throughout the year – check with the pub for details.

Open all day all wk 11am-11.30pm **Food** Lunch Mon-Fri 11-3, Sat-Sun 11-9 Dinner Mon-Fri 5.30-9, Sat-Sun 11-9 Av main course £10 ⊕ FREE HOUSE ◀ Butcombe Bitter, Wadworth 6X, Moles Best, local guest ales Ò Black Rat, Ashton Press. ☕ 13 **Facilities** Non-diners area ❤ (All areas) ♦♦ Children's menu Children's portions Family room Garden Outside area ⊫ Beer festival Cider festival Parking WiFi 🚍 (notice required)

BRADFORD-ON-AVON
Map 4 ST86

NEW The George

tel: 01225 865650 **67 Woolley St BA15 1AQ**
email: thegeorgeatwoolley@gmail.com
dir: From Trowbridge take B3105 to Bradford-on-Avon. Left at Woolley Grange Hotel into Woolley St. Pub 500yds

Home from home with tip-top food

New owners and a complete refurbishment have worked wonders here. The building was originally three Georgian houses, so the interior is comfortably spacious. Furnishings mix modern and period styles, with chesterfields and winged armchairs placed beside open fires. Half a dozen upholstered stools at the bar testify to the welcome awaiting drinkers, who choose between Butcombe and Bath ales, or Ashton Press and Thatchers ciders. From the open-fronted kitchen, chef-proprietor Alexander Venables produces tip-top dishes such as a starter of bouillabaisse with

garlic aïoli, rouille and croûtes, followed by beef Wellington and seasonal vegetables; or slow-braised pork belly with a spiced herb crust.

Open all wk 9.30-3 5.30-11 (Fri-Sat 9.30am-11pm Sun 9.30-6) **Food** Lunch Mon-Sat 12-2, Sun 12-3 Dinner Mon-Sat 6.30-9 Av main course £16 Set menu available Restaurant menu available all wk ⊕ FREE HOUSE ◀ Abbey Ales Bellringer, Butcombe Bitter, Bath Ales, Fuller's London Pride Ò Ashton Press, Thatchers. ☕ 10 **Facilities** Non-diners area ❤ (Bar Garden) ♦♦ Children's menu Children's portions Garden ⊫ Beer festival Cider festival Parking WiFi

The Tollgate Inn ★★★★ INN
PICK OF THE PUBS

See Pick of the Pubs on page 525

BRINKWORTH
Map 4 SU08

The Three Crowns
PICK OF THE PUBS

tel: 01666 510366 **SN15 5AF**
email: info@threecrownsbrinkworth.co.uk
dir: From Swindon take A3102 to Royal Wootton Bassett, take B4042, 5m to Brinkworth

Traditional village inn serving not-so traditional food

The Three Crowns is a thriving community pub, welcoming locals and their dogs, and families set on celebrating a special occasion. Lots of greenery inside and out here, with the little village green at the front and the conservatory restaurant hosting some large pot-plants. The village sits in rich farming countryside on a low ridge above the River Avon and there are lovely views from the pub's secluded beer garden and tree-shaded patio, where heaters bring additional comfort as the evenings draw in. Amiable staff greet you in the cosy, beamed bar, where ales include Fuller's London Pride. The menu has long been recognised for its ambition and variety. Expect starters like cauliflower cheese beignet with tomato sauce; or home-smoked duck and orange, walnut and watercress salad. Follow that with Parma ham wrapped monkfish loin, crushed potatoes, samphire and smoked bacon cream; roasted butternut risotto; or confit pork belly, wholegrain mustard mash, cream leeks and baby vegetables.

Open all day all wk 10am-mdnt **Food** Lunch Mon-Sat 12-2.30, Sun 12-9 Dinner Mon-Sat 6-9.30, Sun 12-9 Set menu available ⊕ PRESTIGIOUS RESTAURANTS ◀ Sharp's Doom Bar, Fuller's London Pride, Greene King IPA Ò Westons Stowford Press. ☕ 27 **Facilities** Non-diners area ❤ (Bar Garden) ♦♦ Children's menu Children's portions Play area Garden ⊫ Beer festival Cider festival Parking WiFi 🚍 (notice required)

BROUGHTON GIFFORD
Map 4 ST86

The Fox

tel: 01225 782949 **The Street SN12 8PN**
email: alexgeneen@gmail.com
dir: From Melksham take B3107 towards Holt. Turn right to Broughton Gifford. Pub in village centre

Showing a commitment to home-grown and home-reared produce

There are excellent ales and good food at this village inn. The owners raise their own chickens, ducks and pigs, tend an extensive vegetable and herb garden, and barter with villagers for wildfowl and other produce. Bread is either baked in the kitchen or provided by the ethical Thoughtful Bread Company, and The Fox produces cured hams, charcuterie and sausages from its pigs. Typical dishes on the menus are smoked haddock Scotch egg with truffled cream leeks; and fillet of beef, boulangère potato, curly kale, garlic and shallot purée.

Open 12-3 5-9.30 Closed 26 Dec, 1 Jan, Mon ⊕ FREE HOUSE ◀ Bath Ales Gem, Butcombe Bitter. **Facilities** ❤ (Bar Restaurant Garden) ♦♦ Children's menu Children's portions Garden Parking WiFi

BURTON
Map 4 ST87

The Old House at Home ★★★★★ INN

tel: 01454 218227 **SN14 7LT**
email: office@ohhcompany.co.uk **web:** www.ohhcompany.co.uk
dir: On B4039 NW of Chippenham

Family-run, traditional ivy-clad free house offering a warm welcome

This ivy-clad, stone built free house (also known as OHH) dates from the early 19th century and is run by the Warburton family. Dad David has been here for years and still happily pulls pints of Maiden Voyage, Wadworth 6X and Thatchers Gold in the low-beamed bar. The finest seasonal ingredients are used to create impressive menu favourites like sausages, mustard mash, spinach and red wine onion gravy; tomato, basil and pine nut risotto; or roast hake fillet, crab mash and cockle vinaigrette. Try white chocolate and honeycomb cheesecake or hot chocolate fondant for afters. The beautifully landscaped gardens feature a waterfall and six high quality bedrooms are available in a stylish annexe.

Open all day all wk **Food** all wk 12-9.30 ⊕ FREE HOUSE ◼ Ales of Scilly Maiden Voyage, Wadworth 6X, guest ales Ò Thatchers Gold & Traditional. ☝ 12 **Facilities** Non-diners area ❄ (Bar Restaurant Garden) ♦ Children's menu Children's portions Garden ⊟ Parking WiFi ☞ (notice required) **Rooms** 6

CALNE
Map 4 ST97

The Lansdowne ★★★ INN

tel: 01249 812488 **The Strand SN11 0EH**
email: lansdowne@arkells.com **web:** www.lansdownestrand.co.uk
dir: On A4 in town centre

Traditional food and local ales a short detour from the M4

Just 15 minutes from the M4 in the heart of Calne, this 16th-century former coaching inn was once home to the local brewery and the courtyard still retains the medieval brew house. Owned by Arkell's, the bar showcases that brewery's beers including Moonlight, alongside monthly guest ales. The straightforward and appealing food menu focuses on traditional pub meals and old favourites. Typical dishes include honey-roasted ham with eggs and chips; Jack Daniels' chicken with seasoned wedges; cod, spinach and cheddar fishcakes; and red onion and gruyère cheese tartlet. At lunchtime, there is also a well-priced choice of sandwiches and jacket potatoes.

Open all day all wk **Food** Lunch all wk 9-2 Dinner Mon-Sat 6-9 Av main course £7.95 Restaurant menu available all wk (except Sun evening) ⊕ ARKELL'S ◼ 3B, Moonlight, guest ale Ò Westons Stowford Press. **Facilities** Non-diners area ❄ (Bar Outside area) ♦ Children's menu Children's portions Outside area ⊟ Parking WiFi ☞ **Rooms** 25

The White Horse Inn ★★★★ INN ◉

tel: 01249 813118 **Compton Bassett SN11 8RG**
email: info@whitehorse-comptonbassett.co.uk
web: www.whitehorse-comptonbassett.co.uk
dir: M4 junct 16 onto A3102, after Hilmarton turn left to Compton Bassett

Civilised drinking and dining

A stone-built, whitewashed village pub, named after the equine figure cut out of the chalk on a nearby hillside in 1870. The bar's log-burner keeps customers warm in winter, while a year-round attraction is the ever-changing roster of local and national real ales. The kitchen relies on seasonal ingredients – their source, the closer to home the better   for braised oxtail, confit beef tongue, creamed mash,

spinach and olive jus; braised shoulder of Wiltshire lamb with curly kale and ratatouille; and fillet of Cornish hake with risotto nero. Pecan tart with organic vanilla ice cream makes for a good finish.

Open all day all wk **Food** Lunch Mon-Sat 12-9, Sun 12-6 Dinner Mon-Sat 12-9, Sun 12-6 Restaurant menu available ⊕ FREE HOUSE ◼ Bath Ales Gem, Sharp's Doom Bar, Wadworth 6X, Adnams Ò Westons Old Rosie. ☝ 16 **Facilities** Non-diners area ❄ (Bar Garden) ♦ Children's menu Children's portions Garden ⊟ Parking WiFi ☞ (notice required) **Rooms** 8

COATE
Map 5 SU18

The Sun Inn ★★★★ INN

tel: 01793 523292 **Marlborough Rd SN3 6AA**
email: sun-inn@arkells.com **web:** www.suninn-swindon.co.uk
dir: M4 junct 15, A419 towards Swindon. At 1st rdbt take A459 signed Swindon & hospital. Left lane at lights. Pub on left before next rdbt

Ideal watering hole for families

The third Sun public house on this site since 1685, today's pre-war building is close to Arkell's Swindon brewery, which bought its predecessor in 1891. With a large garden and playground, and with Coate Water Country Park nearby, it is understandably popular with families, for whom the menus have clearly been designed. For example, there are takeaway fish and chips, sandwiches and hot drinks; chicken nuggets; giant fish fingers; cheeseburgers; and filled deli rolls. Main dishes include home-made three-cheese macaroni; Wiltshire pork sausages and mash; and scampi, chips and peas. An ever-changing specials board adds to the wide-ranging tally.

Open all day all wk **Food** Mon-Sat 12-9, Sun 12-7 ⊕ ARKELL'S ◼ 3B, Wiltshire Gold, guest ale Ò Westons Stowford Press. ☝ 10 **Facilities** Non-diners area ❄ (Bar Restaurant Garden) ♦ Children's menu Play area Garden ⊟ Parking WiFi ☞ (notice required) **Rooms** 10

COLLINGBOURNE DUCIS
Map 5 SU25

The Shears Inn

tel: 01264 850304 **The Cadley Rd SN8 3ED**
email: info@theshears.co.uk
dir: Just off A338 between Marlborough & Salisbury

Delightful thatched pub with modern British menu

Dating from the 18th century, this traditional country inn (now in new hands) was once a shearing shed for market-bound sheep. The original part of the building is thatched, while inside you'll find wooden and slate floors, low-beamed ceilings and a large inglenook dominating the restaurant. Typical choices from the tasty modern British menu may include starters like haggis and black pudding with apple chutney; or smoked duck, Waldorf salad and beetroot sorbet; mains like sausage and mash with broccoli, smoked haddock kedgeree with soft egg; or garlic-infused mushrooms with linguine and truffle oil. Look out for lime and ginger cheesecake, or Eton Mess for afters. The enclosed sunny garden is an ideal place for a quiet drink and for the annual cider festival held in late summer.

Open 12-3 6-11 (Sat 11-11 summer, Sun fr 12) Closed Sun eve **Food** Lunch Mon-Sat 12-2, Sun 12-3.30 Dinner Mon-Thu 6.30-9, Fri-Sat 7-9.30 Restaurant menu available all wk ⊕ BRAKSPEAR ◼ Brakspear, Ringwood, local guest ales Ò Aspall. ☝ 8 **Facilities** Non-diners area ❄ (Bar Restaurant Garden) ♦ Children's menu Children's portions Garden ⊟ Cider festival Parking WiFi ☞ (notice required)

CORTON
Map 4 ST94

The Dove Inn
PICK OF THE PUBS

tel: 01985 850109 **BA12 0SZ**
email: info@thedove.co.uk **web:** www.thedove.co.uk
dir: 5m SE of Warminster. Exit A36 to Corton

In the heart of the countryside

A warm welcome is guaranteed at this bustling 19th-century pub, tucked away in the delightful Wylye Valley. Plenty of original features are still in evidence such as the striking central fireplace and flagstone and oak floors. The appealing menu is based firmly on West Country produce, with many ingredients coming from just a few miles away. Popular lunchtime bar snacks give way to a full evening carte featuring well-made and hearty pub classics. Typical starters include whitebait with home-made lemon and tartare sauce; and mussels in creamy white wine and fresh crab sauce. These might be followed by slow-braised lamb shank with mustard mash, or the Dove Inn mixed grill. Fish and chips, and the famous Dove burger and chips are available to take away, traditionally wrapped in newspaper. The garden is the perfect spot for barbecues or a drink on summer days.

Open all day all wk **Food** Lunch all wk 12-2.30 Dinner all wk 6-9 Restaurant menu available all wk ⊕ FREE HOUSE ◀ Otter, Atlantic, guest ale ♂ Aspall.
Facilities Non-diners area ❀ (Bar Garden) ♦♦ Children's portions Garden ⊼ Parking WiFi ▭ (notice required)

CRICKLADE
Map 5 SU09

The Red Lion Inn ★★★★ INN ◉

tel: 01793 750776 **74 High St SN6 6DD**
email: info@theredlioninncricklade.co.uk **web:** www.theredlioninncricklade.co.uk
dir: M4 junct 15, A419 towards Cirencester. Left onto B4040 into Cricklade. Right at T-junct (mini rdbt) into High St. Inn on right

Town pub with its own microbrewery

Many awards, including an AA Rosette, have been bestowed upon this 17th-century pub, just off the Thames Path. The food is noteworthy not only because it's good, but for using locally foraged ingredients, rare-breed meats and sustainable fish. Some of the real ales are from on-site microbrewery Hop Kettle; ciders are Ravens Roost and Jackdaw. On the menu: chargrilled flat-iron steak; confit Wiltshire pork belly with seared king scallops; monkfish tail scampi; and twice-baked smoked cheese soufflé with ratatouille. In addition to ice creams, sorbets and local cheeses,

desserts include orange and cardamom rice pudding. Beer festivals are held on the last weekend of February and in June.

Open all day all wk **Food** Lunch Mon-Sat 12-2.30, Sun 12-3 Dinner Mon-Thu 6.30-9 Restaurant menu available Tue-Sat evenings ⊕ FREE HOUSE ◀ Hop Kettle North Wall & Hoplite, Wadworth 6X ♂ Mates Ravens Roost & Jackdaw. ▾ 9
Facilities Non-diners area ❀ (Bar Garden) ♦♦ Children's menu Children's portions Garden ⊼ Beer festival WiFi **Rooms** 5

CRUDWELL
Map 4 ST99

The Potting Shed

tel: 01666 577833 **The Street SN16 9EW**
email: bookings@thepottingshedpub.com
dir: On A429 between Malmesbury & Cirencester

A warm welcome to all awaits from new owners

In addition to the grown-ups, children and dogs are very welcome at this Cotswold dining pub swhere the new owners offer good ales and ciders and tempting menus. Two acres of grounds allow plenty of space for lawns, fruit trees and vegetable plots which supply fresh produce for the kitchen. Light pastel shades and beams scrubbed down to their natural hue characterise the appealing interior, where typical dishes include smoked pork belly, damson jelly and kohlrabi salad; home-smoked Cornish mackerel on toast with red pepper dressing; wild boar and smoked Applewood burger, apricot mayonnaise and triple-cooked chips; and halibut, slow-cooked ham hock, wild mushrooms, potatoes and kale.

Open all day all wk **Food** Lunch Mon-Sat 12-2.30, Sun 12-3 Dinner Mon-Sat 6-9, Sun 6-8 ⊕ FREE HOUSE ◀ Bath Ales Gem, Timothy Taylor Landlord, Flying Monk Elmers, Butcombe, guest ales ♂ Ashton Press, Orchard Pig. ▾ 25
Facilities Non-diners area ❀ (Bar Restaurant Garden) ♦♦ Children's portions Garden ⊼ Beer festival Parking WiFi ▭ (notice required)

DONHEAD ST ANDREW
Map 4 ST92

The Forester
PICK OF THE PUBS

tel: 01747 828038 **Lower St SP7 9EE**
email: possums1@btinternet.com
dir: From Shaftesbury on A30 towards Salisbury. In approx 4.5m left, follow village signs

Traditional pub specialising in West Country seafood

A dog-friendly watering hole, this lovely 15th-century pub is an ideal place to put your feet up after a long walk with man's best friend if you have one with you. Close to Wardour Castle in a pretty village, The Forester has warm stone walls, a thatched roof, original beams and inglenook fireplace. Local Donhead Craft Cider is a popular addition to the Butcombe and Otter ales served at the bar. An extension houses a restaurant with double doors opening onto the lower patio area. The pub has a reputation for excellent cooking at reasonable prices, and for its use of fresh West Country ingredients, especially seafood. Dishes are constructed with a mix of traditional and cosmopolitan flavours, crispy crumbed local pork with pickled winter vegetables, black pudding and piccalilli is typical. Follow with a main course of pan-fried Cornish cod fillet, squid ink, butternut squash and hollandaise. Special menus for children and vegetarians are available.

Open 12-2 6.30-11 Closed 25-26 Dec, Sun eve, Mon **Food** Lunch Tue-Sun 12-2 Dinner Tue-Sat 7-9 Av main course £14-£18.50 Set menu available ⊕ FREE HOUSE ◀ Butcombe, Otter ♂ Donhead Craft Cider, Westons Wyld Wood Organic. ▾ 15
Facilities Non-diners area ❀ (Bar Restaurant Garden) ♦♦ Children's menu Children's portions Garden ⊼ Parking WiFi ▭ (notice required)

PICK OF THE PUBS

The Fox and Hounds

EAST KNOYLE   Map 4 ST83

tel: 01747 830573 **The Green SP3 6BN**
email: fox.hounds@virgin.net
web: www.foxandhounds-eastknoyle.co.uk
dir: *From A303 follow Blandford/East
Knoyle signs onto A350, follow brown
pub signs*

Traditional pub with lovely views

This partly thatched and half-timbered,
rustic 15th-century inn makes the most
of its stunning Blackmore Vale location.
There are exceptional views from the
patio beer garden and nearby East
Knoyle village green across these
Wiltshire and Dorset boundary-lands,
where Sir Christopher Wren was born
and the family of Jane Seymour (Henry
VIII's third wife) were based. Hidden in a
timeless village on a greensand ridge,
the engaging exterior is well matched by
the atmospheric interior, with lots of
flagstone flooring, wood-burning fires
and restful stripped wood furniture.
Locals eager to partake of Thatchers
Cheddar Valley cider or Hop Back Crop
Circle rub shoulders with diners keen to
make the acquaintance of the eclectic
menu. Blackboard menus increase the
choice, dependant entirely on the
availability of the freshest local fare.
Starters might include lightly dusted
calamari with garlic mayonnaise; and
deep-fried rosemary and garlic crusted
brie wedges with cranberry jelly. When it

comes to main courses, good,
wholesome pub grub like fish pie;
chicken pie with chips and vegetables
and home-made sausages, mash and
gravy share the board with lamb shank
braised in red wine; slow-roasted belly
pork with an apple and cider sauce;
duck breast with damson sauce and
spring onion mash; or murgh makhani,
basmati rice and chota naan. Baked
pizzas and a comprehensive children's
menu add to the fray, whilst desserts
include lemon posset and shortbread or
rhubarb and apple crumble with vanilla
ice cream. There is also a gluten-free
chocolate fondant and ice cream.

Open all wk 11.30-3 5.30-11
Food Lunch all wk 12-2.30 Dinner all wk
6-9 ⊕ FREE HOUSE ◄ Hop Back Crop

Circle & Summer Lightning, Palmers
Dorset Gold & Copper Ale, Butcombe,
Otter Amber, Platform 5 The Coaster
Ŏ Thatchers Cheddar Valley,
Dorset Orchards Apple Bee. ♇ 12
Facilities Non-diners area
♣ (Bar Restaurant Garden)
◗♦ Children's menu Garden ⋒ Parking
WiFi ☒ (notice required)

EAST CHISENBURY
Map 5 SU15

Red Lion Freehouse ★★★★★ INN ⦾⦾⦾
PICK OF THE PUBS

tel: 01980 671124 **SN9 6AQ**
email: enquiries@redlionfreehouse.com **web:** www.redlionfreehouse.com
dir: From A303 take A345 N. Exit at Enford. Left at T-junct towards East Chisenbury. Pub 1m on right

Astonishing cuisine at a beautiful thatched village inn

Secluded in the upper Avon Valley in a fold of Salisbury Plain, this ancient inn shares a sleepy hollow with other eye-catching thatched properties. Elements of the Tudor pub remain, with plenty of character injected by bare brick, log-burner and other rustic flourishes. At the bar, beer-hounds will be delighted with a rolling selection of beers from Stonehenge and Box Stream – there's a May beer festival too. Equally content will be gastronomes seeking out the confident, contemporary menu which has three AA Rosettes. Licensees Guy and Brittany Manning have a distinguished pedigree in the restaurant world and bring particular flair to the range of dishes crafted from local, seasonal ingredients. Kick in with sika venison and pistachio terrine, then look for slow-cooked pig's cheeks (from the pub's own raised pigs) with crisp polenta, roasted fennel, Burbage shiitakes and pork cracker. Tucked behind the Red Lion is a tranquil tree-shaded beer garden. Luxury riverside accommodation completes the dream here.

Open all day all wk **Food** Lunch all wk 12.30-2.30 Dinner Mon-Sat 6.30-9, Sun 6-8 Av main course £22 Set menu available ⦾ FREE HOUSE ◀ Stonehenge Ales, Ramsbury, Cottage, Box Steam, guest ales ⦿ Ty Gwyn, Black Rat, Perry's. ♥ 30 **Facilities** ☙ (All areas) ♦♦ Children's menu Children's portions Garden Outside area ⌂ Beer festival Parking WiFi **Rooms** 5

EAST KNOYLE
Map 4 ST83

The Fox and Hounds
PICK OF THE PUBS

See Pick of the Pubs on page 529

EBBESBOURNE WAKE
Map 4 ST92

The Horseshoe
PICK OF THE PUBS

tel: 01722 780474 **Handley St SP5 5JF**
dir: Phone for detailed directions

Well-kept beers and home-made food

Dating from the 17th century, the family-run Horseshoe is a genuine old English pub in the pretty village of Ebbesbourne Wake. The original building has not changed much, except for a conservatory extension to accommodate more diners, and there's a lovely flower-filled garden. Beyond the climbing roses are two rooms adorned with simple furniture, old farming implements and country bygones, linked to a central servery where well-kept cask-conditioned ales are dispensed straight from their barrels – Bowman Ales Swift One, Otter Bitter and Palmers Copper Ale – plus real ciders too. Good-value traditional bar food is offered from a varied menu. Freshly prepared from local produce, dishes include liver and bacon; local faggots in onion gravy; fresh fish bake; and lunchtime sandwiches. The home-made pies are a firm favourite – venison and mushroom; chicken, ham and mushroom; steak and kidney; and game.

Open 12-3 6.30-11 (Sun 12-4) Closed 26 Dec, Sun eve & Mon **Food** Lunch Tue-Sat 12-2 Dinner Tue-Sat 7-9 Restaurant menu available Tue-Sat evening ⦾ FREE HOUSE ◀ Otter Bitter, Bowman Ales Swift One, Palmers Copper Ale, guest ales ⦿ Appleby, Thatchers Gold, Wessex Cider. **Facilities** Non-diners area ☙ (Bar Garden) ♦♦ Children's portions Garden ⌂ Parking

EDINGTON
Map 4 ST95

The Three Daggers ★★★★★ INN

tel: 01380 830940 **Westbury Rd BA13 4PG**
email: hello@threedaggers.co.uk **web:** www.threedaggers.co.uk
dir: A36 towards Warminster, A350 to Westbury, A303 to Edington

Where locally sourced meals are kept simple

Opened as the Paulet Arms in 1750 by Harry Paulet, the Lord of Edington Manor, locals quickly christened it the Three Daggers, after the family's coat of arms. It has always been well known for its friendly atmosphere, enjoyable meals and Daggers ale. The interesting menus might include Downland's black pudding Scotch egg, braised haricot beans and tomato sauce; lamb and rosemary pie; baked pollock fillet, creamed peas and bacon; and dry-aged 28-day steaks from Stokes Marsh Farm. Next door there is a farm shop and also a microbrewery with a viewing gallery. Excellent B&B rooms with kitchen facilities are available too.

Open all day all wk 10am-11pm **Food** Lunch Mon-Sat 12-2.30, Sun 12-8.30 Dinner Mon-Thu 6-9, Fri-Sat 6-9.30, Sun 12-8.30 Set menu available ⦾ FREE HOUSE ◀ Daggers Ale, Blonde, Edge & Black ⦿ Westons Stowford Press, Orchard Pig. ♥ 14 **Facilities** Non-diners area ☙ (Bar Restaurant Garden) ♦♦ Children's menu Children's portions Play area Garden ⌂ Beer festival Parking WiFi ⛟ (notice required) **Rooms** 3

FONTHILL GIFFORD
Map 4 ST93

The Beckford Arms
PICK OF THE PUBS

See Pick of the Pubs on opposite page

FOXHAM
Map 4 ST97

The Foxham Inn ★★★★ INN ⦾

tel: 01249 740665 **SN15 4NQ**
email: info@thefoxhaminn.co.uk **web:** www.thefoxhaminn.co.uk
dir: M4 junct 17, B4122 (signed Sutton Benger). Onto B4069, through Sutton Benger. Right signed Foxham

Excellent Wiltshire countryside dining inn

This compact brick-built inn stands in a rural village close to the resurgent Wiltshire and Berkshire Canal. Real ales from the local Ramsbury brewery flow from the bar, but it's for the excellent cuisine created by Neil Cooper that customers beat a path to the door. The accomplished menu offers an extensive range of dishes from crispy whitebait with lemon and tartare to nibble before a starter of Irish goats' cheese, beetroot and caramelised walnuts; or Dorset snails, noodles and light soy broth. Then for mains, how about sea bass fillet, creamed potato, spinach and creamy white wine sauce; or calves' liver, mash, carrots and red onion gravy? There are equally fulfilling sweets to finish. Accommodation allows diners to rest easy after a classy repast.

Open 12-3 7-11 (Sun 12-3) Closed 1st 2wks Jan, Mon **Food** Lunch Tue-Sun 12-2 Dinner Tue-Sat 7-9.30 Av main course £14 Set menu available ⦾ FREE HOUSE ◀ Butcombe, Ramsbury ⦿ Ashton Press. ♥ 10 **Facilities** Non-diners area ☙ (Bar Outside area) ♦♦ Children's menu Children's portions Outside area ⌂ Parking WiFi ⛟ (notice required) **Rooms** 2

PICK OF THE PUBS

The Beckford Arms

FONTHILL GIFFORD — Map 4 ST93

tel: 01747 870385 **SP3 6PX**
email: info@beckfordarms.com
web: www.beckfordarms.com
dir: *From A303 (E of Wincanton) follow Fonthill Bishop sign. At T-junct in village right, 1st left signed Fonthill Gifford & Tisbury. Through Fonthill Estate arch to pub*

Excellent food in elegant coaching inn with lovely garden

Just three minutes from the A303, this handsome 18th-century coaching inn is set on the edge of the beautiful rolling parkland of Lord Margadale's 10,000-acre Fonthill Estate. Once a stopping point for weary travellers on the way from London to the South West, this elegant dining pub is now a destination in its own right. You can eat wherever you want, either in the main bar with its huge fireplace and parquet floor or in the separate restaurant. In summer, head out into the rambling garden where hammocks hang between the trees, you can play pétanque and children can do what children do. In winter the huge open fire in the bar is used to spit-roast suckling pigs and warm mulled wine. Whatever the season, Keystone's Beckford Phoenix real ale is a permanent fixture in the bar, with other beers on tap including Dorset Piddle Jimmy Riddle. Sheppy's is one of the real ciders on draught and

there are 12 wines available by the glass including the Fonthill Glebe, a local crisp white wine. An invigorating menu leads in with own-smoked chalk stream trout with peas, pickled radish, pea tops and tarragon mayo as an eye-catching starter. Advance then to traditional pub grub like beer-battered Cornish fish and chips; or Wiltshire ham and Westcombe Cheddar ploughman's, or plump for a seasonal à la carte main, seasonally adjusted. Pan-fried Skrei cod with ricotta dumplings, hollandaise, kale and artichoke crisps may tempt; or enjoy in garlic roast fregola pasta with cauliflower purée, wild mushrooms, sprouting broccoli and a crispy hen egg. Still room, perchance, for apple, pear and cinnamon crumble with vanilla custard.

Open all day all wk **Food** Lunch all wk 12-2.30 Dinner all wk 6-9.30 ⊕ FREE HOUSE ◪ Keystone Beckford Phoenix, Dorset Piddle Jimmy Riddle, Butcombe, Erdinger ☯ Ashton Press, Westons Wyld Wood Organic, Sheppy's. ♀ 12
Facilities Non-diners area ❤ (Bar Restaurant Garden) ✦ Children's menu Children's portions Play area Garden ⊼ Parking WiFi

FROXFIELD
Map 5 SU26

The Pelican Inn

tel: 01488 682479 **Bath Rd SN8 3JY**
email: enquiries@pelicaninn.co.uk **web:** www.pelicaninn.co.uk
dir: *On A4 midway between Marlborough & Hungerford*

Fresh food cooked well at this A4 inn

This 17th-century roadside inn has been serving the needs of locals and travellers alike for over three centuries. Being only 300 yards from the Kennet & Avon Canal, it is also a popular refuelling stop for walkers, cyclists and the boating fraternity. Expect Ramsbury and local guest ales on tap, a raft of wines by the glass, and locally sourced food. The menu offers traditional pub favourites such as home-made pie of the day, beer-battered fish and chips; pan-fried calves' liver and smoked bacon plus modern English dishes flagged up on the specials board.

Open all day all wk 11-11 (Sun 12-10) **Food** Lunch Mon-Fri 12-3, Sat, 12-9, Sun 12-8 Dinner Mon-Fri 6-9, Sat 12-9, Sun 12-8 ⊕ FREE HOUSE ◀ Ramsbury, Wickwar, guest ales Ò Westons Stowford Press. ♈ 12 **Facilities** Non-diners area ✿ (Bar Garden) ♦ Children's menu Garden ⼝ Parking WiFi ⇔ (notice required)

GREAT BEDWYN
Map 5 SU26

NEW The Three Tuns

tel: 01672 870280 **1 High St SN8 3NU**
email: contact@threetunsbedwyn.co.uk
dir: *Off A4 between Marlborough & Hungerford*

Excellent food in bustling village inn

James and Ashley Wilsey saved this village pub close to Marlborough from being turned into housing and they have breathed new life into the place since reopening it in 2012. Roaring fires and a garden with boules pitch make this a family and dog-friendly venue surrounded by excellent canal walks and cycle paths. Chef James used to work in notable London restaurants and almost everything on the menu is made in-house. A starter of cauliflower soup and Perigord truffle butter might be followed by seared fillet of bream, chorizo-braised borlotti beans, rainbow chard and purple sprouting broccoli.

Open 10-3 6-11 (Fri-Sat 10am-11pm Sun 10-6) Closed 25 Dec, Sun eve, Mon (ex BHs) **Food** Lunch Tue-Sun 12.30-2.30 Dinner Tue-Sat 6-9.30 Av main course £16 ⊕ FREE HOUSE ◀ Three Tuns Ale, Otter Bitter Ò Sheppy's, Ty Gwyn. ♈ 10 **Facilities** Non-diners area ✿ (Bar Restaurant Garden) ♦ Children's menu Children's portions Garden ⼝ Parking WiFi ⇔ (notice required)

HEYTESBURY
Map 4 ST94

The Angel

tel: 01985 840330 **High St BA12 0ED**
email: admin@angelheytesbury.co.uk
dir: *A303 onto A36 towards Bath, 8m, Heytesbury on left*

Dining pub in an upmarket village

The Angel has stood at one end of Heytesbury's High Street for over 400 years; a comprehensive makeover a few years ago resulted in today's comfy mix of traditional and contemporary aspects of a village inn. Exposed brick, wooden flooring, beams and on-trend furnishings are the building blocks that welcome visitors. Diners may choose to eat in the bar or restaurant. A typical menu opener may be devilled lamb's kidneys on toast, followed by a seasonal dish — wild mushroom and chestnut cottage pie. There's a strong hand of quality burgers here too, including one called 'mushoumi' for vegetarians. Booking is essential at weekends.

Open all day all wk 11.30-11 (Sun 11.30-8) ⊕ GREENE KING ◀ IPA, Morland Old Speckled Hen Ò Thatchers Gold. **Facilities** ✿ (Bar Outside area) ♦ Children's portions Outside area Parking WiFi

HORNINGSHAM
Map 4 ST84

The Bath Arms at Longleat ★★★★ INN ⊛
PICK OF THE PUBS

tel: 01985 844308 **BA12 7LY**
email: enquiries@batharms.co.uk **web:** www.batharms.co.uk
dir: *Off B3092 S of Frome*

Quirky but stylish country inn on the Longleat Estate

Occupying a prime position at one of the entrances to Longleat Estate and the famous Safari Park, The Bath Arms dates back to the 17th century. An ivy-clad stone property, it features two beamed bars — one traditional with settles, old wooden tables and an open fire, and a bar for dining. In addition to sandwiches and sharing boards look out for main courses such as pan-fried sea bass with mussel, sweetcorn, potato and chive chowder; poached duck egg 'florentine' with buttered spinach on toasted muffin with hollandaise sauce; and pan-roast breast of Hayward Farm chicken wrapped in prosciutto stuffed with white apricot Stilton. Leave a space for elderflower and lime cheesecake and lemon sorbet or Eton Mess with Horningsham berry compôte and vanilla crème fraîche.

Open all day all wk 10am-11pm (Sun 10am-10.30pm) **Food** Lunch Tue-Thu & Sun 12-9, Fri-Sat 12-9.30 (BHs all day) Dinner Mon 5-9, Tue-Thu & Sun 12-9, Fri-Sat 12-9.30 (BHs all day) ⊕ FREE HOUSE ◀ Horningsham Pride & Golden Apostle, Sharp's Doom Bar Ò Westons Stowford Press, Sharp's Orchard. ♈ 10 **Facilities** Non-diners area ✿ (Bar Garden) ♦ Children's menu Children's portions Garden ⼝ Beer festival Parking WiFi ⇔ (notice required) **Rooms** 17

KILMINGTON

Map 4 ST73

NEW The Red Lion

tel: 01985 844263 **BA12 6RP**
email: theredlionkilmington@gmail.com
dir: *On B3092 between Mere & Frome. 1m of NT Stourhead Gardens*

Welcoming old pub on National Trust estate

A National Trust-owned building on the famous Stourhead Estate, The Red Lion dates from the 16th century and has been a pub for around 350 years. The low-beamed, stone-flagged front bar is cosy and inviting, and children are welcome in the larger back bar. They're passionate about beer and food here, and you'll find straightforward honest pub grub on a regularly changing menu. Lunches include sandwiches and jacket potatoes, plus kedgeree, or sausages. At dinner you might find black pudding and tomato salad to start, with braised faggots or scampi and chips for a main. There's always fish dishes and a pie as well.

Open all wk 11-3 6.30-10 (Mon-Tue 11-3 6.30-9 Sun 12-3 7-10) **Food** Lunch all wk 12-2 Dinner Wed-Sat 7-9 Av main course £8 ⊕ FREE HOUSE ◀ Wessex Stourton Pale Ale, Butcombe Bitter Ö Thatchers Heritage. ₹ 11 **Facilities** Non-diners area ❤ (Bar Garden) ♦♦ Children's portions Family room Garden ⊫ Parking WiFi

LOWER CHICKSGROVE

Map 4 ST92

Compasses Inn ★★★★ INN ◉   PICK OF THE PUBS

tel: 01722 714318 **SP3 6NB**
email: thecompasses@aol.com **web:** www.thecompassesinn.com
dir: *On A30 (1.5m W of Fovant) 3rd right to Lower Chicksgrove. In 1.5m left into Lagpond Ln, pub 1m on left*

Charming thatched inn amid beautiful rolling countryside

An old cobbled path leads to the low latched door of this 14th-century inn. Step inside and you walk into a delightful bar with worn flagstones, exposed stone walls and old beams. Snuggle up by the large inglenook fireplace or relax in the intimate booth seating, perfect on a winter's evening. You can be certain to find three or four local real ales on tap, perhaps from Wiltshire brewery Plain Ales, and the wine list is comprehensive. Be sure to try the food: the kitchen team has won an AA Rosette for their seasonal dishes; these are chalked up on a blackboard because they change so frequently. Examples of starters are smoked haddock, salmon, cod and boiled egg fishcake, buttered spinach and clam chowder; or gnocchi, mushrooms, pesto, kale and crispy poached egg. Main dishes could be pork tenderloin stuffed with stem ginger, sage and quince; chicken breast stuffed with sun-dried tomatoes and olives; or sea bass fillet with steamed mussels; saag aloo and masala sauce. Treacle tart or sticky toffee pudding for afters. Five bedrooms are also available.

Open 12-3 6-11 (Sun 12-3 7-10.30) Closed 25-26 Dec, Mon L Jan-Mar **Food** Lunch all wk 12-2 Dinner all wk 6.30-9 ⊕ FREE HOUSE ◀ Keystone Large One, Sixpenny Gold, Plain Ales Inntrigue, Butcombe Ö Ashton Press & Still. **Facilities** Non-diners area ❤ (Bar Restaurant Garden) ♦♦ Children's menu Children's portions Garden ⊫ Parking WiFi 🚌 **Rooms** 5

MALMESBURY

Map 4 ST98

Kings Arms ★★★ INN

tel: 01666 823383 **29 High St SN16 9AA**
email: thekingsarms.malmesbury@arkells.com **web:** www.thekahotel.co.uk
dir: *M4 junct 17, A429 to Malmesbury. Follow town centre signs. Pub on left in town centre*

16th-century coaching inn in a historic Cotswolds town

Close to Malmesbury Abbey, which was founded as a Benedictine monastery in the 7th century, the inn offers two very different bars, separated by a covered walkway: one is the residents' bar, within the Elmer Restaurant, while the other is the more contemporary Bar 29. The latter serves home-cooked meals such as sausages and mash; pie of the day; fish and chips; omelettes; and the house speciality, double egg, Wiltshire ham and chips. There's live entertainment in the bar at weekends. The real ales – 3B, Moonlight and Wiltshire Gold – are from Arkell's, which owns the pub.

Open all day all wk **Food** Lunch all wk 12-3 Dinner Mon-Sat 6-9 Restaurant menu available all wk ⊕ ARKELL'S ◀ 3B, Wiltshire Gold & Moonlight, Angus Bitter (pub's own) Ö Westons Stowford Press, guest cider. **Facilities** Non-diners area ♦♦ Children's menu Children's portions Outside area ⊫ Beer festival Cider festival Parking WiFi **Rooms** 12

The Vine Tree   PICK OF THE PUBS

tel: 01666 837654 **Foxley Rd, Norton SN16 0JP**
email: info@thevinetree.co.uk
dir: *M4 junct 17, A429 towards Malmesbury. Turn left for village, after 1m follow brown signs*

Former mill with great home cooking

This atmospheric pub was once a mill; workers reputedly passed beverages out through front windows to passing carriages. Today ramblers and cyclists exploring Wiltshire's charms are frequent visitors; the inn is situated on the official county cycle route. A large open fireplace burns wood all winter in the central bar, warming a wealth of old beams, flagstones and oak flooring. Here you'll find Flying Monk ales among others, and over three dozen wines served by the glass. The pub is also worth seeking out for its interesting modern British pub food and memorable outdoor summer dining. Nibble on free-range pork crackling with apple sauce while choosing from the carte. Start perhaps with lightly dusted salt and pepper squid with aïoli, griddled lemon and dressed leaves. Typical of the main courses is coq au vin, parsley creamed potatoes and garlic croûtons.

Open 12-3 6-12 (Sun 12-4) Closed Sun eve in Winter **Food** Lunch Mon-Sat 12-2.30, Sun 12-3.30 Dinner Mon-Sat 7-9.30 ⊕ FREE HOUSE ◀ Flying Monk Elmers, Sharp's Doom Bar, Butcombe Ö Westons Stowford Press. ₹ 40 **Facilities** Non-diners area ❤ (Bar Restaurant Garden) ♦♦ Children's menu Children's portions Play area Garden ⊫ Parking WiFi 🚌 (notice required)

MANTON
Map 5 SU16

NEW The Outside Chance

tel: 01672 512352 **71 High St SN8 4HW**
email: enquiries@theoutsidechance.co.uk
dir: *From Marlborough take A4 towards Chippenham. Left signed Manton & The Outside Chance*

Family-friendly and dog-welcoming winner

When, in 2008, two racehorse owners acquired The Oddfellows Arms, the new name they chose became even more appropriate when Champion Jockey (now Sir) AP McCoy later joined them. The pub is full of sporting trophies and artefacts, there's a splendid log fire in the fireplace, fresh flowers all around, evening candlelight and board games to play. Tables-a-plenty are outside. Sample dishes include chicken Caesar salad; beer-battered haddock and triple-cooked chips; tart of the day; and pan-fried potato gnocchi with Marlborough mushrooms. Curry, poker and open mic nights go down well.

Open all day all wk **Food** Lunch all wk 12-2 Dinner all wk 6-9 Av main course £13.95 Set menu available ⊕ WADWORTH ◀ IPA & 6X. **Facilities** Non-diners area ♣ (Bar Restaurant Garden) ♦♦ Children's menu Children's portions Play area Garden ⋤ Parking WiFi ☞ (notice required)

MARDEN
Map 5 SU05

The Millstream

tel: 01380 848490 **SN10 3RH**
email: themillstreammarden@gmail.com **web:** www.themillstream.co.uk
dir: *6m E of Devizes, N of A342*

Peaceful alfresco options here

Set in the heart of the Pewsey Vale, The Millstream is an attractive village pub near Devizes. The large garden is a wonderfully peaceful spot for an alfresco drink or meal. Inside, the three fireplaces make for a cosy and romantic atmosphere in which to sip a regional Thatchers cider and refuel on dishes such as duck leg confit with plum and ginger sauce; double-baked cheese soufflé; pork medallions with green peppercorn sauce; home-made pie of the day; or butterbean and borlotti cassoulet with garlic bread. Fish is delivered daily from St Mawes in Cornwall so a dish from the specials board might be baked crab pancakes with creamy crab sauce.

Open 12-3 6.30-11 Closed Sun eve & Mon eve **Food** Lunch all wk 12-2.30 Dinner Tue-Sat 6.30-9.30 Set menu available Restaurant menu available Mon-Sat ⊕ WADWORTH ◀ 6X, IPA, guest ales ♂ Thatchers Gold, Kingstone Press. **Facilities** Non-diners area ♣ (Bar Garden) ♦♦ Children's portions Garden ⋤ Parking WiFi ☞ (notice required)

See advert on opposite page

MONKTON FARLEIGH
Map 4 ST86

The Muddy Duck ★★★★ INN ⊚

tel: 01225 858705 **BA15 2QH**
email: dishitup@themuddyduckbath.co.uk **web:** www.themuddyduckbath.co.uk
dir: *Phone for detailed directions*

Popular pub flying high

When you venture through the doors of this pub, reputedly Wiltshire's most haunted pub, you will find a fire-warmed, sunken snug, while picnic tables are set out in the wisteria-covered courtyard; the rear garden looks out over farmland. If Wiltshire can grow it or supply it, then that's where ingredients for the kitchen come from, destined for the table, for example, as crispy pork belly with summer vegetable salad, salted peanuts and pork cracker; Goan fish curry with yogurt, lime pickle and toasted flatbread; or chargrilled beefburger with cheese, triple-cooked chips and tartare sauce. A selection of steaks are also available.

Open all day all wk **Food** Lunch 12-2.30 Dinner 6-9.30 ⊕ PUNCH TAVERNS ◀ Butcombe, St Austell Proper Job, guest ales. ♥ **Facilities** Non-diners area ♣ (Bar Garden) ♦♦ Children's menu Children's portions Garden ⋤ Parking WiFi **Rooms** 5

NEWTON TONY
Map 5 SU24

The Malet Arms

tel: 01980 629279 **SP4 0HF**
email: info@maletarms.com
dir: *8m N of Salisbury on A338, 2m from A303*

Pleasingly out of the way

In a quiet village on the River Bourne, this 17th-century inn was named after early Victorian lord of the manor, Sir Henry Malet. Fruit machine and piped music free, it has an enormous inglenook fireplace, and is bedecked with prints, trophies and myriad curiosities. Regional microbreweries are strongly supported, and most of the Mediterranean, Oriental and traditional English dishes on the ever-changing blackboard are locally sourced too. Game is plentiful in season, often shot by deer-stalker landlord, Noel. Other possibilities are scampi with home-made tartare sauce; and green chilli, ginger and cardamom chicken curry. In fine weather you can sit in the garden.

Open 11-3 6-11 (Sun 12-3) Closed 25 Dec, 1 Jan, Sun eve **Food** Lunch all wk 12-2.30 Dinner Mon-Sat 6.30-9.30 ⊕ FREE HOUSE ◀ Butcombe, Ramsbury, Stonehenge, Triple fff, Palmers, Plain Ales, Butts, Fuller's, guest ales ♂ Westons Old Rosie & Stowford Press, Gwynt y Ddraig Orchard Gold. ♥ 9 **Facilities** Non-diners area ♦♦ Children's menu Garden Beer festival Parking

OGBOURNE ST ANDREW
Map 5 SU17

Silks on the Downs

tel: 01672 841229 **Main Rd SN8 1RZ**
email: silks@silksonthedowns.com
dir: *M4 junct 15, A346 towards Marlborough. Approx 6m to Ogbourne St Andrew. Pub on A346*

Village pub with a horseracing theme

A mile north of the bustling market town of Marlborough you'll find this pub, tucked away in rolling downland. The free house's name reflects the racing heritage of the Berkshire Downs (whose western boundary is on the border with Wiltshire). Framed silks of leading racehorse owners and jockeys adorn the walls and the pub offers local Ramsbury ales, fine wines and an informal dining experience. Sample evening dishes run along the lines of mackerel pâté, chicory salad, ginger and chive dressing; fillet of beef with Stilton sauce and potato cake; or Barbary duck breast, red cabbage, sautéed potatoes and thyme jus and finally, vanilla crème brûlée.

Open 12-3 6.30-11 Closed 25 & 26 Dec, 1 Jan, Sun eve & BHs eve **Food** Lunch Mon-Tue 12-2, Wed-Sun 12-2.30 Dinner Mon-Tue 7-9, Wed-Sat 7-9.30 ⊕ FREE HOUSE ◀ Ramsbury Gold, guest ales ♂ Aspall. ♥ 8 **Facilities** Non-diners area ♦♦ Children's menu Children's portions Garden ⋤ Parking WiFi

The Millstream, Marden, Devizes, SN10 3RH • Tel: 01380 848490
E-mail: themillstreammarden@gmail.com • Facebook: Millstreammarden

The Millstream is a family run public house set in the heart of the delightful Pewsey Vale. It is the perfect all-rounder in its serene rural setting which can easily be reached by car, lying roughly six miles south-east of the charming market town of Devizes.

The pub is also well placed for exploring Marden Henge, the largest Neolithic henge enclosure discovered to date in the UK. The village of Avebury is located approximately just 10 miles north, famous for one of the best known prehistoric sites in Britain; it contains the largest stone circle in Europe.

On arrival to The Millstream you are welcomed with cosy log fires, beamed ceilings, a candle lit dining room and an informal bar area. The ambience is relaxed yet retains a professional touch.

Kate and her kitchen team have successfully put themselves on the map locally as a destination for fine dining. For fish lovers, The Millstream boasts an ever changing, vibrant and impressive menu of fresh fish including, oven roasted hake with chargrilled peppers and aioli, steamed fillet of seabass with ginger spring onion and soy sauce. More seasonal fish dishes offered include, whole cracked crab and Cornish lobster, which can be enjoyed in the exceptional beer garden, set on the back of the River Avon.

Striving to attract customers with a different taste, firm favourites on the menu include double baked soufflés and homemade pies made with our local Wadworth ale. Also popular for a lighter lunch, smaller dishes and starters include chicken liver pâté or a borlotti bean cassoulet. Using locally sourced, fresh and fine quality ingredients, The Millstream has rapidly become a notable spot for a home cooked, traditional Sunday lunch. Food is complemented by a choice of pleasant wine and selection of fine Wadworth cask ales.

Dogs are more than welcome in the bar area, hopefully making friends with the two resident English pointers, Sophie and Francesca.

Booking is highly advisable.

PEWSEY
Map 5 SU16

The Seven Stars Inn

tel: 01672 851325 **Bottlesford SN9 6LW**
email: info@thesevenstarsinn.co.uk
dir: *From A345 follow Woodborough sign. Through North Newnton. Right to Bottlesford. Pub on left*

Handsome thatched inn with seven acres of gardens

Close to two of Wiltshire's famous white horses, this 16th-century free house lies in the heart of the Vale of Pewsey between Salisbury Plain and the Marlborough Downs, and is a 15-minute drive from the stone circles of Avebury. The bar maintains its original character with low beams and oak panelling, and you can expect local and guest ales on tap. The menu of home-made classics could list warm goats' cheese with beetroot and walnut salad; followed by roast pork belly; ale-battered haddock; or Stokes Marsh farm steak. The chef's daily specials add to the choice.

Open 12-3 6-11 Closed Mon & Tue L **Food** Lunch Wed-Sun 12-2.30 Dinner Tue-Sat 7-9.30 Restaurant menu available Tue-Sun ⊕ FREE HOUSE ◀ Guest ales ♂ Orchard Pig Reveller. ♀ 18 **Facilities** Non-diners area ♣ (Bar Restaurant Garden) ♦♦ Children's portions Play area Garden ⊨ Parking WiFi ▭ (notice required)

PITTON
Map 5 SU23

The Silver Plough
PICK OF THE PUBS

tel: 01722 712266 **White Hill SP5 1DU**
email: thesilverplough@hotmail.com
dir: *From Salisbury take A30 towards Andover, Pitton signed. Approx 3m*

Friendly village pub on the fringes of the Salisbury Downs

Close to the cathedral city of Salisbury and ideally situated for visitors to Stonehenge, there's a timeless atmosphere to this English country inn. At its heart is an elaborately moulded old dark-wood bar from which diverge rooms and a snug with rustic furniture, ancient beams, log fires and rustic country-style decor, whilst hop festoons are a reminder that this is the place to get a reliable pint of First Call or K&B Sussex from Hall & Woodhouse's Dorset brewery. Local produce is to the fore in the menu of pub favourites given a modern twist, such as a half rack of ribs slow-cooked with BBQ sauce, or garlic and tarragon king prawns with hot ciabatta. Mains may feature oven-baked salmon fillet with herbed new potatoes, sautéed baby spinach and lemon butter sauce. There's a traditional skittles alley here, too, and the gardens offer views over the villages' thatched roofs. Dogs are permitted in the snug bar area, and there are baby-changing facilities.

Open all wk 12-3 6-11 (Mon-Tue 12-3 6-10.30 Sun winter 12-6 summer all day) Closed 25 Dec **Food** Lunch Mon-Sat 12-2, Sun 12-7.30 (Sun winter 12-4) Dinner Mon-Sat 6-9, Sun 12-7.30 (Sun winter 12-4) ⊕ HALL & WOODHOUSE ◀ Badger Tanglefoot, K&B Sussex & First Call, guest ale ♂ Westons Stowford Press. ♀ 15 **Facilities** Non-diners area ♣ (Bar Garden) ♦♦ Children's menu Children's portions Family room Garden ⊨ Parking WiFi ▭ (notice required)

RAMSBURY
Map 5 SU27

The Bell at Ramsbury ★★★★ INN ◉◉ PICK OF THE PUBS

See Pick of the Pubs on opposite page and advert below

THE BELL AT RAMSBURY

The Square, High Street, Ramsbury, Wiltshire, SN8 2PE
Reservations: 01672 520 230
Email: thebell@thebellramsbury.com

Experience a warm welcome as you enter The Bell at Ramsbury. Part of the Ramsbury Estate, this landmark 300-year-old former coaching inn sits at the heart of Wiltshire's 'Best Kept Large Village 2011'. This quintessential country pub excels in offering a superb Modern-British fine-dining experience prepared by Head Chef Jonas Lodge, who worked at a number of prestigious restaurants including the Fat Duck and the Hind's Head in Bray. The Bell's nine luxuriously adorned en-suite double bedrooms are affectionately known by their game bird or freshwater fish names - the complete sanctuary for that overnight stay. The decoration is sensitive to its origins in its retention of all original features, and yet delivers a calming contemporary finish in soft furnishings, accessories and pampering touches. All the while, The Bell retains its approachable and friendly link as the heart of the village community through it's Bar and continental café, Café Bella.

Within 10 minutes, enjoy Marlborough, host to the world-famous seat of learning, Marlborough College, and with reputedly the widest high-street in Europe; browse an abundance of ladies fashion boutiques amongst a chic café-culture atmosphere. Equally near is Hungerford, your centre for countryside outfitters, the departure point for narrow boat excursions along the Kennet and Avon Canal or unearth that elusive treasure in one of the many antique shops.

It takes only 20 minutes to reach Newbury or Swindon for larger commercial retail outlets, and yet you can be in London's West End in just over the hour.

Come in and relax by the fire and enjoy our hospitality ....

We look forward to welcoming you!

PICK OF THE PUBS

The Bell at Ramsbury ★★★★ INN ◉◉

RAMSBURY   Map 5 SU27

tel: 01672 520230 **The Square SN8 2PE**
email: thebell@thebellramsbury.com
web: www.thebellramsbury.com
dir: *M4 junct 14, A338 to Hungerford.
B4192 towards Swindon. Left to
Ramsbury*

Village-centre pub in the picturesque Kennet Valley

From its strategic position in the centre
of the village, this 17th-century
coaching inn can keep an eye on
everything coming up the High Street.
Just outside, on a little green, a lovely
old tree provides shade for a couple of
benches, while on the wall of a building
opposite a pre-war, AA enamel road sign
survives to inform motorists that London
is 68 miles away. The light, spacious
bar serves Ramsbury real ales, brewed
in nearby Aldbourne, and Lilley's Apples
& Pears cider from Somerset. The bar
menu offers Mediterranean-style
nibbles, fish and triple-cooked chips,
and a daily pie. Experienced head chef
Duncan Jones is guardian of the Bell's
two AA Rosettes, awarded for his
modern British fine-dining tradition.
Among the starters, his inventive menus
may suggest duck egg on toast with
Iberico ham and truffle; and smoked Var
salmon with caramelised yogurt, keta
caviar and nasturtium root. Further
insight is given by such mains as
pan-roast turbot with confit potatoes,

artichokes, wild mushrooms and truffle
velouté; Kelmscott pork belly with glazed
cheek, new potatoes, braised red
cabbage and pork sauce; and scorched
vegetables with roast squash, kale and
burnt leek mayonnaise. To conclude,
among the desserts might be pistachio
and marmalade bread and butter
pudding; and rhubarb posset with
honeycomb and rhubarb jelly. France
takes pole position on the wine list,
followed by Spain, Italy and the New
World. Children have their own menu,
but may have a half portion of
something else if they want; high-chairs
are available for toddlers. Breakfast,
lunch, coffee and tea are served in the
Bell's Shaker-influenced Café Bella.

Open all day all wk 12-11 (Sun 12-10)
Food Lunch Mon-Sat 12-2.30, Sun 12-3
Dinner Mon-Sat 6-9, Sun 6-8 🛢 FREE
HOUSE 🍺 Ramsbury Bitter, Gold
🍏 Thatchers Gold, Lilley's Apples &
Pears. 🍷 12 **Facilities** Non-diners area
🐾 (Bar Garden) 👶 Children's menu
Children's portions Garden 🪑 Parking
WiFi **Rooms** 9

ROWDE
Map 4 ST96

The George & Dragon ★★★★ RR ◉◉ PICK OF THE PUBS

tel: 01380 723053 **High St SN10 2PN**
email: restaurant@thegeorgeanddragonrowde.co.uk
web: www.thegeorgeanddragonrowde.co.uk
dir: *1m from Devizes, take A342 towards Chippenham*

Village pub and specialising in fish and seafood

In 1917, the writer Edward Hutton said that Rowde had a 'curious inn', but as this Wiltshire village possessed four at the time, it's not known whether he meant this 16th-century hostelry or another one. Narrowboaters on the nearby Kennet & Avon Canal can spend up to six hours negotiating the 29 locks of the Caen Flight – that's hard work, so no wonder they flock to this modernised pub with its large open fireplaces, wooden floors, antique rugs and candlelit tables that create a wonderful ambience. The reward for the thirsty might be a pint of Butcombe or Bath Ales Gem; for the hungry, maybe a seafood platter or another special featuring fish delivered daily from Cornwall. Other possibilities from the award-winning menu include, as a starter or main, double-baked cheese soufflé with parmesan cream sauce; chargrilled fillet steak with tenderstem broccoli and hollandaise; and roast chicken breast, curried bubble-and-squeak and red wine jus. Three very stylish bedrooms are available if you'd like to stay over.

Open 12-3 6.30-10 (Sat 12-4 6.30-10 Sun 12-4) Closed Sun eve **Food** Lunch Mon-Fri 12-3, Sat-Sun 12-4 Dinner Mon-Sat 6.30-10 Av main course £17-£20 Set menu available Restaurant menu available all wk ⊕ FREE HOUSE ◀ Butcombe Bitter, Sharp's Doom Bar, Bath Ales Gem, Fuller's ESB & London Pride, Ringwood Fortyniner Ō Ashton Press. ♥ 10 **Facilities** Non-diners area ✿ (Bar Garden) ♦♦ Children's menu Children's portions Garden ⊼ Parking WiFi ▰ **Rooms** 3

ROYAL WOOTTON BASSETT
Map 5 SU08

The Angel ★★★★ INN ◉

tel: 01793 851161 **47 High St SN4 7AQ**
email: theangel.wbassett@arkells.com **web:** www.theangelhotelwoottonbassett.co.uk
dir: *M4 junct 16, A3102 towards Royal Wootton Bassett. At 2nd rdbt left signed Royal Wootton Bassett. Pub on right after lights*

Historic coaching inn with good food and local ales

Slap bang on the high street in Royal Wootton Bassett, this former coaching inn is a contemporary establishment with traditional bar serving a range of Arkell's ales and an oak-panelled dining room showcasing local produce. Meat from named local farms and south coast fish, delivered daily, are cooked on a charcoal grill that is the workhorse of the kitchen. Other options might be crispy bacon salad with black pudding, poached egg and blue cheese; salmon fillet with shellfish bisque, lobster tortellini, balsamic caviar and black truffle; or Stilton and pine nut arancini with charred baby leek, butternut squash and pomegranate vinaigrette. Sandwiches are served at lunchtime and throughout the afternoon. Sunday roasts are popular – booking is recommended.

Open all day all wk Closed 26 Dec, 1 Jan **Food** Lunch all wk 11.30-2.30 Dinner all wk 6-9.30 ⊕ ARKELL'S ◀ 3B, Moonlight & Wiltshire Gold Ō Westons Old Rosie. ♥ **Facilities** Non-diners area ✿ (Garden Outside area) ♦♦ Children's menu Children's portions Garden Outside area ⊼ Beer festival Cider festival WiFi ▰ (notice required) **Rooms** 17

SALISBURY
Map 5 SU12

The Cloisters

tel: 01722 338102 **83 Catherine St SP1 2DH**
email: thecloisters83@gmail.com
dir: *In city centre, near cathedral*

A reputation for good honest food

Near the cathedral, the appropriately named Cloisters is a mid 18th-century pub; its Victorian windows look into a beamed interior warmed by a pair of open fires. The choice of ales includes Hop Back Summer Lightning, Sharp's Doom Bar and Butcombe Bitter. Thanks to a well-qualified chef, the menu will please everyone with its popular pub plates, from traditional fish and chips to pork and leek sausages or beef and ale pie, as well as evening dishes like lamb steak with redcurrant sauce, or salmon fillet with mozzarella and pesto. Doorstep sandwiches, baguettes and jacket potatoes are also available.

Open all day all wk 11-10 (Thu-Sat 11am-mdnt Sun 12-10) **Food** Lunch Mon-Fri 11-3, Sat 11-9, Sun 12-9 Dinner Mon-Fri 6-9, Sat 11-9, Sun 12-9 ⊕ ENTERPRISE INNS ◀ Butcombe Bitter, Sharp's Doom Bar, Hop Back Summer Lightning. ♥ **Facilities** Non-diners area ♦♦ Children's menu & portions WiFi ▰ (notice required)

The Wig and Quill

tel: 01722 335665 **1 New St SP1 2PH**
email: theofficialwigandquill2014@outlook.com
dir: *On approach to Salisbury follow brown Old George Mall Car Park signs. Pub opposite car park*

Charming old pub close to the cathedral

Following his mantra of 'traditional, stylish, relaxing and atmospheric', landlord Robert Wood is building on the inherent qualities of this old city pub. The roomy, beamed bar with open fires, flagstones and wood flooring is as welcoming as ever. Ales include the ever-popular 6X alongside newer brews from Wadworth such as Swordfish. Menus proffer happy pub grub, served all day every day. Light bites include hot and spicy chicken wings or jacket potatoes with a range of fillings; or choose plates such as home-made beef lasagne; lemon and thyme marinated spatchcock poussin; or classic French bouillabaisse. A sheltered courtyard garden behind the pub is a restful spot in summer.

Open all day all wk noon-close **Food** 12-10 Av main course £10.95 Set menu available Restaurant menu available all wk ⊕ WADWORTH ◀ 6X, Henry's Original IPA, Horizon & Swordfish Ō Westons Old Rosie, Thatchers, Aspall. ♥ 9 **Facilities** Non-diners area ✿ (All areas) ♦♦ Children's menu Children's portions Garden Outside area ⊼ Beer festival WiFi ▰

SEMINGTON
Map 4 ST86

The Lamb on the Strand

tel: 01380 870263 **99 The Strand BA14 6LL**
email: info@thelambonthestrand.co.uk
dir: *1.5m E on A361 from junct with A350*

Craft brews and interesting tapas

This popular dining pub began life as a farmhouse in the 18th-century, later developing into a beer and cider house. Today, customers can choose a real ale from the Wiltshire craft brewery Box Steam, or a cider from Westons. Food is freshly prepared from locally sourced ingredients, with an appetising choice of hot dishes and open sandwiches at lunchtime. The Wiltshire Tapas menu offers an interesting mix of British and global treats: fried black pudding with butter beans; spiced chicken wings; and salt and pepper squid with garlic aïoli being just three.

Open all wk 12-3 6-11 ⊕ FREE HOUSE ◀ Box Steam Ō Westons Stowford Press, Thatchers. **Facilities** ✿ (Bar Restaurant Garden) ♦♦ Children's menu Children's portions Play area Family room Garden Parking WiFi

SHERSTON
Map 4 ST88

The Rattlebone Inn

tel: 01666 840871 **Church St SN16 OLR**
email: eat@therattlebone.co.uk
dir: *M4 junct 17, A429 to Malmesbury. 2m after passing petrol station at Stanton St Quentin, turn left signed Sherston*

Lively village pub with robust country cooking

With fine beer from Flying Monk Brewery, alley-skittles and a strong menu of both old-style and contemporary dishes, who would ever want to leave this character Cotswold village retreat? Not John Rattlebone, that's for sure; this Saxon warrior's name lives on as does his restless spirit that occasionally manifests itself here. The interior is one of beams, flagged floors, log-burners and golden stone, and walled gardens enclose three boules pistes and sheltered patios, ideal for the July cider festival. Country bistro home cooking is the style here; kick-in with warm salad of seared pigeon breast, then chow down to Gloucester Old Spots pork belly and chorizo cassoulet.

Open all wk 12-3 5-11 (Fri-Sat 12-12 Sun 12-11) **Food** Lunch Mon-Sat 12-2.30, Sun 12-3 Dinner Mon-Sat 6-9.30 Set menu available ⊕ YOUNG'S ◀ Bitter, St Austell Tribute, Flying Monk Elmers, guest ales ♂ Thatchers Gold & Somerset Haze. ⏉ 14 **Facilities** Non-diners area ❈ (Bar Garden) ♦ Children's menu Children's portions Garden ⋒ Cider festival WiFi ▭ (notice required)

SOUTH WRAXALL
Map 4 ST86

The Longs Arms

tel: 01225 864450 **BA15 2SB**
email: info@thelongarms.com
dir: *From Bradford-on Avon take B3109 towards Corsham. Approx 3m, left to South Wraxall. Pub on left*

Character pub in lovely village location

This stunning-looking golden-stone pub commands the centre of a tiny village above the Avon Valley just outside Bath. A log-burner, slab flooring and country prints welcome you to the airy bar; the cosy dining room is pleasingly cottagey in character. The cuisine is proudly British and seasonal, and each meal has a suggested beer to accompany. There's an on-site smokehouse, while the veg and herbs come from the grounds. Consider a starter of cold home-smoked salmon with horseradish, sweet pickled cucumber and seaweed; leaving room for mains like Wiltshire lamb shoulder and cutlet, toasted almonds, Jersey Royals and Wye Valley asparagus. The lavender-scented secluded garden is a summer delight.

Open 12-3.30 5.30-11.30 (Sun 12-5) Closed 3wks Jan, Sun eve & Mon **Food** Lunch Tue-Sat 12-2.30, Sun 12-3 Dinner Tue-Sat 5.30-9.30 ⊕ WADWORTH ◀ 6X, Horizon, seasonal ales ♂ Thatchers. ⏉ 10 **Facilities** ❈ (Bar Restaurant Garden) ♦ Children's portions Garden ⋒ Parking WiFi ▭ (notice required)

SWINDON
Map 5 SU18

The Runner

tel: 01793 523903 **Wootton Bassett Rd SN1 4NQ**
email: runninghorse@arkells.com
dir: *M4 junct 16, A3102 towards Swindon. At 2nd rdbt right signed town centre. Pub on right*

All-day food at this family pub

Arkell's Brewery owns this late 19th-century, family-friendly pub. Every Monday here is Steak Day, but otherwise the menu offers filled baguettes, jacket potatoes and salads, while on Sundays two roasts are always available, as well as a selection of home-made desserts. There's a children's play area and plentiful parking, while on the River Rey, opposite the pub, Swindon's annual Duck Race is held at the end of May on the Bank Holiday. Please note, children are not permitted after 9pm.

Open all day all wk **Food** all wk 12-8.30 ⊕ ARKELL'S ◀ 3B, guest ales ♂ Thatchers Gold. ⏉ **Facilities** Non-diners area ♦ Children's menu Children's portions Play area Family room Garden ⋒ Parking WiFi ▭ (notice required)

The Weighbridge Brewhouse

tel: 01793 881500 **Penzance Dr SN5 7JL**
email: info@weighbridgebrewhouse.co.uk
dir: *M4 junct 16, follow Swindon Centre signs, then Outlet Car Park West signs*

Striking pub and brewery in former railway building

Built in 1906, the former Great Western Railway Weighhouse was transformed by experienced operator Anthony Windle into a stunning pub-restaurant concept, complete with microbrewery. Many original features have been retained and the old railway building boasts brick walls and lofty ceilings, with a vast bar at one end, dispensing the six home-brewed ales and 25 wines by the glass from the extensive wine list, and an airy, smart and very comfortable dining room at the other. Extensive monthly menus may deliver half a smoked chicken, with sweet chilli, balsamic vinegar and Madeira sauce; pan-fried wild boar medallions; and for something a little different, Thai-style crocodile. There are seasonal fresh fish dishes, a wide choice of house-aged steak; and interesting vegetarian options. Portions are very generous but if you have enough room, there's home-made banoffee pie to finish.

Open all day all wk Closed 25-26 Dec **Food** Lunch Mon-Sat 12-2.30, Sun 12-7.30 Dinner Mon-Sat 6-9.30, Sun 12-7.30 Restaurant menu available all wk ⊕ FREE HOUSE ◀ Brinkworth Village, Weighbridge Best, Antsally's, Pooley's Golden, seasonal ales ♂ Symonds Founders Reserve, Westons Mortimers Orchard. ⏉ 25 **Facilities** Non-diners area ♦ Children's menu Children's portions Outside area ⋒ Parking WiFi

TOLLARD ROYAL
Map 4 ST91

King John Inn ★★★★ RR ◉◉

tel: 01725 516207 **SP5 5PS**
email: info@kingjohninn.co.uk **web:** www.kingjohninn.co.uk
dir: *On B3081 (7m E of Shaftesbury)*

Stylish country pub with innovative modern menus

Named after the original hunting lodge built for King John, this brick-built Victorian inn luxuriates in its location on Cranborne Chase deep in stunning countryside outside Shaftesbury. Its airy, open-plan bar and dining areas have a crisp country feel, featuring rugs on quarry tile flooring, pine tables, snug alcoves and winter log fires. The contemporary dinner menu offers starters like devilled venison liver and kidney with fried bread; cauliflower, mustard and gruyère soup; or crispy hare risotto. For the main course the choices are just as tempting – brill fillet and brill ravioli, cherry tomatoes, saffron velouté; twice-baked Westcombe Cheddar soufflé; and smoked tenderloin of pork, Mona Lisa potato mash and black pudding. Finish perhaps with apple doughnuts, mulled cider and toffee sauce; or lemon posset and shortbread.

Open all day all wk 11-11 **Food** Lunch Mon-Sat 12-2.30, Sun 12-3 Dinner Mon-Sat 7-9.30, Sun 7-9 Av main course £16.95 Set menu available ⊕ CIRRUS INNS ◀ Ringwood Best Bitter, Sharp's Doom Bar, guest ales ♂ Ashton Press. ⏉ 20 **Facilities** Non-diners area ❈ (Bar Restaurant Garden) ♦ Children's portions Garden ⋒ Parking WiFi **Rooms** 8

UPTON LOVELL

Map 4 ST94

Prince Leopold Inn ★★★ INN

tel: 01985 850460 **BA12 OJP**
email: info@princeleopold.co.uk **web:** www.princeleopold.co.uk
dir: *From Warminster take A36 towards Salisbury 4.5m, left to Upton Lovell*

Beside the Wylye trout stream

Built here just west of Salisbury Plain in 1878, the Leo was named after Victoria and Albert's popular, but sickly, eighth child, who lived at nearby Boyton Manor. Local craftsman Matthew Burt's elm-topped bar counter is where to order Somerset-brewed Butcombe ale or Warminster-brewed Plain Ales Sheep Dip. There's a log fire, sofas and cameos of village life in the Victorian snug, while from the dining room beyond you can see the Wylye as you enjoy chicken wrapped in Parma ham; confit duck leg with pea and pancetta fricassée; fisherman's pie; or Portobello mushroom, feta and chilli burger.

Open all wk 12-3 6-11 Sat-Sun 12-11 summer (12-3 6-11 Sun 12-3 winter)
Food Lunch all wk 12-2.30 Dinner Mon-Sat 6-8.30, Sun 6-8 ⊕ FREE HOUSE
◀ Butcombe, Plain Ales Sheep Dip ♂ Thatchers Dry, Ashton Press. ♀ 16
Facilities Non-diners area ♥ (Bar Garden) ♦ Children's menu Children's portions
Garden ⊓ Parking WiFi ➡ (notice required) **Rooms** 6

WANBOROUGH

Map 5 SU28

The Harrow Inn ★★★ INN

tel: 01793 791792 **SN4 OAE**
email: info@theharrowwanborough.co.uk **web:** www.theharrowwanborough.co.uk
dir: *M4 junct 15, A419 towards Cirencester. Exit at next junct signed Cirencester & Oxford. Follow Wanborough sign from rdbt*

Great local produce showcased on the menu here

This handsome thatched inn retains plenty of original character including exposed beams and inglenook fire, the grate of which is Grade II listed. Parts of The Harrow date back to 1747 and beer was brewed on site for the next century. Brewing ceased in 1863 but the pub still offers a range of ales such as Otter Bitter, which can be enjoyed with enticing dishes such as home-made parsnip and ginger soup; pheasant, chestnut and bacon terrine; puff-pastry steak and Otter pie; and braised ox cheeks with root vegetables and parsley and chive dumpling.

Open all day all wk **Food** all day ⊕ ENTERPRISE INNS ◀ Timothy Taylor Landlord, Otter Bitter ♂ Westons Stowford Press. ♀ 9 **Facilities** Non-diners area ♥ (Bar Garden) ♦ Children's menu Children's portions Garden ⊓ Parking WiFi ➡ (notice required) **Rooms** 3

WARMINSTER

Map 4 ST84

The Bath Arms

tel: 01985 212262 **Clay St, Crockerton BA12 8AJ**
email: batharms@aol.com
dir: *From Warminster on A36 take A350 towards Shaftesbury, left to Crockerton*

Family- and dog-friendly pub with a landscaped garden

This 17th-century pub was part of the Marquess of Bath's Longleat Estate, until death duties forced its sale in 1923. The bar, serving Hobdens Wessex Crockerton Classic and Potter's beers, has that genuine 'real local' feel; in winter the log-burner can be an especially welcome sight. The Garden Suite, with views across the lawn, provides additional seating on busy weekends. An extensive menu offers light snacks and baguettes; signature dish 'Sticky Beef'; venison steak hâché with white asparagus and fried egg; shepherd's pie with crushed peas; grilled salmon, fennel and salad; and potato gnocchi with artichokes, peas and pecorino cheese.

Open all day all wk 11-11 **Food** Lunch all wk 12-2 Dinner all wk 6.30-9 ⊕ FREE HOUSE ◀ Hobdens Wessex Crockerton Classic & Potter's Ale, guest ales. **Facilities** Non-diners area ♥ (Bar Garden) ♦ Children's menu Children's portions Play area Garden ⊓ Beer festival Parking WiFi ➡ (notice required)

The George Inn

tel: 01985 840396 **Longbridge Deverell BA12 7DG**
email: info@the-georgeinn.co.uk
dir: *Phone for detailed directions*

Family-friendly pub near Longleat Safari Park

A member of the expanding Upham Group, this 17th-century coaching inn overlooks the grassy banks of the River Wylye. Upham started out as a brewery, so it's their beers that sit alongside guest ales and Orchard Pig Philosopher cider. Food is served in the oak-beamed Smithy Bar and in the two restaurants, where menus open with smoked salmon and granary bread; and antipasti. They continue with Upham beer-battered Atlantic cod, chips, peas and chunky tartare sauce; slow-roasted pork belly, creamed potatoes and vegetables; goats' cheese and caramelised onion quiche, new potatoes and salad.

Open all day all wk 11-11 (Sun 12-10.30) Closed 25 Dec from 3pm, 26 Dec (1 Jan open 11-3) **Food** Lunch Mon-Thu 12-2.30, Fri-Sat 12-9.30, Sun 12-9 Dinner Mon-Thu 6-9.30, Fri-Sat 12-9.30, Sun 12-9 ⊕ UPHAM GROUP ◀ Punter & Tipster, guest ales ♂ Orchard Pig Philosopher. **Facilities** ♥ (Bar Garden) ♦ Children's menu Children's portions Play area Garden ⊓ Parking WiFi ➡ (notice required)

WEST OVERTON
Map 5 SU16

The Bell at West Overton

tel: 01672 861099 **Bath Rd SN8 1QD**
email: hannah@thebellwestoverton.com
dir: *4m W of Marlborough on A4*

Well known for good food

Travellers on today's A4 near Marlborough have been passing or preferably stopping at The Bell since it was built as a coaching inn in 1812. Today, it's definitely worth making a beeline for; it's a great spot to just enjoy a drink in the garden or to linger on for a meal after exploring nearby Avebury Stone Circle. The inn's decor still has original features including sarsen stone walls. Hannah McNaughton and chef husband Andrew strongly support Wiltshire producers and suppliers in both the kitchen and the bar. Andrew has travelled the world and cooked in high profile restaurants; his seasonal menus list dishes such as confit duck and potato soup; lamb kofta with Chinese leaf salad, coriander and mint yogurt as starters, followed by roast Loch Duart salmon, Singapore noodles, char sui pork and brown shrimps; or slow-braised beef cheek, sautéed potato gnocchi, Marlborough mushrooms, peas and watercress. Sandwiches and a set lunch menu are available too.

Open 12-3 6-11 Closed Sun eve & Mon (ex BH) **Food** Lunch Tue-Sun 12-2.30 Dinner Tue-Sat 6-9 Set menu available Restaurant menu available Tue-Sat ⊕ FREE HOUSE ◀ Moles Best, Ramsbury Flint Knapper, Twisted Gaucho. ♟ 15 **Facilities** Non-diners area ☘ (Bar Garden) ♦ Children's portions Garden ⌱ Parking WiFi ⛱ (notice required)

WOOTTON RIVERS
Map 5 SU16

Royal Oak
PICK OF THE PUBS

tel: 01672 810322 **SN8 4NQ**
email: royaloak35@hotmail.com
dir: *3m S from Marlborough*

Pretty thatched pub, a favourite with walkers

This much expanded 16th-century thatched and timbered pub is perfectly situated for Stonehenge, Bath and Winchester and for exploring the ancient oaks of Savernake Forest. Only 100 yards from the Kennet & Avon Canal and the Mid-Wilts Way, it has an interior as charming as the setting, with low, oak-beamed ceilings, exposed brickwork and wide open fireplaces. In the bar you'll find Wadworth 6X and local ale, Ramsbury Bitter. The daily-changing menus cover all manner of pubby favourites and beyond. Look for starters like fresh crab cocktail with lemon mayonnaise; or creamy goats' cheese with spiced beetroot and walnuts; then continue with roast topside of beef with Yorkshire pudding; Moroccan-spiced lamb pie; Thai green chicken curry; or pork and potato vindaloo.

Open all wk 12-2.30 6-11 (Sun 12-10) **Food** Lunch Mon-Sat 12-2.30, Sun 12-8 Dinner Mon-Sat 6-9, Sun 12-8 Set menu available ⊕ FREE HOUSE ◀ Ramsbury Bitter, Wadworth 6X, local guest ales Ò Westons Stowford Press & Mortimers Orchard. **Facilities** Non-diners area ☘ (Bar Restaurant Outside area) ♦ Children's menu Children's portions Outside area ⌱ Parking WiFi ⛱ (notice required)

WORCESTERSHIRE

ABBERLEY
Map 10 SO76

The Manor Arms ★★★★★ INN ◉

tel: 01299 890300 **WR6 6BN**
email: info@themanorarms.co.uk **web:** www.themanorarms.co.uk
dir: *From Ombersley take A443 towards Tenbury. After Great Witley right onto B4202. Right into Netherton Ln. Pub on left in village*

Great beers and menus in sublime countryside

Narrow lanes and footpaths thread Worcestershire's secluded Abberley Hills. Several of these meet outside The Manor Arms, where the promise of satisfying meals and local beers awaits explorers. There's more than a hint of the old world here, with inglenook and rustic furniture creating a restful interior. With a rich larder available from local farms, estates and growers, the chefs have gained an AA Rosette for the balanced menu of pub grub meals and contemporary cuisine. Engage with home-made pie-of-the-day with triple-cooked chips; the charcuterie board of cured meats, antipasti veg, pickles and bread; red Thai duck curry; or local game of the day with duck fat confit potato. Luxury B&B is available here, too.

Open all day all wk **Food** Lunch Mon-Sat 12-2.30, Sun 12-5 Dinner Mon-Thu 6-9, Fri-Sat 6-9.30 Restaurant menu available all wk ⊕ FREE HOUSE ◀ Ludlow Gold, Wye Valley HPA, Enville Ale, Hobsons, Wood's, Otter, St Austell Tribute Ò Robinsons Flagon. ♟ 16 **Facilities** Non-diners area ☘ (Bar Restaurant Garden) ♦ Children's menu Children's portions Garden ⌱ Parking WiFi ⛱ (notice required) **Rooms** 6

BECKFORD
Map 10 SO93

The Beckford

tel: 01386 881532 **Cheltenham Rd GL20 7AN**
email: beckfordinn@wadworth.co.uk
dir: *M5 junct 9, A46 towards Evesham, 5m to Beckford*

Cotswold country inn just off the A46

Midway between Tewkesbury and Evesham, this rambling Georgian country inn has the Cotswolds beckoning just to the east and shapely Bredon Hill rising immediately to the north. The Beckford, now owned by the Wadworth brewery, is an enticing mix of contemporary comforts and traditional fixtures throughout. A typical meal might include baked camembert with red onion chutney; or prawn and apple cocktail as starters; pork and leek sausages, root vegetable mash and red wine and onion gravy; shortcrust pastry pie of the day; and home-made butternut squash, courgette, mushroom and spinach lasagne. Pizzas, sandwiches and wraps are also on the menu.

Open all day all wk **Food** Lunch Mon-Thu 12-3, Fri-Sun 12-9.30 Dinner Mon-Thu 6-9.30, Fri-Sun 12-9.30 ⊕ WADWORTH ◀ 6X, Horizon, IPA, guest ales ♂ Westons Stowford Press, Kingstone Press. ♟ 14 **Facilities** Non-diners area ✿ (Bar Garden) ♦♦ Children's menu Children's portions Garden ⊨ Beer festival Parking WiFi 🚌 (notice required)

BELBROUGHTON
Map 10 SO97

NEW The Talbot

tel: 01562 730249 **Hartle Ln DY9 9TG**
email: jane@thetalbotatbelbroughton.co.uk
dir: *M5 junct 4, A491 towards Stourbridge. At lights left onto B4188 signed Belbroughton. Pub on right at T-junct in village*

Corner village pub with beers from far and wide

Believed to have been built in the late 17th or early 18th century, the pub has oak timbers, open log fires, soft furnishings and an enclosed garden with a covered patio. There seem to be no geographical limits on real ale sourcing, with Cocker Hoop from Cumbria sharing the bar with, perhaps, Boondoggle from Hampshire. In addition to old favourites such as blade of beef slowly braised in ale, are the international dishes such as Hungarian pork goulash; yellow Thai fish curry; and coq au vin. Sundays mean roast beef, pork or chicken, as well as hand-made faggots and Moroccan vegetable tagine.

Open all day all wk Closed 1 Jan **Food** all wk 12-9 Restaurant menu available ⊕ MARSTON'S ◀ Pedigree, Jennings Cocker Hoop, Brakspear Bitter, Ringwood Boondoggle, guest ales ♂ Addlestones, Thatchers Gold. ♟ 14 **Facilities** Non-diners area ✿ (Bar Garden Outside area) ♦♦ Children's menu Children's portions Garden Outside area ⊨ Parking WiFi 🚌 (notice required)

BEWDLEY
Map 10 SO77

NEW The Hop Pole Inn

tel: 01299 401295 **Hop Pole Ln DY12 2QH**
email: bookings@thehoppolebewdley.co.uk
dir: *From Kidderminster take A456 towards Leominster. At rdbt take B4190 towards Bewdley. Pub on left*

Culinary hotspot above the Severn Valley

Over the past five years Louise and Daren Bale have lovingly nurtured and matured this destination dining pub, set close to the ancient Wyre Forest at the edge of Bewdley. Inside, shabby-chic meets comfy contemporary in a warmly welcoming environment. Reliable beers from the Marston's brewery empire wet the whistle, whilst the very accomplished menus feature Dexter beef and real ale pie; or smokey bean and spinach burger from the carte, with set menus a popular option. Produce

is largely locally sourced; the pub's kitchen garden, farm shops and an artisan cheesemaker all feature on Daren's culinary radar.

Open all day all wk Closed 26 Dec **Food** Lunch Mon-Sat 12-3, Sun 12-5 Dinner Mon-Sat 6-9.30 Set menu available Restaurant menu available Mon-Sat ⊕ MARSTON'S ◀ EPA, Banks's Sunbeam, Jennings Cocker Hoop. ♟ 10 **Facilities** ✿ (Bar Garden) ♦♦ Children's menu Children's portions Play area Garden ⊨ Parking WiFi 🚌 (notice required)

Little Pack Horse

tel: 01299 403762 **31 High St DY12 2DH**
email: enquiries@littlepackhorse.co.uk
dir: *From Kidderminster follow ring road & Safari Park signs. Then follow Bewdley signs over bridge, turn left, then right, right at top of Lax Ln*

Homely old inn offering local beers and fabled pies

Close to an old ford through the River Severn, this timber framed inn tucked away in Bewdley's web of lanes has been catering for passing trade for over 480 years. It was a base for jaggers and their packhorses; the inside retains much character from those long-gone days, with cosy log fires and wizened beams. Today's time travellers can indulge in fine beers from the town's brewery and a range of ciders. Fulfilling fodder includes a wealth of pies – Desperate Dan Cow Pie with best Herefordshire beef for example – and savoury suet puddings: venison, port, cranberry and Shropshire Blue prove to be a real feast. Light bites cater for the less ravenous.

Open 5.30-close (Fri 12-3 5.30-close Sat-Sun all day) Closed Mon-Thu L **Food** Lunch Fri 12-2.15, Sat-Sun 12-4 Dinner Mon-Thu 5.30-9.15, Fri-Sat 5.30-9.30, Sun 5.30-8 ⊕ PUNCH TAVERNS ◀ Hobsons Town Crier & Twisted Spire, guest ales ♂ Thatchers Katy, Westons Stowford Press & Mortimers Orchard. ♟ 16 **Facilities** Non-diners area ✿ (Bar Garden Outside area) ♦♦ Children's menu Children's portions Family room Garden Outside area ⊨ Beer festival WiFi 🚌 (notice required)

The Mug House Inn & Angry Chef Restaurant ★★★★ INN ⊚
PICK OF THE PUBS

See Pick of the Pubs on opposite page

BISHAMPTON
Map 10 SO95

NEW The Dolphin

tel: 01386 462343 **Main St WR10 2LX**
email: contact@thedolphinbishampton.co.uk
dir: *Take A44 from Evesham towards Worcester. Right into Fladbury Hill signed Bishampton. At T-junct in Bishampton turn right. Pub on right*

Village local with attractive terraces

Head for one of the terraces here on a sunny day, furnished as they are with wicker chairs and circular glass-topped tables, and parasol-sheltered picnic benches. Inside, the updated interior has padded stools along the bar, where handles for Fuller's and Sharp's beers await. Otherwise settle into one of the hip-hugging tub chairs at a low table, or take a menu through to the neatly arranged restaurant. Here plates of honestly-priced and home-cooked fare range from omelettes with side salad; to a rump of Herefordshire lamb with roast winter vegetables and salsa verde; or home-smoked BBQ baby ribs, coleslaw and fries.

Open 12-3 6-11 (Sun 12-9 Mon 6-9) Closed Mon L **Food** Lunch Tue-Sat 12-2, Sun 12-2.30 Dinner Tue-Sat 6-9 Av main course £15 Restaurant menu available all wk ◀ Fuller's London Pride, Sharp's Doom Bar ♂ Aspall, Westons Stowford Press. **Facilities** Non-diners area ♦♦ Children's menu Children's portions Garden Outside area ⊨ Parking WiFi

PICK OF THE PUBS

The Mug House Inn & Angry Chef Restaurant ★★★★ INN ❀

BEWDLEY | Map 10 SO77

tel: 01299 402543
12 Severnside North DY12 2EE
email: drew@mughousebewdley.co.uk
web: www.mughousebewdley.co.uk
dir: *A456 from Kidderminster to Bewdley. Pub in town on river*

Unrivalled riverside location

Although unusual as a pub name today, a 'mug house' was a popular term for an alehouse in the 17th century. The Severnside address is a strong clue to its location – right on that river, with just a narrow cobbled road and some river's edge seating between it and the pub's flower-decked frontage. Purity Brewing Company's Mad Goose may be on duty at the bar alongside guest ales and regulars Timothy Taylor Landlord and Wye Valley HPA. Rosie's Pig cider makes a refreshing alternative, even during the Early May Bank Holiday beer festival which is held in the rear garden. The lunch menu includes a range of tummy-filling crusty bread sandwiches such as the doorstep chip butty; or choose one of the 10 Mug House platters served with salad, coleslaw, sweet pickled onion rings, Mug House pickle and a warm baguette. For those who enjoy a proper lunch, options for all three courses follow classic lines. A typical choice could comprise fresh

mussels in white wine with garlic and cream; pan-fried liver and bacon with creamed potato, a rich onion broth and peas; and a dark chocolate and black berry fondant. The AA Rosette-standard Angry Chef (provenance unknown) restaurant comes into its own in the evening, when an adults-only policy comes into force. Seasonally-based dishes may include a starter of chicory smoked potato and butternut squash gnocchi with apple and celeriac remoulade, caper popcorn and parsley emulsion. Move on to venison fillet medallions, with braised oxtail croquette and fondant potato, buttered harlequin carrots, braised fennel, and red wine and chocolate jus.

Open all day all wk 12-11 **Food** Lunch Mon-Sat 12-2.30, Sun 12-5 Restaurant menu available Mon-Sat evening ⊕ PUNCH TAVERNS 🛢 Bewdley Worcestershire Way, Timothy Taylor Landlord, Wye Valley HPA, Purity Mad Goose, guest ales ♻ Westons Rosie's Pig. ▾ 10 **Facilities** Non-diners area 🐾 (Bar Garden) Garden ⚏ Beer festival WiFi **Rooms** 7

PICK OF THE PUBS

The Fleece Inn

BRETFORTON Map 10 SP04

tel: 01386 831173 **The Cross WR11 7JE**
email: info@thefleeceinn.co.uk
web: www.thefleeceinn.co.uk
dir: *From Evesham follow signs for B4035 towards Chipping Campden. Through Badsey into Bretforton. Right at village hall, past church, pub in open parking area*

An inn steeped in history

For more than 500 years this old inn remained in the same family, all descendants of an early 15th-century farmer called Byrd, who built himself this former longhouse. His last direct descendant was the Fleece's long-serving landlady, Lola Taplin, who on her death in 1977 bequeathed it to the National Trust, making it the first pub among a fair few it now owns or lets. Not licensed until 1848, this beautiful timbered building remains largely unchanged, thanks in particular to skilful restoration following a devastating fire in 2004. Two special things to look out for are a Jacobean pewter dinner service, reputedly Oliver Cromwell's, and big chalk-drawn 'witch circles' on the floor in front of each hearth, supposedly to prevent witches entering through the chimneys, a practice that Lola insisted should continue after her death. Ales change frequently to include, perhaps, Wood's Shropshire Lass, Pope's Hop Market or

Cannon Royal's Fruiterer's Mild, while cider drinkers have a choice of home-brewed Ark or Thatchers Heritage. Food favourites, such as sausage, mash and sweet and sour onions; pork faggots and mustard mash; and pan-seared lamb's liver with onion tarte Tatin, may appear alongside beetroot ravioli with sage and orange butter sauce; pan-fried sea bass with crab and rosemary gnocchi; and oven-roasted chicken supreme with lemon and thyme pudding. Families will enjoy sunshine in the apple orchard, while children let off steam in the play area. Folk music, Morris dancing, an annual asparagus festival and a beer and cider festival in the second half of October are events to catch.

Open all day all wk **Food** Lunch Mon-Sat 12-2.30, Sun all day Dinner Mon-Sat 6.30-9, Sun all day ⊕ FREE HOUSE 🛢 Uley Pigs Ear, Wye Valley Bitter, guest ales ♉ Thatchers Heritage, The Ark, guest ciders. ♟ 20
Facilities Non-diners area 🐾 (Bar Garden) ♦♦ Children's menu Children's portions Play area Garden ᴘ Beer festival Cider festival WiFi 🚌 (notice required)

The Bear & Ragged Staff

tel: 01886 833399 **Station Rd WR6 5JH**
email: mail@bearatbransford.co.uk
dir: *3m from Worcester or Malvern, clearly signed from A4103 or A449*

Well-positioned free house with good reputation for food

Built in 1861 as an estate rent office and stables, this lovely old free house is easily reached from both Malvern and Worcester. The current owners have created a reputation for good food and beers, such as local Hobsons Twisted Spire (named after Cleobury Mortimer's parish church) and Cornish-brewed Sharp's Doom Bar. A typical meal might involve pan-seared scallops, black pudding, wonton crisps, watercress purée and balsamic reduction; and pan-fried duck breast, duck leg bon bon, dauphinoise potatoes, fine beans and passionfruit jus. Sandwiches are available from Monday to Saturday at lunchtime only, and there is an extensive range of wheat-free and gluten-free dishes.

Open 11.30-2.30 6-10.30 (Fri-Sat 11.30-2.30 6-11 Sun 12-2.30) Closed 25 Dec eve, 1 Jan eve, Sun eve **Food** Lunch all wk 12-2 Dinner Mon-Sat 6.30-9 Restaurant menu available Wed-Sun ⊕ FREE HOUSE ◀ Hobsons Twisted Spire, Sharp's Doom Bar ♨ Westons Stowford Press. ♈ 10 **Facilities** Non-diners area ✿ (Bar Garden) ♦♦ Children's menu Children's portions Garden ⊼ Parking WiFi ➡ (notice required)

The Fleece Inn   PICK OF THE PUBS

See Pick of the Pubs on opposite page

Crown & Trumpet

tel: 01386 853202 **14 Church St WR12 7AE**
email: info@cotswoldholidays.co.uk **web:** www.cotswoldholidays.co.uk
dir: *From High St follow Snowshill sign. Pub 600yds on left*

Ideally placed for exploring the Cotswolds

Just behind the green in this internationally-known picture-postcard village is the Crown & Trumpet, a traditional, 17th-century, mellow-stone inn. The classic beamed bar is just the place for a pint of Stroud Brewery's Tom Long or Stanway

Brewery Broadway Artists, or you can take it out into the peaceful patio garden; a winter alternative is a glass of mulled wine or a hot toddy by the fire. Classic, home-made pub food is available at lunch and dinner — try devilled whitebait; a home-made beef and Guinness pie; chilli con carne; venison sausages with mash; or fisherman's pie. There's musical entertainment every Saturday evening, and each Thursday it's their jazz and blues evening.

Crown & Trumpet

Open all wk 11-3 5-11 (Fri-Sat 11am-mdnt Sun 12-11) **Food** Lunch Mon-Fri 12-2.30, Sat-Sun 12-5 Dinner Mon-Fri 6-9.30, Sat-Sun 5-9.30 Set menu available ⊕ ENTERPRISE INNS ◀ Stroud Brewery Tom Long Amber Bitter, Stanway Brewery Cotteswold Gold & Broadway Artists Ale ♨ Black Rat & Black Rat Perry, Orchard Pig. ♈ 9 **Facilities** Non-diners area ✿ (Bar Garden) ♦♦ Children's menu Children's portions Garden ⊼ Beer festival Parking WiFi ➡ (notice required)

See advert on page 547

The Bell & Cross   PICK OF THE PUBS

tel: 01562 730319 **Holy Cross DY9 9QL**
dir: *Phone for detailed directions*

Good food near famous country park

Exploring the hills, wooded dingles and fabulous viewpoints of the remarkable Clent Hills can work up a healthy appetite; who better to help sate this than the former chef to the England football squad, host-patron Roger Narbett? Standing at the heart of a peaceful village, this character pub is the ideal culmination of a visit to this beautiful part of Worcestershire. Head for the bar for a rolling selection of hand-pulled beers and an inviting log fire in winter; the extensive garden, or the covered and heated patio for comfortable alfresco dining on cooler nights. The imaginative menu opens with a substantial range of starters and light bites such as confit duck rillette and beetroot relish; or lamb koftas with tzatziki, flatbread, pomegranate and cashew nut salad. Enticing mains include baked Cornish hake, pumpkin, bacon and chestnut risotto and prawns or shortcrust pie of the day.

Open all wk 12-3 6-11 (Sun 12-10.30) Closed 25 Dec, 26 Dec eve, 1 Jan eve **Food** Lunch all wk 12-2 Dinner Mon-Sat 6.30-9.15 Set menu available Restaurant menu available all wk ⊕ ENTERPRISE INNS ◀ Enville Ale, Marston's Pedigree & Burton Bitter, Timothy Taylor Landlord, guest ales ♨ Thatchers Gold. ♈ 15 **Facilities** Non-diners area ✿ (Bar Garden) ♦♦ Children's menu Children's portions Garden ⊼ Parking ➡ (notice required)

CLENT *continued*

The Vine Inn

The Vine Inn

tel: 01562 882491 **Vine Ln DY9 9PH**
email: info@vineinnclent.com web: www.vineinnclent.com
dir: *Phone for detailed directions*

Cracking pub secluded in marvellous hill country

Tucked into one of the sharp valleys which cleave the glorious Clent Hills, the Vine started life as a watermill at the dawn of the Industrial Revolution. Reborn as a pub in 1851, beers from Wye Valley, supplemented by cider and perry fresh from the Malvern Hills reward ramblers challenging the mini-mountain range that are the Clents. Recover in the tranquil wood-side gardens behind the flower basket-hung pub and consider a tempting menu that specialises in game and fresh fish offering the likes of free-range crispy duck egg with warm chorizo and black pudding salad, followed by Moroccan beef tagine; salmon Wellington; or The Vine's game pie. Leave space for treacle, lemon and stem ginger tart.

Open all day all wk **Food** Lunch Mon-Fri 12-3, Sat 12-9.30, Sun 12-8 Dinner Mon-Fri 6-9, Sat 12-9.30, Sun 12-8 Set menu available ⊕ PUNCH TAVERNS ◀ Marston's Wainwright, Wye Valley Butty Bach ♻ Hogan's & Hogan's Perry, Thatchers Traditional. **Facilities** Non-diners area ❀ (Bar Garden) ♦ Children's portions Garden ⌇ Parking WiFi ☎ (notice required)

See advert below

| DEFFORD | Map 10 SO94 |

NEW The Oak Inn

tel: 01386 750327 **Woodmancote WR8 9BW**
email: oakinndefford@btconnect.com
dir: *On A4104 between Upton upon Severn & Pershore*

Lovely atmospheric setting for classic pub grub

Unspoilt Worcestershire countryside surrounds Defford, a small village between Pershore and Upton upon Severn. Beautifully maintained, the family-run Oak Inn dates to the 17th century and is friendly and informal. Local cask ales featuring in the cosy bar, and there's a quaint lounge with an inglenook fireplace, as well as a contemporary, refurbished restaurant. On the menu are starters such as home-made chicken liver pâté, or devilled whitebait, while mains might include pan-fried breast of guinea fowl with wild mushroom risotto or classic pub grub — Butty Bach-battered fish and chips, maybe.

Open all day all wk **Food** Lunch Mon-Fri 12-2.30, Sat 12-9, Sun 12-7 Dinner Mon-Fri 6-9, Sat 12-9, Sun 12-7 Av main course £10.95 Set menu available Restaurant menu available Mon-Sat ⊕ FREE HOUSE ◀ Wye Valley Butty Bach & HPA, St Austell Tribute, Sharp's Doom Bar, guest ales ♂ Thatchers Heritage & Cheddar Valley. **Facilities** Non-diners area ❀ (Bar Garden Outside area) ⋫ Children's menu Children's portions Garden Outside area ⊼ Parking WiFi ▄ (notice required)

DROITWICH SPA	Map 10 SO86

The Chequers · · · · · · · · · · · · · · · · PICK OF THE PUBS

tel: 01299 851292 **Kidderminster Rd, Cutnall Green WR9 0PJ**
dir: *Phone for detailed directions*

Charming pub that's top of its league

In a former life, Roger Narbett was the England football team chef; his soccer memorabilia can be found in the Players Lounge of this charming pub he now runs with wife Joanne. Its traditional look comes from the cranberry-coloured walls, open fire, church-panel bar and richly hued furnishings. Indeed, some might also make a case for including the range of real ales, such as Otter Bitter, Timothy Taylor and Wye Valley HPA in the bar, adjoining which is the country-style Garden Room with plush sofa and hanging tankards. The menus offer a wide choice, from sandwiches, deli platters and 'bucket food' to pub classics like chicken curry and shortcrust pie of the day. Among the top performers are slow-cooked shoulder of Cornish lamb, chorizo, gratin dauphinoise, pea and mint purée; and baked gnocchi al forno with porcini, dolcelatte and spinach, truffled rocket and pecorino.

Open all day all wk Closed 25 Dec, 26 Dec eve & 1 Jan eve **Food** Lunch Mon-Sat 12-2, Sun 12-2.30 (light bites 2-5.30) Dinner all wk 6.30-9.15 Set menu available Restaurant menu available all wk ⊕ FREE HOUSE ◀ Enville Ale, Greene King Ruddles, Wye Valley HPA, Timothy Taylor, Hook Norton, Otter Bitter, Marston's EPA ♂ Thatchers Gold. ☘ 15 **Facilities** Non-diners area ❀ (Bar Garden) ⋫ Children's menu Children's portions Family room Garden ⊼ Parking WiFi ▄ (notice required)

The Honey Bee

tel: 01299 851620 **Doverdale Ln, Doverdale WR9 0QB**
email: honey@king-henrys-taverns.co.uk
dir: *From Droitwich take A442 towards Kidderminster. Left to Doverdale*

Spacious, modern and friendly pub

Set in four and half acres of grounds, you can go fishing for carp in this pub's two lakes – and even have your meal brought to you. The garden also has a great play area for children and there is a patio for outdoor drinking and dining. The contemporary interior has plenty of areas in which to enjoy freshly prepared dishes which will satisfy small and large appetites alike. Choose from a good selection of steaks and grills, fish and seafood options like swordfish steak, traditional favourites such as half a roast chicken, and international and vegetarian dishes, perhaps vegetable fajitas.

Open all day all wk 11.30-11 **Food** all wk 12-10 Set menu available Restaurant menu available all wk ⊕ FREE HOUSE/KING HENRY'S TAVERNS ◀ Greene King Abbot Ale, Fuller's London Pride, Sharp's Doom Bar, Guinness. ☘ 15 **Facilities** Non-diners area ⋫ Children's menu Children's portions Play area Garden Parking ▄

ELDERSFIELD	Map 10 SO73

The Butchers Arms

tel: 01452 840381 **Lime St GL19 4NX**
dir: *A417 from Gloucester towards Ledbury. After BP garage take B4211. In 2m take 4th left into Lime St*

A real beer-lovers' pub with a concise menu

Dating from the 16th century this is a pub which values its beer-drinking customers. The low-ceilinged, wooden-floored bar offers a good choice of regional beers served from the cask and is the hub of local life (although, sorry, it's not for the under-10s). The seasonal menu may be small, but it sure offers diversity: for example, grilled octopus, pork dumplings and honey-roast pork belly; roast loin of fallow deer with game pie, celeriac purée and game chips; and pistachio and raspberry macarons with pistachio ice cream. A spacious garden adds to its charm.

Open 12-2 7-11 Closed 1wk Jan, 1 wknd Aug, 24-26 Dec, Sun eve & Mon (incl BHs) **Food** Lunch Fri-Sun 12-1 Dinner Tue-Sat 7-9 ⊕ FREE HOUSE ◀ Wye Valley Dorothy Goodbody's Golden Ale, St Austell Tribute, Wickwar Sunny Daze ♂ Westons Stowford Press. ☘ 11 **Facilities** Non-diners area Garden Parking

---

The Crown & Trumpet Inn

Church Street, Broadway, Worcestershire, WR12 7AE Tel:01386 853202
Email: info@cotswoldholidays.co.uk Web: www.crownandtrumpet.co.uk

Situated just behind the village green of BROADWAY this traditional 17th century Inn, built in Cotswold stone, provides pub accomodation with four double rooms for midweek and weekend breaks.

Providing WiFi service. Serving pub lunch and dinners all through the week using locally produced ingredients to make seasonally cooked homemade dishes.
Weekly Thursday jazz or blues evenings as well as musical entertainment every Saturday evening. Having an open fire in the bar with our own mulled wine and hot toddies in the winter, Pimm's in the summer.

Achieving 30 Years in the CAMRA Good Beer Guide.
Awarded 2007 & 2012 Shakespeare branch of CAMRA Pub of the year.
Hope to welcome you to the Cotswolds, we are also situated just off The Cotswold Way and it is a wonderful walking area.

The Crown and Trumpet Inn is very central for touring Shakespeare's Country and both the Cotswold and Malvern Hills.

FLADBURY
Map 10 SO94

Chequers Inn

tel: 01386 861854 **Chequers Ln WR10 2PZ**
email: tspchef85@gmail.com
dir: Off A44 between Evesham & Pershore

River Avon walkers can refuel here

With its beams and open fire, this lovely old inn has bags of rustic charm. Tucked away in a pretty village with views of the glorious Bredon Hills, local produce from the Vale of Evesham provides the basis for home-cooked dishes such as jumbo crayfish and prawn cocktail; boiled ham with two eggs and chunky chips; and a range of home-made desserts. There is also a traditional Sunday roast. The pretty walled garden enjoys outstanding views – a great setting for drinking or dining – and the nearby River Avon is ideal for walking and fishing.

Open 12-3 5-11 (Fri-Sat 12-11 Sun 12-late) Closed Mon L (Jan-May) **Food** Lunch Tue-Sat 12-2.30, Sun 12-3 Dinner Mon-Sat 6-9 Restaurant menu available Mon-Sat ⊕ ENTERPRISE INNS ◀ Purity Mad Goose, Timothy Taylor Golden Best, guest ales Ŏ Aspall, Thatchers Gold, guest cider. ♚ **Facilities** Non-diners area ✿ (Bar Garden) ♙ Children's menu Children's portions Play area Family room Garden ⊼ Parking WiFi

FLYFORD FLAVELL
Map 10 SO95

The Boot Inn ★★★★ INN   PICK OF THE PUBS

See Pick of the Pubs on opposite page

HARTLEBURY
Map 10 SO87

The Tap House @ The Old Ticket Office

tel: 01299 253275 **DY11 7YJ**
email: enquiries@thetaphousehartlebury.co.uk
dir: From A449 follow station signs

Good pub grub in converted railway building

This is the flagship for the Worcestershire Brewing Company, whose Attwood Ales range of draught and bottled beers are brewed across from the pub. Until not long ago, it was Hartlebury's station building, a purpose recalled by the lounge bar's bench seating and railway-style signs. A short concise menu is offered in the oak-panelled restaurant. Tables on the outside terrace overlook the valley.

Open all day all wk ⊕ WORCESTERSHIRE BREWING COMPANY ◀ Attwood Nectar Bitter, Pale Ale & Gold. **Facilities** ✿ (Bar Outside area) ♙ Children's menu Outside area Parking WiFi

The White Hart

tel: 01299 250286 **The Village DY11 7TD**
email: skdiprose@fsmail.net
dir: From Stourport-on-Severn take A4025 signed Worcester & Hartlebury. At rdbt take B4193. Pub in village centre

At the community's centre and with really good food

Owner and top chef Simon Diprose runs this traditional country pub which continues to go from strength to strength. His concise menus might begin with garlic and mozzarella roasted field mushroom; smoked Scottish salmon with potato salad, pea shoots and prawns; or calamari rings with lime mayonnaise and salad leaves. Moving onto something more substantial there's wild mushroom leek and Stilton crumble; chicken with creamed potato, fresh vegetables and pea, bacon and

marjoram sauce; slow-cooked shank of Welsh lamb with vegetables and creamy garlic and thyme sauce; or lemon roast salmon fillet, baby vegetables and light beetroot and horseradish sauce. At lunchtime you could opt for just filled baps, a ploughman's or a burger and chunky chips.

Open all day all wk **Food** Lunch Tue-Sun 12-3 Dinner Tue-Sat 6-9 Set menu available Restaurant menu available Tue-Sun ⊕ PUNCH TAVERNS ◀ Timothy Taylor Landlord, Wye Valley HPA, Purity Mad Goose. **Facilities** Non-diners area ✿ (Bar Garden) ♙ Children's menu Children's portions Garden ⊼ Parking WiFi ➡ (notice required)

KEMERTON
Map 10 SO93

NEW The Crown Inn

tel: 01386 725020 **High St GL20 7HP**
email: thecrownpubkemerton@gmail.com
dir: In village centre

Vibrant village local popular with walkers

At the foot of Bredon Hill with its stunning views of the Malvern Hills, The Crown Inn is surrounded by fields, orchards and ancient paths, making it popular stopping point for Cotswold walkers. A friendly, vibrant village inn, the bar dispenses local Donnington Gold and Wye Valley Butty Bach ales, with Herefordshire-made Old Rosie keeping cider fans happy, perhaps with bar snacks of pan-fried chorizo or hand-made Scotch egg. Alongside sharing boards, enjoyable pub favourites include Meadows Farm faggots, mash, peas and onion gravy; 'deconstructed' chicken Kiev with chips and salad; and a pie of the day.

Open all day Closed Mon L **Food** Lunch Tue-Sun 12-2.30 Dinner all wk 6-9 ⊕ FREE HOUSE ◀ Donnington Gold, Wye Valley Butty Bach & HPA Ŏ Westons Old Rosie. ♚ 15 **Facilities** Non-diners area ✿ (Bar Garden Outside area) ♙ Children's menu Children's portions Garden Outside area ⊼ Parking WiFi ➡ (notice required)

KEMPSEY
Map 10 SO84

Walter de Cantelupe Inn ★★★ INN   PICK OF THE PUBS

tel: 01905 820572 **Main Rd WR5 3NA**
email: info@walterdecantelupe.co.uk **web:** www.walterdecantelupe.co.uk
dir: 4m S of Worcester city centre on A38. Pub in village centre

Village pub known for its personal touch

Just four miles from the centre of Worcester, this privately-owned free house commemorates a 13th-century bishop of that city, although he was strongly opposed to his parishioners brewing and selling ales to raise money for church funds. Whitewashed walls are bedecked with flowers in the summer, while the interior's wooden beams and stone floor testify to the inn's 17th-century origins. The daily menu on the blackboard features fresh ingredients, sometimes supplied by the villagers. Soup with locally baked bread; a fillet of salmon with lemon and dill butter; and warm chocolate brownie with a scoop of ice cream make up a typical three-course selection. The walled and paved garden is fragrantly planted with clematis, roses and honeysuckle, and its south-facing aspect can be a real suntrap. Cask ales include a particularly well-kept Timothy Taylor Landlord, and beer festivals are held at Easter and in October.

Open Tue-Fri 5.30-11 (Sat 12-2.30 5.30-11 Sun 12-9) Closed 25-26 Dec, 1 Jan, Mon (ex BHs) **Food** Lunch Sun 12-5 Dinner Tue-Sat 6-9.30 ⊕ FREE HOUSE ◀ Timothy Taylor Landlord Ŏ Westons Stowford Press. **Facilities** Non-diners area ✿ (Bar Outside area) ♙ Children's portions Outside area ⊼ Beer festival Parking WiFi **Rooms** 3

PICK OF THE PUBS

The Boot Inn ★★★★ INN

FLYFORD FLAVELL   Map 10 SO95

tel: 01386 462658
Radford Rd WR7 4BS
email: enquiries@thebootinn.com
web: www.thebootinn.com
dir: *A422 from Worcester towards Stratford. Turn right to village*

Friendly, family-run old coaching inn

Parts of this family-run, award-winning, traditional coaching inn can be traced back to the 13th century, and for evidence you need only to look at the heavy beams and slanting doorways. Keep an eye out too for the friendly ghost, age uncertain. The large bar area is comfortable, the pool table and TV having been banished to a separate room, while regulars like London Pride and Black Sheep, and an extensive wine list complement the varied and imaginative menus which change every six weeks. You can eat from the lunchtime sandwich and bar snack menu, from the extensive specials board, or from the full à la carte, but no matter which you choose, or indeed where – including the conservatory – only the best and freshest, mostly county-sourced, produce is used. A sample menu therefore may include starters of crispy pulled pork, black pudding, apple crisps and Colston Bassett Stilton with honey-dressed leaves; followed by salmon supreme

with apple, horseradish and hazelnut crust with creamy wild mushroom sauce; pork fillet stuffed with smoked Applewood, crushed walnuts and chilli flakes, wrapped in bacon, Stowford and Braeburn gravy; baked cod and king prawn mornay, mature cheddar, lemongrass and rosemary. Sundays are devoted to roasts – beef, pork and turkey are served, along with the specials menu. Gardens and a shaded patio area are especially suited to summer dining. The comfortable en suite bedrooms in the converted coach house are furnished in antique pine and equipped with practical goodies.

Open all day all wk **Food** Lunch all wk 12-2 Dinner all wk 6.30-10 Set menu available Restaurant menu available all wk ⊕ PUNCH TAVERNS ◧ Fuller's London Pride, Black Sheep, Sharp's Doom Bar Ō Westons Stowford Press. ▾ 8 **Facilities** Non-diners area ❀ (Bar Garden) ⅱ Children's menu Children's portions Garden ⋒ Parking WiFi 🚌 (notice required) **Rooms** 5

KNIGHTWICK
Map 10 SO75

The Talbot
PICK OF THE PUBS

tel: 01886 821235 **WR6 5PH**
email: info@the-talbot.co.uk
dir: *Take A44 from Worcester towards Bromyard. In 8m right on B4197 to Knightwick*

Microbrewery pub in idyllic setting

Sitting in the lee of wooded hills, parts of this rambling building date back 600 years. The peaceful village inn is home to the Teme Valley Brewery, which uses locally grown hops in a range of curiously named cask-conditioned ales called This, That, T'Other & Wot. Ciders from local producers add to the selection on the bar; on a sunny day the perfect place to sup is in the beer garden by a bend in the River Teme; winter sees huge log fires warm the timeless interior. Ingredients used in the kitchen are equally parochial, with everything apart from Cornish and Welsh seafood coming from the inn's own organic plot, nearby farms and estates. From the seasonal menu, starters may include Capria Cheese millefeuille using Worcestershire goats' cheese; mains could be game cassoulet with locally shot muntjac venison, finishing with a cheeseboard with three local cheeses. Beer festivals are held here three times a year; farmers' markets every month.

Open all day all wk 7.30am-11.30pm **Food** all wk 12-9 Restaurant menu available all wk ⊕ FREE HOUSE ◖ Teme Valley This, That, T'Other & Wot ♂ Kingstone Press, Robinsons, Oldfields Orchard. ♟ 12 **Facilities** Non-diners area ❤ (Bar Restaurant Garden) ♦♦ Children's portions Garden ⊼ Beer festival Parking WiFi ⊂⊃

MALVERN
Map 10 SO74

The Inn at Welland
PICK OF THE PUBS

tel: 01684 592317 **Drake St, Welland WR13 6LN**
email: info@theinnatwelland.co.uk
dir: *M50 junct 1, A38 follow signs for Upton upon Severn. Left onto A4104, through Upton upon Severn, 2.5m. Pub on right*

Stylish inn with panoramic views

Close to the Three Counties Showground, there are spectacular views of the Malvern Hills from the stylish terrace of this 17th-century country inn. Appointed to a high standard with an eclectic mix of smart, contemporary furnishings and rustic chic, the pub has a wood-burner and open fire for the winter. Menus centre around seasonal local produce accompanied by Wye Valley or Malvern Hills ales, plus rotating guests. Typical dishes might be pan-seared Cornish scallops, garden pea purée, black pudding crumb and crisp Parma ham, followed by roast fillet of rose veal, deep-fried macaroni cheese, buttered spinach, glazed parsnips and thyme reduction. An alternative option might be grilled fillet of sea bream, artichoke, chorizo, fine beans, straw potatoes and watercress pesto. If there's still room, choose warm stem ginger rice pudding, rhubarb compôte and vanilla shortbread. There is a good children's menu.

Open 12-3.30 6-11 (Sun 12-3.30) Closed Sun eve & Mon **Food** Lunch Tue-Sun 12-2.30 Dinner Tue-Sat 6.30-9.30 ⊕ FREE HOUSE ◖ Otter Bitter, Wye Valley, Malvern Hills, guest ales ♂ Westons Stowford Press & Mortimers Orchard. ♟ 31 **Facilities** Non-diners area ♦♦ Children's menu Children's portions Garden ⊼ Parking WiFi

The Nag's Head

tel: 01684 574373 **19-21 Bank St WR14 2JG**
email: enquiries@nagsheadmalvern.co.uk
dir: *Off A449*

An excellent choice of real ales

From this pub's garden, the looming presence of North Hill, northernmost top of the stunning Malvern Hills, takes the eye — if only momentarily — away from the panoply

of delights at this enterprising free house. 'Real ale, real food, real people' is the motto at The Nag's Head. Fifteen real ales, many from local breweries, adorn the bar; eight are permanent fixtures and include three from the pub's own St George's microbrewery. The interior is dotted with snugs, log fires and a magpie's nest of artefacts to create a cosy atmosphere, and the marvellous menu features 6oz fillet beef Wellington with dauphinoise potatoes; and St George's beer-battered fresh cod, home-made chips and peas. There's an annual beer festival to celebrate St George's Day in April, and also one dedicated to cider.

Open all day all wk **Food** Lunch all wk 12-2.30 Restaurant menu available Mon-Sat 6.30-8.30, Sun 7-8.30 ⊕ FREE HOUSE ◖ St George's Friar Tuck, Charger & Dragon's Blood, Bathams, Banks's, Wood's Shropshire Lad, Ringwood Fortyniner ♂ Thatchers Gold, Westons Family Reserve & Stowford Press, Robinsons. ♟ 10 **Facilities** Non-diners area ❤ (Bar Restaurant Garden) ♦♦ Children's portions Garden ⊼ Beer festival Cider festival Parking WiFi ⊂⊃ (notice required)

The Wyche Inn ★★★★ INN

tel: 01684 575396 **74 Wyche Rd WR14 4EQ**
email: thewycheinn@googlemail.com **web:** www.thewycheinn.co.uk
dir: *1.5m S of Malvern. On B4218 towards Malvern & Colwall. Off A449 (Worcester to Ledbury road)*

Spectacular views and home-cooked food

Start or end a walk in the Malvern Hills in this traditional, dog-friendly country inn, probably the highest in Worcestershire. Indeed, the views from various nearby high points are quite something; from Malvern Beacon, for instance, you can see seven counties. Beers come from Wye Valley among others, while home-cooked dishes include pie of the day, chicken curry and battered cod. Themed food nights feature sirloin steak (Tuesday/Saturday) and mixed grill (Wednesday), and roast lunches are served on Sundays. Well-behaved pets are welcome in the bar, garden and the bedrooms.

Open all day all wk **Food** Lunch Mon-Fri 12-2.30, Sat 12-8.30, Sun 12-3.30 Dinner Mon-Fri 6-8.30, Sat 12-8.30, Sun 6-7.30 ⊕ FREE HOUSE ◖ Wye Valley HPA, guest ales ♂ Robinsons. ♟ 9 **Facilities** Non-diners area ❤ (Bar Garden) ♦♦ Children's menu Children's portions Garden ⊼ Parking WiFi **Rooms** 6

PERSHORE
Map 10 SO94

The Defford Arms

tel: 01386 750378 **Upton Rd, Defford WR8 9BD**
dir: *From Pershore take A4104 towards Upton upon Severn. Pub on left in village*

Popular village pub with much charm

Neil, Les and Sue Overton said a firm 'no' to music, gambling machines and TV in favour of old fashioned hospitality at the Defford Arms and it must surely contribute to the pub's continued success. It's in a great location too, so days out at Croome Park, the Three Counties Showground at Malvern, Cheltenham Racecourse or Pershore's plum festival could all include a welcome break here. Expect traditional home-made food such as home-made shepherd's pie; oven-braised lamb shank, mash with red wine and rosemary gravy; cheesy fish pie; and lemon meringue pie.

Open Mon 12-2 Tue 12-2.30 5.30-9 Wed 12-2.30 5.30-9.30 Thu 12-2.30 5.30-10 Fri 12-2.30 5.30-11 Sat 12-11 Sun 12-4 Closed Sun eve & Mon eve **Food** Lunch Mon 12-1.30, Tue-Sun 12-2 Dinner Tue-Sat 6-8 Restaurant menu available Tue-Sat ⊕ FREE HOUSE ◖ Guest ales ♂ Thatchers Gold & Heritage. **Facilities** Non-diners area ❤ (Bar Garden) ♦♦ Children's menu Children's portions Garden ⊼ Parking ⊂⊃ (notice required)

POWICK
Map 10 SO85

The Halfway House Inn

tel: 01905 831098 **Bastonford WR2 4SL**
email: contact@halfwayhouseinnpowick.co.uk
dir: M5 junct 7, A4440 then A449

A warm welcome at this village pub

Standing halfway between Worcester and Malvern on the main road, this aptly named Georgian free house offers a range of bottled beers, winter log fires and a mature shady garden at the side. Steaks and seafood are a speciality, but the menu also features a good choice of fresh, locally sourced hot dishes such as pork tenderloin medallion, black pudding, mash and creamy course grain mustard; grilled Scottish salmon fillet and sweet pepper ragout; and roasted Mediterranean vegetable, wilted spinach and goats' cheese lasagne. Round things off with chocolate nut sundae with hot fudge sauce; or Bailey's crème brûlée.

Open 12-3 6-11 Closed Mon-Tue **Food** Lunch Sat-Sun 12-3 Dinner Wed-Sat 6-9 Restaurant menu available Wed-Sun ⊕ FREE HOUSE ♨ Westons Stowford Press. **Facilities** Non-diners area ⚬ Children's menu Children's portions Garden ⋈ Parking WiFi ⊜ (notice required)

SEVERN STOKE
Map 10 SO84

NEW The Rose and Crown

tel: 01905 371249 **Church Ln WR8 9JQ**
email: peteanddifryar@googlemail.com
dir: M5 junct 8, A38 (Malvern). In Severn Stoke, by war memorial, into Church Ln

Pub grub in snug surroundings

Breaking a motorway journey to find a pleasant pub doesn't always pay off, but it should do at the 'Rosie'. Leave the M5 at junction 9 and rejoin at junction 8 (or vice versa) and it won't take long to reach this pretty, 500-year-old, black-and-white pub at the end of a short lane leading to the village church. The large inglenook in the intimate bar is studded with horse brasses, although do watch out for low-flying beams. Essentially a pub grub menu listing light bites; fish and meat platters; salads; cottage pie; trio of sausages and mash; lasagne and chip; smoked haddock Florentine; and all-day breakfasts. Chicken nuggets and pizzas for children.

Open all day all wk **Food** all wk 12-9 Av main course £8 ⊕ MARSTON'S ♨ Brakspear Oxford Gold ♨ Westons Stowford Press, Thatchers. ⬤ 10 **Facilities** Non-diners area ⚬ (Bar Garden) ⚬ Children's menu Children's portions Play area Garden ⋈ Parking WiFi ⊜ (notice required)

TENBURY WELLS
Map 10 SO56

Pembroke House

tel: 01584 810301 **Cross St WR15 8EQ**
dir: Phone for detailed directions

Modern menus and shoot dinners

Built as a farmhouse in the 16th century, by the year 1600 this was a cider house. When Andrew Mortimer bought this classic black and white timbered property he created the two intimate restaurants, where today lunch might be butternut squash roulade; slow-roasted belly pork; or smoked haddock and prawn pancake. For dinner, pan-fried king scallops with asparagus purée and crispy pancetta to start; then half a roast duckling with Grand Marnier and honey sauce; or baked salmon steak with dill and cucumber pickle in puff pastry. Cider these days comes from Robinsons of Tenbury; the real ales all come from hereabouts too.

Open 12-3 5-close (Mon 5-close Sat-Sun all day) Closed Mon L **Food** Lunch Tue-Sat 12-2, Sun 12-2.30 Dinner Tue-Sat 7-9.15 Restaurant menu available Tue-Sat evening ⊕ FREE HOUSE ♨ Hobsons, Wye Valley, Three Tuns, Wood's, Cannon Royall, Ludlow ♨ Robinsons, Thatchers Gold. ⬤ 9 **Facilities** Non-diners area ⚬ (Garden) ⚬ Children's portions Garden ⋈ Parking WiFi ⊜ (notice required)

Talbot Inn

tel: 01584 781941 **Newnham Bridge WR15 8JF**
email: info@talbotinnnewnhambridge.co.uk
dir: 3m E of Tenbury Wells

Restored coaching inn in the beautiful Teme Valley

This 19th-century Teme Valley coaching inn, now in new hands, has a contemporary yet rustic style that makes for a relaxed place to stop for a drink or meal if you're exploring local market towns such as Ludlow and Leominster. Sup a pint of Wye Valley or Hobsons ale in the bar or bag a table and tuck into enjoyable dishes such as mackerel, smoked bone marrow and parsley; scallops, cauliflower and black pepper; duck breast, turnip, pear, Robinsons cider fondant potato; Ludlow Blue risotto, pear and walnut; and clotted cream pannacotta, rhubarb, balsamic meringue.

Open all day all wk Closed 1st 2wks Jan **Food** Lunch Mon-Sat 12-2.30, Sun 12-7.30 Dinner Mon-Sat 6-9.30, Sun 12-7.30 Set menu available ⊕ FREE HOUSE ♨ Wye Valley HPA, Hobsons Best Bitter ♨ Robinsons, Westons Stowford Press. ⬤ 11 **Facilities** Non-diners area ⚬ (Bar Garden Outside area) ⚬ Children's menu Children's portions Garden Outside area ⋈ Parking WiFi ⊜ (notice required)

WORCESTER
Map 10 SO85

NEW Cardinal's Hat

tel: 01905 724006 **Friar St WR1 2NA**
email: info@the-cardinals-hat.co.uk
dir: In town centre

One of the city centre's historic gems

Reputedly the oldest watering hole in Worcester's historic heart and located near the cathedral, this fine Georgian building is a handsome example of an English city pub. Three beautiful period interiors, sensitively refurbished a few years ago, impress with leaded windows, flagged floors, timber framing and oak panelling, stone fireplaces and chapel chairs, all warmed by log burners in winter. A secluded garden terrace is an ideal spot for a summer pint — whether it be one of the ever-changing guest ales, a craft cider, or a premium lager. The tasty bar snack menu includes sharing platters; a pork pie served warm with mushy peas; smoked kippers and toast; and Scotch eggs. Please note, children are welcome before 9pm.

Open all wk 12-11 (Mon 4-11 Fri-Sat 12-11.30 Sun 12-10.30) **Food** Contact pub for food times Av main course £12 ⊕ FREE HOUSE ♨ Purity Mad Goose, Malvern Hills Black Pear ♨ Westons Old Rosie. **Facilities** Non-diners area ⚬ (Bar) ⚬ Outside area ⋈ WiFi

NEW The Old Rectifying House

tel: 01905 619622 **North Pde WR1 3NN**
email: matt@theoldrec.co.uk
dir: From A44 bridge over River Severn, into North Parade (one-way). Pub on right

Rejuvenated, river-facing pub and eatery

Historically, the rear of this black-and-white timbered, 18th-century building was used to rectify, or purify, gin on its arrival from the main part of the distillery on the other side of the Severn. The tastefully redesigned interior incorporates sofas in the first-floor bay windows overlooking the river. Lunch might feature a pulled pork, gherkin and home-made slaw sandwich, or a wild boar burger with chorizo, hash browns and deep-fried jalapeño pieces. Plenty of steaks in the evening, as well as pan-seared halibut; sweet potato and black bean chilli; and beef stew and dumplings.

Open all day Closed 25 Dec, Mon **Food** Lunch Tue-Sat 12-3, Sun 12-6 Dinner Tue-Thu 6-9, Fri-Sat 6-9.30, Sun 12-6 Restaurant menu available Tue-Sun ⊕ FREE HOUSE ♨ Otter Ale ♨ Westons Stowford Press. ⬤ 9 **Facilities** Non-diners area ⚬ Children's menu Children's portions Garden ⋈ WiFi

EAST RIDING OF YORKSHIRE

BARMBY ON THE MARSH
Map 17 SE62

The King's Head

tel: 01757 630705 **High St DN14 7HT**
email: rainderpubcoltd@tiscali.co.uk
dir: *M62 junct 37 follow A614/Bridlington/York/Howden signs. Left at A63. At rdbt 1st exit onto A614/Booth Ferry Rd towards Goole. At rdbt 4th exit on B1228/Booth Ferry Rd. Left, through Asselby to Barmby on the Marsh*

Look out for their Yorkshire tapas menu

In the 17th century this inn served a ferry that crossed the Rivers Ouse and Derwent. Nowadays this family-run village pub is a place that appeals to all tastes; from the beamed bar through a bright, modern lounge to the cosy, intimate restaurant. Several members of the family are trained chefs and make the most of Yorkshire's burgeoning larder; braised beef with clementines and ginger wine, herb cobbler and mash is just one of the tempting mains here. Their innovative Yorkshire tapas menu features haddock goujons, confit lamb croquettes, and baked mussels.

Open Wed-Thu 12-2 5-11 (Mon-Tue 5-11 Fri 12-2 5-12 Sat 12-12 Sun 12-11) Closed Mon L, Tue L ⊕ FREE HOUSE ◂ Black Sheep Best Bitter, 3 guest ales.
Facilities ❶ Children's menu Children's portions Outside area Parking WiFi

BEVERLEY
Map 17 TA03

The Ferguson Fawsitt Arms & Country Lodge

tel: 01482 882665 **East End, Walkington HU17 8RX**
email: admin@fergusonfawsitt.com
dir: *M62 junct 38 onto B1230, left on A1034, right onto B1230, on left in centre of Walkington*

Well-positioned traditional inn where time stands still

Three miles from Beverley in the picturesque village of Walkington, there is a timeless quality to this Victorian pub named after two important local families. Parts of the pub used to form the village blacksmith's shop where carriage wheels were repaired. Open fires, dark-wood panelling, carved settles, beams and some decent tiling to the floor welcomes those set on sampling a pint of Black Sheep, or diners a traditional pub meal from the bar food menu.

Open all day all wk 8am-11pm **Food** all wk 8am-9pm ⊕ FREE HOUSE ◂ Black Sheep, guest ales. ♟ 10 **Facilities** Non-diners area ❶ Children's menu Children's portions Outside area Beer festival Parking WiFi (notice required)

BRANTINGHAM
Map 17 SE92

NEW The Triton Inn

tel: 01482 667261 **Ellerker Rd, Brantingham Rd HU15 1QE**
email: thetriton@thetritoninn.com
dir: *From A63 at South Cave follow Brantingham signs*

Elegant dining in welcoming country inn

Handy for the Wolds, the Humber Estuary and Beverley, this honeyed stone and pantiled building occupies a site where a pub has stood for many centuries. A comprehensive restoration a few years ago produced a comfy mix of traditional pub and contemporary dining inn which has ensured the survival of this treasured community favourite. Beers from area breweries like Wold Top and Great Newsome adorn the bar, complementing a seasonal menu of pub favourites and modern dishes utilising produce from local farms, growers and markets. Specials might be sourced courtesy of the village gamekeeper, and there's a coeliac's menu too.

Open 12-3 5-late (Sat-Sun noon-late) Closed Mon (ex BHs & summer holidays) **Food** Lunch Tue-Fri 12-2.30, Sat 12-5, Sun 12-6 Dinner Tue-Sat 5-late, Sun 12-6 Av main course £13 ⊕ ENTERPRISE INNS ◂ Great Newsome Brewery Frothingham Best,

Wold Top Wold Gold. ♟ 15 **Facilities** Non-diners area ❖ (Bar Garden) ❶ Children's menu Children's portions Play area Garden Beer festival Parking WiFi (notice required)

FLAMBOROUGH
Map 17 TA27

The Seabirds Inn

tel: 01262 850242 **Tower St YO15 1PD**
email: philip.theseabirds@virgin.net **web:** www.theseabirds.com
dir: *On B1255 E of Bridlington*

Village pub that keeps it simple

Just east of this 200-year-old village pub is the famous chalk promontory of Flamborough Head and its equally famed lighthouse. The inn has had a major refurbishment and is now an open, welcoming place with inviting roaring fires in winter. With the North Sea so close you'd expect plenty of fish, and there is, namely, spicy Whitby creel king prawns; deep-fried dusted whitebait; salmon steak hollandaise; and battered haddock fillet. The menu keeps to staples like a good choice of steaks; chicken breast with bacon, barbecue sauce and cheese; gammon with egg and pineapple; and steamed suet pudding with spinach, pine nuts, mozzarella cheese and cherry tomatoes.

Open 12-3 5.30-11 Closed Mon (winter) **Food** Lunch all wk 12-2 Dinner Sun-Fri 5.30-8, Sat 5.30-9.30 Set menu available ⊕ FREE HOUSE ◂ Wold Top, Greene King Abbot Ale & IPA, Morland Old Speckled Hen. ♟ 9 **Facilities** Non-diners area ❖ (Bar Garden) Children's menu Children's portions Garden Parking WiFi

GOODMANHAM
Map 17 SE84

NEW Goodmanham Arms

tel: 01430 873849 **Main St YO43 3JA**
dir: *From Market Place in Market Weighton into Londesborough Rd signed Goodmanham. Right signed Goodmanham. Pub on right in village*

Village pub with its own brewery

In the pretty village of Goodmanham on the Wolds Way National Trail, this timeless red-brick inn is popular with walkers and cyclists refuelling on ales brewed by the pub's own All Hallows Brewery. Other Yorkshire breweries including Theakston and Black Dog also make regular appearances and the pub hosts an Early May Bank Holiday beer festival. Real fires, comfortable armchairs and low beams add to the charm of this friendly pub, which specialises in home-cooked dishes like steak and ale pie; spit roasts on Sundays and pheasant stews cooked over the fire in a Victorian cast iron pot.

Open all wk **Food** Lunch all wk 12-2 Dinner Mon 5-7 Av main course £9.95 ⊕ FREE HOUSE ◂ All Hallows (pub's own), Theakston, Hambleton, Elgood's Black Dog, York ♨ Thatchers, Westons Old Rosie. **Facilities** Non-diners area ❖ (Bar) ❶ Children's menu Children's portions Play area Garden Beer festival Parking WiFi (notice required) Notes ⊛

HUGGATE   Map 19 SE85

The Wolds Inn ★★★ INN

tel: 01377 288217 **YO42 1YH**
email: woldsinn@gmail.com **web:** www.woldsinn.co.uk
dir: S off A166 between York & Driffield

Yorkshire Wolds inn with hearty home-made food

Sixteenth century in origin, this family-run hostelry is, at 525 feet above sea level, the highest in the Yorkshire Wolds. Copper pans and gleaming brassware fill the wood-panelled interior, where the open fires still burn good old-fashioned coal. A typical meal in the charming restaurant could start with smoked haddock and spring onion fishcake; or fresh melon with port wine; then progress to Whitby seafood platter; loin of pork cooked in cider with crispy crackling; or mushroom Stroganoff. Leave room for treacle sponge or fruit Pavlova. The overnight accommodation is particularly popular with those exploring the countryside and coastal area.

Open 12-2 5-11 (Sun 12-10.30) Closed Mon (ex BHs) **Food** Lunch Tue-Sat 12-2, Sun 12-8 Dinner Tue-Thu 5-8 Fri-Sat 5-8.30, Sun 12-8 Set menu available Restaurant menu available Tue-Sun ⊕ FREE HOUSE ◀ Timothy Taylor Landlord, Theakston Best Bitter, York Guzzler ♂ Kingstone Press. ♟ **Facilities** Non-diners area ♦ Children's menu Children's portions Garden ⊼ Parking WiFi ⛟ (notice required) **Rooms** 3

KILHAM   Map 17 TA06

NEW The Old Star

tel: 01262 420619 **Church St YO25 4RG**
email: theoldstarkilham@gmail.com
dir: From A614 (between Driffield & Bridlington) follow Kilham sign. Through Ruston Parva. Right at T-junct in Kilham, pub on right opposite church

Community owned inn in pretty Wolds village

Revitalised and reinvigorated following purchase by a consortium of villagers, this ancient pub now goes from strength to strength. It stands opposite the church in a village at the heart of the Yorkshire Wolds. With open fires, log-burners, rustic decor and quirky artefacts to take the eye, it's a champion of local suppliers, with beers from microbreweries and cider from the village; indeed, they have a cider festival here every year. The frequently-changing menu draws on Wolds producers where possible; perhaps sautéed pigeon breast starter leading to a wide selection of steaks, fish dishes and venerable pub grub choices.

Open all wk 5-11 (Thu-Sun 12-11) **Food** Lunch Thu-Sat 12-9, Sun 12-7.30 Dinner Mon-Wed 5-9, Thu-Sat 12-9, Sun 12-7.30 Av main course £12 ⊕ FREE HOUSE ◀ Theakston Best Bitter, local guest ales ♂ Aspall, Colemans Cider. **Facilities** Non-diners area ♣ (Bar Garden) ♦ Children's menu Children's portions Play area Garden ⊼ Cider festival Parking WiFi ⛟ (notice required)

LOW CATTON   Map 17 SE75

The Gold Cup Inn

tel: 01759 371354 **YO41 1EA**
dir: 1m S of A166 or 1m N of A1079, E of York

Attractive, family-run country pub

A charming, family-run free house that is 300 years old but may not look it at first glance. Giveaways are the low beams and open fireplaces in the bar, now complemented by wooden floors, modern fabrics and wall-mounted coach-lamps. Bar meals are served every lunchtime (except Monday) and evening, from the extensive menu. Look out for choices like an 8oz fillet steak; cod goujons with chips and peas; poached salmon salad; leek and Wensleydale potato cakes with spicy relish; or spinach and ricotta cannelloni, rich tomato sauce with parmesan. A paddock adjoining the large beer garden runs down to the River Derwent.

Open 12-2.30 6-11 (Sat-Sun 12-11) Closed Mon L **Food** Lunch Tue-Fri 12-2, Sat-Sun 12-6 Dinner all wk 6-9 Set menu available ⊕ FREE HOUSE ◀ Theakston Best Bitter. ♟ 11 **Facilities** Non-diners area ♣ (Bar Garden) ♦ Children's menu Children's portions Play area Garden ⊼ Parking WiFi ⛟ (notice required)

LUND   Map 17 SE94

The Wellington Inn

tel: 01377 217294 **19 The Green YO25 9TE**
email: tellmemore@thewellingtoninn.co.uk
dir: On B1248 NE of Beverley

Exciting food in quintessential village inn

Occupying a wonderfully rural location, this country pub is popular with locals and visitors alike, whether for a pint of real ale, a glass of wine, or a plate of good food. Nicely situated opposite the picture-postcard village green, inside is a unique blend of old and new where you can choose from the traditional pub menu or from the carte in the more formal restaurant. Expect excellent dishes like steak and kidney suet pudding; fresh crab, chorizo and rocket tagliatelle; pork belly, bacon potato cake, black pudding and Scotch egg; or cumin roast baby cauliflower, roast squash, gnocchi, tomato and coriander dressing. Leave space for spiced sticky orange cake, confit orange and clotted cream.

Open 12-3 6.30-11 Closed Mon L **Food** Lunch Tue-Sun 12-2 Dinner Tue-Sat 6.30-9 Restaurant menu available Tue-Sat evenings ⊕ FREE HOUSE ◀ Timothy Taylor Landlord, Theakston Best Bitter, Great Newsome Sleck Dust, regular guest ale. ♟ 11 **Facilities** Non-diners area ♦ Children's menu Children's portions Outside area ⊼ Parking WiFi

Silver Stars The AA Silver Star rating denotes a Hotel or B&B that we highly recommend. They have a superior level of quality within their star rating, high standards of hospitality, service and cleanliness.

NEWTON UPON DERWENT — Map 17 SE74

NEW The Half Moon Inn

tel: 01904 608883 **Main St YO41 4DB**
email: info@thehalfmoonnewton.co.uk

Convivial village inn serving robust food and local ales

Located in a pretty village off the A1079 in the Vale of York, this charming free house dates back to 1743 but it reopened in 2015 after a major renovation. Next to the Wolds Way and Five Parishes Circular Walk, the pub is a popular stop for walkers and Newton upon Derwent is famous for its barn owls, that fly through the village at dusk. Well-kept Black Sheep and Tetley's beers are dispensed in the bar, where a typical menu might start with Yorkshire puddings filled with caramelised onion gravy and continue with a home-made steak and ale pie.

Open all wk 5-11 (Sat-Sun 12-12) **Food** Dinner all wk 6-9.30 Av main course £15 Restaurant menu available Tue-Sun ⊕ FREE HOUSE ◄ Tetley's, Wold Top, Black Sheep ♂ Symonds. ♀ 10 **Facilities** Non-diners area ▪▪ Children's menu Children's portions Garden ⊼ Parking WiFi

SANCTON — Map 17 SE83

The Star

tel: 01430 827269 **King St YO43 4QP**
email: benandlindsey@thestaratsancton.co.uk
dir: 2m SE of Market Weighton on A1034

Traditional local serving top-notch pub food

This stylishly modernised and extended old village pub stands at the heart of charming Sancton, past which the Wolds Way recreational footpath threads across the tranquil Yorkshire landscape. Beers from local microbreweries tempt ramblers to linger longer; more leisurely visits are rewarded by a reliable bar menu considerably enhanced by an evening restaurant choice. Yorkshire pudding with braised oxtail and caramelised onion; or smoked haddock kedgeree balls for starters; followed by roast monkfish tail with braised lentils and crispy ham; or calves' liver with crispy onions and potato purée with wilted greens; both typical of the satisfying mains which chef-proprietor Ben Cox crafts from local produce. Banana cake with peanut butter parfait, chocolate soil and toffee sauce rounds it all off nicely.

Open 12-3 6-11 (Sun all day) Closed 1st wk Jan, Mon **Food** Lunch Tue-Sat 12-2, Sun 12-3 Dinner Tue-Sat 6-9.30, Sun 6-8 Av main course £14.95 Set menu available Restaurant menu available Tue-Sun ⊕ FREE HOUSE ◄ Black Sheep, Copper Dragon, Wold Top, Great Newsome ♂ Moorlands Farm. ♀ 14 **Facilities** Non-diners area ▪▪ Children's menu Children's portions Garden Outside area ⊼ Parking

SOUTH DALTON — Map 17 SE94

The Pipe & Glass Inn ⊛⊛   PICK OF THE PUBS

tel: 01430 810246 **West End HU17 7PN**
email: email@pipeandglass.co.uk
dir: Just off B1248 (Beverley to Malton road). 7m from Beverley

Smart inn serving quality food and ales

James and Kate Mackenzie's transformation of this part 15th- and part 17th-century inn has helped earn it two AA Rosettes, but it still retains the village pub feel, with Copper Dragon, Scarborough, Great Yorkshire and other local ales, and Moorlands Farm cider all served in the bar. The restaurant is more contemporary in style and the conservatory looks out over the garden. James sources top-notch local and seasonal produce for a range of modern British menus, including one for vegetarians; here you'll find dishes such as pea and mint ravioli with nettle and mint dressing. The dinner menu may proffer fillet of beef, pickled red onion and watercress salad, ox tongue fritter, horseradish hollandaise and chips. Finish with sticky toffee pudding, stout ice cream and walnut brittle. The pub occupies the site of the original gatehouse to Dalton Hall, family seat of Lord Hotham.

Open all day 12-11 (Sun 12-10.30) Closed 2wks Jan, Mon (ex BHs) **Food** Lunch Tue-Sat 12-2, Sun 12-4 Dinner Tue-Sat 6-9.30 Av main course £20 ⊕ FREE HOUSE ◄ Wold Top, Copper Dragon, Black Sheep, York, Scarborough, Great Yorkshire ♂ Moorlands Farm. ♀ 15 **Facilities** ▪▪ Children's menu Children's portions Garden ⊼ Parking WiFi

SWANLAND — Map 17 SE92

NEW The Swan & Cygnet

tel: 01482 634571 **Main St HU14 3QP**
email: anchorpubs@aol.com
dir: E of Hull

Family-friendly dining pub in East Riding

In the picture postcard village of Swanland surrounded by glorious East Yorkshire countryside, The Swan & Cygnet was completely renovated in 2012 and it's now a light and contemporary family-friendly dining pub. Jennings Cumberland Ale is one of three regular ales dispensed at the bar. Regional ingredients gets star billing on a menu that might start with East Coast crab and chilli ravioli with shellfish bisque and continue with slow-roast belly pork, bubble-and-squeak, caramelised apple, black pudding and cider jus. Leave a space for rice pudding with fruit compôte.

Open all day all wk **Food** Lunch Mon-Sat 12-2, Sun 12-7.30 Dinner Mon-Sat 5-9, Sun 12-7.30 ⊕ MARSTON'S ◄ EPA, Jennings Cumberland Ale, Ringwood Best Bitter. ♀ 8 **Facilities** Non-diners area ❀ (Garden) ▪▪ Children's menu Children's portions Garden ⊼ Parking WiFi ▤ (notice required)

THORNGUMBALD — Map 17 TA22

NEW The Camerton

tel: 01964 601208 **Main St HU12 9NG**
dir: From Hull take A1033 (signed Withernsea) to Thorngumbald

Traditional food and hospitality

This inn is located in the pretty East Riding of Yorkshire village of Thorngumbald which was once a Viking settlement; its unusual name might be derived from Thorn (as shown in the Domesday Book) and from a Baron Gumbaud who settled in the area in the 13th century. This newly refurbished pub prides itself on traditional hospitality, good food and well-kept local real ales such as Theakston. A meal here might begin with home-roasted sticky belly pork ribs in rich BBQ and bourbon sauce and continue with home-made fish pie packed with haddock, prawns and salmon. Three cheese and leek sausages with mash is one of the vegetarian options, whilst carnivores also get to choose from a separate grill menu. Time a visit for the August beer and cider festival.

Open all day all wk **Food** Mon-Sat 11-9, Sun 11-8 Av main course £9.50 ⊕ STAR PUBS ◄ Theakston, Timothy Taylor, guest ale. ♀ 24 **Facilities** Non-diners area ▪▪ Children's menu Children's portions Play area Garden ⊼ Beer festival Cider festival Parking WiFi ▤

NORTH YORKSHIRE

AKEBAR
Map 19 SE19

The Friar's Head

tel: 01677 450201 **Akebar Park DL8 5LY**
email: thefriarshead@hotmail.co.uk
dir: *From A1 at Leeming Bar onto A684, 7m towards Leyburn. Entrance at Akebar Park*

Stone-built Dales pub with a lovely conservatory

This 200-year-old pub lies in the heart of Wensleydale, known for its castles, abbeys and waterfalls. Located next to an 18-hole golf course and at the entrance to Akebar Holiday Park, The Friar's Head overlooks beautiful countryside and has grounds where you can play bowls or croquet. Inside you'll find exposed beams and stonework, and hand-pulled Yorkshire ales at the bar. There are lush plants and vines in the Cloister conservatory dining room and in the evening it looks magical in the candlelit. From the frequently changing menu, typical dishes include tapas choices, twice baked spinach and gruyère soufflé; slow-braised lamb shank; Yorkshire farmed venison steak served pink with caramelised onions and juniper sauce.

Open all wk 10-3 5.30-11.30 (Fri-Sun 10am-11.30pm Jul-Sep) **Food** Lunch all wk 12-2 Dinner all wk 5.30-9 ⊕ FREE HOUSE ◧ Cumberland Corby Ale, Theakston Best Bitter, Black Sheep Best Bitter, Timothy Taylor Landlord, Wensleydale Semer Water, Guinness Ŏ Somersby. ♈ 12 **Facilities** Non-diners area ▪▪ Children's menu Children's portions Family room Garden ⊩ Beer festival Cider festival Parking WiFi ▭ (notice required)

ALDWARK
Map 19 SE46

The Aldwark Arms

tel: 01347 838324 **YO61 1UB**
email: peter@aldwarkarms.co.uk
dir: *From York ring road take A19 N. Left into Warehill Ln signed Tollerton & Helperby. Through Tollerton, follow Aldwark signs*

Warm welcomes abound at this family-run community pub

Successfully run by local boys the Hardisty brothers, this friendly free house has an inviting atmosphere. Keen to include locally sourced, season produce on his menus, the chef offers the likes of Doreen's black pudding fritters with home-made apple and cider sauce; Scotch quail's egg Niçoise; venison saltimbocca; and Hodgson's of Hartlepool beer-battered haddock with home-made chubby chips, 'proper' mushy peas and tartare sauce.

Open all day all wk **Food** Lunch Mon-Sat 12-2, Sun 12-7 Dinner Mon-Sat 5.30-9, Sun 12-7 Set menu available ⊕ FREE HOUSE ◧ Black Sheep, guest ales Ŏ Yorkshire Cider. ♈ **Facilities** Non-diners area ▪▪ Children's menu Children's portions Play area Garden ⊩ Parking WiFi ▭ (notice required)

ARKENDALE
Map 19 SE36

NEW The Blue Bell at Arkendale

tel: 01423 369242 **Moor Ln HG5 0QT**
email: info@thebluebellatarkendale.co.uk
dir: *A1(M) junct 47, A59 signed Green Hammerton & York. 1st left signed Boroughbridge & Walshford. At T-junct right on A168 (Boroughbridge). Left signed Arkendale. Pub on right*

Village dining inn handy for York and Harrogate

At the heart of a village of pantiled cottages and grassy verges; both contemporary and traditional styles blend seamlessly at this tastefully modernised country inn. Leather sofas and chairs cluster around a log-burning stove, whilst farmhouse kitchen-style furniture dots the tiled floor. Yorkshire beers from the likes of Timothy Taylor and Copper Dragon keep drinkers happy. Diners can expect a thoroughly modern menu that may feature cider-steamed mussels; wild mushroom and gnocchi gratin or sticky ginger beer glazed pork belly. Seasonal variations and a specials board extend the choice of the best of Yorkshire produce.

Open all day all wk **Food** Lunch Mon-Sat 12-2.30, Sun 12-8 Dinner Mon-Thu 6-9, Fri-Sat 5-9, Sun 12-8 Restaurant menu available all wk ⊕ FREE HOUSE ◧ Theakston Best Bitter, Timothy Taylor Landlord, guest ale Ŏ Symonds. ♈ **Facilities** Non-diners area ▪▪ Children's menu Children's portions Outside area ⊩ Parking WiFi ▭

ARKENGARTHDALE
Map 18 NY90

Charles Bathurst Inn ★★★★ INN ⊛ PICK OF THE PUBS

See Pick of the Pubs on page 556

ARNCLIFFE
Map 18 SD97

NEW The Falcon Inn

tel: 01756 770205 **BD23 5QE**
email: info@thefalconinn.com
dir: *From A65 (N of Skipton) take B6265 to Threshfield. Through Threshfield (road becomes B6160) to Arncliffe. Pub on left*

In the Yorkshire Dales National Park

At the top of the village is the Falcon, a truly unspoilt old inn with an ivy-clad exterior and mullioned bay windows. It once served time as the original Woolpack of TV's *Emmerdale*, while Arncliffe itself doubled as the soap village. Timothy Taylor Boltmaker is dispensed from cask to jug to glass, with the hand pump reserved for guest ales. Snug and back-bar snacks are usually ploughman's; sandwiches; ciabattas; pork pie and mushy peas, warm cheese and onion pasty; soup of the day; and Mother's fruit cake and Wensleydale cheese. Twenty-four hours' notice is needed for an evening meal in the dining room.

Open all wk 12-3 7-11 (Fri-Sat 12-11 Sun 12-10.30) **Food** Lunch all wk 12-2.30 ⊕ FREE HOUSE ◧ Timothy Taylor Boltmaker. **Facilities** Non-diners area ♣ (Bar Restaurant Outside area) ▪▪ Outside area ⊩ WiFi ▭ (notice required)

PICK OF THE PUBS

Charles Bathurst Inn ★★★★ INN ◉

ARKENGARTHDALE Map 18 NY90

tel: 01748 884567 **DL11 6EN**
email: info@cbinn.co.uk
web: www.cbinn.co.uk
dir: *A1 onto A6108 at Scotch Corner, through Richmond, left onto B6270 to Reeth. At Buck Hotel right signed Langthwaite, pass church on right, inn 0.5m on right*

Spectacular dale scenery at remote country inn

This 18th-century inn sits in possibly one of the North's finest dales, and takes its name from the son of Oliver Cromwell's physician who built it for his workers in what was once a busy lead mining area. In winter, it caters for serious walkers tackling The Pennine Way and the Coast to Coast route, and offers a welcome escape from the rigours of the moors, with many a tale being swapped over pints of Black Sheep Riggwelter or Rudgate's Jorvik Blonde. The 'Terrace Room' features handcrafted tables and chairs from Robert Thompson's craftsmen in nearby Kilburn, all with Thompson's unique hand-carved mouse hiding somewhere. English classics meet modern European dishes on a menu written up on the mirror hanging above the stone fireplace: Cogden Hall sirloin steak, field mushroom, tomato and horseradish sauce; loin of venison with home-made game sausage; roast loin of cod, tomato

and prawn fondue, and grilled polenta; and artichoke risotto with glazed goats' cheese and artichoke hearts. The cheeseboard showcases local specialities such as mature and oak-smoked Wensleydale, Mrs Bell's Blue, Yorkshire Ryedale and Monk's Folly. Typical Early Bird dishes (third Friday every month) are fish and chips with mushy peas; smoked loin of bacon with poached egg and chips; and vegetable lasagne with garlic bread. The wine list is excellent, with well-written tasting notes. From April to September the local outdoor game of quoits can be played. The bedrooms have fabulous views overlooking the Stang and Arkengarthdale and are finished to a high standard with exposed beams, cast-iron bed frames and warm colours.

Open all day all wk 11am-mdnt Closed 25 Dec **Food** Lunch Mon-Fri 12-2.30, Sat-Sun 12-6 Dinner all wk 6-9 Restaurant menu all wk (evening) ⊕ FREE HOUSE ◧ Black Sheep Best Bitter, Golden Sheep & Riggwelter, Rudgate Jorvik Blonde, Theakston ♂ Symonds. ♀ 12 **Facilities** Non-diners area ❤ (Bar Garden) ⅰ Children's menu & portions Play area Garden ⊼ Parking WiFi 🚐 (notice required) **Rooms** 19

PICK OF THE PUBS

The Black Bull Inn

BOROUGHBRIDGE   Map 19 SE36

tel: 01423 322413
6 St James Square YO51 9AR
web: www.blackbullboroughbridge.co.uk
dir: *A1(M) junct 48, B6265 E for 1m*

Traditional inn offering true Yorkshire hospitality

Using a false name, highwayman Dick Turpin stayed at this ancient inn which stands in a quiet corner of the market square and was one of the main stopping points for travellers on the long road between London and the North. Today you have to turn off the A1(M), but it's well worth it to discover an inn built in 1258 that retains its ancient beams, low ceilings and roaring open fires, not to mention one that also gives houseroom to the supposed ghosts of a monk, a blacksmith, a cavalier and a small boy. Tony Burgess is the landlord and the man responsible for high standards that exclude anything electronic which makes a noise, so settle back and enjoy a pint of Timothy Taylor Boltmaker, a guest ale from the Rudgate's brewery or a glass of wine from the list that shows all the signs of careful compilation. The hot and cold sandwich selection in the bar is wide (Cajun chicken; smoked frankfurter; and roast pork and apple being just three),

while in the dining room expect a good choice of traditional pub food on menus such as home-made mince and onion pie; tenderloin of pork, new potatoes, seasonal vegetables with pink peppercorn and cream sauce; battered king prawns with sweet chilli dip; pork sausages, creamy mash and onion gravy; and gammon steak, fried egg, chips and salad. Frequently changing blackboard specials widen the choice to include halibut steak with smoked salmon and fresh prawns in white wine sauce; and wild button mushroom ragout with fresh salad. Possible followers are apple pie and custard, or chocolate fudge cake.

Open all day all wk 11-11 (Fri-Sat 11am-mdnt Sun 12-11) **Food** Lunch all wk 12-2 Dinner all wk 6-9 Restaurant menu available all wk ⊕ FREE HOUSE ◀ John Smith's, Timothy Taylor Boltmaker, Cottage, Rudgate guest ale. ⏲ 11 **Facilities** Non-diners area ❖ (Bar Restaurant) ♦♦ Children's menu Children's portions Parking WiFi 🚌

ASKRIGG
Map 18 SD99

The King's Arms

tel: 01969 650113 **Main St DL8 3HQ**
email: info@kingsarmsaskrigg.co.uk **web:** www.kingsarmsaskrigg.co.uk
dir: *From A1 exit at Scotch Corner onto A6108, through Richmond, right onto B6270 to Leyburn. Follow Askrigg signs to Main St*

Stone-built Wensleydale inn on the Herriot Trail

This elegant, 18th-century coaching inn was used as the fictional Drover's Arms, vet James Herriot's favourite watering hole in the BBC drama *All Creatures Great and Small*. Owned by North Yorkshire hotelier Charles Cody, the inn has a big inglenook fireplace in the oak-panelled bar, where photographs show cast members relaxing between takes. The food, written up daily on an impressive mirror behind the bar, is based on top quality produce, such as game from the surrounding moors, and fish fresh from Hartlepool. Look also for loin of local lamb; pan-fried salmon; and wild mushroom risotto.

Open all day all wk **Food** Lunch all wk 12-2.30 Dinner Mon-Sat 5.30-9, Sun 5.30-8 Av main course £11.50 ⊕ FREE HOUSE ◀ Black Sheep, Theakston, Yorkshire Dales ♂ Thatchers Gold. ♀ 13 **Facilities** Non-diners area ♥ (Bar Outside area) ♦ Children's menu Children's portions Outside area WiFi ⇔ (notice required)

BEDALE
Map 19 SE28

The Castle Arms Inn

tel: 01677 470270 **Meadow Ln, Snape DL8 2TB**
email: castlearmsinn@gmail.com
dir: *From A1 (M) at Leeming Bar take A684 to Bedale. At x-roads in town centre take B6268 to Masham. Approx 2m, turn left to Thorp Perrow Arboretum. In 0.5m left for Snape*

Great base for walking or cycling

In the sleepy village of Snape, this family-run 18th-century pub is a good starting point for walking and cycling, and visiting local stately homes, castles and film locations. The homely interior has exposed beams, flagstoned floors and real fires in the bar, which is home to real ales from the Marston's Brewery. A meal in the restaurant selected from the ever-changing menu might feature a pub classic or something more contemporary. Afterwards, there is a range of home-made desserts and liqueur coffees to tempt you.

Open 12-3 5.30-11 (Sun 12-5) Closed Sun eve Mon L **Food** Lunch Tue-Sat 12-3, Sun 1-3 Dinner Mon-Thu 6-8.30, Fri-Sat 6-9 ⊕ MARSTON'S ◀ Pedigree New World, Ringwood Best, Jennings Cumberland Ale. **Facilities** Non-diners area ♥ (Bar Garden) ♦ Children's menu Children's portions Garden ⇌ Parking WiFi ⇔ (notice required)

BIRSTWITH
Map 19 SE25

NEW The Station Hotel

tel: 01423 770254 **Station Rd HG3 3AG**
email: admin@station-hotel.net
dir: *Take A59 from Harrogate towards Skipton. Right into Chain Bar Ln signed Hampsthwaite. In Hampsthwaite at T-junct right signed Birstwith*

Free house in Nidderdale

Originally called The Sebastopol after the Crimean War siege, this family-owned, mid-Victorian pub served the railway station until it closed in 1964. Regularly changing menus feature traditional classics such as fish and chips, and steak and ale pie, as well as plenty of alternatives, such as pan-fried calves' liver, bacon crisp, kurly kale, mash and gravy; duck with Asian noodles; Shetland mussels and other seafood dishes. Vegetarians might strike lucky with wild mushroom linguine; or butternut squash and sage risotto. In the bar are Copper Dragon real ale from Skipton and Golden Sheep from Masham. Events include Thursday steak nights and open mic nights.

Open all day all wk **Food** Mon-Sat 12-9, Sun & BH 12-8 Set menu available Restaurant menu available all wk ⊕ FREE HOUSE ◀ Copper Dragon Best Bitter, Black Sheep Golden Sheep ♂ Aspall. ♀ 11 **Facilities** Non-diners area ♥ (Bar Garden) ♦ Children's menu Children's portions Garden ⇌ Parking WiFi ⇔ (notice required)

BOROUGHBRIDGE
Map 19 SE36

The Black Bull Inn
PICK OF THE PUBS

See Pick of the Pubs on page 557

Crown Inn Roecliffe ★★★★ RR ◎◎
PICK OF THE PUBS

See Pick of the Pubs on opposite page

BROUGHTON
Map 18 SD95

The Bull
PICK OF THE PUBS

tel: 01756 792065 **BD23 3AE**
email: enquiries@thebullatbroughton.com
dir: *3m from Skipton on A59, on right*

Destination dining and free house in an estate setting

The Bull is part of the Broughton Estate, 3,000 acres of prime Yorkshire parkland and countryside, owned by the Tempests for nine centuries; their family seat, Broughton Hall, is close by. While essentially a dining pub, The Bull still loves to see beer drinkers, with a good selection of real ales – Dark Horse Hetton Pale Ale and Thwaites Original for example – and a real cider, Westons Stowford Press. The chefs rely on carefully chosen local producers for their modern English dishes such as baked east coast cod; Waterford Farm pork belly; Nigel Haworth's take on the classic Lancashire hotpot; and Wensleydale cheese and onion pie. You can choose to have your chips fried in dripping, and there's a good selection of sandwiches as well. Finish with a comforting mincemeat and cranberry Bakewell.

Open all day all wk 12-11 (Sun 12-10) **Food** Lunch Mon-Fri 12-2, Sat-Sun & BHs 12-9 (afternoon bites Mon-Fri 2-5.30) Dinner Mon-Fri 5.30-9, Sat-Sun & BHs 12-9 Set menu available ⊕ FREE HOUSE ◀ Dark Horse Hetton Pale Ale, Thwaites Original, Bowland Hen Harrier ♂ Westons Stowford Press. ♀ 12 **Facilities** Non-diners area ♥ (Bar Outside area) ♦ Children's menu Outside area ⇌ Parking WiFi

PICK OF THE PUBS

Crown Inn Roecliffe ★★★★ RR 🌹🌹

BOROUGHBRIDGE   Map 19 SE36

tel: 01423 322300 **Roecliffe YO51 9LY**
email: info@crowninnroecliffe.co.uk
web: www.crowninnroecliffe.co.uk
dir: *A1(M) junct 48, follow
Boroughbridge signs. At rdbt to
Roecliffe*

Wonderful village just off the A1

Beside Roecliffe's neatly trimmed green,
this handsome 16th-century former
coaching inn has been put well and
truly on the map by owners Karl and
Amanda. The couple have worked
wonders on the striking green-painted
pub, which has been lovingly restored.
Stone-flagged floors, oak beams and
crackling log fires feature prominently in
the civilised bar and dining rooms.
Children and dogs are welcome, and
food and drink can be served in the
garden during the summer months. The
bar's beer handles tempt with some top
Yorkshire brewers (Timothy Taylor,
Theakston, Ilkley), but it's the wine list
that may catch the eye — 20 pages long
and a comprehensive choice of 30 sold
by the glass. The two AA Rosettes are
well deserved for the pub's fine
preparation of fresh and local produce,
from salads and vegetables to farm
meats and game, in a clearly focused
modern British menu. Crown Inn
classics are a strong indicator of the
pub's commitment to provenance and
seasonality. How about a plate of

calves' liver with roasted shallots and
Cumbrian bacon, buttery mash and
Madeira jus? Or a foot of proper
Cumberland sausage, perhaps, with red
onion and thyme mash, roast shallot
gravy and home-made apple sauce? It's
worth pushing the boat out for the
exceptional tasting of Yorkshire Dales
pork for two — a double rack, fillet, slow-
cooked belly, and crisp crackling
together with smoked garlic dauphinoise
potatoes, apple sauce and Calvados jus.
Half a dozen desserts, including a rich
Belgian chocolate tart with lime zest
and vanilla cream, exude the same
attention to detail and careful
presentation. Four beautiful en suite
bedrooms are furnished to a high
specification, including solid mahogany
sleigh beds and free-standing baths.

Open all day all wk **Food** Lunch Mon-Sat
12-2.30, Sun 12-7 Dinner Mon-Sat
6-9.30, Sun 12-7 Av main course £14
Set menu available 🌐 FREE HOUSE
🛢 Timothy Taylor Landlord, Ilkley Gold &
Mary Jane, Theakston, Black Sheep
🍎 Aspall. 🍷 30 **Facilities** Non-diners
area 🐾 (Bar Garden) 👬 Children's menu
Children's portions Garden 🎋 Parking
WiFi 🚐 (notice required) **Rooms** 4

CALDWELL
Map 19 NZ11

Brownlow Arms

tel: 01325 718471 **DL11 7QH**
email: bookings@brownlowarms.co.uk
dir: *From A1 at Scotch Corner take A66 towards Bowes. Right onto B6274 to Caldwell. Or from A1 junct 56 take B6275 N. 1st left through Mesonby to junct with B6274. Right to Caldwell*

Family-friendly country inn

In the tiny village of Caldwell amidst the delightful rolling countryside between Barnard Castle and Darlington, this lovely stone inn is a great place to seek out. With 10 wines by the glass, plenty more bins and reliable Yorkshire real ales, time passes easily here. A blend of traditional and modern rooms is the setting for unpicking a phenomenally comprehensive, globally inspired menu. Start perhaps with avocado and chilli tiger prawns; then follow with home-made suet steak and kidney pudding; or smoked haddock and spinach cheese melt with roast tomatoes.

Open all wk 5-11 (Sat-Sun 12-11) **Food** Lunch Sat 12-11, Sun 12-9 Dinner Mon-Fri 5-9, Sat 12-11, Sun 12-8 Restaurant menu available all wk ⊕ FREE HOUSE ◀ Timothy Taylor Landlord, Marston's Wainwright, Theakston Best Bitter, Guinness. ♟ 10 **Facilities** Non-diners area ♦ Children's menu Children's portions Garden Outside area Parking WiFi

CARTHORPE
Map 19 SE38

The Fox & Hounds
PICK OF THE PUBS

tel: 01845 567433 **DL8 2LG**
dir: *Off A1, signed on both N'bound & S'bound carriageways*

Vegetarians have their own extensive menu

In the sleepy village of Carthorpe, the cosy Fox & Hounds has been a country inn for over 200 years, and the old anvil and other tools from its time as a smithy are still evident. Landlady Helen Taylor's parents bought the pub over 30 years ago, and in her hands and that of her husband Vincent's, they have established an excellent reputation for their food which comes from named suppliers and the daily delivery of fresh fish. A typical dinner could begin with duck filled filo parcels and plum sauce, followed by pan-fried fillets of sea bass and stir-fry vegetables, and ending with pear and almond tart with vanilla custard. There is a separate vegetarian menu of dishes that can be chosen as a starter or a main, such as pea mash and asparagus flan with hollandaise sauce. Beers include local Black Sheep, while the wine choice is global in scope. Home-made produce such as jams and chutneys are available to buy. The entire wine list is available by the glass.

Open Tue-Sun 12-3 7-11 Closed 25 Dec & 1st 2wks Jan, Mon **Food** Lunch Tue-Sun 12-2 Dinner Tue-Sun 7-9.30 Set menu available ⊕ FREE HOUSE ◀ Black Sheep Best Bitter, Worthington's, guest ale ○ Thatchers Gold. ♟ **Facilities** ♦ Children's portions Parking

CHAPEL LE DALE
Map 18 SD77

The Old Hill Inn

tel: 015242 41256 **LA6 3AR**
email: sabena.martin@btopenworld.com
dir: *From Ingleton take B6255, 4m, pub on right*

An ancient Dales inn of great character

Beautiful views of the Dales await visitors to this former farmhouse, later a drovers' inn, parts dating from 1615, the rest from 1835. When Winston Churchill stayed here on huntin', shootin', fishin' holidays, he no doubt enjoyed the bar, which these days serves eminent Yorkshire real ales like Black Sheep and Dent Aviator. A family of three chefs run the inn (one of whom makes sculptures from sugar) producing lunchtime snacks of sandwiches and home-made sausages, and typical main

dishes of beef and ale casserole; smoked haddock fishcakes; and specials of home-reared pork dishes and fish specials according to the daily catch.

Open Tue-Sun Closed 24-25 Dec, Mon (ex BHs) **Food** Lunch Tue-Sat 12-2.30, Sun 12-3 Dinner Tue-Fri & Sun 6.30-8.45, Sat 6-8.45 ⊕ FREE HOUSE ◀ Black Sheep Best Bitter, Dent Aviator & Golden Fleece, guest beer ○ Aspall. **Facilities** Non-diners area ♦ (Bar Garden) ♦ Children's menu Children's portions Garden ⊨ Parking WiFi

CLAPHAM
Map 18 SD76

NEW The New Inn ★★★★★ INN

tel: 015242 51203 **LA2 8HH**
email: info@newinn-clapham.co.uk **web:** www.newinn-clapham.co.uk
dir: *From A65 into Clapham. At T-junct right, over bridge, pub straight ahead*

Grade II listed building in conservation village

Set in the Yorkshire Dales beneath the three peaks of Pen-y-ghent, Ingleborough and Whernside, this is an ideal base for all who enjoy outdoor pursuits. In addition to newly refurbished rooms, the inn offers a bistro for relaxed dining, three bars, and seating outside overlooking the river and village. A variety of teas and coffees are much in demand, but the bars are well stocked with local cask ales, international beers, ciders and malt whiskies. In addition to gourmet sandwiches and sharing platters, unexpected dishes such as osso bucco can be found on the menu.

Open all day all wk **Food** Lunch Mon-Thu 12-2.30, Fri-Sun all day Dinner Mon-Thu 6.30-9.30, Fri-Sun all day Av main course £13.95 Set menu available Restaurant menu available all wk ⊕ ENTERPRISE INNS ◀ Hawkshead, Timothy Taylor Landlord, Settle Blonde. ♟ **Facilities** Non-diners area ♦ (Bar Garden) ♦ Children's menu Children's portions Garden ⊨ Parking WiFi ➡ (notice required) **Rooms** 20

COLTON
Map 16 SE54

Ye Old Sun Inn
PICK OF THE PUBS

See Pick of the Pubs on opposite page

CRAYKE
Map 19 SE57

The Durham Ox
PICK OF THE PUBS

See Pick of the Pubs on page 562

CROPTON
Map 19 SE78

The New Inn

tel: 01751 417330 **YO18 8HH**
email: phil@thegreatyorkshirebrewery.co.uk
dir: *Phone for detailed directions*

Own brewery on site draws many real ale enthusiasts

On the edge of the North York Moors National Park, this family-run free house is fortunate to have the acclaimed The Great Yorkshire Brewery at the bottom of the garden. Popular with locals and visitors alike, the pub is a draw to ale lovers and there is a beer festival in November. Meals are served in the restored village bar and in the elegant Victorian restaurant: choices could include Yorkshire coast fishcakes or crisp belly pork with dauphinoise potatoes; an extensive range from the grill; plus lunchtime sandwiches and ciabatta rolls.

Open all day all wk 11-11 (Sun 11-10.30) **Food** Lunch Mon-Fri 12-2, Sat-Sun 12-3 Dinner Sun-Thu 5.30-8.30, Fri-Sat 5.30-9 ⊕ FREE HOUSE ◀ Cropton Yorkshire Classic, Yorkshire Golden, Yorkshire Pale, Yorkshire Warrior, Blackout & Monkmans Slaughter ○ Yorkshire cider. **Facilities** Non-diners area ♦ (Bar Garden) ♦ Children's menu Children's portions Play area Family room Garden ⊨ Beer festival Parking WiFi ➡ (notice required)

PICK OF THE PUBS

Ye Old Sun Inn

COLTON   Map 16 SE54

tel: 01904 744261 **Main St LS24 8EP**
email: yeoldsuninn@hotmail.co.uk
web: www.yeoldsuninn.co.uk
dir: *Approx 3.5m from York, off A64*

Charming country pub

Ashley and Kelly McCarthy took over this 17th-century country pub more than a decade ago and have worked hard to transform it into a thriving inn. They added a bar area and extended the dining area, allowing them more space to increase the excellent themed events, cookery demonstrations and classes that have proved so popular. In the dining room they have a deli where freshly baked bread, home-made jams and chutneys, fresh fish and daily essentials can be bought. A marquee in the garden overlooks rolling countryside and is used for large functions, which includes a summer beer festival and regular farmers' markets. Ashley takes pride in sourcing food and ale from small local producers and suppliers, including salads from his own polytunnel, and his menus are innovative and exciting. Lunches include light bites such as sandwiches, salads and wraps, plus there's an excellent Sunday lunch menu featuring locally sourced roasted meats, chef's specials and a dinner menu. Expect Yorkshire-style main courses such as slow-braised beef daube, venison cobbler, red

cabbage, carrot purée and red wine jus; hay-baked guinea fowl breast, garlic roasted salsify, pommes Anna, bacon crumbs and Wensleydale pastry; or pan-fried plaice fillet, cauliflower pudding, rarebit tartlet, braised chicory and wilted spinach. Precede with open butternut lasagne, sautéed pumpkin in almond butter with nutmeg cream; or tandoori chicken terrine, onion bhaji, cucumber and onion seed raita. Finish with white chocolate and raspberry tart, honeycomb, ice cream, fruit coulis; or banana and pecan French pastry, toffee sauce and vanilla ice cream. All dishes come with a wine recommendation, or look to the handpumps – Rudgate Battle Axe and Timothy Taylor Landlord are among the choice of seven real ales.

Open 9.30-2 6-11 (Tue 6-11 Fri-Sun 9.30am-11pm) Closed Mon, Tue L **Food** Lunch Wed-Sat 12-2, Sun 12-4 Dinner Tue-Fri 6-9, Sat 5-9.30, Sun 4-7 Av main course £15 ⊕ FREE HOUSE
◀ Timothy Taylor Landlord & Golden Best, Rudgate Battle Axe, Black Sheep, Ossett, Moorhouse's, Cottage ♂ Aspall.
♟ 18 **Facilities** Non-diners area ♦♦ Children's menu & portions Garden ☶ Beer festival Parking WiFi 🚌

PICK OF THE PUBS

The Durham Ox

CRAYKE   Map 19 SE57

tel: 01347 821506 **Westway YO61 4TE**
email: enquiries@thedurhamox.com
web: www.thedurhamox.com
dir: *From A19 through Easingwold to Crayke. From market place left up hill, pub on right*

Free house in the beautiful Howardian Hills

They don't do things by halves here. Not only is this 300-year-old, hilltop pub-restaurant named after a 189-stone ox that was exhibited all over the country, but it also features a steel and cast-iron, charcoal-fired oven nicknamed Big Bertha, weighing in at over a ton. The ox was born in 1796 and, as the pub sign shows, he was a hefty beast; his first owner was the Rt Hon Lord Somerville, a print of whom hangs in the bottom bar. Before entering the pub you somehow just know that inside you'll find flagstone floors, exposed beams, oak panelling and winter fires – and indeed you do. Also, this being Yorkshire, that the real ales will come from nowhere else, thus Timothy Taylor Boltmaker from Keighley, and Treboom from York. Sandwiches and pub classics like North Sea fish pie, and 'Ox' burger meet the need for something quick and easy, or if time is less of an issue you might want to work through the menu. Cured beef fillet carpaccio and celeriac remoulade is one starter option; another is home-

cured salmon, capers and horseradish cream. For a main course, there might be venison haunch steak, fondant potato, creamy Savoy cabbage and bitter chocolate sauce; pan-fried sea bass fillet, butter beans, chorizo and basil oil; or steak and ale suet pudding, hand-cut chips and garden peas. Desserts are no less appealing, typically plum and almond tart, mascarpone and Chantilly cream; and hot cherries, cherry ice cream, cherry mousse and a chocolate flake. There are noteworthy Yorkshire cheeses on the cheeseboard. Children have their own choices and there's a Magnificent Seven menu – '7 dishes, 7 pounds each, before 7pm'.

Open all day all wk 12-11.30 (Sun 12-10.30) **Food** Lunch Mon-Sat

12-2.30, Sun 12-3 Dinner Mon-Sat 5.30-9.30, Sun 5.30-8.30 Set menu available ⊞ FREE HOUSE ◀ Timothy Taylor Boltmaker, Black Sheep Best Bitter, Treboom Yorkshire Sparkle, York Guzzler Ⓒ Symonds. ♟ 10
Facilities Non-diners area 🐾 (Bar Garden) ♦ Children's menu Children's portions Garden ㅈ Parking WiFi 🚐 (notice required)

EASINGWOLD
Map 19 SE56

The New Inn

tel: 01347 824007 **62-66 Long St YO61 3HT**
email: info@thenewinnateasingwold.co.uk
dir: *In town centre*

Taste of Yorkshire in small market town

New it isn't, of course, having been a coaching stop in the 19th century. This inn on the aptly named Long Street, is owned by Yorkshire pub group, West Park Inns. The restaurant makes much of the fish and seafood available from the nearby coast, so home in on the grilled sea bass fillets, or the Whitby scampi. Also listed might be steak and ale pie with herb mash and seasonal vegetables; Thai green chicken curry with basmati rice and coriander naan; and the local 10oz rib-eye steak with slow-roasted tomato and garlic field mushrooms.

Open all day Closed Mon-Tue **Food** Lunch Wed-Sat 12-2.30, Sun 12-7 Dinner Wed-Sat 5-9, Sun 12-7 Av main course £10.95 Set menu available ⊕ FREE HOUSE ◀ Theakston Best Bitter, St Austell Tribute, Timothy Taylor Landlord. ¶ 13 **Facilities** Non-diners area ✿ (Bar Outside area) ◀◀ Children's menu Children's portions Outside area ⊟ Parking WiFi ⨿ (notice required)

EAST WITTON
Map 19 SE18

The Blue Lion
PICK OF THE PUBS

tel: 01969 624273 **DL8 4SN**
email: enquiries@thebluelion.co.uk
dir: *From Ripon take A6108 towards Leyburn*

Smart 18th-century hostelry with imaginative food

This well-maintained 18th-century coaching inn, tucked away in an unspoilt estate village close to Jervaulx Abbey, once catered to drovers and travellers journeying through Wensleydale. Ably run today by Paul and Helen Klein, it has built a reputation as one of North Yorkshire's finest inns. The interior is best described as rural chic, oozing stacks of atmosphere and charm. The classic bar with its open fire and flagstone floor is a beer drinker's haven, where the best of the county's breweries present a pleasant dilemma for the ale lover. A blackboard displays imaginative but unpretentious bar meals, while diners in the candlelit restaurant can expect culinary treats incorporating a variety of Yorkshire ingredients, notably seasonal game. A memorable meal may comprise smoked salmon and celeriac remoulade with crispy capers and lemon oil; slow-cooked pork belly with pickled apple purée, black pudding Scotch egg and cider reduction; with yogurt and honey cheesecake with confit fig to round it all off.

Open all day all wk 11-11 **Food** Lunch Mon-Sat 12-2.15, Sun all day Dinner Mon-Sat 7-9.30, Sun all day Set menu available ⊕ FREE HOUSE ◀ Black Sheep Best Bitter & Golden Sheep, Theakston Best Bitter ♂ Thatchers Gold. ¶ 12 **Facilities** Non-diners area ✿ (Bar Garden) ◀◀ Children's portions Garden ⊟ Parking WiFi

Find out more about this county with *The AA Guide to Yorkshire* – see shop.theAA.com

The Cover Bridge Inn

tel: 01969 623250 **DL8 4SQ**
email: enquiries@thecoverbridgeinn.co.uk
dir: *On A6108 between Middleham & East Witton*

Welcoming Wensleydale pub with well-kept draught ales

The Harringtons have now owned this magnificent little pub at one end of a venerable arched bridge on the River Cover for nearly 20 years. The pub's oldest part was probably built around 1670, to cater for the increasing trade on the drovers' route from Coverdale. Watch out for the cunning door-latch, which befuddles many a first-time visitor. The ancient interior rewards with wrinkled beams, a vast hearth and open log fires, settles and wholesome fodder, including home-made pies, daily specials, and their famous ham and eggs. Relax in the riverside garden with your choice from eight ales on tap, three of which are rotating guests.

Open all day all wk **Food** Lunch all wk 12-2 Dinner all wk 6-9 ⊕ FREE HOUSE ◀ Guest ales ♂ Westons Old Rosie, Gwynt y Ddraig Happy Daze & Two Trees Perry. **Facilities** Non-diners area ✿ (Bar Garden) ◀◀ Children's menu Children's portions Play area Garden ⊟ Parking WiFi ⨿ (notice required)

EGTON
Map 19 NZ80

The Wheatsheaf Inn
PICK OF THE PUBS

tel: 01947 895271 **YO21 1TZ**
email: info@wheatsheafegton.com
dir: *Off A169, NW of Grosmont*

Handsome pub at the centre of the community

This modest old pub is very popular with fishermen, as the River Esk runs along at the foot of the hill, and is a big draw for fly-fishers in particular. The pub sits back from the wide main road and it would be easy to drive past it, but that would be a mistake as the welcoming main bar is cosy and traditional, with low beams, dark green walls and comfy settles. The menu offers sandwiches, soup and hot focaccia rolls at lunchtime, as well as a range of light lunches, including mixed mushroom risotto; and fish stew. In the evening, the supper menu might include a starter of pan-fried duck liver with mushrooms and bacon on toast, and main courses such as beef Stroganoff; or Brazil nut and cranberry nut roast. There's a locals' bar too, but it only holds about a dozen people, so get there early.

Open 11.30-3 5.30-11.30 (Sat 11.30-11.30 Sun 11.30-11) Closed Mon **Food** Lunch Tue-Sun 12-2 Dinner Tue-Sat 6-8.30 ⊕ FREE HOUSE ◀ Black Sheep Best Bitter & Golden Sheep, John Smith's, Timothy Taylor Landlord, guest ales ♂ Thatchers Gold. ¶ 10 **Facilities** Non-diners area ◀◀ Children's menu Garden ⊟ Parking WiFi

EGTON BRIDGE
Map 19 NZ80

Horseshoe Hotel

tel: 01947 895245 **YO21 1XE**
email: horseshoehotel@yahoo.co.uk
dir: *From Whitby take A171 towards Middlesborough. Village signed in 5m*

Riverside hotel champions local ingredients and ales

The Horseshoe is an 18th-century country house set in beautiful grounds by the River Esk, handy for visiting Whitby, Robin Hood's Bay, the North Yorkshire Moors Railway and TV's *Heartbeat* country. Inside the welcoming bar are oak settles and tables, local artists' paintings, and plates around the picture rails. Along with some great beers, such as Durham Brewery ale, local ingredients are used to create the varied menu, try wholetail scampi and chips or medallion of pork fillet.

Open all wk 11.30-3 6.30-11 (Sat 11.30-11 Sun 12-10.30) **Food** Lunch all wk 12-2 Dinner all wk 6-9 Restaurant menu available ⊕ FREE HOUSE ◀ John Smith's Cask, Durham, Black Sheep, Theakston, guest ales. **Facilities** Non-diners area ◀◀ Children's menu Children's portions Family room Garden ⊟ Parking WiFi ⨿ (notice required)

EGTON BRIDGE *continued*

The Postgate

tel: 01947 895241 **YO21 1UX**
dir: *Phone for detailed directions*

Walkers, families and dogs are very welcome

Set in the Esk Valley within a stone's throw of the river, The Postgate is a typical North York Moors country inn; it played the part of the Black Dog in TV's *Heartbeat*. Being on the coast-to-coast trail, and becoming known as a food destination, the pub is popular with walkers who chat amiably with locals in the bar over their pints of Black Sheep. The menu offers an array of locally sourced fresh fish and seafood from Whitby fish market, excellent local meats, and game in season.

Open all wk 12-3 6-12 **Food** Lunch all wk 12-2.30 Dinner all wk 6-9 ⊕ PUNCH TAVERNS ◄ Timothy Taylor Landlord, Black Sheep Bitter ⓑ Thatchers. **Facilities** Non-diners area ❁ (Bar Garden) ♠ Children's menu Children's portions Garden ⋒ Parking WiFi ⚍ (notice required)

■ ELSLACK   **Map 18 SD94**

The Tempest Arms

tel: 01282 842450 **BD23 3AY**
email: info@tempestarms.co.uk
dir: *A59 from Skipton towards Gisburn. At rdbt left onto A56. Pub on left*

Hand-pulled Yorkshire ales and a varied menu

A local landmark, the Tempest dates to the coaching days of the 17th century. The Yorkshire Dales and surrounding countryside bring walkers and cyclists, who enjoy the pub's warm welcome and convivial atmosphere. Wood fires, comfy cushions, alcoves and dining spaces set the interior's comfortable mood, completed by an array of Yorkshire ales at the bar and a vast menu of pub food. A Tempest staple is the seafood pancake with creamy sauce, salad and chipped potatoes. But there's no better place for a starter of Yorkshire puddings and onion gravy, with Bolton Abbey lamb and vegetable hotpot to follow.

Open all day all wk **Food** Lunch Mon-Sat 12-2.30, Sun 12-7.30 Dinner Mon-Sat 6-9, Sun 12-7.30 ⊕ FREE HOUSE ◄ Dark Horse Hetton Pale Ale, Theakston, Marston's Wainwright ⓑ Kingstone Press. ♟ 16 **Facilities** Non-diners area ❁ (Bar Outside area) ♠ Children's menu Children's portions Outside area ⋒ Parking WiFi ⚍ (notice required)

■ FELIXKIRK   **Map 19 SE48**

The Carpenters Arms

tel: 01845 537369 **YO7 2DP**
email: enquiries@thecarpentersarmsfelixkirk.com **web:** www.carpentersarmsfelixkirk.com
dir: *From Thirsk take A170 towards Helmsley. Left signed Felixkirk, 2.25m to village*

Unpretentious village pub with lovely views

Felixkirk, in the Vale of Mowbray, has no shops, making this Provenance Inns owned pub the village's only retail establishment. To the east are the Hambleton Hills and the North Yorks Moors National Park, while west are the Yorkshire Dales. Bare stonework, slate flooring and rich red walls characterise the interior, and there are open fires in the dining areas and the bar. The restaurant and tiered terrace offer the best views. Menu descriptions are simple: pan-seared salmon fillet; braised pork cheeks; gourmet burgers; steak ciabattas; herb crusted haddock; devilled chicken livers; and fish and chips. Check out the Before Seven menu – seven main courses, each £7.

Open all day all wk **Food** Lunch Mon-Sat 12-2.30, Sun 12-3 Dinner Mon-Sat 5.30-9.30, Sun 6-8.30 ⊕ PROVENANCE INNS ◄ Black Sheep Best Bitter, Timothy Taylor Boltmaker ⓑ Symonds. **Facilities** Non-diners area ❁ (Bar Garden) ♠ Children's menu Children's portions Garden ⋒ Parking WiFi ⚍ (notice required)

■ GIGGLESWICK   **Map 18 SD86**

Black Horse Hotel

tel: 01729 822506 **32 Church St BD24 0BE**
email: theblackhorse-giggle@tiscali.co.uk
dir: *Phone for detailed directions*

Village centre inn with pub favourites on the menu

Set next to the church and behind the market cross in the 17th-century main street, this traditional free house is as charming as Giggleswick itself. Down in the warm and friendly bar you'll find a range of hand-pulled ales, with a local guest beer sometimes available. The menu of freshly prepared pub favourites ranges from home-made pizzas to main course dishes like home-made steak and ale pie; haddock and chips; and horseshoe of gammon with either eggs, pineapple, or both.

Open 12-2.30 5.30-11 (Sat-Sun 12-11) Closed Mon **Food** Lunch Tue-Sun 12-2 Dinner Tue-Thu 6.30-9, Fri-Sun 6-9 ⊕ FREE HOUSE ◄ Timothy Taylor Landlord & Golden Best, Tetley's, Settle Signal Main Line. **Facilities** Non-diners area ♠ Children's menu Children's portions Garden ⋒ Parking WiFi

PICK OF THE PUBS

The Bridge Inn

GRINTON Map 19 SE09

tel: 01748 884224 **DL11 6HH**
email: atkinbridge@btinternet.com
web: www.bridgeinn-grinton.co.uk
dir: *Exit A1 at Scotch Corner onto
A6108, through Richmond. Left onto
B6270 towards Grinton & Reeth*

Former coaching inn popular with ramblers and discerning diners

Close to one of Yorkshire's finest old churches, known as the Cathedral of the Dales, this 13th-century riverside pub is located in Grinton, which has stood here for almost 1,000 years. Two of the Yorkshire Dales' wildest and prettiest dales meet in Grinton; Arkengarthdale and Swaledale collide in a symphony of fells, moors, waterfalls and cataracts. Lanes and tracks slope down from the heights, bringing ramblers and riders to appreciate the good range of northern beers that landlord Andrew Atkin matches with his fine foods; Jennings Brewery's Cocker Hoop being a casc in point. Locals enjoy the bustling games room and beamed old bar serving baguettes and toasted ciabattas, while a more tranquil restaurant area caters for those after a more intimate meal experience. The kitchen here is inspired by carefully chosen seasonal local game, meats, fish and other produce, including herbs plucked from the garden. Expect traditional and familiar

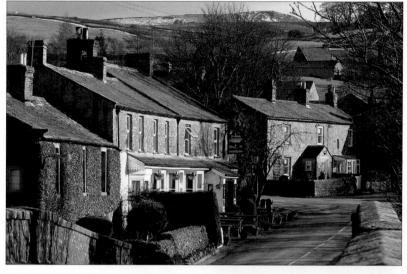

dishes with a modern twist, enhanced by daily-changing specials. Cut to the chase with a starter like ham hock terrine with ciabatta crostini and pickled carrot ribbons; or goats' cheese en croûte with sticky shredded beetroot and raspberry coulis. Mains cater for a wide palate, typically seared pheasant breast with bacon wrapped leg, fondant potato, roasted squash and red wine jus; or bunny burger, herb croûton and tomato, onion and garlic salsa. For non-meat eaters, a vegetarian Moroccan tagine with tabouleh salad and cucumber mint raita hits the spot. End with apple, maple syrup and pecan nut crumble, or home-made ginger sponge pudding.

Open all day all wk **Food** all wk 12-2.30 6-9 Restaurant menu available all wk ⊕ JENNINGS 🛢 Cumberland Ale & Cocker Hoop, Caledonian Deuchars IPA, York Yorkshire Terrier, Adnams ⚙ Westons Old Rosie. ⚲
Facilities Non-diners area 🐾 (Bar Garden) 👶 Children's menu Children's portions Garden 🎪 Beer festival Parking WiFi 🚌

GOATHLAND
Map 19 NZ80

Birch Hall Inn

tel: 01947 896245 **Beck Hole YO22 5LE**
email: glenys@birchhallinn.fsnet.co.uk
dir: *9m from Whitby on A169*

One of the smallest bars in the country

Beck Hole is a tiny hamlet of nine cottages and a pub hidden in the steep Murk Esk Valley close to the North Yorkshire Moors (steam) Railway. This delightful little free house has just two tiny rooms separated by a sweet shop; no more than 30 people plus two small dogs have ever fitted inside with the door closed! The main bar offers well-kept local ales to sup beside an open fire in winter, including the pub's house ale, Beckwatter. The pub has been under the same ownership for over 30 years and the simple menu features the local butcher's pies, old-fashioned flatcakes filled with ham, cheese, corned beef or farmhouse pâté, and home-made scones and buttered beer cake. In warm weather, food and drink can be enjoyed in the large garden, which has countryside views. The local quoits team play on the village green on summer evenings.

Open 11-3 7.30-11 (11-11 summer) Closed Mon eve & Tue in winter ⊕ FREE HOUSE ◀ Birch Hall Inn Beckwatter, Black Sheep Best Bitter, York Guzzler. **Facilities** ❀ (Bar Garden) ♦◾ Family room Garden **Notes** ◉

GRASSINGTON
Map 19 SE06

Grassington House ★★★★★ RR ◉◉

tel: 01756 752406 **5 The Square BD23 5AQ**
email: bookings@grassingtonhousehotel.co.uk web: www.grassingtonhousehotel.co.uk
dir: *A59 into Grassington, in town square opposite post office*

A destination pub with top-notch accommodation

Whoever commissioned this private house in 1760 chose the site well, for this elegant Georgian pub and restaurant stands imposingly in Grassington's cobbled square. Fresh local produce underpins the award-winning menu offering starters of taster slates of tapas-style nibbles; and corn-fed chicken liver pâté with apple jam and warm brioche. Mains might be pheasant breast with prune and pheasant bon bon, apple potato fondant, parsnips and prune jus; or celeriac risotto with trompette mushrooms and truffle pecorino. For lighter options there's an interesting range of open and closed sandwiches, perhaps smoked salmon, salad, lemon and capers will appeal. Thwaites, Dark Horse Hetton Pale Ale and Black Sheep are bar staples.

Open all day all wk **Food** Lunch Mon-Fri 12-2.30, Sat 12-4, Sun 12-8 Dinner Mon-Sat 6-9.30, Sun 12-8 Av main course £13.95 Set menu available ⊕ FREE HOUSE ◀ Dark Horse Hetton Pale Ale, Thwaites Original, Marston's Wainwright, Black Sheep. ☂ 14 **Facilities** Non-diners area ♦◾ Children's menu Children's portions Garden ⋒ Parking WiFi ⬜ (notice required) **Rooms** 9

GREAT HABTON
Map 19 SE77

The Grapes Inn

tel: 01653 669166 **YO17 6TU**
email: info@thegrapes-inn.co.uk
dir: *From Malton take B1257 towards Helmsley. In Amotherby right into Amotherby Ln. After Newsham Bridge right into Habton Ln & follow pub signs. 0.75m to pub*

Enjoyable food in a busy community pub

A welcoming village pub between the Howardian Hills and the North Yorkshire Moors near the bustling market town of Malton. Enjoy a pint of Marston's EPA with the locals in the lively taproom, separated from the dining room – once the village post office – by a double-sided log-burner. Chef-proprietor Adam Myers has gained an enviable reputation in Ryedale for his chargrilled steaks, but other hearty options

are slow-roasted pork belly, black pudding mash with crab apple jus; Cumberland sausages and mash; and wild mushroom and brie tart with slow-roasted tomato and rocket salad. Desserts are no less tempting – ginger sponge with butterscotch sauce and vanilla ice cream.

Open Tue-Fri 6pm-close (Sat 12-2 6-close Sun open all day) Closed from 2 Jan for 2wks, Mon **Food** Lunch Sat-Sun 12-2 Dinner Tue-Sat 6-8.30, Sun 6.30-8.30 ⊕ MARSTON'S ◀ EPA, Wychwood Hobgoblin ⊘ Thatchers Gold. **Facilities** Non-diners area ♦◾ Children's menu Children's portions Outside area ⋒ Parking

GREEN HAMMERTON
Map 19 SE45

The Bay Horse Inn

tel: 01423 330338 **York Rd YO26 8BN**
email: enquiry@bayhorsegreenhammerton.co.uk
dir: *A1 junct 47 follow signs for A59 towards York. After 3m, turn left into village, inn on right opposite post office*

Hearty food in the Vale of York

This traditional inn is part of the original settlement of Green Hammerton, positioned on the old Roman road from York to Aldborough. The pub has served travellers and villagers for over 200 years; many features from those days remain in the beamed, fire-warmed interior. Reliable cask beers accompany home-made meals strong on local produce; excellent matured steaks, gammon and chicken grilled to order are always available. Daily-changing dishes include grilled goats' cheese and pickled star anise beetroot salad; and local sausages with mash, buttered cabbage and onion gravy. Outside is a garden and patio area.

Open all wk 11.30-2.30 5.30-12 (Sat 11.30am-mdnt Sun 11.30-8) **Food** Lunch Mon-Fri 12-2.30, Sat 12-9, Sun 12-7.30 Dinner Mon-Fri 6-9, Sat 12-9, Sun 12-7.30 Av main course £10 ⊕ GREENE KING ◀ Timothy Taylor, Morland Old Golden Hen, guest ale. **Facilities** Non-diners area ❀ (Bar Garden) ♦◾ Children's menu Children's portions Garden ⋒ Parking WiFi ⬜ (notice required)

GRINTON
Map 19 SE09

The Bridge Inn
PICK OF THE PUBS

See Pick of the Pubs on page 565

HARDRAW
Map 18 SD89

The Green Dragon Inn

tel: 01969 667392 **DL8 3LZ**
email: info@greendragonhardraw.com
dir: *From Hawes take A684 towards Sedbergh. Right to Hardraw, approx 1.5m*

If you're in the area, it's worth a visit

Entering the Bar Parlour is like stepping into a Tudor film-set, although parts of the inn are much older – 13th century in fact. Gravestones, forming part of the floor, were washed away from the neighbouring churchyard during floods. In a wooded site behind is Hardraw Force, England's highest single-drop waterfall, which JMW Turner painted while staying here in 1816. The choice of real ales and ciders is good, and pub food includes home-made steak and kidney pie; lamb shank, mash and veg; and a seasonal dish of pheasant bourguignon with horseradish mash and creamed cabbage. Regular live folk music are big draws.

Open all day all wk **Food** Lunch all wk 12-4 Dinner all wk 6-9 ⊕ FREE HOUSE ◀ Timothy Taylor Landlord, Theakston Best Bitter & Old Peculier, Wensleydale, Yorkshire Dales ⊘ Westons Stowford Press. **Facilities** Non-diners area ❀ (Bar Garden) ♦◾ Children's menu Children's portions Family room Garden ⋒ Parking ⬜ (notice required)

HAROME — Map 19 SE68

The Star Inn ◎◎ — PICK OF THE PUBS

tel: 01439 770397 **YO62 5JE**
email: reservations@thestarinnatharome.co.uk
dir: *From Helmsley take A170 towards Kirkbymoorside 0.5m. Turn right for Harome*

Renowned gastro-pub in prime walking country

On the fringe of the North Yorkshire Moors National Park, this 14th-century thatched gem sits in an idyllic village surrounded by wonderful walks. Although renowned as a foodie destination, the genuinely pubby bar is worth seeking out. Here both locals and visitors relax with well-kept pints of Hambleton or Cropton whilst awaiting the call to dine. Chef-patron Andrew Pern changes his dishes frequently according to seasonal availability. A winter menu makes interesting reading. Start off with ballotine of local shot partridge with clementine relish, game forcemeat, pistachio granola and Fridlington beetroot 'borscht'; or duck liver and port 'petite truffe' with sloe gin jelly and garden herb toast; then dive into the mains. Sea turbot fillet with moss parsley, pressed smoked eel and 'Double Fun' potato, apple, lovage and Avruga caviar beurre blanc; or pheasant breast fricassée with 'boozy prunes', leeks, cider cream and wholegrain mustard mash. Look out for specials and veggie choices.

Open all wk 11.30-3 6.30-11 (Mon 6.30-11 Sun 12-11) Closed Mon L **Food** Lunch Tue-Sat 11.30-2, Sun 12-6 Dinner Mon-Sat 6.30-9.30, Sun 12-6 Av main course £22 Set menu available ⊕ FREE HOUSE ◀ Theakston Best Bitter, Black Sheep, Copper Dragon, Hambleton, Cropton ♂ Westons Stowford Press, Ampleforth Abbey. ♟ 20 **Facilities** Non-diners area ◗◗ Children's menu Children's portions Garden ⊓ Parking ▦ (notice required)

HARROGATE — Map 19 SE35

The Fat Badger

tel: 01423 505681 **Cold Bath Rd HG2 0NF**
email: contactus@thefatbadgerharrogate.com
dir: *A59 to Harrogate. A661 3rd exit on rdbt to Harrogate. Left at rdbt onto A6040 for 1m. Right onto A61. Bear left into Montpellier Hill*

Victorian-style grandeur in the heart of Harrogate

In the heart of this spa town's Montpellier Quarter close to the famous Pump Rooms, The Fat Badger has the lofty ceilings, faux gas lamps and leather chesterfields that give the place an elegant, clubby feel. It's a relaxed setting to enjoy a cocktail, a glass of fizz or pint of real ale before choosing perhaps one of the sharing boards (cured and potted meats and smoked fish platter are just two); mussels marinière and frites; steak and Guinness pie; or weiner schnitzel and skinny fries.

Open all day all wk **Food** Mon-Thu 12-9.30, Fri-Sat 12-10, Sun 12-9 Av main course £13.50 Set menu available Restaurant menu available Mon-Sat ⊕ FREE HOUSE ◀ Black Sheep, Timothy Taylor Landlord, Copper Dragon, Golden Pippin. ♟ 18 **Facilities** Non-diners area ◗◗ Children's menu Outside area ⊓ Parking WiFi ▦

HAWNBY — Map 19 SE58

The Inn at Hawnby ★★★★ INN ◎ — PICK OF THE PUBS

tel: 01439 798202 **YO62 5QS**
email: info@innathawnby.co.uk web: www.innathawnby.co.uk
dir: *From Helmsley take B1257 towards Stokesley. Follow Hawnby signs*

Stunning moor views and first-rate food

This charming 19th-century former drovers' inn is perched on top of a hill and offers panoramic country views of the North Yorkshire Moors. Run by hands-on and welcoming proprietors Kathryn and David Young, the pub stocks some great Yorkshire-brewed ales, including Helmsley Howardian Gold and Timothy Taylor Landlord. In the kitchen, local and seasonal produce steers the menu, with accomplished dishes served either in the Mexborough restaurant or in the cosy bar. Typical of dinner starters might be parsley root and cauliflower soup, pickled pear, croûtons and coriander; or home-cured beetroot salmon, blinis, sour cream and caviar. These may be followed by roast rump of lamb, mint roasted chantenay carrots, heritage beetroots and beetroot gnocchi; or ravioli of spinach and ricotta, English asparagus, avocado oil and dukkah. Finish with carrot cake, toffee and Chantilly cream or banana crème brûlée.

Open all wk 10-3 6-11 (Fri-Sun all day) Closed 25 Dec & Mon-Tue Feb-Mar **Food** Lunch all wk 12-2 Dinner all wk 7-9 ⊕ FREE HOUSE ◀ Timothy Taylor Landlord, Black Sheep, Helmsley Howardian Gold ♂ Somersby. ♟ 8 **Facilities** Non-diners area ❀ (Bar Garden) ◗◗ Children's menu Children's portions Garden ⊓ Parking WiFi ▦ (notice required) **Rooms** 9

HELPERBY — Map 19 SE46

The Oak Tree Inn

tel: 01423 789189 **Raskelf Rd YO61 2PH**
email: enquiries@theoaktreehelperby.com web: www.theoaktreehelperby.com
dir: *A19 from York towards Thirsk. After Easingwold left signed Helperby. Approx 5m to village*

No-nonsense pub food at the village inn

Depending on how you approach the village, the signs say either Helperby Brafferton or Brafferton Helperby, an apparent confusion which to locals probably makes perfect sense. At this village inn there is a spacious bar for informal dining, and a barn extension overlooking the rear courtyard for more formal meals. The first of the Provenance Inns, The Oak Tree's menus offer seasonal Yorkshire produce (suppliers are shown on a map on the menu), and locally reared beef (burgers and steaks) cooked, among other dishes, in the charcoal-fired oven. Also on offer are Yorkshire game terrine; pheasant, pancetta and apple spring roll; beer-battered fish and chips; chicken Kiev; and salmon fillet, lemon, garlic and herbs.

Open all day all wk **Food** Lunch Mon-Sat 12-2.30, Sun 12-3 Dinner Mon-Sat 5.30-9.30, Sun 5.30-8.30 Set menu available ⊕ FREE HOUSE/PROVENANCE INNS ◀ Black Sheep Best Bitter, John Smith's Cask ♂ Symonds. ♟ **Facilities** Non-diners area ❀ (Bar Outside area) ◗◗ Children's menu Children's portions Outside area ⊓ Parking WiFi ▦ (notice required)

HOVINGHAM
Map 19 SE67

The Malt Shovel

tel: 01653 628264 **Main St** YO62 4LF
email: info@themaltshovelhovingham.com
dir: *18m NE of York, 5m from Castle Howard*

Friendly roadside village pub

The stone-built 18th-century Malt Shovel offers a friendly atmosphere with well-kept ales and food prepared from quality local ingredients. There are two dining rooms where you can enjoy starters of chestnut mushrooms in rich blue cheese sauce; smoked salmon, spinach and cream cheese tartlet or prosciutto ham and prawns, followed by vegetable and bean goulash; steak pie; or chicken with chorizo sausage and smoked paprika. There is also a large beer garden at the rear of the pub where you can sit and enjoy a pint or two of Black Sheep in lovely surroundings.

Open all wk winter 11.30-2 6-11 (summer 11.30-2.30 5.30-11) Sun all day **Food** Lunch Mon-Sat 11.30-2 (winter) 11.30-2.30 (summer), Sun 12-2.30 Dinner Mon-Sat 6-9 (winter) 5.30-9 (summer), Sun 5.30-7.45 Set menu available ⊕ PUNCH TAVERNS ◀ Copper Dragon Golden Pippin, Theakston Best Bitter, Black Sheep, guest ale Ō Thatchers. **Facilities** Non-diners area ❄ (Bar Restaurant Garden) ⊪ Children's menu Children's portions Garden ⊓ Parking WiFi ▥ (notice required)

The Worsley Arms Hotel
PICK OF THE PUBS

tel: 01653 628234 **Main St** YO62 4LA
email: enquiries@worsleyarms.co.uk
dir: *On B1257 between Malton & Helmsley*

Excellent stop if exploring North Yorkshire

This village hotel and pub form part of the Worsley family's historic Hovingham Hall Estate. Hambleton Stallion from nearby Thirsk, and Black Sheep from Masham are on tap in the Cricketers' Bar (the local team has played on the village green for over 150 years). You can eat here or in the restaurant; lunch and afternoon tea are also served in the large walled garden. Lunchtime choices could include a selection of sandwiches; while the à la carte lists such dishes as Loch Fyne salmon three ways; Goosnargh duck and foie gras terrine; red mullet, green tomato consommé, black olive tapenade, potato gnocchi and Mediterranean vegetables; and Wye Valley asparagus ravioli, 30-month aged parmesan, Morell mushroom broth, pied de bleu mushrooms and basil oil. The pub hosts regular wine evenings and a supper club.

Open all day all wk **Food** Lunch all wk 12-2 Dinner all wk 6.30-9 ⊕ FREE HOUSE ◀ Hambleton Stallion, Black Sheep Ō Ampleforth Abbey. ♟ 20 **Facilities** Non-diners area ❄ (Bar Garden) ⊪ Children's portions Garden ⊓ Parking WiFi ▥ (notice required)

HUBBERHOLME
Map 18 SD97

The George Inn

tel: 01756 760223 **BD23 5JE**
email: visit@thegeorge-inn.co.uk
dir: *From Skipton take B6265 to Threshfield. B6160 to Buckden. Follow signs for Hubberholme*

Dales inn with bags of charm

Stunningly located beside the River Wharfe in the Yorkshire Dales National Park, this pub was built in the 1600s as a farmstead and still has flagstone floors, stone walls, mullioned windows and an open fire. To check if the bar is open, look for a lighted candle in the window. Beers are local, coming from the Black Sheep and Yorkshire Dales breweries. For lunch there's soup, sandwiches and baskets of chips; but the traditional choices for an evening meal are based on locally sourced produce; perhaps try an individual steak and kidney pie, and sticky toffee pudding and ice cream. Enjoy your drink on the terrace in the warmer summer months.

Open 12-3 6-10.30 (summer all day 12-11) Closed last 3wks Jan, Tue **Food** Lunch Wed-Sun 12-2.30 Dinner Wed-Mon 6-8 ⊕ FREE HOUSE ◀ Black Sheep, Yorkshire Dales, Tetley's, local guest ales Ō Thatchers Gold. **Facilities** ❄ (Bar Outside area) ⊪ Children's portions Outside area ⊓ Parking

KETTLEWELL
Map 18 SD97

The Kings Head

tel: 01756 761600 **The Green** BD23 5RD
email: kingsheadkettlewell@outlook.com
dir: *From A65 N of Skipton take B6265 signed Grassington. In Treshfield take B6160 to Kettlewell, right before river bridge. 1st left at maypole. Pub on left*

Family-run pub in Wharfedale

The immense and venerable hearth and chimney breast are difficult to miss in the bar of this traditional family-run pub in the heart of the Yorkshire Dales; it's no wonder visitors and locals alike are drawn here to warm-up on cold wintery nights. Local beers include Dark Horse Hetton Pale Ale. Fresh, seasonal produce is used for dishes on the modern British menus. Seared breast of pigeon with black pudding, Scotch egg, celeriac and truffle, spinach and pancetta is an indicative starter. Follow with pork two ways with bubble-and-squeak croquette, apple, chorizo and sherry sauce.

Open all day Closed 2wks beg Jan, 1wk end Nov, 25-26 Dec, Mon in winter **Food** Lunch 12-3 Dinner 5-9 Set menu available ⊕ FREE HOUSE ◀ Dark Horse Hetton Pale Ale, Wharfdale Blonde, Tetley's Ō Thatchers. ♟ 10 **Facilities** ⊪ Children's menu Children's portions Outside area ⊓ WiFi ▥ (notice required)

KILBURN
Map 19 SE57

The Forresters Arms Inn

tel: 01347 868386 **The Square** YO61 4AH
email: admin@forrestersarms.com
dir: *From Thirsk take A170, after 3m turn right signed Kilburn. At Kilburn Rd junct, turn right, inn on left in village square*

Sturdy coaching inn with hearty food

Next door to the famous Robert Thompson craft carpentry workshop, The Forresters Arms has fine examples of his early work, with the distinctive trademark mouse evident in both bars. A sturdy stone-built former coaching inn still catering for travellers passing close by the famous White Horse of Kilburn on the North York Moors, it has log fires, cask ales and good food. Dishes include starters such as deep-fried brie with Kilburn chutney, and smoked chicken and roasted pepper salad; then there'll be mains like steak and ale pie, and game casserole with horseradish dumplings. There's also a specials board and a selection of lunchtime sandwiches and snacks.

Open all day all wk 9am-11pm **Food** Lunch Mon-Fri 12-3 (out of season 12-2.30), Sat-Sun all day Dinner all wk 6-9 (out of season 6-8) ⊕ ENTERPRISE INNS ◀ John Smith's Cask, Wharfe Bank White Horse Blonde, guest ales Ō Addlestones, Westons Stowford Press. **Facilities** Non-diners area ❄ (Bar Outside area) ⊪ Children's menu Children's portions Outside area ⊓ Beer festival Parking WiFi ▥ (notice required)

KIRKBY FLEETHAM
Map 19 SE29

Black Horse Inn ★★★★★ INN ◉

tel: 01609 749010 **Lumley Ln DL7 0SH**
email: reservations@blackhorseinnkirkbyfleetham.com
web: www.blackhorseinnkirkbyfleetham.com
dir: *Signed from A1 between Catterick & Leeming Bar*

Charming and successful inn

Legend has it that Dick Turpin eloped with his lady from this village pub in the Swale Valley, just off the vast village green; the inn was named after the outlaw's steed in celebration. The pub garden adjoins fields, and the interior, including the seven character bedrooms, is appointed to create a pleasing mix of tradition and comfort. No surprise then that locals and visitors are encouraged to tarry a while, to sup a grand Yorkshire pint and enjoy accomplished food that covers all the bases. Look for starters such as crispy chicken and black pudding bon bon, sweetcorn purée, charred corn and crispy quail's eggs; then a main course of slow-cooked beef, caramelised onions, pancetta, button mushrooms, pan haggerty potato and beef jus; or fish pie with cheddar mash and seasonal veg.

Open all day all wk **Food** Lunch Mon-Sat 12-2.30, Sun 12-7 Dinner Mon-Thu 5-9, Fri-Sat 5-9.30, Sun 12-7 Av main course £16 Set menu available Restaurant menu available all wk ⊕ FREE HOUSE ◀ Black Sheep, Copper Dragon. ☕ 10
Facilities Non-diners area ☆ (Bar Garden) ◕ Children's portions Garden ⌂ Parking WiFi ➡ (notice required) **Rooms** 7

KIRKBYMOORSIDE
Map 19 SE68

George & Dragon Hotel
PICK OF THE PUBS

tel: 01751 433334 **17 Market Place YO62 6AA**
email: reception@georgeanddragon.net
dir: *Just off A170 between Scarborough & Thirsk. In town centre*

Charming and relaxed family-owned favourite

A whitewashed coaching inn that's welcoming and dog-friendly. Affectionately known as the G&D, it's full of charm — from the log fire in the bar, the collection of sporting paraphernalia, to the fountain in the sheltered courtyard — and there are five well-kept, hand-pulled real ales on offer, including an in-house brew. At lunchtime, enjoy a baguette or panini in the bar or, if you fancy contemporary decor and leather seats, Knight's Restaurant's menu offers a great selection of fish dishes — the 'scaddock', that's a combination of golden wholetail scampi and battered haddock; and Whitby Bay thermidor are just two. For meat eaters how about slow-braised shank of Yorkshire lamb; Holme farm venison steak; or a pot of beef lasagne? If you have a sweet tooth, don't pass by their Cadbury's tuck shop cheesecake. The traditional Sunday carvery is hugely popular.

Open all day all wk 10.30am-11pm **Food** Lunch all wk 12-2 Dinner all wk 6-9 Restaurant menu available all wk ⊕ FREE HOUSE ◀ Greene King Abbot Ale, Copper Dragon, Black Sheep, House Bitter, Daleside, guest ales ♨ Westons Stowford Press. ☕ 12 **Facilities** Non-diners area ☆ (Bar Garden Outside area) ◕ Children's menu Children's portions Garden Outside area ⌂ Parking WiFi ➡

KIRKBY OVERBLOW
Map 19 SE34

Shoulder of Mutton

tel: 01423 871205 **Main St HG3 1HD**
email: info@shoulderofmuttonharrogate.co.uk
web: www.shoulderofmuttonharrogate.co.uk
dir: *S from Harrogate on A61 towards Leeds, left for Kirkby Overblow*

Close to Harrogate, Harewood House and other attractions

For those who might be wondering, Overblow is a corruption of oreblow, a reference to the village's iron-smelting past. Built of local stone in the 1880s, this traditional country pub still offers open log fires and the attraction of an enclosed garden. Home-cooked, locally sourced food includes what the menu calls 'Shoulder of Mutton', but is in fact braised Masham lamb in mint and redcurrant gravy; grilled Wensleydale gammon and chips; chicken kohlpari biryani; and a generous selection of gluten-free dishes. On the specials board, look for pan-fried Nidderdale chicken fillet; and squid rings in spicy tomato sauce with tagliatelle.

Open 12-3 6-11 (Sat-Sun 12-10.30) Closed Mon **Food** Lunch Tue-Fri 12-2, Sat 12-9, Sun 12-7 Dinner Tue-Fri 6-9, Sat 12-9, Sun 12-7 Set menu available Restaurant menu available Tue-Sun ⊕ PUNCH TAVERNS ◀ Black Sheep Best Bitter, Timothy Taylor Landlord ♨ Thatchers Gold. ☕ 12 **Facilities** Non-diners area ☆ (Bar Restaurant Garden) ◕ Children's menu Children's portions Garden ⌂ Parking WiFi

KNARESBOROUGH   Map 19 SE35

The General Tarleton Inn ★★★★★ RR ◉◉

PICK OF THE PUBS

See Pick of the Pubs on opposite page

LANGTHWAITE   Map 19 NZ00

The Red Lion Inn

tel: 01748 884218 **DL11 6RE**
email: rlionlangthwaite@aol.com
dir: *From A6108 between Richmond & Leyburn follow Reeth signs. In Reeth follow Langthwaite sign*

Homely pub often used as a film and TV location

The Red Lion Inn is a traditional country community pub that has been owned by the same family for 50 years. It hosts a dart team in winter, a quoits team in summer, and offers only bar snacks, soup, pasties, hot drinks, ice cream, chocolate and sweets. There are some wonderful walks in this part of the Dales and relevant books and maps are on sale in the bar. In the tiny snug there are photographs relating to the various films and TV programmes filmed at this unusually photogenic — they include *All Creatures Great and Small, A Woman of Substance* and *Hold the Dream*.

Open all wk 11-3 7-11 **Food** Lunch all wk 11-3 ⊕ FREE HOUSE ◀ Black Sheep Best Bitter, Guinness ♂ Thatchers Gold. ♈ 9 **Facilities** Non-diners area Family room Outside area ⋈ Parking WiFi

LASTINGHAM   Map 19 SE79

Blacksmiths Arms

tel: 01751 417247 **YO62 6TN**
email: pete.hils@blacksmithslastingham.co.uk
dir: *7m from Pickering & 4m from Kirkbymoorside. A170 (Pickering to Kirkbymoorside road), follow Lastingham & Appleton-le-Moors signs*

Well-loved pub on the southern fringe of the North York Moors

With a cottage garden and decked outdoor seating area, this stone-built, 17th-century free house has a wonderful atmosphere. In the small front bar pewter mugs and beer pump clips hang from the low beams, and copper cooking pans decorate the open range. A snug and two delightful dining rooms make up the rest of the interior. Home-cooked dishes prepared from local supplies include roast

topside of Yorkshire beef with Yorkshire pudding; lamb and mint pie; mushroom and cashew nut Stroganoff; and poached salmon fillet with creamy lemon, dill and prawn sauce. Enjoy the food with Theakston Best Bitter or a guest ale. St Mary's Church, opposite the pub, is renowned for its Saxon crypt.

Open all day all wk **Food** Lunch all wk 12-5 Dinner all wk 6.30-8.45 Av main course £12 Set menu available ⊕ FREE HOUSE ◀ Theakston Best Bitter, 3 guest ales. **Facilities** Non-diners area ⋈ Children's menu Children's portions Family room Garden ⋈ WiFi ⛟ (notice required)

LEVISHAM   Map 19 SE89

Horseshoe Inn ★★★★ INN

tel: 01751 460240 **Main St YO18 7NL**
email: info@horseshoelevisham.co.uk **web:** www.horseshoelevisham.co.uk
dir: *A169, 5m from Pickering. 4m, pass Fox & Rabbit Inn on right. In 0.5m left to Lockton. Follow steep winding road to village*

Family-run pub in tranquil village

On the edge of the North York Moors National Park, this village pub is an ideal overnight stop while touring the area, perhaps by steam train from Levisham station. Charles and Toby Wood have created an inviting atmosphere, especially apparent in the beamed and wooden-floored bar, where a gilt-edged mirror hangs above the open fire, and the real ales are from Black Sheep and Cropton. Local suppliers play a big part behind the scenes so that the kitchen can prepare hearty plates of Whitby scampi and chips, steak and ale pie, and sausage and mash with onion gravy.

Open all day all wk **Food** Lunch all wk 12-2 Dinner all wk 6-8.30 ⊕ FREE HOUSE ◀ Black Sheep Best Bitter, Cropton Yorkshire Moors, Two Pints, Yorkshire Warrior & Endeavour, Wold Top Headland Red, Brass Castle Cliffhanger ♂ Thatchers Gold. ♈ 12 **Facilities** Non-diners area ❀ (Bar Garden) ⋈ Children's menu Children's portions Garden ⋈ Parking WiFi **Rooms** 13

LEYBURN   Map 19 SE19

The Queens Head ★★★★ INN

tel: 01677 450259 **Westmoor Ln, Finghall DL8 1QZ**
email: enquiries@queensfinghall.co.uk **web:** www.queensfinghall.co.uk
dir: *From Bedale follow A684 W towards Leyburn, just after pub & caravan park turn left signed Finghall*

Dales produce is high on the list

This pretty 18th-century country inn with beams and open fires is set on a hillside above Wensleydale and there are stunning views of the countryside from the terrace. The dining room overlooks Wild Wood — believed to be one of the inspirations for Kenneth Grahame's *Wind in the Willows*. Drinkers can quaff a pint of Theakston Black Bull Bitter by the fire and diners can create their own deli board while considering the menu, which demonstrates the kitchen team's passion for Dales produce. As well as sandwiches and pub favourites there are tempting dishes like pan-fried venison steak, port and blueberry sauce and hand-cut chips; and minted pea and leek risotto with asparagus. Spacious accommodation is located in the adjacent annexe.

Open all wk 12-3 6-close Closed 26 Dec, 1 Jan **Food** Lunch all wk 12-2 Dinner all wk 6-9 Av main course £10 Set menu available ⊕ FREE HOUSE ◀ Theakston Black Bull Bitter, Pennine Brewing Co Hair of the Dog, Wensleydale Gamekeeper. ♈ 10 **Facilities** Non-diners area ⋈ Children's menu Children's portions Garden Outside area ⋈ Parking WiFi ⛟ (notice required) **Rooms** 3

PICK OF THE PUBS

The General Tarleton Inn ★★★★★ RR ◉◉

tel: 01423 340284
Boroughbridge Rd, Ferrensby HG5 0PZ
email: gti@generaltarleton.co.uk
web: www.generaltarleton.co.uk
dir: *A1(M) junct 48 at Boroughbridge,
take A6055 to Knaresborough. Inn 4m
on right*

Local produce drives the award-winning menu here

Named in honour of General Banastre Tarleton, a hero of the American War of Independence, this 18th-century coaching inn just north of Knaresborough is an ideal base for exploring the Yorkshire Dales. The renovated interior retains its old beams and original log fires, while the sofas encourage guests to settle down with a pint of Black Sheep. Here you can peruse the seasonal menus that have helped chef-proprietor John Topham and his team earn two AA Rosettes. Championing local produce, east coast fish is delivered daily, local vegetables arrive the day they've been picked, and seasonal game comes from nearby shoots. Food is served in the Bar Brasserie, in the fine dining restaurant, or out in the terrace garden and courtyard when the weather permits. Typical starters include queenie scallops in garlic butter with gruyère and

cheddar; braised pig cheek with black pudding Scotch egg, swede and crisp pig's ear; and guinea fowl and ham hock terrine with foie gras, pease pudding and pickles. These might precede main dishes such as Yorkshire fish pie; slow-braised confit shoulder of lamb with spiced baba ganoush, pistachio goats' curd and white onion purée; or a Waterford Farm beef steak that has been dry-aged on the bone in a Himalayan salt brick chamber. Leave space for one of the accomplished desserts, such as a brandy snap basket with vanilla ice cream and chocolate sauce. Accompanying wines can be selected from a list of 150, with 11 served by the glass.

Open all wk 12-3 6-11 **Food** Lunch all wk 12-2 Dinner Mon-Sat 6-9.15, Sun 6-8.30 Set menu available ⊕ FREE HOUSE ◧ Black Sheep Best Bitter, Timothy Taylor Landlord. ♟ 11 **Facilities** Non-diners area ♦♦ Children's menu Children's portions Garden ⊼ Parking WiFi **Rooms** 13

LEYBURN *continued*

Sandpiper Inn   PICK OF THE PUBS

tel: 01969 622206 **Market Place DL8 5AT**
email: hsandpiper99@aol.com
dir: *A1 onto A684 to Leyburn*

Wensleydale market town inn

The ivy-clad Sandpiper may only have been a pub for 30 years or so, but it's Leyburn's oldest building, dating to the 17th century. Run by Jonathan and Janine Harrison, the bar and snug offer real ales from a small army of Yorkshire breweries, and some 100 single malts. The restaurant, distinguished by a huge stone lintel above an open fireplace, oak floors and candlelit tables, is where Jonathan has built on his excellent reputation for modern British food. Such reputations, of course, require using the finest ingredients, which he does for traditional and international dishes such as pigeon with spinach risotto; tempura fried squid and vegetables with Thai dressing; grilled red mullet with lobster and tiger prawn tagliatelle; and chump of Waterford lamb, dauphinoise potato and roasted vegetables. For dessert, why not one of the Sandpiper's own ice creams or sorbets, or banoffee pie, glazed bananas and shaved chocolate? Daily special, small plates and sandwiches add to the choices.

Open 10.30-3 6-11 (Sun 12-2.30 6-10) Closed 2wks from 1st Jan, Mon & occasionally Tue **Food** Lunch Tue-Sun 12-2.30 Dinner Tue-Fri 6-8.30, Sat 6-9, Sun 6-8 Restaurant menu available ⊕ FREE HOUSE ◼ Black Sheep Best Bitter, Daleside, Copper Dragon, Archers, Yorkshire Dales, Rudgate Brewery, Wensleydale ♂ Thatchers Gold. ♟ 10 **Facilities** Non-diners area ♥ (Bar Garden Outside area) ♦ Children's menu Family room Garden Outside area ⋒ WiFi

▌ LITTON   Map 18 SD97

Queens Arms

tel: 01756 770096 **BD23 5QJ**
email: info@queensarmslitton.co.uk
dir: *From Skipton N on B6265, through Threshfield & Kilnsey. Left signed Arncliffe & Litton*

Secluded village gem at the heart of the community

The whitewashed stone Queens in secluded Littondale radiates its 17th-century character and charm below the limestone crags of the Yorkshire Dales. Enjoy the views from the outside tables, perhaps while you contemplate climbing Pen-y-Ghent at the head of the dale. Inside are slate floors, beams, open fires, contemporary fittings and fabrics, and locally brewed real ales. Reflecting the seasons and the location, traditional food options include chilli con carne with chorizo and rice; steak and ale pie with chips and peas; lamb burger with feta cheese; battered haddock and chips; and vegetable curry. Ginger sponge will help replace the calories lost fell-walking.

Open 11-3 6-11 Closed Mon (winter) **Food** Lunch all wk 12-3 Dinner Tue-Thu 6-9, Fri-Sat 6-9.30 Av main course £12 ⊕ FREE HOUSE ◼ Thwaites Original, Black Sheep, Goose Eye Chinook Blonde, Greene King IPA, Wharfdale Blonde, guest ale ♂ Thatchers. ♟ 10 **Facilities** Non-diners area ♥ (All areas) ♦ Children's portions Garden Outside area ⋒ WiFi ⋙ (notice required)

▌ LOWER DUNSFORTH   Map 19 SE46

The Dunsforth

tel: 01423 320700 **Mary Ln YO26 9SA**
email: hello@thedunsforth.co.uk
dir: *Phone for detailed directions*

Village pub ticking all the right boxes

A modern approach to classic dishes is a mantra of chef-patron Paul Cunliffe at this country inn in a leafy Ure Valley village. It's blessed with open fires, stripped floorboards and homely furnishings; where Paul and his wife Janine tempt with pubby meals at the bar and a perky restaurant menu sourcing produce mostly from local farms and estates and fish from dayboats out of Hartlepool. Line caught haddock may appeal; or look to roast loin of hare or côte du venison from the carte. Beers are mostly from long-established Yorkshire breweries; the wine list has over 50 bins.

Open 12-2.30 5.30-11 (Sat-Sun 12-11) Closed Mon & Tue **Food** Lunch Wed-Sat 12-2.30, Sun 12-6 Dinner Wed-Sat 5.30-9.30, Sun 12-6 Av main course £12 Set menu available Restaurant menu available Wed-Sun ⊕ FREE HOUSE ◼ Theakston Best Bitter & Black Bull Bitter, Adnams Ghost Ship, Timothy Taylor Landlord. ♟ 14 **Facilities** Non-diners area ♥ (Bar Garden) ♦ Children's menu Children's portions Garden ⋒ Parking WiFi ⋙ (notice required)

▌ LOW ROW   Map 18 SD99

The Punch Bowl Inn ★★★★ INN

tel: 01748 886233 **DL11 6PF**
email: info@pbinn.co.uk **web:** www.pbinn.co.uk
dir: *A1 from Scotch Corner take A6108 to Richmond. Through Richmond then right onto B6270 to Low Row*

Lots on offer at this Yorkshire Dales inn

With Wainwright's Coast to Coast Walk on the doorstep, this Grade II listed Swaledale pub dates back to the 17th century. As well as open fires and antique furniture, the bar and bar stools were hand-crafted by Robert 'The Mouseman' Thompson's company (see if you can spot the mice around the bar). Typical food choices include chicken liver and orange pâté; beef and ale casserole with herb dumplings and horseradish mash; and Yorkshire parkin with apple compôte. Local cask-conditioned ales also feature. If you would like to stay over for the Swaledale festivals, the 11 bedrooms all have spectacular views.

Open all day all wk 11am-mdnt Closed 25 Dec **Food** Lunch Mon-Sat 12-2.30, Sun 12-3 Dinner all wk 6-9 Restaurant menu available all wk ⊕ FREE HOUSE ◼ Theakston Best Bitter, Black Sheep Best Bitter & Riggwelter, Timothy Taylor

Landlord ○ Thatchers Gold. ▮ 13 **Facilities** Non-diners area ▮ (Bar) ▮ Children's menu Children's portions Outside area ▯ Parking WiFi ▭ (notice required) **Rooms** 11

MALHAM
Map 18 SD96

The Lister Arms ★★★★ INN
PICK OF THE PUBS

See Pick of the Pubs on page 574 and advert below

MALTON
Map 19 SE77

The New Malton

tel: 01653 693998 **2-4 Market Place YO17 7LX**
email: info@thenewmalton.co.uk
dir: *In town centre opposite church*

Popular town-centre free house for British and European cooking

Overlooking the market place and the part-Norman parish church, the pub's rambling, split-level rooms, wooden floorboards and flagstones declare 18th-century origins. Weekly changing local ales spoil beer drinkers for choice. A comprehensive menu opens with a not unexpected Yorkshire pudding and onion gravy; and a more unusual beef fillet carpaccio with Asian slaw, crisp ginger and Japanese citrus dressing. Lighter dishes include baked bean and corned beef hotpot; and smoked haddock chowder, while mains include roast pork rump; Vietnamese king prawn and glass-noodle salad; and field and wild mushroom 'Kiev'. Vanilla crème brûlée with nutmeg shortbread would round off a meal well.

Open all day all wk Closed 25-26 Dec, 1 Jan **Food** Mon-Sat 12-9.30, Sun 12-8 Av main course £12.50 ⊕ FREE HOUSE ◧ Wold Top Bitter, Great Newsome Prickly Back Otchan, Rudgate Ruby Mild ○ Westons Stowford Press & Wyld Wood Organic. ▮ 9 **Facilities** ▮ (Bar Restaurant Outside area) ▮ Children's portions Outside area ▯ Parking WiFi

---

MARTON (NEAR BOROUGHBRIDGE)
Map 19 SE46

The Punch Bowl Inn

tel: 01423 322519 **YO51 9QY**
email: enquiries@thepunchbowlmartoncumgrafton.com
web: www.thepunchbowlmartoncumgrafton.com
dir: *In village centre*

Village pub with six eating areas

A Provenance Inns group member, the 16th-century Punch Bowl commands a central location in the village. Its beamed, wood-floored bar and tap-room's generous seating includes a settle, and there's a log fire in each of the six eating areas. Kick of a good meal with Yorkshire game terrine, spiced pear chutney and toasted brioche; or Cornish crab cake with Lousiana BBQ dip, then move onto to slow-cooked short rib of beef, wholegrain mustard mash, honeyed parsnips and Black Sheep ale gravy; or truffle honey glazed salmon fillet, cavolo nero and lemon and dill risotto. Summer barbecues are held in the courtyard.

Open all day all wk Mon-Thu 12-3 5-11 (Fri-Sat 12-11 Sun 12-10.30) **Food** Lunch Mon-Sat 12-2.30, Sun 12-8 Dinner Mon-Sat 5.30-9.30, Sun 12-8 ⊕ PROVENANCE INNS ◧ Black Sheep Best Bitter, Timothy Taylor Landlord ○ Symonds. **Facilities** Non-diners area ▮ (Bar Garden) ▮ Children's menu Children's portions Garden ▯ Parking WiFi ▭ (notice required)

PICK OF THE PUBS

The Lister Arms ★★★★ INN

MALHAM　　　　　　　Map 18 SD96

tel: 01729 830330 **BD23 4DB**
email: relax@listerarms.co.uk
web: www.listerarms.co.uk
dir: *In village centre*

Close to majestic Malham Cove

For location alone, this handsome old coaching inn takes some beating, sitting as it does in some of Britain's most impressive cavern-riddled limestone scenery. A dense covering of creepers masks its stone walls, and the old mounting block from coaching days is still in situ. Beyond the attractive tiled entrance are small rooms with original beams, fireplaces, wooden floors and log-burning stoves. One of Thwaites Inns of Character pubs, it's right on the village green, which presents much easier terrain for the fell-walkers, cavers and other outdoor types who drop in here for morning coffee or a pint. If the latter, it could be a glass of Wainwright bitter, named after the fell-walking guide and writer/illustrator Alfred Wainwright, who also hailed from Blackburn; seasonal Dark Horse ales are further options. Traditional home-cooked meals originating from trusted local suppliers might begin with smoked haddock and crab cakes with citrus salad and chilli mayonnaise; or beetroot carpaccio, Yorkshire Blue bon bons. From there the choice broadens to salads, sharing boards, and Lister classics. These comprise firm favourites such as honey-glazed home-cooked ham with free-range fried egg and hand-cut chips; confit pork belly with bubble-and-squeak, sautéed spinach, crispy bacon and cider jus; or local pork sausages with creamy mash, onion gravy and crispy onions. Desserts are home made too, including caramelised bread and butter pudding infused with Yorkshire gin and served with mint custard; and chocolate and hazelnut brownie served warm with chocolate sauce and vanilla ice cream. Feel free to arrive in muddy boots with a well-behaved dog — nobody will object.

Open all day all wk **Food** all wk 12-9 (summer 12-10) Av main course £10 ⊕ THWAITES INNS OF CHARACTER 🍺 Wainwright, Original, Dark Horse Hetton Pale Ale Ŏ Westons Stowford Press & Rosie's Pig. ♟ 8
Facilities Non-diners area 🐾 (Bar Garden) 🧒 Children's menu Children's portions Garden 🪑 Parking WiFi
Rooms 15

MASHAM
Map 19 SE28

The Black Sheep Brewery

tel: 01765 680101 & 680100 **Wellgarth HG4 4EN**
email: sue.dempsey@blacksheep.co.uk
dir: *Off A6108, 9m from Ripon & 7m from Bedale*

Famous brewery site for over 20 years

Set up by Paul Theakston, a member of Masham's famous brewery family, in the former Wellgarth Maltings in 1992, the complex includes an excellent visitor centre and a popular bar-cum-bistro. Don't miss the fascinating tour of the brewery. Next take in the wonderful views over the River Ure and surrounding countryside as you sup tip-top pints of Riggwelter and Golden Sheep; then tuck into a good plate of food, perhaps steak and ale pie with hand-cut chips and seasonal vegetables; locally made Hog and Hop sausages, sage mash, onion gravy and vegetables; or an oak-smoked salmon and prawn sandwich.

Open all wk 10-5 (Thu-Sat 10am-late) Closed 25-26 Dec (Mon Jan-Feb) **Food** Lunch Sun-Wed 12.2.30 Dinner Thu-Sat 6-8.30 Av main course £10.95 Restaurant menu available Mon-Sat ⊕ BLACK SHEEP BREWERY ◀ Best Bitter, Riggwelter Ale, Golden Sheep Ò Aspall, Westons Stowford Press. **Facilities** Non-diners area ❀ (Garden) ◆ Children's menu Children's portions Garden ⊓ Parking WiFi ▦ (notice required)

The White Bear

tel: 01765 689319 **Wellgarth HG4 4EN**
email: sue@whitebearmasham.co.uk
dir: *Signed from A1 between Bedale & Ripon*

Theakston's flagship pub in bustling market town

Theakston Brewery's flagship inn stands just a short stroll from the legendary brewhouse and market square in this bustling market town and provides the perfect base for exploring the Yorkshire Dales. Handsome and stylish, there's a snug taproom for quaffing pints of Old Peculier by the glowing fire, oak-floored lounges with deep sofas and chairs for perusing the daily papers, and an elegant dining room. Menus take in bacon-wrapped pork fillet with black pudding and parsnip and English mustard purée; butternut squash and spinach curry; sausage and mash with onion gravy; and mushroom and sweet pepper risotto with parmesan crisps. Expect live music and 30 cask ales at the late June beer festival.

Open all day all wk **Food** all wk 12-9 ⊕ FREE HOUSE/THEAKSTON ◀ Best Bitter, Black Bull Bitter, Lightfoot & Old Peculier, Caledonian Deuchars IPA. **Facilities** Non-diners area ❀ (Bar Garden) ◆ Children's menu Children's portions Garden ⊓ Beer festival Parking WiFi ▦ (notice required)

MAUNBY
Map 19 SE38

The Buck Inn
PICK OF THE PUBS

tel: 01845 587777 **YO7 4HD**
email: info@thebuckinnmaunby.co.uk **web:** www.thebuckinnmaunby.co.uk
dir: *A1(M) junct 50, A61 towards Thirsk. Left onto A671 (Northallerton). In South Otterington left signed Maunby. Or A1(M) junct 53, A684 towards Northallerton. At rdbt right onto A167 to South Otterington, right signed Maunby*

Chef-led pub for quality eating and drinking

New owners took over The Buck in February 2016. Chef Dave Russell and business partner Jem Jarvis offer a warm and friendly welcome and are keen to keep the classic British country pub atmosphere. In the bar, the menu offers pub classics, from fish and chips to steak sandwiches, while in the restaurant you might start with crab and Granny Smith cocktail, with avocado purée and cumin snaps; or wild mushroom and mascarpone pâté with toasted focaccia. Main courses like pan-roasted breast of duck with courgette ribbons and fondant potatoes; slow-roasted belly of pork with apricot boudin noir, celeriac and apple purée and green peppercorn sauce; or sea bass with lemon risotto and vine roasted tomatoes. Look out for a famous trainer exercising his horses, or the locals playing quoits in the garden.

Open 11-11 (Sun 12-10) Closed Mon & Tue (may open Mon & Tue in high summer; contact pub for further information) **Food** Lunch Wed-Sat all day, Sun 12-4 Dinner Wed-Sat all day Av main course £12 Set menu available Restaurant menu available Mon-Sat ⊕ FREE HOUSE ◀ Theakston Best Bitter, York Guzzler, Pennine Hair Of The Dog. ☘ 12 **Facilities** Non-diners area ❀ (Bar Garden) ◆ Children's menu Children's portions Garden ⊓ Parking WiFi ▦ (notice required)

MIDDLEHAM
Map 19 SE18

The White Swan

tel: 01969 622093 **Market Place DL8 4PE**
email: enquiries@whiteswanhotel.co.uk
dir: *From A1, take A684 towards Leyburn then A6108 to Ripon, 1.5m to Middleham*

Popular and attractive inn

This Tudor coaching inn stands in the shadow of Middleham's ruined castle in the cobbled market square and, like the village, is steeped in the history of the turf, with several top horseracing stables located in the area. Oak beams, flagstones and roaring log fires all feature in the atmospheric bar, where you can quaff tip-top Black Sheep or Wensleydale ales. Using quality Yorkshire produce the menu features modern Italian and English dishes – perhaps pappardelle al cinghiale (gorgonzola pasta parcels with wine and thyme sauce); coniglio (braised rabbit with vegetable risotto); a pizza; or a chargrilled rib-eye steak served plain or with red wine sauce.

Open all day all wk 8am-11pm (mdnt at wknds) **Food** Contact pub for food times ⊕ FREE HOUSE ◀ Black Sheep Best Bitter, Theakston, Wensleydale Ò Thatchers Gold. ☘ 9 **Facilities** Non-diners area ❀ (Bar Outside area) ◆ Children's menu Children's portions Family room Outside area ⊓ Parking WiFi ▦ (notice required)

MIDDLESMOOR
Map 19 SE07

Crown Hotel

tel: 01423 755204 **HG3 5ST**
dir: *Phone for detailed directions*

Family run hotel at the top of the valley

This family-run traditional free house dates back to the 17th century and is in an ideal spot for anyone following the popular Nidderdale Way. There are great views towards Gouthwaite Reservoir from this breezy 900-ft high hilltop village with its cobbled streets. Visitors can enjoy a good pint of local beer and food by the cosy, roaring log fire, or in the sunny pub garden. A large selection of malt whiskies is also on offer.

Open Nov-Apr Tue-Thu 7-11 Fri-Sun all day (May-Oct Tue-Thu 12-2 7-11 Fri-Sun all day) Closed all day Mon, Tue-Thu L (winter) **Food** Lunch Tue-Sun 12-2 Dinner Tue-Sun 7-8.30 ⊕ FREE HOUSE ◀ Black Sheep Best Bitter, Wensleydale Bitter, Guinness ♂ Thatchers Gold. **Facilities** ♥ (Bar Restaurant Garden) ♦ Children's portions Garden ⊟ Parking WiFi **Notes** ⊛

MOULTON
Map 19 NZ20

NEW The Black Bull Inn

tel: 01325 377556 **DL10 6QJ**
email: enquiries@theblackbullmoulton.com **web:** www.theblackbullmoulton.com
dir: *1m S of Scotch Corner off A1, 5m from Richmond*

Great seafood and steaks at this classic country pub

An iconic Yorkshire dining pub for decades, The Black Bull Inn was bought and refurbished by Provenance Inns. With its stone-flagged floors, exposed brickwork and cosy corners, it's a great setting for some classic pub food. Seafood's a speciality, so go for some Lindisfarne oysters, or you could kick off with Black Bull apple and chorizo black pudding with tarragon hollandaise and heritage tomatoes, before moving on to the gourmet fish pie, perhaps, or Yorkshire venison with wild mushrooms, roast parsnip and garlic and herb fondant. Big Bertha, the solid steel and cast iron charcoal fired oven, guarantees perfectly cooked rib-eye, sirloin and fillet steaks.

Open all wk 12-3 5-11 (Fri-Sun 12-11) **Food** Lunch Mon-Sat 12-2.30, Sun 12-3 Dinner Mon-Sat 5.30-9.30, Sun 5.30-8.30 Set menu available ⊕ FREE HOUSE/PROVENANCE INNS ◀ Black Sheep Best Bitter & Golden Sheep, Theakston ♂ Symonds. ♥ 16 **Facilities** Non-diners area ♥ (Bar Garden) ♦ Children's menu Children's portions Garden ⊟ Parking WiFi ▭ (notice required)

NEWTON ON OUSE
Map 19 SE55

The Dawnay Arms

tel: 01347 848345 **YO30 2BR**
email: dine@thedawnay.co.uk
dir: *From A19 follow Newton on Ouse signs*

Great riverside location with a large garden

Right in the middle of a picture-perfect village, The Dawnay Arms dates back to Georgian times. It sits on the banks of the River Ouse, and its large rear garden runs down to moorings for those arriving by boat. The interior, all chunky beams and tables, hosts Black Sheep and guest ales, and the well-chosen wine list also deserves mention. Dishes are mostly British in style and replete with quality ingredients. A menu selection includes Shetland mussel, tiger prawn and calamari risotto; corn-fed chicken wrapped in pancetta with grilled baby leeks, and rib-eye steaks direct from the grill.

Open 12-3 6-11 (Sat all day Sun 12-8) Closed Mon **Food** Lunch Tue-Sat 12-2.30, Sun 12-6 Dinner Tue-Sat 6-9.30, Sun 12-6 Set menu available ⊕ FREE HOUSE ◀ Black Sheep, guest ales ♂ Westons Stowford Press. ♥ 12 **Facilities** Non-diners area ♥ (Bar Garden) ♦ Children's menu Children's portions Garden ⊟ Parking WiFi ▭ (notice required)

NUN MONKTON
Map 19 SE55

The Alice Hawthorn
PICK OF THE PUBS

tel: 01423 330303 **The Green YO26 8EW**
email: enquiries@thealicehawthorn.com
dir: *From A59 between York & Harrogate follow Nun Monkton signs. Pub 2m on right*

Village pub going the extra mile for local sourcing

One of North Yorkshire's renowned village greens fronts this attractive brick-built pub. A duck pond, grazing Highland cattle and England's tallest maypole take the eye here, whilst behind the pub is a tranquil beer garden, fringed by a vegetable and flower garden. The Grade II listed building is around 220 years old and has an airy, contemporary interior and a snug bar where beers brewed in the village take pride of place. Real fires blaze and fresh flowers are dotted here and there; the walls are hung with paintings of the champion Victorian racehorse after which the pub is named. The team of chefs has an uncompromising passion for local sourcing; the result is a thoughtful dining choice including a fixed-price daytime menu and seasonally adjusted evening carte. A starter may be king scallops and chicken wings with cauliflower couscous; mains could be seared mackerel fillet or venison Wellington with braised ox cheek and roasted ceps, finishing with apple crumble.

Open 12-3 5.30-11 (Sat all day Sun 12-6) Closed Mon **Food** Lunch Wed-Sat 12-3, Sun 12-6 Dinner Tue-Sat 5.30-9, Sun 12-6 Set menu available Restaurant menu available Tue-Sat ⊕ FREE HOUSE ◀ Timothy Taylor Landlord, Yorkshire Heart Silverheart IPA, weekly changing local ales ♂ Rekorderlig, Westons Stowford Press. **Facilities** Non-diners area ♥ (Bar Garden) ♦ Children's menu Children's portions Garden ⊟ Parking WiFi ▭ (notice required)

OSMOTHERLEY
Map 19 SE49

The Golden Lion

tel: 01609 883526 **6 West End DL6 3AA**
email: info@goldenlionosmotherley.co.uk
dir: *Phone for detailed directions*

Honest, well-cooked food

Standing in Osmotherley, the 'Gateway to the North Yorkshire Moors', The Golden Lion is a 250-year-old sandstone building. The atmosphere is warm and welcoming with open fires, a wooden bar, bench seating, whitewashed walls, mirrors and fresh flowers. As well as some 45 single malt whiskies, there are always three real ales on offer. The extensive menu ranges through basic pub grub to more refined dishes. Starters might include deep-fried calamari, tartare sauce; or rough pâté with onion and apricot relish. Mains are along the lines of calves' liver, fried onions, mash potato and red cabbage; and whole roast poussin with rosemary and garlic, green salad and chips. A popular dessert is steamed treacle sponge and vanilla custard.

Open 12-3 6-11 Closed 25 Dec, Mon L, Tue L **Food** Lunch Wed-Sun 12-2.30 Dinner all wk 6-9 ⊕ FREE HOUSE ◪ Timothy Taylor Landlord, Salamander, Wall's Brewing Co. **Facilities** ❧ (Bar Restaurant Outside area) ◗◖ Children's menu Children's portions Outside area WiFi

PICKERING
Map 19 SE78

Fox & Hounds Country Inn ★★★★ INN ◉
PICK OF THE PUBS

tel: 01751 431577 **Sinnington YO62 6SQ**
email: fox.houndsinn@btconnect.com **web:** www.thefoxandhoundsinn.co.uk
dir: *3m W of town, off A170 between Pickering & Helmsley*

Great country pub atmosphere with award-winning food

This friendly, 18th-century coaching inn on the edge of the North York Moors is run by resident proprietors Andrew and Catherine Stephens. In the wood-panelled bar, under oak beams and, depending on the temperature, warmed by a double-sided log-burner called Big Bertha, a pint of Copper Dragon Best, or Black Sheep Special, could be waiting, or maybe a rarely encountered whisky. Making full use of locally farmed produce, light lunches (except Sundays) and early suppers (except Saturdays) include smoked haddock, spring onion mash, roast chorizo and poached egg; outdoor-reared roast pork belly, black pudding and apple potato cake, Savoy cabbage and gravy; or a variety of omelettes. The main menu might list warm pheasant terrine, smoked bacon jam and celeriac purée to start, then a seafood platter; or chicken, mushroom and parmesan cobbler, purple sprouting broccoli for a main course; and to finish, dark chocolate and cherry cheesecake. Turn right along the village street past the village green to an ancient packhorse bridge over the gentle River Seven (yes, Seven).

Open all wk 12-2 5.30-11 (Sat 12-2 6-11 Sun 12-2.30 5.30-10.30) Closed 25-27 Dec **Food** Lunch all wk 12-2 Dinner Mon-Fri 5.30-9, Sat 6.30-9, Sun 5.30-8.30 Av main course £15.95 ⊕ FREE HOUSE ◪ Copper Dragon Best Bitter, Black Sheep Ö Thatchers Gold. ♚ 9 **Facilities** Non-diners area ❧ (Bar Garden) ◗◖ Children's menu Children's portions Garden ⊓ Parking WiFi ⌨ **Rooms** 10

The Fox & Rabbit Inn

tel: 01751 460213 **Whitby Rd, Lockton YO18 7NQ**
email: info@foxandrabbit.co.uk
dir: *From Pickering take A169 towards Whitby. Lockton in 5m*

Reliable stop near Dalby Forest

On a wide ridge above wooded dales, the sound of steam trains may drift across pastures to this very traditional Yorkshire Inn near Pickering. The North York Moors Railway is just one of a string of attractions within easy reach of the limestone-built country pub. With beers sourced from nearby craft breweries and menu ingredients with a distinctly Yorkshire pedigree, the Wood brothers have an embarrassment of riches to offer their guests. Seasonally adjusted menus may offer Radford's sirloin steak with home-made chips; or spinach and ricotta cannelonni as filling mains, topped off with a chocolate brownie.

Open all day all wk **Food** Lunch all wk 12-4 Dinner all wk 5-8.30 Av main course £10.95-£13.95 ⊕ FREE HOUSE ◪ Black Sheep Best Bitter, Marston's Oyster Stout, Cropton, Wold Top Ales, Tetley's Smooth Flow, Timothy Taylor Golden Best, guest ales Ö Thatchers Gold, Yorkshire Cider. ♚ 13 **Facilities** Non-diners area ❧ (Bar Garden) ◗◖ Children's menu Children's portions Garden ⊓ Parking ⌨ (notice required)

The White Swan Inn ★★★ HL ◉◉   PICK OF THE PUBS

tel: 01751 472288 **Market Place YO18 7AA**
email: welcome@white-swan.co.uk **web:** www.white-swan.co.uk
dir: *From N: A19 or A1 to Thirsk, A170 to Pickering, left at lights, 1st right onto Market Place. Pub on left. From S: A1 or A1(M) to A64 to Malton rdbt, A169 to Pickering*

Elegant market town inn with award-winning food

At the heart of pretty Pickering, The White Swan Inn fronts the steep main street dropping to the beck and steam railway station. With open fires, flagstone floors, panelling and eclectic furnishings, this sturdy coaching inn oozes character. Far from being a period piece, the owners have skilfully combined good contemporary design to produce a stylish destination dining inn. A creeper-clad courtyard snuggles behind, where browsers can enjoy Timothy Taylor Landlord bitter. It's for the exceptional menus, however, that guests travel to savour. The team led by Derren Clemmit scour the county for the best ingredients. Rare breed meats from the Ginger Pig Farm at Levisham; and lobster and fish from Whitby are crafted into a fine dining experience. A starter of potted crab with celeriac remoulade or poached asparagus, is an appetiser for roast shoulder of Tamworth pork with apple sauce, crackling, goose fat potatoes, Yorkshire pudding and gravy; or spring vegetable risotto with parmesan salad. A local cheeseboard is an ample conclusion, whilst the wine list has 65 bins.

Open all day all wk **Food** Lunch all wk 12-2 Dinner all wk 6.45-9 ⊕ FREE HOUSE ◪ Black Sheep, Timothy Taylor Landlord Ö Westons Stowford Press. ♚ 19 **Facilities** Non-diners area ❧ (Bar Outside area) ◗◖ Children's menu Children's portions Outside area ⊓ Parking WiFi ⌨ (notice required) **Rooms** 21

RIPON
Map 19 SE37

The Royal Oak

tel: 01765 602284 **36 Kirkgate HG4 1PB**
email: info@royaloakripon.co.uk
dir: *In town centre*

Excellent ales and good food in this smart coaching inn

Built in the 18th century, this beautiful coaching inn in the centre of Ripon is an ideal base for exploring nearby Harrogate and York. Well-kept local cask ales from Timothy Taylor and Saltaire breweries can be enjoyed in the bar, as well as wines from a carefully chosen list. Sandwiches and 'pub classics' appear on the menu alongside local steaks and signature dishes such as pheasant en croûte with potato gratin; sticky Ripon beef; and crispy skinned sea trout with Whitby crab cake.

Open all day all wk **Food** Mon-Sat 12-9, Sun 12-8 Set menu available Restaurant menu available ◪ Timothy Taylor Landlord, Best Bitter, Ram Tam & Golden Best, Saltaire Blonde, guest ales Ö Westons Stowford Press, Ampleforth Abbey. ♚ 14 **Facilities** Non-diners area ❧ (Bar Garden) ◗◖ Children's menu Children's portions Garden ⊓ Parking WiFi ⌨

Laurel Inn

tel: 01947 880400 **New Rd YO22 4SE**
dir: *Phone for detailed directions*

On the winding street towards the sea

Given its location it's hardly surprising that this was once the haunt of smugglers who used a network of underground tunnels and secret passages to bring the booty ashore. Nowadays it's the haunt of holidaymakers and walkers, and the setting for this small, traditional pub which retains lots of character features, including beams and an open fire. The bar is decorated with old photographs, and an international collection of lager bottles. This popular free house serves Adnams and Theakston Old Peculier and Best Bitter.

Open all wk 4-12 (winter) 2-12 (summer) **Food** Contact pub for food times ⊕ FREE HOUSE ◀ Theakston Best Bitter & Old Peculier, Adnams. **Facilities** ✿ (Bar Outside area) ♦ Family room Outside area ⊟ WiFi ➡ **Notes** ⊕

The Anvil Inn   PICK OF THE PUBS

tel: 01723 859896 **Main St YO13 9DY**
email: info@theanvilinnsawdon.co.uk
dir: *1.5m N of Brompton-by-Sawdon, on A170 (8m E of Pickering & 6m W of Scarborough)*

Attractive stone-built pub with visible history

There's bags of charm here in what until 1985 was a working forge, its history traceable back to the early 1700s. The bar, with its stone walls and steeply pitched ceiling, was the blacksmith's workshop and the furnace, anvil, bellows and tools are all still in place. Sit on an old pew and enjoy one of the weekly changing Yorkshire beers, such as draught Frothingham Best from the Great Newsome brewery, or a bottle of, ahem, Daleside's Old Leg Over. Locally farmed beef and pork, game from Dalby Forest, and Whitby-landed fresh fish all appear on the bar and dining room menu. Main course choices include slow-braised, Spanish-style shank of lamb with salt-roasted pistachios and creamed potatoes; pan-roasted corn-fed chicken supreme with sautéed garlic mushrooms, wrapped in prosciutto and served with roast butternut squash risotto. Elderflower and rosewater crème brûlée with clotted cream vanilla ice cream and shortcake is a typical pudding.

Open 6pm-11pm (Sat-Sun 12-2.30 6-11) Closed 25 & 26 Dec, 1 Jan, Mon-Tue **Food** Lunch Sat 12-2, Sun 12-2.30 Dinner Wed-Sat 6.30-9, Sun 6-8 ⊕ FREE HOUSE ◀ Scarborough, Cascade, Daleside Old Leg Over, Great Newsome Brewery Frothingham Best Ò Westons Stowford Press. ☙ 11 **Facilities** Non-diners area ✿ (Bar Garden) ♦ Children's portions Garden ⊟ Parking

Downe Arms Country Inn ★★★★ INN

tel: 01723 862471 **Main Rd, Wykeham YO13 9QB**
email: info@downearmshotel.co.uk web: www.downearmshotel.co.uk
dir: *On A170*

Hospitable stone-built hostelry with country-house interiors

A converted 17th-century farmhouse on the edge of the North Yorkshire Moors, within easy reach of the Scarborough coastline and Ryedale. Inside are lovely high ceilings, and large sash windows look down to the attractive stone village of Wykeham. Yorkshire ales populate the bar, and lunchtime plates represent excellent value. In the evening the charming restaurant is transformed into an intimate candle-lit dining room, where a home-made salmon fishcake could precede the pan-fried venison steak served with dauphinoise potatoes. If a rhubarb and custard pannacotta cannot be resisted, one of the inn's 10 en suite and beautifully furnished bedrooms may also prove tempting.

Open all day all wk **Food** Lunch all wk 12-2 Dinner all wk 6-9 Restaurant menu available Mon-Sat & Sun eve ⊕ FREE HOUSE ◀ Black Sheep, Theakston Best Bitter, Wold Top Bitter. **Facilities** Non-diners area ✿ (Bar Garden) ♦ Children's menu Children's portions Garden ⊟ Parking WiFi ➡ (notice required) **Rooms** 10

The Hare Inn ◎◎◎   PICK OF THE PUBS

tel: 01845 597769 **YO7 2HG**
email: liz@thehare-inn.com
dir: *Exit A170 towards Rievaulx Abbey & Scawton. Pub 1m on right*

Historic inn near idyllic moorland dales

Local lore has it that in medieval times a witch lived here. Shape-shifting into a wandering hare, she was pursued home by the hunt, breathing her last in the cottage after changing back into a witch. Other legends and tales – including a resident ghost – abound at this pretty, pantiled pub, which may have been a brewhouse for local abbeys at Rievaulx and Byland. Things are pretty relaxed today at this secluded dining inn in the North York Moors National Park. You'll find low-beamed ceilings and flagstone floors, a wood-burning stove offering a warm welcome in the bar, with beers coming from Rudgate and other Yorkshire breweries. An old-fashioned kitchen range features in the dining area. Chef-patron Paul Jackson's classy, award-winning menu relies on seasonal specialities. So expect the likes of scallop, celeriac, apple and smoked eel as a starter and rabbit with broccoli, eryngii (king oyster mushroom), salsify and black pudding for a main course.

Open Wed-Sat 12-2 6-9 (Sun 12-4) Closed 2wks end of Jan-beg of Feb, 1wk Nov, 1wk Jun, Sun eve, Mon-Tue **Food** Lunch Wed-Sun 12-3 Dinner Wed-Sat 6-9 ⊕ FREE HOUSE ◀ Rudgate Viking, guest ales Ò Thatchers. ☙ 10 **Facilities** Non-diners area ✿ (Bar Garden) ♦ Children's portions Garden Parking WiFi

The Lion at Settle ★★★★ INN

tel: 01729 822203 & 823459 **Duke St BD24 9DU**
email: relax@thelionsettle.co.uk web: www.thelionsettle.co.uk
dir: *Phone for detailed directions*

Stylish Dales coaching inn

Owned by Thwaites and set in the heart of Settle's 17th-century market place, this inn's interior oozes history and atmosphere, with original inglenook fireplaces, wooden floors and a grand staircase lined with pictures that trace the town's history. It's a comfortable base for exploring the Dales or the spectacular Settle to Carlisle railway line. Expect decent cask ales and a classic pub menu offering freshly prepared pub favourites. Typical examples include devilled whitebait; venison cottage pie; the ever popular Settle pudding of beef steak and Wainwright Ale; and one of the deli boards – butcher's or fish maybe. Leave room for banoffee pecan sundae or warm chocolate and hazelnut brownie. There's a beer festival in September.

The Lion at Settle

Open all day all wk 8am-11pm **Food** Lunch all wk bkfst 8am-10am, Sun-Thu 12-9, Fri-Sat 12-9.30 Dinner Sun-Thu 12-9, Fri-Sat 12-9.30 ⊕ THWAITES INNS OF CHARACTER ◗ Original, Lancaster Bomber & Wainwright, guest ales ♂ Kingstone Press. ♟ 9 **Facilities** Non-diners area ✿ (Bar Outside area) ♦ Children's menu Children's portions Outside area ⋒ Beer festival WiFi 🚐 (notice required) **Rooms** 14

See advert below

SKIPTON
Map 18 SD95

Devonshire Arms at Cracoe

tel: 01756 730237 **Grassington Rd, Cracoe BD23 6LA**
email: portalinns@gmail.com
dir: *Phone for detailed directions*

Old beams and warming fires in traditional inn

Close to the famous village of Grassington at the gateway to the Dales, and famed for its association with the Rhylstone Ladies WI calendar. This convivial and

lovingly renovated 17th-century inn is favoured by Three Peaks ramblers who enjoy a rotating selection of real ales; the drinks list also offers a generous choice of wines sold by the glass, and an eclectic collection of rare bottled refreshments. The inn's menu feature pub classics so perhaps after a field mushroom fricassée, Mr Jackson's pork bangers with creamy mash and onion gravy will go down well; or try succulent short-rib of beef and Burgundy stew with horseradish dumplings.

Open all day all wk 12-11 **Food** Lunch Mon-Fri 12-2.30, Sat 12-8.30, Sun 12-7.30 Dinner Mon-Fri 5-8.30, Sat 12-8.30, Sun 12-7.30 ⊕ MARSTON'S ◗ EPA, Pedigree, guest ale. ♟ 12 **Facilities** Non-diners area ✿ (Bar Garden) ♦ Children's portions Garden ⋒ Parking WiFi 🚐 (notice required)

THIRSK
Map 19 SE48

Little 3

tel: 01845 523782 **13 Finkle St YO7 1DA**
email: info@littlethree.co.uk

Bustling haven for real ale fans

Just off the market square in the centre of Thirsk, the quirkily named Little 3 is run by Sean Kirkley, who has turned the place into a haven for real ale drinkers, and diners as well. Yorkshire breweries such as Timothy Taylor and Theakston dominate the hand pumps at the bar, and there is an extensive whisky selection. Away from the bustling bar, the upstairs brasserie serves seasonal dishes and themed specials boards. Look for crispy sweet chilli pork belly; or strips of blackened lamb flank to start; followed by sausages and mash; shepherd's pie; or steak and ale pie. There's a sandwich menu available most lunchtimes.

Open all day all wk **Food** Lunch Wed-Sat 12-2.30, Sun 12-4 Dinner Wed-Sat 5-9, Sun 4-7 Restaurant menu available Wed-Sat ⊕ FREE HOUSE ◗ Timothy Taylor Landlord, Theakston, Rudgate, Bradfield. ♟ 10 **Facilities** Non-diners area ✿ (Bar Outside area) ♦ Children's menu Children's portions Outside area ⋒ Beer festival Parking WiFi 🚐

THORNTON-LE-DALE
Map 19 SE88

The New Inn

tel: 01751 474226 **Maltongate YO18 7LF**
email: enquire@the-new-inn.com
dir: *A64 N from York towards Scarborough. At Malton take A169 to Pickering. At Pickering rdbt right onto A170, 2m, pub on right*

Warm welcome at a Yorkshire favourite

Standing at the heart of a picturesque village complete with stocks and a market cross, this Georgian coaching house dates back to 1720. The old-world charm of the location is echoed inside the bar and restaurant, with real log fires and exposed beams. Enjoy well-kept Theakston Best Bitter and guest ales, bitters, lagers and wines and tuck into beef and ale stew with herb scones; slow-braised lamb shoulder and minted gravy; and beer battered fish and fat-cut chips.

Open all day all wk **Food** Lunch Mon-Sat 12-2, Sun 12-8 (summer Mon-Sat 12-2.30, Sun 12-8) Dinner Mon-Sat 5.30-8.30, Sun 12-8 (summer Mon-Sat 5-8.30, Sun 12-8) ⊕ STAR PUBS & BARS ◖ Theakston Best Bitter, guest ales. **Facilities** Non-diners area ✿ (Bar Garden) ◗◗ Children's menu Children's portions Garden ⊓ Parking WiFi ᴥ (notice required)

THORNTON WATLASS
Map 19 SE28

The Buck Inn
PICK OF THE PUBS

tel: 01677 422461 **HG4 4AH**
email: the-buck-inn@btconnect.com
dir: *From A1 at Leeming Bar take A684 to Bedale, B6268 towards Masham. Village in 2m*

Plenty of choice for real ale fans

Very much the heart of the local community, this traditional pub is welcoming and relaxed. You'll still see cricketing memorabilia in the Long Room, which overlooks the village green and cricket pitch (the pub is part of the boundary). You'll find up to five real ales in the bar with its open fire, including Theakston and a guest ale such as Gun Dog. There are several separate dining areas and the menu ranges from sandwiches and light bites to traditional, freshly prepared pub fare. You might choose deep-fried whitebait or prawn cocktail to start, then mains of steak and ale pie; gammon steak with egg or pineapple, chips and peas; or Masham rarebit with home-made chutney. There's live jazz music once a month.

Open all wk 12-11 **Food** Lunch Mon-Sat 12-2, Sun 12-3 Dinner Mon-Sat 6-9, Sun 6-8.30 ⊕ FREE HOUSE ◖ Black Sheep Best Bitter, Theakston Best Bitter, Gun Dog Ales, 2 guest ales ♂ Westons Stowford Press. **Facilities** Non-diners area ✿ (Bar Garden) ◗◗ Children's menu Children's portions Play area Garden ⊓ Parking ᴥ (notice required)

TOPCLIFFE
Map 19 SE47

The Angel at Topcliffe

tel: 01845 578000 **YO7 3RW**
email: info@theangelattopcliffe.co.uk
dir: *A1(M) junct 49, A168 to Topcliffe. Over river, pub on right*

Bar and grill serving Yorkshire's best

The Angel is a country pub offering the best of Yorkshire's food and drink in relaxed surroundings. Spacious outdoor terraces are furnished with attractive parasol-shaded tables and chairs. The open-plan interior is equally appealing, with a mix of armchairs, alcove seats and stiff-backed chairs around dark wood tables. Hand-pulled Yorkshire ales include Copper Dragon, while menus embrace sandwiches, hot and cold snacks, and classics such as haddock and chips; or lamb and rosemary meatballs. Matured dry-edge Yorkshire beef steaks from the grill come with all the trimmings. Head for the Sports Room, separate from the bar, for the pool table or a big game on the TV.

Open all day all wk **Food** Lunch Mon-Sat 12-2.30, Sun 12-8 Dinner Mon-Sat 5-9, Sun 12-8 ⊕ FREE HOUSE ◖ Copper Dragon, Theakston, St Austell Tribute. ♇ 13 **Facilities** Non-diners area ✿ (Bar Garden) ◗◗ Children's menu Children's portions Garden ⊓ Parking WiFi ᴥ (notice required)

WASS
Map 19 SE57

Wombwell Arms
PICK OF THE PUBS

tel: 01347 868280 **YO61 4BE**
email: info@wombwellarms.co.uk
dir: *From A1 take A168 to A19 junct. Take York exit, then left after 2.5m, left at Coxwold to Ampleforth. Wass 2m*

Enjoyable home cooking in friendly family-run village inn

In the shadow of the Hambleton Hills, this white-painted village pub dates from the 17th century and was built using stones from the ruins of nearby Byland Abbey. One of the two oak-beamed, flagstone-floored bars has a huge inglenook fireplace, the other a wood-burning stove, and the atmosphere is relaxed and informal; popular with locals, walkers and cyclists, all can be found here enjoying a pint of Helmsley Yorkshire Legend. Modern British meals with a South African twist are prepared from high quality produce – sourced locally as far as possible. There's a great selection of sandwiches at lunchtime and for dinner choose one of the Wombwell classics – steak, mushroom and Guinness pie; or try their South African bobotie – a mild and fruity curry with mango chutney. Leave room for one of the comforting home-made desserts, or a plate of local cheeses.

Open all wk 12-3 6-11 (Sat 12-11 Sun 12-10.30) **Food** Lunch Mon-Fri 12-2, Fri-Sat 12-2.30, Sun 12-3 Dinner Mon-Thu 6-8.30, Fri-Sat 6-9, Sun 6-7.30 Av main course £14 Set menu available ⊕ FREE HOUSE ◖ Helmsley Yorkshire Legend, guest ales. ♇ 10 **Facilities** Non-diners area ✿ (Bar Outside area) ◗◗ Children's menu Children's portions Outside area ⊓ Parking WiFi ᴥ (notice required)

WELBURN
Map 19 SE76

The Crown and Cushion

tel: 01653 618777 **YO60 7DZ**
email: enquiries@thecrownandcushionwelburn.com
web: www.thecrownandcushionwelburn.com
dir: *A64 from York towards Malton. 13m left to Welburn*

Traditional stone-built inn serving quality Yorkshire produce

Exposed stone walls and open log fires characterise the comfortable interior of this spacious yet homely village inn. It boasts a traditional tap room, a bar serving York Guzzler ale, and three separate dining areas. Menus are based on carefully sourced local produce, so expect top quality steaks and the likes of confit pork terrine; peppered-cured venison, pickled cucumber and horseradish; a seafood platter; moules marinière; and roast rump of lamb, aubergine purée, sweet potato fondants, home-dried cherry tomatoes, buttered kale and red wine jus. An ideal stop before or after visiting Castle Howard a mile down the road.

Open all wk 12-3 5-11 (Fri-Sun all day from noon) **Food** Lunch Mon-Sat 12-2.30, Sun 12-4 Dinner Mon-Sat 5.30-9.30, Sun 4-8 ⊕ FREE HOUSE ◀ Black Sheep, York Guzzler Ö Symonds. **Facilities** Non-diners area ◆◆ Children's menu Children's portions Garden ⊐ Parking WiFi ▭ (notice required)

WEST TANFIELD
Map 19 SE27

The Bruce Arms
PICK OF THE PUBS

tel: 01677 470325 **Main St HG4 5JJ**
email: info@thebrucearms.com
dir: On A6108 between Ripon & Masham

A family affair at this 18th-century inn

A change of hands introduced new landlady Gil Richardson to The Bruce Arms in the summer of 2015, along with several members of her family. Front of house is run by Maggie (Gil's niece) and Crystal; their husbands are the kitchen's two chefs; additional members of the family help out when needed. The stone-built inn is a comfy and traditional village pub, complete with beams and log fires, where Theakston ales and Yorkshire cider keep the regulars happy. Diners need have no qualms about the quality of the new menu, which is firmly based on the very best of local game, locally reared meat, and North Sea fish. Try a starter of Nidderdale-shot pigeon with wild mushrooms, apple and Doreen's black pudding. Main courses may include oven-roasted east coast darne of salmon with queen scallop fritters, salsa verde and Lyonnaise potatoes. Treacle tart with Brymor clotted cream concludes an excellent repast.

Open 12-3 6-11 (Sun 12-6) Closed 2wks Feb, Mon, Tue, Wed L, Sun eve **Food** Lunch Thu-Sat 12-3, Sun 12-4 Dinner Wed-Sat 6-9 Av main course £14 Set menu available Restaurant menu available Wed-Sun ⊕ FREE HOUSE ◀ Theakston Best Bitter, guest ales Ö Yorkshire Cider. ⦿ 10 **Facilities** Non-diners area ◆◆ Children's menu Children's portions Outside area ⊐ Parking WiFi ▭ (notice required)

WEST WITTON
Map 19 SE08

The Wensleydale Heifer ★★★★★ RR ⊛
PICK OF THE PUBS

tel: 01969 622322 **Main St DL8 4LS**
web: www.wensleydaleheifer.co.uk
dir: A1 to Leeming Bar junct, A684 towards Bedale for approx 10m to Leyburn, then towards Hawes, 3.5m to West Witton

Stylish all-rounder

Built in 1631, this white-painted coaching inn is right in the heart of the Yorkshire Dales National Park. For a morning coffee, head for the Whisky Lounge, where you can indeed also enjoy a malt whisky, or a pint of Heifer Gold or Black Sheep real ale, if you prefer. Of the two dining areas the Fish Bar, with sea-grass flooring, wooden tables and rattan chairs, is the less formal, while the restaurant, which leads to the garden, is furnished with chocolate leather chairs and linen table cloths, and decorated with distinctive artworks by international artist, Doug Hyde. Whichever room you choose, the food is AA-Rosette quality; start with spiced parsnip soup, curry oil and Heifer croûtons; continue with hake fillet and field mushroom and parmesan risotto; or slow-roast beef cheeks, pancetta and mushroom and baby onion jus. There are whole pages of choice for both vegetarians and vegans, and well as a lobster menu, a grill room menu and a fine choice of tapas and sandwiches.

Open all day all wk **Food** Lunch all wk 12.30-2.30 Dinner all wk 6-9.30 Set menu available Restaurant menu available all wk ⊕ FREE HOUSE ◀ Heifer Gold, Black Sheep Ö Aspall. ⦿ **Facilities** Non-diners area ♣ (Bar Garden) ◆◆ Children's menu Children's portions Garden ⊐ Parking WiFi ▭ **Rooms** 13

WHITBY
Map 19 NZ81

The Magpie Café

tel: 01947 602058 **14 Pier Rd YO21 3PU**
email: ian@magpiecafe.co.uk
dir: Phone for detailed directions

Fish-focussed in every way

The acclaimed Magpie Café has been the home of North Yorkshire's 'best-ever fish and chips' since the late 1930s. You could pop in for just a pint of Cropton, but the excellent views of the harbour from the dining room, together with the prospect of fresh, sustainably fished seafood, could prove too much of a temptation. Just what to choose is the question? An exhaustive list of fish and seafood dishes is offered daily; perhaps opt for a traditional Whitby kipper; Whitby crab parcel; seafood St Jacques; or your choice of fish simply battered and served with chips. Desserts include locally made ice creams; sherry and marzipan fruit cake; and a knickerbocker glory.

Open all day all wk 11.30-9 summer (11.30-8 winter) Closed 25 Dec, 6-31 Jan **Food** Contact pub for food times ⊕ FREE HOUSE ◀ Bradfield Farmers Blonde, Brown Cow, Cropton Blackout & Scoresby Stout, The Captain Cook Slipway. ⦿ 10 **Facilities** ◆◆ Children's menu Children's portions WiFi ▭

WIGHILL
Map 16 SE44

NEW The White Swan
PICK OF THE PUBS

tel: 01937 832217 **Main St LS24 8BQ**
email: info@thewhiteswanwighill.co.uk
dir: A64 onto A659 in Tadcaster. At x-roads (at lights) into Wighill Ln signed Wighill. Pub on right in village

Family-run pub with a passion for good grub

If you fish, shoot, forage or grow veg, swap it here for a pint or a meal. That's the promise at this appealing village pub that even rears its own pigs, or Wiglets, as they call them here in Wighill. Tall stools line the corner bar in the Snug, which stocks a real ale named after the pub, as well as Black Sheep, Moorhouse's and Timothy Taylor Landlord. Cosy, in a country-pub way, the restaurant was once used for filming Catherine Zeta-Jones in TV's *Darling Buds of May*. Today it's the location for enjoying cherrywood-smoked salmon salad; braised shin of beef and ale suet-crust pie; and home-made cider and tarragon-battered haddock, chips and smashed peas. Not only vegetarians will opt for Malaysian pumpkin, chickpea and coconut curry. 'On your bike bites!' – for cyclists, you understand – include American pancakes with smoked bacon, and scrambled eggs on toast. Outside is an old telephone box, now the pub's library.

Open all day Closed Mon **Food** Lunch Tue-Sat 12-3, Sun 12-5 Dinner Tue-Sat 5-9.30 Av main course £12-£15 Set menu available Restaurant menu available Tue-Sat ⊕ FREE HOUSE ◀ Black Sheep Ale, Moorhouse's White Swan Ale, Timothy Taylor Landlord Ö Aspall. **Facilities** Non-diners area ♣ (Bar Garden) ◆◆ Children's menu Children's portions Family room Garden ⊐ Parking ▭ (notice required)

Follow us on twitter
@TheAA_Lifestyle

WOMBLETON

Map 19 SE68

The Plough Inn

tel: 01751 431356 **Main St Y062 7RW**
email: ploughinnwombleton@mail.com **web:** www.theploughinnatwombleton.co.uk
dir: *From A170 between Helmsley & Kirkbymoorside follow signs to Wombleton*

A classic Yorkshire pub in a sleepy village setting

When he retired from his previous job, the landlord bought this local, built a complete new kitchen and renovated the rest of it. Today the traditional warm and genuine Yorkshire hospitality continues, with the serving of fine ales and good food – a tradition started in the 15th century when monks brewed beer for weary travellers. Local produce features in the menus, which change seasonally. Starters may include smoked chicken and avocado salad with raspberry dressing, while main courses range from roast sirloin of Harome beef and Yorkshire pudding to tagliatelle, brie, garlic, tomatoes and aubergine croquet.

Open 12-3 5.30-12 (Mon 5-12 Fri-Sun all day) Closed Mon L **Food** Lunch Tue-Sat 12-2, Sun 12-8 Dinner Mon-Sat 5.30-9, Sun 12-8 Restaurant menu available all wk ⊕ FREE HOUSE ◀ Black Sheep Best Bitter, Theakston Best Bitter ᵹ Symonds. **Facilities** Non-diners area 🐾 (Bar Outside area) 🛉 Children's menu Children's portions Outside area ⩊ Parking WiFi 🚍 (notice required)

YORK

Map 16 SE65

The Judge's Lodging ★★★★★ INN ⊛

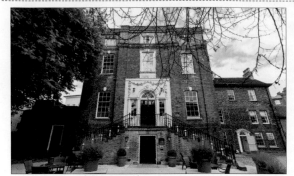

tel: 01904 638733 **9 Lendal YO1 8AQ**
web: www.judgeslodgingsyork.co.uk
dir: *Phone for detailed directions*

Seasonal menu amidst period splendour

Iron-railed steps sweep up to the grand entrance to this former assize court, set off one of York's old town web of narrow lanes and byways. Owning brewery Thwaites carefully and tastefully upgraded this Grade I listed building, incorporating the vaulted cellar bar and secluded cask bar into a stunning period interior. The tree-shaded terrace to the front is a popular place to dine alfresco, selecting from a contemporary, seasonally adjusted menu. Beef and Thwaites ale pie; lobster thermidor; smoked haddock fillet; or barbecue pork ribs may take the eye here; there's also a good range of small plate dishes and sharing boards.

Open all day all wk **Food** Mon-Sat 12-11, Sun 12-10 Av main course £12.95 Set menu available ⊕ THWAITES INNS OF CHARACTER ◀ Wainwright & Lancaster Bomber ᵹ Kingstone Press. 🍷 15 **Facilities** Non-diners area 🛉 Children's menu Children's portions Garden ⩊ WiFi **Rooms** 23

See advert on opposite page

Blue Bell

tel: 01904 654904 **53 Fossgate YO1 9TF**
email: bluebellyork@gmail.com
dir: *At top of Fossgate (near The Shambles)*

A true heritage pub

York's smallest pub, although its vivid red-brick frontage gives its presence away. Serving customers since 1798, it was last refurbished in 1903, thus warranting a Grade II* listing for its hardly-touched interior. The taproom at the front is connected by a long corridor to the snug at the back. Being compact and bijou leaves no room for a kitchen, so it's lunchtime sandwiches only, except on Saturdays (noon-6pm), when you can order beef slow-cooked in Rudgate Ruby Mild beer, with bread and butter. To make up for the culinary limitations, there are seven real ales on tap, and Rosie's Pig and Old Rosie ciders.

Open all day all wk Mon-Thu 11-11 (Fri-Sat 11am-mdnt Sun 12-10.30) **Food** Lunch Sat 12-6 Av main course £4.95 ⊕ PUNCH TAVERNS ◀ Timothy Taylor Landlord, Bradfield Farmers Blonde, Roosters Yankee, Rudgate Ruby Mild, Kelham Island Best Bitter Ö Thatchers Heritage, Westons Rosie's Pig & Old Rosie. ☻ 21
Facilities Non-diners area ☙ (Bar Restaurant) Beer festival WiFi **Notes** ☻

Lamb & Lion Inn ★★★★ INN ◉◉

tel: 01904 612078 **2-4 High Petergate YO1 7EH**
email: gm@lambandlioninnyork.com **web:** www.lambandlioninnyork.com
dir: *From York Station, turn left. Stay in left lane, over Lendal Bridge. At lights left (Theatre Royal on right). At next lights pub on right under Bootham Bar (medieval gate)*

Right in the city's historical centre

Sheltered by one of York's medieval city gates, this inn is close to the magnificent Minster and a handy stop on a circuit of the city walls. The panorama from the elevated beer garden incorporates these historic features; relax here below trees

with Yorkshire craft beers, or settle into one of the cosy snugs in the very atmospheric Georgian interior and peruse the two AA-Rosette menu. A spiced duck pasty with bubble-and-squeak starter, could be followed by braised lamb shoulder, beef cheek, pearl barley, sweet braised red cabbage, carrots and blackberry jelly. Luxury guest bedrooms are available.

Open all day all wk **Food** Lunch Mon-Sat 12-3, Sun 12-8 Dinner Mon-Sat 5-9, Sun 12-8 Av main course £14 Restaurant menu available all wk ⊕ FREE HOUSE ◀ Black Sheep, Copper Dragon, Timothy Taylor, York Guzzler, Saltaire. ☻ 9
Facilities Non-diners area ☙ (Bar Restaurant Garden) ⌗ Children's menu Garden ♒ WiFi ⇌ **Rooms** 12

Lysander Arms

tel: 01904 640845 **Manor Ln, Shipton Rd YO30 5TZ**
email: christine@lysanderarms.co.uk
dir: *Phone for detailed directions*

British menu and a good range of beers

The pub stands on the former RAF Clifton airfield, where Westland Lysander aircraft were based until 1942. The long, fully air-conditioned bar incorporates a pool table, dartboard and large-screen TVs. Restaurant meals range from pan-seared pigeon breast with pickled brambles, spiced ginger waffle and pear purée; and blackened Cajun king prawns with coriander mayo and cherry tomato salad, to chargrilled gammon steak with fresh pineapple, beer-battered onion rings and hand-cut chips; and prime steak pie with button mushrooms, buttered carrots and redcurrant jus. A beer and cider festival takes place over the Early May Bank Holiday weekend.

Open all day all wk **Food** Lunch Tue-Sat 12-2, Sun 12-3 Dinner Tue-Sat 5.30-9 Restaurant menu available Tue-Sat ⊕ FREE HOUSE ◀ Sharp's Doom Bar, York Guzzler, Wychwood Hobgoblin, Copper Dragon, Black Sheep, Theakston, Roosters Ö Rekorderlig. ☻ 8 **Facilities** Non-diners area ☙ (Bar Garden) ⌗ Children's menu Children's portions Play area Garden ♒ Beer festival Cider festival Parking WiFi

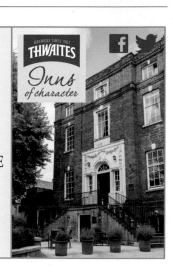

SOUTH YORKSHIRE

BRADFIELD
Map 16 SK29

The Strines Inn

tel: 0114 285 1247 **Bradfield Dale S6 6JE**
email: thestrinesinn@yahoo.co.uk
dir: *N off A57 between Sheffield & Manchester*

Popular free house overlooking Strines Reservoir

Although built as a manor house in 1275, most of the structure is 16th century; it has been an inn since 1771 – the public rooms contain artefacts from its bygone days. The name apparently means 'meeting of waters' in Old English. Locally brewed Acorn Yorkshire Pride shares bar space with ambassadors from the further-flung Marston's, Jennings and Wychwood. Traditional home-made food includes sandwiches, salads, jacket potatoes, hot paninis and burgers then there's pie of the day; giant Yorkshire puddings; liver and onions; butter bean stew; and the 'mammoth' mixed grill. One of the desserts could be their Mars Bar cheesecake. A play area and an enclosure for peacocks, geese and chickens are outside.

Open all day all wk 10.30am–11pm Closed 25 Dec **Food** Lunch Mon-Fri 12-2.30, Sat-Sun 12-9 (summer all wk 12-9) Dinner Mon-Fri 5.30-9, Sat-Sun 12-9 (summer all wk 12-9) Av main course £9.75 ⊕ FREE HOUSE ◨ Marston's Pedigree, Jennings Cocker Hoop, Wychwood Hobgoblin, Acorn Yorkshire Pride. ♟ 10
Facilities Non-diners area ❀ (Bar Restaurant Garden) ♦ Children's menu Children's portions Play area Garden ⊓ Parking ▭ (notice required)

CADEBY
Map 16 SE50

The Cadeby Pub & Restaurant

tel: 01709 864009 **Main St DN5 7SW**
email: info@cadebyinn.co.uk
dir: *A1(M) junct 36, A630 signed Sheffield & Rotherham. At lights, right into Mill Ln signed Sprotbrough. Over River Don, 1st left into Nursery Ln. At T-junct left into Cadeby Rd. Pub on left*

Mid 18th-century village destination pub

The Cadeby stands well back, buffered from the village's main street by a lovely long lawn with tables. Yorkshire-brewed real ales are usually Timothy Taylor Landlord and Black Sheep (plus weekly changing guest ales from the area), while Westons Old Rosie and Stowford Press are on cider duty. Snacks, sandwiches and light meals are available at lunchtime; and the evening menu showcases seasonal dishes prepared in house from the best locally sourced ingredients. Typical choices might be mustard pannacotta, baby beets and goats' cheese crumble to start, followed by lamb rump, cannon and shoulder with smoked pomme purée, baby vegetables and rosemary jus. Certainly leave room for a slice of gin, chocolate and lime cheesecake.

Open all day all wk **Food** Lunch Mon-Fri 12-4.30, Sat-Sun 12-6 Dinner Mon-Fri 6-9, Sat 6-9.30, Sun 12-6 Av main course £13 Set menu available Restaurant menu available Mon-Sat 6-9.30 ⊕ FREE HOUSE ◨ Timothy Taylor Landlord, Black Sheep, guest ales ♥ Westons Old Rosie & Stowford Press. ♟ 9 **Facilities** Non-diners area ❀ (Bar Garden) ♦ Children's menu Children's portions Garden ⊓ Beer festival Cider festival Parking WiFi ▭

PENISTONE
Map 16 SE20

Cubley Hall
PICK OF THE PUBS

tel: 01226 766086 **Mortimer Rd, Cubley S36 9DF**
email: info@cubleyhall.co.uk
dir: *M1 junct 37, A628 towards Manchester, or M1 junct 35a, A616. Hall just S of Penistone*

Impressive building with fascinating history

On the edge of the Peak District National Park, Cubley Hall was built as a country house in the 18th century and became a gentleman's residence in Queen Victoria's reign. It later became a children's home before being transformed into its current role in 1982. Following that, the massive, oak-beamed bar was converted into the restaurant and furnished with old pine tables, chairs and church pews, and the building was extended to incorporate the hotel, which was designed to harmonise with the original mosaic floors, ornate plaster ceilings, oak panelling and stained glass. Food-wise, take your pick from light bites, chalkboard specials and an extensive main menu listing pub classics, a selection of 'proper big' burgers and home-made pizzas. Otherwise choices include meat and potato pie; chicken and mushroom carbonara; chilli con carne; and oven-baked veggie tartlet. The hall is reputedly haunted by friendly Florence Lockley, who married there in 1904 and is affectionately known as Flo.

Open all day all wk 7am–11.30pm **Food** all wk 12-9 Av main course £9.50 Restaurant menu available Sun ⊕ FREE HOUSE ◨ Tetley's Bitter, Black Sheep Best Bitter ♥ Somersby. **Facilities** Non-diners area ❀ (Garden) ♦ Children's menu Children's portions Play area Family room Garden ⊓ Parking WiFi ▭ (notice required)

SHEFFIELD
Map 16 SK38

Broadfield Ale House

tel: 0114 255 0200 **452 Abbeydale Rd S7 1FR**
email: info@thebroadfield.co.uk
dir: *Phone for detailed directions*

An ale house worthy of the name

Silent movie-goers and steam railway passengers were among the first customers at the Broadfield, built just before Queen Victoria died. Millhouses and Ecclesall station no longer exists, but this distinctive pub on the Abbeydale Road is still very much in business. No fewer than nine handles proffer the discerning ale enthusiast a wonderful choice, from the likes of Stancill, Acorn, Black Iris and Blackjack breweries. Pride is taken in the food too, with home-made sausages and pies served with hand-cut chips and mushy peas always in demand; coeliacs, vegans, vegetarians and fish-lovers are also well catered for.

Open all day all wk **Food** all wk 12-10 ⊕ FREE HOUSE/TRUE NORTH BREW CO ◨ Rotating guest ales ♥ Guest cider. **Facilities** Non-diners area ❀ (Bar Garden) ♦ Children's menu Children's portions Garden ⊓ Beer festival WiFi ▭ (notice required)

The Fat Cat
PICK OF THE PUBS

tel: 0114 249 4801 **23 Alma St S3 8SA**
email: info@thefatcat.co.uk
dir: *Phone for detailed directions*

The focus is on the beers

Built in 1832, it was known as The Alma Hotel for many years, then in 1981 it was the first Sheffield pub to introduce guest beers. The policy continues, with constantly changing, mainly microbrewery, guests from across the country, two hand-pumped ciders, unusual bottled beers, Belgian pure fruit juices and British country wines. The pub's own Kelham Island Brewery accounts for at least four of the 11 traditional draught real ales. The smart interior is very much that of a traditional, welcoming back-street pub, with real fires making it feel very cosy, while outside is an attractive walled garden with Victorian-style lanterns and bench seating. Events include the Monday quiz and curry night and an annual beer festival.

Open all wk 12-11 (Fri-Sat 12-12) Closed 25 Dec **Food** Lunch Mon-Fri & Sun 12-3, Sat 12-8 Dinner Mon-Fri 6-8, Sat 12-8 ⊕ FREE HOUSE ◖ Kelham Island Best Bitter & Pale Rider, Timothy Taylor Landlord, guest ales ♂ Thatchers Gold. **Facilities** Non-diners area ✿ (Bar Garden) ⁑ Children's portions Family room Garden Beer festival Parking WiFi ▦

Kelham Island Tavern
PICK OF THE PUBS

tel: 0114 272 2482 **62 Russell St S3 8RW**
email: lewiskelham@gmail.com
dir: *Just off A61 (inner ring road). Follow brown tourist signs for Kelham Island*

City pub with good reputation for its real ales

This 1830s backstreet pub was built to quench the thirst of steelmakers who lived and worked nearby, and in the hands of Lewis Gonda and Trevor Wraith it's become a gem of a busy traditional local. The pub is in a conservation and popular walking area, where old buildings have been converted into stylish apartments, and The Kelham Island Museum round the corner tells the story of the city's industrial heritage. The real ale list is formidable: four residents including Barnsley Bitter and Bradfield Farmers Blonde are joined by 10 ever-changing guests, as well as Westons Old Rosie cider, and a midsummer beer and cider festival at the end of June. Good quality traditional pub food (steak and ale pie, casseroles, veggie choices and a fish dish) is available six days a week. Great in the summer, the pub has won awards for its beer garden and floral displays. Folk nights on Sundays and a quiz night on Mondays pack in the punters.

Open all day all wk 12-12 **Food** Lunch Mon-Sat 12-3 Av main course £6 ⊕ FREE HOUSE ◖ Barnsley Bitter, Bradfield Farmers Blonde, Pictish Brewers Gold, 10 guest ales ♂ Westons Old Rosie & Country Perry. **Facilities** Non-diners area ✿ (Bar Garden) ⁑ Children's portions Family room Garden ☎ Beer festival Cider festival ▦ (notice required)

The Sheffield Tap

tel: 0114 273 7558 **Platform 1B, Sheffield Station, Sheaf St S1 2BP**
email: info@sheffieldtap.com
dir: *Access from Sheaf St & from Platform 1B. (NB limited access from Platform 1B on Fri & Sat)*

Very much on track to serve the best beers

For more than 30 years disused and derelict, the former Edwardian refreshment room and dining rooms of Sheffield Midland Railway Station have become a much praised Grade II listed free house. Painstakingly restored to its former glory by the current custodians, with help from the Railway Heritage Trust, The Sheffield Tap is a beer mecca with its own on-site microbrewery allowing customers to view the complete brewing process while supping a pint or two in comfort. There's 10 real ales, one real cider, 12 keg products and more than 200 bottled beers from around the world. Food is limited to bagged bar snacks, and children are welcome until 8pm every day.

Open all day all wk Closed 25-26 Dec, 1 Jan ⊕ FREE HOUSE ◖ Tapped Brew Company ♂ Thistly Cross. **Facilities** Non-diners area ✿ (Bar Restaurant Outside area) ⁑ Outside area WiFi ▦ (notice required)

TOTLEY
Map 16 SK37

The Cricket Inn
PICK OF THE PUBS

tel: 0114 236 5256 **Penny Ln S17 3AZ**
email: cricket@brewkitchen.co.uk
dir: *Follow A621 from Sheffield, 8m. Right into Hillfoot Rd, 1st left into Penny Ln*

Popular gastro-pub well known for seafood and game dishes

Down a country lane bordered by wooded hills and pastures, this former farmhouse became a pub for the navvies building the nearby Totley railway tunnel in the late 1880s. Walkers and cyclists flock here, while dogs and children are made to feel welcome too. Chef Richard Smith co-runs it with the Thornbridge Brewery in Bakewell, which naturally enough provides the real ales. Richard's kitchen team under Marco Caires produces mixed grill of salmon, sea bass, tiger prawn brochettes, scallops and squid; white bean and chickpea cake with giant couscous and harissa; and a variety of Portuguese dishes, including espetada; Marco's signature dish featuring herby pieces of chargrilled sirloin steak. They also smoke their own fish and meats, and giant feasts are available for groups of eight and over. For a dessert alternative, try a whole-baked Barncliffe Yorkshire Brie — it's enough for two. With three days advance, a feasting menu for a minimum of eight people is available. Summer barbecues are held in the field behind the pub and cricket is played next door.

Open all day all wk 11-11 **Food** all wk 12-9.30 Set menu available ⊕ FREE HOUSE/ BREWKITCHEN LTD ◖ Thornbridge Wild Swan, Lord Marples, Jaipur ♂ Thatchers Gold, Aspall. ☙ 10 **Facilities** Non-diners area ✿ (Bar Restaurant Garden) ⁑ Children's menu Children's portions Garden ☎ Parking WiFi ▦ (notice required)

WEST YORKSHIRE

BRADFORD
Map 19 SE13

New Beehive Inn

tel: 01274 721784 **169-171 Westgate BD1 3AA**
email: newbeehiveinn+21@btinternet.com
dir: *Phone for detailed directions*

Step back in time at an inn with lots of character

Dating from 1901 and centrally situated with many tourist attractions nearby, this classic Edwardian inn retains its period Arts and Crafts atmosphere with five separate bars and gas lighting. It is on the national inventory list of historic pubs. Outside, with a complete change of mood, you can relax in the Mediterranean-style courtyard. The pub offers a good range of unusual real ales, such as Salamander Mudpuppy and Abbeydale Moonshine, and a selection of over 100 malt whiskies, served alongside some simple bar snacks. Music fans should attend the cellar bar, which is open at weekends and features regular live bands.

Open all day all wk ⊕ FREE HOUSE ◀ Kelham Island Best Bitter, Abbeydale Moonshine, Salamander Mudpuppy, Ilkley Mary Jane, Saltaire Cascade Pale Ale ♂ Westons Old Rosie. **Facilities** Non-diners area ♦ Family room Garden ⊟ Parking WiFi ⬛

CALVERLEY
Map 19 SE23

Calverley Arms

tel: 0113 255 7771 **Calverley Ln LS28 5QQ**
email: calverleyarmspudsey@vintageinn.co.uk
dir: *Phone for detailed directions*

Victorian country house in landscaped grounds

Pleasantly located in the gently rolling countryside of the Aire Valley, with the popular Leeds & Liverpool Canal just across the fields. This very substantial village-edge inn makes the most of its situation, with restful views from the leafy beer garden. The rustic theme continues inside, with lots of wood, brick and fireplaces. Part of the Vintage Inns group, the fare reflects their quality menus – sharing and grazing choices; sandwiches; steaks; burgers and stone-baked pizzas sit alongside mains such as pan-fried lamb rump and cheddar shepherd's pie; beef and merlot puff-pastry pie; and Eton tidy cheesecake.

Open all day all wk **Food** all wk 12-10 Set menu available Restaurant menu available all wk ⊕ MITCHELLS & BUTLERS ◀ Leeds Pale, Sharp's Doom Bar, Black Sheep ♂ Aspall. ♟ **Facilities** Non-diners area ♦ Children's menu Children's portions Garden Outside area ⊟ Parking WiFi ⬛ (notice required)

EMLEY
Map 16 SE21

The White Horse

tel: 01924 849823 **2 Chapel Ln HD8 9SP**
email: whitehorse@ossett-brewery.co.uk
dir: *M1 junct 38, A637 towards Huddersfield. At rdbt left onto A636, then right to Emley*

The hub of the community

On the old coaching route to Huddersfield and Halifax on the edge of the village, this refurbished 18th-century pub has views towards Emley Moor Mast and the surrounding countryside. The pub is popular with walkers, cyclists and locals – walking maps are available from the bar, which is warmed by a working Yorkshire range. Of the eight cask ales, four are permanent (including their own Ossett Brewery ales), and four are ever-rotating guests featuring microbreweries. A straightforward menu offers the likes of mushroom Stroganoff; chicken breast stuffed with Wensleydale; vegetable lasagne; and chorizo chicken with rice and salad. Look to the blackboards for daily specials and desserts.

Open all day all wk 12-11 **Food** all wk 12-9 ⊕ FREE HOUSE/OSSETT BREWERY ◀ Excelsior & Silver King, Emley Cross, Yorkshire Blonde, guest ales ♂ Rotating guest ciders. ♟ 9 **Facilities** Non-diners area ♣ (Bar Garden) ♦ Children's portions Family room Garden ⊟ Parking ⬛ (notice required)

HALIFAX
Map 19 SE02

Shibden Mill Inn ★★★★★ INN ⊛⊛　PICK OF THE PUBS

See Pick of the Pubs on opposite page and advert on page 588

HARTSHEAD
Map 16 SE12

The Gray Ox Inn

tel: 01274 872845 **15 Hartshead Ln WF15 8AL**
email: info@grayoxinn.co.uk
dir: *M62 junct 25, A644 signed Dewsbury. Take A62, branch left signed Hartshead & Moor Top/B6119. Left to Hartshead*

Pennine-fringe inn with great views and fine food

Originally a farmhouse that sold ale, this rural inn dating from 1709 occupies a commanding position overlooking the Calder Valley. Ales from Marston's, Jennings and a guest brewery are in the bar, where reminders of the pub's former life can be seen, in winter by the flickering light of the huge log fire. Fine locally-sourced dishes prepared by a five-strong kitchen team include braised pig's cheek terrine, black pudding fritter, apple and vanilla compôte as a starter, followed by roast North Yorkshire venison loin, braised shoulder cottage pie, venison sausage, truffle mash, bubble-and-squeak; or king prawn, cod, sweet potato and chickpea curry. Daily fish specials are also a fixture.

Open all wk 12-3.30 6-12 (Sun 12-10.30) **Food** Lunch Mon-Sat 12-2, Sun 12-7 Dinner Mon-Fri 6-9, Sat 6-9.30, Sun 12-7 Set menu available ⊕ MARSTON'S ◀ Jennings Cumberland Ale, Cocker Hoop & Sneck Lifter, guest ale. ♟ 12 **Facilities** Non-diners area ♣ (Bar Garden) ♦ Children's menu Children's portions Garden ⊟ Parking WiFi ⬛

HAWORTH
Map 19 SE03

The Fleece Inn

tel: 01535 642172 **67 Main St BD22 8DA**
email: info@fleeceinnhaworth.co.uk
dir: *From B6142 in Haworth centre into Butt Ln. Left at T-junct into Main St*

Unchanging town stalwart in Brontë country

Solidly planted on the steep cobbled road in Haworth's old town, this gritstone inn dates from the days when the Brontë sisters were writing their novels in the village vicarage. The enticing pub is owned by the Timothy Taylor Brewery; their award-winning Yorkshire beers as reliable as the steam trains on the famous heritage railway at the foot of the hill. Escape the hurly-burly and indulge in a home-made pie of the day; lamb's liver, crispy bacon, mash and onion gravy; or a warm pulled pork and BBQ sauce sandwich: no-nonsense, filling fare (with some interesting starters) is the staple here. Each Monday evening the town's celebrated brass band practices upstairs.

Open all day all wk **Food** Lunch Mon-Fri 12-9, Sat 10-9, Sun 10am-noon (bkfst) 12-7 Dinner Mon-Fri 12-9, Sat 10-9, Sun 12-7 Av main course £9.25 Set menu available ⊕ TIMOTHY TAYLOR ◀ Landlord, Golden Best, Ram Tam & Boltmaker ♂ Westons Stowford Press, Rekorderlig, Old Mout. ♟ 10 **Facilities** Non-diners area ♣ (Bar Restaurant Garden) ♦ Children's menu Children's portions Family room Garden ⊟ WiFi ⬛ (notice required)

PICK OF THE PUBS

Shibden Mill Inn ★★★★★ INN ❀❀

HALIFAX   Map 19 SE02

tel: 01422 365840
Shibden Mill Fold HX3 7UL
email: enquiries@shibdenmillinn.com
web: www.shibdenmillinn.com
dir: *From A58 into Kell Ln. 0.5m, left into Blake Hill*

Award-winning food in renovated corn mill

The Shibden Valley used to be an important wool production area, the waters of Red Beck powering this 17th-century former spinning mill until the industry collapsed in the late 1800s. Now it's a charming inn with open fires, oak beams, small windows and heavy tiles, happily enjoying a more civilised existence below overhanging trees in a wooded glen that makes Halifax just down the road seem a thousand miles away. The beer garden is extremely popular, not least with real ale fans: a brew called Shibden Mill, made especially for the inn, sits alongside the ever-reliable Black Sheep and three guest ales. With two AA Rosettes, the restaurant attracts those who enjoy excellent food prepared from trusted local growers and suppliers, and a seasonal menu which combines newly conceived dishes with old favourites. Such is the Shibden's focus on customer enjoyment that menu titles such as 'Vegetarian and comforts' and 'Inn fillers' – in addition to the usual three

courses – leave no room for disappointment. From the vegetarian selection may come butternut squash, tomato and Barnscliffe brie lasagne, with pine nuts, roasted beetroots, sweetcorn, candied walnuts and garlic bread. A popular 'Inn filler' is the battered haddock sandwich with lemon and cucumber relish. Otherwise look to a starter of skrei cod if in season, served with cauliflower couscous, sorrel and pomegranate. Rabbit and tarragon pie with crab bisque and roasted langoustine may appear among the main dishes. Finish with a rum and banana baba with its caramelised banana, toffee mousse and banoffee ice cream. Gourmet dinners can be arranged – an ideal opportunity to book one of the inn's luxury bedrooms.

Open all day all wk Closed 25-26 Dec eve & 1 Jan eve **Food** Bkfst Mon-Fri 7am-10am, Sat-Sun 8am-10am Lunch Mon-Thu 12-2, Fri-Sat 12-2.30, Sun 12-7.30 Dinner Mon-Thu 5.30-9, Fri 5.30-9.30, Sat 6-9.30, Sun 12-7.30 Set menu & restaurant menu available all wk ⊕ FREE HOUSE ◀ John Smith's, Black Sheep, Shibden Mill, 3 guest ales ♈ 22 **Facilities** Non-diners area ♦ Children's menu Children's portions Garden ☂ Parking WiFi **Rooms** 11

Shibden Mill Inn

Shibden Mill Fold, Shibden, Halifax, West Yorkshire HX3 7UL • **Tel:** 01422 365840 • **Fax:** 01422 362971
Website: www.shibdenmillinn.com • **Email:** enquiries@shibdenmillinn.com

For over 350 years *The Shibden Mill Inn* has been at the heart of life in West Yorkshire's Shibden Valley. It's a magical place where generation after generation of locals have enjoyed time well spent with friends and family, sharing in life's special moments and shaping memories to last a life time.

The Inn's reputation for warm hospitality, premier gastro dining and first class accommodation draws people to the Shibden Valley from far and wide, and the Mill has naturally become a popular choice for those wishing to savour a sumptuous weekend break or mid-week stay.

Stunning countryside walks are in easy reach, as too are the bright lights and city centre shopping on offer in Leeds. From its unique location, *The Shibden Mill Inn* offers easy access to the very best to be found in this delightful part of West Yorkshire. However there are those who during their stay simply wish to relax and unwind in the beautiful surrounds of this 17th-century property, where once you've arrived and unpacked, there's no reason to leave.

Whatever the occasion *The Shibden Mill Inn* combines first class service and accommodation of the highest order, to ensure a memorable experience that delivers everything you ask of it, and more.

Crowned Yorkshire's Favourite Pub • UK Food Pub of the Year

Inn of the Year • Sunday Lunch Pub of the Year

HAWORTH *continued*

The Old White Lion Hotel

tel: 01535 642313 **Main St BD22 8DU**
email: enquiries@oldwhitelionhotel.com
dir: *A629 onto B6142, 0.5m past Haworth Station*

Charming inn in the Brontë family's home town

This traditional family-run 300-year-old coaching inn looks down onto the cobbled Main Street of the famous Brontë town of Haworth. In the charming bar the ceiling beams are supported by timber posts, and locals appreciatively quaff their pints of guest ale. Food is taken seriously and 'dispensed with hospitality and good measure'. Bar snacks include baguettes, salads and jackets, while a meal in the Gimmerton Restaurant might include belly pork, king scallops with cauliflower purée and dry-cured pancetta, followed by pan-fried pheasant breast wrapped in home-dried bacon with potato rösti and Madeira sauce. Vegetarians are well catered for.

Open all day all wk 11-11 (Sun 12-10.30) **Food** Lunch Mon-Fri 12-2.30, Sat-Sun all day Dinner Mon-Fri 6-9.30, Sat-Sun all day Set menu available all wk evenings only ⊕ FREE HOUSE ◀ Tetley's Bitter, John Smith's, local guest ales. ☻ 9 **Facilities** Non-diners area ♦ Children's menu Children's portions Parking WiFi ⊷

ILKLEY	Map 19 SE14

The Crescent Inn

tel: 01943 811250 **Brook St LS29 8DG**
email: manager@thecrescentinn.co.uk
dir: *On corner of A65 (Church St) & Brook St*

Vast range of local real ales and good food

Part of a hotel dating back to 1861, The Crescent is a landmark building in the centre of Ilkley and it shares the site with its sister restaurant next door. The pub blends original Victorian features such as an open fire with contemporary interiors including handcrafted furniture upholstered in local cloth. Choose from an ever-changing range of real ales from local breweries such as Saltaire Blonde or pick one of the 15 wines by the glass. Unpretentious and enjoyable dishes on the menu include a pulled beef and horseradish sandwich; boneless buffalo wings; a selection of burgers; and tandoori chicken salad.

Open all day all wk **Food** Lunch Mon-Fri 12-3, Sat-Sun all day Dinner Mon-Fri 5.30-9, Sat-Sun all day Av main course £8.95 ⊕ FREE HOUSE ◀ Saltaire Blonde, Ilkley Mary Jane, Copper Dragon Best Bitter, Leeds Pale, guest ales Ö Westons Stowford Press. ☻ 15 **Facilities** Non-diners area ♣ (Bar Restaurant Outside area) ♦ Children's menu Children's portions Outside area ⊓ WiFi ⊷ (notice required)

NEW Friends of Ham

tel: 01943 604344 **8 Wells Rd LS29 9JD**
email: ilkley@friendsofham.com
dir: *From lights on A65 in Ilkley follow Ilkley Moor sign into Brook St. At T-junct left onto B6382 signed Ben Rhydding. 1st right into Wells Rd*

A continental flourish at the heart of Ilkley

This split level charcuterie and bar occupies the skilfully adapted former editorial offices of the Ilkley Gazette. The inspiring choice of real ales from Yorkshire's finest microbreweries and beyond, and the range of carefully selected European wines are themselves newsworthy; the carefully selected grazing menu of the choicest cured meats and artisan cheeses from both home shores and the continent headline the specialist menu. The meats are from high-welfare farms, many of which recognise the Slow Food movement. Special events here can include hands-on cheesemaking. The deli-takeaway provides a fine repast for a ramble on the famous moor above.

Open all day all wk **Food** all wk 10am-close Av main course £10 ⊕ FREE HOUSE ◀ Ghost Spectre, Ilkley Mary Jane, Kirkstall Pale Ale, Summer Wine Teleporter Ö Gwynt y Ddraig Dabinett, Sandford Orchards Fanny's Bramble, Thistly Cross Original. ☻ 22 **Facilities** Non-diners area ♣ (Bar Outside area) ♦ Outside area ⊓ WiFi

Ilkley Moor Vaults

tel: 01943 607012 **Stockeld Rd LS29 9HD**
email: info@ilkleymoorvaults.co.uk
dir: *From Ilkley on A65 towards Skipton. Pub on right*

Proper pub, roaring fire, warm welcome

Known locally as The Taps, it sits at the start of the Dales Way above the old packhorse bridge across the River Wharfe. A popular and stylish establishment, it is equally good for a pint of real ale or a classic dish of pub food – expect the likes of sausage and mash with Yorkshire pudding; rib of beef for two; smoked haddock gratin; and haddock and chips. An ever-changing specials board, full gluten-free menu, impressive children's menu and early bird deals complete the food offerings. A large function room caters for weddings and private parties.

Open 12-3 5-11 (Sat-Sun all day) Closed Mon (ex BHs) **Food** Lunch Tue-Fri 12-2.30, Sat 12-3, Sun 12-6 Dinner Tue-Sat 5.30-9, Sun 12-6 Set menu available Restaurant menu available Tue-Sun ⊕ STAR PUBS & BARS ◀ Timothy Taylor Landlord, Caledonian Deuchars IPA, Theakston Black Bull Bitter. ☻ 9 **Facilities** Non-diners area ♣ (Bar Restaurant Garden) ♦ Children's menu Children's portions Garden ⊓ Parking WiFi ⊷ (notice required)

KIRKBURTON	Map 16 SE11

The Woodman Inn ★★★★ INN

tel: 01484 605778 **Thunderbridge Ln HD8 0PX**
email: chris@woodman-inn.com **web:** www.woodman-inn.com
dir: *1.4m SW of Kirkburton. From Huddersfield take A629 towards Sheffield. Follow brown Woodman Inn signs*

Smart inn with proud Yorkshire provenance

Hidden in a charming hamlet of weavers' cottages in a secluded wooded valley, The Woodman Inn comes up trumps in any search for the perfect Yorkshire inn. Real ales are from county breweries, including the sublime Bradfield Farmers Blonde. Sup this in a long, cosy, log-fire warmed beamed room wrapped around the bar or in the restaurant, where rustic gastro-food makes the most of Yorkshire's produce. Pork belly, ham hock and black pudding terrine with fig and pear chutney; or slow-cooked lamb shoulder, braised red cabbage, potato purée and redcurrant sauce are just two dishes to try.

Open all day all wk **Food** Lunch Mon-Fri 12-2.30, Sat 12-4, Sun 12-7 Dinner Mon-Sat 5-9, Sun 12-7 Av main course £15 ⊕ FREE HOUSE ◀ Small World, Bradfield Farmers Blonde, Timothy Taylor Golden Best. ☻ 14 **Facilities** Non-diners area ♣ (Bar Garden Outside area) ♦ Children's menu Children's portions Garden Outside area ⊓ Parking WiFi ⊷ (notice required) **Rooms** 13

LEEDS
Map 19 SE23

The Cross Keys
PICK OF THE PUBS

tel: 0113 243 3711 **107 Water Ln LS11 5WD**
email: info@the-crosskeys.com
dir: *0.5m from Leeds Station: right into Neville St, right into Water Ln. Pass Globe Rd, pub on left*

Robust food in a historic city centre pub

Built in 1802, The Cross Keys was a watering hole for local foundry workers and it's where steam engine inventor James Watt reputedly hired a room to spy on his competitor Matthew Murray. To learn Murray's trade secrets Watt bought drinks for foundry workers relaxing here after work. This city centre pub has a country pub atmosphere, with hand-pulled pints from local microbreweries complementing food recreated from long lost recipes for traditional British dishes. The best seasonal produce goes into dishes such as braised pig's cheek, mash, braised fennel and cider sauce, which might precede a main course of lamb belly with celeriac purée, celeriac fondant and roasted shallots.

Open all day all wk 12-11 (Fri-Sat 12-12 Sun 12-10.30) Closed 25-26 Dec, 1 Jan **Food** Lunch Mon-Thu 12-3, Fri-Sat 12-9.30, Sun 12-5.30 Dinner Mon-Thu 5-9.30, Fri-Sat 12-9.30 ⊕ FREE HOUSE ◀ North Brewing Co. Prototype, rotating guest ales ♂ Cornish Orchards. ♟ 12 **Facilities** Non-diners area ✿ (Bar Restaurant Garden) ♦ Children's menu Children's portions Garden ⊓ WiFi ▭

NEW Friends of Ham

tel: 0113 242 0275 **4-8 New Station St LS1 5DL**
email: leeds@friendsofham.com
dir: *On one-way street to railway station*

Deceptively small bar with astonishing beers and tapas

This quirky, on-trend bar in the shadow of Leeds railway station lifts experimentation well above the ordinary. It's a charcuterie proffering classic cured meats and rarely seen cheeses gleaned from far-and-wide. Add to this an extravagant selection of 14 draught, craft and cask keg beers; bottled ales and real ciders which change with a frequency that astonishes, as well as 25 wines and sherries and you have an upbeat location well worth seeking out. Look beyond the thin, narrow bar for the basement where there's room to relax and mix-and-match to your heart's content. Horse Cranium stout with paprika boquerones, anyone?

Open all day all wk Closed 25-26 Dec, 1 Jan **Food** all wk 11-11 ⊕ FREE HOUSE ◀ Kirkstall Pale Ale ♂ Lilley's Bee Sting Still Perry, Sandford Orchards Devon Scrumpy. ♟ 25 **Facilities** Non-diners area ✿ (Bar Restaurant) ♦ WiFi ▭ (notice required)

LINTHWAITE
Map 16 SE11

The Sair Inn

tel: 01484 842310 **Lane Top HD7 5SG**
dir: *From Huddersfield take A62 (Oldham road) for 3.5m. Left just before lights at bus stop (in centre of road) into Hoyle Ing & follow sign*

Own-brewed ales and welcoming atmosphere

You won't be able to eat here, but this old hilltop alehouse has enough character in its four small rooms to make up for that; three are heated by hot Yorkshire ranges in winter. Landlord Ron Crabtree has brewed his own beers for over 34 years and they are much sought after by real ale aficionados. Imported German lagers are available, too. In summer the outside drinking area catches the afternoon sun and commands views across the Colne Valley.

Open all wk 5-11 (Sat 12-11 Sun 12-10.30) ⊕ FREE HOUSE ◀ Linfit Bitter, Special Bitter, Gold Medal, Autumn Gold, Old Eli ♂ Pure North Original.
Facilities Non-diners area ✿ (Bar Outside area) ♦ Outside area WiFi ▭ (notice required)

LINTON
Map 16 SE34

The Windmill Inn ★★★★ INN

tel: 01937 582209 **Main St LS22 4HT**
email: enquiries@thewindmillinnlinton.co.uk web: www.thewindmillinnlinton.co.uk
dir: *From A1 exit at Tadcaster/Otley junct, follow Otley signs. In Collingham follow Linton signs*

Historic pub with a diverse menu

Once the home of a long-forgotten miller, this pleasant village pub is made up of small beamed rooms that have been stripped back to bare stone, presumably the original 14th-century walls. A coaching inn since the 18th century, polished antique settles, log fires, oak beams and copper-topped cast-iron tables set the scene in which to enjoy good pub food in the bar or restaurant. A sample dinner menu features starters like chicken liver parfait with toast and plum and apple chutney; and warm pork and apple tart; then mains such as slow-roasted pork belly with black pudding mash and apple jus; or harissa chicken with salad, coleslaw and warm pitta bread. A beer festival is held in July. The Windmill also offers two spacious boutique bed and breakfast apartments.

Open all wk 11-3 5.30-11 (Fri-Sat 11-11 Sun 12-10.30) Closed 1 Jan **Food** Lunch Mon-Fri 12-2, Sat 12-9, Sun 12-5.45 Dinner Sat 12-9 ⊕ HEINEKEN ◀ Theakston Best Bitter, Caledonian, John Smith's. ♟ 12 **Facilities** Non-diners area ✿ (Bar Garden) ♦ Children's menu Children's portions Garden ⊓ Beer festival Parking WiFi ▭ (notice required) **Rooms** 2

MARSDEN — Map 16 SE01

The Olive Branch

tel: 01484 844487 **Manchester Rd HD7 6LU**
email: eat@olivebranch.uk.com
dir: *On A62 between Marsden & Slaithwaite, 6m from Huddersfield*

Highly regarded brasserie-style food

Enter this traditional 19th-century inn on a former packhorse route above the River Colne and the Huddersfield Canal and you'll find yourself in a rambling series of rooms, fire-warmed in winter. The restaurant's brasserie-style food is exemplified by starters of local forest mushroom risotto, parmesan and thyme with white truffle oil; or smoked haddock fish cakes, while typical main dishes include braised lamb shank, black pudding mash with garlic and rosemary jus and black pudding mash; or rosettes of English beef fillet, spinach, fondant and four peppercorn sauce; the beef (proudly sourced from Yorkshire farms) is aged for up to 50 days. Enjoy a pint of Greenfield Dobcross Bitter from Saddleworth on the sun deck and admire the views of Marsden Moor Estate.

Open Tue-Sat 5.30pm-11pm (Sun 12-10.30) Closed Mon eve **Food** Lunch Sun 12-8 Dinner Tue-Sat 6.30-9, Sun 12-8 Set menu available Restaurant menu available Tue-Sat FREE HOUSE Greenfield Dobcross Bitter & Ale, Nook. **Facilities** Non-diners area Children's menu Children's portions Garden Parking WiFi

RIPPONDEN — Map 16 SE01

Old Bridge Inn

tel: 01422 822595 **Priest Ln HX6 4DF**
email: tim@theoldbridgeinn.co.uk **web:** www.theoldbridgeinn.co.uk
dir: *In village centre by church*

Probably West Yorkshire's oldest hostelry

An inn has stood by Ripponden's old bridge, and even earlier ford, since at least 1307. The lower bar is of cruck-frame construction, and the top bar retains its wattle and daub walls, partly later encased in stone. In addition to Timothy Taylor real ales, including Ram Tam and two guests, 14 wines are offered by the glass. Expect main courses like sweet potato, asparagus and spinach Malaysian curry; wild mushroom, pea and sweet pepper risotto; or poached haddock fillet with prawns in creamy cheese sauce. Apparently the salad buffet has been pleasing punters since 1963. Seating outside overlooks the River Ryburn. Booking for meals is recommended.

Open all wk 12-3 5-11 (Fri-Sat 12-11.30 Sun 12-10.30) Closed 25 Dec **Food** Lunch Mon-Sat 12-2, Sun 12-4 Dinner Mon-Thu 5-9, Fri-Sat 5-9.30 Av main course £12.50 FREE HOUSE Timothy Taylor Landlord, Golden Best, Best Bitter, Ram Tam, rotating guest ales Aspall Harry Sparrow. 14 **Facilities** Non-diners area Children's portions Garden Outside area Parking WiFi

SHELLEY — Map 16 SE21

The Three Acres Inn — PICK OF THE PUBS

tel: 01484 602606 **HD8 8LR**
email: info@3acres.com
dir: *From Huddersfield take A629 then B6116, turn left for village*

Welcoming old drovers' inn with a reputation for good food

This old drovers' inn is tucked away in the rolling green countryside of the Pennines, about a 20-minute drive south east of Huddersfield. An ideal stopping off place for travellers heading north to the Yorkshire Dales, the pub has built a reputation for good quality food and a welcoming atmosphere. The spacious interior has a traditional feel with exposed beams and large fireplaces. On summer evenings, sit out on the deck with a pint of Black Sheep (to remind you of the drovers) or a glass of wine and soak up the fabulous views. The food served in both bar and restaurant successfully fuses traditional English with international influences. A typical three-course meal might be Creole-spiced crab gumbo; braised Bolster Moor oxtail; date and sultana pudding with salted caramel sauce and hazelnut ice cream. A wide range of lighter meals is available at lunchtime.

Open all wk 12-3 6-11 (Fri-Sat 12-3 5-11) Closed 1 Jan eve, 25-26 Dec eve, 31 Dec L **Food** Lunch all wk 12-2 Dinner Sun-Thu 6.30-9.30, Fri-Sat 5.30-9.30 Set menu available Restaurant menu available all wk FREE HOUSE Timothy Taylor Landlord, Black Sheep, Copper Dragon, Bradfield Farmers Blonde, Small World. 19 **Facilities** Children's portions Garden Parking WiFi

SOWERBY BRIDGE — Map 16 SE02

The Alma Inn

tel: 01422 823334 **Cotton Stones HX6 4NS**
email: info@almainn.com
dir: *Exit A58 at Triangle between Sowerby Bridge & Ripponden. Follow signs for Cotton Stones*

Country inn with home-cooked food

An old stone inn set in a dramatically beautiful location at Cotton Stones with stunning views of the Ryburn Valley. Outside seating can accommodate 200 customers, while the interior features stone-flagged floors and real fires. The cosy bar serves several ales including a guest, and a vast selection of Belgian bottled beers, each with its individual glass. The appeal of the restaurant area revolves around the wood-burning pizza oven which is on display, the only one in the Calderdale area. Other choices might include hot sandwiches (served from noon to 6pm); home-made meat and potato pie; Thai green curry; and gammon steak, two fried eggs, hand-cut chips and garden peas.

Open all day all wk 12-10.30 **Food** Mon-Thu 12-10, Fri-Sat 12-10.30, Sun 12-9 FREE HOUSE Timothy Taylor Landlord & Golden Best, Tetley's Bitter, guest ales. 10 **Facilities** Non-diners area (Bar Garden) Children's portions Garden Beer festival Parking WiFi (notice required)

How have pubs changed over the last 20 years?
See page 12

CHANNEL ISLANDS
GUERNSEY

CASTEL — Map 24

Fleur du Jardin — PICK OF THE PUBS

tel: 01481 257996 **Kings Mills GY5 7JT**
email: info@fleurdujardin.com
dir: *2.5m from town centre*

Island dining-pub with heaps of awards

Named after a long-vanished breed of Guernsey cattle, this magnificent granite and golden stone property has slumbered here for over 500 years. You can see the evidence in the low, beamed ceiling, old fireplaces and stone features, yet such seasoned charm is cleverly complemented by contemporary decor and design. With the coast so close in all directions, fresh seafood, such as baked Guernsey crab, is an important part of the menu; indeed, you may well see a local fisherman lugging a weighty sea bass through to the kitchen. Pork may come from pigs raised listening to soothing music on a local farm. Other contenders for your enjoyment include Thai red curry; a sizzling chicken, beef or king prawn platter; and specials, such as slow-braised lamb shank, and wild mushroom risotto. After the short walk from Vazon Bay, head for the bar and its ever-changing selection of island and mainland beers, real cider from nearby Castel and carefully selected wines.

Open all day all wk **Food** Lunch all wk 12-2 Dinner all wk 6-9 Av main course £12 Set menu available Restaurant menu available all wk ⊕ FREE HOUSE ◀ Arundel, Liberation Guernsey Sunbeam, Fuller's London Pride, Goose Eye Wonkey Donkey, Sharp's Doom Bar, guest ales ♂ Rocquette. ♀ 12 **Facilities** Non-diners area ♣ (Bar Restaurant Garden) ♦ Children's menu Children's portions Garden ⊟ Parking WiFi ➡ (notice required)

ST PETER PORT — Map 24

The Pickled Pig ★★★ HL

tel: 01481 721431 **Duke of Normandie Hotel, Lefebvre St GY1 2JP**
email: enquiries@dukeofnormandie.com **web:** www.dukeofnormandie.com
dir: *From harbour rdbt into St Julians Av, 3rd left into Anns Place, continue to right, up hill, left into Lefebvre St, archway entrance on right*

Maritime theme and good pub dishes

Part of the Duke of Normandie Hotel, The Pickled Pig attracts a happy mix of Guernsey locals and hotel residents. You can be served your refreshments out in the suntrap courtyard beer garden in warmer weather. The lunch and dinner menus proffer traditional pub favourites, plus the likes of vegetarian red Thai curry; pan-roasted chicken supreme with bubble-and-squeak; and pumpkin and goats' cheese ravioli. At least 80% of the Pickled Pig's produce is sourced locally, including beef from Meadow Court Farm, just a short drive away.

Open all day all wk 11am-11.30pm **Food** Lunch all wk 12-2 Dinner all wk 5.30-9.30 Av main course £13 ⊕ FREE HOUSE ◀ Liberation, Randall's of Guernsey Patois, Puskang ♂ Rocquette. ♀ 14 **Facilities** Non-diners area ♦ Children's menu Children's portions Outside area ⊟ Parking WiFi ➡ (notice required) **Rooms** 37

JERSEY

ROZEL — Map 24

NEW The Rozel Pub & Dining

tel: 01534 863438 **La Vallee de Rozel JE3 6AJ**
email: info@rozelpubanddining.co.uk
dir: *From St Helier to St Martin. At T-junct in St Martin (opposite church) turn right, 1st left signed Rozel Bay. At next T-junct right signed Rozel Bay. Pub on left as entering village*

A country pub by the sea

Now refurbished inside and out, The Rozel is a short stroll from Château la Chaire, its sister property, just inland from Rozel Bay in Jersey's north-eastern corner. A popular community pub, it offers sandwiches, sharing platters and salads, while from the list of starters come quail and black pudding mini Scotch eggs; country-style tomato and basil soup; and prawn and crayfish cocktail. Moving on to mains there's toad-in-the-hole; slow-roasted pork belly with bubble-and-squeak and apple sauce; and cider-battered cod with chunky chips and mushy peas. Ask about chef's daily specials.

Open all day all wk **Food** Lunch Mon-Sat 12-2.15, Sun 12-3.30 Dinner Mon-Thu 6-9, Fri-Sat 6-9.30 Av main course £12 ⊕ LIBERATION BREWERY ◀ Liberation Ale, Bass. ♀ 10 **Facilities** Non-diners area ♣ (All areas) ♦ Children's menu Children's portions Play area Family room Garden Outside area ⊟ Parking WiFi ➡ (notice required)

ST AUBIN — Map 24

Old Court House Inn

tel: 01534 746433 **St Aubin's Harbour JE3 8AB**
email: info@oldcourthousejersey.com
dir: *From Jersey Airport, right at exit, left at lights, 0.5m to St Aubin*

Harbour-side location on Jersey's stunning south coast

Overlooking the stunning bay at St Aubin's Fort, this old inn's medieval origins are testified by the wizened beams and mellow stone walls. The cellars here were once allegedly used to hide contraband, although the restaurant itself is housed in the original court house building. When the sun shines, grab a seat on the terrace and enjoy a pint of Jersey-brewed Liberation Ale or one of 17 wines offered by the glass. Seafood dominates the menu, starting perhaps with seared scallops and saffron risotto before moving on to pan-fried sea bass, crushed potatoes, Jersey crab and sauce vièrge.

Open all day all wk **Food** Lunch all wk 12.30-2.30 (all day May-Aug) Dinner all wk 6-9.30 Av main course £12 Restaurant menu available all wk ⊕ LIBERATION PUB COMPANY ◀ Liberation Ale & IPA. ♀ 17 **Facilities** Non-diners area ♦ Children's menu Children's portions Outside area ⊟ WiFi ➡ (notice required)

ST BRELADE — Map 24

The Portelet Inn

tel: 01534 741899 **La Route de Noirmont JE3 8AJ**
email: portelet@randalls.je
dir: *Phone for detailed directions*

Family-friendly playground with sea views

Parts of this cliff-top building date back to the 16th century. Over time it's developed into a mini theme park for all the family. Today children let off steam while dads sup their pints of international beer or lager and mums relax with a glass of Prosecco on adult-only balconies. Pirate Pete's (seasonal) is popular for kiddies' parties, and the newly opened Mamma's Kitchen furnishes sharing boards along with most flavours of pizza and pasta. Pub fodder from the main menu proffers the likes of crispy salt and pepper squid with dressed mixed leaves and aïoli dip; half a chicken roasted with your choice of glaze; and coconut pannacotta.

Open all day 11-11 Closed Tue (Jan-Mar) **Food** Lunch Mon-Sat 12-2.30, Sun 12-8 Dinner Mon-Thu 4.30-8.30, Fri-Sat 4.30-9, Sun 12-8 Restaurant menu available all wk ⊕ RANDALLS ◼ Wells Bombardier, guest ale. **Facilities** Non-diners area ⋔ Children's menu Children's portions Play area Family room Garden ⊟ Parking WiFi ▭ (notice required)

ST MARTIN — Map 24

Royal Hotel

tel: 01534 856289 **La Grande Route de Faldouet JE3 6UG**
email: johnbarker2806@gmail.com
dir: *2m from Five Oaks rdbt towards St Martin. Pub on right next to St Martin's Church*

Log fires in winter, beer garden in summer

A friendly local in the heart of St Martin, this former coaching inn prides itself on offering quality food and drink. Landlord John Barker has been welcoming guests for many years. A roaring log fire in the spacious lounge warm winter visitors, and there's a sunny beer garden to enjoy during the summer months. On the menu are traditional home-made favourites such as steak and ale pie, chicken curry, beef burgers, pizzas and jacket potatoes, as well as local seafood available according to season and availability. Children's choices are on offer, too.

Open all day all wk **Food** Lunch all wk 12-2.15 Dinner Mon-Sat 6-8.30 Av main course £10-£11 ⊕ RANDALLS ◼ Ringwood Best Bitter, Bass Cask, guest ales Ⓒ Westons Stowford Press. ♇ 9 **Facilities** Non-diners area ⋔ Children's menu Children's portions Play area Garden ⊟ Parking WiFi ▭ (notice required)

ST MARY — Map 24

St Mary's Country Inn

tel: 01534 482897 **La Rue des Buttes JE3 3DS**
email: stmarys@liberationpubco.com
dir: *Phone for detailed directions*

Smart inn with island-brewed ale and global menu

Jersey's Liberation Brewery owns this appealing country inn with smart, contemporary interior. The menu offers imaginative food at reasonable prices, including roasts and grills; espetadas (Portuguese chargrilled skewered meats and fish); and ale-battered cod with chunky chips. There are just three prices on the wine list, but choice extends to half-litre carafes and plenty by the glass. In the bar you'll find continental lagers, island-brewed Mary Ann Special and flagship cask-conditioned Liberation Ale. There's a delightful seating area outside.

Open all day all wk ⊕ LIBERATION GROUP ◼ Liberation Ale, Mary Ann Special, guest ales. **Facilities** ☻ (Bar Garden) ⋔ Children's menu Children's portions Garden Parking WiFi

ISLE OF MAN

PEEL — Map 24 SC28

The Creek Inn

tel: 01624 842216 **Station Place IM5 1AT**
email: thecreekinn@manx.net
dir: *On quayside opposite House of Manannan Museum*

A must for ale lovers

The family-run Creek Inn occupies a plum spot on the quayside overlooked by Peel Hill. A real ale drinkers' paradise, it has locally brewed Okells ales with up to four changing guests. Bands play every weekend, and nightly during the TT and Manx Grand Prix, when the pub becomes the town's focal point. There's a huge selection of dishes on the menu, from local fish, steaks and burgers, to vegetarian options and salads, alongside sandwiches, hot baguettes and toasties. A typical meal might be chilli and garlic crab claws followed by steak and Rory's ale pie with chips and peas.

Open all day all wk 10-late **Food** all wk 12-10 ⊕ FREE HOUSE ◼ Seasonal ales, 4 guest ales Ⓒ Manx Apple, Rekorderlig. ♇ 12 **Facilities** Non-diners area ☻ (Bar Outside area) ⋔ Children's menu Children's portions Outside area ⊟ Parking WiFi ▭

PORT ERIN — Map 24 SC26

Falcon's Nest Hotel

tel: 01624 834077 **The Promenade, Station Rd IM9 6AF**
email: falconsnest@enterprise.net
dir: *Follow coast road S from airport or ferry. Hotel on seafront, immediately after steam railway station*

Family-run pub-hotel with an emphasis on local seafood

The Potts family has run the Falcon's Nest since 1984 and it has become very much a part of life in Port Erin. The magnificent building overlooks a beautiful sheltered harbour and sandy beach, and this waterside location means local seafood dishes dominate the menu in the Victorian-style dining room (once a ballroom). Local 'queenie' scallops turn up on the menu alongside a roast of the day; honey-roast Manx ham and many gluten-free options. Head for the saloon bar or the residents' lounge to sample local ales and over 70 whiskies. A beer festival is held each year in early May.

Open all day all wk 11am-mdnt (Fri-Sat 11am-12.45am) **Food** all wk 12-9 Set menu available Restaurant menu available all wk ⊕ FREE HOUSE ◼ John Smith's, Okells, Bushy's, Bass, Guinness, guest ales. **Facilities** Non-diners area ☻ (Bar) ⋔ Children's menu Children's portions Family room Beer festival Cider festival Parking WiFi ▭ (notice required)

Scotland

CITY OF ABERDEEN

ABERDEEN
Map 23 NJ90

Old Blackfriars

tel: 01224 581922 **52 Castle St AB11 5BB**
email: oldblackfriars.aberdeen@belhavenpubs.net
dir: *From rail station right into Guild St left into Market St, at end right into Union St. Pub on right on corner of Marishal St*

Historic Castlegate-area pub with music nights

Situated in Aberdeen's historic Castlegate, this traditional split-level city centre pub stands on the site of property owned by Blackfriars Dominican monks, hence the name. Inside you'll find stunning stained glass, plus well-kept real ales (five hand pumps) and a large selection of malt whiskies. The pub is also renowned for good food and an unobtrusive atmosphere. The wide-ranging menu has all the pub favourites and more – haggis bon bons; chicken satay skewers; black bean and jalapeño burger; and chilli burritos. There's a weekly quiz on Tuesdays and live music every Thursday.

Open all day all wk 11am-mdnt (Mon 11-11 Fri 11am-1am Sat 10am-1am Sun 10am-11pm) Closed 25 Dec **Food** all wk 11-9 ⊕ BELHAVEN ◀ Inveralmond Ossian, Old Blackfriars, guest ales. ♀ 9 **Facilities** Non-diners area ♦ Children's menu Family room Outside area ⋒ WiFi

ABERDEENSHIRE

ABOYNE
Map 23 NO59

The Boat Inn

tel: 01339 886137 **Charleston Rd AB34 5EL**
email: enquiries@theboatinnaboyne.co.uk
dir: *A93 from Aberdeen to Aboyne. Left in Aboyne centre into Charleston Rd*

On the edge of the Cairngorms National Park

Dating from 1720, this roadside inn stands by the River Dee at the spot where a ferry once operated. Mounted stags' skulls, animal skins and hats adorn the walls of the tastefully modernised, log fire-warmed rooms. You won't often find a real ale from south of the Border in the bar; even some gins and rums are Scottish. Lunch and dinner menus depend extensively on local estates and suppliers for dishes such as battered or grilled North Sea haddock with rustic fries and mushy peas; pan-fried venison with black pudding and Madeira; and Highland-reared sirloin steak. Cream of Galloway ice creams make a great finish.

Open all day all wk Closed 25 Dec, 1-2 Jan **Food** all wk 12-8.45 ⊕ FREE HOUSE ◀ Inveralmond Ossian, Cairngorm Trade Winds, Brewmeister Supersonic IPA, Loch Ness, Ö Aspall. **Facilities** Non-diners area ♣ (Bar Outside area) ♦ Children's menu Children's portions Outside area ⋒ Parking WiFi ☜ (notice required)

BALMEDIE
Map 23 NJ91

The Cock & Bull Bar & Restaurant ◉

tel: 01358 743249 **Ellon Rd, Blairton AB23 8XY**
email: info@thecockandbull.co.uk
dir: *11m N of city centre, on left of A90 between Balmedie junct & Foveran*

Country inn with great food of impeccable provenance

A cast-iron range warms the bar in this creeper-clad, stone-built coaching inn, standing quite alone in open farmland north of Aberdeen. Conversation is easily stimulated by local artist Irene Morrison's paintings, assorted hanging artefacts and good beer. Affordably priced food in the restaurant uses Marine Stewardship Council-approved white fish and Peterhead-landed shellfish; and beef and pork from the region's stock farms. A seasonal menu might list Scottish girolles in garlic butter with pea pancake, broad beans and parsley fritters; the Aberdeen Angus burger; or sweet-spiced breast of Gressingham duck with gooseberries and spätzle. Great wines and whiskies as well.

Open all day all wk 10am-11.30pm (Sun 12-7.30) Closed 2-3 Jan, 26-27 Dec **Food** Mon-Sat 10-8.45, Sun 12-7.30 ⊕ FREE HOUSE ◀ Burnside 3 Bullz Bitter Ale, Guinness. **Facilities** Non-diners area ♣ (Bar Garden) ♦ Children's menu Play area Garden ⋒ Parking WiFi ☜ (notice required)

KILDRUMMY
Map 23 NJ41

Kildrummy Inn ★★★★ INN ◉◉

tel: 01975 571227 **AB33 8QS**
email: enquiries@kildrummyinn.co.uk **web:** www.kildrummyinn.co.uk
dir: *Take A944 from Aberdeen, left onto A97 (Strathdon). Inn on right*

Former coaching inn with an all-round first-rate reputation

Brothers-in-law David Littlewood and Nigel Hake, together with their wives, have fulfilled their long-held ambition to own an inn. Thanks to David's expert cooking and Nigel's amiable hospitality, they have swiftly achieved a reputation for attentive service, highly acclaimed modern Scottish food and excellent accommodation. A sample dinner menu lists goose and chicken liver parfait, compressed apple and beer bread; beef two ways – sirloin and featherblade – horseradish, mash, roots, glazed pearl onions and jus; and North Sea cod with langoustines and shellfish bisque. There are over 50 malts from some of Scotland's smaller distilleries to choose from plus Thistly Cross ciders in the inviting tartan-carpeted bar.

Open 6pm-late (Sun 12-2.30 6-late) Closed Jan, Tue **Food** Lunch Sun 12-2.30 Dinner 6-8.45 Set menu available ⊕ FREE HOUSE ◀ Deeside Swift APA, Macbeth & Talorcan, Atlas Wayfarer Ö Thistly Cross. ♀ 12 **Facilities** Non-diners area ♦ Children's portions Garden Outside area ⋒ Parking WiFi ☜ (notice required) **Rooms** 4

NETHERLEY
Map 23 NO89

The Lairhillock Inn
PICK OF THE PUBS

tel: 01569 730001 **AB39 3QS**
email: info@lairhillock.co.uk
dir: *From Aberdeen take A90. Right towards Durris on B9077 then left onto B979 to Netherley*

A bustling country inn

A 15-minute drive from Aberdeen city centre brings you to this generously beamed inn, part of the scenery in rural Deeside for over 200 years. With all its nooks and crannies, the mot juste for the quarry-tiled interior can only be 'rambling'; in winter, woodsmoke drifts up from the unusual, slab-mounted central fire grate. In the bar Timothy Taylor Landlord is usually accompanied by two guest real ales, while the menu majors on Scottish produce, with starters of haggis, neeps, tatties croquettes, Savoy cabbage and Drambuie sauce; and Cullen skink. Unsurprisingly, Aberdeen Angus steaks have a high profile alongside smoked haddock, Arran cheddar and pea and dill fishcakes; puff pastry pie of the day; and roasted fillet and pulled lamb with honey-roasted parsnips, black pudding potatoes and rosemary and port jus. There's a light, bright conservatory with garden views, candlelit tables, gleaming brass and copper lamps, and bric-à-brac.

Open all day all wk Closed 25-26 Dec, 1-2 Jan **Food** Lunch all wk 12-2 Dinner all wk 6-9.30 ⊕ FREE HOUSE ◀ Timothy Taylor Landlord, 2 guest ales.
Facilities Non-diners area ❤ (Bar Garden) ◆◆ Children's menu Children's portions Garden ⋈ Parking ⊕ (notice required)

OLDMELDRUM
Map 23 NJ82

The Redgarth

tel: 01651 872353 **Kirk Brae AB51 0DJ**
email: redgarth1@aol.com
dir: *From A947 (Oldmeldrum bypass) follow signs to Golf Club/Pleasure Park. Inn E of bypass*

Friendly, family-run inn with attractive garden

Built in 1928 as a house, The Redgarth has been a thriving family owned business for over 26 years. A cask-conditioned ale, such as Highland Scapa Special or Five Ales Jarl, or a tot of the village's own Glen Garioch malt whisky, might precede haggis-stuffed mushrooms with coarse grain mustard dip; an authentic pork goulash with galuska; or catch of the day. Grills are well represented and vegetarians will very likely find a sweet potato, leek and red onion flan, or spinach stuffed cannelloni on the menu.

Open all wk 11-3 5-11 (Fri-Sat 11-3 5-11.45) Closed 25-26 Dec, 1-3 Jan
Food Lunch all wk 12-2 Dinner Sun-Thu 5-9, Fri-Sat 5-9.30 Av main course £12
⊕ FREE HOUSE ◀ Timothy Taylor Landlord, Scapa Special & Orkney Best, Fyne Ales Jarl, Island Hopping Ŏ Aspall. **Facilities** Non-diners area ❤ (Garden) ◆◆ Children's menu Children's portions Garden ⋈ Parking WiFi ⊕

STONEHAVEN
Map 23 NO88

The Ship Inn ★★★ INN

tel: 01569 762617 **5 Shorehead AB39 2JY**
email: enquiries@shipinnstonehaven.com web: www.shipinnstonehaven.com
dir: *From A90 follow signs to Stonehaven, then signs to harbour*

Fresh seafood a speciality

Overnight guests will surely testify that the Ship is in one of the best locations in town, for it overlooks the almost circular harbour, once an important centre of the herring trade. In the blue-carpeted bar you'll find real ales from Inveralmond, Orkney and elsewhere, as well as a hundred-plus malts. Seafood is served in the bar, the air-conditioned restaurant, and on the open-air terrace, all with harbour views. Cullen skink; black haggis parcels, creamed leeks with honey whisky sauce; and breaded haloumi goujons are typical starters, while main dishes include sea bass with tempura prawns and saffron cream sauce; crab claw and mussel platter; nasi goreng; and pan-seared venison steak with spiced cherries.

Open all day all wk **Food** Lunch Mon-Fri 12-2.15, Sat-Sun 12-9 Dinner Mon-Fri 5.30-9, Sat-Sun 12-9 ⊕ FREE HOUSE ◀ Inveralmond Thrappledouser, Orkney, guest ales. **Facilities** ❤ (Bar Outside area) ♦♦ Children's menu Children's portions Outside area 🖛 WiFi **Rooms** 11

See advert on page 597

ANGUS

FORFAR
Map 23 NO45

NEW The Drovers Inn ◉

tel: 01307 860322 **Memus DD8 3TY**
email: info@the-drovers.com
dir: *N of Forfar from A90 follow Memus signs. Through Justinhaugh, follow Memus signs*

A pretty, former drovers' stop-over

With three shapely dormer windows projecting from its slate roof, and an unusual, but very attractive, vaulted interior, the Drovers has few neighbours. The bar's regularly changing real ales have included Northern Light from Orkney and Fair Maid from Perth, while a fine collection of Highland, Lowland, Speyside, Islay and Maritime malts waits alongside. Cullen skink and black haggis Scotch duck egg are listed on the Drovers' Favourites menu, while on the carte are Glenogil pheasant breast with confit legs; pan-fried fillet of salmon; and chestnut, parsnip and Savoy cabbage roulade.

Open all day Closed 25-26 Dec, 1 Jan, Mon-Tue (in Jan-Feb) **Food** Lunch Mon-Sat 12-2.30, Sun 12-4 Dinner Mon-Sat 5.30-9 Av main course £12-£16 Restaurant menu available all wk ◀ Rotating ales Ö Aspall. **Facilities** Non-diners area ♦♦ Children's menu Children's portions Play area Garden 🖛 Parking WiFi 🚌 (notice required)

ARGYLL & BUTE

ARDUAINE
Map 20 NM71

Chartroom II Bistro ★★★ CHH ◉◉ PICK OF THE PUBS

tel: 01852 200233 **Loch Melfort Hotel PA34 4XG**
email: reception@lochmelfort.co.uk web: www.lochmelfort.co.uk
dir: *On A816, midway between Oban & Lochgilphead*

West Coast seafood and far-reaching views out to sea

Seafood lovers flock to this modern bar and bistro, part of the Loch Melfort Hotel, next door to National Trust Scotland's Arduaine Garden. It's not just the langoustines, scallops and mussels they come for – the views over Asknish Bay towards Jura, Scarba and Shuna are a real treat, too. Enjoy Fyne Ales from Cairndow, and perhaps Ayrshire ham and lentil soup; a warm Argyll pork loin, home-made apple sauce sandwich; Isle of Seil oysters; home-made Scottish wild venison burger; or Aberdeen Angus beef and black pudding lasagne. If sitting outside is out of the question, you can watch the waves crashing against the rocks from in front of the fire. Children's dishes include penne pasta, and breaded chicken mini fillets, chips and beans. Sailors can moor free of charge from April to October, hang up their oilskins and freshen up with a shower. The hotel's Asknish Bay Restaurant has been awarded two AA Rosettes.

Open all wk 11-10 Closed Nov-Etr **Food** Lunch all wk 12-2.30 Dinner all wk 6-9 Av main course £12.50 ⊕ FREE HOUSE ◀ Belhaven, Fyne, Tennent's. ☂ 8 **Facilities** Non-diners area ♦♦ Children's menu Children's portions Play area Garden 🖛 Parking WiFi 🚌 **Rooms** 25

ARROCHAR
Map 20 NN30

Village Inn

tel: 01301 702279 **Shore Rd G83 7AX**
email: villageinn.arrochar@stonegatepubs.com
dir: *From Arrochar take A814 towards Helensburgh. Inn in 1m*

Traditional pub in the heart of the Loch Lomond National Park

On the east shore of Loch Long, just a few minutes from Loch Lomond, you'll find the Village Inn. There's a large beer garden and superb views of the 'Arrochar Alps'. Ideally located for the hills and trails of the National Park, the friendly inn, now in new hands, is popular with locals and visitors alike. You'll find three Scottish cask ales in the cosy bar, and if you're hungry you can share a fish deli board, or enjoy something more substantial – start with oak-smoked salmon or duck and apricot terrine and move on to Cumberland sausages and mash; or British beef, Rioja and chorizo slow-cooked pie. There are steaks and burgers as well. Finish with sticky toffee pudding or Manchester custard tart.

Open all day all wk **Food** all wk 12-8.30 (summer 12-9) ⊕ STONEGATE PUBS ◄ Caledonian Deuchars IPA, guest ales Ö Aspall. ♀ 22 **Facilities** Non-diners area ❖ (Bar Garden Outside area) ♦♦ Children's menu Children's portions Garden Outside area ⊼ Beer festival Parking WiFi ▬ (notice required)

CAIRNDOW   Map 20 NN11

Cairndow Stagecoach Inn ★★★ INN

tel: 01499 600286 **PA26 8BN**
email: enq@cairndowinn.com **web:** www.cairndowinn.com
dir: *N of Glasgow take A82, left onto A83 at Arrochar. Through Rest and be Thankful to Cairndow. Follow signs for inn*

An old coaching inn set in glorious scenery

On the upper reaches of Loch Fyne, this old coaching inn offers plenty of fine views of mountains, magnificent woodlands and rivers. Sample one of many malt whiskies in the friendly bar by the roaring fire, or idle away the time in the loch-side garden watching the oyster-catchers while sipping the local Fyne Ales. The menu in the candlelit Stables Restaurant offers steak and Fyne Ale pie; chicken breast stuffed with smoked Scottish cheddar and ham, wrapped in pancetta; roasted pepper, courgette and wild mushroom risotto; and pan-fried venison steak with shallot, mushroom and smoked bacon red wine sauce. Meals are also served all day in the bar and lounges. Accommodation is available if you would like to stay over and explore the area. On your way to the pub you should look out for Britain's tallest tree (Ardkinglas Grand Fir), which is taller than Nelson's Column.

Open all day all wk **Food** Lunch all wk 12-6 Dinner all wk 6-9 ⊕ FREE HOUSE ◄ Fyne Hurricane Jack, Avalanche, Piper's Gold, Maverick, Jarl. ♀ **Facilities** Non-diners area ❖ (Bar Garden) ♦♦ Children's menu Children's portions Family room Garden ⊼ Parking WiFi ▬ (notice required) **Rooms** 18

CRINAN   Map 20 NR79

Crinan Hotel   PICK OF THE PUBS

tel: 01546 830261 **PA31 8SR**
email: reservations@crinanhotel.com
dir: *From M8, at end of bridge take A82, at Tarbert left onto A83. At Inveraray follow Campbeltown signs to Lochgilphead, follow signs for A816 to Oban. 2m, left to Crinan on B841*

Stunning views and the freshest West Coast seafood

This romantic retreat enjoys a stunning location with fabulous views across the Sound of Jura. The hotel stands at the north end of the Crinan Canal, which connects Loch Fyne to the Atlantic Ocean. For over two hundred years this hostelry has been caring for the community needs of this tiny fishing village, and welcoming travellers. This sense of continuity has been lovingly provided by Nick and Frances Ryan for over 40 years. Relax with a drink in the Gallery Bar on a summer's evening, or settle in the Mainbrace, a wood-panelled seafood bar which extends to the patio overlooking the fishing boats. The Westward Restaurant's cuisine is firmly based on the freshest seafood – it's landed daily just 50 metres from the hotel. Look out for hot Arbroath smokie; risotto of crab with cream cheese and chives, and – if meat is preferred – pan-seared Scottish sirloin steak.

Open all day all wk 11-11 Closed 25 Dec **Food** Lunch all wk 12-2.30 Dinner all wk 6-8.30 Restaurant menu available all wk ⊕ FREE HOUSE ◄ Fyne, Tennent's, Caledonian, Guinness. ♀ 8 **Facilities** Non-diners area ❖ (Bar Garden Outside area) ♦♦ Children's menu Children's portions Garden Outside area ⊼ Parking WiFi ▬ (notice required)

INVERARAY   Map 20 NN00

George Hotel

tel: 01499 302111 **Main Street East PA32 8TT**
email: info@thegeorgehotel.co.uk
dir: *On A83*

Town centre pub with a south-facing beer garden

Although built back in 1770 by the Duke of Argyll as two private houses, the George has been, since 1860, a hotel owned by the Clark family. Occupying a prime spot in this historic conservation town, it has been sensitively added to over the years, but without detracting from the original flagstone floors and four alluring log and peat fires. More than 100 whiskies and a range of Fyne Ales from up the road at Cairndow are complemented by a menu that includes dressed Mull of Kintyre crab, Scottish smoked hake, and haggis, neeps and tatties. Beer and music festivals are held on bank holidays in May and August.

Open all day all wk 11am-1am Closed 25 Dec **Food** Lunch all wk 12-6 Dinner all wk 6-9 ⊕ FREE HOUSE ◄ Fyne Ales. ♀ 11 **Facilities** Non-diners area ❖ (Bar Restaurant Garden) ♦♦ Children's menu Children's portions Garden ⊼ Beer festival Parking WiFi ▬ (notice required)

LUSS   Map 20 NS39

The Inn on Loch Lomond ★★★★ INN

tel: 01436 860201 **G83 8PD**
email: inverbeg.reception@loch-lomond.co.uk **web:** www.innonlochlomond.co.uk
dir: *12m N of Balloch*

Scottish hospitality and great views

Today a good road skirts Loch Lomond's western shore, but it wouldn't have been so good in 1814, when this wayside inn opened its doors. Today it incorporates Mr C's Fish & Whisky Bar where the menu might feature haggis, neeps and tatties; Cullen skink; pea and herb risotto; and roast salmon and haddock fishcakes; and for dessert, cranachan (a mixture of whipped cream, whisky, honey and fresh raspberries, with toasted oatmeal soaked overnight in a little bit of whisky) or deep-fried Mars Bars with ice cream. A little shy of 200 whiskies are available, but if you prefer ale, there's Loch Lomond or Sharp's Doom Bar. Live folk music is played on Fridays and Saturdays throughout the summer.

Open all day all wk 11-11 (Fri-Sat 11am-mdnt) **Food** all wk 12-9 ⊕ FREE HOUSE ◄ Loch Lomond, Sharp's Doom Bar. **Facilities** Non-diners area ❖ (Outside area) ♦♦ Children's menu Children's portions Outside area ⊼ Parking WiFi ▬ (notice required) **Rooms** 33

OBAN   Map 20 NM83

Cuan Mor

tel: 01631 565078 **60 George St PA34 5SD**
email: info@cuanmor.co.uk
dir: *Phone for detailed directions*

Delightful views and good home-cooked food

Cuan Mor means 'big ocean', clearly a reference to the Atlantic, which stretches a finger called the Firth of Lorn towards Oban. Restaurant and bars make effective use of reclaimed Ballachulish slate and timbers from the old lighthouse pier. The on-site Oban Bay Brewery produces the real ales, there are 16 wines by the glass, and a hundred or so single malts and special blends – read the Brewery Bar's Whisky Bible for guidance. As you overlook Oban Bay enjoy Isle of Mull scallops, sweet potato mash with smoked bacon and mushroom sauce; or five-hour braised lamb shank with rich Oban ale gravy.

Open all day all wk **Food** Lunch all wk 12-4 Dinner all wk 4-9 (Etr-Sep 4-10) ⊕ FREE HOUSE ◄ Oban Bay. ♀ 16 **Facilities** Non-diners area ♦♦ Children's menu Children's portions Outside area ⊼ WiFi ▬ (notice required)

OBAN continued

The Lorne

tel: 01631 570020 **Stevenson St PA34 5NA**
email: lornebar@maclay.co.uk
dir: *Phone for detailed directions*

A place for refreshment before train or ferry

Handy for both Oban's train station and the Mull ferry terminal, The Lorne is a family-friendly haven with a sheltered and heated beer garden – an ideal spot to enjoy a freshly brewed coffee or a pint of beer from the Oban Bay Brewery before departing the town. The menu offers a good choice of pub classics, like scampi and chips and a selection of burgers, as well as steaks and haggis with neeps and tatties. The 'feast for a fiver' is great value and there are some small plates for smaller appetites. If you're staying in Oban, The Lorne offers a busy programme of pub quizzes, DJ nights and live music, when the party continues into the early hours.

Open all day all wk **Food** all wk 12-9 Av main course £7.95 ⊕ FREE HOUSE ◀ Caledonian Deuchars IPA, Oban Bay. ♟ 12 **Facilities** Non-diners area ♣ (All areas) ♦ Children's menu Children's portions Garden Outside area ⊫ WiFi ⇔ (notice required)

PORT APPIN   Map 20 NM94

The Pierhouse Hotel & Seafood Restaurant ★★★ SHL ⊛
PICK OF THE PUBS

tel: 01631 730302 **PA38 4DE**
email: reservations@pierhousehotel.co.uk web: www.pierhousehotel.co.uk
dir: *A828 from Ballachulish to Oban. In Appin right at Port Appin & Lismore ferry sign. After 2.5m left after post office, hotel at end of road by pier*

Delicious seafood on the shores of Loch Linnhe

Once home to the piermaster (hence the name), this distinctive whitewashed building boasts breathtaking views to the islands of Lismore and Mull. It would be hard to imagine a more spectacular setting for this family-run hotel and seafood restaurant; an AA Rosette being one its many awards, others recognising its green credentials. The popular bar is stocked with Belhaven beers and 50 malt whiskies; a pool room; and a dining area where the finest of Scottish seasonal seafood, meat, game and vegetables are served. Overlooking the pier, the Ferry Bar serves burgers and seafood dishes, plus ciabattas at lunchtime. An evening three-course meal in the restaurant could commence with the Cullen skink, followed by Highland game pie; roast fillet of Scottish salmon; or langoustine platter. For dessert, try the butterscotch pot or a board of local cheeses. Twelve individually designed bedrooms include some with superb loch views.

Open all wk 11-11 Closed 25-26 Dec **Food** Lunch all wk 12.30-2.30 Dinner all wk 6.30-9.30 Restaurant menu available all wk ⊕ FREE HOUSE ◀ Belhaven Best & Export, Guinness. **Facilities** Non-diners area ♣ (Bar Garden Outside area) ♦ Children's menu Children's portions Garden Outside area ⊫ Parking WiFi ⇔ **Rooms** 12

STRACHUR   Map 20 NN00

Creggans Inn   PICK OF THE PUBS

tel: 01369 860279 **PA27 8BX**
email: info@creggans-inn.co.uk
dir: *A82 from Glasgow, at Tarbet take A83 towards Cairndow, left onto A815 to Strachur*

Family-run inn on loch shores

Set between the woods and the water, visitors to the centuries-old loch-side hotel can look forward to losing themselves in the astounding view across Loch Fyne. The reputation of the area's provender is well-established; this is matched by beers from the Fyne microbrewery at the head of the loch. A pint of one of the Fyne ales and a seat on the terrace is a restful way to pass time while considering the menu's seasonally adjusted, daily-changing dishes. Eat outside, dine in the bistro-style MacPhunn's bar or in the more formal Loch Fyne dining room; try Ramsay haggis, creamy mash, buttered neeps and whisky sauce; local venison sausages, leek and smoked bacon mash, and root vegetables with honey; or West Coast fillet of salmon, crushed potato, spinach with white wine and prawn sauce.

Open all day all wk 11-11 **Food** Lunch all wk 12-2.30 Dinner all wk 6-8.30 ⊕ FREE HOUSE ◀ Fyne Ales. **Facilities** Non-diners area ♣ (Bar Garden) ♦ Children's menu Children's portions Garden ⊫ Parking WiFi

TARBERT   Map 20 NR86

NEW West Loch Hotel

tel: 01880 820283 **PA29 6YF**
email: info@westlochhotel.com
dir: *On A83 SW of Tarbert*

On the Gulf Stream-warmed coast

With a backdrop of mature trees, this late 18th-century coaching inn is now a modern hotel, bar and restaurant overlooking the road that skirts West Tarbert Loch, an arm of the Atlantic. Real-ale drinkers enjoy brews from Colonsay, Mull and Oban, while those who prefer a malt can scan the whisky alphabet from Aberlour to Tobermory. Fish and seafood, landed by Scottish boats, includes smoked haddock, salmon and trout, and North Atlantic prawns; other possibilities might be slow-braised Scottish beef cheek with turnip fondant and buttered carrots; venison sausages and baked borlotti beans in rich tomato sauce; and sweet potato tagine.

Open all day all wk **Food** Lunch all wk 12-2 Dinner all wk 5-9 ⊕ FREE HOUSE ◀ Caledonian Best. **Facilities** Non-diners area ♣ (Bar Outside area) ♦ Children's menu Children's portions Outside area ⊫ Parking WiFi ⇔ (notice required)

TAYVALLICH   Map 20 NR78

Tayvallich Inn

tel: 01546 870282 **PA31 8PL**
email: info@tayvallichinn.com
dir: *From Lochgilphead take A816 then B841, B8025*

Popular loch-side pub at the heart of a vibrant community

Established for over 30 years, the inn stands in a picturesque fishing village overlooking the natural harbour of Tayvallich Bay at the head of Loch Sween. There are unrivalled views, particularly from the outside area of decking, where food and a great selection of real ales can be enjoyed. Not surprisingly given the location, fresh seafood features strongly – the catch is landed from the boats right outside the front door. Lobster, crab and langoustine are available in the summer, while typical dishes in winter might be fragrant oven-baked salmon fillet with prawn and caper sauce or line-caught Tarbert haddock in batter with chips.

Open all wk all day in summer (closed 3-6 Tue-Fri in winter) Closed 25-26 Dec, Mon (Nov-Mar) **Food** Lunch all wk 12-2.30 Dinner all wk 6-9 ⊕ FREE HOUSE ◖ Caledonian Best, Loch Ness, Guinness. ♟ 8 **Facilities** Non-diners area ❀ (Bar Garden) ♦ Children's menu Children's portions Garden ⋈ Parking ⇛ (notice required)

EAST AYRSHIRE

SORN
Map 20 NS52

The Sorn Inn
PICK OF THE PUBS

tel: 01290 551305 **35 Main St KA5 6HU**
email: craig@sorninn.com
dir: A70 from S; or A76 from N onto B743 to Sorn

A fusion of fine dining and brasserie-style food

The whitewashed Sorn Inn dates back to the 18th century when it was a coaching inn on the old Edinburgh to Kilmarnock route; today it's a smart gastro-pub that serves ales that include Corncrake from the Orkney Brewery. Menus offer the best of Scottish and seasonal ingredients. Choose crispy pork belly, honeyed celeriac purée, apple gel and pea shoots to start perhaps, then pavé of beef with foie gras, duck liver parfait croûton, Madeira cream, dauphinoise potatoes and green beans; or fillet of salmon with artichoke and saffron risotto, lemon dressing and pea jelly. Half a dozen classic dishes include smoked Ayrshire bacon carbonara; and 'Mum's' steak pie, mash, and buttered cabbage. Finish with coffee pannacotta and chocolate doughnuts, or baked lemon curd cheesecake, lemon purée and mascarpone ice cream.

Open 12-2.30 6-10 (Fri 12-2.30 6-12 Sat 12-12 Sun 12-10) Closed 2wks Jan, Mon **Food** Lunch Tue-Fri 12-2.30, Sat 12-9, Sun 12-8 Dinner Tue-Fri 6-9, Sat 12-9, Sun 12-8 Av main course £15 ⊕ FREE HOUSE ◖ John Smith's, Orkney Corncrake, Guinness. ♟ 12 **Facilities** Non-diners area ❀ (Bar Outside area) ♦ Children's menu Children's portions Outside area ⋈ Parking WiFi ⇛ (notice required)

SOUTH AYRSHIRE

SYMINGTON
Map 20 NS33

Wheatsheaf Inn

tel: 01563 830307 **Main St KA1 5QB**
email: thewheatsheafinnsymington@outlook.com
dir: Off A77 between Ayr & Kilmarnock

Village free house with friendly service

Close to the Royal Troon Golf Course and one of Scotland's oldest churches, this charming 17th-century free house has been run by Martin and Marnie Thompson for over 25 years. Log fires burn in every room of the former coaching inn and the interior is decorated with the work of local artists. The varied menu offers plenty of choice, with dishes like haggis, neeps and tatties with sweet whisky cream; fillet of haddock mornay; gammon steak with egg or pineapple; pan-fried lamb's liver with red wine and onions; or blackened Cajun salmon.

Open all day all wk 11-11 (Fri-Sat 11am-mdnt) Closed 1 Jan **Food** all wk 12-9 Set menu available Restaurant menu available all wk ⊕ FREE HOUSE ◖ Belhaven Best, Morland Old Speckled Hen, Guinness. **Facilities** Non-diners area ♦ Children's menu Children's portions Garden ⋈ Parking WiFi ⇛ (notice required)

DUMFRIES & GALLOWAY

BARGRENNAN
Map 20 NX37

House O'Hill Hotel

tel: 01671 840243 **DG8 6RN**
email: enquiries@houseohill.co.uk
dir: From Newton Stewart take A714 towards Girvan, 8m. Hotel signed

Secluded location in Galloway's forested hills

At the fringe of loch-speckled Galloway Forest and beautiful Glen Trool, this contemporary, homely little hotel makes the most of its setting in Europe's first 'Dark Sky' Park. The House O'Hill attracts cyclists and ramblers on the Southern Upland Way by offering an exceptional combination of local microbrewery beers such as Sulwath and a wide-ranging menu strong on Galloway produce. Local saddle of venison with potato rösti, confit vegetables, chocolate and red wine sauce; or falafel burger with melted cheddar, onion ring and salsa are just two of the dishes on the hit list. There are themed world-food evenings and beer festivals occur in April and September.

Open all day all wk Closed 3-25 Jan **Food** Lunch all wk 12-2.45 Dinner all wk 5.30-8.30 Restaurant menu available all wk ⊕ FREE HOUSE ◖ Sulwath, Stewart's, Ayr, Fyne, Houston. **Facilities** Non-diners area ❀ (Bar Restaurant Garden) ♦ Children's menu Children's portions Family room Garden ⋈ Beer festival Parking WiFi ⇛

BLADNOCH
Map 20 NX45

The Bladnoch Inn

tel: 01988 402200 **DG8 9AB**
email: thebladnochinn@hotmail.co.uk
dir: A714 S of Wigtown to Bladnoch. Inn at rdbt by river bridge

In a charming spot by the River Bladnoch

This traditional country inn is in the heart of the Machars peninsula, just down the road is Wigtown, home to some 20 bookshops. At lunchtime there are sandwiches and filled baked potatoes, while starters include haggis fritters; duck and orange pâté; and garlic mushrooms. Traditional pub favourites make up the mains' choices – home-made chicken curry; pork and leek sausages with mash and honey-roast vegetables; beer-battered fish, pea purée and fries; and macaroni cheese. A carvery is available on Sundays.

Open all day all wk **Food** Lunch all wk 12-3 Dinner all wk 6-9 ⊕ FREE HOUSE ◖ Greene King & IPA, Timothy Taylor Landlord Ŏ Kopparberg. ♟ 15 **Facilities** Non-diners area ❀ (Bar Outside area) ♦ Children's menu Children's portions Play area Outside area ⋈ Parking WiFi ⇛ (notice required)

Find out more about
Scotland on page 16

ISLE OF WHITHORN
Map 20 NX43

The Steam Packet Inn

tel: 01988 500334 **Harbour Row DG8 8LL**
email: steampacketinn@btconnect.com
dir: *From Newton Stewart take A714, then A746 to Whithorn, then to Isle of Whithorn*

Own microbrewery and local seafood a specialty

Personally run by the Scoular family for over 30 years, this lively quayside pub stands in a picturesque village at the tip of the Machars peninsula. Sit in one of the comfortable bars and enjoy a real ale, a malt whisky or a glass of wine. Glance out of the picture windows and watch the fishermen at work, then look to the menu to sample the fruits of their labours. Extensive seafood choices – perhaps salmon and fishcake kebabs, or smoked haddock fillet wrapped with black pudding and bacon – are supported by the likes of wild mushroom risotto and corn-fed chicken breast with haggis and mash.

Open all day all wk 11-11 (Sun 12-11) Closed 25 Dec, winter Tue-Thu 2.30-6 **Food** Lunch Mon-Thu 12-2, Fri-Sun all day Dinner Mon-Thu 6.30-9, Fri-Sun all day Av main course £10.95 ⊕ FREE HOUSE ◁ Belhaven IPA, 5 Kingdoms Blue, guest ales. ♟ 12 **Facilities** Non-diners area ❧ (Bar Garden Outside area) ♦ Children's menu Children's portions Garden Outside area ♩ Parking WiFi ▭

KIRKCUDBRIGHT
Map 20 NX65

Selkirk Arms Hotel

tel: 01557 330402 **Old High St DG6 4JG**
email: reception@selkirkarmshotel.co.uk
dir: *M74 & M6 to A75, halfway between Dumfries & Stranraer on A75*

Choice of two bars and two restaurants

In 1794, when dining at what today is a tastefully appointed town house, Robert Burns reputedly penned and delivered *The Selkirk Grace*. In the bar, Sulwath Brewery's eponymous ale celebrates the occasion. A good choice of dishes is offered in both the homely lounge and bistro, with comfy sofas and a living-flame fire, and the more intimate Artistas Restaurant. Locally sourced specialities include duck leg confit with bubble-and-squeak and game fritter; apple and cider sausages with buttered cabbage, mash and gravy; and haunch of Galloway venison with celeriac purée, sprouts and chestnuts. Finish with clementine verrine, orange sorbet and yogurt foam.

Open all day all wk **Food** Lunch all wk 12-2 Dinner all wk 6-9 Av main course £11.95 ⊕ FREE HOUSE ◁ Timothy Taylor Landlord, Sulwath Selkirk Grace, Dark Horse Hetton Pale Ale, Caledonian Deuchars IPA, Fyne Ales Jarl. ♟ 10 **Facilities** Non-diners area ♦ Children's menu Children's portions Garden ♩ Parking WiFi ▭ (notice required)

NEW GALLOWAY
Map 20 NX67

Cross Keys Hotel

tel: 01644 420494 **High St DG7 3RN**
email: enquiries@thecrosskeys-newgalloway.co.uk
dir: *At N end of Loch Ken, 10m from Castle Douglas on A712*

Great selection of real ales and malts

This 17th-century coaching inn sits in a stunning location at the top of Loch Ken on the edge of Galloway Forest Park, a superb area for walking, fishing, birdwatching, golf, watersports and photography. Part of the hotel was once the police station and in the beamed period bar the food is served in restored, stone-walled cells. The weekly-changing dinner specials feature the likes of deep-fried goats' cheese with caramelised onion relish; minted shoulder of lamb, creamy mash and seasonal vegetables; and home-made Galloway steak pie and chips. If you've still room enjoy hot chocolate fudge cake or sticky toffee pudding.

Open 6pm-11.30pm Closed Sun eve winter **Food** Dinner Mon-Sat 6.30-8.30 Av main course £11 ⊕ FREE HOUSE ◁ Guest ales ♥ Westons Stowford Press. ♟ 9 **Facilities** Non-diners area ❧ (Bar Garden) Garden Parking WiFi ▭ (notice required)

PORTPATRICK
Map 20 NW95

NEW The Crown Hotel

tel: 01776 810261 **9 North Crescent DG9 8SX**
email: crownportpatrick@btconnect.com
dir: *A77 into Portpatrick. At seafront turn right. Hotel on right*

On the water's edge in a picturesque village

With views across Portpatrick's cute harbour and the Irish Sea to Ulster's Mountains of Mourne, the hotel forms an integral part of the historic seafront. The terrace is perfect for a beer – try the town brewery's Fog Horn - although in unsuitable weather the lounge bar or conservatory restaurant would be a better bet. If you expect seafood, you'll have come to the right place, because options include fresh local crab claws in dill cream sauce; Orkney mussels marinière; and West Coast scallops in smoked bacon. Also listed are Galloway venison casserole; Mexican-style chilli beef; and trio of stuffed pasta.

Open all day all wk **Food** all day Restaurant menu available all wk ⊕ FREE HOUSE ◁ Portpatrick Dorn Rock & Fog Horn, Courage Directors. ♟ 8 **Facilities** Non-diners area ❧ (Bar Garden) ♦ Children's menu Children's portions Family room Garden ♩ WiFi ▭ (notice required)

SANDHEAD
Map 20 NX04

Tigh Na Mara Hotel

tel: 01776 830210 **Main St DG9 9JF**
email: mail@tighnamarahotel.co.uk
dir: *A75 from Dumfries towards Stranraer. Left onto B7084 to Sandhead*

Bracing sea air and long sandy beaches

Tigh na Mara means 'house by the sea', which seems appropriate for this family-run village hotel is set in the tranquil seaside village of Sandhead and boasts breathtaking views of the Sands of Luce. A menu created from top-quality local ingredients might include pan-fried piri piri king prawns; haggis lollipops in oatmeal crumb; duo of local pheasant and pigeon, Scotch quail's egg and Arran mustard cream; and pork saltimbocca. Relax with a glass of Belhaven Best in the garden, comfortable lounge or beside the fire in the public bar.

Open all day all wk **Food** Lunch all wk 12-2.30 Dinner all wk 5-9 Set menu available ⊕ BELHAVEN ◁ Best & IPA, seasonal specials. **Facilities** Non-diners area ❧ (Bar Garden) ♦ Children's menu Children's portions Family room Garden ♩ Parking WiFi

CITY OF DUNDEE

BROUGHTY FERRY
Map 21 NO43

The Royal Arch Bar

tel: 01382 779741 **285 Brook St DD5 2DS**
dir: *On A930, 3m from Dundee at Broughty Ferry rail station*

Convivial local by the Tay Estuary

This long established street-corner inn is a pleasing mix of locals' saloon bar, complete with stained-glass windows and an eye-catching Victorian gantry, and a well-maintained art deco lounge long ago converted from the inn's stables. The Royal Arch itself was a monument built to commemorate Queen Victoria's Dundee visit in 1863; a fragment survives on display in the bar. Dispensed from this bar are quality Scottish beers such as from local micro MòR, as well as over 50 malt whiskies; satisfying pub meals can include steak pie or the fisherman's mixed seafood crêpe. There's a pavement terrace canopy for all-weather, alfresco eating and drinking. Beer, cider and sausage festivals are held.

Open all day all wk **Food** Lunch Mon-Fri 11.30-2.30, Sat 11.30-8, Sun 12.30-7 Dinner Mon-Fri 5-8, Sat 11.30-8, Sun 12.30-7 Set menu available ⊕ FREE HOUSE ◀ McEwan's 80/-, Belhaven St Andrews, Caledonian Deuchars IPA, MòR Tea, Vicar?, Black Isle Blonde Ỏ Thistly Cross. ♟ 30 **Facilities** Non-diners area ♦ Children's portions Family room Garden Outside area ⊨ Beer festival Cider festival WiFi ⛟

DUNDEE	Map 21 NO43

Speedwell Bar

tel: 01382 667783 **165-167 Perth Rd DD2 1AS**
dir: *From A92 (Tay Bridge), A991 signed Perth/A85/Coupar Angus/A923. At Riverside rdbt 3rd exit (A991). At lights left into Nethergate signed Parking/South Tay St. Becomes Perth Rd. Pass university. Bar on right*

Edwardian gem with unspoilt interior

This fine example of an unspoiled Edwardian art deco bar is worth visiting for its interior alone; all the fitments in the bar and sitting rooms are beautifully crafted mahogany – gantry, drink shelves, dado panelling and fireplace. Internal doors are all glazed with etched glass. The same family owned it for 90 years, until the present landlord's father bought it in the mid 90s. As well as the cask-conditioned ales, 157 whiskies and imported bottles are offered. A kitchen would be good, but since the pub is listed this is impossible. Visitors are encouraged to bring their own snacks from nearby bakeries. This community pub is home to several clubs and has live Scottish music from time to time on a Tuesday.

Open all day all wk 11am-mdnt ⊕ FREE HOUSE ◀ Caledonian Deuchars IPA, Harviestoun Bitter & Twisted, Williams Bros Seven Giraffes Ỏ Addlestones. ♟ 18 **Facilities** Non-diners area ♣ (Bar) ⊨ Beer festival WiFi ⛟ **Notes** ⊚

CITY OF EDINBURGH

EDINBURGH	Map 21 NT27

The Bow Bar

tel: 0131 226 7667 **80 The West Bow EH1 2HH**
dir: *Phone for detailed directions*

A whisky and beer connoisseurs' delight

If there is one free house that reflects the history and traditions of Edinburgh's Old Town, it's The Bow Bar. With an amazing number of malt whiskies (310 to date), nine real ales poured from traditional tall founts and 50 bottled beers, the focus may be on liquid refreshment but the range of snacks includes haggis, cheese and chilli pies and bridies (meat pastries). Twice a year in January and July, the pub holds ten-day long beer festivals. Tables from old train carriages and a church gantry add to the unique feel of a bar where the sound of conversation makes up for the lack of gaming machines and music.

Open all day all wk Closed 25-26 Dec **Food** Lunch Mon-Sat 12-3, Sun 12.30-3 ⊕ FREE HOUSE ◀ Alechemy, Stewart Fyne Avalanche & Jarl, Tempest, Thornbridge, Fallen Dragonfly, Black Isle Porter, Williams Bros Joker IPA Ỏ Westons Stowford Press. **Facilities** Non-diners area ♣ (Bar Restaurant) Beer festival WiFi

---

The Café Royal ◉   PICK OF THE PUBS

tel: 0131 556 1884 **19 West Register St EH2 2AA**
email: hello@caferoyaledinburgh.co.uk
dir: *Off Princes St, in city centre*

Hearty Scottish fare in historic building

Designed by local architect Robert Paterson and a listed building, The Café Royal (now owned by Greene King) is a glorious example of Victorian and Baroque, with an interior seemingly frozen in time. Elegant stained glass and fine late Victorian plasterwork dominate the building, as do irreplaceable Doulton ceramic murals in the bar and restaurant. They serve local ales such as Kelburn Ca'Canny and Goldihops, wine, coffee and fresh oysters in the bar and restaurant. In the bar there'll be dishes like haggis, neeps and tatties; and wild mushroom risotto while in the restaurant Scottish produce again dominates the menu, from starters of farmhouse pâté with mustard on cider on toast with onion chutney, to mains of Isle of Bute smoked hake, chorizo mash, green beans and crab butter. Please note, only children over five are allowed in the restaurant.

Open all day all wk **Food** all wk 11-9.45 Restaurant menu available all wk ⊕ GREENE KING ◀ Edinburgh Pale Ale, Kelburn Ca'Canny & Goldihops, Williams Bros, Stewart, Broughton Ales Ỏ Aspall. ♟ 9 **Facilities** Non-diners area WiFi ⛟ (notice required)

Doric Tavern   PICK OF THE PUBS

tel: 0131 225 1084 **15-16 Market St EH1 1DE**
email: info@the-doric.com
dir: *In city centre opposite Waverly Station & Edinburgh Dungeons*

Edinburgh's oldest gastro-pub

There's been a dining inn on this site close to the Royal Mile and the Scottish National Gallery since at least 1823. As such it's the oldest food-inn in Edinburgh, and it proudly continues to offer top-quality Scottish sourced produce. The building may be 400 years old and is apparently named from an old language once spoken in north east Scotland, mainly Aberdeenshire. Award-winning Scottish beers are the mainstay here, including brews from Caledonian and micros like Cairngorm, while real whisky-cask cider comes from Dunbar. Public rooms include a ground-floor bar, and a wine bar and bistro upstairs. In this pleasantly informal surroundings, a wide choice of fresh, locally sourced food is prepared by the chefs on site. Favourite starters include Cullen skink; local mussels; and haggis bon bons. Mains could be grilled veal T-bone; crab risotto; home-made shepherd's pie; or baked vegetable gratin. Seafood is delivered fresh each morning; look for hake fillet with chervil crushed potatoes.

Open all day all wk Sat-Thu 11.30am-1am (Fri 11am-1am) Closed 25-26 Dec **Food** all wk 12-10 ⊕ FREE HOUSE ◀ Caledonian Deuchars IPA & Edinburgh Castle, guest ales Ỏ Thistly Cross. **Facilities** Non-diners area ♦ Children's menu Children's portions Family room WiFi ⛟

The Guildford Arms

tel: 0131 556 4312 **1-5 West Register Street EH2 2AA**
email: guildfordarms@dmstewart.com
dir: *Opposite Balmoral Hotel at E end of Princes St*

Late-Victorian classic free house and galleried restaurant

Arrive at Edinburgh Waverley railway station and head straight here; miss a departing train, ditto – it's so close it would be almost criminal not to. Worthy of study are the bar's magnificent Jacobean-style ceiling, and 10 blue porcelain-handled real ale hand-pumps bearing the Stewart family crest. April and October beer festivals, and monthly brewery weekends underscore their commitment to the products of malted barley. The galleried restaurant offers dishes such as fish chowder; confit duck leg with chorizo and bean cassoulet; double loin lamb chops, smoked bacon with caper and red wine sauce; and 21-day aged, 8oz Tweed Valley rib-eye or sirloin steaks. Burgers and sandwiches are there too. Please note, that however fascinated they might be, under-fives are not allowed in the bar.

Open all day all wk Closed 25-26 Dec, 1 Jan **Food** Lunch all wk 12-3, snacks 3-9 Dinner Sun-Thu 5.30-9.30, Fri Sat 5.30-10 Av main course £10 Restaurant menu available all wk ⊕ FREE HOUSE ◀ Orkney Dark Island, Stewart Pentland IPA, Highland Brewing Co & Island Hopping, Alechemy, Fyne Ales Jarl, rotating guest ales Ỏ Westons 1st Quality, Farmer Jims. ♟ 12 **Facilities** Non-diners area ♣ (Bar) ♦ Children's portions Family room Beer festival WiFi

EDINBURGH *continued*

Halfway House

tel: 0131 225 7101 **24 Fleshmarket Close EH1 1BX**
email: stevehwhiting@gmail.com
dir: *From Royal Mile (close to x-roads with North & South bridges) into Cockburn St. Into Fleshmarket Close, or take flight of steps off Cockburn St on right*

Edinburgh's smallest pub is an iconic institution

Hidden down one of the Old Town's 'closes' (a narrow alleyway, often with a flight of steps and enclosed by tall buildings), the cosy interior of this pub is adorned with railway memorabilia and throngs with locals, tourists, lawyers, students and beer aficionados supping interesting ales from Scottish microbreweries, perhaps Houston Peter's Well and Cairngorm Trade Winds. Mop up the ale with some traditional Scottish bar food made from fresh produce – Cullen skink; stovies and oatcakes; or haggis, tatties and neeps perhaps. Look out for the regular beer festivals, but if beer is not your thing, then perhaps sample a few of the 40 or so whiskies displayed behind the bar.

Open all day all wk **Food** all wk all day Av main course £6.50 ⊕ FREE HOUSE ◀ Stewart Pentland IPA, Harviestoun Bitter & Twisted, Cairngorm Trade Winds, Houston Peter's Well, Cromarty, Alechemy, StrathBraan, Knops Ò Addlestones. **Facilities** Non-diners area ❤ (Bar) ♦♦ Outside area ⊼ Beer festival WiFi **Notes** ⊚

The Scran & Scallie ⊚   PICK OF THE PUBS

tel: 0131 332 6281 **1 Comely Bank Rd EH4 1DT**
email: info@scranandscallie.com
dir: *On B900, in Stockbridge area, opposite Inverleith Park & Botanical Gardens*

Top city dining-pub with cutting-edge cooking

From opening in 2013 to becoming an award-winning pub by 2015 is pretty good going, yet the team behind award-winning Edinburgh restaurants, The Kitchin and Castle Terrace have achieved just this for The Scran & Scallie. The name means 'food and scallywag', by the way. Many of the building's original features have been blended with trendy Scandinavian influences, distressed and reclaimed furnishings, Isle of Bute fabrics and wallpapers by Glasgow designers Timorous Beasties. 'Oor menu' of contemporary seasonal dishes and regional classics embraces mussels, seaweed and garlic butter; roasted hake, curried cauliflower and apple; bavette steak au poivre and chips; and spelt and lentil burger. 'Oor puddins & swally' pairs food and drink as, for example, an espresso pannacotta and hazelnut biscotti with Fettercairn Fior malt. Open all week for lunch, bar 'scran' and dinner (with helpful, very late closing times), as well as weekend brunches.

Open all day all wk 11.30am-1am Closed 25 Dec **Food** Lunch Mon-Fri 12-3, Sat-Sun 12-5 Dinner Mon-Fri 6-10, Sat-Sun 5-10 Set menu available Restaurant menu available all wk ⊕ FREE HOUSE ◀ Isle of Skye Skye Red & Skye Black, Harviestoun Ale Ò Thistly Cross. ▼ 40 **Facilities** Non-diners area ❤ (Bar Restaurant) ♦♦ Children's menu Children's portions Play area Family room WiFi ⇝ (notice required)

The Shore Bar & Restaurant

tel: 0131 553 5080 **3 Shore, Leith EH6 6QW**
email: theshorebar@fishersrestaurantgroup.co.uk
dir: *Phone for detailed directions*

Enjoyable food at Edinburgh's bustling port

This old pub at the heart of Leith's bustling waterfront welcomes guests to a memorable wood-boarded and mirrored interior. Locals and visitors are drawn here by the excellent Scottish seafood, meat and game for which the place is famous.

Mains include fish and chips; or hake, seaweed and crab risotto. Scottish-brewed real ales feature, and in summer, from the outside seating you can look out on the promenade beside the Water of Leith.

Open all day all wk noon-1am (Sun 12.30pm-1am) Closed 25-26 Dec **Food** Mon-Sat 12-10, Sun 12.30-10 Set menu available ⊕ FREE HOUSE ◀ Harviestoun Bitter & Twisted, Guinness Ò Aspall. ▼ 14 **Facilities** Non-diners area ❤ (Bar Outside area) ♦♦ Children's portions Outside area ⊼ WiFi ⇝ (notice required)

Whiski Bar & Restaurant

tel: 0131 556 3095 **119 High St EH1 1SG**
email: info@whiskibar.co.uk **web:** www.whiskibar.co.uk
dir: *Phone for detailed directions*

Whisky, music and food galore on the Royal Mile

If you find yourself on Edinburgh's famous Royal Mile and in need of sustenance and a 'wee' dram, then seek out this highly acclaimed bar at number 119. Choose from over 300 malt whiskies (all available by the nip) and tuck into some traditional Scottish food. Served all day, the menu makes good use of Scottish Border beef and daily deliveries of seafood from local fishermen. Typically, try Cullen skink; Haggis tower with neeps and mash; or smoked salmon penne pasta; then cranachan (a blend of whisky, oatmeal, cream honey and raspberries) for pudding. Come for the traditional Scottish music in the evening – The Whiski is famous for its fiddle music.

Open all day all wk 11am-1am (Sat-Sun 9am-1am) Closed 25 Dec **Food** Mon-Thu 11-10, Fri-Sun 10am-10.30pm ⊕ FREE HOUSE ◀ Caledonian Deuchars IPA, Innis & Gunn, Williams Bros Caesar Augustus Ò Thistly Cross. ▼ 9 **Facilities** Non-diners area ♦♦ Children's menu Children's portions Outside area ⊼ WiFi ⇝ (notice required)

See advert on opposite page

RATHO

Map 21 NT17

The Bridge Inn ★★★★ INN 🌸

PICK OF THE PUBS

tel: 0131 333 1320 **27 Baird Rd EH28 8RA**
email: info@bridgeinn.com **web:** www.bridgeinn.com
dir: *From Newbridge at B7030 junct, follow signs for Ratho & Edinburgh Canal Centre*

Canal-side inn offering restaurant cruises

The tree-lined Union Canal between Edinburgh and the Falkirk Wheel runs past this waterside inn, once used by the early 19th-century navvies who dug the cut. In both the bar and restaurant the menu offers dishes based on local produce, including from the pub's kitchen garden, and from its own chickens, ducks and Saddleback pigs, the latter providing a rich supply of pork loin, fillet, belly and sausages. Typical dishes on the menu are starters of seared wood pigeon, crispy lamb haggis, butternut and burnt onion; and Cullen skink, followed by sea bass fillets, lightly spiced sweet potato purée, chorizo, scallop and sauce vièrge; beetroot and borlotti bean risotto; and venison loin, braised and rolled haunch, butternut creamed potato, LBV port gel and bitter chocolate. Guest Scottish cask ales may include Trade Winds from Cairngorm Brewery, Dark Island from Orkney and beers from Arran. The pub's two renovated barges provide Sunday lunch, afternoon tea and dinner cruises. Children and dogs love the big grassy area outside.

Open all day all wk 11-11 (Fri-Sat 11am-mdnt) Closed 25 Dec **Food** Lunch Mon-Fri 12-3, Sat 12-9, Sun 12-8.30 Dinner Mon-Fri 5-9, Sat 12-9, Sun 12-8.30 ⊕ FREE HOUSE 🍺 Belhaven, rotating Alechemy Ales, guest ales ♻ Aspall. ♚ 40 **Facilities** Non-diners area 🐾 (Bar Garden) 👪 Children's menu Children's portions Play area Garden ⚑ Beer festival Parking WiFi 🚐 (notice required) **Rooms** 4

FALKIRK

BO'NESS

Map 21 NS98

NEW Corbie Inn

tel: 01506 825307 **82-84 Corbiehall EH51 OAS**
email: gail@corbieinn.co.uk
dir: *M9 junct 5, A905 signed Bo'ness. Follow Bo'ness signs at next rdbt. Follow A904 signs*

Great beers and good pub grub

You'll find the Corbie Inn on the foreshore at Bo'ness, beside the Bo'ness and Kinneil Railway. Restored, refurbished (and in some places rebuilt) it's a cosy and very friendly little place, where you can tuck into good home cooked bar meals and pub grub – the likes of gammon steak with egg and pineapple, breaded scampi, or home-made steak pie. Real ales on offer include Corbieha' Pale, produced on site at the Kinneil Brew Hoose, an independent brewery located behind the pub.

Open all day all wk **Food** Sun-Wed 12-8.30, Thu-Sat 12-9 Av main course £6.95 ⊕ FREE HOUSE 🍺 Corbieha' Pale, Timothy Taylor Landlord ♻ Thistly Cross. ♚ 9 **Facilities** Non-diners area 👪 Children's menu Children's portions Play area Family room Garden ⚑ Beer festival Parking WiFi 🚐 (notice required)

FIFE

BURNTISLAND
Map 21 NT28

Burntisland Sands Hotel

tel: 01592 872230 **Lochies Rd KY3 9JX**
email: mail@burntislandsands.co.uk
dir: *Towards Kirkcaldy, Burntisland on A921. Hotel on right before Kinghorn*

Family-run hotel just a leap from the beach

Once a highly regarded girls' boarding school, this small, family-run hotel stands only 50 yards from an award-winning sandy beach. Visitors can expect reasonably priced meals throughout the day, including internationally themed evenings. Typical dishes served in the three dining areas include deep-fried breaded mushrooms or king prawns to start; mains like seared tuna steak with lemon butter, or haggis, neeps and tatties; and bread and butter pudding or mint paradise for dessert. Relax and enjoy a Scottish ale in the bar and lounge area, perhaps on a live music night. There is also a patio garden and children can play with the rabbits in the activity area.

Open all day all wk **Food** Lunch Mon-Fri 12-2.30, Sat-Sun all day Dinner Mon-Fri 5-8.30, Sat-Sun all day Set menu available Restaurant menu available all wk ⊕ FREE HOUSE ◀ Caledonian Deuchars IPA, Tennent's, Belhaven Best, Guinness, guest ales. ♟ 12 **Facilities** Non-diners area ✿ (Garden) ♦♦ Children's menu Children's portions Play area Garden ⋒ Parking WiFi ⛼ (notice required)

CULROSS
Map 21 NS98

NEW Red Lion Inn

tel: 01383 881280 **Low Causeway KY12 8HN**
email: david-j-alexander@hotmail.com
dir: *From A985 between Crombie & Kincardine follow Culross signs. Pub in village centre*

Good, honest pub grub in National Trust village

Culross is the most complete example in Scotland of a 17th- and 18th-century burgh, its old, whitewashed buildings and cobbled streets a fascinating time-warp. The step-gabled Red Lion's ceilings were painted by Stirling artist Douglas Cadoo and depict scenes from *Kidnapped* by Robert Louis Stevenson. If you're planning on a meal, haggis, whisky and cream creggans make a good starter; these could be followed by grated cheese and pineapple salad; battered haddock and chips; rotisserie chicken in barbecue sauce; or maybe veggie sausages with beans and chips. A sorbet or a crumble might well tick the dessert box.

Open all day all wk **Food** all wk 12-9 Set menu available ⊕ FREE HOUSE ◀ Inveralmond Fair Maid. ♟ 8 **Facilities** ✿ (Outside area) ♦♦ Children's menu Outside area ⋒ Parking ⛼ (notice required)

ELIE
Map 21 NO40

NEW The Ship Inn ★★★★ INN   PICK OF THE PUBS

tel: 01333 330246 **The Toft KY9 1DT**
email: info@shipinn.scot web: www.shipinn.scot
dir: *A915 & A917 to Elie. From High Street follow signs to Watersport Centre & The Toft*

Great local seafood overlooking the bay

Graham and Rachel Bucknall took over The Ship Inn at the end of 2014 and immediately set about refurbishing it before reopening it in the summer of 2015. Overlooking Elie Bay, the beer garden of this coastal pub is on the beach itself and there is an outside bar and barbecue throughout the summer. With its fabulous bay views, the light and airy upstairs restaurant has a seaside feel and a gallery space showcasing Scottish artists. In winter, grab a sofa or armchair next to the open fires or wood-burning stoves, perhaps with a glass of Edinburgh Gold in hand. Scottish produce, particularly local shellfish and seafood, drives the menu. Typical dishes include smoked haddock, mussel and clam chowder; and braised venison pie with creamy mash potato. Time a visit between May and September and you might well see the pub's cricket team play a match on the beach, all depending on the tide of course.

Open all day all wk Closed 25 Dec **Food** Lunch Mon-Sat 12-3, Sun 12-8 Dinner Mon-Sat 5-9, Sun 12-8 ⊕ FREE HOUSE ◀ Eden Mill The Clock Red Ale, Caledonian Deuchars IPA, Stewart Edinburgh Gold Ŏ Aspall. ♟ 12 **Facilities** Non-diners area ✿ (Bar Garden) ♦♦ Children's menu Children's portions Garden ⋒ WiFi ⛼ (notice required) **Rooms** 6

ST ANDREWS
Map 21 NO51

Hams Hame Pub & Grill

tel: 01334 474371 **The Old Course Hotel, Golf Resort & Spa KY16 9SP**
email: reservations@oldcoursehotel.co.uk
dir: *M90 junct 8, A91 to St Andrews*

Finest Scottish produce at famous golf venue

Part of a famous complex, this pub, with low ceilings, beams and wooden floors, is over the road from the famous Old Course's 18th green. This being one of the 19th holes in the hotel, your fellow diner or drinker might well be a golfing legend, sharing your enjoyment of some of Scotland's best breweries and menus showcasing its finest produce. Freshly landed North Sea fish and seafood is a given, typically shellfish and chorizo gumbo; other dishes include Dornoch rack of pork ribs; Cajun chicken burger; and grilled flat-cap mushroom with garlic potatoes.

Open all day all wk ⊕ FREE HOUSE ◀ Local ales. **Facilities** ♦♦ Children's menu Children's portions WiFi

Silver Stars The AA Silver Star rating denotes a Hotel or B&B that we highly recommend. They have a superior level of quality within their star rating, high standards of hospitality, service and cleanliness.

The Jigger Inn
PICK OF THE PUBS

tel: 01334 474371 **The Old Course Hotel, Golf Resort & Spa KY16 9SP**
email: reservations@oldcoursehotel.co.uk
dir: *M90 junct 8, A91 to St Andrews*

Possibly golf's best-known 19th hole

Golfing history is an all-embracing experience at this former stationmaster's lodge on the now long-disused railway line to Leuchars. It's in the grounds of The Old Course Hotel, the course in question being the world-famous Royal & Ancient Golf Club of St Andrews. Belhaven brewery supplies the appropriately named Jigger Ale, brewed exclusively for both the pub and its sister golfing resort in Wisconsin, USA. Available all day is seafood landed in nearby fishing villages, carefully selected pork, lamb, beef, game and poultry reared by award-winning Scottish producers, and seasonal fruit and vegetables from local farms. Main courses include Cullen skink; rib-eye steak with grilled Portobello mushrooms and béarnaise sauce; and the Jigger burger with Mull cheese, Ayrshire bacon and fries.

Open all day all wk 11-11 (Sun 12-11) **Food** all wk 12-9.30 ⊕ FREE HOUSE ◖ Belhaven Jigger Ale, St Andrews, Guinness. ♟ 8 **Facilities** Non-diners area ♠♦ Garden ⏚ Parking ⬛

CITY OF GLASGOW

GLASGOW Map 20 NS56

Bon Accord

tel: 0141 248 4427 **153 North St G3 7DA**
email: paul.bonaccord@ntlbusiness.com
dir: *M8 junct 19 merge onto A804 (North Street) signed Charing Cross*

An unmissable destination for malt whisky lovers

Visitors from all over the world come to the 'Bon', Paul McDonagh and son Thomas's acclaimed alehouse and malt whisky bar. The reason? To sample some of the annual tally of a 1,000-plus different beers, over 40 ciders (maybe at one of the four beer and cider festivals), or the 350-strong malts collection (a far cry from the original five on offer). Menus display all-day breakfasts, baguettes, giant Yorkshire puddings, chilli con carne, fish and chips, grilled steaks, chicken salads, macaroni cheese and vegetarian Glamorgan sausages (made with leek and Caerphilly).

Open all day all wk **Food** all wk 12-8 Av main course £6.95 Set menu available ⊕ FREE HOUSE ◖ Over 1,000 real ales per year ♂ Over 40 ciders per year. ♟ 11 **Facilities** Non-diners area ♠♦ Garden Outside area ⏚ Beer & cider festivals WiFi ⬛

NEW The Salisbury

tel: 0141 243 0084 **72 Nithsdale Rd G41 2AN**
email: gmthesalisbury@gmail.com
dir: *From A77 (N of Queen's Park), at lights into Nithsdale St (one-way). At rdbt 1st left, pub on right*

A key part of the city's Southside community

The Salisbury was established in 2014 in a former butcher's shop dating back to the early 1900s – an old butcher's rail and some original signage survive. The cosy bar is home to a wide selection of draft and bottled beers and a good range of gins and whiskies. On the monthly-changing menu you might expect to see traditional Cullen skink; West Coast mussels with marinière sauce; beef brisket with Anna potatoes, horseradish dumplings and pickled onions; and roast guinea fowl breast with Stornoway black pudding stack and game jus. If you're in a sharing mood, then opt for a veggie or fish platter.

Open all day all wk **Food** all wk 12-9 Set menu available Restaurant menu available all wk ⊕ FREE HOUSE ♟ 12 **Facilities** Non-diners area ♠♦ Children's menu Children's portions Outside area ⏚ WiFi ⬛ (notice required)

Stravaigin ◉◉
PICK OF THE PUBS

See Pick of the Pubs on page 608

Ubiquitous Chip ◉◉
PICK OF THE PUBS

See Pick of the Pubs on page 609

NEW WEST on the Corner

tel: 0141 332 0540 **160 Woodlands Rd G3 6LF**
email: wotc@westbeer.com
dir: *Phone for detailed directions*

Smart little corner of Bavaria in Glasgow's West End

One of Glasgow's bright new bars, this is part of the WEST brewery, bar and restaurant family, whose company ethos is 'Glaswegian heart, German head'. Thus, their beers - Hefeweizen, Munich Red, Wild WEST and WEST Black - are all brewed in accordance with Germany's 16th-century Purity Law which in updated form still governs their ingredients. The all-day menu will get you started with goulash soup or reibeküchen (crispy potato pancakes), then carry you forward with wienerschnitzel; Nürnburger bratwurst; pan-fried fillet of sea bass; or spätzle (home-made pasta with shallots and emmental cheese). Well-behaved children and dogs are welcome.

Open all day all wk 11-11 (11am-mdnt Fri-Sat) Closed 25-26 Dec, 1-2 Jan **Food** Lunch all wk 12-5 Dinner all wk 5-9 Set menu available Restaurant menu available all wk ⊕ FREE HOUSE ◖ West GPA ♂ Aspall. ♟ 12 **Facilities** Non-diners area ♣ (Bar Outside area) ♠♦ Children's menu Children's portions Outside area ⏚ WiFi ⬛ (notice required)

WEST on the Green
PICK OF THE PUBS

tel: 0141 550 0135 **Templeton Building, Glasgow Green G40 1AW**
email: info@westbeer.com
dir: *Phone for detailed directions*

German-style brewpub in converted carpet factory

As at WEST on the Corner, 'Glaswegian heart, German head' is the strapline this buzzy brewpub and restaurant uses as it's the only UK brewery producing beers in accordance with Germany's Purity Law of 1516, which means no additives, colourings or preservatives. It occupies the old Winding House of a former carpet factory, modelled by its Victorian architect on the Doge's Palace in Venice. Look down into the brewhouse from the beer hall and watch the brewers making artisanal lagers and wheat beers, including GPA, St Mungo, Dunkel and Hefeweizen. Brewery tours are conducted on selected days of the week. The all-day menu has a German flavour too, offering reibeküchen; spätzle; currywurst; bayrischer wurstsalat; brotaufstriche; and jägerschnitzel. If these choices don't appeal you can also choose from grills, burgers and other British pub grub. For dessert there's apple strudel; pear and frangipane tart; and, in a nod to the past, Black Forest gâteau. There is a large beer garden and brunch is available at weekends. October's Fridays are Oktoberfest beer festival days.

Open all day all wk Closed 25-26 Dec, 1-2 Jan **Food** Lunch all wk 12-5 Dinner all wk 5-9 Set menu available Restaurant menu available all wk ⊕ FREE HOUSE ◖ WEST GPA ♂ Aspall. ♟ 12 **Facilities** Non-diners area ♣ (Bar Restaurant Garden) ♠♦ Children's menu Children's portions Garden ⏚ Beer festival WiFi ⬛ (notice required)

PICK OF THE PUBS

Stravaigin ◉◉

GLASGOW Map 20 NS56

tel: 0141 334 2665
26-30 Gibson St G12 8NX
email: stravaigin@btinternet.com
web: www.stravaigin.com
dir: *From A804 into Woodlands Rd. At mini rdbt take 2nd exit into Eldon St. Over river, inn on right*

Popular inner city destination

'Stravaig' is an old Scots word meaning 'to wander', which perfectly fits the Stravaigin's 'think global, eat local' philosophy. In a busy street near the university, this popular bar/restaurant has earned two AA Rosettes and received an environmental award. The newly extended street-level café bar and basement restaurant draw the crowds to eat and drink among the contemporary decor, modern art and quirky antiques. It offers a long list of wines by the glass, a fair few internationally sourced bottled beers and real ales such as Argyll-brewed Fyne Chip 71. Expect innovative and exciting fusion food cooked from top-quality, seasonal Scottish ingredients — the same menu is served throughout. Until late morning you could have a full Scots breakfast or a vegetarian one, even going off-piste with Indonesian fried rice with bacon and king prawns, if you fancy. Slip in for lunch and begin with warm shredded pheasant, sweetcorn salad and salsa verde; lentil, quinoa roasted beetroot and fresh cow's curd salad; or a baozi, namely a 'wee' steamed bun, perhaps filled with pork belly, kimchi, sesame mayo and chilli sauce. Typically available in the evening are tonkotsu ramen with chilli and garlic confit Pentland pheasant leg, slow-poached free-range egg, Asian greens and toasted nori; pan-fried hake, ginger and coriander potatoes, white pickled anchovies and mint relish; and 'spice route curry of the moment'. There might also be award-winning haggis, Islay scallops, Inverurie lamb and Perthshire pigeon. The Stravaigin churns its own ice creams and sorbets, which feature as desserts, alongside milk chocolate and clementine trifle with cinnamon marshmallow.

Open all day all wk Closed 25 Dec, 1 Jan **Food** Lunch all wk 11-5 Dinner all wk 5-11 Restaurant menu available all wk ⊕ FREE HOUSE ◖ Caledonian Deuchars IPA, Belhaven Best, Fyne Chip 71 ♻ Westons Wyld Wood Organic Classic, Addlestones. ♟ 27 **Facilities** Non-diners area ♣ (Bar) ♦♦ Children's menu Children's portions ⊼ WiFi

PICK OF THE PUBS

Ubiquitous Chip ❀❀

GLASGOW　　　　　Map 20 NS56

tel: 0141 334 5007
12 Ashton Ln G12 8SJ
email: reservations@ubiquitouschip.co.uk
web: www.ubiquitouschip.co.uk
dir: *In West End of Glasgow, off Byres Rd. Beside Hillhead subway station*

A Glasgow icon

In a city with an impressive food and drink scene, one of its most intriguing pubs hides down a cobbled Victorian mews in Glasgow's trendy West End. From opening day in 1971, the Chip drew inspiration from regional Scottish dishes, with people's aunties, grannies and even folklore a constant source of inspiration. The main dining area opens into a vine-covered courtyard, while upstairs is the brasserie-style, two AA-Rosette restaurant. A fine-dining menu is on offer in the restaurant and there are lighter brasserie choices in the various bars, mezzanine and roof terrace. There are several drinking areas – the traditional Big Pub, serving real ales such as Fyne Chip 71, nearly 30 wines by the glass and more than 150 malt whiskies, a roof terrace and the Corner Bar which serves cocktails across a granite slab reclaimed from a mortuary; The Wee Pub (the smallest in Scotland) is a great place to stand and chat with a wee dram. Choose the brasserie for Loch Melfort mussels steamed in smoky Chip 71

broth; Inverurie salt beef with celeriac remoulade, sauerkraut and rocket; and seafood platter with smoked fish pâté, organic salmon gravad lax, brown shrimp croquette, puffed capers and lemon aïoli. Scottish provenance is to the fore again in mains that include smoked Finnan haddie, spinach and dill pie with seasonal vegetables; salad of smoked Perthshire pigeon breast with chicory, baby gem, walnuts, cranberries and Lanark Blue cheese dressing; and Galloway venison leg and tomato stew with mash and toasted almonds. Finish with oat and treacle cake, brandy custard and honey syrup. Regular events, such as jazz, whisky and saxophone quartet lunches, offer an insight into a wide range of cuisines, wines and cultures.

Open all day all wk 11am-1am Closed 25 Dec, 1 Jan **Food** all wk 11-11 Av main course £15.95 Restaurant menu available all wk ⬡ FREE HOUSE 🍺 Caledonian Deuchars IPA, Fyne Chip 71 Ꝺ Addlestones. 🍷 29 **Facilities** Non-diners area 🐾 (Bar Outside area) 🚼 Children's menu Children's portions Outside area 🪑 Beer festival WiFi 🚌 (notice required)

HIGHLAND

ACHILTIBUIE
Map 22 NC00

Summer Isles Hotel & Bar
PICK OF THE PUBS

tel: 01854 622282 **IV26 2YG**
email: summerisleshotel@gmail.com
dir: *Take A835 N from Ullapool for 10m, Achiltibuie signed on left, 15m to village. Hotel 1m on left*

Remote, but that's one of its attractions

With its wonderful views of Badentarbat Bay and the Summer Isles, this highly praised hotel is a comforting presence in a truly beautiful place. Real ales come from the An Teallach brewery on a croft a few miles to the south at Dundonnell, and the seafood is equally local, and couldn't be fresher — scallops and lobster come from the bay itself. The bar menu might feature Cullen skink and fish pie, as well as the amazing seafood platters, but there are plenty of alternatives, including wild mushroom risotto; home-made beef burgers; or cottage pie. Desserts might include sticky toffee pudding or chocolate brownie with chocolate ice cream and chocolate sauce. The informal all-day bar serves freshly ground coffee, snacks, lunch, afternoon tea and evening meals, and there's formal dining as well, in the elegant candlelit restaurant. Don't forget that the weather up here can be somewhat changeable, so come prepared, and remember something to deter the midges that the Highlands host from late spring to late summer.

Open all wk 11-11 Closed 31 Oct-3 Apr **Food** Lunch all wk 12-3 (soup & snacks until 5) Dinner all wk 6-9.30 Av main course £12.95 Restaurant menu available all wk ⊕ FREE HOUSE ◀ An Teallach Crofters' Pale Ale, Beinn Deorg. **Facilities** Non-diners area ✿ (Garden) ♦ Children's menu Children's portions Garden ⊟ Parking WiFi ▨ (notice required)

APPLECROSS
Map 22 NG74

NEW Applecross Inn

tel: 01520 744262 **IV54 8LR**
email: applecrossinn@btconnect.com
dir: *From A87 onto A890 signed Lochcarron. Left onto A896, through Lochcarron. Two alternatives routes to Applecross signed in Tornapress*

Superb local seafood served here

Dating from the early 1800s, this former hotel was taken over by current landlady Judith Fish in 1989, since when the pub has been extended and refurbished. Overlooking the stunning Inner Sound of Raasay, looking towards the Isles of Raasay and Skye, it's a magnificent setting to enjoy one of the 50 Scottish malts on offer, as well as local ales like Skye Red. Scottish produce and seafood from local fishermen drives the menu. Peeled local prawns in garlic butter might be followed by Applecross Bay dressed crab salad or rump of Scottish lamb with wild mushrooms and pancetta lardons.

Open all day all wk **Food** all wk 12-9 Av main course £12 ⊕ FREE HOUSE ◀ An Teallach Crofters' Pale Ale, Isle of Skye Skye Red. **Facilities** Non-diners area ✿ (Bar Garden) ♦ Children's menu Children's portions Garden ⊟ Parking WiFi ▨ (notice required)

CAWDOR
Map 23 NH85

Cawdor Tavern
PICK OF THE PUBS

See Pick of the Pubs on opposite page

FORT WILLIAM
Map 22 NN17

Moorings Hotel ★★★★ HL

tel: 01397 772797 **Banavie PH33 7LY**
email: reservations@moorings-fortwilliam.co.uk **web:** www.moorings-fortwilliam.co.uk
dir: *From A82 in Fort William follow signs for Mallaig, left onto A830 for 1m. Cross canal bridge, 1st right signed Banavie*

Canalside spot with panoramic views

The historic Caledonian Canal and Neptune's Staircase, the famous flight of eight locks, runs right beside this modern hotel and pub. On clear days it has panoramic views towards Ben Nevis, best savoured from the Upper Deck lounge bar and the bedrooms. Food, served in the lounge bar, the new Moorings Café and bistro and the fine-dining Neptunes Restaurant, features local fish and seafood, with other choices such as steak and ale pie, and rib-eye of Highland beef. There is access to the canal towpath from the gardens.

Open all day all wk Closed 24-26 Dec **Food** all wk 10-9.30 Restaurant menu available ⊕ FREE HOUSE ◀ Tetley's Bitter, Caledonian Deuchars IPA, Guinness. ♟ 8 **Facilities** Non-diners area ✿ (Bar Garden Outside area) ♦ Children's menu Children's portions Garden Outside area ⊟ Parking WiFi ▨ (notice required) **Rooms** 32

GAIRLOCH
Map 22 NG87

The Old Inn
PICK OF THE PUBS

tel: 01445 712006 **IV21 2BD**
email: info@theoldinn.net
dir: *Just off A832, near harbour at south end of village*

Traditional coaching inn with its own brewery

Specialising in freshly landed local seafood, Highland game produce, Scottish real ales and live folk music, The Old Inn is below the majestic Torridon Mountains, just inland from Gairloch's little harbour. Superb walks to secluded bays and wooded crags, and ravishing views across to Skye and the outer islands abound. Owner Alastair Pearson brews several beers on site, as well as stocking some from other Scottish micros and sometimes English breweries too. The pub also smokes its own meats, fish and cheese, and bread is baked in-house. Start with a pot of spinnies (spiny squat lobster tails) that's a West Coast delicacy, followed by haggis cairn, neeps, potatoes, Drambuie cream and oatcakes; or spinach and ricotta cannelloni with salad. Specials might well include seafood risotto; langoustine and calamari platter; venison steak; and home-made shepherd's pie. Cath's award-winning clootie dumpling — a rich whisky flavoured fruit pudding — makes for a rewarding dessert.

Open all day all wk 11am-mdnt (Sun 12-12) Closed 21 Nov-Feb **Food** Lunch all wk 12-2.30, summer 12-4.30 Dinner all wk 5-9.30 Restaurant menu available all wk evening ⊕ FREE HOUSE ◀ The Old Inn The Erradale, The Flowerdale, The Slattadale, Mike's Mild & Blind Piper, An Teallach Beinn Dearg, Crofters' Pale Ale & Suilven, Cairngorm Nessie's Monster Mash, Trade Winds & Wildcat. **Facilities** Non-diners area ✿ (Bar Garden) ♦ Children's menu Children's portions Garden ⊟ Parking WiFi ▨ (notice required)

PICK OF THE PUBS

Cawdor Tavern

CAWDOR   Map 23 NH85

tel: 01667 404777
The Lane IV12 5XP
email: enquiries@cawdortavern.co.uk
web: www.cawdortavern.co.uk
dir: *Between Inverness and Nairn, take A96 onto B9006, follow Cawdor Castle signs. Tavern in village centre*

Scottish innkeeping at its best

The Tavern is tucked away in the heart of Cawdor's pretty conservation village; nearby is the castle where Macbeth held court. Pretty wooded countryside slides away from the pub, offering umpteen opportunities for rambles and challenging cycle routes. Exercise over, repair to this homely hostelry to enjoy the welcoming mix of fine Scottish food and island microbrewery ales that makes the pub a destination in its own right. There's an almost baronial feel to the bars, created from the Cawdor Estate's joinery workshop in the 1960s. The lounge bar's wonderful panelling came from Cawdor Castle's dining room as a gift from a former laird; log fires and stoves add winter warmth, as does the impressive choice of Orkney Brewery beers and Highland and Island malts. An accomplished menu balances meat, fish, game and vegetarian options, prepared in a modern Scottish style with first class Scottish produce. Settle in the

delightful restaurant beneath wrought iron Jacobean chandeliers and contemplate starting with a trio of Scottish puddings – black pudding, prize haggis and white pudding layered together and served with home-made chutney. Next maybe a venison burger from the grill, topped with smoked bacon, tomato relish and melting mozzarella. Classic sweets include sticky toffee pudding, and chocolate brownie with warm chocolate sauce. Alfresco drinking and dining is possible on the colourful patio area at the front of the Tavern during the warm summer months. Excellent value is a Sunday high tea starting at 4.30pm.

Open all wk 11-11 (high season) (Sat 11am-mdnt Sun 12.30-11 high season)

Closed 25-26 Dec, 1 Jan **Food** Lunch Mon-Sat 12-5, Sun 12.30-5 Dinner all wk 5-9 🛢 FREE HOUSE 🍺 Orkney Red MacGregor, Raven Ale, Clootie Dumpling & Dark Island, Atlas Latitude Highland Pilsner, Three Sisters, Nimbus & Wayfarer 🍏 Thatchers Gold. 🍷 9 **Facilities** Non-diners area 🐾 (Bar) 🚼 Children's menu Children's portions Outside area 🪧 Beer festival Parking WiFi 🚌 (notice required)

GLENCOE
Map 22 NN15

Clachaig Inn

tel: 01855 811252 **PH49 4HX**
email: frontdesk@clachaig.com
dir: *Follow Glencoe signs from A82. Inn 3m S of village*

Real craic at this legendary Highland inn

In the heart of Glencoe, against a backdrop of spectacular mountains, this famous Highland inn has welcomed climbers, hill-walkers, skiers, kayakers and intrepid travellers for over 300 years. Real ales (sometimes as many as 15), over 300 malt whiskies, good food and fresh coffee are served in all three bars, each with its own distinctive and lively character. Local dishes on offer include Stornoway black pudding; oak-smoked West Coast salmon; Highland venison burger; and vegetarian haggis, neeps 'n' tatties. As well as beer, whisky and gin tastings, the pub also holds a Hogmanay beer festival, and two others – FebFest and OctoberFest.

Open all day all wk Closed 24-26 Dec **Food** all wk 12-9 ⊕ FREE HOUSE ◀ Rotating local guest ales ⓣ Thistly Cross, Carn O'Mohr. **Facilities** Non-diners area ☻ (Bar Garden) ♦♦ Children's menu Children's portions Play area Family room Garden ⊨ Beer festival Parking WiFi ▭

GLENUIG
Map 22 NM67

Glenuig Inn

tel: 01687 470219 **PH38 4NG**
email: bookings@glenuig.com
dir: *From Fort William on A830 towards Mallaig through Glen Finnan. Left onto A861, 8m to Glenuig Bay*

A more spectacular setting you couldn't wish for

The Glenuig Inn, on a no-through road and right beside a stunning beach on the Sound of Arisaig, is a popular base for sea-kayakers. The emphasis here is 'as local as we can get it' and this philosophy applies to the bar, where ale from Cairngorm is served, and the kitchen, where menus are prepared using organic seasonal ingredients wherever possible. A typical selection might include Glenuig hot smoked salmon, followed by Skye lamb tagine or home-made venison burger, and chocolate and chilli tart to finish. The inn's owners are committed to 'going green', and since 2015 they have run on 100% renewable energy resulting in zero carbon emissions, so it's no wonder they have a gold award from the Green Tourism Business Scheme.

Open all day all wk **Food** all wk 12-9 ⊕ FREE HOUSE ◀ Cairngorm Trade Winds, Black Gold, Gold, Wild Cat, Highland IPA ⓣ Thistly Cross. ⏴ 9 **Facilities** Non-diners area ☻ (Bar Restaurant Garden) ♦♦ Children's menu Children's portions Play area Family room Garden ⊨ Parking WiFi

INVERGARRY
Map 22 NH30

The Invergarry Hotel

tel: 01809 501206 **PH35 4HJ**
email: info@invergarryhotel.co.uk
dir: *At junct of A82 & A87*

In a tranquil spot, ideal for walking

A real Highland atmosphere pervades this roadside inn set in glorious mountain scenery between Fort William and Fort Augustus. Welcoming bars make it a great base from which to explore Loch Ness, Glencoe and the West Coast. Relax by the crackling log fire with a wee dram or a pint of Garry Ale, then tuck into a good meal.

Perhaps try baked filo parcel stuffed with haggis, bashit neeps, roasted shallot with malt whisky and thyme mayonnaise to start; followed by baked pollock with a sun-dried tomato and herb crust; or a succulent 10oz rib-eye Scottish beefsteak with hand-cut chips. There are, of course, excellent walks from the front door. Please note, booking is required for dinner.

Open all day all wk **Food** all wk 8am-9.30pm Av main course £16.50 ⊕ FREE HOUSE ◀ The Invergarry Inn Garry Ale. **Facilities** Non-diners area ♦♦ Children's menu Children's portions Family room Garden ⊨ Parking

KYLESKU
Map 22 NC23

Kylesku Hotel
PICK OF THE PUBS

tel: 01971 502231 **IV27 4HW**
email: info@kyleskuhotel.co.uk
dir: *A835, A837 & A894 to Kylesku. Hotel at end of road at Old Ferry Pier*

Wonderful local seafood by the loch

This 17th-century coaching inn sits at the centre of the North West Highlands Global Geopark. Surrounded by lochs, mountains and wild coast – and close to Britain's highest waterfall – it's a glorious location. Views from the bar and restaurant are truly memorable – you may catch sight of seals, dolphins, otters, eagles and terns. The fishing boats moor at the old ferry slipway to land the creel-caught seafood that forms the backbone of the daily-changing menu. So settle down with a pint of Isle of Skye, and ponder your choice of the morning's catch, perhaps starting with Ullapool oysters, hot or cold; or Loch Duart salmon gravad lax with cream cheese, cucumber and oatcakes. Next, you could go for chicken Kiev; pie of the day; glazed shallot Tatin with mixed leaves and walnut salad; or seared king scallops with saffron rice, kedgeree and crispy bacon. Gluten-free and vegetarian menus also available.

Open all day all wk Closed Dec-Jan **Food** Lunch all wk 12-6 Dinner all wk 6-9 Av main course £15 ⊕ FREE HOUSE ◀ An Teallach & Beinn Dearg Ale, Isle of Skye. ⏴ 12 **Facilities** Non-diners area ☻ (Bar Restaurant Garden) ♦♦ Children's menu Children's portions Garden ⊨ WiFi

LEWISTON
Map 23 NH52

The Loch Ness Inn

tel: 01456 450991 **IV63 6UW**
email: info@staylochness.co.uk
dir: *Phone for detailed directions*

Comfy village inn in the famous Great Glen

A brisk stroll from here on the waymarked Great Glen Way heads towards the shoreline of the renowned loch. This place, under new ownership, is a hive of activity and there's always an event of some kind going on. The modern menu is based on top Scottish ingredients – haggis and lamb koftas; or Applecross Bay prawns as starters, followed by pan-fried venison steak; or east coast haddock. All this will build an appetite for a loch-side ramble to famous Urquhart Castle. Unusually, a range of Scottish distilled gins is available at the bar – Boe and Caorunn being just two.

Open all day all wk **Food** all wk breakfast-10pm Set menu available Restaurant menu available all wk ⊕ FREE HOUSE ◀ Loch Ness ⓣ Westons Stowford Press. ⏴ 10 **Facilities** Non-diners area ♦♦ Children's menu Children's portions Garden ⊨ Parking WiFi ▭ (notice required)

PICK OF THE PUBS

The Plockton Hotel

PLOCKTON Map 22 NG83

tel: 01599 544274 **Harbour St IV52 8TN**
email: info@plocktonhotel.co.uk
web: www.plocktonhotel.co.uk
dir: *A87 towards Kyle of Lochalsh. At Balmacara follow Plockton signs, 7m*

Award-winning local seafood served here

Set with the mountains on one side and the deep blue waters of Loch Carron on the other, this lovely village is well known for its white-washed cottages and, of all things, palm trees. Dating from 1827, this original black fronted building is thought to have been a ships' chandlery before it was converted to serve as the village inn. Run by Alan Pearson and Mags Pearson, the couple have inherited a successful legacy from Alan's parents who were in charge for two decades. The hotel specialises in seafood — including freshly landed fish and locally caught langoustines (mid afternoon you can watch the catch being landed) — supplemented by Highland steaks and locally reared beef. Lunchtime features light bites and toasted paninis, as well as a good range of hot dishes. Evening dishes might include Talisker whisky pâté; sweet pickled herring and prawns; or grilled

goats' cheese with beetroot chutney to start, followed by Highland venison collops with Cumberland sauce; fillet of monkfish wrapped in bacon; chargrilled Aberdeen Angus steak with whisky sauce; or pan-fried medallions of pork with brandied apricots and cream sauce. Daily specials, written up on the blackboard, add to the tempting choices. There are four Scottish real ales on tap, and a fine range of malts is available to round off that perfect Highland day, perhaps accompanied by one of the 'basket' meals served every evening from 9pm-10pm — try the breaded scampi tails.

Open all day all wk 11am-mdnt (Sun 12-11) Closed 25 Dec, 1 Jan **Food** Lunch all wk 12-2.15 Dinner all wk 6-10 ⊕ FREE HOUSE ◀ Highland Scapa Special & Island Hopping, Cromarty Happy Chappy & Kowabunga.
Facilities Non-diners area ⬥ Children's menu Children's portions Family room Garden ☰ Beer festival WiFi

PICK OF THE PUBS

Plockton Inn & Seafood Restaurant

PLOCKTON Map 22 NG83

tel: 01599 544222 **Innes St IV52 8TW**
email: info@plocktoninn.co.uk
web: www.plocktoninn.co.uk
dir: *A87 towards Kyle of Lochalsh. At Balmacara follow Plockton signs, 7m*

Friendly inn offering great seafood

Located in Plockton which is on Loch Carron in the West Highlands, this inn is owned and run by Mary Gollan, her brother Kenny and his partner Susan Trowbridge. The Gollans were born and bred in the village and it was actually their great-grandfather who built the attractive stone free house as a manse. The beautiful views can be enjoyed from seats on the decking outside. The ladies double up in the role of chef, while Kenny manages the bar, where you'll find winter fires, Plockton real ales from the village brewery, and a selection of over 50 malt whiskies. A meal in the reasonably formal Dining Room or more relaxed Lounge Bar is a must, with a wealth of freshly caught local fish and shellfish, West Highland beef, lamb, game and home-made vegetarian dishes on the menu, plus daily specials. The Plockton prawns (called langoustines here), which Martin the barman catches in the sea loch, are taken to Kenny's smokehouse to the rear of the building to be cured along with other seafood — the results can be

sampled in the seafood platter starter. Other starters include moules marinière; haggis and clapshot; and fish soup of the day. Among the main dishes are hand-dived king scallops pan-fried with bacon and garlic; langoustines, served hot with garlic butter or cold with Marie Rose sauce; grilled fillets of plaice or sea bass with chive, pink peppercorn and lemon butter; and braised lamb shank with Guinness. Desserts include citrus pot, and Scottish cheeses served with Orkney oatcakes. The public bar is alive on Tuesdays and Thursdays with music from local musicians, who are often joined by youngsters from the National Centre of Excellence in Traditional Music in the village.

Open all day all wk **Food** Lunch all wk 12-2.15 Dinner all wk 6-9 ⊕ FREE HOUSE 🍺 Greene King Abbot Ale, Fuller's London Pride, Young's Special, Plockton Crags Ale & Bay.
Facilities Non-diners area 🐾 (Bar Garden) 👪 Children's menu Children's portions Play area Garden 🎍 Parking WiFi 🚐 (notice required)

PICK OF THE PUBS

Shieldaig Bar & Coastal Kitchen

SHIELDAIG Map 22 NG85

tel: 01520 755251 **IV54 8XN**
email: tighaneilean@keme.co.uk
web: www.tighaneilean.co.uk
dir: *Exit A896*

Remote and peaceful lochside pub, hotel and restaurants

Remote enough to make its Inverness postcode look totally inappropriate, the Shieldaig Bar & Coastal Kitchen is part of the famous Tigh an Eilean (House of the Island) Hotel. It's here that the majestic Torridon Mountains meet the western seas. Upper Loch Torridon is just round the corner. Wildlife is abundant, with otters, seals, white-tailed sea eagles, oyster catchers and pine martens. Then there are the deserted beaches and walking trails. From a croft at the magical-sounding Little Loch Broom, the An Teallach Brewery supplies real ales to the traditional bar, where live music and ceilidhs add a weekend buzz. The sea provides much of what appears on the menu, especially the shellfish landed daily by fishermen using environmentally responsible creel-fishing and hand-diving techniques. Ways of sampling this local bounty in the restaurant include gratin of crab with pink grapefruit; seared Hebridean scallops with Serrano ham; and escalope of West Coast sea bream with

Provençal confit. The land also does a pretty good job with food, among other things rack of Scottish Blackface lamb with herb crust and lamb jus. An alternative eating place is the more casual Coastal Kitchen, not that the main restaurant is particularly formal. Here the local seafood is just as imaginatively prepared but with the emphasis on simplicity, such as the hearty seafood stew or one of the speciality pizzas from the wood-fired oven. To watch the often spectacular sunsets, choose a table in the courtyard or one of the first-floor decks. The hotel also owns the village's general store, where you can buy provisions, postcards and most-day-to-day necessities.

Open all day all wk 11-11 **Food** Lunch all wk 12-2.30 (summer all day) Dinner all wk 6-9 (summer all day) ⊞ FREE HOUSE ◀ An Teallach. ♟ 8 **Facilities** Non-diners area ♦♦ Children's menu Children's portions Garden ⊼ Parking WiFi 🚐 (notice required)

LOCHINVER
Map 22 NC02

NEW The Caberfeidh

tel: 01571 844321 **Main St IV27 4JY**
email: admin@thecaberfeidh.co.uk
dir: A837 to Lochinver. Pub on right

Waterfront pub serving great local seafood

Meaning 'stag's antlers' in Gaelic, The Caberfeidh is run by experienced chef-hoteliers Colin Craig and Lesley Cornfield. The Georgian pub's position where the River Inver meets the sea loch makes it a great spot for otter and heron-spotting from the restaurant and beer garden. Its waterfront location is reflected in the menus, which display a strong sense of place with an emphasis on seasonal produce including wild game and locally caught fish and shellfish. Start, perhaps, with Ullapool oysters before moving on to a langoustine platter or wild local venison burger. As opening times vary throughout the year, please check the exact times with the pub.

Open Times vary throughout the year Closed 25 Dec, 1 Jan, Mon in winter **Food** Lunch Tue-Sat 12-2.30, Sun 12.30-2.30 Dinner Tue-Sun 6-8 Av main course £12 ⊕ FREE HOUSE ◀ Isle of Skye Black, Blaven, Gold & Red Ö Thistly Cross, Westons Wyld Wood Organic. ♀ 14 **Facilities** Non-diners area ♦♦ Garden ⴹ Parking WiFi ➡ (notice required)

NORTH BALLACHULISH
Map 22 NN06

Old Ferry Bar at Loch Leven Hotel

tel: 01855 821236 **Old Ferry Rd PH33 6SA**
email: reception@lochlevenhotel.co.uk
dir: Off A82, N of Ballachulish Bridge

Enjoy one of Scotland's most idyllic views

The slipway into Loch Leven at the foot of the garden recalls the origins of this 17th-century inn as one of the Road to The Isles staging points linked to the old ferry. Enjoy a pint of River Leven bitter on the sundeck and drink-in one of the best views from a pub anywhere in Britain, or on chillier days sit beside the open fire. The extraordinary location, near the foot of Glencoe and with horizons peppered by Munro peaks rising above azure sea lochs, is gifted with superb seafood from the local depths. So you can enjoy scallop, sea bass, and mussel dishes and also classics such as an Aberdeen Angus burger with hand-cut chips. Adjoining the bar are family and games rooms.

Open all day all wk 11-11 (Thu-Sat 11am-mdnt Sun 12.30-11) **Food** Lunch all wk 12-3 Dinner all wk 6-9 Restaurant menu available all wk ⊕ FREE HOUSE ◀ River Leven. ♀ 16 **Facilities** Non-diners area ♣ (Bar Garden) ♦♦ Children's menu Children's portions Family room Garden ⴹ Parking WiFi ➡ (notice required)

PLOCKTON
Map 22 NG83

The Plockton Hotel
PICK OF THE PUBS

See Pick of the Pubs on page 613

Plockton Inn & Seafood Restaurant
PICK OF THE PUBS

See Pick of the Pubs on page 614

SHIELDAIG
Map 22 NG85

Shieldaig Bar & Coastal Kitchen
PICK OF THE PUBS

See Pick of the Pubs on page 615

TORRIDON
Map 22 NG95

The Torridon Inn ★★★★ INN
PICK OF THE PUBS

tel: 01445 791242 **IV22 2EY**
email: info@thetorridon.com **web:** www.thetorridon.com/inn
dir: From Inverness take A9 N, then follow signs to Ullapool. Take A835 then A832. In Kinlochewe take A896 to Annat. Pub 200yds on right after village

Idyllic location and definitive Scottish menus

The island-fringed, azure waters of Loch Torridon and the striking mountains across the water are neighbours to this bustling inn. It makes it a convenient base to walk, mountaineer, kayak or rock climb, but its cosy comfortable atmosphere and good home-cooked food very much appeal to the less active too. Painstakingly converted from old farm buildings, a stable block and buttery, there's a good range of Highlands and Islands beer on tap, often from Cairngorm and An Teallach breweries, supplemented by an annual October beer festival. A cosy interior with wood fires and bright decor as well as an airy conservatory-diner is a restful place to consider a fine Scottish menu, much of it from the West Coast area. Chicken liver pâté with chutney and oatcakes to start perhaps; then plump for venison sausages with bean and chickpea cassoulet; chargrilled pork chop with mustard mash; or perhaps Isle of Ewe smoked hake, kedgeree and poached hen's egg.

Open all day all wk Closed Jan **Food** Lunch all wk 12-2 Dinner all wk 6-9 ⊕ FREE HOUSE ◀ Isle of Skye Red Cuillin, Torridon Ale, Cairngorm Trade Winds, An Teallach & Crofters Pale Ale, Cromarty Happy Chappy. **Facilities** Non-diners area ♣ (Bar Garden) ♦♦ Children's menu Children's portions Play area Garden ⴹ Beer festival Parking WiFi ➡ (notice required) **Rooms** 12

NORTH LANARKSHIRE

CUMBERNAULD
Map 21 NS77

Castlecary House Hotel

tel: 01324 840233 **Castlecary Rd G68 OHD**
email: enquiries@castlecaryhotel.com
dir: A80 onto B816 between Glasgow & Stirling. 7m from Falkirk, 9m from Stirling

Friendly family-run hotel

Castlecary House Hotel is located close to the historic Antonine Wall and the Forth and Clyde Canal. Meals plough a traditional furrow with options such as deep-fried haggis balls; home-made steak pie; and daily specials. Home-made puddings include sticky toffee pudding and profiteroles. More formal fare is available in Camerons Restaurant, where high tea is also served on Sundays. There is an excellent and varying selection of real ales on offer, including Arran Blonde and Harviestoun Bitter & Twisted. Live music every Saturday evening.

Open all day all wk Closed 1 Jan **Food** Mon-Sat 12-9, Sun 12.30-9 Av main course £8.50 Set menu available Restaurant menu available all wk ⊕ FREE HOUSE ◀ Arran Blonde, Harviestoun Bitter & Twisted, Inveralmond Ossian's Ale, Houston Peter's Well, Caledonian Deuchars IPA. ♀ 8 **Facilities** Non-diners area ♦♦ Children's menu Children's portions Garden Outside area ⴹ Parking WiFi ➡ (notice required)

EAST LOTHIAN

GULLANE
Map 21 NT48

The Old Clubhouse

tel: 01620 842008 **East Links Rd EH31 2AF**
dir: *A198 into Gullane, 3rd right into East Links Rd, pass church, on left*

Pub favourites overlooking the Gullane Links

Established in 1890 as the home of Gullane Golf Club, this building had a chequered past after the golfers moved on to larger premises, including stints as a disco and as tea rooms. Over 25 years ago the Campanile family took the reins and it hasn't looked back. Roaring winter fires and walls crammed with golfing memorabilia make a good first impression, and the menu delivers a list of international favourites including chilli salt and pepper calamari; Hornigs haggis, neeps and tatties; pot-baked lamb orzo; pork schnitzel, black pudding and fried egg; and Chinese five spice duck salad. For dessert, maybe choose rhubarb and custard pudding.

Open all day all wk Closed 25 Dec, 1 Jan **Food** all wk 12-9.30 ⊕ FREE HOUSE ◀ Timothy Taylor Landlord, Caledonian Deuchars IPA Ó Thistly Cross. ☗ 9 **Facilities** Non-diners area ❀ (Bar Garden) ♦♦ Children's menu Children's portions Garden Outside area ☎ WiFi ☲ (notice required)

LONGNIDDRY
Map 21 NT47

The Longniddry Inn

tel: 01875 852401 **Main St EH32 0NF**
email: info@longniddryinn.com
dir: *On A198 (Main St), near rail station*

Comprehensive menu choices in historic buildings

This combination of a former blacksmith's forge and four cottages on Longniddry's Main Street continues to be a popular spot. Held in high esteem locally for friendly service and good food, it offers an extensive menu featuring the likes of roast chicken platter; pan-fried lamb's liver, crispy bacon, mash, vegetables and onion gravy; Mexican enchiladas; spaghetti carbonara; and haddock mornay. In warmer weather why not take your pint of Belhaven Best, glass of wine or freshly ground coffee outside.

Open all day all wk Closed 26 Dec, 1 Jan **Food** Mon-Sat 12-8.30, Sun 12.30-7.30 ⊕ PUNCH TAVERNS ◀ Belhaven Best. **Facilities** Non-diners area ♦♦ Children's menu Children's portions Garden Parking WiFi ☲

WEST LOTHIAN

LINLITHGOW
Map 21 NS97

Champany Inn - The Chop and Ale House ◉◉

PICK OF THE PUBS

tel: 01506 834532 **Champany EH49 7LU**
email: reception@champany.com
dir: *2m NE of Linlithgow at junct of A904 & A803*

Renowned inn with an award-winning cellar

Spread across a collection of buildings, some dating from the 16th century, Champany Corner is within striking distance of Edinburgh. A talking point in the luxurious bar is a rock pond where oysters and lobsters fresh from the Western Isles take in their new surroundings, while you, glass of St Mungos, Thistly Cross farmhouse cider from Dunbar, or perhaps own-label South African wine in hand, take in the menu. Entirely separate from the restaurant in a former bar is the Chop and Ale House, where starters include marinated herring fillets with crème fraîche; and home-smoked chorizo with apricot and mango chutney. Although the inn is big on Aberdeen Angus steaks and burgers, there's plenty more choice, including best-end-of-neck lamb chops; North Sea cod in home-made batter with 'man-sized' chips; and charcoal-grilled peri-peri chicken. For pudding, hot malted waffles are served with maple syrup and whipped cream; and rich chocolate tart is sprinkled with praline.

Open all wk 12-2 6.30-10 (Fri-Sun 12-10) Closed 25-26 Dec, 1 Jan **Food** Lunch all wk 12-2 Dinner all wk 6.30-10 Av main course £13.50-£25 Restaurant menu available Mon-Fri ⊕ FREE HOUSE ◀ Caledonia Best, St Mungos Ó Thistly Cross. ☗ 8 **Facilities** ♦♦ Children's portions Garden ☎ Parking WiFi

The Four Marys

tel: 01506 842171 **65/67 High St EH49 7ED**
email: fourmarys.linlithgow@belhavenpubs.net
dir: *M9 junct 3 or junct 4, A803 to Linlithgow. Pub in town centre*

Family-friendly pub in historic town setting

This eye-catching building at the heart of Linlithgow has only been a pub since 1981, but its pedigree stretches back a further 500 years to when royalty lived at the nearby palace. The eponymous Marys were ladies-in-waiting to Linlithgow-born Mary, Queen of Scots. Low ceilings, striking dressed-stone walls, and period and antique furnishings give the pub a real sense of atmosphere and history. Caledonian Deuchars IPA and Belhaven St Andrews are on tap along with guest ales; twice-yearly beer festivals are held, whilst robust pub grub includes steak and ale pie, burgers, hot dogs and jacket potatoes.

Open all day all wk **Food** Lunch all wk 12-5 Dinner all wk 5-9 Set menu available ⊕ BELHAVEN/GREENE KING ◀ St Andrews, Caledonian Deuchars IPA, guest ales. ☗ 9 **Facilities** Non-diners area ❀ (Bar) ♦♦ Children's menu Children's portions Garden Outside area Beer festival WiFi ☲ (notice required)

MIDLOTHIAN

DALKEITH
Map 21 NT36

The Sun Inn ★★★★ INN ◉
PICK OF THE PUBS

tel: 0131 663 2456 **Lothian Bridge EH22 4TR**
email: thesuninn@live.co.uk **web:** www.thesuninnedinburgh.co.uk
dir: *On A7 towards Galashiels, opposite Newbattle Viaduct*

A modern dining-pub in five acres of wooded grounds

Opposite a fine Victorian railway viaduct by the Lothianbridge over the River South Esk, this family-run former coaching inn is an expert blend of old and new. The fireplace, oak beams and exposed stone walls are original, while the fine wooden floor owes much to the 21st century. Quite reasonably, Scottish cask ales monopolise the beer pumps, and there is also an extensive wine list. Food in the more formal, AA-Rosette restaurant is modern British and pub classics with a strong Scottish accent. Noteworthy dishes include pan-seared Borders lamb's liver with creamy mash, crispy bacon and onion gravy; turbot fillets, Eyemouth crab and spring onion risotto with chilli and ginger king prawn and red pepper dressing; and free-range hen's egg omelette with Applewood smoked cheddar and spring onion, hand-cut chips, chive cream and dressed leaves. Haggis is one of the optional side dishes. You may take high tea any weekday afternoon.

Open all day all wk Closed 26 Dec, 1 Jan **Food** Lunch Mon-Sat 12-2, Mon-Fri High Tea 2.30-5.30, Sun 12-7 Dinner Mon-Sat 6-9, Sun 12-7 Av main course £15-£20 Set menu available ⊕ FREE HOUSE ◀ Alechemy, Inveralmond, Eden Ales, Stewart Ó Addlestones. ☗ 19 **Facilities** Non-diners area ♦♦ Children's menu Children's portions Garden ☎ Parking WiFi ☲ (notice required) **Rooms** 5

The Howgate Restaurant

tel: 01968 670000 **Howgate EH26 8PY**
email: peter@howgate.com
dir: *10m N of Peebles. 3m E of Penicuik on A6094 between Leadburn junct & Howgate*

Fine food and ales in a former dairy

Formerly the home of Howgate cheeses, this beautifully converted farm building has a fire-warmed bar offering bistro-style meals, while the candlelit restaurant serves a full carte. The kitchen uses the finest Scottish produce, especially beef and lamb, which are cooked on the charcoal grill; other options might include Scotch beef, Belhaven and mushroom pie with chips and veg; salmon fillet, wilted spinach, asparagus and spicy coriander and tomato sauce; smoked haddock and wild mushroom risotto; or chicken Caesar salad with herb croûtons. There are fine beers to enjoy and an impressively produced wine list roams the globe.

Open all wk 12-2 6-11 Closed 25-26 Dec, 1 Jan **Food** Lunch all wk 12-2 Dinner all wk 6-9.30 ⊕ FREE HOUSE ◢ Belhaven Best, Broughton Ales Greenmantle Ale. ▾ 14 **Facilities** ◑ Children's menu Children's portions Garden ⊨ Parking ▭ (notice required)

The Original Rosslyn Inn ★★★★ INN

tel: 0131 440 2384 **2-4 Main St EH25 9LE**
email: enquiries@theoriginalrosslyninn.co.uk web: www.theoriginalrosslyninn.co.uk
dir: *From City of Edinburgh bypass exit at Straiton onto A701 signed Peebles & City Centre. At 2nd rdbt left onto B7006 signed Roslin. At x-roads in Roslin, inn on corner on left*

A perfect city escape that's a stone's throw from Rosslyn Chapel

Just eight miles from central Edinburgh and a short walk from Rosslyn Chapel, this family-run village inn has been in the Harris family for over 40 years. Robert Burns, the famous Scottish poet, stayed here in 1787 and wrote a two verse poem for the landlady about his visit. Today you have the chance to catch up with the locals in the village bar, or relax by the fire in the lounge whilst choosing from the menu. Soups, jackets and paninis are supplemented by main course options like haggis with tatties and neeps; breaded haddock and chips; and vegetarian harvester pie. Alternatively, the Grail Restaurant offers more comprehensive dining options. There are well-equipped bedrooms, four with four-posters.

Open all day all wk **Food** Lunch Mon-Fri 12-3, Sat 12-9, Sun 12-8.30 Dinner Mon-Fri 5-9, Sat 12-9, Sun 12-8.30 ⊕ FREE HOUSE ◢ Caledonia Best. ▾ 14 **Facilities** Non-diners area ❦ (Bar Garden) ◑ Children's menu Children's portions Garden ⊨ Parking WiFi ▭ **Rooms** 7

The Old Mill Inn

tel: 01309 641605 **Brodie IV36 2TD**
dir: *Between Nairn & Forres on A96*

Spacious, family-friendly pub and restaurant

Situated on the Scottish Riviera, officially recorded as one of the sunniest and driest places in the UK, this former watermill has acquired windows, panelling and a beautiful door from a demolished stately home across the Moray Firth. There's a wide choice of food, from 12-hour slow-roasted belly of pork to feta cheese and spinach tart; and pan-fried sea bream with pea and broad bean gnocchi to roast loin of venison with pommes Anna, red cabbage, black kale and 'gin and tonic' scented chocolate jus. There's an ever-changing selection of Scottish real ales at the bar; over 30, all through hand pumps, can be tried during the June beer festival.

Open all day all wk Closed 25-26 Dec, 1 Jan **Food** Lunch all wk 11.30-5 Dinner all wk 5-9 Av main course £12 Restaurant menu available Tue-Sun ⊕ FREE HOUSE ◢ Rotating guest ales. ▾ 9 **Facilities** ◑ Children's menu Children's portions Garden ⊨ Beer festival Parking WiFi ▭ (notice required)

Killiecrankie House Hotel ★★★ SHL ◉◉

PICK OF THE PUBS

tel: 01796 473220 **PH16 5LG**
email: enquiries@killiecrankiehotel.co.uk web: www.killiecrankiehotel.co.uk
dir: *Take B8079 N from Pitlochry. Hotel in 3m*

Historic venue in stunning location

This white-painted Victorian hotel gleams amidst woodland at the Pass of Killiecrankie, the gateway to The Highlands. It is a magnificent gorge, famed for the battle in 1689 when the Jacobites routed the forces of King William III; today it is a stronghold for red squirrels and a renowned birdwatching area. There are walks beside rivers and lochs, and countless hill walks, including on the majestic Ben Vrackie that rises behind the hotel. Standing in a four-acre estate, the hotel retains much of its old character, blended successfully with modern comforts. The cosy, panelled bar is a popular haunt, while the snug sitting room opens on to a small patio. Arm yourself with a Scottish beer such as Blessed Thistle as you study a menu that makes the most of Scotland's diverse produce.

Open all day all wk Closed Jan & Feb **Food** Lunch all wk 12.30-2 Dinner all wk 6.30-8.30 Av main course £13 Set menu available Restaurant menu available all wk ⊕ FREE HOUSE ◢ Orkney Red MacGregor, Cairngorm Blessed Thistle & Trade Winds ♂ Thistly Cross. ▾ 10 **Facilities** Non-diners area ❦ (Bar Garden) ◑ Children's menu Children's portions Garden ⊨ Parking WiFi **Rooms** 10

Meikleour Arms ★★★★ INN

tel: 01250 883206 **PH2 6EB**
email: contact@meikleourarms.co.uk web: www.meikleourarms.co.uk
dir: *From A93 N of Perth, approx 12m take A984 signed Caputh & Dunkeld to Meikleour*

A small country inn set in the heart of a conservation village

Although no longer called a hotel, overnight guests are still very much welcome at this former mail-coach stopover on the old Edinburgh to Inverness road. The flagstone-floored bar offers Perth-brewed Lure of Meikleour, and StrathBraan Due South from Dunkeld. Eat in the bar, the wood-panelled dining room, on the terrace or in the garden and enjoy vegetables, trout and game from the pub's own land; seafood arrives daily from Aberdeen. Menus feature Isle of Mull quiche, roast guinea fowl breast and pearl barley; Scottish haddock deep fried in ale batter; and pear and cider Tatin. A beer and cider festival is held in August.

Open all day all wk 11-11 **Food** Contact pub for food times ⊕ FREE HOUSE ◢ Inveralmond Lure of Meikleour, StrathBraan Due South ♂ Aspall. ▾ 11 **Facilities** Non-diners area ❦ (Bar Restaurant Garden) ◑ Children's menu Garden ⊨ Beer festival Cider festival Parking WiFi ▭ **Rooms** 9

PITLOCHRY
Map 23 NN95

Moulin Hotel
PICK OF THE PUBS

tel: 01796 472196 **11-13 Kirkmichael Rd, Moulin PH16 5EH**
email: enquiries@moulinhotel.co.uk
dir: *From A9 at Pitlochry take A924. Moulin 0.75m*

Hearty local food in prime walking country

Dating from 1695, this welcoming inn, located on an old drovers' road at the foot of Ben Vrackie, is a popular base for walking and touring. Locals are drawn to the bar for the excellent home-brewed beers, with Moulin Ale of Atholl, Braveheart and Light, and Belhaven Best served on hand pump. The interior boasts beautiful stone walls and lots of cosy niches, with blazing log fires in winter; while the courtyard garden is lovely in summer. Menus offer the opportunity to try something local such as mince and tatties; venison Braveheart (strips of local venison pan-fried with mushrooms and Braveheart beer); and Vrackie Grostel (sautéed potatoes with smoked bacon lightly herbed and topped with a fried egg). You might then round off your meal with Highland honey sponge and custard. A specials board broadens the choice further. 25 wines by the glass and more than 30 malt whiskies are available.

Open all day all wk 11-11 (Fri-Sat 11am-11.45pm Sun 12-11) **Food** all wk 12-9.30 Av main course £10 Restaurant menu available ⊕ FREE HOUSE ◀ Moulin Braveheart, Old Remedial, Ale of Atholl & Light, Belhaven Best. ⬤ 25 **Facilities** Non-diners area ⬤ Children's menu Children's portions Garden ⋒ Parking WiFi ⬛ (notice required)

SCOTTISH BORDERS

ALLANTON
Map 21 NT85

Allanton Inn

tel: 01890 818260 **TD11 3JZ**
email: info@allantoninn.co.uk
dir: *From A1 at Berwick take A6105 for Chirnside (5m). At Chirnside Inn take Coldstream Rd for 1m to Allanton*

Informal dining in family-run Borders pub

Wooden floors, contemporary furnishings, artworks, subtle lighting and that all-important log fire characterise this 18th-century coaching inn. A huge silver spoon and fork dominate one wall of the modern bar, a subtle hint perhaps to study the menu, while enjoying that pint of Inveralmond Ossian. Beef may come from the family farm and the fish is fresh from Eyemouth, while receiving the garden smokehouse treatment are pork, salmon, chicken and even cheeses. Daily blackboard specials add to a regularly changing menu that typically features smoked duck breast and soft boiled duck egg; pan-seared scallops with red lentil, coconut and coriander dahl; and apple and caramel turnover with cinnamon ice cream and caramel sauce. A garden with fruit trees overlooks open countryside.

Open all day all wk 12-11 Closed 2wks Feb (dates vary) **Food** Lunch all wk 12-2.15 Dinner all wk 6-8.45 ⊕ FREE HOUSE ◀ Inveralmond Ossian, Scottish Borders Game Bird & Foxy Blonde, Harviestoun Bitter & Twisted, Fyne Piper's Gold, Timothy Taylor Landlord ⬤ Aspall. ⬤ 10 **Facilities** Non-diners area ⬤ Children's menu Children's portions Garden ⋒ Beer festival WiFi

JEDBURGH
Map 21 NT62

The Ancrum Cross Keys

tel: 01835 830242 **The Green, Ancrum TD8 6XH**
email: crosskeysdining@gmail.com
dir: *From Jedburgh take A68 towards St Boswells. Left onto B6400 to Ancrum*

Popular local, destination eatery, enchanting waterside garden

The delightfully large garden bordering the idyllic Ale Water is a huge factor in the favour of this 200-year-old pub, now with new owners. Others are the Front Bar –

proudly unrefurbished for over a century – which serves ales from the Scottish Borders Brewery including Foxy Blonde and Dark Horse. Borders ingredients are the cornerstone of the seasonally-tuned kitchen here. A starter of traditional Scottish Cullen skink might lead on to a main course of game pie packed with local venison, pheasant, rabbit and pigeon. Finish with panettone bread and butter pudding and vanilla ice cream.

Open all wk 5-11 (Fri 5-1am Sat noon-1am Sun 12-11) **Food** Lunch Sat 12-2, Sun 12-3 Dinner Wed-Sat 5.30-9 Av main course £12 ⊕ BORN IN THE BORDERS ◀ Foxy Blonde & Dark Horse. **Facilities** Non-diners area ⬤ (Bar Garden) ⬤ Children's menu Children's portions Garden ⋒ Parking WiFi

KELSO
Map 21 NT73

The Cobbles Freehouse & Dining ◉
PICK OF THE PUBS

tel: 01573 223548 **7 Bowmont St TD5 7JH**
email: info@thecobbleskelso.co.uk
dir: *A6089 from Edinburgh to Kelso, right at rdbt into Bowmont St. Pub in 0.3m*

Accomplished food and well-kept beers

Tucked away in a corner of the town's rather fine square stands this modernised 19th-century coaching inn. For the last few years it has taken on the role as the brewery tap for proprietor Gavin Meiklejohn's Tempest Brewing Co. Gavin is married to Annika, Cobbles' landlady, and his ales – served from keg, cask or bottle – are always perfectly on song in the log fire-warmed bar. The kitchen's AA Rosette was awarded for its mix of cuisines – British pub classics, Pacific Rim and modern European. For thirsty early evening customers, a bar menu is available: chargrilled sourdough toast loaded with imam bayildi (a Turkish recipe for stuffed aubergine); or smoked Scottish salmon with chive crème fraîche. Small bites include Cullen skink and hand-made ravioli. The restaurant main menu beckons with a Hardiesmill Aberdeen Angus steak cooked to your liking, followed by apple and rhubarb crumble with ice cream.

Open all day all wk 11.30-11 Closed 25 Dec **Food** Lunch Mon-Sat 12-2.30, Sun 12-8 Dinner Mon-Sat 5.45-9, Sun 12-8 Restaurant menu available all wk ⊕ FREE HOUSE ◀ Tempest ⬤ Thistly Cross. ⬤ 9 **Facilities** Non-diners area ⬤ Children's menu Children's portions Outside area ⋒ WiFi ⬛ (notice required)

KIRK YETHOLM
Map 21 NT82

The Border Hotel

tel: 01573 420237 **The Green TD5 8PQ**
email: theborderhotel@yahoo.co.uk
dir: *From A698 in Kelso take B6352 for 7m to Kirk Yetholm*

A homely place to stop awhile

Standing at the end of the 268-mile-long Pennine Way walk, this 18th-century former coaching inn is a welcoming and most hospitable place to revive after any journey, be it on foot or by car. The menu features local game and farm meats, perhaps washed down with ales from the Hadrian & Border Brewery. Try spicy Cajun chicken tortilla wrap; vegetable nut roast with herb-scented couscous salad, or a selection of hot open sandwiches. Leave space for sticky date and walnut pudding. The stone-flagged bar has a log fire, and the conservatory dining room looks over the patio and beer garden.

Open all day all wk Closed 25-26 Dec **Food** Lunch all wk 12-2 (winter) 12-3 (summer) Dinner all wk 6-8.30 (winter), 6-9 (summer) ⊕ FREE HOUSE ◀ Timothy Taylor Landlord, Greene King Abbot Ale, Hadrian & Border Pennine Pint. **Facilities** Non-diners area ⬤ (Bar Garden) ⬤ Children's menu Children's portions Garden ⋒ Parking WiFi ⬛ (notice required)

MELROSE

Map 21 NT53

Burts Hotel ★★★ HL ◉◉

PICK OF THE PUBS

tel: 01896 822285 **Market Square TD6 9PL**
email: enquiries@burtshotel.co.uk **web:** www.burtshotel.co.uk
dir: *From A68 N of St Boswells take A6091 towards Melrose. approx 2m right signed Melrose & B6374, follow to Market Sq*

Family-owned, ever popular town-centre fixture

The Henderson family has owned this 18th-century hotel for around four decades. Overlooking the market square, it was built in 1722 by a local dignitary. Its age dictates listed-building status, which restoration, extension and upgrades have all respected in the Hendersons' quest for a modern hotel. After a day out, settle in with one of the 90 single malts, or a pint of Caledonian Deuchars IPA. The restaurant has held two AA Rosettes since 1995, thanks to starters such as herb-crusted hen's egg, confit tomato, spinach and Isle of Mull cheese sauce. This could be followed by harissa-marinated rump of Borders lamb, with lightly spiced couscous, yogurt, and courgette Charlotte. Light lunch specials may list breaded fishcakes with sweet chilli and lime sauce; or breaded chicken goujons with curried mayo dip, salad and fries. Puddings include a range of locally made ice creams, or savour the selection of Scottish and Borders cheeses.

Open all wk 12-2.30 5-11 **Food** Lunch all wk 12-2 Dinner all wk 6-9.30 Restaurant menu available Lunch Sat-Sun, Dinner all wk ⊕ FREE HOUSE ◀ Caledonian Deuchars IPA & 80/-, Timothy Taylor Landlord, Fuller's London Pride, Scottish Borders Game Bird. ₹ 10 **Facilities** ❀ (Bar Garden) ♦ Children's menu Children's portions Garden ⊓ Parking WiFi **Rooms** 20

NEWCASTLETON

Map 21 NY48

Liddesdale ★★★★ INN

tel: 01387 375255 **17 Douglas Square TD9 0QD**
email: reception@theliddesdalehotel.co.uk **web:** www.theliddesdalehotel.co.uk
dir: *In village centre*

Set amidst beautiful countryside

This inn sits in Douglas Square at the heart of Newcastleton (sometimes referred to as Copshaw Holm), an 18th-century village planned by Henry Scott, the third Duke of Buccleuch. An ideal base for exploring the unspoiled countryside in this area, the inn has a bar stocked with over 20 malt whiskies and a different cask-conditioned ale every week in the summer. The menu is full of pub favourites – creamy garlic mushrooms; steak and ale pie; battered haddock and chips; and apple and cinnamon crumble.

Open all day all wk **Food** Lunch all wk 12-2 Dinner Mon-Thu 5-8, Fri-Sun 5-8.30 Set menu available Restaurant menu available Fri-Sun ⊕ FREE HOUSE ◀ Samuel Smith's, guest ale ♂ Samuel Smith's Organic. ₹ 9 **Facilities** Non-diners area ❀ (Bar Garden) ♦ Children's menu Children's portions Garden ⊓ Beer festival Parking WiFi ▦ (notice required) **Rooms** 6

ST BOSWELLS

Map 21 NT53

Buccleuch Arms

tel: 01835 822243 **The Green TD6 0EW**
email: info@buccleucharms.com
dir: *On A68, 10m N of Jedburgh. Inn on village green*

Friendly inn proud to serve locally sourced food

Originally catering for the fox-hunting aristocracy, this charming inn, in the heart of the Scottish Borders, dates back to 1836. It is an attractive brick and stone building with an immaculate garden. Inside, the large and comfortable lounge is warmed by a log fire in winter, while the garden comes into its own during the warmer months. Extensive menus are offered in the both the Blue Coo Bistrot and the rustic Huntsman Bar; the former focuses on local and seasonal produce – in particular, Aberdeen Angus steaks from the area, and the latter on traditional dishes – burgers; haggis, natties and neeps; and baked fish pie for example.

Open all day all wk 12-11 Closed 25 Dec **Food** Lunch all wk 12-2.30 Dinner Mon-Thu 5.30-9, Fri-Sat 5.30-9.30, Sun 5-8.30 Restaurant menu available all wk ⊕ FREE HOUSE ◀ Born in the Borders, Belhaven Best, Guinness. ₹ 20 **Facilities** Non-diners area ❀ (Bar Garden) ♦ Children's menu Children's portions Play area Garden ⊓ Parking WiFi ▦ (notice required)

SWINTON

Map 21 NT84

The Wheatsheaf at Swinton

PICK OF THE PUBS

tel: 01890 860257 **Main St TD11 3JJ**
email: reception@wheatsheaf-swinton.co.uk
dir: *From Edinburgh A697 onto B6461. From East Lothian A1 onto B6461*

Scottish hospitality at its best

This welcoming place is run by husband and wife team Chris and Jan Winson, who have built up an impressive reputation for both their beer and their food. In the bar you'll find Belhaven IPA, draught Peroni, plus Stewarts Brewery and Scottish Borders Brewery bottled beers. Plus there's a whisky map and tasting notes to study before choosing your single malt. There are two dining rooms, one overlooking the village green, and in both the menus feature home-made, locally-sourced food. Dinner might kick off with carpaccio of venison, parsnip purée, and apple and celeriac slaw; or home-made ham hock terrine with toast and pickled vegetables, before moving on to roast chicken breast with a haggis bon bon, fondant potatoes and braised red cabbage; or pan-seared cod fillet with butternut squash purée, olive mash and saffron cream. Desserts might feature orange pannacotta, sticky toffee pudding, or chocolate fondant.

Open 4-11 (Sat 12-12 Sun 12-11) Closed 23-24 & 26 Dec, 2-3 Jan, Mon-Fri L **Food** Lunch Sat 12-3, Sun 12-4 Dinner Mon-Sat 6-9, Sun 6-8.30 Set menu available Restaurant menu available all wk ⊕ FREE HOUSE ◀ Belhaven IPA, Scottish Borders Gamebird & Foxy Blonde, Stewarts Brewing Hollyrood, Peroni ♂ Aspall. ₹ 18 **Facilities** Non-diners area ♦ Children's portions Garden ⊓ Parking WiFi ▦

TIBBIE SHIELS INN

Map 21 NT22

Tibbie Shiels Inn

PICK OF THE PUBS

tel: 01750 42231 **St Mary's Loch TD7 5LH**
email: tibbieshiels@hotmail.com
dir: *From Moffat take A708. Inn 14m on right*

Superbly located famous old inn

The first thing any first-time visitor to this lovely white-painted old inn between two lochs wants to know is: who was Tibbie Shiels? She was a young widow who, determined to support herself and her six bairns, took in lodgers and became the first licensee, catering in due course to Sir Walter Scott, Thomas Carlyle and Robert Louis Stevenson. Her spirit still keeps watch over the bar which serves Broughton ales and over 50 malt whiskies. The majority of the ingredients used in the kitchen are local, including venison, pheasant, partridge, hill-raised lamb and garden-grown herbs. Sandwiches, salads, ploughman's and paninis are all on offer, while the main menu lists Scottish smoked salmon on a toasted crumpet; chicken, leek and smoked bacon pie; battered haddock and chips; and macaroni cheese.

Open all wk 6pm-mdnt Closed Sep-May **Food** Dinner all wk 6-9 ⊕ FREE HOUSE ◀ Broughton The Reiver ♂ Westons Stowford Press. **Facilities** Non-diners area ❀ (Bar Garden) ♦ Children's menu Children's portions Play area Garden ⊓ Parking WiFi ▦ (notice required)

PICK OF THE PUBS

The Inn at Kippen

KIPPEN   Map 20 NS69

tel: 01786 870500 **Fore Rd FK8 3DT**
email: info@theinnatkippen.co.uk
web: www.theinnatkippen.co.uk
dir: *From Stirling take A811 to Loch Lomond. 1st left at Kippen station rdbt, 1st right into Fore Rd. Inn on left*

Quality and caring approach to hospitality

A traditional white-painted village free house at the foot of the Campsie Hills; views across the Forth Valley to the Highlands are stunning. In the capable hands of owners Mark and Alice Silverwood, this popular and caring inn welcomes all comers, along with their children and dogs. In the winter months you'll be warmed by wood fires and entertained by the locals in the stylish bar. If you're a summer visitor, settle in the pretty garden with a pint from the Fallen Brewing Company or Loch Lomond ales. Menus feature the best of regional and seasonal produce. Beef, pork and lamb all come from Cairnhill farms; chicken from Gartmorn Farm just outside Stirling; wild herbs and mushrooms are foraged from the same estate as the game; and seafood from Scottish waters is fully traceable. Special dietary needs can usually be accommodated; the inn bakes its own gluten and dairy-free bread, and at least one dessert is free of both gluten and dairy too. Children have their own

menu, or can be served smaller portions from the carte. The Kippen's sharing boards showcase many of Scotland's natural meat and smoked fish products, such as Great Glen venison salami, hot-smoked Rannoch salmon, Ayrshire Dunlop cheddar, Arbroath smokies (mousse), Perthshire oatcakes and Arran mustard. Main course delights continue with dishes of Shetland mussels in white wine, cream and parsley; beer-battered monkfish tail with hand-cut chips, lemon, tartare sauce and dressed salad; and slow-braised lamb shank with potato purée, baby gem, wild mushrooms, chantenay carrots, salsify and lamb sauce. Finish with ice creams from an award-winning Scottish artisan producer.

Open all day all wk **Food** Lunch all wk 12-6 Dinner Sun-Tue 6-8, Wed-Sat 6-9 Av main course £15 Restaurant menu available all wk ⊞ FREE HOUSE ◖ Fallen, Loch Lomond ♂ Addlestones. ♟ 9 **Facilities** Non-diners area ☙ (Bar Garden) ♛ Children's menu Children's portions Garden ⚟ Parking WiFi 🚌 (notice required)

STIRLING

CALLANDER
Map 20 NN60

The Lade Inn

tel: 01877 330152 **Kilmahog FK17 8HD**
email: info@theladeinn.com
dir: *From Stirling take A84 to Callander. 1m N of Callander, left at Kilmahog Woollen Mills onto A821 towards Aberfoyle. Pub immediately on left*

Ale shop, long beer festival and home-cooked food

In the heart of the Trossachs National Park, the stone-built Lade Inn was built as a tearoom in 1935. The family-owned and run inn is known for its own real ales and for its 16-day beer festival from late August to mid September. There is also an on-site real ale shop selling bottled ales from microbreweries throughout Scotland. The home-cooked menu offers many smaller portions and allergen-free dishes. Typical choices are Scottish smoked salmon with oatcakes; traditional haggis, neeps and tatties; Aberdeenshire pork and leek sausages; beer-battered North Sea haddock and home-made tartare sauce. The beer garden with its three ponds and bird-feeding station appeals greatly to families.

Open all day all wk **Food** Mon-Sat 12-9, Sun 12.30-9 Set menu available ⊕ FREE HOUSE ◖ Waylade, LadeBack & LadeOut, Caledonia Best, Tennent's ♂ Thistly Cross. ☻ 9 **Facilities** Non-diners area ❄ (Bar Garden) ♦♦ Children's menu Children's portions Play area Family room Garden ⋒ Beer festival Parking WiFi ▭ (notice required)

KIPPEN
Map 20 NS69

Cross Keys Hotel

tel: 01786 870293 **Main St FK8 3DN**
email: info@kippencrosskeys.co.uk
dir: *10m W of Stirling, 20m from Loch Lomond off A811*

Warming fires in winter, a garden in summer

The 300-year-old Cross Keys stands on Kippen's Main Street and offers seasonally changing menus and a good pint of cask ale. The pub's welcoming interior, warmed by three log fires, is perfect for resting your feet after a walk in nearby Burnside Wood, or you can sit in the garden when the weather permits. The menus list starters such as smoked haddock Cullen skink and black pudding crumble; and main courses of Highland venison and beetroot stew; slow-roasted Ayrshire pork belly, mustard mash, sticky red cabbage and apple purée. For afters, perhaps choose lemon and lime crème brûlée with shortbread biscuit. Dogs are welcome in the top bar.

Open all wk 12-3 5-11 (Fri 12-3 5-1am Sat noon-1am Sun 12-12) Closed 25 Dec **Food** Lunch Mon-Fri 12-3, Sat 12-9, Sun 12-8 Dinner Mon-Fri 5-9, Sat 12-9, Sun 12-8 ⊕ FREE HOUSE ◖ Belhaven Best, Fallen Brewing Co 1703 Archie's Amber, Guinness, guest ales ♂ Addlestones. ☻ 10 **Facilities** Non-diners area ❄ (Bar Garden) ♦♦ Children's menu Children's portions Play area Family room Garden ⋒ Parking WiFi ▭ (notice required)

The Inn at Kippen
PICK OF THE PUBS

See Pick of the Pubs on page 621

SCOTTISH ISLANDS
ISLE OF COLL

ARINAGOUR
Map 22 NM25

Coll Hotel
PICK OF THE PUBS

tel: 01879 230334 **PA78 6SZ**
email: info@collhotel.com
dir: *Ferry from Oban. Hotel at head of Arinagour Bay, 1m from Pier (collections by arrangement)*

Great for local seafood

The Coll Hotel has some stunning views over the sea to Jura and Mull, and being the Isle of Coll's only inn it is, naturally, the hub of the island community. Come here to mingle with the locals, soak in the atmosphere, and enjoy pints of Fyne Ale and malt whiskies. In the summer months the fabulous garden acts as an extension to the bar and the Gannet Restaurant; watch the yachts coming and going while enjoying a glass of Pimm's or something from the global wine selection. Fresh produce is landed and delivered fresh from around the island every day and features on the specials board. Famed for its seafood, you'll find it in dishes such as crab cakes with wasabi mayonnaise; pan-fried grey sole fillets, lightly spiced Puy lentils, cherry tomatoes and spinach; or scallops with chorizo and cannellini bean ragout. Among the non-fish options, try the roast chicken pie or roasted butternut squash risotto.

Open all day all wk **Food** Lunch all wk 12-2 Dinner all wk 6-9 ⊕ FREE HOUSE ◖ Fyne Ales. **Facilities** Non-diners area ♦♦ Children's menu Children's portions Garden ⋒ Parking WiFi ▭ (notice required)

ISLE OF ISLAY

PORT CHARLOTTE
Map 20 NR25

The Port Charlotte Hotel

tel: 01496 850360 **Main St PA48 7TU**
email: info@portcharlottehotel.co.uk
dir: *From Port Askaig take A846 towards Bowmore. Right onto A847, through Blackrock. Take unclassified road to Port Charlotte*

Beachside hotel displaying Scottish art

This sympathetically restored Victorian hotel is perfectly positioned in an attractive conservation village on the west shore of Loch Indaal. A large conservatory opens out onto the patio and garden and directly onto the beach and lovers of Scottish art will enjoy the work on display in the lounge and public bar. Islay ales and whiskies make a great way to warm up before enjoying menus focusing on local seafood – perhaps pan-fried Scottish salmon fillet with Puy lentils and pancetta, or half an Islay lobster with garlic or lemon butter. Finish with sticky toffee pudding. Regular traditional music evenings are held in the season.

Open all day all wk Closed 24-26 Dec **Food** Lunch all wk 12-2 Dinner all wk 6-9 Restaurant menu available all wk ⊕ FREE HOUSE ◖ Islay Ales Finlaggan, Fyne Ales Jarl ♂ Somersby. ☻ 9 **Facilities** Non-diners area ❄ (Garden) ♦♦ Children's menu Children's portions Play area Family room Garden ⋒ Parking WiFi ▭

ISLE OF MULL

DERVAIG
Map 22 NM45

The Bellachroy Hotel

tel: 01688 400225 **PA75 6QW**
email: info@thebellachroy.co.uk
dir: *Take ferry from Oban to Craignure. A849 towards Tobermory. Left at T-junct onto B8073 to Dervaig*

Oldest inn on Mull specialising in local seafood

Near the foot of a hill road over from Mull's capital, Tobermory, and yards from the pretty sea loch Loch a' Chumhainn, the island's oldest hotel can trace its roots back to 1608. Today's visitors come to experience the wildlife including white-tailed sea eagles, which may well fly overhead as a pint of Fyne Ales Avalanche is being enjoyed on the terrace in front of the inn. The chefs here take full advantage of the generous bounty from Mull's coastal waters and moors. Crab, mackerel and locally smoked haddock all feature on the menus when available, and seasonal dishes include venison and juniper casserole; and locally-sourced lamb shank, plus vegetarian options.

Open all day all wk **Food** Lunch all wk 12-2.30 Dinner all wk 6-8.30 ⊕ FREE HOUSE ◀ Fyne Ales Avalanche, Highlander, Innis & Gunn, BrewDog Punk IPA.
Facilities Non-diners area ❤ (Bar Garden) ❤❤ Children's menu Children's portions Garden ☰ Parking WiFi ☛ (notice required)

ORKNEY

STROMNESS
Map 24 HY20

Ferry Inn

tel: 01856 850280 **John St KW16 3AD**
email: info@ferryinn.com
dir: *Opposite ferry terminal*

Enjoy island ales overlooking the harbour

With its prominent harbour-front location, the Ferry Inn has long enjoyed a reputation for local ales. The pub has racking for a further 10 local ales on top of the five handpulls on the bar and although the beers change regularly look out for the island's own Scapa Special, Dark Island and Orkney IPA. If beer isn't your thing, there are plenty of wines and malt whiskies to choose from, as well as an appealing menu that may include crunchy breaded farmhouse cheese with red onion marmalade, or seafood chowder; followed by prime Orkney steaks and burgers, sausage and clapshot mash, or grilled hot smoked Orkney salmon with vine cherry tomato tartlet and salad. Sticky toffee pudding or hazelnut meringue for afters perhaps.

Open all day all wk **Food** Contact pub for food times Av main course £9 Restaurant menu available all wk ⊕ FREE HOUSE ◀ Swannay Scapa Special & Orkney IPA, Orkney Corncrake, Dark Island, Skull Splitter & Gold. **Facilities** Non-diners area ❤❤ Children's menu Children's portions Outside area ☰ Parking WiFi ☛

ISLE OF SKYE

CARBOST
Map 22 NG33

The Old Inn and Waterfront Bunkhouse
PICK OF THE PUBS

tel: 01478 640205 **IV47 8SR**
email: enquiries@theoldinnskye.co.uk **web:** www.theoldinnskye.co.uk
dir: *From Skye Bridge follow A87 N. Take A863, then B8009 to inn*

Free house attracting locals, tourists and hill walkers

The Old Inn and Waterfront Bunkhouse, on the shores of Loch Harport near the Talisker distillery, is a charming, 200-year-old island cottage very popular among the walking and climbing fraternity. Arrive early for a table on the waterside patio and savour the breathtaking views of the Cuillin Hills with a pint of Pinnacle ale in hand. Inside, open fires welcome winter visitors, and live Highland music is a regular feature most weekends. The menu includes daily home-cooked specials with numerous fresh fish dishes such as hot smoked salmon with lime and herb crème fraîche as a starter. Haggis, neeps and tatties strudel with whisky cream sauce; a Highland burger (beef, venison or spicy bean); or an 8oz sirloin steak and chips could follow.

Open all day all wk Mon-Fri 11am-1am (Sat 11am-12.30am Sun 12.30-11.30) **Food** all wk 12-9 ⊕ FREE HOUSE ◀ Isle of Skye Red Cuillin & Black Cuillin, Cuillin Skye Ale & Pinnacle Ale, Hebridean, guest ales. **Facilities** Non-diners area ❤ (All areas) ❤❤ Children's menu Children's portions Family room Garden Outside area ☰ Parking WiFi ☛

EDINBANE — Map 22 NG35

NEW The Edinbane Inn

tel: 01470 582414 **Old Dunvegan Rd IV51 9PW**
email: info@edinbaneinn.co.uk
dir: *Off A850*

Small country pub and restaurant in converted farmhouse

Some original features of this 150-year-old building were retained during its recent conversion, especially in the stone-walled bar where there's an open fire and a warming stove. Most real ales come from the Skye brewery in Portree, while the guest ale will be from the mainland. In addition to a bar menu, there's a dinner menu perhaps with North Uist crab ravioli with tomato chilli sauce; pan-fried beetroot-marinated Gairloch salmon with dill-crushed new potatoes; and Clava brie, leek and chestnut mushroom filo parcel with leek mash. Local and national performers often play traditional music, sometimes impromptu.

Open all day all wk 12-11 Closed 2nd wk Jan-2nd wk Feb **Food** Lunch all wk 12-2.30 Dinner all wk 6-9 Av main course £14 ⊕ FREE HOUSE ◖ Isle of Skye Gold, Red & Black, guest ale ♂ Thistly Cross. **Facilities** Non-diners area ❖ (Bar Garden) ♦ Children's menu Children's portions Garden ⩑ Parking WiFi ☞ (notice required)

ISLEORNSAY — Map 22 NG71

Hotel Eilean Iarmain ★★★ SHL ◉   PICK OF THE PUBS

tel: 01471 833332 **IV43 8QR**
email: hotel@eileaniarmain.co.uk web: www.eileaniarmain.co.uk
dir: *A851, A852 right to Isleornsay harbour*

Hebridean charm in spectacular setting

In a magnificent coastal location towards the southern end of the Isle of Skye; waterside tables served from the Am Praban bar overlook the Sound of Sleat to an horizon bristling with shapely peaks. Step inside to find tartan carpets and stag antlers in the hallway, whilst elsewhere the decor is mainly cotton and linen chintzes with traditional furniture. Bar meals are served in a relaxed atmosphere, with winter log fires warming the time-honoured interior. It's the ideal place to meet with the local Gaelic speaking community; here, the island's native tongue is weaved into ballads and songs by local musicians who regularly perform here, perhaps fortified by island beers and a considered selection of malts, some very local indeed. The menu is a mix of modern dishes and traditional favourites, so, reason enough to indulge in seafood or venison classics before retiring to a sumptuous residential room, some of which have sea views.

Open all day all wk 11am-11.30pm (Thu 11am-12.30am Fri 11am-1am Sat 11am-12.30am Sun 12-11.30) **Food** Lunch all wk 12-2.30 Dinner all wk 5.30-9 Restaurant menu available all wk ⊕ FREE HOUSE ◖ McEwan's 80/-, Isle of Skye, Guinness. **Facilities** Non-diners area ♦ Children's menu Children's portions Garden ⩑ Parking WiFi ☞ (notice required) **Rooms** 16

Find out more about the AA's awards for food excellence on page 9

STEIN — Map 22 NG25

Stein Inn

tel: 01470 592362 **Macleod's Ter IV55 8GA**
email: angus.teresa@steininn.co.uk web: www.steininn.co.uk
dir: *A87 from Portree. In 5m take A850 for 15m. Right onto B886, 3m to T-junct. Turn left*

Skye's oldest inn set amid beautiful scenery

If your travels take you to Skye, then you just have to visit the Waternish peninsula and the island's oldest inn. Slap-bang in front of it, across a grassy foreshore, are the beautiful waters of Loch Bay. The wood-panelled bar stocks 125 malts and Scottish cask ales on tap, including at times, some from the Isle of Skye Brewery. Daily-changing menus take full advantage of the abundant fresh fish and shellfish, and Highland lamb, venison and beef. Choices include Highland venison casserole with a hint of chocolate; pork loin steak with award-winning black pudding and freshly-made apple sauce; and stuffed aubergine au gratin. The inn offers a very popular, daily-changing crumble which makes an excellent way to finish a meal.

Open all day all wk 11am-mdnt Closed 25 Dec, 1 Jan **Food** Lunch all wk 12-4 Dinner all wk 6-9.30 Av main course £11 ⊕ FREE HOUSE ◖ Isle of Skye Skye Red & Skye Gold, Cairngorm Trade Winds, Caledonian Deuchars IPA, Orkney Dark Island. ☕ 9 **Facilities** Non-diners area ❖ (Bar Garden) ♦ Children's menu Children's portions Play area Family room Garden Parking WiFi ☞

SOUTH UIST

LOCHBOISDALE — Map 22 NF71

The Polochar Inn

tel: 01878 700215 **Polochar HS8 5TT**
email: polocharinn@aol.com
dir: *W from Lochboisdale, take B888. Hotel at end of road*

Cosy island pub overlooking the Sound

Standing virtually alone overlooking the Sound of Eriskay and a prehistoric standing stone, this white-painted inn is the former change-house, where travellers waited for the ferry to Barra. Owned by sisters Morag MacKinnon and Margaret Campbell, it serves Hebridean real ales and specialises in local seafood and meats, as well as pasta dishes, all made with fresh, seasonal ingredients and served in a dining room with outstanding views of the sea. The beer garden is the ideal spot for dolphin watching and for admiring the beautiful sunsets. On summer Saturday nights the sound of live music fills the bar.

Open all day all wk 11-11 (Fri-Sat 11am-1am Sun 12.30pm-1am) **Food** Lunch Mon-Sat 12.30-8.30, Sun 1-8.30 (winter all wk 12-2.30) Dinner Mon-Sat 12.30-8.30, Sun 1-8.30 (winter all wk 5-8.30) ⊕ FREE HOUSE ◖ Hebridean, guest ales. **Facilities** Non-diners area ♦ Children's menu Children's portions Family room Garden ⩑ Parking WiFi ☞ (notice required)

Wales

ISLE OF ANGLESEY

BEAUMARIS   Map 14 SH67

The Bull - Beaumaris ★★★★★ INN ◉◉◉
PICK OF THE PUBS

tel: 01248 810329 **Castle St LL58 8AP**
email: info@bullsheadinn.co.uk **web:** www.bullsheadinn.co.uk
dir: *From Britannia Road Bridge follow A545. Inn in town centre*

Historic and award-winning inn on the island's coast

This 15th-century pub started life as a staging post and inn on the route to Ireland; it's just a stone's throw from the gates of Beaumaris' medieval castle. The bar transports drinkers back to Dickensian times (the man himself stayed here) with settles and antique furnishings; artefacts include the town's old ducking stool. The Bull's location in the midst of a rich larder of seafood and Welsh livestock farms has inspired the multi-talented kitchen team to produce exceptional menus, well deserving of three AA Rosettes. The light and airy Brasserie, created from the former stables, serves a good range of modern global dishes such as chargrilled bacon chop with Welsh cheddar macaroni, tenderstem broccoli, peas and oven-dried tomato. Push the boat out in the intimate Loft Restaurant by ordering grilled wild duck with smoked cabbage, crisp ham, glazed shallots and potato sauce, followed by poached fillet of sea trout with fennel risotto, kohlrabi, confit lemon and ginger velouté. Evening meals are only served in the Brasserie and Loft Restaurant.

Open all day all wk Closed 25 Dec **Food** Lunch Mon-Sat 12-2, Sun 12-3 Set menu available Restaurant menu available all wk ⊕ FREE HOUSE ◖ Bass, Hancock's, guest ales. ♟ 20 **Facilities** Non-diners area ♣ (Bar) ♦ Children's menu Children's portions Parking WiFi **Rooms** 25

LLANFAETHLU   Map 14 SH38

The Black Lion Inn ★★★★ INN ◉

tel: 01407 730718 **LL65 4NL**
email: blacklion.admin@blacklionanglesey.co.uk **web:** www.blacklionanglesey.com
dir: *From A55 junct 3, A5 signed Valley. In Valley at lights right (A5025), 5m to pub on right*

An object lesson in pub restoration

A few years ago this derelict mid-terrace pub was bought by locals Leigh and Mari Faulkner who then restored it using slate and reclaimed oak, and filled it with auction-bought furniture. Even an old water trough found a new home. Today it has a snug, a patio, a bar with Welsh guest ales, an award-winning dining room with views of Snowdonia and AA-rated accommodation. They endeavour to source local produce and much is purchased directly from nearby farmers. One of the starters (i ddechrau) could be beetroot and Y Cwt Caws peli pabo goats' cheese arancini, while mains (prif gwrs) include salmon and cod paupiette, crushed dill potatoes, Menai mussels and prawn broth; and Raymond the butcher's burger, brioche bun, bacon, BBQ sauce and grilled cheddar.

Open Times vary Closed 10 days Jan, Mon & Tue (may open Mon & Tue in high season, contact inn for further information) **Food** Lunch Thu-Fri & Sun 12-2, Sat 12-3 Dinner Wed-Thu 6-8, Fri 6-9, Sat 5.30-9 Av main course £13 ⊕ FREE HOUSE ◖ Marston's Pedigree & EPA, local guest ales ♂ Thatchers Gold. **Facilities** Non-diners area ♣ (Bar Restaurant Outside area) ♦ Children's menu Children's portions Outside area ⋒ Parking WiFi ⛟ (notice required) **Rooms** 2

RED WHARF BAY   Map 14 SH58

The Ship Inn

tel: 01248 852568 **LL75 8RJ**
dir: *Phone for detailed directions*

Walkers' and birdwatchers' favourite with lovely views

Wading birds flock here to feed on the extensive sands of Red Wharf Bay, making the Ship's waterside beer garden a birdwatcher's paradise. In the Kenneally family's hands for over 40 years, this traditional free house proffers carefully tended real ales, including the pub's own brewed by Conwy, and Facer's Flintshire. Local fish and seafood feature in dishes such as Menai mussels served in a classic marinière sauce. Otherwise plump for excellent Welsh beef in the form of a steak and ale pie; a toasted granary bread 'steakwich' with red onion and Dijon mustard sauce; or sirloin steak with home-made chips and pepper sauce.

Open all day all wk **Food** Lunch all wk 12-2.30 Dinner all wk 5.30-8.30 Av main course £11 Set menu available Restaurant menu available Sat ⊕ FREE HOUSE ◖ Conwy Kenneally's Bitter, Adnams, Facer's Flintshire, guest ales ♂ Westons Wyld Wood Organic. **Facilities** Non-diners area ♣ (Bar Garden Outside area) ♦ Children's menu Children's portions Play area Family room Garden Outside area ⋒ Parking WiFi

BRIDGEND

KENFIG   Map 9 SS88

Prince of Wales Inn

tel: 01656 740356 **CF33 4PR**
email: prince-of-wales@btconnect.com
dir: *M4 junct 37 into North Cornelly. Left at x-roads, follow signs for Kenfig & Porthcawl. Pub 600yds on right*

Inn with an intriguing history

Thought to be one of the most haunted pubs in Wales, this 16th-century stone-built free house was formerly the seat of local government for the lost city of Kenfig. Just as remarkably, it is also the only pub in Britain to have held a Sunday school continuously from 1857 to 2000. Welsh brunch; liver and onion casserole; poached cod in cream and tarragon sauce; and beef and Welsh ale pie are amongst the local dishes on the menu, and the daily blackboard specials are also worth attention. A list of suppliers is available for those wishing to check the provenance of the ingredients. HRH The Prince of Wales visited his namesake pub some years ago, which is part of his The Pub is the Hub organisation, and enjoyed half a pint.

Open all day Closed Mon until 4pm **Food** Lunch Tue-Sat 12-2.30, Sun 12-3 Dinner Tue-Sat 6-8.30 Av main course £8.50-£11.50 ⊕ FREE HOUSE ◖ Bass, Sharp's Doom Bar, Worthington's, local guest ales ♂ Gwynt y Ddraig Happy Daze, Tomos Watkin Taffy Apples. **Facilities** Non-diners area ♣ (Bar Garden) ♦ Children's menu Children's portions Garden ⋒ Beer festival Parking WiFi ⛟ (notice required)

CARDIFF

CREIGIAU — Map 9 ST08

Caesars Arms — PICK OF THE PUBS

tel: 029 2089 0486 **Cardiff Rd CF15 9NN**
email: info@caesarsarms.co.uk
dir: *M4 junct 34, A4119 towards Llantrisant/Rhondda. Approx 0.5m right at lights signed Groesfaen. Through Groesfaen, past Dynevor Arms pub. Next left, signed Creigiau. 1m, left at T-junct, pass Creigiau Golf Course. Pub 1m on left*

Country dining inn and farm shop handy for Cardiff

Well established for over 20 years, the Caesars Arms has a lot to offer. Vegetable gardens, polytunnels and a smallholding all form part of this enterprise, supplying a huge variety of greens, rare breed pork, honey, smoked meats and fish to the adjoining thriving farm shop (the former cricket pavilion) as well as the country pub and brasserie itself. The chefs here pride themselves in offering a progressive, modern menu combined with some old favourites, with seafood and exotic fish creating a good range of signature dishes which vary depending on the catch available. Sea bream, turbot or red mullet may feature, whilst a particular favourite is sea bass baked in rock salt then filleted at your table. Welsh game, beef and lamb satisfy the more traditional demands on the menu, whilst free-range chicken and duck come from Madgetts Farm in the Wye Valley. An extensive, quality wine list ensures that finding the perfect companion to your chosen main meal will be a breeze.

Open 12-2.30 6-12 (Sun 12-4) Closed 25-26 Dec, 1 Jan, Sun eve **Food** Lunch Mon-Sat 12-2.30, Sun 12-4 Dinner Mon-Sat 6-10 ⊕ FREE HOUSE ◄ Felinfoel Double Dragon, Brains Smooth, Guinness Ö Gwynt y Ddraig Orchard Gold.
Facilities Non-diners area ✿ Children's menu Children's portions Garden ⊼ Parking ⊟ (notice required)

GWAELOD-Y-GARTH — Map 9 ST18

Gwaelod-y-Garth Inn

tel: 029 2081 0408 & 07855 313247 **Main Rd CF15 9HH**
email: gwaelodinn@outlook.com
dir: *M4 junct 32, N on A470, left at next exit, at rdbt right, 0.5m. Right into village*

Convivial old pub with exceptional views

Whoever built this old ale house chose the location well. On the wooded flank of Garth Hill, high above Taffs Well, the views are great; across the vale, for example, is Castell Coch, built in Victorian Gothic Revival style. The Gwaelod, meaning 'foot of the mountain', has its own brewery – Violet Cottage – nicknamed 'The Brew with a View'. Real ciders are local too. Home-cooked dishes feature daily market mussels, hake, salmon, lemon sole and other fish. Meat alternatives include roasted Gressingham duck breast with kumquat and cassis sauce; chicken wrapped in bacon, stuffed with apricot and brie; and salt marsh leg of lamb.

Open all day all wk 11am-mdnt (Sun 12-11) **Food** Lunch Mon-Thu 12-2, Fri-Sat 12-9.30, Sun 12-3.30 Dinner Mon-Thu 6.30-9, Fri-Sat 12-9.30 Restaurant menu available Mon-Sat ⊕ FREE HOUSE ◄ Wye Valley Bitter, Swansea Three Cliffs Gold, Dark Star, Crouch Vale Brewers Gold, Thornbridge Jaipur, Tiny Rebel, Violet Cottage Shine On (pub's own), Total Eclipse & Zig Zag Ö Gwynt y Ddraig, Abrahalls, Local cider. ♀ 10 **Facilities** Non-diners area ✿ (Bar) ✿ Children's menu Children's portions ⊼ Beer festival Cider festival Parking WiFi ⊟ (notice required)

PENTYRCH — Map 9 ST18

Kings Arms

tel: 029 2089 0202 **22 Church Rd CF15 9QF**
email: info@kingsarmspentyrch.co.uk
dir: *M4 junct 32, A470 (Merthyr Tydfil). Left onto B4262 signed Radyr then Pentyrch. Right at rdbt for Pentyrch. Or M4 junct 34, A4119 (dual carriageway) signed Llantrisant & Rhondda. Into right lane, right at lights signed Groes Farm. Left to Pentyrch*

Traditional Welsh longhouse pub

In a leafy village on the outskirts of Cardiff, this Grade II listed pub is full of traditional features, from the flagstoned snug to the exposed lime-washed walls and log fire of the lounge. The restaurant opens out onto the lovely landscaped gardens. Local brewery Brains supplies the real ales while there is also a choice of New and Old World wines. Promoting seasonal Welsh produce, the menus and daily blackboard specials could include slow-braised squid with red wine, tomato, chorizo and butterbean stew and smoked aïoli; pressed pork belly, Puy lentils, crispy pork and black pudding, crackling and apple relish. The Sunday roasts are very popular.

Open all day all wk **Food** Lunch Mon-Fri 12-3, Sat all day, Sun 12-4 Dinner Mon-Fri 5.30-9.30, Sat all day Set menu available Restaurant menu available Tue-Sun ⊕ BRAINS ◄ Bitter, guest ales Ö Symonds. **Facilities** Non-diners area ✿ (Bar Garden) ✿ Children's menu Children's portions Garden ⊼ Parking WiFi ⊟ (notice required)

CARMARTHENSHIRE

ABERGORLECH — Map 8 SN53

The Black Lion

tel: 01558 685271 **SA32 7SN**
email: georgerashbrook@hotmail.com
dir: *A40 E from Carmarthen, then B4310 signed Brechfa & Abergorlech*

Cosy black-and-white pub in charming Welsh countryside

A drive through the pretty Cothi Valley brings you to this attractive, 16th-century village pub run by George and Louise Rashbrook. Louise does all the cooking and George wisely gives her generous credit for doing so. You can eat from an extensive menu in the flagstoned bar, while the evening menu in the more modern, candlelit dining room offers classic starters like prawn cocktail or fresh garlic mushrooms, followed by vegetable and Stilton crumble; lamb shank with red wine and rosemary gravy; chicken curry; or steak and Guinness pie. If there's room, go for banoffee pie, chocolate and Baileys cheesecake, or sherry trifle. The lovely beer garden overlooks a Roman bridge.

Open 12-3 7-11 (Sat-Sun & BH all day) Closed Mon (ex BHs) **Food** Lunch Tue-Sun 12-2.30 Dinner Tue-Sun 7-9 Restaurant menu available Sun L ⊕ FREE HOUSE ◄ Rhymney Ö Westons Stowford Press, Gwynt y Ddraig. **Facilities** Non-diners area ✿ (Bar Garden Outside area) ✿ Children's menu Children's portions Garden Outside area ⊼ Parking WiFi ⊟ (notice required)

LLANDDAROG
Map 8 SN51

Butchers Arms

tel: 01267 275330 **SA32 8NS**
email: b5dmj@aol.com
dir: *From A48 between Carmarthen & Cross Hands follow Llanddarog/B4310 signs. Pub adjacent to church*

Country pub that's Welsh through and through

David and Mavis James's more than 30 years in this pretty village pub surely make them Old Favourites; as it happens, this is also the term David uses for some of his dishes – beef and ale pie or boiled ham and chips, for example. A further look at the menu reveals chicken in garlic and mushroom sauce; slow-cooked lamb fillet in minted cider sauce; and roast pork in onion gravy with sage and onion stuffing and crackling; or choose from a selection of sandwiches, salads and steaks.

Open 12-3 6-11 Closed 24-26 Dec, Sun & Mon **Food** Lunch Tue-Sat 12-2.30 Dinner Tue-Sat 6-9.30 Restaurant menu available Tue-Sat ⊕ FREE HOUSE ◪ Felinfoel Cambrian Bitter, Double Dragon, Celtic Pride. ☘ 10 **Facilities** Non-diners area ❀ (Garden) ♦ Children's menu Garden ⊓ WiFi ▦ (notice required)

LLANDEILO
Map 8 SN62

The Angel Hotel

tel: 01558 822765 **Rhosmaen St SA19 6EN**
email: capelbach@hotmail.com
dir: *In town centre adjacent to post office*

Reliable base in idyllic Welsh market town

This gabled inn commands a position near the crest of the long hill rising from Llandeilo's old bridge across the Towy, at the fringe of the Brecon Beacons National Park. Popular as both a locals' pub, with some reliable Welsh real ales and a good range of wines, and as an intimate place to dine in Y Capel Bach Bistro, an 18th-century gem tucked away at the rear of the hotel. Most diets are catered for on the ever-changing specials board and fixed price menu; perhaps duck and port liver pâté with spiced chutney; slow-roast pork belly; rich gravy and crackling; and fillet of beef, grilled black pudding with Stilton and bacon cream.

Open 11.30-3 6-11 Closed Sun **Food** Lunch Mon-Sat 11.30-2.30 Dinner Mon-Sat 6-9 Av main course £7.50-£9.50 Set menu available Restaurant menu available Mon-Sat evening ⊕ FREE HOUSE ◪ Evan Evans, Tomos Watkin, Wye Valley ♂ Gwynt y Ddraig. ☘ 10 **Facilities** Non-diners area ❀ (Bar Garden) ♦ Children's menu Children's portions Garden ⊓ WiFi ▦ (notice required)

LLANDOVERY
Map 9 SN73

NEW The Castle

tel: 01550 720343 **Kings Rd SA20 OAP**
email: info@castle-hotel-llandovery.co.uk
dir: *On A40 in town centre*

Top quality cooking in historic coaching inn

Set in a former coaching inn once used by Lord Nelson on his journey to meet the fleet at Pembroke, The Castle is well positioned for exploring the Brecon Beacons National Park. Family-run by chefs, it's no surprise that food is top of the agenda, with everything cooked from scratch using local, seasonal produce. The charcoal grill is the cornerstone of the kitchen, with Welsh beef and lamb getting star billing alongside a curry of the day; lasagne; and Gower Gold battered fish and chips. Time a visit for the cider festival during the last weekend of September.

Open all day all wk **Food** Lunch Mon-Sat 12-3, Sun 12-9 Dinner Mon-Sat 6-9.30, Sun 12-9 Av main course £14 ⊕ FREE HOUSE ◪ Gower Gold, Brains The Rev. James, Boss Black ♂ Thatchers, Gwynt y Ddraig Happy Daze. ☘ 10
Facilities Non-diners area ❀ (Bar Restaurant Garden) ♦ Children's menu Children's portions Garden ⊓ Cider festival Parking WiFi ▦ (notice required)

The Kings Head

tel: 01550 720393 **1 Market Square SA20 OAB**
email: info@kingsheadcoachinginn.co.uk
dir: *M4 junct 49, A483 through Ammanford, Llandeilo onto A40 to Llandovery. Pub in town centre opposite clock tower*

Former coaching inn with family-friendly food

Once the home of the Llandovery Bank, this 17th-century inn overlooks the town's cobbled market square. Step inside and the exposed beams and crooked floors are a reminder of the pub's heritage, with beers from the Gower and Evans Breweries representing the Principality. There's also an excellent choice of local ciders. A good few menus are offered here, including lunchtime specials, light bites and children's. The bar menu offers classics like chargrilled gammon, egg and pineapple; chicken korma; and steak and ale pie. Choices from the à la carte menu include local Welsh lamb rack; or pan-seared salmon fillet with spinach and Dijon mustard sauce.

Open all day all wk 10am-mdnt **Food** Lunch all wk 12-2.30 Dinner all wk 6-9.30 Restaurant menu available all wk ⊕ FREE HOUSE ◪ Sharp's Doom Bar, Gower Gold, Evan Evans Cwrw Haf ♂ Gwynt y Ddraig Black Dragon, Gwynt y Ddraig Orchard Gold, Westons Stowford Press. **Facilities** Non-diners area ❀ (Bar Outside area) ♦ Children's menu Children's portions Outside area ⊓ Parking WiFi ▦ (notice required)

LLANFALLTEG
Map 8 SN12

NEW The Plash Inn

tel: 01437 563472 **SA34 OUD**
email: theplashinn@yahoo.co.uk
dir: *From A40 in Llanddewi Velfrey follow sign for Llanfallteg. 2m, pub on left*

Traditional village in stunning location

Hidden in the beautiful Taf Valley on the Carmarthenshire-Pembrokeshire border, The Plash (it means 'house on the mud') was built in the 1870s as a railway inn and it stayed in the same family for 60 years until the line was closed by Mr Beeching in the 1960s. Log fires in the winter and a lovely sunny beer garden means it's a popular spot all year round, whether it's for a pint of Wye Valley Butty Bach or dinner of vodka-battered calamari and lemon mayonnaise followed by black bean chilli with long grain rice, nachos and sour cream.

Open all wk 12-11 (Mon-Tue 4-11 Sun 3-11) **Food** Lunch Wed-Sat 12-3 Dinner Wed-Sat 6-9.30 Av main course £9.50 Set menu available ⊕ FREE HOUSE ◪ Mantle Cwrw Teifi, Wye Valley Butty Bach ♂ Westons Stowford Press. ☘
Facilities Non-diners area ❀ (Bar Restaurant Garden) ♦ Children's menu Children's portions Play area Garden ⊓ Beer festival Cider festival Parking WiFi ▦ (notice required)

LLANLLWNI
Map 8 SN43

Belle @ Llanllwni

tel: 01570 480495 **SA40 9SQ**
email: food@thebelle.co.uk
dir: *Midway between Carmarthen & Lampeter on A485*

Well-cooked food at this cosy roadside inn

This cosy and welcoming roadside inn sits on the A485 between Carmarthen and Lampeter, surrounded by countryside and with stunning views. It's a great place to dine alfresco on a sunny day. There are two rotating ales here to enjoy along with Weston Stowford Press and local Welsh ciders. In the dining room, pan-seared sewin (sea trout) fillet with chive mash and saffron lemon cream sauce; spinach and mozzarella tart, potato cake and pesto cream; or Welsh beef and mushroom pie with creamed spring onion mash could precede rich chocolate truffle tart; or fresh lemon cheesecake. Expect excellent ingredients including locally reared meats.

Open 12-3 5.30-11 Closed 25-26 Dec, Mon (ex BHs) Food Lunch Wed-Sat 12-3 Dinner Tue-Sun 6-9.3 Set menu available Restaurant menu available Tue-Sun ⊕ FREE HOUSE ◀ Peroni, Guinness, guest ales ♂ Westons Stowford Press, Gwynt y Ddraig. ♀ 9 Facilities Non-diners area ♦♦ Children's menu Children's portions Outside area ⊞ Parking ▭ (notice required)

NANTGAREDIG
Map 8 SN42

Y Polyn ◉◉
PICK OF THE PUBS

tel: 01267 290000 **SA32 7LH**
email: ypolyn@hotmail.com
dir: *From A48 follow signs to National Botanic Garden of Wales. Then follow brown signs to Y Polyn*

Stylish but never stuffy, worth seeking out

Y Polyn is a former tollhouse, now well established as a destination pub for lovers of Welsh food, and handily placed for the attractive county town of Carmarthen and the National Botanic Garden of Wales. The first-floor has been converted to create private dining rooms, ideal for family gatherings and parties. The bounty of West Wales is at the forefront of the uncomplicated, tempting dishes that come from the modest kitchen here, and 'Fat equals Flavour'. Live with it' is the unapologetic ethos. Starters include the famous Y Polyn fish soup with gruyère, rouille and croûtons; and venison ragù, pappardelle, pangritata and parmesan; follow that with roast rump of Welsh lamb, spiced lamb and potato terrine, and yogurt harissa, maybe, or crispy pork belly, braised chicory, roast cauliflower purée and pickled red cabbage. The Black Forest gâteau knickerbocker glory is a winner, or there's white chocolate cheesecake with roast plums. All this has gained the inn two AA Rosettes for its accomplished cooking. The excellent beers come from the local Handmade Brewery.

Open all wk 12-4 7-11 Closed Mon, Sun eve Food Contact pub for food times Set menu available Restaurant menu available Tue-Sun ⊕ FREE HOUSE ◀ Handmade Cwrw Sir Gâr & Pale Ale. ♀ 12 Facilities Non-diners area ♦♦ Children's portions Garden ⊞ Parking WiFi

PENDINE
Map 8 SN20

Springwell Inn

tel: 01994 453274 **Marsh Rd SA33 4PA**
email: springwellinn@btinternet.com
dir: *A40 from Carmarthen to St Clears, onto A4066 to Pendine*

Local seafood a speciality

In the coastal village of Pendine, famous for hosting world land speed records, this 500-year-old pub offers far-reaching beach views and is only four miles from Laugharne, famous for its Dylan Thomas connections. Traditional with a cosy lounge warmed by a real fire in winter, the bar and restaurant offer a range of basket meals and pub classics, as well as main courses such as pan-fried sea bass with white wine sauce; and Gwendraeth Valley gammon steak with pineapple and egg. The Sunday lunch carvery is a popular option and children can choose from their own menu.

Open all day all wk Food Lunch all wk 12-3 Dinner all wk 6-9 ⊕ FREE HOUSE ◀ Sharp's Doom Bar, Brains The Rev. James ♂ Gwynt y Ddraig Black Dragon. ♀ 12 Facilities Non-diners area ♣ (Bar Outside area) ♦♦ Children's menu Outside area ⊞ Parking WiFi ▭ (notice required)

PUMSAINT
Map 9 SN64

The Dolaucothi Arms

tel: 01558 650237 **SA19 8UW**
email: info@thedolaucothiarms.co.uk
dir: *On A482 between Lampeter & Llandovery. From Llandeilo or Llandovery take A40*

An authentic taste of Wales in an old village hostelry

Set in the rolling green Cothi Valley, the Dolaucothi Arms is a Grade II listed building owned by the National Trust. At the helm are David Joy and Esther Hubert who are passionate about Welsh food and drink. Choose an armchair in the cosy lounge bar, or sit at a large table in the main bar where Welsh real ales and Westons and Dunkerton ciders are on tap. Head for the separate dining room with wood-burning stove and eclectic mix of mismatched furniture to enjoy Welsh rarebit with Dave's 'famous' piccalilli; Brynheulog Mangalitza pork and leek sausages, mash, peas and onion gravy; Moroccan lamb pie with chips; an 8oz or 10oz 21-day aged Welsh rump steak. Gingerbread pudding with cider caramel sauce makes a great finish. A beer and cider festival is held over the Summer Bank Holiday weekend in August.

Open all day Closed 25 Dec, Mon & Tue L winter Food Lunch Fri-Sat 12.30-3, Sun 12.30-2.20 Dinner Tue-Sat 6.30-8.30 Restaurant menu available Tue-Sat eve ⊕ FREE HOUSE ◀ Evan Evans Cwrw, Purple Moose Snowdonia Ale, Wye Valley Butty Bach, Jacobi Original ♂ Westons, Dunkertons. ♀ 9 Facilities Non-diners area ♣ (Bar Garden) ♦♦ Children's menu Children's portions Garden ⊞ Beer festival Cider festival Parking WiFi ▭ (notice required)

CEREDIGION

ABERAERON
Map 8 SN46

The Harbourmaster
PICK OF THE PUBS

tel: 01545 570755 **Pen Cei SA46 0BT**
email: info@harbour-master.com
dir: *In Aberaeron follow Tourist Information Centre signs. Pub adjacent*

Delightful quayside hotel overlooking Cardigan Bay

Close to the harbour-mouth, the grand sunsets of Cardigan Bay illuminate the pastel colours of this and other quayside buildings crowding in around the old port. It's an enchanting scene, the ideal culmination of a day's exploring the astonishing coastline and deep countryside here in west Wales. The owners make the most of the wealth of surf 'n turf produce available from this favoured locale. Weekly-changing bar menus might highlight seafood risotto; sweet potato and squash curry, or beer-battered haddock and chips. The fare is an easy medley of traditional and contemporary dishes. The restaurant menu majors on seafood, but also carries local pheasant two ways with creamed Savoy cabbage and bacon; or loin of Brecon venison with pear, carrot and chocolate. Beers are from first-rate microbreweries, whilst the real cider harks from the Ebbw Valley.

Open all day all wk 10am-11.30pm Closed 25 Dec Food Lunch all wk 12-2.30 Dinner all wk 6-9 Av main course £13 Restaurant menu available all wk ⊕ FREE HOUSE ◀ Purple Moose Glaslyn Ale, HM Best Bitter, Seven Bro7thers IPA, Mantle, guest ale ♂ Hallets Real. ♀ 15 Facilities Non-diners area ♦♦ Children's menu Children's portions Outside area ⊞ Parking WiFi

ABERYSTWYTH
Map 8 SN58

The Glengower

tel: 01970 626191 **3 Victoria Ter SY23 2DH**
email: info@glengower.co.uk
dir: *Phone for detailed directions*

Local ales and enjoyable food overlooking the bay

Literally a stone's throw from the beach, the sun terrace at 'The Glen' – as it's affectionately known by the locals – offers fabulous views across Cardigan Bay where you might possibly spot one of the friendly local dolphins. A traditional free house serving a wide range of home-made food all day, from sandwiches and paninis to local butchers' sausages and mash; smoked salmon and asparagus linguine; and home-made chilli con carne, The Glen has a good local reputation for its real ales, including beers from award-winning North Wales brewery Purple Moose. Look out for the pub's Bank Holiday beer festival in late May.

Open all day all wk **Food** Mon-Sat 12-8, Sun 12-6 ⊕ FREE HOUSE ◀ Wye Valley, Purple Moose ♂ Gwynt y Ddraig. **Facilities** Non-diners area ❀ (Bar Outside area) ♦ Children's menu Children's portions Outside area ⊼ Beer festival WiFi

LLANFIHANGEL-Y-CREUDDYN
Map 9 SN67

y Ffarmers
PICK OF THE PUBS

tel: 01974 261275 **SY23 4LA**
email: bar@yffarmers.co.uk
dir: *From Aberystwyth take B4340 towards Trawsgoed. After New Cross left signed Llanfihangel-y-Creuddyn*

Excellent local food in the Welsh hills

Found down winding narrow lanes through stunning countryside, this traditional local is tucked away in Llanfihangel's gorgeous open square alongside listed whitewashed cottages and an imposing church. It has become an oasis for tip-top Welsh beer and quality food. Expect to find a buzzy community vibe and the place packed with local drinkers supping pints of Evan Evans or potent Gwynt y Ddraig cider, farmers from the hills and local foodies in the know. There's distinct Welsh flavour to the short monthly menus (written in Welsh and English, naturally), which champion produce from local farms and artisan producers. Typically, tuck into local honey and duck samosas with plum sauce; Ystwyth Valley lamb cutlets with dauphinoise potatoes, and warm gooseberry and almond cake with stem ginger ice cream. Don't miss the Sunday roasts.

Open 12-2 6-11 Closed 2-12 Jan, Mon (ex BH & school hols) ⊕ FREE HOUSE ◀ Evan Evans, Felinfoel ♂ Gwynt y Ddraig, Westons Stowford Press. **Facilities** ❀ (Bar Garden) ♦ Children's menu Children's portions Garden WiFi

LLWYNDAFYDD
Map 8 SN35

The Crown Inn & Restaurant

tel: 01545 560396 **SA44 6BU**
email: thecrowninnandrestaurant@hotmail.co.uk
dir: *Follow Llwyndafydd signs from A487, NE of Cardigan*

Amid exquisite countryside

A village pub since the 1800s, this traditional Welsh longhouse is only a short walk from Cwm Tydu beach and National Trust-owned cliffs. The award-winning garden is a delight, while inside are original beams, fireplaces and a pretty restaurant. Mains here include beef or three-cheese vegetarian lasagne; fillet of breaded or battered cod and chips; Thai-spiced fillet of salmon; and beetroot and butternut squash cupcake pie. There's a carvery every Sunday. Blackboard specials, a children's menu, light snacks and bar food are also available. Buckleys, Cottage, Evan Evans, Sharp's and guest breweries do the honours in the bar. Please note, opening times depend on the season.

Open all day 12-close (high season) Closed Sun eve, Mon (winter) **Food** Lunch all wk 12-3 (high season) Dinner all wk 6-9 (high season) ⊕ FREE HOUSE ◀ Buckleys Best Bitter, Evan Evans, Cottage, Sharp's Doom Bar, guest ales. ♔ 9
Facilities Non-diners area ❀ (Bar Garden Outside area) ♦ Children's menu Children's portions Play area Garden Outside area ⊼ Beer festival Parking WiFi ▭

PENRHIWLLAN
Map 8 SN34

NEW The Daffodil Inn

tel: 01559 370343 **SA44 5NG**
email: info@thedaffodilinn.co.uk
dir: *On A475, 4m E of Newcastle Emlyn*

Welsh produce drives the menu here

An inn since the 16th century, The Daffodil is run by retired police officer Hugh Matthews and his wife Gill, who grew up nearby. Close to Newquay beach and Llandysul canoeing centre, this village pub is popular with walkers and cyclists stopping off for a glass of Abbot Ale or Stowford Press cider. Diners can eat in the bar or in the restaurant with its valley views and open kitchen. Welsh produce is showcased in dishes like Rhydlewis smoked salmon and lemon confit, perhaps followed by braised lamb shank with white wine, tomato and cannellini beans.

Open 11.45-3.30 5.30-11 Closed Mon-Wed (Jan to mid Feb) **Food** Lunch all wk 12-2.30 (Thu-Sun 12-2.30 Jan-mid Feb) Dinner all wk 6-9 (Thu-Sun 6-9 Jan-mid Feb) Av main course £9.50 Set menu available Restaurant menu available all wk ⊕ FREE HOUSE ◀ Greene King Abbot Ale, Hancock's HB ♻ Westons Stowford Press. **Facilities** Non-diners area ❖ (Bar Outside area) ♦ Children's menu Children's portions Outside area ⊨ Parking WiFi ➡ (notice required)

PONTRHYDFENDIGAID
Map 9 SN76

The Black Lion Hotel

tel: 01974 831624 **SY25 6BE**
email: alynjpugh@gmail.com
dir: *On B4343 N of Tregaron*

Where drovers, pilgrims and travellers have stayed for centuries

A mile away from this white-painted hotel lies the ruined abbey at Strata Florida, a most un-Welsh-sounding place-name that's actually a corruption of Ystrad Fflur, meaning 'valley of flowers'. Walkers, cyclists, fishermen and nature lovers attracted by the abbey and the other scenic delights of west Wales visit here and enjoy its Welsh-farmhouse-like interior, where Llandeilo brewery Evan Evans satisfies no doubt the many real-ale drinkers among them. Home-made food depends to a great extent on local produce, typical examples being Welsh beef lasagne; breaded wholetail scampi; and chickpea curry and rice.

Open 12-late (winter Mon-Wed 4-late Thu-Sun 12-late) Closed L Mon-Wed in winter ⊕ FREE HOUSE ◀ Evan Evans ♻ Westons Stowford Press. **Facilities** ❖ (Bar Garden) ♦ Children's menu Garden Parking WiFi

TREGARON
Map 9 SN65

Y Talbot ★★★★ INN ⊛

tel: 01974 298208 **The Square SY25 6JL**
email: info@ytalbot.com web: www.ytalbot.com
dir: *On B4343 in village centre. (NB take caution in winter on mountain road from Beulah)*

Timeless village inn with great Welsh beer and food

An arresting inn which dominates the compact square at the heart of bustling Tregaron, Y Talbot is surrounded by a web of footpaths and drovers' roads. This idyllic location also guarantees first class provender from local farms, lakes and the Afon Teifi which flows through the town at the fringe of the Cambrian Mountains. Enjoy dishes such as slow-cooked Tregaron ox cheek bourguignon with smoked mash; or Cardigan Bay lemon sole, spinach, new potatoes and sauce Americaine from the contemporary Welsh menu. Ales are usually from local breweries, augmented by an early October beer and cider festival.

Open all day all wk **Food** Lunch all wk 12-2.30 Dinner all wk 6-9 Av main course £12 Restaurant menu available all wk ⊕ FREE HOUSE ◀ Purple Moose Glaslyn Ale, Wye

Valley HPA, Cwrw Teifi, Otley 02 Croeso, Celtic Experience ♻ Gwynt y Ddraig Scrumpy, Snails Bank, Hogan's Poacher's Perry. **Facilities** Non-diners area ❖ (Bar Garden) ♦ Children's menu Children's portions Garden ⊨ Beer festival Cider festival Parking WiFi ➡ (notice required) **Rooms** 13

CONWY

ABERGELE
Map 14 SH97

The Kinmel Arms ★★★★★ RR ⊛⊛   PICK OF THE PUBS

tel: 01745 832207 **The Village, St George LL22 9BP**
email: info@thekinmelarms.co.uk web: www.thekinmelarms.co.uk
dir: *From A55 junct 24a to St George. E on A55, junct 24. 1st left to Rhuddlan, 1st right into St George. 2nd right*

Family-run pub away from the crowds

This award-winning, 17th-century pub is secreted in a secluded hamlet between the coastal plain and the beautiful Elwy Valley. The original sandstone frontage and mullion windows disguise a contemporary, slightly quirky interior, which features a log-burning stove and an eclectic choice of decor, with pictures and collages by host Tim Cunnah-Watson. Whilst beers from local microbreweries and Welsh cider quench a walker's thirst; hungry guests are rewarded with a stylish menu that has gained two AA Rosettes for chef Chad Hughes. Local produce is the baseline for dishes that can include a starter of wood pigeon breast with braised cabbage, white apple purée and granola. Mains might be fillet of beef, duck liver, pickled carrot, onion and truffle; or hake with cauliflower, trompette and shiitake mushrooms, salsify and pickled grape. Finish with chocolate tart with salted caramel and passionfruit sorbet. Four sumptuous rooms are available for guests seeking to incorporate a short break.

Open all day 12-11.30 Closed Sun & Mon **Food** Lunch Tue-Sat 12-2 Dinner Tue-Sat 6-9.30 Set menu available Restaurant menu available Tue-Sat ⊕ FREE HOUSE ◀ Facer's Flintshire, Great Orme, Thwaites Original, Facers DHB ♻ Gwynt y Ddraig. ♟ 15 **Facilities** Non-diners area ❖ (Bar Garden Outside area) ♦ Children's menu Children's portions Garden Outside area ⊨ Parking WiFi ➡ (notice required) **Rooms** 4

COLWYN BAY
Map 14 SH87

Pen-y-Bryn   PICK OF THE PUBS

tel: 01492 533360 **Pen-y-Bryn Rd LL29 6DD**
email: pen.y.bryn@brunningandprice.co.uk
dir: *1m from A55. Follow signs to Welsh Mountain Zoo. Establishment at top of hill*

Character interior and friendly atmosphere

A self-guided walk from the pub makes the most of the wooded hills and lanes here above Colwyn Bay. Alternatively, grab a seat in the garden and appreciate the views across to the gigantic headlands of The Little and Great Orme hills jutting out into silvery Liverpool Bay. The interior is a pleasing mix of Edwardian parlour and country inn. Beer festivals are regularly held, complementing the already generous selection of real ales, many from North Wales breweries. The food side of the business is equally appealing, with daily-changing menus offering a liberal choice, from sandwiches upwards. Breeze in with a starter like seared pigeon breast, wild mushroom sausage and beetroot fondant; or charcuterie board for two or three to share. Mains cover all the bases: Sicilian fish stew; slow-braised lamb shoulder; and roasted squash, leek and chestnut Wellington are typical quality choices on the all-day menu. There is a private dining room for small parties.

Open all day all wk 12-11 (Sun 12-10.30) **Food** Mon-Sat 12-9.30, Sun 12-9 Av main course £12.95-£15.95 ⊕ BRUNNING & PRICE ◀ Original, Purple Moose Snowdonia Ale, guest ales ♻ Aspall. ♟ 14 **Facilities** Non-diners area ❖ (Bar Garden Outside area) ♦ Children's menu Children's portions Garden Outside area ⊨ Beer festival Parking WiFi

CONWY
Map 14 SH77

The Groes Inn ★★★★★ INN
PICK OF THE PUBS

tel: 01492 650545 **Ty'n-y-Groes LL32 8TN**
email: reception@groesinn.com **web:** www.groesinn.com
dir: Exit A55 to Conwy, left at mini rdbt by Conwy Castle onto B5106, 2.5m inn on right

Historic pub blessed with stunning views

This 450-year-old, creeper-smothered inn — the first licensed house in Wales - overlooks the sweeping Conwy estuary. The rambling, oak-beamed rooms are so full of careworn settles, log fires, military hats and historic cooking utensils that, mercifully perhaps, there's no room for jukebox or pool table. Study the nicely balanced menu in the well-groomed bar over a leisurely Welsh Black beer from Llandudno's Great Orme brewery, or one of the 14 wines by the glass. Start with grilled aubergine, feta cheese and olive salad; or seafood and shellfish chowder. Main dishes often have clear local provenance, such as Welsh lamb cutlets, root vegetable dauphinoise, wilted spinach, roast cherry tomatoes, redcurrant and rosemary gravy. Round things off with sweet pancake filled with melted ricotta and raspberries, topped with brandy butter. Luxurious accommodation is also available.

Open all wk 12-3 6-11 **Food** Lunch all wk 12-2 Dinner all wk 6.30-9 Av main course £11 ⊕ FREE HOUSE ◼ Groes Ale, Great Orme Welsh Black, Orme, Tetley's Ò Westons Stowford Press. ♟ 14 **Facilities** Non-diners area ♣ (Bar Garden) Children's menu Children's portions Family room Garden ⌐ Parking WiFi ▄ (notice required) **Rooms** 14

DOLWYDDELAN
Map 14 SH75

Elen's Castle Hotel

tel: 01690 750207 **LL25 0EJ**
email: stay@hotelinsnowdonia.co.uk
dir: 5m S of Betws-y-Coed, follow A470

Relaxed and welcoming atmosphere at this village hostelry

Elen's Castle was once owned by the Earl of Ancaster, who sold it to his gamekeeper. The latter opened it as a coaching inn around 1880, specialising in hunting parties. Now a family-run free house, it boasts an old-world bar with a wood-burning stove and an intimate restaurant with breathtaking views of the mountains and Lledr River. Sample dishes include sweet potato and spinach curry; local Welsh chops with new potatoes and seasonal vegetables; and deep-filled shortcrust Welsh Black beef pie. The chocolate fudge cake or raspberry Pavlova should round things off nicely. Water from the on-site Roman well is said to have healing properties. Check with the pub for their opening times, especially in winter.

Open times vary seasonally Closed 1st 2wks Jan, some week days in winter **Food** Dinner 6.30-9 Av main course £10 ⊕ FREE HOUSE ◼ Shepherd Neame Spitfire, Wychwood Hobgoblin, Brains, Worthington's, Wadworth 6X Ò Westons Stowford Press. **Facilities** Non-diners area ♣ (Bar) ♦ Children's menu Children's portions Play area Family room Garden ⌐ Parking WiFi ▄ (notice required)

LLANDUDNO
Map 14 SH78

The Cottage Loaf

tel: 01492 870762 **Market St LL30 2SR**
email: thecottageloaf@hotmail.co.uk
dir: From A55 onto A470, then A456. Into Mostyn St, left into Market St

Quirky seaside pub with good food and local ale

With a log fire for winter and a large garden for summer, this welcoming pub in the heart of Llandudno attracts visitors all year round. This former bakery only became a pub in 1981 and much of its interior is made up of salvaged materials from a ship-wrecked coal schooner. Conwy Welsh Pride is one of several ales on rotation, alongside a large range of whiskies and wines. Pan-fried fillets of hake and grey mullet with braised fennel and fish stew; and grilled maple-glazed pork chop with sweet potato and bacon mash are typical menu choices. A change of hands.

Open all day all wk **Food** all wk 12-9 Av main course £11.95 ⊕ FREE HOUSE ◼ Courage Directors, Conwy Welsh Pride, guest ales Ò Gwynt y Ddraig Black Dragon, Firey Fox, Dog Dancer & Happy Daze, Westons Old Rosie. **Facilities** Non-diners area ♦ Children's menu Children's portions Garden ⌐ WiFi ▄ (notice required)

LLANDUDNO JUNCTION
Map 14 SH77

The Queens Head ★★★★★ INN ⬡
PICK OF THE PUBS

See Pick of the Pubs on opposite page

LLANELIAN-YN-RHÔS
Map 14 SH87

The White Lion Inn

tel: 01492 515807 **LL29 8YA**
email: info@whitelioninn.co.uk
dir: A55 junct 22, left signed Old Colwyn, A547. At rdbt 2nd exit onto B5383 signed Betwys-yn-Rhos. In 1m turn right into Llanelian Rd, follow to village. Pub on right

One of the oldest country inns in north Wales

Incredibly parts of this attractive family-run inn are reputed to date back over 1,200 years. It still retains a slate floor and oak-beamed ceiling, and there is an old salt cellar by the inglenook fireplace. The Cole family have been running the inn for more than 25 years and have restored and preserved many aspects of traditional village life revolving around the pub, including reinstating the snug next to the bar (dogs are allowed in here). The food is traditional, home cooked, and wherever possible locally sourced. Look out for grilled fillet of plaice; chicken curry; goats' cheese, mushroom and leek tart; or roast lamb shoulder. Sandwiches, hot baguettes and jacket potatoes are also available.

Open 11.30-3 6-11 (Sat 11.30-4 5-11.30 Sun 12-10.30) Closed Mon (ex BHs & school summer hols) **Food** Lunch Tue-Sat 12-2, Sun 12-9 Dinner Tue-Sat 6-9, Sun 12-9 ⊕ FREE HOUSE ◼ Marston's Pedigree & Burton Bitter, guest ale. ♟ 11 **Facilities** Non-diners area ♦ Children's menu Children's portions Garden ⌐ Parking WiFi ▄ (notice required)

LLANNEFYDD
Map 14 SH97

The Hawk & Buckle Inn

tel: 01745 540249 **LL16 5ED**
email: garethandsiwan@googlemail.com
dir: Phone for detailed directions

Old inn situated high in the hills of north Wales

From high in the north Wales hills, this lovingly restored 17th-century coaching inn enjoys spectacular views across the local countryside to Blackpool Tower and beyond. The real ale selection includes Heavy Industry and Purple Moose Glaslyn Ale, while a regularly changing menu uses the best of fresh local produce. Here's just a sample of what you might find — grilled salmon fillet with sweet chilli sauce; vegetable or beef lasagne; beef and ale pie; or gammon steak with fried egg, grilled pineapple, peas and chips.

Open all wk 6-11 (Sat 3.30-12 Sun 5-11) **Food** Dinner all wk 6-8.30 Av main course £11 ⊕ FREE HOUSE ◼ Heavy Industry, Purple Moose Glaslyn Ale, guest ales. **Facilities** Non-diners area ♦ Children's menu Children's portions Garden Outside area ⌐ Parking WiFi ▄ (notice required)

PICK OF THE PUBS

The Queens Head ★★★★★ INN ❀

LLANDUDNO JUNCTION — Map 14 SH77

tel: 01492 546570
Glanwydden LL31 9JP
email: enquiries@
queensheadglanwydden.co.uk
web: www.queensheadglanwydden.co.uk
dir: *A55 onto A470 towards Llandudno.
At 3rd rdbt right towards Penrhyn Bay,
2nd right into Glanwydden, pub on left*

A warm welcome, effortless charm and excellent service

This charming, 18th-century country pub, a former AA pub award winner, was once the storehouse of the Llangwestennin Parish and is located in a pretty rural village just a five-minute drive from the Victorian seaside town of Llandudno. It is ideally placed for anyone enjoying country walks, cycling, or a day on the beach. The Queens Head continues to attract discerning customers with its warm welcome, effortless charm and excellent service. The stylish terrace is just the place to join friends on warmer summer evenings, whilst on colder nights the relaxed atmosphere in the bar is perfect for a pre-dinner drink by the log fire; or arrive early to bag a seat in the cosy snug. Real ales come from the Great Orme and Wild Horse breweries, located in the hills nearby, and you'll find that the lip-smacking wine list with helpful

description notes has plenty of choice. The dedicated kitchen makes excellent use of local produce in varied menus that might include a starter of smoked salmon and trout mousse; grilled local goats' cheese tart; or crispy lamb and feta salad. Local fish and seafood is the cornerstone of the menu and typical examples are Conwy moules marinière; and monkfish and king prawn curry; and baked fillet of cod topped with Welsh rarebit. Meat-lovers are certainly not overlooked, with the likes of home-made lasagne; chicken korma; braised Welsh lamb shoulder with redcurrant and rosemary gravy; and sautéed calves' liver and crispy bacon.

Open all day all wk 12-10.30 Closed 25 Dec **Food** all wk 12-9 ⊕ FREE HOUSE ◀ Great Orme, Wild Horse ♂ Thatchers Gold. ♟ 15 **Facilities** Non-diners area ♦♦ Children's portions Garden ⊼ Parking WiFi 🚐 (notice required) **Rooms** 1

DENBIGHSHIRE

GRAIGFECHAN
Map 15 SJ15

NEW Three Pigeons

tel: 01824 703178 **LL15 2EU**
email: threepigeonsinn@btconnect.com
dir: A949 from Ruthin towards Mold. Right onto B5429 signed Graigfechan

Possibly haunted, definitely worth a visit

From the 12th to the 19th century drovers broke their journeys here on their way to market, and their livestock would graze on the adjacent field, now a campsite. The interior of this 1777 building is warm and traditional, with oak beams, open fires and brassware. Local brews are served in jugs straight from casks in the rock-hewn cellar, a practice that nostalgic regulars appreciate. Rosie's Triple D (Drovers at Dafarn Dywyrch) cider is local too. In the restaurant, enjoy curried cod loin with sag aloo; pan-fried Gressingham duck; and five-spice vegetables in plum and hoi sin sauce. Beer festivals are in March, July and October.

Open 12-3 5-11 (Sat-Sun 12-11) Closed Mon (ex BH), Tue L (Winter only) **Food** Lunch Tue-Fri 12-2.30, Sat 12-3, Sun 12-8 Dinner Tue-Sat 6-9, Sun 12-8 ⊕ FREE HOUSE ◀ Heavy Industry Diawl Bach, Purple Moose Madog's Ale, Sharp's Doom Bar, Brimstage Trapper's Hat ⚫ Rosie's Black Bart & Triple D, Gwynt y Ddraig Orchard Gold. ♟ 10 **Facilities** Non-diners area ✿ (Bar Garden) ♦ Children's menu Children's portions Garden ⊼ Beer festival Parking WiFi ➡ (notice required)

RUTHIN
Map 15 SJ15

The White Horse

tel: 01824 790218 **Hendrerwydd LL16 4LL**
email: enquiries@whitehorserestaurant.co.uk
dir: From Ruthin A494 (Mold Rd). Left at Llanbedr-Dyffryn-Clwyd onto B5429 (Llandyrnog). Right signed Gellifor. At x-roads in Hendrerwydd, pub on left. Or from Denbigh, A525 (Ruthin road). Left onto B5429 to Llandyrnog. Left to Hendrerwydd

16th-century country pub deep in the Vale of Clwyd

Surrounded by the sublime scenery of the Clwydian hills, this pretty, whitewashed pub is the 'charming and friendly retreat from the world' that owners Lucy Hughes and Jason Stock set out to create. For the modern British food their unshakeable maxim is 'locally sourced', typically extra-mature Welsh steak, roast tomatoes, scrumpy-battered onions and grilled field mushrooms; baked haddock fillet on crushed new potatoes with white wine sauce; and spinach and ricotta tortellini, smoked cheese with wilted baby spinach and wild mushroom sauce. It follows then that real ales, such as Porthmadog's Purple Moose, should come only from local microbreweries.

Open 12-2 5-11 (Sat-Sun 12-11) Closed Mon & Tue **Food** Lunch Wed-Sat 12-2, Sun 12-8 Dinner Wed-Sat 5.30-9, Sun 12-8 ⊕ FREE HOUSE ◀ Local micro-brews. **Facilities** Non-diners area ✿ (Bar Garden) ♦ Children's menu Children's portions Garden ⊼ Beer festival Parking WiFi ➡ (notice required)

ST ASAPH
Map 15 SJ07

The Plough Inn

tel: 01745 585080 **The Roe LL17 0LU**
email: ploughsa@gmail.com
dir: Exit A55 at Rhyl & St Asaph signs, left at rdbt, pub 200yds on left

A former coaching inn combining modern and traditional

The bar here is a quirky blend of modern and traditional, with open fires, blackboard menus, an unusual trompe l'oeil bar and real ales from north Wales; the restaurant, though very modern, retains a vaulted ceiling from its days as a ballroom. Dine here on Welsh cask ale-battered cod with chips and mushy peas; roasted butternut squash and pea risotto; or Spanish chicken breast filled with chorizo and garlic,

wrapped in bacon with mustard mash. There's live music on Friday and Saturday nights, as well as a cocktail bar and a wine shop.

Open all day all wk **Food** all wk 10-9 Set menu available ⊕ FREE HOUSE ◀ Conwy, Great Orme, Facer's Brewery Flintshire, Heavy Industry Brewery, Weetwood Ales, Coach House Brewing Company. ♟ 10 **Facilities** Non-diners area ✿ (Garden Outside area) ♦ Children's menu & portions Garden Outside area ⊼ Parking WiFi ➡

FLINTSHIRE

ALLTAMI
Map 15 SJ26

NEW The Tavern

tel: 01244 550485 **Mold Rd CH7 6LG**
dir: A55 junct 33B onto A494 towards Mold. Pub right on right at x-roads

Confident cooking of local produce

A listed stone building in the village of Alltami, on the outskirts of Mold, The Tavern is a welcoming family-run pub serving its own Tavern's Tipple and Gold ales. With an open fire warming the bar in winter and a garden popular in the summer, this all rounder appeals to locals and visitors to Flintshire. Everything on the menu is made from scratch by the chef-proprietor and his team. Start with wild mushroom ravioli, sage butter and parmesan before moving on to Welsh Black beef and ale pie with mash and greens.

Open 12-2 5.30-9 Closed Mon **Food** Lunch Tue-Sun 12-2 Dinner Tue-Sun 5.30-9 Set menu available Restaurant menu available Tue-Sun ⊕ FREE HOUSE ◀ Alltami Gold, Tavern's Tipple. **Facilities** Non-diners area ♦ Children's portions Play area Garden Outside area ⊼ Parking WiFi ➡ (notice required)

CILCAIN
Map 15 SJ16

White Horse Inn

tel: 01352 740142 **CH7 5NN**
email: christine.jeory@btopenworld.com
dir: From Mold take A541 towards Denbigh. After approx 6m turn left

Traditional inn, the hub of village life

This 400-year-old pub is the last survivor of five originally to be found in this lovely hillside village, probably because it was the centre of the local gold-mining industry in the 19th century. Today, the White Horse is popular with walkers, cyclists and horse-riders. Food here is home made by the landlord's wife using the best quality local ingredients, and is accompanied by a good range of local real ales. A typical meal might start with crispy duck spring rolls, home-made soup or Southern fried chicken goujons, followed by home-made chilli con carne; grilled ham and eggs or, one of the many tempting curries – hot Madras; Goan fish curry or vegetable biriyani.

Open all wk 12-3 6-11 (Sat 12-11 Sun 12-10.30) **Food** Lunch Mon-Sat 12-2.15, Sun 12-3 Dinner all wk 6.30-9 ⊕ FREE HOUSE ◀ Timothy Taylor Landlord, Great Orme, Ringwood, Black Sheep, Liverpool Organic ⚫ Thatchers Gold. ♟ 9 **Facilities** Non-diners area ✿ (Bar Garden) Garden ⊼ Parking WiFi

HAWARDEN
Map 15 SJ36

The Glynne Arms

tel: 01244 569988 **3 Glynne Way CH5 3NS**
email: manager@theglynnearms.co.uk
dir: From North Wales Expressway junct 36a onto B5125 to Hawarden. Or from A550 or B5125 to Hawarden. Pub in village centre

Excellent food and very dog-friendly too

This fine-looking old coaching inn's success is down to Charlie and Caroline Gladstone. Charlie's great-great grandfather was 19th-century prime minister Sir William Ewart Gladstone, who married into Hawarden Castle's Glynne dynasty.

Meat, fruit and vegetables come from the couple's Estate Farm Shop down the road. Real ales are local too. At the menu's simpler end are sandwiches, gourmet burgers and grills, while greater sophistication comes courtesy of black pudding bon bons; salmon and plaice rouleaux, fennel choucroute, potato croquette, butter sauce, dill ketchup; Thai green curry; and pecan tart with salt caramel ice cream. This is a dog-friendly establishment.

Open all day all wk **Food** Mon-Sat 12-9, Sun 12-8 Av main course £14 ⊕ FREE HOUSE ◀ Purple Moose, Spitting Feathers, Facer's Flintshire ♂ Rosie's. ♈ 16 **Facilities** Non-diners area ❀ (Bar Garden) ▪♦ Children's menu Children's portions Garden ⋒ Parking WiFi ▭ (notice required)

MOLD
Map 15 SJ26

Glasfryn
PICK OF THE PUBS

tel: 01352 750500 **Raikes Ln, Sychdyn CH7 6LR**
email: glasfryn@brunningandprice.co.uk
dir: *From Mold follow signs to Theatr Clwyd, 1m from town centre*

Hill views, heavenly ales and great menus

This imposing dining pub enjoys magical views from the gardens over the Alyn Valley towards the rippling hills of the Clwydian Range Area of Outstanding Natural Beauty. The edifice was originally a judge's country residence, converted some years ago by the Brunning & Price group. Their hallmark style of polished wood, country and quirky prints, quality antique furnishings and largely wood flooring complements the building's original Arts and Crafts style. The pub's real ale pumps find Purple Moose Brewery and Timothy Taylor side by side, and there's a great wine selection to match the plates of fine pub grub coming from the kitchen. Typical of these are a starter of pheasant, rabbit and prune faggot with celeriac purée and wild mushroom gravy; and Sicilian fish stew with salmon, prawns, mussels, squid, and red mullet served with aïoli. Newly introduced is a choice of children's meals and smaller portions of some adult dishes. Beer festivals in March and October coincide with national food weeks.

Open all day all wk **Food** Mon-Sat 12-9.30, Sun 12-9 ⊕ BRUNNING & PRICE ◀ Purple Moose Snowdonia Ale, Timothy Taylor ♂ Aspall. ♈ 16 **Facilities** Non-diners area ❀ (Bar Garden) ▪♦ Children's portions Garden ⋒ Beer festival Parking WiFi

NORTHOP
Map 15 SJ26

The Celtic Arms

tel: 01352 840423 **Northop Country Park CH7 6WA**
email: info@thecelticarms.co.uk
dir: *A55 junct 33a (W'bound), left into Northop Country Park. Or A55 junct 33 (E'bound) through Northop. At lights left (signed A5126) into Connah's Quay Rd, right signed Northop Country Park*

Pub and restaurant in a beautiful country park

Transformed into a free house by Neal Thacker when he took over in 2015, this former golf clubhouse is set in the beautiful surroundings of Northop County Park. The entrance to this popular place leads into a long bar with areas each end for drinking and eating. Among the eight cask beers are Piffle & Balderdash, brewed by Conwy Brewery. Chargrilled steaks; fish pie; toad-in-the-hole; lobster thermidor gratin; and roasted red pepper, tomato and spinach gnocchi are among dishes on the comprehensive menu. Modestly priced wines include 22 by the glass. Children eat well here and have an outdoor play area.

Open all day all wk 12-11 (Sun 12-10.30) Closed 25 Dec & 1 Jan **Food** Mon-Sat 12-9.30, Sun 12-9 ⊕ FREE HOUSE ◀ Woodward & Falconer Piffle & Balderdash, Conwy. ♈ 22 **Facilities** Non-diners area ▪♦ Children's menu Children's portions Play area Garden ⋒ Parking WiFi ▭ (notice required)

GWYNEDD

ABERDYFI
Map 14 SN69

AA PUB OF THE YEAR FOR WALES 2016–2017

Penhelig Arms ★★★★★ INN ⊛
PICK OF THE PUBS

See Pick of the Pubs on page 638

BEDDGELERT
Map 14 SH54

Tanronnen Inn ★★★★ INN

tel: 01766 890347 **LL55 4YB**
email: guestservice@tanronnen.co.uk **web:** www.tanronnen.co.uk
dir: *In village centre opposite river bridge*

Great hospitality at the heart of Snowdonia

Originally part of the Beddgelert Estate, this stone building was the stables for the passing coach trade in 1809; after conversion to a cottage, it opened as a beer house in 1830. By the end of that century, it had two letting bedrooms and was serving meals for visitors; so setting the style of operation we see today. Today's inn has two attractive small bars serving Robinsons ales, a large lounge with open fire, a dining room open to non-residents in which to enjoy a wide range of home-cooked meals on a daily-changing menu, and attractive accommodation.

Open all day all wk **Food** Lunch all wk 12.30-2 Dinner all wk 7-8.30 Av main course £11.50 Restaurant menu available all wk ⊕ ROBINSONS ◀ Unicorn & Double Hop ♂ Westons Stowford Press. **Facilities** Non-diners area ▪♦ Children's menu Children's portions Outside area ⋒ Parking **Rooms** 7

BRITHDIR
Map 14 SH71

Cross Foxes

tel: 01341 421001 **LL40 2SG**
email: hello@crossfoxes.co.uk
dir: *At junct of A470 & A487, 4m from Dolgellau*

Strikingly modern inn, certainly worth finding

Grade II listed the Cross Foxes may be, but what an interior! It's true that traditional Welsh materials like slate and stone are used in the design, but the effect is light years from being Welsh Traditional. In the impressive bar you'll find regional real ales and ciders, and in the café a multiplicity of teas (including one from Wales), fresh coffees and finger sandwiches; here they also serve a traditional Welsh cream tea and a champagne afternoon tea. A meal in The Grill dining room might be potted Welsh cockles with laverbread; Betws-y-Coed venison goulash; and cheesecake of the day. Gaze at Cader Idris from the large decked area.

Open all day all wk ⊕ FREE HOUSE ◀ Cader Ales, Evan Evans ♂ Kingstone Press. **Facilities** ❀ (Bar Garden) ▪♦ Children's menu Children's portions Garden Parking WiFi

Find out more about the AA's awards for food excellence on page 9

PICK OF THE PUBS

AA PUB OF THE YEAR FOR WALES 2016–2017

Penhelig Arms ★★★★★ INN ❀

ABERDYFI   Map 14 SN69

tel: 01654 767215
Terrace Rd LL35 OLT
email: info@penheligarms.com
web: www.penheligarms.com
dir: *On A493, W of Machynlleth*

Small hostelry with a big reputation

This popular waterside inn has been serving travellers and locals since 1870 and offers spectacular views over the mountain-backed tidal Dyfi Estuary, a nature reserve rich in birdlife. Aberdyfi is a charming little resort with a championship golf course, and sandy beach and harbour, making it a favourite with golfers and watersports enthusiasts; the Penhelig Arms is also perfectly situated for visitors to Cader Idris, the Snowdonia National Park and several historic castles in the area. Music and TV-free, the wood-panelled and log-fire-warmed Fisherman's Bar is a cosy and friendly bolt-hole to enjoy Brains real ales and bar meals such as gourmet burgers and bloomer sandwiches. The waterfront restaurant offers a more brasserie-style experience with views over the estuary and menus showcasing the abundant Welsh seafood (a Penhelig speciality) and Welsh beef and lamb. The kitchen team emphasises the freshness of ingredients and fuse local and cosmopolitan influences in a style of cooking that allows natural flavours to shine through. A typical menu might include Thai chicken cakes and Asian chilli mayonnaise; pork belly, colcannon, braised leeks and apple and fennel sauce; or spinach and ricotta ravioli, pine nuts, pesto and pea shoots. Leave room for salted caramel cheesecake and vanilla pod ice cream; or Bakewell tart, clotted cream and toasted almonds. Daily specials are listed on the blackboard. On Sundays, expect a set menu featuring a traditional roast. The short wine list is attractively priced and complements the excellent food. In warmer weather, you can sit outside on the sea wall terrace.

Open all day all wk **Food** Lunch all wk 12-2.30 Dinner all wk 6-9 ⊕ BRAINS 🍺 Bitter & The Rev. James & SA, guest ale ♻ Symonds. ♟ 25
Facilities Non-diners area 🐾 (Bar Outside area) 👶 Children's menu Children's portions Outside area Parking WiFi **Rooms** 15

CAERNARFON

Map 14 SH46

Black Boy Inn ★★★★ INN

tel: 01286 673604 **Northgate St LL55 1RW**
email: reception@black-boy-inn.com **web:** www.black-boy-inn.com
dir: *A55 junct 9 onto A487, follow signs for Caernarfon & Victoria Docks. Within town walls between castle & Victoria Dock*

Old-fashioned values in the shadow of Caernarfon Castle

Character oozes from the very fabric of this ancient gabled inn, one of the oldest in Wales (built 1522). Relax with a pint of local ale in the fire-warmed, low-ceilinged rooms strewn amidst beams and struts rescued from old ships. Meat and other products are generally local, and dishes from the long menu might include field mushrooms and red onion compôte; vegetable cobbler; black pudding-stuffed chicken breast; and braised lamb shank. The well-proportioned bedrooms are ideal for those wishing to stay on and explore Mount Snowdon, the Lleyn Peninsula or catch the Welsh Highland Railway.

Black Boy Inn

Open all day all wk **Food** all wk 12-9 ⊕ FREE HOUSE ◀ Bass, Cwrw Llŷn ♂ Aspall. ♟ 10 **Facilities** Non-diners area ♦ Children's menu Children's portions Play area Garden ⌁ Parking WiFi ⊟ (notice required) **Rooms** 26

See advert below

Black Boy *Inn*

Northgate Street
Caernnarfon
Gwynedd
LL55 1RW
Tel 01286 673604
reception@black-boy-inn.com

Since the early 16th century The Black Boy Inn has been welcoming weary travellers and visitors to the Town of Caernarfon. Some things don't change, whether you want to drink, dine or unwind, you will find The Black Boy Inn the perfect base to explore the beautiful Snowdonia Mountains of North Wales and Anglesey. We have thirty nine comfortable guest rooms all with private bathrooms and all individually styled and furnished. Free Wi-Fi is available for all our guests throughout the entire inn.

Our celebrated restaurant is awarded a Visit Wales Bronze Award and has a menu to suit all tastes. Each dish is devised and perfected by our head chef and is designed to utilise local ingredients from local suppliers. Whether it's a light lunch or an evening meal, The Black Boy Inn offers a warm welcome and good food to those in search of a relaxed and traditionally welsh experience and environment. Our Caernarfon B&B, hotel style stay is handy for Snowdonia and we strive to provide a personal service. From the moment you arrive our friendly inn staff are always on hand to assist and share their local knowledge.

LLANBEDR
Map 14 SH52

Victoria Inn ★★★★ INN

tel: 01341 241213 **LL45 2LD**
email: vicinn@chessmail.co.uk web: www.vic-inn.co.uk
dir: *On A496 between Barmouth & Harlech*

Close to the beach and many mountain walks

Fascinating features for pub connoisseurs are the circular wooden settle, ancient stove, grandfather clock and flagged floors in the atmospheric bar of the Victoria. Home-made food is served in the lounge bar and restaurant, complemented by a range of Robinsons traditional ales. A children's play area has been incorporated into the well-kept garden, with a playhouse, slides and swings. Situated beside the River Artro, the Rhinog mountain range and the famous Roman Steps are right on the doorstep. If you would like to explore the area, there are five spacious and thoughtfully furnished bedrooms to stay in.

Open all day all wk 11-11 (Sun 12-10.30) **Food** Lunch Mon-Fri 12-3, Sat-Sun 12-9 (all wk 12-9 summer) Dinner Mon-Fri 5-9, Sat-Sun 12-9 (all wk 12-9 summer) ⊕ ROBINSONS ◀ Unicorn, guest ales Ö Westons Stowford Press. ♥ 10
Facilities Non-diners area ◖ Children's menu Children's portions Play area Garden ⋒ Parking ⛟ (notice required) **Rooms** 5

PENNAL
Map 14 SH60

Glan yr Afon/Riverside

tel: 01654 791285 **Riverside Hotel SY20 9DW**
email: info@riversidehotel-pennal.co.uk
dir: *3m from Machynlleth on A493 towards Aberdovey. Pub on left*

Stylish 16th-century inn between sea and mountains

In the glorious Dyfi Valley close to Cader Idris and Cardigan Bay this family-run inn has slate floors, modern light oak furnishings and bold funky fabrics. There's a wood-burning stove pumping out heat in winter, Dark Side of the Moose ale on tap, and a good range of modern pub food. Relax and opt for a starter of melon, crayfish and prawns with Thai spiced mayo; crisp fried whitebait; or a sharing board, then chicken Kiev and sweet potato fries; spiced Mediterranean fish stew; or gammon, egg, pineapple, peas and chips. There's a riverside garden, with views to the hills, for summer enjoyment.

Open 12-3 6-11 (Sat-Sun all day) Closed 25-26 Dec, 2wks Jan, Mon (Nov-Mar)
Food Lunch all wk 12-2 Dinner all wk 6-9 Set menu available ⊕ FREE HOUSE ◀ Cwrw Cader, Tiny Rebel, Purple Moose Dark Side of the Moose & Snowdonia Ale, Salopian Golden Thread, Stonehouse, Brewdog Ö Kingstone Press. ♥ 12
Facilities Non-diners area ◖ (Bar Garden) ◖ Children's menu Children's portions Garden ⋒ Parking WiFi ⛟ (notice required)

TREMADOG
Map 14 SH53

The Union Inn

tel: 01766 512748 **7 Market Square LL49 9RB**
email: mail@union-inn.com
dir: *From Porthmadog follow A487 & Caernarfon signs; then Tremadog signs. Inn on right before T-junct in village centre*

Freehold, family-run pub in historic setting

Hefty local stones were used to build this early 19th-century pub, part of a row of cottages facing the main square of Wales' first planned town. Customers can thank these stones for the snugness of the interior, not least the bar, which offers a really good choice of Welsh real ales (mostly from local microbreweries) and ciders. Home-made food is fresh, locally sourced and seasonal, with Welsh lamb and beef

dishes held in particularly high regard. You'll also find authentic curries, steak and ale pie, fresh fish, scampi and vegetarian dishes, such as roast vegetable lasagne, and daily specials.

Open all wk 12-2 5.30-11.30 (summer 12-2 5-11.30) **Food** Lunch all wk 12-2 Dinner all wk 5.30-9 (summer 5-9) Av main course £8.50-£18.95 Set menu available ⊕ FREE HOUSE ◀ Purple Moose Snowdonia Ale & Madog's Ale, Great Orme, Big Bog, local guest ales Ö Gwynt y Ddraig Happy Daze, Dog Dancer & Farmhouse Scrumpy.
Facilities Non-diners area ◖ (Bar Restaurant Outside area)
◖ Children's menu Children's portions Outside area ⋒ Beer festival Parking WiFi ⛟ (notice required)

TUDWEILIOG
Map 14 SH23

Lion Hotel

tel: 01758 770244 **LL53 8ND**
email: martlee.lion@gmail.com web: www.lionhoteltudweiliog.co.uk
dir: *A487 from Caernarfon onto A499 towards Pwllheli. Right onto B4417 to Nefyn, through Edern to Tudweiliog*

Family-run pub offering good-value dining

Standing at a tangent to the road, fronted by a garden with tables and chairs, the 300-year-old Lion has been run by the Lee family for the past 40 years or so. The bar features an extensive list of whiskies, alongside real ales from Big Bog, Cwrw Llyn and Purple Moose breweries, all Welsh of course. Typical pub meals include spare ribs in barbecue sauce; lamb or chicken balti; sweet chilli, prawn and cod fishcakes; and leek and mushroom crumble. Ample parking and a children's play area both help to make it popular with the many families holidaying in the beautiful Lleyn Peninsula.

Open all wk 11-3 6-11 (summer all day) **Food** Lunch all wk 12-2 Dinner all wk 6-9 ⊕ FREE HOUSE ◀ Cwrw Llyn Brenin Enlli, Big Bog, Purple Moose, Guinness.
Facilities Non-diners area ◖ Children's menu Children's portions Play area Family room Garden ⋒ Parking WiFi ⛟ (notice required)

WAUNFAWR
Map 14 SH55

Snowdonia Parc Brewpub & Campsite

tel: 01286 650409 & 650218 **LL55 4AQ**
email: info@snowdonia-park.co.uk
dir: *Phone for detailed directions*

Own microbrewery, wholesome food, beautiful location

In the heart of Snowdonia, a short drive from Mount Snowdon, this popular walkers' pub is located at Waunfawr Station on the Welsh Highland Railway. There are steam trains on site (the building was originally the stationmaster's house), plus a microbrewery and campsite. Home-cooked food ranges from chicken, leek and ham pie to vegetable curry or roast Welsh beef with all the trimmings. All real ales served are brewed on the premises. The Welsh Highland Railway Rail Ale Festival is held in mid-May.

Open all day all wk 11-11 (Fri-Sat 11am-11.30pm) **Food** Contact pub for food times ⊕ FREE HOUSE ◀ Snowdonia Welsh Highland Bitter, Carmen Sutra, Cais, Gwyrfai, Theodore Stout, Dark & Delicious, Gold, Trithro, Capital T, Ixion Addiction. **Facilities** Non-diners area ✿ (Bar Garden) ♦ Children's menu Children's portions Play area Family room Garden 🪑 Beer festival Parking WiFi 🚌 (notice required)

MONMOUTHSHIRE

ABERGAVENNY
Map 9 SO21

Clytha Arms
PICK OF THE PUBS

tel: 01873 840206 **Clytha NP7 9BW**
email: theclythaarms@btinternet.com
dir: From A449 & A40 junction (E of Abergavenny) follow Old Road Abergavenny & Clytha signs

Excellent beers and stunning views

This converted dower house on the old Abergavenny to Raglan road stands on the edge of parkland dotted with small woods. From the large garden, captivating views embrace the lush and shapely Vale of Gwent. The main bar is full of character, with old pews, tables and rustic furnishings, as well as posters and a wood-burning stove. The pub is renowned for its ever-changing range of real ales which number more than 300 in any given year, along with some great artisan ciders and perrys; a beer and cider festival hosted over the Spring Bank Holiday coincides with national food and drink events. Grazers can sift through a list of 20 tasty tapas dishes, or choose a simple ploughman's with Welsh cheeses. The restaurant menu delights with its flavour combinations; some dishes, such as cockles with bacon, leeks and black pasta, can be served as either a starter or a main course.

Open 12-3 6-12 (Fri-Sun 12-12) Closed 25 Dec, Mon L **Food** Lunch Tue-Sun 12.30-2.30 Dinner Mon-Sat 7-9.30 Set menu available ⊕ FREE HOUSE ◀ Langham Sundowner, Wye Valley Bitter, 4 guest ales (300+ per year) Ó Gwynt y Ddraig Black Dragon, Ragan Perry, Clytha Perry. ▼ 12 **Facilities** Non-diners area ✿ (Bar Garden) ♦ Children's menu Children's portions Play area Garden Beer festival Cider festival Parking WiFi 🚌

LLANGATTOCK LINGOED
Map 9 SO32

The Hunters Moon Inn

tel: 01873 821499 **NP7 8RR**
email: thehuntersmooninn@btconnect.com
dir: Phone for detailed directions

Family-run village pub popular with walkers

In the peaceful village of Llangattock Lingoed on the Offa's Dyke Path, the Hunters Moon dates back to the 13th century and is now run by three generations of the Bateman family who have returned it to its former glory. Dog-friendly and with a large beer garden, this traditional inn focuses on doing the simple things well, from well-kept Wye Valley ale to unpretentious, good quality home cooking using local produce. Try the sizzling flash-fried prawns in garlic, chillies and parsley before moving on to home-made steak and ale pie or pheasant casserole.

Open all day all wk **Food** Mon-Sat 12-9, Sun 12-7 Restaurant menu available all wk ⊕ FREE HOUSE ◀ Wye Valley HPA & Butty Bach, Sharp's Doom Bar Ó Addlestones, Westons Stowford Press. **Facilities** Non-diners area ✿ (Bar Garden Outside area) ♦ Children's menu Children's portions Play area Garden Outside area 🪑 Parking WiFi 🚌 (notice required)

LLANGYBI
Map 9 ST39

The White Hart Village Inn

tel: 01633 450258 **NP15 1NP**
email: info@whitehartvillageinn.com
dir: M4 junct 25 onto B4596 (Caerleon road), through Caerleon High St, straight over rdbt into Usk Rd, continue to Llangybi

Good food and good ales

With no fewer than 11 fireplaces, a 'warm' welcome is assured at this picturesque Usk Valley inn. Oliver Cromwell based himself here during local Civil War campaigns; so add a priest hole, Tudor plasterwork and a mention in T S Eliot's poem *Usk* and this is a destination to savour. Reliable ales from the likes of the Wye Valley Brewery are offered, as well as farmhouse ciders from Gwynt y Ddraig. Representative choices on the menu could include fishcake with creamed leeks; braised pork belly with mustard mash and honey-glazed vegetables; or vegetarian lasagne. Extensive seating is available outside.

Open all day 12-11 (Sun 12-6) Closed Mon **Food** Lunch Tue-Sat 12-2.30, Sun 12-4 Dinner Tue-Sat 6-9 Set menu available Restaurant menu available Tue-Sat ⊕ FREE HOUSE ◀ Wye Valley Butty Bach, Kite Brewery Cwrw Gorslas Ó Thatchers Gold, Ty Gwyn, Gwynt y Ddraig Farmhouse Scrumpy. ▼ **Facilities** Non-diners area ✿ (Bar Garden) ♦ Children's menu Children's portions Garden 🪑 Parking WiFi 🚌 (notice required)

LLANTRISANT
Map 9 ST39

The Greyhound Inn
PICK OF THE PUBS

tel: 01291 672505 & 673447 **NP15 1LE**
email: enquiry@greyhound-inn.com
dir: M4 junct 24, A449 towards Monmouth, exit at 1st junct signed Usk. Or from Monmouth A40, A449 exit for Usk. In Usk left into Twyn Sq follow Llantrisant signs. 2.5m, under A449 bridge. Inn on right

Charming country inn surrounded by farmland

In the 17th century a typical Welsh longhouse, then from 1845 an inn, the family-owned Greyhound stands just outside the town between the Rivers Usk and Wye. Free-house status ensures a range of real ales and ciders in the log-fire-warmed Stable Bar, where the tiled floor remains steadfastly impervious to muddy boots and soggy dogs. You can play darts, crib and dominoes here or just watch them being played. Owner Nick Davies heads the kitchen team, whose skills you can enjoy in the candlelit restaurant, or in one of three other dining areas. Among the starters are garlic mushrooms; farmhouse pâté and hot toast; and prawn cocktail, while an idea of the main courses is conveyed by liver and bacon with fried onions; grilled local trout with a choice of chips, jacket potato, mash or salad; and Brazil nut and spinach roast with coconut korma sauce. Outside are two acres of lovingly-nurtured, award-winning gardens and a large paddock.

Open all day 11-11 Closed 25 & 31 Dec, 1 Jan, Sun eve **Food** Lunch all wk 12-2.15 Dinner Mon-Sat 6-10 ⊕ FREE HOUSE ◀ Greene King Abbot Ale, Bass, guest ale Ó Gwynt y Ddraig, Kingstone Press. ▼ 10 **Facilities** Non-diners area ✿ (Bar Garden) ♦ Children's menu Children's portions Family room Garden 🪑 Parking WiFi 🚌 (notice required)

The Woodlands Tavern Country Pub & Dining

PICK OF THE PUBS

tel: 01633 400313 **NP16 6LX**
email: info@thewoodlandstavern.co.uk
dir: *5m from Caldicot & Magor*

Modern British food and Welsh beers

Below Gray Hill, near the Roman fortress town of Caerwent, this friendly pub is popular with walkers, cyclists and fishermen. They like it, not just because it's close to the Wentwood Forest and plentiful rivers, but also because it has a good selection of Welsh real ales, such as Wye Valley, Felinfoel and regularly changing guests. In addition, there's the food, with baguettes, all-day breakfasts, jacket potatoes and sausage and mash in the bar, and a menu inviting you to try baked mushrooms with goats' cheese and red onion marmalade; hake fillet with roast cherry tomatoes and pesto; or calves' liver with smoked bacon, creamy mash and red wine sauce. Sunday roasts are always well received, especially out on the patio.

Open 12-3 6-12 (Sat all day Sun 12-4) Closed 25 Dec, 1 Jan, Sun eve, Mon **Food** Lunch Tue-Fri 12-2, Sat 12-2.30, Sun 12-4 Dinner Tue-Fri 6-9, Sat 6-9.30 Set menu available Restaurant menu available Tue-Sat ⊕ FREE HOUSE ◖ Felinfoel, Marston's & Pedigree, Wye Valley Butty Bach, guest ales Ö Westons Old Rosie, Thatchers Gold. ♟ 10 **Facilities** Non-diners area ❄ (Bar Outside area) ⦿ Children's menu Children's portions Outside area ⊼ Parking WiFi ⛟ (notice required)

The Crown

tel: 01873 853314 **Old Hereford Rd NP7 7HR**
email: crown@pantygelli.com
dir: *Phone for detailed directions*

Family-run free house with fine views

A charming family-run free house dating from the 16th century, The Crown has fine views of Skirrid (in Welsh, Ysgyrid Fawr) known also as Holy Mountain. Walkers and cyclists love it, but it's a genuine community pub too, serving Bass, Rhymney, Wye Valley HPA and guest real ales as well as Mortimers Orchard cider, all ideal before or with garlic mushrooms on crostini or deep-fried squid with harissa mayo and rocket; venison sausages with mash, green beans and red onion gravy; or tenderloin pork with mange tout and Calvados sauce; and a dessert of sticky toffee pudding with butterscotch sauce; or poached pear with vanilla ice cream.

Open 12-2.30 6-11 (Sat 12-3 6-11 Sun 12-3 6-10.30) Closed Mon L **Food** Lunch Tue-Sun 12-2 Dinner Tue-Sat 7-9 ⊕ FREE HOUSE ◖ Rhymney, Wye Valley HPA, Bass, guest ales Ö Westons Stowford Press & Mortimers Orchard.
Facilities Non-diners area ❄ (Bar Garden) ⦿ Children's portions Garden ⊼ Parking WiFi

The Inn at Penallt

PICK OF THE PUBS

tel: 01600 772765 **NP25 4SE**
email: enquiries@theinnatpenallt.co.uk
dir: *From Monmouth take B4293 to Trellech. Approx 2m, left at brown sign for inn. At next x-roads left. Right at war memorial*

Village green dining inn in stunning countryside

Narrow, winding lanes drop steeply from tiny Penallt's trim village green into the River Wye's famous gorge, which strikes along the foot of thick woodlands close to this appealing stone inn. It's very family and dog-friendly and a favourite stop with ramblers on the area's many footpaths. Although there's been a change in ownership here, the business is essentially unaltered; the inn remains packed with promise, both for drinkers seeking beers and ciders made just a few miles away and for diners keen to sample the generous larder of Monmouthshire and the southern Marches. The flagstone-floored bar, with log-burner and pine settles is a restful place to sit and peruse a menu ranging from starters like crayfish tail risotto with roasted garlic and Herefordshire double cream; or straight to a main of pan-roast salmon steak with beurre blanc, fresh asparagus and new potatoes. Seasonal availability is reflected in the choices. There's a popular supper and drink club on Wednesdays, whilst it's the steak and wine supper on Thursdays.

Open 11-11 (Tue 6-11 Sun 12-9.30) Closed 4-21 Jan, Mon (ex BHs) **Food** Lunch Wed-Sat 12-2.30, Sun 12-3 Dinner Tue-Sat 6-9 Set menu available Restaurant menu available Tue-Sat ⊕ FREE HOUSE ◖ Wye Valley Butty Bach, Kingstone Classic Bitter, Kite Brewery Cwrw Gorslas, Purity Ö Ty Gwyn, Gwynt y Ddraig Black Dragon. ♟ **Facilities** Non-diners area ❄ (Bar Garden) ⦿ Children's menu Children's portions Play area Garden ⊼ Parking WiFi ⛟

Goose and Cuckoo Inn

tel: 01873 880277 **Upper Llanover NP7 9ER**
email: gooseandcuckoo@gmail.com
dir: *From Abergavenny take A4042 towards Pontypool. Turn left after Llanover, follow signs for inn*

Remote and peaceful – a walker's haven

Popular with walkers, this friendly, whitewashed pub in the Brecon Beacons National Park has a garden with views of the Malvern Hills and a traditional interior with flagstoned bar area and a wood-burning stove. Little has changed since the new owners aarived in late 2015. So, it's still the perfect setting for a pint of well-kept Rhymney Bitter or one of around 60 single malt whiskies behind the bar. Good, home-cooked food is the order of the day. The pub hosts two beer festivals – in May and August.

Open 11.30-3 7-11 (Fri-Sun all day) Closed Mon (ex BHs) **Food** Lunch Tue-Sun 11.30-3 Dinner Tue-Sun 7-9 ⊕ FREE HOUSE ◖ Rhymney Bitter, Celt Iron Age Ö Kingstone Press. **Facilities** Non-diners area ❄ (Bar Garden) ⦿ Children's portions Family room Garden ⊼ Beer festival Parking **Notes** ✉

TAL-Y-COED
Map 9 SO41

NEW Warwicks country pub

tel: 01600 780227 **NP7 8TL**
email: warwickscountrypub@outlook.com
dir: From A40 in Monmouth take B4233 signed Rockfield. Through Rockfield. Approx 5m to pub on right

Robust food popular with walkers

Halfway between Abergavenny and Monmouth on the B4223, this wisteria-clad family-run pub occupies a lovely spot in the pretty hamlet of Tal-y-Coed. Surrounded by stunning countryside, it's a popular haunt for Offa's Dyke walkers, who can refuel with a glass of Otter Bitter by the open fire or in the sunny garden. Chef Mark Edwards keeps things simple and his menus have broad appeal. Chicken wings cooked in honey, sesame seeds and smoked BBQ sauce might precede a main course of braised lamb shank in red wine, mint and rosemary sauce with potato and parsnip mash.

Open 12-2.30 6-11 (Wed 6.30-10.30 Sat 12-11 Sun 12-10) Closed Mon & Tue **Food** Lunch Thu-Sat 12-2.30, Sun 12-6 Dinner Wed-Sat 6.30-9.30, Sun 12-6 Restaurant menu available Thu-Sun ⊕ FREE HOUSE ◀ Otter Bitter ○ Westons Stowford Press. **Facilities** Non-diners area ✿ (Garden) ♦ Children's menu Children's portions Play area Garden ☰ Parking WiFi ▬ (notice required)

TINTERN PARVA
Map 4 SO50

NEW The Anchor Inn

tel: 01291 689582 **Chapel Hill NP16 6TE**
email: contact@theanchortintern.co.uk **web:** www.theanchortintern.co.uk
dir: Take A466 N from Chepstow to Tintern. Approx 4m. Pub adjacent to Tintern Abbey ruins

Historic pub in the Wye Valley

Set against the stunning backdrop of Tintern Abbey next to the River Wye, this historic stone-built inn dates back to the 12th century. In the bar, locally brewed ales from Wye Valley and Kingstone breweries are joined by up to three local ciders. Once the ferryman's cottage and boat house, the cosy restaurant showcases local produce in dishes of Caerphilly, leek and minted pea risotto; beef, Wye Valley ale and mushroom pie; or pork, cider and apple sausages with caramelised onion mash. Finish with apple and blackberry oat crumble and bara brith ice cream.

Open all day all wk 10am-11pm **Food** Lunch Mon-Sat 12-3, Sun 12-4 Dinner Mon-Sat 6-9, Sun 5.30-7.30 ⊕ FREE HOUSE ◀ Otter Ale, Kingstone Classic Bitter, Wye Valley Butty Bach ○ Westons Old Rosie, Severn, Ty Gwyn. ▼ 9 **Facilities** Non-diners area ✿ (Bar Garden) ♦ Children's menu Children's portions Play area Garden ☰ Parking WiFi ▬

Fountain Inn

tel: 01291 689303 **Trellech Grange NP16 6QW**
email: fountaininntrellech@btconnect.com
dir: From M48 junct 2 follow Chepstow then A466 & Tintern signs. In Tintern turn by George Hotel for Raglan. Bear right, inn at top of hill, 2m from A466

Good food and well-kept ales at this village pub

A fine old inn dating from 1611 in lovely countryside, with a garden overlooking the Wye Valley. The pub offers several curries, including chicken kashmiri, and fruit and vegetable jalfrezi; and Welsh Black beef, Welsh lamb and roasted ham, all with fresh vegetables, roast potatoes, Yorkshire pudding and beer gravy. There is also a fresh fish menu with whole griddled flounder; sizzling crevettes; and beer-battered cod and chips. The owners' passion for real ales and ciders is evident both in the great bar line-up, and at the September beer festival.

Open Tue-Sun all day Closed Mon **Food** Lunch Tue-Sun 12-2.30 Dinner all wk 6-8.30 Set menu available ⊕ FREE HOUSE ◀ Kingstone Gold Fine Ale, Untapped Border, guest ales ○ Thatchers Gold. ▼ 9 **Facilities** Non-diners area ✿ (Bar Garden) ♦ Children's menu Children's portions Family room Garden ☰ Beer festival Parking WiFi ▬ (notice required)

TREDUNNOCK
Map 9 ST39

Newbridge on Usk ★★★★ RR ◉
PICK OF THE PUBS

tel: 01633 410262 **NP15 1LY**
email: bookings@celtic-manor.com **web:** www.celtic-manor.com
dir: M4 junct 24 follow Newport signs onto B4237. Right at Toby Carvery onto B4236 to Caerleon. Right over bridge, through Caerleon to mini rdbt. Straight ahead into Usk Rd towards Llangybi. In approx 4m turn right signed Tredunnock. Through Tredunnock, down hill, inn car park on left

Two hundred-year-old inn now a smart gastro-pub

The River Usk swings lazily beneath the eponymous bridge beside this country inn in deepest Monmouthshire. From the gardens are restful views across to the forested heights of Wentwood and riverside knolls; the Usk Valley Walk passes nearby and it's handy for the renowned Roman heritage of Caerleon. Part of the Celtic Manor Resort family, the interior is a pleasing blend of traditional beamed ceilings, snug corners and rustic ambience with modern touches and furnishings adding a certain élan. Beers from Brain's Cardiff brewery are the ales of choice, or Welsh cider may hit the spot. The fresh, zingy menu here has the award of one AA Rosette and is influenced by the availability of premium products from local suppliers. Starters may include mackerel, pepper and crayfish terrine, leading to roasted Madgett's Farm duck breast with salt-baked swede and garlic barley; or pan-roasted brill with curried lentils, carrot and coconut.

Open all day all wk 12-12 **Food** Lunch all wk 12-2.30 Dinner all wk 5-10 Set menu available ⊕ FREE HOUSE ◀ Brains The Rev. James & Smooth, guest ale ○ Tomos Watkin Taffy Apples. ▼ 12 **Facilities** Non-diners area ♦ Children's menu Children's portions Garden ☰ Parking WiFi ▬ **Rooms** 6

TRELLECH
Map 4 SO50

The Lion Inn
PICK OF THE PUBS

tel: 01600 860322 **NP25 4PA**
email: debs@globalnet.co.uk
dir: *From A40 S of Monmouth take B4293, follow Trellech signs. From M8 junct 2, straight across rdbt, 2nd left at 2nd rdbt, B4293 to Trellech*

A traditional inn with nautical links

Built in 1580 as a brewhouse and inn by a former sea captain, the Lion consists of two rooms, both with open fires; one is a traditional bar, the other a restaurant. Although best known for its food and drink, the pub also once showed true versatility by providing the best-dressed entry in the Monmouth raft race. Debbie Zsigo who runs it knows instinctively what works. In the bar the answer is Wye Valley Butty Bach and Felinfoel Double Dragon, and a number of local ciders including Raglan Cider Mill Snowy Owl. In the restaurant Debbie provides bar snacks, baguettes, ploughman's, omelettes, light meals and a range of main dishes, typically home-made lasagne; mild chicken curry; locally sourced faggots; and wild mushroom, brie and cranberry Wellington. There's a stream and an aviary in the garden, and beautiful views from the suntrap courtyard. Time a visit for the beer festival in June or the cider festival in August.

Open all day all wk 12-11 (Thu-Sat 12-12 Sun 12-10.30) **Food** Lunch Mon-Fri 12-2, Sat-Sun 12-2.30 Dinner Mon 7-9.30, Tue-Fri 6-9.30, Sat 6.30-9.30 Restaurant menu available all wk ⊕ FREE HOUSE ◀ Felinfoel Double Dragon, Wye Valley Butty Bach, Tiny Rebel Cwtch ♂ Springfield Red Dragon, Raglan Cider Mill Snowy Owl Sweet Perry. **Facilities** Non-diners area ♣ (Bar Garden) ♦️ Children's menu Children's portions Garden Outside area ⋒ Beer festival Cider festival Parking WiFi ⛟ (notice required)

USK
Map 9 SO30

The Nags Head Inn

tel: 01291 672820 **Twyn Square NP15 1BH**
email: keynags@tiscali.co.uk
dir: *On A472*

Bustling hostelry in the Vale of Gwent

Fronting Usk's old market place mid-way between the castle and fine priory church, parts of this inn date from the 15th century. Three generations of the Key family have been running it for over 50 years, lovingly caring for the flower-filled baskets above the pavement parasols in summer, and the beams, polished tables, rural artefacts and horse-brasses that create the traditional interior. Take your pick of the Brains and Buckley's ales at the bar while perusing the menu. 'Local and seasonal' are watchwords for most of the classic dishes, but snails in garlic butter or frogs' legs in hot provençale sauce can be ordered by the more adventurous.

Open all wk 10.30-2.30 5-11 Closed 25 Dec **Food** Lunch all wk 11.45-1.45 Dinner all wk 5.30-9.30 Restaurant menu available all wk ⊕ FREE HOUSE ◀ Brains Bitter, Buckley's Bitter, The Rev. James & Bread of Heaven, Sharp's Doom Bar ♂ Westons Stowford Press. ♚ 9 **Facilities** Non-diners area ♣ (All areas) ♦️ Children's menu Children's portions Garden Outside area ⋒ Parking WiFi ⛟

The Raglan Arms
PICK OF THE PUBS

tel: 01291 690800 **Llandenny NP15 1DL**
email: info@raglanarms.co.uk
dir: *From Monmouth take A449 to Raglan, left in village. From M4 take A449 exit. Follow Llandenny signs on right*

Peaceful setting for good food in the Vale of Gwent

Whether eating in, or just enjoying a pint brewed just three miles away, visitors are sure of a warm welcome at this stone-built 19th-century pub, which was taken over by William Brown in 2015. At the heart of a small village tucked between Tintern Forest and the Usk Valley, this neat inn continues to receive praise for its varied

and frequently changing menu. The head chef and his team use high quality ingredients for the imaginative menu. The pub is keen to reduce food miles and most suppliers are within a nine mile radius; from further afield, the fish is delivered from Cornwall each day. So try a starter of sautéed handpicked forest mushrooms, garlic focaccia and black truffle hollandaise, then follow on with oven-roasted Falmouth Bay cod fillet, Newquay lobster risotto, roast fennel, mussel, caper and lemon dressing. Finish with carrot and wildflower honey cake perhaps.

Open Tue-Sat 12-3 6.30-11.30 (Sun 12-2.30) Closed 25-28 Dec, Sun eve & Mon **Food** Lunch Tue-Sat 12-2.30, Sun 12-2.30 Dinner Tue-Sat 6.30-9 Set menu available Restaurant menu available Tue-Sat ⊕ FREE HOUSE ◀ Untapped ♂ Somersby. **Facilities** Non-diners area ♣ (Bar Garden) ♦️ Children's portions Garden ⋒ Parking

NEWPORT

CAERLEON
Map 9 ST39

The Bell at Caerleon

tel: 01633 420613 **Bulmore Rd NP18 1QQ**
email: thebellinn@hotmail.co.uk
dir: *M4 junct 25, B4596 signed Caerleon. In Caerleon before river bridge right onto B4238 signed Christchurch. Left into Bulmore Rd (follow brown pub sign)*

Ancient riverbank inn with great range of local ciders

Close to an ancient Roman burial ground (believed by some to be the location of King Arthur's Camelot), this 17th-century coaching inn has stood on the banks of the River Usk for more than 400 years. Local produce drives the menu, which might include duck leg confit with orange and thyme polenta cake, beansprout salad and duck jus; or honey and soy belly pork with roasted onion bread and butter pudding and parsnip purée. The pub is particularly well known for its range of local ciders and perrys. It holds annual real ale and cider festivals with barbecues.

Open all day all wk **Food** Lunch Mon-Sat 12-2.30, Sun 12-4 Dinner all wk 6-9.30 Set menu available ⊕ ENTERPRISE INNS ◀ Wye Valley HPA, Timothy Taylor Landlord, Tiny Rebel Cwtch ♂ Gwynt y Ddraig Black Dragon & Happy Daze, Hallets Real. ♚ 10 **Facilities** Non-diners area ♣ (Bar Garden) ♦️ Children's portions Garden ⋒ Beer festival Cider festival Parking WiFi ⛟ (notice required)

NEWPORT
Map 9 ST38

The Ridgeway Bar & Kitchen

tel: 01633 266053 **2 Ridgeway Av NP20 5AJ**
email: theridgeway@storyinns.com **web:** www.storyinns.com
dir: *M4 junct 27, B4591 towards Newport. At rdbt 1st left into Fields Park Rd. 1st left into Ridgeway Ave*

Breezy New England looks and British dishes

Set in a quiet suburb of Newport, just a few miles from Cardiff, and handily situated just a couple of minutes from the M4, the Ridgeway was given a New

England-style makeover a few years ago. There's a breezy coastal atmosphere, beautiful tiled floors and clever contemporary touches. The south-facing patio is a popular spot for a drink, and their varied menus offer something for everyone; starters might be butternut squash and blue cheese en croûte with honeyed walnuts or potted oak-smoked salmon with pickles and grilled brioche; followed by lemon and fennel marinated lamb rump, or chargrilled steak with triple-cooked chips. Finish with treacle tart.

The Ridgeway Bar & Kitchen

Open all day all wk **Food** Lunch Mon-Sat 12-2.30, Sun 12-3 Dinner Mon-Fri 5.30-9.30, Sat-Sun 6-9.30 Set menu available Restaurant menu available all wk ⊕ ENTERPRISE INNS ◀ Wye Valley HPA, St Austell Tribute, Fuller's London Pride Ŏ Aspall, Westons Old Rosie. ♇ 12 **Facilities** Non-diners area ♣ (Bar Outside area) ♦♦ Children's menu Children's portions Outside area ╔ Parking WiFi ▦ (notice required)

See advert below

AMROTH Map 8 SN10

The New Inn

tel: 01834 812368 **SA67 8NW**
email: paulluger@hotmail.com
dir: *A48 to Carmarthen, A40 to St Clears, A477 to Llanteg then left, follow road to seafront, turn left. 0.25m on left*

Old inn specialising in Welsh beef dishes

Originally a farmhouse, this 16th-century inn has been family run for over 40 years. The pub has old-world charm with beamed ceilings, a Flemish chimney, a flagstone floor and an inglenook fireplace. It is close to the beach, with views towards Saundersfoot and Tenby from the dining room upstairs. Along with Welsh beef, home-made dishes include slow-roast belly pork with mustard mash; pasta and meatballs; three bean smokey chilli; and tempura battered hake, chips and mushy peas. There is even a toddlers' menu in addition to the children's menu. Enjoy food or drink outside on the patio or large lawn complete with picnic benches.

Open all day all wk Mar-Oct 11-11 (Oct-Mar eve & wknds only) **Food** Contact pub for food times ⊕ FREE HOUSE ◀ Sharp's Doom Bar, Hancock's, Preseli Ales, Guinness, guest ales. **Facilities** Non-diners area ♣ (Bar Garden Outside area) ♦♦ Children's menu Children's portions Family room Garden Outside area ╔ Beer festival Parking WiFi ▦

ANGLE
Map 8 SM80

The Old Point House

tel: 01646 641205 **East Angle Bay SA71 5AS**
email: info@theoldpointhouseangle.co.uk
dir: *From Pembroke take B4320 signed Monkton & Hundleton. Right signed Angle. At T-junct left signed West Angle Bay. 1st right at pub sign on wall into narrow lane. Follow lane round bay to pub*

Remote but well worth tracking down

It's all angles round here – Angle village, Angle Bay, Angle RNLI. Indeed, the 15th-century Old Point has been the lifeboatmen's local since 1868, when their boathouse was built nearby. The track from the village skirts the foreshore and occasionally gets cut off by high spring tides. At its uneven-floored heart is the snug, its walls covered in old photos and memorabilia, and where Worthington's, Guinness, guest ales and real cider from Honey's in Somerset and Gwynt y Ddraig from Pontypridd are served. There was a change of hands in April 2016 and they continue to serve good, traditional pub food. There are picnic tables at the front with views across Angle Bay.

Open all day 11-11 Closed Mon-Tue & Thu (all wk in summer) **Food** Wed, Fri-Sun 11-11 (all wk in summer) ⊕ FREE HOUSE ◀ Worthington's, Guinness, guest ales ♂ Honey's Midford Cider, Gwynt y Ddraig. **Facilities** Non-diners area ✿ (Bar Garden Outside area) ♦ Children's portions Garden Outside area ⊼ Parking WiFi ☜ (notice required)

BOSHERSTON
Map 8 SR99

NEW St Govans Country Inn

tel: 01646 661311 **SA71 5DN**
email: mallikatucker@yahoo.co.uk
dir: *From Pembroke take B4319 signed Castlemartin, then follow Bosherston & brown pub signs*

Hearty food close to stunning beaches

Surrounded by breathtaking scenery on the Pembrokeshire coast, this friendly free house was named after the local monk who hid from smugglers by living in a tiny chapel built into the side of a cliff. On the edge of the Bosherton Lily Ponds on the Stackpole Estate, the pub is just a mile from the stunning beaches of Broadhaven South and Barafundle Bay. Enjoy pints of Evan Evans Cwrw and Gower Gold as you choose from a menu that might include a bowl of home-made cawl; bacon and leek pie; and a surf and turf featuring an 8oz Welsh sirloin.

Open all wk 12-3 6-10 (Apr-Oct 12-close) **Food** Lunch Mon-Fri 12-3, Sat-Sun all day (summer all wk all day) **Dinner** Mon-Fri 6-9, Sat-Sun all day (summer all wk all day) Av main course £11 ⊕ FREE HOUSE ◀ Evan Evans Cwrw, Gower Gold, Fuller's London Pride, Adnams Broadside. **Facilities** Non-diners area ✿ (Bar Restaurant Outside area) ♦ Children's menu Children's portions Outside area ⊼ Parking WiFi ☜ (notice required)

DALE
Map 8 SM80

Griffin Inn

tel: 01646 636227 **SA62 3RB**
email: info@griffininndale.co.uk
dir: *From end of M4 onto A48 to Carmarthen. A40 to Haverfordwest, B4327 to Dale. In Dale (with sea on left) pub on corner by slipway*

By the sea in a hidden corner of west Wales

Standing opposite the sea wall in a pretty coastal village, the Griffin offers the pleasure of roaring log fires in the winter and, in the summer, the joy of eating out on the water's edge, looking across Dale Bay. On tap in the bar you'll find Buckleys Best Bitter, The Rev. James and Evan Evans Cwrw Haf (koo-roo - it's Welsh for beer). The kitchen's sourcing policy demands that produce is both local and sustainable: for example, the Griffin now has its own fishing boat to supply fresh fish and seafood from the bay. Arrive there when they land and you can perhaps choose from the catch.

Open all wk Apr-Sep all day (winter opening times vary) Closed Nov **Food** Lunch 12-2.30 Dinner all wk 5-8.30 summer, 6-8.30 winter ⊕ FREE HOUSE ◀ Brains The Rev. James, Evan Evans Cwrw Haf, Buckleys Best Bitter ♂ Westons Stowford Press, Thatchers. **Facilities** Non-diners area ♦ Children's menu Children's portions Outside area ⊼ Parking WiFi ☜ (notice required)

LETTERSTON
Map 8 SM92

The Harp Inn

tel: 01348 840061 **31 Haverfordwest Rd SA62 5UA**
email: info@theharpatletterston.co.uk
dir: *On A40, 10m from Haverfordwest, 4m from Fishguard*

Modernised hostelry in the heart of Pembrokeshire

Formerly a working farm and home to a weekly market, this 15th-century free house remained largely unchanged for 500 years. Owned by the Sandall family for over 30 years, the building has a stylish conservatory restaurant where diners can enjoy local favourites like Welsh fillet steak; venison Roquefort; and whole sea bass. Alternatively, the bar lunch menu offers classic pub meals including crispy battered cod and chips. Enjoy lunch in all areas with your children.

Open all day all wk **Food** Lunch all wk winter 12-3, summer 12-9 Dinner all wk winter 6-9, summer 12-9 Set menu available Restaurant menu available all wk ⊕ FREE HOUSE ◀ Tetley's, Greene King Abbot Ale ♂ Thatchers Gold. **Facilities** Non-diners area ♦ Children's menu Children's portions Play area Garden ⊼ Parking WiFi ☜ (notice required)

LITTLE HAVEN
Map 8 SM81

St Brides Inn

tel: 01437 781266 **St Brides Rd SA62 3UN**
email: malcolmwhitewright@hotmail.com
dir: *From Haverfordwest take B4341 signed Broad Haven. Through Broad Haven to Little Haven*

Great walkers' refuelling stop

An ideal stop for walkers on the nearby Pembrokeshire coastal path as it runs through the seaside village of Little Haven, the St Brides Inn has the added attraction of an indoor ancient well, as well as a pretty floral beer garden. Food-wise expect the likes of deep-fried breaded camembert with warm cranberry sauce; black pudding-stuffed pork loin with cider sauce; and home-made rhubarb and ginger crumble. Lunchtime light bites include a bacon and black pudding bap; and pork and apple sausage and mushroom bap with fried potatoes. Fresh fish is always available, together with locally caught lobster and crab, in season.

Open all day all wk **Food** Lunch all wk 12-2 Dinner all wk 6-9 ⊕ FREE HOUSE ◀ Brains The Rev. James, Hancock's HB, Pembrokeshire guest ales ♂ Westons Stowford Press, Tomos Watkin Taffy Apples. ♟ 10 **Facilities** Non-diners area ✿ (Bar Garden Outside area) ♦ Children's menu Children's portions Garden Outside area ⊼ Beer festival WiFi ☜ (notice required)

PICK OF THE PUBS

The Stackpole Inn

STACKPOLE   Map 8 SR99

tel: 01646 672324 **SA71 5DF**
email: info@stackpoleinn.co.uk
web: www.stackpoleinn.co.uk
dir: *From Pembroke take B4319, follow Stackpole signs, approx 4m*

A real find in beautiful Pembrokeshire

This traditional inn is a walker's delight, set in pristine gardens at the heart of the National Trust's Stackpole Estate and close to the spectacular Pembrokeshire coastal path. There's a rare George V postbox in the mellow stone wall outside, a survival from the time when one of the two original stone cottages was a post office. Nowadays the pub offers facilities for walkers, cyclists, fishermen and climbers, as well as those who simply prefer to relax and do nothing. Once inside, you'll find a slate bar, ceiling beams made from ash trees grown on the estate, and a wood-burning stove set within the stone fireplace. The pub's free house status means that there's always a guest beer from around the UK to accompany two Welsh ales, a couple of real ciders and a varied wine list. Chef Mark Dowding oversees the creation of menus that use the best of local produce from the surrounding countryside and fish from the coast. Three-course appetites might begin with duck confit terrine with red

onion marmalde; home hot-smoked salmon with duo of beetrrot; or roasted red pepper houmous with charred pitta bread. Main course options range from roast rump of Welsh lamb with dauphinoise potatoes, butternut squash purée, kale, carrots and rich lamb jus, to creamy tagliatelle with Madeira, roasted onions and mushrooms. Round things off with a light vanilla pannacotta served with poached rose-scented rhubarb; indulgent sticky toffee pudding with toffee sauce and clotted cream ice cream; or rich Belgian chocolate, pecan and cranberry slice with cherry yogurt ice cream. Walkers may enjoy the 'Walkers lunch', a selection of local Welsh cheeses, ham, pickles, salad and bread.

Open all wk 12-3 6-11 (summer 12-11) Closed Sun eve (winter) **Food** Lunch Mon-Sat 12-2.15, Sun 12-2.30 (summer 12-11) Dinner all wk 6.30-9 (summer 12-11) ⊕ FREE HOUSE ◀ Brains The Rev. James, Felinfoel Double Dragon, guest ale ⓧ Gwynt y Ddraig, Westons Stowford Press. ⬙ 12
Facilities Non-diners area ☙ (Bar) ♙ Children's menu Children's portions Garden ⌁ Parking WiFi 🚌

NEWPORT
Map 8 SN03

Salutation Inn

tel: 01239 820564 **Felindre Farchog, Crymych SA41 3UY**
email: johndenley@aol.com
dir: *On A487 between Cardigan & Fishguard*

Top local produce served in former coaching inn

This tastefully modernised, 16th-century coaching inn stands on the River Nevern in the Pembrokeshire Coast National Park. Owners since 2000 are John Denley, a veteran of 20 years in restaurants in North Africa and the Middle East, and his wife Gwawr, born two miles away on the slopes of Carningli Mountain. There is an emphasis on fresh locally sourced produce for the menu, which lists pork liver pâté with home-made chutney; paprika chicken breast with tagliatelle; and grilled fillet of fresh salmon with lemon butter. Felinfoel, Brains and local guests are on tap.

Open all day Closed Tue in winter, (reduced hours out of season) **Food** Lunch all wk 12.30-2.30 Dinner all wk 6.30-9 Av main course £10.50 ⊕ FREE HOUSE ◀ Felinfoel, Brains, local guest ales ♻ Thatchers Gold. **Facilities** Non-diners area ❀ (Bar Garden) ♠ Children's menu Children's portions Garden ⋈ Parking WiFi ▭ (notice required)

PORTHGAIN
Map 8 SM83

The Sloop Inn

tel: 01348 831449 **SA62 5BN**
email: matthew@sloop-inn.freeserve.co.uk
dir: *Take A487 NE from St Davids for 6m. Left at Croesgooch for 2m to Porthgain*

Cosy pub with a maritime history

Possibly the most famous pub on the north Pembrokeshire coast, The Sloop Inn is located in the beautiful quarrying village of Porthgain and is especially enticing on a cold winter's day. The walls and ceilings are packed with pictures and memorabilia from nearby shipwrecks. The harbour is less than 100 yards from the door and there is a village green to the front, a large south-facing patio and a children's football pitch. With ales like Felinfoel and The Rev. James on the pump, a varied menu includes breakfasts, snacks, pub favourites, steaks and home-caught fish. Just the place to call into when out for one of the amazing nearby walks.

Open all day all wk 9.30am-11pm (winter 11.30-10) Closed 25 Dec eve **Food** Lunch all wk 12-2.30 Dinner all wk 6-9.30 Restaurant menu available all wk ⊕ FREE HOUSE/B G BETTERSPOONS LTD ◀ Hancock's HB, Felinfoel, Brains The Rev. James, Sharp's Doom Bar ♻ Gwynt y Ddraig. **Facilities** Non-diners area ❀ (Garden Outside area) ♠ Children's menu Children's portions Garden Outside area ⋈ Parking WiFi ▭

ROSEBUSH
Map 8 SN02

Tafarn Sinc

tel: 01437 532214 **Preseli SA66 7QT**
email: briandavies2@btconnect.com
dir: *Phone for detailed directions*

Free house maintaining its nostalgic originality

Built to serve the railway that no longer exists, this large red corrugated-iron free house stands testament to its rapid construction in 1876. This idiosyncratic establishment refuses to be modernised and boasts wood-burning stoves, a

sawdust floor, and a charming garden. Set high in the Preseli Hills amid stunning scenery, it is popular with walkers, who can refuel on traditional favourites like local lamb burgers; prime Welsh sirloin steak; home-cooked ham; and Glamorgan sausages with chutney.

Open all day 12-11 Closed Mon (ex BHs & summer) **Food** Lunch Tue-Sat 12-2 Dinner Tue-Sat 6-9 Av main course £10.50 ⊕ FREE HOUSE ◀ Worthington's, Tafarn Sinc, guest ale. **Facilities** Non-diners area ♠ Children's menu Children's portions Garden ⋈ Parking ▭ (notice required)

ST DOGMAELS
Map 8 SN14

The Teifi Netpool Inn

tel: 01239 612680 **SA43 3ET**
email: jennyspangles@aol.com
dir: *From A487 follow St Dogmaels signs (B4546). Left signed St Dogmaels, Llandudoch & Poppit (B4546). Left into Maeshfryd St, to end, pub on left*

Family-friendly and dog-friendly inn

This pub offers local guest ales as well as Greene King Abbot Ale, and serves food for all the family from midday until mid evening. It's on the banks of the River Teifi near the village green — a little off the beaten track but a good place to find for anything from a Welsh beef pie to a chicken New Yorker. Sunday lunches are popular.

Open all wk winter 5-10.30 (summer 12-11.30) **Food** Lunch all wk 12-3 Dinner all wk 5-8.30 ⊕ FREE HOUSE ◀ Greene King Abbot Ale, local guest ales ♻ Addlestones. **Facilities** Non-diners area ❀ (Bar Outside area) ♠ Children's menu Children's portions Play area Outside area ⋈ Parking WiFi ▭ (notice required)

Webley Waterfront Inn & Hotel

tel: 01239 612085 **Poppit Sands SA43 3LN**
email: webleyhotel@btconnect.com
dir: *A484 from Carmarthen to Cardigan, then to St Dogmaels, right in village centre to Poppit Sands on B4546*

Seafood in a magnificent setting

This long-established family business is spectacularly situated at the start of the Pembrokeshire Coast National Park, a haven for birdwatchers and watersports enthusiasts. The inn offers outstanding views across the River Teifi and Poppit Sands to Cardigan Bay, which supplies the daily catch for the menu. King scallops with crispy bacon and carrot purée, perhaps to start, followed by pan-seared salmon and sautéed new potatoes. The specials board might feature dressed lobster and crab. Other dishes include rump steak and five bean chilli. The bar serves Gwynt y Ddraig Welsh cider together with a selection of ales.

Open all day all wk **Food** Lunch all wk 12-2.30 Dinner all wk 6-8.30 ⊕ FREE HOUSE ◀ Brains Buckley's Bitter, Felinfoel, guest ales ♻ Gwynt y Ddraig. ♟ 8 **Facilities** Non-diners area ❀ (Bar Garden) ♠ Children's menu Children's portions Play area Family room Garden ⋈ Parking WiFi ▭

STACKPOLE
Map 8 SR99

The Stackpole Inn
PICK OF THE PUBS

See Pick of the Pubs on page 647

TENBY
Map 8 SN10

Hope and Anchor

tel: 01834 842131 **Saint Julians St SA70 7AX**
dir: *A478 or A4139 into Tenby. Into High St, becomes Saint Julians St. Pub on left*

A popular pub with a good choice of fish dishes

Heading down towards the harbour and the beach at Tenby and you can't miss the blue Hope and Anchor pub. Traditionally a fishing pub it has remained popular with locals for years and years. They offer seven real ales that change throughout the week and the menus and special boards feature lots of fish. Tenby mackerel, pan fried in butter or with a Cajun seasoning; sea bass with rocket and couscous salad; or mussels cooked with bacon, onions, cider and cream; even locally caught lobster is featured. Meat eaters might choose minted lamb or rib-eye steaks; steak and ale pie; or rosemary and garlic chicken.

Open all day all wk Closed 25 Dec L **Food** all wk 12-9.30 ⊕ FREE HOUSE ◀ Sharp's Atlantic, Felinfoel Double Dragon, guest ales ♂ Westons Scrumpy, Old Rosie, Orchard Pig The Hog Father. ♀ 13 **Facilities** Non-diners area ♦♦ Children's menu Children's portions Garden ⋒ WiFi ⛟ (notice required)

POWYS

BEGUILDY
Map 9 SO17

The Radnorshire Arms

tel: 01547 510634 **LD7 1YE**
email: radnorshirearmsbeguildy@gmail.com
dir: *8m from Knighton on B4355 towards Newtown*

Enjoyable food and local ales in a former drovers' inn

Tucked away in the Teme Valley, this centuries-old black and white timber framed pub started life as a drovers' inn and it retains an old world charm with mind-your-head beams, inglenook fireplace and wood-burner. Sup on pints of local Ludlow Best or Stonehouse Station Bitter and choose between the bar menu with its pub classics or the main menu. Typical dinner choices include leek and crab tartlet, which might precede venison haunch steak with braised red cabbage, herb mash and red wine sauce, or chicken and mango stir-fry with noodles and sweet chilli sauce.

Open 12-2.30 6-11 Closed Mon **Food** Lunch Tue-Sun 12-2 Dinner Tue-Sat 6.30-9, Sun 7-8 Restaurant menu available Tue-Sun evenings ⊕ FREE HOUSE ◀ Stonehouse Station Bitter, Ludlow Best ♂ Thatchers Gold. **Facilities** Non-diners area ♦♦ Children's menu Children's portions Garden ⋒ Parking WiFi ⛟ (notice required)

BRECON
Map 9 SO02

The Usk Inn
PICK OF THE PUBS

tel: 01874 676251 **Talybont-on-Usk LD3 7JE**
email: stay@uskinn.co.uk
dir: *6m E of Brecon, just off A40 towards Abergavenny & Crickhowell*

An ideal stop for visitors to the Brecon Beacons

Well-positioned on the picturesque Abergavenny to Brecon road, not far from the village centre, The Usk Inn attracts both locals and visitors to the Brecon Beacons National Park and the canal. The inn opened in the 1840s just as the Brecon to Merthyr railway line was being built alongside it. Expect a choice of guest ales at the bar, including Evans Evans Cwrw, along with ciders and popular wines. Typical dinner dishes, based on carefully sourced ingredients, are roasted fillet of monkfish; venison steak with shallot and red wine sauce; and tenderloin of pork with apple sauce and black pudding.

Open all day all wk 11am-11.30pm (Sun 11-10.30) Closed 25-26 Dec eve **Food** Lunch all wk 12-2.30 Dinner all wk 6.30-9.30 Set menu available Restaurant menu available all wk ⊕ FREE HOUSE ◀ Evan Evans Cwrw, Guinness, guest ales ♂ Thatchers, Robinsons. ♀ 11 **Facilities** Non-diners area ♦♦ Children's menu Children's portions Garden ⋒ Parking ⛟ (notice required)

COEDWAY
Map 15 SJ31

The Old Hand and Diamond Inn

tel: 01743 884379 **SY5 9AR**
email: moz123@aol.com **web:** www.oldhandanddiamond.co.uk
dir: *From Shrewsbury take A458 towards Welshpool. Right onto B4393 signed Four Crosses. Coedway approx 5m*

One for all the family

On the Powys-Shropshire border, this 17th-century inn retains much of its original character, with exposed beams and an inglenook fireplace. Its reputation for good quality food owes much to local farmers who supply excellent meats, including lamb and mutton from rare-breed Jacob sheep. Enjoy local Shropshire Lad and guest real ales in the bar, while choosing from an extensive menu that lists grilled lamb chop and shepherd's pie; butternut squash stuffed with cannellini beans, mozarella, peppers and tomato; and Stonehouse ale and beef pie. Among the desserts are fresh fruit Pavlova and ginger and lime cheesecake. The beer garden has plenty of seating and a children's play area.

Open all day all wk 11am-1am **Food** Lunch Mon-Thu 12-2.30, Fri-Sun 12-9.30 Dinner Mon-Thu 6-9.30, Fri-Sun 12-9.30 Restaurant menu available all wk ⊕ FREE HOUSE ◀ Worthington's, Wood's Shropshire Lad, guest ales. **Facilities** Non-diners area ❀ (Bar Garden) ♦♦ Children's portions Play area Garden ⋒ Parking WiFi ⛟

CRICKHOWELL
Map 9 SO21

The Bear ★★★★ INN ❀
PICK OF THE PUBS

tel: 01873 810408 **Brecon Rd NP8 1BW**
email: bearhotel@aol.com web: www.bearhotel.co.uk
dir: *On A40 between Abergavenny & Brecon*

Quintessential market town coaching inn

This imposing white-painted inn, dating from the 15th century, has been run by the Hindmarsh family for over 35 years. The rug-strewn, antique-laden bar offers sandwiches and baguettes on top of the main menu, and Welsh real ales take the lead at the pumps. Alternatively, dine in the original D Restaurant, intimately dressed with linen and fresh cut flowers, or at a table in the restored former kitchen. Head chef Adam Littlewort makes good use of Welsh produce, as in a starter of traditional Welsh stew made with shoulder of lamb and seasonal vegetables, followed by home-made faggots with onion gravy; or Cornish fish pie. For vegetarians, perhaps potato gnocchi with garlic sautéed wild mushrooms and parsley. Finish with sticky toffee pudding with caramel sauce and rich clotted cream.

Open all day all wk Closed 25 Dec **Food** Lunch all wk 12-2.15, afternoon menu 2.15-6 Dinner Mon-Sat 6-10, Sun 7-9.30 Restaurant menu available Mon-Sat ⊕ FREE HOUSE ◀ Brains The Rev. James, Wye Valley Butty Bach, Hancock's HB, guest ales Ò Westons Stowford Press. ♟ 10 **Facilities** Non-diners area ✿ (Bar Garden) ♦ Children's menu Children's portions Family room Garden ㆴ Parking WiFi ⛟ (notice required) **Rooms** 34

DEFYNNOG
Map 9 SN92

The Tanners Arms

tel: 01874 638032 **LD3 8SF**
email: info@tannersarmspub.com
dir: *From Brecon take A40 towards Llandovery. Left onto A4067 to Defynnog*

Old inn not far from the glorious Brecon Beacons

In a tiny village and overlooking open countryside, this 17th-century inn derives its name from the tannery that was once in business up the road. In the foothills of the Brecon Beacons National Park it makes a good stopping point for those setting off to explore this mountain area. The pub has real ales and ciders changing very regularly and the menus offer whole prawns in tempura batter; home-made pâté and toast; French brie and tomato quiche; sweet and sour chicken; rack of roasted BBQ pork ribs; and pan-fried sea bass fillet with buttered new potatoes. Lunchtime quick bites and sandwiches are offered too.

Open all wk 5-12 (Fri 4-12 Sat-Sun 12-12) ⊕ FREE HOUSE ◀ Constantly changing ales Ò Constantly changing ciders. **Facilities** ✿ (Bar Garden) ♦ Children's menu Children's portions Garden Parking WiFi

GLASBURY
Map 9 SO13

The Harp Inn

tel: 01497 847373 **HR3 5NR**
email: info@theharpinn.co.uk
dir: *In village centre on B4350, approx 3.5m from Hay-on-Wye*

Country pub with a long history

A pub since the 17th century, this comfortable inn overlooks the River Wye and is just a few miles from Hay-on-Wye itself. In the bar, grab a table and enjoy a pint of one of several local real ales, including Mayfields Glasbury Undaunted specially brewed for the pub. The tempting menu offers classics of spicy meatballs and spaghetti; steak and ale pie; and oven-baked vegetable lasagne. There's also a range of tasty pizzas and a specials board to watch out for. Regular music events include monthly folk and Irish sessions, and occasional jazz nights.

Open 12-3 6-12 (Sun 12-3 7-11 Mon 6-11) Closed Mon L **Food** Lunch Tue-Sun 12-2 Dinner Tue-Sat 6.30-8.30, Sun 7-8 ⊕ FREE HOUSE ◀ Wye Valley Dorothy Goodbody's Golden Ale & Butty Bach, Mayfields Glasbury Undaunted Ò Westons Stowford Press. **Facilities** Non-diners area ✿ (Bar Garden) ♦ Children's menu Children's portions Garden ㆴ Parking WiFi ⛟ (notice required)

HAY-ON-WYE
Map 9 SO24

The Old Black Lion ★★★★ INN ❀
PICK OF THE PUBS

tel: 01497 820841 **HR3 5AD**
email: info@oldblacklion.co.uk web: www.oldblacklion.co.uk
dir: *From B4348 in Hay-on-Wye into Lion St. Inn on right*

Historic inn with very good food

Close to Lion Gate, one of the original entrances to the old walled town of Hay-on-Wye, parts of this charming whitewashed inn date from the 1300s, although structurally most of it is 17th century. The oak-timbered bar is furnished with scrubbed pine tables, comfy armchairs and a log-burner – perfect for savouring a pint of Wye Valley Bitter. The inn has a long-standing reputation for its food, and the pretty dining room overlooking the garden terrace is where to enjoy grilled mackerel and rhubarb chutney followed by roast pork chop, bubble-and-squeak and Calvados gravy; or roast fillet of salmon, crushed potatoes, mushroom and white wine sauce. Hay, of course, has bookshops at every turn, and it is also home to a renowned annual literary festival.

Open all day all wk 8am-11pm Closed 1st 2wks Jan **Food** Lunch all wk 12-2.30 Dinner Sun-Thu 6.30-9, Fri-Sat 6.30-9.30 ⊕ FREE HOUSE ◀ Old Black Lion Ale, Wye Valley Bitter, guest ales Ò Westons Stowford Press. ♟ 8 **Facilities** Non-diners area ♦ Children's portions Garden ㆴ Parking WiFi **Rooms** 10

The Three Tuns

tel: 01497 821855 **4 Broad St HR3 5DB**
email: info@three-tuns.com
dir: *In town centre*

Stylish town pub with a warm welcome

This 16th-century, possibly older, pub has attracted an eclectic roll-call of famous, even infamous, visitors, from singer Marianne Faithfull and pianist Jools Holland, to the Great Train Robbers. In the bar is an old settle, reclaimed from a fire at the pub, and restored so that visitors can continue to sit and enjoy a welcome pint of Wye Valley Bitter or Butty Bach. The menus range from a home-made pizza, baked ciabatta or beer battered haddock and chips to choices such as sirloin steak with field mushroom, beef tomatoes and triple-cooked chips; roasted pumpkin with hazelnuts, salad and ricotta cheese; and apple and blackcurrant strudel, toasted pine nuts and clotted cream.

Open 11-3 6-11 Closed 25 Dec, Mon & Tue (winter) **Food** Lunch all wk 11-2 Dinner all wk 6-9 ⊕ FREE HOUSE ◀ Wye Valley Bitter, Butty Bach ♻ Westons Old Rosie. **Facilities** Non-diners area ♦♦ Children's portions Garden ⋒ WiFi ▄▄

LLANDRINDOD WELLS   Map 9 SO06

The Laughing Dog

tel: 01597 822406 **Howey LD1 5PT**
dir: *From A483 between Builth Wells & Llandrindod Wells follow Howey signs. Pub in village centre*

Village centre inn with adventurous cooking

All you'd expect from a thriving village local, from pub games in the fire-warmed bar to real ales from respected Welsh microbreweries such as Rhymney and The Celt Experience. Originating as a drovers' stopover some 300 years ago and reputedly haunted, this pub is located in superb walking countryside. The varied menu combines the best of Welsh ingredients with influences from Europe and further afield. Start with five spice pulled pork, hoi sin sauce and Chinese pancakes; or button mushroom escabeche with roasted red peppers; follow that with Welsh shoulder of lamb, pot-roasted with Moroccan spices, honey and ginger and couscous; or Bengali fish stew.

Open all wk Mon 7pm-10.30pm Tue-Thu 6-11 (Fri 5.30-11 Sat-Sun all day) **Food** Lunch Sun 12-2 Dinner Tue-Sat 6.30-9 ⊕ FREE HOUSE ◀ Wye Valley Bitter & Butty Bach, The Celt Experience Celt-Bronze Ale, Felinfoel Double Dragon, Rhymney Bevan's Bitter & General Picton. **Facilities** Non-diners area ♥ (Bar Garden) ♦♦ Children's menu Children's portions Garden ⋒ ▄▄ (notice required)

LLANFYLLIN   Map 15 SJ11

Cain Valley Hotel

tel: 01691 648366 **High St SY22 5AQ**
email: info@cainvalleyhotel.co.uk
dir: *From Shrewsbury & Oswestry follow signs for Lake Vyrnwy onto A490 to Llanfyllin. Hotel on right*

Traditional food in long-established hotel

A watering hole since the 17th century, this hotel offers the choice of an oak-panelled lounge bar and a heavily beamed restaurant. A full bar menu is available at lunchtime (sandwiches, salads, pub classics, vegetarian and children's choices) and the evening menu typically offers Thai fishcakes or breaded whitebait, which might be followed by grilled double lamb chop; steak and ale pie; oven-cooked rainbow trout; or roasted vegetable bake topped with goats' cheese. Lovers of mild ale will find The Rev. James in the bar along with Westons Stowford Press cider.

Open all day all wk 11.30am-mdnt (Sun 12-11) Closed 25 Dec **Food** Lunch all wk 12-2 Dinner all wk 7-9 Av main course £10 Restaurant menu available all wk ⊕ FREE HOUSE ◀ Worthington's, Ansell's Mild, Brains The Rev. James, Guinness ♻ Westons Stowford Press. **Facilities** Non-diners area ♥ (Bar) ♦♦ Children's menu Children's portions ⋒ Parking WiFi ▄▄ (notice required)

LLANGYNIDR   Map 9 SO11

The Coach & Horses

tel: 01874 730245 **Cwmcrawnon Rd NP8 1LS**
email: coachandhorses222@outlook.com
dir: *Take A40 from Abergavenny towards Brecon. At Crickhowell left onto B4558 to Llangynidr (NB narrow river bridge), or from Beaufort take B4560 through Brynmawr to Llangynidr*

Beer garden with lovely views

Just two minutes' walk from the nearby Monmouthshire & Brecon Canal and surrounded by the Brecon Beacons, this early 18th-century free house is a popular

meeting place for car club members. Wye Valley Butty Bach is a bar staple, while on the menu steak and Stogs stew with dumplings features real ale Betty Stogs, a Cornish folklore character. Other possibilities include sautéed lamb's liver with mash, onion rings, vegetables and red wine gravy; steak and kidney pie or pudding; and baked salmon fillet in watercress sauce. Toasted sandwiches, fresh crab and prawn tian, and salads are on the bar menu.

Open all day 12-12 Closed Sun eve (Winter) **Food** Lunch all wk 12-2 Dinner all wk 6-9 Av main course £9.50-£12.50 ⊕ FREE HOUSE ◀ Wye Valley Butty Bach, Sharp's Doom Bar, Bass. **Facilities** Non-diners area ♥ (Bar Garden) ♦♦ Children's menu Children's portions Play area Garden ⋒ Parking WiFi ▄▄ (notice required)

OLD RADNOR   Map 9 SO25

The Harp   PICK OF THE PUBS

tel: 01544 350655 **LD8 2RH**
email: mail@harpinnradnor.co.uk
dir: *Old Radnor signed from A44 between Kington & New Radnor*

Enjoyable food in a Welsh longhouse with lovely views

With magnificent views across the Radnor Valley, this stone-built Welsh longhouse dates from the 15th century. Open the plain wooden door and you step into a cosy lounge and bars with original oak beams, crackling log fires, semi-circular wooden settles and slate floors; books, board games and hop bines complete the warm, traditional appeal. The food focus is on fresh and seasonal produce, and local sourcing is highlighted on the concise, refreshingly no-frills menu. Roasted red pepper and tomato soup with herb oil makes for a tasty starter, and to follow perhaps roast lemon sole, Welsh rarebit, ham and caper potato cake, green beans and parsley cream; a classic steak and chips; or home-cooked ham, egg and chips. Finish with maple syrup cheesecake, praline crumb with vanilla and pecan ice cream. Real ales from Shropshire and Herefordshire breweries are rotated, and an annual June beer festival is hugely popular.

Open 6-11 (Fri-Sun 12-3 6-11) Closed Mon (ex BHs) Tue **Food** Lunch Fri-Sun 12-2.30 Dinner Wed-Sat 6-9 ⊕ FREE HOUSE ◀ Three Tuns, Wye Valley, Hobsons, Ludlow, Salopian ♻ Dunkertons. **Facilities** Non-diners area ♥ (Bar Garden) ♦♦ Children's portions Garden ⋒ Beer festival Parking WiFi

PAINSCASTLE   Map 9 SO14

The Roast Ox Inn

tel: 01497 851398 **LD2 3JL**
dir: *From Hay-on-Wye take B4351, through Clyro to Painscastle*

Classic pub food in restored rural local

In stunning countryside close to Hay-on-Wye and Brecon, the Roast Ox is traditional through and through – a country pub fully restored using venerable building materials and methods. Expect rustic brick floors, stone walls, old fireplaces and a classic pub atmosphere alongside comfortable furnishings and local Wye Valley Butty Bach ale tapped straight from the barrel. Head for the dining room, originally a blacksmith's workshop, for home-cooked and locally sourced fodder. Typical are twice-cooked pork spare ribs in barbecue sauce; Welsh faggots with creamy mash; and a board of Welsh cheeses to die for, served with apple chutney and oat biscuits.

Open all wk Closed Mon-Tue Jan-Mar **Food** Lunch all wk 12-2 Dinner all wk 6-9 ⊕ FREE HOUSE ◀ Sharp's Doom Bar, Wye Valley Butty Bach, guest ale ♻ Thatchers. ▮ 8 **Facilities** Non-diners area ♥ (Bar Outside area) ♦♦ Children's portions Outside area ⋒ Parking WiFi ▄▄ (notice required)

| TALYBONT-ON-USK | Map 9 SO12 |

Star Inn

tel: 01874 676635 **LD3 7YX**
email: anna@starinntalybont.co.uk
dir: *Take A40 from Brecon toward Crickhowell. 6m to pub in town centre*

An astonishing number of beers at Brecon Beacons' pub

In the National Park, with a garden right next to the Monmouthshire & Brecon Canal, and an ever-changing choice of real ales – over 500 guests a year – Ian and Anna Bell's village pub is extremely popular, and even that could be an understatement. Beer festivals pull in even more fans in mid-June and mid-October. But, of course, there's food too, in the shape of local venison faggots with creamed mash and winter greens; fresh beer battered fish and chips; and roast pumpkin and squash gnocchi. Under-12s have their own selection and the under-2s eat for free.

Open all wk 11.30-3 5-11 Fri-Sun 11.30-11 (summer all wk 11.30-11) **Food** Lunch Mon-Fri 12-2, Sat-Sun 12-2.30 Dinner all wk 6-9 (no food Sun eve) ⊕ PUNCH TAVERNS ◾ Wye Valley, Brecon Brewing, rotating guest ales Ö Gwynt y Ddraig, guest ciders. **Facilities** Non-diners area ❤ (Bar Restaurant Garden) ⬩ Children's menu Children's portions Garden ☴ Beer festival WiFi

| TRECASTLE | Map 9 SN82 |

The Castle Coaching Inn   PICK OF THE PUBS

See Pick of the Pubs on opposite page

RHONDDA CYNON TAFF

| PONTYPRIDD | Map 9 ST08 |

Bunch of Grapes   PICK OF THE PUBS

See Pick of the Pubs on page 654

SWANSEA

| LLANGENNITH | Map 8 SS49 |

Kings Head ★★★★ INN

tel: 01792 386212 **SA3 1HX**
email: info@kingsheadgower.co.uk **web:** www.kingsheadgower.co.uk
dir: *M4 junct 47, follow signs for Gower A483, 2nd exit at rdbt, right at lights onto B495 towards Old Walls, left at fork to Llangennith, pub on right*

A pub with it all, near glorious coastline

A lane to Rhossili Bay's magnificent beach starts just along from this 17th-century village inn, which still displays plenty of old beams, exposed stonework and a large open fire. The bar serves a weekly rotating schedule of real ales from the Gower Brewery, which pub landlord Chris Stevens co-founded. Expect much praised home-made food using local produce that includes Vietnamese, Goan and Thai curries; pizzas; gourmet burgers; salt marsh lamb; and Welsh beef and venison. Comfortable and stylish accommodation is available. A beer and cider festival is held during the last weekend of October.

Open all day all wk 9am-11pm (Sun 9am-10.30pm) **Food** all wk 9am-9.30pm ⊕ FREE HOUSE ◾ Gower Gold, Lighthouse & Power, Guinness, rotating guest ales Ö Gwynt y Ddraig Black Dragon. **Facilities** Non-diners area ❤ (Bar Garden) ⬩ Children's menu Children's portions Garden ☴ Beer festival Cider festival Parking ⬛ **Rooms** 27

| LLANMADOC | Map 8 SS49 |

Britannia Inn

tel: 01792 386624 **SA3 1DB**
email: enquiries@britanniainngower.co.uk **web:** www.britanniainngower.co.uk

Welcoming pub adding to the attractions of the Gower

After years of experience in cooking and hospitality around the world, Martin and Lindsey Davies returned to home territory more than a decade ago, applying their skills at the Britannia. The pub's whitewashed and flower-bedecked exterior features a terrace with lovely Gower views. Inside, chunky wooden furniture and beamed ceilings make a welcoming ambience. Martin's fixed price lunch menu is indicative of the quality fare on offer: smoked confit duck pot with home-made fig and date chutney could be followed by Moroccan slow-braised Welsh lamb tagine. Beer gardens front and back are home to a variety of pets.

Open all day all wk **Food** Lunch all wk 12-3 Dinner all wk 6-9.30 Set menu available Restaurant menu available all wk ⊕ ENTERPRISE INNS ◾ Gower Gold, Wadworth 6X, Marston's Pedigree. **Facilities** Non-diners area ❤ (Bar Garden) ⬩ Children's menu Children's portions Play area Garden ☴ Parking WiFi ⬛ (notice required)

| REYNOLDSTON | Map 8 SS48 |

King Arthur Hotel

tel: 01792 390775 **Higher Green SA3 1AD**
email: info@kingarthurhotel.co.uk
dir: *Just N of A4118, SW of Swansea*

A warm welcome and a delightful setting

Sheep graze on the village green opposite this charming inn set in a pretty village at the heart of the beautiful Gower Peninsula. Inside you'll find real log fires, bare wood floors and walls decorated with nautical memorabilia. Eat in the restaurant, main bar or family room, where choices range from pub favourites such as fillet of cod in a lager batter with home-made tartare sauce, or a Welsh Celtic Pride steak through to healthy salads (maybe Greek, ham or chicken Caesar). Enjoy the food with a choice of well-kept local ales, or one of 11 wines served by the glass.

Open all day all wk Closed 25 Dec **Food** Contact pub for food times ⊕ FREE HOUSE ◾ Felinfoel Double Dragon, Tomos Watkin OSB, Worthington's, Tiny Rebel, Mumbles. ♟ 11 **Facilities** Non-diners area ⬩ Children's menu Children's portions Family room Garden Parking WiFi ⬛ (notice required)

PICK OF THE PUBS

The Castle Coaching Inn

TRECASTLE   Map 9 SN82

tel: 01874 636354 **LD3 8UH**
email: reservations@castle-coaching-inn.co.uk
web: www.castle-coaching-inn.co.uk
dir: *On A40, W of Brecon*

Ideal base for walking in the Brecon Beacons

Privately owned and run by the Porter family, this Georgian coaching inn sits on the old London to Carmarthen route in the northern part of the Brecon Beacons National Park. It makes an ideal base for the pursuit of outdoor activities or, for the less energetic, the simple appreciation of mountain views, lakes, waterfalls and wildlife. The inn has lovely old fireplaces and a remarkable bow-fronted window looking out from the bar, where an open log fire burns throughout the winter. The focus on customer satisfaction makes this a relaxing hostelry, even at weekends when it becomes especially lively. Two real ales on tap change weekly, ensuring a pint in tip-top condition; wines and a good selection of Scottish and Irish whiskies are also served. While settling back to enjoy your drink and the great atmosphere, take a look at the menu and specials board. Some guests prefer to stay in the bar to eat; the menu is the same both here and in the restaurant, although additional bar food includes fresh sandwiches, jackets, seafood,

steak and ale pie, and lamb casserole. Starters range from home-made soup of the day with crusty bread, to duck and orange pâté; deep-fried camembert; and a salmon, cod and prawn fishcake served with home-made tartare sauce. Main courses typically include Welsh sirloin steak cooked to your liking with mushrooms, cherry tomatoes and onion rings; supreme of chicken stuffed with Stilton, wrapped in bacon, with white wine and cream sauce; and slow-roasted Welsh lamb. Desserts press all the right buttons with the likes of Belgian triple chocolate praline torte with vanilla ice cream; and lemon posset with shortbread. Outside, the peaceful terrace and garden beckon on sunny days.

Open all wk 6-11 (Sat 12-3 6-11 Sun 12-3 7-11) **Food** Lunch Sat-Sun 12-2 Dinner Mon-Sat 6.30-9, Sun 7-9 ⊕ FREE HOUSE ◖ Guest ales ♨ Westons Stowford Press. **Facilities** Non-diners area 🐾 (Bar Garden) 👫 Children's menu Children's portions Garden 🪑 Parking WiFi

PICK OF THE PUBS

Bunch of Grapes

PONTYPRIDD　　　　Map 9 ST08

tel: 01443 402934
Ynysangharad Rd CF37 4DA
email: info@bunchofgrapes.org.uk
web: www.bunchofgrapes.org.uk
dir: *From A470 onto A4054 (Pentrebach Rd to Merthyr road) into Ynysangharad Rd*

Excellent beers and good local food in The Rhondda

Eight hand pumps lining the bar are the first clue that this pub is an ale lover's paradise. It's owned by the local award-winning Otley Brewing Company, and is a previous winner of the AA Pub of the Year for Wales. The brewery's flagship 02 Croeso is one of four regular Otley ales on offer, alongside guests from other UK microbreweries and imported bottles and kegs from Europe and America. Beer festivals are hosted every two months, when the choice expands to more than 20; and two annual cider festivals showcase Welsh draught ciders among others. To complete the refreshments line-up, the wine list is no also-ran, with quality choices from around the world and seven served by the glass. Surrounded by the striking, wooded landscapes of South Wales, this 160-year-old market town pub includes many of the region's best ingredients in its dishes. The lunchtime bar menu keeps things simple with quality pub-grub offerings such as sandwiches,

ploughman's, deep-fried haddock fillet in Otley ale batter, and Breconshire beef or lamb burgers, perhaps topped with maple-cured streaky bacon and melted Welsh Cheddar. In the evening the kitchen steps up the pace. Indicative starters are carpaccio of wood pigeon, chestnut and pickled girolle salad; or terrine of pork, duck and cranberry with cranberry purée and pecan nut salad. Main courses, too, reflect the kitchen's serious credentials: typical are pan-fried fillet of sea trout, smoked mackerel and potato hash, brown shrimp and herb butter with pickled celeriac; and roasted leg of Breconshire lamb, black pudding and caramelised shallot croquette, roasted carrot and white wine braising jus.

Open all day all wk **Food** Lunch Mon-Fri 12-2.30, Sat 12-3, Sun 12-3.30 Dinner Mon-Sat 6-9.30 Restaurant menu available all wk ⊕ FREE HOUSE ◀ Otley Ales, guest ales ♂ Gwynt y Ddraig, Blaengawney. **Facilities** Non-diners area ❀ (Bar Garden) ♦ Children's menu Children's portions Garden ⌒ Beer festival Cider festival Parking WiFi

VALE OF GLAMORGAN

BARRY — Map 9 ST16

Fox and Hounds ★★★★ INN

tel: 01446 781287 **Llancarfan CF62 3AD**
email: foxandhoundsllancarfan@gmail.com **web:** www.foxandhoundsllancarfan.co.uk
dir: *Contact pub for detailed directions*

Lovely surroundings and good beer

Beautiful countryside surrounds the little village of Llancarfan, and the church houses medieval paintings dating back to the 15th century. The pub was rescued from threat of closure by the villagers, and bought by the Millards. There's a light and airy restaurant and an ornate glass-roofed canopy means you can eat outside even if it happens to be raining. There's Butcombe Adam Henson's Rare Breed and Gold bitter on tap in the bar, while on the menu you'll find starters like avocado, crab and prawn cocktail or rillettes of duck with red onion marmalade, followed by cannon of Welsh lamb; or roasted butternut squash, spinach and pine nut risotto.

Open 12-2.30 6-11 (Sun 12-2.30 7-10.30 Mon 7-11) Closed Mon L **Food** Lunch Tue-Sat 12-2 Dinner Tue-Sat 6-9 Restaurant menu available Tue-Sat ⊕ FREE HOUSE ◀ Butcombe Adam Henson's Rare Breed & Gold ⍥ Ashton Press. 🍷 9
Facilities Non-diners area 👪 Children's portions Outside area ⛩ Parking WiFi
Rooms 8

COWBRIDGE — Map 9 SS97

Cross Inn — PICK OF THE PUBS

See Pick of the Pubs on page 656

Victoria Inn

tel: 01446 773943 **Sigingstone CF71 7LP**
email: oleary445@aol.com
dir: *From Llantwit Major N on B4270. Right to Sigingstone*

Bright and welcoming village inn with extensive menu

This inn stands near the top of an old village tucked away along country lanes in the Vale of Glamorgan, with the captivating coastline of the Bristol Channel just a short hop away. The eye-catching exterior beckons villagers and explorers into a cottagey, beamed interior with lots of prints, brass and antiques. The locally sourced menu, which is strong on seafood dishes, may start with prawn cocktail with brandy-infused Marie Rose sauce, or deep-fried brie wedges with mild cranberry salsa; followed by the inn's popular fish pancake; home-made steak and kidney pie; or port and mushroom braised steak.

Open all wk 9.30-3 6-11.30 **Food** Lunch all wk 11.45-2.30 Dinner all wk 6-9 Set menu available Restaurant menu available Mon-Sat ⊕ FREE HOUSE ◀ Worthington's Creamflow, Evan Evans, Sharp's Doom Bar ⍥ Magners Golden Draught. 🍷 10 **Facilities** Non-diners area 🐾 (Bar Garden Outside area) 👪 Children's menu Garden Outside area ⛩ Parking WiFi 🚌 (notice required)

EAST ABERTHAW — Map 9 ST06

Blue Anchor Inn — PICK OF THE PUBS

tel: 01446 750329 **CF62 3DD**
email: blueanchor@gmail.com
dir: *From Barry take A4226, then B4265 towards Llantwit Major. Follow signs, turn left for East Aberthaw. 3m W of Cardiff Airport*

14th-century pub in the same family for generations

The grandfather of the present owners, Jeremy and Andrew Coleman, acquired this pretty stone-built and heavily thatched inn in 1941, when he bought it from a large local estate. The inn has been trading almost continuously since 1380. The interior is warmly traditional, with a warren of small rooms and low beamed ceilings; open fires include a large inglenook. The selection of well-kept real ales includes national treasures from Brains and Theakston. Dishes from the enticing and reasonably-priced menu are served in both the bar and the upstairs restaurant. Starters may include Pantysgawn goats' cheese arancini with beetroot salad; or confit duck leg samosa with barbecue sauce. Robust main courses feature the likes of roasted haunch of venison with celeriac mash and baby carrots; and pan-fried hake supreme with olive, caper and anchovy linguini. Steaks grilled to your liking are served with home-cut chips, mushroom, home-dried tomato and mixed salad.

Open all day all wk 11-11 (Sun 12-10.30 25 Dec 12-2) **Food** Lunch Mon-Sat 12-2, Sun 12-2.30 Dinner Mon-Sat 6-9 Set menu available ⊕ FREE HOUSE ◀ Theakston Old Peculier, Wadworth 6X, Wye Valley HPA, Brains Bitter. 🍷 9
Facilities Non-diners area 🐾 (Bar Restaurant Garden) 👪 Children's menu Garden ⛩ Parking WiFi 🚌 (notice required)

PENARTH — Map 9 ST17

The Pilot

tel: 029 2071 0615 **67 Queens Rd CF64 1DJ**
email: pilot@knifeandforkfood.co.uk
dir: *Phone for detailed directions*

Contemporary community pub with harbour views

Set on a hillside overlooking the watery wonder that is Cardiff Bay, The Pilot has seen immense changes since it originated as a dock-workers' pub. Transformed like the harbour and docklands at its feet, the pub is now a popular destination where drinkers and diners are equally welcome. With craft beers from the respected Otley Brewery in Pontypridd and ciders from Gwynt y Ddraig to slake a thirst, attention can turn to the ever-changing fare outlined on the chalkboard. Pub classics mix with modern British dishes on a pleasing choice that may feature pan-seared scallops, squash purée and truffle salad; and an 8oz Welsh rib-eye.
A beer and cider festival is held twice a year.

Open all day all wk **Food** all day ⊕ BRAINS ◀ Otley, Tiny Rebel, The Celt Experience, Grey Trees, Vale of Glamorgan ⍥ Gwynt y Ddraig, guest ciders. 🍷 17
Facilities Non-diners area 🐾 (Bar Outside area) 👪 Children's menu Children's portions Outside area ⛩ Beer festival Cider festival WiFi 🚌 (notice required)

PICK OF THE PUBS

Cross Inn

COWBRIDGE Map 9 SS97

tel: 01446 772995
Church Rd, Llanblethian CF71 7JF
email: artherolry@aol.com
web: www.crossinncowbridge.co.uk
dir: *Take B4270 from Cowbridge towards Llantwit Major, pub 0.5m on right*

Ever popular country pub

Much loved by visitors, this 17th-century former coaching inn is set in a picturesque corner of the Vale of Glamorgan's countryside on the fringe of the ancient town of Cowbridge, just a few miles from the splendid Heritage Coast. A family-run pub, Cross Inn has a cosy restaurant and comfortable, character bar with welcoming log fires and a convivial atmosphere. The chefs take great pride in developing daily menus of essentially British food with European influences. Fresh produce is sourced from local farmers and other reliable suppliers, with fish, prime Welsh steaks, poultry and other ingredients delivered every day to supply the bar meals, children's meals and the frequently changing restaurant menu. Expect choices to include pub favourites such as home-made curried chicken, crispy beer battered fillet of cod, wholetail scampi, pies and steaks, local pork and leek sausages and mash.

Other choices could be ham hock terrine with red onion marmalade; and home-made lasagne al forno with hand-cut chips. The regularly changing specials board features a variety of fish, meat and game dishes, and the traditional Sunday lunch are always popular. There is a good wine list of regularly selected, quality wines. On arriving at Cross Inn particularly noticeable are the lovely hanging flower baskets which have won the pub several awards. Dogs are very welcome, and the pub, with a good sized car park, is an ideal starting and finishing point for walkers who enjoy exploring the many delightful country walks the area has to offer.

Open all day all wk 11-11 ⊕ FREE HOUSE ◪ Hancock's HB, Wye Valley Butty Bach, Evan Evans Crwr, Shepherd Neame Bishops Finger, Thornbridge Jaipur ♨ Westons Stowford Press, Thatchers Gold, Gwynt y Ddraig. **Facilities** ✿ (Bar Garden) ♦♦ Children's menu Children's portions Garden Parking WiFi

WREXHAM

ERBISTOCK
Map 15 SJ34

The Boat Inn

tel: 01978 780666 **LL13 0DL**
email: info@boatondee.com
dir: *A483 Whitchurch/Llangollen exit, towards Whitchurch on A539. After 2m turn right at signs for Erbistock & The Boat Inn*

Local ales and modern food at riverside gem

A no-through lane past the Victorian church leads to the 13th-century Boat, in an unrivalled position on the banks of the River Dee; there was once a ferry crossing here. Expect to find a cosy flagstoned and oak beamed bar and several rambling rooms with open fires, stone walls and charming nooks and crannies. It's a fine spot for a pint of local Weetwood Cheshire Cat and some modern pub food, best enjoyed in the glorious riverside garden. From the extensive menu choose tapas: Scotch egg with piccalilli; or hoisin duck spring roll with cucumber and spring onion salad to start; follow with steak, mushroom and ale pie; pan-fried sea bass with saffron mash potato, salsify and broccoli; or Welsh lamb cawl (soup) with crushed carrot and swede. A selection of steaks and sandwiches are also available.

Open all day all wk **Food** Contact pub for food times ⊕ FREE HOUSE ◀ Weetwood Best & Cheshire Cat, Black Sheep Ò Hereford Dry. ☗ 10 **Facilities** Non-diners area ♣ (Bar Garden Outside area) ♦ Children's menu Children's portions Garden Outside area ⌷ Parking WiFi

GRESFORD
Map 15 SJ35

Pant-yr-Ochain
PICK OF THE PUBS

tel: 01978 853525 **Old Wrexham Rd LL12 8TY**
email: pant.yr.ochain@brunningandprice.co.uk
dir: *From Chester towards Wrexham on A483 take A5156 signed Nantwich (dual carriageway). 1st left into Old Wrexham Rd. Pub 500yds on right*

Good ale and good food in an elegant setting

Just outside Wrexham, but set in a country estate of gentle hills, woods and meres, this astonishing Tudor manor house stands at the end of a long, sweeping drive. Timber framed gables overlook award-winning gardens, whilst the interior retains many characteristics of its origins. Brick fireplaces, nooks and crannies, alcoves and quiet corners all help to create an overriding feel of an Edwardian country house. Splendid real ales from breweries like Stonehouse and Weetwood head up a great selection of ales, with real ciders adding local colour. From the kitchen emerge contemporary British dishes. Starters chime in with venison, rabbit and pheasant terrine with black cherry compôte, which might be followed by pan-fried sea bass fillets with linguine, confit cherry tomatoes and samphire; or game suet pudding with mash and red wine gravy. A range of sandwiches and wraps offer lighter lunchtime options.

Open all day all wk 11.30-11 (Sun 11.30-10.30) **Food** Lunch all wk 12-5 Dinner Mon-Sat 5-9.30, Sun 5-9 Av main course £14 ⊕ FREE HOUSE/BRUNNING & PRICE ◀ Brunning & Price Original Bitter, Purple Moose, Weetwood Ales Eastgate Ale, Stonehouse Off The Rails Ò Tomas Watkin Taffy Apples, Aspall, Gwynt y Ddraig Farmhouse Scrumpy. ☗ 22 **Facilities** Non-diners area ♣ (Bar Garden) ♦ Children's menu Children's portions Play area Garden ⌷ Parking WiFi

LLANARMON DYFFRYN CEIRIOG
Map 15 SJ13

The Hand at Llanarmon ★★★★ INN ◉ PICK OF THE PUBS

See Pick of the Pubs on page 658

West Arms

tel: 01691 600665 **LL20 7LD**
email: info@thewestarms.co.uk
dir: *Exit A483 or A5 at Chirk, take B4500 to Ceiriog Valley*

New owners still offering warm hospitality

Set against a stunning backdrop of Berwyn Mountain and originally built as a drovers' inn, the West Arms has been offering visitors a warm welcome for the past five centuries, and this continues with new owners at the helm. Slate flagged floors, low beams and an original inglenook fireplace add to the charm of this lovely old free house, where ales are on tap in the lounge bar. In summer, the riverside gardens are an ideal spot for lunch, from a menu packed with local produce – starting with smoked mackerel, crayfish and watercress salad; or white pudding fritters, pancetta, apple and mustard dressing. Then, on to a main dish of medallions of Welsh beef, dauphinoise potato, asparagus ravioli, wilted spinach and Madeira sauce; or pan-fried chicken breast, coconut and vegetable danska and wild basmati rice.

Open all day all wk **Food** Lunch Mon-Sat 12-2.30, Sun 12-6 Dinner all wk 6.30-9 ⊕ FREE HOUSE ◀ Stonehouse, Black Sheep Ò Somersby. **Facilities** Non-diners area ♣ (Bar Garden) ♦ Children's menu Children's portions Garden ⌷ Parking WiFi ➠ (notice required)

ROSSETT
Map 15 SJ35

The Golden Lion

tel: 01244 571020 **Chester Rd LL12 0HN**
email: goldenlion@hydesbrewery.com
dir: *From Chester take A483 towards Wrexham, left onto B5102 signed Rossett, left onto B5445, pub on left in Rossett*

Attractive village inn with interesting heritage

Haunted by the mischievous ghost of a murderous ploughman, this village-centre pub in the northern Welsh Marches is an engaging mix of old and new. Lots of beams, trusses and wooden flooring offer great character within, melding seamlessly with tasteful decor, countless prints and framed ephemera amidst eclectic furnishings. The regularly changing fare has much for seafood fans, a good vegetarian choice and may feature meaty mains like cottage pie or a fillet steak; platters and bar nibbles prove popular too. An impressive wine list shows 16 by the glass. Dogs are very welcome in the bar, and outside is an immense, tree-shaded beer garden. A change of hands.

Open all day all wk 12-11 (Sun 12-10.30) Closed 25 Dec & 1 Jan **Food** Contact pub for food times ⊕ Hydes of Manchester ◀ Theakston Best Bitter, Hydes Original, Marston's Wainwright, Brains The Rev. James, Fuller's London Pride, guest ales. ☗ 16 **Facilities** Non-diners area ♣ (Bar Garden) ♦ Children's menu Children's portions Play area Family room Garden ⌷ Parking WiFi ➠ (notice required)

PICK OF THE PUBS

The Hand at Llanarmon ★★★★ INN ❀

LLANARMON DYFFRYN CEIRIOG Map 15 SJ13

tel: 01691 600666 **LL20 7LD**
email: reception@thehandhotel.co.uk
web: www.thehandhotel.co.uk
dir: *Exit A5 at Chirk follow B4500 for 11m. Through Ceiriog Valley to Llanarmon Dyffryn Ceiriog. Pub straight ahead*

Imaginative food and well-kept local ales

Jonathan and Jackie Greatorex spent years visiting this 16th-century free house and inn, once a rest stop for drovers and their flocks on the old road from Anglesey to London. Its warm atmosphere and delicious food really struck home, so when the opportunity arose, they bought it. Up the remote Ceiriog Valley, known as The Valley of the Poets, in the shadow of the Berwyn Mountains, is where you'll find it and its original oak beams, plum-coloured walls, large fireplaces and mix-and-match furniture. The well-stocked bar offers Weetwood Cheshire Cat and Big Hand Bastion real ales and plenty of malt whiskies, including a Welsh one. Head chef Grant Mulholland and his team have earned an AA Rosette for their impressive modern European dishes. Everything is prepared on the premises from fresh ingredients — everything, that is, except the steak and ale, and chicken and gammon pies that McArdle's of Chirk make specially for The Hand. Frequently changing menus

include one for the bar, on which you're likely to find classics like ale-battered haddock and home-made chips; steak ciabatta with onions and mushrooms seasoned with Worcestershire sauce; and chicken, gammon and white wine pie. From the dinner menu, typical examples are sautéed wood pigeon, confit duck beignet and cauliflower purée; smoked and fresh haddock fish pie with Welsh Cheddar and smoked paprika mash; and marinated duck breast with burnt apple purée, cherries and cider reduction. There's always at least one vegetarian option. To follow, caramel syrup and orange poached pear with red wine and apple sorbet; or Bramley apple and wild berry crumble with vanilla custard. Few places can be quieter than the sunny terrace garden.

Open all day all wk **Food** Lunch Mon-Sat 12-2.30, Sun 12.30-2.45 Dinner all wk 6.30-8.45 Set menu available ⊕ FREE HOUSE ◖ Weetwood Cheshire Cat, Big Hand Bastion. **Facilities** Non-diners area 🐾 (Bar Garden) 👶 Children's portions Garden 🪑 Parking WiFi 🚌 (notice required) **Rooms** 13

Beer festivals

Beer festivals, or their equivalent, are as old as the hills. The brewing of hops goes back to the beginning of human civilisation, and the combination of a common crop and a fermenting process that results in alcoholic liquid has long been a cause of celebration. Beer festivals officially began in Germany with the first Munich Oktoberfest in 1810. Wherever in the world beer is brewed, today and for the last few millennia, admirers, enthusiasts, aficionados – call them what you will – have gathered together to sample and praise its unique properties. It happens throughout Europe, in Australia, New Zealand, America and Canada, and annual events are held in pubs all over Britain.

Beer festivals are often occasions for the whole family, when entertainment is laid on for children as well as adults. Summer is naturally a popular season for festivals, when the action can take place outdoors, but many are held in October, traditionally harvest time. Beer festivals are sometimes large and well-advertised gatherings that attract a wide following and last several days;

or they might be local but none the less enthusiastic neighbourhood get-togethers.

For up-to-date information, please check directly with the pub.

Abbreviations
Early May BH (1st monday in May); **Spring BH** (last monday in May); **Summer BH** (last monday in August); **wk** week; **wknd** weekend

Public Holidays 2017
New Year's Day January 1; Good Friday April 14; Easter Monday April 17; Early May Bank Holiday May 1; Spring Bank Holiday May 29; Summer Bank Holiday (August Bank Holiday); August 28 (August 7 Scotland only); St Andrew's Day November 30 (Scotland only); Christmas Day December 25; Boxing Day December 26

ENGLAND

BERKSHIRE

CURRIDGE
The Bunk Inn
01635 200400
Jun-Jul

HAMPSTEAD NORREYS
The White Hart
01635 202248
Last wknd Jun

HERMITAGE
The White Horse of Hermitage
01635 200325
Jun

KNOWL HILL
Bird In Hand Country Inn
01628 826622
Jun & Nov

READING
The Flowing Spring
0118 969 9878
Midsummer & Autumn

WALTHAM ST LAWRENCE
The Bell
0118 934 1788
Annually (30 real ales, 10 ciders)

WOKINGHAM
The Broad Street Tavern
0118 977 3706
Twice a year

BRISTOL

BRISTOL
The Alma Tavern & Theatre
0117 973 5171
Jul (summer fayre)

The Cross Hands
0117 965 7759

BUCKINGHAMSHIRE

AMERSHAM
Hit or Miss Inn
01494 713109
Mid Jul wknd

BEACONSFIELD
The Royal Standard of England
01494 673382
Summer BH

BOURNE END
The Garibaldi
01628 522092
Easter & Summer BH

BRILL
The Pheasant
01844 239370
St George's Day (23 Apr)

CHESHAM
The Swan
01494 783075
Summer BH

DENHAM
The Falcon Inn
01895 832125

DORNEY
The Palmer Arms
01628 666612

FARNHAM ROYAL
The Emperor
01753 643006

GREAT HAMPDEN
The Hampden Arms
01494 488255
Summer

GREAT MISSENDEN
The Polecat Inn
01494 862253
Summer

HEDGERLEY
The White Horse
01753 643225
Easter, Spring BH & Summer BH

LACEY GREEN
The Whip Inn
01844 344060
May & Sep

LITTLE KINGSHILL
The Full Moon
01494 862397
Last wk Jun

MOULSOE
The Carrington Arms
01908 218050
Jun

NEWTON LONGVILLE
The Crooked Billet
01908 373936
Early May BH

SEER GREEN
The Jolly Cricketers
01494 676308
Easter & Summer BH

TURWESTON
The Stratton Arms
01280 704956

CAMBRIDGESHIRE

BALSHAM
The Black Bull Inn
01223 893844

BOURN
The Willow Tree
01954 719775
Summer

COTON
The Plough
01954 210489
Summer

DRY DRAYTON
The Black Horse
01954 782600
Apr (St George's Day wknd)

GLINTON
The Blue Bell
01733 252285

HARDWICK
The Blue Lion
01954 210328
Summer

HEMINGFORD GREY
The Cock Pub and Restaurant
01480 463609
Mid Aug wknd

HISTON
Red Lion
01223 564437
Easter & 1st wk Sep

OFFORD D'ARCY
The Horseshoe Inn
01480 810293
Midsummer

PETERBOROUGH
Charters Bar & East Restaurant
01733 315700
Easter Thu-Easter Mon

SPALDWICK
The George
01480 890293

STRETHAM
The Lazy Otter
01353 649780
Jul

WHITTLESFORD
The Tickell Arms
01223 833025
May

CHESHIRE

CHESTER
Old Harkers Arms
01244 344525
Mar (Pie & Champion Ale Wk)

CHRISTLETON
Ring O'Bells
01244 335422
Summer

GOOSTREY
The Crown
01477 532128
Summer

KNUTSFORD
The Dog Inn
01625 861421

MOBBERLEY
The Bulls Head
01565 873395
Jun & Oct

SPURSTOW
The Yew Tree Inn
01829 260274
Easter wknd

STYAL
The Ship Inn
01625 444888
Summer

TARPORLEY
The Swan, Tarporley
01829 733838
Summer

CORNWALL & ISLES OF SCILLY

ALTARNUN
Rising Sun Inn
01566 86636
Mid-late Nov

BOLINGEY
Bolingey Inn
01872 571626
Apr & Oct

CADGWITH
Cadgwith Cove Inn
01326 290513
Oct

CHAPEL AMBLE
The Maltsters Arms
01208 812473
Spring BH

CONSTANTINE
Trengilly Wartha Inn
01326 340332

CUBERT
The Smugglers' Den Inn
01637 830209
Early May BH wknd

GUNNISLAKE
The Rising Sun Inn
01822 832201
Every 2-3 months

GWITHIAN
The Red River Inn
01736 753223
Easter wknd

HALSETOWN
The Halsetown Inn
01736 795583
Aug

MITCHELL
The Plume of Feathers
01872 510387
Oct

PENZANCE
The Coldstreamer Inn
01736 362072
Sep

The Turks Head Inn
01736 363093

PHILLEIGH
Roseland Inn
01872 580254
1st wknd Sep

ST AGNES
Driftwood Spars
01872 552428
Mid Mar (mini beer festival) &
Early May BH wknd

ST IVES
The Watermill
01736 757912
Jun & Nov

ST MAWGAN
The Falcon Inn
01637 860225
Jul (last full wknd)

ST MERRYN
The Cornish Arms
01841 532700
Mar (annual beer & mussel
festival)

TRESCO (ISLES OF SCILLY)
The New Inn
01720 422849
Mid May & early Sep

CUMBRIA

BOOT
Brook House Inn
019467 23288
Early Jun

CONISTON
The Black Bull Inn & Hotel
015394 41335

ELTERWATER
The Britannia Inn
015394 37210
2wks mid Nov

HAWKSHEAD
Kings Arms
015394 36372
Jul & Dec

The Sun Inn
015394 36236
May

LOW LORTON
The Wheatsheaf Inn
01900 85199 & 85268
Late Mar

LOWESWATER
Kirkstile Inn
01900 85219

RAVENSTONEDALE
The Black Swan
015396 23204
Summer

SATTERTHWAITE
The Eagles Head
01229 860237

SEATHWAITE
Newfield Inn
01229 716208
Oct

STAVELEY
The Beer Hall
at Hawkshead Brewery
01539 825260
Mar & Jul

ULVERSTON
The Farmers
01229 584469

WASDALE HEAD
Wasdale Head Inn
019467 26229

WINSTER
The Brown Horse Inn
015394 43443
Late Jul

DERBYSHIRE

ASHOVER
The Old Poets Corner
01246 590888
Mar & Oct (Thu-Sun, 40 beers &
ciders, live music)

BAKEWELL
The Monsal Head Hotel
01629 640250
Sep

BAMFORD
The Yorkshire Bridge Inn
01433 651361
May

BIRCHOVER
The Druid Inn
01629 653836
May

Red Lion Inn
01629 650363
Mid Jul

BONSALL
The Barley Mow
01629 825685
BHs (3-4 times a year)

CASTLETON
The Peak Hotel
01433 620247
BHs

Ye Olde Nags Head
01433 620248
Summer

CHINLEY
Old Hall Inn
01663 750529
3rd wknd Sep

The Paper Mill Inn
01663 750529
3rd wknd Sep

DALBURY
The Black Cow
01332 824297

EYAM
Miners Arms
01433 630853
3 times a year

HAYFIELD
The Royal Hotel
01663 742721

HOPE
The Old Hall Hotel
01433 620160
BHs

LITTON
Red Lion Inn
01298 871458

MATLOCK
The Red Lion
01629 584888

REPTON
The Boot
01283 346047

ROWSLEY
The Grouse & Claret
01629 733233
Aug

SHARDLOW
The Old Crown Inn
01332 792392
Apr & Oct

WILLINGTON
The Dragon
01283 704795

DEVON

BLACKAWTON
The George Inn
01803 712342
Early May BH & Summer BH

BRAMPFORD SPEKE
The Lazy Toad
01392 841591
Spring BH

BRANSCOMBE
The Fountain Head
01297 680359
Mid Jun

BROADHEMBURY
The Drewe Arms
01404 841267
Easter

CLYST HYDON
The Five Bells Inn
01884 277288
2nd wk Aug

COCKWOOD
The Anchor Inn
01626 890203
Easter & Halloween

EAST ALLINGTON
The Fortescue Arms
01548 521215

HONITON
The Holt
01404 47707

IDDESLEIGH
The Duke of York
01837 810253
Aug

KILMINGTON
The Old Inn
01297 32096
Spring BH Sat

KINGS NYMPTON
The Grove Inn
01769 580406
Jul

MEAVY
The Royal Oak Inn
01822 852944
Summer BH

PLYMTREE
The Blacksmiths Arms
01884 277474
Jul wknd

RINGMORE
The Journey's End Inn
01548 810205
Twice a year

ROBOROUGH
The New Inn
01805 603247
Last wknd Sep

SANDFORD
The Lamb Inn
01363 773676

SLAPTON
The Tower Inn
01548 580216

TAVISTOCK
The Cornish Arms
01822 612145
Summer BH wknd

TOTNES
The Durant Arms
01803 732240
1st wknd Sep

Royal Seven Stars Hotel
01803 862125

Beer festivals *continued*

Steam Packet Inn
01803 863880
Mid May (3 days)

TUCKENHAY
The Maltsters Arms
01803 732350

WOODBURY SALTERTON
The Digger's Rest
01395 232375
May

DORSET

BUCKHORN WESTON
Stapleton Arms
01963 370396

CRANBORNE
The Inn at Cranborne
01725 551249
Jun

HINTON ST MARY
The White Horse Inn
01258 472723
Summer

IWERNE COURTNEY OR
SHROTON
The Cricketers
01258 860421
Early May BH

MILTON ABBAS
The Hambro Arms
01258 880233
Jul

STUDLAND
The Bankes Arms Hotel
01929 450225
Mid Aug

WEST STOUR
The Ship Inn
01747 838640
Aug

WORTH MATRAVERS
The Square and Compass
01929 439229
1st Sat Oct (beer & pumpkin
festival)

DURHAM, COUNTY

BARNARD CASTLE
The Morritt Hotel
01833 627232

CASTLE EDEN
Castle Eden Inn
01429 835137
May-Jun

FROSTERLEY
The Black Bull Inn
01388 527784

LONGNEWTON
Vane Arms
01642 580401
Jul (mini beer festival)

STANLEY
The Stables Pub and
Restaurant
01207 288750
3rd wknd Sep

THORPE THEWLES
The Vane Arms
01740 630458
Jun

ESSEX

BELCHAMP ST PAUL
The Half Moon
01787 277402
Summer BH

CASTLE HEDINGHAM
The Bell Inn
01787 460350
3rd wknd Jul

CHRISHALL
The Red Cow
01763 838792
Spring BH

COPFORD GREEN
The Alma
01206 210607
Spring BH wknd

FEERING
The Sun Inn
01376 570442
End of Jun & Sep

FYFIELD
The Queen's Head
01277 899231
Summer BH

GOLDHANGER
The Chequers Inn
01621 788203
Mar & Sep

HASTINGWOOD
Rainbow & Dove
01279 415419
Sep

LITTLEBURY
The Queens Head Inn
Littlebury
01799 520365
Easter

LITTLEY GREEN
The Compasses
01245 362308
2nd last wknd Aug

MARGARETTING TYE
The White Hart Inn
01277 840478
Jul & Nov

MATCHING TYE
The Fox Inn
01279 731335
Jul

MOUNT BURES
The Thatchers Arms
01787 227460

STOCK
The Hoop
01277 841137
Spring BH

WOODHAM MORTIMER
Hurdlemakers Arms
01245 225169
Last wknd Jun (25+ real ales
& ciders)

GLOUCESTERSHIRE

ALDERTON
The Gardeners Arms
01242 620257
Aug

ALMONDSBURY
The Swan Hotel
01454 625671
Jul

BROCKHAMPTON
Craven Arms Inn
01242 820410
Sep

CHELTENHAM
The Gloucester Old Spot
01242 680321

The Royal Oak Inn
01242 522344
Spring BH

CLIFFORD'S MESNE
The Yew Tree
01531 820719
Oct

COATES
The Tunnel House Inn
01285 770280
1st wknd Aug

DURSLEY
The Old Spot Inn
01453 542870
May & Oct

EBRINGTON
The Ebrington Arms
01386 593223
Early Oct

EWEN
The Wild Duck
01285 770310
Summer

LECHLADE ON THAMES
The Trout Inn
01367 252313
Jun

LEIGHTERTON
The Royal Oak
01666 890250

MEYSEY HAMPTON
The Masons Arms
01285 850164
Jun

SAPPERTON
The Bell at Sapperton
01285 760298

TETBURY
The Royal Oak Tetbury
01666 500021
Spring BH

GREATER MANCHESTER

CHORLTON CUM HARDY
The Horse & Jockey
0161 860 7794

MANCHESTER
Marble Arch
0161 832 5914
Aug

OLDHAM
The White Hart Inn
01457 872566

SALFORD
The King's Arms
0161 839 3605
Sep

WALMERSLEY
The Lord Raglan
0161 764 6680
Summer & Autumn

HAMPSHIRE

BALL HILL
The Furze Bush Inn
01635 253228

BEAULIEU
The Drift Inn
023 8029 2342

BISHOP'S WALTHAM
The Hampshire Bowman
01489 892940
Last wknd Jul

BRAISHFIELD
The Wheatsheaf
01794 368652

BRANSGORE
The Three Tuns Country Inn
01425 672232
Last wk Sep

BROUGHTON
The Tally Ho
01794 301280
Summer BH

CHALTON
The Red Lion
023 9259 2246
Last wknd Jul

CHARTER ALLEY
The White Hart Inn
01256 850048

CLANFIELD
The Rising Sun Inn
023 9259 6975
Sep

EAST BOLDRE
Turfcutters Arms
01590 612331
Aug

EASTON
The Chestnut Horse
01962 779257
Jul

EAST STRATTON
Northbrook Arms
01962 774150
Spring BH

EVERSLEY
The Golden Pot
0118 973 2104

EVERSLEY CROSS
The Chequers
0118 402 7065

HANNINGTON
The Vine at Hannington
01635 298525
Jul

HAWKLEY
The Hawkley Inn
01730 827205
1st wknd Jun

HURSLEY
The Dolphin Inn
01962 775209
Apr

The Kings Head
01962 775208
Summer BH

LITTLETON
The Running Horse
01962 880218

LYNDHURST
New Forest Inn
023 8028 4690
2nd wknd Jul

PETERSFIELD
The Old Drum
01730 300208
1st wknd Aug

RINGWOOD
The Railway
01425 473701
Early May BH

SELBORNE
The Selborne Arms
01420 511247
1st wknd Oct

SWANMORE
The Rising Sun
01489 896663
Mid Sep

TICHBORNE
The Tichborne Arms
01962 733760
Summer BH

TWYFORD
The Bugle Inn
01962 714888

HEREFORDSHIRE

HOARWITHY
The New Harp Inn
01432 840900
BHs

MICHAELCHURCH ESCLEY
The Bridge Inn
01981 510646
Summer BH

ORLETON
The Boot Inn
01568 780228
Last wknd Jul

WELLINGTON
The Wellington
01432 830367
Jun

WELLINGTON HEATH
The Farmers Arms
01531 634776

WOOLHOPE
The Crown Inn
01432 860468
Early May BH

HERTFORDSHIRE

ARDELEY
Jolly Waggoner
01438 861350
Aug

HERONSGATE
The Land of Liberty, Peace and Plenty
01923 282226
Mid Feb, Easter, Oct & Xmas

HITCHIN
The Highlander
01462 454612
Late May

WATTON-AT-STONE
The Bull
01920 831032
May & Oct

WESTON
The Cricketers
01462 790273

WILLIAN
The Fox
01462 480233
Jul

ISLE OF WIGHT

NITON
Buddle Inn
01983 730243
Jun & Sep

NORTHWOOD
Travellers Joy
01983 298024
Oct

KENT

BADLESMERE
The Red Lion
01233 740320

CANTERBURY
Duke of Cumberland
01227 831396
Jul or Aug

CHILHAM
The White Horse
01227 730355
Jul

FAVERSHAM
Albion Taverna
01795 591411
Early Sep (annual hop festival)

HALSTEAD
Rose & Crown
01959 533120
Spring, Summer & Autumn

HAWKHURST
The Great House
01580 753119

HOLLINGBOURNE
The Windmill
01622 889000

LOWER HALSTOW
The Three Tuns
01795 842840
Summer BH

MATFIELD
The Wheelwrights Arms
01892 722129

ROLVENDEN
The Bull
01580 241212

SISSINGHURST
The Milk House
01580 720200
Summer BH wknd

STALISFIELD GREEN
The Plough Inn
01795 890256
Summer

TUNBRIDGE WELLS (ROYAL)
Sankey's
01892 511422

WEST PECKHAM
The Swan on the Green
01622 812271
Oct

LANCASHIRE

BASHALL EAVES
The Red Pump Inn
01254 826227

BILSBORROW
Owd Nell's Tavern
01995 640010
1st wknd Jul (American Beer Festival); 1st wk Sep (Oyster Festival); last wk Oct (Oktoberfest)

CHORLEY
The Yew Tree Inn
01257 480344
Good Fri

LANCASTER
The Sun Hotel and Bar
01524 66006
Summer

Toll House Inn
01524 599900
Oct

The White Cross
01524 33999
Late Apr (beer & pie festival)

PARBOLD
The Eagle & Child
01257 462297
Early May BH

RAMSBOTTOM
Eagle + Child
01706 557181

LEICESTERSHIRE

BLABY
The Bakers Arms
0116 278 7253
Summer BH

LEICESTER
The Rutland & Derby
0116 262 3299

LONG WHATTON
The Royal Oak
01509 843694
Summer BH

MOUNTSORREL
The Swan Inn
0116 230 2340
May BHs & Summer BH

SHAWELL
The White Swan
01788 860357

SUTTON CHENEY
Hercules Revived
01455 699336

LINCOLNSHIRE

BASTON
White Horse Baston
01778 560923
1st wknd Jul

CLEETHORPES
The Nottingham House
01472 505150
Spring & Autumn

DRY DODDINGTON
Wheatsheaf Inn
01400 281458

INGHAM
The Inn on the Green
01522 730354
Summer

LITTLE BYTHAM
The Willoughby Arms
01780 410276
Summer BH

SCAMPTON
Dambusters Inn
01522 531333
May

THEDDLETHORPE ALL SAINTS
Kings Head Inn
01507 339798
Jul

LONDON

E14
The Gun
020 7515 5222

EC1
Ye Olde Mitre
020 7405 4751
May, Aug & Dec

NW1
The Prince Albert
020 7485 0270
BHs

SE1
The George Inn
020 7407 2056

SE22
The Palmerston
020 8693 1629

SW6
The White Horse
020 7736 2115
4 times a year (American, Great British, Old Ale & European)

SW10
The Hollywood Arms
020 7349 7840

W4
The City Barge
020 8994 2148

W5
The Grove
020 85672439
Feb & Oct

W8
The Windsor Castle
020 7243 8797

W14
The Albion
020 7603 2826
Aug

GREATER LONDON

CHELSFIELD
The Five Bells
01689 821044
Easter & Oct

HAREFIELD
The Old Orchard
01895 822631

NORFOLK

BRANCASTER STAITHE
The Jolly Sailors
01485 210314
Jun

The White Horse
01485 210262

BURSTON
The Crown
01379 741257
2 or 3 times a year

CASTLE ACRE
The Ostrich Inn
01760 755398
Jun

HEYDON
Earle Arms
01263 587376
May

HUNSTANTON
The Ancient Mariner Inn
01485 536390
Jul

HUNWORTH
The Hunny Bell
01263 712300

KING'S LYNN
The Stuart House Hotel, Bar & Restaurant
01553 772169
Jul

LARLING
Angel Inn
01953 717963
Early Aug

NORWICH
The Reindeer Pub & Kitchen
01603 612995
Summer

THOMPSON
Chequers Inn
01953 483360

WINTERTON-ON-SEA
Fishermans Return
01493 393305
Summer BH

NORTHAMPTONSHIRE

FOTHERINGHAY
The Falcon Inn
01832 226254

NORTHAMPTON
Althorp Coaching Inn
01604 770651

OLD
The White Horse
01604 781297
Summer BH wknd

OUNDLE
The Chequered Skipper
01832 273494
Twice a year

THORNBY
The Red Lion
01604 740238
Last wknd Jul

TOWCESTER
The Saracens Head
01327 350414

UPPER BODDINGTON
Plough Inn
01327 260364
Summer BH

NORTHUMBERLAND

BEADNELL
The Craster Arms
01665 720272
Last wknd Jul

CARTERWAY HEADS
The Manor House Inn
01207 255268
Last wknd Aug

HEDLEY ON THE HILL
The Feathers Inn
01661 843607
Easter

HEXHAM
Battlesteads Hotel
& Restaurant
01434 230209
Summer

Miners Arms Inn
01434 603909

MILFIELD
The Red Lion Inn
01668 216224
Last wknd Jun

NOTTINGHAMSHIRE

BEESTON
The Victoria
0115 925 4049
Easter; last 2wks Jul (beer & music) & Oct

KIMBERLEY
The Nelson & Railway Inn
0115 938 2177
BHs

NEWARK-ON-TRENT
The Prince Rupert
01636 918121
Mid May & late Jun

NOTTINGHAM
The Hand and Heart
0115 958 2456
Spring & Autumn

Ye Olde Trip to Jerusalem
0115 947 3171
2 or 3 times a year

SOUTHWELL
The Hearty Goodfellow
01636 919176
Jul

OXFORDSHIRE

ABINGDON-ON-THAMES
The Brewery Tap
01235 521655
Mar & Oct

ASHBURY
The Rose & Crown
01793 710222
Jun, Jul & Sep

BANBURY
Ye Olde Reindeer Inn
01295 270972
Easter, Summer BH

BLOXHAM
The Elephant & Castle
01295 720383
Early May (part of Bloxfest Music Festival)

BRIGHTWELL-CUM-SOTWELL
The Red Lion
01491 837373
Summer (2 days, local beers & musicians)

BURFORD
The Angel at Burford
01993 822714
Summer

The Highway Inn
01993 823661
Early Jun

CUMNOR
The Vine Inn
01865 862567

DEDDINGTON
The Unicorn Inn
01869 338838

DORCHESTER
The George
01865 340404

FRINGFORD
The Butchers Arms
01869 277363
Jun

GALLOWSTREE COMMON
The Reformation
0118 972 3126
May & Oct

GREAT TEW
The Falkland Arms
01608 683653

HENLEY-ON-THAMES
The Cherry Tree Inn
01491 680430

KINGHAM
The Wild Rabbit
01608 658389
Spring BH

MARSH BALDON
Seven Stars
01865 343337
Summer BH

MILTON
The Plum Pudding
01235 834443
Apr & Oct

NORTH HINKSEY VILLAGE
The Fishes
01865 249796

NORTHMOOR
The Red Lion
01865 300301

OXFORD
The Old Bookbinders Ale House
01865 553549
Jun

PISHILL
The Crown Inn
01491 638364
Late Sep

TETSWORTH
The Old Red Lion
01844 281274
Easter (mini festival)

THAME
The Thatch
01844 214340
Late Sep-early Oct (National Cask Ale Week)

UFFINGTON
The Fox & Hounds
01367 820680
Summer BH

WEST HANNEY
Plough Inn
01235 868909
Easter, Spring BH, Summer BH

WYTHAM
White Hart
01865 244372

RUTLAND

NORTH LUFFENHAM
The Fox Country Pub
01780 720991
Summer

OAKHAM
The Grainstore Brewery
01572 770065
Summer BH

SHROPSHIRE

BISHOP'S CASTLE
The Castle
01588 638403
Jul

The Three Tuns Inn
01588 638797
2nd wknd Jul (town festival)

CLUN
The White Horse Inn
01588 640305
1st wknd Oct

PAVE LANE
The Fox
01952 815940
Summer

PULVERBATCH
The White Horse Inn
01743 718247
Summer BH Sun

SHREWSBURY
The Prince of Wales
01743 343301
Feb & Spring BH

UPTON MAGNA
The Haughmond
01743 709918
October Fest

WENTNOR
The Crown Inn
01588 650613
Jul

SOMERSET

BATH
The Star Inn
01225 425072
Twice a year

BISHOPSWOOD
Candlelight Inn
01460 234476

CHEW MAGNA
The Bear and Swan
01275 331100

CORTON DENHAM
The Queens Arms
01963 220317
Jul

CROSCOMBE
The George Inn
01749 342306
Mid Oct

DULVERTON
The Bridge Inn
01398 324130
Spring BH

DUNSTER
The Luttrell Arms Hotel
01643 821555

HASELBURY PLUCKNETT
The White Horse at Haselbury
01460 78873

HINTON ST GEORGE
The Lord Poulett Arms
01460 73149

ILCHESTER
The Bull Inn
01935 840400

Ilchester Arms
01935 840220
BHs

LOWER GODNEY
The Sheppey
01458 831594
Aug

PITNEY
The Halfway House
01458 252513
Mar

PORLOCK
The Bottom Ship
01643 863288
1st wknd Jul

SHEPTON BEAUCHAMP
Duke of York
01460 240314
Sep (occasionally)

SHEPTON MALLET
The Three Horseshoes Inn
01749 850359
Easter, Summer BH

WEDMORE
The George Inn
01934 712124

WEST HUNTSPILL
Crossways Inn
01278 783756
Summer BH

WINSCOMBE
The Woodborough Inn
01934 844167

STAFFORDSHIRE

CAULDON
Yew Tree Inn
01538 309876
Mid Jul

HAUGHTON
The Bell
01785 780301
Late Aug

STAFFORD
The Holly Bush Inn
01889 508234
Jun & Sep

SUMMERHILL
Oddfellows in the Boat
01543 361692

WALL
The Trooper
01543 480413

SUFFOLK

BURY ST EDMUNDS
The Old Cannon Brewery
01284 768769
Summer BH wknd

DUNWICH
The Ship at Dunwich
01728 648219
BH Sundays

ELVEDEN
Elveden Inn
01842 890876
Spring BH

FRAMLINGHAM
The Station Hotel
01728 723455
Mid Jul

LAXFIELD
The Kings Head
(The Low House)
01986 798395
May & Sep

NAYLAND
Anchor Inn
01206 262313

SIBTON
Sibton White Horse Inn
01728 660337
Jun & Aug

SOMERLEYTON
The Duke's Head
01502 733931

SWILLAND
Moon & Mushroom Inn
01473 785320
Summer

WOODBRIDGE
Cherry Tree Inn
01394 384627
Early Jul

SURREY

CARSHALTON
The Sun
020 8773 4549

CHIDDINGFOLD
The Swan Inn
01428 684688
Sep

CRANLEIGH
The Richard Onslow
01483 274922

FARNHAM
The Bat & Ball Freehouse
01252 792108
2nd wknd Jun

LONG DITTON
The Ditton
020 8339 0785

NEWDIGATE
The Surrey Oaks
01306 631200
Spring BH & Summer BH

TILFORD
The Duke of Cambridge
01252 792236
May (CherryFest, charity beer
& music festival)

WEST END
The Inn West End
01276 858652

WINDLESHAM
The Half Moon
01276 473329

SUSSEX, EAST

BLACKBOYS
The Blackboys Inn
01825 890283

EWHURST GREEN
The White Dog
01580 830264

HARTFIELD
Anchor Inn
01892 770424
Early May

ICKLESHAM
The Queen's Head
01424 814552
Easter, Early May BH, Summer
BH

RYE
The Ypres Castle Inn
01797 223248
Aug

THREE LEG CROSS
The Bull
01580 200586

SUSSEX, WEST

EARTHAM
The George
01243 814340
Mid Apr

EAST GRINSTEAD
The Old Dunnings Mill
01342 821080
Jun & Sep

KINGSFOLD
The Dog and Duck
01306 627295
Annual charity event; contact
pub for details

KIRDFORD
The Half Moon Inn
01403 820223
Summer wknd

OVING
The Gribble Inn
01243 786893
Summer & Winter

SLINDON
The Spur
01243 814216

WEST DEAN
The Dean Ale & Cider House
01243 811465
Early May

TYNE & WEAR

NEWCASTLE UPON TYNE
The Bridge Tavern
0191 261 9966

Crown Posada
0191 232 1269
Feb

WARWICKSHIRE

BROOM
The Broom Tavern
01789 778199
Summer BH

EDGEHILL
Castle at Edgehill
01295 670255
Summer BH

WEST MIDLANDS

WEST BROMWICH
The Vine
0121 553 2866
Oct

WILTSHIRE

ALDBOURNE
The Blue Boar
01672 540237
1st wknd Jun

The Crown Inn
01672 540214
3rd wknd May & 3rd wknd Sep

BOX
The Quarrymans Arms
01225 743569
6 times a year

BRADFORD-ON-AVON
The George
01225 865650

BRINKWORTH
The Three Crowns
01666 510366

CRICKLADE
The Red Lion Inn
01793 750776
Last wknd Feb & Jun

CRUDWELL
The Potting Shed
01666 577833
Summer BH

EAST CHISENBURY
Red Lion Freehouse
01980 671124
May

EDINGTON
The Three Daggers
01380 830940

HORNINGSHAM
The Bath Arms at Longleat
01985 844308
Mid Jun

MALMESBURY
Kings Arms
01666 823383

NEWTON TONY
The Malet Arms
01980 629279
Jul

ROYAL WOOTTON BASSETT
The Angel
01793 851161
Sep

SALISBURY
The Wig and Quill
01722 335665

SEMINGTON
The Lamb on the Strand
01380 870263

WARMINSTER
The Bath Arms
01985 212262

WORCESTERSHIRE

BECKFORD
The Beckford
01386 881532
Oct

BEWDLEY
Little Pack Horse
01299 403762

The Mug House Inn
& Angry Chef Restaurant
01299 402543
Early May BH wknd

BRETFORTON
The Fleece Inn
01386 831173
Mid-late Oct

BROADWAY
Crown & Trumpet
01386 853202
Xmas & New Year

HARTLEBURY
The Tap House @
The Old Ticket Office
01299 253275

KEMPSEY
Walter de Cantelupe Inn
01905 820572
Easter & Oct

KNIGHTWICK
The Talbot
01886 821235
Apr, Jun & Oct

MALVERN
The Nag's Head
01684 574373
Wknd closest to St George's Day
(23 Apr)

YORKSHIRE, EAST RIDING OF

BEVERLEY
The Ferguson Fawsitt Arms
& Country Lodge
01482 882665

BRANTINGHAM
The Triton Inn
01482 667261
Summer & Oktoberfest

GOODMANHAM
Goodmanham Arms
01430 873849
Early May BH

THORNGUMBALD
The Camerton
01964 601208
Aug

YORKSHIRE, NORTH

AKEBAR
The Friar's Head
01677 450201

COLTON
Ye Old Sun Inn
01904 744261
Summer

Beer festivals *continued*

CROPTON
The New Inn
01751 417330
Nov

GRINTON
The Bridge Inn
01748 884224

KILBURN
The Forresters Arms Inn
01347 868386

MASHAM
The White Bear
01765 689319
Late Jun

SETTLE
The Lion at Settle
01729 822203
1st wknd Sep (folk festival)

THIRSK
Little 3
01845 523782

YORK
Blue Bell
01904 654904

Lysander Arms
01904 640845
Early May BH wknd

YORKSHIRE, SOUTH

CADEBY
The Cadeby Pub &
Restaurant
01709 864009

SHEFFIELD
Broadfield Ale House
0114 255 0200

The Fat Cat
0114 249 4801
Aug

Kelham Island Tavern
0114 272 2482
Late Jun wknd

YORKSHIRE, WEST

LINTON
The Windmill Inn
01937 582209
Jul

SOWERBY BRIDGE
The Alma Inn
01422 823334
Late Sep (Oktoberfest)

ISLE OF MAN

PORT ERIN
Falcon's Nest Hotel
01624 834077
Early May

SCOTLAND

ARGYLL & BUTE

ARROCHAR
Village Inn
01301 702279

INVERARAY
George Hotel
01499 302111
Late May BH & Summer BH

CITY OF DUNDEE

BROUGHTY FERRY
The Royal Arch Bar
01382 779741
1st wknd Oct (charity event)

DUNDEE
Speedwell Bar
01382 667783
1st wknd Oct (Rotary Charity
Oktoberfest)

CITY OF EDINBURGH

EDINBURGH
The Bow Bar
0131 226 7667
End Jan & end Jul (plus German
Beer Festival)

The Guildford Arms
0131 556 4312
Apr & Oct (plus monthly brewery
wknds)

Halfway House
0131 225 7101

RATHO
The Bridge Inn
0131 333 1320

CITY OF GLASGOW

GLASGOW
Bon Accord
0141 248 4427
4 times a year (90 beers &
ciders)

Ubiquitous Chip
0141 334 5007
Twice a year (dates vary)

WEST on the Green
0141 550 0135
Oct Fridays (OktoberFest)

DUMFRIES & GALLOWAY

BARGRENNAN
House O'Hill Hotel
01671 840243
Apr & Sep

FALKIRK

BO'NESS
Corbie Inn
01506 825307
Summer wknd

HIGHLAND

CAWDOR
Cawdor Tavern
01667 404777

GLENCOE
Clachaig Inn
01855 811252
FebFest, OktoberFest &
Hogmanay

PLOCKTON
The Plockton Hotel
01599 544274
May

TORRIDON
The Torridon Inn
01445 791242
1st wknd Oct

LOTHIAN, WEST

LINLITHGOW
The Four Marys
01506 842171
last wknd May & Oct

MORAY

FORRES
The Old Mill Inn
01309 641605
Jun

PERTH & KINROSS

MEIKLEOUR
Meikleour Arms
01250 883206
Aug

SCOTTISH BORDERS

ALLANTON
Allanton Inn
01890 818260
2nd wknd Jun

NEWCASTLETON
Liddesdale
01387 375255
1st wknd Jul

STIRLING

CALLANDER
The Lade Inn
01877 330152
late Aug-mid Sep

WALES

BRIDGEND

KENFIG
Prince of Wales Inn
01656 740356

CARDIFF

GWAELOD-Y-GARTH
Gwaelod-y-Garth Inn
029 2081 0408
Easter

CARMARTHENSHIRE

LLANFALLTEG
The Plash Inn
01437 563472
Spring BH & Summer BH

PUMSAINT
The Dolaucothi Arms
01558 650237
Summer BH wknd

CEREDIGION

ABERYSTWYTH
The Glengower
01970 626191
Spring BH

LLWYNDAFYDD
The Crown Inn & Restaurant
01545 560396

TREGARON
Y Talbot
01974 298208
Early Oct

CONWY

COLWYN BAY
Pen-y-Bryn
01492 533360
Beer & bangers week; pie &
ale week

DENBIGHSHIRE

GRAIGFECHAN
Three Pigeons
01824 703178
Mar, Jul & Oct

RUTHIN
The White Horse
01824 790218
Jul

FLINTSHIRE

MOLD
Glasfryn
01352 750500
Mar (Welsh Food & Drink
week); Oct (Great British Pie &
Champion Beers of Britain week)

GWYNEDD

TREMADOG
The Union Inn
01766 512748

WAUNFAWR
Snowdonia Parc Brewpub
01286 650409
Easter week & mid May (Welsh
Highland Railway Raleigh
Festival)

MONMOUTHSHIRE

ABERGAVENNY
Clytha Arms
01873 840206
Spring BH

RHYD-Y-MEIRCH
Goose and Cuckoo Inn
01873 880277
May BH & end Aug

TINTERN PARVA
Fountain Inn
01291 689303
Easter & Sep

TRELLECH
The Lion Inn
01600 860322
Jun

NEWPORT

CAERLEON
The Bell at Caerleon
01633 420613

PEMBROKESHIRE

AMROTH
The New Inn
01834 812368
Jun-Jul

LITTLE HAVEN
St Brides Inn
01437 781266

POWYS

DEFYNNOG
The Tanners Arms
01874 638032
End May

OLD RADNOR
The Harp
01544 350655
Jun

TALYBONT-ON-USK
Star Inn
01874 676635
Mid Jun & mid Oct

RHONDDA CYNON TAFF

PONTYPRIDD
Bunch of Grapes
01443 402934
Every 2 months (20+ ales)

SWANSEA

LLANGENNITH
Kings Head
01792 386212
Last wknd Oct

VALE OF GLAMORGAN

COWBRIDGE
Cross Inn
01446 772995
Late Apr & Sep (mini beer &
cider festival)

PENARTH
The Pilot
029 2071 0615
Twice a year

Cider festivals

ENGLAND

BEDFORDSHIRE

WOBURN
The Black Horse
01525 290210

BERKSHIRE

HERMITAGE
The White Horse of
Hermitage
01635 200325

READING
The Flowing Spring
0118 969 9878
Midsummer & Autumn

WOKINGHAM
The Broad Street Tavern
0118 977 3706
Summer

BRISTOL

BRISTOL
The Albion
0117 973 3522
Early May BH

The Alma Tavern & Theatre
0117 973 5171
Late Dec (Xmas fayre)

The Cross Hands
0117 965 7759

BUCKINGHAMSHIRE

AMERSHAM
Hit or Miss Inn
01494 713109
Mid Jul wknd

BEACONSFIELD
The Royal Standard of
England
01494 673382
Summer BH

BOURNE END
The Garibaldi
01628 522092
Easter & Summer BH

BRILL
The Pheasant
01844 239370
Spring BH

DENHAM
The Falcon Inn
01895 832125

MOULSOE
The Carrington Arms
01908 218050
Jun

CAMBRIDGESHIRE

BOURN
The Willow Tree
01954 719775
Summer

HISTON
Red Lion
01223 564437
Easter & 1st wk Sep

PETERBOROUGH
Charters Bar & East
Restaurant
01733 315700

SPALDWICK
The George
01480 890293

STRETHAM
The Lazy Otter
01353 649780
Jul

THORNEY
Dog In A Doublet
01733 202256
Early May BH

CHESHIRE

CHESTER
Old Harkers Arms
01244 344525
Mar (Pie & Champion Ale Wk)

CORNWALL & ISLES OF SCILLY

CADGWITH
Cadgwith Cove Inn
01326 290513
Oct

CHAPEL AMBLE
The Maltsters Arms
01208 812473
Spring BH

CONSTANTINE
Trengilly Wartha Inn
01326 340332

GUNNISLAKE
The Rising Sun Inn
01822 832201
Every 2-3 months

GWITHIAN
The Red River Inn
01736 753223
Easter wknd

ST MAWGAN
The Falcon Inn
01637 860225
Jul (last full wknd)

TRESCO (ISLES OF SCILLY)
The New Inn
01720 422849
Jun

CUMBRIA

ULVERSTON
The Farmers
01229 584469

DERBYSHIRE

ASHOVER
The Old Poets Corner
01246 590888

BAMFORD
The Yorkshire Bridge Inn
01433 651361
May

BIRCHOVER
Red Lion Inn
01629 650363
Mid Jul

BONSALL
The Barley Mow
01629 825685
BHs (3-4 times a year)

CASTLETON
The Peak Hotel
01433 620247
BHs

CHINLEY
Old Hall Inn
01663 750529
3rd wknd Sep

The Paper Mill Inn
01663 750529
3rd wknd Sep

HOPE
The Old Hall Hotel
01433 620160
BHs

MATLOCK
The Red Lion
01629 584888

SHARDLOW
The Old Crown Inn
01332 792392
Oct

DEVON

BRAMPFORD SPEKE
The Lazy Toad
01392 841591
Summer BH

CLYST HYDON
The Five Bells Inn
01884 277288

DODDISCOMBSLEIGH
The NoBody Inn
01647 252394

EAST ALLINGTON
The Fortescue Arms
01548 521215

KINGS NYMPTON
The Grove Inn
01769 580406
Jul

MEAVY
The Royal Oak Inn
01822 852944
Summer BH

RINGMORE
The Journey's End Inn
01548 810205
Twice a year

ROBOROUGH
The New Inn
01805 603247
Last wknd Sep

TAVISTOCK
The Cornish Arms
01822 612145
Summer BH wknd

TOTNES
Royal Seven Stars Hotel
01803 862125

WOODBURY SALTERTON
The Digger's Rest
01395 232375
May

DORSET

CHEDINGTON
Winyard's Gap Inn
01935 891244
Aug

STUDLAND
The Bankes Arms Hotel
01929 450225

WEST STOUR
The Ship Inn
01747 838640
Aug

WORTH MATRAVERS
The Square and Compass
01929 439229
1st Sat Nov

DURHAM, COUNTY

CASTLE EDEN
Castle Eden Inn
01429 835137
May-Jun

FROSTERLEY
The Black Bull Inn
01388 527784

STANLEY
The Stables Pub and
Restaurant
01207 288750
2nd wknd Dec

ESSEX

BELCHAMP ST PAUL
The Half Moon
01787 277402
Summer BH

FEERING
The Sun Inn
01376 570442
End of Jun & Sep

GLOUCESTERSHIRE

ALDERTON
The Gardeners Arms
01242 620257
Aug

ALMONDSBURY
The Swan Hotel
01454 625671
Jul

CHELTENHAM
The Gloucester Old Spot
01242 680321

The Royal Oak Inn
01242 522344
Summer BH

Sandford Park Alehouse
01242 574517

CLIFFORD'S MESNE
The Yew Tree
01531 820719
Oct

COATES
The Tunnel House Inn
01285 770280

DURSLEY
The Old Spot Inn
01453 542870
May

EBRINGTON
The Ebrington Arms
01386 593223
Late Oct (cider pressing day)

TETBURY
The Royal Oak Tetbury
01666 500021
Spring BH

GREATER MANCHESTER

SALFORD
The King's Arms
0161 839 3605
Sep

HAMPSHIRE

BEAULIEU
The Drift Inn
023 8029 2342

BISHOP'S WALTHAM
The Hampshire Bowman
01489 892940
Last wknd Jul

BRAISHFIELD
The Wheatsheaf
01794 368652

BRANSGORE
The Three Tuns Country Inn
01425 672232
Summer holidays (contact pub
for details)

BROUGHTON
The Tally Ho
01794 301280
Summer BH

EAST STRATTON
Northbrook Arms
01962 774150
Sep

EVERSLEY
The Golden Pot
0118 973 2104

LEE-ON-THE-SOLENT
The Bun Penny
023 9255 0214
Summer BH weekend

LYNDHURST
New Forest Inn
023 8028 4690
Last wknd Mar

RINGWOOD
The Railway
01425 473701
Summer BH

ROMSEY
The Three Tuns
01794 512639
Wknd in Aug

HEREFORDSHIRE

HOARWITHY
The New Harp Inn
01432 840900
Summer BH

MICHAELCHURCH ESCLEY
The Bridge Inn
01981 510646
Summer BH

ORLETON
The Boot Inn
01568 780228
Last wknd Jul

WELLINGTON HEATH
The Farmers Arms
01531 634776

WOOLHOPE
The Crown Inn
01432 860468
Early May BH

HERTFORDSHIRE

WATTON-AT-STONE
The Bull
01920 831032
May & Oct

KENT

LOWER HALSTOW
The Three Tuns
01795 842840
Summer BH

SISSINGHURST
The Milk House
01580 720200
Summer BH wknd

LANCASHIRE

BILSBORROW
Owd Nell's Tavern
01995 640010
Last wk Jul

CHORLEY
The Yew Tree Inn
01257 480344
Good Friday

LANCASTER
Toll House Inn
01524 599900
Oct

LEICESTERSHIRE

BLABY
The Bakers Arms
0116 278 7253
Summer BH

LEICESTER
The Rutland & Derby
0116 262 3299

LONG WHATTON
The Royal Oak
01509 843694
Summer BH

LINCOLNSHIRE

CLEETHORPES
The Nottingham House
01472 505150
Spring & Autumn

LONDON

NW1
The Prince Albert
020 7485 0270
BHs

SE22
The Palmerston
020 8693 1629

SW10
The Hollywood Arms
020 7349 7840

W4
The City Barge
020 8994 2148

W8
The Windsor Castle
020 7243 8797
Jul

NORFOLK

CASTLE ACRE
The Ostrich Inn
01760 755398

WINTERTON-ON-SEA
Fishermans Return
01493 393305

NORTHAMPTONSHIRE

OLD
The White Horse
01604 781297
Summer BH wknd

NORTHUMBERLAND

BEADNELL
The Craster Arms
01665 720272
Last wknd Jul

CARTERWAY HEADS
The Manor House Inn
01207 255268
Last wknd Aug

HEDLEY ON THE HILL
The Feathers Inn
01661 843607
Summer BH

NEWARK-ON-TRENT
The Prince Rupert
01636 918121
Summer BH

NOTTINGHAM
The Hand and Heart
0115 958 2456
Summer

SOUTHWELL
The Hearty Goodfellow
01636 919176
Feb

OXFORDSHIRE

ABINGDON-ON-THAMES
The Brewery Tap
01235 521655
Mar & Oct

ASHBURY
The Rose & Crown
01793 710222
Jun, Jul & Sep

BANBURY
Ye Olde Reindeer Inn
01295 270972
Summer BH

BLOXHAM
The Elephant & Castle
01295 720383
Early May (part of Bloxfest
Music Festival)

NORTH HINKSEY VILLAGE
The Fishes
01865 249796

WYTHAM
White Hart
01865 244372

RUTLAND

MARKET OVERTON
The Black Bull
01572 767677
Last wknd Jun

OAKHAM
The Grainstore Brewery
01572 770065
Spring BH

SHROPSHIRE

BISHOP'S CASTLE
The Castle
01588 638403
Jul

PAVE LANE
The Fox
01952 815940
Summer

SOMERSET

CHEW MAGNA
The Bear and Swan
01275 331100

DUNSTER
The Luttrell Arms Hotel
01643 821555

The Stags Head Inn
01643 821229
Dec

HASELBURY PLUCKNETT
The White Horse at
Haselbury
01460 78873

HINTON ST GEORGE
The Lord Poulett Arms
01460 73149

ILCHESTER
The Bull Inn
01935 840400

Ilchester Arms
01935 840220

LOWER GODNEY
The Sheppey
01458 831594
Aug

PITNEY
The Halfway House
01458 252513
Aug

PORLOCK
The Bottom Ship
01643 863288
1st wknd Jul

SHEPTON MALLET
The Three Horseshoes Inn
01749 850359
Easter, Summer BH

WEDMORE
The George Inn
01934 712124

STAFFORDSHIRE

CAULDON
Yew Tree Inn
01538 309876
Mid Jul

HAUGHTON
The Bell
01785 780301
Late Aug

STAFFORD
The Holly Bush Inn
01889 508234
Jun & Sep

WRINEHILL
The Hand & Trumpet
01270 820048
Aug

SUFFOLK

ELVEDEN
Elveden Inn
01842 890876
Mid Aug

SOMERLEYTON
The Duke's Head
01502 733931

SURREY

FARNHAM
The Bat & Ball Freehouse
01252 792108

LONG DITTON
The Ditton
020 8339 0785

SUSSEX, EAST

BLACKBOYS
The Blackboys Inn
01825 890283

EWHURST GREEN
The White Dog
01580 830264
Late Sep (cider & book festival)

HASTINGS & ST LEONARDS
The Crown
01424 465100
Autumn

SUSSEX, WEST

HORSHAM
The Black Jug
01403 253526
Jul

KINGSFOLD
The Dog and Duck
01306 627295
Annual charity event

WARWICKSHIRE

BROOM
The Broom Tavern
01789 778199
Summer BH

EDGEHILL
Castle at Edgehill
01295 670255
Aug-Sep

WEST MIDLANDS

WEST BROMWICH
The Vine
0121 553 2866
Oct

WILTSHIRE

ALDBOURNE
The Blue Boar
01672 540237
1st wknd Jun

The Crown Inn
01672 540214
2nd week Jul

BOX
The Quarrymans Arms
01225 743569
Jul

BRADFORD-ON-AVON
The George
01225 865650

BRINKWORTH
The Three Crowns
01666 510366

COLLINGBOURNE DUCIS
The Shears Inn
01264 850304
Late summer

MALMESBURY
Kings Arms
01666 823383

ROYAL WOOTTON BASSETT
The Angel
01793 851161
Sep

SHERSTON
The Rattlebone Inn
01666 840871
Jul

WORCESTERSHIRE

BRETFORTON
The Fleece Inn
01386 831173
Mid-late Oct

MALVERN
The Nag's Head
01684 574373
Summer

YORKSHIRE, EAST RIDING OF

KILHAM
The Old Star
01262 420619

THORNGUMBALD
The Camerton
01964 601208
Aug

YORKSHIRE, NORTH

AKEBAR
The Friar's Head
01677 450201

YORK
Lysander Arms
01904 640845
Early May BH wknd

YORKSHIRE, SOUTH

CADEBY
The Cadeby Pub & Restaurant
01709 864009

SHEFFIELD
Kelham Island Tavern
0114 272 2482
Late Jun wknd

ISLE OF MAN

PORT ERIN
Falcon's Nest Hotel
01624 834077
Early May

SCOTLAND

CITY OF DUNDEE

BROUGHTY FERRY
The Royal Arch Bar
01382 779741
Last wknd Apr

CITY OF GLASGOW

GLASGOW
Bon Accord
0141 248 4427

PERTH & KINROSS

MEIKLEOUR
Meikleour Arms
01250 883206
Aug

WALES

CARDIFF

GWAELOD-Y-GARTH
Gwaelod-y-Garth Inn
029 2081 0408
Aug

CARMARTHENSHIRE

LLANDOVERY
The Castle
01550 720343
Last wknd in Sep

LLANFALLTEG
The Plash Inn
01437 563472
Spring BH & Summer BH

PUMSAINT
The Dolaucothi Arms
01558 650237
Summer BH wknd

CEREDIGION

TREGARON
Y Talbot
01974 298208
Early Oct

MONMOUTHSHIRE

ABERGAVENNY
Clytha Arms
01873 840206
Spring BH

TRELLECH
The Lion Inn
01600 860322
Aug

NEWPORT

CAERLEON
The Bell at Caerleon
01633 420613

POWYS

DEFYNNOG
The Tanners Arms
01874 638032
Late Aug

RHONDDA CYNON TAFF

PONTYPRIDD
Bunch of Grapes
01443 402934
Twice a year

SWANSEA

LLANGENNITH
Kings Head
01792 386212
Last wknd Oct

VALE OF GLAMORGAN

PENARTH
The Pilot
029 2071 0615
Twice a year

How to find a pub in the atlas section

Pubs are shown in the gazetteer under the name of their nearest town or village. If a pub is in a very small village, or in a remote rural area, it may appear under a larger town that is within five miles of its actual location.

The black dots in the atlas section match the location name in the gazetteer.

The county map shown opposite will help you identify the counties within each country. The county names are shown at the top of each page in the gazetteer.

The atlas section and the index that follow will help you find the towns featured in the guide.

Key to County Map

England

1 Bedfordshire
2 Berkshire
3 Bristol
4 Buckinghamshire
5 Cambridgeshire
6 Greater Manchester
7 Herefordshire
8 Hertfordshire
9 Leicestershire
10 Northamptonshire
11 Nottinghamshire
12 Rutland
13 Staffordshire
14 Warwickshire
15 West Midlands
16 Worcestershire

Scotland

17 City of Glasgow
18 Clackmannanshire
19 East Ayrshire
20 East Dunbartonshire
21 East Renfrewshire
22 Perth & Kinross
23 Renfrewshire
24 South Lanarkshire
25 West Dunbartonshire

Wales

26 Blaenau Gwent
27 Bridgent
28 Caerphilly
29 Denbighshire
30 Flintshire
31 Merthyr Tydfil
32 Monmouthshire
33 Neath Port Talbot
34 Newport
35 Rhondda Cynon Taff
36 Torfaen
37 Vale of Glamorgan
38 Wrexham

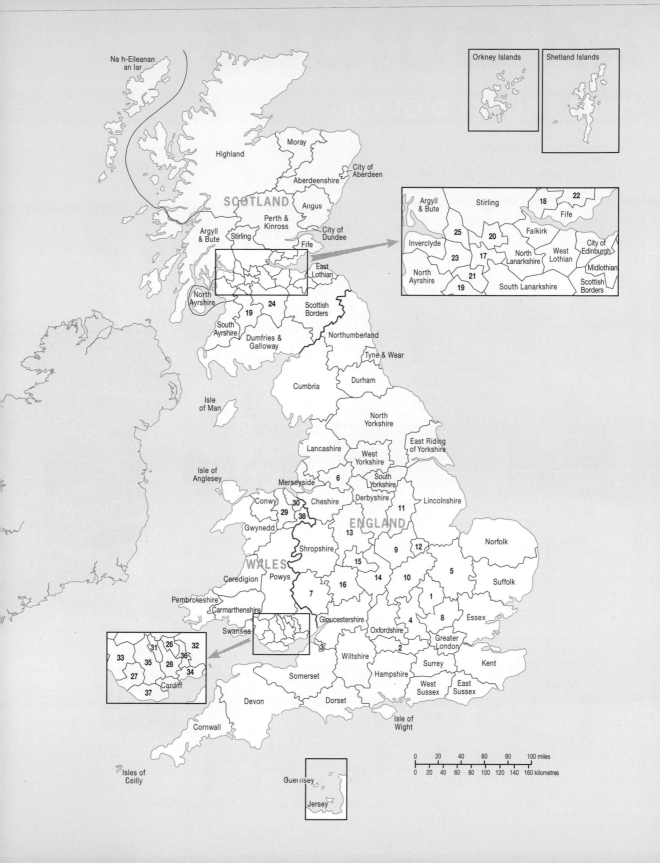

AA GUIDES

YOUR TRUSTED GUIDE

▶ THE BEST PLACES TO VISIT

▶ CLEAR TOWN PLANS AND MAPPING

▶ WRITTEN BY LOCAL EXPERTS

▶ RECOMMENDED PLACES TO EAT

▶ TRUSTED LISTINGS

THE AA GUIDE TO
Yorkshire

THE AA GUIDE TO
Cornwall

THE AA GUIDE TO
Durham & Northumberland

THE AA GUIDE TO
The Cotswolds
with Oxford & Stratford-upon-Avon

SECOND EDITION
THE BEST PLACES TO VISIT ◀
WRITTEN BY LOCAL EXPERTS ◀
RECOMMENDED PLACES TO EAT ◀
CLEAR TOWN PLANS AND MAPPING ◀

THE AA GUIDE TO
Lake District & Cumbria

THE AA GUIDE TO
Norfolk & Suffolk
with Cambridge

SECOND EDITION
THE BEST PLACES TO VISIT ◀
WRITTEN BY LOCAL EXPERTS ◀
RECOMMENDED PLACES TO EAT ◀
CLEAR TOWN PLANS AND MAPPING ◀

THE AA GUIDE TO
Wales

YOUR TRUSTED GUIDE
SECOND EDITION
THE BEST PLACES TO VISIT ◀
WRITTEN BY LOCAL EXPERTS ◀
RECOMMENDED PLACES TO EAT ◀
TOWN PLANS AND MAPPING ◀

THE AA GUIDE TO
The Peak District

SECOND EDITION
THE BEST PLACES TO VISIT ◀
WRITTEN BY LOCAL EXPERTS ◀
RECOMMENDED PLACES TO EAT ◀
CLEAR TOWN PLANS AND MAPPING ◀

THE AA GUIDE TO
Scotland

YOUR TRUSTED GUIDE
A–Z OF PLACES ◀
THE BEST THINGS TO DO ◀
WRITTEN BY LOCAL EXPERTS ◀
RECOMMENDED PLACES TO EAT ◀
CLEAR TOWN PLANS AND MAPPING ◀

THE AA GUIDE TO
Ireland

YOUR TRUSTED GUIDE
A–Z OF PLACES ◀
THE BEST THINGS TO DO ◀
WRITTEN BY LOCAL EXPERTS ◀
RECOMMENDED PLACES TO EAT ◀
CLEAR TOWN PLANS AND MAPPING ◀

🐦 Follow @TheAA_Lifestyle

KEY TO ATLAS

Shetland Islands

24

Orkney Islands

22

Inverness

23

Aberdeen

Fort William

Perth

Edinburgh

20 Glasgow **21**

Newcastle upon Tyne

Stranraer

Carlisle

Middlesbrough

Isle of Man

Kendal

18 **19**

24 Leeds York Kingston upon Hull

Liverpool Manchester **16** **17**

Holyhead Sheffield

14 **15** Lincoln

Nottingham

Birmingham

Norwich

10 **11** **12** **13**

Aberystwyth Cambridge

8 **9** Gloucester Colchester

Carmarthen Oxford LONDON

Cardiff Bristol Guildford **6** **7**

4 **5** Maidstone

Barnstaple Taunton Southampton Brighton Dover

2 **3** Bournemouth

Plymouth Exeter

Penzance

Isles of Scilly

Channel Islands **24**

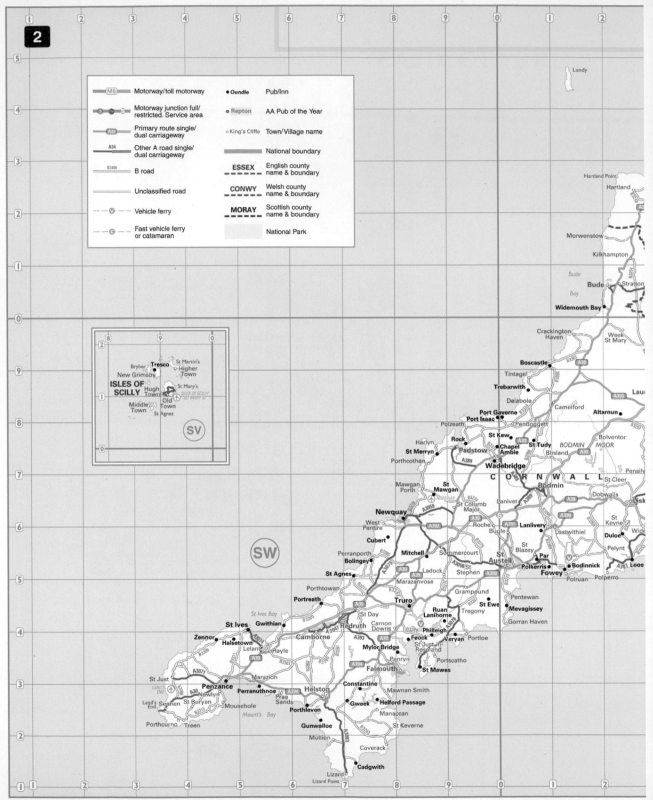

2

	Map Legend
M6	Motorway/toll motorway
	Motorway junction full/ restricted. Service area
A55	Primary route single/ dual carriageway
A34	Other A road single/ dual carriageway
B3400	B road
	Unclassified road
ⓥ	Vehicle ferry
ⓒ	Fast vehicle ferry or catamaran
● Oundle	Pub/Inn
● Repton	AA Pub of the Year
○ King's Cliffe	Town/Village name
	National boundary
ESSEX	English county name & boundary
CONWY	Welsh county name & boundary
MORAY	Scottish county name & boundary
	National Park

ISLES OF SCILLY
Bryher · Tresco · St Martin's · Higher Town
New Grimsby
Hugh Town · St Mary's · ISLES OF SCILLY (ST MARY'S)
Middle Town · Old Town
St Agnes

SV

SW

Lundy

Hartland Point
Hartland

Morwenstow

Kilkhampton

Bude
Bay · **Bude** · Stratton

Widemouth Bay

Crackington Haven · Week St Mary

Boscastle
Tintagel
Trebarwith
Delabole · Camelford · **Altarnun**
Laun
Bolventor
BODMIN MOOR

Polzeath
Port Gaverne
Port Isaac · Pendoggett
Harlyn · **St Kew**
Rock · **Chapel Amble** · **St Tudy** · Blisland · Pensilv
St Merryn · **Padstow**
Porthcothan · A389 · **Wadebridge** · St Cleer
C O R N W A L L
Mawgan Porth · **St Mawgan** · **Bodmin** · Dobwalls · Lisk
St Columb Major · Lanivet · St Keyne
Newquay · Roche · **Lanlivery** · Lostwithiel · Wide
West Pentire · Bugle · St Blazey · **Duloe**
St Day · Pelynt
Cubert · **Par** · **Bodinnick** · **Looe**
Perranporth · **Mitchell** · Sommercourt · **St Austell** · **Polkerris** · **Fowey** · Polperro
Bolingey · Ladock · St Stephen · Polruan
St Agnes · Marazanvose · Grampound · Pentewan
Porthtowan · Carnon Downs · **St Ewe** · **Mevagissey**
Portreath · St Day · **Truro** · **Ruan Lanihorne** · Tregony · Gorran Haven
St Ives Bay · **Gwithian** · Redruth · **Phylleigh** · Portloe
St Ives · **Camborne** · A393 · **Feock** · **Veryan** · Portscatho
Zennor · Lelant · Hayle · **Mylor Bridge** · St Just-in-Roseland
Halsetown · Penryn · **St Mawes**
St Just · Marazion · **Falmouth**
LAND'S END · **Penzance** · **Helston** · **Constantine** · Mawnan Smith
Newlyn · **Perranuthnoe** · Praa Sands · **Gweek** · **Helford Passage**
Land's · Sennen · St Buryan · Mousehole · **Porthleven** · Manaccan
End · **Gunwalloe** · St Keverne
Porthcurno · Treen · Mullion
Mount's Bay · Coverack
Cadgwith
Lizard
Lizard Point

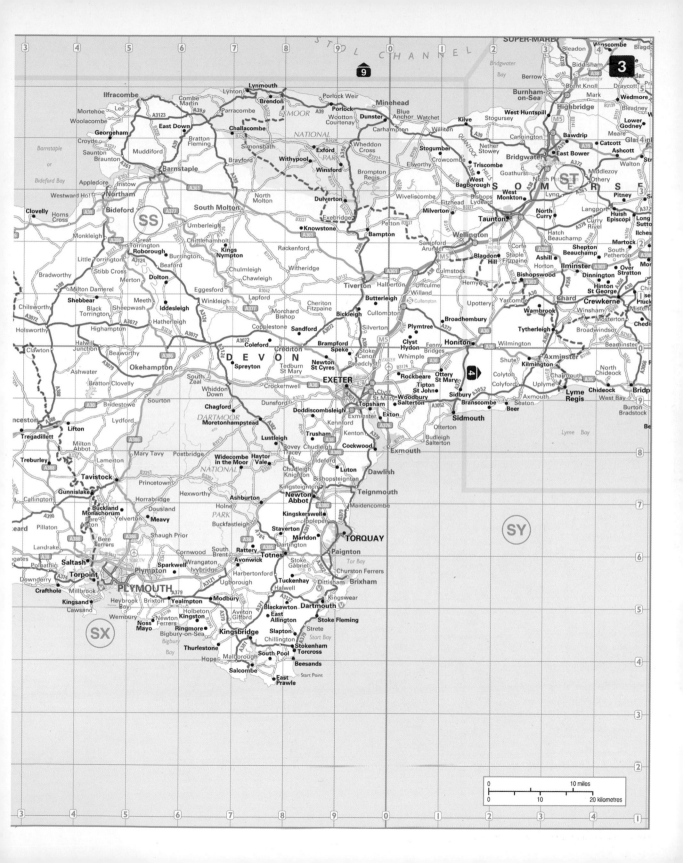

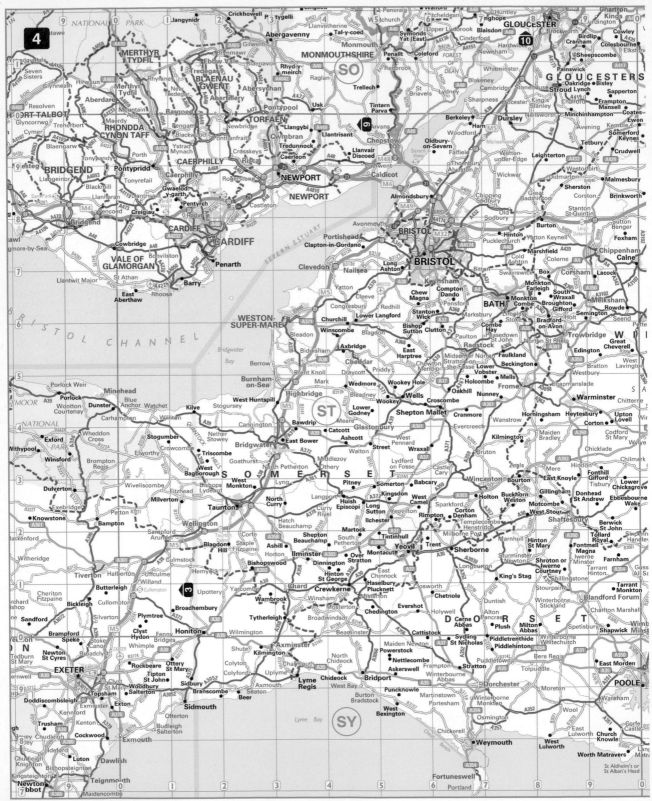

For continuation pages refer to numbered arrows

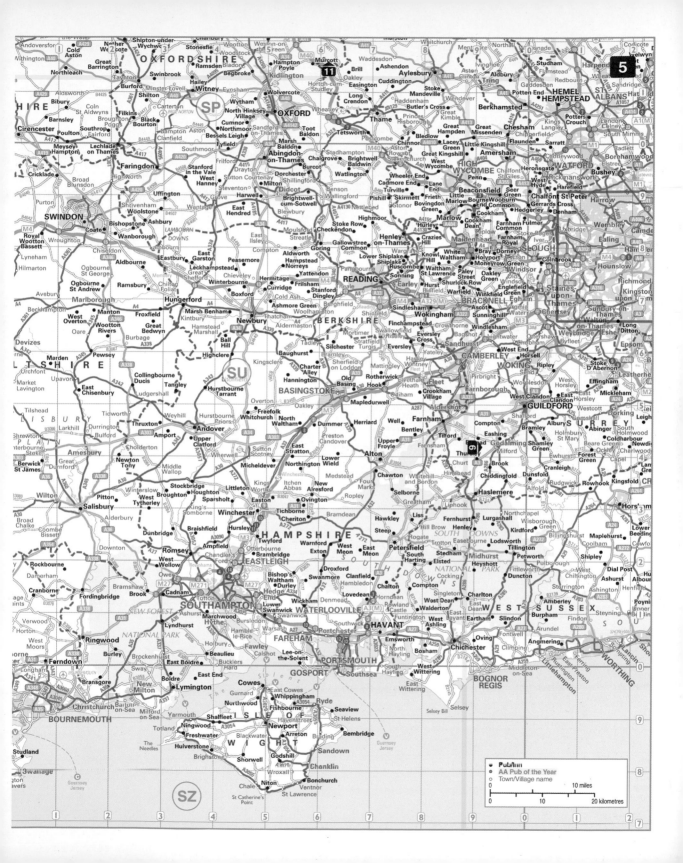

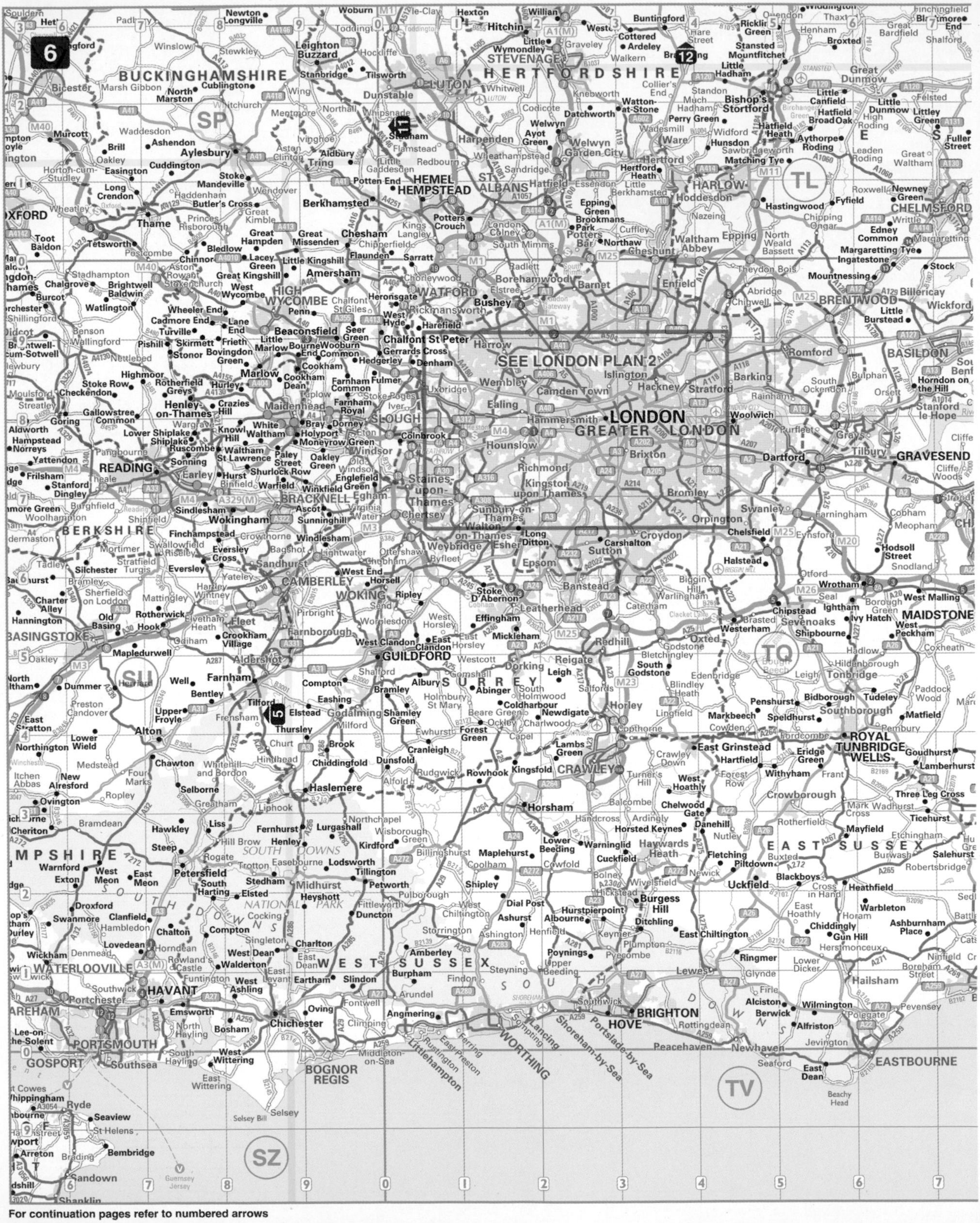

For continuation pages refer to numbered arrows

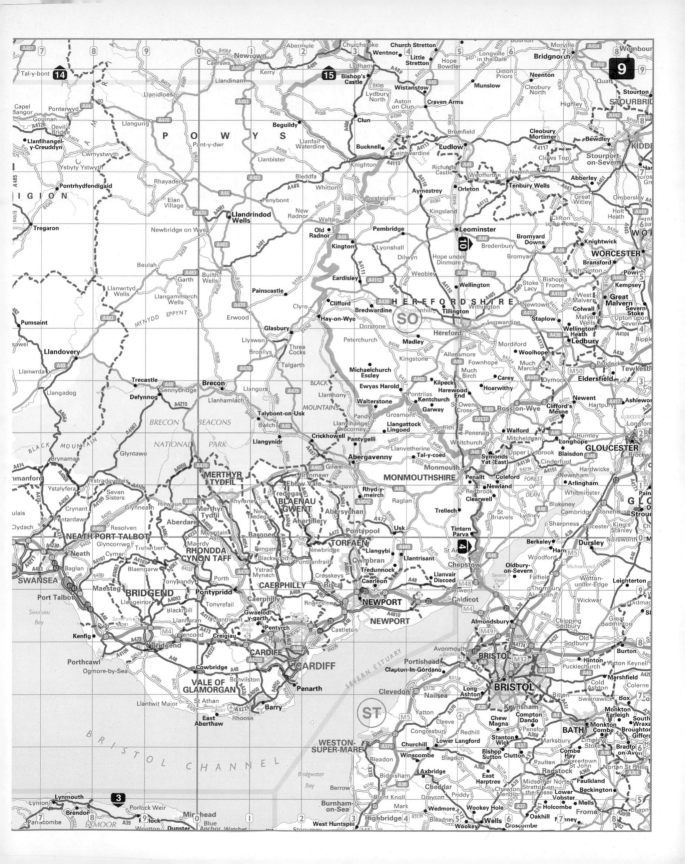

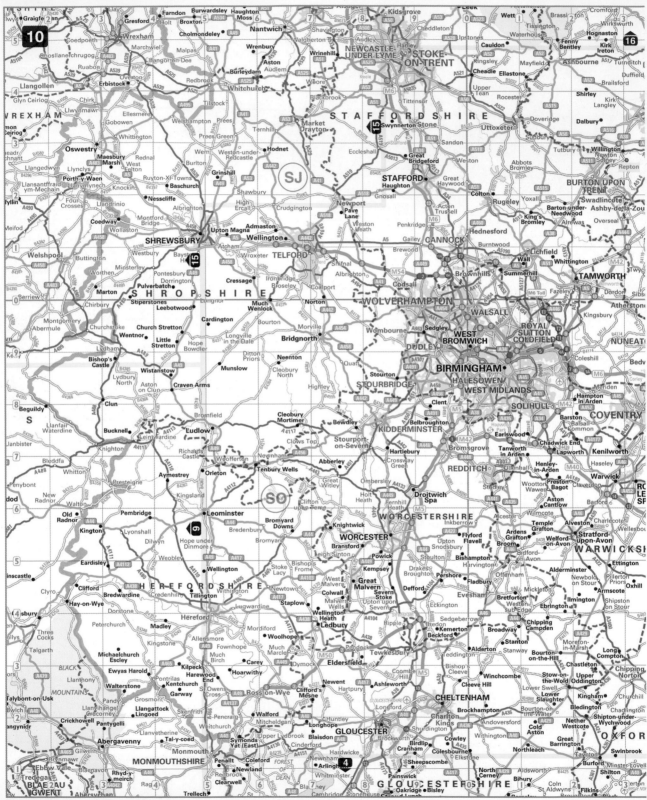

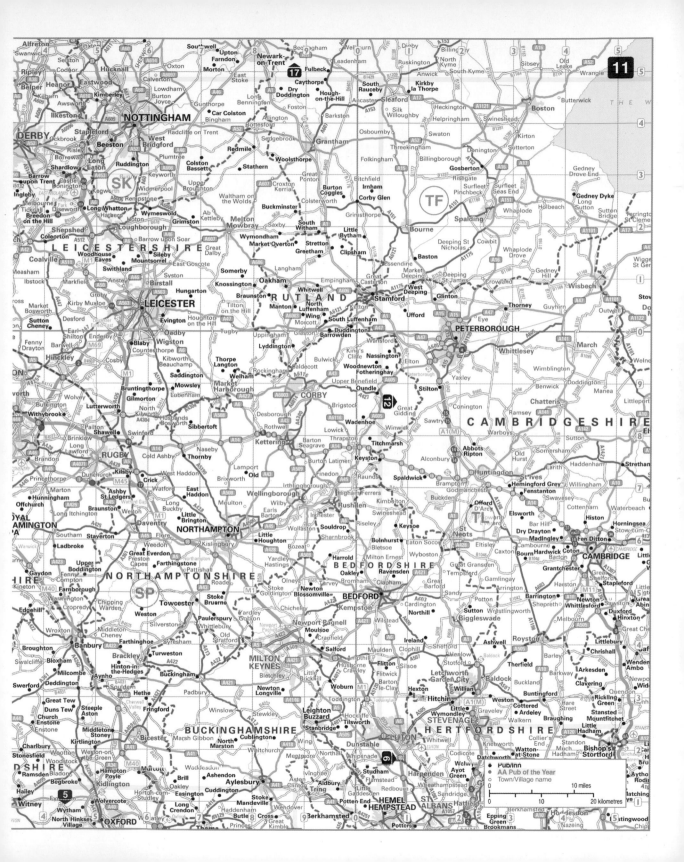

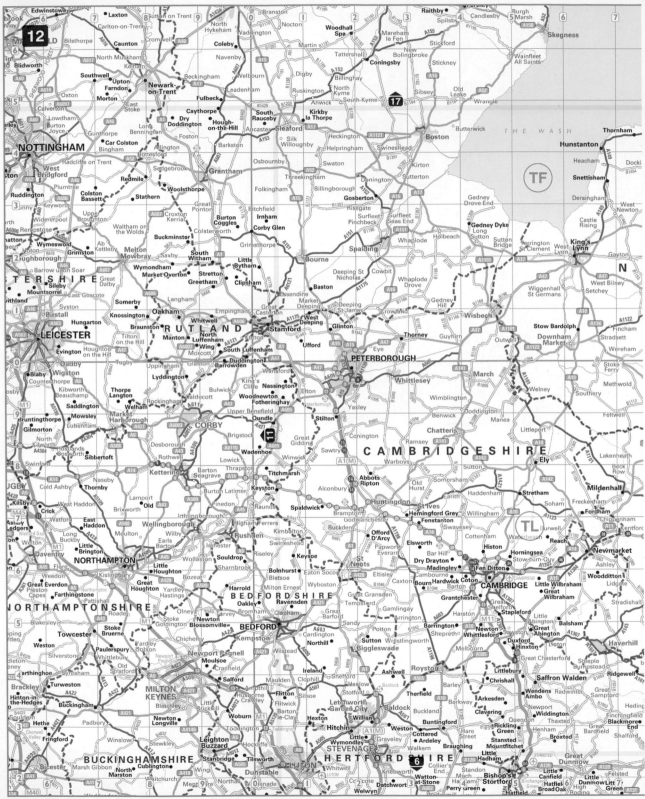

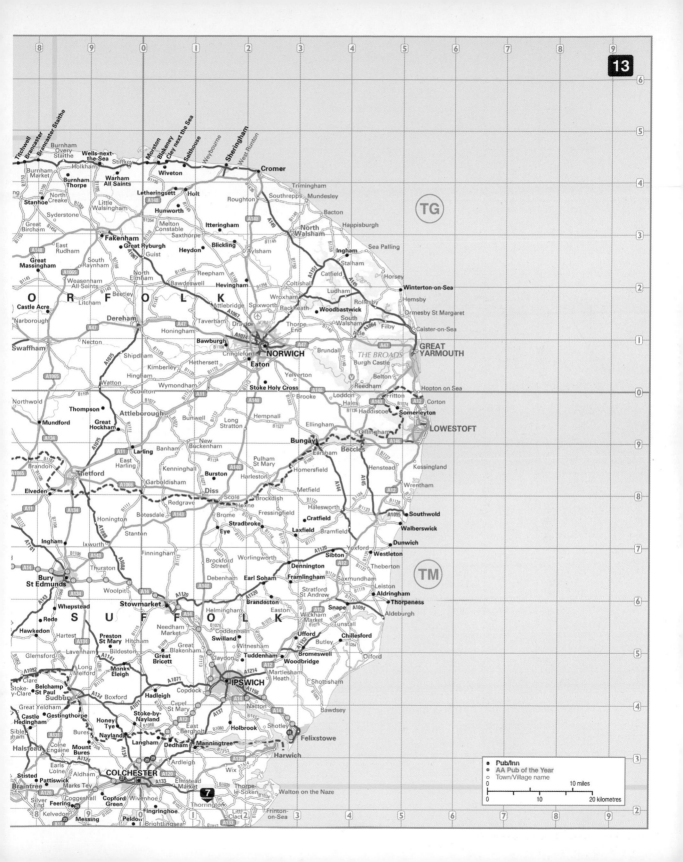

14

ISLE OF
ANGLESEY

Cemaes
Amlwch
A5025
Llanfaethlu
Llanerchymedd
Llanfachraeth
Red
Wharf Bay
Holyhead
Benllech
Llangoed
Llandudno
Rhôs-
on-Sea
Colwyn Bay
Rhyl
B5109
Pentraeth
Deganwy
Trearddur Bay
A55
A5
B5108
B5109
Llandudno Junction
Llanddulas
Abergele
Holy
Island
B4080
Llangefni
Penmaenmawr
Conwy
Llansantffraid Glan Conwy
Llanelian-
yn-Rhôs
Rhosneigr
B4422
A5
Menai
Bridge
Beaumaris
Llanfairfechan
Llannefydd
Aberffraw
B4419
Llanfair
P.G.
Bangor
Llanllechid
Betws-
yn-Rhos
Llanfair
Talhaiarn
Llansannan
Y Felinheli
A4080
Bethesda
Tal-y-Cafn
Llangernyw
A5
Newborough
A4087
Llanrug
Tal-y-Bont
A470
A548
Henl
Caernarfon
Llanberis
Trefriw
Llanrwst
Bylchau
Bontnewydd
Waunfawr
A4086
Capel Curig
CONWY
Llandwrog
Llanwnda
A4085
Betws-y-Coed
A5
Caernarfon
Bay
B4418
Rhyd Ddu
Dolwyddelan
A470
Penmachno
Pentrefoelas
Cerrigydrudion
Gw
Clynnog-fawr
A487
Penygroes
A498
SH
Beddgelert
A4086
Blaenau Ffestiniog
B4501
Y Maerd
Llanaelhaearn
A499
Prenteg
B4410
Ffestiniog
A5
Morfa Nefyn
Nefyn
A4354
Tremadog
Maentwrog
B4391
Llanddern
Tudweiliog
B4417
A487
Llanystumdwy
Porthmadog
Penrhyndeudraeth
A4212
Bala
PENINSULA
Bodfuan
A497
Criccieth
Borth-y-Gest
Talsarnau
SNOWDONIA
Per
Sarn
LLEYN
B4415
A499
Pwllheli
Trawsfynydd
NATIONAL
GWYNEDD
Y Rhiw
Llanbedrog
A496
Harlech
PARK
Llanuwchllyn
Aberdaron
Abersoch
Llanbedr
Ganllwyd
Llanwdd
Bardsey
Island
Dyffryn Ardudwy
A470
A494
Tal-y-bont
A496
Brithdir
Llanwd
Barmouth
Dolgellau
A470
Dinas-Mawddwy
A458
Fairbourne
A493
Mallwyd
Llangadfan
Llwyngwril
Corris
A487
Bryncrug
Cemmaes
Road
Llanbrynmair
Tywyn
Pennal
Machynlleth
A470
N
Aberdyfi
A493
Carno
SN
A487
Borth
Tal-y-bont
9
Llandre
Capel
Bangor
Llanidloes
5 berystwyth
6
7 Ponterwyd
0

Pub/Inn
AA Pub of the Year
○ Town/Village name

0   10 miles
0   10   20 kilometres

For continuation pages refer to numbered arrows

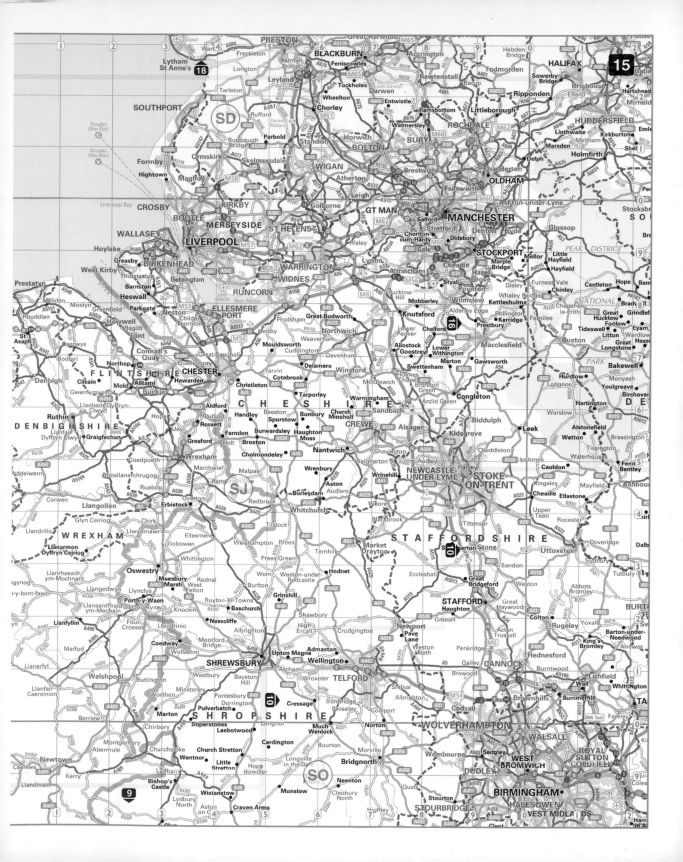

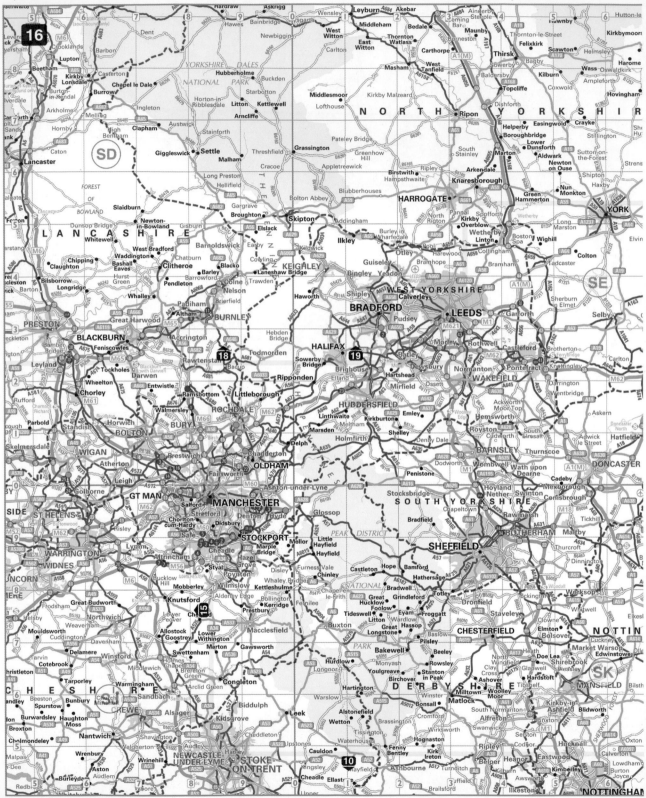

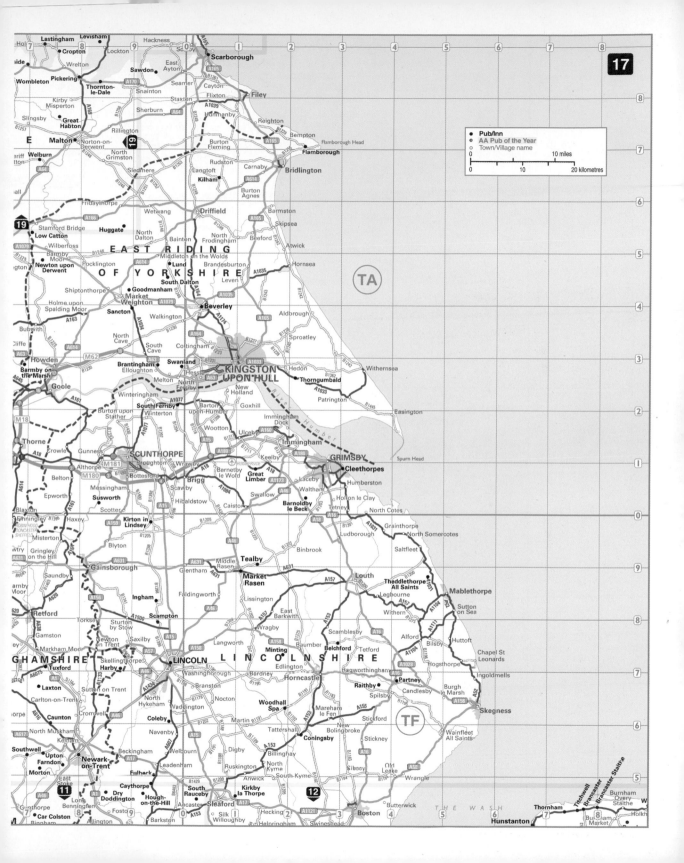

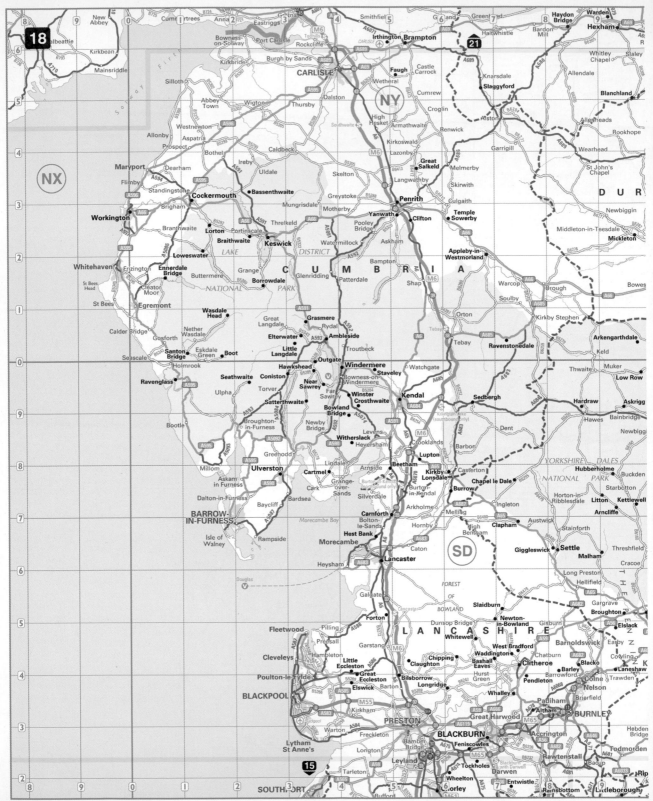

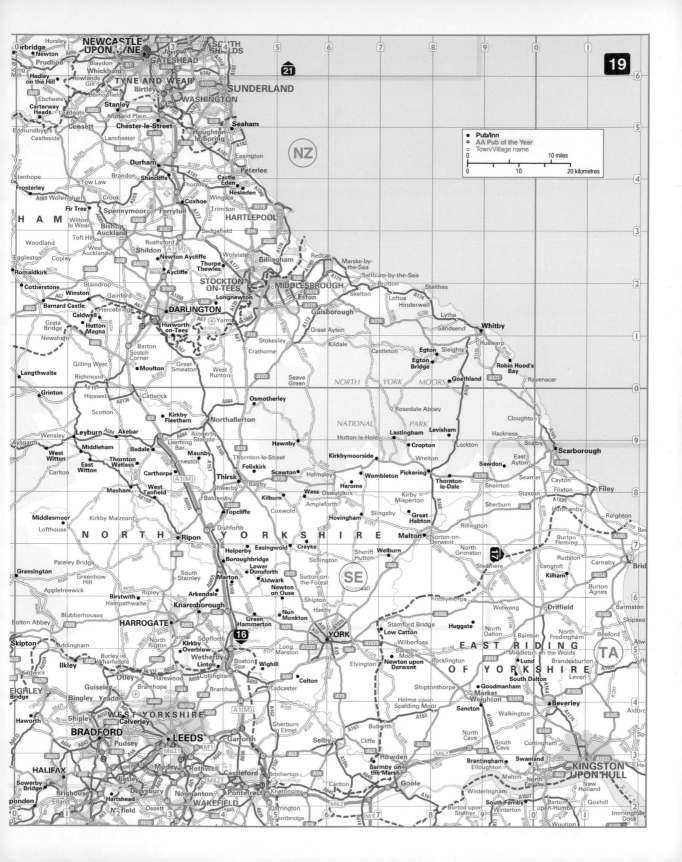

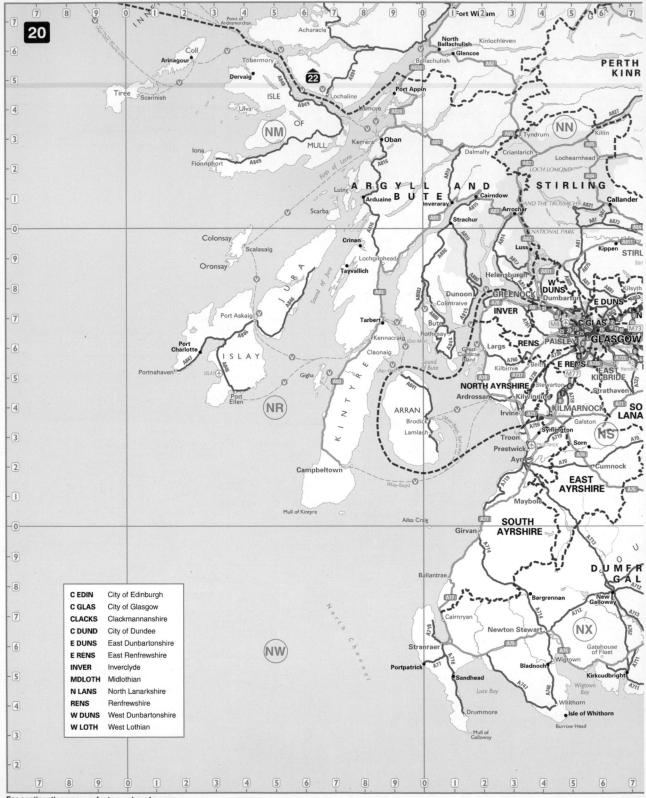

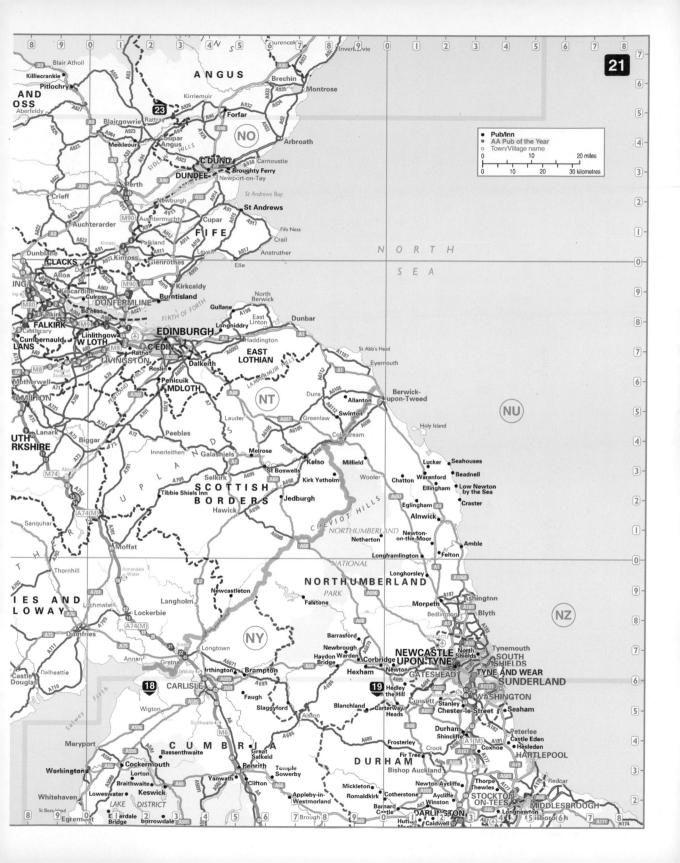

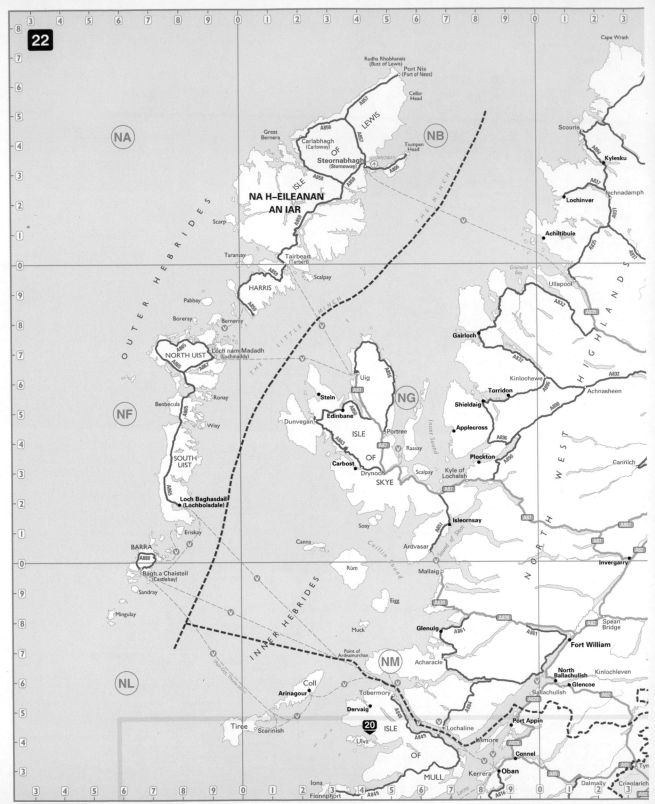

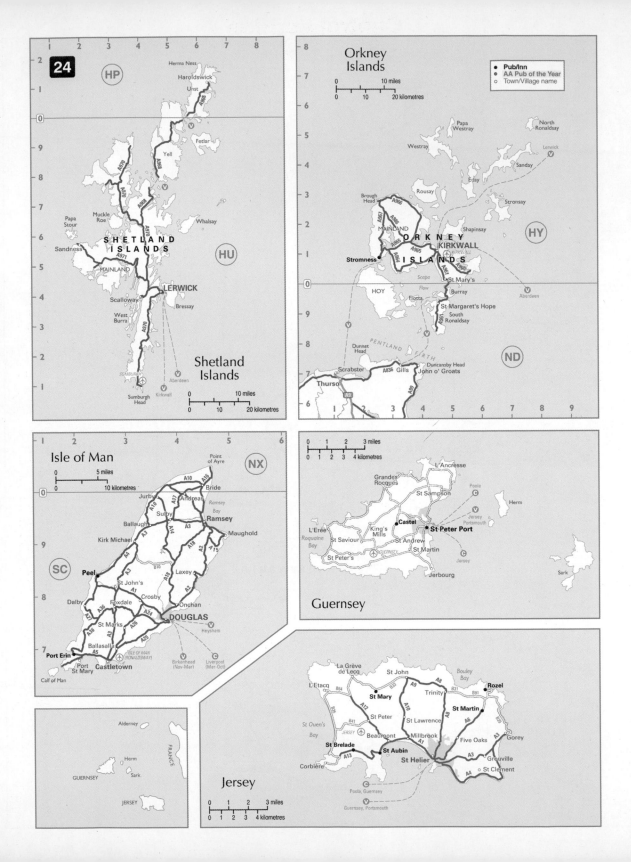

Central London

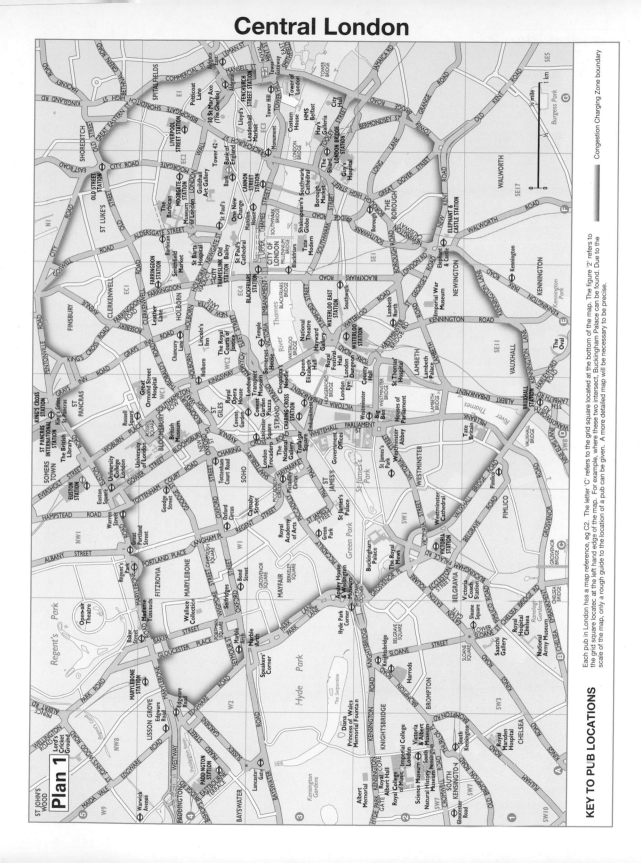

Plan 1

KEY TO PUB LOCATIONS

Each pub in London has a map reference, eg C2. The letter 'C' refers to the grid square located at the bottom of the map. The figure '2' refers to the grid square locatec at the left hand edge of the map. For example, where these two intersect, Buckingham Palace can be found. Due to the scale of the map, only a rough guide to the location of a pub can be given. A more detailed map will be necessary to be precise.

— — — Congestion Charging Zone boundary

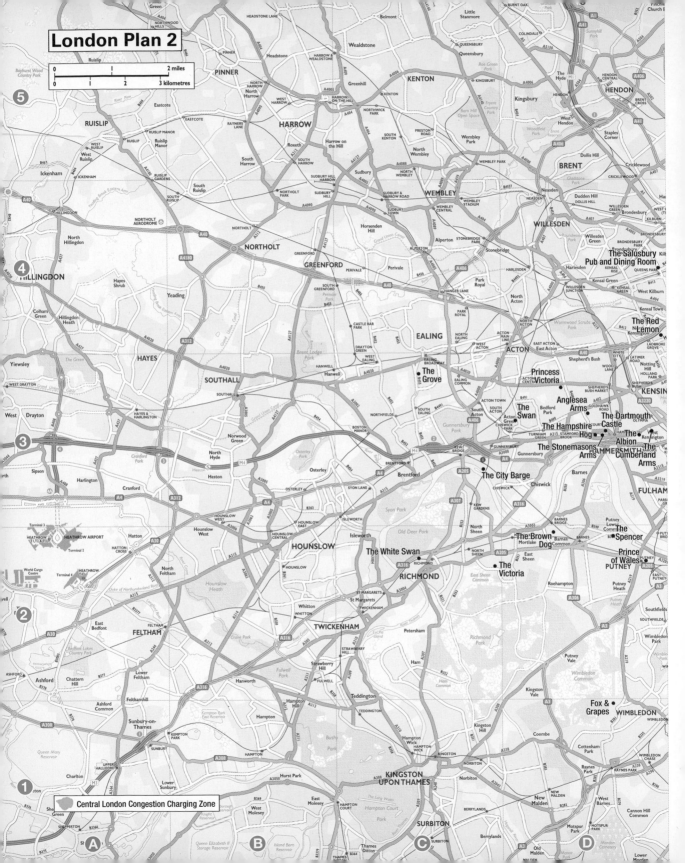

London Plan 2

0   1   2 miles
0   1   2   3 kilometres

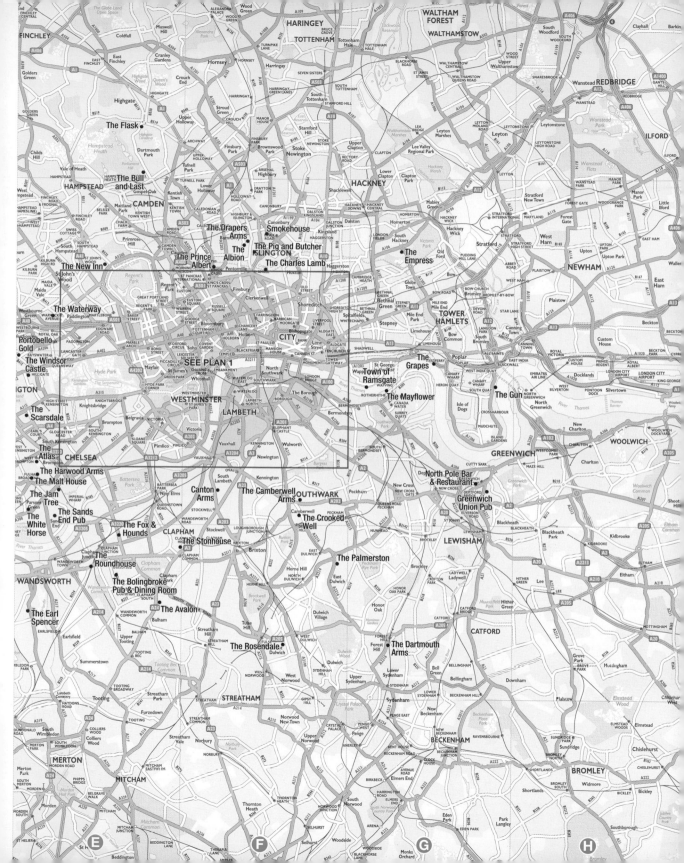

Index

Red entries are Pick of the Pubs

Acknowledgments

The Automobile Association would like to thank the following photographers, companies and picture libraries for their assistance in the preparation of this book.

Abbreviations for the picture credits are as follows – (t) top; (b) bottom; (c) centre; (l) left; (r) right; (AA) AA World Travel Library

Front & Back Cover: © Aleksandr Bryliaev / Alamy

England Opener 22-23 AA/J Wood;
Scotland Opener 594-595 AA/S Anderson;
Wales Opener 626-627 AA/C Molyneux

3 Courtesy of The Maytime Inn, Oxfordshire; 4 Courtesy of The Lord Crewe Arms, Northumberland; 8 Courtesy of The Pheasant Inn, Cheshire; 9 Courtesy of The Cock Pub, Cambridgshire; 10–11bg AA/C Sawyer; 10 Courtesy of The Boot, Derbyshire; 11l Courtesy of The Ship Inn, Fife; 11r Courtesy of The Penhelig Arms, Gwynedd; 12 geogphotos/Alamy Stock Photo; 13l AA; 13r AA; 14 Courtesy of The Cholmondeley Arms, Cheshire; 15 Courtesy of The Flitch of Bacon, Essex – Photo Credit: Rob Whitrow; 16–17 AA/J Smith; 18 AA/M Hamblin; 19l AA/M Hamblin; 19r AA/M Hamblin; 20 AA/J Smith; 21 AA/K Blackwell; 625 AA/J Henderson; 659 AA/M Bauer

Every effort has been made to trace the copyright holders, and we apologise in advance for any unintentional omissions or errors. We would be pleased to apply any corrections in a following edition of this publication

Readers' Report Form

Please send this form to:–
The Editor, The AA Pub Guide,
AA Lifestyle Guides,
8th Floor,
Fanum House,
Basingstoke RG21 4EA

e-mail: lifestyleguides@theAA.com

Please use this form to tell us about any pub or inn you have visited, whether it is in the guide or not currently listed. We are interested in the quality of food, the selection of beers and the overall ambience of the establishment.

Feedback from readers helps us to keep our guide accurate and up to date. However, if you have a complaint to make during a visit, we do recommend that you discuss the matter with the pub management there and then, so that they have a chance to put things right before your visit is spoilt.

Please note that the AA does not undertake to arbitrate between you and the pub management, or to obtain compensation or engage in protracted correspondence.

Date

Your name (BLOCK CAPITALS)

Your address (BLOCK CAPITALS)

Post code

E-mail address

Name of pub

Location

Comments

(please attach a separate sheet if necessary)

Please tick here ☐ if you DO NOT wish to receive details of AA offers or products   PTO

Readers' Report Form *continued*

Have you bought this guide before? ☐ YES ☐ NO

Do you regularly use any other pub, accommodation or food guides? ☐ YES ☐ NO
If YES, which ones?

_____

_____

What do you find most useful about The AA Pub Guide?

_____

_____

_____

Do you read the editorial features in the guide? ☐ YES ☐ NO

Do you use the location atlas? ☐ YES ☐ NO

Is there any other information you would like to see added to this guide?

_____

_____

_____

What are your main reasons for visiting pubs (tick all that apply)

Food ☐   Business ☐   Accommodation ☐
Beer ☐   Celebrations ☐   Entertainment ☐
Atmosphere ☐   Leisure ☐
Other _____

How often do you visit a pub for a meal?
more than once a week ☐
once a week ☐
once a fortnight ☐
once a month ☐
once in six months ☐